North American Elk:
Ecology and Management

A Wildlife Management Institute Book

North American Elk: Ecology and Management

Compiled and edited by
Dale E. Toweill and Jack Ward Thomas

Technical editor Richard E. McCabe

Original illustrations by Daniel P. Metz

SMITHSONIAN INSTITUTION PRESS
Washington and London

The Wildlife Management Institute is a private, nonprofit, scientific and educational organization based in Washington, DC. The Institute's sole objective, since its founding in 1911, has been to help advance restoration and proper management of North America's natural resources, especially wildlife. As a part of the Institute's program, scientific information generated through research and management experiences is consolidated, published and used to strengthen resources decision making and management. *North American Elk: Ecology and Management* is one of the more than twenty-five wildlife books produced by WMI, including the award-winning *Ducks, Geese and Swans of North America, Elk of North America, White-tailed Deer, Ecology and Management of the Mourning Dove* and *Ecology and Management of the Wood Duck.* Also published by Smithsonian Institution Press is WMI's *Ecology and Management of the North American Moose* (1997), edited by Albert W. Franzmann and Charles C. Schwartz. For additional information about the Institute, its programs and publications, write to: Wildlife Management Institute, 1101 14th Street, NW, Suite 801, Washington, DC 20005, or visit www.wildlifemgt.org.

Copyright © 2002 by the Wildlife Management Institute

Library of Congress Cataloging-in-Publication Data

Elk of North America
    North American Elk : ecology and management / compiled and edited by Dale E. Toweill and Jack Ward Thomas ; technical editor Richard E. McCabe ; original illustrations by Daniel P. Metz.—1st ed.
        p.   cm.
    Originally published: Elk of North America. Harrisburg, PA.: Stackpole Books, c1982.
    Includes bibliographical references (p.).
    ISBN 1-58834-018-X (alk. paper)
    1. Elk—United States.   2. Elk—Canada.   3. Wildlife management—United States.   4. Wildlife management—Canada.   I. Toweill, Dale E.   II. Thomas, Jack Ward.   III. Metz, Daniel P.   IV. Title.
    QL737.U55 E42   2002
    599.65.42.0973—dc21   2001049467

British Library Cataloguing-in-Publication Data available

Manufactured in the United States of America
09 08 07 06 05 04 03 02   5 4 3 2 1
First edition

♾ The paper used in this publication meets the minimum requirements of the American National Standard for Information Sciences—Permanence of Paper for Printed Library Materials ANSI Z39.48-1984.

Dust jacket photo by Milo Burcham.
Endsheet artwork by Daniel P. Metz.

Copy editor: Danielle Ponsolle
Production editor: Ruth G. Thomson
Designer: Janice Wheeler
Typesetting and layout: Blue Heron
Production manager: Martha Sewall
Production coordinator: Alan Burchell

Dedication

This book is dedicated to the members of the Rocky Mountain Elk Foundation–past and present–who cared enough about elk and elk hunting to put their time, money and influence on the line. They are people who shared the vision that elk numbers could be increased, long vacant habitats could be reoccupied and elk habitat could be maintained in the face of growing numbers of people and development. Their own growing numbers and ever-increasing efforts have paid off for the welfare of elk over the past two decades and give hope for more of the same in this new millennium.

We also dedicate this effort to our friend Robert Munson, co-founder and first chief executive officer of the Rock Mountain Elk Foundation, who dared to believe that impossible dreams can become reality if one just cares enough and works hard enough.

Contents

Figures

Tables

In Memoriam

MICHAEL W. GRATSON
1952–2000

Wildlife management lost a talented and good friend on December 28, 2000, when the helicopter carrying Michael Gratson struck a snag. Michael and helicopter pilot Mike Haygens died as a result. Wildlife technician Matt Lucia survived the crash.

At the time of his death, Michael was employed by the Idaho Department of Fish and Game as a lead investigator into causes of the elk decline in the Clearwater River Basin of central Idaho. He died in the line of duty, serving a profession he loved, among "those who walk in the Leopold tradition."

Preface

The *Elk of North America* was published a little more than a half century ago. It was authored by Olaus J. Murie and produced by the Wildlife Management Institute. That 1951 volume—now a rare species, indeed—was recognized when it appeared as the first comprehensive treatise on the "monarch of the West" based on "adequate field study." The book was characterized as "extremely significant and worthwhile." Readers were advised that it "is, and will be for a long time to come, the last word on the behavior and characteristics of the elk." Given that the field of wildlife science was less than a score of years old, Dr. Murie's research and presentation of it were as astounding then as they seem now.

A long time to come proved to be just about 30 years. In 1982, *Elk of North America: Ecology and Management* appeared. Authored by 25 wildlife professionals, edited by Jack Ward Thomas and Dale E. Toweill, and produced by the Wildlife Management Institute, that book was regaled as "Surely the finest book ever written about a single species." Another reviewer wrote that "The wildlife community and the Wildlife Management Institute will have a hard time putting together a more informative, interesting and attractive work as this." The Thomas/Toweill book, some of its information too dated, was allowed by the Institute to go out of print a few years ago. Copies in good or better condition are treasures . . . and scarce.

A hard time proved to be 20 years. *North American Elk: Ecology and Management* has been the labor of 40 wildlifers, steered by editors Dale Toweill and Jack Ward Thomas, and again produced by the Wildlife Management Institute. This Toweill/Thomas volume is to *Elk of North America: Ecology and Management* what that 1982 book was to Murie's *The Elk of North America*. They are separate, unique works, vastly changed and improved in content—reflections of the advances of the still-young and emerging science of wildlife ecology and of the importance that the elk holds for scientist, hunter, sightseer alike and for the landscape itself.

In the pages of this new treatise are threads of the past, benchmarks of current resource management and footholds for the future—for elk and, so, for all of us. In the Foreword of Murie's *The Elk of North America*, Wildlife Management Institute president Ira N. Gabrielson wrote: "The Institute is proud to present this interesting and enlightening report. . . ." Of this book, I echo WMI's continuing pride of association with the "report," but more so, with the many extraordinary people, including and since Murie, who provided the substance of it, with the authors, editors, photographers and artist who fashioned it, with the resource agencies, organizations, companies, ranchers, sportsmen and sportswomen, and others in the private sector who strive to ensure that elk are not only symbols of wild North America, but a permanent part of it. To them, to us, the monarch of the West is a touchstone species, and few things are as rare and treasured as that.

Rollin D. Sparrowe
President
Wildlife Management Institute

Acknowledgments

Not surprisingly, several hundred people contributed substantially and directly to this book. The authors, editors and Wildlife Management Institute wish to thank all and identify many. They are listed below.

At least several thousand other people contributed substantially and indirectly. They are the folks who helped with the fieldwork and research. They are the ones who helped draft the reports and management plans. They are the administrators who allowed senior personnel the scope to be involved in this enormous undertaking. They are colleagues who provided information, perspectives and critiques to improve the chapters. They are the photographers, cartographers and computer specialists, artists all—who fashioned the visuals. And, at the top of the list, is Olaus J. Murie, whose work and monograph, *Elk of North America,* was the cornerstone of elk science and management. And, of course, there are the authors of the 1982 book, *Elk of North America: Ecology and Management,* who not only helped pull an extraordinary mass of research data, management experience and professional insight into a coherent and useful volume, but they also were part of the crafting of a publication that set a new standard for professional wildlife literature.

Special thanks are extended to Daniel P. Metz, one of the very best wildlife artists of any place and any time, for creating the pencil and ink wash artwork featured in the book. As when he illustrated the 1982 tome, Dan put into this assignment much more than he was asked or we could afford.

With any creative enterprise of the complexity of this book project, there are persons whose names do not appear on the text pages but who were greatly responsible for those pages getting to press in the first place. This book would not have been completed were it not for the considerable time, energy and talents of Jennifer Rahm of the Wildlife Management Institute and Kelly Wadsworth of Saco, Maine.

In various places in the pages of this book, there is mention of the role of the Rocky Mountain Elk Foundation, not only in the conservation of North American elk, but also conservation of the landscape and habitats that allow elk and other wildlife to prosper. The Foundation also gave early and enthusiastic endorsement of this book and provided support that enabled the investment to get underway.

We salute those named above and below for being integral to this book and a bright future for North American elk.

D. Bruce Banwell, Canterbury, New Zealand

Ludek Bartos, Research Institute of Animal Production, Czech Republic

Louis C. Bender, Washington Department of Fish and Wildlife, Cle Elum

E.T. Bennett, Missoula, Montana

Mark Boyce, University of Alberta, Edmonton

Kevin Brown, Rocky Mountain Elk Foundation, Missoula, Montana

Will Brown, Oregon Department of Fish and Wildlife, La Grande

Gary C. Brundige, South Dakota Department of Game, Fish, and Parks, Custer

George Bubenik, University of Guelph, Guelph, Ontario

Milo Burcham, Missoula, Montana

Vincent Burke, Smithsonian Institution Press, Washington, DC

James Burns, The Provincial Museum of Alberta, Edmonton

Jerry Conley, Missouri Department of Conservation, Jefferson City

Andrew B. Cooper, University of Washington, Seattle

Dan Davis, Clearwater National Forest, Orofino, Idaho

Craig Ely, Oregon Department of Fish and Wildlife, La Grande

Yolanda Finney, Wildlife Management Institute, Washington, DC

John Firebaugh, Montana Fish, Wildlife and Parks, Missoula

Douglas Gober, Clearwater National Forest, Orofino, Idaho

Taylor M. Goodman, Annapolis, Maryland

Russell W. Graham, Denver Museum of National History, Denver, Colorado

Michael Gratson, Idaho Department of Fish and Game, Lewiston

Calvin Groen, Idaho Department of Fish and Game, Lewiston

Bette Gutierrez, Wildlife Management Institute, Washington, DC

John Hafner, Rocky Mountain Elk Foundation, Missoula, Montana

Dick Hancock, Buckley, Washington

Kim Hart, Weatherford, Oklahoma

Alex Irby, Commissioner, Idaho Department of Fish and Game, Orofino

Don Jones, Troy, Montana

David Koehler, Idaho Fish and Game Department, Idaho Falls

Lonn Kuck, Idaho Department of Fish and Game, Star

Kevin Lackey, Rocky Mountain Elk Foundation, Missoula, Montana

Thomas Lemke, Montana Fish, Wildlife and Parks, Livingston

Chunyi Li, AgResearch, Mosgeil, New Zealand

Ed Lindahl, Clearwater Elk Recovery Team, Moscow, Idaho

Samantha Loos, Atlanta, Georgia

Jerry Mallet, Idaho Department of Fish and Game, Boise

Donna McDaniel Skovlin, Reflections Publishing Company, Cove, Oregon

Mia McGreevey, Rocky Mountain Elk Foundation, Missoula, Montana

Steve Mealey, Boise Cascade Corporation, Missoula, Montana

L. David Mech, U.S. Fish and Wildlife Service, Minneapolis, Minnesota

James H. Noyes, Oregon Department of Fish and Wildlife, La Grande

John Ormiston, U.S. Forest Service, Hamilton, Montana

Carol Peddicord, Wildlife Management Institute, Washington, DC

Glenn Plumb, US National Park Service, Yellowstone National Park, Wyoming

Danielle Ponsolle, Orlando, Florida

Margo J. Pybus, Alberta Environment, Edmonton

Bruce Richards, Enumclaw, Washington

Robert Riggs, Booise Cascade Corporation, La Grande, Oregon

Archie Roach, FTE Enterprises, New York, New York

Mary M. Rowland, U.S. Bureau of Land Management, La Grande, Oregon

Rod Sando, Idaho Department of Fish and Game, Boise

Robert Lee Sappington, Department of Anthropology, University of Idaho, Moscow

Lance Schelvan, Rocky Mountain Elk Foundation, Missoula, Montana

Gregg Servheen, Idaho Department of Fish and Game, Boise

John R. Skalski, University of Washington, Seattle

Nicole Sloan, Smithsonian Institution Press, Washington, DC

Bruce Smith, U.S. Fish and Wildlife Service, Jackson, Wyoming

Rocky D. Spencer, Washington Department of Fish and Wildlife, Mill Creek

Christine M. Stalling, Rocky Mountain Research Station, U.S. Forest Service, Missoula, Montana

Jimmy Suttie, AgResearch, Mosgeil, New Zealand

Richard D. Taber, Missoula, Montana

Ruth G. Thomson, Smithsonian Institution Press, Washington, DC

William L. Toweill, John Day, Oregon

Tracey T. Trent, Idaho Department of Fish and Game, Boise

Brian E. Washburn, University of Missouri, Columbia

Janice Wheeler, Smithsonian Institution Press, Washington, DC

Scot J. Williamson, Wildlife Management Institute, North Stratford, New Hampshire

Michael Wisdom, U.S. Forest Service, La Grande, Oregon

Rick Wishcamper, Missoula, Montana

Murray Woodbury, University of Saskatchewan, Saskatoon

John Woods, University of British Columbia, Vancouver

Rami J. Woods, University of Missouri, Columbia

BART W. O'GARA

Taxonomy

Excellent contributions to the study of taxonomy are now being made by specialists in biochemistry, immunology, and cytogenetics. These buttress the accomplishments in anatomy, physiology, and mathematics. Because of the difference in the background of specialists, it is necessary to keep in mind two basic and oft repeated warnings: (1) newly-discovered characters of taxonomic units must be evaluated with caution and with judgement before suggesting significance; and (2) accurate species identification and knowledge of precise localities of capture of source animals are prerequisites of acceptable results. Adequate reference study specimens should always be preserved.

Johnson (1968:29)

Taxonomy is the naming and classification of organisms. Simpson (1990) defined it as the theoretical study of classification, including its bases, principles, procedures and rules. Thus, the subjects of classification are organisms, and the subjects of taxonomy are classifications. A taxon is a group of any rank that is sufficiently distinct to be worthy of assignment to a definite category.

The "father" of taxonomy—Carl von Linnaeus, a Swedish physician and celebrated botanist—developed the system of binomial nomenclature used today. This system, enunciating principles for defining each organism by a scientific name (genus and species) and used worldwide, probably will last as long as the study of biology endures.

The so-called Linnean classification hierarchy includes seven taxonomic ranks—kingdom, phylum, class, order, family, genus and species. In fact, Linnaeus used only five of these; Phylum and Family were added from other sources. The number and kinds of organisms to be classified have now become so enormous that seven levels rarely are enough in practice (Simpson 1990). The deficiency has been made up, for the most part, by adding levels designated as super- above the basic levels, and adding sub- and infra- below them. Proposals have been made to add to the seven basic taxonomic levels, but they have not been standardized. The only ones in general use are cohort, between class and order, and tribe, usually but not always placed between family and genus. The use of any particular number of levels is completely arbitrary, except that use of the seven basic Linnean levels is required by convention.

The most common cause of instability in nomenclature has been the fact that, occasionally, with zoologists working all over the world, more than one specific name has been independently applied to the same, or nearly the same, taxon. The International Code of Zoological Nomenclature (see Ride 1985) established the basic rule of priority, according to which the name of a genus or species is the first name that was validly published in connection with it since 1758. That conventional zero date marked the tenth edition of Linnaeus's (1758) *Systema Naturae*. Even now, some obscurely published old name turns up with priority over a name that has been universally accepted by zoologists. The International Commission on Zoological Nomenclature, under the auspices of the International Union of Biological Sciences, is empowered to suspend the priority rule in a particular case and designate names in general use to continue (Simpson 1990). Note, this applies only to species names. The only commonly used taxon below the species is the subspecies—designated by a third Latin name after the generic and specific name.

The primary criterion in modern taxonomy is phylogenetic relatedness, that is, organisms that share recent common ancestry are grouped together, separate from others with more distant common ancestry. This can be considered the same as evolutionary relationships among taxa as they change over time.

The morphological species definition, based on the typological species concept (a typologist disregards variation and regards the members of a population as replicas of the type specimen), dominated taxonomy during the 19th and early 20th centuries, but is steadily losing ground (Mayr 1970). Thus, at the time most North American big game were being named, an inordinate number of species and subspecies were designated purely on their appearance— mostly slight variations in color and size. It was under this system that an albino red deer was named *Cervus. e. albus,* a tame variety was named *C. e. albifrons* and a partial albino was named *C. e. varius* (see Ellerman and Morrison-Scott 1951). Even the great Linnaeus originally named the male mallard *Anas boschas* and the female *A. platyrhynchos,* apparently because they were recognizable as different by their colors and voices.

Nomenclature

Common Names

Theodore Roosevelt (1905:259) wrote of the elk: "This splendid deer offers a good instance of the difficulty of deciding what name to use in treating of our American game. On one hand it is entirely undesirable to be pedantic; on the other hand, it seems a pity, at a time when speech is written almost as much as spoken, to use terms which perpetually require explanation to avoid confusion. . . . There is little use in trying to upset a name which is imprinted in our geography in hundreds of such titles as Elk Ridge, Elk Mountain, Elkhorn River."

Internationally, the common name "elk" exists for two distinct big game species. What North Americans commonly call "moose" (*Alces alces*) generally are called "elk" in Europe. Henceforth in this chapter, moose will refer to *A. alces* and elk will designate the large *Cervus elaphus* of North America and parts of Asia.

One explanation of how or why New England colonists adopted the term elk for *C. elaphus* was provided by Merrill (1916). He hypothesized that early settlers in eastern North America—probably in Virginia—met two species of deer. They called the first (whitetails) "deer," probably because they were familiar with the small roe deer of England. The other species (our elk) was not recognized as similar to the red deer of Europe because of its great size. Knowing the European elk (moose) was a large animal, the colonists gave it the name "elk." When Englishmen met the true elk in the more northern woods, they named it moose, a name apparently adopted from the Algonquin-speaking Indians of Quebec (see Reeves and McCabe 1997).

What North Americans commonly call elk often are called wapiti in scientific writings to avoid confusion with the European word for moose. Barton (1806:51) established the name of wapiti when he wrote: "As the elk has not to my knowledge been described by any scientific writer on zoology, I have assumed the liberty of giving it a specific name. I have called it Wapiti which is the name by which it is known among the Shawnese Indians." Thus, Eurasian writers came to use an American Indian name to avoid confusion with the common name for European moose (see Bryant and Maser 1982).

Scientific Names and Conventions for This Chapter

The species name for elk was changed from *C. canadensis* to *C. elaphus* by Jones et al. (1973) and others. Thus, in the current checklist of North American mammals north of Mexico (Jones et al. 1991), the elk is considered conspecific with the red deer.

In this chapter, I use *C. elaphus* to refer to the entire red deer/elk species complex; "red deer" will mean European red deer and "elk" will refer to the *C. elaphus* of North America and certain Asian subspecies; "Maraloid" will be used when describing certain intermediate Asian taxa that resemble *C. e. maral* of the Middle East. Because this book is entitled *Ecology and Management of North American Elk* and will be read primarily by Canadians and Americans, elk will be used throughout to avoid confusion, although most Eurasian writers use the word "wapiti" for American elk. I would like to use maral for Asian elk, as do many Asians, but the subspecific name for one taxon is *C. e. maral*, which could cause more confusion. For consistency, bull and cow will designate the sexes, although stag and hind generally are used to refer to male and female red deer in Eurasia and New Zealand. To avoid confusion, hybridization will refer to crosses between animals from different species or genera, and crossbreeding will mean crosses between individuals of the same species but different subspecies. Unless designated as per antler or each antler, number of tines will refer to tines on both antlers.

One of the first non-Native illustrations of North American elk was this lithograph entitled "Alce," It helped to illustrate *Historiae Canadensis sev. Novae-Franciae* by Du Creux (1664). Lydekker (1901:42) wrote that the name "elk" for "the great stag" came from the ancient Greek work αλκε and subsequent Greek alce. Other plausible etymological derivations include from the Latin alces to old high German elaho to the modern German Elk, Elch and Elen and old Norse elgr to the Lithuanian elnis and old Irish elit to the old English eolh to the middle English alke to the modern English elk. *Photo courtesy of the Public Archives of Canada (D-99221).*

Difficulties arise in dealing with placenames in China, where Chinese, Tibetan, Mongolian and Turkic languages use non-Arabic script. Such names have been variously translated into English over the years—apparently as the spoken word struck the western ear. Standard Hanyu pinyin (as used by modern Chinese) will be used when possible. However, a few commonly used western words will be used (for instance, China instead of Zhongguo). For simplicity, The People's Republic of China will be referred to simply as China, and The Republic of China will be called Taiwan. Heilongjiang Province of China will be called Manchuria; the Tibetan Autonomous Region of China will be Tibet; the Nei Mongol Autonomous Region of China will be Inner Mongolia; and the Mongolian People's Republic will be referred to as Outer Mongolia. Also, shan will be used for mountains in China because that is how they will be found on maps, and to use, for instance, Tien Shan Mountains as sometimes seen in American literature is redundant.

Importance of Contemporary Taxonomy

One must be able to identify in Court under oath the identity of individuals of protected subspecies, expose misidentifications, rule whether hybrids between subspecies constitute protected wildlife or not, as well as explain what constitutes, objectively, a subspecies.

Geist (1989a:2)

Taxonomy has long involved basic research by professors at institutions of higher learning and curators of museums. For many people, taxonomy seems little more than the sorting of dead specimens according to a few rather superficial morphological characters, writing out labels and stowing the specimens away in drawers. Those people seldom recognize the importance of taxonomy in understanding the way in which species arise and relate to one another. Wildlife professionals often have regarded taxonomy as of little interest to them except that resource managers, researchers and the general public needed to know names of plants and animals well enough to communicate. Thus, the need to communicate—whether with a hunter who must know what game is legal or with a researcher half way around the world who speaks a different language—is justification for the time, money and expertise spent on taxonomy.

Due to international agreements and national laws to protect endangered species and regulate trade in and hunting of rare species, the taxonomic literature should serve to identify individuals of species and subspecies unambiguously. Legislation such as the Convention on International Trade in Endangered Species (CITES) and the United States Endangered Species Act of 1973 made species, subspecies and even populations legal entities. Thus, taxonomy became relevant to the conservation of officially designated threatened and endangered wildlife. It also is very relevant to persons charged with infractions of laws designed to protect wildlife. Their reputations and economic and social circumstances may be affected adversely by court decisions. Moreover, conservation efforts tend to be guided by taxonomy, which thus decides what may or may not be protected (Geist 1989a).

Decisions with important conservation implications increasingly require more understanding of the systematics of populations, subspecies and species than is currently available. As Ryder (1986:9) observed concerning conservation of biodiversity, "The 'subspecies problem' is considerably more than taxonomic esoterica." The importance of taxonomic relationships, at the species level and below, also looms increasingly important because of translocations of wildlife among countries, provinces and states, such as by those interested in elk farming—a growing industry in Canada and the United States.

Another problem that requires knowledge of taxonomy is that of inbreeding. Although inbreeding is less of a problem for elk than for many species, fragmentation of elk habitat has resulted in some small island populations. Knowledge of the phenotypic and genotypic norms for a subspecies are needed if genetic exchange with other populations is needed for long-term survival of island populations.

Taxonomic authorities sometimes are characterized as splitters or lumpers. Simpson (1945:23) exaggerated the differences slightly: "Splitters make very small units—their opponents say that if they can tell two animals apart, they place them in different genera, and if they cannot tell them apart, they place them in different species. Lumpers make large units—their opponents say that if a carnivore is neither a dog nor a bear they call it a cat."

With taxa being legal units in today's judicial systems, one might think that either splitting or lumping would have more utility than the other. That is not the case. Splitting can result in taxa from which the world's expert on that group often could not, under oath in court, positively identify a specimen. In such instances, neither conservation objectives nor law enforcement is served. On the other hand, if a lumper placed all red deer or elk of a continent into one taxon, most taxonomists could positively identify an individual from that taxon. However, the specimen could have come from such a broad area that law enforcement and other conservation officials may receive little assistance for their cause.

Therefore, although taxonomy is important in regulating trade in threatened and endangered wildlife and in many other conservation concerns, it is not a magic bullet. Even with advances in biochemical techniques, common sense and carefully researched and worded regulations with detailed descriptions of subspecies are a must. Regulations related to a subspecies should cite who named it and (if different) whose description is relevant. This seems necessary because disagreement often exists among "experts" concerning classification of subspecies. Also, in a few cases, more than one group of animals has been given the same name. Naming a species to be protected within a geographic area involves less margin for error than does designating a potentially controversial subspecies.

"For purposes of identification, all members of a subspecies must be *recognizable* as such or lose the protection of the law. . . . Put another way, subspecies are distinguished by at least one consistent taxonomic difference" (Geist 1991a). Geographic location as an integral part of the definition of a subspecies, as proposed by O'Brien and Mayr (1991), presents legal problems. Geographic origin is not a part of a specimen and normally must be accepted on faith (Geist 1991b).

Cervinae (including *Cervus*) are found in the Eurasian fossil record from the Pliocene epoch (5.2–1.8 million years ago). Most North American elk fossils were from the Wisconsin glacial (90,000–10,000 years ago) stage and later; those dated to earlier times are relatively rare (see Chapter 2). Alaskan elk were confluent with those of Siberia and probably represent reciprocal migrations and mixing of populations (Guthrie 1966). Late Pleistocene (200,000–10,000 years ago) fossil *Cervus* were found above the Arctic Circle in Siberia (Flerov 1952).

Recession of the glaciers during the last interglacial stage (10,000 years ago) allowed Alaskan elk to spread southward and eastward across North America (and southward and westward in Asia) as suitable habitat became available (Guthrie 1966). Vegetational changes probably contributed to extirpation of elk in Alaska, but produced prairies, open forests and meadows favorable to their survival in Canada and the United States. Available evidence indicates that some elk of the New and Old Worlds have been separated geographically for only about 10,000 years—an exceedingly short period of geologic time.

Evidence Used in Cervid Taxonomy

Formal classifications of deer have been inadequate, yet through repetition have become regarded as unquestionable primary sources of knowledge
Groves and Grubb (1987:22)

In any attempt at a taxonomic review, the philosophies, methods and findings of earlier authors must be considered. That is no easy matter when important papers are in German, Norwegian, Polish, Russian, Chinese, etc. Few people are fluent in enough languages that they do not have to depend on translations and accept the interpretations offered, often by nonbiologists. Unfortunately, this can perpetuate mistakes and elevate them into dogma.

Comparative anatomy has been the primary method of classification and the method on which much of our present knowledge of deer phylogeny depends.

The Fossil Record

When one looks at a phylogenetic (evolutionary) tree, living species and subspecies constitute the twigs and leaves. Fossils indicate the roots and trunk, and often, main branches and sub-branches—usually corresponding to orders and families. A complete review of the fossil record leading to Cervidae is beyond the scope of this chapter (see Chapter 2).

Size and Weight

Sizes and weights are poor indicators of relationships among species or subspecies, because habitat conditions can easily mask differences or similarities. Not only does habitat affect weights and measurements, but expertise, methods and equipment available to field personnel complicate comparisons. Greer and Howe (1964) obtained various weights from 1,100 Rocky Mountain elk, which were shot during December, January and February in the winter of 1961 to 1962. They found differences in dressed weights from December to February of about 10%. Differences, no doubt, would have been greater had whole weights been available; much fat is lost with evisceration. Also, a large weight loss from summer to December had already taken place. A bull may lose 20% of his normal weight during the rut and only attain full size and development by 4 or 5 years of age (Heptner et al. 1961). However, weights often are reported for younger animals.

Vogt (1936, 1948) increased the weights of red deer from Poland and Hungary to those of medieval bulls—353 to 772 pounds (160–350 kg). This happened over a period of four generations with food high in protein, calcium and phosphate. In the early days of World War II, Vogt could not get the experimental food, and the weights of his deer consequently regressed (see Geist 1989b).

Another example of how habitat conditions can affect weight in *C. elaphus* was given by Reinders (1960). During 1900 to 1914, red deer from various countries of Europe were gathered into a 25,755-acre (10,423 ha) park. By 1929, the population reached 1,300 deer, and 631 were shot. The population then was held at about 650 head. Average weights of bulls during 1921 to 1923 had been 195 pounds (88.5 kg). They increased to 228 pounds (103.6 kg) by 1936 to 1939 and to 250 pounds (113.6 kg) by 1953 to 1956. These variances illustrate the difficulty in using weights when comparing subspecies.

An animal born to a nutritionally stressed mother suffers low levels of growth hormones throughout life, which stunts its growth and thus its measurements, even if it receives good nutrition following birth. This effect also is passed on to its offspring (Winner 1996). Grandchildren of malnourished dams are lighter than those of well-nourished dams, even if their own mothers had adequate food (Mech et al. 1991). The offspring stay lighter until 2 years of age. Such animals undoubtedly retain some juvenile characteristics, such as short, narrow muzzles, throughout their lives. Schultz and Johnson (1995) indicated that white-tailed deer bucks with greater body mass at birth continued to have greater body mass at older ages. On the other hand, Watkins et al. (1991) and Wairimu et al. (1992) found that elk in Alberta that were underweight in spring because they did not receive supplemental nutrition gained weight faster on summer range than did those on supplements, and they attained similar weights and frame measurements by late summer. Crossbred vigor also can alter skull morphology (V. Geist personal communication:1997).

Body measurements of ungulates can be affected by nutrition, but to a lesser degree than are weights, thus are preferable to weights for comparison of populations. However, standard measurements for many subspecies are few or lacking.

Craniometry

Taxonomic criteria should reflect hereditary differences between taxa. In practice, few do. The cause seems to be the unwarranted assumption that within taxa variations are statistical in nature, without inquiry into the biological basis of variation. The foremost method used today in large mammal taxonomy—craniometry—is an invalid taxonomic criterion; nutrition can cause skulls to vary in size and shape, as can the work of cranial musculature, according to Geist (1989a). Although this is true, all evidence available should be used—giving craniometry some value in overall considerations and decisions. When cranial characteristics are used, choosing those that are least affected by nutrition and other habitat parameters is important.

As Simpson (1945) observed, the typical statement of classifiers that, for instance, the skull of a given species is 2.36 inches (60 mm) long, 1.18 inches (30 mm) wide and 0.59 inches (15 mm) deep, aside from being untrue (it can only apply to an average in a sample or to one individual and cannot be true of a species or population), is inadequate and misleading. Variation within a species may be more characteristic than any demonstrable constancy; variation is difficult to measure and can only be estimated from a given sample. Yet, samples can be compared by means and standard deviations.

Wallace (1948) demonstrated that growth of the skull of domestic ewes is intimately associated with that of the brain, and that growth of the latter persists to a remarkable degree under an adverse nutritional regime. With limited nutrition, the facial and forward portions of the skull may be more severely restricted in growth than are the bones of the posterior portion of the skull.

Wallace (1948) pointed out that considerable caution must be exercised in describing growth patterns solely in terms of allometric growth without consideration of the animal's nutritional plane or the rate at which it has grown. Differential growth rates may apply to individual bones, depending on the degree of development of the bone before birth. Thus, the skull of a poorly fed ungulate may exhibit juvenile characteristics of a shortened snout and reduced rostrum. Although such a poorly fed animal could eventually equal the growth of an animal on a high plane of nutrition, Klein (1964) has shown this equalization may not be realized. Therefore, considerable variability may be expected in the forward regions of ungulate skulls sampled from a broad geographic range (see Hutton 1972).

Antlers

Crania and antlers are environmentally plastic; only the antlers of large, mature males have limited taxonomic utility (Geist 1989a); antlers are not as predictable in growth as often thought. Antler characteristics were an imprecise predictor of age in harvested Michigan elk (Bender et al. 1994).

Nutrition influences antler size as well as body weight. Studying farm-raised red deer in New Zealand, Muir and Sykes (1988) found antler weight related to body weight. Within an age group, velvet antler weight increased 0.26 pound (0.12 kg) with each 22-pound (10 kg) increase in pre-rut body weight.

Vogt (1936) was impressed by the enormous antlers of medieval bulls in central Europe. He analyzed the chemical composition of red deer antlers, calculated the quantity of mineral and protein needed to grow 22 pounds (10 kg) of

antler mass in 120 days, analyzed natural forages for their mineral and nutrient content and calculated the amounts in a daily ration of forage of a heavily feeding bull. He concluded that the forage available to deer in the managed forests of central Europe was so deficient in protein and minerals that no modern bull could possibly grow the large antlers of its forebears. After considerable trial and error, Vogt found that pressed sesame seed, left as a cake after the oil was pressed out, exceeded his calculated requirements for protein, calcium and phosphate, and also was acceptable and wholesome to deer. He chose an experimental site with a cold climate, high snowfall, sandy soils and poor plant growth in the mountains of Bohemia, where red deer grew to modest size, and bulls in enclosures, under exceptional care, rarely grew more than 13.2-pound (6 kg) antlers. All cast antlers were weighed and measured. At the end of the 12-year experiment, 7 of 34 bulls had exceeded the prevailing world record in size, and all but one exceeded the one-hundredth best. Antler weights reached nearly 44 pounds (20 kg).

In general, there are three main types of *C. elaphus* antlers (see Heptner et al. 1961). Figure 1 shows the conventional names for antler parts.

Central European (elaphoid) type. This type has numerous tines, primarily because the antler tips branch into tines set in different planes, usually called crowns or cups. European

An example of the extent to which habitat and nutrition can influence the size of antlers. These antlers are from 12-year-old bulls shot in Scotland and England during 1981 and 1982. The upper (inside) set is from the degraded, treeless highlands of Scotland. Its bearer apparently was of pure or nearly pure Scottish stock. The lower antlers are from an area of England with fertile pastures, considerable tree cover and abundant acorns. It probably was a crossbreed of Scottish and continental red deer, and crossbreeding could have contributed to the large size. However, Scottish deer introduced to good habitat in New Zealand became large deer within a few generations and grew antlers as large as the lower one. *Photo by Bart W. O'Gara.*

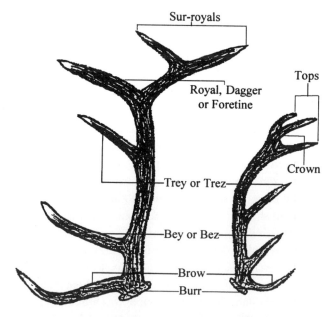

Figure 1.   Comparative elk (*left*) and red deer (*right*) antlers, with nomenclature of parts as used in this chapter. *Illustration by Bart W. O'Gara.*

Antlers of a European red deer (*left*) and a North American elk (*right*). *Left photo by Irene Vandermolen. Right photo by Milo Burcham.*

deer sport such antlers, in which the number of tines can be particularly high. Red deer in good habitat produce heavier antlers in relation to body weight than do elk.

Elk type. With six or seven (occasionally more) tines per side on large bulls, elk antlers can attain extraordinary lengths and generally are widespread (see Chapter 4). Crowns ordinarily do not form, and terminal tines are set in a single plane (sagittal or nearly so). The brow tine arises just above the burr or coronet. The bez about 6 inches (15 cm) above the brow tine, and is equal to or sometimes larger than the brow tine. Together, the bez and brow tines extend out above the muzzle in a formation of four points sometimes called lifters. The trez point is located higher on the beam, and the royal (fourth) tine arises still higher. The latter is the dominant point—quite heavy, long and somewhat flattened; it sometimes is called the dagger point. The remaining points, called sur-royals, generally form a fork at the end of the beam. Usually, at the point of deviation of the fourth tine, the main beam bends backward (downward), sometimes quite sharply. This type is characteristic of elk in North America as well as the Tien Shan of China and Kazakhstan and the Altai Mountains and surrounding areas of Outer Mongolia and Siberia. Although smaller, the antlers of elk in eastern Siberia, Inner Mongolia and Manchuria also possess this type of antler.

Hangul (central Asiatic) type. The hangul is the simplest of *C. elaphus* antler types (Figure 2). The antlers are relatively short although quite massive and usually with no more than five tines per side (brow, bez, central and two terminal that form a fork). Sometimes, a sixth tine (terminal) occurs, but does not form a crown. The fork often forms a wide angle, and sometimes is almost perpendicular to the sagittal plane of the body. The bez and central tines often are quite high on the main beam.

Figure 2. Hangul antlers in the collection of Sir Edmond Loder (from Van der Byl 1915). This type is characteristic of several subspecies in central Asia and typical of the maraloid group. *Illustration by Bart W. O'Gara.*

Pelage and Color

Pelage varies seasonally with molts, growth and wear and may change drastically in only a few weeks. Thus, taxonomic judgments should not be rendered without intimate knowledge of the subject animal's life cycle and exactly when a specimen was collected, a picture taken, etc.

The most highly evolved subspecies of *C. elaphus* exhibit sexual and seasonal dimorphism in color. Sometimes, the primitive red summer tint is completely absent in the more highly specialized subspecies. The central Asian and American elk are multicolored with darkening on the neck and in the lower regions of the body and extremities, and the large rump patches have dark borders. This differs greatly from the red deer and some intermediate subspecies, which are lighter below with generally smaller rump patches and, in some cases, spotted pelage (Flerov 1952). As with pelage, color can change quickly with shedding and regrowth of hair.

Behavior

Social signals may be useful. These include differences in urination postures, courtship, herding, dominance displays and mating calls (see Geist 1989a; see also Chapter 7).

Social Insignia

Taxonomic criteria that reflect genetic differences are the social insignia affecting mate selection, namely nuptial pelage of socially mature adults (Geist 1991a), color, antlers, and—in the case of *C. elaphus*—size, shape and color of rump patches (Dolan 1988). Geist (1989a, 1991a) defined subspecies as those populations united by the same social organ characteristics.

Crossbreeding

The crossbreeding of red deer and elk, producing fertile offspring in the wild, indicates a close relationship, but may not indicate what would happen with wild populations under *natural* conditions. Crosses are known between North American elk and hangul, Manchurian elk and Altai elk, as well as hybrids between red deer and axis, sika, fallow and Père David's deer (Gray 1972) as well as red and sambar deer (Harrington 1973). Most of these crosses took place under captive conditions.

Mallard ducks will hybridize with black ducks, pintails, gadwalls, shovelers and green-winged teal. The wood duck has crossed with 14 other species. Hybrids of closely related ducks (such as mallard and black duck) generally are fertile and the sex ratio is normal (Kortright 1962), but there is no rush to classify any two species of ducks (which are easily recognized as different) as one species because they hybridize. Despite the large number of ducks that will cross, few hybrids are seen in the wild. Apparently most of them, even if fertile, are less well adapted than either of their parent species. The greatest number of misalliances are reported from mixed, semidomesticated flocks brought together from various regions and maintained in park lagoons or zoological gardens (Kortright 1962), a situation not unlike those from which most red deer/elk crosses arose.

Caughley (1971) studied free-ranging populations of Eurasian red deer and North American elk in New Zealand and concluded: (1) crossbreeding is most frequent where the ratio of red deer to elk approaches even numbers, and (2) crossbreeding is less frequent where an area of overlap is inhabited primarily by one or the other subspecies. Crossbreeding can begin on gamefarms and continue in the wild if crosses escape.

Karyotypes

The processes of egg and sperm formation normally require matched sets of chromosomes. Individual animals have matched pairs of chromosomes, one from each parent. The X and Y sex chromosomes are an exception; males have an X and a Y, and females have two X chromosomes. As long as a set matches, meiosis (two consecutive special cell divisions in the developing germ cells characterized by the pairing and segregation of homologous chromosomes) is normal. However, if the two sets of chromosomes differ in number or structure, abnormal meiosis and attendant fertility problems are possible. A more subtle type of problem results from interactions between specific gene loci (as apparently occurs in crosses between white-tailed and mule deer) rather than chromosome number or configuration (Tempelton 1986).

The number and form of chromosomes have been used extensively in determining the relationships among families, genera and species. This technique is useful but not consistent in determining relationships. For instance, closely related species of wild sheep possess different numbers (52 to 58) and configurations of chromosomes, although the species crossbreed and produce fertile offspring (Valdez 1982). On the other hand, mule deer and white-tailed deer, which will crossbreed but produce offspring with limited fertility, have similar numbers and configurations of chromosomes (Hsu and Benirschke 1967). Thus, like almost all criteria used in taxonomy, chromosome maps are helpful but should only be used in conjunction with other evidence.

Genetics

Most biologists agree that genetic relationships should provide the foundation for taxonomy. More specifically, *phylogenetic*, or evolutionary relationships, are the basis of classification of plants and animals. Traditionally, subspecies designations of mammals have been based on morphological variation and geographic distributions. However, morphology may not reflect phylogenetic relationships. Differences in size or color of pelage often are used in subspecies classification, but overlap between populations makes quantification of differentiation difficult. In addition, natural selection can result in rapid divergence of morphology, even when two populations share a recent common ancestry or continue to exchange genes (Ehrlich and Raven 1969, Slatkin 1987). Conversely, natural selection may cause populations that differ in their phylogenetic ancestry to undergo convergence of characters, leading to morphological similarity (Lansman et al. 1983). Finally, morphological characters may be affected by environmental factors, such as diet (Geist 1987, Klein et al. 1987). Locality may be dominant in determining size and shape (Beninde 1937). Geographic discontinuities in distribution as a basis for differentiating taxa does not help in identifying taxa that are legal entities and must be recognizable.

Simpson (1945) observed that morphological and paleontologic data (which also are largely, but not exclusively morphological) always have been and (barring some wholly unheralded and most improbable achievement in some other field) always will be the principal basis for the study of phylogeny. The improbable has come to pass and phylogenetic relationships can now be studied through molecular genetics. Two molecular approaches that have been used extensively in systematics are protein electrophoresis and analysis of deoxyribonucleic acid (DNA).

There now are laboratories conducting commercial deer genotyping to confirm the genetic background and parentage of particular animals. The intensification of deer management in the past decade has brought new genetic problems as well as the application of advanced biomedical techniques in addressing them. Plasma proteins, isozymes and mitochondrial DNA (mtDNA) have provided markers that document hybridization and crossbreeding in wild deer and captive breeding programs. As some deer species receive increased protection and others are bred for commercial purposes, biochemical and molecular techniques are bound to have a growing role in deer management and taxonomy (Dratch and Pemberton 1992).

The higher ruminants are closely related genetically; all species share some alleles at some loci (Mross and Doolittle 1967, Baccus et al. 1983, Irwin et al. 1991, Kraus and Miya-

moto 1991, Allard et al. 1992, Gatesy et al. 1992, Cronin et al. 1996). Apparently, this fact can complicate biochemical studies and may call for large sample sizes to derive statistically significant conclusions on the taxonomy of cervids.

Protein Electrophoresis

With protein electrophoresis, different alleles for a given protein gene are identified by separating the protein molecules by size and electric charge in a gel subjected to an electric field. For example, a common protein—serum albumin—has two alleles in deer. In most geographic areas, a fast allele predominates in mule deer and a slow allele predominates in white-tailed deer. The former migrates faster in the electrophoretic gel than does the slow allele. In some areas where the two species hybridize, the alleles are not clearly segregated between the species (Stubblefield et al. 1986). The frequencies of different alleles can be compared to infer the relationships and level of gene flow between populations or the degree of genetic divergence of different species.

In general, protein electrophoresis is more appropriate for assessing relationships of populations of the same species than for interspecies comparisons. Using this method, many protein genes can be assessed, which is a requirement for accurate comparisons of populations or species. In addition, the method is relatively inexpensive compared with more sophisticated DNA methods. A weakness of the method is that the level of resolution of genetic variation is limited to simple identification of different alleles. Not all alleles are identifiable with protein electrophoresis, and no information is available on how different the protein alleles are from each other (M. Cronin personal communication:1997). Strandgaard and Simonsen (1993) found it difficult to define subspecies of *C. elaphus* based on electrophoresis of isozymes. They proposed that rapidly developing methods using DNA may be more efficient for separating subspecies. However, protein electrophoresis remains a valuable method for assessing genetic relationships of populations or closely related species.

The fossil record generally is poor for closely related populations or species. For a typical pair of species within a genus, for example, only in exceptional cases can one estimate from fossil evidence whether the last common ancestor lived 1 million or 10 million years ago. Electrophoretic methods proved most suitable for comparing recently diverged species, and genetic distances are measured by differences in gene frequencies. However, relationships can be confounded if extant alleles also preexisted in the ancestral species (see Wilson et al. 1985).

Electrophoretic studies comparing deer species have identified abundant protein differences that can be used to refine deer phylogenies (see Dratch and Pemberton 1992). Intraspecific biochemical variation is quantified in three ways: heterozygosity (the proportion of individuals that have different alleles from each parent at a particular locus); percentage of polymorphic loci; and the average number of alleles per locus.

DNA Analysis

During the past several decades, new methods in molecular biology have revolutionized the study of genetic variation. Analyses of DNA allow inference concerning allele frequency differences among populations and species, but they also allow assessment of differences in the DNA itself. DNA consists of a long double helix chain of nucleotides, which contain the genetic code for proteins, as well as noncoding stretches. There are four nucleotides (abbreviated A, G, C and T) that are arranged in linear fashion to form the DNA strand. The sequence of nucleotides varies among genes and, for a given gene, the sequence will vary among different alleles. For example, the two serum albumin alleles mentioned previously, which can be identified in deer with protein electrophoresis, have different DNA sequences. Thus, the frequency of the alleles can be determined, as with electrophoresis, but differences in DNA sequence also can be quantified. This allows inference about the time since the two alleles (and possibly the species possessing them) diverged.

Analysis of DNA variation is quite complex and is evolving into its own science. There are many interesting dynamics involved in DNA evolution that are beyond the scope of this chapter. The main points relevant to taxonomy are that DNA analysis allows very high resolution of the genetic differentiation of alleles of a gene, individual animals, populations and species.

The DNA sequences of alleles that are unique to each species can be compared to estimate the relatedness and time of divergence of the species. This method relies on the general existence of a molecular clock, whereby differences in DNA sequence (caused by random mutations) accumulate over time; therefore, DNA sequence divergence reflects the amount of time since two alleles (and possibly the species possessing them) diverged. This method is reasonable for species that diverged long ago (e.g., species in different genera or families), but not to closely related species or populations of the same species. This is because closely related species or populations often share the same alleles (Pamilo and Nei 1988). In these cases, comparisons of the frequencies of alleles, regardless of their DNA divergence, is a more conservative and reliable way to assess relationships (Cronin 1993).

Comparison of DNA variation among individual animals is becoming well known, as the application of DNA fingerprints expands from human forensics into the study of animal populations. There are stretches of hypervariable DNA that do not code for any particular gene for which there are multiple alleles within most species. The large number of alleles results in individual-specific genotypes when several DNA stretches are considered. The most common DNA used for these analyses are known as minisatellite DNA or microsatellite DNA. This is a greatly expanding field with most applications in family and population studies, but not taxonomy.

As mentioned, the relationships of populations and closely related species are best assessed with comparisons of allele frequencies at several genetic loci, whereas comparisons of DNA sequences are informative for comparisons of different species. Various DNA sequences have been used in taxonomic studies, including mtDNA. The mtDNA is maternally inherited in the mitochondria of the egg cell and evolves rapidly relative to the primary DNA complement in chromosomes in the cell nucleus (Avise 1994). It is inherited separately from the DNA in the nucleus, directly from mother to offspring. There are 37 different genes in the mtDNA molecule, but it is inherited as a single linked set of genes and is very useful to study evolutionary relationships (Wilson et al. 1985, Shields and Wilson 1987, Avise 1994). The mtDNA sequence has been used to infer the relationships of several deer species (Cronin 1992a), and mtDNA allele frequencies have been used to assess relationships of deer populations and subspecies (Cronin 1991a, 1991b). These mtDNA studies have been very informative, but should be combined with studies of nuclear DNA for a thorough assessment of taxonomic relationships. This is because mtDNA represents a small part of the total genome inherited along matriarchal lines, and assessment of many genes is necessary for accurate phylogenetic inference (Pamilo and Nei 1988).

Studies of nuclear (chromosomal) DNA are less numerous than those of mtDNA, but are increasing rapidly. For example, a study of the DNA sequence of a milk protein gene (κ-casein) showed relationships of several deer species to be similar to those shown with mtDNA (Cronin et al. 1996). Assessments of allele frequencies of the same casein gene showed varying levels of divergence among caribou herds, and between caribou and reindeer (Cronin et al. 1995). The study of nuclear DNA variation can be expected to increase greatly in the future, clarifying the relationships among many populations and species.

Relationships inferred from DNA often conflict with those indicated by traditional species or subspecies designations. Some species or subspecies do not have phylogenetically distinct DNA, and each sequence reflects a limited part of the gene pool of populations. Thus, sequence divergence may not provide an assessment of overall genetic differentiation. This leads to the question of how to integrate different types of information. For example, should groups be considered distinct if they show morphological differentiation, but little or no molecular genetic differentiation? In many cases, the answer is yes. For example, some well-known species—including mallards and black ducks, mule deer and whitetails, and polar and brown bears—do not have distinct mtDNA sequences. From a management standpoint, it would be ridiculous to consider mallards and black ducks, mule deer and white-tailed deer or polar and brown bears as the same units because they do not have distinctive mtDNA (Cronin 1993).

An important point is that the use of frequencies of mtDNA genotypes to assess genetic differentiation requires that sample sizes be adequate to characterize a species or a population. The typological thinking of 19th century taxonomists allowed a few individuals of a species, subspecies or population to represent the entire group. If this practice is applied with molecular genetic data, important relationships will not be detected. Assessment of within-group variation cannot be stressed enough for valid comparisons at the species, subspecies or population levels (Cronin 1993). M. Cronin (personal communication:1996) indicated that populations or subpopulations from each taxon should be sampled when using mtDNA to estimate taxonomic relationships. This is especially true when members of the taxa being considered are scattered and occupying varied habitats. Twenty specimens from each population or subpopulation sampled generally are accepted as adequate, but the larger number sampled the better. In many cases, hundreds of individuals should be sampled during molecular taxonomic studies.

In summary, DNA data are very informative, but need to be used with care because they represent a small part of the genome and may not reflect overall phylogenetic relationships of taxa. However, by assessing genetic variation of many genes (mtDNA and nuclear) with representative sample sizes, molecular genetic analyses can allow accurate inference of phylogenetic relationships of populations and closely related species (Cronin 1993).

Higher Taxa

Taxonomy is a science, but its application to classification involves a great deal of human contrivance and ingenuity, in short of art. In this art there is leeway for personal taste, even foibles, but there also are canons that help to make some classifications better, more meaningful, more useful than others

Simpson (1990:107)

Superfamily, family, subfamily, tribe and subtribe names are derived from an included genus by adding the following terminations (examples from *Cervus* in parentheses): superfamily—oidea (Cervoidea); family—idae (Cervidae); subfamily—inae (Cervinae); tribe—ini (Cervini); and subtribe—ina (Cervina). There are no standard terminations for names of groups higher than superfamilies, and such names do not need to be derived from names of included genera (Simpson 1945). Not all of the possible taxa named above will be discussed in this chapter.

Many of the characters used to construct phylogenetic relationships (e.g., antlers, morphology, color) are subject to convergent or parallel evolution. Some of the characters used may not be good indicators of evolutionary change (e.g., hybridization and geographic distance). However, karyotypes and morphology provide independent assessments of phylogenetic relations of deer that generally are in agreement (Groves and Grubb 1987). Table 1, compiled from a number of sources, presents a nested classification leading to *C. elaphus*.

The Artiodactyla—hooved animals in which the axis of the foot passes between the third and fourth toes—are known from the early Eocene. The first (inner) toe is lost or vestigial; the second and fifth toes may form dewclaws. Artiodactyls have unique paraxonic limb (ankle) structure with a double-pulley astragalus (Dawson and Krishtalka 1984).

The relationships of the Cervidae to other artiodactyl families have been assessed with both mtDNA and κ-casein sequences. The deer family grouped closest to either bovids or giraffids. The pronghorn family seemed more distantly related to these groups and the pig family still more distant (Figure 3). This is in contrast to morphology of extant and fossil forms indicating that Giraffidae is a sister group to a clade (a set of species derived from a single remote ancestral species) containing Antilocapridae and Cervidae (Leinders and Hcintz 1980, Groves and Grubb 1987, Janis and Scott 1987) or a clade containing Antilocapridae and Bovidae (Stirton 1944, Simpson 1945, Romer 1966, O'Gara and

Table 1. Nested classification of *Cervus*

KINGDOM—Animalia
  SUBKINGDOM—Metazoa (many-celled)
    PHYLUM—Chordata (hollow dorsal nerve cord)
      SUBPHYLUM—Vertebrata (spinal cord protected by a backbone)
        CLASS—Mammalia (hair and mammary glands)
          ORDER—Artiodactyla (even-toed ungulates, herbivorous diet)
            SUBORDER—Ruminatia (possessing ruminant digestive system)
              FAMILY—Cervidae (true deer, antlers in most males)
                SUBFAMILY—Cervinae (*Axis, Cervus, Dama, Elaphurus,* "Old World deer")
                  GENUS—*Cervus*

Matson 1975, Hamilton 1978). Molecular taxonomy is progressing rapidly, and the current results likely will be amended as more studies are completed.

Cervidae have oligo-cotyledonary placentae and fenestrated lachrymal bullae (Harrington 1985). Adult males

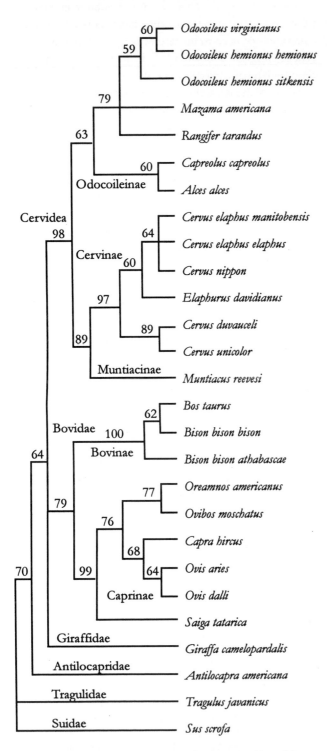

Figure 3. A strict consensus tree or dendrogram derived from phylogenetic analysis of κ-casein DNA sequences of artiodactyls (from Cronin et al. 1996). The numbers are bootstrap values.

generally have large antlers. This family has a very high degree of karyotypic evolution (Neitzel 1987). Although cervids are a young mammalian family with comparatively few recent species, no other mammalian taxon has so extreme an extent of chromosomal diversification (Fontana and Rubini 1990).

Some investigators divide the Cervidae into subfamilies according to the degree of regression of the lateral metacarpals—the Telemetacarpi and the Pleisometacarpi (Figure 4). Telemetacarpi generally are considered most primitive. This group is very diverse, including all the New World, musk, roe and water deer as well as caribou and moose. Pleisometacarpi include only the muntjacs and Cervinae (Harrington 1985). The Telemetacarpi are mostly r-strategists—primarily browser or concentrate feeders with high reproductive potential. The Pleisometacarpi (especially *Cervus*) tend to be k-strategists—generally mixed grazers/browsers with low reproductive potential. Females mature at 2 to 3 years and normally have single births.

The κ-casein DNA sequencing indicated that the subfamilies Cervinae, Muntiacinae and Odocoileinae occurred as monophyletic groups within the Cervidae, agreeing with conventional systematics for dividing the family (Figure 5). These subfamilies have distinct κ-casein lineages (Cronin et al. 1996), as well as mtDNA (Cronin 1991b), repetitive DNA

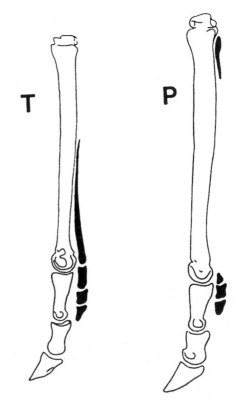

Figure 4. Diagram of the foot of Telemetacarpi (T) and Pleisometacarpi (P), showing the different degrees of lateral metacarpal regression (from Harrington 1985).

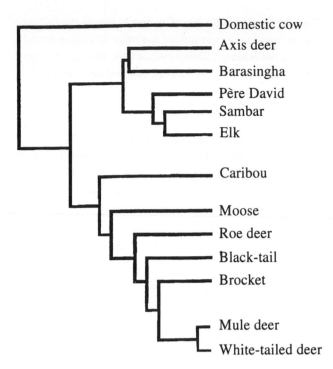

Figure 5. A dendrogram of cervid taxa generated with mtDNA distance estimates by use of the KITSCH computer program (from Cronin 1991b). This program requires the assumption of an evolutionary (molecular) clock, and that distances from the tree root to the tips are equal for all taxa.

(Lima-de-Faria et al. 1984) and allozymes (Baccus et al. 1983). Muntiacinae is particularly distinct. Therefore, little controversy seems to exist concerning the classifications leading to *Cervus* at the subfamily level or above.

In the subfamily Cervinae, the hog deer (*Axis*) and fallow deer (*Dama*), which are known to interbreed, have identical karyotypes that, in turn, are identical to those of elk and red deer (see Wurster and Benirschke 1967). The phylogenetic relationships within and among the genera of Cervinae (*Axis, Cervus, Dama* and *Elaphurus*) remain controversial (Groves and Grubb 1987), particularly within the genus *Cervus* (Putman 1988). According to Herzog (1988), the lack of electrophoretic differences between sika deer, red deer and even fallow deer in 10 enzyme systems provides evidence that these species are closely related. Also, studies of chromosomes and various other evidence suggest that the curious Père David's deer (*Elaphurus*) is closely related to *Cervus* (Cronin et al. 1996, Fontana and Rubini 1990). Harrington (1985) maintained that *Elaphurus* and *Cervus* were related closely enough that the two should be considered congeneric. Hybridization between Père David's and red deer occurs in captivity (Tate et al. 1995) and is being used in breeding programs to "improve" farmed red deer stock (see Putman 1988). However, imprinting (raising red deer

hinds with Père David's deer males) seems necessary to achieve breeding between the two species (Krzywinski 1993).

The evolutionary relationships among 10 taxa from the four genera of Cervinae were examined for comparison of their allozyme (protein) types separated by electrophoretic techniques (Emerson and Tate 1993). The findings contrast with taxonomy of these species that is based largely on studies of comparative morphology. *Cervus* split into two distinct groups, with red deer, elk and sika in one clade, and rusa and sambar (*C. timorensis* and *C. unicolor*) in another. A close genetic relationship again was indicated between Père David's and red deer, elk and sika, whereas rusa and sambar were more similar to members of the genera *Axis* and *Dama* than to other members of the *Cervus*. Lydekker (1894), Koopman (1967) and Lekagul and McNeely (1977) regarded the axis deer as *Cervus,* but Ellerman and Morrison-Scott (1951) placed them in a separate genus, *Axis,* as did Nowak and Paradiso (1983).

Karyotype information from a variety of sources may provide the most comprehensive genetic comparison of the Cervinae, according to Fontana and Rubini (1990). The karyotypes of all *Cervus* species and that of Père David's deer indicated close relationship irrespective of the phenotypic peculiarities that have caused the latter to be placed in a different genus. Karyological evidence indicates that the rusa/sambar group is distinct from the red deer/elk/sika group, although sambar and red deer have hybridized in captivity (Harrington 1973). Such captive hybridization does not necessarily indicate a very close relationship. During recent studies in New Zealand, artificial insemination of 400 red deer hinds with sambar semen resulted in only 31 pregnancies at 40 days and only one live birth (Muir et al. 1997). Gel electrophoresis of three blood proteins confirmed the live calf was a red deer × sambar hybrid, but it proved infertile (P. Muir personal communication:1998). Artificial insemination of 10 sambar females with red deer semen resulted in five pregnancies at 40 days, but none went to term.

DNA sequences indicate that *Cervus* is a paraphyletic (does not include all the descendants of its common ancestor) genus that encompasses Père David's deer when considering κ-casein (Cronin et al. 1996) and mtDNA results (Cronin 1991a). The κ-casein result suggests a clade with elk and red, sika and Père David's deer, and another with sambar and barasingha. This agrees with the allozyme but not with some mtDNA data in which red deer and sambar occur together as a clade. The κ-casein results also are consistent with allozyme data that show close relationships of red and sika deer (Baccus et al. 1983, Emerson and Tate 1993, see Cronin et al. 1996).

Thus, biochemical evidence indicates that Père David's

A one-year-old red × sambar deer hybrid created through artificial insemination of a red deer female with semen from a sambar bull at the New Zealand Pastoral Agricultural Research Institute Ltd. The purpose of such a cross was to produce a farmed deer with a longer breeding season and an improved alignment of food supply with available annual energy requirements. However, this animal proved to have vestigial ovaries (P. Muir personal communication: 1998). *Photo by Paul Muir.*

deer should be classified with *Cervus,* and either *Axis* and *Dama* should be returned to *Cervus,* or rusa and sambar should be moved to a genus reflecting their close relationship with *Axis* and, possibly, *Dama.*

Within the genus *Cervus,* males bear large antlers with all points directed forward from the main beam except for the crowns of some red deer. The neck and gait often makes these deer appear camel-like. The teeth are somewhat low crowned, according to some researchers, but A. Lister (personal communication:1997) regards them as higher crowned compared with many other cervid genera. The dental formula is: incisors—0/3; canines—1-0/1; premolars—3/3; and molars 3/3 × 2 = 32 or 34.

Species

With increasing knowledge of animals it is inevitable that two or more species thought to be distinct will be found to represent in fact only one species, or that what was supposed to be one species will be found to be two or more

Simpson (1990:28–29)

The occasional transference of species to subspecific status, and the converse are not serious disturbances so long as we keep the fundamental differentiation in mind and remember that in many cases intergradation is hypothetical and still awaits demonstration

Taverner (1920:124)

Species are groups of actually or potentially interbreeding natural populations that are reproductively isolated from other such groups. Similarities may arise by homology, parallelism, convergence, mimicry and chance. A major problem is distinguishing between homology, which reflects contiguity of descent, and convergence, which does not (Simpson 1990). Linnaeus named the red deer of Sweden *Cervus elaphus* in 1758. In 1777, Erxleben described and named the Eastern elk of North America from a specimen in Quebec as *C. e. canadensis.* In 1780, Borowski elevated this subspecies to full specific rank—*C. canadensis*—(see Hall and Kelson 1959). However, Caton (1877:337–338) wrote: "After the best investigation and consideration I have been able to give the subject—and my opportunities have not been stinted—I am inclined to fall back into the ranks of those naturalists who first compared the two animals, who failed to find sufficient differences to justify the erection of a new species to accommodate the new variety found on this continent, and I should have been well justified in dropping the specific name of *Cervus canadensis* and returning to that of *Cervus elaphus.*"

Some populations, although as different morphologically as legitimate species, interbreed indiscriminately where they come in contact. However, numerous cases have been described in which natural populations acted toward each other like legitimate species (in areas of contact) as long as their habitat was undisturbed. Yet, reproductive isolation broke down when the characteristics of these habitats were changed—usually by humans.

The European red deer was long considered a different species (*C. elaphus*) from *C. canadensis*—the American and Asian elk (often called maral, izubr or wapiti in Asia). Based partially on observations of previous researchers, such as Caton (1877) and Barclay (1934), Ellerman and Morrison-Scott (1951) and Flerov (1952), it is proposed that red deer and elk were conspecific—an idea that gained credibility as evidence was gathered on crossbreeding and the Holarctic clinal nature of morphological changes in *C. elaphus* populations reported by Caughley (1971).

Those who favor conspecific status point to fertile crossbreeding between Eurasian red deer and North American elk, especially in New Zealand (McCullough 1969, Caughley 1971, Hutton 1972, see Bryant and Maser 1982). By such classification, the specific name *elaphus* Linnaeus 1758 has priority over *canadensis* Erxleben 1777, and the Asian and North American elk now are considered *C. elaphus,* as are the whole red deer/elk complex of Eurasia.

Amino acid sequence electrophoretic studies on fibrinopeptides A and B of elk indicated the same composition as that of red deer in Sweden (Mross and Doolittle 1967). Mross and Doolittle concluded that a close relationship between red deer and elk is borne out by complete identities in both fibrinopeptides. Johnson (1968) found certain proteins from sera and hemoglobins of red deer and elk indistinguishable in their electrophoretic behavior, supporting conspecificity. Dratch and Gyllensten (1985) indicated that an electrophoretic survey of 28 enzyme loci in 388 animals showed significant differences, but supported the argument that red deer and elk should be considered subspecies of *C. elaphus.* They indicated that genetic distances were less than those found in similar comparisons between European and North American moose and caribou.

Sixteen cranial characters among 250 adult North American and 24 Eurasian *C. elaphus* were analyzed by Schonewald (1994:431). She concluded: "Major intercontinental differences do exist between clinal extremes in behavior, in cranial size and sexual dimorphism in addition to semilethal F_1 hybridization. All suggest *C. elaphus* and North American *Cervus* are different species." Also, based on mtDNA—without intermediate subspecies—Polziehn and Strobeck (1998) proposed that elk and red deer should not be considered conspecific.

Hemoglobin from North American elk has a higher isoelectric point than that of red deer. Dratch (1986) used isoelectric focusing—confirmed by starch gel electrophoresis—on blood samples from 159 red deer, 27 North American elk and 38 F_1 crossbreeds from red deer hinds sired by elk bulls in an effort to find a biochemical marker that could discriminate among the three groups. All red deer × elk F_1 crossbreeds tested showed a double-banding pattern representing both parental types. This blood test is useful to verify crossbreeding in farmed elk or in wild populations, and should be helpful in studies of other *C. elaphus* subspecies. Other genetic differences have been reported.

Dratch et al. (1992) found two plasma proteins, transferin and post-transferin, useful in differentiating red deer

Top: first cross (F_1) red deer × elk crossbreeds on a New Zealand farm. Improved yields of meat and velvet antler are the purposes of most such crosses. Note somewhat intermediate characteristics of tails, rump patches (high on the croup, but different coloration on the dorsal portion) and sparse mane. *Bottom:* red deer × elk crossbreeds in New Zealand. These animals show more elk than red deer characteristics. Except for the antlers, they could pass for elk. *Photos by Bruce Banwell.*

Red deer females, such as the Norwegian red deer cow (*left*), on an island off the coast of Norway, do not have manes, unlike cow elk (*right*). Note longer ears on the red deer, compared with the elk's ears. This may reflect the former's greater requirement for hearing acuity in a forested environment. *Photos by Bart W. O'Gara.*

and elk. Stern et al. (1992) indicated that the group-specific component vitamin D-binding globulin was as discriminating between red deer and elk as was the hemoglobin method reported by Dratch (1986). Also, Tate et al. (1992) reported that the frequency of three alleles of C3c were different in New Zealand (European) farmed red deer and elk introduced from North America.

Red deer occupy the western-most portion of the species' geographic distribution, generally using dense cover extensively, and are one extreme for the species in adaptation. They are saltatorial/cursorial runners with a mixed feeding strategy and considerable weight dimorphism between sexes. High sexual dimorphism is typical of mixed and concentrate feeders in semi-open landscapes (Geist and Bayer 1988). In weights reported by Dzieciolowski (1970) for 4-year-old and older red deer in Poland, cows weighed only 55% as much as bulls—139 pounds (63 kg) compared to 254 pounds (115 kg). In red deer, only males have neck manes, which are smaller and shorter haired than those of elk. Red deer are quite uniform in color. The tail is about the length of the ear and contains a scent gland (Murie 1951). Female red deer crouch when urinating. The rump patch is comparatively small and a line of dark hair, continuing onto the tail, bisects it dorsally (Figure 6). Red deer bulls retain their antlers, which have radial terminal branching, for only about 150 days (Geist 1982). Cows have a gestation period of about 232 days. Red deer, generally, are quite nervous and difficult to handle in captivity (A. Moodie personal communication:1995, Geist 1998).

In red deer, roaring is largely restricted to harem-holding bulls during the rut according to Clutton-Brock and Albon (1979). However, Banwell (2000) witnessed and heard roaring from eastern European red deer cows. Roars are produced by vibration of the larynx caused by exhaling rapidly. One to three roars typically are given on the same exhalation, and bulls may average two roars per minute throughout the day. The roar of red deer sounds like a combination of roaring by an African lion and bellowing of a domestic bull when challenging another bull. Sonograms by Nikolski and Wallschläger (1983) indicated that European red deer roaring consists of many harmonics (see Chapter 7).

On the other hand, elk occupy the eastern part of the species' geographic distribution, using open country extensively where humans allow it, and are the other extreme in adaptation for the species. They are open country cursors and, generally, are grazers when grasses and forbs are avail-

Figure 6.   Rump patches of European red deer (*left*), sika deer (*center*) and North American elk (*right*). Rump patches of intermediate taxa in Asia generally are intermediate and reflect relationships with other taxa. *Illustration by Bart W. O'Gara.*

Red deer tend to be uniform in color as illustrated by the bull (*left*) of wild-caught stock on a New Zealand farm. He probably carries genes from at least Scotland and Germany. Elk (*right*) tend to have dark-colored heads, necks, bellies and legs in contrast to their light-colored bodies. *Left photo by Bart W. O'Gara. Right photo by Leonard Lee Rue III.*

able. They have reduced weight sexual dimorphism—a characteristic of animals in open habitat (Geist and Bayer 1988). In weights reported by Quimby and Johnson (1951), Blood and Lovaas (1966) and Flook (1970), cows were 77% to 78% as heavy as bulls. Both bulls and cows have extensive neck manes and, like other open-country ungulates, are quite colorful. Even calves in their first adult coats grow manes. Bodies are light, whereas their heads, manes, bellies and legs are dark—sometimes almost black. The large rump patch generally is not divided by a dorsal line and varies from almost white to almost orange. The short (about half the length of the ear) tail is the same color as the rump patch (Figure 6) and contains a smaller scent gland than that of red deer. Elk tend to quickly adjust to captivity and become tractable, but they resist being chased and will turn on humans (Pearse 1992, Geist 1998).

Elk cows not only are more nearly the same size as bulls, they have other malelike characteristics. Besides having manes, cows do not crouch to urinate, occasionally carry antlers and sometimes bugle (Murie 1951).

Elk bulls retain their antlers, which have linear terminal branching, for about 185 days—35 days longer than do red deer (Geist 1982), and cows have a gestation period of about 248 days—16 days longer than red deer.

The rutting call of the North American elk, its most fa-

mous call, is the bugle of the bull (Boyd 1978). This call varies with age and conditions. Normally, the bugle begins on a low note, slides upward until it reaches high, clear, buglelike notes, which are prolonged, then drops quickly to a final grunt. The call frequently is followed by a series of grunts. Murie (1932:334) represents the call thus:"A-a-a-a-ai-e-eeeeeeeee-eough!e-uh!e-uh!e-uh!e-uh!" A reedy quality changes rapidly as the high note is struck. A deep resonance from the capacious chest accompanies it all. At close range, the low notes are clearly heard. At a distance, the low, hoarse notes are lost to the ear to a great extent, and the high bugle notes are especially clear, much like a whistle (see Chapter 7).

Why cows bugle is unknown, but it may involve the feeling or hormonal state caused by the approach of parturition (Murie 1951).

Rutting calls are related to affinities among subspecies, or supposed subspecies. Crossbreeds between red deer and elk often utter intermediate calls, as do some central Asian taxa—apparently close relatives of the stock from which red deer and elk evolved. Nikolski and Wallschläger (1983) analyzed the intermediate whistle of the Bactrian red deer, and their sonograms showed two frequencies or frequency parts.

All *C. elaphus* have hollow hair that is long and coarse. Shedding in most subspecies takes place twice a year—during spring and autumn. The few subspecies that molt only once a year occupy cold, high altitude ranges of the Tibeto-Himalayan region, where summers are very short. Before the rut, red deer stags develop manes of longer hair than that on the body, and their necks swell (Whitehead 1993). The rump patches of various subspecies of red deer vary in size and color, but as previously indicated, are smaller than the rump patches of elk.

Other differences between red deer and elk were noted by Banwell (1991a) as follows, using the elk as the standard of difference. Ears of elk are comparatively short. The elk's muffle (fleshy bare part of the upper lip) is narrower at the base—not extending laterally underneath for more than one-third of the lower nostril; in red deer, it is larger. The heels of the elk's front hooves are separated or loosely united at their bases; those of red deer tend to be closely united at their bases. The mane of elk is silken to the touch, whereas that of red deer feels coarse and stiff. In some elk, particularly bulls, a hump is evident above the shoulders; it is not so evident in red deer, if discernable at all. While feeding or standing alert, elk tend to hold their tails horizontally; red deer hold theirs against their bodies, unless excreting.

Widespread species may have terminal populations that behave toward each other as distinct species, although they are connected by a chain of interbreeding populations (Mayr 1970). Red deer and elk are morphologically, ecologically and behaviorally quite different. They are not presently connected by interbreeding populations—although the intermediate subspecies will crossbreed in captivity and under disturbed habitat conditions—but by a mosaic of intermediate populations. Some of those might have interbred in the

Red deer bulls do not grow extensive manes except before the rut. Also, not only do occasional adults show spotting reminiscent of sika deer, but red deer calves retain spots longer than do elk calves. *Photo by Leonard Lee Rue III.*

wild before the human reduction of deer numbers eliminated connecting populations, especially in Asia and eastern Europe.

In conclusion, red deer and elk differ in many characteristics, blood proteins are different enough to differentiate between the two groups, and their crossbreeding is hardly a natural phenomenon. Crossbreeding of introduced animals in a country without predators, such as New Zealand, does not necessarily mean red deer and elk would produce a viable population of crossbreeds in either of their native habitats. Thus, combining them seems to stretch the species concept rather thin.

On the other hand, no interbreeding cline now exists between red deer and elk, but intermediate forms progress across Asia—a strong argument for conspecific status. Also, if elk and red deer were considered separate species, the intermediate populations would present a taxonomic nightmare. To determine how many species to recognize and to identify subspecies within those species would require many arbitrary decisions.

If, at some future date, findings prompt reversion to *C. elaphus* and *C. canadensis,* consideration should be directed toward naming a third species. The deer of western Asia and the Himalayas seem to form a quite distinct group, somewhat intermediate to red deer and elk. B. Banwell (personal communication:1997) called this group maraloids as opposed to Atlantics or elaphoids of western and central Europe and North Africa, and wapitoids—the elk and elk-like deer of Asia and North America.

Taxonomy is in something of a state of flux. New and more sophisticated biochemical findings frequently are reported. Also, opportunities to study and test the intermediate populations are increasing. Thus, any change at this time seems premature, and red deer and elk should continue to be considered conspecific.

Subspecies

For evolutionary study and descriptive purposes, many kinds of variation come into consideration, but the only regular infraspecific taxon is the subspecies. Subspecies are widely but not universally useful, and problems of their definition yield to the same sorts of criteria as for dividing other phylogenetic continua.

Simpson (1990:147–148)

Taxonomy can be very complicated, especially if one tries to distinguish between races or subspecies. In recent years, however, the tendency has been to lump groups together, rather than split them into smaller categories

Gilbert (1978a:3)

Too many subspecies of deer are recognized, including those within the genus *Cervus* (Groves and Grubb 1987). Morphological differences in size and shape that are much affected by nutrition are of little value taxonomically. Unfortunately, this includes cranial measurements (Geist 1989a) and the size and shape of antlers, except on robust adults. Good taxonomic criteria must be based on hereditary factors that are expressed despite the environment.

Lengths of tooth rows and tooth morphology are criteria (generally considered little affected by nutrition) often used in classifying small mammals. Unfortunately, such data seldom have been recorded for large samples from subspecies of *C. elaphus*. Also, the numbers of skins and skulls available for study in museums are limited. A museum that has hundreds of study skins and skulls of a given subspecies of small rodent may have none or a couple of a large ungulate. Thus, although thousands of red deer and elk are killed annually by hunters, and the animals' behaviors are well studied, conventional taxonomic criteria are scarce.

Wallace (1915a) maintained that the distribution of *C. elaphus* could clearly be traced along a southern and western line from the Himalayas to Europe, and a northern and eastern line from the Tien Shan to the Rocky Mountains. The latter line of travel now is inundated by the Bering Strait, and desert has obliterated the ancient river system formerly linking Transcaspian forests with those of the Himalayas. Upthrust of the Tibetan Plateau severed the elaphine stock into two principal branches along the line of the Gobi depression. The southern branch found a center of evolution in the Himalayas, while the northern branch—ancestors of elk—found a center of evolution in the Siberian watershed. This seems an oversimplification, but is a useful concept to keep in mind when trying to understand relationships among the many variations of *C. elaphus*.

The subspecies of *C. elaphus* can be segregated by size and color of the tail and rump patch or caudal disk, the presence and extent of neck manes in males and females, the distribution of body color, spotting and the antler morphology (Dolan 1988). These are essentially the social insignia Geist (1989a, 1990) found important in specific and subspecific classification of deer. According to Ryder (1986), a combination of information—including morphology, behavior, natural history, distribution, and mitochondrial and nuclear genetic data—should be used in classification below the species level.

Mutations, genetic drift due to small population size and natural selection favoring adaptations to local environmental conditions eventually lead to genetic differentiation of local populations. Gene flow—the movement of individuals or groups of individuals from population to population—may either constrain evolution by preventing adaptation to local conditions or promote evolution by spreading new genes and combinations of genes throughout the range of a species (Slatkin 1987). Geographic distribution of *C. elaphus* being wide, phenotypic variations are numerous and the range of those variations are broad. Despite extensive study, and more extensive speculation, the subspecific structure has not been completely explained (Groves and Grubb 1987). An extensive literature search, plus on-the-ground observations have convinced me that much of this problem relates to mixing of subspecies through translocations, local extirpations that mask continuity of natural populations, and the political and physical problems of doing research in central Asia. The *C. elaphus* of Asia seem to act as legitimate subspecies where they and their habitat are undisturbed by humans, but mixing now seems fairly common.

Disagreement among evolutionary taxonomists is not over the question of whether species have distinguishable geographic subgroups—most of them obviously do—but about the practicability and advisability of recognizing such subgroups as taxa and naming them as trinomials (subspecies) in the usual formal classifications, according to Simpson (1990). Simpson also indicated that it is no argument against subspecific classification that recognizable subgroups do not occur in all species and the subspecies is a nonobligate category that need not be used; also subspecies often are arbitrary. Classification below the species level often has been subjective because there are no standard criteria for naming subspecies or populations. However, most investigators agree that subspecies designations should be based on phylogenetic relationships, the same as for species (see Bryant and Maser 1982, Ryder 1986, Avise 1989, O'Brien and Mayr 1991, Cronin 1993). In practice, they seldom are.

P. Dratch (personal communication:1997) proposed, as follows, a contemporary approach to classifying subspecies: (1) subspecies initially named on the basis of morphometric characteristics should be retained unless additional analysis by morphological, biochemical or molecular methods indicate that two groups do not show significant genetic differences; (2) when two independent methods show significant genetic differentiation (for example, morphology and biochemical tests on Roosevelt elk), such subspecies distinctions should be maintained; and (3) because these are subspecies and not species differences, sometimes it will not be possible for every member of a subspecies to have significant coherence.

However, when subspecies become legal entities, individuals must be classified with a particular taxon. The confidence of that assignment will depend on the particular characteristics (whether they be alleles or attributes of antlers) of the individual elk.

C. elaphus antlers are highly variable—individually and geographically. In exceptional cases in several subspecies, the tines per side may exceed 20. Diversity also is seen in length, weight, size of tines, their position in relation to each other and shape of main beam. Antlers may be fairly vertical and close-set or widely spread. Individual variability in structure of antlers is fairly high, but each subspecies has a characteristically predominant antler type that is somewhat diagnostic in subspecific classification. Heptner et al. (1961) believed that *C. elaphus* is distinctly separable into three groups—Western, Siberian and Middle Asiatic—corresponding to the three antler types (elaphoid, elk and hangul) described earlier. The principal problem with using antlers in classification is that only the antlers of adult bulls in good habitat fully express the characteristics of a subspecies.

Fontana and Rubini (1990) listed 17 articles in which chromosome maps of various *C. elaphus* subspecies had been published. All but one supposed subspecies yielded a diploid chromosome number of 68 and had 32 pairs of acrocentric (rod-shaped chromosomes with the centromere at or near one of the ends), and one medium-sized pair of metacentric (with the centromere somewhat centrally located—characteristic of chromosomes that are J- or V-shaped during metaphase) autosomes. The sex chromosomes were similar in all subspecies studied—the X chromosome large and acrocentric and the Y small and metacentric. The exception will be discussed under *C. e. bactrianus.*

Animals for which chromosome maps were available and for which authors provided place of origin, came from Sweden (Gustavsson and Sundt 1968), America (Koulischer et al. 1972, Platt and Soukup 1977, Saskatchewan Research Council unpublished data), Gansu Province, China and Manchuria (Wang et al. 1982), Siberia (Graphodatsky and Radjabli 1985), northeastern Italy (Goldoni et al. 1984) and Germany (Herzog 1987). Thus, karyotypes seem of little value at the level of subspecies, except that it will be very interesting if the chromosome number proves to be truly different in *C. e. bactrianus.*

Civilization has greatly reduced overall numbers and restricted distribution of *C. elaphus.* Populations now are mostly isolated and small, and subspecies, especially in Eurasia, often have been mixed through introductions into hunting reserves and "antler farms." Surprisingly, after studying 12 European red deer populations—including one red deer × sika deer hybrid population—Herzog (1991) concluded that mixing of animals from different origins does not necessarily mean increased genetic variability.

Numbers of red deer and elk subspecies vary greatly, depending on the classifications of splitters and lumpers. Whitaker (1970) would not recognize populations located along segments of geographic clines as subspecies. This concept is followed here, and an average specimen from a subspecies must be recognizable—phenotypically or genotypically—from other subspecies. "It is not useful to set up a classification in which groups with different names can not be distinguished" (Simpson 1945:17).

Descriptions and Ranges of Presumed Subspecies

Figures 7 through 11 provide placenames used in discussing ranges of subspecies. Not because so many subspecies should be recognized, but because a basis is needed for discussing the combination of subspecies, the most commonly recognized extant *C. elaphus* subspecies (generally following Dolan 1988, Trense 1989 and Whitehead 1993) are listed in Figures 12 and 13 and below. Subspecies are listed and discussed roughly as they occur from west to east. This facilitated discussing and comparing similar subspecies. Supposed subspecies are in close approximation in places. Whitehead (1993) treated the elk in his list as *C. canadensis,* but it was modified to *C. elaphus* to be consistent with the rest of the chapter. Common synonyms are in parentheses after the area. For historic and present distribution of elk in North America, see Chapter 2.

Cervus elaphus

 scoticus—(Lönnberg 1906) England, Ireland and Scotland

 atlanticus—(Lönnberg 1906) southwestern Norway

 elaphus—(Linnaeus 1758) southern Sweden (*typicus,* Lydekker 1898)

 hippelaphus—(Erxleben 1777) continental Europe (*germanicus,* Desmarst 1822, *montanus,* Botezat 1903, *Brauneri,* Charlemagne 1920)

 hispanicus—(Hilzheimer 1909) Spain and Portugal (*bolivari,* Cabrera 1911)

 corsicanus—(Erxleben 1777) Corsica and Sardinia (*minor,* Wagner 1855)

 barbarus—(Bennett 1833) northern Africa

 maral—(Gray 1850) Asia Minor

 bactrianus—(Lydekker 1900) northern Afghanistan, Tajikistan, Turkmenistan, Uzbekistan

 yarkandensis— (Blanford 1892) Xinjiang Province, China

 wallichi—(Cuvier 1823) eastern Tibet, possibly Bhutan (*affinis,* Hogson 1841)

 hanglu—(Wagner 1844) Kashmir

 macneilli—(Lydekker 1909) Tibetan/Chinese border area

 kansuensis—(Pocock 1912) Gansu to Shanxi provinces, China and surrounding areas

 alashanicus—(Bobrinskii and Flerov 1935) border of southeastern Inner Mongolia and Ningxi Province, China

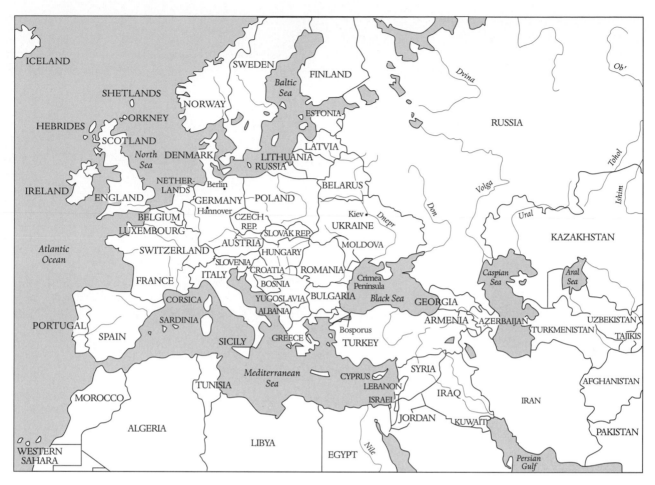

Figure 7.   Europe and the Middle East, with political names used in this chapter. *Map produced and provided by the Rocky Mountain Elk Foundation.*

songaricus—(Severtzov 1873) Tien Shan and surroundings

sibiricus—(Severtzov 1873) Altai to Transbaikalia and western Outer Mongolia (*asiaticus,* Lydekker 1898, *wachei,* Noack 1902)

xanthopygus—(Milne-Edwards 1867) northeastern Asia

roosevelti—(Merriam 1897) coastal areas of northern California to Vancouver Island

nannodes—(Merriam 1905) Sacramento and San Joaquin valleys of central California

manitobensis—(Millais 1915) Saskatchewan and southwestern Manitoba

nelsoni—(Bailey 1935) Rocky Mountains

In the descriptions of presumed subspecies that follow, measurements, coloration, antlers, ranges and status are from Dolan (1988), unless otherwise stated. Length and circumference of the largest antlers listed in the 1997 Safari Club International's record book of trophy animals (Schwabland 1997), as well as the inside spread and total number of tines for that trophy, will be listed for each sub-

species if available. Sample sizes are not large, but measurements are of large, wild bulls. These measurements and numbers will be noted as Safari Club International records. Schwabland (1997) endeavored to ensure that trophy candidates were not crossbreeds, but the possibility exists of crossing at some time past for virtually all extant trophy red deer. Measurements could not be found for females of most subspecies, and weights often were not available for either sex. When weights are given only for bulls, elk cows can be estimated to weigh about 73% as much elk bulls and red deer cows are about 56% as heavy as red deer bulls (Geist and Bayer 1988). What weight differences there are in subspecies of the Middle East and western Asia are unknown. Variations in size, color and antlers always are present, even within closely related members of small populations. General coloration is especially variable by season and may change rapidly at different times of year. Also, individual observers see colors differently, especially subtle shades and mixtures of browns, reds and grays. Thus, general coloration is given primarily as interesting information with minor importance as a taxonomic criterion.

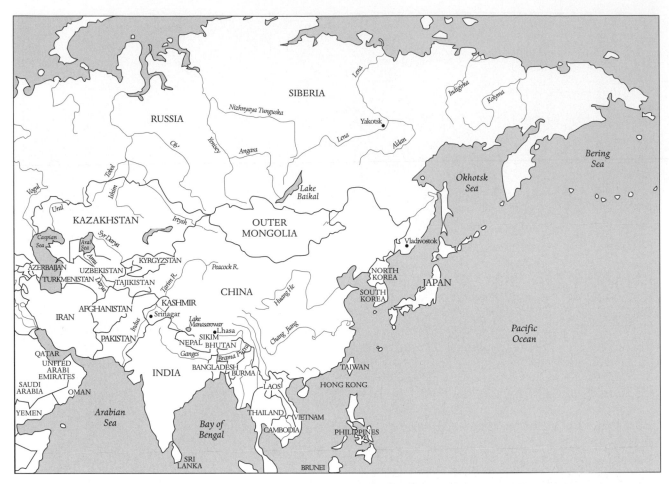

Figure 8.   Asia, with political names used in this chapter. *Map produced and provided by the Rocky Mountain Elk Foundation.*

"European red deer subspecies may no longer exist because of genetic pollution. This is more than a mere impediment to an academic interpretation of the evolution of this species; the difficulties in establishing specimen identity make it difficult to protect remnant populations from illegal exploitation"(Geist 1998:173).

C. e. scoticus

The Scottish red deer is a small subspecies in most of its native habitat, standing about 43 inches (110 cm) at the shoulder and weighing 170 to 220 pounds (77–100 kg) (McElroy 1989), with females being somewhat shorter and about 45% lighter in weight. Introduced into good habitat in New Zealand, the Scottish red deer changed from a small subspecies with poor antlers to a large subspecies that produced handsome trophies (Donne 1924).

Considerable variation among individuals is seen in the intensity of body coloration as well as the amount of gray in the pelage. The insides of all four legs are white with an admixture of reddish hair. The rump patch is rather narrow. The lower two-thirds usually is white, whereas the upper one-third, including the tail, is fox red, lighter than the

Antlers of Scottish red deer on good habitat in New Zealand are large, and usually carry six to eight points per side. The Safari Club International record for Scotland was 37 inches (94 cm) long, with a circumference of 9 inches (23 cm) and inside spread of 52 inches (132 cm). The trophy carried 25 points and was shot in 1993. *Photo by Bruce Banwell.*

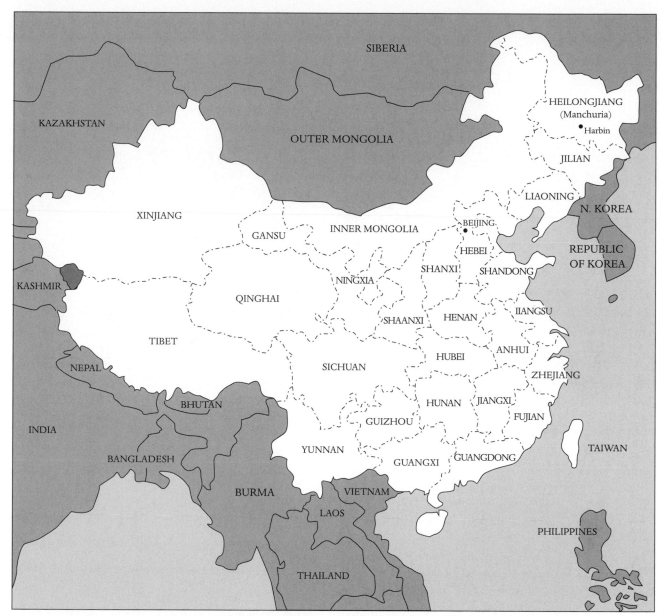

Figure 9.   China, with political names used in this chapter. *Map produced and provided by the Rocky Mountain Elk Foundation.*

coloration of the croup. The lower half of the patch is edged by darker hairs, more conspicuous in some individuals than in others, but the patch seldom is completely framed. A dark brown dorsal stripe extends from about the crown of the head to the level of the shoulder. Because the body coloration is darker during winter, the edging of the rump patch seems to disappear. An ocular ring is present in both sexes. This subspecies is quite distinct in coloration from the red deer of Sweden and central Europe.

During winter, the coat of both sexes is a dark gray-brown with a reddish cast. The lower neck, breast, face and belly have infusions of grayish hairs. Summer pelage changes to a bright, reddish, cinnamon brown, with very little color dimorphism obvious between the sexes. The

forelegs and lower portions of the hind legs often are lighter colored than the body because of an admixture of whitish hairs. The face, lower neck and rear surface of the ears are gray. The belly appears whitish, but has an admixture of reddish hairs.

The main concentrations are in the mountains of Scotland north of about 56 degrees latitude and many of the west coast islands (Whitehead 1982). Native stocks apparently persist only in County Kerry of Ireland and in Scotland and northwestern England (see Harrington 1973). Even in those areas, some crossbreeding has occurred according to B. Banwell (personal communication:1997). The integrity of the Ireland red deer subspecies began diminishing in 1244, when Norman barons introduced red deer

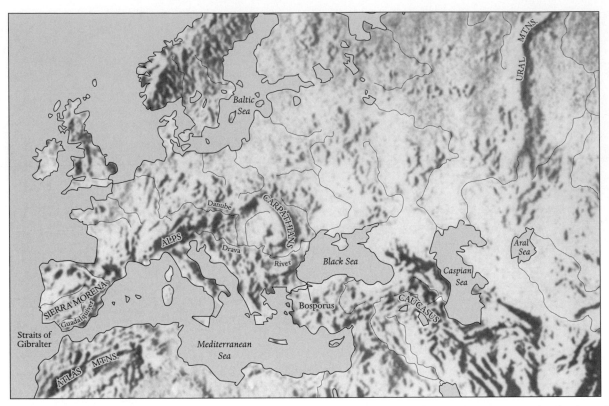

Figure 10. Europe and the Middle East, with names of mountains and bodies of water used in this chapter. *Map produced and provided by the Rocky Mountain Elk Foundation.*

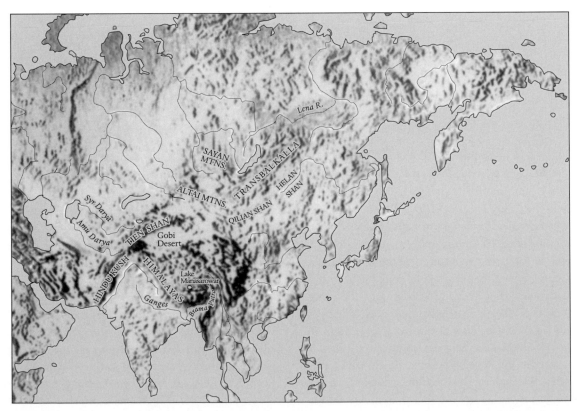

Figure 11. Asia, with names of mountains and bodies of water used in this chapter. *Map produced and provided by the Rocky Mountain Elk Foundation.*

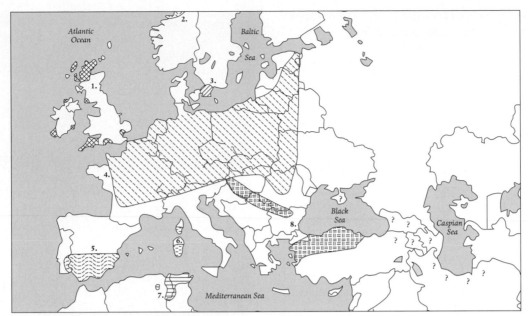

Figure 12. Ranges of presumptive subspecies of red deer (*Cervus elaphus*) in Europe, North Africa and the Middle East (primarily from Whitehead 1993). 1. *C. e. scoticus* (British Isles); 2. *C. e. atlanticus* (Norway); 3. *C. e. elaphus* (Sweden); 4. *C. e. hippelaphus* (Europe); 5. *C. e. hispanicus* (Spain); 6. *C. e. corsicanus* (Corsica and Sardinia); 7. *C. e. barbarus* (North Africa); and 8. *C. e. maral* (eastern Europe and Asia Minor). Ranges shown for *C. e. elaphus* and *C. e. hippelaphus* reflect historic distribution more than present. Small and large populations are scattered (some of them fenced) throughout the areas, and most animals are crossbreeds. The area to the east, particularly in Russia, has scattered herds in what apparently was historic range of *C. e. elaphus* (*C. e. hippelaphus*); most are fenced, but few—if any—are native. Many of those herds have been crossed with Asiatic or North American elk. Also, historic data indicate that *C. e. maral* was found in the Crimea, around the southern coast of the Caspian Sea and in the Caucasus. However, recent travelers in those areas indicate that the animals resemble *C. e. elaphus* (*C. e. hippelaphus*). Translocations may have replaced or mixed with the native deer. *Map produced and provided by the Rocky Mountain Elk Foundation.*

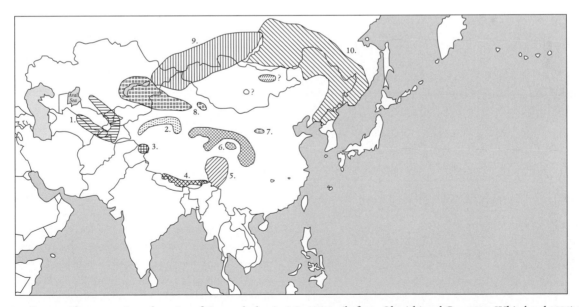

Figure 13. Ranges of presumptive subspecies of *Cervus elaphus* in Asia (primarily from Ohtaishi and Gao 1990, Whitehead 1993). 1. *C. e. bactrianus* (North Afghanistan, Russian Turkmenestan, Uzbekistan); 2. *C. e. yarkandensis* (Chinese Turkestan); 3. *C. e. hanglu* (Kashmir); 4. *C. e. wallichi* (East Tibet); 4. *C. e. affinis* (East Tibet); 5. *C. e. macneilli* (Tibetan/Chinese border); 6. *C. e. kansuensis* Gansu, (China, and vicinity); 7. *C. e. alashanicus* (Ninaxia Province, China); 8. *C. e. songaricus* (Tien Shan and vicinity); 9. *C. e. asiaticus* (Altai to Transbaikalia); and 10. *C. e. xanthopygus* (eastern Siberia, Manchuria and Outer Mongolia). As shown, the range of *C. e. bactrianus* is merely an approximation based on fragmentary reports. Apparently, the animals are in small, scattered groups within the area shown. *Map produced and provided by the Rocky Mountain Elk Foundation.*

from mainland Europe, and additional introductions apparently were made up to the mid-19th century.

C. e. atlanticus

The Norwegian red deer is similar in size to the red deer of Scotland. During summer, the upper portion of the body is colored like that of the Scottish deer, but with a greater intensity of gray-brown on the neck and foreparts of the shoulders; the face is of the same shade but is not quite as dark. The front and hind legs are colored like the neck, becoming darker brown on the anterior surfaces of the forelegs and on the lower portions of the hind legs. In winter, the coat changes to grayish-brown. The forehead and ears are dark, reddish-brown, as is the dorsal stripe, which forms a dark patch on the croup. The belly is white with an admixture of gray and reddish hairs. The tail is a fox red color the year-round and may have a dark line on the dorsal surface.

Norwegian red deer frequent steep, wooded mountainsides during spring and summer, but take advantage of the mild, coastal climate during winter. They range primarily between Boknfjorden in the south and Namjos in the north, including many large and small islands off the coast. Their range seems to be increasing, and wandering animals appear away from their main center of distribution, according to Whitehead (1982).

The Norwegian red deer's antlers are similar to those of the Scottish red deer, being somewhat thin and with a total number of points seldom exceeding 14, less than those in central and southeastern Europe. This could reflect a subspecific characteristic or simply the influence of climatic and habitat conditions in Scotland and coastal Norway. *Photo by Bart W. O'Gara.*

C. e. elaphus

The Swedish red deer is a comparatively large subspecies. Weights of 660 pounds (300 kg) and shoulder heights reaching 55 inches (140 cm) have been reported for bulls (Dolan 1988). As in other red deer, cows weigh only about 55% as much as bulls. Because these animals live near cultivated fields and sometimes feed in them, their heavy weights may reflect good nutrition.

Females are more brightly colored than males. The dorsal surface of the face, from the muzzle to between the ears, upper surface of the neck, upper shoulder and trunk to approximately the center of the flank are dark, dull red. The sides of the face, lower neck, breast and belly are dark blue-gray. The lower shoulder and forelegs are blue-gray mixed with fox red. A dark patch separates the color of the trunk from that of the belly. From the middle of the flanks down the length of the hind legs, the blue-gray coloration is mixed with reddish hairs. A white line encircles the tops

The rump patch of the Norwegian red deer is large and reddish, margined by dark brown hairs that vary in intensity of color. The entire rump patch, or only its lower half, may be framed. *Photo by Bruce Banwell.*

The antlers of Swedish red deer are large and robust in adults, tending to crown formation. *Photo by Anders Jarnemo.*

of the hooves. Light ocular rings are present in both sexes at all seasons. Females generally have a more distinct edging to the rump patch than do males.

In summer, the pelage of both sexes changes to a reddish-yellow, which is rather uniform over the entire body, although somewhat lighter on the legs. There is no appreciable difference in color between the sexes. The rump patch is almost the same color as the body. The dorsal stripe, which is dark brown, extends from between the ears to the level of the croup. In some individuals, white spots parallel the dorsal stripe.

During winter, males are a more or less uniform dark brown—darkest on the legs, flanks, belly and neck. The sides of the face are somewhat lighter, whereas the anterior portion of the face, from the eye to the muzzle, is similar in color to the body. The rump patch varies from light fox red to yellowish-red. In bulls, the dark border may be lacking or very indistinct. The population of pure native Swedish red deer apparently amounts to only several hundred animals, owing primarily to lack of habitat and damage to agricultural crops in southern Sweden (Whitehead 1982). Trense (1989) indicated the presence of about 2,000 red deer in Sweden. Like the Scottish red deer, the Swedish variety has been extensively subjected to crossbreeding with red deer from mainland Europe.

C. e. hippelaphus

The central European red deer is a medium- to large-sized subspecies, standing approximately 47 to 49 inches (120–125 cm) at the shoulder and reportedly weighing 220 to 772 pounds (100–350 kg), depending on location and quality of forage. Some of the larger, heavier animals reported could be *C. e. maral* or crosses with that subspecies.

The winter coat is brown with a reddish cast, although there is considerable variation between individual animals. At the height of winter, a dark brown dorsal stripe is broad on the neck. In males, the lower portion and sides of the neck vary in color from reddish-brown to deep brown, and the hairs form a mane that is most prominent during the rut. The lower portions of the hind legs and the entirety of the forelegs are lighter in color than is the body, often with a grayish cast. The insides of all four legs vary from white to grayish-white. Females are similarly colored, although the face and lower neck are decidedly gray in color.

The summer coat is considerably different. In females, which are more brightly colored, the pelage is a reddish-cinnamon on the dorsal surface of the neck and shoulders, extending back over the trunk onto the flanks. On the lower flanks, the color changes to a silvery grayish-white, lightest on the lower legs. The forelegs from the lower part of the shoulder, as well as the breast, are grayish-white with a slightly reddish wash. The sides and ventral surface of the body and sides of the face are light bluish-gray. The forehead and the area between the ears are fox red. A light ocular ring is present during both seasons. Adult males are darker than females, with an admixture of brown hairs on the sides and lower portion of the neck. The dorsal stripe, extending from between the ears along the back, is darker than the body, but not as dark as in winter. The rump coloration is lighter during summer, and the framing of dark hairs is less apparent, particularly along the upper border. The line dividing the rump patch often is invisible during summer.

Distribution is patchy, but this subspecies occurs from the Normandy coast to the Ukraine, from Denmark to southern France and from Estonia to Romania, but few—if

The upper portion of the rump patch of the European red deer is fox red, as is the tail. The lower portion grades to white between the buttocks. Some individuals have a greater proportion of white hairs in the upper portion of the patch. A fox red line divides the rump patch, which is framed by dark brown hairs. The animals exhibit extensive individual variation, but often carry 12 to 14 points per antler. Antlers from 1400 to 1700 AD, when these animals roamed the greater part of Europe east to the Don and Volga rivers, were huge. Some were up to 50 inches (127 cm) long, with circumferences up to 10 inches (25.4 cm). The spread on one was 74 inches (188 cm). Some heads carried 24 to 50 points (Lydekker 1898). B. Banwell (personal communication:1996) expressed belief that the only pure stock of this subspecies are those in the Royal Danish Park at Jaegersborg, where this photo was taken. The first 25 trophies listed for this subspecies in Safari Club International records are from game ranches or areas of Europe where mixing with *C. e. maral* is likely. The next trophy, from Denmark, had an antler 40 inches (102 cm) long and 10 inches (25 cm) in circumference. The inside spread was 37 inches (94 cm), and the trophy carried 20 tines. *Photo by Bruce Banwell.*

any—areas have not received transplants from other areas. They now are found mostly in forested, hilly country, but will occupy almost any habitat they are allowed to invade.

C. e. hispanicus

The Spanish red deer is one of the smaller subspecies, with bulls standing about 44 inches (112 cm) at the shoulder and weighing 180 to 220 pounds (82–100 kg). On males, a dark dorsal stripe is conspicuous on the neck to about the level of the shoulders. It then fades along the midline of the back, bisecting the rump patch to the root of the tail. The lower legs, flanks and belly are earth brown.

Females are much lighter in color, being pinkish-fawn

This Spanish red deer bull in southern Spain roared almost constantly throughout the rut. During winter, males are grayish-brown with a purple sheen on the face, shoulders, trunk, upper flanks and croup. The latter may have an admixture of darker brown hairs. The neck, lower jaw and rear surfaces of the ears are fawn brown, and creamy white ocular rings are apparent on the dark face. *Photo by Bruce Banwell.*

gray on the upper surfaces of the face and neck, shoulders, trunk and flanks. Hairs that edge the dorsal line have a reddish cast. On the croup, an admixture of sepia hairs forms a dark patch. The interior surfaces of the legs are whitish, whereas the exterior surfaces are lighter than the body, having a strong pinkish cast. Sides of the face and the lower surface of the neck are light bluish-gray. Ocular rings are less conspicuous on the light-colored face than on that of bulls. The rump patch also is less intense in color. During summer, the pelage of both sexes varies from dark cinnamon to sorrel on the upper neck, shoulders, trunk and thighs. This color darkens to a clearer brown on all four legs. The lower portion of the neck and face are deep bluish-gray.

Antlers generally form a crown—sometimes by lateral branching of the fourth tine and sagittal branching of the elongated fifth (terminal) tine. The bez tends to be large and low on the beam, and the trez is short. These antlers often resemble those of *C. e. angulatus,* a fossil form from the Saale (formerly called Riss) Glacial Period of Europe. Unlike European red deer bulls, the neck hair is neither darker nor longer than that of the body, except for the red-brown mid-dorsal stripe on the neck.

These deer are found in southern Spain—an area known as Andalucia—and on the Sierra Morena, occupying overstocked range with scattered cork oak and alder trees. Large areas of sterile rock and scree are interspersed with shoulder high thickets of sticky-leaved, thorny shrubs (Whitehead 1982).

The upper portion of the rump patch and the upper surface of the tail of Spanish red deer are pale ochre, as seen on these bulls on a hunting reserve near La Garganta, Spain. The rump patch is broadly edged with sepia hairs on the lower half, the edging fading as it proceeds up the sides of the patch. The inner sides of the thighs and the scrotum are white, with the white hairs infringing on the color of the lower portion of the rump patch. The largest free-ranging Spanish red deer in the Safari Club International records had antlers 38 inches (97 cm) in length, with a 9-inch (23 cm) circumference and a 30-inch (76 cm) inside span. The trophy sported 19 points. This concentration of bulls reflects management and conditions on an arid hunting reserve. The forage is heavily used and animals concentrate, especially after the rut, where feeding conditions are best. Such concentrations of bull elk seldom are seen except when movements from summer to winter range begin in areas such as Yellowstone National Park or the Sun River Game Range in Montana. *Photo from La Garganta, Spain, by Christian Oswald.*

C. e. corsicanus

The Corsican red deer is the smallest of the red deer. Males stand from 33.5 to 39.4 inches (85–100 cm) at the shoulder. Females vary from 31.5 to 35.4 inches (80–90 cm). Coloration is considerably darker than that of the European form, being dark brown in summer and blackish in winter. Males are darker than females during both seasons. There is a dark dorsal stripe, often bordered by spots. Whitish or reddish spots also may be found on the body as well. B. Banwell (personal communication:1996) indicated that about 2,000 head populated Corsica and Sardinia by the mid-1990s. They range primarily in parks and reserves, on mountains and foothills.

C. e. barbarus

The Barbary red deer generally is considered smaller than the red deer of central Europe, but Burthey et al. (1992) indicated that the females are slightly heavier built for their size than the latter. Males stand approximately 44 inches (112 cm) at the shoulder and weigh 331 to 485 pounds (150–220 kg). Females stand 35.4 to 43.3 inches (90–110 cm) at the shoulder and weigh 220 to 331 pounds (100–150 kg). During winter, the coat of both sexes is brown-gray. In summer, the coat varies from light yellowish-brown to reddish-brown—described as auburn by Burthey et al. (1992), who indicated faint, white spotting—which varies among individuals—can be seen year-round but is most common on females. A dark grayish-brown dorsal stripe runs from the neck along the length of the back but does not continue to the rump patch. The belly and the internal surfaces of the upper legs are lighter than the upper surface of the body.

As the Barbary red deer is similar to other red deer in characteristics of the mane and antlers as well as coloration of the rump patch, it probably originated from populations in which there was selection for size reduction in relation to changes in forage quality (see Groves and Grubb 1987). The possibility that European red deer were transported to North Africa by humans cannot be ignored.

The Barbary red deer was widely distributed in Algeria

The upper surface of the tail of the Corsican red deer is the color of the dorsal stripe. The rump patch is yellowish-red dorsally, but whitish from the root of the tail down, and is edged on either side by a dark stripe. The antlers are simple in form, rarely exceeding four points to a side and the bez tine usually is absent. Perhaps the small body and antler sizes of this island dwarf reflect nutritional stress. *Photo from Parc Naturel Regionale De Corse, Corsica, by Bruce Banwell.*

The Barbary red deer has thin antlers with relatively short tines, with the bez tine usually absent. The brow tine can be very short. Nevertheless, a three-tine crown can occur. The rump patch, much lighter in color than the body, is straw yellow—sometimes with a slight admixture of red. It is framed on either side by a darker line that is more apparent in the winter coat. The surface of the tail is darker in color than the rump patch. *Photo from Tunisia by James Dolan.*

and Tunisia—west to at least the Moroccan border—during the period of Roman rule. Numbers were very low by 1961; how many were in Algeria was unknown, but only 10 remained in Tunisia. These deer recolonized an area about 124 miles (200 km) long on the Mediterranean coast in northeastern Tunisia and numbered about 2,000 by the early 1990s, with about the same number in Algeria. However, the subspecies still is considered endangered. The animals now are found in cork oak forests interspersed with scrub and a few grassy glades (Burthy et al. 1992).

C. e. maral

The Caucasian red deer is a large subspecies. Bulls stand 53.1 inches (135 cm) at the shoulder and weigh as much as 750 pounds (340 kg). Cows are slightly more than half as heavy. During winter, the color varies from brownish-red in the females to dark, slate gray in the males. The predominant color is more gray than that of central European red deer; the antlers are large, but sometimes lack crowns (Heptner et al. 1961). Absence of a mane and dark spot on the rump patch further differentiates this subspecies according to Groves and Grubb (1987). The belly is smoky brown, and the feet, shoulders and hips are of a saturated grayish-brown color, sometimes almost black. The upper

part of the head, from the bridge of the nose to the forehead, is grayish-brown with a reddish tint. The sides of the face are gray, and the space between the rami of the lower jaw is grayish-white. The forehead area between the antlers and the upper part of the neck are brownish-red; the neck is gray below. The ears are light reddish-brown.

During summer, the hair has a distinct yellowish cast. The back and sides often have yellowish flecking or white spotting, and the overall tone of the body is a light, sandy brown. The lower part of the trunk and the neck are a light, dirty gray. An indistinct stripe passes down the neck to the shoulders. The dark lateral lines of the rump patch are less distinct, and the anterior portion is faded.

The skull is narrow, with muzzle breadth about 50% of muzzle length. Barclay (1934) referred to supposed elk-like characters in the Caucasus population, some of which also are shared by Asian populations to the east. In some heads, the fourth antler tine is very large, with the next tine of the crown placed posteriorly rather than mesially to it (Figure 14). This feature is suggestive of elk, and genetic introgression from elk dispersing from the east could have occurred (Geist 1971). However, this subspecies seems to represent a distinct radiation of European red deer, with adaptations toward grazing and life in the open.

Figure 14. (*Top row*) Antlers of red deer from the Caucasus (from Barclay 1934). The left antler is from Armenia and was donated to the British Museum in 1854. Unfortunately, the brow and bez tines were sawn off. Such antlers seem typical of well-nourished red deer in western Europe. The right antler could pass for that of an elk, and the center one has intermediate characteristics. Others depicted by Barclay were very similar to the hangul antlers in Figure 2. (*Bottom row*) Antlers of *C. e. maral* (from Heptner and Tsalkin 1947). The one on the left somewhat resembles a fossil from *Cervus elaphus angulatus* and present-day *C. e. hispanicus.* The one on the right had a single, long, terminal point on one side—apparently a common characteristic of some *C. e. maral* antlers. *Illustration by Bart W. O'Gara.*

The Caucasian red deer is characterized by a short tail (about equal in length to the ear, and colored like the back), short pelage and lack of mane during the rut. The large rump patch reaches high on the croup, and its lower area is white or nearly white—compared with the rufus or cream color in European red deer. It is yellowish-red anteriorly. The brow and bez tines are of equal length, and the bez bifurcates more often than in other subspecies (B. Banwell personal communication:1996). The large antlers form crowns more frequently than do those of *C. e. maral* farther south and east. This specimen, photographed in New Zealand, came from Croatian stock, and was considered from a separate subspecies by Banwell (1993). An Austrian bull in Safari Club International records probably was of this subspecies. It was shot in 1995 and carried 18 points. Its longest antler measured 55 inches (140 cm) in length and had a 12-inch (30 cm) circumference. The inside span was 59 inches (150 cm). *Photo by Bruce Banwell.*

Banwell (1993) gives the western range of what he considers a separate subspecies, *C. e. pannoniensis* (but what I consider a westward extension of *C. e. maral*) as between the Drava and Danube rivers, including southeastern Austria, southwestern Hungary, northern Yugoslavia and further along the Danube toward Romania. Dobroruka (1960) also considered the deer of this general area a separate subspecies, *C. e. montanus;* a genetic study is warranted. Centuries ago, those deer apparently migrated northward during spring across the Hungarian plains to spend summers on mountains and hills along what is now the border between Czech Republic and Hungary. That movement has been blocked by agriculture and invading red deer from central Europe (see Banwell 1993).

The largest herds of Caucasian red deer in Turkey live in the forested triangle formed by Ankara, Eskisehir and Bolu. The animals also are found in forested ranges in the Aegean and Black sea regions (Ogurlu 1992). The range extends north from Turkey along the east coast of the Black Sea

and east to the Caspian Sea—encircling the south coast as far as Turkmenistan (Whitehead 1982).

C. e. bactrianus

The Bukharan or Bactrian stag stands 47 inches (120 cm) at the shoulder. McElroy (1989) gave 440 to 500 pounds (200–227 kg) as the body weight of adult bulls. The winter pelage is a dull, light and sandy gray, darker on the forehead

The rump patch of the Caucasian red deer is bordered on either side by a dark stripe that fades dorsally. Anteriorly, the color of the rump patch fades into that of the back. A dark, poorly outlined dorsal stripe extends to the root of the tail. The coat sometimes is spotted, especially during summer. The face of deer of this subspecies is long and narrow. Antlers are heavy, sometimes ending in a crown, sometimes in a simple fork, and the number of tines is less than in central European red deer. According to Safari Club International records, a 14-point bull shot in North Ossetia, Russia, during 1984 had a 45-inch (114 cm) antler with a circumference of 11 inches (28 cm) and inside spread of 45 inches (114 cm). *Photo from the Kiev Zoo by James Dolan.*

Some Bactrian deer show yellowish-white spotting along the sides of the body and along the dorsal line. The rump patch is sandy white and reddish anteriorly, gradually mixing with the color of the croup. Laterally, the rump patch is bordered by a blackish-brown stripe that does not extend to the level of the tail. The rump patch is divided by an indistinct line. The antlers are of medium size, usually with five tines per side. They generally end in two tines that form a fork; crowns are rare. The only Bactrian deer in Safari Club International records had 12-point antlers 35 inches (89 cm) long with 10-inch (25 cm) burrs and a 23-inch (58 cm) inside span. *Photo from Berlin Tierpark by James Dolan.*

and between the antlers, where there is a considerable admixture of a reddish tone. An indistinct line of the same color extends down the neck to its midpoint, where it nearly disappears. An indistinct grayish stripe extends posteriorly from the shoulders. It gradually widens and merges with the darkish color of the hips. The body coloration grows paler toward the belly. The shoulder area is darker than the body and grayer than the back. Down the anterior surface of the legs to the level of the hooves, there is a dark stripe similar in color to the region around the shoulders. In general, the legs are of a lighter color than the body. The entire upper lip and area around the nostrils and chin are whitish. A spot on the lower lip, near the corner of the mouth, is brownish—the same color as the upper muzzle. The summer coat is brighter in tone than the winter coat.

This subspecies lives in an extreme environment, where annual rainfall is less than 7.9 inches (20 cm), and summer temperatures exceed 113°F (45°C). Historic range in the former USSR was mainly in riparian forests of Tajikistan

and Uzbekistan, but also in parts of Turkmenistan and Kazakhstan (Pereladova 1993). Bactrian red deer probably never were numerous throughout their range, but numbers reached a low of 350 to 400 in Tajikistan by 1960. Complete protection brought that country's population to about 1,000 by 1988. The range of the Bactrian deer included the Syr Darya and Amu Darya valleys, ranging up into northern Afghanistan, where the animals subsist in reed beds and thick, shrubby riparian vegetation. No information is available from Afghanistan, but constant conflict in that country bodes ill for populations there.

C. e. yarkandensis

The Tarim deer or Yarkand stag is a large subspecies standing 53.1 to 55.1 inches (135–140 cm) at the shoulder. Gao and Hu (1993) indicated that adult males weigh about 440 pounds (200 kg). During summer, the dorsal surface of the neck, the area between the antlers and the upper forehead are slightly rufous, as are the shoulders, trunk and flanks.

Most of the head, ventral neck and chest are light gray. The anterior surface of the front legs are a darker rufous with an admixture of dark brown hairs, but the hind legs are somewhat lighter in color. An area immediately above the hooves, inner surfaces of the legs and belly are white. In some individuals, the legs may be more clearly gray. Some individuals show an indication of white spotting. A dark dorsal stripe extends from the crown of the head along the back. A description of the animal in winter pelage apparently does not exist, but Wallace (1915b) reported the animals grew a long, shaggy coat.

Habitats include poplar forest, shrubland, reeds and agricultural lands. Air temperatures in this extremely arid region reach 130°F (40°C), and surface temperatures can exceed 166°F (60°C).

Although listed as endangered under the U.S. Endangered Species Act, recent studies carried out in semidesert habitat along the lower reaches of the Tarim and Peacock rivers of Xinjiang Province, China, indicate a population of approximately 15,000 animals. This does not include animals on antler farms.

C. e. wallichi

Wallichi's deer was named and described by Cuvier (1925) from a drawing that had been sent to him of an animal in a menagerie (Pocock 1912). Pocock described a male specimen, thought to be from the vicinity of Lake Manasarowar (now called Mapam Yumco), Tibet, close to the northwestern corner of Nepal, that was donated to the Zoological Society of London. He believed it to be the same species described by Cuvier. It stood about 51.2 inches (130 cm) at the shoulder and had a long face, small eyes and long ears with emarginated upper edges near the tips. The hair on the neck formed a small mane, and the general body color (in March) was very light, uniform yellowish or sandy brown. However, portions of hair not exposed directly to the sun were grayish-brown on the body, but darker on the neck. The tail was short and the white rump patch extended to the summit of the croup without a dividing line. London Zoological Society photos of that specimen in Dolan and Killmar (1988) show a broad nose (almost like that of caribou), heavy legs and broad hooves.

Anonymous (1982) reported that a large bull was seen in the Ha Valley of Bhutan, being chased by dogs, and later was found dead in a military camp. It had been in good condition, with very large antlers. It was designated a shou, *C. e. wallichi,* but details concerning coloration, size of rump patch, configuration of antlers, etc., were not given. People living in the valley reported quite often seeing herds of the animals.

Hogdson (1841) described *C. e. affinis,* the shou or Sikkim stag, from a skull with antlers and later from "abundant

The rump patch of the Yarkand stag is white except at the anterior portion, where it is mixed with light rufous hairs, and a light rufous line extends onto the dorsal surface of the tail. The rump patch is bordered by blackish-brown hairs. The antlers are massive but relatively short—a record class head was about 40 inches (102 cm) long. The main beam bends only near the middle tine. Above and below this bend, the beam is straight. *Photo from the Tarim Basin, Xinjiang Province, China, by James Dolan.*

supplies" collected north of Sikkim (Pocock 1942:301). Those specimens were shot during February and included both sexes and various ages. The backs, necks and heads were yellowish-earthy brown, but the necks were paler below. The flanks were conspicuously lighter colored, and the bellies were darker, forming a striking contrast (Pocock 1912). The legs were earthy brown on their anterior and exterior surfaces. Hogdson (1841) described the rump patches as remarkably small but conspicuous because of contrasting dark hairs around the patches that surrounded short, white tails. However, Pocock (1942) maintained that the patch was divided by a more-or-less pronounced darkish median line that was strongest on the upper half of the tail. Antlers of the type specimen had long brow tines, projecting forward with sharply up-turned tips. The bez tines were only 2.5 inches (6.4 cm) higher, and were parallel to the brows and had up-turned tips. Above the bez, the beam bent backward and outward for a short distance, then bent sharply upward below the origin of the trez and ended in a pair of subequal terminal tines. Other shou antlers proved quite variable (Pocock 1912), illustrating the limited value of this characteristic.

Pocock's (1912) description of Wallichi's deer, or shou, does not fit with the description provided by Dolan and Killmar (1988) of four captive bulls kept at the Norbulingka—the former summer palace of the Dalai Lama—in Lhasa, Tibet, during the late 1980s. Those animals were molting in late May 1987, when photographed, and some individuals showed a dark median line on the dorsal surface of the tail. Dolan and Killmar (1988) noted the rump patches of the captive bulls were extensive. The parents of those bulls were captured near the Brahmaputra River (Yarlung Tsangpo) south of Lhasa. *Photo by James Dolan.*

Dolan (1988), Dolan and Killmar (1988), Geist and Francis (1991), and Whitehead (1993) used the common name shou with the scientific name *C. e. wallichi,* apparently considering them the same animals.

The antlers of a shou in the collection of Sir Edmond Loder (Figure 15), have five points per side, a beam length

Figure 15.   Antlers of the shou typically are large, have 10 tines and the brow tine is low on the burr and inclined over the face (from Van der Byl 1915). The tips of the fifth tines are inclined toward each other. *Illustration by Bart W. O'Gara.*

of 52.5 inches (133.4 cm) and circumference of 7 inches (17.8 cm). The widest inside measurement is 38 inches (96.5 cm) and, tip to tip, it is 18.5 inches (47 cm). The main beam terminates in large forks, but the other points are comparatively short and weak. The specimen was obtained on the Indian–Tibetan border (see Van der Byl 1915). The antlers bend more forward than in most red deer and elk. Their shape is somewhat reminiscent of mule deer antlers without the forward fork.

According to Van der Byl (1915), the shou (*C. e. affinis*) inhabited what was once part of Sikkim and was called the Chumbi Valley, which is a basin of the Ammu River that

The supposedly same *C .e. wallichi* bulls photographed at the Norbulingka in October 1987 (*previous photo*) were variable in color when photographed in 1991. One (*left*) was grayish on the sides, but a sandy brown on the neck, back, rump and upper hind legs. Another (*right*) was reddish-brown with a nearly black area above the rump patch and as wide as the rump patch, and blackish hairs continued onto the dorsal surface of the tail. This animal appeared nearly similar to M'Neill's deer, which brings into question whether the four bulls actually were those photographed in 1987. *Photos by Christian Oswald.*

projects south between the present Sikkim and Bhutan. Shou were reported to exist in the valleys on both sides of the Brahmaputra River (Yarlung Tsangpo) to the east and southeast of Lhasa, Tibet.

Schaller et al. (1996) described the color of wild Tibetan deer found about 75 miles (121 km) east of Lhasa, Tibet, during October. The general pelage of adult males was gray brown with reddish overtones, the flanks paler than the back. Gray tended to be more prominent than brown on the face, neck and shoulders. Bellies were dark brown, almost black. Rump patches were white, divided by a dark median line that extended to the root of the white tail and occasionally onto its dorsal surface. The large ears were either gray or white. Schaller et al. did not notice any manes, possibly because the animals had not yet grown their full winter coats. Females and young males were more pale than adult bulls. The ventral surface from chin to belly, as well as the insides of the legs, were light gray to white. This, together with the white rump patch, made it conspicuous at a distance. Young in October were a darker gray brown than were the females at that time, and the skin of a fawn, said to have died in July, was colored like a female in winter coat except for white spots and a faint dorsal stripe from neck to rump.

Apparently, the surviving animals are being protected by the Tibetan government, but Schaller et al. (1996) postulated that the entire population in the area they surveyed may not exceed 200. The animals were found on rolling hills at 14,100- to 16,075-foot (4,300–4,900 m) elevation, covered mainly with alpine meadow and patches of willow, rhododendron and other shrubs.

C. e. hanglu

The hangul or Kashmir stag stands about 53.1 inches (135 cm) at the shoulder, and mature males weigh approximately 397 pounds (180 kg). During winter, the males are uniform brownish-gray, with white bands on the dark-tipped body hairs making the coat minutely striated. A reddish-brown dorsal stripe extends from the crown of the head along the back, and is most distinct on the neck and foreportion of the trunk. The head is colored like the body, but the forehead and the area between the antlers are reddish-brown. The upper muzzle and a spot above the nose are dark brown. The interior of the ear is white, the posterior is reddish-brown. The sides of the body lighten in color approaching the belly, being demarcated from the white belly by a horizontal brownish-black band. This band is absent in the females. The groin and scrotum are white to creamy white. The lower shoulder, breast and flanks are blackish-brown. The legs are light, reddish-brown, and darker anteriorly. In summer, the pelage lightens, taking on a more reddish hue, although dark individuals also can be found during summer.

This subspecies is mostly confined to mountain forests north and east of the Vale of Kashmir, India—summering as high as 16,000 feet (4,875 m) and wintering in willow and oak shrublands at 5,500 to 6,000 feet (1,675–1,830 m), according to Gee (1965). Some animals winter in brushy hills close to the valley. Bulls I heard vocalizing during the rut near Shrinigar started with a low roar—such as I had heard in Scotland and Norway—and rose in pitch to finish in a bugle like that of a Rocky Mountain elk. Gee (1965:391) described the sound as "Aaaungrieeeew."

More than 100 Tibetan deer were observed north of the Brahmaputra River and east of Lhasa, Tibet. Only one bull among them had five tines per side, the others having four or three tines or only spikes; however, Schaller et al. (1996) described the antlers as massive and observed that variation in the antlers was greater than in most other subspecies of deer. Note that the narrow rump patches extend slightly above the tails of these animals. *Photo by George Schaller.*

The rump patch of the hangul is comparatively small, extending just above the root of the tail. It is divided by a blackish-brown median line that extends onto the dorsal surface of the tail. The rump patch is creamy white; the anterior portion is yellowish. It is bordered by a wide blackish-brown stripe forming a dark caudal disk at the anterior end. *Photo taken in an enclosure at Srinagar, Kashmir, by Bruce Banwell.*

Most antlers of the hangul are elk-like but usually have only 10 points; however, more points with a crown—as seen here—are not unusual. The brow tine rises high on the burr and generally is shorter than the bez. The fourth tine is shorter than the fifth. The beam usually is curved inward near the middle, so that the terminal tines of the opposing antlers grow slightly toward each other. *Photo taken at Dachigam Sanctuary, Kashmir, by George Schaller.*

Until 1947, Kashmir was a princely state, and 1,000 to 2,000 hangul were protected to provide sport for the Maharaja and his friends (Gee 1965). Following the constitutional accession of Kashmir to India and objections of Pakistan to Kashmir being administered by India, hangul numbers were depleted by poaching. Gee estimated that perhaps 180 head remained in 1965. Recent numbers are unreliable, but Dolan (1988) speculated that the total population did not exceed 1,000.

C. e. macneilli

M'Neill's deer males have an average height of about 53 inches (135 cm) at the shoulder. From personal observation of this presumed subspecies together with Gansu deer at antler farms and from conversation with the farmers, I believe the two are of similar weight. M'Neill's deer are found in rough, brushy country in the Chinese provinces of Qing-

M'Neill's deer has heavy antlers with large brow and bez tines growing forward and slightly downward, then turning upward slightly to the tip. The main beam spreads outward and upward; usually at the level of the trez tine it curves inward. The trez tine originates from the front face of the beam, which again forks at a distance above the trez tine about equal to the distance of the latter from the bez tine. The terminal fork is variable, sometimes resembling those of elk but occasionally having terminal radial branching. Along the China/Tibet border, Tibetans gather cast antlers of M'Neill's deer for sale. Of truckloads picked through by the author, about 5% of the largest showed some crowning. This set of antlers—from a M'Neill's deer shot near the Tibetan border in Qinghai Province, China—has main beams 42.7 and 41.3 inches (108.5 and 105.0 cm) in length. The greatest outside spread is 32.7 inches (83 cm). *Photo by Bruce Banwell.*

The general coloration of M'Neill's deer is silvery-gray, with a reddish cast to the upper portions of the legs. There also is a reddish cast to the flanks and the hair of the face, forehead and between the antlers. This bull was courting white-lipped deer females in Qinghai Province, China. This is one of the few known photographs of *C. e. macneilli* in the wild. *Photo by Cai Guiquan.*

hai, Sichuan and south to Yunnan, as well as adjoining areas of eastern Tibet. Little is known concerning numbers in the wild, but they are common on antler farms. The call of the male seems intermediate to that of red deer and elk (Wallace 1915b).

The white rump patch extends just above the root of the tail on M'Neill's deer, and a dark line extends from the croup to the root of the tail or, variably, onto its dorsal surface. During winter, the dorsal line is blackish. Females in the winter coat are a more or less uniform gray with reddish casts to the neck, flanks and legs. In summer, the females can turn decidedly reddish. The throat mane is weak or absent. *Photo taken in the Kanazawa (Japan) Zoo by Bruce Banwell.*

C. e. kansuensis

The Gansu deer stands about 53.1 inches (135 cm) at the shoulder in a large male, which weighs about 530 pounds (240 kg), according to McElroy (1989). The antlers are of the elk type, with well-developed tines. Female Gansu deer are a lighter gray than males, with less black pigment in the coat. The legs are silvery gray. The darkest pigmentation is on the flanks and hips. The dorsal line and rump patch are as in the male. Both sexes have light ocular rings and light

During winter, the neck and trunk pelage of Gansu bulls are steel gray, with the hairs tipped with black. The face is brownish-gray, and the throat is gray with a reddish cast. The belly and breast are black, as is a dorsal stripe beginning between the antlers proceeding along the entire length of the back. The flanks and hips are darker than the body, with a greater admixture of black hairs. The legs are darker gray than the trunk, and in certain light conditions appear black. *Photo taken in the Beijing (China) Zoo by James Dolan.*

Normally, each Gansu bull antler has 5 tincs, but as many as 12 have been recorded. The top tines ordinarily do not bend inward so much, as do those of M'Neill's deer. Only three sets of Gansu antlers, all from animals shot in 1994, are in Safari Club International records. The largest, an 11-pointer, had a 42-inch (109 cm) antler with 9-inch (23 cm) burrs and an inside spread of 37 inches (94 cm). *Photos by Christian Oswald.*

gray ears edged with black. Summer pelage takes on an overall and rather uniform rufous coloration, darker on the flanks. The sides of the face and lower portion of the neck are grayish-white.

Two rather young Gansu deer shot in western Gansu had antlers 41.25 and 43.75 inches (104.8 and 111.1 cm) long, spreads of 34.75 and 38.5 inches (88.3 and 97.8 cm) and circumferences of 5.75 and 5.5 inches (14.6 and 14.0 cm).

Wallace (1915b) reported that Lydekker wrote in the September 27, 1913, *Field* issue that the call and antlers did not enable Gansu deer to be ranked as elk. Lydekker maintained that the Gansu deer, like the M'Neill's deer, was not an elk but a relative of the hangul, which has a call to some extent intermediate between red deer and elk. However, rump patch size, use of open country when permitted and the fact that they grade into Alashan and Manchurian elk characteristics, along with their calls and antlers, seem to taxonomically associate them with elk, not maraloids.

Gansu deer occur in one county in Sichuan Province, China, through Gansu to Shaanxi Province, according to Dolan (1988). Groves and Grubb (1987) suggested that they continue into Shanxi Province and intergrade with Manchurian elk. These deer generally stay in montane and hill forests or rough badland areas, but they forage into grasslands or croplands at night.

C. e. alashanicus

The Alashan elk is small for an elk. The shoulder height of a bull was 51.2 inches (130 cm) (see Groves and Grubb 1987). Until recently, it was poorly known and of uncertain status. It is distributed in the Helan Shan on the border of southeastern Inner Mongolia and Ningxia Province, China (Ohtaishi and Gao 1990), where they range in partially wooded foothills. Westerners apparently had misunderstood the location because of the name. It originally was reported from the Alashan. Shan means mountains in Chinese, but the Alashan on maps, in Inner Mongolia near the Outer Mongolian border, means happy face—apparently in Mongolian—not Ala mountains (C. Oswald personal communication:1997).

Dolan (1988) considered *C. e. alashanicus* synonymous with *C. e. kansuensis,* and Allen (1940) and Groves and Grubb (1987) have indicated that the Gansu deer, in the northeast of its range, showed signs of hybridizing with elk. Wang and Schaller (1996) noted that about 186.4 miles (300 km) separate the Helan Shan and Alashan elk from the

The Alashan elk is the most conservative in pelage marking of any elk (Geist and Francis 1991). This bull was on a small deer farm in Ningxia Province, China, where only one subspecies, derived from locally caught deer, was kept. His legs and belly were a darker brown, and a small eye ring was obvious. A dark dorsal line continued to the tail, the mane was small, the rump patch was rufous and its lower half had narrow, blackish borders. *Photo by Christian Oswald.*

This Alashan bull, shot during the rut, had one antler freshly broken off at the head. The nearly white bib on the mane was evident on all of the many rutting bulls. Some antlers showed a tendency to crown as shown here—somewhat unusual in a subspecies generally considered to be an elk—but most were typical 12-point elk antlers. The largest typical antlers from an animal shot by Christian Oswald has main beams 35.4 and 35.0 inches (89.9 and 88.9 cm) in length, and the greatest spread is 32.3 inches (82 cm). This may be the first-ever photo of a shot-in-the-wild Alashan. Its maraloidlike antler indicates that this practically unknown subspecies may be genetically closer to southern subspecies than generally believed, or the antler may represent an anomaly. Also, the bull's white bib has not been reported in the literature heretofore, but C. Oswald (personal communication:1997) advised that it is usual for rutting bulls in the wild. *Photo by Christian Oswald.*

Qilian Shan and Gansu deer. The region's climate during the Pleistocene and Holocene oscillated between warm, moist and cold, dry phases. Some 2,500 to 3,000 years ago, forests probably were more or less continuous between these mountain ranges. Now, the intervening area is steppe and desert. The two populations have been separated long enough to become morphologically distinct.

At a deer farm with animals from the Helan Shan and Qilian Shan, Wang and Schaller were shown how the animals from the two ranges differed. Compared with the Gansu deer, the Alashan elk were rangier in build, had longer legs, their summer pelage was less gray and more red, and their rump patches were pale rust rather than white. In summer coat, a bull on another farm was a uniform gray-brown with grayish on the shoulders and lower neck. His legs and belly were a darker brown, and a small eye ring was obvious (C. Oswald personal communication:1997).

The Alashan elk apparently was low in numbers until about 1980. Proximity to Chinese population centers bodes ill for any deer. Velvet antlers, placentas, fetuses and tails are valuable for traditional Chinese medicine, and almost any wild meat brings several times the price of that of domestic animals. However, 15 to 20 years of protection apparently have brought the population back to more than 1,000 head in its limited habitat (C. Oswald personal communication:1997).

C. e. songaricus

The Tien Shan elk is the largest of Asian elk, according to Whitehead (1993) who gave 838 pounds (380 kg) as maximum weight and shoulder height as up to 59 inches (150 cm).

During summer, its color is a rather uniform reddish-brown, darker on the flanks and legs. The neck is red with gray undertones. The face is similarly colored, but somewhat lighter in shade. At this season, the dark blackish-brown dorsal stripe is clearly defined. Gao and Hu (1993) described Tien Shan elk as yellow-brown with nearly white rump patches.

Their range covers the Tien Shan and surrounding mountainous areas of Xinjiang Province, China and Kazakhstan, mostly at altitudes between 4,600 and 9,845 feet (1,400 and 3,000 m) (see Ohtaishi and Gao 1990). This supposed subspecies is contiguous or continuous with the Altai elk and appears identical with it (Heptner et al. 1961). The population in China was estimated at 50,000 in the wild, plus 4,000 to 5,000 in captivity for antler production (Ohtaishi and Gao 1990).

C. e. sibiricus

The Altai elk stands between 59 and 61 inches (150–155 cm) at the shoulder and weighs up to 661 pounds (300 kg), according to Heptner et al. (1961). However, information published by Erepb and Aeeb (1994), plus information from workers on an antler farm in the Altai Republic of Siberia gave average weights of 730 pounds (331 kg) for bulls and 604 pounds (274 kg) for cows. These weights indicate less difference in weight between the sexes than Geist and Bayer (1988) found for North American elk. Time of year when the animals were weighed could account for the difference. Gao and Hu (1993) indicated that Altai elk are larger than Tien Shan elk. Height measurements, which are much less variable than weights, support that contention.

During winter, most bulls are light, yellowish gray-brown on the back and sides of the body. They have large rump patches that extend onto the croup, varying in color from dull, fox red to straw to almost white. Gao and Hu (1993) described the bulls as dark brown with a light yellow rump patch. This patch is framed on the sides and anterior end by a dark stripe, which is quite variable. The legs and stomach are of an intense cinnamon brown color, contrasting sharply with the color of the rump. The well-developed neck mane also is cinnamon brown. The head is either

During winter, the rump patch of Tien Shan elk is primarily white, although the anterior portion is suffused with reddish hairs. The patch is framed with blackish hairs. During winter, males and females are yellowish-gray on the shoulders and trunk, resembling the North American subspecies. The neck, face and forehead, as well as the area between the antlers, are dark gray-brown, with the flanks showing an infusion of this color, which is individually variable. A dark dorsal stripe is hardly visible during winter. *Photo taken in Xinjiang Province, China, by George Schaller.*

Dolan (1988) reported that antlers of Tien Shan elk were distinguished by the length and massiveness of the tines. Whitehead (1993) maintained that the largest Rocky Mountain elk antlers and those of Tien Shan elk are similar. Lydekker's (1915) description indicated the same. This Kazakhstan bull, the largest in Safari Club International records, carried 56-inch (142 cm) antlers with 9-inch (23 cm) burrs. The 14-point trophy had an inside spread of 48 inches (122 cm). *Photo by Richard Castle.*

brown or cinnamon brown, with a light eye ring. The lower lip varies from gray to cinnamon brown.

Altai elk cows somewhat lack the color contrast characteristic of bulls. The basic color on the back and sides is gray-brown, and is darker than that of the bulls. The legs are gray or cinnamon brown. The stomach and the interior portions of the upper legs are lighter in color than the body. The neck mane, which is less strongly developed, is a deep cinnamon brown.

Typical elk habitat in the mid-Tien Shan of Xinjiang Province, China. This mountain range has very similar habitats to those of the Rocky Mountains of the United States and southern Canada in terms of climate, elevation and genera—even species—of trees and forage plants. *Photo by Christian Oswald.*

A dark dorsal stripe runs along the neck and the back of Altai elk, either along the entire length of the back or ending just behind the shoulder blades. In some cases, especially in the southern part of its range, it continues onto the rump patch as a brown stripe, as seen on some animals in this photo, but the tail usually is colored like the rump patch. Such stripes could indicate crossbreeding with other subspecies; more than 100 elk seen on an antler farm in the Altai Republic did not have them. That farm was managed by biologists of the Russian Academy of Science to maintain the genetic purity of Altai elk (V. Yeger personal communication:1995). However, wild elk shot by meat hunters in Siberia had similar stripes (J. Dolan personal communication:1996). *Photo taken near Ulan Bator, Outer Mongolia, by Christian Oswald.*

B. Warren (personal communication:1996) has observed elk in most of their range in Asia and North America. He indicated that coloration of elk in Kazakhstan and Siberia generally resembles that of Rocky Mountain elk, but farther north and west, in the Altai region of Siberia, the animals are browner. Also, V. Yeger (personal communication:1996) stated that elk in the mesic high Altai are darker, whereas those in lower elevation foothills (especially in dry, open areas) are more tan. However, Whitehead (1993) maintained that Tien Shan elk are the darkest Asian elk.

There is more uniformity to the summer coat, and the dimorphism between the Altai elk sexes is less apparent. Generally, the body coloration is cinnamon brown without the darkening of the neck, stomach and legs. This color is somewhat more intense in the bulls. The rump patch edging is more distinct during summer than in the winter pelage.

Vladimer Nicolaevich Yeger (personal communication:1996), Chief Technology Expert for Antler Deer Breeding of the Russian Federation, maintained that large wild bulls in the Altai region had antlers up to 60 inches (1.5 m) in length. He also said that most large heads had 12 points, but 14 points was not uncommon—exactly the same as trophy imperial North American elk. He had never seen cupping or crowns on the antlers of Tien Shan or Altai elk.

Thirty-six Altai elk, all but one from Outer Mongolia, are listed in Safari Club International records. The largest elk listed had antlers 47 inches (119 cm) in length, with 10-inch (25 cm) burrs and 18 tines. The inside span was 40 inches (102 cm). It is not surprising that elk antlers from Mongolia, documented in Safari Club International records, are not as large as the minimum for Boone and Crockett records. Thousands of elk are shot annually in North America by trophy hunters; only a few are shot in Mongolia.

In China, Altai elk primarily are found at 3,280 to 6,560 feet (1,000–2,000 m) above sea level (Gao and Hu 1993). They range in the Chinese, Siberian and Outer Mongolian Altai and the Sayan mountains. Those in western Mongolia were called *C. canadensis wachei* by Whitehead (1993). Scientific endeavor has been limited in this area, perhaps because the ancient line of demarcation between the Chinese and Russian empires runs through it. The Altai elk was considered rare by 1898 because of excessive hunting. As a result of protective legislation, it no longer is considered so. Large numbers are kept on farms in Siberia for antler production; in 1996, the Russian Academy of Science indicated 23,157 Altai elk on 120 farms in just the Altai Republic.

C. e. xanthopygus

The Manchurian elk or isubr adult bulls stand 57.5 to 59.1 inches (146–150 cm) at the shoulder and weigh about 551 pounds (250 kg). However, larger specimens have been recorded. Weight and height measurements of cows could not be found, but these cows appear slightly smaller in relation to bulls than do Tien Shan, Altai and North American elk cows in relation to bulls of their respective subspecies.

Geist and Francis (1991) observed that bulls appear elk-like, and cows appear red deer-like, lacking the mane that is present on cow elk of most subspecies. However, C. Oswald (personal communication:1997) found that females grew a small mane during cold weather. The only Manchurian elk

Some Altai elk bulls observed on a gamefarm in the Altai Republic had typical Rocky Mountain elk coloration (*left*); more than half were a chocolate-brown color with grayish tints (*right*). In those animals, the color of the manes and legs were less different from that of the body than was evident in the lighter-colored animals. However, during mid-May the animals were shedding and colors naturally were faded. *Photos taken in the Altai Republic of Siberia by Bart W. O'Gara.*

in the Safari Club International records had a 34-inch (86 cm) antler with a 5-inch (13 cm) burr. The inside span was 21 inches (53 cm), and the number of tines was 11.

Winter coats of Manchurian bull elk resemble those of the North American elk, being creamy fawn on the trunk and shoulders, darker toward the dorsal line with an inconspicuous dorsal stripe. The forelegs and belly are brown; the rear legs are similarly, but lighter colored. The flanks are like the trunk, with a greater admixture of brown hairs. The face is brown, and the neck and mane gray-brown, sometimes with a reddish cast. Female Manchurian elk are a uniform gray-brown with a reddish cast. They do not have darker colors on their bellies and legs.

During summer, the pelage color of both sexes changes to a bright yellowish-red. The reddish dorsal stripe, now very apparent, extends onto the tail, bisecting the yellowish-white upper portion of the rump patch. The framing of the rump patch is less noticeable at this time of year. Males have a grayish-brown neck and face. In some individuals, faint spotting can be seen along the dorsal line.

According to Allen (1940), this subspecies does not bugle during the rut, but roars like red deer. However, detailed investigations by Nikolski and Wallschlager (1983) contradict this. Nikolski and Wallschlager indicated that the Man-

Altai elk antlers are large with thick beams without crowns, according to Heptner et al. (1961), who reported that these antlers resemble those of American elk. Dolan (1988) maintained that Altai elk have the largest antlers of all *Cervus elaphus*. This bull was shot in the Altai Mountains of southern Siberia. *Photo by Bruce Warren.*

The rump patch of Manchurian elk is fox red, but in some individuals it tends to whiten between the buttocks. The rump patch is bordered by a line of blackish-brown hairs, which is broadest on the lower buttocks. Note the near lack of mane on the cow. *Photo by Bruce Banwell.*

churian elk, like all elk, usually has only one call—not a series of calls as is typical of red deer. The call tends to last 2 to 4 sec, and the sound spectrum shows strong harmonics that follow one another—characteristics of elk calls. However, unlike most elk calls, there are few high frequencies. Thus, the calls of Manchurian elk seem like the calls of other elk, modulated in frequency, so that a maximum of sound penetrates foliage.

The Manchurian elk is a forest animal, and often found in river valleys. Winter food habits—principally poplar, willow and birch (Chen et al. 1993)—reflect such habitat. The elk's range is wide—from northern North Korea through eastern Liaoning and Jilin provinces of China, most of Manchuria and northeastern Inner Mongolia (Ohtaishi and Gao 1990)—and its preferred habitat apparently is dense larch forests interspersed with marshes. The range continues beyond 60 degrees north along the Lena River system, and to the eastern Siberian coast near Vladivostok and at least one offshore island (Egorov 1965).

The antlers of Manchurian elk are relatively short and lightly built, with lightly constructed beams growing more or less vertically from the head. The number of tines per antler varies, but five or six per side is usual. The fourth tine is not particularly well developed and sometimes is shorter than the others. The largest set of Manchurian elk antlers in the Cerviden Museum, Munich, Germany (measured by Christian Oswald), has main beams 38.2 and 37.4 inches (97

and 95 cm) in length, and its greatest spread—at the tips—is 29.5 inches (75 cm).

In a survey of the Yakutia District of northeastern Siberia, Egorov (1965) reported that the *C. elaphus* were neither Manchurian nor Altai elk, but most resembled the latter. V. Geist (personal communication:1996) expressed belief that these were Manchurian elk, but Egorov's description presented the possibility that *C. e. sibiricus* × *C. e. xanthopygus* crossbreeding occurred in that area.

C. e. canadensis

The Eastern elk, the nominal North American subspecies, formerly of eastern North America, was described by Erxleben in 1777 from Quebec (Hall and Kelson 1959). Height measurements and weights seem not to have been taken. Reportedly, the last specimen was a bull killed in Pennsylvania (if indeed it was similar to the animals of Quebec) by an American Indian in November 1867. It supposedly was light colored with long, lightly built antlers. Bryant and Maser (1982) suggested that a remnant population might still occur in Ontario. This has never been conclusively proven, but remains a possibility worth pursuing (see Stalling 1994).

C. e. merriami

Merriam's elk is the second presumed subspecies to become extinct since the arrival of Europeans in North America. The historic range included the mountains of western Arizona, New Mexico, Texas and northwestern Chihuahua, Mexico (Hall and Kelson 1959). It became extinct within a few years of its being described (Dolan 1988). Only antler and skull measurements were taken when this (presumed at the time) species was named (see Nelson 1902).

C. e. roosevelti

The Roosevelt or Olympic elk often is considered the largest of extant elk. Adult bulls stand, on average, about 63 inches (160 cm) at the shoulder. Harper et al. (1967) indicated that bulls in California averaged 561 pound (254 kg) and cows averaged 474 pounds (215 kg). Perhaps the heaviest weights recorded for wild elk are from bulls at the beginning of the rut on Afognak Island, Alaska. The field dressed weight of a 4-year or older bull was 1,094 pounds (496 kg) (Troyer 1960), indicating a whole weight of about 1,300 pounds (590 kg). However, B. Banwell (personal communication:1997) maintained that ranch-raised Manitoban elk in New Zealand are as large. Some Roosevelt individuals are darker than Rocky Mountain elk. They have comparatively short tooth rows and the teeth tend slightly more toward bunodonty than those of other North American elk (McCullough 1969); these seem to be adaptations to a suc-

The rump patch of Roosevelt elk is quite large, extending up on the croup. It is cream colored, bordered laterally by a dark brownish-black stripe that extends only about halfway up the rump patch length. Antlers of Roosevelt elk bulls tend to be short and heavy. On some specimens, the terminal points form crowns somewhat resembling those of red deer. *Photo taken at Prairie Creek, California, by Bruce Banwell.*

culent diet. However, a survey of food habits indicated that, like other elk, Roosevelt elk used a wide variety of vegetative types (Jenkins and Stanky 1991).

During summer, Roosevelt elk are a rich cinnamon buff. The head, neck and belly are dark brown with an admixture of black. In winter, the coat color changes to dark gray, with dusky dorsal stripe, neck, face and belly.

The Boone and Crockett Club's *1993 Records of North American Big Game* listed 127 Roosevelt elk (Reneau and Reneau 1993). Antler lengths of those trophy bulls were from 39 to 55.5 inches (99–141 cm). Most antlers had 12 to 14 points, but 18 had 15 points, 8 had 16, 2 each had 17 or 18 points and 1 had 19 points.

The historic range extended from about the Russian River in California to Vancouver Island, British Columbia, and inland from the Pacific Ocean to the Cascade Mountains (D. McCullough personal communication:1997). Today, Roosevelt elk live along the coast of Humboldt and Del Norte counties, California, northward through western Oregon and Washington to Vancouver Island. McCullough (1969, personal communication:1997) noted that Roosevelt elk reach their greatest density in areas of thick timber with small clearings and high rainfall, their favored habitat; although, they also use clear-cuts. Happe et al. (1990) found

that shrubs in clear-cuts of the Northwest had higher concentrations of astringent tannins, which eliminated much of the available proteins, than did those in old-growth forests.

Radio-collared Roosevelt elk on the Olympic Peninsula selected 6- to 15-year-old clear-cuts and old-age spruce forests during winter (Schroer et al. 1993). They preferred mature deciduous forests on valley floors during spring, summer and autumn.

C. e. nannodes

The Tule elk was named by Merriam (1905) as the smallest of the New World subspecies. Adult bulls stand about 61 inches (155 cm) at the shoulder and weigh on average about 551 pounds (250 kg) in their native grasslands. McCullough (1969) reported a Tule bull weighing 680 pounds (308.5 kg). This subspecies is paler in color than the Rocky Mountain animal, as befits animals in a semiarid environment.

Body coloration is reddish during summer. The neck is dark reddish-brown, and legs are golden fulvous. Conspicuous, and more extensive than in other subspecies, are the white posterior bases of the ears. The rump patch is creamy buff with dark brown lateral lines that extend halfway up the sides of the rump patch. There is little seasonal varia-

Although smaller, Tule elk antlers are similar to those of Rocky Mountain elk in their proportions and spread. Both the main beams and the tines tend to arch from the points of divergence. In the fresh state, they have rugose (wrinkled) surfaces (which are weathered away on exposed specimens). The antlers have a distinctly distorted appearance, as if they were forcefully twisted during growth. There is a tendency toward palmation in large antlers. *Photo taken in Owens Valley, California, by Dale McCullough.*

tion, but in winter, the coat becomes quite tan (D. McCullough personal communication:1997).

McCullough (1969) noted that autumn pelage, antlers and teeth of Tule elk are light colored compared with those characteristics of other elk subspecies. However, most habitats where Tule elk survive are nutritionally and climatologically harsh. In lush habitats, they increase in size—but not quite to the size of other North American subspecies according to D. McCullough (personal communication:1997)—and show deeper pigmentation of teeth and antlers. They then look more like Rocky Mountain elk (D. McCullough personal communication:1996). Personnel of the California Department of Fish and Game obtained whole weights of Tule bulls at Grizzly Island State Wildlife Area, a wetland area including salt marshes and reverted croplands. The heaviest was 910 pounds (413 kg). Six bulls weighed more than 800 pounds (363 kg), and 10 to 15 were more than 700 pounds (318 kg). Cows from the same area averaged 350 to 450 pounds (159–204 kg) according to J. Fischer (personal communication:1998).

On average, Tule elk have the longest tooth rows of the North American elk. The cheek teeth also show subtle differences. The crowns tend more toward selenodonty, with reduction of the cingula (zone near the gum) and more complex folding of the enamel. There also is a tendency toward later eruption of the last molars and slower replacement of premolars (McCullough 1969). These apparently are adaptations to coarse, fibrous forage.

C. e. manitobensis

The Manitoban elk was named *C. canadensis manitobensis* by Millais (1915:281) while on a hunting trip in Canada: "The darkest form of wapiti, with very dark neck and sandy brown upper parts and small horns, rarely exceeding 50 inches. Habitat Manitoba and Eastern Saskatchewan." Adult bulls stand, on average, 61.4 inches (156 cm) at the shoulder and weigh 778 pounds (353 kg); cows average 606 pounds (275 kg). Blood and Lovaas (1966) reported the shoulder height of a 2-year-old cow as 46.8 inches (119 cm) and the mean for two yearling heifers as 52.1 inches (132 cm).

During summer, the Manitoban elk's coat is rich chestnut brown, darker on the legs, head, neck and belly. The winter pelage is lighter colored than that of summer.

The Manitoba elk supposedly was an inhabitant of the Great Plains (Dolan 1988). Where its range terminated and that of the eastern, or Rocky Mountain, elk began was only speculative. V. Geist (personal communication:1997) contended that, during early contact times, elk in Alberta were continuous along river valleys from mountains into prairies.

Although small antlers were one of the characteristics for which Manitoban elk were named, heavy antlers are

The rump patch of Manitoban elk is creamy buff, sometimes with a slight reddish tint, with dark lateral lines extending about one-third the way up its sides. The antlers are quite similar to, but usually shorter (when in the prairie habitat where they were named) than those of Rocky Mountain elk. *Photo taken during September near Baldy Lake in Riding Mountain National Park, Manitoba, by Jim Wilke.*

grown when these elk are provided good nutrition (see Petersen 1993). Manitoban elk on good nutrition also become heavier than Rocky Mountain elk and are favored in New Zealand as a meat animal. Canadian elk farmers keep many Manitoban elk because of the heavy velvet antlers they produce, which are sold primarily to Asians for traditional Chinese medicines. Also, the largest elk antlers listed in the Boone and Crockett records as of 1996 were from a Manitoban bull (Reneau and Reneau 1996). That bull had nontypical antlers that scored 447⅛ Boone and Crockett points. It was shot during 1961 near Gilbert Plains, Manitoba, by Bob Howard.

The largest skull of a bull elk on record—19.9 inches (50.6 cm) condylobasal length and 8.8 inches (22.4 cm) orbital width—was from a Manitoban elk at Riding Mountain National Park (Geist 1998).

C. e. nelsoni

The Rocky Mountain elk generally was classified as *C. canadensis* until being renamed *C. e. nelsoni* by Bailey (1935), who had never seen an eastern elk, only a figure drawn by John James Audubon. The type specimen was from Yellowstone National Park, Wyoming. Rocky Mountain elk stand about 62.2 inches (158 cm) at the shoulder. Whole weights of 43 bulls taken in Banff Park during October through January by Flook (1970) averaged 734 pounds (333 kg); those of 130 cows in the same collection averaged 571 pounds (259 kg). Murie (1951) recorded the live weight of a bull taken in August 1928 in Yellowstone Park at 1,032 pounds (468 kg). He reported the average weight for 29 mature cows from Jackson Hole, Wyoming, was 510 pounds (231.3 kg).

More than 300 trophy Rocky Mountain elk and related subspecies (Manitoban and Tule) are listed in the 1993 *Records of North American Big Game* (Reneau and Reneau 1993). Most antler lengths range from 52 to 61 inches (132–155 cm). The vast majority have 12 to 14 points, but three have 17 points. The extra points are small and do not greatly influence the general conformation of the antlers. The largest antlers in Boone and Crockett club records as of 1998—both typical and atypical—apparently are Rocky Mountain elk (J. Reneau personal communication:1998). The typical antlers scored 442⅝ points. The animal was shot by Alonzo Winters in the White Mountains of Arizona. The atypical antlers scored 465¼ points. The animal died of unknown causes, and the antlers were picked up at Upper Arrow Lake, British Columbia. Both antler sets were be featured in the Boone and Crockett Club's 23rd (1998) awards book. Bryant and Maser (1982) indicated that the historical range included the Rocky Mountains and adjacent mountain ranges from the 55th parallel southward to the 35th parallel.

The summer pelage of Rocky Mountain elk varies from light buffy fawn to creamy buff. The neck, head, legs and belly are dull rusty brown to dark umber. The eye ring is buff. The rump patch is orangish to whitish, generally framed by blackish hairs along its lower half. *Photo taken in Yellowstone National Park by Bart W. O'Gara.*

During winter, the coat color of Rocky Mountain elk changes to buff gray with lavender overtones in dim light—apparently owing to the reflection qualities of hair tips. As the dusky tips of the hairs wear off, the pelage takes on a tan to dirty whitish cast. The tail and large rump patch become more whitish with a conspicuous dark framing. The head and neck are dull rusty brown with a dark brown mane, darkest on the throat. The ears are dull light brown, lined with pale buff. *Photo taken in Yellowstone National Park by Bart W. O'Gara.*

Subspecies Classification

To help understand the relationships of red deer populations in various parts of Europe and Asia Minor, see Figure 25 (Chapter 2) concerning geologic changes in the area and possible movements of ancestral deer.

Red deer were indigenous throughout the British Isles at least until 1,000 years ago (Whitehead 1964). During most of that time, they lived in a forested environment, although tracts of open country probably were present. As a result of clearance and exclosure, Scottish red deer have been progressively confined to open moorland in the highlands (Clutton-Brock et al. 1982). Deforestation and sheep farming greatly altered the habitat by the end of the 18th century, and the size of deer declined (Clutton-Brock and Albon 1989). Apparently, red deer are forest-adapted and do not adapt well in open country, especially in cold climates—the opposite of some elk subspecies.

Mystkowska (1966) tabulated reported maximum weights for red deer across mainland Europe, excluding Swedish red deer. Weights increased from northwest to southeast; a maximum of 309 pounds (140 kg) was reported for those on an island off the coast of Norway, and 772 pounds (350 kg) was reported for deer in Yugoslavia. Mystkowska also compared cranial measurements of red deer from western Europe, Poland and eastern Europe and found the same general trend in size as he reported for weights. A north/south clinal trend in transferrins (serum proteins) of German red deer also was detected (Bergmann 1976), indicating the cline was not just a function of nutrition. In addition, neighboring populations were more similar than those separated by longer distances. Red deer in Hungary, Yugoslavia and Bulgaria have about 2 to 2.5 times the body weight and about 3 to 4 times the antler weight of those in the Scottish highlands (Mitchell et al. 1977); Asian elk have body weights about 3 to 4 times those of western European red deer. Thus, the temptation has been great to introduce eastern deer and elk into western Europe. Such mixing of subspecies has not always produced the desired results. In the days of the Czars, elk from Asia and North America were brought to Poland to increase the size of red deer. The antlers of the crossbreeds had fewer points, poorly developed burrs and less spread than did those of the native deer. Hunters did not like the antlers of the crossbreeds, but it took Polish game managers until the 1930s to weed out the undesirable characteristics by selective hunting (Lindemann 1956). Translocating deer to stock, restock or improve blood lines is an old tradition in European game management, but its extent is inadequately documented. American elk introduced to Scottish deer forests apparently died out (Whitehead 1960).

Geographic variation in European red deer is unlikely to have represented a primary cline, as populations apparently dispersed over the continent from more than one direction since the last glaciation. The true pattern of geographic variation may now be obscured by local extinction (Heptner et al. 1961), restocking and other management activities (Groves and Grubb 1987). In fact, looking at the names of European red deer, one might think that these animals recognized national boundaries.

About 75 red deer from Europe are listed in the Safari Club International Record Book of Trophy Animals (McElroy 1989). Antler lengths range from 35 to 46 inches (89–117 cm), and numbers of tines or points vary from 11 to 23, but most of the larger heads have 18 points or more. The largest head is from Hungary. Lydekker (1901) maintained that red deer antlers in the typical western subspecies attained the maximum degree of complexity. However, he noted that few deer today have so fine or numerously pointed antlers as those that are, from time to time, dug up in peat or other superficial deposits of the British Isles and the Continent—or even as many as those carried by bulls killed two or three centuries ago on the Continent.

The red deer of Hungary, Bulgaria, Romania and Yugoslavia still produce large antlers. They frequently carry a total of 20 or more tines, weigh more than 22 pounds (10 kg) with frontal bone and measure 47.2 inches (120 cm) or more in length. In contrast, antlers from the degraded habitat of Scotland seldom weigh more than 4 pounds (1.8 kg) or exceed 35.4 inches (90 cm) in length. Scottish red deer antlers occasionally bear 14 or even 16 tines, but a head of 12 tines—the royal—is considered a typical quality trophy in Scotland.

Considering skull measurements with principal component analysis and canonical analysis, Lowe and Gardiner (1974) wrote that none of the features of the skulls measured for their study supported the concept of subspeciation in European red deer, although the *atlanticus* subspecies had an overlap of less than 10% with other supposed subspecies. Despite introductions into Scottish deer forests, natural selection appeared to favor the native genes so strongly that no modifications to skull characteristics could be determined.

Flerov (1952) treated all European populations, except for some Mediterranean ones, as a single subspecies—*C. e. elaphus*.

There are two main groups of continental red deer—western and eastern. The western deer are smaller, and bez tines are less common and shorter than the brow tines. Differences in rump patches and voices also exist. On the basis of social organs, western Eurasian red deer segregate into three groups—western European, Spanish and eastern European—all with long tails and split rump patches with dark yellow above the tail and a lighter lower portion. The western European males have well-developed neck manes and the crowns of large bulls often have eight tines. Spanish red deer bulls have manes and somewhat primitive antlers, as described previously. Eastern European bulls nearly all lack neck manes, and often have four tines in the crown, according to V. Geist (personal communication:1997).

Groves and Grubb (1987) suggested that only one subspecies of red deer be recognized for western Europe, *C. e. elaphus* (synonyms *scoticus*, *hippelaphus*, *atlanticus*, *bolivari*). However, *bolivari* (synonym *hispanicus*) seems definitely different.

Allozymes in populations of pure *C. e. elaphus* were not

found to differ genetically from Swedish populations, expected to harbor genes from other supposed subspecies because of translocations (Gyllensten et al. 1983). This could mean that the supposed subspecies were not genetically different in a substantial way, or the genomes of translocated animals were swamped or selected against.

Summing up conclusions relevant to taxonomy in a study of subfossil (from the Quaternary period) teeth, antlers, skulls and skeletons, Ahlen (1965) concluded the following. Differences between Danish and Swedish populations of red deer are so slight that presumed subspecies *C. e. elaphus* and *C. e. hippelaphus* should be combined. Norwegian red deer *C. e. atlanticus*—which differed in several characters—is a legitimate subspecies by criteria set forth by Mayr et al. (1953). Ahlen's study was intensive but not extensive—only Scandinavian material was available.

In an electrophoretic study of red deer from Great Britain, Norway, Sweden and West Germany, Gyllensten et al. (1983) found those from Great Britain and Norway were closely related, but more distantly related to German and Swedish deer , which are closely related. The investigators postulated that the estimated genetic distance would correspond to an approximate divergence time of 60,000 years, indicating differentiation between the two groups was initiated before the end of the last glaciation rather than afterward.

A common origin for the Scottish and Norwegian deer was explained by immigration of red deer from the British Isles to Norway (Cameron 1923). Those deer supposedly survived on glacial refuges on the Norwegian west coast. Gyllensten et al. (1983) suggested that assigning subspecific names to segments of the European red deer population was problematic because the low morphological divergence actually reflects a low level of genetic divergence. However, Gyllensten et al. observed that, if subspecies are to be recognized in Europe, the major branching described above should be reflected. Geist (1971) and Groves and Grubb (1987) apparently considered this difference insufficient for subspecific recognition. Antlers of red deer in Norway and Scotland differ markedly from those in Germany and Sweden (personal observations), but the differences probably could be explained by nutrition.

Further genetic testing seems in order, but with present knowledge, Norwegian and Scottish red deer should be united as *C. e. atlanticus* (both were named in the same year, but *atlanticus* was named first). Central European and Swedish red deer should remain *C. e. elaphus*. Individual variations are great enough that differences in coloration would hardly stand up in court as positive evidence to identify any one of the four supposed subspecies. Also, differences in sizes, weights and antlers generally are correlated with habitat conditions. However, the genetic differences

noted by Gyllensten et al. (1983) appear great enough to identify the two subspecies proposed above. On the other hand, biochemical tests are so new to taxonomy that few standards or precedents are available for use of genetic distance and diversity in determining subspecies.

The deer of southern Spain in the Guadalquivir Basin, Sardinia, Corsica and North Africa were lumped together by Flerov (1952) as a subspecies *C. e. corsicanus,* which has relatively small, simple antlers with three to four tines and often no bez tine or crown. However, such antlers can be seen on European red deer on degraded habitat. Genetic testing seems in order to determine whether these island and coastal deer, whose ancestors apparently survived the last glaciation in coastal refugia, have differentiated enough to be classified as three distinct subspecies.

Geist and Francis (1991) noted that the Spanish red deer, ibex, chamois and roe deer of southern Spain appear to be relicts, similar to ungulates that inhabited Europe before the Saale Glaciation. These relict deer deserve subspecific status. The presence of *C. e. elaphus,* whether by natural expansion or introduced by humans, apparently threatens the long-term survival of *C. e. hispanicus* and complicates the subspecific classification of red deer in Spain. Extinction of a subspecies can be caused by crossbreeding as surely as by extirpation. It is to be hoped that wildlife managers in Spain will recognize the uniqueness of their relict deer and manage for their survival.

Dark color and small size support Flerov's (1952) contention that *C. e. corsicanus* could be consubspecific with the Spanish red deer. On the basis of social organs, these deer seem closely related to *C. e. elaphus.* However, with the information available, it seems premature to combine this dwarf island subspecies with any other until genetic studies indicate its true relationship.

The Barbary red deer could be correlated to the *C. e. elaphus* group on the basis of social organs, but with the information available at present, such a move seems presumptuous. Retaining it as *C. e. barbarus* until genetic studies or other evidence indicate otherwise seems prudent.

Flerov (1952) indicated that red deer in the Carpathians and Caucasus were larger than those in western Europe, although he retained them within his broad concept of *C. e. elaphus.* Skull measurements indicate larger eastern and smaller western animals (see Groves and Grubb 1987). Also, the former are more diverse than western populations, with an admixture of elk-like characters—occasionally an enlarged fourth tine.

Red deer were extirpated so long ago from parts of eastern Europe (probably in the first millennium AD or earlier) that it is hardly possible today to reconstruct their habitation with any degree of certitude (Heptner et al. 1961). Lydekker (1901) noted that red deer were almost unknown in western Russia and were missing from almost the entire extent of the Ural Mountains. Thus, the continuity between European and Asian *C. elaphus* in Russia apparently was severed, if it existed, and differences between the two may have increased during the past 1,000 to 2,000 years. Also, intergrades between what we now call subspecies probably were exterminated.

Groves and Grubb (1987) suggested that the larger eastern European deer—characterized by the lack of a mane and the absence of a dark mark on the rump patch, according to Dobroruka (1960)—extending not only from the Carpathians but also the Baltic coast, and as far as the Crimea, should be termed *C. e. montanus* (synonym *brauneri*). Groves and Grubb (1987:47) admitted, however, that "Published data are ambiguous as to where *montanus* should be regarded as giving way to the equally large form from still further east, *C. e. maral.*"

In contrast to Dobroruka's claims, recent observers reported that the deer of the Carpathians have manes and are reddish-brown like *C. e. hippelaphus* (B. Banwell and C. Oswald personal communications:1997). However, large, gray, maneless (at least during summer and the rut) deer do occur in Europe as far west as the Austrian–Slovenian border (see Banwell 1993). These are not animals of the mountains, but of low, dry, brushy country interspersed with marshes—much like the habitat Vereschagen (1967) described for *C. e. maral* near the Caspian Sea. Banwell called these European deer Pannonian Maral because their habitat, between the Drava and Danube rivers and eastward toward Romania, was ruled by Augustus Caesar as the state of Pannonia. Considering the type of habitat they live in, *C. e. pannoniensis* certainly seems more appropriate than *C. e. montanus*. Comparative DNA studies of deer from eastern and western Europe, as well as the Middle East, probably would resolve the relationship of the eastern European maraloids to their counterparts from farther east and west.

The deer of the Crimea (named *C. e. brauneri* by Charlemagne in 1920) supposedly is somewhat intermediate to *C. e. hippelaphus* and *maral*. Whitehead (1982) reported that *hippelaphus*-like animals were nearly exterminated and *maral* were introduced. On his range maps, the Crimea is shown as part of the range of *maral*. However, C. Oswald (personal communication:1997) says these deer have manes and appear *hippelaphus*-like. Any judgment concerning these deer would require on-the-ground investigations.

Lydekker (1898, 1915), among others, considered that *C. e. maral* ranged northwestward to the Carpathians, whereas Flerov (1952) restricted its distribution to Turkey, the Caucasus and Kurdistan. Geist and Francis (1991) maintained that subspecific designation of red deer in eastern Europe,

west of the Black Sea, as a separate subspecies besides *C. e. maral* was questionable. The described characteristics of *C. e. montanus* and *C. e. brauneri* closely resemble those of *C. e. maral*. Recognizing them as subspecies would be to ignore the clinal nature of those characteristics.

Widely distributed remains of red deer—for the most part resembling the extant *C. e. maral*—have been found in the Caucasus from the Upper Pleistocene to the present. During the 16th century, Persian shahs sometimes killed thousands in organized hunts. By 1888, numbers were so diminished that red deer were introduced from Austria. By the 1920s, red deer survived in only four or five isolated areas, and introductions of exotic deer continued during the 1930s and 1940s (see Vereschagen 1967). Thus, present-day deer could owe much of their variability to introduced genes.

Within the presumed range of *C. e. maral* in the Carpathian Mountains, deer with marked differences sometimes are shot within short distances of one another (Lydekker 1898, 1915, Wallace 1915a). Large, gray, maneless bulls with long-beamed but poorly crowned antlers seem to prefer rolling plateaus and open spaces. Smaller, browner bulls with conspicuous manes and short, crowned antlers seem to prefer steep slopes and valley bottoms (Geist 1998). These types could have evolved together in the differing, but interspersed habitats. Possibly, maraloids remained in this route of entry from Asia into Europe, and western European deer naturally followed preferred habitat back toward the east. Or introductions of western European red deer, when the native *maral* were in low numbers (Vereshchagin 1967), may have led to the intermingling of subspecies.

Antlers from the Carpathian Mountains show a stronger tendency to form a crown than do those from the Caucasus (Wallace 1915a). However, no meaningful dividing line between ranges or significant differences between characteristics attributed to *C. e. montanus*, *brauneri* and *maral* seem to have been proposed. Thus, most researchers have lumped them under the oldest name—*C. e. maral*.

At the beginning of the 20th century, Lydekker (1901:218) noted: "Probably . . . there is a complete gradation from the Persian to the Scandinavian animal." However, Groves and Grubb (1987), Geist and Francis (1991) and others point to differences in western European red deer and eastern European *maral*, saying those differences are great enough to warrant separate subspecific classification. The most convincing evidence for the legitimacy of the subspecies *C. e. maral* lies in the timing of the rut. That of *maral* apparently is much earlier than that of *hippelaphus*. Also, an anecdotal account indicates that *maral* females in the wild violently reject the overtures of rutting *hippelaphus* males (see Banwell 1993).

Fossil elaphine deer are known from what is presently a gap between the natural distribution of red deer and elk

(Heptner et al. 1961), but their affinities do not appear to have been ascertained; some might have been crossbreeds (see Groves and Grubb 1987).

As observed by Lydekker (1898), the red deer of central Asia generally have comparatively simple, uncupped antlers. Such antlers closely approximate those of the sika group, from which *C. elaphus* apparently evolved. Central Asia may be regarded as the original home of red deer and elk, but those of China and the bordering Himalayan nations are the least known and least studied (Dolan and Killmar 1988).

The lone subspecies that did not conform to the numbers and configuration of chromosomes of other *C. elaphus* was the Bactrian deer from the Beijing Zoo (Wang and Du 1981). Four of those animals had diploid chromosome numbers of 66 or 67 instead of 68. Wang and Du indicated that their chromosome maps were more similar to those of the sika deer (2n = 64–68) than to those of other *C. elaphus* subspecies.

Fontana and Rubini (1990) observed that some intraspecific chromosome polymorphisms may be attributed to inexact taxonomic placement, and animals from parks or zoos could have racially mixed origins. The validity of the above findings should be investigated comparing a karyotyping of another, preferably wild, population of Bactrian red deer.

If the chromosome number of all Bactrian red deer proves to be 66 or 67, the possibility must be considered that these deer are closely related to their progenitors, the sika deer, and they are a missing link on the line of evolution from *C. nippon* to *C. elaphus*. Conceptually, that would make the Bactrian deer closely related to *C. e. acoronatus*. The possibility also exists that speciation took place in isolation, and hybridization occurred naturally on secondary contact with sika deer.

Banwell (1991b) reported that a *C. e. bactrianus* in the San Diego Zoo roared like a red deer, but with a falsetto finish. On other occasions, the bull's call was a little closer to that of an elk. Also, Bactrian deer sometimes bear spots—another characteristic that could indicate a close relationship to sika deer.

Little evidence is available to indicate that *C. e. bactrianus* should not be considered a legitimate subspecies, especially until its chromosome numbers and configuration are studied further.

C. e. yarkandensis usually is regarded as a distinct subspecies. It is similar to *bactrianus* in the relatively straight antler beams. The principal differences are, first, the rump patch is larger and reddish-white with no dark stripe bisecting it and no black edging. Second, a crown of three to five tines is usual, although not formed in quite the same way as in true red deer. Banwell (1991a) maintained that the Yarkand deer shows strong elk-like characteristics, especially in the rump patch and tail size. C. Oswald (personal communication:1997) indicated that the rutting call, like that of the Bactrian deer, began with a roar but elevated into a whistle.

C. e. yarkandensis also should remain a subspecies until further genetic testing (not only of it but also of *C. e. bactrianus*) is accomplished.

The deer of the southern and eastern flanks of the Tibetan Plateau form a distinct group, with variable rump patches, dull earthy colors and large antlers in which the beams generally terminate in two tines that are directed inward and are of similar dimensions (Groves and Grubb 1987). They usually occupy brushy habitat on steep hillsides, and their coloration, long ears and gaits are somewhat reminiscent of mule deer. Flerov (1952) put them all, with the exception of *wallichi*, into a single subspecies, *C. e. affinis*, but Pocock (1942) carefully compared the Himalayan populations and recognized *affinis, hanglu* and *wallichi* as valid taxa.

Geist (1971) acknowledged two taxonomic subgroups of Asian deer—a northern one with large elk-like rump patches and short tails of the same light color, and a southern one from the Himalayan area, with small sika-like rump patches circled by black bands and broad, long, dark tails. Such acknowledgments are logical, and undoubtedly reflect close relationships among those subgroups. However, with present knowledge, these broader groups probably should not be coalesced into only two subspecies without confirming evidence from biochemical or molecular tests.

These animals seem somewhat similar to the primitive forms from which both red deer and elk evolved (Groves and Grubb 1987). Under the form *acoronatus*, they resemble the first representatives of *C. elaphus* to appear in the fossil record from the early middle Pleistocene about 500,000 years ago (Kurtén 1968).

Concerning the deer of Asia, Wallace (1915a) wrote that confusion long prevailed because different names commonly were used to designate the same animal, and different animals had more than once been designated by the same scientific name. Perhaps this is illustrated best by the case of Wallichi's deer and the shou. Cuvier (1825) described and named *C. wallichi* from a sketch of a deer in a menagerie that was sent to him. The only description by scientists was of a captive bull, supposedly from the environs of Lake Manasarowar (now called Mapam Yumco), Tibet (Pocock 1912, 1942). However, Ludlow (1959) maintained that no large deer occurred during recent times in the vicinity of Manasarowar Lake, which he described as barren, elevated country unsuitable for deer. From 1936 to 1947, Ludlow saw what he called shou (*C. e. affinis*) in southeastern Tibet and in wooded country near Lhasa.

C. e. wallichi was characterized by Pocock (1912) as having a short, white tail and a large, sharply bordered, white rump patch extending far up onto the back without a median line. Also, on the body and over the croup, a large number of hairs curl forward. *C. e. affinis* was described from what was then Sikkim. Except for differences in rump patches, *affinis* and *wallichi* seemed closely allied, and Lydekker (1915) considered them subspecies of *C. wallichi*. Pocock (1942) maintained the two were different taxa, with the smaller rump patch of *affinis* being divided dorsally by a more-or-less pronounced, darkish, median line extending onto the tail.

Pocock (1912) referred to these two supposed species as *C. wallichi* or Wallichi's deer and *C. affinis* or the shou. Lydekker (1915) called Wallichi's deer *C. w. wallichi* and the shou, *C. w. affinis*. More recent investigators often have combined the two, retaining the vernacular shou with the scientific name *wallichi* (Dolan 1988, Dolan and Killmar 1988, Geist and Francis 1991, Whitehead 1993).

If Pocock's (1942) sketches and descriptions are accurate, it appears no more than two Wallichi's deer have been seen and described by scientists (Groves and Grubb 1987). Possibly, the originally named Wallichi's deer is extinct, was a crossbreed or hybrid raised in captivity, was a captive animal transported a long distance or was one extreme in a cline of color and rump patch size, whereas the shou was the other, and the intermediate animals are extinct or have not been described.

Ohtaishi and Gao (1990) concluded that, if there are two subspecies, they inhabit the same area. Such a situation seems unlikely. Two closely related subspecies in low numbers and close proximity could hardly fail to crossbreed. Using the common name shou with *C. e. wallichi,* is reminiscent of using elk for North American *C. elaphus.* However, shou seems the generally accepted common name, and *wallichi* is the oldest scientific name.

I concur with Groves and Grubb (1987) that the hangul should be considered a valid subspecies. The minute striations on the coat and sika-like rump patch of the hangul or Kashmir stag seem distinctive. Also, the Himalayas separating it from other *C. elaphus* are characterized by very deep canyons carrying mighty rivers and sharply stratified habitat zones. These exceed almost anything in North America as barriers, which would encourage subspeciation.

M'Neill's and Gansu deer are quite similar with identical rump patches; Gansu deer are slightly darker than M'Neill's and have antler tips that turn in less. However, both groups have significant numbers of bulls with six-pronged, elk-like antlers. Groves and Grubb (1987) observed that *kansuensis* may lie within the range of variation of *macneilli,* and that specimens from Shanxi Province, China, indicate there is intergradation with the Manchurian elk. Indeed, the range of the Gansu deer probably was, at one time, continuous with

that of the Manchurian elk, but a wide gap now separates the two (Allen 1940).

The characteristics of these two presumptive subspecies seem to present a cline that has been broken by reduction in numbers and possibly extinction of intermediate populations. Although they occupy a large area, numbers in the wild generally are low. Captures to stock antler farms—capturing young and using baited pitfalls for adults—have taken a heavy toll, and still do. Wallace (1915b) indicated that, when these animals were more numerous, both sounded intermediate to red deer and elk when calling, and the two forms seemed identical except in gradations of color. Barriers to movements between these presumed subspecies seem fairly recent and human induced, and combining them as *C. e. macneilli* seems most logical.

The Altai and Tien Shan elk of Asia, along with all North American elk, are the largest members of the species, with characteristic antlers and large rump patches. Elk resembling those in North America appear to be confined to high, subalpine ecosystems in Asia. Although Geist (1971, 1990) contended that all North American elk and some Asian elk are similar—one subspecies, *C. e. canadensis*—he recognized at least two other subspecies, *C.e. alashanicus* and *C.e. xanthopygus,* of elk in Asia.

Dolan (1988) made *C. e. alashanicus* consubspecific with *C. e. kansuensis,* but he showed the latter with a comparatively small, divided rump patch and dark tail. Geist and Francis (1991) showed the Alashan elk with a larger, but still divided rump patch and a tail of color similar to the patch. Groves and Grubb (1987) also described *C. e. alashanicus* as having a large rump patch, and classified this small subspecies with the elk group. Antlers of an Alashan bull in the possession of Christian Oswald in Munich, Germany, have the typical 12-point configuration of other elk. C. Oswald (personal communication:1997) indicated that the Alashan bull's rutting call was somewhat intermediate to that of the Yarkand deer and Tien Shan elk.

Available evidence indicates that the Alashan elk is a legitimate subspecies. The small size could simply reflect habitat conditions, but the white bib, sometimes crowned antlers and somewhat different bugle seem to set it apart. Zoological investigations are increasing in China, and it seems premature to do anything but leave it as *C. e. alashanicus.*

C. e. wachei supposedly was distinguished from Altai and Tien Shan elk by incurving of the upper portion of its stout antler beam (Lydekker 1915). Also, the trez tine bends upward and inward, and is separated by a shorter distance from the fourth tine than from the bez. The supposed range of this form in western Outer Mongolia is continuous with those of Altai and Tien Shan elk (see Whitehead 1993). Inspection of at least 20 sets of antlers from mature elk in western Outer Mongolia, and twice as many photos of the same, did not reveal one that would look out of place in Yellowstone National Park.

Altai and Manchurian elk are known to crossbreed in the general area where *C. e. wachei* is supposed to occur (Flerov 1952). Some antlers of the Manchurian elk show characteristics similar to those described for *C. e. wachei* (personal observations). Many recent researchers (e.g., Groves and Grubb 1987) have simply ignored this presumptive subspecies. Others, for example, Dolan (1988), have made it synonymous with *C. e. sibiricus*. I have seen photos of supposed female western Mongolian *C. e. wachei* that were similar to wild elk cows in Manchuria but slightly grayer. The Manchurian cows are monocolored except for rump patches and surrounding darker hair. They also have little sign of manes. Apparently, the presence of two subspecies of large cervids (with some crossbreeding) in close proximity has caused confusion leading to the naming of *C. e. wachei*.

Heptner et al. (1961) maintained that the Tien Shan and Altai elk were identical. V. Yeger (personal communication:1996) said that the elk of the Altai Mountains of Outer Mongolia and Siberia, as well as those on the Kazakhstan side of the Tien Shan mixed naturally in the wild. And, although some variation in color is evident, these two groups of animals could be considered one subspecies. Severtzov named both in 1873, apparently on the same page of a Russian journal (see Dolan 1988). Thus, determining a proper name for this group is beyond the scope of this chapter. However, this may be a moot question because many investigators (e.g., Geist 1990) believe that these elk and some North American elk should be considered one subspecies.

Discontinuous phenotypes, such as brown Altai elk, commonly occur in the animal kingdom. The term polymorphism often is used for any kind of discontinuous variation. These morphs sometimes are so strikingly different from the normal type of a population that they have been mistakenly described as separate species. But they are not separate species or subspecies, just as silver red fox, brown black bears and Rh-negative humans are not subspecies (Mayr 1970).

C. e. xanthopygus seems a legitimate subspecies, quite unlike but closely related to the Altai elk, with which it apparently crossbreeds in some areas of overlap. Adapted to forested habitat, it seems almost intermediate to red deer and elk. Less color differentiation than other elk, sparse manes on cows and low frequency calls of bulls separate this subspecies from other elk. Crossbreeding with *C. e. sibiricus* apparently occurs under natural conditions on mountain ranges flanking the eastern shore of Lake Baikal (Flerov 1952). However, the zone of crossbreeding seems

This nearly white elk on an Alberta gamefarm represents a fairly common morph among ruminants. Red deer, pronghorn and springbuck occasionally show this coloration (author's personal observations). Apparently, such color usually results from a mutated recessive gene, which is only expressed when inherited from both parents. *Photo by Bart W. O'Gara.*

narrow, indicating that Manchurian elk are better adapted to lowlands and forests than the crossbreeds, whereas Altai elk are better adapted to open, montane habitat.

Because of the fragmentary nature of the fossil record, the exact time of appearance of *C. elaphus* in North America is not known (see Chapter 3). Nor is it clear whether the first fossils represent the ancestors of present-day elk. During the Late Pleistocene, *Cervus* populations may have been isolated in what now is the eastern and western United States—south of the Wisconsin Glacier. Elk occupied the unglaciated areas of Alaska and the Bering–Chukchi Platform at the same time. They apparently colonized terrain almost as soon as it was deglaciated, and from the Early to Late Holocene epoch (about 10,000 to 500 years ago), they were distributed from coast to coast in the northern United States.

Whether pioneering elk came from northern or southern refugia as glaciers melted would be difficult to prove. Because North American and Siberian elk are so similar, some portion must have come from Alaska and the Bering–Chukchi Platform. Thus, separation of Asian and North American elk, like the continents themselves, seems to have occurred within the past 10,000 years.

Bryant and Maser (1982) speculated that further study of elk subspecies in North America may be an academic quest. They assumed that the six named subspecies were legitimate, and that each evolved in and occupied habitat different from that of the other five. Habitat undoubtedly influenced the morphology of elk, but elk are generalists and most supposed subspecies thrive in the habitats of other presumptive subspecies. Over most of North America, variations caused by habitat and clines between ecotypes seem more likely than do discrete subspecies. Perhaps, if the splitters of the late 1800s and early 1900s had specimens at their disposal from every state where elk once roamed, most of those states would now boast their own subspecies. What the elk of southern states, such as Louisiana, were like is unknown. Intuitively, it seems they would have been quite different from those of Quebec, where North American elk first were named. Naming subspecies on the basis of habitat serves little purpose if all individuals of two supposed subspecies cannot be positively differentiated, morphologically or genetically, from each other.

"Elk are morphologically conservative and differ little from the ancestral wapiti stock in Asia. Over much of North America, they occupied areas that combined forest cover and open land. . . . The eastern subspecies are of doubtful validity (Groves and Grubb 1987). Differences between these subspecies and *nelsoni* were minor from modern-day perspectives, and well within the range of variation of *nelsoni*. These former elk subspecies should be considered demes or ecotypes, because they surely differed genetically in adaptations to local environmental conditions, but not sufficiently to warrant a separate subspecific designation" (McCullough 1993:332).

Few remains of Eastern and Merriam's elk are available, and an attempt to determine subspecific status with available data would remain speculative. Some insight into the relationship of Eastern and Merriam's elk to extant subspecies or populations might yet be gained by DNA analyses. Such research seems worth the attempt using faunal remains found at archaeological sites throughout the historic ranges (see Heffelfinger et al. 1999). However, samples would be needed from numerous (now extinct) populations to determine whether any differences found simply represented points in clines among extant and extinct elk or if differences were abrupt, indicating subspeciation.

According to Bryant and Maser (1982), North American elk were segregated in four groups—along northwestern coastal United States, western and interior California, southwestern United States and east of the Cascade and Sierra Nevada mountains—during the Sangamon interglacial stage (before the Wisconsin glacial stage) about 70,000 years ago (now considered 100,000 years ago). These four groups supposedly occupied four southern refugia (depicted by Guthrie 1966) during the Wisconsin glaciation.

If subspeciation did begin in southern refugia during the

Wisconsin glacial stage, mixing of those previously segregated populations with animals moving south from the Alaska–Yukon refugium and Bering–Chukchi Platform certainly must have occurred during the ensuing 10,000 years.

Bryant and Maser (1982) postulated that the Great Plains interrupted gene flow between eastern and western populations of elk, but they presented a map indicating continuous distribution of Eastern, Manitoban and Rocky Mountain elk. Riparian zones of rivers such as the Missouri, Yellowstone, Platte, Arkansas and their tributaries apparently provided winter habitat for elk, which used vast prairies during other seasons and promoted east–west gene flow. Lewis and Clark found elk to be numerous in the Missouri River bottoms running through the Great Plains (see Chapter 2).

Theodore Roosevelt (1905:271) wrote: "In the old days, when the mighty antlered beasts were found upon the open Plains, they could be followed upon horseback, with or without hounds." During the 1870s, Plains elk were pursued and killed from horseback by soldiers (Dodge 1959). The open prairies were extensive and elk could be pursued for many miles until they were exhausted and could be killed at close range with a pistol. No vegetation was available in which they could hide or outmaneuver a horse. However, Caton (1877) noted that elk hunters on the prairies expected to find their quarry along creek or river bottoms, where they found shade and arboreous food to mix with the herbaceous.

Elk may have been more numerous on the Great Plains, where bison bore the brunt of aboriginal hunting, than in the western mountains. Kay (1994) maintained that, where a differential accumulation of snow occurred on mountains, Native Americans on snowshoes could simply run ungulates uphill into deeper and deeper snow. There, they could kill the floundering animals with hand axes or clubs. Kay hypothesized that elk occurred in very low numbers in the western mountains during prehistoric and early historic times (see Chapter 3).

Were it not for agricultural conflict, elk probably would still feel at home on the Great Plains. However, because of sparse cover on the Plains, elk populations there were extirpated before those in mountainous areas, according to Skovlin (1982).

Elk of the river systems probably met on summer ranges. During a study designed to delimit the summer and winter ranges of the Northern Yellowstone elk herd, Craighead et al. (1972) fitted 1,448 cows with collars that allowed individual animals to be identified. Elk wintering near Gardiner, Montana, occupied most of the Park during summer and usually returned to the same general areas of the summer and winter ranges each year. Four other herds that wintered outside the Park—Gallatin, Sunlight Basin–Crandall Creek, North Fork of the Shoshone and Jackson Hole—also had summer ranges inside the Park. A few Gardiner cows that summered with animals from other herds accompanied those animals to their winter ranges and wintered as much as 100 airline miles (161 km) from the winter range where they were collared. Also, breeding took place on the summer ranges before the five herds returned to their winter ranges. Cows show much greater fidelity to their home ranges and travel less than do young bulls.

Van Dyke et al. (1998) compared home ranges of radio-collared elk from three populations during two time periods separated by about 10 years. Range use differed significantly in two of the three populations. Changes in range use tended to increase spatial separations and reduce densities of elk populations. If such changes occurred within a 10-year period, populations surely occupied all suitable habitat in the course of thousands of years of evolution.

Among elk biologists, almost everyone who has radio-collared bull elk has a story concerning one that moved hundreds of miles to join another herd. The "grandmother" of all such stories was published by Olson (1991). A yearling bull was collared during February 1987, in the Sweetgrass Hills—approximately 100 miles (161 km) north of Great Falls, Montana. The bull was sighted near Independence, Missouri, in March 1990. The radio collar was removed in October 1991 by Missouri Department of Conservation personnel and positively identified as that of the bull from the Sweetgrass Hills. He apparently had trekked along the Missouri River for at least 1,740 miles (2,800 km). With such mobility and the animal's adaptability to varying habitats, it seems doubtful that the Great Plains seriously disrupted gene flow between eastern and western elk populations.

Nelson (1902) named Merriam's elk *C. merriami* primarily from two specimens he obtained near the head of the Black River in the White Mountains of Arizona. The species was named from skull characteristics and color—darker than the Rocky Mountain elk and lighter than Roosevelt elk. Compared with Rocky Mountain elk, the skull was "more massive with nasals broader and much more flattened, and upper molar series more curved" (Nelson 1902:8). However, data presented by McCullough (1969) and Hutton (1972) contradicted this observation. Also, Anderson and Barlow (1978) found it very doubtfully distinct on the limited evidence available on this extinct, supposed species, and lowered it to *C. e. merriami,* saying that even on the most distinct measurement (breadth across the premaxillae) the standard deviations overlapped widely. The antlers of Merriam's elk were said to be most like those of Rocky Mountain elk but very large with tips straighter, giving a longer chord from base to tip. However, antlers pic-

tured and sketched in Bryant and Maser (1982) appeared representative of Rocky Mountain elk, although the tops were rather small compared with the brow and bez tines. Elk from Yellowstone Park introduced into the presumptive range of Merriam's elk now grow enormous antlers (as did the supposed Merriam's elk) and are much sought after by hunters. The possibility seemed to exist that scattered Merriam's elk survived and contributed genes for large antlers to the present population (see Phillips 1992). On the other hand, preliminary mtDNA data suggest that elk now in Arizona did not come from any place other than Yellowstone National Park (J. Heffelfinger personal communication:2001).

That elk were, indeed, isolated in the mountains of Arizona, New Mexico, Texas and northwestern Chihuahua, Mexico—leading to speciation or subspeciation—seems open to question. Before Spanish settlers moved into those areas from Mexico about four centuries ago, much of what now is desert was grasslands until ravaged by European livestock (Leopold 1949). Elk in the comparatively flat, open country around mountain ranges would have been vulnerable to hunters on horseback; a good horse can outrun an elk in such country. However, preliminary analysis of a short (111 base pair) sequence from the mtDNA control region of a "Merriam's elk" specimen indicates that native Arizona elk may have differed from those farther north. This specimen had more base pair differences from elk representing all other presumed, extant subspecies, than did the other subspecies from one another (J. Heffelfinger personal communication:2001).

The idea that montane and prairie elk are different and do not mix seems groundless. Although they noted that elk have excellent dispersal capabilities, Wisdom and Cook (2000) depicted the historic distribution of the three subspecies flowing directly into one another on broad fronts—an unlikely possibility. Elk in the mountains of Wyoming traveled as far as 200 miles (322 km) to reach winter rangelands in the Little Colorado and Red deserts (Sura 1967). As elk numbers increased in the Rocky Mountains, movements onto prairies and shrub steppes, and across such vegetation to isolated mountain ranges, have been common. Also, elk translocated from Yellowstone Park to prairie or eastern deciduous forest habitats have fared well. Clearly, elk are extremely adaptable. However, with the paucity of evidence available, no judgment will be made here concerning classification of extinct animals, except that *canadensis* will not be reserved for the Eastern elk.

C. roosevelti, the elk of the Olympic Mountains in Washington State, was named by Clinton Hart Merriam, who was famous for naming species and subspecies based on slight differences in appearance. Merriam (1897:272) wrote: "I deem it a privilege to name this splendid animal Roosevelt's Wapiti. It is fitting that the noblest deer of America should perpetuate the name of one who, in the midst of a busy public career, has found time to study our larger mammals in their native haunts and has written the best accounts we have ever had of their habits and chase." The new species was named primarily on the basis of its large size, dark color and short, heavy antlers (compared to Rocky Mountain elk, which Merriam apparently regarded as *C. canadensis*).

Merriam (1897) speculated whether the aborted condition of the terminal portion of the antlers was the result of long residence in dense Pacific Coast forests or an indication of closer relationship with red deer. Geist and Francis (1991) discussed the Roosevelt elk and concluded that it is a large-bodied ecotype whose antlers reflect the West Coast habitat in which it lives. One aspect of that habitat is the abundant but rather poisonous, fast-growing and quickly fibrous vegetation. They speculated that abundant spring vegetation promotes growth of heavy main beams and large brow and bez tines, but as the quality of vegetation deteriorates, growth of the royal and sur-royal tines is retarded. Some Roosevelt elk antlers form a crown, but crowned antlers occasionally are seen on Rocky Mountain elk in Yellowstone Park (author observations) and Tule elk in California (D. McCullough personal communication:1997).

Bailey (1936) maintained there were no records to indicate that the range of Rocky Mountain elk ever connected with that of the Roosevelt elk, but Murie (1951:41) wrote "Although the original ranges of *C. c. nelsoni* and *C. c. roosevelti* were separated by territory unoccupied by elk, there was a good chance for limited intermingling of the two races through parts of southern British Columbia and adjacent parts of Washington. There may have been some contact too, by way of the Columbia River Valley. This intermediate country, however, was not ideal elk range." Also, McCullough (1969) indicated that an unusually good record existed concerning the historic distribution of elk in California. He presented a map indicating the confluence of animals considered to be Tule, Rocky Mountain and Roosevelt elk in northern California.

Apparently, when Native Americans secured horses or when Europeans with firearms entered an area, elk in most flat, open terrain soon were decimated (see Chapter 2). Thus, scientists never saw the connecting links among supposed subspecies. Many of those animals occupied the first lands appropriated for agriculture; thus, being in the most fertile habitat, they may have been the largest elk in a great mosaic of populations with different characteristics. Millais (1915) lamented the lack of trophy elk in North America in the 20th century. He indicated that many really large heads had been brought to England by returning 19th century

hunters. He mentioned a head carrying "thin" antlers that measured 69 inches (175 cm) in length with a 70-inch (178 cm) spread from the Olympic Mountains—hardly a typical Roosevelt elk. Millais also referred to antlers from Rocky Mountain states with 18, 21 and 28 points, and Dodge (1959) reported a set of antlers from an elk shot during the 1800s that weighed (with frontal bone) 61 pounds (27.7 kg)—such heads are nearly unheard of today.

Geographic variation of 16 cranial measurements for 95 specimens of Roosevelt and Tule elk was compared with subspecific taxonomy for populations of Pacific Coast elk (Schonewald-Cox et al. 1985). Principal component analysis indicated that Roosevelt elk in northern California differed as much from those in Washington (mostly Olympic Peninsula) as they did from Tule elk in California. A population of Roosevelt elk on Vancouver Island showed marked differences in size from those on the mainland. Compared with other Roosevelt elk, Vancouver Island animals were characterized by small nasal breadth relative to other cranial measurements, approaching measurements similar to Tule elk. This could be the result of poor nutrition or founder effect if a small number of animals started the island population. Thus, it appears that the presumed Roosevelt subspecies is quite variable, as would be expected of a population that occupies a comparatively narrow strip of habitat hundreds of miles long, north to south, including an island.

The Rocky Mountain elk of the Canadian and U.S. Rockies and Roosevelt elk of coastal Oregon, Washington and British Columbia differ in ways primarily governed by the ecological conditions in which they live—not the genes they carry—according to Geist (1990). Geist maintained that animals of these supposed subspecies, raised under similar ecologic conditions, become indistinguishable from one another.

However, genetic data point to differences between Rocky Mountain and Pacific Northwest elk (Dratch and Gyllensten 1985) (Figure 16). Although the difference lies primarily with one locus, Glenn and Smith (1993) considered it great enough to indicate that elk translocated to Michigan must have included Roosevelt as well as Rocky Mountain elk. Polziehn et al. (1998), using sequences from the control region of mtDNA, found the subspecific status of Roosevelt elk supported. All of her Roosevelt elk tissues (five samples) were from only one source, Vancouver Island, and she sampled only 28 individuals from four presumptive subspecies. Although highly significant differences can be found between subspecies, it does not follow that all individuals of that subspecies can be attributed to it with certainty (P. Dratch personal communication:1997). This is because gene frequencies are attributes of populations, not individual animals.

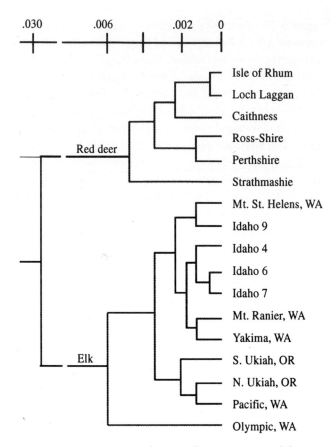

.030   .006   .002   0

Red deer
— Isle of Rhum
— Loch Laggan
— Caithness
— Ross-Shire
— Perthshire
— Strathmashie

Elk
— Mt. St. Helens, WA
— Idaho 9
— Idaho 4
— Idaho 6
— Idaho 7
— Mt. Ranier, WA
— Yakima, WA
— S. Ukiah, OR
— N. Ukiah, OR
— Pacific, WA
— Olympic, WA

Figure 16. Dendrogram of genetic distance among red deer (from 6 locations in Scotland) and elk (from 11 locations in the Pacific Northwest of the United States) as determined by electrophoresis of 28 enzyme loci (from Dratch and Gyllensten 1985). This shows both the genetic distance between subspecies at the extremes of *Cervus elaphus* distribution (D = 0.0248), and the genetic distance between the often accepted Roosevelt subspecies and other Pacific Northwest elk (D = about 0.006).

During a study of elk survival in the Cascade Mountains of Oregon, Stussy et al. (1994) noted that the region hosted an intermixed population of Rocky Mountain and Roosevelt elk. Natural mixing apparently has been augmented by translocations; more than 1,200 animals of both subspecies had been translocated to 50 or more release sites throughout the Cascades since 1947 (Harper 1987).

C. nannodes, the Tule or "dwarf" elk, was named by Merriam in 1905. Principal characteristics were small size, short legs, pale coloration, small, narrow rump patch, and soft (almost woolly) fur on ears. That these elk are small may seem unusual, because, as McCullough et al. (1996:375) observed, "For thousands of years the Tule elk (*Cervus elaphus nannodes*) thrived on arguably the richest agriculture land in the world." However, irrigation was required for that land to reach its potential. Merriam's descriptions and measurements mean little as they were mostly of yearling and 2-year-old animals.

Millais (1915) presented the following observations concerning Tule elk. Before 1840, enormous bands of elk roamed the San Joaquin and Sacramento valleys of central California, living entirely in the open as were bison. Gold seekers made great inroads on them as they were tame and easily shot. Corrals with lateral fences, miles in length, were used by market hunters to capture immense numbers of wild horses, cattle, elk and pronghorn. Meat was sold fresh or dried. Harassment associated with drives to corral traps caused elk to retreat to tule beds along marshes and lagoons, where men on horseback could not pursue them because of mud.

This multitude of elk vanished in the 25 years after the 1849 gold rush. From perhaps 500,000 animals, the Tule elk population crashed to possibly as few as two (McCullough 1969). Protected on a private ranch, they increased to 28 head in 20 years. McCullough et al. (1996) estimated that perhaps five individuals had survived. Thus, the characteristics of extant Tule elk are those of a small segment of the former population, and we will never know what type of a cline (if any) led to that small segment.

McCullough (1969) considered the Tule elk to be the most specialized elk in North America, living as it does in open country under semidesert conditions. Other North American subspecies (now) typically live in temperate climates and use heavy cover at least seasonally. Differences in antler sizes between Tule and other North American elk are substantial. In 1998, the Boone and Crockett Club started recording Tule elk antlers separate from those of Roosevelt and "American" elk (J. Reneau personal communication:1998). The minimum score for the 23rd awards book was 270 Boone and Crockett points. The same scores for American and Roosevelt elk are 360 and 275 points, respectively. Although the Tule elk are comparatively small, their tooth rows were longer, on average, than those of any other presumed subspecies of North American elk—including the supposedly large Merriam's elk (Murie 1951).

D. McCullough (personal communication:1996) can differentiate unlabeled Tule elk museum specimens from those of other North American elk. This subspecies is monomorphic, as indicated from 23 allozyme loci from blood of 76 individuals in two populations (Kucera 1991). There was variation in only 2 of 30 allozymes from livers and kidneys from one population. Another study also indicated extensive loss of genetic variation in Tule elk (R. Denome personal communication:1996). Apparently, bottlenecking—many years of small population size and small founder numbers for translocated herds—resulted in a depauperate genome.

Yearling Tule elk cows reach adult size by midsummer as yearlings and are then indistinguishable from adult cows. In most elk, young cows can be recognized through their second summer. Tule cows also may mature reproductively as yearlings—three of four female yearlings taken in legal hunts were pregnant; the fourth had a corpus luteum, but no fetus was found (McCullough 1969). Other elk cows usually first breed at 2.5 years of age. Also, Tule elk ordinarily rut during August, about 1 month before the rut onset of other elk (McCullough 1969). Differences in breeding times can result in reproductive isolation, as surely as geographic isolation, and remain an isolating factor on secondary contact under natural conditions.

Because of morphological and genetic differences, Tule elk merit subspecific status.

Hutton (1972) compared 272 skulls of Rocky Mountain elk with 25 skulls of Manitoba elk. Nasal width and crown thickness in bulls and cows and pedicel diameters in bulls were highly variable within populations. The width of nasals has been found to be highly variable in other artiodactyl species. Hutton concluded that subspecific status for *manitobensis* could not be substantiated by cranial morphology.

The Alberta Wildlife Management Division does not differentiate between Manitoban and Rocky Mountain elk for management purposes because: "Recent studies of subspeciation using mitochondrial DNA at the Department of Zoology, University of Alberta suggested no detectable differences between *manitobensis* and *nelsoni* (C. Strobeck, personal communication). This led to a decision that genetic mixing from elk transplants was not a concern in Alberta (B. Rippin, NRS wildlife manager, memorandum, 1996). Elk from Elk Island National Park may be transplanted to western locales" (Gunson 1997:150).

Polziehn et al. (1998), using sequences from the control region of mtDNA, concluded that Manitoban and Rocky Mountain elk either are now a complex of relocated and indigenous animals or the two were not historically distinct from each other.

DNA was extracted from 225 elk tissue samples, and genotyped for microsatellite markers using polymerase chain reaction and high resolution gel electrophoresis (Denome 1998). Denome noted that microsatellite alleles are inherited biparentally, whereas mtDNA is inherited maternally and, thus, is poor at assessing gene flow in species of which males are the major mechanism of gene flow.

Tissue samples used in Denome's study were collected from elk in California, Manitoba, Minnesota, North Dakota, Utah and Wyoming, from populations considered to represent Manitoba, Rocky Mountain and Tule subspecies. The patterns of genetic variation and population differentiation were low. "These trends are consistent with a single large population of elk in North America, at least in the recent past. . . . Given these data, it is difficult to justify

the maintenance of the Manitoba subspecies designation" (Denome 1998:1).

The near extinction of elk in the late 19th century, followed by widespread reintroductions from Yellowstone National Park (Murie 1951), could have obliterated much of the historic diversity of North American elk, causing problems in determining the validity of North American subspecies. Protein products of 24 loci from the genomes of Yellowstone Park elk were analyzed by electrophoresis (Cameron and Vyse 1978). Heterozygosity was detected in only one system, indicating elk naturally had little genetic diversity. The Yellowstone elk had not experienced a serious bottleneck, therefore such homozygosity seemed difficult to explain. Also, only one mtDNA haplotype was found in North American elk by Cronin (1992a). However, microsatellite mtDNA data indicate that Yellowstone National Park hosts one of the most genetically diverse elk populations in North America. Polziehn personal communication:1999). This is what one would expect of the herds that survived—in good numbers—the slaughter of elk in Canada and the United States from the 1600s through the 1800s.

After observing that some regard the elk as a separate species from red deer and recognize up to 13 subspecies, Putman (1988:19) wrote: "Within the US, for example, different subspecies are identified in *C. e. roosevelti, C. e. nelsoni, C. e. manitobensis* and *C. e. nannodes*. (Subdivision can, however, continue indefinitely: every ecological population differs subtly in some way from every other, and each could perhaps lay claim to subspecific status. One wonders to what extent finer and finer recognition of such subspecies reflects more local patriotism than any real taxonomic significance!)"

In 1935, Barclay renamed *C. merriami* and *C. nannodes* as *C. elaphus merriami* and *C. e. nannodes*. Apparently, this was the first major publication of the 20th century proposing conspecifity of red deer and elk. McCullough (1969) brought further sense and order to taxonomy of North American elk when he renamed *C. roosevelti* and *C. canadensis nelsoni* as *C. e. roosevelti* and *C. e. nelsoni*. Apparently, the Manitoban elk was ignored in taxonomic revisions. If it was changed from *C. canadensis manitobensis* to *C. elaphus manitobensis* when *C. elaphus* and *C. canadensis* were combined, the publication was not found.

Few barriers to gene flow among elk populations seem to have existed in North America. West Coast elk apparently were somewhat isolated, and populations were evolving to cope with habitat conditions quite different from those faced by most elk. Because intermediate populations were exterminated, we can only speculate on how isolated populations were, and no clinal variation can be established. However, Tule elk were geographically isolated from Rocky Mountain elk before the arrival of Europeans and, at minimum, had a strong genetic filter with Roosevelt elk (D. McCullough personal communication:1997).

Had Roosevelt elk been reduced to only a few animals in the thickest, wettest habitat of the Olympic Peninsula and had not human influences promoted mixing, that population apparently would now constitute a subspecies. Although Roosevelt elk populations are recognizable by biochemical tests, and some individuals can be identified by color and antlers, many could not be differentiated from Manitoba or Rocky Mountain elk. Comments from biologists in the Pacific Coast states harboring Rocky Mountain and Roosevelt elk bear this out.

In California, according to a two-page letter from the California Department of Fish and Game, dated March 25, 1997, and signed by Wildlife Management Division chief T. M. Mansfield: "Geographical location has been the primary means of differentiating between subspecies, but general characteristics, as described by McCullough (1969), also have been used to help differentiate them. In a court of law, it is likely that statements made by Department employees regarding subspecies classification of a given specimen would be based primarily on geographic location and such statements would be more qualified than absolute."

In Oregon, there is natural mixing of Rocky Mountain and Roosevelt elk across the crest of the Cascade Mountains (D. Edwards personal communication:1996). Translocations also contribute to crossbreeding. Heavy, narrow antlers characterize some bulls west of the Cascade crest, but the same sometimes are seen east of the crest in typical Rocky Mountain elk habitat.

The Washington Department of Fish and Wildlife manages elk east of the Cascade crest as Rocky Mountain elk and those west of the crest as Roosevelt elk. However, some Rocky Mountain and Roosevelt elk cross the crest from one year to the next. Thus, the border between subspecies is soft. Also, several translocations of elk from Yellowstone National Park into native Roosevelt elk habitat occurred during 1915 through 1925. Many of the elk from Interstate Highway 5 to the Cascade crest and in the Willapa Hills are intergrades. The only pure Roosevelt elk are on the Olympic Peninsula, according to R. Johnson (personal communication:1997): "I do not think there is a biologist who could examine a western Washington elk and swear in court it was a Roosevelt or a Rocky Mountain elk, except in rare instances where the elk clearly shows the type characteristics. Even then, the biologist will have a difficult time making the call."

The distinctiveness of each extant (presumed) North American subspecies of *C. elaphus* was tested using craniometric data from 250 adult elk. Schonewald (1994:431) wrote: "Morphometric variations in size, shape and sexual dimorphism of adult crania were analyzed using combined male–female principal component analyses. North American subspecies do not represent natural biogeographic variation as earlier presumed."

Considering the elk of North America to constitute two subspecies, *C. e. canadensis* (vernacular names Roosevelt, Manitoban and Rocky Mountain elk) and *C. e. nannodes* (Tule elk), is the only classification consistent with criteria suggested in this chapter. Murie (1951) accepted two species of elk in North America—*C. nannodes* and *C. canadensis* (including Roosevelt, Manitoban and Rocky Mountain elk). Before red deer and elk were considered conspecific, such classification was logical. Groves and Grubb (1987:50) wrote: "We accept *nannodes* as valid but think the other North American subspecies should all be lumped as *C. e. canadensis.*"

The Boone and Crockett Club lists the boundaries for Roosevelt elk as: Del Norte and Humboldt counties, California; west of Highway I-5 in Oregon and Washington; Vancouver Island, British Columbia; and Afognak and Raspberry islands, Alaska. The Alaskan animals were translocated from the Olympic Peninsula of Washington (Reneau and Reneau 1993). Whether the subspecies *C. e. roosevelti* is recognized or not, those boundaries do delineate a group of elk that produces trophies differing in length and number of points from those of other North American elk populations. Thus, eliminating *C. e. roosevelti* as a formal subspecies should, in no way, preclude maintaining the present recognition of Roosevelt elk (common name) as a separate trophy category.

Heptner et al. (1961)—despite elucidating no detectable biological differences—chided Flerov (1952) for suggesting that Siberian and Rocky Mountain elk should be united into one subspecies—*C. e. canadensis*. To Heptner et al. (1961), the sheer geographic distance between these forms (although explainable by late Pleistocene events) justified subspecific segregation. After examining Siberian and North American elk, Geist (1989a) concurred with Flerov (1952).

Guthrie (1966) noted that elk exhibited little speciation during the latter part of the Pleistocene epoch. Lack of speciation resulted in a circumpolar group exhibiting no major morphological discontinuities. The elk of Asia and North America apparently have been separated for only about 10,000 years, so one should not expect a great deal of genetic differentiation in these highly mobile and comparatively monomorphic animals. Phenotypic changes, resulting in apparent subspecies, can occur within a few generations.

It is no surprise that Flerov's (1952) theory, that some elk in Siberia were the same subspecies as were elk in North America, met stiff resistance at the time. With little study of the situation, common sense told most taxonomists that Old and New World elk were separate species—let alone subspecies. Typical of his time, Murie (1951) maintained that elk of Asia and North America differed little, but because of the geographic interruption of range between Old and New World populations, he believed it hardly proper to consider them forms of the same species.

Alaska and eastern Siberia had the same animals before the Bering Land Bridge sank below the waves of the Bering Straits at the end of the last Ice Age, some 10,000 years ago. Therefore, not only are the Inuit people on either side of the Bering Strait closely related, so is almost everything else. "The elk from northern Mongolia, Transbaikalia and the lofty Altai Mountains look exactly like our elk, sound like our elk, and some currently unpublished evidence from molecular biology indicates that they are virtually identical to our elk" (Geist 1990:102). If the elk of North America have not changed genetically in a significant way, as indicated by Cronin's (1992a) work, it should be no surprise that elk in Asia derived from the same stock still are similar.

B. Warren (personal communication:1996), an experienced hunter of elk in Asia and North America, uses the same bugle and hunting techniques on elk of both continents. He reported that he cannot detect differences in rutting behavior or voices of the two groups, but Asian bulls seem to respond best to bugling as opposed to cow calls.

Cronin (1992a) found a lack of significant variation in mtDNA among North American elk populations from four supposed subspecies. He noted a small difference between the geographically disjunct Asian elk from outer Mongolia and North American elk. M. A. Cronin (personal communication:1997) has since seen a unique mtDNA genotype in Vancouver Island elk. Unpublished data of the Saskatchewan Research Council indicated little genetic difference among elk of Canada and the Altai Republic of Siberia. Polziehn and Strobeck (1998) compared the control regions of mtDNA among Asian and North American elk (Figure 17); they found the nucleotide difference in the consensus sequences differed by 1.23%. The same differences between red deer and elk, red deer and sika, and elk and sika were 5.60%, 5.02% and 5.19%, respectively. Larger sample sizes and other genetic studies are needed to verify the apparent closer relationship between sika and either elk or red deer than that between elk and red deer.

An extensive literature review indicated that Altai and Rocky Mountain elk are similar in many ways not already noted in this chapter (Table 2).

The only reason to place Tien Shan, Altai and New World (*C. e. canadensis*) elk into separate subspecies at this time would involve the geographic distance between them. According to Mayr (1970), discussing intelligently the na-

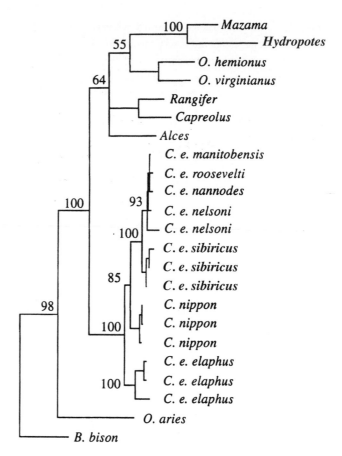

Figure 17. A majority-rule consensus tree for North American and Siberian elk, European red deer and Asian sika deer, as defined by the outgroups domestic sheep and American bison (from Polziehn and Strobeck 1998). The tree is based on six parsimonious trees analyzed using sequence data from the control region of mtDNA. It required 1,173 steps, has a consistency index of 0.705 and the frequency of each branch is given at each node. For example, if 100 equally likely or parsimonious trees were found to describe the relationship among a set number of taxa, then a node with 100 suggests that this bifurcation is found in all 100 trees, and similarly, a node with 75 suggests that this branching pattern is found in 75 of the trees.

ture and origin of isolating mechanisms is impossible if one includes with them so extraneous an element as geographic isolation. Indeed, one of the objectives of taxonomy is to enable identifying a specimen and placing it in the proper taxon. If that cannot be done without knowing where the specimen came from, the whole concept of taxonomy is suspect. However, Polziehn and Strobeck (1998) estimated, from mtDNA, that North American and Siberian elk diverged about 52,000 years ago. If that is correct, further DNA analyses may provide a dependable criterion for differentiating elk from the two continents. Then, Altai and Tien Shan elk should be considered *C. e. sibiricus* or *C. e. songaricus*, whichever was named first.

Altai and Tien Shan elk display more variation in color

Table 2. Apparent similar physical and behavioral characteristics of Altai and Rocky Mountain elk

Characteristics	Source
Gestation period	Boyd (1978), Flerov (1952)
Parturition (timing, behavior, twinning)	Johnson (1951), Murie (1951), Flerov (1952), Taber et al. (1982)
Size of calves	Johnson (1951), Heptner et al. (1961)
Growth and development of calves	Murie (1951), Flerov (1952)
Social units	Flerov (1952), Altman (1956a), Heptner et al. (1961), Shoesmith (1978)
Seasonal movements	Flerov (1952), Heptner et al. (1961), Grkovic (1976), Leege and Hickey (1977)
Feeding behavior	Murie (1951), Flerov (1952), Heptner et al. (1961), Nelson and Leege (1982)
Rutting behavior (timing, fighting, urine spraying, wallowing, harems, etc.)	Murie (1932, 1951), Flerov (1952), Heptner et al. (1961), Struhsaker (1967), Boyd (1978), Geist (1982)
Predator avoidance	Flerov (1952), Altman (1956b), Heptner et al. (1961), Craighead et al.(1972), Geist (1982)
Pelage and molts	Flerov (1952), Boyd (1978)
Antler growth and casting	Murie (1951), Flerov (1952), Boyd (1978)
Longevity	Heptner et al. (1961), Walker et al. (1975)

and antler configuration than do elk in North America. This could be natural or human induced. Most Asian subspecies of *C. elaphus* have been raised in captivity for centuries, perhaps millennia. Crossbreeding has been common, and some captives always escape. However, variations are within the range of those occasionally seen in North America. There seem to be more reasons than not to make Altai and Tien Shan elk consubspecific with all North American elk, except the Tule elk.

Summary and Conclusions

Identification of the units of conservation requires thoughtful integration of available information of all types (Ryder 1986, Dowling et al. 1992). A combination of information including morphology, antler configuration and size, pelage, color, social insignia, behavior, voice, natural history, blood proteins and DNA were considered when evaluating the taxonomic status of *C. elaphus* at specific and subspecific levels.

Bryant and Maser (1982) submitted that studying museum specimens is unwise if any doubt exists concerning purity of the genetic stock. Unfortunately, introductions have so contaminated native gene pools in the ranges of many *C. elaphus* populations that one can only wonder whether we are naming purebreds or mixed gene pools.

A number of what we call subspecies today perhaps should be called human-induced subspecies. Large groups of animals occupying major segments of continents have been reduced to island populations with small founder numbers. This is especially a problem with large ruminants when the dominant bull displaces others from breeding and after breeding several cohorts of daughters, is displaced in turn by his larger sons (Geist 1992). Some Asian subspecies listed here, especially in the Tibeto-Himalayan region, probably should be combined. However, reliable data are scarce, and all chances to evaluate such populations in their natural relationships to other subspecies and clines among them have been lost. Also, the chance exists that subspecies or crossbreeding swarms in Asia remain to be identified.

The following is what some will call a lumper's list of *C. elaphus* subspecies. Actually, it is a lumper's list for Europe and North America, but a splitter's list for the Mediterranean and Tibeto-Himalayan areas. Without adequate information to make changes, the status quo should not be disturbed. Genetic studies and greater access to Asian populations may lead to unification of more presently recognized subspecies. Common synonyms are in parentheses after areas occupied by proposed subspecies.

Cervus elaphus

  elaphus, central and western Europe (*typicus, hippelaphus, germanicus,* at least 17 more)

  atlanticus, British Isles, Norway (*scoticus*)

  hispanicus, southern Spain, Portugal (*bolivari*)

  corsicanus, Corsica, Sardinia (*minor, mediterraneus*)

  barbarus, Algeria, Tunisia

  maral, eastern Europe, Asia Minor (*montanus, pannoniensis*)

  bactrianus, northern Afghanistan, Tajikistan, Turkmenistan, Uzbekistan (*hagenbeckii*)

  yarkandensis, Xinjiang Province, China

  hanglu, Kashmir (*C. casperianus, C. cashmeriensis, C. casmeerianus, C. cashmirianus*)

  wallichi, eastern Tibet, possibly Bhutan (*C. Tibetans, C. narrowness, C. e. affinis*)

  macneilli, northern Tibet, Sichuan, Dinghai, Gansu and Shaanxi provinces, China (*kansuensis*)

  alashanicus, Ningxia Province, China

  xanthopygus, northern North Korea, northeastern China, Outer Mongolia, eastern Siberia

  canadensis, Altai, Sayan and Tien Shan of Asia; all occupied elk range of North America except southern California; see Chapter 2 (*songaricus, sibiricus, asiaticus, wachei, roosevelti, nelsoni, manitobensis*)

  nannodes, southern California

Rump patches—one of the diagnostic characteristics of *C. elaphus* subspecies—of the above named subspecies are illustrated in Figure 18. Like all biological characteristics, individual and seasonal variations occur. Also, emaciated deer, such as those often seen on Asian antler farms or anywhere in menageries, have exceedingly small rump patches compared with those of deer in good condition.

The reduction in the number of commonly recognized subspecies from 22 to 15 was not to reduce numbers, but to satisfy two criteria: (1) an individual from a subspecies should be identifiable as a member of that taxon by mor-

phological or genetic criteria, or both; for instance, almost any competent zoologist could identify a specimen of *C. e. canadensis* as defined here, but few if any could swear in court that a specimen was *C. e. manitobensis, nelsoni* or *sibiricus*; and (2) although very different from each other, populations at the extremes of clines are not subspecies (or species); conspecific status for red deer and elk depends heavily on this principle. At the subspecies level, populations along a cline ordinarily would interbreed to some extent.

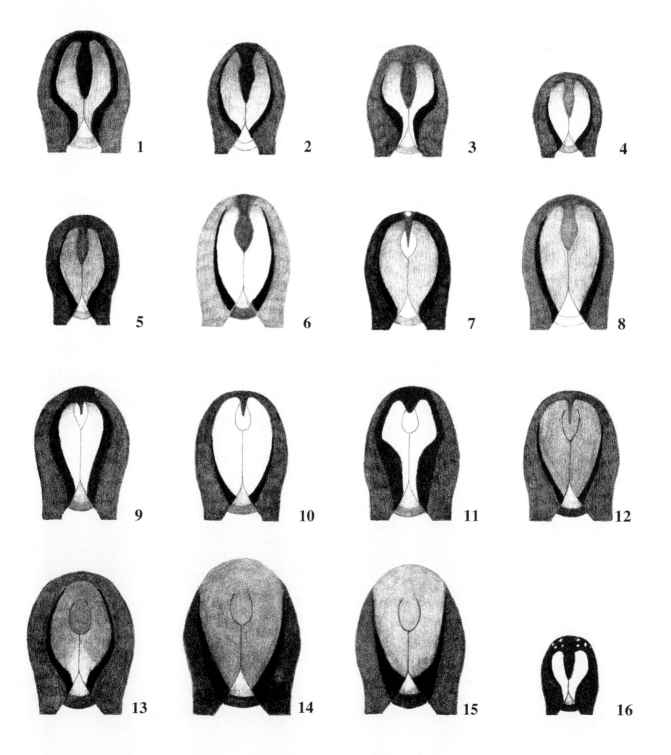

Before subspecies became legal entities, naming ecotypes as subspecies had a purpose. That purpose should not be lost. Slight differences in animals and set geographic areas were recognized. Conservation efforts should focus below the species level because of concerns about the fitness, evolutionary potentials and locally adapted gene pools of natural populations (Soulé 1986, Hedrick and Miller 1992). This can be considered the morphological and genetic component of biodiversity. Common names, if standardized, could serve the same purpose in some cases. Scottish red deer and Rocky Mountain elk will remain in the vocabulary and reflect sets of physical characteristics and habitats as well as did *C. e. scoticus* and *C. e. nelsoni*. However, communication among scientists or others who speak different lan-

Figure 18.   Rump patches characteristic of 15 presumptive subspecies of *Cervus elaphus,* with a *C. nippon* for comparison. *Illustrations by Rex McGraw.*

1. During winter, the upper portion of *C. e. elaphus* rump patches are fox red, as is the tail. This coloration varies to yellowish-red in some Swedish deer. Patch coloration is lighter during summer, and the dividing line often is less visible at that time. The entire patch usually is framed by dark hairs, but borders are less apparent during summer—especially along the dorsal edge. The bellies and inner back legs vary from grayish-white to reddish-yellow, depending on area and time of year.

2. The rump patches of *C. e. atlanticus* are rather narrow. The upper portion is fox red—lighter than the dark croup from which a stripe generally extends onto the root of the tail. The lower two-thirds, as well as the inner back legs, is white or nearly so. The lower patch is edged by dark hairs, more conspicuous in some individuals than others. The patches are not completely framed in Scottish animals, but some are in Norway.

3. The upper portion of the rump patch and dorsal surface of the tail are pale ochre in *C. e. hispanicus*. The narrow lower portion and inner legs are white. The lower half of the patch is framed by sepia hairs.

4. Rump patches of the tiny, dark-colored *C. e. corsicanus* are yellowish-red dorsally, but whitish from the root of the reddish tail down. It is edged on either side by a dark stripe.

5. The rump patch of *C. e. barbarus* is straw yellow, with an admixture of red in its upper portion. Dark lines, framing the lower part, are not apparent during winter. The dorsal surface of the tail is darker and redder than the patch.

6. *C. e. maral* has a comparatively short tail that is nearly the same color as the grayish-brown back. The large rump patch reaches high on the croup and is yellowish-red anteriorly. From the tail down, it is white or nearly so, and the inner hind legs are smokey brown. The dark lateral lines are indistinct.

7. The *C. e. bactrianus* rump patch is bordered ventrally by blackish-brown stripes that do not extend quite to the tail, and is divided by an indistinct line. The patch is sandy white but becomes reddish anteriorly, mixing with the color of the croup.

8. The rump patch of *C. e. yarkandensis* is white except that the anterior portion is mixed with rufous hairs. A line of the same color extends onto the tail. The patch is edged by blackish-brown hairs.

9. The rump patch of *C. e. hanglu* is comparatively small, extending just above the root of the tail—much like that of the sika deer, *C. nippon*. It is divided by a blackish-brown median line that terminates on the tail. The patch is creamy white, but yellows anteriorly. The comparatively wide, blackish-brown stripes bordering the patch join on the croup.

10. The white rump patches of *C. e. wallichi* extend well onto the croup. Apparently, some individuals have a dark median line dividing the rump patches and extending onto the tail. Available descriptions and photos indicate only slightly darkened hair bracketing the patches.

11. The white rump patch of *C. e. macneilli* extends just above the root of the tail. Dark hair on the croup joins with the broad stripes bracketing the patch and extending to the root of the tail or, variably, onto its dorsal surface. In the northern part of this subspecies' range, the general body color is so dark that the lateral and dorsal stripes are barely noticeable.

12. The rufous rump patch of *C. e. alashanicus* has narrow, blackish borders around its lower half. A dark dorsal line continues to the tail, dividing the upper portion. As in all elk, the belly is dark.

13. The rump patch of *C. e. xanthopygus* is fox red, but tends to lighten between the buttocks. It is bordered by lines of blackish-brown hairs, broadest on the lower buttocks.

14. The large rump patch, with matching tail, of *C. e. canadensis* has little variation in color on an individual. However, over the subspecies' vast range—and sometimes within one herd—color varies from fox red through orange, buff, straw and cream to white. The patch usually is framed with blackish hairs around its lower half. In parts of the Altai Mountains and surrounding country, a dark dorsal stripe divides the rump patch on the croup, and something extends onto the tail. This may indicate mixing—natural or human-induced—with other subspecies.

15. The rump patch of *C. e. nannodes* generally is creamy buff, with dark brown lateral lines extending about half way up its sides. It is comparatively light, but similar to patches of *C. e. canadensis*.

16. The rump patch of a sika deer, *C. nippon* is depicted here for comparison. *C. elaphus* generally is considered to have evolved from a sika-like ancestor, and subspecies intermediate to western European red deer and elk show some sika-like characteristics. These include small, white rump patches and spotted summer coats. Although small, sika rump patches are erectile—much like those of pronghorn.

guages will suffer. Perhaps placing a former subspecific name in parentheses—*C. e. atlanticus (scoticus)*—could help in communication as long as rule makers do not try to make them legal entities.

Further study is needed concerning the clinal nature—or lack of it—of *C. e. elaphus* from Great Britain to North America. This preliminary survey indicates three major groupings: (1) the deer of central and western Europe, Great Britain and North Africa—the red deer or elaphine group; (2) the animals from eastern Europe to the Tibeto-Himalayan region and north into central Asia; and (3) the elk of central to eastern Asia and North America. Banwell (2000) proposed the same grouping of subspecies, which he distinguished as Atlantics, Maraloids and Wapitoids. He presented an up-to-date summary of the range and status of *Cervus elaphus,* based to a great extent on his personal observations.

Probably with genetic studies, *C. e. barbarus* and *corsicanus* will be combined with *C. e. elaphus.* The elaphine group does not noticeably grade into the deer of the Middle East. The deer of western Asia are a diverse group, some of which resemble forms ancestral to both red deer and elk. Animals of the Himalayan area with small rump patches and large, dark tails seem to grade toward the north into forms having larger rump patches and shorter tails of the same light color. Possibly, some of these forms graded into each other and even into the elk of central Asia before intermediate populations were exterminated. Modern genetic studies are indicated for this group, but obtaining tissues from the wild will be especially difficult. Tissues from zoos and antler farms may be obtainable, but their genetic purity probably would remain questionable.

Whitehead (1993) used the old classification—*C. elaphus* and *C. canadensis.* Within *canadensis,* he included subspecies *asiaticus, songaricus, xanthopygus, alashanicus, kansuensis* and *macneilli.* This review indicates that those six groups do represent the elk in Asia; although, they should be in four rather than six subspecies. Groves and Grubb (1987) proposed that *macneilli, kansuensis* and *xanthopygus* be graded into each other. This seems possible, but *alashanicus* probably should be in the gradient between *kansuensis* and *xanthopygus.*

While preparing this chapter and conferring with colleagues and reviewers, I was reminded of Futuyama's (1979:viii) comments on evolution, the basis of taxonomy: "Evolution is, to me, the most exciting subject in biology, partly because it is so all-encompassing, partly because it is the study of dynamic processes rather than static facts, and partly because it's a lot of fun to argue about. Almost any question in evolution—Is geographic isolation a prerequisite for species formation?—is approached more by logic or circumstantial evidence than by direct observation, and so often is never quite resolved. Very often no single 'right' answer applies universally. The literature of evolutionary biology reflects the dynamic changes in ideas that the complexity of the subject compels."

Distribution: Past and Present

Geologic time can be subdivided in many ways. Numeric dates, such as 40,000 years ago, are the most useful, but placing numeric ages on fossil localities or specimens is not always possible. Therefore, geologists have devised various means of establishing relative dates to make correlations. Land mammal ages (LMA) are based on the first and last appearances of taxa (Woodburne 1987). For this discussion, three North American LMA—Blancan, Irvingtonian and Rancholabrean—were used. Figure 19 illustrates the relationships between these LMA and the numeric time scale as well as different glacial and interglacial events for North America and Europe.

Historic biogeography can be studied in a variety of ways, including analyses of deoxyribonucleic acid (DNA) sequences and the distributions of fossil sites through time. Both methods have their strengths and weaknesses. With the distribution of fossil sites, it is possible to confirm the presence of a taxon at a certain time in a specific area. However, the absence of sites does not necessarily mean that the organism was not present in an area at a given time. Paleontologists try to filter the biases of the fossil record by understanding the processes involved in the accumulation and preservation of fossils. Unfortunately, these studies, known as taphonomy, were initiated in a formal sense only during the mid-20th century (Efremov 1940). Standardization of taphonomic data and their reporting has developed in the past few decades (Behrensmeyer and Hook 1992). Taphonomic pathways must be considered in evaluating the past distribution of any fossil organism. For *Cervus* in North America, its utilization as a resource by prehistoric people during the Holocene—the past 10,000 years—has created an abundance of Holocene localities. The Pleistocene distribution is much sparser and may be the result of low numbers of elk at that time or poor preservation of their remains.

The ability to identify a taxon on the basis of different skeletal elements also is a critical factor in evaluating the fossil record. Because of the diversity of medium to large cervids during the Pleistocene in North America (Table 3), identification of *Cervus* from Pleistocene deposits, especially on the basis of size of postcranial skeletal elements, can be problematic. Antlers are one of the most distinguishing features used in recognizing *Cervus elaphus,* although considerable variability exists in their morphology. However, when antlers are preserved, they frequently are fragmentary. Antlers of *Cervus* generally are rare in the Pleistocene of the midcontinent of North America compared with the same time in Europe (Lister 1986) and Alaska (Guthrie 1966). The reasons for this are uncertain. They could involve preservational differences related to depositional environments (e.g., bogs, lakes, stream deposits, caves). The possibility also exists that the animals were relatively scarce.

In this analysis, for sites older than 40,000 years, the scientific literature was reviewed for localities containing *Cervus.* For sites in the United States younger than 40,000 years, there was reliance on the FAUNMAP database—FAUNMAP is an electronic database derived from a review

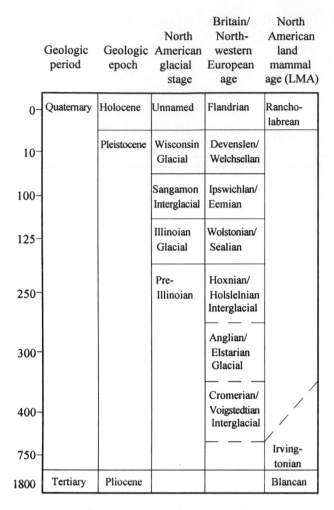

Figure 19. Relationship between land mammal ages (LMA), geologic time intervals, glacial/interglacial fluctuations and numeric ages. The time when the Irvington LMA merged into the Rancholabrean remains controversial.

Table 3. Temporal distribution of genera of North American cervids for land mammal ages (LMA) of the Pliocene epoch, Quaternary period (65–1.8 million years before present [ybp]) and Cenozoic era (65 million years ybp to present)

	Epochs			
	Pliocene	Pleistocene		
	Blancan LMA (4.5 million– 1.8 million ybp)	Irvingtonian LMA (1.8 million– 400,000 ybp)	Rancholabrean LMA (400,000– 10,000 ybp)	Holocene
Cervalces		X	X	
Alces				X
Cervus	?	?	X	X
Rangifer	X	X	X	X
Navahoceros			X	
Odocoileus	X	X	X	X
Bretzia	X	?	X	
Torontoceros			X	
Blastoceros			X	X

Note: Taxa are listed by relative body size, with largest at the top.

elaphus is known from European deposits 500,000 years before present (Lister 1986), and the species may have entered North America about then (Lundelius et al. 1987). However, the fragmentary nature of American fossils precludes firm conclusions. Positive identification of *C. elaphus* in North America is possible only from fossils dated at about 40,000 years before present or later (see Guthrie 1966). Records of elk fossils became numerous only within the past 10,000 years because of utilization of the animals by humans and preservation of remains in archeological sites.

Miocene to Early Pleistocene Evolution

Most orders, or main groups, of placental mammals originated in Europe and Asia during the Late Paleocene (60.9–55.6 million years before present). Great diversification occurred within these orders during the Oligocene and Miocene (see Table 4 for approximate geologic times). According to Groves and Grubb (1987), phylogenetic relationships of deer have been confusing because workers have tended to study fossil or recent material independently, using different morphological characters. Fossil cervids occur across Asia, but knowledge of these forms is limited by the primitive state of geologic correlation over vast areas. Also, political and other practical problems have confounded researchers.

The reconstruction of the evolutionary history of any group is dependent to a great extent on an adequate fossil record. Armed with some knowledge of available fossils, it is possible to look at extant species and make an educated

of the scientific literature (Faunmap Working Group 1994). Criteria for incorporation into the database include a published account, geologic or stratigraphic age known and younger than 40,000 years, geographic location of site known and specimens placed in a public institution (museum, university, etc.). Unpublished specimens and specimens of unknown age or location are not in the database. For Canadian records, the Saskatchewan Radiocarbon Dates and Vertebrate Faunas database (Morlan et al. 1996) and Canadian Museum of Civilization database (Morlan 1999) were used. For both of those databases, *Cervus* specimens had to be associated with radiocarbon dates. Because all *Cervus* specimens do not come from dated sites, other published localities were included.

Cervus evolved and diversified in Eurasia during the Pliocene—4.5 to 1.8 million years before present. The genus may have reached North America by the end of the Pliocene, but fossils are few, fragmentary and controversial. *C.*

Table 4. The geologic time scale since mammals became abundant during the Cenozoic era, or Age of Mammals

Period	Estimated time since beginning of each epoch (millions of years)	Epoch	Mammals
	0.010[a]	Holocene	Modern species and subspecies; extinction of some mammals; dominance of humans
Quaternary	1.8	Pleistocene	Appearance of modern species and subspecies; extinction of some large mammals; widespread glaciation
	5.2	Pliocene	Appearance of modern genera
	23.0	Miocene	Appearance of modern subfamilies
	33.4	Oligocene	Appearance of modern families
	55.6	Eocene	Appearance of modern orders
Tertiary	65.1	Paleocene	Primitive marsupials and placental mammals dominant

Note: Taxa typical of each epoch are indicated (after Romer 1970 and Woodburne 1987); times are from Janis and Manning (1998).

[a] 10,000 years.

guess concerning the most probable sequence of evolutionary change (Eisenberg 1987).

The Eocene epoch *Archeomeryx,* fossil remains of which have been found in Outer Mongolia, generally is placed at the root of all cerviforms. Ancestral forms, apparently close to the roots of the phylogenetic tree of cervids, had four-toed limbs and were omnivorous. They inhabited a vast area of wet tropical and subtropical forests from western Europe to central Asia. *Amphitragulus* appeared in the Late Oligocene (29.4–23.0 million years before present) and may be considered ancestral to the Miocene *Dremotherium* and *Paleomeryx,* which constitute the source of the branch of the Cervidae of Eurasia. *Dremotherium* bears some resemblance to contemporary musk deer. In the Middle Miocene (some 14.5 million years ago), the first true deer, *Dicrocerus,* appeared and resembled the present day muntjacs and probably were ancestral to them (Figure 20). During this period, deer apparently moved from the damp, marshy thickets into drier forests with open areas as such habitats evolved. Changes in the morphology of teeth indicate that coarse foliage and grasses entered the diet (Eisenberg 1987).

Tertiary deer moved from tropical forests into tree-studded savannah—then into treeless steppe, cool temperate

Cervus elaphus acornatus
Middle Pleistocene

Pseudaxis
Late Pliocene

Axis-like
Early Pliocene

Dicrocerus
Mid Miocene

Dremotherium
Miocene

Figure 20. Conception of the appearance of fossil deer leading to *C. elaphus,* from descriptions by various investigators (dating and names from Flerov 1952).

Table 5.   Dates of early, middle and late time classifications in epochs referred to in the chapter

Geologic era	Geologic period	Geologic epoch	Millions of years ago
Cenozoic	Quaternary	Holocene	0.01
		Pleistocene	1.8
	Tertiary	Pliocene	
		Late	2.4
		Early	5.2
		Miocene	
		Late	11.0
		Middle	16.8
		Early	23.0
		Oligocene	
		Late	29.4
		Early	33.4
		Eocene	
		Late	37.1
		Middle	50.4
		Early	55.6
		Paleocene	
		Late	60.9
		Early	65.1

Sources: Miocene and Pliocene data from Janis and Manning (1998); Pleistocene and Holocene data from Faunmap Working Group (1994).

zones, high cold mountains and finally into harsh glacial landscapes of the Ice Ages (between 1.8 million and 10,000 years ago). Progressive adaptations to increasingly seasonal climates spun off new species (Geist and Francis 1991).

Eustylocerus (Cervulinae) lived during Late Miocene/Early Pliocene times and the Middle and Late Miocene apparently saw development of the true Cervidae in Eurasia (see Table 5 for dates of early, middle and late periods of the four most recent epochs). Cervulinae divided into two branches at the end of the Miocene; one led to the muntjacs, and the other bifurcated to lines leading to *Capreolus* and *Cervavitus.* The latter, in a group known as the Pliocervini, were the first representatives of the subfamily Cervinae. These deer possessed more complex antlers, their feet still bore unreduced lateral toes, and grassy plants became frequent in their diets as they came to dwell in savannas and littoral zones. During the Early Pliocene, *Cervavitus* died out and was replaced by more evolved groups—including deer that were closely allied to the now living axis and rusa deer. In the Late Pliocene, *Axis*-like deer evolved to a form closely resembling contemporary sika deer that have occupied parts of Asia to the present time. Sika deer have four tines, not three as in *Axis,* through forking of the superior point (Flerov 1952). *Pseudaxis grayi,* strikingly similar to contemporary sika deer, was a common element of fossil fauna in the Middle Pleistocene of China (Young 1932).

Animals similar to present-day sika apparently gave rise to the base stock from which elk and red deer diverged. Protein and DNA studies tend to support the fossil record in linking *Cervus nippon* to *C. elaphus.* The spotted summer coat is retained in calves of both groups, as is the reddish summer coloration in calves and adults. Increased body size, as well as that of antlers and rump patches, ensued. *Photo by Leonard Lee Rue III.*

Early Pleistocene Distribution of *Cervus*

A considerable proportion of research on Quaternary cervids has been devoted to antler remains, which are often abundant as fossils and are generally the most taxonomically diagnostic elements

Lister (1987:82)

Segments of mitochondrial cytochrome b gene and the mitochondrial control region from five subspecies of sika were amplified using the polymerase chain reaction and sequenced (Cook 1993). Calculated divergence times suggested that sika radiated from a common cervid ancestor about 2 million years ago. *Cervus elaphus acornatus,* the most ancient known subspecies of *C. elaphus,* apparently evolved from a sika-like deer, but was still closely allied to them. A simple fork terminated the upper antler, but brow and bez tines (as is characteristic of most *C. elaphus*) were present (Flerov 1952) (Figure 21). Mitochondrial DNA studies indicate that *C. elaphus* and sika deer have been separated for about 1.3 million years (Li 1996).

Figure 21. The apparent line of evolution within *C. elaphus*. Perhaps in central Asia, where somewhat similar deer still exist, early red deer with five-point per side antlers (*top*) were ancestral to elk (*center*) and western red deer (*bottom*). The dashed line indicates the documental transformation, at least of antlers, as indicated by the fossil record in Europe. The solid line indicates the apparent transformation within Asia. Changes there have not been documented through the fossil record, but seem roughly similar to the sequence of subspecies—from the hangul in northern India to the elk of Siberia—documented in Chapter 1.

The genus *Cervus* arose in the Old World during the Pliocene and diversified with numerous species evolving in Eurasia. The first evidence of *C. elaphus* in Europe is from the early Middle Pleistocene Cromerian interglacial at west Runton and Voigtstedt (Lister 1986). It was widespread throughout Eurasia by the Middle Pleistocene. An early form, *C. e. acoronatus* (Beninde 1937, Di Stefano and Petronio 1992), is characterized by tops of antlers with a simple two-point transverse fork occasionally bearing a small accessory point between and in the plane of the two main points (Lister 1986). From the Hoxnian until present day, the tops of European *C. elaphus* antlers are many pointed and form a three-dimensional crown, although not expressed in all individuals of all populations. The transition between these two forms occurred sometime during Europe's Anglian/Elsterian glacial age (Lister 1986).

Cervus may have dispersed to the New World some time during the Late Pliocene or Early Pleistocene (Irvingtonian LMA) (Lundelius et al. 1987). Unlike the Eurasian record of *Cervus* that is documented by fossil antlers, the early remains from North America are primarily sparse and fragmentary skeletal elements. Consequently, many of these early records of *Cervus* are somewhat equivocal. In fact, numerous fossil

species of *Cervus* have been described for North America, for example, *C. fortis* (Cope 1878), *C. lucasi* (Hay 1927), *C. aguangae* (Frick 1937) and *C. ? brevitrabalis* (Cope 1889), but most of these are considered to be based on material too fragmentary to be valid (Kurtén and Anderson 1980).

The earliest apparent record of *Cervus* from North America is from the Blancan LMA Grand View local fauna of the Glenns Ferry Formation, Idaho (Table 6, Figure 22). The fragmentary jaw of a juvenile individual (Shotwell 1970) and numerous skeletal elements best compare with *Cervus*. Shotwell (1970) noted many differences in the morphology of the dentition of this lower jaw fragment in contrast to modern *C. elaphus*. In fact, he indicated that many of the dental features are more similar to *Odocoileus* than to *Cervus*. Shotwell also wrote that astragali, a humerus fragment, phalanges and a naviculor-cuboid are close in size and character to those of *Cervus*. Hibbard (1959) reported a *Cervus*-like antler fragment from the Grand View local fauna; but according to Guthrie (1966), Hibbard later questioned this assignment. In his later review of the Grand View fauna, Shotwell (1970) did not discuss the antler fragment other than to mention the Hibbard reference. Finally, Shotwell (1970:100) noted, "The new material [described by Shotwell] indicates a cervine with dental characteristics close to *Odocoileus* but in size similar to *Cervus*. Its assignment to either genus seems unlikely unless the genus *Cervus* is viewed in the broadest way. In this broad sense it is possible to include the new material in *Cervus*." This statement is confusing, considering that nothing was mentioned concerning sizes of either genus at that time. The sika-like *Cervus* of Asia were small deer. Geist (1998:185) observed that "In North America the assignment of the genus '*Cervus*' to animals with large cervid-like teeth obscures the paleontological record of wapitis, the habit of taxonomists to take size differences seriously leads to a muddling of the record."

Conrad (1980) described new material from Grand View and, in his assessment, several antler bases appear to have patterns characteristic of *Cervus*, branching of two major tines immediately above the burr. He also reported additional teeth and skeletal elements. The jaw originally referred to *Cervus* by Shotwell (1970) was accepted by Conrad, but he did not mention the antler described by Hibbard (1959). On the basis of paleomagnetic evidence (Conrad 1980) and microtine biochronology (Repenning et al. 1995), the Grand View local fauna is considered to be about 2.1 million years old. This would be about 800,000 years before *C. elaphus* and bez tines evolved in Eurasia (Li 1996). Conrad (1980) also assigned a right distal radius to *Cervus* from the Flatiron Butte local fauna—Glenns Ferry Formation, about 22 miles (35 km) east of Grand View—based on its

The winter coats of sika, like those of most *Cervus elaphus,* tend to be darker and grayer than the summer pelage. Unlike red deer and elk, the small rump patch of sika is erectile. These patches flare when the animals become excited. *Photo by Leonard Lee Rue III.*

size and morphology. He considered the Flatiron Butte fauna to be about 2.9 million years old.

A naviculor-cuboid and upper fourth premolar was assigned by Guthrie and Matthews (1971) to *Cervus* of the Cape Deccit fauna from the Seward Peninsula of Alaska. Repenning (1992) considered the Cape Deceit fauna to be 1.3 million to 1.6 million years old (Irvingtonian), based on faunal correlations with Russian microtine sequences. *Cervus* also is known from numerous faunas (i.e., assemblages of animal communities) within the area of Fairbanks, Alaska (Guthrie 1966). These faunas have been assigned to the early Rancholabrean LMA, although a more precise age is not known at this time (Péwé 1975, Kurtén and Anderson 1980).

Cervus also has been assigned to fossils from Irvingtonian deposits at Cumberland Cave in Maryland (Gidley and Gazin 1938) and at Conard Fissure in Arkansas (Brown 1908) (Figure 22), but are based on relatively few specimens. At Cumberland Cave, *Cervus* is recorded for a pair of fused metatarsals from a juvenile individual. Generic identification of this specimen should be considered with reservation because of its immaturity, as suggested by Kurtén and Anderson (1980). Two calcanea and two naviculor-cuboids from Conard Fissure may be more diagnostic elements, but they should be reexamined because they have not been studied since Brown's (1908) original description.

Because of the fragmentary nature of the fossil record, the exact time of appearance of *Cervus elaphus* in North America is not known. If, as presumed, North American *C. elaphus* was derived from the Old World, then *C. elaphus* probably appeared in North America during the Middle

Pleistocene, the time of earliest record of the species in Europe. This would be about 800,000 years after *C. elaphus* diverged from *C. nippon,* according to Li (1996). If, on the other hand, the early records of *Cervus* in North America can be substantiated, then it is possible (although unlikely) that *C. elaphus* evolved in the New World and dispersed to the Old. In any case, by the late Rancholabrean, *C. elaphus* was widespread and well established in North America.

Late Pleistocene Distribution of *Cervus elaphus*

A well-preserved, but recently damaged fragment of a skull and antlers were discovered in a northwestern Albanian swamp during 1978. Fistiani (1991) identified it as a very large, robust *C. elaphus* from the Late Pleistocene.

Lister (1987) described and illustrated fossilized *Cervus* antlers from the Pleistocene in Europe. Antler remains often are abundant as fossils and generally are taxonomically diagnostic elements. In contrast to the relative conservatism of other skeletal elements, antlers display a great variety of form and a tendency to evolve. The variation is in the size, direction and curvature of the beam as well as in the number, position and form of tines. However, imperfections in fossil antlers mean that descriptions of some species are incomplete, most often with regard to the orientation of antlers in relation to skulls and the morphology of distal parts. The high intraspecific variability of antlers among age classes and populations is evident among present-day species. This, in combination with small sample sizes

Figure 22.   Distribution of Pliocene and Early Pleistocene fossil sites reported to contain *Cervus* in North America (numbers correspond to Table 6).

and the typological approach of many past paleontologists, has resulted in excessive subdivision of fossil material into genera, species and subspecies (Lister 1987).

Figure 23 illustrates how antlers of European *Cervus elaphus* evolved from the Middle Pliocene to recent time. Body sizes of these deer varied from about that of recent roe deer to that of large recent red deer. The bez tine of red deer antlers gradually was reduced and a crown evolved at the

Table 6.   Pliocene and Early Pleistocene sites in North America reported to contain *Cervus*

Locality[a]	State	Land mammal age	Reference
1. Cape Deceit	Alaska	Blancan/ Irvingtonian	Guthrie and Matthews 1971
2. Grand View	Idaho	Blancan	Conrad 1980
3. Flatiron Butte	Idaho	Blancan	Conrad 1980
4. Conard Fissure	Arkansas	Irvingtonian	Brown 1908
5. Cumberland Cave	Maryland	Irvingtonian	Gidley and Gazin 1938

[a] Numbers correspond to those in Figure 22.

antler top (see Lister 1984, 1987). The reason for the apparent decline in strength of the bez tine is difficult to deduce. However, in recent *C. elaphus* bulls, bez tines act along with the brow tines to protect the eyes and face during combat. Reduction of the bez might reflect a change in fighting technique or adaptation for better survival during fights. The bez also has been shown to be sensitive to nutrition. The selective advantage (if any) leading to development of the crown probably lies in its role in visual display and in goring opponents, as the crowns seldom interlock during combat.

Antlers of red deer in Europe lacked a crown during the early Middle Pleistocene (Beninde 1937, Kahlke 1956). These are the earliest known red deer, living 500,000 to 600,000 years ago. The subspecific status of *C. e. acornatus* was confirmed from analyses of long bones and skulls (Di Stefano et al. 1992). These osteological specimens showed no substantial differences from present populations of red deer. The best known acoronate fossils are from Mosbach, Germany. In a large sample of antlers (from their size, mass and features of attached skulls, clearly antlers of mature bulls) the majority had only two top tines, forming a stout, simple fork

The crowns of red deer antlers (*left*) seldom interlock during combat, whereas the tops of elk antlers (*right*) sometimes do as bulls try to twist the necks of their opponents and throw them off balance. Lister (1987) speculated that the origin of the crown lies in its role in fighting or display. He also noted that the latter probably was more important because crowns rarely came into play when stags clash. The interlocking of antlers seems to allow elk bulls to test the strength of opponents or overpower them, with reduced chance of serious wounds. Deer farmers in New Zealand told O'Gara that the small, quicker red deer tended to intimidate elk by their aggressive stab and dodge style of fighting. *Photos by Bart W. O'Gara.*

(see Lister 1984, 1987). Such deer were found at the same fossil site northeast of Heidelberg as a primitive human mandible—the so-called Heidelberg jaw (Nilsson 1982).

In contrast, fossil red deer from the late Middle Pleistocene localities show well-formed, cuplike crowns of up to six tines; examples from 400,000 years ago included finds at Steinheim, Germany (Beninde 1937) and Swanscomb, England (Lister 1986). At Steinheim, the remains were accompanied by those of the so-called Steinheim Man—a variant of the Neanderthaler (Nilsson 1982).

Apparently, the crown originated in Europe during the Middle Pleistocene. Well-dated intermediate samples are not available, but a few specimens from Mosbach possibly show the beginnings of crown evolution. The evolution of the bez tine and crown modified the form of the red deer antler, but did not greatly affect its overall shape and stature. In none of these examples could one be certain whether evolution was taking place in situ or if waves of already-evolved new types entered western Europe from elsewhere (Lister 1987).

The crown has spread only minimally into populations in central Asia. This might be explained by breaks in distribution and, hence, in gene flow (Lister 1987). The antler tops of *C. elaphus* in China are quite similar to the acoronate ones of the European early Middle Pleistocene (Kahlke 1956). Widely distributed remains of red deer—ancestral mainly to *C. e. maral*—have been found in the Caucasus from the Late Pleistocene to the present (Vereshchagin 1967).

Geologic evidence clearly indicates that Asia and North America represent a single continental mass, separated by a segment currently submerged—the Bering–Chukchi Platform (Péwé 1975). The latest exposure was during the Wisconsin glacial stage of the Late Pleistocene (Colbert 1973). The often-heard term, Bering Land Bridge, evokes an image of a narrow strip of land that animals crossed—not something they lived on. However, during maximum glaciation, the Bering–Chukchi Platform formed a flat isthmus about 1,000 miles (1,600 km) wide between Alaska and Siberia (Figure 24), until it again was inundated by rising seas at the close of the Wisconsin glacial stage (Hopkins 1959). During the Wisconsin glacial stage, a northern refugium was formed by lowland areas of central and coastal Alaska that remained free of glaciers and held the Alaskan/Platform/Siberian mammal populations.

When the acoronate ancestors of red deer began to move westward from Asia, their path was determined by geographic conditions, according to Cameron (1923). North of the Caucasus, all routes from Asia to Europe were barred by an immense sheet of water, the Aralo-Caspian Sea, which—uniting the Black, Caspian and Aral seas—flooded the southern Russian and Siberian steppes. Finding no outlet at the Bosphorus, it discharged northward. South of the Caucasus, successive mountain ranges rose steeply along the southern shores of the Aralo-Caspian Sea and extended without a break from the Hindu-kush to the Caucasus. From the Caucasus through Asia Minor, they extended to

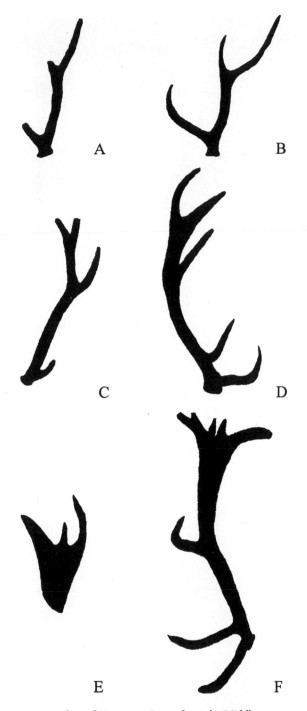

the Balkans and finally into vast forest-clad heights—the Alps and Carpathians. By this path, ancestral red deer traveled to central Europe from Asia. The Caucasus, reaching out as a great promontory into the heart of a broad sea, formed a halfway house on the journey. The forests of Austria and Hungary, which today with the Caucasus, produce the finest trophies, became a center of dispersion. Herds of deer, in the natural expansion of a vigorous subspecies, gradually pushed their way southward to the Mediterranean and westward to the Atlantic (Figure 25).

Southward, on the Mediterranean seaboard, an irregular tract of now-submerged land united southern Italy, Sicily and Tunisia with the Balkan peninsula in the east and with Sardinia and Corsica in the west. In Cameron's (1923) opinion, red deer reached the Atlas Mountains by this Sicilian route rather than by Gibraltar through Spain, although Spanish and African herds probably intermingled across the straits at a later date. Sardinia and Corsica received red deer at the same period and by the same route (Cameron 1923).

The British Isles, including the Hebrides, were joined across the Netherlands to Germany and, by way of the Orkneys and Shetlands, to Norway. Red deer apparently entered southern Sweden from Denmark at a later date, when seas were lowered by proliferation of Arctic ice. Also, Gyllensten et al. (1983) reported that protein electrophoresis indicated that the deer of Norway had been separated from those of continental Europe since the last glacial period. Contemporaneously with these movements in the north and west, red deer entered Russia from Poland, although destined to make little progress until climatic conditions lowered water levels, being checked in the direction of the Baltic by glacial cold and in the direction of the Black Sea by submergence of the steppes (Cameron 1923).

Guthrie (1966) recorded several Pleistocene sites in central Alaska and the Yukon that contain *C. elaphus* remains, including antlers. Many of these fossil antlers have a supernumerary proximal tine that is unusual because proximal tines are the most consistent in pattern and size among individuals of a population, according to Guthrie (1966). However, proximal tines are sensitive to nutrition (see Chapter 1). The fossil *C. elaphus* antlers from Alaska and the

Figure 23. Antlers of European *Cervus* from the Middle Pliocene to recent time (from Lister 1987): A = *C. pardinensis,* from the Late Pliocene of France, had antlers about 23.6 inches (60 cm) in length. They were more or less round in cross section and straight, with somewhat pearled ridge-and-furrow ornamentation. B = *C. philisi,* from the Early Pleistocene of western Europe, was quite similar to *C. pardinensis* but with a longer first tine (Heintz 1970). C = *C. perrieri,* from the Late Pliocene of France, had round to slightly oval antlers—about 31.5 inches (80 cm) long—with mild ridge-and-furrow, slightly pearled ornamentation (Heintz 1970). Possibly, this was the form nearest the ancestry of *C. elaphus.* D = *C. e. acornatus,* from the Middle Pleis-

tocene of Germany, had antlers about 35.4 inches (90 cm) long, with pearled ornamentation that were similar to extant red deer, but with a simple fork at the end of the beam (Kahlke 1959). E = In about 10% of *C. e. acornatus* antlers, from the Middle Pleistocene, a small third point occurred between the two tines of the terminal fork—apparently the beginning of a crown (*see* Lister 1987). F. = *C. e. elaphus,* from Late Pleistocene of Germany, with a five-point crown. Crowns of up to six tines occur on fossils found in England as well as Germany from that time.

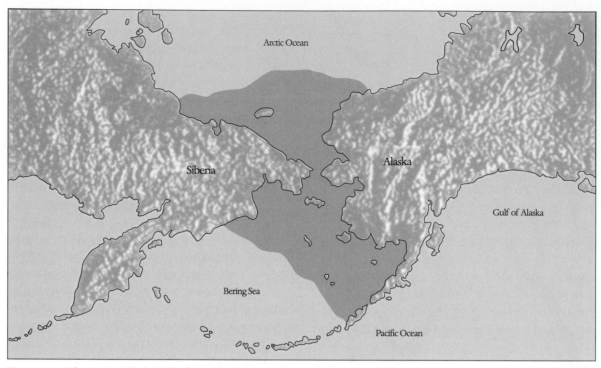

Figure 24. The Bering–Chukchi Platform (shaded area), along with interior Alaska and Siberia, apparently provided suitable habitat for elk during the Wisconsin glacial stage of the Late Pleistocene. It was last inundated about 10,000 years before present (redesigned from Hopkins 1959 by the Rocky Mountain Elk Foundation).

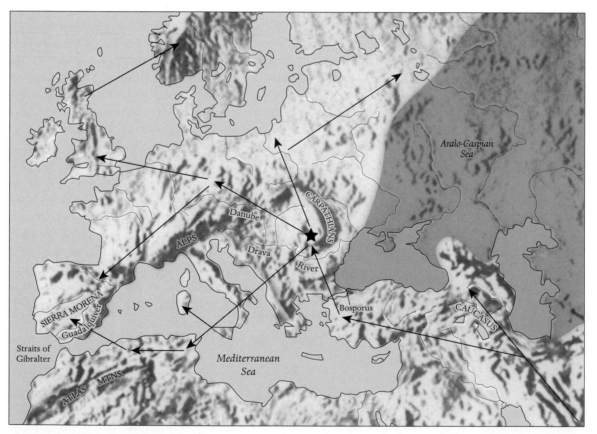

Figure 25. Probable lines of dispersion of *C. elaphus* into Europe during the Pleistocene (redesigned from Cameron 1923 by the Rocky Mountain Elk Foundation).

Yukon are of the acoronate morphology, as are those of present-day elk of Asia and North America.

As previously noted, the age of many of the Alaskan fossils is poorly known. Many of them may predate the Wisconsin glacial stage, but the specimen from Lost Chicken Creek was dated at 10,050 years ago (Harington 1980). Likewise, many *C. elaphus* localities in the Yukon are poorly dated or of unknown age (Table 7), although Harington (1977) believed that many of the specimens from the Dawson area are of the Late Wisconsin glacial substage (40,000–10,000 years before present). Fossils associated with *C. elaphus* from the Sixtymile Locality 3 and surrounding area have been dated from more than 40,000 years ago (beyond radiocarbon) to about 23,000 years ago (Harington 1989). *Cervus* also is known from the Blue Fish Caves, which contain fossil mammals that date to about 16,000 to 13,000 years before present (Cinq-Mars 1979, Harington 1988).

C. elaphus did not occur historically in Alaska or the Yukon (Hall and Kelson 1959). Modern populations have been introduced into the Yukon (Youngman 1975), and elk have been moving into the Yukon from British Columbia since 1975 (M. Hoefs personal communication:1998). Guthrie (1982) believed that the combination of shorter growing season, wet substratum, deep snows, and reduced distribution and complexity of nutritious herbaceous plants

Table 7. Late Pleistocene sites in Alaska and Canada reported to contain *Cervus*

Time/locality	Province/state/territory	Age or years ago	Reference
Undifferentiated Pleistocene			
Sulphur Creek	Yukon	Pleistocene	Guthrie 1966
Dawson Locality 15	Yukon	Pleistocene	Harington 1977
Dawson Locality 28	Yukon	Pleistocene	Harington 1977
Eldorado Creek	Yukon	Pleistocene	Harington 1977
Cripple Creek	Alaska	Pleistocene	Guthrie 1966
Engineer Creek	Alaska	Pleistocene	Guthrie 1966
Fairbanks Creek	Alaska	Pleistocene	Guthrie 1966
Gold Hill	Alaska	Pleistocene	Guthrie 1966
Dome Creek	Alaska	Pleistocene	Guthrie 1966
Lower Gold Stream	Alaska	Pleistocene	Guthrie 1966
Koyuk River	Alaska	Pleistocene	Guthrie 1966
Gertrude Creek	Alaska	Pleistocene	Guthrie 1966
Chicken Creek	Alaska	Pleistocene	Guthrie 1966
Ingle Creek	Alaska	Pleistocene	Guthrie 1966
Rainbow Mine	Alaska	Pleistocene	Guthrie 1966
Late Wisconsin			
Sixtymile Locality 3	Yukon	40,000–23,000	Harington 1988
Blue Fish Caves	Yukon	25,000–10,000	Harington 1988
Broken Mammoth (Cultural Zone 4)	Alaska	11,800–11,000	Yesner 1996
Lost Chicken Creek	Alaska	10,050	Harington 1980

drove the distributional limits of elk and bison south in North America during the Holocene.

Churcher (1968) originally reported a fragmentary dentary of *C. elaphus* associated with radiocarbon dates at about 11,000 years ago from the Griffin North Gravel Pit near Cochrane, Alberta. Shackleton and Hills (1977) reexamined this specimen in 1975 and referred it to *Bison* sp. (C. R. Harington personal communication:1996). Therefore, *C. elaphus* currently is not known from the glaciated regions of central Alberta during the Late Wisconsin glacial stage, but there are several Early Holocene records from the province.

Late Pleistocene records of *C. elaphus* indicate that, south of the Laurentide Ice Sheet, the species ranged from east to west coasts (Figure 26). The Late Pleistocene sites can be divided into two categories: sites that are not well dated or restricted to the past 40,000 to 20,000 years and sites that can be assigned to the Late Wisconsin glacial substage. No full Wisconsin glacial sites are known (Faunmap Working Group 1994). The undifferentiated Late Wisconsin glacial stage sites occur in both the eastern and western United States as well as Alaska and the Yukon (Figure 26). The Late Wisconsin glacial sites are restricted to the eastern United States and Alaska (Figure 27).

The absence of sites in the Plains region is of interest. If this cannot be attributed to lack of preservation or failure of discovery, it would suggest two distinct Late Wisconsin glacial stage populations of *Cervus* in North America—eastern and western populations. The abundance of sites in the midcontinent without *Cervus* (Faunmap Working Group 1994), especially during the Late Wisconsin glacial period, suggests that the Late Pleistocene separation of these two populations may be real.

Holocene Distribution of *Cervus elaphus*

The number of Holocene sites for *C. elaphus* in North America is much greater than the number of Late Pleistocene sites. This difference is partially the result that almost all of the prehistoric Holocene records of *C. elaphus* come from archeological sites (Faunmap Working Group 1994) where humans were responsible for the accumulation of the bones. Obviously, *Cervus* was an important resource for prehistoric humans (discussed later). Throughout the Holocene, *C. elaphus* was distributed from coast to coast, including the midcontinent region (Figures 28 and 29).

From the Early and Middle Holocene, *C. elaphus* is known from the northern areas of its distribution in British Columbia, Alberta, Saskatchewan and southern Ontario (Figure 28, Table 8). A remarkably complete skeleton of *C. elaphus* was recovered from deposits along the Smoky River, near Watino, Alberta. Bone and antler from this skeleton

Figure 26. Distribution of Late Pleistocene fossil sites in North America reported to contain *C. elaphus*. Open circle, 40,000 to 10,000 years ago (3 in the western United States and 1 in the Yukon); cross, 20,000 to 10,000 years ago (1 in the eastern United Sates and 1 in the Yukon); closed circle, unknown age (11 in Alaska and 4 in the Yukon). Ybp, years before present. Sites in Alaska and the Yukon are from Table 7; the rest are from Faunmap Working Group (1994)

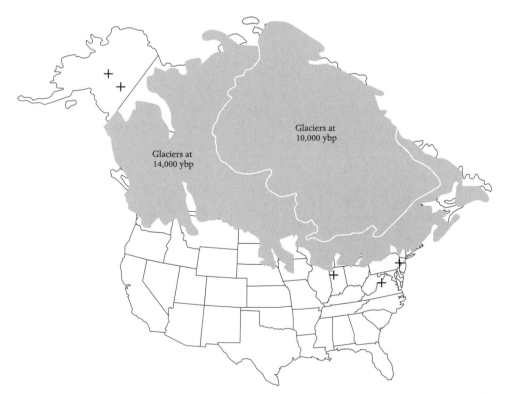

Figure 27. Distribution of Late Glacial (15,000–10,000 years before present [ybp]) fossil sites with *C. elaphus* in North America. The two sites (crosses) in Alaska are from Harington (1980) and Yesner (1996), and the four sites in the eastern United States are from Faunmap Working Group (1994).

Figure 28. Distribution of Early (10,000–8,000 years before present [ybp]) and Middle (8,000–4,000 years before present) Holocene fossil sites with *C. elaphus* in North America. Open circle, Early Holocene (10 in the contiguous U.S., 1 in Alaska, 1 in Alberta); cross, Middle Holocene (26 in the contiguous U.S., 5 in British Columbia, 1 each in Alberta, Saskatchewan and the Yukon) (from Faunmap Working Group [1994] and Table 8).

Figure 29. Distribution of Late (4,000–500 years before present) Holocene fossil sites with *C. elaphus* in North America, including 251 in the contiguous U.S., 19 in British Columbia, 16 in Ontario, 8 in Saskatchewan and 4 in Alberta (from Faunmap Working Group [1994] and Table 8).

have been dated at about 9,000 to 10,000 years ago (Burns 1986). Early Holocene records also have been recorded from numerous other areas in Alberta and British Columbia (Figure 28). All of these records indicate that elk recolonized landscapes almost immediately after those landscapes were deglaciated. Whether the colonizing elk came from northern or southern refugia is unclear; however, the close similarities—morphological, behavioral and genetic—between North American and certain Asian subspecies seem to indicate those from the north predominated. Elk remained in the Old Crow Basin, Yukon Territory—north of its historic distribution (Figure 28)—as late as 4,570 years ago (Harington 1977). Harington (1980) believed that *Cervus* withdrew from the Yukon sometime during the Late Holocene.

The southernmost distribution limits of *C. elaphus* during the Early and Middle Holocene were southern Kansas and northern Arkansas (approximately 36 to 37 degrees north latitude) (Figure 28). For the southeastern U.S., absence of elk sites farther south may be a function of the lack of paleontological sites for this region (Faunmap

Working Group 1994). However, there are numerous fossil sites from Oklahoma, northern Texas and southern and eastern New Mexico that do not contain elk. These sites suggest that its absence from this region may be real, although taphonomic reasons cannot be excluded. If this pattern does reflect the actual distribution of *Cervus*, then elk may not have spread to the southern Plains until the Late Holocene (Figure 29).

C. elaphus is known to have occurred by the Late Holocene, in almost all areas of its historic range in North America. Sites in Canada document elk throughout most of its distribution (Table 8, Figure 29). However, sites are not known from the northernmost limits of the historic range. Sites probably are not known from northern Manitoba and northeastern Saskatchewan because of the marshy nature of the landscape, which prohibits easy and extensive exploration of this area for fossil and archeological sites. Absence of sites in northern Alberta and northwestern Saskatchewan is perplexing, especially because Early and Middle Holocene sites are known from this area.

Records of *Cervus* also are not known from the south-

Excavation of the Watino wapiti in the Peace River District of northwestern Alberta, Canada, April 1985. The oldest radiocarbon date on it is 9,920 ± 220 years before present. Lying in typical death pose, with head and neck curved up and back due to the drying of the neck tendons, the skeleton lies in backwater silts and sands deposited by subsequent spring floods. Likely, the elk fell through thin, late-spring ice on the Smoky River and drowned, unable to find a breathing hole. Examining the carcass are Dr. Jim Burns (*right*), paleontologist at the Provincial Museum of Alberta in Edmonton, and Dr. Desh Mittra, former geology instructor at Grande Prairie Regional College, Grand Prairie, Alberta. The find is the oldest dated elk in Alberta, a fact that supports Burns' (and others) contention that wapiti (*Cervus elaphus*) reached the lower 48 states only after the continental glaciers melted. The similarity of the bones and antlers to those of present-day elk indicates the stability of the elk genome. *Photo courtesy of the Provincial Museum of Alberta, Edmonton.*

Table 8. Holocene sites with *Cervus elaphus* in Alaska and Canada

Time/locality	Province/state/territory	Years ago	Reference
Early Holocene			
Broken Mammoth (Cultural Zone 3)	Alaska	10,300–9,300	Yesner 1996
Watino	Alberta	9,920	Morlan 1999
Peace River	Alberta	9,880	Morlan 1999
Three Hills	Alberta	9,670	Morlan 1999
S. Milan Farm	Alberta	9,630	Morlan 1999
Wakaluk Quarry	Alberta	9,920–9,075	Burns 1986
Middle Holocene			
Drynoch Slide	British Columbia	7,530	Morlan 1999
Glenrose Cannery	British Columbia (Vancouver Island)	8,150–5,730	Matson 1976
Oregon Jack Creek	British Columbia	4,850	Rousseau and Richards 1988
Charlie Lake Cave	British Columbia	4,270–1,400	Driver 1988
Old Crow Locality 1	Yukon	4,570	Harington 1977
Glenrose Cannery	British Columbia (Vancouver Island)	4,290–3,280	Matson 1976
Rats Nest Cave	Alberta	7,060–2,500	Burns 1989
Late Holocene			
Williams Lake	British Columbia	3,625	Morlan 1999
Bowker Creek	British Columbia	2,910	Morlan 1999
Glenrose Cannery	British Columbia (Vancouver Island)	2,340–2,030	Matson 1976
Kelowna	British Columbia	2,225	Morlan 1999
Dionisio Point	British Columbia	2,160–1,400	Morlan 1999
Kamloops	British Columbia	1,740	Morlan 1999
Keatley Creek	British Columbia	1,505	Lepfsky et al. 1996
Shoemaker Bay	British Columbia (Vancouver Island)	1,450–1,130	McMillan and Claire 1982
Dominic Lake	British Columbia	1,430	Morlan 1999
Squak Lake	British Columbia	1,200	Morlan 1999
Chezacut	British Columbia	1,105	Morlan 1999
Deep Bay	British Columbia (Vancouver Island)	900	Monks 1977
Littel Qualicum River (Dry Midden)	British Columbia (Vancouver Island)	730	Bernick 1983
Littel Qualicum River (Wet Midden)	British Columbia (Vancouver Island)	780	Bernick 1983
Moose Meadow	British Columbia	615	Morlan 1999
Upper Loon Lake	British Columbia	367	Morlan 1999
Pennask Lake	British Columbia	184	Morlan 1999
Goose Point	British Columbia	245–170	Wilmeth 1978
Maze Lake	British Columbia	110	Morlan 1999
Hitching Post	Alberta	3,600	Morlan 1999
DjPp-8	Alberta	3,480–2,260	Morlan 1999
Fort Saskatchewan	Alberta	3,385	Morlan 1999
Kenney	Alberta	1,600	Morlan 1999
Sjovold	Saskatchewan	2,500	Morlan et al.1996
Crown	Saskatchewan	4,330–3,330	Morlan et al. 1996
Eastcott	Saskatchewan	2,490	Morlan et al. 1996
Lebret	Saskatchewan	1,635	Morlan et al. 1996
Garrat	Saskatchewan	1,400	Morlan et al. 1996
Bushfield West	Saskatchewan	475–280	Morlan et al. 1996
Lloyd	Saskatchewan	610–195	Morlan et al. 1996
Opimihaw Creek	Saskatchewan	<100	Morlan et al. 1996
Donaldson	Ontario	2,535–1,400	Wright and Anderson 1963
Thede	Ontario	2,240–1,180	Finlayson 1977
Cayuga Bridge	Ontario	1,155	Stothers 1977
Van Besien	Ontario	1,010–1,005	Noble 1975
Wolf Creek	Ontario	580	Morlan 1999
Baumann	Ontario	490	Stopp 1985
Cleveland	Ontario	410	Morland 1999
Christianson	Ontario	340–330	Fitzgerald 1982
Hood	Ontario	320–310	Lennox 1984b
Bogle I	Ontario	320–310	Lennox 1984a
Walker	Ontario	320–300	Wright 1981
Hamilton	Ontario	320–300	Lennox 1981
Plater-Martin	Ontario	311–300	Hamalainen 1983
Cedar Swamp	Ontario	270	Morlan 1999

ernmost parts of its North American range (e.g., northern Georgia and Louisiana, southern New Mexico and Arizona, and central California). Late Holocene sites are known from most of these areas, especially for Arizona, New Mexico and northern Texas (Faunmap Working Group 1994). Therefore, absence of *Cervus* in the fossil record actually may reflect its absence from these regions during the Holocene.

Dixon and Lyman (1996) conducted an extensive analysis of Holocene records of elk in eastern Washington. The modern distribution of elk in this part of Washington is not continuous, but elk are conspicuously absent from the Columbia Basin. On the basis of the maps of Dixon and Lyman (1996), elk appeared to be widespread across the Columbia Basin in the Early and Middle Holocene, but during the last 4,000 years they appear to have occurred only on the southeastern and northwestern edges of the Columbia Basin (Figure 28). Dixon and Lyman warned about accepting these distribution maps at face value, and suggested that the maps might reflect the history of zooarcheological research rather than the actual prehistoric distribution of elk. However, environmental changes during the Middle and Late Holocene cannot be totally eliminated as being responsible for these geographic patterns. Further research is needed on sites of the Columbia Basin.

In Europe, *C. elaphus* showed significant size changes through the Middle and Late Pleistocene (Lister 1981). During the Eemian or last interglacial age, *C. elaphus* populations on the island of Jersey demonstrated an 85% decrease in body size in less than 6,000 years (Lister 1989). This reduction in size was attributed to resource limitation and freedom from predation (Lister 1989), because the island was isolated by rising sea levels. Dwarfing of *C. elaphus* on the European continent during the Flandrian or current interglacial age has been thought to be in response to habitat deterioration caused by human populations (Stuart 1982).

The remains of Pleistocene *C. elaphus* in North America are sparse, therefore it is not possible to obtain a detailed analysis of body size changes through time. Late Pleistocene postcranial elements from the Yukon are larger than modern specimens (Harington 1977). Analyses of elk bones from archeological sites in eastern Washington and other parts of the Pacific Northwest suggest that, 700 to 250 years ago, elk may have been slightly larger than those that inhabit this area today (Dixon and Lyman 1996). However, there is considerable overlap in size. Dixon and Lyman (1996) indicated that hunting pressure by prehistoric human populations may have reduced competition and caused the elk to respond as in colonizing populations, which frequently contain larger individuals (Geist 1971, 1986, McCorquodale et al. 1989). Environmental change cannot be completely excluded as a cause of these size changes.

Models of Speciation and Subspeciation

The fossil record is incomplete, but it can provide a basis for constraining models for geographic isolation and differentiation. Guthrie (1966) proposed a model for the immigration of *C. elaphus* to North America and its differentiation in response to Quaternary environmental fluctuations. This model was used by subsequent investigators (e.g., Bryant and Maser 1982). Since Guthrie (1966) proposed his model, more has been learned, as previously discussed, about the temporal and spatial distribution of *Cervus* in North America. Also, models for climate change have been significantly revised.

Guthrie (1966) proposed that *Cervus* did not appear in North America until the Illinois glacial stage, which was the third glacial event in the prevailing classic chronology (see Zeuner 1959, Hibbard et al. 1965). These Illinois stage specimens presumably were restricted to Alaska. Guthrie (1966) believed then that *Cervus* did not disperse into the central part of North America until the third interglacial, Sangamon, or during Early Wisconsin interstadial—a warm interval of the fourth and last glacial event. Both of these times represent intervals in the Late Pleistocene when continental glacial ice was significantly reduced, allowing plants and animals to move freely northward and southward. A Sangamon record of elk near Medicine Hat, Alberta (Stalker and Churcher 1970), supports the hypothesis of an early dispersal (Figure 30).

During maximum Wisconsin stage glaciation, the corridor between Alaska and the Yukon and the midcontinent of North America was closed by the coalescence of the Laurentide and Cordilleran ice sheets. North American *Cervus* populations then were divided into two isolated refugia. In fact, Guthrie (1966) thought that it might be possible that the central part of North America was not occupied by *Cervus* until the Holocene, after the ice sheets had melted significantly. He did note that there were a few isolated records of *Cervus* in this region during the Wisconsin glacial stage, but they may have been representative of low population levels. In any case, Guthrie (1966) made several inferential suggestions about the discontinuous distribution of *Cervus* south of the continental ice sheets during the Wisconsin stage based on presumed barriers.

According to Guthrie's model, northern and southern populations of *Cervus* were reunited in the Holocene, with Alaskan and Yukon populations becoming extinct (R. D. Guthrie personal communication:1996). Guthrie (1966) believed that the modern northern boundary of the distribution of *Cervus* was then maintained by competition with caribou. However, by the 1990s, elk had moved north into habitat occupied by caribou of western Canada.

Figure 30. A fossil elk antler from Sulphur Creek, Yukon Territory (from Guthrie 1996). If the antler was from a symmetrical set, the rack would be a world record by Boone and Crockett trophy standards (the check marks indicate broken tines). This antler and two others in the Frick Alaskan Collection have supernumerary tines between the brow and bez tines.

In light of new dates and climate reconstructions, Guthrie's model now can be revised. Specimens, especially antlers, from the Grand View local fauna described by Conrad (1980) indicate *Cervus* in the central part of North America sometime during the Blancan LMA. If so, *Cervus* had to be in Alaska by that time, as well. The age of the Cape Deceit material is debatable, but it is at least 1.3 million to 1.6 million years old, from the Irvingtonian LMA (Repenning 1992) and may be as old as 2.1 million years, from the Blancan LMA (Repenning et al. 1988). These dates are significantly older than the Illinois glacial stage, the time frame originally proposed for the Alaskan fossils (Guthrie 1966).

Although identification of materials from Cumberland Cave and Conard Fissure are nebulous, if those specimens do represent *Cervus,* they suggest that the genus was fairly widespread in central North America by the Irvingtonian LMA. These sites document occupancy of midcontinental North America more than 600,000 years ago, before the Wisconsin glaciation. The survival of such early *Cervus* to contribute genes to present-day elk seems unlikely. The fossil record indicates that *Cervus* was distributed from coast to coast by the late Rancholabrean (Figures 28 and 29).

Repeated fluctuations in sea level over the Bering Land Bridge during the Pleistocene would have allowed for exchange of genotypes between populations from Alaska, the Yukon and Siberia, also known as Beringia (see Sher 1984).

However, the fossil record of *Cervus* in Siberia is scant and poorly understood (A. Sher personal communication:1996).

Current knowledge of fluctuations of climates and ice sheets throughout the Pleistocene as determined from deep sea records indicate that the classic models of four glacials and four interglacials are not correct. Instead, it appears that there may have been more than 50 glacial/interglacial fluctuations during the Pleistocene (Rudimann and Wright 1987, Dansgaard et al. 1993). Furthermore, during the early parts of the Pleistocene, glacial/interglacial fluctuations occurred on a 41,000-year cycle, whereas during the Late Pleistocene, the cycles had a period of 100,000 years (Rudimann and Wright 1987). Finally, numerous fluctuations in ice sheets and climates occurred within the Wisconsin glacial stage (Bond and Lotti 1995).

The classic model of four glaciations apparently is an oversimplification. These more complex environmental models would suggest that, with their early appearance in North America, *Cervus* populations were subjected to a much greater degree of geographic, and perhaps genetic, reshuffling than previously presumed. Unfortunately, the chronology of *Cervus* fossil sites does not allow for fine-scale documentation of geographic shifts in response to these earlier events.

As previously indicated, the Late Pleistocene distribution of *Cervus* may have been divided into eastern and western populations (Figures 22 and 26). This pattern would be consistent with the establishment of the *C. e. canadensis* and *C. e. nelsoni* and *roosevelti* populations during the Late Pleistocene. As yet, the fossil record does not provide insight into the mechanisms isolating *C. e. nelsoni* and *C. e. roosevelti.* Guthrie (1966), as well as Bryant and Maser (1982), offered speculations about such mechanisms.

The eastern and western differentiation of Late Pleistocene elk may be supported by distribution patterns of other mammals. Cluster analyses of Late Pleistocene mammal faunas (Faunmap Working Group 1996) resulted in the definition of eastern and western faunal provinces that would have facilitated the longitudinal differentiation of *Cervus.* The environments and faunas of these Late Pleistocene provinces are quite different from modern ones. In fact, many of them do not have modern analogs (Graham 1979, Lundelius et al. 1983, Faunmap Working Group 1996). In most cases, Late Pleistocene sites with *Cervus* contain a mixture of boreal forest species with either deciduous forest and grassland species in the east or with alpine and desert/grassland species in the west. Because *C. elaphus* is quite adaptable to different types of environments today, and appears to have a preference for open habitats, the Late Pleistocene savannas and parklands (Graham and Mead 1987) may have been prime habitat for *Cervus.*

The Late Pleistocene geographic distribution may have been controlled more by competition with other Late Pleistocene ungulates than habitat distribution. Specifically, south of the continental ice sheets in North America, there were numerous extinct cervids (Table 3) as well as other extinct grassland taxa such as camels, horses and mammoths that may have been potential competitors. It is interesting to note that elk and a potential competitor, caribou, co-occurred in both Beringia and south of the ice sheet during the Late Pleistocene.

The modern grasslands of the Plains region probably did not develop until the end of the Pleistocene or Early Holocene. Several faunas from the southwestern Plains region (e.g., western Texas, eastern New Mexico and eastern Colorado) suggest there was a relatively treeless grassland in this area by the end of the Pleistocene (Graham 1981, 1987). The appearance of modern grasslands and the megafauna extinction at the beginning of the Holocene may have been critical in establishing the Holocene geographic distribution of elk. In fact, rather than serving as barriers to dispersal (e.g., Bryant and Maser 1982), the development of grasslands may have facilitated the interchange between western and eastern populations, which appear to have been joined in the midcontinental United States by the Early Holocene (Figure 28). As suggested by Bryant and Maser, riparian environments would have been critical habitat on the Plains. In fact, they cited Pengelly (1963), who noted that Lewis and Clark reportedly observed more elk on the Plains than in the mountains (see also Chapter 1).

The southernmost distribution of elk (presumably *C. e. merriami*) in Mexico and the southwestern United States may not have been achieved until the Late Holocene. Possibly, these southern populations were derived from the isolation of Pleistocene populations by Holocene climate change (Bryant and Maser 1982). However, no fossil sites document such refugia. Late Holocene fossils do indicate that elk extended across northern Texas and into Oklahoma (Faunmap Working Group 1994, Pfau 1994, Shaffer et al. 1995), which is contrary to Bryant and Maser's (1982) assumption.

In summary, *Cervus* probably entered North America during the Pliocene and spread from Alaska to the central part of North America (i.e., Idaho) at that time. If the taxonomic assignments are correct for the fossils from Cumberland Cave and Conard Fissure, they would indicate that *Cervus* was widespread in midcontinental North America by the Early to Middle Pleistocene (Irvingtonian). Climates and ice sheets fluctuated more than 50 times throughout the Pleistocene, allowing for the potential of multiple periods of isolation, reshuffling or extinctions of *Cervus* populations. Unfortunately, the fossil record does not permit fine-scale documentation of these events for *Cervus*. DNA analyses indicating close relationships between elk in the mountains of northern Asia and all North American elk (Cronin 1992a, Polziehn and Strobeck 1998) seem to refute the possibility that such early *Cervus* were ancestral to present-day elk in North America.

During the Wisconsin glaciation, *Cervus* appears to have been divided into northern and southern refugia. South of the North American continental ice sheets, *Cervus* may have been further subdivided into eastern and western populations, although the absence of sites in the Plains region may result from unrecognized biases in the fossil record. The mechanisms differentiating western populations of Roosevelt and Tule elk are not apparent in the fossil record. Also, it is unclear what role other Pleistocene cervids and grassland ungulates, especially extinct ones, may have played in limiting the distribution of elk.

Fossil elk records irrupt in the Holocene because of prehistoric human utilization of elk and the preservation of their remains in archeological sites. Also, Pleistocene extinctions of competitors or predators may have allowed a rapid increase in numbers. Holocene records indicate that formation of the Plains environment did not serve as an isolating mechanism. Instead, it appears that Holocene Plains environments may have reunited eastern and western populations. The most southern populations of elk may not have appeared until the Late Holocene. Finally, the demise of elk in the Yukon (Harington 1988) probably did not occur until the Late Holocene. Therefore, much of the historic distributional pattern of elk probably was not established until the Late Holocene.

During prehistoric times, the domain of *C. elaphus* included an enormous range in Europe and Asia south of 60 degrees north latitude, reaching the Arctic Circle in Scandinavia and Siberia. Fossil remains indicate that *C. elaphus* were spread over a large part of the former USSR, Europe, western Siberia and midcentral Asia (Flerov 1952). Eastern Siberia was a part of the range, and the radiation from Asia to North America apparently passed through what is now the Bering Straits. On the south, the range may have passed farther than the contemporary range, for remains are known from caves in Israel (Flerov 1952).

The distribution of *C. elaphus* still is wide. It encompasses a large but patchy belt of the temperate zone, chiefly hilly forest areas of Europe, Asia and North America between 30 and 60 degrees latitude. The northern limit of range coincides neither with the limits of the Plains and hilly country nor with the forest landscape zones. It is situated in such a way that it does not encroach on the line of an average yearly maximum of snow cover of 15.7 to 19.7 inches (40–50 cm). The species is encountered in particularly large numbers in places where winter snow accumulations are no deeper than 7.9 to 11.8 inches (20–30 cm) (Formozov

1946). See Chapter 1 for maps depicting distribution of *C. elaphus* in Africa and Eurasia.

Historic and Present Distribution of Elk in North America

Provinces and states with more than one presumptive subspecies of elk were contacted concerning differences in management between those subspecies. Except for Tule elk in California, replies indicated extensive mixing—natural and through translocations—and that subspecies, if recog-

nized, were primarily administrative categories. Thus, subspecies generally are disregarded when discussing historic distribution. In this section, if no citation is given for data concerning a province or state, the information was taken from Bryant and Maser (1982).

"When white men first came to this continent, the American elk, or wapiti, was the most widely distributed of the deer, as it was found across what is now the United States from the Pacific Ocean almost, if not quite, to the Atlantic, northward far into parts of Canada, and south almost to what is now Mexico [Figure 31]. . . . Elk were miss-

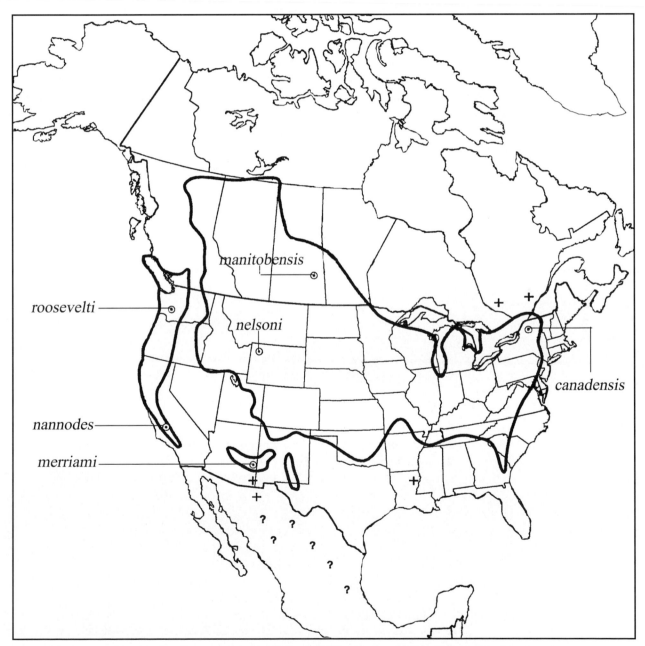

Figure 31.   Supposed historic distribution (solid, thick line) of elk in North America by subspecies. U = Type locations; + = extra limital records; ? = questionable distribution (redesigned from Murie [1951] by the Rocky Mountain Elk Foundation).

ing or were scarce, however, in some parts of the Atlantic coast . . . though there are no available precise records showing Atlantic seaboard distribution, early writers expressed the opinion that elk did at one time reach the sea, and it is at least probable that at some early date elk occupied Atlantic coastal areas" (Murie 1951:19). Hays (1871:388) reported that: "The Wapiti deer (*Cervus canadensis*) was found all along the coast from Canada to the Gulf of Mexico."

"There were other gaps in elk distribution. In the Pacific coast region, elk occupied the Coast and Cascade Ranges from Vancouver Island southward through Washington, Oregon, and into the southern part of California; but curiously enough, much of the Great Basin of the West, including most of Arizona and Nevada and parts of Utah, Oregon, and Washington, appears to have been unoccupied by elk. . . . Undoubtedly elk have occurred in many other areas. The historic record cannot be complete. At the boundaries of the mapped ranges, in particular, more extensive data probably would show a somewhat wider distribution. On the whole, however, it is believed that the elk range as here defined gives a reliable impression of the animal's early distribution and natural choice of territory" (Murie 1951:19–21). The extensive movements sometimes made by radio-collared bulls today (see Chapter 1) certainly

fit with Murie's statement that historic records (or present ones) cannot be complete.

Figure 31 (from Murie 1951:20) suggests nearly continuous distribution among all supposed subspecies of North American elk during early historic times. Present (as of 1995) distribution of elk in western North America is shown in Figure 32. Small, reintroduced populations also occur in eastern provinces and states.

Historically, the natural range of elk in North America (except for introductions and reintroductions) was reduced, for all practical purposes, to Manitoba, Saskatchewan and the Rocky Mountain and West Coast provinces and states of Canada and the United States. Because extirpation of elk in many parts of the species' range occurred after European colonization, estimating that natural range is easier than determining that of red deer.

Elk figured prominently as a food source during the exploration and early settlement of much of the United States and southern Canada. The large herds on open Plains reported by early explorers apparently were reduced in numbers after Indians secured firearms and horses, even before the era of transcontinental migration and settlement. During settlement, elk populations were further reduced or extirpated. Today, elk have been restored to carrying capacity

Spanish explorers probably first saw elk grazing in coastal grasslands in settings very much like that seen above, featuring Tule elk in California. *Photo by Jim D. Yoakum.*

Figure 32. Distribution of elk in North America in 1995 (based on maps drawn by personnel of provincial and state wildlife agencies [Bunnell 1997] and compiled by the Rocky Mountain Elk Foundation). Locations in Mexico provided by D. Doan-Crider.

of available habitat in many areas, and populations generally are stable or increasing slightly (see Bunnell 1997).

Alberta

Elk were observed on the Plains of southern Alberta in 1754 by Anthony Henday, and were reported from the Plains along the Peace River between Vermillion Falls and Fort St. John in 1792 and 1810 (Stelfox 1964). The Wapiti River south of Grand Prairie probably also contained an elk population as its name was derived from this species. During 1792 to 1810, elk were distributed throughout Alberta to within 50 to 100 miles (80–161 km) of the Northwest Territories. However, by 1894, they had been greatly reduced and were practically eliminated north of the North Saskatchewan River. After further reductions between 1897 and 1908, the elk were restricted to a few herds in the Saskatchewan and Brazeau river valleys. By 1913, the remnants of Alberta's once large herds consisted of probably not more than 365 animals, of which a dozen or so were located in the Brazeau, 20 to 50 in the Highwood River drainage and 150 to 300 in the Old Man River drainage. Stelfox (1964) listed the severe winters, development of farms and ranches, excessive meat hunting and widespread fires as the decimating factors. From the early 1900s to 1995, 2,391 elk were translocated, mostly to western Alberta and from Yellowstone National Park or Elk Island National Park (Gunson 1997).

In artist Daniel Beard's illustration "Evicted Tenants of the Adirondacks," printed in an 1885 issue of *Harper's Weekly,* the elk is distinctly featured in the upper left scene. Well before, Henry David Thoreau lamented in his journal for March 23, 1856, the "sweeping" landscape alterations in the slightly more than 200 years since first European settlement on the continent: "When I consider that the nobler animals have been eliminated here,—the cougar, panther, lynx, wolverine, wolf, bear, moose, deer, the beaver, the turkey, etc., etc.,—I cannot but feel as if I lived in a tamed, and, as it were, emasculated country" (Torrey 1906:220–221). *Photo courtesy of the Library of Congress.*

As of summer 1997, about 26,000 elk roamed Alberta (M. W. Barrett personal communication:1998).

British Columbia

During the 1860s, elk could be found on Vancouver Island and several islands in the Gulf of Georgia, on the east and west slopes of the Cascades and on the western slope of the Rocky Mountains to an altitude of 7,000 feet (2,134 m) (Lord 1866). Anderson (1882) concluded that a large portion of the province was frequented by elk. Spalding (1992) provided more than 160 elk sighting and evaluations in all

British Columbian ecoprovinces from prehistoric times to present. He reported 21 translocations of elk to and within British Columbia during 1917 to 1989. In 1914, a small herd of red deer was shipped to British Columbia from New Zealand. They were released on Graham Island in the Queen Charlotte Islands during June 1918. About 1929, elk were released on the same island. They survived but have not done well. As of 1992, only about 200 animals—probably a mixture of red deer and elk—were present.

Elk once occupied the coastal mainland (Fraser River Delta), but disappeared by the early 1880s. Spalding (1992:18) concluded: "The elk is an indigenous animal to British Columbia and when Europeans arrived, was numerous and widespread. Although the provincial population dropped dramatically during the 1880s, sizable native herds remained on Vancouver Island, in the Kootenays and in the northern Rocky Mountains. Further, they were not entirely eliminated from the northern, central and southern interior, or from the mountainous area between southwestern British Columbia and northwestern Washington State. Although elk populations in these latter areas were very low, some animals did remain, sufficient in number to breed and maintain their presence. They apparently moved extensively and were generally secretive, explaining the few, and often unconfirmed, sightings."

By early autumn 1998, the preharvest elk population was estimated at 43,000 (I. Hatter personal communication:1998).

Manitoba

Fossil elk are unknown from Manitoba, but elk apparently occupied much of the province in presettlement times. William B. Miller, who settled in the Dauphin district in 1890, reported elk numerous in the Riding Mountains at that time, although their numbers evidently had been much greater (see Green 1933). They drifted down to the surrounding lowlands during winter.

Millais (1915) indicated that elk roamed the southwestern portion of the province, but were decreasing rapidly until 1895, when they received a measure of protection. He further reported that the elk survived in the natural protection of dense forests and muskeg; during severe winters, such as 1906, they were forced into open country and cultivated lands, where great numbers were killed despite game laws. From 1860 to 1920, agricultural settlement and uncontrolled hunting eliminated most of the elk. The remaining concentrations were in the Riding Mountain National Park and Duck Mountain Provincial Park.

As of 1997, approximately 8,000 elk were to be found in Manitoba (R. Stardom personal communication:1998).

New Brunswick, Newfoundland, Northwest Territories and Nova Scotia

Credible records could not be found indicating that elk had occupied any of the four "N" provinces during historic times (see Bryant and Maser 1982). Also, no fossil *Cervus* have been documented from those provinces (Tables 6–8). However, Caton (1887) reported that a Mr. H. Y. Hind, in his account of explorations of Labrador, said that elk remained in the seclusion of that peninsula (in Newfoundland) until much later than they did in Quebec, New Brunswick and Nova Scotia. Caton was not confusing elk and moose as he noted that their ranges overlapped, and that moose survived the advent of Europeans better than did elk because the former evaded pursuit more readily in deep snow. Caton appeared to publish hearsay without critical review.

Elk appeared in the Fort Liard area of the Northwest Territories during the 1990s. They were fairly rare, but were seen regularly by local people traveling on the Liard River. During autumn 1997, elk could be heard bugling by people in Fort Liard, and at least five animals have been harvested during 1995 to 1998. The elk presumably are from expanding herds in British Columbia. No substantial increases or decreases are evident in this marginal population on the northern edge of the species' range. Personnel of the Northwest Territories Department of Renewable Resources reported no plans to manage elk in the Territories (M. Bradly personal communication:1998).

Ontario

Subfossil antlers (i.e., those that last 50–300 years or more in swamp mud or other environments protected from oxygen and animals) and verbal accounts by Indians and "old-timers" indicate that elk roamed southern Ontario between lakes Huron and Erie during the 1700s (Smith 1901, Wintemberg 1926, Landon 1931). Subfossils also have been found near Ottawa and Sudbury and farther north into central Ontario (J. Hamr personal communication:1998). At least 16 sites in Ontario have yielded elk fossils, some as late as 270 years ago (Table 8). The cause or causes of their extirpation undoubtedly will remain speculative (see Wintemberg 1926). However, when the first settlers arrived in 1832, no observations of elk were recorded.

During the early 1930s, 24 Rocky Mountain elk were introduced from Alberta into the province. Six additional translocations brought the number of elk introduced during the 1930s to about 200. By the mid-1940s, the population had increased to an estimated 300 individuals, and because of an infestation of giant liver flukes, an attempt was made to eliminate the population. During the late 1940s

Elk in Manitoba survived the 19th century destruction of North American elk in perhaps as high numbers as any place outside Wyoming and Yellowstone National Park. Dense forests and muskeg afforded the animals a measure of protection. However, during severe winters, such as 1906, they moved into more open habitat to search for food and came into conflict with agriculture. Millais (1915) estimated that, in 1906 alone, not less than 1,000 head were killed by hunters and farmers, who paid little attention to game laws. This supposed subspecies still subsists in habitat that seems to overlap those of moose and pronghorn. *Photos taken near Baldy Lake in Riding Mountain National Park, Manitoba, by Jim Wilke.*

and early 1950s, about 1,000 elk were killed (J. Hamr personal communication:1998).

By 1955, only a few small herds remained in the province, but they seemed stable-to-increasing. No distinction was made in the hunting regulations between elk and white-tailed deer until 1978; animals of either species could be harvested—a continued effort to eliminate the larger species. With the help of the Ontario Federation of Anglers and Hunters, hunters from across the province petitioned to remove elk from the deer license and protect the remaining animals (Ranta 1998). After 1978, elk were protected (M. Hall personal communication:1998).

Bryant and Maser (1982) speculated that a remnant population of Eastern elk could have contributed to the Ontario population (see also Stalling 1994). However, DNA testing of 40 to 50 blood and antler samples at the University of Alberta indicated no significant genetic differences between the Ontario elk and those from populations of Manitoban and Rocky Mountain elk (J. Hamr personal communication:1998).

A remnant population of about 50 elk remained in the Borwash-French River area south of Sudbury as of early 1998. Restoration of elk to historic range by the Ontario Ministry of Natural Resources is underway (M. Hall personal communication:2001), using excess animals from Elk Island National Park in Alberta. During 1998 to mid-2001, 182 animals were released in the Sudbury area. During 2000 and 2001, 120 were released near Bancroft, and 108 were translocated to the Kenora area. During 2001, 50 elk were released in the Blind River area.

Prince Edward Island

Fossil elk are unknown from Prince Edward Island (Tables 6–8), and the animals have not been present during historic time.

Quebec

Although the North American elk first was named in 1777 by Erxleben from a Quebec specimen, no fossil elk are known from the Province (Tables 6–8). Elk occupied the southern portion of Quebec but were extirpated by the 1830s, and none occupied the Province as of 1995.

Saskatchewan

Elk apparently occupied most of Saskatchewan before the arrival of European settlers, but historic data are lacking. The major concentration occurred within Prince Albert National Park and eastward.

Translocation programs were initiated in Saskatchewan during 1937 to restore Cypress Hills populations in the southwestern corner of the province. The elk came from Wainwright Buffalo Park, Alberta. Other efforts to reintroduce elk took place during 1952 and 1953, with animals captured from the Fort a la Corne Forest in northcentral Saskatchewan. Those animals were released into the Cypress Hills to supplement that population and to the Flotten Lake area near Beauval to create populations in unused habitat (Loran et al. 1997).

Beginning in 1982, elk were translocated from Elk Island National Park and Cypress Hills Provincial Park to various areas in Saskatchewan. By the end of 1994, 696 elk had been relocated to restock historic, forested habitat, restore populations depleted by hunting, supplement small populations, reduce undesirably high populations of elk in protected areas and reduce depredations on agricultural lands. During January through March 1995, 347 elk were translocated to the Sled Lake area—54 from the Cypress Hills and 293 from Elk Island National Park. No elk were translocated during 1996 (Loran et al. 1997).

During February 1998, 45 elk from the Cypress Hills were released at Cumberland Delta. During January through March 1999 and 2000, 689 elk were translocated to the Candle Lake/Cub Hills area, with source animals from Elk Island National Park, Alberta (A. Arsenault personal communication:2001).

The elk population in Saskatchewan was estimated at more than 20,000 animals during the late 1700s. By about 1900, the population was at a low—possibly 1,500 to 1,800. By 1982, the provincial posthunt population was estimated at 5,100. The posthunt population in 1996 was about 12,000 elk (see Arsenault 1998) and, based on population growth projections and limited surveys, the 1997 to 1998 wintering population was about the same (A. Arsenault personal communication:1998).

Yukon Territory

No historic records exist of elk in the Yukon Territory, but fossil evidence indicates the existence of a population in the Alaska/Yukon refugium during Wisconsin glaciation that became extinct at the period's close, probably as a result of vegetational changes (Guthrie 1966). These were large-antlered forms, with a comparatively high frequency of supernumerary proximal tines.

In 1951 and 1954, 49 elk were obtained from Elk Island National Park in Alberta and released about 50 miles (80 km) north of Whitehorse, near Braeburn. Surveys conducted in the late 1960s indicated that these introduced elk had split into two groups: one occupying a large burnt area along the Takhini River west of Whitehorse; the other occupying the Nordenskiold River drainage some 31 miles (50 km) to the north. Both herds were estimated at 35 to 40 head at that time. They remained static until the late 1980s, when the Yukon Fish and Wildlife Branch initiated an enhancement program over a period of 5 years (1989 through 1994). A total of 117 elk from Elk Island National Park were released to build up both herds to viable numbers. This initiative, however, had limited success. By 1997, the Takhini herd was estimated at 55 to 60 elk. The Nordenskiold herd was widely dispersed and difficult to census; its minimum number was around 60, but may have been as high as 80 to 100. Lack of increase in these herds was attributed to high predation rates on calves. Wolves are known to be preying on elk, but to what extent other predators are involved is unknown. Black and grizzly bears, as well as coyotes, also share the elk habitat. Their preying on elk calves has been documented in other areas, so the possibility of such predation cannot be ruled out in the Yukon (M. Hoefs personal communication:1998).

In 1975, an elk was observed along the Liard River near Watson Lake, and there have been a number of additional sightings of individual elk or small groups from the Liard drainage in more recent years. These elk came from British Columbia and may be reflective of an expanding population in northern British Columbia (M. Hoefs personal communication:1998).

Alabama

There are no records of elk in Alabama during historic times, but three archeological sites provide evidence that elk once roamed that state as late as 2,500 years ago (Curren 1977).

In February 1916, 55 Rocky Mountain elk from Jackson Hole, Wyoming, were brought to Alabama to establish a herd. Release locations were in Tuscaloosa, Sumter, Pickens and Calhoun counties. The last known elk was killed in 1921. Poaching, disease and landowner intolerance of severe crop depredation by elk were the primary reasons for failed herd establishment (Allen 1965). The Alabama Department of Conservation reportedly had no plans for further introductions of elk (K. Guyse personal communication:1997).

Alaska

Pleistocene fossils indicate that elk shared Alaska with mammoths, horses and bison. The latest confirmed date for native elk was about 9,300 years ago (Murie 1951).

In 1925, Alaska's Department of Fish and Game implemented an introduction program to establish Roosevelt elk. For several years, elk were translocated on Kruzof, Revillagigedo, Gravina and Afognak islands. The translocations on the Kruzof, Revillagigedo and Gravina islands were unsuccessful and eventually terminated (Batchelor 1965).

In spring 1929, the Afognak Island translocation consisted of three male and five female calves that originated from the Olympic Peninsula in Washington. "From the beginning, the herd thrived and five calves were reported in the spring of 1930" (Burris and McKnight 1973:20). During an aerial census in 1948, 148 elk were observed. By 1965, the population of 1,200 to 1,500 elk had exceeded the habitat's carrying capacity, and the population subsequently declined. Despite liberalized hunting seasons and a series of hard winters that caused heavy mortality among young and old alike, the population continued to exceed carrying capacity. In 1962, the U.S. Forest Service and Alaska Department of Fish and Game attempted again to introduce elk onto Gravina Island near Ketchikan. Eleven calves were captured on Afognak and Raspberry islands and penned on Gravina Island. Eight survivors were released after about 3 months in captivity. Subsequently, they were shot by a homesteader because they had repeatedly damaged his garden (Burris and McKnight 1973).

The elk populations on Afognak and Raspberry islands dropped to an estimated low of less than 500 animals by about 1971. Mild winters during the rest of the 1970s and 1980s allowed the elk to recover. In 1988, they reached an estimated peak of 1,400 animals. Another moderate decline occurred during 1989 and 1990 because of severe winters. Hunting access to certain herds on Afognak was a problem, but some herds were regulated by nature. When commercial logging began about 1975, this situation changed—necessitating smaller management areas with set harvest quotas. Nearly all of both islands became Native corporation property by the early 1980s, and logging by those corporations accelerated to the extent that roads transected or at least bordered the ranges of all Afognak elk herds by 1998.

Public access for hunters may become an issue. Alaska Native Claims Settlement Act regulations governing the lands—almost 50% of the island—awarded to Native corporations contain no provisions for public access. In 1997, prehunting season elk populations again increased and were collectively estimated at about 1,300—200 on Raspberry Island and 1,100 on Afognak Island (R. Smith personal communication:1998).

Occasional sightings of elk, but not established herds, on Kodiak Island were reported as early as 1940. The sightings continued and increased in frequency after 1983. R. Smith (personal communication:1998) believed that a small herd—probably 15 to 20 animals—was becoming established on the Kupreanof Peninsula of northwestern Kodiak. Public support is high for more elk. However, they may compete with deer, and access to the interior of Kodiak is insufficient to manage elk there.

A bill passed during the 1985 legislative session directed the Alaska Department of Fish and Game to translocate not fewer than 30 or more than 150 elk into a suitable site in southeastern Alaska. Etolin Island was selected, and 33 Roosevelt and 17 Rocky Mountain elk from Oregon were released on the island during 1987. Less than half of the animals survived to June 1988; wolf predation apparently was a major cause of mortality (Land and James 1989). Surveys during 1994 and 1995 indicated that the Etolin Island elk population had been growing slowly. Emigration also had occurred and a herd was established on Zarembo Island. Reports were received of elk on Wrangell, Mitkof, Kupreanof and Kashevaroff islands (Dinneford 1995). Alaska's southeastern elk management plan called for hunting when the population reached 250, which it did during 1997. Thus in October, 29 permit holders took eight large bulls—seven on Etolin Island and one on nearby Zarembo Island. According to Crain (1998), if the elk population continues to grow, the number of hunting permits likely will continue to increase.

Arizona

Elk, presumably of the extinct Merriam subspecies, once roamed throughout the mountainous areas of eastern Arizona. The principal range appears to have been the White Mountains, but elk were recorded along the Colorado River above the Grand Canyon in 1826 and in the general vicinity of Flagstaff as late as 1884 (see Murie 1951). Mearns (1907) reported that they used the upper transition and boreal zones during summer, descending to the lower transition and upper austral zones in winter—probably crossing to the high mountains of northeastern Sonora, Mexico. However, Nelson (1925) maintained that elk, like pronghorn, inhabited the foothills and adjacent plains until the 1880s, when they learned to follow the great herds of range cattle through heavy pine forest to summer on grassy plateaus at about 8,000-foot (2,438 m) elevations. No specimens of native elk are known from the San Francisco Mountains, although the habitat seems favorable (Davis 1982). Native elk were extirpated from Arizona during the early 1900s (Cahalane 1939).

Robert Looney of Prescott read an article in the August 1912 *Outdoor Life* magazine about elk translocations (Arizona Game and Fish Department 1972, R. Lee personal communication:1997) and his elks lodge (#536 of Winslow, Arizona) spearheaded a reintroduction. Although later reimbursed, Looney paid the $1,265 required for capture and freight of 80 Rocky Mountain elk from Yellowstone. In February 1913, the elk were released in Cabin Draw near Chevelon Creek, 45 miles (72 km) south of Winslow, after being hauled there in 12 wagons. In 1918, 56 head were shipped to Clifton. Of these, 22 were put in the Grahams, where they were unsuccessful, and 34 were sent to Cutter. In 1927, 23 elk were released at the Campbell Blue area south of Alpine. During that year, 23 elk were released near Kingman and hazed up to the Hualapais. In 1928, 55 elk were released near Williams, and during 1963, 36 were released on the Hualapai Reservation. As a result of translocations, an elk population of approximately 22,000 posthunt adults on non-Reservation land occupied Arizona in 1998 (R. Lee personal communication:1998). As of then, the Game and Fish Department had no plans for further relocations of elk. About 14,400 elk were reported on the Fort Apache/White Mountain Apache, Hualapai Wildlife and San Carlos Apache reservations in 1998 (J. Jojola, R. Riley and A. Moors personal communications:1998)

"The reason for the surprising phenomenon of elk being less in evidence in presettlement times than are the present introduced populations can only be a matter of conjecture. The extirpation of the wolf and grizzly from Arizona has been suggested as a factor in the later success of reintroduced elk, and it is remotely possible that the original elk herds were decimated by disease prior to arrival of the Americans. These factors are not known to have affected elk numbers elsewhere in North America, however, and these explanations appear forced. That the native elk were somehow unable to exploit the forested habitats west of the White Mountains is also difficult to imagine. One is led to speculate that elk may have only recently arrived in Arizona from northern New Mexico and had not yet spread west from the White Mountains before being extirpated by settlers" (Davis 1982:180–181). Davis apparently did not consider that equestrian Indians and Spanish settlers could have extirpated elk in some areas 100 or more years before Europeans arrived.

Records of elk are unknown from Arizona during the Holocene (Figures 28 and 29). Late Holocene sites are known from that area, so the fossil record appears to reflect an absence of elk in the state during the Holocene (Faunmap Working Group 1994). However, historic accounts from early settlers indicate elk were more common in central and western Arizona than previously thought or reported. It is unlikely that elk populations, for whatever reason, were ever very large in Arizona (R. Lee personal communication:1998).

Arkansas

One record exists (Featherstonhaugh 1835) to suggest that herds of elk roamed northeastern Arkansas near the Missouri boundary as late as 1834. It is reasonable to suppose that elk once had a wider distribution in the state, but available literature does not reflect it. Archeological records indicate elk in that area, but more in the western part of the state along the Oklahoma border (Figure 29; Faunmap Working Group 1994). No subspecies of elk was named from the central or eastern United States, therefore the taxonomic status of elk there is undetermined.

The U.S. Forest Service introduced three bull and eight cow elk from Wichita National Wildlife Refuge, Oklahoma, into the Black Mountain Refuge, Arkansas, during 1933. The population grew to 125 by 1948, but by then, wildlife biologists were concerned for the herd's future because of the extremely slow increase. The herd reached an estimated 200 head by the mid-1950s and then vanished. Exact reasons are unknown, but illegal hunting, natural mortality and habitat succession probably contributed to the extermination, according to Cartwright (1995).

In 1981, the Arkansas Game and Fish Commission, in cooperation with private citizens, initiated another elk restoration project in the Ozark Mountains of northwestern Arkansas. Between 1981 and 1985, 112 elk from Colorado and Nebraska (most of them originally from Wyoming) were released at five sites near the Buffalo River in Newton County. State, federal and private interests (including the Rocky Mountain Elk Foundation) have worked together to expand and improve elk habitat along the Buffalo River. An estimated 450 wild elk roamed Arkansas as of 1998, occupying about 225,000 acres (91,058 ha). Between 1981 and 1996, 83 elk deaths were investigated; poaching (32%) and disease (32%) were primary factors in these losses. As of 1998, herd expansion onto private land was not planned, but additional public lands were to be evaluated for possible translocations. The first hunting seasons for elk in Arkansas were held during September 21 to 25 and December 7 to 11, 1998. Eight hunters took seven bulls during September. Three bulls and seven cows were harvested in December (M. Cartwright personal communication:1999).

California

Before 1840, enormous bands of Tule elk roamed the Sacramento, Central and San Joaquin valleys, as well as the Coast Range. According to Millais (1915), they lived almost entirely in the open, and before the advent of miners in 1849, they were practically free from molestation (see Chapter 1). "Because of their large size and stately appearance, and because they were less common than deer, elk were mentioned in the diaries and journals of early explorers and emigrants whenever they were encountered. These accounts lead one to believe that in primitive times elk were much more limited in range and abundance in California than were deer. But in some areas, such as the San Francisco and Monterey Bay areas, and the Concord, Livermore, Gilroy, Sacramento and San Joaquin valleys, they were very numerous. There also are early records of an abundance of elk in Marin County. Some individual herds that numbered at least 2,000 head were reported in the San Joaquin Valley in 1846" (Dasmann 1958:19).

Farther north, between the Cascade Mountains and the Pacific coast, Roosevelt elk also were common before the country was settled (McCullough 1969). Eastern and southern California apparently were without elk (Murie 1951).

In 1849, the California Territorial Legislature adopted common law of England as the rule in all state courts (Anonymous 1980). Before that, Spanish and then Mexican laws applied. In 1852, the first California game law was enacted for 12 counties; it protected elk as well as other game mammals and birds. Game laws were extended to all counties in the state during 1854.

Once the settlement of land began in earnest, and the growing towns and settlements provided customers for market hunters, the elk population in California declined rapidly (Dasmann 1958). Consumption of crops and destruction of fences led to campaigns of extermination. The last elk in the Suisun area reportedly was shot in 1868. Elk had disappeared from Marin County before 1872, and only a few were left in the San Joaquin Valley in the 1870s.

Rocky Mountain elk were introduced into the state in 1916, when 50 elk from Yellowstone National Park were released into the Pit River area of Shasta County. In 1967, a private endeavor was undertaken to establish an elk population on the Ellsworth Ranch, Kern County. Again, Yellowstone National Park supplied the elk; 277 were released into a ranch enclosure. A small number escaped and established themselves on several large ranches. The enclosure was removed and several herds became established throughout adjacent ranches (Dasmann 1975).

The Department of Fish and Game has translocated about 1,000 Tule elk to new areas since 1975, and will continue to do so as suitable new locations are identified (J. Fischer personal communication:1997). Roosevelt elk have been released into historic range in Siskiyou, Trinity and Humboldt counties. Further translocations of Roosevelt elk into suitable historic habitat are planned. About 8,400 elk were reported in the state as of autumn 1998 (J. K. Fisher personal communication:1998).

Tule elk are the most specialized of North American elk, living as they do (or did) in open country under semidesert condition (*left*). Sometimes called dwarf elk, these animals have teeth more specialized for chewing coarse fibrous vegetation than do elk of other subspecies. "Competition from Spanish livestock, heavy hunting by fur trappers, meat demands of the 49ers, and finally development of the land by settlers came in quick succession, reducing the Tule elk almost to the point of extinction" from herds in the San Joaquin and Sacramento valleys that once numbered upward of 2,000 head, according to early explorers (McCullough 1961:1). Tule marshes (*right*) provided these elk with some protection, because the mud restricted human and horse movements. *Left photo by Leonard Lee Rue. Right photo by Bruce Keegan; courtesy of the Committee for Preservation of Tule Elk.*

From the present-day distribution, it is apparent that Roosevelt elk reach their greatest density in thick timber with small clearings in areas of high rainfall, according to McCullough (1969). However, these elk frequently are seen in open meadows such as these in Del Norte County, California. *Photo by Bart W. O'Gara.*

Colorado

Elk were plentiful in the mountains and on the plains of Colorado before exploration and during early settlement (see Murie 1951). Brewer (1871) saw elk in South Park during 1869. Allen (1874) reported that elk in Park County—which stayed near the upper limit of timber during summer, descending occasionally into the valleys in winter—were becoming rare in 1874. Ingersoll (1882) referred to elk in Middle Park as formerly numerous but scarce in the 1880s. Humans usurped the valleys for farms, thousands of miners flowed into the Rockies and, in the absence of game laws, elk were shot indiscriminately (Swift 1945). By 1909, elk numbers had been reduced considerably and were divided about equally between northern and southern Colorado (Cary 1911). Estimates ranged from 200 to 300 to twice that many in Routt and Rio Blanco counties and 460 to 500 in the mountains of Gunnison County. In addition, small bands were known to range in the San Juan and La Plata mountains.

During 1910, the U.S. Forest Service estimated the elk population in Colorado to be 500 to 1,000. The animals were scattered throughout the mountainous areas in 10 small herds, the largest of which existed in the White and Gunnison river watersheds (Swift 1945). The rough topography of those montane refugia offered natural sanctuary for these herds. Murie (1951) also noted the importance of remote, undeveloped wilderness areas for the protection of native animals. Without such areas, elk in Colorado (and elsewhere) probably would have been exterminated by hide and meat hunters.

From 1912 to 1928, the Colorado Division of Wildlife's predecessor agency reintroduced elk from the Yellowstone area to areas from which they had been extirpated. It also supplemented declining herds. Fourteen introductions, totaling approximately 350 head, were made during this span (Swift 1945). During postseason 1998, 220,000 to 240,000 elk were estimated in Colorado (R. Kahn personal communication:1998), and no further translocations or expansions were planned. In fact, reduction of some pioneering herds was being considered.

Connecticut

Physical evidence for the existence of elk in Connecticut is lacking. However, because of records documenting the presence of elk in adjacent states, Goodwin (1935) supposed that the animals occurred in the state during the 16th and 17th centuries. Also, Whitaker and Hamilton (1998) present a range map that includes northwestern Connecticut. In the text, they simply indicate that the original range included west-central New England. Some captive elk existed in the state (regulated by the state's Department of Agriculture) as of 1998, but no free-ranging elk were present (D. W. May personal communication:1998).

Delaware

A calcaneum identical in size and form to that of a modern elk was recovered near Newark, Delaware (Hatt 1949). Records found by the Delaware wildlife section's Heritage Program indicated that elk were observed by early settlers, but the animals were extirpated during the early colonial period (H. L. Alexander personal communication:1998). No wild elk were present during 1998.

Florida

Elk are not known to have been native to Florida, but during the late 1960s, six were brought into the state for the filming of a television series. They then were placed on exhibit in West Palm Beach. In 1968, they were purchased and released on a ranch in Highlands County, south-central Florida. Eleven elk were observed in 1972. Other sightings occurred about 10 to 15 miles (16–24 km) from the release site, and the last recorded sighting was in February 1973 (Bryant and Maser 1982). As of December 1998, a few elk were maintained on fenced and permitted gamefarms, but no free-ranging elk were known to Florida Game and Fresh Water Fish Commission personnel (A. L. Egbert personal communication:1998).

Georgia

Elk remains have not been reported from archaeological sites in the state (Laerm et al. 1993). Also, records do not indicate general distribution of elk in Georgia during exploration and settlement. Of his travels in Georgia during 1773, Bartram (1928) wrote that elk were few and only found in the Appalachian Mountains. Whitaker and Hamilton (1998) indicated that elk were extirpated during the 1870s. No wild elk had been translocated to the state as of 1998 (K. Kammermeyer personal communication:1998).

Idaho

Early historic records indicate that elk occurred throughout most of Idaho, but Murie (1951) maintained they seldom were found on the arid plains of the southern part of the state; they were most plentiful in the eastern portion of the state in and adjacent to the mountains. Elk were specifically recorded from the Salmon River, Crags, Pahsimeroi, Lemhi, Sawtooth, Blackfoot, Bruneau and Elk mountains, as well as the Henry Lake area (Murie 1951). Large herds apparently were absent from the narrow, northern portion of the state. On their return from the Pacific coast, Lewis and Clark spent approximately 50 days crossing the state in

1806, and Lewis reported the following: "June 27 . . . The Indian informs us that there is a great abundance of elk in the valley about the fishery on the Kooskooske [*sic* Kooskia] River" (Humbird 1975:16). The expedition had hunters continuously searching for wildlife, but Lewis or Clark did not report seeing or killing an elk while in Idaho.

With discovery of gold at Pierce in 1860, and subsequent settlement of the state, the elk population declined because of unrestricted, year-round hunting (see Edson 1963, Bryant and Maser 1982). By 1914, only a few scattered herds existed (Edson 1963). The first recorded estimate of elk numbers was published in the U.S. Forest Service census during 1918 (see Edson 1963); it estimated 610 elk present on national forest lands.

A translocation program was initiated in 1915 and proceeded through 1946. During that time, 675 elk from Yellowstone National Park and Jackson Hole, Wyoming, were translocated throughout Idaho (Humbird 1975). Elk reestablished in 40 of Idaho's 44 counties. About 124,000 elk were estimated in the state after the 1998 hunting season (L. Kuck personal communication:1998).

Illinois

Elk remains in archeological sites of Illinois are known from the total Holocene, except for 1,300 to 800 years before present (Purdue and Styles 1986).

In 1673, Jesuit missionary Jacques Marquette's party found elk common along the Illinois River, and in 1712—according to Father Gabriel Marest—the prairies on either side of that river were covered with bison, elk and deer (Kip 1846). Some accounts indicate that heavy snows during the 1760s were detrimental to the species (Hoffmeister 1989). Fonda (1907:215) related seeing elk along the Illinois River in 1825 and killing a large bull from his canoe with a long-barreled gun "loaded with a heavy charge of powder, and seven slugs or pieces of bar lead." Lacewood (1903) wrote of Winnebago and Menominee half-breeds hunting elk in western Illinois during 1830 to 1831. In 1876, Kingston (1908) recalled that buffalo, elk, deer, and turkey were abundant in Illinois and provided food for the settlers. Elk were uncommon and probably nearly gone in northern Illinois by the 1820s and in southern Illinois by the 1830s (see Hoffmeister 1989).

The Illinois Department of Natural Resources conducted a series of studies during 1996 to determine the feasibility of reintroducing elk into the southern part of the state. The studies indicated that habitat was available, but the potential for agricultural damage was high. Benefit/ cost analysis showed that potential benefits outweighed potential damages. Opinions of southern Illinois citizens were equally split concerning reintroduction, but the opposition was very vocal. As of 1999, the Department of Natural Resources had decided not to move forward with an elk reintroduction, but will closely monitor elk introduction efforts in other states (J. Buhnerkempe personal communication:1999).

Indiana

Elk of the late Pleistocene were recorded from eight counties (Lyon 1936) and the animals were found throughout Indiana historically, but had become relatively scarce by the time of the first settlements (Mumford 1969). In a letter written during January 1712, Father Marest recounted a journey down the east shore of Lake Michigan in which elk were seen in what is now Indiana (Kip 1846). Elk were recorded along the Kankakee River in 1712 (Lyon 1936), an elk was killed near Richmond about 1811 (Plummer 1844), and individuals were recorded in Knox County in 1829 and 1830 (Butler 1895)—apparently the last reported sighting of a native elk in the state (Mumford 1969).

During the late 1950s and early 1960s, attempts were made to introduce Rocky Mountain elk into Brown, Jefferson, Jennings and Ripley counties. The efforts failed and were terminated in 1966. Reasons for the failure could not be ascertained (J. Olson personal communication:1997).

Iowa

Early Iowa settlers reported that elk were plentiful, being found in herds of up to 500 head. The elk scattered out during summer, but herded together in October and remained so until spring. During winter storms, they took refuge in and around ponds where the reeds and rushes were 10 feet (3 m) or more in height. At other times, the elk would lie on the highest hills. Elk antlers could be picked up by the wagonload in 1856 (Spurrell 1917).

Allen (1871:185) gave the following account: "During the early settlement of this part of Iowa [Greene County, in west-central Iowa] they were of great value to the settlers, furnishing them with an abundance of excellent food when there was a scarcity of swine and other meat-yielding domestic animals. But, as has been the case too often in the history of the noblest game animals in this continent, they were frequently most ruthlessly and improvidently destroyed. In the severer weather of winter they were often driven to seek shelter and food in the vicinity of the settlements. At such times the people, not satisfied with killing enough for their present need, mercilessly engaged in an exterminating butchery. Rendered bold by their extremity, the elk were easily dispatched with such implements as axes and corn-knives. For years they were so numerous that the settlers could kill them whenever they desired to, but sev-

eral severe winters and indiscriminate slaughter soon greatly reduced their numbers, and now only a few linger where formerly thousands lived, and these are rapidly disappearing. Their home here being chiefly the open country, they much sooner fall a prey to the 'westward march of civilization,' through the most merciless treatment they received at the hands of the emigrant, than does the deer."

Snow was so deep during the winter of 1855 to 1856 that elk could not escape the pursuit of humans and dogs. Despite the incredible numbers killed when overtaken by men, boys and women and beaten to death with clubs, the rapid and sudden disappearance of elk nonetheless astonished everyone (see Spurrell 1917). No wild elk are known to have existed in the state since about that time (R. Bishop personal communication:1997).

Kansas

Knox (1875:20) wrote that elk were " . . . quite common in the west part of the state."

Letters written in 1892 by James R. Mead of Wichita, Kansas, to a Professor L. L. Dyche documented elk in Kansas between 1859 and 1864, and indicated the eastern range of most elk in Kansas was a line drawn north and south through Eldorado in Butler County (Hoffmeister 1947). All country west of that was ranged over by them, and they occasionally were found to the east. Elk followed the timbered creeks, probably for the browse. Mead only saw them during summer or autumn, but old bulls were found in hills between the Saline and Solomon rivers all winter. The elk occurred mainly in broken country with timbered canyons and streams and were not plentiful in the level treeless country adjacent to the Arkansas River. Elk were much more numerous north of the Smoky Hill River in Kansas than south of it. During the 1850s and 1860s, Mead witnessed a drove of 1,000 animals cross the Saline River at the ford right where the town of Lincoln now stands. He only saw them in herds of 1,000 or more during summer and autumn. He killed elk on the Solomon, Saline, Smoky Hill and Arkansas rivers and their tributaries, and knew of elk killed in Butler County on the Walnut River. Mead occasionally saw the animals in what are now Lincoln, Mitchell, Osborne, Smith, Phillips and Rooks counties.

In western Kansas, elk still were fairly abundant in 1871. Reporting on mammals observed chiefly in the vicinity of Fort Hays, Allen (1874) wrote that elk were more or less common near the streams, especially on Paradise Creek, and as far east at least as Fort Harker in Ellsworth County.

Elk apparently were extirpated from Kansas about 1900. In 1951, a private landowner gave the state some 4 square miles (10.4 km²) in central Kansas to facilitate preservation of large prairie animals. The area was surrounded by a high fence, named the Maxwell Wildlife Area and three to six elk were released into the enclosure. The source of these elk is unknown, but reproduction was excellent. By 1973, fear of inbreeding prompted removal of all adult bulls. They were replaced by two from a private herd in Nebraska. Since then, other introductions to broaden the genetic base apparently have led to some disease problems. About 70 head are kept at Maxwell, and surplus animals have been used for translocations within Kansas and to other states (L. Fox personal communication:1998).

From 1981 through 1990, 33 elk from the Maxwell Wildlife Area and from Colorado, Montana and Oregon were released on the Cimarron National Grasslands in the southwestern corner of Kansas. The herd thrived and spread to adjacent areas of Colorado and Oklahoma. From an estimated 42 head in 1988, the herd increased to about 102 in 1994. When translocations began, nearby agricultural crop production was limited, but center-pivot irrigation soon brought cornfields to southeastern Colorado and alfalfa fields to other nearby areas. Crop depredations by elk followed. From 1987 through 1995, 35 elk from this herd were harvested in Kansas, 72 to 77 in Colorado and 12 in Oklahoma. During 1994 and 1995, the harvest of 80 to 83 animals in the three states brought the herd down to 28 head. Hunting seasons were not held in 1996 or 1997, and no elk were seen in Kansas during a spring 1998 survey. However, 13 were then just across the border in Oklahoma. As of 1998, the Kansas Department of Wildlife and Parks had no plans for additional releases of elk (L. Fox personal communication:1998).

During 1986 through 1992, Fort Riley military reservation in northeastern Kansas received 36 elk from the Maxwell Wildlife Area and from Colorado and Montana. This herd has not caused substantial damage on private lands off of Fort Riley, and the state has not authorized a season off the military reservation. Hunting seasons were held on the reservation from 1990 through 1997; and 29 elk were harvested (L. Fox personal communication:1998). Surveys early in 1998 indicated some 142 to 152 on Fort Riley (H. Able personal communication:1998).

Kentucky

Elk apparently roamed nearly the entire state of Kentucky in late prehistoric and early historic times, but they were gone by the mid-1800s (Murie 1951). Shoemaker (1939:22) wrote: "Daniel Boone is always pictured as encountering vast herds of Wapiti and Bison in Kentucky, where he first went in 1769, but John Strader and James Yager, who were there several years earlier, had already described the myriad

heads of game about the salt licks. Colonel Thomas Walker of 'Castle Hill,' who made an expedition over the Cumberland Mountains to Kentucky from his estate in Virginia in 1769, killed Wapiti and Bison. A century after Strader's first appearance, followed by Boone, Kenton, Wetzel, Birty, Colonel Crepps and other great killers, big game was gone from the dark and bloody ground. . . . "

During November 1998 through mid-2001 the Kentucky Department of Fish and Wildlife Resources released 1,046 elk in the central Appalachians. The animals were mostly from Utah, but some were from Arizona, Kansas, North Dakota and Oregon (J. Gassett personal communication:2001).

Louisiana

Elk once occupied the northern portion of Louisiana, but this was the southern boundary of their native range, and they probably were not abundant. According to a letter written by Dr. Milton Dunn in 1918, elk were present when Louisiana was surveyed in 1829 (see Murie 1951). A bull was shot near Mounds in Madison Parish between Roundaway Bayou and the Mississippi River in 1842; little is known concerning the appearance of southeastern elk, but that bull weighed 704 pounds (319 kg) and measured 11 feet (335 cm) from the tip of its nose to the end of a hind foot (see Lowery 1974).

An attempt to establish 20 elk in LaSalle Parish, Louisiana during 1916 failed (Lowery 1974). Causes for this lack of success are unknown. The Department of Wildlife and Fisheries has no plans to establish wild elk populations in Louisiana (D. Moreland personal communication:1997).

Maine

No record was found of elk occurring in Maine during historic times, but Wyman (1868) noted that elk bones were found in shell-heaps at Frenchman's Bay on Mount Desert, the largest of the islands on the indented coast of Maine. Wyman might have been referring to moose, or the bones could have been carried to the coast by the Native Americans who formed the shell-heaps.

Maryland

At one time or another in the prehistoric and historic past, elk roamed in all parts of the state (Paradiso 1969). Early references indicate elk were found in the tidewater as well as the mountains, and their prevalence within the state is suggested by the numerous places that bear the animal's name. As early as 1635, an anonymous contributor to *A Re-*

lation of Maryland stated that elk were to be found in the "upper parts of the country" (Mansueti 1950). Alsop (1666) reported that the three main commodities Maryland afforded for traffic were tobacco, furs (including elk skins) and meat, which were first made vendible by the Indians of the region (see Mansueti 1950). Maryland's native elk apparently were extirpated before the 1850s and reintroductions have not been attempted (Mansueti 1950, Bunnell 1997).

Massachusetts

Only one account could be found of native elk in Massachusetts (see Morton 1883). It indicated that, early in the 1700s, 15 elk were seen near a brook in South Lancaster, and one was shot. The antlers were kept by the family of the lucky hunter. Introductions have not been initiated in the state (Bunnell 1997).

Michigan

Elk once ranged over the southern peninsula of Michigan, and were said to be as common as deer (Murie 1951), but no records of sightings are available for the upper peninsula. An unknown Frenchman (Anonymous 1907) recorded the voyage of Father Emanuel Crespel from Canada into Michigan. Delayed by wind for 2 days during early August 1726 on the northeast coast of Lake Michigan, Indians in the party had time to hunt, and they killed several elk and moose. Roosevelt (1905) indicated that elk survived in northern Michigan—presumably the northern part of the lower peninsula—after the last elk was killed in Pennsylvania during 1869. Caton (1877) previously indicated that some elk remained in the northern lower peninsula as late as 1877.

Twenty-three Rocky Mountain elk from Yellowstone National Park, Wyoming, were translocated into Michigan in 1915. Fifteen or so of the animals were released at various localities, but never became established. The seven to nine other elk were released along the Sturgeon River in Cheboygan County between the towns of Wolverine and Vanderbilt. The animals prospered and continued to increase until the early 1960s, at which time they numbered approximately 1,500 and ranged over three additional counties—Otsego, Montmorency and Presque Isle (Moran 1973). These elk caused crop damage and reforestation problems. Controlled hunts were held in 1964 and 1965, and 477 elk were killed. Elk numbers stabilized during the late 1960s, but began to decline in the early 1970s—primarily because of poaching. Also, the elk range was threatened by exploration for and development of oil and gas deposits. By 1975, the herd numbered about 200 animals. The Department of Natural Resources expanded enforcement efforts, enlisted

public support and intensified habitat improvement. The herd expanded to an estimated 720 elk in 1980. Beginning in 1981, the wildlife agency began developing a management plan with a goal of a viable elk population in balance with the available habitat and one that could sustain optimal recreational opportunities. Elk hunting seasons were held during 1988 through 1995, except for 1991 (Michigan Department of Natural Resources 1996). Hunting seasons resulted in the harvest of 868 elk during 1996 through 1998. An estimated 1,000 elk roamed the state as of January 1998 (J. Urbain personal communication:1999).

Minnesota

Historically, elk were found throughout Minnesota, but were most numerous on the prairies and in hardwood forest transition zones of the south, west and northwest (Fashingbauer 1965). Zebulin Pike wrote of elk in the vicinity of Homer and swimming the Mississippi River near Monticello in 1805. Pike and his men frequently encountered bands of 150 or more elk on the west side of the river in prairie country with scattered scrub oak. A missionary to the Sioux Indians believed elk were becoming rare along the Minnesota River by 1834. In 1840, two herds totaling about 1,000 animals were seen in southern Minnesota. The next year, Indian hunters killed more than 50 in Dodge and Mower counties and adjacent areas of Iowa. Most reports of elk after 1850 were from western Minnesota. Newspapers reported elk in Aitkin, Itasca, Roseau and Kittson counties during the 1870s. A report from Kittson County in 1890 indicated that a group of half-breed Indians had prepared four tons of dried elk meat and were continuing their killing. The last native elk was believed to have been killed in Minnesota during 1908. Three were seen in Beltrami County in 1917, and a band of elk was seen near the Manitoba border in 1932.

The state legislature appropriated funds in 1913 for reintroduction of elk. In autumn 1914, 56 elk were received from Jackson Hole, Wyoming, and James J. Hill of Ramsey County, Minnesota, donated 14 elk (origin unknown). The elk were retained in a 700-acre (283 ha) enclosure at Lake Itasca. Injuries and the poor physical condition of the animals caused by their transportation to the release site resulted in a die-off until only 13 animals remained (Fashingbauer 1965). In 1929, eight elk were released in northeastern Minnesota, but failed to establish a herd. In 1935, 24 elk were released in the Red Lake Game Preserve in northwestern Minnesota. In the mid-1940s this population reached a peak of about 250 animals, but because of the damage they inflicted on agricultural crops, the elk were reduced steadily by landowners (D. Schad personal communication:1997). By 1976, only 15 elk remained in Minnesota.

In 1985, at the urging of landowners, the state legislature ordered removal of the remaining elk from the northwestern counties. An effort to do so failed and eventually was halted by a court injunction. Subsequent legislation authorized a compensation program for elk damage to agricultural crops. Also authorized was a hunting season in years when the precalf population exceeds 20 elk. Elk apparently are not isolated in the northwestern part of the state. There is periodic infusion of new animals, likely from the Pembina Hills in northeastern North Dakota or southern Manitoba. The absence of large areas of suitable habitat without adjacent agricultural lands was given as the primary factor that would preclude expansion of elk range in Minnesota (Minnesota Department of Natural Resources 1997).

Although the current herd uses the same core area from year-to-year, sightings are reported from fairly far afield on a regular basis. A herd has become established along the Minnesota/Manitoba border during recent years. The animals are found on either side of the border during a year (J. Huener personal communication:1998).

Limited hunting seasons were held in 1987, 1996 and 1997. The precalf population was estimated at 35 to 40 elk in 1997 (D. Schad personal communication:1997).

Mississippi

No literature was found to indicate that elk ever were present in Mississippi. However, elk did occur in northern Louisiana as previously noted, and given the similarity of natural vegetation in adjacent portions of the two states (Küchler 1964), elk may well have occupied the northern half of Mississippi.

Missouri

Elk were common throughout Missouri at one time. Herds still occurred in the southeastern part of the state along the Arkansas border in 1834 (Featherstonhaugh 1835), and they were abundant near New Madrid as late as 1859 (see Murie 1951). "One of the wonders of wild life tenacity was the way in which the eastern wapiti held on in Missouri. If an effort had been made to protect them they would be affording grand sport today, but though they lasted until about 1898, they are all gone now" (Shoemaker 1939:26).

In 1951, an introduction program was initiated. Two bulls and eight cows were obtained from Yellowstone National Park, Wyoming, and released in Tyson Park, a 2,372-acre (960 ha) oak/hickory forest enclosure owned by the U.S. Defense Corporation in St. Louis County, Missouri. The population increased to 103 elk in 7 years. In 1958 and early 1959, the herd was exterminated because of over-grazed range and lack of funds for supplemental winter feed (Murphy 1963). Although no wild elk now occupy the state, occasional migrants from northeastern Oklahoma do enter (Bunnell 1997).

Montana

The earliest records of conditions in historic Montana are from the journals of the Lewis and Clark expedition of 1804 to 1806. The vast expanses of prairie grass, cottonwood bottoms and occasional badlands rendered eastern and central portions of the state a paradise for game animals. Compared with the Plains, the heavily timbered country of extreme western Montana was relatively poor in game (see Koch 1941). Elk were widely distributed during the period of exploration, especially in eastern, central and southwestern Montana.

The large herds of elk in Montana started declining in the late 1800s, with the advent of settlement. Within several decades, only small herds occurred in the vicinity of Yellowstone National Park, along the Continental Divide and a few other mountainous areas. The animals were eliminated completely from the ranges in eastern Montana. Elk increased and spread after hunting season closures in 1913. Beginning in 1910, translocations from Yellowstone created herds where they had been extirpated (Rognrud and Janson 1971), and 975 elk were trapped from the northern Yellowstone herd in the Gardiner area and moved to other parts of the state (Robbins et al. 1982).

Although most suitable habitat in Montana is occupied by elk, occasional translocations are made to augment herds in northwestern Montana as excess animals become available on the National Bison Range. Such translocations are popular with hunters because many of the animals are mature bulls.

About 150,000 elk occupied Montana during December 1997 (G. Erickson personal communication:1998).

Nebraska

Elk apparently were fairly numerous throughout Nebraska before settlement. Various writers from the 1800s reported they were: equally abundant in the thinly wooded Missouri region, the open sandhills and the rugged Pine Ridge and badlands; especially abundant in the western part, where immense herds roamed as late as 1870; in large herds along the Niobrara and Elkhorn rivers of eastern Nebraska in 1866 and 1867 (see Jones 1964).

Jones (1964:309) wrote: "Historical accounts are commonplace that record bands numbering in the hundreds and indicate that the species was yet common in some places in the state as late as the early 1870's. The last large herd to be reported was one containing 84 individuals seen in eastern Wheeler County in December, 1877." During spring 1882, a lone bull was seen in Dawson County by an early settler (Kinch 1998). By the late 1880s, the elk were gone, or nearly so.

"Occasional sightings of individual elk and small herds were reported in the 1950s and 1960s, with increasing numbers of elk sighted in the Pine Ridge in northwestern Nebraska. Elk trapping and relocation in Wyoming apparently played a role in the increased number of elk seen in the Pine Ridge, and carcasses found near Hay Springs in 1967 and Harrison in 1969 were animals that had been tagged and released near Rawhide Buttes southwest of Lusk, Wyoming.

"By the 1970s a growing herd in the Bordeaux Creek drainage near Chadron led to increasing landowner complaints of elk depredation. In 1985, the Nebraska Game and Parks Commission received a petition from landowners in the Bordeaux area requesting the complete removal of elk by means other than public hunting [trapped and moved or taken by Game and Parks sharpshooters].

"The Nebraska Legislature granted authority to the Commission to set an elk season for 1986, and an elk management plan adopted that year by the Commission included hunting as the method of control. Following public hearings, the Commission established Nebraska's first modern elk season" (Grier 1995:34).

The Game and Parks Commission established an elk season for 1995. That announcement prompted more than 2,000 applications for the 38 authorized permits (Grier 1995). Popularity of elk hunts has continued. In 1997, 54 permits issued resulted in 38 elk being taken; 84 permits during 1998 netted 42 elk. Elk licenses are for residents only and once-in-a-lifetime, except for a few landowner permits that are available every 3 years. Crop depredations prevent elk from proliferating in much of the state. As of 1998, 80 to 100 elk occupied Sioux County, 80 to 100 were in Dawes County, 40 to 60 roamed the Boyd-Gregory County/South Dakota border, 10 to 20 were to be found in Cherry County and Sheridan County claimed that 15 plus occasional transients—mainly bulls—appeared in other areas (K. Menzel personal communication:1999).

Nevada

"Elk were native to Nevada. Archaeological excavations document the post-Pleistocene presence of elk in the Great Basin at Fort Rock Basin in Oregon, Smith Creek in White Pine County, South Fork in Elko County, Gatecliff in Nye County, and Last Supper Cave on the Sheldon NWR in Humboldt County. Elk dispersed into the other areas of the state over time, but their densities probably were kept very low by Native American hunters wherever they occurred. Historic sightings were reported in the Jarbidge, Bruneau and Independence Mountains in Elko County, and the Schell Creek and Snake Mountains in White Pine County. Newspaper accounts report hunter kills at Lake Tahoe and Honey Lake Valley in the west, and in the Jarbidge and Independence Mountains in the northeast" (Nevada Division of Wildlife 1997:5).

In July 1859, two elk were seen in the Snake Range a little north of the 39th parallel. During winter 1897 to 1898, seven elk ravaged a haystack, from which they were driven with difficulty, in the wild Bruneau Mountains near Mountain City. Dr. C. Hart Merriam reported that elk formerly were found in the Charleston Mountains, some of which are high and with pine forests (see Murie 1951).

"Elk were extinct in Nevada by the end of the 19th century. Human over-exploitation of natural resources—before the passage of protective legislation—contributed to this extinction. Also, introduced diseases devastated many native species.

"Nevada sportsmen reintroduced the first elk in the early 1930s. Through 1996, elk have been released at eight sites scattered throughout Nevada. These are the Spring Range, the Schell Creek Range, Pilot Peak, the Monitor Range, the Goshute Reservation, the South Egan Range, the Bruneau River and the Jarbidge Mountains" (Nevada Division of Wildlife 1997:5). A total of 1,045 elk were translocated at 11 sites in Nevada from 1932 to 1997—more than 80% of them during 1988 to 1997. Most released populations have done well. No releases were planned for 1998 and 1999 (Hess 1997).

Since about 1987, Nevada's rangelands have improved as a result of better management, and elk populations have blossomed. The first elk hunt was held in 1945. Since 1975, hunting seasons have emphasized trophy animals, except where population control was needed. Trophy quality of animals killed has been high, resulting in an average of 62 applications for each available bull tag (Nevada Division of Wildlife 1997).

Several releases in the 1990s showed tremendous potential for population establishment and growth. During the mid-1990s, immigration from Utah resulted in several new elk populations, near Wendover and Pioche. The Schell Creek population numbered about 2,355 animals by spring 1998, and was increasing. The Spring Range population seemed static. The Monitor Range release grew rapidly, numbering 368 in 1998. The statewide spring, precalving population was estimated at 5,300 elk during 1998 (G. A. Tanner personal communication:1999).

New Hampshire

Although a perfectly preserved, shed elk antler was found in a New Hampshire pond, Silver (1957) maintained that it was extremely doubtful that elk were native to the state because Cahalane (1947) gave the original range as from the Berkshires in Massachusetts westward. The antler could have been carried in by humans or be that of a straggler bull.

In 1903, the state was awarded 12 elk (origin unknown)—eight cows and four bulls—from the Corbin heirs. These animals were released on Ragged Mountain by the Andover Fish and Game Club. The population thrived for a number of years, and as many as 40 elk were observed in one herd by 1912. However, crop depredations caused landowners to apply political pressure to the state legislature, which forced the Fish and Game Department to reduce the herd so the animals would no longer threaten agricultural crops. An open season was held in 1941, and 46 elk were killed, including 18 bulls and 28 cows. But this hunt did not relieve enough depredation pressure, and landowners still complained. Finally, in 1955, conservation officers killed 14 cows and two bulls outside of Lempster. As of 1997, Fish and Game personnel were not aware of any free-ranging elk in the state. Elk occasionally escape from a large private hunting preserve in west-central New Hampshire, but there is no record of free-ranging elk reproduction in the state (S. Weber personal communication:1997).

New Jersey

Elk probably visited the northwestern corner of New Jersey in the 1700s and 1800s. This view is strengthened by the presence of elk in Monroe and Pike counties, Pennsylvania (adjacent to New Jersey), and because Stone (1908) reported bones from aboriginal refuse heaps near Trenton. Elk apparently were extirpated in the state by the early 1800s.

New Mexico

Concerning the elk in New Mexico, Bailey (1931:42) wrote: "Forty-years ago it was common in the Sacramento, White and Guadalupe Mountains east of the Rio Grande, in the Mogollon group of mountains west of the Rio Grande, and in the White Mountains of Arizona. There are old records for the Datil and Gallina Mountains of Socorro County and a doubtful record for the Manzano Mountains. To the north there are no more elk records until the Jemez and Pecos River Mountains are reached, where the Colorado elk comes down from the north."

In a letter from Blue, Arizona, dated May 26, 1906, D. B. Rudd, Assistant Forest Ranger, wrote to the U.S. Forest Service: "In the year 1876 when my father moved to this part of the country the elk were very plentiful and could be found in large bands in the White Mountains and in the Blue Range, more particularly on the head of Black River. As late as 1890 elk could be found but not so plentifully. Since the year 1895 I can not find that any have been seen. Whether they were killed or whether the coming of cattle and sheep into their range caused them to leave might be a question" (Bailey 1931:42).

E. D. Mecham of Ogden, Utah, spent 20 years as a trapper and guide in the Rocky Mountains. He told J. A. Allen that he had seen elk as far south as the Mexican border and in herds of 2,000 head in southern New Mexico (Allen 1874). Native elk of the southern mountains apparently were extirpated by about 1900, and those of the northern ranges were last reported in 1909 (Lang 1958).

Shortly after elk were gone from the state, reintroduction of the species was initiated. In 1911, J. B. Dawson of Routt County, Colorado, sold 12 Rocky Mountain elk (nine cows and three bulls) to the state of New Mexico. Yellowstone Park donated 50 elk in 1914 to help with the reestablishment. Ranchers in the Pecos Mountain area used their private lands as refuges until movement of the elk onto public lands (Bailey 1931). By 1998, approximately 80,000 elk were estimated, primarily in the north-central portion of the state as well as mountainous national forests and Indian reservations of southwestern and south-central New Mexico (D. Weybright personal communication:1999).

New York

"Positive records of elk in New York are not numerous, but they are sufficient to show that the animals at one time ranged through the State" (Murie 1951:33).

"In 1654 Father LeMoine made a journey to the western part of New York and speaks of the astonishing number of the deer, and of the great numbers of elk, many of which were killed while crossing the rivers. . . . As late as 1826 a few elk were killed on the Saranac, in New York" (Hays 1871:388–389).

Tome (1854) wrote of hunting elk in New York near the Pennsylvania border during the first two decades of the 19th century. He reported they were quite numerous and gathered in large bands during August and again in late winter.

Shoemaker (1939:19) wrote: "In the broken, densely wooded regions of southwestern New York, Wapiti were numerous. There is a fine set of antlers at Letchworth Park, New York, the stag having been killed, it is said, in the Genesee Valley, about 1843; and another was formerly in the Albany Museum, taken in Cattaraugus County the same year. It is likely that the range of the Wapiti extended to the western edge of the Adirondack wilderness, but they disappeared about 1847."

Between 1893 and 1906, 332 elk (origin unknown) were introduced into the Adirondack Mountains. The translocations were thought to be a success at first, but a decline began and lasted until 1953, when the last elk was observed. Poaching and infection with the meningeal worm, *Parelaphostrongylus tenuis,* were identified as the decimating factors (Severinghaus and Darrow 1976).

North Carolina

Concerning elk in North Carolina during the early 1700s, John Brickell (1737:108–109) wrote: "The Elk is a monstrous, large, strong and swift Beast, in shape exactly like a Deer, but bigger than a Horse. . . . These Creatures may be made Domestick, and it is said, that they are so swift, that they will run more Miles in one day than a Horse can in two. . . . Their Horns generally weigh twelve or fourteen Pounds. These Beasts are plentifully to be met with in the Savannas near the Mountains, and Heads of Rivers: It is reported that some of them are seventeen Hands high. . . . The Stags are swift in Motion, and are said to be a long-liv'd Creature, they are plentifully to be met with in or near the Mountains."

Cope (1870) indicated that elk antlers were found in the Canadian zone of the Black Mountains. O'Berholser (1905) stated that elk survived in North Carolina until about 1750.

North Dakota

"Originally elk ranged over all of what is now North Dakota, and were equally at home in the timber and over the open prairie. On his trip up the Red River in 1800, Alexander Henry . . . found them abundant and wrote in his journal of September 5: 'Large herds were seen at every turn of the river and the bulls were bugling all through the woods. The rutting season was at its height.' During the next six years he frequently mentioned them, and next to the buffalo they seem to have been the main source of meat supply for him and his parties of trappers in the Red River Valley and adjacent country.

"In 1804–5, Lewis and Clark . . . recorded elk along the Missouri River all the way through North Dakota. On October 19, 1804, they reported three herds seen from a point 11 miles above the site of Fort Rice, and the next day great numbers on the wide river bottoms below where Bismarck now stands. At Fort Clark, where they [Lewis and Clark] wintered with the Mandans, elk meat was an important part of their winter provisions. On one hunting trip below the fort, February 21, 1805, they killed 14 elk, and on another trip on April 2, 21. Many herds were noted on the way up the river to Fort Union and beyond in the following April, and the Missouri River Valley seems to have been the great winter resort of the elk of the prairie region at that time. . . .

"In 1915, Remington Kellogg was told of six elk killed in 1883 near Elkton, in Cavalier County. At Towner he was told by Mr. Lymburner that in 1884 elk horns were very plentiful in that section and that as late as the nineties the Sioux Indians had elk meat for sale that had been procured somewhere farther west. Near Plaza, in Mountrail County, he was told that a Mr. Hart had killed an elk in the summer of 1913, but no one could tell where it had come from. . . .

"To what extent the elk were migratory in this open country will never be fully known, but their great abundance along the river valleys in fall, winter, and spring would indicate that these valleys were their wintering grounds. With a dense cover of timber and undergrowth and an endless supply of choice browse, they certainly afforded ideal conditions for elk winter range, just as the high windswept prairies gave equally ideal summer conditions. The shed horns of the elk are found mainly along the valleys or in the timbered areas around the lakes. . . . As the horns are shed mainly during March and April, they are usually left on the winter grounds, but a few are carried back to the summer ranges and widely scattered.

"Next to the buffalo, the elk at the height of their abundance were the easiest to hunt and hence the most rapidly killed of the large game, but when much hunted they become very wild, and it is probable that besides the vast numbers killed in the State, many were driven out of its borders" (Bailey 1926:33–35).

Over the years, several private endeavors attempted to establish Rocky Mountain elk in North Dakota. Citizens of the town of Killdeer made an application in 1941 to obtain translocation stock from Yellowstone National Park. In 1942, 25 elk were released in the Killdeer Mountains (North Dakota Game and Fish Department 1942). None of the translocation programs was successful.

During 1977, 51 elk were brought to the Berthold Indian Reservation in McKenzie County from Wind Cave National Park in South Dakota. An accidental release from the reservation rodeo grounds allowed them to escape to the Killdeer Mountains, where they prospered. The first hunting season on the herd was in 1982. By hunting, the herd— some 100 to 150 head—is held within the tolerance levels of local ranchers (W. Jensen and J. McKenzie personal communications:1998).

During 1985, 47 elk from Wind Cave National Park were translocated to the south unit of Theodore Roosevelt National Park in the Badlands of western North Dakota. That herd increased rapidly and, in 1997, 45 controlled hunt permits were issued during August, when bulls were out of the park; 35 mature bulls were killed on those permits (W. Jensen and R. Rostvet personal communications:1998). Aerial surveys during spring 1998 indicated 228 elk in the park (R. Runge personal communication:1998).

About 100 years after the last native elk was killed or driven out of North Dakota, they began trickling back from Manitoba. The natural route for elk to travel was through the Pembina Hills of the Pembina River Valley in the northeastern corner of the state, where the last hunts took place. During the late 1970s, Manitoba opened a hunting season in the Spruce Woods Provincial Forest. Some of the elk apparently funneled south and east to elude hunters. A colonizing herd found its way to the Pembina River Valley and became resident. By 1983, the herd had become a viable hunting population (McConnell 1993), and has been held at 50 to 100 head to minimize depredations to farming operations in the surrounding area (W. Jensen and R. Rostvet personal communications:1998).

Ohio

Archeological investigations reveal that elk were at least periodically prevalent and widespread in Ohio prehistorically, as summarized by Shriver (1991).

During early settlement of the region, Moravian John Heckewelder (1796) reported that such game as elk, deer, turkey and raccoons abounded near an Indian mission he had started on the Cuyahoga River near Tinker's Creek.

"The elk was frequently to be met with in Ashtabula County, until within the last 6 years [ca. 1830]. I learn from Col. Harper of that County, that one was killed there as recently as October of the present season" (Kirtland 1838:177).

Brayton (1882 in Murie 1951) cited an 1838 history of Ohio saying that about 50 elk skeletons were scattered about on the ground when Circleville was first settled. Although Ohio falls within the former range of elk, records do not indicate its abundance. Kirtland's (1838) account of an elk kill may approximate the extirpation date for Ohio.

Oklahoma

From the records available, the early distribution of elk in Oklahoma apparently was patchy (see Murie 1951). Bailey (1905) mentioned that, during 1852, elk were reported in the Wichita Mountains, apparently their favored habitat in the state. Five elk were bagged during a 2-day hunt near Mount Sheridan in 1869 (Keim 1885). James H. Gaut wrote in 1904 that Mr. A. T. Hopkins killed an elk on Rainey Mountain in Kiowa County during 1881. That apparently marks the last record of an indigenous elk in the Wichita Mountains (Halloran 1963). Halloran and Glass (1959) noted that a notation in the files of the Wichita Mountains Wildlife Refuge indicates the last elk on what is now the Refuge was killed by General William Sheridan on the mountain that bears his name. Commenting on the abundance of elk in 1850s and 1860s, James R. Mead of Wichita, Kansas, reported seeing 50 to 100 elk in a drove near Burlington in Alfalfa County (Hoffmeister 1947).

Reintroduction of elk was started in 1911 with one bull and four cows from Jackson Hole, Wyoming. The animals were released on the 59,000-acre (23,877 ha) Wichita Mountains National Wildlife Refuge. In 1912, 15 more elk were secured. The herd stagnated for a number of years, but in the 1930s it started to increase and peaked in 1967 with a population of about 600. From this population, 405 elk were translocated into eastern Oklahoma from 1969 to 1972. By 1982, it was evident that the effort was not successful in most of the nine release sites due to parasites and poaching. However, four wildlife management areas continued to support elk populations that totaled about 168 animals in 1998. The elk population on the Wichita Mountains National Wildlife Refuge is maintained at around 500 animals by hunting offered through annual public drawings. The Oklahoma Department of Wildlife Conservation's elk management plan includes maintaining elk numbers at current levels for aesthetic purposes and to provide as much hunting opportunity as the resource will allow (M. Shaw personal communication:1998). There were no plans for additional translocations or herd expansion as of 1998.

Oregon

Neahkahnie Mountain, sometimes spelled Necarney, is a bald-faced, grassy butte facing the Pacific Ocean in northwest Tillamook County, Oregon. Its name is derived, so the story goes, from the abundant deer and elk that populated it during the 1500s. At that time, Spanish explorers would put ashore to hunt and replenish their ship's larder. Hence, the butte was dubbed La Carne (the meat). Through the years, the original Spanish name assumed its present spelling (Young 1956).

Elk was one of the main sources of meat for the Lewis and Clark expedition during their stay at Fort Clatsop, just inland from the Pacific Ocean during the winter of 1805 to 1806 (Bakeless 1964).

Oregon was well supplied with elk, which roamed all through the coastal ranges and eastward to the Cascade Mountains. Some early narratives report an abundance of elk in the Willamette Valley, and others record animals throughout the Cascades. Elk also occupied the Blue Mountains, the Wallowas and neighboring localities—as far west as the headwaters of the Deschutes River.

The Wichita Mountains were the favored habitat of elk in Oklahoma during historic times. The animals were extirpated in the state by the early 1880s. Reintroduction to the Wichita Mountains National Wildlife Refuge began in 1911, with a bull and four cows from Jackson Hole, Wyoming. Taken there about that time, the top photo was entitled "King of the Wichita." During the 1990s, the largest elk population in the state roamed the Wichita Mountain and the open grasslands surrounding them. Numbers stood at about 650 head on the Wichita Mountains National Wildlife Refuge (*center*) before the 1998 hunting season. At that time, a herd of about 200 occurred on the adjacent Fort Sill military reservation and an estimated 250 elk were scattered on private lands in the state (M. Shaw personal communication:1998). Small herds also were found in heavily forested habitats on four wildlife management areas in eastern Oklahoma, including (*bottom*) the Cookson Wildlife Management Area. *Top photo courtesy of the New York Zoological Society. Center and bottom photos courtesy of Outdoor Oklahoma.*

The Pleistocene presence of elk in the Great Basin of Oregon was documented by archeological excavations in Fort Rock Basin (Nevada Division of Wildlife 1997). The arid districts were not elk habitat according to Murie (1951), but thriving herds occupy the area today (T. Keegan personal communication:1997).

Market hunting for meat, hides, teeth and antlers took a heavy toll on elk populations in Oregon during the late 1800s (Mace et al. 1995). With settlement of the state and unrestricted hunting, elk were reduced to very low numbers by the beginning of the 20th century. Less than 100 years after Lewis and Clark wintered in Oregon, restrictive hunting regulations were imposed to protect the herds. Elk hunting was closed during 1900 through 1903, opened from 1904 through 1908, and closed again during 1909 through 1932 (Mace et al. 1995).

The remaining elk populations in eastern Oregon were supplemented with elk from Jackson Hole, Wyoming. In 1911, two adult bulls, seven cows and six calves were translocated to Billy Meadows near Joseph, Wallowa County, and released in a 2,500-acre (1,012 ha) enclosure. A second translocation occurred in 1913; it was financed primarily by the Benevolent and Protective Order of the Elks. By 1916, 50 to 60 elk were in the enclosure. Beginning in 1917, several translocations of the progeny of these elk were made to various parts of the state, including Crater Lake, Clackamas River and Clatsop County—raising the possibility of intermixing with Roosevelt elk (Mace et al. 1995).

The Oregon Department of Fish and Wildlife has an ongoing, small-scale translocation program, involving capturing elk at two or three feed sites and releasing them in areas with few elk. Releases generally have been in extreme southwestern Oregon, the northern Cascades near Mount Hood and in extreme northeastern Oregon. Elk have been translocated in these areas as a way to alleviate crop damage and bolster herds that have declined or appear slow to populate the available habitat. The number of elk moved annually probably is less than 100 (T. A. Keegan personal communication:1999). About 120,000 elk roamed Oregon as of April 1998.

Pennsylvania

"Records indicate that elk at one time wandered over nearly all parts of Pennsylvania and their favorite ranges were in the middle of the state, particularly the Allegheny Mountains" (Murie 1951:36). Tome (1854:123) devoted considerable discussion to the elk and its habits and distribution in northwestern Pennsylvania: "Before the axe of the settler had leveled the forests in which they ranged, their most fre- quented resorts in the interior of Pennsylvania were between the Allegheny and Susquehanna, from the Loyalsock Creek to the New York State line." Apparently, elk were common there during the early 1800s. Cope (1870) reported that elk were absent or rare in the low countries south of Philadelphia.

In a summary of the history of elk in Pennsylvania, Gerstell (1936:6) wrote: "The opening of the last century found the wapiti exterminated in southeastern Pennsylvania; rare west of the Allegheny River and in the Blue Ridge and Cumberland Mountain Ranges; numerous on the Pocono Plateau; and abundant throughout the Allegheny Mountain and Plateau sections.

"By 1830, the archives show that the animals had disappeared from the southwestern section of the State, an area once among their favorite haunts. Extermination in the Pocono Plateau district in the diagonally opposite corner of the Commonwealth was completed between 1835 and 1845.

"During the 1840's and up until the early 1850's, a fair number of elk yarded and were annually hunted in those sections of Elk, Cameron and McKean Counties lying between the headwaters of Bennett's Branch of the Susquehanna on the southeast and the Clarion River on the north and west. It was due to the presence of these animals in the region that Elk County received its name when established in 1843.

"During the winter of 1852, a herd of twelve elk are reported to have yarded along the Clarion River near the present town of Ridgway. Seven of these animals were taken by two Indian trappers and following their slaughter, a band of native elk apparently never again yarded within the State.

"From 1855 to 1865, history tells us that elk were occasionally seen and taken at various points in the north-central part of the State. Steadily pushed back into the wilderness areas, the last survivor in the Black Forest region was taken in 1862. This left only one small area in the State harboring the pitiful remnants of wildlife species widespread throughout the Commonwealth only little more than a century previous.

"Along the headwaters of the Clarion River in the eastern half of Elk County the wapiti made its last stand. There, in November 1867, one Jim Jacobs, a full-blooded Indian, killed the last known Pennsylvania elk. It appears that this animal was also the last individual of the species to live in the vast Allegheny Mountain section of eastern North America."

During 1913 through 1926, 145 elk from Yellowstone National Park were translocated to seven Pennsylvania counties. Some moved as much as 40 miles (64 km) within a week of release; 22 elk (probably the presumed eastern subspecies) also were obtained from a private preserve in Monroe County, Pennsylvania. Ten were released in Centre County and 12 in Monroe County. These animals suffered

Elk inhabit the Allegheny Plateau region of Pennsylvania, primarily in forested landscapes (*top*) ranging in elevation from 900 to 2,300 feet (274–701 m). Much of the elk habitat is located along a transition zone between the mixed oak and hickory forest to the south and the northern hardwood forest of beech, birch, cherry and maple (Cogan and Diefenbach 1998). Arial census taking of elk in such habitat (*bottom*) is most practical after the deciduous trees have lost their leaves and snow covers the ground. *Photos by Hal. S. Korber; courtesy of the Pennsylvania Game Commission.*

less mortality and did not travel as far as the western animals (Gerstell 1936). The elk prospered at first, and bulls were hunted from 1923 through 1931; 98 were killed. An additional 78 elk were killed either illegally or in reaction to crop depredation (George 1974). A small herd remains in the north-central part of the state in Elk County, near Saint Mary's. By 1974, the herd included 38 animals. During the 1980s, it varied between 117 and 154 animals. Poaching limited population increases, as did crop depredation. Landowners could legally kill elk that were damaging crops, and depredation kills accounted for about one-third of all known mortality (Wathen et al. 1997).

Elk in Pennsylvania increased to about 312 head by the winter of 1997 to 1998. Because of the increase and public interest, personnel of the Pennsylvania Game Commission plan to translocate up to 60 elk from Elk County to Sproul State Forest in Clinton County—east of the current elk range. The first 16 elk were transferred during February 1998. The project should increase the size of Pennsylvania's elk range from 200 to 800 square miles (518–2,072 km^2) (D. Diefenbach personal communication:1998).

Rhode Island

No records have been found to indicate that elk occurred in Rhode Island during historic times. However, a right pre-molar, two right molars, a left calcaneum and two tail vertebrae of an elk, associated with artifacts, were found at an archaeological site in Scituate, Providence County (Waters and Mack 1962). The site was estimated at 6,000 to 1,600 years old. If these bones and teeth were not transported by Native Americans, a possibility that cannot be dismissed, they represent an eastward extension of about 100 miles (160 km) in the former range of elk in New England, as proposed by Allen (1942) and Hall and Kelson (1959).

South Carolina

Elk are known to have occupied the western portion of South Carolina until the late 1700s or early 1800s, but records of their distribution and abundance are scarce. Hays (1871) reported that elk were plentiful in the Carolinas as late as 1737. True (1883) reported that the last elk in South Carolina was killed in Fairfield County.

South Dakota

Available records, although not voluminous, are sufficient to indicate statewide distribution in primitive times. In the early 1800s, the animals were abundant, especially in the Black Hills (Murie 1951). Chronicling the journeys of travelers to California via the Oregon Trail, Parkman (1910:228)

Clearings comprise about 5% of the landscape on public lands occupied by elk in Pennsylvania. Such forest openings primarily are clearcuts and vacated strip mine sites. On private property, clearings—mainly farm fields and reclaimed strip mines—represent about 15% to 20% of the land. Clearings are important feeding grounds for elk. *Photo by Hal S. Korber; courtesy of the Pennsylvania Game Commission.*

called the Black Hills a hunter's paradise and wrote of "the broad dusty paths made by the elk, as they filed across the mountain-side." By the 1870s, only scattered herds remained east of the Missouri River, and by 1875, only a few elk remained outside of the Black Hills (Dodge 1877). After the gold rush into the Black Hills in 1876, elk populations decreased drastically.

In the 1870s, the Black Hills region of South Dakota was a Lakota Indian reservation, which few non-Indians had penetrated. The Lakota regarded the 111,370-square kilometer (43,000-mile²) track as a religious sanctuary and inviolate hunting ground. For these reasons and because of the region's rugged topography, expeditionary forces to the West made a concerted effort to skirt the region, despite rumors of abundant game, timber and evidence of gold. Concerned, too, about growing unrest among the Lakota and their Cheyenne allies, the U.S. Army undertook to purportedly explore and survey the Indian stronghold. The duty fell to 2 companies of infantry and 10 companies of the Seventh Cavalry, under the leadership of Lieutenant Colonel George Armstrong Custer. The Black Hills Expedition of 1874 was a revealing and successful probe of unchartered wilderness. Wildlife was found in great numbers and, although only few elk were sighted, there was evidence of a large population. More significantly, gold was found. Within months of that revelation, miners rushed into the reservation in violation of the prevailing treaty. Besides inciting the Indians to fateful defense of the region, the miners decimated wildlife populations, including elk, in the Black Hills within just several years. Custer is shown in this photograph by William H. Illingworth, with one of several elk bagged. *Photo from the Elizabeth B. Custer Collection; courtesy of the Custer Battlefield National Monument (Montana), U.S. National Park Service.*

Early, unpublished records of the South Dakota Department of Game, Fish and Parks indicate that about 100 elk were translocated from Yellowstone National Park to the Black Hills around 1911. This was a joint effort by the conservation agencies of South Dakota and Wyoming. During 1912 and 1913, an additional 42 Yellowstone elk were released on the South Dakota/Wyoming border of the Black Hills (B. Hauk personal communication:1997).

In 1914, 25 elk were received from Jackson Hole, Wyoming, and released in what is now Custer State Park in the Black Hills. Subsequent releases were made during 1915 and 1919. By 1920, some 200 elk had been translocated into the Black Hills. Eight years later, the animals were firmly established, and the herd was estimated at 1,000 head, and complaints of crop depredations prompted the opening of an elk season that year.

The last elk translocation in South Dakota occurred in 1990, when 58 head from Wind Cave National Park were released into Black Hills National Forest. As of 1998, the South Dakota elk population was approximately 5,100 head, and the goal was to allow expansion to about 5,600 free-roaming elk in the state. Huntable populations included 3,500 elk on national forest and private lands plus 1,200 in Custer State Park. Four hundred nonhuntable elk roamed Wind Cave National Park. No further translocations were planned (B. Hauk personal communication:1997).

Tennessee

On a trading expedition to the Cherokee towns in southeastern Tennessee during 1673, James Needham reported that, while traveling down the valley bounded by the Holston River and Bays Mountains, he observed a great store of game, including elk (see Kellogg 1939). Other early reported dates and locations of elk in Tennessee are: 1779 and 1780, the plains surrounding Nashville; 1783, upland prairie of Cumberland County; 1785, between Nashville and Holston river settlements (numerous antlers but only one elk); 1785, Lauderdale County south of Forked Deer River; and 1795, around Nashville.

Concerning a road built through the Cumberland Mountains in 1783, Ramsey (1853:501) reported: "The top of the mountain is described as being then, a vast upland prairie, covered with the most luxurient growth of native grasses, pastured over as far as the eye could see, with numerous herds of deer, elk and buffalo, gamboling in playful security over these secluded plains, scarcely disturbed in their desert wilds at the approach of man, and exhibiting little alarm at the explosion of his rifle or fright at the victim falling before its deadly aim."

Rhoads (1897:180–181) wrote: "At the beginning of the

present century, this noble animal was probably a visitant to every county in the State [Tennessee]. It not only abounded in the high passes and coves of the southern Alleghenies; but, associated with the buffalo, it frequented licks near the present site of Nashville, gave its name to some of the rivers and creeks of the southern counties of Middle Tennessee, and roamed through the glades and canebrakes of the Mississippi bottoms. The redoubtable Crockett, during his residence in Obion and Dyer Counties, gives repeated instances of the occurrence of the Wapiti in the bottom lands, and it formed no small part of his larder in the period between the years 1820 and 1830.

"Mr. Miles, after careful inquiry about the elk in his region writes me, 'The last elk killed in West Tennessee that I can learn of was at Reelfoot Lake about 1849. The late David Merrywether of Madison County, Tennessee, killed it. In 1865 I heard that an elk was killed in Obion County.'"

In 1996, personnel of the Tennessee Wildlife Resource Agency began evaluating the possibility of returning elk to that state. One of the goals was to establish a herd with adequate numbers to hunt. Tennessee does not have the potential to establish elk over a wide geographic area, but the possibility exists to situate small herds in selected areas. Such areas could provide suitable habitat, public access for viewing and hunting, as well as minimal conflicts with agricultural and other private interests.

The first reintroduction area to be considered was the "Land Between the Lakes" in western Tennessee. Because of intense opposition, primarily related to concerns with potential crop damage and introduction of diseases, this area apparently will be dropped from consideration. As of February 1998, Tennessee biologists were considering sites in the eastern portion of the state where agricultural interests are not so predominant (G. Wathen personal communication:1998).

Texas

Most of Texas apparently was not in the original range of elk. Bailey (1905:60) wrote: "There are no wild elk to-day in the State of Texas, but years ago, as several old ranchmen have told me, they ranged south to the southern part of the Guadalupe Mountains, across the Texas line. I could not get an actual record of one killed in Texas, or nearer than 6 or 8 miles north of the line, but as they were common to within a few years in the Sacramento Mountains, only 75 miles farther north, I am inclined to credit the rather indefinite reports of their former occurrence [*sic*] in this part of Texas. Specimens of horns and a part of a skull from the Sacramento Mountains indicate that the species was very similar to and probably identical with the Arizona elk de-

scribed by E. W. Nelson who has aided me in making the comparison."

In 1993, the distal portion of a tibia, identifiable as an adult elk, was found in a cut bank in Baylor County (Pfau 1994). That bone was radiocarbon dated at 295, ±50 years before present. Shaffer (1994) cited the recovery of a proximal phalange of an elk recovered from a garbage midden in Delta County in northeastern Texas. The midden was dated at 980 to 520 years before present.

Judge J. C. Hunter, of Abilene, acquired 44 elk in 1927 from the Black Hills of South Dakota and released them in McKittrick Canyon in the Guadalupe Mountains, Culberson County (Texas Game, Fish and Oyster Commission 1945). An estimated 700 elk were in 24 counties in 1976, but the majority were in Brewster and Culberson counties. The Texas Parks and Wildlife Department evaluated the possibility of a program to manage elk as a game species within the state, but encountered: (1) potential competition between deer and elk for available forage and habitat; and (2) potential interbreeding of red deer and elk producing an offspring of uncertain status—exotics not generally being classified as game animals in Texas (C. Winkler personal communication:1976 to Bryant and Maser [1982]).

In 1997, elk were designated as exotic livestock by the 75th Texas legislature. Approximately 3,000 privately owned elk (mostly confined on high-fenced property) reside in 70 counties. The Texas Parks and Wildlife Department has no plans to translocate or introduce elk to any portion of the state.

Approximately 300 free-ranging elk were estimated in Texas during 1995. Then and since, most were found in the Guadalupe and Eagle mountains of the western portion of the Trans-Pecos Region (J. Cook personal communication:1998), although author O'Gara saw a band of 12 to 15 free-ranging elk in the Davis Mountains during spring 1994.

Utah

Records show that, in primitive times, elk were found in largest numbers in the northern Wasatch and Uinta mountains (Murie 1951). Yet, they evidently occupied other parts of Utah. Orange Olsen informed Olaus Murie (1951) that elk formerly ranged on the Mount Nebo Range, but disappeared from there about 1880. Also, the animals were more or less common in the mountains bordering the Salt Lake Valley (Allen 1874). And at one time, elk were native to the Zion-Bryce and Cedar breaks, as indicated by (1) the Paiute name "Paria" (meaning elk) for the stream that drains south from Bryce to the Colorado River; (2) discovery of a weathered elk antler in Willis Creek, Bryce, in 1932, according to Presnall (1938); and (3) an elk reportedly killed at Willis

Creek by a Mr. Johnson of Cannonville sometime between 1900 and 1910. Elk in Utah were extirpated around the turn of the 20th century, with the possible exception of a small number in the Uinta Mountains (N. V. Hancock personal communication:1976 to Bryant and Maser [1982]).

From 1912 to 1915, a reintroduction program was initiated and 152 elk were obtained from Jackson Hole and Yellowstone National Park, Wyoming. By 1925, the elk population increase was of concern to many cattle and sheep ranchers, causing the Utah Legislature to form the Board of Elk Control to reduce elk competition with livestock on national forest land. Elk have been hunted in Utah since that time.

By 1976, the Utah Division of Wildlife Resources had introduced elk into about half the native range, according to N. Hancock (personal communication:1976 to Bryant and Maser [1982]). By 1997, about 60,000 elk occupied all suitable mountain ranges in the state (M. Welch personal communication:1997).

Vermont

Elk antlers often were found in southern and east-central Vermont by settlers, indicating the animals occupied the state in earlier times (Thompson 1853). Perry (1964) proposed that elk were extirpated around 1800.

Virginia

The first permanent English settlers in North America—colonists in Virginia—encountered elk (Merrill 1916). "In 1666, twelve years after Colonel Wood and fifty years before Governor Spottswood, Governor Sir William Berkley, says Arthur, dispatched an exploring party across the mountains to the west, under Captain Henry Butte, with fourteen Virginians and fourteen Indians. They also started from Appomattox. In seven days they reached the foot of the [Blue Ridge] mountains. After crossing them, they came to level, delightful plains, with abundant game, deer, elk, and buffalo, so gentle as not to be frightened by the approach of man" (Hale 1886:21–22). Hays (1871) reported a few elk were in the mountains of Virginia as late as 1847. The last native elk were killed in 1854 and 1855 by Colonel Gos Tuley. Those two specimens were preserved in the U.S. National Museum (Cross 1950).

The Virginia Commission of Game and Inland Fisheries obtained 110 to 150 elk from Yellowstone National Park, Wyoming, in 1917. By 1922, the population had more than doubled, and seemed to warrant a 15-day regulated harvest of bulls. An additional 43 elk were introduced in 1935. A limited season was continued in various forms until the early 1940s, when harvest was suspended for about 10 years. Although elk numbers never were high, substantial damage to crops was noted (Wood 1943). Limited harvests were allowed during 1956 and 1958 through 1960 (Parkhurst 1997). Elk numbers progressively declined and stood at about 165 by the mid-1960s (Gwynn 1977).

The last season, in 1960, was only 3 days in length and only for the four counties that included the core areas for the largest herds of introduced elk—the Bland/Giles and Boteourt/Bedford herds. The last season was limited to antlered bulls and the harvest was reported at only three animals. A remnant number of elk remained in the Bland/Giles area for perhaps a few years. The last few were taken with crop damage permits.

Considerable interest in and support for another reintroduction of elk to the Commonwealth has been expressed. A feasibility study supported by the Rocky Mountain Elk Foundation was undertaken to evaluate the advantages and disadvantages of such an undertaking (see Parkhurst 1997). As of February 1999, plans were to survey public attitudes and opinions—as well as costs and benefits—before making a decision to or not to reintroduce elk. Meanwhile, elk stocked in eastern Kentucky were making their way into Virginia (R. W. Duncan personal communication:1999).

Washington

Archeological evidence indicates that elk once were widely distributed in eastern Washington. However, Lewis and Clark were the first white explorers to travel through the area, and they found little sign of elk there when they crossed Washington during 1805 and 1806, although the elk was an important part of the culture of Indians they met along the way (see Chapter 3). Lewis and Clark indicated that Indians near Clarkston on the Snake River were dressed in elk skins, Indians around White Salmon presented them with a dressed elk skin and the robes of the Indians were elk skin. Along the Columbia River, the Scaddals, Squannanos, Shanwahpaums and Shallatas (all Klickitat bands) depended on hunting deer and elk. Few Rocky Mountain elk were found in eastern Washington by the late 1800s, and by 1900, they were nearly eliminated from that part of the state (see McCall 1996).

The Pacific Coast of Washington was occupied by elk, which have persisted there to the present. The Olympic Peninsula was the stronghold for these animals, but they ranged over the entire coastal forested area and inhabited the Cascade Range to the east. Elk on the west side of the Cascades, except for the Olympic Peninsula, were almost entirely extirpated by the early 1900s (see Murie 1951).

Several reintroductions of Rocky Mountain elk into Washington made significant contributions to the remnant animals. In 1912, 106 elk from Montana were released in Skagit and Snohomish counties, but they caused considerable damage and were eliminated by 1939. Also in 1912, 84 additional elk were released in King County—44 at North Bend and 40 at Enumclaw. Many of those released near Enumclaw survived and became the nucleus of the Mount Rainier herd in that area. In 1913, 50 elk from Montana were released in the Naches River area of Yakima County, resulting in the Yakima herd. Between 1913 and 1930, 145 Montana elk were released in Columbia, Garfield and Walla Walla counties, and now form the Blue Mountain herd. In 1915, 45 elk from Montana were released east of Ellensburg and became the Colockum herd. From 1913 to 1930, 52 Montana elk were moved to the northeastern corner of the state in Pend Oreille and Stevens counties—they formed the Selkirk herd. In 1932, an additional 30 elk were released in Pierce County near Mount Rainier National Park. At various other times since 1932, additional elk have been imported or translocated within the state (McCall 1996).

Elk in the central part of Washington are crosses between Roosevelt and Rocky Mountain elk. Historic data are not clear on whether native Roosevelt elk crossed the Cascade Crest into the eastern part of the state, but elk occupied both sides of the Cascade Crest before 1900 (R. Johnson personal communication:1997). About 62,000 elk occupied Washington State during 1998, but a good method to estimate elk in dense habitat is lacking (R. Johnson personal communication:1998).

Washington, D.C.

Bailey (1896) indicated that elk formerly occurred in the District of Columbia.

West Virginia

The elk once was common in the higher mountain regions of West Virginia, according to Brooks (1911). Cope (1870), writing of the fauna of the southern Alleghenies, mentioned elk remains during European habitation. Hale (1886) reported that herds of elk roamed through the Kanawha Valley and over the hills of western West Virginia in the late 1700s. According to Hale, the last elk along the Kanawha—and perhaps the last native elk east of the Ohio River—was killed by a Billy Young in 1820. The kill was made about 5.5 miles (8.8 km) from the present town of Charleston. However, Brookes (1911:12–13) wrote: "One was shot by the wife of Thomas B. Summerfield at a deer lick near the Sinks of Grandy, probably about 1830. Abraham Mullenix killed one near the same place sometime near 1835. About the year 1840 an elk was killed in Randolph County near

the mouth of Red Creek. According to Maxwell, three elk were killed in Caanan Valley (now Tucker County), by the Flanagans and Joab Carr about 1843. This is the last killing of elk in West Virginia that is recorded. The killing of the three in Caanan Valley was two years previous to the seeing of the herd of seven, near Durbin, by Moses Arbogast and it is probable that others were killed later of which no records were kept." Also, Audubon and Bachman (1851) reported during a visit to West Virginia in 1847, they heard of a small herd of elk surviving in the high mountains about 40 miles (64 km) west of the Red Sulphur Springs. Shoemaker (1939) indicated that elk were known on the headwaters of the Tygart and Greenbrier rivers as late as 1875—the last recorded occurrence in the state if true.

No reintroductions have been attempted in West Virginia, although a feasibility study was conducted during the 1970s (P. Johansen personal communication:1999).

Wisconsin

There is reason to believe that elk once occurred throughout most of Wisconsin. Records indicate their historic presence in 50 of the 71 counties (see Schorger 1954). Jackson (1961) speculated that, although elk occurred in favorable habitat throughout the state, they were more abundant in the southern and western two-thirds than in the northeast corner. Schorger (1954) indicated that elk were most numerous in open woodlands, oak openings and at the borders of grasslands and forests; travelers during 1661, 1662, 1700 and 1766 reported elk within the state; and Copely observed 500 in 1837 along Lake Pepin.

In 1876, Shea (1908:111 and 115) wrote: "two hundred years ago, a little bark canoe that had threaded the marshy maze between the fox and Wisconsin, glided from the latter of these rivers into the clear broad bosom of the Mississippi . . . that current bears them on to a change of scene. Wood and mountain give place to the wide stretching prairie, with herds of elk and deer."

During Pierre Le Seur's voyage up the Mississippi in 1700, hunters killed many rutting bulls in Lacrosse County. They reported the animals were easy to kill from early September to October. Subsequently, Le Seur passed the mouth of the (now) Chippewa River. The region so abounded with elk that it was called Bon Se Cours, literally good stream itself (see Schorger 1954).

Reporting on northern Wisconsin in 1820, Doty (1908:196) wrote: "The moose, elk, rein [sic] and common deer . . . are found in different parts of the country." On a trip from Green Bay to what is now Chicago in 1827, Fonda (1907) noted that the country along the western shore of Lake Michigan teemed with deer, wild turkey and elk.

A report in the *Janesville Gazette* of December 10, 1866, read: ". . . while two hunters were standing in the road about 15 miles [24 km] west of Menomonie, twelve elk, old and young, came onto the road a few rods from them. A dog caught one of the calves, the old ones rushed to the rescue, while the hunters shot down nine of the animals and the other three made off with the hunters in close pursuit" (Jackson 1961:411).

Schorger (1954) believed that the elk of Wisconsin were not extirpated until 1868.

In 1913, elk from Yellowstone National Park were released into an enclosure at Trout Lake, Wisconsin. Additional elk from Jackson Hole were brought to the enclosure in 1917 to supplement the declining population. Only 15 elk remained in 1932. These animals were released and the introduction program was terminated (Jackson 1961).

During January 1995, 25 elk were captured in Michigan. By May, they had been tested for diseases and shipped to Wisconsin, where they were released in the northwestern part of the state near Clam Lake. This is a wooded area, fairly remote from agriculture, where some logging for aspen occurs. Two very severe winters followed. However, by February 1999, 50 elk comprised the herd—the only free-ranging elk in Wisconsin—an experimental population. A decision was made and money appropriated to maintain an elk herd in the state, which may entail introductions of more animals (B. Mytton personal communication:1999).

Wyoming

Historically, Wyoming probably was more densely populated with elk than any other state. The herds, which were widely scattered throughout the state, persisted longer and, apparently, in greater numbers than in other states during settlement (Murie 1951). However, as of the late 1990s, Idaho had more elk and Colorado hosted nearly twice as many (Bunnell 1997)

Elk, at one time abundant in the Black Hills and Bear Lodge Mountains of northeastern Wyoming, had become scarce by the mid-1880s. A few elk ranged in the limestone country of the Black Hills and hence northwestward to Sundance Mountain. In 1885, an elk was killed on Sundance Mountain, and another in the region encompassing the heads of the Stockade, Beaver and Inyankara creeks (Cary 1917). Apparently, they were gone soon thereafter.

The Big Horn Mountains harbored elk in abundance, but by the 1880s, the frontier hunters considered it scarce and had given up hunting for a living. On an autumn hunt to supply the Fort McKinney garrison with meat, the heads of many tributaries of the Powder River were first visited, without success (Hatch 1886). The party then proceeded southward to the Casper Mountains, where 72 elk, 102 mule deer and 45 pronghorn were killed. Elk apparently were extirpated in the Casper Mountains about 1904 (Murie 1951).

Hunting in the Bighorns in 1886, Millais (1915) said that elk were getting scarce. After hunting part of August and most of September, he found and missed a bull. Ten days later, he found another and the next day a herd of about 50.

At one time, the Casper and Laramie mountains were among the best elk ranges in Wyoming, according to accounts of old-timers (see Murie 1951). Parkman (1910) saw a herd of about 200 elk near Fort Laramie in 1846. Also, large heaps of elk antlers found during the early 20th century at most ranches from Laramie Peak north to Douglas and from Laramie Peak west to Toltec testified to the truth of the assertion (Murie 1951). However, the animals were extirpated by about that time.

Elk were abundant in Carbon County, particularly about Elk Mountain and the Medicine Bow Range, in the early 1870s (Allen 1874). However, as early as 1888, they had largely disappeared and, by 1911, apparently were extirpated (Murie 1951).

Elk came into the northern foothills of the Uinta Mountains when snowfall in the mountains was heavy (Crampton 1886). By 1911, there was no evidence of these animals, which apparently had summered in the Uinta Mountains of northern Utah.

The somewhat isolated group of mountains including the Green Mountains and neighboring ranges were formerly occupied by elk. During June 1877, Ingersoll (1882) noted pronghorn and bands of elk accompanied by young calves in sagebrush-covered ridges along the southern edge of the Sweetgrass Hills. The Shirley, Rattlesnake and Green mountains once were elk range. On an expedition north from Rawlins in 1877, Ingersoll (1882) observed elk, including a newborn calf, sharing the rangelands with pronghorn where the Plains met the Rattlesnake Range, as well as in the mountains themselves. He also noted elk on the Plains near the southern branch of the Sandy River. By 1909, Cary (in Murie 1951) reported that elk were scarce in those mountains as well as the Granite and Ferris mountains.

The mountain ranges surrounding Jackson Hole and Yellowstone National Park—the Tetons, the Absaroka, Salt and Wind River ranges, the Caribou, Hoback and Owl Creek mountains as well as Hoback Basin—were a center of abundance for elk and have remained so. While climbing Fremont's Peak in the heart of the Wind River Range in 1877, Ingersoll (1882:183) reported "any quantity of elks . . ." These elk also frequented the lowlands, especially during winter. They wintered on the flats about Pinedale, sagebrush Plains at Big Piney, near Fontenell and on the Red Desert (Murie 1951). A large herd of cows and calves were reported near Bitter Creek in 1868 (Lexden 1914). Sura (1967) indicated that elk traveled as far as 200 miles (322 km) from mountainous summer ranges to the semiarid Little Colorado and Red deserts.

Explorers in Yellowstone National Park during the early 1870s and earlier reported very few game animals. They apparently became more abundant during the late 1870s, prompting Rush (1932:16) to write, "As the period 1870–1878 coincides with the last great killing on the plains, it seems quite likely that the surviving animals retreated more and more into the mountains, especially in the summer, to escape the slaughter. For a time, probably until a large part of the lowland outside the Park was taken up and fenced, these animals that summered in the Park were driven by snow each winter to the plains and lower valleys outside."

Had it not been for the many inaccessible mountain ranges in Wyoming, and establishment of Yellowstone National Park and the Jackson Hole Refuge, elk herds that now thrive in many parts of North America would not exist. Hide hunters and settlers eliminated elk in some areas that still had elk habitat. After game laws and their enforcement became realities, the animals were reintroduced to many such areas. Most of the stock for translocations—

especially the early ones—came from Yellowstone National Park.

That many elk were available from Yellowstone for reintroductions is shown by the following. By 1891, Harry Yount, gamekeeper, reported: "The elk have increased enormously, and most conservative estimates place their number at 25,000" (Rush 1932:17). However, as numbers remained high, range conditions apparently deteriorated. The Park Superintendent's report for 1920 included the following: "Last June, after the most disastrous winter which our wild animals have ever had to face, our rangers estimated the survivors in the northern herd of elk at 11,000, and I am reliably informed that the southern herd fared but little if any better. This loss of nearly 60 percent in one winter is alarming and indicates most forcibly the possible danger of complete extermination of this most noble race of animals" (Rush 1932:23).

Although Wyoming had the most elk of any state at the time, many elk were translocated from the National Elk Refuge to other areas of the state. During the 1960s, elk also were translocated from Yellowstone Park (Robbins et al. 1982). As of 1997, more than 102,000 elk were estimated to roam Wyoming after the hunting season; the predicted posthunt population for 1998 was estimated at 94,990 (R. Rothwell personal communication:1998).

Rocky Mountain elk once summered in what is now Yellowstone National Park and wintered at lower elevations in the Green River Valley of Wyoming. Fences, roads and hunters eventually blocked seasonal movements of the herd between those two ranges. Establishment of the National Elk Refuge at Jackson Hole, Wyoming, in 1912, prevented near extirpation of the so-called south Yellowstone or Jackson Hole herd (see Chapter 14). Without the park and refuge, elk herds that now thrive in many parts of North America simply would not exist. Most elk for early translocations throughout North America and other parts of the world came from Yellowstone and the National Elk Refuge. *Photo by Bart. W. O'Gara.*

Mexico

Bryant and Maser (1982) depicted elk as occurring along the Continental Divide as far south as the state of Durango and along the crest of the Sierra Madre Oriental to the state of Hidalgo, citing Bailey (1905), Gilmore (1947), Baker (1956) and Hall and Kelson (1959). Most of the evidence was gleaned through Spanish accounts from 1549 to the 1800s of hunts in which pronghorn, deer and "large stags" were killed. The large stags may have been elk, or the deer may have been whitetails and the large stags may have referred to mule deer. Spanish writers indicated the stags were large, like the *Cervus elaphus* of Spain (Nelson 1925). One Spanish writer even considered the large stags to be moose (see Gilmore 1947). *C. e. hispanicus,* the Spanish red deer, is about the size of a large desert mule deer. Dolan (1988) gives 44 inches (112 cm) as average shoulder height for Spanish red deer bulls, and Anderson (1981) recorded 42 inches (106 cm) for a large desert mule deer buck.

Four elk bone specimens, including three teeth, apparently were carried into a cave in central Coahuila during pre-Spanish times (Gilmore 1947). Aboriginal peoples used the cave, and an elk jaw or other bones could have been carried from farther north—or traded from people farther north. If elk did extend into Mexico as far as Durango and Hidalgo, they apparently were not numerous and were quickly exterminated after the 16th century. Possibly, elk were invading Mexico at the same time as the Spanish. This view also was expressed for apparently suitable habitat in Arizona unoccupied by elk during presettlement times (Davis 1982). Baker (1956) stated that elk once occurred in the mountainous parts of northern and central Coahuila, but gave no accounts concerning where or when they had been seen. He did cite Gilmore's (1947) report of four bone fragments.

Leopold (1972) indicated that elk occurred along the extreme northern border of Mexico. However, they were exterminated by the late 1880s (Leopold 1947). Leopold (1972) also wrote that there was no evidence to suggest that native elk ever penetrated far into the Sierra Madre. Mearns (1907), on the other hand, reported that, in 1892, a cook for a survey party saw two huge deer with enormous antlers on San Jose Mountain in Sonora. The man had never seen an elk, but his description convinced Mearns that the ani-

Elk introduced into private ranches in Mexico generally have survived but have not spread into the wild. These, on a ranch in Coahuila, seem to remain on or near the valley floor, where water is provided for livestock by improved springs and large storage tanks. The elk also are plagued by parasites, especially ticks, and are medicated in manners similar to those used for cattle. Elk numbers on Mexican ranches generally are increasing and must be managed through sales or meat and recreational harvests. However, they have not spread into the wild, apparently because well-watered habitat usually supports numerous people, including poachers. Rural Mexicans often depend on small fields of varied crops; elk would be extremely destructive under such circumstances. *Photo by Bart W. O'Gara.*

mals were elk. Mearns believed they were traveling to the nearby Sierra Madre Mountains. However, Anderson (1972) doubted that elk occurred in Chihuahua during historic times, and he knew of no acceptable historic records.

Elk from the Wichita Mountains National Wildlife Refuge, Oklahoma, were introduced west of Pieda Blanca, Coahuila, in 1941. Elk from Yellowstone National Park also were released in Mexico during 1952 and 1955. The 1952 shipment—5 bulls, 15 cows and 10 calves—was released 30 miles (50 km) west of Ciudad Muziquiz, Coahuila, on the west side of Sierra Hermosa de Santa Rosa. Where the 1955 shipment—2 bulls, 14 cows and 14 calves—was released is uncertain, but it is believed to have been in western Nuevo Leon. During March 1977, David Garza Laguera brought 6 bulls and 20 cows from Wichita Mountains National Wildlife Refuge to his ranch 35 miles (56 km) northeast of Ciudad Muziquiz, Coahuila. Although mountain lions killed several calves, the herd increased to 56 head in 1980 (see Bryant and Maser 1982).

By 1998, the Garza Laguera herd had spread to several adjoining ranches and numbered some 300 to 500 head. In addition, official Mexican records indicate: 100 to 200 head at Sierra la Encantada, Coahuila; an unknown number near Ocampa, Coahuila; about 100 (mostly crossbred with red deer) at Sierra del Nido, Chihuahua; and a few (probably less than 25) near Monterrey, Nuevo Leon. This information was gathered from the Caesar Kleberg Wildlife Research Institute, the Asociación de Ganaderos Diversificados and the Instituto de Ecología—Secretaria de Medio (D. Doan-Crider personal communication:1998).

Distribution of Introduced *Cervus elaphus* in the Southern Hemisphere

Numerous red deer and a few elk were translocated to the Southern Hemisphere from about 1850 to 1925, primarily to provide sport for European immigrants in Argentina (Flueck and Smith-Flueck 1993), Australia (Bentley 1967) and New Zealand (Donne 1924). Sportsmen among the well-to-do settlers supported or made direct efforts to introduce deer.

Argentina

At the beginning of the 20th century, red deer were brought to Argentina from Austria and the Carpathian Mountains. They prospered and expanded their range. Later, animals were brought from Germany, England and the Ukraine (Whitehead 1982). By 1993, a continuous population occupied the provinces of Neuquen, Rio Negro and northern Chubut (Figure 33). They spread to the east into treeless

Figure 33. General distribution of red deer in Argentina and Chile (as depicted by Flueck and Smith-Flueck [1993] and compiled by the Rocky Mountain Elk Foundation). Some of the shaded area does not support continuous distribution.

steppe and to the west across low Andean passes into Chili. Additional introductions and commercial interests created scattered populations and deer farms in the provinces of San Luis, Buenos Aires, Salta and Jujuy (Flueck and Smith-Flueck 1993).

The animals seem to do well in dense rainforests, steppe and the intervening ecotone, but a small Peruvian herd—estimated at less than 200 in 1982—produced poor antlers (Whitehead 1982), indicating some nutritional deficiency. Flueck and Smith-Flueck (1993) predicted that red deer would spread another 186 miles (300 km) north of the 1993 distribution and as far south as the Strait of Magellan.

Four elk were shipped from Yellowstone National Park to zoos in Buenos Aries, Argentina, from 1937 through 1939 (Robbins et al. 1982). They or their offspring apparently were liberated in an Argentine park (Pargue Dianna), but later were shot (Whitehead 1982). They probably did not get a chance to breed with red deer, but some huge antlers have been collected. This probably reflects excellent nutrition for pioneering red deer, but also might have been influenced by crossbreeding.

Australia

Sambar and other south Asian deer have become established in Australia, but red deer have not faired especially well (Bentley 1967). The first red deer—presented to Queensland by Queen Victoria from her Windsor Park herd—arrived in 1873 (Whitehead 1982). Records seldom were kept or have been lost, but another early introduction apparently was made to the Melbourne area (Bentley 1967).

As of 1982, red deer were found in five Australian states—Victoria, New South Wales, Queensland, South Australia and Western Australia (Figure 34). Apparently,

their presence in the latter two states was somewhat precarious. A later map by Cause (1995) indicated a substantial population of free-ranging red deer only in Queensland. Some 15,000 to 20,000 were to be found there by 1995 (McGhie and Watson 1995). An estimated 1,000 to 2,000 head ranged in the Grampian Mountains of Victoria as of 1999, and a small herd—numbering in the hundreds—was in and around the Snowy Mountains of New South Wales near the South Australia borders. Successful (although illegal) releases took place in at least eight other areas within those states during the late 1990s (C. McGhie personal communication:1999).

Red deer were protected in Queensland under the Fauna Conservation Act, from 1974 through 1989. Shooting and capture permits were issued annually for limited numbers of deer within specified areas during restricted time periods. After capture, deer were considered domestic livestock. Under the Lands Act 1994, all deer were classified as domestic animals. Accordingly, deer hunting and capture no longer were controlled by the Queensland National Parks and Wildlife Service (B. Porter personal communication:2001).

Droughts, predation by wedgetail eagles and dingos,

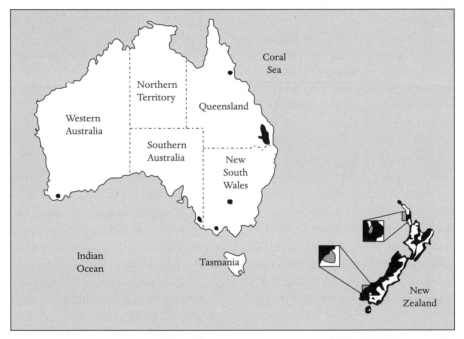

Figure 34.   General locations (*dark shaded areas*) of red deer in Australia and New Zealand during the 1990s. Localities do not depict population sizes for occupied areas—only general areas where the animals occur. Also, stragglers (many from illegal releases and farm escapes) travel widely outside the indicated areas. The southernmost New Zealand area, on the west coast of the south Island, is inhabited by a cross-breeding population (*light shaded area*) of American elk and European red deer. A population of elk was established north of Auckland (*also light shaded*) during the 1990s (McGhie and Watson 1995). New populations may have been established since these data were gathered, especially in Queensland, Australia, where management of deer was transferred from the National Parks and Wildlife Service to the Agriculture Department in 1994. Since then, deer have increased and spread on cattle stations (M. MacKay personal communication:1998). Deer are considered livestock in Australia and New Zealand, therefore translocations seldom are documented. *Information from McGhie and Watson (1995) and New Zealand Department of Conservation (1997); map compiled by the Rocky Mountain Elk Foundation.*

scrub ticks and poaching apparently prevented red deer eruptions, such as occurred in New Zealand, during the species' 125-year history on The Island Continent (McGhie and Watson 1995).

Disappearance of native flora and fauna, widespread erosion and soil depletion are linked with traditional agricultural practices in Australia. McGhie and Watson (1995:315) offer at least a partial solution: "One extremely important fact to consider is that deer and other game animals can be successfully managed, harvested and improved without the need for them to be penned or handled. There is also little need to clear, burn or improve habitat for game animals in fact, in the vast majority of cases, game species play a vital role in the promotion of habitat retention. It has been clearly shown that deer are the only introduced wild animal within this part of Queensland that can produce a significant return to both the landowners and the community without the risks associated with other feral animals such as pigs, goats and foxes. While landowners have a reason to manage and preserve wild deer, they will preserve the habitat, which in turn benefits the native animals. Landowners who have fostered good relations with hunters have found them to have a positive impact on the overall management of their properties."

New Zealand

A pair of red deer was shipped from England to New Zealand in 1851 (Brander 1971). The female died on the journey, but 220 recorded releases of red deer from Australia, England and Scotland followed. The deer were released on both the North and South islands. Eighteen North American elk were released at the head of George Sound in Fiordland National Park on the South Island of New Zealand in 1905 (Whitehead 1982). They soon became established and spread over some 500,000 acres (202,000 ha) of mountainous habitat where they crossbred with red deer. Various exotic animals were imported by Acclimatisation Societies, the New Zealand Government and private individuals. Some liberations took, others failed. The exotic deer were protected by law, hunted under license for a couple months each year and owned in varying proportions by Acclimatisation Societies and the Crown. Beginning about 1910, farmers, foresters and botanists saw deer as a nuisance (Caughley 1983). More important was a change in public attitudes—away from the ideal of recreating the motherland and toward the notion of building a country that was valid in its own right. Native plants and animals became fine and worthy, whereas the exotic deer became deemed less worthy. Deerstalking accordingly smacked of aristocratic power and privilege.

By 1921, destruction of trees by an estimated 300,000 deer caused government officials to consider destroying all wild deer (Donne 1924). Beginning in 1927, a bounty of two shillings per tail was paid to private hunters. Three years later, all protection was removed and, in 1931, government control efforts commenced. During the 1960s poisoning was added to shooting. Between 1931 and 31 March 1975, the number of deer killed on official operations reached 1,124,297 (Whitehead 1982).

Commercial hunting became profitable about 1960, after overseas markets for venison had been located (Caughley 1983). The Forest Service—then in charge of deer extermination—ignored this development at first, but was forced to take notice as the trade expanded. The venison hunters perfected the techniques of killing and recovering deer by helicopter, thereby squeezing the Service out of deer control. The rising price of venison triggered attempts at farming red deer, although it was against the intent of legislation that designated deer as pests not to be harbored. The Wild Animal Control Act of 1977 did not make any provision for harvesting wild deer on a sustained-yield basis. The Act also had the effect of handing ownership of deer on occupied land to the owner or leaseholder of that land. This introduced to New Zealand the European crime of poaching—a throwback to English statutes of the 17th century, which led to the present English legal doctrine that wild animals are private property (Caughley 1983).

The first deer-farming license was issued in 1970, and live capture began in earnest about 1975 (Caughley 1983). It evolved rapidly from corral traps to helicopter net-gunning. Deer farms were established so swiftly that the Forest Service received about five applications a day during much of the 1970s and early 1980s. By the 1990s, wild deer were greatly reduced in numbers and generally scattered in inaccessible country (Figure 34), and most venison was produced from deer farms. Because no restrictions exist concerning how, when or how many red deer can be killed, even without extensive aerial gunning, reinvasion of roaded and settled areas seems unlikely.

As of 1997, approximately 1.8 million deer occupied some 4,600 deer farms in New Zealand. About 250,000 wild deer roamed conservation land, other Crown lease lands, private forests and Maori land. Red deer were the most widespread and numerous species, occupying most forested lands where helicopter hunting is least effective (Department of Conservation 1997).

The New Zealand Department of Conservation (1997) sent a questionnaire to be returned by March 1998 to commercial and recreational hunters, conservation and recreation groups, farmers and forest owners. Input was sought

A lucrative commercial market for venison emerged in New Zealand about 1960, prompting private enterprises to contribute their resources to the government's deer eradication/control program. Because the commercial participants used the efficiencies of aerial gunning and carcass removal, the government operation proved unnecessary. Above, a Hughes 500D helicopter hoists a bull-dogged stag and its shooter from the dense bush for delivery to a base camp. *Photo by Rex Forrester.*

Forest and crop depredations by an extraordinary proliferation of introduced red deer and elk in New Zealand prompted official sanction and undertaking of an extensive deer eradication program beginning in 1931. By 1975, more than 1.1 million deer had been eliminated in official operations. In the early years, New Zealand deer hides—many bound for the automobile upholstery market in the United States—were removed from remote montane parts of the country by backpack (*top*), horseback (*center*) and dray (*bottom*). The dray load above contained 260 hides. *Photos by Ted Porter; courtesy of D. Bruce Banwell.*

for developing a new management plan. Issues involving the most disagreement included the following:

- Whether deer-induced changes in forest ecosystems are always unacceptable.

- Whether deer should be viewed as a pest or a resource that needs to be controlled (or both).
- Whether recreational hunting can be an effective means of controlling the impacts of deer in any circumstances.
- Whether management of hunting and hunters should be the responsibility of the Department of Conservation or hunting organizations.
- Whether recreational hunting areas are justified and whether their status needs to be reviewed.

- Whether poisons should be used to control deer and under what circumstances.

The New Zealand Department of Conservation's (1997) approach to deer management included the following:

- The Department is responsible for managing the lands it administers to protect natural and historic resources for controlling the impacts of introduced animals.
- Unless the impacts of introduced animals are managed, an ongoing decline in indigenous biodiversity is inevitable.
- Deer continue to change forest composition by browsing seedlings and inhibiting regeneration. Selective browsing by deer causes a decline in species diversity and, in some areas, is contributing to forest canopy collapse.
- Because the health and regeneration of forests and natural areas is paramount, the Department must ensure that deer are controlled to levels that maintain and enhance forest health and ecosystem processes.

- To protect indigenous ecosystems from further browsing impact and to safeguard against future control costs, the feral range of any species of deer should be confined to the present limits. (The feral range does not include new and isolated populations.) The Department, therefore, will attempt to remove deer completely where they have been illegally or accidentally released outside of their feral range.
- In some areas within their current feral range, deer may need to be controlled to very low levels or removed completely. The Department will take direct control measures, including poisoning, where an urgent need is identified and other control methods would not be effective.
- The Department acknowledges that recreational and commercial hunters make an important contribution to deer control and should be a part of the overall management regime.

3

Elk and Indians: Then Again

It is the elk, which is the emblem of beauty, gallantry, and protection. The elk lives in the forest and is in harmony with all his beautiful surroundings.

Frances Densmore (1918:176)

Long before European explorers, fur trappers, traders, miners, adventurers and settlers began to probe the continent's interior, the elk was an important aspect of the North American Indians' subsistence economy. Generally less essential to Indians than were bison and deer, elk nevertheless often served as a vital source of food, clothing, implements, weapons, decoration, spiritualism and medium of exchange. Its significance as a necessity in Indian life is a matter of conjecture; that it was an integral part of many Natives' social, cultural, political and material lifestyles is certain.

Prehistoric Indians and Elk

Prehistory was not a time; it was a series of times, marked by complex climatic, ecological, social and cultural shifts, and multiple shifts within shifts. Interpretation of long-ago conditions and dynamics, based on mere point-in-time fragments, is enlightened conjecture by professional archeologists. By any others, it is little more than fantasy. Thus, with respect to elk and Indians prehistorically, little is certain except that both human and faunal numbers and distributions changed often, sometimes slowly, sometimes abruptly, in the 10 or so millennia after the retreat of continental ice sheets. So too, evidently, did their relationship. Any char-

acterization of Indian use of or other association with elk in the following is specific to a particular time and place, and is not intended to reflect a universal or homeostatic circumstance.

Paleo-Indians represent the earliest human culture (circa 18,000–8,000 years ago) in North America, followed by the Archaic Indians (±8,000–500 years ago). Separate groups within each culture usually are distinguished by time period, geography or cultural traits, of which projectile point type is the most common. The Paleo-Indians generally were hunting-oriented and are classified loosely, if at all, by time or region. Archaic Indian groups, on the other hand, were more highly adapted, populous and diverse in subsistence patterns. Therefore, they frequently are equated with or named for specific regional or local environments and technological characteristics, as well as time periods.

The aboriginal record of elk in North America comes from widely scattered assemblages of bones, bone fragments and tools carved from elk bones and antlers. Remnants have been found in archaeological sites across North America, but the earliest clues linking elk and humans are from Alaska and the Great Plains (see Chapter 2).

In Alaska, the first indisputable evidence of humans is heterogeneous sets of stone artifacts, dominated by microlithic blades, wedge-shaped cores, bifacial knives and scrapers, and projectile points. Radiocarbon dating placed their age at 11,000 to 8,000 years ago. Thus, these artifacts represent a Paleo-Arctic tradition (Sherratt 1980, Fagan 1995). They were found in unglaciated regions and on the terminal edges of glaciated areas. In one location (Trail Creek Caves), a collection of horse, bison, elk and caribou bones suggests the debris of a campsite. At another midden site (Dry Creek), remains of elk, mountain sheep and bison were clearly preserved.

Elk remains are fairly common finds in at least some Plateau region archaeological sites dating back approximately 10,000 years ago (e.g., Sappington and Carley 1989, Schuknect 2000). Only deer are shown to have been more significant (by number and live weight) than elk throughout the time of Indian occupation of major portions of the region prehistorically, as determined by midden recoveries (see Sappington 1994).

On the Great Plains, elk antler parts recovered in 1979 from several levels of a Folsom site in extreme eastern Wyoming were dated at about 10,800 and 10,300 years ago (Frison and Bradley 1981). The Folsom complex was an Archaic culture (characterized by migratory or nomadic hunting and gathering, using more diverse tools and dependent on smaller and more varied fauna than did Paleo-Indians) that occurred east of the Rocky Mountains between Alberta and southern New Mexico (Spenser and Jennings 1965). It is characterized in part by leaf-shaped flint projectile points that have a concave base with side projections and a longitudinal groove or channel on each side or face. Among elk antler parts recovered from the site is a first brow tine, ostensibly used for fluting or grooving projectile points (Figure 35).

Except for the Folsom discoveries, elk rarely appear in archaeological sites on the Great Plains until the Late Prehistoric period (1,500–500 years ago), and even then only in small numbers. Until about 8,000 to 9,000 years ago, the Great Plains featured vast coniferous forests and hardwood forests (see Gleason 1922, Dunbar 1949). As modern bison increasingly became the major faunal resource, the Plains Archaic economy apparently shifted from generalized big game hunting to specialized bison hunting and at least nominal dependence on plant foods (see Fagan 1995).

Frison (1978:274) wrote: "The evidence from archeological sites indicates that the elk was not of much significance on the Northwestern Plains until the Late Prehistoric period." Frison noted, however, that his assumption about prehistoric elk populations of the region was subject to revision, depending on the examination of additional data, such as reported by Davis (1973). On the other hand, in reference to the aboriginal economy throughout the whole of the Great Plains and eastern Plateau, Sherratt (1980:357) asserted that "there is no reason to deny that antelopes, mule deer, whitetailed deer, elks and black bears, as well as smaller mammals, were not important from earliest [postglacial] times. . . ."

The discovery of a large number of elk antler digging tools from quarry sites near the Missouri River headwaters in Montana ushered the next important finding of prehistoric elk remains in the Great Plains/Plateau region (Davis 1973). These sites dated back to both the Early Plains Archaic (7,600–4,900 years ago) and Late Plains Archaic (3,000–1,500 years ago) periods. Frison (1978) reported finding a pair of elk mandibles from the Middle Plains Archaic period (4,900–3,000 years). They were found at the Dead Indian Creek site in the Sunlight Basin of the Absaroka Mountains in Wyoming. The same site yielded a small quantity of elk bones and antler remnants from Late Prehistoric and early historic periods. Elk remains also were located in an

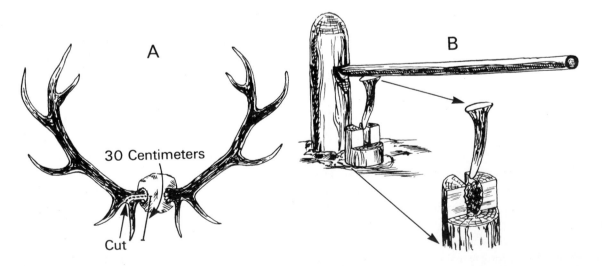

Figure 35. Elk antler tine (*A*) recovered from a Folsom site in eastern Wyoming. The tine was chopped from the antler of a freshly killed, mature bull elk—or shortly after shedding—to ensure maximum tensile strength. The tine likely was used as a fluting tool in conjunction with a simple leverage device similar to that shown at *B. Modified from Frison and Bradley (1981).*

excavated cave (Elk Bone Cave) in Wyoming (Nelson 1942). Camp and bison kill areas of the Big Goose Creek site in northcentral Wyoming produced evidence of elk, particularly antler tools and decorative items. Elk remains also were found at the Piney Creek Buffalo Jump in northcentral Wyoming, about 30 miles (48 km) south of Big Goose Creek (Frison 1967). Two elk antler flaking hammers were recorded from Late Prehistoric sites on the eastern slope of the Absaroka Mountains, occupied by Shoshonean Indians. In the same vicinity, near Cody, Wyoming, elk antlers were recovered from log structures that also are believed to have been Shoshonean (Frison 1978).

West of the Red River, just south of Winnipeg, Manitoba, Anderson focus refuse sites from 2,500 to 1,500 years ago included bones of elk, hare, deer, bison and fish (Vickers 1945, MacNeish 1958). (A focus is a group of archaeological components with a high degree of frequency of common cultural traits.) Overlaying those finds were deposits from the Nutimik focus—1,500 to 1,000 years ago—in which elk, deer, beaver, bear and fish bones outnumbered those of bison (Wedel 1961). Thereafter, bison bones were relatively numerous in the northeastern periphery of the Great Plains.

The Great Plains Middle Missouri tradition, beginning 1,500 to 500 years ago, gave rise to village-dwelling Indians in the Dakotas. Hunting and gardening were their basic occupations, and their principal sources of meat were bison, deer, elk, pronghorn, small mammals and birds (Wedel 1961).

Also dating from within Late Prehistoric time (again 1,500–500 years ago), elk teeth were located in numerous North Dakota archaeological sites (Wood 1957) and from at least one site in South Dakota (in the vicinity of Mobridge) (Wedel 1955).

In the Great Lakes region, the first humans were Early Paleo-Indians who lived there from about 13,000 to 8,000 years ago. These probably were nomadic mammoth and mastodon hunters, whose general way of life was represented by stone implements and weapons that often included fluted projectile points of the distinctive Clovis (New Mexico) type. About 9,000 years ago, climatic and vegetational conditions changed in the region, eliminating mammoths and mastodons, and a different flora and fauna complex populated the region.

Replacing or absorbing the Early Paleo-Indians were the Aqua-Planó Indians, a Late Paleo-Indian group, who inhabited the area from about 9,000 to 4,500 years ago. Of them Oswalt (1966:189) wrote: "The people involved in this chipped stone industry must have hunted deer, caribou and elk as important species of large game animals."

During the period of occupation by Aqua-Planó, two cultural patterns emerged, known as Boreal Archaic (circa 8,000–3,500 years ago) and Old Copper (circa 5,000–4,500 years ago) bridging the Paleo- and Archaic Indian periods. Both cultures adapted to forest environments and introduced woodworking devices (such as the ax, adz and gouge) in addition to use of stone tools. The originators of these new traditions were fishermen, hunters and foragers. Boreal Archaic Indians may have been the first people to hunt elk to any great extent, and they are known to have hunted with spears or *atlatls* (a bifurcated throwing stick) with flint points fluted on one or both sides (Potter 1968).

In the 1960s, archeologists found the tip of a flint point embedded in what has been recognized as an elk bone. The finding was from Silver Lake in Logan County, Ohio, and probably is attributable to the time of domination by the Boreal Archaic. It represents the first reliable evidence of elk hunting. Also, two elk tooth beads were found in a burial site on Frontenac Island, New York (Ritchie 1944), which dates back to somewhat less than 5,000 years ago (F. Johnson 1951).

Subsequent aboriginal cultures of the Great Lakes region, and those first represented as Eastern Woodland Indians, included the Glacial Kame (3,500–3,100 years ago), Adena (3,000–2,700 years), Hopewell (2,100–1,200 years ago), and Intrusive Mound, Cole, Fort Ancient and Erie (1,200–400 years ago). These, too, were predominantly hunting-oriented people, but they abandoned a nomadic existence in favor of villages, some of which remained occupied for a number of generations. Remains from small village sites of Adena Indians in the Ohio River Valley indicate that these people were proficient hunters of elk, deer and raccoons (Quimby 1952, Maxwell 1978, Whitacre and Whitacre 1986).

At the Late Mississippian (circa 850–500 years ago) Reve village site in Lake County, Ohio, more than 1,000 animal bones were found among refuse of this Whittlesay focus village (Greenman 1935). Most numerous were those of bear, deer, elk, bobcat, beaver, porcupine, fox and raccoon. At another Whittlesey village site in Lake County, more than 5,400 animal bones were excavated (Goslin 1948). Among the most numerous were white-tailed deer (1,160), raccoon (794), elk (324), beaver (304), black bear (285) and gray squirrel (149). Moorhead (1899) identified mainly bison, bear, deer, elk, raccoon, wild turkey, turtle, fish and snake from about 5,000 bone fragments from the Baum village site in Ross County. And at the Grahm Village Site along the Hocking River near present Logan, Ohio, elk was represented by 9.7% of identifiable bone fragments (84.9% were white-tailed deer) from the village refuge pit (Prufer and McKenzie 1967).

Except for the high probability that elk served the eastern aboriginal economy as an occasional source of food and likely were taken opportunistically (see, e.g., Goslin

1975, Howard 1995), few other conclusions can be made about the Indians' use of the elk during this period.

Guilday (1971:21) wrote: "Elk remains, while common finds in sites from eastern United States, are never abundant at any one site." From the Mount Carbon Site in Fayette County, West Virginia, once occupied by Fort Ancient Indians, composite remains of deer outnumber those of elk by a 34:1 ratio (Guilday and Tanner 1965). On the basis of food value (weight), that ratio becomes 9:1. At the Escheman Site in Lancaster County, Pennsylvania, which was a Susquehannock village, investigators recorded the remains of 182 deer, 33 bear and 21 elk (Guilday et al. 1962). Again, based on weight, elk represented about 27% of the diet. In Putnam County, West Virginia, archaeological evidence at the Buffalo Site indicated 746 deer and only two elk (Guilday 1971). From investigations at the Carlson Annis Mound (Archaic) in Butler County, Kentucky, Webb (1950) found no elk remains among more than 3,500 midden and burial site excavations. Likewise, Converse (1978) made no report of elk remnants in association with Glacial Kame Indians of the Ohio region. Elk, prehistorically, were not abundant or even present in all places at all times, but the evidence of food value by weight suggests that elk, however occasional, was not an insignificant source.

Another possible link between elk and prehistoric Indians east of the Mississippi River involves the mound-building phenomenon. The construction of burial and effigy mounds, frequently in the configuration of animals, may have begun with the Adenas, but it became a common practice by later cultures, particularly those of the Upper Great Lakes region and principally in the Mississippi River valley. Hopewells, apparently, were the most prolific mound builders.

Virtually thousands of emblematic mounds were built in Wisconsin, Ohio, Illinois and surrounding states from about 3,000 to 800 years ago, and a large percentage were shaped as animals. It is probable that the effigies were personal or tribal totems. And, although time and the forces of nature have impaired reliable identification of shapes, there were attempts in the 1800s to classify them accordingly. In his comprehensive study, Peet (1890:6) reported that "horned" animals often were represented in effigy, and that bison were most common: "The buffalo so nearly resembles the elk and moose that it is difficult to distinguish it, but generally the attitude and the general shape will . . . show what animal was intended." Peet somehow specifically identified elk mounds in two locations in central Wisconsin, and speculated that others represented elk (Figure 36).

Fishing was a principal form of subsistence for many of the aboriginal people of North America. A common means of securing fish and eels was by spearing, and in the lower

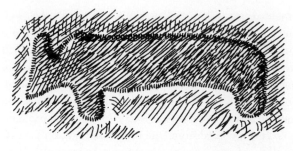

Figure 36. The exact configuration of a supposed "elk" mound constructed by prehistoric Indians in Sauk County, Wisconsin. "It shows how accurately the effigy-builders were able to imitate the shape of this animal. The location of the mound shows that the effigy was placed on the very spot where elk were accustomed to feed, and that effigy-builders were true to nature in every respect" (Peet 1890:298). The mound is more than 30 meters (100 ft) in length and about 9 meters (30 ft) in width. *Redrawn from Peet (1890).*

parts of the eastern Canadian provinces and in the northern Great Lakes and New England regions, spears or harpoons frequently were outfitted with elk antler points (Beauchamp 1902, Wintemberg 1906). These points, particularly numerous in Ontario and New York, were of four major types: single, unilaterally barbed; multiple, unilaterally barbed; multiple, bilaterally barbed; and toggle-heads indicating the effectiveness of elk antler points for a wide range of purposes.

As eastern prehistoric Indians evolved a subsistence pattern that increasingly included farming, their uses of elk appear to have expanded. Fort Ancient Indians in southern Ohio, for example, are known to have cultivated fields with digging sticks and hoes, some of which were fashioned from the shoulder blades of elk. In other states east of the Mississippi River, elk artifacts (especially teeth, beamers and scapulae hoes) have been found in villages and encampment sites dating back as much as several thousand years (see Foster 1873, Wintemberg 1936, McMichael 1963, Brose 1978). In nearly all instances, these remains are small in relation to the amount of remains of other wild animals harvested. This would indicate that the animals, while widespread, either were not extremely abundant or else their seasonal habits were such that they were not readily or easily taken, or that "aboriginal overkill" (discussed later) served to keep elk numbers depressed (Kay 1994, 1995b). In the Late Woodland period of the 1500s and 1600s, deer, elk and beaver were the common animal foods in portions of the Great Lakes region (Cleland 1966, Cowan 1987). Griffin (1978:552) added that, for Late Prehistoric Indians of the Ohio River Valley, "There was a strong dependence upon deer (80 percent at some sites), elk, bear and raccoon. . . ."

In the Southwest, identifiable elk remains are scarce, but

some were found in Chaco and Santa Fe archaeological sites of the Eastern Anasazi in north-central New Mexico (Vivian and Mathews 1964, Traylor 1977). Renaud (1930) reported elk, deer and rabbit remains in Fumarole culture deposits on the southern Plains of northeastern New Mexico outnumbered those of bison. Plog (1979) reported that in northeastern Arizona, western New Mexico and southern Utah, elk was one of the principal hunted species of Western Anasazi from 12,000 to 2,000 years ago. Wormington (1964) indicated that the elk was one of the meat animals hunted by "Developmental Pueblo" Anasazi of Arizona and New Mexico between 700 and 1100 AD.

Indians of California and the Pacific Northwest hunted elk extensively (see Heizer 1978). Elk bones constituted about 50% of the ungulate bones unearthed from archaeological sites along the coasts of Oregon, Washington and British Columbia (Kay 1990). The abundance of prehistoric artifacts from the region—including digging tools, hoes, skin scrapers, hooks, war clubs, fleshers, wedges and adz handles made of elk bone or antler—would indicate a large population of elk, at least in relation to other large wild ungulates, during at least some significant period of Indian occupation. Elk bones found in caves in the River of No Return Wilderness in Idaho date back 4,000 years, and the human inhabitants of those caves were thought to be "efficient hunters" (U.S. Department of Agriculture Office of Governmental and Public Affairs 1982:2, Miles 1963). Kay (1994) attributed the abundance of elk along the coast to thick, protective forests too wet to burn and open—which would have made hunting easier year-round (see Lewis and Ferguson 1988)—and to limited snowfall that prevented Indians from chasing the animals into deep snow where the animals could have been easily killed.

Archaeological evidence accumulated at the American Museum of Natural History (New York City) shows that elk also were used prehistorically in California, Arizona and New Mexico, although recovered artifacts have not been dated.

The three major influences on aboriginal life in North America were (1) arrival of European explorers, trappers, traders, miners, adventurers and settlers, (2) exogenous pandemics, and (3) introduction of the horse (Wissler 1914, see Strong 1933, Devoto 1953, Utley 1984, Washburn 1988). These circumstances occurred almost simultaneously, in a bittersweet eyeblink of anthropologic time. All three were to have an enormous impact on virtually every aspect of the Indians' lifestyle, including their relationships to elk.

Influences of Indians on Elk Populations

As noted elsewhere, elk were more widespread than any other single deer species in North America. Seton (1927) es-

Emigration of elk across the Bering–Chukchi platform and movement southward is detected, in part, by the finding and dating of elk artifacts used by prehistoric Indians. The two eroded elk antler parts, from an archeological site on Fidalgo Island, Skagit County, Washington, appear to be fleshers or chisels. The bone joint, from the same site, may have been an arrow straightener. The artifacts are thought to date from 2500 to 500 BC. In other nearby sites, such as Glenrose Cannery (Matson 1981), circa 8200 to 3250 BC, elk remains, including implements, "are common" (Carlson 1990:65). *Photo by Jerry L. Gildmeister; courtesy of Mr. Winston Banko and the Thomas Burke Memorial Washington State Museum.*

timated that at one time there may have been 10 million elk on the continent. Archaeological evidence and early historic records suggest that Seton's calculation was liberal. Even so, perhaps only a few centuries ago there may have been several times the nearly 1 million elk accounted for today (see Chapter 2; Rocky Mountain Elk Foundation 1997). Furthermore, elk of the Late Prehistoric and early historic period seem to have favored riparian areas within grasslands' broadleaf forest/grassland ecotones, as opposed to the coniferous forestlands typically occupied by elk at present.

Based on pre- and early settlement conditions of browse vegetation and calculated aboriginal subsistence patterns, Kay (1990, 1992) argued that elk were scarce in the Yellowstone ecosystem and, along with other native ungulates, rare throughout the Intermountain region. He observed that elk remains represented only 3% of more than 52,000 bones identified from 200 archaeological sites in the region (see also Frison 1978, cf. Sappington 1994). Wright (1984) conjectured that large numbers of elk did not inhabit the Jackson Hole area of Wyoming until the late 1800s (cf. Houston 1982, Despains et al. 1986). The idea that elk may not have been as abundant historically or prehistorically where they are concentrated today does not preclude the possibility (and, in many cases, certainty) of past elk abundance in many areas where there now are few or none.

The number of Indians that occupied North America in

protohistoric and early historic time is a matter of continuing debate among anthropologists. Claims range from fewer than 2 million to more than 18 million (see Kroeber 1934, 1939, Wissler 1966, Dobyns 1966, 1983, Snow 1995). Using regional density calculations of Oswalt (1966), Driver (1968) and Denevan (1992), and recognizing that most early estimates occurred decades and even centuries after some Indian groups were decimated by European diseases (see Dobyns 1966, 1988, 1989, Swagerty 1988, Roberts 1989), a population of 1.2 to 3.5 million is projected for the United States and Canada at the time of Columbus's "discovery."

And within the vast range of elk at the time, the Indian population at its peak would have been no more than 2.25 million (Figure 37) and probably less than 1.75 million (Mooney 1928, Baumhoff 1978, Ubelaker 1988, Denevan 1992). By the early 1800s, a large percentage of the conti-

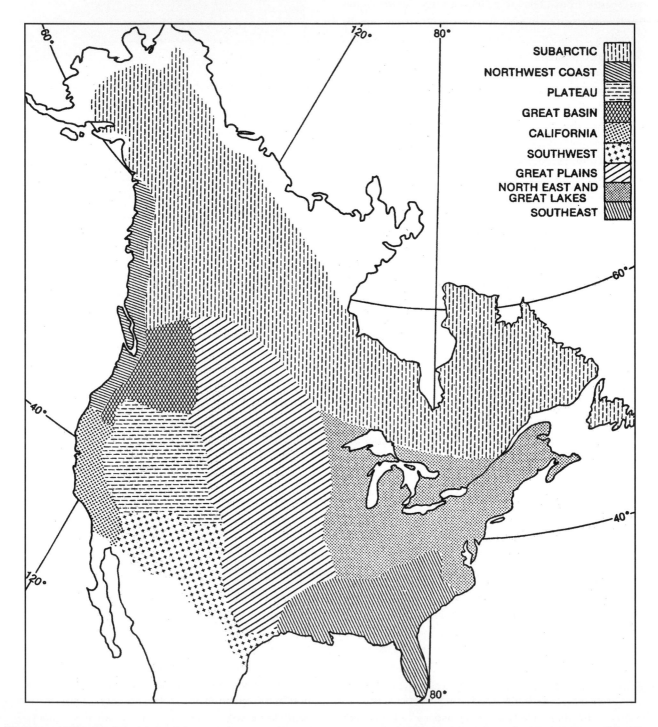

Figure 37. Ethnographic regions of the United States and Canada, circa 1500. *Adapted from Voegelin and Voegelin (1966) and Maxwell (1978).*

nental elk population was concentrated in northern California, the Pacific Northwest, and the northern and central Great Plains regions (see Murie 1951). The species was virtually extirpated east of the Mississippi River.

Despite the presumed low density of Indians on elk range, the Native peoples apparently exerted considerable impact on elk numbers and distribution at least within historic time. Their major influences were by fire and hunting and, in many areas and times, their effects appear to have been in opposition.

Fire

One of the most pervasive impacts of Indians on elk was that of habitat modification by fire. This was a favorable influence in that it set back plant succession to stages that produced a variety and abundance of forage palatable to elk. Incendiary practices combined with lightning-produced fires probably affected tens of thousands of acres of elk habitat annually.

Before the large-scale invasion of white settlers west of the Appalachian Mountains (see Day 1953, DeGraaf and Miller 1996), elk apparently thrived in Plains and prairie habitats (Figure 38). Until the late 1800s, Indians of these regions intentionally set fires to manipulate vegetational stands. Such burning has been ascribed as a means of clearing for agricultural use (Allen 1967, Schmidt 1978b, Cowan 1987), controlling insects (Kniffen 1928, Stewart 1954, Allen 1970, Lewis 1977), fireproofing (Barrett 1980), clearing understory and undesirable vegetation (Stewart 1954, Mutch 1976, Lewis 1977), stimulating growth of medicinal plants (see Barrett 1980), improving forage for horses (De Smet 1843, Johnson 1969, Thwaites 1969), modifying weather (DeVoto 1953), warfare (Inman 1897, Dengler 1923, Garth 1953), clearing campsites and travel routes (Johnson 1969, Lewis 1977), signaling (Phillips 1940, Thwaites 1969), tracking and hunting (Van der Donck 1841, Mullan 1861, Hodge 1907, Lowie 1963, Oswalt 1966, Chittenden and Richardson 1969, Curtis 1970, Garth 1978, McHugh 1979), and aiding food gathering, particularly of berry-producing plants (Clouser 1974).

The Indians' desire to stimulate growth of forage to attract big game animals also motivated them to set fires (Maxwell 1910, Steward 1941, Longhurst et al. 1952, Thwaites 1969, Arthur 1975, Sauer 1975, Feest 1978, Feest and Feest 1978, Olmsted and Stewart 1978, Silver 1978).

California Indians used fire extensively, usually from July through October, to stimulate growth of seed-producing plants, control forest brush and facilitate hunting (Crespí 1927, Harrington 1932, Driver and Massey 1957, Galvan 1968, Lewis 1973, Baumhoff 1978, Olmsted and Stewart

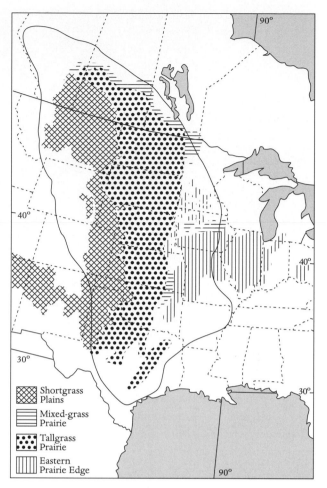

Figure 38. Principal native grassland of central North America. Dotted line surrounds the Great Plains region. *Adapted from Allen (1967), Voegelin and Voegelin (1966), Capps (1973) and Maxwell (1978).*

Legend:
- Shortgrass Plains
- Mixed-grass Prairie
- Tallgrass Prairie
- Eastern Prairie Edge

1978). Eastern Miwok, for example, annually burned lands in the Sacramento Valley in August, reportedly to ensure ample forage for Tule elk (Levy 1978).

From two Kutenai Indians, early Montana forest ranger Bert Davis learned that "In the woods, when trails become blocked by blow-down or the wreckage left by snow slides, the natives simply clear the way with fire. If the fire went wild and destroyed a few million trees, the Indians know that the burn would soon grow up to grass and small brush, which made for good grazing and browsing for deer and elk, and in later times for horses" (Johnson 1969:199–200). Lewis (1985:75) wrote that "fires set by hunter-gatherers differ from [lightning] fires in terms of seasonality, frequency, intensity, and ignition pattern." Kay (1995a) suggested that lightning fires tended to be high-intensity blazes compared with Native burning, which was more frequent and tended to create vegetative mosaics more attractive to elk (see also White 1975, Pyne 1982, 1993, Blackburn and Anderson 1993).

The extent to which brush and forest fires were inten-

Natural fires and those set intentionally or accidentally by Indians maintained vast expanses of grassland that supported enormous populations of native ungulates, including elk. Higgins (1986:5) argued that Indians of the northern Great Plains "generally did not subscribe to annual wholesale or promiscuous burning practices, but used fire as a tool to aid hunting and gathering of food and materials." *Photo from Dengler (1923), after a drawing by Rudolph Friederich Kurz.*

tionally started before the 1700s is uncertain. In the West, there is indication that Indians inhabited large burned areas immediately after fire 8,000 years BP, but whether these infrequent fires were set is unknown (Barrett 1980). Also, the archaeological record shows only limited evidence of human occupation coincidental to small, frequent fires. It is speculated that migration or territorial movements of some prehistoric Indian tribes or bands followed major natural-occurring fires, and "unintentional fires probably were set occasionally during prehistoric time" (Barrett 1980:20). On the other hand, pictographs by ancient Indians in central Idaho reveal a fear of wildfire, which could burn out canyons that supported a variety and abundance of big game (Thompson 1964). Also, C. E. Kay (personal communication:1995) indicated that research has correlated shorter fire cycles with increased Native activity. Thompson (1964) noted that these Indians customarily fought fire on winter game range.

Acquisition of horses by Plains Indians in the 1600s (Haines 1938a, Ewers 1955, Holder 1974, Maxwell 1978) and by mountain tribes about 1730 (Haines 1938b, Roe 1955, Lowie 1963) may have prompted an increase in the use of set fires (Higgins 1986, cf. Barrett and Arno 1982), at least in grasslands. Large numbers of horses likely taxed vegetational resources around traditional encampment areas, and fire was a means of rejuvenating or maintaining suitable forage resources in these locations (Wells 1970, Barrett 1980). Also, the Indians' increased mobility because of horses imposed fewer hardships and constraints on tribal

movements to and from burned areas. Fires, therefore, could be set and left to burn freely, because the use of the horse made possible broader movement and less dependence on the maintenance of geographically confined seasonal campsites (see Grinnell 1972).

Moore (1972) listed 25 tribes on the Plains known to deliberately set prairie fires. East of the Mississippi River and on the Plains, fires frequently were set along riparian habitats and on rolling grasslands. In the mountainous West, fires were started primarily in valley grasslands and Ponderosa pine, Douglas-fir and western larch forests at low elevation, and only rarely in forests at higher elevation (see also R. D. Reynolds unpublished:1959). As Mails (1972:10) pointed out: "Elk made extensive use of the grasslands, but were found most commonly in the summer near forested and mountain country."

Generally, fires were set during spring and autumn when groups of Indians relocated to new seasonal areas (Higgins 1986, Turner 1991). These times also were most appropriate for staging low-intensity fire conducive to seral stage plant growth when the sites were revisited, particularly those on grasslands.

Setting fires was just one of many land-use subsistence techniques, and the Indians probably regarded fire as an unremarkable and commonplace force and advantage of nature (M. Loscheider unpublished:1975, Barrett 1980). Despite the number of reports previously cited of Indian use of fire to attract elk and other wildlife, there is no convincing evidence that burning was done to conserve game animals per se. In any case, fires set by Indians undoubtedly were beneficial to the populations of native large ungulates on which most of the Natives depended. These benefits resulted from setting back vegetative succession and reducing overstories, thereby allowing a greater variety and quantity of palatable forage to flourish (Higgins 1986) and reducing the incidence of lightning-generated fires (Pyne 1982, 1993, 1995, Reid 1987), whose intensity could serve to sterilize soils for long periods.

Hunting

It is reasonable to assume that most Indians killed elk, whether by purposefully hunting them or incidental to pursuing other wildlife or just opportunistically, throughout the pre-Columbian and historic ranges of the species. The only hint that a tribe may not have hunted available elk was an indication by Goddard (1924) and Curtis (1970) that the Mono, a Northern Pauiotso tribe in Nevada, did not hunt them, probably for spiritual reasons. However, those records are suspect because elk were absent or very scarce in the Mono homeland, and because the information came from interviews with tribal members well after their displacement from the traditional territory in the Great Basin. Other Indians within elk range did not hunt them, but these exceptions were due to totemic, social, military or religious group affiliation or personal spiritualism, which are discussed later.

That the elk likely was taken by most Indians does not necessarily mean that it was an important game animal to all or most Indians. In fact, elk was consistently vital to the Indians' economy in only a few areas of the northern California and Plateau regions; conversely, it was sought with only limited enthusiasm by some Great Basin and Subarctic Indians. The year-round availability and overall huntability of elk compared with other animals (especially other big game) appear to have been the primary factors determining the extent to which elk were harvested, used and valued from region to region and even from tribe to tribe within a particular region.

As will be discussed later, the elk generally was hunted as a secondary source of food, for the unique characteristics of its hide and to secure specialty items from other of its body parts. In some instances, hunting and killing elk also was a matter of enhancing prestige and honing war and hunting skills.

This section will identify, on a regional basis, tribes of Indians that hunted elk within recent historic time (since about 1700) and some of the methods used in that activity. Because of the radical changes of Indian lifestyles, cultural and economic emphases, and territories within historic time, and because of the equally significant concurrent decrease and geographic shift of elk populations, the information is only a partial record. Also, most tribes used a variety of techniques to hunt elk, and those cited were not necessarily unique to the tribe or tribes with which they are identified in the literature and this synopsis.

Eastern Woodlands and Prairies

Despite the fact that elk were common in presettlement portions of the East and Mid-Atlantic states (see, e.g., Johnston 1898, Caruso 1959), they were never known to have been the mainstay of any Indian tribe in the East (see Wissler 1966, Driver 1969, Curtis 1970, Mails 1972, Maxwell 1978, Trigger 1978). North and east of the Allegheny Mountains elk was, at most, an occasional food and of less importance than deer, fish, moose, bear, waterfowl, gathered vegetation and cultivated crops. This also was true in the Great Lakes region, where the Indians subsisted primarily on deer, fish, small mammals, waterfowl, other birds and cultivated and uncultivated plants (see Trigger 1978).

A review of the literature revealed only a small number of eastern elk-hunting tribes relative to the number of tribes that existed within the known pre-Columbian and early historic elk range (Table 9). The rapid extirpation of elk from the East after colonization and westward settlement may account for the partial record. In addition, some

Table 9. Elk-hunting Indian tribes from east of the Mississippi River, 1500 to 1850[a]

Known[a]	Assumed[b]
Oneida	Mohawk
Sauk	Onondaga
Fox	Delaware
Cree	Wyandot
Menominee	Seneca
Chippewa	Brulé Sioux
Ottawa	Abenaki
Susquehanna	Kickapoo
Potawatomi	Coyuga
Miami	Shawnee
Huron	Mascouten
Winnebago	
Iroquois	
Southeastern Ojibwa	
Cheyenne[c]	
Pawnee[c]	

Source: From literature survey. It is not expected that the listings are inclusive.

[a] Tribes or tribal subdivisions identified by name.

[b] Assumed from mention of elk hunting in an area known to have been occupied at the time by the tribe indicated, as examined against Hodge (1907, 1910) and Driver (1972); see also Norton (1974) and Trigger (1978).

[c] Before shift to the central Great Plains.

of the early records about Indian elk hunting in the East are not specific or discernible as to place or tribal affiliation. And, as indicated in Chapter 1, frequent reference to moose as elk by early chroniclers precludes certain identification of some tribes that may well have been elk hunters.

Cooper (1938), Oswalt (1966) and Warner (1975) reported that such Eastern and Northern Woodland Indian tribes as the Iroquois, Huron, Southeastern Ojibwa and Oneida were sedentary agriculturists, but adept big game hunters. These tribes broke into smaller groups or family units during winter, and for hunting elk, bear, deer, moose, beaver, fox, wild turkey, porcupine and muskrat during particular seasons (Trigger 1978). This also was the pattern among semiagriculturists, including the Ottawa, Potawatomi, Menominee, Sauk, Fox and Miami.

The hunting techniques used by Indians east of the Mississippi River specifically to hunt elk are not well documented. Most information addresses big game hunting in general. Organized driving through forests, snaring (twitchup), impounding, gang shooting from breastworks and surrounds along game trails and chasing animals to deadfalls are methods frequently identified (Lahontan 1703, Keith 1890, Cooper 1938, MacGregor 1946, Fundaburk 1958, Driver 1969, Grinnell 1972). The fire surround was used by the Southeastern Ojibwa, Ottawa, Winnebago, Illinois and Miami tribes (Feest 1978, McHugh 1979). Dengler (1923:64) wrote: "When heavy snow covered the country [eastern prairie states] the hunters went on the chase armed with spears and bows and arrows. Quickly and easily they glided over the soft white surface on their snowshoes, while the heavy buffaloes and elks often sank up to their bellies in the snow and thus fell an easy prey to the hunters."

According to Lahontan (1703), when the Cheyenne lived in eastern forests, they hunted deer and elk by surrounding herds and driving them into enclosures. Regarding the effigy mounds of prehistoric Indians of the Great Lakes region, Peet (1890:6) noted: "It is remarkable that effigies of buffaloes, moose and elk are more frequently associated with game drives than any other animal." Grinnell (1972[I]:273–274) wrote in 1923: "... in ancient times when they [Indians of unidentified forest tribes in the East] found, in the timber, a place where an elk trail passed under a tree, they tied a rope of rawhide or sinew to a branch arranging the rope so that the noose would hang down over the trail at about the height of an elk's head. If an elk in passing ran it's [sic] head into the noose and became frightened, it gave a quick jump, drew the rope tight, and so was strangled."

Driver (1969) and others have indicated that the Eastern Woodland Indian was a capable stalker of big game and extremely proficient in the use of the bow and arrow, although some preferred using spears for hunting big game.

Fenton (1978) revealed that the essential big game hunting gear of Woodland Indians included bow and arrow, knife and ax (later the tomahawk). As a hunting device in the East before the extirpation of elk, the gun was too primitive for effective use in most hunting situations and, because of its noise and the scarcity of ammunition and gunpowder, many Indians opted for their traditional weapons even when guns were available (see Camp 1957, McCabe and McCabe 1984, Utley 1984, Lohse 1988).

Great Plains

On the Great Plains, two Native lifestyles and economies emerged in the past millennium. By 1775, the nomadic hunter/gatherers and semisedentary hunter/agriculturalists were distinct cultural groups, each well adapted to the physiographic and biotic opportunities presented by the vast region (Mails 1972). On the eastern Plains—the tall and mixed grass vegetative zones—the soil conditions, topography and moisture regimes enabled most Indians to erect villages and cultivate certain riparian areas, as well as hunt. Farther west on the Plains, into the shortgrass region, the wandering herds of bison were so numerous as to preclude the need for crop cultivation or even the development of farming technology. Shifting intertribal and intracultural social relationships (mainly conflict and trade) also influenced the lifestyle and economic distinctions (see Ewers 1954, 1955, 1968, Newcomb 1955, Lowie 1963, Meyer 1977). Because of the abundance of bison and other wildlife, neither group depended on elk, but both hunted elk as a secondary source of food and for parts of the animal that were as useful as, or supplemental to, similar parts of bison. Acquisition of the horse, however, had momentous influence on the predatory relationship of Indians to elk populations in the West. It precipitated another and final major geographic and cultural shift of Indians, especially in the Plains and Plateau regions (Mishkin 1940, Oswalt 1966, Holder 1974, Klein 1980). "The historic village tribes extended their hunting range in summer with a mounted trek after buffalo, although they continued to cultivate their fields of maize. Other tribes . . . completely abandoned their villages and farming and reorganized to move their belongings by horse caravan. Now highly mobile, they could pursue their . . . quarry with ease, shifting camps to keep up with the largest herds" (McHugh 1979:9). Lowie (1963:45) added that the economic utility of horses lay in enabling Plains hunters "to kill large numbers of big game animals more rapidly and efficiently than was otherwise possible and in facilitating transport." The value and usefulness of horses intensified intertribal relationships and competition for space and resources, making hunting a dangerous occupation (Ewers 1955, Meyer 1977). The horse also enabled Indians to remain longer, year-round or to make hunting forays in elk winter ranges. It heightened intertribal trading, and certain parts of elk increased in importance as commodities of exchange. Horse acquisition also signaled the imminent and sweeping ingression of whites, and a resulting concentralization of Indians and many big game populations.

There is little question about the hunting ability of Plains Indians. Burnett (1880:114) wrote: "The Indian always considered wild game as much their property as they did the country in which it was found. Though breeding and maintaining the game cost them no labor, yet it lived and fattened on their grass and herbage, and was as substantially within the power of these roving people and skillful hunters as the domestic animals of the white man."

To understand elk hunting by Indians of the Great Plains, one must realize that, although there were 30 major tribes and an even greater number of political subdivisions, with more than 30 different tongues derived from five linguistic families (Figure 39), all of the aboriginal Plains people relied on the bison, although in varying degrees.

The bison dictated their social organization, daily activities and seasonal rhythms. The bison was their cultural link from generation to generation as well as tribe to tribe, and provided nearly all material needs. During his expedition on the Plains in the 1830s, Alexander Philipp Maximilian zu Wied observed: "The numerous Indians subsist almost entirely on these animals [bison]. . . . The consumption . . . is immense in North America, and [bison] is as indispensable [*sic*] to the Indians as the reindeer is to the Laplanders, and the seal to the Esquimaux." (Thomas and Ronnefeldt 1976:52). At least on the Great Plains, other items of subsistence, such as elk, tended to be incidental except in years or seasons of bison shortage; "all in all hunting of the buffalo and to a lesser extent of the elk, deer and antelope, was a major occupation, while other animals were sought for only sporadically" (Flannery 1953:55).

Bison hunts necessarily were organized and structured events in which large numbers of Indians or entire tribal bands participated. The Indians reorganized the efficacy of

The horse greatly aided the Plains Indians' ability to follow the seasonal movements of big game herds, particularly bison. Although some northern Plains Indians considered hunting on horseback for elk too dangerous and unnecessary, others were not so reluctant, especially on portions of the central and southern Plains where elk were fairly numerous in early historic time. *Photo courtesy of the U.S. Library of Congress.*

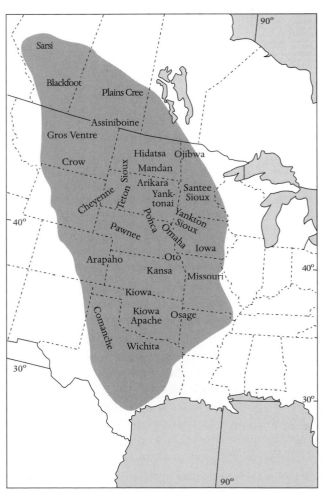

Figure 39. Some principal Indian tribes of the Great Plains. *Adapted from Voegelin and Voegelin (1966), Maxwell (1978) and Lowie (1963).*

communal bison hunting and the impracticality of killing more animals than were needed. In fact, many tribes did not permit individuals or small parties to hunt alone for bison (Capps 1973).

Hunting other big game, especially elk and deer, frequently involved different motivations, skills and techniques. The basic difference was that most elk hunts were by individuals or small groups. These hunts generally lacked the organization of bison hunts: "As neither the elk nor the deer stood in similar vital relation [as the bison] to the people, hunting these animals was attended with less ceremony" (Fletcher and La Flesche 1972[I]:271). This probably was due to the seasons in which elk were most available and the flight behavior of elk in contrast to bison. Again, most elk were found in foothills and mountainous areas during autumn and winter months. Weather conditions, terrain and the relative size of elk populations would have made it difficult and inefficient for large groups of Indians to plan and coordinate their hunts. Although bison could be stampeded en masse, or small groups isolated on flat or rolling grasslands, elk were known to escape by fleeing into dense timber, by climbing hills and sometimes by running great distances (Thwaites 1969).

Among the Great Plains elk hunters (Table 10), there was another factor that dictated different hunting strategies. On the southern and eastern Plains, many Indians actively sought elk in summer. They could afford this selectivity because of the year-round availability of, and relatively unrestricted (by weather) access to, the bison. These Indians, including Pawnee, Yankton Sioux, Oto and Kiowa tribes, concentrated on yearling elk, whose meat was more tender than bison or older elk. Elk cows were hunted shortly after the calving season because their hides were most pliant at that time. Farther north and west, Indians hunted bison primarily during the summer months. This was a matter of economy because winters often were extremely difficult times. Game could be scarce, the Indians' mobility and foraging range were limited and the season was sometimes prolonged by late autumn or early spring blizzards. Consequently, the Indians usually were forced to take whatever animals they could. According to C. E. Kay (1994, personal communication:1995), when there was a choice between genders of elk killed for food, the Indians invariably took females except in spring, when the overwinter rigors of gestation and springtime lactation placed cows in poor condition (see Teit 1928, Kinietz 1940, Wright and Miller 1976, Alvard 1993). Kay (personal communication:1997) subsequently observed that his opinion on Indian selection for cow elk was based on information in the literature regarding Indian selection for bison cows (see, e.g., Howard 1995), and he was not aware of similar information about elk. I

am also unaware of such information, yet believe that Kay's crossover presumption may have some validity for some tribes.

The regional/seasonal pattern of elk harvest had considerable variation. For example, the eastern Plains Omaha preferred to hunt elk in early winter, when the animals were at peak size for the year. Southern Plains tribes, such as the Wichita, hunted in June and again in autumn (Haines 1976). Many northern tribes, notably the Crow, Blackfeet and Teton Sioux, hunted elk at every opportunity regardless of season. The Assiniboine, Gros Ventre and Hidatsa frequently killed elk in spring (primarily to obtain hides suitable for particular uses), but usually hunted them for meat and implements in autumn and winter (Lowie 1913, Flannery 1953, Ewers 1974). In addition, just as marginal tribes periodically visited the Plains to hunt bison, hunting parties of western Plains tribes (including the Crow, Gros Ventre and Blackfeet) regularly traveled to the Plateau region in search of elk (Mails 1972). Most of the techniques used by the Plains Indians to hunt bison also were used to kill elk.

Elk jumps and surrounds are mentioned occasionally in the literature, but it is probable that most elk were taken by individual hunters or small groups. Also, mass killings of

Table 10.   Elk hunters of the Great Plains, 1500 to 1900

Typical ("true") nomads	Semi-nomads	Marginal[a]		
		West	Southeast	North
Arapaho	Arikara	Bannock	Caddo[b]	Beaver
Assiniboine	Hidatsa	Cayuse[b]	Quapaw	Chippewa
Blackfeet	Iowa	Coeur d'Alene		Plains Cree
Cheyenne	Kansa[b]	Flathead		Plains Ojibwa
Comanche	Mandan	Kalispel		Slave
Crow	Missouri	Kutenai		Woods Cree
Gros Ventre	Omaha	Nez Percé		
Kiowa	Osage	Northern Shoshone		
Kiowa Apache	Oto	Umatilla[b]		
Sarsi	Pawnee	Yakima[b]		
Teton Sioux	Ponca			
	Santee Sioux			
	Yankton Sioux			
	Wichita[b]			

[a] Tribes that periodically hunted on the Plains but did not totally assimilate the Plains culture.

[b] Not directly indicated in the literature as being elk hunters on the Plains, but implied or otherwise suggested by examination of clothing, implements, decorations and language, plus historic photographs and artwork.

big game usually took place in autumn, when the animals were of optimal size and their hides in top condition and when fires could be set most advantageously. Also, the weather then was sufficiently cool to accommodate efficient preparation and quantity storage of meat for winter.

The jump was one of the more spectacular communal hunting techniques, in terms of its drama and results, and it appears to have been widely used, despite the fact that few if any elk jumps have been archaeologically identified. In 1923, Grinnell (1972[I]:276) wrote: "The Cheyennes appear to have no definite traditions of a time when they were accustomed to drive elk over a bank or cliff . . . yet no doubt this was done, for affiliated Arapahoes tell of the capture of elk in numbers by this method in old times, and Blackfoot stories refer to the practice. The ungulates, which collect in great herds, readily lend themselves to this method of capture. . . . It is altogether probable that all the Plains Indians . . . captured elk by this method."

After acquisition of the horse by the Plains Indians, the surround became an increasingly popular tactic for hunting elk (Driver 1969). It was favored by the Hidatsa, Mandan and Arikara tribes (Meyer 1977), and commonly used by Northern Cheyennes (Hoebel 1962, Grinnell 1972) and tribes of the central Plains (Dodge 1882). Lowie (1963:18) wrote that "Cree and the Assiniboin were especially expert at impounding, a method likewise reported for the Blackfoot, Gros Ventre, Crow and some other tribes." The Assiniboine sometimes used scarecrows (stone or tree branch stanchions) to drive big game to buffalo parks, or enclosures, in narrow gorges (Thomas and Ronnefeldt 1976). Allen (1876) documented the Indian hunting technique of entrapping elk and bison in impoundments along the Upper Yellowstone River.

Hunting elk from horseback was not an unusual practice. However, before the widespread use of guns, the Chippewa and Sarsi considered it dangerous and inefficient (see Curtis 1970). Plains tribes that regularly hunted elk on horseback included the Comanche, Plains Cree, Cheyenne, Crow and Kiowa. Curtis (1970) noted that the Crow chased elk on horseback in the same way that they hunted bison—splitting into two groups and flanking both sides of a fleeing herd (see also Raynolds 1868). Dodge (1882) observed that Kiowa and Comanche once were very skillful horseback hunters of elk. The Sioux, Gros Ventre and Arapaho likely were mounted elk hunters as well, but I found no conclusive record of this activity.

Denig (1930) wrote that hunting elk on foot was the general practice of all Upper Missouri tribes. Although the Mandan traveled to and from elk hunts on horseback and occasionally used horses in communal drives, most elk hunting was done afoot in forest areas (see Wills and Spin-

den 1906, Thomas and Ronnefeldt 1976, Meyer 1977). Ewers (1955) learned that elk hunting by Blackfeet was almost never done on horseback, but David Thompson reported on mounted hunting of elk by Piegans around 1800 (Tyrrell 1916).

Dodge (1882:577) described a "wonderfully successful" method of horseback hunting for elk "used formerly" by "one or two small fragments of tribes now living in the Indian Territory [Oklahoma]. . . . Each hunter was armed with a long pole, light but strong, the smaller end of which was split and forced open for about a foot, forming a Y. About six inches from the open end was fastened a knife-blade, sharpened to the keenest edge, and set diagonally in the Y, the whole being secured and strengthened with raw-hide.

A herd being discovered, the hunters approach against the wind, and dash suddenly upon the frightened beast, which, confused by the onslaught, and having no leader, crowd together. Running up behind an elk the hunter sets the crotch of his pole against the hind leg just above the knee. A sharp push severed the hamstring. The other leg was quickly served in the same way, and the game secured."

Among the noncommunal elk hunting methods used by Plains hunters were ambushes, concealed traps, pitfalls and deadfalls. Except among the Cheyenne and Assiniboine, snaring elk was absent from the Plains Indians' repertoire. The bow and arrow, lance, knife, tomahawk and club comprised the Plains Indian's total hunting and warfare arsenal, until enough guns were acquired to supplement this arsenal. Writing about Cheyenne hunters, Grinnell (1972[I]:277) noted: "It is well understood that most hoofed game—buffalo, antelope, deer, elk, and sheep—usually travel by certain established trails. In the days of their abundance, they always followed such trails and were not turned from them except by some alarming object. The Indians, who were constantly studying the habits of the animals on which they subsisted, were well informed to their ways, and commonly built their pens, pitfalls, and other traps, lay in wait for, and laid their snares on or near these trails. The Indians expected the game would come to them, instead of their being obliged to search for the animals and bring them to the traps. This was not only a labor-saving practice, but also added greatly to the probability of success in securing food."

In the first half of the 19th century, many Plains Indians had secured rifles (the majority of which were .52 caliber) or smoothbore muskets (approximately .66 caliber) by means of capture, trade, purchase, smuggling or as gifts. Although the rifle was more accurate and had a longer range than the musket, many Indians preferred muskets for hunting because they were comparatively inexpensive, easy to load, shot almost any kind of ball and were effective at

Trapper Osborne Russell made several interesting observations about elk hunting: "its [elk] speed is very swift when running single but when running in large bands they soon become wearied by continual collision with each other and if they are closely pursued by the hunter on horse back they soon commence dropping down flat on the ground to elude their pursuers and will suffer themselves to be killed with a knife in this position: when the band is first located the hunters keep at some distance behind to avoid dispersing them and to frighten them the more a continual noise is kept up by hallooing and shooting over them which causes immediate confusion and collision of the band and the weak Elk soon begin to drop on the ground exhausted" (Haines 1955:137). Such an exhaustion scenario, although possible for calves of a cow/calf band, seems farfetched. Also, no credible account of similar outcome of horseback hunting for elk has surfaced. The literature does support the contention that Crow Indians on horseback chased elk in the same way that they hunted on horseback for bison—by splitting the herd into two groups and flanking both (Raynolds 1868, Curtis 1970). *Painting by Alfred Jacob Miller; photo courtesy of the Public Archives of Canada C-411.*

short range (see Linton 1940, Wallace and Hoebel 1952, Mails 1972). Breech-loading firearms began to be acquired by the Indians in the late 1860s, and so were various repeating rifles (Winchester, Sharp, Spencer, Springfield) during the next decade (Hanson 1955, 1960). The single-shot Henry and Remington Rolling Block also became favored big game weapons, but the gun that ultimately replaced the bow and arrow as the Indian's primary weapon was the Winchester carbine (Mails 1972). It was lightweight, short barreled and easily maintained and repaired. However, it did not appear until after 1873, by which time the Western big game herds of bison, deer, pronghorn and elk had been seriously depleted. Guns, therefore, were not used extensively to hunt elk on the Great Plains, except by the Northern Cheyenne, Blackfeet, Assiniboine, Oglala Sioux, Crow and perhaps the Gros Ventre and Arapaho (see, e.g., Denig 1930). The gun's principal drawbacks were: (1) the difficulty

of getting ammunition in quantity (available ammunition was prudently reserved for bison hunting and warfare); (2) trade muskets were difficult to load on horseback or shoot with sufficient rapidity (Lowie 1963); (3) most guns (particularly cap or percussion locks [see Bidwell 1937]) were unreliable in the cold or damp weather when most elk hunting was done; (4) gunshots in mountainous habitats caused elk and deer to disperse and flee too far to be pursued easily (Ewers 1958); and (5) gunshots could alert enemies. Because guns generally were inefficient for mass killing of elk, some tribes, such as the Pawnee, opted for bows and arrows even when rifles and ammunition were readily available (Denig 1930, Oswalt 1966, Curtis 1970). The aforementioned Indians who used guns to hunt elk overcame the problem of ammunition scarcity by reloading shell casings as many as 50 times and using lead shot or projectiles broken up from cartridges of other calibers (Dodge 1882).

Crow Indians wait in ambush as a column of elk migrates along a game trail. Note that the lead Indian (center) is holding two sticks in the same hand that cradles his rifle. Such sticks typically were stuck in the ground to form an X and served as a mount to steady the gun when shooting. *1887 painting by Charles M. Russell; courtesy of the Amon Carter Museum.*

Guns were used in a communal hunt by unmounted Assiniboine in pursuit of elk "in droves of 100 to 300 . . . found in the large timber bottoms of the Missouri and Yellowstone," according to Denig (1930:537). The hunt involved ceremony and was led by a "divining woman" who had had a dream or vision of hunt success. At the head of a group of 15 to 25 hunters, the woman, stripped to the waist, barelegged, painted yellow and wearing an antler-resembling wreath of bushes with leaves, proceeded to where she dreamed the elk would be. There, she commenced to sing an incantation, while the hunters went in search of the elk. When the animals were located, the hunters separated and flanked the herd on opposite sides. The hunters "commence firing and running toward them, loading and firing while running, in quick succession, when the elk become confused, scatter and turn in different directions, presenting at times a mark for each of the hunters. Every shot bewilders them more, and instead of running in any one direction they keep turning every way until a great many are killed." (Denig 1930:537)

Lowie (1963) indicated that fire was used by the Santee Sioux, Miami and other prairie tribes to surround elk and other big game and to drive the animals to pits or enclosures. Kiowa Apache, Gros Ventre and Cheyenne hunted "by stalk-ing or by ambush as they [elk] came to a waterhole . . ." (Capps 1973:101, see also Flannery 1953). This strategy also was widely used on the central Plains by other tribes to hunt pronghorn, bighorn sheep and deer, and likely was used to kill elk as well.

Sarsi Indians of the northern Plains hunted bison primarily by decoying them into impoundments and shooting them from horseback. However, elk "were never hunted with horses, because they would turn and gore their pursuers. Animals of the deer kind were never driven into corrals" (Curtis 1970[18]:94–95). They hunted elk only occasionally and used stalking, pitfalls and driving over cliffs as the usual tactics. The Sarsi held that elk were not as wary as moose. When elk were approached they sometimes simply stared at the hunter, who was then able to move close enough to shoot. Disguises were not used. Hunters generally approached behind cover and, when ready to make the kill, advanced rapidly into the open. Unlike their neighbors, the Blackfeet and Plains Cree, Sarsi Indians did not use impoundments to capture elk (Curtis 1970).

"Whistles made of wood like the mouthpiece of a clarinet are used [by Assiniboine] to call both deer and elk . . . and are then a useful decoy" (Denig 1930:537).

Northern Blackfeet hunted elk as much as did the Sarsi,

Some Indians were loathe to use firearms to hunt big game because shooting was noisy; it scared off other potential quarry and could alert nearby enemies. Also, most guns available to Indians before the 1860s were inefficient and difficult to maintain. Thereafter, even with better guns, ammunition of the proper caliber frequently was scarce and usually was kept in reserve for warfare. Also thereafter, it was not long before elk were scarce. Nevertheless, many Indians on the Plains eagerly embraced the powerful hunting weapons. *Artwork by Making Medicine, a Cheyenne prisoner at Fort Marion, Florida, in 1875; courtesy of the Smithsonian Institution Anthropological Archives.*

The Assiniboine was one of the few Plains tribes that used dogs to hunt big game, although many tribes used dogs as pack animals. Assiniboine hunters reportedly were skilled marksmen with the bow and arrow and were particularly accomplished at snaring big game. They occasionally held communal hunts for bands or herds of elk but also stalked single animals. Traps or pits were not methods of elk capture used by the Assiniboine (Denig 1930). *Photo by Edward S. Curtis; courtesy of the Amon Carter Museum.*

whereas the Piegan and Blood subdivisions (particularly in Montana) hunted them more often. Ewers (1974) indicated that elk was much less important than were bison and beaver in the Blackfeet economy. As noted, Blackfeet hunters frequently used impoundments and were not averse to shooting elk from horseback, especially after acquiring rifles. Osborne Russell observed Blackfeet Indians drive elk to water where the animals were shot with guns (Haines 1955). Interestingly, according to Welch (1944:136), Blackfeet who first saw horses in the 1730s referred to them as elk-dogs, because the "horse looked something like an elk" and, like a dog, "could be domesticated to carry things."

The Assiniboine hunted elk year-round, but preferably during winter, when the animals could be pursued easily on snowshoes (Lowie 1963). These Indians made effective use of dogs to chase big game and to transport the meat and other carcass parts. The Plains Cree also used dogs to hunt elk that were plentiful in the parklands of Alberta, Saskatchewan and Manitoba, when deep snow facilitated short

chases. Only occasionally were elk hunted from horseback or impounded, which were the usual practices for killing bison and moose, respectively.

Except for the Assiniboine and Plains Cree, most Plains Indians did not use dogs to hunt big game or else abandoned their use after horses were commonplace. With big game herds easy to locate, dogs were of limited usefulness (see Driver 1969, Thomas and Ronnefeldt 1976).

Only the Assiniboine, Plains Cree, Sarsi and Arapaho are known to have worn snowshoes to hunt elk in deep snow on the Great Plains, although it may have been a technique of the Sioux, Ponca, Mandan, Blackfeet, Hidatsa and Gros Ventre who hunted bison in this manner (see Curtis 1970). Oto hunters chased elk to rivers covered with thin ice, where the animals fell through and were killed while struggling futilely to reach shore. Ponca hunters similarly drove elk to ice, where the animals had difficulty keeping their footing and were more easily pursued and killed (Howard 1995).

Although the horse and rifle greatly enhanced the ability of Plains Indians to kill elk, their advent does not seem to have appreciably altered the status of elk as a secondary resource. The innovations also improved the Indians' ability to harvest sufficient numbers of bison to meet most of their needs (Paine 1935, Gard 1968, Rorabacher 1970). C. E. Kay (personal communication:1995) opined that, although the horse certainly increased Native Americans' hunting efficiency, disease had so decimated the Native populations by the time horses appeared that ungulate kill rates declined and ungulate populations increased (see also Geist 1998, Martin and Szuter 1999).

Southwest

Elk were hunted by a number of southwestern tribes, but apparently were not a regular or important feature of the Indians' diet in this region (see Ortiz 1979). To varying degrees, Indians of the Southwest were farmers or gatherers first and hunters second (Goddard 1975). Wild plants, jackrabbits, pronghorn and deer were the primary nonagricultural foods. Some tribes, such as the Santa Clara, Taos and Rio Grande Pueblos, made periodic visits to the Plains to hunt bison and trade with the Comanche and Kiowa (Ford 1983). The tribes known to have hunted elk include the Santa Ana, Santa Clara (Tewa), Taos (Tiwa), Pecos and Picuris Pueblos, Zuni, and the Havasupai, Jicarilla, Central Chiricahua, and Western Apache (see Ortiz 1979, 1983). Bourke (1891:129) reported that "some elk" were found by Apaches (probably Chiricahua) in the San Francisco Mountains and high elevations of the Sierra Mogollan Mountains of New Mexico (see also Cremony 1868). Among these tribes, the elk was an important game animal only to the Santa Ana Pueblo (Strong 1979). Given the limited historic distribution of elk in the Southwest and the big game hunting tendencies of Indians of the region, elk likely were hunted only occasionally by subtribes of the Hopi (before the 1600s) and Navajo. The same may have been true of Mexican Indian tribes including the Jocome, Jano, Suma and Concho.

Little is known of the Southwestern Indians' elk hunting methods. Goddard (1975) noted that the elk that occupied the region were not easily killed. The Tiwa reportedly killed elk driven to and trapped in narrow pits excavated in game trails (Curtis 1970). Santa Clara Pueblos often pursued big game, possibly including elk, on horseback and brought the animals down with bow and arrow at close range (Arnon and Hill 1979). Other Pueblo hunters—Taos, Pecos and Picuris, at least—hunted elk communally under the command of "war chiefs" (Goddard 1975:87). Jicarillo and Mescalero Apaches also hunted elk communally. A leader stationed shooters at advantageous ambush sites along well-used trails, and the animals were driven. The Central Chiricahua hunted elk for both hides and meat. Unlike Eastern Apaches, the Chiricahua commonly hunted big game alone or in groups of two or three, and women were discouraged from participation. They used deer antler disguises to approach deer, but they found elk antlers too heavy, cumbersome and unnecessary in elk hunting because the elk "is not as smart as the deer and is easier to get" (Opler 1941:325, see also Haley 1981). Elk were hunted in autumn when they were fat and their hides in prime condition.

California

Methods used to hunt elk in California appear to have been as varied as the habitats in which elk were found and nearly as numerous as the Indian tribes that cohabited their range (Figure 40).

On California's Central Valley grasslands, Tule elk, wild horses, pronghorn and deer were abundant, and especially so in the San Joaquin and Sacramento valleys during winter months (see Marsh 1840, Millais 1915, Cook and Heizer 1951, McCullough 1971). However, the principal Indian inhabitants of the region—the Yocuts and Miwok—were not particularly proficient big game hunters (Cutis 1970). They subsisted primarily on acorns, other nuts, rabbits, ground squirrels and small birds. Nevertheless, attempts were made to capture big game. Levy (1978) noted that Tule elk and pronghorn were the terrestrial animals most important to the Plains Miwok, located in the area between present-day Sacramento and Stockton, but it must be remembered that big game was of limited consequence to these Indians. According to Wallace (1978b, 1978c), big game hunting was only a marginal subsistence activity of the Northern Valley Yocuts and Foothills Yocuts. The Foothill Yocuts—a group of about 15 tribes occupying the western slopes of the Sierra Nevada from the Fresno River southward to the Kern River—traveled north to the territory of the Plains Miwok to hunt Tule elk (Olmsted and Stewart 1978). Elk were somewhat more important to the Southern Valley Yocuts in the upper end of the San Joaquin valley from the lower Kings River to the Tehachapi Mountains, who rarely hunted elk in open country, preferring to shoot the animals as they came to drink at sloughs and lakes (Mayfield 1929). These Yocuts also set snares on springpoles along Tule runways that elk traveled to reach water. Elk were caught in the snares by their antlers, then dispatched by spears or bows and arrows. Cummins (1978) reported that the Yocuts' arrows often were unable to kill an elk outright, so

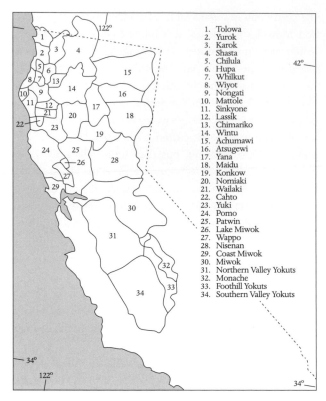

1.	Tolowa
2.	Yurok
3.	Karok
4.	Shasta
5.	Chilula
6.	Hupa
7.	Whilkut
8.	Wiyot
9.	Nongati
10.	Mattole
11.	Sinkyone
12.	Lassik
13.	Chimariko
14.	Wintu
15.	Achumawi
16.	Atsugewi
17.	Yana
18.	Maidu
19.	Konkow
20.	Nomiaki
21.	Wailaki
22.	Cahto
23.	Yuki
24.	Pomo
25.	Patwin
26.	Lake Miwok
27.	Wappo
28.	Nisenan
29.	Coast Miwok
30.	Miwok
31.	Northern Valley Yokuts
32.	Monache
33.	Foothill Yokuts
34.	Southern Valley Yokuts

Figure 40. Some principal Indian tribes of California. *Adapted from Maxwell (1978) and Heizer (1978).*

it became necessary for groups of Indians to chase down wounded animals. John Work led a fur company brigade into California's Central Valley in the early 1830s and observed: "The people are rather short of food and . . . are not able to kill the elk. There are a good many [Tule elk] along the marshy borders of the lake but they seldom venture out on the hard ground and when any of them happen to be found out, they fly immediately in among the water and bulrushes where they cannot be pursued" (Maloney 1945:62). However, when floodwaters forced elk to higher ground, the Natives were able to kill them with reported ease (Mayfield 1929).

Both the Yocuts and Miwok commonly used the drive-to-ambush method. In the southernmost portion of the Yocuts' territory, fire was used to drive elk (Curtis 1970). The Miwok still-hunted from brush blinds along game trails, attempted to drive their quarry over precipices, stalked them wearing deer skin heads with wooden antlers and used snowshoes to chase down elk that foundered in deep snow.

North and west of the Yocuts and Miwok, to the northern reaches of the Central Valley, were the Patwin, Nisenan, Konkow and Yana tribes. Patwin hunters—either singly or in small groups—pursued Tule elk (Johnson 1978). The Nisenan usually killed elk along waterways as the animals la-

bored in soft ground (Wilson and Towne 1978). Yana Indians ambushed elk and other big game at salt and mineral licks.

Curiously, neither snares nor pitfalls were used extensively by any of the Central Valley tribes to capture elk (Olmsted and Stewart 1978), although they were used by Southern Valley Yocuts (Mayfield 1929).

Immediately to the east of the Yana and Konkow were the Maidu, who occupied a portion of the Sierra Nevadas. They hunted big game and purportedly were somewhat more skillful at this than were their neighbors to the west and south (Dixon 1905, Curtis 1970). As did most California Indians, the Maidu drove elk past concealed hunters. In addition, they caught elk and other large ungulates in nets, and stalked them wearing deer masks, rabbit skin blankets and gypsum body paint. Riddell (1978) stated that Maidus sometimes hunted elk by persistent chasing, until the animals were exhausted. In the mountainous region of their territory, both they and their Konkow neighbors chased elk and deer to long, V-shaped, brush-lined chutes, where the animals were shot by bowmen. Whether the chutes led to an enclosure is uncertain. According to Curtis (1970), the most common method of killing big game was the collective drive to water. The swimming animals then were caught by the hind legs and their throats cut. Contrarily, Kroeber (1925) wrote that elk were taken most frequently by being run down over the course of several days by men on snowshoes.

North of the Maidu, still within Sierra Nevada forest habitat and in the northeastern corner of California, lived the Achumawi. These riverine Indians made use of pits to capture elk, deer and bear (see Voegelin 1942). In fact, early settlers of the region found such an extensive network of pitfalls excavated by Achumawi that they named a major waterway through the region the Pit River (Olmsted and Stewart 1978).

Just to the south of the Achumawi were the Atsugewi Indians. Eastern Atsugewi, or Apwaruge, used fire drives and surrounds in mountainous areas to take elk "charmed" by special songs sung the night before a communal hunt (Garth 1978).

West of the uppermost Central Valley, in an area encompassing the northern end of the California chaparral habitat, was the homeland of the Wintu, Yuki and Nomiaki tribes. In this region of the contiguous Cascade/Sierra Madres mountain ranges, elk were fairly common, but not easily hunted. The Wintu hunted elk only in winter, when they could chase them down on snowshoes (Curtis 1970). Nomlaki Indians reportedly hunted deer and elk by running them down in relays (Goldschmidt 1978). To supplement a diet staple of fish, Yuki Indians used snares and nets to trap birds and mammals. Elk, however, were difficult to ensnare and generally found only in places of limited access. Still, the Coast Yuki set snares on elk trails, often after blocking openings in adjacent undergrowth (Kroeber 1925).

North of the Wintu, also occupying primarily mountain forestland, were the Chimariko, Karok, Chilula, Hupa and Shasta. Salmon was the primary food of these tribes, and it was supplemented by nuts, berries, roots, upland game-birds and big game. The Chimariko, who lived along the Trinity River, were unique in that they used converging fires to hunt big game, including elk (Silver 1978). The Karoks, occupying lands along the middle course of the Klamath River, sometimes used dogs to herd elk into ravines (Bright 1978). The Shasta hunted elk in winter by stalking, but more commonly by wearing snowshoes and chasing the animals into deep snow. Both these techniques were used by the Hupa and Chilula as well, although these hunters also used deer masks with natural antlers for stalking, drove elk with trained dogs and forced the elk to water, where they were killed by men in canoes (Wallace 1978a). In addition, they devised snares that were hung along trails at the elk's head height. The noose end was held open by thin strings that broke when any pressure was exerted, and thick iris-fiber rope end was fastened securely to a strong sapling. Elk then were driven along the trail, ensnared and shot with short sinew-lined bows and stone-tipped arrows (Mason 1889).

Wistar (1914:196) recounted an episode in California that is convincing testimony to the effectiveness of the Indians' snares set to capture elk: "before taking leave . . . I must not forget to mention the extraordinary skill of those Indians in snaring elk and other large animals in nooses of stout rope made by themselves from bark, which sometimes got them into trouble with the whites as in the following case: At Durkee's some of his friendlies once confided to me with much secrecy a mysterious accident they had met with which they feared would peril their friendly relations with Durkee. Accompanying them therefore at their urgent request some miles to the top of the ridge they pointed out an unlucky ox belonging to Durkee which must have been dead for a fortnight and still lay just as he perished in a running noose set for an elk on a well-marked runway. The noose had been skillfully arranged by placing a log for the game to step over and a branch necessary to stoop under, the two together well calculated to divert attention from the snare itself. Two long brush fences extended from the spot on either hand obtuse angled toward each other so that any animal traversing the runway would surely be a led directly to the noose and get entangled while avoiding the obstacles placed to distract his attention. Unfortunately Durkee's ox, unaccustomed to such fiendish contrivances in the far-off Missouri prairies of his youth, had in this case

fallen an easy victim and perished by a lingering and solitary death."

Elk hunters of California's coastal region included the Pomo, Sinkyone, Mattole, Wiyot, Yurok and Tolowa. The Pomo sometimes hunted elk in teams, traditionally including several drivers, packers and a stalker wearing a deer hide and mask. They also drove elk to brush fence surrounds. Mattole and Sinkyone Indians depended greatly on Columbian black-tailed deer and Roosevelt elk, even more so than on fish and other wildlife (Kroeber 1925, Elsasser 1978a). Elk and deer were the most important land mammals for the Wiyot (Elsasser 1978b). Tolowa Indians usually captured elk in deep, U-shaped pits that were narrow at the bottom and filled with crossed stakes to prevent the animal from jumping out. These Indians also used dogs to drive elk into snares (Du Bois 1936). And on rare occasions, Tolowa archers stalked or still-hunted elk at dusk. On the other hand, Wiyot hunters commonly set snares to hunt elk. These snares were placed in timber around clearings in which elk fed. Dogs were used to chase the feeding animals into the snares, which were attached to the middle of a pole that prevented the ensnared elk from running off (Curtis 1970).

Chasing big game was a ritualistic procedure for the Yurok (Waterman 1920, Spott and Kroeber 1942). In preparation for an elk hunt of this kind, a hunter often lived apart from his wife for as long as 8 weeks. The hunt itself consisted of setting dogs on a recent or fresh elk trail and chasing the animal. Although the pursuit might last as long as 2 days before the elk was brought to bay by the dogs, the hunter did not eat. After the elk was killed by bow and arrow, it was quartered and hung. The hunter then returned to the village to send others to retrieve the carcass, hide and antlers. This manner of hunting was called *raqhlii^ra*, which also signified pack hunting of deer and elk by wolves (Curtis 1970).

Pacific Northwest Coast

According to La Farge (1957:193), the Pacific Northwest coastal region had "poor to good hunting of deer, bear, mountain sheep and elk . . . [and] hunting land animals was something of a luxury . . . as well as hardy sport." (Note: this mention of hunting big game as sport was one of few such references found in the literature. Other historians suggest just the opposite, typified by Grinnell's (1972[I]:257) statement that, "To the Indian, hunting was work, and often work of the hardest kind" [see also Kohl 1860].)

Elk hunting in this region was reserved, for the most part, for autumn and winter "when snow drove the animals from the mountains to the lower coastal areas" (Maxwell 1978:289). Among Southern Coast Salish, Twana villages conducted community drives in autumn and dried the meat for winter (Elmendorf 1960). However, Quileute Indians, who hunted terrestrial animals infrequently (see Hodge 1910), sought Roosevelt elk in the mountains in July (Frachtenberg 1916, Reagan 1922). Some Coastal Salish Indians did not wait for elk to descend, and pursued them in high mountainous areas where they could be surrounded in deep, crusted snow. Muchalat and Opetchesaht—Nootkan groups from Vancouver Island—used snowshoes to run down elk in deep snow and dispatched the animals with yew spears (Sproat 1868, Drucker 1951).

Indians of the Pacific Northwest were efficient and capable elk hunters (Figure 41), and they relied primarily on communal drives to snares, pitfalls, nets and deadfalls. In the first decade of the 1800s, Meriwether Lewis and William Clark observed Indians use all of these measures (Thwaites 1969). Cooper (1860:170) noted that, "In some places the Indians formerly surrounded the herds, and gradually narrowing their circle, succeeded in killing many. It is almost useless to hunt them [elk] in the forest, where the dense underbrush gives them every advantage over their persuer [sic]."

A common method described by Lewis and Clark involved pits: "Their [Chinook, Clatsop and Tillamook Indians] pitt [sic] are employed in taking [sic] the Elk, and of Course are large and Deep, Some of them a Cube of 12 or 14 feet. [T]hese are usually placed by the Side of a large fallen tree which as well as the pit lye [sic] across the roads frequented by the Elk, these pitts [sic] are disguised with the Slender boughs of trees and moss; the unwary Elk in passing the tree precipitates himself into the pitt which is Sufficient deep to prevent his escape, and is thus taken" (Thwaites 1969[3]:347–349). This technique also was mentioned by Jedediah Smith in 1828, who observed its use in an area (southwestern Oregon) inhabited by Coos and Suislaw Indians (Harper 1980).

Coastal Salish Indians also used pitfalls and usually placed sharpened stakes at the bottom. Their pits were carefully concealed by mats of brush and moss, and considerable care was taken to assure that the pit covers blended with the surrounding ground cover. Elk then were driven cautiously—in such away as to encourage them to move steadily, without scattering or leaving the trail—to the pit or pits.

Stillaguamish hunters used a mountain pass to drive elk over a cliff (W. Suttles personal files).

Bella Coola, Nootka and Kwakiutl hunters placed long, flat, wide-meshed sinew nets across elk runways and anchored the ends to resilient fir saplings. Elk then were driven along fences or barriers to the nets, where they were entangled and easily dispatched (Driver 1969, 1972, Curtis 1970). These Indians also used spring traps and deadfalls (Boas 1906a, Goddard 1924).

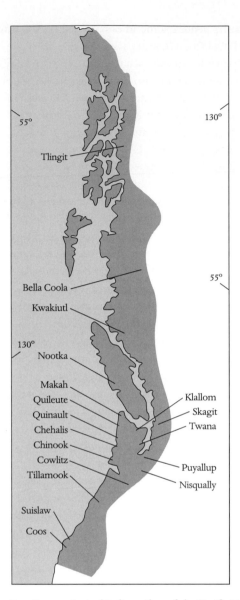

Figure 41. Some principal Indian tribes of the Pacific Northwest. *Adapted from Voegelin and Voegelin (1966) and Maxwell (1978).*

Lewis and Clark recorded that Clatsop and Tillamook Indians used small dogs to drive elk (Thwaites 1969). Curtis (1970) cited use of medium-sized dogs by Twana and Upper Chenault hunters to trail elk and noted that different breeds of dogs were used to hunt other wildlife (primarily deer and bear).

Puget Sound Salish (Skagit, Klailam, Lummi, Puyallup and others) made a practice of chasing elk to water, often using dogs, occasionally human drivers and sometimes fire (Chittenden and Richardson 1969, Suttles 1990). Once in the water, the elk were clubbed or shot with bows and arrows by men in canoes. And it was not unusual for a group of women to use this method if an elk was caught swimming between islands in the Sound (Underhill 1944). Miller and Seaburg (1990) reported that southwestern Oregon

Athapaskan hunters sometimes drowned elk swimming in winter.

The primary hunting implements of the Pacific Northwest Indians were the spear or gig, bow and arrow, metal-tipped club, and gun (Boas 1906a, Curtis 1970, Suttles 1990). The Kwakiutl and Makah were quite successful with bows and arrows, bringing down elk driven to ambush by beaters. However, Lewis and Clark observed that not all coastal Indians were accomplished at hunting elk with these weapons: "Elk was [*sic*] plenty in the mountains, but they could not kill many of them with their arrows" (Thwaites 1969[3]:326). The two expedition leaders further noted that many of the elk taken by their own party had been wounded by arrows, with bits of barb remaining in the animals and flesh growing around it. (Ironically, less than 8 months later [August 1806], Lewis was to regret the mediocre elk hunting skill and superior marksmanship of one of his own men. Somehow mistaking Lewis for an elk, Pierre Cruzatte shot him in the thigh.)

Guns used at the time were old muskets, with limited killing power or range. The Hudson's Bay Company produced these lightweight, short-barreled, cheaply constructed muskets, known as trade guns or fusees, specifically for the Indians (Mails 1972). When ammunition from traders was in short supply the Indians substituted gravel or pieces of pot metal that, according to Lewis and Clark, had minimal effect on the elk but was devastating to the guns.

Great Basin

Much of the Great Basin and Intermountain region is an amalgam of physiographic features generally inhospitable to people and animals alike. It is comprised of numerous alkaline and salt basins and sagebrush-dominated plains, bordered by steep mountains. The region contains few permanent sources of water. Except where the Great Basin grades into the semiarid steppe regime of the central Rocky Mountains to the north and east and the Blue Mountains of Oregon to the northwest, it is not the type of landscape popularly associated with Indians or elk. Nevertheless, both Indians and elk persisted there, although elk "were very scarce . . . [and] could not be regularly relied upon as a primary source of food and raw materials for food and necessities" (Malouf 1966:3).

Most of the Indian inhabitants were of Shoshonean stock, and there existed a sharp contrast between tribes occupying the northern and eastern montane belts and those in or around the lowlands to the south and west (Figure 42). The latter, including the Gosiute, Southern Paiute, Paviotso, Washo, Western Shoshone and Mono, were gatherers (popularly referred to as Diggers), who eked out a meager subsistence primarily from roots, berries, nuts, seeds,

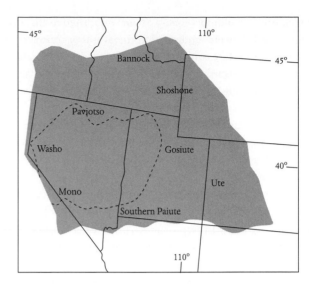

Figure 42. Some principal Indian tribes of the Great Basin region. The Great Basin is outlined by dash line. Other geomorphic provinces within the region include the Colorado Plateaus to the east, the Wyoming Basin to the northeast, the Columbia Plateaus to the north and the Intermountain zones of the northern, middle and southern Rocky Mountains. *Adapted from Voegelin and Voegelin (1966), Maxwell (1978) and Beck and Haase (1989)*

greens, insects and small mammals (Wissler 1966). Only rarely and in small numbers were elk found within the territories of these tribes. Plus, there is little evidence to suggest that these Indians, with the exception of the Gosiutes, had much opportunity to hunt elk. However, given the fact that most of them secured whatever food they could whenever possible, it is possible that elk were hunted at some time by all but the Mono (see Goddard 1924, Curtis 1970).

The Bannocks and Northern Shoshone (along with the Northern Paiute sometimes collectively known as the Snakes) to the north, and the Utes to the east, who resided in the mountains overlapping the Plateau and Great Plains regions, respectively—principally were hunters. Although these tribes are linked ethnologically to the Great Basin, they actually were geographically and culturally more akin to Indians of the Plateau region. In any case, big game, such as elk, mountain sheep, deer, bear and pronghorn, was sufficiently plentiful to constitute a significant portion of their diet, according to Hultkrantz (1974a). The Bannocks and many Shoshones and Utes opted to make seasonal bison hunting expeditions to the Great Plains (Haines 1977).

For the Gosiute, Paiute and Western Shoshone, considerable ritual was attendant to communal hunts for elk (see Malouf 1974). Steward (1941) reported that ambushing, stalking and trailing were the preferred hunting techniques. Elk also were captured in pits and driven to surrounds, although these methods were used more frequently to hunt pronghorn. Stalking often was accomplished using disguises, and elk were ambushed from natural or constructed concealments. Fire sometimes was used to drive animals to enclosures (Steward 1941, 1943, Fowler 1986). Most characteristic of the big game hunting by these Indians were communal drives (to pits, surrounds and enclosures) that involved participation by all members of tribal units, including women and children, and nearly exclusive use of bow and arrow (Malouf 1974). Few, if any, of these Indians had horses.

Most subtribes of the Bannocks, Northern and Southern Ute, and Northern Shoshone were experienced elk hunters, particularly the Northern Bannock (in southern and central Idaho), the Wind River, Fort Bridger, Mountain and Prairie Shoshone, and the Northern Ute. Emmitt (1954) wrote that Ute Indians in the vicinity of Meeker, Colorado, easily dispatched elk that came to water sources. He added that fire was used to drive elk from forests into the open. Callaway et al. (1986) observed that individual Utes typically stalked elk. Dodge (1882:578) reported that "mountain Indians made a sort of surround of elk in winter which is said to be very successful. During the deep snows, this animal collects in great herds on the high exposed slopes from which the wind has driven the snow. A herd being discovered in such position, the Indians creep around and drive them into a deep snow-drift, where they are butchered at leisure" (see also Smith 1974).

Hoebel (1938) labeled a group of Shoshone, who lived just east of the Teton Mountains, as elk eaters. Hultkrantz (1974a), however, denied that such a distinctive tribal group existed (although there was a subtribe—the Lemhi Shoshone or Northern Snakes—known as the sheep [bighorn] eaters) and noted that, in all areas rich in elk and deer, Shoshones hunted both (cf. Kay 1994).

For the northern Great Basin Indians, elk was important winter meat (see Malouf 1974), but bison, mountain sheep, deer, pronghorn, hares and particularly wild plants were of greater year-round subsistence value. These Indians had horses and guns, and both were used in hunting elk by the Northern Ute and Wind River Shoshone. Stalking, ambushes, drives and snares were used regularly to kill elk, and there is a suggestion that some Bannocks also used pits (Curtis 1970). Hultkrantz (1974b) indicated that small groups of Northern Shoshone hunted elk on snowshoes. And, Lowie (1963) reported their use of dogs to chase elk (see also Driver 1969).

The Northern Ute and Wind River Shoshone were especially competent trackers and stalkers of elk and deer (see Wilson 1919). Sir Rose Lambert Price, a retired British army officer, raconteur and member of the Seward Webb elk hunting party in the late 1800s, provided a first-hand ac-

This extraordinary historical photograph by F. Jay Haynes in 1874, shows Emerson Hough in Yellowstone National Park's Hayden Valley, on assignment for George Bird Grinnell, to observe and report on the ease with which elk could be and were being killed by poachers on skis or snowshoes during winter. Hough, a New Mexico attorney and writer, produced a series of articles that Grinnell published and used successfully to promote enactment of the Yellowstone Park Protection Act, which provided protection for all birds and animals in the park and prosecution of violators. Except perhaps for the Yellowstone Organic Act (which established the park), the Yellowstone Park Protection Act is regarded by some as the first important piece of federal legislation pertaining specifically to wildlife conservation (Trefethen 1975). Dramatically and ironically, the scene shows the technique of "crusting"—approaching big game in or chasing big game to deep snow in which the animals floundered and could not escape pursuers on snowshoes. Crusting for elk was widely practiced among subarctic, Pacific Northwest and Rocky Mountain Indian hunters. *Photo courtesy of the Montana State Historical Society.*

count of the character and hunting capability of the Shoshone: "I recall the delicate way he [his Shoshone guide, Tigee] avoided wounding my *amour propre* when I was so frequently toiling after him up some semi-perpendicular mountain, thickly strewn with fallen timber, following a hot trail of elk. He himself would go like a steam engine, and 'stay' almost forever, but I could not. So Tigee, when he saw that I was about played out, would pretend that he was tired and would sit down with an air of extreme lassitude and asked me if I could rest a bit." (Tilden 1964:242).

Plateau

There were four basic subsistence patterns in the Plateau or Columbia River basin region (Figure 43), and elk was a component of each. Virtually all tribes hunted elk, which were common in the mixed coniferous-deciduous mountain forests that characterized this habitat province (cf. Kay 1994, Kay and White 1995). As elk hunters, Plateau Indians were unique in several aspects.

First, the Plateau tribes tended to be acculturated to the lifestyles and economics of tribes in proximate ethnographic regions (Maxwell 1978, Ruby and Brown 1972). On the western Plateau, the Indians were villagers who adopted the subsistence traits of the Pacific Northwest coastal Indians. Fish (salmon in particular) constituted as much as 80% of their diet (Haines 1970a) and was supplemented by wild plants in summer and big game (deer, elk, bear) in winter. Southern and southwestern Plateau Indians were influenced by the harvesting and food gathering practices of the northern California and northern Great Basin tribes. They also traded extensively with Pacific Northwest coastal tribes. Wild plants were especially important in their diets, followed closely by fish, deer, elk, mountain sheep

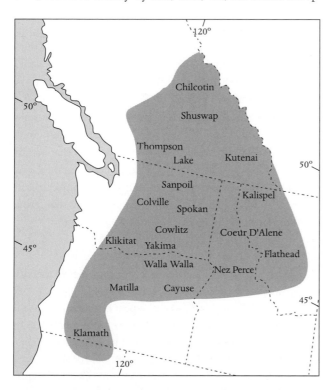

Figure 43. Some principal Indian tribes of the Plateau region. *Adapted from Voegelin and Voegelin (1966) and Maxwell (1978).*

and bear (see Driver and Massey 1957, Maxwell 1978). To the north, the Plateau Indians favored the subsistence role of their subarctic neighbors, splitting their time between fishing and hunting for moose, deer, caribou and elk. Boas (1906b:220) noted that deer, elk, moose, mountain goats, mountain sheep and other game mammals were "infinitely more important in the domestic economy of the [northern Plateau] people than . . . among the coast tribes." In the eastern portion of the Plateau, most tribes' customs and traditions reflected those of the western Plains Indians. These Indians tended to be seminomads, frequenting the Plains for short periods in summer and longer in autumn and winter to hunt bison, and gathering wild plants and hunting deer, elk and mountain sheep in summer on the Plateau west of the Rockies (Ewers 1974, Warner 1975). Fahey (1974:20) observed that pursuing bison on the Plains by Plateau Indians was a matter of preference because "hunting for other animals was seasonably good in their montane homeland." Only on the central Plateau were tribes culturally distinct. These Indians lived year-round on salmon supplemented with deer, elk, wild plants and sometimes bear, mountain sheep and birds.

Second, for many of the Plateau tribes, elk was important as a secondary food source, although some tribes relied on it as a primary source in late winter and early spring. The region typically experiences severe winters with heavy snowfall. This, combined with rugged terrain and a seasonal scarcity of primary and secondary foods other than elk, made elk a significant, if not necessary, food resource. Lewis and Clark—who spent considerable time in the region, observing the widespread and intensive use of elk and experiencing for themselves that animal's subsistence and material importance—reported that, along the Columbia River, "the Scad-dals, Squan-nan-os, Shan-wah-pums and Shallattas [Klikitat and Yakima tribes] . . . depend on hunting deer and Elk" (Thwaites 1969[4]:305). In reference to Indian subsistence on the eastern Plateau, Driver (1969:57) wrote that "a number of animals, such as moose, elk and deer, combined to make meat the staple."

Just as the Plateau Indians loosely identified with the subsistence economies and material cultures of regionally adjacent tribes, so too did they borrow hunting techniques and strategies. Communal drives to enclosures, pits and deadfalls were usual elk hunting methods (see Johnson 1969, Thwaites 1969, Fahey 1974). Colvilles and others also drove the animals over cliffs. And a number of tribes, including the Cowlitz, Klamath, Kutenai and Flathead, used dogs to drive or chase elk (see, e.g., Lowie 1963); fire was used almost exclusively by tribes in the eastern areas, including the Kutenai, Coeur d'Alene and Kalispel. Kalispel hunters sometimes surround an area several miles in circumference, around a scattered herd of elk. By predetermined schedule or signal, the hunters, either mounted or afoot, moved toward the center, gradually driving the elk ahead. When the "noose" was tight, the confused, milling elk were dispatched with arrows and spears. Snaring was practiced throughout the southwestern and western Plateau, and netting was used by some tribes to the north and west. Such northern Plateau tribes as the Chilcotin, Shuswap, Okanagan, Lake and Thompson were known for their ability to drive big game, including elk, to water, where the animals were shot with bows and arrows from horseback or canoes. The Nez Percé did the same in the southern part of the region.

Indians of the Klikitat and a number of Interior Salish tribes chased elk through mountainous forests where other hunters were stationed behind large trees. When the elk ran past the hidden hunters, they were speared. The hunters did not pursue a wounded animal immediately. Instead, they returned a day later when the elk was too weak to escape.

Eastern Plateau tribes, including the Flathead, Kutenai, Nez Percé and Coeur d'Alene, reportedly were extremely skillful elk hunters (Chamberlain 1906, Curtis 1970, Fahey 1974). They were experienced horsemen who had been introduced to the gun by trappers and traders in the first decades of the 1800s. Chamberlain (1906) noted that the gun quickly replaced the bow and arrow as a hunting and warfare weapon. Elk hunts typically were communal operations, featuring surrounds, decoying, fire and horseback drives to water, traps and ambush (Walker 1978), although Johnson (1969) indicated that elk hunting on horseback was unusual because of the rough terrain and heavily timbered country in which elk were sought. Elk were available year-round on the Plateau, but most accessible in autumn and spring. They were at least as numerous and, because of the comparatively open countryside, more easily hunted on the western Plains, where the Plateau tribes traveled to hunt bison. However, Plateau Indians opted not to make summer forays to the Plains for elk because of the marauding, warring Blackfeet who also visited the Plains in that season, usually in numbers far exceeding that of Plateau hunting groups (Ewers 1958, Haines 1970a).

Perhaps the most complete and authoritative record of elk hunting techniques used by the eastern Plateau Indians is the writing and artwork of Jesuit missionary Father Nicolas Point (1967), who lived and worked with the Flathead, Coeur d'Alene, Nez Percé, Pend d'Oreilles (a Kalispel division) and Piegan Blackfeet, and traveled extensively in the region from 1840 to 1847. Among the methods Father Point observed the Indians using to capture and kill elk (which he called red deer) were drives by fire, dogs and "callers" to corrals, pits and waterways, ambushes (sometimes with constructed blinds) along trails when the animals descended from mountains, stalking by individual hunters or small groups and chasing elk in deep snow while wearing snowshoes.

Johnson (1969:65–66) reported that "Kutenais and Flatheads, and other Plateau peoples living even farther west [probably Nez Percé, Spokane, Cayuse and Walla Walla] had long used surrounds and jumps for elk and other big game." In the Mission Range of Montana, historically occupied by Pend d'Oreilles and Southern Flatheads, was a lowland that contained a natural brush enclosure. This feature was known as *Sinyalemin,* or The Surround, because the Indians surrounded elk there (McDonald 1917).

Baker (1955:33) noted the participation of entire "villages" in elk drives to enclosures: "A place was found where the animals could be driven into a narrow place such as between hills or mountains. Sometimes it was necessary to erect a barricade. The men who were more active would go out a distance and start the animals toward the barricade. The children, older men and women would be stationed in such a way as to herd the animals into the proper enclosure. Men had been appointed to do the killing when the animals got to the barricade."

As previously noted, the eastern Plateau Indians hunted bison on the Plains as a matter of preference and seldom out of necessity, given the abundance of deer, elk and other wildlife available year-round on the Plateau. This preference may have been influenced at least slightly by vanity. When Lewis and Clark (Thwaites 1969) wrote that mountain men became like the typical Northern Shoshone (many of whom lived on the southern Plateau in the warm months), who felt degraded if compelled to walk even a short distance, they revealed indirectly that at least some Indian horsemen disdained hunting afoot, which was the most practical way of securing elk in the mountainous, forested Plateau region. If true, despite the fact that Northern Shoshone and their eastern Plateau neighbors were exemplary elk stalkers, this would help to explain their willingness to make long, arduous and sometimes dangerous seasonal treks to the Plains to hunt bison.

Subarctic

The North American subarctic is geographically divided into three zones—Yukon, MacKenzie and eastern (see Helm 1981). Elk hunting was an aspect of Indian life in the latter two. The MacKenzie subarctic was inhabited by Northern Athapaskans, or Denes, and the elk-hunting clans included the Carrier, Slave, Chipewyan, Beaver and Sekani. The eastern subarctic was dominated by Central Algonquian Indians, of whom the Plains Cree and Western Ojibwa were elk hunters.

In the two zones—where the landscape has limited relief and is poorly drained (with numerous glacial lakes), and where coniferous forest is the dominant vegetation—big game (principally caribou and moose) was the most important food (see Reeves and McCabe 1998), followed by fish (salmon, whitefish, pickerel). The eastern subarctic Algonquians were seminomadic, whereas most Northern Athapaskans were relatively sedentary (Driver and Massey 1957, Murdock and O'Leary 1975). To both groups, the elk was of minor importance (Gillespie 1981).

In the MacKenzie subarctic, elk were found in and around present-day Wood Buffalo National Park in northern Alberta. They were hunted only on occasion as far north as the southern Yukon, and usually only to acquire food during shortage or to acquire hides for trade (Maxwell 1978). Samuel Hearne (1795:337), a British employee of the Hudson's Bay Company, who spent several years among the Northern Athapaskans while exploring the Canadian interior in the 1790s, wrote that elk "are the most stupid of all the deer kind, and frequently make a shrill whistling, and quivering noise . . . which directs the hunter to the very spot where they are. . . . Those deer are seldom an object of chace [sic] with the Indians . . . except when moose and other game fail."

The appearance of fur trappers and traders in the region, particularly at the northern Plains fringe, heightened the Indian kill of elk, because the hides, canine teeth and meat, in that order, were trade commodities.

Elk is rarely mentioned as a food item of the Western Ojibwa and Woods Cree in the eastern subarctic, but it was hunted north of Lake Superior and in Manitoba (Grant 1907, Gillespie 1981, Smith 1981). These Algonquians, as noted, were in perpetual pursuit of the migratory caribou, and the limited seasonal overlap of elk and caribou historically may explain why elk was a rarity in the Indians' diet.

Throughout most of the subarctic, subsistence was especially a matter of feast or famine. Consequently, all the Indians' skills and resources were used to kill available game, including the less-preferred elk (Morrice 1906). The two most characteristic methods of hunting big game in the subarctic were driving to water and chasing on snowshoes (see Driver 1969).

Oswalt (1966) reported that Chipewyan, as typical Athapaskan hunters, drove big game to water, where the animals were killed with lances by men in canoes. In reference to Ojibwa hunting in this manner, Jones (1906:140) wrote: "Moose, caribou, elk, and deer were slain with the bow and arrow; they could be overtaken by canoe when swimming, and killed by cutting the throat. . . ." Jones also indicated that the Indians were able to punch holes with a paddle between the ribs of some swimming animals. Water then entered the puncture wound, causing the animal to weaken and drown.

Winter hunting on snowshoes, known as crusting, was common to all the MacKenzie and eastern subarctic hunters. With the aid of dogs, animals were chased to exhaustion by small hunting parties (see Reeves and McCabe 1998). This was the usual tactic for securing moose, and was used only infrequently to hunt deer and elk. Other hunting methods included surrounds and deadfalls. Elaborate funnel traps, some extending for as much as 3 miles (4.8 km) were used to drive caribou, bison and deer, but whether elk ever were captured in this fashion is unknown. Beaver and Carrier Indians made effective use of snares to kill big and small game (Keith 1890).

Hunting in the subarctic was the domain of adult tribal men (Newton and Hyslop 1995, see also Helm 1981). However, women and children assisted in drives and chasing animals in water. The primary hunting weapon was a powerful bow and arrows with unbarbed points of stone or bone. Lances, clubs and knives were other usual armaments.

Aboriginal Overkill

Kay (1994:385) claimed "a major paradigm shift of how ecosystems and aboriginal peoples should be viewed." The centerpiece of the proposition was an aboriginal overkill hypothesis. Although the data do not appear to be weighty enough to support a paradigm shift as encompassing as proposed, they invite a shift in ethnohistoric perspective and serve as the basis for the discussion of this section.

The aboriginal overkill hypothesis holds that predation by Native Americans—not fire or nonhuman predation—was the major factor limiting the number and distributions of ungulates in the Intermountain West. In essence, Kay considered that, for some length of time prehistorically and until European contact, aboriginals were the region's ultimate keystone species (see Mills et al. 1993). His investigations and analyses showed that, in concert with nonhuman predation, aboriginal killing of large ungulates could and did depress some populations of those species to levels far below that generally accepted as having been the case. In particular, Kay revealed that elk were uncommon or rare in at least large portions of the Intermountain region before Native Americans were eliminated or removed as an ecological factor in the late 1800s.

Contradicting the traditional notion that parts of the West, such as Yellowstone National Park, were "teeming" with wildlife (e.g., Randall 1980:188), including elk, before about 1870, Kay (1994) declared a lack of both archaeological evidence (cf. Sappington 1994, Schuknecht 2000) and documented first-hand observations (1790–1850) of large ungulates by early white explorers (the contention was emphatically rejected by Whittlesey [1998; see also Schullery 1996]) and presented vegetation analyses in support of his view that elk were "relatively rare for the past 10,000 years" in the Yellowstone region (see also Robbins 1998).

In support of his hypothesis that aboriginals were the ungulates' foremost limiting factor, Kay cited a number of theoretical considerations: prey switching and use of nonungulate foods; optimal foraging theory; age and sex structure of kills; synergism between Native Americans and carnivore predation; and the absence of aboriginal practices of sustained yield conservation. To these must be added the concepts of buffer zones and game sinks.

Prey Switching and Use of Alternative Foods

Despite the fact that Native Americans preferred meat when it was available (Webster 1983), 80% to 90% of the prehistoric and historic aboriginal diet was of vegetal foods and fish except for Arctic Eskimos and "perhaps" horse-culture Plains Indians, according to Kay (1994:370, cf. McCabe and McCabe 1984). Being able to switch to alternative foods, aboriginals presumably were able to exploit and even overexploit preferred prey and were willing to do so because the scarcity of game was viewed as a supernatural phenomenon, not an ecological consequence of overharvest.

Optimal Foraging Theory

Essentially, this theory holds that predator populations tend to exploit most opportunistically and profitably the prey base that best serves their dietary needs—a compromise of food volume, nutritive value and efficient acquisition. For Natives, ungulates and other large mammals represented the highest ranked foods. Aboriginal hunter-gatherers also sought the nonfood benefits (i.e., hides and tools made from body parts) of large ungulate prey. The fact, according to Kay, that aboriginal diets in the Intermountain region were skewed greatly toward nutritionally low-ranked vegetal foods, small mammals and fish was a priori evidence that populations of the large and high-ranked ungulates were depressed and, by presumption, depressed by aboriginals themselves.

Contrary to assertions otherwise, there is evidence that elk were neither absent nor scarce in the prehistoric Intermountain/Plateau region. Nez Percé Indians and their Paleo ancestors in the Clearwater River region of north-central Idaho, for example, exploited elk for 10,000 years or more (Sappington 1994, R. L. Sappington personal communication:2000). Archeological investigations showed that, in each of the Early (14,000–6,000 years ago), Middle (6,000–3,000 years ago) and Late (3,000–500 years ago) Prehistoric periods, plus in protohistoric time, elk were ex-

ploited by the indigenous people and an important dietary component (Sappington and Carley 1989, Schuknecht 2000). A species that is a regular and significant part of the Native diet for thousands of years in a particular region probably cannot be said to have been overkilled. And although fish and plants were the main subsistence items of the region, game animals still accounted for 15% to 25% of the Natives' diet, and among the dozen or so game species, only the white-tailed deer and mule deer were exploited more than elk (Marchal 1977).

Age and Sex Structure of Kills

Ungulate mortality profiles provide an estimation of predator effectiveness and mortality rates. Carnivores tend to take a disproportionate number of young, aged and otherwise weakened animals from a prey population, which Temple (1987:669) indicated "seems to be a direct function of how difficult it normally is for the predator to capture and kill individuals of that species." Also, where more than one predator species is taking animals from a prey population, the less-efficient predators tend to kill fewer prime age animals (Okarma 1984). Unlike carnivores, according to Kay, Native Americans primarily killed prime-aged ungulates (see Frison 1971, Nimmo 1971, Frison and Walker 1984, Roper 1986); therefore, they were arguably more efficient as an agent of mortality than were the Intermountain carnivores. The emphasis on killing prime age animals is counter to any strategy of sustained yield (Michod 1979, Hastings 1983, 1984), indicating that aboriginals could have had major impacts on ungulate populations.

Kay also noted that ungulate populations are most sensitive to mortality of breeding females; if too many are killed, the population will decline, sometimes precipitously. He observed that, whereas carnivores such as wolves and mountain lions take a disproportionate number of male prey (L. D. Mech [personal communication: 2000] wrote: "I don't believe there is good evidence that wolves tend to take more males than females."), some archeological data and historic accounts indicate that Native Americans preferred to take female ungulates (see Teit 1928, Ewers 1939, Wright and Miller 1976, Alvard 1993), as previously mentioned and because of a desire (see Speth and Spielmann 1983, Speth 1987) and perhaps even necessity (see Speth 1989, 1991, Spielmann 1989) for animal fat—prime age female ungulates tend to have greater fat stores than do other cohorts (see Flook 1970, Anderson et al. 1972, Johns et al. 1984). Accordingly, many investigators have reported the inclination of Native people, during particular hunts, to emphasize the take of animals of sex and age classes with highest fat levels (see Nelson 1973, 1983, Binford 1978, Speth 1983). Cow elk are in prime condition, with highest fat deposition, in autumn and early winter. In these seasons, elk congregate most frequently and at relatively huntable elevations, which (not coincidentally) was when hunting of elk by aboriginals was a relatively strategic subsistence enterprise, compared with killing elk in other seasons when the taking was primarily opportunistic. (Conversely, a number of investigators and chroniclers noted that the amount of meat that an animal provided was of paramount importance [Roberts 1932, Chittenden 1935, Heizer 1955, Wissler 1966], from which one might infer that Natives predominantly selected prime-aged elk and perhaps especially prime age bulls. Further inference of selectivity for bulls, or at least nondiscrimination toward taking adult elk is in the fact that the bulls' bugler teeth were highly prized, as discussed later.)

Kay argued that, by focusing on the animals of highest reproductive value (i.e., prime age females), Native Americans had greater impact on ungulate populations than did carnivore predators, whose prey was disproportionately the animals with least reproductive value (cf. Pimlott 1967, Mech 1970, Stalling 2000).

Synergism Between Natives and Carnivore Predation

Kay explained that wolves and other carnivores limit ungulate populations by reducing recruitment (mainly by taking calves or fawns) and increasing adult mortality, and that such limiting is additive, not compensatory (cf. Smith 1974). According to ungulate population models (Haber 1977, Walters et al. 1981), when predation on ungulates by native carnivores (such as wolves and bears) is in concert with human harvest of the ungulate population, the limiting effect is not only additive, but synergistic, and can cause a collapse of both the ungulate and carnivore populations. This would be true particularly where human predation emphasized the taking of prime age female ungulates.

Besides his continuous-time analysis (see Hastings 1983) of first-person explorer journal documentations of ungulates observed in the Yellowstone ecosystem (1835–1876), Kay (1995b) did not note a single, reliable observation of wolves, which was further indication of a small prey base. "Moreover," wrote Kay (1994:377), "if carnivore predators can limit ungulate numbers, and if they are less efficient predators than Native Americans . . . then it is easy to see how aboriginal peoples could have had a major impact on . . . ungulate populations."

The continuous-time documentations contained 53 references to Native Americans (Kay 1990, 1995b). The relative number of recorded sightings of ungulates, predators and aboriginals seems to validate that the diminishing returns of predation serve as a homeostatic mechanism of limitation of some predator populations, but not neces-

In nearly all period artwork of elk hunting by Indians—such as this 1830s painting by Alfred Jacob Miller, featuring "Snake" (Northern Shoshone) Indians shooting elk from ambush—the animals being chased and shot are mature bulls. This may indicate some degree of artistic license, but it suggests that, as a matter of practicality, Indians often attempted to take the largest elk—prime bulls. Cow elk hides were preferred and cows were relatively fatty during autumn and winter, when elk were most readily available. But, bulls had the most meat and the prized bugler teeth. There is some reliable documentation that certain Indians regularly selected cow bison over bull bison, but similar evidence regarding elk has not been identified. *Photo courtesy of the Walters Art Gallery.*

sarily the human predator (Cohen 1977), who readily adapts to alternative foods.

Finally, Kay supposed that another synergistic effect of carnivore and human predation competition for ungulates was that it likely precluded Indians from developing hunting territories (Bishop 1970, Dyson-Hudson and Smith 1978, Albers and Kay 1987, cf. McLeod 1936, Heizer 1955, Feit 1987) and other practices specifically to conserve ungulates (Smith 1974, cf. Elder 1965).

Sustained Yield Conservation

Kay made a determined effort to debunk the popular notion of the Native American as the original conservationist or a conservationist of wildlife at all, at least in modern connotative context. That the aboriginals disproportionately killed prime age (high-ranking) female ungulates was cited as proof.

Although Native Americans held belief of spiritual kinship with wildlife (see, e.g., Speck 1913, Martin 1978, Bettinger and Baumhoff 1982, Feit 1987), this did not preclude them from exploiting their resource base (Kay 1985a, 1985b). On the contrary, Kay (1995:123) wrote: "Since Native Americans saw no connection between their hunting and game numbers, their system of religious beliefs actually fostered overexploitation of ungulate populations. Religious respect for animals does not equal conservation." Kay noted as well that Indians did not have a concept of maximum sustained yield, therefore had no strategies to "manage" ungulate herds to produce the greatest "offtake." Instead, they acted in ways to maximize their own individual well-being regardless of environmental impact (Simms 1984, 1992). If accurate, these points—more comprehensively addressed by Kay (1994)—are not a harsh indictment of the aboriginals. They are an indictment, however, of the perpetuation of anthropological/ecological myth—a frequent by-product of overinterpreting the ideologies and behavioral motivations of extinct or remnant cultures.

Buffer Zones and Game Sinks

These concepts propose that abundance and distribution of ungulate populations in early historic and probably prehistoric times could have been influenced more by intertribal conflict than by habitat productivity (Martin and Szuter 1999, see also Hickerson 1965, 1970). Accordingly, where Indian tribes were in conflict, before significant European contact, there was between them a war zone or neutral zone where opposing factions avoided each other. In the absence of native predation, large mammal populations irrupted. As William Mark wrote on August 29, 1806: "I have observed that in the country between the nations which are at war with each other the greatest numbers of wild animals are to be found" (Moulton 1993[8]: 328). Where tribes were at peace, enabling the people to forage freely, game became scarce. Noteworthy game sinks on the Lewis and Clark expedition were on the Columbia plateau and in the Columbia basin. Exploration literature also tells of game sinks within known historic elk range, such as found by Jedediah Smith in the central Rockies and Great Basin in 1826, Joseph Walker in northern and central California in 1833, Stephen Long on the southern Plains in 1819 to 1820, to name a few.

Summary

Kay's proposed paradigm shift likely is discomforting to some ethnohistorians and biologists because it is diametrically opposed to long-held assumptions about former abundance and distribution of wildlife populations (such as elk in the Intermountain West)—what Geist (1998:4) called the "Pre-Columbian fallacy"—and the limiting role of aborigi-

nals, and because his arguments have theoretical merit at least. However, again, elevating the hypothesis to paradigm may require more evidence than is available in this case.

A caution advised in adopting and applying Kay's intriguing proposition is analysis based on cross-referencing anthropological information (or interpretations of that information) from one culture or cultural condition to others geographically or temporally distinct. And as Kay (1996:79) himself wisely noted: "With selective quotations, however, there is always a question of whether or not the author included only those passages that supported his or her preconceived notions."

Influence of Elk on the Material Culture of Indians

Food

As food, the elk typically was sought by North American Indians as a secondary source. In all the regions encompassed by the elk's vast historic range, elk meat and its other edible parts were less important to the Indians in terms both of availability and their food preference. Several other food items, including at least one other big game ungulate species were more sought after (Table 11). Only for a few tribes in the Pacific Northwest and Plateau regions was elk a staple, and it held that status only seasonally. To my knowledge, there was just one tribe—the Southern Kwakiutl (Goddard 1924)—and one tribal subunit—the Omaha's Elk clan (Fletcher and La Flesche 1972)—that hunted elk but did not eat it. Also, there were a number of Indians, including the Northern Blackfeet, Ojibwa, Chiricahua, Chipewyan and Slave tribes, who actively hunted and ate elk but did not greatly esteem the meat. In portions of California and the Plateau, northern Great Basin and Pacific Northwest, elk regularly was part of the Indian diet. In all other regions, it appears to have been periodic-to-infrequent fare.

As a secondary food source (and not always a favorite food), the elk was nevertheless quite important to the Indians' subsistence economy in most western regions of North America. Its most significant value in this respect was as a supplement to, or substitute for, primary foods during lean seasons. In some years and seasons, principal food resources were scarce, and they never were as predictable as the Indian appetite. The Indian saying, "When there is no meat, starvation stalks the camp" (Wissler 1966:247), accurately characterized their situation during those times.

The elk served a vital role because of its relative abundance and availability in months when primary foods were

Table 11.   Approximate rank of importance of elk and other nonvegetal foods in diets of historic North American Indians, 1500 to 1850

	Rank[a]			
Region	First	Second	Third	Fourth
Plains				
Northern	Bison	Beaver	Deer	*Elk*
Central	Bison	Deer	*Elk*	Pronghorn
Southern	Bison	Deer	Pronghorn	*Elk*
Pacific Northwest				
Northern	Fish; sea mammals	Deer	*Elk;* mountain goat	Bear; small mammals
Southern	Fish	Shellfish; *elk*	Small mammals; deer	Bear; birds
Plateau				
Eastern and northern	Bison	Deer; fish	*Elk;* bighorn sheep	Caribou; mountain goat
Western and southern	Fish	Deer	Bear	Bighorn sheep
California				
Northern	Fish	Birds	Bear	Small mammals
Central	Rodents	Fish	Deer	Pronghorn
Northeast	Deer	Small mammals	Bear	*Elk*
Great Lakes	Deer	Small mammals	Birds	Bear
Subarctic	Caribou	Fish; moose	Birds; rodents	*Elk*
Great Basin	Jackrabbit	Reptiles; insects	Deer; pronghorn	Bighorn sheep; deer
Southwest	Jackrabbit	Pronghorn; deer	Bison	*Elk*

Sources: Interpolated primarily from Driver (1969), Curtis (1970) and Maxwell (1978).

[a] Based on amount eaten, seasonal significance and preference, in that order.

difficult to locate and obtain. On the central Plains and eastern Plateau, for example, "The flesh and other edible parts of most of the animals hunted . . . were appreciated if there happened to be a dearth of buffalo, or as a welcome change during the winter months from the dried buffalo meat. . . . So far as additional meat diet is concerned . . . elk, deer, and antelope were the most important" (Flannery 1953:59). Chittenden (1935[2]:816) added that the elk's "wide distribution, large size, and comparative ease of capture made it a great resource when buffalo could not be had." Barsness (1985:104) observed that "most Plains Indians seldom ate deer, elk or pronghorn when bison meat was available. The preference was not merely cultural, as evidenced by the fact that members of the Long expedition on the Plains in 1854 discarded their supplies of elk meat whenever bison was to be had."

Except for a number of tribes in the Southwest and the Great Basin, the Indians who hunted elk were mainly meat- or fish-eaters, including the semiagriculturists. They depended on diets that invariably were high in protein, fat and minerals, and which reportedly were healthier than those of Indians in the East, Southeast and Southwest, who lived mainly by farming (Driver 1969). When elk was eaten as a supplement to or substitute for primary foods, the Indians' nutritional intake was not appreciably altered. Elk provided suitably high levels of protein, minerals, fat, salt and vitamins, including ascorbic acid in blood and raw meat.

One reason that Indians were able to derive sufficient nourishment from diets predominately of meat was the quantity consumed. Most ate at least two meals a day when game was plentiful, and they ate as much as they could; it likely was contrary to the provident nature of most to discard any part of an animal that could be eaten (Conrad 1890). Except during winter, in most regions it was not possible to store fresh meat for any length of time and impractical to transport it. Travelers in the West during the 1800s noted with amazement the Indians' willingness and ability to gorge themselves, especially at the peak of hunting seasons and before the onset of winter (see Berkeley 1861, Audubon and Bachman 1851, Hoffman 1896, Wislizenus 1912, McHugh 1979, cf. Catlin 1973).

A daily ration of fresh meat for an Indian has been estimated at 2 to 10 pounds (0.9–4.5 kg), depending on the season of the year and availability of other foodstuffs (Irving 1835, Wissler 1966, Haines 1970b). Nutritionists have suggested that 2 pounds (0.9 kg) was the daily average. However, records of fur trappers' provisions and observations indicate that an average of 4 pounds (1.8 kg) of meat per man, woman or child was a more probable figure (see Thompson 1916, Chittenden 1935, Phillips and Smurr 1961). At one point during the winter of 1805 to 1806, when the Lewis and Clark expeditioners were living with Indians of the lower Columbia River (and all but starving), Lewis wrote: "[O]n the morning of the eighteenth we issued 6 lbs. of jirked [*sic*] Elk [roughly the equivalent of 24 to 36 pounds (10.9–16.3 kg) of fresh meat] pr. man, this evening Sergt. reported that it was all exhausted; the six lbs. have therefore [*sic*] lasted two days and a half only. [A]t this rate our seven Elk [killed eight days earlier] will last us [at that time, there were 31 members of the party] only 3 days longer" (Thwaites 1969[3]:362). Wissler (1966) and Fahey (1974) estimated meat yields from bison (1,000 pounds: 454 kg), moose (800 pounds: 363 kg), elk (350 pounds: 159kg) and deer (100 pounds: 45 kg). However, neither writer revealed the bases of their estimates, and both ignored several important facts.

First, animals were taken year-round, and there were considerable weight fluctuations by animals of each species. Second, the figures ignore the weight differences between age and sex classes within each species. Third, a significant portion of each of these animals' live weight is visceral content (about 25%–40%), much of which was used as food by the Indians. Fourth, the weights given seem to represent maximum hog-dressed weights rather than average meat yields. And fifth, particularly for elk, no distinction is made for gross differences in size of different species.

Table 12 is a reappraisal of the food value (measured by quantity) to Indians and shows hypothetical rates of subsistence utilization of elk and other big game animals. It is for speculative purposes only. The table assumes that most animals killed were adults and that food was gained from viscera and other parts of the animals, as well as meat. The live weight figures were computed as approximate averages of the combined year-round mean weight of adult males and females. Food yields were approximated from combined percentages of dressed carcass weight and visceral content.

The Indians' daily consumptive rate was arbitrarily set at 3 pounds (1.4 kg) per Indian per day of animal food. As previously indicated, the most reliable records reveal that Indians may have consumed an average of about 4 pounds (1.8 kg) of meat per day. However, these records do not appear to be calculated or projected on a year-round basis. And because most tribes periodically experienced times when meat was in short supply, the smaller figure (combining meat and other edible parts) seems appropriate.

In estimating the number of animals of the featured species that would have been necessary to sustain a band of 100 Indians over various time intervals, an assumption was made that the Indians concentrated solely on one species. This, of course, is far from accurate. As Capps (1973) noted, despite the Indians' spartan subsistence regimen and preoccupation with a limited number of primary foods, their diets were surprisingly varied. Plant foods usually were a significant part of the daily fare in all seasons, and small mammals, fish and birds were regular additions. In a band

of 100 Indians in the 1800s, there were approximately 7 to 20 adult men (lowest among the warring factions of the northern Plains; highest among the more sedentary tribes and clans of the central Plains and California coast, respectively) on whom fell the major burden of procuring animal food (Wissler 1966, Driver 1969, Catlin 1973, Heizer 1978). Calculating a consumptive rate of 300 pounds (136 kg) of animal food per day per 100 Indians, this would mean that each hunter would need to secure 15 to 43 pounds (6.8–19.5 kg) per day. It was prudent, therefore, that the able-bodied hunters concentrate on large mammals, particularly herding species that were vulnerable to mass slaughter. And, as noted earlier, the food value of animals corresponded to their sizes. Although Table 12 suggests a food value of elk based on its relative size, it omits the essential parameters of the elk's comparative seasonal availability, abundance and huntability. One must consider that, for most North American Indians, elk were (1) not available as a year-round food source, (2) in less abundance than at least one other big game species in most regions, and (3) difficult to hunt in large numbers during the months when they were most available and necessary. Interestingly, a review of the literature reveals a definite meat-gathering pattern by Indians based as much on food preference as on logistical efficiency. From numerous accounts, it is apparent that, despite the high yield of an elk and the fact that its carcass provided nearly as many utilitarian items as did the bison (discussed later), when Indians had a choice between pursuing elk and animals of another big game species (including pronghorn, mountain goat, mountain sheep, bison, deer and caribou), they invariably opted for the other species. Also from the literature, it appears that the Indians' palatability regard for elk ranked close to that for bear and perhaps moose. If, in fact, elk meat was not preferred (see Greer 1968c), one explanation may be that near-total dependence on elk during winter hardship periods by some Plateau and Pacific Northwest Indians may have diminished their taste for it. Other Indians who hunted elk in autumn and, for whatever reason, killed adult bulls, were securing meat that was relatively tough and tasteless.

Addressing elk as food for fur trappers in the West, Chittenden (1935[2]:816) wrote: "Its meat is excellent, and a good elk steak ranked well with domestic beef." James Mead (1986:63), who lived and hunted in the Indian Territory and Kansas from 1859 to 1875, wrote of his first taste of elk that "I had never eaten sweeter meat in my life" (see also Webb 1872). Even earlier, in the East, Brickell (1737:108), in his history of North Carolina, wrote of elk that "Their Flesh is not near so sweet as the Fallow-Deer [*sic*: whitetail], being much courser [*sic*] and stronger." Daniel Boone, who roamed the wilderness of Kentucky in the 1760s, disdained

Table 12. Approximate number of mature big game animals of various species hypothetically necessary to support 100 North American Indians

Species	Approximate mean live weight[a]		Approximate food yield[b]		Number of animals needed per unit of time[c]			
	Pounds	Kilograms	Pounds	Kilograms	Day	Week	Month	Year
Bison	1,382.0	627.4	937.0	425.4	0.32	2.2	9.7	116.9
Caribou	295.0	133.8	212.0	96.2	1.41	9.9	42.4	516.5
Deer	165.0	74.9	115.0	52.2	2.60	18.2	79.0	949.0
Elk								
Manitoban	692.0	314.2	469.0	212.9	0.63	4.4	19.2	230.0
Rocky Mountain	600.0	272.4	407.0	184.8	0.73	5.1	22.2	266.5
Roosevelt	842.0	382.3	571.0	259.2	0.52	3.6	15.8	189.8
Tule	363.0	164.8	246.0	111.7	1.21	8.5	36.8	441.7
Moose	1,105.0	501.7	759.0	344.6	0.39	2.7	11.9	142.4
Pronghorn	104.0	47.2	43.0	19.5	6.97	48.8	211.9	2,544.1

Sources: From McCabe 1982, Reeves and McCabe 1998.

[a] For both sexes of adults (3 years and older).

[b] Calculated on the basis of 90% of dressed carcass weight (minus most bones), plus 60% of viscera. This calculation also assumes a 7% higher take of meat and fat per animal and a 95% higher take of viscera by pre–1850s Natives than by modern hunters.

[c] Based on a conservative year-round animal food consumption rate of 3.0 lb (1.4 kg) per person per day.

the frontiersmen's preferred delicacy, beaver tail, in favor of elk liver (Farragher 1992). During the Powder River campaign of 1876, U.S. Army Lieutenant John Bourke (1966:48) proclaimed that elk heart boiled in salt water was "good enough for anybody," and fresh elk liver was not unlike raw oysters.

Denig (1930:537) wrote that, "the meat, though eaten, is not relished much by most of the Indians." Like Boone, the Indians found elk meat too much like beef—"unpalatably sweet" and greatly inferior to bison (McHugh 1979:286, Taylor 1975). Several other potential explanations are derived from statements by Lewis and Clark. In February 1806, they wrote that elk were retreating to the mountains, and "[T]his is very unwelcom [*sic*] information for as poore [*sic*] as the flesh of this animale [*sic*] is, it is our principal dependence for subsistence" (Thwaites 1969[4]:102–103, see also Ruxton 1861). In August of that year, Clark wrote that "their [elk] flesh & fat is hard to dry in the sun, and when dry is much easir [*sic*] spoiled than either the Buffalow [*sic*] or Deer" (Thwaites 1969[5]:322). Members of Major Stephen Long's Great American Desert expedition in 1819 to 1820 discarded elk meat when bison was available.

Also, Curtis (1970[4]:115) quoted a Crow Indian as saying: "too much elk-meat is not good." There was no explanation for that statement, nor did a review of the literature confirm it as a universal sentiment.

The animals were butchered and prepared as food in ways that differed slightly from region to region. Typically, an elk was skinned and butchered where it was killed. Generally, skinning, butchering and transporting the elk was the duty of women and boys in areas where elk were hunted communally or during seasons other than winter (see Denig 1930). However, division of labor in this regard varied considerably, even among tribes of the same region (see Driver 1969).

To prepare the carcass for skinning and butchering, the first step was a straight incision from the underlip to the anus. The carcass was then rolled on its back and propped, either against trees or rocks or by twisting the head (except those with antlers) back and around to wedge under one side. Skinning commenced with perpendicular cuts from a body length incision down the inside of each leg and around the ankles. A final cut was made around the mouth, up the bridge of the nose, and around the base of the antlers. The skin then was carefully stripped away in a single piece, which necessitated rolling the animal to one side. Once removed, the hide served as a tarpaulin on which flayed meat was placed and in which it was transported.

Butchering began by disjointing and removing the hind legs and then opening the body cavity to remove the entrails. Some Indians, including the Mandan, Cree, Blackfeet, Pawnee, Flathead, Apache and Miami, picked out choice morsels—such as the liver, heart, kidneys, testicles, eyes, stomach fat, brains and virtually all other minor parts to which fat adhered—to eat as they dressed out the carcass. (Some Plains Indians ate the fleshy inner parts of bison hoofs and the gristle from the bison's nose, but whether the same parts of elk were eaten is not known.) Blackfeet ate the animal's testicles in the belief that it heightened their own virility, and fresh kidneys were thought to aid the infirm (see Ewers 1958, Wissler 1910). All Indians removed the long (tibia) bones, from which marrow was extracted. Other special parts included the tongue, gall, intestines and stomach (Table 13). Blood also was salvaged by many subarctic, Plains and Plateau Indians.

In his diary for December 11, 1876, Army Lieutenant Bourke (unpublished) wrote: "Colonel [Richard Irving] Dodge told us yesterday that one of the Pawnees [Army scouts] had approached him with something in his handkerchief, telling him it was 'heap good.' An examination showed the granulated liver of an elk chased for so long a time before being killed that it had lost the semblance of itself and had turned into big clots of blood. Over this had been sprinkled the gall of the animal and of this blood, greenish looking mixture, the fastidious Colonel was invited to partake. He felt compelled to decline. [The Pawnee] looked at him with an air of compassion and then swallowed the mess himself, leaving nothing but the dirty handkerchief."

Some Northern Coast Salish typically partially roasted venison after an animal was butchered, so that the meat was lighter to transport (see Kennedy and Bouchard 1990).

William White, a private with the 2nd U.S. Cavalry patrol that located and buried Custer and other 7th Cavalry soldiers 2 days after they were killed at Little Big Horn in the Montana Territory, and who married and lived among the Crow for 60 years after his discharge from the military, stated that: "Veal meat was favored by the Indians. They liked best the unborn young—buffalo, elk, deer, antelope, or other animal" (Marquis 1975:169).

After the primary meat cuts were stripped away, the elk carcass usually was quartered and transported to a camp or village. The most frequently discarded parts were boned skulls, backbones and antlers (see Ewers 1968, Fahey 1974), although the existence of any remains was exceptional. Indians of a few Plateau tribes (such as the Kutenai) did not

eat most of an animal's visceral contents, and some Pacific Northwest and Plains Indians left the heart as spiritual atonement. In a similar animistic vein, Flatheads closed the eyes of a slain elk before butchering (Johnson 1969). Cree drank blood from the carcass believing it would prevent them from being disturbed by the sight of blood during battle (Curtis 1970). Upper Coquille (southwestern Oregon Athapaskan) hunters also reportedly drank the blood of slain elk (Miller and Seaburg 1990).

Fletcher and La Flesche (1972) listed the main butcher parts of an elk and their value ranking by Omaha Indians. Valuated most highly was side meat, followed in order by hindquarters, ribs, viscera, back (including muscles, fat and sinew), breast and forequarters. This ranking (primarily for purposes of distribution) was fairly consistent among tribes and regions, although in northern and coastal areas an elk's tongue, marrow, fetuses and entrails were the favored parts.

A great many tribes throughout North America observed strict rituals of food distribution within a tribe, village or group. Among the Flatheads, for example, a hunter who killed an elk held a feast for his neighbors. If he killed more than one elk, he fed his entire village, gave his own kin only a small share and gave the rest away.

Unlike the flesh of bison, elk meat usually was eaten fresh (Wissler 1906), perhaps because it normally was sought when other foods were scarce and the Indians at their hungriest, or because, as Lewis and Clark noted, elk meat putrefied relatively quickly (Thwaites 1969). Some Carrier Indians preferred semispoiled elk meat, because this condition supposedly improved the taste.

Several generalizations can be made about the cooking and consumption of elk meat by Indians in all regions. First, boiling was the most universal cooking method, although the implements used in the process varied considerably (see Driver 1969). For example, Plateau tribes constructed a boiling "kettle" by lining a hole in the ground with rawhide, filling it with water and heating the water with hot stones. The Kutenai preferred elk meat boiled in this fashion, and they seasoned the meat with wild peppermint and onion. Stone-boiling was extensively used by the nomadic Plains Indians, some of whom also boiled food with similar effect by suspending a hide or paunch kettle from four sticks driven into the ground. The Blackfeet added dried fruit and bone fat to produce soup or stew. The seminomadic Plains Indians boiled elk meat in crude earthenware pots. Boiling elk ribs, bone joints and marrow produced a soup enjoyed by most Plains Indians. Plateau and Pacific Northwest Indians prepared soups of fleshy ribs, bones fractured to release marrow, neck fat, and plant roots and berries. Miller and Seaburg (1990) indicated that, during late winter, when other food was scarce, Oregon Atha-

Table 13. Some visceral parts and organs of elk used as food by some North American Indians

Liver	Milk
Bone marrow	Kidneys
Fetus	Testicles
Lungs	Eye
Gristle	Stomach
Fetlock	Stomach contents
Muscle	Fat
Ribs	Hooves (fleshy inner part)
Joints (for soup)	Brains
Hides (starvation fare)	Heart
Gall contents	Tongue
Blood	Intestines

paskan women made soup from elk and deer bone that had been saved. In the subarctic and East, most cooking was by boiling in earthen, wooden or bark vessels. Southwestern Indians invariably boiled elk meat as a stew in earthen pots placed over a fire. In California, fresh elk meat usually was stone boiled in watertight baskets. Baskets and boxes were the boiling vessels used by Pacific Northwest tribes. Also elk blood was boiled to jellylike consistency and consumed as hot broth, or, with added ingredients, a stew. And elk hides sometimes were eaten during periods of food shortage.

A second generalization is that fresh elk meat was never purposefully cooked well-done, as its texture and taste would suffer as a result. Furthermore, the Ojibwa and others believed that it "lost strength in the cooking, and that the longer it cooked the less nourishing it became" (Jones 1906:140).

Third, nearly as universal as boiling elk meat was the practice of drying it. Most elk meat was prepared in this manner, and the ultimate products were jerky and a substance widely known as pemmican—a Cree word loosely translated to mean manufactured grease (Oswalt 1966:28).

Jerky was strips of lean meat, usually taken from the base of the tenderloin. The meat was placed on a platform (out of reach of dogs and other four-footed scavengers) and sun-dried, or, if insects were prevalent, smoke-dried. William Clark identified this procedure when he wrote: ". . . fish and elk (when they [Clatsop and Chinook Indians] are fortunate enough to get it) are hung on sticks in the smoke of their fires to cure" (Thwaites 1969[3]:348). When dried and hardened, jerky weighed as much as one-sixth the amount of fresh meat and had a barklike texture. Although bulky, difficult to chew and moisture absorbent, it was highly portable and a favorite of Indians on the move. William Hornaday described the taste as "quite good," although the lack of salt in the curing gave it a "'far-away' taste which continually reminds one of hoofs and horns" (McHugh 1979:88).

Pemmican essentially was jerky pulverized to a powdery or flaky substance on which soft melted fat (usually bone grease) was poured. It typically was shaped into slabs, but sometimes loaves or flat cakes. Bison meat ordinarily was used for plain or summer pemmican, featuring equal weights of jerky and fat. Because its process of drying was difficult and lengthy, elk meat most often was prepared as winter pemmican—a slightly damp form to which dry fruit (saskatoonberries, chokecherries or buffaloberries) or wild peppermint leaves were added. The additives increased the possibility of spoilage but greatly enhanced the taste and nutritional value.

Roasting and broiling were other common cooking methods, although roasting was infrequent among north-

Among all North American Indians, boiling was the most universal method of cooking elk and other venison. This was done in a variety of containers, from earthen pots to buckskin- or vegetation-lined depressions to, eventually, metal pots secured from traders. There was also a variety of boiling techniques. The technique of stone-boiling was especially popular and it reached its pinnacle of ingenuity with the Assiniboine, whose name supposedly was given them by neighboring Ojibwa, in whose language it meant stone boilers. The custom was described by George Catlin (1973[I]:54): ". . . when they kill meat, a hole is dug in the ground about the size of a common pot, and a piece of the raw hide of the animal, as taken from the back, is put over the hole, and then pressed down with the hands close around the sides, and filled with water. The meat to be boiled is then put in this hole or pot of water; and in a fire, which is built near by, several large stones are heated to a red heat, which are successively dipped and held in this water until the meat is boiled. . . ." Above, the Blackfeet women are stone-boiling meat in iron pots. The "stones" likely are the bricks. The fast that the kneeling woman is wearing an elk tooth dress is certain indication that the photo was staged, as garments so decorated were not worn during routine daily labors by any of the tribes for whom such vestments were treasured. *Photo by Edward S. Curtis; courtesy of the Smithsonian Anthropological Archives.*

ern Plains tribes except when traveling. Broiling generally was accomplished by placing food in coals, and roasting was done by placing meat on spits over an open fire or putting it in small covered pits heated by stones from a campfire.

Before metal kettles and pots were widely available, Sioux and other Plains tribes commonly stone-boiled meat in hide pouches or paunches. The hide or paunch container was suspended from four sticks and partly filled with water. Meat to be cooked was cut into thin strips and placed nearby. Stones were heated in a fire and dropped into the container; not many were needed to make water boil. While the water bubbled, the meat was dropped in to cook for just a few minutes. Cooked meat usually was scooped out on dull sticks or antler rather than stabbed with sharper utensils, to avoid puncturing the container and releasing the liquid, which was quite palatable, having drawn juice from both the meat and the container. This broth was first offered to those without teeth. If paunches of bison or elk were used as containers, they too were cooked by the stone-boiling technique, and were readily consumed when the meat was depleted. *Photo by John A. Anderson; courtesy of Henry W. Hamilton and the University of Oklahoma Press.*

Elk lungs, when eaten (by the Pawnee, Cheyenne, Chiricahua Apache and others), were cut open, dried, and roasted or boiled (Curtis 1970). Elk tongue, a particular favorite of all Indians, usually was roasted. Intestines were cleaned, turned inside out, and either blown full of air and roasted or filled with meat and blood and broiled. Dodge (1882:276-277) wrote that the "liver of a very fat buffalo or elk will not infrequently become granulated and broken up by overheating in a long chase. This, with the contents of the gall-bladder sprinkled over it, is one of the most delicious morsels that can titillate an Indian palate" (see also Wallace and Hoebel 1952).

Newcomb (1961) observed that Comanches delighted in

Although less durable than plain or summer pemmican made from bison meat, which could last indefinitely (McHugh 1979), winter pemmican made with pulverized elk meat, grease and dry fruit or flavored leaves, if properly protected from moisture and air, could last a number of years. If excessively or repeatedly exposed to air, elk pemmican tended to turn rancid. Pemmican, as being prepared above by a Nez Percé woman in 1871, had the bulk and weight of one-third to one-half that of an equivalent amount of fresh meat, and was "acceptable if not exciting to the taste" (Branch 1962:50). *Photo by William Henry Jackson; courtesy of the U.S. Bureau of Outdoor Recreation.*

elk marrow, raw liver flavored with gallbladder contents, warm blood of a freshly killed elk and milk and blood from slashed udders.

As previously indicated, fresh elk meat was not easily preserved. What little was cached was placed in hides or surrounded by grasses, wild bergamot, peppermint or pineapple weed, and then buried in the ground or deep snow.

Uses of Elk Hide

As meat and fish were principal nutriments that sustained most North American Indians, animal hide was the fabric that maintained them. It was their shelter, clothing and handmaiden in a variety of other essential ways. As a source of hides for certain leather articles, the elk was highly esteemed, and there were marked geographic and cultural patterns for this valuation; it was more important to tribes that occupied regions with severe winters and those that were nomadic. The tough, thick, expansive elk hide served many useful purposes that skins of other animals could not, or at least not as well.

Throughout the literature pertaining to Indians and their uses of elk is a recurrent message summarized pointedly by Wissler (1906:163–164), who wrote that "elk were hunted more for their skins than for their flesh." Flannery (1953:59) also indicated that elk usually "were exploited for purposes other than food." However, these statements do not necessarily imply that only the hides were taken, even infrequently, from killed elk. As Dengler (1923:64) further clarified, elk were ". . . pursued chiefly in order to obtain . . . hides although fresh meat was also desired." Ashbrook and Sater (1945:20) wrote that, "The Indian considers it a sacrilege to kill any edible animal and throw away the carcass." (Such pragmatic utility may have been the case for some Indians at times, but the anthropological literature contains so many exceptions as to suggest that the view is, at best, an overstatement or, at worst, sentimentalist pap [see, e.g., Hutchinson 1972, Barnard 1977, Cronan and White 1986, Sherwood unpublished, see also Callicott 1982].)

As a rule, hides of elk killed in spring and summer were used for such items as parfleches, ropes, lodge or tepee covers, moccasin soles and shields. Hides for robes and most other articles of clothing were taken from elk killed in autumn and winter. And whereas hide from bison was equated with warmth, pronghorn and bighorn sheep with regal appearance, deer with strength and flexibility, the principal advantage of elk hide was its durability (Koch 1977). The thickness of elk skin accounted for its durability, but also made it difficult to dress because of its resistance to tanning (Fahey 1974).

Dressing Elk Hides

The task of dressing elk and other hides invariably fell to female Indians, both young and old. It was a laborious process that seems to have been fairly similar from tribe to tribe and even among regions, with the principal difference being the amount of time devoted to working each hide (see Jones 1906, Wissler 1906, Flannery 1953, Catlin 1973). Deer and elk hides did not require the labor that "harsh" bison hides did (Fletcher and La Flesche 1972:345).

Most elk hides tanning involved removal of the outer hair. Usually the first step in the process was soaking the hide for several days in plain water or preparations of elk brain and water, or brain, sagebrush and water, or lye from ashes and water. Parker (1954) noted that ashes were required to remove hair from bison, elk and moose hides, but not from deer hide. A dehaired hide then was stretched taut on a pole frame and attached with leather thongs or spread on the ground skin side up and held in place by wooden stakes. Hides dressed to retain the pelage were framed or staked out usually for 1 or 2 days, during which time the skin side treated with a coating of brain and water. Hewitt (1970:261) noted that the brain of deer was "finer" and primarily used in the preparation of hides except those of elk. Taylor (1975) wrote that the coating mixture was one part brain, two parts liver and a little fat, thoroughly boiled.

Next was graining—the arduous job of removing flesh and other matter from the skin. For this, a "well contrived" scraping tool was used (Thomas and Ronnefeldt 1976:27). Known as a scraper or a dubber (Inman 1897:262), this instrument was made of elk leg bone, shaped like a chisel and serrated at the end or tipped with sharpened stone or metal with sawlike teeth. Describing the skin dressing technique of the Sioux, Mason (1889:569–570) referred to the implement as a webajabe: ". . . hides were stretched and dried as soon as possible after they were taken from the animals. When a hide was stretched on the ground pins were driven through holes along the borders of the hide. These holes had been cut with a knife. While the hide was still green the women scraped it on the under side by pushing a webajabe over its surface, thus removing the superfluous flesh, etc. The webajabe was formed from the lower bone of an elk's leg, which had been made thin by scraping or striking. The lower end was sharpened by striking, having several teeth-like projections. . . . A withe was tied to the upper end, and this was secured to the arm of the woman just above the wrist. When the hide was dry the woman stretched it again upon the ground and proceeded to make it thinner and lighter by using another implement called the weubaja, which she moved toward her in the manner of an adze. This instrument was formed from an elk horn, to the lower end of which was fastened a piece of iron (in recent times) called the weu-hi" (see also Belitz 1973). If the hair was to be removed the hide was turned over, retreated with the brain matter paste, and the scraping sequence repeated. This essentially completed the process of making rawhide.

For hides or skins dressed further for clothing, the next step was curing, and several techniques were used depending on tribal preference and the type of clothing for which the hide was intended. The Ojibwa and Gros Ventre, for example, rubbed the skin side (or sides) with an oily compound made from sagebrush and elk or bison brain. The hide then was left in the sun, giving the oil time to soak in. When dry, the hide was moistened with warm water and rolled up tightly. Once the skin was fully saturated and damp, it was unrolled and stretched to its original shape. To complete the process, the hide was dried by placing it through a thong loop hung from a pole and "sawing" it

Graining was the first labor-intensive job of tanning elk and other big game hides. With the use of scraping tools, including fleshers or dubbers and depilators or beamers, women performed the arduous task of removing extraneous flesh and skin from the hide. To grain a hide, a mixture of diluted, pasty brain matter was applied and the skin was allowed to soak for several days; then the women staked it to the ground, knelt directly on it and, holding the flesher in both hands, bore down with as much weight as possible, shaving away several centimeters of connecting tissue with each stroke. (Shavings of flesh and fat usually were used for making soup.) Once the hide was free of extraneous tissue and dried, it was again staked out. In much the same fashion as the flesher was held and pressure exerted, the depilator was scraped one way along the grain to work the skin down to the desired thickness. This, essentially, was the process for producing rawhide. Subsequent tanning involved repeated treatment with the brain matter, depilating, smoking and drying. Elk skin reportedly was easier to treat than was the coarser bison hide (Fletcher and LaFlesche 1972). Behind the Dakota women, who are graining hides (likely not elk), are racks of meat strips probably drying for jerky or pemmican. The meat is hung out of the reach of dogs and close to the tepees for additional safeguarding and convenience. *Photo by S. J. Morrow, courtesy of the Smithsonian Institution Anthropological Archives.*

back and forth. This stripping action generated friction with sufficient heat to evaporate the moisture eventually and uniformly distribute the oil. The result was a soft, dry, clean, white skin. On the other hand, some Indians smoked rawhide to prepare it for articles of wear. Such skins were placed in small, enclosed tepee- or conical-shaped structures (similar to sweat lodges) and smoked for a day or more by means of a wood (frequently sumac) pot fire that generated little or no flame (Hodge 1907, Catlin 1973). This

The best scrapers, or dubbers (*top*), were fashioned from the lower leg bone of elk. The end was serrate to remove hair in particular, but also other adherent matter. Handles were wrapped in rawhide and a wrist strap attached at the heel of the chisel-like tool provided the users with control and additional pressure. A flesher, or beamer (*bottom*), was made of elk antler bent at a right angle with a sharp chipped flint or piece of field metal lashed across the short end. A relatively delicate instrument, it was used to hack and shave hides to the desired thinness. "Its proper use is a high skill, and a good fleshing tool is a cherished heirloom. [George Bird] Grinnell acquired a flesher that had passed through the hands of five mothers and daughters (all known) and had been in continuous use for about a hundred and fifty years when he received it" (Hoebel 1960:62). *Photo courtesy of the Museum of the American Indian, Heye Foundation.*

procedure produced a skin that retained its soft texture and flexibility even after continual wearing and soaking. It also darkened the finished skin. Dark brown or gray-black leather was a distinctive characteristic of Blackfeet clothing (particularly moccasins and leggings), from which the appellation black foot probably originated (Catlin 1973, Koch 1977).

Clothing and Accessories

The major uses of elk hide for clothing were as dresses (for women), shirts (for men) and robes (both sexes). Because its thickness and weight made it too cumbersome for most daily activities (Taylor 1957, cf. Mails 1972), elk hide was less commonly used than bison on the Plains, caribou in the subarctic, jackrabbit and pronghorn in the Southwest and Great Basin and deer in all other regions. However, it was treasured for cold weather, ceremonial wear and smaller articles such as moccasins and leggings.

Most widespread among the clothing items made from elk hide was the robe. Tanned elk skins were used as summer robes by the Fox, Sauk, Arapao, Cheyenne, Crow, Mescalero Apache, Taos Pueblo, Northern Shoshone, Nez Percé, Wasco-Wishram, Yakima, Costanoan, Puinnault, Chinook and Tsinshian, but Indians of other tribes, including the Plains Cree, Ojibwa, Cayuse, Interior Salish, Blackfeet, Pawnee and Kutenai, used them almost exclusively in cold seasons and often with the fur intact (Wissler 1906, Thwaites 1969, Curtis 1970, Paterek 1994). The Kutenai, who adopted the Plains Indian fashion of dress, preferred elk and mountain goat robes to those made of bison for everyday use, although this was exceptional; their mantles and blankets usually were elk hide as well (Curtis 1970).

Among a number of Great Plains tribes (Gros Ventre, Assiniboine, Teton Sioux, Mandan, Ponca and others), the elk hide robe was seldom worn other than as ceremonial garb. The Nez Percé, Blackfeet and Crow wore particularly attractive white (unsmoked) ceremonial robes (Mason 1889, Curtis 1970). However, the robe was one of the first pieces of clothing to be replaced by the colorful wool blankets received in trade with whites. In the Pacific Northwest and California, elk robes were worn mostly by men in earliest historic time, but later by both sexes (see Voegelin 1942). Among the Delta and Coastal Salish, ownership of such a robe was a sign of prestige or nobility (Hill-Tout

1906). Men of several California tribes, including Winton, Yuki and Nomlaki, and Pacific Northwest and western Plateau tribes, including the Tillamook, Clatsop, Chinook and Klamath, wore elk hide tunics as armor on war excursions (Curtis 1970).

As with elk hide robes, shirts were not for everyday use because of their thickness (Taylor 1957), except by some men of the Gros Ventre, Pawnee, Kutenai, Fox, Western Woods Cree, unidentified Athapaskan tribes and perhaps Northern Shoshone. Also, like elk hide robes, shirts were generally made from the skins of "young" elk (Curtis 1970[18]:65) or cows, and were for purposes of ceremony and warfare (Figure 44).

Elk skin armor shirts or double-layer vests were worn in battle by the Nez Percé, Clatmop, Coastal Salish, Itupa, Tsimshian, Northern and Southern Valley Maidu, Tolowa, Tutuni, Achuwami, Wailaki, Hupa, Wintun, Yurok, Haida,

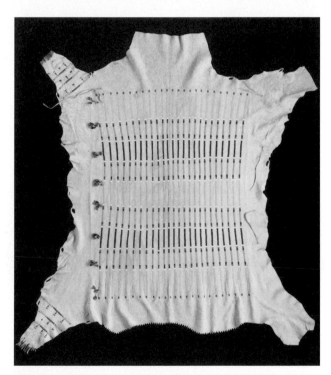

The ceremonial Piegan Blackfoot robe above features a pictographic narrative of an important event in the owner's life, including bear hunting, horse raids, battles, coups and ownership of horses. Except among some Indians of the Pacific Northwest, Plateau and Great Basin, elk robes for daily use were not common. The preferred winter robe was bison "in the hair," and tanned deer hide for the other seasons. Elk hides are relatively difficult to tan and lack the warmth and pliability of bison hide robes, and bison also were more readily obtained and easier to kill (Ewers 1939). Therefore, fewer elk hides were tanned for robes, giving those that were special value and use as ceremonial wear. *Photo courtesy of the Museum of the American Indian, Heye Foundation.*

The Absaroke, or Crow, were widely acknowledged as having the finest (and whitest) tanned hide clothing (see Mason 1898, Catlin 1973). The painstaking treatment and ornamentation of hides were more than mere fancy or pride; they were important in social relations. Crow marriage was an alliance of families, not only the conjoining of a man and a woman. The bond was formalized by family exchanges of garments for the bride and groom. The 75- by 79-inch (190 by 200 cm) robe above, collected in Montana about 1880, was of a type frequently presented to a young bride by the groom's family (Merritt 1988). The robe's beaded embroidery simulated a decorative pattern "used by the Crow long ago" and featured porcupine quills (Wildschut and Ewers 1959:20). *Photo courtesy of The Detroit Institute of Arts.*

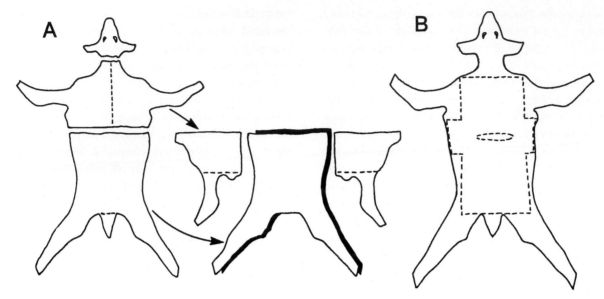

Figure 44.   The general design of two types of elk hide "warshirts." When completed, pancho-style A was a ceremonial garment typical of those worn by Blackfeet, Cree, Omaha, Sioux, Crow, Mandan and Assiniboine. They were called binary (Conn 1974:59) because two hides matched for size were required to complete the poncho. This is thought to be the earliest style of Plains shirt (Wissler 1915), which hung to midthigh (redrawn from Koch 1977). Style B represents the preparation design for a waist-length, poncho-type shirt worn by men of such tribes as the Cheyenne, Thompson, Shuswap, Lillooet and Gros Ventre. *Patterned from a shirt drawn by Rudolph F. Kurz in 1851 (from Hewitt 1970).*

Quinault, Klamath and Modoc and, reportedly, were effective protection against primitive weaponry (Curtis 1970, Olmsted and Stewart 1978, Suttles 1990). On the Northwest coast, the Tlingit wore armor (only in ceremony after the 19th century) in the form of shirts made from moose or elk hides, on which the wearer's clan symbol was painted. Most elk hides were acquired by the Tlingit in trade. A Tlingit suit of armor made of cedar and other wood slats and held together front and back by elk hide cords was collected at Sitka, Alaska, sometime before 1859 (De Laguna 1990). Elk hide armor with painted designs was worn by Noota war chiefs (Jewitt 1815). Tsimshians made cuirasses of two or three elk skin layers fashioned "in a large, flat rectangle with an opening for the head; it was partially sewed together or tied on the sides" (Pasterek 1994:3,365). The Nez Percé shirt of mail, with half-length sleeves and fastened in the front with leather thongs, was manufactured of rawhide taken from the neck of bull elk.

Clatsops of the Oregon coast wore double-layered elk hide armor tunics, which were said to be, along with those of the Chinook farther north, the finest protective wear along the coast.

Similar in function to the warshirt was the corselet worn by Coastal Salish warriors including Nootka, Chinook, Makah and Kwakiutl (Curtis 1970, Paterek 1994). It usually consisted of an overlapping double row of ironwood or yew slats or rods fastened by laced cords. These strips, interlaced and covering the entire upper body except the head

and neck, were backed by deer skin and occasionally covered with elk rawhide. The corselet also was impenetrable by primitive arrows.

Frontiersman, hunter, trapper and guide "Uncle Dick" Wooten discovered to his chagrin and near demise another Indian use of elk skin in warfare. While prospecting in the 1840s in mountains bordering the San Luis Valley in south-central Colorado, Wooten and a companion espied an elk herd, and approached with the intent of killing several for food. At closer range, the animals began to look "rather queer." "We turned back," Wooten wrote, "and had barely gotten started when . . . the harmless looking elk turned out to be Ute Indians. They threw off their disguises, and . . . started in pursuit of us" (Conrad 1890:240). Wooten and friend escaped and prudently abandoned prospecting in that region.

Dresses for women of the Blackfeet, Sarsi, Arikara, Comanche, Ute, Yakima, Coastal Salish, Northern Shoshone, Arapaho, Apache, Plains Cree, Cheyenne, Ojibwa, Crow, Gros Ventre, Hidatsa, Mandan, Kiowa, Nez Percé, Teton Sioux and other tribes commonly were fashioned from two cow elk hides (Wissler 1915) in a manner similar to that for binary elk skin shirts illustrated in Figure 44, except that on skins for dresses the tail was retained (being the only fur part of the garment). Also, such dresses were worn in reverse, with the tail and part of the hind leg skin forming a yoke (Driver 1969). Wissler (1906:165–166) provided an excellent description of elk hide dress construction: "In making a garment, the two skins were brought together so that the extensions for the hind limbs overlapped each other, the tails coinciding. Leaving an opening between the tails long enough for the head to slip through, the two skins were sewed together along the upper edges of the leg pieces. At the bottom the two skins were sewed up at the sides to the point where the skin begins to come outward to the extensions of the hind limbs. Through these openings the arms were passed. When the completed garment is seen on a woman, the skin from the front limbs of the elks hangs down on each side almost to the ground while in front and behind the skirt scarcely reaches the ankles. Out from the shoulders and down from the arms to the elbows hangs a cape-like extension, made by sewing together the skins of the hind limbs. The skirt, or that part of the garment below the belt is usually covered with strings of deer skin from four to ten inches in length, giving the whole a fringed appearance. . . . The edges of the skin at the bottom and around the arm holes were often notched and fringed. . . . [These] dresses . . . did not have true sleeves . . ." (see also Hail 1980).

In the collections of Brown University's Haffenreffer Museum of Anthropology is a three-elk skin ceremonial dress of an Oglala Sioux woman. It is essentially a binary dress with the third skin, entirely beaded, sewn as a yoke at the top and right angle to the other skins. It weighs 13 pounds (5.9 kg).

Elk skin dresses are not known to have been worn regularly, except by Blackfeet, Cayuse and Ojibwa women (see Jones 1906, Wissler 1906, Thwaites 1969, Curtis 1970). Their sheer bulk made them impractical for most warm-weather activities. They generally were reserved for festive and ceremonial occasions, and were counted among a woman's most treasured possessions. Karl Bodmer, artist for the 1833 to 1834 Maximilian zu Wied Expedition on the Upper Missouri River, attempted to purchase from a Teton Sioux woman a leather dress thought to have been made of elk hide. She refused to part with the dress, but was willing to sell her bison robe (Wied 1843). Elk skin gowns owned by women of Coastal Salish bands were evidence of great wealth.

Women of some tribes, including the Blackfeet and Shoshone, wore chemises made of elk hide, and others, including Cheyenne, Arikara and Sioux, sometimes dressed in elk skin smocks.

Elk skins and elk hide clothing, as previously suggested, were featured aspects of many Indians' ceremonial proceedings. Elk leggings and dancing skirts, for example, were worn on such occasions by men and women of the Haidu, Chinook and Kwakiutl tribes. Aprons and dresses of elk hide were part of Arapaho and Crow ceremonies, respec-

tively, and Blackfeet women wore colorfully decorated elk skin dresses during the medicine pipe ceremony. For the Blackfeet sun dance, bison and elk hides were spread out for the participants, and the event was presided over by a "sacred woman" who wore an elk skin medicine robe and bonnet (McClintock 1968).

Members of the Kiowa's highest military order—the Real Dogs or Horses—wore three types of insignia sashes, two of which were elk skin (Mooney 1898).

Nearly all North American Indian tribes (and some subdivisions) had distinctive footwear designs, but composition generally was of two types: hard-sole and soft-sole. The ankle-high soft-sole moccasin, usually restricted to use in summer, commonly was made of deer skin and rarely fashioned from elk hide except by some Plateau tribes, including the Ute, Cayuse and Northern Shoshone (see Paterek 1994). Most hard-sole moccasins were knee-length and made from hides of two animal species. Elk rawhide from skin on the animal's neck was frequently used for soles, with tanned deer, pronghorn or bighorn sheep hide uppers for summertime wear. Elk skin soles and uppers of bison hide *in the hair* (sewn with the fur inside) commonly were worn in winter by Shoshone and Plains Indians including the Teton Sioux, Southern and Northern Cheyenne, Arapaho, Crow, Sarsi, Comanche, Gros Ventre and Blackfeet. Zuni Indians in the Southwest had deer skin moccasins with elk or bison rawhide soles. For daily footwear by Chickasaw Indians of the Southwest, elk hide was well-dressed and smoked to prevent hardening (Adair 1775). Mails (1972) noted that some Plains Indians, including the Plains Cree or Plains Ojibwa (see Hails 1980), used soft, tanned elk hide scraps to make moccasin uppers, but this probably was not a common practice. Clark (1884) observed that moccasin uppers featuring elk hide used by Sioux, Cheyenne and Arapaho typically were from subadult animals. Also, some Athapaskan and Eastern Algonquian Indians made boot-length moccasins from a single piece of elk hide (Wissler 1906), but this too was unusual. The Nez Percé, like many other Indians, wore moccasins of bison skin and elk skin, but preferred deer hides because the former "were of coarse texture and were not so durable" (Curtis 1970[8]:43). Many Coastal Salish in the Pacific Northwest and the Hupa, Shasta, Tachi and Karok in California wore elk rawhide moccasins on hunts or journeys in all seasons through rocky or brush country, but seldom used footwear otherwise. Quinault and other Puget Sound Indians made crude moccasins from elk hock hide. Curtis (1970) wrote that elk skin moccasins were highly prized among Chinookan Indians. The Wintun and Nomlaki reportedly wore elk hide sandals, but not moccasins (see Goldschmidt 1978). And among members of the Omaha elk society, for whom eating bull elk meat was taboo, wearing moccasins made of elk hide also was ascetically forbidden (Fletcher and La Flesche 1972). However, deceased members of that society were buried in male elk skin moccasins (as were cult members of the Osage) and dressed in bull elk hide clothing, so they could be recognized by relatives in the afterlife. Other Omahas wore elk skin moccasins "blackened with smoke and usually with an ornamental seam across the back of the foot. The flaps turned outward" (Hewitt 1970:64). During his trip up the Missouri River in May 1833, Maximilian found noteworthy a Ponca man "with a pair of shoes, made of elk leather, which were dyed black with the juice of a white walnut" (Werd 1906 [22]:285).

Leggings were worn primarily by men as insulation during cold weather, as protection against scraping against brush when traveling and to enhance their costume by allowing more spacing for decorative ornaments, totemic displays and markings (see Conn 1955, Taylor 1961, Feder 1962). Deer skin was generally preferred, but elk hide was used by some tribes, including the Brule and Teton Sioux, Hidatsa, Crow, Cree, Fox, Flathead, Kutenai, Blackfeet, Carrier, Tahltan and presumably the Gros Ventre and tribes of the Oregon coast (Paterek 1994). Typically, each elk skin legging was a single piece of tanned hide, with a seam (often fringed) on the outside, and fit to cover the hip. It was attached to a thong belt or girdle that also contained breechclout. Leggings, such as worn by Blackfeet girls and women, extended to the thigh and were tied around the ankles and above the knees or held up by thongs attached to a waist cord (Grinnell 1962). Some Cayuse, Nez Percé and Wailak men wore lightweight, tanned elk hide breechclouts.

Yana men and both sexes of Puget Sound Salish wore hair-on elk hide hats (see Paterek 1994).

As previously discussed, elk hide once was habitually used for shirts and corselets worn in battle by Indians in California and the Pacific Northwest and, to a lesser extent, on the Plateau and Plains. It also was featured in the construction of shields used by many warrior Indians in those same regions, plus the Southwest. Warshields, like many other North American Indian accouterments, linked the pragmatic and spiritual. On the Great Plains, most shields were made of horse or bison hide treated with heat and moisture, shrunk to a saucer-shaped diameter of about 18 inches (46 cm) and increased in thickness to 0.5 inch (1.8 cm)—about twice its original thickness (Mails 1972). A soft, dressed skin usually of elk or deer was used as a removable cover.

Although some tribes and societies decorated shield covers with uniform designs or commonly shared symbols, most shields were decorated individually. Medicine bag items were attached to the shield, and the cover was painted, burned or beaded with pictures of animals or physical elements that represented the owner's totem or dream spirit and whose attributes the bearer was assumed to possess in battle (Dodge 1882). The strength, speed and gallantry of elk made the animal a popular totem and talismanic shield cover design (Mails 1972). As acme of warring paraphernalia, shields were displayed with prominence inside or in front of a warrior's tepee or lodge when not in use.

On the west coast and in the northern Great Basin and Plateau regions, shields were somewhat larger and often made only with skin from the necks of bull elk. Nez Percé, Bannock and Shoshone shields, for example, were made of two layers of unshrunken elk rawhide stretched over oblong wooden hoops and held together with glue and sand. A warrior's exploits in battle sometimes were painted on the cover. As guns and metal-tipped weapons became available, shields decreased in popularity as tools of war.

Shelter

Only a few tribes are known to have used elk skins for lodge or tepee coverings. As a rule, hide-covered dwellings were used by the nomadic tribes, whereas the relatively sedentary Indians built structures with more sturdy and permanent materials. Thus, it was the Great Plains and some peripheral Indians who used hides for this purpose, and the most readily available source was bison, whose hides were relatively coarse, fibrous and elastic, therefore quite durable. Furthermore, 6 to 20 skins were necessary to cover a single dwelling. With elk less abundant than bison, there is little doubt that elk skin probably was not used for shelter on a much broader scale than the literature indicates, although attention to this aspect of the Indians' material culture came after many tribes had access to and adopted the use of canvas. Some of the Plains and Woods Cree lived in tepees of elk skin, although bison and moose hide structures were more common. Clark (1884) observed that tepees covered with bison or elk hide were the best. Elk skin summer houses were owned by some of the wealthier Kutenai, and Curtis (1970[4]:90) reported that the Northern Shoshone "had beautiful lodges of elkskin."

In the Pacific Northwest, central Plains and Plateau region elk skin frequently was used for small temporary shelter by small hunting parties and war bands. The Indian practice of using elk hides in this way was borrowed by trappers, explorers and others who traveled beyond reach of the creature comforts east of the Mississippi during the early and mid-1800s. The American West was particularly tantalizing to European noblemen and aristocrats who were enraptured by romanticized accounts of "savages, beasts, and spectacles." Travel to the West for adventure and excitement "was the ruling passion for a whole species

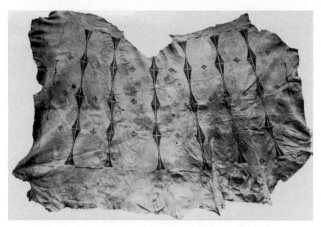

The elk skin tepee (from a Siouan term for place to live) was not commonplace, but they apparently were not rare. Among the Kutenai, for example, elk skin tepees were owned only by the wealthiest tribal members. Throughout the regions, bison hide was the usual fabric. From 6 to 20 elk hides were required to make a tepee cover, depending on tribal affinity and custom and the use of the shelter; 12 to 20 elk hides per tepee was most typical. For tepee covers, "winter" hides of elk were used; they were treated by soaking, stretching and drying repeatedly, but were not smoked. Generally, Plains tepees were of three- (e.g., Crow, Blackfoot, Cree, Arikara, Nez Perce, Comanche, Shoshone) and four-pole (e.g., Lakota, Cheyenne, Arapaho, Pawnee, Kiowa, Kiowa Apache) construction (the number of poles tied together), with as many as 30 poles (preferably cedar or lodgepole pine) to support the conical dwelling that could have a diameter of 24 feet (7.3 m) or more. Eight to 12 poles for dwellings 16 feet (4.9 m) in diameter or less and 10 to 14 feet (3.0–4.3 m) high were most prevalent. Although elk hide was not in widespread use for tepees, coverings of elk skin were popular for "summer lodges"—small, expediently raised shelters used during travel away from villages. The elk skin tepee cover above was purchased in 1879 by U.S. Army General A. W. Greeley from an Oglala Sioux at Fort Laramie. *Photo courtesy of the Museum of the American Indian, Heye Foundation.*

of 19th Century Europeans" (Wheeler 1976:148–149). Few of the foreigners returned unenlightened or dissatisfied. Among these tireless and wealthy enthusiasts was Windham Thomas Wyndham-Quin, the fourth Earl of Dunraven and Mountearl. Dunraven's journey to the upper region of the Yellowstone in 1874 so enthralled him that he subsequently wrote *The Great Divide*, a popular and insightful travelogue. In it, he recounted an occasion when, in present-day Yellowstone National Park, he and his entourage were forced to take refuge under an elk hide lean-to for their afternoon tea during a downpour. While elk hide may have served Indians well for such purposes, the Earl lamented: "If a wise man wishes to be comfortable in camp . . . let him give up the idea of being *too* comfortable" (Dunraven 1967:215).

The Lewis and Clark expeditioners, on the other hand, showed no reluctance to use elk hide as protective clothing, footwear, cordage, shelter or for storage. Repeated reference is made in their journals to dependence on elk hide to keep their gear and themselves dry. Clark reported on one occasion that "[W]e made a camp of the Elk skin to keep off the rain which continued to fall . . ." (Thwaites 1969[2]:214). And it is of no small consequence to American history that, during much of the expedition, the journals were wrapped in elk skins (Moulton 1986–1999).

Weltfish (1965) wrote that, for sleeping in warm weather, many Pawnee Indians used a hide blanket, preferably well-tanned elk or deer skin.

Tepee linings or dew cloths were semicircular and about 6 feet (200 cm) wide. Fastened about the inside of tent poles, they deflected dew that accumulated on the tent cover and water that dripped down the tent poles. The lining shown above (folded in half) was made of "summer" elk skins and owned by Piegan Blackfeet. A summer skin simply was one from an animal killed during summer, when its pelage was less dense and the hide easier to work. Cured elk hide dew cloths reportedly were more water repellent than similarly treated hides of other large ungulates. At least within historic time, painting of linings often was done by women, whose art was abstract, geometric and skilled. *Photo courtesy of the Museum of the American Indian, Heye Foundation.*

Other Uses

In addition to clothing, accessories and shelter, other widespread uses of elk hide by Indians were ropes, drag lines (safety ropes around horses' necks), harnesses, quirt lashes, belts, bedding, tack belts, ceremonial mats, tobacco pouches, backing for cradleboards and pictographs. Leftover scraps of tanned elk hide invariably were cut for fringe and sewn into small bags and pouches. Marquis (1975) indicated that elk skin thongs were a favorite for closing bags and other containers. Less universal were the elk skin rifle scabbards, quiver linings and wrist guards found among some tribes of the northern Plains. Pawnee quivers and bow cases often were made of elk hide dressed to be nearly impervious to moisture.

Parfleches (thick rawhide with hair removed, painted and typically envelopelike storage sacks and bags) were made primarily of bison hide on the Plains and in the Southwest, but also of elk, moose and horse hide in the intermountain region (Torrence 1994) and parts of the Pacific Northwest (Haeberlin and Gunther 1930). After the near extinction of bison by 1883 and termination of the Indian's nomadic horse culture, parfleche making virtually ceased, until revived about 1900 as a Native art form using cowhide.

Among the most unique utilizations of elk skin were for glue and boats. The Comanche, Crow and other tribes made a strong glue from elk hide scrapings (especially the neck skin) and shavings of the animal's antler tips and hooves. These materials were boiled to a thick liquid consistency and placed on sticks. When dry, the substance could be carried in quivers and made usable when needed by softening in hot water.

Clark (1884:188) wrote: "Indians . . . make a very good glue from the neck muscles and muscular tissue found on each side of the neck of a buffalo bull or bull elk. This is boiled in water for two or three days, and when of a thick,

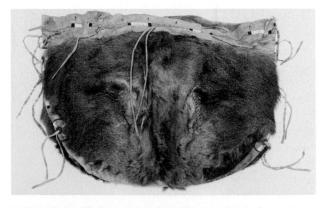

A Gros Ventre elk skin storage bag, also comprised of deer skin, porcupine quills and glass trade beads. *Photo courtesy of the Chandler-Pohrt Collection of the Buffalo Bill Historical Center.*

sticky consistency, or as they say, 'when it gets ripe,' a small stick with notches on the end is twisted and turned in the contents of the vessel, until a large amount adheres to it; this hardens on cooling and exposure to the air, and the glue is kept in this way for long periods of time. . . . It is used for fastening the feather-guides to arrows, fastening sinew on the back of bows, fastening the feathers of a war bonnet, etc. . . . It is whitish in color, unless stained or colored, as is sometimes done, with ochre."

Boats and canoes made with elk hide were not uncommon in the Plateau region. The Kutenai, for example, sewed together fresh elk hides that had been stretched to shape. They dried stiff and hard and then were fitted to a frame of split fir. "This formed a remarkably seaworthy craft, very wide of beam and so bulging amidships as to be, in effect, rather more than half-decked. Both ends were noticeably rounded and upcurving, the canoe giving the impression of being closely patterned on the lines of a waterfowl" (Curtis 1970[7]:127). Pirogues covered with elk skin were used by a number of tribes along the Columbia and Upper Missouri rivers. Meriwether Lewis noted that as many as 28 elk skins and four bison skins were needed to encase these vessels (Thwaites 1969). In most instances, the fur side of a skin used for this purpose was singed rather than scraped, as scraping tended to decrease the hide's thickness and strength. As previously stated, bison skins also were used, but as in other instances, were neither as strong nor durable as elk skin and, in the drying process, shrunk to a smaller size than did elk skin. Pieces of elk hide were used as well to patch damaged or leaking boats.

Crow and other Indians of the central Plains cut shoots or rods for arrows in late autumn. The sticks were tied tightly in bundles with elk skin and hung over a fire for several weeks to harden and straighten the wood (Clark 1884).

Nootka Indians used elk rawhide to make twisted ropes approximately 20 to 23 feet (6–7 m) in length, which attached to harpoons for whale hunting. Hodge (1910) wrote of elk skin fishing line.

The Chinook conducted a healing ceremony that centered on an elk skin attached to a pole in front of a platform covered by another skin. The event lasted several days, featuring a game in which invited adult men, on signal, rushed for the elk skin and tried to wrest it from other competitors. Water was thrown on the hide to make it slippery and difficult to grasp. When the fun was called to a halt, the contestants were given whatever portion of the skin they held onto at that moment. "As elkskin for moccasins was scarce, the efforts to get possession of the prize were real" (Curtis 1970[8]:103). Shortly thereafter, individuals performed sacred songs and imitated the sick person, apparently to invest in him the performer's healing spirit. Two medicine men officiated to determine whether the singer/actor was possessed of evil power, and if they determined it was the case, the performer was not allowed to step on an elk hide covering the ceremonial platform. This supposedly prevented the wrong power from reaching the sufferer.

The importance of elk hide in rituals was not exclusive to the Chinook. McClintock (1968) reported that it was a feature of the Blackfeet's brotherhood ritual. Members of the Omaha elk society used elk skin to make medicine bags in which to protect pipes and sacred articles. Beldon reported that tanned elk hide was used as a bandage by Indians of the Upper Missouri region and that elk hide was used by Arapaho, Cheyenne, Pawnee and Sioux to cover their sweat lodges (Brisbin 1974). And among the items in the sacred war bundle (from the Peabody Museum of Archaeology and Ethnology, Cambridge. Massachusetts) of an Omaha shell society warrior were skins of seven elk fetuses and a wolf skin to which tufts of elk hair were attached.

Item of Trade

Intertribal and even interregional trading was commonplace long before the appearance of European voyagers. Virtually all the Indians within the range of elk engaged in trading (Driver 1969). Among themselves, the Indians were shrewd traders, skillfully bartering fair exchange for commodities important to their various lifestyles, such as food, furs, decorative items, horses. Except in California and the Pacific Northwest and Plateau regions, trade of hides apparently was limited, although McNitt (1962) reported on accounts of Utes exchanging bison robes and elk hides for Navajo horses and blankets.

The arrival of white trappers and traders had a marked affect on the material economy of most Indian tribes. The role of trade between whites and Indians was a primary catalyst in the rapid and dramatic diffusion of North American Indian culture, significantly influencing the number and distribution of many native wildlife populations, including elk (see Martin 1978, Krech 1981, Washurn 1988).

Hide painting was a medium not exclusive to the Great Plains Indians, but it seems to have reached its zenith as an art form there in the 1900s. Selection of elk hide for paintings does not appear to have been related to the merit of its surface or "canvas." Also, most such paintings were done on bison hide, probably because it was in greater supply, particularly for the types of articles on which art was regularly featured, including tepee covers, tepee linings, parfleches, calendars, shields, robes, shirts, instruments and toys. However, because many articles of tanned elk hide were ceremonial or had some spiritual or social significance, selection of elk hide probably was rarely arbitrary. At left is a biographical Shoshone pictograph on elk hide, probably from the late 1800s. The images are unusually stylized and artistic and the documentation quite abbreviated; all suggests that the painting may have been commissioned. At right is a Hopi (Arizona) elk skin painting with mythological figures. In general, southwestern Indians were more prolific, stylistically diverse and skilled artists than Plains Indians, but not necessarily so as hide painters. The Hopi artist was Homovi. For a number of years, the hide painting hung in the office of the Secretary of the U.S. Department of the Interior. *Left photo courtesy of the Joslyn Art Museum. Right photo courtesy of the Museum of the American Indian, Heye Foundation.*

In the Indians' subsistence industry, white traders saw and exploited any opportunity to tap a vast and profitable reservoir of temporarily fashionable goods for which there were ready markets in the East and Europe. These goods were resources on which the Indians depended, but with which they naively parted in exchange for baubles, guns, metal, alcohol and promises. Unaccustomed to the luxury and novelty of the white man's wares, many Indians (particularly in the Plains, western Plateau and Southwest regions) engaged in a lively commerce that redirected their subsistence energies and compromised their independence, all within a span of about 100 years.

When sighted after white traders were in business, the animals that previously had been the Indians' food, fiber and spiritual kin were "apt to look to the native woodsman less like a fellow creature, and more like a price; in the gleam of eye and fur could be seen the gleam of a musket barrel or a brass kettle or a hank of beads; on the forest air the trapper could almost sniff the potent fragrance of the White man's tobacco. . . . Even bears, who already seemed a little less awesome, because of their vulnerability to bullets, the Indians began to regard not so much as reverenced fellow beings, but as wearers of hides for which the traders might give good exchange" (Johnson 1969:187).

Among Indians of the Pacific Northwest, eastern Plateau, northern Plains and subarctic, elk was important as a medium of exchange and value index. Boas (1906a) explained that canoes, slaves and curried elk skin blankets were the standards of value against which other trade or sale items were appraised, although actual payments frequently were made with the elk skin blankets. This is borne out by the experiences of the Lewis and Clark expeditioners, who at various times traded with Indians as follows: one elk skin for a canoe; a dressed elk hide and handkerchief for one sea otter pelt; two elk skins for one bighorn sheep hide; two robes and four elk skins for two canoes; two elk skins for a gun; and old tin canisters for one elk hide. Clark reported that the Indians attempted to trade wapato roots, rush mats, dried fish, "She-ne-tock-we" (black) roots and elk hides, "all of which they asked enormous prices for, particularly the Dressed Elk Skins" (Thwaites 1969[3]:299).

Elsewhere, the presence of whites prompted an enormous marketing of hides. In just 1 year (1831) the Sioux alone traded 50,000 bison robes to the American Fur Company (Morgan and Harris 1967). At first elk was not part of the intemperate harvest and commerce. "The elk," wrote Maximilian in 1833, "is not properly comprehended in the trade [by Mandan, Arikara, Hidatsa, Sioux, Assiniboine, Iowa, Kansa, Osage, Piegan Blackfeet and others], as its skin

The frequent inequity of trade between whites and Indians is characterized in this lithograph published in an 1871 issue of *Leslie's* magazine. Although this Plains Indian's expression reflects skepticism about exchanging an elk carcass for alcohol, other Indians, in actuality, eagerly accepted the traders' pots, pans, buttons, mirrors, needles, knives and stimulants. Those who opted not to be smitten by geegaws, addictives and promises generally were labeled renegades or hostiles. *Photo courtesy of the U.S. Library of Congress.*

is too thick and heavy, and is, therefore, used for home consumption" (Thomas and Ronnefeldt 1976:52). Chittenden (1935) suggested that, except for special purpose, elk hide was of less general use than the skins of other wild animals.

By the time wholesale slaughter of bison had reached a peak in the mid-1870s, elk figured prominently in the harvest wherever it was available. Reduction first of beaver and then of bison, plus a continued demand for furs and hides, had a direct and significant bearing on the increased kill of elk and other animals—a shift of attention easily accommodated by the repeating rifle and transcontinental railroads (see Madson 1966, Kelsall 1968, Schmidt 1978b, McCabe and McCabe 1984). In the winter of 1869 to 1870, for example, in an area about 15 square miles (39 km²) in northwestern Wyoming, more than 4,000 elk were killed by hunters, and "the only part of most of them saved was the tongue and hide" (Norris unpublished; see also Chapter 14).

To what extent hide-hunting Indians contributed to the decline of elk is uncertain, but it is clear that many elk were killed by these often unwitting accomplices (see Johnson 1969, Haines 1955). In 1926, an aged Swampy Cree Indian reported that, as a young man, he hunted elk on the parklands around present-day Dauphin, Manitoba, and elk number then were likened to those of bison (Green 1933). The ancient hunter added that, Indians turned to killing elk—for hides to barter with European traders—to such an extent that the elk population was nearly decimated *before* the first white settlers arrived. Concerning elk in southwestern Ontario, Wintemberg (1926:58) wrote: "The extinction of

the Wapiti, if caused by man, may have been due either to Iroquois Indian hunters, who came into the country from what is now New York State, after the dispersion of the Hurons, Tabacco Nation Indians, and Neutrals (1649–1951), or the Missisauga, who succeeded the Iroquois in the occupation of the country. The later comers probably hunted with guns instead of bows and arrows of the earlier Indians, and this may have led to the speedy extinction of the animal; at any rate, it appears to have disappeared from the country before the beginning of British settlement, late in the eighteenth century."

Rorabacher (1970) estimated that, for approximately every bison hide that reached market, five bison were killed. Furthermore, 99% of the meat of animals killed by hide hunters was wasted. There is very little reason to believe that the statistics for elk were any different. Among Plains Indians (principally Sioux, Crow and Pawnee) in the 1850s, a bison robe from the Indians brought $1.25, whereas an elk skin was worth $1.00 (Brisbin 1974). However, one of the latter decorated with porcupine quills was valued at $5.00. In the 1870s, a bison hide was worth less than $4.00 (Gard 1968) and an elk hide about $7.00 (Haines 1977). At about that time, the per-capita annual income in the United States was about $170 (U.S. Census Bureau Public Information Office personal communication:1981). One elk hide, therefore, was much more readily and profitably sold than was the animal's meat, which was considerably more difficult to process, transport and market before spoilage occurred.

Some Indians resisted the temptation of white traders' goods and professed goodwill in exchange for hides when game was plenty, but too many did not. A few were forced or duped into participation; most did so heedless of the consequences. In a three-decade frenzy of killing elk that extirpated the species from much of its western range, the Indians "worked toward their own destruction willingly and well" (Matthiessen 1959:149). For Indians, unlike whites, the slaughter of game was an inequitable proposition; it

proved to be a fateful and wholly expensive paradox. The resulting depletion of game not only broke down the Indians' role of subsistence hunting, but, combined with the ravages of exogenous diseases and the appropriation of Native lands, it precluded any opportunity for recovery of traditional lifestyle (Lowie 1963). *Lithograph illustration by R. Caton Woodville, published in the November 6, 1886 issue of* The Illustrated London News; *courtesy of the U.S. Library of Congress.*

Instrumental in the rapid decline of elk in the West was the transcontinental railroad. It brought an invasion of settlers, ranchers, miners, soldiers and others whose activities fragmented and reduced elk range. The iron horse prompted and serviced an untempered commercial harvest of elk for meat, hides and specialty parts. *Top left photo courtesy of Paramount Pictures. Top right photo courtesy of the Union Pacific Railroad Museum. Bottom photo courtesy of Doris Whithorn and the Park County (Wyoming) Museum.*

To be sure, the greatest share of responsibility for the decline of elk and other wildlife rests with white professional hunters and the people they clothed and fed with the spoils of their labor. Even as late as 1881, with bison and elk herds seriously diminished, *more than 5,000* of these hunters and their skinners still plied their skill in Wyoming, Montana, the Dakotas and southern Canada—the area in which most remaining elk were confined (Sandoz 1978). In addition, settlers, miners, soldiers and sport hunters exacted a heavy toll on wildlife resources in the West. "No sooner does the pioneer encroach upon these districts of unrivaled agricultural resources than the larger animals at once and forever disappear. The elk, the buffalo and the beaver are the first to exterminated" (Allen 1871:8). On the Great Plains, English explorer and adventurer Sir George Gore reportedly killed 2,000 bison and 1,600 elk and deer in a portion of 1854 (Barsness 1985). In any case, the fact remains that from a subtle and salubrious beginning, trade in animal hides and flesh very nearly eliminated elk and other wildlife and, in so doing, permanently undermined the North American Indians' way of life.

Although some Indians, dazzled by trade goods and promises, contributed significantly to the extirpation of elk and other big game, the rapid and wanton depletion of wildlife resources was accomplished mainly by market gunners, pioneers (*top*) and self-styled sportsmen (*bottom*) from the East and abroad, most exercising their talents, weaponry and tenacity in advance of any notion of or concern about conservation and the advent of laws to prevent overexploitation. *Photos courtesy of the Montana State Historical Society.*

Teeth

No other aspect of elk, including hide and food parts, was more highly prized by North American Indians than its upper canine teeth, the so-called buglers, ivory teeth, whistlers, tushes or tusks (Greer 1968c). The canines are rounded and about the size and shape of the tip a man's thumb, although flatter. They are well developed in both sexes of adult elk, but more specialized in bulls (Murie 1951). The size, shape and color determined their value; the larger and dark-stained (brownish) teeth had greatest worth (see Madson 1966). To most Indians the permanent canines—and in some instances the milk teeth (Hodge 1907, Koch 1977) and lower incisors (Hewitt 1970)—were, in the words of a Gros Ventre, "like pearls to the whites. They were our greatest decoration" (Flannery 1953:80).

As discussed earlier, elk teeth were found in archaeological sites as far east as Ohio (Mills 1922) and Ontario (Wintemberg 1936), as far south as West Virginia (McMichael 1963), and dating back 3,000 to 5,000 years ago (F. Johnson 1951), although they were most common to Late Woodland Indians (the Erie and other Iroquoian tribes) in Ontario, eastern Michigan, and Northeastern Ohio. The teeth were used primarily as decorative beads, pendants and necklaces.

Prehistorically, elk tusk ornaments also were found on the northern Great Plains, but were absent from the southern and central Plains. The earliest recorded finding dates to 530 to 630 years ago and was located at the Fort Yates archaeological site along the Missouri River in south-central North Dakota—an area occupied, at least in part, by Mandan Indians or their ancestral predecessors (Hurt 1953, Wood 1957).

Until about 1800, elk canines—as characteristic clothing decoration on the Great Plains—appear to have been used almost exclusively by the Mandan, and perhaps the Hidatsa, Crow and Arikara. This is supported in part by Curtis' (1970) assertion that elk teeth were not used by the Blackfeet before the acquisition of guns. In the mid-1880s, German artist and adventurer Rudolph Kurz remarked that Crow Indians originated the use of elk teeth-decorated apparel (Hewitt 1970), but this is confirmed neither by archaeological records nor elsewhere in the literature. The Crow may have adopted the practice (in eastern Montana) before contact with whites (Mulloy 1942). Cheyenne, Arapaho and Sioux subsequently borrowed the trait and its associated values, and introduced it to other regions, particularly the central Plains and western Plateau.

Lewis and Clark made frequent reference to the use of elk teeth by tribes of the Columbia River basin in both the Plateau and Pacific Northwest regions. The teeth obviously were an established tradition there before 1800. The mode of use was similar to that found on the Plains, therefore it seems impossible to generalize about the historical uniqueness of elk teeth as a tribe- or region-specific cultural element (see Sapir 1916).

Wood (1957:385) tentatively concluded: "Elk teeth are part of a trait complex which reached its most complex expression among the Mandan, Hidatsa, Crow, Blackfoot and Dakota." Elk teeth quickly became a distinctive and wide-

This unusual scene shows a Cheyenne woman with dog and travois. The travois willow basket features the woman's collection of elk teeth. Because any garment with elk teeth was a prized and well-guarded possession, this display likely was made for the photographer's benefit. *Photo by T. M. Galey; courtesy of the Smithsonian Institution Anthropological Archives.*

spread ornamentation in the late historic period. A review of the literature artifacts and period photographs in the Anthropological Archives of the Smithsonian Institution (Washington, DC) indicated use of elk teeth in the 1800s by the Mandan, Pawnee, Crow, Cheyenne, Comanche, Blackfeet, Assiniboine, Sioux, Arapaho, Omaha, Arikara, Hidatsa, Atsina, Northern, Eastern and Western Shoshone, Bannock, Ute, Nez Percé, Kiowa, Flathead, Yakima, Hupa, Shasta, Gros Ventre, Gosiute, Tillamook, Cowlitz, Clatsop, Kalispel, San Juan Paiute, Chinook, Klamath and Kutenai. This, however, must be considered only a partial list because of inconsistencies in the historic record and the only cursory attention given to this aspect of ornamentation in ethnographic accounts.

Actually, teeth for decorative purposes were obtained from a variety of animals—including bear, mountain lion, horse, moose, wolf and bison—but elk canines were the most popular and highly valued. Elk tusks were valued by what might be considered a primitive gold standard. Each elk has but two canines and not all of these tusks were suitable and, until the final decades of the 1800s, it supposedly and arguably was anathematic for Indians to kill animals solely for their most desirable part or parts. It, therefore, took considerable time to accrue large quantities of the teeth, even in regions where elk were plentiful (Flannery 1953). As Denig (1930:589) noted: "The elk are not killed in great numbers by any one hunter, so that much time and bargaining is required for an individual to collect . . . the number usually wrought on a . . . woman's dress." Rudolph Kurz remarked that elk teeth were "very expensive . . . due to their being so rare" (Hewitt 1970:80 and 252).

A sense of the worth of elk tusks can be gained by examining dollar values and quid pro quo exchange rates in the early and mid-1800s. For example, Franqois Larocque (1910), who traveled through the Rocky Mountains in 1805, indicated that Flathead Indians gave one horse for 70 to 80 elk canine teeth. In 1833, Maximilian reported that the Mandan equated one horse with 150 tusks (Thomas and Ronnefeldt 1976). Audubon and Bachman (1851) made reference to a gift from Indians of a pronghorn robe decorated with 56 elk tusks. The Indians who gave the robe to Audubon were not identified by tribe, nor was a specific date mentioned, but presumably the event took place during Audubon's trip up the Missouri River in 1843. In any case, the robe reportedly was equal in value to 30 horses. Edwin Denig (1930), a clerk at the Fort Union trading post in the 1840s, indicated that, to Crow Indians, 100 elk canines were worth 10 ermine skins or one horse. Denig (1953) further noted that a Crow woman's frock with 300 elk teeth (and other ornaments) could not be purchased for less than $200—thousands of dollars in modern terms.

Among the Crow at Fort Berthold (now covered by Lake Sakakawea in North Dakota) in 1851, Rudolph Kurz cited the worth of 100 elk teeth as a pack horse or $20 (Hewitt 1970). In 1854 a fancy dress of bighorn sheep hide adorned with 300 elk teeth was worth 25 bison robes or $75 (Greer 1968c). Grinnell (1972[I]:224) wrote that, among the Cheyenne, "One hundred elk-teeth used to be worth a good horse." Dodge (1882) valued a Cheyenne dress decorated with elk teeth at eight ponies or $200. Dodge (1882:308–309) also reported that, on the southern Plains where elk then (1870s) were "rare," teeth "could scarcely be bought for less than two ponies ($50–$60)." And according to Ewers (1955:220), the Blackfeet valued a dress ornamented with elk teeth at two good horses, expressed as "the best buffalo horse" or "the best horse you have."

Catlin (1973[II]:74) observed that Comanche and "Pawnee Picts" (Wichita) women "are always decently and comfortably clad . . . generally with a gown . . . of deer or elk skins; often garnished very prettily with long fringes of elk's teeth, which are fastened on them in rows, and more highly valued than any other ornament they can put upon them."

Indicating another measure of value, Hilger (1952) noted that elk teeth were items of inheritance among the Arapaho. The same was true of other tribes, particularly on the Great Plains. And whereas many Indians obtained "medicine" by visions, the Crow did not, but were able to purchase it for as much as 500 elk teeth (Curtis 1970). The Crow also used elk tooth counters in at least one game of chance.

Francis LaFlesche (1890:215), an Omaha, noted that, as a youth in a village "among the bluffs of the Missouri River"—in the vicinity of present-day Omaha, Nebraska and Council Bluff, Iowa—he took part in a game that involved gambling "for feathers, necklaces of elk-teeth, beads and other valueless articles that were the treasures of the Indian boy." The statement that elk teeth necklaces (ergo, elk teeth) were valueless articles is curious because it is contrary to virtually all other references and evidence on the worth of elk teeth. However, it cannot be dismissed, because LaFlesche was a highly credible informant. Omaha villages at the time (mid-1800s) were, at most, at the fringe of elk range. And because the elk was not a regular or otherwise important source of food or other goods for the semisedentary Omaha, the teeth may not have had (and apparently did not have) anywhere near the worth that they did among tribes (including other village tribes) only a few hundred miles away but more within prevailing elk range.

There are a number of references in the literature suggesting that Indians were seldom willing to part with their elk tusks. Given the eagerness with which Indians of some

Pacific Northwest and Plateau tribes attempted to trade elk teeth to the Lewis and Clark expeditioners (Thwaites 1969, Moulton 1986–1999), it might be more appropriate to say that most Indians were reluctant to sell or trade tusks except among themselves and always for very high prices.

On the Plains and eastern Plateau, elk teeth were used primarily as decorative pendants on dresses worn by women and children (usually girls). In California, the Pacific Northwest and the eastern Plateau, elk teeth commonly were strung as necklaces, anklets and armbands. In all cases, the teeth were prestige items and heirlooms that signified family wealth and rank (Bailey 1926, Mails 1972).

To make the teeth suitable for attachment, the Indians perforated them biconically at the root, through the labial and lingual aspects. Unlike the canine teeth of many other mammals, which have convex surfaces and relatively thick roots, elk canines are flat and thin. Once the tooth was drilled, the perforation was reamed out to allow for threading with sinew thread or a narrow leather thong. Most teeth were polished to a high gloss, and a very few were lightly inscribed with simple geometric designs.

Elk tusks usually were seen as costume embellishments on the upper portions of one piece sleeveless dresses or on capes or mantles of two-piece dresses worn by women and girls (Dorsey 1903, Wood 1957). These dresses were worn or given as gifts (Denig 1953) on such special occasions as weddings, which often was when a bride acquired such a garment (Lowie 1913). Curtis (1970[4]:22) wrote that "no self-respecting [Crow] man presumed to marry unless he and his family could furnish the elk-teeth necessary to adorn a wife's dress."

Concerning dresses worn by Cheyenne women, William Clark observed: "[T]hose dresses usually [*sic*] fall as low as mid leg, they are frequently ornamented with beads [*sic*] and shells and Elk tuskes [*sic*] of which all Indians are very fond of" (Thwaites 1969[5]:357). Grinnell (1972) added that such a dress could weigh 10 pounds (4.5 kg) or more.

Dresses generally were decorated front and back or just on the front with elk teeth in curved lateral rows or series; the Nez Percé were an exception, attaching the teeth with "no studied care" (Spinden 1908:216). Some attached elk teeth as bangles to fringe at the hem. The Lakota and others also decorated dress sleeves with vertical rows of teeth (Hodge 1910). Meriwether Lewis noted, in 1805, that "[T]he tusks of the Elk are pierced [and] strung on a throng [*sic*] and woarn [*sic*] as an ornament [*sic*] for the neck, and is generally woarn by the [Shoshone] women and children" (Thwaites 1969[3]:5).

There is little evidence that men wore elk teeth before the 1870s, except as pendant charms, bracelets, earrings and choker-type necklaces. Bailey (1926) and Johnson (1923)

An elk tooth dress symbolized a husband or father who was a good hunter and provider or who had wealth enough in horses to trade for the coveted upper canine teeth of elk (Hail 1980). Above, the Lakota mother's dress is decorated with what appear to be elk teeth. However, their size and lack of staining suggest elk teeth manufactured of bone or carved from wood and painted. The child's hide dress also is ornamented, but with cowrie shells, which were more common and considerably less valuable than elk bugler or whistler teeth. *Photo courtesy of The Field Museum (#15328), Chicago.*

pointed out that the wearing of elk canine teeth on clothing was scorned as feminine ornamentation by most Indian men, who preferred bear claws and eagle talons for decoration. Generally, the only cases where men are known to have worn garments with elk teeth attached involved ceremonial costumes, and costumes worn by transvestites and "clowns" or woman impersonators. The transvestites were male homosexuals who adopted the clothing and roles of a woman and, among most tribes, were highly regarded (see Hoebel 1962, Driver 1969). Lowie (1913:207) discussed the apparel and behavior of a Crow clown: "One of the clowns is dressed up as a woman, wearing a fine elk-tooth dress; he is obliged to walk, talk, and sit like a woman, and is stuffed so as to simulate pregnancy."

Whatever aversion Indian men had to wearing elk tooth clothing appears to have dissolved after the 1870s. Apparently, the sudden interest in elk canines by the whites (see Chapters 14 and 17), combined with the erosion of the In-

Crow, Winnebago, Lakota, Cheyenne, Blackfeet, Shoshone and probably other tribes wore elk tooth pendant necklaces, chokers, earrings and bracelets. Such charms were thought to bring good luck and health to the wearer or bearer (Ewers 1955, Matthiessen 1959) or indicated that the wearer, such as Absaroke Chief Plenty Hawk (aka Little Light) was a good hunter (Hails 1980). *Photo by Fred E. Miller; courtesy of The University of Montana Museum and Northwest History Collection.*

The number of elk teeth per dress depended on family wealth and standing, but, commonly, was 100 to 300 on a finished garment. Denig (1930, 1953) indicated that 300 was the usual amount on a Crow woman's dress and that a frock was not complete unless it had that many. Catlin (1973), on the other hand, witnessed two Mandan women wearing single rows of elk teeth, and Wissler (1910) reported the same for a Blackfoot dress. Other writers variously cited use of as many as 600, 740, 900 to 1,000 and 1,500 elk teeth on single garments (Wilson 1924, Burroughs 1961, Lowie 1963, Greer 1968c, Grinnell 1972). A Chicago *Record-Herald* reporter who visited a Shoshone village in southern Montana in 1901 estimated that the Indians there had 20,000 elk teeth in possesssion. More than 140 elk teeth can be counted on the white dress of this young Arapaho woman. *Photo courtesy of The Field Museum (#13489), Chicago.*

dians' corporeal resources and economic identity, encouraged the alteration of certain traditional discriminations. The photographic record in the Smithsonian Institution's Anthropological Archives reveals this transformation; men of at least 12 tribes are shown wearing some form of clothing ornamented with elk tusks. The most common article was a cloth vest. (Elk teeth remained tangible evidence of prestige and wealth, as well as being liquid assets.)

Elk tusks also were displayed on shields, pipe bags, bandoleers, medicine pouches, and harnessings for horses and dogs (see Steward 1943, Curtis 1970, Mails 1972, Koch

1977). Dorsey (1896) mentioned an Omaha rattle in which elk molars were used.

As elk were increasingly scarce and difficult to obtain in the late 1800s, some Plains and Plateau Indians became expert at producing imitation tusks from elk antler or bone. These "teeth" were cut, filed and sanded to proper size and shape, then meticulously carved to remove all cancellous tissue. The imitations were painted with brown earth paint to simulate tartar (Hail 1980). Wilson (1924) reported that an Indian could make five artificial teeth in a day, and the final product was nearly indistinguishable from the genuine article.

The reason for the popularity of elk tusks among Indians is difficult to trace. One possible explanation was given by a Sioux elk dreamer, Shooter, who told that these teeth survive when all else of the elk carcass "crumbled to dust," therefore symbolizing long life (Densmore 1918:176). Hidatsa lore held that the first elk ate people. Spirits decided to punish elk by removing all but the upper two canines (see Curtis 1970). The elks' behavior was modified, and the animals were given back their teeth but gave up their tusks at death.

Under a porcupine quill breast plate, an Oglala Sioux wears a vest ornamented with elk teeth. There is little if any evidence of Plains Indian men wearing elk tooth clothing before about 1870. After 1880, there were few elk and fewer opportunities for Indians to hunt elk or other wildlife that provided traditional clothing and decoration. Men may have adopted the elk teeth ornamentation of clothing as an extension of the former use of such teeth as jewelry charms or because of their universal value and the associated spiritual, mythical characteristics of their source animal. *Photo courtesy of The Field Museum (#15950), Chicago.*

Antlers

During the 1830s and 1840s a number of white travelers on the northern Great Plains noticed a curious phenomenon—the occurrence of enormous stacks of elk antlers, obviously constructed by aboriginal residents. At least three such mounds existed in northeastern Montana before 1850.

In 1833, Maximilian zu Wied (1843) located a large pyramid of antlers near the Missouri River above the mouth of the Yellowstone River. The Elkhorn Steeple was then about 18 feet (5.5 m) high and 15 feet (4.6 m) in diameter at its base, and contained more than 1,000 antlers. Father De Smet also witnessed this mound in 1846. Another formation was sighted approximately 50 miles (80 km) above the mouth of the Yellowstone River. Denig (1930:398) described it as "an immense pile of elk horns [*sic*], covering an area of about one acre of ground, and in height about 30 feet. . . . From the state of decay the horns [*sic*] are in it must be very ancient." Thaddeus Culbertson explored the

region in 1850 and reported another such mound on what became known as Elk Horn Prairie, above Fort Union in northwestern North Dakota (McDermott 1952).

Of the mounds along or near portions of the Upper Missouri River, Bradley (1966:349) remarked: "The Elkhorn monuments are among the mysteries of the West destined never to be unraveled. They were three in number, situated on Elkhorn Prairie, on the south side of the Missouri river, just below the mouth of Poplar Creek. The largest was about twenty feet high and twelve feet in diameter at the base, tapering gradually to a rounded top; the other two were somewhat smaller, and all stood within a few hundred yards of each other, about two miles from the Missouri. They contained many thousand horns [*sic*], all evidently shed by living animals. They were first discovered in 1831, and appeared to have been built a good many years, as the horns were somewhat decayed and the superincumbent weight had pressed the base of each mound several inches into the hard prairie soil. Major Culbertson made diligent inquiries concerning them among all the surrounding tribes, Assiniboines, Blackfeet and Crows, but none were in possession even of a tradition concerning their origin. Such a number of horns could only have been gathered by great labor from a vast area, and it seems improbable from the known character of the neighboring Indians that they could have been the architects of the mounds. There is nothing to indicate the purpose of the monuments, which remains wrapped in as deep mystery as their origin. They seem not to have been discovered by Lewis and Clark in 1805 or 1806, but must then have been in existence. A belt of timber partially interposed and they might readily have been overlooked by men toiling at the line of a keel boat or seated upon its low deck. There is but one known monument of a similar form within a radius of hundreds of miles, which is of stone and located near Belly river [Montana]. Like the Elkhorn mounds, no account of it could be obtained from the surrounding Indians and the builders of all must evidently be sought among another people."

In 1850, the mounds were taken down by employees of the American Fur Company. The best antlers were taken to St. Louis in an attempt to sell them to horn workers and dealers. The speculative venture apparently proved unremunerative.

The objective of these elk antler assemblages is not clear, although some writers have suggested that they were benchmarks, totems or some other means of spiritual supplication—or charms for successful hunting. In all likelihood, the various mounds were constructed for different reasons and, over time, served a variety of purposes for the successive generations and tribes occupying their vicinities (see Connor n.d.).

Early explorers of the Upper Missouri River were amazed and confounded by large piles of elk antlers, several that included hundreds if not thousands of antlers and apparently of decades or centuries in the making. Their precise origin and purpose or purposes have never been adequately explained. One possible explanation for an elk antler mound in the Black Hills of the Dakota Territory (*top left*) was provided by George Bird Grinnell (1972). Prehistorically, according to legend, the Arapaho killed elk by driving the animals over a cliff at that location. After the carcasses were dressed, the hunters heaped the antlers on a pile, which continued to increase in size with subsequent drives over the course of many years. Grinnell indicated that the practice of creating such accumulations was common to most Plains tribes, but particularly to the Arapaho, Cheyenne and Blackfeet. Near Fort Sanders, in Albany County, Wyoming, a cairn of elk, bison, mountain sheep and wolf skulls and bones (*top right*) was thought to have served Indians as a travel marker. Along the Missouri River above the mouth of the Yellowstone River was the famous Elkhorn Steeple, first observed and documented by Maximilian zu Wied (1843) in 1833. It reportedly had been built up by hunting and war parties of Blackfeet, who added a brace of antlers each time they passed the site. Karl Bodmer, Maximilian's artist on the expedition painted the scene, which was later copied as a lithograph (*in detail above*) and printed as "The Elkhorn Pyramid on the Upper Missouri" in London in 1842. *Top left photo taken by William Illingworth on the Black Hills Expedition of 1874, led by George Armstrong Custer; courtesy of the South Dakota State Historical Society. Top right photo taken in 1870 by William Henry Jackson; courtesy of the U.S. Geological Survey. Bottom photo from the InterNorth Collection; courtesy of the Joslyn Art Museum.*

Further indication of the quantity of elk antlers on the Great Plains is, again, drawn from Maximilian's observations in the 1830s. Overlooking the prairie near the confluence of the Missouri and Milk rivers in Montana, the adventurer–naturalist remarked that "as far as the eye could reach there were the bleached bones of the buffaloes and elks, and their immense horns" (Thomas and Ronnefeldt 1976:78). It is apparent that there was no shortage of antlers shed annually by bull elk, or left over from bulls killed by Indians, predators, accident or natural cause.

Addressing the role of elk in the trade between whites and Indians in the West during the early and mid-1800s, Chittenden (1935[2]:816) revealed that elk antlers "were not used except in ornamentation." Although this comment may have been accurate with respect to some whites, it was not true for the Indian, for whom elk antlers served a variety of utilitarian purposes—as weapons, implements, and even medicines and decorations.

Weaponry

Most noteworthy of the elk antler weapons was the so-called horn bow, which was popular among Indians of the Plains and eastern Plateau before guns were in great supply. Bows also were made of wood and from horns of bison and bighorn sheep, but the short, recurved, sinew-backed bows fabricated from elk antler were reported to be "stronger, tougher, more elastic, and more durable than a bow of any other materials" (Dodge 1882:417).

Elk bows were made in two ways. The first was described in 1875 by James Belden, a white trapper and hunter who lived among the Crow: "They take a large horn or prong and slice off each side of it; the slices are then filed or rubbed down until the flat sides fit nicely together, when they are glued and wrapped at the ends. Four slices make a bow, it being jointed. Another piece of horn is laid on the center of the bow at the grasp where it is glued fast. The whole is then filed down until it is perfectly proportioned, when the white bone is ornamented, carved and painted" (Lowie 1963:74). In his classic study of the Cheyenne, Grinnell (1972[II]:73) wrote: "Another method was to take a whole long, more or less crooked, antler and treat it in one piece. If such a bow was to be made, an antler as nearly straight as possible was chosen, and was then whittled, scraped, and rubbed until fairly thin. It was soaked in water, and little by little more of it was taken off until it had become quite thin. It was still crooked, but by heating it before the fire and greasing and working it, it became more or less limber. In this crooked form, the bow was finally completed, being shaped, the nocks cut for the string and the whole implement finished. During all this time it was constantly being worked and made more pliable and, finally, when it had be-

come quite flexible, the bow was firmly lashed to a straight stick and left there until entirely dry and straight. Sinew was now applied to the back, and when this had been done and the glue had dried and hardened, the implement was complete and ready for use. They did not last very long, but were likely to break when they became old." Brisbin (1974) noted that such bows took about 3 months to fashion, were of unexpected beauty and were not articles of trade or sale. However, Garretson (1938) indicated that, among Comanche, a bow of this type was valued at 6 to 20 ponies.

Indians who used one or both of these styles of elk antler weapon included the Sarsi, Blackfeet, Crow, Shoshone "sheepeaters," Assiniboine, Mandan, Hidatsa, Sioux, Cheyenne, Comanche, Nez Percé, Gros Ventre and Tewa.

Elk antlers were also used by Indians in the making of spears, harpoons, gaffs, knives and tomahawklike clubs. The hard consistency of the elk antler made it an ideal point or blade for these formidable weapons and hunting or fishing devices (see Wintemberg 1906). Many Indian fisherman of California and the Pacific Northwest, such as the Totowa and Tututni, used elk antler-tipped gaffs to spear trapped fish. The Nootka used a whaling harpoon that consisted of a heavy yew shaft approximately 14 feet (4.3 m) long and a mussel shell blade bound with sinew and spruce gum to a barbed socket of bone or elk antler. A shorter harpoon with a barbed, detachable elk antler tip was used for seal hunting by the Wiyot. Some Indians, including the Kutenai, Shoshone, Northern Assiniboine, Central Miwok, Wisham (a Chinookan subtribe of central Oregon) and a number of Delta Salish tribes, made knives with split elk antler blades and wooden handles. Conversely the Ute, Sarsi and Hidatsa sometimes made knives with bone blades and elk antler handles. The Sarsi, Kutenai, Tsimshian, Washa and others had war clubs tipped with elk antler, and some Crow warriors carried spears or lances with similar tips. In battle, Western Shoshones sometimes used "sharp hooks of elk-horn fixed on the ends of poles, which they used to disembowel the enemy" (Curtis 1970[8]:179).

To my knowledge, arrow points of elk antler were not widely used except in northwestern California (Miles 1963), the Ohio River valley (Beauchamp 1902) and perhaps by the Conoy Indians of Maryland and Pennsylvania (Hodge 1907). However, these antlers were extensively used as chisels to shape points from bone, flint or obsidian. Meriwether Lewis commented on this activity by the Shoshone: "[W]ith the point of a deer or Elk's horn they also form their arrow points of the flint, with a quickness and neatness that is really astonishing" (Thwaites 1969[3]:19–20).

Mandan and Pawnee Indians devised an arrow shaft straightener from an oval section of elk antler with a bored hole. And the Cheyenne placed feathers for arrow fletching

A carved Tsimshian elk antler war club, 15.5 inches (39.4 cm) in length, is meant to represent a bear. *Photo courtesy of the Museum of the American Indian, Heye Foundation.*

on a flat piece of elk antler, which served as a cutting board so that the feathers could be trimmed evenly.

Saddles

For general mounted travel, Indians used frame (riding) saddles. As opposed to the pad saddle, frame saddles produced less chafing and facilitated transport of accessories. Many of these saddles consisted of portions of elk antler. The Kutenai, for example, had three types of elk antler frames—a man's saddle, a woman's saddle and a pack saddle (Walker 1978). The basic construction was antler pommel and cantle with wood sideboards. The whole was held together by thongs. Wet rawhide was placed over the sideboards and stitched; when subsequently fitted and dried, it was compact, solid and light. It also was comfortable and especially popular for riding long distances (Mails 1972). The Blackfeet called the design a "prairie chicken snare saddle" (Ewers 1955:92).

The essential point of variance among frame saddles was the bow or front portion made of antler. Most were Y-shaped, made from a forked section of antler, with the stem serving as the pommel. Some pommels were wood, but antler was more durable and, by steaming or boiling, could be bent to desired shape.

Indians who used elk antler to make at least some of their frame saddles included the Crow, Blackfeet, Kiowa, Cheyenne, Sioux, Nez Percé, Ponca, Mandan, Kutenai, Shoshone, Sarsi, Ute, Bannock, Thompson, Hidatsa, Plains Cree and perhaps the Caddo, Mescalero Apache, Omaha and Winnebago. The Kiowa used elk antler for both pack and riding saddles (Hail 1980).

Implements

Strong and durable tools and utensils used in the Indian's daily life were manufactured from elk antlers. Antler was

fashioned into useful shapes after months of soaking in still, backwater pools warmed by summer sun (Stands in Timber and Liberty 1967). Probably the most widespread of the antler tools was a wedge used primarily to split firewood. It was found in all the regions in which elk were hunted, but especially in California, the Pacific Northwest and western Plateau (see Miles 1963). The wedge featured a sharpened end that was jammed into the wood and a wider, flattened or rounded opposite end that was struck with a rock or stone mallet. Lewis reported in 1806 that the elk antler wedges the Clatsop and Coastal Chinook used to hollow out canoes "appear to answer extremely well" (Thwaites 1969[4]:20). The Cahto (or Kato) Indians of California used such wedges to cut wooden slabs for lodge roofing, and the Nootka used them on Vancouver Island to fell trees.

Nearly as prevalent as wedges were elk antler chisels and adzes, used to chip and shape stone and wood items. Chisels of elk antler were particularly common on the Plateau, as were elk antler adzes in the Pacific Northwest. Whereas Indians of the Columbia River frequently used elk antler wedges to build canoes, as previously noted, the Klamath and other Indians farther inland used elk antler adzes and fire to fashion shovel-nosed canoes from pine, cedar or Douglas-fir logs.

Unique to California was the elk antler "purse" (Hodge 1907). Valuables of wealthy members of the Hupa, Yurok and Karok tribes were placed in an oblong hollow piece of elk antler 6 to 7 inches (15–18 cm) long. The outsides of these purses usually were elaborately carved and covered with a thin piece of antler held in place by thongs. Hupa men were noted for their skill in working elk antlers (Wallace 1978a).

In California, the Pacific Northwest and on portions of the Plateau and Plains as well, spoons were made of elk

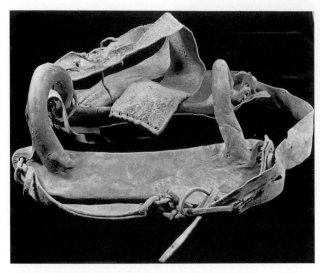 

The so-called elk horn saddle (*left*) was widely but not exclusively used by mounted Indians in the West. A Spanish-style saddle, with pommel and cantle fashioned from steamed elk antler, typically was placed on a hide or cloth pad and another hide covered the saddle seat for the rider's comfort (*right*). Elk horn saddles, "more recent than either wood or pad saddles" (Hails 1983:227), were used for daily horseback riding by men and women, for extended travel and as pack saddles stabilized with the aid of a martingale and crupper. The rawhide that was shrink-wrapped around the saddle was usually from bison, but elk skin was used on some saddles. *Left photo courtesy of the Haffenreffer Museum of Anthropology, Brown University, Bristol, Rhode Island. Right photo of Standing Hawk (Omaha) and woman by William Henry Jackson; courtesy of the Union Pacific Railroad Museum.*

A Karok elk antler wedge (*top*) and a Snoqualmu elk antler adze (*bottom*). *Photos courtesy of the Museum of the American Indian, Heye Foundation.*

Elk horn purses, such as the Hupa artifact above, were used by a number of California Indians to secure and transport currency of the day—strings of dentalium shells (Fane et al. 1991). Wafer-thin strips of antler or bone, held in place by wrapped straps of rawhide, served to cover the purse opening. *Photo courtesy of the Museum of the American Indian, Heye Foundation.*

antler. Among the Wiyot Indians: "The best spoons were of elkhorn and were ladle-shaped with handles decorated with incised geometric figures, especially on the edges" (Curtis 1970[13]:77). The Sarsi used elk antler for both spoons and ladles. Some southwestern Oregon Athapaskan men (especially chiefs) used elk antler spoons, but the women of those tribes did not (Miller and Seaburg 1990). Elk antler was used extensively by most western Indians in making handles for cutlery and other tools on which considerable weight or pressure was regularly exerted, and it continued to be used even after metal implements were available (Lowie 1963, Mails 1972).

Quirt handles of elk antler tines were popular among the

About 7 inches (17.8 cm) in length, Hupa spoons (*above*), like those of the nearby Yuroks, were used by men for eating acorn mush (women used spoons of mussel shell or fashioned from animal skull). Wealthy Indians kept especially elaborate sets of such spoons for entertaining guests. To make such spoons, elk antler was steamed and bent into shape. "Their handles were then carved into a variety of geometric shapes, in a more or less free expression of the carver's personal creativity" (Fane et al. 1991:182). *Photo courtesy of the Museum of the American Indian, Heye Foundation.*

Assiniboine, Mandan, Sarsi, Sauk, Fox, Crow, Shoshone and Osage. Brisbin (1974) described an elk horn whip (probably quirt) beautifully carved and painted. The usual construction of quirts involved removal of a tine's spongy core, a hole bored at one end for a wrist strap and a second hole bored at the other end to accommodate a wooden pin that passed through a perforation in the end of a leather sash or strop (see Penney 1992).

Elk antler digging tools, which resembled pick axes, were used on the northern Plains prehistorically (Davis 1973). Within historic time, elk antler hoes and rakes were made and used by the Hidatsa (see Edmonds and Clark 1989). Also within the historic period, digging tools made from elk antlers were used by Salish tribes of the Pacific Northwest, Plateau and Great Basin regions. Likewise attributed to the Salish is an elk antler basketry awl recovered in British Columbia (Fane et al. 1991). Its specific function in basket or mat making is uncertain, but it may have been used to separate the layers of cedar bark that served as fabric.

Fleshers and hide scrapers, or dubbers, were among the most important tools manufactured of elk antler, as discussed earlier in relation to hide preparation. Especially common on the Great Plains (Taylor 1975), these tools were used to remove meat, fat and other extraneous tissue from animal skins. They tended to be curved less acutely at the scraping end, but were otherwise quite similar.

Among the Cheyenne, when a man died, his shield and war bonnet traditionally were left to his son or best friend; a woman's flesher was left to her daughter, and other property of the deceased usually was distributed among nonrelatives (Llewelyn and Hoebel 1941).

Medicine

A piece of elk antler reportedly was used by some Sioux doctors (herbalists) as a remedy for broken bones, but its curative agent and method of use are unknown (Mails 1972).

Most Indians placed considerable stock in the medicinal and spiritual values of visions and tokens or sacred objects symbolic of those visions. Such objects were accumulated in bundles or carried or worn as ornaments, charms or medicines. These usually were individual possessions and had a variety of different symbolic meanings. However, there were some tribal bundles, and certain tokens had broadly recognized meaning and value. Among the Crow and Lakota, for example, headdresses featuring elk antler were considered to be potent love medicines.

Decoration

The feathered headdress was one of the most prestigious items earned and owned by a Plains or eastern Plateau war-

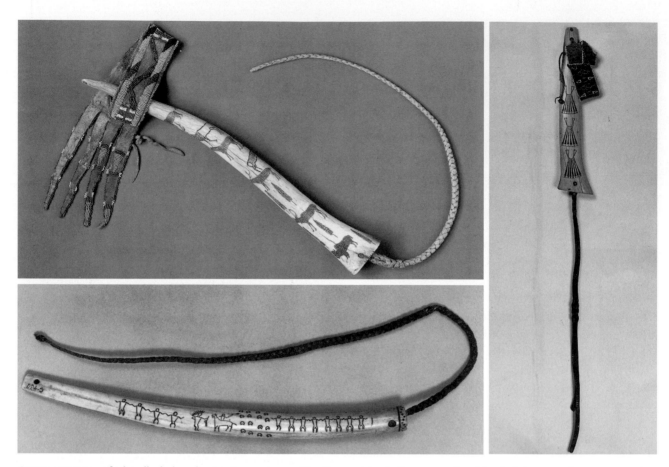

Quirts, consisting of a handle, lash and wrist strap, were used by all equestrian Indians to prod or drive their horses and, on rare occasion, as a coup weapon. The handles were made of bone, wood or antler and generally were about 14 to 18 inches (36–46 cm) long. Quirts made from elk antler tines were favored, in part because they were especially durable and could be attractively incised. Lashes were rawhide (sometimes elk skin), about 20 to 24 inches (51–61 cm) in length, often braided. The top left quirt is Crow, featuring a fringed and beaded wrist strap and fairly stylized artwork on the elk antler handle. It dates from about 1875. The bottom left elk antler quirt is Osage, from the southern Plains and illustrates the owner's coup record. The incising style shows the quirt to be pre-1850. The right elk tine quirt is Sac and Fox , and its geometric handle design probably was simply decorative. *Top left photo courtesy of the Founders Society of the Detroit Institute of Arts. Bottom left photo courtesy of the Chandler-Pohrt Collection of the Buffalo Bill Historical Center. Right photo courtesy of the Museum of the American Indian, Heye Foundation.*

rior. It symbolized his accomplishments in warfare and represented his stature and rank. The base of such a headdress—known as a roach spreader, and to which plume holders were attached—often was carved from elk antlers (Feder 1958, Howard 1960). According to Hail (1980), east-

ern Plains and Woodland tribes made roach spreaders from elk antler until about 1870.

The grizzly bear was considered powerful medicine by many tribes in the West. Its claws symbolized the animal's strength and ferociousness in battle and were adopted as

A Salish digging stick, features an elk antler tine as the blade. *Photo courtesy of the Museum of the American Indian, Heye Foundation.*

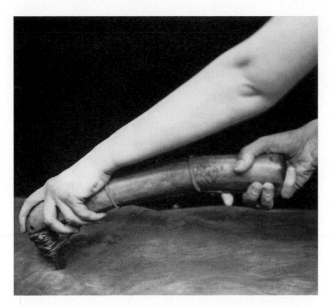

The typical fleshing tool was "a piece of elk-horn, bent at a right angle, and armed anciently with a cutting edge of flint and in modern times with a more or less keen steel blade" (Grinnell 1972 [I]:213), such as the Kutenai flesher above, minus only a wrist strap. Other dubbers, such as those used by the Sarsi and some Blackfeet, were entirely of elk antler, with the scraping end filed to a fine edge or thinly serrated. *Photo courtesy of the Museum of the American Indian, Heye Foundation.*

clothing ornamentation and necklaces in particular by warriors, chiefs and other prominent male tribal members (Feder and Chandler 1961). Natural yellow claws were prized most highly. When the grizzly became scarce after the mid-1800s, imitation claws were carved from elk antlers (Koch 1977).

Other Antler Uses

Members of the Cheyenne elk horn scrapers warrior society (also known as hoof-rattle and elk soldiers) carried a piece of elk antler "carved to imitate a snake and notched on one side, over the notches of which they rapidly drew a piece of bone. The elk-horn [*sic*] rattling instrument was painted yellow below and dark blue above, with a snake's head carved on one end and the tail on the other. These rattles represented the blue racer [snake] which came from the sun. It is from this instrument that they received the name Elk-horn Scrapers" (Grinnell 1972 [II]:58). Stands in Timber and Liberty (1967) confirmed that the "Elks" were a Southern Cheyenne military society, which had as its insignia an elk antler and a crooked-ended spear wrapped with otter skin and hung with eagle feathers. Dorsey (1905 [I]:18–19) wrote that the elk antler emblem was formed like a rattlesnake: "It has a straight body about two inches thick and about eighteen inches long. It has a head and tail. . . .

Whenever the tribe desired large herds of buffalo, elk, or deer to come near their camp the warriors [horn scrapers] would come together and chew the herb used in making the sacred arrow ceremonies and blow it upon the elk antler to make it effective."

Kane et al. (1991) reported on the elk antler daggers of a bear-doctor of the northern California coast Pomo tribe (see also Barrett 1917, Cody 1940).

Boiled pieces or scrapings of elk antler also were part of the formula used by Comanche Indians in the process of making glue (Lowie 1963), but Clark (1884) noted that the antler parts were unnecessary.

Elsewhere, antler tip pestles were used by Indians of northwestern California (Miles 1963). Mandan Indians used elk antler as lodge decoration and for hanging items off the floor (Boller 1972). From an intrusive Hopewellian burial site (the Mound City Group), Mills (1922) excavated an elk antler comb with eight teeth.

Curtis (1970) reported that the Wiyot had a *grass game* that sometimes involved the use of sections of elk antler.

"The Elk (Hoof-Rattle or Horn-Scraper) Society has more than one hundred warriors and four Cheyenne maidens. . . . Each warrior carries a rattle. The rattle is a stick about a foot long, covered with tanned buckskin, to which are sewed or tied several dry dew-claws of elk, deer, or antelope" (Dorsey 1905 [I]:18). *Photo courtesy of The Field Museum (#A102776a), Chicago.*

Players wrapped bundles of sticks in grass, into one of which a marked piece of antler was placed. The object was for the opponent to guess which bundle contained the antler. Much gambling for high stakes was involved. Mandan and Hidatsa played a game called snow snake, which used elk antler with feathers attached (Marriott 1963). It was similar to modern lawn darts. Cheyenne women had a throwing sticks game (Miller 1985). Played on smooth ground, elk antler-tipped sticks about 6 feet (1.8 m) long were hurled underhand to slide a long distance. The Oglala Sioux had a game called *kagu woskate* or *haka heciapi* (Meeker 1901) or *hehaka woskate* (Walker 1905), meaning the elk game. Meeker (1901) described the activity as a hoop game, although Wissler (1907) disagreed with this designation. Lakota women called the rawhide ring implement of the game *cangleskan*, meaning hoop, or *taoga canleska*, meaning web hoop. In some versions of this popular gambling game, the rings—about 3.5 inches (8.9 cm) in diameter—may have been netted or webbed. This game was played by tossing a ring in the air and another player attempting to catch it on a hehaka stick (Figure 45). Points

were awarded according to the projection on which the ring was caught, and the game was played to a number of points agreed to by the players. Walker (1905) wrote that the game was played to ensure success of an elk hunt, but the gaming and hunting correlation is vague. Jones (1989:12) implied that "association of hoop and stick games such as the elk game with sexual organs and intercourse" was not uncommon among Plains tribes, but the associative evidence for the elk game is not convincing. Hoop and pole (or stick) games were played throughout the continent north of Mexico (Culin 1975), but there is no hint in the literature of their universal or widespread sexual connotation.

Exploitation

As indifferent toward elk antlers as white men may have been when elk and their antlers were found in abundance, this attitude changed in the latter half of the 19th century. At that time, antlers were used in the manufacture of as knives, tobacco pipes, buttons and other decorative items. "Fences were made of them, doorways were ornamented with them and in a variety of ways the stately antlers of this

In this 1875 photograph of a Wyoming encampment of the famed Shoshone chief Washakie, elk antlers are visible in the left foreground, near the entrance of Washakie's tepee. In review of thousands of 19th century photographs of Native Americans, this is the only scene found in which whole elk antler or other unused elk parts are plainly visible. Washakie's band was the easternmost division of the Shoshone proper, and its territory was roughly bordered by the Wind River Range, the headwaters of the North Platte River and South Pass in Wyoming and Brown's Hole in Colorado. *Photo by William Henry Jackson; courtesy of the Smithsonian Institution Anthropological Archives.*

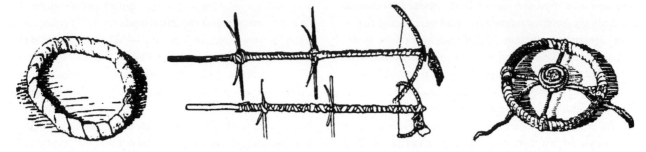

Figure 45. The Oglala Sioux's elk game was a gambling contest in which points were awarded to players who caught tossed rings (*left*) on specially made hehaka (elk) sticks. The rings, sometimes webbed, were 3.5 to 11.5 inches (8.9–29.2 cm) in diameter and the sticks were 36 to 40 inches (91–102 cm) long with two sets of crossbars. The tops of some sticks had an arced piece and featured small, colored flags, as shown above. Catching rings on the top was most difficult, so held the highest point value. Meeker (1901:26) stated that contest winners were awarded a hair ornament (*right*) that was "a miniature gaming hoop or wheel . . . as small as the matter can make it, with spokes like a wheel, ornamented with porcupine quills and tied to a small lock of hair on one side of the crown by a buckskin string fastened to the center of the ornament." The ornament was similar to that worn by elk dreamers (Jones 1989). *Illustration from Culin (1907).*

noble animal did service in adorning the abodes of men" (Chittenden 1935[2]:816). In less than 50 years, the value of elk antlers changed from prairie litter to objet d'art and status symbol. The railroad, which permitted lucrative transport of elk meat and hides to eastern markets, invited transcontinental distribution of antlers, which began to appear in and around households and business establishments across the United States.

Unlike the commercial slaughter of elk for hides, meat or teeth, killing elk solely for their antlers does not appear to have occurred to any great extent between 1850 and 1900. And there is no evidence known to me to indicate that this ever was done by Indians.

However, Indians did trade antlers, and some devoted their energies to antler crafts, selling the products to white artifact seekers. And when elk were in short supply and the Indians were forced to adopt the unfamiliar circumscription of reservation life, some Indians took to scouring the prairie for bones, horns and antlers, which then were sold for shipment to St. Louis and Philadelphia to be ground into phosphorous fertilizer or glue or converted into knife handles, combs and other sundries. The bone pickers, both Indians and whites, gathered virtually hundreds of tons of these remains (mostly bison) at $4 to $30 per ton (see Inman 1897, Branch 1962, Taylor 1975, McHugh 1979, Russell 1981).

For the Indians, it was a bitterly ironic and ignoble sequel to their relationship with the animal on whom they had depended and with whom they had lived symbiotically for hundreds and, in some regions, even thousands of years.

Bones

As discussed earlier, marrow extracted from elk leg bones was considered a delicacy. Other bones, such as the ribs and

When the Plains were all but depleted of big game, some Indians cruised the empty sagebrush and grasslands in rude carts, picking up bone and antlers, to sell them for just a few dollars per ton (Russell 1981) or swap them at trading posts for canned meat. A writer of the era noted that, "allowing 40 feet for a freight car, the bones that went East would make a string of cars 7,575 miles long—enough to fill two tracks from New York to San Francisco" (Tilden 1964:225). *Photo by F. Jay Haines; courtesy of the Montana State Historical Society.*

joints, were also used in soups or were chopped and boiled to produce grease for the preparation of pemmican. Bones were a base for vermilion and other body-paint dyes. In addition, tallow removed from boiled bones was used as an ungent or salve by the Quinault and other Coastal Salish (Curtis 1970), and to rejuvenate dried leather, caulk boat and tent seams and polish decorative items of bone or quill. William Clark observed that "After eateing [*sic*] the marrow out of two shank bones of an Elk, the Squar [Sacajawea or Bird Woman—a Shoshone who was captured as a young girl and raised among the Hidatsa, she served as guide and interpreter for the Lewis and Clark Expedition] choped [*sic*] the bones fine boiled them and extracted a pint of Grease, which is Superior to the tallow of the animal" (Thwaites 1969[3]:264).

In nearly all regions, except portions of the Southwest and Great Basin, elk bones were used in the making of awls, bodkins, needles and forklike utensils. These items, as well as bone pipes, were relatively common among village (non-nomadic) Indians of the Plains and Eastern Woodland tribes.

The elk ham-bone reportedly made a very good axe head (Brisbin 1974:118).

Indicative of other widespread uses of elk bone by historic North American Indians are the following artifacts, most of which are on file with the Smithsonian Institution's Department of Anthropology: chisel points (femur)—Nootka; arrow points—Iroquois; fish hooks—Pomo; arrow straighteners—Ute; knife handles—Mandan; drawblades—Blood Blackfeet; fleshers (hind leg)—Woods Cree; knives (rib)—Cheyenne; hoes (shoulder blade)—Omaha; beamers (tibia)—Sarsi; netmesh measures—Chilula; scrapers—Teton Sioux; hair scrapers for crushing lice—Hupa; harpoon points—Winton; and club handles—Coastal Salish and Bannock. (It must be emphasized that this is only a partial list of artifacts and tribes that used them.)

Hair

According to Ewers (1958), Blackfeet Indians used buffalo hide pad saddles filled with the hair of elk and moose.

The stiff hair of elk tails had several applications. Wissler (1966) indicated that it was used for ornamentation and embroidery. It also was fashioned into eyeshade visors by some Arapaho and Plains Cree (Kroeber 1902, Koch 1977).

Miscellaneous

Other parts of the elk that figures in the material culture of North American Indian tribes included: the paunch

One of the more intriguing elk bone artifacts located is a tubular smoking device identified as a squaw pipe from an unidentified Plains tribe. Bone pipes, according to Miles (1963:220), were not unusual, "but seldom used in comparison with other forms," such as bowl or elbow-shaped pipes. Because straight pipes (bone or stone) were less bulky and generally smaller than stem pipes, according to Grinnell (1972:208), they were relatively easy to transport, so were taken on war and raiding expeditions for "ordinary" smoking. McGuire (1899) noted that the tube pipe was the most conti-

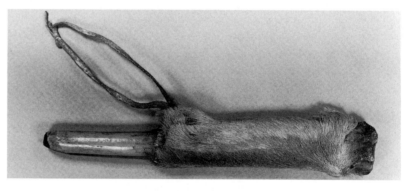

nentally widespread and primitive form. Known to use elk, deer and pronghorn shin bones for tube pipes were the Kiowa, Comanche, Arapaho, Crow, Winnebago, Cheyenne and Lakota. Adams (1990), however, noted that Oglala "bone" elbow pipes actually were fashioned from deer or elk antler. Typically, to keep bone pipes from splitting, they were wrapped with moistened rawhide that shrunk tightly around the bone when dried. The intrigue of this particular pipe is its "squaw pipe" designation, which would suggest that it was owned or used by an Indian woman or women. However, the term squaw is or was antecedent to a wide variety of articles (e.g., squaw ax, squaw horse, squawberry, squaw medicine, squaw wood) and conditions or circumstances (e.g., squaw winter, squaw side) that were not necessarily specific to or associated with Indian women (Blevins 1993). Squaw, incidentally, was derived from an Algonkian word for wife, but often was used as a pejorative by whites and became (and remains) objectionable in nearly all contexts to most Indians and specifically so to Plains Indians (see Hoxie 1996). Accordingly, the term squaw pipe would not have been applied to the artifact by Indians themselves. Smithsonian Institution anthropologist Candice Greene (personal communication:1997) advised that squaw pipes were the only ones used by Indian women but were smoked by some men as well. They were secular devices. Although Hodge (1910) indicated that, among most tribes, tobacco was cultivated and smoked only by men, Dr. Greene stated that recreational (nonceremonial) smoking was commonplace among women as well as men (see also Steinmetz 1984, Paper 1988). Another intrigue is that this pipe is wrapped in hair-out hide. The significance of this uncommon wrap is unknown, but the treatment probably was decorative in purpose, suggesting that the pipe may have had a ceremonial function. A nearly identical straight pipe in the Museum of the American Indian, Heye Foundation collections is a Cheyenne artifact. *Photo courtesy of the Union Pacific Railroad Museum.*

Billowing engines of the "bad medicine wagons" and their spidery tracks and trestles came to symbolize to Native Americans the futility of resisting the white invasion. The U.S. government sponsored, greatly subsidized and, in countless essential ways, supported construction of the transcontinental railroad. In its initial considerations of the outlandish proposal for a transcontinental railway, Congress hardly considered the consequences to Indian life, except for consensus that the "numerous, powerful and entirely savage" Indians and the western wildlife that supported them were obstacles to manifest destiny and needed to be moved, bought out or driven away (Brown 1977:29, see also Phillips 1974). *Photo courtesy of David R. Phillips.*

(Wissler 1966), bladder (Orchard 1916, Parker 1954) and intestines (Flannery 1953) as bags; hooves for glue (Lowie 1963), rattles (Opler 1941) and necklaces (Clark 1884); split dewclaws for rattles and jinglers (Lowie 1913, Hoebel 1962, Mauer 1992); and fecal matter for fertilizing tobacco plantings (Lowie 1920, Curtis 1970). Elk droppings also were scattered as part of the female ritual attendant to the Crow sun dance ceremony (Marquis 1974). McClintock (1968) reported Blackfeet use of the skins of elk fetuses for berry bags. Blackfeet quill workers were said to keep quills in cigar-shaped elk bladders (Ewers 1958). Thick muscle from the neck of a bull elk sometimes was twisted and dried for use as a pipe (Clark 1884). Morrow (1975) reported that Wasco Indians, who resided on the south side of the Columbia River near The Dalles, used *sizings* to weatherproof rawhide. The sizings were a mixture of cactus juice, hide scrapings, antler glue, fish roe, beaver tail wax or liquid from the eyes, fish lymph and secretions from the glands of a bison or elk.

Sinew fibers from the elk's leg and backbone tendons were used as string and thread. Lewis and Clark observed elk sinew thread being used by Shoshone, to sew skins, and by Clatsop and Chinook Indians, to sew robes (Thwaites 1969). Indians of California, the Pacific Northwest, and the Plateau and northern Plains used elk sinew to attach beadwork and other ornaments to their clothing. Weltfish (1965) noted the practice among Pawnees of tying feathers to their scalplocks with elk sinew.

Threads were obtained by drawing strands from a length of dried sinew with an awl or piece of flint. It was moistened in the mouth and then twisted by rolling it between the palms of the hands with one end held by the user's teeth. The moistening and twisting caused the sinew to expand. Once sewn, the stitches would dry and shrink, creating a strong and tight seam (Wissler 1906).

Because of the strength of elk sinew, some California Indians used it in the construction of snares. Twisted sinew strings also served some horsemen of the eastern Plateau and northern Plains tribes as cinches. Pawnee (Brisbin 1974) and Crow (Clark 1884) reportedly fastened arrowheads to shafts with moistened elk sinew. Also, as previously noted, some Indians, such as the Flathead, used sinew taken from near the spinal column of an elk or bison to wrap around bows, reportedly adding to the weapons' elasticity, strength and distinctive appearance.

Omaha Indians made bowstrings with sinew taken from the elk's shoulder to the base of its spine. "This sinew was prepared by soaking it over night in water slightly mixed with glue, after which the sinew was stripped into strands and all the water squeezed out. A strand composed of many threads was measured off twice the length of the bow. A pole having on it a small branch was driven into the ground and the strand looped over this branch. The maker of the bowstring took the ends in one hand, twisted them between his fingers, and swung them twisting until the two strands tightened; then he twisted the cord firmly together into one string and knotted the ends. A loop remained where the cord was over the branch on the pole; this loop was for the head notches on the bow; the other end was left free for convenient adjustment. . . . Every man kept two strings for his bow—one fastened on the bow, the other carried in the quiver for use in emergencies" (Fletcher and La Flesche 1972[2]:449).

As with most wildlike hunted, the elk could be and probably often was thoroughly utilized (Figure 46). What was not eaten or converted to some manner of tool, decoration, instrument or fabric probably was fed to camp dogs. If not quite the "commissary" that the bison was said to represent to Indians (Cook 1989:113), the elk, by virtue of its size, number and distribution, was nearly so for many Natives.

1 Antlers
Spear points
Harpoon points
Fluting/grooving tool
Digging tools
Flaking hammers
Horn bows
Gaff points
Knife blades
War club heads
Lodge hangers
Hooks
Arrow points
Arrow shaft straighteners
Arrow fletchers
Saddle pommels
Saddle cantles
Pestles
Chisels
Hoes
Adzes
Adze handles
Wedges
Purse
Pipes
Spoons
Basketry awls
Ladles
Quirt handles
Fleshers
Hide scrapers (beamers)
Medicine for broken bones
Roach spreaders
Imitation bear claws
Imitation elk teeth
Rattles
Glue
Games
Tool handles
Cutlery handles

2 Brain
Tanning and curing hides

3 Teeth
Beads
Pendants
Necklaces
Anklets
Gambling counters
Medium of exchange
Bangles
Earrings
Charms
Bracelets
Decoration on: shields,
 armbands, bags,
 medicine pouches,
 harnessings, women's
 and girl's dresses,
 men's cloth vests

4 Neck muscle
Pipes

5 Bone marrow
Grease to prepare pemmican,
 base for body paint dyes

6 Dewclaws
Rattles
Jinglers

7 Hooves
Glue
Rattles
Necklaces

8 Stomach (paunch)
Bags

9 Intestines
Bags

10 Bones
Digging sticks
Hoes
Awles
Bodkins
Needles
Fork-like utensils
Pipes
Chisel points
Arrow points
Fish hooks
Arrow straighteners
Knife handles
Drawblades
Fleshers
Knives
Ax head
Beamers
New mesh measures

Bones (continued)
Hair scrapers
Harpoon points
Club handles

11 Tail hair
Ornamentation
Embriodery
Eyeshade visors

12 Bladder
Quill bags

13 Hair (general)
Pad stuffing

14 Hide
Parfleches
Ropes
Lodge and tipi covers
Sweatlodge covers
Moccasin soles
Moccasin uppers
Shields
Shield covers
Robes
Soup (shavings)
Dresses
Shirts
Leggings
Moccasins
Ceremonial wear:
 leggings, dancing
 skirts, aprons,
 dresses, medicine
 robes
Mats
Mantles
Blankets
Armor shirts or vests
Tunics
Corselets

Hide (continued)
Chemises
Smocks
Burial robes
Sandals
Warshields
Temporary shelter
Harnesses
Bedding
Tobacco pouches
Cradleboards
Pictographs
Fringe
Small bags
Rifle scabbards
Quivers
Quiver linings
Bow cases
Glue
Boats
Cordage
Quirt lashes
Belts
Thongs
Bandages
Fishing line
Disguises
Canoes
Pirogues
Boat patches
Medium of exchange
Value index
Drag lines
Tack belts
Medicine bags
Ceremonial rugs
Dew cloths

15 Fat
Tallow: salve, rejunenate
 dried leather,
 caulk boat and
 tent seams, polish
 items of bone
 or quill

16 Sinew
Horn bowwraps
Bowstrings
Cinches
Harpoons
Thread
String
Snares

17 Hide from bull elk neck
Moccasin soles
Shields
Glue
Armor shirts

Figure 46.   Some uses of elk and elk by-products by North American Indians. *Illustration by Charles W. Schwartz.*

Art and Ideography

Native Americans were very adept at converging concrete images and ideas in both tangible and visual expressions (Mallery 1972). Their paintings, drawings, sign language and use of colors, shapes and forms tended to be highly allegorical. As an important economic, spiritual and cultural milieu, the elk was not uncommonly featured in the Indians' various ideograph mediums.

At least until Native American art was stylistically, technically and commercially influenced by whites in the 1800s (see Ewers 1939, Gebhard 1974), most of it was simplistic in design and both complex and evocative in symbolic gist. It found expression in a wide variety of mediums, including rock art, sculpture, bone and wood carving, quill and beadwork, costume and painting.

Holmes (1908) described four reasons for Native art: technique or the technical factors of art (or craft) itself; aesthetics; ideography; and spiritualism. Also, Native art can be divided into two stylistic categories, namely, geometric and representational. As a subject of Indian artwork, the elk was representational (a life form) and its executions certainly were within the purview of Holmes' last two reasons and probably the former two as well. The vast majority of elk art reviewed in the literature and from collections clearly was rendered consequent to spiritualism. Also remarkable is the fact that most elk art extant is from the northern Plains and Plateau regions and of the historic time period.

There are, however, examples of elk art from prehistory, and these are primarily petroglyphs (Figure 47). Petroglyphs and rock paintings of elk tend to be difficult to discern, particularly from deer and caribou renderings, and those believed with fair certainty to be elk are uncommon (see Mallery 1972, Keyser 1987, 1992, Ragnovich 1994). Nevertheless, some of the best examples are found at Legend Rock in central Wyoming and Castle Gardens in west-central Wyoming (Mauer 1992). Some of the elk images are pecked (chipped with a stone hammer) and rather crude, but others are pecked, incised and relatively anatomically accurate. Both types are considered ceremonial, as opposed to biographical (see Keyser 1987), and date from 1000 to 1775 AD, with the Castle Gardens elk likely postdating 1625.

Most historic period Indian art featuring elk is found as painting on hides. Although hide painting was widely practiced during the period of early European contact, Ewers (1939) suggested no reason to believe that the artform was not of ancient origin. As far as can be determined, all representational painting was accomplished by men, whereas most geometric painting was executed by women. (In certain other mediums, including quill and beadwork and embroi-

Represented in pecked, incised and painted forms throughout the species' prehistoric and historic ranges, elk petroglyphs were neither common nor rare. Most rock art symbols, images and characterizations are difficult to type, but where elk appear, they usually are quite distinctive and discernable from other representations (Mallery 1893), including deer, with which elk sometimes are confused. The origin of most petroglyphs is uncertain, but anthropologists agree that worshiping, ceremonial healing, chronicling, chronologizing, mapping, sign posting and story telling were the usual purposes (see Rajnovich 1994). Also, rock art was of local rather than general or universal significance (Hodge 1910). The elk images in the top photo were incised between 1000 and 1700 AD at Legend Rock in central Wyoming. Also at Legend Rock, the bottom image is a larger, more anatomically detailed bull elk created by pecking and incising between 1625 and 1775. *Photos by E. M. Maurer; courtesy of The Minneapolis Institute of Arts.*

dery women produced both styles.) The representational painting was of three types—time counts or calendars, biographical, and vision record (Hall 1926) (Figure 48).

Figure 47. Six examples of late prehistoric and early historic picture writing featuring what are believed to be elk (all but last extracted from complex illustrations): (a) pecked and colored petroglyph—Pipestone Quarry, Minnesota (Winchell 1884); (b) painted petroglyph—Shinumo Canyon, Utah (Mallery 1893); (c) unknown medium—vicinity of Fort Snelling, Minnesota (Eastman 1849); (d) petroglyph—Oak Canyon, Utah (Steward 1941); (e) rock painting—Pecos River region, Utah (Newcomb 1967); and (f) Assiniboine pen drawing in 1853 at Fort Union, North Dakota (Denig 1930).

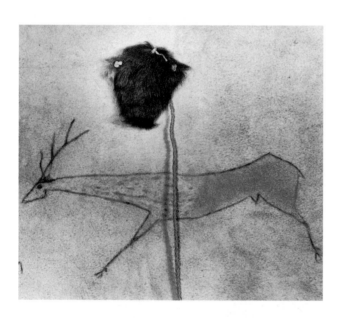

On authentic, historic, painted hides of Plains Indians (and exclusive of the horse—after about 1750), the bison, eagle, bear and mythical thunderbird were the primary representational animals featured (Mauer 1992). The next most commonplace were the wolf, coyote, elk, deer and turtle. However, even the mainstay bison was depicted on only 7% of such hides; the other animals less so (Ewer 1939). The above elk painting is a 13-inch (33 cm) long detail of a Crow elk skin love blanket. *Photo courtesy of the Museum of the American Indian, Heye Foundation.*

Figure 48. Besides through music and stories, the primary method used by most elk-hunting Plains tribes (Mails 1972) to document their traditions and chronologies was by means of what the Lakota referred to as "winter counts," which were calendrical histories. Each winter, the designated keepers of winter counts painted successively on hide (later, muslin) a subjective image of a monumental event that came to represent the past year of the tribe or tribal division. The images typically were arranged linearly across the hide or cylindrically from the outside in. Hide calendars were tribal treasures and most that have survived record the annual dramas of several generations. According to Hodge (1910), pictographs done by the Kiowa and Lakota, among Indians of the United States, reached the highest development in the calendars of. At left above is the pictographic image from a winter count by Yanktonais Sioux *Shunka-ishnala* (Lone-Dog). It commemorates a successful hunt in 1837 to 1838 when 100 elk reportedly were killed. On the winter count of Brulé Sioux *Wa-po-ctan-xi* (Brown-Hat aka Battiste Good), the winter of 1860 to 1861 was signified by the death of Female-Elk-Walks-Crying (*right*). *Wa-po-cta^n-xi*'s winter count is somewhat unique in its extensive use of epigrammatic symbols. *Illustrations from Mallery (1893).*

(All clockwise from upper-left) ◆ *Page 1* "Wapiti (wild calf)" by Karl Bodmer (1833), courtesy of the InterNorth Art Foundation and the Joslyn Art Museum, Omaha, Nebraska; Untitled by Rudolph Kurz (1852), courtesy of the Smithsonian Institution, Washington, D.C.; "Female Elk or Wapiti" by John Dean Caton (ca. 1875), courtesy of the Library of Congress, Washington, D.C.; "Cow and Bull Elk" by Frederic Remington (1888), courtesy of the Amon Carter Museum of Western Art, Fort Worth, Texas; "Young Elk or Wapiti" by John Dean Caton (ca. 1875), courtesy of the Library of Congress, Washington, D.C.; "Elk—Rocky Mountain" by Alfred Jacob Miller, courtesy of the InterNorth Art Foundation and the Joslyn Art Museum, Omaha, Nebraska. ◆ *Page 2* "Gang of Elk, Saline River" by Vincent Brooks (ca. 1866), courtesy of the Amon Carter Museum of Western Art, Fort Worth, Texas; "The Exalted Ruler" by Charles M. Russell (1912), courtesy of the Benevolent and Protective Order of the Elks Lodge 214, Great Falls, Montana; Untitled dust jacket and frontispiece of Murie's *The Elk of North America* (1951) by Walter A. Weber (ca. 1950), courtesy of the Wildlife Management Institute, Washington, D.C.; "Elk" by Ernest Thompson Seton (1894), courtesy of the Philmont Museums Collections, Cimarron, New Mexico. ◆ *Page 3* "Worldly Possessions" from Custer County, Nebraska, 1886, from the Solomon D. Butcher Collection, courtesy of the Nebraska State Historical Society, Lincoln; "Montana Hunters" (1890s), photo by DeCamp, courtesy of Daniel A. Hilger; "Ranch on the Yellowstone" (1880s), photo by William Henry Jackson, courtesy of the U.S. Geological Survey, Reston, Virginia; "B and E Ranch" outside Billings, Montana (1885), photo by F. Jay Haines, courtesy of the Montana Historical Society, Helena. ◆ *Page 4* "The Al Wise Ranch" of Callaway, Nebraska (1892), from the Solomon D. Butcher Collection, courtesy of the Nebraska State Historical Society, Lincoln; "Hermit Fisherman's Cabin" on Grand Lake, Colorado (1870s), by William Henry Jackson, courtesy of the U.S. Geological Survey, Reston, Virginia; "F. Jay Haynes Home and Studio" in Yellowstone National Park (1884), by F. Jay Haynes, courtesy of the Montana State Historical Society, Helena; "Western Ranch" (?) photo from the Phillips Collection, courtesy of the Amon Carter Museum of Western Art, Fort Worth, Texas; "Scout's Rest," home of William "Buffalo Bill" Cody near North Platte, Nebraska (Cody and members of the visiting Bostonian Opera Company), courtesy of the Nebraska State Historical Society, Lincoln. ◆ *Page 5* "Elk in Harness" at Edgeley, North Dakota (1893), by F. Jay Haynes, courtesy of Doris Whithorn and the Park County Museum, Livingston, Montana; "Steamboat Benton" (1880) plied the Missouri River between St. Louis, Missouri, and Fort Benton in Montana Territory (both the steamboat and fort were named after Thomas Hart Benton, U.S. senator from Missouri from 1820 to 1850, and a leading advocate of expansionism and the westward crusade of Manifest Destiny), photo by F. Jay Haynes, courtesy of the Montana State Historical Society, Helena; A "Winton" in the Elks parade in Minneapolis, courtesy of the Minnesota Historical Society, St. Paul; "Diamond-Stacked Engine No. 23" of the Union Pacific Railroad, at a waystop west of Laramie, Wyoming (1868), photo by A. J. Russell, courtesy of the Union Pacific Railroad Museum Collection, Omaha, Nebraska; "Northern Pacific Railroad Western Survey Team's Return" (1867), photo courtesy of the Minnesota Historical Society, St. Paul; "Oscar Soderholm and Team" west of Laramie, Wyoming, on the Big Laramie River (ca. 1900), courtesy of the Union Pacific Railroad Museum, Omaha, Nebraska. ◆ *Page 6* "Glory Enough for One Day" in the Yellowstone National Park vicinity of Wyoming (1882), sportsman/publisher George O. Shields killed a fine elk bull, and as he and companion L. A. Huffman, famed western photographer, began skinning the animal, a sow grizzly and her two cubs charged, twice, and had to be killed, photo by Huffman, courtesy of the Montana State Historical Society, Helena; "Trophy Hunt near Jackson Hole" in September 1896, by a member of railroad magnate W. Seward Webb's "sporting expedition" to the Yellowstone region via a ten-car luxury train that made the trip from Shelburne, Vermont, to Cinnabar, Montana, in the fastest rail time to date, photo by F. Jay Haynes, courtesy of the Montana State Historical Society, Helena; "The Prize Shot" by Charles M. Russell (190?), courtesy of the Amon Carter Museum of Western Art, Fort Worth, Texas. ◆ *Page 7* "American Elk—Wapiti Deer" by John James Audubon (1845), courtesy of the Library of Congress, Washington, D.C.; Untitled by Daniel P. Metz (1981), dust jacket art for Thomas and Toweill's *Elk of North America: Ecology and Management* (1982), courtesy of the Wildlife Management Institute, Washington, D.C.; "The Sierra Nevada in California" by Albert Bierstadt (1868), courtesy of Helen Huntington Hall and the Smithsonian American Art Museum, Smithsonian Institution, Washington, D.C.; "Buffalo and Elk on the Upper Missouri" by Karl Bodmer (1833), courtesy of the InterNorth Art Foundation and the Joslyn Art Museum, Omaha, Nebraska; "Bugling Elk" by Carl Rungius (undated), courtesy of the Glenbow Museum, Calgary, Alberta. ◆ *Page 8* "Elk" by Francis Lee Jaques (undated), courtesy of the James Ford Bell Museum of Natural History, Minneapolis, Minnesota.

Nearly all early Indian painting of elk (and most other life forms) on hides, rock, pottery and skin is two dimensional, showing length and height. Whole animals invariably are shown in profile. The same is true for animals in petroglyphs and quill and beadwork. Also noteworthy are that elk and other wild mammals generally are shown in some form of motion or stereotypical behavior. Their coloration lacks shading and realistic background features are absent. These conditions suggest that less emphasis was placed on artistic representation than on tactical, zoomorphic characterization of an event, time or personal or group relationship, either secular or spiritual.

A depth dimension in elk art is found in sculpture, carving and costume (particularly ceremonial masks), but most such objects are rare finds and date from the 1830s and later. At important medicine ceremonies, Cheyenne priests directed children to make 2- to 3-inch (5.1–7.6 cm) high mud sculptures of elk and other important food animals (Dorsey 1905). These small effigies were placed around a central alter in the medicine lodge to honor the animals that gave themselves as sustenance to the tribe.

The following Native artifacts from various museum collections feature elk images: cradle decoration (quills on hide), spoon (carved cow horn), whistle (carved wood), pendant (rawhide cutout), pipe bowl (carved stone), vest (beads on hide), moccasins (quills and beads on hide), storage bag (beads on hide), effigy pipe stem (carved wood), tips (painted hide), shield cover (paint on hide), drum head (painted hide), pipe bag (beads and quills), tepee liner (painted canvas).

Among the Kiowa and Blackfeet, medicine tepee designs were vision inspired and became heraldic symbols for the visionary's offspring (Hails 1980). And, except among the Kiowa and Blackfeet, tepee painting was not commonplace. The model tepee cover above is Kiowa, and the painting style and design of bison and a bull elk postdated the introduction of ledger art (circa 1880). *Photo courtesy of the Smithsonian Institution Anthropological Archives.*

Pipe smoking was an integral part of western Indian life and particularly so among Plains people. Smoking tended to have a ceremonial component, but most pipes were everyday pipes (McGuire 1899). Tobacco was placed inside the mouth of the large end of the tube, lit and inhaled by the smoker tilting his head and the pipe slightly upward. ("Tobacco" on the Plains included sumac leaves and bark of red willow, bearberry, red osier dogwood, ironwood, wahoo, arrowwood, laurel, manzanita in various mixture or combined with wild tobacco.) The few that were used solely or primarily for specific functions or by select persons tended to be decorated with beads, horsehair, feathers and quills. Some wood pipe stems of ash, sumac or other wood (with a soft, pithy core that could be removed easily) were carved to feature effigy, totem or spirit animals. The Lakota pipe stem, circa 1880, is made of ash, decorated with porcupine quills and features a bison, turtle and elk, animals frequent and important in Lakota mythology and oral traditions (Ewers 1986). *Photo courtesy of the Peabody Museum of Archaeology and Ethnology, Harvard University.*

The elk image also had a place in sign language, the North American Indians' well-developed means of universal communication. Margry (1886 [vi]:518) recording for the early 18th century, observed that the elk was symbolic of the Hictoba or "Scioux de la Chasse" (possibly the Santee Sioux). According to Clark (1884), the sign for elk was made by bringing both hands along the sides of the head, palms outward, with fingers and thumbs extended, separated pointed upward. Then, by wrist action, the hands were moved forward then backward three or four times parallel to the head. Also, among the Plains and Prairie Indians who symbolized other tribes, primarily on calendar pictographs (winter counts), the acknowledged emblem for the Ponca was an elk hair ridge or roach (Mallery 1893:387).

The Crow, like many other peoples of the central and northern Plains, believed in the power of medicines and charms to win the affections of the opposite sex. Such power was used mainly by men to entice or seduce a new love, restore faithfulness of a spouse or regain lost love (Wildschut 1975). The bull elk was acknowledged as the primary giver of love medicine, appearing in dreams to instruct in the making of charms, such as the rawhide cutout above. The elk silhouette has a yellow bead eye. The pendent has blue beads, and there is a blue heart line from the animal's heart to mouth. Blue and yellow are common colors on various Absaroke love medicines. *Photo courtesy of the Peabody Museum of Archaeology and Ethnology, Harvard University.*

Some Lakota cradle decorations featured real and mythical animals whose powers would protect the child (Hunt 1982). The elaborate quill work on tanned leather, from about 1870, features spiders, thunderbirds, bison, bighorn sheep and the heads of what are thought to be elk or deer. *Photo courtesy of the Joslyn Art Museum.*

Excellent examples of Plains sculpture are these two horn spoons on which elk heads were carved. (*Left*) A Lakota spoon predating 1885; (*right*) a Crow spoon, circa 1900. After big game herds were extirpated from much of the West, Indian carvers worked with cow horn (Ewers 1986). *Left photo courtesy of the Museum of the American Indian, Heye Foundation. Right photo courtesy of the Montana State Historical Society.*

Mythology and Ethnoethology

Besides the numerous ways that elk served Indians as a material resource, it also contributed to the social organization of many tribes and to the personal and spiritual identity of many individuals and groups (Figure 49). Intertribal societies and cults were common, and many were based on veneration of a particular animal species. Societies generally were male-oriented and functioned as fraternal or governmental units. Cults were quasireligious affiliations of men who believed they learned or were vested with supernatural power as construed through vision quests. The animals served as personal and cult patrons, although the mystical relationship fell short of zootheism. Societies and cults both had distinctive rituals, social responsibilities, ceremonies, and ceremonial clothing and props associated with the animals from which the groups drew their identities.

In general, many cultures (especially those of the Great Plains) mythologically and spiritually held that the bull elk represented gallantry (Eastman 1904), masculine charm, virtue and beauty (Deloria 1932), sexual prowess (Miller 1985), virility (Powers 1978), longevity (Densmore 1918), strength (Newcomb 1961), courage, tenacity and protectiveness (Brown 1992). To the Arikara, the bull elk's power was not confined to prospective suitors of available females, but also accounted for seduction and infidelity (see Dorsey 1904). In addition, the elk was thought to have a beneficial influence on the reproductive functions of women and was protective in childbirth and during a child's infancy (Hail 1980). Miller (1985:236) reported that Sioux and Cheyenne elk dreamers distributed elk teeth to newborn babies "as tokens of good luck." Cheyennes believed that elk were difficult to kill, and any man who dreamed of elk acquired such power of endurance (Grinnell 1972). The elk's power in this

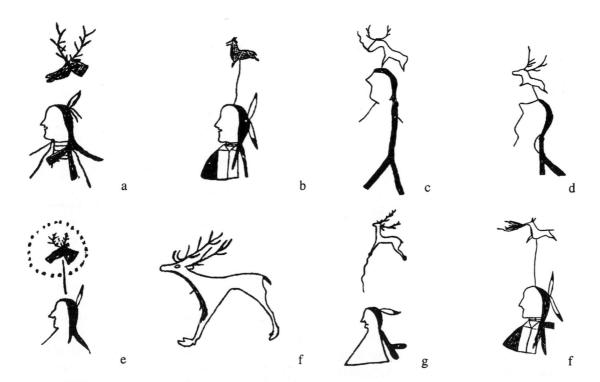

Figure 49.   Personal names of Indians of most Plains tribes commonly borrowed from personal, clan or fraternity totems or spirits, among which the elk was powerful and popular. Names, which tended to be given or changed at critical junctures in the life of an Indian man or woman, could symbolize the supernatural or mythical figures, remarkable events, circumstances, or personal or totemic characteristics. They could be given to or borrowed from others, mainly distinguished relatives, and were highly respected forms of identity. Nineteenth-century picture writings revealed names primarily by ideogrammic figures connected by a line to the mouths of human heads illustrated in profile. The line indicated speech. Above are names of Lakotas, which were recorded by Garrick Mallery from 1876 to the late 1880s. They include (a) Elk-Head, (b) Spotted-Elk, (c) White-Elk, (d) Fast-Elk, (e) Afraid-of-Elk, (f) Lean-Elk, (g) Little-Elk and (h) Elk-Walking-With-His-Voice. *Illustrations from Mallery (1893).*

regard was like that of a mule deer, but stronger. The same belief was held by Comanche (Wallace and Hoebel 1952). Omaha Indians held that an elk vision granted fleetness to the witness (Fletcher and La Flesche 1972, see also Mails 1972). And Gosiute Indians believed that shamanistic stature could be gained through visions, and the spirit vision of elk conferred doctoring powers (Malouf 1974).

According to Hodge (1910), most Indian people throughout North America made sacrifices to deities, spirits or totems. The acts of making sacred—giving up something of personal value—mainly were forms of homage rather than tokens of supplication. Among the articles sacrificed by Algonquian and Iroquois Indians were elk hides.

Because of the nearly universal anthropomorphic kinship regard for animals, all or most tribes familiar with elk accounted for the species in their mythological traditions. Mythology deified cultural origins and norms, natural phenomena, interspecific associations and morality. The Dakota, for example, believed in "Elks," a mythical people who appeared from the north "and once held dominion over all this country, from the Mississippi r., E. and N., to the great waters" (Pidgeon 1853:162). Crow traditions indicated that elk (and bison and deer) were ordained as a tribal food source (Clark 1884).

Tribes known to have had elk societies or cults, or in whose mythology elk figures prominently, included the Hidatsa, Piegan, Nez Percé, Delta Salish, Nootka, Upper Chehalis, Haida, Mandan, Keres, Hopi, Tewa, Cheyenne, Sarsi, Arikara, Chinook, Oto, Pawnee, Omaha, Plains Cree, Fox, Crow, Lakota, Kiowa, Osage, Wichita, Quapaw, Kutenai, Flathead, Washo, Yurok and Kwakiutl.

The following is, despite its length, a cursory examination of the Lakota's complex metaphysical and ethnoethologic relationship with elk and their attendant habitual and ceremonial practices. Of this relationship, Wissler (1902:261) wrote: "The elk is taken as the incarnation of the power over females, the real (i.e., physical) elk is regarded only as the recipient of such power. The power itself is conceived of in the nature of an abstraction similar to our own conception of force. The fact that the elk seems to act in conformity with the laws governing this power is taken as evidence of its existence. Then the idea of the Indian is that the elk possesses the knowledge necessary to the working of the power." Blish (1967:199) added: "The Elk was closely associated with the Indian idea of love and sexual passion. Supernatural power lay behind manifestations of sex desire; consequently, numerous mythical creatures were thought to control such power, and of these, the bull elk was the most important."

A number of male animals—bull bison, spiders and stallions, as well as bull elk—were believed to have particularly

The beaded Lakota pipe bag features two elk, which were protective designs of the Oglala. The top elk is light blue and yellow, with a small red square on its side from which extends a wavy line and eagle feather. Such a square (or triangle or circle) indicated an opening where the heart of a mythical or spirit animal would otherwise be; according to Wissler (1907:43), "The conception seems to be that an animal without a heart is immortal and supernatural." The eagle feather was a fairly universal symbol of courage and exploit. The line joining the elk and the feather shows connection and association, probably emphasizing the species' innate bravery. The dotted line behind the top figure's front leg represents tracks that, in turn, possibly signify a real or metaphorical journey. The lower animal is beaded navy blue and, with symbolic heartlessness, it denotes a nonmythical animal. Inasmuch as all bull elk were perceived as possessing great power, the artistic presentation of two elk—one a spirit animal, one not—may simply have been an expression of the same animal's dual role as patron and provender. Until the late 1800s, representative artwork among Plains Indians was the exclusive prerogative of men, who were not beadworkers. By about 1885, Indian women were producing life forms in beadwork, often for non-Indian patrons (Hail 1980). This reflected not only their boredom and frustration with reservation life, but a disintegration of traditional values, customs and ethos. Interestingly, the bag dates from 1870, at which time only some of the Lakota were on reservation land, pursuant to the Laramie Treaty of 1868. *Photo courtesy of the Pennsylvania Museum, Philadelphia, S4-140487.*

potent seductive power over females of their respective species (Wissler 1905, 1907), but the bull elk's power in this regard was unparalleled, as evidenced by its ability to attract females by calling (bugling) and to maintain and defend a harem. For the Lakota, seductiveness in courtship was ascribed more to supernatural power than to personal allure. Consequently, young men sought to acquire such seductive tutelage and supremacy through images of the mystical or hypothetical, *wakan* elk dreamed about during religious fasting. Those who succeeded became part of a dream society or cult, and were known as elk men or elk dreamers. Elk dreamers were exclusively male, but youth was not prerequisite as with mule deer dreamers (Powell 1992).

So strong was the elk's charismatic power that, as a Lakota medicine man related to a sick man, "If one dreams of an elk he will be very sick. If a young girl will give him a pipe, this will cure him" (Walker 1991:135–136).

The animal dreamers (bison, wolf, bear, mule [black-tailed] deer and white-tailed [long-tailed] deer dreamers, besides elk dreamers [Blish 1967]) were required to perform in a ceremony on a day called Medicine Day (Blish 1967), to celebrate, test or validate, and display their associative power (Wissler 1912a). The ceremony was designed, according to Oglala shaman Black Elk, to represent "the source of life and the mystery of growing" (Neihardt 1959:177).

The rite was initiated by purification in a sweat lodge. Apparently when a young man received an elk vision, or in conjunction with other ceremonies, such as the fourth day of the Lakota's sun dance (Walker 1991), a tepee, replete with various liturgical objects in prescribed places (Fletcher 1882), was erected outside and on the west side of the camp (Jones 1989), and participants—masked dancers—were ushered inside by way of an east-facing entryway.

At least some of the dancers' masks were triangular pieces of rawhide, with horns (Densmore 1918) or a willow branch framework to represent elk antlers (Fletcher 1882), and with a circle made of eagle feathers on the right side. Branches sometimes were wrapped with otter fur to represent bull elk antlers in velvet (Powell 1992). According to Blish (1967), the masks (head gear) differed by individual taste and dream perception (see also Wissler 1912a). Although masks in general were not greatly used in religious and semireligious ceremonies of the Indians of the Great Plains, elk masks were an exception, and actually were used by many tribes within the elk's historic range. Hodge (1910) described the mask as made from the animal and realistic, but that it did not represent the elk itself, merely the totemic or supernatural power associated with the species.

The same was true of shields featuring painted elk figures. According to Hail (1980:43), such shields were carried during ceremony "in honor of the favored animal."

"Early in the 19th century, a Crow named Travels went into the mountains to fast after being rejected repeatedly by the woman he wished to marry. On the fifth day of the fast, he had a vision in which an elk-man wearing a painted elk-skin robe spoke to him. 'When you go home make a robe like that which I am wearing now,' the elk-man told him. 'Paint it as this one is painted. Put it on and walk in front of the girl you love. Sing my songs and whistle. She will not refuse you again.' Travels did as instructed. He killed a large bull elk and fashioned its skin into a replica of the robe he had seen in his vision. He wore the robe for a single day. The following morning, Travels related, the woman who had spurned him came to his tipi and said she would be his wife" (Newton 1994:88-89). The Crow elk skin "love blanket" (*top*) features a painting of a cow elk in estrus and a bull elk in a premount posture. The Indian artist (unknown) accurately depicted the cow "looking back"—typical of cow elk courtship behavior (*bottom*). *Top photo courtesy of the Museum of the American Indian, Heye Foundation. Bottom photo by Jim Wilkie.*

 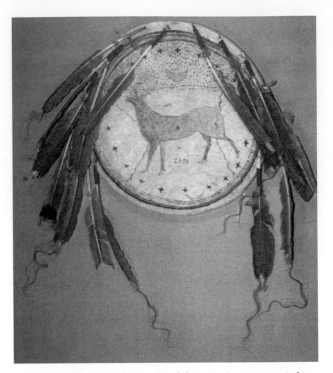

The Lakota elk dreamer's dance shield was strictly ceremonial; although, individual members of this animal dreamers' society carried in battle shields with elk images as a display of power gained through tutelage and spiritual association with the elk. With the advent of the horse culture on the central and northern Plains, war shield use diminished. The elk dreamer dance shield was carried when the society performed (with other dream societies) on a Medicine Day to honor the elk and initiate a new member or simply demonstrate and celebrate connection with their guardian animal. The dance shield at left is painted muslin stretched over a willow hoop. The shield's surface background is light blue. The rectangular white center features three concentric rows—red, blue and red. The elk head is blue (a sacred color). Hawk bells and a sweetgrass bundle are tied under the elk's nose, and fastened to the border of the shield are great horned owl wing feathers, sage grouse tail feathers and hawk bells. The elk dreamer's shield at right, of white, tanned hide with a wooden hoop frame and rawhide disk insert, dates from after the Sioux wars, therefore probably was made for ceremony rather than warfare. It was designated as a sacred object that should not be handled by menopausal women. The shield's pictograph features a bull elk with two human feet, indicating the totemic association. Also in the painted scene are sky stars, a human figure, power lines, two rattlesnakes and a spider. The colors are blue, red, green and yellow. Attached to the turkey feathers are red cloth ties, red-dyed horse hair and gray breath (down) feathers. All parts of Native ceremonial devices and wardrobe had special significance beyond decoration to the user or wearer, but the particular meanings of the various articles on this shield are not known. Elk dreamers held their last ritual dance ceremony in 1888, by which time the Lakota had to acknowledge that the supernatural powers of the elk no longer favorably affected Lakota warfare and hunting success. *Left photo from the George H. Bingenheimer Collection; courtesy of the Haffenreffer Museum of Anthropology, Brown University, Bristol, Rhode Island. Right photo courtesy of the South Dakota State Historical Society's Cultural Heritage Center, Pierre.*

The dancers' bodies were painted yellow, with black or blue (the two colors were interchangeable in Lakota art) on the lower limbs in characterization of the bull elk's pelage coloration. Walker (1991:135) reported from an anonymous source that "Those who dream of the elk must wear sticks like elk horns with hide branches and rawhide ears. They must paint yellow. They must paint their hands and feet black and have black paint on their breast and back." Neihardt (1959) wrote that yellow was considered a masculine color and was associated with the south wind, the source of light and life, which was where the power of the bull elk—the patron of virility—resided.

The dancers' accouterments, paintings and animations presumably enabled them to experience physical and spiritual transformation to the tutelary animal.

Mirrors and hoops were important embellishments (Figure 50). By reflecting light, the mirror symbolically held supernatural charm, and the dancers could "shoot their influence into all they oppose" (Wissler 1912a:88), "catch the eye of a girl and bring back her heart" (Brown 1992:67) and place spectators and opponents "under the power of the Elk Dreamers Society" (Powell 1992:84, see also Blish 1967).

Some dreamers had a circle drawn on their backs to signify personal strength and the nation's cosmological hoop

Figure 50. Oglala Sioux drawing of an elk dreamer society (cult) ceremonial dance, featuring two elk dancers with hoops and directly connected to the power emitted by the patron elk, indicated by the wavy (spirit) lines. Also shown are single members of the buffalo and black-tailed deer (mule deer) cults and a woman who may be a holy woman or the mythical Two-Face. Both of the elk dancers and the black-tailed deer dancer hold mirrors, the flashing of which was integral to their respective cults' magic. Neither of the elk dancers' hoops are webbed, although most apparently were. Also noteworthy is that the elk is not depicted with a heart, typically symbolic of supernatural association. The elk's symbolic nature was based, at least among the Lakota, on its earthly traits less so than supernatural manifestations. In other words, the bull elk's power was metaphysical, but not so the animal or its behaviors. *Illustration from Wissler (1912).*

ordination. Actual hoops, carried by hand or worn around the neck or shoulders were sacred, exemplifying a spider web, again the nation's hoop and, both metaphorically and linguistically, the rainbow. The hoop was the emblem of fork-horned animals and intricately associated with the rituals and regalia of fork-horned cults (Blish 1967). Antlers, such as those of adult bull elk tend to form near circles, or hoops, when viewed frontally. As with rainbows, even the largest bull elk antlers were not full circle, with part of the circumference invisible, but clearly perceptible in the abstract. (Petersen [1989] noted that a Lakota headdress with elk antlers was a love charm.) Elk dancers' hoops were somewhat individualistic, and at least one reportedly was wrapped with elk hide (Densmore 1918). To each hoop was attached a single eagle feather, representing honor, and various amulets—usually parts of animals that were believed to import protective powers for the wearer. Part of a hoop might be made of aromatic varieties of horsemint, or beebalm, known to the Lakota as elk herb, elk food or elk medicine (Fletcher 1882, Densmore 1918).

From the tepee constructed for the ceremony, after songs were sung within and two pipes were purified with incense, the masked dancers were led out by two virgins—holy women or Double Woman—who may have had visions and who possessed exceptional singing voices and magic (Wissler 1907, 1912a, Howe 1953, Blish 1967, Powers 1986). Two other virgins followed. The young women carried the pipes (perhaps symbolically linked to the cure previously mentioned) and wore ceremonial dresses, sometimes green, as observed by Fletcher (1882), to represent fertility and cow elk. The dancers were led on a circular path, making offerings at the cardinal compass points, beginning to the west and rotating clockwise to the south. (Miller [1985:236] reported that elk dreamers distributed elk bugler teeth to newborn babies, "as tokens of good luck," but whether this was part of the ceremony was not clarified.) As they moved, the elk dancers would "crouch, trample the dirt, or glide noiselessly along" (Fletcher 1882:286) in the manner of elk (Brown 1992). The dancers impersonated elk vocalizations and stamped their feet (leaving tracks), mak-

Young Lakota men commonly used elk "medicine" to ensure their success in romance. The bull elk's bugle was such medicine, produced by wooden whistles and flutes, some of which were elaborately carved. "The cry of the male elk, in the rutting season, is very singular," wrote Prince Maximilian zu Wied (1906:176) in 1832. "It is a shrill whistle, which, for the most part, runs regularly up the scale, and then suddenly falls to a low, guttural note. The notes perfectly resemble a run upwards on the flageolet." The ability of the bull elk to attract cow elk was viewed by a Lakota as demonstration of control over the wind (Brown 1992, see also Capps 1973), and it was the sound that men tried to simulate to borrow or develop the power of enchantment. This flute, made of ash, features a whistling, or bugling, elk. *Photo courtesy of the University of Pennsylvania Museum, Philadelphia, S4-140541.*

ing magic to overcome their principal rivals, the Thunderers—*Heyoka* or contraries (Laubin and Laubin 1977). Other dreamers (non-elk), including the Heyoka, lined the dancers' route and tested the potency of the elk's medicine by shooting stones, fingernails, grasshoppers and bird claws at the dancers (Hasserick 1964:239). Grasshoppers and bird claws were considered poison to elk dreamers (Walker 1991). By dodging the missiles and turning a mirror toward the magic shooter, an elk dreamer avoids injury and deflects the evil, thereby "proving the superior power of his spirit elk guardian" (Powell 1992:85). Women and children followed the procession at a discrete distance.

After one ceremonial rotation, which covered a distance of 6 to 7 miles (9.7–11.3 km), including "sometimes doubling back, as wild game does" (Laubin and Laubin 1977:364), the elk dreamers reentered the tepee for a feast. The last to enter was the candidate for membership. There they sang and concocted medicine (aphrodisiacs) "for procuring women" (Wissler 1912a:28). One formula for a lover's stew (Powers 1978:42) consisted of sclerotic of the elk eye, gristle from the fletlock and musk from the metatarsal glands.

To be an elk man was a great compliment to the Lakota, as the designation connoted association with the elk's ascribed masculine virtues. Dichotomously, an elk woman—one who was easily seduced by an elk man—lost respectability (Eastman 1904, Deloria and Brandon 1961) and was subject to ridicule (Powers 1986, 1988).

Nonceremonial dress of elk dreamers included a hoop, an eagle plume—which represented the people (Neihardt 1959:177)—and a courting blanket that bore a painting of a spider, elk or whirlwind (Wissler 1905). The whirlwind—the playful young brother of the four winds (Brown 1992)—embodied the essence of allusiveness and unpredictability, desirable traits for keeping rivals and enemies off guard. The whirlwind also signified a bull elk's sexual advertisements, as in the pawing up of mud and dirt during

wallowing, dominance displays and fights. (Jones [1989] pointed out the parallel of dominance sparring and fights among bull elk in the rut and warfare distinction as prerequisite to successful courtship by Lakota males.) "Standing in the blanket" was a common courtship practice among the Lakota. A suitor attempted to engage a woman in conversation and envelop her in his courting blanket, symbolic of the spider web or envelopment of elk power. Often, the suitor resorted to further persuasive power of flute (flageolet) music, also correlated with the elk and its whistling or bugling to entice prospective mates.

Wissler (1905) indicated that dreamers successful in conquest wore their robes with the design on the outside, advertising the strength of their elk power or medicine. And with each additional conquest—analogous to harem-gathering—the blanket was silhouetted on the edge with the drawing of a woman.

The Lakota also believed that, improperly channeled, the elk power could be detrimental. Myths held that an elk dreamer who seduced married women or too many women was a danger to the tribe (Deloria 1932).

Adams (1990) reported that, among the Oglala Sioux, elk pipe smokers had their own society, which was thought to have unusual power in matters of romance. She told that her grandfather, as a young, single man, asked for a love potion from a medicine man who had elk power. The medicine man obliged by mixing herbs, powdered elk bone and crushed, dried eye of an elk. Small amounts of the potion were secretly added to the food of the young woman who was the object of the grandfather's attention. The young woman already was engaged, but the grandfather persisted in speaking with her and surreptitiously administering the potion. He also sought additional medicine to discourage the fiancé. This medicine was straight elk bone powder. When the grandfather was near his rival, the grandfather put some of the powder in his hand and discreetly blew it at the man. After 3 years, the woman married the grandfather.

An ochre-colored, stone (pipestone or catlinite?), elbow-shaped pipe bowl (shown upside down) made by a Lakota carver about 1860 features the image of an elk on the underside. The circle or hoop carved in similar shallow relief behind the elk's foreleg suggests association with the Elk Dreamer Society. During this society's dance ceremonies, members carried hoops of twined willow branches, fur or horsemint and other herbs (Mauer 1992). The hoops (often in conjunction with mirrors) were symbolic protection against the power of other animal dreamers (Wissler 1907). Whether the pipe actually was used in elk dance rituals or if it was truly connected to the Elk Dreamer Society are unknown, inasmuch as the pipes used by elk dreamers were mainly yellow in color, according to Wissler (1912), and catlinite pipe bowls of the Lakota "were occasionally carved with a great range of effigy images" (Denney 1992:269). *Photo courtesy of The Minneapolis Institute of Arts.*

From oral histories, eyewitness accounts and interviews, variation is seen in the elk cults' rituals among tribal divisions and temporally, but the basic mystical orientation was universal among the Plains Lakota. The same is true of similar elk fraternities of the Pawnee, Cheyenne and others.

Among the Indian tribes whose women had elk societies was the Assiniboine. Such affiliations were predominantly quasireligious and social, and the association logically seems to have been with cow elk, source of provender and agent of delivery of the bull elk's substantial power. Long (1942:190) described the ceremony of an Assiniboine female elk society: "When a band camped near a wooded creek, the women of this society went into the timber and changed their garments to short dresses with short sleeves. Then they would smear their exposed legs from the knees down and their arms to the elbows, with white clay. Headdresses of leaves were placed over their hair. An elderly woman, who was the Medicine Woman, led the group in which young women and girls were considered as young female elk and the older women represented the older female elk.

"Two men, as bull elk, with wooden horns fastened to their heads, stayed far behind the females and danced, blowing on whistles at frequent intervals. They never joined the group of women but always kept far in the rear.

"As the parade passed within the camp circle it was customary for warriors to join it. They would walk on each side and shoot arrows at the 'Female Elk,' being careful not to hit any of them. When an arrow fell among them, the group ran and scattered just as a herd of elk would do.

"After a parade completed the camp circle, they returned to the woods and changed their costumes. The Female Elk Dance was then over until the same time a year later."

Mentioned early was the Assiniboine communal elk hunt ceremonially led by a divining or elk dreamer woman (Denig 1930:302).

During a portion of the Blackfeet sun dance, a sacred woman was assisted by other women who "sang the Elk song, making signs with their hands, imitating the movements of elk, swaying their bodies like trotting elk and giving the elk call" (McClintock 1968:302).

All Kiowa boys under instruction to be warriors belonged to a Rabbit Society, the insignia of which was a piece of hair-on elk hide with an erect feather attached (Newcomb 1961). Also among Kiowa, the highest military order—the Koisenko—was a fraternity restricted to the bravest warriors. "It was their duty to lead the most dangerous charges, and they were not allowed to retreat in battle. Around his neck their leader wore an elk skin sash which trailed on the ground at his right side. In battle it was his duty to dismount in front of his comrades, thrust a ceremonial arrow through a hole in the elkskin and into the ground, and remain in this spot throughout the battle" (Newcomb 1961:203, see also Mooney 1898).

The elk dance of the Shongopovi Hopi was part of an unmasked social ceremony. The Shongopovi Pueblo of the middle mesa of Tusayan in northeastern Arizona probably was built around 1680. *Painting by Marshall Lomakema; photo courtesy of the Museum of the American Indian, Heye Foundation.*

For the Lakota's grass or war dance—a ritual originating with the Omaha—long *heȟaka sí yotanka* or elk whistle (Densmore 1918). It actually was made of wood (such as boxelder), but its use produced a series of harmonics audibly similar to and indicative of a bugling elk (see Lauber and Lauber 1977).

In more secular ways, the live elk performed a number of unusual services. For example, a Portuguese manuscript chronicling early exploration of the California coast reportedly made reference to the use of small (Tule) elk by Indians in the San Francisco Bay area (probably Coastal Miwok) as beasts of burden, to haul things in primitive carts (B. Edmiston personal communication:1981). Pawnee and Cheyenne had ceremonies that featured elk dancers as part of healing/medicine rituals (Clark 1884, Grinnell 1961). Wild bergamot beebalm—elk medicine—was used in

Lakota healing practices (Densmore 1918). Winnebago Indians of the Great Lakes region called the sixth of 12 moon periods of the year *Ho-waw-zho-ze-raw,* meaning time of whistling elk (Minor and Minor 1978:388). Blackfoot Indians sang a song to elk when they opened their sacred pipe bundle—a symbolic source of power (see Ewers 1958)—which was wrapped in elk hide (Wissler 1912b). And one of the 12 major sacred bundles of the Pawnee was *Arikariki,* the elk bundle (Weltfish 1965). Finally, Mails (1972) observed that a vital and emphasized aspect of Plains Indian boys' education was the scrutiny of animal habits and behaviors. They were taught, for example, that deer showed how to withstand thirst, hawks revealed how to strike quarry or an enemy with stealth, speed and accuracy, frogs taught watchfulness, bears strength, kit foxes cunning, coyotes elusiveness and elk gallantry.

Native American's last hope for a return of their traditional way of life ended calamitously with the failed Ghost Dance movement of 1888 to 1890. The movement actually was a revival of previous uprisings, military and spiritual, against white suppression (see Northrop 1891, Mooney 1896). It gained final momentum through the teachings, prophesies and sorcery of a Paiute dreamer named Wovoka. Known to whites as Jack Wilson (Hodge 1910), Wovoka, or "Cutter," reputedly had a vision that, if a Ghost Dance was widely and properly performed, a new world would be ushered in following a great earthquake and flood. In the new world, nonbelievers (most whites) would be eliminated and the land transformed into a paradise, free of disease, war and famine, and teeming with wildlife. Wovoka's self-aggrandizing proclamations had prompt and widespread appeal to Indians suffering the indignity and confusion of reservation confinement. The Ghost Dance "religion" was readily adopted by Great Basin, Intermountain and Plains tribes desperate to reclaim their pre-white culture and freedoms. Although the dance itself was fairly uniform among the many wishful believers, certain attendant rituals and costumes were tribally specific. Fairly universal clothing articles of Great Plains Indians were the Ghost Dance shirt worn by some men and the Ghost Dance dress worn by some female dancers. However, most tribes adopted individual styles, materials and decorations for such shirts. Above is an Arapaho Ghost Dance shirt, fashioned in the style of a war tunic (as was commonplace), made of elk skin, painted sacred blue and ornamented with eagle feathers and painted symbols. "Their [Arapaho] Ghost Dance shirts and dresses were of the finest buckskin and beautifully painted," wrote Lauber and Lauber (1977:67). The Arapaho's

messianic vision was that a wall of fire preceding a massive landslide would drive whites away forever. Eventually, Indian fervor for success of the Ghost Dance alarmed whites, at least in part because Lakota Ghost Dancers believed that their Ghost Dance shirts were bulletproof, which whites construed as a portent of war. The reaction culminated in the killing of Sioux chief Sitting Bull at the Standing Rock Agency in North Dakota in 1890 (Utley 1993) and the massacre of Sitting Bull's Hunkpapa confederate Big Foot (formerly Spotted-Elk) and many of his band at Wounded Knee on the Pine Ridge Reservation in South Dakota several months later (Jensen et al. 1991). Ghost dancing continued for a brief time thereafter, but the momentum and credibility of the movement collapsed under the weight of Indian disillusion that a new old beginning could occur. *Photo courtesy of the Buffalo Bill Historical Center, Cody, Wyoming; artifact from the Chandler-Pohrt Collection, a gift of the Searle Family Trust and the Paul Stock Foundation.*

Conclusion

The nearly complete eradication of bison from the Great Plains in the last decades of the 1800s mirrored the end of the Plains Indian culture that had evolved over the course of centuries. Perhaps not as dramatic, but equally telling and over an even greater range, was the simultaneous eclipsing of elk populations and traditional Indian life.

Before smoking a pipe, Lakota Indians held the stem to the cardinal compass points, to invite the directional spirits to be present—West was thunder, North was the big spirit (that sent bison), South was the sun, earth or spirit mother, and East was where the "spirit of the elk lives" (Cook 1923:209, cf. Pidgeon 1853, Neihardt 1959). Ironically, it was from the East that the end came.

As victims of the growth and sprawl of the civilization that overwhelmed them, remnant populations of elk and Indians were treated similarly, but separately. Lands were set aside—parks and refuges for elk, reservations for Indians—as concessions to reconstituted humanity. The former and the subsequent emergence of scientific management and public sensitivity have enabled the elk to prosper. Native Americans continue to seek adaptation to evolving societal expectations and cultural circumstances.

ROBERT J. HUDSON AND JERRY C. HAIGH
with contributions by ANTHONY B. BUBENIK

4

Physical and Physiological Adaptations

The physical and physiological adaptation of elk, specifically the interaction of body form and function, contribute greatly to the evolutionary fitness of the species. Understanding of the physical and physiological adaptations of elk has grown substantially during the past two decades (Bubenik and Bubenik 1990, Brown 1992). Expansion of the international red deer/elk industry has provided both the opportunity and renewed need for physiological research with special attention devoted to nutrition, growth, reproduction and antler development (Haigh and Hudson 1993).

Nevertheless, we view studies on the new agricultural role of elk in the context of understanding and managing them in the wild. We begin by exploring the evolutionary history of elk to determine selective forces and identify important adaptive gradients. We then examine the correlation of body size and reproductive and metabolic adaptations to seasonal environments. The chapter concludes with sections on stress and assessment of physiological status.

In this chapter, red deer and North American elk are referred to as stags or hinds and bulls or cows, respectively. When referenced collectively, males and females will be the gender-distinguishing terminology.

Evolutionary Biology

Dispersal Theory

Members of the red deer/elk group form a cline of body size, conformation, coloration and antler development (Dolan 1988). The wapitoid (elk-like) pole of the gradient expresses larger body size and antlers, heavier manes, more contrasting rump patch and smaller tails than for conservative such forms as the Kashmir or Yarkand stags (see Chapter 1). Geist (1987) argued that this pattern reflects the presumed path of dispersal during the Pleistocene (Ice Age) from northern India to Europe and then back eastward across Asia into North America. The association of geography, size and physical traits is the basis of Geist's (1987) dispersal theory (Figure 51), which provides a useful context for understanding morphological and physiological adaptation.

Wapitoid subspecies living northeast of the Ural Mountains and eastward into North America developed during the Pleistocene dispersal. These subspecies adapted to more open and seasonal habitats and grassier diets than did red deer. Today, throughout their range, elk generally occupy parkland ecotones except in areas where human pressures force them into forested habitats. Many elk are migratory, and their diets have a predominantly grass/forb composition. Some elk populations have readapted as forest ecotypes (Murie 1951). Adaptation to open periglacial environments involves changes in body size and conformation, sensory capacity, trophic adaptation to grass forb diets and strong seasonal cycles of reproduction, growth and metabolism. Although described separately, morphology, physiology and behavior are intimately linked in adaptive suites (sets of variable factors) honed by the operational environment.

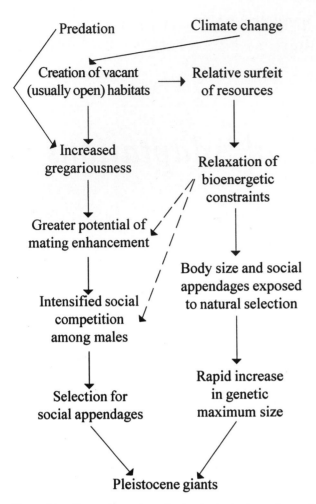

Figure 51. Factors hastening selection for body size and sexual dimorphism of elk and other ungulates in Pleistocene environments (adapted from Hudson 1985). Following the creation of new habitats accompanying climatic change associated with glaciation (see Chapter 1), dispersing populations enjoyed abundant high quality forage in previously unoccupied habitat (see Geist 1987). This abundance of resources allowed elk and other ungulates to approach their maximum genetic potential for body size, antler development and reproduction. In response to predation in open periglacial landscapes, most ungulates likely lived more gregariously (see Chapter 7). This tendency to live in groups, along with more sharply defined breeding/calving peaks on the more seasonal environment, offered greater potential mating enhancement for males. This, in turn, intensified mating competition and hastened selecting for other traits that augment dominance of males, and hence, participation in mating.

Operational Environment

Environmental structures have a powerful impact on the welfare, productivity and ultimately the evolution of elk (Bubenik 1982). The German word Umwelt (literally translated the world around) refers to the operational environment—the network of environmental factors affecting a species. The Umwelt concept allows stratification and qualification of environmental factors in a comprehensive manner (Figure 52).

The first division of Umwelt is based on the salience of environmental factors. Ausserwelt describes the potentially important but nonperceived elements of the environment (cosmic radiation, disease, etc.). This contrasts with Merkwelt—the world of perceived stimuli. Some of its factors (e.g., weather) are not influenced by the animal, whereas with others, the animal participates in some way. These other factors belong to Nutzwelt, which refers to the world of resources, and Mitwelt, which encompasses the social world of interactions within and between species.

Physical Adaptation

Umwelt is a powerful stimulus for adaptation and evolutionary change. Dispersal of *Cervus* during the Pleistocene caused rapid changes in adaptive suites in physical, physiological and behavioral features. The dispersal theory is based mainly on such visually apparent traits as size, antlers, conformation and coloration. However, it makes predictions about such functional traits as social, trophic (feeding level) and sensory adaptation.

Mature Size

Mature body sizes of elk vary widely by subspecies and environment. Under optimal conditions, mature bulls of the widespread mountain ecotypes may exceed 1,100 pounds (500 kg) and cows may exceed 660 pounds (300 kg). Mature body size is highly adaptive and seems to stay within relatively narrow limits. Suboptimal nutrition slows growth rates, but only persistent nutritional deprivation early in life greatly reduces mature lean body mass. Mature size presumably is shaped by thermal environment, locomotion, predation and seasonal forage availability and quality. At least, this holds for females who are not subject to competition for breeding opportunities (Jarman 1983, Georgiadis 1985, Geist and Bayer 1988).

Body mass can be considered a primary adaptive strategy. Thus, much of the interspecific variation in nutrition, life history and ecology can be explained (Hudson 1985). Large ungulates tend to occupy more open habitats, carry relatively larger horns or antlers, and have longer gestation periods and lower reproductive and mortality rates. Hence, their population changes at a slower rate than populations of smaller ungulates.

Large ungulates typically exhibit lower metabolism and reduced demands of gestation and lactation (Oftedal 1985, Gordon 1989). Allometric scaling of metabolic parameters means that large animals can subsist on lower quality forages and persist longer on body reserves (Lindstedt and Boyce 1985). On the other hand, small animals often can subsist on sparser forage resources, reproduce faster and respond more rapidly to environmental change. Although this holds true in analysis of members within families or higher taxonomic units, the evidence is less clear over the narrow range of mature weight among subspecies and ecotypes of elk.

Red deer and elk generally conform to interspecies scaling of most productive traits (Figure 53), performing like other animals of equivalent genetically determined mature weight (Table 14). Although not firmly established in comparative studies, elk seem to have slightly longer gestation periods, lower maintenance costs and do better on lower quality forages than do red deer.

Sexual Dimorphism

One of the most striking characteristics of cervids is their strong sexual dimorphism of body and antler size. Polygynous (one male mates with several females during one breeding season) ruminants are most dimorphic because larger size improves competitive ability and confers greater opportunities for males to breed (Jarman 1983). The greatest difference (about twofold) between male and female weights (Figure 54) occurs in species weighing between 110 and 220 pounds (50–100 kg) (Georgiadis 1985). Within the subfamily Cervinae, red deer are more dimorphic than elk, but fallow deer are even more dimorphic (Table 15).

Antlers scale hyperallometrically (antlers of larger species, subspecies or ecotypes make up a larger percentage of body weight) and are related to relative polygyny (ratio

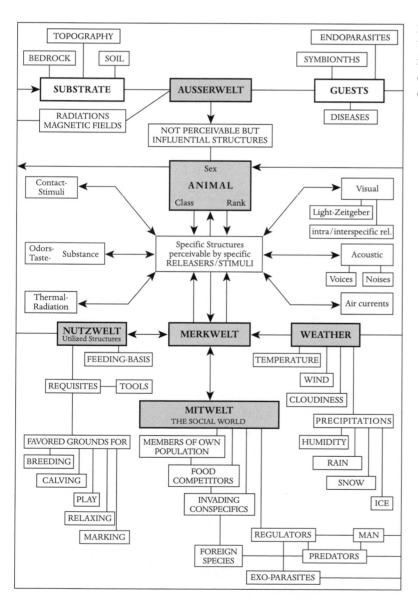

Figure 52. The Umwelt concept (Bubenik 1982). Umwelt describes the network of environmental factors affecting a species. In elk, each maturation class and gender can prefer different operational environments in different seasons.

Table 14.   Productive traits of New Zealand red deer and Rocky Mountain elk

Traits	New Zealand red deer		Rocky Mountain elk	
	Female	Male	Female	Male
Mature weight[a]	220 (100)	441 (200)	683 (310)	992 (450)
Birth weight[a]	18.7 (8.5)	19.2 (8.7)	37.5 (17)	41.9 (19)
Daily gain of nursing calves[b]	11.4 (322)	12 (362)	28.2 (800)	30.0 (850)
Gestation length (days)	233		<255	
Peak milk volume[c]	2.4 (2.5)		3.8 (4)	
Peak milk energy yield[d]	12		22	
Velvet yield of average mature male[a]		6.6 (3)		17.6–22.0 (8–10)

Source: From Haigh and Hudson 1993.

[a] In pounds (kilograms).

[b] In ounces (grams) per day.

[c] In quarts (liters) per day.

[d] In kilojoules per day.

of breeding females to breeding males) (Clutton-Brock 1980, 1982). The scaling parameter varies from $W^{1.35}$ to $W^{1.6}$ (W is live weight), although some data sets selected to approach genetic maxima for each species can be approximated by a simple linear relationship (Haigh and Hudson 1993). The relationship $Y = 0.0026X^{1.6}$ between antler weight (Y) and dressed weight (X) calculated by Huxley (1931) for red deer overestimates the antler size of elk (Geist and Bayer 1988). Well-nourished male red deer have antlers that usually weigh 4% to 6% of the dressed weight, with some exceeding 8%. Only unusual elk bulls of prime age can accomplish such production (Bubenik 1966).

Dimorphism of both body and antler size tends to be a parabolic function of openness of habitat, increasing from forested to savanna habitats and diminishing in species adapted to open grassland (Geist 1991a). Perhaps in large, loose aggregations, dominant males are not effectively able to restrict mating choices of females. Geist and Bayer (1988)

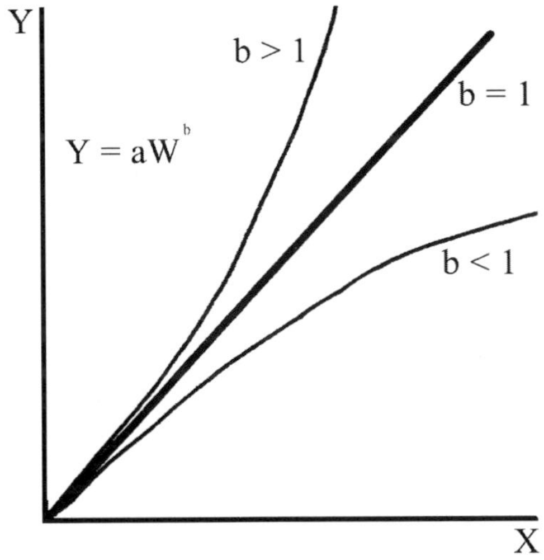

Figure 53.   Allometry and scaling by body size. Allometry originally was applied to relative growth of parts of animals to their whole weight. This principle extends beyond mechanical considerations to metabolic phenomena, ecological and social characteristics, and population dynamics (see Hudson and White 1985). Mathematically, such relationships are described by the allometric equation: $Y = aW^b$ where Y is the trait, a is the intercept, W is live weight, and b is the slope. The value of b describes curvature: values of 1 describe isometric (linear) scaling (e.g., gut capacity); values of greater than 1 describe disproportional increases with body size (e.g., antler size); values of less than 1 describe traits that do not increase as quickly as size (e.g., metabolic rate).

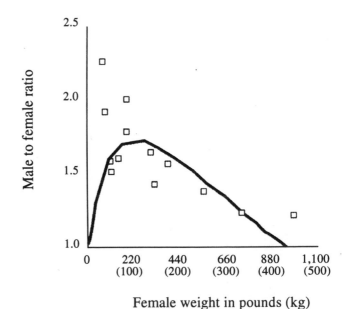

Figure 54.   Sexual weight dimorphism (expressed as the ratio of adult male weight to adult female weight) in relation to female body weight among the world's deer (Haigh and Hudson 1993).

Table 15. Sexual dimorphism in body size of selected Old World deer and Rocky Mountain elk

Species or subspecies	Typical male mature weight in pounds (kg)	Typical female mature weight in pounds (kg)	Male to female ratio	Hard antler weight in pounds (kg)
Fallow deer	194 (88)	86 (39)	2.25	7.7 (3.5)
Sika deer	257 (117)	161 (73)	1.60	5.5 (2.52)
Scottish red deer	339 (154)	180 (82)	1.88	6.6 (3.0)
European red deer	352 (160)	198 (90)	1.78	13.9 (6.3)
Yugoslavian red deer	572 (260)	330 (150)	2.00	19.8 (9.0)
Père David's deer	473 (215)	330 (150)	1.43	17.4 (7.9)
Elk	992 (450)	683 (310)	1.45	27.5 (12.5)

Source: From Haigh and Hudson 1993.

and Geist (1991a) added that nutritional limitations in open habitats may reduce the adaptiveness of oversized weapons such as antlers. For any given fighting style, there also may be an optimal mechanical size that is surpassed in larger species (Kitchener 1985, 1991).

The penalty of striving for mating enhancement is heavier mortality among males (Georgiadis 1985). The sex ratio of dimorphic species such as *Cervus elaphus* is skewed in favor of females, and the distortion increases under harsh environmental conditions (Flook 1970a).

Antlers

Antlers are secondary sex characteristics in male cervids (Clutton-Brock 1982, Bubenik and Bubenik 1990, Lincoln 1992) (Figure 55). Aristotle (384–322 BC) recorded effects of castration on antler growth (Peck and Forster 1961), as did Turbeville (1576). Antlers have been used for medicinal purposes in both Europe and Asia since ancient times.

Function

Antlers primarily serve as rank indicators, display organs and weapons during intraspecific combat (Clutton-Brock

1980, 1982). They are important means of establishing dominance among males. Changes in hard antler structure, either through accidental fracture or experimental removal, can alter a male's status. Breeding males losing their antlers are immediately challenged (Lincoln 1972a). In fact, an older male's dominance deteriorates when he loses his antlers (mature stags cast antlers before younger stags). Younger males assert dominance temporarily until their own antlers are cast, and then the normal hierarchy is reestablished (Bubenik 1983).

Males of unequal rank seldom fight, as they establish their relative social position by complex visual displays,

Display behavior of bull elk includes carrying vegetation and other materials in the antlers, enhancing their apparent size. *Photo by Pete and Alice Bengeyfield.*

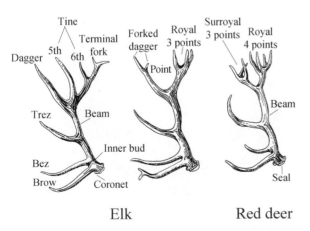

Figure 55. Terminology for elk and red deer antlers (Bubenik 1982). *Illustration by A. B. Bubenik.*

Antlers are not only symbols of social rank, but also may be used as tools to create scrapes or rubs on trees or shrubs to advertise dominance and to create wallows. *Photo by Leonard Lee Rue III.*

which include parallel walking and brandishing antlers. The display behavior may include carrying vegetation on antlers, which apparently enhances the antlers' appearance (Lincoln 1992). Antlers also are used for making scrapes and wallows and for marking by thrashing vegetation. Occasionally antlers will be invoked for defense against predators (including humans), and in secondary uses such as back scratchers and tools for knocking down fruit.

Although antlers provide a visible expression of dominance, other social and individual factors are of similar importance. For example, antlerless males can successfully defend a harem and breed. There are no reports of free-ranging antlerless male elk; however, in Scotland, antlerless red deer are known as hummels and occasionally are seen in the wild. Their ability to breed is an important factor for the deer farmer because an antlerless stag is considerably easier to manage during the rut, and it inflicts less damage to fences, other deer and humans. However, for the breeding stag to maintain control of his harem, it is essential that no antlered male be in the same paddock.

Generally, the male with the largest antlers is dominant, but threatening and intimidating behaviors also contribute to assertion of dominance. There is also some evidence that females in estrus will seek males with the largest antlers (Bubenik 1983).

General Structure

Red deer have a greater propensity than elk to produce secondary tines (Figure 56). Only the frontal half of the antler beam has the potential to divide into tines (Bubenik and Pavlansky 1965, Bubenik 1966). Brow tines in prime elk bulls are nearly parallel, and only the tips are bent slightly upward. Bez tines (the first tine above the brow tine) have the same shape as brow tines, but in good specimens, the bez is longer. In elk, the royal tine (dagger or fourth tine) is flattened and sometimes bent slightly inward. A fifth and sixth tine can develop before the beam ends with one or two points, known as the terminal fork. In the Roosevelt elk, the dagger can build a fork (bifurcate), and the beam's

Figure 56.   Comparative configuration of fairly typical elk and red deer antlers (Bubenik 1982). *Illustration by A. B. Bubenik.*

end can branch (ramify) into a royal. The dorsal part of the beam ramifies only at the top into a fork of three or more points building a cuplike crown.

This difference in antler structure between elk and red deer appears related to the taxon typical openness of habitat and consequent use of antlers in display and combat (Figure 57). The length of the antler beam in elk indicates that antlers serve as a long-distance, visual signal. The slightest head nodding is reinforced visually by movement of the elongated antlers. This nodding of antler beams advertises the bull's presence and rank. In short-distance displays there is remarkable difference between elk and red deer in terms of amplitude of head nodding, perhaps due to differences in architecture of the terminal parts of their respective antlers.

Ontogenesis

Antler ontogenesis is the history of individual antler sets in terms of size and configuration. Antler size increases from the first to the fifth set. From the sixth set onward, each new growth is slightly slower; a peak is reached at about the twelfth set. The best trophy antlers are expected in bulls with eleventh or twelfth antler sets. In Banff National Park, Alberta, maximum antler sizes of elk occur at about 8 years of age (Figure 58). Velvet antler weights of farmed elk appear to increase until 10 years of age (Woodbury and Haigh 1996).

Antler configuration is more or less specific for each individual, making the antlers an important part of the bull's

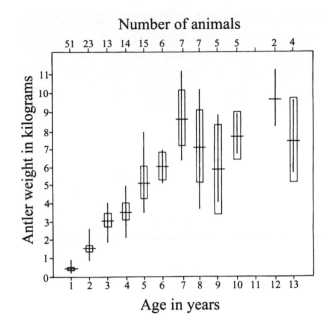

Figure 58. Weight of elk antlers of each age removed in winter in Banff National Park, Alberta (Flook 1970a). Median horizontal lines represent means; vertical bars show 95% confidence limits; and vertical lines show ranges.

gestalt (a unified whole with properties that are more than the sum of its parts). Bulls seem to recognize each other by their antlers, and the more experienced animals seem to estimate social class and rank of conspecifics.

Figure 57. Elk and red deer antlers as visual stimuli (Bubenik 1982). The slightest head nod is enlarged many times at the ends of the antlers. In elk (*left*), it is perceived best from the side view, because of the bull's long beam. In red deer stags (*right*), it is seen best from the front, because of the numerous points of the royal. *Illustration by A. B. Bubenik.*

The first set of antlers usually is simple spikes. In bulls of healthy populations, these spikes are usually at least 15.75 inches (40 cm) long. Branching of first antler sets is infrequent. However, small brow tines sometimes occur in wild yearlings (Murie 1951). This occurred relatively frequently in the White River elk herd (Boyd 1970), where 28% of yearling bulls had tines, 12% had forked antlers (2/2) and some had three to five points on each side (Figure 59). On gamefarms where heavy supplemental feeding is practiced and animals are selected for early antler growth, the frequency is higher.

Malformations

Malformed antlers in males and antlered females are seen occasionally. Trauma is often a factor. Malformed antlers with extra tines and points frequently are the result of animals injured when their antlers are in velvet. Malformations resulting from injuries may be repeated in many subsequent antler cycles (Figure 60).

Sometimes when part of a velvet antler is broken but held to the beam by a piece of velvet, the two pieces grow together. Otherwise, a cartilaginous tissue (or callus) forms and the broken piece swings when the callus gets wet.

Corkscrew antlers also are unusual. Some of these antlers have points bent downward as a result of retarded mineralization. The immediate cause is a disturbance in calcium/phosphorus metabolism during the period of antler growth. The beam rotates or bends down from its own weight and becomes mineralized in that position.

There is a rare anomaly of unknown etiology called rubber antlers. The osteon (bone) of such antlers is poorly mineralized. They seldom are cleaned of velvet. When dry, these antlers are hard, but when wet, they can be bent like semihard rubber.

The rarest anomaly involves unilateral or bilateral peruques, eo-antlers in males with normally developed testicles. The antler tissue on one or both beams, or only the lower part of the beam, apparently has no receptors for testosterone (Bubenik 1966).

One of the most peculiar manifestations of abnormal antler development is the relationship between damage to legs and growth of antlers. The evidence is mainly anecdotal and comes from different species of deer. Marburger et al. (1972) reported that 69% of white-tailed deer with abnormal antlers had either old gunshot wounds or healed leg fractures. One experiment has been conducted in white-tailed deer that were in hard antler (Marburger et al. 1972). When hind legs were amputated, or neurectomies performed, the contralateral (opposite) antler grew small and abnormally shaped. In one case in a Sambar stag, amputation for medical reasons, before any antler growth had

Figure 59. Multiple-branched yearling elk from White River Plateau, Colorado. *Illustration by A. B. Bubenik.*

started led to marked differences in antler size throughout the five years of the animal's life, although all the events of the cycle happened in synchrony (T. A. Davis 1982). The level of amputation may play a role, because author Haigh observed an elk bull with a lateral digit amputated for medical reasons that grew normally balanced antlers for several years. Fracture of the scapula in a white-tailed deer is reported to have led to a complete ipsilateral (same side) failure of antler growth for two successive years (Marburger et al. 1972).

The reason for the discrepancy in antler conformation after injury has not been determined. There are two hypotheses. Marburger et al. (1972) considered that complex neural pathways are involved. T. A. Davis (1982) thought the relationship to be mechanical. He postulated that the imbalance in gait in the Sambar stag led to a structural adaptation of the head to reestablish bilateral balance.

Hemi-castration (half castration) has peculiar and contradictory effects on antler growth (Chapman 1975). Fowler (1894) reported that this led to abnormal ipsilateral antler development in a fallow deer. However, it resulted in antler deformity in a sika deer on the contralateral side (Penrose 1924).

Depending on the degree of hermaphroditism (possession of both male and female sex organs), males with external female characteristics can produce antlers. A few elk cows carry eo-antlers (Buss and Solf 1959, Bubenik 1982). In an unusual case, a fertile antlered female elk went

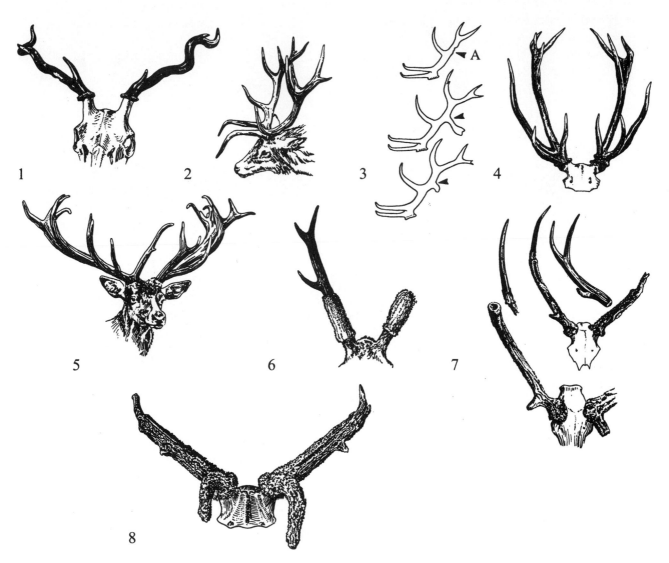

Figure 60. Antler anomalies (Bubenik 1982): 1. corkscrew antlers, result of osteomalacia (softening of bones often due to inadequate intake of calcium, phosphorus or vitamin D); 2. downward bent brow tines, the result of partial osteomalacia at the beginning of antler growth; 3. accessory tine developed after injury in year "A" and retained in the trophic (growth) memory of the antler center for two successive antler cycles (arrowheads = injury site and accessory tines in subsequent 2 years); 4. accessory tines over the bez tine, result of bilateral injury of growing antlers; 5. partial osteomalacia affecting only the ends of tines and points; 6. and 7. rarest anomalies in cervids— the lower part of the beam is not susceptible to testosterone but remains alive, and the upper part has its yearly cycle of cast; and 8. true eo-antler of the castrated bull. *Illustrated by A. B. Bubenik.*

through a complete but abnormal antler cycle. In another case, antlers were seen in a whitetail doe with a possibly masculinizing (steroid-producing) tumor (Dout and Donaldson 1959).

Body Conformation

Body size and conformation (shape) are related. This is partly a biomechanical issue involving ratios such as surface/volume and weight/cross-sectional area and factors such as gait and other adaptations to life in open country. Red deer and elk are adapted to running on hard ground and have Laufer (runner) body conformation. Smaller forest-dwelling species, such as white-tailed deer, have Schlupfer (diver) conformation. Laufer traits include more rigid spines, longer dorsal spinal processes at the withers, longer legs and shoulders higher than the hips (Estes 1974).

Skeleton

Conformation or shape is determined largely by the skeleton (Figure 61). Cervinae and other Old World deer belong to the plesiometacarpal group (i.e., rudiments of the lateral metacarpals are present only at their proximal ends) (Harrington 1985).

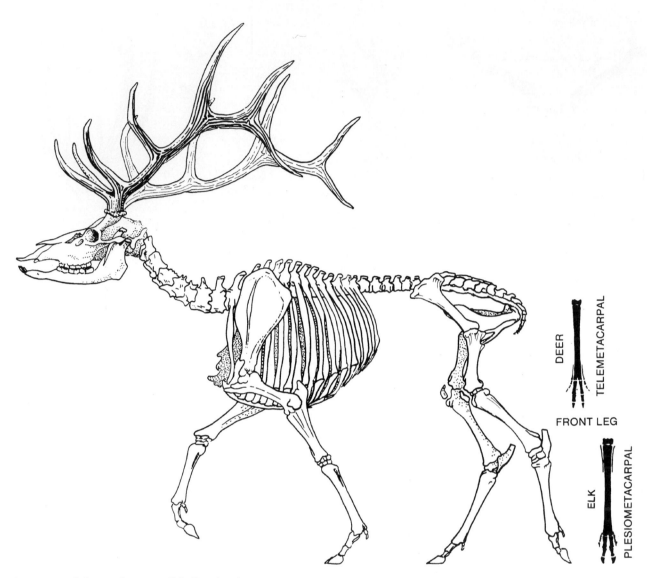

Figure 61.   Skeleton of a prime elk bull (Bubenik 1982). *Illustration by A. B. Bubenik.*

Although the skeleton is considered refractory to nutrition, there is substantial phenotypic variation. Red deer respond quickly and positively to improved feeding or social conditions by changing phenotype (Vogt 1947, Geist 1986c). Populations of phenotypically small animals may be either malnourished, socially distressed or both.

As in other animals, the mature conformation of elk derives from waves of skeletal growth. Generally, waves of growth are along the axial skeleton from the ends of the spine to the middle of the back and along the appendicular skeleton from the distal (farthest from the body) to the proximal (nearest) ends of the limbs. Growth from the center of the forehead along the nasal bones imparts an adult facial appearance. Maturation influences mineralization and structure of bones as well as their relative dimensions (Knight 1966a).

Nutritional effects on maturation have long been studied in the livestock industry to control carcass characteristics with feeding programs (Berg and Butterfield 1976). The ratio of distal to proximal bones (both axial and appendicular skeletons) has been evaluated as a method of reconstructing nutritional history, although this technique is not sensitive enough to detect anything but the most severe nutritional conditions during early life.

Limbs and Hooves

Limb and hoof structure reflects the adaptation of elk to firm ground. Compared with many other deer (particularly in the telemetacarpalia [New World deer]), elk have a tight hoof structure that splays little, even on soft ground.

Snow has been a factor in the adaptive radiation of limb and hoof structure. Incorporating both morphological and behavioral traits, Telfer and Kelsall (1984) ranked ungulates according to their ability to cope with snow. Morphological adaptations relevant to snow include foot loading (body weight divided by the area of the four feet contacting the ground or snow surface) and chest height (leg length) (Telfer and Kelsall 1979). Foot loading is important only where the snow crust provides consistent support. Where it does not, large hooves simply increase drag. Long legs (chest heights) enable animals to wade in deep soft snow.

Foot loadings vary little among ungulates, perhaps because snow seldom provides sufficient consistent support. Foot loadings of elk are less than of bison but greater than those of moose or deer. Mean foot loadings increase from 6.5 pounds per square inch (457 g/cm²) in young male elk to 10.5 pounds per square inch (738 g/cm²) in adult bulls. Adult cows have foot loadings of approximately 9.1 pounds per square inch (640 g/cm²).

Chest height of elk bulls ranges from 31 to 37 inches (78–95 cm), with an average of 35 inches (88 cm). Adult elk cows average 33 inches (83 cm). Shoulder height for elk bulls is about 59 inches (150 cm), with a maximum of 64 inches (162 cm); for cows, shoulder height is about 53 inches (135 cm).

Elk are forced to dig (crater) through snow to access winter forage, and adaptations of hooves and limbs are obviously important. Although hoof and limb adaptations for foraging have been studied in other northern ungulates (Collins and Smith 1991), little biomechanical work has been done specifically on such adaptations in elk despite their importance in seasonal migrations (Boyce 1991b).

Sensory Adaptation

Evolutionary dispersal into open habitats influenced the way many animals, including elk, oriented themselves in their environment, selected food (Provenza et al. 1992), detected predators and communicated among themselves. Some of these influences and their outcomes are detailed in Chapter 5. Here we set the stage by considering the sensory capacity and sensory signals of elk.

Sensory perception has remained relatively unstudied, because of the obvious difficulty of evaluating an animal's capacity to discriminate stimuli. The simplest but least certain way to evaluate sensory systems is anatomical analysis—a common approach used to evaluate spectral sensitivity in vision (Jacobs et al. 1994). According to K. L. Risenhoover (http://lutra.tamu.edu/klr/hearing.htm), acoustic spectra can be evaluated by measuring brain waves when anesthetized animals are exposed to sounds varying in frequency and intensity. Finally, it is possible to assess sensory perception by operant conditioning (stimulus–response learning).

Vision

In elk and most other ruminants, the wide placement of the orbits and elliptical pupil oriented horizontal to the ground provides a wide field of view but limits depth per-

The elk's long legs and tight hooves give it advantage over most other native ungulates in terms of accessing forage during periods of deep snow. *Left photo by Charles Shaw; courtesy of the U. S. Forest Service. Right photo by Herman B. Wilsey.*

ception and perhaps shape discrimination. This reflects the importance of predator detection in evolution.

Information on visual acuity of elk and related species is largely anecdotal. Visual acuity can be determined from the ability to distinguish shapes of different sizes at different distances. Few studies have been conducted on shape discrimination, yet such discrimination seems to be similar among domestic bovids (cattle, sheep and goats). Ruminants seem to be quite capable of detecting movement, but they apparently are not able to make sense of detail. Nothing is known about how elk interpret and generalize visual patterns and structure; however, the wide placement of eyes on an elk would indicate that they have rather poor depth perception.

In mammals, visual receptor cells, rods and cones, typically are distributed over the retina. Cones located within the fovea (central part of the retina) are responsible for color vision. Most ruminants have cones, which suggests that they can discriminate color (Jacobs 1993). Jacobs et al. (1994) studied spectral mechanisms in the retinas of both white-tailed deer and fallow deer. Both species have two classes of photoscopic receptors on the cones, and thus have the requisite retinal basis for dichromatic (two-color) color vision.

Experiments on color perception usually are conducted in pair-wise tests of colors of equivalent luminosity. Using operant conditioning, Scott (1981) documented discrimination of blaze orange by captive elk. In domestic ruminants, yellow and orange appear most readily discriminated (Arave 1996). Sheep and cattle have greater difficulty discriminating longer wavelengths (e.g., red versus blue).

Hearing

Elk have sharp hearing, although the lower threshold has not been determined. Their response to acoustic spectra probably is comparable to that of white-tailed deer, which are sensitive to a range similar to humans (K. L. Risenhoover personal communication:1996). Consequently, use of high frequency whistles on vehicles to reduce highway collisions is unlikely to be effective. There are, of course, other issues such as the unlikely assumption that animals are killed because they were not aware of approaching traffic.

Chemoreception

The chemical senses of taste and smell are used in a variety of contexts. They are important in food selection (Provenza et al. 1992) and communication (Walther 1984). Most work on sensory sensitivity has been conducted with odocoileine deer (Crawford and Church 1971, Rice and Church 1974).

Taste depends on chemoreceptors that detect dissolved

The eyes of elk are large and prominent with elliptical pupils oriented horizontal with the ground, providing a visual arc of approximately 270 degrees. Ears are large and hearing is acute. Ears may be individually rotated, allowing elk to pinpoint the direction of sounds of interest. *Photo by Leonard Lee Rue III.*

molecules. The four basic tastes are sweet, bitter, salty and sour. Chemoreceptor cells also detect airborne molecules (olfactory) that are an important complement of taste. However, little data exist on either taste or olfaction in elk. In domestic ruminants, studies on the role of sensory perception in food selection often are conducted either by offering water or other neutral carrier tainted with various tastes or odors or by selective ablation of senses of touch (lidocaine), taste, smell (osmic acid) or sight (blindfolds or colored lights). Generally, senses are used in concert mainly to identify foods rather than fix a preference.

Signals

Animals signal one another in a variety of ways (see Chapter 7). Body size, color, rank indicators (such as manes and antlers), and expressive postures and movements are important releasers of behavior of conspecifics. Here, we emphasize pheromones, that is, odors that convey social meaning (Duvall et al. 1986, Müller-Schwarze 1987).

Chemical signals emanate from many parts of the body—feces, urine, breath and specialized skin glands

The ability to discriminate among odors is especially important to elk with regard to food selection, detection of danger, social signals and reproduction. At right, olfactory clues are not always as revealing as they might be, as evidenced by this elk's porcupine "whiskers." *Left photo by Leonard Lee Rue, III. Right photo by Erwin Bauer.*

(Walther 1984). Excreta convey information about physiological status. Urine of females is tested by breeding males to detect estrus, apparently using the vomeronasal organ in the palate, which is exposed during flehmen or lip-curl (a grimace associated with sniffing socially meaningful odors). Urine of rutting males is strongly scented with ketone bodies (e.g., acetone) arising from rapid mobilization and incomplete combustion of fat; it may reveal rutting status to

conspecifics (Miquelle 1990).

The most highly differentiated skin glands possessed by elk are the metatarsal, tail and preorbital glands (Murie 1951, Lincoln 1971a). The metatarsal gland (situated on the external part of the hind leg, just below the hock) and an area around the penis (belly patch) are true apocrine glands as are hair follicles of the pedicle skin, velvet of developing antlers, and areas around the vagina and anus in females.

Scent glands in elk are highly differentiated and occur on the external rear legs (metatarsal glands), ventral side of the tail, and ahead of each eye (preorbital glands) of both sexes. In addition, bulls produce glandular secretions around the penis and near the base of developing antlers, and cows produce glandular secretions around the vagina and anus. *Photo by Irene Vandermolen.*

Fat-producing (sebaceous) glands surround the hair follicles of velvet antler. On the ventral side of the tail are two large, modified sweat gland tissues, highly prized for traditional Oriental medicine. Interdigital glands (between the hooves) are rudimentary or absent in red deer and elk, although pronounced in many other wild ruminants.

One of an elk's most striking glands is the preorbital gland in the hollow cavity (antorbital fontanela) anterior to the eye. This gland produces copious secretion—comprised more of fermented epithelial cells than a true apocrine secretion. Typically, the preorbital gland flares when elk are aroused by alarm, anger, fear or even eager anticipation. The extreme development of this gland occurs in sambar stags. Many antelope use the preorbital gland to mark territories (e.g., gazelles) or mates (e.g.,wildebeest). In cervids, rather than conveying a specific intention, the preorbital gland seems to complement other signals to indicate emotional tension.

Trophic Specialization

Forage type has been an important selective force in evolution of ruminants. Of the world's 160 living ruminant species, 25% are grazers, 40% are browsers and 35% are mixed feeders. Red deer and elk are extraordinarily adaptable mixed feeders (Church and Hines 1978, Hofmann 1985, 1989). Consistent with their evolutionary history and preference for more open habitats, elk appear marginally better adapted than red deer to grass diets. Although the relative importance of morphological specialization and size remains controversial (Gordon and Illius 1994, Robbins et al. 1995), this classification involves differences in all parts of the alimentary tract including dentition, salivary glands, foregut and hindgut.

Dentition

The selenodont dentition (zigzag enamel pattern) of ruminants shows striking adaptation to diet. To compensate for greater wear caused by their diet of coarse dusty grasses, grazers have high crowned (hypsodont) molars and premolars that usually provide an effective occlusal (contact) surface during the reproductive life of the animal (Janis and Fortelius 1988).

As in all ruminants, the upper incisors of elk have been replaced with a dental pad (Figure 62). The outer pair of so-called lower incisors are technically incisiform canines. The first premolar was lost during the evolution of ruminants, therefore the remaining premolars are numbered 2 to 4. The dental formula of red deer and sika deer is similar to that of most other cervids. Upper canines are found only in

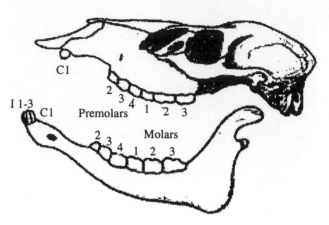

Figure 62. Dentition of elk and red deer. Upper incisors have been lost. Lower incisors are accompanied by an incisorform canine on the lower jaw. Premolars are numbered 2 to 4 because the first premolar was lost during evolution. *Illustration from Haigh and Hudson (1993).*

elk (and caribou). The upper canine is nonfunctional for feeding and masticating, but still is used in threat displays as a relic of its ancestral use as a weapon. The female's canines

Like all ruminants, elk lack upper incisors. The tongue is used to pull vegetation into the mouth, where it is clipped by pressure from the lower incisors against the upper dental pad. *Photo by Verna R. Johnston.*

are smaller; they can be used to determine the gender of skulls (Greer and Yeager 1967).

Grazers have larger muzzles relative to mandible length than do browsing species (Janis and Ehrhardt 1988). The width of the incisor bar of ruminants generally scales to weight $(W)^{0.35}$ and, therefore, is proportionally smaller in larger animals. At any given body size, the incisor bar is wider in grazers $(8.96W^{0.35})$ than in mixed feeders $(7.17W^{0.35})$ and browsers $(6.84W^{0.35})$ (Gordon and Illius 1988). The incisor bar also is more curved among browsing ruminants. These differences confer appropriate selectivity to these groups. The dental characteristics of red deer and elk place them in a mixed feeder or grazer category.

Salivary Glands

Ruminants produce prodigious volumes of saliva from parotid, submaxillary, buccal and sublingual glands. Despite differences in the size of the parotid and other salivary glands, there is little difference among ruminants in salivary secretion rate, which, in elk, is about 0.4 to 0.5 $g/kg^{0.75}$ per minute (Robbins et al. 1995). The saliva buffers the rumen contents for microbial fermentation. Tannin-binding serous proteins in saliva of deer and several other browsers may be part of a defense mechanism against antinutritive substances in plants (Austin et al. 1989). Dietary tannins are not always detrimental; high tannin materials (e.g., oak leaves) sometimes are purposely added to diets of captive deer. Certain levels may improve performance by optimizing the proportion of a ruminal bypass protein (discussed later).

Salivary glands appear particularly well developed in browsers and mixed feeders such as red deer and elk (Kay 1987, Robbins et al. 1995). Parotid glands are three times larger in concentrate selectors (1.4–2.2 g/kg) than in roughage feeders (0.5–0.7 g/kg) (Kay 1987, 1989). There are exceptions such as the kudu, which browses but has salivary glands like a grazer.

Digestive Adaptation

Mammalian herbivores depend on a symbiotic relationship with microorganisms to digest cellulose (Kay 1987). Although nutritional adaptation involves most parts of the digestive tract, the most important differences are in the four-chambered stomach (Figure 63).

Forage enters the atrium of the first chamber, the rumen. After regurgitation of the coarser matter for further mastication and further mixing and fermentation in the rumen, finer particles spill over the reticular fold into the reticulum. Particles of suitable dimensions and specific gravity pass through the reticulo-omasal orifice to the omasum where much of the liquid is removed. The digesta is then subjected to acidic enzymatic digestion in the abomasum.

The rumen in *Cervus* has three blind sacs. The atrium—a chamberlike entrance between the esophagus and rumen and the reticulum—is relatively large. The capacious rumen of elk shows well-developed ruminal compartments divided by strong pillars, papillae that are longest in the bottom of the ventral sac, indicating nonhomogeneous distribution of digesta (Prins and Geelen 1971, Nagy and Regelin 1975, Church and Hines 1978).

The reticulum, the second compartment of the ruminant stomach, has a mucous membrane in the form of ridges that divide the inner surface into many sided, honeycomb ridges (polyhedrals), which occasionally have smooth papillae. Considerable absorption of end products of digestion occurs here but the functional significance of the unusual honeycomb pattern is not understood.

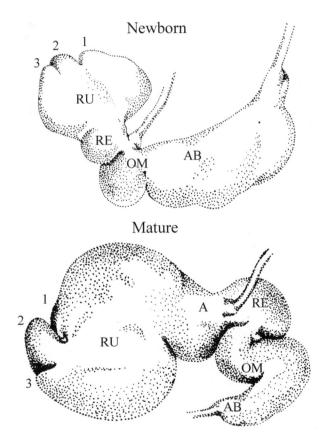

Figure 63. Development of the four-chambered ruminant stomach (Bubenik 1982). RU = rumen with 1, 2, 3 blind sacs; RE = reticulum; AB = abomasum; OM = omasum; and A = atrium of the rumen. *Illustration by A. B. Bubenik.*

The omasum has many folds, with granular, partly keratinized (hornlike tissue) papillae. Inside the folds are muscular and vascular tissues. By muscle contractions, considerable amounts of water are pressed out and reabsorbed. The abomasum is the ruminant's true glandular stomach, along with the bottom (fundic) portion and the outlet between the stomach and the duodenum (pyloric region or portion of the small intestine).

In newborns, the forestomach is small compared with the large abomasum. The forestomach begins to develop when the first solid food is eaten (including soil, feces of older conspecifics and, from the second week on, fresh plants). By about 4 months of age, mature proportions of all the stomachs are achieved.

Allometry Versus Digestive Specialization

Because of differential scaling of digestive capacity and metabolic rate, grazing ruminants are expected to be large and browsing ruminants small (Hudson 1985). But there are many exceptions—the world's largest ruminant (giraffe) and largest cervid (moose) are browsers. For this reason, Hofmann (1989) doubted the significance of body size in digestive adaptation. However, issues such as food distribution influence optimal body size, and these may account for the observed exceptions and lack of a consistent pattern.

Ruminoreticular volumes in ruminants average about 20% of body weight but vary widely from 8% to 36% depending on species, diet and season. Values for elk vary seasonally but decrease in the upper part of this range. Although fermentation volume scales isometrically (i.e., is a constant proportion of body weight), grazers tend to fall above the interspecies relationship and browsers below (Van Soest 1982); Gordon and Illius (1994) questioned the significance of this difference.

The overall size and proportions of the four-chambered stomach are more consistent correlates with dietary adaptation (Hofmann 1989). Roughage grazers have relatively large rumens and omasa but small reticula and abomasa. Compared with that of browsers, papillae of grazers are less evenly and densely spaced, which provides a less effective absorptive surface. Roughage grazers have capacious ruminoreticula with well-developed delaying structures that slow passage and expose digesta to prolonged fermentation. Because fermentation progresses slowly, papillation is relatively undeveloped. Papillae are heteromorphic (uneven) in distribution because of the digesta being layered. The papillae in the upper parts of the rumen are cornified to protect the rumen wall from injury by coarse floating material.

In contrast, browsers (concentrate selectors) have relatively small, well-papillated ruminoreticula with rather open communication among stomach compartments. Rates of fermentation and passage are quicker. Their well-developed salivary glands, ventricular groove (which remains functional into adulthood), hydrochloric acid-producing parietal cells in the abomasum and extensive hindgut fermentation suggest a bypass mechanism. It seems likely that the saliva of browsers washes cell solubles down the ventricular groove to the abomasum where tannins (chemically bound with salivary protein) are dissolved in the acidic environment. This is an adaptation to the chemical defenses of plants as well as the high cell solubles of browse diets. These contrasting digestive strategies are appropriate given the fermentation patterns of grass and browse diets. Grasses ferment slowly but completely, whereas the highly differentiated tissues of browse plants ferment quickly but plateau at a lower level. The optimal retention time when gut fill constrains intake is when about 50% of the fermentable portion has disappeared. Therefore, digestion coefficients—a standard agricultural measurement of the completeness of digestion—mean little to the success of wild animals whose optimal strategy involves the trade-off of completeness of digestion and throughput.

Elk and, to varying degrees, other members of *Cervus* fall between these two extremes in anatomical and functional design.

Functional Correlates

Although empirical evidence is scanty (Westra and Hudson 1981, Baker and Hobbs 1987, Spalinger and Robbins 1992, Spalinger et al. 1993), roughage feeders are predicted to have longer retention times, larger gut fills and opt for more complete digestion of forage than do concentrate selectors (Hofmann 1989). Attempts to corroborate these predictions (Baker and Hansen 1985, Baker and Hobbs 1987, Renecker and Hudson 1990) have been complicated by seasonal changes and interactions among diets. Questions have even been raised about the overriding importance of body size (Gordon and Illius 1994, Robbins et al. 1995).

The rumen fill of grazers is generally higher and fermentation and passage rates are lower than those of browsers. Because of the larger size and strongly subdivided foregut, the movement of food through the digestive tract of grazers is delayed, permitting relatively complete microbial fermentation before fine particles pass through the omasum to the lower tract for gastric digestion. Longer exposure of digesta to fermentative microorganisms means more complete digestion—a significant factor for hand-fed livestock but not necessarily for survival of wild animals whose success is linked more directly with daily digestible nutrient intake. The diet of browsers is passed rapidly and, consequently, is lightly fermented.

Fermentation rates of grazers, browsers and mixed feeders seem to differ largely because of their diets. Ruminants of all types ferment food in a similar manner, as suggested by comparisons of red deer and sheep (Kay and Goodall 1976). Although differences in digestion rates and ruminal microbial populations (Cederlund and Nystrom 1981) may contribute to observed differences among browsers, mixed feeders and grazers, the most important factors contributing to differences in digestion appear to be related to the kinetics of passage (Huston et al. 1986, Renecker and Hudson 1990).

Passage rates of feed particles by elk range widely. Differences of feed types, marker kinetics and computational methods make comparison of studies almost meaningless. On constant diets, passage rates change surprisingly little despite a 30% range of feed intakes from winter to summer (Milne et al. 1978, Domingue et al. 1991). Fractional outflow rates of food particles (turnover of digestive contents) are in the order of 5% to 6% per hour and liquid outflows are about 16% per hour. The high outflow rate of liquid from the rumen may partly explain why deer are less susceptible to frothy bloat (Freudenberger et al. 1994a, 1994b) and are able to graze alfalfa pastures under conditions that would be unwise for cattle grazing.

Photoperiod and Seasonality

During dispersal to higher latitudes and more open habitats, the evolving genus *Cervus* faced strongly seasonal environments that encouraged tightly synchronized calving and breeding seasons and seasonal growth and metabolism. Day length provided the most reliable cue of changing seasonal resources.

Physiological rhythms are intrinsic, but entrained by photoperiod (Lincoln 1985, Loudon and Brinklow 1992). Deer from temperate zones, when moved across the equator, gradually shift cycles of antler development, breeding, hair molt, appetite and energy expenditures to adapt to the new seasonal synchrony (Marshall 1937, Bedford and Marshall 1942). The period of seasonal cycles can be reduced to 6 months by artificially controlling light (Pollock 1975). Tropical deer, on the other hand, usually do not develop cycles when moved to high latitudes and are not responsive to melatonin treatment (Loudon and Curlewis 1988). Near the equator, day length is less important to physiological rhythms. Feed availability and other poorly defined environmental cues may influence seasonal synchrony of breeding and antler cycles among equatorial species (Loudon and Curlewis 1988).

Melatonin controls hypothalamic release of gonadotropin-releasing hormones and various metabolic hormones. Metabolic and reproductive hormones initiate physiological changes characteristic of specific points in the seasonal cycle (Table 16). The significant metabolic hormones are the thyroid-stimulating hormones prolactin and growth hormone, whose action seems to be mediated through insulin-like growth factor (IGF) or other somatomedins (Milne et al. 1990). Among males, the important seasonal reproductive hormone is testosterone. Among females, progestins and estrogens regulate seasonal patterns. Reproductive hormones also have profound metabolic effects.

Highest annual values of both prolactin and thyroid hormones in most adult northern cervids (Lincoln 1985, Loudon et al.1989) fall quite precisely on the summer solstice. Melatonin, which is secreted during hours of darkness, is at its lowest annual levels at this time. The exception among seasonal cervids is Pére David's deer, which has a prolactin peak in early May in association with its early calving (Sibbald et al. 1993). The close association of prolactin and thyrotropin is not entirely unexpected because both are released by thyroid-releasing hormone (Fraser and McNeilly 1982).

Photosensitivity and Melatonin

Seasonal rhythms are under endocrinological control, and melatonin is the key mediator (Lincoln 1985, Reiter 1991). The pineal gland is a neuroendocrine transducer that translates day length into an endocrine message; it works in concert with the superior cervical ganglia and suprachiasmic nuclei (Figure 64).

The pineal gland synthesizes a variety of hormones and indoleamines, of which melatonin is best understood and presumably most important. The pineal gland produces melatonin during the hours of darkness but the pattern varies. For example, in some species, melatonin increases abruptly and subsides before dawn. In other species, melatonin increases throughout the period of darkness (Reiter 1991). The pattern of melatonin production throughout a 24-hour cycle, rather than average blood concentrations, seems to transduce day length into a biochemical signal. The duration of the nighttime increase in circulating melatonin relays information about photoperiod.

Circadian melatonin rhythms can be eliminated by exposure to constant light, pinealectomy (removal of the pineal gland) or superior cervical ganglionectomy (removal of the neural pathway that enervates the pineal gland) (Yellon et al. 1992). However, the rhythm of melatonin secretion, driven by the suprachiasmatic nucleus, persists in animals kept in darkness. In adult cervids removal of both the pineal gland and the suprachiasmatic ganglia affect the synchrony but does not completely suppress seasonal cycles. However, in younger animals these interventions may disrupt such endogenous seasonal cycles as antler growth, pelage and appetite (D'Occhio and Suttie 1992).

Table 16.   Important seasonal metabolic and reproductive hormones and their origins and functions in cervids

Primary origin	Hormone	Function	Key reference
Pineal gland	Melatonin	Transduces photoperiod; entrains circannual rhythms	Reiter 1991, Yellon et al. 1992, Ebling and Hastings 1992
Hypothalamus	Releasing and release-inhibiting hormones acting on adenophypophysis (e.g., gonadotropin-releasing hormone and thyrotrophin-releasing hormone)	Hormones delivered via portal circulation to adenohypophysis functions	
Pituitary	Adrenocorticotropin (ACTH)	Stimulates adrenal cortex	
	Thyrotropic hormone (TSH)	Stimulates thyroid	
	Follicle-stimulating hormone (FSH)	Stimulates ovarian follicle development; seminiferous tubule development in testes	
Pituitary	Luteinizing hormone (LH)	Stimulates conversion of ovarian follicle to corpus luteum; stimulates progesterone and testosterone production	
Pituitary	Prolactin	Stimulates appetite and milk production	Meier 1977, Loudon et al. 1983, Suttie et al. 1989, Milne et al. 1990, Curlewis 1992
Pituitary	Growth hormone (GH)	Stimulates growth via somatomedin (IGF_1 and other growth factors); Lipolytic	
Liver (and other tissues)	Insulin-like growth factor 1 (IGF-1) and other somatomedins with endocrine, paracrine or autocrine action)	Stimulates growth of lean tissue and antler matrix (effector for hypophyseal growth hormone)	McGuire et al. 1992, Suttie and Webster 1995
Thyroid	Thyroxin and tri-iodothyronine (most active form in cervids)	Stimulates oxidative metabolism; inhibits TSH	Ryg and Jacobsen 1982, Shi and Barrell 1992
	Calcitonin	Inhibits excessive rise in blood calcium	
Adrenal cortex	Glucocorticoids (cortisol, corticosterone, etc.)	Regulates carbohydrate metabolism	
	Mineralocorticoids (aldosterone, deoxycorticosterone, etc.)	Regulates sodium metabolism and excretion	
	Cortical androgens, progesterone	Stimulates secondary sexual characteristics, predominantly male	
Adrenal medulla	Adrenalin, noradrenaline	Augments sympathetic function; vasodilation in muscle, liver, lungs, vasoconstriction in many visceral organs; increases blood sugar	
Parathyroid	Parathormone	Increases blood calcium	
Pancreas	Insulin	Reduces blood glucose, stimulates formation and storage of carbohydrates	
Pancreas	Glucagon	Increases blood glucose by mobilization of glycogen from liver	
Ovary	Estrogen	Initiates and maintains female secondary characteristics; initiates periodic thickening of uterine mucosa; inhibits FSH	
Ovary	Progesterone	In cooperation with estrogens, stimulates female secondary characteristics; supports and glandularizes uterine mucosa; inhibits LH and FSH	
Testis	Testosterone	Initiates and maintains male secondary sexual characteristics	

Manipulation of Seasonality

Manipulation of photoperiod can be used experimentally to improve understanding of seasonal adaptations of wild elk or commercially to advance breeding or enhance growth in farmed animals. The intensity of light required to precipitate an endocrine response varies among species. Reindeer seem to require more than 1,000 lux (lx) (Eloranta et al. 1995), which is between the threshold in humans (more than 2,000 lx) and in hamsters (200 lx) (Reiter 1991).

Administration of melatonin in feed or by implant can be used to manipulate the timing of physiological cycles,

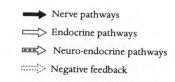

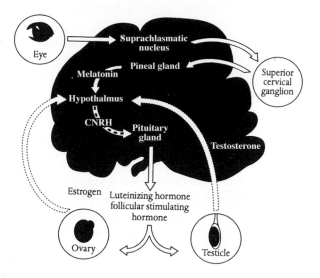

Figure 64. Neuroendocrine response to photoperiod. Light synchronizes the endogenous rhythm to the external day and night cycle and sets the duration of nocturnal secretion. Light, perceived by the retina, stimulates nerve pathways through the brain (shaded) and the superior cervical ganglion to the pineal gland, with subsequent 24-hour cycles mediated by the hypothalamus. The suprachiasmatic nucleus (bilateral cluster of neurons in the anterior hypothalamus) control pineal melatonin production through a multisynaptic pathway. This center generates 24-hour rhythms that are entrained by photoperiod. GNRH = gonadotropin-releasing hormones. *Illustration by J. Deubner, from Haigh and Hudson (1993).*

particularly to advance breeding and calving dates (Adam and Atkinson 1984, Lincoln et al. 1984, Adam et al. 1989, Asher 1990, Heydon et al. 1995). Oral administration of melatonin late in the afternoon advances puberty (Webster and Barrell 1985). Increasing baseline levels of melatonin with a slow-release implant creates a short-day signal with the same effect. Immunizing animals against melatonin also has been explored as a way of sustaining rapid growth of farmed red deer during winter (Duckworth and Barrell 1989).

Initiation of melatonin treatments less than 100 days after the winter solstice delays puberty by impinging on a possible photoperiod entrainment period. Initiation after 100 days advances puberty, with later dates resulting in progressively less advancement (Asher et al. 1993). Longer days in early spring seem to be part of the entrainment process.

Not all animals need to receive melatonin, as there is a

degree of social reproductive synchrony. In particular, advancing rutting dates of red deer stags also advances conception dates of hinds (McComb 1987, Fisher et al. 1988).

Digestive and Metabolic Adaptation

Elk face strong seasonal cycles of forage quality and availability. Seasonal intake can be adjusted by feeding selectively and by feeding longer or faster. These responses often are conflicting, therefore optimization involves complex trade-offs (Chapter 5). In addition to behavioral modifications, elk invoke a variety of physiological adaptations to adjust maintenance requirements and productive processes to seasonal environments.

Like most other northern wild ruminants, the seasonal metabolic cycles of elk affect growth, appetite and energy expenditures (Kay 1985, White 1992). These cycles are particularly striking in *Odocoileus,* the subject of much of the early work (Wood et al. 1962, Bandy et al. 1970). However, these cycles have proven an important feature of the nutritional physiology of red deer (Pollock 1975, Simpson et al. 1978) and elk (Hudson et al. 1985, Watkins et al. 1991, Jiang and Hudson 1992, 1994).

Appetite and Digestive Function

Regulation of Forage Intake

Dry matter intakes vary severalfold depending on forage quality/availability and on seasonal metabolic rhythms. Peak appetite during antler development and summer weight gain coincides with the summer solstice and peak circulating levels of prolactin. Reproduction is a prime determinant of seasonal energy requirements and, hence, feed intakes of both genders.

Elk cows fed ad libitum during winter generally consume medium- to high-quality feeds (metabolizable energy contents of 8–10 kJ/g) at maintenance levels. These requirements are usually met by a daily dry matter intake of approximately 40 to 65 $g/kg^{0.75}$ body weight to adjust for the scaling of energy requirements and body size. Despite rapid growth of the fetus in the third trimester of pregnancy, intakes remain low but increase sharply to about 100 $g/kg^{0.75}$ per day during lactation, exceeding intakes of dry cows by more than 50%. The picture, of course, is complicated on seasonal ranges where forage quality and availability change throughout the year. Also, young or underweight animals may continue to grow during winter or gain exceptionally quickly on summer ranges after high winter weight losses. This compensation occurs largely through greater feed intake (Wairimu and Hudson 1993).

Intakes of elk bulls ranges from less than 20 g/kg$^{0.75}$ per day during the rut to more than 100 g/kg$^{0.75}$ per day in early summer. Minimum seasonal intake in red deer stags is highly correlated with circulating testosterone (Ryg 1986). Fasting during the rut induces ketosis, which imparts the smell of acetone to the male's breath and urine but seems not to precipitate the metabolic disorders seen in cattle.

Digestive Function

When food is scarce or otherwise associated with high foraging costs, a digestive system that selectively retains feeds is adaptive, even if the mechanism may constrain gut capacity. In summer with abundant forage and relatively low foraging costs, rapid passage of digesta enables elk to take advantage of the fast decline phase of digestion, and rapid passage relieves the constraint of digestive capacity on intake.

Physical properties of feed appear to explain most seasonal variation of digestion. Among domestic ruminants, passage rates are influenced by intake level and forage type and quality (Warner 1981, Van Soest et al.1988). However, the relationship appears weak in deer (Milne et al. 1978, Renecker and Hudson 1990, Domingue et al. 1991, 1992, Sibbald and Milne 1993).

The simplest explanation is that digesta fill increases either by changing distension set-points or digestive tract dimensions. Evidence for the former comes from Sibbald and Milne (1993) who found higher dry matter proportions and weights of digesta and water-filled capacity of the rumen when feed intake by red deer was high. However, they did not find differences in the weight of gut tissues. Domingue et al. (1991) also found that higher feed intake was accommodated by higher digesta loads. In a subsequent experiment with melatonin implants to mimic seasonal photoperiod, Domingue et al. (1992) found that rumen capacity remained about the same throughout the year. However, the rumen dry matter pool as a proportion of rumen capacity was found to increase with feed intake and decreasing melatonin.

Rumination frequency and gut motility also may play a role in seasonal patterns of digestive function (Stafford et al. 1993). As in most ruminants, the so-called A-sequence of contraction commences with a biphasic pressure wave in the reticulum (reticular doublet) followed by a B-sequence, a monophase positive pressure wave in the dorsal rumen sac (with one or more waves in the ventral sac). Although eating and rumination times and rumen boli per day increases from winter to spring, A-sequence contractions (1,800 per day) and B-sequence contractions (500 per day) varied little by season. The frequency of A-sequence contractions is similar in red deer and elk (Kay 1987).

Although digestibility does not change seasonally with intake, rumen fermentation may (Domingue et al. 1991). Molar proportions of acetate relative to propionate are higher in summer (4.2) than in winter (3.62). Also, rumen

Forage intake by elk bulls reaches a maximum of more than 100 g/kg$^{0.75}$ per day during the summer solstice and coincides with peak circulating levels of prolactin and the period of maximum antler growth. *Photo by George Wolstad; courtesy of the U.S. Forest Service.*

ammonia concentrations, pool size and outflow, and whole body nitrogen retention are higher in summer. The larger rumen pool size and this higher rumen ammonia concentration may maintain fiber digestion when intake increases in summer (Freudenberger et al. 1994a).

Energy Metabolism

Exactly how seasonal cycles of energy expenditure confer an adaptive advantage is not clear. Once popular interpretations included: (1) winter bioenergetic dormancy that spares energy during times of hardship; and (2) a mechanism for minimizing grazing pressure of populations on limited winter feed resources. Both interpretations are rather unlikely. What is unusual about northern wild ruminants is their high summer energy expenditure rather than the winter minimum, which simply falls toward the interspecies mean. More likely, the cycle primes animals to use the brief seasonal pulse of plant growth.

Ecological Maintenance

Energy expenditures of free-ranging animals in natural environments are termed ecological metabolism. This quantity has been measured in small mammals using doubly labeled water (Nagy 1987). The high costs of the isotope and certain problems with its application in ruminants (methane production, rapid seasonal growth) have limited its application in cervids (Fancy et al. 1986, Midwood et al. 1989). Metabolizable energy requirements for maintenance and gain can be calculated more directly (and inexpensively) by regression of intake (kilojoules per kilogram$^{0.75}$ per day) against daily gain (grams per kilogram$^{0.75}$ per day) (Figure 65).

Published estimates for winter requirements of red deer and elk are in the order of 450 to 550 kJ/kg$^{0.75}$ per day (Fennessy et al. 1981, Suttie et al. 1987, Jiang and Hudson 1994, Cool and Hudson 1996). Summer and fall values increased to 720 and 876 kJ/kg$^{0.75}$ per day (Jiang and Hudson 1994). The incremental costs of free-existence increase this by about 200 kJ/kg$^{0.75}$ per day.

This seasonal cycle is strongly developed even in the first 18 months of life. Summer maintenance requirements of adult cows are lower than those of yearlings, but lactation demands of adult cows increase apparent requirements by at least 25%. Bulls generally have higher requirements than cows, except perhaps for lactating cows.

Ecological metabolism usually is estimated using a factorial approach based on summing fasting metabolism, with incremental costs of thermoregulation and activity. The focus of this chapter is on the physiological basis of these costs rather than construction of energy budgets.

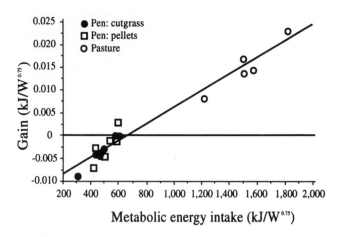

Figure 65. Estimation of energy requirements for maintenance and gain (Jiang and Hudson 1992). The intercept (zero weight [W] change) represents the maintenance requirement (in kilojoules per kilogram$^{0.75}$ per day). The slope estimates the costs of depositing or mobilizing body tissues in units of kilojoules per gram.

Maintenance Metabolism

Basal metabolic rate represents the minimal energy expenditure required for such essential physiological processes as cardiopulmonary function, protein turnover, and ion gradients and substrate transport. This state is difficult to achieve experimentally, therefore a standardized measurement—fasting metabolic rate—at 72 hours after feeding commonly is used. Metabolic rates of animals that have not been subject to a nominal fast but are at rest include energy related to digestion and nutrient metabolism (or resting metabolic rate). Winter fasting metabolic rates of temperate zone hoofed mammals tend to be slightly above the interspecies mean of 295 kJ/kg$^{0.75}$ per day (Table 17). The fasting metabolic rate of red deer is 330 to 400 kJ/kg$^{0.75}$ per day, similar to cattle but higher than sheep. Summer fasting metabolic rates of most temperate zone wild ruminants are considerably higher.

One problem with these seasonal comparisons is that they are confounded by previous feeding levels that can prime tissue metabolism and influence the size of metabolically active organs such as the liver and gut (Koong et al. 1985). The British Metabolizable Energy System requires up to 6 weeks of maintenance feeding before determining fasting metabolic rate (Hudson and Christopherson 1985). This condition is seldom observed in studies on deer. Pekins et al. (1992) suggested that, when activity and thermal conditions are carefully standardized, the apparent seasonal cycle in white-tailed deer is lost.

Table 17. Seasonal daily fasting metabolic rate (in kilojoules per kilogram$^{0.75}$) of elk, red deer and other wild and domestic ruminants

Species	Season	
	Winter	Summer
Cattle	320	320
Domestic sheep	210	230
Bighorn sheep	256	
Mountain goat	319	
Bison	305	
Roe deer	382	416
White-tailed deer	339	585
Mule deer	372	
Reindeer	427	536
Moose	310	450
Red deer and elk	330–400	

Source: Updated from Hudson and Christopherson 1985.

Activity

Wild ruminants spend more than 90% of their day foraging, resting/ruminating or walking between bedding and feeding sites. Thus, energy budgets can be easily calculated from activity budgets if the incremental costs of standing, traveling and foraging are known.

Energy costs of standing in most domestic ruminants are in the order of 9% higher than for energy expenditures by those animals while bedded. Experiments on cervids suggest increments of 18% to 23% (Cohen et al. 1978, Gates and Hudson 1979, Parker et al. 1984, Regelin et al. 1986). The disparity may be related to body conformation but must be at least partly due to the greater alertness of wild species. Metabolic rates are measured opportunistically, and animals are more likely to bed when relaxed and stand when aroused.

Energy expenditures during locomotion scale linearly with velocity but vary little per unit distance (Fancy and White 1985). Therefore, incremental costs can be conveniently expressed as energy expenditures associated with moving 1 kg of body mass for 1 km. Studies on both red deer (Brockway and Gessamen 1977) and elk (Cohen et al. 1978, Gates and Hudson 1978, Robbins et al. 1979, Parker et al. 1984) suggest that the energy cost of their walking on a firm horizontal surface is similar to that of domestic animals; about 2.6 kJ/kg per kilometer regardless of the speed at which the animal travels. On inclines, this increases to almost 10 times the cost per equivalent unit of elevation (Parker et al. 1984).

Differences are more striking when ungulates ascend and descend slopes or are on different substrates such as snow

or wet tundra (Cohen et al. 1978, Fancy and White 1987). Energy costs of locomotion in snow increase exponentially with sinking depth, approximately doubling by 60% of brisket height (Dailey and Hobbs 1989).

The incremental cost of eating is less than 1 kJ/kg$^{0.75}$ per hour. However, free-grazing animals expend 3 to 5 kJ/kg$^{0.75}$ per hour because of the additional costs of searching for and selecting forage (Fancy and White 1985). Because animals may spend 30% to 50% of their day foraging, daily energy requirements may increase about 30% (Hudson and Christopherson 1985).

Thermoregulation

Over a wide range of thermal conditions, heat exchange with the environment can be regulated by physical and behavioral means. Above the upper critical temperature, additional heat is released through such mechanisms as panting. Below the lower critical temperature, the metabolic rate increases to produce heat to offset that lost to the environment. The slope of the line relating metabolic rate to ambient temperature below the lower critical temperature defines conductance or reciprocally thermal insulation (Figure 66).

One complication is that metabolic rates sometimes decline with falling temperatures as observed in bison (Christo-

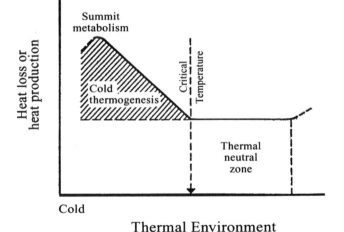

Thermal Environment

Figure 66. Estimates of heat loss and resistance to heat loss (insulation) usually are made from steady state measurements of metabolic rate using induced respiration calorimetry and measurements of deep-body (core) and surface and air temperatures (Christopherson and Young 1981). For temperatures below the lower critical temperature, whole body insulation (I), ignoring evaporative heat loss, can be crudely estimated by I – (Tr – Ta)/H, where Tr is the core temperature, Ta is ambient temperature and H is metabolic heat production (watts per meter^2, where 1 watt = 1 J/meter^2 per second). Insulation (slope of relationship between metabolic rate and degrees below the lower critical temperature and metabolic rate) is influenced by body size, condition and pelage characteristics.

pherson et al. 1979) and moose (Renecker et al. 1978, Schwartz and Renecker 1997). This has not been found in elk (Gates and Hudson 1979, Parker and Robbins 1984).

Cold Stress

Elk are quite resistant to cold. Lower critical temperatures approximate –4°F (–20°C), but this changes with season (Parker and Robbins 1984). In winter, the metabolic rate of elk drops to an operative temperature of –4°F (–20°C), at which point piloerection or shivering first occurs (Figure 67). In summer, the lower critical temperature of yearlings is approximately 50°F (10°C).

Lower critical temperatures are determined by both thermoneutral metabolic rates and insulation. Thermoneutral metabolic rate is influenced mainly by feeding level. However, not all increments of thermoneutral heat production substitute for the heat of thermoregulation; ac-

tivity increases metabolic rate and makes animals feel warmer, but thermal insulation is destroyed (Figure 68).

Heat Stress

Disproportionate attention probably has been paid to cold stress, because there are many more days each year when elk are exposed to heat stress sufficient to depress feed intake and productivity. Upper critical temperatures of elk in winter are 59° to 68°F (15°–20°C). In summer, upper critical temperatures generally are higher but variable. Elk tolerate heat better than do mule deer (Parker and Robbins 1984), but a particularly difficult time for heat stress is spring, when the animals are still in winter coats.

Elk respond to high temperatures both by panting and sweating, particularly the former. Respiratory rates increase gradually at 50°F (10°C) in winter and sharply at 86°F (30°C) in summer (Parker and Robbins 1984). Panting pro-

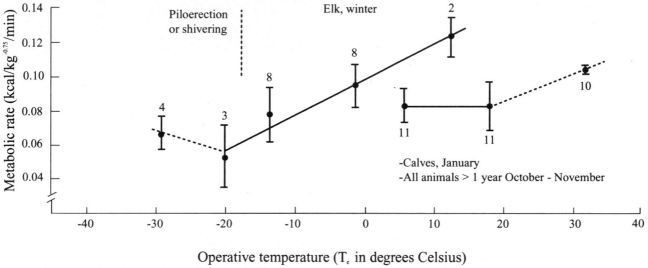
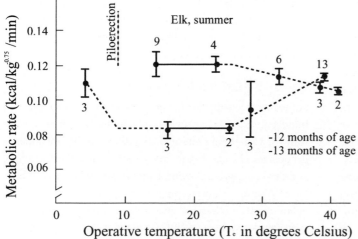
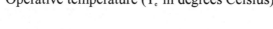

Figure 67. Critical temperatures of elk in winter (*top*) and summer (*bottom*) (Parker and Robbins 1984).

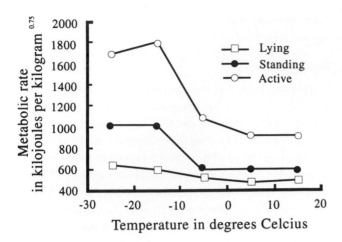

Figure 68. Energy expenditures in relation to ambient temperature for weaned elk calves, which were bedded, standing or active (Gates and Hudson 1979). Although weaned elk calves have lower critical temperatures of –4° F (–20°C) when bedded, it increases to 23°F (–5°C) when they are standing or active.

vides cooling both by evaporative and nonevaporative means. Cutaneous water loss (sweating) is much greater in elk than in mule deer and increases sharply at seasonal upper critical temperatures. On hot summer days, cutaneous water loss can approach twice the metabolic heat production.

Hair Coat

Thermoregulatory responses change rapidly throughout the year in response to temperatures and the hair coat. Elk molt twice a year (Kay and Ryder 1978), shedding duller winter coats throughout May and June to expose reddish summer coats. The autumn molt is less obvious, with the gradual development of a winter coat with woolly underhairs. This coat cycle (or, at least, guard hair production) is controlled by photoperiod. The woolly undercoat may be also influenced by temperature. When annual changes in day length are compressed into 6 months, red deer double the frequency with which they shed and regrow their coat, although changes sometimes are obscured by incomplete shedding of the previous coat (the time required for a coat to develop is constant). Melatonin-treated red deer replace summer coats with thick grayer winter coats in late summer and possess normal summer coats during winter (Domingue et al. 1992). This reversed coat cycle persisted for a year after experimental melatonin treatment concluded.

The metabolic hormones prolactin and triiodothyronine appear to play a central role in the hair coat cycle. A seasonal increase in plasma prolactin in spring facilitates normal molt of the winter coat and subsequent growth of the summer coat (Curlewis et al. 1988). Thyroid hormones also may be important; thyroidectomy disrupts the cycle and tri-

Elk molt twice a year, shedding dull winter coats during May and June to expose short, reddish summer coats and gradually developing longer summer coats with a dense mat of wooly underhairs during autumn. *Photo by Leonard Lee Rue III.*

iodothyronine replacement restores it (Shi and Barrell 1992, 1994). However, the timing suggests predominance of prolactin (Curlewis et al. 1988).

Metabolic Regulation

Metabolic rate generally follows day length and, consequently, appetite to which it may be causally linked. It still is not certain whether appetite or energy requirements drive the cycle. This coupling is regulated by still poorly defined neuroendocrine factors.

Linkage of Appetite and Metabolism

Some research supports the primacy of the appetite cycle. In reindeer, variation in previous feed intake seems to account fully for variation in energy expenditure, therefore appetite is considered to be the primary cycle (Nilssen et al. 1984). Seasonal changes in fasting energy expenditures of white-tailed deer also may simply reflect activity and thermal insulation rather than an endogenous cycle of energy requirements (Mautz et al. 1992, Pekins et al. 1992). However, a problem with basing evidence on energy expenditures is that they are not quite the same as energy requirements.

On the other hand, Loudon and Brinklow (1992) concluded that seasonal changes in metabolic requirements (1) are real and (2) precede changes in appetite. Seasonal changes in intake and growth probably are a direct consequence of an underlying seasonal rhythm in metabolic rate and energy requirements. Changes in metabolic rate precede those of appetite, suggesting that animals are eating to meet their requirements. In Soay and some modern sheep breeds, there is a sinusoidal seasonal change of more than 20% in requirements for maintenance (Argo and Smith 1983). Similar studies on white-tailed deer (Holter et al. 1979b) suggest an underlying cycle. Simpson et al. (1978) detected a slight seasonal cycle in maintenance requirements (as opposed to energy expenditures) of red deer. This has since been confirmed for elk (Jiang and Hudson 1992, 1994).

An interesting question is whether primary cycles of appetite and expenditure are out of phase as they may be in domestic sheep (Walker 1991). This may give seasons of unexpected weight loss (spring) or high efficiency of gain (autumn). Neuroendocrine control of seasonal cycles suggests this possibility.

Melatonin and Metabolic Hormones

Endocrine control of growth, reproduction and lactation in deer is complex and the photoperiodic changes in intake and energy metabolic rates remain unresolved (Ryg 1986).

Although melatonin transduces light cycles into physiological rhythms, metabolic and reproductive hormones initiate subsequent physiological changes characteristic of specific points in the seasonal cycle (Figure 69).

Prolactin

The most dynamic of the metabolic hormones is prolactin, which may increase 1,000-fold from the seasonal nadir in winter to its peak at the summer solstice (Bubenik 1990a, Sibbald et al. 1993). Administration of exogenous prolactin increases feed intake (Ryg and Jacobsen 1982, Ryg 1986). Conversely, suppression of prolactin secretion by the dopamine agonist bromocryptine diminishes food intake and subsequent live weight gain during spring (Curlewis et al. 1988, Milne et al. 1990). The dopamine antagonist domperidone has the reverse effect, which apparently is not completely countered by exogenous prolactin. The fact that the effects of prolactin reduction by bromocryptine and melatonin are different confirms that melatonin affects other hormonal systems.

Thyroid Hormones

Whereas appetite seems linked most closely to prolactin, metabolic rates are linked to the thyroid hormones—thyroxin (T_4) and especially its active form triiodothyronine (T_3) (Ryg and Jacobsen 1982, Ryg 1986). As previously noted, thyroidectomy suppresses the amplitude of seasonal

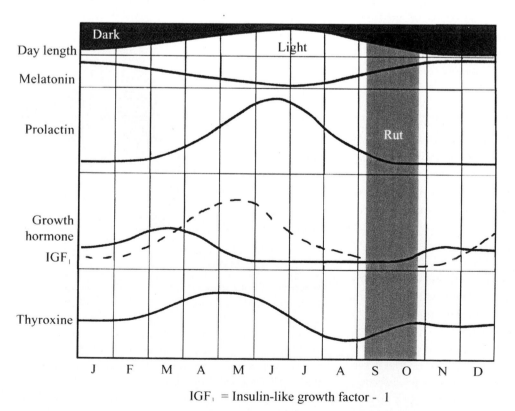

Figure 69. Patterns of metabolic hormones influencing seasonal changes in appetite, weight and energy expenditure of elk and red deer of either gender (Haigh and Hudson 1993).

IGF_1 = Insulin-like growth factor - 1

changes in appetite, growth, pelage, antler development and rutting behavior, and thyroid hormone replacement restores these cycles (Shi and Barrell 1992, 1994).

Triiodothyronine and T_4 appear to influence metabolic rate and usually decline during nutritional deprivation (Ryg and Jacobsen 1982, Hamr and Bubenik 1990). Generally, T_3 is a more active metabolic regulator (Bubenik et al. 1986). Release of both prolactin and thyrotropin (TSH) is stimulated by thyrotropin-releasing hormone (Fraser and McNeilly 1982). Like prolactin, plasma T_3 declines both with melatonin and bromocryptine treatments (Milne et al. 1987).

Gonadal Steroids

The amplitude of seasonal cycles of appetite and activity also are enhanced by gonadal steroids—especially among mature stags (Loudon and Brinklow 1992). Intake and testosterone levels are inversely related, as expected from the known effects of the rut.

Environmental Modulation

Despite the central importance of photoperiod, metabolic cycles are modulated by the environment. For example, chronic malnutrition suppresses metabolic cycles. Supplementing elk with concentrates in winter may increase apparent maintenance requirements (Kozak et al. 1994, Case 1994). In red deer, the timing of the onset of the breeding season and winter coat growth differ detectably in their sensitivity to nutrition and lactation. The feedback is mediated by hormones such as prolactin, insulin, thyroid hormones, growth hormone and IGF_1, which respond to nutritional plane (Breier et al. 1986, McGuire et al. 1992).

Antler Cycle

The most striking seasonal phenomenon is the antler cycle (Bubenik and Bubenik 1990). The physiology of this rapidly regenerating bone is of immense scientific and medical interest, and strong international markets for velvet antlers have given new impetus to research on antler development.

Innervation and Blood Supply

The nerve supply to the growing antler is derived from branches of the trigeminal and facial nerves. Two branches of the trigeminal nerve supply parasympathetic (sensory) branches to the pedicle (Wislocki and Singer 1946, Woodbury and Haigh 1996). In about 20% of red deer and elk, fibers of the auriculopalpebral branch of the facial nerve also supply the lateral part of the pedicle. Careful dissection

of the heads of red deer, elk and fallow deer have failed to show any innervation to the pedicle from branches of the second cervical nerve (Adams 1979, Woodbury 1995).

Blood supply to the pedicles and growing antler is from the superficial temporal artery, which arises directly from the carotid artery and travels over the orbital part of the frontal bone (Suttie et al. 1985, Waldo et al. 1949) (Figure 70). In radiographic studies of the head of a single red deer stag, Suttie et al. (1985) found that the medial branch of the superficial temporal artery supplied only the pedicle, and that only one branch of the lateral superficial temporal

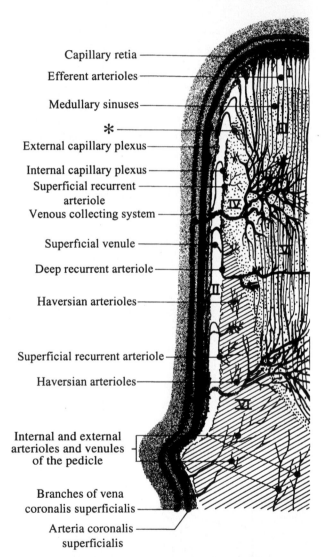

Figure 70. Vascularization of growing antler in cross section: (I) germinal cap; (II) fibrocellular periostal layer; (III) preosseous zone; (IV) peripheral cancellous bone; (V) core of coarsely trabeculated bone with wide medullary spaces; (VI) compact Haversian bone. The asterisk indicates capillary beds where superficial recurrent arterioles and medullary sinuses are interposed. *Redrawn from Waldo et al. 1949.*

artery supplied the antler itself. This branch divided at the antler/pedicle junction and supplied the rest of the developing structure—subdividing branches supplying the various antler beams.

The arterioles submerge in corkscrew fashion into the core of the antler beam then divide into a network of very narrow vessels (capillary plexus). The capillaries join in venules inside the beam and tines. They conduct the blood back to the surface, penetrating the cortical bone in the canals of the so-called Haversian system of the antler.

Mineralization

The beam and tines mineralize only slightly during the first half (about 60 days) of the growing period. Dynamic mineralization occurs in the second half, but most mineralization occurs in the last third of velvet growth. Under the influence of testosterone, which begins to increase after the summer solstice (Lincoln 1971a, 1971b, Haigh et al. 1984), mineralization starts at the base of the antler and proceeds toward the tip. Both testosterone and estradiol receptors have been demonstrated in the periosteum (connective tissue covering the bone) and cartilaginous tissue of the growing antler (Li 1987, Lewis and Barrell 1994). Other steroid hormones cause the velvet antler of castrates to mineralize and clean. Both progesterone and estradiol-17β will cause the velvet antler to mineralize (Jaczewski 1979). The mineralizing effects of estradiol, whose chemical structure is closely related to testosterone, are thought to be indirect (Lewis and Barrell 1994). In vitro studies show that insulin-like growth factor-1 (IGF_1) binding in cartilage declines in the presence of testosterone (Elliott 1994). Testosterone probably reduces antler growth by preventing IGF_1 stimulation of cell division. Finally, when construction is finished, the points are remodeled into ivorylike bone, and the compact core has been reinforced (Bubenik 1966).

Meanwhile, some superficial growth occurs. Ridges and pearls are formed (which make the surface rougher) and, just above the pedicle, a rim of bone—the coronet—appears. This is a specific feature of subsequent antlers. When the mineralization process between the top of the pedicle and the base of the antler is nearly complete, the antler blood supply is cut off and the velvet becomes necrotic. The necrotic process apparently is accompanied by sensation. The bulls rub the antlers on branches and trees, and the velvet is shed within hours. Bulls sometimes eat parts of the shed velvet. Fresh, cleaned antlers are ivory white except for a few spots where blood comes out of microscopic openings of the Haversian system among lamellae of the cortex. In dead antler, liquid blood is trapped in the

As soon as antlers are fully mineralized, the antler blood supply is cut off at the pedicle and the velvet begins to strip off. This process may be accompanied by sensation; bulls begin rubbing antlers against vegetation almost immediately, and may rub all velvet from antlers within hours. Freshly cleaned antlers are nearly white; however, all but the antler tips (which are comprised of extremely dense ivorylike bone) are soon stained brown due to the reaction of bone, fluids from plants, and soil. *Photo by Len Clifford.*

medullary bone and is well-preserved for months, probably due to the high citrate content of the antler.

A dark pigment develops on the antlers due to the reaction of oxygen with juices of plants rubbed during shedding and thrashing. The denser the cortex, the thinner this pigment layer. The points, which are ivorylike in well-developed antlers, are not pigmented.

Composition

As specific gravity of antler increases, first a stronger cortex results, followed by a stronger entire antler. A low specific gravity usually results from inadequate calcium in the diet (Magruder et al. 1957). The specific gravity of red deer antlers varies from 1.15 in the central part of the beam and 1.67 in the tips of the tines.

The mineral substance—bone salt—that impregnates the bone matrix is a tricalcium phosphate with a calcium/phosphorous ratio of 1.667:1. Its hydroxyl group (oxygen/hydrogen link) is replaced mainly by fluorine, carbonates, phosphates or citrates of magnesium.

The fresh, cleaned antler is dead bone with 40% to 50% water content. It remains attached to the pedicle until the pedicle begins to regenerate its surface. The dry air weight is approximately 80%. The dry matter has about 22% calcium and 10% phosphorous (Bernard 1963).

In response to the market for traditional medicines and interest in nutriceuticals in the Western world, composition of velvet antler has received more attention (Fennessy 1991, Zhao et al. 1992, Hoon et al. 1995). Commercial velvet usually is cut-off about 65 to 80 days after "button drop" (loss of the base of the previous year's harvested antler) when the fourth tine (royal) begins to bulb. Composition of commercial velvet varies from the tip to the base (Table 18). Dry matter, collagen and ash decrease from the base, whereas protein and lipid increase. The C18:3ω6 fatty acid (18 carbons with double bond at the 3 position) is found only in the tip. Chondroitin sulfate is the major glycosaminoglycan and may contribute to the purported usefulness of antler in the treatment of arthritis (Hoon et al. 1995).

Velvet elk antler harvested commercially is cut before significant mineralization occurs, about 65 days after "button drop" (loss of the base of the previous year's harvested antler), when the fourth (or dagger) point begins to bulb. *Photo by Milo Burcham.*

Table 18. Chemical composition of elk antler velvet at about 65 days after button drop

Chemical component[a]	Antler tip	Antler base[a]
Dry matter[b]	14.36	42.05
Protein	69.08	49.27
Collagen	10.01	31.99
Lipid	18.94	0.50
Uronic acid	1.24	0.11
Sulfated GAGb	3.73	0.26
Sialic acid	0.61	0.09
Ash	9.40	48.04
Calcium	0.42	16.50
Phosphorus	0.39	8.59
Magnesium	0.04	0.29[c]
Aspartic acid[c]	6.64	6.78
Glutamic acid	10.52	11.20
Serine	3.04	3.51
Histidine	2.11	1.57
Glycine	7.63	17.42
Threonine	3.29	2.90
Arginine	5.15	7.26
Alanine	5.74	8.87
Tyrosine	2.11	1.62
Valine	4.34	3.69
Phenylalnine	3.34	3.18
Isoleucine	2.37	1.76
Leucine	6.42	5.11
Lysine	3.87	3.96[d]
Fatty acids[d]		
$C_{14:0}$	1.18	1.06
$C_{16:0}$	16.27	12.19
$C_{16:1\omega7}$	4.26	0.83
$C_{18:0}$	7.79	9.61
$C_{18:1\omega7 \text{ and } \omega9}$	55.72	59.31
$C_{18:2\omega6}$	2.58	4.61
$C_{18:3\omega6}$	0.16	0.00
$C_{18:3\omega3}$	0.86	0.87
$C_{20:1\omega9}$	0.19	0.18
$C_{20:2\omega6}$	1.98	0.45
$C_{20:3\omega6}$	0.73	0.64
$C_{20:4\omega6}$	2.99	5.62
$C_{22:4\omega6}$	0.39	0.82
$C_{22:6\omega3}$	1.29	1.37
Total SAFA	27.15	25.12
Total MUFA	61.89	60.50
Total ω-3 fatty acids	2.15	2.25
Total ω-6 fatty acids	8.82	12.14
Ratio ω-6: ω-3	4.19	5.41

Source: Hoon et al. 1995.

Note: GAGb = glycosaminoglycan b; MUFA = monounsaturated fatty acids; SAFA = saturated fatty acids.

[a] Percentage of dry matter, except where noted as otherwise.

[b] Percentage of fresh weight.

[c] Amino acid composition percentage of dry matter.

[d] Fatty acid composition percentage of total fat.

Development

Antlers are actually two structures—the pedicle and the deciduous antler that develops from it. These structures develop in different ways and under different hormonal environments. The initial growth, during the onset of puberty, is of the pedicle, which grows under the influence of testosterone. The first true antler tissue develops when testosterone concentrations decline, normally in the spring of the first year of life. Regulated by changes in secretion of testosterone from the testicles, the antlers then undergo an annual cycle of growth, calcification, cleaning, casting and regeneration.

Antler Cycle and Maturation Process

The antler cycle changes with age (Figure 71). Calves rarely exhibit a complete antler cycle. In yearlings, antler growth begins in June/July and terminates when velvet is shed between the end of August and mid-September. The growing period usually is 90 ± 10 days, including the hardening phase of about 2 weeks, during which only mineralization occurs. Some yearlings with delayed antler growth (whether from late birth or poor body condition) cease trying to clean antlers, and then the velvet dries up and remains in place.

In 2-year-old bulls, growth of the second set of antlers begins during late April or early May. Once completed, the velvet begins to shed in late August for a period of 115 ± 10 days. Their antlers are cast from March to mid-April (Murie 1951). The uppermost tines may be brittle because their mineralization could not be completed before velvet shedding. These "raghorn" bulls often exhibit broken tines after the rut.

Three-and 4-year-old bulls living in well-organized populations where sexual stimulation is not prolonged are ca-

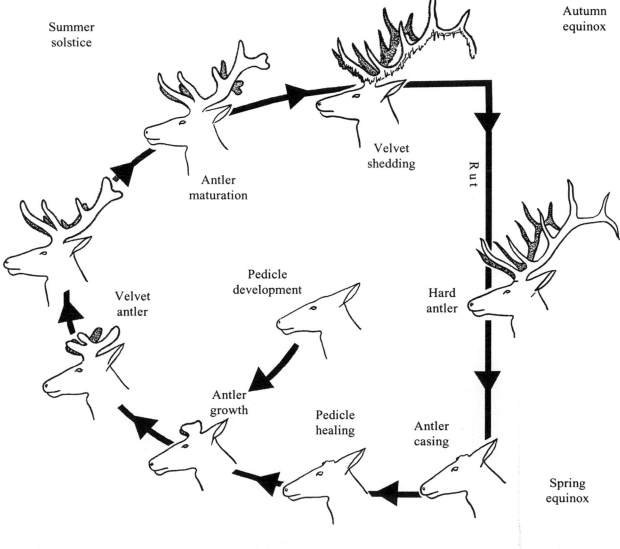

Figure 71. The antler cycle. *Illustrated by J. Deubner, from Haigh and Hudson 1993.*

pable of casting their antlers in February to mid-March. Velvet is shed in the first half of August, thus the growing period lasts about 140 ± 10 days, minus 10 to 14 days for healing of the pedicle surface.

Prime bulls, if well-fed and sexually inactive since mid-October, can cast their antlers as early as mid-January to late February (Murie 1951). Velvet is shed in late July or early August, indicating a growth period of 150 ± 10 days, minus 10 to 14 days for healing the pedicles. Prime bulls that join cow herds in midwinter may delay casting their antlers by about 10 to 20 days due to renewed sexual stimuli. Senior bulls exhibit the same pattern as other prime bulls. However, aged animals will not completely shed velvet.

Factors affecting the synchrony of antler casting are not clear. Topinski (1975) suggested that intervals of days or weeks between the casting of both antler beams may occur in socially stressed males. However, Bartos and Perner (1991) found that the incidence of asynchronous casting was almost as high as synchronous casting (both antlers cast in less than 24 hours). Furthermore, older and higher ranking stags were more likely to cast asynchronously.

Elk bulls shed their antlers after the rut is concluded and from January to April, depending mainly on age and health. Sexually relaxed prime bulls tend to cast antlers earlier than young, sexually repressed bulls. Also, older, higher ranking males tend to drop their antlers asynchronously, days or weeks apart. *Photo by Len Rue, Jr.*

Pedicles and First Antlers

The pedicles are permanent bony outgrowths of the frontal bone of the skull (Chapman 1975). Pedicle development is stimulated by secretion of testosterone (Wislocki et al. 1947), whereas development of the first deciduous antler arises after the pedicle has reached a certain critical length, but cannot occur if testosterone levels fail to decline.

The potential for development of pedicles and antlers lies in the periosteum of the frontal lateral crest of the skull (Goss et al 1964, Hartwig and Schrudde 1974, Goss 1987). Pedicles are normally only grown by intact male deer, and castration before about 6 months of age entirely prevents the appearance of pedicles (Bubenik 1990a). Female cervids have antler growth potential if sufficiently stimulated by exogenous androgen hormones, but antlers are seen normally only in the female reindeer. Both the cellular and the fibrous layer of this anterogenic periosteum are much thicker than those of periosteum of cranial bones or even the periosteum at the margin of the anterogenic region (Li and Suttie 1994). The ossification process in the region of the lateral crest is intramembranous.

The first signs of pedicle development occurs between 60 and 100 days of fetal life and probably reflects a surge in testosterone secretion during sexual differentiation. During this time, both testicular size and neck girth also increase. Later, as surrounding tissue grows and gonadal testosterone levels decrease, fetal pedicles become more difficult to see (Lincoln 1973).

During the first few months after birth there is no further growth of the pedicle. In red deer, development can be detected between 6.5 and 7.5 months of age (Li et al. 1994) and, early in spring of the first year of life, some 9 to 10 months after birth, the pedicles are first visible at the onset of puberty, at about 0.79 inches (20 mm) in height in red deer (Li and Suttie 1996).

The skin of the pedicle and the skin of the antler differ in appearance and structure. The pedicle skin and hair resemble that of the skull, whereas the antler hair is only 0.039 or 0.079 inches (1–2 mm) in length and smooth (Li and Suttie 1994). Histologically, their appearance also differs. Antler skin lacks the sweat glands and erector pili muscles of the pedicle, but it contains large sebaceous glands (Li and Suttie 2000). The transition from pedicle to antler skin is considered to occur due to mechanical expansion by the developing osseocartilaginous tissues underlying the tip of the pedicle (Li and Suttie 2000).

The microscopic appearance of velvet differs among cervid species (Bubenik 1992). It is also richly innervated.

A surge and subsidence in testosterone levels in the first spring of life create the hormonal environment that changes the ossification patterns in the developing pedicle. Although testosterone plays a crucial role in the development of the pedicle, its continued presence inhibits antler growth (Jaczewski 1990, Suttie et al. 1994).

The pedicles grow in diameter once a year by deposition of new lamellae. They reach a maximum height in the first antler cycle and are shorter with each antler casting. Attempts to use pedicle length and circumference for accurate aging of red deer were unsuccessful (Bubenik 1966). Pedicle diameter predetermines beam diameter, as antlers grow only in length. A distinct increase in diameter can occur only by additional bone apposition among the superficial arteries, which produces ridges, pearls and the coronet (the ringlike rim on the edge of the pedicle). These form after the antler cortex is partly mineralized. The casting of antlers shortens the outer length more than the inner length of the pedicles (Schuhmacher 1939), yielding a greater spread of the antler beams (Figure 72).

Antlers grow from the tip, rather than the base as do horns. The cells at the tip of the growing antler contain receptors for IGF$_1$ and IGF$_2$ (Elliott et al. 1992). The former are more concentrated in the chondroblast zone of the antler tip, whereas the latter are found in greatest concentrations in reserve mesenchyme and perichondrium tissues, which are undergoing rapid differentiation and proliferation (Elliott et al. 1993).

Antlerogenic cells in the periosteum at the tip of the pedicle change their differentiation pathway from the formation of bone to the formation of cartilage. The ossification pattern changes from the intramembranous type seen in pedicle growth, through a transition stage to endochondral ossification in the pedicle, which starts when the pedicle is from 2 to 5.9 inches (5–15 cm) in height. In the developing antler, a modified endochondral type of ossification occurs (Li and Suttie 1994). The term modified is used because nonantlerogenic ossification involves creation of bone by osteocytes, whereas ossification in antler occurs by the deposition of mineralized material within the cartilaginous matrix. Furthermore, in nonantlerogenic cartilage, vascularization is limited in contrast to the antler cartilage, which is well-vascularized.

The primary bone is remodeled by bone-resorbing (osteoclastic) and bone-building (osteocytic) activity in the bone plates (lamellae), which are oriented in parallel fashion and create the outer shell or cortex of the antler. Inside are the small beams or crossbars (trabeculae) of woven or medullary bone. Growth by apposition and remodeling of osteoid into osteon is very rapid in antlers. Antler is unique tissue because both intramembranous and modified endochondral ossification occur at the same time in different areas (Chapman 1975, Banks and Newbrey 1982).

By the time the pedicle is 0.98 to 1.57 inches (25–40 mm) in height, it consists of four regions. From distal to proximal, these are perichondrium, cartilaginous tissue, osteocartilagenous tissue and osseous tissue (Li and Suttie 1994).

Subsequent Antlers

The development of subsequent antlers involves casting, regrowth, mineralization, cleaning, gradual change in physical properties during the hard antler phase and completion of the cycle by another casting (Figure 73).

The preparative period before casting involves reactivation of osteoclastic (bone-resorbing) activity below the compact bridge separating the hard antler and pedicle (Frankenberger 1961, Goss 1992). After a few weeks, the pedicle medullary bone is restored, and a small cavity develops below the bridge. At the time of casting and in the space of a few hours, the compact ring between the antler and the pedicle cortex is destroyed and the antler drops (Bubenik 1966). A crust of dried blood forms over the exposed pedicle, which then proceeds to heal from the periphery. Under this scab, velvet starts to grow and, within a few days, the wound is healed. Antler casting occurs between January and March in most mature bulls, and between March and May in 2- to 4-year-old bulls, depending on the sexual cycle length, nutritional status of the individual and the amount of time spent with females during winter (Bubenik et al. 1977a). The growing period is about 90 days in yearlings and 130 to 140 days in prime bulls.

The seal is the round base of antler bone, surrounded by the coronet. It may be convex, flat or concave. In general, as long as the seal remains convex and good health prevails, a bull will improve his antler size each year. A flattened seal

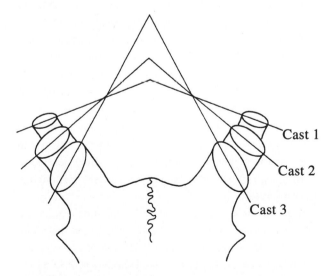

Figure 72. Antler spread and size is determined by changes in pedicles during subsequent casts of antlers (Schumacher 1939). *Illustration by A. B. Bubenik.*

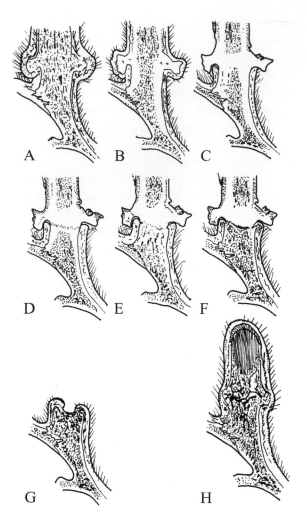

Figure 73.   The antler cycle as seen in cross section of the beam and pedicle (Waldo et al. 1949, Bubenik 1966, 1982). To begin the velvet phase, the medullary bone of the pedicle is completely regenerated (A). Later the mineralization process concentrates to the cortex of the pedicle and the basal portion of the beam (B) until the blood supply between the medullary core of the pedicle and beam is cut off (C). As soon as the tips of antlers also are mineralized, the antler bone begins to die, and the velvet is dead. Soon osteoclastic activity in the pedicle is activated, the medullary bone appears (D), and, below the dead antler, the compact bridge begins to be resorbed along the antler base. At the end of this process, the antler loses connection with the pedicle and falls off (E–F). Velvet regenerates from pedicle skin (G), and a new velvet and antler growth period begins (H). *Illustration by A. B. Bubenik.*

indicates the stage before the quality begins to decline with age. Concave seals indicate poor or declining antler quality.

Antler Growth Regulation

Antler growth is under both endocrine and neural control. The degree to which the nervous system is involved in

antler development has been the subject of considerable scientific debate.

Hormonal Factors

The timing of antler growth and its subsequent mineralization is linked to the annual cycle of testosterone (Lincoln 1971a, 1992, Suttie et al. 1995). Testosterone, dihydrotestosterone and estradiol, or its derivatives, are the only steroidal hormones whose roles have been identified definitely (Bubenik et al. 1974, Morris 1980). At least in *Cervinae* and *Odocoileinae*, testosterone is the most important hormone of antlerogenesis. Bubenik (1982) implicated other hormones, such as growth hormone, thyroxine, calcitonin and parathormone.

Whereas timing of the antler growth cycle in relation to day length is controlled by testosterone, the trophic control of growth is regulated by growth factors including IGF_1 and IGF_2, which are mitogenic for antler-tip cells (Elliott et al. 1992, 1993, Price et al. 1994). Several other growth factors also may be involved, but have not been studied sufficiently (Suttie and Fennessy 1992).

During pubertal development that culminates in the hardening of spike antlers and development of fertility (although not sexual maturity), the pedicles and antlers are under the influence of testosterone derived from interstitial cells of the testicle, which, in turn, are under the influence of luteinizing hormone derived from the pituitary gland. As serum testosterone concentrations increase, mineralization of antler tissue proceeds until, at maximum testosterone levels, the antler is fully mineralized.

Testosterone also appears to be responsible, at least in part, for velvet shedding, but the mechanism has not yet been demonstrated. Other hypotheses include a role for estradiol (Bubenik 1982) and the catecholamine 5-hydroxytryptamine, which may be released from the mast cells of the antler velvet, and cause blood vessel constriction and velvet shedding (Rayner and Ewen 1981). Bubenik (1982) postulated that the death of the velvet can be compared to a myocardial infarct. If there is heavy deposition of fat in velvet arteries (similar to atherosclerotic plaques), then resulting hypoxia will cause temporary arterial spasm and death of the velvet. Overaged adults or underdeveloped yearlings do not always shed their velvet completely (Bubenik 1966).

Testosterone levels decline after the rut and show a transient low-grade increase in early spring (Bartos 1980, Bubenik 1982, Haigh 1982, Haigh et al. 1984). This increase may trigger the casting of old antlers and growth of a new set (Bartos et al. 2000).

Among the most compelling evidence of the direct influence of testosterone on antlers is the effect of castration.

As previously noted, Aristotle recognized this effect and, in 1576, Turbeville wrote: "For you muft underftand that if you geld an Hart [red deer stag] before he haue an heade, he will neuer beare heade. . . . In lyke manner, if you gelde him when he hath a veluet head, for it will remayne fo alwayes, and neyther freye [to clean velvet] or burnifhe."

Physical or chemical castration deprives the organism of testicular testosterone or blocks testosterone receptors in the target tissue (Bubenik 1990). Because the antlers of castrated white-tailed deer and intact roe deer did not grow when receptors were blocked with cyproterone acetate, Bubenik et al. (1974) and Bartos (1980) considered that small amounts of testosterone were necessary for antler regeneration. Bartos et al. (2000), in an experiment with fallow deer, comparing the effects of castration with those of castration combined with cyproterone acetate (1,000 mg on alternate days for 24 days), concluded that low levels of circulating testosterone (<0.1 nanogram per milliliter [ng/mL]) play a biological role in antler growth and suggested that this might be by sensitization of antler cells to the effects of IGF_1. With relatively lower doses (150 or 350 mg once a week) of cyproterone acetate in intact red deer stags, Suttie et al. (1995) demonstrated that velvet antler continued to grow. This dose may not have been sufficient to entirely suppress the effects of testosterone. This is supported by the fact that, in those red deer, antlers grew longer than in controls, which may have been because mineralization was delayed or prevented at the partially suppressed concentrations of testosterone. Suttie et al. (1995) also considered that the conflicting results may have been due to species differences.

Bubenik (1990) and Bartos et al. (2000) suggested that small amounts of androgen are produced in the adrenal gland and play a role in antler growth. It has been shown that progesterone is produced in the adrenal gland of red deer (Jopson et al. 1990), and progesterone also has been shown to be able to cause mineralization of velvet antler (Jaczewski 1979).

If a newborn male elk is castrated, no pedicle will develop until a testosterone booster is applied (Wislocki et al. 1947, Lincoln et al. 1970). If the booster will not help, then antler growth in castrates can be induced by traumatization of the antlerogenic perioseum (Jaczewski and Krzywinska 1974). A testosterone booster or trauma can induce pedicle and eo-antler growth (remains in velvet) in females (Bubenik 1966, Chapman 1975, Jaczewski 1976).

Eo-antlers of castrates or females can freeze at the tips as soon as mineralization of the beam is so advanced that thermoregulation of the top zone of the eo-antlers is impaired. In such cases, the frozen part is separated and regenerated.

Elk and red deer translocated across the equator change their seasonality and their antler cycles to match the local light cycle (Bedford 1942, Marshall 1937). This change can occur in as little as 5 months (Otway 1985). Under experimental conditions, when subjected to altered or reversed light cycles, deer also change the antler cycle to match day length, although older animals may not always respond to such manipulations (Goss 1969, Jaczewski 1954). Deer can respond to artificially accelerated passage of years by light manipulation, but there is a limit. It seems that in "years" of 3 months or less, the animals do not perceive day length changes and the antler cycle reverts to the intrinsic rhythm (Goss 1969).

Although the rapid change in serum testosterone concentrations in late summer is evident, there is a much more subtle and transient elevation after the winter solstice in late January or February (Bubenik 1982, Haigh et al. 1984). For a few days, the duration of day length is the same in February as it is in August, and the light signal during this period may be stimulatory until its increasing duration is recognized.

Neuronal Factors

Velvet is heavily enervated (Vacek 1955), although no nerves develop under the periosteal layer (Woodbury 1995). Nerves perform a role in determining antler size and shape, but the mechanisms are not understood (Fennessy and Suttie 1985, Bubenik 1990b, Suttie 1990, Li et al. 1993).

Marked hypertrophy of developing antlers may occur in response to injury and, in some cases, it is not only the antler on the side that sustains damage that grows excessively. Accidental damage in nonanesthetized animals has produced tremendous abnormal growth that has persisted for several years (Bubenik 1990b). Experiments to reproduce these abnormalities in anesthetized animals failed and, the degree of deformation appeared directly related to the level of consciousness at the time of injury (Bubenik 1990b).

Bubenik and Pavlansky (1965) postulated the presence of antler growth centers within the central nervous system, perhaps in the hypothalamus. This possibility is suggested by several cases in which damage to a growing antler caused abnormal growth on the damaged side. This persisted in the growth of similarly abnormal antler in subsequent years. Bubenik and Pavlansky cited examples of accidental damage to several antlers and, in three unreplicated experiments, they unilaterally damaged the antler of two fallow deer and an elk. In one fallow deer, the damage was created at the very outset of antler growth. For four antler cycles, the antler on the injured side grew more than did the antler on the control side—in the first instance, as much as 180% more. By the fourth cycle, it had reverted to match the control antler. In a second fallow deer, a ring of velvet 0.4 inches (1 cm) wide was excised from a region below the antler tip. This region and the antler of that same side in the following cycle developed abnormally. By the third cycle, it matched the contralateral control. In the elk, damage was created when the antler was about 40% grown. A supernumerary tine developed and persisted for three cycles. It was suggested that there are bilateral centers that normally are synchronized and interactive but could become disjointed. Bubenik and Pavlansky also suggested that the proposed antler growth centers governed species-specific antler shape and development.

In support of this hypothesis, G. A. Bubenik (1990b) described several experiments in which the transplant of antlerogenic periosteum to other sites on the body led to development of antlerlike tissue. The farther away from the normal site that the antlerogenic periosteum transfer was conducted, the less the structure developed its species-specific shape. The only occasions in which the species-specific shape was seen were those in which the transplant took place into areas supplied by nerves that normally provide antler innervation.

Bubenik (1990b) cited the numerous reports of antler anomalies seen by hunters. Many of these anomalies involved unilateral damage and the development of velvet antler on one side only. For none of these hunter-killed animals is there record of previous injury or the shape of the previous set of antlers, but all are intriguing. As Bubenik pointed out, the critical experiment of denervation of future pedicle areas in prepubertal male deer had not been conducted at that time (1990). Results of experiments in which neurectomy was performed to test the role of nerves were reported in pedicle (Li et al. 1993) and antler development (Suttie et al. 1995).

In the first of these experiments in 4-month-old red deer stag calves, only the sensory nerve branches of the trigeminal nerve to the pedicle were sectioned either unilaterally or bilaterally. At postmortem, all animals were checked for success of the operation in removing all innervation to the pedicle. In 10 of 12 animals, there was partial regeneration of the nerves, but there was no difference in pedicel size and growth rate in those 10 or in the 2 animals in which no regeneration occurred. There was no difference in pedicle size or growth rates between treated and control sides in the unilaterally or bilaterally operated animals and the control group. However, antler size was impacted negatively by unilateral treatment (Li et al. 1993).

In the second experiment, the unilateral section also was performed on 4-month-old red deer stag calves. The neurectomy involved removal of both branches of the trigeminal nerve as well as the auriculopalpebral branch of

the facial nerve and removal of any possible sympathetic supply by superior cervical ganglionectomy. At all operated sites of parasympathetic nerves, there was limited regeneration, estimated to have been no more than 5% compared with the nerve tissues on the control side of the head. Unilateral neurectomy did not prevent pedicle growth in any animal, and denervated pedicles developed at the same time as control ones. However, neurectomy had a marked effect on both pedicle growth rate and length, as well as the initiation of the change from pedicle to first antler growth. Denervated pedicles grew more rapidly than controls (Suttie et al. 1995).

The results of these two experiments support the role of nerves in pedicle and antler development, but differ in relation to rate of pedicle development. Suttie et al. (1995) argued that deer in the second experiment were kept outside on a lower plane of nutrition. Hence, the control pedicles may have grown more slowly, rather than the operated pedicles more rapidly.

Goss (1991) performed further experiments on young fallow deer bucks. He removed disks of frontal bone periosteum and replaced them either in their original orientation or 180 degrees from it. On the side in which polarity had been changed, the pedicles grew forward instead of backward, and the antlers were abnormal, particularly lacking palmation. The antler growth of the deer was followed for several years and the ratio of antler length between the two sides was recorded. The cumulative length of the rotated antlers was less than half the length of their contralateral controls, although on neither side were normal antlers grown. Goss concluded that the pedicle bone contains the morphogenetic information responsible for shaping the succession of antlers.

The earlier experiment of Suttie and Fennessy (1985), in addition to the findings of Li et al. (1993) and Suttie et al. (1995), implies that a continuous neural connection is not a prerequisite for any aspect of the antler cycle, but that it is essential for normal size and growth rates of these tissues and, in some way, governs the species-specific trophic memory for each species of deer. However, signs of pedicle development occur early in fetal life (Lincoln 1973), therefore the possibility remains that neural connection plays a role before the age of 4 months (when neurectomy studies were conducted). None of these experiments explain the peculiar trophic memory described in several reports (Magruder et al. 1957, Bubenik and Pavlansky 1965, Bubenik 1990).

Reproduction

Delivery of a calf is timed late enough to avoid inclement weather and ensure plenty of high quality forage but early enough for the calves to attain sufficient weight to survive the subsequent winter. Throughout much of the elk's range, this occurs at the end of May or early June. There are, however, minor modulations that account for the year-to-year variation in rutting and calving dates (Harper et al. 1967, Struhsaker 1967). Weather or forage quality and availability leading up to the rut are likely candidates.

Reproductive Anatomy

Females

The female reproductive tract of the elk is very similar to that of the domestic cow or sheep (Figure 74). In nonpregnant adult elk, the entire tract usually lies within the pelvic cavity. The vagina is about 7.9 inches (20 cm) in length. The cervix is about 4 to 6 inches (10–15 cm) long and 0.6 to 2.0 inches (1.5–5 cm) in diameter, with the smaller measurements being obtained before the first pregnancy. When it is opened longitudinally one can see that it has a complex arrangement of four to six rings (Greer and Hawkins 1967, Glover 1985).

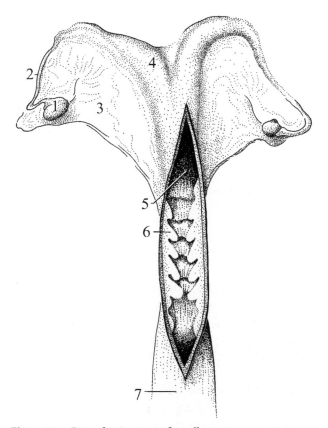

Figure 74. Reproductive tract of an elk cow: 1. ovary; 2. uterine tube; 3. broad ligament; 4. uterine horn; 5. uterine body; 6. cervix; 7. vagina. *Illustration by J. Deubner, from Haigh and Hudson (1993).*

The overall length of each uterine horn before the first pregnancy is about 2 to 3 inches (5–7.5 cm). The body usually is not more than about 1 inch (2.5 cm) long (Fisher and Fennessy 1985). There are from 6 to 14 caruncles (Fisher and Fennessy 1985). Morrison (1960a) reported five of these in each horn, with the proximal ones being 0.9 inch (2.3 cm) long, 0.7 inch (1.8 cm) wide and 0.5 inch (1.2 cm) high.

The ovaries are small, ivory-colored, egg-shaped organs on the ends of the fallopian tubes (oviducts). In the nonbreeding season, the ovaries are somewhat spheroid in shape and usually not more than about 0.4 inch (10 mm) across in any direction. Even during the estrous period, they are small, 0.2 by 0.3 by 0.6 inch (5 × 8 × 15 mm), but follicles and corpora lutea can be palpated easily (Glover 1985). Follicles have been measured in postmortem studies. Mature follicles average about 0.33 inch (8.5 mm) in diameter and range from 0.3 to 0.4 inch (8–11 mm), although a maximum of 0.67 inch (17 mm) has been recorded. The corpus luteum in the nonpregnant ovary grows to about 0.4 to 0.55 inch (10–14 mm) in size before regressing. In the pregnant animal, growth of the corpus luteum continues until about 70 days of pregnancy, with an average diameter of 0.55 inch (14 mm) and a range of 0.5 to 0.7 inch (13–18 mm) (Morrison 1960b, Greer and Hawkins 1967). A secondary corpus luteum of pregnancy is seen in more than half of pregnant reproductive tracts (Morrison 1960b).

Males

The reproductive organs of the elk bull consist of the testicles, epididymes, ductuli deferentia, accessory glands, penis and prepuce (Lincoln 1971a, Haigh 1982, Wallace and Birtles 1985) (Figure 75). The testicles undergo considerable change in size during the year. A threefold increase in size between early summer and autumn has been noted in red deer stags, and the scrotal circumference of male elk increases by about 50% between May and September (Haigh et al. 1984). The testes contain the semen-producing canals (seminiferous tubules), and the interstitial (Leydig) cells that produce testosterone.

Cellular changes in the testis and the production of spermatozoa occur seasonally. As testosterone levels increase after the summer solstice, activity within the testicular parenchyma increases. The diameter of the tubules increases, and development of the cycle of seminiferous epithelium occurs. This process depends on luteinizing hormone and follicle-stimulating hormone in the pituitary and the subsequent development of the Leydig cells of the interstitium of the testis, which produce testosterone (Lincoln 1971b, Haigh et al. 1984).

At the onset of the rut, the interstitial cells of the testis are of maximum size and number, as is the activity of the

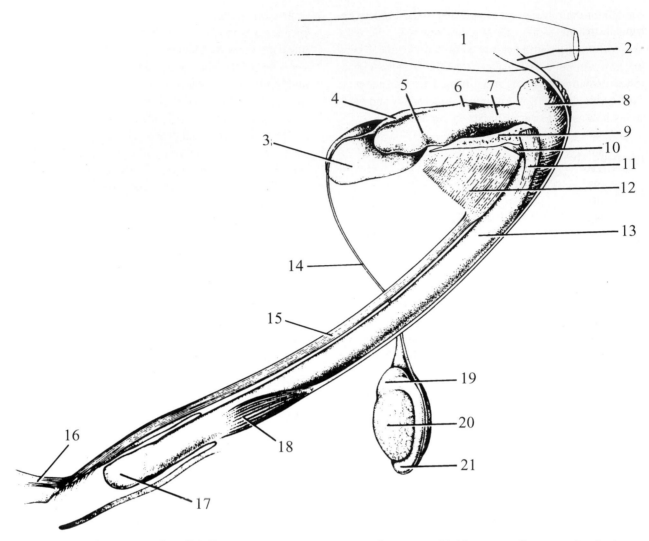

Figure 75.   Reproductive tract of an elk bull: 1. rectum; 2. retractor penis muscle; 3. urinary bladder; 4. ampulla; 5. vesicular gland; 6. prostate body; 7. pelvic urethra; 8. bulbospongius muscle; 9. pelvis (cut ischium); 10. suspensory ligament of the penis; 11. ishius cavernosus muscle; 12. symphyseal tendon; 13. penis; 14. vas deferens; 15. caudal preputial muscle; 16. cranial preputial muscle; 17. glans penis; 18. expansion of retractor penis muscle; 19. caput epididymus; 20. testis; 21. cauda epididymus. *Illustration by J. Deubner, from Haigh and Hudson (1993).*

seminiferous tubules. When reproductive activity has ceased in the spring at about the time of antler casting, the interstitial cells are small and inactive. No mature spermatozoa are visible in the lumen and cells of the seminiferous epithelium show almost no differentiation beyond the very earliest forms of sperm precursor (Lincoln 1971b, Hochereau de Riviers and Lincoln 1978, Haigh 1982). These changes are reflected in measurements of scrotal circumference.

The walls of the semen-producing canals are furnished with Sertoli cells, among which the germ cells for semen (spermatogonia) are imbedded. By the process of multiple division, spermatogonia develop into mature sperm (spermatozoa). The spermatozoa of the elk and red deer have the same appearance as those of other ruminants (Haigh 1982, Haigh et al. 1984).

Ejaculates with a high percentage of abnormal forms appear in July and August. By the beginning of September, ejaculate of mature elk bulls contains a high proportion of normal sperm (Haigh 1982, Haigh et al. 1984). A wide range of spermatozoal abnormalities have been found in both elk and red deer (Haigh and Hudson 1993). They are similar to those seen in cattle, and the same classification can be used.

The epididymis, which is the principal location for the storage of sperm, also undergoes seasonal changes. In autumn, it is lined by a tall pseudostratified columnar epithelium. By spring, the height of this epithelium has declined sharply, and the nuclei of the epithelial cells are condensed. In autumn, the cauda epididymis is densely packed with sperm. In May, no sperm are visible in the lumen (Lincoln 1971b, Haigh 1982).

The accessory glands (the part of the reproductive tract lying in the pelvis of the elk) include paired ampullae, paired vesicular glands, the prostate and its disseminate part, and small bulbourethral glands (Lincoln 1971a, Haigh 1982, Wallace and Birtles 1985) (Figure 76).

At their distal ends, the *ductuli deferentia* enlarge to form the ampullae. These organs lie in a common bundle of connective tissue in close apposition to one another throughout most of their length. They are 1.6 to 2 inches (4–5 cm) long and about 0.4 inch (1 cm) in diameter at their widest (Haigh 1982). Each ampulla opens separately into the duct of the adjacent seminal vesicle, forming short ejaculatory ducts (Haigh 1982, Wallace and Birtes 1985). Their epithelium exhibit changes that are correlated with the sexual cycle. Histologically, the ampullae have the appearance of a branched tubular gland with saclike dilatations, the crypts of which contain secretion. In May, the epithelial height has not changed, but the nuclei have condensed. At this time, some crypts contain densely packed degenerative sperm (Haigh 1982).

The paired seminal vesicles are attached to the anterior end of the pelvic urethra, lateral to the ampullae, and are joined medially by a genital fold. They are 2.4 to 2.8 inches (6–7 cm) long and have a slightly lobulated appearance (Haigh 1982). In autumn, they contain a thick yellow secretion. Each gland opens separately into one of the paired ejaculatory ducts. The glands show increased epithelium from July into the rutting period in October. They regress by November and contain little or no secretion in spring (Haigh 1982).

The prostate gland consists of two parts. It has a discrete, bilobed body lying anterior to and continuous with the disseminate prostate. This body is visible on the dorsal part of the pelvic urethra as two small discrete hemispherical masses just caudal to the ligamentous band that connects the vesicular glands. It opens ventrally into the pelvic urethra. The epithelium of the prostate body is of a tall, columnar type during the rut and shortens markedly, appearing cubelike by November (Lincoln 1971a, Haigh 1982). The widest part of the prostate can be identified throughout most of the pelvic urethra, underlying the urethral muscle. It has numerous ducts opening into the urethra (Haigh 1982). There appears to be little seasonal change in epithelial height (Haigh 1982, Wallace and Birtles 1985).

The bulbourethral glands are extremely small; their combined weight is 0.02 ounce (0.6 g). These glands are found at the junction of the urethral and bulbourethral muscles under a layer of connective tissue on either side of midline. In one study comparing epitheleal heights before and after the rut, no differences were found (Wallace and Birtles 1985).

The penis is a rod-shaped structure that undergoes very little increase in circumference during erection, but increases in length by about 40% (Haigh 1982). The urethra, which lies on the ventral surface of the penis through its length, curves dorsally at its extremity and permits the ejection of urine in an upward direction (Haigh 1982). The prepuce has well developed muscles that are responsible for the remarkable rapid forward and backward movement—

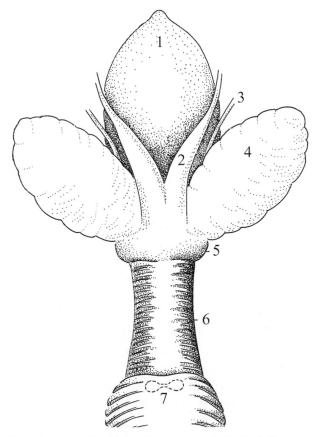

Figure 76. Pelvic organs and accessory sex glands of elk: 1. urinary bladder; 2. ampula; 3. ureter; 4. vesicular gland; 5. prostate body; 6. urethral muscle surrounding disseminate prostate and bulbourethral gland distally; 7. bulbourethral gland; 8. bulbospongiosus muscle. *Illustration by A. B. Bubenik, from Haigh and Hudson (1993).*

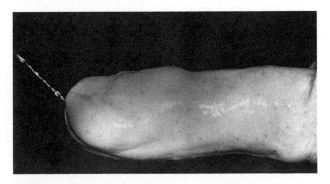

The urethra at the tip of the penis of an elk points upward, directing the spray of urine or ejaculate upward relative to the long axis of the penis, as shown here. *Photo courtesy of Jerry C. Haigh.*

often called palpitation—of this region, as observed during the rut (Haigh 1982).

Reproductive Cycles

Reproductive parameters of red deer and elk are summarized in Table 19. Hormonal events during the estrous cycle and through pregnancy have been studied in greatest detail in the red deer.

Females

Puberty and conception rates are strongly related to body weight (Fisher and Fennessy 1985, Hudson et al. 1991) (Figure 77). About half of red deer hinds and elk cows will come into estrus for the first time at a threshold weight of about 70% of the mature weight. In well-nourished populations, first estrus normally occurs in the autumn of the second year of life. This is particularly common in farmed elk and red deer (Haigh and Hudson 1993). In free-ranging populations, a smaller proportion of yearlings have full-term pregnancies (Green 1950, Morrison 1960a). Puberty may be delayed another year in undernourished animals (Fisher and Fennessy 1985). There also are records of both wild red deer and farmed elk calves coming into estrus in the spring of their first year (Daniel 1963, Haigh and Hudson 1993). Cows 2 years of age and older can have ovarian cycles that lead to pregnancy rates of 85% to 95% (Flook 1970a).

The onset of breeding is highly synchronized (Struhsaker 1967, Guinness et al. 1971). Red deer hinds that do not have a calf at foot tend to come into estrus about 10 days before those that are suckling (Loudon et al. 1983, Adam et al. 1985). The presence of a stag also affects the date at which hinds come into estrus; the sight, sound and smell of a stag has been shown to advance estrus by as much as 6 days (Lincoln 1985). The nutritional state of the adult hind also can have a profound effect if and when she comes into estrus. Hinds in poor condition, especially if they are nursing a calf, may not show heat, or may only come into estrus late in the breeding season (Hamilton and Blaxter 1980, Loudon et al. 1983). The latter effect may be carried over from year to

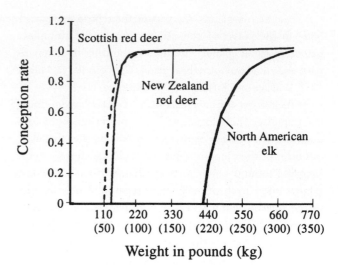

Figure 77. Conception rates of Scottish red deer, New Zealand red deer and North American elk (Hudson et al. 1991) in relation to live weight (Haigh and Hudson 1993).

year, thus late calving may be a self-perpetuating phenomenon (Morrison 1960a).

A transitional period from the anestrous phase of spring and early summer to the estrous period occurs in adult cows (Glover 1985) (Figure 78). Regular palpation of the reproductive tract and study of progesterone profiles show that activity starts in late July or early August. The uterus increases in tone and size, and small follicles and corpora lutea sometimes can be palpated. As in other seasonally breeding ruminants, serum progesterone concentrations are irregular and slightly elevated before the first estrus in both red deer and elk (Morrison 1960b, Adam et al. 1985, Glover 1985, Jopson et al. 1990). These early cycles are irregular and may be anovulatory (ovulatory without estrus). This stage is known as silent heat and is common in domestic ungulates (Thomas and Cowan 1975).

Silent heat probably synchronizes estrus and thus shortens the rut and calving period. Evidence comes from trials in which red deer synchronized to come into estrus before the normal season had an effect on control animals in the same paddock (Moore and Cowie 1986). Some of the controls came into heat, although they had not received hormonal treatments. Progesterone, secreted by the small, first generation corpora lutea may have a priming effect on other females, who then come into fertile estrus just before the second ovulation.

Progesterone secreted during silent heat apparently is sufficient to induce secretion of pheromones—odoriferous substances that trigger sexual responses to bulls. Observing red deer stags, Bubenik (1982) concluded that pheromones are in urine and secretions of the vagina and perineal glands. In silent heat, the estrogen level seems too low to

Table 19. Reproductive parameters of female elk and red deer

Species	Duration of estrus (hours)	Estrus interval (days)	Gestation length (days)
Elk	6–10	19–25	247 ± 3
Red deer	6–30	21.2	233

Sources: From Morrison 1960a, 1960b, Guiness et al. 1971, Fisher and Fennessy 1985, Haigh 1998.

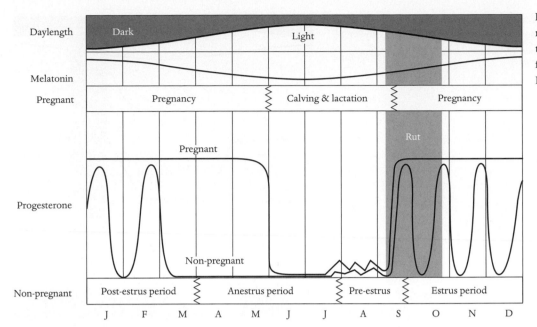

Figure 78. Seasonal reproductive changes in the red deer hind (modified from Haigh and Hudson 1993).

elicit the cow's sexual drive. She will avoid being courted, and this agitates the bulls.

During the early part of the breeding period, estrous cycles are about 21 days in length, but the length is not constant either between animals or during the breeding season (Morrison 1960a, Fisher and Fennessy 1985, Glover 1985). After the winter solstice another transition period occurs. Estrous cycle length increases and becomes irregular. Some animals cease earlier than others, but all activity appears to cease by the spring equinox or a little sooner.

Hormonal events during the estrous cycle are very similar to those of other polyestrus seasonal spontaneously ovulating ruminants. Before the onset of the breeding season, progesterone concentrations are less than 1 ng/mL. After the first estrus, they increase to a peak of 3 to 4 ng/mL by about day 10 or 11. If the animal is not pregnant, the concentrations decline to baseline levels before the next estrus. High progesterone levels have been measured at about the time of estrus (Kelly et al. 1982), but it seems likely that they may have been an artifact caused by the handling procedure (elevated progesterone of adrenal origin has been seen in ovariectomized hinds stressed by handling [Jopson et al. 1990]). A luteinizing hormone surge occurs just before estrus (Kelly et al. 1982). In elk, this occurs about 20 hours before the onset of estrus. Estrogen also appears to follow the general ruminant pattern, being highest just before and on the day of estrus (Fisher and Fennessy 1985). Hinds usually are in estrus for no more than 24 hours, and the period may be as short as 12 hours (Morrison 1960a, Fisher and Fennessy 1985, Glover 1985).

An anestrous period occurs annually for about 4 months

from about the time of the spring equinox. During this time, serum progesterone levels are minimal, the ovaries are small and inactive and the uterus is flaccid and at its smallest (Glover 1985).

Males

Seasonal reproductive changes are most striking in the male (Figure 79). During the rut, testosterone concentrations, scrotal circumference and percentage of normal sperm increase sharply. Secondary sexual characteristics also change. The most obvious are antlers, which are used to establish dominance and breeding privileges during the rut. Also, in preparation for rutting battles, the neck swells due to massive development of the muscles, giving the rutting stag a very distinctive appearance (Lincoln 1971b, Loudon et al. 1983).

Puberty in the male has been defined as the period when secondary sexual characteristics and accessory organs develop under the influence of the testis (Lincoln 1971a). It is a continuous process that begins when the stag has reached a critical weight and is reflected in the initiation of pedicle growth. Puberty ceases temporarily when the stag is growing his first set of antlers, but resumes again at about 13 or 14 months of age. Onset of puberty at this stage is more related to body weight than to photoperiod, and there are records of undernourished free-ranging red deer not reaching puberty until 3 years of age (Lincoln 1971a, Fennessy et al. 1985).

Suttie et al. (1991) described the events that occur in the testis of young red deer stags. During autumn, when a male calf is about 3 months old, testicular diameter begins to in-

Figure 79. Seasonal reproductive changes in the red deer stag (modified from Haigh and Hudson 1993).

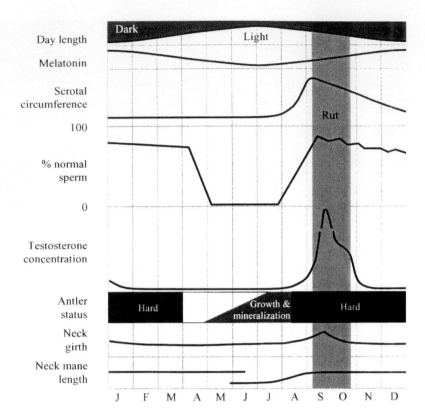

crease. The following spring, the increase is arrested, but size does not decline. About midsummer, at the start of the second year, testicular size again starts to increase as the calf approaches puberty.

From the time that the calf is 3 months of age, pulses of luteinizing hormone increase to about three per 24 hours. These lead to discrete pulses in testosterone. From the time of the summer solstice, the number of pulses of both hormones increases to about eight per day. There is a subsequent decline in spring and, after the spring equinox (by the time that the animals are 11 months old), pulsatile secretion of luteinizing hormone is almost undetectable. After the summer solstice, when males are 13 months old, frequent low-amplitude pulses of luteinizing hormone are accompanied by frequent discrete pulses of testosterone. In late summer, the frequency is maximal and accompanied by recurrent large amplitude pulses of testosterone, which persists for 2 months (Suttie et al. 1991).

Although 15-month-old stags may be fertile, they usually are not able to breed successfully in the presence of older males (Lincoln 1971b, Fisher and Fennessy 1985). However, in experimental situations, they can and will breed hinds in estrus (Follis 1972).

The exact details of physiological activity after puberty have been described in red deer. Elk follow the same pattern, but events occur some 3 weeks earlier, because the elk

gestation length is that much longer. It also is important to note that juvenile animals develop their sexual activity more slowly than do adults, at least until about 3 years of age (Turbeville 1576, Lincoln 1971b, 1985). Accordingly, the sequence of events in an individual mature elk bull can be summarized as follows.

At the spring equinox, pituitary activity and testosterone concentrations are minimal. At about the summer solstice, the weight of the pituitary gland begins to increase and, with it, the output of gonadotrophin-releasing hormone. By August, pituitary weight is at its maximum, as are luteinizing hormone concentrations. Testosterone concentrations begin to increase in response to the luteinizing hormone activity. In September, although luteinizing hormone levels are not as high, the responsiveness of the target cells in the testis to luteinizing hormone is much more marked, and testosterone levels are at a peak in late August and most of September. At this time, testicular testosterone concentrations may be 1,000 times higher than those measured in spring and early summer. Trials with synthetic gonadotrophin-releasing hormone have shown that the pituitary gland will respond to injections of this hormone at any time of year (Fennessy et al. 1988). However, the responses to gonadotrophin-releasing hormone are greatest just before and at the time of antler velvet cleaning. The consequent testosterone increases occur most markedly at the time of the rut, to a limited extent, while the animal is in hard antler and hardly at all between casting and antler cleaning. Lincoln (1971a, 1971b, 1985) likened this annual change from an inactive and infertile state to full reproductive readiness to a seasonal puberty. By mid-October, testosterone levels have declined to near baseline levels, where they remain for most of the winter.

Translocated Animals

As mentioned previously, elk and red deer translocated across the equator change their seasonality to match the local light cycle (Marshall 1937, Bedford and Marshall 1942), and change can occur in as little as 5 months (Otway 1985).

Although the rapid change in serum testosterone concentrations in later summer is clearly seen, there is a much more subtle and transient elevation after the winter solstice in both elk and red deer (Blaxter et al. 1974, Haigh et al. 1984, Suttie et al. 1984). Biannual increases in testosterone also have been detected in white-tailed deer, sika deer, roe deer and pudu (Bubenik et al. 1982, Sempere and Boisson 1982, Brown et al. 1983a, 1983b, Reyes et al. 1997).

On deer farms, males that are well-nourished can exhibit two rutting seasons a year (Suttie 1980). In the northern hemisphere, the principal one occurs in autumn, whereas the second one, in which some fighting and bugling is heard for about 10 to 14 days, occurs in late January or early February. The duration of day length is the same in February as it is in August. The light signal during this period may be stimulatory until its increasing duration is recognized.

There also are differences in concentrations of prolactin receptors according to season. Recent work has shown seasonal fluctuations of prolactin receptors in the testis and epididymis of red deer (Clarke et al. 1995). The role of prolactin in the testis has not been fully determined, but it may have both stimulatory and inhibitory functions. In the epididymis, a receptor was detected only during the breeding and early nonbreeding season.

Scrotal circumference increases markedly and peaks at the onset of rut. It subsequently declines steadily until it reaches its nadir in spring (Haigh et al. 1984). The percentage of normal sperm in ejaculates, the scrotal circumference and the concentrations of serum testosterone all increase and decline in synchrony.

However, seasonal changes also are likely to be governed by active programmed cell death (apoptosis) and proliferation is a genetically governed, signal-induced process. The genetic markers for both proliferation and apoptosis have been demonstrated in other seasonally breeding animals such as the roe deer and the European brown hare (Blottner et al. 1995).

Rut

The period of maximum reproductive activity in stags is called the rut (Lincoln 1985). It starts about 2 weeks before the autumnal equinox, but the onset may depend on the nutritional state of the animals.

The behavior of stags changes quite abruptly when antler velvet is shed. Rutting behaviors include antler rubbing or thrashing, wallowing, preputial palpitation with or without urine spraying, bugling or roaring, dominance displays, and sparring (Struhsaker 1967). Fighting changes from boxing to a complex of displays that may culminate in clashes involving engagement of antlers. The underside of

Elk may begin to demonstrate rut behavior as soon as antler velvet is shed. Rut behavior may include scent marking, antler display, wallowing, bugling, and other advertisement by individual bulls. *Top photo courtesy of the Wyoming Game and Fish Department. Bottom photo by Tom W. Hall.*

the belly, the forelegs and the neck become darkly stained due to the frequent spraying of fluid from the penis, usually accompanied by preputial palpitation, which is known in elk as thrash urination (Struhsaker 1967, McCullough 1969). The urethra at the tip of the elk's penis points upward, which allows for a spray that is almost at right angles to its long axis (Haigh 1982). This fluid does contain sperm (Lincoln 1972b).

The rut may last only a few weeks, with peak activity as few as 20 days (Struhsaker 1967). A resurgence of activity may occur if hinds do not conceive during the first period (Rapley 1985). If a free-ranging stag is exhausted by this time, he likely will be usurped by another (Struhsaker 1967). As indicated above and noted by Turbeville (1576), the young stags come into the peak of their rut later than do the mature stags (Lincoln 1971b).

Rutting males spend little time feeding. A mature elk bull may lose as much as 20% of his body weight in 6 weeks, and losses of 25% have been recorded in red deer (Struhsaker 1967, Lincoln 1971b, Rapley 1985). Bulls that are markedly debilitated after rutting must soon regain condition to survive a harsh winter.

Pregnancy

Elk and red deer females normally carry a single calf. Twinning probably occurs in no more than 1% of the overall population, but there are occasional farm records of an increased incidence (Guinness et al. 1971, Haigh and Hudson 1993, Fyffe and Fyffe 1995). When twins of opposite sex are carried, freemartinism (female of the pair is sterile and masculinized) may occur (Stewart-Scott et al. 1990). Reports of triplets are rare. Quadruplets have been reported from a carcass, although one of the fetuses showed signs of resorption (Follis and Hancock 1975).

The placenta is epitheliochorial. The cotyledons are visible by 31 days of gestation and implantation is well advanced by 34 days (Morrison 1960b). The placenta extends through both horns of the uterus, even if there is a single fetus (Fisher and Fennessy 1985).

Endocrine Changes

Changes in progesterone, estradiol and estrone sulfate concentrations associated with pregnancy are similar to those of other ruminants (Kelly et al. 1982, Adam et al. 1985, Glover 1985, Barrell and Boss 1989). Progesterone levels increase after conception in a fashion similar to that of the estrous cycle, but do not decline again until near birth. Through pregnancy, until about 30 days before calving, they fluctuate between 3 and 15 ng/mL, and there appears to be a correlation between the number of corporal lutea

present on the ovaries and the concentration of progesterone (Kelly et al. 1982). In red deer with a single corpus luteum, progesterone concentrations show little change from early pregnancy until day 220 of gestation. Kelly et al. (1982) suggested that luteal tissue provides most, if not all, of the progesterone of pregnancy. Decline in progesterone concentrations before calving occurs at the time that estradiol concentrations are rising. Estradiol levels reach an average concentration of 34 picogram per milliliter (pg/mL) just before calving (Kelly et al. 1982). Estrone sulfate levels in pregnant red deer increase about 30 days after conception, peak around 60 to 80 days and decline thereafter (Barrell and Bos 1989).

Fetal Development

Among ungulate species, birth weight scales to $weight^{0.79}$, whereas gestation length scales to $weight^{0.19}$ (Robbins and Robbins 1979). The average daily rate of synthesis of fetal tissues, expressed as birth weight divided by gestation length ($W^{0.79}/W^{0.19}$), scales with an exponent of 0.60 (0.79 − 0.19) slightly less than the metabolic exponent (Robbins and Robbins 1979, Oftedal 1985, Gordon 1989). Because of this scaling, the demands of gestation appear proportionately smaller for elk than for smaller deer.

Fetal development has been used both to determine time since conception (Morrison et al. 1959) and to estimate nutrient requirements throughout pregnancy (Adam et al. 1988a, 1988b). Table 20 shows simple field measurements

Elk normally give birth to a single calf. Twins, such these Tule elk calves, probably occur in no more than 1% of the population. *Photo by Leonard Lee Rue III.*

Table 20. Weights and measurements of known-age elk embryos

Fetal age in days	Weight	Body length[a]	Contour length	Foreleg length	Hindleg length	Head width	Head length	Tail length
25	0.00014	0.24						0.79
	(0.004)	(6.2)						(2.0)
30	0.0012	0.32		0.03	0.028			0.10
	(0.035)	(8.2)		(0.8)	(0.7)			(2.5)
37	0.0086	0.57		0.14	0.12			0.10
	(0.243)	(14.4)		(3.5)	(3.0)			(2.5)
43	0.039	0.94		0.24	0.20			0.79
	(1.1)	(24)		(6.0)	(5.0)			(2.0)[b]
59	0.39	2.56	4.41	0.91	0.79	0.64	0.96	0.15
	(11)	(65)	(112)	(23)	(20)	(16.2)	(24.5)	(3.7)
90	6.91	6.61	10.51	2.87	2.95	1.42	2.50	0.41
	(196)	(168)	(267)	(73)	(75)	(36.0)	(24.5)	(10.5)
123	51.68	12.00	18.11	6.06	7.05	2.23	4.31	0.57
	(1,465)	(305)	(460)	(154)	(179)	(56.6)	(109.6)	(14.5)
182	190.9	21.25	31.34	12.60	14.90	3.19	7.03	1.26
	(5,412)	(540)	(796)	(320)	(378)	(81.0)	(178.5)	(32.0)

Source: From Morrison et al. 1959.

Note: Weights given in ounces (g), and measurements given in inches (mm).

[a] Crown–rump (early stages) and forehead–rump (later embryonic stages) measurements.

[b] Possible printing error in original data.

of known-age elk fetuses. Figure 80 details accumulation of energy and protein in the developing red deer conceptus.

Pregnant wild ruminants vary in their sensitivity to nutritional stress. Species such as pronghorn and white-tailed deer resorb multiple embryos. However, for most, the effects of undernutrition are expressed as undersized neonates that experience heavy mortality. In some circumstances, nutritional stress seems to alter the sex ratio at birth in ways that cannot be explained by differential fetal mortality (Clutton-Brock and Iason 1986).

Gestation Length

Gestation lengths of *Cervus* conform to interspecies allometric relationships (Brinklow and Loudon 1993). Generally, cervine deer have longer gestation periods than New World deer of similar size. Gestation lengths are often quoted as 255 days in elk, considerably longer than the 233 days in red deer. Using DNA percentage testing after artificial insemination, Haigh (1998) suggested a shorter gestation of 247 ± 3 (n = 47) in elk. Among cervids, the longest gestation periods are in the roe deer (300 days including a preimplantation diapause) and Pére David's deer (280 days) (Brinklow and Loudon 1993).

Birth Weights

Birth weights of healthy elk calves range from 33.1 to 48.5 pounds (15–22 kg) (Hudson et al. 1991). Male calves are slightly heavier than female calves. Birth weights are directly related to maternal age and size (Blaxter and Hamilton 1980, Hudson et al. 1991). Good nutrition increases birth weights slightly (Hamilton and Blaxter 1980); severe malnutrition during late gestation may reduce birth weights (Thorne et al. 1976).

Birth weight, for a number of reasons, seems to be a good predictor of neonatal survival. Calves below a certain minimum threshold weight at birth are unlikely to survive,

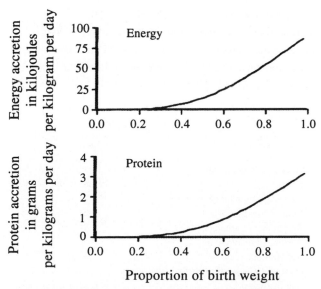

Figure 80. Daily deposition energy and protein in the conceptus (fetus plus associated maternal tissue and fluids) of red deer (from Adam et al. 1988a, 1988b).

and those that are excessively large may induce dystocia (difficult birth), which can lead either to stillbirths or to reduced viability due to calving stress and exhaustion. Increasing calf weight of Scottish red deer calves from less than 8.8 pounds (4.0 kg) to 13.2 to 15.4 pounds (6–7 kg) reduced calf mortality from 100% to 5%, respectively (Hamilton and Blaxter 1980). Elk calves that weighed more than 35 pounds (16 kg) at birth had a 90% chance of surviving to 4 weeks of age under captive conditions, whereas newborns weighing less than 25 pounds (11.4 kg) had less than a 50% chance of survival (Thorne et al. 1976).

Birth Dates

The peak of the calving season of elk generally is the first of June, with variations from year to year and from place to place. Out-of-season calving is more common on elk farms (Haigh and Hudson 1993) than in the wild, and dates as late as November 23 have been recorded. The latest conception date reported in northern parts of elk range, which should have produced a September calf, is January (Wishart 1981).

Male calves tend to be born several days later than female calves, although this might be due to the slightly greater proportion of male calves born to first-time calvers (Hudson et al. 1991). This seems contrary to the sex ratio bias of red deer on the Isle of Rhum, where sons predominate among older dominant hinds (Clutton-Brock et al. 1982).

Birth date affects the coat cycle, seasonal cycles of appetite, live-weight change and timing of estrus. Late-born calves may remain lighter even at 18 months of age (Sibbald et al. 1993).

Parturition

Whether the dam or the calf initiates parturition has not been investigated. Circumstantial evidence suggests that it may be the calf, as red deer hinds carrying embryos transferred from elk carry them for the full elk gestation period.

Apart from the distended abdomen, there are a few visual clues of impending calving in red deer and elk (Arman et al. 1978, Church and Hudson 1996). In adult hinds the udder may begin to enlarge as early as 4 weeks before calving, whereas in first calvers, this may not be seen until 2 weeks before delivery (Cowie et al. 1985).

There are two periods of restlessness. The first occurs from 7 to 10 days before calving, the second within about 48 hours (Cowie et al. 1985). Restlessness and solitude seeking are characteristic of imminent parturition. Preparturient free-ranging elk may move away from the main herd a few days before giving birth; they may not rejoin the herd for about a month. Female farmed deer usually are held in paddocks before calving to permit close observation.

The calving sequence of farmed elk is summarized in Table 21. By the end of first-stage labor, the expectant mother usually separates from the herd. As labor advances she may look at her flanks and frequently change position from standing and laying. She may even start to strain, stop and move away, and then graze briefly before starting again. Normal calving can take as long as 2 hours from the start of second-stage labor (when the head of the calf engages in the pelvis). Fetal membranes rupture at some time during this stage, and calving usually occurs within 45 minutes of this event if presentation is normal.

The normal presentation is anterior, dorsal with the forefeet coming first, followed by the head (Arman et al. 1978, Cowie et al. 1985). During delivery, the dam will turn and lick herself, the emerging calf or ingest fetal fluids that have splashed on the ground. She also will eat any parts of the placenta within her reach. In normal presentations, passing the calf's head through the pelvis is the rate-limiting step. Once this is achieved, complete delivery usually occurs in a matter of seconds. The dam changes position often during the birth and final delivery may take place when she is either lying or standing. As soon as the calf is born, the mother attends to it by licking and drying it, but the dam may rest if parturition has been prolonged (Cowie et al. 1985, Church and Hudson 1996).

Third-stage labor—the detachment and ejection of the placenta—usually occurs within approximately 4 hours of delivery, but it may occur as soon as 15 minutes (Church and Hudson 1996). The placenta usually is eaten by the hind. There are several possible reasons for this widespread behavior. Most often assumed is that this removes odors that may attract predators, but there may be nutritional, endocrine or even social reasons (Kristal 1980).

Disturbance of a dam during calving may delay the process considerably. Dams may rejoin the herd and subsequently seek a new calving site. Inexperienced dams may leave the calving site altogether or even abandon the newborn.

Table 21.   Calving behavior of farmed elk

Observations	Mean ± SE
First stage (minutes before birth)	
Pacing	365 ± 38
Second stage (minutes before birth)	
Contractions first seen	122 ± 24
Appearance of amniotic sac	97 ± 21
Bursting of amniotic sac	79 ± 17
Appearance of calf	45 ± 5
Third stage (minutes after birth)	
Calf first stand	49 ± 5
Calf first suckle	76 ± 5

Source: Church and Hudson 1996.

As labor advances, the elk cow may frequently change position. As her calf begins to travel down the birth canal, she usually stands and strains to aid the process. Normal presentation of the calf is anterior, with the hooves of the forelimbs first to emerge from the vulva. *Photo courtesy of Jerry C. Haigh.*

Detachment and ejection of the placenta usually occurs shortly after birth (as soon as 15 minutes, although it may be delayed for up to 4 hours). The placenta usually is eaten by the cow soon after it is expelled. *Photo by Erwin Bauer.*

Bonding and Abandonment

Because newborn elk calves hide from predators (versus newborns that follow a herd), they may be separated from their dams for long periods of time. During a 24-hour period, a calf may only spend a few minutes with its mother during short suckling bouts. Therefore, it is important for both animals to establish recognition of one another. This bonding is initiated when the mother first licks the calf after birth, but it is reinforced on subsequent occasions. After a suckling bout, she attempts to lead her calf away with repeated vocalizations and nose-to-nose contact. At some point, the calf will leave its mother and seek cover. After grazing, the mother may return to the calf and initiate contact with a soft mewing. Alternatively, the calf may squeak and even stand up when seeking its mother. If it does this, several females may approach and sniff the calf to identify it. It is possible that a dam may have "labeled" her calf with olfactory signals so she can recognize it later (Cowie et al. 1985).

On farms, where several females may be close together and give birth in a short period, calves may be indiscriminate in choosing a source of milk and, if not repulsed, will nurse any cow that will accept it. This leads to mistakes in matching dams and calves that have only been uncovered through subsequent DNA microsatellite testing. Females that have lost calves may be willing to let other calves suckle, and may even adopt the calf of another hind.

Mismothering may occur in first-time calvers as well as those with difficult births. This usually is attributed to maternal inexperience, but also may be due to endocrinological immaturity. There are theoretical evolutionary reasons why young mothers should invest less heavily in their offspring and be more willing to abandon them in favor of trying again the following year. Hinds that lose their calves shortly after parturition cease lactating in a few days and recover quickly.

Lactation and Neonatal Development

Peak milk yields measured in energetic terms scale approximately to $W^{0.52}$ in ungulates suckling single young (Robbins and Robbins 1979, Oftedal 1985), which implies a greater demand (relative to maintenance metabolism) on small animals. This consistent relationship holds despite wide differences in the chemical composition of milk (Table 22). Ungulates differ mainly in the amount of water they provide their nursing young. Among the world's ungulates, large ruminant species that nurse their young frequently ("followers" such as bison) produce less concentrated milk than do smaller ruminants, such as elk, that hide their young (Arman et al. 1974).

During the first month of lactation, red deer milk contains 20% to 25% total solids, 8% to 13% fat, 7% to 9% protein and 4.5% lactose (Arman et al. 1974). Elk milk is slightly more dilute at a comparable stage of lactation (Parker et al. 1984, Watkins et al. 1985, Kozak et al. 1995). As milk production declines through lactation, the energy concentration of red deer milk increases from 4.5 to 7×10^6 J/kg. Elk milk seems marginally less concentrated in well-fed high-yielding animals—less than 8.8 pounds (4 kg) per day—but

Table 22. Percentage of milk constituents of domestic livestock, elk and red deer

Species	Stage of lactation	Solids (%)	Fat (%)	Whey protein (%)	Total protein (%)	Lactose (%)	Ash (%)
Cow		12.7	3.7		3.4	4.8	0.7
Sheep		19.3	7.4		5.5	4.8	1.0
Goat		13.2	3.5		4.5	5.1	0.8
Cow	Colostrum	25.0	7.5		14.0	3.0	0.8
Elk	Average through 84 days	19.8			6.2	4.1	1.3
	Days 22–47		7		6.5–7	5–6	
	Days 91–154		10–12		7.5–9	4–4.5	
Red deer	Colostrum just postcalving	34.4	11.05	12.7			
	Colostrum 15 hours postcalving	25.8	10.65	3.4			
	Days 3–30	21.1	8.5	1.1		4.45	1.18
	Days 31–100	23.5	10.3	1.2		4.45	1.11
	Days 100+	27.1	13.1	1.3		4.46	1.10

Source: Haigh and Hudson 1993.

energy concentration averages about 5×10^6 J/kg and increases as volume decreases toward the end of lactation.

Milk production reaches a peak several weeks after parturition and gradually declines thereafter. A well-conditioned elk cow nurses intensively (four to five times per day) during her calf's first 6 weeks. In September, milk production declines. Elk wean gradually so that nursing bouts become quite infrequent by early winter. Flook (1970a) and Kittams (1953) reported that 36% to 60% of cow elks had milk in December, and 14% to 18% had milk in February. The frequency and duration of nursing bouts are poor indicators of the amount of milk transferred because larger and older calves drink much more rapidly (Hudson and Adamczewski 1990).

For obvious technical reasons, few lactation curves for cervids have been published (Arman et al. 1974, Hudson and Adamczewski 1990). On good nutritional planes, red deer produce about 0.66 gallons (2.5 L providing 10 megajoules [1 megajoule = 10^6 joule, J] of energy) of milk per day and elk produce more than 1 gallon (4 L providing 25 megajoules) per day at peak lactation. Nutritional plane has modest effects on milk production, which, in turn, has even less effect on the growth of calves. Differences have been seen in Scottish red deer grazing hills and improved pastures (Loudon et al. 1984), but supplementation had little effect in elk grazing moderately stocked aspen parkland ranges in western Canada (Hudson and Adamczewski 1990) (Figure 81).

If dietary energy is converted to milk energy with an efficiency of 0.64, hinds need to increase intake by 16 (red deer) to 40×10^6 J (elk). This doubles their daily energy requirement. If the diet is deficient in energy, body tissues (about 18×10^6 J/kg) can be mobilized to support lactation. One kilogram of mobilized tissue allows the secretion of

about 15×10^6 J as milk and, thus, replaces 23×10^6 J of dietary energy. Milk production declines under severe nutritional stress to prevent excessive draw on body reserves.

Calves nurse four to five times daily and consume up to 35 ounces (1,000 g) of milk at each nursing bout during peak lactation (i.e., at 4–6 weeks of age when elk calves weigh about 110 pounds [50 kg]) (Hudson and Adamczewski 1990). Although calves spend less time nursing as summer progresses, they nurse more quickly (calf weight is the main determinant of drinking rate). This level of milk production supports an average daily rate of gain of about 9.9 ounces (280 g) per day in Scottish red deer, 11.3 ounces (320 g) per day in New Zealand red deer and 30.7 ounces (870 g) per day in elk calves, until prerut weaning in early September. The interspecies mean milk conversion effi-

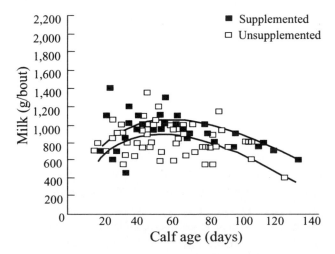

Figure 81. Milk production of elk on supplemented and unsupplemented pastures over the summer grazing season (Hudson and Adamczewski 1990).

ciency among wild ungulates is about 33.5×10^6 J/kg gain at peak lactation.

The most powerful effect on calf performance is birth weight. In farmed elk, every 2.2 pounds (1 kg) of increase in birth weight compounds to 8.2 pounds (3.7 kg) of body weight by weaning at 110 days. By the beginning of the rut, weaning weights (corrected to 110 days of age) are in the order of 88 pounds (40 kg) for Scottish red deer, 110 pounds (50 kg) for New Zealand red deer and 265 pounds (120 kg) for farmed elk. Gender differences are not great at this age, although stag calves grow one-third faster during their first winter (Freidel and Hudson 1994).

Assessment of Reproductive Status

Pregnancy determination can be made by transrectal manual palpation of the uterus, blood sampling for estrone sulfate, blood sampling for pregnancy-specific protein, blood or fecal sampling for progesterone or its metabolites, transrectal ultrasonography or ovarian analysis.

Rectal Palpation

The simplest and least expensive method of pregnancy determination is rectal palpation, which can only be accomplished in animals large enough to permit the insertion of a hand. It is a relatively easy procedure with elk if restraint is adequate and the operator's hand and forearm is small enough. The uterus of nonpregnant elk lies almost entirely within the pelvic cavity. The uterus of a nonpregnant yearling is small, with a horn diameter of about 0.6 inch (1.5 cm) and a length of 3.1 to 3.9 inches (8–10 cm). Enlargement in the pregnant horn can be detected readily by 42 days postconception, at which time it lies over the pelvic brim. The uterus then may be about 8 to 10 inches (20–25 cm) in length, and the first two of the cotyledons on the dorsolateral surface of each horn can be felt. They are about 0.5 inch (1.3 cm) in height and 2.0 inches (5 cm) in diameter (compared with the caruncles of the nongravid uterus, which are about half that size). At this stage, the fetus is about 0.94 inch (2.4 cm) in length and often can be felt by finger tapping of the fluid-filled uterus. By 75 days postconception, the uterus has considerably enlarged, its weight has pulled it down into the abdominal cavity and the fetus may be as much as 11.8 inches (30 cm) in length (Haigh and Hudson 1993).

Blood Tests

Elevations of serum progesterone do occur during pregnancy, and some early scientific papers suggested that this was a sufficient test (Weber and Wolfe 1982). Unfortunately, this hormone also is produced in the adrenal gland under stress and during the normal nonpregnant estrous cycle, therefore care must be used in interpretation (Adam et al. 1985, Jopson et al. 1990). Willard et al. (1994) found that during the rut, progesterone concentrations in nonpregnant and pregnant animals (as determined by later calving) were 3.2 ± 0.7 and 5.5 ± 0.4 ng/mL, respectively. Although these figures were significantly different, progesterone concentration was only 85.8% accurate in diagnosing pregnancy. After 120 days, progesterone in pregnant animals increased markedly to mean values of 10.3 ng/mL and was 100% accurate.

Willard et al. (1994) also found that estrone sulfate was of no use in pregnancy determination during the rut. By 12 to 20 days postrut, the concentrations had risen almost sixfold and were 100% accurate. At that time, the levels in nonpregnant and pregnant animals were 107 ± 2.7 pg/mL and 632.3 ± 46.5 pg/mL, respectively.

A protein similar to the pregnancy-specific protein of cattle, which is produced by the binucleate cells of the placenta, has been detected in pregnant red deer and elk. This protein cross-reacts in the bovine test and can be used as a reliable indicator of pregnancy in red deer and elk from about 32 days of gestation (Haigh et al. 1984, Hein et al. 1991, Willard et al. 1994).

Fecal Tests

A relatively new and completely noninvasive method of determining pregnancy is through measuring of estrone conjugates, pregnane-3-glucuronide (PdG) and free progesterone in feces (White et al. 1995). Pregnant animals have higher concentrations of both pregnane-3-glucuronide and free progesterone from December until the end of April, whereas estrone conjugate concentrations do not differ between pregnant and nonpregnant animals until March. Of the three components, pregnane-3-glucuronide proved to be the most reliable indicator of pregnancy status. All 11 pregnant animals in the White et al. (1995) study were correctly classified. However, five of the eight nonpregnant animals were misclassified. Possibly, the enzyme immunoassay method of measurement used in this study contributed to these inaccuracies. Radioimmunoassays of fecal metabolites in caribou were able to distinguish pregnancy status accurately (Messier et al. 1990). Although less accurate, enzyme immunoassays are less expensive than radioimmunoassays, do not require disposal of radioactive material and have the potential for rapid on-site determination (White et al. 1995).

Ultrasound

Transrectal real-time ultrasound examination, in the hands of an experienced operator, also is highly accurate (Revol and Wilson 1991a, 1991b). Best results are obtained between 30 and 130 days of gestation. However, the tests still are 71% accurate when taken at 21 to 23 days. Willard et al. (1994) used ultrasound 120 days after the rut and found it to be 100% accurate in detecting pregnancies of 15 animals. However, they detected intrauterine fluid in two animals that did not subsequently calve. Although Williard et al. did not discuss possible reasons for this apparent misdiagnosis, it may have been due to early embryonic death.

After 100 days of pregnancy, when the fetus has dropped into the abdominal cavity, transrectal examination of the reproductive tract may be difficult. Later in gestation, transabdominal evaluation may be used, but this requires the placement of the probe over an area devoid of hair, which would require examination in the hairless region anterior and lateral to the udder.

Ovarian Analysis

Ovaries can be located easily, after a cautious opening of the abdomen, by following the meanderlike path of the fallopian tubes. Ovarian analysis can play an important role in population forecasts by identifying the cows' maturational status, the timing of ovarian cycles and possible fertilization success at times when the embryo cannot be easily seen. Standard methods are described by Morrison (1960).

Corpora lutea of pregnancy regress to form corpora rubra and eventually corpora albicantia. These structures allow estimation of reproductive history (Langvatn 1992a, 1992b). The corpus rubrum allows an unbiased assessment of age-specific natality rates. However, attempts to trace reproductive history using corpora albicantia in progressive stages of regression give increasing underestimation of past productivity of older animals (Langvatn et al. 1994).

Growth and Development

Compared with other mammals, young ungulates have very high growth rates. These rates reflect evolutionary pressures to (1) pass quickly through the vulnerable early postnatal period when predation pressures are high and (2) attain sufficient body size and nutritional reserves to cope with hardships imposed by seasonal environments.

Growth Cycles

Throughout life, animals grow toward a genetically determined maximum size. However, even in constant nutri-

tional environments, both genders exhibit seasonal cycles of body weight and composition, particularly as they approach prime age (Figure 82).

In good nutritional environments, elk calves continue to grow, albeit more slowly during their first winter, reaching about 310 to 350 pounds (140–160 kg) by spring. They may gain an additional 220 pounds (100 kg) over the next summer, with females entering the rutting period at 485 pounds (220 kg) and males at 550 pounds (250 kg). Red deer stags continue to grow slowly during their second winter gaining 3.5 ounces (100 g) per day, about 1.35 times as much as hinds. This differential seems slightly lower in elk. An additional summer brings females close to their mature weight but males may not reach mature weight until they are 4 or 5 years of age.

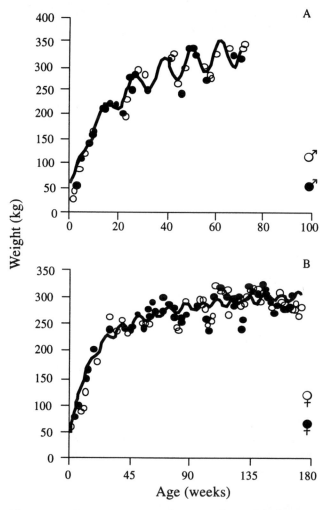

Figure 82. Representative growth curves of two elk bulls (A) and two elk cows (B) on aspen parkland rangelands in western Canada with minimal winter supplementation (R. J. Hudson personal files).

Elk calves grow rapidly throughout their first year, reaching a weight of about 300 pounds (136 kg) by the following spring. *Photo by Len Clifford.*

Seasonal weights of adult females are related mostly to pregnancy and the demands of lactation. During winter, pregnant hinds may lose as much as 10% of their autumn weight, because the developing conceptus contributes little to winter live weight. Delivery of the calf causes an abrupt loss of approximately 66 pounds (30 kg). On most summer ranges, lactating cows are able to gain weight, thus achieving the same rut weights as cows without calves.

Body weight changes are most dramatic in mature bulls, which are at their maximum just before the rut when they may weigh more than 1,100 pounds (500 kg). Within 6 to 8 weeks, rutting bulls may lose more than 20% of their body weight, mainly due to reduced appetite and heightened physical stress.

The amplitude of seasonal weight cycles is greatest in animals on good planes of nutrition. On low planes of nutrition, weight loss and rutting activity are subdued, and growth may ensue during the usual period of weight stasis if nutritional conditions improve. Restoration of good nutritional conditions leads to rapid compensatory growth.

Elk gain weight at rates that suggest they have seasonal target weights. Potential gains vary with both current body weight and seasonal growth impetus. Just how these two determinants interact is not known.

Winter Weight Loss

Winter weight change is strongly related to peak autumn weights (Figure 83). Elk given unlimited access to good di-

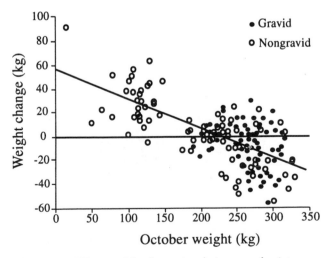

Figure 83. Winter weight change in relation to peak winter weight (Hudson et al. 1985). Heaviest animals entering the winter experience the most profound weight losses. Smaller animals may even gain weight despite the short day lengths.

ets gain slowly during winter, except those that are larger than about 551 pounds (250 kg). Hand-reared calves weighing less than 175 pounds (80 kg) in October may grow without obvious interruption throughout the winter. However, animals (particularly males) entering winter at high weights experience profound weight loss. The contrast in performance is particularly marked when food resources are scarce.

Several explanations can be offered for the propensity of small animals to grow and large animals lose weight during winter. Large animals with greater body reserves simply may not strive to maintain positive energy balance. This is unlikely, however, because large males often are in poor condition at the end of winter, and their weight loss is ameliorated by supplemental feeding. This suggests that larger animals simply have greater difficulty meeting their vastly greater nutrient requirements when foraging rates are limited by forage availability.

Summer Weight Gain

During summer, when the photoperiodic stimulus is high, rates of weight gain vary inversely and linearly with spring weight, regardless of whether weight is determined by age or nutritional history (Figure 84). Weight stasis or loss during winter is followed by compensatory growth (Hudson et al. 1985, Renecker and Samuel 1991), as previously noted.

Although gains on summer pastures are inversely proportional to weights at the end of winter, red deer may not completely recover from the setback of winter nutrition, depending on the quality and persistence of summer pasture (Suttie and Hamilton 1983, Suttie et al. 1983, Adam

and Moir 1985). Heavy winter feeding on farms often benefits late-born calves and ensures adequate size of males that are to be slaughtered at 1 year of age. It also can improve the frame development of females in their first breeding season.

Although they have not been compared directly, elk seem to compensate more completely for winter weight loss than do red deer (Hudson et al. 1985, Watkins et al. 1991). Yearling bulls on spring/summer pasture rapidly recover weight (Figure 85). Such compensatory growth may result from a combination of higher voluntary feed intake, improved efficiency of feed utilization and increased body water. Of these, higher feed intake seems to be most important (Watkins et al. 1991, Wairimu et al. 1992, Wairimu and Hudson 1993).

Body Composition

Body composition changes with age, weight, nutrition and perhaps (independently) season. For the animal, the significance of these changes in body composition confer functional (adult conformation and composition) and bioenergetic (body reserves) benefits. For the hunter and elk farmer, these changes relate directly to carcass yield and venison quality.

Priorities for Growth

As an animal matures or gains/loses weight, tissues are deposited or mobilized in a consistent order. The earliest to develop and most protected is nervous tissue. The skeleton also is an early priority. Muscle and other lean tissue are

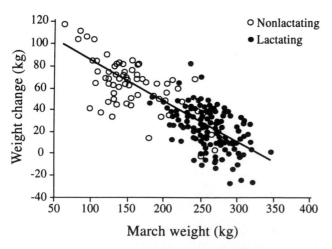

Figure 84.   Summer weight change of elk in relation to spring weight (from Hudson et al. 1985).

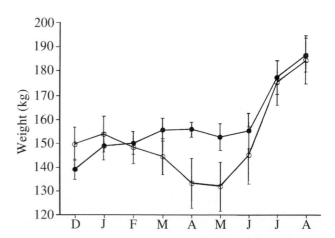

Figure 85.   Compensatory gain of yearling elk bulls on summer pastures (Wairimu et al. 1992, Wairimu and Hudson 1993). Supplemented animals (closed circles) maintained weight in late winter but entered the rut at the same weight as bulls that were not supplemented.

more sensitive, and fat (at least the triglyceride portion) in fat depots is most labile (capable of being changed). Although both protein and fat are mobilized together, initially the greatest proportion is fat (Torbit et al. 1985a, 1985b, Adamczewski 1987). As winter progresses and fat deposits are depleted, lean tissue becomes increasingly important as a potential source of metabolizable energy. However, the energy content of muscle tissue is low, and considerably more muscle than fat must be mobilized daily to fuel maintenance demands. As a result, if an animal is metabolizing muscle tissue to meet energetic demands, weight declines precipitously. With spring green-up, elk rapidly rebuild reserves, replacing tissue deposits in the reverse order they were mobilized.

Although body composition at specified weights generally is similar regardless of age or rate of growth, both environmental and physiological factors may cause short-term deviations from simple allometric rules. Animals on exceptionally high planes of nutrition tend to be fatter at similar live weights because lean tissue growth is rate limited. The proportion of water associated with lean tissue growth may change with maturity and season. Homeorhetic controls (controls influencing the whole body) also may influence the seasonal partitioning of energy between lean and fat tissue growth (Owens et al. 1993). In white-tailed deer, short days appear to promote fat accretion (Abbott et al. 1984, Verme 1988). However, Suttie et al. (1991a) were unable to find photoperiod-linked differences in fatness despite rapid growth among reindeer on long-day photoperiod, and we are aware of no data specific to elk.

From a bioenergetic standpoint, the most important compositional aspect is the amount of body fat because it is the principal energy depot. The propensity of animals to fatten (percentage carcass fat) varies widely among species. Absolute amounts of fat scale crudely to $W^{1.0}$. Along with their relatively low metabolic rate, these reserves should enable large animals to wait out periods of acute starvation as long as these are preceded by ample opportunity to accumulate reserves (Lindstedt and Boyce 1985). This may be a partial explanation for Bergmann's rule, which posits that warm-blooded animals from colder climates tend to be larger, because northern environments tend to be more strongly seasonal. However, it probably does not extend to the high Arctic, where periods of forage abundance are too short and sieges of winter too long to make this a viable adaptive strategy.

Fat levels in elk and red deer depend on nutritional and social conditions, sex, age and season. Rump fat thickness can reach 2.76 inches (70.1 mm) in August (Flook 1970a). Fat is stored first in bone marrow, then by deposition around the kidneys, intestines and stomach cavity (Figure 86). Mobilization of fat generally proceeds in reverse order.

Energy Content and Cost of Gain

Energy content of lean or fat tissue reflects changing body composition, particularly fatness. Fat has an energy content of approximately 39 kJ/g, whereas lean tissue contains only 5 kJ/g. Because protein and fat are deposited and mobilized together, the energy content of each unit of gain usually falls between 6 and 20×10^6 J/kg. Too little is known to calculate precise values from weight and rates of gain as is done for conventional farm livestock.

Most of the variation in the energy content of gain in immature animals is explained by live weight. Irrespective of age or nutritional history, there is a tendency for animals of the same weight to have similar body compositions. The most relevant illustration of this principle is work on white-tailed deer by Robbins et al. (1974). However, McCullough and Ullrey (1983) suggested that this oversimplifies more complex relationships.

The efficiency of converting metabolizable energy in feed to gain (kf) is similar in red deer and sheep, which is about 0.55 (Simpson et al. 1978). It is slightly higher for concentrates and lower for forages. By calculation, requirements for growth are expected to range from 16 to 55×10^6

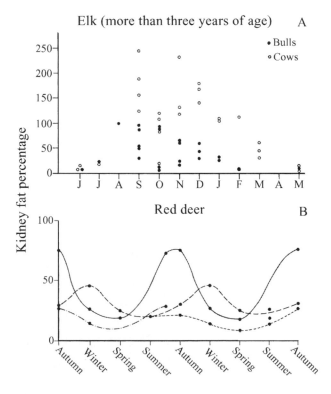

Figure 86. Kidney fat indices in elk (*A*) (Flook 1970a) and red deer (*B*) (Riney 1955).

J/kg live weight gain. Empirical work on red deer gave values of 37×10^6 J/kg for 6- to 18-month-old stags and 55×10^6 J/kg live weight gain for hinds, the higher value perhaps reflecting deposition of (mainly) fat (Fennessy et al. 1981, Suttie et al. 1987). Efficiencies of weaned red deer calves may vary through the winter months (55×10^6 J/kg in November and December, 87×10^6 J/kg in January and February and about 50×10^6 J/kg in March and April), but these estimates were indirect and might be partially explained by changing maintenance requirements (Milne et al. 1987). In adult Pére David's deer, the rapid increase in live weight in mid-to-late summer was associated with a steep decline in feed intake, suggesting improved efficiency (Loudon et al. 1989). For elk, estimates of the energy costs of gain are in the range of 16 to 37×10^6 J/kg, with some evidence of seasonal variation with high values in summer (Jiang and Hudson 1992, 1994, Wairimu et al. 1992, Cool and Hudson 1996).

Carcass Composition

Although carcass yields are of interest to hunters (Field et al. 1973), most of the interest stems from the international venison industry, which is based mainly on red deer (Drew 1985, 1992).

The carcass yield of most cervids is slightly higher than conventional ruminant livestock (Table 23). Gender and age influence dressing percentage (Table 24). The main variables influencing dressing percentage are diet and gut content. Ingesta-free body weight averages 90% of live weight, but varies with season and diet. Blood loss is a minor factor in yields. Total blood volume in mammals averages 5.5% of body mass—approximately 5.3 gallons (20 L) for an adult elk. However, bleed-out percentages range from 2% to 3% of whole body weight.

Deer carcasses usually are more than 70% lean and less than 10% fat with a very high lean to bone ratio (Drew

Table 23. Weight conversions for a 772-pound (350 kg) adult bull elk

Component	Weight in pounds (kg)	Proportion of live weight
Live weight	770 (350)	1.00
Bled weight	750 (340)	0.97
Field-dressed weight (eviscerated carcass)	503 (228)	0.65
Clean dressed weight (skin, lower legs and hide removed)	417 (189)	0.54
Retail cuts (bone in)	269 (122)	0.35

Sources: Adapted from Field et al. 1973, Hudson personal data.

Table 24. Elk gender and age differences in dressed weight percentage of live weight

Age	Bull	Cow
2 years	45	48
2–4 years	44	46
Mature	42	51

Source: Madson 1966.

1992). Part of this leanness stems from the age at which farmed deer are slaughtered (usually at 15 or 27 months). The ingesta-free body mass is 20% to 25% protein over a wide range of body weights. Body water decreases from 75% to 60% with increasing body weight, whereas fat increases from 0% to 18%. The proportion of fat increases linearly with carcass weight.

The skeleton comprises 6.4% to 7.2% of the dressed weight, or about 99 pounds (45 kg) for bulls and 88 pounds (40 kg) for cows.

Venison

Fresh venison is 75% to 78% water and 22% to 25% protein. It has many characteristics that make it nutritionally superior to conventional meats (Tables 25–28). Fat content averages 3% to 4%, and the energy content (about 5.5 kJ/g) is lower than beef and particularly lamb. Cholesterol levels (55 mg per 100 g) are slightly lower than conventional meats, according to the U.S. Nutritional Data Laboratory (http://www.nal.usda.gov/fnie/). Iron levels in venison are high, at 2.76 mg per 100 g.

The lipid fraction is comprised of two main groups—membrane-associated phospholipids and depo-triglycerides. The triglyceride component of elk differs strikingly from that of other deer (Garton and Duncan 1971, Garton et al.

Table 25. Percentage composition of ingesta-free body weight of Scottish red deer stags

	15-month-old stags	27-month-old stags
Empty carcass[a]	119.00 (54)	147.00 (67)
Protein	24.00	0.23
Fat	0.35	0.096
Water	68.00	0.64
Ash	18.00	0.14
Carcass energy[b]	6.76	8.77
Gut contents	0.10	0.13

Source: Kay et al. 1981.

[a] In pounds (kg).

[b] In kilojoules per gram.

Table 26. Nutrients in 3.5 ounces (100 g) of trimmed free-ranging and farmed red deer leg meat

	Free-ranging	Farmed	Farmed
Age (months)	27	12	27
Carcass weight [a]	95.0 (43.1)	89.7 (40.8)	166.9 (75.7)
Lean meat[b]	3.4 (95.6)	3.4 (95.6)	3.1 (88.0)
Fat[b]	0.1 (3.3)	0.1 (3.3)	0.4 (10.9)
Minerals[b]	0.04 (1.1)	0.04 (1.1)	0.04 (1.1)
Polyunsaturated fatty acids[b]	0.02 (0.5)	0.01 (0.3)	0.01 (0.3)
Polyunsaturated: saturated fatty acid ratio	0.18	0.10	0.03

Source: From Drew and Seman 1987.

[a] In pounds (kg).

[b] In ounces (g).

Table 27. Triglyceride composition of venison loins (grams per 100 g total fatty acids ± SD) compared with published data for lamb loins

Fatty acid	Venison	Lamb
C14:0	7.0 ± 0.59	5.0 ± 1.26
C16:0	39.4 ± 1.16	20.2 ± 1.11
C16:1	13.3 ± 2.53	3.4 ± 0.27
C18:0	10.8 ± 2.08	24.5 ± 1.35
C18:1	27.1 ± 1.74	38.1 ± 2.42
C18:2	1.3 ± 0.83	1.3 ± 0.54
C18:3	1.0 ± 0.41	1.0 ± 0.24
Polyunsaturated	2.3	2.3

Source: From Drew and Seman 1987.

Table 28. Venison loin phospholipid composition (grams per 100 g fatty acids ± SD)

Fatty acid	Amount
C14:0	0.7 ± 0.37
C16:0	13.9 ± 1.36
C16:1	2.9 ± 0.42
C18:0	14.9 ± 1.76
C18:1	17.0 ± 1.70
C18:2	22.6 ± 1.91
C18:3	12.3 ± 1.55
C20:4	8.8 ± 1.09
C20:5	7.0 ± 1.60
Polyunsaturated	50.7

Source: From Drew and Seman 1987.

1971, McClymont 1979). The adaptive significance is unknown, but it does offer another forensic marker.

Work on commercial venison quality includes Seman et al. (1988), Stevenson et al. (1992), and Barry and Wilson (1994). It focuses on both palatability and nutritional value. Cholesterol and lipid composition of meats and other animal products have received considerable attention in relation to heart disease and strokes. Emphasis on cholesterol and saturated fats has moved to the ratio of 3:6 fatty acids because this seems to influence how cholesterol is metabolized and how it influences cardiovascular disease.

Regulation

Growth of northern cervids must be maximized for the brief pulse of annual forage production (Suttie and Webster 1995). This is regulated by complex and poorly defined endocrinological interrelationships.

Somatotropin and Somatomedins

Studies on neuroendocrine control of growth has centered on growth hormone (or somatotropin) and IGF_1. Growth hormone is a polypeptide with a variety of anabolic and metabolic effects closely related to prolactin, and is similarly depressed by bromocryptine treatment. Growth hormone secretion is pulsatile (it must be sampled every 15 minutes over a 24-hour period), and the pattern of its blood concentration seems to stimulate IGF_1 production by the liver and perhaps other tissues (Suttie et al. 1989). In autumn and early winter, growth hormone pulses are frequent but of low amplitude. In spring, growth hormone pulses have high mean concentrations (i.e., they have a high amplitude) that decrease by midsummer when the frequency but not the amplitude increases.

Under normal nutritive conditions, growth hormone stimulates IGF_1 production by the liver (the relationship uncouples during nutritional stress). IGF_1 has both endocrine (distant) and paracrine (local) effects. Pulses of growth hormone increase in late winter and early spring, stimulating a subsequent increase (approximately 1-month lag) in IGF_1, which coincides with summer growth and velvet antler development (Suttie et al. 1989, 1991a).

A manipulated photoperiod of 16 hours of light (L) and 8 hours of darkness (D) stimulates out-of-season growth in reindeer during winter. This growth is associated with an increase in the plasma levels of IGF_1 (Suttie et al. 1992). Conversely, a photoperiod of 8L:16D delays the spring rise in growth. Melatonin treatment of red deer also advances seasonal patterns of increasing and decreasing of plasma IGF_1 and of weight gain and loss. The effect of melatonin treatment on IGF_1 differs seasonally. Initially, melatonin does not influence the seasonal increase in IGF_1, although its amplitude is lowered. Later, melatonin treatment advances the seasonal decrease in IGF_1 to shorten the duration of elevated IGF_1.

Although IGF_1 plays a central role in seasonal growth regulation, other hormones appear to be important. Growth hormone may have independent effects on adipose tissue and perhaps bone.

Insulin

Insulin facilitates uptake of glucose by cells and generally is lipogenic through its effect on adipose tissue. Insulin reduces protein breakdown and also has a permissive effect on IGF_1 production by the liver. When insulin is low during modest undernutrition, IGF_1 also declines. Under these conditions, protein synthesis is uncoupled from growth hormone, and the feedback inhibition of growth hormone by glucose and IGF_1 is abolished. Severe undernutrition (starvation) leads to decreasing IGF_1, even if growth hormone increases. Food restriction decreases protein synthesis and increases fat deposition.

Prolactin

Prolactin also has liporegulatory effects (Meier 1977, Curlewis 1992) and may contribute to the propensity of deer to deposit lean tissue growth in summer and fatten in autumn (Verme 1988). These homeorhetic controls have not been specifically addressed in elk.

Adrenal Hormones

Beta-adrenergic agonists, structurally related to epinephrine and nor-epinephrine, stimulate lipolysis and decrease protein degradation (Owens et al. 1993). Glucocorticoids, produced in the adrenal cortex, enhance protein degradation. The gluconeogenic potential of body protein is 1 to 2 ounces (30–55 g) of glucose per 3.5 ounces (100 g) of protein (Lobley 1992). The main glucocorticoid in ruminants is cortisol, which influences growth of cartilaginous tissue. Corticosterone is found in smaller quantities and has a less clear metabolic role. The adrenals also produce androgens such as testosterone and androstanedione.

Gonadosteroids

Estrogens stimulate growth hormone and IGF_1 release, whereas androgens protect muscle from degradation. Androgen receptors are widely distributed in muscle tissues (especially the neck), explaining the typical sexual dimorphism in muscular hypertrophy (increase in size).

If circulating in high doses, androgens or androgen-like corticoids can stimulate mineralization of bone cartilage,

close the growth plate and stop bone growth. Mineralocorticoids prevent depletion of sodium and potassium reserves in the cell. Glucocorticoids participate in the control of carbohydrates.

Stress

The concept of stress was developed by Selye (1973) to explain adaptive biochemical mechanisms to cope with different kinds of pressure. Because all organisms are challenged constantly, they adapt to stress and, to a certain degree, are capable of controlling or counteracting it. Because life produces exhilaration as well as stressful situations, normal stress (eustress) is distinguished from harmful overexposure (distress).

Wild elk face distress from social interactions and from predation, hunting and industrial/recreational disturbance. Managed elk also are stressed by translocation, transport and mixing of social groups. Concern for the welfare of farmed red deer and elk has stimulated a number of studies on assessment, consequences and amelioration of stress (Pollard et al. 1992, 1994a, 1994b, Griffin and Thomson 1994).

Neurophysiological Response

Stress triggers a neurophysiological response that involves many target organs (Figure 87). The limbic system of the brain evaluates stressful signals in the context of experience, and activates three distinct response axes: (1) hypothalamic-adrenomedullary axis; (2) sympathetic-medullary axis; and (3) neuropeptide axis involving opioids, enkephalins and endorphins.

The main long-term stress hormones are the adrenocorticoids, cortisol and corticosterone (Smith and Bubenik 1990). Cortisol is considered the most physiologically relevant in ruminants. Lengthy stress periods cause enlargement of the adrenals, and continued high level of corticoids can stop skeletal growth and reduce disease resistance. Flook (1970a) used adrenal weight as an index of social stress. However, size and function of adrenal glands are not necessarily related. Administration of adrenocorticotropic hormone offers a better way to assess the response to stress (Smith and Bubenik 1990) and perhaps could be used to select stress-resistant individuals for commercial production (Bubenik and Bartos 1993).

Physiological Parameters

The acute response to stress involves basic physiological parameters such as core temperature and respiration and

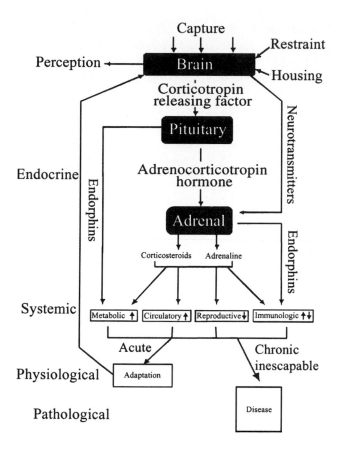

Figure 87. Neurophysiologcal response to stress (redrawn from Griffin and Thomson 1994).

heart rates (Table 29). More attenuated responses include endocrine and immunological changes.

Core and Surface Temperatures

Rectal and tympanic (ear drum) temperatures (normally 102.2°F [39°C]) respond quickly and have been used to evaluate alerting responses of several species. Although

Table 29. Physiological normals

Physiological parameter	Unit	Number of animals	Mean ± SD or SEM	Management
Respiration rate	Breaths per minute	27	27.8 ± 8.5	Farmed
		5	13.0 ± 0.5	Bottle-raised
Heart rate	Breaths per minute	27	80.4 ± 13.1	Farmed
		5	70.0 ± 4.4	Bottle-raised
Rectal temperature	Degrees Celsius	27	40.2 ± 0.5	Farmed
		5	38.7 ± 0.08	Bottle-raised

Source: From Haigh and Hudson 1993.

Note: SEM = standard error of the mean.

changes in body temperature involve only fractions of Celsius degrees, they are well within the reliable range of electronic sensors. Surface temperature, as measured by infrared imagery, also is used in stress research with animals. Infrared imaging has been particularly valuable to detect physiological responses of animals and perhaps even in estimation of energy expenditures.

Respiration and Heart Rates

Cardiovascular function is a highly sensitive index of emotional state. One component of cardiovascular function, respiratory rates (normally 13 breaths per minute) can be measured visually (especially in cold weather). However, the value of respiratory rate is limited because panting—an important thermoregulatory behavior—also may influence respiratory rate. Thus, as an index of stress, respiration rate is difficult at best.

A better measure of cardiovascular function is heart rate, which can be measured remotely by telemetry. Comprehensive data on elk heart rates were collected by Lieb and Marcum (1979), and were shown to vary from 36 to 65 beats per minute, with a seasonal and circadian rhythm. The minimum average heart rate occurred in winter and maximum in summer. Mean monthly maximum resting heart rate varied from 1.13 to 1.28 times the mean monthly minimum resting heart rate. Maximum resting heart rates occurred on the average 2.7 hours after maximum ambient temperatures. For minimum ambient temperatures, minimum heart rates lagged 1.9 hours.

Telemetry data by Ward et al. (1976) showed heart rate to be much lower in elk cows than in bulls. A mature cow exhibited a heart rate of 46.8 ± 8.2 beats per minute when resting and 60.3 ± 9.2 when feeding. A yearling bull's heart rate was 68.3 ± 7.8 beats per minute in a resting period and 84.3 ± 9.9 when feeding. The yearly averages were 54.3 beats per minute for the cow and 75.7 for the bull.

Pauls et al. (1981) used heart rate to estimate energy expenditures associated with various activities, with a view to calculating daily expenditures. Consistent and interpretable estimates of energy expenditure were obtained from individually calibrated animals. Chabot (1993) found that the calibration was reasonably stable seasonally, but the cause of the change (feed intake, thermal stress, activity or alarm) influenced the relationship between heart rate and energy expenditure.

Immune Function

Bidirectional links exist between the brain and the immune system (Griffin and Thomson 1994). Lymphocytes complement endocrine tissues by producing adrenocorticotropic

Heart rate provides an important measure of cardiovascular function and emotional state, including stress. Above, researchers implant a heart monitor in a drugged elk. *Photo by Michael H. Francis.*

hormone, thyroid-stimulating hormone, prolactin and endorphins. In return, hormone receptors are widely distributed on cells of the lymphoreticular system (lymphocytes, monocytes and granulocytes). Disease stimulates a generalized stress response and stress may influence disease resistance. Chronic stress (e.g., nutritional deprivation or transport) suppresses immunity, but acute stress sometimes enhances it (Griffin et al. 1992a).

The effects of distress on immune function can be measured directly as disease resistance. Distress also may be measured indirectly as ability to develop antibodies to novel antigens (humoral immunity) or by lymphocyte transformation in response to specific antigens or nonspecific mitogens (Griffin and Thomson 1994).

Neutrophil/lymphocyte ratios have been used as a sensitive index of chronic stress because lymphocytes decrease and because neutrophils increase with the glucocorticoid response to stress (Murata et al. 1987). Their usefulness for evaluating stress in elk needs to be studied.

Assessment

Measurement of physical and physiological parameters helps managers in several ways: (1) assessment of diseases and disorders; (2) identification of species, gender, age, location and genetic relatedness; (3) assessment of reproductive status; and (4) evaluation of nutritional status or stress. These are detailed in other chapters. In this section, physical and physiological baselines for normal animals are summarized.

Blood Parameters

Blood parameters may vary with temperament, tameness and prior experience with the restraint system. Blood parameters can reveal a great deal about physiological, nutritional and emotional health and social status. However, care must be taken to minimize spurious effects of stress. Despite this general knowledge and specific data on other cervids (Seal et al. 1972), little similar work has been done on elk (Table 30).

Genetic Markers

Identification of species, subspecies and closer genetic relationships has important applications in taxonomy and wildlife forensics. It has become increasingly important in regulating the emerging deer/elk industry. Paternity determination both in wild populations and on elk farms where single-sire mating is not used has become particularly relevant.

Blood tests to distinguish red deer and elk were developed in the 1980s, using the distinctive post-transferrins, hemoglobins and serum enzymes (Dracht and Gyllenstein 1985). The most definitive differences are in post-transferrins and hemoglobin. Pure elk are always post-transferrins type 1-1 and hemoglobulin type BB, and their gametes carry allele 1 and allele B. Red deer are type 2-2 and AA and form gametes with allele 2 and allele A (Dracht and Gyllenstein 1985). Therefore, first-cross hybrids are 1-2, AB. One of four second generation hybrids would have the type of a normal elk and mating double hybrids will produce, on average, 14 hybrid types for every 1 pure elk type and 1 pure red deer type.

Two other proteins provide information on subspecific differences—transferrin and superoxide dismutase. These substances do not allow absolute distinctions between elk and red deer, but they can enhance discrimination. These proteins contain two variants—transferrins A and B and superoxide dismutase F and S. Transferrin AA is rare in wild elk but frequent in red deer. The frequency of superoxide dismutase type SS is low in elk but high in red deer.

Table 30. Hematological, serum enzyme and serum chemistry data on physically restrained elk and red deer

Constituent	Elk	Red deer
Hemoglobin (g/L)	114–189	159–207.6
Hematocrit (%)	0.3–0.52	0.45–0.63
MCH (pg)		17.04
MCHC (g/L)		330
MCV (L)	42.1–44.6	52.7
RDW (%)		30.56
WBC ($\times 10^9$/L)	4.57–7.76	4.4–5
Neutrophils ($\times 10^9$/L)		1.933
(%)	19–69	
Lymphocytes ($\times 10^9$/L)		2.608
(%)	15–77	
Monocytes (%)	0–4	1.1
Eosinphils (%)	0–11	4
Basophils (%)	0–1	3
Platelets ($\times 10^9$/L)	195–451	
Total protein (g/L)	71–76	55–72
Albumin (g/L)	39–41	27–46
Globulin (g/L)	31	39.7
Alpha$_1$	4	1.0–6.2
Alpha$_2$	7.5	2.5–6.7
Beta	10.5	4.6–10.4
Gamma	22.0	10.6–25.6
A/G ratio	1.55	1–2.2
Fibrinogen (g/L)		2.70
Aldolase (U/L)		26
ALP (U/L)	305	287
AST (U/L)	90–96	40–82
ALT (U/L)		96
CK (U/L)	349	51–197
GGT (U/L)		19.5–47
LDH (U/L)	903	491
Pepsinogen (U/L)		0.91–0.99
Superoxide dismutase (u/g Hb)		1,022
SDH (U/L)		2
β-Hydroxybutarate dehydrogenase (U/L)		491
Glutamate dehydrogenase (U/L)		25 (12–61)
Calcium (mmol/L)	2.25	2.1–2.78
Phosphorus (mmol/L)	2.28	1.75–2.83
Sodium (mmol/L)	141	138–154
Potassium (mmol/L)	5.48	4.43
Magnesium (mmol/L)	0.96	0.71–1.04
Chloride (mmol/L)	8	
Urea (mmol/L)	7.7–8.3	8.56–11.06
Creatinine (μmol/L)	165	
Glucose (mmol/L)	7.5–12.8	6.9–10.1
Vitamin E (μmol/L)	5.09	

Source: From Haigh and Hudson 1993.

Notes: MCH = mean corpuscular hemoglobin; MCHC = mean cell hemoglobin concentration; MCV = mean cell volume; RDW = red cell distribution; WBC = white blood cells; ALP = alkaline phosphatase; AST = aspartate aminotransferase; ALT = alanine aminotransferase; CK = creatine phosphatase; GGT = gamma-glutamyl transferase; LDH = lactic acid dehydrogenase; SDH = sorbitol dehydrogenase.

The number of informative proteins is quite small, therefore attention has turned to analysis of DNA. Portions of DNA can be sampled using restriction endonucleases, DNA probes and specific DNA hybridization techniques. Restriction endonucleases scan the DNA for specific nucleotide sequences and cleave the DNA at these restriction sites. These restriction fragments offer an informative polymorphism, which can be used to distinguish taxa. Labeled DNA probes that hybridize to specific or homologous DNA fragments can be used to compare specific regions. There are several classes of probe for mitochondrial and DNA markers.

Mitochondrial DNA exists as a closed circular chromosome within the mitochondria. It evolves rapidly and is inherited maternally. Nuclear DNA probes can detect single-copy gene sequences or polymorphic anomalous DNA sequences. Single-copy gene sequences can give insight into the evolution of species and subspecies. There is more variation at anomalous loci termed VNTRs (variable number of tandem repeats) or minisatellites. A third type of nuclear DNA probe is satellite DNA. These highly repetitive sequences are clustered in specific regions of the chromosomes. Unlike fingerprinting probes, satellites have only limited ability to discriminate among individuals within a species.

Skeletal Differences Associated With Age and Gender

Although antler pedicles are predominately used to distinguish gender in skeletal remains, pelvic bones are diagnostic. Mature animals whose pubic region of the pelvic bone has fused and exhibit diameters averaging 6.1 inches (15.5 cm) or less probably are bulls; those exhibiting larger diameters probably are cows (Denney 1957).

Age can be crudely estimated from skeletal size and proportions, but more precisely by closure of the growth plates, cartilaginous pads separating the epiphysis and diaphysis of the long bones. Details are provided by Knight (1966).

Aging by Tooth Replacement, Wear and Cementum Annuli

Age can be crudely determined by elk size, conformation, coloration, antler and mane development, and, on remains, by closure of skeletal growth plates. The most reliable and practical for captured animals is dental replacement and wear.

Replacement

Sequence of incisor eruption provides a reasonable estimate to about age 2 years for red deer and age 3 years for elk. All permanent incisors (including the incisiform canine) erupt by 12 to 24 months in red deer and a bit later in elk (Table 31). However, replacement patterns are variable and strongly influenced by nutrition. Generally, dental replacement is complete by the time the animal is 27 months of age.

The important features in elk older than 2.5 years are replacement of the incisors and absence of the fourth premolar. However, there is considerable variation. For instance, at Glensaugh, Scotland, among red deer 21 months of age, roughly one-third had two, three or four pairs of permanent incisors (Blaxter et al. 1974).

Wear

Wear patterns (after all permanent teeth have appeared) reflect age (Figure 88). However, use of tooth wear information is inexact because it is governed by a number of factors, including diet, soil type and substrate.

Tooth rows of mature elk bulls measure 5.16 to 5.83 inches with a mean of 5.51 inches (131–148 mm with a mean of 139.9 mm). In mature elk cows, tooth rows measure 5.08 to 5.83 inches with a mean of 5.47 inches (129–148 mm with a mean of 138.9 mm) (Flook 1970a).

With progressive wear, the tooth row becomes shorter because the crown base is shorter than the crown top. To avoid gaps between teeth, wearing crowns are pushed together by pressure on the roots in the direction of the second premolar (the first in the row).

By 10 years of age, elk incisors are typically well-worn. Progressive tooth wear is seen with reduction in the size of the tooth tops as the roots become exposed and the central teeth tend to fall out.

The cheek teeth are more difficult to see in the live animal and have little application for age estimation, although they are used for this purpose in dead animals. Casts can also be made of cheek teeth to aid in estimation. In older animals, these teeth take on special significance, as the third premolar and first molar tend to wear out first, sometimes causing malocclusion.

Table 31. Eruption pattern of incisors and canines

	Wild elk (months)	Farmed red deer (months)
All deciduous	Birth–17	Birth–13
1 pair permanent incisors	16–23	10–14
Upper permanent canines	15–19	
2 pairs permanent incisors	18–24	14–22
3 pairs permanent incisors	25–29	19–22
4 pairs permanent incisors	27–33	19–26

Source: From Haigh and Hudson 1993.

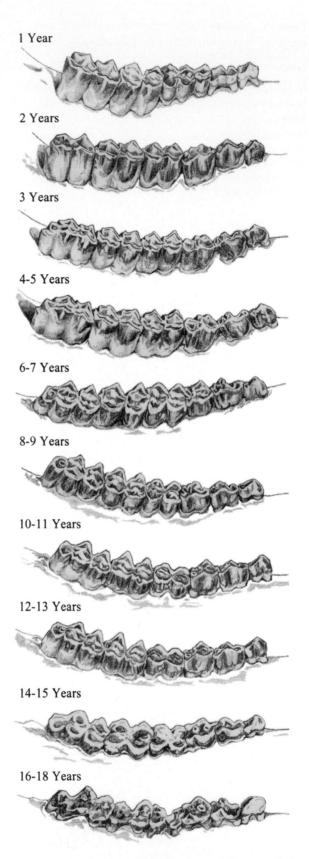

1 Year

2 Years

3 Years

4-5 Years

6-7 Years

8-9 Years

10-11 Years

12-13 Years

14-15 Years

16-18 Years

Figure 88. Tooth wear in elk (Bubenik 1982). *Illustration by A. B. Bubenik, based on Greer and Yeager (1967).*

Cementum Annuli

Cementum annuli are deposited between the roots and the cavity in the jaw (alveolus) of the first molars (Mitchell 1963, Keiss 1969). These are unaffected by differences in tooth wear and counting annuli is the preferred method for aging. Staining thin sections of tooth gives the most reliable results, but polished thick sections allow simpler and more rapid assessment.

Conclusion

Elk are marvelously adaptable generalists, with a well-developed capacity to adjust physically, physiologically and behaviorally to a variety of habitats and disturbances. The adaptability will continue to be tested in their ever-changing and increasingly artificial environment.

5

JOHN G. COOK

Nutrition and Food

Nutrition can have substantial effects on virtually every aspect of physiology related to productivity of animals. For a species such as elk, the nutritive value and quantity of forage can have an inordinate influence on the number of animals that breed and successfully reproduce. Nutrition, therefore, plays a fundamental role in determining population growth rates, carrying capacity of elk ranges, the number of elk that can be harvested each year by hunters and abundance of trophy-sized animals. Severe undernutrition has potential to limit herd productivity to the extent that populations cannot sustain themselves through time. Nutrition also may influence the effects of predation on elk populations.

Plants generally are a poor source of essential nutrients because nutrient concentration and availability typically are low during substantial portions of the year. Moreover, plants have evolved a myriad of adaptations that induce toxic effects or impede digestion and assimilation of nutrients when consumed. Large ungulates, in turn, counter low nutrient levels and plant defenses using a variety of anatomical, physiological and behavioral adaptations. Nevertheless, large ungulates often face considerable challenges to obtain sufficient nutrients to survive, particularly during periods of harsh weather, and to reproduce successfully during relatively short periods of nutritional abundance. Thus, it is not surprising that nutrition often is a primary influence on elk distribution, abundance and productivity.

Nutritional issues also present large ungulates biologists and managers with important challenges. The effects of nu-trition usually are subtle and can be masked by a variety of factors, including predation or hunting practices. Research has contributed insights on relationships between nutrition and productivity of herbivores. But much of this information has been collected on livestock. Moreover, much of the nutritional research on large ungulates has been conducted under captive conditions and has focused on North American white-tailed deer and European red deer (Cook et al. 1996). We know little about the practical relevance of nutrition's influence on wild elk herds. Yet effective habitat management requires skillful integration of nutritional information with that of other habitat components to provide for the needs of wild elk.

This review is intended to be moderate in depth and scope. Focus is primarily on forage characteristics that influence nutritional value, foraging strategies used by elk to acquire daily nutritional needs, effects of nutritional deficiencies on individuals and populations, estimates of nutritional requirements during each season for various productive stages and methods to assess the nutritional status of elk. Relevance of nutrition to management of elk herds is briefly discussed as well.

Nutrition-related Definitions

Some ambiguity exists regarding the meaning of a number of terms used in wildlife nutrition. Two key terms—nutrition and nutritional condition—were defined in the techniques manual of The Wildlife Society (Harder and Kirkpatrick 1994). Nutrition was defined as the rate of ingestion of assimilable energy and nutrients. Nutritional condition was defined as the state of body components (principally fat and muscle protein) controlled by nutrition, which influences an animal's fitness. Saltz et al. (1996) proposed to alter the definition of nutritional condition by substituting the term future fitness for fitness, because fitness refers to lifetime reproductive success and condition does not affect past reproductive success. I concur with this suggestion. In this chapter, *condition* is used interchangeably with nutritional condition.

Other terms used frequently include nutritional status and nutritional plane, which probably are intended to be analogous, although it appears that nutritional status has been used as an equivalent term to nutritional condition (see Harder and Kirkpatrick 1994). In this chapter, nutritional status and nutritional plane refer to the level of intake of assimilable nutrients in relation to daily nutrient requirements of the animal. Thus, nutritional status would be high if daily nutrient intake equaled or exceeded nutritional requirements, regardless of the animal's nutritional condition.

Also in this chapter, *nutritive value* of food is defined as the amount of assimilable nutrients contained within a food item. *Assimilable* is the key term of this definition; nutritive value of a food item may not be the same for different herbivore species. I use the term nutritive value equivalently to the term forage quality. Forage quality has been used by some to mean the amount of biomass of key forage species (e.g., Thomas et al. 1988a). Here, forage quantity, not forage quality, refers to the amount of available food.

Some clarification of food energy terms also is in order. The total amount of energy contained in food is called gross energy. A substantial portion of gross energy typically is not available to the herbivore; gross energy, therefore, has marginal biological relevance. Digestible energy (DE) refers to the amount of energy that can be digested and is equal to the gross energy of the food minus that excreted in the feces. A certain portion of digestible energy is lost in urine and in methane produced primarily in the rumen; DE minus this lost energy is referred to as metabolizable energy (ME). Both DE and ME are useful measures of the food's energy value. Large ungulate ecologists often use digestibility of the forage (measured either using feeding trials with live animals, in vivo [in the laboratory] or in vitro [using rumen fluid from donor animals]) as a surrogate of DE, because digestibility of the forage is linked closely to its DE content. The product of digestibility and gross energy provides an approximate measure of DE (Hobbs et al. 1982). Digestibility of forage usually is expressed as dry matter digestibility or digestible organic matter. Dry matter digestibility refers to the digestibility of the entire food; digestible organic matter refers to the digestibility of the food less the ash content (i.e., minerals).

Intake of energy and food typically is expressed on a metabolic weight (MW) basis (kilocalories per pound or kilogram of metabolically active tissue). Metabolically active tissue requires considerable energy; whereas, metabolically inactive tissue does not. Large animals contain proportionally less metabolically active tissue than do smaller animals. Stating energy requirements, for example, on a MW basis provides a useful approach for comparing energy requirements among animals of different sizes and is frequently used in this chapter. MW usually is calculated simply as MW = body weight$^{0.75}$. The $^{0.75}$ scales body weight in a manner that reflects surface area-to-volume ratio, relative cross-sectional area or body composition (Haigh and Hudson 1993), but why the factor $^{0.75}$ is not completely understood.

Digestion

Digestive Anatomy

Elk, like other true ruminants, have a single large stomach that is divided into four compartments—the rumen, reticulum, omasum and abomasum (see Figure 63). The rumen and reticulum serve as a storage tank for undigested and partially digested food matter and culture chamber where fermentation of food and absorption of nutrients occurs. The inside surface of the rumen contains papillae (small fingerlike projections) that increase the absorptive surface of the rumen wall. Size and shape of the papillae often vary as content of diets change. Muscular layers in the rumen wall contract rhythmically, mix the rumen contents and enhance digestion. The inside surface of the reticulum contains reticular ridges arrayed in a distinctive honeycomb pattern. These ridges may be important for sorting and handling food particles and regulating passage of food out of the reticulum (Van Soest 1994).

The next compartment, the omasum, is a small, compact, oval structure. The specific role of the omasum is somewhat unclear and seems to differ among ruminant species. Water and some nutrients are absorbed to the bloodstream from the omasum. This compartment also moves fine food particles and liquid for passage into the next compartment, the abomasum, and filters coarse, poorly digested food particles for return to the reticulum (Van Soest 1994). The omasum is a regulator of food passage and may limit food intake in many ruminants (Hofmann 1988). The final compartment of the ruminant stomach is the abomasum. Its structure and function are similar to that of stomachs in nonruminant species. Hydrochloric acid, pepsin and, in milk-fed juveniles, renin, induce chemical digestion in the abomasum before food is passed into the small intestine.

The midgut and hindgut (small and large intestine) also are similar anatomically and functionally to that of non-ruminant herbivores. The small intestine consists of three sections—the duodenum, jejunum and ileum, in order of occurrence from the terminus of the abomasum to the large intestine. The small intestine is the primary organ for enzymatic digestion and nutrient absorption of ingested food that escapes the rumen. Biliary and pancreatic secretions neutralize the low pH from gastric secretions in the abomasum. Bile homogenizes fats; pancreatic enzymes, including amylase, trypsin and lipase, digest starch, protein and fats and aid absorption of nutrients. In ruminants, the primary nutrients digested and absorbed in the small intestine are amino acids that arise mostly from microbes passed through the forestomach; only small amounts of sugars, fats and glucose reach the small intestine (Van Soest 1994).

Water, minerals and nitrogen are absorbed from the large intestine. Moreover, despite fermentation in the rumen and reticulum, there appears to be appreciable escape of fermentable ingesta, particularly hemicellulose, from the rumen to the large intestine. This ingesta is fermented in the cecum and large intestine and may provide a source of energy to the animal. Absorption of water from ingesta in the large intestine varies among species. Those that are adapted to dry environments excrete considerably less water through the feces (Van Soest 1994).

Digestive Processes

Limited digestion of food begins when food enters the ruminant's mouth. Food is pushed back to premolars and molars on both the upper and lower jaws. These teeth have ridges of alternating hard enamel and softer dentin (Short 1981). Jaw movement is lateral, resulting in a grinding rather than a cutting process. Chewing immediately after acquisition of food is limited, but it is effective in breaking down up to 50% of the food ingested into particles of less than 0.039 inch (1 mm) in size. Cattle typically may chew up to 50,000 times per day (Welch and Hooper 1988). Chewed food particles are aggregated into a bolus that facilitates swallowing.

Salivary excretions from several sets of glands in the mouth wet the food, enhancing bolus formation and swallowing. Saliva contains enzymes useful for breaking down

Food ingested by elk is rapidly ground between the molars by lateral movement of the jaws, then swallowed. *Left photo by Don Ballard. Right photo by Carol Polich.*

certain fats. Also, enzymes that initiate breakdown of starches are produced in glands located in the muzzle and mix with saliva in the mouth. The extent of digestion from these enzymes is limited and probably is most important for suckling juveniles (Church 1988). In addition, saliva in some species of ruminants contain proline-rich proteins that bind with plant compounds, namely tannins (described later), which have inhibitory effects on digestion of nutrients. Such binding proteins can block the inhibiting effects of tannins and enhance digestion of plant material (Robbins et al. 1991).

After chewing, food is swallowed into the rumen, where microbial fermentation and rumination begins. Rumination is a process where food contained in the rumen is regurgitated to the mouth, rechewed and swallowed again. Rumination enhances microbial digestion primarily by reducing the size of food particles; rechewing during rumination is the primary mechanism for reducing food particle size (Spalinger and Robbins 1992). Food is regurgitated from a concentrated mass of ingesta that floats in the rumen near the cardia (area around the esophageal opening of the rumen). This ingesta is sucked into the esophagus and transported by antiperistaltic esophageal contractions to the mouth. Liquid in the regurgitated mass is swallowed, and chewing the food commences. Saliva again is added to the chewed mass, serving to extract soluble contents of food and aid formation of a bolus. This food is then reswallowed.

Rumination probably is induced by tactile stimulation of coarse material in certain areas of the rumen and reticulum. Considerably more rumination time is required to break down coarse plant fragments. Ruminants may spend 10 to 11 hours daily ruminating if foods are high in structural tissues, which can be a factor in limiting the amount of food an animal eats each day (Van Soest 1994). The ability to regurgitate and remasticate food has survival benefits. Ruminants can quickly fill their rumen in habitats with abundant food and spend more time bedded while processing their food (ruminating) in habitats protected from predators and harsh weather.

Muscles in the rumen and reticulum contract and relax throughout the day. This mixes the ingesta and prevents accumulation and clogging in the rumen. Large, coarse material floats and is regurgitated from the rumen and rechewed. Particles that have been reduced in size become waterlogged and sink. These denser particles are passed out of the rumen and reticulum (Van Soest 1994)

Fermentation in the ruminant stomach provides an efficient means to digest plant material, particularly cellulose and other plant structural tissues. Nonruminant mammalian digestive systems are unable to digest and acquire energy from cellulose because it is impervious to normal acid/pepsin digestion. The rumen and reticulum provide a fermentation vat of relatively constant temperature and pH for a variety of anaerobic bacteria, fungi and protozoa (Van Soest 1994). These microorganisms ferment simple and complex chemical compounds of the diet, including cellulose and other plant structural tissues. Fermentation products from the microbes, then, are used by the ruminant primarily as a source of energy. The microbes also are digested in the abomasum and small intestine, providing a variety of other essential nutrients.

Bacteria are the primary contributors of fermentation products that are used by the animal; protozoan and fungal contributions are relatively minor. Protozoa, due in part to their predation on rumen bacteria, actually might contribute to a lower net availability of nutrients for use by the animal. Bacteria typically account for 60% to 90% of total rumen microbial mass, ciliated protozoa account for 10% to 40% and fungi account for 5% to 10% (Van Soest 1994). McBee et al. (1969) estimated 57.5 to 66.9 billion bacteria per 0.04 ounces (1 g) of rumen contents in four Yellowstone elk. *Bacterioides* spp., principally *B. succinogenes* and *B. ruminicola*, comprised 48% of the bacteria. *Butyrivibrio* spp. made up the major portion of the remaining 52%.

Many species of microbes require specific plant constituents (e.g., cellulose, hemicellulose, starch, sugars, lipids and proteins) to use as substrate (a source of energy). Some survive using fermentation products produced by other microbes. The numbers and species composition of rumen organisms depend on the amount and kind of food ingested by the ruminant and the rate of passage through its digestive system. In turn, the amount and kind of food that a ruminant can efficiently digest depends on numbers and species composition of the rumen microbial community. Rapid changes in diets, particularly from highly fibrous diets (roughages) to those high in energy and low in fiber (concentrates), can induce changes in the rumen environment that, in turn, may drastically alter the species composition and abundance of microbes. Such changes may make the animal sick or be fatal, but usually they are a problem only for animals fed processed rations.

Fermentation of vegetative carbohydrates in the rumen and reticulum results in synthesis of large quantities of volatile fatty acids. Most of these are absorbed directly through the rumen wall into the bloodstream and comprise the major source (70% to 80%) of ME for the animal. Acetic, propionic, butyric, isobutyric, valeric and isovaleric acids are the principal volatile fatty acids found in ruminants (Van Soest 1994). Dietary substrate and microbial organisms influence the relative production of these acids. For example, the molar ratios (moles of acetate to propionate to butyrate) range from 71:16:8 for roughage diets to

53:31:11 for concentrate diets of cattle (Fahey and Berger 1988). Nowlin (1974) studied volatile fatty acid production in elk digestion in vitro (artificial digestion in the laboratory using digestion flasks and freshly collected rumen liquor) for several northern Idaho browse species. His findings suggested that the relative production for each of the principal volatile fatty acids is similar to that found in deer and cattle.

Relative proportions of the various volatile fatty acids influence energy status of the ruminant, because each provides different levels of energy. Acetate contains about 70% of the energy in propionate and about 58% of that in butyrate (Robbins 1983). Fermentation of cellulose primarily results in production of acetate (about 70% acetate and 12% to 30% propionate and butyrate). Cellulose ferments slowly, therefore ruminant species with a relatively large rumen size (e.g., cattle and bison) use cellulose more effectively because rumen retention time is longer. Fermentation of hemicellulose, also a component of cell walls, proceeds more rapidly and produces more propionate and butyrate (57% acetate and 38% propionate and butyrate). Fermentation of starches and simple sugars (e.g., glucose, fructose and sucrose) produces about 50% acetate and 35% to 50% propionate and butyrate (Short 1981, Fahey and Berger 1988).

Soon after eating commences, volatile fatty acid concentration in the rumen increases and ruminal pH decreases. Fermentation peaks about 4 hours after feeding on a roughage diet, but sooner on a concentrate diet. As volatile fatty acids are absorbed across the rumen wall, the concentration of volatile fatty acids declines and pH increases. Buffering compounds such as bicarbonate from saliva introduced when swallowing food and secretions from cells in the rumen wall help to neutralize acid production and minimize reductions in pH. This buffering effect is critical for maintaining a hospitable environment for microbes in the rumen (Van Soest 1994).

Ruminal microbes also play a key role in processing protein for ruminants. The microbes remove proteins and nonprotein nitrogen from consumed plants, break them down into amino acids and peptides and use these products to synthesize microbial protein. Ruminal microbes contain 20% to 60% crude protein (dry matter basis), which, along with some dietary protein that escapes ruminal degradation, are digested into peptides or amino acids and absorbed in the abomasum and small intestine (Owens and Zinn 1988). Forage protein varies in quantity and digestibility throughout the year, whereas microbial protein remains of good quality and digestibility. This provides a nutritional advantage to ruminant versus nonruminant herbivores. Nevertheless, a certain amount of nitrogen (a key ingredient of all proteins) is required in the diet to support growth of the microbial population (Short 1981). And, protein synthesis by rumen microbes may not always be sufficient to meet the essential amino acid needs for rapid growth and high production, at least in domestic animals (Owens and Zinn 1988).

Wild ruminants have a well-developed capability to conserve nitrogen during periods when nitrogen levels in forage are low. In general, feces and urine account for the majority of nitrogen lost from the body. Nitrogen in feces includes undigestible dietary nitrogen, nitrogen contained in microbes originating primarily from the large intestine and sloughed cells of the endothelial layer of the alimentary tract. Nitrogen in urine, mostly contained in urea, is removed from the blood by the kidneys. During periods of low nitrogen consumption, ruminants have little ability to reduce loss of fecal nitrogen, but nitrogen loss in the urine declines considerably due to renal reabsorption (DelGiudice 1996). Ruminants also recycle various products of protein metabolism (ammonia, for example) that are converted to urea in the liver and then are shunted back to the rumen for use by rumen microbes. The primary pathways for urea recycling are through saliva and diffusion from the blood across the rumen wall (Owens and Zinn 1988). Conservation and recycling of nitrogen help to maintain the viability of the rumen microbial community during times of severe food shortage, which, in turn, helps to ensure that the animal can digest food when food is next available (Short 1981).

Fats, or lipids, contained in plants have potential to contribute disproportionately to the energy balance of the ruminant because of their high caloric content (about twice that in carbohydrates) (Short 1981). But lipid concentration in plants normally is low (1%–4%), and adult ruminants generally are poorly adapted to processing large amounts of ingested fat. Lipids in plants chiefly occur as triglycerides in seeds, galactolipids and phospholipids in leaves, and in other forms in waxes, carotenoids, chlorophyll and essential oils. Ruminal microbes alter substantially chemical properties of ingested fats; plant fats are mostly unsaturated, but are rapidly hydrogenated to saturated fats. Lipids are readily absorbed in either the rumen or the small intestine (Van Soest 1994).

Rumen microbes provide another key function for the ruminant vitamin synthesis. Water-soluble vitamins (B-complex vitamins, vitamin C) are synthesized by microbes from consumed plant matter. These microbes and their by-products are digested in the intestinal tract, releasing vitamins and other nutrients for absorption by the ruminant. Fat-soluble vitamins (vitamins A, D, E and K) cannot be synthesized by the rumen community and must already be present, at least in precursory form, in the elk's food. Except among captive elk, a deficiency of any vitamin probably is uncommon. A vitamin A deficiency could arise in winter if carotene is leached by rain from naturally cured herbaceous vegetation. Carotene, the precursor to vitamin A, occurs in super-quantities in green vegetation. Browse is a principal source of vitamin A in winter. Vitamin A is stored in animal fat and can be used during periods of shortages.

Development of the Alimentary Tract and Digestion in Juveniles

The rumen, reticulum and omasum at birth are non-functional and poorly developed. The abomasum is well-developed and highly functional, however, and its weight equals that of all other forestomach compartments. This is an adaptation for efficient digestion of milk (Lyford 1988); the rumen, reticulum and omasum contribute little to the digestion of milk.

During the first several weeks of life, milk provides nearly all nutrients required by the neonate (i.e., a juvenile to 1 month of age). Total dry matter content of elk milk averages about 20%, which is considerably more concentrated than that of cattle and similar to that of domestic sheep and deer. During midlactation, fat, protein, sugar and mineral content average 6.7%, 5.7%, 4.2% and 1.1%, respectively, and energy content is 27.5 kilocalories per ounce (1.1 kcal/g) (expressed on a wet weight basis) (Robbins 1983). Over the course of the lactation period, concentration of constituents generally increases slightly, compensating to some extent for declining milk production (Robbins et al. 1981).

Colostrum (i.e., milk first consumed after birth) plays a critical role in protecting immunologically immature neonates from diseases to which they are particularly susceptible. Colostrum contains a variety of immunological components, such as antibodies and phagocytic cells. During the first 24 to 36 hours after birth, newborns are able to absorb these immunological components intact, without digestive breakdown, through the lining of the alimentary tract. These components provide passive immunity, and some may remain effective 3 to 4 weeks after ingestion. Ability to absorb these immunological components wanes after 24 hours. But milk continues to provide some immunological protection against diseases of the alimentary tract throughout the neonatal period (Robbins 1983).

Growth of the gut during the first 2 months after birth typically proceeds rapidly in relation to that of other tissues. Much of this rapid growth is accounted for by the rumen, reticulum and small intestine after the first 3 weeks of age. Inoculation of microbes in the rumen begins several hours after birth, upon contact with the mother, dirt, vege-

Colostrum, the first milk consumed by an elk calf following birth, contains phagocytes and antibodies, and it plays a critical role in providing immunological protection from diseases to the newborn animal. Ability of the calf to absorb these elements through the lining of the alimentary tract declines rapidly within 24 to 36 hours after birth. *Photo courtesy of the Oregon Department of Fish and Wildlife.*

tation and a variety of other sources. Consumption of vegetation begins within the first 2 weeks after birth. Rumination begins, and volatile fatty acid production typically is well-developed within 3 weeks after birth (Lyford 1988, Lyford and Huber 1988).

At about 8 weeks of age, rate of growth of the rumen is at a maximum, rumen papillae are well-developed, the rumen microbial population is similar to that in adults, and young ruminants typically are greatly dependent on products of fermentation. Juveniles may be fully functional ruminants at this time. Development of rumination patterns similar to those in adults requires another 4 weeks or so (Lyford 1988, Lyford and Huber 1988).

Rapid development of the ruminant stomach depends on intake of solid food early in life. Consumption of digestible food is key for stimulating ruminoreticular growth; virtually no growth or development will occur if juveniles consume only milk. This is because milk is shunted directly to the abomasum through the esophageal groove during nursing, thereby contributing little fermentable mass to stimulate ruminoreticular development. Consuming ade-

During the first 3 to 4 weeks of an elk calf's life, mother's milk provides all nutrients needed for rapid growth. It also protects the neonate from gastrointestinal diseases. Although elk calves can be successfully bottle raised in captivity, bottle raising can be a challenge because of (1) difficulties with providing a milk formulation that adequately mimics the composition of elk milk and (2) problems associated with reduced protection from diseases. *Photo by John G. Cook.*

quate quantities of milk, however, is required to provide the nutrients to support rapid growth of alimentary tract (Lyford 1988).

The nature and extent of forestomach development depend on the type of food consumed. Bulky, undigestible food induces expansion and muscular growth of the rumen and reticulum, but has little effect on epithelial development (and, thus, absorptive capability). Readily digestible concentrates stimulate epithelial development, but the presence of coarse dietary fiber may be required for normal rumen development and function (Lyford 1988).

When milk production is high, ruminoreticular development can be retarded because juveniles may be reluctant to switch from milk to vegetation (Lyford 1988). Reluctance to switch to solid food has been observed in hand-raised elk calves (Cook et al. 1994a, 1996). Data from Hudson and Adamczewski (1990) suggested that maternally raised elk calves increase solid food intake earlier in life if milk production is depressed. Milk production of cow elk begins to

decline about 4 weeks after parturition although nutrient intake of the mother may remain high (Robbins et al. 1981). Declining milk production even when nutrition is good, therefore, may be an adaptation to force juvenile elk calves to increase intake of solid food and ease the lactation burden of the dam.

Although forced switching to solid food, due to depressed milk yields, may enhance ruminoreticular development, growth may suffer (Lyford 1988). Reduced growth was demonstrated with red deer (Loudon et al. 1984) and hand-reared elk calves (Cook et al. 1994a, 1996), but other elk studies showed that this does not always occur (Robbins et al. 1981, Hudson and Adamczewski 1990). Timing and magnitude of reduced milk production, size of the juvenile and nutrient content of vegetation likely mediate effects of reduced milk production on calf growth.

Foraging Dynamics

The acquisition of nutrients each day is a complex process that reflects characteristics of both the vegetation and the herbivore. The foraging environment presents many options from which herbivores must select in some optimizing manner to acquire energy and nutrients that meet requirements. During some seasons, considerable selective effort on the part of the herbivore may be required to consume sufficient nutrients and energy; in others, herbivores may be unable, despite selection, to consume energy and nutrients to meet daily requirements.

Forage Nutritional Characteristics

Useful features of plants related to nutritive value are the relative amounts of cell contents, or cell solubles, and structural components, or cell wall. Cell contents include soluble sugars, starch, organic acids, lipids, soluble minerals and protein. Structural components include cellulose, hemicellulose, lignin, cutin, silica and other compounds. Cell contents are highly digestible and nutritious, whereas cell wall is moderately to poorly digestible (Table 32).

Relative amounts of cell solubles and cell wall and characteristics of cell wall influence the amount of time required to digest food and, in turn, how much food animals can consume each day. Elk require 5 to 10 hours to digest food containing 10% to 30% cell wall, and require 20 to 30 hours to digest food with 40% to 60% cell wall (Figure 89A). Time required for cell wall digestion in elk largely depends on lignin (an indigestible component of cell walls), cell wall content and thickness of cell walls. Lignin has classically been considered the most important of these digestive inhibitors because it hinders microbial attack on cell

Calves must begin to consume vegetation and other materials (including dirt) soon after birth to stimulate rumen development. *Photo by D. Robert Franz.*

wall (Jones and Wilson 1987). Spalinger et al. (1986) concluded, however, that cell wall thickness apparently is the most important of these factors (Figure 89B). Due to greater time requirements to digest cell wall, herbivore species with relatively large rumen capacity, and thus, longer food retention time, digest cell wall constituents more efficiently.

Table 32. Bioavailability of selected forage components to ruminant herbivores

Component[a]	True digestibility (%)
Class 1	
Soluble carbohydrate	100
Starch	90+
Organic acids	100
Protein	90+
Pectin	98
Class 2	
Cellulose	Variable
Hemicellulose	Variable
Class 3	
Lignin	Indigestible
Cutin	Indigestible
Silica	Indigestible

Source: Adapted from Van Soest 1994.

Note: Class 1 = completely available; Class 2 = partly unavailable due to lignification; Class 3 = unavailable.

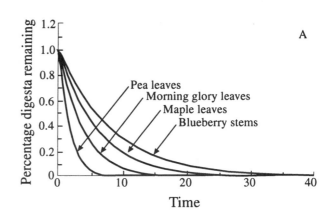

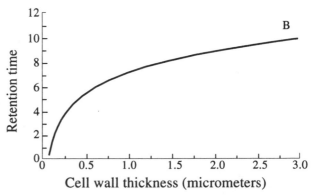

Figure 89. Digestion times of four forages (*A*) in the rumen of elk, and the relationship (*B*) between mean cell wall thickness of forage and mean retention time in the elk rumen (adapted from Spalinger et al. 1986).

Total gross energy content of plants is primarily a function of the amount and energy content of various plant constituents. These vary considerably. For example, oxalic acid contains 0.7, glucose 3.7, cellulose 4.2 and fat 9.4 megacalories of energy per 2.2 pounds (1 kg) of forage (Minson 1990). In practice, however, gross energy content of most plants is relatively constant (Jones and Wilson 1987). The amount of this energy that is available to the herbivore varies in proportion to the digestibility of the forage, and forage digestibility is largely a function of cell wall digestibility (Jones and Wilson 1987). For ruminants, the digestibility of food is virtually synonymous with digestibility of energy in the food (Robbins 1983). Equations relating digestibility of dry matter and DE content for mule deer, elk and moose are:

$$Y = -7.90 + 1.08X \text{ (Schommer 1978 for elk;}$$
$$r^2 = 0.99)$$
$$Y = -0.61 + 0.98X \text{ (Mould and Robbins 1982 for elk;}$$
$$r^2 = 0.98)$$
$$Y = -2.42 + 1.04X \text{ (Schwartz et al. 1988 for moose)}$$
$$Y = -1.48 + 1.04X \text{ (Milchunas et al. 1978 for deer;}$$
$$r^2 = 0.99)$$

where Y = percentage digestibility of gross energy and X = percentage digestibility of dry matter.

Nitrogen is another key nutritional attribute of forage often measured in nutrition studies. The forms of nitrogen ingested by ruminants include true proteins (60%–80% of total plant nitrogen), soluble nonprotein nitrogen and a small amount of lignified nitrogen that is unavailable to the animal. Ruminal microbes use plant nitrogen to synthesize their own protein (which the herbivore digests to acquire necessary amino acids to create its own protein). Nitrogen content of plants typically is reported as crude protein content. This approach involves determining total nitrogen (N) content and converting the nitrogen estimates to crude protein (CP) by the equation CP = N × 6.25 (milk protein is calculated using the factor 6.38; Haigh and Hudson 1993). This conversion factor (6.25) is based on the average nitrogen content of plant proteins and is a general approximation (Van Soest 1994).

Proportion of crude protein available to the animal is largely a function of the amounts of crude protein and nondigestible fiber-bound protein and the extent of protein precipitation by plant tannins (plant defensive compounds that can form indigestible protein/tannin complexes) (Robbins et al. 1987a). For plants that do not contain appreciable plant defensive compounds, digestible protein (DP) content is highly correlated to crude protein (CP) content and can

be estimated using the following equations from deer studies (Robbins et al. 1987a):

$$DP = -3.87 + 0.9283 \times CP \text{ (for grass and legume diets)}$$
and
$$DP = -4.27 + 0.9365 \times CP \text{ (for winter deciduous shrub diets).}$$

Calculation of digestible protein for tanniniferous forage is more complicated and discussed later in this chapter.

Growth stages, or phenology, of plants result in marked differences in nutritive value among seasons (Figure 90), and account for more variation in plant nutritive value than any other environmental or plant factor. When plants begin growth, new plant matter predominantly contains products of photosynthesis (cell solubles) and digestible structural components. As plants mature, poorly or undigestible structural components such as lignin are added, thus reducing the nutritive value of the whole plant. The proportion of stems relative to leaves increases as the plant matures. In many plant species, but not all (Van Soest 1994), increasing proportion of stems reduces the digestibility of the entire plant because cell wall content is high in stems (Minson 1990).

After plants reach maturity, the above-ground portion of

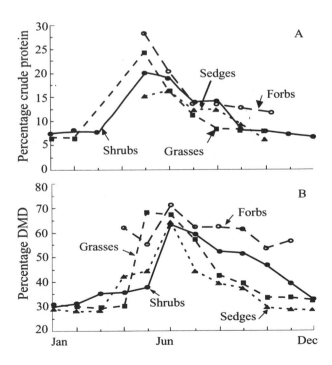

Figure 90. Seasonal levels of crude protein (CP) (*A*) and digestible dry matter (DMD) concentration (*B*) of four forage classes eaten by moose in boreal forests of Alberta (adapted from Renecker and Hudson 1988).

many plant species, including grasses and some forbs, dies. Such plants generally transport energy and nutrients to underground storage structures (roots, tubers), which reduces nutritive value of above-ground foliage. The above-ground foliage may break apart and disappear by early autumn. For herbaceous plant species that are more persistent, nutritive value typically declines gradually during late autumn and winter, mostly due to leaching. Nutritive value of shrubs generally remains constant throughout winter (Hobbs et al. 1981).

During the growing season, several environmental variables affect nutritive value of forage (Table 33). Relatively high temperature increases lignification of cell wall and enhances plant metabolic activity, which reduces the pool of cell solubles. Digestibility may decline by a half unit or more per 1.8°F (1°C) increase in temperature. Increasing sunlight enhances nutritive value by enhancing photosynthetic rate, which increases cell solubles. Increasing levels of sunlight also increase metabolism of nitrogen, which increases protein synthesis; however, this effect is inconsistent and probably small (Wilson 1994). Increasing water availability may decrease nutritive value, contrary to popular belief (Wilson 1994), because rate of plant growth and advancement to maturity and thus cell wall development is enhanced (Van Soest 1994). Conversely, drought conditions may terminate plant growth earlier than normal during the growing season, reducing nutritive value and plant production. Drought conditions also may cause death or injury to plants, an effect that may persist several years after the drought (Frank and McNaughton 1992). Finally, nutrient content of soils, which can be altered with fertilizer applications, have a variety of effects on plant nutritive value (Van Soest 1994).

The effects of weather on nutritive value can be complex and difficult to predict. On the northern shortgrass prairie in Colorado, plant nitrogen and dry matter digestibility were lower when water was added to simulate wet years,

compared with that during years of normal precipitation (Milchunas et al. 1995). Bø and Hjeljord (1991), however, reported greater nutritive value of a key moose browse after a cool, wet June than after a dry, warm June in southern Norway. Cloudy and wet conditions variably affect ruminant performance. For moose, Sæther (1985) reported heavier yearling bull weights after a cool, dry summer in a humid region of Norway, but heavier weights after wet summers in a drier region of the country. A more detailed analysis of yearling bull moose weight dynamics in northern Norway confirmed the trend toward heavier weights after a cool, dry summer (Solberg and Sæther 1994).

There are few studies that have attempted to identify weather effects on forage nutritive value on elk summer ranges in drier regions of the western United States. Elevated levels of precipitation help to maintain plant growth longer during the growing season (Sauer and Uresk 1976), probably postponing declines in nutritive value due to plant senescence. Skovlin (1967) reported lower crude protein levels in several species of grasses in late summer/early autumn during dry years, and Vavra and Phillips (1980) reported lower nutritive value of cattle diets during dry years in foothill ranges in northeastern Oregon (Figure 91). Merrill and Boyce (1991) reported significant correlations between precipitation, green plant abundance in summer and abundance of elk calves. It has long been perceived that relatively dry conditions reduce reproductive performance of large ungulates in much of the western U.S. However, the relative effects of changes in plant production versus changes in forage quality on animal performance are unclear. Data of Coe et al. (1976), regarding African ungulates, suggest the former; data of Vavra and Phillips (1980), regarding cattle in northeastern Oregon, suggest the latter is more important.

Nutritive value also varies among different classes of vegetation, such as, grasses, forbs and shrubs (see Figure 90). In general, forbs and grasses, compared with shrubs, tend to be higher in quality early in the growing season and lower in quality late in the growing season and during the dormant season (Jones and Wilson 1987). In practice, exceptions occur to these simple rules.

During winter, DE content of grasses typically is higher than that of shrub twigs. The higher lignin and cutin content of shrubs reduce the digestibility of cellulose and hemicellulose. Protein content, however, is quite low in grasses, compared with that of shrubs in winter (Hobbs et al. 1981), because grasses translocate greater portions of nutrients to roots for storage than do shrubs (Van Soest 1994). On winter range in Colorado, digestibility of grasses in elk diets varied from 40% to 50% and that of shrubs varied from 23% to 40%; crude protein was 3% to 5% in

Table 33. Influences of environmental variables on plant production (yield), constituent composition and digestibility of forage

	Temperature	Light	Water supply	Nitrogen fertilizer
Yield	+	+	+	+
Cell solubles	−	+	−	−
Cell wall	+	−	+	±
Lignin	+	−	+	+
Digestibility	−	+	−	±

Source: Adapted from Van Soest 1994.

Note: Positive association is indicated by +, negative association is indicated by − and variable association by ±.

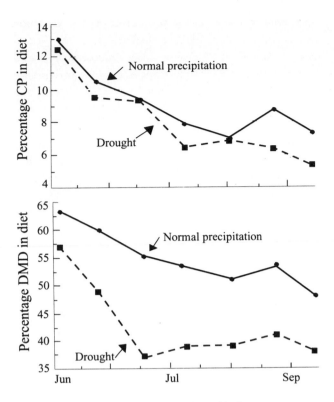

Figure 91. Crude protein (CP) and digestible dry matter (DMD) of cattle diets during summer on lower montane forest and grassland plant communities in northeastern Oregon. Data were collected during two summers with roughly normal precipitation and during a drought year with precipitation about 59% of normal (from Vavra and Phillips 1980).

grasses and 4.6% to 8.1% in shrub twigs (Hobbs et al. 1981). These protein and digestibility levels for shrubs during winter appear representative across a variety of elk studies (Geis 1954, Boll 1958, Ward 1971). Other studies have reported lower grass digestibility (25%) and protein (1.5%–2%) on elk ranges in late winter (McReynolds 1977, Bryant 1993). Higher protein in browse and higher energy in grasses suggest that dietary mixes of the two forage types may improve overall nutritional plane (Otsyina et al. 1982). Such mixes may help maintain viability of ruminal microbe populations and enhance utilization of the unlignified cellulose and hemicellulose contained in grasses (Hobbs et al. 1981).

During spring, some species of grasses and forbs initiate growth quite early, providing forage of high nutritive value. Crude protein and digestibility of such plants are as high as 20% and 70%, respectively, providing nutrient content well in excess of that required for gestation. The transition from cured, dormant vegetation to young, green vegetation tends to be gradual because abundance of new growth is initially limited; no records exist of digestive disorders due to a rapid diet change for elk at this time. Other plant

species, including shrubs, generally initiate growth later, thereby extending this lush period into late spring.

During summer and autumn, differences in nutritive value among shrubs, forbs and grasses again become apparent. Plant species that initiate growth early and species with shallow root systems reach maturity relatively early and enter dormancy. Deeper-rooted species, including shrubs and some species of forbs, may continue growth and actively photosynthesize substantially later in the season. For example, dry matter digestibility of forbs averaged 15 percentage units higher than in grasses and 5 units higher than in shrubs in early summer, but digestibility of shrubs and forbs were equivalent and about 15 percentage units higher than in grasses by late summer in a Wyoming study (Cook 1990). Crude protein levels generally followed a similar pattern in this study. Marked differences in nutritive value between shrubs and grasses late in the growing season (see Figure 90) also were reported in central Alberta (Renecker and Hudson 1988). In addition, digestibility of grasses tends to be greater than that of sedges throughout summer, due to lower cell solubles and greater cell wall concentrations in sedges (Renecker and Hudson 1988).

However, such generalizations are not always valid. For alpine tundra and subalpine forests in Colorado, Baker and Hobbs (1982) reported greater crude protein and dry matter digestibility in grasses compared with that in shrubs during summer (Table 34). Cell wall and lignin content of shrubs were relatively high, apparently accounting for lower shrub digestibility. Sedges tended to be higher in nutritive value than grass, which also was in contrast to results reported by Renecker and Hudson (1988). Causes of inconsistencies in sedge/grass/forb/shrub nutritive value differences among studies are unclear.

Certain plant species, particularly bluebunch wheatgrass, Sandberg's bluegrass, crested wheatgrass (an introduced perennial grass) and cheatgrass (a winter annual introduced from Eurasia), often reinitiate growth during autumn and remain green during winter, although growth in winter

Table 34. Percentage crude protein (CP) and dry matter digestibility (DMD) of graminoids, forbs and shrubs consumed by elk during summers of 1977 and 1978 in alpine and subalpine habitats in Colorado

	Graminoids		Forbs		Shrubs	
Date	DMD	CP	DMD	CP	DMD	CP
Early June	70	15	76	9	43	14
Early August	69	14	65	15	38	12
Mid-September	62	11	55	9	34	9

Source: Adapted from Baker and Hobbs 1982.

By late summer, digestibility of shrubs (such as these willow shoots) and forbs may average about 15% higher than the digestibility of grasses. Both elk and moose may select shrubs during this period, but there is little evidence of significant competition between the two species for forage. *Photo by Judd Cooney.*

Sedges may have a high nutritive value in some seasons, and they are frequently selected by feeding elk. *Photo by Len Clifford.*

usually is suppressed. Some agricultural crops, such as winter wheat, act similarly. Nutritive value of these plants typically is high, remains high throughout winter despite freezing temperatures and has potential to elevate nutritive value of diets substantially. For example, crude protein averaged about 20% and dry matter digestibility ranged from 60% to 85% in bluebunch wheatgrass during winter on a northeastern Oregon elk wintering area (Bryant 1993). Crude protein and digestibility of crested wheatgrass ranged from 15% to 23% and 50% to 60%, respectively, during autumn and winter in northern Utah (Urness et al. 1983).

The amount of autumn growth available to herbivores, however, is variable from year to year, undoubtedly a function of a variety of factors including precipitation, temperature regimes following growth initiation and snow accumulation. For example, autumn growth of bluebunch wheatgrass apparently fails to occur unless at least 2.4 to 3.15 inches (6–8 cm) of precipitation fall in late September and October (Bryant 1993). Also, the presence of species that initiate growth in autumn may be rare or completely absent on some winter ranges (e.g., see Hobbs et al. 1981). Finally, the amount of this autumn growth may be low and variable even during autumns when precipitation is adequate to initiate growth. Bryant (1993) reported about 18 pounds per acre (20 kg/ha) dry-matter basis of new growth of bluebunch wheatgrass, 10% of the amount of cured bluebunch bunchgrass, on elk winter range in northeastern Oregon. Elk may have to spend considerable time and effort to consume appreciable amounts of this high-quality forage.

The effect of forest overstory on forage nutritive value is of interest to elk managers, but is not clearly defined across a variety of ecological settings. Dense forest overstories greatly reduce solar radiation inputs to understory vegetation. Therefore, photosynthesis, accumulation of cell solubles and digestibility might be expected to be lower under forest overstories (Van Soest 1994). Soil moisture dynamics under forests probably differ to some extent as well, in part because snow melt during spring is delayed under forest overstories. Krueger and Bedunah (1988) reported that forest cover delayed plant phenology 2 to 3 weeks in a Montana study. Late summer declines in forage quality probably are delayed as well.

Findings of Hanley et al. (1987), Van Horne et al. (1988) and Happe et al. (1990) apparently have established several trends regarding clear-cutting effects on nutritive value in the very wet, coastal regions in western North America. Higher solar radiation in clearcuts apparently increased cell solubles by increased photosynthesis (Tables 35 and 36). But this effect was counteracted by increased concentrations of tannins, which inhibit digestibility of forage. Results from these studies suggest that DE concentrations are little affected by clear-cutting, but protein, particularly digestible protein, may be reduced significantly (Hanley et al. 1987, Van Horne et al. 1988).

However, results of other studies indicate that patterns from the coastal studies may not be universal. In Texas, Blair et al. (1983) reported significantly higher dry matter

Table 36. Percentage dry matter digestibility (DMD), nonstructural carbohydrates (NSC) and crude protein (CP) of a shrub and three forb species in clearcut (CUT) and hemlock/spruce forests (FOR) during summer in southeastern Alaska

Species	Treatment[a]	NSC	DMD	CP[b]
Bunchberry dogwood	CUT	10.4	63.2	14.4
	FOR	5.4	62.4	16.3
Skunk cabbage	CUT	15.1	74.6	26.3
	FOR	12.6	75.5	32.5
Trailing bramble	CUT	9.0	57.4	12.5
	FOR	6.3	55.9	16.3
Alaska blueberry	CUT	18.7	52.8	17.5
	FOR	11.5	53.8	23.1

Source: Modified from Van Horne et al. 1988.

[a] Nutritive value estimates for clearcuts were the average of 5- and 11-year-old cuts; estimates for forested sites were the average of 80-year-old and old-growth stands.

[b] Van Horne et al. (1988) presented percentage nitrogen (N) rather than percentage CP; I converted N to CP using the equation CP = N × 6.25 to enhance comparability among studies.

digestibility in several deer forages grown in full and moderate sunlight than in plants grown in complete shade. As in the coastal studies, crude protein was higher in shade. Regelin et al. (1974) found no statistically significant difference in digestibility or crude protein content in deer forage collected in clearcuts and unharvested lodgepole pine/spruce/subalpine fir forests in Colorado, although weak trends suggested higher nutritive value of plants in forests by late summer (Table 37).

Biologists' understanding of timber harvest effects on nutritive value appears incomplete because relationships between forest cover and forage nutritive value may vary considerably across regions occupied by elk. For example,

Table 35. Percentage cell wall content, dry matter digestibility (DMD) and crude protein (CP) of leaves of four forages in elk and deer diets in clearcut (CUT) and old-growth (ODG) forests

Species	Treatment[a]	Cell wall		DMD		CP	
		Summer	Autumn	Summer	Autumn	Summer	Autumn
Vine maple	CUT	23.9	35.8	41.4	38.0	9.2[a]	6.1
	ODG	32.2	40.8	45.0	40.6	11.3[b]	3.8
Salmonberry	CUT	30.4	34.2	35.4[a]	31.2[a]	9.5[a]	8.9
	ODG	37.7	42.0	30.3[b]	36.0[b]	14.7[b]	10.5
Huckleberry	CUT	25.5	26.9	47.9[a]	44.2	10.4	7.2
	ODG	35.6	34.7	37.8[b]	47.7	14.3	10.4
Swordfern	CUT	58.9[a]	59.6[a]	21.5[a]	24.6[a]	6.7[a]	6.9
	ODG	65.4[b]	66.7[b]	16.4[b]	17.6[b]	8.2[b]	8.2

Source: Adapted from Happe et al. 1990.

Note: Data were collected at Olympic National Park in western Washington State.

[a] Within columns and plant species, different lower-case letters indicate significantly different nutritive levels.

Table 37. Percentage dry matter digestibility (DMD) and crude protein (CP) of shrubs and forbs in deer diets during summer in clearcuts (CUT) and unharvested lodgepole pine, spruce and subalpine forests (FOR) in Colorado

| | DMD | | | | CP | | | |
| | Forbs | | Shrubs | | Forbs | | Shrubs | |
Date	CUT	FOR	CUT	FOR	CUT	FOR	CUT	FOR
July 6	63.3	63.1	48.9	46.1	19.2	19.4	18.1	19.9
August 13	66.9	69.4	50.5	49.0	12.3	14.3	12.4	13.5
September 20	64.5	69.2	50.0	50.1	7.7	8.3	9.4	10.5

Source: Adapted from Regelin et al. 1974.

Note: No statistically significant effects of logging treatment on dietary quality were reported.

plant defense compounds may be less likely to accumulate if light, soil nutrients and water are abundant compared with conditions where light is abundant but nutrients are not (Shure and Wilson 1993). Moreover, the coastal studies of Hanley et al. (1987), Van Horne et al. (1988) and Happe et al. (1990) were conducted using plants that contained tannins; plant nutritive value responses to shading might differ in plants lacking these compounds. In some areas of the western U.S., nontanniferous forage may predominate in large ungulates diets (e.g., Irwin et al. 1993). Finally, different silvicultural harvesting strategies have potential to affect forage nutritive value, including tannin content, perhaps providing options for increasing forage production without increasing tannin content (Shure and Wilson 1993).

Plant Toxins and Digestive Inhibitors

Plants have evolved a fantastic variety of defensive strategies, mostly at the chemical level, that discourage plant consumption by herbivores. More than 12,000 compounds have been identified in the plant kingdom that can interfere with digestion, growth, reproduction, and neurological and tissue function (Robbins 1983). Groups of these compounds germane to the nutritional ecology of wild ruminants are summarized in Table 38.

Several plant defenses such as lignin, cutin, suberin and silica have important functions for the plant. Lignin provides support and rigidity to cell walls of higher plants. Its chemical composition differs among types of plant to the point that a concise and universal definition has eluded scientists (see Van Soest 1994). Lignin is resistant to normal enzymatic and acid digestion in the stomach and small intestine and microbial fermentation in the alimentary tract. As a result, lignin is a primary factor limiting cell wall digestion. Cutin and suberin are important for healing plant

injuries, reducing water loss and limiting plant diseases. Although quantitatively insignificant in grasses, they are mostly indigestible and block digestion of some cell wall components in shrubs. Silica is deposited in hairs on the plant surface and cuticle edges and may complement lignin to strengthen cell walls primarily in grasses, sedges and horsetail. Silica also reduces cell wall digestibility (Robbins 1983, Van Soest 1994). When silica in forage is high and water intake is low, siliceous urinary calculi (kidney stones) may form and block urinary excretion. Although urinary calculi are an occasional problem for livestock operators, implications for elk are unknown.

A wide variety of other inhibiting compounds are loosely referred to as secondary compounds because they generally have little metabolic value to the plant and were viewed as by-products of plant metabolic systems (Robbins 1983). Terpenoids are one of the largest classes of secondary compounds and include the volatile, aromatic oils of sagebrush, conifers and other evergreens. These terpenoids have antimicrobial properties, particularly to bacteria that ferment cellulose. For example, Striby et al. (1987) reported that removal of monoterpenes from sagebrush increased its in vitro digestibility 12 percentage units. Hobbs et al. (1986) found that including sagebrush with grass significantly reduced digestion of grass cell wall. The extent to which terpenoids affect digestion of food is debated, how-

Table 38. Defensive compounds in forage plants

Compound	Plants	Effect
Phenylpropanoids		
Lignin	All higher plants	Limits digestibility of cell wall
Proanthocyanidins (condensed tannins)	Many broad-leaved plants	Limits carbohydrate and protein digestion
Isoflavones	Legumes	Estrogenic; antifungal
Gallate esters		
Hydrolyzable tannins	Many broad-leaved plants	Toxic; limit protein digestion?
Terpenoids		
Terpenes	Conifers	Toxic?
	Sagebrush	Toxic (adaptable)
Saponins	Legumes, etc.	Toxic; bloat?
Waxes and wax polymers		
Cutin	Many broad-leaved plants	Reduces cell wall digestion
Suberin	Many broad-leaved plants	Reduces cell wall digestion
Biogenic silica	Grasses, sedges and lower plants	Limits digestion; sharp edges (lowers intake)

Source: Adapted from Van Soest 1994.

ever, because the rumination process releases much of the aromatic terpenoids (Cluff et al. 1982). Many of the studies showing terpenoid effects on forage digestibility did not account for the volatilization of these compounds. Terpenoids also can be toxic, although the adapted ruminant can detoxify small quantities of these compounds.

Alkaloids encompass a wide class of nitrogen-containing secondary compounds including nicotine, caffeine and morphine. These can induce pharmacological effects and inhibit digestion. Alkaloids are present in several species of pasture grasses and may cause problems for livestock operators (Van Soest 1994). Alkaloids comprise the toxic agent in several species of larkspur, lupine and groundsel and occur in hound's-tongue, false hellebore and poison hemlock—plants that can be common in western mountain ranges. A wide variety of toxic effects has been reported in free-ranging livestock, including deformaties in juveniles and death in adults (Manners et al. 1992, Molyneux and Ralphs 1992, Panter et al. 1992). Practical implications to large ungulates are generally unknown, but are unlikely to be of major importance in most situations.

Alkaloids also comprise the toxic agent in true locoweeds, of which there are 13 species in North America (Wolfe and Lance 1984). Locoweed poisoning resulting in death has been reported for elk in northern New Mexico and south-central Colorado (Wolfe and Lance 1984). Wolfe and Lance concluded that locoweed poisoning likely was a function of low precipitation and poor range condition, and probably is not an important mortality factor of elk on most ranges.

Glucosides include a variety of compounds in higher plants that have little effect on ruminal microbes, but are toxic to herbivores (Van Soest 1994). Majak (1992) identified two types that occur in relatively common western plants: miserotoxin, an aliphatic nitrotoxin present in many milkvetch species, and prunasin, a cyanogenic glucoside found in Saskatoon serviceberry, chokecherry and many other species in the Rosaceae plant family. Cyanogenic glucosides also have been reported in skunk cabbage, an important deer forage in southeast Alaska (Van Horne et al. 1988). Enzymatic degradation of these compounds may result in toxic by-products (aglycone and hydrocyanic acid) that can be absorbed into the blood of the animal. These by-products, particularly aglycone, can be detoxified by microbes, but hydrocyanic acid is readily absorbed (Majak 1992). Practical implications relative to wild elk are unknown, but serious problems are unlikely.

Soluble phenolics include flavonoids, isoflavonoids, and hydrolyzable and condensed tannins. Soluble phenolics inhibit digestion and can be toxic (Robbins 1983, Van Soest 1994). The two groups of tannins generally have different chemical properties and functional activity (Hagerman et al. 1992).

During the past 15 years, tannins have received considerable attention in large ungulate research, due to their widespread occurrence and pronounced effects on digestion. Tannins are present in about 17% of herbaceous annuals, 14% of herbaceous perennials, 79% of deciduous woody perennials and 87% of evergreen woody perennials (Rhoades and Cates 1976). Tannins are found in many plants commonly eaten by elk or at least common on elk ranges (Table 39). Plants that lack tannins include the foliage of many pastoral crops, foliage of grasses and sedges, all plants in the Asteraceae family (e.g., sagebrush, asters, thistles and many others), fungi, algae, mosses and liverworts. In addition, tannin content of twigs of many deciduous shrub species is low and probably biologically inconsequential during winter, even in shrubs that have high foliar tannin content during summer (Robbins et al. 1987a).

Several key studies have been conducted to assess the effects of tannins on digestion in mule and white-tailed deer. Tannins significantly reduced the digestibility of crude protein in a wide variety of forages fed to deer (Robbins et al. 1987a). They had minimal effect on cell wall digestibility, but significantly reduced digestibility of cell solubles (Robbins et al. 1987b). Total DE, therefore, was reduced by tannins, particularly in young, nutritious foliage. Digestibility of cell wall also was shown to be unaffected by tannins in elk (Mould and Robbins 1982).

Wild ruminants have evolved strategies to reduce the effects of tannins. For example, certain salivary proteins (proline proteins) chemically bind with tannins primarily in the mouth and can render tannins inert in the alimentary tract. When ruminants consume diets high in tannins, production of these proline compounds may increase due to increasing size and output of salivary glands. These compounds, absent in the saliva of cattle and sheep, are important in North American deer, yet unstudied but probably important for elk (Robbins et al. 1987a). This absence of proline compounds probably explains why tannins appear to reduce cell wall digestibility in livestock but not in deer (Robbins et al. 1987b).

In addition, ruminal microbes adapt to and degrade tannins. Several groups of bacteria produce tannases capable of breaking down hydrolyzable tannnins (Deschamps 1989), including the bacteria *Streptococcus caprinus* in goats (Nelson et al. 1995). Seven anaerobic, tannin-tolerant bacteria have been isolated from rumen fluid of elk. These bacteria grew in the presence of relatively high levels (8 g of quebracho and 3 g/L of tannic acid per liter of rumen fluid) of hydrolyzable and condensed tannins (Woolston 1995). Appropriate habituation of ruminal microbes might reduce effects of tannins on digestion of nutrients and perhaps reduce tannin toxicity.

Table 39. Presence of tannins in forages used by big game in western North America

Plant family and species[a]	Season or month	Astringency or content[b]	Location	Sources
Aceraceae				
Vine maple (S)	Summer	0.7[f]	W WA	3
	Autumn	0.6[f]	W WA	3
	Winter	0.0[f]	W WA	3
	Spring	1.2[f]	W WA	3
Maple (S) sp. uncertain		0.12[e]		8
Araceae				
Skunk cabbage (F)	May, July	4.0[c]	SE AK	1
	October	2.5[c]	SE AK	1
Asteraceae				
Big sagebrush (S)	July	0.0[d]	S WY	4
Fringed sagewort (S)	July	0.0[d]	S WY	4
Green rabbitbrush (S)	July	0.0[d]	S WY	4
Hawksbeard (F)	July	0.0[d]	S WY	4
Hairy goldaster (F)	July	0.0[d]	S WY	4
Groundsel (F)	July	0.0[d]	S WY	4
Rose pussytoes (F)	July	0.0[d]	S WY	4
Western yarrow (F)	July	0.0[d]	S WY	4
Betulaceae				
Red alder (S)	Summer	0.46[e]	SE WA?	6
Caprifoliaceae				
Red elder (S)	Summer	0.08[e]	SE AK	5
Cornaceae				
Bunchberry dogwood (F)	May, July	7.2[c]	SE AK	1, 2
	October	5.5[c]	SE AK	1, 2
Red-osier dogwood (S)	Summer	0.49[e]	SE WA?	6
Cruciferae				
Tansy mustard (F)	July	0.0[d]	S WY	4
Ericaceae				
Alaska blueberry (S)	May, July	1.9[c]	SE AK	1, 2
	October	3.5[c]	SE AK	1, 2
	Summer	0.10[e]	SE AK	5
	Winter	0.10[e]	SE AK	5
Red huckleberry (S)	Summer	0.1[f]	W WA	3
	Autumn	0.2[f]	W WA	3
	Winter	T[f]	W WA	3
	Spring	T[f]	W WA	3
Fabaceae				
Alfalfa (F)	Summer	0.0[e]	SE WA?	6
Lotus (F)		+		7
Lucerne (F)		0		7
Red clover (F)	Summer	0.0[e]	SE WA?	6
Sainfoin (F)		+		7
White clover (F)		0		7
White clover flowers (F)		+		7
Fagaceae				
Gambel oak (S) (juvenile)	Summer	0.23[e]	N UT	9
Gamble oak (S) (mature)	Summer	0.18[e]	N UT	9
Grossulariaceae				
Wax current (S)	July	0.022–0.095[d]	S WY	4
Hydrophyllaceae				
Silverleaf phacelia (F)	July	0.0[d]	S WY	4
Onagraceae				
Fireweed (F)	Summer	0.32[e]	SE AK	5
Fireweed flowers (F)	Summer	0.64[e]	SE WA?	6

Table 39 continued

Plant family and species[a]	Season or month	Astringency or content[b]	Location	Sources
Pinaceae				
Western hemlock (T)	July	4.1[c]	SE AK	1
	October	7.1[c]	SE AK	1
Polygonaceae				
Sulfur buckwheat (F)	July	0.009–0.058[d]	S WY	4
Rosaceae				
Antelope bitterbrush (S)	July	0.009–0.058[d]	S WY	4
Bigflower cinquefoil (F)	July	0.022–0.095[d]	S WY	4
Trailing bramble (F)	May, July	4.1[c]	SE AK	1
	October	3.1[c]	SE AK	1
Salmonberry (S)	Summer	1.0[f]	W WA	3
	Autumn	1.0[f]	W WA	3
	Winter	0.1[f]	W WA	3
	Spring	1.4[f]	W WA	3
	Summer	0.30[e]	SE AK	5
Saskatoon serviceberry (S)	July	T–0.014[d]	S WY	4
True mountain mahogany (S)	July	T[d]	S WY	4
Polypodiacaea				
Swordfern (F)	Summer	0.5[f]	W WA	3
	Autumn	0.5[f]	W WA	3
	Winter	0.5[f]	W WA	3
	Spring	1.6[f]	W WA	3
Salicaceae				
Sitka willow (S)	Summer	0.18[e]	SE AK	5
Willow (mixed spp.) (S)	Summer	0.23[e]	SE AK	5
Scrophulariaceae				
Green penstemon (F)	July	0.0[d]	S WY	4

Sources: 1. Van Horne et al. 1988; 2. Hanley et al. 1987; 3. Happe et al. 1990; 4. Cook 1990; 5. Hanley et al. 1992; 6. Robbins et al. 1987b; 7. Barry and Blaney 1987; 8. Robbins et al. 1987a; 9. Dick and Urness 1991.

[a] S = shrubs; F = forbs; T = trees.

[b] Either astringency (level of protein precipitation) or content of tannins presented as per cited study. Plant species for which only presence or absence was presented in source: 0 indicates no tannins present; + indicates tannins present; T indicates trace levels. A variety of different methods were used for tannin analyses; thus, direct comparison of tannin levels generally is not possible among studies. Identification of units and methods to determine astringency or tannin content is provided by footnotes c through f.

[c] Milligrams of tannic acid equivalents per gram forage: astringency determined using BSA (bovine serum albumin) technique modified from Martin and Martin (1982) and converted to tannic acid equivalents.

[d] Milligrams of tannin per gram forage; tannin content determined using radial diffusion assay of Hagerman (1987), which provides estimates of protein-complexing tannin content; ranges in content result from uncertainty about relative amounts of hydrolyzable versus condensed tannins; the lower value assumes 100% hydrolyzable tannin, and the greater value assumes 100% condensed tannin.

[e] Milligrams of precipitated BSA per milligram forage; astringency determined using BSA technique of Robbins et al. (1987a).

[f] Units not given; probably milligram tannic acid equivalents per gram forage; astringency determined using the dye-labeled protein method of Asquith and Butler (1985).

Toxic phenolics that are absorbed can be detoxified and excreted in the urine. Rate of ingestion and absorption of toxic phenolics must be balanced by detoxification rate to avoid poisoning. Thus, animals may limit intake of tanniferous forage—a response reported by Robbins et al. (1987a) in mule and white-tailed deer. There is evidence that deer at least have some capability to increase tolerance to toxic tannins and other soluble phenolics over several weeks of adaptation (McArthur et al. 1993).

Results of two studies by Robbins et al. (1987a, 1987b) cast some doubt regarding the validity of conclusions from earlier forage studies in which nutritive value of tanniferous plants were evaluated. Standard crude protein assays, in vitro determinations of dry matter digestion and digestibility estimated from sequential detergent analyses may provide misleading assessments of nutritive value of tanniniferous forage, particularly during late spring through early autumn. Both studies presented new protocols to determine nutritive value more adequately using in vitro techniques. These protocols were validated in subsequent work with black-tailed deer (Hanley et al. 1992).

Foraging Strategies

Not all ruminant species are equal in their ability to acquire and digest different types of food. This observation has led to development of several descriptive categories of foraging characteristics that reflect anatomical and digestive attributes of ruminant herbivores. These morphophysiological feeding types include concentrate selectors or browsers, intermediate feeders or mixed feeders and roughage feeders or grazers (Hofmann 1988).

Concentrate selectors typically have narrow muzzles that aid in selecting the most nutritious parts of plants rich in easily digested cell solubles. They also have a relatively poor capacity to digest cell wall. North American examples include mule, white-tailed and black-tailed deer (although mule deer also have been regarded as intermediate feeders [see Hobbs et al. 1983]). Roughage feeders, which include cattle and bison, have an enhanced capacity for digesting cell wall and large muzzles efficient for consuming large volumes of food rapidly. Intermediate feeders show adaptations to one or the other extreme. They tend to be highly flexible in their choice of food, and their digestive efficiency of cell wall tends to be intermediate between concentrate and roughage feeders (Hofmann 1988). However, this classification system has been criticized; many of the characteristics attributed to the various categories may simply be a function of body size (Robbins et al. 1995).

Elk and red deer are classified as intermediate feeders. Compared with mule or white-tailed deer, elk tend to digest cell wall more efficiently (especially if lignin content is relatively low), digest cell solubles slightly less effectively and retain food particles in their rumen longer (Mould and Robbins 1982, Baker and Hansen 1985, Baker and Hobbs 1987). Longer retention time of food in the elk rumen probably accounts for greater cell wall digestion. Lower metabolic rates of elk, due to larger body size, lessen to some extent the need for highly digestible food (Baker and Hobbs 1987). Such differences may contribute to the perception that elk are digestively more like cattle than deer. But many of these digestive differences between deer and elk appear to be quite small (Mould and Robbins 1982), and research that might explicitly establish greater similarity between elk and cattle is lacking.

There also may be differences between deer and elk in response to declining nutritive quality of forage. Baker and Hobbs (1987) reported that mule deer have a greater capacity than elk for increasing ruminal food volume and forage intake rates to compensate for declining forage quality (Figure 92). Other evidence indicates that the ability to increase intake to compensate for declining forage quality, even in deer, is weak. In fact, just the opposite pattern probably is more common (Figure 93) (Minson and Wilson 1994). Passage of large amounts of slowly digested, large particles into the omasum apparently risks impaction of digesta in the rumen, ultimately placing limits on increasing forage intake rates as nutritive value declines (Spalinger et al. 1993).

Being a large-bodied intermediate feeder, elk would be expected to have a greater tendency than deer to consume more grasses than forbs or shrubs (Baker and Hobbs 1987). Food habits data from elk and several species of deer generally support this prediction during most seasons of the year across a variety of vegetative biomes (Collins and Urness 1983, Leslie et al. 1984, Leslie et al. 1987, Jenkins and Wright 1988, Ngugi et al. 1992). Such differences between elk and deer diets can be pronounced (Ngugi et al. 1992) or negligible (Mower and Smith 1989). On the other hand, elk diets show considerable plasticity even within a seasonal range (Merrill 1994), and forbs and shrubs often constitute very high proportions (80%–90%) of diets (Irwin and Peek 1983, Leslie et al. 1984, Edge et al. 1988). Elk diets are largely a function of differences in forage availability, particularly in winter (Jenkins and Wright 1988), and relative nutritive value in other seasons (Figure 94) (Merrill 1994). Thus, the contention that elk are primarily grass grazers often is not a valid generalization.

Maximizing net intake of energy and nutrients, or specific combinations, appears to be a basic foraging goal of herbivores such as elk (Hanley et al. 1989). Net intake of ME in particular is simply the difference between energy provided by forage consumed and energy expended while foraging. The amount consumed is a function of nutritive value, amount of time required to acquire and digest the food and the abundance of food across the landscape. The amount of energy expended relates to the amount of time and distance traveled while searching for food and the amount of time chewing food, both of which can result in substantial energy expenditures. Herbivores may vary their diets to some extent to obtain a suitable mix of nutrients and to avoid overconsumption of toxic plant chemicals. It is generally advantageous for elk to minimize time spent foraging, to reduce susceptibility to predators and hunters and reduce exposure to adverse weather.

It has long been known that herbivores tend to select forages of high nutritive value. Recent information on effects of tannins and other toxic or digestion-inhibiting compounds make clear that selection of food presents the herbivore with complex decisions. McArthur et al. (1993) reported that deer may select plants as a trade-off between the benefit derived from digestible dry matter and the cost of nontannin phenolics that presumably induce toxicity when absorbed. Tannins influenced diet choice only as one of the factors reducing digestible dry matter.

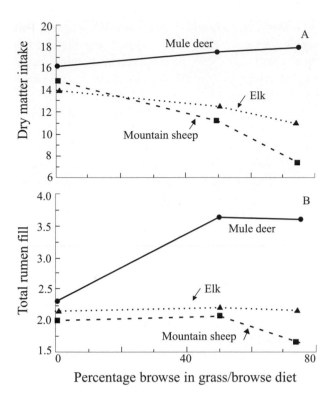

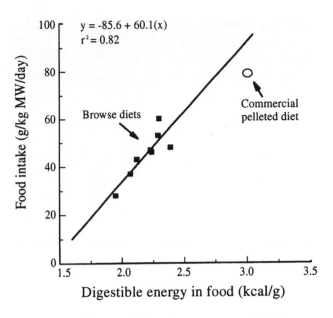

Figure 93. Influences of digestible energy on total daily intake of food (expressed on a metabolic weight [MW] basis) of white-tailed deer (adapted from Gray and Servello 1995). The data values representing the pelleted diet were not used to calculate the regression equation.

Figure 92. Influence of browse on dry matter intake (grams of food per kilogram of body weight per day) (*A*) and total rumen fill (percentage of body weight) (*B*) (adapted from Baker and Hobbs 1987). Results indicate that total food intake of elk and mountain sheep declines as lignin content (due to increasing browse) in diets increases. Mule deer seemed capable of maintaining intake as lignin intake increases, by increasing amount of food held in the rumen.

sizes may be preferred, particularly by a large herbivore such as elk (Riggs et al. 1996).

During bouts of feeding, an elk circulates through its home range making decisions about where and what it eats. Vegetation assemblages typically are distributed heterogeneously across landscapes, due to effects of soil type, land management, topography, soil moisture, forest overstory canopy cover and snow. Elk generally would be expected to select those patches that would allow them to consume nutrients at a relatively high rate (Langvatn and Hanley 1993) and remain in a patch until nutrient intake

Mechanisms used by ruminants to decide if a food is good or bad is not completely clear. Ruminants apparently have minimal ability to assess nutritional value and toxicity of plants never before consumed based on smell and taste (Provenza 1995). The primary mechanism guiding diet selection may involve postingestive feedback systems. Herbivores apparently quickly establish a link between foods responsible for discomfort or malaise and avoid overeating them. Conversely, foods that are nutritious and nontoxic contribute to a feeling of satiety, and animals acquire preference for them (Provenza 1995). Learning plays a role in the food selection process, starting with lessons of food selection from the mother early in life (Provenza 1995). Herbivores also tend to remember locations of patches with abundant, suitable food (Gillingham and Bunnell 1989).

The amount of time required to bite, chew and swallow food also may be an important factor affecting food choices. The amount of food an animal may obtain per bite can vary considerably in elk (e.g., 0.002–0.11 ounces [0.05–3 g] of dry matter per bite). Plant species providing large bite

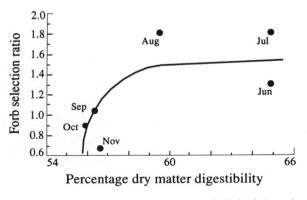

Figure 94. Relationship of selection ratios of elk for forbs and digestible dry matter of forbs (adapted from Merrill 1994). The selection ratios are a measure of preference—values greater than 1.0 suggest preference, and values less than 1.0 suggest avoidance.

An intermediate or mixed feeder, the elk is less selective in its diet than are browsers (such as deer), but more selective than grazers (such as bison). *Top left photo by Randy Flament. Top right photo by James Shuey. Bottom left photo by Jack Ballard. Bottom right photo by Conrad Rowe.*

rates begin to decline (Jiang and Hudson 1993), because movement among patches increases energy expenditure. Theoretically, therefore, elk should allocate time within patches and time traveling between patches so as to enhance energy balance, that is, maximize energy intake and minimize energy expenditure (Jiang and Hudson 1993). Studies of elk during summer in Idaho and Montana suggest that elk select sites with relatively abundant succulent forbs and shrubs, particularly in late summer (Irwin and Peek 1983, Edge et al. 1988).

Intake rates of elk within a patch are largely a function of the abundance of plants that elk will consume, bite size, cropping rate, amount of time required to bite the plant and prepare the food for swallowing ("handling" time), fiber content and the extent of physical obstructions, such as woody material associated with forage (Gross et al. 1993). Particularly if intake is calculated during the course of the entire day, rumination time to break down cell wall can be a factor affecting intake; it often is considered to be a component of handling time (Spalinger et al. 1986). Cropping rate generally increases when bite size declines (Gross et al. 1993) and, in some habitats, elk may be able to in-

crease cropping rate sufficiently to maintain intake rates despite declining bite size (Wickstrom et al. 1984).

Field studies with elk have shown that intake rate within patches is nonlinearly correlated to forage abundance (Figure 95), and that the specific relationship varies across seasons and vegetative types (Hudson and Watkins 1986). Greater intake rates have been reported for elk on cured pastures than on lush green pastures, apparently due to greater water content of lush vegetation and a greater tendency of less fibrous feeds to break at the point clipped by incisors rather than at ground level (Hudson and Watkins 1986). Several studies have indicated that elk typically can consume as much as 0.7 ounces (20 g) per minute on a dry matter basis if forage is abundant (Collins and Urness 1983, Wickstrom et al. 1984, Hudson and Watkins 1986). Intake rates may range as low as 10% to 20% of this level in some vegetative communities, such as dense coniferous forests (Collins and Urness 1983).

Abundance of acceptable forage also is related nonlinearly to rate of travel as animals are feeding (Figure 96) (Wickstrom et al. 1984). Rapid travel will increase energy expenditures that can reduce foraging efficiency. Relatively

Elk, reportedly, have greater intake rates on cured pastures than on lush grasslands because the lush vegetation has greater water content and because less fibrous plants tend to break where clipped by incisors, rather than at ground level. *Left photo courtesy of the Oregon Department of Fish and Wildlife. Right photo courtesy of the Wyoming Game and Fish Department.*

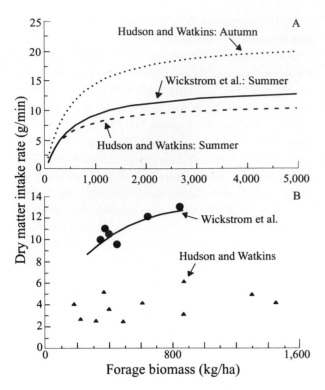

the greatest forage abundance. This is because there can be an inverse relationship between abundance of forage and its DE content in many ecological settings (Hobbs and Swift 1985). Wilmshurst et al. (1995) concluded that, in grassland habitats of Alberta, elk maximized energy intake in patches with intermediate levels of plant abundance and intermediate forage quality (Figure 97).

The rather strong relationships between forage biomass and intake rates (Wickstrom et al. 1984, Hudson and Watkins 1986) appear most applicable to simple grass-dominated plant communities (see Figure 95A). Spalinger and Hobbs (1992) pointed out that these relationships are weaker when forbs and shrubs predominate in diets. When animals feed on discrete leaves, which often is the case when grazing forbs or shrubs, the physical dimensions or weight of the leaf may regulate bite size. Intake, therefore, is determined largely by cropping rate under these conditions and may remain rather constant until leaf biomass declines to low levels (Spalinger and Hobbs 1992). This may account for the poor relationship between intake rate and biomass in forested communities, as noted by Hudson and Watkins (1986) (see Figure 95B).

Daily intake of food plays a key role in determining the nutritional status of herbivores over a seasonal period (Minson and Wilson 1994). Amount of time spent foraging each

Figure 95. Relationship between forage biomass and instantaneous dry matter intake rates of elk in grassland (*A*) and mixed forest communities (shrubs, forbs and grasses) (*B*) (adapted from Wickstrom et al. 1984, Hudson and Watkins 1986). In mixed forest communities, Wickstrom et al. found a significant relationship between forage biomass and intake rates, whereas Hudson and Watkins did not.

rapid rates of travel also may indicate that the habitat is relatively unsuitable and its foraging value to the grazing animal is relatively low.

Although increasing abundance of forage relates to increasing intake rates of forage, elk may not always be able to maximize intake rates of DE by grazing in patches with

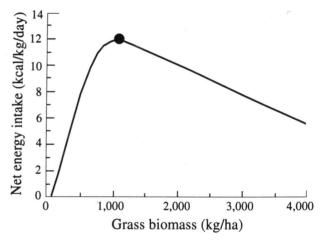

Figure 97. Predicted net energy intake of elk in relation to grass biomass. Because digestible energy content of forage can decline as forage abundance and density increase, herbivores such as elk might choose to graze in vegetative patches with moderate levels of forage biomass. For this graph, elk would "optimize" diets in plant communities of 1,100 kg/ha (adapted from Wilmshurst et al. 1995). Such relations probably vary considerably among ecological settings, however. For example, in many areas, native plant communities used by elk produce far less than 1,000 kg of forage per hectare; the relationship in this graph (developed for planted pastures), therefore, may not be apply for such areas.

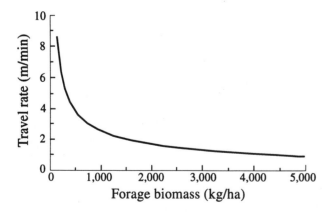

Figure 96. Effect of forage biomass abundance and travel rate of grazing elk in grassland and forest plant communities (from Wickstrom et al. 1984).

day is limited by rumination time (up to 10–12 h/day), predator surveillance, nursing and caring for offspring during summer and fatigue (9–13 h/day seems to be the upper limit on daily foraging time of elk [Hudson and Nietfeld 1985]) (Wickstrom et al. 1984). Such constraints may preclude elk from feeding in areas of low forage abundance. For example, a lactating cow elk during mid-summer will consume nearly 18 pounds (8.2 kg) of good quality forage a day (Robbins et al. 1981). At an intake rate of 0.35 ounces (10 g) per minute, a moderately high average for elk summer range (Collins and Urness 1983, Wickstrom et al. 1984, Hudson and Watkins 1986), the cow would have to eat 13 to 14 hours per day. Abundance of forage in many summer range habitats apparently support intake rates considerably lower than 0.35 ounces (10 g) per minute (Collins and Urness 1983, Hudson and Watkins 1986). Apparently, elk cannot afford to spend much time foraging in habitats with low forage abundance.

Food Habits

Knowledge and understanding of large ungulate food habits can be important to interpret animal behavior and ecology. It is useful in the management of large ungulates to evaluate habitat preference, potential for interspecific competition, habitat management planning and management practices. A wealth of information has been developed on elk food habits and is summarized here.

The food habits summaries presented below build on those of Kufeld (1973). Kufeld's techniques for listing and evaluating food preferences are followed. The main difference between this review and that of Kufeld is the additional information now available for Rocky Mountain elk and inclusion of food habits data for Roosevelt and Tule elk.

Several conditions had to be met before a reference was included in the summaries: (1) diet had to be listed by plant species and in a manner that would allow estimation of its content in the diet; (2) season of use had to be indicated; (3) plant species preference had to be for elk only; and (4) sample sizes needed to be large enough so the findings were reliable.

Kufeld (1973:106) explained some of the problems involved in summarizing food habits, including differences in methods of data collection and presentation that create difficulties comparing relative preference among various studies: "In every study, however, some plants were consumed more extensively than others," providing some means to categorize plants according to whether they were used lightly, moderately or heavily in relation to other species consumed in the study. Measures of relative plant preference such as amount consumed and amount available to elk were considered in assigning plants to use categories.

Plants comprising less than 1% of elk diets were excluded from this review. Kufeld's (1973:106) terminology regarding value of the plant to elk was used: "*Highly valuable plant*—one avidly sought by elk and which made up a major part of the diet, or which was consumed far in excess of its vegetative composition. These had an average ranking of 2.25 to 3.00. *Valuable plant*—one sought and readily eaten but to a lesser extent than highly valuable plants. Such plants made up a moderate part of the diet in food habits studies where encountered. Valuable plants had an average ranking of 1.50 to 2.24. *Least valuable plant*—one eaten by elk but which usually made up a minor part of the diet in studies where encountered, or which was consumed in a much smaller proportion than it occurred on the range. Least valuable plants had an average ranking of 1.00 to 1.49."

Even a low value of 1.00 indicates that elk made some use of a particular species and may suggest greater preference for that species than for those not mentioned at all. The numerical value does not reflect nutrient quality, but does suggest relative palatability or quantity consumed.

Elk food habits were divided into four seasons of use— winter (December through February), spring (March through May), summer (June through August) and autumn (September through November).

Food habits of Rocky Mountain elk are extremely variable (Tables 40–42) because the subspecies occurs in many different vegetative types in the United States and Canada (Table 43). Forage preferences vary among ranges, seasons and years, and appear strongly related to forage availability and phenology.

The winter diet is influenced by forage availability, mainly as affected by snow conditions. Elk move to ranges where snow depth is reduced, and exist there on whatever forage is accessible. On predominantly grass ranges in Montana, elk primarily eat grass. The other extreme is the winter shrub ranges in northern Idaho, where the majority of the diet is woody plants. Increasing snow depth typically alters choice of food: use of low-growing herbs and shrubs declines when snow depth increases, whereas the use of tall shrubs, conifers and often arboreal lichens increases as snow depth increases (Claar 1973, Hash 1973, Singer 1975).

In spring, elk typically direct most grazing to species that begin growth early, usually grasses, and then increase their consumption of forbs or shrubs during the summer. By autumn, dried grass and grass regrowth (if available) and shrubs may become prominent in elk diets.

Diets of Roosevelt elk also vary considerably among locations and seasons according to forage availability and palatability (Table 43). In northern California, grasses typically make up more than half the diet during all seasons, but are especially important during winter, when they con-

Table 40. Relative seasonal values of forbs, ferns and lichens eaten by Rocky Mountain elk

Plant	Winter Rank[a]	Value[b]	Number of references[c]	Spring Rank[a]	Value[b]	Number of references[c]	Summer Rank[a]	Value[b]	Number of references[c]	Autumn Rank[a]	Value[b]	Number of references[c]	References[d]
Fringed sagewort	2.00	+	1	2.00	+	1							43
Prairie sage	3.00	++	1	2.00	+	1	2.00	+	1	3.00	++	1	43
Northwestern mariposa							1.00	−	1				44
Common pipsissewa										1.00	−	1	4
Thistle	1.00	−	2	1.00	−	3				2.00	+	3	10, 14, 15, 18, 33, 38
Canada thistle				1.00	−	1							39
Elk thistle				1.00	−	1	1.00	−	1	3.00	++	1	24
Queen's cup beadlily							1.00	−	1	1.00	−	1	44
Commandra										1.00	−	1	18
Pale commandra							2.00	+	1				29
Common commandra							3.00	++	1				25
Western goldthread	1.00	−	1	2.00	+	1	1.67	+	3	2.00	+	2	20, 21, 22, 44
Bunchberry							1.00	−	1				21
Scouler corydalis							2.00	+	1				44
Low hawksbeard							1.00	−	1				40
Larkspur							2.00	+	1				2
Little larkspur				1.00	−	1	2.00	+	1				12, 14
Sierra larkspur				2.00	+	1	2.00	+	2				7, 44
Slimpod shootingstar							3.00	++	1	3.00	++	1	44
Darkthroat shootingstar				1.00	−	1							14
Fireweed	3.00	++	1				2.00	+	4	2.00	+	1	3, 4, 13, 23, 44
Horsetail	1.00	−	2				1.00	−	1	1.00	−	1	16, 17, 21
Fleabane				2.00	+	1	1.50	+	2	2.00	+	1	12, 24
Eriogonum	2.00	+	1							1.50	+	2	13, 17, 18
Sulfur eriogonum							1.00	−	1	1.00	−	1	41
Wyeth eriogonum							1.00	−	1	1.00	−	1	27, 34
Buckwheat	2.00	+	1										26
Strawberry	1.50	+	2	2.00	+	1	1.00	−	3	1.00	−	2	13, 18, 24, 44
European strawberry				1.00	−	1							4
Virginia strawberry							1.00	−	2				35, 41
Bursage							2.00	+	1				2
Common perennial gaillardia							1.00	−	1				44
Rough bedstraw							1.00	−	1				27
Northern bedstraw	1.00	−	1										38
Geranium				2.00	+	1	1.50	+	2	1.00	−	1	2, 18, 23, 24
Richardson geranium				3.00	++	1							24
Sticky geranium				1.67	+	3	2.33	++	9	2.00	+	2	12, 23, 24, 35, 36, 37, 39, 41, 44
Avens							2.00	+	1				6
Prairiesmoke avens				1.00	−	1	2.00	+	1				12, 14
Ross' avens				1.00	−	1							9
American licorice							2.00	+	2	2.50	++	2	25, 38
Sulfur sweetvetch							2.00	+	1				23
Maximilian sunflower										2.00	+	1	28
Common cowparsnip				1.00	−	1	1.00	−	2				7, 44
Hawkweed							2.00	+	1				2
Western hawkweed							1.00	−	1				40

Table 40 continued

Plant	Winter Rank[a]	Value[b]	Number of references[c]	Spring Rank[a]	Value[b]	Number of references[c]	Summer Rank[a]	Value[b]	Number of references[c]	Autumn Rank[a]	Value[b]	Number of references[c]	References[d]
White hawkweed							1.50	+	2	1.00	−	1	27, 44
Woolyweed							1.50	+	2				34, 44
Houndstongue hawkweed				1.00	−	1	1.00	−	1				41
Smooth alumroot							2.00	+	1	2.00	+	1	44
Ballhead waterleaf							3.00	++	1				44
Streambank globemallow							3.00	++	1	3.00	++	1	44
Rocky Mountain iris										1.00	−	1	8
Chicory lettuce				2.00	+	1							28
Prickly lettuce							1.50	+	2				25, 28
Peavine	1.00	−	1	2.00	+	2	2.00	+	1				3, 6
Aspen peavine							2.00	+	1				5
Labradortea ledum	2.00	+	1										3
Korean lespedeza										2.00	+	1	31
Dotted grayfeather	1.00	−	1							3.00	++	1	24, 38
Grays licoriceroot							1.00	−	1				34
Canby's licoriceroot							2.00	+	1	1.00	−	1	44
Fernleaf licoriceroot							2.00	+	1	1.00	−	1	44
Wayside gromwell	1.00	−	2										13, 38
Lupine				2.00	+	1	1.00	−	8	2.14	+	7	4, 10, 11, 12, 16, 17, 18, 19, 23, 33, 36, 38, 40, 44
Velvet lupine							3.00	++	1				29
Oread lupine							2.00	+	1				35
Ornate lupine	2.00	+	1										13
Silky lupine	2.67	++	3	2.00	+	2	1.50	+	2				7, 14, 24, 38, 40
Alfalfa							3.00	++	1	3.00	++	1	1, 29
Yellow sweetclover	2.00	+	2	1.00	−	1	2.50	++	4	3.00	++	2	25, 26, 28, 29, 43
Mountain bluebells							3.00	++	1	3.00	++	1	44
Microseris				1.00	−	1	1.00	−	2				24, 41
Miterwort							1.00	−	1	2.00	+	1	44
Cord-leaved montia							3.00	++	1	3.00	++	1	44
Siberian montia							3.00	++	1	3.00	++	1	44
Leafy musineon				2.00	+	1							26
Alpine forget-me-not							3.00	++	1	3.00	++	1	36
Yellow evening primrose										2.00	+	1	36
Pricklypear cholla				2.00	+	2							19, 42
Alpine oreoxis							3.00	++	1				9
Sweet anise							3.00	++	2				34, 44
Crazyweed							1.00	−	1				18
Showy crazyweed				1.00	−	1							23
Yellowhair crazyweed				3.00	++	1							24
Fern-leaved lousewort							2.00	+	1				12
Elephanthead pedicularis							2.00	+	1				44
Sickletop pedicularis							2.00	+	1	1.00	−	1	44
Penstemon	1.00	−	1	1.50	+	2	1.00	−	1				4, 10, 13
Sulfur penstemon							1.00	−	1				40
Yellow penstemon										1.00	−	1	44

Continued on next page

Table 40 continued

Plant	Winter Rank[a]	Value[b]	Number of references[c]	Spring Rank[a]	Value[b]	Number of references[c]	Summer Rank[a]	Value[b]	Number of references[c]	Autumn Rank[a]	Value[b]	Number of references[c]	References
Wilcox penstemon							3.00	++	1	3.00	++	1	44
Littleflower penstemon							1.00	−	1				34
Yampa							2.00	+	1				35
Arrowleaf				2.00	+	1							3
Phacelia				1.00	−	1							4
Silverleaf phacelia							1.00	−	2	2.00	+	1	40, 44
Phlox	1.00	−	1							1.00	−	1	18, 33
Hood's phlox	1.00	−	1										36
Jacob's ladder							2.00	+	1	1.00	−	1	44
Pokeweed fleeceflower							2.50	++	2				34, 44
Cinquefoil				1.33	−	3	1.25	−	8	1.50	+	2	4, 9, 12, 18, 23, 24, 36, 41
Varileaf cinquefoil							3.00	++	1				35
Gland cinquefoil				1.00	−	1	1.33	−	1	2.00	+	1	34, 39, 44
Northwest cinquefoil							1.00	−	1				23
Western bracken				1.00	−	1							20
Pyrola	3.00	++	1							1.00	−	1	4, 30
Buttercup							2.00	+	1				24
Sagebrush buttercup				1.00	−	1	1.00	−	1				7
Mountain sorrel				2.00	+	1	2.00	+	1				7
Sitka burnet							2.00	+	1				34
Lesser club-moss				1.00	−	1							41
Groundsel	1.50	+	2	2.00	+	1	1.00	−	3				3, 13, 32, 36, 39
Columbian groundsel							3.00	++	1				44
Arrowleaf groundsel							2.50	++	2	3.00	++	1	34, 44
Feather solomonplume							2.00	+	1				44
Starry solomonplume							2.00	+	1				44
Goldenrod	1.00	−	1										13
Creek goldenrod	1.00	−	1										4
Field sowthistle							2.00	+	1				3
Starwort	1.00	−	1										24
Dandelion				1.00	−	2	3.00	++	3				12, 23, 41
Common dandelion	1.00	−	1	1.75	+	4	2.17	+	6	2.00	+	2	3, 4, 7, 24, 35, 39, 40
Mountain thermopsis							1.00	−	1				36
Pine thermopsis										1.00	−	1	8
Salsify										1.00	−	1	15
Yellow salsify	2.00	+	1	2.00	+	1	2.00	+	1				14, 28, 38
Falsebugbane							2.00	+	1				27
Clover				1.50	+	2	2.00	+	3				12, 20, 24, 37
Whiproot clover							3.00	++	1				9
Hayden clover				2.00	+	1	2.00	+	1				7
White clover							3.00	++	1				41
Rydberg clover				2.00	+	1	2.00	+	1				7
Cattail										1.00	−	1	18
Sitka valerian							3.00	++	1	3.00	++	1	44
California falsehellebore							1.00	−	1				27
Escholtz falsehellebore							1.00	−	1				44
American falsehellebore	1.00	−	1				2.00	+	1	2.00	+	1	20

Table 40 continued

Plant	Winter			Spring			Summer			Autumn			References[d]
	Rank[a]	Value[b]	Number of refer-ences[c]	Rank[a]	Value[b]	Number of refer-ences[c]	Rank[a]	Value[b]	Number of refer-ences[c]	Rank[a]	Value[b]	Number of refer-ences[c]	
American vetch				2.00	+	2	2.00	+	1				3, 26, 28
Nuttall violet				1.00	−	1	1.00	−	1				7
Wyethia							2.50	++	2	2.50	++	2	33, 36, 37
Common cocklebur	3.00	++	1										28
Common beargrass	1.50	+	1				1.67	+	3	2.50	++	2	4, 13, 20, 44
Heart-leaved Alexanders				3.00	++	1	3.00	++	1				24
Mountain deathcamus							2.00	+	1				35

Source: Partly from Kufeld 1973.

[a] Calculating relative value involved arbitrary assignment of numerical ratings: 1.00 (light use); 2.00 (moderate use); or 3.00 (heavy use).

[b] Value symbols: − = limited value; + = valuable; ++ = highly valuable.

[c] Number of references on which seasonal ranking is based.

[d] References: 1. Anderson et al. (1956); 2. Baker et al. (1953); 3. Blood (1966); 4. Bohne (1974); 5. Boyd (1970); 6. Boyd (1972); 7. Brazda (1953); 8. Burt and Cates (1959); 9. Capp (1967); 10. Claar (1973); 11. Constan (1972); 12. Eustace (1967); 13. Gaffney (1941); 14. Gordon (1968a); 15. Greer (1959a); 16. Greer (1960a); 17. Greer (1960b); 18. Greer et al. (1970); 19. Hansen and Reid (1975); 20. Hash (1973); 21. Jenkins and Wright (1987); 22. Kingery et al. (1996); 23. Kirsch (1963); 24. Knight (1970); 25. Knowles (1975a); 26. Komberec (1976a); 27. Korfhage (1974); 28. Mackie (1970); 29. Martinka (1969); 30. Moran (1973); 31. Murphy (1963); 32. Nichols (1957a); 33. Peek (1963); 34. Pickford and Reid (1943); 35. Probasco (1968); 36. Rouse (1957); 37. Rouse (1958); 38. Schallenberger (1965b); 39. Singer (1975); 40. Stark (1973); 41. Stevens (1966); 42. Wing (1962); 43. Wydeven and Dahlgren (1983); 44. Young and Robinette (1939).

stitute more the 75% of the diet (Tables 44–46). Forbs are used during summer and autumn, but are unimportant in winter and spring. Some browse is eaten during all seasons (Harper et al. 1967).

Batchelor (1965) found that, on Afognak Island, Alaska, grasses, sedges and perennial forbs are important in Roosevelt elk diets during spring and summer. When these plants mature in autumn, browse becomes more important. During winter months, these elk feed almost exclusively on shrubs.

In western Oregon, browse comprised about 70% of elk diets in spring and summer and declined to about 50% during autumn and winter. Forbs were most important in autumn and winter, when they constituted about 30% of the diet. Autumn use dropped to about 15% during spring and summer. Grass consumption ranged from 12% to 15% during all seasons, except during winter, when it increased to approximately 20% (Harper 1971).

Diets of Roosevelt elk on the Olympic Peninsula of Washington are similar to those of elk on Afognak Island, Alaska. Grasses and forbs constitute 75% to 90% of the spring diet. As the season progresses, browse becomes more important, but makes up less than half of the summer and autumn diets. During winter, elk of the Olympic peninsula herd feed almost exclusively on browse, presumably because of the effect of snow on forage availability (Schwartz and Mitchell 1945).

Distribution of Tule elk is limited to California (U.S. Bureau of Land Management 1980). The most complete year-round information about their food habits was reported by McCullough (1969). He found that annual forbs were extremely important in spring and early summer. Plant

Forage availability and palatability vary widely in the diets of Roosevelt elk across the subspecies range. In northern California, for example, elk mainly eat grasses (50%–75%); forbs are important in summer and autumn but are insignificant in winter. In western Oregon, on the other hand, Roosevelt elk were shown to eat more forbs (15%–30%) than grasses (12%–20%). *Photo courtesy of the Oregon Department of Fish and Wildlife.*

Table 41. Relative seasonal values of grasses and grasslike plants eaten by Rocky Mountain elk

Plant	Winter			Spring			Summer			Autumn			References[d]
	Rank[a]	Value[b]	Number of references[c]	Rank[a]	Value[b]	Number of references[c]	Rank[a]	Value[b]	Number of references[c]	Rank[a]	Value[b]	Number of references[c]	
Wheatgrass							2.00	+	1				30
Crested wheatgrass	2.00	+	1	2.00	+	1							18, 25
Thickspike wheatgrass				1.00	−	1							18
Intermediate wheatgrass	2.00	+	1				1.00	−	1				35, 25
Slender wheatgrass	3.00	++	1										10
Scribner wheatgrass							2.00	+	1				5
Bluestem wheatgrass	2.33	++	3	2.00	+	3	1.50	+	4	2.67	++	3	20, 21, 23, 33, 35
Bearded bluebunch wheatgrass	2.75	++	12	2.09	+	11	1.67	+	6	2.00	+	3	2, 4, 6, 8, 9, 10, 11, 14, 15, 16, 18, 19, 22, 24, 25, 32, 33, 34, 35, 36
Bearded wheatgrass							1.00	−	1	3.00	++	1	9, 31
Slender wheatgrass							1.00	−	1	2.00	+	1	31
Stiffhair wheatgrass							1.00	−	1				22
Spike bentgrass							3.00	++	1	2.00	+	1	39
Idaho bentgrass				2.00	+	1	1.00	−	2				15, 27
Oregon bentgrass							1.00	−	1				15
Bluegrama				1.00	−	1	1.00	−	1	1.00	−	1	14
Big bluestem	1.00	−	1	1.00	−	1	3.00	++	1				38
Little bluestem	1.00	−	1	1.00	−	1	1.00	−	1				38
Threeawn	1.00	−	1										25
Brome	1.00	−	2				1.75	+	4	2.00	+	1	9, 16, 26, 30, 36
Mountain brome	3.00	++	1	2.00	+	1	2.25	++	24	2.00	+	2	10, 15, 22, 30, 35, 39
Smooth brome	3.00	++	1	2.00	+	1	2.00	+	2	2.00	+	2	14, 18, 24
Cheatgrass brome	2.00	+	3	1.00	−	1							4, 7, 15, 25
Columbia brome				3.00	++	1	2.00	+	1	1.00	−	1	15, 16
Bluejoint reedgrass	2.50	++	2	1.00	−	1	1.50	+	2	1.00	−	1	10, 15, 19, 35
Pinegrass	2.00	+	2	2.00	+	2	2.00	+	2	1.33	−	3	10, 15, 19, 39
Prairie sandreed	1.50	+	2										16, 21
Sedge	2.00	+	6	1.30	−	3	1.92	+	12	1.80	+	5	1, 9, 10, 13, 14, 15, 16, 17, 19, 22, 27, 28, 29, 30, 31
Threadleaf sedge	3.00	++	1										10
Elk sedge	2.40	++	5	2.00	+	2	2.00	+	7	2.50	++	2	2, 7, 10, 15, 18, 19, 20, 22, 28, 35, 39
Cloud sedge				2.00	+	1	2.00	+	1				3
Raynolds sedge				2.00	+	1	2.00	+	1				3
Orchardgrass				2.00	+	1	1.50	+	2				15, 17, 22
Danthonia	2.00	+	1	1.00	−	1	2.00	+	1	1.00	−	1	14, 19
Timber danthonia	3.00	++	1				2.00	+	1				10, 30
Parry danthonia	2.00	+	1										18
Onespike danthonia	2.00	+	1										6
Tufted hairgrass							2.00	0	2				15, 27
Mountain hairgrass							1.00	−	1				15

Table 41 continued

Plant	Winter			Spring			Summer			Autumn			References[d]
	Rank[a]	Value[b]	Number of references[c]	Rank[a]	Value[b]	Number of references[c]	Rank[a]	Value[b]	Number of references[c]	Rank[a]	Value[b]	Number of references[c]	
Smooth crabgrass										2.00	+	1	26
Hairy crabgrass										2.00	+	1	26
Inland saltgrass	2.00	+	1				2.00	+	2				23
Canada wildrye							2.00	+	1				30
Yellow wildrye	3.00	++	1	3.00	++	1							37
Blue wildrye	1.33	−	3	1.50	+	2	3.00	++	1	2.50	++	2	16, 31, 33, 39
Fuzzyspike wildrye										1.00	−	1	31
Fescue				2.00	++	1	3.00	++	1	2.00	+	1	14
Meadow fescue							1.00	−	1				22
Idaho fescue	2.27	+	11	2.33	++	9	1.75	+	4	2.50	++	4	2, 3, 4, 6, 8, 9, 10, 11, 12, 16, 18, 19, 29–36
Sheep fescue				2.00	+	1	1.50	+	2				3, 22
Rough fescue	2.00	+	7	2.80	++	5	1.00	−	3	2.50	++	2	6, 9, 10, 11, 16, 17, 18, 19, 32, 33, 35
Spike fescue							2.00	+	1				3, 22
Baltic rush							3.00	++	1				27
Parry rush							3.00	++	1				28
Prairie junegrass	1.67	+	6	1.50	+	4	2.00	+	3	2.50	++	3	6, 9, 10, 11, 20, 21, 23, 29, 35, 36
Millet woodrush							3.00	++	1	3.00	++	1	39
Showy oniongrass							1.50	+	2				30, 31
Alaska oniongrass				1.00	−	1	1.00	−	1				15
Muhly	1.50	+	2										6, 29
Stonyhills	1.00	−	2				1.00	−	1	2.00	+	1	20, 21, 23
Pullup muhly							2.00	+	1				15
Mountain muhly	1.00	−	1	1.00	−	1	1.00	−	1				14
Indian ricegrass	2.00	+	1							3.00	++	1	21, 37
Alpine timothy				2.00	+	1	1.67	+	3				3, 27, 30
Timothy	2.00	+	3	2.33	++	3	1.20	−	5	3.00	++	1	3, 10, 19, 22, 33, 36
Bluegrass	1.71	+	7	2.38	++	8	1.88	+	8	2.50	++	4	7, 8, 9, 11, 14, 18, 19, 24, 30, 32, 33, 35, 36
Alpine bluegrass							2.00	+	1				19
Bulbous bluegrass	2.00	+	1										25
Rattlesnake mannagrass	3.00	++	1										10
Canada bluegrass	2.00	+	2	2.50	++	2	1.50	+	2	2.00	+	1	10, 15, 22, 23
Skyline bluegrass				2.00	+	1	2.00	+	2				3, 27
Kentucky bluegrass	3.00	++	1	2.00	+	1	2.33	++	3	3.00	++	1	17, 22, 38
Sandberg bluegrass	2.00	+	1	2.00	+	3	1.33	−	3	2.00	+	2	2, 3, 20, 22, 23
Bottlebrush squirreltail							1.00	−	2				28, 35
Needlegrass	2.25	++	4	2.50	++	2	2.00	+	2	2.00	+	2	6, 14, 15, 19, 29
Subalpine needlegrass	3.00	++	1				1.00	−	1				10, 28
Needle-and-thread	1.50	+	2	2.00	+	2	1.00	−	1	2.00	+	2	21, 37, 25
Green needlegrass	1.00	−	1	2.00	+	1							23
Spike trisetum							2.00	+	1	2.00	+	1	9, 18

Continued on next page

Table 41 continued

	Forage value												
	Winter			Spring			Summer			Autumn			
Plant	Rank[a]	Value[b]	Number of refer-ences[c]	Rank[a]	Value[b]	Number of refer-ences[c]	Rank[a]	Value[b]	Number of refer-ences[c]	Rank[a]	Value[b]	Number of refer-ences[c]	References[d]
Wolfs trisetum							2.00	+	1				27

Source: Partly from Kufeld 1973.

[a] Calculating relative value involved arbitrary assignment of numerical ratings: 1.00 (light use); 2.00 (moderate use); or 3.00 (heavy use).

[b] Value symbols: − = limited value; + = valuable; ++ = highly valuable.

[c] Number of references on which seasonal ranking is based.

[d] References: 1. Anderson et al. (1956); 2. Bohne (1974); 3. Brazda (1953); 4. Buechner (1952); 5. Capp (1967); 6. Casgranda and Janson (1957); 7. Cliff (1939); 8. Constan (1972); 9. Eustace (1967); 10. Gaffney (1941); 11. Gordon (1968a); 12. Greer (1959b); 13. Greer et al. (1970); 14. Hansen and Reid (1975); 15. Hash (1973); 16. Jenkins and Wright (1987); 17. Kingery et al. (1996); 18. Kirsch (1963); 19. Knight (1970); 20. Knowles (1975a); 21. Komberec (1976a); 22. Korfhage (1974); 23. Mackie (1970); 24. Martinka (1969); 25. Mower and Smith (1989); 26. Murphy (1963); 27. Nichols (1957a); 28. Pickford and Reid (1943); 29. Picton (1960b); 30. Probasco (1968); 31. Rouse (1957); 32. Schallenberger (1965b); 33. Singer (1975); 34. Snyder (1969); 35. Stark (1973); 36. Stevens (1966); 37. Wing (1962); 38. Wydeven and Dahlgren (1983); 39. Young and Robinette (1939).

species of greatest significance in the diet included eriogonum, tidytips, blazing-star, scalebud, cryptantha, gilia and storks-bill. As these forbs mature in early summer, late-curing annual forbs such as fivehook bassia, white sweet-clover and common sunflower are important. Perennial forbs are important in summer and autumn and include American licorice, alkalimallow and alfalfa. Browse is particularly important to Tule elk in winter, although some is eaten throughout the year. Selected species include antelope bitterbrush, big sagebrush, rock eriogonum, common winterfat, black greasewood, big saltbush and willow.

Annual and perennial grasses are eaten throughout the year. Some preferred species include desert needlegrass, bottlebrush squirreltail, Indian ricegrass, pine bluegrass, galleta, foxtail barley and knotgrass. Sedges also are eaten. October contents of rumens of elk from Owens Valley, California, contained nearly 50% grass, indicating the importance of that forage class during autumn (Ferrel 1962, 1963).

Most large ungulates studies have moved beyond standard food habit evaluations during the past decade, focusing instead on relative energetic and nutritive contributions of plants and assemblages of plants and strategies used by ruminants to extract nutrients from plant communities across landscapes. This in part is because food habits data per se generally have little direct relevance to dietary quality, foraging efficiency and population demographics except perhaps under specific, local settings (Hanley 1997). Because of the cost and difficulty in directly measuring forage quality of plant assemblages, there is temptation to equate forage quality to some measure of forage abundance (e.g., Thomas et al. 1988a). Although there may be

an association between abundance and quality under some conditions (Hobbs and Spowart 1985), equating forage quantity to forage quality confuses the important distinction between the two variables. Moreover, actual forage quality at any given point in time generally is not a predictable function of forage quantity, in part because the inverse relation between quantity and quality (Hobbs and Swift 1985) does not necessarily hold across a variety of ecological settings and seasonal periods.

Effects of Inadequate Nutrition

Nutrition can affect productivity of elk by influencing the timing of estrous and subsequent birth date, probability of conception, fetal growth rates, probability of fetal survival, birth weight, resistance to disease and parasites, growth of juveniles, probability of juvenile survival, age at puberty and probability of adult survival. Undernutrition in any given season may have effects on key life processes during that season or carry-over to subsequent seasons or years. Thus, undernutrition has a cumulative aspect; large ruminants such as elk can tolerate seasonal undernutrition to some extent, but eventually must be able to alleviate accumulating deficits to avoid pauses in reproduction or reductions in their ability to survive winter conditions.

In the following, the impacts of inadequate nutrition on various aspects of productivity are reviewed. Data on elk are emphasized, but because of a dearth of such data, some of the discussion relies on information collected from other large ruminants. Much of the nutrition information concerns energy and protein effects; little information on other nutrients is available for wild ruminants.

Table 42. Relative seasonal values of shrub and tree species eaten by Rocky Mountain elk

	Forage value												References[d]
	Winter			Spring			Summer			Autumn			
Plant	Rank[a]	Value[b]	Number of references[c]	Rank[a]	Value[b]	Number of references[c]	Rank[a]	Value[b]	Number of references[c]	Rank[a]	Value[b]	Number of references[c]	
Grand fir	1.00	−	3										15, 27, 53
Subalpine fir	2.00	+	1										29
Bigtooth maple	2.00	+	1										41
Rocky Mountain maple	2.00	+	6	1.00	−	1	3.00	++	2	2.00	+	2	6, 15, 16, 26, 32, 39, 57
Mountain maple							2.00	+	1				5
Alder										1.00	−	1	24
American green alder	1.00	−	1							1.00	−	1	6
Thinleaf alder	1.00	−	1				1.50	+	2	2.00	+	1	7, 15, 57
Saskatoon serviceberry	2.40	++	11	1.67	+	3	2.20	++	5	2.00	+	5	1, 5, 6, 7, 15, 16, 23, 26, 27, 30, 32, 39, 41, 48, 49, 51
False indigo							2.00	+	1				55
Bearberry	1.00	−	3	1.00	−	1				1.67	+	3	5, 6, 31, 48
Silver sagebrush	2.00	+	1										37
Big sagebrush	1.56	+	9	1.20	−	6	1.00	−	2	1.80	+	5	7, 8, 13, 16, 18, 19, 22, 24, 26, 37, 41, 43, 45, 47, 49, 50, 54
Threetip sagebrush	3.00	++	1	2.00	+	1							47
Barberry	1.00	−	1										13
Creeping mahonia	1.50	+	6	1.83	+	7	1.00	−	3	2.00	+	13	1, 2, 6, 8, 12, 15, 18, 20, 21, 22, 24, 25, 27, 28, 29, 31, 32, 44, 47, 53
Bog birch	2.00	+	2				3.00	++	1				15, 32
Water birch	1.00	−	1										15
Jerseytea ceanothus							3.00	++	1				4
Redstem ceanothus	3.00	++	5	2.00	+	1	2.00	+	2	2.00	+	2	15, 27, 39, 53, 56, 57
Snowbrush ceanothus	2.34	++	9	2.00	+	1	2.50	++	2	2.20	+	5	6, 12, 13, 15, 16, 27, 32, 38, 39, 41 56, 57
True mountain mahogany	2.67	++	3	2.00	+	1	2.00	+	1	2.00	+	1	24, 26, 36
Curlleaf mountain mahogany	2.00	+	3	2.00	+	1				2.40	++	2	1, 12, 13, 41
Rabbitbrush	1.00	−	1	1.00	−	1				1.00	−	1	24
Rubber rabbitbrush	2.00	+	3	1.00	−	1							11, 13, 50, 54
Green rabbitbrush	1.40	−	5	3.00	++	1				1.67	+	3	11, 17, 33, 34, 37, 50, 54
Redosier dogwood	2.23	+	9				3.00	++	1	1.50	+	2	5, 6, 16, 26, 27, 29, 49, 53, 57
Silverberry elaeagnus	2.50	++	2										15, 32
Winterfat	2.00	+	1							1.00	−	1	24
Ash	2.00	+	1										23
Galax	2.00	+	1				2.00	+	1				4
Wrights silktassel	3.00	++	1										36

Continued on next page

Table 42 continued

Plant	Winter			Spring			Summer			Autumn			References[d]
	Rank[a]	Value[b]	Number of references[c]	Rank[a]	Value[b]	Number of references[c]	Rank[a]	Value[b]	Number of references[c]	Rank[a]	Value[b]	Number of references[c]	
Checkerberry wintergreen	2.00	+	1				2.00	+	1				4
Creambush rockspirea	1.00	−	2				1.50	+	2	1.00	−	1	35, 39, 56, 57
Juniper	1.75	+	4	2.00	+	1				1.50	+	2	21, 24, 29, 36
Common juniper	1.00	−	3							1.00	−	1	15, 31, 48
Creeping juniper	1.00	−	3										10, 32, 48
Sierra juniper	2.00	+	1										13
Rocky Mountain juniper	1.50	+	2	1.00	−	1				1.00	−	1	15, 37
Labradortea ledum	2.00	+	1										5
Twinflower				1.00	−	1				1.00	−	1	28
American twinflower	1.00	−	1										15
Bearberry honeysuckle	2.00	+	1				2.00	+	1				15, 57
Utah honeysuckle							3.00	++	1	1.00	−	1	57
Rusty menziesia							2.00	+	2	1.00	−	1	27, 57
Myrtle pachistima	1.67	+	3	2.00	+	1	1.00	−	1	2.20	+	5	2, 6, 13, 15, 27, 28, 36, 41
Lewis mockorange	1.00	−	2										15, 39
Spruce	1.00	−	1										29
Mallow ninebark	1.00	−	2				2.00	+	2	1.00	−	1	35, 39, 57
Pine	1.00	−	3							1.00	−	3	8, 21, 47, 53
Jack pine	1.00	−	1										40
Lodgepole pine	1.50	+	6	1.00	−	1				1.33	−	3	6, 15, 18, 22, 29, 32, 48, 49
Limber pine										1.00	−	1	44
Ponderosa pine	1.00	−	2										13, 15
Poplar	1.00	−	1										6
Southern poplar	2.00	+	1										5
Quaking aspen	2.33	++	9	2.25	++	4	1.74	+	4	2.50	++	8	2, 5, 7, 8, 9, 15, 22, 26, 32, 36, 44, 48, 49, 57
California poplar	2.00	+	3							1.00	−	1	15, 29, 49
Cinquefoil							1.00	−	1				9
Bush cinquefoil	1.00	−	2										15, 32
Cherry	1.50	+	2							1.00	−	1	4, 6
Common chokecherry	2.44	++	9	2.00	+	3	2.00	+	3	1.50	+	2	5, 11, 15, 18, 23, 26, 33, 37, 39, 47, 48, 54, 57
Bitter cherry	1.00	−	1				3.00	++	1	3.00	++	1	39, 57
Pin cherry	2.00	+	1										5
Douglas-fir	1.43	−	16	1.00	−	4	1.00	−	1	1.33	−	3	6, 7, 8, 12, 13, 14, 15, 18, 21, 22, 27, 31, 56, 39, 48, 53
Antelope bitterbrush	3.00	++	4	2.00	+	1				2.25	+	2	2, 11, 13, 26, 54
Common apple	2.00	+	1										40, 43
Scarlet oak	2.00	+	1										4

Table 42 continued

Plant	Winter Rank[a]	Winter Value[b]	Winter Number of references[c]	Spring Rank[a]	Spring Value[b]	Spring Number of references[c]	Summer Rank[a]	Summer Value[b]	Summer Number of references[c]	Autumn Rank[a]	Autumn Value[b]	Autumn Number of references[c]	References[d]
						Forage value							
Gambel oak	3.00	++	4	2.00	+	1	2.00	+	1				7, 23, 24, 26, 41
Nothern red oak	2.00	+	1										40
Cascara buckthorn	2.00	+	1				1.00	−	2				27, 57
Sumac	2.00	+	1										41
Staghorn sumac	1.00	−	1										40
Currant	1.00	−	1				1.00	−	1				15, 51
Wax currant							1.00	−	1				7
Umatilla gooseberry							3.00	++	1	2.00	+	1	57
Gooseberry currant							3.00	++	1				45
Western black currant							1.00	−	1	1.00	−	1	57
Sticky currant							3.00	++	1	2.00	+	1	57
Rose	1.50	+	2	1.00	−	1	2.00	+	2	2.00	++	1	15, 27, 48, 57
Prickly rose	1.00	−	2				3.00	++	1	3.00	++	1	5, 46
Arkansas rose							1.00	−	1				33
Blackberry	3.00	++	1							1.00	−	1	22, 29
Red raspberry							2.00	+	1				5
Western thimbleberry							2.00	+	2	2.00	+	1	51, 57
Willow	2.10	+	11	2.00	+	1	1.75	+	8	2.25	++	8	5, 6, 8, 13, 16, 18, 19, 22, 31, 32, 38, 44, 47, 48, 52, 56, 29
Bebb willow	3.00	++	1										15
Coyote willow	2.00	+	1										15
Geyer willow	2.00	+	1										15
Yellow willow	3.00	++	1										15
Dusky willow	2.00	+	1										15
Scouler willow	2.00	+	5	1.50	+	2	1.00	−	1	2.00	+	1	15, 27, 41, 49, 53
Blue willow	3.00	++	1										15
Elder				2.00	+	1	2.50	++	2	1.00	−	1	3, 27
Blueberry elder							2.50	++	2	2.50	++	2	27, 57
Blackbead elder	3.00	++	1				3.00	++	1	3.00	++	1	15, 57
Silky sassafras	2.00	+	1										4
Russet buffaloberry	2.00	+	1				1.00	−	1	1.50	+	2	22, 24, 38, 48
American mountain ash							3.00	++	1	3.00	++	1	57
Western mountain ash	2.00	+	1										15
Greenes mountain ash										2.00	+	1	27
Spirea	1.00	−	1				1.00	−	1	1.00	−	1	15, 31
Birchleaf spirea	2.00	+	1										48
Shinyleaf spirea							2.00	+	1	2.00	+	1	57
Menzies spirea							2.00	+	1	2.00	+	1	57
Snowberry	1.40	−	5				1.50	+	2	1.83	+	6	13, 20, 21, 26, 31, 37, 38, 44, 48, 56
Common snowberry	2.00	+	2	1.00	−	1	1.67	+	3	1.67	+	3	5, 6, 15, 27, 35, 51, 57
Western snowberry	1.00	−	1				1.00	−	1	2.00	+	1	33, 47
Indiancurrant coralberry										2.00	+	1	42
Utah snowberry				1.00	−	1	1.00	−	1				7

Continued on next page

Table 42 continued

Plant	Winter Rank[a]	Winter Value[b]	Winter Number of references[c]	Spring Rank[a]	Spring Value[b]	Spring Number of references[c]	Summer Rank[a]	Summer Value[b]	Summer Number of references[c]	Autumn Rank[a]	Autumn Value[b]	Autumn Number of references[c]	References[d]
	Forage value												
Pacific yew	2.00	+	5	1.00	−	1	3.00	++	1	1.33	−	3	27, 35, 40, 47, 53, 54
Eastern hemlock	1.00	−	1										40
Blueberry	1.75	+	4				1.00	−	3	1.00	−	4	6, 8, 12, 13, 22, 32, 40, 44, 52
Big whortleberry	1.00	−	1	1.00	−	1	3.00	++	1	1.50	+	4	15, 27, 31, 38, 57
Grouse whortleberry	1.00	−	1				1.00	−	2	1.75	+	4	9, 15, 27, 31, 36, 57
Small soapweed	2.00	+	1	1.00	−	1				1.50	+	2	24, 33, 34

Source: Partly from Kufeld 1973.

[a] Calculating relative value involved arbitrary assignment of numerical ratings: 1.00 (light use); 2.00 (moderate use); or 3.00 (heavy use).

[b] Value symbols: − = limited value; + = valuable; ++ = highly valuable.

[c] Number of references on which seasonal ranking is based.

[d] References: 1. Anderson (1958); 2. Anderson et al. (1956); 3. Baker et al. (1953); 4. Baldwin and Patton (1938); 5. Blood (1966); 6. Bohne (1974); 7. Boyd (1970); 8. Boyd (1972); 9. Burt and Cates (1959); 10. Casgranda and Janson (1957); 11. Chadwick (1960); 12. Claar (1973); 13. Cliff (1939); 14. Cowan (1947a); 15. Gaffney (1941); 16. Geis (1954); 17. Gordon (1968a); 18. Greer (1959a); 19. Greer (1959b); 20. Greer (1960a); 21. Greer (1960b); 22. Greer et al. (1970); 23. Greffenius (1938); 24. Hansen and Reid (1975); 25. Harper (1971); 26. Harris (1958); 27. Hash (1973); 28. Hoskins (1952); 29. Jenkins and Wright (1987); 30. Kingery et al. (1996); 31. Kirsch (1963); 32. Knight (1970); 33. Knowles (1975a); 34. Komberec (1976a); 35. Korfhage (1974); 36. Lang (1958); 37. Mackie (1970); 38. Martinka (1969); 39. McCulloch (1955); 40. Moran (1973); 41. Mower and Smith (1989); 42. Murphy (1963); 43. Ngugi et al. (1992); 44. Peek (1963); 45. Pickford and Reid (1943); 46. Picton (1960b); 47. Rouse (1957); 48. Schallenberger (1965b); 49. Singer (1975); 50. Snyder (1969); 51. Stark (1973); 52. Stevens (1966); 53. Trout and Leege (1971); 54. Wing (1962); 55. Wydeven and Dahlgren (1983); 56. Young (1938); 57. Young and Robinette (1939).

Table 43. Rocky Mountain and Roosevelt elk food habit references by state or province

State or province	References
Alaska	Batchelor (1965), Troyer (1960)
Alberta	Cowan (1947a)
California	Harper et al. (1967)
Colorado	Boyd (1970), Boyd (1972), Capp (1967), Greffenius (1938), Hansen and Reid (1975), Harris (1958), Hobbs et al. (1979), Nichols (1957a)
Idaho	Chadwick (1960), Claar (1973), Hash (1973), Herman (unpublished), Hines (1970), Irwin and Peek (1983), Kingery et al. (1996), McCulloch (1955), Trout and Leege (1971), Wing (1962), Young (1938), Young and Robinette (1939)
Manitoba	Blood (1966)
Michigan	Moran (1973)
Missouri	Murphy (1963)
Montana	Bohne (1974), Brazda (1953), Casgranda and Janson (1957), Constan (1972), Eustace (1967), Gaffney (1941), Geis (1954), Gordon (1968a), Greer (1959a), Greer (1959b), Greer (1960a), Greer (1960b), Greer et al. (1970), Jenkins and Wright (1988), Kirsch (1963), Knight (1970), Knowles (1975a), Komberec (1976a), Mackie (1970), Marcum (1979), Peek (1963), Picton (1960b), Rouse (1957), Rouse (1958), Schallenberger (1965b), Singer (1975), Snyder (1969), Stevens (1966)
New Mexico	Burt and Cates (1959), Lang (1958), Short et al. (1977)
Oregon	Cliff (1939), Harper (1966), Harper (1971), Hines (1970), Korfhage (1974), Korfhage et al. (1980), Pickford and Reid (1943), Skovlin and Vavra (1979), Swanson (1970)
South Dakota	Wydeven and Dahlgren (1983)
Utah	Collins (1977), Mower and Smith (1989)
Virginia	Baldwin and Patton (1938)
Washington	Boltz (unpublished), Buechner (1952), Davitt (unpublished), Jenkins and Starkey (1993), Leslie et al. (1987), McArthur (unpublished), McReynolds (unpublished), Merrill et al. (1995), Schoen (unpublished), Schwartz and Mitchell (1945), Skinner (1936), Stark (1973)
Wyoming	Anderson (1958), Anderson et al. (1956), Baker et al. (1953), Martinka (1969), Ngugi et al. (1992), Probasco (1968)

Table 44. Relative seasonal values of forbs, ferns and lichens eaten by Roosevelt elk

Plant	Winter Rank[a]	Winter Value[b]	Winter Number of references[c]	Spring Rank[a]	Spring Value[b]	Spring Number of references[c]	Summer Rank[a]	Summer Value[b]	Summer Number of references[c]	Autumn Rank[a]	Autumn Value[b]	Autumn Number of references[c]	References[d]
Gooseberry currant							3.00	++	1				45
Pearly-everlasting							1.00	–	1				7
Sea-watch				2.00	+	1							1
Bigleaf sandwort	2.00	+	1	2.00	+	1							2
Ladyfern	2.00	+	1	2.00	+	1							1, 11
Deerfern	1.33	–	3	1.50	+	2	1.00	–	1	1.75	+	4	6, 8, 9, 10
Pacific bleedingheart							1.00	–	1				7
Fireweed							2.33	++	3	2.33	++	3	1, 7, 11
Smooth willowweed							1.00	–	1				7
Watson willowweed				1.00	–	1	1.00	–	1				10
Horsetail				2.00	+	1	3.00	++	1	1.00	–	1	1, 7
Common cowparsnip				2.00	+	1	2.00	+	1				1
Spotted catsear	2.67	++	3	2.33	++	3	2.60	++	5	2.00	+	4	2, 3, 4, 7, 10
Sea lovage							2.00	+	1				1
Lupine										1.00	–	1	7
Nootka lupine							2.00	+	1				1
Indian lettuce							2.00	+	1				1
Siberian montia	1.00	–	1	2.00	+	2	2.00	+	2	2.00	+	2	8, 10
Oregon oxalis	2.00	+	1	2.00	+	3	1.75	+	4	1.75	+	4	3, 6, 7, 8, 10
Buckhorn plantain				1.00	–	1	2.00	+	1	2.00	+	1	3
Western swordfern	1.80	+	6	1.80	+	6	1.40	+	5	1.40	+	5	2, 4, 5, 6, 8, 9, 10
Common selfheal							1.00	–	1	1.00	–	1	3
Western bracken	1.33	–	3	1.50	+	2	1.67	+	3	1.00	–	2	2, 4, 6, 10
California Spanish moss	2.00	+	1										8
Creeping buttercup							1.00	–	1	1.00	–	1	3
Sitka burnet							2.00	+	1				1
Mexican betony				1.00	–	1	1.00	–	1				10
Trefoil foamflower	2.00	+	1	2.00	+	1				2.00	+	1	8
Menzies tolmiea	2.00	+	1	2.00	+	1				2.00	+	1	8
Clover							1.00	–	1	1.00	–	1	7
Bearded usnea	2.00	+	1	2.00	+	1							8
Pleated usnea	2.00	+	1										8
Eschscholtz falsehellebore							2.00	+	1				1

[a] Calculating relative value involved arbitrary assignment of numerical ratings: 1.00 (light use); 2.00 (moderate use); or 3.00 (heavy use).

[b] Value symbols: – = limited value; + = valuable; ++ = highly valuable.

[c] Number of references on which seasonal ranking is based.

[d] References: 1. Batchelor (1965); 2. Harper (1966); 3. Harper et al. (1967); 4. Hines (1970); 5. Jenkins and Starkey (1993); 6. Leslie et al. (1984); 7. Merrill et al. (1995); 8. Schwartz and Mitchell (1945); 9. Skinner (1936); 10. Swanson (1970); 11. Troyer (1960).

Estrous Dynamics and Pregnancy Rates

In temperate regions, numerous studies of ruminants have demonstrated a significant relationship between body weight of females and their probability of successful conception (Hamilton and Blaxter 1980, Cameron et al. 1993). In reality, nutritional condition rather than weight probably is directly related to pregnancy rates (Thomas 1982, Cameron et al. 1993); weight simply is a surrogate measure of condition. Infertility from inadequate nutritional condition may be due to failure to ovulate, resorption of the fertilized ovum or failure to conceive after ovulation (Trainer 1971). Recent elk studies suggest that failure to become pregnant due to nutritional deficiencies during the breeding season result from a failure to ovulate and breed (Cook 2000).

Strong relationships between weight and pregnancy rate

Table 45. Relative seasonal values of grasses and grasslike plants eaten by Roosevelt elk

Plant	Winter Rank[a]	Winter Value[b]	Winter Number of references[c]	Spring Rank[a]	Spring Value[b]	Spring Number of references[c]	Summer Rank[a]	Summer Value[b]	Summer Number of references[c]	Autumn Rank[a]	Autumn Value[b]	Autumn Number of references[c]	References[d]
Bentgrass	1.00	–	2	1.00	–	1	3.00	++	1	2.00	+	2	3, 4, 5
Redtop	3.00	++	1	3.00	++	1	2.00	+	1	2.00	+	1	2
Vernalgrass	2.00	+	1	3.00	++	1	3.00	++	1	3.00	++	1	2
Brome										1.00	–	1	5
Mountain brome							1.00	–	1				2
Bluejoint reedgrass				2.00	+	1							1
Sedge	1.00	–	1	2.00	+	2	1.00	–	2	1.00	–	2	1, 4, 5
Windseed sedge							3.00	++	1	3.00	++	1	8
Dewey's sedge				2.00	+	1							6
Slough sedge	2.00	+	1	1.00	–	1	1.00	–	1	1.00	–	1	2
Orchardgrass	3.00	++	1	3.00	++	1	3.00	++	1	2.50	++	2	2, 5
California danthonia	3.00	++	1	3.00	++	1				2.00	+	1	2
Tufted hairgrass	2.00	+	1							1.00	–	1	1
Slender hairgrass										1.00	–	1	5
Wildrye							3.00	++	1	1.00	–	1	2
Blue wildrye							1.00	–	1	2.00	++	1	5
Fescue	2.00	–	1										3
Meadow fescue	1.00	–	1							2.00	+	1	3, 5
Red fescue	1.00	–	1				1.00	–	1	3.00	++	1	1, 5
Common velvetgrass	1.00	–	1				1.00	–	2	1.50	+	2	2, 3, 5
Rush	2.00	+	1										3
Ryegrass										2.00	+	1	5
Common timothy	1.00	–	1							1.00	–	1	3, 5
Bluegrass	1.00	–	2	1.00	–	1	1.00	–	1	2.00	+	1	3, 4
Millet woodrush	1.00	–	1				1.00	–	1	1.00	–	1	7

[a] Calculating relative value involved arbitrary assignment of numerical ratings: 1.00 (light use); 2.00 (moderate use); or 3.00 (heavy use).

[b] Value symbols: – = limited value; + = valuable; ++ = highly valuable.

[c] Number of references on which seasonal ranking is based.

[d] References: 1. Batchelor (1965); 2. Harper et al. (1967); 3. Jenkins and Starkey (1993); 4. Leslie et al. (1984); 5. Merrill et al. (1995); 6. Schwartz and Mitchell (1945); 7. Swanson (1970).

have been reported for elk (Figure 98). Hudson et al. (1991) indicated that cows weighing less than 420 pounds (190 kg) during the rut generally do not breed, and cows weighing less than 530 pounds (240 kg) have a reduced probability of breeding. However, high pregnancy rates have been observed for first-time bred 2.5-year-old cows that weighed 385 to 440 pounds (175–200 kg) (Figure 98). Differences between studies probably were due to differences in body condition and frame size. The 2.5-year-old cows probably were smaller in stature but in better condition than were younger cows (i.e., yearlings) included in the study of Hudson et al. (1991). At least in deer, very obese animals may not breed, due to accumulation of fat around the ovaries, which can hinder follicular development and result in irregularity or cessation of estrus (Verme 1965).

Reduced nutritional condition during the breeding season results from inadequate nutrition in winter, spring or summer and lactation during summer. In several studies of red deer, supporting a calf during the rut lowered pregnancy rate to 48% to 82%, compared with a pregnancy rate of more than 90% for nonlactating hinds (Lowe 1969, Mitchell 1973, Guinness et al. 1978a). Hamilton and Blaxter (1980), however, reported that supporting a calf during the rut had no effect on pregnancy rates of red deer. Such differences among studies probably reflect differences in nutritional plane sometime during the 5 to 8 months before breeding.

Hudson et al. (1991) and Trainer (1971) reported that lactation during the rut lowered pregnancy rates of elk. Trainer (1971) reported that 54% of prime-age lactating cows and 84% of prime-age nonlactating cows were pregnant in Roosevelt elk studies in Oregon. Differences likely

Table 46. Relative seasonal value of shrub and tree species eaten by Roosevelt elk

Plant	Winter Rank[a]	Winter Value[b]	Winter Number of references[c]	Spring Rank[a]	Spring Value[b]	Spring Number of references[c]	Summer Rank[a]	Summer Value[b]	Summer Number of references[c]	Autumn Rank[a]	Autumn Value[b]	Autumn Number of references[c]	References[d]
Vine maple	1.75	+	4	2.50	++	4	3.00	++	4	2.00	+	4	2, 4, 8, 9, 10
Bigleaf maple										2.00	+	1	9
Red alder	1.00	–	1							2.50	++	2	5, 6, 9
Sitka alder							1.00	–	1			5	8
Kidneywhort baccaris							1.00	–	1				3
Cascades mahonia	2.50	++	2	2.00	+	1	2.00	+	1	3.00	++	1	5, 10
Salal	2.40	++	5	1.75	+	4	1.67	+	3	1.75	+	4	2, 4, 5, 8, 9, 10
American twinflower	3.00	++	1										5
American devilsclub	2.00	+	1	2.00	+	1				2.00	+	1	1, 9, 11
Sitka spruce	2.00	+	1										8
California poplar										1.00	–	1	7
Douglas-fir	2.25	+	4	1.00	–	2	1.00	–	1	2.00	+	1	2, 5, 8, 10
Cascara buckhorn	2.00	+	1	1.00	–	1	2.00	+	1	1.00	–	1	10
California rose							1.00	–	1	1.00	–	1	3
Nootka rose	2.00	+	1										11
Cutleaf blackberry				2.00	+	1	2.00	+	1	2.00	+	1	4
Whitebark raspberry							1.00	–	1	1.00	–	1	10
Western thimbleberry				2.00	+	2	2.00	+	2	1.50	+	2	4, 7, 10
Five-leaved bramble	2.00	+	1										1
Himalaya blackberry	1.00	–	1	3.00	++	1	1.00	–	1				3
Salmonberry	1.17	–	6	2.33	++	6	2.14	+	7	1.75	+	8	1–11, 7, 6, 5
California dewberry	3.00	++	3	2.67	++	3	2.50	++	4	2.33	++	3	2, 4, 6, 10
Grapeleaf California dewberry	3.00	++	1	2.00	+	1	1.00	–	1	2.00	+	1	3
Willow	2.00	+	4				2.00	+	2	2.00	+	4	1, 5, 6, 7, 9, 11
Scouler willow	2.00	+	1	2.00	+	1							8
Sitka willow	2.00	+	1	2.00	+	1							8
European red elder	3.00	++	2	2.00	+	1	2.00	+	3	2.00	+	4	1, 4, 7, 11
Pacific yew	3.00	++	1										5, 6, 7
Western red cedar	3.00	++	3							1.00	–	10	5, 6, 8
Pacific hemlock	2.33	++	6	1.25	–	4	1.67	+	3	1.75	+	4	2, 4, 8, 10
Blueberry	2.00	+	1	3.00	++	1	1.00	–	1	1.00	–	2	5, 6, 7
Big whortleberry				2.00	+	1	2.00	+	1	2.00	+	1	8
Ovalleaf whortleberry	1.33	–	3	1.50	+	2	1.50	+	2	1.50	+	2	1, 8, 11
Box blueberry	1.50	+	2	1.50	+	2				1.50	+	2	2, 9, 10
Red whortleberry	2.33	++	3	2.00	+	3	2.50	++	2	2.25	++	4	4, 8, 9, 10
Moosewood viburnum	2.00	+	1							2.00	+	1	1,11

[a] Calculating relative value involved arbitrary assignment of numerical ratings: 1.00 (light use); 2.00 (moderate use); or 3.00 (heavy use).

[b] Value symbols: – = limited value; + = valuable; ++ = highly valuable.

[c] Number of references on which seasonal ranking is based.

[d] References: 1. Batchelor (1965); 2. Harper (1966); 3. Harper et al. (1967); 4. Hines (1970); 5. Jenkins and Starkey (1993); 6. Leslie et al. (1984); 7. Merrill et al. (1987); 8. Schwartz and Mitchell (1945); 9. Skinner (1936); 10. Swanson (1970); 11. Troyer (1960).

were due to different levels of fat content, ultimately controlled by nutrition levels during summer. Kohlmann (1999) provided an equation to predict the probability of cow elk breeding as a function of a kidney fat index, based on data collected from Roosevelt and Rocky Mountain elk across Oregon (Figure 99).

A number of studies have shown that total nutritional intake on an annual basis can be insufficient to support reproduction, such that the mother must use her body reserves. Under these conditions, the nutritional condition of the mother declines each year (10%–13% per year in caribou [Reimers 1983a]) until reproduction fails, usually by

An elk cow's nutritional status has significant bearing on the conception, fetal growth and survival, general health of offspring, and the survivability of the cow herself. Undernourished cows, as above, are especially vulnerable to parasites. *Photo by Leonard Lee Rue III.*

foregoing breeding (Cameron 1994). Such reproductive pauses probably occur in elk (Cameron 1994), but their frequency is difficult to assess, particularly in herds where juvenile mortality during summer is relatively high. Such mortality will allow compensation in condition before the breeding season and can result in high pregnancy rates despite poor nutrition (Verme 1962, Verme and Ullrey 1984).

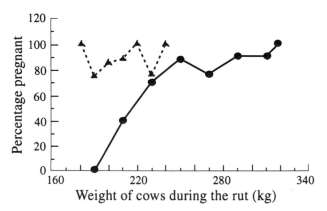

Figure 98. Relationship between body weight during rut and pregnancy rates of elk cows (adapted from Hudson et al. 1991 [solid line] and J. G. Cook personal data for 45 cows [dotted line]).

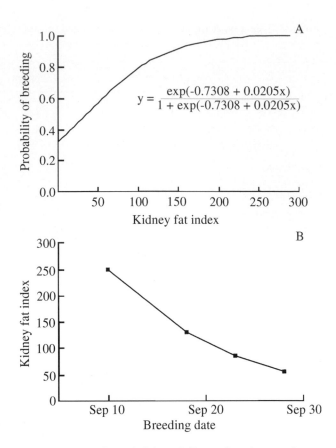

Figure 99. (*A*) The probability of elk cows breeding as a function of kidney fat index (a measure of nutritional condition). The prediction equation was developed from Roosevelt and Rocky Mountain elk data collected from 1965 to 1996 in Oregon by Kohlmann (1999). (*B*) Relationship between kidney fat index and breeding date of 25 Roosevelt cows in western Oregon (Trainer 1971).

Timing of ovulation and breeding may be delayed as well if weight or condition during the breeding season is relatively low. Such effects have been reported for reindeer (Reimers 1983b), red deer (Mitchell and Lincoln 1973, Guinness et al. 1978b), white-tailed deer (Verme 1969) and elk (Trainer 1971, Kohlmann 1999, Cook 2000). In red deer, conception date may be delayed about a week if hinds are supporting a calf at the time of breeding (Mitchell and Lincoln 1973). Hamilton and Blaxter (1980) reported that parturition (and thus conception) of red deer occurred 1 day earlier for every 9 pounds (4 kg) of additional weight in red deer. Trainer (1971) reported a 19-day spread in mean breeding date among Roosevelt elk with different fat levels. Summer forage conditions were believed to play a role in determining breeding dates in this elk study. Kohlmann (1999) presented an equation to predict the mean conception date (CD) of elk: CD = 55.69 − 0.1074(KFI), where KFI is a kidney fat index.

Age at First Breeding

Onset of breeding is quite variable among young females of temperate cervids; it appears to be a function of body weight in red deer (Hamilton and Blaxter 1980), reindeer (Reimers 1983a), white-tailed deer (Verme and Ullrey 1984) and moose (Sæther and Haagenrud 1983, Sæther and Heim 1993). This appears to be true for elk as well; the percentage of yearling cows breeding has been reported to be as low as 0% to 7% (Murie 1951, Cheatum and Gaab 1952, Trainer 1971) and as high as 50% (Hudson et al. 1991). Greer (1968b) reported that no yearling cows weighing less than 335 pounds (152 kg) were pregnant; 10% weighing 334 to 359 pounds (152–163 kg) were pregnant; and 25% weighing 359 to 373 pounds (163–169 kg) were pregnant. Hudson et al. (1991) indicated that cow elk must achieve 65% to 70% of their adult weight before they will breed.

Nutrition during winter or summer may have important effects on yearling breeding rates by controlling condition at the time of rut. Winter weather apparently affected subsequent yearling breeding in a study in Utah (Hancock 1957). Pregnancy rates of yearling cows after a mild winter was 66% at one study area and 11% at another. Yearling cow ovulation rates was zero in both herds after a severe winter. Excessive winter weight loss apparently precluded yearlings from breeding during the following rut because a greater proportion of nutrition in summer was allocated to recovery rather than to growth. In a red deer study, nutritive value of spring and summer food also had important effects on yearling pregnancy rates (Wegge 1975). Sæther and Heim (1993) and Sæther (1985) concluded that abundance of certain forbs on summer home ranges in Norway significantly affected yearling cow moose weights and consequently their probability of breeding as yearlings. Stussy (1993) reported very low pregnancy rates in yearlings, 2.5- and 3.5-year-old Roosevelt cows in western Oregon (Figure 100), an area of mild winter weather, suggesting the importance of nutrition in summer and autumn. Timing of birth may interact with nutrition to affect onset of breeding (Sæther and Heim 1993).

Fetal Survival

Little is specifically known about the extent and causes of fetal mortality in brucellosis-free elk (brucellosis often induces fetal loss). Citing unpublished data, Kohlmann (1999) noted embryonic mortality of at least 4% during the first trimester in Oregon elk. Thereafter, fetal mortality has rarely been documented, but apparently is uncommon except when induced by substantial undernutrition during winter or spring. Thorne et al. (1976) documented three

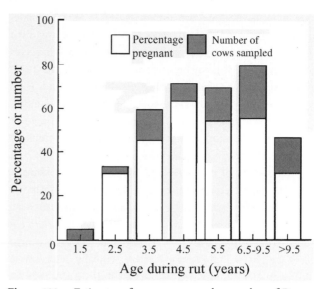

Figure 100.   Estimates of pregnancy rates by age class of Roosevelt elk in coastal environments of western Oregon (adapted from Stussy 1993). The low pregnancy rates of prime age cows and the relatively advanced age required for pregnancy rates to plateau, at 4.5 years of age, are indicative of markedly inadequate nutritional conditions, probably during summer and autumn.

abortions of a total of 12 pregnant cows held in captivity that had lost 14% to 17% of body weight between early winter and just after parturition. No fetal losses were noted of 27 other cows losing less than 14% of their weight. Kozak et al. (1994) also reported fetal losses in elk and linked these losses to poor nutritional condition.

Similar effects of acute nutritional deficiencies on fetal mortality have been reported for white-tailed deer (Verme 1962). In caribou, fetal mortality is uncommon and confined to periods of unusually severe nutritional restriction (Cameron et al. 1993). Substantial nutritional deprivation in winter and in spring may cause death more often during or just after parturition than during gestation (Wegge 1975).

Inadequate nutrition during winter (Skogland 1983) or during late gestation (Cameron et al. 1993) might delay parturition date until the fetus reaches some critical threshold in size (Verme 1965). In white-tailed deer, semistarvation in winter lengthened gestation 4 to 6 days (Verme 1965).

Fetal Growth and Birth Weight

Fetal growth and birth weight can strongly influence neonate survival at or soon after parturition. Livestock young that are too small at birth may lack vigor, tolerance to cold, rainy weather and disease resistance, and ability to survive birthing stress (Holland and Odde 1992). Low birth weight may contribute to inefficient digestion and assimilation of milk, because the alimentary tract may be inadequately developed (Lyford 1988). Growth rate of low birth weight red deer (Blaxter and Hamilton 1980) and elk calves (Cook et al. 1994b) may be suppressed. Thorne et al. (1976) reported that elk calves weighing less than 25 pounds (11.4 kg) at birth only had a 50% chance of survival, despite protection from predators. Newborn calves that are too weak to nurse are abandoned by their mother, usually within 6 to 10 hours after birth, based on my observations.

Birth weight of elk calves can vary markedly. Robbins et al. (1981) reported average birth weights of 46 pounds (21 kg) from captive cows on a high plane of nutrition year-round. Birth weights as low as 15 pounds (7 kg) have been reported (Thorne et al. 1976, Cook et al. 1994b). Average birth weights of free-ranging calves typically are from 30 (Johnson 1951, Smith 1994) to 40 pounds (Schlegal 1976) (14–18 kg).

Fetal growth and birth weight are sensitive to a variety of genetic and environmental factors (Holland and Odde 1992). Birth weight of red deer calves was significantly correlated to the weight of its mother during rut, regardless of the mother's age. On average, for every 22-pound (10 kilogram) increase in the mother's weight during the rut, calf birth weight was 1.1 pound (0.5 kg) higher (Blaxter and Hamilton 1980). Conversely, Hudson et al. (1991) reported that birth weight of elk calves was unrelated to weight of

Although birth weight of elk calves can exceed 55 pounds (25 kg), it typically ranges from 30 to 40 pounds (14–18 kg). Calves weighing less than 25 pounds (11.4 kg) at birth have been shown (Thorne et al. 1976) to have only a 50% chance of survival, even when protected from predators. *Photo by T. W. Daniels.*

mature cows during the rut. Reasons for disparate conclusions from the studies are not clear, but they may be explained by differences between species or the overall nutritional plane of the females studied.

Birth weight of juveniles also is sensitive to weather conditions during the last trimester of gestation in roe deer (Gaillard et al. 1993) and red deer (Clutton-Brock et al. 1982) (Figure 101). Smith et al. (1996) reported that March temperatures were positively correlated to birth weight of elk calves (Figure 101). Although the correlative mechanisms are not clear, warmer temperatures in spring probably hasten snow melt and enhance vegetative growth, resulting in greater forage production earlier in spring (Clutton-Brock et al. 1982, Smith et al. 1996). Smith et al. (1996) also reported that warmer temperatures in December and January were correlated with larger birth weights. The effects of March temperatures apparently were greater, however.

In livestock, the influence of nutritional restriction on birth weight remains unclear. Studies typically show that fetal growth is not responsive to levels of protein in diets, but varying the energy level in the diet can have important effects (Holland and Odde 1992). Maternal mobilization of stored protein and energy apparently compensates for inadequate nutrition and helps to maintain fetal growth rates. Inadequate nutrition during gestation, therefore, may reduce condition and affect the performance of the cow after parturition. However, long-term (i.e., autumn through spring), chronic nutritional deficiencies can have substantial effects on birth weight in livestock (Holland and Odde 1992).

Nutritional influences on elk birth weight likewise are not clearly defined. Thorne et al. (1976) reported a strong relationship between birth weight and the feeding level of alfalfa hay over winter and spring. Conversely, in a similar study in which winter diets were restricted but spring diets were not, birth weight was insignificantly influenced by winter nutrition (Oldemeyer et al. 1993). There seems to be general agreement that nutrition during spring has substantially greater impact on birth weight than does nutrition during winter (Clutton-Brock et al. 1982, Oldemeyer et al. 1993). Even so, severe nutritional deficiencies during harsh winters probably affects birth weight, even if spring nutrition is adequate (Verme 1963, 1977). For example, Keech et al. (2000) reported that birth weight of singletons and twins of moose in Alaska was positively correlated to the fat level of their mothers, measured at the end of winter (March).

So what do we know about the prevalence of low birth weight in wild elk calves? The answer is not much. Studies measuring birth weight of elk calves in an unbiased manner are rare, because few studies have been designed to account

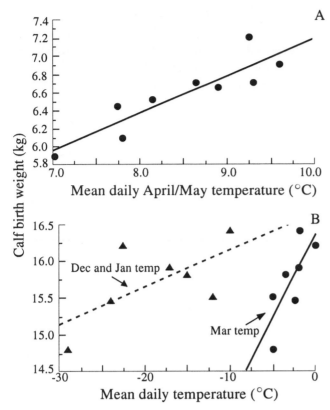

Figure 101. Relationship between birth weight of red deer calves and average daily temperature in April and May (*A*) (from Clutton-Brock et al. 1982a) and birth weight of elk calves and average temperature in March and December/January (*B*) (from Smith et al. 1996). Smith et al. found that (1) temperature in March but not April or May influenced elk calf birth weight, and (2) the effects of December/January temperature were independent of and apparently weaker than the effects of March temperature on birth weight in northwestern Wyoming.

for elevated mortality rates of small calves (low birth weight calves have a greater tendency to die soon after birth and, therefore, not be found). Studies that have reported birth weights (Johnson 1951, Schlegal 1976, Smith et al. 1997) typically have not indicated the portion of the calf crop with low birth weights.

Juvenile Growth

At least during the first 60 days of life, calf growth is linked closely to milk yields of the mother. In turn, milk yields are markedly influenced by the mother's nutrition (Oftedal 1985). The effects of nutritional deprivation on yield can be rapid, substantial and independent of nutritional plane just before the lactation period (Barnicoat et al. 1949, Peart 1968, Loudon et al. 1983). Loudon et al. (1983) reported that milk production in red deer was 1.6 times higher in females maintained on pastures with 1,600 pounds dry matter per acre (1,800 kg/ha) at 69% digestibility than in fe-

males using forages of low density with 60% digestibility (Figure 102). Crête and Hout (1993) reported that caribou ranging on poor quality summer range were unable to metabolize enough energy and protein to sustain lactation during peak milk production during the first month after giving birth. They also reported that nutritional demands of lactation eliminated virtually all fat contained in the dams. In elk, supplementation of diets of cows grazing aspen parkland habitats in Alberta apparently resulted in greater milk consumption in elk calves during summer—1.9 pounds (0.88 kg) per nursing bout for unsupplemented versus 2.38 pounds (1.08 kg) of milk per nursing bout for supplemented cow/calf pairs (Hudson and Adamczewski 1990).

Growth of older juveniles that rely less on milk remain inordinately sensitive to nutrition through mid-autumn. Verme and Ozoga (1980a) showed that weight, skeletal size, size of internal organs and fat depots of white-tailed deer fawns were significantly influenced by even moderate differences in DE content of diets (85 vs. 76.5 kcal/oz [3.0 vs. 2.7 kcal/g] of food fed for 10 weeks). Similarly, Holter and Hayes (1977) found that a 40% restriction in DE intake reduced fat accumulation in white-tailed deer fawns by 76% during a 6-week period in early autumn. Growth of caribou calves on poor quality summer range averaged 30% to 40% below that of calves on high-quality summer range or others held in captivity (Crête and Huot 1993).

The growth rate of calf elk during the first 2 months after birth is closely linked to milk consumption—and therefore influenced by the nutrition and body condition of its mother. *Photo by C. J. Henry; courtesy of the U.S. Fish and Wildlife Service.*

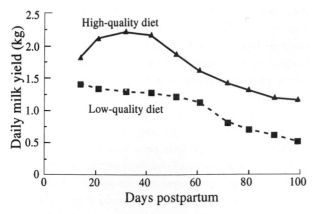

Figure 102. Daily milk yield of red deer dams held on improved pastures (1,580 pounds of forage per acre [1,771 kg/ha], 69% dry matter digestibility) and red deer held on native pastures with lower forage abundance and quality (60% dry matter digestibility) (adapted from Loudon et al. 1983).

Studies with elk calves demonstrate a marked link between nutrition and growth as well. Cook et al. (1996) reported that daily growth of calves increased about 1.4 pounds per day per 100 kilocalories (2.9 g/day per kcal) increase in daily DE consumed per pound of metabolic weight (MW) in late summer. By mid-autumn, these growth rate values declined from 1.4 pounds to 0.88 pound (2.9–1.8 g) of daily gain (Figure 103). Growth ceased when DE feeding level fell to 300 to 352 kilocalories of DE per pound (140–160 kcal/kg) MW, and was highest when DE intake exceeded 770 kilocalories per pound (350 kcal/kg) MW.

The relevance of strong growth–nutrition relationships to free-ranging elk calves is difficult to assess, however, be-

cause little data exist indicating energy content of elk diets during summer and autumn. Cook et al. (1996) developed a model to predict body size of elk calves at the beginning of winter based on DE content of forage available to calves from late summer through autumn. Results of the model indicated that growth of wild elk calves is substantially reduced below potential, based on dietary DE levels reported for wild elk in central Washington (Figure 104). Loudon et al. (1984) found that growth of red deer calves during summer was significantly greater for cow/calf pairs held on high-quality pastures compared with those held on pastures of low nutritive value. Conversely, growth of elk calves ranging in large pastures during summer (through September) in central Alberta was unaffected by supplementing cows with a high-quality pelleted ration (Hudson and Adamczewski 1990). These contrasting results suggest that calf growth in summer and autumn may vary substantially across a variety of ecological settings (Cook et al. 1996). The quality of forage available to juveniles apparently determines the extent to which calves can compensate for the declining milk production of their mothers (Sowell et al. 1996). Performance of calves during summer also may be affected by nutritional factors that determine the mother's condition at the beginning of summer (Hudson and Adamczewski 1990).

During winter, growth of calves typically wanes, but can continue at a reduced level if forage conditions are sufficient to support growth. Studies with captive red deer calves have shown that providing abundant, nutritious food during winter will significantly increase body weight at the end of winter and may provide for larger body size the following autumn (Suttie and Hamilton 1983, Milne et al. 1987). However, the potential for growth declines consider-

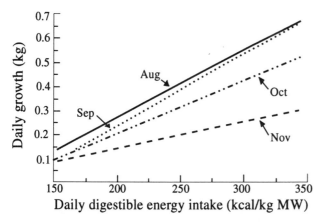

Figure 103. Relationship between daily intake of digestible energy (kilocalories of intake per kilogram of metabolic weight [MW]) and daily growth rate of elk calves from August through November (adapted from Cook et al. 1996). The increasingly horizontal slopes of the lines as season progresses indicate declining growth potential beginning in October.

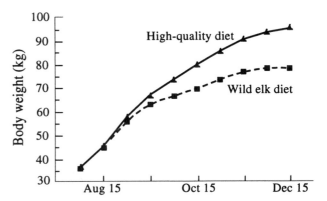

Figure 104. Predicted growth and body size of elk calves over autumn consuming a high-quality diet and of calves consuming diets estimated for wild elk in Washington (Schommer 1978). The prediction equation used here was presented by Cook et al. (1996). The reduced growth performance predicted for wild elk is due to low forage quality levels in autumn.

ably in juveniles by the beginning of winter (see Figure 103). For example, Cook et al. (1996) reported that growth of elk calves in mid-November was half of that in September at equal levels of nutrition. Cessation of growth, apparently in response to changing day length (photoperiod effect), is well-documented in North American deer (Verme and Ozoga 1980b) and European red deer (Sibbald et al. 1993). Reduction in growth results in reduced nutritional requirements—an adaptation to winter nutritional deficiencies. The primary value of relatively high levels of forage quality and abundance to wild elk calves during winter apparently is to minimize loss in condition and mortality, rather than to support rapid growth (Cook et al. 1996).

Juvenile Survival in Summer

Birth weight is a primary factor influencing survival during summer (Verme 1977, Guinness et al. 1978a, Clutton-Brock et al. 1982, Fairbanks 1993). Survival of elk calves in captivity averaged 50% to 66% for those weighing less than 25 pounds (11.4 kg) at birth and about 90% for calves more than 36 pounds (16 kg) at birth (Thorne et al. 1976, Oldemeyer et al. 1993). Most juvenile mortality in summer occurs during the first few days after birth, according to Guinness et al. (1978a) for red deer, Fairbanks (1993) for pronghorn, Verme (1977) for white-tailed deer and Whitten et al. (1992) for caribou. Mortality within the first 2 days of birth can range up to 40% (Whitten et al. 1992).

Juvenile mortality before winter can be partitioned into two general categories: (1) mortality at or near birthing due to low birth weight/viability problems, as discussed above; and (2) mortality due to accidents, inclement weather (e.g., snowstorms occurring during birthing) disease and, particularly, predation. The first category generally is a direct function of maternal nutrition during gestation.

Relevance of nutrition to the second category of mortality is unclear and depends on the extent to which nutrition might predispose to these mortality factors (e.g., predation). Studies of bighorn sheep (Cook 1990) and white-tailed deer (Sams et al. 1996) have linked mortality to disease with deficient nutrition during summer. I am unaware of any studies that have determined the effects of inadequate nutrition during summer/autumn on elk calf survival during these seasons. Emerging evidence suggest that, in predator-rich environments, nutrition before summer/autumn, in fact, does predispose to predation. For example, Keech et al. (2000) reported that the amount of time that moose calves survived after parturition was significantly influenced by birth weight in a region of relatively heavy predation by bears and wolves. Likewise, Singer et al. (1997) reported that probability of summer survival of elk calves in

Yellowstone, where predation by grizzly and black bears and other predators was common, also was significantly influenced by birth weight. Smaller calves may be slower and easier for predators to catch (Singer et al. 1997), and their mothers may be in poorer condition such that frequency of visits and quality of care (e.g., milk production) may be reduced (Keech et al. 2000).

Birth date also may influence survival during summer and autumn (Figure 105). In predator-rich environments, a classic perception is that juveniles born during the peak of parturition are less susceptible. This apparently is due to a swamping effect—the ratio of predators to juvenile prey is lower during the peak of parturition, therefore prey survival is enhanced. Thus, the parturition period should be short and synchronous to minimize summer juvenile mortality; timing of the parturition period generally should be relatively unimportant. An alternative hypothesis that incorporates nutritional influences is that parturition should be timed to maximize the use of high-quality forage available during the growing season, and relatively early births should confer a survival advantage (Keech et al. 2000). However, a variety of studies provide conflicting results regarding birth date's influence. For example, Guinness et al. (1978a) for red deer, Fairbanks (1993) for pronghorn, and Singer et al. (1997) for elk in Yellowstone failed to show a significant relation between birth date and juvenile survival during summer or autumn. Guinness et al. (1978a) did point out that the combined effect of late births and low birth weight is particularly detrimental to red deer calves. In ecological settings where nutritional restriction is sufficiently severe to cause one (e.g., low birth weight), it is likely to cause the other as well (e.g., late birth).

All in all, research suggests that summer and autumn

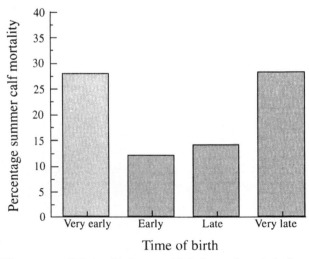

Figure 105. Relationship between birth date and survival of red deer calves during summer (adapted from Clutton-Brock et al. 1982a).

survival of juveniles results from a complex interaction between maternal condition before the summer, predator numbers and density, and probably a variety of other factors, including nutritional status during summer. Relative importance of these factors are poorly understood. Summer/autumn juvenile mortality can be high particularly in predator-rich environments. But new studies, such as Keech et al. (2000) and Singer et al. (1997), clearly show that mortality studies are of questionable value if they succeed only in documenting proximate causes of death and fail to assess underlying, subtle predisposing factors such as nutrition.

Juvenile and Adult Survival in Winter

The effect of nutrition on winter survival is well-recognized. High mortality can occur when snow accumulates and persists to the point that animals starve. The effects of starvation are most pronounced in juveniles, owing to smaller body size, increased susceptibility to cold temperatures and lower endogenous energy reserves available in fat and muscle tissues.

In terms of meeting the energy and nutritional requirements of large ungulates such as elk, the nutritive value of forage on winter range typically is marginal at best, even during relatively mild winters (Wallmo et al. 1977, Hobbs et al. 1980, Irwin et al. 1993). But elk are well-adapted to withstand nutritional deficiencies during winter. Highly insulative pelage and a variety of other physiological adaptations to withstand cold temperatures, reduced activity and reduced energy requirements enhance tolerance to low forage nutritive value and harsh weather (Riggs et al. 1993).

Survival during winter largely depends on the availability of forage as mediated by snow accumulation (Hobbs 1989). As snow deepens, animals may compensate to some extent by spending more time foraging in habitats with a greater abundance of shrubs (Jenkins and Wright 1988, Goodson et al. 1991b). The proportion of green herbaceous plant material, foraging efficiency (i.e., cropping rates and dry matter intake) and nutritive value of diets typically decline, even with relatively minimal snow accumulation (Figure 106) (Hanley and McKendrick 1985, Riggs et al. 1990, Goodson et al. 1991a). In addition, snow accumulations more than 10 to 12 inches (25–30 cm) will increase energy expenditures considerably as animals travel, and juveniles are particularly susceptible owing to their smaller stature (Fancy and White 1985). When snow is deep, elk may expend more energy feeding than they can ingest. Particularly under these conditions, elk must survive using energy stored in fat and muscle.

Because of the dependency on energy stored in fat and muscle during summer, overwinter survival also relates to body size and nutritional condition at the beginning of winter (Figure 107) (Verme and Ozoga 1980a, Hobbs 1989). In calves, size and condition in late autumn may reflect birth

The condition and amount of available winter range are significant determinants of overwinter survival and health of elk. Although elk are well-adapted to withstand winter deficiencies of nutrition, reduced winter range or reduced accessibility of elk to traditional winter range, without a corresponding reduction in herd size, can severely stress the population. *Photo by Donald Schuhard; courtesy of the U.S. Natural Resources Conservation Service.*

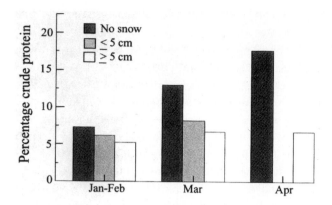

Figure 106. Effects of snow depth on dietary crude protein levels of bighorn sheep during winter in Colorado (adapted from Goodson et al. 1991a).

weight, birth date and nutritional levels during the summer and early autumn. Regarding birth weight, however, Clutton-Brock et al. (1982) reported that birth weight has little influence on body size and condition in late winter and, therefore, differences in weight at birth are insufficient to affect overwinter survival. Festa-Bianchet et al. (2000) argued similarly. But other studies discount this. Bailey and Mears (1990) reported that small cattle calves grew more slowly on an absolute basis (pounds per day) than calves of normal birth weight, although they grew equivalently on an incremental basis (percentage per day). Thorne et al. (1976) also reported this for elk calves. This pattern suggests potential for weight differences existing at birth to actually increase as calves grow, a type of multiplier effect. Keech et al. (1999) reported that birth weight of free-ranging moose calves was related to weight at 10 months of age based on the equation: Y = 6.88X + 36.9, where Y = weight in kilograms at 10 months of age and X = birth weight in kilograms.

The striking aspect of the equation is that each pound increase in birth weight translates to a 6.88-pound (3.12 kg)

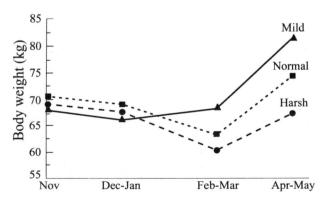

Figure 107. Effects of winter severity on weight of moose calves (from Cederlund et al. 1991). These data point to the importance of large size and abundant fat reserves for surviving normal to harsh winters.

increase in weight at age 10 months, suggesting a dramatic multiplier effect. Pelabon (1997) reported similar responses in fallow deer: a 1-pound (0.45 kg) difference in birth weight translated to a 5-pound (2.27 kg) difference by the onset of winter. Finally, Schultz and Johnson (1995) showed a 1- to 7-pound (0.45–3.17 kg) relation from birth to 1.5 years of age in male white-tailed deer held under captive conditions with good quality and abundant food. The advantage from larger birth weight remained through the 2.5-year-old age class in this study, indicating the multiplier effect provides advantages that hold through mature age classes.

The relation of birth weight to overwinter survival, however, has been reported infrequently. Cederlund et al. (1991) reported that smaller moose calves lost more weight over winter, suggesting greater susceptibility of smaller juveniles to harsh winter weather. Also, Clutton-Brock et al (1987) reported a relation between birth weight and overwinter survival of red deer calves. But Singer et al. (1997) found no relation between birth weight and winter survival of elk calves in Yellowstone, although the majority of calf mortality was due to starvation.

Late birth also may result in smaller calf body size at the onset of winter and therefore, may influence overwinter survival. Late birthing can reduce the synchrony between the peak in forage quality and the peak in nutritional demands of the lactating mother (Clutton-Brock et al. 1982, Festa-Bianchet 1988). Hence, calves born well after the peak in forage quality may have less opportunity to catch up and may be more likely to fall behind (Guinness et al. 1978b, Clutton-Brock et al. 1982). Singer et al. (1997) found that winter mortality of late-born calves was higher than that of earlier-born calves. But few studies have been conducted that identify the practical relevance of birth date's potential effect on overwinter survival of juveniles.

Finally, nutritional status over summer and autumn can strongly influence calf size at the onset of winter, due to the close coupling of calf growth and nutrition (Cook et al. 1996). Nutrition's influence during summer and autumn on juvenile growth and subsequent winter survival, however, has rarely been studied in wild herds. Projections of body size using an elk calf growth model (Cook et al. 1996), with estimates of nutritive value of diets measured for free-ranging elk, suggested that autumn diets can be insufficient to sustain high growth rates across autumn (see Figure 104). Weather's influence on forage quality and quantity in summer and autumn influenced growth performance of cattle calves in the Blue Mountains of Oregon (Skovlin 1962) and calf/cow ratios of elk in Yellowstone (Merrill and Boyce 1991). Information presented later in this chapter suggests that inadequate DE levels after late summer may be a relatively common problem restricting calf growth in many areas.

In adults, size and condition at the outset of winter reflect lactation status during the previous summer, summer/autumn nutritional levels and, for bulls, extent of weight loss during the rut and recovery after the rut. Nutritional demands of lactation can limit the amount of fat that females can accrue before winter, and many of the studies identifying factors that influence breeding, discussed above, indicate lactation's influence on fat accumulation (e.g., Trainer 1971, Cook 2000). There undoubtedly exists an interaction such that the magnitude of lactation's influence depends on levels of nutrition during summer and autumn. Thus, lactating and nonlactating cows should be relatively fat at the onset of winter in areas of excellent summer/autumn nutrition, whereas only nonlactating cows would be fat in areas of marginal to inadequate summer/autumn nutrition. Such interactive relations have been discussed by Verme and Ullrey (1982). As with calf growth, discussed above, the extent to which inadequate summer/fall nutrition appreciably limits fat accretion and contributes to overwinter mortality in wild elk herds in unknown in most ecological settings.

Synthesis

The literature is replete with examples of pathways throughout which nutrition influences demography and productivity of ungulate populations. Much of this work is piecemeal and often contradictory, but general patterns and conclusions seem evident. Foremost, growth and survival of juveniles and subadults are inextricably linked to nutrition. Young animals face considerable challenges to survive against disease, predation, accidents, starvation, and harsh weather. Nutrition plays a crucial role by affecting resistance to disease, rate of development and thus capability to evade predators, and growth rates that determine body size and fat levels during their first winter. Particularly in northern climates, the latter is crucial; young must race with time their first summer to grow sufficiently to survive winter. Elk calves have an enormous propensity to grow, from 30 pounds (14 kg) to more than 320 pounds (145 kg)—a 10-fold increase, during their first 5 months of life (Hudson and Adamczewski 1990). Early birth and large birth weight provide important advantages, particularly in terms of early neonatal mortality, but such growth requires enormous nutritional inputs (discussed later) that probably are unavailable in many ecological settings (Cook et al. 1996, Parker et al. 1999).

Nutrition also influences the ability of ungulates to maximize lifetime reproductive success, a result of becoming reproductively mature at a relatively early age and, for elk, successfully producing a calf each year thereafter. Many of the factors that affect calf performance may affect lifetime reproductive success. Low birth weight may delay the age at first breeding (puberty) and result in lifelong disadvantages (Schultz and Johnson 1995, Keech et al. 1999). Festa-Bianchet et al. (2000) reported that growth during summer and autumn influenced adult weights and lifetime reproductive success in bighorn sheep. In elk, cows can first breed as yearlings, but the majority in the wild apparently do not. Yet, I have found that captive elk maintained on a high nutritional plane in summer and autumn their first and second years of life can easily attain 450 pounds (204 kg) and virtually all breed when yearlings, even when fed winter starvation diets that induce 20% weight loss when calves. In some herds, many cows fail to breed until 3.5 or even 4.5 years of age (e.g., Stussy et al. 1993), suggesting severely restricted nutritional conditions.

Nutrition's greatest influences on adults include overwinter survival and fat accumulation dynamics of lactating cows during summer and autumn. How well habitat provides for these needs determines probability of survival and successful reproduction. The adult female faces important tradeoffs: (1) sacrifice her body reserves (fat levels) to maintain her calf during the summer and autumn and face greater probability of dying in winter; (2) breed in autumn despite marginal fat reserves and face greater probability of winter mortality; (3) sacrifice her body reserves to provide for the well-being of her current calf and lower the probability of breeding and raising a calf the next year; and (4) sacrifice her body reserves during winter to maintain fetal growth and viability and face a greater chance of dying that winter. In nutritionally optimum environments, these tradeoffs are inconsequential. In nutritionally marginal environments, the tradeoffs between reproduction and survival must be balanced in some optimal manner, or herds risk extirpation.

What has been learned about nutritional influences contributed to theory that links nutrition, survival and reproduction of individuals, and dynamics and productivity of herds. This theory generally is referred to as density dependence (although density dependence may operate by mechanisms other than nutrition). It postulates that negative feedback relations exist between herbivores and the vegetation on which they depend. As populations increase, competition for forage increases and abundance of the more palatable forage declines. It also predicts that there is some dynamic stable state of equilibrium between herbivores and vegetation, referred to as ecological carrying capacity (Caughley 1970, 1977). Empirical examples suggest that, as population numbers increase, juvenile survival declines first, followed by pregnancy rates and birth rates and, finally adult survival (Caughley 1977).

Many examples exist of density dependence in large herbivore populations (Fowler 1987), most from populations on islands with no predators or parks and preserves with no hunting and often with few predators. Fowler (1987) argued that density-dependent effects of nutrition are mostly expressed when populations approach carrying capacity. The importance of density dependence in predatory-rich environments, or for ungulate populations that are heavily hunted, has been infrequently studied, often debated and generally is unclear.

Nutrition's effects also may occur well below carrying capacity and independently of density. These effects reflect the inherent capability of different landscapes to support elk. For example, precipitation, temperature and other climatological conditions on elk winter ranges vary considerably (see Cook et al. 1998), as does vegetation. Rate of weight loss, survival and other such demographic characteristics undoubtedly vary among these winter ranges as well, regardless of animal density. Differences in climate and vegetation on summer ranges also probably induce density-independent nutritional influences.

Although concepts of density dependence provide a framework linking the many piecemeal studies of nutritional influences, important unanswered questions remain. From a management perspective, foremost among these is how nutritional conditions among different seasons contribute to the dynamics of wild populations. Effects of winter nutritional deficiencies have long been recognized as key influences because of easily observed, often dramatic die-offs. Winter ranges, therefore, usually are considered the principal determinant of carrying capacity across the entire annual range of herds (e.g., Wallmo et al 1977).

Influences of late spring, summer and autumn ranges are more subtle, and their influences often are discounted (e.g., Wallmo et al. 1977, Lyon et al. 1985, Christensen et al. 1993, Unsworth et al. 1998). Moreover, the nutritional effects arising during these seasons often are manifested in other seasons, particularly winter. These carry-over effects (e.g., Picton 1984, Novellie 1986) are not well documented or well understood. Julander et al. (1961) provided some of the earliest information from western summer ranges that summer/autumn nutrition can be a key determinant of productivity. Since then, we have learned that large ungulates, such as elk, are adapted to nutritional deficiencies during winter and that the probability of survival (Hobbs 1989) and recovery after winter is linked to spring/summer/autumn nutrition. Studies also have shown that elk demography, particularly calf survival and recruitment, is linked closely with abundance of green vegetation during summer in the Yellowstone area (Merrill and Boyce 1991).

The upshot is that relative effects of seasonal nutrition

levels on productivity can vary substantially among herds and among years within herds. Verme (1969) recognized this and, for Upper Midwest deer ranges, proposed a classification system that reflected the differential role of nutrition on deer productivity among regions and herds and the differential role of nutrition among seasons. Such a scheme for elk has yet to be developed.

Nutritional Requirements

Nutritional requirements of elk vary markedly among seasons and age classes, primarily as a function of growth, gestation, lactation and antler growth. Energy requirements also vary as a function of activity levels and weather. Reasonable estimates of requirements are needed to understand functional relations between nutrition and dynamics of ungulate populations, evaluate carrying capacity and habitat quality, and assess the need for and results of habitat manipulations such as prescribed fire and timber harvest. In this section, estimates of nutritional requirements are calculated for adult cows across an annual cycle and for calves and subadults during key seasonal periods (in this chapter, subadults includes yearlings, 2- and 3-year-old elk—animals that are, or potentially can be, reproductively mature but are still growing). Calculations are based on a factorial approach that reflects nutritional requirements for various activities and stages of production. Readers should be aware that estimates of energy requirements deviate markedly from those presented in Thomas and Toweill (1982). As such, conclusions about probability of deficiencies in diets of elk herds differ markedly as well.

Energy Requirements: Adults

Maintenance and Activity

Animals must expend considerable energy for physiological homeostasis, which primarily involves energy for cellular respiration and maintenance. A reasonable estimate of energy expended each day for this is 77 kcal/kg MW (National Research Council 1984). ME requirements for maintenance can be calculated by dividing energy expended by the efficiency of utilization of ME for maintenance. This efficiency ranges from 0.64 to 0.75, the lower value for lower quality diets (Hudson and Christopherson 1985). For calculations here, the lower value was used in winter, the higher value in spring, 0.71 in summer and 0.68 in autumn.

Activity also induces important energetic costs to animals. On the basis of elk activity data (Craighead et al. 1973) and energy expenditure rates determined for domestic livestock (Moen 1973), estimates of total daily energy expenditures for basal metabolism and activity were estimated. The ME conversion factors listed above for maintenance were used to estimate ME requirements for activity.

An elk weighing 520 pounds (236 kg) would expend between 6,500 and 7,500 kcal/day during the year for metabolism and activity (Table 47). ME required for these expenditures would range from 9,500 to 10,500 kcal/day, or about 70.3 to 77.1 kcal/lb (155–170 kcal/kg) MW per day, with the highest value occurring in summer. However, Jiang and Hudson (1992) estimated that summer ME requirements for live-weight maintenance of nonlactating cows was 104.3 kcal/lb (230 kcal/kg) MW compared with 77.1 kcal/lb (170 kcal/kg) MW indicated in Table 47. For prediction purposes here, the average of the two estimates (200 kcal) was assumed to be the ME requirement for live-weight maintenance during summer. Finally, because data in Table 47 were based on activity levels of nonmigratory elk and no adjustment for migration was incorporated, spring/autumn energy requirements for activity probably are underestimated for migratory elk herds.

Gestation

Gestation increases energy requirements for gravid (pregnant) cows. Greater requirements are due to accumulation of energy (net energy) contained in the tissues of the growing fetus and energy required to grow the fetus. ME requirements include net energy and efficiency of ME conversion to net energy. Accretion of fetal tissues occurs slowly during the first 150 days of gestation and increases thereafter (Figure 108). Energy for pregnancy can be estimated using an equation from the National Research Council (1984) for cattle, with an adjustment for gestation length:

$$Q_{ne} = PW(0.0149 - 0.0000407t/GT)e^{[0.05883t - 0.00008804(t/GR)^2]}$$

where Q_{ne} = net energy required for pregnancy in kilocalories per day, PW = average elk calf weight at parturition (assumed to equal 18 kg for Rocky Mountain elk), t = elk gestation time in days and GT = ratio of elk–cattle gestation time (256 days/280 days = 0.91).

The amount of ME required to provide Q_{ne} can be estimated by dividing Q_{ne} by 0.65 for forage of moderately good quality. Thus, ME requirements for pregnancy (Q_{pe})

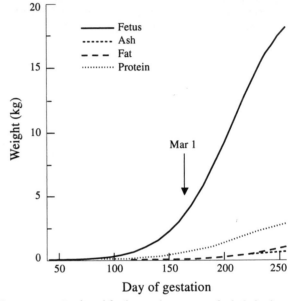

Figure 108. Predicted fetal growth patterns of whole-body (wet weight basis) and body constituents (dry matter basis) of Rocky Mountain elk. Appreciable tissue accumulation begins to occur in late February and early March, increases rapidly during the third trimester and declines slightly during the last week before parturition.

Table 47. Estimated daily activity pattern, energy expenditure rates in kilocalories and metabolizable energy (ME) requirements for activity and standard metabolic rate (SMR) in kilocalories by seasons for a 520-pound (236-kg) cow elk

| | Daily activity | | | | | | | | | | | |
| | Foraging | | Bedding | | Traveling[a] | | Standing | | Ruminating | | | | |
	hours	kcal	hours	kcal	hours	kcal	hours	kcal	hours	kcal	SMR[b] plus activity	ME[c]	ME/MW[d]
Winter	9.2	1,172	13.5	0	0.9	301	0.4	7	6.0	340	6,456	10,088	167.5
Spring	13.0	1,657	9.6	0	1.1	368	0.3	5	6.0	340	7,006	9,341	155.1
Summer	9.7	1,236	9.8	0	3.1	1,036	1.0	23	6.0	340	7,271	10,241	170.1[e]
Autumn	12.7	1,618	9.8	0	0.8	267	0.7	12	6.0	340	6,873	10,107	167.9

Sources: Activity pattern, Craighead et al. 1972; energy expenditure rates, Moen 1973.

[a] Based on an average rate of speed of 1.5 miles (2.4 km) per hour on level terrain.

[b] SMR for 520-pound (236-kg) elk is 4,636 kcal/day.

[c] Metabolizable energy requirements to met SMR and activity energy expenditures.

[d] Metabolizable energy requirements calculated on a metabolic weight basis (kilocalories per kilogram of weight$^{0.75}$).

[e] Jiang and Hudson (1992) estimated metabolizable energy requirements for live-weight maintenance of six subadult cow elk during summer to be 230 kcal/kg of metabolic weight, 64% higher than during winter.

equals $Q_{ne}/0.65$, and units are kilocalories of ME per day. Although the base formula for Q_{ne} was developed using cattle fetal energy needs for growth, the adjustment using GT scales estimates for differences in gestation length. Substantial increases in energy requirements begin to occur in late February or early March, assuming a June 1 birth date, and continue to occur until birth (Figure 109).

Lactation

Energy needs for lactation are markedly greater than those for pregnancy. During the course of lactation, mothers will expend about four times more energy for lactation than for pregnancy (Price and White 1985). Energetic costs of lactation include the energy contained in milk and the efficiency of energy conversion from maternal sources to milk. This rate of efficiency averages about 65% in wild ruminants (Price and White 1985).

Energy costs of lactation can be computed as the product of milk yield and energy content of milk:

$$Q_{el} = [(MY)(EC)]/0.65$$

where Q_{el} = energy (kcal/day) required for lactation, MY = milk yield (g/day), EC = energy content of milk (kcal/g) and is based on caloric values of 9.25, 5.85 and 3.69 kcal/g of fat, protein and lactose, respectively (Robbins et al. 1981) and 0.65 = efficiency of ME conversion.

Milk yields were presented by Robbins et al. (1981) for captive cow elk in good condition raising rapidly growing calves on abundant feed. Two equations were presented: milk yield increase and milk yield decline.

MY = 3055.5 + 50.1t (for 1–25 days after birth, when milk yields increase)

and

MY = 5578.9e$^{(-0.0125t)}$ (for 26–80 days after birth, when milk yields decline)

where MY = milk yield in grams per day and t = number of days after birth.

Energy concentration (EC) of milk during the first 3 weeks was estimated as the product of caloric value and proportional content of fat (6.5%), protein (5.5%) and lactose (4.1%). After the first 3 weeks, I used an equation presented by Robbins et al. (1981) that provides a direct estimate of energy content of elk milk:

$$Q_{el} = 5691e^{-0.0084t}/0.65$$

On the basis of these equations, daily ME requirements for lactation peak at about 7,000 kcal in late June or early July (assuming a June 1 birth date) and decline to 3,200 kcal at 120 days after birth (Figure 110). It is assumed that calves are weaned at 120 days after birth, but some nursing likely continues through much of autumn. The abrupt lactation peak 3 to 4 weeks after birth (Figure 110) is an artifact of switching between the two prediction equations and, in reality, change is more gradual.

Replacement of Winter Weight Loss

Fat and muscle catabolized during winter must be replaced during spring through autumn if the animal is to maintain itself from year to year, and substantial winter weight loss has been shown to reduce milk yields the following sum-

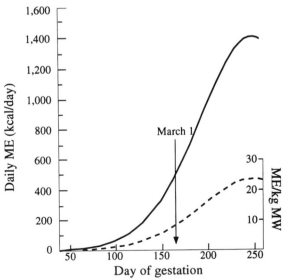

Figure 109. Predicted daily metabolizable energy requirements in kilocalories per day (solid line) and on a metabolic weight (MW) basis (dash line) to support fetal growth in gestating elk during winter and spring.

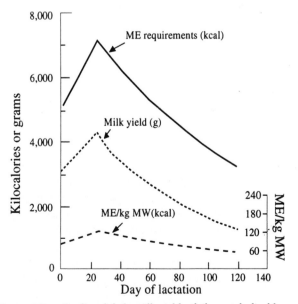

Figure 110. Predicted daily milk yields, daily metabolizable energy (ME) requirements of lactation and daily ME requirements expressed on a metabolic weight (MW) basis.

mer (Kozak et al. 1995). Elk may lose 25% or more of their body weight during very severe winters and 10% during moderate to normal winters. For a 520-pound (236 kg) cow, this represents about 130 and 52 pounds (59 and 24 kg) of tissue, respectively.

Jiang and Hudson (1992) estimated that 9.31 kcal of ME are required per gram of gain in large, subadult cow elk. Although ME requirements for gain may not be identical to requirements to replace winter-catabolized tissue, I assume that this value provided a reasonable approximation of ME required to replace tissue catabolized in winter. A 520-pound (236 kg) cow elk losing 10% of her body weight during winter would require about 219,480 kcal ME to replace this lost tissue (based on Jiang's and Hudson's estimate of ME requirement). Daily ME intake would have to average 1,330 kcal for a 520-pound (236 kg) cow or 10 kcal/lb (22 kcal/kg) MW, assuming this gain would occur over 165 days. (The 165 days is based on the assumption that gain would occur in April and May, when forage nutritive value is high, and between mid-July and early November, after peak lactation and before snow begins to accumulate.) After atypically harsh winters that induce 25% weight loss, the cow elk would require a total of 549,290 kcal ME, or about 3,330 kcal/day spread over 165 days, or about 25 kcal/lb (55 kcal/kg) MW per day.

Winter Maintenance

Estimates of winter energy requirements, including those of maintenance and activity in Table 47, assume that animals occur in thermoneutral conditions (i.e., range of temperature in which animals do not have to increase metabolic rate to maintain body temperature). If temperature falls below thermoneutrality, then energy requirements increase to maintain body temperature because the animal shivers to generate heat. The temperature at which energy expenditure begins to increase to maintain body temperature is referred to as lower critical temperature. Lower critical temperature of elk calves was estimated to be −4° to −13°F (−20° to −25°C) (Parker and Robbins 1984). These temperatures were measured as operative temperatures, which adjust air temperature based on humidity and radiation flux (e.g., solar radiation). Lower critical temperature of adult elk probably is much lower—at least −30°F (−35°C).

Factoring in the effects of cold temperature on ME requirements is quite difficult. Wind and solar radiation have important influences on lower critical temperature (Parker and Gillingham 1990). For example, during clear days, air temperature may drop substantially below lower critical temperature, but solar radiation can effectively compensate for cold temperatures. Elk also have a number of behavioral options to avoid elevated heat losses, including bedding down and selecting areas with reduced wind. Estimates of ME requirements presented here for winter assumed that thermoneutral conditions prevail across winter. Swift et al. (1980), for elk, and Gasaway and Coady (1974), for moose, concluded that cold temperatures likely had minor impacts on energy balance during winter. Even so, if temperatures are exceedingly cold, winter ME requirements probably will be somewhat higher than predicted here.

Predicted Seasonal Requirements

Estimates of combined ME requirements for each season are presented in Figure 111. Winter estimates include ME required for maintenance and activity, spring estimates add

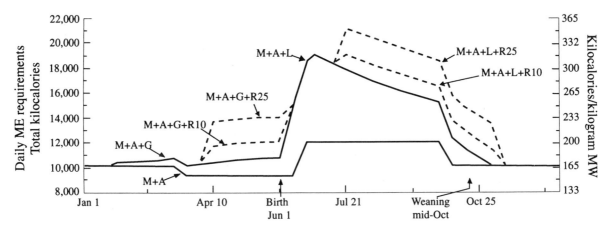

Figure 111.   Estimated daily metabolizable energy requirements for an adult cow elk to meet maintenance (M), activity (A), gestation (G), lactation (L) and winter catabolism replacement (R10 and R25) needs during each season. Data are presented for a 520-pound (236 kg) cow and on a metabolic weight (MW) basis. R10 and R25 are based on 10% and 25% winter weight losses, assuming a normal winter and an unusually harsh winter, respectively. The replacement increments were based on total metabolizable energy requirements divided by 165 days; replacement tissue accretion was assumed to occur primarily in April, May and mid-July through early November. The M + A + G and M + A + L lines indicate spring, summer and autumn metabolizable energy requirements after a mild winter, in which winter weight loss is insignificant.

gestation requirements, and summer and autumn estimates include ME requirements for maintenance, activity, lactation and replenishment of catabolized tissue in winter. ME requirements for replenishment are presented for 10% and 25% weight loss levels during winter.

Estimates of ME requirements vary among studies (Table 48), but generally corroborate predictions in Figure 111. Estimates of ME for maintenance generally range around 130 kcal/kg of MW under penned conditions and 160 to 180 kcal when costs for free-ranging activity levels are included in maintenance estimates. The low requirements for domestic sheep (Table 48) apparently reflect low metabolic rates of sheep (Hudson and Christopherson 1985). Estimates of ME requirements for late gestation range from 10 to 25 kcal/kg of MW per day above that estimated for winter maintenance. Estimates of nutritional

Table 48. Estimates of daily metabolizable energy requirements of mature gravid or lactating female ruminants

Species	Maintenance[a]	Mid-gestation[b]	Late gestation[c]	Early to mid-lactation[d]	Mid- to late lactation[e]	Source
Elk	165	165	170	300	265	Figure 109
Elk	145	150	195	285	285	Haigh and Hudson 1993[f]
Elk		132	149	250	250	Robbins et al. 1981[g]
Elk	132					Jiang and Hudson 1992[h]
Elk	168					J. G. Cook personal data[i]
Elk	173					Hobbs et al. 1982[j]
Red deer	136					Kay and Staines 1981[k]
Caribou	205	205	225			Adamczewski et al. 1993[l]
Caribou	160	162		235	220	Boertje 1985[m]
Caribou	200					McEwan and Whitehead 1970[n]
Roe deer	166					Papageorgiou et al. 1981[o]
White-tailed deer		131				Ullrey et al. 1970[p]
Black-tailed deer				273		Sadlier 1982[q]
Moose	131					Schwartz et al. 1988[r]
Cattle	138	147	173	227	227	National Research Council 1984[s]
Sheep	100	110	157	243	157	National Research Council 1985[t]

Notes: Units are kilocalories per kilogram metabolic weight. Metabolizable energy requirements to replace winter-catabolized tissues are not reflected in estimates.

[a] Early winter period before gestation requirements become important.

[b] February and March assuming a June 1 birth date.

[c] April and May assuming a June 1 birth date.

[d] June and July assuming a June 1 birth date.

[e] August and September assuming a June 1 birth date.

[f] From Figure 11-2 in Haigh and Hudson (1993); I converted total daily ME requirements for a 550-pound (250-kg) cow to calculate requirements on a MW basis.

[g] I calculated from reported intake and energy content of food during each period. In this study, penned elk gained an average of 33 pounds (15 kg) during lactation. I subtracted ME associated with this gain from total energy intake to estimate requirements for live weight maintenance during lactation. This calculation assumed that about half of gain was due to increasing intake, i.e., gut fill (Cook et al. 1998), and ME required for remaining gain (9.3 kilocalories per kilogram of gain [Jiang and Hudson 1992]) was subtracted from observed ME intake to estimate ME requirements for lactation.

[h] Study used penned subadult nongravid cows averaging 515 pounds (234 kg) of body weight.

[i] Study used penned three-year-old nongravid cows averaging 440 pounds (200 kg) of body weight.

[j] Estimated requirements included ME for activity of free-ranging animals.

[k] Requirement for nongravid adult females held indoors during winter.

[l] I calculated from net energy requirements presented for caribou assuming ME use efficiency of 0.65 (National Research Council 1984). Study included energy requirement increments for activity of free-ranging animals.

[m] I calculated to incorporate weight homeostasis. Data from this study were based on a model that included energy requirements for activity.

[n] Estimate for penned caribou and reindeer.

[o] Study used mix of nongravid females and males held in pens.

[p] Study used penned mature, gravid white-tailed deer does.

[q] Study used penned lactating deer and data value is metabolizable energy consumption at the peak of lactation.

[r] Study used penned male and female yearling (n = 2) and adult (n = 8) moose.

[s] I calculated from data for 1,212-pound (550-kg) cattle cow (National Research Council 1984).

[t] I calculated from data for 154-pound (70-kg) ewe with a single lamb (National Research Council 1985).

requirements during lactation for elk (Robbins et al. 1981) and black-tailed deer (Sadlier 1982) are lower than that predicted for elk in Figure 111. The elk and blacktail studies were conducted under penned conditions, and therefore do not reflect greater energy requirements for activity of free-ranging elk.

Confirming the estimates of ME requirements to replace winter-catabolized protein and fat during summer is difficult because no studies apparently have measured this, although the greater energy requirements for replacement accretion is recognized (Kozak et al. 1995). Accurate estimates depend on knowing the relative amounts of protein and fat lost in winter and replaced in summer, because ME requirements for gain vary in relation to the ratio of protein to fat of the gain. Estimates of this ratio in winter-catabolized tissue vary, from 1:5 in caribou (Parker et al. 1993b) to 4:6 in white-tailed deer (Torbit et al. 1985a).

Data I have collected from elk recovering from winter weight loss suggest that ME requirements to replace winter-catabolized tissue may be underestimated in Figure 111. Three year-old cow elk forced to lose 11% of their body weight during winter gained 121 pounds (55 kg) the following summer, compared with 77 pounds (35 kg) gained by well-fed cows of the same age that did not lose weight over winter (Figure 112). The difference in gain—44 pounds (20 kg)—can be considered compensatory growth to replace winter-catabolized tissue. The difference in ME intake during the compensatory growth period (April through Sep-

tember) divided by the amount of compensatory growth provides a rough estimate of ME requirements to replace winter-catabolized tissue. ME requirement calculated in this manner was 13.5 kcal/g of compensatory gain, about 45% higher than ME requirements used here to estimate the R10 and R25 increments for gain in Figure 111.

Energy Requirements: Lactating Subadults

The ME requirement for growth in subadults was not included in the estimates of ME requirements in Figure 111. The ME increment required to sustain growth from spring through autumn for a 2-year-old cow is quite high, substantially increasing nutritional burdens during reproduction if the cow becomes pregnant as a yearling. For example, a nonpregnant, subadult cow will gain about 88 pounds (40 kg) from autumn when she is a yearling to the following autumn when she is 2 years old. Total ME requirement of this gain is 372,000 kcal, assuming ME requirements for gain of 263.6 kcal/oz (9.3 kcal/g) (Jiang and Hudson 1992). Spread over 165 days from spring through autumn (assuming the cow is lactating), the cow will require about 2,255 kcal/day, or about 20.4 kcal/lb (45 kcal/kg) of MW. This represents roughly a 40% to 50% increase in production ME requirements due to the additional costs of growth compared to those of a mature lactating cow. Therefore, a cow breeding as a yearling has greater difficulty acquiring all ME requirements, and her performance and that of her calf would

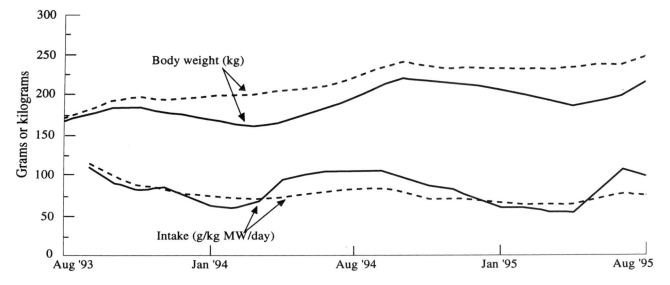

Figure 112.   Body weight and daily food intake (in grams of dry-matter food per kilogram of metabolic weight) for two experimental groups of nongravid, nonlactating elk cows over a 2-year period (J. G. Cook personal files). In one of these groups (solid lines), nutritive value and amount of food fed were reduced during autumn and winter to induce a 10% weight loss; the other group (dashed lines) received high-quality (2.9 kcal of digestible energy per gram of food) food fed ad libitum during the entire study. Greater levels of intake during April through September 1994 enhanced weight gain (i.e., compensatory growth) of the winter-restricted group, yet these cows were unable to catch up completely. Six cows were included in each group, all 2 years old at the study's outset.

more likely be depressed than that of a mature cow if forage conditions are marginal.

Energy Requirements: Calves

The ME requirements for rapid growth in calves is high during their first 6 months of life. Indeed, the greatest weight-specific requirements of ME over the course of the animal's life typically occurs during this time. The mixture of protein and energy in the mother's milk is about optimum for growth of young calves (Lyford and Huber 1988). If nutrition of the mother is adequate, calves can satisfy most nutritional requirements from milk during the first 3 or 4 weeks after birth. After this neonatal period, acquiring adequate nutrition from milk becomes more problematic, because calf requirements are greater and forage nutritive value typically declines (Schingoethe 1988).

During the first 4 or 5 months of life, growth of well-fed calves is roughly constant and ranges from 1.5 pounds (0.7 kg) (Cook et al. 1996) to 2.0 pounds (0.9 kg) (Robbins et al. 1981) per day. The range in these growth rates is largely due to different sizes of calves; for instance, large calves grow more rapidly than small calves (Cook et al. 1996). These growth rates, in combination with live-weight maintenance requirements, can be used to estimate ME requirements for calves. The ME requirement for calf growth averages 113.4 kcal/oz (4 kcal/g) of gain based on red deer (Simpson et al. 1978) and cattle calves (calculated from Lyford and Huber 1988). Calculations from data of hand-reared elk calf from Cook et al. (1996) suggest a slightly higher ME requirement—142 kcal/oz (5 kcal/g) of gain in August and increasing to 284 kcal/oz (10 kcal/g) in late October/early November. Live-weight maintenance for penned calves is about 61.2 to 70.3 kcal of ME per pound (130–155 kcal/kg) of MW, as calculated from Cook et al. (1996) for elk calves in early autumn and from Lyford and Huber (1988) for cattle calves.

Satisfying the increasing ME requirement for gain in autumn induces greater demand for high-quality food if growth is to be maintained; this is a period when forage is unlikely to be of sufficient nutritional value to provide for this demand. Perhaps for this reason, juveniles of the deer family, including elk, apparently have evolved to reduce growth in mid-autumn to late autumn, and may cease growth altogether by early winter, even if food quality and quantity are high (Verme and Ozoga 1980a, Sibbald et al. 1993, Cook et al. 1996). The upshot is that calves will not grow much in winter regardless of foraging conditions; thus, nutritional goals in late autumn and winter should focus on maintaining condition and minimizing starvation losses, rather than on providing for growth (Cook et al. 1996).

With estimates of body weight, growth rates, mainte-

During the initial 4 or 5 months of life, well-nourished calf elk gain weight at a relatively constant rate of 1.5 to 2 pounds (0.7–0.9 kg) per day. However, calves will grow little, if at all, during the winter regardless of forage conditions. Older, larger calves have higher maintenance requirements than do younger and smaller calves, not only because of the former's bigger size, but because they are more active. *Photo by Joe Rosone.*

nance requirements and requirements for gain, ME can be estimated for calves from late spring to early winter. Weight of calves can be predicted during summer and autumn based on the following equation:

$$W = BW + \sum_{i=1}^{n} [GR_i - (GR_i/75)a_i]t_i$$

where W = weight at time t in kilograms, BW = birth weight in kilograms, GR = growth rate in kilograms per day, 75 = number of days between September 30 and December 15, a = number of days past September 30, when growth rate begins to subside, or 0 if on or before September 30, t = number of days past parturition and n = number of days during period of consideration. This equation gradually reduces growth rate after September 30 such that growth ceases in mid-December. Daily ME requirements for calf growth can be predicted from June 1 through mid-December with the following equation:

$$ME = 145(W^{0.75}) + [GR - (GR/75)a] \times \{2 + [0.0400(b)]\}$$

where ME = daily ME required for maintenance and growth in kilocalories per day, W = body weight from above equation, 145 = maintenance ME requirements per kilogram of MW for penned elk calves (from Cook et al. 1996), 2 = kilocalories required per gram of gain at the time of birth, 0.0400 = daily increase in kilocalories required per gram of gain (calculated assuming that 2 kcal/g required in early June increasing linearly to 10 kcal/g in late October), b = number of days postpartum (June 1), and GR and a as in equation to calculate W above.

Assuming a growth rate (GR) of 1.65 pounds (0.75 kg) per day during summer, a 40-pound (18 kg) calf at birth will weigh about 143.3 pounds (65 kg) in early August and 298 to 309 pounds (135–140 kg) when growth ceases in late autumn (Figure 113A). These predictions (1) agree quite closely with weights of calves reported by Robbins et al. (1981); (2) are within 22 pounds (10 kg) of that reported by Hudson et al. (1991) in mid-October; and (3) are within 11 to 22 pounds (5–10 kg) of that reported by Jiang and Hudson (1994) in late autumn and early winter. Growth of calves in these three studies apparently was not restricted by nutrition.

The ME requirements to achieve these predicted growth rates increase rapidly as weight increases, then decline as growth potential declines in autumn (Figure 113B, C). From the end of the neonatal period through early October, predicted ME requirements were about 300 kcal/kg of MW, closely matching estimates of ME requirements needed for rapid growth in elk calves reported by Cook et al. (1996) (i.e., 315 kcal). However, the decline in requirements in autumn (Figure 113B,C) may be too rapid; Cook et al. (1996) reported ME intake of elk calves in November was about 265 kcal/kg of MW compared with about 200 kcal/kg predicted here. Moreover, a ME increment for activity of free-ranging calves is not included in Figure 113B or C, further suggesting that predicted ME requirements were conservative, particularly from mid- to late autumn.

Estimated ME requirements for calf maintenance at the beginning of winter were just under 150 kcal/kg MW, and decreased within the range reported in a variety of studies. For example, 150 kcal is equivalent to that estimated for white-tailed deer fawns (Holter et al. 1977), slightly lower than that estimated for mule deer fawns (158 kcal) (Baker et al. 1979) and higher than that for penned elk calves in two studies—118 kcal (Jiang and Hudson 1994) and 136 kcal (Cool 1992). In a series of four winter experiments using 60 penned elk, calves and yearling cows lost 5% to 10% of their body weight on diets providing 125 to 130 kcal ME per kg of MW (Cook et al. 1998). Therefore, the predicted requirement of 150 kcal appears to be reasonable.

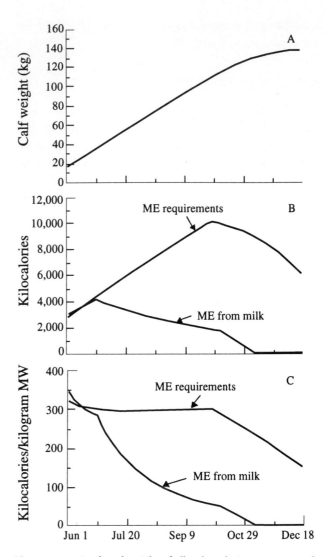

Figure 113. Predicted weight of elk calves during summer and autumn (*A*); estimated total daily metabolizable energy (ME) requirements to support predicted growth of calves and daily ME available from milk (*B*); and estimated ME requirements and ME in milk expressed on a metabolic weight (MW) basis (*C*).

On the basis of data from Robbins et al. (1981), ME obtained by milk (ME of milk was assumed to be 90% of total milk energy) provides for the elk calf's needs only through the first month after parturition (Figure 113B,C). The ME intake from milk and solid food calculated from Robbins et al., when compared with ME requirements, suggests there may be lag time after the first month when calves experience important ME deficiencies, because calves in that study failed to eat sufficient solid food to compensate for declining milk energy (Figure 114). The ME deficiency depicted in Figure 114 suggests that growth would decline in July and increase in August. Robbins et al. (1981) reported that calf growth was 30% lower in July, compared with that in June and August, supporting the suggestion.

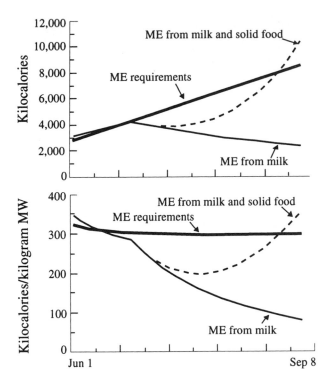

Figure 114. Predicted daily metabolizable energy (ME) requirements for calf growth and observed ME intake of elk calves from milk and solid food (adapted from Robbins et al. 1991) during the first 100 days postpartum. (*Top*) Total daily ME requirements and intake; (*bottom*) Daily ME on a metabolic weight (MW) basis. Robbins et al. (1991) observed a moderate decline in calf growth during July, apparently due to inadequate ME intake, as the graphs indicate.

Protein Requirements: Adults

Deriving estimates of protein requirements is more difficult than deriving estimates of energy requirements because dietary protein use depends on its amino acid composition, relationships between protein usability and energy intake, and total food intake (Robbins 1983). As such, protein estimates from the following equations are general approximations.

Maintenance

Protein requirements for adults also can be factored into several subcomponents and added together to estimate total requirements in different seasons. For maintenance, ruminants must replace endogenous protein lost in feces. This is primarily a function of food intake and includes protein lost through sloughing of cells of the alimentary tract, digestive enzymes and undigested microbial protein. Protein also is disposed in urine and through dermal (e.g., hair) losses.

Metabolic fecal protein is roughly a constant function of

food intake—about 0.53 oz/lb (33 g/kg) of dry matter intake (Mould and Robbins 1981, National Research Council 1985). Calculating fecal protein losses, therefore, requires estimates of amount of food eaten. Urinary endogenous and dermal losses can be estimated based on body weight (National Research Council 1984). Daily crude protein (CP) needed for maintenance can be estimated using the formula (National Research Council 1984):

$$CP_m = [33I + (2.75W^{0.5}) + (0.2W^{0.6})]/(TD \times BV)$$

where CP_m = protein required for maintenance in grams, I = daily food intake (dry matter basis in kg/day); 33I estimates endogenous fecal protein loss, $2.75W^{0.5}$ = estimated urinary protein losses based on body weight (W), $0.2W^{0.6}$ = estimated dermal protein losses based on body weight (W), TD = true protein digestibility (assumed 0.9) and BV = biological value of protein (assumed 0.65).

Daily food intake was estimated based on intake levels reported for mature gravid and lactating captive cow elk by Robbins et al. (1981). These elk consumed about 0.96, 1.09, 1.41 and 2.10 ounces of alfalfa hay per pound (60, 68, 88 and 131 g/kg) of MW during winter, the last 2 months of gestation (April and May), the first month of lactation and the second 2 months (July and August) of lactation, respectively. For calculations here, intake of 1.76, 1.44 and 0.96 ounces of food per pound (110, 90 and 60 g/kg) of MW during September, October and November, and December, respectively, was assumed.

Biological value refers to the value of the protein to the animal and is mostly a function of amino acid composition. The BV averages about 65% in livestock when true protein digestibility is 90%, largely because of the high nucleic acid content of microbial cells digested in the small intestine (National Research Council 1984). Calculation of crude protein requirements for maintenance also must account for the truc digestibility (TD) of the food (National Research Council 1984). Estimates of TD vary considerably, typically are related inversely to protein content of the food and can exceed 100% due to urea recycling. A TD of 90% is assumed here (National Research Council 1984). Although the apparent digestibility of elk foods have been estimated (Schommer 1978), TD of protein throughout the alimentary tract is higher and provides a more realistic estimate of ingested protein available to the animal (National Research Council 1984) and therefore was used here.

On the basis of the seasonal intakes listed above, an adult cow elk weighing 520 pounds (236 kg) would have to consume a low of 10 ounces (284 g) in winter and a high of 18.55 ounces (526 g) CP during mid-summer each day to meet maintenance requirements (Table 49).

Table 49. Estimated daily protein requirements (dry matter basis) for maintenance of an adult cow elk weighing 520 pounds (236 kg)

Period	Food intake[a]	Total food intake[b]	Protein lost[c]	Crude protein required (g/day)[d]	
				Total	Metabolic weight
December–March	60	3.61	166.6	284.8	4.73
April–May	68	4.09	182.5	312.0	5.18
June	88	5.30	222.4	380.2	6.31
July–August	131	7.89	307.9	526.3	8.74
September	110	6.62	266.0	454.8	7.55
October–November	80	4.82	206.6	353.2	5.87

[a] Food intake in grams per kilogram of metabolic weight per day (calculated and extrapolated from Robbins et al. 1981).

[b] Total food intake calculated for a 520-pound (236-kg) elk in kilograms per day.

[c] Protein lost by endogenous fecal and urinary nitrogen and dermal sloughing in grams per day.

[d] Crude protein requirements to replace lost protein expressed as total requirements (grams) and on a metabolic weight basis (g/kg of metabolic weight).

Gestation

Total protein deposited in the fetal body at any point in time during the last 3 to 4 months of gestation can be estimated using an equation presented for cattle by Prior and Laster (1979):

$$TP_g = \{0.000586e^{[(0.0589t/GR) - 0.00009334(t/GR)^2]}\}BWR$$

where TP_g = total protein content in fetus in grams (dry matter basis), t = day of gestation, GR = gestation length ratio (256/280 = 0.91) to adjust for shorter gestation length in elk compared with cattle and BWR = birth weight ratio (18/36 = 0.50) to adjust for smaller birth weight of elk calves (assumes 80-pound [36 kg] cattle calf weight, from study of Prior and Laster [1979]). TP_g was adjusted up by 5% to account for nonfetal products of pregnancy (e.g., placental and uterine development). From TP_g, an equation was derived to predict the amount of protein required by the fetus for growth each day and to convert this to estimates of daily CP requirement for gestation (CP_g):

$$CP_g = 0.01267e^{(0.07072t - 0.00016133t^2)}/(TD \times BV)$$

where t = day of gestation for a cow elk, TD = true digestibility and BV = biological value.

Daily protein accretion for pregnancy maximizes at 1.06 ounces (30 g) per day in late gestation, resulting in a CP requirement of about 1.76 ounces (50 g) CP consumption per day (Figure 115). Daily rate of protein accretion in the fetus declines slightly during the last 2 to 3 weeks of gestation. This decline has been observed in some but not all cattle studies (Prior and Laster 1979). It occurs concurrently with increasing fetal fat accretion. Whether these declining

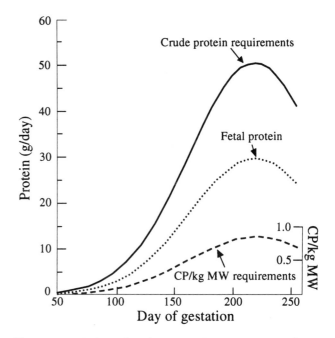

Figure 115. Estimated crude protein (CP) requirements of a 520-pound (236 kg) cow (including requirements expressed on a metabolic weight basis [CP/kg MW]) to meet daily protein needs for growth of the fetus and other products of conception.

protein and increasing fat accretion patterns hold in elk is unclear.

Lactation

Daily protein needs for lactation require estimates of milk yield and protein content of milk. These data were obtained from Robbins et al. (1981) for elk fed a nutritious ration. Daily CP requirements then can be estimated with the following equation:

$$CP_l = (MY \times PC)/(TD \times BV)$$

where CP_l = crude protein requirement for lactation (g/day), MY = milk yield (g/day, wet weight basis), PC = protein content of milk (averages 6.2% in elk [Robbins et al. 1981]), TD = true digestibility coefficient (0.90) and BV = biological value coefficient (0.65).

The CP requirements for lactation peak at 15.87 ounces (450 g) per day 3 to 4 weeks after birth and decline to about 5.29 ounces (150 g) per day 3 to 4 months after birth (Figure 116). At peak lactation, CP requirements are about twice that during late gestation.

Replacement of Winter Protein Loss

Summer and autumn protein requirements to replace muscle mass catabolized in winter depend on amount of weight lost in winter and the protein content of lost weight. Assuming a protein-to-fat catabolism ratio of 40:60 (Torbit et al. 1985a), a cow losing 25% of her body weight would have to replace 23.15 pounds (10.5 kg) of protein, and a cow losing 10% would have to replace 9.26 pounds (4.2 kg) of protein. Spread over 165 days in April, May and mid-July through early November, daily CP requirements would be 3.84 and 1.53 pounds (108.8 and 43.5 g) or 0.03 and 0.01 oz/lb (1.81 and 0.72 g/kg) of MW, respectively.

Predicted Seasonal Protein Requirements

The CP requirements vary considerably among seasons (Figure 117). During winter, a 520-pound (236-kg) cow elk requires about 10.6 ounces (300 g) CP, or about 0.08 oz/lb (5 g/kg) of MW daily to meet maintenance and gestation needs. Gestation increases protein requirements moder-

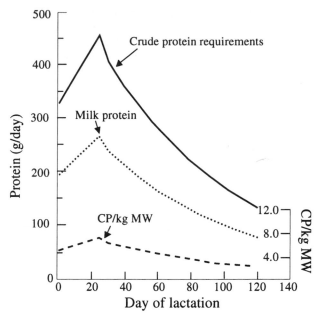

Figure 116. Estimated crude protein (CP) requirements of a 520-pound (236 kg) cow (including requirements expressed on a metabolic weight basis [CP/kg MW]) to provide for protein contained in milk during late spring through early autumn.

ately during the last trimester, whereas lactation induces a marked increase in CP requirements—up to 31.75 ounces (900 g) per day or about 0.24 oz/lb (15 g/kg) of MW daily. The CP increments for replacement of winter-catabolized muscle mass represent a moderate but important increase in protein requirement from spring through autumn (Figure 117). These estimates of CP requirement are generally consistent with other published estimates (Table 50).

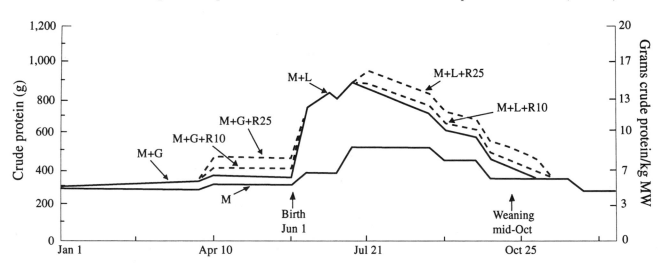

Figure 117. Estimated daily crude protein requirements for an adult cow elk weighing 520 pounds (236 kg) to meet maintenance (M), gestation (G), lactation (L) and winter catabolism replacement (R10 and R25) needs during each season, and predicted crude protein requirements expressed on a metabolic weight (MW) basis. R10 and R25 are based on 10% and 25% winter weight loss, respectively. The replacement increments were based on total crude protein requirements divided by 165 days; replacement tissue accretion was assumed to occur primarily in April, May and mid-July through early November. The M + G and M + L lines indicate estimates of spring, summer and autumn crude protein requirements after a mild winter.

Table 50. Estimated grams of crude protein required daily per kilogram of metabolic weight of mature gravid or lactating female ruminants

Species	Maintenance[a]	Mid-gestation[b]	Late-gestation[c]	Early to mid-lactation[d]	Mid- to late lactation[e]	Source
Elk	4.9	5.5	6.0	13.5	12.0	Figure 115
Elk	4.2					Hobbs et al. 1982
Caribou	5.1					McEwan and Whitehead 1970
Roe deer	4.1					Papageorgiou et al. 1981
White-tailed deer	4.8					Holter et al. 1979[f]
Moose	3.9					Schwartz et al. 1987
Cattle	5.6	5.8	6.9	12.0	12.0	National Research Council 1984[g]
Sheep	4.7	5.4	8.0	13.8	8.0	National Research Council 1985[h]

Notes: Crude protein requirements to replace winter-catabolized tissues are excluded from estimates.

[a] Early winter period before gestation requirements become important.

[b] February and March assuming a June 1 birth date.

[c] April and May assuming a June 1 birth date.

[d] June and July assuming a June 1 birth date.

[e] August and September assuming a June 1 birth date.

[f] Estimates determined using yearling does during summer.

[g] I calculated from data for a 1,212-pound (550-kg) cow.

[h] I calculated from data for a 155-pound (70-kg) ewe with a single lamb.

Protein Requirements: Lactating Subadults

Protein deposition during growth is the multiple of the rate of growth and the protein content of tissue accretion (National Research Council 1984). Protein content of gain can be variable, depending on age, season and dietary factors.

For subadult and adult cattle, protein content of gain can be estimated with the following equation (National Research Council 1984):

$$P = G[268 - 29.4(E_g)]$$

where P = protein content of gain in grams, G = gain in kilograms and E_g = energy content of gain in kilocalories per gram (estimated to be 6.2 kcal in subadult cows by Jiang and Hudson [1992]).

For a 2-year-old cow growing a total of 88.2 pounds (40 kg) during summer and autumn, total protein accretion would be 7.56 pounds (3.43 kg), requiring consumption of about 12.92 pounds (5.86 kg) CP. When spread over 165 days (assuming the cow is lactating), daily CP requirement for gain would be 1.25 ounces (35.5 g), or about 0.011 oz/lb (0.72 g/kg) of MW.

Protein Requirements: Calves

Content of gain in neonates tends to be relatively high in protein and low in fat, and content of gain during autumn tends to be reversed. For example, Verme and Ozoga (1980a) reported that deer fawns shifted to a fat storage mode in autumn regardless of nutritional levels. Prediction of CP requirements for summer and autumn calf growth was based on several assumptions. First, protein was assumed to comprise 80% (wet weight basis) of gain during the neonatal period, 40% by late autumn and the transition among the two periods was assumed to be gradual and linear. Also, BV of milk protein was assumed to be 90% and 65% for protein in solid food. True protein digestibility was assumed to be 90% for all food. Metabolic fecal nitrogen was assumed to be 0.13 ounces of protein per pound (8 g/kg) of dry matter milk intake (Robbins 1983), and the usual 0.53 ounces of protein per pound (33 g/kg) of dry matter solid food intake. Total dry matter intake was estimated based on data from Robbins et al. (1981) during the first 100 days postpartum, and from Cook et al. (1996) during the second 100 days postpartum. Growth patterns used to calculate CP requirement were identical to that used to predict calf ME requirements. The CP prediction equations presented above were used.

Predicted CP requirements of calves on a MW basis were high during the neonatal period, declined and then stabilized by mid-July, increased in early autumn and declined in late October (Figure 118B). Protein from milk satisfied requirements through mid-July. Thereafter, increasing CP from solid food plus that from milk provided protein well in excess of requirements. The CP from solid food is based on elk data from Robbins et al. (1981). The CP content of solid food in their study was about 19%—higher than that in forage typically consumed by free-ranging

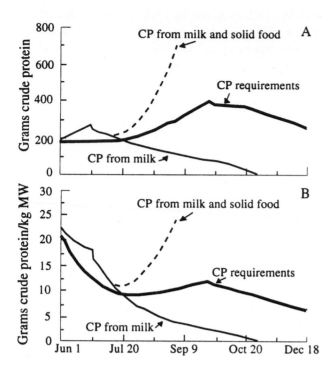

Figure 118. Predicted total daily crude protein (CP) requirements and intake of elk calves during summer and autumn (*A*); predicted CP requirements and intake expressed on a metabolic weight (MW) basis (*B*). Estimated intake of CP is based on data from Robbins et al. (1981). The levels of crude protein requirements indicated for mid-summer may be underestimated to some extent.

calves after mid-summer. Even so, comparisons of Figure 114 and Figure 118 suggest that ME potentially is more limiting to calf growth than protein is, a contention supported by studies of deer fawns (Verme and Ozoga 1980a). Estimated CP requirements for maintenance were 7.05 ounces (200 g) per day, or about 0.096 oz/lb (6 g/kg) of MW. This requirement on a MW basis is similar to that predicted for adults in winter.

Accuracy of the estimates of CP requirements for calves is difficult to judge because published estimates for juveniles tend to be variable and generally are restricted to autumn. Earlier estimates of deer fawn requirements ranged considerably higher than predicted here for autumn. Smith et al. (1975), for example, indicated that deer fawns required 0.30 ounces of digestible CP per pound (19 g/kg) of MW per day—nearly double that predicted in Figure 118B. Ullrey et al. (1967) reported that deer fawns grew significantly faster when fed 0.24 ounces CP per pound (15 g/kg) of MW than did fawns fed about 0.136 ounces CP per pound (8.5 g/kg) of MW, and that fawns fed 0.384 ounces CP per pound (24 g/kg) of MW did not grow appreciably faster than those on the moderate level.

Conversely, Verme and Ozoga (1980a) indicated that deer fawns fed about 0.352 ounces CP per pound (22 g/kg) of MW grew at about the same rate as fawns fed only about 0.136 ounces CP per pound (8.5 g/kg) of MW. The National Research Council (1984, 1985) recommended feeding cattle calves and domestic sheep lambs 0.144 to 0.208 ounces CP per pound (9–13 g/kg) of MW to maintain incremental growth rates of 0.5% to 1.0% per day—levels similar to that reported for rapidly growing elk calves during autumn (Cook et al. 1996). These estimates agree closely with those predicted here during autumn.

The relatively low levels of CP requirements during the mid-summer period relative to that in early summer and autumn (Figure 118) may be slightly low. The low level was a result of low solid food consumption observed in elk calves by Robbins et al. (1981), who suggested that free-ranging calves probably begin eating solid food earlier. If so, predicted CP requirements in mid-summer would be higher. It is likely that after the neonatal period, CP requirements for calf growth range from 0.16 to 0.208 oz/lb (10–13 g/kg) of MW through mid-autumn.

Forage Nutritive Value Requirements

Concentrations of energy and protein in forage required to meet nutritional requirements were calculated simply by dividing total daily requirement (Figures 111 and 117) by daily forage dry matter intake rates. Intake rates were estimated for each season (Table 51), based on data presented for mature lactating cows (Robbins et al. 1981) and nongravid, nonlactating 2- to 4-year-old cows (J. G. Cook personal data) (see Figure 112). The highest intake rate of each of the three groups of cows (Table 51) in each seasonal period was assumed to provide the best estimate of what cow elk are able to consume during that period.

Forage energy content was expressed as DE, rather than ME, to enhance comparability with measures of dietary energy levels reported in a variety of studies. The ME was converted to DE by dividing ME by 0.82 (National Research Council 1984). Forage nutrient content requirements for calves during late summer through autumn also are presented. Intake rates presented by Cook et al. (1996) were used to estimate required forage nutrient content for elk calves. For calculations here, I increased intake estimates of Cook et al. (1996) about 15% early in this time period and reduced intake about 20% in the late portion of this period to account for relatively small body size of their calves.

Digestible Energy Concentrations

During winter, estimated DE concentration to satisfy maintenance and activity requirements of adult gravid cows was

Table 51. Estimates of daily food intake rates of cow elk

Months	Intake[a]	Status of cows[b]
November to March	60	Adult gravid cows
	62–85	Two- and three-year-old cows; HQAD feeding
April	68	Adult gravid cows
	64–72	Two- and three-year-old cows; HQAD feeding
	93	Two-year-old compensating cows, HQAD feeding
May	68	Adult gravid cows
	72–77	Two- and three-year-old cows; HQAD feeding
	101	Two-year-old compensating cows; HQAD feeding
June	88	Adult lactating cows
	78–80	Three- and four-year-old cows; HQAD feeding
	104–106	Three- and four-year-old compensating cows; HQAD feeding
July to August	125	Adult lactating cows
	75–82	Three- and four-year-old cows; HQAD feeding
	99–104	Three- and four-year-old compensating cows; HQAD feeding
September	120	Adult lactating cows (extrapolated)
	79	Three-year-old cows; HQAD feeding
	96–111	Two- and three-year-old compensating cows; HQAD feeding
October	100	Adult lactating cows (extrapolated)
	70	Three-year-old cows; HQAD feeding
	82–87	Two- and three-year-old compensating cows; HQAD feeding

[a] Units are grams of food per kilogram of metabolic weight on a dry-matter basis.

[b] Two- to 4-year-old cows were not pregnant or lactating and were fed a high-quality, ad libitum diet (HQAD) (J. G. Cook personal data). The "compensating" cows were undergoing catch-up growth due to 10% weight loss during winter. Data for alfalfa hay-fed adult gravid and lactating cows are from Robbins et al. (1981).

65.2 kcal/oz (2.3 kcal/g) of food (Figure 119A). This is equivalent to 50% to 55% dry matter digestibility of alfalfa hay, for example. Required concentration of DE declined to 62.4 kcal/oz (2.2 kcal/g) during gestation in late spring because calculated activity requirements declined (see Table 47) and estimated intake rates increased substantially. Food DE concentration requirements for spring would be higher if the herd was migratory. Required DE levels increased markedly during the 3 to 4 weeks postpartum to 102.1 kcal/oz (3.6 kcal/g) during peak lactation, declined and then stabilized at 70.9 to 76.5 kcal/oz (2.5–2.7 kcal/g) of food through early autumn. The latter is equivalent to 56% to 60% dry matter digestibility. Requirements for replacement of winter-catabolized tissue increased required DE concentration in forage considerably through summer and autumn (see Figure 118).

The very high estimated level of required DE—99.2 to 102.1 kcal/oz (3.5–3.6 kcal/g) of forage—during peak lactation is inordinately high and was due to the moderate level of food intake used for calculations. Robbins et al. (1982) indicated that lactating cows will consume about 1.408 oz/lb (88 g/kg) of MW during the first month postpartum (June), which is substantially lower than the 1.696 oz/lb (106 g/kg) of MW used here. In contrast, Jiang and Hudson (1994) reported that subadult nonlactating cows consumed 2.464 oz/lb (154 g/kg) of MW during May (followed by declines to 1.648 oz/lb [103 g/kg] of MW in July and August). Wairimu et al. (1992) reported that yearling male elk undergoing compensatory growth consumed 0.80, 2.0 and 0.80 ounces of forage dry matter per pound (50, 125 and 50 g/kg) of MW in April, May and June and July, respectively. Thus, it is probable that cow elk can eat more forage than assumed here during June, suggesting that actual forage DE requirements are closer to 1.4 kcal/oz (3 kcal/g) of MW than 1.6 kcal/oz (3.5 kcal/g) of MW as indicated in Figure 119A.

In calves from August through autumn, DE content of forage required above that supplied by milk ranged from 73.7 to 85.1 kcal/oz (2.6–3.0 kcal/g) of forage consumed through early November and declined to 65.2 kcal/oz (2.3 kcal/g) at the beginning of winter (Figure 120). The relatively high DE content requirement in August and September reflects the relatively moderate contribution of milk to total energy requirements during a period of rapid growth.

Crude Protein Concentrations

Required CP concentrations in forage followed a similar seasonal pattern calculated for DE (see Figure 119B). Differences would be expected, however, because CP requirements change little as a direct function of elk activity, and increasing forage intake also increases CP requirements. This largely accounts for increasing rather than declining (see Figure 119A) CP forage concentration requirements across spring. Estimated CP requirements for winter were 7% to 7.5%, 14% to 15% for a short time during peak lactation and 9% to 12% for lactation during most of summer and autumn. Increments for replacement of winter-catabolized tissue increased forage CP requirements 1 to 3 percentage units (see Figure 119B).

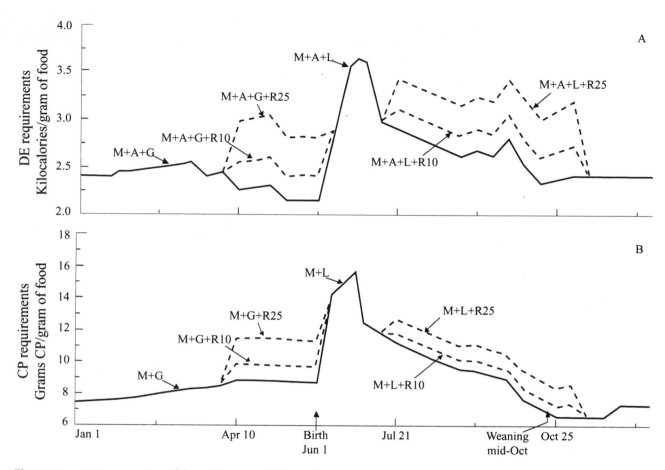

Figure 119. (*A*) Concentration of digestible energy (DE) and (*B*) concentration of crude protein (CP) in forage required to satisfy daily metabolizable energy and protein requirements of adult cow elk for maintenance (M), activity (A), gestation (G), lactation (L) and replacement of winter-catabolized tissues, assuming either 10% (R10) or 25% (R25) winter weight loss. The DE requirements probably are overestimated for June (early lactation) and underestimated in April, May (third trimester).

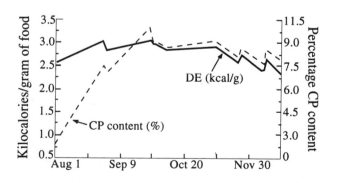

Figure 120. Concentration of digestible energy (DE) (kcal/g of food) and crude protein (CP) in forage required to satisfy daily metabolizable energy and protein requirements of calves from early August through mid-December. The estimates are required in solid food, in addition to that received in milk from the mother. The estimates of DE requirements are based on data collected from captive calves and therefore, may not completely account for activity levels of free-ranging calves.

Milk apparently was able to supply much of a calf's CP requirement through August, as required CP content of forage during this time was only about 4% of forage dry matter. After milk intake declined, required CP increased to 9%, then declined to about 7% at the beginning of winter (see Figure 120).

Caveats

Estimates of DE and CP forage content requirements are sensitive to estimates of daily food intake rates. Reliable estimates of intake rates of free-ranging elk, therefore, are paramount for determining forage quality requirements. Unfortunately, there are no estimates of daily intake rates for wild elk in native habitats during any season. Moreover, observations of food intake from studies not included in Table 51 may deviate substantially from that used to develop Figure 119. For example, estimates of winter dry matter intake of calves range from 0.56 oz/lb (35 g/kg) of MW less (Jiang and Hudson 1994) to 0.80 oz/lb (50 g/kg) more (J. G. Cook personal data) than used here. Dry matter forage intake in late spring (May) ranges from 1.04 oz/lb (65 g/kg) of MW (Robbins et al. 1981) in gravid cows to 2.46 oz/lb (154 g/kg) in subadult nongravid cows (Jiang and Hudson 1994), compared with 1.60 oz/lb (100 g/kg) used here. In summer, reported intake ranges from 1.20 oz/lb (75 g/kg) of MW in 3- and 4-year-old nonlactating cows to 2.32 oz/lb (145 g/kg) in lactating adult cows (J. G. Cook personal data), compared with 2.0 oz/lb (125 g/kg) of MW used here.

The apparent upper limit of the amount of food that an elk can consume each day is quite variable (e.g., up to about 2.5 times more in summer than in winter) due to influences of photoperiod (seasonal effects), age, productive stage and prior nutritional effects on condition. Specific influences of each of these are poorly understood, in part because effects of one depend on effects of the others (Weston and Poppi 1987). The ability of elk to vary intake as the need for food varies likely is accounted for by (1) changes in appetite, apparently due to changes in metabolic patterns (Bines and Morant 1983); (2) changes in gut fill, due in part to changes in the size of the rumen (Minson 1990); and (3) perhaps changes in rumination patterns (Spalinger et al. 1986).

In addition, daily food intake declines as food quality declines, because digestion and passage of food from the rumen slow, and amount of time spent ruminanting rather than feeding increases. High levels of digestible and indigestible components of cell wall reduce daily intake, as do deficiencies in DE, CP and a variety of minerals in food, if their levels are insufficient to maintain a productive ruminal microbial population (Spalinger et al. 1986, Minson 1990, Seoane et al. 1991, Minson and Wilson 1994, Nandra et al. 1995). The effect can be substantial. For example, declines in CP content from 12.5% to 6% reduced food intake of a grass hay by 30% (Minson 1990, see also Figure 93).

Minson and Wilson (1994) noted that the amount of food a ruminant can consume each day has profound influences on the animal's nutritional status. The effect of forage quality on daily food intake, therefore, may equal or exceed the direct effect of nutrient content of forage on nutritional status; the combined effects appear particularly influential (Figure 121). Other forage characteristics, including plant defense compounds, abundance and availability, affect intake as well. The role of forage abundance for elk has been reported by Collins and Urness (1983), Irwin and Peek (1983), Wickstrom et al. (1984) and McCorquodale (1991).

The estimates of required DE and CP concentration requirements (Figure 119) would have been lower if the highest intake rates reported for elk in late spring and early summer—i.e., 2.46 and 2.32 ounces of food per pound (154 and

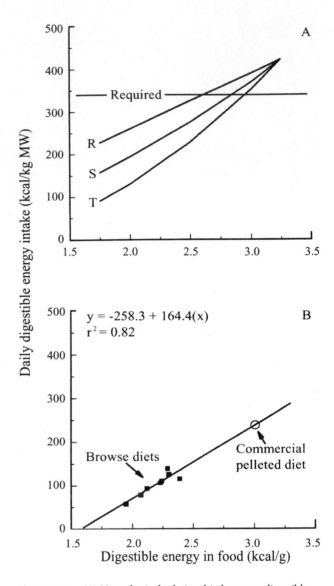

Figure 121.   (A) Hypothetical relationship between digestible energy consumption on a metabolic weight basis and digestible energy in food, assuming maximum intake rate of 130 g of food per kilogram metabolic weight during midsummer. Line R assumes constant food intake across food digestible energy levels; line S assumes a 10% decline in food intake per 0.5 kcal decline in food digestible energy levels; and line T assumes a 20% decline in food intakes per 0.5 kcal decline in food digestible energy levels. Differences among lines illustrate that declining food intake, as forage quality declines, can markedly increase the deleterious effects of declining forage quality on nutritional status. These relations have not been developed for elk, leaving uncertain the magnitude of the effect. (B) Empirical data for white-tailed deer in winter (adapted from Gray and Servello 1995). These data indicate that daily digestible energy intake declines about 80 kcal/kg of MW per 0.5 kcal decline in food digestible energy content, similar to that depicted by line T in graph A. This suggests a very strong effect of declining digestible energy content on daily food and digestible energy intake.

145 g/kg) of MW—were used to develop estimates of forage nutrient concentration requirements. This does not mean, however, that estimates in Figure 119 are too high, because the approach used here to estimate required nutrient concentrations ignores the effect of forage quality on daily food intake (see Figure 121). Indeed, use of elk intake rates of forage presumably of high quality to calculate the lowest levels of forage quality necessary to provide their requirements probably is not completely reliable. Thus, (1) the highest estimates of requirements in Figure 119 (June) probably are too high; (2) the estimates of requirements after mid-summer and before winter may be slightly low; and (3) the estimates of requirements during the third trimester of gestation (May) probably are too low. On the basis of my experience with feeding gravid and lactating cow elk, consumption of food with a DE content less than 2.5 kcal of DE, at any time during late spring through mid-autumn, induces weight loss.

Required Versus Observed Forage Nutritive Value

Results of studies that have identified nutrient concentration in diets of ungulates in the western United States and Canada are summarized in Table 52. To compare reported estimates of dietary quality to requirements, I converted data in Table 52 to units of DE and CP per unit of forage dry matter and plotted them with DE and CP requirements in Figure 122. Obtaining estimates of DE from the dietary quality studies generally required converting estimates of dry matter digestibility to DE. This was done by multiplying the digestibility coefficient by gross energy—4,600 kcal/g of forage from April through October (J. G. Cook personal data on spring, summer and autumn elk diets in northeastern Oregon) and 4,200 kcal/g in the dormant season (Schommer 1978). A few studies presented results on an organic matter basis. These estimates for both CP and DE were adjusted to a digestible dry matter basis assuming that forage ash content was 10% of dry matter.

Estimates from about 20 studies indicate considerable variation in dietary quality of large ungulates across western ranges (Figure 122). Particularly regarding summer DE estimates, some of the variation may be due to differences in techniques, because forage sample preparation and laboratory assay protocol influence nutritional estimates. On the basis of the majority of the studies, comparison of DE requirements and observed dietary DE suggests substantial deficiencies from midautumn through early spring, and slight to moderate deficiencies during much of summer through early autumn.

The effect of deficiencies during the summer and early autumn lactation period may largely depend on extent of weight loss in winter. Cows that lose just 10% of body weight in winter may be hard-pressed to replace this tissue during the growing season and simultaneously satisfy demands for gestation and lactation. Reproductive pauses (Cameron 1994), perhaps alternate year breeding, may be widespread under these conditions unless summer forage quality is relatively high. It may be impossible for gravid cows losing 25% of the weight during winter to replace this tissue and raise a large calf in the following seasons on most summer/autumn ranges. Milk yield and growth of calves undoubtedly would suffer, and reproductive pauses would be probable. Results of several of the studies reviewed by Cameron (1994) suggest that, even without appreciable winter weight loss, DE intake in summer and autumn may be insufficient to satisfy demands of lactation in some areas and calf growth in most areas. White (1983) pointed out that even seemingly small deficiencies in diets may induce a greatly enhanced, or multiplier, effect on animal production, largely due to accumulation of deficiencies over time.

At first glance, the substantial deficiencies apparent for winter and marginal deficiencies for summer (Figure 122A) support the widespread notion that nutrition in winter has the greatest potential to limit elk populations. However, deficient dietary quality resulting in weight loss in winter is typical, and elk are well adapted to these conditions. Recovery of these tissues must occur during spring through autumn, thereby placing the burden of replenishing weight lost in winter on summer ranges. Moreover, deficiencies during late gestation and much of the lactation period can have immediate, deleterious effects on birth weight, milk yields and calf growth. Thus, it may be that a 10% deficiency in forage DE across summer and autumn may have greater implications than a 20% to 25% deficiency in winter.

The amount of variation in DE levels among studies in spring (Figure 122A) suggests that there may be considerable variation in ability of various elk ranges to support fetal growth during the last trimester. At one extreme, forage DE content increases before the third trimester begins and greatly exceeds all springtime nutritional requirements (including winter-catabolism replacement costs). On some ranges, however, increasing forage quality apparently is delayed to the point that substantial deficiencies may occur throughout most of the third trimester (Figure 122A). This may explain why birth weight is correlated to spring weather and apparently, in some herds, timing of green-up (Smith et al. 1997b), despite the fact that third trimester DE requirements are not particularly high.

Results of studies that reported dietary crude protein levels (Figure 122B) suggest that protein probably is not limiting to elk populations on most ranges except during late au-

Table 52. Nutrient content of large ruminant diets in western North America

Nutrient[a]	Species[b]	Apr.	May	June	July	Aug.	Sept.	Oct.	Nov.	Dec.	Jan.	Feb.	Mar.	Location	Reference[e]
Interior Rocky Mountain region															
CP	RME				17.30	15.50	13.00							SE ID	1
DDM	RME				71.30	62.80	58.80							SE ID	1
CP	RME				15.00	13.60	10.80							CO	4
DDM	RME				61.00	60.30	50.50							CO	4
CP	RME								5.70	5.30	5.10	4.90	4.70	CO	7
DDM	RME								44.80	41.30	39.00	38.00	37.80	CO	7
CP	RME	24.00	22.00	21.20	17.40	11.50	9.20	10.60	6.20	5.90		4.20	18.60	C WA	17
DP	RME	18.90	17.10	16.30	12.70	8.00	5.80	7.00	3.30	3.30		2.10	13.90	C WA	17
DE	RME	3.05	3.15	3.07	2.84	2.57	2.28	2.18	2.08	1.77		1.52	2.66	C WA	17
DDM	RME	73.80	76.20	72.50	68.80	65.70	59.00	57.50	53.80	47.80		45.50	65.30	C WA	17
CP	RME	23.20	20.30	20.60	14.90	12.00	9.70	8.00	6.20	8.80		5.30	20.20	C WA	18
ADF	RME	30.40	28.80	26.60	29.10	35.60	37.00	38.90	46.40	45.90		52.00	40.50	C WA	18
ASH	RME	11.00	10.10	9.90	10.00	13.20	12.30	10.50	6.90	12.20		12.90	12.60	C WA	18
Ca	RME	0.31	0.35	0.24	0.38	0.37	0.33	0.21	0.33	0.32		0.39	0.39	C WA	18
P	RME	0.31	0.31	0.18	0.19	0.17	0.14	0.12	0.20	0.25		0.05	0.30	C WA	18
CP	RME		14.10		11.00		8.20							NE OR	20
DE	RME		2.94		2.74		2.41							NE OR	20
CP[c]	RME	7.70									3.50	3.80	5.80	NC NM	19
DOM	RME	49.00									36.00	36.00	44.00	NC NM	19
CP[c]	RME	7.50									5.10	5.10	6.00	NC NM	19
DOM	RME	39.00									33.00	36.00	35.00	NC NM	19
CP	MD				15.00	11.50	9.40							C CO	6
DDM	MD				36.80	38.90	38.10							C CO	6
CP	MD	16.70						8.80	6.50		5.10	6.20	6.10	CO	10
DDM	MD	54.10						32.50	29.00		27.50	31.50	29.50	CO	10
CP[c]	MD		22.50						6.30		7.80		8.60	CO	12
DOM	MD		72.00						32.10		35.00		40.10	CO	12
CP	BHS			13.40	11.80	11.10	9.00	8.20	7.30	8.90	9.00	7.00		S WY	8
DDM	BHS							49.00	38.00	44.50		38.00		S WY	8
CP	BHS	8.00	15.00		11.80	12.00	9.20	8.50	5.20	6.40		3.00	5.00	S WY	21
CP	BHS	18.60	19.30								[—[d]	8.00]	12.00	NC CO	11
DDM	BHS	68.00	73.40								[—	51.40]	57.40	NC CO	11
NDF	BHS	60.80	54.60								[—	66.90]	66.00	NC CO	11
CP	BHS[c]		23.50						5.80		6.50		7.00	CO	12
DOM	BHS		71.30						34.70		39.90		46.30	CO	12
CP	BHS							4.70	3.40	4.10	3.30	6.90	16.30	C WY	13
CP	MOO	5.30	19.80		12.90			7.70		6.50	5.500	6.70		Alb	5
DDM	MOO	48.00	68.00		59.00			59.00		49.0	39.00	47.0		Alb	5
CP	CAR	[—	4.40]	16.90	[—	14.40]	[—	7.80]	[—	—	4.40	—	—]	AK	16
DDM	CAR	[—	60.00]	69.00	[—	70.0]	[—	63.00]	[—	—	60.00	—	—]	AK	16
LIG	CAR	[—	5.00]	3.00	[—	5.00]	[—	5.00]	[—	—	5.00	—	—]	AK	16
NDS	CAR	[—	3.00]	61.00	[—	61.00]	[—	44.00]	[—	—	30.00	—	—]	AK	16
ASH	CAR	[—	3.00]	0.00	[—	2.00]	[—	3.00]	[—	—	3.00	—	—]	AK	16
Ca	CAR	[—	0.38]	0.47	[—	0.79]	[—	0.56]	[—	—	0.38	—	—]	AK	16
CEL	CAR	[—	12.00]	12.00	[—	13.00]	[—	12.00]	[—	—	12.00	—	—]	AK	16
HEM	CAR	[—	5.00]	24.00	[—	19.00]	[—	36.00]	[—	—	50.00	—	—]	AK	16
P	CAR	[—	0.08]	0.38	[—	0.25]	[—	0.15]	[—	—	0.08	—	—]	AK	16
CP[c]	CAT				12.60	10.50	11.20	11.10						NE OR	2
DOM	CAT				60.00	56.40	53.30	51.40						NE OR	2
LIG[c]	CAT				12.90	13.10	15.40	15.60						NE OR	2
ADF[c]	CAT				55.10	54.90	60.10	63.40						NE OR	2
Coastal forests															
CP	RME		20.00			10.60		10.60						W WA	9
DDM	RME		84.90			78.70		79.40						W WA	9

Table 52 continued

Nutrient[a]	Species[b]	Apr.	May	June	July	Aug.	Sept.	Oct.	Nov.	Dec.	Jan.	Feb.	Mar.	Location	Reference[e]
CP	RE			15.60	14.70	12.30	9.80	8.90	7.10					SW WA	14
DDM	RE			61.80	57.80	52.20	47.20	45.50	44.20					SW WA	14
CP	RE	[—	18.80]	15.90			13.40			8.80				W WA	3
DDM	RE	[—	38.00]	41.00			38.50			27.50				W WA	3
P	RE	[—	0.42]	0.32			0.25			0.19				W WA	3
CP	BTD	[—	20.70]	16.70			14.10			8.00				W WA	3
DDM	BTD	[—	38.00]	37.00			35.00			26.50				W WA	3
P	BTD	[—	0.44]	0.27			0.22			0.20				W WA	3
CP	BTD	15.00	19.00	17.50	14.00	12.00	11.50	11.00	11.80	10.90	10.90	12.00	13.80	SE AK	15
DDM	BTD	52.00	56.00	57.50	57.50	54.00	51.00	54.00	64.00	58.00	58.00	56.00	56.00	SE AK	15
P	BTD	0.30	0.38	0.35	0.24	0.18	0.18	0.20	0.21	0.22	0.21	0.24	0.28	SE AK	15

Note: For references that presented nutrient content of individual forages but did not calculate an overall dietary nutritive value, the unweighted average of the different forages is presented here. Cattle and domestic sheep values are presented only if data were collected on a range likely used by elk in that particular season.

[a] Abbrevations are CP = crude protein; DP = digestible protein; DDM = in vitro digestible dry matter; DOM = in vitro digestible organic matter; DE = digestible energy; ASH = ash (minerals); Ca = calcium; P = phosphorus; NDS = neutral detergent solubles; NDF = neutral detergent fiber; ADF = acid detergent fiber; LIG = lignin.

[b] Abbreviations are: BTD = black tailed deer; MD = mule deer; WTD = white-tailed deer; RE = Roosevelt elk; RME = Rocky Mountain elk; BHS = bighorn sheep; CAT= cattle; CAR = caribou.

[c] Units are expressed on an organic matter rather than a dry matter basis.

[d] [—] = Values enclosed in brackets indicate data collected over multiple months.

[e] References: 1. Canon et al. 1987; 2. Holechek et al. 1981; 3. Leslie et al. 1984; 4. Baker et al. 1982; 5. Renecker and Hudson 1985; 6. Regelin et al. 1974; 7. Hobbs et al. 1981; 8. Cook 1990; 9. Hanley 1984; 10. Bartmann 1983; 11. Goodson et al. 1991b; 12. Hobbs et al. 1984; 13. Irwin et al. 1993; 14. Merrill et al. 1995; 15. Hanley et al. 1985; 16. Boertje 1990; 17. Schommer 1978; 18. McArthur 1977; 19. Rowland 1981; 20. J.G. Cook (personal data) collected from grazing trials using tame elk at four sites on elk summer range in northeastern Oregon. Corrections for tannin effects were included; 21. Arnett 1990.

tumn through early spring. Emerging evidence supports the contention that energy generally is more limiting than protein (e.g., Lyford and Huber 1988, Cook et al. 1996, Parker et al. 1999). Even during the peak in lactation in late June, reported CP content of diets generally exceeded estimated requirements. Some caution is appropriate, however. First, my estimates of CP requirements do not reflect declines in daily intake as forage CP levels decline, as discussed above, and therefore, may underestimate CP requirements. Second, diets high in tannins reduce the availability of dietary protein to the ruminant herbivore—a problem potentially most important from mid-spring through mid-autumn. Virtually none of the dietary quality studies reviewed here accounted for the effects of tannins. Thus, there may be greater potential for protein to be limited during the growing season than indicated in Figure 122B.

Inadequate CP in forage during winter probably has detrimental effects on elk. In particular, viability of rumen microorganisms and their ability to digest food may be depressed (Minson and Wilson 1994). However, the extent of the effects are unclear. Diets highly deficient in DE will induce catabolism of both fat and lean body mass and increase urea inputs to the rumen via urea recycling. Recycling of urea to the rumen may postpone the potentially debilitating effects of low dietary CP content on viability of ruminal microorganisms and may reduce to some extent the detrimental effects of inadequate CP content of forage during winter.

Mineral Requirements

Although minerals play a key role in many aspects of production, they have largely been overlooked in large ungulate nutrition studies. Required minerals include calcium, cobalt, copper, iodine, iron, magnesium, manganese, molybdenum, phosphorus, potassium, selenium, sodium, chlorine, sulphur and zinc. Specific roles of minerals in ruminant physiology are highly variable, often interactive, and excessive mineral intake can be toxic. The National Research Council (1984, 1985) provided a useful summary of the role of minerals, requirements and toxicity levels for ruminant livestock. Although not well-recognized, many minerals also have strong influence on daily food intake. This is due largely to the mineral requirements of ruminal microbes; inadequate minerals in animal diets may reduce their productivity and, in turn, reduce the rate of forage digestion (Minson and Wilson 1994).

A summary of mineral requirements based on beef cattle requirements is presented in Table 53. These are "suggested," because specific requirements for many of the

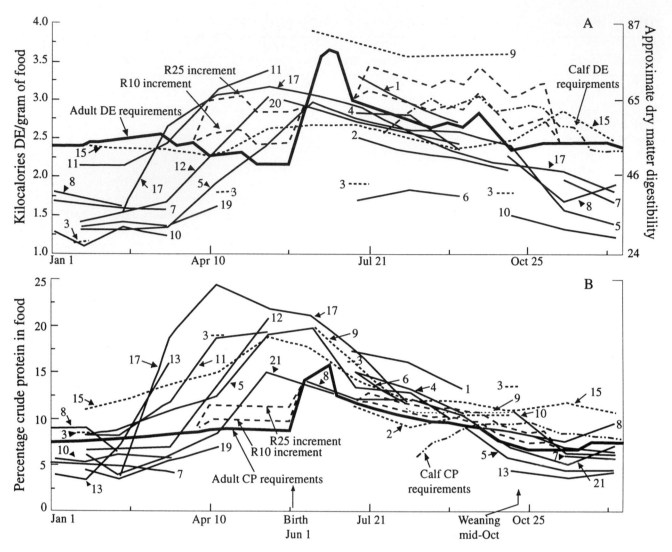

Figure 122. (*A*) Concentration of digestible energy (DE) and (*B*) crude protein (CP) in forage required for adult gravid/lactating cows and 3- to 6-month-old calves, compared with observed DE and CP levels reported in a variety of field studies in the western United States (calculated from Table 52). The narrow solid lines are estimates from studies conducted in interior (noncoastal) environments; the narrow, short dash lines are from studies in coastal environments. The R10 and R25 increments refer to additional DE and CP requirements to replace fat and lean muscle catabolized during winter (10% and 25% weight loss, respectively). Numbers associated with each line identify the reference source, indicated in Table 52.

minerals have not been determined. Moreover, how well mineral requirements for beef cattle match those for elk is unclear. Haigh and Hudson (1993), for example, indicated that copper requirements for elk are substantially greater than for livestock. In contrast, selenium requirements of elk apparently are lower than that of cattle (Stussy et al. 2000). Table 53 provides *approximate* guidelines, however, for female and juvenile elk.

Antler growth requires a considerable investment of minerals and may require higher mineral content in diets than the Table 53 guidelines suggest. Calcium comprises about 22% and phosphorous 11% of antlers, with protein making up much of the rest (Robbins 1983). Elk require approximately 3.5 ounces (100 g) of protein per day for antler

growth (Robbins 1983), increasing their daily crude protein requirements by roughly 50% over that needed for maintenance. Forage crude protein levels should range from 10% to 13% during the antler-growing season (April through July). Estimates of calcium and phosphorus forage concentration requirements for antler growth range from 0.40% to 0.64% and 0.26% to 0.54% (dry matter basis), respectively (Robbins 1983, Ullrey 1983). The higher estimates exceed those for beef cattle presented in Table 53. The ME requirements for antler growth are considered to be insignificant in relation to the daily energy budget of elk bulls (Haigh and Hudson 1993).

The estimates of calcium and phosphorus in large ungulates diets summarized in Table 52 and presented

Table 53. Suggested mineral requirements and maximum tolerable levels of essential minerals in diets of beef cattle

| Diet content | Requirement | | Maximum tolerable level |
	Suggested value	Range[c]	
Calcium[a]		0.16–0.58	2
Cobalt[b]	0.10	0.07–0.11	5
Copper[b]	8.00	4.00–10.00	115
Iodine[b]	0.50	0.20–2.00	50
Iron[b]	50.00	50.00–100.00	1,000
Magnesium[a]	0.10	0.05–0.25	0.40
Manganese[b]	40.00	20.00–50.00	1,000
Molybdenum[b]			6
Phosphorus[a]		0.17–0.39	1
Potassium[a]	0.65	0.50–0.70	3
Selenium[b]	0.20	0.05–0.30	2
Sodium[a]	0.08	0.06–0.10	10[d]
Chlorine[e]			
Sulfur[a]	0.10	0.08–0.15	0.40
Zinc[b]	30.00	20.00–40.00	500

Source: National Research Council 1984.

[a] In percentage.

[b] In parts per million.

[c] The listing of ranges recognizes that requirements for most minerals are affected by a variety of dietary factors and animal characteristics. For example, the high calcium levels are most applicable for young, lactating cows; the low calcium levels are most applicable for mature animals in some stage of maintenance.

[d] Sodium chloride (salt).

[e] No values for chlorine were presented.

On occasion, elk are seen chewing on bones or shed antler. It may be, as in other animals, that the behavior is related to a need for additional calcium. *Photo by Michael H. Francis.*

Approximately 3.5 ounces (100 g) of protein is required per day to support antler growth in bull elk. As a result, the dietary demand for crude protein is increased by about 50% over requirements for basic body maintenance. *Photo by Jim Yoakum.*

for Alaskan forages by Hanley and McKendrick (1983) suggest deficiencies for maximum antler growth in areas the studies were conducted. However, the extent and implications of inadequate minerals for antler growth are poorly understood.

Game Ranching and Nutrition

A fundamental goal of game ranching elk—maintaining high levels of production while keeping production costs relatively low—should differ little from that of ranching livestock. Although similarities exist between ranching cattle, for example, and ranching a large ungulate species such as elk, some important differences in the context of nutrition may exist. These relate to a stronger tendency for physiological processes to be entrained by photoperiod, perhaps greater differences in performance and requirements between males and females (Fennessy et al. 1991), and differences in forage preferences, tolerance to harsh weather, and animal products (such as antlers for Oriental markets).

The nutritional requirements presented above have useful relevance to game ranching operations. However, depending on the type of operation, energy requirements for maintenance of ranched game may be lower than that presented for wild animals. The winter-catabolism replacement increments also should not be relevant, as long as winter weight losses in captive herds are held to less than about 7% to 8% (this estimate excludes the products of conception; weight loss based on live weight [including products of conception] should not exceed 5% by early March, particularly if cows are at a moderate level of condition at the beginning of winter). Otherwise, estimates should be applicable, particularly in the context of differences in requirements among seasons.

A primary area of nutritional concern in a game ranching situation involves strategies necessary to produce rapid growth and development in calves and subadult animals. Early birth dates, large birth sizes and rapid growth will hasten the transition of calves to solid food, freeing dams earlier to recover from the nutritional stress of lactation. This, in turn, will help to maintain early breeding of adult cows and may reduce to some extent the dependence of cows on food of high quality late in the summer. Early births also may improve calf growth by synchronizing the greatest nutritional demands of cows and calves with the highest levels of forage quality and quantity.

Maintaining rapid growth of females during their first 1.5 years of life is key for maximizing their pregnancy rates as yearling cows. Pregnancy rates of yearlings vary considerably and are linked strongly to the cows' size. Thus, although costs may be relatively high, ensuring a high plane of nutrition during this first 1.5 years of life may be a wise investment.

Cows that breed as yearlings will have relatively high nutritional requirements to support growth and reproduction simultaneously. Energy requirements will be higher than those presented above for adults, to ensure normal growth of the yearling cow and her calf and the mother's return to estrous relatively early in the breeding season as a 2.5-year-old cow. Pregnant and lactating 2- to 3-year-old cows also will continue to grow, although at a reduced rate compared with that of cows breeding as yearlings. Requirements presented above may be slightly inadequate for this age group as well.

Some supplementation may be required during seasons when requirements are high. Nutritional needs for late gestation in spring tend to be moderate, but captive cows grazing vegetation that initiates growth relatively late (e.g., late April) may produce small calves, and moderate levels of supplementation may be useful. Cows grazing on vegetation that initiates growth relatively early (e.g., late March) should require little or no supplementation for fetal growth, unless abundance of vegetation is low relative to stocking levels. Spring nutritional requirements of calves born the previous summer are higher than that of adult, gravid cows. Enhancing the probability that calves will be sufficiently large for breeding as yearlings may require supplementation during early to mid-spring, until vegetative growth is well underway. A high-quality pellet (at least 85.1 kcal DE per ounce [3 kcal/g] and 12% to 16% crude protein) may provide the best type of supplementation, particularly because intake rates tend to be low in early to mid-spring (J. G. Cook personal data).

The very high nutritional requirements of lactation in summer coincide with a period of high forage quality and quantity. But adequacy of summer vegetation to meet requirements should not be assumed. This is particularly true if calves are born relatively late (e.g., during or after the second week of June). Appropriate levels of supplementation from July through October may enhance calf growth (cf. Hudson and Adamczewski 1990), induce earlier breeding dates and increase pregnancy rates. The need for and extent of supplementation will depend on the quality and abundance of available forage. Supplementation with a formulated ration with high energy—at least 85.1 kcal of DE per ounce (3 kcal/g)—and moderate levels of protein (12%–16%) may be necessary to ensure optimum performance.

After mid-autumn, a unique set of conditions exist in which it may not be clear how best to manage a captive elk herd nutritionally. At this time, calves are presumably weaned, forage quality has declined to low levels and photoperiod apparently is responsible for a reduction in calf growth. Some growth in calves can be maintained during late autumn, but a high feeding level of high-quality forage probably will be required, and the resultant growth rates may be relatively low. Therefore, providing adequate supplementation to maintain growth in November and December may not be worth the costs. The nutritional requirements of cows at this time of year will be quite low; relatively low levels of supplementation to maintain body weight may suffice or not be necessary.

Winter nutritional requirements particularly of adult cows are the lowest of any time during the year, but forage quality and quantity may be inadequate to prevent substantial weight losses. Low levels of weight loss—less than 7% to 8%, excluding products of conception, or 5% including products of conception—should have little detrimental effect on herd productivity. Substantially greater winter weight loss will increase nutritional requirements the following growing season because of compensatory growth. Supplementation with a moderate quality hay—68.0 to 73.7 kcal/oz (2.4–2.6 kcal/g), with 55% to 60% digestibility and at least 10% crude protein—should be adequate during winter. Feeding of lower quality grass hays may induce substantial weight loss, because elk do not seem to accept such hay to the extent that cattle do. Supplementation with urea and minerals, however, may ameliorate rejection to some extent. Supplementing high energy rations in winter can enhance female calves' size in their first breeding season, but benefits may be marginal (Brelurut et al. 1995), and winter supplementation may not be as effective as supplementation in early spring and late summer.

Pellets are an unnatural food for wild ruminants, and pellet feeding can induce poorly recognized problems for elk. First, high-energy pellet formulations often contain inadequate fiber (Baker and Hobbs 1985). Unless pellets are specially formulated to provide sufficient fiber, elk must consume hay or native forage along with the pellets to avoid enteritis. On the basis of my experience, elk diets must contain at least 40% long hay if high-energy, grain-based pellets are being fed. Switching from a high fiber to a high concentrate diet without an adequate transition period will make elk sick and can be fatal. Gradual transitions of 4 to 7 days are required to avoid illness. The potential for illness seems to be highest during winter or early spring, when the switch to a "hot" diet follows an extended period of feeding a low-quality diet.

Also, grain-based pellets typically have low calcium-to-phosphorous ratios (less than 1:1), which can cause formation of kidney stones. This is considered a problem primarily in castrated males (Blood and Radostits 1989), but also may affect intact males (National Research Council 1985). Affected males may be unable to pass kidney stones (calculi) through the urethra, resulting in urinary blockage and death. A calcium-to-phosphorus ratio of at least 1.2:1 in cattle diets is recommended (Blood and Radostits 1989). Haigh and Hudson (1993) presented information regarding pelleted ration formulations for red deer and elk.

Nutritional objectives for bulls may differ from those of cows because the economic incentive for achieving very large body size early in life may be lower than for cows. Moreover, if operators choose to market antler products from their bulls, nutritional objectives will include maximizing antler growth and will focus, to a greater extent, on providing adequate protein and minerals.

In conclusion, specific feeding strategies will vary considerably among operations and must reflect to a large extent the amount and quality of forage available to the captive herd. Haigh and Hudson (1993) pointed out that, above all else, supplemental feeding should be based on good judgment, because the need for supplementation will reflect the unique characteristics of the farm. Efficiency in the long run will depend on sufficient monitoring of elk per-

Pellets are an unnatural food for wild ruminants and often contain inadequate fiber. If elk are not provided hay or allowed to consume native forage to obtain sufficient fiber, many may become ill with digestive enteritis. *Photo courtesy of the Colorado Division of Wildlife.*

formance and forage characteristics, and by making appropriate adjustments in feeding strategies to achieve performance objectives. A good example of such monitoring by elk growers in Hawaii was provided by Smith and Peischel (1991). Valuable information on nutrition and animal production is available for domestic livestock in National Research Council (1984, 1985). Haigh and Hudson (1993) provided useful guidelines based on considerable practical experience and academic research. Proceedings of several International Wildlife Ranching Symposia provide a wealth of information (see Renecker and Hudson 1991), as do several commercial magazines, including *The Deer Farmer* (P.O. Box 2678, Wellington, New Zealand), *The Canadian Elk and Deer Farmer* (P.O. Box 6016, Federal Way, Washington 98063) and *North American Elk* (7301 NW Tiffany Springs Road, Kansas City, Missouri 64153).

Assessing Nutritional Status

Two general approaches exist to assess the nutritional status and condition of elk: those that depend on collecting samples of the animal (e.g., weight, tissues, urine, feces);

and those that depend on samples of vegetation consumed by the animal. Samples of the animal provide relatively direct measures of condition or nutritional status that can only be inferred from vegetative approaches. Data of dietary quality and intake, however, may provide greater insights regarding fundamental characteristics of the environment that influence the nutritional status of the animal. Coupled information from both approaches would be of greatest value, but both have rarely been collected simultaneously. Simulation modeling also provides a means to link data on forage conditions to the nutritional status of the animal.

Samples collected directly from animals provide information either on nutritional condition of the animal, a direct result of relatively long-term nutrition, or information on very recent nutrition (e.g., 1–7 days before sample collection). Thus, the type of information desired will determine to some extent what type of data should be collected from the animal. Moreover, some of the approaches require slaughter, others capture and handling (which are highly invasive and usually expensive), and others require only collection of feces or urine, with virtually no trauma or even disturbance to the animals. Finally, accuracy and reliability vary considerably among different types of samples collected from animals.

Given the current state-of-the-art, the most reliable and accurate approaches, particularly of nutritional condition, apparently are those that are most invasive. Increasing societal concern for animal welfare may impede slaughter or even capture of animals and is perhaps one factor spurring research of less-invasive techniques of nutritional status. At any rate, elk managers and researchers clearly are faced with a myriad of decisions regarding methods to assess condition and nutritional status of elk. The following is a brief review of a variety of techniques.

Body Composition

Probably the most useful measure of an animal's nutritional condition is its whole-body composition (i.e., the amount of fat, protein, ash and water, excluding the ingesta contained in the alimentary tract) and energy content. Direct estimation of these measures requires sacrificing the animal, homogenizing the body and extracting samples. Total energy content then can be calculated. Because fat contains appreciably greater concentration of energy than do other body components, fatter animals and, thus, animals in better condition contain greater weight-specific levels of energy. Degen et al. (1990) presented an approach modification that reduces costly and time-consuming fat and protein determinations. Gross energy content of samples from the homogenized mass is determined by

Assessing physical condition in free-ranging elk is difficult, particularly as the most accurate methodologies require that elk must be either killed or immobilized using drugs delivered by a dart gun similar to the one shown here. *Photo by Jim D. Yoakum.*

bomb calorimetry, and simple equations are used to predict body composition.

Used to estimate whole-body energy content and composition are several approaches that do not require sacrificing the animal. These are generally referred to as dilution techniques. They involve (1) injecting a measured amount of an inert chemical that readily diffuses through the body in body water; (2) collecting a sample of body water from either blood or urine after the tracer reaches equilibrium; and (3) determining the concentration of the tracer. Because water in fat and protein is quite constant and different, it can be used to calculate fat and protein content of an animal. For white-tailed deer, regression equations have been developed that are used to calculate fat, protein and ash content from body water estimates (Robbins et al. 1974).

Most dilution techniques used for large ungulates involve one of two general approaches. In one, animals are chemically immobilized, the inert chemical tracer injected (usually into the jugular vein), the animal held several hours until the tracer reaches equilibrium throughout the body and a blood sample taken to determine tracer concentration. This is referred to as the single-point equilibrium approach (Watkins et al. 1990). The other involves collecting multiple samples after tracer injection. Animals are immobilized, the tracer injected and blood or urine samples collected periodi-

Large grinders are used to provide homogenized samples of carcasses of large animals that, in turn, can be used to estimate fat, protein, ash and water content of the whole body (body composition). Such estimates are key for understanding nutritional condition of an animal, but determining body composition in this manner is expensive and labor intensive, and it requires sacrificing the animal. Thus, wildlife biologists have conducted research for decades to find alternative approaches, using relatively easy-to-acquire samples, such as feces, blood, urine, and bone marrow, to index body composition or nutritional states. *Photo by Rachel C. Cook.*

cally over the next several days. Because tracer concentration in body water declines gradually and predictably, estimates of tracer concentration from the serial samples can be used to calculate the tracer concentration in body water by extrapolating back to time = 0 (see Torbit et al. 1985b).

Compared with the multisample approach, the single-point approach may overestimate body water, for reasons that are not completely clear (Watkins et al. 1990). Moreover, the amount of time required for the tracer to reach equilibrium is uncertain, and mistakes in estimating this time can introduce bias. Several deer studies allowed 2 hours for equilibration (DelGiudice et al. 1990, Watkins et al. 1990), but other researchers indicated that up to 10 hours are required in large-bodied ruminants (see Nagy 1983). In elk calves, 5 hours were required for equilibration (Cook et al. 1998). The multisample approach requires substantially more handling for 4 to 5 days for collection of adequate samples. Laboratory costs are two to four times greater using the multisample approach, which is an important consideration depending on the specific tracer used.

Deuterium oxide and tritium seem to be the most accepted inert chemical tracers used for large ungulates studies (Torbit et al. 1985b, Watkins et al. 1990). Both have different advantages and disadvantages. Body composition

using tritium is inexpensive, but tritium is radioactive and its use is regulated. Deuterium is not regulated, but cost is considerably greater than that of tritium. Urea is an additional tracer receiving attention for body composition work with livestock (Rule et al. 1986). It has rarely been used for wild ungulates and will require testing and development before routine use with elk. Urea and its laboratory assays are inexpensive, and animal handling requirements using urea are relatively minor compared with those using tritium or deuterium.

A number of difficulties exist with dilution techniques that restrict their use. First, multiple recaptures for the multisample approach are difficult with wild animals. Second, equations for calculating fat, protein and ash content once water content is estimated have not been published for elk. Appropriate studies will have to be conducted to develop these equations using procedures that require slaughter (Torbit et al. 1985b). Finally, a fundamental problem of the dilution techniques is that weight of water and dry matter contents of the alimentary tract must be estimated and subtracted from total live weight to calculate ingesta-free body weight. These estimates are difficult to obtain from wild animals unless they are sacrificed, which, of course, defeats the purpose of dilution techniques. Ingesta content can vary considerably among age classes, type of diet, amount of food consumed and among animal species.

Other approaches have been considered for estimating body composition. Ultrasound is based on differences in electrical conductivity between fat versus lean body and other tissues and can be used to measure depth of fat depots, for example. Ultrasound has been used for estimating body composition in small species of wildlife, with varying accuracy (Harder and Kirkpatrick 1994), and with livestock (e.g., Bullock et al. 1991). Stephenson et al. (1994) used ultrasound to assess condition of moose, by measuring subcutaneous rump fat depth and correlating this measure to total body fat. Initial results indicated a high level of correlation.

Ultrasonography has more recently been developed to assess condition of elk as well (Cook 2000). As with moose, ultrasound is used to measure thickness of subcutaneous fat deposits on the rump. Detailed evaluation indicates that rump fat thickness is highly ($r^2 = 0.87$) and linearly correlated to total ingesta-free body fat ranging from 5% to more than 20% (Cook 2000). Ultrasound is exclusively a live-animal evaluation technique. It can be used on elk sedated with drugs or elk that are immobilized using hobbles without sedation, which normally is the case in net-gunning capture operations. However, rump fat in elk is depleted when body fat declines below about 5%, so rump fat thickness fails as an index of condition when body fat is below

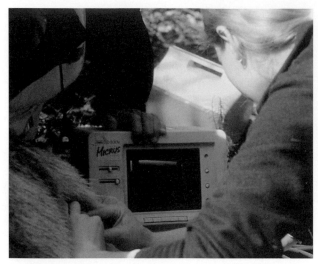

Ultrasound has been used to measure the depth of fat deposits on the body of live elk. The rump fat layer in elk is highly correlated to total body fat level. Ultrasound has the advantage of not requiring invasive sampling. *Photo by John G. Cook.*

this level (Cook 2000). Practical experience with six herds in the northwestern U.S. indicates that this limitation is a critical shortcoming during winter and early spring, because most elk have less than 5% body fat (R. C. Cook personal data). Another limitation has been cost of portable ultrasonographs. New units were costing about $15,000 (1995 prices), but several companies are now manufacturing and selling them for about half this amount (1999 prices). Refurbished machines can be purchased for less. They are reasonably compact and light—about 22 pounds (10 kg)—and can be operated using batteries. They can be placed in a backpack and transported and loaded/unloaded in a helicopter with reasonable ease during field operations, even in remote, rugged areas.

Body condition scoring (BCS) based on visual and hands-on approaches provides a rapid and inexpensive means to assess condition—an approach that has proven to be useful in the dairy and beef industries. Gerhardt et al. (1996) introduced probably the first rigorously tested BCS for wild ungulates. This was a hands-on version developed for caribou. They reported good correlation between body fat and an arithmetic combination of weight and their BCS. A BCS based on visual assessment was reported for game-farmed elk by Zebarth (1995), but it has not been rigorously tested. Furthermore, visual approaches probably suffer from lack of precision when applied to wild animals with long, thick pelages (Gerhardt et al. 1996) such as elk in winter. More recently, a hands-on BCS, modified from Gerhardt et al. (1996), was developed and tested for elk (Cook 2000). It is well-correlated ($r^2 = 0.87$) to ingesta-free body fat levels ranging from about 0% to 20%, and thus covers virtually the

entire range of nutritional condition likely to be encountered in wild herds (Cook 2000). Potential problems are that BCS can be subjective such that different observers may derive different scores for the same animals. This BCS also is more affected by animal position and immobilization technique (e.g., sedation versus hobbling) than is rump fat thickness as measured by ultrasound (R. C. Cook personal data).

Cook (2000) also developed and tested an elk condition evaluation system that was an arithmetic combination of rump fat thickness and BCS (Figure 123). This combination index, referred to as LIVINDEX, eliminates the rump fat depletion problem mentioned above and reduces to some extent the potential implications of BCS subjectivity. It is more correlated to ingest-free body fat ($r^2 = 0.90$) than is either rump fat or BCS alone, and it covers the entire range of condition likely to be encountered in wild elk. This index probably is the most accurate, rigorously tested technique to evaluate nutritional condition currently available for live, free-ranging elk. However, the potential subjectivity concerns of BCS still hold, and both BCS and ultrasound techniques require adequate training (Cook 2000).

Bioelectrical impedance analysis is a relatively new technique that has been shown to work well on monogastrics, such as bears (e.g., Hilderbrand et al. 1998). Bioelectrical impedance analysis measures resistance to the flow of weak electrical current—the greater the water content of the body, the less resistance. This technique, therefore, indirectly measures fat level by measuring water content, as does the dilution techniques described above. The value of

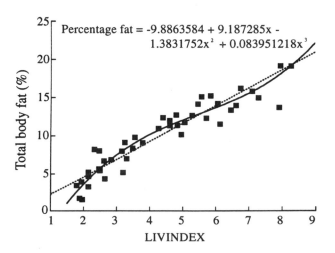

Figure 123. Relationship of LIVINDEX and total ingesta-free body fat of 43 yearling and adult cow elk (adapted from Cook 2000). LIVINDEX was calculated as a combination of subcutaneous rump fat depth, measured using ultrasonography, and a body condition score developed for elk. It accounted for 90% of the variation in body fat, based on the polynomial equation, over virtually the entire range of body condition likely to occur in wild elk (Cook 2000).

bioelectrical impedance analysis to measure fat content of elk apparently is low, based on preliminary assessments by Cook (2000), probably because the ruminant stomach contains a very large and variable amount of water that hinders the technique.

Fat Indices

Fat indices serve as an index to body composition and nutritional condition. They involve sampling from various areas in the body where fat accumulates. Fat indices require dead animals and, therefore, have largely been applied using hunter returns. Accordingly, use of hunter-harvested animals restricts to some extent the time period during which nutritional condition can be evaluated. Two fat indices—fat located around and attached to the kidneys and marrow fat in several bones—have received considerable attention (see Harder and Kirkpatrick 1994).

Kidney fat is obtained by removing the kidney and its surrounding fat and trimming excess fat extending beyond the ends of the kidneys. The weight ratio of remaining fat to the kidney multiplied by 100 is the kidney fat index (KFI). Expressing kidney fat as a ratio to kidney weight adjusts for differences in size of the animal. With red deer, Riney (1955) believed that KFI was a robust index across seasons, ages and a wide range of environmental conditions. Finger et al. (1981) reported that KFI accounted for 75% of the variation in whole body fat in white-tailed deer. Some biologists no longer trim excess fat from the ends of the kidneys (e.g., Kohlmann 1999).

However, kidney weights fluctuate seasonally, thereby distorting true differences among seasons. Dauphiné (1975) argued that, to account for gross differences in body weight, there was little reason to divide the weight of perirenal fat by the weight of the kidneys as long as animals were grouped by age class. Anderson et al. (1990) proposed a kidney fat weight index that excluded kidney weights. Harder and Kirkpatrick (1994) concluded that dividing kidney fat by the weight of the kidneys probably should be avoided when comparisons among seasons are of major interest. For elk, Cook (2000) found that an index based only on kidney fat weight was substantial better correlated to total body fat than were KFIs derived by dividing by kidney weights. This study included a wide range of ages and body sizes, confirming that dividing by kidney weight did little to account for differences in body weight.

Bone marrow indices of nutritional condition were first described for white-tailed deer nearly 60 years ago and have received considerable attention since then. Because marrow fat appears to be one of the last fat stores used, low values of marrow fat tend to be indicative of long-term or acute nutritional deprivation (Harder and Kirkpatrick 1994). Mech and DelGiudice (1985) reported that any loss of this fat reserve is indicative of poor condition in white-tailed deer. For red deer, Bubenik (1982) indicated that fat percentages greater than 80% before winter and greater than 60% in late winter were indicative of excellent condition. Percentages lower than 75% before winter and less than 55% in late winter indicated marginal to inadequate condition.

Additional work (Cook 2000) suggests that recommendations of Mech and DelGuidice (1985), rather than those of Bubenik (1982), apply to elk (Figure 124). Femur marrow fat in elk apparently is unresponsive to changes in total body fat levels until the latter falls below 6%, which corresponds to a femur fat level of 80% to 85% (Cook 2000). Thus, percentages greater than 85% at the beginning or end of winter indicate only that elk are not in poor to very poor condition. Percentages less than 80% at the beginning of winter indicate severe nutritional restrictions over the previous summer or autumn (or perhaps very old age or even disease problems), and percentages less than 80 in late winter indicate poor to very poor condition.

Fat content of femur marrow has been used traditionally for condition assessments. Marrow of the mandible also appears suitable for assessing marrow fat levels, and mandibles typically are easier to collect than femur bones from freshly killed animals and animals found dead (Cederlund et al. 1989). Cederlund et al. (1986, 1989) indicated that fat

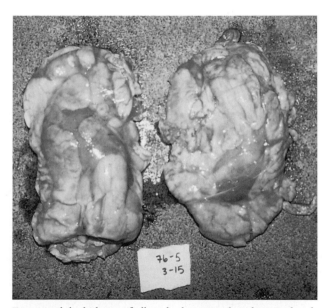

Fat around the kidneys of elk and other animals is deposited and metabolized in a reasonably predictable sequence, and kidney fat indices have been widely used as an indicator of body condition for animals that have been harvested by hunters. However, the weight of the kidney, as well as the surrounding fat, fluctuates seasonally, making between-season comparisons difficult. *Photo by Rachel C. Cook.*

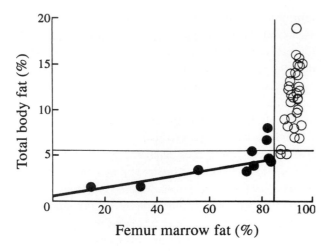

Figure 124. Relationship of femur marrow fat to total ingesta-free body fat of 43 yearling and adult cow elk (adapted from Cook 2000). In this study, femur marrow fat was virtually constant (indicated by open circles) until total body fat decreased below about 6% (indicated by closed circles). Thus, this technique by itself is of little value as a condition index except for elk in poor to very poor condition (Cook 2000).

content of femur and mandibles respond similarly as nutritional condition of the animal varies. In elk, mandible fat may have more value as a condition index over a greater range of total body fat than does femur fat, but mandible fat levels, as a predictor of total fat, (1) seems to be confounded by age and (2) within an age class, an imprecise predictor (Cook 2000).

A number of visual schemes have been used to assess marrow fat content, but they tend to be subjective and have largely been replaced by more quantitative procedures. One of the quantitative approaches involves oven drying marrow to a constant weight and dividing dry weight by the initial wet weight and multiplying by 100 to estimate percentage fat content (Neiland 1970). This approach is simple, objective, inexpensive and has been recommended as practical method useful for a variety of wildlife studies (Hunt 1979).

A second method involves mixing marrow fat with a solution of chloroform and methanol (Verme and Holland 1973). The marrow fat dissolves in the chloroform, and the water dissolves in the methanol. The mixture then is set near a low heat source, and water evaporates rapidly. The remaining material contains fat and some nonfat residue, the latter of which usually is ignored but can be estimated and subtracted from the total residue (Harder and Kirkpatrick 1994).

A final technique that has received little attention involves visual scoring of fat deposits of carcasses and the viscera. For deer, Kistner et al. (1980) developed such a score that was modified and tested for elk by Cook (2000). This

score is based in part on fat levels of the heart, kidneys, viscera, subcutaneous rump fat and subcutaneous brisket fat. With modifications for elk, this score was highly ($r^2 = 0.90$), linearly correlated with total body fat (Figure 125), and it covered the entire range of body fat levels likely to be encountered with wild elk. Use of the technique in many field settings may not always be practical. But Cook (2000) found that scoring based on a subset of fat deposits (heart, pericardium and kidneys—easily identified and thus easily obtained from hunter-harvested animals, for example) predicted total body fat as well as the entire Kistner score. This provides a much simpler, practical approach to such a scoring system.

Fat deposition in various areas of the body generally follows a set priority, although it is not mutually exclusive (Cederlund et al. 1989). In red deer, fat is first stored in the bone marrow, then deposited around the kidneys, intestines and stomach cavity and, finally, stored subcutaneously over the rump and saddle (Riney 1955). Catabolism of fat under nutritionally limited conditions apparently follows in reverse order. Therefore, the relative value of fat indices may differ among seasons.

Such patterns of sequential fat deposition has led to combinations of different indices that cover different ranges of condition, ultimately to cover a greater range of nutritional condition. The LIVINDEX described above is an example for live animals. For dead animals, several workers

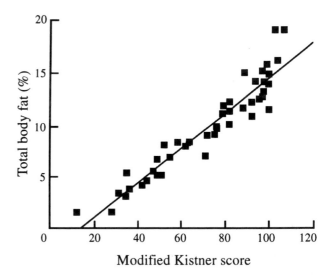

Figure 125. Relationship of a carcass evaluation scoring system, originally developed for deer (Kistner et al. 1980) and modified for elk (Cook 2000), and total ingesta-free body fat of 43 yearling and adult cow elk (adapted from Cook 2000). Although this technique has mostly been overlooked, it offers greater precision and accuracy ($r^2 = 0.90$) over a wider range of nutritional condition than more traditional techniques developed for dead animals.

recommended using a combination of kidney fat and bone marrow fat indices (Ransom 1965, Connolly 1981, Kie et al. 1983). Kidney fat indices (those wherein fat weight is divided by kidney weight) should be used as long as KFI exceeds 15% to 30%, and femur marrow fat probably should be used when KFI falls below 15% to 30%. Connolly (1981) discussed a formal approach for deer based on an arithmetic combination of KFI and femur marrow fat, referred to as CONINDEX.

In elk, however, such a combination of indices apparently is only partially effective. Kidney fat indices in elk are correlated to total body fat in a highly nonlinear manner (Figure 126), such that they are hypersensitive to changes in body fat at very low levels of condition, and they are hyposensitive to body fat changes at middle and high levels of condition (i.e., >12%–13% total body fat). Thus, for elk at least, KFI is marginally useful at low levels of condition, as has been shown for deer, and is marginally useful above moderate levels of condition. Moreover, Cook (2000) showed that, although the CONINDEX for elk is well-correlated to body fat levels when body fat is below 12%, it loses virtually all predictive capability above this level.

Cederlund et al. (1989) noted that marrow and other body fat deposits rarely have been proven to be related to condition and survival. Considerably more knowledge is needed of fat deposition and mobilization in various tissues of the body. Robbins (1983) noted that few studies have attempted to assess reliability of various fat indices by comparing with total body fat. He concluded that KFIs are poor predictors of body composition, and he argued against converting marginally relevant biological relations to highly

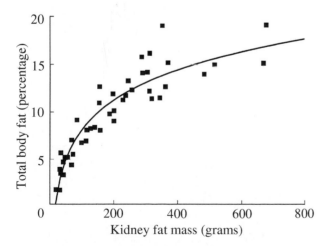

Figure 126. Relationship of kidney fat mass and total ingesta-free body fat of 43 yearling and adult cow elk (adapted from Cook 2000). The markedly nonlinear relation weakens the value of kidney fat indices as a condition indicator (Robbins 1983). For example, the predictive value of this technique appreciably declined for elk with more than about 12% total body fat.

significant statistical relations using mathematical transformations (e.g., "linearizing" highly nonlinear relations, such as that in Figure 126). For elk, Cook (2000) demonstrated that standard bone and kidney fat indices generally suffer from these problems, and she showed that the reduced subset scoring of the Kistner system, as modified for elk (Cook 2000), may be a practical alternative for dead elk condition evaluation, although further development and standardization of the scoring system may be needed.

Body Weight

Body weight and changes in weight have long been used as general measures of condition and performance in large ungulates studies. Changes in weight in particular provide a useful measure of nutritional effects (Jiang and Hudson 1994) and disturbance effects of hunting (Austin et al. 1989). Some state wildlife agencies use dressed carcass weights of 1.5-year-old male deer taken by hunters (Harder and Kirkpatrick 1994). Such measurements taken over a number of years can provide useful insight regarding trends in habitat conditions.

Use of weight as a measure of condition and animal performance has limitations. Substantial changes in the amount of food eaten can change live body weight by 8.8 to 11 pounds (4–5 kg) within several days of diet changes in adult elk (Cook et al. 1998). In addition, weight may be a poor indicator of nutritional condition, because it is a function of a variety of factors including ingesta weight, level of dehydration and animal stature (e.g., skeletal size). Finally, body composition and, thus, condition, may change with little concomitant change in body weight (Torbit et al. 1985a). For example, Verme and Ozoga (1980b) reported that small deer fawns often contained as much fat as did larger deer fawns in late autumn. Nevertheless, some of these confounding factors can be accounted for, and body weight can be a useful measure for a variety of applications (Harder and Kirkpatrick 1994).

Blood Chemistry

There has been a long-term, intensive search for components of blood or urine that are reliable and sensitive indices of nutritional condition or short-term nutritional status. Much of this work has focused on white-tailed deer; very little has been conducted using elk. Results of the search have been somewhat disappointing in that blood and urine studies have not provided the panacea for which many researchers hoped (Franzmann 1985). There are advances, however, and the search is not over. Further work, particularly with several new variables, may yet provide more useful indices of condition or nutrition that have widespread, practical applications.

The total number of blood variables scrutinized for wildlife applications is quite long and has been summarized by Harder and Kirkpatrick (1994) and specifically for elk and red deer by Haigh and Hudson (1993; see Chapter 4). Updated summaries including all known data for elk are presented by season for serum constituents in Tables 54 through 56 and for whole blood in Table 57. Many of the blood variables have useful diagnostic value for veterinary work but little value for assessing condition or nutritional status. Blood variables emphasized in a variety of large ungulate studies for assessing nutrition or nutritional condition are briefly reviewed.

Glucose

Glucose in the blood is a primary source of energy for a variety of cellular functions in nonruminant animals. In ruminants, volatile fatty acids from microbial degradation in the rumen serve this function, although glucose is required as an energy source for red blood and brain cells. Moreover, before ruminal digestion develops appreciably, glucose serves as the primary source of energy in juvenile ruminants. Reduced serum (portion of the blood minus red and white blood cells) levels of glucose can be indicative of inadequate energy consumption.

Seal et al. (1978) reported significant nutritional effects on glucose levels in white-tailed deer fawns, but, in adult white-tailed deer (Kie et al. 1983) and adult elk (Weber et al. 1984), glucose did not respond to differences in condition or nutritional status. Because young ruminants that still consume milk rely more on glucose as an energy source than adults do, glucose may have greater diagnostic value for young animals. For example, in elk calves, glucose levels were significantly correlated with growth rate of maternally raised neonates; they were two to three times higher in large versus small calves at birth and 15% to 20% higher on average in well-fed, rapidly growing calves compared with nutritionally restricted calves during late summer and early autumn (Cook et al. 1994b).

One of the difficulties with serum glucose is that various capture techniques have considerable effects on glucose levels. Both xylazine hydrochloride and carfentanil citrate—drugs frequently used to immobilize large ungulates—significantly elevate serum glucose levels (Cook et al. 1994b). Excitement that occurs during capture also increases glucose levels (Wesson et al. 1979). Effects of capture, therefore, may preclude useful applications of glucose data for work with free-ranging elk.

Serum Urea Nitrogen

Serum urea nitrogen, often referred to as blood urea nitrogen, is one of the most widely assessed blood indices of condition and nutritional status (Harder and Kirkpatrick 1994). Serum urea nitrogen is a by-product of protein digestion, and increasing levels of protein in ruminant diets are associated with increasing levels of serum urea nitrogen. Serum urea nitrogen levels also are insensitive to immobilization with drugs (Mautz et al. 1980, Cook et al. 1994b) and capture stress (Wesson et al. 1979).

Working with live elk, immobilized by drugs, allows biologists to collect blood, fecal matter, and other samples from free-ranging elk with little risk of side effects, although biologists must consider any potential effect of the drugs on variables measured. *Photo by Jim D. Yoakum.*

Table 54. Blood serum reference values for elk in winter

Serum constituent	Calves[a] Mean	SE	Yearlings[a] Mean	SE	Adult cows[a] Mean	SE	Mixed age/sex[b] Mean	SE	Adult cows[c] Mean	SE	Adults mixed sex[d] Mean	SE	Adults mixed sex[e] Mean	SE
Cholesterol (mg/dL)	50.90	3.56	58.80	4.06	65.40	4.79			72.40	13.59				
Glucose (mg/dL)	103.50	4.41	97.10	2.58	109.00	3.50	146.40	46.69	170.6	51.73	183.00	44.00	233.00	53.00
Triglycerides (mg/dL)	7.30	0.66	9.20	0.68	11.70	0.88								
Urea nitrogen (mg/dL)	30.70	1.51	30.30	1.12	32.80	0.78			24.60	7.31	36.00	15.24	23.40	9.88
Uric acid (mg/dL)									0.30	0.22				
Triiodothyronine (ng/dL)	135.20	6.87	279.30	23.02	152.70	11.95								
Thyroxine (μg/dL)	3.30	0.18	4.60	0.15	4.10	0.33								
Insulin-like growth factor (ng/mL)	283.20	32.22	305.1	16.44	298.1	19.77								
Total protein (g/dL)	6.20	0.07	6.40	0.12	6.70	0.10	5.60	2.40	6.30	0.77	7.10	0.96	7.60	1.03
Albumin (g/dL)	4.50	0.06	4.90	0.05	4.80	0.10	2.30	0.99	1.00	0.20	3.80	0.97	2.80	0.72
Globulin (g/dL)							3.40	1.45						
Total bilirubin (mg/dL)	0.20	0.03	0.30	0.02	0.30	0.03			1.20	0.52				
Creatinine (mg/dL)	1.30	0.04	1.70	0.04	1.90	0.04								
Alanine aminotransferase (IU/L)	32.80	4.15	22.30	2.46	18.70	2.17								
Alkaline phosphatase (IU/L)	247.60	24.22	167.00	22.04	79.40	24.72			215.8	121.91	2.10[f]	1.27	3.10[f]	1.88
Aspartate aminotransferase (IU/L)	46.80	3.28	36.20	2.94	38.10	3.23			110.9	42.00	90.60	33.96	89.70	33.66
Gamma glutamyltransferase (IU/L)	21.30	0.88	20.60	0.81	25.30	1.32								
Lactate dehydrogenase (mg/L)									373.0	91.00	892.0	312.00	903.0	316.00
Calcium (mg/dL)	9.9	0.12	9.7	0.13	9.4	0.06	9.4	0.44	7.3	0.93				
Inorganic phosphorus (mg/dL)	8.6	0.28	7.6	0.28	6.4	0.18			4.8	1.80				
Sodium (mEq/L)	141.3	0.92	141.0	0.29	141.3	0.53	148.2	8.62						
Potassium (mEq/L)	4.0	0.09	4.2	0.12	4.2	0.08	5.5	0.65						
Chloride (mEq/L)	101.8	0.62	101.7	0.44	102.4	0.44								

[a] Data from tractable, bottle-raised female calves, yearlings and adult cows (six elk, each sampled twice, in each age group) in a study designed to establish reference values of elk fed high-quality food ad libitum. Blood samples were collected from calm elk lightly sedated with low doses of xylazine hydrochloride within 5 to 8 minutes after xylazine injection to avoid analgesic effects. No animals in this study were pregnant or lactating (from Quinlan-Murphy 1998).

[b] Data from wild elk (19 to 39 elk for each variable) restrained in a squeeze chute without drugs (from Herin 1968).

[c] Data from wild adult cow elk (21) restrained in a squeeze chute without drugs (from Vaughn et al. 1973).

[d] Data from adult free-ranging elk (9 to 61 elk for each variable) apparently restrained in a squeeze chute without drugs (from Follis 1972).

[e] Data from adult captive elk (11 to 107 elk); method of restraint unstated (from Follis 1972).

[f] Data are sigma units.

But the relationship of serum urea nitrogen to nutrition is complicated. High energy intake reduces serum urea nitrogen, apparently because protein is used more efficiently by rumen microbes and, therefore, less urea is produced (Harder and Kirkpatrick 1994). This effect has been reported for white-tailed deer (Kirkpatrick et al. 1975) and elk calves (Cook et al. 1994b). In adult elk, serum urea nitrogen ranged from 37 to 45 mg/dL in cows fed a high-protein, low-energy diet compared with 32 to 38 mg/dL in cows fed a high-protein, high-energy diet for 2 years (J. G. Cook personal data). Nutrition/serum urea nitrogen relationships also are confounded when animals are on submaintenance diets. Catabolism of body protein and conservation of nitrogen (urea) by the kidneys will elevate serum urea nitrogen considerably (Harder and Kirkpatrick 1994). Such confounding interactions weaken the diagnostic value of serum urea nitrogen, although its value is enhanced if used in combination with other indices.

Alkaline Phosphatase

Alkaline phosphatase is a hormone concentrated in the osteoblasts (cells from which bone tissue develops). Elevated alkaline phosphatase serum levels are associated with various growing processes such as pregnancy and body and antler development. For example, alkaline phosphatase levels average greater than 300 international units per liter (IU/L) of serum in 2- to 4-month-old elk calves, and range from 150 to 300 IU/L in 5- to 14-month-old juvenile elk and from 75 to 150 IU/L in adult nonpregnant, nonlactating adult cows (J. G. Cook personal data). Nutritional restrictions that limit growth processes may induce declines in alkaline phosphatase levels. Seal et al. (1978) reported that alkaline phosphatase differed significantly in relation to dietary energy intake of white-tailed deer fawns. Seal and Hoskinson (1978) found higher levels in free-ranging pronghorn fawns believed to be in good condition than in fawns

Table 55. Blood serum reference values for elk in spring and autumn

	Autumn						Spring					
	Calves[a]		Yearlings		Three-year-old-cows		Calves		Two-year-old cows		Three-year-old cows	
Serum constituent	Mean	SE	Mean	SE	Mean	SE	Mean	SE	Mean	SE	Mean	SE
Cholesterol (mg/dL)	46.10	2.84	60.00	3.91	63.80	3.21	50.20	2.77	60.70	3.59	59.30	4.07
Glucose (mg/dL)	115.20	9.07	94.20	3.80	104.30	6.09	91.30	5.60	83.20	2.96	97.20	2.52
Triglycerides (mg/dL)	6.70	1.01	10.70	1.11	13.80	1.16	11.70	0.80	13.20	0.70	10.80	1.22
Urea nitrogen (mg/dL)	30.30	1.28	33.30	1.03	34.40	1.03	27.50	1.15	34.00	0.58	34.00	1.13
Triiodothyronine (ng/dL)	140.60	13.6	170.00	7.75	92.60	9.21	140.80	11.43	133.80	9.77	160.00	12.79
Thyroxine (μg/dL)	3.00	0.21	5.70	0.22	4.80	0.27	5.40	0.28	5.20	0.27	4.30	0.27
Insulin-like growth factor (ng/mL)	273.70	9.72	411.30	21.38	356.80	22.80	526.40	48.96	385.10	25.23	535.00	34.98
Albumin (g/dL)	4.20	0.05	4.70	0.04	4.60	0.12	4.60	0.09	4.50	0.06	4.30	0.08
Total protein (g/dL)	6.00	0.05	6.40	0.07	6.70	0.11	6.00	0.12	6.30	0.10	6.60	0.11
Total bilirubin (mg/dL)	0.20	0.02	0.20	0.01	0.30	0.02	0.40	0.03	0.40	0.06	0.30	0.05
Creatinine (mg/dL)	1.30	0.04	1.40	0.03	1.80	0.07	1.30	0.04	1.70	0.06	1.90	0.06
Alanine aminotransferase (IU/L)	38.30	3.70	29.30	3.78	21.50	1.88	30.00	3.25	26.00	2.77	20.30	1.61
Alkaline phosphatase (IU/L)	189.70	25.6	192.80	36.33	69.00	14.73	210.30	23.47	108.20	16.96	84.50	18.75
Aspartate aminotransferase (IU/L)	45.90	2.58	37.50	3.08	35.90	2.66	30.20	2.24	34.20	1.45	40.20	2.37
Gamma glutamyltransferase (IU/L)	22.80	0.63	23.50	1.23	23.40	1.00	19.50	1.06	20.50	0.81	24.50	1.52
Calcium (mg/dL)	10.10	0.11	9.60	0.08	9.40	0.07	10.30	0.11	9.50	0.11	9.20	0.07
Chloride (mEq/L)	98.70	0.54	99.30	0.040	100.40	0.27	102.00	0.97	105.5	0.34	101.80	0.31
Inorganic phosphorus (mg/dL)	8.4	0.23	8.1	0.14	7.0	0.23	8.7	0.37	6.9	0.32	6.6	0.35
Potassium (mEq/L)	4.4	0.10	4.1	0.03	4.2	0.08	4.1	0.06	60.7	3.59	4.0	0.07
Sodium (mEq/L)	138.7	0.43	139.9	0.51	139.3	0.28	142.8	0.95	144.3	0.21	140.8	0.17

Note: All data were from tractable, bottle-raised female calves, yearlings and 2- or 3-year-old adults (6 elk, each sampled twice, in each age group) in a study designed to establish reference values of elk fed high-quality food ad libitum. Blood samples were collected from calm elk lightly sedated with low doses of xylazine hydrochloride within 5 to 8 minutes after xylazine injection to avoid analgesic effects. No animals in this study were pregnant or lactating (from Quinlan-Murphy 1998).

[a] Xylazine hydrochloride, used for sedation, may have influenced these calf data, because methodology to eliminate xylazine influences had not yet been adopted in this study.

believed to be in poorer condition. Kie et al. (1983) reported lower levels in free-ranging deer maintained at high densities (and probably with lower nutritional status) than in deer occurring at lower density. Weber et al. (1984) noted higher alkaline phosphatase levels in elk consuming higher quality diets in burned areas than elk without access to the burns. Wolkers et al. (1994) observed that alkaline phosphatase was one of the three most useful indices of nutrition in a study using young adult female red deer. Cook et al. (1994b) found that alkaline phosphatase was significantly higher in neonatal and 3- to 6-month-old elk calves with rapid growth versus calves growing relatively slowly; it also was higher in large versus small elk calves at birth.

Even so, alkaline phosphatase has received relatively little attention as a key indicator of condition or nutritional status. One of the difficulties with alkaline phosphatase is that variation of levels appears to be quite high. Ninety-five percent confidence intervals (a measure of sample variation) are generally ±30% to 40% of the mean in young elk—roughly two to three times greater than that for most other serum variables (Cook et al. 1994b). Multiple sources of alkaline phosphatase in the body (see Wolkers et al. 1994)

may account for this high variation. There is potential for distinguishing between alkaline phosphatase from osteoblasts and that of other sources such as the liver. Further work in this area has potential to improve the value of alkaline phosphatase as an indicator of nutritional status (Cook et al. 1994b).

Thyroid Hormones

Two thyroid hormones—thyroxine (T_4) and triiodothyronine (T_3)—induce many direct and indirect influences on physiology, particularly in relation to metabolism, growth and thermogenesis (heat production). Thyroid hormones are important for digestive development and bone growth in juveniles, and they influence digestive kinetics (Westra and Hudson 1981). T_4 is a precursor to T_3, and T_3 is the primary physiological regulator (Hadley 1984). In general, increasing levels of T_3 are associated with increasing metabolic activity that usually is associated with growth or other productive processes (Newsholme and Leech 1983). T_3 declines as energy intake declines, mainly due to a reduced rate of conversion of T_4 to T_3; T_4 does not necessarily decline under nutritional restriction (Newsholme and Leech 1983).

Table 56. Blood serum reference values for elk in summer

Serum constituent	Yearling females[a] Mean	SE	Three-year-old cows[a] Mean	SE	Yearling males[b] Mean	SE	Yearling females[b] Mean	SE	Adult cows[b] Mean	SE
Cholesterol (mg/dL)	60.60	3.14	70.10	4.08	83.50	18.51	82.00	10.29	88.40	10.49
Glucose (mg/dL)	81.90	2.53	80.90	2.26	107.30	31.80	100.80	65.22	167.10	49.04
Triglycerides (mg/dL)	11.50	0.73	14.10	1.10						
Uric acid (mg/dL)					0.60	0.79	0.30	0.17	0.30	0.10
Urea nitrogen (mg/dL)	33.90	0.94	37.00	1.37	27.50	8.64	26.10	7.44	25.80	6.54
Tri-iodothyronine (ng/dL)	115.70	9.21	92.90	3.94						
Thyroxine (μg/dL)	4.90	0.15	4.80	0.13						
Insulin-like growth factor (ng/mL)	472.30	19.72	470.60	17.34						
Albumin (g/dL)	4.40	0.06	4.50	0.04	1.20	0.32	1.10	0.31	1.10	0.25
Total protein (g/dL)	6.30	0.10	6.40	0.06	6.80	0.75	6.70	0.41	7.60	0.75
Total bilirubin (mg/dL)	0.30	0.02	0.40	0.03	1.00	0.43	1.30	0.31	1.30	0.53
Creatinine (mg/dL)	1.20	0.02	1.60	0.070						
Alanine aminotransferase (IU/L)	37.20	4.31	32.7	3.14						
Alkaline phosphatase (IU/L)	169.90	29.50	120.20	23.62	269.60	39.06	195.80	61.23	148.70	95.34
Aspartate aminotransferase (IU/L)	39.20	3.49	40.10	2.54						
Gamma glutamyltransferase (IU/L)	21.00	1.34	22.30	1.35						
Calcium (mg/dL)	10.20	0.09	9.50	0.05	9.20	0.86	9.40	1.08	9.00	0.89
Chloride (mEq/L)	100.1	0.45	102.5	0.51						
Inorganic phosphorus (mg/dL)	8.50	0.16	7.10	0.37	6.60	1.31	6.00	4.43	4.70	1.33
Potassium (mEq/L)	4.10	0.05	4.00	0.07						
Sodium (mEq/L)	139.20	0.44	140.60	0.63						

[a] Data from tractable, bottle-raised yearlings and adult cows (6 elk, each sampled twice, in each age group) in a study designed to establish reference values of elk fed high-quality food ad libitum. Blood samples were collected from calm elk lightly sedated with low doses of xylazine hydrochloride within 5 to 8 minutes after xylazine injection to avoid analgesic effects. No animals in this study were pregnant or lactating (from Quinlan-Murphy 1998).

[b] Data from 33 wild elk (10 yearling males, 6 yearling females and 17 adult cows) captured during June and July in panel traps and chemically restrained with succinylcholine chloride (from Pedersen and Pedersen 1975).

Both thyroid hormones have been examined in a number of studies of juvenile ruminants. Seal et al. (1978) and Watkins et al. (1982) reported substantial effects of nutrition on T_3 levels in white-tailed deer fawns. Watkins et al. (1991) found that T_3 was significantly correlated with body fat and gross energy content of deer fawns, and that this hormone was correlated with body composition more so than was any other blood variable measured, including T_4. Cook et al. (1994b) reported that serum T_3 levels were two to three times higher in well-fed elk calves than in calves receiving 45% to 50% less food. Results of these studies regarding T_4 responses were mixed.

Bahnak et al. (1981) reported moderately lower levels of both thyroid hormones in adult deer fed slightly restricted energy diets year-round and markedly lower levels of the hormones in deer fed a highly restricted diet during winter. Hamr and Bubenik (1990) reported that T_3 and T_4 levels averaged three to five times higher in deer fed concentrate diets compared with that in severely malnourished deer, and that levels of both hormones for deer fed natural winter diets averaged two times higher than that in the malnourished deer. Weber et al. (1984) found no differences in T_4 in

free-ranging elk using recently burned areas compared with those without access to the burned areas (T_3 was not measured in this study). In a controlled study using nongravid cow elk in winter, serum T_3 levels of cows forced to lose 10% to 12% of their body weight averaged about half of that of cows that maintained their weight (Figure 127). However, T_4 levels did not differ appreciably in this study (J. G. Cook personal data).

Serum thyroid hormones thus show promise as indicators of condition or short-term nutritional status in large ungulates. Some evidence suggests that T_4 may be most indicative of nutritional condition, whereas T_3 may be most diagnostic of short-term nutritional status (Franzmann 1985, Cook 2000). Much remains to be learned about their general applicability and reliability across age and production classes, season and species.

Insulin-like Growth Factor

Research into endocrine control of growth has led to identification of several additional hormones that might be useful indices of condition or nutritional status, particularly in young animals. One of these, growth hormone, has been

Table 57. Hematological values of elk blood

Sex	Mean corpuscular volume[a]		Percentage mean corpuscular hemoglobin concentration		Percentage packed cell volume		Percentage hemoglobin		White blood cells[b]		Red blood cells[c]		Drug sedative	Source
	Mean	SD	Mean	SD	Mean	SD	Mean	SD	Mean	SD	Mean	SD		
Both[d]					46.300	2.100	18.300	0.800	5.559	1.902			None	Herin 1968
Both[e]	62.000	2.400			67.600	5.700	19.000	1.600	8.628	2.492	11.000	1.000	SSC[f]	Pedersen and Pedersen 1975
Both					49.000		17.800		3.140		8.500			Boyd 1970
Female[d, h]					52.000	33.200	19.100	16.600	6.849	1.780	10.700	1.340	None?	Follis 1972
Male[d, h]					52.400	33.500	19.000	16.500	8.140	2.116	11.400	1.420	None?	Follis 1972
Female[d, g, i]					53.900	1.200	17.000	0.400	4.000	0.510	6.90	0.710	M99	Vaughn et al. 1973
Male[d, g, f]					50.200	3.700	16.000	1.600	3.900	0.780	4.800	1.990	M99	Vaughn et al. 1973
Both[j]	44.300	6.600	38.300	3.900	44.900	5.500	17.100	2.100	5.346	1.450	9.900	1.700	Mixed	Weber 1973

[a] μM^3.

[b] Multiplied by $10^3/mm^3$.

[c] Multiplied by $10^6/mm^3$.

[d] Winter.

[e] Summer.

[f] Succinylcholine chloride.

[g] Spring.

[h] A mix of age classes and captive/wild elk.

[i] Captive elk.

[j] A mix of age, gender, captive/wild, seasons and capture techniques (including use of SCC and M99).

shown to be unreliable as an indicator of nutritional status because it is released within the body in a pulsatile fashion, and it tends to vary widely among animals receiving the same diet (Gluckman et al. 1987). In contrast, a compound referred to as insulin-like growth factor-1 (IGF_1) appears to

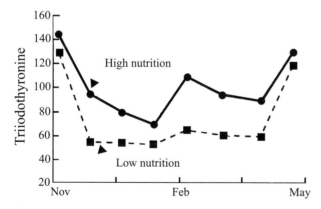

Figure 127. Serum triiodothyronine levels (in nanograms per deciliter of serum) in two groups (six animals in each) of 2-year-old nongravid elk cows, one fed a high level of nutrition that provided for constant weight across winter (high nutrition) and the other fed a submaintenance ration that induced 10% to 12% weight loss between late November and mid-March (low nutrition) (Quinlan-Murphy 1988). Elk were allowed to consume similar diets during the first and last sampling periods.

be strongly tied to nutritional status in both juvenile and adult domestic ruminant animals (Gluckman et al. 1987, McGuire et al. 1992). Preliminary work with elk suggests that serum IGF_1 levels are sensitive to changes in diet of elk calves (Figure 128) and subadults (Quinlan-Murphy 1998). Cook (2000) reported significant, nonlinear correlation to total body fat in adult elk.

Laboratory determinations of IGF_1 levels require radioimmunoassay techniques that are not yet widely available. Also, some evidence suggests that, although IGF_1 may be fundamentally linked to various growth processes, serum levels of this hormone may not be particularly diagnostic of its activity in the body. Levels of IGF_1 depend on age (Kerr et al. 1991), at least in cattle. Thus, routine applications for management purposes may require age-specific comparisons. As with the other hormones, considerable research is needed before widespread practical applications are possible.

Other Serum Indicators

A variety of other serum and whole blood variables have been investigated. Serum cholesterol, nonesterified fatty acids, triglycerides, electrolytes, ketones and others have been shown to be useful indices of nutrition in some studies but not in others. Whole blood variables, such as packed cell volume and hematocrit, also have been inconsistent in their diagnostic value (Franzmann 1985, Harder and Kirkpatrick 1994).

Urine Chemistry

Assessments of condition and nutritional status based on urine chemistry have received a high level of attention since the 1980s. Urine can be collected from snow, greatly reducing costs and stress associated with capture. Moreover, urine chemistry may be more diagnostic than blood chemistry. Animals tend to hold constant various constituents in blood in part by regulating excretion through the kidneys. Thus, urine chemistry may exhibit greater range and sensitivity to changes in diet than blood exhibits (DelGiudice et al. 1989). (However, this argument may not hold for blood hormones.) Restriction of condition/nutrition assessments to periods when snow is present, however, limits the technique, although urine can be acquired at any time of the year from captured females using catheters.

Urinary assessments for large ungulates have been limited mostly to urea nitrogen, cortisol and various electrolytes contained in urine. Estimates of each of these variables are calculated by dividing their urinary concentration by the concentration of urinary creatinine. Creatinine output from the body is believed to be relatively constant and unaffected by diet. This calculation, therefore, accounts for differences in urinary concentration due to the animal's state of hydration or mixing with water in snow after being voided (DelGiudice et al. 1990).

Urinary urea nitrogen is one of the primary urine constituents that has received much scrutiny. As with serum

urea nitrogen previously described, increasing urinary urea nitrogen is indicative of increasing dietary protein and of increasing catabolism of body protein when nutrition is inadequate (DelGiudice and Seal 1988). Cortisol in urine also may be indicative of nutritional status and condition. Cortisol in the body influences catabolism of fat and protein. Under nutritional restriction, cortisol levels are elevated, permitting increased catabolic rates, and elevated cortisol levels in the urine should reflect this condition (Saltz and White 1991). The diagnostic value of urinary electrolytes (calcium, sodium, potassium and phosphorus) is lower. Urinary electrolyte levels are strongly linked to electrolyte intake, which may or may not be related to condition or nutritional status. However, high levels of potassium in the urine, particularly if urinary urea nitrogen also is elevated, generally indicates elevated muscle cell breakdown during protein catabolism, because cellular breakdown releases potassium that ultimately is excreted in the urine (DelGiudice et al. 1991a).

An intensive study was conducted on urine chemistry of free-ranging elk in Yellowstone National Park (DelGiudice et al. 1991b). Decreasing potassium to creatinine ratios and increasing urinary urea nitrogen to creatinine ratios indicated progressive nutritional deprivation and increasing catabolism of lean body tissue. Urine chemistry most indicative of severe energy deprivation was collected from elk believed most nutritionally stressed. DelGiudice et al. (1991b) concluded that sequential collection and analysis of urine samples from snow provided a direct, quantitative assessment adequately sensitive to detect subtle differences in condition or nutritional status of elk across vast winter ranges.

However, urinary indices are not without problems and limitations. Considerable unexplained variation, inadequate sensitivity over a range of nutritional conditions, ambiguous interpretation and important differences among sex and age classes have been identified (Parker et al. 1993b, Harder and Kirkpatrick 1994, White et al. 1996). Criticisms of urinary urea nitrogen include: (1) urea nitrogen levels can be high due either to very high-quality or low-quality diets (Saltz et al. 1996); (2) within-animal variability is high over short time periods; (3) urinary urea nitrogen is unreliable unless the subject animals have lost at least 20% of autumn weight (White et al. 1996); and (4) there may be more reliable urinary variables for assessment (Saltz et al. 1992). Presently, urinary urea nitrogen appears to be a general index that requires large sample sizes, sequential sampling and substantial supporting information (e.g., other indices, range condition and weather data) to be useful (Harder and Kirkpatrick 1994, DelGiudice 1996). Although urinary cortisol levels may provide a superior alternative (Saltz et al.

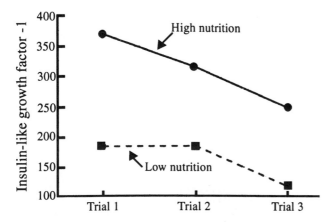

Figure 128. Serum insulin-like growth factor-1 levels (in nanograms per milliliter of serum) in two groups of elk calves (six calves in each)—one fed a high level of nutrition that supported rapid growth and the other fed a low level of nutrition that reduced growth, in late summer and autumn. Each trial lasted 18 days and consisted of different calves randomly allocated to each dietary group (Quinlan-Murphy 1998).

1992), this has not been conclusively demonstrated (Del-Giudice 1996).

Another urinary index apparently well-suited for assessing short-term nutritional status (Garrott et al. 1996, Vagnoni et al. 1996) involves the measurement of purine derivatives, particularly allantoin, which comprises the largest proportion of total purines excreted. Purine derivatives in the urine arise primarily from intestinal digestion of microbial protein originating in the rumen. As nutrition increases, ruminal microbial growth increases, as do purine derivatives such as allantoin in the urine (Vagnoni et al. 1996).

Research with wild and captive elk provided preliminary indications that allantoin is well-correlated with daily intake levels of dry matter digestibility—a surrogate measure of DE (Vagnoni et al. 1996)—and that allantoin is diagnostic of observed changes in weather severity and expected changes in dietary quality (Garrott et al. 1996). Additional work with captive elk has shown that allantoin/dry matter digestibility relationships are robust across a wide variety of experimental manipulations of dry matter digestibility feeding rates, across a substantial range of intake levels—15.9 to 131.5 kcal of ME per pound (35–290 kcal of ME/kg) MW per day—and across at least two age classes (yearlings and 3- to 4-year-old cows) (Figure 129) (Garrott et al. 1997). At least for elk, allantoin may be the best urinary index of short-term nutritional status currently available. However, it is unsuitable as an index of nutritional condition. Pils et al. (1999) provided insights and guidelines for reducing bias from snow–urine samples of wild elk.

One of the difficulties associated with using blood and urine chemistry is that normal levels for adequately fed animals across a variety of seasons, ages and productive stages often are unknown (Franzman 1985). This is particularly true for elk, which have been used infrequently in blood and urine chemistry studies, and for all North American large ungulates in seasons other than winter. The available data of blood and urine constituents for elk are summarized in Tables 54 to 59.

Fecal Chemistry

The level of nitrogen in the feces (fecal nitrogen) has received much scrutiny as an index of dietary quality. In ruminants, fecal nitrogen may vary with dietary quality primarily because variations in dietary nitrogen (National Research Council 1985) or energy (Merchen 1988, Lyons and Stuth 1992) influence productivity of rumen microbes. Wehausen (1995) indicated that fecal nitrogen is mainly influenced by energy rather than by protein intake. Undigestible forage volume also influences concentration of microbial and endogenous nitrogen in the feces (Merchen 1988).

A variety of studies have demonstrated that fecal nitrogen is correlated with dietary nitrogen (Leslie and Starkey 1985, Howery and Pfister 1990), dietary digestible dry matter (Leslie and Starkey 1985, Wofford et al. 1985) and weight change of adult ruminants (Gates and Hudson 1981, Hebert et al. 1984). Hodgeman and Bowyer (1986) and Irwin et al. (1993) used fecal nitrogen to compare nutritional status among herds of free-ranging ruminants. The technique is noninvasive, samples are relatively easy to collect and laboratory assays are inexpensive (Figure 130).

However, estimates of fecal nitrogen tend to vary more than concomitant estimates of dietary quality, and the relationship between fecal nitrogen and dietary quality may change with season or other conditions (Hobbs 1987) and

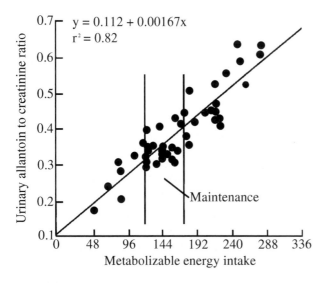

Figure 129. Relationship between allantoin to creatinine ratios of urine and metabolizable energy intake (in kilocalories per kilogram MW per day) of adult nongravid elk cows during late winter and spring (adapted from Garrott et al. 1997).

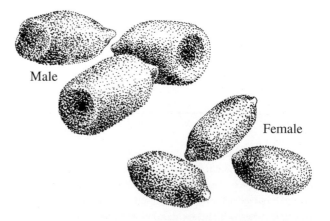

Figure 130. Hard pellets of elk showing sex-related size and shape differences. *Illustration by A. B. Bubenik.*

Table 58.   Urinary reference values for elk in spring, summer and autumn

| | Spring | | | | | | Summer | | | | Autumn | | | | | |
| | Calves | | Two-year-old cows | | Three-year-old cows | | Yearlings | | Three-year-old cows | | Calves[a] | | Yearlings | | Three-year-old cows | |
Urine constituent[b]	Mean	SE	Mean	SE	Mean	SE	Mean	SE	Mean	SE	Mean	SE	Mean	SE	Mean	SE
Cortisol:cr × 10	0.50	0.13	0.30	0.03	0.40	0.10	0.60	0.09	0.60	0.03	0.90	0.22	0.60	0.08	0.60	0.13
Urea nitrogen:cr	9.50	0.40	8.90	0.48	8.10	0.15	11.40	0.34	9.90	0.34	12.40	0.63	10.20	0.35	8.90	0.32
Calcium:cr × 1,000	3.40	1.73	12.70	6.48	29.60	4.09	57.90	9.67	35.80	7.32	87.40	14.32	18.80	6.61	7.70	3.93
Potassium:cr × 100	225.10	24.04	194.50	9.70	166.70	12.11	263.10	10.66	200.30	8.17	311.50	22.57	212.40	9.68	196.10	13.69
Sodium:cr × 100	5.80	0.43	6.80	0.52	6.30	0.54	14.30	4.60	8.50	0.98	43.80	15.92	8.20	0.46	10.90	1.50
Phosphorus:cr × 1,000	3.90	0.43	10.80	4.56	3.40	0.44	19.30	13.45	24.40	11.95	24.50	7.35	22.2	15.84	5.60	1.57

Note: All data were from tractable, bottle-raised female calves, yearlings and 2- or 3-year-old adults (6 elk, each sampled twice, in each age group) in a study designed to establish reference values of elk fed high-quality food ad libitum. Urine samples were collected from elk held in feeding stalls without the use of physical or chemical restraint of any kind (except for those data referenced by the footnote a). No animals in this study were pregnant or lactating (adapted from Quinlan-Murphy 1998).

[a] Xylazine hydrochloride, used for sedation, may have influenced these calf data, because methodology to eliminate xylazine influences had not yet been adopted in this study.

[b] Urinary variables are presented as ratios with urinary creatinine (cr) and multiplied by an adjustment factor following current conventions.

consumption of tannins induces substantial bias in dietary quality predictions (Robbins et al. 1987a). Cook et al. (1994a) also showed that fecal nitrogen could not be used as an index of dietary quality in elk calves. Growth and development of the alimentary tract and changes in milk intake relative to solid food intake greatly altered relationships between quality of solid food consumed and fecal nitrogen.

Such criticisms apparently have effectively eliminated the fecal nitrogen technique as a viable option for assessing dietary quality, unless improvements are made. Bias induced by tannins probably precludes using the technique for herds and seasons during which tannin intake is appre-

Table 59.   Urinary reference values for elk in winter

| | Calves[a] | | Yearlings[a] | | Three-year-old cows | | Mixed sex/age[b] | | Mixed sex/age[c] | | Three-year-old cows[d] | | Two-year-old cows[e] | | Adult cows[f] | |
Urine constituent[g]	Mean	SE	Mean	SE	Mean	SE	Mean	SE	Mean	SE	Mean	SE	Mean	SE	Mean	SE
Allantoin:cr											0.36	0.05	0.28	0.05	0.22	0.03
Cortisol:cr × 10	0.50	0.08	0.60	0.05	0.60	0.08										
Urea nitrogen:cr	10.10	0.50	8.20	0.39	7.50	0.20	4.40		73.50	30.50						
Calcium:cr × 1,000	40.00	17.33	36.00	5.29	26.00	3.79										
Potassium:cr × 100	272.30	12.99	191.40	6.64	172.00	8.06	423.00	19.00	334.00	118.00						
Sodium:cr × 100	7.90	1.52	11.00	0.80	15.90	2.04	5.70	2.00	1,175.00	744.00						
Phosphorus:cr × 1,000	6.20	1.47	21.50	15.49	5.90	1.65	12.30	2.50	1,948.00	895.00						

[a] All data were from tractable, bottle-raised female calves, yearlings and 2- or 3-year-old adults (6 elk, each sampled twice, in each age group) in a study designed to establish reference values of elk fed high-quality food ad libitum. Urine samples were collected from elk held in feeding stalls without the use of physical or chemical restraint of any kind. No animals in this study were pregnant or lactating (adapted from Quinlan-Murphy 1998).

[b] Reference values from urine snow samples of 10 captive elk held on pasture and supplementally fed good-quality hay and a protein supplement and were intended to represent elk in good nutritional condition (from DelGuidice et al. 1991a).

[c] Reference values from urine snow samples of 10 elk found at the time of death from starvation in Yellowstone National Park. These data were intended to apply to elk in very poor nutritional condition (from DelGuidice et al. 1991a, see also DelGuidice et al. 1991b for additional data on Yellowstone elk).

[d] Data from tractable cows fed high-quality rations ad libitum. Reference values were estimated for January through early March (from Vagnoni et al. 1996). Urine samples were collected from elk held in feeding stalls without the use of physical or chemical restraint of any kind. No animals in this study were pregnant or lactating.

[e] Data from tractable cows on restricted rations designed to induce about 10% weight loss over winter. Reference values were estimated for January through early March (from Vagnoni et al. 1996). Urine samples were collected from elk held in feeding stalls without the use of physical or chemical restraint of any kind. No animals in this study were pregnant or lactating.

[f] Data collected via multiple snow sampling from five wild radio-collared cows over three winters in Yellowstone National Park. Reference values were estimated for January and February using data from Garrott et al. (1996).

[g] Urinary variables are presented as ratios with urinary creatinine (cr) and multiplied by an adjustment factor following current conventions.

Collection and analysis of fecal material have been used widely, particularly for measurement of fecal nitrogen as a measure of diet quality. Although samples can be easily obtained and laboratory assays are inexpensive, this technique has been criticized because the relationship between diet and fecal nitrogen is not constant. *Photo courtesy of the Wyoming Game and Fish Department.*

ciable. However, Irwin et al. (1993) reported that tannins generally comprise insignificant portions of bighorn sheep diets from late autumn through early spring in Wyoming, and concluded that, under these conditions, fecal nitrogen provides a general index of dietary quality that might be used for prioritizing winter range forage improvements or for identifying the need for more detailed evaluations of nutrition. Even so, assessments using fecal nitrogen without collateral knowledge of tannin levels in diets should be avoided. Table 39 provides an indication of tannin content of many plants found on western ranges.

Wehausen (1995) indicated that the fecal nitrogen index might be improved with several changes in technique. These changes would improve the index for diets lacking appreciable tannins; others would be required for diets containing tannins. Another approach using feces is referred to as near infrared reflectance spectroscopy (Lyons and Stuth 1992). Initial research with cattle suggests that near infrared reflectance spectroscopy may be quite useful for predicting protein and energy of diets. Considerably more work will be needed to assess the value of this technique for elk grazing a variety of vegetation during different seasons.

Dietary Quality

Nutritional status also can be evaluated based on what animals eat. One of the advantages of this approach is that a variety of measurements can be taken of plant community characteristics and directly linked to forage selection processes and dietary quality. Few options exist to directly measure dietary quality of free-ranging large ungulates in a

reliable, precise manner unless they are relatively approachable. Therefore, measurement of dietary quality typically involves observations of tractable animals transported to habitats used by free-ranging animals. Data collected from tractable animals are assumed to be representative of forage selection and dietary quality of wild animals.

A general approach often used for either wild or tractable animals involves determining the relative amounts of each forage species consumed (i.e., dietary composition), collecting samples of each forage species in a manner that simulates the parts of plants selected and analyzing each species for nutritional content (e.g., crude protein, energy, minerals). Dietary quality can be calculated based on the nutritional content and the relative amounts in the diet of each forage species.

For wild animals, three common approaches have been used to estimate dietary composition: the feeding site technique, bite counts and microhistological examination of feces. The former two techniques are considered to be biased and may offer only general descriptions of diets (Schwartz and Hobbs 1985). Both require counting the number of individual stems or leaves (feeding site technique as described by Cole 1956) or bites (bite count method) consumed where animals were observed feeding. Bias of the bite count approach is reduced when grazing animals allow close observation. Because weight of bites or individual stems and leaves differ among forage species, potential for bias can be reduced by determining dry weights of bites of each species and calculating dietary composition using these weights (Gill et al. 1983). Use of radio-marked animals to locate feeding sites also may reduce bias, by minimizing oversampling in habitats where animals are easiest to find. Microhistological examination of feces for estimating dietary quality of free-ranging animals probably is the more common approach. It also can be biased due to different levels of digestion of each plant species (Gill et al. 1983, Schwartz and Hobbs 1985).

Regardless of the dietary composition technique used, researchers collect forage species contained in the diet, analyze them for appropriate nutritional constituents and calculate dietary quality based on dietary composition. In addition to bias from inaccurate estimates of dietary composition, bias may result from failure to collect parts of plants actually consumed by grazing animals, or by collecting plant parts in habitats different than typically used by animals.

Other sources of potentially serious bias in dietary quality estimates may result from handling and assay procedures of forage samples. For example, allowing clipped forage to air-dry before further processing reduces estimates of DE, because plants continue to metabolize cellular carbohydrates after clipping (Robbins 1983). Cook (1990) reported that air-drying forage before analysis reduced estimates of digestible dry matter 10 percentage units in early summer and 3 units in mid-autumn. The decline in bias among seasons probably reflected differences in cell soluble content; biases in winter, therefore, probably are minimal. Finally, effects of tannins on estimates of available protein and DE content also may introduce important biases (discussed above) (Robbins et al. 1987a, 1987b). Neither of these key sources of bias appear to be widely recognized, thereby raising concerns about reliability, particularly regarding summer forage quality estimates from many studies. Protocol for collecting, storing and analyzing forage samples for nutritional content should be given careful consideration; Haufler and Servello (1994) provided useful guidelines for handling forage samples before nutritional analysis.

Use of tame animals offers several distinct advantages for dietary quality investigations: identification of plant parts selected by animals is reasonably accurate; intake rates and foraging efficiency can be estimated; and tame animals can be used for rigorous experimentation. How well foraging of tame animals represents that of wild animals is a fundamental question, however. Procedures for rearing, training and maintaining tame animals may affect the extent to which tame animals simulate wild animals (Schwartz and Hobbs 1985).

Determining dietary composition and dietary quality with tame animals involves either a bite count technique or fistulation. The bite count technique used for tame animals is similar to that used for wild animals described above, except that tame animals allow very close observation as they forage. Good agreement has been reported between the bite count and fistulation techniques, at least for determining dietary composition (Schwartz and Hobbs 1985). Parker et al. (1993a) suggested several areas for improvement of the bite count technique for tame animals.

Fistulation involves surgical placement of a cannula either in the esophagus or rumen. Sampling using an esophageal fistula requires attaching a collection bag at the cannula. Swallowed forage is deposited in the collection bag. Sampling using a ruminal cannula involves collecting consumed forage directly out of the rumen. Samples collected either way can be used to estimate dietary composition and dietary quality. Dietary quality estimates may be affected by contamination with saliva or initial digestion that reduces estimates of dietary quality. Holechek et al. (1982) provided a review of fistulation techniques.

Forage and Nutrient Intake Rates

Although dietary quality provides useful information, concomitant estimates of nutrient intake are required to assess

nutritional status more completely. Efforts to determine forage or nutrient intake have been limited to tame animal studies, because intake rates of free-ranging wild animals are virtually impossible to measure. Approaches for determining intake basically fall into two categories: (1) those that assess instantaneous intake (e.g., amount of food per minute) and (2) those that assess intake over 24-hour periods. The former is useful for assessing foraging efficiency and environmental variables that affect foraging efficiency, and it may provide an important index of habitat quality (Hanley et al. 1989). Instantaneous intake rates, however, may have limited relevance to nutritional plane and can give a misleading index of habitat quality, because they do not reflect gut fill and ingesta passage rates, which constrain intake on a daily basis (Wilmshurst and Fryxell 1995). Daily intake rates of various nutrients provide a direct measure of how well animals satisfy total daily nutritional requirements and, therefore, are key for assessing nutritional status.

Either the bite count method or fistulation approaches can be used to estimate instantaneous intake rate. The bite count method requires estimates of bite size, bite rate and the amount of time spent foraging. Bite size is determined by clipping representative samples of each consumed plant species, and drying and weighing them. Bite size can be

When tractable elk are available, a biologist may accompany the animals and carefully record the plant species selected and volumes consumed. After each feeding bout, the biologist may then collect a similar sample and analyze it for nutritional content as a means of assessing dietary quality. *Photo by John G. Cook.*

somewhat difficult to estimate reliably (Parker et al. 1993a). Fistulation approaches do not require separate estimates of bite size or bite rate, and may be more accurate, but whether greater accuracy justifies fistulation must be considered. Estimates of instantaneous intake rates also depend on the appetite and relative state of hunger of the animal. Hence, results from any given study probably depend on level of food restriction before experimentation. Wickstrom et al. (1984), for example, conducted grazing experiments using hungry, food-deprived elk. Results using very hungry animals might not be representative of free-ranging elk.

The bite count method can be modified to assess total daily food or nutrient intake simply by incorporating an estimate of amount of time during the day and night the animals spend foraging. Jiang and Hudson (1992) provided an example of this approach using elk. Even for tame animals, daily foraging time may be difficult to estimate accurately. Radio-telemetry using transmitters with activity sensors may be the most practical approach. Fistulation techniques for total daily intake perhaps could be used for estimating total daily intake, but are not very practical for extended periods in the field (Parker et al. 1993a). Automated systems are being developed using new technology that may greatly advance capabilities to study grazing dynamics (e.g., Rutter et al. 1997).

Assessing total daily intake using tame animals also can be assessed using inert markers. A variety of internal (undigestible naturally occurring plant constituents) and external markers exist. Chromic oxide is one of the most commonly used external markers (Holechek et al. 1982) and has been used to estimate forage intake in elk (Jiang and Hudson 1992). Generally, the approach using external markers involves delivering a known amount of marker to the animal's digestive tract, either by feeding in food or by inserting a bolus into the rumen, and measuring the concentration of the marker in the feces. The method also requires calibration across a wide variety of forage types. In general, chromic oxide provides a relatively convenient and reliable method for measuring forage intake of captive elk in the field (Jiang and Hudson 1992). Holechek et al. (1982) reviewed a number of other approaches using feces to estimate intake.

Nutrition and Management

Elk and land managers face several areas of uncertainty regarding how best to manage elk populations and habitats in a practical and cost-effective manner to maintain highly productive, abundant herds. It is clear from a relatively extensive set of literature that nutrition plays a fundamental role in determining productivity of wild ruminants. But the majority of this literature emanates from captive animals; little information is available from wild herds of elk across a variety of ecological settings (Cook et al. 1996). Thus, most managers considering management decisions relevant to herd productivity and abundance have little information with which to assess the extent of nutritional deficiencies, the effects of nutritional status and the relative influence of nutritional status among seasons on productivity and abundance. Yet, such information is essential for developing appropriate management strategies designed to enhance productivity through nutritional mechanisms.

Across a variety of ecological settings and climatic regimes, inherently different areas have different potential to support elk at any given level of productivity and abundance. In general, elk managers are faced with finding approaches that improve elk habitat given various societal and environmental constraints. Despite substantial research, it is still not clear how best to manage landscapes to elicit vegetative responses that, in turn, will elicit a measurable response in productivity and abundance. One primary difficulty is scale of application. Although several techniques can improve the nutritional status of herbivores, it is not clear how much and which portion of landscapes used by elk have to be treated to induce a measurable herd response that will be maintained over a worthwhile period of time.

Techniques such as fertilizing and planting may provide useful nutritional benefits to elk herds. Fertilization and planting have improved winter diets of elk in northwest Oregon (Mereszczak et al. 1981). However, neither may be realistic options for enhancing nutritional plane on many ranges used by elk, because costs are high and the techniques may not be practical because of topographic, soil and other limitations.

The value of prescribed burning for enhancing forage conditions also can be substantial. Prescribed burning often improves forage and dietary quality, although effects typically are short-lived (Hobbs and Spowart 1984, Cook et al. 1994c, Riggs et al. 1996). Fire can increase forage quantity as well—an impact that probably persists longer than the forage quality effect. Difficulties with fire are that vegetative responses are not always beneficial and, more important, prescribed fire usually is conducted at such small scales that benefits to elk tend to be spatially and temporally limited (Riggs et al. 1996). The area that must be burned to produce or sustain a population effect increases with the size of the herbivore population and with its density. Accordingly, the large elk populations common across the West may not be particularly responsive to prescribed burning at the scale usually applied (Riggs et al. 1996). Because of scale, the value of prescribed fire probably is greatest where elk are highly concentrated, such as on winter ranges. Even so, Peek (1989) reported that 20 years of prescribed burning on northern Idaho shrub fields yielded no demonstrable increase in elk herd productivity (although such burning may have prevented or reduced productivity declines). And, burning in areas where elk are concentrated risks subsequent damage to the plant community due to herbivory effects, particularly if size of burns are small (Riggs et al. 1996). Prescribed burning of small areas on summer range probably will provide little benefit in terms of population response because few animals are affected. Large-scale prescribed burning on summer ranges may be beneficial, but likely will not be a viable option in most management settings.

Costs and benefits of habitat improvement projects such as burning and fertilizing are rarely evaluated. For such projects, it is unclear if benefits justify the costs because costs typically are high relative to the amount of area treated, and amount of area treated may be too small to affect the population appreciably. Formal assessment of cost/benefit relationships may improve allocation of scarce funding among such projects (Daniels and Riggs 1988). Unfortunately, costs and benefits typically are difficult to estimate reliably due to uncertainty of the project's effect on population dynamics (i.e., additional animals produced due to the project) and uncertainty of the economic value of the additional animals. Such a process, however, may stimulate more consideration of what may be accomplished by habitat improvement projects and stimulate monitoring efforts to ascertain whether intended goals (in terms of population response) are achieved.

Because of scale and cost/benefit limitations, large-scale, planned manipulations of elk habitat generally are restricted to activities that occur for other purposes, primarily timber harvesting and livestock grazing. These activities can change habitats in a manner that improves or reduces quality of elk ranges. Considerable effort during the past 30 years has resulted in habitat evaluation models (see Wisdom et al. 1986, Thomas et al. 1988a, Christensen et al. 1993) that were primarily designed to minimize the negative effects of timber harvest (e.g., increased roads, loss of cover) on elk. Such models have received widespread acceptance and application (Edge et al. 1990), but they were not developed to account directly for the nutritional changes stemming from timber harvest, nor were they intended to be relevant to population productivity (Thomas et al. 1988b). As such, they do not adequately account for the potential nutritional benefits of timber harvest.

Potential benefits from timber harvest largely emanate from inverse relations between forest cover and understory forage production (Pase 1958, McConnell and Smith 1970). Timber harvest that substantially reduces forest overstory typically increases forage production that, in turn, can substantially increase forage intake rates of elk (Collins and Ur-

ness 1983). The effects of timber harvest on forage quality are variable, as previously discussed. Specific relationships among timber harvest, forage quality, forage quantity and elk nutritional status remain unclear. Detailed studies of the influences of a variety of silvicultural practices, and relationships between silviculture and a variety of site factors (e.g., aspect, precipitation, soil type) on nutritional status are needed to understand more fully how timber harvest can be used best to provide for the nutritional needs of elk.

Inverse relationships between forest overstory canopy and forage production suggest that carrying capacity, particularly that of summer ranges, can be enhanced by means of timber harvest as long as human access is controlled and adequate security cover is retained. Indeed, large increases in elk populations in response to huge wildfires in the western U.S. during the early part of the 20th century (Pengelly 1963b) support this contention. The trend toward restricting timber harvest on federal lands in the western U.S. may over the long-term reduce carrying capacity of elk ranges that, in turn, may have detrimental effects on elk productivity and abundance (Hett et al. 1978).

Although timber harvest may have beneficial influences on nutritional status, concomitant loss of cover is an important consideration. Cover potentially provides security from predators and humans and protection from weather. The need for security cover is well-accepted; the need for thermal cover is strongly debated (Peek et al. 1982b, Riggs et al. 1993). Thermal cover generally refers to stands of trees of sufficient density to moderate harsh weather conditions in summer or winter. Thermal cover, therefore, is linked to nutrition because it may reduce energy expenditures and thereby reduce dietary energy requirements. No controlled scientific study has yet shown that thermal cover provides energetic benefits that translate to improved condition or performance of large ungulates. In contrast, three controlled deer studies (Robinson 1960, Gilbert and Bateman 1983, Freddy 1985), a computer simulation modeling study of mule deer (Hobbs 1989), and a 4-year experimental elk study (Cook et al. 1998) failed to demonstrate benefits of thermal cover. These studies indicated that elk managers should *not* assume that good quality thermal cover has potential to appreciably compensate for inadequate forage conditions.

Influences of livestock grazing on elk nutrition can be either beneficial or detrimental. Removal of forage by livestock increases the potential for competition with and reduced nutrient intake by elk. On the other hand, it has potential to improve quality through effects on plant growth patterns (i.e., enhancing regrowth) and by changing ratios of live to dead plant material.

The potential for using cattle grazing to improve the nutritional status of elk was proposed at least 25 years ago (Anderson and Scherzinger 1975). The quality of blue-bunch wheatgrass—an important winter forage plant—can be improved on rangeland winter ranges in the interior Northwest by cattle grazing in spring if the timing of grazing is carefully controlled (Clark 1996). This process involves moderate defoliation that can result in reduced reproductive stem development, reduced translocation of nutrients into the roots and adequate regrowth of foliage to meet forage biomass needs of elk in winter (Anderson and Scherzinger 1975, Westenskow-Wall et al. 1994, Clark 1996). The magnitude of forage quality improvements by spring grazing on winter diets are small but can be significant (Clark 1996). In addition, livestock grazing of bunch-grasses in particular can reduce accumulation of old, standing, dead plant material, thereby increasing the availability of young, nutritious growth. This growth has considerable potential to improve the quality of elk diets (Bryant 1993, Westenskow-Wall et al. 1994). On Oregon's coast range, Rhodes and Sharrow (1990) demonstrated that summer grazing by sheep can improve forage quality of herbs the following October, by stimulating regrowth of plants (Table 60). The following spring, they were unable to show improvements in forage quality, but forage quantity was enhanced about 70%, apparently due to earlier green-up in the grazed areas. Examples exist showing that elk use of winter ranges increases after livestock grazing the previous summer (see Anderson and Scherzinger 1975, Jourdonnais and Bedunah 1990, Frisina and Morin 1991). This probably is due mostly to reductions in standing dead litter (Clark 1996).

Although grazing by livestock can be controlled to limit reductions in total forage availability, reductions typically occur. Excessive stocking rates and inappropriate grazing seasons probably have negative effects on elk nutrition, particularly on autumn, winter and early spring ranges. Under judicious livestock grazing programs, reductions in forage may not be particularly detrimental, and enhancements of forage quality may compensate for reductions in quantity. The potential ability of forage quality enhancements to compensate for reduced quantity depend on a host of factors, such as the magnitude of forage quality improvements and forage quantity reductions, whether or not elk populations are limited by forage quality or forage quantity, the extent of overlap of elk and livestock diets, season, weather and ecological setting. These and other factors were reviewed in detail (Clark 1996, Wisdom and Thomas 1996).

Feeding also is an option for elk managers to directly affect the nutritional status of wild elk. There is a widespread conception that large ungulates cannot be fed on an emergency basis during harsh winters, based on a substantial number of unsuccessful attempts (Baker and Hobbs 1985). Many of these failures were due to feeding hay of inadequate quality, pelleted rations that may have been too "hot" (Baker and Hobbs 1985) or efforts that were "too little and too late." Past failures have led to improvements that demonstrate most species of large ungulates including elk can be successfully fed during winter.

A fundamental problem in developing suitable rations

Table 60.   Effects of summer sheep grazing on selected elk forages the following October and March in a Douglas-fir plantation in coastal forests of western Oregon

Category/plant	October CP G	October CP U	October DDM G	October DDM U	March CP G	March CP U	March DDM G	March DDM U
Grasses								
Orchard Grass	12.8*	5.1	60*	32	24.2	24.0	73	72
Bentgrass	9.7*	3.9	51*	35	17.6	17.3	68	56
Velvet grass	6.8	5.6	44*	35	16.7	16.1	75	71
Forbs								
Pearly everlasting	9.5*	5.4	41*	27	22.7	23.5	60	60
Big lotus	13.2	11.2	22*	9				
California figwort	14.6*	12.3	68*	50	25.3	22.3	70	69
Shrubs								
Thimbleberry	8.0	7.9	34	36	21.1	22.6	46	46
Salmonberry	8.5	8.0	31	29	24.4	21.6	38	38
California dewberry	9.8	7.1	30	31	20.2	20.0	42	43
Vine maple	6.5	5.4	40	36				

Source: Adapted from Rhodes and Sharrow 1990.

Note: Data are 2-year averages of percentage crude protein content (CP) and percentage in vitro dry matter digestibility(DMD) of plants from grazed (G) and ungrazed (U) portions of the study area (* indicates significant differences between grazing treatments, i.e., within rows).

for feeding large ungulates involve simultaneously providing adequate fiber and high levels of soluble carbohydrate (high levels of energy) (Baker and Hobbs 1985). Rations that have inadequate fiber and high DE can result in overeating disease (Blood and Radostits 1989). Acute cases often are fatal. This occurs when ruminants consume too much of the ration to which they are not adapted. This initiates a cascade effect in which species composition of rumen microbes change, increased acid production overwhelms various buffering systems and blood pH declines to abnormal levels. I have found that captive elk on submaintenance diets in winter are surprisingly susceptible and quickly succumb to overeating disease. Undoubtedly, wild elk under starvation conditions also are susceptible, paticularly if natural forage is scarce.

Many grain-based, high-energy pelleted formulations do not provide adequate fiber for elk. Many feeds also have low calcium to phosphorous ratios (less than 1:1, which can induce formation of urinary calculi and cause death in males, as previously discussed). Maintaining a calcium to phosphorus ratio of at least 1.2:1 in formulated rations should be considered (Blood and Radostits 1989). Baker and Hobbs (1985) presented a pellet formulation that apparently works well for mule deer and might work well for elk during emergency winter feeding operations. Many permanent elk feeding stations hold elk overwinter on high-quality alfalfa hay fed in a variety of forms including pellets or as unprocessed long hay. Alfalfa hay with *at least* a 58% level of digestibility probably is suitable; lower quality hay may not effectively provide for DE needs. The calcium to phosphorous ratio of alfalfa hay—5:1 (National Research Council (1985))—will not induce formation of urinary calculi. Crude protein content of food is less of an issue for winter feeding (Baker and Hobbs 1985). Protein levels should provide for maintenance needs of the animal and ruminal microbes (at least 9% to 10% crude protein).

Nutrition of elk also can be managed through manipulation of population size and animal density. The details of such an approach are embodied in the concept of harvest or yield theory (McCullough 1984). The smaller the population in relation to carrying capacity, or K (carrying capacity is defined here as the total number of animals an area of land can support based on available nutritional resources), the greater the nutritional plane of individual animals and the greater the reproductive output. Therefore, for any population, there is a point at which the total number of animals recruited each year into the population is maximum (Figure 131), and this point usually occurs well below K.

This concept clearly indicates there are important trade-offs between abundance and herd productivity. When populations are near K, nutritional plane for individual ani-

mals should be low, and the population should experience poor growth rates, moderate pregnancy rates and relatively high mortality, particularly of juveniles. Maintaining elk populations well below K, near the level at which maximum yield occurs, should result in a more vigorous herd with a greater level of reproductive success. In practice, K and the point of maximum yield are unknown for elk herds, and predation can mask or override the productivity enhancements expected when populations are reduced relative to carrying capacity.

Habitat improvement practices, such as planting, burning and fertilization, can be undertaken to change K. And if K is enhanced appreciably, the total number of animals the land area can support and population level at which maximum yield occurs can be expected to increase as well (Figure 131). Viewed from this perspective, the problem of

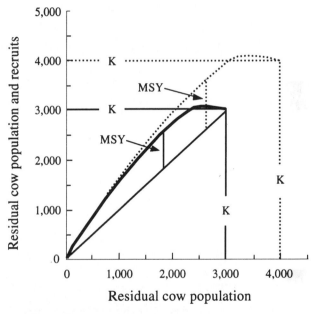

Figure 131.   Relationship between carrying capacity (K) and herd productivity (number of animals recruited into the population) of a hypothetical elk population. Maximum sustained yield (MSY) is the point at which the largest number of young (recruits) are added to the population. Solid lines indicate relationships when K is 3,000 adult cows; dotted lines indicate relationships when K is 4,000 cows. These relations illustrate that: (1) reductions in the residual herd below K to the point at which MSY occurs will result in the greatest number of animals produced each year in the population, likely due to improved nutritional status; and (2) increasing carrying capacity increases both the number of animals that can be supported and the MSY (i.e., increasing K from 3,000 to 4,000 cows increases MSY from 600 to 900 animals in this hypothetical setting). Maintaining populations near MSY also may reduce damage to forage from overgrazing and may reduce elk use of croplands. These relationships were developed based on white-tailed deer data of McCullough (1984), with adjustments for elk reproductive characteristics.

scale becomes more apparent, particularly for elk herds that occupy hundreds of square miles of habitat. Planting, burning or fertilization of several hundred acres at a time may have very little impact on K for the entire herd. This, in part, is why such costly projects typically are limited to winter range, where animals are concentrated. It also is why large-scale improvements, such as those required to improve nutrition of elk on summer range, for example, generally must be linked to such landscape-scale activities as timber harvest.

Additional nutritional issues that have been of minimal concern during the 20th century may begin to arise. Elk populations throughout much of the western U.S. have risen to some of the highest levels since the late 1800s. Numerous examples from a variety of large herbivore species worldwide indicate an inverse relationship between productivity and population size, or density dependence (Fowler 1987), which contributed to development of the maximum sustained yield concept. The general idea is that as large herbivore populations approach carrying capacity, competition for palatable and nutritious forage increases,

Winter feeding is an option for affecting the nutritional status of free-ranging elk, provided that elk are sufficiently concentrated in an area where feed can be provided, an adequate feed ration is provided, and animals are in reasonably good condition when feeding is initiated, allowing time for rumen bacteria to adjust to the feed provided. To be successful, feed rations must contain adequate fiber and high levels of soluble carbohydrates. Inadequate fiber provided with high levels of digestible carbohydrates may cause a cascade effect resulting in increased acid production in the rumen. Various buffering systems then are overwhelmed, leading to abnormally low pH level in the blood. Elk on sub-maintenance diets are very susceptible to this overeating disease, which often is fatal. *Left photo courtesy of the Colorado Division of Wildlife. Photo below courtesy of the U.S. Fish and Wildlife Service.*

preferred forages may decline in abundance and reproductive success and survival decline due to increasing nutritional constraints (McCullough 1984). Buechner and Swanson (1955), in northeastern Oregon, and Houston (1982) and Sauer and Boyce (1983), in the Yellowstone region, reported examples of density dependence in elk populations.

Productivity as measured by calf production and survival has been declining in some areas of the West (e.g., Irwin et al. 1994, Bomar 2000), which suggests that density dependence is beginning to exert important influences. In the Blue Mountains of northeastern Oregon, where elk productivity has been declining since the 1960s, there is evidence that herbivory by elk, deer and cattle is altering vegetative composition and structure, that these effects occur in the absence of livestock grazing and that changes in vegetation may have detrimental impacts on other wildlife species and basic ecosystem processes (Irwin et al. 1994, Cook et al. 1995). Changes in vegetative composition and structure are predictable results of high-density populations at or near carrying capacity (Caughley 1979, McCullough 1984). Declining productivity, however, is a multifaceted issue that may result from density–nutrition effects, increasing predation, skewed sex and age ratios (Noyes et al. 1996), increasing human activities or a combination of these and other factors. Causes of productivity declines, at least in the Blue Mountains, are poorly understood (Cook et al. 1995).

Although most admirers of elk prefer relatively high abundance of elk, reduced abundance may enhance reproductive success and production of trophy-sized animals and reduce landowner conflicts and detrimental impacts to wildland vegetation (McCullough 1984, Irwin et al. 1994). Increasing forage quality and quantity through habitat improvements provides some potential to maintain abundance and productivity concurrently at reasonable levels, but such improvements will have to be both extensive and effective. The importance of these density issues currently are unclear, but may present elk managers with difficult decisions in the future.

Conclusions

It is clear that, without abundant food of good quality, reproductive success and productivity of elk will suffer. However, despite 50 years of research on elk in the western U.S., the explicit mechanics, extent and magnitude of nutritional influences on productivity of free-ranging elk herds are poorly understood. In part, this is because slight to moderate nutritional deficiencies have subtle influences that often are difficult to detect or identify. The effects of moderate nutritional deficiencies may influence elk populations through multiple pathways, including reduced pregnancy rates, puberty attainment of young females, and fetal, neonatal and winter survival. Nutritional deficiencies may have relatively minor effects on any one of these productivity variables, but their cumulative impact can be considerable; just a 5% reduction in each would result in roughly a 25% decline in total herd productivity. Moreover, nutritional issues are inextricably linked to animal density. Elk populations have increased markedly over the past 60 years across much of the western U.S. Nutrition apparently did not appreciably restrict growth of many of these herds 40 years ago when populations were lower, but the probability of nutritional limitations likely has increased as elk densities have increased.

Development of reliable management strategies that can improve the foraging environment for elk and, in turn, enhance productivity requires considerable advances in our understanding of the nutrition/productivity relationships of free-ranging herds. Several research questions are of special concern:

- What nutritional levels are required to sustain optimum growth and reproductive performance? Research emphasis should be on determining the magnitude of effects of different levels and timing (e.g., seasonal effects) of nutritional deficiencies on growth and reproduction in elk.
- What are the fundamental, mechanistic relationships between vegetative characteristics (e.g., structure, composition, quantity and quality) and total daily nutrient intake in habitats used by free-ranging elk?
- What are the effects of various habitat manipulations on vegetative characteristics that are key determinants of total daily nutrient intake?
- What are the effects of large herbivore density on vegetative conditions and long-term elk productivity trends?
- If density manipulations are used to manage nutrition, what levels of density changes are necessary to elicit desired responses in vegetation or herd demographics?

Greater understanding of these questions in the context of nutrition/productivity relationships of wild elk will provide a valuable basis to develop reliable, cost-effective models designed to help elk managers (1) assess and monitor nutritional conditions across landscapes; (2) select appropriate habitat management approaches to improve foraging conditions; (3) predict population responses to changes in foraging conditions; and (4) provide for the nutritional needs of elk and, concurrently, a host of other uses and products desired from western wildlands.

6

E. TOM THORNE, ELIZABETH S. WILLIAMS,
WILLIAM M. SAMUEL AND T. P. KISTNER

Diseases and Parasites

Historically, diseases (including parasitic, bacterial, viral, nutritional, neoplastic, toxic and anomalous conditions) were noted as curiosities of little importance to elk until the 1950s, when several publications addressed diseases as management considerations (e.g., Cowan 1951, Murie 1951, Honess and Winter 1956). Since that time, significance of diseases in management of elk has increased as elk have been forced to exist on reduced habitat of poorer quality, including winter feedgrounds; domestic livestock marketing and grazing practices have exposed elk to increasing varieties of formerly exotic diseases; and, an emerging game-farming industry brings not only livestock diseases but previously inconsequential wildlife diseases closer and closer to free-ranging elk.

Although interests and biases of individual authors influence selection of diseases discussed in literature, a cursory examination of Murie's book *The Elk of North America* (1951), Thomas and Toweill's *Elk of North America* (1982), this volume and appropriate journals, such as the *Journal of Wildlife Diseases,* reveals a change over time in perception about which diseases are important with regard to elk and their management. Murie (1951) introduced brucellosis as a disease of elk and a factor reducing calf production. And in *Elk of North America,* Kistner et al. (1982:188) prophetically acknowledged that elk of western Wyoming "must be considered, along with bison and cattle, in the national brucellosis eradication program," but remained pessimistic regarding resolution of the problem. In the same book

Robbins et al. (1982) questioned the validity of tests used to establish the presence of brucellosis. Currently, brucellosis arguably could be the most important bacterial disease occurring in elk, but its importance is based on social and political rather than biological considerations (which will be discussed further). Murie (1951) clearly believed necrotic stomatitis was the most problematic disease of elk, especially for those elk that use winter feedgrounds. Now, thanks to greatly improved feedground and winter habitat management, necrotic stomatitis is uncommon to the extent that it barely merits mention.

Murie (1951) described biting flies and winter ticks as nuisances and the latter as a drain on the vitality of elk. He also did not feel psoroptic scabies was a significant problem, although it resulted in death of a few animals most winters, and he did not ascribe significance to internal parasites.

In addition to brucellosis and necrotic stomatitis, Kistner et al. (1982) devoted considerable space to parasites of elk, notably meningeal worm, carotid artery worm, lungworms and tapeworms. That work also dwelt on several bacterial diseases—such as actinomycosis, anthrax, bacterial-induced arthritis, clostridial infections and leptospirosis—which (from our current perspective) have been replaced in importance by bovine tuberculosis, paratuberculosis and pasteurellosis. Similarly, we place less importance on certain parasites but increase emphasis on others, such as elaphostrongyline worms. Viral diseases, remarkably, remain relatively unimportant in elk. An entirely new disease, chronic wasting disease (a transmissible spongiform encephalopathy), has been recognized in elk and also will be addressed further.

Emergence in the past two decades of the commercial gamefarming industry, especially elk and deer farming, has forced some changes in emphasis concerning diseases that merit attention (e.g., bovine tuberculosis and elapho-strongyline worms). Elk farming, in particular, now requires consideration of the effects of diseases on captive commercial elk in addition to free-ranging elk in any review of diseases and parasites. Prudence also dictates that attention be paid to spread of diseases by elk and deer in national and international commerce, providing a new threat to free-ranging elk.

Diseases addressed in this chapter will include those that have current or potential elk management implications, are of zoonotic importance, result in significant conflicts with livestock and influence sporting qualities or edibility of elk. Consequently, a number of diseases that may have fascinating epidemiologic and etiologic stories or are important to an individual adversely affected elk, but which are very unlikely to be encountered by the average wildlife manager, elk enthusiast or sportsman, will not be discussed, but are included in Table 61.

Necropsies by well-trained biologists or veterinarians provide valuable opportunities to learn more about diseases and parasites of free-ranging elk. *Photo courtesy of the Wyoming Game and Fish Department.*

Bacterial Diseases

Brucellosis

Brucellosis in elk is a contagious, infectious disease caused by *Brucella abortus* (Thorne et al. 1978b, Thorne 1982b), which is a worldwide pathogen of cattle and humans. Brucellosis also is known as Bang's disease in cattle, and as undulant fever and Malta fever in humans. Brucellosis is known to occur only in free-ranging elk of the Greater Yellowstone Area of Wyoming, Montana and Idaho (Adrian and Keiss 1977, Thorne et al. 1978a, McCorquodale and DiGiacomo 1985, Davis 1990), where it also occurs in free-ranging bison. It is not currently known to occur in farmed elk; the only known brucellosis-infected farmed herd was in North Dakota and it was depopulated to eliminate the disease. Brucellosis is regarded as an exotic disease of elk and bison in the Greater Yellowstone Area, and was introduced directly or indirectly by cattle around the turn of the century (Honess and Winter 1956, Thorne and Herriges 1992, Meagher and Meyer 1994).

Human brucellosis caused by *B. abortus* found in elk generally is not as severe as brucellosis caused by *Brucella suis* (*B. suis*) acquired from swine, caribou and reindeer, and *Brucella melitensis* (*B. melitensis*) acquired from domestic goats and not present in North America. Currently, about 100 human cases of brucellosis occur annually in the United States, and most are due to *B. suis*. Most human cases occur in slaughterhouse workers who become infected by direct contact with contaminated tissues, splashing contaminated fluids into their eyes or aspirating them into their lungs. Although human brucellosis is rare in the Greater Yellowstone Area where brucellosis occurs in elk, at least two poorly documented cases are believed to have originated from contact with an elk. One was a hunter who killed a pregnant elk during a late-season hunt in Montana and handled the fetus extensively. Numerous elk that are infected or exposed to brucellosis undoubtedly are harvested in Wyoming each year, yet no case of brucellosis acquired from an elk has been documented. This likely is because *B. abortus* is an intracellular parasite and, therefore, not readily available for transmission to hunters, even when eviscerating a carcass. In addition, most hunting seasons occur very early in the course of pregnancy of elk, when the bacterium generally is located in low numbers in the lymphatic tissues and not yet present in large numbers in the uterus, as occurs late in pregnancy. The threat to nonhunting elk enthusiasts is essentially nonexistent.

Bovine brucellosis is worldwide in occurrence and, where common, it is of significant economic and public health importance. Abortion is the most common and sig-

Table 61.   Miscellaneous diseases, infections and conditions reported in *Cervus elaphus*

Disease or infection	Etiology	References
Viral		
Contagious ecthyma, dermatitis	Parapoxviruses	Lance et al. 1983, Horner et al. 1987
Malignant catarrhal fever	Herpesvirus	Huck et al. 1961, Reid et al. 1979, Fletcher 1982, Li et al. 1996
Louping-ill, serologic evidence of infection	Louping-ill virus	Reid et al. 1978, Fletcher 1982
Keratitis, serologic evidence of infection	Cervid herpesvirus–1	Inglis et al. 1983, Nettleton et al. 1986, Thiry et al. 1988
Serologic evidence of infection	Parainfluenza–3 virus	Kingscote et al. 1987, Aguirre et al. 1995
Serologic evidence of infection	Bovine herpesviruses	Lawman et al. 1978, Kingscote et al. 1987, Thiry et al. 1988, Aguirre et al. 1995
Serologic evidence of infection	Respiratory syncytial virus	Aguirre et al. 1995
Virus isolation, serologic evidence of infection	Bovine viral diarrhea virus	Lawman et al. 1978, Nettleton et al. 1980, Kingscote et al. 1987, Aguirre et al. 1995, Frölich 1995, Van Campen and Williams 1996, Tessaro et al. 1999
Serologic evidence of infection	Adenovirus	Darbyshire and Pereira 1964, Lawman et al. 1978
Serologic evidence of infection	Vesicular stomatitis virus	Webb et al. 1987
Serologic evidence of infection	California serogroup virus	Eldridge et al. 1985
Serologic evidence of infection	Jamestown Canyon virus	Grimstad et al. 1986
Bacterial		
Epiphysitis and endocarditis	*Actinomyces pyogenes*	Badger 1982
Kerato-conjunctivitis, keratitis, conjunctivitis (pinkeye)	Various bacteria (*Moraxella* sp., etc.)	Wilson et al. 1981, Pearson 1984
Meningo-encephalitis	*Streptococcus zooepidemicus*	de Lisle et al. 1988
Salmonellosis	*Salmonella* spp.	McAllum et al. 1978, Fletcher 1982
Bacterial isolation	*Listeria monocytogenes*	Martyny and Botzler 1975
Mycotic		
Systemic mycosis	Phycomycetes	Munro et al. 1985
Pulmonary mycosis	Zygomycete (probably *Absidia* sp.)	Jensen et al. 1989
Nutritional		
Acidosis	Overeating	Fletcher 1982
Enzootic ataxia	Copper deficiency	Fletcher 1982, Gogan et al. 1989, Peet and Hepworth 1993

nificant sign of brucellosis in cattle. Abortions occur in the last half of pregnancy due to *Brucella*-induced placentitis. A retained placenta may follow abortion, leading to temporary or permanent infertility (Crawford et al. 1990). Transmission of the disease occurs by contact with contaminated reproductive tissues such as fetuses, fetal fluids and placentas from infected cows. Susceptible cattle become infected after bacterial invasion through the mouth or conjunctival membranes of the eyes (Crawford et al. 1990). Few cows abort more than one time due to brucellosis, but they may remain infected and shed *B. abortus* with subsequent birth events. Although bulls are susceptible to infection and the organism may localize in the reproductive tract, sexual transmission does not occur because the vagina is a hostile environment to *B. abortus*.

Numerous tests using blood serum have been developed to diagnose brucellosis in cattle (MacMillan 1990). Positive reactions to serologic tests do not always indicate that animals are currently infected or what stage of the disease the animals are in, but they do confirm that the animals were at one time exposed and infected. Isolation in a laboratory of

B. abortus from tissues, reproductive products, milk or uterine fluids is the only means of definitive diagnosis. However, because culture of the microorganism is difficult and time consuming, serologic tests are effectively relied on for management of brucellosis.

A living strain of *B. abortus* isolated from a cow and referred to as strain 19 is used as an effective vaccine in cattle. Strain 19 establishes transient infection and causes good immunogenicity, and it is stable and of low virulence (Nicoletti 1990). The primary disadvantage associated with use of strain 19 vaccine is that it may cause persistent antibodies that interfere with serologic tests to detect cattle infected with *B. abortus*. Because calves have greater resistance to brucellosis and shorter persistence of serum antibodies after vaccination than do adults, strain 19 usually is administered to calves at 4 to 12 months of age (Nicoletti 1990). Strain 19 vaccine may be administered to adult cows to reduce intraherd infection and transmission rates when other means of quickly eliminating the disease are not feasible and residual serum antibodies are acceptable (Arza et al. 1989, Nicoletti 1990). Although protection afforded by strain 19 to vaccinated cattle is not complete, it does significantly reduce infection and abortion rates in vaccinated cattle compared with nonvaccinated cattle exposed to *B. abortus* (Nicoletti 1990). In a vaccinated herd, fewer abortions occur that result in less shedding of *B. abortus* into the environment and fewer exposed cattle. Exposed animals are less likely to become infected, abort and expose other cattle (Dietrich et al. 1991).

Brucellosis was first detected in elk based on serologic tests in 1930 at the National Elk Refuge (Murie 1951) and in 1933 at Yellowstone National Park (Tunnicliff and Marsh 1935). Years later, high prevalence of brucellosis was demonstrated by serologic tests and culture of *B. abortus* from elk at the National Elk Refuge and Grey's River Feedground in extreme western Wyoming (Thorne et al. 1978b). Extensive research at the Wyoming Sybille Wildlife Research Unit demonstrated the effects and transmission of brucellosis in elk (Thorne et al. 1978a, Thorne et al. 1979, Morton et al. 1981). Brucellosis is not known to occur in free-ranging or farmed elk anywhere outside the Greater Yellowstone Area.

Brucellosis in elk is similar but not identical to the disease in cattle. Fifty to 70% of affected cow elk loose their first calf after infection, due to abortion or birth of a nonviable calf (Thorne et al. 1978a, Herriges et al. 1989). The calf loss due to brucellosis in elk has been estimated at 12.5% on extensively infected Wyoming elk feedgrounds (Herriges et al. 1989) and at 7% on the National Elk Refuge (Smith and Robbins 1994).

Retained placenta and infertility after abortion or parturition do not appear to occur in elk, likely because elk are quite fastidious and agile and may be able to remove the placenta themselves. Chronic brucellosis sometimes causes bursitis and synovitis, which may be characterized by lameness (Thorne et al. 1978a); it also may have been responsible for some of the arthritis described by Murie (1951). As with cattle, brucellosis is transmitted among elk primarily by oral contact with *B. abortus*-contaminated reproductive tissue or feed.

Controlled studies at the Sybille Wildlife Research Unit demonstrated that, under appropriate conditions, brucellosis may be transmitted from infected elk to susceptible cattle. For transmission to occur, there must be an abortion or birth event by an infected elk in close temporal and spatial contact with cattle (Thorne et al. 1979). These conditions could occur if infected elk used cattle feedlines during winter and early spring. However, transmission of brucellosis to cattle is unlikely to occur through normal calving, because elk seek seclusion and are meticulous at cleaning up the placenta and fetal fluids (Geist 1982), leaving little or no contamination to serve as a source of infection for cattle.

Serologic tests conducted on blood sera collected from

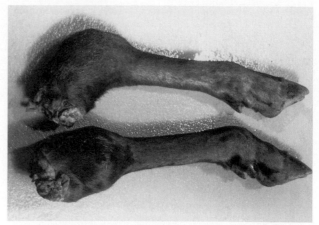

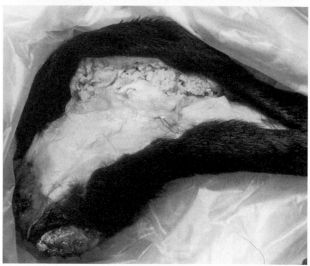

Bilateral chronic carpal arthritis, due to brucellosis (*top*), causes lameness that predisposes affected elk to predation or winter mortality. Inside, a carpal joint of the leg from an elk with chronic brucellosis (*bottom*). The puslike material contained in the distended arthritic joint cavity harbors large numbers of *Brucella*. *Photos by Elizabeth S. Williams.*

hunter-killed and trapped elk can be used to detect previous exposure to or current infections of *B. abortus* (Thorne et al. 1978b, Morton et al. 1981). It is recommended that a battery of up to four tests be used, with criteria established for elk rather than cattle, and that there be no suspect category. Although serologic tests may fail to detect a few recently infected elk or old, chronic infections, they are suitable for surveys to determine the presence or absence of brucellosis in a population, provided a sufficient number of elk are tested.

Controlled studies demonstrated that elk responded to strain 19 vaccine in a manner similar to cattle (Thorne et al. 1981, Herriges et al. 1989). Protection is not complete, but vaccination before exposure reduced both infection and abortion rates. And although high doses of strain 19 induced abortion in some pregnant elk, this problem was remedied by reducing the dose. As with cattle, vaccination

Winter feedline comingling of cattle and elk likely has led to the transmission of bovine diseases, including brucellosis, to elk. In the Greater Yellowstone Area, it could serve as a source of transmission of brucellosis to cattle and is discouraged. *Photo by A. Lorin Ward.*

of elk considerably lowers the rate of abortion due to brucellosis and, therefore, reduces shedding of *B. abortus* that could cause intra- and interspecific transmission. Reduced transmission combined with increased resistance among elk that do become exposed results, over time, in lowered prevalence of brucellosis within a herd or population.

The occurrence of brucellosis as a self-sustaining endemic disease among elk of the Greater Yellowstone Area is a reflection of use of winter feedgrounds, especially in Wyoming, and possibly of contact with infected bison. Although elk use of feedgrounds is not unique to Wyoming, feedgrounds are more extensively used there by state and federal wildlife managers than in any other state, province or region. Approximately 25,000 elk use 23 feedgrounds in western Wyoming each winter; about one-third of these animals use the National Elk Refuge.

In the early 1900s, a few elk in scattered locations likely became infected with *B. abortus* through exposure to cattle. Subsequent crowding that occurred when elk began to use winter feedgrounds resulted in high rates of intraspecific transmission on a few feedgrounds. Subsequent movement of elk from one winter feedground to another the following winters likely led to establishment of brucellosis on most, if not all, feedgrounds in Wyoming. In the early 1990s, the average rate of infection among mature cow elk, based on serologic tests, was estimated at approximately 37% (Herriges et al. 1991).

Although brucellosis causes reduced reproductive poten-

Artificial crowding that occurs on feedgrounds, even for relatively short periods, results in abnormally high rates of transmission—such as on the National Elk Refuge at Jackson, Wyoming—of brucellosis among elk. In the absence of feedlines, brucellosis probably would not be a self-maintained disease among elk of the Greater Yellowstone Area. *Photo by Orane A. Olsen; courtesy of the U.S. Forest Service.*

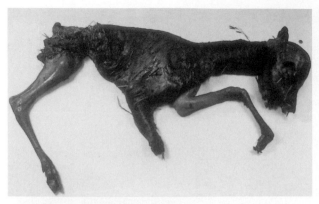

This elk fetus, aborted because of brucellosis, appears mutilated because of attempts by the dam, and perhaps other cow elk, to consume the fetus. Consumption of placentas and fetuses reduces environmental contamination and opportunity for transmission of brucellosis to cattle and other hosts, but it enhances transmission of brucellosis among elk on feedgrounds. *Photo courtesy of the Wyoming Game and Fish Department.*

tial among infected feedground elk herds, it does not significantly affect overall elk production. However, the disease does makes feedground management inefficient because of the costs associated with feeding elk that will not produce viable calves. The significance of brucellosis among elk of the Greater Yellowstone Area is due to the conflicts it generates between elk and cattle, and its potential impacts on a national program to eradicate brucellosis from the United States (Thorne et al. 1991a, 1991b, Thorne 1992, Thorne and Herriges 1992, Keiter and Froelicher 1993). The brucellosis eradication program was initiated in the 1930s and has cost more than $3.5 billion. The program has been very successful and is administered by the U.S. Department of Agriculture Animal and Plant Health Inspection Service's Veterinary Services and State Veterinarians. By the end of 2000, no infected cattle herd or ranched bison herd remained in the United States. The states of Wyoming, Montana and Idaho have eradicated brucellosis from cattle, and increasing attention is focused by animal health officials and cattle industries on brucellosis-infected elk and bison of the Greater Yellowstone Area. Although most of the attention has been focused on bison of Yellowstone National Park (Thorne et al. 1991b), there are approximately 116,000 more brucellosis-infected and -exposed elk in the Greater Yellowstone Area than bison, and many of them use winter feedgrounds in Wyoming during winter.

Brucellosis has been successfully eradicated from most cattle and bison herds by applying techniques of the eradication program. Measures applied consist of identifying infected herds through tests on milk, market and slaughter cattle, or herds exposed to known-infected herds. Within an infected herd, blood test-positive animals are slaughtered,

and the herd is periodically retested until no blood test-positive cattle or bison are detected. In states that already have eradicated the disease or when rapid and certain elimination of brucellosis is desired, depopulation is the preferred eradication method. When a herd is depopulated, all animals are sent to slaughter, regardless of blood test status.

Since the 1940s, strain 19 vaccine has been used very effectively to reduce *B. abortus* infections within cattle herds and avoid large numbers of infected animals within a herd when it is exposed. Consequently, proper use of strain 19 vaccine markedly reduces the number of cattle that must be sent to slaughter to eradicate brucellosis. Strain 19 is generally given to heifer calves, but under special circumstances, adult cows may be vaccinated. In either case, the larger the proportion of females within a herd that is vaccinated, the more beneficial the vaccination program.

It is generally agreed that traditional test and slaughter or depopulation techniques used on cattle would not be logistically possible or politically acceptable with publicly owned free-ranging elk or bison of the Greater Yellowstone Area. The Wyoming Game and Fish Department and Veterinary Services have conducted extensive controlled and feedground trials using strain 19 vaccine in elk (Thorne et al. 1981, Angus 1989, Herriges et al. 1989, 1991), and the Game and Fish Department has implemented a program intended to vaccinate feedground elk ballistically, using an airgun system that shoots biobullets containing absorbable strain 19 vaccine. Experience has demonstrated that once feedground elk are acclimated to the report of the airgun, 50% to 70% of the mature cows and 95% to 100% of the calves on a feedground can be vaccinated. Preliminary evaluation at Grey's River Feedground—where about 1,000 elk spend each winter and the vaccination program was initiated in 1985—showed that, based on blood tests, the prevalence of brucellosis has declined from 40% in mature cows in the 1970s to less than 10% (Wyoming Game and Fish Department unpublished files:2000). Many researchers believe that brucellosis cannot be eradicated by vaccination alone. However, widespread vaccination of feedground elk appears to be the only way the current high prevalence of brucellosis in feedground elk can be lowered dramatically.

It is likely that the relatively rare occurrence of brucellosis in elk of the Greater Yellowstone Area where they are not fed is a reflection of brucellosis among feedground elk and the occasional movement of exposed feedground elk to nonfeedground areas (Thorne et al. 1979). If brucellosis is absent among feedground elk, the disease probably will disappear from nonfeedground elk without intervention by managers.

Because of the clear relationship between feedgrounds and high prevalence of brucellosis, the Wyoming Game

Airguns are used by the Wyoming Game and Fish Department to remotely vaccinate free-ranging elk against brucellosis. Vaccination has been demonstrated to reduce dramatically the prevalence of brucellosis among feedground elk. The upper barrel propels vaccine-loaded methycellulose bio-absorbable bullets; the lower barrel propels paint balls to mark vaccinated elk. *Photos courtesy of the Wyoming Game and Fish Department.*

and Fish Department also has implemented its Brucellosis-Feedground-Habitat Program. This is an attempt to integrate the vaccination program with habitat enhancement and management of feedgrounds to encourage elk to spend less time on feedgrounds and more time on native winter ranges. This will reduce the rate of transmission among elk and, therefore, augment the vaccination program. The Brucellosis-Feedground-Habitat Program also seeks, through activities such as elk-proof fencing of haystacks for cattle, to reduce elk/cattle conflicts and opportunities for elk-to-cattle transmission of brucellosis. This nontraditional approach to brucellosis control depends on partnerships between the Wyoming Game and Fish Department, U.S. Forest Service, U.S. Bureau of Land Management, Veterinary Services, landowners, and the Rocky Mountain Elk Foundation.

To coordinate and enhance brucellosis control and eradication activities for both elk and bison throughout the Greater Yellowstone Area, the governors of Wyoming, Montana and Idaho, along with the Secretaries of the U.S. Departments of the Interior and Agriculture signed a Memorandum of Understanding forming the Greater Yellowstone Interagency Brucellosis Committee in 1995. This committee consists of state and federal wildlife and land management agencies and animal health regulatory agencies. Its objective is to develop plans for elimination of brucellosis while protecting the integrity of elk and bison herds and the viability of the region's livestock industries.

Bovine Tuberculosis

Bovine tuberculosis is caused by the bacterium *Mycobacterium bovis* (*M. bovis*) and is an important disease of cervids, including elk (Clifton-Hadley and Wilesmith 1991). The organism has a thick, waxy cell wall and, hence, is relatively resistant in the environment. Organisms survive protected in feces for months, but in an environment with exposure to sunlight (ultraviolet light), variable temperature and desiccation, the organism may only remain viable for days or weeks (Mitscherlich and Marth 1984, Jackson et al. 1995).

Bovine tuberculosis historically has been an important disease of domestic cattle. There is currently a state/federal program in place to rid the United States of this disease in cattle and commercial cervids, and that goal is close to being accomplished. Many countries, including Canada, have successfully eradicated bovine tuberculosis from their cattle herds. Historically, bovine tuberculosis has been reported rarely from cervids generally and even less frequently in elk. It was reported in elk, bison and moose from Elk Island National Park in Alberta in the 1950s, but was not maintained among those species after population reduction (Corner and Connell 1958). More recently, bovine tuberculosis was diagnosed in free-ranging elk from Manitoba (Doré 1999). Free-ranging elk, red deer and hybrids have been reported to have bovine tuberculosis in New Zealand, and the source of infection may have been cattle with tuberculosis, or brush-tailed possums, which are an important nonruminant reservoir of infection (O'Neil and Pharo 1995).

Humans are susceptible to bovine tuberculosis, but it is not nearly as common in humans as is tuberculosis caused by *Mycobacterium tuberculosis*. In part, the drive to eradicate bovine tuberculosis came about because of concern over public health. Some humans in contact with gamefarm elk affected by tuberculosis have become infected and skin-tested positive for the disease (Fanning 1992, Stumpff 1992).

Bovine tuberculosis is currently only known to be present in one population of free-ranging elk in North America (Williams et al. 1995, Doré 1999). It has been reported in free-ranging red deer, elk and hybrids in other parts of the world (Clifton-Hadley and Wilesmith 1991), and has been a serious problem for the gamefarm industry in North America (Stumpff 1982, Miller et al. 1991, Essey 1992b, Thoen et al. 1992, Haigh and Hudson 1993, Whiting and Tessaro 1994) and elsewhere, particularly New Zealand (Beatson 1985, O'Neil and Pharo 1995), although it now appears to be mostly under control. Bovine tuberculosis is a serious management problem in free-ranging white-tailed deer in Michigan (Schmitt et al. 1997).

Bovine tuberculosis in elk is characterized by a long incubation period. Years may pass from the time the animal is infected until clinical signs of illness are observed (Beatson 1985, Clifton-Hadley and Wilesmith 1991). Usually, only animals in the terminal stages of systemic disease show obvious signs. Clinically affected animals may develop a wasting condition, poor hair coat, respiratory difficulty and a tendency to lag behind the herd. Duration of illness also may be prolonged, difficult to detect and, because the clinical signs are not specific, may be confused with many other infectious and noninfectious diseases. Sudden death is rare, but may occur.

Lesions of bovine tuberculosis have been described in gamefarm elk depopulated due to the disease (Miller et al. 1991, Rhyan et al. 1992, Thoen et al. 1992, Whiting and Tessaro 1994, Rohonczy et al. 1996). Grossly, bovine tuberculosis is characterized by the presence of numerous variably sized granulomas or tubercles, from which the disease gets its name. These vary from tiny nodules to very large, firm masses, often with a laminated appearance on the cut surface. Elk with bovine tuberculosis may develop subcutaneous abscesses that contain thick, chalky-white to yellow pus (Beatson 1985, Clifton-Hadley and Wilesmith 1991, Haigh and Hudson 1993). The formation of subcutaneous abscesses is somewhat different than signs of the disease in domestic livestock. Tubercles are common in the lymph nodes of the head (parotid, mandibular and retropharyngeal), thoracic cavity (tracheobronchial and mediastinal), abdominal cavity (pancreatic and mesenteric) and dorsal portions of the lungs (Miller et al. 1991, Rhyan et al. 1992, Whiting and Tessaro 1994). Mammary glands may be severely affected (Miller et al. 1991), and other organs occasionally are involved. Although there are subtle differences, microscopic lesions usually are similar to those of bovine tuberculosis in domestic cattle. Some variation does occur among affected individuals. The organisms may be difficult to detect within the lesions, and lesions sometimes resemble other diseases. Diagnosis of mycobacterial infection may be difficult (Clifton-Hadley and Wilesmith 1991, Rhyan et al. 1992, Rhyan and Saari 1995). Because humans are susceptible to bovine tuberculosis, animals suspected of having tuberculosis should be necropsied only by appropriate veterinary authorities.

Bovine tuberculosis is transmitted primarily by the animal's respiratory system. When an affected animal coughs, it expels bacteria in an aerosol. If a susceptible animal then breaths in the bacteria, colonies of the bacteria may form in the lungs. The bacteria are distributed to the lymph nodes and lungs within macrophages (Thoen and Himes 1986, Thoen 1992). High densities of animals increase the probability of transmission between infected and susceptible animals. Elk also may contract the disease orally by consuming forage and feed contaminated with the bacteria, in which case the bacteria probably first infect the tonsils or lymph nodes associated with the digestive tract. Concentration of animals around feeding troughs likely facilitates transmission (Clifton-Hadley and Wilesmith 1991). Calves may become infected by nursing from dams shedding the bacteria in milk due to lesions in the mammary glands.

Important nonruminant reservoirs of *M. bovis* are not known to occur in North America. However, European badgers in the United Kingdom (Clifton-Hadley et al. 1993) and brush-tailed possums and possibly feral ferrets in New Zealand are important sources (Morris and Pfeiffer 1995).

None of the antemortem diagnostic tests are completely reliable (Haigh and Hudson 1993). Diagnosis of the disease in captive elk is by skin testing (single cervical test or comparative cervical test) (Griffin and Cross 1989, Corrin et al. 1993, Haigh and Hudson 1993), which must be conducted by an accredited veterinarian and requires a 3-day holding period between injection and evaluation of the test. The lymphocyte blastogenesis test, which is a measure of cell-mediated immunity, shows poor correlation with bacterial

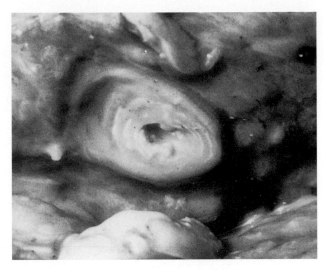

Typical tubercle caused by *Mycobacterium bovis* in the mammary gland of a gamefarm elk. *Photo courtesy of M. W. Miller.*

isolations (Hutchings and Wilson 1995). The blood test for tuberculosis is a combination of a test for antibodies (enzyme-linked immunosorbent assay, or ELISA), lymphocyte blastogenesis and nonspecific measures of inflammation (Griffin and Cross 1989, Griffin et al. 1992b, Haigh and Hudson 1993, O'Neil and Pharo 1995). This test commonly is used in New Zealand and recently in North America. Although none of these tests is perfect on an individual elk basis, they are useful in detecting infected herds.

Culture and identification of *M. bovis* are required for definitive diagnosis of bovine tuberculosis. The bacterium grows slowly in culture, although new technology may reduce the time needed for identification of the organism (Gross and Hawkins 1985).

Bovine tuberculosis in gamefarm elk has been a serious problem in North America (Stumpff 1982, Miller et al. 1991, Essey 1992b, Haigh and Hudson 1993, Whiting and Tessaro 1994) and New Zealand (Beatson 1985, O'Neil and Pharo 1995). In the United States, the multiple cases of tuberculosis identified in bison and elk in the 1980s and 1990s may have resulted from elk obtained from a menagerie in Iowa (Essey 1992a). Identification in South Dakota of bovine tuberculosis involving elk and bison in the 1980s (Essey 1992a) was important because it was the first alert for North America that these species are quite susceptible to infection. It was recognized that the diagnostic tests were not ideal, regulations inadequate to deal with movement and handling of animals infected or exposed to this disease, and tuberculosis in gamefarm animals could impact national tuberculosis eradication programs for domestic livestock. Herds of elk and bison involved in this outbreak were depopulated, and many domestic cattle and gamefarm animals were tested and slaughtered as a result.

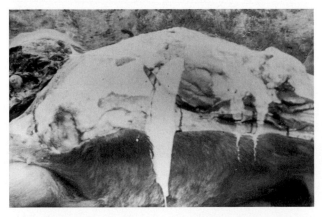

Although uncommon in domestic livestock, large subcutaneous abscesses appear to be more common in gamefarm elk and can serve as a source of human exposure to tuberculosis. White pus from the abscess is flowing down the side of this elk with tuberculosis. *Photo by M. W. Miller.*

After nearly 10 years without a recognized outbreak of bovine tuberculosis in elk, the disease was identified in gamefarm elk in Canada that originated in Montana (Essey 1992a). Canada then closed the border to importation of cervids from the United States, and extensive testing of elk and other deer in herds in Canada and the United States was implemented. The subsequent testing and heightened awareness of the problem, coupled with increased state and federal regulation of the gamefarm industry, revealed that many herds had been infected or exposed to tuberculosis. Infected elk herds, for the most part, were depopulated or subjected to repeated skin testing. Depopulation was difficult because of lack of government compensation programs at adequate market value for elk that were killed. Several states lost tuberculosis-free status when cattle became infected from elk (Essey 1992a) or other cervids, resulting in considerable hardship to livestock producers in affected states. Gamefarm cervids are now included in the Cooperative State-Federal Bovine Tuberculosis Eradication Program in the United States. As of 1998, only two captive cervid herds in the United States were identified as infected with bovine tuberculosis (Thompson and Willer 1998).

Of great concern to wildlife managers was the spread of bovine tuberculosis from elk on a gamefarm in Montana to free-ranging mule deer (Rhyan et al. 1995) and coyotes (Hillman and Thompson 1994) found near the facility. Surveillance of the free-ranging deer, elk and predator/scavenger populations continues. It is believed that the disease did not become established in these populations.

Surveillance for bovine tuberculosis in herds of free-ranging elk has been conducted with culture and gross and microscopic examinations of lymph nodes of the heads of hunter-killed elk from Wyoming (Williams et al. 1995). This technique was estimated to be approximately 55% sensitive (Williams et al. 1995) and to be a practical method for free-ranging populations (Miller et al. 1991). To date, there is evidence that bovine tuberculosis occurs in only one population of free-ranging elk of North America.

The consequences of having bovine tuberculosis become established in free-ranging elk populations could be severe (Thorne et al. 1992). Management of brucellosis in free-ranging elk illustrates the types of conflicts that could arise. In many ways, bovine tuberculosis is a more difficult disease to manage than brucellosis, because diagnosis is more difficult and vaccination for tuberculosis is not possible at this time. As a worst-case scenario, whole herds of elk might be depopulated. Restrictions on hunting, conflicts with livestock industries and changes in management of public lands likely would follow. Prevention of spillover of bovine tuberculosis from gamefarm cervids to free-ranging populations of elk is a critical management issue.

Paratuberculosis

Paratuberculosis, or Johne's disease, is a bacterial disease caused by *Mycobacterium paratuberculosis* (*M. paratuberculosis*). This organism, which is related to *M. bovis* (the cause of bovine tuberculosis), also is highly resistant in the environment. It may persist in soil for a year or longer (Mitscherlich and Marth 1984), but it is relatively sensitive to exposure to ultraviolet radiation from sunshine, drying and high temperatures and, under natural conditions, probably remains viable for less than a year in the environment. As with all the mycobacterial pathogens, this bacterium is slow growing and may take many weeks before it can be isolated in culture.

Paratuberculosis is a disease of many ruminants, including most domestic livestock, and particularly dairy cattle. In cattle, the disease may cause considerable economic loss due to decreased milk production, loss of body condition and mortality. It is common in livestock in the Northeast, Midwest and West Coast of the United States. Paratuberculosis has been reported in many species of wild ruminants (Williams and Spraker 1979, Chiodini et al. 1984), but in North America, it is only known to be endemic in a herd of Tule elk in California (Jessup et al. 1981), herds of bighorn sheep and mountain goats in one area of Colorado (Williams et al. 1979), and Key deer in Florida (C. Quist personal communication:2000). Paratuberculosis has never been diagnosed in elk sympatric with these affected bighorn and mountain goat herds. Paratuberculosis has been maintained in Tule elk at Point Reyes National Seashore, California (Jessup et al. 1981) for at least 20 years (Cook et al. 1997). These elk probably contracted the disease through contact with pastures contaminated by dairy cattle infected with *M. paratuberculosis* (Jessup et al. 1981). Elk are susceptible to experimental infection orally (Williams et al. 1983a), but clinical disease has not been observed in free-ranging elk other than at Point Reyes.

This disease is of concern in the gamefarming industry, where it is currently relatively uncommon (Gilmour 1984, Griffin 1988, Haigh and Hudson 1993, Power et al. 1993); this could change in the future.

Chiodini et al. (1984) reviewed paratuberculosis in ruminants. It is a disease of the intestinal tract. The slow-growing bacteria proliferate in the intestine, causing inflammation that results in thickening of the intestinal wall and impaired function. Because of this damage, digestion and assimilation are disrupted; the animals lose condition and may become emaciated. Some animals develop diarrhea, but often only in the terminal stages of disease. Bacteria are shed in the feces and transmitted to susceptible animals by ingestion of contaminated feed or forage. High densities of susceptible animals, such as occur on gamefarms, contribute to transmission of this infection. The incubation period (time from infection to development of clinical disease) is prolonged and may take years. Thus, young animals seldom are clinically affected, although they may be infected; the disease is primarily observed in young adult and mature animals.

Diagnosis of paratuberculosis in the live animal is difficult, as is true of many mycobacterial diseases (Thoen and Haagsma 1996). There are several types of blood tests (ELISA tests, complement fixation tests, immunodiffusion tests) that measure antibody production (Colgrove et al. 1989, Collins et al. 1991, Sweeney et al. 1995) and other blood tests (lymphocyte blastogenesis tests) that detect cell-mediated immunity (Williams et al. 1985). However, none of these tests is ideal, and false-negative and false-positive results are possible. Culture of feces for the bacteria is a definitive method of diagnosis. This method is useful on a herd basis, but lacks sensitivity on individual animals because of sporadic shedding of the organism in the feces of subclinically infected individuals. Newer tests for detection of *M. paratuberculosis,* including radiometric detection (Cook et al. 1997), polymerase chain reaction (de Lisle and Collins 1995) and DNA probes (Thoen and Haagsma 1996), are now available. Radiometric detection techniques were used to diagnose the presence of paratuberculosis in Tule elk at Point Reyes, although clinical disease had not been observed for years.

Gross lesions of paratuberculosis are emaciation and variable thickening of the wall of the small intestine, particularly the ileum (lower small intestine). Mesenteric lymph nodes and ileocecal lymph nodes usually are enlarged and may contain foci of gritty mineralization. The lymphatic vessels that link the intestine to the mesenteric lymph nodes may be thickened, opaque and surrounded by clear edema fluid in the mesentery (Jessup et al. 1981, Williams et al. 1983b). Microscopic examination of the tissues is important for diagnosis of the disease and, at a minimum, sections of mesenteric lymph nodes and distal small intestine should be collected for histopathology. With minor variations, the microscopic lesions of paratuberculosis in elk are similar to those in domestic livestock (Jessup et al. 1981, Williams et al. 1983b). Distal small intestine and mesenteric lymph nodes are preferred for culture of the organism, which is a definitive method of diagnosis. Demonstration of the etiologic agent is important because some other mycobacterial diseases, with different management implications, may look very similar to paratuberculosis. For example, avian tuberculosis (caused by *Mycobacterium avium-intracellulare*) may occur in red deer and elk, but is not likely to be significant to populations. However, it may cause confusion on some antemortem diagnostic tests for paratuberculosis and bovine tuberculosis.

Because paratuberculosis is a serious infectious disease of both domestic and wild ruminants, elk from affected populations should not be used for translocation stock. Subclinically affected elk could be carriers of the bacterium, possibly exposing susceptible animals at another location. Thus, the Tule elk at Point Reyes are not used for translocations. This has become a problem due to limited habitat and continued growth of the herd. Similar problems are experienced by gamefarm managers. Movement of elk from herds with paratuberculosis runs the risk of distributing the disease to new herds.

Leptospirosis

Leptospirosis is a bacterial disease caused by several serovars of *Leptospira interrogans* (*L. interrogans*). It is not considered an important disease of free-ranging elk, but it has been the subject of considerable study because of its importance to the domestic livestock industry. Humans also may contract leptospirosis, but these cases are not related to contact with elk. In cattle, some serovars, especially serovar *pomona,* may cause abortion and systemic disease leading to economic loss. The bacteria often causes damage to the kidneys—a preferred location for replication of the organism. Leptospires are excreted in urine.

Elk probably can become infected with various serovars of *Leptospira* but clinical disease has not been reported. Serologic evidence of infection in elk has been reported from many areas in North America (Kistner et al. 1982, Kingscote et al. 1987, Aguirre et al. 1995, Bender and Hall 1996). Leptospirosis can be a problem in captive red deer, and the clinical disease has been associated with serovars *pomona* (Fairley et al. 1984, 1986) and *ballum* (Corrigall 1978). Clinical signs of leptospirosis may include sudden death, depression, hemolysis and jaundice, bloody urine and kidney disease. The disease organism is shed in urine, and leptospiruria has been detected in red deer for at least 8 months (Fairley et al. 1984). Sometimes, very concentrated elk urine—a normal physiologic response to dehydration—may have the appearance of bloody urine, especially on snow, but this should not be confused with the urine of clinical leptospirosis.

Animals infected with *L. interrogans* develop antibodies that can be detected by blood tests (microscopic agglutination and ELISA), but determination of the specific infecting serovar requires isolation of the bacteria by culture and identification. This is because of considerable cross-reactivity between antibodies to many of the serovars. Animal health regulatory agencies frequently require testing of ruminants for leptospirosis before importation, although there is no evidence that elk have served as reservoirs for this disease. Leptospirosis has implications for the commercial elk industry and the game manager translocating elk and answering questions from concerned livestock owners.

Septicemic Pasteurellosis

Septicemic pasteurellosis in free-ranging elk has been reported only a few times. This bacterial disease is caused by particular serotypes of *Pasteurella multocida* (*P. multocida*) A3 and A4 (Franson and Smith 1988, Wyoming Game and Fish Department unpublished files:1992, Wilson et al. 1995). Septicemic pasteurellosis, which involves all body organs in an affected animal, has been confused at times with hemorrhagic septicemia (Murie 1951), another systemic disease caused by serotypes of *P. multocida* (B2, E2). It is important to distinguish between these two diseases because hemorrhagic septicemia—a highly fatal disease of cattle and other ruminants—is considered exotic to North America except for a few outbreaks in bison in the Greater Yellowstone Area in the early part of the 20th century (Carter and DeAlwis 1989, Gochenour 1924). It has not reoccurred. Septicemic pasteurellosis has been diagnosed in elk on the National Elk Refuge (Thorne 1982e, Franson and Smith 1988) and on feedgrounds in northwestern Wyoming (Wyoming Game and Fish Department unpublished files:1992). It is

Blood samples obtained from trapped elk can be used to monitor the prevalence and severity of certain diseases. *Photo by D. E. Worley.*

likely that *P. multocida* is carried by normal elk and, at times of significant stress on the animal, possibly nutritional or environmental, the bacteria proliferate and cause severe systemic disease.

Septicemic pasteurellosis is not considered to be a major management problem. The clinical disease is acute, with some animals showing severe depression and excessive salivation before death; otherwise, affected animals are usually in fair to good body condition. Some affected animals are just found dead. Lesions include pinpoint to paintbrushlike areas of hemorrhage on the surfaces of organs, swollen hemorrhagic or edematous lymph nodes, and exudation of cloudy fluid in thoracic and abdominal cavities. The bacteria are easily cultured from affected lymph nodes, spleen, lungs and other organs using standard techniques.

P. multocida also may cause pneumonia in elk (Kistner et al. 1982, Thorne 1982e, Rhyan et al. 1997). In these instances, the anterior-ventral portions of the lung were firm and purple, in contrast to the remainder of the lung tissue. Layers of fibrin were on the surface of the lung, and there was increased cloudy fluid in the thoracic cavity and the pericardial sac. Lymph nodes of the lung, including the tracheobronchial and mediastinal nodes, were enlarged and edematous, and many contained areas of hemorrhage. Stress, due to a variety of factors, probably is responsible for many of these cases. As with septicemic pasteurellosis, local increases in mortality may occur, but these diseases do not appear to threaten elk populations.

Abscesses and Miscellaneous Bacterial Infections

Abscesses due to bacterial infection are common in elk. *Actinomyces pyogenes* (*A. pyogenes*) is most often the cause, and this bacterium induces abscesses in domestic (Timoney et al. 1988) and other wild ruminants. A variety of other bacteria have been cultured from abscesses, including *Streptococcus* spp., *Actinomyces bovis*, *Enterobacter* spp., *Yersinia pseudotuberculosis*, *Edwardsiella* spp., *Actinobacillus* spp. and *Fusobacterium necrophorum* (Thorne 1982d, Haigh and Hudson 1993). *Yersinia enterocolitica* has been isolated from clinically healthy Roosevelt elk (Martyny and Botzler 1976). *Yersinia pseudotuberculosis* was cultured from tissues of Rocky Mountain elk (Thorne 1982f, Sanford 1995) and red deer (Fletcher 1982, Jarrett et al. 1990, Sanford 1995); however, yersiniosis does not appear to be as severe a problem in North America as it is in stressed red deer from New Zealand (Henderson 1983).

Abscesses usually have a fibrous connective tissue wall of variable thickness, which contains creamy off-white to yellow or green pus. Elk usually are able to wall off these infections, but may have some difficulty completely ridding the body of them. These abscesses usually are not of any great significance to the individual elk unless they occur in a critical area, such as the heart or brain. They are most common in skin, lungs and peripheral lymph nodes. *Actinomyces*-caused abscesses are common in the mandibular and pharyngeal lymph nodes of the head of Rocky Mountain elk (Williams et al. 1995) and Tule elk (Kistner et al. 1982).

Abscesses often are found by hunters in the process of dressing or cutting an elk carcass. The meat is considered safe to eat if the abscess is thoroughly trimmed away. Any meat that has come in contact with pus from the abscess should be discarded. A carcass with multiple abscesses may not be suitable for human consumption.

If there is doubt as to the nature of an abscess, it should be examined by culture and histopathology. This is because abscesses caused by *M. bovis* in elk may look very much like *Actinomyces*-caused abscesses. Differentiation between these diseases is very important.

Necrobacillosis (Necrotic Stomatitis)

Necrobacillosis, or necrotic stomatitis, is caused by the anaerobic bacterium *Fusobacterium necrophorum*. This pathogen infects a wide variety of domestic (Timoney et al. 1988) and wild ruminants. Historically, the organism has caused considerable mortality, and Murie (1930,1951) considered it the most important disease of elk.

The bacteria produces a toxin that causes tissue necrosis and results in damage to the soft and bony tissues of the feet and mouth, often with extension to the forestomachs, lungs and liver. The yellow, firm, dry, sharply demarcated appearance of the necrotic tissues is characteristic of this infection. Clinical signs vary depending on the location of lesions. Oral lesions result in swelling of the face, reluctance or refusal to eat, loss of condition and death; in domestic calves, this disease is called calf diphtheria. Lameness may occur due to infection of the joints, bones and soft tissues of the feet (foot rot).

F. necrophorum is shed in feces and remains viable in the soil for weeks to many months (Mitscherlich and Marth 1984).The bacteria probably is introduced into the soft tissues of the mouth through damage from rough forages. Another possible route of entry into the body is through the rumen wall following a bout of rumenitis. In the past, necrotic stomatitis was associated with feeding coarse hay to elk on the National Elk Refuge and on state feedgrounds in Wyoming (Murie 1951). Observations suggest that stressed animals may be predisposed to the infection, and high densities and unsanitary conditions may favor winter losses due to necrotic stomatitis.

Currently, necrotic stomatitis is relatively uncommon,

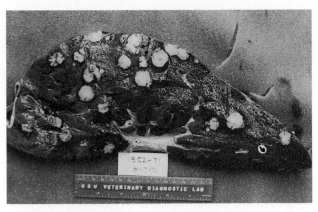

Multiple necrobacillosis lesions, caused by *Fusobacterium necrophorum*, in the liver of an elk, often are secondary to damage in the rumen. *Photo by D. H. Helfer.*

probably due to improved feeding practices on feedgrounds maintaining elk throughout winter. Free-ranging elk not on feedgrounds probably have little problem with this disease, but it has been reported occasionally. Necrobacillosis is a potential problem in elk maintained on gamefarms where management is poor. With good nutrition and management, however, it is not a serious problem.

Foot Rot and Arthritis

Foot rot is a generic name for a variety of infections of the joints and soft tissues of the feet. Arthritis refers to inflammation and damage to any joint. These clinical entities may be caused by a variety of bacteria organisms, but *A. pyogenes* and *F. necrophorum* and *Staphylococcus* spp. are most commonly identified. Bacteria are introduced into the foot from abrasions or puncture wounds with consequent proliferation of the bacteria, inflammation, swelling, lameness and occasional joint involvement. In severe cases, the entire hoof may slough. Arthritis secondary to bacteria introduced through the navel (navel ill) and that circulate through the bloodstream and lodge in joints, may occur in young calves, and multiple joints often are involved (polyarthritis). Arthritis secondary to *B. abortus* septicemia occurs in elk herds where brucellosis is endemic. The carpal, stifle and fetlock joints are involved most often. Affected elk may have difficulty foraging, which can lead to secondary loss of condition. Frequently, only one foot or joint is involved, although damage to multiple feet or joints is possible.

Foot rot and arthritis are relatively uncommon in elk and generally reflect the occurrence of unsanitary conditions on feedgrounds or in captivity; arthritis due to *B. abortus* occurs only in elk of the Greater Yellowstone Area, primarily on feedgrounds in Wyoming. Antibiotic treatment may be given to captive elk. Response to treatment is variable, es-

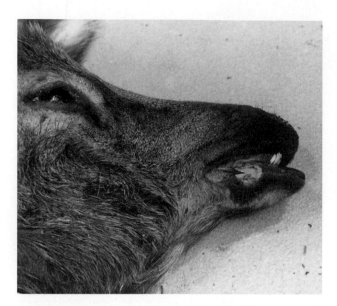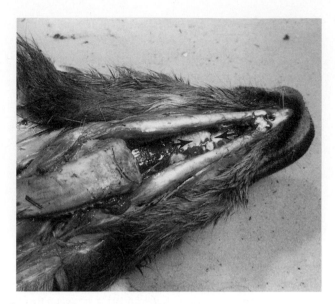

An ulcer on the lower lip (see arrow) of an elk calf is an external sign of extensive necrotic stomatisis. This is seen occasionally in elk that consume coarse woody browse or hay containing awns. Although necrotic stomatisis once was common among feedground elk in Wyoming, it now is rare. Irregular areas of necrosis (see arrows) on the hard palate of an elk calf with severe necrotic stomatisis (necrobacillosis) due to *Fusobacterium necrophorum. Photos courtesy of E. S. Williams.*

pecially if there has been significant damage to the bones and joints.

Clostridial Infections

Clostridium spp. are toxin-producing anaerobic bacteria that cause a variety of infections in animals, including livestock and wild ruminants (Timoney et al. 1988). These bacteria are common in soil and intestinal tracts of animals. Clostridial diseases occur sporadically in elk and are not considered important to populations.

Enterotoxemia, or purple gut, is a disease of neonatal animals caused by *Clostridium perfringens* (*C. perfringens*) type C. It has been diagnosed in elk calves on gamefarms, and the manifestations were similar to those found in domestic beef calves and lambs (E. S. Williams personal files:1994). Affected calves usually are less than a week old and die acutely. Postmortem examination reveals extensive hemorrhage in the small intestine, often with bloody contents in the lumen. Microscopic lesions are characteristic and consist of severe mucosal necrosis and hemorrhage, with numerous large bacilli that stain gram-positive lining remains of villi. Bacteria are numerous in the intestine and can be readily cultured from the gut if collected shortly after death. It is important to recognize that *C. perfringens* is a normal inhabitant of the intestinal tract, and isolation of the organism alone is not enough to confirm enterotoxemia. Purple gut has not been reported in free-ranging elk and is uncommon in gamefarmed elk.

Another uncommon form of enterotoxemia—pulpy kidney disease—caused by *C. perfringens* type D, has been reported in red deer in New Zealand (Haigh and Hudson 1993). It often follows abrupt change of diet, especially to concentrates, in domestic livestock. Clinical signs are acute onset of diarrhea, depression and loss of appetite. Animals dying acutely may have few gross lesions. Vascular congestion, foci of hemorrhage on the heart and increased pericardial fluid may be present. The pulpy kidney designation refers to the rapid decomposition that follows death due to enterotoxemia, rather than a direct manifestation of clostridial infection.

Clostridium septicum (*C. septicum*), *Clostridium chauvoei* (*C. chauvoei*) and *Clostridium novyi* (*C. novyi*) cause malignant edema and blackleg. In ruminants, these infections are characterized by acute illness, high fever, rapid death, vascular congestion, hemorrhage, gas formation, fluid exudation and rapid carcass decomposition. These systemic diseases, usually secondary to contamination of deep wounds, such as punctures following darting, are rarely reported in elk (Howe 1981).

When a dart hits and injects drugs into the heavy muscles of the hind leg, considerable tissue damage may occur. Bacteria may be carried into the wound when the needle goes through the coat and hide, and result in a nidus of infection. If the wound is anaerobic, which may occur due to disruption of blood flow to the damaged tissues, the bacteria proliferate and produce potent exotoxins.

Prophylactic treatment of elk with long-acting penicillin

or other antibiotics active against gram-positive organisms is recommended following darting or other activity that may cause tissue necrosis or anaerobic wounds. Efficacious, multivalent vaccines against these clostridial diseases are used in domestic livestock and have been used in elk (Haigh and Hudson 1993).

Anaplasmosis

Anaplasmosis is caused by a rickettsial organism, *Anaplasma marginale* (*A. marginale*), with several other species known but not thought to be significant pathogens in cervids. Anaplasmosis is a significant disease of cattle, in which it causes acute or chronic disease, anemia, jaundice, and possible death (Timoney et al. 1988). It normally is transmitted between animals by ticks and biting flies. This rickettsia infects and results in the destruction of red blood cells. Packed cell volumes may decline severely during acute infections.

Elk are susceptible to natural and experimental infection with *Anaplasma* spp., but significant clinical disease has not been reported (Post and Thomas 1961, Howe et al. 1964, Harland et al. 1979, Zaugg et al. 1996). Elk have been considered possible reservoirs of this infection for domestic cattle because they may harbor *A. marginale* in their blood for up to 1 year (Post and Thomas 1961), but experimental evidence suggests that they probably are insignificant in the epidemiology of this infection (Kuttler 1984).

Exposure to *Anaplasma* may be detected by testing blood for antibodies. Some surveys have detected exposed elk (Howe and Hepworth 1965, Vaughn et al. 1976, Kuttler 1984). However, some tests, such as various agglutination and complement fixation tests may be inaccurate (Post and Thomas 1961, Howe et al. 1964). Currently, the rapid card agglutination test often is used (Harland et al. 1979), but false negatives may be a problem (Magonigle and Eckblad 1979). However, this test still is valuable as a screening test (Zaugg and Kuttler 1985, Zaugg et al. 1996). The indirect immunofluorescence test overcomes some of the problems associated with other serologic tests. Tests for antibodies against *Anaplasma* often are required for transporting elk across jurisdictional lines.

Viral and Prion Diseases

Hemorrhagic Disease

Hemorrhagic disease is a generic name for diseases caused by two viruses—bluetongue and epizootic hemorrhagic disease. Both are closely related orbiviruses transmitted by bites of midges or no-see-ums (*Culicoides variipennis*) in North America (Hoff and Trainer 1981). Elk and red deer

are not known to develop significant clinical disease associated with infection of either of these viruses, but they do become serologically positive (Trainer and Jochim 1969, Aguirre et al. 1995) and carry the virus in their blood for weeks (Murray and Trainer 1970, Hoff and Trainer 1973, Gibbs and Lawman 1977, E. S. Williams personal files:1985). During this time, biting midges could ingest elk blood containing the virus, become infected and, after suitable incubation periods, transmit the virus to a susceptible host.

Although hemorrhagic disease is not an important clinical entity in elk, bluetongue and epizootic hemorrhagic disease are serious diseases in other North American wild ruminants, including white-tailed deer, mule deer, pronghorn antelope and bighorn sheep (Hoff and Trainer 1981, Thorne 1982a, 1982c, Thorne et al. 1988). These diseases may reduce local populations and disrupt hunting seasons, particularly because hunting seasons usually occur in autumn, when these diseases are most active. The epizootiology of these diseases has been studied intensively in the southeastern U.S. (Nettles and Stallknecht 1992). Clinical disease and death may occur in sheep, but serious disease in cattle is rare (Timoney et al. 1988). Also, reproductive loss may occur in cattle and has been suspected in pronghorn (Thorne et al. 1988).

The concern about bluetongue and epizootic hemorrhagic disease in elk relates to the potential for their spread as a result of elk translocations or by movement in commercial channels. Many animal health regulatory agencies require that imported elk be tested for bluetongue antibodies; seropositive animals and even entire herds may be excluded. Currently, several serologic tests are used, including the competitive ELISA test (which is very specific for bluetongue antibodies), the serum neutralization test (which is very useful for epidemiologic purposes) and the immunodiffusion test (which is inexpensive to run and good for screening, but lacks in specificity). With the immunodiffusion test cross-reactions are common between bluetongue and epizootic hemorrhagic disease antibodies.

Chronic Wasting Disease

Chronic wasting disease, classified as a spongiform encephalopathy, was recognized in elk housed at wildlife research facilities in the early 1980s in Colorado and subsequently in Wyoming (Williams and Young 1982). It was first diagnosed in mule deer (Williams and Young 1980) in these same facilities, and it is possible that transmission occurred between these species in captivity (Williams and Young 1992). Chronic wasting disease occurs in captive as well as free-ranging elk in localized areas of northeastern Colorado and southeastern Wyoming (Williams and Young

1992, Spraker et al. 1997). It has been reported from elk on gamefarms in Saskatchewan, South Dakota, Nebraska, Oklahoma, Montana and Colorado, but may be found elsewhere in the future with improved surveillance (Williams et al. in press). The disease is not known to occur elsewhere in the world.

The cause of chronic wasting disease is not known, although it is a member of the transmissible spongiform encephalopathy group of diseases that include bovine spongiform encephalopathy in cattle, scrapie in sheep and goats, transmissible mink encephalopathy in mink and Creutzfeldt-Jacob disease in humans. Although some of the characteristics of these diseases are similar, they are not directly related, and the epidemiology is quite different. The etiologic agent of spongiform encephalopathies is theorized to be an infectious protein or prion that is devoid of nucleic acids and replicates in the host by inducing conformational changes in inherent cellular proteins that render them nearly indestructible (Prusiner 1991). Accumulation of this extremely resistant protein in the brains of affected elk leads to central nervous system disease and death. The infectious agents of spongiform encephalopathies are unique in their extreme resistance to environmental factors and usual disinfectants. Sodium hypochlorite (bleach) and sodium hydroxide at high concentrations for prolonged periods are used as disinfectants for these agents.

Clinical signs of chronic wasting disease include weight loss (usually over a period of weeks to months), behavioral changes that may be quite subtle except to those familiar with individual animals, increased drinking and urination, grinding of teeth, and excessive salivation. Some elk have head tremors and may be uncoordinated. The clinical course in free-ranging animals maybe more rapid than in captive animals (Spraker et al. 1997), although that is difficult to assess reliably. The disease is progressive and, in uninterrupted cases, the animals die of emaciation and hypothermia, often with secondary aspiration pneumonia. This is a disease of young adults and mature animals; calves are not clinically affected. The natural incubation period is not specifically known but is thought to be more than 18 months. The longest period of incubation is not known, although a duration of years is probable.

The mode of transmission of chronic wasting disease is unknown. However, epidemiologic information from observation of captive animals and occurrence of the disease in the wild suggests that transmission occurs from animal to animal (Williams and Young 1992) and through environmental contamination. Oral transmission of chronic wasting disease probably is the natural route of exposure. There is no evidence that the disease is associated with consumption of contaminated rendered concentrates, as has been

Although early signs of chronic wasting disease are difficult to detect by people unfamiliar with it, depression, marked emaciation, drooling and unsteadiness are apparent in animals in advanced stages of the disease. *Photo courtesy of the Colorado Division of Wildlife.*

hypothesized for bovine spongiform encephalopathy (Wilesmith et al. 1991). Direct transmission from a cow elk to her calf also is possible, but has not been proven.

There is no evidence available to date that the agent causing chronic wasting disease of elk and deer is infectious to humans (World Health Organization 2000). However, several human diseases are spongiform encephalopathies (e.g., kuru and Creutzfeldt-Jakob disease), and bovine spongiform encephalopathy has been linked to an unusual variant of Creutzfeldt-Jakob disease (Will et al. 1996). Thus, prudence dictates that elk with clinical chronic wasting disease should not be eaten.

Diagnosis of chronic wasting disease is relatively difficult in comparison with diagnosis of many other infectious diseases. Gross examination of an animal that has died of chronic wasting disease frequently shows only an emaciated carcass, sometimes with increased amounts of fluid, sand and gravel in the rumen. The urine often is extremely dilute, due to damage to the portion of the brain that regulates urine concentration. Aspiration pneumonia may kill an elk that has chronic wasting disease before significant loss of body condition. The pneumonia in these cases is due to inability of the animal to control swallowing and rumination. None of the gross lesions is specific to chronic wasting disease, and all of them may be seen in other infectious diseases or noninfectious conditions. Definitive diagnosis of chronic wasting disease requires microscopic examination of the brain or testing of central nervous system tissue for the presence of the abnormal protein. Thus, it is very important that the brains of all animals suspected of having chronic wasting disease are collected and examined specifically for spongiform encephalopathy. In chronic wasting disease surveillance, it is extremely important that particular areas of the brain are examined (medulla oblongata); the diagnostic laboratory should be consulted if chronic wasting disease is a consideration.

The implications of this disease are significant for both managers of free-ranging elk and for the gamefarm industry. The disease currently is very localized geographically; however, it is important to be vigilant for its presence outside the known endemic area. The impact of chronic wasting disease on elk populations is not yet known, although epidemiologic studies and modeling efforts are underway (Miller et al. 2000). On the basis of low prevalence in free-ranging elk, the current direct impact of the disease is insignificant. Although there is no known association of chronic wasting disease with human disease, public health concerns related to the spongiform encephalopathies may lead to restrictions on human consumption of elk from affected areas or even from areas where the disease is not known to be present if appropriate surveillance has not been conducted. Concerns in the gamefarming industry are similar but amplified because ranched elk often are destined for venison markets. Another concern for the gamefarming industry is loss of export markets for meat and live animals should chronic wasting disease become widely established in the commercial elk industry. If chronic wasting disease becomes established in farmed elk, it easily could be moved with asymptomatic elk in commerce throughout the country and, possibly, the world. However, state, provincial and federal animal health and wildlife management agencies have developed chronic wasting disease control and surveillance programs.

For the wildlife manager, concern about chronic wasting disease relates to the potential impact of this disease on populations of elk, impact on domestic livestock industries, should evidence be found that cattle and sheep are naturally susceptible, and the concerns of hunters about human susceptibility. Research on chronic wasting disease is ongoing, and more information on distribution, impact and implications of this disease in elk will be available in the future.

Parasites

Every elk in North America likely is infected with one or more species of parasite. Parasites have been the focus of many surveys and reviews (see bibliography of Worley and Greer 1976, for early reports and, more recently, Kistner et al. 1982, Thorne et al. 1982 and Haigh and Hudson 1993). Recent studies of specific parasites of elk have focused on liver flukes (Foreyt 1996a), abomasal parasites (Van Baran et

al. 1996), psoroptic mites (Ziccardi et al. 1996), *Sarcocystis* spp. (Foreyt 1995), coccidia (Foreyt and Lagerquist 1994), meningeal worms (Samuel et al. 1992) and ectoparasites (Samuel et al. 1991). Nonetheless, and despite many other parasitological studies, it is apparent that: (1) relatively few species of parasites—approximately 54 (Table 62)—in relatively low numbers, have been reported from elk of North America; (2) clinical disease is rare; and (3) there is little evidence that multiple parasitism, although common, results in mortality (however, see discussion of mitigating factors such as host nutrition by Murie 1951, Cowan 1951, Kistner et al. 1982). Fifty-three parasites reported from elk is a remarkably small number in contrast to the 111 species of parasites reported from white-tailed deer (Samuel 1994a) and the 79 species reported from mule deer (Samuel 1994b). However, this does not indicate that parasites of elk are benign and, as such, unworthy of further consideration. Several species are very important for elk and, as a result, have become the focus of controversies important to wildlife managers and sportsmen. These parasites and the issues that surround them will be emphasized. They include: (1) meningeal worm, *Parelaphostrongylus tenuis* (*P. tenuis*), and translocation by game ranchers of elk from enzootic areas of eastern North America to parasite-free areas of the West, and impact of neurologic disease on isolated populations of elk relocated to former ranges in eastern North America; (2) liver fluke, *Fascioloides magna*, and translocation by game ranchers and wildlife agencies within or between jurisdictions of western North America; (3) several ectoparasites, such as winter tick, *Dermacentor albipictus*, and mange mite, *Psoroptes* sp., that have current or potential implications for elk management; (4) several immature tape worm cysts, such as hydatid cysts of *Echinococcus granulosus* and bladderworm stage of *Taenia hydatigena* that, due to their size and location in elk or zoonotic implications, may have a negative influence on sportsmen regarding edibility of harvested elk; and (5) several parasites such as lungworm, *Dictyocaulus viviparus*, that are potentially transmitted between elk and domestic livestock.

Meningeal Worm and Elk Translocation

The meningeal worm belongs to a small group of lungworms, the elaphostrongylines, associated with connective tissues of the central nervous system and musculature of members of the Cervidae. Its usual definitive host is white-tailed deer. Meningeal worm is found throughout the deciduous mixed-wood forest of eastern North America (Anderson and Prestwood 1981, Comer et al. 1991); it has not been recorded west of 105 degrees west longitude (Figure 132).

Table 62. Parasite species reported from free-ranging elk of North America

Species (former name)	Common name	Location in host
Protozoa		
Sarcocystis sybillensis	Sarcocysts	Muscle tissues
S. wapiti	Sarcocysts	Muscle tissues
S. miescheriana[a]	Sarcocysts	Muscle tissues
Eimeria wapiti	Coccidia	Intestine
E. zurnii	Coccidia	Intestine
E. wassilewskii (*hegneri*)[a]	Coccidia	Intestine
Eimeridae	Coccidia	Semen/epididymis
Trypanosoma cervi	Flagellate	Blood
Entamoeba sp.	Amoeba	Intestine
Cestoda		
Echinococcus granulosus	Hydatid tapeworm	Lungs (occasionally liver)
Taenia hydatigena (*Cysticercus tenuicollis*)	Bladderworm	Mesenteries/liver
Moniezia benedeni	Tapeworm	Small intestine
M. expansa	Tapeworm	Small intestine
Thysanosoma actinioides	Fringed tapeworm	Hepatic ducts/ intestine
Trematoda		
Fasciola sp.[a]	Liver fluke	Liver
Fascioloides magna	Liver fluke	Liver
Zygocotyle lunata	Cecal fluke	Cecum
Dicrocoelium dentriticum	Fluke	Hepatic ducts
Nematoda		
Marshallagia marshalli	Stomach worm	Abomasum
Mazamastrongylus odocoilei (*Ostertagia odocoilei*)[b]	Stomach worm	Abomasum
M. pursglovei	Stomach worm	Abomasum
Ostertagia leptospicularis/ Ostertagiakolchida	Abomasum	Abomasum
Trichostrongylus axei	Threadworm	Abomasum
Cooperia oncophora	Threadworm	Intestine
Nematodirella alcidis (*longissimespiculata*)	Thread-necked worm	Intestine
Nematodirus helvetianus	Thread-necked worm	Intestine
Teladorsagia circumcincta (*Ostertagia circumcincta*)	Threadworm	Intestine
Ostertagia ostertagi	Threadworm	Intestine
Trichostrongylus colubriformis	Threadworm	Intestine
Capillaria sp.	Capillarid worm	Intestine
Oesophagostomum venulosum	Nodular worm	Cecum, large intestine
Trichuris sp.	Whipworm	Cecum, large intestine
T. ovis	Whipworm	Cecum, large intestine
Parelaphostrongylus tenuis	Meningeal worm	Central nervous system
Othostrongylus macrotis (*Protostrongylus* sp.)	Lungworm	Bronchioles
Dictyocaulus viviparus (*Dictyocaulus hadweni*)	Lungworm	Bronchioles
Setaria labiatopapillosus	Filariid worm	Abdominal cavity

Table 62 continued

Species (former name)	Common name	Location in host
Elaeophora schneideri[b]	Arterial worm	Carotid and other arteries
Onchocerca cervipedis (*Wehrdikmansia cervipedis*)[b]	Legworm	Subcutaneous
Arthropoda		
Cephenomyia jellisoni	Botfly larvae	Retropharyngeal recesses, naso-pharyngeal area
Otobius megnini	Soft tick	Ear canal
Psoroptes sp. (*P. cervinus, P. equi* var. *cervinus, P. equi* var. *cervinae, P. commununis* var. *cervinae*)	Scab mite	Skin
Lipoptena cervi[b]	Louse fly	Skin
L. depressa[a]	Louse fly	Skin
Bovicola equi[a]	Chewing louse	Skin
B. longicornis[c]	Chewing louse	Skin
B. concavifrons (*americanum*)[c]	Chewing louse	Skin
Tricholipeurus parallelue (*Damalinia parallelus*)[a,b]	Chewing louse	Skin
Tricholipeurus lipauroides[a,b]	Chewing louse	Skin
Linognathus sp.[a]	Sucking louse	Skin
Solenopotes ferrisi	Sucking louse	Skin
Dermacentor albipictus	Winter tick	Skin
D. andersoni	Rocky Mountain tick	Skin
Ixodes pacificus	Hard tick	Skin

[a] Identification suspect.

[b] Deer parasite. *Onchocerca cervipedis* common in deer and moose. *Lipoptena cervi* introduced from Europe.

[c] Genus often called *Damalinia* in older literature.

The meningeal worm is one of four closely related species known from ungulates of North America. The other three are *Parelaphostrongylus andersoni* (*P. andersoni*) of the musculature of white-tailed deer and caribou (Lankester and Hauta 1989), *Parelaphostrongylus odocoilei* (*P. odocoilei*) of the musculature of mule and black-tailed deer (Platt and Samuel 1978) and *Elaphostrongylus rangiferi* (*E. rangiferi*) of the musculature and central nervous system of caribou and moose in Newfoundland (Lankester and Fong 1989). All four elaphostrongylines use terrestrial snails and slugs (gastropods) as intermediate hosts. *Parelaphostrongylus tenuis* is the only elaphostrongyline known from American elk.

Meningeal worm causes little pathology in white-tailed deer, but it can cause a serious neurologic disease in many ungulates. Free-ranging hosts are known to include moose (Anderson 1965a), caribou (Bergerud and Mercer 1989), reindeer (Anderson 1970), elk (Carpenter et al. 1973), red deer

Figure 132. Approximate distribution of meningeal worm, *Parelaphostrongylus tenuis,* in the United States and Canada.

(Woolf et al. 1977) (presumptive), black-tailed deer (Nettles et al. 1977a) and fallow deer (Nettles et al. 1977b). Captive animals reported with neurologic disease include reindeer (Nichols et al. 1986), eland (see Anderson and Prestwood 1981), sable antelope (Nichols et al. 1986), scimitar-horned oryx (Nichols at al. 1986) (presumptive), bongo (Nichols et al. 1986) (presumptive), llama (Baumgartner et al. 1985), guanaco (Brown et al. 1978), domestic sheep (Jortner et al. 1985) and domestic goats (Kopcha et al. 1989). Neurologic disease has been caused by experimental infection in caribou (Anderson and Strelive 1968), elk (Samuel et al. 1992), fallow deer (Pybus et al. 1992), moose (Anderson 1964), mule deer (Tyler et al. 1980), bighorn sheep (Pybus et al. 1996), pronghorn antelope (see Anderson and Prestwood 1981), llama (Rickard et al. 1994), domestic sheep (Anderson and Strelive 1966) and domestic goats (Anderson and Strelive 1972).

The life cycle of this parasite, along with host susceptibility, are pivotal to the practice of relocating elk from one area to another. Elk become infected as the parasite cycles between white-tailed deer (adult life stage) and terrestrial snails and slugs (larval life stages).

Anderson (1964, 1965b) and Anderson and Strelive (1967) elucidated the life cycle in white-tailed deer, the usual host. Adult meningeal worms live in the cranial cavity associated with the spaces and blood sinuses provided by the connective tissue coverings (the meninges) of the brain. They deposit eggs into the venous blood circulation. Eggs are carried to the lungs where they develop to characteristic dorsal-spined larvae. These larvae, called first-stage, pass from the lung toward the throat where they are swallowed and carried with ingesta to be shed with feces about 3 months after the deer becomes infected, completing the cycle (Figure 133).

Larvae in the external environment are quite resistant to freezing but not desiccation (Shostak and Samuel 1984). They penetrate the foot of a variety of land snails and slugs (Table 63) and, in several weeks, develop to the infective third stage. Ungulates, such as white-tailed deer, become infected by accidentally ingesting infected gastropods. Larvae leave the gastropods, penetrate the stomach wall, enter the abdominal cavity and migrate to the posterior spinal cord. This takes between 1 to 2 weeks. Migrating larvae enter the dorsal horns of the gray matter of the spinal cord and begin maturing. About a month and a half after infection, subadult worms move outside the spinal cord and migrate to the cranium. There, they become sexually mature adult worms and, after mating, females lay eggs.

Thus, for meningeal worms to become established in a new area, first-stage larvae in feces of introduced ungulate definitive hosts (i.e., the host with adult life stage in which sexual reproduction occurs) must reach local terrestrial gastropods and develop to the infective stage in these gastropods. The gastropods, in turn, must be ingested by suit-

able ungulate hosts. Although 24 species of gastropods are known intermediate hosts of meningeal worms, only three or four are important hosts in nature (Lankester and Anderson 1968, Lankester and Samuel 1997). They include the small brown-to-black slug, *Deroceras laeve,* and woodland snails, such as *Zonitoides* spp., that are widely distributed in North America. These gastropods occur widely across the West, where *P. tenuis* does not occur.

With the recent interest and growth in game ranching and the associated transport of ungulates throughout North America, the risk of accidental introduction of *P. tenuis* to susceptible ungulate populations has generated concern and controversy (Samuel 1987, Samuel et al. 1992, Miller and Thorne 1993). According to Samuel and Demarais (1993:445), "This controversy pits the private sector,

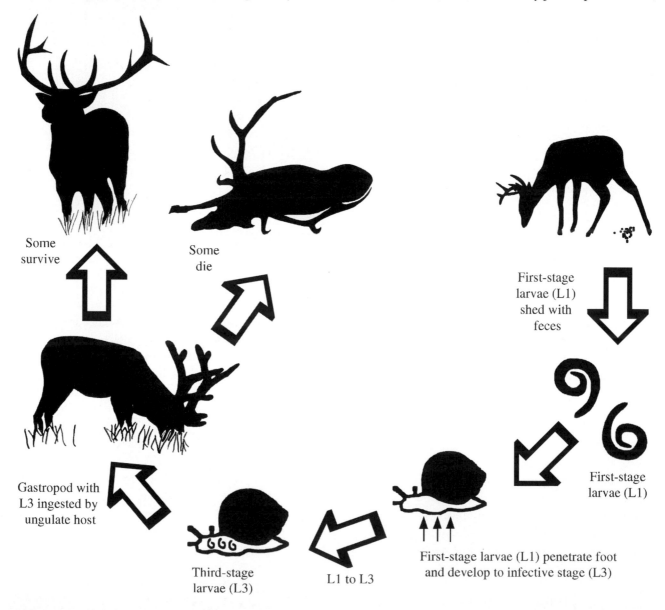

Some survive

Some die

First-stage larvae (L1) shed with feces

First-stage larvae (L1)

Gastropod with L3 ingested by ungulate host

Third-stage larvae (L3)

L1 to L3

First-stage larvae (L1) penetrate foot and develop to infective stage (L3)

Figure 133.   Schematic life cycle of meningeal worm.

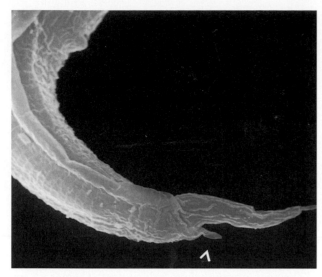

Scanning electron micrograph shows the posterior portion of the first-stage larva of *Parelaphostrongylus* (sp.) and its characteristic posteriorly directed dorsal spine (see arrowhead) near the tip of the tail. First-stage larvae of *P. tenuis* are shed in variable and intermittent degrees in the feces of elk. *Photo by T. R. Platt.*

eager to diversify its agricultural base, against traditional sportsmen and government agencies, worried about impacts of such activities on indigenous free-ranging wildlife, particularly ungulates and their habitats." Elk have been the focus of this controversy because they are the primary ranched species being transported within and between many jurisdictions.

In addition, many wildlife management agencies frequently relocate wild ungulates to restock former ranges or supplement dwindling herds. Typical examples include moose to Michigan (Aho and Hendrickson 1989), elk to Michigan and Pennsylvania (Moran 1973, Eveland et al. 1979) and caribou to former ranges (Bergerud and Mercer 1989). "Contemporary wildlife scientists have come to recognize that the relocation of wild animals never consists of the movement of a single species. Rather, it always entails relocation of a 'biological package' consisting of the animal itself (host) and its passenger organisms, potentially including viruses, bacteria, fungi, protozoans, helminths, arthropods or other pathogens" (Davidson and Nettles 1992:467). The implications for meningeal worm in the translocation of elk are twofold. Moving *P. tenuis*-infected captive elk from eastern to western North America may facilitate the movement of this parasite across the natural ecological barrier that currently restricts it to east of the Great Plains (Wasel 1995). And moving noninfected elk from western to eastern North America will result in exposure to meningeal worm.

The meningeal worm can only become established in western North America if there are suitable densities of

Table 63.   Known intermediate hosts of meningeal worm, *Parelaphostrongylus tenuis*

Phylum Mollusca	
Class Gastropoda[a]	
Subclass Prosobranchia (Streptonsura)	
Order Archaeogastropods	
Suborder Neritopsina	
Family Helicinidae	*Helicina orbiculata*
Subclass Pulmonata	
Order Geophila (Stylommatophora)	
Suborder Orthurathra	
Family Cionellidae	*Cionella (Cochlicopa) lubrica*
	C. (Cochlicopa) spp.
Suborder Heterurethra	
Family Succineidaa	*Succinea ovalis*
Suborder Sigmurethra	
Infraorder Aulacopoda	
Family Discidae	*Discus cronkhitei*
	D. patulus
	Anguispira alternata
Family Philomycidae	*Philomycus carolinianus*
Family Arionidae	*Arion circumscriptus*
Family Vitrinidae (Zonitidae)	*Mesomphix cupreus*
	Zonitoides (Ventridens) collisella
	Z. arboreus
	Z. nitidus
	Nesovitrea electrina
Family Limacidae	*Deroceras laeve*
	D. reticulatum
Infraorder Hoplopoda	
Family Mesodontidae	*Mesodon (Inflectarius) inflectus*
	Polygyra dorfeuilliana
	P. jacksoni
	Stenotrema fraternum
	S. stenotrema
	Triodopsis (Neohelix) albolabris
	T. divesta
	T. tridentata

[a] Gastropod classification after Burch and Pearce (1990).

overlapping populations of white-tailed deer and terrestrial gastropods and optimal conditions for the parasite. Samuel et al. (1992:629) observed that "The abundance of suitable intermediate and definitive hosts in western North America suggests that meningeal worm could become established in white-tailed deer populations if it were introduced." For example, in Alberta, 8 of 33 recorded species of terrestrial gastropods are known intermediate hosts of *P. tenuis* (W. M. Samuel unpublished files:1996) and are widely distributed in North America.

Regarding the effect of climate on survival of first-stage larvae or activity and survival of gastropods, Wasel (1995) predicted an 88% probability that, if introduced, *P. tenuis* could become established in Edmonton, Alberta, based on a summer precipitation model for North Dakota and Manitoba where *P. tenuis* is present. This posed the question, can eastern-source elk survive infection and, thus, become transmitting hosts for this parasite? Samuel et al. (1992) examined elk as a potential host for meningeal worm by infecting 26 calves with few to many larvae of *P. tenuis*. All 13 calves given many larvae (i.e., 125, 200 or 300 larvae) developed neurologic disease and died; 2 calves shed larvae in feces. Of 13 calves given fewer larvae (i.e., 15, 25 or 75), 6 became clinically ill and 4 survived; 7 of these 13 calves shed parasite larvae in feces. Shedding of larvae was variable and intermittent (Welch et al. 1991a), and elk with clinical disease sometimes went into remission. This suggests that infected elk could go undetected.

Anderson et al. (1966) infected two elk calves with meningeal worm of white-tailed deer origin. Both developed neurologic disease; one died, and the second survived and shed first-stage larvae in its feces. Worms were recovered from the subdural space and seen in cross section of the dorsal (and ventral) horns of gray matter. Karns (1966) and Pybus et al. (1989) reported first-stage *P. tenuis*-like larvae in feces of elk in northwestern Minnesota and southwestern Manitoba, respectively. Pybus et al. (1989) confirmed the finding by experimentally passing the larvae through snails and then white-tailed deer, and recovering adult *P. tenuis*.

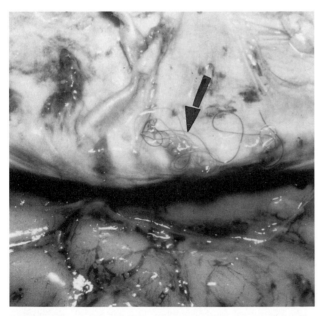

Meningeal worm (see arrow) in the subdural space overlying the brain of an experimentally infected elk. The dura matter has been peeled back to expose the adult worm. Note a lack of cellular inflammatory response. *Photo by M. J. Pybus, from Samuel (1994).*

Samuel et al. (1992) successfully infected white-tailed deer with elk-origin larvae, proving that transmission from elk to deer is possible. This suggests that, if infected elk were transported to meningeal worm-free areas in the West, they could potentially spread infection to white-tailed deer. Samuel et al. (1992:636–637) concluded that "a few infected elk could provide sufficient larvae to establish infections in white-tailed deer that would then amplify and spread meningeal worm on a much broader scale. Such a situation likely would put a variety of free-ranging and captive species at risk." They recommended that translocations of elk into western North America not be done until methods for successful detection or treatment of *P. tenuis* become available.

One frequent comment is that meningeal worm can be eliminated using anthelmintic treatment. There is no evidence for this. In fact, treatment of white-tailed deer with ivermectin for members of the genus *Parelaphostrongylus*, although likely killing some worms, merely resulted in temporary cessation of larval shedding in deer feces (Kocan 1985, Samuel and Gray 1988).

Restocking elk to areas where they once occurred in eastern North America may not be as successful as desired, because of the presence of meningeal worm in resident white-tailed deer. The potential impact of *P. tenuis* on elk is not really known, but for several translocations, some information suggests that infection and neurologic disease occurred in elk soon after they were released at the translocation site. A brief historic perspective follows.

Twenty-four elk were relocated from Jackson Hole, Wyoming, to indigenous habitat in northern Lower Peninsula of Michigan in 1918. Failing (1951:23) described clinical signs, general in nature but consistent with neurologic disease caused by *P. tenuis*, as follows: "During the last few years, sick elk have been found throughout the range and to date no cure has been found. Some of the symptoms are partial or total blindness, loss of fear and loss of appetite." Failing (1951) thought that cobalt deficiency might be the cause, but Fay and Stuht (1973:11) were more specific: "A neurologic disease which cannot be attributed to bacterial or viral infection has been observed in 39 individuals since 1938. . . . A clinically affected individual tends to leave its herd and remain near a road, field or woodland clearing and becomes less wary. In some instances vision seems impaired. In advanced cases, the animal often walks aimlessly or in circles and may carry its head in a tilted position. . . . Since the initial finding in 1969, meningeal worms are regularly found in neurologically stricken animals. . . . It is concluded . . . that the neurologic disease in Michigan wapiti is caused by nematode *P. tenuis*." Similarly, B.S. McGinnis observed sick elk in Virginia (Anderson et al. 1966). It should be remembered that it was only in 1965 that Anderson (1965a) confirmed that a neurologic disease known in moose for about 50 years was caused by *P. tenuis.*

Carpenter et al. (1973) described lesions and recovered mature and immature *P. tenuis* from four elk that were part of a 1969-to-1971 translocation program involving almost 400 elk from Wichita Mountains Wildlife Refuge in southwestern Oklahoma, where meningeal worm did not occur in white-tailed deer, to eastern Oklahoma, where it did occur (Kocan et al. 1982). Clinical signs were later observed in elk at all of the five state-owned management areas (Raskevitz et al. 1991). Carpenter et al. (1973) described clinical signs in live elk, including the four mentioned, between June 1970 and February 1971. Animals were circling and showed signs of ataxia, adipsia and impaired vision. There were associated histologic lesions in the central nervous system. Carpenter et al. indicated that relocating elk to eastern Oklahoma would be of limited success because of the presence of meningeal worm. They advised, as had Karns (1967) for moose management in Minnesota, that "an increase in the number of infected deer on range managed for wapiti would likely increase the number of infected intermediate hosts and consequently increase the probability of infecting wapiti" (Carpenter et al. 1973:152).

Raskevitz et al. (1991) documented that re-establishment of elk was seriously hampered at four of the five release sites in Oklahoma. In the fifth site, Cookson Hills Wildlife Management Area, deaths from *P. tenuis* were observed annually, but the population continued to increase to around 100 to 150 elk. Raskevitz et al. attributed this success in part to reduced availability of infected gastropods in areas used by elk. Furthermore, none of 48 elk feces had meningeal worm larvae, nor was any evidence of subclinical infection detected.

Reports of meningeal worm-related deaths in two elk populations in western and north-central Pennsylvania, respectively, appeared in the mid-1970s (Woolf et al. 1977, Eveland et al. 1979). In the late 1960s, clinical signs attributed to meningeal worm were observed in red deer first introduced in the early 1950s to the enclosed Rachelwood Wildlife Research Preserve (approximately 5,000 acres [2,100 ha]) in western Pennsylvania. Introductions of elk were begun in 1959 and, by the mid-1970s, their numbers peaked at around 70 animals, whereas red deer were nearly gone. Between 1968 and 1973, cerebral nematodiasis was demonstrated in 12 of 15 elk (or elk/red deer hybrids) found dead in the preserve. Adult worms and histologic lesions attributable to infection with *P. tenuis* were seen in 8 (18%) and 20 (45%), respectively, of 44 elk or elk/red deer hybrids shot at random, 1973 through 1975. Therefore, Woolf et al. (1977) found histologic evidence of infection in

elk that did not display clinical signs. Prevalence in 2.5-year-old and younger elk was 59%, versus 21% in older animals, suggesting that greater susceptibility of younger elk to disease and harvest would have a detrimental effect on population recruitment and might limit the growth of elk living sympatrically with white-tailed deer. These prevalences are comparable to the prevalence of meningeal worms in white-tailed deer in Rachelwood Preserve, 1972 through 1975—141 (62%) of 229 (D. R. Anderson unpublished data:1993).

Olsen and Woolf (1978), also working in the Rachelwood Preserve, recorded development of clinical signs of the neurologic disease in six naturally infected elk. Initial signs were decreased flight distance, seclusion and listlessness. Other signs included stiff or hackney gait; propensity for using established trails; circling; tolerance of human contact; aimless wandering; general and lumbar weakness; ataxia; staggering; excessive salivation; bulging eyes; paraplegia; "held head low"; and turning of the head and neck to one side (torticollis) (Olsen and Woolf 1978:264). Animals went into remission between 18 and 140 days after initial observation of signs. They suffered superficial abrasions from staggering against trees, fences, etc. Mean time from initial observation of clinical signs to death was 100 days (range, 35 to 191 days). This compares with a range in time of death in the Samuel et al. (1992) experimental study in which elk given 125 larvae or more died between 60 and 122 days. Olsen and Woolf (1978) speculated that elk with disease are more susceptible to predation, including shooting by humans, because of a tendency to use trails and fields and decreased flight distances. They also suggested that neurologic disease might have a detrimental effect on the social organization of an infected population of elk, including failure of infected cows to care for young, failure of infected young males to participate in rutting activities in autumn and secluded infected cows not being bred. Because all evidence of a lack of growth in the population pointed to *P. tenuis*-caused deaths of calves, Olsen and Woolf suggested that neurologic disease would continue to limit the population even if hunting was halted. The elk population in Rachelwood Preserve appears to have increased slightly since the 1970s, with a few cases of neurologic disease occurring annually, whereas the number of white-tailed dear has declined significantly (from more than 1,000 to 300) (Woolf and Harder 1979, D. R. Anderson personal communication:1996).

In north-central Pennsylvania, where elk were relocated from Yellowstone National Park in the early 1920s, cerebral nematodiasis attributed to meningeal worms was seen from 1975, when clinical and pathological studies began, to 1992 (Eveland et al. 1979, Cogan 1993). During that time, *P.*

A twisted neck (i.e., torticollis) is a common sign in terminal cases of parelaphostrongylosis caused by infection with meningeal worm. *Photo by A. Olsen, from Samuel (1994).*

tenuis-caused mortality was 28 (12%). From 1971 to 1993, the number of elk increased from about 40 (1974) to about 205 (1993) (D. Devlin and W. Drake unpublished report:1989, Cogan 1993).

In summary of elk relocations from western areas of the United States, where *P. tenuis* is absent, to the eastern U.S. (or in Oklahoma from west to east), where *P. tenuis* is present, several points are obvious. Only a few populations,

Incoordination and circling, two common clinical signs of parelaphostrongylosis infection, can lead to injuries when an animal encounters a fence, as with this wild elk in Pennsylvania. *Photo by A. Olsen.*

particularly the one in north-central Michigan, have achieved good growth in numbers, whereas others in Pennsylvania, Minnesota and Ontario have struggled. Many elk sharing range with *P. tenuis*-infected white-tailed deer become infected with meningeal worms and some die. However, the exact involvement of *P. tenuis* in success (or lack thereof) of these populations is unknown.

Large American Liver Fluke and Elk Translocation

The parasite known as the large American liver fluke, *Fascioloides magna (F. magna)*, causes severe infection in many wild and domestic hosts, including all five North American members of the Cervidae—elk, moose, caribou, white-tailed deer and mule deer (Foreyt 1981, 1996b, Lankester 1974, Lankester and Luttich 1988). This trematode is reviewed here for several reasons. It is a classic example of a parasite that has become established in new areas by means of its translocated infected elk hosts. The American liver fluke is large and easily seen, and when found in high numbers, it can produce extensive lesions in the liver. Host mortality often is attributed to this parasite. Elk and white-tailed deer are considered to be the natural or usual hosts.

F. magna was first described by Bassi (1875:104) from "stag of Canada, *Cervus canadensis*" translocated from the United States to the "Royal Park" by the King of Italy in 1865. It is transmitted between vertebrate herbivores and aquatic snails. Specifically, the main definitive hosts capable of transmitting infection are deer and elk, and the main snail intermediate hosts in North America are many species of the genus *Lymnaea* (listed by Foreyt 1981).

Elk become infected by feeding at the air/water interface of low-lying marshes or permanent ponds and sloughs where vegetation harbors the metacercarial life stage of the parasite (the metacercaria is the final larval stage of digenetic trematodes; it forms when the tailed, free-swimming cercarial stage settles on vegetation, loses its tail and encysts). After being eaten by elk, metacercariae excyst in the gut, penetrate the gut wall and likely migrate across the body cavity where they penetrate the liver and become established in hepatic parenchyma. Flukes mature about 30 weeks later in white-tailed deer, mule deer and elk (Foreyt and Todd 1976, Foreyt 1996b). Mature flukes, usually in groups of two or three, are found in host-produced whitish fibrous capsules in the liver, where the capsules connect to bile ducts (Foreyt 1996b). Eggs exit the host in the feces.

Eggs are shed with elk feces about 6.5 to 8 months after ingestion of metacercariae (Foreyt 1996b). Under appropriate conditions, miracidia hatch from eggs in water in several days and penetrate the foot of lymnaeid snails. Miracidia transform to the sporocyst stage, the first of several multiplying larval stages in the snail. The result is the potential for hundreds of cercaria to leave a snail that was originally infected with one miracidium. The cercariae settle on vegetation, lose their tail and secrete a protective mucous coat.

Fascioloides magna has been reported from Cervidae in five major wetland-associated areas of North America: woodland caribou of northern Quebec and Labrador (Lankester and Luttich 1988); white-tailed deer of the southeastern U.S. (Pursglove et al. 1977); white-tailed deer and moose around the Great Lakes (Lankester 1974, Addison et al. 1988); elk and moose of the Canadian Rocky Mountain parks (Kingscote et al. 1987, Pybus 1990a, 1990b) and game-ranched elk of western Montana (Hood et al. 1997); and Roosevelt and Rocky Mountain elk and Columbian black-tailed deer from the Pacific coast of Canada (i.e., Vancouver Island and British Columbia) and the United States (Oregon and Washington) (Cowan 1951, Dutson et al. 1967).

Foreyt (1996a, 1996b) groups definitive hosts of *F. magna* in three classes based on host response. The first class consists of hosts that usually are not affected clinically by the parasite and in which the parasite matures and sheds eggs to the external environment. The best North American examples are white-tailed deer and elk. Hosts that usually survive infection but do not transmit parasites make up the second class. In these hosts, the parasite can mature and produce eggs, but rarely does. Mature flukes are encapsulated in hepatic tissue, and eggs do not pass in feces, because they become trapped in hepatic tissue. The best examples in North America are bison, cattle, moose and llamas. The final class is aberrant hosts in which infection usually is lethal because developing flukes migrate through and severely damage hepatic tissue. The best North Ameri-

can examples are bighorn sheep, domestic sheep and domestic goats.

Swales (1936) indicated that walls of capsules were thinner and damage was less in white-tailed deer (see Addison et al. 1988) and elk than in bison, cattle and sheep. Swales (1936:85) wrote that "The large Bovidae are completely resistant, the Cervidae are tolerant and *O. aries* is partially resistant to *F. magna.*"

Within any of the three groups of hosts, it is likely that some individuals with many flukes will have severely affected livers. This is because maturing flukes move through liver tissue causing extensive damage. Wobeser et al. (1985:242) described infected elk livers as having "variable number of cystic fibrous tracts filled with brown-black debris and trematodes, with black pigmentation of the hepatic parenchyma adjacent to these tracts." The black pigmentation, which often is extensive, is seen in virtually every infected animal regardless of species, and is hemosiderin as a result of red blood cell digestion by the parasite. Haigh and Hudson (1993:281) described lesions in elk as follows: "The surface of the liver is often pitted and contains fibrous scars . . . when infection is heavy, the liver may take on a bizarre form and there may be adhesions to adjacent tissues. . . . Large pockets of blood and parasite eggs, seen as viscid black fluids, are formed in most infected livers. Infected livers are larger than normal." Livers of infected moose and woodland caribou also are enlarged (Lankester 1974, Lankester and Luttich 1988).

Foreyt (1996b:605) described livers of experimentally infected elk as having "numerous subcapsular branching fluke migratory tracts on the surface." He attributed death in one of four infected elk to "severe acute fibrinous peritonitis," resulting from intestinal rupture near the liver associated with hemorrhage and fibrin deposition. In sum-

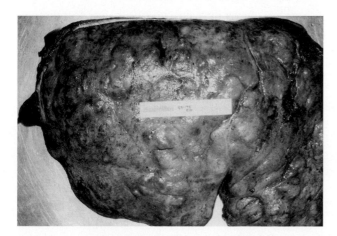 

Superior aspect (*left*) and undersurface (*right*) of the liver of an elk infected with more than 600 liver flukes, *Fascioloides magna*. Such livers usually are enlarged, with extensive areas of black pigmentation and a roughened surface caused by capsules that contain adult flukes. *Photos by M. J. Pybus.*

mary, three predictable outcomes of severe infection with *F. magna* are pigment-laced lesions, an enlarged and often distorted liver, and fibrin deposition.

No clinical signs have been reported for elk, as one might suspect given the above grouping of host response. But Pybus (1990b) mentioned a new focus of infection in elk in and near Banff, Alberta, in Banff National Park. Prevalence of fluke infection in these elk is very high, about 80% to 90%, and up to 600 flukes have been recorded, as have several deaths of elk attributed to severe infection (M. J. Pybus unpublished files:1997). Signs in three experimentally infected bighorn sheep and three experimentally infected mule deer were described as "depression, weight loss, weakness, or loss of appetite" (Foreyt 1996a:557) and "depression, had droopy ears, and were anorectic and weak for 1 to 2 wk before death" (Foreyt 1996b:604). Foreyt suggested that rapid death was due to massive hemorrhage resulting from blood vessels ruptured by migrating flukes.

The first documented translocation of *F. magna* was in the early 1860s with American elk from the United States to the Royal Park in Turin, Italy (Bassi 1875). Erhardova (1961:91) stated that this fluke was "introduced to Europe at the end of the 19th century by wapiti and Virginia deer [white-tailed deer], imported for zoological gardens, parks and enclosures." Reference to white-tailed deer likely refers to a separate introduction of liver fluke to Czechoslovakia. In Europe, the parasite occurs in many hosts, including red deer, elk, fallow deer, introduced sambar deer, introduced bluebuck, roe deer, cattle and domestic sheep (Erhardova 1961, Erhardova-Kotrla 1971). Roe deer are particularly susceptible, and death can result from infection with few flukes (Erhardova 1961).

At the Canadian Forces Base, Camp Wainwright (formerly National Buffalo Park) in east-central Alberta, liver flukes once were abundant there, but now are gone. This one-time Park was founded as a refuge for Plains bison in the early 1900s. It was fenced and, by 1920, held 7,000 bison, numerous elk, moose, deer, yak and a few pronghorn (Lothian 1981). Liver flukes were first noticed in the livers of a few bison by Cameron (1923). By 1933, many elk and deer were heavily infected (Swales 1936). Some elk, likely infected with *F. magna,* were translocated to Ontario. Infected elk, cattle, bison and domestic sheep were later reported from the area of the introduction (Kingscote 1950).

Because of the presence of liver flukes and high prevalence of tuberculosis in Camp Wainwright, an extensive animal reduction program was initiated just before World War II. It resulted in the slaughter of 2,900 bison, 1,800 elk, 115 moose and 250 deer (Lothian 1981). In addition, dead aquatic vegetation was burned, and there was extensive chemical control of aquatic snails. This apparently eradicated liver flukes, because many white-tailed deer and mule deer have been shot by hunters since the 1960s and examined superficially or in detail for liver flukes; none has been found (Stock 1978, Pybus 1990b).

Recently, mortality of captive elk on a ranch in Montana was attributed to the presence of *F. magna,* and the presence of *F. magna* was noted in elk on 4 of 28 other game ranches (Hood et al. 1997). Spread of infection from one ranch to another was documented. Lymnaeid snails were common on some ranches, and the overlap of elk ranches and lymnaeid snails in Montana was considerable.

New foci of liver fluke infection in elk can occur through natural dispersal of elk from one area to another. Green (1946) found no liver flukes in livers of 550 elk from near Banff, Alberta, but half of 52 elk later examined there in 1964 and 1965 were infected (Flook and Stenton 1969). Flook and Stenton (1969) suggested that infected immigrants from Kootenay National Park in British Columbia were the source of infection.

At least one other new focus is more difficult to explain. *F. magna* were found for the first time in elk and moose of Elk Island National Park in central Alberta in 1987 (Pybus 1990a). This followed approximately five decades of extensive reduction by slaughter of deer, moose, elk and bison, during which federal veterinary inspectors did not record *F. magna* in livers (Blyth 1995). W. M. Samuel (unpublished files:1974, 1977) and Samuel et al. (1976) found no flukes in

Typical habitat for elk and aquatic snail, which are intermediate hosts of the large American liver fluke (*Fascioloides magna*) in Banff National Park, Alberta. *Photo by M. J. Pybus.*

livers of 34 bison, more than 150 moose, 64 elk and 15 white-tailed deer, 1969 through 1983 (Table 64). Elk Island, near Edmonton, is a fenced park surrounded by farmland. There have been no recent translocations of ungulates to the park. Habitat for aquatic snails is abundant. Presence of *F. magna* in this elk population has confounded what had been extensive use of these animals as sources for translocations to other areas, but a treatment protocol using triclabendazole has been developed (Pybus et al. 1991). Elk are drenched at 50 to 60 mg/kg, with no chance of reinfection for 1 month (Pybus et al. 1991). "This protocol should result in death of most, if not all, adult *F. magna* and a large portion of the immature flukes. A second drenching after seven days probably would improve the efficacy" (Pybus et al. 1991:603–604). Control of liver flukes in nature is virtually impossible, given the abundance of snail habitat, aquatic snails, white-tailed deer and elk, and prevalence and numbers of flukes in white-tailed deer or elk in enzootic areas.

Implications of Mange Mite (*Psoroptic* sp.) and Winter Tick (*Dermacentor albipictus*) for Elk Management

Psoroptic mange mites of the genus *Psoroptes* are obligatory, nonburrowing, surface-feeding parasites of many species of domestic and wild mammals, including elk. They live on the skin surface, where they cause a disease known variously as scabies, scab and mange. The disease is progressive and often becomes a severe exudative dermatitis seen mainly in adult male elk during late autumn and winter (Smith 1985). Scabies has a long history with elk in and near the National Elk Refuge, Jackson, Wyoming (Skinner 1928, Mills 1936, Murie 1951, Worley et al. 1969, Smith 1985, Samuel et al. 1991).

The taxonomy of the elk scab mite, and other species of *Psoroptes*, remains unclear (c.f. Boyce et al. 1990, Boyce and Brown 1991). The mite on elk (here called *Psoroptes* sp.) has been given many scientific names in the literature, including *Psoroptes cervinus* (*P. cervinus*), *Psoroptes equi* (*P. equi*) var. *cervinus*, *Psoroptes equi* (*P. equi*) var. *cervinae*, and *Psoroptes communis* (*P. communis*) var. *cervinae*.

Mites

Species of psoroptic mites tend to be grouped by host and location on the body (i.e., body mites or ear mites) (Sweatman 1958). Mites spend their entire life on the host, with all life stages (see Sweatman 1958, Meleney 1985, Muschenheim 1988) occurring on one animal. Transmission is by direct contact. The life cycle from egg to adult is completed in 2 to 3 weeks (Sweatman 1958). Female *Psoroptes ovis* (*P. ovis*) lay up to 80 eggs (Kirkwood 1986). This suggests that if *Psoroptes* sp. on elk are similarly prolific, elk can become severely infested in approximately 2 months.

Table 64. Helminths in elk from Elk Island National Park near Edmonton in central Alberta, and Ya Ha Tinda Ranch on the Red Deer River east of Banff Park in west-central Alberta, 1973 to 1974

	Elk Island			Ya Ha Tinda		
	Number infected	Number inspected	Percentage	Number infected	Number inspected	Percentage
Cestoda						
Echinococcus granulosus	15	70	21	13	36	36
Taenia hydatigena	1	64	2	0	36	0
Moniezia sp.	11	59	19	1	37	3
Thysanosoma actinoides	0	58	0	3	37	8
Trematoda						
Fascioloides magna	0	64		0	17	
Zygocotyle lunata	2	62	3	0	37	0
Nematoda						
Trichostrongylus axei	51	56	91	4	36	11
Cooperia oncophoro	2	62	3	0	37	
Nematodirella alcidis	3	62	5	0	37	
Nematodirus helvetianus	1	62	2	0	37	
Ostertagia sp.	1	62	2	0	37	
Trichuris sp.	22	62	36	7	37	19
Dictyocaulus viviparus	13	62	21	0	36	
Setaria sp.	1	64	2	0	14	
Onchocerca cervipedis	0	42		0	26	

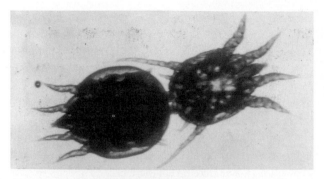

Psoroptes (sp.) mites (magnified ×100). *Photo by T. P. Kistner.*

There are virtually no experimental details on basic biology of psoroptic mites on elk, but a lot of comparable information is available for similar mites on cattle and sheep (Kirkwood 1986, Stromberg and Fisher 1986, Stromberg and Guillot 1989). Some species of *Psoroptes* suck fluids by means of pseudorutellae, feeding on superficial lipid emulsion at the surface of the skin; others feed on blood obtained from leakage rather than by skin puncture with mouth parts (see Kirkwood 1986). The resulting scablike lesions consisting of inflammation and edema at the site of infestation on the skin of the host are basically a host reaction to antigenic material from the mites (Kirkwood 1986).

Stromberg and Fisher (1986) described gross lesions as wet and crusty, and microscopic lesions as chronic exudative superficial perivascular dermatitis. Lange (1982:245) stated that, "As the inflammatory process progresses, sheets of epidermis are shed by the host. . . . These sheets are layered in the hair coat of the body." Animals lose hair, body fluids and heat. Samuel et al. (1991) found up to 6.5 million mites as-

Severe cases of scabies caused by infestation with psorptic mites, *Psorptes* (sp.) involves extensive loss of hair over the shoulders and sides with crusting of the skin. *Photo courtesy of U.S. Fish and Wildlife Service from Samuel et al. (1991).*

sociated with dense, often moist scabs on the dorsal and lateral thoracic regions of the body of individual elk.

Murie (1951) noted that scabies had a long history on elk from the Jackson area of Wyoming, and that it was most common in mature bulls and old cows. Murie, and later Lange (1982), suggested that this probably was because bulls lost body condition, hence resistance, during and after the rut. Muschenheim (1988) cited cases of malnourished elk from the National Elk Refuge developing scabies, suggesting that nutritional stress might result in development of scabies. However, she also noted that captive well-fed elk became reinfested with psoroptic mites; stress associated with captivity may have been involved.

Except for incidental reports from northern Idaho (Colwell and Dunlap 1975) and Minnesota (Fashingbauer 1965), clinical disease and mortality have only been reported from northwestern Wyoming and adjoining parts of Montana. However, Ziccardi et al. (1996) found serological evidence of infestation in elk from six of nine populations sampled. These included elk from North Dakota (two populations), Utah, Washington and Wyoming (two populations including the National Elk Refuge). Because the original source of the populations in North Dakota was northwestern Wyoming, an enzootic area for *Psoroptes,* Ziccardi et al. (1996) recommended treating elk from enzootic areas with an acaricide before relocation.

It is important to determine whether elk from recently developed high density populations, such as Elk Island National Park (Blyth 1995), are seropositive, because they frequently are translocated to other areas. The recent very high densities of elk that occur in and near the towns of Banff and Jasper, in Banff and Jasper National Parks, also should be examined.

Psoroptic mange is an important domestic animal disease, but there is no evidence that mites from elk are transmissible to domestic livestock. Hepworth and Thomas (1962) were unable to infest cattle and sheep with mites from elk.

Treatment of mite infestation with ivermectin has received a lot of attention in recent years, particularly for mangy bighorn sheep (see Foreyt 1993). Administration of ivermectin in pelleted feed for 7 consecutive days was completely effective. However, subcutaneous or intramuscular injection is the more usual route of administration, and has been successful in treating captive elk (Muschenheim 1988). Ivermectin also could be delivered by projectile syringe or biobullet.

Ticks

Ticks are external parasites that feed on blood of vertebrates. The only tick known to cause problems for elk is the winter tick, *Dermacentor albipictus* (*D. albipictus*). It is a parasite of ungulates, mainly North American members of the family Cervidae. Moose are the most severely affected of the cervid hosts (Welch et al. 1991b).

Dermacentor albipictus is unique among ticks reported from elk in that all three parasitic blood-feeding life stages—larva, nymph and adult—feed on the blood of one host (Figure 134). Elk in Alberta, and likely in most western populations of elk except perhaps those most southerly in location, become infested in late summer and autumn when they contact clumps of tick larvae (seed ticks less than 1 mm in length) on tips of vegetation. Once on elk, the larvae feed on blood and molt to the nymph life stage. In mid-winter, nymphs begin blood-feeding and molt to the adult stage. During late winter and early spring, adults (particularly females) engorge on blood and become the large, grayish, grape-sized ticks commonly seen on elk. In Al-

berta, they drop from elk in March and April. Elk are tick-free during summer. Winter ticks lay eggs in the vegetative litter layer in late spring; the eggs hatch to larvae in late summer, thus completing the life cycle.

Although winter ticks have been reported only from elk in the four provinces of western Canada and in seven states of the United States (Samuel et al. 1991), most elk in western North America likely become infested each year of their life. This is based on observations of many elk from many locations with a characteristic, tick-induced, damaged hair coat at the dorsal base of the neck. *Dermacentor albipictus* were recovered from all of 47 and 9 elk hides from Elk Island and Jasper National Parks, Alberta, and the National Elk Refuge, Wyoming, respectively (Samuel and Welch 1991, Samuel et al. 1991). The mean estimated numbers of ticks per elk from these populations was 3,400 and 3,960, respectively. For comparison, mean tick numbers for

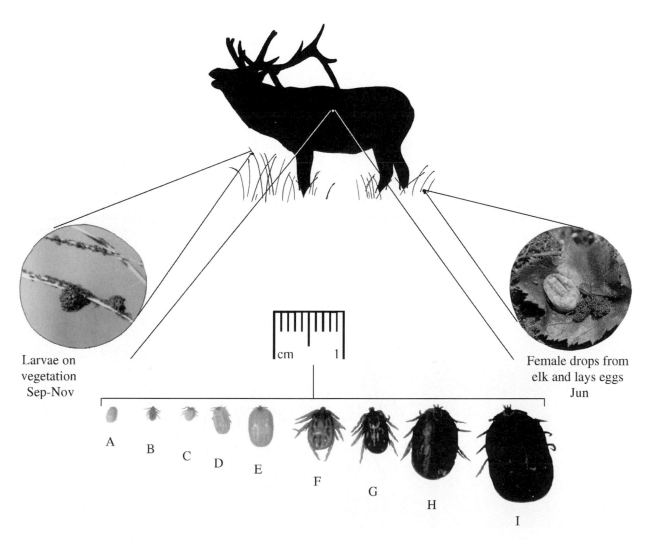

Figure 134.　Schematic life cycle of winter tick, *Dermacentor albipictus,* for elk in Alberta. The line-up at the bottom of the figure features A = blood-fed larva (Oct–Nov), B = unfed nymph (Nov–Jan), C, D and E = blood-fed nymphs (Jan–Apr), F = adult male (Feb–Apr), G = adult female (Feb–Apr), and H and I = blood-fed adult females.

other hosts in Elk Island National Park were 37,070 (moose), 1,450 (white-tailed deer) and 175 (plains and wood bison) (Samuel and Welch 1991).

One consequence of winter tick infestation on elk is grooming, which causes the characteristic pattern of damage to the winter hair coat. Elk also lick the anal region. Grooming, mainly in the form of oral grooming and scratching with the hind feet, occurs on areas of the body with highest tick densities. In most cases, elk have a damaged hair coat at the dorsal base of the neck, which produces a characteristic notch or collar of broken hair. Sometimes, the damage to the coat is more extensive.

The exact relationship between winter ticks and elk is not known. Infestation of winter ticks on elk may cause morbidity and mortality (Banfield 1949, Cowan 1951, Murie 1951, Stelfox 1962a), but no critical studies have been done. Nonetheless, strong statements appear in early literature. Murie (1951:165–6), for example, stated that "the winter tick is a never-failing scourge that visits the elk each spring, its numbers varying from year to year. . . . Ticks are a heavy drain on an animal's vitality and may be a contributing factor in the death of some diseased elk." Results of experimental (McLaughlin and Addison 1986, Glines and Samuel 1989), observational (Hatter 1950, Cowan 1951, Berg 1975, Garner and Wilton 1993) and other field studies (Samuel and Barker 1979, Samuel and Welch 1991) strongly support the idea that winter ticks kill many moose, but moose tend to have almost 10 times more ticks than do elk.

There is a growing body of literature suggesting that ectoparasites, such as ticks, frequently harm their hosts (Lehmann 1993). Perhaps winter ticks operate as proposed by Blyth (1995), as follows. At low densities, hosts have abundant food and few ticks. As hosts reach higher densities, they saturate the environment with egg-laying female ticks to be picked up as larvae from vegetation the next autumn. High-density host populations lose condition because of forage limitations and high numbers of ticks. Many hosts in poor condition die in spring. The numerous female ticks that drop from hosts in the spring produce many more ticks that will infest hosts the next autumn.

Typical tick-induced damage to an elk's winter hair coat usually is restricted to a "notch" at the dorsal base of the neck (*left*), but may be more extensive (*right*). *Left photo (elk silhouetted against Old Faithful geyser in Yellowstone National Park) by Irwin and Peggy Bauer. Right photo by William M. Samuel.*

Thus, ticks still are very numerous 1 year (winter) after a die-off. Dead elk in northern areas in late winter usually are malnourished, with several thousand ticks and much tick-related damage to their hair. Severe winters are involved, suggesting that a complex interaction of winter ticks, host density, nutrition and weather is involved in die-offs.

For captive game-ranched elk, infestation probably causes more aesthetic problems for buyers (due to the tick-induced damaged coat) than actual problems for the elk themselves. Haigh and Hudson (1993) discussed treatment and control measures used by game ranchers to treat winter tick infestation of elk, but measures described appear fairly ineffectual.

Echinococcus granulosus and Other Tapeworm Cysts: Aesthetic Concerns

Elk hunters, particularly in northern areas, commonly see immature tapeworm cysts in elk, particularly the hydatid cyst of *Echinococcus granulosus* (*E. granulosus*) in the lung. A second tapeworm cyst, *Taenia hydatigena* (*T. hydatigena*), called the thin-necked bladder worm, occasionally is observed in the liver. Both immature tapeworm cysts are large, conspicuous and readily visible during dressing of the carcass.

Adult tapeworms of these species are found primarily in the small intestine of wolves, but also in coyotes and other carnivores, including dogs. Wolves often carry many thousands of adult *E. granulosus*. Eggs pass from the canid with feces. Elk become infected by eating ground-level vegeta-

tion contaminated with eggs from canid feces. Embryos (called onchospheres) hatch from eggs in the gut, penetrate the gut wall, and make their way to the lung (*E. granulosus*) or liver (*T. hydatigena*) through the circulation, where they develop to the hydatid or cysticercus life stages, respectively. In general, wherever wolves and elk share range, *E. granulosus* is prevalent in elk (Flook and Stenton 1969, Pybus 1990b).

In North America, the wild hosts most commonly infected with hydatid cysts are moose, elk and barren-ground caribou. Hydatid cysts, found primarily in the lung and secondarily in the liver, vary in size, but often are the shape and sizes of a pea or golf ball. The cyst consists of the vesiculated oncosphere, which becomes a unilocular bladder with a germinal epithelial lining and an outer connective tissue capsule of host origin. Many thousand young tapeworms, called protoscoleces, bud off from the internal epithelial lining. Hydatid cysts grow over time. Canids become infected by feeding on infected elk lung.

Echinococcus granulosus is the only tapeworm of elk that can infect humans, but humans do not become infected through direct handling of an elk carcass (Figure 135). Dogs that become infected with *E. granulosus* by eating lungs of infected ungulates are generally considered to be the source of human infection. Thus, humans become infected the same way elk become infected, through exposure to tapeworm eggs. The rule of thumb here is to avoid providing dogs access to the viscera of elk. In addition, precautions should be taken (e.g., wearing gloves and mask) when han-

Typical grooming postures of elk against winter ticks include oral grooming to posterior body regions using the tongue and teeth (*left*) and to the anterior regions with the hoof (*right*). *Left photo by Leonard Rue, Jr. Right photo by Valerius Geist.*

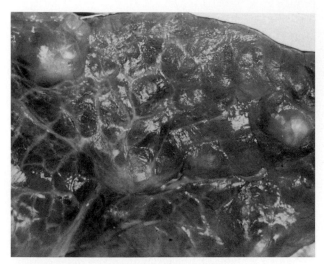

Golf ball-sized hydatid cysts of *Echinococcus granulosis* in the lung of a moose (*left*) and an opened cyst (*right*) with small white brood capsules. Both the cyst and brood capsules contain many future tapeworms. Infections in elk are similar. *Photo by J. C. Holms.*

dling wolves or coyotes, and especially having contact with their feces.

In publications, virtually all researchers of hydatid-infected ungulates discuss the effect of the cyst on host survival, particularly increased susceptibility to predation by reduction of host stamina during pursuit (Cowan 1947b, 1951, Green 1949a, Flook and Stenton 1969). There is no recent information for elk, but Messier et al. (1989:218) antici-

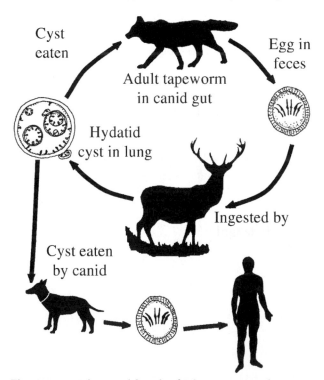

Figure 135.   Schematic life cycle of *Echinococcus granulosus,* showing that humans could not become infected from contact with elk, but rather from contact with eggs in the feces of canids. The larval life stage in the lung of elk is called the hydatid cyst.

pated "that individuals [moose] harboring heavy pulmonary infections are recognized as vulnerable by wolves." Rau and Caron (1979) presented data suggesting that moose heavily infected with *E. granulosus* were more susceptible to hunting by humans.

In New Zealand, a case of fatal hepatic cysticercosis was reported in a captive 3-week-old red deer (McKenna et al. 1980). Several hundred bladderworms of *T. hydatigena* were found in the grossly enlarged liver. The friable and grossly enlarged liver covered in hemorrhagic tracts was the result of developing cysticerci migrating through the liver. Such cases are quite rare.

In summary, presence of parasitic cysts in the lungs or liver is unsightly, but of no great concern for sportsmen. Viscera should not be fed to pets because these animals may become infected with tapeworms and become the source of *E. granulosus* infection for humans.

A third immature tapeworm, *Taenia ovis krabbei,* found as small pea-sized cysts in cardiac and skeletal muscle of moose, mule deer and caribou of North America, rarely has been reported in elk (Sweatman and Henshall 1962, Haigh and Hudson 1993).

Lungworm in Elk

Dictyocaulus viviparus (*D. viviparus*), called the cattle lungworm or thread lungworm, is a cream-colored lungworm about 2 to 4 inches (5–10 cm) in length that is common in many species of ruminants the world over. North American hosts include elk, muskox, bison, moose, mule deer, black-tailed deer and white-tailed deer. *D. viviparus* is the only common lungworm in elk, and in elk, it has widespread distribution (Table 65).

Table 65. Reports of *Dictyocaulus viviparus* in elk, which illustrate the widespread distribution of the parasite and variable prevalence

Geographic location	Percentage prevalence	References
Alberta (southwestern)	32	Kingscote et al. 1987
Alberta and British Columbia (Mountain. Parks)	4	Flook and Stentson 1969
Alberta (southeastern)	54	Stock and Barrett 1983
Alberta	2	Pybus 1990a
Alberta (Elk Island National Park)	21	W. M. Samuel unpublished files: 1974, 1977
Alberta (near Banff National Park)	0	W. M. Samuel unpublished files: 1973, 1974
Montana (south-central)	8	Barrett and Worley 1966
Montana (western)	35 (calves) 44 (adults)	Worley et al. 1969
New Mexico	23	Wilson 1969
South Dakota	10	Boddicker and Hugghins 1969
Wyoming (Yellowstone National Park)	43	Worley and Barrett 1964
Wyoming (northwestern)	58	Bergstrom and Robbins 1979
Wyoming (northwestern)	60	Bergstrom 1975

Note: Synonyms include *Dictyocaulus hadweni* and *D. eckerti.*

D. viviparus has a direct life cycle. Adult worms, which live in the bronchi and bronchioles of the lung, produce eggs that contain a vermiform larva that hatches to first-stage larvae during passage to the outside with feces. On vegetation and soil, larvae molt twice to the infective third-stage. Fungi of the genus *Pilobolus* apparently are involved in dissemination of infective larvae from feces to surrounding vegetation. These fungi grow on elk feces (Foos 1989). When sporangia discharge, larvae on them are dispersed several meters. Elk are infected by accidental ingestion of infective larvae with vegetation. Larvae penetrate the gut wall, enter the enteric lymph circulation and migrate to the lungs. Adult worms are capable of producing larvae that are shed in elk feces within 1 month (Presidente et al. 1972).

Lungworm is thought to be a problem in free-ranging and captive elk and captive red deer (Worley 1979, Bergstrom 1982, see Mason 1994), but clinical signs have not been described for elk. Mason (1994:40), described the early signs of lungworm infection in red deer as being "vague, including loss of condition, retarded growth, and roughened coat." The hacking cough common in infected cattle was not reported by Mason, but was reported for captive black-tailed deer with dictyocauliasis (Presidente et al. 1973). Ac-cording to Mason (1994:40) "Severely affected animals (red deer) will die suddenly" (see also Charleston 1980).

Prominent lesions occur in the lumen of the major air passages. Worms in elk lungs usually are found in a foamy blood-tinged mucus in smaller bronchioles toward the periphery of lung lobes (Worley and Barrett 1964). Bergstrom (1975) saw lesions in infected elk lungs that ranged from a slight interstitial hyperplasia to large areas of fibrosed, non-functional tissue with extensive emphysema in areas where large masses of worms blocked the bronchioles.

Morbidity or death of elk with lungworms usually is tied to other factors, such as overstocking and forage depletion (Banfield 1949), abnormally severe weather, poor nutrition or heavy tick infestations (see Worley 1979). Honess and Winter (1956) thought that even light infections with lung-worms were a drain on vitality that predisposed elk to winterkill.

The question of strain differences between *D. viviparus* found in cervids and domestic cattle has been answered. Cross infections can occur but strain differences exist. Thus, although data are limited, lungworm from cattle have been shown to infect elk, moose and black-tailed deer more readily than cervid lungworm infect cattle (Gupta and Gibbs 1971, Presidente et al. 1972, Presidente and Knapp 1973).

Summary

Generally speaking, parasites are not much of a problem for elk. Total worm numbers in individual elk usually are few, and associated problems are minimal. An elk can be expected to host several and perhaps many species of parasites during its lifetime. In most situations, the host is little the worse for wear. Although, in times of stress from poor

Infections of lungworms, *Dictyocaulus viviparus,* in the smaller airways of the lung of an elk can be common in overwintering calf elk. *Photo courtesy of William M. Samuel.*

nutrition or severe weather, the role of parasites in host morbidity and mortality increases.

More commonly, specific parasites become important for elk in specific situations. For that reason, the issues of translocation of meningeal worms and liver flukes along with elk and aesthetic concerns of hydatid cyst and bladderworm are emphasized. In addition, the biologies of locally important psoroptic mites and potentially important winter ticks were reviewed because of these parasites' real or perceived importance. There is little doubt that meningeal worm, psoroptic mites and liver flukes cause mortality of elk, but significant impacts on populations of hosts have not been documented. Of these, *P. tenuis* of elk in eastern North America is likely the major parasite of management concern because of its impact on eastern elk and potential to be introduced into the West with farmed elk.

Miscellaneous Conditions

Capture Myopathy (Exertional Myopathy)

Capture myopathy is a noninfectious condition arising from prolonged or extreme muscular activity. It could more correctly be termed exertional myopathy, because the condition does not occur only following capture. Muscular damage is related to such physiologic imbalances as decreased blood and muscle pH, hyperthermia associated with intense activity, and localized hypoxia (Williams and Thorne 1996). Unfortunately, capture myopathy is an all too common sequel to capture of elk (Lewis et al. 1977, Smits 1992, E. S. Williams unpublished files:1995), although it generally is avoidable with proper management. Capture operations should be planned carefully to assure that (1) the amount of the time elk are highly stressed and directly handled is kept to a minimum, (2) elk are not worked in hot weather or during the heat of the day, and (3) transport of the animals, if required, uses appropriate enclosed trailers. Exertional myopathy appears to be associated closely with elevated temperatures during trapping, pursuit, restraint and immobilization.

Clinical signs observed in elk with capture myopathy are variable. Occasionally, animals may die suddenly after capture or handling; this may be due to systemic acidosis and shock. The more usual presentation is stiffness or lameness, reluctance to move, weakness, inappetence and depression. Muscle damage usually is symmetrical. The onset of signs may occur hours to days after capture, and duration of clinical signs is variable, possibly lasting weeks to as long as a month. Some affected animals may progress to recumbency, insensibility to surroundings and death. Severely affected elk may become emaciated. Rupture of the gastroc-

Capture or exertional myopathy generally can be avoided with proper management and planning. Efficient capture, minimal handling, cool temperature and animal comfort (minimized stress) are important considerations. Perhaps most important is that persons capturing or otherwise handling captive or immobilized animals be trained in the best techniques, are aware of the disease's symptoms and have knowledge of remedial responses. *Photo courtesy of Harold C. "Red" Palmer.*

nemius tendons, with resultant dropping of the leg and loss of weight bearing may occur in severely affected elk (Lewis et al. 1977, Haigh and Hudson 1993).

Prognosis for elk with clinical capture myopathy is poor; severely affected elk often die. If this disease affects free-ranging elk, such as those trapped or translocated, they undoubtedly are predisposed to predation.

Significant changes in blood chemistry occur in elk with capture myopathy (Lewis et al. 1977). Although a variety of alterations occurs, measurement of enzymes circulating in the blood commonly is used to assess degree of muscle damage in the live animal. Greatly increased values of enzymes found in the blood due to necrosis of muscle cells, creatine kinase and aspartate aminotransferase, may be detected in affected animals (Williams and Thorne 1996). High serum levels of creatine kinase presumably reflect active or very recent muscle degeneration and damage. Normal mean values of creatine kinase and aspartate aminotransferase in elk are approximately 349 and 90 to 96 units/L, respectively (Haigh and Hudson 1993), although normal animals may have values that fall within a large range. In animals with capture myopathy, values of creatine kinase and aspartate aminotransferase may exceed 10,000 units/L. Absolute diagnostic values cannot be given, because there are causes of increased enzymes other than capture myopathy. These enzymes are relatively labile in the blood. Therefore, for accurate testing, blood samples must be collected and handled properly.

The lesions of capture myopathy have been well described (Bartsch et al. 1977). Elk that die acutely after severe exertion may appear essentially normal on gross examination. Typical gross lesions of capture myopathy are bilateral areas of hemorrhage, edema and paleness of muscle masses. The most commonly affected muscles are the large muscles of the thigh, hip, shoulder and back. In advanced cases, muscles may appear pale, dry and chalky, in marked contrast to normal, adjacent muscles. The microscopic lesions in affected muscles are characteristic.

Diagnosis of capture myopathy usually is relatively straightforward: history of capture, immobilization, transport or exertion; onset of clinical signs within several weeks; typical elevations in blood enzymes; and typical gross and microscopic changes in the musculature.

Handling elk in conditions that lead to development of capture myopathy should be avoided; treatment of severe capture myopathy is seldom successful (Wallace et al. 1987, Spraker 1993). Immobilized elk can be monitored for hyperthermia and the animals should be cooled when their body temperatures increase above approximately 107°F (41.6°C). Cooling an animal the size of an adult elk obviously is very difficult; water or snow can be rubbed into the coat to the skin, and captured animals should be shaded. Administration of intravenous fluids to maintain hydration and sodium bicarbonate to ameliorate physiologic acidosis also have been attempted. These treatments—which have been of variable value—should be given only by individuals experienced in veterinary treatment and with appropriate physiological monitoring.

Routine treatment of elk with vitamin E/selenium injections also has been suggested because of the pathologic similarities between capture myopathy and a nutritional disease related to vitamin E or selenium deficiency called white muscle disease. Selenium injected at the time of capture is unlikely to prevent development of capture myopathy because damage already may have been triggered. Selenium deficient soils are found in some areas of elk range, and supplementation may be helpful in those areas. However, many elk ranges have adequate or excessive amounts of selenium, and supplementation of animals from those areas is not appropriate.

It is the responsibility of those handling elk to prevent capture myopathy; capture and handling of elk should al-ways be conducted using techniques to minimize occurrence of this disease. The danger should be weighed carefully against the scientific or management benefits to be gained when wild elk are handled (Williams 1993).

Neoplasia (Tumors)

Tumors are not commonly reported in elk. This probably is not due to a lack of susceptibility, but because neoplasias usually occur in older animals. The age structure of hunted populations of elk, or where significant predators are present, tends to be skewed toward younger animals. In general, tumors are only significant to the individually affected animal and not to the population. They are of interest to comparative medicine and to hunters that might find tumors in harvested elk.

Benign tumors, which grow by gradual enlargement, are of little consequence unless they occur in such critical areas as the eye or brain. Malignant tumors (sarcomas and carcinomas), which grow by local invasion and metastases, may cause life-threatening disease. Diagnosis of the type of tumor and determination of malignancy usually requires microscopic examination of formalin-fixed tissues. Inflammatory lesions may be confused with neoplastic disease if histopathologic examination is not conducted. For example, a case of osteogenic sarcoma (malignant tumor of bone) was thought to be actinomycosis (lumpy jaw) on gross examination (Drake 1951).

Generally, localized tumors do not harm the quality of

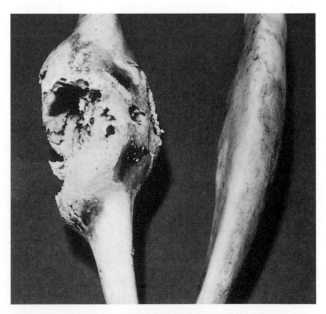

Ventral view of an elk's mandible showing boney lesions of lumpy jaw. Lumpy jaw is usually caused by infection by bacteria, such as *Actinomyces,* and can cause the elk to have difficulty chewing. *Photo by Bart W. O'Gara.*

vension, but animals with systemic or disseminated neoplastic disease that cause visible abnormalities in visceral organs or the carcass should not be consumed. The cause of neoplastic disease in elk, with the exception of fibromas, is not known.

Fibromas (warts) are benign, usually small, pigmented tumors of the skin and occasionally the digestive tract of elk (Kistner et al. 1982, Williams 1982, Moar and Jarrett 1985). They are relatively uncommon in elk, in contrast to deer, in which they are frequently observed (Fay 1970, Sundberg and Lancaster 1988). Fibromas in deer are caused by a papillomavirus, which probably also is the case in elk. Fibromas are removed from the carcass with the hide and do not affect the quality of the meat.

A variety of other tumors have been diagnosed in elk. Benign tumors include melanoma (Williams 1982), embryonal nephroma (Snyder et al. 1979b), seminoma (Seefelt and Helfer 1980), Leydig cell tumors (Haigh and Hudson 1993), uterine myxoma (Williams 1982), and thyroid adenoma (Boyd 1970). Malignant tumors include undifferentiated carcinoma involving the pericardial sac and epicardium (J.D. Herriges and E. S. Williams unpublished files:1986), astrocytoma (Snyder et al. 1981), meningeal sarcoma (Snyder et al. 1981), nephroblastoma (Snyder et al. 1979b), lymphoma (Kistner et al. 1982, Haigh and Hudson 1993), osteogenic sarcoma (Drake 1951), myxosarcoma (Snyder et al. 1979a), myxofibrosarcoma (Haigh and Hudson 1993), hepatic tumors (Haigh and Hudson 1993), and renal carcinomas (Haigh and Hudson 1993). Some of these were incidental findings at necropsy; others caused death of the animal.

Intoxication

Intoxication, or poisoning, rarely is reported in elk. However, elk undoubtedly are susceptible to a variety of toxins, as are domestic ruminants. The best documented toxicologic problems in elk are related to consumption of locoweed. Most cases have been reported from Colorado and New Mexico (Adcock and Keiss 1969, Wolfe and Lance 1984). An outbreak of "locoism" in New Mexico was associated with poor range conditions. Clinical signs included emaciation, weakness, incoordination, muscular trembling, posterior ataxia, lethargy and blindness. Although gross lesions are not specific, microscopic lesions were characteristic and consisted of finely vacuolated cytoplasm in many epithelial and nervous system cells. Locoism was not considered to be a significant mortality factor in the herd, but Wolf and Lance (1984) believed that locoweed intoxication could impact herds restricted to ranges with abundant locoweed.

Tule elk died after ingestion of poison hemlock (Jessup et al. 1986). Sixteen elk (which represented 13% of a herd) died

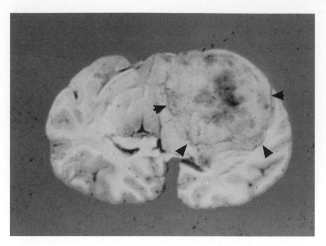

Arrows above delineate an astrocytoma (brain tumor) in the brain of a 12-year-old cow elk. Tumors are rarely recognized in free-ranging elk and do not have significant impact on elk populations. *Photo by R. B. Davies.*

over a 50-day period. Affected elk were depressed, uncoordinated or recumbent, and unaware of their surroundings. Some elk had convulsions, and others made groaning vocalizations. The mortalities were believed to be associated with unusual conditions that included early emergence of poison hemlock, limited range for the elk and overpopulation.

Although not recognized as a problem in elk in North America, "ryegrass staggers" has been reported in elk in New Zealand (Mackintosh et al. 1982, Brooks and Cahill 1985). This disease is caused by ingestion of a neurotoxin produced by an endophyte fungus that grows on perennial ryegrass pasture. The toxin damages the cerebellum, resulting in staggering, incoordination and occasionally death in affected elk. Elk appear to be more susceptible to poisoning by this plant than red deer (Brooks and Cahill 1985).

An unusual outbreak of foxglove intoxication was reported in farmed red deer in Scotland (Corrigall et al. 1978). Clinical signs included weight loss and unexpected mortality with fluid and often bloody intestinal contents. This plant intoxication is unlikely to cause problems in free-ranging elk in North America.

Fluorosis or ingestion of increased amounts of fluoride may result in damage to teeth and bones (Shupe et al. 1984, Vikoren and Stuve 1996). Reported cases have been associated with smelters, causing downwind disposition of fluoride particulates on vegetation consumed by elk.

Anomalies

Anomalies usually refer to defects in development; they frequently are present at birth, but others may become apparent as the animal grows. The cause of developmental defects usually is not known. Some may be genetic defects; others may be the result of toxic, nutritional or infectious insults during gestation. Anomalies are not commonly reported, and generally only affect single animals.

Murie (1951) reported anomalous antler development and an antlered cow. Some antler deformities may be due to previous trauma resulting in damage to the germinal cells at the base of the antler or due to hormonal disturbances (Carrasco et al. 1997). Copper deficiency may have been the cause of antler anomalies in Tule elk (Gogan et al. 1988). Other reported anomalies in wild elk include abdominal hernias (Murie 1951), corneal dermoid (R. B. Davies personal communication:1977), cleft palate (Gogan and Jessup 1985) and brachygnathia inferior (undershot jaw) (Gogan and Jessup 1985).

Snake Bite

An unusual case of snakebite was reported in captive elk in Colorado (Miller et al. 1989). Seven of 11 elk were bitten by prairie rattlesnakes; clinical signs included painful swelling of the face and muzzle, submandibular edema, difficult breathing, bloody nasal discharges, tearing, loss of appetite, anxiousness and depression. All elk survived after treatment, and the lesions resolved within 3 to 5 days. Snakebite undoubtedly occurs in free-ranging elk, but its occurrence must be rare and mortalities even less common.

7

Adaptive Behavioral Strategies

To explain the behavior of elk, one must logically link elk actions to their morphology, anatomy, companions, environments and history. Behavioral ecology now casts animal behavior into a systems perspective, legitimizing the notions of strategy and tactics, as a way of organizing processes coherently. This is taken from military planning, a good introduction to which is *Strategy,* by military historian Lidell Hart (1967). A strategy aims to fulfill a goal, which is the outcome, product or result of a strategy. Biologists have been shy to use these words on the mistaken fear that they imply teleology, or the conscious setting of goals. Unfortunately, the terms strategy and tactics often are confused—the latter being merely the enabling actions of the former. Tactics, in turn, depend on tactical requirements, which, translated into biology, mean habitat factors. As shown below, there is utility to organizing adaptations logically within strategies, or better, *adaptive syndromes* (as I prefer to label them to avoid confusing strategy with tactics).

The elk evolved into a fairly competent long-legged "cursor" (Gambaryan 1974, Geist 1998). Its goal is to escape predators by a strategy of rapid and sustained flight while trying to disorient pursuers by various tricks and, thereby, to lose itself in vast expanses. This security adaptation typically is found in ungulates from fairly open plains, where flight is impeded by low irregularities (e.g., small shrubs, rock rubble, tussocks, gullies and gentle changes in elevation) in the flight path. This strategy minimizes costly body lift and directs expended energy into forward propulsion, while allowing runners to avoid obstacles that might impede speed or block flight. This strategy generates a characteristic body form or morphology, which identifies long-legged cursors as such. It differentiates them from short-legged cursors, which seek flat, unobstructed ground for flight, from "saltors," which combine fleeing in long jumps with hiding in thickets, and from "rock hoppers," which seek security in cliffs. Cursors evolved from saltors. Saltors lift their bodies high with each jump to clear obstacles, but at great cost in energy. Consequently, saltors are short-winded. The sika deer, a species similar to the ancestors of elk, is a classic saltor (Gambaryan 1974).

Long-legged cursors, characteristically, keep their heads high when running, probably to see, identify and avoid obstacles. They appear to place their legs with great precision, but in variable fashion so as to avoid obstacles or gain better footing. That requirement has consequences to leg and shoulder structure, as great and complex muscular forces are required to place the hooves in a fraction of a second on exactly the spot identified visually, or face the possibility of a stumble and near-certain death from the predators in pursuit. Cursors, as open plains dwellers, thus, are likely to have larger eyes and, presumably, better vision than do saltors, which typically dwell in forests. Cursors are expected to exhibit superior endurance and speed, and this demands proportionately larger chests to accommodate large lungs and heart, with large diameter tracheas for quickly conducting respiratory gasses. As plains-adapted cursors, elk may rely less on scent orientation during flight do than savannah-adapted European red deer, which have large tail glands to leave scent trails; the tail glands of elk are small.

The adaptive syndrome of a cursor also requires highly developed, large young at birth, high milk production and quick growth rates, so that the young quickly reach "survivable" size (Geist 1986b, 1991a). That demand biases against twinning; it favors maternal investment in only one young. It also favors an extended gestation period, so as to grow a large neonate and extend maternal protection to the young as long as possible. In nonterritorial breeding species, for example, hierarchically breeding species, the demand to produce a highly developed young favors large antlers or horns on breeding males, as these are a proxy for the male's ability to gather resources above the basic needs of maintenance, body repair and growth. These are, of course, just the qualities required by a female to ensure that her daughters will be good exploiters of available resources; therefore, they will be able to bear large babies and give abundant milk. To be effective, courting males advertise

their ability to live in luxury (virgin habitats or those with highly seasonal plant communities) and grow large horns or antlers, and successful females must select such mates. The following constellation of attributes is a related adaptation: endurance, high speed, running with elevated head, large lungs and heart, a specific body form, a specific choice of open habitats, large babies, rich milk, luxury display organs in males and concomitant, showy courtship displays. Attributes that appear out of place when viewed in isolation are logical and integral parts of a security strategy, or an adaptive syndrome. An adaptive strategy, when treated as a hypothesis, enables a classic hypothetico-deductive approach to test the hypothesis, which in turn, leads to discovering new facts about a species. It is a means of organizing unequal elements into meaningful, logical patterns.

Cursorialism is not the only security strategy of elk. Like other species frequenting open spaces, elk also adopted the security strategy of the selfish herd, in which individuals associate closely to minimize the prospect of selection by predators. Many characteristics of elk attest to this strategy (Dehn 1990). When dwelling in thickets, however, neither cursorialism nor selfish herd behaviors are adaptive, and the elk relies on hiding for security (Roosevelt 1902, Van Dyke

Elk are long-legged cursors, well adapted for running with their heads held high to better identify and avoid obstacles. *Photo courtesy of the Wyoming Game and Fish Department.*

Bearing a single, highly developed calf that grows to "survivable" size quickly is correlated with the survival strategy of being a cursor. This demand favors an extended gestation period for calf development and giving birth to a single calf that has sole access to its mother's milk. *Photo by Dave Daughtry, courtesy of the Arizona Game and Fish Department.*

1902). This is not a strategy evolved by elk, but one inherited from its forest-dwelling ancestors, as is the elk's strategy of hiding newborn young in cover—a widespread and presumably ancient and successful means of seeing young through the critical first month of life (Lent 1974). The presence of these traits, as well as its large, but not very specialized teeth, implies that the elk still is in the process of becoming a cursor. Because they live on open plains, cursors commonly are faced with dusty grass and herbs as food, and such grit is abrasive on teeth. Consequently, dwellers of grassy plains can be expected to have teeth greatly specialized to deal with the abrasive food. However, the elk, while having the largest teeth relatively and absolutely among the *Cervus elaphus,* has rather modest teeth compared with those of grazers such as bison or horses.

Also, for elk to grow large, "bragging-size" antlers, they require a diet of mineral- rich plants. However, grasses are highly deficient in nutrients for antler growth (Vogt 1936, 1948). These conflicting demands may slow elk adaptation to open steppe and cursorialism, because elk must revisit areas with mineral-rich forage during antler growth, and such forage consists primarily of the foliage of shrubs, trees and meadow herbs. That is, elk must live a significant part of their lives in cover to meet growth demands. As a result, they must be adapted to both forest and plains. Accordingly, elk should be opportunistic and thus likely to spread rapidly in space given the opportunity. In fact, and as should be expected, elk are more widely spread and occupy a greater range of biomes than do the more primitive Eurasian red deer races.

The foregoing illustrates another point about adaptive syndromes: following one syndrome limits further evolutionary options. Cursorialism and the selfish herd place the elk into the realm of abrasive food. Consequently, both security strategies help move the elk from browsing to grazing, with implications for the shape and function of teeth and other feeding organs. Cursorialism places the elk in wide open spaces, which also has consequences for social signals. Most signals must reach farther and, therefore, increase in strength. Life in the open promotes noisier, showier and smellier actions. Elk also are the least sexually dimorphic of *C. elaphus,* with females being closer to the male in external appearance and size. This, too, is typical of plains-dwelling ungulates (Geist and Bayer 1988)—a consequence of competition between males and females within the herd. Females mimic the age class of males with which they most likely compete (Geist 1974a). Yet, for all the "pull" of the open plains, elk also retain old, proven adaptations, such as hiding neonates and a mixed feeding strategy.

The sexes also may differ in their respective emphasis on adaptive syndromes due to differing behavioral goals. The

To grow large antlers effective for self-advertisement, elk require a diet of mineral-rich plants. However, grasses are relatively deficient in the nutrients needed for antler growth. *Photo by Leo E. Barthelmess.*

primary goal of the female appears to be to ensure security for the calf. Thus, female elk should favor security over food. Bulls, however, must favor food over security if they are to grow large body size and massive antlers. Otherwise, they chance failure in the breeding season. In all this, females have an advantage here over males—they must only optimize, never maximize, the size of young at birth, as maximization would lead to dystocia and possible death of both mother and child. Bulls, however, must maximize forage throughput to reach large body and antler size. This difference in emphasis ecologically segregates females from males (Geist 1982).

The adaptive syndrome also helps clarify in ecology the meaning of niche. Adaptive syndromes or strategies deal with processes and are equivalent to "Elton's niche," or the profession of the species (Elton 1933). The *result* of these processes places the animal into specific locations at specific times, which can be abstracted quantitatively by the "Hutchinson's niche" (Hutchinson 1958). Elton's niche is *process;* Hutchinson's niche is the *result* or *end product* of that process. Elton's and Hutchinson's niches are complementary, inasmuch as the latter is the logical consequence of the former. Elton's and Hutchinson's niches are different sides of the same coin. Elton's niche (process, activity or *strategy*) invariably generates Hutchinson's niche (space, dimension, habitat quality or *result of strategy*). Elton's niche predicts and explains; Hutchinson's does neither, but it offers a technique for precise quantitative comparisons of niches. Grinnell, who was the first to use niche, described niche as both process and place (Pianka 1994).

Adaptive syndromes also arbitrate an old debate in animal behavior, namely, to what extent animals are driven haplessly by reflexes, as opposed to adjudicating between several possible options and, thus, acting "intelligently" (Marler and Hamilton 1966). One begins by identifying the primary goal of organisms—maximizing reproductive fitness—as evolutionary theory suggests. One can deduce at least seven enabling goals that help maximize reproductive fitness.

1. The individual must minimize expenditures of energy and nutrients on maintenance, so as to have maximum resources available for reproduction. Whenever possible, the individual must apply Zipf's (1949) Law of Least Effort, because metabolic energy is difficult to obtain, expensive to process and inefficient in use (Brody 1945, Kleiber 1961).

2. The individual should maintain homeostasis (that is, a functioning body) by avoiding danger from all sources (predators, parasites, pathogens, climatic calamities, etc.).

3. The individual must create and maintain access to scarce resources essential for reproduction (and, by definition, succeed in obtaining more than an equal share to maximize reproductive fitness). Interspecific and intraspecific competitions, thus, are unavoidable (see Geist 1978b).

4. It must directly reduce the reproductive fitness of potential competitors by whatever means (see Geist 1978b).

5. It must take advantage of opportunities to use resources (and move opportunistically to capture these resources)

6. It must support individuals with identical genes in proportion to relatedness (this is the kinship hypothesis of sociobiology, as reviewed in detail by Wilson [1975]).

7. It must mate with individuals of equal or, preferably, superior abilities to itself in fulfilling the enabling goals identified above.

The number or kind of enabling goals is not important. Important to note, however, is that, although these goals apply simultaneously to maximize reproductive fitness, they cannot possibly be executed simultaneously. Consequently, individuals must choose which rule to follow—or even whether to follow any of the rules. They cannot be deterministic, but must be fundamentally judgmental. Whatever the dictatorship of reflexes and instincts, there must be a broad field of choice and options about what behavior to use. There is evidence to suggest that, the more extreme and unpredictable in climate the habitats they inhabit, higher terrestrial mammals rely increasingly on options and less on instincts. This is reflected in increases in brain size with latitude (Geist 1978b).

Much of the ecology and behavior of elk is explained by adaptations to seasonal occupation of cold, high latitudes and altitudes. Timing of births is set by the availability of high-quality food needed for late gestation and lactation. Thus, births must occur just before the vegetative green-up in early summer. In turn, this dictates the timing of mating, which depends on the length of the gestation period. With a gestation period of about 250 days and a peak of calving in early June, courtship and breeding must occur in the latter part of September. Because calving must occur during a narrow window of opportunity (calves born too early would suffer from poor milk yield—a result of poor forage available to cows—whereas those born too late may fail to grow to survivable size by late autumn), the rut must be relatively short, which demands tremendous energy expenditure by the bull. This selects for bulls storing large depots of fat during summer. Fat deposition by bulls is required not only to subsidize energy demands during the rut, as bulls reduce feeding, but also to heal massive injuries they sustained during battles over breeding opportunity. Each bull can expect about 50 antler punctures per rutting season, and each cow about half a dozen (Geist 1986a). Thus, the "exhaustion" of bulls after the rut may reflect more than the depletion of fat; it may also be due to bulls healing from injuries and infections. The costs of rutting and injuries are reflected in reduced body and antler growth by red deer (Vogt 1948); severe injuries are likely to express themselves as asymmetries in subsequent antlers (Davis 1987). Females fatten less and use their reserves to subsidize energy requirements in winter.

Many differences between elk and other ungulates trace back to the origin of elk as an Old World deer. Social behavior is very resistant to change, as both the sender and receiver of signals must change simultaneously and concurrently (Hofer 1972). Consequently, elk share much of their social behavior with other Old World deer, despite great morphological and ecological differences between them. Old World deer differ greatly in social behavior from New World deer. Findings valid for elk need not be valid for such distant, New World cousins as moose, caribou or white-tailed deer.

Also, differences between elk populations are expressions of differences in environmental quality. The red deer, as a species, is remarkably plastic in growth and behavior and is able to adjust itself to a great extreme of environments.

Body mass in males from poor, infertile habitats may be only one-fifth of that of males from very favorable habitats. Translocations have demonstrated that small red deer brought to regions that held big deer, assume the size and characteristics of those big deer. Conversely, deer translocated from regions with large deer to regions with small deer change to small body size within a few generations (Beninde 1937). Nutritional experiments have shown that it takes about five generations to change small-bodied into large-bodied deer and that large-bodied deer placed on poorer forage quickly respond with poor, asymmetrical antler growth, low rates of reproduction and illness (Vogt 1948).

A subsequent analysis of these nutritional experiments showed that enlargement of body size also led to increasing distinctness of subspecific antler characteristics (Geist 1998). An earlier review of this phenomenon (Geist 1978b) showed that consistent resource shortages under maintenance conditions led not only to environmental dwarfing, but also reduced reproductive performance and produced deep changes in individual behavior. Similarly, provision of luxury conditions, rapidly resulted in large body size, high reproduction, luxurious development of secondary sexual organs and exuberant behavior. Nutritional changes thus reflected, at one extreme, the common maintenance conditions and, at the other, the rare conditions of colonization of favorable habitats. In other words, the respective morphological and behavioral changes are adaptive under conditions of maintenance versus colonization. Consequently, these phenotypic extremes were labeled maintenance and dispersal phenotypes. They are not genetic, but normal epigenetic expressions of genomes in response to resource availability in the environment. This plasticity of response to environment has great practical implications to taxonomy (Geist 1991b, 1992), management and even to human health (Geist 1978b, 1989b).

As a general rule, elk increase in body mass from south to north. Because their geographic range ends at about 60 degrees north, one cannot see the decline in body size that befalls other ungulates and carnivores that live north of that latitude. Accordingly, body size increases up to about latitude 60 degrees north and, contrary to Bergmann's rule, rapidly declines at higher latitudes (Geist 1987a, 1990a). The elk may be too mobile to reflect an expectation arising from this; as altitude and latitude compensate, we expect mountain elk to be bigger than sessile, lowland elk at the same latitudes. In Canada, the reverse is found; lowland populations in Manitoba and Alberta are larger bodied than Rocky Mountain or Roosevelt elk. Whereas Eurasian red deer are smaller in maritime than in continental climates (Beninde 1937, Mitchell et al. 1977), elk from North America's moist Pacific coast are some of the largest. It appears that local environmental factors, such as quality and temporal patterning of nutrition, override the expected differences.

History is vital to understanding elk. The elk of North America, along with populations of red deer in Outer Mongolia and southern Siberia, are the most highly evolved of the *Cervus elaphus,* as they are the most cursorial, the most divergent in social characteristics, the most cold-adapted and the largest (Geist 1998). These are consequences of the species having lived and evolved in Beringia, an area of contiguous land, encompassing (during glacial times) what is today Alaska and eastern Siberia (see Chapter 1). Modern elk evolved here in the late Pleistocene. From Beringia, it spread west into Asia and east into North America. Along with other eastern Siberians, elk colonized North America after megafaunal extinction, where, freed from competition with the primitive forest elk (Izubr stag) and other red deer subspecies, elk spread widely across many habitat types, including Pacific rainforest, prairie, high mountains, eastern hardwoods and even sagebrush deserts. Only North America's southern deserts barred elk dispersal. In its native northeastern Asia, the elk is narrowly confined to the open, high, subalpine steppe, as found in the Tien Shan Mountains, the High Altai and northern Mongolia. The lowlands to the east and north are occupied by the primitive Manchurian forest elk, and the valleys draining the Tien Shan are occupied by the small, primitive Lop Nor stag, a close relative of the better known Buchara stag. Both of these red deer subspecies are closely tied to dense riparian vegetation. Their closest relative, the Manchurian forest elk, spread postglacially northward, wedging between the Asiatic and North American populations of advanced, cursorial elk (Geist 1998).

The ecological difference between advanced elk on the two continents is explained by elk entering lower North America after megafaunal collapse. Elk had previously been part of the late Pleistocene fauna of Alaska and eastern Siberia. They became benefactors of the demise of North America's species-rich Rancholabrean fauna. With the extinction of many specialized herbivores and predators after the last glaciation, elk entered into an "ecological vacuum" and prospered. The narrow habitat range occupied by advanced elk in Asia today reflects competition with other red deer subspecies. These subspecies, distinct in social organs and behavior, act much like good species by occupying different habitats. In North America, however, the few native species that survived megafaunal extinction did not preclude elk from colonizing virtually every plant community between the southern deserts and the boreal forest. The ecological differences between advanced elk in Asia and in North America illustrate, therefore, the opportunism of the elk: unless excluded by competitors or carnivores, elk can live virtually anywhere, provided there is security and abundant food year-round (irrespective of its adaptations to eastern Siberia). Elk that were bred, born and raised within the city of Banff in Banff National Park, Alberta, are benefactors of an artificial urban environment and demonstrate the same point.

As a high latitude/altitude deer evolving in cold climates, elk must change food habits seasonally. They are forced to do so by snow, ice, blizzards, floods, phenologic changes, dryness and wetness, but also by seasonal plant productivity. Elk must have the physical attributes to forage for and digest a multitude of foods. Elk thrive where there is no dense species-packing, because northern areas are inherently poor in species diversity, and megafaunal extinctions made them even more so. Consequently, North American elk must have been under reduced selection for interspecific food competition.

It appears that elk were unable to colonize North America as long as the Rancholabrean fauna was intact, although there may have been an unsuccessful southward advance by elk from Alaska about 40,000 years ago judging from a recent skeletal find in Alberta. Elk remains become abundant in North America only after megafaunal extinction. However, the inability of elk to colonize North America in earlier interglacials is not a complete surprise. In addition to evolving under highly seasonal northern conditions, elk apparently were subjected in Eurasia to fundamentally different selection pressures than were large Rancholabrean herbivores. Eurasian and North American Pleistocene faunas apparently were controlled by different factors. The Eurasian fauna appears to have been resource (food) limited, whereas the North American fauna appears to have been predator limited (Geist 1998). In a food-limited fauna, herbivores are expected to improve feeding organs progressively and to exhibit progressive declines in body size via efficiency selection. In a predator-limited fauna, extremes in antipredator adaptations are expected, plus large body size, large luxury organs, but little improvement in organs of feeding. Also expected is that severe predation pressure selects for relatively clever, large-brained prey and predators (Jerison 1961). That expectation is met in the comparison of Rancholabrean survivors and East Siberian post-Pleistocene immigrants. Today, the old Americans (Rancholabrean faunal elements) are remarkably competent at coexisting with humans, whereas the East Siberians and European introductions are not. Old Americans, such as coyotes, black bears, cougar, white-tailed and black-tailed deer, pronghorn and peccaries, have little difficulty coexisting closely with humans, even in suburban and urban areas. The same cannot be said of East Siberian immigrants and other introduced European species, such as gray wolves, grizzly bears, wolverines and Russian wild boar. And, unlike American deer, roe deer and red deer do not thrive in European urban settings.

Elk act more like American fauna than Eurasian fauna in that, compared with the European red deer, they are more tractable in captivity and form urban populations when protected in national parks. Elk mingle readily with harmless humans. Therefore, elk behave similar to American bighorn sheep, but unlike European mouflon. That suggests that elk in Alaska met and coevolved with the northern extension of the Rancholabrean fauna and its large, specialized carnivores. However, unlike bison and moose, the elk was not capable of greater success. Bison and moose penetrated the North American fauna in mid-Pleistocene times and quickly evolved into huge, ornate species with distinctly improved security adaptations, represented by the long-horned bison and the stag-moose, respectively. Both species evolved much more quickly than their Siberian

As a species that developed in eastern Siberia and colonized North America in the absence of competition from related but more primitive species, elk spread rapidly across the northern portion of the continent, literally from coast to coast. These Tule elk feed on dune grasses along the coastline of northern California. Only the deserts of the American southwest and Mexico provided an effective barrier to elk colonization. *Photo by Jim D. Yoakum.*

counterparts in terms of ornate hornlike organs, but both lagged distinctly behind their Siberian counterparts in improvements to feeding adaptations. Siberian moose continued to evolve a specialized muzzle, whereas bison improved cheek teeth. When the next and last wave of Siberians entered North America postglacially, the bison had advanced teeth and the moose a very distinctly shaped muzzle that apparently was suitably adapted to feeding on aquatic plants (Geist 1998). Thus, both were advanced in feeding adaptations over their deceased Rancholabrean counterparts, but were primitive in antipredator adaptations and possessed much smaller horns and antlers.

North American elk also act like old Americans by competing poorly when confronted by Eurasian forms. This can be deduced from the fate of North American and Eurasian deer introduced to New Zealand and Europe, or the fate of native deer when facing feral Asiatic species (Geist 1995a, 1998). Furthermore, elk were not abundant when many potential competitors were alive, such as in Pleistocene Alaska (Guthrie 1966) when elk shared the range with mammoth, bison, horses, camels, etc. Elk were hunted by early hunters, beginning about 11,800 years ago (Hoffecker et al. 1993). Elk probably entered southern North America during the Younger Dryas cold spell (11,000 to 10,000 years before present) along with a wave of Siberian bison, but archeological data suggest that they were not common until post-Colombian times, after European diseases and warfare eliminated most of the American native people in the 16th century (McCabe 1982, Cronon 1983, Kay 1990, Cowan 1995). Pre-Colombian North America appears to have supported human populations dense enough to exploit, severely, the larger big game species, including elk. Once freed from the predation pressure of Native people, wildlife flourished in unprecedented numbers during the next 250 years, until the heavy hand of white man nearly depleted many species of North American wildlife (McCabe and McCabe 1984, Geist 1996; see also Chapter 3).

The recent influx of elk into southern North America also is revealed by adaptive deficits. One would expect that elk in California, experiencing short winters, would have an antler retention time no longer than do red deer, about 150 days; however, Tule elk retain antlers about 185 days after the rut (McCullough 1969), as do the elk along the Pacific coast (Harper et al. 1967). Red deer shed the velvet as early as late July and then move about with cleared antlers for some 60 to 80 days before rutting. North American bull elk begin to rut right after casting velvet. Tule elk, however, do something that their recent Siberian ancestry and incomplete "adaptation" to warm climates can explain—bulls begin to join females and rut *before* they have cast velvet (McCullough 1969).

This may be explained as follows: if one assumes that females maximize neonatal security by dispersing neonates in *time* (as well as in *space*), one would expect a temporal spread of the birth season in southern latitudes. That spread requires an extension of the rutting season, which can be accomplished by advancing the beginning and retarding the end of rutting activities. That is, as cow elk come into heat *earlier* as well as *later* in the year, bulls, to be successful, are obliged to follow to reproduce. That, however, pushes the beginning of the mating season progressively closer to velvet shedding (and eventually *ahead* of velvet shedding). Consequently, bulls must begin courting and fighting before they complete antler development and before velvet shedding.

There is expectation that, while evolving as exploiters of ecotones in highly seasonal environments and in periodic contact with the species-rich Rancholabrean megafauna (Martin and Klein 1984, Van Valkenburg and Hertel 1993), elk adjusted rapidly by learning. This expectation was fulfilled in part by elk adjusting to humans in North America, but also by the enlarged size of cervid brains, with respect to latitude (Kruska 1970). Also the brain size of Ice Age mammals generally was larger than those of species from earlier epochs (Jerison 1961). Moreover, experimental studies suggest that brain size increases with the diversity or complexity of environmental stimulation (Krech et al. 1960, Cummins et al. 1973, Zimmerberg et al. 1974, Greenough 1975). Experimental studies in New Zealand by Batcheler (1968) and Douglas (1971) on red deer showed that the animals' ecology could be profoundly altered by experience. Craighead et al. (1973) and Mitchell et al. (1977) emphasized the same for elk and red deer, respectively.

Therefore, postglacial elk in North America became part of a new, low-diversity, megaherbivore-free fauna of Siberian immigrants and small-bodied surviving Rancholabrean opportunists. Due to the fauna's recent assemblage, there has been neither close coevolution between species nor close adaptation of the Siberians to North American climates and landscapes. That is, today's North American large mammal fauna is much less closely adapted to the land and to each other than are older faunas (i.e., those in Africa and Asia). In evolutionary terms, North American fauna is immature.

Accordingly, overlap in food habits between American deer and elk is expected. Compared with the findings on food habits and morphology in species-packed African herbivores (Owen-Smith 1988), elk are a plastic, opportunistic ecological generalist, with mouth and rumen morphology not much refined by efficiency selection. Also, considerable seasonal change in the structure of the elk digestive tract is expected, because the species frequents many types of habitat, and moves about seasonally. Local differences in food quality may contribute to these movements, shown by Bützler (1974) for red deer.

For many reasons, elk are expected to adjust behaviorally to climatic and edaphic changes. Consequently, it should not be "hard wired" in its behavior, but instead, be a "learning machine." As such, elk will defy rigidity in its ecology, and perform inexplicably, unless an investigator knows what the elk had learned and was putting to good use. Yet, elk, as ecological generalists, actually are specialized to survive ecological change.

General Foraging Strategies

Compared with the ancestral red deer, elk are more Plains adapted, have a greater preference for grasses, possess absolutely and relatively larger cheek teeth and have a rumen as large as grazers (Prins and Geelen 1971, Hobson et al. 1975, Van de Veen 1979). The rumen structure is complex and the papillae reminiscent of grazers (Hofmann 1985, Hofmann et al. 1976). Nevertheless, the elk is classified as an *intermediate feeder*—a forager not fully adapted to a diet of coarse, fibrous forage (Church and Hines 1978; see also Chapter 5). The massive need for minerals during antler growth may keep the elk tied to forests and highly digestible foliage and forbs, despite its adaptations to open Plains (Mitchell et. al. 1977). Moreover, as cold-adapted Siberians, elk should select only relatively fine-fibered plants, C-3 (northern, cool climate, alpine) grasses and foliage only modestly defended by secondary compounds (Johnson et al. 1968, Jordan 1971, Klein 1986). The size of elk demands a large, absolute amount of food that, in cold climates, would be relatively more digestible than food in warmer climates. Therefore, elk, which were originally adapted to high-quality northern forage, should struggle with coarse, toxic forages common to low latitudes and altitudes. It is thus significant that the phenotypically small California elk has, on average, the largest tooth rows and most complex molars (McCullough 1969). Did the tough-fibered C-4 (warm climate) grasses and well-defended plants of the American Southwest stop the southward expansion of the ubiquitous elk beyond northern Mexico (see Bryant and Maser 1982)? Other northern grazers, such as bison, mountain sheep, mountain goats, euceratheres, forest musk oxen and mammoths, also failed to spread beyond northern Mexico. (Note: advanced elk occupy high elevations in central Asia and New Zealand; whereas, red deer and primitive Manchurian elk occupy low elevations [Heptner et al. 1961, Smith 1974]. Compared with red deer, elk have spread little in New Zealand [Smith 1974, Challies 1985], a fact which may relate to competitive inferiority.)

Seasons of the North generate great forage abundance and scarcity, which leads to an opportunity for large herbivores to store energy and nutrients during seasons of abundance for use during seasons of scarcity. In addition, such savings are used by bulls to pay the high cost of rutting. Thus, red deer intake of food in summer is three times the winter intake (Van de Veen 1979). In Alaska moose, the winter intake is six times the summer intake (Gasaway and Coady 1974). Because food is very inefficiently converted to fat, relatively large amounts of food need to be processed to fatten northern elk. This may be relevant to understanding why bull elk are shorter-lived than red deer stags. A northern form, such as the elk, adapted to fine-fibered forage is likely to suffer severe tooth wear on forages from southern latitudes. Bulls suffer much greater tooth wear than do cows (Flook 1970a). Also, red deer males grow larger and store more fat than do hinds. The size of the bull elk's dentition apparently has not kept up with the demands placed on it. Tooth row length in bulls exceeds that of cows by about 3% (McCullough 1969, Hutton 1972), or 6% to 9% in mass. However, elk bulls have a body size about 28% larger than cows, or a "metabolic" size 21% larger than that of cows. This means that the demand placed on the bulls teeth exceeds that of cows by about 15%. However, no differential tooth wear by sex was found in red deer (Mitchell et al. 1977).

By virtue of being larger, elk ought to have a lower metabolic cost than red deer and use their fat stores more efficiently. Thus, a 575-pound (260 kg) cow elk, with 20% of her body weight as fat, is expected to survive 72 days on that fat (assuming 100 kcal of maintenance costs per kilogram$^{0.75}$ of lean body mass), compared with 56 days for an equally fat red deer female weighing 220 pounds (100 kg). Because elk may be two to three times heavier than red deer, they are expected to survive a winter one-third longer. Conversely, elk could survive on much poorer forage than red deer could in a winter of equal length and severity, as elk would require a smaller fraction of the daily food intake to be satisfied by winter forage. These theoretical expectations suggest that elk are driven to high food consumption in summer. One possible correlate is that, to maximize food intake, elk may take chances with predators.

As indicated above, elk appear to be able opportunists that readily take advantage of circumstances. Food is not a defendable resource for elk, and they are not expected to expend much effort contesting feeding by other elk. Rather, they are expected to move on to feed wherever possible. Also, elk are not indicators of "wilderness." On the contrary, they are benefactors of human-made ecological havoc. This is a legacy of the Ice Ages, with the great oscillations in climates and young ecosystems on disturbed, fertile soils. The deer family may have done better during the

Ice Ages than other ruminants, because the nutrient demands of antler growth made them flourish in habitats with high nutrient densities. Disturbed sites tend to be covered by plants of early ecological successions, as are glacial landscapes that are fertilized continually with glacially eroded loess and silts (Geist 1978b). Whereas nonmigratory elk kept a recognizable kinship structure on permanent patches of grassland on California's coastal beaches (Franklin and Lieb 1979), elk in logged-off areas were socially quite labile (Harper et al. 1967), as were nonmigratory elk in Michigan (Moran 1973), both of which exploited small forest clearings created by heavy snow falls. Elk also may move opportunistically to patches of high-quality forage, because as cursors that invest in large young at birth and high milk production, increased maternal care by the cow toward her calf demands a high plane of nutrition. This may extend even to yearlings in the absence of calves (Altmann 1963a, Lowe 1966, Schloeth 1966, Smith 1974).

Law of Least Effort

Although foraging strategies aim at maximizing the intake of nutrients, the law of least effort (maintaining energy expenditure) ensures economic expenditures of ingested energy and nutrients. Individuals must strive to satisfy the opposing demands. The law of least effort results in testable predictions:

1. Repetitive, predictable routines by individuals and a fidelity to seasonal home ranges, minimizing costly exploration and arousal,

2. Choosing to feed where the snow has been blown away, or is shallow and soft,

3. Moving in single file through deep snow,

4. Changing food habits with snow depth and hardness (Formozov 1946, Geist 1971c),

5. Abandoning ranges when food is scarce and search time is long (so that waves of dispersal follow food shortages [Heptner et al. 1961]),

6. Remaining with patches of abundant food and abandoning lengthy migrations (as do elk that use hot springs in winter in Yellowstone National Park [Craighead et al. 1973]),

7. An inverse relationship between roaming and forage density (if so, individual home ranges in summer ought to be smaller than in winter and spring, as was verified for elk [Knight 1970 and Craighead et al. 1973]), and

8. Minimize expenditures in social interactions (this has not been quantitatively investigated in elk, but in bighorn sheep, the cost of social behavior, as measured in heart beats, follows Zipf's law entirely [MacArthur et al. 1982]); that is, behaviors are used predominantly in inverse proportions to their cost.

Whether elk seek out dense coniferous cover to conserve energy (Beall 1976) or to ensure security cannot be decided at present. One can argue that, in choosing a roof over its body, an elk avoids exposure to the great heat sink of the sky on cold, clear winter nights (Folk 1966). However, this may be incidental to seeking out cover for hiding. Sunlight increases in intensity with elevation (Hamilton 1973), so an

Elk, bulls that enter the winter after the stresses of the mating season and cows that enter the winter after the stresses of lactation, must maximize energy conservation during the winter. The law of least effort predicts that elk should, therefore, establish and maintain predictable routines during winter, choose to feed where search time is minimal, move single file through snow, and abandon ranges when food is scarce and search time is long. *Photo courtesy of the Wyoming Game and Fish Department.*

animal exposing itself at higher elevation in winter would absorb more radiant energy. However, that is hardly an explanation for why bulls in winter are found at higher elevations than cows.

Following Hamilton's (1973) color theory, elk should have a problem getting rid of heat during exertions. Consequently, during warm, sunny weather, they would be better off with a coat that reflects, rather than one that absorbs the sunlight. Elk that need to be active in the open on warm days should avoid loading solar heat into their bodies. Elk, as Siberians from open landscapes and rutting in early autumn, would be subjected to high ambient temperatures and high solar load during the mating season. Because rutting bulls are expected to shed more heat than do cows, Hamilton's color theory predicts a lighter, dorsal body coloration in bulls, and that is the case. Tule elk are exposed to the highest ambient temperatures and solar incidence, therefore ought to be the lightest in color, and that appears to be true (Murie 1951). Other large mammals to cross open Beringia into America, which mate during warm seasons, such as moose, bison, musk oxen and grizzly bear, also have light-colored backs. In contrast, caribou and Stone's sheep, which rut later in the year, during cold weather and short days, have dark backs, as does the Alaskan coastal brown bear, a dweller of dense forests.

Security Strategies

As previously indicated, elk are cursors (runners), whereas the ancestral sika deer, at the opposite end of the spectrum, are saltors (jumpers). European red deer, judging from body form, occupy a position in between (Gambaryan 1974, Geist 1998). The primitive sika deer is a skilled hider, but it runs with little endurance and may be exhausted in 20 minutes or less (Gambaryan 1974). European red deer and elk, however, are very enduring. This is known from records of European parforce hunts, in which stags were chased by hounds and horse, and from occasions in North America when elk were pursued by horse. Probst (1737) warned that up to three rallies of hounds and horses may be required to chase a red deer stag to bay. Döbel (1754) expected a chase to last 2 to 5 hours, except those for fat red deer stags during August, which could be brought to bay in as little as half an hour. Even with several rallies of horses and hounds, chases could last several hours, and failed chases could be expected. Red deer stags often bested horses and hounds. There is a record of one stag hunt (Roedle 1971) that covered 10 Prussian miles (1 Prussian mile = 7,532 m); the Count of Anhalt Dessau killed eight horses while bringing that stag to bay. A description of 19th

century parforce hunting in England (The Duke of Beaufort and Morris 1886) suggested that it was less demanding than earlier hunts on the continent. The English stags were smaller, and English hunters were likely to be mounted on thoroughbred horses that were faster and with greater endurance than possessed by horses from earlier centuries. The hunt master at Exmoore in England, nevertheless, needed two horses for each hunt, as the chases could last for hours. In a recent study of red deer hunted with horses and hounds, Bateson and Bradshaw (1997) reported that the mean distance traveled by 64 hunted red deer was 11.87 miles (19.1 km [standard deviation = 7.39]), and the mean duration of the hunt was 3.12 hours (standard deviation = 1.21). The chase was episodic, with deer running hard for short periods followed by hiding or relative inactivity. Deer hunted during spring (with low body fat) ran more extensively than did deer hunted during autumn.

Aroused red deer had three tactics to shake pursuing horses and hounds: run into a group of other deer; double back along their own flight path; or run into water. Between patches of cover, the stags ran rapidly over open ground. Cover appears to be a vital tactical requirement for red deer to shake pursuing predators. Yet, without the keen participation of the huntmaster in deciphering the ruses and leading the dogs quickly back on track, the pack would very likely lose the stag, although running stags give off large amounts of scent that dogs may detect several hundred yards downwind. Eventually, persistent hounds and experienced huntmasters usually brought a stag to bay, often in water, where it confronted the dogs with lowered antlers. Experienced hounds stayed back, allowing hunters to perform the coup de grace. Small red deer could be killed by the pack, even by a few hounds that strayed from the pack.

The experiences of the parforce hunters suggest that it would be difficult for a wolf pack to catch any but exhausted, injured or ill red deer. However, they might be able to capture fat stags during August. During their long history, red deer have had to deal not only with wolves, but with many other predators, such as tigers, lions, leopards, lynx, various saber-toothed cats, dholes, hyenas, many forms of bears and canids, as well as humans. In North America, the small puma is a surprisingly effective predator of elk (Hornocker 1970), but only where elk depend on forest.

In North America, mounted hunters did not have an easy time with elk that departed at a trot into hilly, rocky, broken terrain. Such escapees were difficult to catch up with, even for hunters mounted on very good horses. There are anecdotes of mounted hunters following fleeing elk for days. Elk, clearly, used the vastness of that landscape to their advantage as they kept on moving, not returning to where they had been spooked, as mule deer or whitetails are likely to do. However, on level, dry, unobstructed Plains, the old Spanish Californians, mounted on spirited horses, readily ran down and lassoed elk. Cavalry officers in the West used greyhounds to chase elk and were quite successful at it. Bull elk were more easily run down than cows or yearlings. Mounted hunters were at a disadvantage once elk reached broken terrain where they maintained speed for a long time; whereas, horses had difficulty with the footing (Caton 1877, Roosevelt 1902, Van Dyke 1902).

Selfish Herd

As expected in an ungulate from savannah and steppe, elk use the selfish herd strategy as a means to avoid predation. Advantages and disadvantages of this antipredator strategy are as follows:

Dilution Effect. Because the chance of being taken by a predator for any individual is diluted in proportion to the number of companions in a group, the larger the group, the lower the chances of any single individual being taken. At least theoretically, this appears to be the most important effect (Dehn 1990).

Position Effect. Because predators are more likely to take an individual at the periphery of a group than at the center, the safest position to be in is the middle. Also, the larger the group, the smaller its periphery to the area it covers, and the lesser the chances for an individual to be on the periphery.

Straggler Effect. In a large herd, there is a high likelihood that one or several weak members occur and in flight, will rapidly fall to the rear and become prey. Consequently, being healthy is prerequisite to life in the selfish herd; injured individuals are expected to leave the herd and seek security in hiding.

Many-eyes Effect. The more individuals in a group, the greater the potential for predator detection. However, vigilance per individual drops in herds, so this effect contributes minimally to security (Dehn 1990). Moreover, it operates best during daylight, whereas the sounds made by many individuals at night may serve to mask a predator's approach.

Confusion Effect. This sets in when many individuals run in different directions past a predator, obliterating the individual initially targeted.

As anticipated from the above, the more open the landscape, the larger the groups of elk or red deer (Lowe 1966, Clutton-Brock 1974, Franklin et al. 1975, Redgate 1978). Elk tend to avoid obstacles to running, such as logging slash (Black et al. 1976), deep snow (Craighead et al. 1973) and boggy ground (Murie 1951). Flight leadership falls to a calf-leading cow, one with many social bonds; cows hanging

When aggregating in open terrain, elk use a selfish herd strategy, grouping to reduce the risk that any given elk will be attacked by a predator, offering the greatest protection to elk near the center of the group, maintaining maximum likelihood of detecting a predator before it comes near enough to launch an attack, and maximizing the confusion confronting a predator when many elk flee in different directions. *Photo courtesy of the U.S. National Park Service.*

Classic confusion effect of elk behavior just commencing during the charge of a grizzly, which unsuccessfully chased one group after another for more than 10 minutes (see Chapter 9). *Photo by Kim Hart.*

back and watching tend to have few social bonds (Franklin and Lieb 1979).

Although elk are large, they rarely confront and attack large predators. Also, bull elks do not defend calves against predators, as do musk oxen or American bison bulls. Only one observation of a cow elk turning to face a wolf is available (Cowan 1947b), and no ganging up on wolves has been observed (Carbyn 1975). However, cow elk, alone or in company, readily turn on and chase the smaller coyote, striking with front hooves at the small, but often persistent predator.

Safeguarding Calves

To safeguard calves, elk have retained the ancient strategy of hiding calves until the calves reach a size at which they are capable of escape by running. For elk, it is adaptive—climate permitting—to disperse their calves as much as possible in time and in space. Such dispersal minimizes the likelihood of encounters between predators and young. A long birth season is only possible in southern climates, such as in California, where calving lasts about 50 days (McCullough 1969). In the North, the relatively short productivity pulse demands synchrony of calving, lest milk production falls outside the most productive time of the year. Timing of births lasts some 22 days in Montana (May 21 to June 12) (Johnson 1951) and 20 days in Banff, but 45 days in Jasper National Parks (Flook 1970a).

The elk calf is a typical hider with a spotted coat, a crouch or prone response in the face of danger, and a minimum of scent that predators can detect (Johnson 1951). It probably selects its own hiding place, as do other hiders, such as neonate deer, except caribou and moose (Dathe 1966, Bromley 1976, Walther et al. 1983). The calf normally blends into its surroundings as it lies flat on the ground.

The mother removes evidence of its presence by ingesting its urine and feces (Youngson 1970, Arman 1974), and also eats the birth membranes and licks off the birth fluids. She visits the calf relatively rarely while it is in hiding and may attack minor predators or decoy away larger ones (Altmann 1963a, McCullough 1969). She may lead the calf to a safer site if predators become conspicuous. However, faced with a pack of cooperating coyotes, a cow elk is likely to lose her calf. While some pack members engage the cow, distracting her, others kill the calf.

Cows and their calves vocalize with each other. The alarm bark of a cow makes small calves drop to a prone response, but causes older calves to run to her. A cow locates her hidden calf by a nasal whine, which may be repeated until the calf responds; the calf may bleat loudly in distress (Murie 1951, Harper et al 1967, McCullough 1969).

The elk calf is a typical hider, with a spotted coat and a minimum of scent, that depends on hiding silently in the face of danger during the initial 4 or 5 days after birth. *Photo by T. W. Moran.*

As expected in a classic hider, the suckling periods of elk calves are few, but long (Lent 1974). In the closely related red deer, there are only four to six visits per day (Bubenik 1965). This compares with more than 10 sucklings per day for caribou (Lent 1966, 1974). For California's Tule elk, suckles averaged 40.3 seconds (range, 15–120 seconds) (McCullough 1969); in caribou, 32 seconds (Lent 1974). For reindeer Skogland (1989) found much longer suckling durations (94.1–61.5 seconds in the first week), which varied with forage availability to the female. Cow elk usually initiate and terminate suckles (Harper et al. 1967, McCullough 1969). And, elk milk is as rich as that of red deer (Geist 1998).

There is one exception elk have made in their neonate's biology to cursorial life on cold, coverless Plains—they bear fairly large calves. The elk calf at birth is relatively as large or larger than the follower-type caribou calf, although some African antelope bear noticeably larger hider-type young (Geist 1998).

The elk hiding phase lasts probably as long as in red deer—about 4 days (Bubenik 1965). Following the hider phase, elk calves may be bedded together while the cows graze close by (Altmann 1963a). Confronted with danger during the calf's hiding phase, a cow typically will flee. The transition from hiding to a normal mode of security—which is to group in the open, outrun predators and relocate distantly in space—takes about 16 days (Wallace and Krausman 1991). As a calf grows, the amount of attention paid to it by its mother appears to diminish. The cow may join other cows in the vicinity of the birth site within a day after birth (Harper et al. 1967). Nursery herds reach their maximum size within 6 weeks after birth (Franklin and Lieb 1979).

The hider strategy of the elk would be compromised should the offspring of the preceding year, now a yearling, follow its mother to the birth site of the new calf. By doing so, it could attract predators and cause the calf to miss-imprint on the yearling instead of the mother. And it might compete with the calf for milk. Consequently, there is a sharp separation of the cow and the yearling about 2 weeks before the cow gives birth (Altmann 1963a). Cow elk are more hostile to male yearlings than to female yearlings, and also are hostile to other cows about the time of parturition (Franklin and Lieb 1979). Whereas male elk and red deer yearlings are more likely to wander or join other male yearlings, bull groups or strange nursery groups, female yearlings are likely to be found close to their mothers once the latter return with their calves to normal herd life (Lowe 1966, Mitchell et al. 1977, Franklin and Lieb 1979).

Clearly, once a calf joins a herd, it must not detract from the efficiency of this unit in escaping predators. It is very much on its own in the herd and must learn to avoid harm on its own; there is little assistance from the mother. Calves may suffer some abuse from adults, such as displacement from good feeding spots (Murie 1951, Harper et al. 1967). Cows in nursery herds are minimally involved in strife and do not intervene on the side of their calf if it is attacked. Cows repulse strange calves and allow only their own to suckle (Altmann 1952, McCullough 1969). On rare occasion, a yearling may suckle, but it is not known if nourishment is gained, or whether it suckles on dry teats, as documented for mountain goats (Hutchins 1983). In all this, elk do not differ from European red deer (Linke 1957, Bubenik 1965).

During alarm and flight, calves "heel" and stay close to their mother (Altmann 1963a). When separation does occur, the cow appears to return to where she last saw the calf (McCullough 1969). The distress call of the calf may attract not only its mother, but other elk as well (Altmann 1963a). The calf has some difficulties recognizing its mother for at least the first 2 weeks of its life (Altmann 1963a, Harper et al. 1967). The female appears to recognize her calf by its scent. Zoo experience suggests that ungulate mothers improve in mothering with subsequent births (Hediger 1955). Observations of captive moose indicate that females virtually imprint on the mothering process (Lent 1974, Knorre 1974, Baskin 1987).

Calves form groups within the somewhat dispersed, grazing nursery herd. The calf group appears to focus attention on a particular female for protracted periods of time, much as happens in mountain sheep (Geist 1971c). This gives rise to the notion of "baby sitting" (Altmann 1952, Harper et al. 1967). I suggest that calves baby sit adults, not vice-versa. To focus on one adult would, in the event of sudden danger, minimize confusion. Alarmed calves initially would bolt after the adult on which they had been focusing, and locate their respective mothers later. In emergencies, this would minimize indecision and waste of precious time by calves.

When something unusual is detected by elk, they do not necessarily bolt, but instead explore the unusual stimulus. This allows them to match the response to the danger, in accordance with the law of least effort. An alarmed elk usually assumes an erect alert posture, keeps its eyes on the source of disturbance and struts in a stiff, rather unusual gait. It may "bark" repeatedly. Alarm barking ceases once it takes flight. Because alarm strutting and barking are relatively rare events and contrast sharply with usual elk behavior, they are expected to attract attention (Figure 136).

Elk illustrate the basic, ancient way in which deer have safeguarded their young. The greatest deviations from this model are found in caribou and moose. Caribou, as good cursors, evolved follower-type young, rich milk and facultative (nonobligatory), synchronized, saturation calving; cari-

A young cow elk in alarm posture, with head held high and strutting in an unusual, stiff gait in which the forepart of the body is raised on the forelegs. Alarm barks, not uncommonly, are uttered from this posture. *Photo by Valerius Geist.*

bou also may disperse at parturition and hide in inaccessible areas such as forests or on high, bare mountain ridges (Bergerud et al. 1984, Bergerud 1985, Skogland 1989). Moose deviate from the hider model as large, aggressive females defend their young. That defense fosters the close maternal bond of moose and much of the characteristic biology of moose. Nevertheless, when hard-pressed, caribou and moose calves revert to the old way of avoiding harm and drop into a stiff recumbent position, preferably within cover (Lent 1974, Skogland 1989, S. Mahoney personal communication: 2000).

Newborn calves of elk, moose and caribou—all large cold-adapted species—do not appear to be affected much by hypothermia. For small-bodied young, however, hypothermia does matter (Geist 1971c). Tiny young must be born into fairly high ambient temperatures, therefore birth may be deferred to a warm season, as with roe deer, or to a warm nest, as with wild boar (Briedermann 1986). By constructing a large, sheltered nest in which the sow broods her tiny young, wild boars are freed from seasonal constraints on giving birth, and may farrow anytime, even in winter—provided food is available (Oloff 1951).

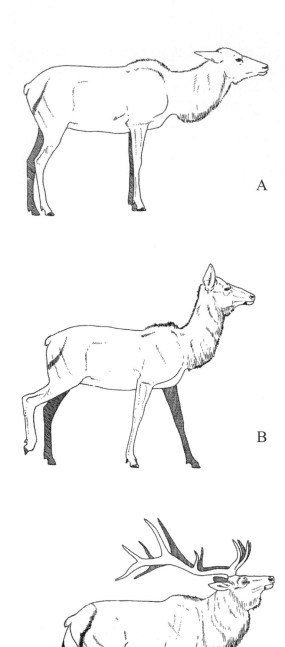

Figure 136. Social signals are conspicuous deviations from the everyday activities of a species. (*A*) The normal stance of a calm, secure female elk. It has no direct signal function and is paid no attention by other members of the herd. However, (*B*) draws attention at once. It is the stance of an alarmed cow elk investigating something unusual in the distance, and may be accompanied by hair raised on the tail and rump patch (and possible release of tail gland scent) and a very loud alarm bark. (*C*) A bull elk in full flight. Its behavior not only alerts other elk, but is likely to trigger imitation. All run away. *Illustration by Valerius Geist.*

Antipredator Strategies of Bulls

The ecology of male and female elk follows different interests. To maximize inclusive fitness, females must rear a maximum number of calves beyond the dangerous neonate stage. Because males do not contribute material resources toward raising their offspring, they must inseminate as many females as possible to maximizing fitness. If females are unable to select consistently the male they will accept for mating, then males must dominate competing males to breed. Consequently, they must prepare themselves before sexual competition for the stresses and strains of conflict. Body mass is very important in winning combat (Clutton-Brock et al. 1982, Miura 1984), therefore, to grow large, males must *maximize* their forage intake.

Females, however, must *not* maximize forage intake during gestation. If they did, their neonates would likely be so large as to get stuck in the birth canal or die of dystocia (become damaged internally by passing through too narrow a birth canal); either of which might also kill the female (see Geist 1971c). Instead, females must always *optimize,* but never maximize, birth size. Accordingly, food intake is less critical to pregnant cow elk than to bulls. Therefore, cows can compromise food in favor of security. However, to maximize body growth, bulls must compromise security in favor of food. Consequently, males may tend to exploit rich pockets of forage of questionable security.

Although this trade-off accounts for many differences in behavior between sexes in dimorphic ungulates (Geist 1982, Shank 1982, Jakimchuk et al. 1987, Sukamar and Gadgill 1988), it is not the only factor. There may be straightforward differences in resource requirements between sexes, such as the need for more water by lactating mule deer, which requires them to stay closer to water sources (Bowyer 1984), or the ability of the males (due to relatively larger rumen) to digest fiber better (Bell 1971, Staines et al 1982, Bowyer 1984, Beier 1987), which allows them to compensate and feed on coarser forage (Dziciolowski 1969, McCullough 1979, Shank 1982, Clutton-Brock et al. 1987a). It may also be that females, by close grazing, preclude males from obtaining enough forage on core female ranges, analogous to small-bodied sika or fallow deer grazing an area so closely that red deer cannot share the area (Kiddie 1962, Challies 1985). Females, needing absolutely and relatively less food, have more time to be selective and can exploit smaller bits of high-quality forage. Therefore, they can live in areas with low forage density and need to move less than males (Ordway and Krausman 1986). Males may be evicted outright by females, as in mountain goats (Geist 1978b), decline to compete for food

with the females they inseminated (Geist and Petocz 1977) or, in long mating seasons, segregate from active social life to recover body condition (Geist 1974a, Prins 1989). It may also be that stags, crowned by sensitive velvet antlers, select open areas where antlers are unlikely to be irritated (Verme 1988a).

Sexual segregation is evident in elk at spring green-up, when the elk diet shifts from grasses to forbs and foliage (Knight 1970), which are richer in nutrients and minerals (Vogt 1936, 1948). This predicts that elk should shift from open to shrubby areas, as Knight (1970) showed. One also expects group size to decrease as elk move into cover. That, however, was found only for bulls; cows remained in relatively large groups (Knight 1970). The postcalving gregariousness of cows is understood best as a security strategy to protect calves; bulls are free to take chances.

As calves grow and become better runners, cow herds decrease in size and cows move progressively farther into bush (Knight 1970). The hypothesis also predicts that cows without calves should act as bulls do in their choice of company and foraging areas. That remains to be verified for elk, but cow moose without calves did join bull groups (Geist 1963).

To maximize body and antler growth and fattening, bull elk can choose small, productive forest meadows. There, surrounded by nutritious forbs and foliage and hidden by cover, bulls live solitary and secluded, and minimize contact with predators. Compared with cows, bulls roam farther afield in search of rich forage pockets, have larger home ranges and are less attached to those ranges.

Elk males behave independently (Altmann 1952, Lowe 1966, Franklin and Lieb 1979). Male yearlings only rarely make contact with their mothers after segregation (Linke 1957, Lowe 1966, Schloeth 1966, Bützler 1972). Adult bulls colonize an area well-before cows (Flook 1970, Mitchell et al. 1977), are seen less frequently than cows in open areas (Franklin and Lieb 1979), have larger home ranges in summer (Lowe 1966, Franklin and Lieb 1979) and appear to have less home range fidelity (Mitchell et al. 1977). In hiding, bulls appear to be less vocal than cows. Cows can be very noisy in nursery groups.

Generally, bulls practice a less secure antipredator strategy than cows and should suffer higher mortality (Flook 1970a). After the rutting season, however, when there is very little body growth, bulls do not choose the security of large cow groups, as do caribou, roe deer, even mule and white-tailed deer males, because the bulls, being Old World deer, retain antlers long after the mating season, which would be conspicuous in female company. Exhausted bulls, healing their many injuries (Geist 1986a), are not likely to have the stamina that cows have in running,

Large elk and red deer stags (Raesfeld and Vorreyer 1978) go into seclusion after the rut. Subsequently, bulls band together, choosing terrain laden with obstacles for culling predators. Compared with cow/calf band habitat at that time, bulls may be found at higher elevations, on steeper slopes and in deeper snow. In dense rainforests of the Pacific coast, bull elk may remain alone in winter (Franklin et al. 1975).

This behavior of elk and other Old World deer contrasts sharply with that of the New World deer that normally shed their antlers soon after rutting terminates. In addition,

To maximize antler growth, bull elk generally select small productive forest meadows, maximizing potential nutrition by selecting a variety of forbs and foliage and minimizing energy expenditure. *Photo by Jim D. Yoakum.*

Large elk bulls, like red deer stags, typically go into seclusion after the rut. Bulls band together, selecting terrain laden with obstacles to detain potential predators, allowing the bulls to recuperate from rut-associated injuries and energy expenditures. *Photo by Ray Rogers; courtesy of the Idaho Department of Fish and Game.*

which surely would be detected and targeted by predators (Bromley 1976, Geist and Bromley 1978). Not only would large bulls be vulnerable to culling predators, but each bull caught would teach the successful predator to look for more bulls in mixed herds. Consequently, exhausted males, or any ill, injured or otherwise conspicuous elk should shun female company. Young bulls not exhausted by the rut are safe in female herds as they can run as fast and as far as females. Therefore, many small bulls but not many large bulls are expected to occur in cow herds after the rut, and that is found universally in the red deer species. And it is expected that cow and bull elk are vulnerable differentially to predation, and they should flee in different directions when disturbed by predators, and that often is the case (Altmann 1952). Also, bulls avoid cows, such as when bulls vacate an area they colonized *after* cow elk move in (Flook 1970a).

caribou shed the long-haired, white neck mane. Without their gender markings, the males join female groups. That is, males appear to camouflage their presence in the herd by means of *female mimicry*. Antler and horn shedding in New World deer and pronghorn (Bromley 1976, Geist and Bromley 1978), display hair shedding in bison (Lott 1979) and subsequent joining of female herds by the males appear to be antipredator strategies in all these species. Moose, however, upon shedding antlers, do not become more social. Rather, antler shedding appears to trigger discord and dispersal among males. That is ecologically significant: antler shedding takes place just before the snow increases in height and hardness, thereby impairing the movement of moose. Consequently, each bull faces the long period of deep, hard snow *in isolation*. Moose in deep snow can move little and closely crop the limited supply of browse. This limited food supply could be shared by several moose only to the detriment of all.

Bull elk casting antlers, as in moose, become aggressive and disperse (Knight 1970). Keeping antlers all winter, consequently, allows bulls to live in the security of the selfish herd with a minimum of strife—an option foreclosed to moose. As Lincoln (1972a) showed for red deer stags, the experimental removal of antlers led others to attack the deantlered stag. There is at once a drop in gregariousness after red deer stags cast antlers; stags with cast antlers are subject to harassment by antlered companions (Linke 1957, Lincoln et al. 1970, Bützler 1972, Raesfeld and Vorreyer 1978). Stags without antlers also are disadvantaged when feed is in short supply. Retaining antlers in winter thus allows a male to keep its identity among companions and compete for forage. It is noteworthy that antler casting in elk coincides with green-up and appears to initiate dispersal from wintering grounds. In a large enclosure in Czechoslovakia, red deer stags dropped their antlers in relation to rank; the more aggressive, larger antlered stags shed earlier (Bartos and Hyanek 1982, Bartos 1985).

If performing sparring matches creates a stable, low-cost social milieu among wintering bulls, then it benefits elk and red deer to retain antlers until spring. That is, retention of antlers should be directly proportional to the average length of winter. This, of course, predicts that antler casting and green-up should be correlated. Elk, as eastern Siberian mammals adapted to long winters, ought to have longer antler retention than do red deer. In fact, red deer retain their antlers for about 140 to 170 days after the rut, and elk bulls retain theirs for about 180 to 190 days (Geist 1982, 1998). Tibetan red deer, which also face long winters, also retain antlers a long time and start to rut right after shedding velvet, as do elk (see Engelmann 1938).

Cows and Calves Versus Bulls

As indicated above, cow elk appear to maximize security at the expense of nutrition, whereas bulls do the opposite. Consequently, cows should make do with the forage in secure areas, and bulls should roam and seek out the best forage. If so, cows should vary in size between populations more so than bulls, because bulls should equalize growth between populations. This is confirmed by smaller skull size differences in bulls between populations than in cows (Hutton 1972).

Calf elk feed more selectively than do cow elk because the former need less food and thus have more time to select it (Harper et al. 1967, Dzieciolowski 1969). Also, feeding patterns of calves are more erratic than those of adults (Harper et al. 1967). Calves appear to take advantage of the vigilance of their mothers and pay less attention to security, which might help explain why they are caught more frequently by cougars than are adults (Hornocker 1970). Another factor affecting the manner of calf foraging is the long lactation time in red deer and elk (Smith 1974). A long period of diet supplement by milk ensures a calf of a maximum of time of selective foraging under the watchful eyes of the mother.

Compared with bulls, cows should keep a body weight favorable to sustained running and should not fatten maximally. This, along with smaller body size (and to preclude dystocia, cows must *not* maximize birth weight), implies that cow elk should be more selective in their grazing and consume less food than do bulls. Also, obese animals probably are run down by predators more readily than lean ones. This is confirmed by the experience of par-force hunters running down red deer with horses and hounds—fat stags may be brought to bay within half an hour, whereas lean ones may run for several hours (Probst 1737, Döbel 1754). Spitsbergen reindeer, which evolved in the absence of culling predators, show the reverse pattern—stubby legs and the accumulation of much greater masses of fat than in other caribou.

Unlike some African antelope that rut year-round and convert ingested forage to work without first storing surplus energy as fat (Geist 1974b), bull elk are seasonal breeders that depend heavily on stored fat for breeding. Elk may carry 18% to 25% of their body weight as fat, whereas African antelope rarely have more than 5% carcass fat (Ledger and Smith 1964). Males that lose their fat deposits in the rut tend to become casualties (see Geist 1971c, Knaus and Schroeder 1975, Mitchell et al. 1977). Converting food to fat is energetically expensive, because for every calorie stored as fat, one calorie is thrown away as heat (Blaxter

Elk calves feed more selectively than elk cows and, on a diet supplemented by mother's milk, grow very rapidly. However, they are less alert to potential predators than cows, and many do not survive to their first birthday. *Photo by Frank and John Craighead; courtesy of the U.S. Forest Service.*

1961). Converting ingested energy and nutrients to work directly minimizes wastage. Fattening is so wasteful of forage that it could only evolve in seasonal climates in which the annual vegetative growth period far exceeds the capacity of herbivores to consume that production (Geist 1974b, 1978b, 1987a). This suggests that the quality and quantity of summer nutrition must be of paramount importance to bull elk. Its importance can be gauged in some alpine chamois populations in which bucks *defend* summer feeding territories (Knaus and Schröder 1975) or, in essence, "fattening territories."

Because lipogenesis generates waste heat, one expects that males, which fatten more than cows (Mitchell et al. 1977), will also need to lose more body heat in summer. Whether wallowing in summer in moist soil or water by bull elk and red deer stags is done to remove heat, ward off insects or serve some unknown function remains obscure. However, as predicted by the lipogenesis hypothesis, females rarely wallow (Darling 1937, Raesfeld and Vorreyer 1978).

After the rut, only bull elk that have retained sufficient fat deposits to ensure overwinter survival ought to associate freely with cows. The others should hide or form groups of their own in terrain containing obstacles for predators. At this time, bulls are debilitated not only by fat loss, but also by upward of 50 deep punctures from dirty antler tines (Craighead et al. 1973, Geist 1986a). Such wounds and their infections are costly, as shown by reduced antler growth in the summer after severe wounding (Vogt 1948).

Fires play an important role in the biology of elk. Burns

may generate patches of superior forage in climax forests. Such burns may generate habitat patches too small to exploit securely by nursery herds, but which may be acceptable for single bulls. Because wildfires cannot be predicted,

Wallowing is practiced primarily by bulls, and may aid in dissipation of excess heat during the summer. However, elk wallows are strongly identified by scent, and likely serve to advertise the presence of a dominant bull. *Photo by Michael H. Francis.*

it pays for bulls to roam, more so than cows (Franklin and Lieb 1979). Bulls should and do pioneer dispersals (Flook 1970a, Mitchell et al. 1977). Wanderings are maximum in bulls about to grow maximally (i.e., 2- and 3-year-olds) (Franklin and Lieb 1979). Young bulls (but not cows) ought to leave the maternal home ranges, as females are expected to compromise forage resources in favor of security and deplete forage on cow ranges. Consequently, a young bull cannot maximize body growth on his mother's range. Accordingly, cows encourage their male offspring to disperse by being more aggressive to those males (Franklin and Lieb 1979).

Yearling bulls are dispersed a second time by older bulls during the rutting season. Dispersal is linked to risk, as the relatively higher mortality of young bulls indicates (Flook 1970a). The mortality of bulls that are prevented from dispersing, such as among elk held in large enclosures, should be relatively lower. For free-ranging unhunted elk in Siberian nature reserves, Heptner et al. (1961) reported 27 to 33 bulls per 100 cows. For elk in Banff and Jasper National Parks, Flook (1970a) noted 37 bulls per 100 cows (Flook 1970a); in the securely enclosed Elk Island National Park, the ratio was 85 bulls per 100 cows (Flook 1970a); and in another enclosed population in Missouri, it was 55 bulls per 100 cows (Murphy 1963). However, this does not explain the great sex ratio differences between the red deer and elk. For red deer, Heptner et al. (1961) recorded 63 to 83 stags per 100 cows in protected reserves. It may be that elk rut more intensely than red deer and have a greater chance of dying. That hypothesis has yet to be investigated.

Knuckle Cracking

Although forest-dwelling ungulates emphasize stealth, silence and inconspicuousness, ungulates from open landscapes indulge in noise and conspicuousness. Elk, as ecotone dwellers, should act like hiders in cover and like gregarious cursors in the open. Indeed, elk in cover can act with deliberate stealth. However, a gregarious form that moves occasionally into cover must solve a problem, namely, how to distinguish, in cover, friend from foe. In the open, the typical noises and sights of companions keep individuals informed. In cover, however, when all are silent and out of sight or obscured, distinguishing between moving companions and moving predators when they are screened by vegetation is difficult.

The solution for elk, as well as for red deer, Père David's deer, white-lipped deer and caribou appears to be knuckle cracking. With every step, the animal emits an unmistakable click, which remains distinct no matter on what substrate the animal walks. It also differs between species. No predator emits such sounds. Consequently, friend can be distinguished from foe. In caribou, the clicking sound is heard with the placement of each foot. In red deer, I have heard it produced only by front legs. And in elk, the clicks are dull and not nearly as audible as in caribou.

Cessation of knuckle cracking or feeding noises is a signal to be on the alert. It signifies that others have become alert. This ought to arouse alarm. In addition, in response to predators elk may utter loud warning barks, a vocalization they share with other Old World deer, particularly sambar, chital and muntjacs. When highly alarmed, elk assume an erect stance, hold the head high, fixate the object of suspicion with side to side movement of the head, move off initially in a halting "warning" gait (Altmann 1963a) and then break into a hackneyed trot. In flight, elk are not at all vocal.

Harassment

There is a good body of investigation and theory on the ability of elk to adjust to human disturbance (see Stemp 1983, Chabot 1992). Batcheler's (1968) experiments are particularly noteworthy. He harassed red deer in New Zealand using hunters, and focused on red deer in good habitat, leaving those in poor habitat undisturbed. The harassed deer abandoned the disturbed areas (virtually) permanently. Because these deer shifted from good to poor ranges, their reproduction, body growth and population sizes all declined. Experimental harassment of mule deer also indicated that reproduction as well as daily activity could be disrupted (Yarmolloy et al. 1988).

Elk have remarkable learning ability, which makes possible their "domestication" on deer farms (Heptner et al. 1961, Stubbe 1972, Yerex 1979). Their actions in and out of refuges are astounding to many laymen. Away from such sanctuaries as towns and national parks, elk tend to be quite wary of humans and the danger they pose. Conversely, elk seek out secure areas and, in those areas, are generally tolerant of even close human proximity. Secure from predators, elk enter towns to feed on lawns, cross busy streets and rest among buildings. Their habituation to traffic makes them a road hazard, particularly at night. Along busy roads, there is an avoidance zone that varies in width depending on the extent and nature of the activity and the amount of cover. Once disturbed, however, elk disperse, become nocturnal, seek cover or vacate the area. I found elk in captivity to be more tolerant of humans than are most captive red deer. In harassed red deer, rutting activity may become silent and inconspicuous.

Heavily hunted elk also may "stalk" through forest, moving a few steps at a time, then stopping to look and listen.

Elk have a remarkable ability to adapt to situations where people are a regular element of their surroundings and where the actions of people are not perceived to pose a threat, as in national parks. Away from such settings, however, elk tend to be very wary of human activity. *Photo by Milo Burcham.*

Pursued elk become very dependent on cover, and their movements may become erratic.

Elk bedded down in dense pine forests are almost impossible to approach by stalking, because they detect the hunter and quickly move off, rarely even offering a glimpse. However, a hunter who rushes into a bedded elk herd can cause such confusion that the animals are vulnerable for a minute or two before they manage to organize for joint escape. The conspicuous smell of elk can be used as a guide to approach them (Frison 1991).

In heavily forested areas, elk may be quite tolerant of human activity. With their keen senses, they are able to detect and maintain vigilance of disturbance sources and are good judges of danger. Moving vehicles usually are tolerated, but those that stop cause an increase in heart rate, especially when a door is closed loudly. Heavy hunting pressure may cause elk to abandon migrations and ranges (Craighead et al. 1973), but so can disturbance by mountain lions (Hornocker 1970).

Signals

Most signals of elk are directed at companions. There are certain rules in the use of these signals, as addressed extensively by Walther (1984). Signals would not evolve unless they enhanced the fitness of the sender. In competition for material resources, for example, signals of aggression are much more economical than aggression itself, which costs energy, wounds, infections and lost opportunities. This conforms with the law of least effort. The simplest signals to indicate imminent violence are the *intention movements* to use weapons. Such movements are *threats*.

The weapons most commonly used by elk and other deer to gain access to *material* resources are the front hooves. While standing, elk may strike with one leg at companions or they may rear and flail with both front legs (Figure 137). Bulls resort to front legs as weapons when their antlers are cast or in velvet. Even bulls with hard antlers normally respond to a front leg attack by rising and flailing (McCullough 1969, Clutton-Brock et al. 1982); although, bulls may react with an antler thrust, as in red deer (Lincoln et al. 1970, Lincoln 1972b). Older mule deer does may dominate antlerless bucks, particularly young ones (Geist 1981). I have seen antlerless bull moose chase off antlered bulls in the wilds, and cow moose with young calves may also chase off large bulls in velvet (Geist 1963). Similarly, aggressive adult cow elk may dominate bulls up to 3 years of age, as McCullough (1969) observed in California elk. In all such cases, aggressive females signal a front leg weapon threat.

Because the posture using front legs for fighting requires an upright stance on both hind legs, with head held up and ears folded back and out of the way of the opponent's weapons, the *front leg threat*—universal among deer—is just the first action of fighting. An elk may snap the front hooves down hard on the ground. A moose may look back at an intruder, lay back its ears, and cock a hind leg well-before striking with that leg, in the same manner as a horse kicks. Only rarely will an elk strike out with a hind leg.

Elk retain rudimentary canines—the so-called elk tusks or bugler teeth—in the upper jaw. They may expose these in a *biting threat* by raising the upper lips and emphasize the threat audibly by grinding their teeth and hissing from a raised head with the ears laid back, and eyes rolled forward as if maintaining the pupil slit in a horizontal position (Geist 1966a, 1982, McCullough 1969, Lincoln et al. 1970, Clutton-Brock et al. 1982) (Figure 138). This threat is precursor to biting, occasionally used by cow elk on one another. In the primitive sika deer, biting is common, whereas in the tusked muntjac, severe wounds may be inflicted with the long, sharp canines (Barrette 1977c). The biting threat is found in Old World deer, but not in New World deer (although functional upper canines are found in the Andean deer). In elk, the hissing/biting threat may suddenly be followed not by a bite, but by the elk leaping upward and flailing with its front legs.

Another weapon threat is used by antlered bulls. In this threat, the antlers are snapped forward toward opponents. Invariably, it is larger bulls that threaten younger bulls in this manner. Among bulls of equal rank, threats are frequent, but for such bulls, antlers snapped forward may be less a threat than an invitation to spar. Bull elk outside the

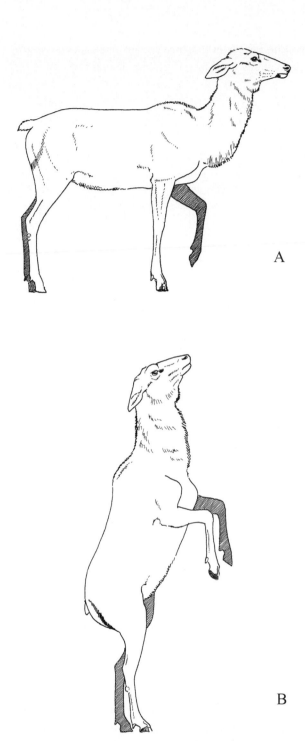

Figure 138. The bull elk, in velvet or in hard antlers, may use a head-high biting threat, usually against other bulls, in which he exposes the regressed, blunt upper canine (elk tusk) by raising the upper lip. He reinforces or draws attention to this threat by hissing. Because this head-high threat is used normally by dominant bulls approaching subordinates, the common response is to withdraw from the dominant. Elk habituated to people tend to use all or part of this threat when passing a person closely. Because subordinates ignoring this threat may be hit with antlers, it is good practice to give habituated elk always a wide berth. *Illustration by Valerius Geist.*

Figure 137. Female elk (*A*) is signaling that it is about to rise on her hind legs and (*B*) flail with her powerful front hooves at an opponent. In *A*, she performs an intention movement to use a specific weapon—her front legs. In addition, she is changing the physiognomy of her head by laying back ears, a most noticeable departure from the ear position in a normal, calm elk. Threats are intention movements with a given weapon, be it front legs, canine teeth or antlers. Cow elk and males in velvet antlers commonly use their front legs as weapons on other elk as well as on predators. Exceptionally, elk have also been seen to kick with a hind leg at predators. *Illustration by Valerius Geist.*

rutting season spar frequently and, as in other Old World deer, sparring is initiated by bulls with antlers pointing at one another, with the contestants acting as if they were of equal rank (or symmetrical sparing, discussed later).

In a head-to-head aggressive engagement, the winner may leap after the departing foe and, with its antlers, jab the foe in the side or rear. Or it may terminate the charge by slapping the ground with the front hooves, while uttering a series of sharp grunts—the "Sprengruf" of the German hunters' language. Such a ground-slapping termination to fighting is common to Old and New World deer alike. It also may be used by a rutting bull to head off cows departure from his "herded" harem. A bull occasionally catches up with a departing female and strikes her with his antlers, inflicting punctures. Mule deer use their antlers in this fashion when chasing off defeated rivals, but in its similar rush courtship, the call accelerates into roars emitted by the buck with each jump (Geist 1981).

Observations on captive elk, red deer and sika stags indicate that threatening males will pounce forward with lowered antlers in an attempt to gore an opponent whose eyes

The weapons most commonly used by elk to gain access to material resources (such as food) are the front hooves. Elk may strike out at a companion with only one leg, or two animals may stand on their rear hooves and flail away at each other. *Photos courtesy of the Wyoming Game and Fish Department.*

The biting threat is typical for many deer species. In elk, the upper lip is curled to expose the upper canine tooth while the elk grinds its teeth and hisses audibly from a raised head, with ears held well back and eyes rolled forward. *Photo courtesy Wyoming Game and Fish Department.*

are averted or who appears to be inattentive. Although female elk do not have antlers, they still "horn threat" occasionally and butt an opponent (Harper et al. 1967). I have seen red deer hinds at rutting wallows act as if they had antlers. Between bouts of frolicking, they "horned" the wallows with nonexistent antlers. They used the identical weaving motions that stags use before making antler contact when sparring.

Although elk are large, they have no distinct *defensive threat,* such as is found in moose (Geist 1963), nor diverse defenses against predators. The defensive threat in moose, its dark body color, its lashing out with front and hind legs, its carnivorelike roar during confrontations, may be related to a propensity to stand and defend itself against predators, particularly when mired in deep, hard snow in late winter. Unlike moose, elk normally do not disperse and hole up in deep snow. Consequently, elk would not be regularly tested by wolves in deep snow as is the case for moose. Elk are restricted to lower snow blankets than are moose, where they can retain mobility.

Cow elk attack coyotes with a *rush threat.* Red deer apparently grind their teeth during rush threats (Raesfeld and Vorreyer 1978). Large elk bulls occasionally use the rush threat with head elevated against smaller bulls. In wintering herds, overt aggression is not common, but it may flare up

Generally, elk are fairly tolerant of human behavior, but, when threatened, startled or aggravated, likely can respond quickly and aggressively. Rut bulls are particularly dangerous. They also may display an antler threat, whereby the antlers are snapped forward toward perceived threats (*top*), or in actual attack (*bottom*). *Photos by Kim Hart*.

if access to concentrated food is blocked by companions. Cow elk and yearling bulls have high rates of aggression (Franklin and Lieb 1979). Overt aggression also flares when elk become excited and crowded, as in response to the herding of a rutting bull (McCullough 1969). Cow elk may aggressively chase off their yearlings in spring (Altmann 1963a).

Observations suggest that, during grazing, dominant elk usurp the feeding spots of subordinates (Harper et al. 1967). It would be to their benefit to detect signs (e.g., momentarily intensified feeding or movement to another site) that subordinates have found superior forage and then locate and take over such areas, just as it would be in the subordinates' interest to hide such signs. Most material resources required by elk cannot be defended economically, therefore elk must compete with efficiency in finding, ingesting and processing forage.

Submission

Because combat is costly to elk, it pays for them to fight as little as possible. This applies even to dominants, because subordinates could retaliate tit for tat. The effectiveness of retaliation limits overt aggression (Geist 1966b). Subordinates should terminate fighting as quickly as possible. In the selfish herd, injury may be costly to the group, as injured members attract predators and the loss of each group member reduces security. Even species that are often solitary, such as white-tailed or roe deer, may group opportunistically when feeding in the open. At that time, it is in each individual's interest to minimize strife so as to maximize security and, therefore, efficiency of feeding (Geist 1978b).

To accommodate social harmony, elk have signals of "courtesy," nonaggression and submission. Submissive behavior involves a posture with depressed head, as in all deer, but similarities end there. The submissive posture is seen mainly during courtship when cows avoid bulls; while running ahead of a bull, a female, with extended muzzle and depressed ears, makes rapid chewing motions (Figure 139). There is no vocalization, as in sika or fallow deer; also, sambar females neither "jaw" nor vocalize. Jawing, as discussed later, may be more than submission. It may be a cut off signal that stops a bull's courtship advance at the cow's behest.

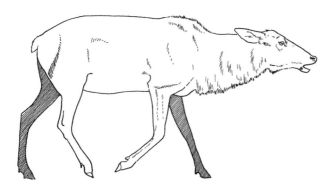

Figure 139. The submissive behavior of a cow elk withdrawing from a molesting or courting bull is conspicuous, not only because of the lowered head and neck, but also because she may twist her head from left to right while making exaggerated chewing motions. It is as if she shows the bull that she is chewing. This chewing behavior, in which the horizontal movements of the jaw are exaggerated, is a submissive signal that elk share with red deer, sika and fallow deer. Submissive elk are silent, but sika and fallow deer are not. Fallow deer females, in particular, are very loud, yapping steadily during submissive withdrawal. *Illustration by Valerius Geist.*

In deer, submissive behavior has two basic manifestations—a lowering of the body and head, and a signal that symbolizes nonaggression. The latter normally is "feeding" and, vocally, the "distress" call of the fawn. In olfaction, it is the mimicking of female odors as well as female signals by subordinate males. Muntjacs not only will crouch, but lie flat on the ground (Barrette 1977b), a posture sometimes assumed by red, fallow, sika, mule deer and sambar females confronted by aggressively courting males. This happens in captive and wild deer, such as mule deer (Geist 1981). The crouch is essentially an infantile hiding posture, which may be accompanied by distress calling in fallow and sika deer females. Red deer hinds and fawns moving rapidly away in a head-low posture may also squeak. I witnessed a captive cow elk, relentlessly pursued in a small enclosure by a large, deantlered bull. He assumed the threatening herding posture and she only opened her mouth as if to call. She crouched while urinating, in the manner of a primitive Old World deer and in sharp contrast to the normal urinating posture of female elk (Figure 140). Cow moose also vocalize softly, not unlike a distressed calf, and lower the head when withdrawing from courting bulls. Cow moose do not crouch. White-tailed deer may assume extreme submissive postures by crouching low on the ground and crawling past an opponent in this posture. Whitetail does moving through a group of mule deer does also may crouch low. When passing one another, white-tailed deer tend to crouch a little, keeping the head low.

A common courtesy behavior in deer (including elk) is *eye aversion,* which, in mule deer, is almost a ceremony (Figure 141). It is striking if big bucks avert eyes when a subordinate looks at them; it is conspicuous during breaks in sparring matches. Eye aversion initiates the turning away of subordinates from approaching dominants.

Submissive postures used by dominant deer toward subordinates become *appeasement* postures (Barrette 1977b). These may be seen when dominant mule deer bucks pursue subordinates to solicit a sparring match (Geist 1981). Because sparring matches in *Odocoileus* run by very different rules than do those in *Cervus,* in which sparring partners act as "equals," there are no appeasement postures by elk bulls. An extended distress call, however, may form part of the subordinate's behavior in sparring in Old World deer, elk included.

Feeding as a social signal is widespread in ungulates; it is especially well-described in the rituals of territorial Thomson gazelle bucks (Walther et al. 1983). In perhaps its most primitive form, the behavior is evidenced by submissive muntjacs that pick up a leaf and chew it in an apparently exaggerated manner in front of a dominant (Barrette 1977b).

Figure 140. The urination postures of the advanced elk subspecies are significant insofar as the female uses the same urination posture as does the male. In this behavior, as in aspects of her morphology and relatively large size, she is a male mimic. This is common in gregarious ungulates from open plains, whose females tend to mimic the class of young males they need to defeat in intraspecific competition. Caribou have gone even further than elk in this regard, in that female caribou have antlers and are virtually indistinguishable from yearling and 2-year-old males. *Illustration by Valerius Geist.*

Figure 141. A behavior that promotes peaceful coexistence in deer is eye aversion. It is seen nowhere more clearly than in a tight group of resting individuals. Everyone avoids looking into the face of the other. Consequently, the heads diverge as far as possible, and individuals rest so as to look at the back of heads of companions. Eye aversion also takes place in sparring matches, in which it signals a break. Here two red deer stags have just paused in sparring (from a photo by Ludek Bartos). *Illustration by Valerius Geist.*

Sparring

Sparring is a sporting engagement in which there are no winners or losers; it is neither fighting nor contest (Geist 1974a, 1981, 1982, 1998, Kitchen and Bromley 1974, Barrette 1977b, 1977c, Miura 1984, Peek et al. 1986, Barrette and Vandal 1990a, 1990b). Sparring—significant advance in social behavior—is absent in the primitive territorial species (e.g., duiker, water deer, pudu, mazama, mountain goat) whose weapons are specialized to inflict severe damage to the opponent's body surface. Sparring has evolved with gregariousness as an adaptation to the selfish herd, and functions to bond males with harmless wrestling (Figure 142). Hornlike organs in gregarious species evolved so as to function not only as weapons, but to allow the locking of heads for wrestling. Thus, wounding is unusual in sparring. A common form of antler contact, sparring must not be confused with the very rare fights. Barrette and Vandal (1990a) recorded six fights in 1,502 instances of frontal antler contact in caribou. While observing thousands of sparring matches among mule deer in seven rutting seasons, I have seen only 10 serious dominance fights.

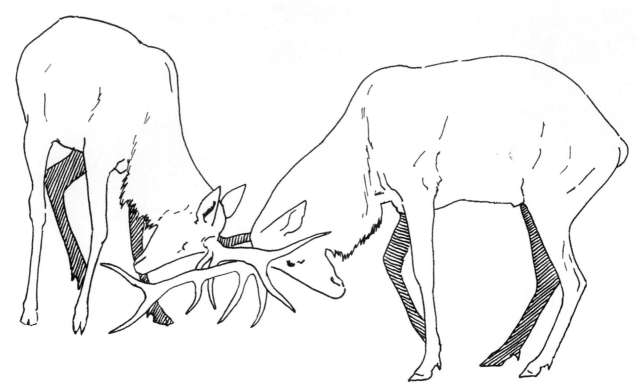

Figure 142. Sparring, a sporting engagement of weapons without loss of rank to either participant, is a consequence of life in a selfish herd (i.e., grouping with others against the threat of predation), leads to the evolution of complex antlers. Sport is a social dimension that escapes primitive resource defenders. It is engaged in by bull elk as long as they carry hard antlers. *Illustration by Valerius Geist.*

Sparring matches are often confused with fighting. When sparring, elk display and then carefully engage antlers; therefore, sparring is a means of each animal learning about his own antler size and strength relative to others. Sparring invariably is initiated with a slow approach and eye aversion by both opponents (*above*) and deliberate bobbing of antlers (*top opposite photo*). The Tule elk bulls shown are virtual mirror images. Once the sparring partners engage antlers, they twist their necks, push and evade, which leads to some circling (*second opposite photo*). This typically involves loud vocalizing. After a period of sparring, the subordinate animal (in this case, the bull on the left will initiate disengagement by moving backward slowly (*third opposite photo*), but keeping his antlers protectively pointed at his opponent. Disengagement is gradual, with neither showing any signals indicative of submission. The bulls act with restraint, as if both were dominant, and they may rejoin for further sparring (*bottom opposite photo*). *Photos by Verna R. Johnston.*

Sparring varies considerably among deer species. However, in all its variants, the social rank of the two participants is maintained, but beyond that, similarities end. Sparring in its most primitive form is found in muntjacs; it appears to allow several males to cooperate in holding a common territory (Barrette 1977a, 1977b, 1977c). In mule and white-tailed deer, sparring is a means of bonding (Geist 1981)—an activity that allows young and old, large and small to interact without loss of status or wounding. Although "rules" of sparring differ between species, they are adhered to closely by sparring partners in all cases. Sparring undoubtably fosters familiarity between males, and allows some gain in fighting skills. It probably is a low-cost, low-risk form of assessment of fighting ability (Barrette and Vandal 1990a, 1990b). It appears to ensure retention of a stable rank order in male groups.

Among red deer, with antler shedding and the loss of ability to spar, the old dominance hierarchy collapses to give rise to a much less stable hierarchy based on fighting with front legs (Lincoln et al. 1970).

Among elk, sparring matches commence with the shedding of velvet in early autumn (Altmann 1952) and continue after the rut. In wintering bull groups, sparring increases in frequency toward spring, just before the antlers are shed (Franklin and Lieb 1979). Much the same can be said of moose, except for differences in the schedule of antler shedding. Mule deer also have the pre- and postrutting peaks in sparring; in chital in the wilds, it is an ongoing activity among hard-antlered males, and thus continues year-round. Sparring matches in mule and white-tailed deer usually are extended over some time and may last even an hour. Although older bucks spar primarily before and after the rut, yearlings spar throughout the rut.

Rarely, sparring occurs among male deer in velvet. Such males appear to avoid touching the soft, growing points of antlers. A large bull moose, who accepted to spar with a yearling calf, quickly struck it with a front hoof when the latter butted vigorously into the former's growing antler stub. The calf wheeled away, stood momentarily and departed from the bull it had followed previously. Exceptionally, a mule deer fawn without antlers, may engage in a sparring match with a yearling buck. Sparring invitations by bucks to does happen rarely and, in every instance I observed, were misunderstood as a threat by the participants. There is no sparring among female deer or fawns except in antlered female caribou and calves.

In elk, sparring is *symmetrical,* in that each bull acts in the same fashion regardless of its actual dominance rank. The bulls act as equals (Struhsaker 1967, McCullough 1969, Franklin and Lieb 1979). This is derived logically from the manner in which the ritual is conducted: the participants almost exactly mirror one another's behavior, and each acts as if dominant. With experience, an observer can learn to tell which is the real dominant. The lesser male will do a few things differently (e.g., vocalize more, act less secure), and this is most evident among sparring partners that differ greatly in size and age.

Sparring partners among elk may initially approach slowly with a head-high dominance display similar to that of primitive Old World deer such as sambar, chital or barasingha. This leads to one of the actors slowly lowering its antlers toward the other, so that the other may engage. This is *soliciting.* However, the dominance approach may be absent, and antler lowering, coupled with nodding (all intention movements), may initiate the sparring match. The latter probably occurs only among well-acquainted, not very excited bulls. A soliciting bull does not spread his front legs in anticipation of a forceful lunge. Partners engage antlers carefully with weaving motions of the head; such weaving may commence when the bulls are several feet apart. Once engaged, opponents push and twist heads, but neither is very forceful. Disengagement is followed by eye aversion by one or both bulls, and one of the sparring partners may remain standing with the antlers lowered until the other again squares off.

During sparring, a bull elk (usually the smaller partner) may emit squealing sounds (Harper et al. 1967, Struhsaker 1967), as also is found in red deer (Bützler 1972), sika deer and barasingha. In red deer, the same sound is emitted occasionally by a courting stag or a small stag running from a large one (Bützler 1974).

Sparring often has a decidedly playful quality. This is particularly so in young males, who may disengage by a backward jump, followed by bobbing and weaving of antlers, and frolicling. Bull elk occasionally run side by side, frolicking, bobbing and weaving at one another (Altmann 1952, Struhsaker 1967). In spring, a large group of elk bulls moving out to feed in the evening may contain many pairs of frolicking, sparring bulls.

In elk as in red deer (Lincoln et al. 1970), sparring may escalate into a short fight, from which one opponent flees; this is a logical derivative of opponents acting as equals when engaged in sparring. However, it obscures somewhat the differences between sparring and fighting in Old World deer. Also, sparring among large bulls is noticeably more forceful than among paired small bulls. Both red deer (Bützler 1974) and elk may engage in sparring during the rut. These are relatively forceful engagements, intermediate in frequency between undoubted sparing and violent dominance fights, and lack both the extended parallel marches and runs of males about to erupt into violent dominance fights. Thus, without the intense preliminary

Sparring is almost always symmetrical; that is, it is characterized by participation by bulls of nearly identical antler size. *Top photo by Leonard Lee Rue III. Center photo courtesy of the National Park Service. Bottom photo by Len Rue, Jr.*

displays that normally precede violent combat, herd bulls in rut do engage in brief fights with other bulls (McCullough 1969).

Dominance Fights

Elk dominance fights are very much colored by a bull's need to attend to his harem. Because the bull advertises, it maximizes competition for itself by attracting rivals (Geist 1982). In red deer, most dominance fights occur at the height of the rut (Clutton-Brock et al. 1979).

A large bull elk will unhesitatingly chase off yearling bulls by rushing them in a *nose-up posture,* exposing canines and hissing—behavior not dissimilar to its herding behavior of females. However, with large rivals, a harem-tending bull acts noticeably different; he resorts first to displays instead of overt aggression. Because fighting can be very costly as a result of the high probability of wounding (Geist 1986a), the cost of healing and the possibility of losing the next fight due to sheer exhaustion, the bull must protect his gains at the least cost. If dominance displays achieve the same end as fighting, then displays or aggrandized appearance ought to be used. Sighting a rival, a bull may spray urine, horn the ground and small trees with great vigor, and bugle loudly. Large bulls differ somewhat from younger, smaller ones in that, due to their more frequent urine spraying and wallowing, the former distribute more rut odor and look darker. Red deer stags may carry soil debris and vegetation on their antlers (Lincoln 1972b).

Does such a display intimidate? When rapidly walking toward rutting bulls in dense timber while imitating the bugling of a urine-spraying (i.e., aggressive) bull, I noticed that young bulls were intimidated if I imitated vigorous horning with an elk antler. Horning is done mainly by large bulls ready to fight, and my vigorous horning apparently projected this intimidating, aggressive image (the young bulls and I were invisible to one another in the dense forest). Replies to my vocal challenges changed noticeably in volume; the young bulls moved off and would not allow me to approach closely. Nevertheless, they continued to reply well to my bugling.

Even when a herd bull makes contact with a rival, it pays to fight as little as possible. Most clashes of harem-holding bulls are quite brief. Escalation is avoided, particularly early in the rut (Clutton-Brock et al. 1979). Not every defeated rival is gored, despite opportunity to do so. Moreover, as McCullough (1969) observed, a herd bull may interrupt a dominance fight and chase off lesser bulls before continuing the fight. Full-blown dominance fights, which appear to be identical in elk and red deer, are rare. A description based

on my own observations, those of Bützler (1974) and Clutton-Brock et al. (1979, 1982)—for red deer—and Harper et al. (1967) and McCullough (1969)—for elk—was published in Geist (1982). It is refined here with insights gained when challenging rutting bull elk in densely forested foothills of the Alberta Rockies with a call and an antler.

A dominance fight between large bulls, such as a harem-holder and a challenger, are preceded by loud calling until the opponents sight one another. Both horn small conifers, bugle and urine spray during the approach. They approach frontally, but turn sharply and circle 5 to 20 paces apart. Typically, they avoid looking at one another. Their antlers are tilted forward during the circling or the subsequent "parallel march" (Figure 143). Bulls that tilt antlers at the opponent are likely to be the losers. The parallel march may start at a walk, but it can accelerate into a trot. In this dominance display, there is no stiffness or "foot dragging," as seen in mule deer, white-tailed deer and moose. In the parallel march, both bulls may bugle; one may trot ahead of the other. They may follow a straight path or a winding one. I have seen repeated parallel marches continuing for up to 200 paces along mountain slopes. When turning, before retrac-

Figure 143. Before serious fighting, both rivals display to one another with sound, smells and conspicuous visual performances. Thus, upon meeting, they tend to march rapidly side by side, occasionally even trotting, in which the full size of the body is displayed to the opponent. The bulls hold their heads fairly low and the antlers tilted slightly forward. They avoid staring directly at one another; although, they do glance at each other. The least secure bull, often the smaller and likely looser of the engagement, may tilt his antlers toward the larger, as if anxious to catch the attack that is likely to follow, as the bulls swing toward one another at the end of a parallel march. *Illustration by Valerius Geist.*

A large bull elk will chase off subordinates by rushing them with a nose-up posture, displaying its canines and hissing. *Left photo by Irene Vandermolen. Right photo by Jack Ballard.*

If the nose-up threat is insufficient intimidation of an opponent, a bull will often thrash the ground with his antlers. *Photos by Leonard Lee Rue III.*

ing their march, one or both bulls, while momentarily facing one another, may sweep the antlers low over the ground. The bulls also may bugle and horn a small conifer before resuming the parallel march. I have witnessed herd bulls, at this point, quickly grasp the opportunity and move uphill of challengers and hold that position. Clutton-Brock et al. (1979) also observed this. (When, with a call, I approached bull elk in cover, one response to my challenge was to move uphill of my position before approaching me.) The parallel march leads suddenly to a clash, often after a short pause in which opponents square off with lowered antlers. Some bulls rake the ground with their antlers just before lunging.

From extensive observations of red deer, Bützler (1974) suggested that the signal for lunging is a tipping of the antlers by one of the opponent. Although highly variable, fights generally are forceful pushing contests, in which each bull tries to gain an uphill position. Once a bull pushes another downhill, there may be little for the downhill combatant to do except disengage and flee as quickly as possible. A bull elk may shove a rival downhill several hundred meters. On level terrain, shoving may be followed by circling and large sideway bounds as the combatants strive to retain balance. Bull elk with engaged antlers also twist their necks powerfully from side to side and, on rare occasion, a combatant may die from a broken neck (Flook 1970a).

Fighting bulls breathe heavily. They spread their legs and crouch low to the ground. Should a rival stumble, it may be gored. Quick attacks by one bull on another's unprotected flank may occur. Combatants may disengage by backing off and pause before clashing again. One of the bulls may use the disengagement as opportunity to turn and flee. Disengagement and flight from violent combat invariably leads to the "winner" vigorously pursuing with half a dozen vigorous jumps uttering several short sharp barks and goring the quitter. Then, the winner will stop and bugle after the vanquished rival, who may bugle back. Both bulls may show every sign of exhaustion. Despite this, the winner inevitably will spray urine on himself, bugle and horn the ground or a small conifer before returning to the harem.

Elk, red deer, Père David's deer, fallow deer and, to some extent, sika deer show a break with the behavior of their more primitive relatives. It appears that the advertisement strategy has been adopted independently and has led to similar deviations. The old dominance display of hard-antlered males to one another has been transformed into herding behavior directed at females. It is most divergent in fallow deer, with which it has evolved into a dominancelike broadside display, from which the buck may nevertheless charge and gore females. The ancient head-high dominance display with the stiff walk is replaced by the parallel march and a loose, agile manner of walking in the red as well as

When bulls do engage in dominance fights, antlers serve as offensive weapons, but their construction minimizes risk of serious injury. A dominance fight generally begins as a strength-test of wrestling, with the combatants' royal tines interconnected. The brow and bez tines are important to the protection of eyes during the violent lunging, twisting and circling episode. In contrast, the parallel beams above the trez tines reduce the chance of locked antlers by foes whose antler spreads usually are nearly identical. Often, only single antlers are interconnected, causing the bulls to whirl more so than shove back and forth. Unless all antlers are re-engaged, the outcome of the fight will likely depend on whether one of the animals slips down and is vulnerable to being gored. *Photo by Gary Leppart.*

the fallow deer. The old head-low dominance display of males in velvet is so rare as to be unreported except for bull elk in summer (Altmann 1956a).

Wounds and Combat Mortality

Fighting leaves visible and invisible wounds. A rutting bull annually receives on average 30 to 50 wounds. Most are on the neck, shoulders and rear. Some exceed 10 inches (25 cm) in length (Geist 1986a). After the rut, some bulls limp, some carry broken antlers, and some die of festering wounds. Wounded bulls are among the first victims of winter (Craighead et al. 1973). The wound of a punctured bull may become contaminated with soil, urine, plant debris, glandular secretions and the concomitant bacterial growth, increasing the likelihood of massive internal infections.

Fighting mortality is by no means insignificant; about 5%

of red deer stags in Germany's Rominten Heath died annually of fighting wounds (Müller-Using and Schloeth 1967). In Russia, studies indicated that about 13% of 208 stags found in the Woronesh Sanctuary had died of combat, as had 10 of 33 stags found in the Krim Sanctuary (Heptner et al. 1961). The cost of fighting can be high in other deer species as well. Of 50 moose bulls, 4 years and older, shot and autopsied at the Petschora-Illitsch moose reserve in Russia, six had fresh antler punctures (Heptner and Nasimovitsch 1967), almost certainly an underestimation. In another Russian reserve, 7 from 14 bull moose found dead had died of combat (Heptner and Nasimovitsch 1967).

Advertisement as a Rutting Strategy

The behavior of rutting bull elk, as well as that of a number of other Old World deer species (i.e., sika, fallow, white-lipped, Père David's, axis, Eld's deer and barasingha) follows closely an "advertisement" strategy. Instead of finding an estrous female, then guarding her as inconspicuously as possible (the essence of the "tending-bond" strategy used by many deer species), the rutting bull elk appears to rely on attracting females by noisy, smelly and showy advertisements (Geist 1982). This strategy is developed even further in fallow deer; bucks may form leks, so that each buck on a small area supports the advertisements of the other (Apollonio et al. 1989, Clutton-Brock et al. 1989, Langbein and Thirgood 1989).

Central to the advertisement strategy is the female choosing the mate. In the tending-bond strategy the female also "sifts" the males, so as to be mated by the "best," but she does so indirectly. In white-tailed deer, for instance, does rely on a combination of estrus and roaming to attract many males. After stringing them out as they follow her at high speed, she lets aggression sort out the winner among the remainder. Estrus is a means of maximizing male sexual competition (Geist 1978b). In the advertisement strategy, a showy estrus would interfere with the female's choice if her estrus attracted other males and the chosen male were disabled in a fight over the female. For females of species that practice the advertisement strategy, neither a showy estrus, nor a period of high mobility is expected. This is true for elk; although, bulls do detect the estrus period (Morrison 1960a).

Large antlers signal a male's superior abilities at foraging and, indirectly, at avoiding predators. They also signal a superior efficiency in using ingested resources to spare a maximum from maintenance and growth for reproduction. That would ensure superior milk production in the female's daughters.

Symmetrical antlers are a proxy for health. The more symmetrical the antlers, the healthier the bull and, consequently, the better its systems of defense against pathogens and parasites. Asymmetrical antlers also could prevent a bull from fighting effectively and, thus, losing contests (Lincoln 1972b).

In deer, antler size and antler display behavior in courtship are directly correlated (Geist 1991a). Lincoln (1972b) and Lincoln et al. (1970) showed experimentally that red deer pay close attention to the shape of antlers of companions, who they recognize by their antlers. Lincoln (1972b) also showed that stags deprived of most of their antlers were not able to retain hinds. During antler-growing periods, gaining dominance by red deer stags (Bartoň et al. 1987) and fallow deer stags (Bartoň and Losos 1997) over other stags resulted in increased antler growth. Clutton-Brock et al. (1979) found that the number of antler points correlated with a stag's ability to hold a harem. It should be noted that antler points are added during the terminal growth of antlers. Miura (1984) showed that, in sika deer, antler length was correlated with fight success. Thus, a male's success in dominating others during the antler-growth period is advertised by the structure of his antlers. Deer farmers have noted that hinds choose stags, rather than vice versa (Lucas 1969, Yerex 1979), which makes plausible the social significance of antlers, but does not clinch the argument for female choice or that antlers are subject to female choice as Darwin (1872) suspected. One also needs to consider what would halt the evolution of features chosen by the female. There is no evidence in the paleontologic record of run-away selection for antler size. Frevert (1977), who managed red deer for trophies in the Rominten Heath, noted that stags with very large and complex antlers could not defend themselves in battle against stags with normal antlers, and such trophy stags frequently locked antlers and died.

Large antlers, vigor in behavior and high dominance might also signal heterosis, a favorable trait in variable environments. Dominance usually is related to size, and deep, resonating sounds can only be produced in a large body. Thus, low-frequency sounds can be a proxy for size or mass. A male that advertises frequently, despite close proximity to other males, is one that likely is successful in warding off other males and one to stop harassment of his females by lesser males. Such a male should have a better chance of attracting and mating females. Therefore, the volume of advertisement should be attractive to females, as was verified for European red deer by McComb (1987, 1991).

The advertisement hypothesis explains the loud rutting calls of males and the manner in which they are used. The bull, to maximize advertising, must reach as far as possible with its call. In open areas, high-frequency sounds travel better than do low-frequency sounds. Low-frequency sounds travel better in thickets of plants because they lose less energy to leaves than do high-frequency sounds. Red deer, adapted to forest and riparian thickets, uses only a low-frequency roar. Elk, as open country herders, have a complementary rutting call—a high-frequency whistling bugle that can be heard far away. However, they terminate the rutting call with a very deep, guttural sound, which would indicate the caller's body size. The calling of young and old males can be distinguished.

Elk bulls, unlike the red deer stags, do not form a resonating chamber with their lips, but call with the mouth open, as do sika deer bulls (Figure 144). The bugling elk retracts the lips, exposing the upper palate and lower incisor teeth; it does not retract the tongue deep into the throat, as does the red deer. The difference in shaping the mouth during the call is associated with the fleshier muzzle of the red deer, compared with that of the elk.

Geist (1982) set out expectations about when bull elk call as advertisement. The advertisement call ought to be uttered mainly when cows are most active and, therefore, should closely track the cows' daily activity, as found by Struhsaker (1967) and Bützler (1974). Bulls should silence advertising competitors in close proximity. Consequently, harem bulls should approach nearby calling bulls and "out-advertise" competitors. Bulls holding harems ought to advertise more than bulls without harems, or they might lose cows to the competition. Accordingly, older bulls should bugle more than younger bulls, because the former are most likely to hold harems and less likely intimidated by rivals.

A harem master is expected to "bind" cows to him, so that they come to and remain with him rather than follow another bull. For instance, a bull elk allows a courted cow to "reinforce" her control over him by halting in response to the cow's cut-off signal by working her jaws (the cow rapidly moves her lower jaw left to right and reverses in the horizontal plane). Young bulls that managed to get to females act in the opposite fashion; they ruthlessly pursue cows no matter how often the female sends the jawing cut-off signal. A halted herd bull then turns around and bugles away from the female. This would reinforce (in Pavlovian fashion) the female experience of "controlling" the bull. A large bull can be very gentle in courtship. Conversely, a young bull making the most of what little time he has before a big bull chases him off, is eager and not gentle. Thus, there is a distinction between the hasty, rough pursuit of the cow by the young bull (a pursuit she cannot dissuade) and the courting experience she has with a large bull. To retain a loyal harem, a bull must differentiate his behavior from that of his rivals. His advertisements should condition

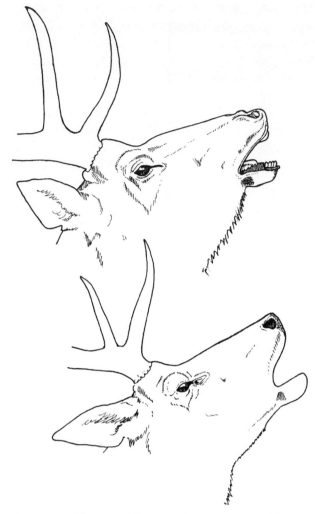

Figure 144. There is a difference in how European red deer stags and bull elk shape their mouths during the rutting calls. The red deer stag, uttering a deep, resonating roar, forms a resonating chamber with his mouth and restricts the orifice through which it exhales. To do that, it must pull the lips and the rhinarium over the upper and lower jaws. The bull elk does the opposite when bugling its high notes. It pulls the lips back, exposing its upper palate, tongue and teeth. However, there is variation in the position of the bull elk's mobile lips as it not only whistles, but also roars. The difference in lip positions results in the red deer stag having more "fleshly" lips and a muscular snout, as well as having a deep skin fold between the rami of the lower jaws, that, in elk, is replaced by a row of long hairs extending onto the mane. *Illustration by Valerius Geist.*

the female positively to his presence. This makes bugling an integral part of the courtship sequence (Bützler 1974).

Another prediction of the advertisement hypothesis is that bulls should have individualized calls. That would permit females to distinguish between different bulls and their associated behavior. In red deer, there are distinct patterns

Bull elk advertise their location and dominance by bugling. Unlike red deer stags, elk do not form a resonating chamber with their lips, but rather call with their mouth open. *Photo by Len Clifford.*

Urine spraying by bull elk is scent advertising. The intensity of the rut scent tends to signal a bull's dominance rank. *Photo by Len Rue, Jr.*

of vocalization that the stags retain over years (Bützler 1974). Also, the earlier that elk bulls start to advertise before the rut, the more likely that they can condition females favorably. However, to start too early would be to squander precious, stored resources prematurely. Bulls begin advertising about 2 weeks before cows come into heat. Also, bulls in good condition advertise earlier than bulls in poor condition (Heptner et al. 1961, McCullough 1969).

Advertising should be carried on all channels of the sensory system—by sound, sight, smell and touch. Closely linked to vocal advertisement are *urine spraying* and opening of the preorbital gland. At the end of the bugle, the bulls usually emit a series of yelps. These vocally mark the act of urine spraying. When so engaged, the elk pulls up his belly in quick succession, he "palpitates." This palpitation can be readily seen even at dusk, because the light part of the belly behind the penis orifice bobs up and down. The belly ahead of the penis orifice is soaked in urine and colored a very dark brown. It can be assumed that the more a bull bugles, the more he sprays and smells. The sheer intensity of a bull's rut scent should signal his rank.

Urine spraying is variable in elk and red deer. There may be no more than a dribble or large, rhythmic discharges of urine from the erected penis. Urine may be sprayed in a fine, solid stream between the front legs at the neck, or it may be sprayed like a cone of fine mist against the belly or, with penis withdrawn, it may fall as a stream to the ground.

From the erected penis, urine may be sprayed at right angles. When urine falls straight to the ground, it usually is at a wallow that the bull has churned with his front legs, his horns and his antlers (Figure 145). The bull also lowers itself into the wallow where he rubs his neck mane on the wallow's edge. This is a behavior found in all Old World deer that wallow. The bull cakes the sides of his face, neck, chest

Figure 145. Bull elk copiously "perfume" themselves with urine—apparently a potent attractor for cows. Large rutting bulls have their underparts forward of the penis orifice, as well as their long-haired neck mane, soaked in urine. Urine spraying and horning the soft earth tends to proceed wallowing in the urine-soaked mud. This sequence is initiated by the bull pawing open a pit in soft soil, frequently next to a spring in the forest. *Illustration by Valerius Geist.*

belly, flanks and legs with urine-soaked mud. The penis remains erect in the wallow and, while wallowing, the bull may continue to spray urine. Urine spraying has been mistaken for ejaculation (Darling 1937, Struhsaker 1967, Raesfeld and Vorreyer 1978). Ejaculation does occur, but it is very rare and looks quite different from urine spraying (Figure 146).

After wallowing, a bull may move to a tree and vigorously rub his neck on the trunk—another behavior common to most species of deer, even those that do not wallow, such as mule deer. The elk bull tends to return to the same wallow, and may lie in it for minutes or even hours. Not all wallows form mud; some in subalpine forests may be pawed in deep layers of moss and dark organic matter close to seeps. While wallowing is done mainly by older bulls, as expected from the advertisement hypothesis, cows also are attracted to the wallow, albeit rarely. Yearling bulls in the vicinity of wallows may become excited, as evidenced by their frolicking and exuberant jumps (Struhsaker 1967). This also is confirmed for red deer (Raesfeld and Vorreyer 1978, Bützler 1974), which have been seen to rise on their hind legs and thrash overhanging branches with their antlers—a behavior known as preaching (see Schaller 1967).

Wallowing was reported to be infrequent in California Tule elk (McCullough 1969), probably because, at the time and place of observation, there were few places available with soft soil. Horning of vegetation while urine spraying is common in Tule elk. It begins early in the rut, and is part of the challenge ritual of bulls. However, like wallowing,

horning may be engaged in spontaneously. It is a noisy activity that leaves a conspicuously debarked young tree, usually a pine or a spruce. It also may include scraping the tree with the incisors (McCullough 1969), and rubbing the head and neck on the debarked stem (Graf 1955). Horning is part of the dominance display of bull elk, not a territorial marking activity.

Harem Herding and Courting

After a bull has attracted females, he may not be able to hold his harem together by advertisement alone. Cows attempting to escape from the harem are discouraged from leaving by *herding*. In absence of herding, females would join and remain with a bull strictly of their own volition, as seen in the pseudoharems of mule deer (Geist 1981). Herding tends to keep straying cows in the bull's control. However, a bull cannot succeed in holding back a cow that is determined to leave.

The herding posture is a threat posture derived from the head-high biting threat, as seen in the more primitive behavior of sika deer. In this species, there is little distinction between the head high threat and the herding posture; in the red deer, there is some distinction; in elk, distinction is most pronounced. A herding bull assumes a low-stretch posture with the head below the level of the withers. Averting his head slightly, the herding bull circles the straying female at a rapid walk or trot. His eyes are wide open, as are

Figure 146.   All cervid males occasionally ejaculate in the absence of females. This behavior in elk is virtually identical to that in other Old and New World deer. *Illustration by Valerius Geist.*

After an elk bull has attracted cows, advertising his location by bugling increases the risk that a larger, more dominant bull might challenge his harem ownership. Often, cows are discouraged from leaving a harem by the bull's vigilant herding or blocking. *Photo by Leonard Lee Rue IV.*

the preorbital glands. He may yelp, palpitate and drip urine while approaching. McCullough (1969) heard teeth grinding by a bull during a herding approach. If the cow does not run back to the harem the bull may rush her and even slam his antlers into her. A bull's rush at the cow may terminate with two to four loud coughs, the same sounds bulls make when rushing after a departing rival. Thus, the herding posture is a serious threat. Moreover, many mature cows carry a complement of scars on their bodies, confirming that bulls gore cows when herding (Geist 1986a). After herding, a bull elk often stops, turns away from the harem and bugles while the herded cow slips back into the harem.

A variation on herding is a bull's attempt to block an escaping cow's way. The bull turns broadside to do the blocking. He may arch the back, as if attempting to look bigger. His stretch is extreme and he rolls his eyes out sideways to observe the cow. He may whirl, rush the cow and snap his antlers toward her. I have seen young bulls herd cows using a head-high threat posture outside the rutting season.

The posture of a *courting* bull elk is the opposite of the *herding* posture (Geist 1966a) (Figure 147). It also is an elegant solution to a vexing problem the harem-holding bull must solve. As indicated, the herding posture is a serious threat. Yet, to breed, a bull also must approach in a manner that not only does not repel the cow, but attracts her.

The courtship posture of the elk is somewhat more pronounced than that of red or sika deer (Figure 148). Its elements are a frontal approach (as opposed to a tangential one in herding), a raised head and elevated antlers (as opposed to a low-stretched one with reclined antlers in herding), a slight crouching in the rear, thus emphasizing the elevation of the head, and a flicking of the tongue and, thus, a soft plopping sound (as opposed to yelping, coughing and tooth grinding in herding). The tongue flicking is an intention movement toward licking the croup, tail and perianal region of the cow, the antithesis of goring with antlers. If the cow stands, the bull may lick her on the back, withers, neck and head, and the two may touch muzzles. Usually, however, the cow withdraws in a submissive posture, at which the bull stops, turns and bugles. After courting, and presumably tasting some of the cow's urine, the bull performs the lipcurl.

When a cow is being followed closely by a bull, she intensifies the submissive posture by making snakelike motions with her head. The cow also will work her jaw while looking back at the bull. Resting cows approached by bulls may respond similarly. McCullough (1969) suggested that jawing was a signal of the cow's impending flight, and I concur. It is a logical signal only in the context of an advertisement system; it would be useless in a tending-bond system.

Figure 147. The courtship behavior (*A*) of a bull elk is antithetical (opposite in posture, motion and sound) to his harem-herding behavior (*B*). *Illustration by Valerius Geist.*

Unlike fallow or sika deer females, courted cow elk do not vocalize, nor do they assume a crouched urination posture. Normally, there is no distinct urination posture assumed by cow elk in herds, which may be related to the female elk's male mimicry (see Figure 140). Bull elk do not assume a distinct urination posture either. Failure to signal urination appears to be a means of reducing sexual harassment by young bulls.

The display of a herding bull elk (*top*) is much different from than that of a courting bull (*bottom*). Although the former is a threat behavior, the courting bull usually approaches a cow frontally, with a head-up posture and elevated antlers, while crouching slightly in the rear and making a soft plopping sound with his mouth. *Top photo by Len Clifford. Bottom photo by Leonard Lee Rue III.*

Figure 148. In sika (*left*) and red deer (*center*), the distinction between herding (*A*) and courtship (*B*) postures is less pronounced than in the more highly evolved elk (*right*). *Illustration by Valerius Geist.*

Breeding

A cow approaching estrus reduces her overall activity. She tends to stand about as if ill, and periodically licks her side, hind quarters and vulva. She tolerates the courting bull, who approaches her periodically and licks her. The cow licks her vulva frequently, which may dilate and close (Morrison 1960a). Bützler (1974) observed that red deer stags, at this stage of courtship responded with jawing if the female jawed. Clearly, the males use appeasement behavior.

Before breeding, a receptive cow assumes a slightly spread-legged stance, lifts her tail and spreads the hair about the perianal region. She may quiver in the haunches and twitch her legs. The bull slides his chin, neck and chest onto the cow's back, while his erect penis makes searching motions and slides back and forth in the sagittal plain. The bull does not clasp the cow with the front legs, which hang down along the cow's flank. The bull keeps his weight on his hind legs. He normally slides off to repeat the procedure. These are precopulatory mounts of which there

An elk cow typically responds to a bull's courting behavior by assuming a submissive posture and making snakelike motions with her head. *Photo by Irene Vandermolen.*

likely are to be several. The bull is most attentive to the female between mounts and licks her on the croup, withers, neck, vulva, etc. Morrison (1960a) counted 1 to 16 precopulatory mounts, with 4 as average, for captive elk. McCullough (1969) observed 1 to 33 precopulatory mounts in free-ranging Tule elk, but typically there were 5 to 8 before successful copulation.

Copulation is a conspicuous event. The mounted bull suddenly coils backward, in extreme cases throwing his head and neck straight up. At the same time, he clasps the cow with the front legs and bounds upward in the rear, leaving the ground completely (Figure 149). Morrison (1960a) suggested that semen transfer may occur in the absence of the bull's copulatory jump.

Occasionally, a cow is knocked down by the bull's thrust, but usually she jumps forward from beneath him. She stops with back arched, head lowered and tail raised. Some blood may flow from her vagina. Often, urine and mucous are voided (Morrison 1960a, Harper et al. 1967). Other cows,

Bull elk detect a cow's onset of estrus by about a day and will periodically approach her (*left*) to ascertain, by scent, taste and the cow's behavior, her readiness to breed. The lip curl or urine-testing behavior of a rutting bull elk includes retraction of the upper lip (*right*). This permits the orifice to open to the Jacob's organ in the upper palate, where the urine of a cow may be tested for signs of hormones of estrus. In elk, this behavior has no known social function. *Left photo by Erwin Bauer. Right photo by Wes Keyes; courtesy of the Arizona Game and Fish Department.*

Figure 149. The copulatory jump of bull elk erupts from the (A) mounting posture. The copulatory jump (B) appears to be common to many, but not all deer. It is not found in caribou, roe deer or the muntjacs. A bull elk copulates with, then carefully guards an estrous cow for about a day. *Illustration by Valerius Geist.*

yearlings and calves may approach the estrous female, sniff her body, vulva and the spilled fluids on the ground. The estrous cow may lick her flanks and lie down or commence grazing. Her arched back posture, or lordosis, may last up to half an hour (Figure 150). Lordosis tends to excite red deer and elk bulls sexually. This is evidenced from incidents when gut-shot stags, exhibiting similar postures, were mounted by companions (Beninde 1937, Bützler 1974).

Right after copulation, bull elk may show a high level of aggression toward other bulls in their vicinity and go into a bout of advertising. The bull may return periodically to the female to lick and groom her. This postcopulatory attention is a pronounced part of the bull's behavior.

The copulatory behavior of elk is exceedingly similar to that of other Old World deer and some New World deer. A captive sambar stag I observed apparently did not touch the female at all with his front legs during mounting, while the female, upon copulation, pushed first rearward and then jumped free of the stag. The copulatory jump is widespread, but not ubiquitous; it is not found in caribou, roe deer or muntjac. The latter mates during postpartum estrus (Barrette 1977a), and the vagina may be rather open at that time. Nor did MacNamara and Eldridge (1987) report copulatory jumps by South American brocket deer and pudu. Caribou, in their short, synchronized rut, mate but once (Bergerud 1974), and this may be true for moose as well (Baskin 1987, Bubenik 1987).

Figure 150. Lordosis is the postcopulatory, arched back posture commonly assumed by cow elk for some minutes after copulation. Besides elk, only the mule deer is known to go through up to an hour of postcopulatory contraction and strong lordosis. *Illustration by Valerius Geist.*

Female Courtship

Courtship of the male by the female is not a common event, but it is spectacular. It is exceedingly similar in all deer species. It has been described for elk by Struhsaker (1967) and Morrison (1960), for red deer by Darling (1937) and Bützler (1974), and for mule deer by Geist (1981). I have also seen it in captive fallow deer, sambar, sika deer, red deer and free-ranging chital. Female courtship is the most powerful expression of female choice, directed in all instances at a large male. Morrison (1960a) observed an estrous cow elk attack yearling bulls, and I have seen two estrous fallow does run from yearlings and press themselves against the sides of a large, foot-sore buck, who eventually bred both.

Female courtship universally entails tactile, aggressive and flight components to arouse a bull into copulation. This includes nibbling and licking his face, neck and body, diving under his neck to rub the body along his neck and chest, rubbing her neck along his body, as well as "horning" and butting him. The courting cow also may mount the bull, perform lordosis and "coquette runs" away from and around the bull. She may threaten the bull with a lowered head, jump away, buck, gambol and kick. This sequence may trigger the bull into following. Morrison (1960a) observed cow elk present in lordosis to the bull, prance before him, move off a few steps, look back at him, twitch the hocks and quiver in the hind quarters. This eventually gets tired bulls to mount. However, female courtship also may be intense when old males are somehow slow to copulate with the first estrous female of the year.

Breeding is initiated by the cow who, in response to a light touch to her hindquarters by the tending bull, straddles her legs slightly and lifts her tail. The bull then positions himself behind the cow, slides his chin (*top*), neck and chest onto the cow's back as he seeks penetration. The bull then mounts, keeping his weight almost entirely on his rear legs (*center*). There may be a number of precopulatory mounts. Intromission occurs when the mounted bull suddenly clasps the cows hindquarters with his forelegs while thrusting and bounding forward, often leaving the ground completely, and in extreme cases throwing his head and neck skyward (*bottom*). *Top left photo by Irene Vandermolen. Other photos by Len Rue, Jr.*

Female courtship behavior tends to be aggravated and highly tactile, to arouse a bull to perform copulation. *Photo by John Trout, Jr.*

Behavior Applied

The study of free-ranging creatures is demanding of time, discipline, endurance and finances. The apprentice observer needs time to develop the ability to observe critically, gain competence in the hypothetico-deductive approach to the testing of ideas and develop confidence in dealing with qualitatively unequal data. Studies of short duration, in particular by inexperienced personnel, are likely to lead to flawed conclusions. Such researchers lack adequate familiarity with the animals and likely have not mastered identification of critical detail. Also, environmental conditions may vary between years, and what was observed in one year may not be observable in another. Comparative studies between years, populations and species are important, because they cross-fertilize and alert to oversights.

Errors in interpretation of animal behavior are not uncommon in management or policy formulation. Some mistakes lead to badly damaged wildlife populations or extirpations, others lead to the courts, hospital wards or the grave. Professional biologists should know, for example, that, as primates, we are destined to misread the intentions of big game, because those animals do not communicate by the rules of primates. Consequently, the *very* dangerous dominance displays of ungulates and large carnivores are meaningless to us because, *during the display, those animals do not address us with their eyes*. Most large mammals depart from this rule of primate communication: *when poised to attack from a dominance display, ungulates and carnivores do not look at the object of their aggression*. Therefore, the uninformed observer is at high risk of injury or death. Large mammals tend to look at us during *defensive* threats and attacks. In dominance displays, however, they address us with their bodies, occasionally with a show of armaments and olfactory marking, all of which we fail to intuit. We can only know about this very dangerous threat intellectually.

Even defensive threats may be misread, as happened to a warden in a busy national park. The warden did not recognize the threat signals of a moose blocking a trail through deep snow. When the moose cocked a hind leg in preparation for a kick, the warden mistook the lifted leg for an injury. Nor did he know that the hard trail surface was for moose a high-quality defensive area that, due to good footing and the lack of deep snow, allowed it to spin about, lashing out with front and hind legs at opponents. Thus the warden tried to spook the bull into deep snow, unaware that the moose would be most unlikely to give up its precious defensive position. He agitated the bull with explosive devices, then sent tourists past the moose. The bull charged causing a near-fatal injury to a visitor (*Tippett and Rand v. United States of America* 1995). Misreading threats by large mammals—elk included—has lead to fatalities and serious injury to zoo staff. Wildlife biologists must *not* trust their intuition when dealing with large mammals, but instead learn how these animals communicate. Otherwise, those biologists, like other citizens, need to stay distant.

The city of Banff, Alberta, in Banff National Park, has long become a retreat for elk from wolf predation. Savannahlike golf greens there attract cow elk and calves as feeding and resting areas. Rutting bulls, also attracted to these areas, are potential "problems," because they can challenge people who inadvertently get between bulls and their harems. A televised National Geographic Society report showed wardens removing dangerous bulls from the town. However, removal does not deal with the root of the problem, because other bulls take the place of those taken away. Only removal of the cows can reduce the presence and potential danger of bulls in town. This cannot be done easily or cheaply on a golf course, but it can be done in small parklike areas by permanently alienating the cows, fencing them out or removing the attractants. Such an approach, combined with luring cows to attractive, alternative areas (and with some visitor control), would lead to a spatial segregation of elk and humans, and enhance the prospect of peaceful coexistence.

An insightful example of repeatedly misapplied animal behavior and its related subject—suffering and animal welfare (Dawkins 1980)—is provided by an ongoing controversy in Great Britain over the hunting of red deer with horses and hounds. Because there were charges that this is a cruel sport, the National Trust, on whose land deer were hunted, commissioned Professor Patrick Bateson, Department of Zoology, Cambridge University, to study the matter. When Bateson's report (1997) was submitted, the National Trust banned deer hunting on its lands within hours. However, some readers, scientists included, took umbrage at Bateson's report, pointing to a surprisingly large number of serious shortcomings, including the absence of peer review before submission, as noted in the July/August issue of *Hunting*. A paper based on the report was subsequently published in the *Proceedings of the Royal Society* (Bateson and Bradshaw 1997), but perpetuated its elementary errors.

A study team formed by several universities, funded by the Country Alliance, subsequently repeated and extended the research done by Bateson and, in September 1999, after appropriate peer review, delivered a scathing indictment (Harris et al. 1999).

Bateson had assumed a priori that red deer, by their evolutionary past, were not equipped for sustained running, but were forest creatures, which typically move but short distances during the day, and which wolves catch by ambush or a short chase. The red deer's chief antipredator strategy as a cursor (scientific references and centuries of hunting experience to the contrary) was thus misrepresented. The reference to short daily movements confounded *adaptation* with *adjustment,* and further misled. Undisturbed red deer, faithful to Zipf's Law, are not expected to run long distances spontaneously. The reference to wolves also was misleading. Indeed, wolves, after testing prey, are likely to kill after a short chase; they give up quickly on competent runners. They, too, can be expected to be faithful to Zipf's Law, particularly where prey is common, which is a logical criterion of study areas for scientists studying wolves. How wolves hunt where prey is scarce might have been relevant, but no systematic examination of this subject exists. At least one observation by Mech and Korb (1978) indicated that a wolf can pursue a deer for more than 13 miles (20.8 km) in less than 2 hours. Thus, Bateson's research was off on the wrong foot from the outset. It led to the measure of physiological functions, and finding these functions in the range of competent runners, they were judged (falsely) as excessive for red deer.

In addition to a false standard, the physiological work was found to be marred by incorrect theoretical premises and inadequate methodologies. The joint universities study team showed that the muscle physiology of red deer is similar to that of another able cursor, the horse, and has good lactate tolerance and a high oxidative capacity (Harris et al. 1999). Consequently, the muscle physiology data support those from comparative anatomy, locomotion studies and hunting experience showing that red deer are able cursors. Deer sustained minimal, if any, damage from hunting—a very important point when trying to judge *animal suffering.* Because, in principle, subjectivity is not within the domain of science, we can only infer that suffering has occurred if there is evidence of *lasting* damage to individuals and possibly to populations as well. If hunted deer recover from the run, akin to an athlete recovering from a run, there is no case for suffering. If there were heedless flight from the pursuers—with deer crashing into obstacles, slashing bodies, breaking bones or rupturing internal organs—then there would be prima fascia evidence for suffering. However, hunted red deer acted circumspect. They eluded the hounds regularly, gaining time, so that the average time for a hunt was 3.21 hours and the distance covered was 12 miles (19.3 km). This is slow progress indeed—3.37 miles per hour (6 km/h)—for a species that can run as fast and enduring as a red deer. Bateson might have argued plausibly for suffering had he demonstrated negative population responses by red deer, such as had been found by Batcheler (1968) in New Zealand, where intensive stalking led to home range abandonment, reduced reproduction, survival and body growth. However, Bateson argued that stalking and shooting were relatively benign compared with hunting—a conclusion put in doubt by Batcheler's findings. Yarmollov et al. (1988) found that chasing before the rut led, in mule deer, to aberrant behavior of affected deer and to a drop in fecundity, evidence not without welfare implications. It may be concluded from all this that, for the formation of public policy, the mere reputation of scientists, or the institutions employed, must never justify skipping a disinterested review of the work by peers.

"Quality deer" management historically has focused on antlers as indicators of population and individual quality (Raesfeld and Vorreyer 1978, Miller and Marchinton 1995). This is matched by the popular objective of managing deer populations for trophies. However, observations of massively antlered red deer stags have indicated that those animals were reproductively disadvantaged compared with stags with normal antlers (Frevert 1977). My field observations of mule deer indicate that bucks with the most massive antlers are nonparticipants in the rut. Furthermore, management experience and experimental work have shown that large body and antler size can be achieved in red deer by reducing the participation of males in the rut (Frevert 1977, Stubbe and Passarge 1979:282), whereas the increased growth in body and antler size of older stags (Neumann 1968) coincides with their decreased rutting activity. Huge antlers, therefore, do not necessarily identify high-quality males, but may identify males whose heredity favored body and antler growth over costly reproduction. Furthermore, trophy management focused only on antler size may degenerate and punish males that succeed in living under marginal conditions and those that have been highly successful in earlier mating seasons (which may have resulted in diminished body and antler growth). Males that fight and breed during the rut must heal out numerous, costly antler punctures (Geist 1986a), therefore are unlikely to grow large, symmetrical antlers (Vogt 1948, Davis 1987). Behavior is the key to understanding the biology of males with exceptional trophy antlers.

8

WILLIAM MILLER

Elk Interactions with Other Ungulates

Past successes of elk reintroduction and management across much of the western United States have resulted in increasing elk numbers. With this success came increased demands on the land resources to accommodate many species of herbivores. These additional pressures have produced conflicts not only among wildlife populations, but also with livestock, all of which are competing for the range resource.

This land-use conflict is not a new phenomenon. Hall (1955) wrote that the interaction of wildlife and livestock had been an issue since the turn of the century. He further indicated that, instead of decreasing in intensity, the conflict had become broader and more bitter as time passed. He suggested that "we must face the facts, and the fact is that at the present time, all of the other conflicting interests on our rangelands must force us to work out some mutual solution to the problem of livestock versus wildlife" (Hall 1955:4). These demands continue today, and they emphasize the need for a more thorough understanding of multiple species management.

Multiple species management is the practice of managing for two or more large herbivore species, domestic or wild, on the same pasture or range during the same year (Nelson 1984). Multiple species utilization of a common resource generally results in more efficient use of the forage resource. However, this use of a common resource may increase the likelihood of interspecific interaction and the possible abuse of the grazing resource.

Multiple species interaction can be classified into two major components, competition and facilitation. According to Birch (1957), competition exists when (1) a number of organisms use common resources that are in short supply, or (2) organisms seek a resource that is not in short supply, harming each other in the process. Miller (1967) and Nelson (1984) suggested that the first half of this definition should be characterized as exploitation; whereas, Nelson (1982) suggested that the second half should be characterized as disturbance, which has been referred to as social interaction (see Denniston 1956, Schladweiler 1974, Mackie 1976).

Wisdom and Thomas (1996) further described exploitative competition as the common use of a limited resource by two or more species, resulting in the reduction of population performance of one species because of competition for the limited habitat resource. Potential limiting resources generally are cover, space, water and food. Cover and space are resources seldom limiting in a competitive sense and are nonconsumptive because they become immediately available with the departure of the individual animal. And, although water is consumptive, there have been no reported instances of exploitative competition between elk and other large herbivores. This would suggest that the most exploitative competition between elk and other species focuses on food.

Competition for food between large herbivores involves several factors (Nelson 1984, Vavra et al. 1989), the most important of which are diet similarity, consumption equivalence, range overlap, timing of forage use, forage height, quantity and quality and density of competing species. It is the interaction of these factors that determines the extent and intensity of exploitative competition.

Nelson (1984:491) indicated that disturbance competition results in "an individual of one species [being forced to leave] the vicinity of an individual or group of another species. The animal which leaves the area may simply be intimidated or annoyed by the mere presence of the other species." McNaughton (1985, 1991) suggested that this type of competition may be minimal among species of wild herbivores that have evolved together. Elk have been reported to have a minor negative impact on bighorn sheep, while responding in a negative fashion to the presence of cattle (Lonner and Mackie 1983, Knowles and Campbell 1987, Wallace and Krausman 1987, Frisina 1992, Yeo et al. 1993).

Although the definition and characteristics of competitive interactions have been established, the definition of facilitation has received only limited attention. One functional definition of facilitation is the improvement in resource availability for one species as a result of prior use of the resource by a second species (Anderson and Scherzinger 1975, McNaughton 1985, 1991, Anderson et al. 1990a, 1990b). As with competition, the resource could be space, cover, water or food. Generally, the impact of one species on space and cover is minimal as these resources tend to revert to their original state with the departure of the first species. Food resources, however, have the potential to be changed as a result of their use by one species, thereby possibly improving their condition for another species. For this reason, food also may be the center of any facultative response.

Range Relationships of Elk and Other Large Herbivores

Elk and Livestock

Cattle

Competition between most large herbivores centers around food. Competition for forage between elk and cattle is more intense than with any other large herbivores in the western United States (Cooperrider 1982). Both species are dietary opportunists, using a variety of grasses, forbs and shrubs (Kufeld 1973, Nelson and Leege 1982, Kingery et al. 1996). Because of their body sizes, thus high forage intake, each species has potential for a high impact on the forage availability. In addition, the timing of forage utilization is such that cattle may consume forage essential to elk survival during critical periods. Conversely, heavy winter and

No other large herbivore species competes more intensively for forage resources in the western United States than elk and cattle. Because grass is the main forage of both species, competition can be most significant in foothill areas of concentrated dual use, such as on south-facing slopes and ridge tops. These areas are used most heavily by elk in winter and spring and by cattle in summer and autumn. In particular, cattle grazing reduces cured grasses and other desirable browse for winter use by elk. Placement of salt blocks on ridge tops to distribute cattle also increases the competitive impact. Elk tend to avoid close contact with cattle, but this intolerance or disturbance competition is not hard and fast, or universal. The degree of direct interaction depends on the season, the density and breed of cattle, the number of species and age of elk, the forage type, the topography and the proximity or intensity of human activity. Note the pronghorn in the upper right of the scene; all three species are attentive to the others. *Photo by A. Lorin Ward; courtesy of the U.S. Forest Service.*

spring foraging of grazing allotments by elk can create an adverse situation for cattle (Hobbs et al. 1996).

Although the diets of both elk and cattle contain large amounts of grass, competition between the two species may not be significant as long as the individual grass species eaten or the intensity of use of common species are dissimilar. Kingery et al. (1996) reported the dietary composition of elk and cattle using conifer and mixed conifer forest types in northern Idaho. They found that cattle diets contained 91% to 99% grass, less than 3% forbs and less than 4% shrubs during a grazing season. During the same period, elk diets contained 33% to 93% grass, 2% to 37% forbs and 4% to 28% shrubs. Dietary overlap between the two herbivores ranged from 37% to 88%, depending on forest type and timing. Similarly, Brown (1990) reported on a 4-year study of the impact of a "savory grazing method" on big game in central Arizona. In this study, he found that the average cattle diet contained 84% grass, 11% forbs and 5% shrubs/trees; whereas, the average elk diet contained 33% grass, 28% forbs and 39% shrubs/trees, with a dietary overlap of about 31%.

Competitive interaction between elk and cattle is greatest on winter and spring/autumn ranges (Nelson 1982, Wisdom and Thomas 1996). The nature of the interaction on winter range is dependent on both spatial and temporal factors. Generally, elk winter range is very limited in size, creating a situation whereby elk numbers are concentrated. Throughout much of the West, elk winter range constitutes spring/autumn cattle range. Heavy cattle use of this range in autumn has potential to reduce the availability of herbaceous forage and, in some cases, the more desirable browse species, thereby reducing the quantity and quality of already limited forage resources for wintering elk. Conversely, in late winter/early spring, elk are present when the more desirable forage species initiate new growth. Hobbs et al. (1996) studied the impact of wintering elk on spring cattle production in Colorado and reported as much as a 10% decrease in beef calf performance (growth) as a result of prior use of the forage resource by elk.

Distribution and habitat utilization by elk are influenced greatly by forage quality and quantity. In early spring, elk begin moving to higher elevations in response to emergence of new vegetative growth. New growth is very high in protein and digestibility and is essential for the increasing nutrient requirements of gestating elk cow. Elk continue moving toward higher elevation summer range in response to the continued emergence and growth of forage species. Normally, during this movement from winter to summer range, elk are undisturbed by cattle. In many regions, those portions of the range used by elk during spring migration also are used by cattle as part of their summer range. Al-

though the prior use of these ranges by elk has potential for negative impact on subsequent cattle use, the continued growth of the vegetation through early summer most likely offsets any impact.

On summer range, competitive interaction between elk and cattle generally is minimized. For the most part, elk summer range is located on large areas of public land. These areas are relatively undisturbed, have a wide diversity of habitats and potential for production of large amounts of forage. During summer, cattle typically spend a large portion of time grazing autumn range of elk, sometimes causing a negative impact on elk.

During autumn, elk move from summer range to lower elevation winter range. The rate of movement depends on the timing of inclement weather. The potential for competitive interaction between elk and cattle at this time of year is the reverse of that observed in the spring. Again, most elk grazing takes place in the absence of cattle, because cattle normally already will have moved to lower elevation pasture. Although prior use of these ranges will have reduced the amount of cured forage available to elk in autumn there is potential for a facultative effect of prior cattle use. Anderson and Scherzinger (1975) found that prior grazing of areas by cattle stimulated regrowth of some of

On shared summer range, exploitive competition for habitat resources, especially space and food, between cattle and elk, usually is not significant. In fact, association of the two species during this season would be somewhat unusual in most areas. All of the bull elk are on alert as they move quickly past the cattle. *Photo courtesy of the Oregon Department of Fish and Wildlife.*

the herbaceous species, thereby enhancing the forage quality available for elk. A similar response has been observed on autumn elk range in central Arizona (Miller et al. 1995). It is the combination of these traits that limits potential interaction of elk and cattle.

Spatial patterns of habitat use also play an important role in elk and cattle interaction. A number of researchers have reviewed the spatial pattern of habitat use by cattle and agree that they select areas with gentle slopes in close proximity to water, without apparent or significant regard for security cover, and cattle are unaffected by the presence of roads (Nelson and Burnell 1975, Holechek et al. 1989, Hart et al. 1993, Sheehy and Vavra 1996). Conversely, elk use steeper slopes at greater distance from water and limited distance from security cover, and elk avoid areas with roads (Nelson and Burnell 1975, Perry and Overly 1976, Hart et al. 1991, Sheehy and Vavra 1996).

A number of studies has shown an avoidance response on the part of elk to the presence of cattle (Mackie 1970,

Wallace and Krausman 1987, Yeo et al. 1993), but this avoidance is not universal. Ward et al. (1973) found elk and cattle to cohabit areas in southeastern Wyoming. Although the data are inconclusive, Yeo et al. (1993) suggested that the response of the elk might not be avoidance of cattle as much as a reaction to increased human activity associated with the presence of cattle.

Domestic Sheep

The potential for interaction between elk and domestic sheep is less than that observed between elk and cattle. Competition for food and space is limited mostly to summer range. Pickford and Reid (1943) reviewed the composition of elk and sheep diets in northeastern Oregon and found that elk consumed 13% grasses, 81% forbs and 6% shrubs, whereas sheep ate 33% grasses, 66% forbs and less than 1% shrubs during the same summer period. This amounted to a 65% diet similarity—somewhat less than the potential observed with cattle. However, Pickford and Reid

Competition with domestic sheep is limited over most elk range, where the species primary forage in summer is grasses and sedges. Where forbs and shrubs are the major part of the elk summer diet competition with sheep can be significant. In Nelson Park, on Wyoming's Medicine Bow Range, elk feed in early July (*top*) and sheep graze the same location in August (*bottom*). *Photos by A. Lorin Ward, courtesy of the U.S. Forest Service.*

concluded that, because of the strong diet similarity between the two species, common grazing of an area constituted dual use of the forage resource.

One aspect that mitigates the potential interaction of elk and sheep is domestic sheep management. Usual sheep grazing practices confine sheep to small areas on high elevation ranges. Rhodes and Sharrow (1990) indicated that, in western Oregon, this practice extended the availability of high-quality grass well into late summer and autumn for subsequent elk use. This was similar to vegetative response to cattle grazing reported by Anderson and Scherzinger (1975), Anderson et al. (1990a, 1990b), Frisina and Morin (1991) and Frisina (1992).

Finally, elk appear to respond to the presence of sheep in much the same way as they respond to cattle. Several studies have reported that elk move out of an area whenever a large flock of sheep move in (Culbreath 1948, Nichols 1957b, Stevens 1966); although, this response may be related as much or more to dogs, horses and humans tending the sheep as to the sheep themselves.

Elk and Native Ungulates

Mule Deer

Mule deer also are present on most western rangelands that support elk. Because of this cohabitation, the potential for competition between these two species does exist. Generalizations about the similarity or dissimilarity of the diet of these two species are difficult to make. Hofmann's (1988) classification of the morphophysiological feeding types places the mule deer into the concentrate selector class and the elk, on the grass roughage end of the intermediate types. This classification suggests that mule deer have a much higher shrub component in their diet. However, the diet composition for both elk and mule deer largely depends on forage availability.

Many studies have shown that mule deer diets contain predominantly forbs in spring and summer and browse in winter (Cowan 1947a, Mackie 1970, Hansen and Reid 1975, Hobbs et al. 1983, Singer and Norland 1994). Forbs also may comprise a significant part of the elk diet in early spring (Nelson and Leege 1982, Brown 1990), although grass is the predominant component throughout much of the year (Nelson and Leege 1982). Under these conditions, the time period for highest potential dietary overlap is in spring.

Sheehy and Vavra (1996) reviewed the potential for ungulate interaction based on foraging area in northeastern Oregon. They found that elk preferred grassland community types at high elevations and in close proximity to forest edge. In contrast, mule deer preferred foraging areas in grassland/shrub transition zones at any elevation and moderate distance from forest edge. The findings indicated that the potential for foraging area overlap was 35% to 67%.

During the long winters of deep snow, elk can outcompete mule deer on the same range. Elk can tolerate a wider array of foods and, because they are larger (and consequently, more mobile under those circumstances) than mule deer, they have greater access to scarce forage. *Photo courtesy of the Wyoming Department of Game and Fish.*

Sheehy and Vavra concluded that temporal and spatial separation of ungulates reduced the potential for forage resource conflict.

There appears to be no negative social interaction between elk and mule deer. They are frequently observed feeding in close proximity to one another. Because of their dietary and general habitat differences, elk and mule deer apparently do not seriously affect one another. However, in instances where severe overpopulation of an area by one or the other species occurs, a serious interaction could develop.

White-tailed Deer

Elk and white-tailed deer cohabit range in mountainous areas of the Northwest and adjacent portions of Canada (Kellogg 1956). Hofmann (1988) classifies the white-tailed deer feeding type, like that of the mule deer, as a concentrate selector. This was substantiated further by the diet compositions reported by Kingery et al. (1996), in which white-tailed deer diets contained 33% to 61% browse and only 3% to 26% grasses. Elk diets in the same study contained only 2% to 25% browse and 33% to 93% grasses. With this type of forage selection pattern, the potential for diet similarity and competition is extremely low.

Differences in habitat selection by elk and white-tailed deer further contribute to low potential for interaction between these species. As described, elk generally prefer foraging areas at high elevations in grassland communities near forest edge (Sheehy and Vavra 1996). Whitetails generally prefer foraging areas in scrubland and riparian communities near the forest edge at any elevation (Sheehy and Vavra 1996). These characterizations indicate a general spatial separation of the two species and, therefore, limited opportunity for significant competition.

Bighorn Sheep

Whenever elk and bighorn sheep occupy the same foraging area, the potential for competitive interaction is high. Hofmann's (1988) feeding classification places both elk and bighorn sheep in the grass/roughage-eating class. A study of niche relationships of ungulate species in Yellowstone National Park reported that elk diets contained 86% grasses and sedges, 11% forbs and 3% shrubs; whereas, bighorn sheep diets contained 67% grasses and sedges, 25% forbs and 8% shrubs, for a 73% diet overlap (Singer and Norland 1994).

Another element contributing to potential competition of these two species is habitat overlap. In the same study of niche relationship, Singer and Norland (1994) reported a 68% overlap in foraging area selection and a 78% similarity in topographic selection. They concluded that a combination of habitat use and diet similarity might reflect interspecific competition. The potential of this competition would be limited impact of bighorn sheep on elk, but a much larger impact of elk on bighorn sheep.

Bison

The potential for competition between bison and elk is the greatest because of similarities in the physiology, size and

Studies have indicated that elk and bison offer great potential for competition, although elk are more specialized feeders than bison. However, the restricted range of bison precludes substantial exploitive interaction. Note the elk bedded down on the hillside in the background. There is a bison bedded there as well, within only a few yards of an elk. As a rule, the species tend to be intolerant of each other in close proximity. *Photo by Richard Vesey; courtesy of the Wisconsin State Historical Society.*

habitat selection. However, because of the limited distribution of bison, studies of their interaction with elk are few. The greatest prospect of their interaction is in Yellowstone National Park. Singer and Norland (1994) reviewed the niche relationship of these two species. They reported that the diet of elk contained 86% grasses and sedges, 11% forbs and 3% shrubs; whereas, bison diets were composed of 99% grasses and 1% forbs, for a diet similarity of 47%. Habitat selection similarity in the same study was 75%, and topography selection similarity was 57%.

Moose

Moose have been found in large portions of elk range in the western United States and adjacent Canada. Compared with the potential for elk competition with cattle and deer, the competitive interaction between elk and moose is minimal. In most areas where elk and moose populations overlap, there is a difference in habitat and diet selection by the two species (Boer 1997). During winter months, elk seem to prefer open grass or brush/grass vegetation (Gordon 1968b). Moose, on the other hand, seem to prefer riparian habitat with an abundance of willows and other preferred deciduous browse (Harry 1957, Knowlton 1960, Huston 1968, Dorn 1970). During spring and summer, elk diets shift to higher amount of forbs and grass (Stevens 1970), and moose diets continue to be dominated by browse species (Huston 1968, Dorn 1970). Accordingly, it appears that competition between elk and moose is extremely limited, but during winter conditions of deep snow and limited forage availability, there is a likelihood that competition could occur.

Evaluation of Competition

One of the major problems facing wildlife managers is the ability to quantify animal competition for the purposes of

Even where elk and moose share rangeland—almost exclusively in western Canada and a portion of the Rocky Mountain range in the United States—competition for food generally is not significant. Elk, as grazers, and moose, as browsers, tend to occupy different habitats, especially during periods of resource scarcity, such as winter (see Boer 1998). On cohabited range, where elk are allowed to increase dramatically in number, competition between the species is possible. Where preferred elk foods are limited, elk readily shift to other foods, some of which are important to moose. Even when in close proximity, elk and moose rarely interact. *Photo by Michael H. Francis.*

resource allocation. A number of methods have been used, but with only limited success (Nelson 1984). The underlying concept of any approach for the evaluation of competition is that individuals of one competing species may be substituted for those of another at a rate described by the Lotka (1925) and Volterra (1931) equation: $\alpha = [K_1 - N_1]/N_2$ and $\beta = [K_2 - N_2]/N_1$, where α is the number of individuals of species 1 that is replaced by an individual of species 2; $K_{1\ or\ 2}$ is the carrying capacity for species 1 or 2 and $N_{1\ or\ 2}$ represents the stocking rate for species 1 or 2. Similarly, β describes the response of species 2 in terms of a change in the number of individuals of species 1. Both α and β have been referred to as trade-off values, coefficients of competition, marginal substitution rates (Smith 1965, Nelson 1982, 1984) or niche overlap (McArthur and Levins 1967) depending on the researcher.

In this equation, α and β can be determined empirically by comparing changes in population numbers of one species with changes in another species. This type of determination requires a highly controlled environment, which limits the size of animal populations to which this approach can be used. The size of large herbivores practically precludes using this approach. Instead, researchers of competition between large animals have sought ways of determining α and β indirectly through the evaluation of factors that may affect competition. As previously described, these factors include diet similarity, consumption equivalence, timing of use, social interaction, animal distribution patterns, forage availability and range overlap.

Diet Similarity

In any situation where two or more large herbivores use the same general area, either concurrently or at different times, the similarity of the diets of these species is of importance. As a result, the most studied aspect of competition among large herbivores has been diet similarity. There have been a wide range of diet similarity methods developed (Oosting 1956, Stark 1973, Hansen and Reid 1975, Howes 1977, Olsen and Hansen 1977), but all produce a single similarity value ranging between 0 (no similarity) and 1 (total similarity). Although these methods provide estimates of diet similarity, they all suffer from the same problem—the output of a single value does not allow for unequal trade-off between the species being evaluated.

The importance of α and β inequality in evaluating competition and replacement of one species by another has been reviewed by McArthur and Levins (1967). They proposed that if all factors (other than food consumption) affecting competition were disregarded, the impact of one species on another could be described as:

$$\alpha = \frac{\sum_{n+1}^{n} D_{i1}\, D_{i2}}{\sum_{n+1}^{n} D_{i1}{}^2}$$

In this equation, α is the impact of species 2 on species 1, based on quantities of food species consumed; D_{i1} is the quantity of food resource (i) consumed by species 1; and, D_{i2} is the quantity of food resource (i) consumed by species 2. Similarly, β can be described as:

$$\beta = \frac{\sum_{n+1}^{n} D_{i1}\, D_{i2}}{\sum_{n+1}^{n} D_{i2}{}^2}$$

Although the McArthur and Levins (1967) method allows for unequal competitive effects between species, it disregards all other factors influencing competition. Before any meaningful evaluation of competition can be made, diet similarity must be modified to account for these other contributing factors.

Consumption Equivalence

The daily consumption rate (CR) of an animal is defined as the amount of food consumed by an individual animal per unit of body weight per day, and usually is expressed in term of grams of forage dry matter per kilogram of animal weight, or as a percentage of body weight. The consumption rate is used to determine the total daily dry matter intake (DMI) of an individual animal. Consumption rate varies as a function of a wide range of physical and physiological factors related to the species. All of these factors are related to the nutritional requirements of the animal and also may be influenced by diet quality (see Chapter 5).

When the average total daily DMI of one species is expressed as a proportion of the DMI from of another species, the resulting quotient is the consumption equivalence (E_1), where $E_1 = (DMI_2/DMI_1)$. By convention, consumption equivalence has been expressed in terms of a standard 1,000-pound (454 kg) beef cow (Stoddart et al. 1975), with the commonly used equivalencies of five deer = five sheep = two elk = one 1,000-pound (454 kg) beef cow.

Use of such a standard exchange rate is subject to a number of errors, not the least of which is that all animals of a particular species vary in body size and, therefore, have a different daily intake. For example, if one assumes that the mean body weight is 452 pounds (205 kg) for elk and 1,000 pounds (454 kg) for cattle, and one also assumes that they consume 2.5% of their body weight daily, the consumption equivalence for the impact of cattle on elk (E_1) would be 2.2, and the impact of elk on cattle (E_2) would be 0.45. These values are different from the 2.0 and 0.5 that would come from the standard consumption equivalence. By convention, consumption equivalence has been expressed in terms of a "standard" 1,000-pound (454 kg) beef cow (Stoddard et al. 1975), with the commonly used equivalences of five deer or five sheep or two elk. This equivalence would indicate that the average deer and sheep would have a body weight of 200 pounds (90 kg) and the average elk would weigh 500 pounds (227 kg).

Timing of Use

It is generally accepted that competing animal species need not occupy the same area simultaneously for competition to occur (Nichols 1957b, Nelson and Burnell 1975, Mackie 1976, Nelson 1984). In a study of elk and cattle interaction, conducted in central Arizona, the timing of use was regulated by a combination of management practices and behavioral interactions (Miller et al. 1995). The management pattern for cattle was to maintain the herd on low elevation pastures until late May, early June or such time that range conditions permitted their introduction into the grazing units. Under these conditions, the only forage utilization observed during spring and early summer was by elk. Similarly, almost immediately after introduction of cattle into a grazing unit, elk were observed to move to adjacent areas and not return until 2 to 3 weeks after the cattle departed the unit. Once the elk returned, they remained in the area until moving to lower elevation range in late autumn.

With this type of grazing pattern by both elk and cattle, the potential for competitive interaction for forage resources was unilateral. Because the grazing of one species occurs without the other species being present, timing of use is a significant factor. In this situation, spring elk use of the resource impacted summer cattle use, whereas summer cattle use impacted elk use in autumn.

Range Overlap

A number of researchers have recognized the effect that the pattern of animal distribution has on determining competition between large herbivores (Julander 1958, Mackie 1970, Nelson and Burnell 1975, Sheehy and Vavra 1996). If the potential competing species do not use the resource at the same location, then the potential for competition between the species does not exist. Nelson (1982) indicated that the amount of range overlap (area of joint use) could be estimated using field data, such as pellet group counts and forage utilization samples, as input to an R-factor estimator:

$$R_{12} = \frac{\sum_{h=1}^{s} U_{h1} U_{h2}}{\sum_{h=1}^{s} (U_{h1})^2}$$

Here, R_{12} is the R-factor, showing distribution of competitive impact of species 2 on species 1 in s number of habitats, and U_{h1} and U_{h2} are proportions (or percentages) of time spent in habitat (h) by species 1 and 2, respectively. The R-factor for species 1 on species 2, or R_{21}, is estimated by reversing the subscripts for animals 1 and 2 in the equation.

As a result of the greater availability of geographic information system (GIS) technology, estimation of the R-factor for one competing species on another is easier. Using GIS, display of the amount of habitat used by the competing species is possible, as is determination of the extent of overlap between the competing species by a number of overlay techniques. The R-factor is then estimated as:

$$R_{12} = \frac{OA_{21}}{U_1}$$

where R_{12} = R-factor, showing distribution of competitive impact of species 2 on species 1, OA_{21} = area used by species 1 and also used by species 2, and U_1 = the total area used by species 1. The corresponding R-factor R_{21} again is estimated by reversing the subscripts for species 1 and 2 in the equation.

Trade-off Values

Nelson (1984) defined trade-off as the change in the number of one species with the addition or deletion of individuals of a second species within an interspecific dynamic. Trade-off can be expressed in terms of α and β, where α is the change in the number of species 1, with the addition or removal of an individual of species 2, and β is the change in the number of species 2, with the addition or removal of an individual of species 1.

As previously indicated, interspecific interaction is a complex relationship between two species, and it includes range overlap, dietary overlap, timing of use and consumption equivalence. On a quantitative basis, the trade-off is the product of the interaction of all of these components and can be calculated using the equation: $\alpha = R_i \times E_i \times \alpha$ and $\beta = R_i \times E_i \times \beta$. Here, R_i is range overlap for species i, E_i is the consumption equivalence for species i and α and β are the dietary overlap for species i (Nelson 1982). Trade-off values have the potential of ranging from 0 (no competitive effect) to more than 1 (an individual of one species will replace more than one individual of a second species). Situations wherein the trade-off value equals 1, the competitive interaction is equivalent to intraspecific competition.

It is important to understand that, although there exists potential for competitive interactions between two species

Bison generally dominate interspecies, social association with elk. Large bull elk may displace bison cows, calves and even yearling bulls in the absence of bison resistance. However, any bison aggression, even by calves, is likely to reverse elk dominance. The rut bull elk's antagonistic threat behavior, involving the aversion and antler tilting (see Chapter 7) is a prelude to submissiveness in this instance. *Photo by Don Zippert.*

for a resource, if that resource is present in adequate amounts to meet the needs of the two species, then the competition is minimal. Smith and Julander (1953) suggested that even if there is sufficient forage resource to meet both species' needs, the addition or removal of an individual of one species still impacts the number of individuals of the second species that the habitat can support.

One means of evaluating the competitive effect of multiple grazing species on one another and the ability of the resource to meet the needs of the two species is through the use of trade-off curves. The lines on a trade-off curve reflect the change in the number of one species with the addition of an individual of the second species (Figure 151). In this process, α and β become the slope of the lines, with K_i being the grazing capacity of the area, including proper use considerations. The point of intersection is the point of optimum numbers of both species that the area can support. This value also can be calculated using the Lotka-Volterra equation:

$$N_{1max} = \frac{K_1 - \alpha K_2}{1 - \alpha\beta}$$

and

$$N_{2max} = \frac{K_2 - \beta K_1}{1 - \alpha\beta}$$

where N_{1max} and N_{2max} are the optimal number of species 1 and 2 that the area can support, K_1 and K_2 are the grazing capacity for species 1 and 2 and α and β are the trade-off values for species 1 and 2. Under proper management, stocking combinations of species 1 and 2 could be max ($N_1 + N_2$), as proper use of the key forage for both species would not be exceeded.

Management Application

An example of the application of the aforementioned concepts is the competition potential between elk and cattle in

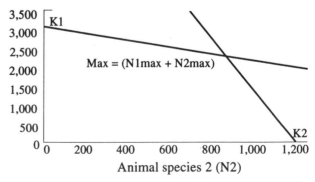

Figure 151. Trade-off curve showing the change in the number of species an area can support with the addition of a given number of species 2.

a portion of a grazing allotment in the Ponderosa pine type of central Arizona (Miller et al. 1995). Elk use of the area begins in early spring, with the melting of the snow, and continues until early summer, when the cattle are brought onto the allotment. At that time, the elk are displaced to adjacent areas, where they remain until 2 to 3 weeks after cattle are removed. The elk will remain on the allotment until late autumn, when they move to lower elevation range. Under these conditions, the timing of use pattern indicates unilateral competition of spring elk on cattle and of cattle on autumn elk.

Analyses of diet composition are presented in Table 66. As the result of the management practices on this allotment, coupled with the social interaction response of elk to the introduction of cattle, the competitive trade-off value for diet similarity would be based on the spring elk diet compared with cattle diet for β, and cattle diet compared with autumn elk diet for α. Using these data as input into the diet similarity estimator presented results in an α of 1.07 and β of 0.63. As indicated in the previous discussion, the McArthur and Levins (1967) method allows for unequal diet similarities.

Table 66. Summary of plant species composition in elk and cattle diets, and forage availability in central Arizona

	Percentage diet composition[a]			Percentage forage availability[b]
Plant species	Spring elk	Cattle	Autumn elk	
Grass				
Wheatgrass spp.	2.85	2.65	3.79	2.37
Pine dropseed	1.85	1.13	1.86	6.81
Sedge spp.	2.80	3.56	2.99	1.46
Orchardgrass	4.83	6.83	2.54	0.79
Arizona fescue	21.98	39.35	32.24	31.28
Mountain muhly	14.96	13.50	12.99	11.73
Muhly spp.	0.00	2.70	3.27	2.28
Bluegrass spp.	9.48	16.12	4.99	3.45
Little bluestem	2.87	2.70	4.27	2.89
Squirrel-tail	6.83	5.38	2.58	6.13
Other grasses	4.00	0.42	3.51	3.79
Subtotal	78.65	98.13	76.32	NA
Forbs				
Bur clover	2.10	0.76	2.33	1.91
Other forbs	0.00	1.11	11.33	23.13
Subtotal	2.10	1.87	13.66	NA
Shrubs/trees				
Ponderosa pine	15.20	0.00	7.30	NA
Gambel oak	3.23	0.00	2.72	NA
Other shrubs	0.80	0.00	0.00	NA
Subtotal	19.23	0.00	10.02	NA
Total	99.98	100.00	100.00	NA

[a] Values are a proportion of the total herbaceous production.

[b] NA = value not available.

Consumption equivalence values are based on the species of animal and on physical and physiological factors influencing the consumption rate. In this example, assumed mean body weight for elk is 452 pounds (205 kg) and 1,000 pounds (454 kg) for cattle, with a daily consumption rate averaging 2.5% of their respective body weight. This would equate to a daily DMI of 11.2 pounds (5.1 kg) for elk and 25.1 pounds (11.4 kg) for cattle. Therefore, the consumption equivalence for the impact of cattle on elk (E_1) would be 2.2, and the impact of elk on cattle (E_2) would be 0.45.

The third element necessary to calculate the competitive trade-off coefficient is the range overlap value. Data of habitat use and overlap are presented in Table 67. During spring, elk utilization appeared to be distributed evenly throughout the study area, with elk using 2,785 acres (1,127 ha), or 45.1% of the area. Cattle use was 3,637 acres (1,472 ha), or 58.9% of the allotment. Finally, autumn elk use was limited to 1,507 acres (610 ha), or 24.4%. Using GIS, it was possible to determine the degree of range overlap between spring elk and cattle and between autumn elk and cattle (Table 67). The data indicate that, of the area used by cattle, 1,811 acres (733 ha) or 49.8% had been previously grazed by elk. Likewise, 605 acres (245 ha) or 40.2% were previously grazed by cattle. These are the data required to account for the influence of range overlap on competitive interactions.

Using these data, it is possible to estimate the total trade-off coefficient for the interaction of elk and cattle (Table 68). Under the conditions described in this example, the trade-off coefficient for cattle on elk would be 0.94, or for every unit of change in the number of cattle on the allotment, there would be a change of 0.94 elk that the area could support without exceeding proper use. Similarly, the trade-off coefficient for elk on cattle would be 0.14, or with a unit of change in the number of elk on the area, there would be a change of 0.14 cattle the area could support.

Taking the example one step farther and incorporating forage availability, while assuming a proper-use rate of 50% of available forage, the allowable forage crop for cattle on the allotment was 690,688 pounds (313,296 kg), or a total grazing capacity for cattle of 1,148 cattle-unit months. Similarly, the allowable forage crop for elk in autumn at a 50% proper-use rate, would be 1,017,432 pounds (461,507 kg), or

Table 67. Summary of amount of range used and overlap for elk and cattle in central Arizona

Species	Range use in acres (ha)	Area of overlap in acres (ha)	Percentage of relative overlap
Spring elk	2,785 (1,127)	Not applicable	Not applicable
Cattle	3,637 (1,472)	1,811 (733)	49.8
Autumn elk	1,507 (610)	605 (245)	40.2

Table 68.   Coefficients used to estimate competitive trade-off for elk and cattle interaction in central Arizona

Competition factor	Competition coefficients	
	Cattle/autumn elk	Spring elk/cattle
Diet similarity (α or β)	1.070	0.630
Consumption equivalence	2.200	0.450
Range overlap	0.402	0.498
Trade-off coefficient	0.940	0.140

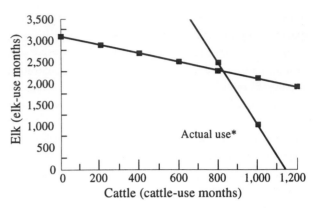

Figure 152.   Trade-off evaluation in the number of elk an area can support with the addition of a given number of cattle.

a total grazing capacity of 3,076 elk-unit months. Using the trade-off coefficients derived with the given grazing capacities by species would yield the trade-off curve shown in Figure 152. Furthermore, if the data on grazing capacity were integrated with the trade-off coefficients, the resulting N_{max} would be 826 for cattle and 2,291 for elk. The combined optimal stocking of elk and cattle (3,117) would be greater than either of the individual grazing capacities.

However, the ultimate question is, what is the intensity of the competition between elk and cattle in this example? The year these data were collected, a total of 578 cow/calf pairs used the allotment for 45 days, and a total of 952 elk-use months were determined to have taken place on the allotment. Plotted data on the trade-off curve (Figure 152) in-

dicate that the actual number of elk and cattle using this allotment are well below any serious competitive threshold.

Outlook

Almost 50 years have passed since Hall (1955) indicated that the issue of elk competition with other ungulates was an increasing problem. Little has happened to change this situation. In fact, increases in elk numbers throughout most of the western United States during the past few decades have

Elk and mule deer cohabit major portions of their respective ranges and their habitat-use patterns, including food habits, also tend to overlap. However, elk move more and discriminate less, regarding the selection of habitat types, and their food habits are broader and more flexible. *Photo by Hugh Hogle; courtesy of the Rocky Mountain Elk Foundation.*

only increased the potential for competitive interactions between elk and other ungulates.

An area in which the potential for competition may not be as severe as once thought is that of elk and cattle interaction. Previous logic of competition for the forage resource between these two species was that one cow was equivalent to two elk and, conversely, two elk were equal to one cow. As demonstrated, there are several factors that serve to reduce the relative impact of these two species on one another. Although their interaction still is a factor in management of these two species, the magnitude of their interaction is far less significant than previously believed.

Of greater concern is the developing competition of elk with native ungulates, such as mule deer. Throughout much of the western United States, there is concern about the decline in mule deer numbers. One possible explanation for this decline is the increase in elk numbers on traditional mule deer range. Two major reasons for increased interaction of the species relate to changes in habitat use by elk.

Throughout much of the historic elk range, there has been extensive habitat modification, which has had both a positive and negative impact on elk distribution. In many areas of the West, substantial human development has occurred on what was once elk winter range. This has forced elk to winter in areas that were once predominately used by mule deer. In addition, past land management policy has resulted in the conversion of large areas from moderately dense forest predominately used by mule deer, to nearly open, parklike forest, which is highly favored by elk. The combination of these two events has significantly increased the potential of competitive interaction for both forage and space resources.

Effective management of elk in the future will have to incorporate considerations to minimize their competitive interactions with other ungulates. An understanding of how and when potential competitors use available resources will aid in management decisions that should facilitate multiple species utilization of shared range.

9

KENNETH J. RAEDEKE, JOSHUA J. MILLSPAUGH
AND PATRICK E. CLARK

Population Characteristics

The basic data necessary for an understanding of any population are birth and death rates, age and sex composition, numerical abundance and the nature and form of regulatory mechanisms (Eberhardt 1971, 1985). However, seldom is all of this information about the dynamics of a population available for management decisions. Instead, the data likely consist of limited information on age and sex structure and reproductive rates of the population. These rates and variables typically are pooled collections of data gathered from a subsample of individual elk from a given population. Although it is the individual that dies and the individual that reproduces, the ecological effect of these individual events must be evaluated from a sample subset representing the entire population.

For purposes of this chapter, an elk population is defined as a group of animals that share a particular environment and occupy a contiguous region, such as a management unit. Such a population has characteristics that may be modeled and described mathematically. These include production, abundance, survival and mortality, age and sex composition and movement. These processes do not occur in isolation, but are interrelated with biotic and abiotic attributes of the animals' surroundings.

Analysis of the interaction of these characteristics can provide estimates of elk population growth, population regulation and individual life expectancy—information important to wildlife managers. Therefore, collecting and analyzing information concerning elk population characteristics and the subsequent managerial decisions based on that information play essential roles in the conservation of elk populations.

Natality

Breeding and Conception

This section deals with estimates of reproduction for elk populations. Natality is defined as the number of calves born each year in a population. Although commonly used in a similar context, fecundity refers to reproductive output from an individual cow elk. Knowing an elk population's natality is important to managers because reproductive output often is related to population health and status.

Elk are seasonal breeders whose reproductive strategy is adapted to seasonal fluctuations in forage quantity and quality (Sadlier 1987). Cows are bred in early autumn after the peak of nutritional demands from lactation, while there is time to improve body condition before the stressors of winter. In early spring, increasing nutritional demands on cows in late gestation tend to coincide with increasing availability of high-quality forage. Calves are born in late spring when forage quantity is rapidly increasing and forage quality peaks.

Evidence of conception may be found in ovaries of cow elk harvested during the autumn hunting season. Interpretation of such evidence requires understanding of the processes of Graafian follicle development, shedding of ova, fertilization and formation of corpora lutea.

Ovulation and Conception

Graafian follicles are spherical groups of cells in the ovary, with each follicle containing one ovum. Immature follicles normally are not more than 0.08 inch (2 mm) in diameter. Activity begins 6 to 8 weeks before estrus; several follicles in each ovary increase to 0.28 to 0.35 inch (7–9 mm) in diameter early in this period. As estrus approaches, all but one follicle per pair of ovaries regress. The active follicle pair may increase to 0.31 to 0.43 inch (8–11 mm) in diameter the days before estrus, and to 0.39 to 0.71 inch (10–17 mm) in diameter immediately thereafter. There is then a second period of follicular development, during which follicles may grow to more than 0.20 inch (5 mm) in diameter. One may rupture, resulting in formation of a secondary (or postconception) corpus luteum, 0.20 to 0.39 inch (5–10 mm) in diameter. The ovum shed at this time ordinarily is not fertilized. In one study, two-thirds of sexually active cows exhibited two corpora lutea of pregnancy—one primary and one secondary—although there was only one fetus in every case (Halazon and Buechner 1956). The presence of large follicles or corpora lutea in the ovaries of an elk harvested between early autumn and spring probably indicates fertilization and implantation of a single ovum during the previous estrus.

Timing of Conception

Peak periods of conception vary among subspecies, populations and years (Table 69), but most elk are bred from mid-September through mid-October. Breeding may begin as early as mid-August and extend into early or mid-November (Trainer 1971). Anomalies in the timing of conception will be explored later in this chapter.

Conception dates are related to a number of variables, including forage conditions, bull age, cow lactation status and cow condition (Trainer 1971, Noyes et al. 1996). McCullough (1969) observed that the onset of the rut in Tule elk occurred earlier in good forage years than in poor forage years. Based on 25 Roosevelt elk cows 3 to 10 years of age, Trainer (1971) reported that cows with high kidney fat indices (indicating good physical condition) conceived earlier than cows having low kidney fat indices. Similarly, Noyes et al. (1996) reported that nonlactating cows were in better condition and bred earlier than lactating cows. Lactating cows conceived later than nonlactating cows, presumably due to the high nutritional demands of lactation and typically poorer body condition of lactating cows.

Some research also suggests that conception dates tend to be later and more asynchronous in herds with predominately yearling sires (Hines et al. 1985, Squibb et al. 1991). Hines and Lemos (1979) reported that, among captive elk, births of yearling-sired calves peaked in the first half of July; whereas, calves sired by mature bulls were born in late May and early June. Nearly two-thirds of the conceptions in cows bred by yearling bulls occurred in October, whereas three-quarters of conceptions from breeding by 3.5-year-old and older bulls occurred in September. Follis (1972) reported a similar delay in conception when yearling bulls were the primary breeders. In northeastern Oregon, Noyes et al. (1996) observed that conception dates of Rocky Mountain elk cows bred by bulls older than 3 years of age were earlier than conception dates of cows bred by bulls less than 2 years of age. Mean conception date among cows sired by 5-year-old bulls was September 21, whereas the mean conception date for cows bred by yearling bulls was October 7 (Table 70). The possible reason for delays in births of yearling-sired bulls was discussed by Prothero et al. (1979), who suggested that yearling bulls were sexually active about 1 month later than mature bulls.

Bull age also may alter the length of the rut, which influences the synchrony of cow conception. Noyes et al. (1996) reported that, when 5-year-old bulls were the primary breeders, length of the rut was 41 days, with 90% of the

Table 69. Conception dates of elk from various locations

State	Location	Subspecies (sample)	Mean conception dates (range)	Source
Washington	Olympic Peninsula	Roosevelt	Oct. 1 (Sept. 15–Oct. 15)	Schwartz and Mitchell (1945)
	Mount St. Helens	Roosevelt (29)	Oct. 4 (Sept. 11–Oct. 23)	Merrill (1987)
Oregon	Western	Roosevelt (37)	Sept. 23 (Aug. 19–Oct. 30)	Trainer (1971)
	Northeast	Rocky Mountain	Oct. 1 (Sept. 10–Oct. 27)	Trainer (1971)
	Starkey Experimental Forest and Range Station	Rocky Mountain	Sept. 21 (Sept. 9–Oct. 19)[a]	Noyes et al. (1996)
Montana	National Bison Range	Rocky Mountain (40)	Early Oct. (Sept. 16–Nov. 4)[b]	Morrison et al. (1959)
Utah	Cache Management Unit	Rocky Mountain (44)	Mid-October (end Sept. and beg. Nov.)[c]	Squibb et al. (1986)

[a] When 5-year-old bulls were sires.

[b] 65% bred between September 26 and October 10.

[c] Bimodal, with peaks at the end of September and beginning of November.

Table 70. Conception dates of Rocky Mountain elk at Starkey Experimental Forest and Range Station, Oregon, 1989 to 1993

Bull age in years	Number of bulls	Mean conception date (range)[a]	90% of cows bred
1	26	Oct. 7 (Sept. 15–Nov. 24)[x]	Oct. 21
2	26	Oct. 3 (Sept. 15–Nov. 8)[x]	Oct. 12
3	27	Sept. 25 (Sept. 11–Oct. 22)[y]	Oct. 6
4	28	Sept. 27 (Sept. 15–Nov. 8)[y]	Oct. 3
5	33	Sept. 21 (Sept. 9–Oct. 19)[z]	Sept. 28

Source: Noyes et al. 1996.

[a] Dates were statistically different at $p < 0.05$; x versus y and z, y versus x and z, and z versus x and y.

cows bred by September 28. However, the rut lasted 71 days when yearling bulls were the primary sires (Table 70), with 90% of the cows being bred by October 21.

It has been hypothesized that heavy hunting pressure on mature bulls may influence conception dates. In Utah, Squibb et al. (1986) reported a bimodal distribution of conception dates for a heavily hunted elk herd and a decrease in the frequency of conceptions around the opening dates of the regular bull hunting season. The period between peak conception frequencies coincided with the hunting season and was not explained by age or condition of cows. It is important to note that, although heavy hunting interfered with breeding by delaying conception, conception was not prevented in this population.

Estrous Cycle Length, Recurrence and Seasonality

For conception to occur, copulation must take place during the short period of sexual receptivity (estrus) of cow elk. This period may be less than 12 hours, but generally ranges from 12 to 24 hours (Frandson and Whitten 1981). Morrison (1960a) reported that the duration of estrus in cows from a captive Rocky Mountain elk herd ranged from 12 to 17 hours, although the actual duration could not be determined due to logistic constraints. For these same elk, the duration of an estrous cycle ranged from 19 to 25 days, with a mean duration of 21 days (Morrison 1960a). Similarly, Frandson and Whitten (1981) reported an estrous cycle of 21 to 22 days.

If fertilization does not occur during this short period, a second estrus occurs about 21 days later (Morrison 1960a). The number of recurrent estrus cycles and the maximum period over which estrus occurs varies among elk populations. The factors responsible for termination are unknown, but likely are related to the condition of the cow. Wallace et al. (1988) reported conception of a cow within the first week of March in Arizona, meaning that as many as to

eight estrous cycles may have occurred before conception. Morrison (1960a) documented four recurrent estrums, and Wishart (1981) reported that one cow had six.

The potential for recurrent estrous periods relates directly to the potential for late births of elk calves. For instance, a cow that mates successfully during her fourth estrous cycle could produce a calf 9 weeks later than the presumed birth date of a calf conceived during the first estrous cycle. Such late births could have important ramifications to the subsequent survival of late-born calves and population dynamics of the herd. Consequences of late parturition will be discussed later.

Fecundity by Age Class

Fecundity rate is the number of live births per female during a specified time interval. In ungulates, fecundity rates are strongly related to female body size, condition and age (Blaxter and Hamilton 1980, Hines et al. 1985, Albon et al. 1986, Cameron et al. 1993), which are further related to the nutritional plane of females (Albon et al. 1983). Mean fecundity rates of each female age class in an elk population can provide valuable insight into the status of that population. Elk populations under stress due to poor habitat conditions or high population density may display lower mean fecundity rates than do less-stressed populations. Typically, lower fecundity rates in stressed populations would be most evident in the youngest and oldest age classes (Caughley 1977). Colonizing populations, which typically are not limited by habitat or density constraints, may exhibit higher mean fecundity rates, especially in the yearling age class (e.g., McCorquodale et al. 1988).

Breeding Success of Yearling Cows

There is no evidence to suggest that cow elk breed during their first autumn, that is, at 3 to 4 months of age. However, cow elk may become sexually mature during their second autumn, although the proportion of yearling females that successfully conceive is highly variable between elk populations and between years (Tables 71 and 72) within the same population (Flook 1970b, McCorquodale et al. 1988). There are four lines of evidence on the reproductive contribution of yearling cows (to 15 months old): (1) the state of the reproductive tract in their second winter (when they are 16 to 23 months old); (2) the presence of pigmented corpora lutea in the ovary; (3) placental scars on the wall of the uterus; and less reliably (4), evidence of previous lactation when they enter their third winter (at about 28 months of age).

The likelihood of a yearling cow successfully breeding presumably is influenced by her condition and state of matu-

Table 71.   Proportions of pregnant yearling cows in various elk populations

State and location	Subspecies (sample size)	Percentage pregnant	Reference
Wyoming			
Yellowstone	Rocky Mountain (large number)	0	Murie (1951:123)
Yellowstone	Rocky Mountain (14)	7	Cheatum and Gaab (1952)
Yellowstone	Rocky Mountain (39)	2.7	Kittiams (1953)
Yellowstone	Rocky Mountain (104)	12	Greer (1966)
Yellowstone	Rocky Mountain	0–34	Houston (1982)
Adjacent to Grand			
Teton National Park	Rocky Mountain (108)	15	Cole (1969)
Utah			
Logan	Rocky Mountain (41)	12	Follis and Spillett (1974)
Nebo	Rocky Mountain (117)	13	Hancock (1957)
Oklahoma			
Wichita Mountains	Rocky Mountain (14)	14	Buechner and Swanson (1955)
Colorado			
Rocky Mountain			
National Park	Rocky Mountain (6)	17	Buechner and Swanson (1955)
Washington			
Yakima-Wenas	Rocky Mountain (6)	17	Buechner and Swanson (1955)
Mount St. Helens	Roosevelt (16)	31	Merrill (1987)
British Columbia	Rocky Mountain (82)	21	Flook (1970)
Michigan			
Pigeon River	Rocky Mountain (30)	23	Moran (1973)
Montana			
Sun River	Rocky Mountain (19)	26	Knight (1970)
Oregon			
Eastern	Rocky Mountain (15)	33	Trainer (1971)
Blue Mountains	Rocky Mountain (85)	48	Buechner and Swanson (1955)
Western	Roosevelt (25)	12	Trainer (1971)
California			
Owen's valley	Tule (4)	75	McCullough (1969)

ration, which is affected, in turn, by the environment. Hancock (1957) reported that female calves that experienced a hard winter were less likely to breed as yearlings than were those that did not experience a stressful winter (Table 73). Greer (1968) speculated that much of the variation in yearling cow pregnancy rates was attributed to the relative severity of the preceding winter. Similarly, Houston (1982) reported that yearling pregnancy rates were nega-

tively correlated with the severity of the previous winter and population density.

Additional factors, such as body size, probably influence the likelihood of successful breeding in yearling female elk. Greer (1968) reported yearling Rocky Mountain elk in the Northern Yellowstone herd weighing less than 335 pounds (152 kg) who did not become pregnant; whereas, only 10%

Table 72.   Annual variation in breeding by yearling Rocky Mountain cow elk from the Northern Yellowstone elk herd

Year	Number examined	Number pregnant
1961–1962	70	6
1962–1963	13	0
1963–1964	32	9
1964–1965	35	3
1965–1966	27	1
1966–1967	44	15
1967–1968	92	12
Total	313	46

Source: Greer 1968.

Table 73.   Yearling Rocky Mountain cow elk ovulation after a mild winter (1950–1951) and a severe winter (1951–1952) in Utah

Year	Herd	Percentage of yearling cows with current corpora lutea	Percentage of yearling cows ovulating[a]
Autumn 1951	Cache	33.0	66.0
	Nebo	18.2	10.7
Autumn 1952	Cache	0.0	0.0
	Nebo	3.3	0.0

Source: Hancock 1957.

[a] As shown by pigmented ovarian scars on the subsequent year.

Several environmental factors, such as forage quality and availability, which influence body condition, may affect yearling cow breeding success. *Photo by Rocky Spencer.*

Table 74. Percentage of breeding in 2-year-old cows of five elk herds

Location	Subspecies (sample size)	Percent breeding	Source
Western Oregon	Roosevelt (289)	33	Trainer (1971)
Sun River, Montana	Rocky Mountain (14)	64	Knight (1970)
Pigeon River, Michigan	Rocky Mountain (35)	74	Moran (1973)
Eastern Oregon	Rocky Mountain (105)	92	Trainer (1971)
Mount St. Helens, Washington	Roosevelt (13)	69	Merrill (1987)

of yearling females weighing 335 to 359 pounds (152–163 kg) and 25% of yearlings weighing 359 to 373 pounds (163–169 kg) became pregnant. Similarly, Buechner and Swanson (1955) suggested that yearling pregnancy rates of Rocky Mountain elk in southeastern Washington may be dependent on the nutritional status of juveniles and lactating cows, as influenced by population density and range condition. These observations support the hypothesis that breeding by yearling cows is influenced strongly by differences in their growth and development, which is influenced by nutritional and environmental factors.

Breeding Success of Adult Cows

Successful breeding in 2-year-old cows is less variable (Table 74) than in yearlings (Knight 1970, Trainer 1971, Moran 1973). Nutritional and environmental factors also influence the reproductive maturity and success of 2-year-old cows, but not to the extent that they influence yearling cows.

Cow elk 3.5 to 7.5 years of age generally are regarded as the major contributors to the productivity of elk populations (Table 75). In cows more than 3 years of age, reproductive success is influenced largely by body condition, environmental stresses and recent reproductive history. Lactating cows (cows that successfully raised a calf to the breeding season) may be less likely to conceive than nonlactating cows, especially after severe winters or those on poor quality rangelands. Harper (1971) evaluated pregnancy rates and lactation status of Roosevelt elk in western

Oregon and Rocky Mountain elk in northeastern Oregon. He found that lactating Roosevelt elk cows (n = 52) exhibited a 48% pregnancy rate compared with a 75% pregnancy rate in nonlactating Roosevelt elk cows (n = 50). The pregnancy rate of lactating Rocky Mountain elk cows (n = 56) was 82%; whereas, 100% of the nonlactating Rocky Mountain elk cows examined were pregnant (n = 9).

Although an 80% pregnancy rate may seem adequate for prime-age breeders, such a rate actually is quite poor. Elk managers documenting pregnancy rates less than 80% should attempt to determine the cause of such low rates. Considering that nearly 95% of adult cows are fertile in most populations, an observed pregnancy rate of 80% indicates a significant rate of pregnancy failure. Pregnancy failure in conceiving females may be due to a number of factors, including early embryonic mortality as a result of endocrine imbalances and aged gametes. Abortion caused by severe malnutrition or toxins is another possibility.

Table 75. Reported pregnancy rates of prime (3.5- to 7.5-year-old) cow elk in different populations

State or province and area	Subspecies (sample size)	Percentage fertile	Reference
Oregon			
Western	Roosevelt	49	Harper (1971)
Michigan	Rocky Mountain (112)	84	Moran (1973)
Oregon			
Eastern	Rocky Mountain (105)	90	Trainer (1971)
Alberta			
Banff-Jasper	Rocky Mountain (358)	93	Flook (1970)
Wyoming			
Yellowstone	Rocky Mountain (269)	94	Greer (1968)
Gallatin	Rocky Mountain (73)	98	Greer (1965)
Yellowstone	Rocky Mountain (88)	99	Cheatum and Gaab (1952)
Sun River	Rocky Mountain (52)	81	Knight (1973)
Washington			
Mount St. Helens	Roosevelt (62)	87	Merrill (1987)

Mature elk cows (those more than 3.5 years old) are the primary contributors to elk populations. Cow elk typically segregate themselves to calve, but rejoin the herd within a few weeks. *Photo by Bruce Richards.*

Table 76. Fertility of various older age classes of Rocky Mountain cow elk in the Northern Yellowstone herd, as shown by presence of corpora lutea

Age in years[a]	Sample size	Number with corpora lutea	Percent with corpora lutea
7.5	102	100	98
8.5	75	72	96
9.5	74	74	100
10–14	100[b]	94	94
15–21	37[c]	17	46

Sources: Cheatum and Gaab 1952, Greer 1966, Greer and Hawkins 1967.

[a] All elk aged by tooth wear in lower jaw.

[b] Greer's 10–15 age class combined with Cheatum and Gaab's 10–14 age class.

[c] Greer's 16–21 age class combined with Cheatum and Gaab's 15–21 age class.

Reproductive Longevity of Cows

The reproductive longevity of cow elk varies between populations because of geographically variable genetic and environmental factors. Rocky Mountain elk cows from the Northern Yellowstone herd typically begin to decline in reproductive fitness after reaching 14 years of age (Table 76). In Michigan, Moran (1973) reported that Rocky Mountain elk cows older than 7 years had pregnancy rates of 53% compared with 84% for cows 3 to 7 years of age. Trainer (1971) observed that Rocky Mountain elk cows in northeastern Oregon maintained high reproductive capacity through 11 years of age. In western Oregon, he examined eight Roosevelt elk cows older than 11 years and reported that none was pregnant. Also in western Oregon, Harper (1971) reported that pregnancy rates for 3- to 7-year-old Roosevelt cow elk averaged 49%, whereas cows 8 to 10 years old averaged only 30% pregnancy rates.

Influence of Bull Age on Pregnancy Rates

Some studies suggest that pregnancy rates are lower in elk herds with fewer older bulls, in which yearling bulls do most of the breeding. Smith (1980) indicated that pregnancy rates declined from 77% to 61% for Roosevelt elk in Washington and, at the same time, the number of preseason branched bulls declined from 8 to 5 per 100 cows. Hines et al. (1985) also reported that pregnancy rates declined in Roosevelt elk in Oregon (from 67%–47%) when the number of preseason branched bulls declined from 39 to less than 10 per 100 cows. Squibb et al. (1991) reported that pregnancy rates of Rocky Mountain elk in northern Utah were higher in an area with 41 bulls per 100 cows preseason versus another with 15 bulls per 100 cows and few older bulls.

Kimball and Wolfe (1979) discussed a comprehensive study on the effects of "any-bull" hunting on elk population dynamics in northern Utah. Before 1968, bull harvest in northern Utah was restricted by limiting the number of hunters. After initiating any-bull hunting in 1968, hunter numbers increased nearly 500%. Yearling bulls in the male component of the harvest increased from 35% to 75%, and few mature bulls remained in the herd. However, productivity of the herd remained unchanged from pre-1968 levels at 48 calves per 100 cows, and pregnancy rates averaged 12% for yearlings and 85% for adult cows.

Perhaps the most comprehensive and experimental approach taken thus far to examine the role of yearlings and mature bull breeding efficiency was conducted with a closed, but free-ranging elk population within the 30-square-mile (78 km²) big game enclosure at Starkey Experimental Forest and Range Station near La Grande, Oregon. Noyes et al. (1996) reported an increase in pregnancy rates of Rocky Mountain elk cows from 89% when yearling bulls were the primary sires to 97% when 5-year-old bulls were the primary breeders. However, the increase was not statistically significant. Noyes et al. (1996) considered the 89% pregnancy rate they observed to be maximum breeding potential for yearling bulls. Follis (1972) reported similar pregnancy rates of 86% and 93% for captive elk cows bred by yearling bulls and 3.5-year-old bulls, respectively.

Pregnancy

Timing of Birth

Reported gestation length varies by subspecies and region. Lantz (1910) reported that the gestation length of elk ranged from 249 to 262 days. On the basis of a known conception date, Morrison et al. (1959) reported a captive bred Rocky Mountain elk calf was born following a 247-day gestation. Harper (1971) concluded that the gestation period of Roosevelt elk was approximately 250 days; Harper et al. (1967) reported a gestation range of 258 to 265 days.

Given a normal gestation length of about 250 days, with the peak of conception occurring from the middle to the end of September, calves typically are born in late May and early June. Variation of mean parturition dates between elk populations may be related to variations in plant phenology, timing of peak forage quality between geographic areas or, as previously mentioned, differences in the age of the primary sires or cow body condition. Rust (1946) reported that June 1 was the mean parturition date for Rocky Mountain elk in northern Idaho. Parturition dates for the Northern Yellowstone herd ranged from May 13 to June 10 (Rush 1932a). Johnson (1951) reported the peak parturition date for the Gallatin herd in West Gallatin river drainage of southwestern Montana was June 1; parturition ranged from May 21 to June 12. Schwartz and Mitchell (1945) observed that Roosevelt elk on the Olympic Peninsula calved between May 14 and July 10. Flook (1970b) reported that the peak dates for Rocky Mountain elk were May 24 in Banff National Park and June 1 in Jasper National Park, both in Alberta. Roberts (1974) reported May 15 to June 15 parturition dates for Rocky Mountain elk in Idaho, peaking the last week of May and first week of June. Reichelt (1973a) reported similar patterns of parturition for Rocky Mountain elk on the West Fork of the Madison River in Montana; of 13 calves, 6 were born between May 17 and May 24, and 7 were born between May 25 and June 4.

There is an implicit assumption that late breeding is a rare occurrence, but this may not be the case (Freddy 1987). Hamilton and Blaxter (1980b) and Asher and Adam (1985) reported that only 60% to 65% of the calves were born in a 20- to 30-day period. The remaining 35% to 40% were born primarily during the 45 days following the peak calving period. Thus, it appears that some fraction of an elk population may naturally breed late. Such late breeding may reflect influences of social behavior involving rank and dominance (Clutton-Brock et al. 1987b), in addition to the aforementioned reasons.

Multiple Pregnancies

Multiple pregnancies in elk are extremely rare. Of 1,186 pregnant cow elk examined by Flook (1970b), only two multiple pregnancies (0.2%) were observed. Kittams (1953)

Twinning is rare enough (approximately one-third of 1% of all pregnancies) that it is not a significant factor in elk population dynamics. *Photo by Bruce Richards.*

reported only five twinnings in 1,690 pregnancies (0.3%). McCullough (1969) reported twins in 1 of 63 Tule elk in Owens Valley, California. Twins were evident in less than 1% of more than 3,000 elk from the Yellowstone area (Houston 1982). Mitchell (1973) reported twinning rates of red deer in Scotland as 1 in 600, and Mitchell et al. (1981) reported twinning rates of 1 in 400 among red deer. Because of their rarity, multiple pregnancies probably are not an important factor in elk population dynamics.

Out-of-season Births

Although the majority of elk calves are born in May and June, there are reports of out-of-season births. However, seasonal breeding and poor survival of out-of-season births limit the prevalence of asynchronous reproduction of ungulates in northern latitudes (Sadlier 1987, Smith 1994).

Smith (1994) reported five out-of-season elk births on the National Elk Refuge; four in autumn and one in early spring. He speculated that out-of-season births occur with some regularity on the refuge and that more out-of-season births probably are not witnessed, due to the secretive nature of cows and the hider strategy used by calves. Four of the out-of-season births reported by Smith (1994) occurred approximately 5 months after the normal peak of parturition. Given a 250-day gestation, calves born in mid-November would have been conceived in early to mid-March.

Wallace et al. (1988) also reported conception of an elk cow within the first week of March in Arizona. If this cow entered estrus during September, as many as eight estrous cycles may have occurred before conception. Wishart (1981) reported a near-term fetus recovered from an Alberta elk on September 21. Murie (1951) reported an April birth of an elk near the National Elk Refuge.

Role of Bulls in the Breeding Ecology of Elk

Many elk populations in the western U.S. have been subjected to intensive hunting pressure, and the proportion of mature bulls in these populations relative to proportions in unhunted herds is low. Declines in posthunting bull-to-cow and cow-to-calf ratios in many western states have prompted concerns that reductions in the number of mature bulls has impaired the breeding capability of many elk populations.

In general, it is hypothesized that some of the reproductive burden has shifted to yearling bulls, who are less efficient breeders than bulls older than 2 years. It is further hypothesized that, when yearling bulls are the primary sires, pregnancy rates decline and conception dates are later and more spread out, resulting in later-born calves and higher overwinter calf mortality (Follis 1972, Prothero 1977, Kim-

As with other young ungulates, elk calves blend into their environment very well. Such camouflage helps reduce predation. *Photo by Dick Hancock.*

ball and Wolfe 1979, Prothero et al. 1979, Squibb et al. 1986, Freddy 1987a, Noyes et al. 1996). Also, Follis (1972), Prothero (1977), Kimball and Wolfe (1979), and Prothero et al. (1979) speculated that a cycle of later-breeding cows may be perpetuated from the potentially later and less-efficient breeding cycle of yearling bulls.

Yearling Bull Breeding Efficiency

Given the previously discussed data regarding bull age and conception dates and rates, a few questions arise. First, are yearling bulls as physiologically capable of breeding as efficiently as older bulls? Trainer (1969) concluded that most yearling bulls show viable spermatogensis and are physiologically capable of successful conception. Conaway (1952:314) examined 12 yearling bulls and reported that all had "well developed" epididymal tubules that contained "abundant sperm." Harper (1971) examined testes of yearling bulls collected during the first week of November; 96% of the testes contained sperm, and almost 70% had sperm content similar to bulls older than 3 years of age. Therefore, based on empirical data, it appears that yearling bulls are at least physiologically capable of breeding.

Another question is whether yearling bulls are sexually active as early in the rut as are mature bulls. Observations

The prevalence of mature bulls in an elk population may influence the synchrony of cow elk conception and pregnancy rates, which may alter population characteristics. *Photo by Bruce Richards.*

suggest that yearling bulls and possibly 2-year-old bulls do not achieve the "hypersexual" rutting behavior of older bulls (Lincoln 1971, Follis 1972, Hines and Lemos 1979). Prothero et al. (1979) reported that yearling bulls were sexually active 1 month later than mature bulls, and the duration of their sexual activity 1 month shorter. Similarly, Struhsaker (1967) reported that bulls 3 years of age or older were more sexually active than younger bulls: of 368 heterosexual approaches observed, 348 (94%) were made by bulls older than 3 years. Six (2%) were by 2-year-old bulls and 14 (4%) were by yearling bulls.

Even if yearling bulls are sexually active and physiologically capable of breeding, behavioral factors may preclude yearling bulls from breeding. Older bulls tending harems often restrict breeding opportunities of yearling bulls by preventing them access to cows in estrus through intimidation and by physically driving them away from the cows (Conaway 1952, Struhsaker 1967, Squibb 1985). Also, cows in estrus exhibit a preference for older bulls and may not allow mounting by yearling bulls if older bulls are present (Morrison 1960a).

However, in the absence of older bulls, yearling bulls may breed cows. In fact, Squibb (1985) reported that mating by yearling bulls was common in the absence of mature bulls. Yearling bulls apparently served estrous cows through a mating system identical to that exhibited by older bulls. Squibb concluded that mating by yearlings represented a considerable contribution to the reproduction in a northern Utah herd, and that yearling bulls may compensate for the absence of older bulls. However, it also is important to note that, although mature bulls constituted less than 25% of the total bull population, they performed more than 70% of the completed copulations, indicating that, even in low proportions, mature bulls may do the majority of the breeding.

Hunting Regulations, Antler Restrictions and Effects on Elk Population Dynamics

The aforementioned declines in posthunting season bull-to-cow and cow-to-calf ratios have stimulated concerns in many states that reductions in the number of bull elk have impaired the breeding efficiency of many elk populations across North America. As a result, since the 1970s, states have implemented a number of regulatory changes that have focused primarily on varying the structure and number of seasons and placing minimum antler point restrictions on bulls that may be legally harvested. In hunted populations, the majority of mortality among bulls is due to hunting (Unsworth et al. 1993), therefore harvest regulations targeting specific age classes can have a substantial influence on the age structure of an elk population.

Generally, antler point restrictions are viewed as an effective way to fulfill the demands of hunters for elk hunting opportunities while simultaneously reducing the bull harvest. In the White River elk herd in Colorado, Freddy (1987) reported that regulations controlling bull harvest through antler restrictions were relatively more successful in increasing recruitment of bulls older than 2 years into the population than were regulations allowing any antlered bull to be harvested. However, if the objective is to produce trophy bulls, antler point regulations without restriction of hunter numbers does not appear to be a viable option (Carpenter 1991). Weigand and Mackie (1987) reported that most elk biologists believed that the only way to maintain trophy class bulls was to avoid hunting them altogether.

Many western states have used antler point restrictions in an attempt to increase bull recruitment. Antler point regulations were first implemented for elk in Colorado in 1931 (Carpenter 1991). In 1971, all spike bulls were protected statewide. However, during the 1971 experimental season that protected spike bulls, nearly half the branch-antlered bulls shot were yearlings. Posthunt counts showed 1.7 branch-antlered bulls per 100 cows—the lowest ratio in 5 years (Carpenter 1991). Therefore, in 1972, antler point regulations restricted harvest to bulls with four points or better in 10 selected areas in Colorado. This shifted pressure from yearling bulls to 2-year-olds, and reduced hunter harvest. In 1985, antler point regulations were used for the White River elk herd and, in 1986, as a result of low postseason bull-to-cow ratios, antler point regulations were implemented statewide. Data from the White River elk herd demonstrated that beginning in 1985, the impact of antler point regulations on total postseason bull-to-cow ratios was "positive, immediate and pronounced" (Carpenter 1991:21).

Several states also have instituted spike-only bull hunts, thus focusing harvests on recently recruited bulls. In the Elkhorn Mountains in Montana, a spike-only harvest regulation was in effect from 1987 through 1993 (Vore and DeSimone 1991). This regulation change resulted in a fourfold increase in the total number of bulls in the herd postseason and an increase by 40 times the number of bulls older than yearlings over the course of this 7-year period. Concern was raised that a spike-only regulation might significantly reduce the number of hunters. Harvest surveys indicated an initial decline in hunter numbers after the new season, although numbers of hunters returned to former levels within 2 years (Vore and DeSimone 1991).

In response to high elk harvest vulnerability due to extensive clearcuts, high road densities and low topographic relief, a spike-only regulation was instituted in Game Management Units 60, 61 and 62A in Idaho (Hughbanks and Irby 1991). The rationale was that spike-only regulations would focus hunting pressure on spike bulls, while enabling the protection of yearling bulls with branched antlers. Therefore, even if all yearling spike bulls were harvested, recruitment of bulls into the 2-year age class would still occur, because 24% of yearling bulls had branched antlers. Subsequent winter herd composition counts indicated that the spike-only regulation in these units was successful in increasing bull recruitment into the older age classes.

Regulations based on antler configurations, not the number of antler points, also have been used in areas such as Montana. Low cow-to-calf ratios in the Gravelly-Snowcrest Mountains in southwestern Montana in the early 1980s coincided with high mortality rates of bulls under any antlered bull harvest regulation (Hamlin and Ross 1991). Concern over these low ratios and potential impacts on the breeding biology of these populations caused changes in hunting regulations during 1981. The general elk season was limited to branch-antlered bulls, which were defined as any elk having at least one antler with a branch of at least 4 inches (10.2 cm) from the main beam. Hamlin and Ross (1991) observed substantial increases in bull-to-cow ratios in the spring of 1982, following implementation of the branch-antlered bull regulation. Calf-to-cow ratios improved to 44:100 from lows of 25:100 before increased numbers of breeding bulls could have influenced those ratios. Subsequent concern about illegal mortality of spike bulls resulted in implementation of a brow-tined bull regulation in 1990 (Hamlin and Ross 1991).

Antler restrictions have their opponents. Some argue that regulations limiting harvest to three-, four- or five-point bulls fall short because they protect only yearlings and perhaps 2-year-olds. Furthermore, it is argued, such regulations have a tendency to increase pressure on the first legal age class, merely postponing the heavy harvest of a generation. Harper (1985) commented that remedies such as antler-point restrictions were ineffective in the long term. They asserted that limited-entry hunting was the best option for controlling harvests of bull elk.

It is worth pointing out that, for antler restrictions to be effective, the population must be below carrying capacity (Carpenter and Gill 1987, Ueckermann 1987). Controlling the cow segment of the population is of paramount importance for the management of large bulls, which may be accomplished effectively through antlerless permits in many hunting areas (Raedeke and Taber 1985). Carpenter and Gill (1987) noted that increasing the number of cows may result in decreased bull survivorship, due to the reduction of preferred forage species.

Population Consequences of Few Mature Bulls

Although a few studies have reported a correlation between the lack of older bulls and declines in pregnancy rates and later conception dates, there is little evidence relating low mature bull numbers to declines in calf production, survival or recruitment. Freddy (1987), studying Colorado's White River elk herd, concluded that, although there was a decline in postseason calf counts, coupled with declining mature bull numbers, the definitive cause of the declining cow-to-calf ratios could not be determined. He hypothesized that declining herd nutrition, as related to increased elk numbers, was the most likely factor affecting reproduction. Hamlin and Ross (1991) also indicated a correlation between bull-to-cow and cow-to-calf ratios, but concluded that other factors were involved and a convincing relationship between mature bulls and calf production and subsequent survival could not be determined. DeSimone et al. (1993) described a similar relationship in the Elkhorn

Mountains in Montana. After a change from open bull hunting from 1982 through 1985 to spikes-only or older bulls by permit only from 1987 through 1993, significant increases in the number of bulls were recorded. During the same period, the average number of calves per 100 cows increased from 32 to 37—a difference that was not statistically significant. Despite such correlative data, further research is necessary to determine population consequences of few mature bulls.

Consequences of Late Conception and Parturition

If yearling bulls are the primary sires and conception dates are a month later, what are the potential impacts on herd dynamics? Late conception and parturition dates could substantially influence elk population structure and dynamics. Calves born in July, a month later than normal, may not have enough time during the remainder of the summer and autumn to grow adequately and build fat reserves before forage becomes limited and environmental conditions worsen in winter. These late-born calves may enter winter in less than optimal body condition and are more likely to suffer winter mortality than are calves born during the typical peak of parturition. For example, B. L. Smith et al. (1997) reported that winter calf survival and mean birth weights were correlated positively for calves that entered winter. However, supplemental feeding in some herds likely contributes to the survival of late-born calves, such as in the National Elk Refuge, where overwinter calf mortality averaged only 2.4% for 30 years (Smith 1994b).

The effect of bull age on conception dates has implications for calf survival, inasmuch as the timing of conception and birth date may affect calf survival. Therefore, elk managers should attempt to maintain enough mature bulls to ensure short, synchronous and early calving seasons. Also, late conception during one year can disrupt the long-term reproductive success of cow elk by perpetuating late breeding in subsequent years. Late conception and consequent late parturition may not allow cow elk enough time to recover lost fat reserves after the nutritional demands of lactation. As a result, cows in poor condition at onset of the rut may not ovulate until their condition improves later in the rut, thus perpetuating the late breeding cycle (Laflamme and Connor 1992). It is possible that, in years of exceptional late season forage quality, late-breeding cows may improve body condition enough to ovulate and conceive earlier in the rut. However, most late-breeding cows that return to early breeding probably do so by failing to conceive during one year. Consequently, achievement of an early synchronous rut, by increasing the number of mature bulls in elk populations where yearling bulls previously have

The ability of calves to survive their first year depends, in part, on individual physical maturity and vigor when entering the winter period, particularly on crowded or otherwise poor range. *Photo courtesy of the American Museum of Natural History.*

been the primary sires, may take several to many years to accomplish (Squibb et al. 1986).

Evolutionary Concerns

There also are evolutionary concerns related to the reduction of mature bulls in elk populations. In the polygynous mating system of elk, which is based on male advertisement and female choice (Geist 1982), the bull must be able to seek out females and maximize his advertising (Geist 1982, 1991, Clutton-Brock et al. 1987b). Therefore, the male is required to advertise his presence and dominance, while the female must have a way of determining which mate is best. In the case of elk, maximizing efficiency is related to several advertising activities, including vocalizations (i.e., bugling) and antler size (Geist 1982; see Chapter 7). Large antlers and large body size indicate that bulls are proficient at obtaining necessary resources, thus presumably possessing superior genes (Geist 1982). However, reductions in large bulls may extinguish this adaptive genetic selection process (Geist 1991).

Acceptable Bull-to-Cow Ratios

As previously discussed, there are potential effects of bull age on conception dates and calf survival, because the timing of conception and birth date may affect calf survival. Therefore, efforts may be necessary to maintain enough mature bulls to ensure synchronous and early parturition dates. However, the mature bull-to-cow ratio necessary for early synchronous breeding is questionable. Bubenik (1985) suggested 25 mature bulls per 100 cows, although Noyes et al. (1996) observed synchronous breeding with 18 bulls (older than 3 years) per 100 cows. Hines et al. (1985) concluded that 3 to 10 bulls (older than 2 years) per 100 cows during the rut were necessary.

In the attempt to determine the minimum and optimal numbers of mature bulls in free-ranging elk populations, several questions arise. First, what are natural bull-to-cow ratios? Second, what is an acceptable bull-to-cow ratio to ensure efficient reproduction? Essentially, there are two perspectives on the issue—European and North American. From the European standpoint, red deer sex ratios should approach unity (Geist 1982). Bubenik (1982) reported that elk herds should have 67 to 83 males per 100 females. Furthermore, males should live 14 to 16 years and female life spans should range from 15 to 17 years. Under this scenario, males seldom breed until 6 to 8 years of age (Bubenik 1982). Given the high densities of males, the rut presumably is shorter, and males lose less weight, improving their potential to survive harsh winters (Geist 1982) but also allowing nonbreeding younger males to put more energy into growing large bodies and antlers (Geist 1991).

At the opposite end of the spectrum are many North American elk herds that are heavily hunted, with sex ratios highly skewed toward females. In some areas, postseason ratios are less than 10 bulls per 100 cows. Are such bull-to-cow ratios detrimental to elk populations? In Colorado, Freddy (1987) found that below a threshold of about 10 bulls per 100 cows, calf-to-cow ratios declined.

DeSimone et al. (1993) summarized data from seven national parks and found that these populations usually have about 50 bulls per 100 cows, with about two-thirds of the bulls older than yearlings. This sex ratio is similar to those found in the studies of unhunted European red deer herds, where about two females per male have been commonly reported (Mitchell et al. 1977).

Mortality

Intrauterine Mortality

Nutritional status of cow elk during gestation can substantially influence reproductive success and the potential of intrauterine mortality. Thorne et al. (1976) conducted a winter feeding trial on gestating, mature cow elk and reported that all observed abortions occurred in two groups of cows that were on the lowest plane of nutrition and had suffered the greatest weight loss (Table 77). McNeil (1972) also reported that cows wintering on poor-quality diets exhibited higher incidences of reabsorption or abortion of fetuses.

Diseases that affect intrauterine and neonatal mortality rates have perhaps the greatest potential of any elk diseases for influencing elk population structure. Brucellosis (*Brucella abortus*) is a highly contagious reproductive disease affecting many wild ungulate species (see Chapter 6). Abortions and stillbirths are common manifestations of brucellosis in elk (Thorne et al. 1978b). Murie (1951) suggested that brucellosis, coupled with necrotic stomatitis, may have accounted for the "many" winter abortions observed in Rocky Mountain elk at Jackson Hole, Wyoming. The potential of brucellosis to impact elk populations is well illustrated by Thorne et al. (1978a). Under controlled conditions, 54% of naturally infected cows (n = 13) aborted or produced nonviable calves due to brucellosis. Artificially infected cows (n = 66) suffered a 61% calf loss to brucellosis (Thorne et al. 1978a). In free-ranging elk wintering on feedgrounds managed by the Wyoming Game and Fish Department, calf losses due to brucellosis were estimated at 12.5% (Herriges et al. 1989); whereas, a 7% calf loss was reported on the National Elk Refuge (Smith and Robbins 1994). Occurrence of brucellosis in elk seems to be localized to herds that fre-

Table 77.   Relationship of overwinter weight loss by pregnant Rocky Mountain elk cows to calf birth weight and survival

Diet quality	Number of cows[a]	Percentage of overwinter weight change[b]	Fetuses reabsorbed	Fetuses aborted	Mean calf birth weight		Percentage of live-born calves alive at 4 weeks	Percentage of fertilized ova at 4 weeks postpartum
					Pounds	Kilograms		
Low	22	−19	7	3	27.1	12.3	4	23
Medium	12	−6	0	0	34.2	15.5	92	92
High	12	+4	0	0	39.9	18.1	100	100

Source: Based on Thorne et al. 1976.

[a] Assumed by present authors that all cows conceived.

[b] Products of conception excluded from live weights.

quent winter feedgrounds of northwestern Wyoming (Thorne et al. 1978a). Brucellosis-related calf losses appear to be negligible in nonfeedground elk (Thorne et al. 1997).

Bacterial diseases such as *Listeria monocytogenes* have been linked to late-gestation abortions and weak calves in red deer (Brown 1986) and in Roosevelt elk in California, but this pathogen did not appear to have a substantial effect on elk populations (Martyny and Botzler 1975). McCullough (1969) suspected the 63% mortality rate he observed in Tule elk calves between conception and 1 month of age was due largely to infectious bovine rhinotracheitis.

Calf Mortality

Physiological maturity, body condition, sex, population size, age of the cow, birth date, birth weight, disease, severity of environmental conditions and predation influence calf survival and subsequent recruitment into the population (Schlegal 1976, Guinness et al. 1978c, Sauer and Boyce 1983, Singer et al. 1997, Smith and Anderson 1998). Combinations of these factors also may have important impacts on calf mortality. For example, substantial winter mortality of elk calves may occur when malnutrition operates in concert with disease and heavy parasite loads (Schwartz and Mitchell 1945, Murie 1951).

Calves of yearling cows, older cows and cows in poor body condition during pregnancy experience substantially higher mortality rates than do calves of healthy, prime cows. Prime cows produce the heaviest, earliest born, healthy

A suite of variables, including body condition, birth date, birth weight, predation, diseases and environmental conditions, affect whether or not calves are recruited into an elk population. *Photo by Bruce Richards.*

calves, which, in turn, have comparatively high survival rates. Flook (1970b) reported calf mortality in Banff National Park between 3 months postconception and 6 months postparturition as 38% in yearling cows, 27% for 2- to 13-year-old cows, and 44% in cows older than 14 years.

As elk populations increase beyond some optimal size, cows compete for forage, lose weight and conceive later, ultimately resulting in later birth dates and lighter calves. Late-born calves, presumably, are at an energetic disadvantage (Clutton-Brock et al. 1982, 1987), thus reducing their ability to survive winter (Smith and Anderson 1998). A similar density-dependent response in reproductive timing and calf survival has been observed in red deer (Guinness et al. 1978c, Clutton-Brock et al. 1982, 1987b). In Yellowstone National Park, summer calf survival was correlated positively with birth weight. Calf survival there in the winter was related positively to early calving and mildness of winter, and it was inversely correlated to population size (Singer et al. 1997). Cook et al. (1996) discussed the importance of nutrition in late summer and autumn for growth of elk calves, and they suggested a link between dietary quality during this time and winter survival. Cows wintering on poor quality diets produced more weak, nonviable calves than cows wintering on adequate diets. Thorne et al. (1976) reported that cows experiencing greater than normal weight losses during winter tended to produce calves with lighter birth weights and lower survival rates (Table 77). In contrast to these reports, Smith and Anderson (1998) found no difference in survival rates of elk that summered inside versus outside Grand Teton National Park, although densities of elk in Grand Teton National Park were more than two times higher—15.3 elk per square mile (5.9/km²) inside, compared with 6.2 elk per square mile (2.4/km²) outside.

The sex of the calf may also influence survival. Smith and Anderson (1998) noted sex-biased survival rates among elk calves in northwestern Wyoming (n = 164). Neonatal survival (birth to July 15) was higher among females (90%) than males (74%); annual calf survival also was higher among females (66%) than males (50%). Smith and Anderson listed three factors as probable reasons for this sex-based survival: (1) male-biased neonatal mortality (B. L. Smith et al. 1996a); (2) sex bias in winter range attendance; and (3) calf mortality off the National Elk Refuge exceeding mortality on the refuge, suggesting an effect of supplemental feeding. Contrary to what other researchers have reported, birth weight was not important in calf survival, but weather severity and birth date were important.

Many observed estimates of calf mortality are likely low because significant perinatal mortality may occur, but goes unobserved (B. L. Smith et al. 1996b). For instance, stillbirths, rejected and abandoned calves and immediate, postpartum calf mortality are missing from samples of captured neonates. In red deer calves, more than half of all preweaning mortality occurred within 24 hours of birth (Blaxter and Hamilton 1980).

Predation on Calves

Evidence concerning predation on newborn calves by black and grizzly bears, wolves, mountain lions and coyotes has emerged in recent years (Gese and Grothe 1995, Myers et al. 1996, Singer et al. 1997, Smith and Anderson 1998). In addition, more information on summer predation is now available, indicating that predation on elk calves within the first few months of life may substantially influence cohort mortality rates. Singer et al. (1997) reported that predation was the greatest source of calf mortality (43.9%), and all but one instance of predation occurred during summer in Yellowstone National Park (Table 78). In southeastern Washington, of 192 elk calves that were captured and fitted with radio collars between June 1992 and September 1996, 48 died (Myers et al. 1996). Predation by cougar (42%), black bear (21%), coyote (4%) and unknown predators (11%) caused 78% of the total mortality of marked calves. The remaining 22% of calf mortality was attributed to state-licensed hunters (5%), other human causes (4%) and unknown causes (13%). Smith and Anderson (1998) re-

ported that predation in northwestern Wyoming accounted for 19 of 22 (86%) deaths caused from birth to July 15. They also reported that predators selected early born calves, whereas late-born calves typically died from other causes.

Black bears have been the most common predator in many areas throughout elk range during the past several decades and may cause a substantial amount of mortality among elk calves. B. L. Smith et al. (1996a) reported that 22 of 145 (15%) marked calves in northwestern Wyoming died before July 15, of which 10 of 22 (45%) were killed by black bears. Johnson (1951) reported black bear predation accounted for 2 or possibly 4 of the 10 calf mortalities observed during his study of Rocky Mountain elk calves from the West Gallatin herd in Montana. Schlegel (1976) reported that 38 of 53 (72%) marked calves in north-central Idaho were killed by black bear and 11% by cougar. Most mortalities (n = 21) occurred during summer, when calves were 3 to 10 days of age; the remaining losses (n = 18) occurred when calves were 16 to 42 days old. A single case of mountain lion predation occurred on a calf that was nearly 1 year old (Schlegal 1976). These data also demonstrate that calf age may influence predation rates. As calves mature and become more mobile, they enter the relative security of cow to calf nursery groups, minimizing losses to predators.

Mountain lions have been increasing in number in many

In Yellowstone National Park's Willow Park, a subadult grizzly bear, having spied an elk band feeding in a meadow, immediately charged, including crossing a creek at a dead run. The elk watched the bear approach until it was within about 60 yards (66 m) and then they scattered. The bear pursued the largest group of elk around the large meadow at full speed for fully 10 minutes or more before turning its attention to a calf that broke from the group. It was unable to catch this animal either, but finally managed to catch another that, with some cows, ran into a willow thicket. The tenacity and speed of the young grizzly also reflects the speed and elusiveness of elk, including calves, against a determined and lethal, if not somewhat inept predator. Adult grizzlies are much more efficient hunters, but grizzly numbers in most of elk range are too few to represent a significant impact on any elk population. *Photo by Kim Hart.*

Table 78. Survival rates and cause of mortality of elk calves in Yellowstone National Park, 1987 to 1990

Period	Number calves collared	Survival rate (SE)	Number of deaths					
			Predation	Unknown	Disease	Accident	Starvation	Hunter harvest
Summer	127	0.646 (0.132)	28[a]	5	3	2	1	0
Winter	82	0.719 (0.325)	1[b]	4	1	1	15	4
Annual	127	0.427 (0.179)	29	9	4	3	16	4

Source: Singer et al. 1997.

[a] Grizzly bear (n = 11); black bear (n = 1); mountain lion (n = 0), unknown bear species (n = 1); coyote (n = 11); eagle (n = 1); unknown predator (n = 1).

[b] Mountain lion.

areas throughout elk range and may be an important predator on elk calves (Myers et al. 1996). Schwartz (1942) reported that cougars were the major predator of Roosevelt elk on the Olympic Peninsula. In Idaho, mule deer and elk accounted for 70% of the prey item occurrences in 198 cougar scats examined (Hornocker 1970). Fifty-three elk killed by cougars were examined during that study, and 28 (53%) of those kills were calves.

Recent efforts to reestablish wolves in parts of their former range could have significant impacts on elk calf predation, elk population dynamics and the region's predator complex as a whole. Carbyn (1983) reported that elk were the primary prey species of gray wolves in Riding Mountain National Park, Manitoba, constituting 26% of the wolf kills examined. Boyd et al. (1994) reported that wolves killed more elk calves than hunters in the area of Glacier National Park, Montana, and colonizing wolves killed a higher proportion of elk calves than did wolf populations establishing themselves elsewhere.

Although bears, wolves and mountain lions are the primary predators of elk calves, coyotes also kill elk calves and have the potential to be significant predators. For example, coyote predation accounted for roughly 30% of the early mortalities (conception to early postnatal) observed among Tule elk calves (McCullough 1969). Toweill and Anthony (1988) reported remains of three Roosevelt elk calves among the seven recorded incidents of elk being fed on by coyotes during spring in Oregon's Cascade Mountains. Singer et al. (1997) noted that 11 elk calves were killed by coyotes during summers from 1987 to 1990 in Yellowstone National Park. Elk density on calving grounds, behavior of cows, calf vigor, duration of the calving period and amount and types of hiding cover probably influence the effectiveness of coyote predation on newborn calves.

Coyote predation on older elk calves occurs and may become significant, especially during winter. Body size, condition and snow conditions probably are the principal variables influencing the effectiveness of coyotes preying on older calves. Small calves have a relatively larger surface-to-volume ratio that may predispose them to larger energy losses (Hudson 1985) and greater rates of decline in body condition. Small calves also have more difficulty traveling and foraging in deep snow because of their relatively lower chest height and small hoof surface area. Surface crusting of snow can make travel in even moderate snow depths difficult and energetically inefficient for elk (Parker 1983). Coyotes are uniquely suited for calf predation in elk winter range habitats where surface crusting of snow occurs. Because of their relatively light body weight and large paws, coyotes often are able to run on top of the surface crust in pursuit of elk calves that break through the crust, flounder and collapse in exhaustion.

A mountain lion cache site. Mountain lions can be significant predators on elk calves. In southeastern Washington, 42% of the deaths of radio-marked elk calves were attributed to cougars (Myers et al. 1996). *Photo by Rocky Spencer.*

Wolves can be a significant source of elk calf mortality, particularly colonizing wolves. Efforts to reestablish wolf populations in elk range need to consider this fact. *Photo by Pete and Alice Bengeyfield.*

The elk calf, at left, was wounded by a coyote and sought refuge in a stream. His survival depends on waiting out the coyote—a marginal prospect. Note that ice already had formed just below the calf's knees. At right is an elk calf severely wounded by coyotes. The injuries to the throat, nose and jaw are typical of coyote attacks. *Left photo by Michael H. Francis. Right photo by John D. Cada; courtesy of the Montana Department of Fish, Wildlife and Parks.*

Because elk population characteristics are strongly affected by variations in calf survival, predation loss should be considered an important factor influencing elk populations. Additional research is needed to provide natural resource managers with a better understanding of the magnitude and ecology of predation on elk calves.

Disease Impacts

Several bacterial diseases working in concert with other stressors can impact calf survival and significantly influence elk populations (see Chapter 6). Diarrhea and enteritis caused by infections of the bacteria *Escherichia coli* can result in substantial mortality in newborn elk calves (Smits 1991). Development of *E. coli* infections into a serious disease, however, generally requires predisposing conditions, such environmental stress or infection by other pathogens or parasites.

Fusobacterium necrophorum is the causal organism of necrobacillosis, which can result in high mortality rates in elk, especially calves (Allred et al. 1944, Rosen 1981). Damage to skin, hooves or mucous membranes provides a point of entry for the organism. Depending on the site of infection, necrobacillosis can manifest itself as laryngitis, stomatitis, reticulorumenitis or footrot (Smits 1991). In calves, necrobacillosis often spreads from primary infection sites to the lungs and liver tissue, with death usually resulting from purulent pneumonia or toxemia (Kistner et al. 1982, Smits 1991). Epizootic occurrences of necrobacillosis often are linked to mouth injuries sustained while feeding on coarse, poor quality hay or on overstocked ranges.

Few diseases that affect elk calves are caused by viruses, but enteritis resulting from infections of coronavirus may cause calf mortality in newborns (Smits 1991). Also, rotavirus may be a causal agent in elk calves dying from pneumonia and diarrhea (Smits 1991). And as previously noted, McCullough (1969) suspected that the high mortality rate observed in Tule elk calves to 1 month of age was due largely to infectious bovine rhinotracheitis (bovine herpesvirus 1).

Environmental Influences

Environmental factors, such as temperature and precipitation may influence calf survival (Coughenour and Singer 1996). Generally, severe winter weather conditions are considered the limiting environmental factors for elk calves. Sauer and Boyce (1983) reported that calf survival in winter was negatively correlated with November precipitation. The added influence of precipitation early in winter further stressed juveniles, which, in turn, may have increased early winter mortality. In addition, environmental conditions during other seasons may have substantial influence on calf population dynamics. For example, Sauer and Boyce (1983)

also reported that calf survival was correlated with high summer (July) temperatures. They suggested that inclement summer weather decreases foraging efficiency, thus energy intake, and leads to decreased energy reserves for winter. As a result, these climate effects of spring and summer may cause direct or delayed density-independent mortality.

Adult Mortality

Mortality in adult elk is due largely to hunting, predation, disease, malnutrition, harassment, accidents and extreme environmental conditions. Mortality commonly is assumed to be density dependent. If mortality in elk operates in a density-dependent fashion, losses due to hunting and predation should decrease losses due to malnutrition and old age (Caughley 1976). Thus, elk populations can be divided roughly into two groups: (1) those in which hunting is a major cause of mortality; and (2) those in which debilitation (disease, parasitism, malnutrition, old age, etc.) is a major cause of mortality. In both cases, mortality during any particular year is influenced strongly by weather, because early autumn storms can result in heavy hunting harvest and severe winters are associated with heavy losses in debilitated individuals. Even young, vigorous adults undergo a decline in physical reserves during winter, although this usually does not result in death.

Where elk are not hunted, as in many parks and refuges, winter mortality due to debilitation appears to be greater among adult bulls than among adult cows. Flook (1970b)

Severe or sustained abnormal weather conditions in all seasons can impact calves' energy reserves and influence their overwinter survival. *Photo courtesy of the U.S. National Park Service.*

Radiotelemetry is the best available technique to study elk mortality. Using radio-collars equipped with mortality sensors, elk biologists can determine the place, cause and possibly timing of death. *Photo by Bruce Richards.*

Black bears, even large males, are unlikely to kill adult elk, but these bears are very capable predators of young calves. Black bears will readily scavenge wounding-loss elk and those succumbing to other injuries. A black bear "set up" on or near an elk carcass it has cached should be given a wide berth. *Photo by Kim Hart.*

studied bull and cow mortality and reasoned that adult bull elk should suffer higher mortality rates than adult cows because: (1) the comparatively larger bulls require a greater annual food intake than do cows; (2) compared with cows, bulls eat more food with about the same dental equipment, and the primary food-processing equipment characteristic of bulls—tooth row length—is not substantially greater than that of cows; and (3) older bulls use much of their stored energy during the rut, therefore are likely to enter winter with reduced fat reserves. McCullough (1969) reported that, of 41 Tule elk more than 1 year old found dead, 28 (68%) were bulls. He attributed a higher mortality rate among adult bulls, compared with adult cows, to their greater aggressiveness and range of movement and to injuries and energy depletion associated with the rut.

Predation

For much of the 20th century, predation on adult elk was not considered an important mechanism of population regulation because of the limited number of large predators in many areas. Recently, wolves and other predators are reported to be increasingly influential in limiting or regulating ungulate populations (Gasaway et al. 1992, Messier 1994). Predation now is viewed as an important mechanism of elk population regulation in many areas (e.g., Kunkel 1997), and a tremendous amount of effort has gone into determining the effects and rates of predation on elk populations (Gunther and Renkin 1991, Hamer and Herrero 1991, Huggard 1993a, 1993b, Boyd et al. 1994, Gese and Grothe 1995, Kunkel 1997, Mattson 1997). Despite this recent

work, more research is necessary to determine the role of predation on elk population dynamics.

Natural predators may exert a substantial influence on specific adult age and sex classes of elk populations. In Idaho, Hornocker (1970) found that bulls and calves were more susceptible to mountain lion predation than were adult and yearling cows. Also, half of the lion-killed elk were in good physical condition, illustrating that elk condition did not appear to be a factor in cougar prey selection. Boyd et al. (1994) also found that bull elk were killed by wolves at a disproportionately high rate relative to their occurrence near Glacier National Park, Montana. Also in Glacier, Kunkel et al. (1999) reported that both wolves and cougars predated on more older and younger elk than did hunters. Carbyn (1983) reported elk older than 11 years of age represented nearly half of the 53 (47%) observed elk kills recorded for one wolf pack in Riding Mountain National Park, Manitoba. Increasing numbers of adult cow elk were killed by this pack during late winter, compared with early and midwinter.

Coyotes are not known to kill healthy adult elk, but are quick to scavenge remains of any elk carcass (*top*). Wolves, in groups or packs, will kill elk of either sex and the young, prime or senior. Grizzlies, which hunt independently and rarely during periods of deep snow, mainly take calves or enfeebled elk. Wolves will defer to a grizzly at a kill site (*bottom*), but a grizzly is unlikely to defer to wolves. *Photo by Lance Peck.*

Disease Impact

Few diseases or parasites directly cause mortality of adult elk (see Chapter 6), but most reduce an infected elk's capacity to cope with severe weather, malnutrition or predation (Kistner et al. 1982). Murie (1951) reported that necrotic stomatitis (*Fusobacterium necrophorum*) was an important disease in elk wintering at Jackson Hole, Wyoming. Necrotic stomatitis (*F. necrophorum*) may become epizootic on overstocked elk winter ranges (Schwartz and Mitchell 1945, Murie 1951); whereas, foraging and browsing on coarse material may cause penetrating injuries to the mouth that provide infection sites for the causal organism of necrotic stomatitis. Also, elk suffering from malnutrition may exhibit a depressed immune response to the disease and debilitation or mortality may result (Kistner et al. 1982).

Even heavy parasite infections do not directly cause mortality in adult elk. However, several roundworm species exhibit acute pathogenicity in elk and are capable of causing mortality. Meningeal worms (*Parelaphostrongylus tenuis* [*P. tenuis*]), which coevolved with the white-tailed deer of eastern North America and do little damage to their natural host (Eckroade et al. 1970, Prestwood 1970), may cause severe neurological damage and mortality in elk (Carpenter et al. 1973). Gastropods, such as snails and slugs, serve as intermediate hosts in the life cycle of *P. tenuis*. Elk sharing range with white-tailed deer and the intermediate host are potentially susceptible. Occurrence of the disease in elk populations seems to be limited to eastern and some midwestern states in the United States and eastern provinces of Canada (Carpenter et al. 1973, Thompkins et al. 1977, Smits 1991). Public desire for elk reintroductions in the eastern states has raised concerns regarding the risk of these introduced populations to *P. tenuis* (Anderson 1972). Absence of *P. tenuis* in western populations likely is due to limited populations of the native hosts.

Arterial worms (*Elaeophora schneideri*) are nonpathogenic inhabitants of the carotid and internal maxillary arteries of mule deer, but they are major pathogens in Rocky Mountain elk (Kistner et al. 1982). Immature lung worms (*Dictyocaulus viviparus*) cause extensive damage to the lungs of most cervids, including elk. Inflammation caused by the presence of the parasites or by secondary bacterial infections may result in pneumonia and death (Kistner et al. 1982).

Psoroptic scabies caused by parasitic mites (*Psoroptes equi* var. *cervinae*) can severely debilitate bulls and old (postprime) cows during winter (Murie 1951). Winter ticks may occur in sufficient numbers on adult Rocky Mountain elk to cause substantial declines in body condition and, under severe environmental conditions, may cause high mortality (Cowan 1951, Murie 1951).

Brucellosis and tuberculosis (*Mycobacterium bovis*) are likely the two most important diseases affecting elk population management today. Both brucellosis and tuberculosis are zoonotic (transmittable to humans), transmittable to domestic livestock and represent a significant economic concern to the livestock industry (Frye and Hillman 1997).

Although brucellosis in elk once occurred in several areas of North America, the disease currently seems to be confined to the Greater Yellowstone area in Wyoming. It appears to have been transmitted from cattle to elk in the Greater Yellowstone area around 1900 (Thorne and Herriges 1992, Smith and Roffe 1994). Concentration of elk on winter feedgrounds apparently allows for perpetuation of brucellosis in this elk population. Wyoming elk wintering on native winter range in the Greater Yellowstone area average 2.2% seropositive for brucellosis (Thorne et al. 1997); whereas, feedground elk in the Greater Yellowstone area average 37% seropositive (Herriges et al. 1991). Consistently low or zero seroprevalence for brucellosis has been reported for free-ranging elk in other parts of the United States (McCorquodale and DiGiacomo 1985).

Brucellosis is transmitted primarily by oral contact with vaginal exudates, aborted fetuses and fetal fluids from infected cows (Thorne et al. 1978a). The high concentration of elk that occurs on a feedground may disrupt the normally seclusive birthing behavior of cow elk. Abortions and nonsynchronous births have been recorded among the feedlines. Elk are curious and may be very fastidious regarding birthing events in other elk. Cows commonly will smell, lick and attempt to consume placenta and aborted fetuses that are not their own. Consequently, an abortion on the feedline by an infected cow can potentially expose many other elk to brucellosis. When not concentrated on a feedground, elk seek seclusion during birth and thoroughly clean up birth products (Thorne et al. 1997). An infected cow aborting on native winter range or calving on normal calving grounds during spring would provide very little opportunity for exposure of other elk (or any other ungulate) to brucellosis.

Not only does brucellosis have the potential to impact elk herd productivity significantly, causing calf losses as high as 61% (Thorne et al. 1978a), but it is an economically significant livestock disease. The National Cooperative Brucellosis Eradication Program was initiated in 1934 (then known as the Cooperative State–Federal Brucellosis Eradication Program) to eradicate the disease from livestock in the United States. In 1934, brucellosis cost the livestock industry an estimated $50 million annually (Fitch 1934). Good herd management, disease surveillance and vaccination programs steadily reduced the prevalence of brucellosis in livestock. By 1994, 33 states plus Puerto Rico and the Virgin Islands were classified as brucellosis Class-Free. The Class-Free classification indicates that a brucellosis case has not been diagnosed in the state for at least 1 year (U.S. Animal and Plant Health Inspection Service 1992). However, even with the success of the National Brucellosis Eradication Program, current economic losses from brucellosis are estimated at $10 million annually (Frye and Hillman 1997).

The potential for interspecific transmissions of brucellosis between elk or bison and cattle is a significant economic concern to the livestock industry, particularly in the Greater Yellowstone area. Transmission of brucellosis from elk or bison to cattle in or near the Greater Yellowstone area could result in loss of Class-Free status, leading to economically devastating export restrictions and herd depopulations in the affected states. If brucellosis is not eliminated from elk and bison in the Greater Yellowstone area, the cattle surveillance program for brucellosis in Idaho, Montana and Wyoming will have to continue indefinitely at great expense.

The brucellosis problem in the Greater Yellowstone area actually is only a symptom of a larger problem—inadequate winter habitat to maintain the elk population at the size desired by the public (Thorne et al. 1997). Elimination of the feedgrounds in the Greater Yellowstone area likely would eventually eliminate the brucellosis problem in free-ranging elk, but the feedgrounds maintain elk populations in western Wyoming at higher levels than the existing winter ranges can support. Eradication of brucellosis from elk populations in the Greater Yellowstone area will require natural resource managers to design and implement management programs that reduce feedground dependency of elk and increase winter range carrying capacity. Thorne et al. (1997) suggested shortened feeding periods and winter habitat enhancement as means to disperse elk off winter feedgrounds. Habitat enhancement efforts, such as those included in Wyoming's Brucellosis-Feedground-Habitat Program (S. G. Smith et al. 1997), likely will increase the carrying capacity of elk winter range, making room for at least some former feedground elk. If elimination of Wyoming's feedgrounds becomes a management goal, however, these habitat improvements may not be large enough to accommodate all the elk currently dependent on the feedgrounds. Consequently, elimination of the feedgrounds may require population reductions to bring elk numbers into balance with an ecologically sustainable winter range forage supply.

Dispersal of elk off feedgrounds will increase the potential for elk depredation on stored crops. Consequently, efforts to decrease the feedground dependency of Wyoming elk will have to occur in concert with intensified management approaches to control and prevent crop depredation by elk (Thorne et al. 1997).

Bovine tuberculosis (*Mycobacterium bovis* [*M. bovis*]) is a highly contagious, zoonotic disease found in cervids. The severe pathogeny of *M. bovis* in humans and potential of elk to human transmission of the pathogen make bovine tuberculosis potentially more important than brucellosis in terms of elk populations and management. Although tuberculosis does occur in elk (Hadwen 1942, Stumpff 1982, Rhyan et al. 1995), it currently is rare in free-ranging elk populations (Williams et al. 1995, Rhyan et al. 1997). Habitat conditions and management practices—including supplemental feeding (Schmitt et al. 1997) and gamefarming (Stumpff 1982, Thoen et al. 1992)—that concentrate wildlife populations appear to promote the prevalence of tuberculosis. An epidemic occurrence of the disease was recorded in free-ranging white-tailed deer in Michigan (Schmitt et al. 1997); high deer densities, poor habitat quality and extensive supplemental feeding were thought to have contributed to this epizootic.

Because of the long-term concentration that occurs on the winter feedgrounds, elk in the Greater Yellowstone area are particularly at risk for rapid transmission of tuberculosis throughout the herd. The effect such an epidemic would have on the structure and dynamics of the elk population still is unknown, but the human health hazard it would create, particularly for hunters, is quite alarming. Also, cross-the-fence transmission of tuberculosis between gamefarm elk and free-ranging elk of the Greater Yellowstone area has become a serious concern. For example, in 1991, tuberculosis was diagnosed in a captive elk herd located near the northern border of Yellowstone National Park (Thoen et al. 1992).

Given the current situation in the Greater Yellowstone area, the question regarding a tuberculosis epizootic is not whether it will occur in the feedground herds, but rather when will it occur. Management options for response to such an epidemic likely would be limited to quarantine and depopulation of the affected area, which would be distasteful and politically volatile. As with the brucellosis problem, dispersal of wintering elk on the Greater Yellowstone area by reducing or eliminating feedground dependency through habitat enhancement should substantially reduce the potential for tuberculosis outbreaks in free-ranging elk.

Environmental Factors

Environmental factors, such as snow depth and temperatures, that vary geographically and temporally impact adult elk populations differently. Generally, harsh winter weather causes increased mortality of adult bulls and cows that enter the winter season in poor condition. Cow survival is correlated positively with January temperatures and negatively with May temperatures and total July precipitation (Sauer and Boyce 1983).

Elk have the capability to respond to increasingly severe environmental conditions by migrating to another area or shifting forage sources. Houston (1982) suggested that fidelity to winter range of the Northern Yellowstone elk herd was related in part to environmental conditions. However, other herds may not have the capacity or opportunity to migrate to areas more hospitable and, as a result, mortality rates may be higher.

Harvest

Hunting is the major source of mortality in most hunted elk populations (Peek et al. 1967, Kimball and Wolfe 1974, White 1985, Leptich and Zager 1991, Unsworth et al. 1993). Hunter harvest may account for 90% of bull elk mortality in areas open to rifle hunting. Of the 22 deaths recorded among elk older than 1 year of age in northwestern Wyoming by Smith and Anderson (1998), 21 (95%) were related to hunting. Unsworth et al. (1993) reported that 86% of all radio-marked elk mortalities in north-central Idaho occurred during September and October, were the result of hunter harvest (Table 79). The 40% annual bull mortality rate (compared with 11% for cows) observed in Idaho by Unsworth et al. (1993) was similar to the 42% annual rate reported by Kimball and Wolfe (1974) for a harvested herd in northern Utah during 1951 through 1972. White (1985) reported a mortality rate of 45% among elk in the hunted portion of his study area of New Mexico, and Leptich and Zager (1991) estimated a mortality rate of 55% for bulls in central Idaho. Leptich and Zager (1991) reported a 12% mortality rate for hunted cow elk in northern Idaho; all of the deaths were associated with hunting or poaching.

In areas not hunted, annual elk survival generally is much higher. White (1985) reported survival rates of 91% for the unhunted portion of his study area in New Mexico. The annual survival rate for resident unhunted Roosevelt cow elk in the Cascade Mountain Range in Oregon was 89% (Stussy et al. 1994). Poaching was the dominant source of the 11% mortality.

Wounding loss also may be a significant source of mortality among hunted elk populations. Smith and Anderson (1998) reported a wounding loss of 21% of the recovered take of antlerless elk. Similarly, in Colorado, Freddy (1987) reported a wounding loss equivalent to 18% of the antlerless harvest. Leptich and Zager (1991) noted wounding losses of 27% of the total reported cow harvest and 12% of total bull harvest in northern Idaho. Also in Idaho,

Table 79. Annual survival rates of radio-collared bull and cow elk in north-central Idaho, 1986 to 1991

Year[a]	Number of bulls radio-collared	Bull survival (SE)[b]	Number of cows radio-collared	Cow survival (SE)[c]
1986–1987	30	0.733 (0.060)	9	1.000[c]
1987–1988	40	0.589 (0.058)	9	0.875 (0.093)
1988–1989	42	0.560 (0.070)	11	0.808 (0.118)
1989–1990	28	0.585 (0.070)	9	0.778 (0.130)
1990–1991	29	0.552 (0.092)	8	1.000

Source: Unsworth et al. 1993.

[a] Year starts July 1 and ends June 30.

[b] Surival rates did not differ for bulls by year.

[c] Surival rates did not differ for cows by year.

Unsworth et al. (1993) reported that 21% of bulls harvested in north-central Idaho were lost to wounding.

Road access greatly influences elk vulnerability to harvest and has great potential to influence herd dynamics. The issue of elk vulnerability and harvest has received a tremendous amount of attention in recent years (Christensen et al. 1991). Increased harvest pressure, coupled with losses in hiding cover and increased elk exposure because of road access, led to a posthunting bull-to-cow ratio decline from more than 15:100 to less than 5:100 in northeastern

Although hunter harvest comprises the majority of mortality of mature bull elk in hunted populations, other forms of mortality, including poaching, wounding losses, predation and environmental conditions, may be significant. *Photo by C. H. McDonald; courtesy of the U.S. Forest Service.*

Elk wounding loss rates of 15% or more can be very limiting to a given population. Any such loss is extraordinarily wasteful and almost always unnecessary. Improved marksmanship and better shot selection are the primary ways to minimize wounding losses. *Photo courtesy of the U.S. National Park Service.*

Oregon in the early 1980s (Leckenby et al. 1991). Unsworth and Kuck (1991) reported an annual survival rate of 41% for bulls older than 2 years in a roaded area and 78% for bulls in an unroaded area of north-central Idaho encompassed 618 square miles (1,600 km²). Yearling bull survival also differed—44% in roaded areas versus 79% in unroaded areas. Cole et al. (1997) studied survival of female Roosevelt elk before, during and after limited vehicle access in southwestern Oregon, and found that survival increased with limited vehicle access. The work of Leptich and Zager (1991) in Idaho demonstrated how elk vulnerability in roaded areas skewed mortality rates (Table 80), age structure and mature bull-to-cow ratios.

Accidents

Compared with mortality from winter stresses and predation (both natural and human), accidental deaths of elk are relatively uncommon. However, recent reviews indicate that injury and mortality among rutting elk bulls may be more common than once thought (Clutton-Brock 1982, Leslie and Jenkins 1985). Elk antlers are highly developed and, as such, have the potential to inflict severe wounds. Traditionally, it was believed that conspecifics avoid inflicting lethal injury to one another (Lorenz 1966) and that combat between antlered males was highly ritualized to minimize fatalities (Maynard and Price 1973). Leslie and Jenkins (1985) noted four mortalities of mature (5 years and older) male Roosevelt elk during the rut. Two of the mortalities were accidental but occurred during combat, whereas two strongly suggested direct combat-inflicted causes.

Generally, older (5 years or older) bulls die from rut-related combat more often than younger bulls. This probably is related to their greater activity and to the intense harem-tending behavior exhibited by older bulls. Although many more bulls are removed from an elk population by winter mortality than by combat mortality, it tends to affect bulls exhibiting the most intense rutting behavior and may exert an influence on population structure (Flook 1970b).

Reliable estimates of survival are critical to effective management (Caughley 1977), because small discrepancies (5%) in survival rates for elk may have serious consequences to overall elk population dynamics (Nelson and Peek 1982). Unfortunately, these data often are elusive.

Population Structure

Age Structure

Female elk typically live longer than male elk. Flook (1970b) reported that the oldest bull examined in an unhunted Rocky Mountain elk population was 14 years old, and the oldest cow examined was 21 years of age. Picton (1961) examined the records of 254 ear-tagged elk harvested by hunters in Montana and found that the maximum age for bulls was 12.5 years versus 18.5 years for cows. Smith (1985) reported that three cows older than 20 years died on the National Elk Refuge.

In unhunted elk populations, debilitation losses of adult bulls are more commonplace than among adult cows. More so than cow elk, bulls suffer from accelerated tooth wear. Because of their larger body size, bulls consume a greater quantity of forage annually. However, as previously noted, tooth row lengths of cows and bulls are quite similar. Consequently, bulls must process a higher quantity of forage with about the same amount of dental surface as cows, thus accelerating tooth wear. Worn or lost teeth may cause bulls to have difficulty meeting their nutritional demands at a younger age than in cows (Flook 1970b).

Bulls also suffer reduced fat reserves and disabling injuries as a result of the rut (Flook 1970b). Rutting activity may be a direct and an indirect cause of sex-specific mortality in bull elk. Also, rutting activity may remove more older bulls than younger bulls from the population. Flook (1970b) reported that bulls of 7 years of age and older may be more sexually active than younger bulls, based on the relationship of age to testicular size and harem-tending activity. Intense rutting activity by older bulls generally results in more of a decline in body condition during autumn and winter than is experienced by cows or younger bulls. For example, kidney fat indices for cows typically are high from September through December; whereas, kidney fat indices for adult bulls exhibit a decline from high levels during August to relatively low levels by mid-October. Kidney fat indices of yearling and 2-year-old bulls tend to be highest in October and begin to decline in November (Flook 1970b).

Table 80. Percentage of elk mortality in the Coeur d'Alene River drainage, Idaho, 1988 to 1990

Area	Bulls	Number of bulls	Cows	Number of cows
Roaded[a]	61.7	26	9.1	33
Unroaded[b]	32.3	19	5	20
Managed access[c]	44.7	12	16.3	13

Source: Leptich and Zager 1991.

[a] 5.9 miles of road per square mile (2.3 km/km²) of habitat and open road density of 4.5 miles of road per square mile (1.7 km/km²).

[b] 1.3 miles of road per square mile (0.5 km/km²) of habitat and open road density of 1.0 miles of road per square mile (0.4 km/km²).

[c] 5.3 miles of road per square mile (2.0 km/km²) of habitat and open road density of 2.6 miles of road per square mile 1.0 km/km²) as a result of permanent and hunting season road closures.

Compared with other forms of mortality, such as harvest, winter stresses and predation (both natural and human), accidental death of elk is relatively uncommon. At top left, an elk died after miring in a mud hole. At top right, a cow dies of exhaustion, trying to extricate itself from a river it and the young bull tried to cross on thin ice. At center left, a cow reaching for leaves slipped off the bank and suffocated. At center right, a slip while trying to leap a three-strand fence snared this cow who then died of exposure or starvation. At lower left, a cow elk is rescued from a grate it fell into with both fore- and hind legs. At lower right a bull standing to feed on a paneled haystack wedged its hoof between two slats and, unable to pull free, died of injuries. *Top photo courtesy of the U.S. National Park Service. Center left photo courtesy of the Arizona Game and Fish Department. Center right photo by Dale R. Potter. Bottom left photo by Rocky Spencer. Bottom right photo courtesy of the Wyoming Department of Game and Fish.*

An elk calf gored by a bull elk apparently took to the stream (*top left*) after being attacked by coyotes the next morning, as evidenced by injury around its muzzle in addition to the goring wound. The day of the goring, the calf's mother remained in the vicinity after the elk band left and the calf failed to follow; she periodically checked on the calf, which became too weak to stand. An adult coyote with a den somewhere nearby appeared to have smelled the injured calf, searched it out and initially scared it up. At each subsequent approach of the calf that day, the coyote and others were chased away by the cow. When in the water the next morning, and rapidly failing, the calf again was occasionally sought out by the cow (*top right*), who appeared to call to her young, but the calf did not respond. The coyote did not approach the calf until the calf died (*bottom left*), and then it came in below the bank, apparently to avoid detection by the cow. The coyote gorged itself on the calf (*bottom right*), then disappeared, only to return shortly and gorge and leave once again. On another trip to the carcass, an adult coyote was joined by a pup, which ate what the adult regurgitated for it. Before leaving the area, the cow made a final visit to the site after the coyotes had finished feeding. Although the mortality in this case can be credited to predation, it more accurately resulted from conspecific aggression—a rarity among elk, especially so among elk not involved in dominance fights. *Photo sequence by Kim Hart.*

The timing of the decline in kidney fat indices of younger bulls may coincide with the waning of rutting activity by mature bulls, at which time younger bulls are allowed to join cow herds and participate in breeding cows that did not conceive during their earlier estrous cycles. Kidney fat indices of cows, younger bulls and older bulls all typically decline from early or mid-winter to spring, but the kidney fat indices of all bulls tend to be consistently lower than those of cows (Stuhsaker 1967, Flook 1970b). Intense rutting activity and the consequential reduction in body condition of older bulls may predispose those bulls to greater winter mortality than that experienced by either cows or younger bulls.

Competition between cows and bulls for forage during winter would be expected on rangelands stocked to carrying capacity (Caughley 1976). Because natural regulatory factors appear to cause higher mortality in bulls than in cows, bull-to-cow ratios should decline as range-stocking rates approach carrying capacity. Houston (1982) reported a decline in the bull-to-cow ratio from 62:100 during 1968 (when the population contained 5,000 elk) to 47:100 in 1972 (when the population had increased to 12,000 head in Yellowstone National Park).

Sex Ratios

Sex Ratio at Birth

Information on fetal sex ratio comes principally from winter collections of embryos from pregnant cows, so that the fetal sex ratio is neither the primary sex ratio (i.e., sex ratio at conception) nor the secondary sex ratio (i.e., sex ratio at birth), but something in between. One difficulty in deriving primary sex ratio from data collected on fetal sex ratio during winter is that no reliable estimate exists of intrauterine loss for the time between conception and collection. This could be done readily, because ovarian structure reveals, by the presence or absence of current corpora lutea, whether or not conception occurred in that year. In addition, Flook (1970b) stated that, in early pregnancy, male elk fetuses are recognized more easily than female fetuses.

Reported sex ratios of elk at birth vary considerably. The long-held view that sex ratios of ungulates at birth are at or near parity has been the subject of considerable debate (Hoefs and Nowlan 1994). In several studies of ungulates, fetal sex ratios exhibit a preponderance of males (Chapman et al. 1938, Robinette et al. 1957, Verme 1983). For example, from a sample of 462 Rocky Mountain elk fetuses collected in Banff National Park from 1944 to 1948, Green (1950) reported a male-to-female sex ratio of 111:100. Flook (1970b) reported a sex ratio of 113 males to 100 females among 1,159 fetuses collected from Rocky Mountain elk cows be-

tween 1957 and 1967 in Jasper, Banff, Waterton Lakes and Elk Island National Parks. However, Kittams (1953) examined reports from Yellowstone National Park, Banff National Park and Jackson Hole, Wyoming, and found substantial variability in sex ratios for fetuses 2 to 5 months postconception. Fetal sex ratios ranged from 88 to 121 males per 100 females, but no statistically significant deviations from parity were detected for fetal sex ratios in composited samples for each location or for all three locations combined (n = 828 males to 801 females). Flook (1970b) speculated that the nearly even sex ratio obtained by Kittams (1953) may have been the result of higher intrauterine losses of male fetuses in Yellowstone, Banff and Jackson Hole elk (86% pregnancy rate) when compared with the elk examined by Flook (1970b) from the four Canadian national parks (93% pregnancy rate).

In some cases, supplemental feeding and timing of feeding may influence sex bias at birth in elk. B. L. Smith et al. (1996b) investigated sex bias at birth among 165 young elk born to free-ranging, supplementally fed females in northwestern Wyoming and an additional 86 young born to females confined and supplementally fed in pastures. They reported that sex ratios of neonates in Grand Teton National Park were not sex biased. However, sex ratios were biased toward males on calving areas in a population of elk that existed at lower density outside that park. The proportion

The sex ratio of a new elk calf crop often can be assessed by examination of calves caught by hand, which can be accomplished until a few days after birth. *Photo courtesy of the Utah Division of Wildlife Resources.*

of males born in seven cohorts increased with earlier initiation of supplemental feeding and with increased feed digestibility. They speculated that males may be favored by nutritional supplementation early in gestation. Boyce (1989) reported a tendency toward an overall 1:1 sex ratio for elk calves in Jackson Hole, although differences in specific areas and years were evident (Table 81).

Sex ratios of newborn calves may differ between elk populations and possibly between subspecies. From 155 Rocky Mountain elk calves captured in the West Gallatin River drainage of Montana and Yellowstone National Park, Johnson (1951) reported a sex ratio of 96 males per 100 females. Angstman and Gaab (1950) reported a calf sex ratio of 97:100 for the West Gallatin herd (n = 470). The sex ratio of 472 calves captured in the Sun River drainage of Montana was 102:100 (Picton 1961). Schwartz and Mitchell (1945) examined 94 Roosevelt elk calves on the Olympic Peninsula and observed that the sex ratio was 64 males per 100 females.

Immigration, Dispersal and Range Fidelity

Immigration and emigration rates of individual elk can be examined using either radiotelemetry or observations of marked individuals; either way, the time and resources necessary to monitor dispersal may be considerable (Boyce 1989). Potentially, population loss due to emigration and gain by immigration represent a significant factor in elk population dynamics. For example, the lack of young bull dispersal in Michigan may explain, in part, the high bull-to-cow ratios (greater than 50–60:100) observed by Bender (1992), compared with elk populations in the western states. Similarly, Flook (1970b) reported bull-to-cow ratios of 85:100 within fenced areas of Elk Island National Park, Alberta; whereas, bull-to-cow ratios of 37:100 were observed in nearby Jasper National Park, Alberta, where elk may readily disperse. Flook (1970b) believed that the lack of yearling bull dispersal and lack of mortality as a result of dispersal

(Clutton-Brock et al. 1982, Geist 1982) in Elk Island National Park were the main reasons for the differences in bull-to-cow ratios.

In general, female offspring tend to establish ranges in or adjacent to their mother's group. However, in polygynous mammals such as elk, dispersal of males is a regulating mechanism (Boyce 1989), and limited evidence suggests that dispersal among yearling bull elk is density dependent (Boyce 1989). Also, bull offspring often are driven away by harem bulls from their mothers' range (Franklin and Leib 1979). In some cases, juvenile males may not be forced to disperse until they are 2.5 years old (Hurley and Sargeant 1991), as in Michigan, where harem bulls tolerate the presence of young bulls (Bender 1992). However, the absence of dispersal behavior in Michigan likely is due to limited range (Bender 1992).

Bull elk dispersal often occurs at 2.5 years of age. Hurley and Sargeant (1991) reported dispersal among 2.5-year-old bulls in the Bob Marshall Wilderness area of western Montana. They reported a mean distance of 15.3 miles (24.6 km) between pre- and postdispersal activity centers for bulls, compared with 2.2 miles (3.6 km) for cows. It also is important to note that Hurley and Sargeant (1991) reported that mortality rates were higher for dispersing bulls than for other sex or age classes in Montana. Millspaugh (1999) reported similar findings for bull elk in the southern Black Hills of South Dakota. Radio-collared bulls dispersed at 2.5 years, and mortality due to legal harvest resulted in lower survival rates among dispersers than nondispersers.

A number of studies have reported strong philopatry of female elk for seasonal and annual ranges (Craighead et al. 1972, Rudd et al. 1983, Edge and Marcum 1985a, Edge et al. 1986, Smith and Robbins 1994). Edge et al. (1986), for example, reported that only 3% of marked and 2% of radio-collared elk dispersed. Furthermore, only 4 of 58 (7%) radio-collared adult cow elk made temporary movements between herds. Smith and Robbins (1994) reported a 98% rate of fidelity among summer ranges for the Jackson elk

Table 81. Male elk calves derived from sex ratios (calves 0–1 year) at Jackson Hole, Wyoming, 1951 to 1985

Period	Teton Wilderness		National Forest (south of Teton Wilderness area)		Grand Teton National Park and National Elk Refuge		Jackson herd	
	Percentage	Number	Percentage	Number	Percentage	Number	Percentage	Number
1951–1975	54.5	602[a]	49.6	1,393	51.5	1,309	53.4	6,245[a]
1976–1985	54.4	217	46.6	1,174[a]	39.8	1,369[a]	44.0	2,761[a]
Total	54.5	819[a]	48.2	2,567	45.5	2,678[a]	50.5	9,006

Source: Boyce 1989.

[a] Denotes sex ratio not equal to 1:1 ratio.

herd. Such strong fidelity, tradition and learned behavior among cow elk likely contribute to the stability of social groups (Edge et al. 1986; Van Dyke et al. 1998).

Although tradition and learned behavior are important, other factors, such as population abundance, may influence range fidelity. Van Dyke et al. (1998) evaluated home range fidelity of three elk populations in south-central and northwestern Montana during two time periods (1979–1982 and 1988–1991). They reported a significant shift in range boundaries and range use between the two time periods for two of the three elk populations. Their data suggested that, where shifts in range use were correlated positively with population growth, those changes likely were density-dependent. These results have important implications for elk population management and the structure of elk populations. For instance, if elk shift range use, harvest quotas may need to be considered (Van Dyke et al. 1998). Also, if two previously disjunct subherds coalesce into one herd, the age and sex structure of the population could change.

Population Growth and Regulation

The role of natural regulation in elk populations is widely debated. Perhaps, part of the dispute stems from confusion about the various definitions of natural regulation. The most basic description of population growth is given as: $N_{t+1} + 1 = N_t + B + I - D - E$, where N_{t+1} = the population size at time $_{t+1}$, N_t = the initial population size, B = births, I = immigration, D = deaths and E = emigration. The basic tenet here is that population growth is a function of the interaction between B, I, D, E and N_t. Populations increase due to births and immigration and decrease due to emigration and deaths. In the absence of limiting factors and with unlimited resources, ungulate populations typically grow exponentially (Caughley 1970). Population growth is said to be density independent when birth and death rates are not dependent on population size. The factors affecting population growth when populations are large are termed density-dependent factors. As population size increases, resources become limited, and birth rates and survival decline. This idea of resource limitation and subsequent limits to population growth is known commonly as natural regulation. Boyce (1991a) provided an excellent discussion on problems inherent in these terms.

Role of Density Dependence and Compensation

Regulation of elk populations may occur through a variety of processes, such as competition for food (Houston 1982, Merrill and Boyce 1991), predation, disease and weather (Merrill and Boyce 1991, Coughenour and Singer 1996). A

variety of density-dependent processes have been reported in elk populations, including declines in pregnancy rates (Thorne et al. 1976, Houston 1982, Merrill and Boyce 1991), declines in calf survival due to low birth weights (Clutton-Brock et al. 1987b, Singer et al. 1997) and declines in juvenile survival at high elk densities (Houston 1982, Merrill and Boyce 1991). These data suggest that population regulation is achieved most consistently through effects on juveniles rather than on adults (Coughenour and Singer 1996).

Generally, the limitation of food and competition for that food in winter are cited as the mechanisms that create density-dependent effects in ungulate populations (Merrill and Boyce 1991, Coughenour and Singer 1996). In the Northern Yellowstone elk herd, population numbers appeared to be regulated by density-dependent competition for food (Houston 1982, Merrill and Boyce 1991). Coughenour and Singer (1996) suggested two hypotheses to provide evidence that the Northern Yellowstone elk herd was nutritionally limited. First, elk responded to precipitation, which caused variations in forage productivity. Second, elk populations grew more slowly when elk were more abundant, suggesting that elk were competing for a limited resource, presumably forage.

Body condition, which may be dependent on competition for food during winter and spring, influences female reproductive performance, birth dates, birth weights and, subsequently, juvenile survival (Thorne et al. 1976, Guinness et al. 1978c, Clutton-Brock et al. 1987b). Poor cow condition increases weight loss, depressing calf birth weight and delaying birth dates (Thorne et al. 1976, Merrill and Boyce 1991). Houston (1982) identified undernutrition at high densities and subsequent effects on reproduction, calf birth mass and survival of calves (in summer and winter) as critical features in the population growth of the Northern Yellowstone elk herd.

Benefits of winter feeding on female condition and neonatal growth may help mask negative effects that current densities of elk may impose on calf survival. For example, elk calves supplementally fed on the National Elk Refuge had a survival rate of 88.6% compared with 71.4% for calves unfed during the same period (Smith and Anderson 1998). These percentages compare closely with the 71.9% survival rate reported by Singer et al. (1997) for elk calves in Yellowstone National Park. Thus, the effects of density dependence may be somewhat offset by supplemental feeding.

Juvenile mortality is among the most sensitive responses to increasing population density (Eberhardt 1977, Fowler 1987, Coughenour and Singer 1996). Knight (1970), Houston (1982) and Sauer and Boyce (1983) reported that density-dependent recruitment rates are due to changes in

Competition for food in winter may be an important density-dependent process, helping to regulate elk populations. Survival of calves on winter feedgrounds is dependent, in part, on the distribution of feed relative to the number of elk present. Bull elk displace cows and calves. Cows displace calves. Unless supplemental feed is well distributed, calves may not be able to compete for it. *Photo by H. L. Shantz; courtesy of the U.S. Forest Service.*

fecundity or survival of young, which could be due to lower energy reserves as a result of more dominant individuals excluding calves from food sources. Boyce (1989) concluded that both recruitment and juvenile survival were density dependent in the Jackson elk herd, despite the intensive management program. Sauer and Boyce (1983) found that calf survival was negatively correlated with cow census data, which suggests that elk density affects calf survival. Therefore, large elk populations in winter may decrease the chance of calf survival until the next spring. Sauer and Boyce (1983) suggested that, when elk were concentrated on feedlots or winter ranges, density-dependent mortality among juveniles could be an important mechanism of population regulation. Coughenour and Singer (1996) found that cow mortality was independent of elk population density, and density-dependent processes acting on bull and calf mortality were sufficient to regulate population numbers. Similarly, Singer et al. (1997) reported that winter survival of calves was inversely related to elk population size during winter. Summer survival of calves also was inversely correlated with population size during the previous winter.

Singer et al. (1997) also observed a unique density-dependent relationship in summer calf mortality due to predation in Yellowstone National Park. Severe droughts during 1988, subsequent large fires and the severe winter of 1988 to 1989 had large influences on elk populations by reducing forage biomass availability. Consequently, elk calved later in spring 1989; calves were lighter and thus more vulnerable to predators. Predators may have searched harder for elk calves, as other food sources were reduced. Because fire reduced groundcover, elk calves were less likely to hide effectively, and predator search efficiency likely increased (Singer et al. 1997). Moreover, smaller calves may be easier for predators to capture.

Recognition of density-dependent processes also are important, because modeling exercises involving harvest regimes should be based on an inverse relationship between population density and fecundity and juvenile survival. Fowler (1981) reported that age specificity of density-dependent mortality and reproduction changes the shape of the yield curve, which affects maximum sustained yield.

Role of Density-independent Processes

Elk survival also is affected by density-independent features of the landscape. Environmental conditions are density independent and consequently operate as a random factor on elk populations. Two consecutive years of extreme environmental conditions may have cumulative effects on population mortality rates. Harsh, long winters may reduce the fitness of pregnant cows, resulting in low-weight neonates that fail to achieve adequate size and body condition to survive a second harsh winter.

A variety of density-independent features may be important to the function and structure of elk populations. In Yellowstone National Park, the density-independent factors important to elk survival were spring precipitation, forage production and snow depth (Coughenour and Singer 1996). Cow and bull mortality rates were higher, and rates of increase typically lower, after a year with a wet spring. Singer et al. (1997) also reported strong influences of environmental factors on calf survival. Winter survival of calves and cow-to-calf ratios were relatively low for calves born late in spring after deep snow years.

The importance of density-dependent and density-independent mortalities varies geographically and temporally, and these factors should not be considered mutually exclusive mechanisms of population control. Climate tends to punctuate density-dependent factors during severe winters and to mitigate them in mild winters (Sauer and Boyce 1983). That is, density-dependent factors interact with density-independent factors and increase mortality during severe winters and decrease mortality during mild winters. Winter weather also may modify density-dependent factors or act independently in elk populations (Merrill and Boyce 1991). Picton (1984), for example, found that weather can significantly influence calf recruitment when population numbers are high. Calves were at a competitive disadvantage because they began winter with less fat reserves and were more susceptible to mortality as a result of density-independent processes.

Precipitation also can play an important role in adult and juvenile elk population dynamics. For instance, recruitment of juveniles in Yellowstone National Park was correlated with precipitation (Coughenour and Singer 1996). Adult mortality rates were not correlated significantly with elk numbers, but were correlated with precipitation.

Early spring green-up typically results in cow elk establishing a high nutritional plane during the latter stages of gestation, which, in turn, increases birth weight and juvenile survival (Merrill and Boyce 1991). Precipitation may result in rapid plant growth and an increase in the nutritional value in forage, leading to subsequent improvement in the body condition of cows (Coughenour and Singer 1996). Increased nutritional level allows cows to reduce maternal weight loss, obtain a threshold body weight necessary for conception and enter the winter with large fat reserves (Merrill and Boyce 1991). Winters with high snow accumulation and consequent delayed plant phenology may provide a higher quality diet for a longer period in late summer and autumn than in years with average phenological development.

Density-independent processes also may operate differently on males and females. Coughenour and Singer (1996) speculated that bull mortality rates were regulated primarily by density-independent factors. Singer et al. (1989) found that the susceptibility of bull mortality to density-independent factors was illustrated when severe snow, coupled with reduced forage caused by the 1988 Yellowstone fires and dry summer led to high bull mortality rates in the winter of 1988–89. Such mortality was thought to have been related to the high energy demands on bulls during autumn rut and use of more marginal habitats.

The timing of bad weather events also may have a variety of impacts on elk populations. Coughenour and Singer (1996) reported that winter severity was more detrimental late in winter than during early winter. Elk in Yellowstone National Park were affected by severe winter weather as illustrated by die-offs in 1974–75 (Cole 1983) and 1988 to 1989 (Singer et al. 1989, Coughenour and Singer 1996).

Rates of Increase

Estimates of rates of increase are essential for efficient wildlife management (Eberhardt et al. 1996) because they provide a measure of population performance. Several variables, such as age and sex structure, are important in understanding estimates of rate of increase. Equally important to elk population growth rates are differences in

The availability of rapidly greening vegetation in spring is important to meeting the nutritional needs of elk. At this time, bull elk begin developing antlers and cow elk must meet nutritional demands of late gestation. *Photo by Bruce Richards.*

Years with high snow accumulation, followed by delayed plant phenology, may provide a higher quality diet for a longer period in late summer and autumn than do years with average phenological development. *Photo by George Wolstad; courtesy of the U.S. Forest Service.*

survival rates. Nelson and Peek (1982) found that small changes in adult survival, which may be difficult to detect, can have dramatic effects on the rate of increase in all populations. For elk, survival rates have greater impact on rates of increase than do fecundity rates, a reflection of the narrow range of fecundity in elk.

The absence of tree cover on the Arid Lands Ecology Reserve in central Washington shrub-steppe has made it possible to make accurate counts of elk since the early 1980s (McCorquodale et al. 1988, Eberhardt et al. 1996). Subsequently, reliable data are available to estimate rates of increase in this herd. McCorquodale et al. (1988) estimated a rate of increase of 0.30. However, Eberhardt et al. (1996) believed this rate was above the feasible maximum rate of increase and suggested that a rate of increase of 0.28 represented a maximum for elk. This value is similar to that calculated for the Northern Yellowstone elk herd by Eberhardt (1987) using data from Houston (1982).

Rate of increase for other colonizing elk herds is variable. Gogan and Barrett (1987) reported rates of increase for reintroduced Tule elk in California at 31% on Grizzly Island and 29% at Point Reyes. These high rates of increase were a result of low calf and adult mortality rates, high natality rates and calf sex ratios favoring females (Gogan and Barrett 1987). Differences in the growth rates of the two introduced Tule elk populations in Point Reyes and Grizzly Island reportedly reflected the importance of density-independent environmental factors on elk population processes (Gogan and Barrett 1987). Moffitt (1934) reported a rate of increase of 0.18 for elk in Alaska; Burris and McKnight (1973) reported an increase rate of 0.37 for elk in Yosemite National Park in California. Merrill (1987) reported a rate of increase of 0.34 for colonizing elk at Mount St. Helens in Washington. All of these data suggest that elk populations have great growth potential in a diversity of habitats.

Assessing Elk Population Characteristics

Attempts to assess elk population characteristics are limited by constraints well described by Eberhardt (1971:457–458): "The basic ingredients for a study of any population are birth and death rates, age and sex composition, and numerical abundance. Given good estimates of these essentials, few complications of mathematics, logic, or terminology are involved in understanding population behavior in general terms. Unfortunately, a complete array of the needed data is never available, and all sorts of difficulties arise in trying to get along with the observations that can be obtained."

The elk population attributes of greatest interest from the standpoint of conservation and management are size and productivity. It is important to know whether, under some particular management plan, a population is increasing, stable or declining. For hunted populations, it is vital to estimate the annual recruitment as a base for establishing a proper annual level of harvest. For determining both of these population attributes—size and productivity—knowledge of still another attribute, namely population structure is useful.

Population Structure

Population structure refers to the relative abundance of males and females of different ages in the population. Population structure data are important because, coupled with birth and death rates, growth rates can be ultimately estimated (Boyce 1989). There are two techniques to assess population structure, each of which is useful in its own way. The first is that structure can be detected through herd composition counts—recognition and enumeration of four

or five age and sex classes in a population. Eberhardt et al. (1996) reported herd composition data and subsequently estimated survival rates for elk on the Arid Lands Ecology Reserve in Washington from aerial counts (Table 82). From these data, other information vital to elk management, such as reproductive rates also may be calculated from cow-to-calf ratios. The second way to assess population structure is through the use of mathematical models. Such analyses will be explored later in this chapter.

Herd composition counts depend on an observer's ability to distinguish between age and sex classes—ordinarily adult (2 years and older) bulls, yearling bulls, cows and calves. In intensive studies, it is possible to distinguish yearling cows from older cows, at least during summer. For a herd composition count to be representative of an entire population, all sex and age classes should be equally observable. This, perhaps, is never entirely true, but it is more likely to occur in some seasons but not in others. For instance, when elk are aggregated in large herds during the winter, observability usually is best, or at least most convenient, but it may be difficult then to distinguish between yearling and adult cows.

Herd composition counts are one of the few types of data regularly collected on elk populations. Although herd composition counts commonly are used to assess population status, the assumptions, strengths and weaknesses of the technique are poorly documented in the literature (Caughley 1974b, McCullough 1994). McCullough (1994) provided the assumptions for using and applying composition counts to big game management, reemphasized the shortcomings and suggested ways in which those counts can be used within a larger population management strategy.

Herd composition counts often are made during early autumn to ascertain the composition of the prehunt popu-

Table 82. Herd composition and estimated survival rates for adult elk on the Arid Lands Ecology Reserve in Washington

Year	Adult	Yearling	Total	Estimated bull survival	Adult	Yearling	Total	Estimated cow survival	Number of calves	Adult bull: Adult cow ratio
1983	5	3	8		16	3	19		13	31:100
1984	7	12	19	0.88	20	1	21	1.00	15	35:100
1985	18	7	25	0.95	21	8	29	1.00	17	86:100
1986	22	8	30	0.88	29	9	38	1.00	21	76:100
1987	14	5	19	0.47	32	16	48	0.84	27	44:100
1988	12	13	25	0.63	33	14	47	0.69	23	36:100
1989	18	10	28	0.72	38	13	51	0.81	23	74:100
1990	22	12	34	0.79	49	11	60	0.96	21	45:100
1991	19	12	31	0.56	70	9	79	1.00	23	27:100
1992	30	11	41	0.97	93	12	105	1.00	44	32:100
1993	33	19	52	0.80	102	25	127	0.97	59	32:100

Source: Eberhardt et al. 1996.

Note: Estimated survival rates for each year are calculated as the ratio of adults to totals in the previous year.

lation. Subsequent counts often are conducted after the autumn hunt to determine composition of the posthunt population and assess the level of harvest of different segments of the population (e.g., change in the number of branch-antlered bulls). Herd composition counts also may be conducted during late winter to determine overwinter calf survival. Generally, management goals are stated as desirable ranges of sex and age ratios obtained from herd composition counts. Desired ratios are typically a high ratio of males to females and a high ratio of young to females. Because these ratios are not necessarily coupled with population size (Caughley 1974b), some other independent assessment of population performance, such as population size, should be collected using the techniques described in this chapter (see McCullough 1994). A least two seasonal phenomena influence herd composition counts:

1. Although calves are born during late May and early June, they are not routinely observable until about 1 month old. Therefore, the number of calves observed per 100 cows may be higher during July than during June, although the actual total number of calves may be lower.

2. Although elk are more readily observable during the rut than at other times of the year, due to increased activity of bulls, the clumped distribution of bulls with harems of cows during autumn tend to make count results erratic.

In addition, there may be a relationship between seasonal behavior and observability. Knight (1970), for example, suggested that Rocky Mountain elk cows who lose their calves may not need as much feed as do cows who still are suckling calves, therefore they may not appear in open foraging areas as consistently as adult cows with calves. Thus, they may not be counted as accurately as some other more observable groups. In studies of Rocky Mountain elk in western Washington, yearling elk are believed to be exceptionally observable in May and June, when they are newly separated from their mothers. There undoubtedly are other ways that seasonal visibility of elk is affected by the interaction of behavior and habitat. As those ways are identified in specific herds, herd composition counts can be made more reliable.

Data from herd composition counts can be used in conjunction with reproductive data to provide estimates of calf survival from summer and through the following winter. For example, on the western slope of the Cascade Mountain range in Washington, Rocky Mountain elk cows had a reproductive rate of 0.1 in their second year, and older cows had a rate of 1.0 (Schoen 1977). If, in early June, each 100 cows include 10 two-year-olds and 90 older cows, the expected calf production would be: $(10 \times 0.1) + (90 \times 1.0) = 91$. Actual counts for July and August 1976 are presented in Table 83. By combining the July and August counts to obtain a larger sample, there is a ratio of 66 calves to 100 cows. The estimated loss of calves between birth and August is 91 minus 66, or 25 calves per 100 cows. This also may be expressed as approximately a 27% loss of the calf crop between birth and August 1976.

Herd composition counts taken at intervals throughout the year are influenced by adult losses as well as by adult gains through immigration. Composition counts are most useful for comparing events in a population from season to season or year to year. Life tables, described later in this chapter, are most useful in comparing the demographics of one population with another.

Population Abundance

Management of elk requires sound data on population size. However, as Peek (1985) pointed out, estimating the number of elk is difficult. Nonetheless, when developing elk management plans, biologists invariably are expected to provide estimates of the number of elk in a given population. In most cases, management decisions can be made with the help of systematically calculated indices of population density.

Animal abundance estimates can be characterized in three ways: relative density (the density of one population relative to that of another or to the same population from one year to the next); the number of animals within a population; and absolute density (the number of animals per unit area). A brief summary of some of the techniques commonly used to estimate elk population numbers follows. More detailed discussion of this topic is given in Caughley (1977), Seber (1982), Skalski and Robson (1992), and Lancia et al. (1994), among others.

Total Population Counts

Total population counts for big game evolved from "deer drives" of pioneer days and have been used to estimate elk

Table 83. Summer herd composition of Rocky Mountain elk in western Washington, 1976

| Month | Number observed | | | | | |
	Adult bulls	Yearling bulls	Adult cows	Yearling cows	Calves	Total
July	13	4	79	13	46	155
August	15	9	78	5	58	165
Total (%)	28 (9)	13 (4)	157 (48)	18 (6)	104 (33)	320 (100)

Source: Schoen 1977.

population numbers (Lovaas et al. 1966, Houston 1982). These counts generally are limited to populations within fenced areas or populations with very limited geographic range and that occupy relatively open habitats (i.e., elk on the Arid Lands Ecology Reserve in south-central Washington). McCullough (1979) used drive counts to census white-tailed deer within the fences of the George Reserve in Michigan. Annual censusing of the big game populations on the National Bison Refuge in Montana also has been conducted using drive counts. Winter counts of elk on the National Elk Refuge in Wyoming, corrected for variations in winter weather, have been conducted regularly since the early 1960s, and provide useful information about the dynamics of that elk population (Boyce 1989).

Before 1964, most censuses of elk populations used line-transect or strip-transect flight patterns to cover the entire study area in an attempt to count all animals present. However, these methods involve two important assumptions: the probability of spotting an elk was 100%; and bias associated with the counts was consistent among surveys. However, both assumptions are unrealistic in most situations. Considerable variation among counts could occur due to differences in the amount of cover, group size and weather, each of which influence population counts. Because of these problems, methodology involving sightability (Samuel et al. 1987) and mark–recapture methods (Bear et al. 1989) have been developed. In addition, improvements in sampling techniques (Otten et al. 1993) have greatly improved estimates of elk population numbers.

Thermal Scanners

Several attempts have been made to conduct counts of big game using thermal infrared scanners (Croon et al. 1968, Garner et al. 1995, Naugle et al. 1996). However, variables such as canopy cover, the presence of multiple species and bias in sampling strategies have made interpretation of thermal scanning results difficult (Garner et al. 1995, Naugle et al. 1996).

Garner et al. (1995) used a commercially available thermal infrared-scanning system to survey populations of several wildlife species. They reported marked differences in counts by untrained and trained analysts. Computer-assisted analysis of infrared imagery recorded 52% fewer deer compared with drive counts, and densities of moose were five times those estimated from conventional aerial methods. They reported that, with the aid of computer-assisted analysis, infrared themography may become a useful wildlife population tool. More research is needed to verify the actual efficiency of detection by combining aerial scans with ground truthing for a variety of species and habitats.

Estimates of Relative Density (indices)

An index of relative population density is some measure of population numbers that is functionally related to the number of animals in the population or area in question (Eberhardt 1978, Lancia et al. 1994). Some of the most commonly used indices in elk management include roadside counts (including spotlight counts), track counts, fecal pellet group counts, hunter success (catch-per-unit-effort) and aerial surveys. To be most useful, the methods used to calculate the index should be standardized as much as possible, so that changes in the index values reflect changes in the population rather than changes in measurement techniques. Where possible, replicated samples should be used so that estimates of sample variance can be calculated (Seber 1982). In addition, researchers should determine how all indices track abundance in different habitats.

In some cases, population indices can be calibrated to actual estimates of population abundance. An index that is developed in conjunction with a total population estimate can be used to estimate total elk population at a later time. A sightability index provides an estimate of the percentage of the population that is observable under defined conditions, often based on censuses of marked animals (Samuel et al. 1987). If, for example, a population estimate of 1,000 elk is calculated using mark–recapture techniques, but an average of only 250 elk are observed from the air during the field surveys, a sightability index of 0.25 can be calculated, implying that, for every elk seen, there were 3 additional elk that avoided detection. In subsequent years, the average number of elk observed in similar aerial surveys could be multiplied by four to get an expanded population estimate for the area surveyed, based on the sightability index calculated for that population and area. Other variations involving radio-marked animals (Samuel et al. 1987) will be discussed later.

In any such censusing effort, the prudent biologist would recalibrate the sightibility index periodically to be sure that habitat changes or other conditions have not altered the sightibility of elk in the area. Population indices are most useful in answering questions, such as, what is the relative percentage change in an elk population from one year to the next? What is the proportional reduction in density of elk that results from increased or decreased hunting pressure? What is the trend in numbers of an elk herd over time?

Sample-area Counts

Many forms of sample-area counts to estimate population size have been developed for big game, including elk. An animal density estimate is calculated by counting all the elk within a given area divided by the size of area sampled, resulting in estimates of elk per square mile or square kilometer. Common forms of this approach are aerial censusing and road transects.

Aerial censusing of elk routinely is conducted in many states and provinces using both helicopter and fixed wing aircraft. Counts usually are conducted before the autumn hunting season or during winter or spring, when snow cover improves visibility and elk group size is maximized. In many cases, particularly in forested areas, aerial surveys should be treated as an index of the population, as it is unlikely that all elk will be counted. Counts can be adjusted when the proportion of elk not counted in an area can be accounted for by other data sources, such as telemetry studies, in which the number of marked elk in the area is known (Samuel et al. 1987).

Mark–recapture

Mark–recapture techniques, also known as the Petersen Index or Lincoln Index, have a long history of use in assessing big game populations. A large body of scientific literature describes the many variations of the technique (see Seber 1982, Skalski and Robson 1992, Lancia et al. 1994). In many cases, mark–recapture population estimates are calculated as part of radiotelemetry studies, where collared elk are the "marked" elk. Certain assumptions must be made in mark–recapture projects for them to be effective (Skalski and Robson 1992): (1) sighting probabilities of marked and unmarked elk are the same; (2) each animal has an identical but independent probability of being resighted; (3) marked and unmarked animals are classified correctly; (4) no markers are lost or unaccounted; (5) the population is closed; and (6) resighting is randomly distributed throughout the population.

The extent to which these assumptions are met depends on the population being surveyed. For instance, population closure between populations will be highly variable. In addition, one might suspect differences in elk visibility due to aggregation size (Bear et al. 1989). Also, because of habitat variability, a similar probability of sighting for each animal is unlikely. Random and selective sampling may not be an appropriate sampling strategy because of relatively low capture rates. This results in low proportions of animals marked, and a large proportion of the total population must be marked for this method to provide reliable population estimates (Bartmann et al. 1987, Skalski and Robson 1992). Instead, adaptive sampling procedure may be more appropriate (Thompson and Seber 1996).

Mark–recapture methods all have the same basic format. A sample number of elk are captured, marked and released. Then, a second sample of elk is collected, and the numbers of marked and unmarked elk are recorded. In most studies of elk and other big game, the "recapture" is based on visual observations rather than physically capturing the elk. The proportion of the number of marked and unmarked elk, relative to the number originally marked, is used to calculate the number of individuals in the population at the time of capture. The population size, then can be estimated using one of several techniques, such as Chapman's (1951) modified Lincoln–Peterson Index or a maximum likelihood estimator as described by Bear et al. (1989).

The elk population size (N) is related to the number of elk captured and released (M) in the sample, as the total number of elk observed (n) at a subsequent time is related to the number marked that are recaptured or resighted (m) in the simplest form by the following equation: $N = (M)(n)/(m)$. For example, if 28 elk are captured, marked and released and, on a subsequent aerial survey, 200 elk are counted and 15 of the 200 elk were marked, then the estimate of (m) is 15, the estimate of (n) is 200 and the elk population estimate is calculated as follows: $N = (28)(200)/(15)$, or $N = 373$.

Capturing and marking elk may be an expensive venture (Otten et al. 1993). The high costs of capture and marking can be reduced using other marking techniques. Recent efforts conducted by the Washington Department of Fish and Wildlife have involved marking elk with paintballs fired from a helicopter (Myers et al. 1995, Spencer 1997). Subsequent surveys were flown to resight elk marked with paint and document herd composition. Mark–resight estimates of elk numbers were reliable and precise (Myers et al. 1995, Spencer 1997). Further refinement of this technique and evaluation of biases could provide a cost-effective and precise procedure for estimating the abundance of elk and other ungulates.

Still other possibilities exist for the identification of marked elk during surveys. Using a mark–resight method for individuals that possessed unique scars, pelage and antler configurations, Weckerly (1996) estimated Roosevelt elk abundance. He suggested that improvements in the reliability of estimates may be obtained by increasing the number of resight episodes and observing a large proportion of the population.

Sightability Models

Animal counts based on mark–recapture theory may provide a highly variable underestimation of actual population size due to visibility bias (Caughley 1974, Samuel et al. 1987, Singer and Garton 1994). Visibility bias (i.e., bias introduced as a result of not observing all animals) is a commonly recognized problem in the counts of elk and other

Aerial surveys are often conducted in the autumn, before hunting seasons to determine herd composition. *Photo courtesy of the Colorado Division of Wildlife.*

ungulate populations (Caughley 1977, Pollock and Kendall 1987, Bear et al. 1989). The probability of spotting elk, called the sighting probability, depends on animal body size, group size (Bear et al. 1989, Unsworth et al. 1990), observer fatigue and experience (LeResche and Rausch 1974, Samuel et al. 1987), search speed, habitat, animal behavior, snow cover and altitude, among others. Generally, two approaches are used to improve the accuracy of aerial surveys for elk—refinements in survey methodology (Otten et al. 1993) and application of correction factors (Samuel et al. 1987, Unsworth et al. 1990).

Samuel et al. (1987) calculated a sightability index from a ratio of radio-collared elk observed in a survey versus those not seen but known to be present in north-central Idaho. Using this methodology, researchers have the ability to evaluate various factors that might influence sightability, allowing a better estimate of population size. They found that elk visibility was influenced significantly by group size and vegetative cover. Snow cover, search rate, animal behavior and different observers did not significantly affect elk observability in their study. Similarly, Cogan and Diefenbach (1998) reported that group size and percentage canopy closure affected the probability of sighting elk in Pennsylvania.

Unsworth et al. (1990) validated the Samuel et al (1987) model for elk against a control population of known size on the National Bison Range in Montana, using the following logistic regression model, predicting elk sightability: $y = [\exp(u)]/[1 + \exp(u)]$, where y = sighting probability, and $u = 2.24 + 1.57 \ln(\text{group size}) - 0.86$ vegetation cover class. To ensure the most accurate estimates when using the sightability techniques for elk, Unsworth et al. (1990) rec-

Elk are commonly marked to determine important population characteristics, such as population size. Here, the front elk has just been marked in its rear flank by a paint ball fired from a helicopter. Subsequent surveys are flown to determine the number of elk marked versus the number unmarked. *Photo by Bruce Richards.*

ommended that surveys be conducted when group sizes are largest and elk are using the most open habitats, which typically occurs during winter.

Eberhardt et al. (1998) compared the use of visibility curves described by Samuel et al. (1987) with Petersen Index estimates of abundance in Yellowstone National Park. They reported that estimates based on Petersen estimates may provide a suitable alternative, and recommended that researchers use both techniques to estimate abundance.

Although most sightability surveys are conducted during winter months, Anderson et al. (1998) reported on the development and evaluation of sightablity models for summer surveys. Anderson et al. (1998) found that, as with winter models, the amount of vegetative cover strongly affected the probability of sighting elk herds during summer. Elk group size also influenced sightability in summer, as did elk behavior. Previously, Samuel et al. (1987) reported that elk behavior did not influence elk sightability in Idaho, but Anderson et al. (1998) believed that herd behavior during summer surveys may be more important than during winter, because the lack of snow cover makes sighting elk more difficult. Anderson et al. (1998) recommended application of the Idaho elk model in summer, when elk were less gregarious (less than 20 elk), and recommended "summer Model B," which accounts for the influence of group size and vegetation classes for high-density elk populations where elk occur in larger groups. To obtain the most precise abundance estimates, surveys should be conducted when sighting conditions are best. In summer, this means conducting surveys early in the morning, and avoiding surveys when elk are solitary (i.e., calving season).

Abundance Estimates Based on Harvest Data

Removal Methods

For a long time, hunter harvests have been used to estimate the size of big game populations. This approach is attractive because harvest data are routinely collected as part of standard population monitoring efforts of most management agencies, and the elk herd manager does not need to capture elk or conduct other expensive studies. However, such a technique is not used that often.

For big game populations, a common estimation technique is the change-in-ratio method (Paulik and Robson 1969, Lancia et al. 1994), popularized for deer by Kelker (1940). The method involves measuring changes in the proportions of males and females in the population before and after hunting seasons. It is based on the concept that, if one identifiable sex or age class (such as antlered males) is hunted more heavily than another, selective removal will be reflected in differences in the prehunt and posthunt sex ratios. It is assumed that the change in prehunt and posthunt ratios is a function of harvest only. If prehunt and posthunt ratios can be estimated, along with the number of animals killed, both the prehunt and posthunt population can be calculated. In addition to estimating population abundance, survival rates, productivity and exploitation rates may be computed using change-in-ratio techniques (Paulik and Robson 1969). An example of the use of the change-in-ratio method for elk was given by Boyd (1970). The preseason elk population in two Colorado management units was calculated as follows, where: $N = K (P1 - b)/(P1 - P2)$, $N = 1,268 (0.052 - 0.676)/(0.052 - 0.173)$ and $N = 6,539$ elk, where K = total harvest of 1,268 elk, $P1$ = fraction of bulls in the postseason count (0.052), $P2$ = fraction of bulls in the preseason count (0.173), b = fraction of bulls in the harvest (0.676) and N = total prehunt population estimate. To calculate the number of bulls, cows and calves in the preseason population, the total population estimate was multiplied by the percentage of each these groups in the preseason herd composition counts.

Use of Age-harvest Data to Estimate Demographic Parameters

Many state agencies routinely collect age-harvest data through mandatory check stations or tooth returns. Such data often are more cost effective and less labor intensive to collect than other forms of data. Gove (1997) developed a model based on age-harvest data and a multinomial likelihood function that was used to estimate annual abundance, survival and recruitment for elk in Washington and Idaho. The model requires data on abundance or survival rates from one or more age classes before the remaining parameters are estimated. The model also provides estimates of precision not available in other techniques.

Other available techniques to analyze harvest data include population reconstruction techniques, such as virtual population analysis or cohort analysis (Roseberry and Woolf 1991) and sex-age-kill (SAK) modeling (Eberhardt 1960, Creed et al. 1984). However, these methods are used infrequently for elk populations, although the data to conduct such an analysis are generally available.

The basic data needed to conduct a SAK analysis are harvest numbers, adult sex ratio, juvenile-to-adult female age ratio, annual survival and the conditional harvest mortality rate (i.e., proportion of total mortality associated with harvest). Roseberry and Woolf (1991) listed three assumptions of the model: (1) the proportion of deaths accounted for is relatively constant over time; (2) age determination is accurate; and (3) estimates of adult sex ratio and fawn-to-doe ratio are accurate.

The following is an analysis presented by Bender and Spencer (1999:643) for elk in Michigan and Washington, using the SAK approach. Bender and Spencer estimated preseason elk populations by:

$$N_T = N_B \times (1 + R_{C/B} + R_{C/B} \times R_{C/C})$$
$$= (K/M_B \times P_H) \times (1 + R_{C/B} + R_{C/B} \times R_{C/C})$$
$$= (K/M_H) \times (1 + R_{C/B} + R_{C/B} \times R_{C/C})$$

Individual bull, cow and calf population parameters were estimated by:

$$N_B = K/M_B \times P_H \text{ or } K/M_H$$
$$N_C = N_B \times R_{C/B}$$

and

$$N_J = N_C \times R_{C/C}$$

where N_B = number of bulls, N_C = number of cows, N_J = number of calves, N_T = total number of elk, M_B = mean annual total bull mortality rate, P_H = the proportion of M_B due to harvesting, M_H = the bull elk harvesting rate, $R_{C/B}$ = the ratio of cows to bulls in preseason composition, $R_{C/C}$ = the ratio of calves to cows in preseason composition and K = the number of bulls harvested.

In the example provided by Bender and Spencer (1999), M_H = 0.14, $R_{C/B}$ = 100/61, $R_{C/C}$ = 0.51 and K = 57. Substituting into the total preseason estimator above,

$$N_T = N_B \times (1 + R_{C/B} + R_{C/B} \times R_{C/C})$$
$$= (K/M_H) \times (1 + R_{C/B} + R_{C/B} \times R_{C/C})$$
$$= (57/0.14) \times [1 + (100/61) + (100/61) \times 0.51]$$
$$= 1,414$$

Using these data, estimates for the total number of bulls (N_B), cows (N_C) and calves (N_J) also can be computed as:

$$N_B = K/M_H = 57/0.14 = 407$$
$$N_C = N_B \times R_{C/B} = 407 \times (100/61) = 667$$

and

$$N_J = N_C \times R_{C/C} = 667 \times 0.51 = 340$$

The approximate variance expressions for the total abundance estimator, N_T, is:

$$\text{Var}(N_T) \approx N_T^2 \times [CV(K)^2 + CV(M_H)^2] + N_{J+C}^2 \times CV(R_{C/B})^2 + N_J^2 \times CV(R_{C/C})^2$$

where CV is the coefficient of variation. Assuming $CV(M_H)$ = 0.11, $CV(R_{C/B})$ = 0.07, $CV(R_{C/C})$ = 0.08 and $CV(K)$ = 0, as Bender and Spencer (1999) did, the variance for the total abundance estimator would be:

$$\approx 1,414^2 \times [0^2 + 0.11^2] + [(667 + 340)^2 \times 0.07^2]$$
$$+ [340^2 \times 0.08^2]$$
$$\approx 29,901$$

with SE $\approx$ 173, CV $\approx$ 0.12 and approximately 95% confidence interval of 1,068–1,760.

Approximate variance expressions for individual population components also may be computed. In addition to revealing how confident one may be about a population estimate, these variance expressions can be used to optimize the sampling strategy to achieve the highest precision for a fixed amount of money. Researchers should consider the use of such reconstruction techniques in conjunction with other enumeration approaches (Bender and Spencer 1999). Also, additional effort should be placed on identifying variance structures of these reconstruction techniques to determine the precision of the estimates.

Life Tables

Patterns of mortality among age classes can be summarized in a life table (Caughley 1977). A life table, when complete, is a tabular representation of the age distribution of an entire population by year class. For each age class (x), there is one value (l_x) for the number of live individuals entering the age class and another value (d_x) for the number dying during the class interval, usually expressed as 1 year. The l_x value for any age class, less the d_x value, equals the l_x value of the succeeding age class. Any d_x value, divided by the l_x value for that age class, gives the proportion dying (q_x), which is expressed as a percentage (Caughley 1977).

Theoretically, there are three ways of developing a life table. One is to start with a generation (cohort) of newborn and monitor the fate of its individuals each year until the last individual is dead. This has not been done for elk. Another method is to determine the mortality of each age class in a population during the course of 1 year (Eberhardt 1971); this, too, has not been done for elk.

Instead, a collection of all available data on age-specific productivity, seasonal herd composition counts, and age and sex of individuals that die has been done. Ideally, this is done for a period of years, spanning the usual variation in climatic conditions and during which time, seasonal population numbers and herd structure remain the same. A life table can then be constructed representing average reproduction and mortality patterns during the span of years.

Although available data often fall short of the ideal, an attempt to construct a life table can lead to useful insights, such as the estimation of values that cannot be measured directly. Because somewhat different patterns of mortality often are found between males and females, life tables generally are separated by sex. Most often, only the productive (female) segment of the herd is presented.

Examples of life tables for the Northern Yellowstone elk herd (Houston 1982) are presented in Tables 84 and 85. These life tables clearly demonstrate the contrast in mortality patterns of male and female elk—male elk typically suffer much higher mortality in all ages and, as a result, have a much shorter life span. The differences would be even greater in elk populations in which hunting mortality is concentrated on males.

Biomanagement Models for Elk Populations

The use of modeling in the management of elk populations has increased tremendously since the early 1980s. Models have been used to address several questions related to elk population dynamics, including effects of predation (Mack and Singer 1993, Vales and Peek 1993), harvest (Williams 1981, Peek and Garton 1987, Smith and Yuan 1991, Thelen 1991, Vales and Peek 1993), environmental influences (Turner et al. 1994, Wu et al. 1996), and various survival and reproductive outputs. Simulation models afford insight into the complexity inherent in population characteristics and can provide timely information about alternative

Table 84. An example of a life table for cow elk in Northern Yellowstone herd

Age in years	f_x	d_x	l_x	q_x
0	—	0.323	1.000	0.323
1	17	0.013	0.677	0.019
2	2	0.002	0.664	0.003
3	2	0.002	0.662	0.003
4	4	0.004	0.660	0.006
5	3	0.004	0.656	0.006
6	7	0.009	0.652	0.014
7	2	0.003	0.643	0.005
8	2	0.003	0.640	0.005
9	5	0.009	0.637	0.014
10	3	0.007	0.628	0.011
11	5	0.012	0.621	0.019
12	5	0.013	0.609	0.021
13	13	0.041	0.596	0.069
14	9	0.034	0.555	0.061
15	5	0.020	0.521	0.038
16	13	0.059	0.501	0.118
17	14	0.075	0.442	0.170
18	15	0.093	0.367	0.253
19	12	0.082	0.274	0.299
20	7	0.057	0.192	0.297
21+	15	0.135	0.135	1.000
Total	160	1.000		

Source: Houston 1982.

Table 85. An example of a life table for bull elk in Northern Yellowstone herd

Age in years	f_x	d_x	l_x	q_x
0	—	0.639	1.000	0.639
1	34	0.022	0.361	0.061
2	5	0.004	0.339	0.012
3	5	0.005	0.335	0.015
4	5	0.005	0.330	0.015
5	15	0.016	0.325	0.049
6	40	0.048	0.309	0.155
7	47	0.064	0.261	0.245
8	28	0.042	0.197	0.213
9	23	0.041	0.155	0.265
10	9	0.020	0.114	0.175
11	15	0.031	0.094	0.330
12	11	0.028	0.063	0.444
13	4	0.012	0.035	0.343
14	4	0.013	0.023	0.565
15+	3	0.010	0.010	1.000
Total	248	1.000		

Source: Houston 1982.

courses of management (Williams 1981, Starfield 1997). Figure 153 provides an example of model output and the different population characteristics that can be modeled.

Data of a model may be adjusted annually, when actual harvest information becomes available and other demographic information, such as survival rates, are estimated. The model can be continually tested and updated by comparing population projections with those observed in the field. In this fashion, a useful working model for a particular herd can be built, and a great deal of insight obtained about the dynamics of that population.

Predictions from models should be compared with measurements obtained for the real population. This process is called model validation, and predictions will be correct only to the extent that the model and input data are valid. Incorrect predictions will show that the model or data used in the model are incorrect in some aspect, and will direct attention back to the assumed relationships and data used. Some of these parameters will be based on better evidence or data. Suspected inaccuracies can be checked, and data that are weak may be collected through further field investigation. The overall result will be improvement of the model, better predictive capability and better elk management.

Leslie Matrix Model

A common approach to population simulation is possible through a modeling procedure described by Leslie (1945).

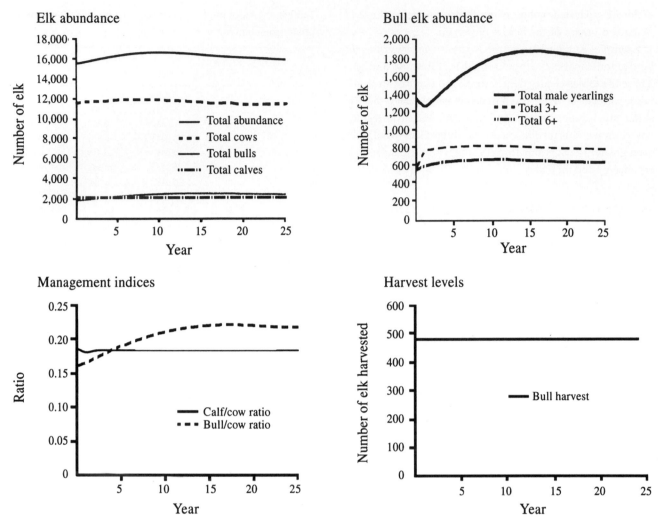

Figure 153.   Population projection and management indices under designated population demographics, no cow harvest and no calf harvest. Annual harvest is 481 bulls, 3 years and older.

This model essentially is a bookkeeping system that accounts for the relative abundance in each age class. The population is projected from some starting age structure for any number of generations desired. Although an element of variability in these rates may be incorporated, the model is structured as a matrix of mortality and productivity rates multiplied by an initial distribution of age frequencies. All values in the model can be obtained from field investigations, therefore the model conforms as closely as possible to the actual population. Variations in harvest patterns can be added, and population consequences on structure and abundance may be derived. Leptich and Zager (1991), for example, modeled the effect of road densities and subsequent harvest on elk population age structures.

Hypothetical Population

In this section, we model a hypothetical elk population, using estimates based on various field studies of Rocky

Mountain elk cited earlier in this chapter. Using the Leslie Matrix Model, reasonable values are assumed for the distribution of ages in the cow cohort of the population, average fertility rates and a rate of mortality that might be expected in a stable and unhunted population (Table 86).

The cow cohort of this population numbers 1,263 and remains constant year after year. About 67% of the cow calves produced each year die, along with a scattering of adult cows. As discussed previously, mortality in adult cows is assumed to be heaviest in the older age classes.

To calculate the effect of a cow harvest on herd stability, it is assumed that a harvest will increase calf survival, as winter competition will be reduced and the number of cows without calves in the population will decrease. Mortality rates in adult cows are assumed to be constant, that is, density independent, with the exception of older cows. Also, various age classes are not equally vulnerable to hunting. It will be assumed that animals in the 0 to 1 class are

Table 86.   The cow cohort of a hypothetical, stable, unhunted elk herd

Age class in years (x)	Number of elk entering age class (l_x)	Percentage producing female calves	Percentage surviving through class intervals (s_x)[a]
0–1	374	0	33
1–2	125	15	75
2–3	94	47	75
3–4	89	47	95
4–5	85	47	95
5–6	81	47	95
6–7	77	47	95
7–8	73	47	90
8–9	66	47	90
9–10	59	47	90
10–11	53	45	70
11–12	37	45	65
12–13	24	45	65
13–14	16	45	65
14–15	10	35	0
Total	1,263		

[a] Percentage surviving through class interval: $s_x = 1 - q_x$

Table 87.   Number and percentage of bulls entering various age classes of hypothetical elk herds in which various percentages of antlered bulls have been harvested

Age class in years	Harvest percentage of antlered bulls			
	0%[a]	25%[a]	40%[a]	80%[a]
0–1	325 (29.1)	325 (35.6)	325 (46.7)	325 (64.0)
1–2	146 (13.0)	146 (16.0)	146 (21.1)	146 (28.7)
2–3	110 (9.8)	100 (11.0)	90 (13.0)	29 (5.8)
3–4	96 (8.6)	83 (9.1)	63 (9.1)	8 (1.5)
4–5	84 (7.5)	69 (7.6)	42 (6.0)	0 (0.0)
5–6	73 (6.5)	55 (6.0)	15 (2.2)	0 (0.0)
6–7	64 (5.7)	45 (4.9)	9 (1.3)	0 (0.0)
7–8	56 (5.0)	35 (3.8)	6 (0.8)	0 (0.0)
8–9	46 (4.1)	23 (2.5)	0 (0)	0 (0.0)
9–10	38 (3.4)	16 (1.7)	0 (0)	0 (0.0)
10–11	31 (2.8)	12 (1.4)	0 (0)	0 (0.0)
11–12	22 (2.0)	4 (0.4)	0 (0)	0 (0.0)
12–13	14 (1.3)	0 (0.0)	0 (0)	0 (0.0)
13–14	9 (0.8)	0 (0.0)	0 (0)	0 (0.0)
14–15	6 (0.1)	0 (0.0)	0 (0)	0 (0.0)
Total	1,120	913	692	508

[a] Number of bulls entering age class (%).

half as vulnerable as adults, and animals in the 1 to 2 class are twice as vulnerable. By experimenting with different harvest rates, a stable cow cohort of 1,120 can be produced at a continued annual harvest rate of 10%.

The annual harvest is equivalent to 112 cows, and the overwintering number of cows is reduced by 94 individuals, or 8%. The calf mortality through hunting is 50%, but annual calf mortality is reduced from 67% to 55%. The proportion of cows more than 10 years old is reduced from 140 to 82, or 41%.

A similar model could be constructed for the male component of this hypothetical elk population. For simplicity, it has a male cohort similar to the female cohort and the former is subjected to hunting harvest rates of 25%, 40% and 80% of the antlered bulls (those 1 year of age and older). The number of male calves entering the male cohort is constant at 325 per year, and their survival rate is 45%, because it is dependent on the harvest rates for antlerless elk. All age classes are assumed to be equally vulnerable to hunting, except males in the 1- to 2-year class, which are assumed to be twice as vulnerable as the older bulls. Simulations are continued until the population has stabilized at 15, 10 and 5 years. The changes in age structure and size of the male cohorts are given in Table 87.

The addition of hunting mortality has two principal effects on these male cohorts. First, the total size of the cohort is reduced and stabilizes at a lower number. Second, the percentage of bulls in the older age classes declines, and

the cohorts have a younger average age. With a hunting harvest rate of 25%, the male cohort is reduced from 1,120 to 913, or 18.5%. With a hunting harvest of 40%, the reduction is from 1,120 to 692, or 38%. Both bull cohorts could be harvested at these levels indefinitely, with no further reduction in cohort size or age structure. Because these cohorts have stabilized and recruitment is constant, the harvest for both populations must equal recruitment into the antlered bull cohort, or 146 elk.

When hunting mortality is increased to 80% of the antlered bulls, a similar but more extreme pattern arises. The bull cohort stabilizes after 5 years at this harvest level, at 508 bulls, for a reduction of 55%. Few bulls survive beyond 3 years of age, leaving the yearling bulls to do most of the breeding. The ratio of antlered bulls to adult cows after the hunting season is now 5:100.

Black-box Models

There are several, generic, population models available to predict consequences of various harvest or management options on elk populations. An example of such a model commonly used by management agencies is POP-II (Bartholow 1995), the origins of which arose from ONEPOP (Gross et al. 1972). POP-II takes the form of many menu-driven computer-simulation models used to simulate wildlife populations. The user is prompted to enter a series of demographic data, including such variables as initial population structures, age-specific fecundity rates, sex ratios and sex-, age- and season-specific mortality rates. Other parameters—such as percentage wounding loss, or effort values placed on specific age classes to be harvested, sex- and age-specific harvests and a weather severity index—also may be entered. Once the necessary data have been entered, the model is run to verify that it is performing realistically.

The model begins with a population size at the start of the biological year, which corresponds to calf drop, then subtracts age- and sex-specific preseason natural mortality (e.g., predation, disease), harvest mortality and age- and sex-specific postseason natural mortality. Finally, recruitment information based on age-specific natality rates is added to estimate population size. After the model is suitably calibrated, it may be used to estimate the effects of changing various parameters, such as harvest rates. Outputs that may be evaluated include management indices, such as population abundance, age and sex structures, and pre- and postseason sex ratios. Such models are called black-box models because users often are not readily aware of the algorithms or relationships assumed in the simulation. As with other models, there are assumptions inherent in each, and the user must be aware of these assumptions and determine the effects of violating them. Although black-box models generally are user-friendly, the elk managers should consider building their own model. This would ensure that the manager is aware of each assumed relationship and calculation. Such models can be developed using readily available computer software.

Spreadsheet Modeling

In contrast to black-box models, models may be built by elk managers, using variations of Leslie matrices within commonly available spreadsheet software. Spreadsheets originally were developed to keep track of business inflows and outflows. As such, they are applicable and well-suited to monitor elk population inflows (birth and immigration) and outflows (death and emigration). Given current capabilities, spreadsheet models may contain density-dependent processes, stochastic events, such as winter weather, a variety of hunt options and allow the evaluation of several aspects of elk biology. In addition, these spreadsheet models allow managers to designate which algorithms and relationships to use and incorporate in the simulation exercise. Cooper (1994, 1996), for example, described simulation models that take a Leslie matrix form with fecundity and postharvest survivorship keyed to habitat and weather. These spreadsheet models have allowed Idaho wildlife managers to test the effects of harvest levels on elk population dynamics.

Similarly, Raedeke et al. (1998) used a Leslie-type model to evaluate the effects of various harvest strategies (3+ and 6+ bull harvest, cow and calf harvest) on elk herd demographics in the Kootenay region of British Columbia. The model was programed in spreadsheet software and allowed users the ability to incorporate density-dependent recruitment, effects of low bull-to-cow ratios on pregnancy rates and environmental stochasticity, among others. See Starfield and Bleloch (1991), Starfield et al. (1994) and Starfield (1997) for further aspects of model building for wildlife applications.

Modeling the Effects of Forage and Weather

Other models may be used to evaluate the effects of density-independent processes. Wu et al. (1996) used a modeling approach to identify the relative contributions of fire pattern, winter snow conditions and initial ungulate density to ungulate survival on the northern winter range of Yellowstone National Park. Turner et al. (1994) documented the development and validation of their model (NOYELP), and demonstrated that winter severity may play a dominant role in elk survival. Fire effects also were important in average or severe winters; ungulate mortality was increased with a clumped random-burn pattern compared with a clumped dispersion of burned sites. They also evaluated the effects of weather, fire pattern and population abundances on elk winter survival and found that spatial pattern and location of burned areas had significant effects on elk population dynamics.

Regardless of the model type used, the model should be tested continually and updated by comparing population projections with those observed in the field. In this fashion, a useful working model for a particular herd can be built and a great deal of insight obtained into the dynamics of elk populations.

Outlook

The current volume of information on elk population characteristics is impressive. We have accumulated a remarkable amount of information regarding basic population characteristics (e.g., expected fecundity by age class, gestation length), yet we remain relatively ignorant of several important population mechanisms. How do declines in posthunting bull-to-cow ratios affect population success? How does predation influence the characteristics of elk populations? Are elk regulated in a "bottom-up" or "top-down" fashion? Certainly there is good correlative evidence for each of these important population processes in populations throughout North America. However, reliable causal relationships are few and far between. Undoubtedly, the experimental work conducted at research sites, such as the Starkey Experimental Forest and Range Station, is invaluable by providing such cause and effect data; information that is crucial to effective elk management. Other areas, such as Yellowstone National Park and Jackson Hole, offer long-term data that are equally important for teasing apart the abiotic and biotic factors affecting elk population characteristics. We encourage the continuance of experimental work and also suggest that research move beyond experimental studies and test hypotheses in natural field settings (e.g., nutritional effects on population characteristics; Cook et al. 1996).

Many important challenges remain to supplement our understanding of elk population characteristics. Expansions of predators (e.g., wolves in western North America) will create new formidable challenges in managing elk populations. For example, recent literature (Kunkel and Pletscher 1999) suggests that wolves may be a primary limiting factor of elk populations in the Glacier National Park area of Montana. Although debates of population regulations are not new to wildlife management, implementation of ecosystem management requires that we understand the processes regulating wild populations (Estes 1996). Further studies of disease impact on elk population characteristics may also be beneficial. In particular, understanding the spa-

tial and temporal relationships among bison, elk and cattle movements may provide insight into brucellosis infections (Berger and Cain 1999). As these examples demonstrate, there is much room for future elk population characteristics research. Researchers will need to consider multiple system states and how competing factors act in concert with one another to influence elk population characteristics.

We suggest that population characteristics are an important response variable to determine the consequences of management actions on elk populations. By monitoring key population characteristics (e.g., pregnancy rates), managers can readily assess the effects of their management actions over time. Other research (e.g., resource selection, habitat use) could benefit elk management by linking population characteristics with choices made by elk. That is, radio-tracking studies that involve elk movements, resource selection, and survival patterns also should consider simultaneously monitoring population characteristics of the populations (Millspaugh and Marzluff 2001). In this way, researchers can help elucidate the underlying mechanisms affecting animal population characteristics within different landscapes. We contend that population demographics is the key response variable that should be monitored to determine the success of an individual based on the resource choices it makes.

10

LARRY L. IRWIN

Migration

One of the animal kingdom's most fascinating behaviors is that of long-distance migration. From whales to birds to butterflies, numerous examples exist of seemingly heroic annual migrations, often covering tens of thousands of miles. Among terrestrial mammals, annual migrations of herds of African plains game are spectacular due to the sheer numbers of animals involved (Sinclair 1985). In North America, with the great bison herds long since extirpated, the barren-ground caribou reign as the champion traveler (Hemming 1971). For example, Fancy et al. (1989) documented annual movements of barren-ground caribou up to 3,159 miles (5,055 km)—the longest migration of any terrestrial mammal. Although not as impressive as those of caribou, migrations of elk herds also can be spectacular, often exceeding 5,000 animals and covering more than 50 miles (80 km).

This chapter examines several basic questions about elk migration. First of all, why do elk migrate? Also, what factors stimulate migration? How far do elk travel annually, and how fast do they go? How do human activities, such as logging, road building and hunting, influence elk migrations? In answering these questions, this chapter aims to clarify evolutionary aspects and identify the influences that are important to elk biology and management.

Migration has been defined as animal movement, "usually periodically, from one region or climate to another for feeding or breeding" (Gove 1969:537). Migratory elk herds generally are found in mountainous regions where they are able to move up or down in elevation and up or down river

drainages, apparently in response to seasonal changes. The area traversed in migration between winter and summer ranges commonly is referred to as spring/autumn (or transitional) range. Because such extensive movements occur annually, one might reasonably assume that migration is important to survival of elk populations. Therefore, detailed knowledge about elk migration should be important to elk enthusiasts, as well as to wildlife researchers and managers.

Variations in Migration

For several reasons, the biological underpinnings for elk migrations appear to be complex. First, not all elk migrate. Murie (1951) believed that the original eastern elk populations of North America did not migrate. Rocky Mountain elk successfully introduced to some restricted portions of the eastern elk range similarly did not display migratory behavior (Moran 1973). The Tule elk of California do not migrate, and there is no evidence that they ever did (Madson 1966). Harper et al. (1967) suggested that, originally, there were two kinds of Roosevelt elk in California—one migratory and the other nonmigratory. Taber (1976) reported that Rocky Mountain elk introduced to the Cedar River area near Seattle, Washington, were nonmigratory and remained in lowland areas year-round.

Seasonal movements of many elk herds may not actually be true migrations. For example, most herds of Roosevelt elk in the Pacific Northwest and California make seasonal

493

movements in response to changes in forage conditions (Graf 1943); such movements are not considered true migrations. The Tule elk also make seasonal movements in response to changes in local conditions, but are not considered migratory (Madson 1966, McCullough 1969). Such movements resemble migration in that the elk involved generally move to higher elevation habitats during summer and to valleys and lower elevations during winter. However, these movements differ from migration for several reasons: (1) the summering areas often are accessible during winter; (2) movements are not consistent among herds; and (3) the timing of movements differs among herds (McCullough 1969). If good supplies of forage, water and cover are available, elk may remain in an area year-round. If forage cures or if the forage supply dwindles for various reasons, elk will move to an area with more suitable conditions.

Adding to the complexity, the overall patterns of migration among elk may have been obscured by exposure to hunting. For example, it seems certain that some populations of elk that probably were nonmigratory have been greatly reduced or eliminated by shooting. Such removal by shooting was documented for Rocky Mountain elk in Wyoming (Allred 1950). Similarly, Rudd et al. (1983) concluded that unequal harvesting of resident elk was responsible for an increased percentage of migratory elk—from 20% in the mid-1960s (Craighead et al. 1972) to more than 81% by 1981, among herds that wintered in Sunlight Basin and the North Fork of the Shoshone River areas near Cody, Wyoming. Also, Boyce (1991b) concluded that shifts in the percentage of Rocky Mountain elk using various migratory routes to Jackson Hole, Wyoming, resulted from heavy culling along certain routes open to hunting. On the other hand, hunting pressure generally is insufficient to halt migrations from refuge areas, such as Yellowstone National Park, where harsh weather apparently induces migrations (Adams 1982, Rudd et al. 1983).

A second reason for the complexity of elk migration is the variable ways that different populations use winter and summer ranges. For example, some segments of populations migrate, whereas others do not. Martinka (1969) reported on four relatively nonmigratory portions of the Rocky Mountain elk population wintering in Jackson Hole, Wyoming, along with their migratory counterparts. One part of the herd did not migrate, remaining on the refuge all year. In 1964, the proportion of elk that spent the summer within the valley was about 23% of the total wintering population. Three other segments spent the summer within 20 miles (32 km) of the refuge, and one segment of the herd moved as far as 60 miles (97 km).

Changes in areas closed to hunting and shifts in distribution of hunters contributed to the increase of the resident Jackson Hole population segments (Anderson 1958). These

Not all elk migrate, and not all seasonal movements of elk in response to changing forage conditions represent migrations. Here, what appears to be a spectacular migration of elk at the National Elk Refuge is actually a response to disturbance by people on the valley floor. True migration is characterized by traditional patterns and timing of movement by a majority of the population, with movements connecting warm season and cold season ranges. *Photo by Roger LaVake.*

subpopulations were not stable in composition, and complex interactions occurred between members of the migratory and resident elk herds (Martinka 1969). Significant numbers of yearling bulls from the migratory group remained with the resident animals each year (Smith and Robbins 1994). When older, some bulls rejoined the migratory herds, but others did not. The same pattern occurred for some cows, but the shift was less pronounced. The causes and consequences of such changes in migratory habitats of individual elk are not understood.

A similar situation was found among six Rocky Mountain elk herds using Yellowstone National Park (Craighead et al. 1972). Five of those herds were migratory, but a portion of the Madison River drainage herd was nonmigratory (Craighead et al. 1972). The nonmigratory animals wintered at elevations of more than 7,000 feet (2,134 m), with snow depths often exceeding 4 feet (1.2 m). Elk were able to remain in the area because thermal springs and warm water streams resulted in less snow cover, providing access to forage. Another example was demonstrated in Colorado, where approximately 16% of the elk herd from the White River Plateau remained year-round on winter range (Boyd 1970); whereas, the majority migrated to distinct summer ranges.

Importance of Migration

Despite the variability in elk migration patterns and, conversely, because of their consistency, migrations have had far-reaching effects on the status and condition of many elk populations. Winter snow accumulation and resultant inaccessibility of forage make it infeasible for elk to remain on summer ranges during normal winters. Under such conditions, migration becomes a basic mechanism for survival: elk must move or die.

Increases in Available Range

Migration provides the means by which more elk can be maintained than would be allowed by year-long use of a single range. Only about 10% of the mountainous national parks of Alberta and British Columbia is comprised of winter ranges, which are used by thousands of big game animals, including Rocky Mountain elk (Cowan 1950). Also, Rocky Mountain elk of the Big Prairie herd in Montana migrate to and occupy a winter range that is only 17% of the size of their summer range of more than 420,000 acres (169,975 ha) (Gaffney 1941). Such migration provides for rapid replenishment of the weight and fat reserves depleted during winter. Widely distributed on relatively large summer and spring/autumn ranges, elk groups seek areas away from human activity, where they can feed and rest undisturbed.

Although the area of summer ranges is relatively large, the area actually occupied by individual elk on summer range may be smaller than that occupied on winter range (Knight 1970, Compton 1975). Forage is more nutritious on summer range than on winter range, therefore the animals do not have to move as much during summer to satisfy their requirements.

Protection of Winter Ranges

Migration away from winter ranges allows for maximum summer growth, recovery and accumulation of forage on winter ranges. On ranges occupied by elk during summer and winter, summer use of important forage plants by elk can reduce forage supplies during winter (Martinka 1969). This can limit the number of animals supported on that range through winter. In some cases, efforts to improve forage conditions on winter ranges, such as by weed control, have met with increased use by elk during summer, possibly reducing the overall benefits of the range improvements (L. Marcum personal communication:1995). Where only limited numbers of elk spend summer on what normally would be winter range, the impact may not be as noticeable (Craighead et al. 1973). In fact, there is evidence from studies of domestic cattle that light spring grazing actually might improve forage quality on elk winter ranges (Anderson and Scherzinger 1975).

Recognizing the importance of protecting elk winter range from summer use, wildlife managers in Idaho hypothesized that scattering salt blocks on summer and transitional ranges might lure elk away from winter ranges. If so, the salting would retard autumn movements to winter ranges and promote early returns to summer ranges. It was hoped that the salting program would give the winter range maximal opportunity to recover from winter browsing. However, the program did not achieve this goal (Dalke et al. 1965a), because no differences could be detected in the rate of elk movements to higher elevations from the winter range between salted and unsalted portions of the study area.

Establishment of New Ranges

Migration may be a factor in elk emigrating to new ranges or recolonizing formerly used ranges. Elk usually show high fidelity to winter ranges used in previous years. For example, Smith and Robbins (1994) found that 97% of 85 radio-tagged elk returned to the National Elk Refuge each year. Roosevelt elk on the Olympic Peninsula in Washington habitually used the same wintering areas each year. Even when faced with severe food shortages, these elk did not move to nearby drainages where forage was abundant (Schwartz and Mitchell 1945).

On the other hand, several studies of Rocky Mountain elk demonstrated that some marked animals moved to winter ranges different from the ones where they were marked (Johnson 1951, Brazda 1953, Craighead et al. 1972). Such movements actually are emigrations that might result in establishment of new winter ranges or reestablishment of elk herds on formerly used ranges. For example, McCorquodale et al. (1986) described the establishment of a new population of Rocky Mountain elk in a semidesert area of central Washington, after a severe winter.

Another example was provided by Rocky Mountain elk migrations of the Northern Yellowstone herd. Houston (1982) questioned whether the Northern Yellowstone herd normally migrated as far as the 80 miles (129 km) that Skinner (1925) suggested. However, Lemke (1989) and Lemke et al. (1998) documented that a portion of the Northern Yellowstone herd (2,000–3,000 elk) began reusing historic winter ranges in the Dome Mountain and Sixmile Creek areas in Montana, some 12.4 miles (20 km) north of Yellowstone National Park. In that instance, elk migrated early in 1988, apparently in response to the severe drought (Lemke 1989, Vales and Peek 1996), and continued moving (that is, emigrating) beyond the winter ranges that usually were occupied. In subsequent winters, these elk continued to return to the former winter ranges, involving migrations up to 93.2 miles (150 km), according to Vore (1990).

Reestablishment of winter use by elk on the Dome Mountain Wildlife Management Area probably was aided by delaying the opening date of hunting seasons in the area to avoid overharvesting local, nonmigratory elk (Lemke 1989) and by habitat acquisition that placed 1,236 acres (3,500 ha) of key winter range into public ownership (Lemke et al. 1998). The importance of such emigrations probably has not been as great in recent years as it was in the past, when elk numbers were lower and some potential winter ranges were unoccupied. Although such colonizations and recolonizations by migrating elk have occurred after severe winters or drought, most cases of individual animal emigration probably involve juvenile males.

Migration and Hunting

Probably the most important aspect of elk migration is its well-known effect on hunting success. On many traditional ranges, with normal autumn weather, elk are scattered over a large area at high elevation. These high country lands often are inaccessible to hunters who do not have the time or means to reach them. For example, Schwartz and Mitchell (1945) found that Roosevelt elk that remained on their summer range were less harassed by hunters than were those on transitional or winter ranges. The total harvest under Indian summer conditions generally is low, although hunters who gain access to the high country may enjoy success both in terms of harvest and satisfaction.

At the other extreme, severe weather conditions during hunting seasons sometimes force elk to concentrate prematurely on lower elevation winter ranges, where they are relatively accessible to hunters. Rocky Mountain elk are extremely vulnerable to hunters under such conditions. In Idaho, for example, an increase in harvest of the St. Joe River elk herd from a near normal of 984 in 1954 to 1,839 in 1955 resulted when deep snow and cold weather in November forced earlier than normal concentration of the animals on accessible winter range (Rogers 1957). A sudden autumn snow in 1970 in Montana resulted in a harvest of 92 cows and calves above the Sun River elk herd quota of 325, despite the fact that the season was closed 48 hours after the quota was met (Picton and Picton 1975). Similarly, an unusually heavy snowstorm contributed to high harvest of elk that had begun migrating from northwestern Yellowstone in October 1946 (Lemke 1995). When the late season began on January 1, 1947, an estimated 1,180 elk were killed between 8:00 A.M. and 12:00 noon. The season was closed 3 days later after 3,000 to 4,000 elk had been taken.

Where elk can find protection afforded by national parks or refuges on summer and transitional ranges, they tend to stay within those sanctuaries until the hunting season is over or they are driven out by deep snow (Lovaas 1970, Picton and Picton 1975, Brown 1985). Lovaas (1970) provided many examples of the variable harvest of Rocky Mountain elk from the Gallatin herd in Montana, due to the timing of autumn migration. Many early reports of overharvests of elk resulted from the fact that "early day hunters, like today's, often thought that a scarcity of elk during a mild fall was due to a reduced herd rather than to the actual cause, which was nearly always delayed migration" (Lovaas 1970:9).

A study of the productivity of the Sun River Rocky Mountain elk herd in Montana, where part of the population occupies a refuge during summer, found that autumn migrations often were delayed relative to other herds (Knight 1970). As a result, the herd largely escaped harvest. The Jackson Hole, Wyoming, herds of Rocky Mountain elk spent most of their time on Yellowstone and Grand Teton national park lands and, consequently, were vulnerable to hunting only during the short period of their migration to the National Elk Refuge at Jackson Hole (Anderson 1958). In herds that migrated east from Yellowstone National Park to other areas in Wyoming, some elk delayed their migrations and remained inside the park until January, well after hunting seasons had closed (Rudd 1982). Similarly, Rocky Mountain elk from western Yellowstone National Park migrated later than did resident elk, and moved quite rapidly to winter ranges in southeastern Idaho (Brown 1985); consequently, they often were unavailable to most hunters.

When elk migrate along traditional travel routes, they generally are more vulnerable to hunting than when they remain widely dispersed on their summer range. Elk hunting during autumn migrations may result in heavy harvests in localized areas. For example, a study of marked elk of the Sun River herd in Montana revealed that 67% of 49 tag returns of hunter-killed elk were from the vicinity of passes in upper portions of drainages bordering elk winter range (Picton 1960).

Factors Affecting Elk Migration

One might generalize that elk learned to migrate annually in response to severe winter weather, such as cold temperatures and deep snow or to changes in availability and quality of food supplies associated with deep snow or the curing of vegetation (Schwartz and Mitchell 1945, Murie 1951, Troyer 1960, Madson 1966, Sweeney and Steinhoff 1976, Adams 1982, Rudd et al. 1983). Similarly, spring migrations apparently are triggered by receding snow and the onset of succulent green-up, which proceeds upward in elevation with advancing day length (Dalke et al. 1965b). If migration is indeed a learned behavior, then knowledge of migration routes is passed down from generation to generation by habitual use of the same routes (Boyce 1991b).

Although learning clearly is involved in migratory behavior, migration also is widely believed to have an instinctive or genetic basis (Baker 1978). Under this belief, the ultimate factor driving the evolution of annual migratory behavior is seasonal variation in forage quality and availability (McCullough 1985, Boyce 1991b). Another theory holds that evolution of migration in ungulates was shaped by pressure from predators. For example, the common pattern among ungulates of migrating in large herd groups may constitute an evolved antipredator strategy to compensate for less familiarity with locations of secure habitats and escape routes along migratory routes (Walther 1977), as suggested for migrating Serengeti ungulates subject to predation by African lions (Fryxell et al. 1988). The effects of predators on elk migration have not been examined, although Boyce (1989) speculated that predation by wolves

likely was not a factor driving evolution of migration in elk. The reintroduction of wolves to Yellowstone National Park and other areas may provide new insights in that regard.

Methods of Studying Elk Migration

Any discussion of factors influencing migration among elk should begin with a description of the methods used to gather information, because each method has advantages and disadvantages relative to the conclusions that can be made. These techniques include aerial fixed-wing and helicopter surveys (e.g., Anderson 1958), observations of neck-banded individuals (e.g., Knight 1966a), ear tag returns (Straley 1968), radio tracking (e.g., Rudd et al. 1983, Smith and Robbins 1994) and track counts (Anderson 1958, Cole 1969, Boyce 1989). In general, track counts and aerial surveys provide the most voluminous observations about general migratory patterns. Frequent observations of a relatively large number of marked individuals (for example, using radio collars) provide greater ability to detect details of specific factors that influence elk migrations.

Aerial surveys have proved very practical for locating migration routes where animals can be seen or tracks can be observed in snow (e.g., Robel 1960a). Hunters also have helped to identify autumn migrations by returning numbered ear tags to wildlife agencies. The date and location of kills provide detailed information on distributions and relative frequency of interchange among adjacent elk herds.

Track counts have been used since 1945 by the Wyoming Game and Fish Department and the National Park Service to count elk crossing snow-covered road transects from Beaver Creek in Grand Teton National Park to Twogotee Pass, Wyoming (Boyce 1989). After counting, tracks are obliterated to ensure that they are not recounted during subsequent surveys (Anderson 1958, Cole and Yorgason 1964, Boyce 1989). Such counts have documented shifts in the geographic distribution and timing of annual migrations. However, conditions for conducting track counts vary among years, and the transects have not always been sampled the same number of times, complicating data analyses. However, such a long record of data collection has proven to be very useful in understanding elk migrations in Jackson Hole (see Boyce 1989).

In general, radio transmitters are expensive, therefore most radio-tracking studies afforded only a limited sample size, which proved to be too small to provide much confidence in the migration data acquired. However, Rudd (1982) successfully combined observations of 41 radio-tagged and 164 neck-banded elk to determine factors that influenced migrations to and from Sunlight Basin and the

North Fork of the Shoshone River in Wyoming. And to gather details about migrations to and from the National Elk Refuge in Wyoming, Smith and Robbins (1994) tracked 85 radio-tagged elk older than 2 years of age.

Preferred Ranges

Among the many factors influencing elk migrations is their apparent preference for spring/autumn and summer ranges over winter ranges. In spring, elk seem to be eager to begin migration to summer ranges at higher altitudes, often venturing through deep snow and leaving behind relatively abundant forage resources. In autumn, elk often delay migration to winter ranges until forced to move because of weather conditions, although food supplies are more accessible and energetic costs of movement are less at lower elevations.

Groups of Rocky Mountain elk, especially mature bulls, often are observed at the spring snowmelt line (Gaffney 1941, Murie 1951, Anderson 1958, Boyd 1970), suggesting preference-related behavior. Such groups were noted by Compton (1975) in some snow-covered areas where new growth on vegetation was not yet available. Some early migrating groups of bulls of the Jackson Valley herd in Wyoming were found on summer range when it still was covered with snow (Altmann 1956b). Food apparently was scarce, although some was available on exposed south-facing slopes. Wintering elk of the Pete King herd in Idaho moved to higher elevations when weather moderated and snow conditions permitted (Leege and Hickey 1977). By the end of April, snow at high elevation of the South Fork of the Flathead River in Montana usually was hard-packed and, in some instances, elk were able to move on top of the snow to get to exposed patches of forage (Gaffney 1941).

Habitual Behavior

The role that habitual behavior plays in elk migrations needs more clarification. Murie (1951) believed that elk occupied certain areas during particular times of the year because they learned to do so as calves, following their mothers. Ear tag returns from translocated Jackson Hole Rocky Mountain elk partially corroborated Murie's conjecture (Anderson 1958).

Several studies have shown that elk possess a relatively high tendency to return to the same ranges year after year (Murie 1951, Brazda 1953, Anderson 1958, Picton 1960a, Tanner 1965, Knight 1970, Craighead et al. 1972, Smith and Robbins 1994). This suggests that habitual or repetitive, learned behavior is an integral part of the mechanisms governing elk migration. Rocky Mountain elk of the Soldier

Mountain herd in Idaho returned to the same feeding grounds annually once they became accustomed to being fed during winter (Tanner 1965). Also, these elk remained in relatively stable social groups year after year.

Translocated elk provide support for the belief that learned and habitual behavior influence migration. Translocated mature elk commonly attempt to return to their original home range, often traveling long distances to do so (Anderson 1958). How such translocated elk navigate or whether they possess any real "homing" abilities is not known. Adult Rocky Mountain elk translocated from Jackson Hole to semidesert areas of Wyoming—in an effort to reestablish an extirpated herd—left their new surroundings in an apparent attempt to return to the feeding yards at Jackson Hole from which they were originally trapped (Allred 1950). Those elk wintered at scattered locations north of the translocation site. However, when calves were used for translocations, they established new migrational routes as yearlings in the semidesert area. The calves apparently had not developed a strong enough imprint of migration routes to return to the winter range where they were captured.

Elk have a strong tendency to follow the same migrational routes each year (Altmann 1952, Brazda 1953, Anderson 1958, Boyce 1989), often using the same routes for both spring and autumn migrations (Skinner 1925, Anderson 1958, Compton 1975). Clearly, adults recognize familiar areas and remember specific routes used in previous years. Anderson (1958) found that some Rocky Mountain elk used the same river crossings year after year, although easier crossings were nearby.

Habitual use of the same travel routes probably is due largely to topography, which has influenced the locations of natural travel corridors and trails. For example, elk of the Green River herd in Wyoming, which normally migrated to Jackson Hole, were forced to change their migratory path in 1943 because of a severe winter with deep snow (Allred 1950). They changed the direction of migration and traveled on the same migrational routes that extirpated herds had followed to the desert in previous years. The aforementioned translocated calves from Jackson Hole to semi-desert area in Wyoming also followed these same routes (Allred 1950), suggesting that natural movement pathways are identified by traveling elk.

Although most migratory elk show a high degree of fidelity to traditional migration routes, Rocky Mountain elk have changed their migration routes in response to human settlement and hunting (Boyce 1989), especially on winter ranges (Anderson 1958, Picton 1960a, Kimball and Wolfe 1974, Hurley 1994). Thus, there seems to be an interaction between conditioned or habitual behavioral patterns on

Traditional use of travel routes is a hallmark of migration, such as these trails used by elk crossing between Pelican Creek and the Lamar River in what is now Yellowstone National Park. Trails such as these may represent decades or even centuries of use by elk. *Photo by George M. Wright.*

one hand and response to immediate circumstances encountered during migration on the other. If weather and forage conditions and hunting pressure are normal, the migration routes followed appear to be habitual. That various circumstances, such as hunting, may cause elk to use alternative routes has value for possibly establishing new migration routes and pioneering new ranges. This topic will be discussed later.

Weather

As noted previously, weather—specifically, deep snow—usually is the most important influence on time and rate of autumn elk migration, primarily through its influence on forage availability. This has been documented repeatedly for Rocky Mountain elk in Washington (Mitchell and Lauckhart 1948), Wyoming (Anderson 1958, Rudd et al. 1983, Boyce 1989), Montana (Lovaas 1970, Picton and Picton 1975), Idaho (Leege and Hickey 1977, Brown 1985) and for Roosevelt elk in Washington (Schwartz and Mitchell 1945) and Alaska (Troyer 1960).

One might speculate that migration is triggered by changes in day length, or photoperiod, because photoperiod is known to influence physiological and behavioral changes, such as those occurring during the rut. If pho-

toperiod exerts a similar influence on migration in elk, one would expect that the timing of migrations would be predictable during both spring and autumn. However, Anderson (1958) reported that the start of autumn migration of the Jackson Hole herd of Rocky Mountain elk was not predictable. Its timing was almost entirely dependent on the depth and type of snow cover; snow cover had to be nearly complete for elk to begin large-scale migration. Rudd et al. (1983) correlated the timing of autumn migrations of Rocky Mountain elk from Yellowstone National Park to winter ranges in the North Fork of the Shoshone River and Sunlight Basin, Wyoming with about 8 inches (20 cm) of snow measured at Yellowstone Lake. Boyce (1989) confirmed that snow accumulation played a major role in the timing of autumn migration of Rocky Mountain elk in the Jackson Hole herd unit. Therefore, it does not appear that photoperiod has a measurable influence on the timing of elk migrations.

Other studies reported the strong influences of snow and forage availability on migrations in elk. Autumn migrations by the Sierra Madre herd of Rocky Mountain elk in Wyoming were "probably initiated by a combination of occurrences including snow accumulation and food availability" (Compton 1975:67). Marked elk remained at intermediate elevations until snow accumulation forced them downslope to winter range. In a study of the Pete King drainage in north-central Idaho, by Leege and Hickey (1977), Rocky Mountain elk moved to relatively poor forage areas when snow depth exceeded 1.5 to 2.0 feet (46–61 cm). Even in nonmountainous areas, such as Michigan, snow cover influences the distribution of elk herds; it causes the animals to congregate on wintering areas (Moran 1973). The range of areas elk used in Michigan was greatly restricted when snow was deeper than 1.5 feet (46 cm).

In Montana, mature Rocky Mountain elk were able to move without apparent difficulty in loose snow up to about 3.3 feet (101 cm) deep (Gaffney 1941). Where the snow was packed or crusted, they were able to move through snow about 2.5 feet (76 cm) in depth (Gaffney 1941); deeper snow greatly restricted their movements. Although elk were seen in deeper snow, 4 feet (122 cm) was the maximum depth in which mature elk could move efficiently. Calves and weak animals could not move freely in snow more than 2.5 feet (76 cm) deep (Gaffney 1941). Schwartz and Mitchell (1945) documented that groups of as many as 15 Roosevelt elk bulls on the Olympic Peninsula in Washington were found in snow depths of 5 to 6 feet (152–183 cm).

Leege and Hickey (1977) found that only 1% of Rocky Mountain elk observed during eight aerial surveys on Idaho's Pete King drainage were located in snow more than 2 feet (61 cm) deep, although 36% of the area had snow

Weather plays a significant role in elk migration. Increasing snow depth appears to be one factor triggering migratory movements, both by covering otherwise available forage and by causing elk to travel as a group, thereby conserving energy as they follow in the path broken by others. *Photo by Winson E. Steurewald; courtesy of the U.S. Forest Service.*

cover of that depth or greater. The elk showed an apparent preference for areas with snow depths of less than 1.5 feet (46 cm), and the greatest densities usually were found in areas with the least amount of snow. A similar response was noted in Montana's Glacier National Park, where Rocky Mountain elk made extensive use of shrub fields with snow depths up to about 2 feet (61 cm) (Martinka 1976). Deeper snow forced elk to use forests where forage was available under deep tree crowns that intercepted much of the snow.

Other weather factors do not affect elk migration di-

Elk may move without difficulty in loose snow about 2 feet (61 cm) deep. However, even at lesser depths, snow accumulation tends to concentrate elk in areas where forage is most readily accessible. *Photo courtesy of the U.S. National Park Service.*

Bull elk tolerate greater depths of snow than do elk cows and calves, and may be found where snow depths exceed 3 feet (91 cm) or, on occasion, 4 feet (122 cm). On the Olympic Peninsula, small groups of bulls have been located in "yards" where snow depth exceeded 6 feet (183 cm). *Left photo by Red H. Mass; courtesy of the U.S. Forest Service. Right photo by Brian M. Wolitski.*

rectly to the extent that snow depth does. Spring storms have little effect on elk migration, except that they influence the rate of snowmelt (Anderson 1958). Streams flooded from heavy spring runoff usually coincide with spring migrations of Rocky Mountain elk and may limit the animals' movements temporarily, particularly soon after calving. Anderson (1958) found no strong correlation between temperatures and the onset of autumn migration of the Jackson Hole herds of Rocky Mountain elk. And Boyce (1989) found that temperature was not a reliable predictor of the number of elk that migrate to the National Elk Refuge in Jackson Hole. However, Rudd et al. (1983) found that peak eastward migrations of elk from Yellowstone National Park into Sunlight Basin and the Northfork of the Shoshone River coincided with deep snowfall and rapid temperature decreases from about 23 to –4°F (–5 to –20°C).

Forage

Often in concert with weather, forage quality and quantity affect elk migrations. For example, the timing and amount of rainfall influence the volume and nutritional value of forage, which can bear on the amount of time elk spend on summer ranges. Vales and Peek (1996) found that Rocky Mountain elk in Yellowstone National Park migrated much earlier than usual in the severe drought year of 1988. Similar early migration during a drought year also was observed in Jackson Hole by Yorgason and Bendt (1960). Ostensibly, such migration before deposition of significant snow is due to the likelihood that drought and probably hard frosts render succulent mountain meadow forbs (herbaceous plants) unpalatable and less nutritious. Albon and Langvatn (1992) observed that plant protein levels at high elevation sites declined in September. In responding to such changes, elk that migrate early to transitional ranges or winter ranges would find cured grasses, which are more nutritious than cured forbs.

Forage may exert an even stronger influence on migration among elk than does weather. As Boyce (1991b) and McCullough (1985) theorized, the driving evolutionary force behind migratory behavior of elk probably involved the length of time that elk can acquire high-quality succulent forage. If so, elk should enjoy much greater dietary quality on high elevation summer ranges. In fact, studies

When snow is deep, elk tend to move under tree canopies where snow depth is reduced and forage is more readily available. *Photo by Jim Weiss; courtesy of the Utah Division of Wildlife Resources.*

have found that vegetation from high elevation summer ranges is much higher in nutritional quality than is forage from lower elevations (Klein 1965a, Hebert 1973, Albon and Langvatn 1992). Morgantini and Hudson (1989) found that, by migrating to high elevation alpine summer ranges, Rocky Mountain elk in western Alberta acquired a diet that was higher in protein, due to succulent willow leaves. Such access to higher quality diets should result in increased survival. In red deer, for example, migratory females gained more weight than did sedentary animals of the same population (Langvatn and Albon 1986). Larger body mass enhances the likelihood of surviving the rigors of winter.

However, overall elk densities on summer range may dictate whether migrant elk acquire higher quality diets than do sedentary elk. Relatively heavier culling by hunting may reduce densities of sedentary elk outside of parks and other refuges, allowing the remaining elk to acquire relatively high-quality diets, compared with those of migrating elk herds that enjoy less hunting pressure. For example, Rudd (1982) found that Rocky Mountain elk that migrated to Yellowstone National Park from Sunlight Basin and the North Fork of the Shoshone River in Wyoming were less productive than were elk that did not migrate. Similarly, reduced densities might be responsible for observations made by Woods (1991) of equal quality of diets obtained by sedentary and migratory elk in Banff National Park, Alberta.

Observations implicating nutrition as a strong influence on migration among Rocky Mountain elk have been made most frequently in association with refuge settings (Knight 1970, Brown 1985, Hurley 1994, Smith and Robbins 1994, Vales and Peek 1996). In some of these cases, early migrations might be characterized as a "bull pasture concept," because mature or old-age bulls often were the *first* to migrate after the rut was completed in October and *before* significant snowfall occurred. After the rut, some adult bulls traveled to winter range, such as Yellowstone National Park (Vales and Peek 1996) and Grand Teton National Park (Smith and Robbins 1994), or they returned to summer ranges, as in Banff National Park (Morgantini and Hudson 1988, Woods 1991). In two instances, elk migrated from relatively inaccessible wilderness areas in Montana (Hurley 1994) and Yellowstone National Park (Brown 1985) to winter ranges where hunting pressure was light because of strictly limited permits. In many of these cases, some cows migrated early as well.

New research is needed to clarify whether such early migrations occurred because the elk were searching for higher quality forage or in response to hunting pressure. Clearly, however, hunting was not involved in early migrations within Yellowstone National Park, where nutrition appears to have been the primary driving factor (Vales and Peek 1996). Some early migrating adult bull elk in Jackson Hole risked encounters with hunters as they moved through areas with open hunting seasons in an apparent attempt to gain access to cured grasses on winter range (Smith and Robbins 1994). Gaining access to preferred resources might allow adult bulls to regain some of the energy reserves lost during the rut. If so, such early movements could increase overwinter survival of adult bulls and, thereby, would have implications for management.

The timing and rates of spring elk migration from lower to higher elevations also are related closely to availability of succulent forage, which is associated with snow conditions. Food availability was thought to be the primary stimulus for initiating the spring migration of Rocky Mountain elk in the western Sierra Madre area of Wyoming (Compton 1975). The migratory period for the majority of observed elk coincided with spring green-up each year. According to Ward et al. (1973:330), spring movements of Rocky Mountain elk in the Medicine Bow National Forest of Wyoming were "mainly influenced by availability of new, succulent forage." Finally, movements away from the National Elk Refuge occurred within a few days after supplemental feeding was stopped each spring (Smith and Robbins 1994), supporting a view that forage availability strongly influences spring migrations.

The rate of green-up in the Selway River drainage of

Idaho dictated the pace of Rocky Mountain elk migration back to summer range (Dalke et al. 1965b). As a result, upward progress was rather slow. Elk showed a definite selection for drainages with an abundance of succulent vegetation. Reverse, or downward, spring migrations often occurred in response to emergence of succulent green herbaceous vegetation at lower elevations. The Selway drainage elk returned to lower elevations in April, after they had traveled to higher elevations. Skinner (1925) made similar observations in Jackson Hole, Wyoming.

Sex and Age

The timing and extent of migrations vary by sex and age groups of elk, which have implications for management of hunting seasons and for conducting elk censuses. When spring migration begins, large wintering groups of elk break into smaller groups and begin to drift gradually upward, following the receding snowline (Altmann 1956b). In the Jackson Hole area of Wyoming, mature bulls, along with a few cows, normally begin to migrate first and rapidly, often crossing snow-covered areas (Anderson 1958). Groups of bulls of the Jackson Hole herd remained separate from one another throughout the summer, until the beginning of the rutting season in September (Altmann 1956b). Old bulls of Colorado's White River plateau herd reached summer range several weeks ahead of the cows (Boyd 1970).

In winter, mature bulls may not migrate at all, tending to spend winter at higher elevations than do other sex and age classes. Or, if they do migrate, mature bulls often do not move as far as other classes. Large, old bulls in various Rocky Mountain elk herds in Colorado usually were located in separate groups at higher elevations than were other groups (Riordan 1948). In Colorado's Rocky Mountain National Park, old bull elk spent winter on high, open alpine meadows, where they were subject to harsh climatic conditions that generally were avoided by elk of other sex and age classes (Packard 1947). Similar observations of Roosevelt elk on the Olympic Peninsula in Washington were reported by Schwartz and Mitchell (1945), who found groups of bull elk in snow depths up to 5 to 6 feet (152–183 cm)—areas not used by other herd groups. By virtue of their larger body size, bulls are better able to withstand such rigorous conditions than are other sex and age groups.

Migrating elk groups with pregnant cows halt temporarily for calving in late May and early June (Altmann 1956b, Smith and Robbins 1994). At this time, barren cows (including yearlings and 2-year-olds) of the Jackson Hole herd separate from pregnant cows and cows with calves. This segregation commonly extends throughout the summer (Anderson 1958). It led Brazda (1953) to suggest that the calving period was more important in governing the rate of upward movement than was plant development.

Rocky Mountain cow elk with calves typically do not resume migration until late June or July. In Montana's Gallatin herd, only 3 of 31 marked calves moved away from the drainage (location where they were marked) before calving season was over, and all movements were less than 1 mile (1.6 km) (Brazda 1953). Newborn calves were limited in their ability to migrate, and they and their mothers accordingly migrated slowly (Brazda 1953). Similar migratory behavior was observed by Rudd (1982) in Sunlight Basin and the North Fork of the Shoshone River, and by Anderson (1958) and Smith and Robbins (1994) in Jackson Hole, Wyoming.

In the White River Plateau herd in Colorado, spike (probably yearling) bulls usually stayed with the cows until

Although bull elk may winter at higher elevations and in deeper snow accumulations than do other sex and age groups of elk, they also may migrate earlier and travel farther than cow and calf elk to seek out security from hunters or high-quality seasonal ranges. For example, mature or old-age bulls were among the first to migrate from summer ranges after the rut to winter ranges in Yellowstone and Grand Teton National Parks, and they often did so before the first significant snowfalls. *Photo courtesy of the U.S. Fish and Wildlife Service.*

Migratory patterns appear to be learned over the course of succeeding generations, although there is some indication that there also is an instinctive component to some migratory behavior. Here, in the Gallatin National Forest near Yellowstone National Park, an adult cow leads a band of elk through newly emergent shrub–grasslands to higher elevations, where pregnant cows will shortly give birth to their calves. *Photo by George Wolstad; courtesy of the U.S. Forest Service.*

calving season approached, at which time they were "kicked out of the group" (Boyd 1970: 63). Altmann (1956b) reported that when pregnant cows of the Jackson Hole herd dropped out of the spring migration to higher elevations, yearlings remained with them. Smith and Robbins (1994) observed that yearling bulls often remained on winter range during summer.

These partially conflicting views of the migration of various elk groups once again point out that migration is a complex process, and variation is to be expected in all of its phases. An example of such variation was displayed by yearling Rocky Mountain elk in a study of Montana's Gallatin River herds in Montana (Peek and Lovaas 1968). Yearling males and, to a lesser extent, yearling females were found in decreasing numbers as distance increased from winter range. The proportion of these younger elk that migrated to the extremities of either summer or winter ranges was less than the proportion for other age groups. This behavior suggests that both social behavior and learning play a large role in migration.

Insects

Insect infestations have been reported as a nuisance to elk on summer ranges and influence habitat use and local movements (Johnson 1951, Murie 1951, Brazda 1953). High, windswept ridges are used by elk in an apparent attempt to elude swarms of insects. Some elk at lower elevations attempt to avoid insect attacks by bedding down in tall sedge meadows. However, the emergence of flies evidently does not affect the upward migration of elk, because the elk are on summer range before tabanid flies appear at lower elevations. Also, in the Gallatin River drainage of Montana, there was no apparent effect of insects on the autumn migration, because elk still were on the summer area nearly a month after the last flies were recorded (Brazda 1953).

Darling (1937) stated that, in Scotland, small flies attacked red deer in early spring, causing the animals to move to higher country; although, vegetation there was not yet developed. The deer moved back to lower elevations to feed at night when the insects were not active. Later, when larger tabanid flies emerged, the deer moved higher and remained for the season, coming down to feed only when the flies were inactive during rainy periods.

A similar pattern of daily activity relative to insect attacks may be exhibited by elk. Insects may influence the daily movements, activities and distribution of elk on summer ranges. And, in some instances, insects may accelerate upward movement of elk during spring migration. However, insects generally have little or no major influence on the timing or speed of either autumn or spring migration.

Hunting

How and to what extent hunting affects migration is not clearly understood. Certainly, hunting can influence local distributions of elk. When elk are disturbed by hunters, they may travel 2 to 3 miles (3.2–4.8 km) before stopping, and are neither as evasive nor as quick to seek hiding cover as are deer. Thus, elk tend to be more vulnerable to hunters than deer, and some elk populations have been greatly reduced or eliminated by hunting pressure.

Until the late 1800s, for example, thousands of animals, including Rocky Mountain elk, wintered in the semidesert area of Utah's southern Sublette and Fremont counties and northern Sweetwater County, and spent the summer in the Upper Green River Basin to the north. In the 1880s, ranchers commented on the "direct routes taken by migrating game herds from the mountains to the winter range" (Allred 1950:599). Huge losses of cattle during the severe winter of 1886–1887 made the ranchers change their operations from winter grazing of cattle to raising hay for feed. This brought changes in the use of meadows—fences were installed to protect the growing hayfields—the migrational routes for elk were narrowed as a result.

With this change, elk hunters had only to wait along a migration route. In this manner, thousands of elk were killed for meat and many just for their bugler teeth (see Chapter 3). Killing by market gunners caused a marked decline in the numbers of elk. However, the remaining population continued its habitual migrations along remnants of the original route. When the homestead grazing law was enacted in 1914, more fences were erected, and the migration corridors probably were narrowed even more. By 1917, elk were no longer using winter range in the desert (Allred 1950).

A similar situation in California was described by Harper et al. (1967). A population of Roosevelt elk once was centered in the area from the Siskiyou Mountains to Mount Shasta, and migrated to winter ranges at lower elevations, probably along river bottoms. This population also crossed settled areas and was vulnerable to shooting. Consequently, it was extirpated or greatly reduced.

Hunting near national parks and refuges presents particular problems for wildlife managers, because hunting pressure can reverse early migrations before significant snow depths occur (Brown 1985, Vore 1990). Also, heavy hunting can reduce and change the sex and age composition of herds adjacent to such refuges (Knight 1970, Rudd et al. 1983). Moreover, elk quickly learn the locations of areas that have low or no hunting pressure, often leading to population increases in such areas. Rocky Mountain elk groups disturbed by shooting in the vicinity of Yellowstone National Park, Wyoming, made 3- to 8-mile (4.8–12.9 km) movements to reach the sanctuary of the park (Altmann 1956b).

Similarly, Anderson (1958) suggested that Rocky Mountain elk disturbed by hunters might not have been able to

Although elk may winter in very open country, such as this snow-blown Colorado hillside, disturbance by hunters has caused elk to abandon many such areas in favor of areas that provide greater protection. In fact, recent increases observed among fully protected herds in open country have indicated that freedom from disturbance by humans may be more important than the thermal protection provided by forests in determining where elk will spend the winter. *Photo courtesy of the Colorado Division of Wildlife.*

get back on their habitual migration route for some distance. He believed that such changes in migrational routes due to hunting would not persist in subsequent years because of habitual use of alternative routes. Anderson (1958:111) concluded that "hunting probably has more influence as a means for regulating the number of elk using particular routes by reducing or increasing the number of animals using those routes rather than causing them to change their habitual migration patterns."

On the other hand, evidence of hunting pressure causing a shift in the numbers of elk using various migrational routes was reported for the Cache herd of Rocky Mountain elk in Utah (Kimball and Wolfe 1977). Tag returns from animals marked on winter range revealed that only 7% of marked elk harvested before 1951 had migrated in a southerly direction. The percentage of marked animals harvested from southern areas increased to 11% in 1955 to 1960, 27% in 1961 to 1966 and 26% in 1967 to 1969. The southern portion of the Cache range was private land with closely controlled hunting, whereas the central and northern areas were public lands open to hunting. The shift in elk distribution was "perhaps due to differential hunting pressure in various areas of the Cache Unit" (Kimball and Wolfe 1974:166).

In 1961, severe weather conditions, including deep snow, arrived much earlier than normal to Yellowstone National Park, forcing Rocky Mountain elk of the Gallatin herd to migrate during the hunting season, and hunters harvested large numbers of elk (Lovaas 1970). The remaining elk, however, continued migrating downward to winter range. Also, Rudd et al. (1983), evaluating responses of radio-tagged and neck-banded elk to a 2-week hiatus during hunting season, concluded that hunting pressure was insufficient to halt eastward migrations from Yellowstone National Park. In these instances where migrations were induced by harsh weather, the needs to escape deep snows and find forage were stronger influences on the timing and route of migration than was hunting pressure along the way.

The overall timing of autumn migration by Rocky Mountain elk of Jackson Hole, Wyoming, apparently has not been changed by hunting. Current migrations occur in November, as they have since at least 1911 (Anderson 1958, Boyce 1989). However, Boyce (1989) found changes due to hunting in the relative numbers of elk that used various migration routes by the Jackson Hole herd.

Because the restructuring of historic elk ranges—brought about by changing distributions of people, acquisition and establishments of national parks, winter ranges and reserves, and the subsequent management of elk populations on the basis of individual herds—hunting probably does not directly affect elk migrations to the extent that it may have in the past. Elk migration routes generally have been shortened by these changes; consequently, the time needed to migrate is less. Hunting seasons are much shorter, and usually are set to provide the desired harvest based on normal autumn weather and migrational trend. Only when these conditions differ markedly from anticipated or projected norms is the influence of hunting significant. Under current elk management practices, regulated hunting has little effect on elk migrations. Conversely, elk migration significantly affects hunter success.

Forest Management

Extensive loss of forest cover, such as from heavy wildfires or timber harvests, may play a role in elk migration, primarily by increasing the vulnerability of elk to shooting by hunters. For example, management of the Sand Creek, Idaho, herd of Rocky Mountain elk was complicated by high road densities, reduced cover from extensive timber harvesting and gentle topography—conditions that promoted easy hunts (Brown 1985, Pauley 1991). Under those conditions of relatively easy access, where hunter densities were as high as 13.2 hunters per square mile ($5.1/km^2$), the majority of elk were brought out whole because hunters were able to drive to the carcasses. Such conditions resulted in declining numbers of elk and concomitantly declining hunter success, which was exacerbated when the remaining elk increasingly eluded hunters by retreating to Harriman

Management of migratory elk herds has included acquisition and protection of critical winter ranges as parks and refuges, protection of migration corridors by such actions as forest road management, timing of hunting seasons, development of a suitable forage base and protection of farm and ranchland (including paneling or fencing of stackyards) to reduce the potential for elk damage. As a result, most herds, whether protected on a winter range refuge or located on federal lands, are more or less in balance with available habitat, usually a mix of low elevation forest and grassland affording food, water, hiding cover and protection from adverse weather. *Photo courtesy of the Wyoming Game and Fish Department.*

National Wildlife Refuge and by establishment of a resident herd on the Sand Creek winter range (Pauley 1991). Pauley (1991) believed that the lack of security cover contributed to an early migration to winter range. However, permit-only or lack of hunting on the winter range also may have contributed to the early migrations, as was the case noted by Hurley (1994) for the Clearwater Game Range in western Montana.

Management response to the combined effects of reduced security cover and high hunter densities and pressure on the Sand Creek herd included the following: (1) developing a hunt on winter range to reduce the resident herd there; (2) delaying hunting season until migrations were well underway (Brown 1985); and (3) subsequently restricting hunting of bulls to spikes only (Hughbanks 1993). Hunting pressure decreased, and many yearling bulls escaped harvest, apparently because hunters perceived the heavily roaded areas as unlikely to contain many elk (Hughbanks 1993).

Loss of security cover has prompted suggestions for providing "leave" strips of timber, assuming that migrating elk will use such strips as migration corridors. In fact, elk have been observed to use such timber "stringers" in some areas during summer and autumn. However, elk migrate across vast expanses of open country, such as sagebrush flats, at night, therefore the potential value of timber strips as migration corridors probably is more perception than reality.

Barriers to Migration

Elk will tolerate considerable exposure to human habitation, such as roads, fences and fields used by livestock, on winter range. Most elk herds faced these potential barriers when settlers moved onto elk winter ranges to raise crops or graze domestic livestock. Then and now, however, human tolerance of elk has not always been as reciprocal. The invariable result of fences and human disturbances has been a restriction of elk to relatively small and less desirable portions of traditional winter ranges. Migrational routes may be shortened and elk forced to winter at higher elevations in what generally is not considered their prime winter habitat.

In most instances, migrating elk are able to negotiate humanmade obstacles, such as highways, logging slash, canals and fences, although movements may be delayed. Altmann (1956b) observed the initiative exhibited by mature Rocky Mountain elk cows to negotiate such obstacles when leading groups en route to summer range from winter feeding grounds in Jackson Hole, Wyoming. If part of a social group was delayed by a disturbance, such as highway traffic, the two subgroups appeared to search for each other, sometimes for days. However, Knight (1970) found little or no evidence of such group cohesiveness in Montana's Sun River herd of Rocky Mountain elk. He found that, with but few exceptions, no two individuals—other than cows with their calves—were closely associated for more than several days.

Rocky Mountain elk of the Sun River herd followed a well-used trail during migration (Picton 1960a). This trail crossed from one canyon to another over a series of passes in the upper reaches of the wintering range. An easier route following along the Sun River was avoided, probably because of human habitation and associated hunting pressure.

Rocky Mountain elk of the Jackson Hole herd, which once migrated through an area known as Antelope Flats, changed their route to the foothills above the flats because of settlement before 1911 (Anderson 1958). After Antelope Flats was acquired by the government and agricultural activity decreased, many elk again moved directly down the flats and without detouring to the foothills. Changes in hunting pressure since acquisition of the flats, due to changes in hunting regulations, also may have been a factor in restoration of this migration route.

Although elk often migrate across broad expanses of open country, barriers across migration routes, such as fences and human development activities, can concentrate animals, and force them to hasten their migration or stop entire herds short of their destination. When this occurs, elk may damage fences, croplands or be forced onto roadways, with the attendant risks to both elk and vehicle operators. *Photo courtesy of the Oregon Department of Fish and Wildlife.*

Examples of geographic barriers to elk migrations are relatively few inasmuch as elk are adaptable to rough terrain. For example, Rudd (1982) recorded that elk migrating eastward from Yellowstone National Park negotiated very deep snow while crossing the crest of the rugged Absaroka Divide in midwinter. Elk generally are not widespread on the upper extremes of such high mountain ranges, however, because these rocky, tree-free habitats are not preferred range.

Conversely, the fact that there are fewer than a dozen passes across the 60 miles (96.6 km) of the Continental Divide west of the Sun River in Montana somewhat restricts migration of Rocky Mountain elk between the Sun River and South Fork of the Flathead drainages (Picton and Picton 1975:35). Two segments of the Northern Yellowstone herd were prevented from rejoining during migration by rough country along the Yellowstone River within Yellowstone National Park (Craighead et al. 1972). Considerable intermingling of these two segments did occur on the winter range, however, especially during severe winters with deep snow.

Apparently, autumn migration by the Gallatin herd of Yellowstone National Park also is limited by terrain. Lovaas (1970:5) wrote: "the elk are discouraged from moving completely out of the mountains and into the lower valley by the precipitous and rugged lower portions of the canyon, which is bounded on the west by the great mass of the Spanish Peaks and on the west by the deeply cut and heavily timbered drainages of Levinski, Portal, Moose, Swan, and Squaw Creeks." This area also was virtually impassable to elk during spring thaws, because of high water, and during winter, because of deep snow.

High water in streams from spring runoff may slow or stop an elk migration (Altmann 1956b, Anderson 1958). Although adults are good swimmers, elk calves may require several days of coaxing before they cross larger streams at floodstage. However, Johnson (1951) observed an elk calf, approximately 4 days old, swim across a swollen river about 4 feet (1 m) deep and more than 59 feet (18 m) wide.

Parameters of Migration

It is difficult to generalize about the parameters associated with elk migrations. As noted previously, there are large differences in the annual migrations of individual elk herds, largely caused by weather, forage conditions and physiographic settings. The safest generalization that can be made is that elk, as individuals, groups and herds, are quite adaptable to a wide range of environmental conditions and, although creatures of habit, they are not inflexible. Tables 88 through 92 illustrate the diversity of elk migrations.

Spring migrations generally occur during May, depending on weather conditions (Table 88); autumn migrations may occur September through December (Table 89). Migrations may cover from less than 1.5 miles (2.4 km) (Dalke et al. 1965b) to more than 93.2 miles (150 km) (Vore 1990) (Table 90).

Elevation

Elk tend to disperse in irregular groups on summer ranges and, in the course of a summer, may be located in almost all suitable habitats at all elevations (Table 91). An exception was reported by Taber (1976), who found that Rocky Mountain elk near Seattle, Washington, generally were widespread on summer ranges from 1,500 to 3,000 feet (457–914 m) in elevation. However, elk there avoided elevations above 3,000 feet (914 m), although such elevations accounted for more than 39% of the area studied. Drying vegetation at higher elevations should not have been a limiting factor in the elk distribution in Taber's (1976) work, leading one to hypothesize that this elk herd, which had been introduced into the area only a short time before the study, may have been too small to use the available summer range.

Elevation of elk winter ranges (Table 92) per se is not of great importance, because elk must use whatever range is available. They often are forced to use winter ranges at elevations higher than probably is optimal. However, elevation

Table 88.   Time of spring migrations of various elk herds

Elk herd	State	Time of spring migration	Reference
Afognak Island	Alaska	May and June	Troyer (1960)
Jackson Hole (North)	Wyoming	May	Anderson (1958)
Jackson Hole	Wyoming	April and May	Smith and Robbins (1994)
North Yellowstone	Wyoming–Montana	April and May	Craighead et al. (1972)
Blackfoot–Clearwater	Montana	April and May	Hurley (1994)
Selway	Idaho	May and June	Dalke et al. (1965b)
Sierra Madre	Wyoming	Late April–early May	Compton (1975)
White River Plateau	Colorado	April and May	Boyd (1970)

Table 89. Time of autumn migrations of various Rocky Mountain elk herds

Elk herd	State	Time of autumn migration	Reference
Jackson Hole	Wyoming	Late October into December	Anderson (1958)
		November	Boyce (1989)
		Late October–November	Smith and Robbins (1994)
North Yellowstone	Wyoming–Montana	Arrived in November	Craighead et al. (1972)
Absaroka–Yellowstone	Wyoming	November	Rudd et al. (1983)
Selway	Idaho	Began late September	Dalke et al. (1965b)
Sierra Madre	Wyoming	Late October and early November	Compton (1975)
White River Plateau	Colorado	Late October to early January	Boyd (1970)
Banff National Park	Alberta	September–November	Morgantini and Hudson (1988)

Table 90. Distances of migration of various elk herds

Elk herd	State	Migration distance	Reference
Afognak Island	Alaska	Rarely over 10 miles (16.1 km)	Troyer (1960)
Fremont County	Idaho	>30 miles (48.3 km)	Mohler et al. (1958)
Sand Creek	Idaho	50–70 miles (47–117 km); average 51.3 miles (82 km)	Brown (1985)
Selway	Idaho	Does not exceed 20 miles (32.2 km)	Dalke et al. (1965b)
North Fork Salmon River	Idaho–Montana	25.3 miles (40.5 km)	Grkovic (1976)
Jackson Hole North	Wyoming	60 miles (96.5 km)	Anderson (1958)
North Yellowstone	Wyoming–Montana	Normal maximum 80 miles (128.7 km)	Skinner (1925)
North Yellowstone	Wyoming–Montana	Maximum 93.8 miles (150 km)	Vore (1990)
Absaroka–Yellowstone	Wyoming	Average 30 miles (48.3 km)	Rudd et al. (1983)
Sun River	Montana	Maximum 28 miles (45.1 km)	Picton (1960)
White River	Colorado		
North Fork		4 miles (6.4 km)	Boyd (1970)
South Fork		4–13 miles (6.4–20.9 km)	Boyd (1970
Banff National Park	Alberta	16–42.5 miles minimum (26–68 km)	Morgantini and Hudson (1988)

Table 91. Elevations of summer ranges of various Rocky Mountain elk herds

Elk herd	State	Summer range elevation	Reference
Big Prairie	Montana	4,300–8,500 feet (1,311–2,591 m)	Gaffney (1941)
Cache	Utah	3,937–9,843 feet (1,200–3,000 m)	Kimball and Wolfe(1974)
Cedar River	Washington	1,500–3,000 feet (457–914 m)	Taber (1976)
Jackson Hole[a]	Wyoming		Altmann (1952)
May 5		6,000 feet (1,829 m)	
June 5		7,500 feet (2,286 m)	
July 5		9,000 feet (2,743 m)	
August 1		10,000 feet (3,048 m)	
Madison[b]	Wyoming–Montana	>7,000 feet (2,134 m)	Craighead et al. (1973)
North Yellowstone	Wyoming–Montana	7,000–10,000 feet (2,134–3,048 m)	Craighead et al. (1972)
Sun River[c]	Montana		Knight (1970)
May		5,295 feet (1,614 m)	
June		5,470 feet (1,667 m)	
July		7,079 feet (2,158 m)	
August		7,400 feet (2,256 m)	
White R. Plateau	Colorado	Above 8,500 feet (2,591 m)	Boyd (1970)

[a] Monthly means in 1949–1950.

[b] Year-round.

[c] Monthly means 1963–1965.

Table 92. Elevations of winter ranges of various elk herds

Elk herd	State	Winter range elevation	Reference
Big Prairie	Montana	4,300–6,500 feet (1,311–1,981 m)	Gaffney (1941)
Cache	Utah	<6,890 feet (2,100 m)	Kimball and Wolfe (1974)
Cedar River	Washington	1,500–2,500 feet (457–762 m)	Taber (1976)
Fremont County	Idaho	About 5,499 feet (1,676 m)	Mohler et al.(1958)
Gallatin	Wyoming–Montana	6,500–7,500 feet (1,981–2,286 m)	Johnson (1951)
Jackson Hole	Wyoming	6,500 feet (1,981 m)	Altmann (1952)
Madison[a]	Wyoming–Montana	>7,000 feet (2,134 m)	Craighead et al. (1973)
North Yellowstone	Wyoming–Montana	5,200–7,500 feet (1,585–2,286 m)	Craighead et al. (1972)
Olympic Peninsula	Washington	A few hundred to 2,000 feet (to 610 m)	Schwartz and Mitchell (1945)
Pete King[b]	Idaho		Leege and Hickey (1977)
Adult bulls		3,072 feet (936 m)	
Spike bulls		2,802 feet[c] (854 m)	
Cows without calves		2,859 feet (871 m)	
Cows with calves		2,770 feet (844 m)	
Rocky Mtn Park	Colorado	7,800–8,500 feet (2,377–2,591 m)	Packard (1947)
Sun River[d]	Montana		Knight (1970)
December		5,228 feet (1,594 m)	
January		5,105 feet (1,556 m)	
February		5,259 feet (1,603 m)	
March		5,095 feet (1,553 m)	

[a] Year-round.

[b] 1969 average elevations.

[c] Error in original read 2,982 feet.

[d] Monthly means 1963–1965.

In the spring, elk migration tends to parallel streams and timber stringers as the animals move to higher elevations as soon as snow melts, allowing the sun to warm the soil and highly nutritious grasses to emerge. *Photo courtesy of the Oregon Department of Fish and Wildlife.*

is an important factor, as it influences the extent and depth of snow and the growth and availability of vegetation. The distribution of elk on winter ranges is governed by snow depth and cover and forage availability, not by elevation. Dalke et al. (1965b) reported that elevations at which elk were found during late winter and early spring were not the same for any 2 years during a 4-year study of the Selway River herd in Idaho.

Speed

The speed of elk migrations also is variable and has not received much study. Spring migration often begins with a hurried, single-file mass movement as soon as snowmelt permits (Anderson 1958). Well-defined trails, often along stream courses, generally are followed. When elk reach intermediate elevations, they tend to disperse over large areas. The Northern Yellowstone herd originally had a normal maximum movement of 80 miles (129 km), according to Skinner (1925). This distance was covered in about 50 days for an average daily rate of 1.6 miles (2.6 km) per day. The movement was not believed to be steady and was affected by weather. Vales and Peek (1996) radio-tracked migrating elk in the Northern Yellowstone herd, which completed their migrations in 2 to 5 days. Rocky Mountain elk that summered in the eastern Gros Ventre drainage, Teton Wilderness, northwestern Grand Teton National Park (the areas west of Jackson Lake) and Yellowstone National Park took from several days to 8 weeks to reach the National Elk Refuge in Wyoming (Smith and Robbins 1994).

Brazda (1953) found that migratory movements of the Gallatin herd in Montana generally were short—2.5 to 3.5 miles (4.0–5.6 km)—during the month of June after calving. From July 1 to July 15, the average individual movement increased to 11.4 airline miles (18.3 km), and to an average of 14.8 miles (23.8 km) from July 16 to July 31. Maximum elevations were reached in July.

Dalke et al. (1965b) calculated the average rate of vertical migration of the Rocky Mountain elk herd of the Selway River drainage in Idaho to be 55 feet (16.8 m) per day during spring migration in 1959 and 30 feet (9.1 m) per day in 1960. These estimates would suggest rather leisurely movements, given the well-known proclivity for disturbed elk to cover such distances in a few seconds.

Downward migrations to winter range tend to be completed more swiftly, prompted by severe weather or hunting pressure, or both. The same routes used during spring generally are followed in return migrations to winter range. Robel (1960a) reported a decline in elevation of concentrations of Idaho's Selway herd from 4,189 feet (1,277 m) in early October 1957 to 3,232 feet (985 m) in the latter part of

October 1957. This was an average daily change of approximately 32 feet (9.7 m) per day—not much different from the spring migration rate in 1960 reported by Dalke et al. (1965b). However, because these estimates were made by dividing total elevation moved by the total number of days between observations, and not from readings taken daily, it is possible that movements occurred more rapidly.

Habitat Used During Migration

Few studies have specifically measured habitat conditions used by migrating elk, other than to notice that elk tend to use the same routes habitually. Brown (1985) identified relatively specific migration corridors for some segments of Idaho's Sand Creek elk herd. In particular, Brown identified important bottlenecks of migration through the Sheep Falls crossing of Henry's Fork of the Snake River and the point at which they crossed U.S. Highway 20. Boyce (1989) and Smith and Robbins (1994) indicated that elk in the Jackson Hole herd unit in Wyoming tended to cross ridges and mountain slopes while migrating during normal autumn weather, but used more direct routes along drainages during severely adverse weather.

Elk Migration and Management

Proper management of elk requires reliable information on population size and sex and age composition of the various segments of each identified population within a delineated management unit. Preferred seasonal habitats should be identified and the behavior of elk understood, including migratory behavior. An understanding of migrational patterns should lead to increased accuracy in the collection of biological data to support management. For example, snow deep enough to concentrate elk at elevations below 10,000 feet (3,048 m) was considered essential for accurate aerial surveys in counting and obtaining sex and age ratios of elk herds in Colorado (Riordan 1948).

Differential patterns of migration by particular sex and age groups need to be identified and analyzed. Accurate determinations of numbers and sex and age ratios of Rocky Mountain elk of the Jasper National Park region of Alberta and British Columbia were difficult to obtain because elk often were segregated by sex and age groups (Cowan 1950). Extensive reconnaissance covering each of the different types of range occupied by elk in that area was required to obtain reliable estimates of numbers and sex ratios of the herds. Younger age classes of Montana's upper Gallatin herd were found not to migrate to the limits of either winter or summer ranges in proportion to their occurrence in the population (Peek and Lovaas 1968). In western Washington, adult Rocky Mountain elk bulls were segregated from the rest of the herd during most of the year, leading Taber (1976) to conclude that their numbers probably were underestimated in population counts. Similar findings have been reported in Idaho (Leege and Hickey 1977), Washington (Schwartz and Mitchell 1945) and Colorado (Packard 1947).

Timing of autumn migration and hunting season dates may influence the sex and age composition of elk harvested under an any-elk hunting season. Anderson (1958:142) showed such a differential rate of kill among particular sex and age groups of the Jackson Hole herds, depending on the stage of migration: "Invariably, more bulls than cows are killed during the early part of the season when the elk are scattered and high. The reverse is true after the elk have grouped along the migration routes; many more cows than bulls are taken." More recently, these relationships may vary due to regulations that specify harvesting only spike bulls in some areas.

Regulated harvest of elk populations can be complicated further where there is differential migration by various age and sex components of the population. For example, the complexity of herd management at Jackson Hole, Wyoming, during the autumn hunting season was increased by the presence of a resident herd through which migratory elk passed on their way to the Jackson Hole Refuge (Martinka 1969). The same was true in areas east of Yellowstone National Park, Wyoming (Rudd et al. 1983), north of the park in Montana (Lemke 1989) and west of the park in Idaho (Brown 1985).

Identification of migratory patterns also aids in specifying management strategies for particular herds. For example, a study of migrational patterns of six discrete Rocky Mountain elk herds within Yellowstone National Park revealed that, although there was some mingling of the herds on the summer ranges, "the majority of these animals return to specific winter and summer ranges. Thus, they could be managed as separate herds" (Craighead et al. 1972:41). Robel (1960a) plotted migrational routes of Rocky Mountain elk in the Selway district of Idaho, and determined the summer range of a large herd that was causing damage on its winter range. He believed that, "since the time of migration was also determined, it might well be possible to set the hunting season to intercept the migratory herd as it moves from its summer range to the wintering area" (Robel 1960a:103).

The relationship of Rocky Mountain elk using particular summer areas and those migrating to specific wintering areas was tested for the Sun River elk herds in Montana using marked animals (Knight 1970). If use of specific summer and winter ranges is constant within a herd, such knowledge would be a valuable aid to management. For example, the desired harvest of elk causing damage on summer range could be taken on winter range, when the animals were grouped and the harvest could be controlled with greater efficiency. However, distribution of marked animals in the study showed that summering areas apparently were independent of wintering areas, and "it would not be feasible to formulate a management plan whereby animals from a summering area could be harvested through a hunting season on a specific wintering area" (Knight 1970:48).

In the majority of instances, population manipulation of elk must be geared to a specific management unit in which the condition of the winter range is critical. The number of animals it can support without damage must be known. Harvest of a portion of an elk population from a particular winter range should be undertaken, whenever possible, on summer and transitional ranges to increase the challenge of the hunting experiences (see Chapter 18). However, when the desired level of harvest cannot be met under these conditions, additional harvest of specific sex and age groups must be conducted on winter range. Such a strategy was developed for the Northern Yellowstone herd in Montana (Lemke 1995). In that situation, harvests beginning the first Friday after New Year's Day were regulated carefully by permit-only entry and by alternating 3-day rest and 4-day hunt periods to allow elk to migrate. These management activities avoided overharvesting resident elk populations and also the "firing line" conditions that occurred during migrations before a moratorium on late-season harvests from 1968 to 1976 (Lemke 1995).

Game refuges, national parks and large ranches that do not permit hunting and other land management activities, often present difficulties for management of hunting seasons (Knight 1970, Brown 1985, Smith and Robbins 1994). In some cases, desired levels of harvest often are difficult to obtain because elk learn the locations of such refuges along their migration routes or at the ends of those routes. However, as in the case of the Northern Yellowstone herd described by Lemke (1995), managers might use adaptive management experiments to exploit knowledge about elk migrations in controlling herd size and composition. For example, temporarily delineating relatively small refuges on or adjacent to winter ranges might be an effective means for increasing escape of adult bulls in areas where adult bull-to-cow ratios are low. Such refuges, which might be on the order of 10 square miles (25 km²), might be helpful in areas where vulnerability of elk to hunters may have been temporarily increased due to a large wildfire or extensive timber harvests. Or, if there is evidence that nutritional quality of autumn forage increases overwinter survival of adult bulls, such temporary refuges would contribute to population health. If such experimental refuges indeed are considered useful, they could be designated as such follow-

Where it occurs, elk migration is often critical to the ultimate survival of herds seasonally dependent on widely dispersed portions of their habitat—areas typically under the jurisdiction of a wide array of private, federal and state land managers. To ensure perpetuation of the magnificent annual parade that is necessary for the continued existence of these herds the land managers must work together. *Photo courtesy of the Wyoming Game and Fish Department.*

ing public review and through cooperative agreement with appropriate landowners, changing hunting unit boundaries or involving limited-entry permits. For example, the Blackfoot–Clearwater Game Range in western Montana, a wintering area on which security cover was low due to past timber harvests, was managed under limited-entry hunts (Hurley 1994).

Unanswered Questions About Migration

Although scientific research has expanded knowledge about elk migrations, several questions remain to be answered. Research clarification would improve the scientific basis for management of elk and their environments. Questions needing additional scientific inquiry include the following:

1. Does postrut migration by bulls increase their likelihood of overwinter survival?
2. How does weather interact with nutritional value of forage to influence timing and extent of elk migrations?
3. Do those elk that migrate to high elevation summer ranges enjoy longer life spans or produce more young than do those that do not migrate?

4. If young elk learn migratory routes from their mothers, what are the mechanisms by which translocated elk establish migratory routes?
5. How do interactions between hunting pressure, extensive logging, exploration for oil and gas reserves, highways or other human activities influence migration?
6. How do state and national parks and other refuges influence migratory patterns among elk?
7. Will reintroducing wolves and grizzly bears to formerly occupied areas change migratory patterns of elk?

Conclusion

Since the classic volume edited by Thomas and Toweill (1982), new research has clarified evolutionary and immediate factors that influence the timing and extent of migrations. This research also has elevated the influence of summer/autumn forage supplies in migrations and the likely importance of these supplies to overwinter survival. The additional information has strong implications for blending management of elk hunting seasons with management of areas reserved from hunting and other land management activities, such as grazing and timber harvesting.

11

ALLEN Y. COOPERRIDER

Elk and Ecosystem Management

Perhaps it is not even proper to speak of 'elk management' by itself. It needs to be integrated with management of other species.

Olaus J. Murie (1951:348)

The context in which elk and other game species are being managed is changing and will continue to change. This is a result of the differing values that the public places on elk as well as newer approaches to managing wildland landscapes, which have come to be termed ecosystem management.

For at least 10,000 years, Native Americans "managed" elk through harvest traditions and habitat manipulation of which the most pervasive was burning (McCabe 1982). The extent to which Native Americans, in combination with native predators, limited numbers, density and distribution of elk is a subject of continuing debate (Kay 1990, 1994, 1995a, 1995b, Cannon 1992; see Chapter 2). With the arrival of European settlers in North America, elk were subject to heavy hunting and these settlers are believed to be responsible for widespread decline in distribution and density of elk, although some biologists have hypothesized that elk were never numerous (Kay 1990, 1994).

Early management strategies for elk and other game species focused on population management, as reflected in such practices as bag limits, closed seasons, banning of market gunning or restriction on sex and age classes that could be hunted. As game management became more sophisticated, the importance of habitat management was recog-

nized, and game managers intensified efforts to describe, quantify, enhance or conserve habitat for particular species, such as elk. Thus, both population management and habitat management tended to be focused on single species (or closely related species groups, such as ducks or waterfowl). As a result, game management (later, wildlife management) tended to evolve as a collection of single-species management programs.

Since the mid-1980s, the need for more comprehensive management of ecosystems has become compelling. This need derived, in part, from efforts in wildlife management, particularly efforts to save threatened and endangered species. However, those working in forestry, range management, water management and many other resource management fields also have recognized the need for more holistic approaches to management of landscapes.

In the field of wildlife management, single-species approaches have become increasingly unwieldy, if not ineffective. This has become most evident when applying single-species management to threatened species. Many biologists have concluded that it would be easier to protect intact, functioning ecosystems, with their full complement of species, rather than attempt to rehabilitate species one-by-one after the ecosystem were degraded to the point where species became endangered (Hutto et al. 1987, Scott et al. 1988, Noss and Cooperrider 1994). In wildlife management, the limitations of single-species management for common game species such as elk also became evident. For one thing, managing habitat for one species was likely to be

The traditional focus of elk management featured the contact between wildlife managers and hunters relative to elk harvested during annually established hunting seasons. *Photo courtesy of the Wyoming Department of Game and Fish.*

detrimental to other species. More important, land-use practices, such as logging, were altering ecological processes in ways that were likely to affect many species.

The move toward ecosystem management did not derive solely from concerns for endangered species or even from wildlife management. Foresters and range managers also have come to realize that the resources they manage are dependent on healthy, functioning ecosystems. Furthermore, increasing understanding of the biology of single species— be it a tree species, wildlife species or rangeland grass species—began to reveal the complexity of ecosystem-level interactions that governed the health and viability of all such populations. For example, cutting trees was demonstrated to decrease hiding cover for elk. When this decrease was coupled with increasing densities of roads (allowing increased human disturbance), elk were shown to make less use of habitat lacking such cover. This resulted in less totally usable habitat that elk could use for foraging and other activities. Logging and roads also made elk more vulnerable to hunting and poaching. Thus, the ability of an area to support elk involved a complex interaction of logging, cover, road density and human disturbance (including hunting pressure), as well as forage supply. Manipulation of any of these factors is likely to have more widespread effects on the ecosystem and ecological processes and, thus, on many other species.

Ecosystem management has been interpreted in many ways. A generalized framework for an ecosystem approach is shown in Table 93. Grumbine (1994) listed 10 dominant themes of ecosystem management (Table 94). Because elk

often move wide distances across the landscape and use many different habitats, some themes of ecosystem management, such as Theme 2 (the need to work across administrative boundaries) and Theme 7 (the need for interagency cooperation) will be familiar to elk biologists and managers. Other themes may be less familiar, such as some of the conservation biology concepts (native diversity, viable populations, etc.) inherent in Theme 3—ecological integrity.

For purposes of this chapter, ecosystem management integrates scientific knowledge of ecological relationships with a complex sociopolitical and value framework toward the general goal of protecting native ecosystem integrity over the long term (Grumbine 1994). In the future, elk management is likely to be carried out in this context.

Role of Elk in the Ecosystem

A key concept of ecosystem management and managing landscapes for conservation of biodiversity is the zoning of the larger regional landscape into areas dedicated to differing biological and socioeconomic goals (Noss and Cooperrider 1994, U.S. General Accounting Office 1994, Interagency Ecosystem Management Task Force 1995, Hunter 1996). At one extreme are dedicated natural areas, relatively undisturbed by human activities, such as mining and grazing, and relatively unmarked by human artifacts, such as buildings and roads. These natural areas often have been given administrative designations and managed as national parks and monuments, wilderness areas or wildlife refuges.

Table 93. Framework for an ecosystem approach

Stage	Description
1. Define the regional ecosystem (ecoregion) of concern	Ecoregions may be defined based on watershed boundaries, vegetation types or other criteria.
2. Involve stakeholders	Stakeholders include the various governments, agencies, organizations and citizens affected by or otherwise concerned about the land management policies and practices adopted for the ecoregion.
3. Develop a shared vision or goal	A vision statement is a clear conceptual picture of the desired future state. Vision statements usually are long term in nature and tend to be broad and general. However, they should be specific enough to guide the development of objectives in Stage 5.
4. Characterize the historic ecosystem as well as the present ecosystem status	Characterizing the historic ecosystem requires a description of the composition, structure and function of major ecosystem elements and their variability over time. Understanding and describing the role of indigenous people in this system is critical. Characterizing present ecosystem conditions should include both ecological and socioeconomic conditions and trends.
5. Establish ecosystem objectives	Objectives need to be more specific than the vision or goal of Stage 3. Objectives need to be quantifiable or verifiable so that one can measure progress and eventual success. More specific subobjectives may be established as part of a plan, as identified in Stage 6.
6. Develop and implement a plan to achieve the above objectives	A plan should include detailed steps for achieving objectives, plus a clear statement of how progress will be monitored and evaluated.
7. Monitor conditions and evaluate results	Monitoring is necessary to determine whether the plan is being implemented properly, expected results are being achieved and underlying assumptions are sound.
8. Adapt management to new information	Adaptive management is a process of adjusting management actions and directions after obtaining new information systematically collected as part of a management program.

Source: Interagency Ecosystem Management Task Force 1995.

Table 94. Dominant themes of ecosystem management

Theme	Description
1. Hierarchical context	A focus on any one level of the biodiversity hierarchy (genus, species, populations, ecosystems, landscapes) is not sufficient. When working on a problem at any one level or scale, managers must seek the connections between all levels. This often is described as a systems perspective.
2. Ecological boundaries	Management requires working across administrative/political boundaries (i.e., national forests and parks) and defining ecological boundaries at appropriate scales.
3. Ecological integrity	Managing for ecological integrity implies protecting total native diversity (species, populations, ecosystems) and the ecological patterns and processes that maintain that diversity. Most authors discuss this as conservation of viable populations of native species, maintenance of natural disturbance regimes, reintroduction of native and/or extirpated species, representation of ecosystems across natural ranges of variation, etc.
4. Data collection	Ecosystem management requires more research and data collection (i.e., habitat inventory/classification, disturbance regime dynamics, baseline species and population assessment), as well as better management and use of data.
5. Monitoring	Managers must track the results of their actions so that success or failure may be evaluated quantitatively. Monitoring creates an ongoing feedback loop of useful information.
6. Adaptive management	Adaptive management assumes that scientific knowledge is provisional and focuses on management as a learning process or continuous experiment, in which incorporation of results of previous actions allows managers to remain flexible and adapt to uncertainty.
7. Interagency cooperation	Ecological boundaries require cooperation between federal, state and local management agencies, as well as private parties. Managers must learn to work together and integrate legal mandates and management goals.
8. Organizational change	Implementing ecosystem management requires changes in the structure of land management agencies and the way they operate. Changes may range from the simple (e.g., forming an interagency committee) to the complex (e.g., changing professional norms or altering power relationships).
9. Humans embedded in nature	People cannot be separated from nature. Humans are fundamental influences on ecological patterns and processes and, in turn, are affected by them.
10. Values	Regardless of the role of scientific knowledge, human values play a dominant role in ecosystem management goals.

Source: Grumbine 1994.

At another extreme are lands dedicated to extractive activities, such as commercial forestland and grazing land. The latter are wildlands in the sense that they are not urbanized or farmed, but typically are managed with the primary goal of producing such amenities as livestock forage or timber.

All sorts of gradation exist between these extremes. For example, many areas, such as U.S. Forest Service wilderness areas, allow light touch human activities, such as nonmotorized hunting and recreation. Similarly, many areas, such as commercial forestland, dedicated primarily to extractive activities, are managed with a secondary purpose of supporting fish and wildlife.

A central goal of ecosystem management is to determine the mix and spatial arrangement of such areas within a regional ecosystem (hereafter termed ecoregion) that will allow the perpetuation of the biodiversity of each area, while still allowing some level of extractive activities to provide for human needs.

Within such an ecoregion, elk may be managed for different purposes. The purposes will depend on the ecology of the ecoregion, the degree to which the ecosystem has deteriorated or is in need of restoration, and the socioeconomic needs and desires of humans. Wherever viable populations of elk were native to an ecoregion, the goal of maintaining or restoring viable populations of elk within the ecoregion follows from the ecosystem management goal of protecting or restoring species composition, just as it does for all other native species. However, as elk are wide ranging, they may occupy portions of the regional landscape that are managed for quite different purposes. For example, the elk herds in and around Yellowstone National Park move from natural areas within the park out toward private and national forestland managed for livestock grazing or timber production.

Because elk may play quite different roles in an ecoregion, public expectations of management as well as management techniques may vary considerably from area to area. In the next sections some of these various roles are described, recognizing that, even within a given ecoregion, the role may vary.

Elk in the Natural Landscape—A Keystone Species

Ideally, a "natural area" serves, by human design and designation, as a repository of the world's ecological processes and, thus, as "living, interim definition of relative naturalness" (Maser 1990:129). Therefore, human intervention in the form of deliberate manipulation of elk or any other organism is normally kept to a minimum. If natural areas were large enough to contain viable populations of all the species present and if unnatural or human-induced prob-

lems from outside were negligible, then no human intervention would be necessary. However, most natural areas are too small and too affected by outside activities, such that elk (and many other large, migratory ungulates) often require some management (Noss and Cooperrider 1994). But, before discussing these situations, I examine briefly a few of the important ecological roles that elk play in the natural ecosystem, because an understanding of those roles should guide development of management goals and practices in all systems.

Keystone species are species that play pivotal roles in ecosystems and on which a large part of the biotic community depends (Noss and Cooperrider 1994). Although designation of a species as a keystone is an arbitrary one and of questionable scientific validity (Mills et al. 1993), the concept is quite useful in management. Elk, like other large, migratory herding ungulates, such as bison and caribou, often are considered keystone species, especially in North America where there are relatively few ungulate species. In many ecoregions of North America, elk, together with mule or white-tailed deer, are the predominant ungulates in the system.

Some of the ecological functions that elk play include competition with other herbivores, food sources for scavengers and large predators, modifiers of habitat and transporters of plant propagules.

First, elk compete with other herbivores in the natural ecosystem, particularly with other ungulates in the system, such as mule deer and bighorn sheep (see Chapter 8).

Second, elk may serve as a food or prey base for many species, especially large carnivores and omnivores. Wolves, for example, are highly dependent on large ungulates for food over large portions of their range, and the biomass of elk usually is much larger than that of other ungulates, such as deer and pronghorn (e.g., elk outnumber the other six ungulates in Northern Yellowstone National Park by a ratio of 16:1). Winter-killed elk also provide a food source for such scavengers as grizzly and black bears. Although the importance of food for scavengers is not well understood in most systems, it is reasonable to expect that winter-killed elk may provide a critical, concentrated source of energy and protein for many carnivores, omnivores and scavengers in early spring when food often is in limited supply.

Third, elk can modify habitat necessary for their own survival, although the role, specifically the degree, of modification is controversial. Several authors (Kay 1985, 1990, 1994, Kay and Chadde 1992, Kay and Wagner 1994, Wagner et al. 1995) have provided evidence of changes in plant species composition and vigor at the site, watershed and ecoregion scale as a result of elk foraging. Conversely, other researchers maintain that the effect of elk on plant species composition is minimal, at least at the ecoregion scale, and that other factors, such as drought and changes in fire regimes, may be more important (Singer et al. 1994, Singer and Cates 1995).

Finally, ungulates that move great distances, such as elk, likely serve a role in dispersal of other species by moving plant seeds, disease organisms (such as ectoparasites) and other small organisms or reproductive stages of species. This has not been well-documented for elk, but it also has not been extensively studied.

These are but a few of the potential or observed roles of elk in ecosystem functioning. Some of these roles, such as dispersing plant seeds, have not been studied and, based on extrapolation from studies of other ungulates, one can only speculate about their importance. Other roles, such as the impact of elk on plant community composition and structure have been studied in many places and are a subject of continuing controversy with herds such as the Northern Yellowstone elk herd (Kay 1990). In all likelihood, many other roles still are undiscovered. The relative importance of the ecological roles of elk may vary considerably from place to place, and the discussion is intended to be exemplary rather than exhaustive.

Elk as Threatened or Endangered Species

Due to the success of elk management throughout North America, elk are not threatened or endangered except in local areas. However, with continuously increasing pressure on land and resources, more and more elk populations may become threatened with extirpation. Experience with other species suggests that elk populations may be particularly vulnerable in the following situations.

1. Island populations, where small, isolated populations exist with little or no interchange with other populations. These may be actual islands or they may be islands of habitat surrounded by habitat that is naturally unsuitable or has been made unsuitable by human action.
2. Populations where habitat fragmentation from highways, logging, urbanization or other human factors is causing both loss of habitat and division of large contiguous blocks of habitat into smaller, discontinuous patches.
3. Peripheral populations near the edge of the geographic range of elk or at the limits of their ecological tolerance.

Studies have shown that elk, by their selective feeding habitats in areas where they are abundant, dictate to a large degree the variety of plant species that may exist. *Photo by Jim D. Yoakum.*

In situations 1 and 2, populations are subject to what has been termed the perils of small populations (Wilcove 1987), and may be subject to a variety of problems that range from genetics (e.g., inbreeding) to vulnerability to chance events. Considerable study has been devoted to estimating the risk of extinction of such populations (see Primack 1993, Meffe and Carroll 1994, Hunter 1996).

In contrast, populations near the edge of their geographic range or ecological tolerance (e.g., some populations that winter at higher elevations) may always have been vulnerable. Over long periods of time, local extirpation followed by recolonization at a later time may have been the natural pattern. Such populations may be vulnerable to extirpation from both random events, such as harsh winters, and also long-term trends, such as global warming.

The degree to which resources are or should be devoted to saving these marginal populations from extirpation will depend on how concerned people are with maintaining natural populations and how much value people place in conserving such populations, regardless of the naturalness of their condition.

Elk as Candidate for Restoration

As mentioned earlier, a central goal of ecosystem management is to protect or restore the species composition of an ecosystem. If viable (self-sustaining) populations of elk were historically present within an ecosystem, it follows that they should be restored to such an ecosystem. This sort of goal is appropriately applied at the ecoregion level. Thus, it does not demand that elk be restored on every acre of the ecoregion, but rather that viable populations be restored to portions of that ecoregion. For example, the U.S. Fish and Wildlife Service (1994) has designated the Central Valley of California (including San Francisco Bay) as an ecoregion. This area coincides well with the historic range of Tule elk (McCullough 1969). Much of this area now is occupied by agriculture (the Central Valley) or urban development (the San Francisco Bay area). At one point, only one remnant population existed within this historic range. However, as a result of an active program of restoration, viable populations of Tule elk now are well distributed throughout this ecoregion, thus meeting the bottomline criteria of ecosystem management. Similarly, the goal for the eastern United States, from which elk had been extirpated, would be to ensure that viable populations of elk were reestablished within each ecoregion.

One of the concerns about reestablishing elk populations is the degree to which the reintroduced populations contain the same genetic material as the extirpated population. Ideally, from the standpoint of conserving genetic diversity, reintroduced populations would be from the same subspecies or race. In the case of eastern elk, however, such stock are no longer available. The question arises: Should closely related subspecies (of elk) be reintroduced so that their ecological roles in the ecosystem can be reestablished? From the standpoint of biodiversity, conservation arguments can be made both for and against such reintroduc-

Restoration of Tule elk required management efforts to identify the genetic material characteristic of this subspecies, to protect it from being diluted by mixture with genetic material from other subspecies and to restock Tule elk widely within its native range. Potential for restoring this (or any other) native race of elk would have been seriously jeopardized if elk from other races had been introduced into Tule elk range. In all likelihood, the less well-adapted species would not have fared as well as the site-adapted Tule elk. *Photo by Joseph F. Dixon; courtesy of the University of California—Berkeley Museum of Vertebrate Zoology.*

Within the past few decades, elk have been reintroduced into many areas from which they had been long extirpated, such as these elk, which are part of a population currently flourishing in Pennsylvania. Such populations must be afforded a high degree of protection when first translocated, but reestablished populations can contribute toward restoration of native ecosystems. *Photo by James H. Shuey.*

tion. What most conservation biologists would agree on is that when reintroductions (of any species) are being planned, the reintroduced stock should be as similar genetically as possible to the population that formerly occupied the area.

Elk in the Managed Landscape— A Featured Species

Within the managed landscape, elk often are treated as a featured species, i.e., one that is managed to achieve particular population goals (Thomas 1979b). This is because elk are both highly valued and manageable. These goals may be expressed in terms of elk numbers, density or harvest. Elk are one of the most manageable species in North America, because habitat requirements are understood, and their populations respond predictably to both habitat and population management. The most common goal of elk management is for recreational hunting (see Chapter 18). However, elk also are valued for other purposes, such as viewing, listening to bugling and photography.

Elk as Commercial Species—Game Ranching

Elk are becoming part of commercial enterprises termed game ranching. The term game ranching can denote quite different enterprises, therefore it is important to be clear about which is being discussed. One is that of ranchers or other landowners managing their lands to provide elk habitat, with the intent of receiving revenue through guiding, or access fees or other elk-related recreation. The base herds are native, and movements of elk are not restricted. This form of game ranching generally is done within the context of existing hunting and property rights laws and regulations. Management objectives and practices parallel those on public lands, and such enterprises are compatible with and often encouraged by state wildlife agencies.

The other enterprise is the raising of elk in semicaptivity, which also may be termed gamefarming. In this type of gamefarming, elk are confined on private property where they are raised for sport shooting or the sale of meat and other products. The elk often are derived from non-native stock and may not be genetically similar to native herds on surrounding lands. Gamefarming has caused great concern among conservationists and wildlife agencies. It is similar to livestock production in its goals and practices. Like traditional livestock enterprises, such operations can overuse rangeland forage supplies and spread disease to native wild elk herds. In addition, animals escaping from such enterprises (an everpresent possibility) can interbreed with native animals, thus affecting the latters' genetic purity, with potential adverse effects.

Elk are big animals and can cause severe damage to farm crops, tree saplings in reforestation efforts and ornamental plants, as well as cause damage to fences and other structures. In most instances, wildlife management agencies must strive to prevent such damage and, in some states, must reimburse private landowners for damage if it occurs. *Left photo by Milo Burcham. Right photo courtesy of the Oregon Department of Fish and Wildlife.*

Elk have been used as flagship species to focus attention on preservation of open space around western communities, such as Mt. Jumbo, outside of Missoula, Montana. *Photo by Nelson Kenter.*

Elk as Pest Species

People value elk for many reasons, but there are situations in which elk cause considerable economic damage. In particular, elk can damage agricultural crops, particularly orchards, and raid and consume considerable quantities of stored hay. Elk also can cause damage to forest species, particularly newly planted trees in plantations. Such situations usually are limited to localized areas. Furthermore, some situations, such as damage to haystacks, can be minimized easily and economically through the use of protective paneling or fencing. Nevertheless, damage problems are real and must be dealt with within the context of ecosystem management.

Elk as Flagship, Umbrella or Indicator Species

Elk may play other roles within the context of ecosystem management. These roles are more social than ecological, that is, they reflect human perceptions about elk and how elk can be used to shape or gauge a conservation strategy. Flagship species, umbrella species and indicator species often are confused with keystone and featured species, as described earlier.

Flagship species are those that are popular and charismatic, and thus attract popular support for their conservation (Noss and Cooperrider 1994). Conservationists often use such flagship species as bears and eagles to help gain public support for more holistic conservation programs. Elk certainly qualify as "flagships" and have adorned the covers of many publications promoting conservation. Flagship species, such as elk, that require large areas frequently are used as umbrella species to enhance conservation of other elements of the ecosystem.

Umbrella species are those that require large areas to maintain viable populations, and protection of their habitat may protect the habitat and populations of many other more restricted or less wide-ranging species (Noss and Cooperrider 1994). The philosophy is that, if habitat for a species such as elk can be conserved, then many other species, such as birds and small- and medium-sized mammals, also will be protected. Elk, being both popular and charismatic as well as wide ranging, would appear to be an ideal umbrella species in some ways. However, caution needs to be used in applying this philosophy, because there have been situations in which elk have thrived and other species were lost from that system. For example, in the forests of the Pacific Northwest, elk generally have maintained or increased in density and distribution since the mid-1900s. At the same time, many forest species, such as

spotted owls, marbled murrelets, pine martens and Pacific fishers, have declined in numbers to the point of endangerment or near endangerment. As discussed later, presence or abundance of elk may not correlate well with presence of other species.

Indicator species are those that have such a narrow ecological tolerance that the size and health of their populations are an indication of environmental conditions (Hunter 1996). For example, certain species of lichens are indicators of air quality, because they are sensitive to pollution. At one time, biologists thought that a given species might be an indicator of quality of habitat for other species that use a similar habitat. This use of indicator species has been shown to be of limited validity or usefulness (Landres et al. 1988). Therefore, elk population size or health is unlikely to be an indicator of habitat quality for other species. Furthermore, elk are unlikely to be a good indicator species. They are an adaptable species and relative generalists in use of habitat and forage. Furthermore, they are quite responsive to management. Thus, the density or health of an elk population is most likely to indicate the in-

Elk have been used as an indicator species in some national forest plans. In the Clearwater National Forest in Idaho, elk population decline called attention to forest succession that had resulted in a significant reduction in openings in the forest canopy—therefore, a reduction in forage for elk and other species that required grass and shrub forage to survive. *Photo courtesy of Idaho Department of Fish and Game.*

tensity and effectiveness of elk management, rather than trends in other environmental conditions or other species.

Despite much evidence to suggest that elk are not good indicator species, many land management agency plans and programs continue to use elk as an indicator species or a management indicator species. This apparently is a result of confusion between the concepts of featured species and indicator species. Future elk management within the context of ecosystem management would be improved if biologists would make clear distinctions between those concepts.

Managing Elk with an Ecosystem Approach

Ecosystem management is an evolving approach to land management. At this time, ecosystem management is more a philosophy than a well-developed set of procedures. Thus, elk management within the context of ecosystem management is likely to change as more formal ecosystem approaches are developed. However, general stages, as shown in Table 93, are likely to form the basic framework for most ecosystem approaches.

Issues, Questions and Objectives in the Natural Landscape

Under ideal circumstances, vast intact acreages of pristine wildlands, virtually unaltered by humans of the past 500 years, similar natural landscapes and the elk within the landscapes would require nothing more than laissez faire management. Unfortunately, most reserves are too small and too influenced by human activities to justify such an approach. Therefore, before objectives being set for elk within such a system, one must examine to what extent the reserve area is operating as an intact ecological system. The data gathered in Stage 4 of the ecosystem approach—characterize the historic ecosystem—should provide essential, useful information for addressing elk issues. Examples of the types of questions that should be addressed include the following:

1. Are viable populations of elk essentially self-contained within the natural area?
2. Are the ecological processes that maintained or regulated the elk populations (e.g., fire regimes and large native predators) still present within the natural area?
3. What was the role of indigenous people in maintaining or controlling elk habitat and numbers?
4. In the natural landscape, are there human-caused processes, such as livestock grazing or disease transmission, that need to be mitigated?
5. Is natural connectivity of the landscape being main-

tained so that both population viability and normal genetic exchange are being maintained?

The primary objective for elk management within the natural landscape should be maintenance of elk habitat, numbers and distribution through natural processes augmented when necessary by light touch management that mimics natural processes. Light touch management would include such practices as prescribed burning where necessary to mimic the natural fire regime within the ecoregion. The degree to which active management of elk numbers or habitat is required will depend on the degree to which the herds and habitat are self-contained.

Issues, Questions and Objectives in the Managed Landscape

Elk management objectives within the managed landscape may vary from minimizing damage problems to enhancing habitat and elk numbers to maximizing recreational hunting. As with the natural landscape, the questions addressed in Stage 4 of the ecosystem approach should provide a useful baseline to gauge the degree of management that is economical or desirable. For example, landscapes that historically supported few elk or whose ecological functions have been severely impaired may require extensive (and costly) management to achieve high-density elk populations for recreational hunting.

In areas managed to optimize elk hunting, the objectives may vary considerably, as discussed in Chapters 17 and 18. For example, management to provide maximum high-quality trophy hunting opportunities will require different population or habitat management strategies than will management aimed at providing a maximum number of hunter or viewer days.

Managing Elk within the Mixed Landscape

Most ecoregions contain a complex mosaic of ownerships and lands, for which the management objectives may vary considerably. The challenge of ecosystem management is to find the mix of management techniques and prescriptions that will achieve ecosystem management goals and objectives. In terms of elk management, one of the key questions to ask up front is whether more or less discrete subpopulations or herds exist, such that clear objectives can be set for each herd unit (i.e., manage for trophy hunting, maximum harvest, minimal damage, etc.). When that is determined, then elk management may be focused on achieving a clear and unambiguous goal.

More typically, however, population units will occupy

Elk, provided with a desirable mix of cover and feeding areas such as provided by well-designed timber harvest rotations, often are highly productive. These herds can provide a source of animals able to colonize less productive habitats. *Left photo courtesy of the Oregon Department of Fish and Wildlife. Right photo by Jack Ballard.*

several different areas during the year with differing owner-ship patterns and managed by a mix of private individuals and government agencies with different attitudes about elk. Determining objectives in these cases can be difficult and contentious, and there is no cookbook approach that can be prescribed for resolving such conflicts. Ecosystem manage-ment, however, provides a context and evolving set of tools, both biological and social, for dealing with these issues by looking at the whole ecosystem that the elk occupy.

Issues of Scale (Temporal and Spatial)

One of the underlying themes of ecosystem management is that humans need to look at problems in the proper per-spective. In particular, resource management often has suf-fered from focusing on short time spans (1 to 10 years in-stead of decades to centuries) and small geographic scales (sites or stands instead of watersheds or ecoregions). Elk management often has suffered from such myopia.

Within both managed and natural areas, elk managers often have been concerned with wide fluctuations in elk numbers and habitat condition. The underlying, but often unstated assumption is that elk numbers and habitat should remain relatively stable (e.g., not vary more than ±20%) from year to year. Yet, such conditions frequently are not achieved; severe winters, diseases and other factors lead to substantial fluctuations in numbers and habitat conditions.

It may be time for elk biologists to be more concerned about relative stability over larger areas and longer periods of time.

Elk biologists have long recognized the importance of dealing with year-round habitat for herds. However, one continues to see elk habitat goals developed internally by land management agencies that control only a portion of the year-round range. Elk biologists have been less prone to look beyond the herd units to view elk populations in a larger context.

An important question to ask about any herd is the quality of its natural habitat relative to adjacent herds. If a herd is occupying marginal habitat (e.g., at latitudinal, climatic or elevational limits of elk range) compared with that of adja-cent herds, then its management opportunities may be quite different than for herds on prime habitat.

A related question deals with source and sink herds. From studies of many vertebrate species, it is known that, across a species' range, there may exist subpopulations that reproduce prolifically on prime habitat. These subpopula-tions may produce many animals that emigrate to other ar-eas (source populations). In contrast, there are other popu-lations on marginal habitat whose net reproduction may be inadequate for many years to maintain population numbers (sink populations). These latter populations may be aug-mented by individuals immigrating from other areas.

Such an augmentation phenomenon is likely to occur in

areas such as the northern Rocky Mountains, where there are large areas of contiguous elk habitat and at least some interchange between elk herds. This phenomenon has not been well documented for elk, partly because most studies have focused on individual herds. However, identification of herds as source or sink populations will be quite useful in clarifying management opportunities for and constraints of each.

Agency Roles and Responsibilities

In recent years, wildlife agency mandates have changed to reflect different demands from society and increased understanding of the complexity of ecosystems and ecological relationships. New approaches, collectively termed ecosystem management, have required that agencies redefine their missions in terms of elk management as well as many other activities. This differs somewhat from agency to agency and, although some agencies such as the U.S. National Park Service appear to have clear missions, most federal and state agencies have a variety of missions and responsibilities that overlap and are inconsistent.

The National Park Service has had a general mandate to manage lands and wildlife to emulate the "natural landscape" conditions described earlier. Thus, in most national parks, recreational hunting of elk has been prohibited, and such artificial enhancement as winter feeding is avoided. However, the Park Service also has mandates to provide for recreation. As a result, developments for recreational access and use, such as roads and trails, often conflict with the habitat needs of elk. More important, most national parks are not large enough to contain year-round habitat for many of the elk herds that occupy them seasonally. For example, Yellowstone National Park, the oldest and largest national park in the contiguous 48 states, is not large enough to contain many of its large elk herds year-round. Furthermore, the National Park Service clearly has established its right to prohibit hunting within parks, despite the fact that, on most lands, this is a prerogative of state wildlife agencies. However, once the elk leave the park, the Park Service has no control over hunting, and elk born and raised in national parks frequently and legally are hunted once they cross the park boundaries.

One of the missions of national parks is to provide visitors with the opportunity to see native wildlife, such as this bull in Yellowstone National Park. Animals in parks tend to become somewhat habituated to human presence, allowing people to view them in natural settings. *Photo by Milo Burcham.*

The so-called multiple use agencies also have mixed missions. The U.S. Forest Service has operated for many decades with a mandate to manage its lands for multiple uses. However, there has been continuing controversy about the meaning and interpretation of that multiple use mandate. Although, in theory and by law, multiple use can be construed to mean that all resources such as timber, wildlife and recreation, is equally important, in practice now and historically timber harvest has been given priority over other resources and uses of the National Forest System. Thus, when timber harvesting operations have conflicted with needs to conserve elk habitat, timber harvesting usually has been chosen at the expense of elk habitat.

A similar situation has existed historically with the other principal multiple use agency, the U.S. Bureau of Land Management. Since 1976, the Bureau has had a mandate to manage for a variety of uses, including wildlife. Historically, however, livestock grazing has been given priority over other resources and uses on the public domain. Because elk often compete with livestock for forage, giving priority to livestock grazing frequently has resulted in less than optimal forage available for elk.

In general, most federal agencies now have a mandate to move away from management dominated by commodity production to some form of management that recognizes the primacy of maintaining healthy ecosystems (Interagency Ecosystem Management Task Force 1995). Thus, the role of these agencies, with regard to elk, is generally to manage within managed or mixed landscapes in a way that is consistent with maintaining the health of the larger ecosystem of which their lands compose a part.

The situation with state wildlife agencies is less clear and varies considerably from state to state. Few such agencies have formal mandates for ecosystem management or to manage wildlife by means of an ecosystem approach. Furthermore, most still derive a substantial portion of their funding from sale of hunting and fishing licenses and have a strong mandate to manage lands and wildlife for benefit of hunters and anglers. However, most state wildlife agencies have few areas that are large enough to manage for migratory ungulates such as elk. Thus, these state wildlife agencies must rely on the cooperation of private landowners and federal land management agencies to provide for adequate elk habitat. On the other hand, the states have clear authority over elk population management, which includes setting hunting seasons, harvest quotas, permissible hunting methods and permit requirements. This interdependency of landowners managing elk habitat and state agencies managing elk hunting has required the agencies to work with landowners to maintain elk populations. Emerg-

ing ecosystem management approaches will continue this tradition, albeit in perhaps a broader ecological context and a more participatory environment. Thus, state agencies likely will need to work within a context of ecosystem management regardless of whether they have such a mandate.

Setting Goals and Objectives

Setting goals and objectives usually is the most critical part of any management program. Without a clear goal or vision and verifiable objectives, a program is likely to drift in random directions depending on prevailing political, governmental and societal whims. Ensuring early, inclusive participation in setting goals and objectives can help a program be resilient to ephemeral political pressures. Elk are likely to be an important species in many ecosystems; therefore, setting goals and objectives for their management and that of other ungulates in an ecoregion should be done thoughtfully and openly, with input from the public, from scientists and from those directly affected by such management decisions.

However, as most ecoregions will have areas that range from relatively untouched reserves to highly developed urban or agricultural areas, objectives for elk may have to vary, depending on the portion of the ecoregion in which they reside or move. Table 95 provides example goals and objectives for an ecoregion, followed by objectives for elk management appropriate for inclusion within an ecoregion plan.

Developing goals, objectives and action will be dependent on asking appropriate questions regarding elk and the landscape they inhabit. And these questions will be quite different depending on whether the elk reside primarily within a natural or managed landscape.

Role of Citizens and Elk Proponents

One of the key elements of ecosystem management is that human values play a dominant role in developing ecosystem management goals (see Table 94). Thus, modern practitioners of ecosystem management have recognized the need for meaningful and continuous input from citizens in developing and implementing land and resource management programs. Because elk are valued by many people for a variety of reasons, citizens need to be involved actively in elk management. Similarly, others within organizations and agencies may serve roles as advocates for elk. For example, wildlife biologists within land management agencies often serve both as experts on wildlife biology and as in-house advocates for wildlife resources. Table 96 illustrates the various roles of citizen/advocates, biologists and managers in the various stages of an ecosystem approach.

Citizens, such as the group (*left*) comprising the Clearwater Elk Recovery Team, in central Idaho's Clearwater National Forest, play a major role in interacting with land and wildlife management agencies to ensure that wildlife resources are considered in management decisions. *Photo by Dale E. Toweill.*

Table 95. Examples of elk management objectives for Klamath Ecoregion of California and Oregon

Area	Subspecies/movement pattern	Primary land manager[a]	Objectives[b]
Point Reyes National Seashore	Tule elk—nonmigratory	U.S. National Park Service	1. Manage as natural keystone species. 2. Minimize damage by elk and by animals that move outside seashore boundaries to local holdings.
Coastal mountains of Sonoma and Mendocino counties (generally west of Highway 101)	Historically, probably contained Roosevelt elk	Primarily private lands, including several tracts of large industrial forestlands	1. Reintroduce Roosevelt elk onto private lands. 2. Manage as a featured species for recreational hunting and other values. 3. Manage to minimize damage to agriculture.
Coastal mountains of Mendocino and Sonoma counties (generally east of Highway 101)	Tule elk—mostly nonmigratory	Primarily private lands; some larger tracts of BLM lands; portions highly populated	1. Manage as featured species. 2. Minimize damage to agriculture.
Coastal mountains of Humboldt and Del Norte counties (outside parks)	Roosevelt elk—both resident and migratory patterns	Mix of private, tribal and USDA Forest Service lands	Manage as featured species for recreational and subsistence hunting and for other values.
Redwood National Park (and adjacent state park lands)	Roosevelt elk—primarily nonmigratory	U.S. National Park Service and California Department of Parks and Recreation State Park	Manage as natural keystone species.
Mountains of central Klamath Basin	Probable intergradation between Roosevelt and Rocky Mountain elk—mostly migratory	Mix of private, tribal and USDA Forest Service lands	1. Reestablish migratory traditions and herds in lower basin. 2. Manage as featured species for recreational and subsistence hunting and for other values.
Forestlands of upper Klamath Basin (Oregon and California)	Rocky Mountain elk—migratory	Predominantly USDA Forest Service lands, with some private and tribal lands	Manage as featured species for recreational hunting.
Crater Lake National Park	Rocky Mountain elk—migratory	U.S. National Park Service	Manage to mimic as much as possible the natural role of elk in the area given the migratory pattern where mostly elk are present only during summer.

Note: The Klamath ecoregion consists of the hydrobasins that drain into the Pacific Ocean south of the Oregon border and north of the San Francisco Bay, including the Smith, Klamath, Trinity, Eel and Russian rivers, as well as many smaller streams (U.S. Fish and Wildlife Service 1994).

[a] BML = Bureau of Land Management; USDA = U.S. Department of Agriculture.

[b] The suggested objectives in this table are those of the author and are presented here as possible alternatives only. They do not necessarily represent the views of the respective fish and game agencies (Oregon and California) nor of any or all of the primary land managers listed.

Table 96. Role of elk proponents (citizens, biologists, managers) in planning for elk management within an ecosystem approach

Stage	Role
1. Define the regional ecosystem (ecoregion) of concern	Ecoregions can be defined based on many criteria, of which the most common are watershed or hydrobasin boundaries and vegetation types. One criterion for delineation can be ranges of large migratory animals such as elk. Biologists should consider elk movements and herd boundaries when deciding how to delimit ecoregions.
2. Involve stakeholders	Active involvement.
3. Develop a shared vision or goal	Those concerned with elk will want to ensure that a shared vision is compatible with and complementary to visions for elk habitat and populations.
4. Characterize the historic ecosystem as well as the present ecosystem status	Primarily, this is a task for biologists. Historic elk numbers, patterns or distribution and habitat condition, as well as the current situation, should be included in any characterization.
5. Establish ecosystem objectives	Biologists and advocates will want to ensure that objectives are complementary and supportive of elk management objectives.
6. Develop and implement a plan to achieve the above objectives	Stages 6 to 8 are tasks to be shared by all stakeholders. This would include elk advocates, biologists and managers. It also should include a diversity of agency representatives, ranchers and other landowners and foresters. In the past, certain groups often have been excluded from some of the stages of developing a plan and program. In moving to ecosystem management, the trend is to be inclusive rather than exclusive at all stages.
7. Monitor conditions and evaluate results	See Stage 6.
8. Adapt management to new information	See Stage 6.

Conclusion

The context in which elk and elk habitat is being managed is changing from one of single-species management to one in which elk management is part of a larger integrated effort to sustain ecosystems. This will require that those concerned about elk development implement management actions in a way that is consistent with larger goals for an ecoregion. Learning about the ecological roles that elk play in the ecosystem is an important and critical step in developing such actions. An ecosystem approach to elk management also likely will require considerably more interaction with more diverse constituencies and interests than has been the norm.

12

JON M. SKOVLIN, PETER ZAGER
AND BRUCE K. JOHNSON

Elk Habitat Selection and Evaluation

The traditional definition of habitat includes four basic components—food, cover, water and space. The spatial arrangement of these components relates closely to how elk distribute themselves. How well wildlife biologists and managers understand the behavior/habitat relationships of elk may determine how well they are able to maintain and improve the essential habitat elements necessary for elk survival. As human activities make greater demands on shared natural habitats, it becomes increasingly important to have a scientific basis for developing management decisions that affect elk habitat.

Historic Considerations

Range of Habitat Tolerance

Before settlement of North America, principally by Europeans, members of the genus *Cervus* showed wide habitat tolerance over their range on the continent. The remarkable variety of ecosystems once occupied by elk confirms their adaptability. Roosevelt elk were at home in the dense, coastal, coniferous rainforests of the Pacific Northwest, whereas Tule elk preferred the nonforested inland valleys of California. Merriam elk occupied the dry forest and chaparral mountains of the Southwest, whereas Manitoban elk inhabited cool shrub forests of the northern lakes region and extended onto the North American prairie. At one time, Eastern elk occupied mixed conifer/hardwood forests of the eastern U.S. and southeastern Canada. Rocky Moun-

tain elk occurred in the vast interior region of inland mountains and plains. The few regional habitats apparently unoccupied by elk were the western deserts and the humid ecosystems of the Southeast (see Chapters 2 and 3).

Conflict with settlement, unregulated hunting in the late 19th century, and agricultural alterations of habitats once used by elk during winter spelled the end for many herds of mountain-dwelling elk—a process documented for the Gallatin elk herds in Montana (Lovaas 1970).

Today, free-ranging elk are found in 21 states and six provinces (see Chapter 2). In the western states and provinces, these elk populations are found primarily in coniferous forests associated with mountain, foothill or canyon rangelands. That elk range is restricted to rugged, broken terrain and related cover types probably is the result of their extirpation from areas of human settlement.

Human Influence on Elk Habitat

With the settlement of North America and concomitant alteration of natural ecosystems, most of the traditional winter range of Rocky Mountain elk was cultivated or grazed by domestic livestock. Livestock grazing in the foothills surrounding agricultural lands altered the native plant composition. During autumn and winter, when grass was in short supply, the livestock turned to shrubby browse and, in severe winters, riparian shrubs were cut for emergency cattle feed. Because elk rely heavily on shrubs for forage and, to a lesser degree, for shelter, the combination of these fac-

Exploration and settlement of the West accelerated following the Civil War, and wildlife populations plummeted. Funding of the Ferdinand V. Hayden Expedition of 1871—first of the great geographic surveys of the American West under the auspices of the Department of the Interior—were interpreted in the September 12, 1874 edition of the *New York Herald*, including the statement: "Game of all kinds abounds in great profusion in the mountains. You may, in fact, call the Rocky Mountains the hunters paradise. Elk, which have superb antlers and weigh from 400 to 700 pounds when dressed are stupid in the presence of the hunter, generally following their leader regardless of the consequences. Mountain sheep are easy game to kill, and make delicious meat, as do the deer and fawn. About the middle of September the high mountain game are driven down into the valleys and onto the plateaux by the approach of winter and then the slaughter of the hunter is at its height" (Taylor 1975:109). The article ended "May many come and see for themselves in 1875." Here members of the Hayden Expedition pack elk quarters into camp in the vicinity of Yellowstone National Park. *Photo by W. H. Jackson; courtesy of the U.S. Geological Survey.*

tors drastically influenced elk habitat, particularly the food component.

Elk habitats and food supplies also have been modified through human control of wildfire on elk range (Figure 154). For eons, fire was responsible for creating a mosaic of patchlike forest landscapes highly preferred by elk. Even-aged, unburned timber stands were bounded abruptly by burned-over stands of different age, structure and, often, different plant composition. Postfire succession of herbs and shrubs provided excellent forage and cover for elk for 20 to 30 years, until forest canopy again closed out the understory (Figure 155).

In cool, temperate forests with high annual rainfall, such as those of the coastal range or northern Idaho, stands of Douglas-fir, hemlock and cedar were burned less frequently and, thus, were relatively unproductive communities that provided little elk habitat. However, when conditions were right for fires, crown fires burned vast areas. Elk subsequently were found largely in ecotones along the edges of unburned habitats. In the drier intermountain areas, however, topography, soils and variable rainfall contributed to discontinuous vegetative communities and mixed-species stands. In these areas, more frequent but small, cool fires

provided diverse habitats with great amounts of community edge, which supported larger populations of elk.

Fire control permitted increased growth and survival of seedling trees. Because these seedlings were not thinned regularly, overstocked stands of coniferous forest became the norm (Arnold 1950). Likewise, mountain shrub communities matured and became decadent. More recently, effective fire control has led to timber stands maturing with closed canopies, causing further reduction of the understory forage supplies (Pace 1958, Irwin et al. 1994).

Because of logging, much of the managed forest used as elk summer range is now in various stages of secondary succession, resulting in a dynamic mix of ecotones and forage-producing areas (Skovlin et al. 1989). Within the Columbia River Basin, there is an apparent shortage of early and late successional stages and an abundance of mid-successional stages of forest ecosystems, due in part to fire suppression and logging (Hann et al. 1997). Since about 1935, the numbers of sheep, horses and cattle—competitors with elk for forage—have been reduced substantially on public lands (Wagner 1978). Thus, spring and summer range forage generally is assumed to be adequate for most populations of elk. However, quality of summer forage may limit

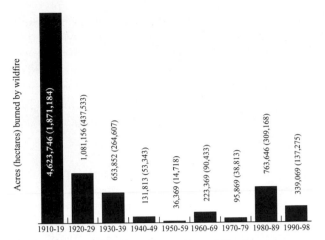

Figure 154. Acres (hectares) burned by wildfire from 1910 to 1989 in national forests of Region 1, U.S. Forest Service (Leege 1968). Formerly the Northern Region, this area includes eastern Washington, northern Idaho and western Montana. In the 1950s, less than 1% of the area burned during the 1910–1919 period was affected. This reduction in burned forest, due to improved fire technology and accessibility, reduced the diversity of elk habitat drastically.

productivity of elk under certain conditions, such as drought (see Chapter 5; Cook et al. 1998).

Winter habitats are critical for elk, but forage conditions on winter ranges may not have improved proportionately to conditions on summer ranges. One example of declining winter range is central Idaho's Lochsa River region. There, a pattern of successional events involving both fire and logging apparently has begun to limit the elk population. After thousands of acres were burned by wildfires in the early 1900s, excellent browse became available for elk, and populations expanded. However, few large-scale fires have occurred since and maturing shrub fields and forest encroachment have resulted in an apparent decline in habitat quality. Without fires to create or rejuvenate shrub fields, natural succession is reducing the forage base (Young and Robinette 1939, Leege 1968, Luman and Neitro 1980) and contributing to a declining elk population.

Pressures are increasing on the remaining elk winter range on both public and private lands. Human developments—such as reservoir impoundments, subdivisions, ac-

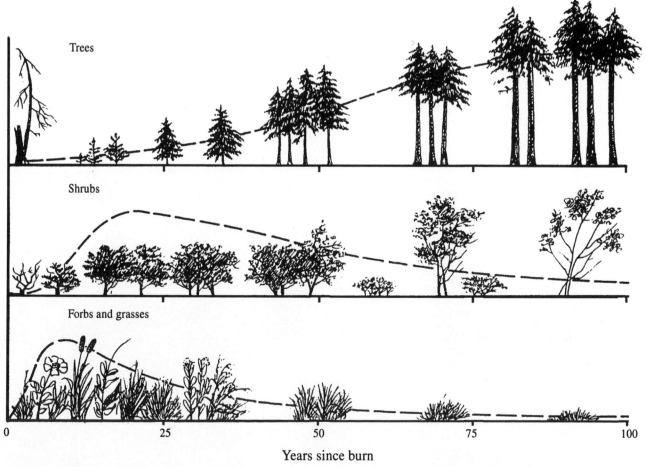

Figure 155. Natural postfire succession provides an immediate surge and subsequent rapid decline of forbs and grasses in the herbaceous layer, a somewhat slower but prolonged shift in the shrub layer, and a slow but steady return of the forest that eventually dominates the plant community (Lyon and Stickney 1966).

cess roads, highways and cultivation of land for agriculture and intensive livestock grazing—curtail elk herd expansion and make it difficult to maintain certain herds under natural conditions (see Chapter 17). Livestock enterprises on low elevation private land further diminish opportunities to balance the year-round elk forage supply. Also, much of the timber on these elk winter ranges is harvested, leaving depleted cover conditions.

The shrub fields that developed after the wildfires in the northern Rocky Mountains provided abundant forage for elk for decades. However, the passage of time and natural patterns of plant succession have resulted in large and decadent plants that provide little elk forage and screen sunlight from formerly productive understory plants, as in the old shrub field at left along Idaho's Lochsa River. *Photo courtesy of the Idaho Department of Fish and Game.*

Seasonal livestock grazing patterns on low elevation lands and development of travel corridors, as shown below along Interstate 80 near Pole Mountain, Wyoming, may diminish the supply of forage available to elk during critical periods of the year in some areas. *Photo by A. Lorin Ward.*

Greater demand for wood fiber has led to new harvest techniques that allow access to land previously impractical to log. In some areas of scattered forest, cover on elk summer range is becoming inadequate for optimal elk production.

Although logging generally has increased elk forage supplies, associated road construction has improved accessibility for recreationists, and these human impacts significantly reduce elk security. Today, there is easy access to what once were elk sanctuaries as the recreational vehicle industry provides rugged, all-terrain forms of mobility. Where regulations restrict human activity, elk soon change their distribution patterns (Irwin and Peek 1983) and increase their use of former sanctuaries (Rickard et al. 1977, Lyon 1983).

During the first half of this century, hunting regulations, reintroduction of elk, wildlife preserves, predator control, reductions in livestock grazing and wildland improvement measures permitted elk populations to increase. Since mid-century, enlightened forest management practices, more adaptive hunting regulations and further reduction in the number of sheep, cattle and horses grazing on public land accelerated the growth and expansion of elk populations.

By the late 1990s, elk numbers probably reached an all-time high, at the same time as their natural habitat was being reduced and altered (Bunnell 1997). Bull/cow and calf/cow ratios were departing from desirable levels. Natural predation was increasing. Bull escapement was down in many areas, and the older-age cohort of bulls was in short supply. Although elk densities increased, productivity decreased, leading to questions of density-dependent regulation based on too many animals for the available habitat.

Elk Habitat Use

Elk habitat use is conditioned by topography, weather, cover, the need to avoid predators, biting insects and hunters, and biological factors—such as forage quality and cover quantity. Habitat use also is a characteristic of its availability (Hobbs and Hanley 1990).

Topographic Influences

Topographic features, such as elevation, slope and aspect, affect local vegetation and, consequently, the patterns of elk use. Elevation is the most important feature because of its relationship to temperature and precipitation. For each increase in elevation of 328 feet (100 m), temperature declines about 0.9°F (0.5°C) (U.S. Army Corps of Engineers 1956). Although elevation does not affect elk behavior on a day-to-day basis, it is important in terms of habitat use because precipitation, snow accumulation and plant phenology are related directly to elevation.

Elk use certain terrain features consistently. In a study of slope preference on spring, summer and autumn ranges in the Wasatch Mountains of Utah, Julander and Jeffrey (1964) found that elk use gradually increased on slopes up to 30%, after which use dropped sharply. For ease of comparison, a slope of 100% represents 45 degrees above horizontal. Similarly, on a summer range in western Montana, Zahn (1974) observed higher elk use on moderate slopes—15% to 30%—than on slopes greater than 30% or less than 15%.

Marcum (1975) showed that, on summer range, moderately steep slopes—27% to 58%—received somewhat more feeding and bedding use by elk than did lesser slopes. Slopes of more than 58% received considerably less use. Leege et al. (1975), working on summer range in north-central Idaho, found slightly more elk use on slopes of 20% to 40% than on those of 0% to 20%. Very little use was made of slopes greater than 40%. In a subsequent study in the same geographic range, Hershey and Leege (1982) found use of steeper slopes progressed with advance of season, but that slopes of more than 60% were seldom used. Reynolds (1964a) found that, on pinyon/juniper summer range in New Mexico, elk used slopes up to 40% as readily as level topography.

Nelson and Burnell (1975) reported that elk use of slopes in central Washington varied considerably among years. Mackie (1970) also found that slopes used by elk in central

Although Rocky Mountain elk demonstrated some preference for slopes between 20% and 40%—and avoided slopes greater than 100% (45 degrees)—slopes of less than 80% had little effect on Roosevelt elk, shown here on an alder slope. *Photo by Jim D. Yoakum.*

Montana were quite variable among seasons and years. In general, he found that nearly 60% of all elk use was on slopes less than 18%; less than 1% of elk use occurred on slopes greater than 100% (45 degrees). About half of all elk use was in the 0% to 18% slope class during spring and autumn, whereas more than two-thirds of summer and winter use was in this class. Komberec (1976b) also found most winter and spring elk use in east-central Montana to occur on slopes less than 18%. Harper (1971) suggested that, until it exceeded 80%, steepness of slope had little effect on Roosevelt elk use in western Oregon.

Elk use of slopes and their position on slopes vary by season. Beall (1974) showed that, on western Montana winter range, elk generally used upper, middle and lower slopes, in that order. This also was reported for elk on summer range in Utah (Julander and Jeffrey 1964). Beall (1974) further noted that use occurred on north-facing as well as south-facing slopes during winter, but the latter were used twice as heavily as the former. Ridge tops were not especially used on this study area.

Topographic features, such as terrain, have been correlated with elk habitat preference (Edge and Marcum 1991). Julander and Jeffrey (1964) found that elk on Utah summer range preferred ridge tops to lower spur ridges. Dalke et al. (1965b) observed that elk preferred lower spur ridges on spring range in central Idaho. Marcum (1975) noted that, drainage bottoms on western Montana summer range were used frequently by elk, but no particular preference was shown for ridge tops. McLean (1972) also stated that stream bottoms often were used during summer months in Idaho's Lochsa River area, and ridge tops commonly were used for bedding in winter and late spring. Pedersen et al. (1980) reported that elk used riparian stream bottoms more so than all other montane forest communities of northeastern Oregon.

Elk tend to use upper slopes regardless of season. In winter, elk prefer upper south-facing slopes that, because of wind, sun angle (radiation) or shade pattern are the first to become bare of snow. Elk use of upper landscape positions in summer may be related to cooling wind patterns, visibility or cover type. Valley drainage bottoms also are used during summer, most likely because of their association with riparian habitat as a source of late-summer food and water.

Southerly aspects commonly are used by elk during winter. Many investigators have reported that elk used southern to southwestern exposures in winter and spring (Flook 1962, Kirsch 1963, Dalke et al. 1965b, Schallenberger 1965, Lovaas et al. 1966, Stevens 1966, McLean 1972, Bohne 1974, Simmons 1974, Ward et al. 1975, Komberec 1976b, Martinka 1976, Sweeney and Steinhoff 1976). McLean (1972) observed that elk forage about 500 to 700 feet (152–213 m)

higher on the southern aspect than on other aspects in the Lochsa River area in central Idaho during winter months. The reason most often cited for elk preference for this aspect is the greater availability of forage, due principally to lower snow depth.

South-facing aspects seldom are used in summer. Nelson and Burnell (1975) found high and significant elk avoidance of southerly aspects during summer in the mountains of central Washington. In Utah, Julander and Jeffrey (1964) noted that elk used northeastern exposures during summer, but shifted to southwesterly exposures later in the year. This seasonal pattern also was reported for elk in western, northwestern and eastern Montana (Bohne 1974, Simmons 1974, Knowles 1975, Komberec 1976b). Although aspect was not especially important to elk in central Washington, Bracken and Musser (1993) found that, during winter, elk preferred northeasterly exposures. They also found that elk frequently used level areas during all seasons.

Marcum (1975) found that use of aspect differed between sexes of elk on western Montana summer range. Although no significant difference existed between overall use of northwesterly and southeasterly exposures, bulls preferred southerly through easterly exposures, and cows made more use of southwesterly through northwesterly and northeasterly exposures. Mackie (1970) found that elk in central Montana concentrated on northerly exposures in summer and on westerly and northerly exposures in winter; moderate snow depths did not affect use during the latter period.

In winter, elk select areas high on south-facing slopes, where solar radiation and the effects of wind tend to eliminate snow cover before that of other areas. *Photo courtesy of the Wyoming Game and Fish Department.*

Forests on north-facing slopes generally provide the highest levels of cover and the coolest microhabitats for elk during summer and early autumn. In many areas, these circumstances are highly favored by elk during these seasons, although they often provide relatively little forage. *Photo courtesy of the Oregon Department of Fish and Wildlife.*

Spring use centered on southerly to easterly exposures. In a study of Roosevelt cow elk in the coastal range of Oregon, Witmer and deCalesta (1983) found that southerly aspects were used year-round.

Seasonal use of aspect is determined largely by forage availability, thermal factors and cover type. Forest cover on upper north-facing slopes provides the coolest habitat during summer and the most-succulent, high-quality forage into autumn months. Because of their relatively moist conditions, north-facing slopes usually furnish the highest levels of cover. Under continuous crown cover, however, these stands may not provide abundant forage.

Meteorological Influences

Meteorological or weather features play a significant role in elk habitat use. Apart from physiological and behavioral responses, selection of microsites for thermal protection is the only effective means elk have of adapting to the wide range of temperatures and weather conditions experienced during the year. Elk seek habitats that moderate weather conditions to minimize energy expenditure (Beall 1974).

During winter, snow depth restricts elk distribution and movement. During autumn and early winter, accumulation of snow on summer range determines duration of use by elk (Banfield 1949, Anderson 1954, Simmons 1974). Murie (1951) suggested that snow accumulation triggers elk migration (see Chapter 10).

Elk movements begin to be restricted by snow depths in excess of 18 inches (46 cm) (Beall 1974, Sweeney and Steinhoff 1976, Leege and Hickey 1977). Sweeney and Steinhoff (1976) found that in the San Juan Mountains of Colorado, snow depths in excess of 16 inches (41 cm) produced noticeable elk movement to areas with less snow. Accordingly, they considered 16 inches (41 cm) of snow to be a "response depth." Beall (1974), working in western Montana, observed that, when depths approached 18 inches (46 cm) elk began moving to lower areas. Energy expenditures for locomotion increase exponentially as snow depths increase. When snow depth equaled 23 inches (58 cm), energy expenditure for a 220-pound (100 kg) elk calf is about five times greater than that of travel on a snow-free surface (Parker et al. 1984).

From work in central Idaho, Leege and Hickey (1977) suggested that snow depths in excess of 18 to 24 inches (46–61 cm) caused elk to move into vegetative types with less snow. In Glacier National Park in Montana, elk made extensive use of fire-induced shrub fields where snow depths were less than about 24 inches (61 cm) (Martinka 1976). At greater depths, they made nearly exclusive use of nearby conifer stands.

Sweeney and Steinhoff (1976) found that snow depths above 28 inches (71 cm) usually prohibited use by elk—this was considered to be the critical snow depth. Their observations of snow depth and pawing behavior of elk suggested that snow depths of 16 to 28 inches (41–71 cm) caused elk to cease grazing herbaceous forage and turn to browsing shrubs. Gaffney (1941) also found a switch from grazing to browsing habits by elk on the Flathead River in Montana when depths exceeded about 36 inches (91 cm). He noted the added difficulty for elk to forage when snow was crusted or packed.

Temperature and wind velocity also influence elk movements and habitat use. In studying temperature effects on elk, Murie (1951) observed that extreme cold apparently does not affect elk distribution, but that they are quite susceptible to heat. Abrupt temperature change alone may initiate a temporary local elk response, and cold weather seldom initiates a general or lasting response unless it is extreme, prolonged or accompanied by snow (Anderson 1954). However, Gaffney (1941) observed that elk stayed largely in heavy timber when temperatures fell below 0°F (−18°C). Elk usually return to previous activities and locations after temperature changes that last only 2 or 3 days (Murie 1951).

Norberg and Trout (1957) suggested that, in central Idaho, extreme cold could drive elk to lower elevations. Skovlin (1982) observed that elk migrated from summer to winter range in a 1-week period throughout the Blue Mountains of northeastern Oregon and southeastern Washington in response to cold weather. This was in mid-November 1955, when temperatures dropped abruptly from daytime highs of 50°F (10°C) to highs of –40°F (–40°C). Snow depth was not a factor during this event.

Diurnal temperature variation seems to influence daily movements of elk. Harper (1971) found sightings of Roosevelt elk to be related inversely to average daily temperatures of 40 to 70°F (4–21°C). In a study of winter habitat selection in western Montana, Beall (1974) discovered that elk selected bedding sites that appeared to aid body temperature control, hence energy conservation. More than 80% of all bedding sites were associated with clumps of timber on upper slopes. During cold periods, day beds were on south-facing exposures and night beds were on north-facing exposures. During warm periods, the bedding locations were reversed. Also, as temperatures increased, day beds tended to be found under dense canopies, and night beds were in more open-canopied stands. Beall also found a correlation between elk use of winter habitat and thermal and solar radiation intensities, although not with ambient temperature.

Humidity and cloud cover affect elk activity. Harper (1971) showed sightings of Roosevelt elk to increase in direct proportion to humidity increases of 50% to 100%. Beall (1974) found that cloudy skies reduced Rocky Mountain elk activity levels on western Montana winter range.

Beall (1974) also found no apparent reaction by elk to barometric pressure changes during winter in western Montana. Harper (1971, 1962), working with Roosevelt elk in western Oregon and California, respectively, reported more elk activity when barometric pressure was low than during periods of normal pressure. When pressure was falling, elk showed signs of restlessness and anxiety—feeding and movement were intermittent. When pressure was rising or static, feeding and bedding activities were normal.

The influence of wind on elk use of habitat takes two forms. First, in terms of chill factor, effective temperature is proportional to wind speed. Second, wind has the effect of creating noise that reduces the ability of elk to hear or locate potentially alarming sounds. This may lead to their search for protective cover and to inactivity when in such cover. Harper (1971, 1985) suggested that high wind velocity had the effect of decreasing Roosevelt elk activity. Beall (1974) found that Rocky Mountain elk sought shelter

whenever wind speeds exceeded 30 miles (48 km) per hour or when wind speeds produced chill factors below –25°F (–32°C).

In a review of cover use by big game in the northwestern U.S., Peek et al. (1982b) concluded that the use of "thermal cover" by elk is only required during extreme winter conditions involving high winds. Cook et al. (1998) were unable to document any energetic benefits of forest cover for elk in a controlled study under natural conditions in the Blue Mountains of Oregon.

Biological Influences

The effect of elk on their habitat has been the center of controversy for decades (see Casebeer 1961, Cook et al. 1996, Hobbs 1996). A classic example is near Yellowstone National Park, where unnaturally high densities of elk have been maintained. The supposition of the U.S. National Park Service that high elk densities are natural was challenged by Kay (1990), who suggested that present population levels of herbivores have entirely eliminated the shrub component on some winter ranges.

Romme et al. (1995) concluded that the lack of aspen regeneration in Yellowstone could not be explained by any single factor, such as fire suppression or excessive elk numbers. Rather, regeneration of aspen involved a complex interaction among factors of low numbers of elk, relatively moist weather patterns, widespread fires and the presence of large mammalian predators. Houston (1982) suggested that elk were not adversely affecting grassland communities, but were impacting shrubs, aspen and willow. Other studies have demonstrated that, during periods of drought, elk adversely affect the shrub component (Singer et al. 1994) and grasslands (Frank and McNaughton 1992).

These findings have corroborated studies of secondary succession in intermixed forests and grasslands of the Blue Mountains of northeastern Oregon (Skovlin 1982, Irwin et al. 1994). The role elk play in determining secondary succession through selective grazing for shrubs has been well documented by exclosure studies on changes in plant composition (Edgerton 1972, 1987) and by research on diet selection by tame elk in the same study exclosures (Riggs et al. 1993, Irwin et al. 1994, Cook et al. 1996).

Thermal Cover

Thermal cover—a habitat feature usually related to vegetative structure—is used by elk to ameliorate the effects of weather (Lyon and Christensen 1992). Although they have an extensive sweat gland system, elk may respond to unusually warm weather by selecting cool or shaded habitat.

Some research has tried to quantify stand structure in

▼ D. Robert Franz   ▲ D. Robert Franz   ▼ Donald M. Jones

▲ Ken Archer ▼ Erwin Bauer ▼ Kim Hart

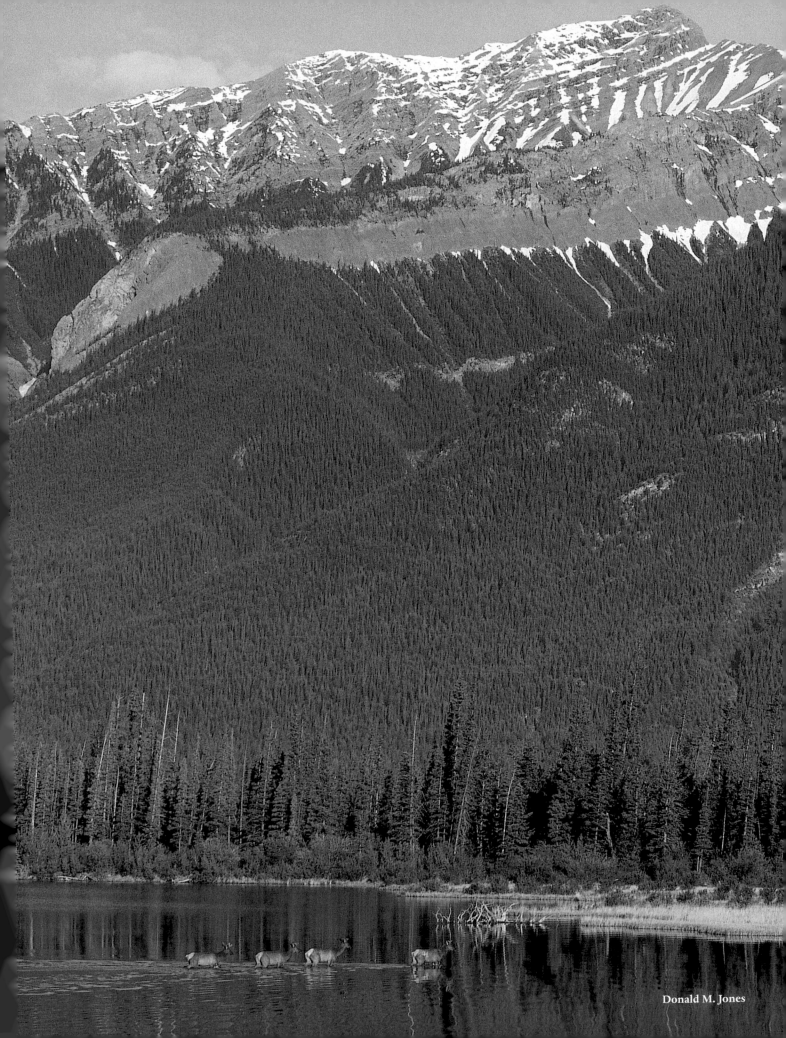

Donald M. Jones

▲ Milo Burcham   ▼ Donald M. Jones   ▲ Debi Ottinger

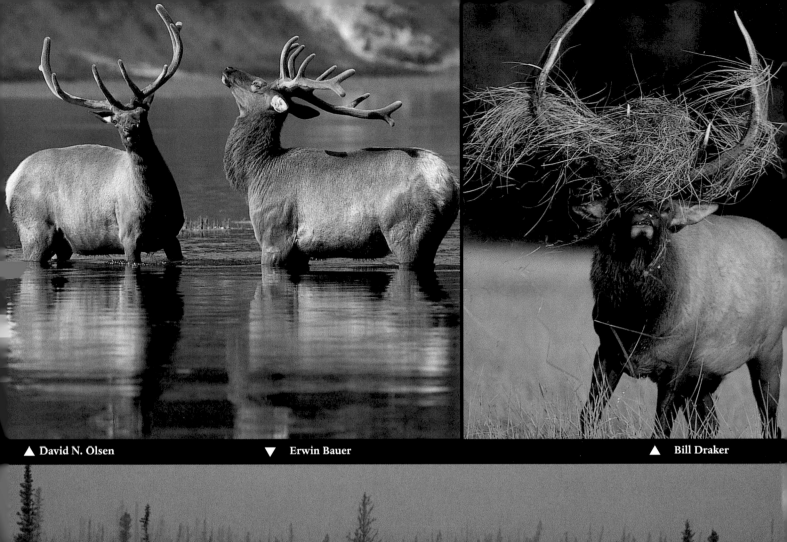

▲ David N. Olsen   ▼ Erwin Bauer   ▲ Bill Draker

▲ Debi Ottinger   ▼ Donald M. Jones   ▲ Kim Hart

▲ Brian Hay

▼ Dusan Smetana

▲ **Michael S. Quinton**　　　▼ **Debi Ottinger**　　　▲ **Milo Burcham**

▲ Don Kesler ▼ Michael H. Francis ▲ Kim Hart

▲ Erwin Bauer   ▼ Michael S. Quinton   ▲ Milo Burcham

Rodney Schlecht

terms of optimal thermal cover. Black et al. (1976) and Thomas et al. (1979) suggested that, to meet thermal cover needs, coniferous trees should be 40 feet (12.2 m) tall, with a 70% crown closure. These structural characteristics, however, have not been validated experimentally. Winn (1976) found that elk avoided stands with trees less than 30 feet (9.1 m) tall on summer range in Utah's Uinta Mountains.

Thermal cover provided by timber stands presents elk with a wide selection of daytime and nighttime temperatures (Beall 1974), which vary depending on the size and number of forest stand openings (Edgerton and McConnell 1976) and height and density of the canopy (Bergen 1971). Different stand conditions also provide varying degrees of thermal protection (Gohre and Lutzke 1956) and cover from snow and rainfall (Ovington 1954). Understory vegetation provides an additional windbreak (Ozoga and Gysel 1972), making a stand of timber more effective as thermal cover.

In summer, upland forests provide shade from direct solar radiation (Muller 1971), thereby lowering energy demands of the body (Moen 1973). Relatively cool soil and microclimatic conditions typical in the shade of large trees help elk conserve energy and dissipate heat (Mueggler 1971, Moen and Jacobsen 1974). However, older, well-developed forest stands with naturally pruned lower branches permit considerable wind movement under the canopy (Bergen 1971), which disturbs the layer of warm air surrounding the body surface of the elk, thereby lowering body temperature.

Elk thermal cover requirements probably are lowest on spring/autumn ranges. Edge et al. (1990) suggested that thermal cover, as described by Thomas et al. (1979), was not required for optimal production of elk on such ranges in northwestern Oregon.

In an attempt to test cover guidelines developed for the Blue Mountains in northeastern Oregon (Thomas et al. 1979, Thomas et al. 1986), Leckenby (1984) quantified environmental factors at daytime elk activity sites. Like Parker (1983) and Parker and Robbins (1984), Leckenby found that, when ambient temperature exceeded 55°F (13°C) elk actively searched for more effective cover. Beyer and Haufler (1994) highlighted one problem in validating the guidelines by illustrating that daytime habitat use by elk is quite different than 24-hour habitat use. Although many assumptions of cover were correlated with observations of elk distribution in Leckenby's 5-year study (1984), few actually were validated through cause–effect research.

In contrast, Irwin and Peek (1983) showed increased use of timbered stands during autumn. Furthermore, elk displayed no habitat selection patterns during winter. In addi-

Thermal cover is a term used to describe microhabitats that ameliorate effects of wind and temperature during climate extremes of heat or cold. It usually is described in terms of vegetation stands that disrupt or provide barriers to prevailing winds, reducing the effect of wind chill on the body, or providing shade during warm days. Although shade may be provided by a single tree (*left*), thermal cover is more generally indicated at the level of blocks of vegetation at least 6 feet (1.8 m) tall (*right*). *Left photo by P. E. Farnes; courtesy of the U.S. Soil Conservation Service. Right photo by Jim D. Yoakum.*

tion, Williams (1962) concluded that snow and temperature were the principal features influencing elk behavior during winter, but that these factors did not greatly influence selection of habitat cover types. Beall (1974) concluded that winter habitat selection was correlated more closely with thermal and solar radiation intensities than with ambient air temperatures.

When used in management plans, thermal cover has been reduced to guidelines that imply satisfactory quality (>70% canopy cover) or marginal quality (40% to 70% canopy cover) (Thomas et al. 1988a). Some scientists have questioned the applicability of such cover requirements as applied to forest plans because the requirements restrict timber management options (Riggs et al. 1993). After 4 years of summer and winter elk field trials, Cook et al. (1998) could find no evidence to support the hypothesis that thermal cover provided positive energetic benefits affecting elk body mass or condition when tested under various controlled environments.

Finally, regarding summer thermal conditions and Rocky Mountain elk habitat, recent studies in the shrub steppe of south-central Washington (McCorquodale 1991) and southeastern Idaho (Strohmeyer and Peek 1996) have demonstrated that Rocky Mountain elk populations can prosper with cover types not at all associated with a coniferous forest structure. Moreover, Merrill's (1991) study of Roosevelt elk on Mount St. Helen's does not support the hypothesis that elk require forest cover in summer to maintain body temperatures, at least in Pacific coastal climates. Because elk populations successfully establish in areas lacking classically defined thermal cover, cover requirements need further quantification.

Hiding or Escape Cover

Hiding cover is a feature of habitat that provides elk with security or a means of escape from the threat of predators or harassment (Lyon and Christensen 1992). Like thermal cover, hiding cover usually is some form of vegetation, but it also may be a variety of topographic features.

A qualitative measure of escape cover in forest, woodland or shrub communities is sight distance, that is, the distance at which 90% or more of an adult elk is hidden from view (Lyon and Christensen 1992). Sight distance typically is a function of tree stems per acre and understory forest vegetation. In younger second-growth stands with crown cover less than 75%, sight distance often is related to shielding effects of low-growing understory vegetation.

Several researchers have reported increased elk use of timber cover during autumn (Nichols 1957a, McLean 1972, Lonner 1976), coincidental to the rut, and especially during hunting season (Bohne 1974, Marcum 1975). Coop (1971)

Escape cover is measured by the distance at which 90% or more of an elk is hidden from view of an observer, as calculated from a "cover board" blocked from view at a particular distance. Like thermal cover, escape cover is most often a measurement of vegetation—usually a combination of tree stems per acre plus understory vegetation. *Photo by Jon Skovlin.*

also found that, in central Montana, elk use of open glades decreased in autumn. This was particularly notable with the onset of hunting season. Lonner (1976) found that, during autumn in southwestern Montana, elk used older timber stands that had dense understory regeneration—at least two structural layers—as opposed to stands with scarce regeneration. In northeastern Oregon, Leckenby (1984) noted that elk used denser stands in summer than in winter and when "influenced" by an observer.

Elk avoid disturbances created by active logging and road construction operations (Stelfox 1962a, Marcum 1975, Pedersen and Adams 1976, Ward 1976, Lyon 1979a). Findings in Montana suggested that topographic relief may provide sufficient cover to give elk security from such harassment (Montana State University 1975, Lyon 1979b). Thus, a line-of-sight barrier may be useful in planning landscape disturbance activities that interfere with high-use elk habitat.

Several investigators have proposed timber stand density guidelines for elk cover (Smith 1987, Thomas et al. 1988a). Thresholds have been proposed between stands dense enough to provide thermal and escape cover and stands

Tree overstory and canopy coverage are primary determinants of understory herbage productivity—and, therefore, elk forage. Pole-sapling forests with a high number of stems per acre and a high degree of canopy closure, as in this lodgepole pine stand, often equate to little or no elk food under the canopy. *Photo by Len Rue, Jr.*

open enough to allow the growth of forage (Black et al. 1976, Thomas et al. 1979).

Arnold (1950), Pace (1958) and McConnell and Smith (1971) showed that overstory stand density determines the understory herbage productivity of foraging areas within forested habitats. Arnold (1950) found that growth of tree regeneration, as well as natural crown closure of second-growth timber stands, rapidly depletes forage biomass. Skovlin et al. (1976) reported that natural crown closure of second-growth ponderosa pine and Douglas-fir in the Blue Mountains of Oregon proceeded at nearly 2% per year. This, in turn, depleted understory herbage production by about 7.2 pounds per acre (8.1 kg/ha) per year between 20 and 30 years after a heavy selection harvest.

Working in the ponderosa pine-type of the Southwest, Clary (1972) suggested the need for undisturbed thickets as bedding cover. On the basis of earlier work of Reynolds (1962a, 1966a), Clary (1972) proposed that pine stands of less than 40 square feet basal area per acre (9.2 m²/ha) do not provide adequate escape cover and that stands of more than 80 square feet (7.4 m²) do not provide sufficient understory forage to be of use as feeding areas. Clary, therefore, recommended retention of stands of 40 to 80 square feet per acre (9.2–18.4 m²/ha) with sufficiently unthinned thickets for bedding.

Crown density of forest overstory influences elk use of cover. Marcum (1975) related summer range feeding and bedding activities of elk in western Montana to four crown cover classes and showed that the most frequently used bedding sites occurred in high (75%–100%) cover. Feeding occurred most often in low (0%–25%) cover. Nelson and

Guidelines recommending a ratio of 40% hiding and thermal cover to 60% forage area, as typified in the Bridge Creek area of northeastern Oregon, have been widely accepted as optimal for elk. However, to be effective, such general guidelines also depend on the on-site configuration of open space and cover, providing elk with openings that are not too large, short line-of-sight distances in hiding and thermal cover areas, and cover distribution that affords secure travel routes. *Photo courtesy of the Oregon Department of Fish and Wildlife.*

Burnell (1975) found highest elk use in the heaviest (75%–100%) crown canopies on central Washington summer range. They suggested that thickets functioned as elk resting and escape areas, whereas more open canopies were used for feeding.

Guidelines proposed by Thomas et al. (1976) and Black et al. (1976) for Oregon's Blue Mountains Ponderosa pine/mixed conifer types suggest a 40:60 ratio of hiding and thermal cover to feeding areas. This suggestion was based on: (1) optimal opening size for maximum elk foraging use developed elsewhere (Reynolds 1962a, 1966a, Harper 1971); (2) minimum-sized security screen in terms of sight distance; and (3) optimal configuration of forage opening surrounded by patches of escape cover.

Black et al. (1976) suggested maintaining 20% hiding cover, 10% thermal cover and 10% either thermal or hiding cover. This prescription called for stands of hiding cover having four to eight sight distances of 200 feet (61 m), which yielded patches of 6.5 to 26 acres (2.6–10.5 ha). Optimal cover patches on summer and spring–autumn range were estimated at 30 to 60 acres (12.1–24.3 ha) of timber at least 40 feet (12.2 m) tall, with a 70% crown cover. These calculations were based on the entire land management impact area, not on forested portions of the impacted area only.

Whereas earlier guidelines on habitat quality emphasized thermal cover, it is currently defined more broadly to include security considerations (Peek et al. 1982b, Hillis et al. 1991, Christensen et al. 1993, Cook et al. 1998).

Habitat Diversity

Ecotones—areas where different types of vegetation are juxtaposed—and early successional communities are important components of elk habitat. Ecotones provide a higher diversity and greater quantity of forage plants used by elk than do either of the adjacent communities individually. Winn (1976) demonstrated that both frequency of plant species and herbage biomass at an edge was two times greater than 50 yards (46 m) into a meadow. Plant frequency and biomass continue to decline farther into open meadows, but at a reduced rate.

Levels of elk use decrease with increased distance from the interface of forest and nonforest communities (Reynolds, 1962a, 1962b, 1966a, Kirsch 1963, Coop 1971, Harper 1971, Marcum 1975, Winn 1976, Leckenby 1984) (Figure 156). Leckenby (1984) found that at least 80% of elk use in summer forage areas occurred within 300 yards (274 m) of this ecotone in the Blue Mountains of Oregon.

An important, related feature of elk habitat is the juxtaposition or interspersion of vegetative types, that is, the degree to which plant communities are intermixed within an

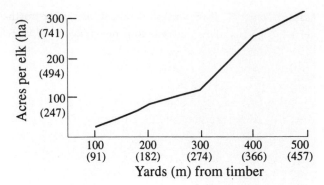

Figure 156. Comparison of elk use (density), expressed in acres (ha) per elk, with yards (m) from standing timber. Heavy use occurs near the forest edge and disproportionately lighter use is found as distance increases toward the center of openings (Harper 1971).

area (West 1993). Habitats with high interspersion provide large amounts of edge per unit area. When contiguous cover types are forest/grassland or forest/meadow communities, such areas are potentially high elk-use areas.

Reynolds (1964a) found that, on sampled summer ranges in New Mexico, Rocky Mountain elk use of an area was considerably higher where shrubs were intermixed with pinyon/juniper stands than where shrubs were absent. Lonner (1976) showed that two-layered forest stands were used more frequently by Rocky Mountain elk than were single-layered stands. Lonner (1977) also found a close, positive relationship between the density of regenerating trees and elk use across several forest habitats. Edgerton and McConnell (1976) noted that old-growth timber stands provide better thermal protection from winter weather than do adjacent partially cut stands.

Timber harvest and other habitat alterations may be used to improve elk habitats. In the short term, logging and attendant roading diminish elk use (Beall 1974, Lyon 1979a, Pedersen et al. 1979, Edge and Marcum 1985b), but in the longer term, judicious logging can be designed to enhance diversity of forage and cover. For example, in the upper slope types of the Blue Mountains in Oregon, Skovlin et al. (1989) showed small clearcuts of 5 to 20 acres (2–8 ha) were highly attractive to elk. They found that these clearcuts received more elk use than did partially cut or adjacent uncut stands, even with open roads and unlimited access. This increase, however, only lasted for about 5 years before elk use returned to prelogging levels. Restricting vehicle access may have extended the number of years of heavy elk use (Perry and Overly 1979).

Properly conducted selective logging can improve habitat for elk (Reynolds 1964a). Edge and Marcum (1985b) found that elk use of home ranges remained about the same if adequate cover was left. Other studies in the northern Rocky Mountains were less convincing (Lyon and Ward 1982). Lyon (1979b) warned that the disturbance associated with frequent logging reentry could cause elk to shift home ranges.

The effects of logging on habitat must be evaluated on a case-by-case basis because of the multitude of natural and human-caused variables entering into any logging activity. The consequence of logging on elk habitat and behavior, however, depends largely on the attendant roading and postlogging management.

Physiological Requirements

Water

Water in the form of dew, in succulent forage and that produced by metabolic processes helps to offset the amount of surface water needed by elk. Lactating cows probably have a seasonal dependency on surface water (Miller 1974, Marcum 1975, Thomas et al. 1976).

Elk use habitats near water when surface water is limited. Jeffrey (1963) suggested that, on summer range in Utah, Rocky Mountain elk preferred areas within 0.33 mile (0.53 km) of water. In the central Washington Colockum herd analysis areas, Bracken and Musser (1993) found that elk greatly preferred habitat within 0.12 mile (0.2 km) of water during spring, summer and autumn.

During one exceptionally dry year of a 3-year study also in central Washington, Nelson and Burnell (1975) found that Rocky Mountain elk remained within 0.5 mile (0.8 km) of water. Cattle also showed very high dependence on the same water sources in all 3 years. Similarly, Mackie (1970) found close elk dependency on water as measured by habitat use rates in relation to distance from permanent water in the Missouri Breaks of central Montana. Both Nelson and Burnell (1975) and Mackie (1970) showed that elk use of summer range declined markedly beyond 0.5 mile (0.8 km) from water. Mackie also found that elk needs for water varied considerably from season to season and year to year. All three studies—Jeffrey (1963), Mackie (1970) and Nelson and Burnell (1975)—showed that, even on livestock ranges, elk relied on permanent water sources during dry summers. Kirsch (1963), working on range used by both elk and sheep in central Montana, indicated that elk favored habitats closely associated with water.

In the aforementioned studies, elk use of habitats near water may have been even more pronounced if the range was not shared with livestock, inasmuch as many researchers have demonstrated that the presence of cattle discourages elk use of surrounding habitat (Reynolds 1962a, Jeffrey 1963, Blood 1966, Skovlin et al. 1968, 1983, Mackie 1970, Lonner 1974, Knowles 1975, Yorgason et al. 1975, Burbridge and Neff 1976, Neff 1980, Painter 1980, Wallace and Krausman 1987).

In arid environments, water development can change elk

Ecotones are areas where different types of vegetation are juxtaposed, such as this Tule elk habitat in Cache Creek, California. Ecotones feature a mixture of forest and openings with a high diversity of plant species and easy access to either cover or forage. Studies have shown that elk use of both forage and cover areas decreases as distance from ecotones increases. *Photo by Jim D. Yoakum.*

Elk seem to enjoy water, and their use of summer range has been shown to decline in inverse proportion to distances greater than 0.5 mile (0.8 km) from water. *Photo by George Wolstad; courtesy of the U.S. Forest Service.*

distribution patterns. Providing a new source of water from reservoirs coincided with elk colonization at the Idaho National Engineering Laboratory in arid southeastern Idaho (Strohmeyer and Peek 1996). Although water was not the sole motivation for summer movements of elk, Strohmeyer and Peek (1996:85) suggested that, "obviously, surface water was important." Similarly, McCorquodale et al. (1986) suggested that, in the sagebrush steppe of south-central Washington at the Arid Lands Ecology Reserve, the distribution of natural springs was an important determinant for habitat use patterns for lactating female elk, but bull elk habitat use was less constrained by surface water availability.

In an Arizona study, DelGiudice and Rodiek (1984) could not demonstrate elk dependence on water, but they found a high preference in elk for habitat within 0.25 mile (0.41 km) of permanent water during early spring. Less concentrated use during summer was attributed to greater seasonal rainfall, presence of cattle and passage of the elk calv-

ing period, which reduced water demands by lactating cows.

Marcum (1975), working on summer Rocky Mountain elk range in western Montana, found that more than 80% of all elk use in July was within 0.25 mile (0.41 km) of a permanent water source. On a nearby mountain summer range, a distance-to-free-water relationship was detected in one of two seasons (Lyon 1973). In northwestern Montana, Simmons (1974) also suggested that late-summer water needs restricted elk distribution. A study of elk summer range use in northeastern Oregon showed that a high proportion of elk use was within riparian habitat (Pedersen and Adams 1976, Pedersen et al. 1979). However, the extent to which water played a role in riparian habitat use by elk is unknown. None of the three Montana studies or the Oregon study was conducted in areas with traditional cattle grazing.

Salt

Salt use by elk, as with many other ungulate species, is primarily a habit-formed luxury. There is no doubt that Rocky Mountain elk are attracted to salt; that they thrive without it seems equally certain. Opportunities for use of salting in management and influencing the distribution of Rocky Mountain elk have been studied at length (Rush 1932a, Young and Robinette 1939, Stockstad et al. 1953, Dalke et al. 1965a, Guest 1971). Little has been reported on salt use by Roosevelt elk. Working with the Olympic Peninsula Roosevelt elk herd in Washington, Schwartz and Mitchell (1945) concluded that coastal elk may have little desire for or need of salt.

Use of salt was determined to be ineffective as a means of altering the migratory habits of elk (Dalke et al. 1965a). It was found, however, that as a means of inducing localized forage use, salt is perhaps one of few good attractants. Salt also has been suggested as a means for redistributing heavy elk grazing in the vicinity of historically used licks (Williams 1960).

In a study using coarse granulated salt and dyes to stain elk feces on an isolated summer range plateau in the Blue Mountains of Oregon, the rate of salt use by a resident herd of 50 to 70 elk was calculated (Skovlin 1982). During June, it was in excess of 50 pounds (22.7 kg) per station. The herd used an average of 11 pounds (5.0 kg) of granulated dye-mixed salt per station during July, 2 pounds (0.9 kg) in August, 1 pound (0.44 kg) in September and 6 pounds (2.7 kg) in October. The increased October consumption resulted from autumn rains in September, which affected a regrowth of grass forage commonly occurring in grassland openings in this region. That the rate of salt intake by elk is

Mineral salts of many kinds (including sodium) are eagerly sought by elk, which often seek out and consume mineralized soils or salt-bearing waters. As a result, many natural salt licks have been used by elk for centuries, and distribution of sodium is one of the few effective means of attracting elk to a specific site—to the extent that nearly all states have laws against using salt to attract elk during hunting seasons. *Photo by Lawrence Clark.*

related to seasonal forage succulence and phenology agrees with the findings of elk studies elsewhere (Young and Robinette 1939, Dalke et al. 1965a) and for ruminant use of salt in general (Chapline and Talbot 1926).

Special Behavioral Requirements

Calving Areas

Some studies infer that cow elk select specific types of habitats in which to calve (Altmann 1952, 1956a). Other investigators indicate no apparent search for such particular cover types (Stevens 1966, Marcum 1975, Sweeney and Steinhoff 1976). Although there seems to be wide variability of what constitutes calving habitat, certain habitats appear to be used more frequently than others.

Roosevelt elk often calve in dense timber or heavy brush thickets (Graf 1943, 1955, Batchelor 1965). At the southern terminus of their range, however, Roosevelt elk apparently are not so selective. Harper et al. (1967) found no special calving habitats in northern California studies. Most calving was observed in the ecotone between open prairie or meadow and scattered conifers with mixed hardwood shrubs. In Oregon, Roosevelt elk used benches, stream bottoms and areas of gentle terrain for calving (Harper 1971). Troyer (1960) found that Roosevelt elk on Afognak Island, Alaska, used treeless areas for calving.

Although calving usually occurs on spring/autumn transitional range, it also may occur on upper reaches of winter range (McLean 1972) or on lower summer range (Roberts 1974). In a comprehensive review, Sweeney (1975) suggested that elevation of calving grounds may vary inversely with latitude.

In general, calving habitat depends largely on the availability of succulent and nutritious vegetation during the month-long calving season (mid-May through mid-June). This, in turn, is related directly to the receding snowline and plant phenology. Where sagebrush is available and intermixed with conifer types, there seems to be selection by elk for the ecotone between types (Johnson 1951, Anderson 1954, Picton 1960a, Boyd 1970, Coop 1971, Reichelt 1973). Although open sage parks or meadows frequently are used for calving, Johnson (1951) and Reichelt (1973) reported the distance from the forest edge to be especially important, and that newborn calves often were found a short distance into the forest community.

On other ranges, open areas somewhat removed from forest cover were selected for calving (Picton 1960a, Dalke et al. 1965b, Phillips 1966, Roberts 1974). On several calving grounds west of the Continental Divide in central Idaho, Rocky Mountain elk calved in the ecotone between sagebrush and open timber (Phillips 1966, 1974, Davis 1970, Roberts 1974). It also was suggested that cows give birth to their calves in the timber and probably do not move them to the sagebrush-covered openings until several days after birth.

Where sagebrush does not occur, interspersion of small openings in otherwise moderately dense timber appears to be important (Marcum 1975, Sweeney 1975). Rocky Mountain elk in the Sawtooth Mountains of Idaho calved in areas with a timber overstory ranging from 20% to 60% cover and averaging 37% (Phillips 1974). Few other studies have identified overstory cover on traditional calving grounds. Roberts (1974) described hiding places for Rocky Mountain elk calves in Idaho that had sagebrush cover of about 20% to 40%. They usually were in slight depressions on long slopes. These microhabitat characteristics for calving grounds were similar to those reported for Rocky Mountain elk on the Gallatin Range of Montana (Johnson 1951). Phillips (1974) found newborn Rocky Mountain elk calves on slopes with grades averaging about 35%.

Roosevelt elk calving areas have been reported on gentler slopes (Harper 1971). Also, gentle slopes reportedly have been used by Rocky Mountain elk in Montana (Reichelt 1973, Marcum 1975), Wyoming (Johnson 1951, Ward 1973) and Oklahoma (Waldrip and Shaw 1979). Slope probably is not a critical factor, based on the variability reported, but elk seem to prefer gentle slopes for calving.

Several studies have suggested that slash, downed logs or

Cow elk become solitary just before calving, often selecting small secluded openings in the proximity of forest ecotones—the interface between forest canopy and larger openings. *Photo courtesy of the Arizona Game and Fish Department.*

other woody material is important to elk as cover in calving areas (Young and Robinette 1939, Phillips 1966, Winn 1976). In terms of preference or dependence, such requirements often have not been quantified. Waldrip and Shaw (1979), however, found calf bed sites in the Witchita Mountains of Oklahoma that were consistently associated with boulders, woody vegetation and overhead tree cover.

Aspect also is commonly referenced in studies assessing calving habitat. As with slope, preference for aspect probably is more a function of what is available at calving time than as an element specifically selected by a pregnant cow. Some investigators have found that southerly exposures are used most frequently during calving (Altmann 1952, Reichelt 1973, Sweeney and Steinhoff 1976, Waldrip and Shaw 1979), but others have found that cow elk use northwesterly exposures (Phillips 1974, Roberts 1974).

There is little evidence of annually repeated use of calving areas by specific cows beyond the normal happenstance of a herd being at about the same locality during migration in successive years. There are exceptions, however, that show habitual use of calving areas by certain elk cows (Zahn 1974).

It appears that Rocky Mountain elk are somewhat more selective in calving habitat than are Roosevelt elk, although there are few in-depth studies of Roosevelt elk calving requirements. Cow elk probably select hiding cover for the calf and nutritious foraging areas reasonably close to water to meet their lactation demands.

Wallows

Wallows are important for identifying high-use habitat of mature bull elk. Wallows are used primarily by mature rutting bulls and may have some territorial behavioral purposes (Seton 1927, Young and Robinette 1939, Murie 1951, Altmann 1956a), such as for advertisement or dominance display. Bull activities at wallows apparently are the same for Roosevelt elk (Graf 1943, Murie 1951, Harper et al. 1967) and Rocky Mountain elk (Young and Robinette 1939, Murie 1951).

Wallows usually are associated with antler rubbing on small nearby trees. These "rub trees" are important territorial markers. Bushy saplings or shrubs may show results of repeated rubbing. Torn-up cutbanks and signs of ground pawing show evidence of simulated combat. Abandonment of wallows often signals the disappearance of mature bulls from the general area. With the reduction in number of mature branch-antlered bulls in heavily hunted areas, old wallows may become grassed over on many ranges, indicating declining use.

Travel Lanes, Corridors and Trails

Little study has been made of the importance of travel lanes to the movement and distribution of elk. Winn (1976), however, suggested that forested travel lanes adjacent to open meadows were especially important for efficient use of intermingled meadow complexes by Rocky Mountain elk. Research on Rocky Mountain elk in the Blue Mountains of northeastern Oregon revealed that a grassland complex with corridors of timber was an important habitat type (Pedersen and Adams 1976). The timber permitted elk to cross from one canyon to another under protection of continuous forest cover. In addition to their use as travel lanes, these landscape features serve as feeding areas. Methods have been outlined to protect elk habitat through selective logging in relation to travel lanes (Lyon 1975, Black et al. 1976, Leege and Hickey 1977, Pedersen et al. 1979).

Trail crossings between drainages are important elk travel routes. These often are located in low saddles and immediately beneath ridge tops. In timbered areas, elk movements often keep old trails and stock routes open.

Evaluating Elk Habitats

Many studies referenced in this chapter provided site-specific information describing habitats used by elk; other studies attempted to evaluate the consequences of a particular management activity on elk distribution. Skovlin (1982) provided a detailed approach for evaluating elk habitat on a site-specific basis. However, it is difficult to apply site-specific information to other similar areas or to evaluate cumulative effects of various land management practices, such as roading, timber harvest or habitat improvement.

Consequently, in the 1970s, biologists began synthesizing the findings of many studies to develop models that describe the relationships between elk and their habitats, to rate numerically the quality of elk habitats and to develop guidelines for managing elk habitats.

Models were based on studies to test specific hypotheses or to correlate elk distributions or population levels with attributes of the environment (Johnson 1980). The output of these models was a habitat suitability index or habitat effectiveness index. Habitat suitability is defined as the potential of an area to support a species and is represented by an index ranging from 0 (completely unsuitable) to 1 (optimal) (U.S. Department of the Interior 1981). Habitat effectiveness was defined as the percentage of available habitat that is usable by elk during the nonhunting season (Lyon and Christensen 1992).

Habitat Effectiveness Index Models

A multitude of habitat effectiveness models have been developed since the late 1970s for a variety of habitat types and geographic locations in the West. Habitat effectiveness models are based on the assessment of physical and biological characteristics of a study area, with the assumption that habitat rating is proportional in some way to the carrying capacity of the landscape (K. H. Berry 1986, Raedeke and Lehmkuhl 1986). Models developed since 1980 range in complexity from simple (single) function to multivariate models that predict elk distributions.

Working in western Montana, Lyon (1983) developed a habitat effectiveness model for elk based on road density. Also in Montana, Lonner (1984) presented a model predicting elk distributions during five time periods for Montana, based on 33 independent variables that were either dynamic and site specific (e.g., cattle use), static and site specific (e.g., percentage slope), or static and related to surrounding terrain (e.g., amount of wet meadows within a circular plot).

A habitat effectiveness index was developed for Rocky Mountain elk summer range in eastern Oregon (Thomas et al. 1979), which served as a prototype for Roosevelt elk summer range models (Wisdom et al. 1986) and Rocky Mountain elk winter range in the Blue Mountains of Oregon and Washington (Thomas et al. 1988a). Brunt and Ray (1986) and Brunt (1990) developed habitat effectiveness models for Roosevelt elk on Vancouver Island, British Columbia. Bracken and Musser (1993) developed a summer habitat effectiveness model in Washington with three variables: distance to cover/forage edge; slope; and distance to water. These models use similar approaches to calculate a habitat effectiveness index score. Coefficients ranging from

0 to 1 that rated habitat quality were assigned to variables describing study areas. Variables and their coefficients differed among models for rating habitats for elk.

The habitat effectiveness model for Blue Mountains winter range (Thomas et al. 1988a) has four components: size and spacing of cover and forage areas; roads open to traffic per unit of area; cover quality; and forage quantity and quality. Variables of the model and coefficients for the variables were based on research describing elk ecology. Leckenby (1984) found that elk used edges between cover and foraging areas. Preferred habitats were those that were near foraging areas (<40% canopy cover) and cover (>40% canopy cover).

Effects of density of open roads on elk distribution were based on pellet group data collected by Perry and Overly (1979) and summarized by Thomas et al. (1979) and Lyon (1983). As open road density (miles of open roads per square mile of habitat) increased, the probability of elk using the area declined. Coefficients of cover quality were based on two categories—more than 70% canopy closure, and 40% to 70% canopy closure. The forage variable was based on the quantity and quality of bunchgrasses on winter range, and the values were summarized by Leckenby et al. (1986).

Numeric scores (from 0.05 to 1.0) were assigned to classes for each variable. Rating for each variable was the sum of products of the scores and percentages of the analysis unit with each class. Ratings for each variable then were multiplied, and a geometric mean was calculated. The geometric mean provided an overall rating of the analysis of each unit within each class. Ratings for each variable then were multiplied and a geometric mean was calculated. The geometric mean provided an overall rating of the habitat. An example to calculate a habitat effectiveness (HE) index score for elk winter range in the Blue Mountains of Oregon (from Thomas et al. 1988a) is as follows: the HE variable score, $HE_{SRFC} = 0.62$ is defined as HE index with all four model components $(HE_S + HE_R + HE_F + HE_C)^{1/N} = (0.61 \times 0.42 \times 0.71 \times 0.80)^{1/4}$, where $HE_{S(pacing)} = 0.61$ is derived from the size and spacing of cover and forage areas; $HE_{R(oads)} = 0.42$ is derived from the density of open roads; $HE_{F(orage)} = 0.71$ is derived from the quality and quantity of forage available to elk; $HE_{C(over)} = 0.80$ is derived from the cover quality; and $1/N$ is the nth root of the product. Habitat effectiveness models were not designed to predict population levels, but instead, to describe the capability of the habitat, on a relative score, to meet the habitat needs of an elk population. The higher the score, the better the habitat. Analysis units were subwatersheds of 5,000 acres (2,023 ha) or less.

Although variables of habitat effectiveness models were based on many studies, the models themselves have not been validated because neither the coefficients assigned to classes for each variable nor the interactions of the variables have been fully tested. Instead, the values were based on expert opinion, after review of supporting studies (Thomas et al. 1988a, Holthausen et al. 1994). Brunt (1991) attempted to validate models developed in British Columbia for summer, mild winters, and severe winters. He found that elk were selecting for areas modeled to have higher habitat suitability. Laymon and Barrett (1986) stressed that habitat suitability models not validated (untested) should not be used to evaluate habitats.

Wolff (1995) and Hobbs and Hanley (1990) suggested that a weakness of habitat effectiveness models is that measures of use versus availability, which provide the basis for many of the variables, do not necessarily measure carrying capacity of the habitat. Wolff (1995) emphasized the importance of understanding behavioral as well as ecological factors that determine a species' distribution. Hobbs and Hanley (1990) stressed the need to understand the mechanisms of resource acquisition and subsequent population responses to availability. Wisdom (1998), working at the Starkey Experimental Forest and Range Station in northeastern Oregon (Johnson et al. 1991), found that the rate of motorized traffic on forest roads accounted for significant variation in distribution of elk. It was not the road, but traffic on the road, that elicited the response by elk.

When first implemented, habitat effectiveness models were used to evaluate cumulative effects of forest management practices on elk habitat, but the models were cumbersome because of time needed to complete the required mapping. The time required for analysis was shortened only after land management agencies began producing digitized maps of roads, and techniques were developed to determine size and spacing of cover through Landsat imagery (Leckenby et al. 1985). Geographic Information System (GIS) capabilities made the analysis easier to complete and allowed for analysis of a variety of alternatives.

It was not until Ager and Hitchcock (1992) and Hitchcock and Ager (1992) developed computer programs specific to habitat effectiveness models that the process of calculating habitat effectiveness index scores became relatively quick, allowing foresters and wildlife biologists to work together to evaluate the effects of timber harvest and road-closure options on elk habitat relative to desired management objectives.

Simulation Models for Elk in Forest and Rangeland Management

Simulation models differ from habitat effectiveness models in that the levels of complexity can be much greater in the former, and, if properly formulated, a simulation model can provide insight into complex ecological processes. Raedeke and Lehmkuhl (1986) linked a model of Roosevelt elk and black-tailed deer carrying capacity in the Olympic Peninsula to a model of forest succession. They were able to predict the effects of various silvicultural processes on elk and deer carrying capacity of forested lands. They stated that the weakness of their model was its inability to adapt to changes in road densities, patch size and other landscape features.

Forage allocation models based on linear programming (Van Dyne et al. 1984) or deterministic models (Cooperrider and Bailey 1984) described animal stocking rates, but outputs from both models were difficult to interpret and did not incorporate the spatial distribution of animals or vegetation into the results. Consequently, the usefulness of the simulation models was limited because the models were not readily adaptable to change, and interpretation of results was difficult.

Landscape-level Planning, Monitoring and Analysis of Elk Habitat

The need to conduct planning and monitoring of natural resources on a landscape scale has led to the development of powerful computer software (e.g., ARC/INFO [Environmental Research Systems, Inc. 1990], FRAGSTATS [McGarigal and Marks 1995] and UTOOLS [Ager and McGaughey 1997]). Specific software has been developed that allows watershed-level planning and monitoring for assessment of elk habitat (Ager and McGaughey 1997). This software provides a flexible framework for the analyses of spatial and temporal relationships of vegetative structure and composition, roads, topography, water, soils and other variables that can describe or affect elk habitat. What was state-of-the-art for modeling elk habitats only a few years ago (Cooperrider and Bailey 1984, Raedeke and Lehmkuhl 1986, Brunt 1990), now has been augmented by three-dimensional images and analyses showing how and where changes are occurring on the landscape.

Only when tested simulation models incorporate spatial and temporal distribution of vegetation and animal behavior will managers be able to evaluate habitat treatments on distribution of elk and carrying capacity of the landscape. Turner et al. (1993) developed an individual-based spatial model for elk and bison in Yellowstone National Park. Their model linked vegetation, landscape features and winter weather conditions to foraging dynamics and winter survival of elk.

Two models currently being developed in Oregon represent new approaches that biologists can use in evaluating carrying capacity and elk survival on a landscape scale. An elk vulnerability model uses GIS to evaluate the effects of topographic diversity, cover, access and hunter numbers on elk harvest rates and subsequent bull-to-cow ratios (Vales et al. 1991, Vales 1996). This model allows land managers to evaluate how changes in cover, road density or hunter numbers may influence elk harvest rates.

A forage allocation model using GIS to link landscape characteristics (slope, aspect, distances from water, roads, cover/forage edge and plant community) with estimates of seasonal quality and quantity of forage has been developed that addresses limitations of earlier allocation models. The forage allocation model predicts distributions of elk, mule deer and cattle, and estimates forage utilization on the landscape (Johnson et al. 1996). Both the elk vulnerability and forage allocation models need to be validated.

Grazing Lands Applications—a highly deterministic model—evaluates animal performance and vegetative response (Ranching Systems Group 1994), and represents an alternative to simulation modeling. This program was developed for the livestock industry, but it can be applied to elk habitats and performance. This program requires detailed measures of vegetative composition and production (Skovlin 1982).

Although research and management continue to focus on how changes in habitat affect elk population distribution and performance, there is an increased interest in understanding the effects of elk populations on the structure and composition of their habitat (Irwin et al. 1994) and on the ability of habitats to maintain elk populations (Coughenour and Singer 1996). Irwin et al. (1994) presented empirical evidence that persistent grazing by large ungulates—primarily cattle, elk, mule deer and domestic sheep—has changed ecosystem processes, resulting in moderate to severe decreases in composition and abundance of shrubs in forest communities in northeastern Oregon. Productivity of elk herds has declined in many of the same game management units, concurrent with increases in elk populations. Irwin et al. (1994) identify adaptive management strategies that could clarify the complex relationships between herbivores, vegetation, productivity and ecosystem processes.

(*Left*) Grazing pressure by elk and other ungulates (including livestock such as cattle and domestic sheep) has been shown to have a major influence on both the species and amount of vegetation present. It appears that grazing is a major driving force in patterns of plant succession on lands occupied by grazing animals. (*Right*) An elk exclosure in Washington State. Elimination of weeds by elk outside the exclosure produced better growth of plants outside. *Left photo courtesy of the Oregon Department of Fish and Wildlife. Right photo courtesy of the U.S. Forest Service.*

As understanding of elk ecology has increased, along with the development of high-speed personal computers and associated computer programs; the complexity of models has increased, evolving from habitat effectiveness index models to simulation models integrating ecological processes. Ultimately, the potential exists to develop models that allow biologists to consider the cumulative effects of manipulating elk habitats over spatial and temporal scales, and to devise management options. For a review of modeling wildlife habitat relationships, see Verner et al. (1986). Advances in modeling processes and developments in computer technology allow rapid analyses of landscapes and display of results in three-dimensional graphics (J. K. Berry 1986, Ager and McGaughey 1997).

The full potential of landscape-level habitat analysis and monitoring for elk has not been realized. Habitat effectiveness models, such as those published by Wisdom et al. (1986), Thomas et al. (1988a) and Brunt (1990) represent the habitat capability of various landscapes to support elk populations. Other habitat effectiveness models weigh the variables differently or include different variables, such as density of cattle in calculating a habitat effectiveness score (Lonner 1984). Consequently, the final form of the habitat effectiveness model has not been determined. Although elk vulnerability models (Vales et al. 1991, Unsworth et al. 1993) predict population-level responses of harvest to the habitat conditions, Vales' (1996) model begins to incorporate variables found in habitat effectiveness models into elk vulnerability models.

Future landscape-scale monitoring of elk habitats will incorporate models that predict elk distribution, population size and productivity. These models will use harvest theory evolving from elk vulnerability research to estimate harvest rates based on current landscape condition and population size. Models will be interactive so that range conservationists, wildlife biologists and foresters can assess impacts of various resource management decisions affecting elk habitats and herd productivity.

Before these models are operational, however, they will have to be validated, and the underlying assumptions of the models will need to be stated clearly so that users will know the limitations of the models. Forethought on implementing these models and monitoring the responses of elk populations will be required with the ongoing process of developing, testing and improving the models over many years. Data that accurately describe vegetation will need to be gathered systematically and relatively frequently. Remote sensing will provide broad categories of forage classes and must be validated by intensive on-the-ground vegetational measurements. Accurate population estimates also will be required. Agencies responsible for estimating population composition and size will need to follow rigorous sampling protocols to ensure that samples are adequate to develop population models.

Development of Elk Vulnerability Models

Beginning in the early 1900s, combinations of protective regulations, law enforcement, translocations and changes in habitat allowed for increased elk populations throughout western North America. In some areas, this eventually led to conflicts with livestock and habitat capabilities (Picton 1991). To balance big game populations with habitats and competing land uses, some states and provinces initiated liberal hunting seasons and bag limits. Timber harvests and their associated roads were considered beneficial because canopy openings created diversity and enhanced elk habitat. Logging roads provided better access for hunters who, in turn, helped wildlife managers achieve elk harvest goals (Lyon et al. 1985, Picton 1991).

By the early 1970s, a new set of problems was emerging. The elk populations in some areas were static or declining, whereas the number of hunters using an expanding system of forest roads was increasing (Potter 1982). To counter this decline, most states shifted to bull-only hunting seasons or otherwise moved to restrict cow harvest. The rationale was that protecting the reproductive segment of the population would allow populations to continue to expand. Concurrently, Wyoming was promoting antlerless elk harvest to control populations and attempting to improve the proportion of bulls in the population and harvest.

Declines in bull populations and overall elk populations were suspected to be the result of habitat changes and improved hunter access. This led to several major investigations to determine the effects of logging and associated activities on elk (e.g., Pedersen et al. 1980, Leege 1984). To enhance elk survival, Hillis et al. (1991) suggested retaining blocks of at least 250 acres (101 ha) of hiding cover at least 0.5 mile (0.8 km) from open roads over 30% of the evaluation area. Lyon and Canfield (1991) showed that elk moved to large blocks of contiguous habitat with low open road densities during the hunting season in Montana. Also, Hurley and Sargeant (1991) showed that hunting pressure often displaced elk from areas near roads to more dense and homogeneous cover. In Montana, Marcum and Edge (1991) found that bulls occupied habitats farther from roads and disturbance than did cows. Similarly, Lyon (1983) showed that potential elk use of habitats declined with increasing road density. Others demonstrated that elk actively avoid areas near open roads (e.g., Hershey and Leege 1976, Perry and Overly 1979). The results of these studies formed the basis for management guidelines to maintain suitable summer habitat for elk populations and, at the same time, enhance hunting opportunity.

Because most early research was based on pellet group surveys and marked cow elk, the results largely reflected cow elk ecology and habitat use. Information pertaining specifically to bull elk ecology often was lacking. Observed differences usually were ignored, either because managers assumed that bull elk used their habitat in a manner similar to cows or that limited management resources should be focused on the reproductive segment of the herd. Although direct observations suggested differential distribution between bulls and cows, they did not address differences in how bulls used their habitat. Data began to accumulate questioning the assumption that bull elk ecology was the same as cow elk ecology (Pedersen et al. 1980).

In Montana, Marcum's (1975) telemetry-based study provided substantial documentation of cow versus bull habitat use. He found that bulls used comparatively southerly aspects, higher elevations, steeper slopes and forest stands with denser canopies, and resided farther from ecotones than did cows from June through November. Marcum also found that bulls moved farther from clearcuts and disturbances associated with roads than did cows.

Bull Elk Mortality

By the mid-1980s, many elk populations had expanded and extended their range considerably. A new problem emerged—adult sex ratios were skewed heavily toward females. Either the habitat management guidelines did not fit bull elk ecology or a decade of bulls-only hunting had taken its toll. This was cause for concern among wildlife managers and served as impetus for research focusing specifically on bull elk, particularly in Montana and Idaho. Hurley and Sargeant (1991), Leptich and Zager (1991), and Unsworth and Kuck (1991) reported that such traditional mortality factors as winter loss and predation were not as significant as formerly believed. Idaho researchers (Leptich and Zager 1991, Unsworth and Kuck 1991, Unsworth et al. 1993) found that at least 90% of the mortality among bulls in northern and north-central Idaho was related to hunting during September and October (Figure 157). Moreover, they discovered that mortality rates for yearling bulls essentially were equal to those for adult bulls. Thus, to manage bull elk was to manage hunting season mortality.

Research shifted to assessing elk vulnerability by measuring variables that influenced mortality of bulls during the hunting season. Lyon and Christensen (1992) defined elk vulnerability as a measure of the susceptibility to being

Studies of elk survival indicate that bulls select different kinds of habitats than do cow elk—habitats characterized by more southerly aspects, steeper slopes, denser forest canopies and farther from ecotones. *Photo by Dan Walters.*

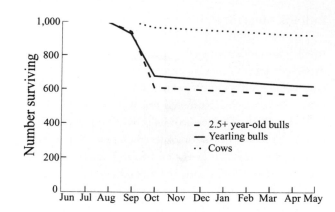

Figure 157. Survival curves for adult cow, yearling bull and adult bull elk in northcentral Idaho (J. W. Unsworth unpublished data).

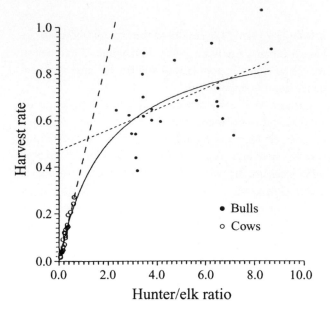

Figure 158. A relationship between elk harvest rate and the hunter-to-elk ratio. Dash and dot lines show separate relationships for cows and bulls (Vales et al. 1991).

killed during the hunting season. Thomas (1991) identified several factors related to elk vulnerability (density of open roads, number and density of hunters, number of hunter days, availability of security cover, habitat fragmentation, no antler or age harvest restrictions on buls, hunting season structure and length, improved hunting technology, and rugged versus gentle terrain), many of which are interrelated. For example, the number of hunters and hunter days are likely to increase with increasing open road density and, conversely, security cover often is reduced.

Some biologists have tried to address elk vulnerability indirectly by using elk habitat effectiveness guidelines. Some of the variables, such as roads, which are important in habitat effectiveness models, also are important in elk vulnerability models. However, some of the data necessary to evaluate elk habitat effectiveness and elk vulnerability are very different. Habitat effectiveness focuses on elk distribution, whereas elk vulnerability represents a population-level response based on the fate of elk during the hunting season and on the habitat and hunter-related factors associated with that outcome. These two concepts should not be confused.

Vales et al. (1991), working in Oregon, developed a functional relationship between harvest rate and sex-specific hunter-to-elk ratios (Figure 158). They suggested that the slope of the line formed by this equation could be interpreted as a vulnerability coefficient. Harvest rate (and vulnerability) increased with increasing hunter-to-elk ratios up to a point, beyond which the number of hunters became overwhelming and the harvest rate flattened out. The equation and shape of the curve would vary with cover characteristics, hunter/elk encounter rates, hunter effectiveness and other factors. Thus, it would be necessary to develop a series of curves representing different combinations of many factors, such as road density, access, cover, terrain, season structure and method of take. An important man-

agement implication of this effort is that vigorous management of hunters is necessary to manage elk populations effectively (Vales et al. 1991, Christensen et al. 1993).

Lyon and Burcham (1995) approached elk vulnerability from a somewhat different perspective in Montana. Using global positioning system (GPS) units, they closely monitored hunter activity and movement in relation to topography, roads, cover types and elk density. They anticipate developing a series of models to predict the influence of hunter strategy and density on elk vulnerability.

Weber (1996), also working in Montana, used landscape elements to differentiate the sites at which elk survived the hunting season from those where elk were harvested and random sites. Surviving elk occupied areas that were not close to roads, had low road density and contained large patches of forest that provided hiding cover. Weber also pointed out that hunting pressure can overwhelm the most secure landscapes.

Biologists currently are investigating yearling and mature bull mortality in relation to vulnerability factors in west-central Colorado (Freddy 1997). Researchers in Idaho evaluated elk vulnerability or bull mortality by monitoring the fate of radio-collared bulls during the hunting season. Corresponding habitat and hunter-related variables also were measured. Preliminary analyses demonstrated a relationship (Figure 159) between bull elk survival and the density of open and closed roads (Kuck and Unsworth 1987, Leptich and Zager 1994). Although not surprising, this response represented the first quantitative relationship of

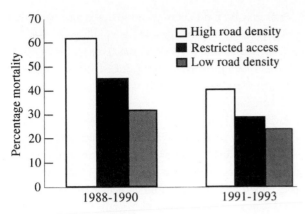

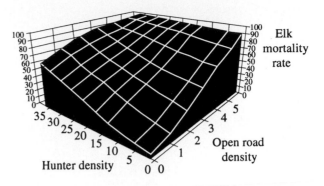

Figure 159. The relationship between open roads and bull elk mortality rates in northern Idaho (Leptich and Zager 1994). High road density is about 4.5 miles per square mile (2.8 km/km²); low road density is about 1 mile per square mile (0.6 km/km²), and restricted access is about 2.6 miles per square mile (1.6 km/km²). The 1988 to 1990 and 1991 to 1993 bars represent different season structures.

Figure 160. Bull elk mortality in relation to hunter density and open road density, derived from research in north-central Idaho (Unsworth et al. 1993).

road density to vulnerability. This work also represented the first documented link between elk population parameters and habitat variables.

Analysis Concepts

When habitat and hunter data were subjected to multivariate analyses, logistic regression models were developed wherein variables of habitat and hunter density were used to predict bull elk hunting season mortality. Unsworth et al. (1993) found that open road density, hunter density and an index of topographic roughness (circular standard deviation of aspect [Zar 1984]) were significant predictors of elk mortality in north-central Idaho. Hunting season mortality of elk increased with increasing open road density and hunter density and decreasing topographic roughness. The logistic regression relationship is: $m = e^u / (1 + e^u)$, where m = mortality, e = the exponential function and u = 4.784 + 1.050 × open road density (km/km²) – 0.035 × index of topographic roughness + –0.169 × hunter density (hunter days/km²). This bull elk mortality relationship to hunter density and open road density is illustrated in Figure 160.

In heavily canopied cedar/hemlock forests of northern Idaho, predictors of bull elk mortality include interior hiding cover, an index of hunting pressure and hunting season structure. Leptich et al. (1995) proposed a model where u = –0.760 × the plan type – 1.547 × the percentage interior hiding cover ≥67% hiding cover value + 0.177 × the hunting pressure index. The hunting pressure index equaled hunter density × a road density index (ERD) where ERD = total road density –0.5 × closed road density. "Plan" was a categorical variable differentiating two season structures.

The interior hiding cover variable attempts to address habitat fragmentation. Elk vulnerability decreases as interior hiding cover increases. Interior hiding cover was based on the average hiding cover (Lyon 1987, Lyon and Christensen 1992) for each vegetative type that was at least 98 feet (30 m) from the edge of that vegetation type.

The index to hunting pressure combines hunter density and a road density index. The logic behind this is that hunting pressure is a function of hunter number and distribution. An extensive road network distributes hunters throughout an area, leaving few refuges for elk. With fewer roads, hunter distribution and movement are restricted, and elk are more secure. Closing a road does not restore an area to an unroaded condition, because the closed road continues to offer easy access for nonmotorized hunters.

Access management plays a key role in reducing elk vulnerability. A measure of open road density was by far the most important variable in the model proposed by Unsworth et al. (1993). At some point, however, hunter density may overwhelm the efforts of access management, and resource managers will be forced to reduce hunter density or otherwise improve elk escapement opportunities (Unsworth and Kuck 1991, Vales et al. 1991).

For most managers, hunting season mortality rates alone are not very useful. But they are an important input for the widely used Leslie Matrix-based population models or simpler "home-grown" spreadsheets used to predict population size and composition. Unfortunately, managers have incomplete data and virtually no control over the biological parameters, such as minimum breeding age and age-specific fecundity, that drive these population models. But, as recent research has demonstrated, managers can measure and control hunting season mortality through access management, regulation of hunter density and habitat management. Recognizing that at least 90% of the annual mortality for antlered elk occurs during the hunting season

Management of hunter access—especially access by vehicle, whether by road or off-road—plays a significant role in elk vulnerability to hunters during the hunting season. Hunter efficiency is related to both the number of hunters and the speed with which hunters can travel in elk habitat. Increasing sophistication of off-road vehicles increases the speed with which hunters can access distant elk habitat, often forcing elk managers to reduce hunting opportunity to reduce elk vulnerability. *Photo by Stu Murrell; courtesy of the Idaho Department of Fish and Game.*

is a powerful management tool. The utility of this tool depends largely on cooperation between managers of elk populations and managers of elk habitat.

Elk mortality models used in conjunction with population simulation models offer a tool to predict the results of such management actions as strictly regulated access. For example, applying the Unsworth et al. (1993) model developed in central Idaho, an open road density of 2 miles per square mile (1.3 km/km²), a hunter density of 0.8 hunter days per square mile (0.3/km²) and a topographic index of 111.3225 will result in a bull mortality rate of about 27%. By reducing road density to 1 mile per square mile (0.6 km/km²), bull mortality declines to about 16%. Therefore, if the objective is to improve bull-to-cow ratios or bull age structure, managers should strive to reduce bull mortality by reducing access or hunter density (Unsworth et al. 1993). The mortality models offer quantitative guidelines that will help agencies responsible for habitat and those responsible for population management achieve their goals.

Models, when based on realistic situations, provide important insight into the effects that proposed management

activities may have on elk populations. A key factor is that elk vulnerability models provide a quantitative link between elk habitat and elk populations. Hence, the utility of elk vulnerability models is related directly to the degree of commitment and cooperation between land managers and population managers.

As with most models, caution must be exercised to apply the model only within the range of the data on which it was based. Because elk occur in a variety of ecosystems, it will be necessary to develop comparable models for each region. These efforts should be coordinated, at least in a general way, so the data sets and models can be compared and more generalized theories can be developed. It is easy to envision a "family" of models addressing the relationship between elk mortality and habitat factors across the distributional range of elk subspecies. Researchers currently are exploring other approaches to developing elk vulnerability models, such as using large-scale, coarse-grained habitat evaluation in conjunction with good population data to link population parameters with habitat requirements. (Course- or fine-grained habitat evaluations refer to the resolution of the habitat variables.)

Elk vulnerability research represents a significant first step in understanding of bull elk ecology and management. It offers managers a useful set of tools with which to manage elk and their habitat.

Evaluating Elk Habitats of the Future

Elk are highly adaptable; they flourish in habitats as diverse as remote high mountainous wilderness, managed industrial forests, cold deserts and moist coastal forests. They constantly search for high-quality forage to meet nutritional demands of reproduction and survival. Consequently, habitats selected vary seasonally. When the routine habits of elk are disrupted by activities of predators or humans, they seek out habitat that provides security. This security may be found in vegetative cover, terrain features or escape from the point of actual or perceived threat.

Wildlife biologists and land managers struggled in early studies to develop methods and techniques to answer such questions as: "What do elk eat?" "Where do elk go?" "What is their life history?" Findings of early studies allowed elk management to move forward to identify critical habitats and ranges.

More recently, biologists have addressed such questions as: "How do elk respond to human activities associated with roading, logging, cattle grazing, hunting and recreation?" "How do we evaluate habitats?" "What are the limiting habitat factors for specific herds?" From these questions, models have been developed for evaluating timber sales and the effects of road density on elk habitat and estimating elk habitat quality.

Biologists now are attempting to answer such questions as: "How do we manage elk populations to maintain productive herds?" "What is the carrying capacity of this habitat analysis unit?" "What are the impacts of elk on their habitat?" "How does habitat management affect how we manage elk populations through hunting?" "How do we manage elk populations and their habitats as part of ecosystems?" We have only begun to answer those questions (Wisdom and Thomas 1996).

The future is promising. Useful tools are in place and being further developed to enhance landscape-scale habitat and population evaluations. Studies are being conducted to examine cause and effect mechanisms underlying habitat use. It is up to biologists and researchers to rethink their concept of the scale at which elk should be managed.

There is need to synthesize, test and validate new and existing habitat effectiveness index models and other appropriate data into a "family of models" that can be applied at broad geographic scales. There also is a need to integrate management objectives (numbers) for elk with those of other components of the ecosystem at a landscape level.

Elk vulnerability research is in its infancy, but it has tremendous potential to link population parameters with harvest rates, hunting methods, and landscape and habitat factors such as road density, cover and terrain features. Ultimately, habitat effectiveness index and elk vulnerability models will be merged to address sustainable population management. One can envision spatially explicit population models that are based on predator/prey theory and linked to GIS, describing elk habitats that allow elk and land managers to estimate harvest rates based on landscape condition, population size and hunting regulations.

Models need to be interactive so that wildlife biologists, range conservationists and foresters can assess the impacts of various management decisions on elk habitats and population dynamics. Because these models are spatially explicit, they also may provide an understanding of how elk impact their habitat, and further define the carrying capacity of the analysis unit.

Remote sensing and GIS are important tools whose applications remain to be standardized. Accurate population estimates continue to be required. Agencies responsible for estimating population composition and size will need to follow rigorous sampling protocol to ensure that samples are adequate to develop accurate population models.

Research and accurate interpretation will need to be transferred quickly into management prescriptions for immediate application. Administrators, researchers and managers must work closely to develop monitoring and feedback systems for rapid adjustment and fine tuning of management scenarios. The keys to success are planning, forethought and commitment within an adaptive management program.

In future elk habitat evaluations, ecosystem management will require broader interpretation than in past management activities (see Chapter 11). Rather than planning for individual species within landscapes or watersheds, planning will need to be carried out on a regional basis. Emphasis will be placed on community patterns, processes and function to assure proper ecosystem health and stability (Quigley et al. 1996). Habitat research and management, however, will continue to focus on sustaining yields of featured species, such as elk, but more concern will be given to how elk fit into multispecies management schemes and what their function is for improving habitat conditions for all wildlife.

13

L. JACK LYON AND
ALAN G. CHRISTENSEN

Elk and Land Management

The North American elk once was the most widely distributed member of the deer family on this continent. Elk were found from the Atlantic to the Pacific coasts and from Mexico to Alaska. By the end of the last century, they had been virtually extirpated, except in Yellowstone National Park. Today, elk distribution is limited by the fact that elk are too large to coexist successfully with intense agriculture and settlement (see Chapter 2). Lands available to elk do not generally support suburban housing or high value cash crops. However, the story of elk recovery, in numbers and range occupied since the early 1900s, truly is one of the significant success stories in wildlife management. Past success has bred new challenges in elk management, and it is certain that elk will continue to be a prominent consideration in land management within the species range in the West.

The last time a chapter on elk and land management was written, the authors assumed that commodity production uses of nonagricultural land, such as intense timber management and grazing, were in direct competition with elk management (Lyon and Ward 1982). Until sometime in the 1980s, budgets and management staffs of public land management agencies reflected the direct commercial values of timber and grazing on public lands, while comparatively small professional staffs and budgets were allocated to wildlife functions. In the late 1980s and early 1990s, public recognition and increased demand for management of all resources on public lands led to significant budget and manpower increases for recreation and wildlife. Where multiple uses are considered, elk have become increasingly important.

Concurrent with the increased elk management interests of public agencies, some private and tribal management programs were being developed. Managers of the Vermejo Ranch in New Mexico, the Deseret Ranch in Utah and the White Mountain Apache and Mescalero Apache reservations all began to manage elk as significant economic enterprises. This transition continues to develop and, as a result, there has emerged a better balance of resource concerns on both public lands and large private holdings.

Today, federally managed public lands provide millions of acres of suitable elk habitat. National forest system lands produce "nearly 80 percent of all elk killed by hunting in the United States each year" (Barton and Fosburgh 1986:102). On these and other public lands, and on many adjacent private lands, hunters pursue elk in autumn. Year around, millions of people observe wildlife, and elk are a primary attraction on public lands in the West. Elk represent major social and economic factors in many of the areas where they are found. Some small communities and small businesses survive on the economic benefits of elk. Elk license sales often represent the largest single revenue source for western state wildlife agencies.

In addition to high social and economic values, elk fulfill a number of ecological roles. As a large, mobile herbivore, elk influence vegetation either directly or indirectly. Their social behavior and survival strategies affect other ungulates that may occupy the same habitats. As a large prey species, elk contribute to the support of predators capable of killing them, including mountain lions, bears, wolves

Because of the active (hunting) and passive (viewing, photography) recreation that elk afford, and because of the favorable impacts those recreational activities have on local businesses, elk are important economic and social factors throughout nearly all of the species' range. In most situations, people should not be allowed to approach elk as close as in this photograph (the photographer used a telephoto lens and was at a safe distance; the people were not at a safe distance). *Photo by Milo Burcham.*

An elk killed by wolves in Yellowstone becomes an important source of food for bald eagles, ravens, magpies and a host of other scavengers, as well as the wolves. *Photo by Milo Burcham.*

and perhaps coyotes. Elk carrion, from winter mortality, combined with hunting mortality and viscera left in the field, represent a significant source of food for a host of avian and mammalian predators and scavengers, some of which are considered threatened or endangered.

Clearly, the management of elk habitat has ramifications that reach far beyond the public perception of elk as a magnificent and desirable wildlife species. The recovery of elk from near extinction in the late 1880s to present numbers approaching 1 million (Bunnell 1997) has occurred largely on public lands. Since the mid-1970s, accompanied by increased realization of the adaptability of elk, private lands have played an increasing role in supporting elk and elk habitat. In the future, public and private lands both will play key roles in providing elk habitat. There will be challenges and opportunities unique to each ownership but linked by a common public interest in and ownership of this magnificent species.

Elk Management in North America

The increasingly positive public perception of elk has been accompanied by changes in management philosophy almost as great as the changes in elk populations. Following the near disappearance of elk in the late 1800s, management efforts concentrated on reestablishing herds in suitable wildland areas and protecting those animals as their nucleus populations increased in density and expanded to occupy additional habitat. For much of the past 100 years, direct control of hunters and hunting seasons has been the primary technique of elk management in North America. Management into the 1950s reflected the view of elk as a limited resource highly dependent on large blocks of unroaded, wild country.

During the 1960s and 1970s, as timber harvests increased on public lands, managers began to envision producing elk in conjunction with other activities. The initial assumption proposed that livestock grazing likely was incompatible with increases in elk numbers; whereas, timber harvest, by improving hunter access and creating new foraging areas, likely was beneficial. Also, winter range was considered to be *the* significant habitat variable in elk management, and summer range was not perceived as a limiting factor.

When too much access proved to be a problem, much of the research and most of the management during that period assumed the need for mitigation of conflicts between mutually exclusive uses. It was also found that, in some elk populations, hunting mortality accounted for over 95% of all mortality (Leptich and Zager 1991), thus questioning whether winter range was the most significant variable in elk management.

By the mid-1980s, the assumption that elk were depen-

dent on large blocks of wildland was weakened in the growing recognition of elk as relatively tolerant habitat generalists. Managers increasingly recognized the importance of habitats managed at a landscape scale and, most importantly, had identified the direct connection between hunter access and mortality of bulls. As a result, management of elk is no longer deemed possible without cooperation between those who control hunters and those who control land. In most of the West, this cooperation has produced large numbers of elk.

However, the ability to produce elk may not be a completely positive accomplishment. Most elk herds range over a mosaic of public and private lands on which management objectives are not oriented to elk production alone. Because of the size, adaptability and mobility of elk, there is substantial potential for conflicts between elk use of certain habitats and other uses. The latter decades of the 20th century produced an array of political and ecological problems never envisioned when the century began. For elk, as well as humans, the world has become smaller and more crowded each year. The human population of the United States has grown relatively slowly during the past 50 years, but a large part of recent movement and growth has been into the Rocky Mountain region—the main stronghold of elk on this continent. This movement has been accompanied by development of human habitations where there previously was open space, and by increased human mobility facili-

For many years, elk were viewed as a limited resource, dependent on large blocks of unroaded habitat. This concept has changed slowly as wildlife managers have come to recognize the tolerance and adaptability of this species. *Photo by Milo Burcham.*

Residential development in areas that were once open space has constricted elk habitat. In some places, this has created severe conflicts, as habituated elk move through suburban landscapes. *Photo by N.A. Lyon.*

tated by increased access and new technologies that have effectively reduced the vastness of a West formerly considered secure.

Another unanticipated result of burgeoning elk populations has been the new problem of population control. Elk in close proximity to people produce hunting conditions that either are aesthetically unfulfilling for hunters or seen by the public as "unfair" to elk. Hunter habitat—land where elk and hunters can both freely move across the landscape—may be increasingly in short supply in the future. Merely having more elk, without land that is compatible

with the maintenance of elk habitat and appropriate population levels through regulated recreational hunting, is not desirable.

The 1990s also produced changes in management philosophy, which included a new awareness and appreciation for all wildlife values, especially on public lands. The overall view of public land management was broadened to a concept including total ecosystem management rather than management for any specific single purpose. Even the single-purpose holdings of many large timber companies currently are managed within this broader view.

All of these changes were important for elk and for land management. The elk now is a featured, or key, species in most of the national forest plans in the West. Management of elk habitat, which once was a constraint on commodity uses of public land, has become a constraint on other uses in some areas. Elk now are recognized as a far more adaptable species to changing habitats than was imagined only a few years ago. And finally, it is known that increasing elk populations, however desirable they may appear to be, create some increasingly complex problems in land management.

Land Management Problems in Elk Habitat

Historically, any approach to management problems involving elk has been a direct and positive action based on one or two relatively simple assumptions. Early studies and

Elk have become a featured species in the majority of national forest plans in the West. They are also an important consideration in the management of many large, private forestland holdings. *Photo by Len Clifford.*

solutions to elk management problems often were perceived as cause and effect related. Researchers identified a problem and then sought a straightforward, pragmatic solution. Although land management problems still exist with respect to elk, the complexities of those problems have been deciphered and treated in many new ways. Whether the changes are a function of new knowledge, new technology or both is not the point. As increasing numbers of humans use a fixed resource of space and assets, the relationships that formerly existed are compressed and complicated. Elk and other wildlife get caught up in these changes.

Boiled down to fundamentals, the major factors that define elk and land management consider (1) how vegetation that defines elk habitat is managed, (2) how human access and use patterns are managed, (3) how livestock are managed on ranges shared with elk, and (4) how people and their use of the land and elk are influenced and managed. These elements have long been the subject of studies and research, largely on public lands, but they are so fundamental that what has been learned on public land can be transferred to private and tribal lands.

In attempting to describe the development of the current level of understanding, it was helpful to examine changes in management perspectives that have developed since publication of *Elk of North America: Ecology and Management* (Thomas and Toweill 1982). The evolution of solutions for elk management problems is particularly interesting because it has been influenced almost as much by widespread changes in philosophy as by research accomplishments. In no way does that statement disparage the pertinent research done before the early 1980s, but it is important to point out that the philosophy and approach to gathering and using information in land management has changed vastly since the time of Murie's (1951) classic work, and a large part of the change has been brought about by concern for elk and other wildlife on public lands.

Vegetation Management and Elk Habitat

The increasing complexity of vegetation management solutions using landscape analysis, prescribed fire, new silvicultural methods and new harvesting equipment has paralleled the evolution in elk management since the 1980s. Just as land managers can no longer conduct site-specific actions that ignore interactions with adjacent lands, it has become necessary to recognize that the management of any elk herd is not solely the responsibility of the wildlife agency, which normally controls only the hunting season. In their movement from land of one ownership to another, elk achieve the peculiar status of a common property resource that can be mismanaged by many and managed for the

common good only by "mutual coercion, mutually agreed upon by the majority of the people affected" (Hardin 1968:1,247).

In North America, there are few successful free-ranging elk herds not associated with forested lands (Allen 1972). Because of this association, the practice of forestry probably has a greater potential for either negative or positive influence on elk habitat than does any other land management activity. On the roughly 25 million acres (10.1 million ha) of the U.S. Department of Agriculture Forest Service Northern Region, for example, about 5 million acres (2 million ha) have been altered by logging since the 1960s (U.S. Department of Agriculture 1994). Because these acres virtually define elk range, understanding of the ecological relationships involved in management of forests as elk habitat has developed through a provocative and difficult process (Lyon et al. 1985).

Before 1970, the primary theory of habitat management for elk was a simple extension of the historical responses of elk herds to large northern Rocky Mountain forest fires. Between 1910 and 1920, more than 4.5 million acres (1.82 million ha) in northern Idaho and western Montana were burned; within 30 years, the recovering seral vegetation produced spectacular increases in big game populations. In the Pacific Northwest, a somewhat comparable situation prevailed where vast areas of Douglas-fir old growth were logged. The postlogging seral vegetation produced a midcentury expansion of Roosevelt elk populations and the first elk hunting seasons in nearly a century in both Oregon and Washington.

The presumption that timber harvest could provide a logical alternative to fire-created seral habitats was widely accepted during the 1960s (Pengelly 1963b, Lyon 1966, Mueggler 1967), but successful improvement of productive elk ranges after timber harvest was much harder to document than some of the obviously adverse effects.

Silvicultural Practices

In part, differences between silvicultural theory and practice were inherent in the orientation of forest managers. By definition, silviculture is "the science and art of cultivating forest crops, based on a knowledge of silvics" (Society of American Foresters 1983:240–241). Until very recently, the only recognized forest crops were wood products and, in practice, silvicultural techniques that influenced elk habitat were logging methods. It has yet to be demonstrated that any one silvicultural system is more desirable than another for management of elk habitat. No matter what system is used, the practice of forestry has two general effects on elk: (1) during the logging operation, there is direct and substantial disturbance of animals and their habitat and (2) in the long term, there is modification of habitat structure that can either improve or downgrade conditions for elk.

Initially, at least, disturbance caused by logging was considered a passing event, and tree removal was considered largely beneficial because forage supplies were increased. However, by 1970, it had become apparent that something was not quite consistent in the logic that logging could be substituted for fire as a tool of habitat manipulation. Among other things, a fair number of biologists had begun to notice that habitat modification through logging did not result in any apparent increase of elk populations (Allen 1972, Lyon et al. 1985). To the contrary, it was reported "that forage in openings created by timber harvest is not actually used by elk; that the disturbance of the logging operation drives elk out of the logged area; and that post-logging access increases vulnerability to hunting and leads to harassment" (Lyon 1971b:448). In some places, the increased access accompanying logging made it easier to attain hunting season harvest goals, but even that became a mixed blessing when too many elk were killed too quickly, or too easily, to provide the desired objectives for population management or recreation opportunity.

Elk and Logging Studies

During the 1970s, repeated protests initiated by wildlife managers became the driving force for an array of new studies about elk response to logging. For a few years, the perceived effects of logging on elk became an environmental cause, with lots of conflicting claims and plenty of opportunity to point the finger of blame (Lonner and Cada 1982, Leckenby et al. 1991). As a direct result, major research projects were initiated in Montana, Oregon, Wyoming, Alberta and elsewhere in the West, with the objective of obtaining more and better information about elk habitat requirements and animal responses to environmental modification by logging. These studies have provided a spectacular increase in knowledge about elk behavior outside the hunting season. Virtually every state and several provinces in which elk are found have conducted one or more studies either to collect basic information or to verify the results of studies conducted elsewhere. In some respects, no matter where they are found, elk respond to disturbance and demonstrate underlying characteristics of habitat selection with uncanny similarity. In other respects, the detected differences only serve to emphasize the incompleteness of understanding in elk ecology.

In the following summary of results from studies of logging on elk populations, there is heavy reliance on the Montana Cooperative Elk/Logging Study (Lyon et al. 1985) because it was active longer (15 years) than most other studies and embraced most of the recommendations included in other studies. Major research efforts also were underway in Oregon and Washington during this time period. Most of the research conducted in those studies was framed around a few primary questions concerning the immediate disturbance, cover loss, road construction and slash disposal.

Disturbance by Logging

Much of the forestland occupied by elk in western North America was relatively unaccessed until about 1950. Thus, when commercial logging occurred, the initial entry involved the use of heavy equipment, large trucks and gasoline-powered chain saws. Elk reaction to the noise and activity of logging varied widely depending on season, cover, topography, kinds of equipment and type and duration of human activity. On both summer and winter ranges, the recorded reaction was movement away from logging activity to areas without such disturbance. Measured displacements have ranged up to 5 miles (8 km), with the greatest movement detected when heavy equipment operating on or near a ridgeline was visible over a large area (Lyon 1979b). Most often, the distance elk moved appeared to be the minimum necessary to avoid contact with people and equipment. In timber sale areas where traffic was limited to logging equipment, there was little elk response beyond 1 mile (1.6 km) (Lonner 1985). Edge (1982) reported displacement to 0.67 mile (1.1 km) and Lieb (1981) found average displacement of 0.9 mile (1.45 km).

Under most circumstances, displacement of elk by human activities during logging is temporary. Some animals may return during night and weekends, when logging activity ceases (Beall 1974, Edge 1982), and a few even become habituated to logging activity during daylight hours. Lonner (1985) reported displacement was greater in autumn than in July, and Edge and Marcum (1985b) described a buffer zone of 1,640 to 3,281 feet (500–1,000 m) between the disturbance and areas of high elk use.

The most common postlogging sequence involves the return of at least some displaced elk within a few days to weeks after the disturbance has ended. Marcum (1975) suggested that animals that move greater distances to find security are less likely to return immediately. Lyon (1979b) showed that disturbance in the same drainage over several consecutive years will imprint an avoidance behavior lasting beyond the completion of the timber sale, although Edge et al. (1985) reported that home ranges of individual animals were not permanently altered as long as adequate cover remained.

Although there has been no indication that elk will *not* eventually return to logged areas, the movement away from active logging operations is a management concern, because even temporary displacement represents a reduction in usable habitat and an increase in stress for individual animals (Ward and Cupal 1979). Evaluating a different kind of disturbance, Kuck et al. (1985) found that simulated mining operations resulted in abandonment of traditional calf-rearing areas. In some cases, movement away from a disturbance may create additional management problems if the displaced elk move onto private lands.

Opening Size

Logging, especially clear-cutting, creates openings in the forest. If forage is gained and cover is lost, one of the essential questions in the management of elk habitat is how large such openings should be. Thomas et al. (1979) showed that openings larger than 7.0 acres (2.75 ha) will receive less than 50% utilization by deer and elk. However, depending on elk management objectives, the size of an opening probably is not the overriding concern. Elk use of high elevation parks, meadows and other large natural openings has been reported wherever such openings occur—in Yellowstone National Park (Murie 1951), Teton Wilderness (Anderson 1958), Flat Tops Primitive Area in Colorado (Boyd 1970) and the Medicine Bow Range and the Bighorn Mountains in Wyoming (Ward 1973a, Ward et al. 1975). McCorquodale (1991) reported habitat studies of elk on the Arid Lands Ecology Reserve in eastern Washington, where the only cover is sagebrush. And Merrill et al. (1987) reported a healthy elk herd and extremely high reproductive rates in the revegetated blast zone of Mount St. Helens. In all these situations, however, the large openings were acceptable because the elk population was either unhunted, undisturbed or both.

In areas where tree cover is almost continuous, there is some evidence that elk prefer smaller openings, but this is not unequivocal. Reynolds (1962a, 1964b, 1966a) presented a series of reports suggesting that 45 acres (18.2 ha) in Ponderosa pine types and 20 acres (8.1 ha) in spruce/fir types probably were the maximum openings that would be used fully by elk. Lyon and Jensen (1980) confirmed that clearcuts larger than 40 acres (16.2 ha) were used less than smaller clearcuts. However, in an area where natural grassland openings were relatively large, elk showed no particular preference for small clearcuts.

A study in Idaho showed that large clearcuts less than 10 years old were more acceptable to elk than were smaller but older cuts (Hershey and Leege 1976). In Montana, Lyon and Jensen (1980) found that vegetative height in forest types where understory plants were not suppressed corresponded with increased elk use of any size opening. In these types, cover inside the opening provided desirable security for elk. In some other forest types, however, overstory canopy shaded and reduced forage production, and elk use declined as cover height in the opening increased. In these types, forage production was greatest during the early stages of seral vegetation development. In the absence of

Elk generally prefer forest openings and clearcuts smaller than 40 acres (16.2 ha), except where natural grassland openings are large, then no such preference is indicated. *Left photo by Jim D. Yoakum. Right photo by George Wolstad; courtesy of the U.S. Forest Service.*

Increases in forage production in clearcuts can make an important contribution to elk habitat quality. However, lack of disturbance, size of opening and road management are important considerations in determining whether forage actually is available to elk. *Left photo courtesy of the U.S. Bureau of Land Management. Right photo by Len Rue, Jr.*

hiding cover inside an opening, cover at the edge of the opening became the controlling variable of elk use. This security cover was particularly important when clearcuts were accessible to motor vehicles (Lyon and Jensen 1980).

Generally it has been assumed that elk use of openings is related to those area's higher forage production. Where moisture is adequate, the level of forage production has typically been enhanced by direct seeding of grasses and forbs. However, the effectiveness of forage seeding for reducing elk browsing on conifers remains questionable (Becker et al. 1996). In many forest types, cover, forage quality and roads determine elk use of clearcuts. Many investigators have reported increases in understory forage production after cutting or thinning of forest stands (Reynolds 1962b, 1964a, 1969, Pearson 1964, 1968, McConnell and Smith 1965, Clary and Ffolliott 1966, Basile and Jensen 1971, Clary and Larson 1971, Ffolliott and Clary 1972, Hooven 1973, Ward 1973a, Irwin 1976, Regelin and Wallmo 1978). Some have reported that, in addition to measurable increases in forage production, higher protein content and greater palability of forage plants occur when the plants grow in the open, rather than in shaded condi-

tions (Einarsen 1946, Dealy 1959). However, other researchers have found no nutritional differences other than those related to greater species diversity in openings (Regelin et al. 1974) or increases in variety and total production (Pengelly 1963b, Basile and Jensen 1971, Wallmo et al. 1972).

One point that should not be overlooked is that few investigators have reported increases in elk populations corresponding to forage increases in openings. The value to elk of any increase in forage production depends on whether food is limiting and whether the added forage is actually available. Reynolds (1969:4), for example, observed that although thinning produced increases in forage production ranging up to 30%, "The fallen trees proved as effective barriers for deer and elk as for cattle." Pearson (1968) recorded greatest use by elk where Ponderosa pine was thinned to zero basal area—a clearcut.

Management of Logging Debris

After timber sales, the cut-over areas contain variable amounts of materials in the form of discarded logs, branches and tops. Within limits, this dead material (slash) left on the ground may provide certain benefits to elk. Black et al. (1976) suggested that slash might be piled or windrowed to provide cover and reduce long sight distances. Reynolds (1966b) found that cut-over areas with undisturbed slash on the Kaibab Plateau, Arizona, were used more heavily by deer than were cleared areas. Elk, being a larger ungulate, would presumably be less affected than deer by the thinly scattered debris that Reynolds recorded (7% of the ground covered by slash). On the other hand, elk would almost certainly avoid the slash coverage exceeding 50% after some logging operations as in the Oregon Cascades (Dyrness 1965).

Where slash is piled in windrows or otherwise is enough to be a barrier to animal movement, it may restrict the way elk are able to use their habitat. Lyon and Jensen (1980) reported that numbers of pellet groups in clearcuts in western Montana declined by at least 50% where slash was more than 1.5 feet (0.5 m) deep. This restriction also affected elk use of uncut forest areas that contained substantial amounts of dead and down materials as a result of past fires, insect infestations or disease. Although elk are not excluded from areas with large amounts of down timber, they apparently prefer to avoid such situations.

Even if waste material is removed, any habitat improvement for elk after timber stand thinning is temporary. Following removal of 33 and 66% of the basal area from lodgepole pine stands, Lyon (1986) reported losses of 50% and 90% of the hiding cover, respectively, and 30% and 60% of the thermal cover, respectively, without producing a perceptible increase in forage production.

Habitat Improvement

Despite the demonstrated relationships between timber management and elk habitat quality, habitat improvement practices for elk often have concentrated on nonforestry options. Most commonly, habitat improvement has involved a variety of techniques to increase or improve forage production without much regard for other components of elk habitat.

Controlled burning, particularly in the Intermountain West, is a common technique for improving big game winter ranges and, despite some disparity in reported results, burning in most western habitats has been favorable for elk. Leege and Hickey (1971) reported that burning brushfields in northern Idaho increased browse available to wintering elk by reducing the height of tall shrubs and promoting sprouting of desirable forage plants. Similarly, an intense prescribed fire in a Douglas-fir forest in Idaho increased shrub forage for mule deer and elk (Lyon 1971a). The benefits were expected to last for more than 20 years.

In addition to modifying shrub communities, prescribed fire has been used to increase herbaceous vegetation in grand fir habitat types (Leege and Godbolt 1985). Broadcast seeding of grasses after prescribed fire further increased forage production on these sites. Elsewhere, fire has been used to reduce plant litter that inhibited grazing by elk on a Montana fescue/wheatgrass winter range (Jourdonnais and Bedunah 1990) and to prevent incursion by seedling trees into grassland winter ranges.

Peck and Peek (1991) reported that elk in British Colum-

Untreated logging slash can be a major barrier to animal movement. Where such debris is dense and more than 1.5 feet (0.5 m) deep, it may even prevent elk from using habitat. *Photo by Dick Hancock.*

Prescribed fire is a commonly applied technique for improving elk habitat on many areas in the West, by increasing the amount, structure and diversity of postfire forage. *Left photo by Stu Murrell. Right photo by Tom Leege.*

bia wintered primarily in postfire grass and shrub communities, except during severe weather, when conifer stands were used. Canon et al. (1987) found that elk preferred to forage in aspen stands that had been burned. However, Romme et al. (1995) noted that burned aspen stands in Yellowstone National Park following the 1988 fires were no more attractive to elk than were unburned stands.

Skovlin et al. (1983), in addition to burning, experimented with fertilization and spring livestock grazing in attempts to increase elk winter use of bunchgrass ranges in Washington. In this situation, only the fertilized range attracted elk. Long (1989) reported elk in Wyoming attracted to burned and fertilized meadows after treatments of public land designed to reduce damage on private pasturelands.

Some of these experiments have been interpreted as demonstrating increased palatability of burned and fertilized plants, but it seems equally possible that the attraction to these areas was simply due to availability. Rowland et al. (1983) detected no difference in the nutritive quality of winter forage in burned and unburned Ponderosa pine range in New Mexico. However, there were differences in the nutrient content in the diets of elk using the burned and unburned ranges, and elk using the burned winter range had greater body weights. Irwin and Peek (1983a:443) described elk as generalist feeders that "maximize energy intake through mechanisms of habitat selection rather than food selection." Other investigators have confirmed that feeding site selection by elk optimizes food intake relative to energy expenditure (Irwin and Peek 1983b, Hanley 1984, Wambolt and McNeal 1987, McCorqodale 1993). If generally true, habitat manipulations that allow elk to optimize food in-

take efficiency should both attract more elk and result in relatively increased body size.

Access Development and Use

Development of roads and trails effectively shrinks the landscape by facilitating travel into and through it by both humans and wildlife. For humans, the ability to access an area by roadway may change a daunting cross-country trek into a pleasant excursion. For elk, using closed roads may save energy.

If mechanized transportation is allowed, areas that were challenging to travelers on foot can become trivial in scale. A day's travel on foot becomes a distance traveled in minutes, and the resulting "shrinkage" assures the presence of more people at more times on more landscapes. When a network of roads is transposed on a landscape and mechanized travel is used in hunting elk, the result has been a rapid decline in the number of mature bulls (Leege 1976, Thiessen 1976, Leckenby et al. 1991, Leptich and Zager 1991, Youmans 1991).

Access—mainly that facilitated by roads—is perhaps the single most significant modifier of elk habitat and a factor that will remain central to elk management on public and private lands.

Roads

Of all the factors related to logging, the construction of roads and the subsequent vehicle traffic on those roads has proved to be the most significant modification of elk habitat.

In the short term, construction activities are a major (although usually temporary) disturbance. The long-term influences of roads on elk use of forest environments appear to fall into two general categories. First, the roadbed itself, or associated debris, may alter the topography of specific areas or create a physical barrier to elk movement. Second, roads increase the probability of contact with humans, whether or not associated with motor vehicles, because they create energy- efficient travel corridors for both elk and humans.

Road Construction

The creation of physical barriers during road construction can be particularly critical in forested areas with steep slopes. As slope becomes more acute, road construction requires larger cuts and fills and greater amounts of slash are created, and adequate slash treatment becomes increasingly difficult.

The common recommendation from virtually all studies of this problem is to create the fewest possible roads, and to use standards that minimize road width, cuts and fills as initial criteria of road design and location. Lyon (1975), Black et al. (1976), Lyon et al. (1985), Marcum (1976), Perry and Overly (1976), Ward (1976), and Lyon et al. (1985) recommended that roads be located away from openings and in dense timber except where such locations bisect cover areas or moist habitat areas preferred by elk.

Road construction also creates a wide variety of problems related to watershed drainage and aesthetics. Because solutions appear to be about the same for all aspects of the problem, these disciplines also confirm that the smallest

Roads that remain open to vehicle access constitute the single most significant negative modification of elk habitat by human activities. *Photo by L. Jack Lyon.*

scale road appropriate to the job will be least damaging to the environment (Gardner 1971, Wyoming Forest Study Team 1971).

Road Management

During the 1960s, when many elk herds were located in unroaded areas and elk harvests were below the considered potential in most states, construction of new roads was viewed as a positive contribution to more intensive elk management. Concurrently, timber harvest increased greatly on previously unroaded segments of national forests, and the resulting network of roads became a major wildlife management problem rather than an asset. Wildlife biologists throughout the West became concerned that "road access makes elk more vulnerable to hunters and leads to year-round harassment by picnic parties, motorcyclists, Sunday drivers, and snowmobiles. As road densities increase, elk retreat from this disturbance until, eventually, there is no escape left" (Wyoming Forest Study Team 1971:48).

The number of reports showing consistent year-round influence of roads on elk use of the environment is overwhelming. Among the reports demonstrating a decline in elk use of areas adjacent to roads are Marcum (1975, 1976), Burbridge and Neff (1976), Hershey and Leege (1976), Perry and Overly (1976, 1977), Ward (1976), Lyon (1979a, 1979b, 1983), Morgantini and Hudson (1979), Rost and Bailey (1979), Edge (1982), Lonner (1985) and Witmer and deCalesta (1985). The width of the area avoided by elk has been reported as 0.25 to 1.8 miles (0.4–2.9 km), depending on the amount and kind of traffic, quality of the road and density of cover adjacent to the road.

High-quality unpaved roads generally receive greater use by people and represent a larger area of avoidance by elk (Hershey and Leege 1976, Perry and Overly 1976, 1977, Rost and Bailey 1979). However, Burbridge and Neff (1976) reported that slowly moving vehicles on primitive roads were more disturbing to elk than were rapidly moving vehicles on an improved forest highway. Witmer and deCalesta (1985) reported a 50% decline of elk use in a 1,640-foot (500 m) band around paved forest roads in Oregon, but Ward et al. (1976) found elk to be tolerant of the constant high-speed traffic on Interstate 80 in Wyoming. Actually, none of the reported studies is inconsistent with Ward's (1976) observation that elk prefer to be at least 0.5 miles (0.8 km) from people engaged in out-of-vehicle activities, and they tend to be undisturbed by repeated events of a predictable nature, such as vehicle traffic that does not stop.

The importance of elk avoidance to humans and human activity can be substantial where open road densities are high (Figure 161). Although the area nearest a road is avoided by elk, this habitat will still receive some use. It sim-

Vehicular access on a proliferation of roads in many parts of elk range gives people nearly unlimited access to elk. Elk are vulnerable to the harassment by humans as a result of this rangewide, year-round access. As the number of miles of road per square mile increases, vehicular disturbance prevents full use of otherwise available habitat. Two miles of open road per square mile (1.24 km/km²) will reduce elk habitat effectiveness by as much as 50%. Above, a large and damaging clearcut reveals the extent of roads through forested elk range. *Photo courtesy of the Montana Cooperative Elk/Logging Study.*

ply becomes less effective than it might be if elk could use it without disturbance (Lyon 1979a). Thomas et al. (1979) indicated that habitat effectiveness for elk in Oregon can approach zero when open road densities reach 6.1 miles per square mile (3.8 km/km²), and Lyon (1983) calculated that an open road density of 3 miles per square mile (1.9 km/km²) would leave less than 40% effective habitat for elk in western Montana.

Reductions in habitat effectiveness cannot be prevented if forest roads remain open to *any* level of motorized traffic. However, management actions that eliminate vehicle traffic

on forest roads virtually always increase habitat effectiveness. Marcum (1975, 1976), for example, found that elk used closed logging roads more than would be randomly expected, and Witmer and deCalesta (1985) reported increased elk use of habitat near roads closed to vehicles.

Generic Habitat Models

As each influence (logging, roads, etc.) on elk habitat was recognized and described, it produced a management recommendation designed to reduce negative impacts on elk populations (usually with some effort to minimize sacrifice of commodity production goals). The studies—Hershey and Leege (1976), Ward (1976), Lyon (1979b), Edge and Marcum (1985b)—demonstrated that adequate security during the active period of a timber sale could mitigate much of the disturbance, whereas lack of security could result in undesirable displacement of elk to less desirable habitat or to undisturbed private land. It was shown that a timber sale area design could be modified to enhance (or destroy) home range characteristics and that roads could be designed to reduce immediate disturbance and long-term effects as well.

Most recommendations required managers, when evaluating impacts on elk habitat quality, to address an area larger than just that of direct manipulation for road con-

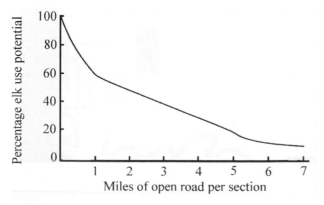

Figure 161. Elk habitat utilization in relation to miles of open road per section (in square miles) (from Lyon et al. 1985).

Paved roads not only give people easy access to elk, but they usurp tremendous amounts of landscape, usually along topographic paths of least resistance, which were the normal travel routes of populations of animals such as elk. Roads that do not necessarily block elk travel lanes or corridors at least fragment or dissect the species' range. And where there are paved roads and vehicles, there will be costly collisions with animals that must cross those roads to access other areas for their biological and social needs. *Top photo by Don Domenick; courtesy of the Colorado Division of Wildlife. Bottom photo courtesy of the U.S. National Park Service.*

struction or timber harvest. Of the 11 recommendations produced by research in Montana, for example, only two addressed site-specific concerns—protection of moist sites and design of clearcuts (Lyon et al. 1985). Another recommendation addressed an apparent elk behavioral response to cattle. The remaining eight all referred in one way or another to the influences of logging and roads over an area larger than that directly impacted by the logging.

The significance of these results is that the research conducted during the 1970s and early 1980s produced a broad definition of what elk habitat should look like—not just in a project management area, but in a larger area surrounding the treatment area. In this step, managers moved from site-specific habitat improvement to treatment of larger landscapes to reach specific goals. Another result of this research was modification of the perspective that elk needed wilderness to survive and prosper and a somewhat grudging acceptance that elk could be produced in logged areas if certain things were done. This change was important because it caused research to refocus on the more significant issues—access and security during autumn and quality of the habitat during summer.

The most common approach to applying such recommendations in land management has been through the creation of generalized models describing the essential components of elk habitat. Considering that "typical" elk ranges in North America extend from Olympic rainforest to open, sagebrush steppe of eastern Washington, and include mixed conifer habitats from Arizona north into Canada, it is difficult to describe any common formula for optimal elk range. However, somewhere between the unknown maximum and minimum limits, there is a range of environmental conditions capable of supporting elk. And although the precise description of the optimal condition is elusive, it is possible to describe in general terms a combination of habitat components acceptable as elk range.

The first attempts to describe such an acceptable combination were presented by Black et al. (1976) and Thomas et al. (1976). These models were incorporated into the Blue Mountains guidelines (Thomas et al. 1979), and have since proliferated into many additional versions designed to fit local conditions, local land management objectives and even local biases in land-use plans.

The significance of summer range as a factor in preparing elk for overwinter survival was underestimated for many years. It is now recognized that high-quality forage during summer is essential to winter survival of most herds. *Photo by Leonard Lee Rue III.*

The initial logic for all generic elk habitat models was the concept that an elk summer range with too much forest cover probably was no better for elk than a situation with all forage and no cover. Removal of some cover would result in increases of forage production, and optimization simply was a matter of achieving an appropriate balance. Deviation from full habitat utilization, usually ascribed to disturbances by motor vehicles, produced *habitat effectiveness* as an expression of expected actual habitat utilization by elk. Winter range was not considered in this model, although similar models later were developed for winter range application (Thomas et al. 1988a).

Conceptually, this was a relatively simple model. In actual application, it tended to become very complex. Thomas et al. (1979) provided separate definitions for hiding cover and thermal cover as well as a wide range of forage production responses within different vegetative types. In addition, early versions tended to imply precision about road quality, the amount of actual traffic on a road and the effect on elk use of available habitats.

Despite these variations, most models of elk habitat in the northern Rockies and the Pacific Northwest (e.g., Thomas et al. 1979, Leege 1984, Witmer et al. 1985, Wisdom et al. 1986) are basically similar. To a greater or lesser degree, all have been developed from the same two basic assumptions. First, elk habitat quality is a function of cover and forage. Second, full utilization of elk habitat is limited by the extent of forest roads open to vehicles. And, although these limits are substantial, the losses in habitat effectiveness associated with open roads can be reduced if the roads are closed to motorized vehicular traffic.

In developing locally applicable modifications of the generic habitat model, biologists have considered a wide variety of additional parameters. Leege's (1984) widely used habitat model for forestlands in northern Idaho, for example, included provisions for reducing habitat effectiveness where cover next to roads was poor, where cattle were grazing and for situations using gates rather than permanent closure for traffic control. Similarly, Wisdom et al. (1986) developed a range of coefficients to credit or penalize various cutting, burning, seeding and fertilization practices.

Additional modifications and changes in model application have involved the use of LANDSAT and GIS (Leckenby et al. 1985, Eby and Bright 1986) to supply the vegetation information needed, revisions to include sizing and spacing of cover and forage patches (Wisdom et al. 1986) and use of specialized computer software to handle the calculations (Hitchcock and Ager 1992, Ager and Hitchcock 1994).

The proliferation of these many different, but similar models has had a positive influence in elk habitat management, but positive results do not necessarily confirm the models as an accurate reflection of habitat requirements for elk. Thomas et al. (1988b) proposed that models are more important for assuring communication between biologists and land managers than for their effect on elk. Predictions derived from an elk habitat model were almost certainly a contributing factor in the observation by the supervisor of the Nez Perce National Forest that "our wildlife resources are as or more important than timber" (Kovalicky and Blair 1991:245).

Although the conceptual habitat model for elk has been field tested only a few times (Leckenby 1984, Lyon 1984), the real tests are that (1) so many versions have been developed and (2) those versions that survived are ones that generally coincided with the original model. Where objectives other than optimizing elk habitat have been used as drivers, the models have mostly failed and been replaced.

Another important effect of elk habitat models has been a change from management of individual habitat components to more objective management of complete elk ranges. For many years, the primary method of habitat improvement for big game was to increase forage production, usually on the winter range. When the evaluation area for most elk habitat models was arbitrarily set at somewhere between 3,000 and 10,000 acres (1,200–4,000 ha), it helped to emphasize the requirement that productive elk habitat includes a broad range of integrated components over a larger landscape.

There also were some negative aspects to the proliferation of elk habitat models. One major problem, for example, was the occasional unique modifications of either a model or descriptive terminology to favor commodity production rather than elk habitat. Such subterfuges usually lacked any basis in research or even observational data, with the result that they were confusing to the public and to biologists and managers alike. By the late 1980s, the situation had become so confused that it was necessary to conduct an "Elk Management Terminology Workshop," and produce a glossary defining a number of misused terms in elk management (Lyon and Christensen 1990, 1992).

Another problem was the inappropriate extrapolation of habitat effectiveness models, which are based on elk summer range relationships, to winter range, hunting seasons and other situations outside the scope of the original research. By the late 1980s, both habitat and population biologists had begun to recognize that the application of habitat models designed to measure the capability of land to *support* elk could not be applied effectively in evaluation of hunting season scenarios. Habitat models considered adequate to provide quality elk habitat in a forest managed for

timber production did not and never were designed to provide adequate security for elk during the hunting season.

Elk and Livestock Grazing Relationships

Although timber harvest has been the center of major controversy involving elk at least since the mid-1970s, grazing and perceived competition between elk and domestic livestock have been controversial almost continuously since the early 1900s. Preble (1911) reported competition between cattle and elk in Jackson Hole many years before there were significant numbers of elk recovered anywhere else in the West. And, as elk herds in the western states increased in size, there was a continuing series of studies of elk and livestock relationships, of range damage by elk on winter ranges in Yellowstone National Park and elsewhere and of continuing management concern about competition between elk and other wildlife species for range forage.

In the early 1900s, elk were damaging agricultural crops on Jackson Hole ranches and starving on winter ranges used by cattle in the summer. The cause and effect seemed so obvious that the U.S. Bureau of Biological Survey (Preble 1911) recommended establishment of a winter range for elk where forage could be maintained by excluding cattle. On a broader scale, studies of elk and livestock relationships have produced dozens of scientific reports (see Lyon and Ward 1982, Nelson 1982) and, although many investigators have recognized differential grazing habits and habitat selection patterns, there is strong implication throughout the literature that whatever problem exists can be solved only by forage allocation. In short, when two ungulates eat the same forage plants, direct action requires division of the available resources.

Much research has suggested that this is the management action least likely to benefit elk. The original and obvious conclusion has been modified over time, often into a quite different conclusion. The elk is a large and versatile herbivore, and one that usually grazes so lightly that use of vegetation may be difficult to detect. However, when elk populations are large, or when they are crowded into limited winter range areas, elk can be extremely destructive of vegetation. Virtually every western state can provide examples of winter ranges so badly depleted that animals have starved and damage to forage plants and watersheds has been extensive (Lyon 1966, Rognrud and Janson 1971).

Winter Range

Klemmedson (1967:268) reported that big game winter range had been declining in size and productivity at least since the 1930s; he concluded that, "while something must be done to counteract the trend of dwindling winter habitat . . . it seems unlikely that existing priorities will greatly change." Among the factors Klemmedson considered significant in this trend were winter range overuse by livestock and big game, wildfire, insects, disease, rodents, flood and soil erosion, ecological succession, forestry and range management, urban expansion, recreation, roads, highways and water development projects. Although virtually all of these factors still are present and important in determining the quality of elk winter range, management of elk and elk range has changed radically in the intervening years, with the result that the winter range situation seems not nearly as desperate as it did when described by Klemmedson.

One major change has developed from an increasing understanding of the role herbivory plays in ecosystem function. Possibly, it should not have been a revelation to wildland managers that grazing, at some nondestructive level, is virtually essential to the continued health and maintenance of grasslands in North America. Nevertheless, widespread acceptance of the conclusion that some grazing is better than no grazing has resulted in major philosophical changes in range management. In addition, another long-standing and successful approach has been substantially expanded through the purchase of designated winter range areas by state wildlife agencies, the federal government and even by private agencies. During the late 1980s, for example, the Rocky Mountain Elk Foundation joined with other private interests to provide a catalyst for federal purchase of the OTO Ranch and other large holdings important to the Northern Yellowstone elk as they migrate out of Yellowstone National Park each winter. These lands, now managed by the U.S. Forest Service, provide a winter home for a herd that has exceeded 19,000 animals in some years (Lemke 1994).

Range Damage by Elk

The history of elk use in Yellowstone National Park (Kittams 1959, Pengelly 1963b), on Big Game Ridge in the Teton Wilderness, Wyoming (Croft and Ellison 1960, Gruell 1973), in the Selway-Bitterroot Wilderness, Idaho (McCulloch 1955), the Bob Marshall Wilderness of Montana (Gaffney 1941) and many other areas where livestock use does not regularly occur, indicates the potential for destructive overgrazing by elk. Elk have been accused of causing serious damage by tracking and trampling, and there is no doubt that this damage can occur where elk activity is concentrated. In recent years, with elk numbers expanding throughout the West, range damage by elk has been reported wherever there seems to have been potential for competition with livestock.

However, there are conflicting interpretations of the

When elk population sizes exceed the capacity of available winter range to provide nutritious forage, both the elk population and the winter range will be significantly damaged. *Photo courtesy of the U.S. Forest Service.*

severity of such damage. In a study of the ecology of Big Game Ridge in the Teton Wilderness, Gruell (1973) failed to substantiate earlier conclusions by Croft and Ellison (1960) that overutilization and trampling by elk were responsible for vegetation deterioration and accelerated soil erosion. He concluded that the harsh, high-altitude environment is incapable "of supporting a vegetal cover more lush than that present [and] . . . that a significant deterioration in the plant cover has not occurred" (Gruell 1973:47). Similarly, since at least the mid-1960s, there have been two diametrically opposing views of elk management and the resulting range condition in Yellowstone National Park. Pengelly (1963b) argued that herds should be reduced to protect the range resource, but the park instead developed a policy of "natural regulation" (Cole 1971), which has been denounced for causing range deterioration and criticized as an unsatisfactory, "alternative solution to the problem. This has been to view signs of heavy habitat use—i.e., changes in plant composition, reduction in plant vigor, increases in soil exposure, increases in accelerated soil erosion and the like—as representing a 'Zootic disclimax' rather than 'elk damage'"(Taber and Raedeke 1987:576).

The alternative view is the argument that grazing animals have not greatly modified these ranges (Houston 1982). It is supported by studies concluding that no permanent damage to the Yellowstone grasslands has been caused by grazing (Cayot et al. 1979, Coughenour 1991, Frank and McNaughton 1992). Given the unique situation of Yellowstone National Park, there may never be an agreement between science and politics.

Where there is agreement, wildlife managers have explored a variety of responses to range overuse by elk, but there is little evidence of a solution without controversy. One obvious alternative, for example, is herd reduction to prevent permanent damage to vegetation and soils. Where recreational hunting can be used, some states have successfully conducted hunting seasons exceeding 90 days in areas of poor access and large elk populations. However, "it is much more difficult to get public support to protect soil and plants than to protect elk, perhaps because the consequences of grave errors are not as visibly dramatic" (Pengelly 1963b:23).

Competition with Livestock

Competition among grazing animals of different species can take place at several different levels. Historically, relationships between elk and domestic livestock were viewed simplistically in terms of direct competition for a limited forage resource. The potential for competition has produced an array of food habits studies showing that virtually all ungulates eat grasses, forbs and browse in some combination. Nelson (1982) mentioned the strong diet similarities between cattle and elk as possible evidence of competition.

Lyon and Ward (1982) tabulated 37 studies conducted between 1911 and 1979 on rangeland interactions between cattle and elk. There is no absolute consensus in these studies, but a general implication throughout is that, because elk and domestic livestock compete for a common forage base, they may be incompatible. Such a conclusion is supported by Mackie's (1978) observation that year-long elk population densities in Montana habitats where livestock grazing was practiced were about half that of elk densities in similar habitats without livestock. Also, Skovlin et al. (1968) found that elk preferred pastures where the fewest cattle were present. However, some reversal of this implication was suggested by concurrent use of pastures in Wyoming by elk and cattle (Ward et al. 1973). Such simultaneous use of winter ranges has been documented throughout the West, but it generally has been interpreted as a forced relationship brought on by competition for limited forage.

In addition to competition with cattle on winter range, elk have been repeatedly observed moving out of spring or summer grazing areas as an immediate response to the introduction of cattle (Mackie 1970, Lonner 1975b, Nelson and Burnell 1976). It has been assumed that this movement indicated competition for space, in which the elk were being displaced. However, Mackie (1978:462) concluded that "Much current thinking is rooted largely in inference and speculation and is controversial at best."

Livestock as a Management Tool

Anderson and Schertzinger (1975) possibly were the first to introduce the idea that appropriate management of cattle

The controversy over range damage by elk in Yellowstone National Park has continued for more than four decades. Trampling and overuse are evident in some areas, but whether these examples represent permanent, long-term damage has been interpreted in various ways. *Photos courtesy of the U.S. National Parks Service.*

could benefit elk on winter ranges. In the climate of the times, their proposal seemed quite radical. Since 1975, however, an increasing number of studies have confirmed that grazing by domestic livestock can provide a positive contribution to range management for elk. Scotter (1980:23) reported that, "Available evidence supports the generalization that dual use by livestock and wild ungulates, when properly planned, can benefit both classes of animals. . . ."

The majority of the research required to develop this suggestion into useful management techniques was conducted during the 1980s. It showed, for example, that elk prefer spring grazing of grasslands previously grazed by cattle (Grover and Thompson 1986, Jourdonnais and Bedunah 1988, Frisina 1992). It repeatedly demonstrated that, by selecting the unused pasture of rest rotation systems during the summer, elk avoid cattle (Wallace and Krausman 1987, Frisina 1992, Yeo et al. 1993). And, finally, techniques proposed by Anderson and Schertzinger (1975), using managed cattle grazing to increase forage on elk winter ranges, were tested and confirmed (Frisina 1986, Alt et al. 1992). In several areas, the coordinated management of elk winter range and private ranches has increased both elk and cattle numbers (Frisina and Morin 1991) and reduced damage on private property (Frisina 1986, Alt et al. 1992). Similarly, Rhodes and Sharrow (1990) demonstrated that sheep grazing can improve big game forage in Oregon's coast range by improving forage quality in autumn and the quantity of high-quality forage in spring.

While these research investigations were occurring, there was a nearly simultaneous development of philosophy that privately owned livestock should be removed from publicly owned grazing lands of the West. In part, this position developed because historically low grazing fees appeared to have subsidized the livestock industry at public expense. Very little of the associated rhetoric considered the potential effects on elk and other wildlife if livestock were to be removed entirely.

Low-density human occupation of western rangelands that support elk and other wildlife has been the circumstance for more than a century. Where the continued existence of a cattle ranch depends on grazing on public land, there is almost always a corollary dependence of a public elk herd on winter range on private land. Simultaneously, existence of the ranch provides protection from suburban development. Loss of viable ranch operations and replacement by subdivisions, recreation developments and other uses that preclude wildlife are a far greater threat to the ability of the environment to support elk than is continuation of livestock grazing. Henderson and O'Herren (1992:20) stated that "The most perilous change for wild ungulates is the conversion of relatively large agricultural

holdings to relatively small residential tracts." And although it seems obvious that grazing is a process necessary for the existence of grasslands, Frisina and Mariani (1995:24) suggested that "management strategies should move away from attempts to resolve immediate species-specific (cattle vs. wildlife) land use conflicts and begin to develop long-term approaches designed to sustain grassland systems."

Resolving Rangeland Conflict

There are no easy, obvious solutions to wildlife/livestock grazing conflicts. It is abundantly clear that unilateral resolution of two conflicting positions, with the land manager serving as referee, will benefit neither party and can only harm the resource. It is equally clear that political and court-ordered solutions are indefensible often on reasonable biological grounds.

Collaborative problem solving has been promoted by the Nevada Cattlemen's Association, in conjunction with most of the federal land management agencies, the Rocky Mountain Elk Foundation and many state wildlife agencies in the West. They sponsored two symposia, "Seeking Common Ground" (Nevada 1991) and "Sharing Common Ground" (Evans 1996), to explore some cooperative relationships and management techniques involving livestock and elk. As a result of these initiatives, progress has been made. There are on-the-ground demonstration projects

Residential development and conversion of winter range from ranches to subdivisions is far more harmful to elk than any amount of grazing by cattle. *Photo by Marty Holmes.*

throughout the West that document the feasibility of protecting range resources, supporting cattle ranching, and maintaining huntable elk populations. Some typical examples include the Owl Mountain Partnership in Colorado (Roath 1996), the Upper Muddy Creek Project in Wyoming (Hicks et al. 1996), the Monroe Mountain Project in Utah (Shiverdecker et al. 1996), the Blue Mountains Elk Initiative in Oregon (Mullarkey 1996) and the Devil's Kitchen Management Plan in Montana (Hibbard 1996). In each of these situations, local ranchers, sportsmen's organizations, outfitters, state departments and federal agencies have combined efforts to build trust and cooperation between livestock and wildlife management. The common denominator of most of the successful projects has been collaboration to enhance the range resource, rather than competition to control the grazing.

People Management

Early elk management models largely attempted to explain only habitat changes, but, with increased access on public lands, expansion of elk hunter numbers, increased public use of elk habitats during all seasons and proliferation of popular articles about elk, the expansion of models to incorporate human dimensions into elk management has become increasingly important. Concurrent with expanded understanding of the role of summer range in supporting elk populations (compared with the role of these same habitats in protecting elk during the hunting season) was recognition of hunting mortality as the single greatest factor in controlling elk numbers (Zager and Leptich 1991). As the importance of these two factors was recognized, it became increasingly apparent that any overall understanding of management of land and elk would require the integration of elk habitat models with regulated hunting—involving management of people, as well as elk, into the framework for land management decisions.

Elk Vulnerability

A lack of adequate security from disturbances increases stress on elk during all seasons. During much of the year, management to provide security merely requires provision of adequately distributed cover and control of road densities. During the elk hunting season, however, even the best cover may not be adequate, and unlimited human or vehicle access can create unacceptable management situations. Thiessen (1976) and Leege (1976) reported overharvest and elk population declines in Idaho where new roads constructed for timber harvest increased hunter access. Morgantini and Hudson (1979) and Basile and Lonner (1979),

on the other hand, reported that elk avoided or left traditional ranges during the hunting season. Janson (1973) and Basile and Lonner (1979) reported that open roads changed the character of the hunting experience, and both Coggins (1976) and Basile and Lonner (1979) found that road closures improved the quality of the hunt experienced by participants.

Hunter use of extensive road systems has been shown to increase the elk harvest significantly (Youmans 1991), reduce the number of days required to harvest an allowable number of animals (Leckenby et al. 1991) and to change population structure (Leptich and Zager 1991). In summary, unlimited vehicle access has resulted in too many kills too quickly, changed the population structure or reduced the size of the herd and, in many cases, required reduced season length and restricted hunter numbers (Leckenby et al. 1991).

Of all the problems associated with elk vulnerability during the hunting season, the most difficult to deal with has been the widespread reduction in the number of mature bulls. Early in this chapter, the importance of elk as a source of recreation visitor days to public lands was mentioned. Whether for hunting or viewing, the quality of the recreation experience is very much linked to the presence

Closure of road to motorized vehicular traffic is an important means of reducing the vulnerability of elk and other game to disturbance and hunter harvest. Such management practice is highly controversial within the hunting community. Some hunters feel that road closures are discriminatory, in that they give greater hunting and harvest opportunity to young hunters with limited physical impairments, or to those who can afford guides, outfitters and other relative conveniences. Other hunters insist that road closures enable a better and more level "playing field" for the hunter, the hunted and the landscape—the essence of fair chase. *Photo by Milo Burcham.*

of mature bull elk. However, in most western states, despite record-high total numbers of elk, there has been a continuing decline in the number of mature bulls. Carpenter (1991), for example, described a decline from 35 to fewer than 6 bulls per 100 cows in the White River elk herd in Colorado between 1960 and 1980. Leckenby et al. (1991) reported several elk management units in Oregon with 3 or fewer bulls per 100 cows.

This is a disturbing trend, and research has confirmed that the most compelling objections are no longer conjectural. It is known, for example, that there are elk herds in which most of the breeding is done by bulls that were calves only the year before. Potential biological consequences include a relaxation of natural selection (Geist 1991c), reduced pregnancy rates and increased probability of calves born late (Noyes et al. 1996). For hunters, it is clear that no trophy bulls will be available if all bulls are killed before they reach maturity. And, for the non-hunter, it is equally clear that the mature bull as a visual resource will have ceased to exist.

As the decline in numbers of mature bulls became more widely recognized across the West, the paradox of expanding elk numbers and extensions into ranges not occupied since the 19th century became increasingly apparent. Out of this paradox, the concept of elk vulnerability gained wide acceptance as an important management approach that combines habitat conditions with the reality of regulated hunting.

In April 1991, a symposium on elk vulnerability was held in Bozeman, Montana. Attended by more than 400 biologists from throughout the United States and Canada, this watershed event marked a conceptual change in the management of elk and elk habitat (Christensen et al. 1991). Lonner (1991:2) set the theme for the symposium by pointing out that the initial concerns of the sponsors were: "good habitat security that would protect elk from becoming easy prey during the hunting season"; "desired elk population characteristics in the face of intensifying land management practices"; and "satisfying the growing demand for quality elk hunting and nonhunting experiences."

The symposium also served to galvanize both habitat and wildlife population managers to recognize that, without cognizance of factors that control the population, elk habitat management alone does not manage for elk. Within the framework of elk vulnerability, habitat managers and population managers now find it necessary to recognize the interdependence of habitat parameters and regulated sport hunting. Leptich and Zager (1991) reported a study in Idaho in which 6% of bull mortality was natural, 18% of cow mortality was traced to poaching and the rest was associated with legal hunting.

There is, of course, the obvious simplistic solution to the problem of reducing elk vulnerability—i.e., reduce the number of hunters. However, the social significance of elk hunting and the fiscal dependence of many wildlife management agencies on hunting license revenues weigh

Although the yearling bull is sexually capable, recent research has shown that breeding by young bulls can have negative population consequences. *Above photo by Ernest Lindsay; courtesy of the U.S. Forest Service. Right photo courtesy of the Wyoming Game and Fish Department.*

against this approach. No solution can be simple if basic management objectives include maintaining a high number of hunter recreation days and maintaining reasonable control over elk population levels. The symposium *Proceedings* provided a broad overview of research on roads, cover and hunter densities among the management strategies to enable survival of a larger proportion of the mature bull population through the hunting season. The majority of that research was done on public land and in the context of regulated public hunting.

Increased hunter access, often using roads constructed to facilitate timber harvest, has always been a major influence on the numbers of elk killed. Youmans (1991) presented graphic evidence for five hunting units on the Bitterroot National Forest, Montana, indicating that sharp increases in numbers of bulls harvested coincided with sharp increases in miles of forest road constructed. Over a 36-year period in this area, the numbers of hunters increased from about 2,000 to 10,000, and hunter success declined by two-thirds.

Several studies examined the influence of roads on hunters' behavior and bull survival over shorter time periods. Leptich and Zager (1991), for example, reported bull mortality rates in Idaho decreasing from 61.7% in highly roaded areas (more than 4.5 miles of open road per square mile [2.8 km/km²] of habitat) to 31.3% in areas with fewer roads (less than 1.0 mile of open road per square mile [0.6 km/km²] of habitat). In the roaded area, no bull survived more than five hunting seasons, whereas in the unroaded area, some bulls lived in excess of 10 years. In a similar study in another part of Idaho, Unsworth and Kuck (1991) found that bull elk in areas with more than 4 miles of open

road per square mile (2.5 km/km²) of habitat were more than twice as likely to be killed during autumn hunting seasons than were bulls in areas with less than 0.5 mile of open road per square mile (0.3 km/km²) of habitat. In Montana, Hurley and Sargeant (1991) reported that although only 14% of their radio-equipped elk were located on the 25% of the study area with open roads (124 square miles: [321 km²]), those elk sustained 43% of the total hunting season mortality.

Lyon and Canfield (1991) reported that elk not only moved to areas of lower road density when hunted, but also that they consistently selected a conformation of habitats providing access to the larger, continuous forest communities in the environment. This behavior was interpreted as evidence of elk response to habitat fragmentation rather than selection for hiding cover. At the same time, Hurley and Sargeant (1991) reported that elk in areas with open roads increased their use of dense timber during the hunting season by 50%.

The primary implications of these elk behaviors during the hunting season are that security for elk can be increased through appropriate landscape design. Canfield (1988, 1991) described the use of radio-telemetry to locate appropriate security areas, and Hillis et al. (1991) provided descriptions of security areas, suggesting that unroaded hiding cover blocks of at least 250 to 300 acres (101–121 ha) were about the minimum needed to provide hunting season security.

Hiding cover alone cannot satisfy hunting season security requirements, and neither can road closures and prevention of habitat fragmentation. Leckenby et al. (1991) reported that road closure programs only provided short-term mitigation for loss of habitat and increased harassment and vul-

Reducing elk vulnerability requires cooperation of landowners to produce landscapes in which the needs of both elk and elk hunters can be satisfied. *Photo by Len Rue, Jr.*

nerability. As shown in Idaho, even wilderness areas may not provide adequate protection if hunter numbers and persistence are high and season timing is inappropriate (Rybarczyk and Unsworth 1991). Research of the kind required to provide definitive limits on hunter numbers is extremely difficult to design and implement. However, research by Vales et al. (1991, 1996) suggested that elk vulnerability becomes very high when the number of hunters per legal animal exceeds a threshold of about three; it probably is unacceptable when the ratio of hunters to legal animals surpasses one.

An additional consideration that may further confound the problem of low bull/cow ratios is the high (and often increasing) overall population of elk. Managers striving to protect bull numbers must also seek to achieve desirable harvest objectives of females to maintain populations at appropriate levels. This can focus hunting pressure on the cow elk population segment and result in undesirable hunting situations. Road closures intended to reduce bull harvest may preclude adequate cow harvests (K. Hamlin personal communication:1990). Elk vulnerability can be viewed only as a complex relationship in which hunting pressure and habitat conditions must be considered simultaneously.

Growth and Zoning

Another powerful change that has taken place since the 1960s is the expansion of human occupation into elk range, and most notably those geographic locations supporting elk winter ranges at lower elevations. People, drawn to these areas by open lands and attractive lifestyles, have created a boom of human growth and sprawl within many of the prime elk habitats of the mountainous West. Associated development often results in direct conflict with expanding elk herds. In Colorado alone, more than 90,000 acres (36,422 ha) of open land are being developed annually (deBuys 1996).

Given low-density human populations, abundant public lands, and general human tolerance of wildlife in the West, historically, many of the areas undergoing rapid development have weak or nonexistent land-use plans and few effective forums for dealing with such development. This has resulted in increased complaints about elk depredation on private lands, elimination of some elk herds, rapid loss of key habitats and widespread misunderstanding among many new residents about elk management.

With the growth and development that has occurred in many areas of the West has arrived or emerged a human population either unfamiliar or intolerant of traditional land management practices. State and federal management agencies face new questions about traditional management

actions. Grazing, timber harvest and traditional hunting practices are increasingly being publicly challenged, and management of elk and elk habitat is caught up in this new debate. Both state and federal agencies have responded with new management plans and approaches, setting elk population goals as well as identifying habitats and habitat management practices. This change in public attitude also has led to polarized views about the management of public lands as a bastion of wildlife habitat and equally polarized views of the management of elk, a public resource, on large tracts of private land not open to the public. Nevertheless, these plans and the public forum they provide will become increasingly important as elk continue to expand in numbers and public pressure for access and use of elk habitat increases.

Beginning in the late 1980s, many states developed elk management plans that identify elk population goals and define areas of habitat for elk. These plans have become increasingly important as elk habitat has been developed for human use and occupation. Proximity to wildlife is a major attraction to open lands, but when those wildlife, including elk, come within what is perceived as too close proximity to development, the animals are viewed as problems. And the ability to control their population numbers or habitat use on private land can be complex and contentious.

All too frequently second home, suburban and exurban developments, as well as ski resorts, golf courses, airports and myriad other artificialities—and the roadways to connect them all—sprout up in western landscapes that were elk winter range or portions of traditional migration routes. *Photo by Hugh Hogle; courtesy of the Rocky Mountain Elk Foundation.*

Ecosystem Management

In 1992, the U.S. Forest Service announced that "ecosystem management" henceforth would be the driving policy on national forests. The concept of ecosystem management has since been embraced by most other federal land management agencies, many state agencies and many larger private landowners.

Briefly, ecosystem management involves recognition of ecological processes that substantially shape and define the land and vegetation (see Chapter 11). Rather than a site-specific or even drainage-specific approach to land management, an ecological perspective is largely a process of looking at major watersheds or landscape units and recognizing how site-specific conditions fit and function within the context of the larger environment.

Ecological processes such as climate, fire and hydrological cycles are largely responsible for shaping the land and vegetation that support elk. As knowledge of how these processes shape habitat improves, understanding of how elk respond to habitat changes will become more important. Elk will continue to be seen as a species of primary interest, but increasingly included within a mosaic of other species and their habitat needs. Management likely will shift from modifications intended to benefit a single species to maintenance of desirable habitat conditions within a recognized range defined by ecological processes and site conditions. As a relative habitat generalist, elk likely will continue to prosper, but managers will need to embrace elk and elk management within a larger and more complex context.

Land and Elk

In 1890, only about 100,000 elk existed in the United States, and these were confined to Yellowstone National Park, and their safety from poachers provided by patrols of U.S. Army cavalry (Robbins et al. 1982). Perhaps the long-standing perception of elk habitat being largely wilderness was cast from that circumstance. For whatever reason, 20th century elk were perceived as requiring vast acreage of undeveloped, largely mountainous and essentially pristine country. This perception was honed by efforts to reestablish elk where areas of this description were preferred sites, and preserves often were established to ensure their safety. In general, people came to associate elk with "rugged, high" country and described elk in terms related to a wilderness setting.

Only as data were generated from radio-collared elk did biologists begin to recognize the more plebeian nature of elk habitat. Elk herds have prospered in managed forests that undergo frequent disturbances and are accessible by roads. Elk herds in designated wilderness areas, where human access is limited and habitat disturbance is driven by natural processes, have some of the poorest demographics, confounding the earlier perceptions of elk habitat. Also, elk have begun to occupy habitats ranging from desert steppe in southeastern Washington to Conservation Reserve Program lands in Colorado—both nontypical under former elk habitat definitions that relied heavily on forest parameters that included coniferous cover for temperature control and security. When Mount St. Helens severely damaged 150,000 acres (60,705 ha) of Roosevelt elk habitat in Washington State, biologists were amazed at the rapid recovery in an area essentially *devoid* of cover (Merrill et al. 1987).

These cases and other examples have resulted in a much changed or expanded perception of what defines elk habitat. It now is recognized that land capable of supporting elk not only includes the important publicly owned habitats, but also vast tracts of privately owned lands that now appear to be major factors in the future management of elk.

Coupled with the new perception of landscape capable of supporting elk is recognition of how land features contribute to the thrift of elk herds as well as their security under hunting conditions. Separation of the ability of land to nurture elk from the ability of land to shield elk from hunters is another very powerful change that has occurred in elk management within the past decade. It is particularly significant on public lands where hunting is the primary means of population management.

These two shifts in the way land and elk relate have resulted in significant changes in how managers look at and manage the land, and who owns the land. In general, the result has been an expanded definition of elk habitat, a perception that elk can and will occupy ranges formerly not considered suitable and an increased role and responsibility for private lands in elk management. New habitat definitions consider vegetation, terrain, access, hunting regulations and management intent of the owner. Four of these five factors are human-related and subject to social and economic forces that affect both public and private lands.

For much of the 20th century, public lands were perceived as the bastion of elk habitat, but in recent years, the role of private and corporate lands has taken on increased significance. Included in the expanded role of privately owned lands is recognition of economic considerations as both positive and negative factors in the way land is managed with regard to elk. Elk and elk hunting have rapidly evolved as significant economic factors and directly affect management of privately owned lands. What has evolved in many areas in the West is a quilt work of land ownership and land-use patterns across which elk move and are influenced. Affected by public policy and multiple uses on public lands, expanding numbers of elk have increased their use

Elk have been popularized as a montane wilderness animal, but history indicates that many presettlement populations were habituated mainly to foothill, plains and prairie habitats. Experience within the time of modern wildlife management—essentially 1935 to present—has shown that elk are adaptable to a wide range of habitat types and ecological disturbances, particularly where such types are part of a larger ecological unit rather than a unique vegetative type. Some currently occupied elk ranges include southwestern desert chaparral (*top*), sagebrush steppe (*second photo*), coastal forests in California (*third photo*) and rolling grasslands (*bottom*), as well as mountain meadows and valleys. *Top photo courtesy of the Arizona Game and Fish Department. Second photo courtesy of the Wyoming State Archives. Third and bottom photos by Jim D. Yoakum.*

of adjacent private lands where the habitat may have different attributes and where disturbance patterns are different and reduced from those associated with multiple uses on public lands. Increasingly, year-round human use of public lands for recreation, management of vegetation, extractive activities, livestock grazing and maintenance activities is thought to influence elk movement to nearby private lands where these types of activities are much reduced. This has led to concern about the fate of a public resource that uses private land and is not available to the public for either hunting or other uses. Elk management on larger acreage of private land has increasingly been influenced by economic considerations, and resulted in expanded managed hunting programs and elk ranching. Elk managers frequently get caught between the public that financially supports agencies that have responsibility for elk and for elk habitat, and the private landowners who may provide important seasonal or year-long range and seek an economic return from elk to sustain their operations. At best, these situations have resulted in coordinated efforts that allow elk herds to thrive and meet both public and private needs; at worst, these situations have resulted in relegating elk to the role of "merchandise" in a land-use shell game based on financial considerations devoid of philosophic or conservation ethic.

According to Lonner (1991), "wild" elk are defined by remote and wild country where patterns of use have long-standing traditions largely controlled by natural processes. Here, elk are seen as important components of the ecosystem, valued as a species and inherently worthy. "Mild" elk are products of many competing uses on both public and private lands that are heavily influenced by human economic and social needs. Elk are an important and valued component of a landscape managed to meet people needs, but subject to the vagaries of public opinion and demographics. Elk do well in managed timberlands and national parks, but they are not the same as wild elk in a remote backcountry setting. "Defiled" elk are those largely confined by fences, in close proximity to people, managed mainly according to economic considerations, and whose fate may be determined by market conditions. These elk contribute to public misunderstanding and are fodder for conflict between public values. Their frequently sad fate lowers esteem for both humans and elk.

Ultimately, there is a defining relationship between elk and the land. The land and its attributes largely define the elk that are found there, just as elk reflect the nature of the land on which they live and the way it is managed. Both reflect the health of the environment and the values and prevailing temper of the people who are its stewards.

Elk defined by remote and wild country and natural processes are seen as important components of the ecosystem and a worthy representative of the species. Conversely, elk produced within enclosures are managed according to market demands that have no relationship to their status as a magnificent game species. The antlers of the bull above right have been removed and sold for medicinal purposes. *Photos by Milo Burcham.*

14

MICHAEL L. WOLFE, JOHN F. KIMBALL, JR.
AND GREGORY T. M. SCHILDWACHTER

Refuges and Elk Management

The calamitous decline of wildlife populations throughout the United States by the end of the 19th century posed serious concerns for conservation-minded sportsmen (Hornaday 1913, Trefethen 1975, Reiger 1986). Some of these citizens began working to reverse the trend, largely by attempting to eliminate poaching and regulate hunting, but the declines continued. Later, sportsmen teamed with other interest groups in support of land reserves, intended to protect commodities, scenery and recreational opportunities, in addition to wildlife. These first refuges—including Yosemite and Yellowstone national parks—served multiple purposes. Subsequent reserves were more specifically designated as wildlife refuges, such as the Afognak Forest and Fish-Culture Reserve created in Alaska by President Harrison in 1892. It was in 1903, when President Theodore Roosevelt invoked executive power to reserve land specifically and solely as a national wildlife refuge, that Americans began systematically using the conservation tactic of creating refuges for wildlife. Elk figured prominently both in the first general land reserves and in the first specific refuges for wildlife.

Refuges were part of a larger set of conservation tactics, including establishing management agencies, restricting hunting and interstate transport of game and reserving land for the protection of wildlife and for other purposes. Sportsmen and other conservationists worked to halt the slaughter of wildlife for trade in meat, feathers and other parts (Oldys 1910). State-level efforts were reinforced by passage of the federal Lacey Act of 1900.

Early conservationists also developed the concept of wildlife held in a public trust overseen by public agencies that managed public lands (Bean 1983). By reshaping federal law, they reserved lands for federal supervision, such as the National Elk Refuge, where hunting was prohibited (Gilbert 1993). Aesthetics was a popular attribute of reserved lands and some of the proponents for reserving lands were railroad companies seeking to deliver tourists to places such as Yellowstone National Park.

By approximately 1930, sportsmen's conservation actions and initiatives reflected a strategy that remains familiar to the same movement today. It included citizen advocates, scientific experts and institutions, such as public trust ownership, reserved lands, regulations and technical schools and agencies. In the first textbook on the subject, Leopold (1933) credited Theodore Roosevelt with consolidating the strategy under the unified rubric of "conservation through wise use." The Roosevelt doctrine, said Leopold, offered three formative ideas to the future of conservation: all outdoor resources are one integral whole; conservation of those resources is a public responsibility and their private ownership is a public trust; and science is the tool for carrying out that responsibility. The first conservation strategy was equivocal on the respective responsibilities and roles of public and private landowners and it remains an issue today.

This chapter reviews the birth and development of reserved lands as refuges and their role in the management of elk and conservation in general. The first national park—

President Theodore Roosevelt deserves much of the credit for the creation of a system of national refuges in the United States for the protection and management of wildlife under the banner of "conservation," a term coined by his good friend and the first Chief of the U.S. Forest Service, Gifford Pinchot. Conservation, as applied to natural resources including wildlife, meant "wise use"—and the management of renewable natural resources including timber, forage for wildlife and livestock in such a way as to ensure it's renewal. Roosevelt's strategy for the conservation of renewable resources became known as the Roosevelt Doctrine. *Photo of Roosevelt camping with naturalist John Burroughs (standing at right); courtesy of the Theodore Roosevelt Collection, Harvard College Library.*

Yellowstone National Park—is perhaps the most notable both in the history of conservation and also in the specific field of elk management. Elk management also is featured at the National Elk Refuge. Together, these areas symbolize the theory and practice of refuges in elk management. This review focuses on these two refuges, but touches on other relevant refuges, ideas and theories of conservation.

The Refuge Idea

Ideas have changed over time about what a refuge is and why we should have them. During these changes, public interest in the opportunity to see wildlife has remained high.

Ideas, goals, organizations and abilities for managing wildlife in the field also have changed. The combined effects of political, ecological, institutional and practical forces have resulted in refuges of differing sizes and purposes. For example, national wildlife refuges, state and national parks, state and national forests and other public lands are either designated as refuges or are providing refuge functions.

Ecology and Aesthetics

In conservation, the idea of a refuge began with dual ecological and aesthetic purposes. Ecology is the study of the relationship between living beings and their environments and the gist of the word refuge is that living beings find security in a designated place. However, in providing a safe environment for wildlife, refuges also can protect scenery and open space for recreation and these related benefits were among the goals of the first refuges that harbored elk in America. Sportsmen, politicians and other citizens shared aesthetic desires with their ecological notions that declining elk and other wildlife would benefit from protections on reserved lands. As a result, the idea of refuge has changed with changes in ecology and aesthetic ideals.

Elk were one of the species of prime concern in the late 19th century; their numbers were believed to have declined dramatically throughout their historic range. Seton (1927) estimated the size of the original elk population at as many as 10 million animals. By 1910, the total population probably did not exceed 50,000 animals, with isolated herds occurring in only a few mountainous areas of the West. The largest remnant herds were in Yellowstone National Park, Jackson Hole and adjacent areas of northwestern Wyoming. Although these numbers have recently been challenged, with arguments that Native Americans contributed to the herds' decline (see Chapter 3), no one disputes the decline of elk was a concern behind the creation of refuges.

Ironically, elk became overabundant in the refuges established to help the species recover from scarcity. Some of today's most contentious refuge issues involve arguably overabundant elk. For example, as elk herds rebounded, elk spread out from refuges and ate private stores of hay. It was soon apparent that, just as refuges can help elk avoid harm from people, they also can enable elk to create problems for people. One of the continuing purposes of refuges is to lure elk away from private lands and hay stores, but people now are concerned that the elk population is artificially high and, because of feeding programs, elk are too tolerant of human presence. Some refuges have resulted in elk numbers overbrowsed feedgrounds and other seasonal ranges.

Refuges also were part of a national concern about

scenery, wildlife and such commodity resources as minerals, water and timber. Frederick Law Olmstead, a key figure in Yosemite National Park as well as New York's Central Park, saw the purpose of parks as "the preservation and maintenance as exactly as is possible of the natural scenery" (Hampton 1971:133). Congress, when regulating uses in Yosemite, Sequoia and General Grant national parks, took a broader utilitarian view by ordering the parks to, "provide for the preservation from injury of all timber, mineral deposits, natural curiosities, or wonders[,] . . . provide against wanton destruction of the fish and game . . . [and provide] a public park or pleasure ground" (Hampton 1971:145).

Today, as more than 100 years ago, elk and other wildlife provide a meeting point between ecological management and aesthetics. Nineteenth-century Americans' interests in recreational hunting (Reiger 1986), scenic travel (Aselson and Moore 1985), bird watching and sustainable use of resources (Trefethen 1975) began at least as early as the 19th century. Today, the public remains strongly interested in watching elk and other wildlife in a wild setting. Most of these concerns and changes collide in the current technology and policy debate about whether people should intervene in the management of refuges at all or allow these ecosystems to regulate themselves "naturally."

Institutions

The refuge idea emerged as basic laws, organizations and customs developed around it. In the early days of refuge thinking, the United States was conducting war with Native peoples, rebuilding society and national government after the Civil War, building railroads and canals and other transportation networks, settling and watering the West, establishing nationwide newspapers and telephones, boosting literacy and structuring America's industrial economy of corporations, monopolies, trusts, unions, and union-breakers. These institutions over time affected what people knew about land and wildlife, how they thought about these resources, how accessible the resources were and what people were able to do with them.

Canada was also in formative stages of government (the provinces formed the Dominion of Canada in 1867) and western transportation (the Canadian Pacific Railroad developed and benefited from park tourism). However, unlike in the United States, the setting aside of parks and other reserved lands was accomplished by government officials without social movement.

It was not a foregone conclusion in the United States that reserved lands would be governed by federal authorities as most of them are today, but it was in Canada (Paehlke

1989). When the idea of a preserve for wildlife, scenery and Native people occurred to the artist George Catlin in 1832, he naturally assumed it would be "a nation's park." On the other hand, where state governments were in place, reserved lands were the property of state or local government. New York City created Central Park in 1856 and California received a grant of land from Congress to make Yosemite the first state park in 1864. Even after Congress named Yellowstone the first national park in 1872, the idea of state parks continued, as New York set aside the Adirondack preserve and Niagara Falls in 1885. In following years, the federal government began reserving lands for different purposes, including forest reservations (1891) and fish culture reservations (1892).

The debate about authority for reserved lands overlay the debate of authority for fish and wildlife. Like many issues of states rights, authority for fish and wildlife was assumed to rest with states because it was not among the enumerated powers in the Constitution and the Tenth Amendment states that "powers not delegated to the Federal Government by the Constitution are reserved by the States or to the people." In 1871, however, Congress created the U.S. Fishery Commission, presumably under the authority of the Constitution's property clause "respecting the territory or other property belonging to the United States." In 1896, the Supreme Court supported the states' custodial authority for wildlife (*Geer v. Connecticut*). On the other hand, later (1928) rulings established that the federal government could reduce wildlife populations on federal lands to prevent damage to the habitat (*Hunt v. United States 278*). A 1976 decision (*Kleppe v. New Mexico*) encroached on states' rights and led some legal observers (Bean 1977, Lund 1980) to contend that, in certain instances, Congress could enact laws that have paramount authority on federal lands and could supercede the wildlife laws of the states (Musgrave et al. 1998). Generally, however, the dual jurisdiction of state and federal authority has been formalized in enabling legislation and policy statements by various federal agencies. The most significant of these were the National Forest Management Act and the Federal Land Policy and Management Act, both enacted in 1976.

As the federal government established and consolidated its authority to reserve lands, private interest groups emerged to lobby these decisions and professional societies and organizations formed to promote their areas of expertise. Several of the major private groups in conservation and environmentalism today were formed in the same years that refuges were being designed and restocked with elk and deer. The 1880s were the first years of the American Ornithologists Union, Audubon Society and Boone and

Crockett Club. In later years, the Sierra Club, Ecological Society of America, Izaak Walton League, and National Wildlife Federation were formed. Many of the professional forums, schools and research institutions were established in the early 1900s. For example, the International Association of Fish and Wildlife Agencies, many schools of forestry, the Wildlife Management Institute, the Cooperative Fish and Wildlife Research Units, and The Wildlife Society were formed between 1900 and 1940.

Definitions and Examples

Driven by a complexity of law, organizations and goals, refuges are commensurately diverse. They differ in ecological characteristics, legal mandates and types of activities permitted; these features on various refuges have changed over time.

Leopold (1933:15) wrote that "the word 'refuge' as a device used in game management did not come into use until about 1910, but the group of ideas now associated with that word was in practice much earlier." In his view of the evolution of game management, refuges might be a half-way point between the basic idea of restricting hunting and the more advanced approach of controlling environmental factors that influence a population.

The words refuge and reserve have had similar meanings, which hint at the overlapping function of wildlife refuges and the forest reserves now called national forests. "Some . . . of the forest reserves," said Theodore Roosevelt, "should afford perpetual protection to the native fauna and flora, safe havens of refuge to our rapidly diminishing wild animals" (Catton and Mighetto 1998:5). The connection between these words also has been opportunistic. In groping through law books for some legal authority to punish violators of unenforceable rules, Yellowstone managers found a law pertaining to "Indian reservations" that they could stretch for the conservation purpose of imprisoning poachers on forest reserves (Hampton 1971:156).

Naturally, many definitions of refuges focus on ecological function. Hewitt (1921:238) noted that Canadian national parks (Banff, Jasper and Waterton Lakes, established in late 1800s) would "serve as unrivaled breeding . . . for the big-game and fur-bearing animals for the adjacent unprotected regions." In his classic text, *Game Management,* Leopold (1933:195) defined a game refuge as "an area closed to hunting in order that its excess population may flow out and restock surrounding areas. A refuge is at all times a sanctuary, and the two terms are synonymous."

The notion of sanctuary was later joined with the idea that refuges also benefit the users of wildlife on the refuge. Robbins et al. (1982:479) defined a refuge as a "designated unit of landscape primarily maintained for seasonal and/or year-round use of wildlife, and in the best interest of those wildlife and their users." Since the 1940s, those users have included hunters. Although hunting in a wildlife refuge has posed a contradiction for some citizens, ecologists and professionals realized that hunting could serve ecological purposes. For example, in refuges where elk numbers exceed carrying capacity, hunters can help reduce the population size. This idea of users helping to provide ecological conditions also includes loggers and livestock grazers. Defining compatible uses of refuges was the focus of the National Wildlife Refuge System Improvement Act of 1997 to draw bounds around acceptable or "compatible" uses of national wildlife refuges. This act established the wildlife conservation mission of the refuge system, provides guidance to the Secretary of the Interior for management of the system, provides a mechanism for refuge-specific planning and gives managers directions and procedures for determining wildlife conservation and public uses of the refuge system. The different activities permitted among refuges create refined differences in types of refuges.

These definitions are not exhaustive—refuges provide other functions, and refugelike functions can be provided by lands designated for other purposes. Refuges provide animals for reintroduction, public recreation and research. Direct and indirect functions of refuges are provided by lands designated for other purposes under a broad range of jurisdictions and management authorities. These include wilderness areas, national and state forests, national and state parks, management areas, military reservations and even industrial lands with limited public access. Some private lands can function as refuges (Burcham et al. 1999). Objectives and methods differ widely among these disparate units of land. Robbins et al. (1982) identified national parks, management areas and national refuges as being particularly important with respect to managing elk in North America. Today, the importance of national forests to elk management also is clear (Thomas 1979).

Discussion in this chapter is limited to refuges that enable populations to roam freely (at least for part of the year), breed freely and where natural mortality and hunting are the principal forms of removal. This excludes any discussion of intensively managed populations of semidomesticated, fenced animals in gamefarm situations (Hudson 1989). This is not to say that such populations could not play refugelike roles in a management situation. Managers of specific elk herds and populations should build their site-specific plans according to where refuge functions are provided for that specific herd instead of assuming that these functions will be provided only by lands specifically designated as refuges.

Refuges typically are designed so that essential wildlife habitat is maintained or enhanced, whether for a single species of particular interest, such as the elk at the National Elk Refuge (*above*), or a diverse assortment of species (such as in Yellowstone National Park). Refuges typically are managed so that wildlife may move freely across refuge boundaries, and are not incompatible with recreational hunting and other wildlife management practices as used to manage both wildlife populations and public uses of the set-aside lands. *Photo courtesy of the U.S. Fish and Wildlife Service.*

Refuge Management in Yellowstone, the National Elk Refuge and Elsewhere

Yellowstone National Park, principally in northwestern Wyoming, and the National Elk Refuge, in Jackson, Wyoming, are the oldest and best-known examples of designated refuges on this continent. Elk featured prominently in the creation of Yellowstone and are the namesake for the National Elk Refuge. Management of elk in these refuges figured prominently in rehabilitating the nation's formerly decimated populations and management of these refuges then changed as wildlife conservation thought developed throughout North America.

In review of the art and science of refuge management, Yellowstone National Park and the National Elk Refuge are useful focal points. Wagner et al. (1995), Wright (1998) and others have proposed slightly differing chronologies to describe the evolution of management approaches that the U.S. National Park Service has applied to the management of ungulates in national parks since the turn of the century. Changes in U.S. Fish and Wildlife Service policy for national wildlife refuges also are open to interpretation. Regardless of the exact sequence one prefers, elk in Rocky Mountain parks and refuges have been a focal point.

The roots of land protection began in the mid-19th century. Next is review of the state of ecological science and ef-

forts to increase numbers of ungulates and public viewing of them from about 1900 to 1940. Between approximately 1940 and 1970, with concern about the capacity of winter range and other habitats, management turned to reducing ungulate numbers in part by culling the herds. Since about 1970, public concerns about culling wildlife eventually precipitated refuge controversy over whether the "natural regulation paradigm" and whether it provides sustainable management.

As described by Fishbein (1989), the Yellowstone Ecosystem, frequently termed the Greater Yellowstone Ecosystem, encompasses 21,622 square miles (56,000 km²), including Yellowstone and Grand Teton national parks, three national wildlife refuges, portions of seven national forests and various other federal, state and private lands (Figure 162).

Protecting Land and Animals in the 19th Century

Reserving Land for Recreation and Wildlife

National parks were established in the United States by an act of Congress known as the National Park Service Act in 1916, "to conserve the scenery and the natural historic objects and the wildlife and to protect for the enjoyment of the same in such manner and by such means as will leave them

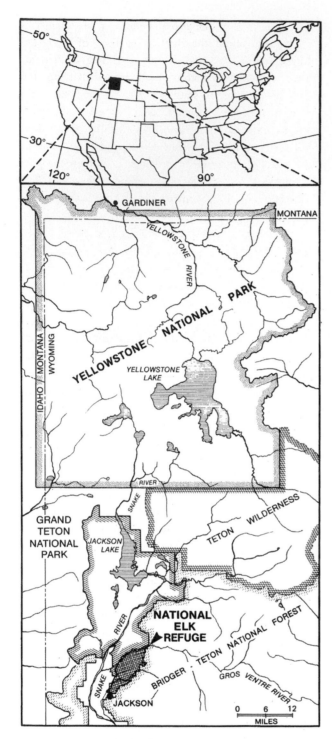

Figure 162. The area used by the Jackson Hole elk herd, including Yellowstone National Park, Teton Wilderness, Grand Teton National Park, Bridger–Teton National Forest and the National Elk Refuge (from Robbins et al. 1982).

unimpaired for the enjoyment of future generations." These areas were not set aside specifically for elk or other big game animals but for the entire assemblage of animals and other biotic and physical features that were part of each park's

ecosystem. This comprehensive motive has deep roots in human history; in America, its most obvious traces emerged in the mid-19th century (Trefethen 1975, Reiger 1986). George Catlin—the artist mentioned earlier who traveled the Missouri River in the1830s and proposed "a nation's park" for the Great Plains—saw the purpose of reserving land as including "man and beast" and the surrounding wilderness (Reiger 1986:94). At midcentury the advocates of reserved lands emphasized the recreational benefits of reserving land. In *Wild Northern Scenes—Sporting Adventures with the Rifle and Rod* (1857), Samuel Hammond described the Adirondack Mountains in New York and advocated preservation of limited wilderness areas as resources for recreation and rejuvenation. In 1860, the *Boston Evening Transcript* ran a series of articles publicizing the Yosemite wilderness (King 1962). Four years later on August 9, 1864, the *The New York Times* published an editorial advocating state acquisition of the Adirondacks for purposes of preservation. When, in 1864, Congress passed "An Act authorizing a Grant to the State of California of the Yosemite Valley," it did so, "on the express conditions that the premises shall be held for public use, resort, and recreation." Such use, resort and recreation by nature lovers and artists already were common in the Hudson River Valley of New York, where railroads provided access. New railroads exposed these travelers to the West, as did the wagon roads to areas such as the headquarters of Yellowstone River. Tourism influenced Yellowstone's eventual network of roads (Pritchard 1999).

Concern and appreciation for wildlife was part of the motivation for tourism in the 19th century. Americans had already seen the extinction of the great auk, extirpation of beaver in the eastern U.S. and many parts of the West and the declines of other game. The passenger pigeon's steady decline would end in extinction in the early 1900s (Schorger 1955). The New York Sportsmen's Club had been advocating game laws since 1846 and other sportsmen and citizens were motivated to prevent such decline in the West (Trefethen 1975).

Belief was widespread that elk, bison, pronghorn and deer were in steep decline in the West by late century. That the elk herd declined steeply seems obvious, although there are questions about the pre-Columbian abundance and distribution of the species. Accounts of early explorers, compiled by latter-day authors such as Haines (1955) and Casebeer (1961), document a substantial presence of elk in the Yellowstone/Jackson Hole area. However, this notion of the "pristine" abundance of elk in the area is increasingly controversial (see Chapter 3).

Apart from the question of historic abundance, there exists some controversy as to whether the Jackson Hole area constituted historic elk winter range or whether animals began using the valley for winter range only after settlers blocked migration routes out of the valley, as was suggested by Anderson (1958). Robbins et al. (1982) evaluated written evidence, including historic evidence presented by Murie (1951) and Cole (1969), and concluded elk actually did winter historically in Jackson Hole. Thus, it appears that the Yellowstone ecosystem has contained two more or less discrete elk populations. The Northern Yellowstone herd summers in the park area and winters in the northern portion of the park and into Montana. The Jackson Hole (or southern Yellowstone) elk herd summers as far north as the southern portion of the park and winters in Jackson Hole, approximately 62 miles (100 km) south of the park (Robbins et al. 1982).

Using the Army for Federal Land Management

Land reservation protected the geysers, rock formations, wildlife and other beauty of the Yellowstone area. Creation of Yellowstone National Park in 1872 and enactment of the Yellowstone Protection Act of 1894 were among the first national efforts to conserve the scenery and wildlife of the West. With the passage of the Yellowstone Organic Act in 1872, Congress set aside more than 3,300 square miles (8,546 km²) of western landscape and established what was to become the first national park in the United States. Yellowstone National Park, located in the northwestern corner of Wyoming but also occupying adjacent parts of Montana and Idaho, currently includes 3,473 square miles (8,995 km²) of spectacular scenery and is one of the largest and arguably most successful wildlife sanctuaries in the world. However, its successful establishment was not without debate and antagonisms.

As a conservation solution, federal land protection was ahead of its time. No agents were employed to supervise and enforce the protective measures. The Yellowstone Organic Act—officially known as An Act to Set Apart a Certain Tract of Land Lying Near the Head-waters of the Yellowstone River as a Public Park—created the park and placed its administration under the Department of the Interior, directing the Secretary to establish regulations "to provide against the wanton destruction of the fish and game . . . and against their capture or destruction for the purpose of merchandise or profit." However visionary the Act was, it failed to provide funds or authority for enforcement of park regulations (Trefethen 1975, Haines 1977), as if the set-aside of land was an appropriation enough. This problem resembled the earlier experience in Yosemite, in which commissioners began with an appropriation of $2,000 through the State Act of 1866, and then had only enough to hire a guardian of the park (Hampton 1971).

Lack of institutional support reflected an underlying disagreement about the rightful legalities of parks and refuges. In an 1886 debate about ending civilian administration of Yellowstone, some argued that the Park should be delegated to state or private control, calling the idea of a park "show business" and "imperial" (Hampton 1971:78). On the other hand, defenders of Yellowstone made clear their feeling that it was a place of "natural objects and . . . magnificent scenery . . . [founded on] the principle that this park was to be kept sacred and held apart for the people of this country" and part of its purpose was for, "strangers from all parts of the world who come hither to see the beauty and grandeur of our country." Others rebutted that "Government ought [not] to engage in the raising of wild animals" (Hampton 1971:117). The Yellowstone Protection Act of 1894 settled this question by formalizing federal jurisdiction and intention to administer the park.

Nevertheless, the park remained virtually unprotected. Poaching of wildlife and other resources continued. Elk were especially targeted because of their relative abundance and vulnerability, especially in deep snows. Poachers for the hide market and "tuskers" killed large numbers of animals, removing only their tongues, hides and ivories (canine teeth). Wholesale slaughter and waste of elk became a symbol of efforts for protection for the park's natural resources. Writers attracted national attention to the situation by publishing detailed accounts (see Chapter 3). The statutory protection by both the federal and Wyoming territorial governments in 1881 was useless to stop the extensive poaching, damage to thermal formations and forest fires started by campers, which led to the assignment of enforcement responsibilities for the park to the U. S. Army in 1886.

The military provided a logical solution (Hampton 1971, Haines 1977). Without creating a more specific federal institution for protecting interests of the United States, Congress had no other body on which to call. Using the military to fill the administrative role was pitched as a common-sense interim measure until the country was ready to invest funds in civilian staff. After all, the soldiers were being paid whether they were working at the parks or not. Not so, said others, who claimed the Army should be in constant readiness for national defense. Interestingly, the Yosemite commissioners, who did not have access to federal troops, solved their funding problem by turning to private enterprise. They offered 10-year leases to people who would build buildings, roads and trails. Tolls were collected on some roads.

It remains a point of speculation as to how this police action assigned to the cavalry sat with the troops and their commanders. Unrestrained killing of big game by public

The great stimulus for the first national parks was protection and preservation of great scenic wonders such as the geysers and grand vistas of Yellowstone, Yosemite, Sequoia and other places. In addition, Congress decreed that the areas set aside must also "provide against the wanton destruction of the fish and game" native to the area. Concern for wildlife was based in part by the wholesale slaughter of elk and other species, many shot within the park boundaries. These elk were killed near Yellowstone Falls in 1875 by Frederick Boettler and his brother Phillip, early settlers whose ranch (located 2 miles south of the present town of Emmigrant) was a base for hunting and prospecting in the region, and by other hunters. The Boettler brothers reportedly killed about 2,000 elk in the vicinity of Mammoth Hot Springs. As reported by Norris (unpublished), "as the only part most of them saved was the tongue and the hide, an opinion can be formed of the wanton, unwise, unlawful slaughter of beautiful and valuable animals in the Great National Yellowstone Park." *Photo by L. A. Huffman; courtesy of the Montana State Historical Association.*

and private agents to feed the army and railroad crews and for private gain may have seemed normal to troops on the trail although Congress and several states had been debating and legislating protection for bison since 1864 and especially through the 1870s. Some have speculated that the killing of bison in particular was a part of an Army's strategy against Native Americans. Frank Mayer, a former buffalo "runner," said this policy would not be documented, but: "What did happen was that army officers in charge of plains operations encouraged the slaughter of buffalo in every possible way. Part of this encouragement was of a practical nature that we runners appreciated. It consisted of ammunition, free ammunition, all you could use, all you wanted, more than you needed" (Mayer and Roth 1958:28).

Cook (1907:113) reported that General Philip Sheridan spoke to the Texas legislature against a measure to curb buffalo hunting, offering the alternative: "Send [the hunters] powder and lead, if you will; but, for the sake of lasting peace, let them kill, skin, and sell until the buffaloes are exterminated." A similar point of view came from Sec-

retary of Interior Delano in 1873, who said in his official report that year that he "would not seriously regret the total disappearance of the buffalo . . . in its effect upon the Indians" (Gard 1959:207). About 10 years later, on the other hand, Sheridan was among the advocates for protection of elk in Yellowstone (Pritchard 1999). He retired 2 years before the Army took charge of the park.

Protection as the First Refuge Policy

Protection, as a policy, was based on strong consensus among the natural resource professionals of the day. It also made sense to a vocal segment of the public and would lead to the effective protection of Yellowstone and, later, the establishment of the National Elk Refuge.

It was roughly when the U.S. Cavalry assumed command at Yellowstone in the mid-1880s that settlement of the Jackson Hole area began. With settlement, conversion of natural elk winter range to domestic livestock production began and continued through the following three decades. Use of most of the bottomlands for haying and grazing removed much of the elk's traditional winter forage and resulted in direct conflict between elk and domestic livestock (Graves and Nelson 1919). This competition, coupled with severe winters that typified the 1890s and early 1900s, caused periodic heavy elk mortality (Smith and Robbins 1994). Wilbrecht and Robbins (1979) cited reports that more than 10,000 elk perished during the winter of 1897, and reported that "old hunters and settlers" remembered unusually heavy winters taking a high toll of game animals even before there was significant agricultural development in the area. These losses were exacerbated by elk killed for their tusks and to prevent damage to ranchers' hay, despite the fact that, in 1895, Wyoming—having only acquired statehood 5 years earlier—enacted a 10-month closed season on hunting elk (Robbins et al. 1982).

The first of Yellowstone's managers saw killing in large numbers. In the mid-1870s, Superintendent Norris and visitor George Bird Grinnell were among those who numbered the dead elk. Norris' annual report of 1877 recommended a large game preserve be established in the northwest corner of the park. His ideas for protection were echoed and amended during the next few years, ultimately leading to the assignment of the cavalry to protect the wildlife (Pritchard 1999:9–10). The protective ideas advanced by Superintendent Philetus Norris in 1877 were picked up by the Secretary of Interior Carl Shurz in 1880, who recommended outlawing hunting altogether. His successor, Secretary Henry Moore Teller, instituted the hunting ban in 1883 (Pritchard 1999).

In 1886, when the U.S. First Cavalry assumed command at Yellowstone to enforce the hunting ban and protect all features of the park, public interest in parks and the protection of wildlife was reaching national prominence. Even under the watchful eye and patrols of the cavalry, poaching of elk continued. Newspapers and magazines told of the violations and raised significant national concern over the plight of wildlife. The Boone and Crockett Club (formed in 1887) and several other citizen groups lobbied to protect wildlife within the park.

On the strength of public and professional opinion, the protection was signed in the Yellowstone Protection Act of 1894, the Lacey Act of 1900, and state laws to limit take. The two federal Acts—1894 and 1900—also served to define further federal trust of wildlife (Pritchard 1999). Specifically, the Yellowstone Protection Act provided the authority, manpower and mechanisms to enforce misdemeanor laws, including those against poaching (Haines 1977, Davis 1983). Robbins et al. (1982) opened that passage of this law effectively marked the belated end of an era of public toleration of overexploitation of public natural resources in general and elk in particular.

When "The Nimrod on the Yellowstone" appeared as a full-page cover on New York City's July 11, 1878, edition of *The Daily Graphic,* viewers were appalled at the destruction it creatively depicted and of which its caption told: "The splendid game in the so-called National Park, on the Yellowstone, is being recklessly destroyed by hunters simply for the pleasure of killing, notwithstanding the laws of Congress and of Wyoming and Montana, intended to protect the region from the spoiler. Elk, of which the Park contains thousands, are shot down, and the carcasses left upon the plain, not even the skin being removed. . . . It is the duty of the prosecuting authorities of the Territories . . . to see that such criminal and wanton waste be punished and repressed." *Photo courtesy of the Library of Congress.*

Focusing on Wildlife

In the early 20th century, conservationists began planning and designing reserved lands specifically as wildlife refuges. The focus on wildlife was accomplished through changes in federal authority and agencies, public debate, an elk problem in Wyoming and the science of the time.

Soon after 1900, certain fundamental concepts of wildlife management were publicly established in North America under the leadership of President Theodore Roosevelt of the United States and Prime Minister Sir Wilfred Laurier of Canada. The concepts found application in the United States' newly created forest reserves, under the management of Gifford Pinchot, and a voice in William T. Hornaday, director of the New York Zoological Society. Federal conservation efforts advanced the concept of efficient use and protection of resources. The Progressive Party's ideal of centralized, rational management (and concentrated power) enabled wildlife managers to focus land reservations on wildlife as a sole purpose. However, scientists and administrators of refuges battled over conflicting notions in their own minds and in the public's view about how to manage confined wildlife and share its habitat with human visitors.

In Canada, the catalysts were Sir Clifford Sifton, chairman of the Commission on Conservation, and C. Gordon Hewitt, Canada's chief entomologist, father of the 1916 Migratory Bird Treaty Act and author of *The Conservation of the Wild Life of Canada* (1921).

Federal Authority and Agencies

Federal land policies reversed course, from disposal to reservation, with the repeal of homestead laws and creation of authorities for the reservation of land. In one important instance, the shift from disposal to reservation was accomplished all in the same congressional act, variously known as the Forest Reserve Act or Creative Act of 1891. The latter provision of this law authorized the president to create forest reserves, but the main purpose of the law, seen in its official title, was to repeal one of the homestead acts—"An Act to Repeal Timber-culture Laws, and for Other Purposes." President Harrison used this authority to create the Yellowstone National Park Timberland Reserve on the outskirts of the park. He also used this authority to create the first functional wildlife refuge in Alaska in 1892.

In 1888, the experiment with state control of reserved lands fell into disfavor. Criticism of California's commissioners of Yosemite resulted in official investigations and, ultimately, the taking of Yosemite Park back into federal jurisdiction (Hampton 1971).

The federal role continued to strengthen under President Roosevelt, who invoked executive power to create the Pelican Island Refuge in 1903. Roosevelt also appointed a commission to evaluate laws pertaining to federal land. At the time, there was no clear presidential authority for what Roosevelt was doing. In 1905, the commission recommended ways of consolidating federal authority and helped build the idea of a centrally planned system of land classification and management (Coville et al. 1905). That same year, Congress provided substance to the president's questionable use of executive power by authorizing the president to create wildlife ranges (Bean and Rowland 1997).

The other institutional change that strengthened the federal role was creation of federal land and resource management. The U.S. Commission of Fish and Fisheries, established in 1871, the Bureau of Biological Survey (1896) and the U.S. Forest Service (1905) all received charge over reserved lands. In 1916, the National Park Service was established for the care of Yosemite as well as Yellowstone, Sequoia and General Grant national parks. (In 1940, General Grant National Park was absorbed into the new Kings Canyon National Park, which was joined with Sequoia and now is managed as one park called Sequoia and Kings Canyon National Parks.)

Public Debate

More Americans were capable of public debate once widespread use of the telegraph enabled quick and easy communication across the United States. Use of the telegraph allowed newspapers and magazines to disseminate news quickly and broadly. By about 1870, major newspapers were established in the United States. After Yellowstone Park was established and by the time the Cavalry was in charge, the *Chicago Evening Journal* and *Scribner's Monthly* carried allegations of ineptitude and destruction under Captain Harris' command (Hampton 1971). People filed petitions urging government officials to protect public resources. The arrest of a Yellowstone poacher named Howell in 1894, who was caught in the act, gave Grinnell strong material to use in *Forest and Stream* to help move the Park Protection Act through Congress that year (Hampton 1971). The management of Yosemite in California by a board of commissioners also drew the attention of users and preservers of the valley, with newspapers taking differing sides and the issue eventually drawing national attention.

Refuges for Wildlife:
Formation of the National Elk Refuge

Elk in Wyoming helped attract attention to the idea of refuges established specifically for wildlife. The species-specific idea for a refuge in the vicinity of Yellowstone began to surface in 1905 when the Wyoming State Legislature established the Teton Game Preserve adjacent to Yellowstone National Park. After 7 years, starting in 1905, the National Elk Refuge was established in 1912 as one of the earliest units in this system of suitable wildlife habitats. Pursuant to the Game and Bird Preserves Act of 1905, its purpose was specifically to protect elk and their winter habitat, as well as private property.

Murie (1951:318) described this preserve as, "an inviolate sanctuary for elk . . . in the heart of the elk summer range . . . [where] after spring migration, a large number of calves are born . . . herds spend the summer, and . . . the rut takes place." The 570,000-acre (230,680 ha) preserve between the southern boundary of Yellowstone National Park and Jackson Hole existed until 1947, when it was abolished by the State Legislature to manage elk more effectively (Anderson 1958, Ise 1961).

One of the first suggestions for an elk refuge in the Jackson Hole area was made in about 1906 by D. C. Nowlin, then a Wyoming State game warden. The concept gained momentum during the severe winters of 1909, 1910 and 1911, when an estimated 20,000 to 30,000 elk were forced into the valley where they raided haystacks and, despite the help of this domestic hay, died in record numbers (Anderson 1958, cf. Cole 1969).

In 1910, the State of Wyoming appropriated $5,000 to buy hay for the elk (Madsen 1985). However, even with that appropriation, the supply of hay was inadequate and many hundreds of elk died that winter (Wilbrecht and Robbins

1979). The following year (1911) the Legislature requested help from the federal government. Congress responded with an appropriation of $20,000, "to be made available immediately for feeding and protecting elk in Jackson Hole and vicinity, and for removing some of them to stock other localities" (Wilbrecht and Robbins 1979: 249). In fact, it proved impossible to carry out this congressional mandate because Wyoming had already purchased, and was feeding, all the hay available in the valley. Consequently, nothing further could be done to remedy the situation except to make arrangements for the following winter.

The loss in 1911 alone was estimated at 2,500 animals (Wilbrecht and Robbins 1979, Madsen 1985). These events attracted national attention when local residents appealed for help in dealing with losses of elk and the corresponding loss of crops and hay.

In August 1912, Congress appropriated $45,000 for the purchase of land for the production of feed for elk and maintenance of a winter elk refuge. An additional $5,000 was appropriated in early 1913. The resultant National Elk Refuge was created with a dual mission: protect and feed elk during the winter and protect local hay and crops from elk depredation. The initial purchase of 1,760 acres (713 ha) was augmented by an additional 1,000 acres (405 hectares) of

Passage of laws to protect elk and other wildlife within refuges was only the first step in restoring elk herds. Poaching continued until monies were found to secure enforcement of game laws, depleted herds required time to rebuild, areas where elk had been locally eliminated required new stock and, in some areas, severe winters forced elk onto winter ranges, such as Jackson Hole, that had been converted by settlers into farmland. Starving elk damaged private property and haystacks. Despite feeding efforts, many elk died. *Photo courtesy of Lee Van DeWater.*

land withdrawn from public domain, which resulted in a refuge of 2,760 acres (1,118 ha) (Robbins and Wilbrecht 1979).

Science of the Day

As management institutions were changing, scientific thought during the early 1900s was phasing in some of its own modern fundamentals. In the 19th century, preserving "wild nature" as parks had fit closely with traditions of natural history studies. Professionals were expert at classifying, cataloguing and preserving specimens, therefore preserving nature made clear sense. But an important change occurred around the turn of the 20th century, as scientists such as Charles Adams branched into new intellectual territory. He was a pioneer in the still new concept of studying relationships among living things and their environments—ecology. Adams (1913) published one of the first ecological texts, *Guide to the Study of Animal Ecology*, and attended the first organizational meeting for the Ecological Society of America in 1914 (Pritchard 1999).

Adams and other ecological thinkers focused their ideas on the management of parks and refuges. Park and refuge "natural conditions" were considered the best setting in which to conduct ecological studies and ecology was gaining a position as the basis for management (Pritchard 1999). The foothold of ecological thought included the concept of equilibrium between population growth and environmental resistance. It also recognized systematic interactions among species and processes. However, turn-of-the-century ecology left plenty of room for contrary thoughts, such as predator control and fire exclusion.

Leopold (1933) included Roosevelt among the revolutionaries who suggested that wildlife populations regenerate and, therefore, can be hunted without necessarily annihilating them. This was a fundamental change, Leopold (1933:17) wrote, from the idea that game existed in a fixed quantity and that game laws were needed as "a device for *dividing up* a dwindling treasure." The old idea of a fixed quantity was the intellectual underpinning for restricting hunting and creating refuges. The new idea of a regenerating quantity became the support for controlling environmental factors to increase, decrease or maintain populations according to policy goals.

Adams advanced the idea that research and management should focus beyond the level of individuals and single species and consider associations (i.e., communities) of species and environmental factors (Pritchard 1999). The National Park Service responded to this concept with very protective policies applied to all elements of the biological communities within park boundaries.

The limits of ecological thinking were both intellectual and political. Intellectually, Adams and his colleagues believed that animal and environmental components were finely balanced in whatever condition the managers found them, yet these scientists believed that adjustments were justified for visitors' sake. Visitors to Yellowstone would see more birds and other wildlife, they reasoned, if managers promoted berry-thickets near campgrounds and built feeding stations in the park. Barrington Moore (one of Adams' colleagues and president of the Ecological Society of America) even embraced the functions of dead trees and downed wood in his concept of natural balance, yet he considered fire wasteful (Pritchard 1999). The primary political limit on ecological management lay with the issue of predators. Adams and Moore and other ecologists argued that predators were part of the balance, but park managers overruled them and continued with policies of predator control. Sam Woodring, for example, as Chief Ranger at Yellowstone and Superintendent of Grand Teton National Park, could not be convinced that game could coexist with predators (Pritchard 1999).

Managing Without Guns: Land Deals, Feeding and Translocation

Between the turn the century and about 1940, refuge managers appeared to wrestle with transition. The fruit of their protective policies was evident in the larger herds and the effectiveness of some of their tactics came into question (feeding, for example, was rarely effective in preventing depredation on nearby private crops). The evidence suggested it was time to change from protective management, driven by concern about extinction, to maintenance management aimed at optimizing herd size.

Transition was slow and incomplete, most notably on the issue of how to enforce an upper limit on the herd size. Likely explanations for the difficulty in transition came down to uncertainty about population dynamics, continuing pressure to protect private hay and political queasiness on the subject of culling elk that were the trophies for a growing number of wildlife watchers. Evidence for these forces is presented in the details below. Another key perspective is that the cavalry (with its mandate of protection) was still in place in Yellowstone until 1916. The institutional memory favoring protection doubtlessly held sway despite the obvious overabundance of elk before and after 1910 when elk die-offs occurred in the region, although neighboring ranchers continued to complain about depredations on their crops.

During this transition, managers expanded refuge sizes, continued with some feeding programs and began translocating elk.

Feeding

The practice of providing hay to bait elk away from privately owned haystacks became routine at the National Elk Refuge by 1910. That practice, combined with continual harassment of the elk feeding on private hay lands, eventually concentrated most of the elk on the refuge. It soon became apparent, however, that the refuge was too small to accommodate the number of wintering elk. Heavy losses of elk around the refuge during the winters of 1917 and 1922 prompted D. C. Nowlin to write: "The past winter has proven conclusively to me, that this place does not, nor can the present Refuge be made to produce enough feed for even the elk that are left that come here for feed in hard winters. Eleven years of continuous feeding have virtually domesticated the elk that annually migrate to the Refuge and they seem to have lost the stamina and all the 'rustling' [foraging] qualities noted in the wild species" (Wilbrecht and Robbins 1979:250).

In fact, the elk had become habituated to the feeding program on the National Elk Refuge. Nowlin expressed concern about any future for the elk unless the refuge was expanded and there was a serious commitment of funds for the program. Depredation problems continued. Nowlin wrote further: "As to elk trespass on ranches adjoining, and in the vicinity of the Refuge, I have this to say: Continuous feeding for several years has served to bring the elk to the Refuge and to the ranches every season, whereas, before regular feeding was started, the elk congregated here only in severe winters. Elk depredations and heavy losses in hard winters influenced a large majority of the settlers to advocate the purchase by the government of the 'swamp' north of Jackson, when Mr. E. A. Preble investigated conditions here in 1911. It was assumed that elk would remain perfectly wild and come to the feeding grounds only when forced to do so by very bad weather conditions. The elk now come for hay regularly and early in the season, and we have been unable to accumulate a supply of hay sufficient for hard winters" (Wilbrecht and Robbins 1979:250).

The limited hay on the refuge was rationed all winter. Refuge records show that at times the animals received as little as 3 pounds (1.4 kg) per elk per day (Wilbrecht and Robbins 1979, Robbins et al. 1982). Later, additional hay was purchased and hauled to the refuge. Other logistical adjustments were made to the feeding program in its first 75 years. Initially, elk were fed loose hay from stacks, later with baled hay and, since 1975, alfalfa pellets. Delivery vehicles have progressed from horse-drawn sleighs to tractor-drawn sleighs to large-capacity trucks currently used to deliver the pellets.

Yellowstone Park managers also fed elk, but on more of an ad hoc basis. The last military superintendent, Major Lloyd Milton Brett, ran feeding programs between 1910 and 1916. Later, superintendent Horace Albright came to Yellowstone just in time for the winter of 1919, which threatened to kill many elk. Albright orchestrated magazine articles and wealthy connections to fund a feeding program in 1919 and 1920 as well, when his purpose was to keep elk inside the park where hunting was prohibited (Pritchard 1999).

As a result of enforcement of game laws and establishment of refuges, soon growing elk herds moved onto privately owned ranches, where they damaged fences and consumed forage and stored hay intended for cattle. Irate ranchers and worried wildlife officials harassed the marauding elk on private lands, forcing them onto the refuges, where increasing numbers of elk soon damaged vegetation and made management ever-more difficult. In desperation, wildlife managers on the National Elk Refuge, Yellowstone National Park, and some other areas began providing artificial feed to wintering elk to keep the animals from damaging private lands, and managers appealed to sportsmen for financial support to purchase elk feed. *Photo courtesy of Howard Schofield.*

Expanding

Early 20th century managers' analysis of the situation at the National Elk Refuge was that of a herd with too little space, instead of a space with too many elk. Surrounding national forests became the focus of attempts to expand.

In 1919, U.S. Forest Service lands adjacent to the east side of the refuge were classified as critical big game winter range, and taken off limits to grazing by domestic livestock (Robbins et al. 1982). The refuge was augmented with an additional 1,760 acres (712 ha) in 1927, when the Izaak Walton League of America donated land purchased with funds solicited from a nationwide subscription campaign (Trefethen 1961). A major increase in refuge area resulted after 1935, when Congress appropriated funds for habitat acquisition for refuges and national parks throughout the United States. As a result of this appropriation, many homesteads were purchased and added to the National Elk Refuge (Wilbrecht and Robbins 1979). Some boundary adjustments occurred, with the enlargement of Grand Teton National Park in 1950. With these additions, the refuge grew to its present size, exceeding 24,710 acres (10,000 ha).

Sportsmen were often very protective of increasing elk herds, and responded to requests for assistance with both financial and political support for efforts to expand refuge boundaries to meet the demands of the growing herds. As a result, the National Elk Refuge grew to encompass more than 24,000 acres (9,713 ha), and cattle were removed from some portions of adjacent national forest lands. *Photo courtesy of the Wildlife Management Institute.*

Enlargement also was a strategy in Yellowstone. These boundary adjustments had the force of the president's Committee on Outdoor Recreation behind them. In 1925 and 1926, a delegation including Charles Sheldon of the Boone and Crockett Club, Chief of the Forest Service W. B. Greeley, Director of the National Park Service Stephen Mather and others investigated several park and forest boundaries. In 1926, the Park Service began negotiating with Wyoming to move the boundary line to topographic divides at the head of river drainages, which was completed in 1929. Lands to the north were added to Yellowstone by 1932, in a land deal involving a private organization called the Gallatin Game Preservation Company (Pritchard 1999).

A similar idea of the time was to capture the habitat values of national forests even without annexing the land into a park or refuge. Forest Service Chief Graves believed that managers would "be best able to maintain and develop game life on areas permanently devoted to forest and park purposes or set aside specifically for wild-life preservation" (U.S. Department of the Interior 1917:187–188). On the basis of this thought, Graves recommended a landscape approach that including feeding as necessary: "The Yellowstone elk problem will never be solved except by applying a plan that includes the entire region, both the park and the surrounding forests. With such a plan and with adequate authority, the respective responsibilities may be distributed and the necessary activities coordinated for effective results. The whole talent and resources of the Government should be used in preparing and carrying out these plans. This would apply to redistributing animals, making plants in depleted areas, killing predatory animals, feeding when necessary, and actual field administration." (U.S. Department of the Interior 1917:191–192).

This plan apparently made sense to E. W. Nelson, chief of the Biological Survey. In his speech to the same Fourth National Park Service Conference in 1917, Nelson described a cross-boundary effort with the Forest Service to provide adequate winter grazing for the present Yellowstone herds and a reasonable increase. The Forest Service invited the Biological Survey to cooperate in a study of what areas in the national forests bordering Yellowstone would be necessary for these purposes. Chief Nelson reported that: "A representative of the Forest Service and one from the Biological Survey made an extended visit to the park and the surrounding forest during the summer of 1915, to learn the summer conditions in relation to the game in and out of the park, and another trip was made last winter to observe the condition at that season" (U.S. Department of the Interior 1917:203).

The inimitable Hornaday (1913:166) had earlier pontificated on this subject, arguing that national forests were so capable of supporting elk that these lands should be stocked with elk from which surplus animals would be, "presently killed according to some rational, working system. . . . In view of the awful cost of beef[,] . . . it is high time that we should consider the raising of game on the public domain on such lines that it would form a valuable food supply without diminishing the value of the forests." Although it is difficult to determine whether or not to take Hornaday's notion seriously, he clearly had a grasp of the concept of culling and the habitat value of nonrefuge lands.

Translocating Elk

Translocation appealed to two of the managers' greatest needs. First, it was a means of reducing the fast-growing herds in the National Elk Refuge and Yellowstone National Park. Second, it fit cleanly into the national belief that elk were near extinction and that more refuges were needed. Naturally, the other newly created refuges needed restock-

ing and the advocacy groups that helped point the federal government to new sites for refuges also highlighted the need for restocking. In some cases, private advocates advanced money for corrals and other expenses of the translocation projects (Trefethen 1975).

Robbins et al. (1982) noted that from 1912 to 1967, more than 13,500 elk were sent from Yellowstone National Park to 38 states and Canada and Mexico (Figure 163). These translocated elk were used to stock ranges as well as to provide animals for zoos and wildlife parks. Elk from the National Elk Refuge area were used to reestablish herds at the Wichita Mountains Wildlife Refuge in Oklahoma and the National Bison Range in Montana. They also were used to restock historic ranges or establish new herds in Arizona, Colorado, Idaho, Montana, New Mexico, Oregon, South Dakota, Utah, Washington and Wyoming. Translocations from the National Elk Refuge and Yellowstone herds were critical to the reestablishment of elk throughout North America after population declines in the late 19th and early 20th centuries.

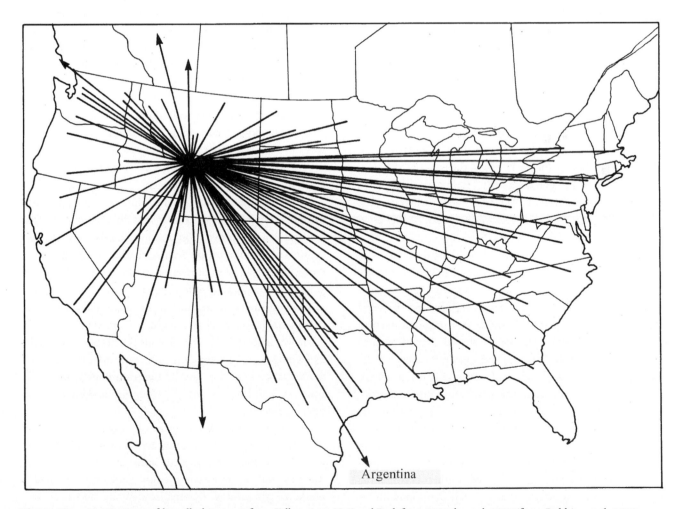

Argentina

Figure 163.   Destinations of live elk shipments from Yellowstone National Park from 1892 through 1967 (from Robbins et al. 1982).

Sportsmen's clubs across the nation were anxious to share in the success of elk restoration programs on major refuges, and refuge managers often welcomed opportunity to reduce their burgeoning herds. The resulting program of translocation sent more than 13,500 elk from Yellowstone National Park alone between 1912 and 1967. Elk were sent, often by railway and horse-drawn wagon (such as these destined for release in Arizona) to 38 states as well as Canada and Mexico. *Photo courtesy of the Arizona Game and Fish Department.*

State Programs: The Utah Experience

The combination of protection, feeding and translocation was used in state as well as federal programs. States across the country—most notably Utah, New Mexico, Iowa and Pennsylvania—established reserves for ungulates about this time and each played a role in restoring deer and elk across the country. Utah's story is especially interesting as an example of what became of elk translocated from the Jackson/Yellowstone area.

In the presettlement and early pioneer times, elk were considered plentiful in mountainous areas of much of Utah (Murie 1951), but by the early 1900s, these herds had been virtually extirpated (Hancock 1955). Reintroduction of elk into Utah was initiated in 1912 by residents who obtained elk from Wyoming and the Yellowstone Park herd (Popov and Low 1950).

Initially, Utah used a preserve or refuge system as a means of protecting big game populations. Biennial reports indicate that, during the period of 1919 to 1923, nearly 1 million acres (405,000 ha) of Utah's best deer and elk range were set aside as refuges to provide year-round protection for big game animals (Utah State Fish and Game Commission 1920–1924). Many states and provinces adopted the concept of setting aside areas of seasonal concentrations, or areas generally defining the year-round distribution of groups of animals, as refuges. In Utah, the concept remains part of the current management program of herd units.

The association of a refuge system and winter feeding program came about in most states, just as in the Jackson Hole/Yellowstone area, as a result of conflicts between big game herds and agricultural and urban developments. A winter feeding program in Utah was instituted in 1939, with a primary purpose being to lure big game away from

farmland and residential areas where they were damaging orchards and shrubbery. Because elk numbers still were low, emphasis was placed on feeding mule deer, but elk also were fed. In some areas, it was necessary to feed deer and elk for as long as 3 months, but even so, deer losses became a problem after about 30 days. Other states were experiencing similar results with feeding programs. The Utah Fish and Game Department reported that it determined, by experimenting with feeding programs to sustain deer for long periods and through practical experience in Utah and other states, that winter feeding of game for long periods of time was not economically sound. However, it had been forced to resort to winter feeding programs to lure the game from areas where they could do damage.

By the late 1940s, most of the winter feeding programs in Utah were in developed areas and directed toward agricultural damage prevention and public relations. One exception was at Hardware Ranch, in the northern part of Utah, which had been purchased by the state in 1945 to act as a refuge and "intercept feeding area" for elk. "During the migration from summer to winter range, the majority of the elk in this area passes through. . . [Hardware Ranch and] . . . it was believed that the elk could be stopped, and held, by feeding . . . to prevent damage to orchards and other cultivated crops near the 'face of the mountain' from Blacksmith Fork to Logan Canyon" (Utah Fish and Game Commission 1954:27).

At the same time, an elk trap was constructed at Hardware Ranch to provide for intensive studies of elk. The objective was "that management information learned from this area could be applied to the other units when refined to workable procedures" (Kimball and Wolfe 1985:192). To a large extent this objective has been realized. There are more than 20 research publications pertaining to Hardware

Utah's Hardware Ranch became a model for many western state agencies as elk herds expanded—and as the potential for damage to private ranchlands increased. The Hardware Ranch was purchased in 1945 and managed specifically to *intercept* migratory elk that might otherwise continue traveling traditional routes to winter ranges that had been converted by private developers to ranchland, farmland and orchards. *Photo by Don Paul; courtesy of Utah Division of Wildlife Resources.*

Ranch elk, on such topics as winter feeding rates, demographics of elk populations under various harvest programs, elk behavior and elk immobilization studies.

Reluctance to Kill

In the 1910s and 1920s, the protection ideal was mixed with a recognized need to control the population size. However, control mentality did not go as far as the idea of purposefully killing elk. Perhaps that concept made no sense to people who were still trying to repopulate a species believed to be near extinction.

That is not to say no one thought of culling elk. The idea appears about 1913, in the writings of Grinnell (Pritchard 1999) and Hornaday (1913). However, the idea of direct killing was not broached as a management tool until 1917 (Pritchard 1999). At that time it was summarily rejected, with reason being the likelihood of protests. Hornaday (1913:169) suggested managers should, "reduce the number, *and the annual birth,* [original emphasis] of females to a figure sufficiently limited that the herds could be maintained on existing ranges." Graves (U.S. Department of the Interior 1917:190) wrote: "In several instances State game preserves have been superimposed upon the national forest,

or blanket laws passed restricting hunting, without reference to the possible increase of the protected animals beyond the available feed, and without reference to the various problems of forest administration. All goes well until the numbers increase beyond the capacity of the land to support them, and then the animals suffer or actually die of starvation. And I fear very much that in the case of our splendid elk herd in the Olympic Mountains that unless the principles of technical game administration are applied there, ultimately that herd will suffer, because it may increase to a point beyond what the feeding grounds will supply to the animals, and then the animals will begin to starve or otherwise suffer. It is just as unintelligent and just as cruel to overstock a range with wild stock as with cattle."

Nevertheless, managers discredited the idea of killing elk at this time. Nelson (U.S. Department of the Interior 1917:202) referenced a "direct-reduction" prescription for Yellowstone but dismissed it as based on faulty data: "[It] has even been proposed that thousands of these elk be killed in order to stop the supposed overstocking of the range and attendant wholesale starvation of the animals during the first severe season. This idea was due to an erroneous belief as to the total number of elk in the park and as to their rate of increase."

The most likely explanations for the reluctance to kill are that (1) prevailing thought could not shift from the desire to protect at all costs to the desire to manage for optimum herd size as quickly as the herd size responded to predator controls, hunting prohibitions and enforcement of poaching laws, and (2) it made more sense to most people to ship surplus elk to depleted ranges rather than to destroy them.

Whatever the cause for confusion in policy, the facts support Leopold's (1933) suggestion that the first refuges—for example, Last Mountain Lake in Canada (1887), Yellowstone (1894), Pelican Island (1903) and Wichita (1905)—mark a halfway point between the idea of restricting take and the idea of producing sustained annual crops of wild game for recreational use. Managers would need to believe that a certain number of animals could be removed—by killing or translocating—without compromising the herd viability. As translocation succeeded in reestablishing herds throughout the West, the need for new populations waned and the idea of culling the source elk herds became a tool of management. The notion of limiting the take of wildlife to less than the annual increase may have appeared as early as 1915. In that year, Wyoming issued "limited licenses" for moose for this purpose (Leopold 1933).

As discussed in the next section, there also was at work the more powerful factor of the basic dilemma in the mission of the National Park Service. Its dual mission from the National Park Service Act—"to conserve the scenery and the natural objects and wildlife therein and to provide for the enjoyment of same"—poses a riddle that remains unsolved: how shall we conserve wildlife without evicting ourselves (Leopold 1933)?

Culling and Hunting in Refuges and Parks

Besides the revelations on population dynamics from the Kaibab deer population irruption and crash in the late 1920s and other research (Leopold et al. 1947), weaknesses in refuge policy were becoming clear. The policies of killing predators, enlarging refuges and feeding and translocating elk were not sustainable. The practices maintained elk numbers for a time and the herds continued to attract public visitors, but both had their limits. Finding alternatives under the increased interest and scrutiny of the public was difficult. The situation in Utah again serves as an example.

Utah Phases Out Feeding

Through the 1950s, Utah's feeding programs were limited to elk and used primarily to prevent agricultural damage. By the mid-1960s, the Department of Fish and Game was feeding at only two locations—Hardware Ranch and on the Ogden River Unit at the Ogden Valley's Monastery near Huntsville. Concerns for private land habitat deterioration, failure to eliminate elk depredation in the immediate area and differences in overall objectives for the elk herd eventually led to termination of feeding at the latter location (Kimball and Wolfe 1985).

With elimination of the supplemental feeding program on the Ogden River Unit, management options for elk were limited to maintaining herds on available ranges. The one exception remained Hardware Ranch, where special research projects (previously discussed) and an active winter recreation program for nonconsumptive wildlife users were in place (Kimball and Wolfe 1985).

The nonconsumptive program at Hardware Ranch has attracted as many as 50,000 visitors during winters and currently supports private sector development of sleigh rides, tours and a cafe through summer, autumn and winter. Given these ancillary interests, termination of the winter feeding program at Hardware Ranch would be difficult, regardless of the objectives established for the elk.

Hunting and Culling Begins

As professional wildlife management continued to establish itself in the 1920s and 1930s, the concept of intervention in nature for management purposes took hold (Pritchard 1999). In Yellowstone, this thinking began to manifest itself in the culling of pelicans as part of fish conservation in 1924 and manipulations of bears by feeding and capturing. A pivotal elk study began in 1928. Rush (1932) triggered concern about overgrazing in Yellowstone and the need to reduce the herd size. This led to realization that elk must be culled and the first direct reductions in 1934. From that year until 1967, when reductions ceased, 67,440 elk were removed from the Northern Yellowstone elk herd. This number included those that succumbed in winter, those shot by rangers and hunters and those shipped to other ranges (Pritchard 1999).

Recreational hunting also became an accepted practice on refuges. As early as 1924, and again in 1949 and 1958, hunters were allowed to hunt on some waterfowl refuges. In 1984, the U.S. Fish and Wildlife Service extended hunting opportunities on refuges (Bean and Rowland 1997).

Revising the Mission for Wildlife Refuges

Possibly, the beginning of culling and opening of refuges to hunting prompted Congress to consolidate activities on refuges into an encompassing mission statement. Despite the early origins of wildlife ranges and refuges, no comprehensive set of administrative rules governed management of the disparate units until passage of the National Wildlife Refuge Administration Act of 1966. This act sought to consolidate all of the different refuge areas into a single "system" and place their management under the administration of the U.S. Fish and Wildlife Service.

Three decades later, the National Wildlife Refuge System Improvement Act of 1997 amended its predecessor in several important respects. The act defined the National Wildlife Refuge System's mission: "The mission of the System is to administer a national network of lands and waters for the conservation, management, and where appropriate, restoration of the fish, wildlife, and plant resources and their habitats within the United States for the benefit of present and future generations of Americans." In addition, the act established new planning requirements for each refuge and clarified the standards and procedures to regulate recreational and commercial uses (Musgrave et al. 1998). Significantly, the act also mandated the Secretary of the Interior to ensure the biological integrity, diversity and environmental health of the national refuge system (Bolen and Robinson 1999).

This broadening of vision for the management of national wildlife refuges reflected a nationwide expansion in ideas about conservation. The new ability and willingness to include in management plans many more parts and processes of ecosystems, and the obvious need for more diverse human uses of refuges, became the context for one of today's remaining debates about refuge management and ecology—natural regulation.

Natural Regulation

The debate underlying refuge management for elk by 1970 was the same debate driving conservation events surrounding Yellowstone and the National Elk Refuge. The all-encompassing question was (and remains) whether, and how, the role of people in ecosystems of reserved lands should be limited. This conundrum was forced on the National Park Service in the agency's organic mission. It was the key issue of the policy debate over compatible uses in national wildlife refuges. Ever since the early 1900s, when the Ecological Society of America's Committee on Preservation of Natural Conditions adopted the motto "An undisturbed area in every national park and public forest" (Pritchard 1999:43) as its goal, the issue of human intervention (or lack thereof) has been the force behind designated wilderness areas in national forests. It has surfaced in deciding whether to feed elk and whether to kill elk in refuges, and it has been at the center of controversy about natural regulation, particularly in Yellowstone.

The National Park Service has applied natural regulation to management of elk and other ungulates in the Rocky Mountain national parks, specifically Yellowstone, Grand Teton, Glacier and Rocky Mountain. The principal impetus for this management direction arose from mounting public opposition to direct removals of elk and other ungulates as a means of reducing excess numbers in Yellowstone National Park (Woolf 1974). As noted previously, culling and translocation of overabundant ungulates had been instituted as control strategies in several western parks in the early 1940s (Wright 1998). Opposition to the reduction programs by various segments of the public, including sportsmen, animal welfare advocates and environmentalists, increased significantly during the 1960s as did media coverage of the events involved.

The issue of "natural regulation" of plants and animals in national parks and refuges became a contentious management issue in the 20th century, particularly in Yellowstone National Park, as scientific studies began to demonstrate that growing populations of elk and other wildlife were clearly influencing patterns of vegetation across large portions of the landscape. Elk severely damaged this heavily browsed aspen on winter range in northern Yellowstone. Damage such as this adversely impacted some ecosystems in ways that affected other species of concern. Fundamental to this issue was the role of humans as active managers of elk (and other species) to achieve specific outcomes within "natural" ecosystems. Although some people advocated reduction of the elk herd by recreational hunters, others advocated a strict "no interference" policy. *Photo courtesy of Yellowstone National Park.*

This opposition provided impetus in 1962 for the Secretary of the Interior to impanel a group of prominent scientists to evaluate a range of wildlife issues in the national parks. This committee, formally designated as the Special Advisory Board on Wildlife Management in the National Parks, resulted in a report—hereafter referred to as the Leopold Report—that advised that, wherever possible, the parks should be managed to maintain a reasonable semblance of a primitive state (Leopold et al. 1963). It concluded that certain situations might warrant human intervention to maintain desired conditions, including control of ungulates. The committee's recommendations were approved by the Secretary in 1963 and incorporated into National Park Service administrative policy.

Direct reductions continued for several years after the Leopold Report, amidst public hue and cry. The mounting opposition culminated in 1967, when the U.S. Senate held field hearings to debate the issue of elk control in Yellowstone (Wright 1998). Facing intense political pressure, including the threat of budget cuts, the Park Service in 1969 banned artificial control in the park. The agency later extended this shift in management policy to other parks.

As the Park Service ended artificial control, it also embraced the theory and philosophy of natural regulation with respect to ungulate management. Wagner et al. (1995) argued that the decision to experiment with natural regulation was prompted by political pressure from local hunters, guides and outfitters interested in causing the park to maintain high elk numbers in the Northern Yellowstone herd, thereby enhancing local elk hunting.

The natural regulation theory is based on observations of ungulate/vegetation interactions in a variety of settings and set forth by Caughley (1976). Natural regulation rests on the assumptions that ungulates are food-limited and diminishing food resources lead to decreased reproduction and survival rates. Conversely, increasing food resources allows for increases in reproduction and survival. Theoretically, a dynamic equilibrium results between large ungulate herbivores and the supporting vegetation (Singer et al. 1998). Also, the theory suggests that predation (other than hunting) is not necessary in regulation of ungulate populations (Kay 1990). Boyce (1991) applied the synonym of "ecological process management"—a term coined by Shepherd and Caughley (1987)—to describe the theory of natural regulation as applied in management direction.

The underlying philosophy was reflected in Houston's (1982:1) assessment: "The primary purpose of natural areas, such as Yellowstone, is to maintain ecosystems in as near pristine conditions as possible. This means that ecological processes, including plant succession and the natural regulation of animal numbers, should be permitted to pro-

ceed as under pristine conditions and that modern man should be restricted generally to nonconsumptive uses."

Since the implementation of natural regulation in management direction, it has become one of the most contentious natural resource management polemics of recent time. In essence, Yellowstone became a proving ground for both the theory and the underlying philosophy. Debate about it has generated a voluminous literature, both from the popular press and the scientific community, including comprehensive treatments by Chase (1986), Hess (1993) and Sellars (1997). The entire Fall 1998 issue *The Wildlife Society Bulletin* was devoted to the subject of ungulate management in national parks. The arguments involved are diverse, complex and far from value-neutral. As summarized by Boyce (1998), the principal questions in the debate include the following: What are the direct effects of herbivory on the vegetation? Is there a loss of biodiversity as a consequence of ungulate herbivory (see Wagner 1994)? What was the pristine abundance of elk and other herbivores and the effect of Native Americans on these populations (see Chapter 3)? And, does Yellowstone National Park constitute a "complete ecosystem"?

The effect of the Yellowstone natural regulation debate on refuge management thinking elsewhere in North America is buried within many parallel influences on refuge managers. As shown by the following evidence, although refuge managers differed on the values and risks of intervention, the political and philosophical growth of the environmental movement was turning the debate against intervention.

The Fish and Wildlife Service has distinguished itself from the Park Service on the role of refuge management. Hunting became an authorized use of refuges mainly as a recreational issue, but legal defenses of the policy by the federal government rely on the usefulness of hunting as part of refuge management. The Refuge Policy Act of 1966 and regulations in 1984 both lay legal groundwork for hunting on refuges. Antihunting groups challenged the 1984 regulations and a decision in 1989 to permit public deer hunting on the Mason Neck National Wildlife Refuge in Virginia, but neither case (nor any other) overcame a Fish and Wildlife Service analysis behind the agency's position that hunting helps control deer populations (Bean and Rowland 1997).

Pritchard (1999) argued that differing professional views on intervention stem from a difference in how professionals construed the terms protection and management in the 1960s. What Starker Leopold called protective activity in Yellowstone, for example, was called management by Adolph Murie—control of predators, fire and insects, and the manipulation of fish and ungulates (Pritchard 1999). Leopold argued for replacing protective intervention with management interventions that create and maintain natural scenes (Pritchard 1999). From his different standpoint, Murie believed Yellowstone had already been overmanaged, therefore he objected to the Leopold Report's urging the Park Service toward further manipulation of the ecosystem.

Whatever potential these professional debates had to change refuge thinking probably is lost under the changes made through the much broader debate in American politics about environmentalism. Many more Americans were brought into the issues of land, water, air and wildlife with Rachel Carson's (1962) exposé of chemical use and pollution shower whose effects were much closer to home than were the remote lands that were the focus of conservationists (Paehlke 1989). The results of the larger debate included the Wilderness Act of 1964, the National Environmental Policy Act of 1970 (NEPA) and the Endangered Species Act of 1973.

Each of these laws represented a shift from the conservationist point of view that resources should be used efficiently, to the environmentalist view that human influence on the environment should be limited (Paehlke 1989). The Wilderness Act recognizes and attempts to maintain areas "where the earth and its community of life are untrammeled by man, where man himself is a visitor who does not remain." NEPA made it the policy of the entire United States government, pursuant to the National Environmental Policy Act (NEPA), "to promote efforts which will prevent or eliminate damage to the environment and biosphere and stimulate the health and welfare of man." NEPA's basic rule is that the human influences on the environment must be studied so as to limit adverse effects. Enactment of this policy began a sequence of more systematic moves away from intervention in ecosystems.

In addition to NEPA policy to document "environmental impacts," the Endangered Species Act of 1973 required federal agencies to promote recovery of listed species or populations largely by prohibitions instead of actions (Yaffee 1982). These mandates soon were joined by the notion that biological diversity must be preserved and that preservation requires broader analysis and reduced human intervention. In 1976, the National Forest Management Act and the Federal Land Policy and Management Acts mandated consideration of biodiversity in the management programs of federal land management agencies, such as the Forest Service and Bureau of Land Management.

Within this web of policy, philosophy and the associated budgeting, inaction has proven easier than action, thereby supporting the spirit of the natural regulation paradigm. Similar changes may be developing on national wildlife refuges, and on the National Elk Refuge in particular, as refuges adopt the directive of the National Wildlife Refuge Administration Improvement Act of 1997 to consider biological integrity and diversity in addition to the featured species on which these units have traditionally focused.

Recent Ideas About Management and Results

Yellowstone National Park and the National Elk Refuge highlight the successes, failures and remaining questions in refuge management. In Yellowstone, the central questions concern the effects of the natural regulation policy on the ecosystem—in particular, the forage conditions and elk. At the National Elk Refuge, debate has focused on effects of feeding elk and the management of separate elk herds.

The history of the National Elk Refuge leaves little doubt that this refuge has fulfilled much if not all of its original mission to carry elk through the winter, prevent depredation and provide elk for translocations. The National Elk Refuge is integral to the Jackson elk herd system (Boyce 1989) and its translocation program clearly has succeeded in restoring many elk herds to areas where elk numbers had been depleted. However, the feeding program remains controversial. This issue has focused on habituation of elk to supplemental feeding, habitat deterioration, problems associated with managing the elk population segments and increasing costs and potential for disease transmission.

Doing the Numbers

Throughout the history of the National Elk Refuge, the size of the Jackson Hole elk population and the number of animals wintering on the refuge have been subjects of controversy among resource professionals, local inhabitants and environmental advocates. In the 1930s, the Wyoming Game and Fish Department and the U.S. Fish and Wildlife Service agreed that the Jackson Hole population should be controlled at 20,000 animals—a figure later reduced to 15,000 (Simpson 1999). In 1943, the two agencies established lower and upper limits of 5,000 and 7,000, respectively, for the number of elk wintering specifically on the refuge. The maximum number was amended to 7,500 animals in 1974 (Robbins et al. 1982)—a target figure that remains in force currently.

Counts of the number of elk wintering on the National Elk Refuge have been conducted in most years since its establishment by observers riding on hay sleds or trucks through the elk herds during the time of maximum number of elk on the feedgrounds. Counts usually have been conducted in such a way that all elk on the feedgrounds were counted and classified by gender and age class in a single day (Boyce 1989).

The numbers of elk on or adjacent to the Refuge from 1912 through 1999 (Table 97) show a statistically significant ($r = 0.44$), positive trend (Figure 164). Despite annual fluctuations, the total number of elk on the National Elk Refuge has increased gradually over time.

Certain periods of decline may have punctuated the overall increase. Boyce (1989) pointed out that winter severity can influence feedground counts and may compromise the reliability of this index of the population. Boyce (1989) concluded that counts were lower during the 10-year period of 1975 to 1985, and attributed this decline to a shift of elk away from the National Elk Refuge to new adjacent feedgrounds in the Gros Ventre area, where the Wyoming Game and Fish Department initiated feeding programs on a regular basis during the late 1950s.

Since the mid-1980s the number of elk on the National Elk Refuge increased sharply, reaching an historic high of nearly 12,000 animals in 1997. The counts have subsequently declined, probably as the result of more aggressive harvests of elk by hunters on the perimeter of the refuge—a result of efforts designed by the Wyoming Game and Fish Department and the refuge to limit herd growth.

During the early years of the program, when the refuge was smaller and feed was limited, the refuge occasionally experienced significant elk mortality. Deaths ranged up to 21% of the 1922 wintering herd of 4,300 elk. As noted earlier, feeding rates were reported to be as low as 3 pounds (1.4 kg) of hay per day per elk. As the refuge expanded and the feeding program became more stable, the mortality rate among elk declined. Robbins and Wilbrecht (1979) reported that the elk mortality rate averaged 3.3% for the period 1927 to 1945.

Winter elk mortalities on the National Elk Refuge from 1941 through 1998 declined still further, to an average of 1.4% (Table 98). Boyce (1989) noted that this loss is very similar to the 1.8% adult mortality reported for cattle on ranches in Wyoming during the early 1980s. A study by Smith and Anderson (1998) revealed that winter survival of juvenile elk (<1 year old) on the National Elk Refuge was higher (88.6%) than comparable rates for animals wintering off the refuge, possibly due to the high plane of winter nutrition provided to pregnant cows wintering on the refuge. However, supplemental feeding may increase the frequency of out-of-season births (Smith 1994), which in turn may result in attendant higher mortality of juvenile elk. The net effect of winter feeding on calf recruitment remains unclear.

In Yellowstone, three decades after managers began the natural regulation experiment, what is the evidence? Most obviously, elk populations in Yellowstone and other national parks have burgeoned. National Park Service records indicate that, between 1968 (when culling stopped) and 1988, the Northern Yellowstone elk herd increased about 2.6-fold, from approximately 4,000 animals to more than 20,000 (Singer and Norland 1994). Although the increase is obvious, the dynamics within the population are not, which helps perpetuate the debate about natural regulation. If natural regulation functioned as expected, then the growth in population would slow down as the density of elk increased. White et al. (1998) cited elk densities of 31 to 65 per square mile (12–25 elk/km²) for Yellowstone and Rocky Mountain national parks and these densities appeared to correlate with the death of more calves and yearlings and, in turn, slower population growth. However, this does not mean that the density of elk alone causes the slowing of population growth. Coughenour and Singer (1996) found that winter weather accounted for 55% of the variation in the per capita population growth rate. Singer et al. (1998) concluded that evidence for the outcome of natural regulation management of ungulates in the park is equivocal and complex. They noted that the natural regulation model for Yellowstone likely was flawed in its assumptions of a single, steady state for the park, based on conditions that were presumed to exist when the park was created.

At the same time, ample evidence exists that elk herbivory has suppressed vegetative communities within Yellowstone, including sagebrush (Singer et al. 1998a, Wambolt 1998), willows (Singer et al. 1998b) and aspen (White et al. 1998). Others (e.g., Wagner et al. 1995) have argued that increased ungulate populations might lead to the suppression or even elimination of certain coinhabitant animal species, including beaver, pronghorn, bighorn sheep and deer. They cited studies demonstrating increased stream bank erosion, reduced avian densities and limited species diversity in these impact areas. Jackson (1992) observed that bird numbers decreased when more than 70% of willows were severely browsed. On the basis of comparison of historic and contemporary photos, Kay and Wagner (1991) argued that increased elk populations and associated habitat alteration began after creation of the Park and were not historic conditions there.

The debate over ungulate management in Yellowstone will likely continue. Boyce (1998) indicated that the arguments advanced against ecological process management in the national parks have some merit but are not sufficient, either individually or collectively, to displace management direction. In 1997, the U.S. House of Representatives recognized in its appropriations report for fiscal year 1998 that a, "number of scientists question the natural regulation management program conducted by Yellowstone National Park as it relates to bison and elk, while others defend the approach." Congress subsequently directed the National Park Service to initiate a National Academy of Sciences review

Table 97. Census and classification of elk on the National Elk Refuge, 1912 to 1999

Year	Date	Bulls Mature	Spike	Cows	Calves	Unclas-sified	On feed	Off feed	Total
1912									7,250
1913									4,000
1914									6,150
1915	No feeding								
1916									8,000
1917									6,000
1918									10,000
1919									3,000
1920									8,000
1921									3,500
1922									4,300
1923									3,400
1924									4,800
1925									5,500
1926	No feeding								
1927		450	258	3,650	1,143		5,521	1,104	6,625
1928									7,500
1929									6,000
1930									7,000
1931		131	41	2,425	513		3,110		3,110
1932		1,160	194	4,305	1,214		6,873	1,527	8,400
1933									7,460
1934	No feeding								
1935		644	315	6,142	1,860		8,961	539	9,500
1936		605	25	3,020	432		4,083	117	4,200
1937									4,000
1938		768	264	4,552	1,071		6,655		6,655
1939									9,500
1940	No feeding								
1941	19 Feb	1,182	530	5,876	2,216	520	10,324	676	11,000
1942	13 Mar	1,177	530	5,947	2,187	9,841	9,841	1,344	11,185
1943	15 Jan					9,779	9,779	1,921	11,700
1944	No feeding								
1945	26 Feb	661	245	3,522	798		5,226	1,217	6,443
1946	07 Mar	833	311	3,929	1,168		6,241	1,759	8,000
1947	Not classified								7,000
1948	Not classified								6,750
1949	25 Feb	1,070	588	3,639	1,572	1,190	8,059	1,364	9,423
1950	Not classified								9,700
1951	Not classified								
1952	07 Feb	1,221	480	4,502	1,148		7,351	1,196	8,547
1953	14 Feb					9,000	9,000	200	9,200
1954	25 Feb	1,155	577	5,000	1,383		8,115	1,415	9,530
1955	15 Jan								8,000
1956	12 Mar	1,489	447	7,362	1,719	595	11,612		11,612
1957	Jan					6,800	6,800	1,200	8,000
1958						5,695	5,695	1,305	7,000
1959	09 Mar	1,020	236	3,204	1,224	363	6,047	496	6,543
1960	29 Feb	996	302	2,413	1,035		4,746	1,030	5,776
1961	13 Jan	696	343	3,683	869		5,591	1,114	6,705
1962	03 Jan	1,070	531	4,191	1,874		7,666	556	8,222
1963	03 Jan	614	365	4,086	762		5,827		
1964	26 Feb	967	307	4,867	1,775		7,916		
1965	28 Jan	930	594	4,889	1,533		7,946		
1966		803	383	4,127	1,243		6,556		

Continued on next page

Table 97 continued

Year	Date	Bulls		Cows	Calves	Unclas-sified	On feed	Off feed	Total
		Mature	Spike						
1967	10 Feb	822	407	4,622	1,518		7,369	296	7,665
1968	15 Feb	689	429	4,465	1,076		6,659	150	6,809
1969	31 Jan	886	573	5,523	2,223		9,205		
1970	19 Feb	864	533	5,428	1,596		8,421	775	9,196
1971	02 Mar	736	580	5,181	1,557		8,054	823	8,877
1972	04 Feb	720	532	4,781	1,582		7,615	835	8,450
1973	28 Feb	740	416	4,745	1,293		7,194	286	7,480
1974	28 Feb	716	557	5,233	1,372		7,878	678	8,556
1975	03 Mar	745	522	4,768	1,415		7,450		
1976	05 Mar	980	511	4,725	1,643		7,858	515	8,373
1977	15 Mar	616	459	3,511	1,146			5,732	
1978	23 Feb	1,393	424	5,073	1,523	82	8,495	396	8,891
1979	23 Feb	1,503	544	4,347	1,434	130	7,958	594	8,552
1980	04 Mar	1,680	441	4,443	1,185	25	7,774	206	7,980
1981	No feeding							6,300	
1982	24 Feb	1,261	405	3,801	1,063	216	6,746	489	7,235
1983	24 Feb	1,118	488	3,312	960	45	5,923	346	6,269
1984	23 Feb	1,073	345	2,886	706	45	5,055	311	5,366
1985	22 Feb	984	293	3,500	981	106	5,758	408	6,166
1986	20 Feb	819	350	4,039	1,222	0	6,430	296	6,726
1987	17 Feb	928	569	4,889	1,434	93	7,820	528	8,348
1988	18 Feb	922	574	4,785	1,472	203	7,753	1,106	8,859
1989	09 Feb	1,200	601	5,715	1,970	306	9,486	604	10,090
1990	14 Feb	1,053	532	5,312	1,234	187	8,131	1,251	9,382
1991	11 Feb	1,232	503	5,356	1,223	230	8,314	1,155	9,239
1992	13 Feb	1,162	436	5,823	1,379	570	8,800	1,069	9,869
1993	04 Feb	1,116	448	5,414	1,317	555	8,295	1,634	9,929
1994	02 Feb	1,033	381	4,747	829	0	8,500	1,715	10,215
1995	02 Feb	1,362	445	6,171	1,458	0	9,436	855	10,291
1996	13 Mar	1,301	635	6,801	1,267	0	10,004	385	10,389
1997	13 Feb	1,405	493	7,498	1,340	0	10,736	1,232	11,968
1998	19 Feb	1,456	398	5,691	949	0	8,494	1,015	9,509
1999	24 Feb	1,188	234	4,947	931	0	7,300	1,151	8,451

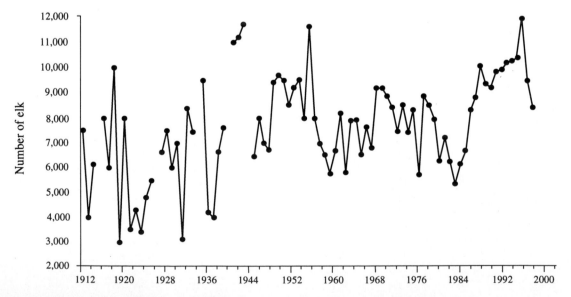

Figure 164. The number of elk wintering on the National Elk Refuge from 1912 through 2000.

Table 98. Elk mortality on the National Elk Refuge, 1941 through 1998

Year	Classified mortalities					Unclassified	Total mortalities	Elk on Refuge	Percentage mortality
	Bull	Spike	Cow	Calf	Total				
1941	13	6	41	74	134	166	300	11,000	2.70
1942							400	11,185	3.60
1943	84		94	813	991	66	1,057	11,700	9.00
1944	16		13	7	36		36	6,000	0.60
1945							Unknown	6,441	
1946	17		17	35	69	40	109	8,000	1.40
1947	31		18	13	62		62	7,000	0.90
1948	21		10	4	35	6	41	6,750	0.60
1949	33		28	117	178		178	9,423	1.90
1950	21		24	112	157		157	9,700	1.60
1951	28		23	92	143		148	9,500	1.50
1952	60		36	145	241		241	8,447	2.90
1953	27		19	4	50		50	9,000	0.60
1954	22		14	13	49		49	9,530	0.50
1955	15		14	3	32		32	8,000	0.04
1956	20		22	45	87		87	11,612	0.07
1957	33		32	15	80		80	8,000	1.00
1958	24		15	22	61		61	7,000	0.90
1959	36		11	20	67		72	6,543	1.10
1960	27		21	10	58		58	5,425	1.10
1961	39		15	18	72	5	72	6,705	1.10
1962	62		32	88	182		182	8,222	2.20
1963	9		8	5	22		22	5,827	0.40
1964	40		20	19	79		79	7,916	1.00
1965	7	2	24	21	54		54	7,946	0.70
1966	5	0	15	13	33		33	6,556	0.50
1967	7	0	10	24	412		41	7,665	0.50
1968	19	1	35	19	74		74	6,809	1.10
1969	10	2	13	18	43	11	54	9,205	0.60
1970	17	0	68	27	112	1	113	9,196	1.20
1971	13	3	52	47	115	2	117	8,877	1.30
1972	16	5	30	26	77	2	79	8,450	0.90
1973	5	4	47	17	73	2	75	7,474	1.00
1974	14	3	47	59	123	2	125	8,556	1.50
1975	5	1	36	15	47	3	50	7,330	0.70
1976	26	4	65	36	131	5	136	8,373	1.60
1977	9	0	3	0	12	0	12	5,732	0.20
1978	28	3	60	37	128	5	133	8,956	1.50
1979	41	7	32	75	155	2	157	8,552	1.80
1980	15	2	19	22	58	0	58	7,980	0.70
1981	8	0	1	0	9	2	11	6,300	0.20
1982	33	3	30	26	92	2	94	7,235	1.30
1983	102	6	29	29	166	5	171	6,269	2.70
1984	91	1	54	96	242	3	245	5,366	4.60
1985	43	0	21	2	66	0	66	6,266	1.10
1986	36	4	45	35	120		120	6,726	1.80
1987	30	2	37	12	81		81	8,348	1.00
1988	13	1	18	3	35	7	42	8,859	0.50
1989	28	4	45	43	120	14	134	10,090	1.30
1990	22	2	30	34	88	7	95	9,382	1.00
1991	38	1	43	8	105	15	120	9,239	1.30
1992	45	3	15	16	79		79	9,869	0.80
1993	57	10	102	90	259		259	9,929	2.60
1994	40	1	18	3	62	0	62	10,215	0.60
1995	35	5	65	122	227		227	10,291	2.20
1996	41	2	35	18	96		96	11,968	0.80
1997	63	8	41	89	201		201	9,509	2.10
1998	34	1	28	86	149		149	8,451	1.80

of all available science related to management of ungulates and the ecological effects of ungulates on the park. The study was completed late in 2001, but was not available for analysis when this book went to press. Nevertheless, according to senior wildlife personnel at the Yellowstone Center for Resources at Yellowstone National Park, the advisory report is a much anticipated milestone pertaining to management of wild, free-ranging ungulates, including elk (G. Plumb personal communication:2001). At this point, perhaps the greatest unknown is the influence of predation by recently reintroduced wolves on the park's ungulate populations. Regardless of the findings, undoubtedly public opinion will play an influential role in future deliberations regarding the management of national parks and their elk populations.

To Feed or Not to Feed

Discussing management options for the Jackson elk herd, Smith and Robbins (1994) argued that a supplemental winter feeding is not an absolute necessity in the National Elk Refuge program. They noted that supplemental feeding is costly and that the associated concentration of elk adversely impacts ranges and increases the potential for disease problems. Yet the feeding program continues on the refuge and other western states and provinces run feeding programs as well. The position of most state agencies toward these programs has changed from one of a "necessary evil" to a "valuable tool" (Gill and Carpenter 1985). To some extent this evaluation reflects a change in public attitude, but, increasingly, managers have come to realize that loss of habitat (and particularly winter range) may require such programs to ensure the continued existence of elk herds in some areas (see Chapter 15).

Providing supplemental feed does not reflect a lack of natural forage at the National Elk Refuge (Robbins et al. 1982). Estimates of the amount natural forage available on the southern half of the refuge during the period of 1969 to 1980 average more than 8,490 short tons/7,700+ metric tons per year based on range studies conducted annually. This entire area is available to elk during most winters. The northern portion of the refuge produces an average of about 3,525 short tons/3,200+ metric tons of forage annually. However, the higher elevation and inherently greater snow depths in this area limit free-ranging by elk in many winters.

National Elk Refuge management objectives have been to maintain elk on natural forage for as much of the winter as possible. Robbins et al. (1982) described the typical feeding regimen used and efforts to maximize its effectiveness. In a typical winter, elk occupy the refuge for approximately 6 months (November–May). Within this period, the animals are allowed to feed on natural forage for as long as possible (usually about 4 months) and are administered supplemental feed only when snow conditions or animal numbers necessitate such measures (generally in February or March). The length of the feeding period is correlated with winter severity. Between 1912 and 1975, this period averaged 75 days, with no feeding occurring in five winters with light snow accumulations and a feeding period of 147 days in 1962. Robbins et al. (1982:500) concluded: "Supplemental feeding on the National Elk Refuge, and other refuges as well, is a management expedient necessitated by excessive numbers and restricted distribution of elk on a given winter range where forage supplies are insufficient or inaccessible. Sociopolitical considerations rather than principles of balanced resource management dictate the need for this practice."

Finally, attempts continue to make the feeding program as effective and cost-efficient as possible. In the 1970s, after several years of testing, the use of baled hay to feed elk was gradually phased out and replaced with alfalfa pellets (Robbins et al. 1982), a practice that has continued to present. Madsen (1985) reported that the cost of pelleted hay was about 50% greater than that of baled hay, but estimated that the savings in costs associated with handling efficiency (6 man-hours per day per 7,000 elk feeding on pellets versus 64 man-hours per day per 7,000 elk feeding on hay) decreased overall costs by 8% to 12%. Boyce (1989) reported that the costs for feed alone for the estimated 7,500 elk on the National Elk Refuge was more than $250,000 annually. Although the cost of feed is only one part of the overall budget, Boyce (1989) argued that the cost was offset by several positive factors, including (1) tourism in Jackson Hole, (2) increased harvest of elk by hunters, and (3) enhanced educational and research opportunities.

State experience has paralleled these developments at the National Elk Refuge. As both elk and human populations have increased throughout the West, land-use conflicts have increased. The same problems experienced during the early 1900s suggest the same solutions, that is, limiting elk feeding programs to carry over herds where winter range is unavailable or to lure elk away from situations where they can damage private lands or crops. As a result of this pressure to feed animals, many western states have developed feeding policies to guide these programs.

Although several states currently maintain routine winter feeding programs, the underlying principle of most of these policies is that, although winter feeding can be used to reduce or prevent game damage and to improve survival during severe winters, big game populations should be maintained to the extent possible within existing forage

Debate about natural regulation of wildlife populations is complicated by the fact that weather and other variables that influence in the complex interplay between elk and their environment are constantly changing. Wildfires that raged through much of Yellowstone National Park in 1988 drastically altered forage conditions, and reintroduction of timber wolves in 1994 added a major elk predator—examples of the kinds of changes that result in elk populations constantly adjusting to their environment. Here wolves of the Druid pack in Yellowstone's Lamar Valley pull down a bull elk. *Photos by Pete and Alice Bengeyfield.*

supplies and the ability of the habitat to support self-sustaining populations (Hernbrode 1984, Emerson 1988, Kuck et al. 1988).

Wyoming is unique because of the large number of elk that are artificially fed each winter. In addition to the National Elk Refuge (where there is an agreement to feed 7,500 elk), Wyoming operates 22 feedgrounds where approximately 15,000 elk are fed. The primary reasons for feeding elk in those areas were to prevent agricultural damage and compensate for the loss of traditional winter range.

The Wyoming Game and Fish Department policy recommends moving or scattering feeding areas as an important part of dealing with disease prevention. In addition, the agency's policies recommend keeping animals separated to the extent possible to reduce the opportunity for disease transmission. Widespread concern about the potential for elk to contract and spread brucellosis has resulted in a comprehensive review of elk herd management and feeding practices. Maintaining healthy animals by providing feed in sufficient quantity and quality to wintering animals and minimizing stress on wintering herds probably are the most significant factors in a successful feeding program.

Effects of Feeding

Habitat Deterioration

The question of habitat deterioration caused by supplemental feeding programs and the "artificially supported" population of elk has also been a concern. As early as 1912, Theodore Roosevelt recognized the potential problem of supplemental feeding of elk in Yellowstone Park. He saw that artificial feeding would only "remove the difficulty for two of three years until the elk had time to multiply once more to the danger point" (Beetle 1979:259). Murie (1951:323) expressed the concern that "Establishing an elk feed ground in that area [north end of Jackson Hole in moose wintering area] would inevitably build a herd that would destroy browse resources there sooner or later, and thus compete with the moose." Almost 30 years later Beetle (1979:260) observed that "Aspen in Jackson Hole are so intensely browsed that their suckers produce new trees only within enclosures [areas protected from elk]. . . . Here large ungulates have utilized the aspen community more intensely than and to the detriment of smaller ungulates and nongame animals." Beetle's concern for habitat deterioration extended beyond the National Elk Refuge and into the elk's summer range in Grand Teton National Park and the southern part of Yellowstone Park.

On the other hand, Boyce (1989) concluded that there was no evidence that the Jackson elk herd had caused deterioration of its habitat except on or near winter feed-grounds. And although there seemed to be no question of habitat deterioration on and immediately adjacent to winter feedgrounds on the National Elk Refuge, there was some indication that spring and summer ranges used by elk wintering on the National Elk Refuge may be experiencing damage.

Refuge managers have continued to seek ways to increase the Refuge's winter range carrying capacity, including prescribed burning of sagebrush stands, seeding of desirable forage and the increased use of irrigation systems in grasslands. In addition, attempts have been made through the strategic placement of salt blocks, water developments and feeding sites to control better the distribution and range use patterns of elk on the refuge. The managers also are seeking opportunities to increase winter range on the refuge through conservation easements or acquisitions. Finally, they are critically examining the existing interagency agreements that establish objectives for the number of elk that are on feedgrounds in the area (Wilbrecht and Robbins 1979, Smith and Robbins 1994).

Habituation

Another concern with feeding programs is that elk will grow accustomed to people and lose their instinct to flee. This is called habituation and it is a potential problem wherever elk and people are forced into regular proximity, especially on refuges.

Thompson and Henderson (1999) described the risk of elk habituating to people as highest in those areas where (1) elk gather in high densities, (2) hunting is prohibited, (3) the habitat provides winter range, and (4) humans behave consistently and predictably. Such conditions exist to varying degrees in many refuge situations and some urban fringe areas. Thompson and Henderson noted that the risk of injuries to elk, people and pets resulting from aggressive interactions increases where elk populations are highly habituated to people. Also, where elk and people are in close proximity, people are more likely to see elk dead or dying (for any reason), and object out of concern for the animals or disgust at the sight. To address the concern of habituation and also maintain viewing opportunities, managers need creative alternatives. Alternatives to the traditional quasinatural viewing experience are difficult to devise without resorting to the unpopular option of restricting public access in elk habitat.

Regarding habituation and reacting to the simplistic notion that big game winter ranges can be replaced, or augmented, with artificial feeding programs, Murie (1951:305) observed: "Artificial feeding of game animals is now rightly looked upon as the last resort in wildlife management, a

practice to be adopted only when all efforts to provide suitable winter range have failed. . . . One of the most critical situations the wildlife administrator has to face is a public demand to feed elk on an overstocked range. The temptation is strong to take the line of least resistance, haul in a supply of hay and cottonseed cake and establish a feed ground. The result is a loss of any favorable animal distribution there may have been. The elk become concentrated in an area of feeding. No matter how heavily hay is fed the browse in that vicinity will be destroyed. Once feeding is begun, popular pressure will be such that the supply of hay, rather than carrying capacity of range, will become the measure of the herd." Another perspective was offered by Boyce (1989:239), who considered the National Elk Refuge "a showplace of wildlife management performing a critical role by replacing limited elk winter range previously usurped by land development and offering spectacular opportunities for viewing wildlife."

We conclude that, only when there is virtually no other alternative, then, and perhaps only then, should refuges and artificial feeding programs be considered effective means of maintaining elk populations.

"Habituated" elk are those that lose their fear of humans. When elk are habituated, there is substantial risk that humans—particularly those not accustomed to the behavioral signals of large, wild and potentially dangerous animals—will be injured or killed. *Photo by Kim Hart.*

Managing Various Elk Herd Segments

Improvements in research and management techniques, such as radio telemetry, have lent more precision to refuge management, but this has not necessarily reduced controversy. For example, identifying and managing the several herd segments or subpopulations that compose the Jackson Hole population have also been subjects of continuing controversy.

These herd segments winter at the National Elk Refuge but summer in different areas. On the basis of location estimates of elk equipped with radio collars between 1978 and 1984, Smith and Robbins (1994) defined four distinct summer ranges. Elk summering in Grand Teton and Yellowstone national parks comprised the largest segments—48% and 28%, respectively. Animals summering on the Gros Ventre and Bridger Teton national forests each accounted for another 12% of the total. The fidelity to the summer ranges was 98%, whereas fidelity to winter range on the National Elk Refuge was 97%.

Pursuant to directive of the Wyoming Game and Fish Commission, which established a numerical target of approximately 11,000 animals for the entire herd, responsibility for regulating the annual harvest is borne by the Wyoming Game and Fish Department. A portion of the combined annual harvest—which has averaged 3,200 animals per year—has occurred on lands administered by the U.S. Forest Service, National Park Service and U.S. Fish and Wildlife Service.

Management of these elk is complicated by the fact that agencies have policies and disparate agendas and are subject to the unique socioeconomic and political pressures brought to bear by diverse interest groups. Undoubtedly, the most controversial element of the multiagency arrangement is the harvest occurring in Grand Teton National Park. This controversy dates back to the expansion of the park in 1950. Grand Teton is the only park in the National Elk Refuge system in which regulated hunting of an indigenous species is sanctioned. As stipulated by Public Law 787, hunting in the park is permissible on lands east of the Snake River to maintain elk numbers at acceptable levels. Robbins et al. (1982) observed that continuing efforts to shift elk migration corridors to the east of the park (so that a greater proportion of the regulated harvest can occur on Forest Service lands) have been largely unsuccessful. In fact, Smith and Robbins (1994) expressed concern that the Grand Teton herd segment actually had increased in recent years as a result of low winter mortality and inadequate harvests.

Data support the suspicion that more of the growing elk population is summering on national park lands. Boyce

Studies of radio-collared elk (note the white collar on the cow at uppermost right) have dispelled the myth that elk from any given winter range or summer range all share movement patterns in common. In fact, elk commonly demonstrate site fidelity only within family units—the offspring of any single cow is more likely to use the same ranges summer and winter, but elk that associate on any given winter or summer range may be widely dispersed in other seasons. As a result, it is difficult to manage winter range herd size through the use of hunting seasons on nearby areas at other times (such as during the autumn months). This makes it particularly difficult to manage the size of herds wintering in refuges. *Photo courtesy of the Wyoming Game and Fish Department.*

(1989) determined that, although the winter counts of elk in the refuge area showed a stable or positive trend, elk migration through the national forest lands along the eastern side of the Jackson herd unit had been reduced from 20% to 30% of the herd to less than 5% because of hunting pressure. The reduction in elk traveling through national forests is paired with more elk traveling through the national park. In their review of national park policies and strategies, Wagner et al. (1995:54) reported that, before 1958, few elk summered in Grand Teton National Park, but by the late 1980s, "half of the 7,000–10,000 elk wintering on the nearby National Elk Refuge did so." Smith and Robbins (1994:49) expressed concern that "Growth of the Grand Teton National Park herd segment has resulted from low winter mortality and inadequate harvests in the limited geographical areas in which elk can be hunted." Efforts to manage national park segments of the National Elk Refuge winter herd have involved limited hunting within Teton National Park and on the refuge. Smith and Robbins (1994) argued that additional harvest from these herd segments would be necessary to meet management objectives. Despite long-term objectives of the National Park Service to eliminate hunting within the park, Smith and Robbins contended that continued—and perhaps more aggressive—harvest on National Park Service lands will be necessary to meet management objectives on the National Elk Refuge.

Countering desires by the various agencies for a smaller regional elk herd, strong pressures exist from local guides and outfitters to maintain high numbers of elk for the economic returns associated with outfitting and guiding elk hunters. Rather than the current objective of 7,500 elk wintering on the refuge, many outfitters favor a population objective in the range of 8,000 to 9,000 animals, in the belief that higher elk numbers will result in harvest quotas more in line with demand for elk hunting opportunity.

Preventing Depredation

Management of elk on the National Elk Refuge has accomplished a key objective—the prevention of elk depredation of livestock forage on private lands in the area, but this solution is not likely to be sustainable unless herd size is reduced. By providing hay on the refuge and harassing elk feeding on private hay, managers have concentrated most of the elk on the Refuge. In 1938, managers attempted to contain elk on the refuge with an 8-foot (2.5 m) fence along the western and southern boundaries (Madsen 1985). Despite such efforts, however, completely preventing depredation is unlikely. Elk behavioral patterns, once established, are notoriously difficult to change. Without fencing and given the fidelity of elk to winter feeding areas, elk foraging off the refuge could return to haystack depredation on private lands. To avoid this, Smith and Robbins (1994) estimated that the state/federal agreement would need to reduce the population from 7,500 to 5,500 elk on the National Elk Refuge.

Elk are large, powerful and intelligent animals, capable of breaking through fencing to access winter feed, making impossible complete elimination of elk depredations on private lands. *Left photo courtesy of the Oregon Department of Fish and Wildlife. Right photo by Jim Weiss; courtesy of the Utah Division of Wildlife Resources.*

Preventing Disease

Another point of success is that diseases apparently are not transmitted from these refuge elk herds, nor have epidemic outbreaks occurred on winter feedgrounds. However, the risk of these outcomes continues.

A significant concern is that elk or other indigenous ungulates will transmit disease to domestic livestock on adjacent summer range areas. Brucellosis has been the focus of this concern in the Yellowstone ecosystem, as are psoroptic mange (scabies) and septicemic pasteurellosis (Smith and Roffe 1994; see also Chapter 6).

The incidence of animals testing seropositive for brucellosis among adult female elk in the Western Wyoming feedground complex (including the National Elk Refuge) has averaged 37% since 1970 (Thorne et al. 1991). The rate of seropositive individuals is much lower (0%–2.6%) among animals tested from surrounding states (Colorado, Idaho and Utah). These data suggest that high animal densities, particularly in association with supplemental feeding, can maintain a high prevalence of brucellosis in elk. The mechanism is transmission among animals unnaturally crowded on feedgrounds, where they may be extensively exposed to contaminated reproductive products and tissues. Despite the potential that brucellosis-caused abortions could reduce the annual calf crop by 7%, such losses have not manifested themselves at the Refuge (Smith and Roffe 1994).

Keiter (1997) summarized the political concern and scientific uncertainty about whether wildlife (especially bison) can transmit brucellosis to livestock. Although generally in agreement that livestock introduced brucellosis to wildlife, scientists cite competing studies on the risk of wildlife-to-livestock transmission (Keiter 1997). As a matter of law, courts have concluded that infected wild animals pose a risk to livestock, but no court has ruled that wildlife are responsible for a specific instance of infection (Keiter 1997).

Scabies and pasteurellosis have been implicated in some deaths of elk, although not at disconcerting levels. Significant levels of psoroptic mange in North American elk are confined to Yellowstone National Park and Jackson Hole. Smith and Roffe (1994) reported that approximately 65% of male elk found dead during winters on the National Elk Refuge were afflicted with scabies. Pasteurellosis, which is an acute disease of wild and domestic ruminants, has periodically claimed losses of less than 1% of wintering elk on the refuge.

Recreational Opportunities

Public viewing and enjoyment have become a significant element of the National Elk Refuge program. Boyce (1989) reported that more than 5 million people visited the refuge from 1973 through 1985. Construction of a wildlife art museum and visitors sleigh rides to view the wintering herd are further indications of the importance of the nonconsumptive recreational opportunity. Moreover, the support facilities (motels, restaurants, etc.), which handle approximately 0.5 million visitors annually, represent a significant economic factor in the Jackson area. However, Boyce (1989:145) voiced concern about the artificiality of refuge settings and how the animals in refuge settings may be presented/perceived: "Concentrations of elk on feedgrounds offer considerable opportunity for public viewing and enjoyment. But with this comes a change in attitudes towards the elk. Elk appear to some to be like so many cattle pastured for winter. And too many people know how to manage cattle!"

Sanctuaries: Incidental Refuges and Results of Incidental Management

As noted earlier, refuges incorporate the notions of sanctuary and protection of elk from human disturbance. Although most refuges have been established deliberately, some may be created inadvertently, such as by withdrawal or elimination of public access to certain tracts of land. Examples include shutdown and land transfer of military reserves and other defense or research installations and restrictions on public access to reclaimed tracts of industrial land.

One of the better known examples is the Arid Lands Ecology Reserve, a portion of the U.S. Department of Energy's Hanford Site in south-central Washington. This shrub-steppe site harbors an elk population that appeared in 1972 and has persisted largely without human intervention (Rickard et al. 1977). This herd has increased at an average rate of 20% per year (Eberhardt et al. 1996)—a rate approaching the biotic potential for the species.

Whatever the manner in which sanctuaries are created, it is important to recognize that elk are robust animals with potential for severely affecting the habitats they occupy, particularly where the animals are concentrated. Literature pertaining to elk and red deer populations (both indigenous and introduced) in New Zealand (Veblen 1982), Patagonia (Veblen et al. 1982, 1989, 1992), Germany (Wolfe and Berg 1988) and Yellowstone National Park (Kay 1990) provides ample documentation of these concerns.

In general, elk and red deer combine the advantages of a relatively large body size with a moderately high potential for population growth. A large rumen capacity enables elk and red deer to process and subsist on a broad spectrum of forage species, including cured grasses and other items of relatively low nutritional value (see Chapter 5). The large size of calves (and the related small surface-to-volume ra-

Concentrating elk on feedgrounds has long provided social and economic benefits to communities that have capitalized on elk viewing as a recreational opportunity. In 2000, 924,000 people visited the National Elk Refuge, including 24,664 who took winter sleigh rides through the feedgrounds (J. Griffen personal communication:2001). *Top photo, ca.1912; courtesy of Henry Kitchens, Doris Whithorn and the Park County (Wyoming) Museum. Bottom photo courtesy of the Wyoming Game and Fish Department.*

tio) reduces the animals' potential for heat loss, thereby serving to reduce winter mortality. Consequently, elk may be less affected by density-independent natural mortality such as severe winter weather, than are other species with smaller body sizes, such as deer. The robust nature of elk becomes an important consideration in situations where management relies on natural factors to maintain numbers within the limits of the habitat.

In land management sanctuaries such as national forests, elk management has been driven by the concept of security, but current revelations of declining elk productivity have called into question the assumption that forage will always be sufficient in these sanctuaries.

The Future

Nearly a century after its establishment, perennial questions about the operation of the National Elk Refuge persist. The questions relate to justification for and costs of supplemental feeding of elk and the appropriate size of the herd. These questions are fundamental to virtually all elk winter feeding operations. Questions lingering over Yellowstone National Park are broader than elk management alone, including the scope of acceptable winter recreational uses and bison management (policies for both issues are being developed by park staff).

The need for refuges as sources of elk for repopulating extirpated herds has greatly lessened since 1970. With a few exceptions, elk ranges in the western U.S. have been adequately repopulated by elk (Bunnell 1997). As managers begin to reestablish elk in the eastern U.S., they have a number of refuges and public lands in many states from which to secure surplus animals for translocation.

The need for refuges as wintering grounds will persist, but refuges will not meet that entire need. The majority of elk populations spend summers on lands managed mostly by the U.S. Forest Service. In winter, when these elk move to lower elevations, a growing number of the herds find winter ranges converted to agricultural, residential and urban land uses. In some locations, the future existence of elk populations may depend on refuge areas or feeding grounds.

The role of national forests in complementing refuge management and providing incidental refuge functions may gain more scrutiny. Elk managers on national forests long assumed that amounts of elk forage on their jurisdictions has exceeded minimum requirements, but information in the 1990s suggested that forage on these lands may instead be inadequate and possibly even suppressed by management concepts such as thermal cover (Edge et al. 1990, Cook et al. 1996, 1998). The Clearwater National Forest has initiated management projects with forage production for elk as a central purpose and need. If providing forage for elk in forested habitats stimulates burning and logging, these controversial prescriptions likely will heighten scrutiny to elk management on national forests.

All of these considerations—feeding, establishing new herds and managing summer ranges—are surrounded by the same dynamics in public opinion that surrounded the first ideas in refuge management. The nature of the "conservation ethic" in American society is changing, with a progressively greater portion of the public engaging in nonconsumptive wildlife recreation. A parallel trend is the "new paradigm in ecology" (see Pickett and Ostfeld 1995), with greater emphasis on ecosystem processes and function rather than the production of a given commodity or species. To members of the public, the term ecosystem processes may come across as a euphemism for hunting, burning, grazing and logging because these have been advanced as tools to mimic nonhuman disturbances such as predation, fire and foraging by wild ungulates. Therefore, the future most likely holds continued debate over the central dilemma of how to reserve lands for wildlife, surround these lands with people and sustain the wildlife populations inside.

15

JAMES M. PEEK, KAROLINE T. SCHMIDT,
MICHAEL J. DORRANCE AND BRUCE L. SMITH

Supplemental Feeding and Farming of Elk

Leopold (1933) pointed out that all wildlife are artificialized to some extent, because humans have the capability of destroying populations and habitats of anything, including their own. Therefore elk populations may be viewed as existing at human pleasure and convenience, regardless of where they occur. People may think that elk populations that live in wilderness or national parks and remote from humans are truly wild, and that their lives are free of human effect. However, if people so choose, those same animals can easily be impacted and extirpated, as were wildlife populations in war zones or subjected to unregulated exploitation. Most wildlife biologists and others would consider the degree to which wildlife populations may be left wild to be a fundamental measure of the success of wildlife conservation. In fact, keeping wild things wild is the business of wildlife management.

This chapter covers two situations in which the wildness of elk is extensively compromised—supplemental feeding and private farming. The practice of supplementing wild forage with crops much like those fed to livestock is long-standing and takes on many forms and purposes. The practice of farming privately owned elk for their meat, hides and antlers also is of long-standing, and is increasing across North America.

Supplemental Feeding

Ungulates—including pronghorn, white-tailed deer, mule deer and Eurasian roe deer—may be fed supplementally during winter to prevent malnutrition losses, substitute for inadequate habitat, prevent damage to vegetation and crops, or retain animals in areas where they may be readily observed. However, supplemental feeding reaches its greatest level with North American elk and Eurasian red deer. These animals are well distributed across the temperate regions of North America and Eurasia (see Chapter 2).

Elk and red deer are an extremely valuable resource because they are prized as big game, food and medicine, and because they are readily "farmed" (confined and raised commercially). On all continents, a wide range of elk and red deer habitat conditions exists, ranging from close confinement of paddocks and small pastures to untrammeled wilderness, reserves and parks. In Europe, diets of red deer are regularly or occasionally supplemented in nearly all countries (Gill 1986). Winter feeding substitutes for lost natural winter range, prevents winter starvation, increases range carrying capacity, increases stag density, antler points and weight, controls animal movements, and assists in preventing forest damage (Raesfeld 1920, Raesfeld and Lettow-Vorbeck 1965, Wagenknecht 1980, Hofmann and Kirsten 1982, Bayrische-Staatsforstverwaltung [Bavarian Forestry Department] 1983, Glaser 1983, Bubenik 1984, Nerl 1985, Bützler 1986, Onderscheka 1986, 1991, Linn 1987, Raesfeld and Reulecke 1988, Reimoser 1988a, Colloredo-Mannsfeld 1992, Sackl 1992, Wieselmann 1994).

In Austria and Germany, there is a long tradition of supplementally feeding free-ranging red deer in winter (Stahl 1979). Feeding philosophy and management objectives are

617

very similar in both countries, except that presence of alpine habitat in Austria allows some populations to exist in free-ranging status year-round. In both countries and in Hungary, supplemental winter feeding is legally obligatory (Gill 1986). These three countries have the highest red deer densities (6–7.8 per square mile: 2–3/km²) in continental Europe. Only in the Scottish Highlands, and due to the economic importance of red deer in Scotland, are densities higher (Gill 1991). Austria contains the greatest continental red deer population (Gill 1986), which can be attributed to habitat variety ranging from alpine to lowland plain, a high density of feeding stations and a long tradition of supplemental feeding.

The supplemental feeding system in Austria may be compared with the situation in North America. In Austria, most red deer populations are free-ranging in summer, but diets are intensively supplemented during winter. Only a few herds winter at high elevations beyond human habitation (Schmidt 1993). Several herds and segments of populations are free-ranging during parts of summer, and confined to "winter enclosures" where they are fed until late spring. In North America, elk existence ranges from free-ranging, publicly owned populations to totally confined, privately owned stock. Some populations occupy habitat that is little affected by humans, as in some wilderness areas and national parks where natural dynamic processes ultimately dictate population levels and characteristics. Most elk exist on public and private lands that are managed for multiple purposes, most commonly watershed, timber, livestock, fish, wildlife and recreation. Elk in these situa-

tions ordinarily are not managed according to animal husbandry practices designed for domestic livestock, but instead, according to wildlife management practices designed to perpetuate populations in a wild, free-ranging circumstance. In addition, there are combinations of husbandry and wildlife management, as with the Jackson Hole elk in northwestern Wyoming and the Yakima elk herd in central Washington, both of which free-range for much of the year, but typically are fed during winter. In these cases, winter ranges have been limited or eliminated, and supplemental feed has substituted for natural forage on winter range.

Perspectives on Supplemental Feeding

Supplemental feeding in winter has been controversial for the entire century in North America. Advocates espouse a tradition rooted in livestock husbandry, and visualize the principles associated with managing livestock as being more or less directly applicable to wildlife. In addition, supplemental feeding advocates include those who wish to minimize malnutrition loss during severe winters for altruistic reasons, and those who wish to maintain or increase huntable populations. Supplemental feeding has been used to draw animals away from valuable crops and timber. Those opposed to supplemental feeding as a general policy typically are versed in wildlife management principles and practices stemming from Leopold (1933) and others, which advocate keeping wildlife as independent of humans as possible. The issue was clearly stated by Wyoming State Game Warden D. C. Nowlin in 1909: "If our elk are to remain re-

Austria contains the greatest red deer population in Europe, and winter feeding of red deer is well established. Animals are free-ranging in summer, but are confined to winter enclosures where they are fed until spring, as shown here. Note the growth of velvet antlers on the stags in this photograph. *Photo by T. Gspurnig.*

ally wild and to be hunted under restrictions as wild game, they should not be semi-domesticated and attracted to ranches by continuous supplemental feeding. Such treatment would soon take them out of the category of wild animals and put them in a class with the elk of eastern game parks" (Anderson 1958:48). Economic reasons and ecological issues related to the crowding of animals into small areas, which makes them susceptible to disease and promotes habitat damage, also are involved.

Dasmann (1964) discussed the predilection of humans to provide food for wildlife throughout history. Supplemental feeding to provide more trophies, long in practice in Europe and increasingly popular in some parts of the United States, makes animals dependent on artificial feed and can cause destruction to natural foods by artificially keeping populations at levels higher than the natural forage base would dictate. Ozoga and Verme (1982) pointed out that supplemental feeding of deer to prevent winter-kill has been tried in many states, and many of these trials were ill-conceived ventures undertaken on an emergency basis and with poor quality feed. Neither Dasmann (1964) nor Ozoga and Verme (1982) considered supplemental feeding to be a substitute for habitat restoration. However, as habitats continue to fragment and diminish, supplemental feeding may be the only recourse to sustaining elk, deer and other ungulates where demand is high (Ozoga and Verme 1982).

Supplemental Feeding Policies

Supplemental feeding of red deer in Austria has evolved over centuries. In that country, the primary aim of supplemental winter feeding has been to increase red deer numbers on one's own hunting ground. Originally, winter feeding was used to increase range fidelity of red deer and to attract them to specific hunting grounds. This was readily accomplished by putting out salt licks, as early as 1157 AD, and was subsequently forbidden outside sovereign reviers (hunting units) because of its effectiveness. Eventually, winter feeding was directed at increasing red deer numbers by reducing winter mortality. In some alpine regions as early as 1500 AD, red deer were fed hay to reduce winter mortality (Stahl 1979, Ennemoser 1983). Winter feeding, originally an isolated practice on the hunting grounds of the nobility, became a common practice in the late 19th century. In some areas, fences were erected to block red deer migration into lowland areas to maintain a dense population in the specific hunting ground where they then were fed in winter (Glaser 1983). Many feeding stations were erected where red deer occurred during the hunting season in unsuitable winter habitat (Guggenberger 1981, Greutter 1985, Gossow and Dieberger 1989, Gossow 1990, Kahls and Stadl-

mann 1990, Zeiler and Gossow 1990, Zeiler et al. 1990, Sackl 1992). Gossow (1990) advised use of a few, large feeding stations to concentrate forest damage locally. Feeding management now is planned on a scale large enough to approximate the range of each population in Austria.

Since 1938, winter feeding of red and roe deer is required by law in times of scarcity of natural food. This often is interpreted to mean the entire winter period—from after rut until late spring. In the second half of the 20th century, both game damage to forests and awareness of such damage increased substantially. Supplemental winter feeding was blamed for this, especially for increased bark stripping. However, feeding was and still is regarded as an appropriate measure to prevent forest damage. The impact of deer on forest vegetation depends primarily on the silvicultural system and growing-stock targets (Reimoser and Gossow 1996). Since the 1980s, establishment of a feeding station must be reported to the relevant authorities in most of Austria's nine provinces. Currently in the Austrian Alps, there is approximately one feeding station per 5.8 square miles (15

Many of the Austrian feed stations were used to maintain a dense population of red deer in a specific hunting ground, where they were fed all winter. Free-ranging animals traveling traditional migratory routes found their access to low-elevation winter ranges blocked, and they were then funneled into feeding enclosures through one-way gates (*above*). Holding animals on winter feedgrounds was and is regarded as an appropriate measure to prevent forest and private land damage. In reviers with a feeding station, approximately 80% of the culls (harvest) occurs from November through January, when red deer are using feed stations. *Photo by Karoline T. Schmidt.*

Establishment of a feeding station must be reported to relevant authorities in most of Austria's nine provinces, where feedgrounds occurred at a density of one per every 5.8 square miles (15 km²) in 2000. In some areas, there is a winter feeding station for every 2.5 square miles (6.5 km²). Feeding stations occur in every type of habitat, from low riverine forest to alpine forest above 5,500 feet (1,700 m) in elevation. *Photo by T. Gspurnig.*

km²), with densities of stations in some areas reaching one per 2.5 square miles (6.5 km²). Feeding stations may be found in every type of habitat, from lowland riverine forests to timberline regions at 5,577 feet (1,700 m) above sea level, and may support a few to more than a hundred animals.

In North America, the major elk-producing states and provinces essentially have adopted policies on supplemental feeding of big game in general and elk in particular, which subsume a pragmatic middle ground between pure animal husbandry and pure wildlife management (Table 99). Permanent feedgrounds exist in Idaho, Utah, Washington and Wyoming. In Arizona, supplemental feeding of wildlife is seldom an issue, and habitat enhancement is promoted as an alternative. New Mexico discourages supplemental feeding and advocates depredation hunts when problems occur. In those southern states, supplemental feeding would be one alternative to resolving depredation on agricultural crops, but it is discouraged in favor of other solutions. Mon-

tana and Nevada have no established supplemental feeding programs, and both states promote habitat improvement or acquisition as alternatives. Alberta does not supplementally feed elk, but does use "intercept feeding" to reduce haystack damage and other agricultural depredations.

Idaho and Utah feed wildlife in winter on a case-by-case basis, when emergency or unusual conditions occur, to prevent damage to private property or for public safety, and to prevent excessive mortality during severe winters. Populations on the South Fork of the Boise River in Idaho and at the Hardware Ranch in Utah are fed every winter. Oregon will implement supplemental feeding on a large scale if, on the rare occasion, it is considered to be cost-effective relative to other methods of alleviating problems. Three populations are fed to hold animals away from private lands, and another population is fed to keep elk available for viewing. Wyoming has 23 feedgrounds in the northwestern part of the state where elk are fed annually, but supplemental feeding elsewhere is discouraged. Washington has permanent feedgrounds where winter range has been eliminated, and will feed elsewhere when emergencies occur. Colorado will feed during emergencies, such as severe winters, and has developed quantitative means to determine when and how to conduct feeding programs. British Columbia does not feed wildlife as a policy, but if sufficiently pressed, will authorize private citizens to do so. An instance where private citizens urged the province's Fish and Wildlife Branch to feed an apparently stressed population of bighorn sheep resulted in permission being given for the citizens to do so.

National Elk Refuge Supplemental Feeding

The feeding of elk in Jackson Hole, Wyoming, was initiated in 1907 by state game wardens and institutionalized in 1912 when the U.S. Congress allocated funds to establish the National Elk Refuge to provide winter habitat and feed for the Jackson elk herd (Anderson 1958, Robbins et al. 1982; see also Chapter 4). Feeding of elk in winter served to mitigate losses of historic winter ranges after the settlement of Jackson Hole by Europeans and attendant livestock grazing and haying of elk winter ranges (Smith and Robbins 1994). Anderson (1958) concluded that the Jackson elk traditionally migrated from Jackson Hole to areas with less severe winter conditions, and these migration routes were blocked by settlement and ranching. However, Cole (1969) contended that Jackson Hole was an historic wintering area in which 15,000 to 25,000 elk were estimated to winter during the time of European settlement, 1887 to 1911.

Whether their migration routes were blocked and lost from memory, or their winter ranges in Jackson Hole were usurped by humans, elk progressively became more depen-

Table 99. Summary of big game supplemental feeding policies of western states and provinces

Province or state	Policy	Personal communication sources
Alberta	Does not feed wildlife; has not fed for years	G. Lynch (November 1995)
Arizona	Winter feeding of wildlife seldom an issue; habitat enhancement is promoted	D. Shroufe (September 1994)
British Columbia	Does not feed wildlife; will authorize private individuals on occasion	D. Blower (October 1995)
Colorado	Used as a last resort to prevent damage to private property or to reduce unusually severe winter-related mortality	D. Baker (December 1994)
Idaho	Feeds only in emergency and unusual conditions, on a case-by-case basis. Annual feeding in one area (South Fork Boise River) occurs	L. Nelson (June 1995)
Montana	No established winter feeding program; habitat enhancement is promoted	P. Graham (October 1994)
Nevada	No winter feeding program; habitat enhancement is promoted	W. Molini (October 1994)
New Mexico	Discourages winter feeding; has depredation hunts as an alternative	D. Sutcliffe (September 1994)
Oregon	Feeds on large scale if cost effective relative to alternatives. Four populations are fed to minimize damage to private lands and retain elk for viewing	D. Carleson (October 1994)
Utah	Feeds only in emergency and unusual conditions, on a case-by-case basis. A permanent feeding station occurs at Hardware Ranch	R. Valentine (December 1994)
Washington	Feeds to prevent damage and forage loss during extreme weather conditions	D. Brittell (September 1994)
Wyoming	Feeds on 23 grounds in northwestern part of the state; otherwise, emergency feeding is rare and discouraged	J. Talbott (March 1995)

Note: Survey conducted by James Olson, Idaho Wildlife Federation.

dent on supplemental feed after establishment of the National Elk Refuge in 1912. This became the first large-scale supplemental feeding program in the United States.

Winter feeding maintained larger numbers of elk than available habitat could support, and problems associated with the artificial concentration and densities of elk on the National Elk Refuge soon became apparent. These in-cluded diseases, such as necrotic stomatitis and brucellosis, and range damage (Murie 1951).

Brucellosis currently is the disease of greatest concern, not primarily because of its effects on the elk, but because its causative bacterium can infect a variety of other species, including cattle (Thorne et al. 1979, 1991a). The hallmark clinical sign of brucellosis is abortion (see Chapter 6),

Elk wintering in step terrain along the South Fork of the Boise River in south-central Idaho are fed every winter. In this area, little is left of elk winter range; unfed, elk would either starve or move into residential areas or developed farmland. In this situation, winter feeding is used to intercept and hold animals while they remain on native range and public land. *Photo courtesy of the Idaho Department of Fish and Game.*

Winter feeding of elk on the National Elk Refuge at Jackson Hole, Wyoming, is used to hold animals on historic winter range, sustaining the herds at levels higher than presently available winter range could support. *Photo by courtesy of the U.S. Fish and Wildlife Service.*

which may reduce the annual productivity of elk wintering on the National Elk Refuge by an estimated 7% (Oldemeyer et al. 1993). Maintenance of brucellosis in elk results from the animals' artificial concentration, particularly where they are supplementally fed (Thorne et al. 1991a, Smith and Roffe 1992). The seroprevalence of brucellosis in mature cow elk on the National Elk Refuge has averaged 39%

One detrimental impact often associated with winter feeding of free-ranging elk is damage to vegetation (hedging of shrubs and trees, debarking of trees, etc.) in the vicinity of the feedground, as elk concentrated in a relatively small area seek to satisfy their need for fiber volume. *Photo by courtesy of the U.S. National Park Service.*

(Boyce 1989). However, seroprevalence may not reflect actual occurrence rates. In one study, Thorne et al. (1979) recovered brucellosis bacteria from tissue cultures of just 17 of 45 seropositive cow elk.

The influence of artificial concentrations of elk at feedgrounds on the prevalence of other diseases, such as septicemic pasteurellosis and scabies, is unclear (Smith and Roffe 1992).

Range damage includes creating browse lines on shrubs and trees, debarking of trees, heavy utilization of grasses and shrubs and suppression of aspen regeneration (Boyce 1989).

Feeding elk sometimes was ineffective in substantially reducing winter mortality. In 1920, for example, nearly half of the Jackson population was lost to malnutrition and associated problems (Craighead 1952). Since 1975, mortality has averaged less than 1.5% of elk wintering on the National Elk Refuge (Boyce 1989). Increased emphasis on range management techniques, such as irrigation, prescribed burning and planting of robust varieties of winter forage, is intended to encourage natural foraging by elk as much as possible. Elk are supplementally fed a pelleted alfalfa hay ration (Table 100) when forage becomes depleted or unavailable because of deep or crusted snow. During the 1975 to 1996 period, elk were not fed at all in 2 years (Table 101). Feeding started in December in 3 years, January in 11 years and February in 7 years, and it typically ended in late March or early April.

The population objective for the entire Jackson elk herd is 11,000 wintering elk, with a maximum of 7,500 located on the National Elk Refuge. Both objectives have been exceeded since 1987, despite efforts to control population size

Table 100. Chemical analyses of pelleted feeds provided to elk on the National Elk Refuge, Wyoming, 1971 to 1974

Nutrient	Percentage content	Years
Crude protein	13.0–18.3	1971–1974
Crude fat	1.7–3.75	1971, 1974
Crude protein	25.25	1971
Moisture	6.76–9.4	1971–1974
Calcium	1.02–1.51	1972–1974
Phosphorous	0.19–0.24	1972–1974
Carotene	19.48–30.6[a]	1973–1974

Source: Smith and Robbins 1984.

[a] Milligrams per kilogram.

by hunting (Smith and Robbins 1994). Boyce (1989:238) concluded that "despite an extensive supplemental feeding program for more than 75 years, the Jackson elk herd is generally healthy and viable and provides extensive opportunities for recreational hunting and recreational uses."

Utah and Colorado Histories

Utah

Experiences in Utah and Colorado are typical for western ranges. Winter feeding programs generally have occurred after losses (affecting mule deer primarily) became noticeable, especially during severe winters. Musclow (1984) reported that the severe winter of 1931 to 1932, during which mule deer and elk invaded agricultural areas and caused damage, prompted a major feeding effort in Utah. Loss of winter range on Utah's Wasatch Front to housing and industrial developments exacerbated the problems, and supplemental feeding was common during the 1930s. Work reported by Doman and Rassmussen (1944) adequately identified the problem and established a pattern that wildlife management agencies pursued for the next several decades. They concluded that winter feeding of mule deer was not very successful, because the supplements of alfalfa, grass hay and other rations did not substitute for the native

Table 101. Pelleted alfalfa hay provided to elk wintering on the National Elk Refuge, Wyoming, since 1975

Year	Number of elk	Supplemental feeding			
		Start	End	Number of days	Daily ration in pounds (kg)
1975	6,676	Feb 18	April 20	62	6.5 (2.95)
1976	7,858	Feb 18	April 12	55	7.5 (3.4)
1977	5,732			0	
1978	8,413	Jan 20	April 5	75	6.8 (3.08)
1979	7,828	Dec 26	April 10	106	7.2 (3.27)
1980	7,749	Feb 5	April 11	56	4.3 (1.95)
1981	6,300			0	
1982	6,530	Jan 22	April 16	82	5.8 (2.63)
1983	5,878	Feb 10	April 22	81	5.4 (2.45)
1984	5,010	Jan 4	April 20	108	7.9 (3.58)
1985	5,758	Jan 2	April 10	99	9.6 (4.35)
1986	6,430	Dec 11	March 23	101	7.9 (3.58)
1987	7,820	Jan 13	April 3	81	8.0 (3.63)
1988	7,753	Feb 1	April 2	62	7.3 (3.31)
1989	9,486	Dec 7	April 7	122	8.3 (3.76)
1990	8,131	Jan 23	March 30	67	8.5 (3.86)
1991	8,314	Jan 8	March 24	72	7.5 (3.4)
1992	8,800	Jan 22	March 23	57	6.6 (2.99)
1993	8,295	Jan 11	April 11	91	8.3 (3.76)
1994	8,500	Feb 14	March 20	34	6.7 (3.04)
1995	9,436	Jan 6	April 6	91	6.7 (3.04)
1996	10,004	Feb 27	April 5	38	5.7 (2.59)
1997	10,738	Jan 28	April 6	69	7.2 (3.27)
1998	8,489	Jan 16	April 4	79	7.2 (3.27)
1999	7,300	Feb 16	April 4	48	7.2 (3.27)
2000	5,054	Feb 25	May 31	36	5.8 (2.63)
Mean[a]	7,626	Jan 20	April 6	74	7.07 (3.21)

[a] Means are only for those years during which elk were fed.

forage, and prolonged periods of feeding did not prevent malnutrition losses. Concentrations of animals promoted range damage, which further reduced the ability of native forages to support deer and elk. Concentrations actually became a problem in and of themselves whenever the damage was extensive. Alternatives of habitat acquisition and improvement were emphasized as long-term solutions that were preferable to supplemental feeding.

Experience with elk almost from the start showed that this species could be successfully fed an alfalfa hay diet. In Utah, the purchase of the Hardware Ranch in the Blacksmith Fork River, to provide a place to feed elk to prevent damage and avoid conflicts with mule deer, was accomplished by Utah Division of Wildlife in 1946. Subsequently, evaluations of winter diet for farmed elk in Alberta demonstrated that good winter nutrition can increase milk production of lactating cows during the subsequent summer (Kozak et al. 1995). The composition of the diet fed in winter is presented in Table 102.

In Utah, loss of traditional winter feedgrounds below the Wasatch Front to housing development resulted in overgrazing of existing forage, range damage (which further reduced the ability of native plants to provide winter food), and loss of many elk and deer. *Photo by Hugh Hogle; courtesy of the Rocky Mountain Elk Foundation.*

Table 102. Supplemental food winter diet of adult elk cows at Ministik Wildlife Research Station, Alberta

Ingredient	Percentage dry matter composition	Nutritive component	Percentage composition
Dehydrated alfalfa	25.6	Dry matter	87.1
Barley	31.1	Protein	16.6
Wheat shorts	14.0	Gross energy[a]	17.9
Beet pulp	16.0	Digestible energy[a]	15.4
Soybean meal	8.5	Neutral detergent fiber	32.4
Molasses	4.0	Acid detergent fiber	16.4
Trace mineral salt	0.4	Lignin	2.9
Vitamins A, D, E	0.2		
Permapel	0.1		

Source: Kozak et al. 1995.

[a] Kilojoules per gram.

Colorado

The Colorado experience with mule deer supplemental feeding provides insight into how changes in information also have changed management approaches. Mule deer periodically experience winter mortality regardless of density across the portions of their range where deep snows and severe cold prevail. Habitat improvement and acquisition are the recommended approaches to dealing with the problem (Gilbert et al. 1970), but even on the best habitat, mule deer occasionally will experience high levels of mortality. Early efforts to feed this species in winter typically resulted in high mortality, because poor-quality hay or high-energy concentrates were used, which animals were unable to digest. Supplemental feeding usually was initiated only after deer already were experiencing nutritional stress, and the transition from low-quality natural forage to higher quality supplemental forage exacerbated the problem. The problem in Colorado made national headlines during the severe winter of 1983 to 1984, when private individuals and groups began to feed mule deer throughout the western slopes when the deer began to concentrate where they could be readily observed and accessed. People were feeding a mixture ranging from poor-quality hay to rice and setting the stage for a major die-off. Fortunately, the Colorado Division of Wildlife had been working on deer nutrition and had developed a ration readily accepted by the deer, therefore was able to reduce mortality to low levels during that exceptionally severe winter (Baker and Hobbs 1985). The ration was calculated to provide high levels of easily digestible energy, with sufficient fiber to prevent overeating and digestive upset. Baker and Hobbs (1985) responded to criticisms over the biological and financial costs of the feeding program by indicating no evidence to suggest that mule deer are affected permanently by occasional feeding, and by providing an estimate of the costs of a feeding program. Their estimates were that feeding a 2.0-pound (0.9 kg) ration per deer per day to 5,000 deer probably saved 995, at a cost of $174.81 per deer saved. They concluded that feeding can be a worthwhile investment if winter mortality of unfed populations will be high and populations to be fed are accessible and concentrated on limited areas. Their information did not support routine supplemental feeding to increase survival of mule deer beyond that normally occurring. They indicated that feeding is an effective management technique with a limited range of efficacy.

An investigation concerning white-tailed deer in northern Michigan by Ozoga and Verme (1982) also supported the conclusion that supplemental feeding should be undertaken only as an emergency measure to avoid starvation during harsh winters. A supplemental ration developed by Ullrey et al. (1971) was used to feed these whitetails (Table 103).

Texas White-tailed Deer

Supplemental feeding of white-tailed deer in the East and South is widespread, as illustrated by the ready availability of deer feeders in catalogs of outdoor equipment suppliers. Although much of the activity is similar to feeding birds, involving private parties who wish to see deer on their lands, the practice also is used to enhance deer hunting opportunities, and Texas is a prime example of this. In Texas, a state composed primarily of private lands, whitetails provide extensive income through the sale of hunting leases. Lease rates range from $1.80 to $7.50 per acre ($4.45–18.53/ha) with an average value of $2.20 per acre ($5.44/ha) (for review, see McBryde 1995). Supplemental feeding is practiced in an effort to increase survival, body size and antler size, with highly variable results. Efforts to maximize mature bucks in populations, by using antler size as a criterion to distinguish age, would work in Texas if males less than 2.5 years old could be distinguished from older animals (DeYoung 1990). However Jacobson (see Brown 1988) effectively used antler length as a criterion for increasing age structures in Mississippi, even when the limitations imposed were not completely practiced. Although hunters can reliably identify spike and fork-horned bucks when restrictions on antler size of older males are put in place, success in achieving goals may vary from place to place.

The Austrian Practice

The original aim of feeding stations was to keep red deer on one's own hunting ground. Accordingly, feeding stations typically are erected near rutting grounds (Guggenberger

Table 103. Comparison of a supplemental ration fed to mule deer in Colorado with a ration developed for white-tailed deer in Michigan

Nutritive component	Percentage diet composition	
	Colorado[a]	Michigan[b]
Dry matter	94.6	92.9
Crude protein	23.3	17.6
Neutral detergent fiber	42.7	
Acid detergent fiber	20.6	17.6
Acid detergent lignin	5.2	3.8
Ash	9.5	4.6
Calcium	0.54	
Phosphorous	0.45	
In vitro digestible dry matter	70.50	
Gross energy[c]	4.4	4.2
Ether extract		2.0
Cell wall constituents		40.5

Sources: Colorado, Baker and Hobbs 1985; Michigan, Ullrey et al. 1971.

[a] Ration composed of wheat middlings, brewer's dry grain, cottonseed hulls, sun-cured alfalfa and dehydrated alfalfa.

[b] The Michigan diet was 34.7% corn cobs, 29.5% corn, 18% soybean meal, 10% linseed meal, 3% alfalfa meal, 3% cane molasses, 0.3% corn oil, 0.5% trace mineral salt, 0.5% ground limestone, 0.25% sodium sulfate, and 0.25% vitamins A, D and E.

[c] Kilocalories per gram.

1981, Wotschikowsky 1981, Gossow 1983). Feeding sites also are located to fulfill safety and thermal requirements of red deer. Mixed forest stands with abundant herbaceous plants and shrubs on small, southerly exposed and elevated benches with good strategic view or a strongly varying slope with hollows and ridges are ideal places for stations (Raesfeld 1920, Hofmann and Kirsten 1982, Bayerische-Staatsforstverwaltung 1983, Greutter 1985, Nerl 1985, Raesfeld and Reulecke 1988, Furst 1990, Gossow 1990, Reimoser 1990, Zeiler et al. 1990).

Because most feeding stations were located where little natural winter forage occurred (Glaser 1983, Rossler 1983, Sackl 1992), red deer obtained virtually all of their daily energy demands throughout winter from supplemental feed. Winter energy demands of red deer are shown in Table 104. The starch equivalent system summarizes the nutritive value of feed in terms of one value—the ratio of the ability of a particular feed to promote production relative to production achieved by feeding starch (Gill 1991). One unit corresponds to the amount of fat 1 g of digestible starch will yield and is equivalent to 2.36 kcal or 9.87 kJ (Bubenik 1984). The starch equivalent system is presented to provide a rough comparison with international data.

Feed recommendations were based primarily on experiences at feeding stations, and both quantity and composi-

Table 104. Estimated or calculated metabolizable energy requirements for maintenance of red deer

Sex	Weight in pounds (kg)	Comments	Starch equivalent[a]	Kilocalories per	
				Body weight$^{0.75}$	Day
M		740 g of protein	1,470		3,469
F	220 (100)	200 g of protein	2,000		4,720
F			1,200		2,832
F	154 (70)			125–156	3,025–3,775
F	220 (100)			125–156	3,952–4,932
F		Diet rich in protein	1,400		3,304
F		Diet poor in protein	2,200		5,192
F	187 (85)		1,626		3,837
Calf	110 (50)	140 g of protein year-long	700		1,652
F	187 (85)	200 g of protein year-long	1,000		2,360
M	330 (150)	300 g of protein year-long	1,550		3,658
M	220 (100)		1,250–1,350	400–420	
M	264 (120)	Antler growth	1,200		
M	220 (100)				
M	154 (70)	Undisturbed			
M	154 (70)	Disturbed			
M	220 (100)	200 g of protein	1,400–2,000		

[a] One unit corresponds to the amount of fat yielded by 1 g of digestible starch and is equivalent to 2.36 kcal or 9.87 kJ (Bubenik 1984).

tion vary dramatically (Table 105). Because every revier has unique conditions, universal recommendations are not useful (Raesfeld 1920, Gossow 1983, Drescher-Kaden 1991). Feeding hay ad libitum, with some left over until the next feeding, is practiced at most feeding stations (Raesfeld 1920, Hofmann and Kirsten 1982, Ennemoser 1983, Bubenik 1984, Nerl 1985, Onderscheka 1986, Steiermark 1986, Ueckermann 1986, Furst 1987, Linn 1987, Onderscheka et al. 1990). Although hay alone will support red deer throughout winter (Wolfel 1986), many investigators advised supplementing a hay diet, because hay alone will not prevent forest damage (Raesfeld 1920, Ueckermann 1986, Onderscheka 1991). Most researchers recommended silage, turnips, beer draff, apple draff or potatoes as juicy feed (Hofmann and Kirsten 1982, Nerl 1985, Furst 1987). The ratio of dry-to-juicy feed should be 1:3 or 1:4 by weight (Ueckermann 1986, Wieselmann 1994). Commercial supplemental feed typically is 15% ± 3% crude protein (Sternath 1994). To ensure thorough chewing and salivation of fibrous feed a particle size larger than 1.2 inches (3 cm) is recommended (Bubenik 1984, Raesfeld und Reulecke 1988, Onderscheka 1991, Wagenknecht 1992).

Trophy enhancement was stressed by nearly all commercial feed sellers as an important component of their feed (Sternath 1994). Phosphoric acid was identified in the 19th century as the most important feed component responsible for antler development (Raesfeld 1920). Early in the 20th century, Vogt (1936) achieved exceptional antler growth by feeding sesame cake. Sesame contains a calcium-to-phosphorus ratio of approximately 54:46, as well as 36% protein, which favors synthesis of muscle and bone. Vogt (1937) recommended that feed rich in proteins should be fed after the rut until mid-December and, for antler growth, feed rich in calcium and phosphorus should be fed from February until June. Estimations of mineral requirements for antler growth vary considerably, but managers generally agreed that a calcium-to-phosphorus ratio of approximately 1:1 was necessary (Table 106).

Water has been regarded as an absolute necessity at feeding stations, especially if animals were maintained on a diet mainly of concentrates. Wagenknecht (1992) and Wieselmann (1994) recommended 1.85 to 2.4 gallons per day (7–9 L/day). On the other hand, Raesfeld and Reulecke (1988) and Ueckermann (1986) reported that red deer rarely drink water during winter, because snow and silage (containing approximately 80% water) satisfy water demands.

One of the foremost arguments for supplemental feeding is that, by autumn, most commercial forests (where trees are planted and nutured entirely for lumber or pulp production) lack sufficient natural forage to sustain deer. Therefore, feeding advocates advise starting supplemental feeding immediately after the rut, so that stags may replenish energy reserves (Hofmann and Kirsten 1982, Bayerische-Staatsforstverwaltung 1983, Ennemoser 1983, Bubenik 1984, Nerl 1985, Wieselmann 1994). This recommendation was followed even in areas where natural forage

Table 104 continued

Megajoules per day	Source
14.5	Vogt 1936
19.7	Wagenknecht 1983
11.8	Ennemoser 1983
12.6–15.8	Bubenik 1984
16.5–20.6	Bubenik 1984
13.8	Ueckermann 1986
21.7	Ueckermann 1986
16.5	Ueckermann 1986
6.9	Ueckermann 1986
9.8	Ueckermann 1986
15.3	Ueckermann 1986
12.6–13.3	Drescher-Kaden 1991
11.8	Onderscheka 1976
22.4	Giacometti 1992
10.2	Colloredo-Mannsfeld 1992
15.3	Colloredo-Mannsfeld 1992
	Wieselmann 1994

Feed provided at winter feed stations in Austria includes hay fed ad libitum, usually with a variety of supplements. Feeding of hay alone will not prevent forest damage, therefore hay is routinely supplemented with high carbohydrate silage, turnips, beer draff, apple draff or potatoes, both early and late in the season. Commercial feed supplements, including at least 15% ± 3% crude protein, also are used, and, because development of trophy antlers often is an objective, supplements such as sesame cake, rich in phosphorus and calcium. *Photo by T. Gspurnig.*

was not scarce, such as alpine pastures (Schmidt 1992, 1993). Early and constant feed provision will make red deer accustomed to the feeding place and assure range fidelity (Raesfeld 1920). Red deer use the supplemental food as soon as it is offered (Glaser 1983). Raesfeld (1920) and Vogt (1936) stressed the importance of feeding during late winter and spring. In most Austrian provinces, providing feed until spring (April or May) is legally mandated. Feeding advisedly should end slowly, terminating 1 month after spring vegetation is available, as late as June after some severe winters. A rapid switch to newly sprouting natural vegetation may cause diarrhea and rumen dysfunction (Bützler 1986, Onderscheka et al. 1989, 1990).

Bubenik (1984), Nerl (1985), Onderscheka (1986), Furst (1987) and Ueckermann (1990) reported that dietary intake increased as ambient temperatures declined, therefore the amount of food offered should increase gradually from October to April. This contrasts with the natural decline of feed intake in winter, which reflects endogenous periodicity in response to lower quality and quantity of natural forage. At winter feeding stations where red deer have access to natural forage, consumption will increase in November, reaching a maximum in February or March (Ueckermann 1990). This possibly reflects decreasing availability of natural forage as snow depths increase and red deer become more dependent on supplemental feed. However, during severe winters in an alpine area where the supplementally fed red deer herd used windswept alpine pastures, feed intake at feeding stations was lowest between January and March (Schmidt 1992).

Onderscheka (1986), Raesfeld and Reulecke (1988), and Onderscheka et al. (1989, 1990) advised against abrupt changes in diet composition during feeding periods, which can lead to digestive upset and potentially increase forest damage. Hofmann and Kirsten (1982) and Bubenik (1984) recommended feeding easily digestible carbohydrates, such as apples, pears, chestnuts, beechnuts, acorns and maize during early winter. More fibrous feed, such as hay silage with corn, may be offered during midwinter. The proportion of concentrates was increased again in March. Feeding should take place every day at the same time, regularly and punctually, and feeding places must be accessible for red deer throughout the feeding period (Nerl 1985, Onderscheka 1986, 1991, Steiermark 1986, Raesfeld and Reulecke 1988, Onderscheka et al. 1989, 1990, Wagenknecht 1992).

Feed at feeding stations is locally and temporally concentrated in contrast to the distribution of natural forage. Stags displace hinds; therefore, separate feeding places for hinds and stags have been recommended (Raesfeld 1920, Bubenik 1984, Bützler 1986) but rarely realized. At well-managed feeding stations, many troughs, and hay racks, hay heaps on

Table 105. Feed recommendations and calculated average feed consumed by one red deer per day

Recommended amount of concentrated feed, in pounds (kg)	Feeding period (animal)	Calculated daily average amount of feed in pounds (kg)		
		Hay	Silage	Other
		Ad libitum		3.3–4.4 (1.5–2.0) sesame, 1.1 (0.5) acorns
		1.1 (0.5) or ad libitum		2.2 (1.0) turnips, 1.1 (0.5) grain, 3.3 (1.5) oats, 1.5 (0.7) acorns
1.1 (0.5)		Ad libitum	11 (5.0)	
1.1 (0.5)		2.76 (1.25)		
	October–December 220-pound (100 kg) animal	2.5 (1.15)	3.3 (1.5)	
	January–March	2.76 (1.25)	26.0 (11.8)	
	April	+0.25 cobs		
1.1–1.5 (0.5–0.7)		6.6 (3.0)	5.5 (2.0–3.0)	
1.3 (0.6)		1.1 (0.5)		11.0 (5.0) turnips
		1.1 (0.5)	11.0 (5.0)	0.4 (0.2) soy meal
		1.1 (0.5)		13.2 (6.0) turnips, 1.1 (0.5) maize
2.0 (0.9)		1.7 (0.75)		15.4 (7.0) turnips
1.3 (0.6)	Yearlong (stag)	1.1 (0.5)		11.0 (5.0) turnips
	Yearlong (hind)	2.2–4.4 (1.0–2.0)		6.6–11.0 (3.0–5.0) turnips
1.0 (0.45)				or silage
		2.2 (1.0)	8.8 (4.0)	2.2 (1.0) beer draft
	Mild winters	3.3 (1.5)	9.9 (4.5)	2.2 (1.0) beer draft
1.1 (0.5)	Severe winters	Ad libitum	8.8–11.0 (4.0–5.0)	
1.1–1.7 (0.5–0.75)		4.4 (2.0)		11.0 (5.0) turnips or silage
2.2 (1.0)		3.3 (1.5)	Ad libitum	
0.4 (0.2)		3.3–4.4 (1.5–2.0)	7.7–11.0 (3.5–5.0)	2.2 (1.0) turnips
		4.4 (2.0)	8.8 (4.0)	0.9 (0.4) maize
1.06 (0.48)		2.84 (1.29)	3.57 (1.62)	1.0 (0.45) turnips, 4.76 (2.16) beer draft
		3.3–4.4 (1.5–2.0)	11.0 (5.0)	13.2 (6.0) turnips

Table 106. Estimated calcium and phosphorus requirements for antler growth in red deer

Antler weight in pounds (kg)	Weight in grams per day		Calcium/ phosphorus ratio	Comments
	Calcium	Phosphorus		
22 (10)	54.0	46.0	1.17:1	Total requirements
	8.5	7.5	1.13:1	
21 (9.5)	11.2	5.4	2.07:1	First half of antler growth requirements only; 60% usability of minerals consumed
21 (9.5)	16.8	8.14	2.06:1	Second half of antler growth requirements only
	36.8	26.0	1.41:1	Total requirements for first half of growth
	48.0	31.2	1.53:1	Total requirements for second half of growth
			1.5:1	
			1.7:1	
			2.0:1	

Table 105 continued

Source
Vogt 1937
Raesfeld and Lettow-Vorbeck 1965
Bayerische-StaatsforstVerwaltung 1983
Bubenik 1984
Bubenik 1984
Bubenik 1984
Nerl 1985
Ueckermann 1986
Ueckermann 1986
Ueckermann 1986
Ueckermann 1986
Ueckermann 1986
Pacher 1987
Furst 1987
Furst 1987
Linn 1987
Onderscheka 1986
Onderscheka et al. 1990
Raesfeld and Reulecke 1988
Drescher-Kaden 1991
Volk 1993
Wieselmann 1994

Table 106 continued

Source
Vogt 1936
Glaser 1983
Bubenik 1984
Bubenik 1984
Bubenik 1984
Bubenik 1984
Raesfeld and Lettow-Vorbeck 1965
Ueckermann 1986
Drescher-Kaden 1991

the ground and creep feeders for calves are used to ensure simultaneous access by all individuals (Raesfeld 1920, Hofmann and Kirsten 1982, Nerl 1985, Raesfeld and Reulecke 1988). Only recently has feeding management been planned on a scale large enough to approximate the range of a population in two Austrian provinces (Reimoser 1988b, 1996).

Economics

Evaluating costs of a supplemental feeding program may take many forms, because the ways value is placed on wildlife are many and varied (Steinhoff et al. 1987). The following are several examples, which are necessarily not comparable. One way to assess the cost of feeding is to compare it with the net economic value of an elk hunting trip. Sorg and Nelson (1986) estimated that value to be $99.82 per day in Idaho in 1982. Estimated costs of feeding one deer ranged from $10 to $30 per winter, and for elk, $30 to $80 per winter, but both escalating during the most severe winters in Idaho (L. J. Nelson personal communication:1994). In a situation more predictable than typically occurs elsewhere, the cost of mechanized feeding of a pelleted alfalfa ration to elk on the National Elk Refuge during the 1990s averaged $0.52 per elk per day or $33 per elk during an average 64-day period of feeding.

Another example is the Colorado estimate of $174 per deer provided by Baker and Hobbs (1985), based on how many mule deer were saved when a population of 5,000 was supplementally fed during a severe winter, and not on the direct cost of the feeding program itself.

Elsewhere, Utah estimates were based on feeding an average of 25,044 deer in 1984 at $22 per deer (Musclow 1985). Kimball and Wolfe (1984) reported that feeding elk at the Hardware Ranch and other areas in Utah cost between $0.28 and $0.57 per animal per day, or $25.00 to $51.00 per animal per 90 days in winter. The annual cost to feed approximately 500 elk was $75,000, or $150 per elk at the Hardware Ranch.

In Idaho, hunters provide $1.50 per deer, elk and pronghorn tag toward a depredation alleviation and winter feeding program administered by Idaho Department of Fish and Game. During 1984 through 1993, more than $400,000 per year was provided for these activities (L. J. Nelson personal communication:1994). Annual supplemental feeding expenses have ranged from less than $100,000 to more than $400,000 during the same period, whereas depredation alleviation expenses have ranged from just over $50,000 to more than $550,000. During some years, the combined expenses have exceeded income; during other years, income has exceeded expenses. Funds can be carried over from one year to the next, which helps to cover situations in which supplemental feeding or depredations are increased. Neither income nor expenses in Idaho showed any trend during the 1984 through 1993 period, with both feeding and depredation alleviation being most expensive during severe winters, as the policy would imply.

Supplemental feeding occurs primarily in the southern portions of Idaho, but depredations occur throughout the state. At least 95% of the big game populations in the state are not fed. Kuck (1999) reported that an average of 2,564 elk were fed statewide between 1982 and 1999. Toweill (1999) estimated that costs to feed elk (with the goal of increasing numbers of cows and calves that might survive winter) would be $5,120.60 per elk that survived the winter solely because of supplemental feed and the effect on an elk population of approximately 5,000 would be undetectable.

McBryde (1995) reported costs of supplemental feeding of deer to be $1.34 per acre ($3.31/ha) in a Texas investigation. Feeding consists of supplying feed in commercially produced deer feeders. A comparison between supplemental feeding and developing food plots suggested that food plots would be more cost effective than the feeders except during drought conditions, which reduced food plot yields below 583 pounds per acre (653 kg/ha), or when a farmer did not have tractors and implements already on hand. If lease rates were less than $14.17 per acre ($35.00/ha), less than 2.5 acres (1 ha) in food plots per 2,000-acre (809 ha) unit would maximize profits. The projections assume a deer population of 46 per square mile (17.8/km²).

Average feeding costs are approximately 12 Austrian schillings (approximately $1.20) per red deer per day in Austria (1996 estimates). A feeding period generally will be between 150 and 200 days, depending on location of the feeding place and winter severity. If natural forage is available, feeding costs (feed plus costs for labor) are approximately 800 Austrian schillings (about $80) per deer per winter. In enclosures, where supplemental feed is the sole source of food, feeding costs may be tenfold that estimate. In western Austria, where red deer are supplemented on average for 180 days each winter, feeding costs are 2,500 Austrian schillings (approximately $250) per deer. Because about one-third of the population will be culled, feeding costs result in 7,500 Austrian schillings (approximately $750) per winter per individual culled the following hunting season. A prime trophy stag sold to a trophy hunter will yield approximately 100,000 Austrain schillings (approximately $10,000) (F. Volk personal communication:1995).

However, it is impossible to take all aspects relevant to supplemental feeding into consideration and calculation. One of the foremost goals of supplemental feeding has become the prevention of forest damage, while maintaining red deer at huntable densities. The reduction of forest dam-

Although the cost of feeding per elk in Idaho averaged about $30 to $80 depending on the duration of the winter feeding period, Toweill (1999) estimated that the net gain due to winter feeding, that is, the cost associated with each elk that survived the winter solely because supplemental feed was provided, would exceed $5,000 per elk. Costs per bull elk carried through winter solely due to supplemental feed were estimated to be several times that amount. *Photo courtesy of the Idaho Department of Fish and Game.*

ages, especially reduced browsing pressure on forest rejuvenation, is difficult to calculate because it varies depending on location, management, age and structure of the forest stands, as well as variable timber prices. Older stands without abundant conifer regeneration have little storage capacity for rain and snow melt, and will not be able to prevent snow and mud avalanches. If supplemental feeding reduces browsing and bark-stripping pressure, stands with well-developed understories will not be as subject to avalanches and erosion, but these ecological benefits are impossible to evaluate in economic terms. However, supplemental feeding may pay off in the long term. Other aspects that have to be considered are varying prices paid for trophy stags, and compensation claims for depredation in neighboring forests and on farmland. Some hunting grounds are used as recreational opportunities to establish or enhance business. Furthermore, some revier owners simply enjoy the being able to experience high red deer densities attributable to supplemental feeding. Because of the hunting system in Austria, feeding programs are financed by the owners or lessees of the respective revier, most being private individuals and, thus, are profitable either in the short, medium or long term.

Supplemental winter feeding of big game on both continents can be justified economically regardless of the method by which the economics of the situation are viewed. There is enough experience to anticipate where and when supplemental feeding programs may have to be established. For established programs where feeding is an annual occurrence, the type and formulation of feed to use and how to distribute it among animals are understood.

The efficiency with which supplemental feeding programs can be conducted, and the general support for the activity, make economically based arguments against supplemental feeding controversial. However, where supplemental feeding is occasional and reaches a relatively small proportion of a population, it becomes more difficult to justify under any circumstances.

Where hunting rights are leased for substantial sums, supplemental feeding may be economically justifiable to prevent excessive mortality during the occasional severe winter or drought. On balance, an efficiently executed program of supplemental feeding may be justified for the occasional severe winter for populations that are in balance with or exist below the ecological carrying capacity of their habitat. This may be the case especially when other alternatives prove less effective in reducing mortality or other problems. The problems of habitat damage due to concentrating animals in small areas, feeding small proportions of a population and long-term perpetuation of misplaced public relations are discounted in this conclusion.

Disease

Pathogens thrive where animals and plants concentrate; habitat relationships and population density interact with the various diseases and parasites that are prevalent in wild populations (Herman 1969, Holmes 1982). The potential for diseases and parasites to proliferate where big game animals are concentrated in seasons when they are naturally in poorest condition has been understood for decades, as the Jackson Hole experience demonstrated (Murie 1951). In recent years, increased game-farms have enhanced the potential for disease and parasite transmission between privately owned big game and free-ranging wildlife.

Smith and Roffe (1992) reported that brucellosis, pasteurellosis and scabies were the three diseases most prevalent among elk on the National Elk Refuge. Approximately 37% of elk in the western Wyoming feedground complex tested positive for brucellosis, which is transmissible to bison and cattle (Thorne et al. 1991a). U.S. Department of Agriculture regulations that restrict sale and shipment of brucellosis-infected cattle and domesticated bison herds have created concerns about financial hardship among agricultural interests in the states of Wyoming, Montana and Idaho, which harbor infected wild elk and bison herds. Litigation against state and federal wildlife management agencies, possible transfer of legal authority over free-ranging bison and elk in the Yellowstone area to the Department of Agriculture, and threatened livestock market sanctions against Montana, Wyoming and Idaho are among the recent repercussions of brucellosis in elk and bison (Keiter 1997).

The increased opportunity for intraspecific exposure to brucellosis-causing bacteria shed in the environment where elk are concentrated apparently perpetuates this disease on feedgrounds. Extensive testing of other elk populations have failed to find evidence of brucellosis to any significant degree (Vaughn et al. 1973, Adrian and Keiss 1977, Thorne et al. 1979), including areas of the continent where brucellosis previously was widespread in cattle (Drew et al. 1992).

Pasteurellosis among elk was documented during 1985 to 1986 and 1986 to 1987 on the National Elk Refuge (Franson and Smith 1988). During the protracted winter of 1992 to 1993, an estimated 160 elk infected with septicemic pasteurellosis died on the refuge. This disease can be particularly virulent among immunologically naive or compromised animals, with rapid progression of clinical signs, including lesions of the lungs, heart, spleen and lymphatic system (Franson and Smith 1988).

Of even greater concern to biologists than the cost and manpower required for winter feeding is the risk of disease transmission. The potential for diseases and parasites to proliferate and spread among concentrated animals when they are in their poorest body condition has been understood for decades and is amply supported by evidence. *Photo courtesy of the Idaho Department of Fish and Game.*

Mites of the genus *Psoroptes* cause a progressive and severe exudative dermatitis in adult male elk, and some animals die each winter on the National Elk Refuge (Samuel et al. 1991). This winter mortality may be related to malnutrition and poor physical condition as a consequence of rutting behavior on ranges where high densities of bulls occur (Smith 1985). Few reports of this parasite and the disease it causes occur outside the Yellowstone ecosystem.

Tuberculosis has been among the most important diseases in farmed New Zealand red deer (Griffin et al. 1992c). Standard methods of diagnosis that are applicable to cattle are not sensitive for deer, and more specific testing has been developed in that country for this pathogen. Bovine tuberculosis has been transmitted from captive elk to pigs, cattle and humans in Alberta, and infected elk have escaped to the wild (Geist 1991b).

Although not reported from free-ranging elk to date, bovine tuberculosis was discovered in free-ranging white-tailed deer in Michigan in 1994 (Doster 1996). The 16 affected deer occurred in an 11- by 12-mile (17.7 by 19.3 km) location where high-density populations were maintained with winter-long supplemental feeding by private hunting clubs. The Michigan Department of Natural Resources asked these hunting clubs to stop feeding deer and increase harvests.

In Canada, efforts are underway to prevent the transmission of meningeal worm from eastern provinces where it is indigenous to white-tailed deer. This parasite causes paralysis in moose, elk and caribou, but is tolerated by deer (Karns 1966, Anderson 1972). Efforts to prevent infection by prohibiting importation of captive elk from Saskatchewan and other provinces to the east are in effect for Alberta.

Potential exists for disease transmission to wild elk and deer concentrated on feedgrounds from escaped, infected, privately owned animals. In Alberta, contact is known to occur between wild elk and privately owned elk, and disease transmission is virtually inevitable as a result. Transfer of pathogens between wild and captive animals may or may not produce significant outbreaks in diseases. However, when animals carrying these pathogens concentrate on winter range or on feedgrounds, the probabilities for outbreaks increase. Potentials for outbreaks of diseases and parasites among animals on feedgrounds must be considered in managing supplemental feeding programs. Although the record suggests that outbreaks have been only occasional, conditions predisposing more frequent and more virulent outbreaks have been enhanced in recent years with the proliferation of privately farmed elk. Efforts to monitor farmed elk populations effectively for tuberculosis and bovine spongiform encephalopathy as well as bru-

cellosis will help protect free-ranging populations. This is especially important now that it is apparent that privately held elk come in contact with wild elk.

Does Supplemental Feeding Affect Populations?

Two investigations with white-tailed deer demonstrated that populations of this species respond to supplemental feeding. Ozoga and Verme (1982) and Woolf and Harder (1979) reported on captive white-tailed deer populations that were maintained on artificial forage. On the 5,100-acre (2,064 ha) Rachelwood Wildlife Research Preserve in Pennsylvania, Woolf and Harder (1979) reported densities of 544 deer per square mile (210/km²). Herd productivity was 43.4% over an 11-year period, based on prefawning population size and prerut size. This deer population exhibited low productivity when compared with free-ranging deer outside of the reserve, with density-related effects including nutrition and disease. Nevertheless, a very high density of deer was being maintained in an enclosure with the use of artificial feed.

Ozoga and Verme (1982) demonstrated that fawn production and survival could be increased by supplemental feeding in a 1-square mile (2.6 km²) enclosure in northern Michigan. Bucks grew larger antlers after supplemental feeding was initiated, with males older than 3.5 years changing from 1.06 inch (26.9 mm) beam diameter to 1.66 inch (42.1 mm) diameter. Number of points increased from an average of 7.3 to 9.9 per deer.

The Austrian and North American experiences provide contrasts in the way the effects of supplemental feeding are viewed. Generally, supplemental feeding in North America is viewed as an activity intended to maintain animals during a severe winter or drought, whereas in Austria, efforts to improve animal condition and increase numbers beyond what the natural forage base would allow are incorporated into the feeding programs.

The original motivation of winter feeding (i.e., to restrict red deer movements) is considered a detriment in North America. In Europe, intensive winter feeding has successfully discouraged red deer movements into lowland areas and eliminated the tradition of migration, as well as the use of traditional alpine wintering areas (Guggenberger 1981, Wotschikowsky 1981, Glaser 1983, Gossow 1983, Gossow and Dieberger 1989, Zeiler et al. 1990). Supplemented herds are influenced less by snow regimes, therefore have a much more predictable pattern of home range use than do free-ranging populations (Schmidt 1992, 1993). Supplemental feed may retain and attract red deer to a revier, thereby increasing culling success (Gossow 1983, Sackl 1992). Sackl

(1992) reported that in a 53-square mile (137 km²) revier, almost half the feeding stations were situated less than 1,640 feet (500 m) from the border. In reviers with a feeding station, as much as 80% of the culls take place from November to January, when red deer use the feeding station (Zeiler et al. 1990, Sackl 1992).

A variety of other reasons also are involved in the evolution of the Austrian winter feeding program, and controversy exists. Winter feeding basically is justified as compensation for lost winter range and is viewed as necessary to ensure survival of red deer (Raesfeld 1920, Wagenknecht 1980, Hofmann and Kirsten 1982, Nerl 1985, Bützler 1986, Onderscheka 1986, 1991, Ueckermann 1986, Raesfeld and Reulecke 1988, Wieselmann 1994). However, if not viewed exclusively from a hunter's perspective, winter feeding certainly is not necessary to ensure the survival of the species in the Alps or to maintain red deer populations within their present range (Zeiler 1996). Although it generally is acknowledged that many winter ranges are lost to human encroachment, there is controversy concerning whether the current extent of supplemental feeding is justified. In many Austrian alpine areas, segments of red deer populations had wintered on windblown alpine pastures until supplemental winter feeding in the middle of the 20th century attracted these herds to lower elevations. Herds that could not be bound to the feeding place and, thus, could not be managed were culled (A. Furst personal communication:1989). Only a very few herds still winter above the timberline or on southerly exposed slopes with accessible natural forage (Onderscheka 1989, Schmidt 1993). Changes in forest management, fragmentation of the forest from die-off and increased nitrogen supply due to acid rain may increase summer carrying capacity (Eisfeld 1990), but winter forage remains the limiting factor because of the deep snows that persist on large clearcuts (Reimoser 1990). In many areas, however, forest composition, altered for forestry objectives, is detrimental for red deer nutrition even during the growing season (Donaubauer 1990, Onderscheka 1991), therefore deer enter the winter with insufficient fat deposits (Hofmann and Kirsten 1982, Bützler 1986, Onderscheka 1986). Changes in forestry practices to favor understory development could alleviate this problem in some areas. Uneven-aged silvicultural practices that bring about a proper balance between available food supply and food-independent settling stimuli can greatly decrease the predisposition of the forest to game damage (Reimoser and Gossow 1996). For the present, supplemental winter feeding is seen as the only short- and middle-term solutions to compensate for the lack of natural winter forage. Nonsupplemented red deer could damage forest cultures to such a

Controversy exists regarding winter feeding of red deer in Austria. Some herds, as shown here, continue to exist on alpine winter ranges without supplementation, and feeding is not necessary to insure survival of red deer within their present range (although likely not at present population levels). Feeding has been successful in diverting red deer from areas where damage has historically occurred, but changes in forest management practices to promote development of desirable forage may be required to enable some herds to survive severe winters—particularly now that traditional migratory routes no longer exist. In addition, herds are a valuable economic asset in terms of trophy and meat production. *Photo by Karoline T. Schmidt.*

high degree that forest managers would no longer accept this ungulate species at densities attractive for hunting.

Winter starvation was regarded as a positive selective force by Raesfeld (1920). However, Lettow-Vorbeck's revision of Raesfeld's classic book (Raesfeld und Lettow-Vorbeck 1965) stressed that winter death was not selective, and considered proponents of winter starvation as an appropriate selection force to be an excuse by those who did not want to feed.

Management of red deer or elk for the primary purpose of hunting and selective harvest may strive for maximum sustainable yield. Winter feeding and culling policies were intended to eliminate red deer fluctuations that, in former times, occurred especially in alpine areas. Stable, high densities of red deer deprive natural vegetation of regeneration periods that may have existed when the deer populations fluctuated on a more natural basis (Donaubauer 1990).

The extent to which feeding influences survival is difficult to assess, because selective culling of individuals in poor condition masks effects of winter feeding on winter survival. However, feeding undoubtedly reduces winter mortality rates (Bayerische-Staatsforstverwaltung 1983, Reimoser 1990). Individuals that would be primarily affected by winter mortality (i.e., calves and old males), benefit most from supplemental feeding. Orphaned calves survive at higher rates with supplemental feeding despite their discrimination at the feeding troughs (Rossler 1983). Winter feeding may result in artificial concentrations of animals, which, in turn, reduce the availability of thermal cover for newborn calves. Preparturient hinds will seek solitude from other members of the herd, which may be inferior thermal shelter. Frequently, calves are born next to an enclosure fence (Hoglmuller 1983, Rossler 1983).

After World War II, demands for red deer hunting opportunities grew, as did prices for leasing rights (Anderluh 1990, Colloredo-Mannsfeld 1992). Increased survival was not offset by increased culling rates of hinds, because hunters selected against females. Between 1960 and 1990, red deer populations throughout Austria clearly grew (Greutter 1985, Gossow and Dieberger 1989, Zeiler et al. 1990, Zeiler and Gossow 1990), and culls increased 370% from 1950 to 1990 (Donaubauer 1990). Despite increasing culling levels, red deer expanded their range by 3,089 square miles (8,000 km²) from 1945 to 1975 (Colloredo-Mannsfeld 1992). Natural densities for red and roe deer in alpine forests were estimated as 1.3 to 2.6 per square mile (0.5–1.0/km²), but increased to 52 to 104 per square mile (20–40/km²) under winter feeding regimes (Mayer 1977). Reviers with 0.26 feeding stations per square mile (0.1/km²) support red deer densities of 10.4 to 28.5 per square mile (4–11 deer/km²) (Zeiler et al. 1990, Sackl 1992). A red deer density of 7.8 deer per square mile (3 deer/km²) is regarded as minimum density for reviers considered to be prime red deer habitat and where supplemental winter feeding is approved and encouraged (Kahls and Stadlmann 1990).

Winter feeding conceivably may increase population size by enhancing reproduction and reducing juvenile mortality (Schroder 1985, Gossow and Dieberger 1989). Supplemental feeding may increase percentages of yearling hinds conceiving as well (Ennemoser 1983). Current hunting laws assume a fertility of 80% in adult females (Sackl 1992)—a figure used with estimates of population size and density based on hunter observations to fix red deer bags and culling quotas. Conclusions about densities based on red deer culls may be biased because hind culls are not controlled by authorities (Zeiler et al. 1990, Sackl 1992).

Raesfeld (1920) stressed the importance of adequate nutrition of pregnant hinds in spring, and Vogt (1936) emphasized mineral nutrition to ensure healthy calf production. In some areas, the amount of feed per individual per day increased by 50% from 1975 to 1981, and average carcass weight of calves increased by 22% (from 66.4 to 81.3

pounds: 30.1–36.9 kg) and that of yearling females increased by 9.8% (from 103.2 to 113.3 pounds: 46.8–51.4 kg) (Ennemoser 1983). In other areas, carcass weight of yearling females remained relatively low (109.8 pounds: 49.8 kg), despite intensive winter feeding programs (Sackl 1992). Experimental work by Glaser (1983) showed that body weight changes not only differed between sex and age classes but also depended on whether feeding occurred at a feeding station where red deer roamed free or inside a winter enclosure where the deer were confined until late spring. After 6 years of intensive winter feeding, average stag weight dropped by 18.6% (from 151.5 to 123.2 pounds: 68.7–55.9 kg), average male calf weight dropped by 5.4% (from 96.8 to 91.5 pounds: 43.9–41.5 kg), whereas average adult hind weight increased by 3.1% (from 96.8 to 123.5 pounds: 54.3–56 kg) and average female calf weight increased 6.9% (from 84.7 to 90.4 pounds: 38.4–41 kg).

Inside an enclosure only adults gained weight during 6 years of intensive winter feeding (Glaser 1983). Stags gained 4% (from 170.6 to 177.5 pounds: 77.4–80.5 kg) compared with 2.9% carcass weight increase in hinds (from 111.6 to 114.9 pounds: 50.6–52.1 kg). But both sexes of calves lost weight—male calves lost 3.8% (from 91.3 to 87.7 pounds: 41.4–39.8 kg), and female calves 4.6% (from 85.3 to 81.3 pounds: 38.7–36.9 kg) (Figure 165). Findings differ between studies and, after 20 years of winter feeding, Rossler (1983) reported calf carcass weight had increased by 57%. These strikingly different results in body weight gain, despite little difference in feeding regimens, may be linked partly to different densities: where deer more than doubled (133%) their weight (from 330.7 to 771.6 pounds: 150–350 kg), density was 0.86 per square mile (0.33/km²) (Vogt 1936), whereas in enclosures with little weight gain (5.1 pounds [2.3 kg] or 3.6%) of deer, density was 1 animal per 0.33 square mile (0.13 km²) (Glaser 1983). At high densities, dominant individuals secure high-quality food, whereas subordinates have to make do with remnants (Glaser 1983,

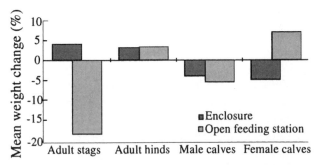

Figure 165. Percentage mean weight changes during 6 years of intensive winter feeding of red deer in an enclosure, compared with the aggregate mean from the previous 4 years when the deer were not fed (Glaser 1983).

Linn 1987, Schmidt 1990). Sociological aspects, such as social stress, also may be involved.

As trophy antlers became a status symbol among hunters in the latter half of the 19th century (Gossow 1983), winter feeding was regarded as the most direct means to increase antler size and weight (Anderluh 1990, Eisfeld 1990). Supplemental feeds contained minerals lacking in managed forests (Vogt 1936, Bubenik 1984), and the elimination of migrations through limestone habitats deprived red deer of 60% to 80% of their phosphorus demands for antler growth (Onderscheka 1991). After 20 years of supplementary feeding between 1960 and 1980, Glaser (1983) and Gossow and Dieberger (1989) reported that the number of medal-winning trophies more than doubled, and quality of trophies increased by 13%. The weight of cast antlers increased more than 100% (Rossler 1983). A 3-year-old stag fed sesame cake increased its antler weight from 3.5 to 13.2 pounds (1.6–6 kg; 273%), antler scoring points from 124 to 171 (37.9%) and antler length from 27 to 39 inches (68.5–99 cm; 44.5%) within 6 years (Figure 166). Antler weight increased relative to carcass weight and may have accounted for up to 8.3% of the carcass weight (or 6.3% of body weight) at the beginning of the rut (Vogt 1936, Glaser 1983). Feeding to increase trophy quality was considered an abuse by Raesfeld and Reulecke (1988), Onderscheka et al. (1989, 1990) and Wagenknecht (1992), but remains an effective advertisement for commercial supplemental feed.

The Austrian history shows that supplemental winter feeding generally increased range fidelity, population density and trophy quality, as well as hunting success rates. As supplemental feeding intensified in Austria, hunting shifted

from efforts to retain deer on hunting grounds to production and management, therefore could no longer be regarded as an example of sustainable use within a forest ecosystem (Zeiler 1996).

Supplemental feeding of some 23,000 elk by the Wyoming Game and Fish Department and the U.S. Fish and Wildlife Service maintains populations at higher densities throughout western Wyoming than the available winter range could support (Thorne et al. 1991b). These winter feeding programs promoted high survival rates (Murie 1951, Boyce 1989, Smith and Robbins 1994, Smith et al. 1997a). Although no difference in winter survival of elk at least 1 year old was detected, survival of calves that wintered on the National Elk Refuge was significantly higher than that of calves not supplemented in winter (Smith et al. 1997a).

Effects of supplemental feeding on reproductive biology have been investigated in the Jackson elk herd. At the rates and duration that supplementation occurs at the National Elk Refuge (see Table 101), winter feeding did not produce larger birth weights than reported for Rocky Mountain elk that are not fed (Smith et al. 1997b). Instead, March temperatures accounted for most variation in cohort birth weights of Jackson elk. This is not surprising, because most fetal growth occurs during the last 2 months of gestation (Nelson and Leege 1982), after winter feeding has ceased at the National Elk Refuge (Smith et al. 1997b). When March temperatures were warmer, vegetative green-up began earlier. Cow elk presumably were able to recover body condition lost during winter and allocate more energy to fetal growth more quickly under these conditions. Cohort birth weight of red deer also varied with annual spring temperatures and consequent growth of new grass during their birth year (Albon et al. 1987).

There was evidence that winter feeding did influence sex ratios of red deer at birth. The proportion of male births was greater after winters when feeding began early in the winter and digestibility of the feed was high (Smith and Anderson 1998). Survival of male fetuses, which are energetically more costly to produce than are females (Clutton-Brock et al. 1982), may be favored by nutritional supplementation in early winter, when prenatal mortality becomes male-biased under nutritional stress (Robinette et al. 1957, Trivers and Willard 1973, Maynard Smith 1980).

Elk and red deer typically lose weight during winter, which they regain during the growing season (Mitchell et al. 1976, Nelson and Leege 1982). When supplementally fed, elk may lose, maintain or gain weight in relation to the ration provided. Adult cow elk maintained in pastures with limited natural forage at the National Elk Refuge lost 6.2% to 10.8% of body weight from late January to early April when fed 5 pounds (2.3 kg) of pelleted alfalfa per elk per

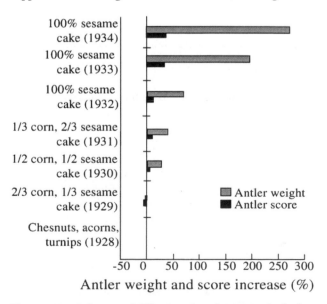

Figure 166. Influence of different ratios of sesame cake feed on percentage increases in antler weight and antler score (in relation to 1928) for 3-year-old red deer (Vogt 1937).

day (0.95–1.03 pounds per 1,000 pounds [0.066 kg/1,000 kg] body weight) (Oldemeyer et al. 1993). Female weight loss averaged 4.2% on a ration of 7.1 pounds (3.2 kg) of pelleted alfalfa per elk per day (1.36 pounds per 100 pounds [3.0 kg/100 kg] body weight) (Oldemeyer et al. 1993). Overwinter weight changes of adult female elk held in paddocks varied from –9.5% when fed 2.2 pounds of baled alfalfa per 100 pounds (4.85 kg/100 kg) of body weight, to +4.2% when fed 1.96 pounds of pelleted hay per 100 pounds (4.32 kg/100 kg) of body weight (Thorne and Butler 1976). At Utah's Hardware Ranch, a ration of 7.1 pounds (3.2 kg) of meadow hay per elk per day was required to maintain body weight during winter (Kimball and Wolfe 1985).

Weights attained by autumn can influence conception rates (Sadlier 1969, Mitchell et al. 1976). There is no evidence that autumn weights differ between fed and unfed elk herds. Likewise conception rates of elk fed in winter averaged 87% in females 2 years of age and older at the National Elk Refuge (Smith and Robbins 1994) and 85% at the Hardware Ranch (Kimball and Wolfe 1979); these were similar to rates reported for unfed elk herds (Houston 1982, Taber et al. 1982). Eight of 50 (16%) yearlings were pregnant in January on the National Elk Refuge (Smith and Robbins 1994), and 16 of 132 yearlings (12%) at Utah's Hardware Ranch were pregnant (Kimball and Wolfe 1979). These are characteristic of pregnancy rates in other Rocky Mountain elk populations (Houston 1982, Taber et al. 1982).

Winter feeding has been demonstrated to increase antler size in Austrian red deer (Glaser 1983, Rossler 1983). Antler mass of 2- to 15-year-old elk that died during winter on the National Elk Refuge between 1989 and 1994 was unrelated to the amount of feed those elk received during the winter before growing their last set of antlers. Instead, early growing season temperatures during March and April preceding their deaths and ambient temperatures when male elk were in utero (which also correlated with cohort birth weights) both were correlated significantly with antler size (Smith 1997). The former effect underscores the sensitivity of antler growth to the prevailing foraging conditions during each year of cervid lives. The latter effect provides further evidence of the persistent influence that environmental conditions during an elk's year has on growth throughout the animal's life (Albon et al. 1983a).

The consequences of supplemental feeding on adjacent vegetation also must be considered. Animals that are concentrated on feedgrounds will not restrict themselves to the artificially provided food, but also will browse plants within the area. If feeding grounds are located with due consideration for this effect on surrounding plants, and if they are not permanently established such that vegetation has an opportunity to recover, effects on habitat may be minimized.

However, severe damage to adjacent vegetation may diminish the ability of the native plants to sustain animals at times when supplemental feeding does not occur, therefore the danger of making animals increasingly dependent on feeding must be taken into account.

Conclusions

A convergence of information and practices is evident in the Austrian and North American records. Initial experiences in Austria were not much different than those in North America, where supplemental feeding programs were inefficient and mortality of animals occurred. Subsequently, experience and studies made the programs more effective in preventing mortality and accomplishing other objectives. The European experience has been further extended toward specific husbandry practices that emphasize antler size or maximum weight and body size, with associated controversy. Objectives of reducing damage to forests and croplands are apparent on both continents. In central Europe, the dramatic loss of winter habitat to a variety of causes and fundamental alteration of red deer habitat due to forestry practices make economical and ecological maintenance of huntable deer populations largely dependent on supplemental feeding. In North America, proper feeding of mule deer, with expectation of the subject's survival, is a fairly recent research success. For the red deer/elk complex in both Europe and North America, this has been demonstrated for more than half a century. At present, high densities of deer of several kinds can be effectively maintained with efficiently executed supplemental feeding programs, and physical attributes, such as body and antler size, can be enhanced.

Also apparent is that, when habitat is severely diminished or eliminated and deer still are present, supplemental feeding is a legitimate practice. Conversely, the practice itself may alter habitat adversely. The purposes for which the animals are maintained are diverse, and all would have to be considered as justifiable in one value context or another (i.e., free-ranging herds versus confined, commercially exploited animals).

Therefore, decisions about supplemental feeding are less a scientific than a philosophical exercise. Technology aside, what are the circumstances in which a certain population will be allowed to exist? If the desire is to keep the wildlife resource as free as possible of human intervention, then supplemental feeding and confinement are discouraged. If the forces of natural selection are encouraged, then the emphasis is on wildlife management.

The opposite view is utilitarian. It specifies that humans must have uses and incentives to provide for wildlife, and the intrinsic biological value of the resource ultimately will not be sufficient to maintain it (Kellert 1976). According to this view, a wildlife population modified from its original nature existing in confinement or heavily modified habitats represents a population that is more apt to be secure because it has an economic value. However, even with a utilitarian point of view, the question arises whether dependence on interventions is useful and sensible. Supplemental winter feeding has substantially subverted red deer ecology in central Europe. For red deer, the immediate effects of winter feeding on deer behavior include use of unsuitable habitat, involuntary shuttling between feeding places and resting places, high rates of agonistic behavior, direct competition, lack of sexual segregation, male dominance and discrimination against hinds and calves at the feeding troughs. In the long term, red deer populations abandon seasonal migrations and lose traditional knowledge of natural winter ranges. Now, reconstruction and reestablishment of natural wintering traditions will result in initial heavy winter starvation and severe forest damage.

The middle ground is where most supplemental feeding policies of western U.S. states lie: some populations will be fed supplementally during severe winters for the purpose of reducing mortality. The Austrian situation represents an extension of this, wherein annual supplemental feeding is necessary to maintain deer populations at desired levels and distributions, under present conditions. Management in Austria and most of central Europe is not aimed at minimizing, but at optimizing anthropogenic interventions for the benefit of wildlife (especially game animals) and forestry. By regarding supplemental winter feeding as a matter of course, foresters and hunters have become dependent on feeding programs much more than have red deer themselves. Without this management measure, integrated red deer hunting/forestry management is scarcely conceivable. More diversified forest management and changes in population management may allow more deer, as well as enable managers to become less dependent on supplemental feeding, and pressures toward that end exist.

Elk Farming

Farming of privately owned elk is well established in Canada and the United States (Tables 107 and 108). Approximately 1,800 farms in Canada raise 46,000 elk and red deer, of which Saskatchewan and Alberta raise approximately 60%. Quebec, Manitoba, Saskatchewan, Alberta, Northwest Territories and Yukon allow farming of native species of deer, whereas other provinces do not. In British Columbia, approximately 15,000 fallow deer are raised on 64 farms.

Approximately 110,000 elk are privately owned in the United States. In the United States west of the Mississippi, approximately 550 farms raise more than 17,500 elk and red deer (Table 109). In the United States, the industry is worth $500 million per year, according to the North American Elk Breeders Association, of Platte City, Missouri (website www.naelk.org: April 24, 1999). In addition, reserves or parks where privately owned elk may be hunted exist in Colorado and Texas, and zoos and other park facilities have captive elk.

Elk antlers and velvet sell to Oriental markets as aphrodisiacs and general medicine. Korea alone purchased approximately 143 tons (130,000 kg) of elk antlers in 1996. Soft antlers and velvet can sell for $35.00 to $110.00 per pound ($15.88–$49.90/kg), with a large-antlered bull producing as much as 40 pounds (18.1 kg) of antlers. Elk venison is sold to restaurants in the United States, and is priced three to four times more than beef. Five-month-old weaned calves sell for $3,000 to $6,000 (1997 prices). A prized breeding bull may sell for up to $60,000, with semen from a top breeding bull selling for up to $6,500. The North American Elk Breeders Association maintains a registration for more than 18,000 elk. The lucrative markets promote commercial growth and bring pressures on the state agencies to allow more game farming. North Dakota, with 52 farms in 1997, had 33 applications pending. In Nebraska, 27 herds were registered with the U.S. Department of Agriculture in May 1996, and 37 in January 1997, reflecting the industry's growth.

The recent increase in farming of elk has encouraged its regulation by the states and provinces. The North American Elk Breeders Association maintains a listing of regulations in Canada, Mexico and the United States. It is available on the internet at www.wapiti.com. Nine states do not permit farming of elk, although some farms that were established before prohibitions exist in several states (see Table 108). The regulations were prompted by concerns about hybridization with wild elk, potential habitat alteration and transmission of disease. As of 1997, there was a moratorium on transfer of elk from the United States into Canada. Under new laws, Saskatchewan allowed the importation of elk from Idaho in March 2000. Mexico allows interchange of elk with the United States, pending disease testing by qualified veterinarians.

In the United States, regulations vary (see Table 108), but typically require that individual elk be identified and tested for disease whenever change of ownership or location occurs. The main concerns are transmission of brucellosis and tuberculosis, but other diseases and the parasite *Parelaphostrongylus tenuis* are considered as well. Fencing regulations are included in 13 states. Farming of red deer, which can

Table 107.   Status of cervid ranching/farming in Canada, 1997

Province	Status	Species permitted	Number of farms	Number of animals[a]
Newfoundland	Not permitted			
Prince Edward Island	Nonnative	Elk	1	12
		Red deer	1	7
New Brunswick	Nonnative only	Elk	4	100
		Red deer	4	600
		Fallow deer	2	100
Nova Scotia	Nonnative only	Red deer	6	300
		Fallow deer	2	100
Quebec	Indigenous and nonnative	Elk		1,400
		Red deer		5,500
		White-tailed deer	850	4,500
		Fallow deer		3,500
Ontario	Nonnative except for white-tailed deer	Elk		3,700
		Red deer		6,500
		White-tailed deer	323	750
		Fallow deer		4,000
Manitoba	Indigenous and nonnative (not regulated)	Elk	31	900
		Fallow deer	2	200
Saskatchewan	Indigenous and nonnative	Elk and red deer		14,500
		Mule deer		400
		White-tailed deer	300	750
		Fallow deer		5,000
		Caribou		20
Alberta	Indigenous except for reindeer	Elk	235	12,000
		White-tailed deer	92	2,800
		Mule deer	24	350
		Reindeer	7	50
British Columbia	Nonnative only	Fallow deer	64	15,000
		Reindeer	8	200
Northwest Territories	Indigenous and nonnative	Reindeer	1	9,000
Yukon	Indigenous except for reindeer	Elk	4	100
		Reindeer	1	50

[a] Total elk = 32,712; total red deer = 12,907; total elk and red deer = 45,619.

hybridize with elk, is prohibited in five of the western states where elk are common; it is restricted to portions of the Dakotas where wild elk do not occur (Table 109). In Massachusetts, red deer may be farmed, but native elk may not. In Texas, elk/red deer hybrids are kept on 19 farms, and 1 farm maintains 100 elk/sika deer hybrids.

Colorado's regulations are elaborate, covering all concerns that typically govern elk farming. Live wildlife possessed in Colorado must go through a mandatory licensing process supervised by the Division of Wildlife. Elk taken in big game hunting parks must be tested for disease. All privately owned animals must be tattooed and marked with ear tags to identify them. Elk farming applications include documentation of employee training, maintenance of business records including profits, development of a business plan, operation of the activity in a businesslike manner, and filing of state and federal income taxes. Licensees must al-

low inspections of captive animals and facilities at any reasonable time. All elk imported into Colorado must be tested for hybridization with red deer, which are not permitted in that state. Veterinarians are authorized to inspect and test animals whenever a transfer of ownership or location is proposed.

Colorado law requires that fences intended to contain private ungulates must be a minimum of 8 feet (2.4 m) above ground level, mesh of 12.5 by 7 inches (30.5 by 17.8 cm) or less up to 6 feet (1.8 m), with the remaining 2 feet (0.6 m) being smooth, barbed or woven wire with strands not more than 10 inches (25.4 cm) apart. Posts must be spaced no more than 50 feet (15.2 m) apart, and be a minimum of 4-inch (10.2 cm) diameter (if wooden), with stays or posts at every 20 feet (6.1 m). Minimum wire gauges are 12½-gauge for conventional fence and 14½-gauge for woven high-tensile fence. The North American Elk Breeders Asso-

Table 108. Nationwide status of elk ranching/farming in the United States, 1997

State[a]	Identification of individuals needed	Fencing requirements
Alabama	Not allowed	
Alaska	Yes	Red deer restricted
Arizona	Not allowed	
Arkansas	Yes	
California	Not allowed	
Colorado	Yes	Yes
Connecticut		
Delaware		
Florida	Yes	
Georgia		
Hawaii		
Idaho	Yes	Yes
Illinois		
Indiana		
Iowa		
Kansas	Yes	
Kentucky		
Louisiana		
Maine		
Maryland	Not allowed	
Massachusetts	Red deer allowed, but not elk	
Michigan	Yes	Yes
Minnesota	No information	
Mississippi		
Missouri	Yes	
Montana	Yes	Yes
Nebraska		
Nevada		Yes
New Hampshire		Yes
New Jersey		
New Mexico		
New York	Yes	
North Carolina		Yes
North Dakota	Yes	Yes
Ohio		
Oklahoma	Yes	Yes
Oregon	Not allowed	
Pennsylvania		Yes
Rhode Island	No information	
South Carolina	Regulations being developed	
South Dakota	Yes	
Texas		
Tennessee	Yes	
Utah	Yes	Yes
Vermont		Yes
Virginia	Not allowed except in zoos	
Washington	Not allowed	
West Virginia	Not allowed	
Wisconsin		Yes
Wyoming	Not allowed	

[a] States with no information have no regulations. Some may not have elk ranches or farms.

ciation recommends an 8-foot (2.4 m) fence, with posts every 20 feet (6.1 m).

Selective breeding for large antlers is a major impetus in the industry. A perusal of the website of The North American Elk Breeders Association shows much discussion about antler size and factors that affect antler growth, including breeding activity, status and nutrition. Captive elk obviously are being bred to produce large antlers, which, in time, may alter the genetic makeup of captive and wild animals.

Hybridization with red deer is a major concern, as indicated by the number of states whose regulations address the issue (see Table 108). Red deer and hybrid red deer/elk crosses have escaped in Ontario and Montana, where they have been culled by provincial and state authorities. The concern involves introduction of genes into the genetic composition of wild animals that alters the ability to adapt in the wild. Although it is in the elk farmers' own interest to make every effort to prevent privately owned elk from escaping, fences inevitably will be damaged and some captively raised animals will intermingle with free-ranging elk. Thus, the potential for disease transmission cannot be dismissed. One incident in western Montana involved privately owned red deer that escaped to the wild and were

The North American Elk Breeders Association recommends that fences for holding elk show reach a minimum of 8 feet (2.4 m) above ground level, with posts no further than 20 feet (6.1 m) apart. In addition, handling facilities need to be constructed so as to allow handlers to closely confine elk during handling. *Photo by James Peek.*

Table 109.   Status and estimated number of elk farms and elk being farmed in the western United States, 1997

State	Status	Number of farms	Number of animals
Arizona	Elk; no more permitted	1	125
	Red deer; no more permitted	1	110
California	Elk not permitted		
Colorado	Red deer prohibited	122	6,037
Idaho	Red deer prohibited	51	1,693
Montana	Red deer prohibited	52	2,800
Nebraska	Red deer prohibited	47	1,684
Nevada	Red deer prohibited		
New Mexico		6	1,118
North Dakota	Red deer restricted	52	
Oklahoma		27	671
Oregon	Red deer prohibited	11	295
South Dakota	Red deer restricted	33	
Texas	Elk	127	2,575
	Elk/red deer cross	19	1,105
	Elk/sika deer cross	1	100
Washington	Elk not permitted		
Wyoming	No more permitted	1	400
Utah	Red deer prohibited	4	40
Total		555	18,753

seen with wild elk (Stalling 1998). Diseased elk were imported into Alberta, resulting in the quarantine of approximately two-thirds of the gamefarms in the province in 1990 (Geist 1991b). During the early 1990s, farmed elk in eight states and four provinces were infected with bovine tuberculosis.

Elk Farming in Alberta

Alberta has the most extensive experience with farming elk. Gamefarming was promoted as an option for agricultural diversification by agricultural interest groups in the 1980s, and opposed by other groups concerned with environmental issues, animal welfare and the well-being of indigenous wildlife. In 1987, after considerable discussion and debate, the Alberta government approved the farming of indigenous big game animals (i.e., white-tailed deer, mule deer, moose and North American subspecies of elk; Table 110). Responsibility for administration of gamefarming was shifted from the Alberta Fish and Wildlife Division to Alberta Agriculture, Food and Rural Development (AAFRD) in 1990.

Number, Size and Distribution of Elk Farms

In 1995, there were 182 elk farms in Alberta, with 2,951 bulls and 4,045 cows older than 1 year of age, and 2,305 calves. Most cow herds were small, with fewer than 20 producing animals, as might be expected in a relatively new in-

dustry. However, there were four farms that had 100 to 110 cows older than 1 year of age. Similarly, most bull herds had fewer than 20 animals, but eight herds had more than 60 bulls. The largest herd had 421 bulls and no cows, and the second largest herd had 257 bulls with no cows.

Most farms were in central Alberta, although many were in forested areas of western Alberta, between the aspen parkland and foothills. There were 69 farms within the range of wild elk in Alberta. About two-thirds of the farms had more than 80 acres (32 ha) fenced, and 85% had fewer than 160 acres (64 ha) fenced. Fencing of the four largest farms varied from 692 acres (280 ha) enclosed to 940 acres (380 ha). The total area fenced was about 18,285 acres (7,400 ha), and farms averaged 101 acres (41 ha). There were about 6,820 acres (2,760 ha) fenced on the 69 farms within wild elk range in 1995.

Management of Privately Owned Elk

Management of privately owned elk in Alberta has been intensive. Pastures are cross-fenced to separate elk by sex and age classes and to handle animals on demand. During winter, elk are fed high-quality forage, grain and a mineral supplement. Calves also are given a supplemental ration after being separated from the cow herd in autumn. Elk are grazed on domestic grasses and legumes during snow-free periods. Pastures are situated primarily on cultivated land with small patches of woody vegetation. Woody vegetation is quickly stripped of available forage, but provides cover

Table 110. Elk farming regulations in Alberta

Permitted	Prohibited	Required
Private ownership of North American subspecies of elk	Farming of subspecies of elk from outside North America	Renew licenses annually
Elk farming on private land	On-farm slaughter	Maintain detailed herd records
Sale of farm-reared meat, antlers and other parts	Hunting on game farms	Provide an annual report of herd inventory
Processing and packaging of velvet antlers		Register and ear tag elk
Transfer of elk from public to private ownership		Report changes in herd inventory within 30 days
Entry and inspection of game farms by government personnel		Have fences and facilities adequate to contain domestic elk and keep out wild elk
Quarantine, isolation and slaughter of diseased domestic animals and herds		Treat elk humanely
Restrictions on the importation of elk into Alberta		Slaughter elk at government-inspected abattoirs
		Identify carcasses
		Obtain permits for importation of live elk and exportation of live elk, meat, antlers and parts
		Notify wildlife officers when wild elk are in elk paddocks

Note: Pursuant to the province's Wildlife Act and the Livestock Industry Diversification Act.

during inclement weather. Provincewide, the stocking rate in 1995 was 2.5 acres (1.0 ha) per adult in 1995.

Herd bulls are placed with the cows during September and October. However, some farmers use artificial insemination to enhance selective breeding. Females normally are exposed to bulls at 15 months of age. They usually do not require assistance when calving. Most farmers ear-tag 1- or 2-day-old calves.

Friedel and Hudson (1993) surveyed 50 farms with 1,084 breeding age females in 1990 to 1991. They reported calving rates of 81% for 2-year-old cows and 96% for mature cows. Weaning rates were 74% for 2-year-old cows and 91% for adult cows. However, the provincewide weaning rate was only 71% in 1994 and 71% in 1995. Most elk are treated with an anthelminthic for internal parasites once or twice each year.

Markets

Breeding stock and velvet antlers were the primary products of elk farming in Alberta. In 1995, meat sales were negligible, although about 50 males were slaughtered in 1994. Breeding stock and bulls for velvet antlers were in great demand. Prices more than doubled between 1994 and 1995, with male calves selling for $2,250 to $3,000, female calves selling for $9,000 to $10,500 and mature cows fetching $10,500 to $18,750 (all in U.S. dollars).

Velvet was harvested 65 to 75 days after the shedding of old antlers in bulls more than 2 years of age. At this time, the first three tines have developed and the top of the antler flattens as the branches of the royals develop. Harvesting antlers earlier reduces antler weight; harvesting later reduces antler quality (Haigh 1987).

Velvet antlers were harvested from 1,861 bulls in 1994. Average production varied from 2.2 pounds (1.0 kg) in yearlings to 17.4 pounds (7.9 kg) in bulls older than 4 years of age. However, velvet antler production varied markedly within all age classes. Mature bulls, for example, produced velvet antlers ranging from 8.8 to 37.4 pounds (4–17 kg).

Prices of velvet antlers depend on antler quality and weight. The highest quality antlers are unblemished with minimum calcification; prices are discounted for antlers that are calcified or have broken points, torn skin and bruises. Price increases with velvet antler weight, and highest prices are paid for antlers from mature bulls.

Velvet antlers usually are sold fresh frozen. In 1995, prices for single antlers larger than 22 pounds (3.5 kg) varied between $62.60 and $90.70 per pound ($138–$200/kg) (U.S. dollars) and averaged about $68 per pound ($150/kg).

Velvet antler must be harvested before significant mineralization of the antler tissue to fetch top price. Careful handling of velvet antler is also required to minimize potential for surface blemishes, which will result in reduced price. *Photo by Theodore Wood.*

The velvet antlers from an average mature elk bull probably sold for about $1,200, although velvet antlers from an exceptional bull could have sold for more than $2,350.

Velvet antlers are dried and processed in several plants in Alberta. Oriental markets, principally Korea and Hong Kong, purchase whole, dried antlers. Ground velvet antlers in gelatin capsules also were sold to health food stores in North America.

Effects on Wild Populations

During the 1980s, big gamefarming was promoted as an economical and environmentally acceptable alternative to conventional agriculture on large tracts of marginal grazing land in Alberta. The elk was promoted as a gamefarm animal because it could use native vegetation without the modification or destruction of wildlife habitat. Benson (1991), Bunnage and Church (1991), Hudson and Dezhkin (1989) and Renecker and Hudson (1993) have identified arguments favoring gamefarming and the privatization of wildlife. On the other hand, opponents regarded gamefarming as a significant threat to the conservation and preservation of wildlife and wildlife habitat (Geist 1985, 1991, 1995, Anonymous 1993, Bunnell 1993). See Table 111 for arguments on both sides of the issue.

Effects on Wildlife Habitat, Wild Ungulates Movements and Public Access to Wild Lands

Most people assumed that elk would be farmed on large tracts of native vegetation (Geist 1985, 1995, Anonymous 1993), but this has not occurred. Extensive areas of native vegetation have not been fenced for elk. Elk farming has neither preserved, modified nor destroyed significant areas of wildlife habitat and is not likely to do so unless management of privately owned elk changes markedly. Movements of wild ungulates have not been markedly affected because elk pastures are on cultivated land and most are less than 158 acres (64 ha), although there may be some exceptions, such as along river valleys.

The cost of fence construction and materials may be the primary deterrent to elk farming on native pastures. In 1995, the cost of materials for a 8.2-foot (2.5 m) high fence was about $9,050 per mile ($5,625/km) (U.S. dollars), and contracted labor was an additional $2,715 per mile ($1,687/km). Thus, the perimeter fence on 158 acres (64 ha) cost about $24,000. Cross-fencing was required, because elk have to be segregated by sex and age classes and handled on demand. Cross-fencing represented about 70% to 100% of the length of perimeter fences. Consequently, the cost of cross-fences somewhat negated advantages gained in fencing large areas.

An Industry and Food Source for Natives

Advocates of gamefarming suggested that the farming of native wildlife could provide a more culturally adaptable

Table 111. Arguments for and against elk farming

For	Against
Diversification of agriculture	Increased poaching
Preservation of native vegetation and wildlife habitat	Diminished access to wildlands
	Restricted public access
	Habitat loss for free-ranging wildlife
Maintenance of genetic stock	Restricted movement of wild ungulates
Industrial development and food source for Indians and Métis	Alteration of native landscapes
	Collection of wild stock by game ranchers
	Genetic contamination
	European and Asian subspecies
	Selective breeding of North American subspecies
	Introduction of diseases to wild stock
	Inadequate containment of domestic stock
	Increased predator control
	Increased "nuisance" elk problems
	Will lead to paid hunting
	Changes in public attitudes toward wildlife
	Inadequate enforcement and monitoring

The costs of land, fencing, and buildings to hold and maintain elk require a considerable investment. Owners must be able to segregate the elk by sex and age, and be able to handle individual animals on demand. *Photo by Jeff Henry.*

form of agriculture for Indians and Métis (Anonymous 1993). In 1995, only four licenses were held by First People, so they have not taken advantage of this opportunity.

Poaching

When very high monetary values are placed on deer products, poaching often poses a threat to local wild populations. The magnitude of the threat depends on development and availability of markets, current status of wild populations, and commitment of governments to protection of the populations (Klein 1991). Wild elk are poached for velvet antlers, meat or as live animals. However, whether gamefarming will add significantly to this problem is not yet known, although poaching may be an important source of mortality in some wild populations.

For a number reasons, poaching for velvet antlers probably yields a poor return for effort expended, so likely does not and will have negligible effect on wild stocks. First, as previously noted, quality is of utmost importance for velvet antler sales. Velvet antlers must be unblemished, and the best comes from mature bulls. Prices are sharply reduced for antlers that have broken points or torn skin, as well as for those from immature bulls. Velvet antlers must be harvested within a time span of only a few days because calcification occurs very soon after the royal point emerges. Antlers deteriorate within a few hours without refrigeration. And legislation requires that antlers be tagged properly, and the tags must remain in place until the antlers are processed.

Most marketable venison is from juvenile males 16 to 27 months of age (Haigh 1991). On the other hand, mature bulls are required for velvet antler production. Consequently, meat sales in Alberta have been negligible and will continue to remain low as long as velvet antler prices remain high. However, there is an opportunity to develop markets for venison in the European Union when velvet antler prices decline. The most likely product would be whole carcasses, boned out, from animals 18 to 24 months of age. Slaughter must be in federally inspected plants approved by the European Union. These factors make it improbable that wild and domestic elk meat could be mixed for these markets.

However, lower quality cuts and ground meat may be sold in domestic markets. Wild and domestic meat can be mixed and sold at local meat markets and butcher shops, but whether this increases poaching or has a significant impact on any wild population is unknown. The opportunity to sell poached animals could increase if on-farm slaughter or paid hunting were permitted without additional regulation and monitoring.

Wild elk are attracted to gamefarms (R. C. Acorn personal communication:1996). Poaching of wild elk in Alberta is possible by registering a poached elk as a gamefarm animal, enticing wild elk into lane ways and pastures and then ear tagging them as if they were domestic animals. However, with relatively few years of selective breeding, wild elk no longer have the traits desirable in domestic herds, therefore they tend to be considered nuisances rather than a source of breeding stock.

Collection of Wild Stock by Gamefarmers

Opponents of gamefarming have expressed the concern that farmers would be permitted to collect elk from the wild and that fewer wild elk would be available for hunting and viewing. In fact, the Wildlife Act of Alberta does permit the collection of wild elk and the transfer of elk from public to private ownership by authorization from the Minister of Environmental Protection. However, no collection permits have been issued since 1986.

Predator Control

Opponents of gamefarming have indicated concern that gamefarming could lead to increased predator control in a single-species management system (Geist 1985, 1993, 1995, Anonymous 1993, Bunnell 1993). Friedel and Hudson (1993) reported a 0.4% predation loss of elk calves on 50 elk farms in 1990 to 1991. However, predator control normally is unnecessary, because domestic elk cows are very aggressive toward dogs and coyotes, and usually kill any canid that gets into fenced elk pastures. Coyote control with toxicants was conducted on only one elk farm in 1995. Thus, predator control in Alberta has not increased as a consequence of elk farming.

Nuisance Elk

Opponents of gamefarming are concerned that problems with wild elk would increase through crop depredation or direct interference with domestic elk management. R. C. Acorn (personal communication:1996) surveyed 80 elk farmers within or near wild elk range in Alberta to evaluate problems with wild elk. Seventy percent of farmers reported wild elk immediately adjacent to perimeter fences of domestic elk pastures on at least one occasion. Bulls commonly were seen in autumn during the rut, whereas cows were seen most often in late autumn and winter. No crop damage was reported. However, wild bulls did cause problems when they fought with domestic bulls through perimeter fences. Light, medium and severe damage to perimeter fences by elk was reported by 16, 7, and 6 farmers, respectively. All damage occurred during the rut. Severe damage required replacement of wire mesh, whereas light and medium damages required repairs without installation of new wire. Severe damage usually was caused by branch-antlered bulls and tended to occur on the edge of wild elk range, where bull harvest was restricted by hunting regulations and branch-antlered bulls comprised a greater percentage of the population.

Fence damage during the rut probably can be minimized by keeping domestic bulls and cow herds in pastures that are not on the perimeter of elk farms. Alternatively, electrified wires on perimeter fences likely can prevent most fence damage.

Disease Transmission

Fence-line contact between wild and domestic elk is common in Alberta (R. C. Acorn unpublished data:1996). Thus, gamefarms could form a bridge for the transmission of diseases to wild populations (Anonymous 1993, Bunnell 1993, Geist 1993). These diseases included bovine tuberculosis, meningeal worm, and chronic wasting syndrome or spongiform encephalopathy.

Tessaro (1986) concluded that the potential importance of gamefarming in the epizootiology of infectious diseases like brucellosis and bovine tuberculosis should not be overlooked. In 1990, bovine tuberculosis was discovered in elk imported into Alberta from the United States. The outbreak was controlled with the slaughter of 2,588 elk, about half of the domestic elk population in Alberta in 1991 to 1992. Compensation of $16.2 million (Canadian dollars) was paid to owners of the condemned animals (Wheaton et al. 1993). Although bovine tuberculosis has not become established in free-ranging wildlife in North America other than bison (Tessaro 1992), current conditions in some locations may allow this disease to be perpetuated in the wild (Miller and Thorne 1993).

Meningeal worm is a nematode parasite that could be transported in domestic elk from eastern to western North America (Samuel et al. 1992). This parasite apparently causes little damage to free-ranging white-tailed deer, but it can cause fatal neurologic disease in other ungulates, including elk, mule deer, moose and caribou. The meningeal worm is common in white-tailed deer in eastern North America and may occur in the aspen parklands of southern Saskatchewan (Anderson and Prestwood 1981), but has not been detected in Alberta as of 2000.

The prairie may act as an ecological barrier to meningeal worm, but the abundance of suitable intermediate hosts (snails and slugs) and definitive hosts suggests that this parasite could be introduced and become established in western North America. Samuel et al. (1992) reported that a few infected elk could provide sufficient larvae to establish infections in white-tailed deer, which then would amplify and spread meningeal worm on a much broader scale and put a variety of free-ranging and captive species at risk.

Alberta prohibited the importation of gamefarm ungulates in September 1988 to prevent the introduction of meningeal worm. This moratorium continues except for limited importation of elk calves from the Yukon, which is free of meningeal worms.

In February 1996, a domestic elk in southern Saskatchewan was diagnosed with chronic wasting disease, a transmissible spongiform encephalopathy. As the name implies, chronic wasting disease causes chronic debilitation and eventual death in elk and mule deer (Williams and Young 1980, 1982). This disease has been reported in domestic elk and deer in Colorado and Wyoming and in wild elk in close proximity to diseased domestic herds in Alberta. The minimum incubation period is about 18 months, but most cases occurred at 3 or 4 years of age. Transmission is lateral and possibly maternal (Williams and Young 1992).

An infected elk in Saskatchewan was imported from the United States in 1989 and probably contracted the disease there. Elk from the same herd also were imported into Alberta, but all had to be slaughtered in the tuberculosis program. However, on farms in Alberta in 1996, there were more than 300 elk that had been imported from the United States before 1988. Chronic wasting disease has not been identified in Alberta, although surveys have not specifically looked for its occurrence before 1997. Williams and Young (1992) wrote that transmission of chronic wasting disease from gamefarm animals into free-ranging conspecifics would be a concern if the disease became established in the captive cervid industry.

The Alberta government has acted responsibly in preventing the introduction and establishment of nonindigenous diseases to the province. The long-term consequences of introducing these diseases into free-ranging wildlife populations are unknown or, if known, are highly undesirable. Moreover, many of these diseases, once introduced, would be virtually impossible to control in free-ranging wildlife populations (Miller and Thorne 1993). For a more detailed discussion of elk parasites and diseases, see Chapter 6.

Genetic Contamination

Legislation limits elk farming to North American subspecies. Regardless of whether farming of nonindigenous subspecies is permitted, domestic elk in Alberta, within a few years, will have a different genetic composition than that of wild stock. Farmers practice selective breeding to achieve what they consider to be desirable traits for domestic animals.

Selection for temperament (increased docility and reduced flight response) is an integral part of deer farming programs (Haigh 1991). Domestic elk are being bred selectively for increased tractability, greater body and antler weight, and increased calving by 2-year-old cows. Artificial insemination has been used in some herds to achieve increased antler size, with semen selected from bulls that produce velvet antlers greater than 39.7 pounds (18 kg).

Interbreeding of differently adapted populations may have detrimental consequences, including loss of adapted genes or gene complexes, homogenization of populations through swamping with a common gene pool and no readaptation to local conditions if introductions continue. It is extremely difficult to predict the outcome of an introduction (Hindar 1996). However, it is safe to assume that not all traits will be desirable in wild elk. For example, Frank et al. (1991) reported that red deer, which appeared to be affected adversely by restraint (i.e., less-tractable animals), had higher levels of immune reactivity in contrast to that of more placid individuals.

Inadequate Containment of Domestic Elk

Problems with elk that have escaped have been minimal in Alberta. From 1990 through 1995, six bulls and one cow escaped and were not recovered. However, inadequate containment of domestic elk may become a serious problem.

Containment of elk on elk farms may become a serious problem for both the landowner, balancing potential loss of valuable stock against increasing costs associated with fence maintenance, and the regulatory agency responsible to ensure that domestic animals do not mingle with wild, free-ranging herds. In many jurisdictions it may be impossible to require farmers to recover elk that have escaped from an enclosure. Where elk ranches are located in proximity to wild herds, selectivity bred domestic elk may interbreed with wild elk. *Photo by Michael Dorrance.*

When prices for elk are relatively high, there is strong incentive to recover escaped animals. In the future, elk herds likely will become larger, and farmers may not notice that animals are missing as readily as now or previously. In addition, fences will require more maintenance as they grow older. And as the price of elk declines, farmers may spend less time attempting to recover elk that escape.

Elk farm fences were fairly new in the early 1990s. A fences age, they require maintenance, and establishing and requiring standards for fence maintenance may prove impossible. Also, it may not be possible to require farmers to recover escaped elk. These circumstances may lead to significant problems with escaped animals. Selectively bred domestic elk are genetically different from wild elk and interbreeding with wild elk may reduce the viability of wild stocks.

Inadequate Enforcement

In 1995, the Alberta Department of Agriculture spent at least 2 person-years to maintain records, monitor and regulate an elk and deer industry with about 280 licensed farms and 12,000 animals. As the numbers of gamefarmers increase, the lobby may be expected to become stronger for deregulation or self-regulation of the industry. Regardless, it will be a challenge to regulate gamefarming adequately by an agency that has neither a history of law enforcement nor a mandate for wildlife conservation. The same is true in the United States for states whose departments of agriculture have primary gamefarm regulatory authority.

Conclusions

Agriculture has benefitted from diversification into game-farming, in that an additional source of revenue has resulted. On the other hand, benefits for indigenous wildlife

"Treating elk as another form of livestock sires a cultural and philosophical clash of values and beliefs. For some, it makes perfect sense. For others, it's an assault on wildness" (Stallings 1998:75, see also Williams 1998). *Photo courtesy of the Albuquerque Tribune.*

populations and the wildlife conservation movement are difficult to ascertain and controversial. To date, the negative impacts of elk farming on wild elk populations appear to be negligible. In the future, in the absence of regulatory authority and enforcement capability, gamefarming disease transmission and genetic contamination could have major impacts on wild populations. Although provinces and states have taken steps to regulate elk farming and protect against the major diseases that could affect other livestock, further monitoring of diseases that could affect wild elk and other wildlife is necessary. Elk farming is prevalent and accepted as a legitimate agricultural endeavor; it will not decline in the foreseeable future. Steps to minimize the effects of elk farming on wild elk and other wildlife should be a priority of those interested in maintaining the wildlife resource in a free-ranging state, with huntable populations.

16

Hunting Red Deer and Elk:
Old and New Worlds

Writers of all sorts and conditions, from the gravest, have not disdained to record the pleasures of the chase, and to expound its mysteries. . . . [It] would be a bold spirit indeed who should sit down now to such a theme with the assurance that he had anything fresh to offer. . . . I know not well what to write, except I should in some sort repeat another man's tale.

Beaufort and Morris (1885:3)

Elk and red deer have been hunted by humans for thousands of years. They still are the favored quarry of a multitude of sportspeople in many Holarctic countries, as well as some areas of the Southern Hemisphere where they were introduced. Large size and highly palatable meat undoubtedly were—and still are—reasons for this popularity. However, ancient cave paintings and modern trophy rooms attest to the awe and appreciation hunters always have had for the animals' lordly beauty and large antlers. This chapter documents human pursuit of and admiration for these magnificent deer.

Because Chapter 3 deals with aboriginal elk hunters in North America, this chapter will be concerned only with prehistoric and historic hunting and management practices in Eurasia and how they influenced exploitation, sport hunting and management of elk in Canada and the United States after the arrival of Europeans.

Prehistory

By flickering torchlight the Stone Age hunter-artist painstakingly applied oxide pigments to a limestone rock face. When the painting was finished, a file of majestic stags decorated a wall of the now famed cavern of Lascaux in southwestern France.

Clutton-Brock (1986:540)

Humans apparently reached Europe more than a million years ago (Gore 1997). These *Homo sapiens* seem to have been capable of advanced behavior, including manufacture of weapons and group hunting. In the cold climate, they could have lived as herbivores during summers, but must have been carnivores during winters. They may have scavenged the remains of some large mammals killed by large carnivores. However, on the fossilized bones of ancient prey, the tooth marks of scavenging animals often are found on top of butchery marks. Mark Roberts, site director for excavations at Boxgrove, England, expressed the belief that scavengers would arrive after humans had left with the best cuts from their kills (Gore 1997). Thus, ancestral humans and ancestral red deer apparently evolved together in a predator/prey relationship (see Chapter 1 for evolution of *Cervus* spp.).

Space does not allow a description concerning the introduction and subsequent hunting of elk and red deer in the Southern Hemisphere. However, substantial populations occur in Argentina, Australia, Chile and New Zealand. Subspecies tend to be mixed in introduced populations, partly because of multiple introductions from different parent subspecies and partly because some introductions were from already mixed European populations. However, pure *C. e. atlanticus* from Scotland are to be found in parts of New Zealand. Scottish and Continental red deer and Rocky Mountain elk have mixed in Fiordland. This elk/red deer crossbreed—shot in Fiordland, New Zealand, during 1953—carries 18 points on 45.5-inch (116-cm) antlers. Oluas Murie described this specimen as probably the finest example of a "son of two continents." *Photo by Bruce Banwell.*

Humans arose as predators, according to Morris (1967). When the so-called killer ape came down from the trees, Morris contends, it had to hunt to survive. To do this efficiently, a bigger brain was needed to compensate for the poor hunting body, and that required a long childhood to educate the better brain. Women had to remain behind and care for babies while the men hunted. To succeed, hunters had to cooperate and communicate, as well as stand erect and use weapons for the hunt.

Thus, hunting supposedly spurred the development of those characteristics that make us human—intelligence, erect posture, language, the spirit of cooperation, construction of tools (weapons) and sexual division of labor. The latter suggests that the hunting way of life was respon-

sible for development of the nuclear family and the idea of home. "That the stories of Man the Hunter and Woman the Gatherer amount to little more than useful (if inaccurate) generalizations about human realities led anthropologists to abandon the hunting hypothesis years ago" (Stange 1997:57). Hunting probably was not the principal force that drove human evolution, but it apparently made occupation of northern areas possible and prepared early man for war, to protect home and hearth.

The grassy steppes and high plateaus of Central Asia and the Middle East were seats of early human culture. At least some of the women in those societies probably were more hunters than gatherers. Archaeologists have found many graves with weapons alongside female skeletons, including one such apparent woman warrior/hunter who was buried with spears and 30 arrows (Edwards 1996).

For 1.5 million years, tribes of hunters apparently roamed the valleys, savannas and forests, killing animals with their primitive weapons. Besides hunting, those ancients caught young animals that they kept for later times of need (Hobusch 1980). The eventual domestication of livestock probably originated with this practice.

The earliest known red deer in Europe lived some 500,000 to 600,000 years ago (Beninde 1937, Kahlke 1956). Remains of those deer were found at the same fossil site northwest of Heidelberg, Germany, as was a primitive human mandible. Remains of Steinheim man—a variant of the Neanderthaler—also were found with those of red deer at another site in Germany (Nilsson 1982). Those fossils were judged to be 400,000 years old. Near Shöningen, Germany, scientists discovered five artfully shaped, wooden throwing spears, about 400,000 years old, that had been preserved in a peat bog (Gore 1997). With fine, narrow points and greatest weight forward, the spears seem designed to be thrown from a distance rather than thrust at close range. The longest was more than 7 feet (2.13 m) in length. Thus, red deer—like those we know today—probably were human quarry for at least half a million years.

Red deer were a common food of Paleolithic hunters in Lebanon, Syria and Israel. Despite their widespread occurrence, red deer in southwestern Asia seem to have been confined to river valleys and wooded slopes (Vereshchagin 1967).

Stone Age and Bronze Age—ca. 1.5 million to 4,400 and 4,400 to 2,600 years ago, respectively (Fagan 1977)—drawings on cliffs—southwest of Baku, Azerbaijan—depicted many animals, but lions and red deer were most common. On the Iranian plateau, 57% of the bones carried into caves by Stone Age hunters were those of red deer (Vereshchagin 1967). Throughout the ages in the Middle East, remains of wild boar, red deer, wisent and horses were the most common species found in kitchen middens. Which species was most numerous apparently depended on the habitat favoring one species or the other. Red deer apparently figured prominently in religious beliefs and rituals, and were a favorite subject of painters and sculptors of the Caucasus. By the Bronze Age, the red deer motif was repeated in pendants, belt buckles and decorations on weapons. During the 7th century BC, legendary Scythian horsemen from the East swept across the steppes of the Trans-Kuban plain and southern Ukraine, and left clues to their culture in finely wrought golden articles depicting red deer and the hunt.

Hunting Methods

From the first habitation of western Europe by man, red deer provided meat to hunting communities. By the end of the Mesolithic, deer constituted the single most important food species. Tools and weapons were fashioned from deer bones and antlers. Sinews and skins made cords. Antlers furnished hoes and picks.

Clutton-Brock (1986:540)

Prehistoric

Ancient rock paintings have been found in more than 120 caves—some of them hundreds of yards long—of northern Spain and southern France. Mostly, they represent hunted animals and the hunt (Figures 167 and 168). Hunting pro-

Antlers and body proportions of the red deer depicted on the walls of caves in Spain thousands of years ago seem similar to those characteristics in present-day deer from eastern Europe. These stags, originally from Croatia, were photographed on a gamefarm in New Zealand. *Photo by Bruce Banwell.*

Figure 167. From a rock gallery in southern Spain is a dark red painting of one or two hunters following cloven-hoofed animal tracks, presumably of red deer (redrawn from Hernandez-Pacheco 1919). Whether the gaps in the trail represent leaping animals or trackless ground remains a 12,000-year-old mystery. The figure in front of the hunter is indistinguishable. Such sketchy detailing is characteristic of Spanish cave art. It deemphasizes anatomical exactness in favor of actions or effects—somewhat like modern impressionism and caricature.

vided the basic needs of Paleolithic humans' existence and also inspired the artist (Hobusch 1980).

There are few real records of human hunting activities until the Sumerian or Chinese cultures some 4,000 to 5,000 years ago. An advanced state of civilization had been attained and probably had existed for some centuries. From that time, hunting methods are depicted on pottery fragments. In the Far East and the Mediterranean area, the dog, horse, elephant, cheetah and falcon had been trained as allies in the hunt. Humans had begun to have a decisive effect on the surrounding fauna, even before emerging from the Stone Age (Brander 1971).

Throughout the Greek and Roman civilizations, hunting was written about extensively. Plato, Virgil, Cicero and

Figure 168. From a cave in Spain near the one featuring the art in Figure 167 is the painted scene depicted above, showing a naked male bowhunter with headdress chasing or driving two red deer stags, one of which is wounded (from Obermaier 1924). Although such period rock art is highly stylized and skilled, the figures tell a story rather than serve as symbolic representations. According to Obermaier (1924), artwork then was not produced for artistic sake. Interestingly, cave painting was not found in many inhabited caves. Where such art was found was invariably in caves not habitable or very difficult to access. This suggests that such artwork had superstitious or other religious or totemic connotations, perhaps not unlike primitive North American rock paintings discussed in Chapter 3.

Horace—among other famous classical writers—all lauded hunting. The use of the horse and hound in the chase and skill with bow and arrow and spear all were acclaimed. The Romans preserved game in parks; apparently, the Greeks did not (see Brander 1971).

"The ancient Greeks seem to have depended largely upon the assistance of nets in obtaining most kinds of game. The Rev. W. Houghton has drawn attention to the fact that the Greek hunters, in the time of Xenophon, anticipated a stag-hunt by setting a number of traps in the covers which were expected to supply a stag. The engine in question resembled the devices used in Africa, India, and even Central Asia, for taking ostriches and deer by the feet. 'It consisted of a circular crown of yew twigs, twisted strongly together. In this were fixed several spikes of tough yew-wood and iron alternately, the latter being the larger; these spikes probably radiated towards the centre of the circle, but we have no accurate information on this point. We are not told what was the ordinary diameter of these circular crowns of yew-wood, but I apprehend it was about two feet. The spikes were equidistant, and so arranged that they permitted the foot of the animal to pass between them and

then closed upon the leg. To the periphery of the Podostrabe (or crown of yew) a strong noose or eye of twisted hemp was firmly attached, to which again was fastened a rope of the same material, bearing at its other end a clog of oak timber perhaps 22 inches long, and 4 inches broad, with the bark still adhering to it. Such was the fashion of this instrument, and it was set as follows: a round hole was dug in the ground, about 1.5 feet deep, equal in diameter at the top to the crown of the Podostrabe, and gradually narrowing below; another hole was made for the clog, and a channel for the rope. The circular part of the snare was then placed in the round hole, and the clog and rope in their respective places, and all was covered over with leaves and earth.' When a stag, trotting through his favourite pass, put one of his feet into the snare, his struggles to get away soon liberated the trap from the earth. The unfortunate animal was therefore obliged to drag the log of wood after him. His efforts to escape from the staghounds were thus cruelly handicapped" (Watson 1896:48–49).

By the time of Christ, the two basic lures—hunger and sex—were used fully in trapping and snaring animals (Figure 169). Herding and mothering instincts also were ex-

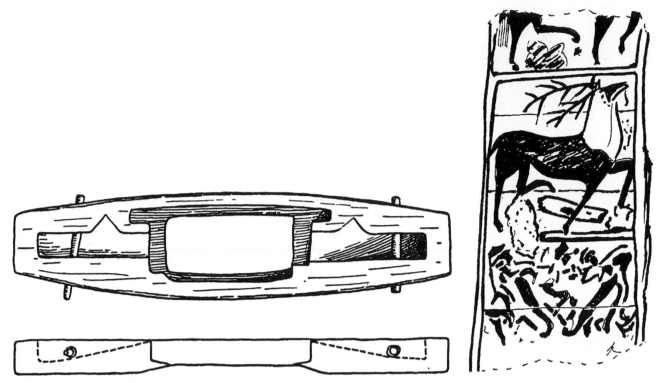

Figure 169. Tread or treadle traps, as depicted on the left above (from Clark 1952), have been dated to as early as 500 BC. They consist of heavy wood frames, 2 to 4 feet (61–122 cm) in length, tapering slightly at squared ends. In the middle, they have one or two oblong apertures fitted with wooden flaps, which are held in a closed position by wooden springs set in grooves cut in the frame and held down by cross pegs. The frames and flaps generally were of oak and the springs of pliable wood such as willow. These curiosities, found along rivers and in bogs, were long thought to be other devices, including musical instruments, machines for making peat bricks, boat models and traps for pike, beaver or otters. The first clue to the real use came from the carved cross slab at left above (from Bateman 1971) at Clonmacnois, County Offaly, Ireland, and dated from about 700 to 900 A.D. It features a red deer caught in an oblong contraption much like the enigmatic antiquities, and especially like one uncovered in a Scottish bog in 1921. Similar traps were found still in use in Poland to capture red and roe deer. The Polish traps were set, flap down, in groups on marshy ground near favored water sites of deer. The trap shown above left from overhead and profile was drawn from one found in Drumacaladerry Bog, County Donegal, Ireland, and is in the National Museum of Antiquities in Dublin. In groups of three to nine, like traps have been found from Ireland to Scotland to Germany and Yugoslavia, and Scandinavia to northern Italy.

ploited. Crops were planted to attract deer to hunters laying in wait, and mating calls were used by bowmen to locate or attract their prey. The cries of young deer, captured by hand, would bring their dams within arrow range. The same young were raised and used as walking blinds for hunters to creep within shooting range of others. As practical naturalists, our ancestors would have little to learn from us today (Brander 1971).

Although rock paintings and petroglyphs provide some indication (Figure 170), prehistoric deer hunting methods remain somewhat a matter of conjecture. However, that deer were an important food source is indicated by their bones around prehistoric human habitations. The development of weapons, especially arrow and spear heads—from stone to bronze to iron—apparently were factors important in the acquisition of venison (Figure 171). The domestication of dogs and horses also contributed to the efficiency of human hunters. Accounts of red deer hunting in England

illustrate how two strong deer hounds can bring down and kill a red deer stag (Chalmers 1935), and in open country, the horse allows the hunter to be at and assist in the kill. An account of catching a live bull elk in Pennsylvania during January 1800 indicates how primitive hunters, with the aid of dogs, might have taken red deer and elk (Tome 1854).

Watson (1896:45–46) wrote: "The sculptured stones of ancient Scotland are eloquent witnesses to the early history of our forefathers. . . . The numerous hunting scenes, in particular, possess a certain fascination for men who sympathise with the hardships and perils of the chase. Full of vigour were the brawney spearmen of those days, as bold in spearing the monarch of the glen as in fighting for the sacred cause of hearth and home. The spear was often replaced by the flight of a well-poised arrow; but whatever weapon served the necessity of the hour, the hunter's success depended largely upon the assistance of the powerful hounds whose strength and courage were relied upon to

Figure 170.   Cave paintings and petroglyphs from Stone Age Italy illustrate various techniques used by Paleolithic hunters to capture large herbivores, mainly red deer (from Bateman 1971), including by treadle trap (*upper left*), snare (*upper right*), netting (*lower left*) and enclosure trap (*lower right*). It may be conjectured that the upper left painting may also indicate impoundment, the upper right scene depicts a pitfall, and the bottom right scene shows a cliff drive (see Rongstad and McCabe 1982).

serve their master in the moment of need—as when a wounded hart stood at bay with head lowered in proud defiance of the horse and his rider." "Hart" was and is the poets' and hunters' name for red deer stags.

"'Oracle Bones' of the Shang Dynasty (1776–1122 BC) shed much light on customs of the people of that period in China and give vivid and true pictures of the way they lived. . . . The pictographic forms depict the stately stag as well as some of the smaller species. Deer were extensively hunted during this period. They were trapped in pitfalls, netted or speared in the chase. They frequently figure as sacrificial animals" (Gibson 1940:169 and 172). Pictographs of pitfalls were very realistic and depicted unwary deer in a pit. Some pictographs featured pits containing water. The character used to signify hunting was modified about 200 AD to include that of a dog, possibly indicating dogs then were used more widely in hunting.

By looking at historic records and methods used by some hunting societies today, a clearer picture emerges of how prehistoric hunters secured large prey. In my conversations with aboriginal hunters in Taiwan during 1988 and 1994, they indicated that, until about 1960, ceremonial hunting parties went into the mountains annually and used all of their ancestral methods to secure game for a holiday feast. Included were nets, snares, iron traps, crossbows, 18- to 24-inch (45–60 cm) bush knives, pitfalls with sharpened stakes and dead falls using rocks or logs. The bush knives were used to dispatch animals in snares, traps or nets. When soil conditions allowed, pits were dug deep enough that deer, serow and boar could not climb out; stakes were not used, and the animals were taken alive for sale to gamefarms. Many of the aborigines still preferred crossbows to rifles, because shots in the jungle seldom exceeded 40 yards (36.6 m) and traditional hunting areas were small enough that rifle fire would scare big game from them.

That hunters of the Middle East—even with primitive weapons—were effective predators of large mammals is illustrated by the following lists of extinctions in the Caucasus: lion, 10th century; primitive bull, 12th century; and kulan (wild ass) and cheetah, 13th century. With the advent of firearms, others were extirpated: moose, early 19th century; tarpan (wild horse), 1880s; wisent, 1920s; and tiger, 1930s (Vereshchagin 1967). This list also indicates the adaptability of the red deer in avoiding extirpation despite its large size, palatability and propensity to damage crops.

Among the earliest elk hunters in North America were the emigrants from Siberia, who pursued large mammals, such as bison and elk, in the Tanana Valley of central Alaska some 12,000 to 10,000 years ago (Hoffecker et al. 1993). Lanceolate stone points—finely crafted and shafted to spear handles—and dogs made it possible for these foot-hunters to subsist primarily on large game.

Figure 171. The bow was the primary weapon of the paleolithic hunter in southern Europe 12,000 to 10,000 years ago (Clark 1952). Hunting scenes painted during that time period on rock shelter walls in eastern Spain support that contention. One of the paintings, redrawn above, originally done in dark red on the walls of a shelter in Cueva de los Caballos, near Albocacer, Castellon, features a herd of red deer being driven to a line of archers (from Obermaier 1924). This drive was depicted to occur in late summer, as evidenced by the large stag and spike to be in hard antler and the calves still spotted. Bows clearly are of a simple type. Arrow shafts evidently are fletched, but details of the tips are not sufficiently discernible. However, barbed and tanged flint arrowheads dating to the period were found in the vicinity of the shelter.

Historic

"French and German archives afford ample proof of the extraordinary pitch to which the love of sport was driven, a pitch to which no parallel is to be found in our history. Great Britain never produced a Landgrave of Hesse who, to the dismay of his clerics, insisted on substituting in the Lord's Prayer an entreaty to 'Give us our daily hart in the pride of grease'" (Baillie-Grohman 1896:168). Pride of grease refers to the very fat red deer stag just before the rut.

"Deer-shooting was in those days as much the principal topic of conversation among the ruling classes, as it was one of the chief subjects of the limited correspondence that passed between crowned heads. Of this ample proof is to be found in the letters of the period preserved in the principal Continental archives. But not only this, the antlers of stags that were in any way remarkable for size, number of points, or on account of abnormal formation, were the most valued presents exchanged by potentates, who, we may take it, understood a good deal more about deer and antlers than most men do to-day. These trophies were conveyed by ambassadors very much in the same way as monarchs now send their portraits or the highest order of their dynastic family, by special envoys of high rank with all the pomp and dignity of a state ceremony. There are extant several interesting accounts of how these ambassadorial bearers of antlers were received at the recipient's court, and as most of these August old hunters were collectors of antlers, we can well believe that these offerings of friendship were a good deal more appreciated than are now the portraits or diamond-set orders which are the modern tokens of esteem" (Baillie-Grohman 1896:174).

During the late Middle Ages, some 600 to 500 years ago, France had a richer literature on hunting than did either England or Germany. "The great hunters of those days found time to enter into their diaries the events relating to the chase; nothing else was worth noting. In France the chase remained the all-absorbing subject of men's thoughts until the actual outbreak of the great upheaval. Louis XVI's diary, under the fatal date of the 14th of July 1789, which witnessed the storming of the Bastille, contains naught but the laconic 'killed nothing.' While on the 5th of the following October, the day the maddened hordes of the 'Great Unwashed' threw themselves upon Versailles, his diary contains but the following: 'Shot at the gate of Chatillon, killed 81 head, interrupted by events; went and returned on horseback.' Nothing more, nothing less. That it was destined to be his last hunt he knew not, or assuredly he would have ended his diary with the grand total of all he had slain in his lifetime, as representing that summary of his career most worthy of perpetuation" (Baillie-Grohman

1896:168–169). After the Revolution, most of the large estates fell into ruins, game preserves ceased to exist and poaching reduced game to low numbers (Brander 1971). France dropped from the van of hunting.

Development of Weapons

"Indeed it seems likely that it was because our precursors hunted that we evolved as men at all. And since they had neither the fangs and claws, nor the speed to hunt like wolves and cats, they must have used a primitive weaponry" (Caras 1970:4).

Before discussing historic hunting practices in various times and areas, a short discussion of the evolution of hunting weapons—primarily from Hobusch (1980)—during that time seems relevant.

Early in recorded history, approximately 3,000 years ago, the hunting spear consisted of a long, leaf-shaped, metal blade on a strong wooden staff. To ensure a firm grip, the staff was wrapped with leather strips, embossed or ornamented with brass nail heads. A crosspiece of horn prevented too-deep entry of the spear into game. A hunting sword with a straight blade and crosspiece was carried by mounted huntsmen during the late 15th and 16th centuries. This was superseded by hunting knives not very different from some carried today.

Laminated bows, apparently manufactured by Greeks, are known from Scythian graves dating to about 400 years before Christ. Edwards (1996) described one as 32 inches (81 cm) long, laminated of strips of willow and alder, joined by fish glue, and double curved. A Greek inscription on a stone in the trading town of Olbia near the Black Sea indicates that a bow such as this one cast an arrow 570 yards (521 m)—very impressive, if true.

The bow and arrow and the crossbow were the typical weapons for killing from a distance. Although the crossbow was known in China since the 2nd century BC, the Romans only began to use similar weapons in the 4th century AD. Crossbows were used increasingly after the Crusades, despite a papal prohibition against the un-Christian weapon for war. With longbows, English archers shot 10 to 12 heavy arrows per minute with fair accuracy up to 164 yards (150 m). With various crossbows, ranges were extended to 328 to 547 yards (300–500 m), and an accurate hit could be assured at 219 yards (200 m). The missile for red deer often was a two-pronged arrow that caused great damage. The crossbow's disadvantages included heavy weight and relatively slow reloading. However, Queen Elizabeth of England (1558–1603) rode her hunting steed and killed animals with a crossbow as late as 1600. She preferred the older weapon to the guns available at that time (Whisker 1981).

Small firearms appeared during the mid-14th century.

Wrought-iron, match-lighted handguns were the first of these new types of weapons. Blunderbuss, arquebus and musket were prototypes of hand-fired weapons that allowed shooting at a distance of 300 paces by the late 15th century. Matchlock muskets did not replace crossbows as hunting weapons, because the "evil-smelling" burning match could be seen and smelled from a distance. At the beginning of the 16th century, the wheel lock was invented—the spark created as in the modern flint lighter. The oldest drawing of the mechanism was by Leonardo da Vinci. By turning a small hardened steel wheel with a key, the huntsman cocked a two-armed leaf spring. When the trigger was pulled, the wheel, with its large teeth, was set in motion. Rifled barrels were introduced in the mid-16th century. Until well into the 18th century, hunting played a greater role in development of weapons than did military interests. Guns were developed with up to four barrels. So, too, were guns with a drum magazine that could fire four shots through one barrel. Also, air guns were made primarily for killing deer and wild boar. They usually had a spherical reservoir of compressed air sufficient for about 20 shots.

In 1548, King Edward VI of England sought to restrict the use of what today would be viewed as a shotgun. Barrels were about 1 inch (2.5 cm) in diameter, and with a heavy load of powder and shot, they could cut a sizeable swath through a flock of birds. The King believed these weapons were dangerous to men (probably the shooters) and animals (Whisker 1981).

Early in the 17th century, the wheel lock was superseded by flintlocks, so the arm fired quickly instead of waiting for the wheel to turn. To this time, firearms were owned primarily by royalty, and were ornate indeed. Gold, silver, ivory and precious woods combined with fine engraving to make many of them true works of art.

The invention of fulminate of mercury during 1786 in France, followed by research in England, led to the primer, making percussion ignition possible, and the first detonating lock was invented in 1807 by a Scottish clergyman. The new gun still was a muzzleloader, but with primer—resembling a little hat and generally called caps—set on a nipple with a hole leading into the barrel and the powder charge. For the first time, the hunter or soldier did not have to worry about his priming powder blowing away or getting wet. Interior parts of percussion guns were similar to those of flintlocks and, from about 1840 on, flintlocks could be reworked to use percussion primers. Long-barrel percussion guns gave good accuracy and had a range of about 766 yards (700 m). However, even an experienced rifleman could only fire about 1.5 shots per minute (Hobusch 1980).

Breech-loaders of various types were known since the 16th century, but cartridges and mercury percussion combined to make them practical. In 1831, the so-called needle-gun was developed (the firing pin was shaped like a needle). Cartridges first were of cardboard and rimfire, but metal cartridge cases and central ignition were soon to follow. Describing the expansion and variety of repeating rifles would require a chapter of its own. By the mid- to late 1800s, many hunters had rifles with which they could accurately fire 10 to 15 rounds per minute (Hobusch 1980).

Express rifles, which came into use during the 1870s, enabled a stalker to make a nearly sure kill and abolished the hound as an essential accompaniment of the stalk; the chase, the bay and the rough-and-tumble with a fighting stag passed into history. The break-loaded, black-powder Express rifle carried stalking far from its early traditions, and smokeless, small-bore, high-velocity rifles carried it a good deal farther still. These weapons have a trajectory so flat that at 200 yards (183 m), it is practically a straight line. They will riddle a 20-inch (51 cm) bull, with suitable allowance for wind, at 600 yards (549 m) and, at that range, will collapse a stricken stag as completely as would the old Express at 60 yards (55 m). Add to these weapons a telescopic sight and it seems a probable conclusion that, just as the Martini-Henry Express rifle eliminated the deerhound from the stalk, so the modern magnums may eliminate the stalk itself (Hobusch 1980).

Great Britain

In Great Britain, the word hunting is reserved for any sport that entails the use of hounds (Whitehead 1982). Thus, deer hunting would indicate hunting deer with hounds, as was being practiced with staghounds and buckhounds of southern England as of 2000. Stalking is the term usually applied to shooting deer, whether on foot or from a high seat. In Scotland, deer terrain always is referred to as forest, although the area may be completely devoid of trees. The professional keeper on a deer forest is called a stalker; his assistant is called a ghillie, or he may be the ponyman should ponies or garrons still be used to bring in the deer. The sportsman generally is referred to as the rifle, although in former days he often went by gentleman. Other terms in common usage are the glass, when referring to the telescope, and piece for the luncheon packet. After the shot, the deer will be gralloched (have the stomach and intestines removed).

Most historic accounts of hunting in Great Britain concern events after the Norman invasion (1066 AD). However, Britain had its own famous hunting monarchs before that time. King Penda (circa 642 AD) coursed red deer with hounds over royal hunting grounds in the Pytehley country, which still were being hunted by British royalty some 13 centuries later. King Brian Boru of Ireland (924–1014 AD)

On many Scottish hunts, ponies have been replaced by all-terrain vehicles for bringing in the game. This detracts from the hunt for those who are nostalgic about tradition. *Photo by Bart W. O'Gara.*

was known as a good administrator, great soldier and master of the hounds. The rough-and-tumble chase after big game with hounds and horse was considered the best training for war in those days (see Barrow 1948).

During the 14th century, Gaston de Foix wrote *Livre de Chasse* (Baillie-Grohman and Baillie-Grohman 1909). In it, very strict conduct rules were applied to red deer hunting. "Rude and furious" cries, such as took place in boar hunting, were forbidden and considered derogatory. Only skilled men were permitted to hunt. Even Louis XV had to hunt hares, roe deer and fallow deer for 5 years before being allowed to hunt red deer (MacPherson 1896).

During the same century, the Hundred Years War with France and the black death (bubonic plague) had considerable effect on British hunting. The first prevented the British from extensively copying continental methods—especially the many forms of trapping and snaring deer. In Britain, deer generally were taken with hounds or other active hunting; for instance, when Edward III was engaged in the French wars, he always had 60 couples of staghounds with him. When not fighting, he was hunting (Beaufort and Morris 1885). The plague reduced the British population by a quarter or a third within 2 years. Whole villages were wiped out, leading to a shortage of laborers. Freemen could command high prices for their labor. The result was a changeover to sheep farming, which required less labor, and the growth of a middle class. Grants of hunting rights to all classes and increased interest in hunting ensued (Brander 1971).

"Barclay, in his *Contra Monarchomachos*, gives the following account of Queen Mary's visit to the forest of Atholl: In the year of our redemption 1564 the Earl of Atholl, a chief of royal extraction, exhibited to the most excellent and illustrious Queen of Scotland a hunt, got up with immense pomp, and at great cost . . . and which our people are accustomed to call a royal hunt. The Earl had about two thousand Scottish Highlanders, to whom he entrusted the duty of raising the stags from the forests and mountains of Atholl, Badenoch, Mar, Moray, and other adjoining regions, and driving them to the place which was destined for the hunting. These men are so nimble and so unencumbered, and so quickly ran up and down, day and night, that in less than two months they drove into one place more than two thousand deer, with does and goats, which they brought before the Queen and the chiefs who were stationed in the valley . . . from which the Queen derived no ordinary pleasure. . . . A very strong and fierce hound having been loosed by the Queen's command, and sent to attack a wolf, while pursuing the flying wolf, so frightened a stag that he again betook himself to flight, and all the others retreating with him, broke through that part where they were most closely surrounded by the mountaineers. . . . So compact was the whole herd, that they would all have escaped, had not some of those who were most expert at the chase followed in their track, and by skill in their art detached some of the stragglers from the main body; those in a short time became the prizes of the hunters—there were killed that day 360 deer, five wolves, and some goats" (McConnochie 1923:21–22).

Queen Elizabeth was a notable huntress. Reportedly, she hunted on horseback every second day during 1575; she was then 77 years old (Beaufort and Morris 1885).

Sir Thomas Cockraine wrote of the increasing scarcity of deer by 1581 and noted an increasing dependence on the chase for sport. This situation apparently contributed to the popularity of fox hunting (Whisker 1981).

Before the advent of firearms, red deer of Great Britain often were driven into compounds, where they were slaughtered by men with spears, bows and arrows, swords or stones (Hart-Davis 1978). Ancient stone dykes exist in Scotland that were wings leading to red deer traps. The deer were driven uphill between two dykes, which were very wide apart at the entrance (bottom) and gradually narrowed, ending in a cul-de-sac (Watson 1896).

During the 18th century, it was the practice to hold "tainchells," or large deer drives, in which many hundreds of men and dogs took part, so that a large number of animals would be driven to concealed marksmen who, with luck, were able to take a considerable toll of the deer.

Chalmers (1935) listed a number of things that the drivers of red deer soon learned: (1) the deer ordinarily cannot be forced or they will break back through the drivers; (2) they prefer to move into the wind and uphill when disturbed; (3) if disturbed, the deer will cross a ridge preferably at a low point, thus passes are natural ambush sites; and (4) if a posted hunter shoots at red deer coming to her/him, the deer invariably will turn—once a fair proportion of beasts are by, the rearguard (most of which are large stags) seem committed to press forward.

"Some interesting particulars concerning the Highland drives for deer are to be gleaned from the MS. of Colonel James Farquharson of Invercauld. The vassals of the chief were bound to give personal attendance on the superior, with eight followers from each davoch of land, with their dogs and hounds, at all his huntings within the bounds of Mar, 'and sall caus big and put up our lonckartis for the hunting, and sall make and put furthe tinchellis at the samen, according to use and wont.' From early times the wilds of Braemar and Glen Dee had been the resort of the scottish sovereigns for purposes of sport, and the great gatherings of the Earl of Mar were on quite a regal scale. John Taylor, the Water Poet, was present at one of these great huntings, in the year 1618. From him we learn that the Lonquhards, which the vassals of the Earl were bound to erect at huntings, were temporary cottages (no doubt made of branches of trees or turf), intended to accommodate those engaged in the sport. The company numbered from fourteen to fifteen hundred men and horses.

"'The manner of the hunting,' says Taylor, 'is this: five or six hundred men doe rise early in the morning, and they doe disperse themselves divers wayes, and seven, eight, or ten miles compasse, they doe bring or chase in the deer in many heards (two, three, or four hundred in a heard) to such or such a place as the noblemen shall appoint them; then when day is come, the lords and gentlemen of their companies doe ride or goe to the said places, sometimes wading up to the middles through bournes and rivers; and then they being come to the place doe lie down on the ground till those foresaide scouts, which are called the Tinckhell, doe bring down the deer; but as the proverb says of a bad cooke, so these Tinckhell men doe lick their own fingers; for besides their bowes and arrows which they carry with them, wee can heare now and then a harquebuse or a musquet goe off, which doe seldom discharge in vaine; then after we had stayed about three hours or thereabouts, we might perceive the deer appear on the hills round about us (their heads making a shew like a wood), which being followed close by the Tinckhell, are chased down into the valley where we lay; then all the valley on each side being way-laid with a hundred couple of strong Irish greyhounds, they are let loose as occasion serves upon the heard of deere, that with dogs, gunnes, arrows, durks, and daggers, in the space of two hours, fourscore fat deere were slaine, which after we disposed of some one way and some another, twenty or thirty miles, and more than enough left for us to make merry withall at our rendevouze. Being come to our lodgings, there was such a baking, boyling, rosting and stewing, as if Cook Ruffian had been there to have scalded the Devil in his feathers'" (Watson 1896:52–54).

The hunt was dear to the heart of both keepers and poachers in "Merry Old England" as attested to by the following epitaphs.

In Memory of Robert Hackett, Keeper of Hardwick Park, who departed this life Decr. ye 21, Anno Dom. 1703.

Long had he chased
    The red and fallow deer,
But Death's cold dart
    At last has fixed him here.

A more ambitious effort found a place in the church of St. Nicholas, Nottingham, to the credit of a once famous poacher:

Here lies a marksman, who, with art and skill,
When young and strong, fat bucks and does did kill.
Now conquered by grim death (go reader tell it)
He's now took leave of powder, gun, and pellet;
A fatal dart, which in the dark did fly,
Has laid him down among the dead to lie.
If any want to know the poor slave's name,
'Tis Old Tom Booth, ne'er ask from whence he came.
He's hither sent; and surely such another
Ne'er issued from the belly of a mother.

"This epitaph was composed some time before the hero's death, and so delighted was he with it, that he had it graven upon a stone in anticipation of his own demise. He died in 1752, in his seventy-fifth year" (Watson 1896:61–62).

In some districts, the deer drive seems to have been an annual event, generally held in August before the harvest, so that the crofters (crofters differ from renters in that they enjoy certain legal protections and can pass their agricultural, grazing and housing rights to their heirs) would be free to participate. It was conducted under definite rules of discipline as exemplified by these orders issued by the Duke of Atholl in 1710 (Whitehead 1993:328) to those taking part:

1. That none shall offer to fire a gun or pistol in the time of the deer-hunting.
2. That none shall offer to break up a deer (cut up), or take out a gralloch, except in his Grace's presence, where they are to be disposed of.
3. That none be drunk or swear an oath.

"Bogs were also sometimes used to trap deer, and when the driven deer became entangled in the soft, boggy ground, such as to be found in Sutherland or Caithness, they were slaughtered by the natives" (Whitehead 1993:329).

A somewhat similar method of taking deer was being practiced in Ireland until the 19th century, when the stags in the woods of Killarney were driven into the lake, where they were either shot or caught with ropes thrown about their antlers (Beaufort and Morris 1885).

Deer driving as it used to be practiced now is obsolete. The later years of the sport were those of muzzleloaders, and a sportsman often sat on his vantage point with a stack of loaded single-barrels beside him.

In addition to driving deer to rifles in an ambush, a much favored former pastime was coursing an unwounded deer with hounds (par-force hunting), a sport still practiced in 2000. Terrain, more than anything else, was the main factor that determined whether a course was worthwhile.

As the deerhound ran by sight rather than by scent, it was essential that the dogs have a good view of the deer both before being slipped (released) and during the course. The preliminary, therefore, to any course was for the hunting party to get as close to the deer as possible—a difficult undertaking with young, eager hounds. Fairly flat, rolling country was the ideal type of terrain, because on such ground, deer would keep running and could be pulled down by the dogs, generally by one seizing a hind leg or flank to knock it off its balance, while another dog seized its throat (Whitehead 1993).

This type of hunting was dangerous for hounds and horsemen. "The Stuart brothers relate how two of 'stout Glengarries' splendid hounds were killed. One on each side they overtook their stag but he, striking with his antlers, left and right, laid each hound dead" (Chalmers 1935:196). Barrow (1948:x) mentioned that "There are ghosts a-many, including that of the execrable Wild Dayrell of sinister Littlecote Hall on the Bath road, hunting his spectral hounds and breaking his spectral neck over a spectral stile."

In those days, the country was comparatively open and without fences, and chases were long. One stag, jumped in Sherwood Forest, reportedly was pulled down 108 miles (174 km) away. Henry the VIII rode 10 horses to a standstill during a 1-day hunt (Barrow 1948). Although this form of hunting formally dates back to the 14th century, legislation involving the keeping of dogs dates back to as early as the 11th century.

By the 19th century, the sport of hunting with staghounds in England had developed into a perfected ritual whose participants took their respective duties very seriously. Beaufort and Morris (1885) indicated that the hunt master at Exmoore needed two horses for most stag hunts, and chases could last for hours. The same traditional methods still were practiced as of 2000. However, during late 1997, the House of Commons sided with animal rights activists and voted overwhelmingly to ban the hunting of fox, deer, hare and mink with hounds. The legislation still could be killed by the Prime Minister (Barr 1997). According to G. K. Whitehead (personal communication:2000), no decision has been made, and red deer were coursed with hounds in southern England in 2000. However, some estates recently have banned such hunting, thus, reducing the available territory. G. K. Whitehead, a dean of English deer stalkers, expressed belief that hunting (driving) is not a suitable method of managing deer.

On the day before a hunt, the "harbourer" must search for deer in the chosen area (MacPherson 1896). He must get near enough to the herd, without disturbing them, to choose the biggest and best stag for the chase. He also has to make sure that the stag is in a suitable area from which to start the hunt. The following day, he leads the hunt to that area, and the "tufters" are let loose. These are dogs that are led to the spot where the stag was last seen, to get his scent (Clutton-Brock 1986). When the scent is discovered, the tufters follow it, attempting to separate the stag from the herd. When they succeed, the rest of the pack is let loose, and the hunt begins. The hunt ends when the deer is standing at bay. It is shot and its entrails fed to the dogs.

Waters of the Bristol Channel are a common resort of deer when hard pressed. Occasionally, when hounds are very close, deer make a mistake and fall or jump over heights that are fatal. The great majority of the runs end in the water, whether it be the Channel or a stream (Watson 1896). There are stories of red deer crossing to the Coast of Wales—some 12 to 14 miles (19–26 km)—and of fishermen finding them swimming 30 miles (48 km) offshore.

Hunting with hounds holds great attraction for some people, as indicated by the following: "On this day a well-known local doctor visited a lady in an interesting condition on his way to the meet, promising to call in again presently; this he had an opportunity of doing early in the course of the run, but finding his services were not yet indispensable, he went on and saw the stag killed, returning to his patient in time to bring a fine boy into the world. It is said that his father once did all this, and gave surgical assistance to a cow as well, in the course of a day's hunting. On September 29, 1884, we tried, though in vain, till 8.45 to kill a young stag found nearly five hours before; but the run of September 22, 1871, was the most remarkable all round, for on that day hounds killed at 8.30 after running through twelve different parishes for over five hours—during the first part of the time at a great pace. Besides the hunt servants only six saw the finish: of the six, three were farmers, all mounted on ponies by Old Port; and of the three, two—Messrs. Bawden and Westcott of Hawkridge—had ridden the whole chase bare-backed and in their shirt-sleeves; the former with nothing but a hemp halter for bridle.

"Such an incident speaks volumes for the sporting instincts of the farmers who are the backbone of our stag-hunting. No class enjoys it more, and no class does more to promote its prosperity.

"The chase of the wild red deer has a very strong hold on the people of the country round Exmoor. Of course the hundreds of tourists and sportsmen whom it attracts bring

English red deer, chased by hounds or not, often take to the water, apparently to cool off and play. *Photo by Bart W. O'Gara.*

Not only deer hunters (those who pursue deer with hounds) but deerstalkers use dogs in England. A well-trained dog at heel will whine when it crosses a fresh track or detects the airborne scent of a deer. The stalker will then attach a short leash to the dog's collar and let it lead the way to the quarry. In dense vegetation, where English deer usually bed, the quiet approach of stalker and dog may bring them to within 50 yards (46 m) or less of their intended prey. The deer, already aware of its pursuers, generally does not bolt before some action by the stalker (stopping, a direct stare, etc.) indicates that it is seen. A gentle tug on the leash causes the dog to set. If the stalker is prepared and quick, a stationary shot is possible. Often, however, it is at an animal virtually exploding from heavy cover. Although the range is short, an occasional poorly placed shot is probable. The experienced stalker relaxes for 20 to 30 minutes before again allowing the leashed dog to follow the deer. Ordinarily, a dead deer is soon found or a wounded one dispatched after a quiet approach. Only under unusual circumstances is a dog released to chase a wounded deer. If a cripple is jumped several times and seems impossible to approach, the dog may be belled (or nowadays even radio collared) and released. Labrador retrievers are the dogs of choice for many stalkers. They are easy to train and control, and they have good noses. Labs, generally, are gentle with people, but capable of catching and holding a wounded stag. *Photo by Bart W. O'Gara.*

money into the district; and nobody is blind to the advantages of that. But the deer do a good deal of damage, and though there is a damage fund, which gets larger every year, the men who benefit most by the sport are very often not identical with those who do most for it. There is no mistake, however, about the feeling of the people of the country; all classes, from the landlord to the labourer, take a keen interest in the hunting. Everyone on the road, as the hounds go home, inquires anxiously about the day's doings, and the huntsman is sure of congratulation or sympathy as the case may be when he answers the inevitable question, 'Hav' ee killed?' which is addressed to him from every house and cottage that he passes" (Watson 1896:247–249).

Another popular sport was hunting carted deer, said to have been founded by George III (reign 1760–1820). It was developed as a substitute to hunting, due to the spread of agriculture and the Enclosure Acts (Whitehead 1980). This involved releasing a captive deer from a cart, waiting 30 minutes, then losing the dogs. The object was to chase the deer until it bayed, but not to kill it. Haviers, castrated males, were considered the best deer for the chase because they did not grow hard antlers, were less likely to injure themselves and usually would run. When the chase was over, the deer was led back to the cart by a rope looped around its neck.

Peasants lost crops to red deer and often could do little about it. However, crop depredations led to reduction or extirpation of red deer in many areas. One account of retaliation foreshadowed similar trapping of elk for research purposes. After the raiding of stacked grain by red deer in Scotland during the 18th century, the farmers opened large doors on both sides of their barn and attached ropes to both in such a way that they could be closed at will by the watchers. Grain was scattered about and into the barn. The evening came, and the frost was very severe. A good many hours passed without any unusual circumstance. At last the welcome sound of the deer approaching was heard. Three or four deer sniffed cautiously around and soon began to nibble at the grain. They seemed scared at finding the barn open but gathered courage on discovering that a passage through was clear. When all the grain on the snow outside the barn had been consumed, the animals followed the trail of grain into the barn. As soon as the unlucky animals had crossed the threshold, both doors were hastily closed. When daylight returned, the fate of the poor wanderers was soon settled (Watson 1896).

Cameron (1923) and Chalmers (1935) provide the following description of the evolution of deer stalking in Scotland. The Scottish highlands, as late as the 15th century, presented a hunting ground scarcely less primitive than the highlands of Alaska in the early 20th century. Mountains and glens now totally denuded of wood then were wrapped in a continuous forest, above which stood a stony sea of desolate peaks, upon the outer skirts of which were thinly dotted the castles of chiefs and the humbler dwellings of clansmen. Within the forest were vast solitudes, remote from human habitation, which gave ideal sanctuary to game. Red deer could browse and bed undisturbed in all the high glens. This hunting ground was called by the Gaels, *am fàsach*—the wilderness.

Highland cattle and hill ponies were pastured at large on the fàsach, and extensive forests were reserved as private hunting grounds by feudal overlords, whether chief or king. Apart from these reservations, the sport and pasturage of the fàsach was shared in common by members of the clan, who paid for the privilege with their sword. Restrictive game laws did not exist in the military organization of the clans, and game had no commercial value beyond its immediate utility as food. The stag of the fàsach was a forest animal widely scattered through dense cover and visible from viewpoints only when at feed on cleared spaces. The sport of kings, chiefs and gentlemen of the clans was the drive and hunt gatherings for the purpose were held annually in autumn throughout the highlands, often on a huge scale. Killing deer by the still hunt, or silent stalk, in the pathless solitudes of the fàsach did not appeal as a sport to highland gentlemen, who replenished their larders by means of professional stalkers. Hence, surprising to modern sportsmen, deer stalking in those days essentially was the sport of clansmen—the rank and file. Successful stalking meant days and nights on the hill, patient watching at dusk and dawn for deer on the feed, much disappointment due to imperfect weapons, and many a rough-and-tumble with wounded stags, for which a well-trained hound gave indispensable aid. Thus, the Highlanders of Scotland were trained for war in the strenuous pursuit of red deer, and

The highlands of Scotland are legendary to deer stalkers throughout the world. This degraded habitat allows spying on deer from long distances. The long, roundabout stalk can be challenging, usually ending with a crawl through wet, tundralike vegetation. The mountains once were forested; when the forests were cut down, heavy grazing and browsing by sheep and, later, by large numbers of red deer continued the degradation. *Photo courtesy of Kenneth Whitehead.*

The roaring of red deer is the primary means of locating the animals in forested areas of Europe. However, on the hills of Scotland, the animals can be seen at farther distances than they can be heard. *Photo by Tom Weir.*

few rewards for distinguished service were more highly valued than permission to kill deer in the reserved hunting grounds of their chiefs.

As late as the 18th century, vast stretches of forest still clothed the slopes and swept into the glens, despite the axe and fire of social progress. There were no fences, and the antlered monarchs, of a weight and beam unknown on bare hills, were free to roam. The gradual extinction of wolves toward the close of the 17th century relieved the red deer of this foe, but prepared the way for the great agricultural discovery that was destined a century later to revolutionize the rural economy of the highlands. Sheep farming proved a profitable industry, and the sheep carried everything before them. Crofter-clansmen were sent to the seaboard or shipped overseas by their chiefs because of the lack of work in the highlands. Black cattle also were banished from the glens; mountain slopes were shorn of their natural woods to make pasture for sheep; and almost without exception, the old deer forests of the highlands were placed at the service of wool and mutton. To the lairds of those days, many of them on the verge of bankruptcy for their fidelity to a lost cause, deer were of no value compared with an industry that turned bogs and rocks into gold. The famous hunting grounds of chiefs and kings were hired out for sheep with the rest, and the old wood stag was threatened with the fate of the wolf.

As sheep replaced red deer in much of the highlands, "Duncan MacIntyre, the forester poet, lover of the deer . . . sung of these days of transition and danger.

> 'Yestreen I stood on Ben Dorain, and paced its dark
> grey path;
> Was there a hill I did not know?—a glen or grassy
> strath?
> Oh! gladly in the times of old I trod that glorious
> ground,
> And the white dawn melted in the sun, and the red
> deer cried around.
> Yestreen I wandered in the glen; what thoughts were in
> my head!
> There I had walked with friends of yore—where are
> those dear ones fled?
> I looked and looked; where'er I looked was naught but
> sheep! sheep! sheep!
> A woeful change was in the hill! World, thy deceit was
> deep!'" (Chalmers 1935:19–20).

However, sheep farming, with its abundant capital and drastic methods, did not oust the deer from their last retreats in the Caledonian forest. That deer could thrive and multiply as well as sheep on bare hills was an important discovery and, in the long-run, was destined to play a still greater role in the economic history of the highlands. The zeal displayed by the sturdy, lowland farmers in pushing their new industry had made them unwillingly the pioneers of a new sport, and land that had been laboriously prepared for sheep rapidly was reclaimed for deer. The adaptive stag had mastered the strenuous life of the open hill and beaten the hardy sheep at their own game (Cameron 1923, Chalmers 1935).

Deer became more valuable to the laird than were sheep. Hills that would carry 5,000 sheep, worth at the best a rent of 500 guineas, would feed 1,500 deer, and stand a killing average of 50 stags, worth three sheep rents. In economic importance, no comparison was possible. The passion for deer and hills that had inspired the poetry of the Gael instantaneously gripped the imagination of the sporting world. It drew boundless stores of southern wealth and enterprise to the stony heart of Scotland. For the highland crofters who still clung to their native glens, it opened up new avenues of employment. It also enlisted young men in permanent occupations for which they had inherited apti-

tude, and which touched their hearts on a peculiarly responsive chord. As stalkers and gillies to the ever-growing host of lessees of deer forests, these dispossessed clansmen once more could pursue the sport of deer slaying that had been the joyful recreation of their forefathers for centuries.

The new deer forests owed their immediate and immense success to humans' love and longing for wild nature and sport. They brought the flavor of a real wilderness, where nothing mattered but mountains and stags, to the door of busy men in populous commercial centers. Leisured hunters of big game responded to that call of the wild, for which they would pitch lonely camps in the least-explored regions of the globe. At the same time, the new deer stalking gained much of its attractive force from the splendor of the Scottish "cloud land"—the romance and mystery of the hills, plus the fragrance and freedom of the rolling moor. Apart from the romantic side of it, the sport possessed a distinctive charm in its appeal to the personal qualities of the stalker. It needed sound heart and lungs, steady nerve, keen perception, great muscular activity and brisk mental calculation. It embodied the joys of hill stalking, which is said by those who have tried everything to be the finest sport in the world, whether the quarry be chamois in the Alps, bighorns among the Rockies, ibex in the Himalayas or Marco Polo sheep in the Tien Shan.

Most stalkers prefer to shoot at stationary deer, but an American millionaire sportsman of the 19th century, Walter Winans, despised easy targets and, being a brilliant shot, could regularly kill stags galloping past him at 200 yards (183 m) (Whitehead 1993). His sport in Scotland generally was at driven game rather than the conventional stalking. This sort of shooting required a vast area of ground and, at one time, Winans held the sporting rights over almost 250,000 acres (101,173 ha).

Germany (including the Holy Roman Empire)

During the 7th century, the right to hunt was the sole prerogative of royal courts. In those days, game in Germany was divided into two groups: *Hochwild* and *Niederwild*—literally high game and low game. Hochwild, which included red deer, was reserved for the sovereign and his guests. Niederwild, which included roe deer, was hunted by people of lesser rank, but then only with the sovereign's permission (Whitehead 1982).

By 1500, more ceremony was being introduced and, to entertain in lavish fashion, large hunting parties assembled for the sport, and great hunting castles (*Schloss*) were erected. Large drives (*Treiben*) were the order of the day, and large numbers of deer and boar were driven into confined areas to be shot at by the assembled hunters (Whitehead 1982).

Peasants had to do forced labor for their feudal lords, lost all privileges and suffered fierce punishments for poaching game that devastated their fields. In 1525, crowds of peasants stormed the fortified houses and hunting castles of the princes. Many of their demands involved freedom to hunt and exemption from labor to support hunting by the princes. The peasants suffered a resounding defeat by the united armies of the princes, and terrible bloodshed followed. Taxes and compulsory labor increased, and the dream of freedom from hunting services died a sad death (Hobusch 1980).

"For a great part of the seventeenth century a father and son occupied the throne, and killed the game of Saxony by the hundreds of thousands. Elector [a prince of the Holy Roman Empire who took part in the election of the emperor] John George the First, who reigned from 1611 to 1656, and Elector John George the Second (1656–1680), were probably the greatest slaughterers of game known in modern history. In the seventy years of father and son's reign, they bagged a total of 110,530 deer.

"It must be remembered, too, that during the reign of the elder Elector, the whole Continent was in the throes of the Thirty Years' War, during which Tilly invaded his territories, while the Swedes, in revenge for his making peace with the Emperor, wrought for ten years terrible havoc throughout Saxony. What his bag would have been in time of continued peace it is impossible even to conjecture; of startling size it was in any case" (Baillie-Grohman 1896:169–171).

"While the nobles attending the Court of their sovereign lord participated to a certain, though limited, extent in the pleasures of the chase, none but personages of princely rank could aspire to slay what might be termed record stags. Even the highest nobles of the land, on becoming aware of the presence of an unusually large stag in their forests, hastened to give their sovereign an opportunity to hunt and kill it. This would be contrived by dint of the most extraordinary exertions and elaborate arrangements. Miles of stout palisades of poles and canvas, or 'stake and binder' fences 8 feet [2.4 m] high, upon which hundreds of peasants laboured for weeks, would be erected so as to enclose that part of the forest to which the great hart had been tracked, and on the day of the royal chase he would be forced to pass the sovereign's stand. The death of such a notable hart was followed by State carousals and festivities that lasted often for a week, and very often seriously impaired the fortune of the host. Marble monuments, some of which are still extant, were erected to mark the spot where the cumbersome firelock or the air-gun, which was then a favourite weapon, particularly for stalking, had brought down the great hart. Many a cloister or monastery, as well as church, owed its origin to the death of a great hart having made the spot famous. Gold and silver medals were struck in commemoration; and foresters were rewarded for tracking a stag, and enabling their master to kill it, with the gift of ducats, bearing on one side the imprint of a hart, on the other the words, 'By this golden ducat I was betrayed'" (Baillie-Grohman 1896:179–180).

"In the seventeenth and eighteenth centuries Saxony, Bavaria, Würtemberg, and many of the smaller Duchies were practically one vast preserve wholly given up to game—principally red-deer and wild boars—which preyed upon the crops of the unfortunate peasants. . . . Poaching was in those days very literally a deadly crime; branding on the face, cutting off the right hand, plucking out the right eye, or getting flogged out of the country, being the usual punishment for a first offence, while hanging or decapitation for a repetition, and other even more inhuman punishments, were occasionally resorted to. Thus, in 1537, one Archbishop of Salzburg, a great Nimrod, as these church dignitaries almost invariably were, caused a wretched peasant, who had killed a stag that was nightly ravaging his crops, to be sewn up in the fresh skin of the stag, and be torn to pieces in the market square of the town by the archiepiscopal hounds" (Baillie-Grohman 1896:181–182).

"In the eighteenth century, the same violation of art and taste which led to the monstrous productions of the rococo period, made itself apparent in venery [the act, art or sport of hunting]. The chase became a mere pageant of stage effect and ludicrous mummery. Princes tried to outrival each other in the invention of the most bizarre *coup de théâtre,* as well as the most extravagant pageantry, which made it a travesty of sport. On such occasions, to give a few instances, huge temples, with great flights of steps, in one instance 240 feet high, leading up to galleries, were erected, and the driven stags and wild boars, by means of hundreds of hounds, would be forced to ascent these flights of stairs, to be shot from the galleries by the invited royal guests and their lords and ladies, amid the blast of trumpets and fanfares of hunting-horns. The preparations for such a *chasse* would literally occupy thousands of men and horses for months; and, notwithstanding the unfortunate peasants were compelled to give their services gratuitously, and that often just at harvest time, the cost of such an entertainment was enormous" (Baillie-Grohman 1896:179–180).

Foraging on the peasants' crops apparently promoted great body size and huge antlers. Stags with as many as 66 points were shot during the 14th to 16th centuries. The largest known stag (now in the castle of Moritzburg near Dresden, Germany) carries only 24 points, but has a spread of 75.6 inches (192 cm). With a very small fragment of skull attached, it weighs 41.5 pounds (18.8 kg). When, where or

This photo shows the size of antlers to be found in Europe during the Middle Ages, compared with those of today (above and below the ancient trophy). The Soboń Family, now in Lódź, Poland, has owned these antlers for nearly 300 years. Before then, it was in the trophy collection of the Prussian King, Fredrick the Great, according to Stephen Saboń. A French knight, de Zolorin, is believed to have been the first owner, during the 7th or 8th century AD. *Photo by Stefan Soboń.*

by whom the deer was killed is unknown. It first appeared in an inventory of Elector Augustus's heirlooms in 1586 (Baillie-Grohman 1896).

Perhaps the most dedicated and active hunters of 18th- and 19th-century Germany were the par-force hunters who pursued red deer—unhindered by fences or stockades—with horses and hounds. European red deer—pampered by foresters of the medieval and rococo periods, well-nourished on peasants' crops, large and brawny—were enduring. Probst (1737) reported that up to three rallies of hounds and horses were required to bring a stag to bay. Apparently, a Count of Anhalt Dessau killed eight horses in the process of running one stag down (Roedle 1971). English par-force hunts seldom lasted as long, perhaps because the smaller deer had less endurance, and English hunters were likely to be mounted on fast thoroughbred horses.

In 1848, the long-delayed revolution in Germany and Austria reduced the power of the feudal aristocracy. For the first time, the commoner had the right to own guns and dogs and to hunt game. Many German sportsmen made up for lost time.

Although hunting no longer is the sole prerogative of royalty, and modern game laws make hunting available to everyone, no other country is so steeped in hunting tradition as is Germany. Many hunting customs dating back to the 7th century still are practiced today. One of the first customs a visitor to Germany or Austria will notice is the plume of hairs worn by hunters in their hats. These hairs—known as Barts—may be from chamois, red deer or wild boar. In red deer (*Hirsch*), the hairs for a *Hirschbart* are taken from the mane of a rutting stag (Whitehead 1982).

"Another custom a visiting hunter is soon to become acquainted with is the use of the greeting *Waidmannsheil* and *Waidmannsdank*—literally hunter's greeting and hunter's thanks. Not only is it a general term of greeting between one sportsman and another, but during the hunt, following a successful shot, the *Jäger* (keeper) or person guiding the hunter, will take a small branch—*Schützenbruch*—(hunter's branch) and after dipping it in the blood of the deer, will place it on his hat or on the blade of his hunting knife and present it to the successful hunter with the word *Waidmannsheil* (hunter's greeting)—who will accept it and after placing it on the right side of his or her hat, will respond with the words *Waidmannsdank* (hunter's thanks). Even when hunting alone, it is customary for a hunter, after making a kill, to place a small branch in his hat, thus informing anyone met on the way home that the hunt has been successful.

"When an animal has been wounded, and finally tracked down by a dog, the dog handler will present the branch to the hunter, who will then break a piece off and hand it back to the dog handler, part of which will then be attached to the dog's collar thus denoting that success has been achieved only by the combined efforts of hunter, dog-handler and dog.

"Branches are also used in many other ways during the course of a hunt, such as to indicate the point where a wounded deer was first hit, and to indicate the direction in which it went off. The branches are always broken from the living tree, and only those trees native to Germany are used. These include oak, alder, pine, fir and spruce.

"The use of the hunting horn is another aspect of the hunt that has persisted through the centuries. At one time the carrying of the hunting horn was the exclusive privilege of the large game hunter. Now, in modern Germany, a social hunt is not complete unless buglers are present with their hunting horns, not only to pass information and instructions to those partaking in a hunt—this is particularly important during a drive—but also to play a *Totsignal* (last post) during the closing ceremony. Altogether there are over forty distinct hunting calls in use in Germany today—some instructive, such as informing beaters and hunters that game has broken back, and the drive will be retaken—others ceremonial, particularly to mark the end of a hunt when all the game will be laid out in proper order, each beast lying on its right side, with Red deer occupying the first row, stags at one end and calves at the other. If any Fallow deer have been killed they will occupy the second row, and in the mouth of every male deer will be placed a small branch as a token of respect, indicating the last bite—*letzter Bissen*. It also is customary to place a branch, referred to as ownership branch—*Inbesitznahmebruch*—over the bullet hole in the body. For male animals, the broken end of the branch points towards the head—for females the branch is reversed with the tip pointing in the direction of the head.

"The buglers take up their position behind and to the right of the rows of game, whilst behind them stand the dog handlers with their dogs. The third row will be taken up by the beaters. To the front of the game, with the host standing in the centre, are the hunters, and after the former has announced the total number and species of game taken, he will hand out a shooter's branch, *Schützenbruch,* to every hunter who has shot a cloven-footed game [see also below]. The host also may name the king of the hunt—*Jagdkönig*—the hunter who has killed most game. The buglers then present the appropriate *Totsignal* for each species killed, and close the ceremony with the two calls—*Halali* and *Jagdvorbei*—the hunt is over. Throughout the ceremony it is customary for the party to stand at ease, with head gear removed, and on no account should anyone step over a carcass, but always walk round.

"Following a day's driving there usually is a festive meal or gathering held at a hunting lodge or guest house—*Schüsseltreiben* or *Knödelbogen*—literally the last drive, and all hunters who have participated in the day's sport are expected to attend.

"The Saint Hubertus holiday is observed by all hunters in Germany on 3 November, and the Hubertus hunt generally is considered the outstanding social function of the hunting calendar. During the hunt practically all the hunting customs are employed, ranging from the various bugle calls to the most commonly used branch signs and display of game" (Whitehead 1982:52–54).

Hubert is said to have been born about 658, the son of the Duke of Aquitania (Hobusch 1980). Legend has it that Hubert, a passionate hunter, lost his way while hunting in the forests of the Ardennes. During his wanderings, he saw a very fine stag, which bore a radiant crucifix between its antlers. At the same time, Hubert heard a voice telling him to abandon unrestricted hunting and profess his Christian faith. Hubert was so impressed, says the legend, that he

The Saint Hubertus holiday hunt on November 3 is the foremost social hunt in Germany. Above, trumpeters sound the call for the mounted hunters and their dogs to assemble for a drive for small game, boar or deer. The call to assemble is the first of two or three dozen signals used in the course of the day's hunt. *Photo by Schleich; courtesy of Anthony Photography.*

gave up all his worldly vanities and entered a monastery. About 700, he is said to have been made Bishop of Liège by Pope Sergius. Hubert died in 727 and was canonized 100 years later. Known as the patron saint of hunters, Saint Hubert's Day (November 3) no longer means the end of the hunting season for big game; however, it is a reminder of proper ways to hunt and practice wildlife conservation (Hobusch 1980). In Europe and North Africa, some hunting clubs are named Saint Hubert's Club, and I found members of those clubs quite willing to let an American join in their boar drives and bird hunts.

Other European Countries

Practically every country of Europe has red deer and red deer hunting. Many animals are as wild and natural as any elk in North America; others are in enclosures, or fenced out of agricultural lands and fed during winter; most are crossbred. North to south, they range from within 100 miles (160 km) of the Arctic Circle in Norway (Pottinger 1910), to the Mediterranean and North Africa (Whitehead 1982); west to east, they are found from the Atlantic Ocean (Caillard 1910) through European Russia (Demidoff 1910) and Greece (Gennadius 1910).

For the most part, stags in Europe are hunted by stalking on foot during the rut, but high-seats, horse-drawn carriages and drives are used depending on the wariness of the deer, density of vegetation, steepness of terrain, weather conditions, personal preferences and local traditions. The drives generally are not large, such as those described for Spain; they typically involve a few men, seldom with dogs, drifting the deer to a few standers. Such drives often are the means for cropping females. Dogs are used to locate wounded animals and sometimes are used in drives. Some countries (Germany, England, Norway, Yugoslavia) require or suggest that a dog be available to track wounded deer. Hunting with hounds and horses is mostly restricted to France, where the term par-force chasse originated. Literally, it means by force (power or strength) hunting. The French *par-force* frequently is used elsewhere in Europe, but *chasse* generally is replaced by hunting, jagd, etc.

The largest trophies generally are produced in areas on and around the Carpathians. In the smaller countries, red deer usually are found on private lands, and hunting is by invitation of (or payment to) landowners. In Austria, red deer were, in the eyes of sportsmen, the principal prize of the chase. They were and are hunted solely during the rut,

Sport hunting for red deer in much of Europe takes place during the rut. At that time, roaring stags, such as this one in Sweden, are comparatively easy to locate and stalk. Most sport hunters in Europe are trophy and meat hunters, but the meat often is sold or the property of the landowner. Some hunters keep the skulls of female deer as trophies. However, the appearance (beauty) of antlers seems more appreciated than in North America, where size seems the most admired characteristic. The Rowland Ward System, currently owned and administered by Game Conservation International (Game COIN), originated in England. It ranks trophies by length of longest antler or horn, with no credit for the other side, secondary tines or mass. The system is easy to understand and apply, but its simplicity does not do justice to deer antlers. Conseil International de la Chasse (CIC) criteria have become the traditional European way of evaluating trophies. The CIC system involves measurements, much like those of the Boone and Crockett Club, but points may be awarded for color, beauty, pearling and antler weight. CIC places top trophies into three medal classes—gold, silver and bronze. *Photo by Anders Jarnemo.*

High seats, such as this one in England, are used in most European countries for hunting red deer and other game. Placed at the edges of clearings or over game trails, the seats enable standing shots at unaware game, often at close range. They also provide shooting rests. Thus, the quarry can be studied, a trophy stag or fat meat animal selected and an instant kill administered. Waiting in a seat is not boring if one enjoys observing birds, hares, squirrels and other wildlife at close range. Early morning and late evening are the ideal times to occupy high seats. *Photo by Bart W. O'Gara.*

because stalking them in the thick woods at other times generally would be a hopeless task.

Stalking red deer on bright moonlit nights during their rut in the Alps was one of Baillie-Grohman's (1882:152–153) favorite sports, and he described it thus: "those memorable half-hours stretched motionless at full length in the grass, pendent with heavy dew, as with beating heart you watch the stag issue from the sombre forest heavy with the fragrant perfume of the pine, stalking forth in all the strength and pride of a monarch on to the little dell where the bright moonlight throws quaint shadows of his noble proportions, his breath issuing from his dilated nostrils upon the frosty air in vapoury clouds blending with the gauze layer of luminous steam which envelopes Mother Earth. No proud call re-echoes through the silent night from crag to crag those welcome seconds during which, with bared feet and

crouching form, the blood rushing wildly through your tingling veins, you stride over fallen trees, cross the dark brook, wending your noiseless step through the maze of lichened pines, as, with your rifle to your shoulder, you approach the heedless quarry, thereby betrayed. And no such experiences as, when you have approached to within a dozen yards and already perceive through the network of brush and pine branches the faint outline of the stag lit up by a fitful moonbeam, you behold him suddenly dash away, and with inflated neck, bristling hair, and head thrown well back, crash through the dense timber: for upon his fine ear there has re-echoed an answering call to his challenge, and long before you have time to feel your discomfiture your quarry is far away, rushing onward to meet his rival in combat."

Early in the 20th century, land in Austria was held by two widely separated classes—nobility and peasantry—and hunting red deer was conducted in much the same manner as during feudal times. Baillie-Grohman (1910) boasted that more men in Austria started after, located, followed, stalked and killed stags entirely unassisted by keepers or gillies than could be found doing so in Scotland. However, by the 1980s, paying to hunt had become a common practice, and tourist resorts—even a few hotels—had their own shooting grounds for use by guests. Gone are the days of hunting for oneself, except for private landowners. Foreign hunters and guests at resorts and hotels—who usually contract for a specified number of days or kills—generally are provided a professional Jäger, whose duty it is to bring the hunter within shooting distance of the quarry (Whitehead 1982).

Although drives were (and are) used to reduce red deer numbers in the thick forests of Europe, stalking while the stags were roaring was the choice of sportsmen. Baillie-Grohman (1896:215) maintained that: "To the stalker, the call of the stag is the essential part of the rut; for by it, at first faintly, then gradually nearer and nearer, he is guided toward the spot where the champion of the forest is roaming through his demesne, bent on love and war."

Baillie-Grohman (1896:234–238) described a hunt in the dense cover of the Carpathian Mountains of Hungary: "If he was coming in our direction we were as favourably placed as we possibly could be, for when shifting ground in the leisurely manner usually observed by a band of deer lorded by a real master-stag, the hinds would be ahead, slowly grazing along, eyes and ears keenly on the watch, while his majesty would stalk some paces behind, heedless of danger, now angrily crushing down a sapling, then throwing up his head and sniffing the air, or with outstretched neck sounding his guttural challenge, the *timbre* of which is of such astonishing force. But of such scenes, though enacted but a few dozen paces off, one sees precious little in these impenetrable forests. My host's warning that one shoots not at stags, but in nine cases out of ten merely at brown patches momentarily visible between trees that hide the rest of the animal's body, was, as I soon found out, strikingly correct. For, though the band was coming my way not more than 40 yards above the trail at the side of which we were crouching, I saw but occasional glimpses of the hinds as they slowly filed past our ambush. Of the stag himself I saw but the upper half of the right antler, but it made my heart beat hard; it was a double royal, five massive points forming the crown, so that it was at the very least a head of fourteen points. The fallen trunk of a beech of great size, behind which the stag passed when I caught the only glimpse I did of his antlers, was a bulwark that effectually shielded the animal, and prevented my taking the random shot which I would probably have been tempted to risk, had merely a bush intervened between the prize and my .450 rifle. Some supremely anxious moments were thus passed, hoping against hope that some fairy hand would turn the herd downwards, and thus lead them to cross the path where there would have been a rare chance for the old rifle to give tongue, but, alas! such would have been too good luck. Two minutes later the advanced guard had got my wind, and, with an angry snort amid loud crashing of dry sticks, the deer took flight, some strong language, in Hungarian and English, tainting the breeze for the next minute or two."

"Experienced old hands use in Hungary, as well as in the Alps, the artificial 'call,' which is, as I have already said, a large sea-shell of the Ammonite order wherewith one can imitate the stag's roar fairly accurately. This call is, as a rule, less successful in bringing the stag up to one, than it is to cause him to betray his whereabouts by an answering note of anger. If dry sticks are about, and the stag is not too near, the efficacy of the ruse is heightened by stamping about on the sticks, as a stag does when breaking cover or when getting ready for a rush. These are tactics which are also observed in Canada when moose-calling. Another ruse which, in the early part of the rut, when stags are still on the lookout for hinds, is often attended by success, is to imitate the squeaking grunt of the hind which she emits when hard pressed by a pursuing stag" (Baillie-Grohman 1896:244).

Hungary was considered one of the finest countries in Europe for hunting red deer early in the 20th century. The deer were large, carried magnificent antlers, and were widely distributed in the hills and lowlands because of strict conservation and the protection afforded by dense vegetation (Széchényi 1910). Large stags on reserves were maintained, mostly to be hunted by communist officials, during the years of domination by the Soviet Union. Since the fall of the Soviet Union, western Europeans and Americans have hunted there and obtained some magnificent trophies. However, the need to make money from the land has resulted in overstocking and overshooting of large stags—resulting in smaller trophies. The largest deer and antlers today are to be found west of the Danube River. The usual methods of hunting are from a high seat, or by stalking on foot or in a horse-drawn carriage. Calling with the aid of a triton shell or ox horn is practiced during the rut; driving is illegal (Whitehead 1982).

The Duke of Frias (1910) stated that he had never heard of anyone stalking red deer in Spain. He also noted that the *podencos* used to drive the deer were powerful and swift-footed greyhounds. The traditional way of hunting red deer in Spain is the *monteria*—a mass drive, and such drives apparently differ from those of ancient times only in details related to improved weapons (Whitehead 1982).

A *monteria* takes place only one day a year—between October 10 and February 20—in any one area. Where game is scarce, 2 years may elapse between such events. Only bulls are shot and most regions are overpopulated, resulting in small animals and degraded habitat. Also, all age classes of bulls are shot, so trophy heads are few. During an average year, about 35,000 stags are killed by this method.

The sizes of monteria differ from one locality to another. On the larger ones, as many as 100 hunters spread over about 2,000 acres (809 ha). Perhaps 200 to 300 dogs, some with bells on their collars, take part, in packs of 20 to 30. The dogs belong to individual hunters, called *perrero*, who carry horns that are blown at frequent intervals to help keep contact with the pack. Some senior perrero carry muskets, which they fire (without projectiles) periodically to encourage the dogs or when game is started. A few beaters participate, but the dogs are better able to penetrate the shoulder-high thickets of sticky-leaved shrubs. To protect their legs from the numerous thorns, many sportsmen and beaters wear leather skirts.

The hunters assemble at about 8:30 A.M. As each one's name is called by the hunt master, a card is drawn from a hat, indicating where his/her stand or blind will be for the day. By 9:00 A.M., the draw usually is completed and the hunters, in groups of about 10, are guided to their blinds—some of which may be 10 miles (16 km) distant. Some stands can be reached only on foot or by mule or horse. The perrero, with their dogs, and beaters will have started long before, to be at their starting points by about noon, when most monterias actually begin. Only one drive, lasting 4 to 5 hours, is made per day.

Depending on the terrain, most blinds are spaced about 400 yards (366 m) apart, encircling the area to be driven. Two lines of hunters generally are posted diagonally through the center—these usually are the most productive

The red deer of eastern Europe are large; some weigh nearly as much as an elk. The antlers are comparatively short but massive. This one was shot in Bulgaria near the Black Sea. Europeans traditionally shot red deer with 7mm or 8mm mausers or mannlichers. Even before World War II, the American 30.06 gained popularity. When the .308 caliber became available, it was adapted to short-bolt actions in Europe. Drillings were used extensively, but mostly for roe deer and small game. Those weapons usually had two 16-gauge barrels above a rimmed 5.6mm or 7mm barrel. Since World War II, most have been 12 gauge over .308. Europeans generally use heavier projectiles than do North Americans. This is understandable because shooting distances usually are less and the deer tend to be in denser cover. Also, the quick knockdown of fragile projectiles is less necessary because dogs are available to find carcasses or wounded game. Primitive weapons generally are legal but not popular. *Photo by Christian Oswald.*

stands. Because the ground is broken and rough, hunters generally can shoot in any direction except when beaters are nearby.

At the end of a drive, successful hunters generally cut off the heads of their quarry and start for home. The headless

In Spain, red deer, such as this one shot near Lagarganta, generally are hunted in drives, but a few estates now cater to hunters who wish to stalk their game. *Photo courtesy of Christian Oswald.*

carcasses were collected later by horsemen, their location being indicated by white pieces of paper attached to nearby bushes to facilitate discovery. Hunters must remain at their stands throughout a drive, and little effort is made to follow-up wounded game. Thus, a complete tally of the results of a monteria seldom is possible. During a monteria, in which Whitehead (1982) participated, 470 shots were counted, and about 80 bulls plus a boar or two were bagged.

Luck of the draw is the most important element. Hunters on poor stands usually will not see legal game, but a favorably placed hunter may, if good at hitting running game with a rifle, kill a dozen red deer and a boar during a drive. A monteria is a social occasion, much favored by many Spanish shooters. Similar drives are conducted on a smaller scale in Portugal.

For further information concerning hunting throughout Europe, see Aflalo (1910) for the early 20th century or Whitehead (1982) for the early 1980s.

Middle East

The Persian kings, with their spectacular hunts about 1300 BC, influenced later court hunts and the art of hunting in general. Hunting was seen as an extension of war, and drives were organized on military lines, employing 7,000 to

8,000 men. Game was driven as far as 62 to 93 miles (100–150 km). Game animals, including red deer, also were kept in large animal parks. Thousands of courtiers accompanied the king on hunts in these "paradise" parks, and after the king had shot the first arrow, the great carnage began. With spear, sabre, bow and arrow, the herded game was killed, mainly from the saddle. The use of horses in hunting saw a peak in Persia. Under the rule of the Sassanidae Dynasty (3rd to 7th centuries AD) and the Arabian khalifs, the hunt occupied an important place as a theme in arts (Hobusch 1980). The following information on the Middle East will be from Vereshchagin (1967), unless otherwise indicated.

The wide distribution of red deer has been documented for nearly the entire Caucasian Isthmus, Iranian Plateau, Lebanon, Syria and Israel from the Pleistocene to the 19th century. For the most part, these belong to the extant subspecies in the area today. Spears and bows were the chief weapons used in big game hunting, and the horse-mounted drive—with permanent or temporary fences or traps placed across gullies and valleys—was the principal hunting method used by nomads during the last three millennia.

In addition to group hunting, solitary hunting was widely practiced in the forests and mountains. A sharp decrease in numbers of large mammals on the Caucasus occurred during the Middle Ages, when the techniques of bow manufacturing and forest and mountain hunting were at a high level.

Large-scale hunting into late medieval time was made possible by conditions in a feudal society and existence of large bands of armed men who provided manpower. During the winter of 1301 to 1302, Ghazin Khan ("King of Islam" and one of the Mongol rulers of Iran) ordered the construction of two wooden fences in the mountains. Each fence was one day's travel long, forming a V, which was one day's travel wide at the open end. At the apex of the V was a corral. The warriors then drove the game—ungulates and carnivores alike—into the corral. Ghazin Khan, seated on a stage in the middle, enjoyed the sight of the animals. Some were killed and some set free.

During the 16th and 17th centuries, large drive hunts continued. Peasants often were called for hunting duty—*Shikari*—to build fences and traps necessary for drives. The hunters—gentry and men-at-arms, often 10,000 or more—assembled on the Shah's orders. In addition to mounted warriors, foot soldiers were used to drive the animals. On some hunts, animals were driven for several days and hundreds, even thousands, were killed during a hunt. Mounds of hundreds of red deer antlers commemorated some hunts.

At the beginning of the 17th century, red deer were reported in herds on the Ukrainian steppes. At the beginning of the 18th century, Vakhtand VI, the 94th czar, and his entourage killed 180 deer in one day, southwest of Tiflis, Georgia.

By the time firearms were introduced and perfected in the Caucasus, the big game population had been considerably reduced. Perpetual wars between tribes and the local custom of blood revenge greatly accelerated distribution of firearms, making them available for hunting. Large-scale drives were no longer feasible, but small-gauge flint and percussion-type shotguns and rifles created new possibilities for individual hunting. Improvements in firearms, arming of shepherds and shipments of large quantities of arms into the mountains during the Civil War (1917–1922) brought about the destruction of bison and most red deer in the area.

Demidoff (1910) wrote of the Caucasus as a part of the Russian Empire and indicated that red deer were kept on reserves or estates of the aristocracy, where they were stalked. However, in the countryside, peasants drove red deer and boar at any time of the year, and few red deer remained.

Today, red deer are mostly protected, and little legal hunting for them is available in the Middle East. Red deer are found in the deciduous forests that lie between the Caspian Sea and the northern slopes—up to about 7,500 feet (2,280 m) of elevation—of the Elburz Mountains in Iran (Whitehead 1982). Ibex horns are used to imitate the roar of the stags.

China

"In early antiquity the Chinese—if we can depend on fragmentary records of their attitudes—were unfriendly toward wild animals. They regarded them as the enemies of civilization—hateful predators that ravaged crops, despoiled barnyards, and attacked human beings. . . . This feeling of the complete alienation of the non-human races has not entirely disappeared in modern times: 'harmful' animals—and the word 'harmful' can be interpreted very broadly—not subject to man ought to be ruthlessly exterminated" (Schafer 1963:319).

"In Chinese mythology the god of longevity is paired with a deer. An early Chinese herbal written around A.D. 200 describes the uses of the growing antler: 'Deer velvet tastes sweet and its property is warm. It is used for treating metrorrhagia . . . febrile disease, and epilepsy, and also for reinforcing vital energy, strengthening memory and will, and delaying the onset of senescence.' In present day Chinese medicine almost 20 different parts of deer are used as tonics to prevent debility" (Clutton-Brock 1986:540).

A reverence for nature runs through literature amassed during the 4,000-year span of Chinese history. The poet found the mountains his most faithful companions; emperors painted finches in bamboo groves and ascended sacred mountains. Attitudes, poetry, paintings and common sayings abound with images of nature and a view of man as part of a greater order of things. Old trees are prized for their antiquity and dignity; flowers are loved and admired; there is a universe of peaks and clouds, snow and wind, waterfalls and ponds, reeds and shores, hills and dense forests (Smil 1984). To stop here, would be to tell only the more appealing half of the story.

Some animals were regarded as heaven-sent symbols of heaven's attitude toward the spiritual condition of the Chinese realm. Malformed mammals, albino birds and many other wonders were treated with circumspection and awe. Generally, however, creatures that could serve the purposes of men, however trivial, were treated in the same way as domestic animals and could be maimed and slaughtered at will. Kings and barons killed leopards and deer, under carefully controlled conditions, to demonstrate their power and glory. Few wild creatures were treated with humanity (Schafer 1963).

The following accounts of ancient Chinese hunting preserves are from Schafer (1963), unless otherwise specified.

The literature of ancient China refers to royal preserves and hunting parks, but interpretations are difficult and sometimes contradictory. Some indicate such reserves provided meat offerings for the temples. Others indicate that restricting movements of wild animals to reservations provided protection from those competitors and enemies that swarmed over potential farmlands and attacked innocent people. "But when the degenerate nimrods who succeeded to the throne of these good rulers took over the people's land for their own selfish purposes, wild beasts flourished again: 'They set aside the cultivated fields, and made gardens and animal preserves of them, so that common folk could not obtain clothing and food'" (see Schafer 1963:321).

Firm historic evidence of preserves is available beginning about 700 BC, during late Chou times. The baronial preserves seem, at that time, to have been primarily hunting parks for recreation of the privileged classes, but the royal preserves had ceremonial functions. Soon after the Chou king Hui Wang took the throne in 675 BC, he seized private land for a royal preserve. A staff of officers and underlings headed by four "preserve men" was obliged to supply appropriate beasts, alive and dead, for religious sacrifices, memorial services for the dead, venison in emergency situations and probably ordinary ones and for entertainment of state guests. The department that levied taxes supplied fodder for the animals, and the public executioner provided mutilated criminals as guards.

Preserves were surrounded by earthen walls high enough to prevent most animals from escaping, but fre-quent references were made to tiger cages. In late Chou times, the feeling arose that the great animal enclosures were harmful to common people, not only because hunting rights were being abrogated, but also because men were required to build the walls around them. Some idea of the size of enclosures is gained from the "Supreme Forest" enclosed during the 3rd century BC. It extended through the countryside south of the Wei River for about 200 miles (322 km).

The grounds of the Supreme Forest were prepared for the great winter hunt (date not given) by the royal foresters. They burned to clear a large open space and cut away brambles. Beaters, hunters and athletes readied themselves. When the royal party arrived, birds and beasts were driven into the cleared area and the slaughter began. Frenzied animals lunged and clawed at each other—tigers fought with buffaloes, part of the display was no hunt at all. There were combats between man and beast and tests of strength. Strong men even grappled with lions, leopards, bears, rhinoceroses, yaks and elephants. At least some of those animals were killed. The scene, apparently, was similar to the exhibitions staged by Emperor Commodus (180–192 AD) in the Roman arena. Two differences between the killing orgies of Rome and China were: the Roman arena was in the city, whereas the Chinese arena was in the country; Commodus killed the rarities of the Orient with sharp and powerful weapons; many of the great beasts of Asia were brought down by the bare hands of the Han athletes. After the blood and battle, the court relaxed with good food, lovely ladies sang in boats on K'un-ming Lake, and acrobats and jugglers provided entertainment. In the time of Wu Ti (140–87 BC), 500,000 laborers worked within the Supreme Forest. Slaves—male and female—as well as poor people who could not buy exemption were pressed into service. At five coins per person daily, by Yüan Ti's time (48–32 BC), 70 billion coins were raised to supply the armies.

A Chinese manuscript from about 1120 BC records a hunt in which, among other animals, 22 tigers, 269 bears, 352 wild boars, 721 yaks, 3,508 sika deer and 5,235 red deer or elk were killed. This hunt apparently was in the hunting park of King Chou Wu-wang (Hobusch 1980).

The Supreme Forest fell into disuse as the Chou Dynasty fell. In the second year of the succeeding Han regime, the grounds were given to the common people to cultivate.

The Han Imperial Park followed and was more than 31 miles (50 km) long and 15.5 miles (25 km) wide, made up of well-watered forest and fields. It apparently contained 36 palaces and hostels, each accommodating 1,000 vehicles and 10,000 horsemen. A later Han Park was 311 miles (500 km) in circumference.

After the disintegration of the Han Empire in 220 AD, evidence for royal parks became fragmentary. Apparently, they still existed, but on a smaller scale. By the 8th and 9th centuries, T'ang rulers again enclosed large parks where animals were killed for pleasure and need, but evidence indicates that indiscriminate slaughters no longer were considered normal.

Perhaps the Imperial Game Park south of Peking (Beijing) was one of the most recent walled preserves in China. In about 1400, it was surrounded by a wall 9.8 feet (3 m) high and 46.6 miles (75 km) long. For nearly 500 years, no trespasser could enter this forbidden city. Little was known in public concerning animals in the park. In 1865, Père David, a Jesuit priest, peeped through a small gap in the wall and saw a species of deer unknown to him. Through the French embassy in Peking, Father David received three of the deer—only one of which survived the trip to Paris. Once that animal was known, zoos in England and Germany soon obtained specimens. The species had long since become extinct in the wild, and it was named in honor of Père David. In 1894, a flood destroyed most of the deer in the park. During the Boxer Rebellion in 1900, European troops killed more than 100 Père David's deer. In 1901, one female Père David's deer remained in the Peking Zoo. It died in 1920 (Hobusch 1980).

Watson (1896) indicated that the Chinese frequently made use of covered pits to capture deer—much as de-picted on ancient oracle bones (1776–1122 BC) and seen in China today. The hunters (trappers?) took care to excavate the soil to such a depth that deer could not jump out. Pits were carefully covered with slender bamboo and grasses. Stags were attracted to the vicinity of the pits by means of a call, made from the skin of an unborn fawn, imitating the cry of a hind. The Chinese also located deer in cover, placed nets around the thickets and drove the animals into the nets with the help of dogs.

Early in the 20th century, Wallace (1915b:156) wrote: "China is so vast a country, travel in the interior is so difficult and uncertain, so vague, and the incursion of foreigners so long discouraged, that there is little wonder it should remain, from the point of view of the big game hunter, the least known of all countries." He noted that, in western China, big game was taken by means of crossbows and arrows set alongside trails, as well as in foot snares. "Deer, particularly the larger species, are being steadily exterminated throughout the Chinese Empire. Were the natives armed with modern rifles, they would quickly vanish altogether. With the weapons they already possess they can make pretty accurate shooting up to 200 yards [183 m]. . . . The usual method of hunting these animals adopted by the natives is to start before dawn and locate a stag by his roar. The hunters, usually four or five in number, return to the

Historically, Chinese caught elk in pit traps, and they still do. These pits, in the Qilian Shan of northern Gansu, were covered with thin branches and dead grass. Wheat and barley were planted around the pits to attract elk. If not seriously injured in the pits, captive animals generally were taken to antler farms. *Photo by Christian Oswald.*

Hunting camps in western China generally are spartan. Traveling through the vast grasslands, one can easily imagine eastern Montana or Wyoming a century ago. The Mongol herder and his family (occupying the white tent) were amazed when a white man—the first they had ever seen—rode up and made camp for the night. However, they were extremely hospitable and asked questions through the Chinese guide and interpreter late into the night. *Photo by Bart W. O'Gara.*

valley, indulge in a hearty meal, talk matters over and start out again in the afternoon. The ridges, extending from the main valley, are clothed on their northern slopes with forests of pine, larch, etc. To these the deer retreat during the daytime. The hunters post themselves round the particular patch of timber in which they think the stag they have seen is located and endeavour to stalk him as he emerges towards evening. Sometimes they attempt a drive. They also catch a few immature animals in native traps. Although their chief aim is to secure a stag with good horns, not for its beauty as a trophy—they care nothing for this—but for its value as translated into terms of pounds, shillings, and pence, they remorselessly slaughter any animal of whatever age or sex which comes within range of their long guns" (Wallace 1915b:169).

Wade (1910) noted that, late in the 19th century, a type of red deer was fairly abundant in the steep hills covered with dense brush along the Yangtze Valley. Those deer spent daylight hours hidden in long grass at the bottom of gullies, where they could neither be seen from afar nor approached quietly. During June, when velvet antlers were most valuable, local hunters made drives, posting 12 to 20 guns in passes around the head of a valley. Drivers came up from below, shouting and rolling rocks into the small gullies. The shooters carried old matchlocks loaded with rough iron shot larger than buckshot. Despite the short range, many deer, of all ages and both sexes, were killed.

Sowerby (1914) noted that securing guides for elk hunt-ing in China was difficult because the hunters hoped to kill the animals the next June, when the velvet was prime. He maintained that the Tien Shan, Gansu and Manchurian elk all were much the same in habits. Various capture–shooting methods were used by the local people including: pitfalls around wallows and on trails—uninjured animals being kept for antler farms; driving to waiting guns; snow tracking; and lying in ambush along the animals' travel routes.

Wilson (1986:156) provided the following description of a Chinese killing device for large mammals: "Two trees growing side by side are selected, and a large, heavy log-beam is attached to a pivot resting in the fork of convenient branches. This beam measures about 8 feet [244 cm] in length, and in the extremity a stout stake about 15 inches [38 cm] long and shod with a barbed spear some 8 inches [20 cm] long is fixed. From the end nearest the pivot a bamboo rope is suspended. The beam is poised by pulling down this rope and attaching it to a cunningly arranged contrivance some 14 inches [35 cm] above the ground. . . . To the stout fixed parts are arranged two collapsible rods, to one of which a trip-rope is attached. This trip-rope is stretched across the 'run' and lashed to a tree on the opposite side, the height above the ground being about the same as the animal's knee-height. The whole trap is a rough and strong yet a delicate and devilish contrivance. An animal coming down the run touches the trip-rope with its forelegs, and is immediately impaled by the spear. The cross-beam, to which the spear is attached, is so heavy that the spear is driven almost through the animal's body behind the shoulder, inflicting a mortal wound. Death may often be slow, but it is always sure, and very seldom can a wounded beast break away. The 'run' is only roughly trampled out, and the bamboo stems and other brush effectually hide the trip-rope. These traps are in common use, and are a source of considerable danger to anyone traversing these runs.

"Dead-falls are also employed by the natives in trapping many animals. . . . These dead-falls are fitted with a treadle arrangement, and the animal stepping upon this causes the whole mass to fall, crushing him to death."

Sowerby (1922) wrote of hunting elk in Manchuria early in the 20th century. He was guided by a Russian hunter, and they used tree stands overlooking trails in the thick birch and coniferous forests. Local farmers also asked them to shoot elk and bears that were raiding their crops, and stands on the edges of fields proved productive. Sowerby met a Russian market hunter who carried only a rifle, knife and blanket, and slept under a tree wherever night overtook him. Moving about the forests was considered somewhat risky, because of prowling tigers and even more dangerous opium growers.

Sowerby (1917) related that sportsmen up and down China's coast planned their annual shooting excursions for the New Year's holidays. A month was needed to reach the best hunting grounds and return. In the old Imperial Hunting Grounds, 90 to 100 miles (145–161 km) north of Tientsin, 50 to 100 birds (mostly pheasants) could be shot in a day. Deer and boar also were numerous in the spruce/oak forest, but cold storage plants were being built in nearby villages, and the market for game was increasing.

Wong-Quincey (1939) noted that Chinese "of the younger generation" had taken up shooting with modern firearms during the 1920s and 1930s with great enthusiasm. These were largely men who had studied abroad.

Today, although hunting big game generally is illegal for residents in China, capture and shooting of elk and their relatives for velvet antlers and other ingredients of traditional Chinese medicines persist. However, in some areas, the animals have increased since about 1975. International hunters are welcome, for a substantial fee, and may provide the principal incentive for conservation, as well as funding for law enforcement (Harris 1995, Liu 1995). Seven subspecies of *C. elaphus,* nearly half of those in the world, are found in China (see Chapter 1). Sport hunting is conducted primarily during the rut by roaring or bugling to locate or attract bulls.

Other Asian Countries

Today, sport hunting for elk and its relatives in Asia, outside China, is centered primarily in Kazakhstan, Outer Mongo-

lia and Siberia. Subspecies to the south and west generally are endangered because of poaching and habitat loss.

When visiting the Court of Kubla Khan in 1298, Marco Polo reported on hunting in the Far East (Brander 1971). The Great Khan had two barons, each with 10,000 men under his command, 2,000 of whom were in charge of about 5,000 mastiff dogs. Polo did not indicate that these men were mounted, probably presuming everyone knew Mongols would be. One baron and his men dressed in red, another in blue, so they could be recognized in the field. When the Khan went big game hunting in his quarters, carried by four elephants, one of the barons with his men and dogs were deployed in a line to the right, the other to the left. They moved along abreast of one another, the line extending a day's journey on horseback from end to end. Game, mostly deer and boar, were run down by packs of the great hounds and dispatched by the huntsmen. Marco Polo described such hunts as a most delightful sport and spectacle. Spectacle seems the best description.

The beautiful Kashmir stag, beset by poaching in an area coveted by two nations, is no longer a trophy to be sought by sportsmen. Accounts from the 19th century indicate that

Some of the largest elk antlers in Asia are to be found in the Tien Shan of Kazakhstan. The country now is open to western hunters, but getting a large bull generally involves lots of horseback riding and considerable bugling. Bugles used for the elk of Kazakhstan, Outer Mongolia and Central Siberia are similar to those in North America. Imitation of the lower frequency roaring of European red deer usually involves a call with a larger resonating chamber than does the whistlelike elk bugle. Large sea shells, as well as cow and ibex horns, have been used for centuries (and still are by some stalkers) to imitate the red stag. *Photo courtesy of James Hetherington.*

Areas around Asian temples often are sanctuaries for wildlife, bringing game animals into close contact with human habitations. This bull elk was photographed in downtown Ulan Bator, the capitol of Outer Mongolia. *Photo by Bern Vetter.*

it was hunted during the rut in a manner similar to that used where elk are somewhat migratory in North America. As the animals came down from the high country, uttering their roar/bugle, stalkers intercepted them on the ridges they had traveled to winter ranges for centuries (Aflalo 1904).

Bactrian deer, occupying riparian areas in the deserts of Afghanistan, Tajikistan, Turkmenistan and Uzbekistan, also suffer from war and lack of protection.

The two subspecies of elk distributed over the Altai district of southern Siberia and all the way to the Pacific Coast were rare by 1910, according to Demidoff (1910), because

Elk in Outer Mongolia, as in North America, are hunted most easily during late September and early October, during the rut. Thus, Russian helicopters (*top*) often are used to move hunters into base camps. Primitive transportation—often camels or horse carts (*bottom*)—is relied on to establish spike camps in prime hunting areas. *Photos by Vetter Bern.*

Gers—a Mongolian term; Russians call them yurts—are comfortable and warm. Nomadic herders of central Asia apparently have used them for thousands of years, and better portable hunting camps can hardly be imagined. Good manners and good luck require that one enter a ger right foot first and move to the left, clockwise, the direction in which the sun travels. *Photos by Bern Vetter.*

of the high prices paid for body parts, especially velvet antlers, in China. Apparently, every Kalmuk that owned a gun spent all of June in the woods, wounding many bulls for every one killed. The Russian government had passed a law against all shooting of elk, and elk antler farms were supplying the Chinese market.

Elk numbers increased under the strict laws of the Soviet Union, but poaching appears to have increased somewhat

This handsome bull was shot in Outer Mongolia near the Siberian border. In fact, the larch forest in the background is in Siberia. Typically in the region, an arriving hunter is met by an interpreter who remains with her/him throughout the hunt. Local guides, wranglers, skinners and camp tenders usually come from the nearest settlement or from nomadic families who use the area. Most of them are herders or wood cutters by trade. The wages and, especially, tips from a few hunts may be the most money they make during a year, and they often receive part of their winter meat supply from the hunt. Thus, international hunters are welcomed with open arms in most areas. Local guides are knowledgeable of game and habitat. Essentially, they are the hunters, and foreigners are the shooters. *Photo by Bill Hintze.*

The horses of central Asia are tough, dependable hunting mounts, but the saddles generally are hard. The silver "conchos" punish a novice rider's inner thighs during a long day in the saddle. The rare, permanent ger in the background, of wood with a cement floor, was near a large spring. *Photo by Bern Vetter.*

An elk in the Altai Mountains of Siberia. This was one of the smaller bulls seen on this hunt, but larger ones eluded the hunters. *Photo by Bruce Warren; courtesy of Cabelo's Outfitters.*

The Kashmir stag was a favored trophy of Indian royalty and British officers stationed in India. Now it is seriously threatened by subsistence poaching. *Photo by Bruce Banwell.*

with the disintegration of that Union. Sport hunting by foreigners has provided income for local people and incentives for conservation in some places. However, the area is immense, and the number of foreign hunters is small.

If information from guides, antler farmers and other local people is reliable, then what Demidoff (1910) reported concerning elk in Siberia apparently applies as well to Kazakhstan and Outer Mongolia.

North America

"The elk is prized for its trophy value, majestic size, and palatable meat. . . . In the wild, and in an appropriate setting, an elk herd is a magnificent sight. Even the sounds made by elk, the shrill bugle and resonating grunts of a bull in rut, are completely unique in the deer family. . . . For the outdoorsman and city dweller alike, the elk is a symbol of wilderness, open space and freedom" (Lyon and Thomas 1987:146).

Christopher Columbus's historic landfall in 1492 preceded the arrival of English pilgrims by 128 years. Exploitation of wildlife during those interim years by the Spanish is not recorded. The Carolinas, New Jersey, Pennsylvania and Rhode Island had been settled by 1682, and development of the New World by English-speaking people had begun in earnest. Settlers adopted the snowshoes used by Indians for pursuing big game on deep and crusted snow. The vast herds of game were so tame that the inadequacy of the early settlers' heavy matchlocks and wheel locks scarcely mattered. As this state of affairs changed, good hounds became an important asset. Early settlers brought dogs with them, but the first pack of hunting hounds was brought from England to Maryland in 1650 (Brander 1971).

Early explorers and settlers slaughtered big game at salt licks, during severe winters and in any other way possible. Extirpation of elk in eastern Canada and the United States is chronicled in Chapter 2. In 1760, 200 settlers in central Pennsylvania participated in a massive circle drive—reminiscent of those described as taking place in the Middle East during the 16th and 17th centuries (Shelford 1963). They killed 98 white-tailed deer, 111 bison, 109 wolves, 41 mountain lions, 114 bobcats and 2 elk. Whether elk were not numerous or they broke back through the lines of drivers, as they are prone to do, is unknown. (An experienced Montana outfitter observed to me that elk can be driven just about any place they want to go.)

During LeSeur's voyage up the Mississippi in 1700, hunters used "whistles" to attract rutting bulls in LaCrosse County, Wisconsin. They reported the animals were easy to kill by that ruse from early September to October. Previous experience with roaring red deer in the forests of Europe probably had prepared some of these explorers to take advantage of rutting bull elk (Schorger 1954).

Tome (1854) wrote extensively concerning elk hunting during the late 1700s and early 1800s in New York and along the western branch of the Susquehanna River and its tributaries in Pennsylvania. Dogs apparently were very important for successful elk hunting in forested areas at that time. Hunting parties followed elk tracks in the snow, sometimes for a day or more, until the quarry was jumped. If a shot was not possible or was missed, a dog—or two—was loosed. After a run, sometimes 12 miles (19.3 km) or more, an elk usually would stand and fight. The stand often was in water or on a large, flat rock. Although a dog or two would worry an elk for only a few hours before returning to the hunters, that elk—now separated from its band—often was doomed. The hunters, on foot, traveled light, carrying only axes or tomahawks, knives, salt, flour and a blanket. They camped on the trail, building shanties of hemlock boughs if the night was especially cold. In this way, the hunters could pursue the same elk as long as it took to overtake it. On one of Tome's hunts, this reportedly involved 4 days and more than 50 miles (80 km).

Tome (1854) gave little information concerning the flintlocks used to hunt elk, except they would not fire when wet. On one occasion, it took him an hour to get his rifle to fire, while the dogs fought an elk. Also, although five or more men and boys often constituted a hunting party, frequently only one or two carried a gun. Apparently, the extra manpower was needed for skinning, cutting, salting, drying and carrying meat. These hunters also scavenged kills made by cougars, which apparently were very numerous. The meat was jerked over a slow fire, while one or two of the party traveled to the settlement and returned with horses to pack the meat and skins home.

Tome (1854) and his brother killed as many as 35 elk each per year, mostly with the aid of dogs. He did not deliberate on the type of dogs used, but said the good ones would remain on any trail they were started on and would not switch species or individuals. Hunting with dogs was especially easy when the snow was deep and crusted. Those conditions made it difficult for the elk to run, whereas dogs could skip along over the crust. August also was a favorite hunting month because the animals were fat and gathered into bands of up to 60, and bugling made the bands easy to locate. Also, instead of fleeing, the bands might face dogs, and a number could be shot without scaring them off.

About June 10, cows would leave their calves and go a short distance to rivers to feed on aquatic vegetation and succulent vegetation along the banks. Hunters plied the rivers in canoes and sent dogs after any cows they saw. The cows would run to where their calves were bedded and return with them to the water. When hard pressed, the cows would face the dogs. Often, the hunters would shoot the cows, and dogs and men would plunge in to capture the calves. Captured elk, calves and adults, soon became tame and were readily handled, except for the bulls during the rut. They were broken to harness, and the cows would stand to be milked. Tome (1854) maintained elk milk was nearly equal to that of a domestic cow in quality and quantity; also, elk were said to be more easily kept in good condition throughout the year than were domestic animals. Large wild-caught bulls sold for up to $500 each at a time when men worked for a dollar a day.

By the 19th century, most elk were in the western states, and the slaughter continued. With the end of the Civil War, the rush West accelerated. Indians were subjugated, and plundering of western game reached staggering proportions. Blair (1987:15) wrote: "In December 1870, the *Laramie Weekly Sentinel* reported that buffalo hunting was a leading amusement of Laramie sportsmen. Ironically, in May of the following year, the *Sentinel* righteously protested against 'the influx of a company of British sportsmen who are here to hunt antelope, elk, buffalo, bear, and deer for sport.'

"For the most part, the settlers and residents of the railroad camps did not hunt and fish. Hunters would bring game in by the wagon load to be sold. Holiday parties were often formed and the buckboards and wagons would return home from hunting and fishing piled high with game to be distributed about the settlement or camp.

"The game herds still seemed endless, but the introduction of breech-loading rifles and brass cartridges had revolutionized big game hunting. The rifled muzzle-loaders had been effective weapons in the hands of men who knew how to use them, but they had limitations."

In July 1873, the *Cheyenne Leader* stated that an estimated 200,000 big game animals were slaughtered the previous year, largely by market hunters, but the area involved was not given (Blair 1987).

"In the case of the wapiti, one factor that helped to ring his death knell was the sudden discovery, made about twenty years ago that the skin of this deer, which formerly was considered the most valueless game hide, because porous, was of use in certain branches of the leather industry" (Baillie-Grohman 1900:30).

As a rule, hide hunters were miners or ranch hands whose regular work ended with the coming of winter, when hide hunting was best. Severe winters sometimes assisted the work of extermination. Near Steamboat Springs, Colorado, a severe blizzard during January 1893 imprisoned about 1,000 elk in deep snow. Ranchmen, prospectors and hide hunters waded in, killing many with clubs (Baillie-Grohman 1900). Apparently, no elk escaped.

The very names of hide hunter and meat hunter conjure up visions of dirty, hard-drinking hermits—more or less frontier soldiers of fortune who would do anything for a price. Some, no doubt, fitted that description, but others were citizens making a living and starting a new life the best way they could. Such vocation was grueling and generally unpleasant, but in that era, it was honest and socially acceptable work.

During his first elk hunt, some 100 miles (161 km) north of Cheyenne, Baillie-Grohman (1882) happened upon a tobacco-chewing boy dressing a bull elk. The 14-year-old, tiny for his age, invited the stranger to spend the night at his family's cabin, as camp was a long way off, and darkness was fast approaching. The boy had killed more than 200 elk and mule deer, plus 2 grizzlies, with the needle gun he carried. He also used the rifle, with its 4.5- to 5-foot (137–152 cm) barrel lashed with rawhide to a homemade stock, as a vaulting pole to mount his Indian pony. The boy's father had moved his family to the neighborhood 3 or 4 years previously, when Indians still were roaming through the Laramie Peak country. He then was making a living selling meat and hides to a buyer in a settlement, 45 miles (72 km) distant. The buyer was an innkeeper, grocer, dry goods merchant, sheriff and postmaster of the settlement. All game—only the hind-quarters were used for food—fetched $0.03 per pound (6.6 cents/kg), which was paid in kind—coffee, sugar, flour, ammunition and other articles of merchandise.

The son had seen a herd of perhaps 2,000 elk on the move from a distance of 9 or 10 miles (14–16 km). Early the next morning, the family set out to find them (Baillie-Grohman 1882:144). "Everybody, except the youngest daughter and the little niece, was going after the 'gang' of elk. The ponies (some nine or ten) were already hitched to posts in front of the shanty, and all the antiquated rifles—the 'Sister Julia,' 'Track-maker,' and 'Greased Lightning,' the latter being the name of my dwarf friend's shooting-iron—were cleaned and laid ready for use. The little hunting party presented a quaint and yet not unpicturesque sight . . . male and female alike, armed with long rifles and revolvers, and mounted on shaggy ponies—and certainly it had about it the spice of novelty." They killed more than 20 elk that day.

Baillie-Grohman wrote extensively of his other hunting experiences. Having killed nine bull elk with large antlers during a 2-day hunt in the Laramie Peak country, although he could have tripled the number, he refrained from shooting more because he considered excess killing a waste. His camp crew was amused by this attitude. Regarding the attitudes of Americans toward game animals at that time, he wrote: "The western hunter seems to fancy the game resources of his home perfectly limitless, and exhibits a supreme indifference to the reverse side of the 'first come first served,' hence is often astonished at what he calls English squeamishness. To a friend a western guide once said, 'You have come a good many thousand miles to shoot, and now that we have at last struck game where it is plenty, you shrink from depriving the rascally Redskins or a parcel of skin-hunters of what is just as much yours as theirs. Certainly you Britishers are strange chaps'" (Baillie-Groham 1882:151).

Although he gloried at the sight of hundreds of splendid bull elk during a hunt in Wyoming, Baillie-Grohman (1882:152) wrote: "Every kind of stalking is much easier in the New than in the Old World, not only on account of the greater quantities and greater fearlessness of the game, but also owing to the nature of the ground, and the fact that during autumn the wind blows constantly from the same point, changing only at the approach of bad weather. All these circumstances combine in making Wapiti hunting a toilless pleasure—in fact, in the long-run rather too much so."

Many of the early sport hunters in North America were wealthy Europeans—often called gentlemen hunters (who came to North America for extended periods to enjoy the nearly unlimited shooting. Many were true sportsmen, but not all of the gentlemen hunters were squeamish about killing simply for the sake of killing. Blair (1987:10–11) gives the following account: "One of the earliest and wealthiest of the 'foreign sportsmen' was Sir George Gore of Ireland. Sir George's income from the family estate was $200,000 a year and he spent a good deal of it hunting all over the world. The Irish nobleman had never hunted in the new world so early in 1854 he decided America would be the site of his next expedition.

"Sir George had heard a lot of tales about the American West and wanted to see for himself. He arrived at Fort Laramie in June of that year with his extensive entourage. The outfit included six wagons, 21 carts, 12 yoke of oxen, 112 horses, 14 dogs and 40 servants.

"Old frontiersmen, trappers and bluecoats at Laramie had never seen anything the like of this. Gore even had gold-plated buffalo guns that took two menservants to carry.

"Sir George hunted to his heart's content that summer, killing everything within range of his guns. Elk, deer, bear, antelope and bighorn sheep all fell before the onslaught. That fall he returned to Fort Laramie. So pleased was the Irish peer with his summer's activity in the American wilds that he had his wagons unhitched and announced that he would spend the winter at Laramie and hunt again next spring.

"Some of the Sioux nation came in from the north to trade and the chiefs were so impressed with this mighty white hunter with his fancy outfit and even fancier thunder sticks that they invited him to come north to hunt next summer.

"That winter Sir George met Jim Bridger. Bridger wasn't impressed by the nobleman's riches or manners and the two hit it off. Sir George decided 'Old Gabe' was just the man to take him north to Sioux country. The two spent a lot of time together that winter and you can bet Bridger bent the Irishman's ear with a lot of confidential and amazing information concerning the wilds of America.

"In the spring of 1955 [*sic*; correct date is 1855] the outfit followed up the North Platte and crossed the plains to the headwaters of the Powder River. Bridger then took the expedition down Powder River to its junction with the Yellowstone. They then turned west up the Yellowstone to the mouth of the Tongue River. Gore and Bridger set up their winter camp about 10 miles up the Tongue.

"This turned out to be a long winter and Sir George was getting tired of roughing it. He longed for the comforts of his mansion in Ireland. When spring rolled around again Sir George headed his train eastward. Even Bridger was impressed when the two years' killing was added up. The count showed the Irish peer had bagged 2,500 buffalo, 40 grizzly bear and more antelope and deer than anyone had cared to count. So ended the greatest single hunting expedition in Wyoming's history."

Elk on the Plains could be run down by mounted riders and shot at close range with pistols. When the animals were only found in mountainous terrain, the era of commercial hunting waned and that of sport hunting waxed. The popularity of hunting elk in the mountains continues to increase to this day.

The size of elk antlers varies, but the largest are never found on the Plains, but always at high altitudes in timber, according to Baillie-Grohman (1882). Perhaps those mountain bulls with huge antlers wintered at lower elevation and enjoyed 2 months or more of green-up as they returned to the high mountains during spring. Not only the size of antlers, but the challenge of the mountains themselves and their beauty makes hunting elk in the mountains a joy. Baillie-Grohman wrote that running elk on horseback on the upland Plains put them on a par with less sporting quarry, such as bison.

The elk adapts well. It is more a creature of different habitats than were his ancestors. The elk was seen on grassy prairies by explorers and early pioneers. A few elk

Early voyagers on the Saint Lawrence and upper Mississippi watersheds probably saw and shot bugling elk in situations similar to this. *Photo by Milo Burcham.*

still occupy such country, but only where breaks or other rough areas offer some escape cover. Most elk today are mountain animals, feeding in meadows and clearings (natural or manmade) and bedding in heavy forest cover. When hunted, elk often resort to almost impossibly dense, tangled timber, areas of downed trees, canyons and precipices. Despite their great size, elk in such cover are capable of rabbit-like concealment. A bull weighing nearly half a ton can move quietly in heavy timber—his antlers back on his withers. How a bull can carry a dozen tines quietly through dense lodgepole, where all but the best hunters sound like bulldozers, is hard to comprehend.

For many years after elk numbers hit bottom, about 1900, and slowly began to increase because of protection and reintroduction, elk hunting was mostly a near-wilderness experience involving tent camps and horses. The exceptions were mostly firing-line situations where elk were intercepted as they were driven from national parks or wilderness areas by autumn or early winter snows. Trophy hunting also was an exception—it was mostly fashionable among wealthy sport hunters guided and outfitted by nearby ranchers who had the needed horses and saw opportunity to make extra money each autumn.

Early in the 20th century, red deer were brought to Argentina from Austria, England, Germany and the Ukraine. Most were released on ranches in the foot hills of the Andes. They spread westward through low passes into Chile and eastward into the vast pampas. Unlike red deer on the degraded, treeless highlands of Scotland, those invading the treeless grasslands of Argentina are large animals with antlers to match. Hunting them in this area (*left*) must be reminiscent of 19th century elk hunts on the Great Plains (*right*). *Left photo by Harry Cornell. Right photo (1891) by L. A. Huffman; courtesy of the Montana State Historical Society.*

Until about the 1950s, most elk hunters would pass a tough old bull for a "blue cow" that provided prime eating. (Some barren, nonlactating cows have a bluish sheen to their coats, hence the appellation.) Even after World War II, many of those meat hunters would shoot the lead cow of a herd and then drop 5 to 10 of the milling animals for friends and family, or even strangers, to tag. During those times, some cattlemen discouraged—via lead—reinvasion of elk on their ranches.

As elk—and logging roads—proliferated, so did road and foot hunting. Anyone with a vehicle and rifle had a fair chance at bagging an elk. Thus, as elk increased, elk hunters increased at a greater rate. This necessitated more restrictions on hunters, usually allowing bull-only harvests at first. By the late 1980s and 1990s, few bulls— except spikes—remained in some herds, and many state wildlife agencies moved to protect bulls. Branch-antlered or brow-antlered regulations protected at least most yearlings and increased the chance of a few bulls reaching maturity. Five point-or-better regulations (often on tribal reservations or large ranches) protected another age class or two.

Hunters changed over the years. Although some still prefer to shoot a cow, most will take the largest bull they see. Thus, the present situation with drawings for cow permits in many areas, drawings for bulls in certain trophy areas, and regulations concerning sizes of bulls, etc., evolved and probably will continue to do so.

Many nonhunters, and especially antihunters, believe that hunters exhibit antlers primarily to impress others with their hunting prowess. This may be true of some hunters, but for most, the antlers represent beauty, a trophy experience, and the mysteries and sanctity of wild things and places. The appearance of this hermit's cabin along the River of No Return, in Idaho, is greatly enhanced by antlers and other memorabilia. Those symbols of wildness and wilderness linger in the eye-mind of beholders, just as they surely contribute to the occupant's satisfaction with his humble abode. *Photo by Bart W. O'Gara.*

Elk rifles need not be of especially large caliber, but projectiles with good sectional density and sturdy construction for deep penetration are important. Shot placement is crucial. Where these large animals are hit and projectile construction are more important than the projectile caliber they are hit with. *Photo by Bart W. O'Gara.*

Few animals can equal a large bull elk for trophy appeal or a fat cow for eating. Except from rutting and postrut bulls, elk venison has a pleasant flavor, much like grass-fed beef. The meat is not marbled with fat as is beef. Thus, after trimming away peripheral fat, elk venison is considered to be a more healthful diet than beef. However, among Germanic people of central Europe, who consume vast quantities of venison as chops, steaks and sausage, elk is not favored. Christian Oswald's family has imported game meat to Germany for seven generations. He says that elk resembles beef too closely, both in size of cuts and flavor, and beef is cheaper than venison. Red deer venison is considered excellent by Germans and, in the author's opinion, tastes much like mule deer or white-tailed deer from forested habitat. *Photo by Jay Higgins; courtesy of the U.S. Forest Service.*

Some ranchers now make considerable income from elk hunters. Large bulls generally are more common on private land than on public land, and out-of-state hunters often book with ranchers. Hunting there may be with horses, but generally involves four-wheel drive pickups, downhill foot hunting from ranch or logging roads and small drives.

Because many nimrods now can hunt elk, generalizing about hunting techniques is difficult. Firing-line hunting generally has been eliminated by limited entry drawings and staggering the periods when individuals can hunt. Horseback hunts from tented camps still are popular with guided hunters and those who own horses. Such hunts and "drop camp" hunts are arguably the most rewarding experiences available to today's elk hunter. Most local hunters hunt on foot.

Lyon and Burcham (1998) examined behavior and movement patterns of elk hunters in an area of western Montana where logging roads were closed to motorized vehicles. They had hunters carry Global Positioning System (GPS) units to record locations at 15-second intervals during 99 hunting expeditions (50 different hunters) in 1993 to 1995. Each unit was carried in a backpack with the antenna protruding on a short cable. At the end of a hunting day, data were downloaded to a personal computer and converted to Universal Transverse Mercator (UTM) coordinates. Subsequent analysis within a global Geographic Information System (GIS) indicated time and motion budgets for hunter effort, and departure distances from roads and hunting camps. Hunter locations overlaid on other GIS layers estimated time spent in different vegetation types and topographic situations. Five archery hunts and 94 rifle hunts were recorded. Most hunting was on foot from a vehicle at a gated road or trailhead, but 15 hunts involved horses. Four hunters reached their hunting sites by bicycle and two by snowmobile. Nineteen hunters started from overnight camps.

Packing into the high country to hunt elk is strenuous when saddle horses have to double as pack horses until camp is established. However, few experiences are more rewarding, whether the hunt is successful or not in terms of elk harvested. *Photo courtesy of Bart W. O'Gara.*

A gentle but lively saddle horse can be the elk hunter's best friend. *Photo by Bart W. O'Gara.*

Hunters averaged 4.7 hours of actual "weapon-in-hand" hunting per hunt. Walking hunters spent an hour less per hunt than did those on horseback. The most experienced walking hunters (n = 11) spent 5.6 hours, and the least experienced (n = 8) spent 4.4 hours. The average distance traveled by hunters on foot was 5.9 miles (9.5 km), but the 10 most experienced hunters walked an average of 7.8 miles (12.6 km). Hunters on horseback averaged 10.4 miles (16.8 km). The sample was very small, but bicycle hunters averaged 11.2 miles (18.0 km) per hunt.

For the 93 hunts in which the maximum distance reached from a trailhead or other starting point could be

Late-season, back-country elk hunting in the Rockies is not for couch potatoes. Hunters, especially elderly ones, should exercise extensively and possibly have a physical checkup before such hunts. *Photo by Bart W. O'Gara.*

determined, the average was 1.6 miles (2.6 km); five walkers, five on horseback and one using a bicycle reached 2.8 miles (4.5 km). Hunters on foot traveled at an average speed of 121 feet (37 m) per minute, and those on horseback averaged 167 feet (51 m) per minute. The average change in elevation during a hunt was 1,004 feet (306 m), with a range of 108 to 2,648 feet (33–807 m).

The average slope on hunter routes was 21%, and hunters spent 60% of their time hunting areas less steep than those of the study area. Closed roads were numerous in the study area, and hunters with the least experience spent 40% of their hunting time on such roads. Even those with the most experience used roads 27% of the time. Elk hunters seemed to favor hunting in mature Douglas-fir, ponderosa pine and western larch timber and avoided lodgepole pine forests and open sagebrush and rangelands.

Management

"The first extant laws on hunting are Roman" (Whisker 1981:41). Hunting, then, as now, was an integral part of management, and management of game animals was primarily for or by hunting. Many early Roman military leaders were granted hunting privileges for service to the expanding Republic, and hunting in certain parks was reserved for the rich. Hunting was restricted in agricultural areas because hunting with horses and hounds could ruin crops and endanger farmers. Only large game was considered worthy of the warrior–hunters, therefore peasants were allowed to hunt small game.

Great Britain

Red deer legislation and management in Great Britain are examined extensively because they influenced the near extinction of elk in North America, as well as present management practices. The following regulations are from Whitehead (1980) unless otherwise stated.

English common law implicitly recognized game management and conservation, but the scarcity of game mitigated against universal hunting rights. Those rights were reserved for the warrior–nobility class, who could share or not share with the peasants. For all intents and purposes, the nobility were their own law in regard to the peasantry–serf class. Common law also recognized an obligation on the peasants to assist the nobility in hunting. They were required to serve as beaters, which involved considerable risk. Eventually, the law recognized at least minimal obligations of the nobility to provide support for those injured and for the families of those killed in the chase (Whisker 1981).

Before the 11th century, red deer were hunted throughout Britain by commoners. Gradually, as forests were cleared for agriculture, red deer became less important as food. In 1016, King Canute issued the *Charta de Foresta,* and forest officers, called verderers, were appointed to enforce laws within royal forests (lands to which kings claimed ownership—not necessarily wooded areas). When offenses were committed therein, punishment usually was a fine or disfigurement. Any subsequent offenses would incur the death penalty.

The *Charta de Foresta* forbade any mean person to keep a greyhound. If a free man wanted to keep a greyhound, he had to live at least 10 miles (16 km) from the boundary of any forest. If the distance was less than that, tendons in the dog's legs had to be cut to prevent it from chasing deer.

For about the following 30 years, forest laws remained virtually unchanged. During that time, a man was permitted to take deer on his own land, provided he did not trespass in the royal forests. However, following the Norman Conquest, this changed. During his reign from 1066 to 1087, William the Conqueror laid claim to large areas. His following three descendants also gradually acquired vast expanses of land, claiming exclusive hunting rights. Harsh hunting laws did much to estrange these monarchs from their subjects. The penalty for hunting in a royal forest was death. The penalty for killing a royal hound was blindness, with the aid of a red hot poker. William I even put to death the owner of a dog that bit a deer.

Predatory animals were long persecuted by "elite" hunters (i.e., nobility). King Edgar (959 to 979) imposed an annual tax on the Welsh of 300 wolf skins per year. This was primarily to destroy wolves and save deer for the nobility (Whisker 1981).

In 1216, King Henry III came to the throne and ended the practice of requisitioning land for hunting privileges. He also granted a *Charta Foresta,* in 1224, requiring that all lands requisitioned by King Richard and King John immediately be freed from forest laws. The death penalty no longer was used to punish those found guilty of killing a royal stag. Instead, offenders were required to pay a fine. If they had no money, they were imprisoned for a year and a day. However, if an archbishop, earl or baron were passing through a royal forest, they were entitled to kill one or two deer, provided the verderer was present.

Although forests were owned by the monarchy, subjects had some rights over certain defined tracts of land. These tracts were called chases, purlieus and warrens. A chase was held by a subject who acquired the land through a royal grant. Chases usually were given to a subject when it was considered to have lost many of the attributes of a forest. Offenses committed therein, such as illegally taking deer, were punishable by common law only, not forest regulations. A purlieu was a tract of land adjoining a forest, after once having been a part of the forest. Those who had freehold lands (an estate held by its owners and heirs forever) within a purlieu were permitted to keep greyhounds, provided that their freeholding's yearly value was 40 shillings. A freeholder then was able to chase deer toward the royal forests adjoining the purlieu, but only allowed to enter the forest if his dogs were in pursuit of deer.

Warrens were tracts set aside for the exclusive hunting privileges of the public. Special licenses or grants were issued by the king to private individuals. Occasionally, the public right was restricted if a favorite stag of the king happened to wander out of the royal forest. Notices were posted in various places, forbidding subjects to hunt until the stag was located. In Scotland, no such tracts existed. Hunting privileges were granted to landowners, rather than assigned to tracts of land.

King Edward I, who ruled from 1272 to 1307, probably was the first to declare a formal hunting season for red deer. Stags were hunted from June 24 to September 14. Hinds were hunted from September 14 to February 2. In addition, King Edward proclaimed that from June 9 to July 9, forests were to be undisturbed so females could raise their young in peace.

During Richard II's reign (1377–1399), many laws were passed designed to keep deer hunting as the sole privilege of landowners. A qualification act was passed, allowing only those of a certain social rank or income to hunt. For the next 400 years, only 50 Acts of Parliament were passed concerning the possession, killing and selling of game. Many of these laws dealt with privileged hunter qualification.

In 1541, a statute was passed regarding the ownership and use of guns and crossbows. It stated, specifically, where and on which animals certain weapons could be used. In 1603, during the reign of James I, taking of deer still was a privilege for those who qualified. A qualifying man was one who had an inheritance of £10, or more per year, a lease for life worth £30, or more per year, worth of £200, in goods, or the son of a baron, knight or esquire.

During the 17th century, poaching became common, and contemporary laws were ineffective. Poaching was punishable by imprisonment, unless the poacher paid 40 shillings to the poor of the area from which the deer was taken. When a member of a poaching fraternity was caught and fined, his fellow members each could make a small monetary contribution to save him. Thus, in 1692, An Act for the More Effectual Discovery and Punishment of Deer-stealers was passed. This act required all those assisting in an illegal kill to pay £20, plus an additional £30, for each deer taken. Poaching continued, however, and punishment grew harsher. During the reign of George I (1714–1727), an act was passed that changed the penalty for deer poaching from a fine of £30, to 7 years of imprisonment or indentureship on one of His Majesty's plantations in America. Another act, passed in 1723, dictated that anyone found with blackened face or in any way disguised in a forest, park or ground where deer were kept, was liable to suffer death without clergy. Man traps—leghold traps, which were 6 feet (183 cm) in length—were used toward the latter part of the 18th century to deter poachers. Poachers strapped wooden slats to their legs to prevent injuries, but legs sometimes were broken.

During the 19th century, three major acts were passed. The chief interest in forests was for timber production for the Royal Navy. Also, people claimed that deer were becoming too numerous, causing considerable damage to crops. In 1851, the Deer Removal Act provided for the total removal of all deer from the forests of England. Although the goal was never achieved, deer were slaughtered for 2 years by any means possible. At first, they were shot with relative ease, but as their numbers dwindled, they had to be driven with dogs into large nets, then shot (Whitehead 1964).

In 1860, the Game Licenses Act was passed and applied to everyone in the United Kingdom except the royal family and her majesty's gamekeeper. The New Forest Act of 1877 did much to curtail the powers of the crown. This act provided commoners with the right to elect forest verderers from among those who owned at least 74 acres (30 ha) to which commoners had rights. Verderers had all the powers of a summary court, so this was beneficial to the commoners. They could elect verderers who would manage forests and deer to satisfy their interests.

Compared with England, Scotland had virtually no royal forests, and the wilder highlands were not so closely guarded until the mid-18th century, when stalking became popular (MacNally 1970). There, land belonged to a clan or to the chieftain of a clan, rather than to the monarchy (Chalmers 1935). Restrictive game laws did not exist within clans, and game had no commercial value other than for food (Cameron 1923). In 1862, a court decision was made regarding the stalking and ownership of deer in Scotland. Although the right to hunt was never exclusive to the crown, proprietors were officially given the right to breed and protect deer on their own land.

During the 19th century, deer stalking grew in popularity. Gradually, the land was cleared of sheep in favor of red deer (Hart-Davis 1978). In the highlands, much land was bought by wealthy people. Hardwood forests of oak, ash and birch were planted (Cameron 1923), and heather was burnt in small patches to create favorable deer grazing and red grouse habitat (Chalmers 1935). Ground was cleared for sporting lodges. Professional stalkers were hired to manage red deer and, in 1860, selling wild game became legal. Deer forests acquired a high commercial value, which helped to bring about a collapse in the sheep industry.

The built-in "inefficiencies" of red deer stalking and deer meat production as products of the land were discussed by Gordon (1910:371–372). "But deer-stalking is a terribly expensive pastime. . . . It has often been fiercely argued by political agitators and others that the preservation of deer was a curse to Scotland and an injustice to the people, but in my humble opinion it has helped in a great measure the prosperity of that country. Where the deer roam on the mountain heights of Perthshire, Rossshire, Inverness-shire, and Aberdeenshire, in nearly every instance nothing could exist but sheep. This at first sight looks bad; sheep are doubtless good for human wants, whilst venison is certainly a luxury. But which brings the most money to a district, sheep or deer? Ten thousand acres of sheep ground can be attended to by one shepherd and two collie dogs. The shepherd lives principally on porridge, washed down occasionally with 'mountain dew'; the same tract of deer–forest means instantly money flowing into the district. There must be stalkers, gillies, ponies, stores and all the necessaries for a rich man's establishment. And Scotland, or at any rate the mountains and glens of Scotland, and the villages and people therein, thrive and exist well, because these great game farms bring money to them."

Management of wild red deer in Scotland has been a contentious issue for some 200 years. Early attention focused on the relationship between agriculture and management of red deer for sport. Plantation forestry expanded following establishment of a Forestry Commission in 1919, and the red deer conflict took on another dimension. Between 1872 and 1954, seven government-appointed enquiries addressed the issues. Relevant legislation was enacted in 1948 with passage of the Agriculture (Scotland) Act, which granted occupiers the right to kill deer marauding on enclosed land. The Deer (Scotland) Act of 1959, as amended, still provides the basic framework for management of red deer. It established closed seasons, increased penalties for poaching and The Red Deer Commission. From its inception, the Commission has argued for a reduction in the red deer population. However, from 1900 to 1989, red deer numbers doubled from about 150,000 to 300,000. Harvests were increased from about 24,000 in 1973 to 70,000 in 1993 and, for the first time, the cull of females approximately equaled annual recruitment. It is not clear to what extent the wild red deer population is approaching carrying capacity of its habitat, but individuals are not

A stalker (*at left*) and a gillie (*on the right*) generally accompany each rifle (hunter; *center*) on the hill in Scotland. Customarily, the rifle (actual) is not uncased and loaded until the quarry has been glassed and the stalk begins. The stalker pictured here had about 50 "trashy" stags and 250 hinds to shoot before the season was over. After the day's hunt, the feet and heads are removed, and a call to the local butcher shop brings a refrigerator truck to pick up the carcasses. Most of them are shipped directly to Germany, where little is wasted. Hides go to tanneries and, except for the choice cuts, much of the meat goes to sausage makers. *Photo by Phil Wright.*

achieving their full potential in growth or reproductive output (see Scottish Natural Heritage Policy Paper 1994).

Forest owners in Scotland never seem to have embraced scientific management of their animals. Tradition seems to be the prime concern. However, the animals were managed by great grandfather, so they will be managed today. Although the best stags were not harvested, stags to be harvested for meat on forests where I stalked were not shot until they were 10 years old or older. Young stags were never culled, and the vegetation showed obvious signs of overuse. Watson (1990:22) observed that, "Some have suggested that, within the deer count areas, present populations may be as much as twice the sustainable ecological carrying capacity of the ground . . . it is the plague of Red Deer that is the real cause of concern."

"One factor has remained constant in the Highland deer forests, the standard of stalking and the impeccable behavior of that small group of professional stalkers. These men have an immense store of knowledge of the Highland environment and without their help it would be much more difficult to manage and conserve the lovely world of deer and

This gillie had been pulling red deer off the hill since he was 14 years old. He said it was hard work but paid better than anything else available to him. He also indicated that he liked being in the country. *Photo by Bart W. O'Gara.*

Introductions to promote large antlers and novel varieties have destroyed much of the genetic integrity of red deer in Britain and Ireland. Red deer are numerous in the historic range of this subspecies, but native deer are endangered because of crossbreeding with non-native red deer and hybridization with elk and sika deer. Unlike the red deer of Scotland, those in England enjoy good thermal cover and nutritious forage. *Photo by Bart W. O'Gara.*

Although Scottish red deer stalking is a famous sport, the bald mountains provide poor thermal cover, and the numerous deer overuse preferred vegetation. The animals are small and often carry antlers with only three or four points per side. Even on the antlers of prime-aged animals, bez tines and crowns are the exception. Compare this photo with the one at lower left of a similarly aged animal. *Photo by Bart W. O'Gara.*

the bare unenclosed hills." So wrote Fraser Darling (1964:ix), an American who conducted a seminal behavioral study of red deer in Scotland during the 1930s and applied his findings to the conservation and management of the species.

Germany

With the beginning and expansion of princely ownership of forests in Germany, hunting laws appeared during the early Middle Ages. The concept of *forestis* appeared for the first time in a parchment from 648 AD, for the royal forests of the Ardennes. The order was made by the Frankish King Dagobert, and belongs to the oldest hunting laws of Europe.

By the early 19th century, royal hunting prerogatives had virtually disappeared, and the title of much of the land, previously controlled by feudal lords, passed to common people. By 1848, hunting rights became connected to real estate titles, and landowners were entitled to hunt on their own property. Soon, uncontrolled hunting seriously reduced red deer populations—almost to a point of extirpation. Fortunately, during the early part of the 20th century, due to sound legislation, Germany's stock of game was restored (Whitehead 1982).

At that time, poachers sometimes were shot on sight. Schönberg (1910:148) noted, "Thirty years ago, when it was the custom to punish a gamekeeper for manslaughter, if he could not prove that he had been fired at first, deaths were frequent. Of late years, the keeper generally gets off free, if his adversary is hit in front and is known to be a poacher: hence matters have improved greatly." However, wealth and leisure time—spawned by the industrial revolution—increased the demand for red deer hunting. This, in turn, resulted in overstocking and deteriorating food supplies, and German deer decreased in body and antler size, as had those in Scotland under the same influences. The Germans resorted to winter feeding with high-protein forage, selective harvests (sparing the best stags until after their breeding years), culling of excess females and all small, weak animals, and introductions of large deer from Hungary or Russia. The result generally has been large, crossbred deer.

Today, the Federal Hunting Law defines hunting rights, open seasons, minimum size of hunting areas, licensing requirements, etc., but the *Länder* (states) are able to impose their own regulations within this framework to suit their own particular needs. Hunting land in Germany is divided into areas averaging 1,000 to 2,000 acres (405–809 ha) called *Revieres*. The right to hunt deer in these areas can be owned or leased by federal or state agencies, individuals, syndicates or communities. Whoever owns or leases hunting property is automatically the holder of the hunting rights. All holders are bound by law to manage and conserve the game so that a reasonable balance is maintained between available feed, cover and crop damage. This is called the *Abschussplan* (shooting plan). To make this plan, the holder of hunting rights must take an annual census—including sex ratios and age classifications—of all cloven-hoofed game except boar on his shooting ground. From this, a shooting plan will be prepared and submitted to a county hunting authority for approval. The shooting plan will indicate the number of deer, including the class of trophy, to be culled. The hunting authority then will evaluate the plans and, in the light of crop damage and any other factors that might have occurred during the previous year, approve or amend accordingly. Holders of hunting rights are required to own or have available a dog capable of searching for wounded game. Many breeds of hunting dogs are used for this purpose. For deer, however, bloodhounds are most popular (Whitehead 1982).

Normally, according to German practice, if a deer is shot in one Revier, but escapes to die on a neighboring Revier, the hunter is not entitled to leave his ground to take possession, but must mark the point where the deer crossed the boundary and, as soon as possible, inform the holder of the hunting rights of the area in question. A number of estates, however, have an agreement that, if a wounded deer is visible on a neighbor's ground, the animal may be given a finishing shot and, although it must then be gralloched (stomach removed), under no circumstances may the carcass be removed.

Other European Countries

Hunters and landowners are the primary practitioners of game management in much of Europe, not only of hunting, but also of conservation and improvement of game habitat, although they must function in accordance with government oversight regulations. Effective deer predators generally have been eliminated; thus, hunting is essential for maintaining population levels in balance with the available habitat and tolerance for crop and forest damage. During the early 1990s, most western European hunting grounds were privately owned, but hunting rights often were leased to hunters or hunting associations. Hunting rights in eastern Europe were leased by governments; countries were divided into units, and each unit was managed by a hunting association under a game management plan. However, several large areas are under communal ownerships or administered by government. Government owns more than 75% of the forests in Ireland and 66% of those in Greece. In Italy, hunting is open to anyone. In Switzerland, hunting is organized by a central administration, but rules applying to each Canton are different (Myrberget 1991).

Hunting is deeply ingrained in France, where 2 million people buy permits each year for various game. Par force hunting takes few animals, but some 10,000 men and women from all over Europe mount up each season to chase red deer through 2 million acres (809,400 ha) of forest scattered across France (Rosenblum 1998). Even more come to watch what has become a spectator sport. Parents and children cruise forest roads in automobiles or chase behind riders on bicycles or afoot to catch a glimpse of the action. Perhaps more hours of recreation are realized for each deer killed in this manner than in any other type of deer hunting.

"If during the last hundred years, the stock of red deer has multiplied tenfold in Central Europe through careful conservation, too great a density of game has already been observed in some reservations. Heavy investment is required today to guarantee the proper management of game, so that animals living in the wild may continue to do so. . . . Game and hunting have moved, with all their ancient traditions and history, into the field of economics" (Hobusch 1980:263).

About 8 million people in Europe, outside the former Soviet Union, are hunters. This implies that 1.6% of the population hunts—about 4.1 per square mile (1.61 km²). Most of them are men. Italy has the highest density of hunters, and Denmark, France, Greece, Spain, Portugal and Great Britain have relatively high hunter densities. Eastern Europe and Finnoscandia have relatively low numbers. About 250,000 red deer are killed annually in Europe. Hunting is of great socioeconomic significance; hunters often redistribute economic resources from densely populated areas to rural districts. Most meat is sold on the international market and represents considerable profit in foreign money (Myrberget 1991).

Early in the 20th century, most of the best red deer shooting areas of Norway were leased by Englishmen. The deer were found mostly on islands off the coast (Pottinger 1910). Currently, visiting hunters must obtain a license, but it does not confer the right to hunt anywhere. Permission to hunt must be obtained from landowners—usually by lease. An effort is made to hold deer populations at about 2.6 per square mile (1/km²) (Whitehead 1982). Red deer hunting generally is conducted by hunting teams consisting of landowners or those that lease hunting rights from landowners, often through local rod and gun clubs. Research has indicated that red deer populations can sustain more hunting pressure, and the government and the Norwegian Association of Hunters and Anglers are working to increase hunter access on private land to increase the harvest levels (S. Brainerd personal communication:1997). Dogs seldom are used for hunting red deer in Norway, in sharp contrast to moose and roe deer hunting. However, the game law requires that hunters have access to dogs to track wounded animals.

According to Poland's Constitution, conservation of the natural environment is a duty and one of the fundamental functions of the state (Pietrzak 1991). Governmental agencies oversee wildlife management, but hunting in Poland is organized by the Polish Hunting Association, a social organization with a membership of more than 60,000 hunters in about 2,400 clubs during the early 1980s. Hunting districts, which varied in size from about 7,413 to 24,710 acres (3,000–10,000 ha) were leased to the clubs for 10-year periods. These clubs were responsible for financing and managing wildlife. They also organized, through the Polish Travel Bureau, hunting by foreign hunters (Whitehead 1982). Game animals in the wild are the property of the state;

Landowners in Norway receive permits for the red deer to be shot on their land. Some sell the permits for approximately the price of the meat. Others shoot the deer themselves and sell the carcasses to a butcher. Antlers generally are saved from all the stags that are shot, even if they are only to be displayed in a barn, as here. *Photo by Bart W. O'Gara.*

however, although landowners do not possess game, they share in the profits from hunting licenses (Pietrzak 1991). The population of big game in Poland increased remarkably during the 1980s (Sikorski 1991).

Bemoaning the reduction in numbers of game animals and extirpation of some in Switzerland by the beginning of the 20th century, Pitard (1910:335) observed: "The fact is democratic governments do not present auspicious conditions for the maintenance of game." He noted, however, that game laws were bringing about improvements, and: "The stag, which seemed to have deserted our country, has returned to it and prospers, particularly in the Jura" (Pitard 1910:335).

Today, two hunting systems exist in different districts of Switzerland. One is similar to that in Germany and is called *Revierkantone*. The other—called *Patenkantone*, which means people's hunting—requires a test of hunting knowledge before acquiring a license. The license specifies the kind and amount of game that can be taken. The average size of a Patenkantone is about 523,858 acres (212,000 ha), where the hunting is available for anyone. Federal reserves, where no shooting is allowed, are scattered among the Patenkantone to conserve wildlife. A Revierkantone generally is about half as large, and cities or villages lease them for 8 years at a time. Specified groups of hunters may shoot and hunt on them (Whitehead 1982).

Red deer apparently have been extirpated in Albania. They also were extirpated in Greece during the 1920s to 1930s, but were reintroduced from Bavaria. As of 1998, some 100 to 200 head roamed the Parnitha Mountains about 19 miles (30 km) north of Athens. A few wild red deer also occur in the Rhodopi Mountains near the Bulgarian border. In Bulgaria and the former Yugoslavian Republics, red deer generally are artificially fed, at least during winter. They are managed to produce large trophies for international hunters. Some are in fenced hunting reserves (G. Giannatos personal communication:1998).

With the rise of the Soviet Union, all land was nationalized during 1918 and, in the first paragraph of the new law, it was stated that private property—land, water and forest, as well as the fauna inhabiting it—is abolished, to be administered and controlled by the state. In a new decree concerning closed seasons and possession of hunting weapons, signed in 1920, every citizen of age was accorded the right to join a hunting society and get a hunting permit after passing a test in biology, knowledge of hunting and nature conservation. Big game especially increased under strict Soviet regulations. By 1959, 2.5 million hunters pursued their sport over an area of some 494 million acres (200 million ha). Soviets hunted primarily for meat, but some were trophy hunters (Hobusch 1980).

Every republic of the former USSR had a board of game management with which regional boards were affiliated. These boards had supervisory and management functions (Sokolov and Baskin 1991). Those functions involved collecting information on population dynamics, approval of annual harvest quotas, hunting regulations and law enforcement. Since the collapse of the Soviet Union, most countries have maintained this general structure; however, law enforcement has weakened, and funds for management have been reduced.

During recent centuries, exploitation has exterminated only one European animal—the great auk. Opposition to hunting is increasing, especially in Italy. There, hunter densities are high, regulations generally are ignored, active game management tactics are lacking and small birds are regarded as game (Myrberget 1991). As Scheibler (1910:212) observed: "Everybody likes to walk through the fields carrying a gun, even with the poor chance of shooting no more than a wretched little sparrow." Growing opposition also exists in Nordic countries, where hunting sometimes is perceived as a hinderance to other recreational activities. Ethical and moral objections are most prevalent among women. Obligatory hunting examinations have been introduced in many countries, partly to decrease opposition to

hunting and partly because they are deemed beneficial to hunters themselves. Examinations include practical exercises, as well as educational programs designed to broaden hunters' understanding of the ecological role of hunting and game management (Myrberget 1991).

China

"The rule of law, inherited from the Romans, is so central to Western Civilization that most of us take it for granted. . . . Another great empire, China, arranged things precisely the opposite of the Roman way. Confucius and his disciples down through the centuries distrusted written laws. . . . Even today the concept of written law and written contract is fairly weak in China" (Reid 1997:64).

In the ancient order of Chinese civilization, wildlife was valued for recreation, food and medicine. Royalty maintained large hunting reserves that protected deer and their habitats. Deer farming has a long history; wild meat was considered extremely nutritious and animal parts, especially of deer, were sought for traditional Chinese medicines. The environment was seen predominantly as a storehouse of riches to be harnessed for human benefit—a source of free goods and marketable commodities (Smil 1984). Peasants harvested wildlife (often illegally) in any way they could. In areas of high human populations, overharvest and loss of habitat eliminated most of the larger wildlife species. Ethnic minorities in less populated areas hunted for centuries, harvesting deer for food and medicine, but no concerted wildlife management programs were developed, either by tribal people or provincial governments, to protect wildlife and promote sustained yield use as human populations increased. In other Asian countries, many royal hunting reserves were converted to national parks during the 20th century. This did not happen in China. As feudal lords fell, wildlife was killed by the peasants, and the land generally was put under cultivation, not a surprising situation considering that China has only 5% of the world's arable land and nearly one fourth of its people.

With a huge and expanding human population, and increasing demands for uses of limited arable land, China faces serious environmental challenges. Any conservation plan must take the aspirations of local people into account; survival of wildlife ultimately depends on those people. China's more than 1.2 billion people create a tremendous market for food and medicines derived from wildlife, but no workable wildlife management program has evolved to protect wildlife and promote sustained yield use.

The Japanese invasion and civil war occupied China at the time wildlife management systems were rapidly evolving in western civilizations. Wars can be destructive of wildlife, but the areas involved generally are limited. However, a government at war puts emphasis on production of war machines and food, not conservation.

Since 1949, industrial growth and energy development have enjoyed high priorities, while the environment was disregarded. When Western and some Third World countries were developing wildlife management as an art/science, isolationism prevented Chinese colleges and universities from keeping up with world trends (He 1991). In 1970, the Chinese government established goals to conserve wildlife; however, contradictions between local needs and national policies weakened conservation efforts. Regulations promulgated in the cities accomplished little in the country.

Local people ordinarily are not allowed to hunt big game in China. Commercial hunting for export of meat prevailed during the 1980s, and poaching for meat and medicine is common. If the local people were allowed to hunt for their own needs (not commercial), scientific management could be pursued to the benefit of local people and wildlife (Dulan Bureau of Agriculture and Animal Husbandry 1987).

China designated its first nature reserve in 1956. By 1986, 333 reserves had been set aside (Li and Zhao 1989). This is encouraging, but, at present, most reserves are paper tigers affording little or no protection to wildlife. Indeed, on some where game guards were provided, the guards were the worst poachers because they had the best weapons. Native people should be given first consideration in use of wildlife, but they also should be educated in sustained yield use of wildlife and its habitats, and values of healthy wildlife populations.

Many areas are densely populated, leaving little habitat for wildlife. Habitat loss is less serious in lightly populated areas, but losses are accelerating. With bans on hunting, wildlife is not valued, and poaching and overexploitation are tolerated. The Ministry of Forestry and Environmental Protection Bureau have commitments to wildlife conservation, but their efforts are impeded by financial problems, lack of trained personnel and lack of cooperation with other agencies. China's environmental problems seem overwhelming, but slow progress in conservation should not reflect negatively on the country's well-meaning environmental scientists, policymakers or administrators. The reasons for present environmental problems are rooted in history and poverty.

During recent years, international hunting in China has provided wildlife agencies with a way of raising funds for wildlife conservation programs (Liu 1995). As pointed out by Child (1990), trophy hunting is a lightly consumptive use of wildlife, killing and removing a small proportion of animals from the population. The "product" sold really is the experience of tracking and killing animals, the services that go with this, and the prestige of taking home the trophy.

This high value means that a trophy-quality animal is worth a great deal more if sold to a sport hunter than if harvested for its meat and hide. In terms of impact on the environment, trophy hunting may be less disruptive than game viewing because it involves far fewer people and vehicles, and the quality of the environment has to be maintained both for aesthetic reasons and to ensure that a wide range of high-quality trophy animals is available (Harris 1995). Trophy hunting is easily managed by local communities because benefits are easily extracted and controlled.

Conservation benefits derived from the Dulan International Hunting Program include: local residents in the Reserve becoming interested in wildlife protection programs and removing nonlocal poaching by patrolling regularly; improving the habitat for wild ungulates through restricted grazing activities; and providing a practical way of raising funds for wildlife conservation, as a large portion of the income from this program is allocated directly or indirectly to wildlife conservation. Since establishment of the Dulan International Hunting Reserve, the wildlife agencies, local people and the local government have benefitted (Liu 1995). Before the hunting program began, nonlocal poaching was nearly uncontrollable on a provincial scale, but Liu (1993) found improvement within the hunting area because of the involvement of local people in wildlife protection activities. When I visited Dulan in 1986 *before* it became an International Hunting Area, I saw Han Chinese and Peoples Liberation Army soldiers poaching almost every day I was in the field. Heads of many recently butchered blue sheep, and a few white-lipped deer and argali, were seen. Liu worked in the area during 1991 and 1992, *after* it became an International Hunting Area, and did not see poachers.

The Ministry of Forestry and the provincial wildlife agencies divided hunting income as follows. The agency that benefitted most was Dulan Agriculture and Animal Husbandry Bureau, an association of local people in two small villages where the hunting occurred. That Bureau received 45% of the gross hunting income. Second was the Qinghai Wildlife Management and Protection Bureau, which received 30% of the income. More than 65% of the hunting income was profit (Liu 1993).

International sport hunting has promoted local involvement in wildlife conservation and management in China. Incentives, cultural or economic, have encouraged local people to cooperate with wildlife managers. Sport hunting in Qinghai, as in other Asian countries, has brought in foreign currency, produced employment for local people and increased game populations for subsistence hunting (O'Gara and Li 1988).

Unfortunately, many officials in Europe and the United States do not understand the value of international hunting related to conservation in China. Trophies of the most desirable species (argali, Tibetan antelope and wild yak) cannot be imported to most western countries. Consequently, money for protection of those species, as well as the will of local people, is insufficient to save them in many areas. Well-meaning legislation to protect these magnificent animals presently is the greatest threat to their survival. Without a hunting program, little money is available for enforcing game laws except in parks. Parks are of local value but, even if properly protected, they tend to create small "island" populations of wildlife. The same can be said of sport hunting if it remains only an international program. Local people throughout China should be allowed equal but limited licenses to harvest or otherwise profit from big game so that management programs are instituted over large areas. When people develop a proprietary interest in a wildlife population, they resent others harvesting more than a fair share and will cooperate to maintain viable populations. Hunting programs are a means to an end, enabling animals to be harvested at a reasonable rate, while maintaining the animals themselves (O'Gara 1988). To be successful, any management program must provide a return for local people.

At present, subsistence hunting is illegal, but it should be legalized and appropriately managed. Without managed hunting, little money will be available for enforcing game laws except in a few national parks. A combination of parks, reserves, international hunting areas and, especially, a managed hunting program for local people is needed. When local people have a reason to support wildlife conservation, wildlife will be assured protection and consideration. If this does not happen soon and nonlocal poaching is not checked, valuable game species may be eliminated from the wild in China. Wildlife may become mostly a memory in the 21st century.

North America

"Unjustifiable as the rapid extinction of the red man will appear to our grandchildren, the extermination of the animals that dwelt on his plains, that roamed his forests, or that filled his rivers, must seem even less excusable, for, in their case, protection should have been as possible, as in civilized communities the enforcement of laws protecting human life. But the frontiersman, as one knew him in those days, was not an ordinary personage.

"In his fierce and utterly selfish attack on Nature, he waged a merciless war the like of which no country has ever seen, for in days of older conquests the scientific means of wreaking destruction in such a wholesale manner were lacking" (Baillie-Grohman 1900:28–29).

According to Regelin (1991:55): "The history of wildlife management in North America comprises four rather distinct areas: the Era of Abundance from the first European settlement until 1850, the Era of Exploitation from 1850 to 1900, and the Era of Conservation Awareness from 1900 to 1935. Since 1935, we have been in the Era of Scientific Wildlife Management" (see also Trefethen 1975, McCabe and McCabe 1984). Regelin's eras of abundance and exploitation seem appropriate for western North America, but somewhat late for the eastern portion of the continent (see Chapter 2).

An estimated 10 million elk roamed North America before the arrival of Europeans. By 1922, habitat loss and unregulated hunting reduced elk to about 90,000 head (Seton 1953). By the mid-1970s, hunters were taking more elk annually than existed in 1922. By 1995, the North American elk population had reached nearly 1 million (Bunnell 1997). Thus, elk management in North America had a dismal beginning, but has entered a golden era that should continue.

Frontiersmen and settlers from Europe generally had received no benefits from the game in the Old World, where the animals had damaged their crops but could only be hunted by the gentry. Those early Americans had little concept of wildlife conservation; indeed, some probably harbored resentment for animals that had complicated their lives. In America, animals on open land could be killed by anyone, and nearly everyone wanted their share, or more, before someone else got it. Mainly in the van of settlement, valuable species were relentlessly and continuously exploited, primarily for hides and meat, and nearly to the point of extinction.

Hunting and management of game animals in Great Britain influenced those practices in Canada and the United States. As previously noted, many colonists were commoners from England, where they had been denied the privilege of hunting—some even had been sent to the New World as punishment for hunting in the king's forest.

"Despite the devastating effects of market hunting on America's wildlife, it was hunters, albeit the recreational sort, who eventually helped create the basis for modern wildlife conservation and protection. . . . The American sport hunter had, in many respects, more in common with the European gentleman hunter than his frontier countrymen" (Kellert 1996:68).

Before 1842, wildlife was considered to be the property of the landowner on whose land it was found, a carryover of English common law. The first important decision concerning wildlife was made in 1842 with *Martin v. Waddell*, wherein Chief Justice Taney decided that the public's right to fish superseded a landowner's claim of personal property. This decision gave birth to the doctrine of public trust, which apparently had not existed in England at the time of the American Revolution. Nevertheless, it now is firmly established in American law (Bean 1978:280).

The next decision important to understanding federal and state wildlife law was *Geer v. Connecticut* in 1896. In this case, a Connecticut man, Edgar Geer, had legally killed game birds within Connecticut, but was accused of possessing them with the intent of illegally shipping them out of the state. Chief Justice White decided that the states had the "right to control and regulate the common property in game," which right was to be exercised "as a trust for the benefit of the people." This case provided the basis for the legal doctrine of states' rights to regulate the use of wildlife within their borders (Bean 1978:280–281).

Thus, federal wildlife regulation before 1900 was limited in scope, but the principles of public trust and of a state's right to regulate the wildlife within its borders had been established. Moreover, there was a steady growth of wildlife legislation at the state level. The appearance of a new monthly newspaper, the *American Sportsman,* in 1871 marked an environmental watershed in U.S. history. It was the country's first periodical to make hunting, fishing, natural history and conservation its primary concerns. Although systematic, commercial exploitation of animal life was everywhere evident, the minority of Americans—who already looked to British "gentlemen" for examples of "correct" manners of hunting—were enthusiastic about the new newspaper. The same economic developments that made wildlife more accessible to market hunters also brought it closer to sportsmen. Indeed, major reasons for the rapid increase of the latter included improvements in transportation and equipment (Reiger 1986). By 1880, some form of game or fish legislation had been passed in every state or territory (Bean 1978).

Intrinsic to the 19th-century concept of game and fish laws was the belief that fish and wildlife were to be preserved as a food supply. Thus, neither aesthetics nor ethics, as they were to emerge in the 20th century, played a part. During the 20th century, the national mood changed. Nash (1968:37) described emergence of "The Progressive Conservation Crusade" of that time as basically the "ending of the frontier," when the "abundance, opportunity, and distinctiveness of the New World" were disappearing; he stated that "The idea of 'ripeness' is useful: Americans were *ready* to be concerned about their environment." This concern was spurred by the decline of wildlife. In addition, the nation's new mood of conservation was focused and directed by her outspoken and energetic new leader, Theodore Roosevelt. Although Roosevelt's Conference of Governors did not meet at the White House until 1908, the president's conservation policies and his words had

been affecting the country since he assumed the presidency in 1901.

Rules establishing public ownership of wildlife apparently were based on Roman legal traditions, which recognized wild animals as ownerless (*res nullius*) or as shared social possessions (Wolfe 1995). "According to Roman law animals in the wild were unprotected, and everyone, except slaves, could catch or kill them. Roman law considered property only that which was under a person's personal power and authority. Hence, an animal belonged to whoever caught or killed it" (Hobusch 1980:68). This concept had been superseded in much of Europe when royalty reserved hunting privileges for themselves.

Roman influence is pervasive in contemporary legal codes of Europe and North America. In the ongoing struggle between the common people of Rome (plebians or plebs) and the governing elites (patricians), the plebs favored written law over the all-too-human whims of their rulers. The first of those written codes—the Twelve Tables—came out in 450 BC. The Romans continued to issue legal codes for nearly a thousand years. The Revised Code, completed in 534 AD, has served as the foundation of western law ever since (Reid 1997).

When the founding fathers of the United States launched their bold experiment in democratic government, they used republican Rome as their model (Reid 1997). Thus, the comprehensive body of statute and case law left behind by the Romans helped to shape laws and thinking in North America. Early Americans drew parallels between their leaders and Roman nobels. A larger-than-life statue of George Washington in a toga and sandals still is on exhibit at The National Museum of American History.

Canada also followed the Roman tradition, and a socialist wildlife management system now is flourishing in freemarket societies with strong commitments to property rights. That such a system works—and it is the envy of wildlife managers throughout the world because it works so well—is a tribute to the dedication of wildlife managers and the tolerance of landowners.

Many elk herds of North America would not exist today were it not for animals translocated from Yellowstone National Park (see Chapter 14). The Park protected elk at a time when they were being overexploited and reduced to exceedingly low numbers throughout the West. More than 13,500 elk were shipped from Yellowstone Park during 1892 to 1967 for restocking public and private lands, as well as to zoos. Those elk went to 38 states, the District of Columbia, 2 Canadian provinces, Mexico and Argentina (Robbins et al. 1982). Many Yellowstone elk also were captured north and south of the Park for translocation. However, just as conservation measures are not popular today with those who anticipate damage to their self interests, the proposal to establish the park was not a popular one in the Wyoming Territory. The Territorial Legislative Assembly sent the following joint resolution to the National Congress in 1884 (Blair 1987:19–20).

"'Whereas, By dispatches from Washington it appears that there is urgent necessity of prompt measures to prevent the loss of the jurisdiction over the Yellowstone National Park; and,

"'Whereas, It is considered that such a loss would be an irreparable one to our Territory and an unmerited humiliation to our people. . . .'

"Another joint memorial pleaded, 'That a joint committee of both houses of the Eighth Legislative Assembly, to be composed of two members of the Council and three members of the House of Representatives, be appointed to prepare suitable legislation for the government of the Yellowstone National Park. . . .'

"Still another memorial read: 'Your memorialists therefore earnestly protest against the transfer of any portion of the park within our limits to any other jurisdiction, as our people would universally regard such action as a humiliation to a prosperous and loyal people, who have manifested their desire to aid the government to preserve and keep intact forever this royal spot within our limits.'

"'We court the fullest investigation as to our financial condition, as, although young and but sparsely populated, yet there is no Territorial debt, and our Territory is abundantly able to meet the large appropriation made for the government of the park without embarrassment.'

"This same memorial went on to ask 'that the park be made to conform to the boundaries of the Territory, or the Territorial jurisdiction be extended over that portion lying outside of its limits, and that the park not be extended in the east and south.'"

During the 20th century, benefits of a rational, government-centered wildlife management system were realized in Canada and the United States (Heberlein 1991). This system evolved during the latter half of the 19th century, as leisure and wealth, resulting from the industrial revolution, spawned urban sportsmen. Those sportsmen believed the appropriate use of wild animals was to provide recreation and meat through regulated sport hunting, and they were willing to pay for the privilege. Sport hunting as used here refers to legally harvesting animals on a sustained yield basis—whether for meat, recreation or trophies—as opposed to subsistence or commercial hunting.

Theodore Roosevelt and other founders of the Boone and Crockett Club won out over those who killed game by any means to provide food for their tables or to sell in markets. Science became involved with wildlife studies, and

wildlife came to be managed by provinces, states and federal governments—largely for hunting. Despite increased urbanization, industrialized agriculture, urban sprawl, habitat loss, pollution and human population growth, game and nongame species generally have flourished. However, some species, especially those dependent on climax vegetation and particularly sensitive to pollution, have not fared well.

Canadian approaches to wildlife management, research and education differ from those in the United States because: the ratio of people to resources is remarkably low in Canada; large expanses of land are publicly owned; provincial governments are responsible for most resource management; and Canadian universities have no clear mandate for extension to resource users and managers (Bunnell et al. 1995). Combined, these four factors have produced an approach to wildlife management that is uniquely Canadian.

The principal problem facing game species in North America during the 19th century and before was overharvest, principally for the market. Hunters responded with restrictions and money for protection and habitat management. Today, the biggest problems are loss and modification of habitat. Because hunters have financed acquisition of habitat and influenced management, especially on public lands, hunted species sometimes are better off than unhunted species.

Three aspects of the managed hunting system have contributed to its great success.

1. Hunters have financed protection, habitat acquisition, research and management expenses through license fees and excise taxes on sporting equipment.
2. Sale and waste of meat were outlawed, reducing the temptation to poach and facilitating enforcement of game laws.
3. Federal, provincial and state governments have cooperated and divided jurisdiction over wildlife in a rational, practicable manner. Federal governments took the lead in management of migratory wildlife that crossed international, provincial and state boundaries, and in management of endangered species. Provincial and state agencies managed resident wildlife.

Wildlife managers have done an excellent job of returning elk and other game species to substantial numbers in Canada and the United States within the past half century, while allowing legal harvests of millions of animals in that time. Such harvests have garnered support for maintaining healthy populations, especially from people who have enjoyed many days of recreation and realized tasty, nutritious venison. Any conservation plan must take the desires of local residents into account. The survival and welfare of wildlife and their habitats ultimately depend on those people.

Many people, laws and circumstances have interacted to

return wildlife, including elk, from the brink of extinction, but one program stands out in the United States. "The Federal Aid in Wildlife Restoration Program, or Pittman-Robertson program as it is called in honor of its legislative sponsors, has proven to be the single most productive wildlife undertaking on record. It has meant more for wildlife in more ways than any other effort. And it is a story of how cooperation gets things done; how states, the federal government, private conservation groups, and the sporting arms and ammunition industry joined hands to give Uncle Sam the best wildlife management scheme in the world" (Williamson 1987:4). The Pittman-Robertson program became law in 1937. It is funded by an 11% manufacturer's excise tax on sporting rifles, shotguns, ammunition and archery equipment (10% percent on handguns). For 1998, those tax receipts were nearly $80 million, and between 1939 and 1998, the total of Pittman-Robertson receipts was more than $3.78 billion.

Just as Gordon (1910) praised the expense and inefficiency of red deer stalking in Scotland during the late 19th and early 20th centuries, Geist (1994:491–492) expressed well the concept of inefficiency as an economic asset. "Like the U.S. automobile industry, which generates wealth and employment from an inefficient but convenient form of transportation, so North American wildlife conservation generates wealth and employment by deliberately rendering the public use of wildlife as inefficient as possible. This inefficiency is legislated; state, provincial and federal restraints on how wildlife may be killed for consumption, or even observed, are directly responsible for the many varied market opportunities that the private sector can exploit. The result is a rich, innovative, job-intensive manufacturing and service industry that supports the tightly controlled use of public wildlife. Unlike conventional economics, which brings the resource to the consumer, North American wildlife economics takes the consumer to the resource.

"The traditional core policies of North American wildlife conservation remain largely intact: the public ownership of wildlife with bans on the private ownership of native species; a ban on trade in dead wildlife (excluding furs); an annual egalitarian allocation of surplus wildlife by legislatures after consultation with the public; a ban on the killing of wildlife without good reason; a ban on the waste of wildlife after killing; and the involvement of scientists and wildlife professionals in management.

"To show how the system works in practice, consider what you would have to do if you wanted to eat grouse. Under the legislation, you could not buy it from a butcher's shop or hire someone else to kill it for you. Rather, you must go to the expense and trouble of equipping yourself for the hunt, learning the art of hunting and its legal aspects, and paying for transport and clothing as well as for the storage of any game that you do not want to eat immediately. Such a requirement demands specialized goods and services. Similarly, if you were a bird-fancier, you would not be able to buy a native species to admire in a cage. Instead, you would have to spend money on the binoculars, clothing and transport required to watch birds in their native habitats. The result? A lively industry in support of bird-watching. Legal restrictions on the kinds of hunting and fishing gear that may be used, although introduced to deter people from participating in these sports, can encourage the development of new market niches. For instance, under legislation, deer have been free for the taking but only with bows and arrows. The result has been an innovative manufacturing industry in archery equipment, private archery ranges, specialized camouflaged clothing and novel lures to attract the quarry, and a deluge of magazines, books and tapes to keep the hobbyist well informed.

"A lot of money is spent by people who hunt, fish or view wildlife in North America. Wildlife, available to anyone for a nominal licence fee, is in reality acquired only after great expenditure. Wyoming, for instance, makes about $1 billion annually from its 960,000 big-game animals. That is, each living big-game animal contributes about $1,000 a year to the state's economy. Although most of this income comes from viewing wildlife, the viewers and the consumers largely overlap."

How can wildlife be considered that valuable in economic terms? Rippe (1997:7–8) explained that "the dollar values of hunting and wildlife play an important role in the economy of Wyoming.

"Whenever money changes hands, whether it be for a fishing reel, a duck call, or fly-tying lessons, economic activity is generated. A dollar spent for a bucket of leeches at Fred's Bait Shop starts a new cycle of activity in the community. Thanks to that purchase, Fred can get his roof fixed. The roofer can then afford that yacht he's been wanting; the boat dealer can buy a Rolex, and so on. Ultimately this rolling snowball effect in the local economy results in new jobs.

"Most important are the 'new' dollars injected into the economy from outside. Something different happens when somebody from out of state or out of town spends money in your city. The visitor's money isn't just a rerun of the same old dollars cycling around town from the bait shop to the grocery to the gas station. It's new money that acts like an infusion, boosting the overall buying power of the community. With respect to wildlife's role in the economy, new dollar infusions come from out-of-state sportsmen and wildlife-watchers and from federal grants. . . .

"In Wyoming, where hunting, fishing, and trapping are traditions, plenty of businesses—outfitters, gunsmiths, and

Many logging roads are closed to motorized vehicles during hunting seasons in elk states. Some hunters consider this an inconvenience, whereas others welcome it as a chance to get away from crowds and for its protection of elk herds. (*Top*) Out-of-state hunters who hire guides and outfitters seem to especially enjoy primitive means of transportation, one of the advantages of inefficiency. (*Bottom*) Tent camps or rustic log cabins also add to the enjoyment of hunts, as these New Yorkers seem to attest. *Photos by Bart W. O'Gara.*

taxidermists, to name a few—rely heavily on wildlife. Sporting goods stores, boat and auto dealers, service stations, motels, restaurants, meat lockers, and other enterprises, while less dependent on wildlife-related activities, clearly profit from them just the same.

"Ironically, hunting and fishing aren't always given full credit for their influence on people's spending patterns. Suppose there were few hunting, fishing, or wildlife-observing opportunities. How might Wyoming commerce be different than it is now? Would the sales of boats, outboard motors, and ATVs [all-terrain vehicles] be as brisk? And how quickly would rifles, scopes, binoculars, and graphite fly rods move off the shelves? Sales of automobiles obviously would continue even in the absence of wildlife,

but it would be pretty naive to think the subject of hunting doesn't come up regularly when four-wheel-drives are sold.

"A survey of hunters' expenditures conducted for the Game and Fish Department by the University of Wyoming found that some sportsmen even buy land in Wyoming for the primary purposes of hunting or fishing. But officially published hunter and angler expenditures don't include major equipment or property purchases of more than $100; only the out-of-pocket purchases made on individual fishing and hunting trips are counted. In terms of its beneficial effects on local and state economies, wildlife doesn't get nearly the credit it deserves."

Geist (1994:492) wrote: "North American wildlife conservation is in principle analogous to the management of wildlife by native tribes, such as the Labrador Cree in Canada or some tribes in Africa. Citizens may exploit wildlife, provided that they follow certain legal rules and regulations; and they may express their opinions on wildlife conservation, individually or through conservation organizations, to management agencies or their elected representatives. Wildlife conservation becomes a very public affair; all may participate."

The foregoing seems to emphasize economies, but Geist (1995b:279) later focused on multiple values: "In the quest for biodiversity, sustainable development and economic models that are environmentally compatible, the North American system of wildlife conservation merits attention. The North American system reversed Garrett Hardins' 'Tragedy of the Commons,' returned species from the brink of extinction, and restored wildlife (including large predators) to modest abundance despite private firearms, people, and livestock outnumbering big game about 7, 9 and 120 to 1, respectively. The system created an extensive continental system of protected areas, fostering biodiversity, while generating from a public resource, wealth and employment by the public sector. The North American system of wildlife management may be the greatest environmental success story of the 20th century."

The antihunting movement has caused some problems in managing certain game species. Kellert (1996:65–66) observed that "The recent emergence of extensive antihunting sentiment constitutes a remarkable development given the evolutionary importance of hunting and gathering. . . . The debate for and against hunting confronts one of the great paradoxes of human existence: on one hand, humans appear equipped with the capacity and will to consume animal flesh; on the other, they remain equally capable of subsisting solely on vegetative and fruit matter."

Antihunting is hardly a new phenomenon. Beaufort and Morris (1885) indicated it was a problem in 19th-century England. They thought it eventually would terminate the sport, although critics of hunting since the 14th century had failed to do so.

"Humanistic antihunters focus on the presumed experience of the individual animal," wrote Kellert (1996:75). "In their view, species population levels or habitat maintenance are irrelevant in defending hunting. The notion of wildlife sometimes needing to be hunted for the 'good' of the species or health of the habitat constitutes an abstraction of little meaning to most humanistic antihunters."

Whisker (1981:vii) indicated that "There is an historic and legal right to hunt. This conclusion is compelled by the overwhelming evidence of man's history as a civilized and rational being. There is little but the rhetoric of an antihunting movement that suggests the contrary." Such historic and legal rights apparently will sustain our management system into the foreseeable future, but managers and hunters should heed Hutton et al's. (1995:274) conclusions that, "Nature-centered concerns are entirely legitimate, but we believe the misguided zeal of many groups has been based on chauvinism, moral righteousness, and a conviction of the superiority of their cause. There is an urgent need to raise public consciousness over the conflict between protecting the interests of individual animals and protecting the environment as a whole, while at the same time, preserving the valuable contributions that animal welfare has to offer."

Roger Caras (1970:113–115), a critic of hunting and wildlife management in general because of the perceived cruelty, conceded that "A great many well-hunted deer and quail die better in this country, at least, than cows, sheep, pigs, chickens, ducks, turkeys and horses do. . . . Who can go to a rodeo and then criticize a hunter? Again an expertly placed bullet would be the best gift a rodeo horse could receive." However, Caras (1970:171, 172–173) maintained, "Big game hunting, both real, as it is in the wild, and imagined, as it is on preserves, will be phased out, not immediately, but eventually. . . . According to Dr. S. Dillon Ripley of The Smithsonian, between 75 percent and 80 percent of all wildlife forms could vanish from the earth in the next quarter of a century."

That 75% of all wildlife forms *did not* disappear during that quarter of a century is not as surprising as the fact that the prediction appeared in a book condemning sport hunting. Antihunters seldom consider the losses associated with habitat destruction or cite even one species extirpated by sport hunters.

Statistics provide little evidence that Caras's prediction concerning big game hunting being phased out will happen any time soon. However, in West Coast states, hunter declines of up to 30% occurred during 1980 to 1990 (Heberlein 1991). Also, the comparative number of older hunters in the hunting population indicates a potential decline early in the 21st century. The good news is that fewer hunters may mean less crowding and more hunting opportunities for those who remain. A smaller number of more committed and knowledgeable hunters may improve their public image, improve hunting quality and provide a stable political and funding base needed to conserve all wildlife in the 21st century.

The American public has varying levels of approval concerning hunting practices. According to Kellert (1996), about 85% of Americans approve of hunting for meat, and 65% approve of hunting for recreation and meat. Only about 38% approve of hunting mammals for recreation/sport, and 20% approve of hunting for a trophy. This seems

For elk hunting in unroaded areas, few substitutes exist for pack horses. Elk hunting is part of the North American heritage, and it is now a regular part of community life for many towns and cities in the western states and provinces. For some, the "true hunt" involves a pack train that penetrates the wilderness to replay a yearly event of getting away from homes, being challenged by nature, associating with companions with common interests and hoping for a chance to bag a trophy. Such a hunt, whether an elk is bagged or not, is the high point of the year for "true hunters." *Photo by C. H. McDonald; courtesy of the U.S. Forest Service.*

strange in a country where meat hunters apparently exterminated a few species and endangered many, but sport hunters caused dramatic increases in many species. Uninformed people seem to believe that trophy hunting depletes wildlife populations. In fact, the reverse is true. Meat hunting can, if poorly managed, deplete game, but marketing of trophy hunting depends very much on the quality of trophies offered, and this, in turn, requires that the population not be overharvested. Also antitrophy hunters with whom I have talked seem to believe the meat is wasted on most trophy hunts, which it generally is not. Drawing fine lines between meat and trophy hunters of big game belies the facts. Many meat hunters suddenly become trophy hunters when they see a large buck or bull, and some trophy

hunters become meat hunters on the last day or two of an unsuccessful trophy hunt.

During the years 1955 to 1985, the U.S. human population 12 years old and older, grew by about 83%. During the same time, the number of hunters increased only 39% (from 11.78 million to 16.34 million) (U.S. Fish and Wildlife Service 1993). Hunters of small game increased only about 13% (from 9.82 million to 11.13 million), apparently reflecting the movement of people from rural areas where rabbits, squirrels and gamebirds are hunted relatively conveniently and provide meat for the table. Waterfowl hunters increased about 62% (from 1.97 million to 3.20 million), approximately the human population increase. Big game hunters increased about 185% (from 4.41 million to 12.58 million), apparently because big game populations generally had increased dramatically. Also, cheap transportation and a comparatively good economy in that time frame afforded hunters greater recreational time and opportunity.

Elk are valued and appreciated by many segments of society—hunters, photographers, wildlife watchers, business persons catering to hunters or tourists, and many others. The animals have prospered and increased tenfold or more under the management practices of the 20th century. Habitat preservation or manipulation and population regulation by hunting, plus funding provided by hunters, brought about this tremendous increase despite escalating human demands on elk habitat for fiber, food and fuel. Hunters' dollars paid for habitat acquisition and improvement, law enforcement, research, and other expenses related to wildlife (game and nongame) management.

The Rocky Mountain Elk Foundation is testimony to the immense popularity of elk with hunters and the general public. This organization began in Montana during 1984, with volunteers and an idea. By 2000, it had funded more than 2,700 conservation projects and land acquisitions in 47 states and 8 Canadian provinces. These projects have enhanced and conserved more than 3 million acres (1.2 million ha) of elk habitat (J. McConnell personal communication:2000). Not only are people in "elk states" enthusiastic about the animals, but thousands of Rocky Mountain Elk Foundation volunteers, who live throughout Canada and the United States, commit their talents, energy and resources toward ensuring the future of elk, other wildlife and their habitats.

Elk managers in the 21st century will face many new challenges and rapidly changing conditions. However, nothing in the foreseeable future indicates that the elk hunter and her/his money and enthusiasm will be replaced as the primary driving force promoting the welfare of the magnificent monarch of the mountains and prairies in North America.

17

S. DWIGHT BUNNELL, MICHAEL L. WOLFE,
MARK W. BRUNSON AND DALE R. POTTER

Recreational Use of Elk

What once was the "Great American Elk Hunt" evaporated with dreamlike speed and is now but a memory of times past—a reminder that there are limits to human aspirations. By the early 1900s, elk had dwindled from a population of perhaps 10 million with a coast-to-coast range to about 90,000 animals that clung to remnant wilderness strongholds of western North America. The story became familiar. Placenames now ring with the nostalgia of the Great Hunt of the 1800s, including Wichitas, Chiricahuas, Mogollons, Big Horns, Sangre de Cristos, Red River Valley, and breaks of the Republican, Canadian, Platte, Arkansas, Missouri, Little Missouri, Green, Flathead and Gallatin rivers. "There remains now but a dim memory of the time when a man might arm himself as he saw fit and go forth at any time of the year and kill what game he liked" (Lovaas 1970:12).

It is easy to condemn the early pioneers' exploitive ways, but they had a job to perform: "manifest destiny" was the charter of the day. Railroaders, timber barons and market hunters performed Herculean labor to supply eastern markets and provision the westward advance of civilization. In San Francisco during the 1850s, for example, elk steaks were found on the menus of most restaurants, and a fat hindquarter sold for $40.00 (McCullough 1969). Natural resources seemed inexhaustible, and the concept and the practice of conservation were little known and of less concern. Some populations and a few species of wildlife could not readily adapt to the intrusions of humans literally and figuratively carving out new nations on a pristine continent.

Other species, such as elk, were able to persist only in deep forests and rough, isolated, mountainous terrains of the West. For pioneers, the "first law" of economics became a reality. "When you've squandered an inheritance and face dire poverty, you quit spending" (Madson and Kozicky 1971:10).

The recovery of elk from the unstable and low population numbers of less than a century ago attests to the success and farsightedness of professional wildlife management and the conservation movement (Figure 172). Some recolonization of elk range resulted from the expansion of scattered populations existing at the turn of the century. However, in most states, and even within states with remnant populations, source herds were not locally available to provide for natural expansion. The recovery of elk during the 20th century is largely the result of translocation by wildlife managers and sportsmen. Today's elk herds are a fitting tribute to men such as Roosevelt, Bailey, Grinnell, Merriam, Murie, Darling, Leopold, Lacey, Pittman and Robertson, to name a few. After a century of recovery, North America north of Mexico is home to almost 1 million elk residing in 25 states and 7 provinces. Elk numbers doubled during the last quarter of the 20th century (Table 112). In 1995, more than 800,000 elk hunters spent nearly 5.3 million recreation days afield hunting elk (Bunnell 1997). Overall interest in elk is very high, and nonconsumptive uses of elk, including photography, viewing and snowmobile trips to observe elk, are popular pastimes.

Where elk once were killed by the thousands for meat,

hides, tallow, and teeth, they now are managed for a wide spectrum of biological and recreational values. Hunting for recreation, according to Leopold (1933), is an improvement over hunting for food because, in addition to a test of skill, an ethical code is introduced. The hunter formulates this ethical code for himself, and must live up to it without the moral support of bystanders.

Research suggests that, although overall participation in hunting has decreased nationwide on a percentage basis, elk hunting participation has risen dramatically. The U.S. Fish and Wildlife Service (1977) reported that, whereas the U.S. population increased by 62% from 1955 to 1996, the number of hunters rose only 41% during that period. These numbers are offset slightly by an increase in the number of

Table 112.   Elk population in the United States and Canada at 5-year intervals, 1975 to 1995

| State/province | Subspecies | Year | | | | |
		1975	1980	1985	1990	1995
Alaska	Roosevelt	500	800	1,100	1,200	1,200
Arizona	Rocky Mountain	15,000	19,000	35,000	50,000	51,000
Arkansas	Rocky Mountain			112	250	350
California	Rocky Mountain	1,000	1,150	1,500	1,000	1,250
	Roosevelt	2,500	2,500	2,500	3,500	4,000
	Tule	600	875	1,470	2,500	2,900
Colorado	Rocky Mountain	105,000	130,000	175,000	220,000	203,000
Idaho	Rocky Mountain	na	90,000	110,000	115,000	116,000
Illinois	No elk					
Kansas	Rocky Mountain			32	145	150
Kentucky	No elk					
Michigan	Rocky Mountain	200	500	950	980	1,200
Minnesota	Rocky Mountain	18		32	18	33
Missouri	No elk					
Montana	Rocky Mountain				90,595	93,401
Nebraska	Rocky Mountain	20	40	80	80	200
Nevada	Rocky Mountain				1,965	3,335
New Mexico	Rocky Mountain	27,500	28,000	32,500	40,000	50,000
North Dakota	Manitoba		4	20	40	100
	Rocky Mountain		16	200	275	550
Oklahoma	Rocky Mountain	600	650	750	1,000	950
Oregon	Rocky Mountain		54,300	51,150	51,500	64,000
	Roosevelt	38,900	36,200	42,800	52,800	56,000
Pennsylvania	Rocky Mountain	45	120	135	150	300
South Dakota	Rocky Mountain	na	950	1,850	1,500	3,350
Tennessee	No elk					
Texas[a]	Rocky Mountain					300
Utah	Rocky Mountain	18,000	25,000	40,000	58,000	60,000
Virginia	No elk					
Washington	Rocky Mountain	23,000	24,000	24,000	24,900	30,700
	Roosevelt	35,000	31,000	31,000	30,000	31,500
Wisconsin	Rocky Mountain					25
Wyoming	Rocky Mountain	43,178	67,465	70,352	82,128	102,439
Alberta	Roosevelt	12,000	12,000	14,000	15,000	21,000
British Columbia	Rocky Mountain	15,000	20,000	30,000	38,000	45,000
	Roosevelt	2,700	2,800	2,700	2,500	3,300
Manitoba	Manitoba		7,900	6,400	8,000	9,300
Northwest Territories	Rocky Mountain					20
Ontario	Unknown					
Saskatchewan	Manitoba			7,000	9,000	11,000
Yukon Territory	Rocky Mountain	80	80	85	90	100

[a] 1975 to 1990 unreported.

[b] Study under way to determine why elk have not prospered and to prepare for reintroduction.

U.S. women who hunt, from 1.5% in 1980 to 2.7% in 1990. However, between 1975 and 1995, the total number of elk hunters in the U.S. and Canada increased by more than 50% from 530,000 hunters in 1975 to 837,000 hunters in 1995 (Table 113).

Sport hunting is certainly one of the dominant uses of today's elk, but other recreational uses including photography and observation are increasing rapidly (Flather and

Table 112 continued

State/ province	Notes/comments
AZ	Prehunt; does not include reservation lands
CA	1982 data for 1985
ID	1975 information not available
IL	Conducting reintroduction feasibility study
KS	1990 average of 138 to 151
KY	Reintroduction under way; no free-roaming elk
MO	No wild elk; occasional immigrants
MT	No reports before 1992, 1992 estimate for 1990
TN	Tentative plans to re-establish
VA	Studying possible reintroduction
WI	Translocated into state in 1995
AB	Rocky Mountain and Manitoban treated as same species
BC	1986 data for 1975
MB	Estimated 1975 population 7,000
NT	Fort Liard area
ON	Remnant population of about 50 elk[b]
SK	Estimated 1975 population 4,000, 1980 population 5,500

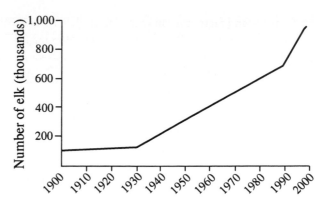

Figure 172.   Elk population trend in the United States, 1900 to 2000.

Cordell 1995). Income derived from the sale of elk licenses, permits and tags provides a significant portion of the total income of fish and wildlife agencies in many western states. This is illustrated in Utah. Not traditionally known as an elk state, Utah has an elk population of about 60,000. In 1996, 35,575 elk hunters paid $1,950,055 to hunt bull elk in Utah. This amounted to 14% of the Utah Division of Wildlife Resource's annual license and permit income of just over $14 million for the year (Utah Division of Wildlife Resources 1997).

Recreationists can enjoy associations with elk either through consumptive recreation (i.e., hunting) or through nonconsumptive activities such as photographing, observing, listening or "bugling" to attract elk. Less is known about the extent of nonconsumptive uses of elk than about hunting, although research in the past two decades has led to an increased understanding of the demographics, motives and satisfactions of nonconsumptive wildlife-related recreation (e.g., Kellert 1980, 1985, Duda and Young 1994). People have enjoyed reading about elk for years, but land managers are increasingly faced with large numbers of people who want to see elk close-up on winter ranges or hear them bugle during the autumn rut. The vulnerability of elk populations to increasing nonhunting uses is not well understood but may be significant (as well as difficult to manage). Management of potentially conflicting uses of elk, that is, uses that might occur at the same time or place and uses that create potential human safety concerns (such as bugling elk for photography or observation and bugling elk to attract trophy bulls for harvest), may become necessary.

In addition to recreation directed primarily toward elk observation, travelers frequently choose routes that afford them the likelihood of seeing elk along the way (Rocky Mountain Elk Foundation 1997). Traffic jams sometimes are reported in national parks such as Rocky Mountain and Yellowstone, where motorists stop to watch and photograph elk near heavily traveled park roads.

Table 113.   Number of U.S. and Canadian elk hunters at 5-year intervals, 1975 to 1995

State/province	Subspecies	Year 1975	1980	1985	1990	1995
Alaska	Roosevelt	123	538	765	672	408
Arizona	Rocky Mountain	5,467	8,824	10,323	12,764	22,124
Arkansas	Rocky Mountain					
California	Rocky Mountain				16	15
	Roosevelt			100	20	35
	Tule				95	110
Colorado	Rocky Mountain	140,202	163,400	139,033	192,907	219,852
Idaho	Rocky Mountain	na	na	67,200	77,700	101,500
Kansas	Rocky Mountain				6	10
Michigan	Rocky Mountain			120	230	316
Minnesota	Rocky Mountain					
Montana	Rocky Mountain	90,682	89,822	89,182	99,852	109,860
Nebraska	Rocky Mountain					38
Nevada	Rocky Mountain	10	12	85	243	306
New Mexico	Rocky Mountain	12,100	13,200	13,266	20,989	27,782
North Dakota	Manitoba			5	5	16
	Rocky Mountain			25	30	34
Oklahoma	Rocky Mountain	142	133	179	261	25
Oregon	Rocky Mountain	73,280	74,655	81,550	66,121	81,905
	Roosevelt	37,550	44,615	52,126	44,383	58,871
Pennsylvania	Rocky Mountain					
South Dakota	Rocky Mountain	261	350	683	371	764
Texas	Rocky Mountain	9	8	2	6	4
Utah	Rocky Mountain	18,904	20,555	29,287	43,263	35,826
Washington	Rocky Mountain	51,500	53,093	53,282	48,074	40,664
	Roosevelt	51,500	51,559	64,692	41,981	43,939
Wisconsin	Rocky Mountain					
Wyoming	Rocky Mountain	49,266	54,272	45,809	48,810	53,041
Alberta	Roosevelt	15,500	29,600	37,300	22,000	19,000
British Columbia	Rocky Mountain	5,700	11,000	15,000	15,000	12,400
	Roosevelt		160	189	192	135
Manitoba	Manitoba	527	2,802	2,798	2,650	2,881
Northwest Territories	Rocky Mountain					
Ontario	Unknown					
Saskatchewan	Manitoba					2,541
Yukon Territory	Rocky Mountain					

Agencies that measure total wildlife-related recreation use do not maintain data for individual species, therefore it is not possible to determine how many people seek out and enjoy elk-related recreational activities. However, some insight into the overall importance of wildlife-related recreation is offered by the U.S. Forest Service's (1990) Public Area Recreation Visitor Study, conducted from 1985 to 1987. This nationwide study found that wildlife observation on federal lands for all species was enjoyed by 14% of the American population. Among those who reported engaging in wildlife-related recreation, the median number of annual participation days in that activity was 18. Participation in nature study or photography was reported by 13% of Americans and big game hunting was reported by 7% of Americans (Cordell et al. 1987).

Nonconsumptive wildlife-related recreation is extremely popular in the United States, although sources differ widely on participation trends. Duda and Young (1994) reported that, between 1981 and 1990, there was a 63% increase in the number of trips taken for the primary purposes of watching, feeding and photographing wildlife. However, the U.S. Fish and Wildlife Service (1997) reported a 12% decrease in wildlife watching from 1980 to 1996. The Service calculated that, in 1996, 62.9 million Americans observed, fed or photographed wildlife and 23.7 million took trips for the primary purpose of nonconsumptive wildlife-related recreation.

There is little doubt that elk are revered. The elk is depicted on the state seals of Idaho, Oregon and Michigan. The British Columbia coat of arms also features elk. The

Table 113 continued

State/ province	Notes/comments
AR	Elk are protected; no hunting at present
CA	1974 data for 1975, 1984 data for 1985
KS	First elk hunting season was in 1987
MN	Only hunt ever held in 1987; seven elk harvested
NE	1986 (75), 1987 (42)
NM	1994 data for 1995
WI	No hunting
BC	1976 data for 1975
NT	Remnant population of about 50 elk
YT	Elk protected

Benevolent and Protective Order of the Elks (a 1-million-member fraternal organization) chose the elk—after rejecting bison, bear, beaver, and fox—as a symbol because it appealed strongly to their ideals: ". . . an animal that lived in peace, but would fight to defend its rights and to protect the weak and helpless" (Fehrenbach 1967:13).

Placenames also testify to the elk's place in human experience. Twenty-six states and four Canadian provinces have towns that contain the name of elk. Kansas and Pennsylvania each have an Elk County. At least eight states have towns named Elkton, and there are several Elk Horn, Elkhart and Elkin towns. There are towns named Elk in Washington and Wyoming , Elk City in Idaho, Kansas, Oklahoma and Oregon, and Elk Ridge in Utah. In other states, there are communities named Elk Grove, Elk Springs, Elk River, Elkville, Elk Run Heights, Elk Falls, Elk Mills, Elk Valley, Elk Hills, Elk Neck, Elk Rapids, Elk Park, Elko, Elkland, Elk Garden, Elkhorn Prairie, Elk Mound, Elkhead, Elk Mountain and Elkview. In Canada, there are the towns of Elk Point and Elk Water (Alberta), Elkford and Elko (British Columbia), Elkhorn (Manitoba), and Elk Creek (Manitoba and Ontario).

Elk also are immortalized in geographic placenames of rivers, lakes, creeks, flats, buttes, ridges, points and mountains. Nearly all these names attest to the historic presence of the antlered ungulate. Theodore Roosevelt (1893) named his North Dakota ranch the Elkhorn. He reported finding a splendid pair of antlers interlocked from an autumn battle of fighting "wapiti" at the spot where he built the ranch house.

The facts that elk populations were severely depleted during the early 1900s, that the remaining elk herds were concentrated in remote areas of sparsely populated states, and that travel was difficult and expensive meant that opportunities for elk-related recreation were limited. However, interest in elk remained high enough to motivate active efforts to return elk to many former habitats. Efforts to return elk to their former ranges continue. Between 1975 and 1995, free ranging elk populations were established in Arkansas, Kansas, North Dakota and Wisconsin. Translocations of elk designed to reestablish elk populations have recently occurred in Kentucky, Wisconsin and Ontario. Elk reintroduction feasibility studies are being conducted in Missouri, Illinois, Tennessee, North Carolina, Virginia and New York (Klaphake 2000:17).

Another evidence of people's continuing high interest in having elk available for recreational use is the fact that, despite the continuing loss of habitat and increasing conflicts between elk and agricultural, elk populations have increased dramatically since about 1970 (Bunnell 1997). Elk can now be observed, photographed and hunted within minutes of several western population centers. For example, virtually every one of Utah's 2 million residents could recreate with elk after driving less than 1 hour from their homes. By taking advantage of today's relatively cheap and efficient travel opportunities, even residents of areas far removed from established elk populations have better opportunities to interact with elk.

The dramatic growth of the Rocky Mountain Elk Foundation (RMEF) since its inception in 1984 further demonstrates that people continue to be interested in elk. For example, more than 25,000 people joined RMEF in 1996, and total membership exceeds 113,000. Between 1984 and 2000, the Foundation completed 2,757 projects that conserved or enhanced almost 3 million acres of wildlife habitat (Klaphake 2000:30). Foundation's quarterly magazine has a

The cultural and historic regard for elk in North America is reflected in the fact that elk are featured on the state seals of Idaho (*top left*), Oregon (not shown) and Michigan (*above*), and on British Columbia's coat of arms (*bottom left*). *Photos courtesy of the respective state and provincial government.*

total circulation exceeding 150,000. Bob Munson, founder and CEO stated, "The RMEF has enjoyed success only because it has tapped into a renewable and perhaps unlimited resource—people who care about wildlife and the land" (Rocky Mountain Elk Foundation 1997).

Although there is high interest in elk, some groups and individuals are adamantly opposed to increasing the reintroduction of elk. Opposition to elk has come from segments of the livestock industry, for example, public land grazing permittees and, in some cases, agency personnel. Many public land grazing permittees view elk as direct competitors for limited and overallocated forage. Because elk have been missing from many ecosystems in the West for roughly 100 years, some people regard elk as non-native and just another problem.

The Rocky Mountain Elk Foundation was founded in 1984 and is headquartered in Missoula, Montana. It has as its mission the conservation of elk, other wildlife and their habitats. With about 115,000 members in 2001 and by virtue of dedication to its mission, the Foundation has become a respected member of North America's conservation community. *Photo courtesy of the Rocky Mountain Elk Foundation.*

The Hudson's Bay Company's Royal Charter of May 2, 1670, granted by Charles II, specified that whenever an English sovereign visited its domain, the "Governor and Company of Adventurers Trading into Hudson's Bay" would pay rent of "two Elkes and two Black beavers" (Reeves and McCabe 1997:68). King George VI visited and accepted payment in 1939 (*above*), as did Queen Elizabeth II in 1959 and 1970. The payment of "Elkes" surely was intended to mean moose, which Europeans call "elk," but the terms of the charter were followed literally, as evidenced by the North American elk antlers that were on display at each of the "rent payment" ceremonies. The confusing provision was eliminated when, in 1970, the Company was rechartered in Canada. *Photo courtesy of the Hudson's Bay Company Archives.*

Elk are also opposed by some ranchers and farmers whose crops and improvements are subject to elk depredation. Elk usually travel in groups especially in winter, and large herds are common. Winter depredation on stacked or stored hay can be very significant in terms of the volume of hay consumed. Also, elk depredations tend to be concentrated at the worst times—during droughts, when forage production is low, and during extreme winters, when replacement forage is expensive and often not available. Some sportsmen also are opposed to the reintroduction of elk because they believe that elk will outcompete and displace mule deer, the animal they have traditionally hunted.

Love and hate feelings toward elk abound among hunters, owners of private property, agriculturalists, residents of rural areas, suburbanites, naturalists, conservationists, hikers, mountain bikers, etc. Almost nobody who becomes involved with elk remains neutral in his or her feelings. The fact that elk evoke strong emotions is both a challenge and an opportunity. The challenge is to bridge the emotional gap between those who favor elk and those who oppose elk; the opportunity is to channel these strong feelings into actions, programs and policies to the benefit of elk and elk habitat.

Elk Hunting and the Hunter

Hunting is one of North America's most popular outdoor recreational activities. More than 14 million people hunted in the United States alone in 1996 (U.S. Fish and Wildlife Service 1997). Nearly 800,000 hunters spent more than 5 million days afield hunting elk in 1995, more than double the number of days that were spent afield hunting elk in 1975 (Bunnell 1997). The trend of increasing hunter pressure on elk, combined with decreased elk range sizes, increased hunter mobility, more effective hunting equipment, increased emphasis on the quality of the hunting experience, various habitat quality problems, and the need to control and even reduce the size of some elk populations had marked impacts on elk and elk management during the last quarter of the 20th century.

People who ranch and farm in elk country tend to embrace the species as a symbol of strength and tenacity in a rugged landscape not unlike themselves. On the other hand, elk depredations of croplands and other inconveniences to humankind, leave very few people neutral in their feelings about elk and elk management. *Left photo by E. P. Haddon; courtesy of the U.S. Fish and Wildlife Service. Right photo by Chris Chaffin; courtesy of the Idaho Department of Fish and Game.*

The elk hunter has been perceived in many ways. Murie (1951:286) described the trophy elk hunter or recreational hunter as one who "organizes a pack train with guide and helpers, and penetrates the wilderness . . . to establish a permanent camp." He also characterized meat hunters are those whose "rule is to get their elk as quickly as possible and return home. Often they are not people of great means. Many of them spend a single day in the field and are satisfied with bull, cow, or calf, the first one that can be had" (Murie 1951:286). Recreational hunters reportedly take to the field in early season when the bulls are bugling and the trophy animals are not wary. According to Murie, the meat hunter follows later in the season when elk are coming down from high country, and hunting success is largely a matter of luck in encountering a traveling band of elk, followed by marksmanship.

Traditionally, hunting has been the dominant utilitarian and recreational use of elk. In recent years, both elk hunt-ing and the nonhunting recreational uses of wildlife, including elk, have increased dramatically (Duda and Young 1994, Bunnell 1997). Because elk hunting has been the dominant traditional use of elk and despite the increasing interest in nonhunting uses of the species, funding for elk management programs continues to come primarily from the sale of hunting licenses, tags and permits by individual states and provinces.

Settlement of North America was motivated in part by a desire for freedom from the feudal systems of Europe that gave ownership of wildlife to the landed gentry. In North America, wildlife has been managed both legally and traditionally by the states and provinces as a public trust. In the United States, the right and responsibility to manage resident wildlife is reserved to the states. Thus, the individual states and provinces have the lead responsibility for elk management except in national parks and Indian reservations (Spaeth 1993).

Wildlife agencies traditionally have served hunters and fishermen within their jurisdictions. Beginning in the late 1800s and early 1900s, states began to charge a fee for hunting and fishing licenses as a funding mechanism for wildlife management and wildlife law enforcement (Trefethen 1975, Bean 1977). Although wildlife agencies are striving to broaden their funding base, the majority of funding for wildlife management in North America continues to come from hunting license sales and excise taxes on sporting arms, ammunition and archery equipment (Kallman 1987).

A commonly accepted axiom among wildlife managers is that elk management programs more than pay their way and, in fact, in states with large elk herds (and especially in states that cater to large numbers of nonresident elk hunters), income from elk hunting can be a very significant portion of the overall funding for agency programs. Among such states, only Wyoming has reported management costs exceeding income from elk license sales. The costs of winter elk feeding at state feeding grounds and the state's share of feeding costs at the National Elk Refuge in Jackson Hole, added to other management costs, has resulted in overall statewide elk management costs that regularly exceeds elk license income (Wyoming Game and Fish Department 1996). However, the value of elk hunting to the total economy of Wyoming still eclipses the cost of management, and Wyoming elk herds also are an important natural resource and tourist attraction. When all factors are considered, management of elk in Wyoming has long *been an economically justified* activity as well as an important component of Wyoming's quality of life.

Montana's Elk Management Plan (Montana Department of Fish, Wildlife, and Parks 1992) indicated that, "In addition to its cultural, aesthetic, social and ecological values, Montana's elk resource is a substantial asset to the state's economy. An economic survey conducted in 1985 by the DFWP [Department of Fish, Wildlife, and Parks], in cooperation with the Bureau of Land Management and the U.S. Forest Service, determined that resident and nonresident hunters contribute $58.4 million to Montana's economy in the form of transportation, lodging, food, guide fees, and other expenditures associated with elk hunting. This figure does not include purchase of elk-hunting licenses."

As previously indicated, 530,000 hunters hunted elk in the United States during 1975, as did more than 21,000 hunters in Canada. Between 1976 and 1985, the number of U.S. hunters increased modestly to about 575,000, but the number of elk hunters in Canada more than doubled, to more than 55,000. During this period, the number of elk hunters in Arizona nearly doubled, to more than 10,000. In Utah, 11,000 new hunters were reported during the period, bringing the state total to nearly 30,000. Compared with

1975, the number of hunters pursuing Roosevelt elk increased by almost 15,000 in Oregon and by more than 13,000 in Washington. By 1995, almost 800,000 hunters hunted elk in the United States—a 50% increase over 1975, with most of the increase occurring after 1985. Also in 1995, almost 220,000 hunters hunted elk in Colorado—more than 25% of the total U.S. elk hunters. From 1986 to 1995, however, the number of hunters in Canada decreased by 18,000 hunters to around 37,000 (Bunnell 1997).

In 1975, elk hunters spent almost 2.5 million days afield hunting elk in the United States. By 1985, there was a 40% increase in hunter-days afield to more than 3.5 million days. An even larger increase in elk hunting recreation occurred between 1986 and 1995—more than 5 million days were spent hunting elk in the United States in 1995 (Table 114). Hunting days afield peaked in Canada in the mid-1980s at about 0.3 million days per year, but decreased to 0.25 million during 1995 (Table 114).

The role of hunting, as a sociological phenomenon in North America, has changed significantly over time. In fact, it differs from place to place and with the species hunted. Consequently, the role of hunters is perceived differently by people in different places. This is important because hunting also is a biological phenomenon. Its actual and potential influences on elk populations, and the public perception of those influences, are linked inextricably to the type and extent of management required to maintain elk numbers and habitat in any given area.

The next several sections of this chapter will examine the role and dynamics of elk hunting and pertinent sociological and demographic characteristics of elk hunters. Information used here is drawn from published literature (Potter 1982) and unpublished survey data from the State of Washington (Potter et al. 1973) supplemented and updated as appropriate by the *1996 National Survey of Fishing, Hunting and Wildlife-Associated Recreation* (U.S. Fish and Wildlife Service 1997) and the *Status of Elk in North America 1975–1995* (Bunnell 1997).

The Washington State survey involved a mail questionnaire that was distributed to a 2% sample of all 1970 resident hunters in Washington State. There was an 85.4% return (5,540), of which more than 1,000 were from elk hunters. In a separate analysis of hunters, Hendee and Potter (1976) demonstrated that Washington State hunters showed major social and economic characteristics similar to those of hunters evaluated in 18 other surveys including 12 states, two regions, and two nationwide studies. In the absence of other comparative data, the 1970 Washington State hunters surveyed are assumed here to be generally representative of other hunters in North America, and particularly so for elk hunters.

Table 114. Total number of elk hunting days in the United States and Canada in 5-year intervals, 1975 to 1995

State/province	Subspecies	Year 1975	1980	1985	1990	1995
Alaska	Roosevelt	593	2,206	3,294	1,727	1,757
Arizona	Rocky Mountain	23,506	49,573	51,195	58,764	100,992
California	Rocky Mountain				65	60
	Roosevelt	200	0	400	80	180
	Tule				380	440
Colorado	Rocky Mountain	680,157	818,767	714,281	963,883	1,147,067
Idaho	Rocky Mountain	na	na	521,100	653,000	846,800
Kansas	Rocky Mountain				20	100
Michigan	Rocky Mountain			209	591	898
Minnesota	Rocky Mountain					
Montana	Rocky Mountain	650,031	566,659	579,772	736,162	884,203
Nebraska	Rocky Mountain					240
Nevada	Rocky Mountain		46	273	1,249	1,384
New Mexico	Rocky Mountain	40,000	69,000	70,320	195,000	288,600
North Dakota	Manitoba			15	25	80
	Rocky Mountain			78	174	170
Oklahoma	Rocky Mountain	355	333	448	653	63
Oregon	Rocky Mountain	514,320	377,435	402,224	375,589	465,281
	Roosevelt	190,800	234,118	247,252	208,924	322,585
South Dakota	Rocky Mountain				2,769	5,106
Texas	Rocky Mountain	100	100	100	100	100
Utah	Rocky Mountain	107,542	99,798	149,508	218,455	214,357
Washington	Rocky Mountain	na	na	233,014	241,302	206,569
	Roosevelt	na	na	285,790	233,328	260,553
Wyoming	Rocky Mountain	279,171	342,824	261,780	280,701	337,974
Alberta	Roosevelt	70,500	150,000	182,650	131,940	127,120
British Columbia	Rocky Mountain	50,000	101,000	133,000	137,000	116,000
	Roosevelt		700	795	1,166	1,014
Manitoba	Manitoba	8,000	33,000	17,000	13,000	17,000
Saskatchewan	Manitoba				14,429	

Entry Into Elk Hunting

Introduction to hunting usually occurs through a family experience at an impressionable age. If a person has not hunted by age 20, he or she probably will never hunt. In Washington, nearly 90% of elk hunters started hunting before age 20, and more than half had hunted elk by age 15. In contrast, only 2.6% of the elk hunters first hunted elk after age 30. These figures are consistent with those for other types of hunters in Washington. Schole (1973) also reported that Colorado hunters began hunting at an early age, with 47% of the hunters having joined the hunting ranks by age 10, and 90% by age 15. Studies of hunters in Wisconsin (Klessig 1970), six northeastern states (Bevins et al. 1968) and Ohio (Peterle 1961, 1967, 1977a) showed similar results.

The initiating agent of a neophyte hunter usually is a family member or relative. About 56% of Wisconsin hunters (Klessig 1970) and 61% of Colorado hunters (Schole 1973) were introduced to hunting by their father, with other family members or relatives contributing heavily in the initiation process. More than 52% of Washington hunters were introduced to hunting by fathers, whereas other family members or relatives were cited as most influential by another 14%. Friends, personal motivation, organized groups, magazines, books, movies, television and other factors also were listed as catalytic influences by elk hunters.

Reasons for taking young people hunting, in order of frequency mentioned, included developing (1) appreciation and knowledge of the outdoors, (2) character of sportsmanship and responsibility, (3) knowledge of gun safety and survival, and (4) father/son relationship (Schole 1973).

Table 114 continued

State/ province	Notes/comments
CA	1974 data for 1975; 1984 data for 1985
ID	1975 and 1980 information is missing
KS	Rough estimates
MN	Only hunt in 1987; 46 hunting days
TX	Unknown, but about 100 days per year
UT	1975 and 1980 information unknown; 1991 totals for 1990
WA	1975 and 1980 information unknown; 1991 totals for 1990
BC	1976 data for 1975
	1976 data for 1975

The vast majority of elk hunters—who collectively spend more than 5 million days annually hunting elk in North America—were introduced to the activity before age 20 and by a relative. *Photo by Donald M. Jones.*

Hunter Satisfaction

The common characterizations of trophy hunters and meat hunters imply that the recreational value of elk hunting is, in large, part contingent upon bringing an animal home. However, social scientists studying outdoor recreation behavior have found that hunting involves various types of satisfaction, of which killing an animal is only one.

Some of the early innovations instituted to gain satisfaction and a sense of achievement in the hunt were both destructive and unsportsmanlike by standards of the mid-1900s. In describing the emergence of sportsmanship, Trefethen (1961:11) listed three innovations of the western sportsmen: "Many attempted to gain satisfaction by running up huge strings of kills, often with two or more hunters competing to see which could kill the greatest number of game with the fewest shots. From the standpoint of the game supply this type of hunting, accepted as legitimate sport in its time, was as destructive as the commercial slaughter by the market hunters. Others found excitement in cutting out and coursing selected bull buffaloes and making the kills from horseback with pistol or carbine. Still others passed up shots at nearby animals and made their kills at extreme range."

The elk was no less immune to "sport" and market hunters than were the bison, passenger pigeon and pronghorn. The "success" of these early hunters can be seen in the drastic decline in elk numbers, culminating in the eventual ban on elk hunting. Whereas elk once had roamed much of North America, they were confined to remote pockets of remaining wildlands in the West after the 1880s. In 1852, California declared the first closed season on elk hunting. Michigan followed suit in 1879, with a complete closure for 10 years. Colorado elk hunting ended in 1903. Washington followed in 1905 and Utah in 1907. By 1910, elk were protected by law throughout their restricted range (Palmer 1912).

Modern wildlife management had its origin in the citizen movements of the late 1800s and early 1900s, but it was not born as a scientific discipline until the 1930s. Its unique character was rooted in the biological principles of animal husbandry (Leopold 1933). This half-century span also marked the emergence of the modern sportsman, who restricted his harvests to surplus and trophy animals (Kimball and Kimball 1969, Trefethen 1978). New hunting preferences, satisfactions and ethics also evolved during this period.

Several writers have suggested that the values and appeal of hunting include development of self-reliance, initiative, instinct, ecological awareness, cultural values and ethics (Anthony 1957, Shephard 1959, 1973, Leonard 1965, Ortega y Gasset 1972). They also suggest that the opportunity to release antisocial impulses and enjoy the thrill of the chase are important lures of hunting. Johnson and Rasmussen (1946:902) identified a common notion that hunting has therapeutic values by providing "certain outlets for energy and the opportunity to release nervous tension common to

modern civilization." Leopold (1949) suggested five components or levels of hunting enjoyment in the following order: (1) the sense of husbandry through the application of land management; (2) the perception and understanding of the principles of ecology; (3) the simple pleasure of breathing fresh air and having a change of scenery; (4) the pleasure of feeling close to nature; and (5) the pursuit of game with their associated symbols of achievement.

Sometimes, however, hunter behavior does not live up to the philosopher's opinion or expectation about the nature of hunting. For example, Wagar (1971:45) related an account of a nonresident elk hunter in Colorado, who stopped at a check station with a spike, bull elk that "didn't look just right. The carcass seemed small, the antlers were very dry, and a moth was found in the hair. Questioning proved that the hunter was unsuccessful and had paid a cowpoke $50 for a cow elk carcass and a pair of old spike

The modern elk camp (*top*) can be an authentic recreation of the first elk camps more than 125 years ago (*bottom*). Hunters now can identify the same rigors, hardships and privations routinely endured in the 19th century. The elk hunters of today also can experience the myriad similar satisfactions from the wilderness hunt of yesteryear. *Top photo courtesy of the Idaho Department of Fish and Game. Bottom photo courtesy of the Wyoming State Archives, Museums and Historical Department.*

bull antlers from the bunkhouse!" It was stories such as this that triggered the sensitivities of nonhunters and led some to question hunting. During the 1940s, Leopold (1949) noted what he believed were two disturbing trends in hunting—increasing reliance on what he termed gadgets and the proliferation of "How to and Where to" hunt magazines—and that both trends tended to erode the hunter's self-reliance and skill.

There has been philosophical opposition to hunting for centuries. Not until recent decades, however, have antihunting and antihunter sentiments grown to sufficient magnitude to cause serious concern among wildlife managers and hunters alike. Peterle (1977b:159) summarized that "Hunters have little room for optimism." Philosophical opposition approaching religious fervor has evoked a vastly different public profile of the hunter, with heavy psychological overtones and ecological implications (Denney 1973, Frodelius 1973, Shaw 1973, Peterle 1977b). Historically, American society has had a strong tendency to view hunters in a positive light in part because most Americans were hunters, were dependent on hunters to provide some of their food, or at least had known hunters personally. In recent years, however, hunters have become a minority and an easy target for mass media antihunting campaigns based on emotion and sensation. As a result, today Americans are more likely to accept negative portrayals of hunters.

Some people have viewed hunters as sadistic cowards, filled with a lust to kill and need to prove their identity or masculinity by wielding a high-powered rifle in contempt for the sanctity of life. Hunters also have been characterized as victims of impotency and high inferiority complexes. Such unsubstantiated, pejorative labels have generated considerable controversy and public scrutiny of the role of hunting and the responsibilities of hunters. There was little research on hunters until the 1960s and 1970s.

A psychological study of Colorado big game hunters negated the notion that hunters are psychologically different from nonhunters (G. C. Thornton unpublished). A motivation analysis test, standardized to the general population, was given to 85 hunters in nine cities in 1972. The test was designed to measure 10 aspects of the normal personality including a person's interests, psychological drive and value system strengths. Test results showed hunters to be essentially no different than nonhunters; test scores showed them to be normal, average people. The results did not support a contention that hunters are maladjusted, overly aggressive or wanton killers.

Davis (1962) did one of the first studies that explored attitudes of modern-day hunters. He interviewed 1,027 Arizona hunters and found that the average hunter was motivated to satisfy several basic needs, including recreational and aesthetic values and physical health. In a subsequent study, Davis (1967) found a complex set of hunter motives, which included exercising, developing an appreciation for nature, sharing companionship with family and friends, reaping the economic values of using game as food, challenging nature, developing character traits and awakening religious beliefs. He concluded that hunters usually are motivated by a package of changing and interrelated satisfactions.

This theme was repeated in thorough explorations by Potter et al. (1973) and Hautaluoma and Brown (1978) of the nature of a hunting experience. In a study of more than 5,500 Washington State hunters—including more than 1,000 elk hunters—Potter et al. (1973) developed a list of 11 "dimensions of hunting satisfactions." The dimensions, in order of overall importance to hunters, were:

1. Nature—appreciation of nature and the outdoors;
2. Escapism—implying search for a change of routine;
3. Companionship—desire for company with fellow hunters;
4. Shooting—getting shots and making difficult kills;
5. Skill—using one's knowledge, ability, or cunning;
6. Vicariousness—indirect participation such as reading, movies, and television;
7. Trophy display—displaying game;
8. Harvest—bagging or possessing game;
9. Equipment—owning, maintaining, and using equipment;
10. Outgroup verbal contact—talking to other hunters; and
11. Outgroup visual contact—seeing other hunters.

Of course, not all hunters are alike. Hautaluoma and Brown (1978) found that all hunters reportedly obtain satisfaction from being in nature, honing their skills, using equipment, meeting other hunters in the field and harvesting game. However, hunters varied in other particulars, such as the importance of bagging trophies to display, giving away game to others and releasing frustration. Using this same approach in Montana, Olsen (1989) identified four categories of hunters—multiple-experience hunters, meat hunters, trophy hunters, and outdoorsmen. Trophy hunters obtained the highest net economic value from elk hunting, and meat hunters the lowest. In a similar study, Schole (1973) asked Colorado hunters why they hunted. The hunters listed love of outdoors, companionship with fellow sportsmen, challenge with the animal, outdoor recreational activity and escape from daily routine, in that order of prevalence of response. Eleven other reasons, with lesser response prevalence, also were given.

Studies that downplay the importance of bagging game in hunter experiences were contributed by Kennedy (1974),

There is a package of satisfactions that provides the positive rational for recreational hunting and distinguishes it from killing (Hendee and Potter 1971, Potter 1982). Succinctly, "one does not hunt in order to kill; on the contrary, one kills in order to have hunted" (Ortega y Gassett 1972:110–111). *Photos by Donald M. Jones.*

who found that killing ranked fourth in a list of reported benefits derived by deer hunters in Maryland, and by More (1970, 1973), who found that killing game neither added to nor detracted from the experiences of Massachusetts hunters. Other researchers agree that other satisfactions exist but feel that "seeing, shooting, and bagging game are still the most central evaluative criteria for the recreationist" (Vaske et al. 1982:197). Vaske et al. (1982) compared satisfaction ratings by consumptive and nonconsumptive recreationists in various studies and found that participants in consumptive activities were more likely to rate their experiences as unsatisfactory. Hautaluoma and Brown (1978) suggested that, although success may not be essential to a hunting experience, the reasonable probability of success is very important.

Stankey et al. (1973) hypothesized that hunting success serves a "catalytic function," such that its presence or absence affects the relative importance of other experiential elements. Social–psychological theory suggests that persons often rate experiences as satisfying in the face of disappointing results due to a psychological phenomenon called cognitive dissonance (Shelby and Heberlein 1986).

According to this theory, individuals are motivated to redefine post hoc outcomes that do not match expectations. Thus, the Massachusetts and Maryland results may be partially explained if the survey respondents who were not successful redefined their experiences in a positive direction by deciding that they had not actually expected to harvest any game on the trip. Changing a hunter's expectations about a trip also can enhance that hunter's satisfaction with the trip. For example, Heberlein (1992) found that deer hunters reported greater satisfaction with a high hunter-density experience if they were told ahead of time that they would encounter numerous other hunters.

There undoubtedly is some low level of harvest success below which most hunters will cease hunting altogether. Empirical evidence suggests that this level is between 5% and 10%. Figure 173 shows the number of visits to national forests by deer hunters and elk hunters between 1950 and 1973, and their harvest success rates. The picture is one of rapidly increasing numbers of hunters accompanied by falling success rates. However, when the success rate dropped to 6%, about 1964, the number of hunter visits stabilized. This suggests that a 6% hunter harvest success is

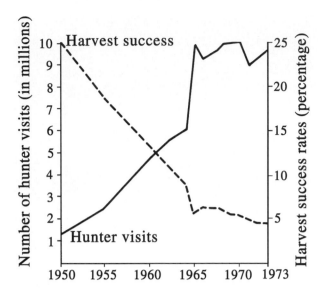

Figure 173. Number of big game hunter visits and harvest success rates for elk and deer on national forests in the United States, 1950 to 1973 (U.S. Forest Service 1975a).

not high enough to attract many new hunters or keep experienced ones from dropping the recreation. If this has validity, wildlife managers can regard 10% as the threshold of acceptable hunter harvest success rate. Complex management techniques are needed to regulate the number of hunters and sustain game populations, as well as to ensure satisfactory harvest success rates. In some situations, maintaining satisfactory harvest success rates is as much a challenge as is developing intensive habitat management programs to maintain or increase elk numbers.

Clearly, hunting satisfactions are many and complex. There is much more to hunting than harvesting game, although harvesting an animal is the ostensible intent of hunting in most cases.

There is a "package" of satisfactions that provides the positive rationale for recreational hunting and distinguishes it from killing (Hendee and Potter 1971). More philosophically and somewhat poetically, Ortega y Gasset (1972:110–111) wrote that "one does not hunt in order to kill; on the contrary, one kills in order to have hunted."

Elk Hunting Satisfaction

In terms of the satisfactions received, elk hunting is generally similar to other types of hunting. McLaughlin et al. (1989), in a study of elk hunters in Idaho, found that the satisfactions of elk hunting included being in a natural setting, feeling uncrowded, perceiving game to be abundant and available, having game populations with healthy age structures, having opportunities for social contact and being

aware of the chance to harvest an animal for trophy or other reasons.

Sanyal and McLaughlin (1993) developed a model of elk hunter behavior that links differences in hunters' goals to variation in hunting strategies. They suggested that *how* a person hunts may be as important as *why* they hunt. For example, Sanyal and McLaughlin pointed out that someone who is highly motivated to put meat on the table may be more likely to use a strategy with a high likelihood of success, such as road hunting, even if it does not achieve other goals, such as physical fitness or honing one's tracking skills. Moreover, hunters adapt their strategies to fit the conditions to avoid undesirable outcomes. Such changes in strategy can occur within seasons, within trips or even within days. For example, hunters may be willing to climb to vantage points early in a trip that they would not approach later on or they may choose to kill a less desirable animal late in the season that they might reject on opening day.

At least two other studies have surveyed elk hunters to determine satisfactions of the hunt or what constitutes quality elk hunting. A Wyoming study asked elk hunters to rank by importance 42 experience items that contribute to quality hunting (Water Resources Research Institute 1975). Ranked extremely important by the hunters were having minimum danger from other hunters, seeing wildlife, being close to nature, being outdoors, making a good shot and bagging good eating game. Again, nature and the outdoor theme ranked high among hunting satisfactions. The results were slightly different in a Saskatchewan survey, in which hunters were asked about the main purpose of their hunting (Ross 1975): 53% listed meat, 35% listed recreation and 11% listed trophy.

Several interpretations may account for differences between the Saskatchewan survey and others. First, there is a subtle difference between "hunting satisfaction" and "purpose for hunting"; the latter implies a motive for hunting, whereas the former implies a product or something received after the fact. Second, the economic role of big game may be significantly more important in Canada than in the United States.

Social–psychological benefits of elk hunting have been identified beyond the satisfactions associated with the experience itself. Baas (1988) surveyed 2,400 Roosevelt elk hunters in Oregon, and then performed a follow-up survey of 170 adolescent children who hunted with those adults. He found that both adults and teenagers believed that hunting positively influenced family relationships. Parents agreed strongly with the statement that "Hunting is a way of passing on important values to my child," whereas adolescents agreed strongly with statements that "Hunting with this relative is important because it gives me a chance to show him/her that I am responsible" and "Hunting is important because it gives us a chance to use teamwork when we hunt." Also, young hunters exhibited higher evaluations than did a national sample of adolescents on a psychological assessment tool for measuring self-concept.

During the 1980s, the lack of mature bull elk, particularly on public lands, was a biological concern as well as a hunter satisfaction concern in several western states. The biological concern stemmed from the fact that most breeding was being done by yearling bulls (Squibb et al. 1986). The lack of mature bulls was a concern to hunters who were not satisfied with hunting elk in areas where no mature bulls were available for harvest. The presence of mature bulls in an elk herd adds to hunter satisfaction even if the harvest of mature bulls is restricted (Stalling 1996). The facts that mature bulls bugle actively, begin to bugle earlier in the season and establish harems all add to the hunting experience. Beginning in the 1980s, several elk states adopted regulations and other practices designed to produce more mature bulls. Yearling or spike-only hunts, road closures, antler point restrictions and other strategies were adopted by several states. Generally speaking, these changes have been successful in producing more mature bulls and in increasing hunter satisfaction on the units where they have been adopted.

Hunter Age

In 1970, elk hunters reportedly were mostly middle-aged, with the modal class between 25 and 34 years old, and more than 50% between 25 and 44 years old. By 1996, the hunter population had aged. The modal class among big game hunters was between 35 and 44 years old (28%) , according to the U.S. Fish and Wildlife Service (1997), and 36% were more than 44 years old, whereas just 15% were under 25 years. In 1970, younger hunters appeared to be underrepresented by about 10% to 12% compared with other types of hunters and the general U.S. population. This suggests that elk hunters, unlike other types of hunters, are more a fraternal collection of middle-aged peers than a father/son or other uneven-aged group. This may become an important consideration in the design of party permit programs. For example, a father/son party permit may be less popular with elk hunters than with hunters of other game.

The elk hunter also was underrepresented in the over-65 age class, compared with the U.S. population. This may be because elk hunting often is strenuous. Resource managers, however, do not deal solely with a middle-aged clientele, because all ages are represented, including individuals ranging from 10 to more than 65 years of age.

That most elk hunters are 35 to 50 years old may be correlated to a combination of factors that include level of hunting maturity (itself related to diverse experiential satisfactions), income (ability to afford attendant services and equipment), leisure time, sociability (relative breadth of acquaintance with other active elk hunters as possible companions or sources of hunting opportunity and reinforcement of the hunting priority) and health (ability to deal psychologically and physically with the experience as a challenge versus intimidation). *Photo by Leland Prater; courtesy of the U.S. Forest Service.*

Education Level of Elk Hunters

Data from the 1996 National Hunting and Fishing Survey (U.S. Fish and Wildlife Service 1997) show that hunters, in general, and big game hunters in particular, are less likely to have earned a college diploma than did the U.S. population as a whole (19% compared with 25%), but more likely to have earned a high school diploma (85% compared with 87%). No data specific to elk hunting were reported in 1997. On the basis of the educational levels of elk hunters, it can be assumed that most have at least an average ability to understand ecological principles and resource management programs.

Hunter Vocation

Most elk hunters (59%), as well as other hunter types (53%), were employed in so-called blue-collar occupations. This compared with 35% in the U.S. population as a whole. This information has important implications in strategies for developing, engendering, gaining public acceptance of and implementing wildlife management programs. New systems to reduce crowded hunting conditions through complicated license or harvest quota programs will be more effective and successful if they are explained to hunters and structured to be compatible with the sociological and demographic characteristics of the prospective participants. Otherwise, programs may not be adopted or adopted readily, to the detriment of the resource and all concerned (Rogers 1962, Rogers and Shoemaker 1971, Muth 1975).

Sales and service vocations were underrepresented by about the same magnitude among elk hunters and other hunter types. This can be explained by the fact that women constitute a large portion of this occupational group, but represent only a small portion of the elk and other hunting publics. In the professional, technical and managerial class, all other types of hunters approximated the percentage represented by the U.S. population, whereas elk hunters were somewhat less well represented.

Hunter Income

The income distribution of elk hunters was skewed toward the higher income brackets, whereas all hunter types and the U.S. population were more evenly distributed through the income levels. On the basis of 1970 and 1971 data, about 11% of elk hunters earned less than $6,000 annually, and 16% earned about $15,000. More than half the elk hunters were in the $9,000 to $15,000 bracket—twice the proportion of other hunters and the U.S. population. In 1991, 49% of all hunters reported earning more than $30,000, whereas only 42% of the general population earned at that level (U.S. Fish and Wildlife Service 1993, 1997).

Hunter Residence

In 1970, elk hunter residence was shown to be predominantly urban, as was the case for other types of hunters and for the U.S. population as a whole. A greater proportion of elk hunters resided in rural areas, however, than did other types of hunters. The percentage of rural elk hunters in Washington (41%) was consistent with the 40% rural elk hunters in New Mexico (Kirkpatrick 1965). These data from the Washington State survey also were consistent with data on elk hunters from other states. The average rural residence for all hunter types was 34% in Washington, 33% in California (Folkman 1963), 34% in Texas (Berger 1974) and 32% for Wyoming big game hunters (Doll and Phillips 1972). However, by 1991, rural big game hunters in the United States outnumbered urban big game hunters, not only in the percentage who participate (14% rural residents versus 5% of urban residents), but also in the total of number of hunters (5.69 million rural big game hunters, compared with 4.78 million urban big game hunters (U.S. Fish and Wildlife Service 1993).

Hunter Gender

Traditionally, women have accounted for less than 10% of all hunters and they were even less represented among elk hunters. In Washington, a 1970 study found that only 5% of elk hunters were women (Potter et al. 1973). Of all women hunters, a clear majority (58%) hunted deer, whereas only 16% hunted elk. In 1991, 8% of U.S. women hunted big game (U.S. Fish and Wildlife Service 1997), and the upward trend of female participation in big game hunting, and hunting generally, continues.

Hunter Race

In 1991, hunters in the United States were overwhelmingly (97%) Caucasian (U.S. Fish and Wildlife service 1997). Eight percent of the total U.S. population hunted, including only 2% African Americans and other races. The authors are not aware of any data that specifically documents elk hunters by race.

Licensing

History

In general, licensing goes back to the early 1900s, although a few states issued licenses in the late 1800s (see Potter

Participation in elk hunting by women is increasing, in part because women are being exposed to the multiple satisfactions and rewards of outdoor activities not previously considered traditional for women, and by gaining confidence in their ability to enjoy these experiences and associated newfound skills, including hunting. The surge of female interest and involvement since the early 1990s can be traced to social and economic factors, but perhaps most of all to the emergence of Becoming an Outdoors Woman (BOW) and similar female-oriented programs adopted by the National Wild Turkey Federation, National Rifle Association and the National Shooting Sports Foundation. *Photo by Donald M. Jones.*

1982). For example, Michigan adopted the first nonresident and resident licensing system in 1895; North Dakota followed suit later the same year (Palmer 1912). Licensing became more universal after legislatures created separate wildlife agencies. The license records are nearly complete since about 1920. In 1876, Manitoba had the earliest recorded elk season requiring a license in North America, and Colorado and North Dakota introduced the first licensed elk seasons in the United States in 1891. Alberta, British Columbia, Montana, Wyoming, Idaho and Washington followed suit around the turn of the century. Colorado, Idaho, Montana, Oregon, Texas, Washington, Wyoming and British Columbia have had continuous licensing since 1920.

South Dakota has a unique and unusual licensing situation. Custer State Park, independent of the South Dakota Department of Game and Fish, sets its own seasons, determines allowable harvest and maintains licensing authority. Records of licenses from 1962 to 1979 show that Custer State Park issued a high of 212 elk licenses in 1973, but averaged 132 licenses annually for the period. This nearly matches the number of elk hunting licenses sold for the rest of the state. Harvest in the park averaged about 100 elk per year—approximately three times the total for the rest of South Dakota. The license fee to hunt elk in the park in 1980 was $200 compared with $16 to hunt elk in other sections of the state.

Texas also has a unique licensing system, which stems from its tradition of closely controlled access to private property. The Texas Parks and Wildlife Department offers free elk permits to landowners who, in turn, control distribution to hunters. The landowners may not sell the permits, but may include them in a package of services. This usually means that the elk hunter pays an access fee to hunt on private lands. The elk hunter in Texas must purchase a general hunting license that entitles him/her to hunt other game as well.

Number of Licenses

The number of elk hunting opportunities (licenses, tags, permits, etc.) issued annually has increased as elk populations have increased. However, elk populations in North America increased more rapidly during the 1980s than did the number of elk licenses issued. This and other factors resulted in an increase in elk numbers during that period (Bunnell 1997). By 1995, the ratio of licenses issued compared with the total elk population exceeded the 1970 ratio. In 1970, states and provinces issued almost 513,000 elk licenses. At that time, the population of elk in North America north of Mexico was estimated at 553,000, a ratio of 0.93 license per elk. In 1995, 947,000 licenses were issued, with an estimated population of 968,000 elk, a ratio of 0.98 license per elk. In order, Colorado, Oregon and Washington issued the greatest number of licenses in 1979, each issuing more than 100,000. In 1995, Colorado (220,000), Montana (177,000), Oregon (159,000), Idaho (114,300) and Washington (94,000) issued the most elk permits. During the 1995 hunting season, Kansas (33), Nebraska (38), North Dakota (16), Oklahoma (24) and Texas (8) each issued less than 50 permits. Fifteen states and four provinces issued elk hunting licenses in 1975. In 1985, 18 states and 4 provinces issued elk licenses. In 1995, the number of states and provinces issuing licenses had increased to 20 and 4, respectively (Bunnell 1997).

Table 115 lists each state and province with the number of elk hunting licenses or permits issued from 1930 through 1995. Since the time that elk hunting licenses first were issued, the number and use of those licenses have increased dramatically, which attests to the success of elk management. That general trend continues. From 1960 to 1979, the number of licensed elk hunters more than doubled in the United States and Canada combined. Alaska, Idaho, Montana, Oregon, Washington, Wyoming and Saskatchewan doubled or nearly doubled their license sales, and sales in Arizona, Colorado and New Mexico increased 4.5 times, and sales in Utah increased almost 10 times.

Between 1980 and 1995, Arizona more than doubled the number of elk permits issued. Idaho and Montana both increased elk tags by nearly 50% and Colorado increased elk permits by 35%, adding 46,000 elk hunters. During this period, Washington decreased elk permits from more than 136,000 in 1980 to slightly more than 94,000 in 1995, a 31% decrease in permits issued.

The outlook in Canada has been similar to that in the United States. The early to mid-1970s showed a decline in licenses issued, but sales increased steadily through 1980. However, between 1980 and 1995, Alberta decreased their elk permits by a third with almost 10,000 fewer permits issued in 1995.

The number of elk-hunting licenses issued is only one indicator of demand for hunting. Another indication is the latent demand—that is, the number of individuals who want to hunt elk but are unable to obtain licenses within existing quotas. Many states and provinces limit the number of licenses issued to keep the harvest of elk herds within prescribed limits. In 1974, for example, there were 10,896 elk hunter applications for the 50 available permits in California. The hunters' odds were 1 in 217 for getting a permit to hunt elk in that state. Michigan had 35,000 applicants for 300 permits in 1965 (Moran 1973). In 1969, the number of applicants in Colorado exceeded the supply by 13,000. And in Nevada, 240 individuals applied for 15 elk-hunting permits (Wildlife Management Institute 1971).

Still another indicator of the popularity of elk hunting is the number of nonresident elk hunters (Table 116). In 1975, Colorado and Montana had 36,545 and 25,584 nonresident elk hunters, respectively. Idaho and Wyoming followed with more than 6,700 and 6,000 nonresident elk hunters, respectively.

Several states restrict or, at times, have restricted the number of nonresident hunters. For example, the Wyoming Game and Fish Department limits the number of nonresident hunters allowed to 7,250 per year. Idaho limits nonresidents to 10% of the elk hunting permits available for a given season, or a maximum of 12,815 elk tags sold on a first-come first-served basis. In 1976, Montana established a limit of 17,000 nonresident elk tags.

It is somewhat surprising that Oregon and Washington had so few nonresident elk hunters in the 1970s because each of these states had herds of some 50,000 to 60,000 elk, equaling those in Idaho, Wyoming and probably Montana, which does not census its elk population. The number of nonresident elk hunters almost doubled (2,767 to 5,531) in Oregon between 1975 and 1995, but nonresident elk hunters in Washington showed only a very modest increase (830 to 1,039) during the same period. Although data are not complete, it is apparent that, in 1995, more than half of all nonresident elk hunting in North America occurred in Colorado (Table 116). Two of the five Canadian provinces with hunted elk populations—Manitoba and Saskatchewan—do not issue out-of-province licenses. Alberta and British Columbia offer nonresident hunters an opportunity to pursue elk. Combined, they sell 500 to 600 nonresident licenses per year. Ontario closed elk hunting seasons in 1979.

The trend of increasing elk license sales has continued through the mid-1990s, but information collected by Bunnell (1997) suggests that, if elk managers reach their goals, elk populations and license sales may stabilize early in the 21st century and could decline somewhat thereafter. Projections made by the U.S. Forest Service (1975) that big game hunters would increase by two-thirds within 50 years may in fact be optimistic. By 1991, approximately one-third of the way through the projection period, the number of big game hunters actually had decreased by about 15%. However, during the period 1975 to 1995, the number of elk hunters in the United States increased by two-thirds, from more than 531,000 to more than 797,000 (Bunnell 1997).

License Fees

Receipts from sales of state hunting licenses are a primary means of support for all state wildlife management programs and activities. Also important to each state wildlife agency is the benchmark Federal Aid in Wildlife Restoration Act of 1937, also known as the Pittman-Robertson Act, after its sponsors. The act provides for a manufacturer's excise tax on sporting firearms, handguns, factory-made ammunition and certain archery equipment. These monies, collected by the federal government, are allocated to the state wildlife agencies on a 3:1 matching grant basis, using a formula that considers each state's land area and number of licensed hunters. In addition to helping finance wildlife programs of the state agencies, the Pittman-Robertson Act safeguards hunting license receipts by basing each state's eligibility to receive federal aid matching funds solely on the

Table 115. Number of resident and nonresident elk hunting licenses or permits issued in states and provinces at 5-year intervals, 1930 to 1995

State/province	\<\-\-\-\-\- Year \-\-\-\-\-\>									
	1930	1935	1940	1945	1950	1955	1960	1965	1970	1975
Alaska	—	—	—	—	50	501	345	309	184	869
Arizona	—	229	229	—	4,250	2,225	2,245	6,086	6,170	7,712
California	—	—	—	—	—	150	—	—	100	50
Colorado	?	?	?	7,517	25,266	24,006	39,495	45,852	93,293	137,312
Idaho	?	3,758	9,759	12,752	33,855	52,257	58,717	59,177	72,793	49,427
Kansas	?	?	?	?	?	?	?	?	?	
Michigan	?	?	?	?	?	?	?	?	?	
Minnesota	?	?	?	?	?	?	?	?	?	
Montana	?	?	?	?	?	62,147	59,497	91,794	87,328	113,464
Nebraska	?	?	?	?	?	?	?	?	?	
Nevada	—	—	—	60	100	60	10	45	15	10
New Mexico	—	?	?	?	?	708	2,436	5,932	6,812	8,078
North Dakota	?	?	?	?	?	?	?	?	?	
Oklahoma	?	?	?	?	?	?	?	?	?	194
Oregon	?	?	4,153	12,625	24,741	29,309	49,134	67,519	73,563	110,924
South Dakota	?	?	?	?	?	?	?	?	50	145
Texas	?	?	?	?	?	?	?	?	?	9
Utah	?	357	928	700	1,680	1,473	2,281	2,505	10,354	19,656
Washington	?	878	5,310	20,376	52,559	37,701	51,640	72,895	98,699	103,615
Wyoming	?	?	?	?	22,495	24,295	25,446	33,650	44,793	54,099
Alberta	?	—	—	?	?	?	?	?	29,761	16,396
British Columbia	?	?	?	?	?	?	?	14,866	10,177	7,229
Manitoba	—	—	—	—	?	?	?	175	1,719	527
Saskatchewan	—	—	—	—	2,392	3,287	1,317	1,067	2,644	2,282

Note: — = closed season; ? = unknown.

Table 116. Number of nonresident elk hunting licenses issued yearly in states and provinces at 5-year intervals, 1950 to 1995

State/province	\<\-\-\-\-\- Year \-\-\-\-\-\>						
	1950	1955	1960	1965	1970	1975	1980
Alaska			22	52	56	9	
Arizona			67	183	185	231	142
California							
Colorado	3,691	3,832	7,265	13,068	24,781	36,545	49,225
Idaho	1,182	3,729	6,725	7,187	11,930	6,746	7,966
Montana	897	2,180	4,279	7,648	9,501	25,584	na
Nevada							
New Mexico		193	301	589	941	1,703	na
Oklahoma							
Oregon				708	1,246	2,767	2,953
Utah						101	na
Washington				193	504	830	939
Wyoming	1,899	2,500	2,532	4,000	5,500	6,000	6,086
Alberta					346	225	na
British Columbia				907	690	339	na

Table 115 continued

State/province	Year			
	1980	1985	1990	1995
AK	1,334	816	1,335	811
AZ	9,380	10,740	13,065	22,500
CA	—	100	120	160
CO	163,400	139,033	192,907	219,852
ID	79,000	85,000	98,000	114,300
KS			6	33
MI		120	230	316
MN		4	—	—
MT	120,978	140,125	155,691	176,631
NE				38
NV	12	97	243	306
NM	?	?	?	?
ND		5	5	16
OK	176	316	312	24
OR	—	136,411	130,158	179,044
SD	350	683	371	764
TX	8	2	6	8
UT	20,621	30,556	46,581	28,877
WA	136,208	89,226	90,935	94,066
WY	62,533	53,596	54,578	59,594
AB	28,900	37,412	21,690	19,140
BC	13,500	17,000	18,000	17,000
MB	?	?	?	2,895
SK	3,250	4,400	4,817	?

Table 116 continued

State/province	Year		
	1985	1990	1995
AZ	228	586	902
CA			1
CO	43,318	79,184	97,232
ID	10,674	13,306	13,436
MT	na	17,048	na
NV			9
NM	na	na	na
OK		13	
OR	4,375	5,795	5,531
UT	na	na	1,100
WA	670	1,001	1,039
WY	7,030	8,763	9,231
AB	na	na	na
BC	na	na	na

fact that the state uses license receipts strictly for wildlife purposes. Although hunters frequently gripe about license funds being "stolen" by state governments, hunters can be assured that, if a state receives any Pittman-Robertson funds, all license and permit money must go for wildlife purposes.

License fees vary widely among states and provinces (Table 117). Some hunters must purchase a general license or firearms permit before obtaining an elk permit. Additional charges may include an application fee, vendor fee or conservation license. Some combination licenses also allow the hunter to fish or hunt other game species. In all cases, there is a price differential between resident and nonresident fees.

In 1980, Texas had the lowest resident fee at $5.25, and Oklahoma charged the least ($50) to nonresident elk hunters. The highest resident fees were paid by Utah and Nevada elk hunters—$40 and $39, respectively. Wyoming charged a high of $250 to 1980 nonresident elk hunters, and Alberta charged $205 to alien elk hunters. These fees are small compared with charges to hunt elk on some Indian reservations, as discussed later in this chapter. In 1995, North Dakota had the lowest resident elk hunting fee ($20) and Colorado ($250) had the lowest nonresident elk hunting license fee.

From 1965 to 1980, more than half the states and provinces doubled their elk hunting fees. Manitoba did not increase its resident fee during this 16-year period. Oklahoma and Texas increased fees by only $1.75 and $2.10, respectively, during the same period. The more popular elk hunting states—Colorado, Idaho, Montana, Oregon, Washington and Wyoming—increased fees by an average of $11, whereas the increase for all states and provinces averaged $9.60. Nevada had the highest raise in resident hunting fees—$24. License fees generally about doubled again between 1980 and 1995, but Montana resident fees rose from $8 in 1980 to $92 in 1995, and Nevada's resident elk hunting fee increased from $39 in 1980 to $130.50 in 1995. Wyoming resident fees remained at $25 in 1995.

Nonresident license fees show a different pattern. Although resident fees increased relatively little in actual dollars paid, nonresident fees to hunt elk in the United States and Canada rose an average of $83 from 1965 to 1980. Ontario increased nonresident fees by only $4 over the 12-year period, but both Alaska and Wyoming charged $150 more in 1980 than in 1965. Between 1980 and 1995, nonresident fee increases ranged from 40% in Wyoming ($250 to $350) and 50% in Arizona ($200 to $303) to more than 100% in Oregon, New Mexico, Washington and Montana, and more than 300% in Oklahoma ($50 to $250) and Idaho ($151 to $425).

Table 117.   Resident (R), nonresident (N) and alien (A) fees, in dollars, paid to hunt elk in states and provinces at 5-year intervals, 1965 to 1995

State/province	Residency	Year			
		1965	1970	1975	1980
Alaska	R	7.00	7.00	7.00	12.00
	N	35.00	35.00	95.00	185.00
Arizona	R	20.00	20.00	20.00	30.00
	N	75.00	75.00	75.00	200.00
California	R				
Colorado	R	10.00	12.50	12.50	16.00
	N	50.00	75.00	75.00	135.00
Idaho	R	6.00	13.00	13.00	14.00
	N	103.00	150.00	150.00	151.00
Michigan	R				
Montana	R	1.00	3.25	3.25	8.00
	N	100.00	151.00	151.00	225.00
Nebraska	R				
Nevada	R	15.00	20.00	22.50	39.00
	N				
New Mexico	R	15.00	15.00	16.50	21.00
	N	50.00	50.00	75.00	176.00
North Dakota	R				
Oklahoma	R		13.25	13.25	15.00
	N		25.00	25.00	50.00
Oregon	R	11.00	15.00	15.00	22.00
	N	70.00	70.00	85.00	180.00
South Dakota	R	8.00	16.00	16.00	16.00
Texas	R	3.15	3.15	5.25	5.25
	N	25.00	25.00	37.50	100.75
Utah	R	18.50	20.00	20.00	40.00
	N			150.00	225.00
Washington	R	12.00	13.00	17.50	18.50
	N	60.00	60.00	92.00	102.00
Wyoming	R	5.00	5.00	15.00	25.00
	N	100.00	125.00	125.00	250.00
Alberta	R	6.00	8.00	9.00	15.00
	N	50.00	100.00	100.00	105.00
	A	100.00	100.00	100.00	205.00
British Columbia	R	6.00	9.00	17.00	17.00
	N	77.00	80.00	107.00	107.00
	A	87.00	90.00	175.00	175.00
Manitoba	R	20.00	20.00	20.00	20.00
Ontario	R	4.50	10.00	10.00	
	N	36.00	40.00	40.00	
Saskatchewan	R	10.00	12.00	15.00	20.00

Note: Values may include application, vendor and other minor fees in addition to the base license fee. This is a ratio of comparison as listed by the states. It may or may not include license fees, application fees and other associated fees, but does not indicate the ratio of resident and nonresident costs.

The total amounts paid for license fees by elk hunters are impressive figures. Nearly all these monies were used for wildlife agency operations and programs that benefit hunters and nonhunters alike. Considering that, between 1980 and 1995, license fees, on the average, more than doubled and the number of elk hunters also doubled, it is probable that income from elk hunting increased roughly 400% during that period. In 1980, resident elk hunters in the United States and Canada contributed more than $12.3 million, whereas nonresidents contributed $13 million—a total of more than $25.3 million paid for the privilege to hunt elk. This included general license or firearms fees that usually were a prerequisite to other hunter privileges, such as bird hunting and other big game hunting. Nonresidents

Table 117 continued

State/ province	Year		
	1985	1990	1995
AZ	60.00	63.00	63.00
	300.00	303.00	303.00
CA	165.00	198.00	236.50
CO	25.00	25.00	30.00
	210.00	210.00	250.00
ID	19.50	19.50	21.00
	226.50	320.00	425.00
MI	104.00	104.35	104.35
MT	52.00	62.50	92.00
	302.00	452.00	480.00
NE			117.50
NV	91.00	105.50	130.50
			610.50
NM	38.00	38.00	41.00
	213.00	213.00	391.00
ND	20.00	20.00	20.00
OK	25.75	35.25	35.25
	150.75	211.50	251.00
OR	23.00	29.00	41.00
	180.00	265.50	343.00
SD	16.00	35.00	35.00
UT	40.00	45.00	55.00
	225.00	225.00	328.00
WA	32.00	32.00	39.00
	225.00	225.00	270.00
WY	25.00	25.00	25.00
	250.00	250.00	350.00
BC	20.00	20.00	25.00
	120.00	120.00	150.00

paid about the same amount in total fees despite being outnumbered by resident elk hunters nearly 8:1. Putting it another way, nonresidents constituted 11% of the elk hunters, but paid 51% of the total fees.

Nonresident hunters make very substantial contributions to wildlife management revenues in several states. Nonresidents paid more than $24 million just in license and permit fees to hunt elk in Colorado in 1995. Nonresident license fees exceeded $8 million in Montana, $5 million in Idaho and $3 million in Wyoming in 1995. Resident hunters paid $8.5 million to hunt elk in Montana and more than $3 million in Colorado, Oregon and Washington. Nonresident fees exceeded resident fees in Colorado, Idaho, Montana and Wyoming.

License fee increases usually mean a drop in license sales. Small increases, however, often have no effect on sale trends. In Colorado, Idaho and Washington, the number of resident elk hunters continued to increase when license fee increases were in the range of $1.00 to $2.50. When increased fees were greater, the number of sales dropped. However, the drop in license sales usually occurs during the first year of a fee increase, then sales start climbing again. Conclusions are similar for nonresident hunters, except that license fee increases are much greater. To avoid decreases in sales and realistically reflect increasing costs for management, states and provinces should consider raising license fees gradually and more often. It is not uncommon to find license fees remaining the same for 5, 10 or even 15 years, then increasing greatly to catch up with increased costs.

Differential license fees were the subject of a 1970 study (Wildlife Management Institute 1971). At that time, nonresident hunters, on average, paid more than seven times as much for elk hunting licenses as did resident hunters. It was believed that a nonresident license fee approximately five times greater than the resident license fee met the test of reasonableness. In 1965, 6 of the 10 elk hunting states were above the 1:5 ratio. Montana—at 1:100—had the greatest differential. Since 1965, there has been an increase in the number of states and provinces exceeding the 1:5 ratio. Only Oklahoma was below the ratio in 1980, and Washington and Utah were slightly above. Table 118 shows the ratio of nonresident to resident elk license fees updated for 1985, 1990 and 1995. Idaho, with a ratio of 20.2 to 1 has the highest differential in fees. Wyoming, at 14 to 1 is the only other state with a ratio more than 10 to 1. Arizona has the lowest ratio at 4.8 to 1. Ratios between 5 to 1 and 10 to 1 are the norm (Montana, British Columbia, Oregon, Colorado, Washington, New Mexico, Oklahoma and Utah).

It seems natural that states with high-quality elk hunting and high nonresident demand for elk hunting permits and licenses should charge what the market will bear. One problem with this is that elk are harvested mainly on federal lands in those states with the largest license fee differentials. For example, in 1970, 85% of the elk harvest in Colorado was on federal land. This was true for 95% of Idaho's elk harvest, 70% of Oregon's, 90% of Utah's, 88% of Wyoming's and 100% of Alaska's (Wildlife Management Institute 1971).

Table 118.   Ratio of nonresident to resident elk hunting costs at 5-year intervals, 1965 to 1995

State/province	Year						
	1965	1970	1975	1980	1985	1990	1995
Montana	100.0	46.5	46.5	28.1	5.8	7.2	5.2
Wyoming	20.0	25.0	8.3	10.0	10.0	10.0	14.0
Idaho	17.2	23.0	11.5	10.8	11.6	16.4	20.2
British Columbia	12.8	8.9	6.3	6.3	6.0	6.0	6.0
Texas	7.9	7.9	7.1	19.2			
Oregon	6.4	4.7	5.7	8.2	7.8	9.1	8.4
Colorado	5.0	6.0	6.0	8.4	8.4	8.4	8.3
Washington	5.0	4.6	5.2	5.5	7.0	7.0	6.9
Arizona	3.8	3.8	3.8	6.7	5.0	4.8	4.8
New Mexico	3.3	3.3	4.5	8.4	5.6	5.6	9.5
Oklahoma		1.9	1.9	3.3	5.8	6.0	7.1
Utah			7.5	5.5	5.6	5.0	6.0

Fee differentials arguably discourage equal access to the resources on federal lands, which are owned in common by all citizens. This viewpoint was expressed by the Public Land Law Review Commission (1970) in the form of a recommendation: "State policies which unduly discriminate against nonresident hunters and fishermen in the use of public lands through license fee differentials . . . should be discouraged." The Commission acknowledged that a reasonable differential was justified, but did not define what was reasonable. However, it viewed the existing situation as "so discriminatory as to raise constitutional questions." The Commission went on to recommend that federal fish and wildlife cost-sharing programs be available only to states with reasonable resident and nonresident fee differentials.

Fee differentials are a likely topic of further debate in the decades ahead. Continued large fee differentials in the United States could trigger congressional reaction if the issue is forced into the courts. The question of how far a state's legal authority extends to federal lands already has been tested. In 1976, the U.S. Supreme Court upheld the right of Congress to legislate control of wild horses and burros on federal land in *Kleppe v. State of New Mexico*. The point is that states may jeopardize traditional management prerogatives by maintaining large resident and nonresident

Nonresident elk hunters constitute less than 12% of all elk hunters, but pay more than 50% of the total elk hunting fees. License and permit revenues from nonresident elk hunters exceed those of resident hunters in Colorado, Idaho and Wyoming. In addition, the economic investment by nonresidents—for travel, lodging, outfitter and guide fees, equipment rental, shipping, and other expenses—is at least several times that of most resident elk hunters. *Photo courtesy of the Wyoming Game and Fish Department.*

fee differentials. If the federal government steps in, the result could be mandatory equal resident and nonresident state license fees or even federal licensing of hunters on federal lands. This likely would not be in anyone's best interest, including that of wildlife, in the long run.

Compounding the problem is the nonresident contribution to wildlife agency income. In some cases, nonresidents pay more than half the revenue received by the agencies from elk hunters. If this revenue was lost or reduced substantially, resident hunters might face large fee increases.

Elk Harvest

During 1995, hunters harvested more than 166,000 elk in 21 states and 3 provinces. Table 119 summarizes elk harvest in the United States and Canada from 1935 to 1995. Colorado has consistently produced the largest elk harvest, including more than 36,000 elk harvested in 1995. Idaho, Montana and Oregon had 1995 harvests exceeding 20,000 elk. Wyoming harvested nearly 18,000 elk in 1995. Arizona, New Mexico, and Utah harvested about 10,000 elk each in 1995. And the state of Washington harvested more than 6,000 elk in 1995. British Columbia (2,800) and Alberta (2,200) had the largest harvests in Canada (Bunnell 1997). The dollar value of elk meat is significant. Assuming that the average elk yields 300 pounds (136 kg) of table meat, the 166,000 elk harvested in 1995 represented 24,900 tons (22,576 metric tons) of potentially high-quality meat. Valuing this meat arbitrarily at $1.50 per pound ($0.68/kg), the estimated value of elk meat taken home by hunters is $74,700,000. Besides

Current, conservative value—$1.50 to $2.25 per pound ($0.68–$1.02/kg) of elk meat taken home by hunters annually is approximately $75 million to $112 million. Elk is higher in protein and lower in fat than beef and is widely considered one of the best (and mildest) of the game meats. *Photo by Don Domenick; courtesy of the Colorado Division of Wildlife.*

having substantial monetary value, elk meat is high in protein and low in fat compared with most beef.

Several states not normally thought of as elk hunting states have supported harvests in the past. Pennsylvania hunters—restricted to still-hunting and to one four-point bull per year—harvested 101 elk from 1923 to 1931. Michigan reported 269 elk harvested in 1964 and 183 in 1965. New Hampshire sponsored its first and only elk hunt in 1941. Although 600 permits were available through lottery, only 293 hunters applied and 200 actually hunted in a 2-day December hunt; 46 hunters harvested elk.

Figure 174 shows harvest trends from 1935 to 1995 for seven states with long traditions of elk hunting. Although

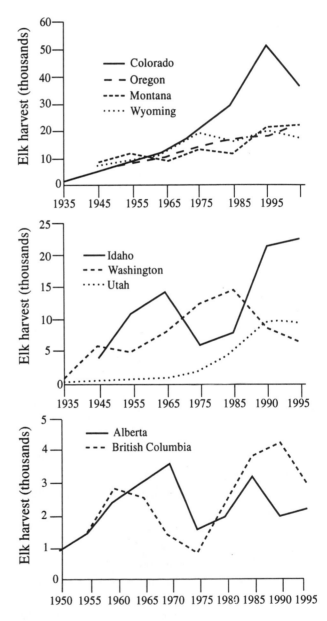

Figure 174. Elk harvest trends in seven states (1935 to 1995) and two provinces (1950 to 1995).

Table 119.   Yearly elk harvest by state and province in 5-year intervals, 1935 to 1995

State/province	Year								
	1935	1940	1945	1950	1955	1960	1965	1970	1975
Alaska	—	—	—	27	26	127	142	62	23
Arizona	145	95	—	1,484	612	637	1,469	924	1,138
California	—	—	—	—	144	—	—	21	26
Colorado	955	2,987	3,361	7,446	7,037	10,839	13,595	17,059	22,111
Idaho	1,821	?	4,392	7,165	15,799	16,545	14,064	14,146	8,981
Kansas	?	?	?	?	?	?	?	?	0
Michigan	?	?	?	?	?	?	?	?	0
Minnesota	?	?	?	?	?	?	?	?	0
Montana	?	?	?	11,300	16,000	10,100	7,700	13,988	15,750
Nebraska	?	?	?	?	?	?	?	?	0
Nevada	—	—	40	30	28	3	10	6	6
New Mexico	?	?	?	?	?	948	1,161	1,589	1,805
North Dakota	?	?	?	?	?	?	?	?	—
Oklahoma	—	—	—	—	—	—	—	104	150
Oregon	?	2,529	2,465	5,391	6,083	10,800	12,266	12,680	15,351
South Dakota	?	?	?	?	?	?	?	28	58
Texas	?	?	?	?	?	9	4	6	5
Utah	205	838	562	1,403	850	1,173	997	1,995	2,366
Virginia	2	5	1	—	—	3	—	—	—
Washington	250	1,800	3,212	10,740	7,000	7,760	11,150	11,150	12,730
Wyoming	?	?	4,987	9,122	9,554	9,383	12,564	18,012	20,970
Alberta	—	?	?	?	2,312	2,050	?	?	850
British Columbia	?	?	?	749	1,705	2,814	1,982	1,836	1,172
Manitoba	—	—	—	?	?	?	?	1,133	174
Saskatchewan	—	—	—	897	304	646	230	936	190

Note: — = closed season; ? = unknown.

harvest fluctuated annually in some states and during some periods, the 5-year trends generally are upward through the entire period. During this period, short-term fluctuations in harvest with generally increasing harvests resulted from weather conditions during the hunts, changing elk management goals, the steady upward trend of elk populations, the steady increase in licensed elk hunters, and other local or short-term factors. Colorado, Wyoming, Montana, Oregon, Washington and Utah showed steady and, at times, large increases in the number of elk harvested from 1935 to 1980. Colorado's harvest increased from less than 1,000 elk in 1935 to a peak at the end of the 1980s with annual harvests around 50,000, and then declined to just slightly more than 36,000 in 1995.

Elk populations and elk harvests in Utah were controlled carefully for a period of 40 years (1925 to 1965) by a unique system involving two citizen boards. The Utah Fish and Game Board was similar to boards and commissions in other western states—setting policy and determining harvest on resident species of game. However, a second board, the Board of Big Game Control, had all authority to determine harvest on big game in Utah. By law, the Board of Big

Game Control was composed of five individuals—a representative selected by the Utah Wool Growers Association, a representative selected by the Utah Cattlemen's Association, a U.S. Forest Service employee representing public land managers, a representative sportsman selected by the Utah Wildlife Federation, and the Director of the Utah Department of Fish and Game (now Utah Division of Wildlife Resources) who also served as secretary of the Board. The secretary voted only to break a tie. During 1925 to 1965, the representatives of the wool growers, cattlemen and public land mangers, in general, shared a goal of controlling elk numbers (Hancock and Bunnell 1985). However, in the mid-1960s, increasing public pressure for more elk-hunting opportunity forced the Board of Big Game Control to adopt an unlimited bull hunting program. Hunter participation increased dramatically after 1966; however, the harvest of cow elk was curtailed sharply and several elk herds were started by translocation and natural migration. The net result was that elk herds grew dramatically (Hancock and Bunnell 1985). The board was abolished in 1995, and Utah now has a single, seven-member Wildlife Board that sets policy, including harvest levels, for all wildlife.

Table 119 continued

State/ province	Year			
	1980	1985	1990	1995
AK	101	200	201	96
AZ	1,902	3,959	5,699	10,139
CA	0	49	92	108
CO	27,623	22,349	51,595	36,171
ID	8,300	15,550	21,500	22,437
KS	0		4	10
MI	0	119	204	256
MN	0	2	0	0
MT	14,841	17,635	20,574	21,961
NE	0	0	0	14
NV	11	84	143	183
NM	2,011	2,919	7,117	12,204
ND	—	21	19	17
OK	88	120	147	21
OR	22,800	20,671	18,336	22,395
SD	145	284	152	474
TX	4	0	3	4
UT	2,633	5,383	10,009	9,470
VA	?	?	?	?
WA	10,820	8,964	8,646	6,429
WY	17,428	13,809	20,086	17,695
AB	2,046	3,238	2,053	2,241
BC	2,370	3,712	4,141	2,893
MB	502	327	436	850
SK	675	650	1,055	—

Elk harvest in Idaho increased rapidly between 1935 and 1955, and then leveled off. Between 1968 and the late 1970s, harvest in Idaho declined steadily. The decline resulted from the degradation of winter range in the Clearwater drainage. However, by 1985, harvest had rebounded to 1960 levels (about 15,000). And the 1995 harvest was more than 22,000 elk.

In general, Canadian harvests increased significantly between 1950 and 1965. From the mid-1960s through about 1980, harvests declined to near or below 1950 levels. However, harvests again increased during the 1980s, only to decrease again during the 1990s. Declines in Canada's elk harvest generally have been the result of restrictive regulations designed to maintain mature bulls and provide uncrowded hunting. The total population of elk in Canada has continued to grow through the mid-1990s. Alberta and British Columbia have consistently produced most of the elk harvested in Canada.

The percentage of hunters bagging an elk reflects the relative success rates for elk hunters in the United States and Canada (Table 120). Nevada, in 1978, and California, in 1961, each reported 100% hunter harvest success. During California's 15 elk hunting seasons from 1975 to 1979, hunters averaged a 57% harvest success, Nevada averaged 77% during that span. These rates, however, are misleading when compared with those of other states. California and Nevada have limited-number, permit-only elk hunting, which wildlife managers say accounts for the relatively high harvest success rates. This is illustrated in Montana; in 1975, hunters without permit limitations showed a 14% harvest success rate, whereas hunters under limited, permit-only hunts experienced a 42% harvest success rate. Under limited permits, elk harvest success in Utah ranged from 39% to 90% through 1966. Utah removed the permit limitations in 1967, allowing unlimited elk tags. Harvest success rates immediately dropped to 23%. In 1979, the rate was 8% for general-season bull elk hunters. However, as herds increased in Utah, bull elk hunter success also rebounded to more than 15% during much of the 1990s.

Table 120 lists harvest success percentages for elk hunters in states and provinces from which data were available. Generally, the proportion of successful hunters, in terms of actual harvest, has declined over the years. The large elk harvest states—Colorado, Idaho, Montana, Oregon and Washington—showed harvest successes of 9% to 17% in 1979 and 8% to 22% in 1995. Wyoming was the exception—elk hunters averaged about 33% harvest success from 1970 to 1995.

The overall trends and relationships of elk harvest success are illustrated by plotting separate curves for total elk harvest and the number of licensed hunters. In Figures 175 and 176, Utah and Washington are used as representative elk hunting states. The general picture is one of rapidly rising numbers of hunters and proportionately fewer elk harvested. Utah showed a fairly high harvest success rate through 1950. However, hunting opportunity was extremely limited (Hancock and Bunnell 1985). After 1950, hunter numbers began to increase slowly. After 1966, hunter numbers increased rapidly due to the adoption of an open, unlimited bull elk hunt. Recreation increased substantially, but harvest did not increase proportionately with hunters numbers, so the hunter success rate decreased. In the 1990s, hunter success in Utah rebounded to near previous levels. Hunter success continues below 10% in Washington.

Figures 175 and 176 demonstrate what wildlife managers have known for a long time: as hunter numbers increase, so do the harvests, but the percentage of harvest success decreases. This relationship allows managers to make recreational hunting opportunities available to larger numbers of hunters, but they do so only within constraints that ensure sustained elk populations and maintain a threshold of hunter success and harvest quality.

Table 120.   Percentage of elk hunting harvest success in some states and provinces at 5-year intervals, 1935 to 1995.

State/province	1935	1940	1945	1950	1955	1960	1965	1970	1975
Alaska	x	x	x	54	25	37	46	34	19
Arizona	54	41	x	35	28	28	24	15	15
California	x	x	x	x	96	x	x	21	x
Colorado	—	—	45	30	29	27	24	18	16
Idaho	48	—	34	21	30	28	24	19	18
Montana	—	—	—	—	26	17	8	16	14
Nevada	x	x	67	30	47	30	22	40	60
New Mexico	—	—	—	—	—	39	20	23	21
Oregon	—	61	20	22	21	22	18	17	14
South Dakota	—	—	—	—	—	—	—	56	40
Utah	57	90	80	84	58	51	40	19	12
Washington	28	34	16	20	19	15	15	11	12
Wyoming	—	—	—	41	39	37	37	40	39
Alberta	x	x	—	—	—	—	—	—	5
British Columbia	—	—	—	—	—	—	13	18	16
Manitoba	x	x	x	—	—	—	—	66	33
Saskatchewan	x	x	x	38	—	49	22	35	8

Note: x = closed season; — = no data.

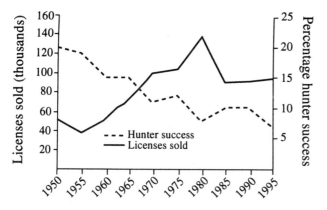

Figure 175.   Trends and relationship of elk hunting license sales and elk harvests in Washington State, 1950 to 1995.

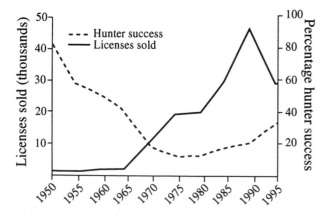

Figure 176.   Trends and relationship of elk hunting license sales and elk harvests in Utah, 1950 to 1995.

This relationship of increased hunter numbers afield and lower harvest success encourages a change in management perspective from one based on harvest to one based on days afield (Potter et al. 1973). Such an orientation assumes that benefits to the hunter are maximized by increasing the number of hunter days afield (Crissey 1971). One shortcoming of the concept lies in the assumption of constant levels of benefits per hunter, regardless of harvest success or quality hunting conditions. That is, if the number of hunters seeking the same number of animals is doubled or tripled, the benefits are doubled or tripled, although the quality of the experience may be altered drastically (Hendee 1974). The consequently more crowded hunting conditions are unpleasant for many hunters; they make some hunters feel unsafe. However, data collected by the International Hunter Education Association do not support the assertion that big game hunting accidents are increasing (D. Knotts personal communication:2001).

In addition to producing altered hunting conditions, a large increase in hunter numbers tends to increase the effort required to bag an elk. For example, in 1974, an average of 21 days of hunting was required to harvest an elk in Colorado (Colorado Division of Wildlife 1974). At the same time, hunters were averaging 4.4 days of elk hunting each year. This means that, on average, a hunter would harvest only one elk for every five seasons of hunting effort. In 1995, almost 220,000 Colorado elk hunters spent 1,147,000 days afield to harvest 36,000 elk—an average of almost 32 days afield per elk harvested.

Table 120 continued

State/ province	Year 1980	1985	1990	1995
AK	19	26	30	23
AZ	21	38	45	46
CA	—	49	70	67
CO	17	16	27	16
ID	—	23	28	22
MT	16	20	21	20
NV	92	99	59	60
NM	15	22	34	44
OR	19	15	17	16
SD	21	42	41	62
WA	210	8	10	8
WY	32	30	41	33
AB	7	9	9	12
BC	21	24	27	23
MB	95	12	16	30
SK	—	—	—	—

Although more hunters are served under the aforementioned conditions, the challenges of managing hunter density and maintaining harvest success rates at or above an acceptable threshold level become increasingly difficult. There is a need to find a balance between hunter numbers, quality experiences and harvest success. One such effort is found in New Mexico. In 1976, in an attempt to provide the hunter with a quality experience and reduce intense hunter pressure on elk, the Department of Game and Fish stratified the elk hunting season. Hunters could apply for an elk license every other year and, for each year that they received a license, they had to specify one of six hunt periods between October and December.

Miscellaneous Hunting Requirements

As more and more hunters take to the field and elk management becomes more intensive, licensing and harvest quotas, as well as additional hunting regulations, are inevitable. Today, there are not only bag limits and restricted seasons, but requirements for hunter age, hunter education courses (including safety), residency and guides. In addition, there is a host of licenses, tags, stamps and permits. The success of a big game management program depends on hunter regulations. This is true for both biological and sociological factors of management.

The minimum age for hunting elk is fairly low in most states and provinces. In Alaska, New Mexico, Texas, Washington and British Columbia, there is no minimum age. In most cases, however, young, prospective elk hunters are restricted from participation by other requirements, such as passing a hunter safety training course. In Washington, less than 1% of all hunters are younger than 12 years old. A random sample of Washington hunters revealed no one less than 9 years of age. During the 1970s, the oldest minimum age for elk hunters was 16 years in California, Oklahoma and Utah. Utah's age requirement was lowered to 14 in 1988.

To obtain a hunting license in most states, the minimal residency requirement is 2 to 6 months. Alaska, California, Wyoming and Alberta both have a residency period of 12 months, whereas Saskatchewan has only a 2-month residency provision. The trend is liberalization of this requirement. As of 1979, there were six states and provinces that required 3 or fewer months to become a resident.

Nearly all hunters must take hunter education or firearm safety courses to obtain their first license. In California, Colorado and British Columbia, every hunter must pass a training course. In other states and provinces, only hunters under a specified age must show evidence of having taken the training. This training will reach most elk hunters at least once, as approximately 90% start hunting before age 20

Hunter education courses are not mere formalities to enable licensing to hunt. Their primary objectives are to give novices an understanding of hunting and its ecological role, to acquaint them with laws, rules and ethical standards of hunter conduct and with their responsibility to the land and its owners and the animals, to familiarize them with hunting weapons and the safe use and care of those weapons, and to instill an appreciation for the opportunity to pursue and perhaps take quarry by fair chase. *Photo by Diane Ronayne; courtesy of the Idaho Department of Fish and Game.*

years. Elk hunters in Alaska, Oklahoma, Texas, Alberta and Saskatchewan are not required to take any courses, although a course often is available and many hunters opt to take the course. For example, 37% of the hunters in Saskatchewan have had firearm safety training (Ross 1975).

Idaho's situation is unique. The public school system cooperates with the Idaho Department of Fish and Game by allowing agency personnel to teach a 1-day firearms safety training course to all sixth graders. Each year, about 16,500 boys and girls are taught gun handling and safety, hunter ethics, survival, wildlife identification and some ecological concepts. This program has many advantages over the programs oriented only toward hunters. First, it reaches an audience at an impressionable age. Second, it provides understanding of the ecological basis for hunting in the framework of wildlife management. Third, it introduces potential participants to appropriate human behavior in the out-of-doors, which applies to a variety of recreational activities.

Professional guide service is required in Wyoming, Alberta and British Columbia. The need for this requirement is questionable, at least from the hunter's standpoint. The requirement does support the guide service industry, however. For example, each nonresident elk hunter in Wyoming during 1970 paid about $360 for a guide (Doll and Phillips 1972). Human safety in hazardous unfamiliar terrain and areas of climatic danger is the primary reason for mandatory guide service. However, severe dangers and serious hazards "are found in relatively few areas," and mandatory use of guide service is unreasonable except when and where there are "overriding reasons of human safety" (Wildlife Management Institute 1971:15).

Hunter regulations generally are accepted if their purposes are understood, and if they are advertised, fair and enforced for all. This principle is illustrated best by a restriction in several wildlife management units in northeastern Oregon. For the purpose of improving hunting conditions, 480 miles (772.9 km) of forest roads were closed to motorized vehicles during the elk hunting season (Coggins and Magera 1973). The management units affected were small enough that they did not restrict access by hunters on foot, but the closures definitely altered the pattern of vehicular traffic and means of transporting meat. These regulations were advertised widely in advance of the hunt, and the restricted units were posted. Enforcement was strict, including aircraft patrol. Hunters even policed their own ranks and often went to great lengths to see that violators were apprehended.

Hunters were asked their opinion of Oregon's program as they passed through check stations (Coggins and Magera 1973). In 1 year, 87% of the hunters voiced approval of the restrictions. A year later, approval increased to 93%. Hunters believed that the quality of hunting was much improved over the no-closure conditions. In addition, vehicular restrictions did not reduce the bull elk harvest significantly. It was governed more by the number of hunters in the woods and weather conditions. This program illustrated that hunter restrictions generally are accepted when the aforementioned principles are followed and opportunities are realized for upgrading the various dimensions of hunter satisfaction.

Another example of a restriction that found favor with hunters was a Monday opening—rather than Saturday opening—of Washington's elk season. Sixty-four percent of hunters surveyed preferred the Monday opening, and another 5% had no preference (Parsons 1975). The intent of this restriction was to reduce crowded hunting conditions. Despite the fact that a Monday opening conflicted with jobs, hunters favored the program because it reduced congestion, which made the elk hunting experience more pleasurable.

Illegal Kills and Other Human-related Elk Mortality

The record is far from complete on elk mortality. Hunting and acts of nature take the largest toll, but a host of other human-caused agents add to elk mortality. Among these are motor vehicle and train collisions with elk, out-of-season poaching and in-season illegal kills, farm-related kills, and harvests for biological collections.

Washington is one of the few states or provinces that has kept records on miscellaneous human-caused agents of elk mortality. By a wide margin, poaching and other illegal kills accounted for the largest number of elk. However, because they represent only the "known" kills, the figures undoubtedly are conservative.

The importance of these mortality factors may have been minor in terms of annual numbers. It represented less than 0.5% of Washington's total 50,000 to 60,000 elk and only about 1% of the state's 1,000 animals harvested by hunters in 1965. However, unaccounted mortality from these sources may increase annual losses and compound the problem of establishing harvest quotas in particular management units.

Hunter Accidents

Hunter accidents are a major concern of wildlife management agencies. Firearms safety legislation and training began in the late 1940s in New York. Every hunter there less than 17 years old was required to take a firearms safety course before purchasing his first license (Laycock 1955). The 4-hour course was designed by the National Rifle Association in cooperation with the National Education Association and, in a much-refined form, is used extensively today. By 1959, 36 states had laws requiring training of young hunters (Bradshaw and Bradshaw 1959) and, by 1962, all states and Canadian provinces had active firearms safety programs. However, not all states require the training.

Hunter education and safety programs have been successful in reducing accidents. Statistics show that the number of accidents relative to the number of participants is lower for hunting than for most other outdoor activities (Edson 1954). In addition, statistics indicate that elk hunters have a better safety record than hunters in general.

Elk hunter accidents accounted for only 5.8% of all hunter accidents. The average accident rate for the seven states and provinces over the 15-year period was 1.4 accidents per 50,000 elk hunters. Even with rapidly increasing hunter numbers during the period of 1975 to 1995, elk hunting remains a relatively safe form of outdoor recreation.

Crowded conditions certainly detract from the elk hunting experience for many hunters, and crowding apparently gives some hunters a feeling of insecurity. However, compared with many common outdoor activities, hunting, including elk hunting, is a relatively safe form of outdoor recreation. For example, 1995 statistics reported by the National Safety Council show that in the United States, there were more than 4,000 injuries and nearly 800 deaths resulting from boating, more than 600,000 injuries and 800 deaths resulting from bicycling and more than 145,000 injuries and 1,500 deaths from swimming. During 1995, there were 1,130 nonfatal accidents and 112 deaths resulting from hunting in the United States. During 1995, only two fatal accidents in the United States were attributed to elk hunters (International Hunter Education Association 1995).

Hunter-related Uses of Elk

Today, recreational hunting is the major consumptive use of elk, but there have been other uses of elk that deserve mention. An important use of elk around the turn of the century was "tusk" hunting. This practice eventually led to a major program of elk conservation, including the establishment of a wildlife refuge.

A more recent concern over elk stems from Indian treaty rights, discussed later in this chapter.

Tusk Hunting

Some of the most wasteful killing of elk was that done by tusk (canine teeth) hunters of the late 1800s and early 1900s. Tusk hunters followed in the path of the mid-19th century market hunters who were after meat, hides and tallow rendered from elk. Between 1885 and 1910, big game populations faded by more than 80% in the wake of unrestricted and unregulated hunting (Madson and Kozicky 1971; see Chapter 3). The tusk hunter, who was partly responsible for the elk decline, was after a prized trophy of the day.

As discussed in Chapter 3, elk teeth were valued highly by many Native Americans, and when Euro-Americans arrived, they too took a fancy to elk tusks. Gold-mounted on a watch fob, these tusks became the unofficial badge of membership in the Benevolent and Protective Order of Elks. Despite laws to protect the elk, hunters and jewelers capitalized on the demand for the valuable canine teeth.

In 1913, a man reportedly killed a bull elk in his orchard in New Hampshire. He sold the two teeth to a firm in South Dakota for $10 (Silver 1957). Another person reported a pair of tusks selling for $85 and others for $50, but the usual price was from $10 to $20 per pair (Leek 1915). In Washington during the 1920s, the going price was $5 per tusk (Johnson 1923). In 1907, the Wyoming State Legislature found that a premium pair of tusks could cost hundreds of dollars. The price probably included mounting, perhaps in a gold setting. Allowing for inflation, a $200 pair of elk tusks in 1907 would have cost about $1,000 in 1980 and nearly $2,000 by the year 2000.

The Elks organization, although implicated as part of the cause for the decline of elk, became a significant force in the protection and return of elk from near extinction. In 1903, the Benevolent and Protective Order of Elks—in response to President Theodore Roosevelt's address to Congress a year earlier, in which he urged legislation to protect elk—issued a "memorial" to the U.S. Congress calling for proper care, protection and maintenance of the animals (Benevolent and Protective Order of Elks 1903). In 1904, the Seattle, Washington, Elks lodge adopted a resolution calling for the Grand Lodge to take steps toward enacting a legal moratorium on the killing of elk for 10 years (Nicholson and Donaldson 1969).

The first official suggestion for establishment of a permanent elk refuge came in 1906 from Wyoming State game warden D. C. Nowlin, but the greatest impetus occurred in 1907. At that time, in an effort to curb illegal tusk hunting, the Wyoming State Legislature (1907:197) passed a resolution asking the Benevolent and Protective Order of Elks's "discontinuance, and decrying of the wearing of elk's teeth as emblems." During that same year, President Roosevelt asked the Elks to abolish the custom of using elk tusks (Fehrenbach 1967). Accordingly, the organization adopted a resolution "requesting the membership of the Order to dis-

Between 1885 and 1910, big game populations reportedly declined by 80% (Madson and Kozicky 1971), although others have suggested that the most significant exploitation of big game populations, including elk, probably peaked by about 1880 (see, e.g., McCabe and McCabe 1984, Reeves and McCabe 1997; see also Chapter 3). Despite some efforts to ban or restrict elk hunting in portions of the species' remaining range during the last decades of the 19th century, hunting of elk mainly went unregulated and unenforced. Hunting interest declined mainly because the elk were few. Nevertheless, certain wealthy "adventurers" managed to find the remnant herds and take what they wished and could. Above is W. Seward Webb and members of his 1896 hunting party in the Teton Country near Yellowstone National Park. According to Tilden (1964:238), "the Webb hunters were not game hogs. They were content with a few trophy heads besides what was needed for food." The "few" trophy bull heads visible in the photo number six, which also indicates there was a rather substantial amount of camp food and appetites. *Photo credited to famed frontier photographer F. Jay Haynes (although Haynes is the man standing just left of the tepee); courtesy of the Montana State Historical Society.*

pense with the use of the elk tooth as an article of personal adornment" (Nicholson and Donaldson 1969:193).

In 1908, following Warden Nowlin's suggestions of 2 years earlier, the Grand Elks Lodge encouraged establishment of what later was to become the National Elk Refuge in Wyoming. The Lodge commissioned one of its own subcommittees to study elk problems and make recommendations. After months spent in the field and dozens of interviews, the subcommittee submitted an 8,000-word report that concluded: (1) "the widespread report that the elk is

[*sic*] being exterminated in order to get their tusks for commercial purposes is without foundation in reason or in fact"; and (2) the elk were dying out primarily because they could not reach winter feeding grounds that had been shut off by the advance of civilization (Nicholson and Donaldson 1969:193). The report further declared that, to preserve elk, steps needed to be taken to provide sustenance in winter, and it recommended the "establishment of ranges" for this purpose. This recommendation was adopted and transmitted to the U.S. Congress (Fehrenbach 1967). It ultimately led to the establishment of the National Elk Refuge near Jackson Hole, Wyoming, which is the only federal refuge devoted exclusively to the preservation of elk (see Chapter 14).

Indian Treaty Rights and Hunting

Indian treaty rights involving natural resource allocations and use continue to be complex and often controversial. The complexity and status of Native American hunting and fishing issues began to change rapidly in the 1970s—change that continues today. The complexity, importance and rapidity of change in these issues are evidenced by the fact that the Conference of Western Attorneys General sponsored publication of the *American Indian Law Deskbook* (Spaeth 1993) to help those involved in Native American law, including hunting and fishing issues, become informed and stay abreast of current issues and legal opinions. The controversy, although not new, is focused on the interpretation of Indian treaty rights and a variety of laws, opinions and values. The following discussion does not intend to indulge in opinion or philosophy concerning Indian use of elk, but rather to stimulate analysis and understanding of the issues. It is clear, however, that conservation and management of any wildlife resource may be complicated by user groups who react to any infringement on what they consider to be their rights. Management can become doubly complex and sensitive when the rights and traditions of different cultural groups are involved.

Cultural and Historical Background

Historically, hunting was much more than a recreation for North American Indians and, to some extent, that remains true today. Agriculture was part of Native culture, hunting, fishing and gathering wild plant food were the primary means of subsistence. For groups such as the Plains Indians, the diet and livelihood of the tribe were greatly dependent on the hunt. Hunting also was an important focal point of identity among and between cultural and tribal functions (see Chapter 3).

The role of hunting in the Indian culture is understood best by looking at the religious and philosophical differences between the Indian and western civilizations. Western civilization has its roots in the Judeo-Greco-Christian heritage, which tends to view nature as impersonal but important because of its potential exploitive value. On the other hand, Indians traditionally have perceived themselves in kinship with nature, and they believe their fate is bound closely to the environment (W. Fairservis personal communication:1973). Wildlife was an important spiritual component of most Indian cultures, as evidenced not only in their mythology, but also in their ceremonies and totems. Hunting, therefore, was more than a pragmatic act of subsistence; it manifested the Indians' religious beliefs, customs and social behaviors. Some researchers argue that Native Americans were active land managers through their use of fire (Pyne 1982), whereas others argue that the Indian was a conservationist only in the sense that he had limited ability to exploit natural resources (Allen 1962). Czech (1995:568) indicated that "two things are obvious. First, Indian tribes as a whole had great respect for wildlife. . . . Second, Indians had wittingly or not, lived in a way that promoted . . . ecological integrity."

For all but a few Native Americans (for example, certain Natives in Alaska), hunting now is predominantly a recreational activity. Nevertheless, hunting is undertaken by some Indians not only or primarily as a matter of subsistence, but also as an important link to their heritage. At a time when hunting represents one of few remaining vestiges of a traditional way of life, and wildlife continues to be a literal and figurative fixture of spiritual kinship and other cultural manifestations for the Indians, Native Americans tend to guard their treaty rights zealously, no matter how contrary their desires may be to the wishes of others.

According to the U.S. Constitution, treaties are "supreme law of the land." They are a contract between sovereigns possessing independent jurisdictions or authorities. However, legislative and legal history has modified the basic status of Indian treaties. Congress determined that it has the power to annul treaties when such action is justified. Therefore, a whole spectrum of opinions about the fundamental status of treaties and their inviolability exists and is the subject of heated debate.

Treaties were made with Native Americans by the U.S. Senate from 1789 to 1871. After 1871, "agreements" were the legal instruments of land cessions. Agreements had to be ratified by both the U.S. Senate and House of Representatives (Kappler 1904). Agreements contained treaty-type terms and conditions, but they were not as detailed and rarely made reference to retained off-reservation hunting and fishing rights.

An agreement was believed to have less authority than a treaty, but a case in 1975—*Antoine v. State of Washington*—put an end to that perception. The case involved an Native American who was arrested for hunting on ceded lands. Washington State contended that an agreement, unlike a treaty, was not the supreme law of the land. And because the state was not a party to the agreement, the federal government did not have the right to abridge the state's policing authority over hunting. The court ruled that the agreement had the force of a treaty, thus establishing the status of an agreement.

In early treaties, diplomacy was the main tool of negotiation, and sovereignty was viewed in a relatively strict sense, which the federal government generally acknowledged. A substantial erosion of sovereignty took place with the 1831 court decision *Cherokee Nation v. Georgia*. In this case, Native Americans were referred to as "domestic dependent nations," which reflected an English interpretation of sovereignty. By the mid-1800s, the United States had become stronger and settlement of the West was underway. Native American "uprisings" were dealt with by armed force, and treaties reflected the attitude of a military superior to its defeated foe, with few acknowledgments of sovereignty (Miller 1994).

A typical treaty with the Native Americans established land cessions and reservations, plus terms of payment by the U.S. government. Other clauses could include rights and privileges of the Native Americans, benefits and annuities from the federal government and the format of their future relationship.

Among the rights and privileges that Indians retained was that of hunting. However, many treaties made no mention of hunting, although it was vital to Native American culture and subsistence. This might have occurred because of the way Native Americans perceived wildlife resources—that is, so intrinsic to life as not to be a negotiable commodity or privilege (E. Blanchard personal communication:1976). However, many treaties do mention hunting. The following is a typical statement on hunting, taken from the 1789 Treaty of Fort Harmar in the Ohio Territory: "It is agreed between the said United States and said nations, that the individuals of said nations shall be at liberty to hunt within the territory ceded the United States, without hindrance of molestation, so long as they remain peaceably, and offer no injury or annoyance to any of the subjects or citizens of the said United States" (Washburn 1973:280).

In the 1800s, the wording of treaties changed. The change was subtle, but it has become the center of recent court battles. An 1885 treaty with the Yakima tribe, similar in wording to others made with tribes in the Northwest, is an example: "The exclusive right of taking fish in all the streams, where running through or bordering said reservation, is further secured to said confederated tribes and bands of Indians, as also the right of taking fish at all usual and accustomed places, in common with the citizens of the territory . . . together with the privilege of hunting, gathering roots and berries, and pasturing their horses and cattle upon open and unclaimed land" (Kappler 1904:699). At issue, among other things, has been interpretation of "usual and accustomed places" in relation to reservation boundaries.

With respect to treaties between Native Americans and the federal government, there is little disagreement over hunting rights. However, reservations lie within state boundaries and are distinct political entities that claim relative immunity from state authority. Traditionally, states have the constitutional authority to manage wildlife and hunting, except in most instances, on reservations. Ceded lands and off-reservation hunting are the chief sources of conflict.

Ceded lands are those lands originally comprising the territory of Native American tribes. On signing treaties, the Native Americans relinquished those lands to the United States, while retaining or gaining reservation lands. After treaties were signed, many Native Americans continued their custom of hunting on their usual territory, including ceded lands, without challenge. The initial problems arose when ceded lands became a part of a state admitted to the Union. The states took a more possessive attitude, on the premise that statehood transferred sovereignty of ceded land to the newly created state. In other words, Native Americans practicing the same customs as before statehood were considered in violation of the state's authority. Early court decisions upheld this premise in the 1896 *Ward v. Race Horse* and the 1916 *New York ex rel Kennedy v. Becker*.

The controversy was far from settled by these court rulings. In *United States v. Winans*, the court ruled that statehood authority does not supersede Native American treaty rights. The U.S. Supreme Court ruled that Native Americans retained any rights not expressly bargained away. This ruling was echoed in 1930 in *Pioneer Packing Co. v. Winslow*. Thus, an important consideration with respect to Native American hunting and fishing rights is that such rights generally are considered not as a grant to the Native Americans, but as a reservation of rights not ceded by treaty (Spaeth 1993).

Court cases since 1930 basically are compromises of the aforementioned legal rulings. For example, the landmark 1942 case from *Tulee v. Washington* (1942) stated that, although Native Americans are not considered totally exempt from state regulations off reservation, the burden is on the state to prove that regulations are necessary for resource preservation. In another case, *Makah Indian Tribes et al. v. Schoettler*, the ruling declared in 1951 that the state can regu-

late Native American hunting and fishing only if conservation cannot be achieved by other means, such as restricting non-Native American hunting and fishing. In a 1976 case, *State of Washington v. Starr et al.*, involving elk kills off reservation lands, the court convicted Native Americans defendants on evidence that the elk resource was underpopulated, and regulation was necessary to ensure conservation and continuation of the elk. An appeal of this decision was dismissed in 1978.

Another complicating factor involved in consideration of treaty rights is that, due to the language of many treaties, the rights conveyed by treaties change over time as circumstances change. For example, *Ward v. Race Horse* established in 1896 that the right to hunt on the unoccupied lands of the United States "was a temporary right which ended when the lands in question became part of the state of Wyoming." The opinion that the right to hunt on unoccupied land is temporary and subject to extinction was upheld by the 10th Circuit Court of appeals in 1995 in a Wyoming case—*Crow Tribe v. Repsis*.

Another problem has been the definition of "open and unclaimed lands." In *State of Washington v. Chambers*, the court established in 1973 that the phrase was defined as "lands which are not in private ownership," and further declared that "private lands must show outward indications of such ownership observable to a reasonable man . . . lest such lands be considered open and unclaimed."

This theme appeared again in the 1975 *State of Washington v. Moses*, which involved the killing of elk—for ceremonial purposes—on private timber company land. The judge's instructions to the jury stated that lands in private ownership and "not in such usage or posted as would warn off a reasonable person" are open and unclaimed within the context of the treaty. The words "unoccupied lands" sometimes replace the phrase "open and unclaimed lands" in treaties. In rulings that have broad application to tribes and involve considerable elk habitat and elk-related recreation, the courts have held and the 10th Circuit Court affirmed in 1995, with *Crow Tribe v. Repris*, that creation of the National Forest System in 1887 resulted in the occupation and claiming of national forest lands. However, the opinion that national forest lands are occupied and claimed is not universally held. National parks and national refuge lands generally are considered as occupied and claimed (Spaeth 1993).

The power of a treaty to affect resource use is seen in the 1968 *Menominee Tribe v. United States*. In this case, the Supreme Court held that Menominee could retain the right to hunt and fish on their former reservations, without complying with the State of Wisconsin's fish and wildlife laws. During the 1950s, it became federal policy to terminate reservations by outright purchase. In this court decision, hunting rights survived termination even on state and private holdings of former reservation lands. Other court cases are using this decision in their own defense.

In summary, the current situation finds reservation hunting by United States Native Americans to be largely immune from state jurisdiction and regulation. However, although state authority to regulate Native American hunting on reservations is subject to federal interests as defined by treaty, the courts have established that states may become involved in regulating on-reservation hunting rights in the following circumstances: when necessary for conservation of resources, on fee lands within the reservation, by reason of the specific treaty involved, by state/tribal agreement, and for other reasons dictated by specific circumstances of treaty and time (Spaeth 1993). When hunting off reservation, Native Americans, unless granted specific rights by treaty, are subject to state regulation. Even when off-reservation hunting rights are established by treaty, the states may subject Native Americans to regulation under the following circumstances: to ensure public health and safety; promote conservation and protect and maintain allocations between Native Americans and other parties.

Hunting by non-Native Americans on reservation lands offers income opportunities to tribes that sell access and hunting privileges, but it complicates state and tribal management of elk hunting. The major legal questions of non-Native American hunting on reservation lands involve state licensing and law enforcement. Generally, the states require a state hunting license for non-Native American hunters on reservations or for transporting harvested animals off reservations. The Navajo Nation of the Southwest asserts that the three states (Arizona, New Mexico and Utah) bordering their reservation contribute little to wildlife conservation on reservations and that multiple-state licensing of non-Indians would drive sportsmen away and decrease income to the tribe.

The U.S. District Court declared, in the 1976 *Confederated Tribes of the Colville Indian Reservation v. State of Washington,* the State of Washington could not require non-Native Americans to abide by state game laws if they were on a reservation. This decision was appealed and reversed in the 1979 *Confederated Tribes of the Colville Indian Reservation v. State of Washington,* thereby giving the state the right to require licensing of non-Native Americans on reservations. Two situations are involved, non-Native Americans hunting on fee land within the reservation and non-Native Americans hunting on reservation trust lands. Generally speaking, non-Native Americans are subject to state jurisdiction when hunting on privately owned land within a reservation. In most situations, a state's jurisdiction extends to non-Native Americans hunting within reservation bound-

aries, but that jurisdiction may be shared with a tribe or assumed by federal action. Each situation must be determined on a case-by-case basis (Spaeth 1993). Case-by-case determination is required for both concurrent jurisdiction or federal assumption of jurisdiction because both situations are determined by specific state, tribal and federal actions. For example, federal actions designed to provide economic benefit to a tribe (such as providing elk for translocation to the reservation for the purpose of providing income to the tribe through the sale of elk hunting permits) may outweigh a state's need for general jurisdiction.

The potential to market access and other hunter privileges is high on some reservation lands. Southwest reservations—namely, the Fort Apache, Jicarilla Apache, Mescalero Apache, Hualapai, San Carlos and Navajo—have taken the lead in this respect. In 1995, non-Native American hunters paid very high fees (more than $8,000 in some cases) to pursue trophy bull elk on reservation lands. The Oglala Sioux in southwestern South Dakota have an extensive range management program and also market fee hunting (Cole 1974). They manage several enclosed pastures totaling 28,000 acres (11,332 ha) for quality hunting of trophy elk. In 1973, non-Native American hunters each paid $1,200 to hunt elk. Income generated from hunting equaled the possible return from raising cattle on the land. Seeing such income potential, other tribes have started building wildlife programs, complete with hunting and fishing codes, law enforcement, animal translocation and animal census.

The situation in Canada is similar to that in the United States. Like the United States, Canada has both treaty and nontreaty Native Americans, and has passed several acts dealing with jurisdiction, classification of Native Americans and clarification or limitations of rights. The Indian Act of 1970 and the Natural Resources Transfer Act of 1929 transferred wildlife law jurisdiction from the federal government to the provinces, except for Native Americans hunting for subsistence. In terms of subsistence hunting, Native Americans are allowed to hunt on unoccupied Crown lands under privileges related to aboriginal property rights. Native Americans in provinces that have elk do not hunt them to any extent. Where they do, the Supreme Court of Canada has held that provincial wildlife laws apply to Native Americans on reserves. In British Columbia, the practice on reservations has been to apply provincial wildlife laws on reservations to non-Native Americans only.

Legal relationship of a state or province to Native American rights and privileges is confusing and often inconsistent. Notwithstanding the frustrations of all parties concerned and the numerous resolution efforts, there is need for continued cooperation between wildlife agencies and various Native American groups, especially where the welfare of the resource is essential to sustain wildlife populations. However, Native American rights involve long-standing power struggles, self-interests and misunderstandings on all sides. The complex legal questions, with a history of nearly 200 years, are complicated by different cultural perspectives and the increasing demand for the use of elk. Resolution in the best interest of the resource, yet compatible with the legal and vested interests of the cultures involved, will require mutual cooperation and understanding.

State Tribal Cooperative Agreements

Actions by states often affect tribal elk herds and vice versa, creating distrust and dissension. A long history of divisive and costly litigation has done little to solve many of these problems. Faced with this situation, many states and tribes

On their reservations, a number of Indian tribes (notably Apache, Sioux and Navajo) have wildlife programs that feature trophy elk production and hunting. The hunting has been marketed to non-Natives, who have been willing to pay large fees to take a trophy bull. At least some of the programs have generated more income than was possible from raising livestock, and generally at less expense. The success of the elk program has given rise to other hunting and fishing operations, which have entailed a strong component of professional resource management on those reservations. *Photo courtesy of the White Mountain Apache Tribe, Wildlife and Outdoor Recreation Division.*

are adopting a policy of cooperation in place of confrontation and litigation (Spaeth 1993). The federal government has adopted a policy of seeking negotiated settlements to reserved Native American water rights and has enacted other provisions that require or authorize states and tribes to negotiate agreements. Other natural resource issues, such as elk herd management, lend themselves to cooperative agreements. Several states have or now are engaged in negotiating cooperative agreements dealing with wildlife management. The western states' Attorneys General suggest that the following considerations should apply when negotiating a cooperative agreement between a tribe and state: find common ground and common interests; be creative and consider involving seemingly unrelated issues to balance outcomes; avoid seeking legal concessions; involve all affected parties; make agreements voluntary and self-enforcing; and consider unique situations (Spaeth 1993).

One thing seems certain—managers of wildlife, including Native American managers, will have to consider Native American hunting rights and how they fit into the total program of their regions and management units. In the management of wildlife in general and elk in particular, neither the Native American nor the non-Native American is living in isolation. Furthermore, recent court decisions will keep the status of Native American hunting rights in flux for the next few decades. Accordingly, this new era of cooperation that seems to be gaining a foothold has an opportunity to be much more productive than the past 200 years of litigation. Elk herd management goals and objectives, including recreational use of the resource, will change over time as circumstances and needs dictate. Cooperative, time-limited agreements between states and tribes have the potential to circumvent many legal problems, build levels of trust, and protect or enhance recreational uses of elk.

Elk Recreation on Private Land

As the number of elk hunters increased during the past 25 years, the demand for trophy bull elk also has increased. One evidence of this is the high odds against drawing a permit to hunt on elk units that are managed as trophy units by several states. This is especially true on units that encompass public lands. These units typically feature a high success rate with many trophy bulls available for harvest to a limited number of hunters. For example, the odds against drawing a permit to hunt the Monroe unit in central Utah were 70:1 in 1996. The Monroe unit is largely public land and has an abundance of large, mature bulls. The odds against drawing a permit exceed 25:1 on several other trophy units in Utah (Utah Division of Wildlife Resources 1997).

Beginning in the 1970s and continuing into the 1990s, a number of factors, including an increased numbers of hunters, resulted in a general decline in the quality of elk hunting on public lands throughout much of the western U.S. This situation created a market for the owners of private lands where hunter numbers could be controlled and the harvest limited. Some hunters were willing to pay considerable sums for access to private lands where there was an uncrowded, reasonable opportunity to harvest a mature bull elk. Landowners also may provide guide services, accommodations, care and handling for trophy heads and meat, and opportunities for other outdoor activities, such as fishing or small game hunting.

A number of private ranches have taken advantage of the demand for trophy animals and uncrowded hunting conditions, and now market access to their lands and various related services to elk hunters who are willing to pay. The fee charged depends on many factors, including size of the hunting area available and number of competing hunters, but the age and trophy quality of the bulls seem to be the prime factors determining hunter fees. Wharff (1996) reported a strong relationship between the average Boone and Crockett score (taken at time of harvest) of previously harvested bulls and the fees charged by various private hunting enterprises. For autumn 1996 hunts, several landowners who cater to trophy bull elk hunters, and whose operations produce bulls averaging more than 320 Boone and Crockett points, charged $7,000 to $10,000 for a trophy elk hunt or elk hunt package, which included some additional services provided by the landowner. Management of wildlife-related recreation on private land can provide economic benefit to landowners. Economic benefits include both cash flow and diversification of income base. Jordan and Workman (1990) reported that the average Utah ranch involved in fee hunting had a gross income from hunter access and service fees of $9,628 resulting in a net (operating expenses except depreciation and value of owner/operator labor) income of $6,649 or $0.66 per acre.

From 1987 to 1996, the wildlife management program at Deseret Ranch near Woodruff, Utah, produced a net profit each year (gross wildlife income minus program salaries and other direct costs) with access fees for elk hunting being the dominant revenue producer on the ranch. During recent years, revenues derived from the sale of access for hunting have accounted for 30% to 40% of the annual total net income for the entire ranch (Wolfe et al. 1996). Profits from wildlife-related recreation have kept the overall ranch operation in the black on more than one occasion. For example, in 1996, when low cattle prices greatly reduced income from livestock production, Deseret's wildlife recreation program produced a net profit of about $1.50 per acre

($0.67/ha) per year with about 60% of that income coming from elk. Wildlife-related recreation also has been very important in other years when drought has reduced forage production for domestic livestock, forcing the ranch to liquidate livestock at low prices (R. Danvir personal communication:1997).

Deseret Ranch has some advantages in producing income from wildlife because it is large—encompassing 250,000 acres (100,000 ha) of private land and 125,000 acres (50,000 ha) of interspersed public land. Smaller ranches also can generate income from wildlife. By joining together through formal and informal arrangements, smaller landowners can increase their opportunity to profit from managing for free-ranging big game, including elk. The Lost Creek Landowner Association in Morgan County, Utah, consists of several neighboring landowners who own private lands in the Lost Creek drainage. The Lost Creek drainage is almost entirely privately owned and provides year-long habitat for a large and productive herd of elk. During the autumn hunting period, the elk herd generally is found on the high elevation ranges, but it winters on the lower elevation ranges in the drainage. The Association recognizes that the elk herd cannot prosper without adequate year-long range. It feels that winter range is the most limited habitat and, therefore, the most critical habitat in the drainage. If lower elevation landowners are not able to profit from wildlife, they may be tempted or forced to change land use on critical winter ranges. The lower elevation ranges in the drainage are only about an hour drive from the majority of Utah's population of more than 2 million people, and many of the ranges could be subdivided for housing. Many of the landowners in the Lost Creek drainage have joined together to protect and enhance wildlife habitat with funds collected from wildlife-related recreation. Funds for habitat improvements are collected by the Association and distributed by an elected Board of Directors. The board selects projects for funding, with winter range protection and improvement being the first priority. The Association spent nearly $4,000 in 1996 and 1997 for seedlings and seed used on the Echo-Henefer Wildlife Management Area, owned by the Utah Division of Wildlife Resources, which provides critical winter range on the unit. Other Association-funded projects on private ranges have been designed to produce and protect wildlife forage on lower elevation ranges (S. Kearl personal communication:1997).

Nonconsumptive Uses of Elk

As previously noted, participation in nonconsumptive wildlife recreation has been growing rapidly in recent decades, and more than four times as many Americans participate in nonconsumptive activities as participate in hunting (U.S. Fish and Wildlife Service 1997). Each year, people discover more ways to enjoy wildlife. Encounters with wildlife may include observing or hearing an animal or seeing evidence of it, such as scats, tracks and signs of browsing. In addition, wildlife is enjoyed vicariously through books, photographs, television programs, movies and just by being in an area where animals are known to occur (Lime 1976, Kellert 1980, 1985).

By virtue of increased public interest in the environmental, conservation and outdoor-oriented leisure activities beginning in the late 1960s and early 1970s, state, provincial and federal wildlife agencies have been compelled to focus additional attention on nonconsumptive uses of wildlife. For example, in testimony before the U.S. House of Representatives' Merchant Marine and Fisheries Subcommittee on Fisheries and Wildlife Conservation and the Environment on October 29, 1979, the Director of the U.S. Fish and Wildlife Service reported that: "In 1951, 3.5 million people visited 100 [national] wildlife refuges. In 1961, visitations had increased to 11 million people on 150 refuges and . . . [in 1979] 26 million people will visit national wildlife refuges." He reported that 75% of visits to refuges are wildlife oriented, and of total visitation, hunting, fishing and trapping account for only 3%. Also, a 1975 nationwide survey in the United States revealed that, of 95.9 million people (above age nine) engaged in recreational activities related to fish and wildlife, only 21.5% were hunters, whereas 64.3% were involved in observing and photographing wildlife (U.S. Fish and Wildlife Service 1978). In autumn 1970, a study of public recreation on 40 areas in 13 states showed that hunting accounted for only 9% of 4.2 million user days (U.S. Fish and Wildlife Service 1972). Of the 10 activities recorded, hunting was fifth in popularity behind sight-seeing (28.3%), fishing (19%), picnicking (18%) and camping (15%).

Most state wildlife agency programs are funded primarily from revenues generated from the sales of hunting, fishing and trapping licenses. Accordingly, their resource management programs have emphasized management of consumptive resource uses. Additional monies to support the nonconsumptive programs have not been easily or readily attainable. The alternatives have been to (1) tap and thereby distribute more widely the limited consumptive resource funds, (2) secure additional general fund revenues from state or provincial treasuries, or (3) develop other fund-producing sources. In most cases, a combination of the alternatives has been used.

Increasingly, state agencies have found sources of funding for nonconsumptive, wildlife recreation. These include

Missouri's constitutional amendment that designates a fraction of a penny of sales tax to conservation programs; nongame tax checkoffs on income tax forms in many states; sales of special license plates and conservation licenses and other innovative sources of funding. Proposals for further funding of nonconsumptive wildlife recreation, and there is evidence of widespread public support for such programs (Duda and Young 1994). In any case, there are many areas where people enjoy elk in the absence of specific programs, which demonstrate the pioneering efforts in nonconsumptive programs involving elk.

Owens Valley

A model of multiagency cooperation is found in the Owens Valley on the western side of the Sierra Nevada Mountains of southern California. Owens Valley contains the largest population of Tule elk in five herds that range freely over

Although hunters provide the majority dollars for wildlife management programs, there are three times as many people who actively take part in wildlife viewing and photography as there are hunters. In the West, elk are popular sighting and photography subjects of the so-called nonconsumptive recreationists in any season. The nonconsumptive users represent a significant pro-wildlife constituency that hunters need to acknowledge, respect and cultivate. *Photo by Bob Schillereff.*

more than 500,000 acres (202,350 ha) of land that is maintained by the federal government and the City of Los Angeles. Although the California Department of Fish and Game manages the herds, eight resource agencies have joined together to develop and offer several observation sites. These sites feature interpretive displays, self-guided trails and guided tour programs.

National Elk Refuge

The National Elk Refuge in Jackson Hole, Wyoming, probably is the most popular nonconsumptive elk program in North America. Visitors come from all over the world. In addition to drive-through viewing areas, the Jackson Jaycees maintain a sleigh ride concession on elk wintering and feeding grounds. The Teton Valley is the traditional winter range for about 8,000 elk, and supplemental feed is provided by the refuge. When the concession began in 1966, 2,593 persons took sleigh rides. By 1971, the number had risen to 4,828 and in 1980, 15,300 persons visited the refuge to enjoy the wintering elk herd.

Visits by drive-through observers also have been increasing on the refuge. In 1972, there were approximately 3,600 drive-through visitors. By 1980, the number had increased to more than 216,000.

Another extremely popular program was the refuge's 200-acre (81 ha) exhibition pasture. A group of elk was fenced and pastured for summer viewing from 1957 to 1975. An estimated 200,000 people stopped to view elk in this setting each summer. Unfortunately, vandals persisted in cutting the fence and made it necessary to terminate this popular program in 1975.

Since 1964, Boy Scouts have collected elk antlers under a special-use permit. At sunrise on the first Saturday in May each year, about 300 scouts and leaders from the Teton Valley line up at the National Elk Refuge. Before the day is over, more than 10,000 pounds (4.5 metric tons) of shed elk antlers have been collected, sorted and tied into bundles, each weighing about 20 to 60 pounds (9–27 kg). Matched pairs go into one pile, old bleached antlers into another and fresh brown ones into still another pile. The community also participates in the activity by donating trucks, lunches, advertising and auctioneers. Eighty percent of the proceeds from the sale of antlers is donated to the refuge to support the elk feeding program. The antler collection campaign also includes a litter clean-up effort (U.S. Fish and Wildlife Service 1997). The project supplies raw materials for an elk antler craft and jewelry industry. Also, large quantities of antlers are sold and shipped to Korea and Japan where the antlers are cured, ground and prepared for sale in the Orient for use in traditional medicines and as a supposed aphrodisiac. The antler collection campaign has earned the scouts from $0.67 per pound ($0.30/kg) in 1968 to an average of $6.00 per pound ($2.72/kg) in 1980. The price per pound exceeded $9.00 per pound ($14.00/kg) in both 1996 and 1997.

Under a special use permit from the U.S. Fish and Wildlife Service, about 300 Boy Scouts annually collect more than 5 tons (4.5 metric tons) of shed elk antler on the National Elk Refuge near Jackson, Wyoming, on the first Saturday in May (*top*). The antlers are sorted and tied into bundles that are put up for auction in downtown Jackson (*bottom*). Some of the bundles go as raw product for antler craft and jewelry business (earrings, bolo ties, necklaces, pendants, cribbage boards, pistol grips, belt buckle, carvings, etc.) and much of the rest is sold to bidders from the Orient, where the antlers are shipped, cured, ground and packaged as medicinal products. At $9.50 per pound ($14.00/kg), the event raised about $99,962 in 2000, 80% of which the scouts give back to the Refuge for the winter feeding of elk. *Photos by John Wilbrecht; courtesy of the U.S. Fish and Wildlife Service.*

Hardware Ranch

One of the most researched and documented sites of non-consumptive elk use is the 12,692-acre (5,136.5 ha) Hardware Ranch southeast of Logan, Utah. Owned and operated by the Utah Division of Wildlife Resources, the ranch provides winter sleigh rides and a visitor center for thousands of people each year. Approximately 650,000 persons visited the ranch between 1960 and 1980. Sleigh rides during this period were free of charge. The cost of this program placed heavy demands on the state wildlife agency. This prompted studies of visitors to determine the program's values (Ashcroft 1967, Wood and Kennedy 1973). The following summary of these studies emphasizes the potential value of nonconsumptive use activities in other programs.

More than half the visitors neither fished nor hunted, thus indicating that sportsmen license fees were supporting a program used primarily by appreciative users. Not surprisingly, most visitors did not object to the use of hunting and fishing license fees to support the ranch, but two-thirds preferred that another source of funds be used, such as an admission fee. The ranch was the primary destination of 95% of the visitors, who drove an average of 136 miles (219 km) to see elk.

Wood and Kennedy (1973) found that visitors to Hardware Ranch generally were satisfied with their experiences at the ranch. The elk, sleigh rides and scenery ranked as the most important features. Nearly half of the visitors said they had no complaints. Most of the unenjoyable features identified had to do with conditions at the parking area and the length of the sleigh ride. Hardware Ranch has remained a popular destination since that study was done. Additional facilities have been added, including a food concession and visitor center. The area also has become a popular trailhead for snowmobilers. As a result, many recreationists who do not join the sleigh rides or stop at the visitor center also are participating in an elk viewing experience, although that may not be their primary reason for visiting. The sleigh rides are run by a concessionaire who charges a modest fee for a longer sleigh ride.

Rocky Mountain National Park

Rocky Mountain National Park in Colorado features one of the best elk bugling and viewing opportunities in North America. Yearly, thousands of visitors are treated to the early autumn mating ritual of elk in the Horseshoe Park area of the park. In 1980, more than 300,000 people visited the area in September and October. The Estes Park Area Chamber of Commerce has advertised elk viewing and listening as a feature event of their Fall Festival. In addition, the U.S. National Park Service offers guided tours.

Elk bugling and viewing have been so popular in recent years that traffic and visitors have posed a disturbance to the natural behavior of elk. To prevent disturbance and harassment of elk and to enhance elk viewing opportunities, the National Park Service closes the Horseshoe Park area to off-road hiking in September and October. It also prohibits "elk calling" with artificial bugling devices and the use of spotlights to view elk at night.

Most sociological studies of wildlife viewing do not focus on individual species. Studies of nonconsumptive, wildlife recreation in general have found that many characteristics of hunting experiences also can be ascribed to wildlife viewing experiences. Like hunters, wildlife viewers differ in activity styles. Martin (1995) classified Montana wildlife viewers as high, medium and low involvement recreationists, based on the number of wildlife viewing trips they take, their use of specialized equipment, such as spotting scopes, their participation in educational courses about wildlife and whether or not they volunteer with a wildlife organization. All levels of visitors expressed interest in viewing large mammals such as elk, whereas opportuni-

The Hardware Ranch, southwest of Logan, Utah, and operated by the Utah Division of Wildlife Resources, is a major elk wintering ground. It also is a popular tourist destination when elk are in residence. Between December 15, 2000 and March 13, 2001, 45,000 people stopped at the Ranch's visitor center. Of those, 28,000 (ages four and older) took sleigh rides on the grounds to see and photograph the close at hand. *Photo by Michael Milbourn; courtesy of the Utah Division of Wildlife Resource.*

ties to view other classes of species tended to be sought only by higher involvement visitors.

Recreational Value of Elk

Economists have devoted considerable effort in recent years to placing monetary values on wildlife, recreation, wilderness and other noncommodity resources to account more accurately for those resources in cost–benefit analyses (e.g., Johnson and Johnson 1990, Payne et al. 1992). Typically, these values are inferred from an analysis of changes in demand for use of a resource at different prices. Such analyses of wildlife-related recreation offer some insight into the importance of elk as a recreational resource.

The ability to engage in either the consumptive or nonconsumptive use of elk is affected by the price of a recreation visit, as well as by the supply of recreation opportunities. For nonconsumptive activities, such as photography or observation of wild elk, recreation supply is determined mainly by access to viewing opportunities. Because elk are most numerous in the states and provinces of the Rocky Mountains and Pacific Northwest (Bunnell 1997), the supply of viewing opportunities in natural habitat is greatest in those regions. Elk can be observed easily in and around national parks and wildlife refuges at appropriate seasons. In most places where elk are found, local tourist businesses can tell visitors of unofficial viewing locations along mountain highways, in farm fields or on the outskirts of towns. Opportunities for consumptive recreation are less readily available, as every state and province regulates elk hunting. However, opportunities to hunt elk somewhere nearly always are present for those willing to pay the price of a nonresident license.

Because the supply of recreation opportunities is not highly constrained, the principal determinant of demand for an elk-related recreation experience is the price—including direct expenditures, as well as opportunity costs—of making the trip. The price of wildlife viewing is associated almost entirely with travel and, therefore, is lower for residents of the western U.S. and Canada than for other North Americans. This regional effect on price also exists for elk hunting, although it is complicated somewhat by the variables of resident and nonresident license fees and permit availability.

Walsh et al. (1992) suggested that demand for nonconsumptive wildlife recreation is more "elastic" than the demand for hunting. Therefore, increases in the price of a trip are more likely to lead to a decrease in the demand for wildlife viewing than to a decrease in the demand for hunting opportunity. However, Walsh et al. also found that recreationists substitute consumptive and nonconsumptive experiences, so that an increase in the price of hunting is likely to lead to an increase in participation in wildlife viewing, as some hunters choose to engage in affordable, nonconsumptive uses of wildlife. As already reported, both nonconsumptive and consumptive uses of elk have increased dramatically since the 1970s.

There are several ways in which economic importance can be estimated for natural resources or ecosystem elements that are not bought or sold as consumer goods. To value wildlife, economists most often choose one of three approaches—expenditure analysis, travel cost method or contingent valuation method. Each method has advantages and drawbacks for valuing wildlife. The following brief descriptions are offered to give readers an idea of the basis for wildlife valuation; full descriptions of these approaches are available elsewhere (e.g., Loomis et al. 1984, Decker and Goff 1986).

Expenditure Analysis

The simplest way to value wildlife is to calculate the total recreation expenditures that are fully or partially attributable to a given species. For elk, that might include money spent on licenses, outfitters and travel required for an elk hunting or viewing trip. Calculations typically are based on data from tourist expenditure diaries or postvisit surveys, as well as from such secondary sources as hunting license records. The focus of such research tends to be on the economic impact of recreation for relevant political jurisdictions (e.g., Dalton 1983, Moisey and Yuan 1990). However, these calculations are seen as only a partial proxy for value, because they do not capture the so-called consumer surplus, that is, the amount people would be *willing to* pay over and above what they *do* pay (Loomis and Walsh 1997). For example, Brooks et al. (1991) calculated that an average Montana elk hunter spent $81 per trip, but they could not measure whether the trips were worth more than that to hunters. A second concern with this sort of analysis is that it is difficult to assign partial values. For example, if a rifle is purchased and used to hunt deer, elk and mountain sheep, what percentage of the expenditure is elk related?

Travel Cost Method

Demand for elk-related recreation trips can be estimated by measuring the probability that a person will make such a trip at various prices (gas and mileage, lodging, outfitter expenses, private land access fees, etc.). These estimates then form the basis for calculating consumer surplus estimates that are better proxies for value than expenditures alone (Clawson and Knetsch 1966, Loomis and Walsh 1997). This method has been applied to valuation of both fishing and hunting experiences (e.g., Wilman [1984] was able to assess the value of deer hunting in forests managed under different silvicultural regimes by measuring hunters' willingness to travel to those locations). The travel cost method does not work well when applied to air travel because airline ticket prices are only correlated loosely with distance. Therefore, it may be more useful in valuing resident elk hunting than nonresident hunting by distant visitors. Also, it can be difficult to estimate how much of the value of a trip is associated with seeing or hunting an elk and how much with other aspects of the recreation experience, such as sharing companionship, being outdoors or camping along the way.

Contingent Valuation Method

Consumer surplus also can be estimated with surveys that ask respondents about their willingness to pay for wildlife or wildlife-related experiences. Such surveys must be crafted carefully to avoid producing biased estimates (Loomis et al. 1984, Loomis and Walsh 1997). Because it is difficult for people to place a value on a good or service for which they do not normally pay, surveys typically ask about willingness to pay for changes in current conditions (e.g., respondents might be asked what they would pay in additional taxes if they knew the money would go toward the purchase of winter range or how much more they would pay for an elk tag if hunting conditions were improved in specific ways).

Most nonmarket valuation studies for wildlife have occurred in the context of hunting or fishing. In a review of 104 fish and wildlife valuation studies, Duffield (1992) found that 40% examined hunting, compared with just 5% that examined nonconsumptive recreation. Consumer surplus estimates for wildlife-related recreation tend to be higher than estimates for wildland recreation in general. McCollum et al. (1990), for example, estimated that values for big game hunting in national forests of the western U.S. ranged from $30 per trip to $105 per trip depending on the region, and values for wildlife observation were $65 to $80. In contrast, general recreation (all trips) was valued at $25 to $61.

Calculated values for individual animals can be high. Fried et al. (1995) found a median value of $333 per harvested elk at Oregon's Starkey Experimental Forest, which is managed for high-quality elk hunting experiences

Economic benefits of elk hunting and nonconsumptive uses of elk to the major elk states and provinces are significant in amount and importance. As essential as elk are for bringing dollars into local and larger economies, the greater value likely accrues to the users simply in the experiences. Something valuable is always gained on a visit in elk country. *Left photo courtesy of the Oregon Department of Fish and Wildlife. Right photo courtesy of the U.S. National Park Service.*

as part of an ongoing U.S. Forest Service research effort. The same study estimated that the average value of an elk hunting trip to the Starkey Forest, over and above expenditures, was $287. Bolon (1994) offered estimates of $235 to $471 per trip based on a variety of data sources. Expenditures for a 6-day Starkey trip averaged about $297 during the same period (Fried et al. 1995). Values for a Starkey hunt were higher than for most elk hunting trips elsewhere, probably because of the quality of the experience and high probability of harvest success. For example, Fried et al. reported that hunter success rates for 1989 to 1990 were 41% at the Starkey Forest, compared with 16% statewide.

Estimates from other locations, although not as high as at Starkey Forest, nonetheless showed that elk are a valuable recreation resource. Sandrey et al. (1983) estimated that the average amount that hunters were willing to pay for an elk tag across Oregon was $90. In Montana, Brooks et al. (1991) calculated that an average elk hunter's expenditures are $81 per trip for Montana residents and $1,399 for nonresidents (including airfare, nonresident license fees and other costs not borne by Montanans). In 1987, the net economic value of elk hunting in Montana—that is, the value over and above expenditures—was estimated at $185 per trip or $66 per day (Olsen 1989). When the $66 per hunter-day estimate is multiplied by the total number of elk hunters in Montana, the aggregate consumer surplus associated with elk hunting in the state was more than $58 million in the late 1980s.

By estimating how the quality of the recreational experience affects wildlife values, economic analyses offer insights to managers on benefits that might be realized by improving or altering elk hunting conditions. As noted previously, Fried et al. (1995) argued that hunting trips on the Starkey Experimental Forest had a high consumer surplus because the likelihood of hunting success was higher than elsewhere in Oregon. Similarly, Park et al. (1991) estimated the mean value of doubling a hunter's chance to obtain a trophy elk in Montana at $179 to $317, depending on the statistical assumptions used in their contingent value model. Enhancing the quality of a hunting trip is most likely to add value when hunters currently perceive a need for improvement. For example, a study in Montana did not find an increase in mean willingness to pay associated with reductions in hunter density (Olsen 1989), apparently because encounters with other hunters are rare enough that they do not detract from the quality of a Montana elk hunt.

In one of the few studies of the nonconsumptive economic value of elk, Duffield (1992) reported results of a study in Yellowstone National Park. His data came from a 1989 survey of Yellowstone visitors who were asked about their willingness to pay to expand winter range for the

Northern Yellowstone elk herd by 10,000 acres (24,710 ha). Survey respondents accepted or rejected a single hypothetical price for elk habitat preservation that ranged from $1 to $500. The probability of a visitor paying a $1 fee was estimated at 92%, compared with $10 at 62%, $50 at 30%, and $500 at 5%. Median willingness to pay for elk range expansion was estimated at $78 (mean) and $18 (median). Extrapolating those figures to the entire population of Yellowstone visitors, the 1989 present value of expanding the Northern Yellowstone herd's winter range totaled $35.9 million. An interesting aspect of Duffield's study was that most of the value was not attributable to the recreational use of elk. On the contrary, Duffield estimated that 83% of that total was existence value (the value associated with knowing that elk thrive in Yellowstone regardless of whether one ever expects to gain any personal utility [recreational value] from their presence). It is interesting to speculate as to the existence value of elk throughout their range. Efforts by states and provinces to reestablish elk into areas where no or very little hunting will ever occur indicates that the nonconsumptive and existence value of elk may be very high.

Most studies that focus on the recreation value of nonconsumptive wildlife recreation have not attempted to as

In various sanctuaries, depending on the time of year and age and sex of the elk, the animals may be habituated enough to the presence and attentions of people that what might otherwise be a dangerous encounter is merely an exercise in mutual curiosity or tolerance. Such habituation is as old as the sanctuaries themselves. *Photo courtesy of the U.S. National Park Service.*

Wildlife managers must be very vigilant about inadvertent human harassment of elk that may cause herd displacement or trigger defensive reactions by individual animals. The consequences of both can be biologically, administratively and economically costly. *Top photo by Leonard Lee Rue III.*

sign values to a particular species. In fact, tourists may be more likely to seek destinations that have many species (e.g., bears, wolves, bison and elk in Yellowstone National Park) than to seek a particular species. This sort of recreation can be very important economically. For example, a University of Montana study found that 11% of nonresident visitors to the state visited a specific area to view wildlife and 23% visited a designated wildlife viewing area (McCool 1996). Wildlife viewing visitors stayed longer in the state than did other groups (4.8 nights compared with 2.6 nights overall) and reported slightly higher expenditures ($67 per day). About 1.5 million visitors to Montana viewed wildlife, including elk, in 1990.

Recreational Impacts

Concerns about the effects of human disturbance on elk date back to the observations of ethologist Margaret Altmann (1956). Altmann observed that elk react to "persecution" by evasion—moving away from persecution and by curtailing rutting activity. Since then, a sizeable body of literature on the effects of recreational and industrial activities on elk behavior has accrued, including studies by Ward et al. (1973) and Morgantini and Hudson (1980), as

well as the proceedings of two symposia (Peek 1976, Christensen et al. 1991). A common theme of many of these studies is the influence of road density in increasing elk vulnerability to hunting and their responses to other human activities.

Recreational activities may be *selective* or *nonselective*, with respect to their impacts on wildlife (Hammitt and Cole 1987). The former comprise those that focus on a particular species and usually are associated with hunting. Nonselective impacts result from coincidental encounters with wildlife by recreationists engaged in any of numerous activities. Traditionally, the primary impacts of recreation on elk have been selective in nature because of the emphasis on hunting. Obviously, some nonconsumptive recreational activities also may be selective (e.g., photography). Undoubtedly, the most significant trend is the phenomenal growth of nonconsumptive outdoor activities (Duffus and Dearden 1990, Flather and Cordell 1995). These include hiking, cross-country skiing and mountain biking, as well as many activities that involve a variety of motorized off-road vehicles. The net effect of this trend is the juxtaposition of elk with people (sometimes in large numbers with potentially disturbing devices) at virtually all times of the year, thereby possibly increasing the nonselective impacts.

A conceptual framework of the major impacts on wildlife associated with recreational activities was proposed by Wall and Wright (1977). Geist (1978) provided a conceptual underpinning for an understanding of human impacts on ungulates. His review focused on two main aspects, namely harassment and learning. Harassment refers to actions that may cause mere excitation in certain situations, but may result in panic, physical exertion, disruption of essential activities, displacement and sometimes even death in other situations (cf. Ream 1979). Harassment can be active or passive. These effects may occur as largely unintended impacts on the nonharvested segments in hunted populations or intentionally on the part of recreationists. However, the major impact is that of unintentional harassment, and herein lies the significance of the burgeoning recreational activity alluded to earlier.

Learned responses of wildlife to human activities include habituation, attraction and avoidance. Habituation is defined as a waning response to a repeated neutral stimulus—one that is associated with neither a positive nor negative outcome (Eibl-Eibesfeldt 1970).

The subject of human disturbance on wildlife has spawned extensive literature, some of which relates to recreational activities. Considering the broad array of potential disturbances caused by recreational activities and the many wildlife species involved, knowledge regarding of impacts of these activities still is in an emerging stage. Knight and Cole (1995) noted that, although numerous studies have been conducted, the results often are disparate and seldom definitive. The majority of studies document immediate (usually individual) behavioral responses rather than long-term, population-level responses. Even in cases that demonstrate physiological changes, such as elevated heart rates, a demographic response may not be observed.

Another problem is that of site-specific variation. A certain activity may constitute harassment in one location, but animals may have habituated to the same activity elsewhere (typically in a sanctuary situation). Site-specific responses will depend necessarily on the particular mix of consumptive and nonconsumptive activities, as well as nonrecreational disturbances to which the animals are subjected. Boyle and Samson (1985) suggested that inadvertent disturbance of large mammals by hikers could cause displacement, but based on the studies they reviewed, such displacement generally has a negligible influence on the animals' distribution and movements.

In some cases, predictions for a species of interest may be based on inferences drawn from studies of another species. Such an approach is fraught with difficulty because the behavioral, psychological and demographic responses of different animals (even those of a particular taxonomic group) may differ substantially. It should be noted that elk are notoriously robust animals and may be more tolerant at a population level to behavioral and physiological stress than are deer. For example, it might be argued that elk on winter range areas may be less sensitive to displacement than cohabitant mule deer because they are larger. Because of their size, elk are better able to cope with deep snow without expending as much energy by virtue of a smaller surface-to-volume ratio.

Although elk can become somewhat accustomed to the sight and noise of snow machines the stay on established trails and travel at designated times, the sudden presence of these vehicles can impose undue energy costs on the animals during a vulnerable season. When conditions are best for snowmobiling, they tend to be are harshest for elk. *Photo by Cecil Stoughton; courtesy of the U.S. National Park Service.*

Despite these many difficulties, some valuable information on the impacts of human disturbance on elk associated with recreational activities does exist, although some accounts are quasi-anecdotal in nature. For example, Anderson and Scherzinger (1975) reported that an expected increase in elk numbers in response to improved winter forage occurred only when snowmobiles were banned. They also noted that the closure of 10 miles (16.1 km) of regular road and all old logging roads and ski trails also may have contributed to the increased use of the area. Squibb et al. (1986) compared mean conception dates between two elk populations in northern Utah subject to differing levels of disturbance associated with hunting regulations. They attributed delays in conception to the disruption of the breeding season resulting both from direct hunting for elk and an indirect, nonlethal disturbance associated with a general mule deer hunting season.

That elk can demonstrate strong population responses in the absence of hunting and other disturbance was amply demonstrated by the herd on the Arid Lands Ecology Reserve, a portion of the U.S. Department of Energy's Hanford site in south-central Washington. This site harbors a population that colonized the area in 1972 (Rickard et al.1977). Largely in the absence of human intervention, the population increased at an average rate of 20% per year (Eberhardt et al. 1996)—a rate approaching the species' biotic potential. It is noteworthy that this herd prospered in a shrub-steppe ecosystem lacking the coniferous cover considered essential by some to protect elk from the extreme summer temperatures that occur in this geographic area. Although this population was not hunted, its remarkable performance was at least partially attributable to the general lack of human disturbance.

Results of studies on the response of elk to winter recreation illustrate well the problems discussed earlier. A study (Cassirer et al. 1992) in Yellowstone National Park demonstrated spatial displacement of elk in areas free from human disturbance, when cross-country skiers approached within 440 yards (400 m). The animals moved to steep slopes with tree cover and sometimes into another drainage. However, an earlier investigation in Alberta showed no negative response in elk numbers to cross-country ski trails (Ferguson and Keith 1982).

The impact of snowmobiles and all-terrain vehicles is even less clear. We are aware of no studies designed specifically to test the effects of these vehicles on elk. A few investigators have examined the effects of these vehicles on white-tailed deer (Dorrance et al. 1975, Eckstein et al.1979, Yarmolay et al. 1988). However, because of the differences in the experimental design of those studies, making generalizations about their results is difficult. At a minimum, the disturbances caused short-term spatial displacement. In addition, the disturbances increased home range size, altered feeding patterns and affected reproductive performance. Gander and Ingold (1997) reported flight responses of varying distances by chamois to hikers, joggers and mountain bikers. The distance fled was influenced by the time of day and type of disturbance. These findings are merely illustrative rather than indicative of the kinds of responses that could occur with elk. One fact does seem fairly clear, any impacts that snowmobiles and all-terrain vehicles have on elk and other wildlife likely have increased in recent years and will continue to increase. Woodbury (1997) reported that snowmobile sales have doubled nationally during the previous 5 years.

Intuitively, it would seem that disturbances resulting from motorized vehicles might be more significant than other types of disturbances, but the results of some studies suggest that animals habituate more readily to vehicles than to persons out of vehicles (see Ward et al. 1973). Moreover, some fraction of pedestrian-based recreationists are accompanied by dogs, which may increase the intensity of interaction.

Disturbances associated with the development of ski areas for the rapidly growing downhill ski industry can impact elk. Such disturbances comprise physical (i.e., habitat modification) and human components, but it is difficult to separate the respective effects of the two. Morrison et al. (1995) documented the responses of two elk populations in Colorado to ski area expansion. Development at one site consisted only of physical disturbances, whereas development at the second location primarily involved increases in human activity. Both areas showed initial decreases in post-development elk use, albeit in varying degrees. Although elk use appeared to increase in subsequent years, presumably as the result of habituation, the authors cautioned against assuming complete recovery.

Conclusion

The burgeoning amount of information on hunters and hunting is impressive. In *The Elk of North America*, Murie (1951) devoted only three pages to the discussion of elk hunting. At that time, little was known about hunters and the role of hunting in elk management. Since then, dozens of studies have been launched to inquire into who the hunter is, why he hunts and what satisfactions he receives. It is not unreasonable to expect a similar quantum increase in such information in future years.

It seems certain that the nonconsumptive use of wildlife will continue to grow. It could become one of the largest line items in wildlife agency budgets; therefore, the importance of nonconsumptive wildlife values to the North American public should not be underestimated. A study of American households reported that 36% of the respondents were unequivocal in their evaluation that hunting has no value (Carpenter et al. 1977). When asked to make a trade-off among hunting, viewing wildlife and the value of just knowing wildlife is present, these respondents unanimously placed hunting last. Hunters—representing 15% of the respondents—saw hunting as extremely important. In the trade off, 51% of the hunters placed viewing at the top. Hunting and the existence value split 43%, and 6% were undecided. This suggests, as do other consumptive versus nonconsumptive attitude surveys, that (1) the sociological role of hunting in elk management is not well understood, (2) nonconsumptive values are important to consumptive users as well as to nonconsumptive users, and (3) there is need and opportunity to improve the capability and scope of elk management through increased emphasis on nonconsumptive use programs.

The concerns of future wildlife managers will shift in emphasis. Although concern for balancing elk populations with available and potential habitat will remain important, additional attention will focus on management of human activities to prevent elk harassment on or displacement from crucial summer and winter ranges. Concern for over-harvested elk populations in a few areas may lead to the closing of heavily roaded areas to vehicular traffic in the name of hunting quality. Native American's role in wildlife management and use will require better definition. It is possible that future hunting seasons may have to be justified by environmental impact statements. Montana submitted an environmental impact statement for big game hunting (Montana Department of Fish, Wildlife and Parks 1972) and prepared a separate statement on a special elk hunt adjacent to Yellowstone National Park (Newby 1975). Another challenge and shift in emphasis will be the movement away from defending hunting toward enlisting the support of a growing segment of the population that is concerned with the welfare of wildlife, independent of their attitudes toward hunting (Shaw 1977).

All of the aforementioned are minor compared with the most fundamental concern: loss of elk habitat. Elk again could be relegated to a few remnant wild places, as they were 100 years ago. This may occur, not because of excessive hunting, antihunting sentiment or harassment from the nonconsumptive users. Instead, it may result from a collapse of the foundation supporting elk habitat. If this sounds alarmist, one must consider the trends in recent years. Critical habitat has disappeared through drainage, dam construction, subdivision development, road building and urban sprawl. A study of land-use trends revealed that, in a 10-year period from the mid-1960s to the mid-1970s, urban sprawl alone consumed 750,000 acres (303,525 ha) annually (Williamson 1973). Roadways and airports usurped 130,000 acres (52,611 ha), and reservoirs claimed 300,000 acres (121,410 ha). Williamson (1973) predicted that, in addition, 34 million acres (13,759,800 ha) of rural land—equivalent to half of Colorado—would be taken over by urban developments early in the 21st century.

Although much elk range may not be affected by human development and expansion, many critical areas and migration corridors will be impacted. This is as true today as it was in 1908, when a study concluded that elk were dying out primarily because the advance of civilization was preventing the animals from reaching winter feeding grounds (Nicholson and Donaldson 1969). For many elk popula-

tions, the slightest change in a critical portion of their ranges can adversely influence the animals' well-being. This was demonstrated during the settlement era, particularly for elk wintering along streams, and during the exploitation era of the late 1800s.

Although some elk ranges may not be lost to human development, they may be altered significantly to accommodate human needs, desires or both. Food and wood fiber production, energy extraction and environmental contaminants are but a few of the potentially detrimental influences on the welfare of elk throughout their range in North America. Furthermore, loss or depreciation of habitat quality may significantly affect opportunities for public uses of elk, particularly hunting. Because hunting indirectly has been and probably will continue to be the primary source of financial support for elk management programs, loss of this recreational opportunity or its lowered quality as an outdoor recreational activity could have a serious effect on the number, distribution and value of elk.

These concerns about the future of elk are not, or at least should not be, solely those of the professional wildlifer. They must be important to the public as well. And although they reflect a possibly bleak scenario, they should be viewed as a reason for developing alternatives to reverse or prevent negative trends. They also should serve as a catalyst for public recognition of the management task ahead and for the application of the scientific know-how at hand.

It is hoped that the mid-1900s saw a rebirth of the "Great American Elk Hunt." However, unlike the Great Hunt of the 1800s, elk hunting now is based on well-founded biological principles and scientific facts. The goal of elk management remains the conservation and sustained yield of elk to produce benefits for the hunter and nonconsumptive user alike. Uncontrolled hunting combined with widespread habitat loss once relegated elk to a few wild places. Hunting now is controlled carefully, but habitat loss actually may be accelerating, especially in the western portions of the United States and in southern Canada.

The recent rebirth of elk is a wildlife management success story of great import and value. However, the reestablished herd may represent only 10% of earlier populations and an even smaller fraction of the original range of elk. The short-term future of elk seems bright, but the long-term future of elk is yet to be determined.

18

DAVID H. STALLING,
GARY J. WOLFE AND DAN K. CROCKETT

Regulating the Hunt

Balancing the Complexities
of Elk Vulnerability

From Kublai Khan to Roosevelt

In the late 1200s, Mongol ruler Kublai Khan, grandson of Genghis Khan, forbade his subjects to hunt during breeding seasons, creating one of the earliest laws designed to protect wildlife from overhunting. Access, too, was controlled and, according to the writings of the 13th century traveler Marco Polo, "anyone who contravenes this rule is made to repent it bitterly" (Bunnell 1993:107). Even before Khan's time, people adhered to self-imposed regulations, often in fear of reprisal from powers even greater than the ruthless Khan. In classical mythology, Artemis, the Greek goddess of wildlife, punished hunters who killed too many animals, slew sacred animals or hunted in sacred places (Hudson 1993). Fear of punishment by deities, barbaric leaders or even kings and queens of Europe kept many red deer herds flourishing, but as human populations increased, hunting, in much of the world, became sport exclusively for the wealthy and influential (Posewitz 1994). Death penalties for killing one of the "king's deer" were not uncommon (Whisker 1981). It is no wonder that, when Europeans first set foot on the wildlife-rich shores of North America, they abjured regulations that might restrict their new-found freedom to hunt (Reiger 1975). Of course, these settlers were not practicing the recreational pursuit engaged in by kings. They hunted for meat and survival, much like the Native Americans who inhabited the continent before their arrival.

Assiniboine hunters, wearing snowshoes, chased elk into deep snow for easy killing, Arapahos drove herds over cliffs,

Lakotas trapped the animals in rings of fire, and Coastal Salish caught elk in snares and pitfalls. From eastern hardwood forests to the Great Plains and from the high Rockies to the West Coast, Native Americans hunted elk for food, clothing, religious ceremonies and decorative purposes (see Chapter 3).

But, there were an estimated 10 million elk (McCabe 1982) and roughly 11 million people (Manning 1995) living in North America before Europeans arrived. Today, more people than that live in Los Angeles, and more than 325 million folks populate North America, while elk number about 1 million (Bunnell 1997). With human populations mushrooming and wildlife habitat dwindling, demand for elk hunting exceeds supply. Laws are necessary to prevent people from killing too many elk; sustainable hunting requires regulations.

In the United States and Canada, hunting regulations were essential to save what remained of commonly hunted wildlife species. In 1646, Rhode Island became the first colony to establish a closed season on deer. By the time the states came together to form a nation in the late 1700s, all except Georgia had closed seasons (Schmidt 1978b). From 1850 to 1900, game laws became increasingly common and more restrictive in response to rapid depletion of wildlife. Westward expansion, more efficient rifles, transcontinental railroads that provided access and a means of hauling animals parts and a booming market for meat, furs, hides and ivories resulted in bison, elk, deer, pronghorn and other wildlife being rapidly reduced in numbers. By the late

1800s, less than 90,000 elk remained, mostly in Yellowstone National Park, but also in Riding Mountain National Park, in Manitoba, and isolated pockets of wilderness in Wyoming, Montana and Colorado (Bryant and Maser 1982).

Maine was the first state to hire full-time game wardens, in 1852, to enforce laws protecting deer and moose (Trefethen 1975). Other states followed, enforcing newly set seasons and bag limits. Many states eliminated hunting during breeding seasons. George Bird Grinnell, editor of *Forest and Stream,* lambasted market hunters and implored people to push for regulations to protect wildlife. Other magazines, such as *American Sportsman* and *Field and Stream,* uncovered and scorned exploitation of wildlife, rallying hunters to conserve the remnants of once-great populations (Reiger 1975). George Oliver Shields, editor and publisher of *Recreation* magazine, William T. Hornaday, director of the New York Zoological Park and C. Gordon Hewitt, of the Canadian Department of Conservation, also publicized the plight of wildlife and were instrumental in crafting legislation to protect what remained of wildlife and their habitat. The highly influential Boone and Crockett Club, whose membership included the nation's leading ornithologists and mammalogists, strongly pushed for laws to protect wildlife species and establish parks and reserves (Trefethen 1975). Canadian Prime Minister Sir Wilfrid Laurier formed a Commission on Conservation and, along with Hewitt and commission chairman Clifford Sifton, published *The Conservation of the Wild Life of Canada* (Hewitt 1921) calling for protective regulations. With Laurier and Sifton working hand-in-hand with U.S. President Theodore Roosevelt and his chief forester, Gifford Pinchot, Canada and the United States emerged with all but identical regulations and policies to conserve wildlife (Trefethen 1975).

Early elk regulations, for the most part, simply made it illegal to kill what few animals remained. But, many people settling the West defied restrictions protecting wildlife. In the absence of efforts to enforce them, wildlife laws were ineffective. Despite regulations that prohibited the killing of elk and other wildlife in newly formed Yellowstone National Park, hide and tusk hunters continued decimating animals within park boundaries (Geist 1991d). So, on August 20, 1886, the U.S. Army took over jurisdiction of the park to protect elk and other wildlife—a date Geist (1993:51) referred to as "the first day of modern wildlife management in North America."

Wildlife protection efforts extended far beyond park boundaries and did more than merely restrict when and where people could hunt or how many animals they could kill. By the late 1800s, some hunters questioned the sportsmanship of commonly accepted hunting practices, such as

At a time when elk numbers had been drastically reduced and the species was protected throughout nearly all of its remnant range in the early 20th century, the carcass of this bull was abandoned after only its two bugler teeth were extracted by poachers. Wrote W. A. Wadsworth (1902:239–240): "There is a great local pretense that they are killed off by 'Eastern dudes,' 'Toorsts,' 'Indians,' etc.; but the majority are taken late in the season by men who go into the mountains for 'meat' for winter use, and by pot hunters wanting the hides or teeth. The former have little value, but the two small tusks called the 'ivories,' found in the upper jaw, have by a strange perversion, and with the approval of its officers, become fashionable as a badge among some of the members of a well-known society. So, many a noble beast has died in the snow, leaving head, hide and carcass to rot untouched, to furnish a foolish ornament to some fat and worthy clubman who never saw forest, mountain, or camp fire, and is so ignorant of the lore of his own fraternity as not to know the difference between the great prehistoric Irish Elk, from which it derives its name, and the American Wapiti. . . . " *Photo courtesy of the Wildlife Management Institute.*

chasing deer with hounds, killing deer from boats and jacklighting (Trefethen 1975). When Theodore Roosevelt helped to found the Boone and Crockett Club in 1887, he defined the rudiments of what he called fair chase (Anonymous 1887). Long before there were laws mandating hunter behavior, he urged people to stop trapping bears, wolves and cougars, chasing moose, elk or deer in deep crusted snow, shooting swimming animals from a boat or methods other than fair stalking or still hunting (Baier 1993). Early day conservationists Madison Grant and Martin Van Buren Ives joined Roosevelt in an effort to outlaw unsportsmanlike hunting methods in the Adirondack Mountains of northern New York, despite strong opposition from hunters, guides and hotel owners who favored generous game laws (Trefethen 1975:112).

Although controversy ebbed and flowed in the East over hunting laws and ethics, conservationists struggled in the West to protect what remained of failing wildlife populations, particularly elk. By 1900, elk were absent from 90% of their original range. Many herds were so small and scattered that productivity was minimized and they could not breed effectively and could no longer sustain population growth to offset losses. In 1873, California made the killing of Tule elk a felony, punishable by 2 years in prison. A few years later, Montana enacted a similar law for its elk populations. New Mexico first closed hunting seasons on elk in 1865. Colorado closed all elk hunting in 1903. In 1905, Washington imposed a 10-year ban on elk hunting. Other states followed and, by 1910, all legal elk hunting came to an end (Madson 1966).

Rigorous efforts to protect herds paid off. Under the protection of federal troops and state game wardens, elk in Yellowstone National Park and other remnant herds began to increase in numbers. State and federal wildlife biologists and land managers successfully translocated elk from refuges, such as Yellowstone, the Teton Game Preserve and the National Elk Refuge, and reintroduced the animals to parts of their former range throughout the West and beyond. Between 1912 and 1967, shipments of more than 13,500 elk radiated out from Yellowstone to various points in the United States, Canada and Mexico (Robbins et al. 1982, see also Chapter 14). By 1941, the United States was home to more than 200,000 elk. Eleven states had resumed elk hunting by 1942 (Madson 1966), managing growing elk populations under evolving ideas of wildlife management.

Evolving Regulations

Modern game management principles first emerged in North America in the 1930s, advanced by forester Aldo Leopold (1933), who promoted the concept of managing for healthy wildlife populations in balance with available habitat, allowing hunters to kill "surplus" animals. As elk populations began to recover, more states gradually reopened elk hunting seasons, with hunting and harvests strictly regulated. A unique system of wildlife management emerged in North America, based on four key principles: (1) public ownership of wildlife, (2) elimination of marketing the meat, parts and products of game mammals and birds, (3) allocation of the material benefits of wildlife by law, not by marketplace, birthright, land ownership or social position, and (4) prohibition of frivolous killing of wildlife (Geist 1993). Public ownership of wildlife formed the cornerstone to this system, giving all citizens a say and a stake in wildlife policies, laws and regulations.

Hunting became the primary method of regulating big game populations in the United States and Canada. Through license sales, excise taxes on hunting equipment and contributions from hunter/conservation organizations, hunting provided the primary source of funding for state, federal and provincial wildlife management programs. The system has been, until recently, remarkably successful. As Geist (1993) pointed out, achievements of wildlife management in North America include recovery of some wildlife populations, development of an identifiable segment of the economy based on appreciation and pursuit of wild animals, emergence of a profession of wildlife management, greater public involvement in decisions affecting wildlife, taxation to benefit wildlife, habitat conservation, establishment of international treaties to protect wildlife, the even-

The Tule elk populations of California were nearly exterminated during and immediately following the California gold rush, which began in 1849. *Photo by Luther C. Goldman; courtesy of the U.S. National Archives.*

When the National Elk Refuge, near Jackson, Wyoming, was officially established in 1912, it was known for a few years as the Government Winter Elk Refuge. *Photo from 1918 courtesy of the U.S. National Archives.*

tual protection of large predators and establishment of effective wildlife law enforcement.

Because money derived from hunting fuels wildlife management efforts—primarily in state agencies—North American wildlife management before 1970 focused on protecting and propagating game species. Leopold (1933:3) defined game management as "the art of making land produce sustained annual crops of wild game for recreational use." Although successful, this hunter-supported system has been increasingly criticized in recent decades for favoring hunted species—purportedly sometimes to the detriment of nonhunted species—and for catering to hunters while discounting the needs and desires of nonhunters (Trefethen 1975, Madson 1993).

But wildlife management is growing to embrace the full spectrum of species, for a variety of goals, not just produc-

ing annual crops of game for hunting. Meslow (1993:36) observed: "As wildlife managers, we have not lost the earlier goals in that we still manage wildlife in order to provide annual crops of game for recreational use. However, our playing field has expanded. We now address the desires of an expanded wildlife conservation constituency. These changes are reflected in such mundane ways as the names of our public agencies; what were formerly called Game Departments are now almost universally called Wildlife Departments. Titles of academic institutions have evolved as well; Departments of Game Management have given way to Departments of Wildlife Management and Wildlife Ecology. These are more than just changes in name. Changes in philosophy and mode of operation have accompanied them."

In fact, the most dramatic alteration in land management plans that ever occurred, in relating to a wildlife ques-

Elk from Yellowstone National Park corralled (*left*) for shipments by rail (*right*) in 1912 to Washington State and western Montana. *Photos courtesy of Doris Whithorn and the Park County (Wyoming) Museum.*

tion, was the "President's Plan" to manage forests of the Pacific Northwest to assure the viability of a threatened species—the northern spotted owl (Thomas et al. 1990, Forest Ecosystem Management Assessment Team 1993).

Wildlife managers and land managers are moving rapidly away from a maximum sustained yield approach—focusing primarily on commodities (timber, grazing, etc.)—and adopting an ecosystem management approach. This evolving philosophy involves restoring, protecting and maintaining all components of a healthy ecosystem while meeting the needs of people—including elk and elk habitat. Game management matured into wildlife management, and wildlife conservation took on new meaning, becoming "the total human effort to maintain and enhance our wildlife heritage for a broad array of public values" (Mackie 1991:1). In turn, wildlife management is beginning to embrace entire ecosystems, while still remaining rooted in the land ethic espoused by Leopold (1949:204–221) more than half a century ago: "The land ethic simply enlarges the boundaries of the community to include soils, water, plants, and animals, or collectively: the land. . . . A land ethic, then, reflects the existence of an ecological conscience, and this in turn reflects a conviction of individual responsibility for the health of the land."

In his landmark book, *The Elk of North America*, Olaus Murie (1951:289) wrote: "Perhaps it is not even proper to speak of 'elk management' by itself. It needs to be integrated with management of other species, for the elk is only one member of the fauna." And in a more recent report, Christensen et al. (1993:1) stated that, "We recognize now that elk are part of a much bigger picture and that elk habitat management must be placed within the context of ecosystem management, biodiversity, state management strategies and goals and shifting public demand and interest that now embrace non-consumptive and consumptive interests."

In summarizing a 1991 symposium concerning the vulnerability of elk to hunting, Thomas (1991:318) said that "merely producing elk is not enough. The hunting experience and the effect of hunting on elk welfare are also important and must be addressed simultaneously with the production of elk. Indeed, the world is changing so rapidly these considerations may already be more important than production."

As wildlife management goals and philosophies change and are subsumed into ecosystem management, so do hunting regulations evolve. Early elk management efforts focused on recovering species. Total prohibitions of hunting in the early 1900s, followed by very limited hunting, coupled with aggressive translocation programs into the 1960s, allowed elk herds to grow and expand. When herds

began to flourish, with rising numbers and expanding ranges, hunting regulations were altered to reflect a policy of maximum sustained yield, producing as many elk as possible and allowing hunters to harvest a perceived excess, or surplus, of animals. Most wildlife managers believed that as long as hunting was reasonably controlled and habitat maintained or enhanced, populations would take care of themselves. They embraced the idea that long, liberal seasons generally were possible, if not necessary (Mackie 1991).

For the most part, hunters could kill bulls but not cows. Regulations simply defined seasons, bag limits and hunting methods. As long as bulls bred cows and produced an annual crop of calves, all seemed well for elk and elk hunters. But as growing numbers of hunters equipped with increasingly high-tech gear penetrated elk country through an expanding network of logging roads, hunted elk—usually bull elk—became *too* vulnerable (Lyon et al. 1985).

When elk hunting seasons were reinstituted in states and units where moratoriums had been in effect for a score of years or more, most hunters were allowed to harvest only bulls. This enabled the herds to continue to recover in number and range. In time, with improved high-tech hunting gear and an extensive road network through much of elk range, the focus on bull-only hunting placed too much pressure on those particular animals, and regulations had to be adjusted. *Photo by L. D. Bailey; courtesy of the U.S. Forest Service.*

Elk Management Objectives

If wildlife and land managers were given the sole task of maintaining healthy, sustainable populations of elk, the challenges of protecting elk habitat and creating hunting regulations would be greatly simplified. However, natural resource professionals are obligated and often required by law to provide for the needs and demands of enormously diverse constituencies and special interest groups, including loggers, miners, ranchers, anglers, hunters, environmentalists, backpackers and photographers. When making hunting regulations, political, economic and social considerations often supersede biological considerations. If elk hunting regulations are not responsive to public interests, and generally understood and supported by the public, they will almost certainly fail. Successful hunting regulations depend on balance, cooperation, understanding and education (Kovalicky and Blair 1991, Moroz 1991).

Desired objectives of elk management are rooted in the land management needs and public attitudes about what constitutes best use of elk populations at a given time and place. Scheffer (1976) listed two dominant public concerns with important bearing on wildlife management in general and on elk management in particular: (1) a growing respect for nature and naturalness (the environmental/ecological movement) and (2) a growing respect for life (the antikill issue). Traditional wildlife management, whose success or failure formerly was measured by the number of hunter days afield and the number of animals killed, is being reoriented to provide experiences demanded by a new generation of recreational users. Production of wildlife to accommodate the hunting of a maximum number of animals may no longer be considered the primary function of wildlife management (Hendee 1974).

Today's wildlife populations, including elk, must be managed to provide not only hunting, but also other recreational benefits (Thomas and DeGraaf 1973, Hendee 1974, LeResche 1974). This does not mean that hunting has no part or only a small role in wildlife management. To the contrary, hunting will continue to be an important component of elk population management. However, wildlife management must provide stewardship and maintenance of natural resources for optimal benefits to all segments of society. Thus, wildlife management also involves people, and their attitudes and preferences with respect to wildlife and its uses (Scheffer 1976). This is especially true in the context of a species as popular as elk.

Within the ecological constraints of the species being managed and public desires and demands, two schools of wildlife management have evolved: (1) management designed to maximize current user satisfactions within bio-logically sound limitations and (2) management designed to meet long-range objectives at some cost to more immediate desires, such as maximal short-term hunting opportunities. These schools are not necessarily mutually exclusive in theory or practice; most management programs combine elements of each.

Discussing management designed to maximize user satisfaction, Hendee (1974) pointed out that traditional theories of wildlife management may no longer be adequate to deal with both an ever-expanding human population (and, thus, increased demands for hunting privileges) and declining wildlife populations. Some wildlife populations, such as elk, have grown and expanded in recent years. However, habitat—particularly critical winter range—has diminished and habitat accessible to public hunting has grown more crowded during hunting seasons. The once-popular notion of measuring hunting success by the amount of animals killed is no longer adequate, especially as demands for hunting privileges increase and harvest success rates decrease. An emphasis on maximum harvest fails to recognize the benefits other than killing elk and has been replaced by a *hunter-days afield* concept, in which it is assumed that the success of hunting regulations can be measured by the number of days hunters spend hunting—a back-to-nature concept. However, this concept also fails in some respects to identify adequately the benefits of hunting. It implies constant levels of hunter satisfaction, regardless of the quality of the hunting experience (Hendee 1974).

Success in modern wildlife management depends, in large part, on a multiple-satisfaction and multifaceted approach that encompasses physical and sociological, as well as biological, factors (Hendee 1974). Although every state manages its elk populations in slightly different ways, with various goals in mind, the approach used in Montana typifies the process.

In 1992, the Montana Fish, Wildlife and Parks Commission and the Montana Department of Fish, Wildlife and Parks developed a statewide Elk Management Plan to guide stewardship of Montana's elk and elk habitat on state, federal and private land (Youmans 1992). The plan divided the state into 35 elk management units, each encompassing one or more hunting districts which share similar ecological characteristics and, in most cases, include the year-round range of major elk populations. While specific goals and objectives differ for each unit, Montana's statewide management goal is to "maintain elk populations in a healthy and productive condition and cooperate with public and private land managers in the management of elk habitat to provide hunting opportunity, a diversity of hunting and viewing experiences and general enjoyment by the public" (Youmans 1992:14).

Statewide habitat objectives are to: (1) identify elk habitats critical to attaining and maintaining objectives for elk populations and elk-related recreation; (2) recognize the contributions of private and public land managers in the management and maintenance of elk habitat and work toward development of cooperative programs to maintain the current amount of productive elk habitat (a little under 27 million acres); and (3) work with land managers to maintain elk habitat offering adequate security so that elk harvest is distributed throughout the hunting season, with no more than 40% of the annual bull harvest taken during the first week of the rifle hunting season.

Recognizing that habitat holds the key to sustaining healthy elk populations and good hunting opportunities, the state plan emphasized habitat research, habitat management strategies and cooperation with state, federal and private land management agencies and property owners. The plan served as a guide to wildlife managers, land managers and others responsible for policy decisions that affect wildlife and wildlife-related recreation in Montana. The Department also relied on the plan to help set priorities for field activities, manage time and budgets and formulate elk management regulations.

While developing the elk management plan, state officials solicited comments at public meetings, informal meetings with interest groups (hunting clubs, landowner associations, conservation organizations, guide and outfitter groups and hunting industry representatives) and meetings with state and federal land management agencies.

The Department also sent out questionnaires and allowed 10 weeks for public review of the draft plan. Throughout, the agency kept the public informed through news releases, brochures, and articles in magazines and newspapers.

Issues considered included: (1) management of elk habitats on public and private lands; (2) desired elk population levels; (3) elk distribution; (4) hunting season regulations; (5) depredation of agricultural crops; (6) public access; (7) resource conflicts between elk habitat requirements and other land uses such as logging, mining and ranching; and (8) competition for (a) elk hunting opportunity, particularly for mature bulls (issues surrounding length and timing of hunting seasons for bowhunters versus the rifle season), (b) special hunting seasons in which only hunters who draw a limited number of tags, available through a lottery system, can hunt, (c) public access, (d) private landowner preferences for special permits, (e) use of licenses that allow hunters to hunt only antlerless elk, and (f) hunting opportunities for Montana state residents in comparison with opportunities for nonresidents, and opportunities for hunters hiring guides, as compared with hunters who do not hire guides, but hunt on their own.

Statewide elk population objectives, as outlined in the plan, were to: (1) maintain the current population of approximately 89,000 elk (as counted during winter, after hunting seasons are over)—although the available habitat could have supported substantially greater numbers of elk,

By statute, elk population goals and harvest management plans must consider citizen interests in the species besides those of hunters. Such consideration has to be more than mere adherence to the law, but a desirable accommodation of a constituency that has a great stake in the well-being of elk herds, whether or not the constituency necessarily realizes or appreciates its stake "ownership." *Photo by Leland J. Prater; courtesy courtesy of the U.S. Forest Service.*

the Department considered this number of animals (which took into consideration adjustments in elk population objectives for individual elk management units) to be compatible with current land uses and landowner tolerance for elk on private lands; (2) maintain an observed ratio of bull elk numbers as compared to cow elk in each elk management unit commensurate with the ability of the habitat to sustain elk even during periods of stress and disturbance from human activities such as hunting (the Department stated that a ratio of 5:100 was too low and would require corrective action through management to increase the numbers of bulls); and (3) maintain the ratio of calves to cow elk at levels commensurate with the ability of the habitat to sustain elk in each elk management unit (a ratio of 20:100, for example, was considered too low in some units and would require corrective action to increase calf numbers). The plan recommended that hunting season regulations for each elk management unit be based on the inherent capacity of the habitat to produce and sustain elk, as reflected by the following parameters: population size and age/sex composition; objectives for late winter population levels and herd composition; habitat carrying capacity (which takes into consideration other land uses occurring in elk habitats); the ability of the habitat to hold elk during the stress and disturbance of hunting season; status of elk population levels in relation to private landowner tolerance for elk; potential for damage on private lands from elk and the potential for an elk herd to support recreation activities, such as hunting and wildlife viewing, as influenced by land ownership and public access (Youmans 1992).

Whatever the management approach, establishing hunting regulations was distinct and separate from obtaining information on the numbers of elk that could be or needed to be harvested to meet population objectives. Hunting regulations would be set for delineated land areas (management units or combinations of units) and only after the desired biological and sociological goals had been identified clearly. Sociological considerations might influence which of a number of possible combinations of hunting regulations could be used, but the objective of a hunting season had to be justifiable strictly on the basis of the information at hand to the wildlife biologist or manager (Lipscomb 1974).

Clearly, designing a hunting season to accomplish stated management goals seldom involves simple choices. To illustrate the complexity involved in developing hunting regulations and aid in identifying the options available, Giles (1969) proposed the decision tree (Figure 177). Each choice on the decision tree offers wildlife managers advantages and disadvantages and each can be blended with others in countless ways to achieve various goals.

Elk Management Regulations

Once wildlife management agencies determine objectives for managing elk, they must devise regulations to achieve those goals. Regulatory options abound, but they can be grouped into five basic categories: (1) who—the number of hunters allowed, and the allocation of licenses among those desiring to participate; (2) what—bag limits, dependent on sex, age and numbers of elk allowed to be harvested; (3) when—seasons, the period during which hunting is permitted; (4) where—management units, areas in which hunting is allowed; and (5) how—type of weapons, hunting equipment and technology to be used.

Within these categories, a vast number of regulation combinations are possible. Selecting appropriate regulations hinges on the relationships among a diversity of factors designed to manage elk—these vary dramatically. What works in one time and place will not necessarily work in another, depending on the vagaries of weather, terrain, vegetation, road densities, hunter densities and elk numbers—to say nothing of shifting biological, social and economic forces (Kuck et al. 1991, Thomas 1991, Vales et al. 1991). In rugged, thickly timbered country with few hunters, maintaining good habitat security by closing roads or restricting logging may be enough to reduce the vulnerability of elk to hunting (Hillis et al. 1991, Unsworth and Kuck 1991). But even in the most remote wilderness, restrictions may be needed if excessive elk mortality due to hunting produces undesirable herd characteristics (Kuck et al. 1991, Vales et al. 1991).

In some areas, it is sufficient to adjust the hunting seasons, reducing hunting pressure during the rut or during mass migration out of the high country to lower elevations with the onset of heavy snows. States such as Montana, Idaho and Wyoming—with substantial elk habitat in relation to hunter densities—still have more management options than states such as Washington and Oregon, with rapidly dwindling habitat and mushrooming human populations. Places such as New Mexico and Arizona—with fewer elk in more open country—have opted for allowing only a limited number of hunters. At the other extreme, Colorado offers unlimited license sales. In 1995, roughly 220,000 elk hunters killed about 36,000 elk from an estimated herd of 203,000 (Bunnell 1997). Still, hunters must choose bow, muzzleloader or rifle. In 1996, if they elected to hunt with a rifle, they had to select one of three seasons—5 days in mid-October, 12 days in late October or 9 days in early November. Harvest on most of Colorado's 116 game management units was restricted to four-point or bigger bulls during all seasons. In some units, hunters could kill spike bulls during the third season. In 26 of the units, hunters could hunt ma-

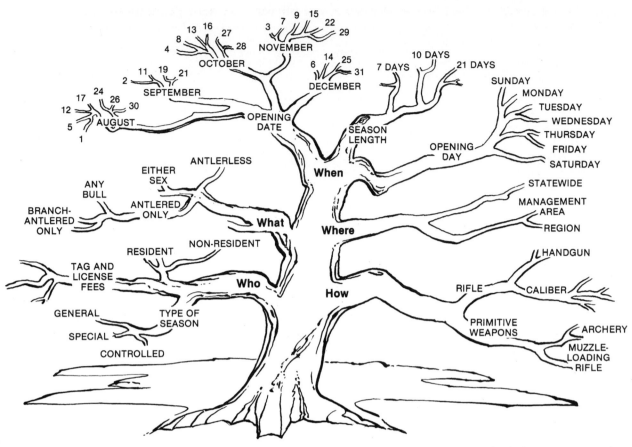

Figure 177. Simplified decision tree for establishing hunting regulations. Each decision must relate to individual management goals and overall management objectives (from Giles 1969).

ture bulls only if they were fortunate enough to draw a limited-entry permit (Carpenter 1991). Between these extremes lie many options, but fitting the right options to a specific place can seem a daunting task. For the most part, wildlife agencies favor less restrictive options. They understandably are reluctant to reduce hunting opportunities and associated license sales that help fund research, management and habitat acquisition and enhancement projects.

Most wildlife management agencies regularly evaluate, revise and update their regulations. Although this sometimes leads to confusion among hunters, effective management of wildlife populations demands it. The size and composition of elk populations, habitat conditions, indeed whole ecosystems, all change constantly. Regulation must change to incorporate the most accurate and recent biological data, as well as citizens' views on the status of the animals being managed. Changing hunter interests and demands require that a maximum variety of hunting experiences be made available. Changing patterns of land use for timber, grazing and agricultural purposes likewise require that regulations be adjustable. Antiquated regulations must be

discontinued to simplify enforcement activities (Baird 1975) and minimize hunter concerns. The simple effects of some types of hunting regulations are presented in Table 121.

Although no other aspect of wildlife management affects most hunters more directly than the establishment of hunting regulations, perhaps none is less understood by them. All too often, hunters find themselves bewildered by the complex stew of opening dates, timing of hunting seasons, season lengths, harvest restrictions, weapons limitations, wildlife management units, hunting permits and license fees. Keeping hunting regulations as simple as possible helps avoid hunter confusion, unintentional game law violations and other misunderstandings that can foster ill will toward the management agency.

Hunter Numbers and License Allocation

With human populations on the rise, demands for elk hunting increasing and elk habitat declining, maintaining a balance between hunter numbers and sustainable elk populations has grown increasingly challenging.

Table 121. General usefulness of hunting regulations in achieving particular management goals and objectives

Regulation	Sex ratio manipulation	Elk damage control	Optimum production	Production of trophies	Quality hunting experience	Achieving hunter distribution
Early season (August to September)	+	+	−	−	+	+
Regular season (October to November)	−	×	+	+	×	×
Late season (December to February)	+	+	+	−	+	−
Long season (more than 30 days)	+	+	−	−	+	+
Normal season (15 to 30 days)	×	−	+	+	×	×
Short season (less than 15 days)	−	−	+	+	−	−
Weekend opening day	+	+	+	−	−	−
Weekday opening day	−	−	−	+	+	+
Bull only	+	−	−	−	+	+
Branch-antlered bull only	×	−	−	−	+	+
Four-point bull only	×	−	−	+	+	+
Spike bull only						
Cow only	+	−	−	+	×	−
Either sex	−	+	+	+	−	−
Rifle only	×	+	+	−	−	−
Primitive weapons only	×	−	−	+	+	+
Entire state open	−	−	−	+	−	−
Unit permits	+	+	+	+	+	+
Unrestricted hunter numbers	+	+	+	−	−	−
Hunter number restrictions	+	−	+	+	+	+
No access restrictions	+	+	+	−	−	−
Road closures	−	−	−	+	+	+

Note: + = useful; × = no significant influence; − = negative influence.

Although the percentage of Americans who hunt has declined steadily in recent decades, the actual number of hunters has increased (Decker et al. 1993). This is especially true for elk hunters. The number of hunters who pursued elk in North America rose from 552,773 in 1975 to 834,402 in 1995, a 51% increase (Table 122).

The amount of time elk hunters spend in the field increased even more. In 1975, hunters spent 2.62 million days afield hunting elk in North America. By 1995, the total number of days elk hunters spent pursuing their quarry jumped to 5.35 million, an increase of 105% (Table 122).

Harvest rates also climbed. In 1975, hunters killed an estimated 104,000 elk in North America. By 1995, this total had risen by 60% to an estimated 166,000 annually. During the same period, the estimated North American elk population increased by 75%—from 553,000 to 968,000 (Table 122).

As demand for elk hunting has increased, state and provincial wildlife agencies have relied on limiting the number of elk hunting licenses issued as an important management technique to help regulate the number of animals harvested. In 1996, only five states and three provinces—Colorado, Idaho, Montana, Washington, Wyoming, Alberta, British Columbia and Saskatchewan—authorized an unlimited number of resident general bull elk licenses, and only Colorado and Washington offered an unlimited number of nonresident general bull elk licenses.

In some states, the demand for elk hunting licenses has

Table 122. Elk hunter participation, harvest and population trends in the United States and Canada, 1975 to 1995

Participation/trend	1975	1980	1985	1990	1995
Number of elk hunters	552,773	618,598	703,001	738,641	834,402
Days afield	2,615,275	2,846,059	3,854,498	4,470,476	5,346,693
Elk harvest	103,793	114,300	120,147	172,318	166,068
Elk population	552,941	560,850	768,718	902,116	967,928

Source: Data from Bunnell 1997.

greatly exceeded the supply. For example, in 1996, there were 158,700 applicants for 20,874 bull elk licenses in Arizona, 70,907 applicants for 440 licenses in Michigan, 11,731 applicants for 170 licenses in Nevada, 11,052 applicants for 80 licenses in North Dakota, 17,161 applicants for 14 licenses in Oklahoma, and 14,289 applicants for 701 licenses in South Dakota (Bunnell 1997). The combined odds of drawing an elk license in one of these six states was only 0.078.

In addition to setting higher license fees for nonresidents, state hunting regulations generally restrict nonresidents' opportunity more so than residents' opportunity to obtain an elk license. In nearly all states, nonresidents are segregated from residents in the license drawings and, in many cases, a cap is established on the total number or percentage of elk licenses available to nonresidents. For example, 138,700 general bull elk licenses were issued in Montana in 1995 (Bunnell 1997). Although the number was unlimited for residents, only 17,000 licenses were available for nonresidents. In many states and provinces with limited elk populations (California, Kansas, Manitoba, Michigan, Minnesota, Nebraska, North Dakota, Saskatchewan and South Dakota), all elk hunting licenses are reserved for residents.

Three states and two provinces (Idaho, Montana, New Mexico, Alberta and British Columbia) further restrict the availability of licenses to nonresidents by reserving a portion of the nonresident license allocation for nonresidents who hunt with an outfitter or guide.

Beginning in 1996, Montana implemented a unique market-based system for allocating elk hunting licenses to nonresidents hunting with professional outfitters. Of the 17,000 licenses reserved for nonresidents, 11,400 were available through a lottery drawing at a price of $475, for which there were 25,995 applicants. Additional licenses then were guaranteed at a price of $835 to those nonresidents who were outfitter-sponsored. The objective was to set the license fee at a level that would result in a target of 5,600 outfitter-sponsored licenses being sold. If the target was exceeded, the fee would be increased the following year; if the license target was not achieved, the price would be reduced the following year. A total of 5,455 guaranteed licenses were sold in 1999, and the Montana Fish, Wildlife and Parks Commission held the license fee at $835 for the 2000 season.

In 1996, the New Mexico state legislature passed Senate Bill 193, which addressed the allocation of certain big game licenses, including elk, among residents, nonresidents and nonresidents hunting with outfitters. Until then, both residents and nonresidents were included in the same lottery for limited elk licenses and no special provisions were made for nonresidents hunting with outfitters. SB-193 specified that 80% of the limited elk licenses would be allocated to residents, 17% to nonresidents hunting with a licensed outfitter and 3% to nonresidents hunting without an outfitter. The nonresidents who hunted without an outfitter were further restricted by a requirement to be accompanied in the field by a New Mexico resident. SB-193 spurred a widespread, vocal outcry from nonresidents who hunted in New Mexico, which resulted in a lawsuit against the state. The case never went to trial. The state legislature amended SB-193 in 1997 and reapportioned the license allocation, with 78% to residents, 10% to nonresidents hunting with a licensed outfitter and 12% to nonresidents hunting without an outfitter. The provision that nonguided nonresident hunters be accompanied in the field by a New Mexico resident also was dropped.

As demand for a limited number of elk hunting licenses increases, the debate over the allocation of licenses among residents and nonresidents and the concept of reserving a set number or percentage of licenses for nonresidents hunting with professional outfitters undoubtedly will become more contentious. Where adequate habitat remains, elk hunting opportunities abound, but opportunities to hunt mature bulls are limited (Bunnell 1997). Given a choice, most hunters want to shoot the largest bull possible (Kuck et al. 1991), but few mature bulls remain in most public areas with general hunting seasons. The challenge for wildlife managers is to protect and maintain healthy age classes and sex ratios while sustaining elk hunting opportunity. This demands ever more creative approaches to designing and implementing hunting regulations.

Harvest and Limit Regulations

Before 1900, most elk harvests were regulated loosely, if at all. Individual bag limits either did not exist or were liberal. Those days are long past. With demand for hunting privileges far exceeding the potential opportunities available, a harvest limit of one elk per hunter per year—set in most states early in the century—has remained in effect. It is highly unlikely that it will be increased in the foreseeable future except in areas where seasonal elk populations are so large as to threaten the optimal carrying capacities of their ranges or cause recurring depredations of crops or cropland. In Utah, hunters who hold antlerless permits can apply for an additional, second antlerless permit, if the permits are available.

Regulations designed to focus harvest on particular sex or age groups of an elk population are necessary in some management systems. Harvest options, controlled by regulated hunting, are available for maintaining, reducing or encouraging growth of any sex or age class within an elk population, depending on the objective for a specific management unit.

Sex-specific Harvest Regulations

The most common type of harvest regulation permits only the taking of antlered elk. Although an occasional cow elk with hormonal imbalances may grow antlers, for all practical purposes, this regulation restricts the legal harvest to antlered bulls. Most states define legal antlers as those of a certain minimum size—for instance, longer than the elk's ears. Hunters must identify the presence and size of antlers before attempting to harvest the animal, thereby reducing accidental shootings of antlerless elk. The converse of this regulation—harvest of antlerless elk only—allows harvest of females, calf elk of both sexes and bull elk with hormonal abnormalities that preclude the growth of antlers. A third general type of regulation allows the harvest of either sex, that is, elk of any sex or age category. This is the least restrictive and least common type of regulation.

Most states and provinces have an antlered-only elk season, followed or preceded by a controlled hunt during which a limited number of licenses are issued for antlerless elk. An antlered-only elk season is easily understood by hunters and relatively easy to enforce. The distinction between elk with antlers and those without is readily apparent.

After the rut, antlerless elk move in groups toward wintering areas. Their movements are more predictable and their collective presence makes them more noticeable; hence, they are more vulnerable to hunters than are bulls. And because cow elk tend to lead these bands, they often are the first to expose themselves to hunters. Following the rut, bull elk lose their aggressiveness and tend to become solitary or follow elk bands led by mature cows.

The primary objective of cow or antlerless hunts is elk population control. As mentioned earlier, North American elk populations have increased by about 75% since 1975. As elk populations have grown in numbers and expanded into new territory, the number of antlerless elk licenses authorized also has increased. In 1975, only 5% (25,610 of 512,838) of all elk licenses issued in the United States and Canada were specified as cow or antlerless. By 1995, this had increased to 15% (142,176 of 947,365 elk licenses issued) (Bunnell 1997).

Whenever large numbers of elk hunters are afield, it is best to use the least restrictive regulations possible. Desirable regulations allow maximum hunting flexibility for the individual hunter, minimize unintentional violations, facilitate enforcement of regulations and minimize accidental and crippling losses of elk. Either sex, antlered-only and antlerless-only elk hunting regulations approach these goals and have been used widely.

Age-specific Harvest Regulations

The second major strategy—limiting harvest to animals of a particular age group—normally is applied only to bulls and is based on antler size and conformation.

A common regulation is the protection of spikes—bulls with unbranched antlers. Spikes are the typical antler conformation of yearling bull elk (Murie 1951). As of 1995, five states and two provinces had regulations protecting spike bulls in at least some hunting units. The premise of such a regulation is to exempt yearling bulls from hunting mortality and allow them to mature. Wildlife biologists analyzed the effectiveness of such regulations in Colorado's White River National Forest and found that regulations prohibiting the harvest of spike bulls did not effectively protect yearling bulls (Boyd and Lipscomb 1976). Almost half (48.6%) of the legal branch-antlered elk checked at hunter check stations were yearlings and the number of spike bull elk shot and abandoned increased markedly.

New Mexico has prohibited the shooting of spike bulls for many years. Wolfe (1982) examined 482 bull elk harvested at the Vermejo Park Ranch in northern New Mexico. In contrast to Boyd and Lipscomb's findings (1976), no yearlings were taken, although 33 of the bulls in the harvest sample had small antlers with four or less points to the side. Apparently, branched antlers were a much more common occurrence in yearling bulls from the White River National Forest. Recognition of geographic variation is important when designing regulations based on such morphological features as antler conformation.

Wildlife managers also have experimented with such strategies as allowing unlimited hunting of spikes but limiting the harvest of branch-antlered bulls and protecting all bulls with less than four or five antler points per side (Wolfe 1985, Freddy 1987b, Vore and DeSimone 1991). A more complete discussion of antler point restrictions to achieve specific management objectives follows later in this chapter.

Hunting Seasons

Types of Seasons

Elk hunting seasons can be grouped into three categories—regular (general), special and managed (controlled) (Mace 1953). Any individual state or province may hold any combination of season types during the course of a year, depending on elk population size and characteristics, public demand and acceptance and management goals and objectives.

General seasons are those designed to allow participation by all interested individuals. Requirements for participation normally only involve purchase of a valid hunting license and elk tag. No restriction is placed on the total number of participating hunters; however, the number of nonresident hunters may be limited. Maximum freedom in choosing a place to hunt is emphasized; although, a few states have formulated restrictions to help ensure hunter distribution. General hunts usually are restricted to bulls only and are held after the rut but before elk concentration on wintering grounds. Hunter acceptance and participation generally are high, but such hunts often are not particularly effective in controlling the number or distribution of animals harvested, as general hunts usually allow hunters to hunt anywhere within the designated management unit or units. Thus, local harvests may fluctuate greatly from year to year, depending on local weather conditions and total hunting pressure.

Special and managed seasons are designed to meet three primary objectives: (1) provide additional management of a resource not attainable during a general season, (2) provide additional recreational opportunities with minimum impact on wildlife populations, or (3) obtain specific population data for research purposes (Tully 1975). In special seasons, the number of participants may or may not be limited; however, the method of harvest is prescribed. Examples of special seasons are those in which hunters must use either archery equipment or muzzle-loading rifles. Recreational values of such hunts are high, although harvest levels generally are low. Special "primitive weapons" elk hunting seasons have been established in most states and provinces. However, archery-only seasons are more common than muzzleloader-only seasons. Those special seasons increase recreational opportunities; thus, they provide a maximal number of hunter days afield without fear of overharvests. Such seasons also may be used to disperse local concentrations of elk before the opening of general seasons or achieve harvests in areas where safety concerns preclude the use of high-powered rifles. They also help distribute hunting pressure over time.

In some states and provinces, hunters may participate in both the primitive weapons season and the general rifle season as long as they have not filled their elk tag. Choose-your-weapon seasons, however, require hunters to decide whether to hunt during archery, muzzleloader or some other special season and restrict them to that season only. Choose-your-weapon seasons effectively have reduced hunting pressure while maintaining hunting opportunities in some places (Carpenter 1991).

Managed hunts limit the number of participants, the area in which hunting is allowed and the sex of animals allowed in the harvest. They are designed to permit harvest of a designated number of animals from a specific area. They also help control agricultural damage (Tully 1975), harvest surplus animals from designated herds and resolve other specific management problems. Because of the broad spectrum of situations in which managed hunts may be used (see Tully 1976), recreational opportunities and values vary widely. Judicious application of managed hunts can make a variety of hunting experiences available to elk hunters. Such hunts are particularly useful in allowing for maximal hunter participation while safeguarding the elk population in management units and areas where elk numbers are low. This is reflected in the fact that managed hunts were offered in all states holding elk seasons in 1996.

Timing

Elk are hunted from late summer through early winter. Hunting seasons may be classified as early, regular and late. Seasons opening before October typically are classified as early and those extending beyond November generally are classified as late.

Early seasons usually begin in August or September. They are preferred for northern elk ranges, where later openings often are impractical because of the strong possibility of inclement weather and reduced access to hunting areas.

Early elk seasons also provide some of the best trophy-type hunting experiences. At this time, elk generally are in prime condition, less wary due to rutting activity and susceptible to being lured into close proximity of the hunter by the use of simulated elk vocalizations (bugling or cow calling). Because of the increased vulnerability of bull elk to hunting during the rut, early seasons almost always are restricted to managed or special types of hunts, particularly those restricted to primitive weapons.

An early elk hunting season, beginning in August or September, also is useful in dispersing elk summering on critical winter ranges or causing agricultural damage. Managed hunts on such areas generally result in dispersing the elk back onto summer range until winter snowstorms or keeping elk away from areas of potential crop damage.

Early hunts may be applied most profitably to management units or localities with limited access, with high elk populations for which a differential harvest by sex may be desirable, or with low elk populations that can withstand only limited harvest, such as through primitive weapons regulations. Most states, even those with early trophy bull seasons in designated management units or areas, hold the main portion of elk hunting seasons in October to mid-November, often after deer hunting seasons close. During this "regular" period, temperatures usually are cool enough to prevent meat loss through spoilage due to heat or insects,

Because elk bulls are especially vulnerable early in the season, during the rut, hunts tend to be restricted to special types, such as with primitive weapons. Modern bows and arrows might not be considered "primitive" by some observers, but bow hunting for elk involves a great deal of the skills and savvy that were necessary before the advent of modern firearms. *Photo by Milo Burcham.*

yet pleasant enough for hunters to enjoy being afield. Also, the first autumn snowstorms often occur during this time and cause elk to begin migration toward winter ranges. The movement of elk and the presence of snow cover improve hunting conditions and harvest opportunities. Wildlife managers generally encounter relatively few problems during October/November hunts. Weather during the regular period rarely inhibits hunter access to hunting areas or elk movements to wintering areas. As a result, harvests can be monitored and managed most effectively. Regular seasons tend to be short and, because the elk and hunters are concentrated, enforcement of regulations is less difficult than at other times of the year

The majority of elk hunts held after mid-November—by which time elk usually are concentrated on winter ranges—are managed hunts, restricted to small areas and small numbers of hunters. Many such late-season hunts actually are reopenings of areas hunted earlier during the regular season. Three kinds of hunts predominate during this period. The managed hunt focuses on reducing elk damage problems and often is held in an area that could not be hunted

earlier in the year because of conflicts with agricultural uses or other activities. A second type of hunt is designed for hunters willing to brave winter storms for a chance at a trophy bull, inaccessible until forced out of the high country by deepening snows. The third type is a cow or antlerless hunt, designed to remove females from the herd to help control overall population size. It is important that late season hunts be managed hunts because elk usually are concentrated on wintering areas at this time and, unless harvest is regulated strictly, overharvest can occur.

Season Length

An important consideration in establishing hunting regulations, season length usually is correlated with four factors: (1) management goal or objective, (2) distribution and number of elk, (3) number of elk hunters, and (4) accessibility of the hunting area.

Accessibility of the hunting area is related closely to the timing of the season. In states such as Colorado, Oregon and Washington, where roads lace much of the available elk habitat, regular seasons—wherein hunter numbers are not regulated strictly—must be short to prevent overharvest. Short seasons also are the rule wherever elk are hunted on crowded wintering areas without readily accessible cover. Elk that are distributed widely, such as on some summer ranges, are better able to withstand long hunting seasons. Season length must be designed to accomplish desired goals without detrimental effects to the elk populations in question. Long hunts held late in the year—including managed hunts—can create additional stresses on elk at a time when they can ill afford them. Combined with forage limitations and stresses of weather, late season hunting can unduly increase winterkill rates. Such hunts also can drive elk from critical winter ranges to areas of inadequate forage and thermal or escape cover. Conversely, managed elk hunts held on or near agricultural lands during winter may be desirable because they tend to disperse elk to other wintering areas, thereby minimizing elk damage to crops or cropland.

Naturally, the purpose for which a hunt is held—whether damage control, herd reduction or sex ratio manipulation—is a vital consideration in the design of hunting regulations, particularly those pertaining to season timing and length. And, this consideration must be evaluated for each situation and management unit or area. Creating appropriate management prescriptions for specific units and areas requires the combined art and skill of competent wildlife managers.

Another consideration, with regard to length of the hunt, is hunter appeal. For hunting seasons designed to attract nonresident hunters, long seasons are preferable. A longer season gives nonresidents better opportunities to

Late season hunts can help alleviate elk concentrations on and damage to agricultural lands, which the animals visit during their autumn migration to winter range. Hunts at that time reduce the number of elk, haze concentrated herds, disperse them to other range or force the animals to denser cover than crop fields. *Photo by Milo Burcham.*

plan their excursions, familiarize themselves with the area being hunted and enjoy the diverse satisfactions of time afield.

The question of whether to open elk seasons on a weekend or weekday has been a major consideration in all states and provinces, particularly as the greatest percentage of total elk harvest occurs during the first days of the season. Many states have elk and other big game season openings on a Saturday to provide equitable opportunity for participation during the first days by city dwellers and many wage earners who often are able to hunt only on weekends. With the increasing demand for hunting, several states have experimented with opening dates other than a Saturday to relieve hunter congestion and diminish pressure on elk populations. Washington, for example, selected a Monday opening date in 1971 to resolve the problem of large numbers of hunters from the densely populated Puget Sound area overcrowding nearby elk hunting areas. This resulted in a 30% reduction of hunting pressure on the season opening. At first, hunters objected to the change and license sales dropped. But after 4 years of Monday openings, the system was accepted and, in fact, favored by most hunters (Parsons 1975). The shift in attitude may have been attributable to an actual change in hunter preference or to a loss of a portion of those hunters favoring Saturday opening dates. Among the reasons listed by Washington hunters favoring a Monday opening date for elk season were: (1) reduction of hunting congestion; (2) elimination of undesirable participants (careless, inexperienced or intoxicated

individuals) and activities (road hunting, herd shooting, etc.); (3) elk conservation (less pressure on elk herds and fewer illegal kills); (4) better sportsmen afield; and (5) increased hunter safety (Parsons 1975).

Idaho used standard calendar dates for most hunting season openings until it moved to a Saturday opening date in the 1950s, except in the more inaccessible areas. Idaho then adopted Wednesday opening dates in 1975 to achieve better hunter distribution and divide hunting pressure between opening date and the first weekend of the elk season (J. L. Thiessen personal communication:1977). Analysis of results of the regulation change revealed that differences in opening dates were evident only in the initial 5 days of the season. Peak hunting pressure under a Wednesday opening date averaged 20% less than under a Saturday opening date. More people hunted the first 5 days of an elk season opening on a Wednesday than during the first 5 days of a season opening on a Saturday. With Wednesday openings, hunter pressure was divided more evenly among each of the first 5 days of the season. Furthermore, harvest success rates per day actually were greater with a Wednesday opening date than with a Saturday opening. This was attributed to the presence of relatively few unskilled hunters for a season opening on Wednesday. A sample of Idaho hunters—stratified to include hunters participating on the Wednesday opening date and those hunting for the first time on the initial weekend of the elk season—revealed that about 55% favored the Wednesday opening (J. L. Thiessen personal communication:1977).

Split seasons have effectively reduced hunting pressure while maintaining hunting opportunities in some places (Carpenter 1991). Such seasons break hunts into distinct segments—for example, an October season, November season or December season—and require hunters to choose when they will hunt. This technique can allow for satisfactory hunting opportunity while decreasing the vulnerability of elk to hunters by ensuring that all elk hunters are not in the woods at once.

In the late 1970s, New Mexico was faced with the challenge of managing an increasing number of elk hunters. From 1969 through 1979, there were no restrictions on the number of elk hunters during the general bull season in the northern half of the state. The New Mexico Game and Fish Commission addressed the problem in 1980 by implementing a regulation that prohibited hunters from obtaining a New Mexico elk license if they held one the previous year. It soon became apparent that, with the growing number of hunters wishing to hunt elk in New Mexico, even limiting hunters to such alternate-year hunting would not be effective in managing the total number of hunters afield. The Commission abandoned the regulation after 3 years. In its place, they established a series of 5-day split seasons and numerous elk hunting units, along with a requirement that hunters choose the season and management unit in which they wished to hunt. In addition, they limited the number of licenses authorized in each season and management unit and adopted a lottery for selecting hunters. This system has remained largely unchanged since, with the exception that, beginning in 1997, nonresident elk hunting licenses were limited to no more than 22% of the total number available (H. F. Olson personal communication:1997).

Management Units

Whereas license holders in most states and provinces formerly had practically a statewide or provincewide choice of where to hunt, various regulations have been developed to distribute hunting pressure as needed. For many years in Colorado, for example, the western slope of the Rocky Mountains had an opening day of elk season 5 days before opening on the eastern slope, which was much closer to larger cities and most of the state's resident elk hunters (Hunter 1957). If a single opening date had been set, many hunters would not have gone to the western slope to hunt. The early opening on the western slope encouraged many to travel the extra distance, thus directing hunting pressure.

In Idaho, three different opening dates were used for many years for much of that state's elk hunting. The Idaho system resembled Colorado's somewhat but had the added feature of an early opening—usually in mid-September—in the backcountry, much of which was roadless. However, in

those two states and others, an individual hunter still was free to hunt wherever he or she chose within the state.

In Oregon, where both Roosevelt and Rocky Mountain elk populations are found, the approach was somewhat different. Beginning in 1964, Oregon initiated regulations limiting the individual hunter to a particular area. These regulations permitted an individual to hunt in either western Oregon for Roosevelt elk or eastern Oregon for Rocky Mountain elk, but not in both areas. Opening dates and season lengths also varied. Similar regulations have been in effect since then and the number of hunters has increased in each area.

Use of large management zones with different opening dates, as practiced in Colorado, Idaho, Oregon and elsewhere, has been one approach to regulating hunter distribution and elk harvest. However, in some states, further division of large zones has proved necessary to resolve specific harvest problems. Because big game populations are not distributed uniformly within a state or province and because animals move without regard for political boundaries, a land unit based largely on the distribution and migrational habits of the animals has proven to be a convenient and frequently necessary tool for the wildlife manager.

Wildlife management units now form part of the regulatory framework in all states and provinces where elk are hunted. Their sizes and shapes depend on local and seasonal conditions, and the number of elk management units per state ranges from just 1 in Pennsylvania to more than 100 in Colorado. Regardless of the size and number of units in a given political jurisdiction, the general purpose of the unit system is to perpetuate elk populations on a sustainable basis, provide and manage elk hunting in each delineated area and facilitate the collection and analysis of biological data required to manage elk populations on a sound basis.

Lauckhart (1954) pointed out that the unit system of big game management can achieve three desirable goals. First, it may be used to direct and disperse hunter pressure and harvest. Second, it allows the manager to respond to specific regional areas of concern, as with depredation problems. And third, the fact that management units allow intensive and responsive management results in improved public relations.

It is important that management units be small enough so that hunting pressure can be focused, as needed, on one or more of the segments of the elk population but not so small that hunters are crowded (Kimball 1955). Hunter accessibility is a prime consideration. Hunting pressure is a function of accessibility. For example, when two management units of equal area are hunted by equal numbers of hunters, hunting pressure is greatest in the unit most heavily roaded or easily traversed.

Managers attempt to define areas that are natural geographic or geologic entities—areas within which an elk population remains for a specific period of time. Examples of such areas are those bounded by ridgetops, large rivers, deep canyons or other natural features. Often, the units are elk population units, but consideration is given to physical boundaries that can be identified by hunters.

Weapons and Technology

Weapons

Weapons used by recreational hunters to hunt elk include modern rifles, muzzle-loading rifles, shotguns, handguns, longbows (traditional, recurve and compound) and crossbows. Each state and province normally requires certain minimum specifications for any weapon used to harvest elk. Such specifications are to assure that projectiles used have adequate killing power to minimize losses of wounded elk. Rimfire cartridges, for example, are prohibited for elk hunting in most states and provinces because they lack the size, muzzle velocity and impact energy to produce clean kills under most conditions at reasonable ranges. Fully automatic rifles are considered unsporting and cannot be safely handled by most hunters, so they are prohibited in all states and provinces.

Killing power of a firearm involves a combination of several factors. Bullets, balls and slugs kill by destroying tissue, hydrostatic shock and hemorrhage. An effective shot is one that either destroys a body organ vital to immediate life maintenance (heart, lungs, liver, brain, etc.), severely fractures a major skeletal component (spine, shoulders, etc.) or produces massive hemorrhaging with resultant blood loss and shock. To immobilize an animal the size of an elk effectively, a firearm must fire a heavy projectile (to break bones and penetrate vital areas) of fairly large dimension (to cause maximum tissue damage) at a high velocity (to impart maximum shocking power).

Handgun projectiles have lower bullet velocities and impact energy at reasonable distances than do minimum-caliber rifles. However, certain handgun cartridges—such as .357 magnum, .41 magnum, .44 magnum, .45 Colt and a number of powerful "wildcat" cartridges—are sufficiently powerful to kill elk effectively. Hunting big game with handguns has increased in popularity and gained general acceptance during the past 20 years. In 1996, handguns were legal for hunting elk in all states with established elk seasons, except Kansas, Nebraska and Oklahoma. The ownership of handguns is highly regulated in Canada, and their use is not permitted in hunting.

Shotguns are effective for shooting elk at close range and are allowed for elk hunting in a number of states and provinces. Although the velocity of a shotgun slug is not great, slugs are large in diameter and generally weigh 0.5 ounce (14.2 g) or more. Their short effective range—approximately 100 to 150 yards (91–135 m)—normally makes them impractical for elk hunting except in brushy or densely populated agricultural areas.

Similar to the shotgun is the muzzle-loading rifle. Although not as effective as modern rifles at long ranges, muzzle-loading rifles can be quite effective to about 100 to 150 yards (91–135 m) and are legal for elk hunting in most states and provinces. For many hunters, hunting with a muzzle-loading rifle is not only a challenge but also serves as a symbolic throwback to a hunting mode of frontier days. This sense of tradition and the constraints of the weapon itself enliven hunts and increase satisfaction among users. Several states annually hold special managed elk hunts for muzzle-loading rifle enthusiasts.

Arrows shot from bows do not produce the hydrostatic shock caused by firearms. Rather, the killing power of arrows is their ability to cause massive hemorrhaging and blood loss due to the cutting effect of arrowpoint blades. Compound bows, recurves and longbows, like muzzle-loading rifles, can be effective short-range weapons in elk hunting. Bow hunting is a popular recreation and, in 1996, all major elk hunting states and provinces provided regular elk hunting archery seasons. Crossbow hunting is less popular and to provide a special crossbow elk season would complicate season structure. Nevertheless, eight states and three provinces permitted crossbow hunting for elk, usually as part of the rifle season or special bow hunting season.

Rifles and bows are effective weapons in the hands of skilled individuals with knowledge of their equipment, hunting area and the animals they hunt. Each weapon requires special and honed skills and a different approach to hunting. In the hands of incompetent, careless or unprepared individuals, any weapon can result in abuse to the user and the animals being hunted. Such abuses invariably stir adverse public reaction toward hunting. Most states now require that beginning hunters take a course in hunter education, ethical responsibility and firearms safety training before obtaining a hunting license. Hunters can help by policing their own ranks against unsafe and unethical individuals and actions.

Technology

The Boone and Crockett Club defines fair chase as "The ethical, sportsmanlike and lawful pursuit of a free-ranging wild animal in a manner that does not give the hunter an improper or unfair advantage" (Poston 1993:1). Madson (1992:59) described it this way, "A good working definition of a game species is one that is fitted with survival equipment enabling it to *take* advantage, while a genuine sport hunter is one constrained by ethics and respect to *give* advantage." Posewitz (1994:58–62) charted the evolution of the concept of fair chase from the days of loincloths and flaked obsidian arrow and spear points to Gore-Tex clothing and bullets propelled at 3,500 ft/sec: "When the hunter with a spear in hand stalked wildlife in the primal forest, the pursuit was well within the bounds of fair chase. That situation is past. Technological advancement, the human population explosion, and the loss of wildlands required a new balancing act between the hunter and the hunted . . . there is a constant flow of products developed to provide advantages to hunters. Sights, scents, calls, baits, decoys, devices and techniques of infinite variety fill the marketplace. In each case an individual choice must be made as to what sustains fair chase and what violates that concept."

Concerns about the impact of technology on wildlife and hunting certainly are not new. As early as 1907, Pennsylvania had outlawed the use of autoloading firearms for hunting and, in 1912, New Jersey banned the use of all repeating shotguns unless their capacity was reduced to two shots (Trefethen 1975). From the turn of the century to modern times, hunting regulations have continually adapted to reflect advancing technology and ensure that hunters do not become *too* proficient.

Increased use of technology poses special concerns to wildlife managers and may be the most difficult variable to regulate. As hunters strive for ways to improve chances of killing elk, a growing hunting industry responds to those demands. A look through most any hunting equipment catalog shows a plethora of technology available to the modern elk hunter: trail devices to photograph, record and store animal movements; game scanners; hearing enhancers; night-vision goggles; range finders; variable rifle scopes; latex bugles; cow-in-heat scents; how-to books and videos; state-by-state hunting unit statistics; all-terrain vehicles with gun mounts and thousands of other gadgets designed to increase the chance of finding and killing elk. When too many people become too proficient at killing elk, regulations must become more restrictive if any reasonable definition of fair chase is to prevail.

The hunting equipment industry and the increasing number of elk hunters have boosted funding for wildlife conservation efforts while, ironically, contributing to reduced hunting opportunities in the long term. Providing enhanced hunting technology is big business—a business that, in part, contributes immensely to wildlife conservation through special excise taxes paid on certain hunting equipment (through congressionally mandated acts, such as the Pittman-Robertson Federal Aid in Wildlife Restora-

Use of technology can virtually eliminate any notion of the concept of fair chase in elk hunting, and can cause discrimination against those who choose not to reduce hunting to a convenience of killing. Abuse of technological advantages demeans recreational hunting and the quarry. *Photo by Bud Journey; courtesy of the Rocky Mountain Elk Foundation.*

tion Act of 1937) and support of nonprofit conservation groups, such as the Rocky Mountain Elk Foundation, National Wild Turkey Federation and Ducks Unlimited. Jobs also are created. And, of course, the technology race would not exist if there were not plenty of hunters willing to spend significant amounts of money to improve their chances of killing an elk. This intimate relationship between the hunting equipment industry, hunters and state wildlife agencies makes it all the more challenging for managers to regulate technology.

Leopold (1949:181) contemplated the relationship between technology, industry, hunters and the hunt: "I have the impression that the American sportsman is puzzled; he doesn't understand what is happening to him. Bigger and better gadgets are good for industry, so why not for outdoor recreation? It has not dawned on him that outdoor recreations are essentially primitive, atavistic; that their value is a contrast-value; that excessive mechanization destroys contrasts by moving the factory to the woods or to the marsh. The sportsman has no leaders to tell him what is wrong. The sporting press no longer represents sport; it has turned billboard for the gadgeteer. Wildlife administrators are too busy producing something to shoot at to worry much about the cultural value of the shooting. . . . I do not pretend to know what is moderation, or where the line is between legitimate and illegitimate gadgets. Yet there must be some limit beyond which money-bought aids to sport destroy the cultural value of sport. . . . Our tools for the pursuit of wildlife improve faster than we do, and sportsmanship is the voluntary limitation in the use of these armaments. It is aimed to augment the role of skill and shrink the role of gadgets in the pursuit of wild things."

Wildlife managers continue to struggle with the question, how far should technology go? In the right hands, a 7mm magnum with a 3- by 9-power variable scope can be consistently deadly to big game at 300 yards (274 m). How about a 50-caliber converted machine gun barrel mounted on a tripod and equipped with a 20-power scope? Such a weapon can be accurate at 1,000 yards (914 m). How about a heat-seeking, laser-guided projectile? How much technology is too much? And who is to decide? Are devices that enhance hearing, such as sound amplifiers, acceptable? What about regular hearing aids? How about devices that enhance vision, such as binoculars and scopes? At what point does the search for quicker, cleaner kills exceed the concept of fair chase?

In some cases, governments decide. In the late 1980s, when Idaho hunters were shooting elk from half-mile (0.8 km) distances using turret-mounted 50-caliber rifles, the Idaho Fish and Game Commission responded by setting weight limits for hunting rifles. In 1995, Idaho prohibited the use of electronic or enhanced illuminating sights, radio transmitters, electronic range finders or magnifying telescopic sights during archery and muzzleloader seasons. Bows that can shoot more than one arrow at a time, bows with more than 65% letoff, and explosive, barbed and expanding broadheads also are illegal (Kuck 1993). In addition, many state wildlife departments are working with land management agencies and private landowners to close roads, and limit the impact of four-wheel drive trucks, trail bikes and all-terrain vehicles.

Educational efforts eventually may prove more effective than regulations in controlling the impacts of technology. By emphasizing the concepts of fair chase and ethics through hunting education classes, brochures, magazine articles and other public outreach programs and by showing hunters the often inverse relationship between technology and hunting opportunities, wildlife managers, conservation groups, hunting organizations and others can help hunters better understand the potential impacts of high-tech gear on elk and elk hunting opportunities.

The Vulnerability Concept

Elk vulnerability is "a measure of elk susceptibility to being killed during the hunting season" (Lyon and Christensen 1992:3). Concerns about bull elk vulnerability originally sprang not so much from high mortality in the bull herd

segment as from low calf numbers. In the 1970s, wildlife biologists noticed that widespread declines in pregnancy rates and spring calf counts coincided with reduced mature bull/cow ratios in many herds (Hines and Lemos 1979, Peek 1985, Freddy 1987b, Leckenby et al. 1991, McCorquodale 1991, Squibb et al. 1991, Vales et al. 1991). Although yearling bulls were known to be capable of breeding females, serious questions remained about their reproductive efficiency and the social and ecological consequences of such breeding (Hines and Lemos 1979, Prothero et al. 1979, Geist 1991c, DeSimone et al. 1993).

Prothero et al. (1979:160) noted that red deer in Europe are managed to sustain age and sex ratios as close as possible to what they would be in unhunted populations and suggested that "with dwindling game herds and reduced game habitat, perhaps the time is not far off when we can, and should, be concerned about the behavioral welfare of our game populations." Even earlier, Murie (1951:331) postulated: "Looking to the future, in view of the needs of elk and the exacting requirements of recreation based on multiple use, the safest course is to model elk management along natural lines, so far as is reasonably possible, to preserve its distinct *habits* as well as its habitat."

A growing body of research (Hines and Lemos 1979, Hines et al 1985, Squibb 1985, Geist 1991c, Johnson et al. 1991, DeSimone et al. 1993, Noyes et al. 1996) affirms the wisdom of Prothero's and Murie's advice. It strongly suggests that, in the absence of older bulls, a lack of social order may lead to more fighting among young bulls and increased harassment of cows throughout an extended rut. Spending even more energy on the rut saps vigor in both bulls and cows, increases susceptibility to predators and tough winters and makes for less healthy calves. And as young bulls tend to breed later than old bulls, their calves are often born later in spring. Such latecomers often miss out on prime growth-boosting forage and do not have enough time to gain adequate body weight before their first winter. Those that are not killed by predators or disease head into winter a bit smaller and perhaps less able to handle the stresses of winter than are calves sired by older bulls.

Perhaps because a large rack suggests a bull's ability to adapt and survive, cows—when given a choice—pick larger, mature bulls with which to breed, ensuring the best genes are passed on (Bubenik 1985, Geist 1991c). Reducing the number of large bulls may inhibit this adaptive genetic selection process. Although cows certainly can produce calves and foster large herds even when yearling bulls are responsible for the majority of the breeding (Squibb 1985, Freddy 1987b), overall pregnancy rates may be slightly reduced, conception dates are delayed and the rut is extended by a month or more (Johnson et al. 1991, Noyes et al. 1996).

When too many prime bulls are removed from an elk herd, the lack of a social hierarchy can stress the young bulls who may not be satisfactorily conditioned for the rigors of the rut, breeding and subsequent overwinter survival. Calves sired by the later-breeding young bulls are born later and may not have the time to gain sufficient size and energy reserves to stave off winter mortality factors, including predation. *Photos courtesy of the Wildlife Management Institute.*

The mature bull/cow ratio required for early and synchronous breeding in free-ranging elk populations is unknown. However, Noyes et al. (1996) documented early, synchronous breeding and high pregnancy rates with 18 3-year-old bulls per 100 cows within a 30-square mile (78 km²) enclosure on the Starkey Experimental Forest and Range in northeastern Oregon. The influence of bull age on the timing and synchrony of the rut became apparent when bulls were 3 years old; it increased as the bulls aged to 5 years. As bull age increased, the rut became more condensed and breeding occurred earlier, ranging from 71 days and a mean conception date of October 7 when yearling bulls were the primary sires, to 41 days and a mean conception date of September 21 when 5-year-old bulls were the sires. This research strongly suggests that elk populations require older bulls to ensure short and early calving seasons. With this as a management objective, Noyes et al. (1996:515) recommended that "hunting regulations should be designed and habitat managed to ensure sufficient bull escapement. Relying on 2-year-old bulls to breed, a situation that results from spike-excluded hunting seasons, may not enhance herd productivity if most 2-year-olds are harvested the following hunting season." To increase the number of older bulls, they suggested a hunting strategy proposed by Vore and DeSimone (1991), allowing unlimited hunting of spikes but limiting the number of licenses issued for branch-antlered bulls.

Concerns about boosting and maintaining mature bull/cow ratios increasingly influence elk hunting regulations. Controlling bull elk vulnerability is the key. As defined earlier, vulnerability is a measure of an elk's susceptibility to being killed during the hunting season. Conversely, security is "the protection inherent in any situation that allows elk to remain in a defined area despite an increase in stress or disturbance associated with the hunting season or other human activity" (Lyon and Christensen 1992:5).

Vulnerability and security are inversely related—as security declines, elk vulnerability increases (Youmans 1992). For example, easy hunter access by roads can make elk less secure, thereby increasing vulnerability (Lyon et al. 1985, see also Chapter 13). Ironically, many state wildlife agencies once supported road-building projects for that very reason (Madson 1966). In the early 1960s, expanding elk populations throughout the West appeared to be growing too large for available winter range. Logging and road building on federal lands seemed good for elk and elk hunting—the large openings in the forest produced forage and roads provided access for hunters to kill more elk (Lyon et al. 1985).

By the early 1970s, however, wildlife biologists throughout the United States and Canada noticed some disturbing trends in elk herd composition data—a decrease in calf pro-

Limiting the number of hunting licenses or permits for branch-antlered elk bulls, but liberalizing the harvest of spike bulls, is a useful way to sustain prime bulls in a herd. The prime bulls establish and maintain social order within their herds or groups. They also represent the best of the male genetic stock. *Photo by Don Domenick; courtesy of the Colorado Division of Wildlife.*

duction, accompanied by low mature bull/cow ratios—despite apparent improvements in the quantity and quality of forage (Lyon et al. 1985). In Oregon, wildlife biologists warned of declining elk populations brought on by loss of habitat security from increased logging, high densities of roads and increased hunting pressure (Bartels and Denney 1969). By 1982, there were only two to four bulls per 100 cows in many hunting units, with virtually no branch-antlered bulls in the posthunt elk population (Leckenby et al. 1991). Hunters simply killed too many mature bull elk and wildlife biologists began to question the effects of logging and roads on the security provided by elk habitat (Lyon et al. 1985). In a game of hide and seek, elk were increasingly the losers because places to hide decreased and the density of seekers (hunters) increased.

In 1969, concern over a proposed timber sale in the Lewis and Clark National Forest, along the Middle Fork of the Judith River in Montana's Little Belt Mountains, proved a catalyst for change in elk management. Forest Service officials viewed the sale as critical to the forest's planned program of timber harvest. Montana Department of Fish, Wildlife and Parks biologists feared disastrous effects on elk. In an effort to resolve conflict, the two agencies met in

March 1970 and agreed to the Montana Cooperative Elk/Logging Study. This 15-year research project involved five government organizations and a timber company (Lyon et al. 1985). About the same time, similar research began in the Blue Mountains of Washington and Oregon (Thomas 1979b). The two projects produced a wealth of crucial information concerning the effects of logging and roading on elk, elk habitat and elk hunting—spawning concepts such as habitat security and elk vulnerability.

In 1989, chronically low numbers of bull elk in many western elk herds combined with concern over the potential problems associated with low mature bull/cow ratios—disrupted breeding seasons and social structures and reduced calf production and survival—prompted wildlife professionals representing state (Montana and Idaho), federal (Forest Service), university and private interests to form an Elk Vulnerability Working Group. In 1991, the group sponsored an elk vulnerability symposium, which brought together biologists, administrators and educators from the United States and Canada to address issues of elk vulnerability and develop methods to monitor and manage elk vulnerability (Christensen et al. 1991). This growing awareness of elk vulnerability has influenced elk hunting regulations throughout the western United States and Canada.

Vulnerability encompasses a diversity of factors, including hunter access and numbers, habitat, timing and duration of hunting seasons, terrain, weather, hunting equipment technology and hunting regulations (Thomas 1991). Elk hunting regulations are increasingly designed to enhance habitat security for elk and reduce the vulnerability of elk to hunting—attempting to strike a delicate balance between elk being too vulnerable to hunting, which may result in an excessive harvest, and being vulnerable enough to permit the desired harvest levels and types.

Because habitat security can influence vulnerability as much as hunter numbers and hunting equipment technology can, relying solely on state or provincial wildlife agencies to solve the problems through regulation of hunting seasons, bag limits and methods of take is almost certainly doomed to fail. More than ever before, hunting regulations, habitat conditions and access provided to hunters are becoming the shared responsibility of land managers, wildlife managers and hunters (Lonner 1997, Thomas 1997). The challenge of modern elk management lies in the interaction of regulations and habitat conditions in maintaining healthy, balanced elk herds, while allowing for continued hunting opportunities and desired population control.

Elk living in rugged, thickly forested terrain generally are more difficult to kill; therefore, they are considered more secure and less vulnerable. In the timbered mountains of western Montana and northern Idaho, simply closing roads might be enough to reduce vulnerability (Hillis et al. 1991, Unsworth and Kuck 1991), whereas in open, flat terrain, this might still leave elk too exposed (Lyon 1979a, Edge and Marcum 1991). Even in the most secure habitats, elk are increasingly vulnerable because more hunters are pursuing them. Deciding which combination of regulations works best to achieve specific goals in a particular place often is a matter of trial and error. Fortunately, the advent of computer models has helped make the decision process a bit easier and the results more predictable.

Computer models help wildlife managers, land managers and the public gain a better understanding of the complex relationships between elk, elk hunting, elk habitat security and the vulnerability of elk to hunting (Vales et al. 1991, Zager and Leptich 1991, Vales 1996). A cooperative project involving the Oregon Department of Fish and Wildlife, Washington Department of Fish and Wildlife, U.S. Bureau of Land Management, Warm Springs and Umatilla tribes, seven private timber companies and the Rocky Mountain Elk Foundation led to the development of a comprehensive "Elk Vulnerability Model" (Vales 1996). By integrating information about hunting and habitat, the model helps bring alternative management schemes to the attention of land and wildlife managers, who are often at odds over elk management issues. Using the model, land and wildlife managers can predict the effects of logging, road construction, hunter access and hunting regulations on elk vulnerability, security and hunting.

Land and wildlife managers provide the computer program with specific information about an area, such as herd size, bull/cow ratios, densities of roads open to hunter use, vegetation types, steepness of slopes and hunter numbers. By experimenting with different management scenarios, the model forecasts results and assists managers in determining the most effective strategy to meet management objectives. For example, will closing a few miles of roads boost bull/cow ratios? How about splitting the rifle season into several shorter seasons? Or switching to archery-only hunting? What about limiting the harvest to branch-antlered bulls only or spikes only? What will be the impact of limiting the total number of bull licenses issued? Should cow elk be harvested? What about the timing of the hunting season—early versus late? In each scenario, the model can help estimate how many hunters can pursue different segments of the herd—cows, calves, spike bulls, young bulls, mature bulls—and still maintain desired sex and age ratios in the herd.

Figure 178 illustrates the use of Vales' (1996) model for predicting elk vulnerability. The horizontal axis depicts the number of hunters per elk that legally may be hunted in a specific area for a given hunt. (If all bulls are legal, the ratio would be the number of hunters per bull in the herd. If only cows may be taken legally by hunters, the ratio would be the number of hunters per cow in the herd.) The verti-

The proliferation of roads throughout elk range, and especially along or near autumn migration routes, represents an increase in the animals' vulnerability to traffic, hunting pressure and stresses caused as a result of forcing the animals to unfamiliar and possibly inadequate winter range. *Photo by Milo Burcham.*

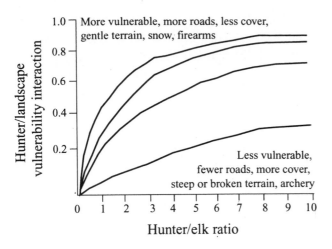

Figure 178. Hunter/landscape vulnerability interaction in relation to hunter/elk ratio (from Stalling 1996f).

cal axis represents harvest rates—the percentage of elk that can be hunted legally, which actually are killed. The lines on the graph define the vulnerability of hunted elk under different situations. The higher the line, the more vulnerable the elk are to being killed by hunters.

If, for example, there were 10 hunters per elk in a densely forested, roadless area incised with steep drainage, elk mortality might be 35%. On the other hand, if there were 10 hunters per elk in a hunting unit laced with open roads in gentle terrain, elk mortality due to hunting might be 85%. Therefore, if wildlife managers wanted to reduce the number of elk killed by hunters in the heavily roaded unit, they could try cutting hunter numbers back to five per elk, but mortality still might be around 80%, or they could close

some roads to vehicles, thereby reducing mortality due to hunting without changing the number of hunters. They also could implement an archery-only hunting regulation or allow only the harvest of cow elk, thereby reducing the number of hunters pursuing bulls, or they could combine several of these options. The model's strength lies in clearly illustrating the options managers have to control harvest rates and reduce elk vulnerability and in helping them predict the effects of their choices.

Management to Meet Particular Goals

Sex Ratio Manipulation

In 1995, Vales' (1996) elk vulnerability model was put to the test in northeastern Oregon, where only 3 bulls per 100 cows survived the hunting season in most management units (Vales et al. 1991). The state's elk management plan, adopted in 1991, called for restoring posthunt bull numbers to at least 10 per 100 cows. The Oregon Department of Fish and Wildlife attempted to reduce hunter density by splitting the rifle season into two separate and distinct periods; however, most hunters opted for the first season and nothing changed—there still were too many hunters pursuing too few bulls. The first season was further restricted to hunters who successfully drew a limited number of tags in a lottery, forcing other hunters (unlimited in number) to hunt the second season, thereby reducing crowding. Still, nothing changed. At this point, the state turned to Vales' model to evaluate its options.

The Oregon Department of Fish and Wildlife held a se-

To be most effective, road closures to reduce elk vulnerability to overharvest must be enacted and enforced in concert with other well-considered (and, ideally, modeled) harvest regulations. *Photos by Bud Journey; courtesy of the Rocky Mountain Elk Foundation.*

ries of public meetings at which citizens were asked what they would like done. Subsequently, a list of options was assembled and analyzed using the vulnerability model. The resulting bull/cow ratios were predicted for future years under different management scenarios. At the public meetings, Oregon hunters said they wanted high-quality experiences, with plenty of hunting opportunities and no overcrowding (B. K. Johnson personal communication:1996). This presented a daunting, but not impossible, challenge to managers. They used the model to graphically demonstrate to hunters the tradeoffs associated with each option. With the model helping to explain how many hunters could be in the field under different types of seasons while still achieving management goals, the hunting public was better equipped to help managers decide what would work best. Hunters responded and, in 1996, most hunting units in northeastern Oregon changed from a situation where an unlimited number of hunters were allowed to kill any bull elk to one in which a limited number of hunters (selected by lottery) could kill only bulls with spike antlers.

Biologists believed the new regulations could boost bull/cow ratios and restore mature bulls into the social dynamics of the herd. In 1996, most hunting units in northeastern Oregon had about 20 spike bulls per 100 cows before the hunting seasons. Only 3 to 5 of these 20 spikes survived the hunting season, and there was a high probability that the survivors would be killed the next year. The state considered going to a restriction whereby it would be legal to shoot only bulls with three or more antler points per side to allow younger bulls to survive another year. But the goal was not to produce just 2-year-old bulls. Managers wanted older bulls. By limiting hunting only to spike bulls, and with 3 to 5 per 20 spikes surviving the hunting season each year, the survivors would not be hunted the following year. If another three to five survived the following year's hunting season and so on, the herd composition should rebound to 10 bulls per 100 cows. As the number of mature bulls increases, the state eventually hopes to offer a limited number of permits for branch-antlered bulls (B. K. Johnson personal communication:1996, R. A. Riggs personal communication:1996, D. J. Vales personal communication:1996). The plan has worked to date (B. K. Johnson personal communication:2000). Bull ratios have risen and there are about 9 to 11 spike and branch-antlered bulls per 100 cows. The state still hopes to reach 10 mature bulls per 100 cows, with mature bulls defined as those 3 years and older.

Maximum Production

Understanding management of any population for maximum production hinges on understanding the basis of

population growth theory. An S-shaped curve depicts population growth in a limited environment (Figure 179) and is arrived at by the equation:

$$\frac{\Delta N}{\Delta t} = N\left(\frac{K - N}{K}\right)$$

where N = population size, t = time; r = rate of increase in population; K = carrying capacity of the environment and Δ = change, that is, ΔN/Δt = change in population size as time increases.

This equation shows that starting with some initial population size, a population will recover over a period of time, based on some reproductive rate, until that population nears the carrying capacity of its environment. As a population reaches its environment's carrying capacity, its birth rate must decrease, its death rate must increase or both, leading to population size stability.

Because maximal production is the goal, plotting net production in relation to density is helpful (Figure 180). The resulting curve will peak at the inflection point between the population's growth and decline phases. The specific shape of this curve is influenced by the annual death rate for each age group of animals, the maximal productivity rate for each age group, the population level that must be reached before productivity declines and the relationship of population density and productivity (Walters and Bandy 1972).

When maximal production is the desired goal of an elk population, several factors immediately become obvious. Maximal production means not only maximizing net production but also harvesting most of that production peri-

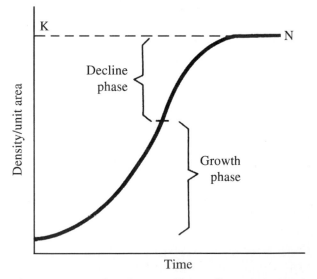

Figure 179. An S-shaped curve reflecting elk population size in a limited environment, where N = population size and K = carrying capacity of the environment.

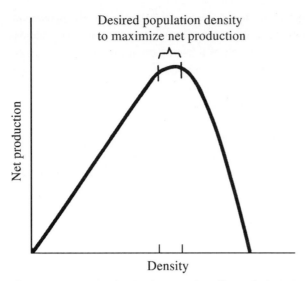

Figure 180. Net production in a growing elk population as a function of population density.

odically to maintain population density at or below the level at which net production is maximized. This keeps population density below the environment's carrying capacity and near the inflection point between the population's growth and decline phases. To go one step farther, this also means minimizing the number of animals that do not contribute directly to population productivity. In elk populations, this implies minimizing the number of bulls, as the sexes are born in approximately equal numbers (Knight 1970) and elk are polygamous (Murie 1951). Bulls must be present in the population in a number sufficient to ensure breeding of all reproductively active females, but, above that number, they can be removed. Thus, maximal production of a population and production of trophy bulls are incompatible goals in management of any given elk population.

Hunting regulations to achieve maximal production in an elk herd commonly include a general antlered-only elk hunting season combined with managed hunts for antlerless elk. Regulations are most effective in areas where access to the elk is not difficult and hunter numbers are high. These conditions allow for most effective harvest. Colorado, for example, generally attempts to achieve maximal production in most of its elk herds.

Producing Trophy Animals

Second only to moose as the largest member of the deer family in North America, with antler beams that may exceed 5 feet (1.5 m) in length, the elk is considered by many hunters as one of North America's outstanding trophy animals. The allure of trophy elk is enhanced by the fact that they inhabit some of the most rugged and picturesque ar-

eas in North America and their native wariness provides the hunter with a unique challenge.

Antler size in cervids is known to be influenced by age, nutrition, health status and genetic factors (Hibler and Adcock 1971, Wolfe 1980, Harmel 1983, Ullrey 1983). Wolfe (1983) evaluated the relationship between age and antler size for 482 bull elk harvested at Vermejo Park Ranch in northern New Mexico and concluded that maximum antler development occurred between the ages of 7.5 and 10.5 years. Antler main beam length, circumference at the base of the main beam and antler weight all increased each year until maximum size was reached at 10.5 years; then those characteristics declined. Trophy quality, as measured by the Boone and Crockett Club's scoring system (Byers 1998), also peaked between the ages of 7.5 and 10.5 years. The highest average Boone and Crockett scores are recorded for bulls that were 9.5 years old. Wolfe (1983) concluded that increased trophy production could be obtained by manipulating the age structure of the bull segment of the herd to increase the number of bulls in the 7.5- to 10.5-year age classes.

The production of trophy-sized antlers requires that an elk not only be on a suitable diet but also fully mature physiologically and sexually—a situation that does not occur often in heavily hunted elk populations. As discussed earlier, the number of mature bulls per 100 cows declined in many herds as a direct result of hunters killing too many bulls (Bartels and Denney 1969, Boyd and Lipscomb 1976, Freddy 1987b, Leckenby et al. 1991, McCorquodale 1991, Vales et al. 1991, DeSimone et al. 1993).

In 1971 and 1972, the Colorado Wildlife Commission experimented with special hunting regulations to increase the number of trophy bulls in the harvest (Boyd and Lipscomb 1976). These regulations protected spike bulls in 1971 and all bulls with less than four points on one antler in 1972.

Hunter check station counts made during the 1971 season, when taking spike bulls was not allowed, revealed that 48.6% of the branch-antlered bulls, as aged by dentition, were 1.5-year-olds. Only six bulls (5.8%) had antlers with six or more points on both sides. The proportion of 2-, 3- and 4-year-old elk in the harvest more than doubled over the previous 5-year average, whereas harvest of 6- and 7-year-old elk nearly tripled. Boyd and Lipscomb (1976) concluded that, if the management objective was to increase the number of trophy bulls, the spike bull protection regulation was not adequate because it shifted the harvest to and increased the kill in those age classes that needed protection to permit young bulls to develop trophy antlers. Posthunt classification counts estimated that there were only 1.7 branch-antlered bulls per 100 cows—the lowest ratio recorded in the population over a 5-year period.

The 1972 regulation—limiting harvest to elk with a minimum of four points on one antler—was in effect on 10 management units. Data showed that the four-point restriction accomplished the objective of transferring the majority of the harvest from yearling bulls to 2-year-old bulls. However, 22 bulls, including 16 yearlings, were reported to have been killed and abandoned by hunters. Harvest success in 1972 was 23.5%—a significant contrast to 32.5% in 1970 when there was unrestricted bull hunting.

On the basis of these data, Boyd and Lipscomb (1976) suggested that such restrictive regulations were not necessary to raise the ratio of mature, large-antlered bulls to cows. They believed that the ratio could be increased under unrestricted bull hunts by simply *reducing hunter pressure.* Reduced hunting pressure also would decrease the number of bull elk killed illegally or accidentally and then abandoned. Boyd and Lipscomb (1976:9–10) further concluded that: "The effect of these regulations on herd production must also be considered because of the limited number of animals that a winter range can carry, and the sex ratio of the winter herd is a critical factor in determining total herd productivity. An increase in males on the winter range requires a corresponding decrease in females if the herd is kept in balance with its habitat. This decrease in females will result in proportional decreases in the next year's calf crop and the surplus available for harvest. Protecting yearling bulls has the effect of increasing the number of males on the winter range and will, therefore, force a decrease in average annual harvest. When considered on a 'per additional trophy harvested' basis, the decrease in total harvest is even more severe. Many bulls 'saved' by a yearling restriction will die before they can be harvested as trophies, but not before replacing cows on the winter range for one or more years. This effect, as well as the increased illegal bull kill, must be weighed against any increase in trophy quality resulting from a 4-point bull restriction."

A 10-year study evaluating strategies to increase the production of trophy-class bull elk (defined as mature bulls 7.5 to 10.5 years of age) at Vermejo Park, a private ranch in northern New Mexico, led to similar conclusions regarding antler point restrictions (Wolfe 1985). Between 1979 and 1983, hunters were encouraged not to shoot bulls with less than five antler points per side (5 by 5). Wolfe predicted that this strategy would increase the average age of the bull harvest and the percentage of mature bulls in the harvest. The percentage of mature bulls in the harvest was used as an indicator of trophy quality. Although the 5 by 5 antler point restriction did reduce the number of bulls smaller than 5 by 5 that were killed by hunters by approximately 53%—as compared with the previous 5-year period (1974 to 1978)—there was no significant change in the average age of the

bull harvest (4.6 years versus 4.7 years). And the percentage of the harvest composed of trophy-class bulls steadily declined from 13.7% in 1979 to 4.6% in 1983. Wolfe (1985:129) concluded that, "if increased trophy production is desired, *limiting the total bull harvest is effective,* but establishing minimum size limits in addition to the harvest limit may be counterproductive."

Wolfe (1985:130) further suggested that "the harvest strategy that would maximize trophy production in the Vermejo Park elk herd would be to limit the bull harvest to trophy-class animals (age 7.5 to 10.5 years), and manage the cow harvest for maximum sustained yield." This is consistent with McCullough's (1979:239) recommendation for white-tailed deer: ". . . the route to producing large numbers of trophy males is to manage females for maximum sustained yield (MSY) and restrict the kill of males to trophy heads." However, such a strategy probably would not be acceptable to the majority of people hunting elk on public lands, because it would require them to give up significant opportunities to hunt bull elk. Boyd and Lipscomb (1976) used a computer simulation model to evaluate the impacts of a four-point restriction on hunter opportunity. They calculated that the trade-off would be a loss of 3.9

Trophy hunting is not a primary elk management goal for any state or province. However, some programs are designed to produce trophy bulls, because trophy animals produce the healthiest offspring and attract the most attention of hunters and non-hunters alike. *Photo by Milo Burcham.*

nontrophy elk (young bulls, cows and calves) for each additional trophy elk produced.

Although production of trophy bulls is not the primary goal in elk management programs of most states and provinces, some management units are managed for trophy production. And in other areas, hunts often are scheduled to provide excellent opportunities to take trophy elk. One example is the hunt held during the rutting season when bulls may be selectively "bugled up," thus offering the hunter an opportunity to select a large bull. Another example is the hunt held late in the winter, when elk tend to be congregated on wintering grounds and all age classes of elk are, therefore, more vulnerable. Trophy hunting also may be emphasized in areas with low elk population levels to provide recreational opportunities from herds unable to tolerate general hunting pressure.

Population Reduction

Although regulations can help reduce bull elk vulnerability, they also are needed to help make elk *more* vulnerable to hunting. Throughout the West, elk have learned to find refuge from hunters, often on private lands off limits to hunting. This diminishes the ability of wildlife agencies to meet harvest objectives and often arouses dissatisfaction among both hunters and landowners. In other places, private lands block public access to public lands, making it extremely difficult for people to hunt elk and all but impossible for states to meet harvest objectives and population goals. In certain localities, elk populations cause problems, such as crop or other property damage, that require prompt action. Local reductions of elk populations are best achieved through use of managed hunts held late in the year, when harvests can be directed at particular segments of an elk population.

As elk populations have grown in numbers and expanded into new territory, the number of antlerless elk licenses authorized also has increased, primarily in response to the need to manage elk population growth rates and address local crop depredation problems. Between 1975 and 1995, the number of hunting licenses issued in the United States and Canada valid for cow or antlerless elk increased from 25,610 to 142,176 (Bunnell 1997). To encourage adequate harvests in certain areas, Colorado works with cooperating landowners and issues special cow elk hunting permits that are valid only on specific privately owned lands. Montana has special cow tags that permit hunters to kill cows only in a specified unit. Most other states have similar programs to encourage the hunting of antlerless elk. The success rate traditionally is high in these units, but in return for better odds of killing an elk (albeit antlerless), hunters must forfeit the opportunity to kill antlered bulls or hunt elk anywhere else in the state.

Types of Hunter Experience

This discussion is confined to regulations designed to achieve adequate distribution of hunters. Other aspects of hunting regulations and hunter satisfactions are discussed in Chapter 17.

Congestion and crowding of hunting areas is one of the most common complaints of elk hunters. Parsons (1975) reported that less congestion of hunting areas in Washington was the most significant reason for hunters favoring an elk season opening on a Monday.

From earliest times, all hunting has contained some element of man pitting himself against nature (Ortega y Gasset 1972). Thus, the *wilderness experience* often is an essential element in the satisfaction of elk hunting. Because of the increasing demand for elk hunting opportunities, this wilderness experience satisfaction is one of the most difficult to achieve. Hunting areas tend to be overcrowded, particularly those relatively close to urban centers (Bider and Pimlott 1973). Residents of rural areas often are upset by the influx of nonresident hunters into what the former consider their own hunting domain (Kimball 1957). As a result, one of the primary considerations in establishment of hunting regulations is to allow for participation by a maximum number of hunters and, yet, distribute hunters so that each has an opportunity to enjoy the wilderness experience, and perhaps harvest an elk.

Thomas et al. (1973) reported that hunters who returned to hunt the same area on consecutive days or years tended to establish home ranges, with specific boundaries for their hunting activities and a sense of territoriality that included defense of these areas against potential intruders. Therefore, establishment of hunting home ranges resulted in hunters spacing themselves across suitable hunting ranges and in their home ranges more efficiently, in part because of increased knowledge of topography and animal habits in the hunted area (Thomas et al. 1973). Hunters who developed home ranges had an increased interest in policies affecting management of their hunting areas and tended to resist any management changes within those areas or in regulations that would have made them inaccessible.

Findings such as these provide a framework within which hunting regulations may be designed to achieve and maintain better hunter distribution. To be effective, individual regulations must be designed for specific goals and objectives in specified management units and areas (Table 121).

Achieving distribution of hunters over time has been a goal of several states, particularly Oregon. In 1976 to 1977,

Oregon held managed elk hunting seasons almost continually from August 28 to February 28, in addition to general and special sessions. Other regulations designed to distribute hunters over time have included split season general hunts, as in New Mexico.

Typical of western states, Colorado has used a combination of techniques to improve elk hunter distribution. These techniques have included a variety of harvest regulations (antlered animals only, either sex and permits validated for a particular sex elk), different season opening dates (opening the less populated western portion of the state earlier than the eastern portion), different season lengths, different types of seasons (general, special and managed hunts), choice of managed hunt areas and use of publicity to direct hunters where recreational opportunities were available (Hunter 1957). Idaho has improved distribution of hunters in backcountry areas through construction and advertisement of access routes (Mohler 1956, Morrison 1960c). The opposite problem—too many hunters in an area laced with roads—usually is handled by a program of road closures during elk hunting seasons. This customarily is done in cooperation with other land management agencies, such as the U.S. Forest Service and Bureau of Land Management. Washington has handled an overabundance of hunters in areas close to population centers by adopting a Monday opening date for elk hunting season (Parsons 1975).

Regulations at Work: Bringing Back the Bulls

Wildlife managers struggle for ways to restore and sustain bull elk numbers, provide hunting opportunities *and* gain and maintain the trust, understanding and support of the public. Following are sketches of five hunting units in Colorado, Montana, Utah, Idaho and Oregon, where wildlife managers have grappled with low ratios of mature bulls to cows.

Colorado: Lessons from White River

Colorado grows elk, lots of them. At 215,000 and growing, no other state boasts a larger herd (Carpenter 1991). Statewide, Colorado's elk annually produce about 50 to 60 calves per 100 cows, with a 90% survival rate. This productivity enables the Colorado Division of Wildlife to manage for maximum hunting opportunities, allowing 219,852 elk hunters to kill 36,171 elk in 1995 (Bunnell 1997) and 246,778 elk hunters who harvested 60,120 elk in 2000 (http://wildlife.state.co.us/hunt/BigGame/bighuntindex.htm).

But when Colorado coal miner John Plute killed the world record elk—as judged by antler size and conformation—near Crested Butte in 1899, elk were almost gone from the state. By 1910, no more than 1,000 elk remained in Colorado (Clifton 1990). After early day conservationists pushed for temporary bans on hunting—especially market

Harvest management success means harvesting enough elk of specified age and sex to maintain the elk population at the desired numerical level and affording hunters enough personal rewards to encourage their participation in future years. *Photo courtesy of the U.S. Forest Service.*

hunting—the herd began to bounce back. In 1929, hunting resumed. By 1960, nearly 40,000 people hunted elk in Colorado (Carpenter 1991). As hunting pressure continued to increase, concerns surfaced once again, particularly in the White River herd.

Colorado's largest elk herd roams a 3,650-square mile (9,454 km²) area shaped roughly like an egg. The towns of Rifle, Glenwood Springs, Yampa, Steamboat Springs, Craig and Meeker perch on the perimeter and the Flattops Wilderness forms the yolk. Comprising a dozen different game management units, the White River country ranges from 12,000-foot (366 m) alpine peaks to sage-covered lowlands, with everything from aspen groves, spruce forests, grassy meadows and steep canyons in between (Freddy 1987b).

In the mid-1980s, Colorado Wildlife researcher David J. Freddy spent 2 years reviewing and analyzing data collected by many other wildlife biologists and compiled his findings in a 1987 report, "The White River Herd: A Perspective, 1960–85." This report documents a 1962 ratio of 24 bulls per 100 cows after hunting season, with 7 of those bulls more than 2 years old. By 1982, those numbers plunged to only 4 bulls per 100 cows, with few, if any, surviving more than two hunting seasons. The low bull/cow ratios coincided with declines in cow/calf ratios—from about 60:100 in the mid-1970s to 43:100 in 1983. The skewed sex ratio and possibly related drop in calf productivity argued strongly for changes in hunting regulations.

In 1986, White River became the first place in Colorado to adopt branch-antlered regulations. Hunters there could kill only bulls with at least four points on one antler, or brow tines longer than 5 inches (12.7 cm). This allowed bulls to survive at least one hunting season—more likely two seasons, as few bulls there grew branching antlers until they were 2.5 years old. To distribute hunting pressure more evenly and further reduce bull vulnerability, Colorado elk hunters had to choose to hunt only during archery season, muzzleloader season or one of three rifle seasons. Except for limited-entry trophy bull units—where diminished hunting pressure allowed more bulls to reach maturity—virtually all of Colorado's hunting units soon followed White River's lead. Similar season structures and antler restrictions soon prevailed throughout the state.

Still, very few bulls in the White River and other open units lived through three autumns. For the most part, the antler point restrictions allowed bulls to live 1 year longer before they were killed by hunters (past harvests comprised mostly yearlings). The brow tine regulations focused the harvest on 2.5-year-olds, a fair amount on 3.5-year-olds and somewhat on 4.5- to 5.5-year-olds. But extending the average bull's life by a year did boost bull/cow ratios significantly and allowed more bulls to live long enough to grow six-point racks. In the White River herd, bull numbers climbed to about 20 per 100 cows (Freddy 1987b), and elk biologists accomplished this feat without cutting hunter numbers.

The only state that sells an unlimited number of elk licenses to nonresidents and residents alike, Colorado remains committed to providing the most elk for the most people. David J. Freddy said, "We would have to really, really restrict hunter opportunities to get a lot of bigger, older bulls. You can cut the hunters, but, if you are going to stay economically viable, the prices of licenses must go way up. So everybody's caught in those economic supply-and-demand curves" (Stalling 1997:60).

Of all the factors elk managers have to balance, the relationship between economy and biology is perhaps the most precarious. "I think concerns about social structure and breeding structure are probably going to come more into the forefront here, because we are going through this period of heavily harvesting elk," Freddy said. "We are going through a very slow process of harvest experimentation, and our first obligation as an agency is to protect the resource. We're learning as we go and there's going to be some changes. I hope hunters don't lose perspective of the long-term values for the resource" (Stalling 1997:69).

The branch-antlered regulations adopted for the White River country have provided a major step in this learning process. State wildlife biologist Gene Byrne emphasized that the genetic and social effects of 2.5-year-old bulls doing the majority of the breeding remain largely unknown. But, he stressed that, compared with spikes, 2.5-year-old bulls can court and impregnate cows more effectively. "It appears that even 2.5-year-old bulls are not as biologically up to the job as older bulls are. There are some implications, but we're certainly a lot better off than we were. We've definitely brought back the bulls with antler point restrictions" (Stalling 1997:69).

Montana: Elkhorn Innovations

In the Elkhorns of Montana, as in the White River of Colorado, wildlife biologists lamented drastic declines in bull/cow ratios during the early 1980s (Vore and DeSimone 1991). But, as briefly described earlier, Montana tried a more radical approach to improve those ratios. Rather than protecting yearlings during the general hunt, spikes became the only legal quarry. Biologists launched this experiment in the most heavily hunted elk country in the state—20 square miles (51.8 km²) in western Montana's Elkhorn Mountains.

From lofty talus slopes and scattered clumps of whitebark pine and alpine fir, down to low, dry hillsides of juniper and sage, very little of the Elkhorn goes unprobed by hunters. Abundant roads and fairly open country make bulls highly vulnerable to hunters. Until 1985, bulls made up less than 2% of the posthunt herd. Some years, bull numbers sank below 1 per 100 cows after the hunting season, with mature bulls virtually nonexistent (Vore and DeSimone 1991). But mature, as defined by Montana wildlife biologist Rich De-Simone, was not synonymous with branch-antlered. Like Wolfe (1983), DeSimone contended that bull elk do not reach physical, sexual and behavioral maturity until they are at least 6 years old. "Two-year-old bulls can certainly maintain calf production," DeSimone said, "and hunters may be satisfied with killing raghorns, but healthy, wild herds require a diverse age-class of bulls, including mature bulls" (Stalling 1997:70).

Reviewing options to boost bull numbers, DeSimone concluded that branch-antlered restrictions would do little to increase the percentage of mature bulls in the herd. Instead, he proposed to let hunters kill spikes, but sharply limit the mortality of mature bulls. During the first year, 1986, hunters could kill only branch-antlered bulls, which assured that most of an entire age class of spikes survived. Then, in 1987, the new regulations took hold. Hunters could kill only spikes during the general rifle season, and a limited number of special permits to hunt branch-antlered bulls were available through a drawing. By 1993, bull numbers climbed to 10 per 100 cows, with more than half those bulls carrying the heavy racks of mature animals. Hunters seemed pleased with the results (Vore and DeSimone 1991). They could continue to hunt, see far more mature bulls than they used to and know they had a chance to someday hunt those big bulls. As mature bull/cow ratios increased, so did the number of limited-entry permits. In 1996, 100 either-sex elk tags were made available to hunters, allowing those hunters to pursue branch-antlered bulls in the Elkhorns (Montana Department of Fish, Wildlife and Parks 1997).

Although the ratio of bulls to cows and the diversity of age classes within the herd do not match those of naturally occurring elk populations (which, according to DeSimone and fellow state wildlife biologist John Vore, range from 40 to 60 bulls per 100 cows, with 75% of the bulls surviving to maturity), the regulations provided significant hunting opportunities while maintaining older bulls in the herd (DeSimone et al. 1993).

"We don't yet understand all the biological implications of low bull-to-cow ratios and young bull age structure, but elk evolved with big bulls as part of the herd for a reason," Vore said (Stalling 1997:71). "What if we had a human population where all we had was 98% 13-year-old boys and maybe a few 20-year-old boys? Sure, we could still get the breeding done, but we wouldn't have a real solid or stable social organization. I think there are consequences to elk populations when you don't have a good complement of older bulls—like increased harassment of cows, disrupted social structures and less-healthy calves. These are theories, but it all makes good sense. We are learning a lot, yet barely scratching the surface of wildlife management. I think we have to admit what we don't know, but some things intuitively make sense. There's a reason to have older bulls around, just as there's a reason to have older males around in a human population."

Utah: Slot Limits

In the early 1990s, unaware that Montana already was experimenting with the idea of spike-only hunting, the Utah Division of Wildlife devised a similar plan for the Manti-La Sal herd, one of the largest in Utah. Roughly 10,000 elk reside within the 1.3-million acre (526,000 ha) Wasatch Plateau of central Utah, mostly on public lands administered by the Manti-La Sal National Forest. This sweep of conifer and aspen forests, grasslands and high desert benches stippled with piñon and juniper contains a healthy balance of winter and summer range. But, with 4.9 hunters per square mile (1.8 hunter/km²) and 1.9 miles of open road per square mile (0.73 km/km²), high densities of both hunters and open roads define the area (J. Karpowitz personal communication:1999). The U.S. Forest Service closed roads to motorized vehicles, whittling road densities to 0.9 mile of open road per square mile (0.35 km/km²). But closing roads often spurred resistance from hunters accustomed to being able to drive most places. As a result of easy access, abundant hunters, low habitat security and regulations allowing hunters to kill any bull, post-season bull numbers languished at 1 or 2 bulls per 100 cows throughout the early 1980s.

In 1992, the Utah Division of Wildlife implemented a spike-only regulation, with limited numbers of branch-antlered bull tags issued through a special drawing. During the winter of 1995–1996, the state counted 10 bulls for every 100 cows in the Manti unit, with half of those bulls carrying six-point racks (J. Karpowitz personal communication:1999). As mature bull/cow ratios rose, hunters embraced the regulations, said Utah wildlife biologist Jim Karpowitz. "They just love the idea that now, even though they go up there and can only kill a spike, they're seeing big bulls and hearing bulls bugle. We used to have a silent elk rut— nothing bugled. There just weren't any mature bulls" (Stalling 1997:72).

Utah also had several limited-entry hunting units that boasted excellent bull/cow ratios. In the San Juan unit during the mid-1990s, for example, bull/cow ratios remained consistently around 25:100 (J. Karpowski personal communication:1999). During that time, however, roughly 10,000 hunters per year pursued elk in the Manti unit, whereas only 15 people hunted elk in the San Juan unit each year. The difference in license revenue was dramatic. And the spike-only regulation gave 10,000 people the chance to hunt elk each year, while 66 hunters per year had the chance to seek mature bulls in the Manti unit.

Idaho: Closing Roads

In parts of northern Idaho's rugged backcountry, where relatively few roads penetrate the steep, thickly vegetated mountains, elk remained fairly secure. But even in these areas, roads open to vehicular use can compromise elk security. Wildlife biologists have studied the relationships between habitat condition, hunter density and elk mortality since the 1970s, when mature bull/cow ratios began declining in the face of increased hunter access on an expanding web of logging roads (Lyon 1979a, Thomas 1979b, Lyon et al. 1985). From 1986 to 1990, Unsworth and Kuck (1991:85) monitored mortality rates of bull elk in both roaded and unroaded areas of the Clearwater Drainage in northcentral Idaho, and reported that "Bull elk in roaded habitat were more than twice as likely to be killed during fall hunting seasons as those in areas with very few roads."

A 5-year study in Idaho's Clearwater Drainage compared bull elk survival in three management units with similar terrain and habitat, each about 100 square miles (259 km²) in size (Gratson and Zager 1993, Leptich 1993, Leptich and Zager 1994). The first unit contained 2.49 miles of open road per square mile (1.54 km/km²), and the roads were left open during hunting season. In the second unit, roads were closed during hunting season, reducing open road densities from 4.08 miles of open road per square mile (2.54 km/km²) to 0.90 miles of open road per square mile (0.56 km/km²). Unit three was mostly unroaded, containing an open road density of 0.37 miles of road per square mile (0.23 km/km²). Researchers radio-collared and monitored the survival of 231 bull elk in the three study units. In the first area, with high road densities, 49.6% of the radio-collared bulls survived hunting season. In the second unit, where roads were closed, 69.6% of the bulls survived. In the third unit, which was mostly unroaded, 71% of the bulls survived. Research in the Clearwater Drainage and elsewhere in northern Idaho provided very strong evidence that managing vehicular access led to significantly improved survival rates of bulls and improved bull/cow ratios. In a 1992 to 1995 hunter

opinion survey, the Idaho Department of Fish and Game found that 60% of hunters in each of the three study units said road closures were "easily acceptable" or "not easy to accept but tolerable" as "a method to maintain good numbers of bulls and branch-antlered bulls" (Leptich and Zager 1994:22).

Oregon: Trade-offs

Just closing roads cannot always achieve desired mature bull/cow ratios. For example, a group of Oregon researchers examined options for reducing bull elk vulnerability, and concluded: "Where sex ratios have been heavily suppressed, hunter/elk ratios are high, and terrain is easily accessed, attempts to enhance sex ratios via light, or moderate hunter restrictions will be ineffective. . . . Vigorous management of hunter numbers and/or hunter effectiveness (e.g., weapons types, antler point restrictions, season lengths, access) is required to enhance sex ratios in most circumstances regardless of habitat conditions" (Vales et al. 1991:180–181).

Beginning in 1989, researchers analyzed 13 years of data on elk populations and hunter harvests in the Sled Springs and Chesnimnus units of northeastern Oregon. The gentle, forested plateaus and steep, rugged grasslands of the 540-square-mile (1,400 km²) Sled Springs unit are heavily logged and veined with roads. Less than 20% of the land is public, administered by the Wallowa-Whitman National Forest. Private timber companies own nearly 40% of the land and allow public hunting on virtually all of it. The rest is private rangeland.

About 2,700 elk inhabit the unit and, until 1978, nearly 5,000 hunters annually pursued them. Few bulls survived. Winter counts revealed sex ratios as low as 3 bulls per 100 cows and almost invariably, those bulls were spikes. Private and federal land managers closed roads and saw no improvement in bull/cow ratios. Even with vehicles excluded, hunters could easily cover the open, logged country, finding and killing nearly every bull elk. State wildlife managers created three different split seasons, in which hunters could choose to participate in only one of the three, thus distributing hunting pressure over a longer period and reducing the intensity of hunting pressure on bulls during any one season. However, bull/cow ratios remained low and failed to recover (Vales et al. 1991).

Finally, in 1991, the Oregon Department of Fish and Wildlife began restricting hunter numbers. They split the season into two rifle hunts and one archery hunt, limiting the first rifle season to 1,100 hunters who could kill any bull. They placed no limit on the number of hunters allowed to hunt in the second season, but hunters choosing this option had to relinquish the opportunity to hunt elk anywhere else in the state. They, too, could kill any bull. The archery season remained unlimited, and any elk was legal—cow or bull. Bull numbers improved slightly to 4 or 5 per 100 cows, but not enough to satisfy a 1990 statewide mandate to manage elk herds for a minimum of 10 bulls per 100 cows.

Wildlife managers had no choice but to restrict hunter numbers further. In 1995, they limited the first rifle season to 900 hunters and the second season to 500. The first season remained "any bull," and the second rifle season changed to spike-only. Three hundred any-elk archery tags were available, along with 200 spike or antlerless tags. Bull numbers finally rose to 9 bulls per 100 cows in 1996, and appeared to be climbing. By 2000, bull numbers had climbed to 11 spike and branch-antlered bulls per 100 cows, as previously indicated, and state officials hoped to achieve a goal of maintaining 10 mature bulls (3 years old and older) per 100 cows (B. K. Johnson personal communication:2000).

As elk habitat continues to dwindle and the ranks of elk hunters grow, such trade-offs will become more common. Before the state implemented these fairly severe restrictions, hunters swarmed the Sled Springs area, outnumbering elk two to one (Leckenby et al. 1991). Not surprisingly, the hunting experience for many was compromised. Still, everyone *did* have the opportunity to hunt elk. That opportunity is gone. But in 1996, there were more elk than hunters, and those who did draw a tag had better odds of killing a bull and experiencing a satisfying hunt.

Ethics, Education, Public Support and Compliance

Hunting regulations work when a majority of hunters understand, respect and embrace them. Such understanding derives from knowledge, skill and ethics. Posewitz (1994:16) defined an ethical hunter as "A person who knows and respects the animals hunted, follows the law, and behaves in a way that will satisfy what society expects of him or her as a hunter."

Wildlife managers cannot regulate ethics. But they can inform and educate the public about the complex relationships between elk, hunters and the land. As human demographics change, along with attitudes about hunting (Decker et al. 1993), and as antihunting groups strive to expand their influence (Horn 1992, Mitchell 1992), a better understanding of and participation in hunting and wildlife management issues among the nonhunting public become increasingly important. Ultimately, however, the future of hunting hinges on the conduct of hunters.

During a 1993 symposium on North America's hunting

Although camaraderie is an important value and benefit of hunting, crowded hunting conditions on an elk hunt diminish the perceived and actual prospect of harvest success, which, in turn, reduces satisfaction with the total experience. Wildlife managers need to propose season regulations that meet herd harvest objectives without negating hunter enthusiasm and interest. ("Crowding," to elk hunters, may be a noncompanion in sight or sound, or any number of other factors—companions or noncompanions, hunters or nonhunters—merely in mind's eye). *Photo by Donald M. Jones.*

heritage, Madson (1993:69–70) observed: "I've heard wildlife professionals say that we're not in the business of dictating ethics to hunters. I agree with about half of that. A wildlife agency probably shouldn't dictate much of anything to anyone. As public agencies, we're generally in the business of finding a consensus that balances a little science with a lot of opinion. However, state wildlife people have a lot to contribute to the ongoing debate over ethics. . . . State wildlife agencies need to stay involved in the ethics dialog. We need to act as a catalyst for it. We need to provide a conduit between hunters and other conservation-minded people so that these groups can discover what they have in common rather than focusing on how they differ."

Critics of hunting and wildlife management often claim that wildlife agencies cater only to the hunting public, to the detriment of nongame species. A brochure printed by the Humane Society of the United States (1981:2) asked:

"Hunters argue that their efforts have increased populations of vanishing wildlife, but to whose benefit? The animals? Or the hunters? Can hunters truly call themselves protectors of wildlife? Are they not merely providing targets and protecting their own interests?" Such questions, more often than not rhetorical fund-raising gambits, dismiss the role of hunters historically and currently of providing the principal wherewithal for wildlife management to succeed. That wildlife populations have been restored through hunter investments and that hunters are primary beneficiaries cannot ignore the simple fact that those wildlife populations probably would not have been restored for anyone's benefit in the absence of hunter support.

Nonetheless, in 1996, voters in eight states cast ballot initiatives and referendums aimed at limiting or ending certain kinds of hunting and trapping. This reflects a rising tide in which individuals and organizations are attempting to steer wildlife management through the ballot box (Horn 1992). Many wildlife managers worry that these initiatives could undermine the ability of state wildlife agencies to be effective stewards. They are troubled by the notion of wildlife management policies and hunting regulations based on public opinion and emotion rather than science and guidance from professional wildlife biologists and state and federal land managers, with input from the public. Supporters of these initiatives, however, say they are necessary because state and federal agencies have failed to consider the desires and opinions of the nonhunting public.

Regulated hunting and wildlife management in North America have resulted in tremendous and undisputable benefits for wildlife habitat and numerous species of wildlife, both hunted and nonhunted (Reiger 1975, Trefethen 1975, Geist 1993), but they are not without fault. In *An American Crusade for Wildlife,* Trefethen (1975:337) wrote: "In spite of its record of accomplishment, the American system of wildlife conservation, like any other manmade institution, is not perfect. It could be vastly strengthened and expanded. Large segments of the American public are demanding that this be done. Many nonhunters, although they benefit from sportsman-financed state and federal programs in which they have little financial investment, resent what they consider the dictatorial powers of hunting and fishing interests over the regulation of America's fish and wildlife populations. Some wildlife administrators and sportsman's groups have actively resisted opening the doors of administrative decision to nonhunters who are concerned for the future of wildlife."

Trefethen (1975:367) recommended efforts to increase communication and mutual understanding between hunters and nonhunters: "Most nonhunters need to learn more about the principles of wildlife management and the biological basis for its existence. . . . On the other hand, sportsmen must admit more freely that not all of the members of their fraternity smell of roses. If sport hunting is to remain socially acceptable, they must do everything in their power to eliminate from their ranks the vandal, the game hog and the slob hunter. They must insist on tough state laws that carry the penalty of automatic license revocation as well as fines for any deliberate violation of the game codes, which, in all states, should be extended to include vandalism, illegal trespass, littering and violation of hunting safety rules. They must insist upon mandatory comprehensive hunter-education programs that extend beyond learning how to cross a fence without shooting oneself into the ethics and etiquette of sportsmanship, wildlife habitats, species identification, and game laws. They must initiate a meaningful dialog with reasonable segments of the nonhunting public with a goal toward resuming cooperation toward mutual goals. In their actions and behavior, they must respect the sensibilities of the nonhunter and recognize that wildlife has public values and uses beyond those for hunting."

An estmated 10% of U.S. citizens oppose hunting; another 10% are hunters. This leaves about 80% who are undecided or unsure about hunting. If America's hunting tradition is to continue, hunters and wildlife managers need to ensure that hunting is conducted with respect for the animals, the species and the land, and that hunting regulations are based on sound, science-based principles of wildlife management. Hunters and wildlife professionals also need to inform and educate the public about the role of hunters in wildlife conservation, and how ethical hunting can deepen people's appreciation for wildlife and wildlands and strengthen society as a whole. *Photo courtesy of the Wildlife Management Institute.*

Beck (1996:200, 209) put it this way: "The philosophies underlying wildlife management have evolved little in the past 60 years, while the philosophies of society have changed greatly. The role of state wildlife agencies has been, and remains, to protect and provide. We protect wildlife in order to provide for an array of human benefits. Dominant among the benefits is hunting. Ironically, even as we have progressed technologically, we've developed a mind-set and jargon that serve to distance us from both wildlife and the social act we call hunting. . . . I want to keep hunting, I want to keep learning about wildlife. I want to keep living with wildlife. These things can only happen if we bring a stronger social conscience to our roles as wildlife managers and hunters. We must change, or we will cease to exist. To help steer our way through the coming years, we must adopt a new paradigm: biology provides the planks to build the boat, but society steers the ship."

Many hunter/conservationists, from Theodore Roosevelt (1893) through Aldo Leopold (1949), James Trefethen (1975), John Mitchell (1979), Ted Kerasote (1993), David Petersen (1996)and others, have eloquently addressed hunter behavior and attitudes. Critical thinkers throughout the past century have explored the need to expand hunter education and encourage more public participation in the wildlife management process, as well as the necessity of improving and upholding hunting ethics and the traditions of fair chase. Such actions could help nullify the effects of the antihunting/antimanagement movement, improve public understanding and support of hunting and wildlife management and possibly reduce the need for more restrictive regulations. Public participation programs in Idaho and Oregon's Master Hunter program offer fine examples.

Encouraging Public Participation and Support in Idaho

Idaho gains about 40,000 new residents each year (Ronayne 1995) and struggles with challenges common to all western states—growing urbanization, increased hunters crowding of less and less wild country, declining mature bull/cow ratios, and diminishing understanding and support of state wildlife programs.

In 1994, the Idaho Department of Fish and Game compiled a report entitled "Keeping People in Mind While Managing Wildlife: Integrating Economics and Socio-Political Issues with Elk Ecology" (Cooper 1994). The report served as a case study on elk management in the Lochsa River watershed, where bull/cow ratios and calf/cow ratios had dropped far below management goals. Wildlife managers winnowed the field of regulatory options to four: (1) change the general antlered-only elk hunt to a controlled antlered-

only hunt with limited permits while retaining the current controlled antlerless-hunts; (2) change the general antlered-only elk hunt to a controlled antlered-only hunt—in which hunters who chose to hunt the unit would be limited to only that unit, and could not hunt elsewhere—with unlimited permits while retaining the current controlled antlerless hunt; (3) change the general antlered-only elk hunt to a general spike-only hunt followed by a controlled antlered-only hunt with limited permits, while retaining the current controlled antlerless hunt; or (4) manage motorized access to the area with seasonal road closures while retaining the current season structure.

The report concluded that, under option (1), annual hunter participation would be lowered from 821 hunters to 686, resulting in an estimated annual loss of $77,800 from the Idaho Fish and Game Department's revenue and a loss of money spent by hunters in the local economy (restaurants, hotels, gas, etc.). Under option (2), the state could only achieve its goal of boosting bull/cow and calf/cow ratios if hunters chose not to hunt the unit. If enough hunters chose to hunt elsewhere, the management goals might be achieved, but local communities would lose an estimated $534,000 and the hunting pressure would almost certainly be manifested in other areas. Option (3) would require a decline in hunter numbers to 474, again affecting wildlife management budgets and state and local economies. And if spike bulls were overharvested, the state would not achieve its management goals. Option (4), on the other hand, would most likely achieve the state management goals without affecting hunter numbers or state and local economies. After examining all the management options, wildlife managers, land managers and the public came to the same conclusion: "Managing motorized access should be attempted before any other options are implemented" (Cooper 1995:7).

Cooper (1995:7), who compiled the report, wrote: "The dominant concern expressed by everyone was having the opportunity to provide input into the decision-making process. *All four management strategies have more to do with managing people than with managing elk themselves* [emphasis added]. As such, the choice of which policy to enact should take the human dimension into account. Local, state and department-level economics, hunter behavior and preferences, the desires of the local community and forest user groups, and the needs of the agency responsible for managing the habitat all are important considerations that should be factored in the decision-making process." This concept, Cooper explained, is one of the fundamental tenets of ecosystem management, based on four principles: (1) manage with people in mind, (2) manage for where you are, (3) manage across political and legal boundaries, and

(4) manage based on an understanding of processes rather than on fixed rules.

The Idaho Fish and Game Commission used Cooper's study to identify a number of flaws in the state's elk management plan, including a "lack of involvement by the broader public in wildlife management decisions that affect their use of the land" (Parker 1995:9). In response, the agency hired a private marketing research firm to develop a prototype public involvement program in Idaho's Clearwater Region. Designed to increase citizen participation in establishing deer and elk hunting seasons, the program called for community meetings throughout the region to identify deer and elk management issues of most concern to the public (Idaho Department of Fish and Game 1995). Then, the Department of Fish and Game helped create the Clearwater Citizen's Advisory Committee, made up of about 20 individuals representing hunting and nonhunting organizations. Wildlife biologists from the Department met twice a month with the committee to discuss aspects of deer and elk management, such as how population data are collected, what is involved in determining the optimum bull/cow ratios for a herd and other technical information.

Then, the Department used the information and comments gathered from the public to draft a set of proposed regulations for deer and elk seasons. A second round of community meetings gave the public an opportunity to comment on these recommendations. The citizens advisory committee then reviewed the draft, examined the second round of public input and forwarded its own recommendations for hunting regulations to the Idaho Department of Fish and Game and the Idaho Fish and Game Commission. The state integrated the advisory committee's report into the annual hunting regulations.

Hunter crowding and the overharvest of mature bulls consistently topped the list of concerns expressed by both wildlife biologists and citizens participating on the advisory committees. In response, in 1996, the Idaho Fish and Game Commission adopted a minimum biological objective of 10 mature bulls per 100 cows, before hunting season, with mature bulls defined as at least 3.5 years old. This objective was recommended by both wildlife biologists and citizen participants as a way to ensure enough adult breeding bulls for optimum calf production. Biologists predicted this prehunt bull/cow ratio would result in a total posthunt ratio of about 20:100, including young bulls and mature bulls (Idaho Elk Management Team 1997). While developing and modifying hunting regulations to achieve its objectives and maintain significant hunting opportunities, the Idaho Department of Fish and Game continues to encourage public participation.

The process was difficult, time consuming and placed tremendous responsibility on all involved—wildlife biologists, the state Fish and Game Commission, advisory committee members, hunters and anyone else with an interest in elk management in the Clearwater region. In turn, it gave all participants a deeper understanding of wildlife management, hunting and hunting regulations. That, Idaho wildlife managers hoped, would lead to the knowledge, support and respect necessary for hunting regulations to be successful and acceptable.

Oregon's Master Hunters: A New Breed of Jägermeister

Sometime around 700 AD, legend has it, a German named Hubert went deer hunting one Good Friday while everybody else went to church. Deep in the beech woods, Hubert came upon a heavy-racked stag in a small clearing. He drew his bow, but before he could shoot, a crucifix appeared between the deer's antlers. Hubert unstrung his bow and hastened toward church. After his revelation, Hubert not only went on to become the Bishop of Maastricht and Liége, he became known as the Patron Saint of Hunters.

In Germany, the stag with a crucifix between its antlers remains the emblem of the *Jägermeister,* which translates to master hunter, a hard-won title of prestige and honor in Germany. To earn the right to hunt, Germans undergo rigorous tests to demonstrate their knowledge and proficiency in wildlife ecology, wildlife protection, hunting traditions and firearms. Only a skilled few pass muster, and there are no apparent hunter-image problems in Germany. Jägermeisters are widely respected (Madson 1993). But this exclusive approach does pose a few drawbacks. For one thing, upon finally becoming a hunter, the initiate needs a fair amount of wealth and influence just to buy a rifle, let alone gain access to hunting grounds. For another, the hunt itself shares more in common with a well-choreographed red deer stalk on a shooting preserve in South Texas than it does with chasing elk in the wild heart of British Columbia.

In much of the western United States and Canada, nearly anyone of appropriate age can purchase a license and hunt on large expanses of public land. But there are drawbacks to that, too. With only conscience and perhaps a rudimentary hunter safety course to guide them, many hunters become *meisters* of poor behavior in the field. They fail to respect private property, fudge on bag limits and shooting hours, ride all-terrain vehicles into walk-in areas, leave trails of trash through the woods, make only the most cursory searches for wounded game and sometimes worse (Kerasote 1993).

A few years ago, a hunter in Maine mistook a woman

hanging laundry in her backyard for a white-tailed deer and killed her. About that same time, a Montana hunter identified a tent as a bear, ventilating the nylon several times before concluding something was amiss. Unfortunately, these flesh-and-blood Elmer Fudds supply the images many people conjure when they hear the word "hunter." Hapless road hunters firing rounds into decoy deer are much more likely to make the evening news than are people who study wildlife, practice shooting, follow the principles of fair chase, pass up questionable shots and kill cleanly.

Can state wildlife and provincial agencies adopt parts of Germany's Jägermeister tradition—including hunter knowledge and proficiency testing—while still retaining North America's uniquely democratic hunting traditions? Oregon's volunteer Master Hunter Program provides genuine cause for hope.

The seeds of the Master Hunter Program were sown in western Oregon's Willamette Valley in the late 1980s when expanding elk populations collided with expanding human populations along the Cascade foothills (Bickler 1995). Although some residents enjoyed watching elk from the back porches of their new country homes, others complained of damage to gardens, orchards and hayfields. In response, the Oregon Department of Fish and Wildlife developed damage-control pool hunts. Hunters who applied for and drew special tags were on standby between September and March to shoot cow elk in response to depredation complaints. But during the first few damage-control hunts, hunters did some damage of their own. One person gutted an elk on someone's front lawn, others discarded gut piles in roadside ditches. Large bones left in hayfields fouled agricultural equipment. Wounded elk hobbled through residential areas. And, a hunter near Springfield shot a hole through the window of a house moments after the homeowner had stepped away from the window (Bickler 1995). Residents were less than thrilled to have hunters in the neighborhood.

In response, the Oregon Department of Fish and Wildlife developed a Hunter Proficiency Program, initiated in 1991, in which district biologists used a mandatory shooting test and written exam to rank hunters who drew tags for the special damage-control hunts. Hunters scoring highest were used for the most sensitive hunts, while those scoring lower were assigned hunting areas where they were less likely to get in trouble. Within a few years, complaints against hunters were nonexistent (Bickler 1995).

About the same time the state was developing this Hunter Proficiency Program, the Oregon Forest Industries Council called a conference to discuss concerns about hunter behavior on private forestlands. The timber companies recognized that hunting helped limit the damage done by deer and elk to their tree farms. But in some areas, hunters were costing them nearly as much—through road and culvert damage, broken gates and fences and vandalized equipment—as the voracious elk and deer.

Similar discussions took place in eastern Oregon, where Oregon Department of Wildlife officials were seeking ways to improve relations between hunters and cattle ranchers. Although ranchers posted more and more land—often because of poor hunter behavior—they lost a higher percentage of their crops and grass to animals, particularly elk. Just over half of Oregon is public land, but most of the historic winter range for elk and deer lies on the private lands at lower elevations (Bickler 1995). Formerly grasslands, parts of many ranches in eastern Oregon's foothills now grow alfalfa and other crops. Such alluring foods make these traditional winter ranges irresistible to elk. Even ranchers who closed their lands to public hunting because they wanted to benefit from fee hunting operations found they had more elk and deer than they were willing to tolerate eating their cattle feed after hunting season ended. The Oregon Department of Wildlife decided to import the Hunter Proficiency Program from the suburbs of the Willamette Valley to eastern Oregon cattle country to help defuse spiraling tensions over private lands and public wildlife. Thus was born the Oregon Master Hunter Program.

The Master Hunter Program has five core objectives: (1) foster positive relations between hunters and private landowners, (2) increase access to private lands by giving landowners a way to identify hunters who have graduated from the program, boosting landowners' comfort level with hunters, (3) improve the public image of hunters, (4) develop a pool of ethical and knowledgeable hunters for possible use in sensitive damage control situations, and (5) offer graduates high-quality hunting opportunities (Bickler 1995).

The path to becoming a Master Hunter began with a 10- to 15-hour home study course and workbook that built on the basic Oregon hunter education manual (Oregon Fish and Wildlife 1992). The workbook quizzed hunters on topics such as hunter responsibilities, wildlife conservation and management, wildlife identification and field care of game. Then, students took a half-day classroom session that stressed hunter ethics and landowner relations, as well as firearms safety. The class also included discussions on the impacts of hunter behavior on nonhunters and antihunters and concluded with a written exam.

Students who passed the exam moved on to a shooting test. Using their own rifles, they could shoot from sitting, kneeling or offhand positions, but could not use any support. To advance to the final phase, students had to place five rounds in an 11-inch (28 cm) group from 100 yards

(91.4 m) (those hunting with bows and muzzleloaders faced equivalent challenges). Hunters who fulfilled the shooting test moved on to the key step in the program—completion of at least 20 hours of volunteer work to benefit wildlife.

The volunteer work could be through the Oregon Department of Fish and Wildlife's volunteer program or with any other natural resource agency or conservation group, such as the U.S. Forest Service, Bureau of Land Management, Fish and Wildlife Service, Rocky Mountain Elk Foundation, The Nature Conservancy, National Audubon Society or other. Students also could work on private land if the project were approved in advance. The work emphasized a tie between responsible land stewardship and responsible hunting. Once students completed the four phases, the state checked their background for game violations. After this final check, Master Hunters advanced to graduation, receiving a letter signed by the Oregon Department of Fish and Wildlife director, a patch, a decal and a lapel pin—all of which, along with the study material, were paid for out of a small enrollment fee. In the process, they also gained hunting opportunities others did not have, such as hunting on private ranches or timberlands where landowners would only grant Master Hunters permission to hunt. These special opportunities offered a significant incentive for people to complete the program. But, a mixture of altruism, pride and deep concern about the future of hunting seemed to be equally important motives for many who became master hunters.

As of 1997, about 750 hunters had completed the program. Tony Burtt, of the Oregon Department of Fish and Wildlife, said: "Hunters who have been through it think it's great, and many of the participating landowners express cautious satisfaction. We are optimistic. We like the way hunters have supported it and have not labeled it as elitism. We are encouraged by the support from the timber industry—we want to get a wider level of acceptance among them as well as cattle ranchers, but this will take time. Perhaps the biggest success will turn out to be peer pressure on the 'ethically disadvantaged' hunter. Students in the program feel strongly the need to self police, and I do not think they will tolerate any misbehavior" (Stalling 1996d:50).

Oregon Department of Fish and Wildlife Hunter Education Coordinator Michael Bickler hopes hunters, non-hunters and landowners all will eventually look to Master Hunters as models of what hunting can and should become. His goal is to expand the program throughout Oregon, and his dream is that states all across the country will adopt similar programs. Concluding a presentation about the program at the 1995 Governor's Symposium on North America's Hunting Heritage, Bickler (1995:9) noted: "The Oregon Master Hunter program offers us challenges as well as opportunities. We know from experience that some will complain that the Master Hunter Program establishes an elitist mentality. But as a hunter, I would prefer to be associated with those who subscribe to only the highest ethical standards and expertise in their endeavors. . . . It is time for hunters to take the moral high ground. It's time for all of us to subscribe to only the highest levels of behavior and commitment. It's time for all of us to become 'Master Hunters,' for our sake as hunters and the sake of all wildlife."

Regulating Ethics

Wildlife managers can regulate seasons, hunter numbers, equipment, bag limits and other tangible factors. And, they can regulate hunter education requirements in hopes of improving hunter behavior and compliance to regulations. Controlling the attitudes and ethics of hunters, however, presents a more ethereal challenge. As Leopold (1949:178) wrote: "A peculiar virtue in wildlife ethics is that the hunter ordinarily has no gallery to applaud or disapprove of his conduct. Whatever his acts, they are dictated by his own conscience, rather than a mob of onlookers. It is difficult to exaggerate the importance of this fact."

But wildlife agencies do, indeed, attempt to regulate ethics. At a 1993 hunting heritage symposium, Madson (1993:70) observed: "Well-meaning hunters and wildlife managers have often legislated hunting morality. As a result, we have to plug our shotguns when we hunt migratory birds; we have to use rifle calibers that some biologist decided were adequate for big game; we have to get out of our vehicles before we shoot, and take upland birds only in the air. It's surprising how many of our hunting regulations have more to do with ethics than with pure management of the harvest. Few hunters find our hunting 'blue laws' to be more than a minor inconvenience, but they do have a disadvantage—they end one path of ethical discussion. When ethics become law, they cease to be ethics. For that reason, I hope state wildlife agencies and hunters can find ways to extend the ethical debate and improve the hunter's behavior without a barrage of new laws. When hunters do right, I'd like to think they chose to do it and can be given some credit for it. If state and federal wildlife managers set about forcing the issue in every case, the hunter's image will continue to deteriorate, not only among casual bystanders but among hunters themselves."

During the 1986 Western States and Provinces Elk Workshop in Coos Bay, Oregon, Thomas (1986:314) appealed to his fellow wildlife biologists to consider morality and values in the management process: "Oh, I fully understand that such things as ethics and cultural values don't fit well into cost/benefit analyses or linear programs. But we ignore those values at our peril and at the peril of elk and other big-game animals. We ignore such considerations because, I think, somewhere in the evolving drama of elk and elk hunting management we have indeed forgotten the welfare of the animals, the deep cultural values of hunting, and the respect that the hunter owes to the quarry. Somehow as professional wildlife managers we have forgotten that elk are really a precious relic of our past preserved as part of the modern world to serve as the spirit of place and a link with hunters and hunted of a thousand generations. Elk and elk hunting are symbols that we, as a society, want to keep with us as we move into the future increasingly dominated by technology and a pervasive tameness and sameness."

Hunter Support and Compliance

No one likes restrictions. Human nature resists dictation of the who, what, where, when and how of any activity—unless the reasons for the restrictions are understood and embraced. This certainly applies to elk hunters, who traditionally cherishing the distinctive freedom associated with high, wild, backcountry haunts. But throughout the West, hunters have accepted restrictions if the purposes are understood and the regulations are fair and intelligently and equally enforced (Kovalicky and Blair 1991, Thompson et al. 1991). As previously mentioned, hunters in the Lochsa area of Idaho overwhelmingly supported access restrictions after examining all other options available (Cooper 1995). In Montana, hunters in the Elkhorn Mountains expressed strong support for hunting regulation changes that limited harvest to spike bulls unless the hunters had special permits to hunt cows or branch-antlered bulls (Vore and DeSimone 1991).

Many proposed hunting regulations initially meet strong opposition. Once hunters experience the improved quality of hunting that often results many become champions of the new regulations. A survey sent to 1,000 randomly selected Rocky Mountain Elk Foundation members turned up the following from 450 respondents: 86% agreed that elk should be managed so bulls can grow to maturity even if that restricts hunter opportunity; 92% agreed that hunting should be restricted if necessary for proper conservation of wildlife and 92% agreed that some roads should be closed on public land to protect wildlife (Rocky Mountain Elk Foundation 1990). A survey conducted by the Montana Department of Fish, Wildlife and Parks to examine hunter opinions on road closures revealed that, before closing roads, 56% of hunters approved of the closures, 22% were opposed. Three years after the closures, 76% of hunters polled supported the access restrictions. Many hunters said

they walked more, saw more elk and enjoyed the experience. Researchers attributed the success of the access restrictions and public support to public participation and consensus building during the planning stage (Thompson et al. 1991).

Public participation and understanding lead to public support. Indeed, they form the cornerstone of the regulatory process, helping to ensure compliance and perhaps aiding law enforcement efforts. At a 1991 elk vulnerability symposium, Kovalicky and Blair (1991:245) of the U.S. Forest Service put it this way: "We can dictate management changes in policy and direction, but we cannot dictate change in an individual's attitude and value system. This change must come from within. The fate of elk and other forest resources rests with people. Laws don't make things work, nor do rules and regulations; it takes the human hand, heart and mind to give them meaning."

Harvest Assessments

Equally important as the setting of elk hunting regulations is the follow-up assessment of harvest results. Harvest assessments are a key tool for evaluating the effectiveness of past management strategies and providing important data for setting new regulations. Harvest assessments seek both biological and sociological data. Wildlife managers have used a variety of methods to measure harvests and each have inherent flaws as well as unique strengths. However, with complex statistical analysis and compensation for biases built into the methodologies, managers are achieving increasingly higher rates of precision. The different methods of harvest assessments include random phone surveys, random mail surveys, check stations, hunter report cards and mandatory reporting.

Random phone surveys and multiple wave mail surveys are the primary methods wildlife agencies use to gather elk harvest data. Many states also use check stations as a cross checking means but not as a source of primary data.

Pitfalls of Harvest Assessments

The consistent underlying factor limiting precision in harvest assessments is sample size. Larger samples cost more money and wildlife agencies across the country are facing tightening budgets. Therefore, agencies cannot afford to sample as large a segment of the hunting population that would provide optimal statistical precision.

The basic premise of using statistics to measure harvests is simple. It is impossible to contact every single hunter, so by sampling a small cross section of the hunting population and analyzing the data with computer-aided statistical methods, managers can infer what is happening with the whole population of hunters. But to get an accurate reflection of the whole, the small sample must be accurate and unbiased (Table 123). The easiest and best way to ensure accurate samples is to have as large a sample as necessary. Thus, statistical methodology may not be as important as the ability and resources to get adequate sample sizes.

An equally frustrating problem for managers stems from the fact that license agents take a long time to remit their sales data (most states require agents to remit within 30 days but enforcement is difficult, and agents have been known to take as long as 6 months). Once the agencies receive the data from the agents, they must enter it in a hunting license database. The database is used by managers to determine the sample size needed to achieve specific confidence levels and where the sample pools—the actual addresses and phone numbers—come from. Preliminary data usually are not available until March, and final data are not available until June (V. Clingman personal communication:1998). In most states and provinces, submissions for the regulation-setting process must be approved by March/April, which means that managers are forced to operate with data that are two seasons old. Although some managers argue that management should be based on trends—using year-old data rather than current data is not a major problem—several state agencies, including those of Montana, Oregon, Idaho and British Columbia, are looking at ways either to streamline the hunting regulation-setting process or hunting license database system.

Many states either have or are planning to implement a point-of-sale on-line database system that is designed to improve the timeliness of the harvest assessment process. The point-of-sale system requires license agents to have a workstation that is connected to a central database. When a license is sold, the information is immediately downloaded to the new license database. In addition to improving the timeliness of harvest assessments, the point-of-sale database will be a useful tool for conservation law enforcement. It will require anyone wanting to purchase a license to present picture identification and a social security number or unique personal identification number (PIN). When the license agent enters the person's drivers license number, social security number or personal identification number, the individual's past hunting history will appear on the computer screen, proving residence and the right to purchase a hunting license. This will help eliminate problems, such as hunters purchasing multiple licenses and past violators purchasing licenses (T. Lonner personal communication:1998).

However, there are disadvantages to the point-of-sale system. The system is considered inconvenient by many hunters and vendors. Common complaints include the fact that the machines are slow and they do not work during busy times or during power outages. Because of technical breakdowns, a paper system should be readily available as a backup.

Random Phone Surveys

The random phone survey is one of the most frequently used methods to assess elk harvests. It is currently used by Oregon, Colorado, Idaho and Montana. There are many reasons managers are using or switching to random phone surveys, the most important ones being cost effectiveness, accuracy and randomness. Because phone surveys use ran-

Table 123. Comparison of actual and field interview-projected harvest results for a hypothetical 9-day hunting season beginning on a Saturday

Day of season	Number of hunter days	Actual harvest	Actual success rate	Number of hunters interviewed[a]	Number of elk checked	Apparent success rate
1	5,000	250	0.05	100	5	0.05
2	4,000	120	0.03	100	3	0.03
3	3,000	60	0.02			
4	1,500	30	0.02			
5	1,000	10	0.01	100	1	0.01
6	1,000	10	0.01	100	1	0.01
7	1,500	15	0.01	100	1	0.01
8	3,000	30	0.01	100	1	0.01
9	1,500	15	0.01	100	1	0.01
Total	21,500	540		700	13	
Mean			0.025[b]			0.019[c]

[a] Assumes a sample of 100 hunters checked each weekend day and on 3 weekdays selected at random.

[b] Elk per hunter per day or 0.108 per hunter per day assuming 5,000 hunters.

[c] Elk per hunter per day.

dom samples they are statistically sound, allowing for a greater measure of statistical precision of responses. There are different methods for carrying out phone surveys, but they all involve a target number of people who must be surveyed (based on the total number of licenses sold) to achieve certain confidence intervals. Confidence intervals are a way of measuring how reliable point estimates are, based on the sample size representing the whole population of hunters. Most agencies shoot for confidence intervals of 80% or more.

Phone surveys work very well for limited draw hunts, for which managers have a known number of hunters and can more easily survey readily and successfully. With general seasons, the results tend not to be as good, because it is difficult to contact a large enough sample size to produce high confidence levels and, thus, precise results (Table 124) (J. Ellenberger personal communication:1998). Colorado, for one, is considering going to totally limited licenses on a statewide basis to improve the precision of random phone surveys (J. Ellenberger personal communication:1998). It did this for mule deer in 1998 and is considering it for elk in the future.

Problems with phone surveys, in addition to sample size, include hunters not knowing exactly where they had been and mistakenly reporting for the wrong management unit; hunters reporting juvenile animals as adults; hunter inconvenience; higher costs than necessary due to hunters relaying information and experiences anecdotally, and hunter exaggeration or fabrication about harvest success. Reporting the wrong management area is not always a significant problem, because herd units often cross many management units, so someone incorrectly reporting an adjacent management unit may still be reporting for the same herd unit. Hunter inconvenience—the intrusiveness of calling people at home—can be intensified in some states in which harvest surveys for multiple species all use this method. Hunters there might be called numerous times if they hunted more than one big game species. This could represent a source of aggravation to an agency's foremost supportive constituency. However, in Montana, phone surveys for multiple

species including elk, deer, pronghorn, bear, upland birds and waterfowl, have identified fewer than 1% of the hunters surveyed being disgruntled by the calls (T. Lonner personal communication:1998).

Multiple Wave Mail Survey

In the past, some managers were reluctant to use mail surveys because of inherent biases in the methodology. However, this has changed as ways of compensating for biases have been built into the survey design. Currently, several states and provinces including Arizona, British Colombia, Wyoming and Washington, are using mail surveys as their primary source for harvest data. In fact, Wyoming, Washington and Arizona have been using mail surveys since they began doing harvest assessments in the 1960s or 1970s. By consistently improving the methodology over such spans of time, many of the problems with mail surveys have been rectified. Also, using the same methodology for so many years is beneficial because it provides for consistent datasets that are especially useful for identifying trends.

Nonresponse bias has historically been the most troublesome problem, but other biases, such as geographic bias, memory bias and general reporting inaccuracies, also have been a concern. Nonresponse bias—whereby surveys are not returned or are returned at a disproportional rate by sampled hunters—is solved by mailing multiple waves of surveys. After the first mailing, surveys are re-sent to hunters who did not return the first survey; agencies continue sending waves of surveys until they reach their target number (percentage) of returned surveys to achieve preset confidence level. Unfortunately, the necessity of mailing multiple waves of surveys to eliminate nonresponse bias offsets mail surveys' historically most attractive characteristics—reaching high numbers of hunters at a relatively low cost.

Mail surveys of the general public are considered satisfactory with a rate of return of less than 40%; hunting and fishing surveys, with only one or two reminders, typically achieve response rates of 60% to 90% (Smith 1959, Aney

Table 124. Magnitude of precision of random phone surveys concerning elk harvests in Colorado

Harvest	Area with large pool	Precision[a]	Area with small pool	Precision[a]
Bulls	4,850	±4	172	±23
Cows	3,400	±3	136	±20
Calves	338	±13	10	±84

Source: J. Ellenberger personal communication: 1998.

[a] Expressed as ± percentage

1974). In a mail survey of elk hunters, Smith (1959) noted an 89% response to an initial survey. A follow-up wave was sent to the nonrespondents, and 83% responded to it. Analysis has indicated that no serious bias results from non-responses when the rate of return is high (Smith, 1959). Rate of response to harvest mail surveys in the 1990s was as good or better than Smith reported in 1959. In 1996, British Columbia sold a total of 13,854 elk licenses and question-naires were sent to 9,260 hunters. Eighty percent (7,408) of the hunters who received the questionnaire completed and returned it, making the total sample size about 70% (I. Hatter personal communication:1998).

Geographic bias occurs when surveys are returned at dis-proportional rates from different geographic areas. This is caused by a myriad of socioeconomic and sociopolitical fac-tors. Geographic bias can easily be compensated for by fac-toring the response rates for different areas into the statisti-cal packages used to analyze the harvest data.

Memory bias typically occurs, when, by the time they re-ceive the survey, hunters have often forgotten what they did in the field. Common memory biases include locations hunted, location of harvest, number of animals seen and number of days hunted.

General reporting inaccuracy includes a broad scope of intentional and unintentional misreporting ranging the wrong management district to misrepresentations about harvest success or location. Other common misreporting includes hunters reporting their party's success as their own, identifying juvenile animals as adults and unwilling-ness to reveal their secret or special spot.

Check Stations

Although check stations are helpful as a means to cross check harvest data gathered by surveyors, they rarely are used as primary sources of data for overall harvest assess-ment. This is because they are too expensive to run on a large enough scale to gather adequate sample sizes. How-ever, a recent study by Steinard (1994), in which hunters leaving North Park, Colorado, were interviewed once at a check station and again 2 or 3 months later by telephone to determine if they had harvested an animal, showed a high degree of consistency ($P > 0.736$).

Most managers still feel that check stations are an invalu-able tool because they allow biologists to get a sense of what is really happening with harvests in the field (V. Cling-man personal communication:1998) and because they are extremely useful for gathering important data on the age and general health of harvested animals. These data help identify changes in sex and age ratios in specific herds. They

are not data than can be gathered on a reliable basis by any-one other than trained personnel. Another benefit of check stations is the personal contact between managers and hunters, and the good will generated for the wildlife agen-cies. The confidence and support of the hunting public for wildlife agencies cannot be overvalued (J. Ellenberger per-sonal communication:1998).

In addition to gathering important harvest and biological data, check stations often are operated in conjunction with conservation law enforcement activities (Low 1951, Thompson 1951, Aney 1974). However, to be an effective tool for conservation law enforcement, check stations must require all vehicles, including those of nonhunters, to stop and be checked for game. This is an inconvenience to the public that can negate any hope of generating good will for wildlife agencies and managers. To counter this, some states require that only successful hunters stop at check sta-tions, which eliminates conflicts with the general public, but this inhibits effective enforcement of conservation laws.

Drawbacks to check stations stem mostly from their high cost. Agencies cannot afford to staff enough stations to cover all game management units or areas with multiple ac-cess routes. Also, agencies are rarely able to staff check sta-tions 24 hours a day, although check stations may be staffed by volunteers, such as wildlife students, who appreciate the opportunity to gain field experience. However, hunters of-ten travel to and from hunting areas at odd hours and may pass a check station when it is closed. As a result, conserva-tion law enforcement activities have been de-emphasize as a check station operation in many jurisdictions.

Hunter Report Cards

Report cards are forms issued with each license or tag to be returned by each hunter at the end of the season. Informa-tion requested may include number of days hunted, loca-tions hunted, game harvested, sex or age of animals har-vested, and location of harvest. All hunters are required to respond in some states and, in others, only those hunters who have successfully harvested game that season.

Like check stations, report cards rarely are used as a pri-mary source of data for elk harvest assessments. However, unlike check stations, which still are used in some form in every western state, report cards use is nearly obsolete. Only Nevada uses a report card system for their primary source of elk harvest data. The decrease in use of report cards is due to their low return rate, high nonresponse bias and definite reporting biases. Many states that once used re-port cards for their primary elk harvest data (Idaho and Ore-gon, for example) have switched to random phone surveys.

From a logistical standpoint, check stations are an expensive way to gather primary harvest data. However, from the standpoint of public relations, as a ground-truthing mechanism for harvest assessment models and statistics, and for spot checking of conservation law compliance, the stations can have considerable merit. *Photos courtesy of the Colorado Division of Wildlife.*

Mandatory Reporting

Mandatory reporting requires all successful hunters to register their elk harvest with state wildlife authorities within a certain time frame. Although mandatory reporting can be an effective technique for states with a limited number of tags, it can be an enforcement nightmare for states with numerous tags. It also has negative public relations implications. Some hunters resent the imposition of having to drag in their elk to be checked within 10 days of harvest. Some hunters do not lend themselves to that sort of expedient reporting. Consequently, mandatory reporting is rarely used, and most managers feel it is unnecessary.

Outlook

Harvest assessments provide important data necessary for managers to determine the effectiveness of past regulations and to set new regulations. Although there are drawbacks to virtually every method, the precision and expediency of harvest assessments will continue to increase as methodologies are refined and computer data management and analysis become more powerful. Improved harvest assessments will be necessary to maintain elk herds in balance with habitats in transition because of human population

growth, sprawl, recreational demands, service demands and other influences.

The Future

Hunting regulations have grown radically more complex since the days when Theodore Roosevelt thrilled to the chase. Concepts of wildlife management have grown and branched continuously since Aldo Leopold planted the seeds more than 50 years ago. Without support for the ideas and visions of those men and the thousands of conservationists who followed their leads, few if any wild elk likely would exist in North America today.

At the beginning of the 20th century, public understanding and support of regulations helped protect the ragged remnants of once-great elk herds. Today, a century later, more and more people are exploring the ways in which changing landscapes make elk more vulnerable to hunting. In the future, wildlife managers almost certainly will be forced to create more complex hunting regulations. The burgeoning commercialization of elk meat, antlers and semen—and elk hunting as well—cast long shadows on the future of wild elk and good hunting. And, if North America's human population continues to grow at present rates, the habitat required by elk and cherished by elk hunters will erode steadily. But land managers, wildlife managers and hunters are joining together in efforts to foster healthy, well-balanced elk herds while sustaining elk hunting as a meaningful and rewarding pursuit. For their efforts to succeed, the public's continued endorsement of intelligent hunting and wildlife management will be essential.

Speaking at the 1986 Western States and Provinces Elk Workshop, in Coos Bay, Oregon, Jack Ward Thomas (1986:314) charted a sound course to guide wildlife managers into the future: "Those of us in elk and elk-hunting management will be forced to regulate hunter numbers, intensify management of hunting, assure elk habitat in more intensively managed forests, control access for hunters and others, increase coordination with land management for timber and grazing, *and* find a way to pay for it in state and federal agencies. New days are upon us and it is up to us, the wildlife management professionals, to devise, sell, and institute the new ways—additional ways—of management and funding that will be required to sustain elk and elk hunting as part of the way of life in the American West."

19

DALE E. TOWEILL AND JACK WARD THOMAS

The Future of Elk and Elk Management

I have but one lamp by which my feet are guided; and that is the lamp of experience. I have no way of judging the future but by the past.

Patrick Henry 1775 (in Platt 1993)

When *Elk of North America: Ecology and Management* was submitted for publication in 1980, the future for elk appeared bright, although prospects were mixed when considered state by state. In sharp contrast with a West-wide decline in mule deer numbers (perhaps not an unrelated occurrence), elk herds numbered approximately one-half million animals in North America and growing. Wildlife managers were beginning to voice concerns that the growth of elk herds evident in the 1970s could not be sustained—or even maintained.

In an effort to evaluate these concerns, elk managers in 16 states and provinces where elk occurred in significant numbers were queried about the future of elk populations in their jurisdictions. In half of those states and provinces (Alberta, British Columbia, California, Idaho, Montana, South Dakota, Utah and Washington), managers predicted that elk numbers would increase from 1975 levels (Peek et al. 1982a).

All were correct (Bunnell 1997). In fact, elk numbers increased by 75% in Alberta, growing from 12,000 in 1975 to 21,000 by 1995. In British Columbia, the increase was 200% during the same period—from 15,000 to 45,000. Increases within the United States were typically of lesser magnitude, although elk numbers in Utah increased 223%, as herds

grew from an estimated 18,000 in 1975 to 60,000 animals in 1995.

In contrast, wildlife managers in six states and provinces (Manitoba, Nevada, New Mexico, Oregon, Saskatchewan and Wyoming) predicted that elk herds would remain stable. All were wrong—dramatically wrong. The elk population in these six jurisdictions increased from about 170,000 elk in 1975 to nearly 300,000 in 1995—an increase of 76%.

Wildlife managers in only two states (Arizona and Colorado) predicted declines in elk populations from 1975 levels. They, too, were very wrong. Instead, the elk population in Arizona increased 340%, from an estimated 15,000 to 51,000 elk in 1995. In Colorado, the number of elk increased 93%, from 105,000 in 1975 to 203,000 in 1995 (Bunnell 1997).

By 2000, the Rocky Mountain Elk Foundation (RMEF) reported that elk in North America numbered some 1.2 million animals. In the last quarter of the 20th century, elk populations increased in every one of the 23 states and 7 provinces where elk populations existed in 1995. The number of elk hunters skyrocketed between 1975 and 1995, increasing 66% (from 531,046 to 797,445) in the United States, and 59% (from 23,971 to 40,385) in Canada. The number of elk harvested by hunters likewise increased—63% (from 100,903 to 160,084) in the United States and 39% (from 2,890 to 7,411) in Canada (Bunnell 1997).

Our primary intent in this concluding chapter is to examine the future of elk and elk management in North America. To do so, it is necessary to review the underlying successes in wildlife and land conservation and the evolution of federal law that made possible the almost incredible achievements in elk management during the 20th century.

These successes are inextricably tied to the evolution of policy related to management of the public lands—primarily in the western states and provinces. To understand our past policies is critical to understand how we have come to our present status related to elk and elk hunting. That understanding is, in turn, critical in divining what the future may hold.

The taproots of these successes are personified in the vision and subsequent actions of a failed cattleman of a century ago (who was to become president of the United States) and to the outcome of an epic philosophical struggle over how natural resources in North America would be treated. That great debate continues to this day over how best to use the natural resources of North America—the appropriate mix of preservation and conservation. This review begins with an overview of the evolution of conservation, wildlife law and wildlife management primarily as it pertained to elk management in the late 19th and the 20th

centuries. Particular emphasis is placed on the closing decades of the 20th century—the score of years that have passed after *Elk of North America: Ecology and Management* was published. The closing section contains our predictions for the future of elk and elk management in the 21st century. As noted by Patrick Henry, we have no way of seeing into the future other than by a careful evaluation of history. Our predictions are based on our own perceptions of historical trends, new developments and personal experiences from 65 cumulative years spent in careers in federal land and state wildlife management agencies.

Overview of Historic Factors Affecting Elk Management

The Beginning of Wildlife Conservation, 1900 to 1940

Conservation and the Roosevelt Doctrine

President Theodore Roosevelt could hardly have chosen a better philosophical basis for the United States' approach

"Opening" of the American West to settlement owed much to a series of survey expeditions in the last three decades of the 19th century. They were undertaken or underwritten by the U.S. government to discover the geologic and geographic nature of the landscape, the customs, temper and malleability of the Native people, opportunities for such enterprises as farming, ranching, mining, and the most practicable routes across the land for overland travelers and for the potential of transcontinental rail lines. One of those important expeditions was headed by Ferdinand V. Hayden. He and his party surveyed the Yellowstone region 4 years before the famous battle of the Little Bighorn not too far north of the expedition route. Above is a bivouac of the survey's photographic division, including soon-to-be-famed photographer William Henry Jackson, who took this photo below Grand Teton Mountain. The moose and elk (on the ground at the base of the left game pole) afforded the men a good bit of camp meat. Jackson wrote: "The game was plentiful in this isolated region; big horned mountain sheep, bears and elk ranged over the high plateau . . ." (Jackson 1947:164). *Photo courtesy of the U.S. Geological Survey.*

(also adopted in Canada) to land management than *conservation*. This approach ensured a long-term future for the management of renewable forest and range resources, and associated wildlife resources, even while striving to ensure careful husbandry of those resources on a local level and in a manner related to the local need. It quickly became obvious, even to the president's opponents, that conservation favored the long-term welfare of states and territories, by ensuring healthy and renewable natural resources in perpetuity.

Well-managed forest and range resources were conceived as the basis on which businesses and communities could be built and sustained over the long term. This philosophy was in sharp contrast to the "boom-and-bust" exploitation typical of rural western economies of the mid and late 19th century—exploitation that had already resulted in catastrophic depletions of nation's wildlife resources.

Roosevelt's chief forester Gifford Pinchot (1947:322–323) detailed how the concept of conservation came to him while he was riding horseback in Rock Creek Park near Washington, D.C., on a winter's day in 1907. "Suddenly, the idea flashed through my head that there was a unity in this complication—that the relation of one resource to another was not the end of the story . . . all of these separate questions fitted into and made up the one great central problem of the use of the earth for the good of man . . . here was one question, instead of many, one gigantic single problem that must be solved if the generations, as they came and went, were to live civilized, happy, useful lives in the lands which the Lord their God had given them."

He took the idea to Roosevelt who "understood, accepted, and adopted it without the smallest hesitation . . . It became the heart of his administration . . . Launching the conservation movement was the most significant achievement of the T.R. Administration, as he himself believed." (Pinchot 1947:326)

Roosevelt, in lock-step with Pinchot constantly maneuvering behind the scenes, worked tirelessly to hammer the conservation message home, championing "conservation through wise use" to governors of the states and members of Congress. By the end of his presidency, Roosevelt had become the chief spokesperson for the concept of conservation—both nationally and internationally. Roosevelt's conservation message and his friendship with Canadian Prime Minister Sir Wilfrid Laurier resulted in development of nearly identical wildlife management policies in Canada and in the United States, championed by such eminent conservationists as Sir Clifford Sifton in Canada. Sifton, despite his role as a developer of the Canadian West (which made him very wealthy), served as chairman of the Commission on Conservation, which focused public attention on issues of forest, fish and wildlife management between 1911 and

1919. Sir Clifford Sifton and C. Gordon Hewitt, Canada's chief entomologist and "father" of the 1916 Migratory Bird treaty, carried the parallel message of wildlife conservation in Canada.

Conservation rested on the assumption that wildlife, forests, ranges and water were renewable resources that might last forever if they were harvested *scientifically* and not faster than they reproduced and grew. Through his efforts, Roosevelt established his concept of conservation as the "Roosevelt Doctrine"—a doctrine that, in turn, established the basis for modern approaches to the management of natural resources. The Roosevelt doctrine consisted of three fundamental principles (Leopold 1933).

1. Natural resources can, and must, be managed as integrated systems. This laid the foundation for what is currently known as ecosystem management;
2. *Conservation through wise use* is a public responsibility, and ownership of wildlife and other natural resources are a public trust; and
3. The best scientific information and judgment were to be the basis for management decisions.

By the end of Roosevelt's presidency, the framework for management of a system of national forests and national wildlife refuges was firmly in place alongside a system of national parks. Although refuges and parks initially contributed significantly to the recovery of elk, their initial importance was dwarfed over time by the 172-million-acre National Forest System that was in place in the West by 1909 and managed under a philosophy that would later become known as multiple use sustained yield.

Wildlife Management

Throughout North America, management of wildlife as a renewable natural resource followed the same general pattern as management of trees and livestock forage, that is, conservation through wise use would allow wild animals to flourish if harvests were scientifically regulated. However, wild animals were unique in that they were a *mobile* resource, capable of moving wide distances and even capable of crossing international boundaries. This ability of animals to move across jurisdictional boundaries has placed wild animals in a unique category of resources since Roman times, when they were recognized as *ferae naturae*—belonging to no one while alive, becoming property only after being captured or killed (Bean 1977a). We see three key elements of overriding importance in the development of modern laws regulating wildlife management: (1) state ownership, (2) elimination of commercial markets, and (3) responsibility for establishment of regulations allowing private citizens to harvest surplus animals.

These elk antlers at the headquarters of Theodore Roosevelt's Elkhorn Ranch near the Little Missouri River in the Dakota Territory evidenced the future president's abiding interest in the species. "In the grove back of my ranch house when we first took possession," wrote Theodore Roosevelt (1896:150) of his Elkhorn Ranch along the Little Missouri in western North Dakota, "we found the skulls of two elk with interlocked antlers; one was a royal, the other had fourteen points. Theirs had been a duel to the death." That and writings about his hunting experiences in the 1880s led the ambitious New Yorker turned ill-fated rancher to an association with George Bird Grinnell, owner and publisher of *Field and Stream* magazine. Their discussions kindled Roosevelt's interest in wise use and preservation of wildlife and other natural resources. With a number of other sportsmen, Roosevelt and Grinnell founded the Boone and Crockett Club in 1887 (Brands 1997). That, in turn, culminated in his encouragement of and support for Gifford Pinchot's formulation of the term and concept of conservation. *Photo taken in 1882 by Theodore Roosevelt; courtesy of the U.S. Library of Congress.*

Ownership of wildlife was assumed by the United States at independence and, by virtue of not being expressly retained by the federal government, passed as a public trust responsibility to the states upon statehood, as clearly stated by Justice Edward White, writing for the majority of the Supreme Court, in *Geer v. Connecticut* in 1896. Justice White declared that states had the "right to control and regulate the common property in game," which was to be exercised "as a trust for the benefit of the people" [161 U.S. 519] (Bean 1977a, see also Horner 2000). The very mobility of wildlife dictates that many species (such as marine mammals and migratory birds) must be managed cooperatively by sovereign states under provisions of international treaties (Hewett 1921, Hayden 1942, Geist 1995a).

The critical importance of this ruling is that it not only declared public ownership of wildlife in law (de jure), but in fact (de facto). Thus, by law, wildlife may be held privately only in trust for the public, the basis for what has come to

be known as the public trust doctrine. Accordingly wildlife has been identified as a valuable commodity—no less than the money in an estate. Like any other trustee, the state is legally obligated (one of the obligations of statehood) to provide benefits to the beneficiary—namely, the citizens of the state (Horner 2000). Resolution of the issue of wildlife ownership (and, in the United States, the state's trust responsibility) is fundamental to the entire framework of wildlife management in North America, because at the heart of the public trust doctrine is the concept that certain natural resources are so valuable to the public and community well-being that the public's interest in these resources warrants legal protection (Blumm et al. 1997). Thus, the states, as trustees, may not allow privatization of wildlife for purposes of domestication or private use. In fact, as trustees, the states must act to prevent the spread of disease into wild stocks and must seek to preserve sufficient habitat for their well-being (Geist 1995a, Horner 2000). Public trust responsibility also dictates that wildlife may not be killed wantonly, either directly or by destruction of critical habitat. As a resource in public trust, wildlife may be harvested only for food, fur, in self-defense or protection of private property (Geist 1995a).

Elimination of markets in the meat, parts and products of wildlife was among the most important factors responsible for the tremendous successes in wildlife restoration in North America. By the end of the 19th century, unregulated market hunting for the table and for bird feathers had resulted in the destruction of the passenger pigeon and the decimation of populations of water birds and big game animals. Although regulations prohibiting sale of some wildlife parts were in place earlier, prohibition of the sale of wildlife meat in New York in 1911 marked the beginning of a nationwide trend. By 1915, all but 1 of the 48 states had passed similar legislation, and Canada followed with prohibition in some provinces beginning in 1920 (Geist 1995a). Subsequent provisions prohibiting international trade in wildlife and wildlife products have appeared in many federal acts and treaties (Bean 1983). Elimination of economic returns to an individual associated with the killing of excess wildlife has removed the danger of concentrated, market-driven harvests of wildlife, as well as market incentives for keeping some particularly desirable species uncommon (their market value increased by enforced scarcity).

The final component underlying modern wildlife management is the harvest of some animals of certain species (i.e., game animals), surplus to healthy and viable populations, to the public as beneficiaries of the state's trust responsibilities. This harvest is allocated, as is the harvest of trees and livestock forage, under provisions of the Roosevelt doctrine—that is, on the basis of public input informed by scientific information and judgment. The allocation of wildlife to the public owners of the wildlife resource makes every citizen a shareholder in resource management (Geist 1995a). As beneficiaries of the public trust and shareholders in wildlife resources, citizens have the right and perhaps a responsibility to make their wishes regarding wildlife management known to the state. Because wildlife management decisions must attempt to represent the desires of all concerned citizens while simultaneously ensuring that each state fulfills its public trust responsibilities, wildlife management has long been and likely will always be controversial—and all the more so because decisions must be made to satisfy a public increasingly divided philosophically on the many values that wildlife provide.

The Great Debate

Throughout the 20th century, both public land and wildlife management battles focused, ultimately, on the balance be-

Markets in wildlife meat, hides and other parts flourished during the last half of the 19th century. Elk were killed, sometimes by the wagonload, for their meat, hides or even just their "bugler" teeth. The elimination of such markets, mainly through promulgation of the Lacey Act of 1900, was a cornerstone of wildlife management, allowing for restoration of wildlife populations that had been jeopardized at the hands of market gunners. *Photo courtesy of the Wildlife Management Institute.*

tween exploitation and preservation of public resources—the Great Debate. In the beginning of the 20th century, the great debate raged among such icons as Gifford Pinchot (speaking for conservation), John D. Rockefeller (speaking for exploitation of forests and public resources for private gain) and John Muir (outspoken spiritual leader of the preservationist movement). The debate focused on land management, but the implications for wildlife management were profound.

The struggle between champions of exploitation and preservation of natural resources was the heart of the great debate and involved developing core values for North American society. Against this stark contrast, conservation—or wise use—was envisioned as a pendulum oscillating between the extreme positions of preservation and unimpeded exploitation driven by the springs of economic need and public opinion. The pendulum was pushed first one way and then another as personalities, policies and circumstances influenced management of natural resources. Throughout the 20th century, proponents of exploitation and preservation defined conservation differently as the pendulum shifted. It is this push and pull of the pendulum that provides a framework for evaluating past actions af-

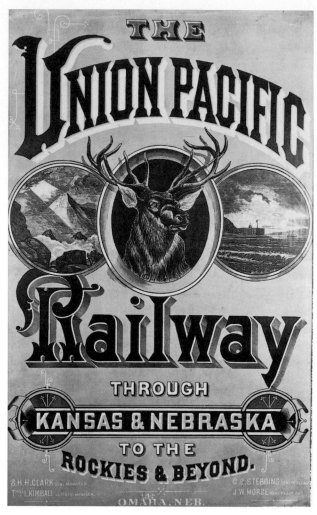

Along with majestic scenery, the image of the elk often was featured on billboards and posters to recruit both riders on newly constructed transcontinental railroad and settlers of prairie lands owned by the railroads. *Photos courtesy of the Union Pacific Railroad Museum.*

fecting elk management in the 20th century and, then, forecasting what is yet to be.

Funding for Wildlife Management

William H. Taft, who followed Theodore Roosevelt as president of the United States in 1909, failed to demonstrate much interest in conservation and became embroiled in the Tea Pot Dome scandal, which led to the firing of Pinchot for his opposition. Roosevelt returned from a prolonged sojourn in Africa, and was appalled at Taft's rejections of his philosophy of conservation. He ran for president for the Bull Moose Party, and so split the vote that Democrat Woodrow Wilson was elected. Woodrow Wilson focused on the First World War and its aftermath. That focus diverted attention from natural resource management and concerns over conservation. However, this was the quarter century (1900–1925) when private sportsmen's clubs became increasingly active in their attempts to reestablish elk

herds throughout the United States (see Chapter 15). Conservation as national policy rested on the laurels of the achievement of the period 1880 to 1910 and was maintained and addressed in a low-profile manner. The need for *conservation action* was forcibly brought to the fore of public attention by the combination of the Great Depression beginning in 1929 and the Dust Bowl Era of the 1930s (Trefethen 1975).

Human suffering brought about by the combined effects of the Great Depression following the stock market crash of 1929 and the Dust Bowl of 1928 to 1931 galvanized the political arena and the public as never before to accept and champion the notion that natural resources must be protected if they were to be maintained and the nations were to return to prosperity. Franklin Delano Roosevelt, sworn in as president in 1933, almost immediately implemented a series of programs that produced tremendous benefits to wildlife. Of particular importance to elk was the Fish and

Wildlife Coordination Act of 1934, which stipulated that wildlife conservation receive equal consideration with water resource development—and as later amended, that construction agencies consult with federal and state wildlife management agencies and provide compensation for wildlife habitat destroyed or impaired as a result of construction activities (Trefethen 1975). Franklin Roosevelt also created the U.S. Soil Conservation Service, and perhaps more important, the Civilian Conservation Corps. The Civilian Conservation Corps created a virtual army of over 3 million young workers who planted trees, fought wild fires, built lakes and trails in national forests, and worked in many other ways to restore wildlife habitat across the nation. Even more important, workers in the Civilian Conservation Corps lived and worked in conservation—and many took the skills and lessons from that work experience back home (Trefethen 1975).

However, of all that happened in the 1930s, perhaps no action was more significant to elk restoration and management than the combination of the passage of federal legislation that secured funding for state wildlife management agencies to restore wildlife populations.

To understand the great significance of a secure funding base for wildlife management, one must realize that unlike the control of lands under several types of ownership, management of wildlife was clearly recognized as the domain of the states since the period of initial settlement by Euro-Americans (Bean 1977a). Still, at the beginning of the 20th century, few states and provinces had any mechanism in place for funding wildlife management. Pioneers and settlers were accustomed to killing or taking wildlife without limitations. All of the early state wildlife agencies relied solely on appropriations by state legislatures, and what limited funding was available usually was directed to a few favored individuals as political patronage (Trefethen 1975). Funding for more comprehensive state programs in wildlife protection and conservation began to appear among the states in 1895, when the first hunting licenses were required in South Dakota. Even this idea took time to take root among the states. By 1922, 14 states still did not require hunting licenses of residents. Wildlife management, where it was practiced at all, consisted almost entirely of ineffective attempts at enforcement of game laws (Trefethen 1975).

With few game laws in place and almost no effective game law enforcement, devastation of America's wildlife resources through illegal hunting or wanton killing and habitat loss continued almost unabated well into the 20th century. Appalled by the devastation of wildlife in the 1920s, Aldo Leopold, a forester trained at Yale and experienced in the Forest Service (and, therefore, well-versed in Gifford Pinchot's concepts of sustainable management),

Franklin Delano Roosevelt initiated the Civilian Conservation Corps to alleviate unemployment brought about by the Great Depression and to rebuild and protect natural systems from drought, fire and neglect. Civilian Conservation Corps workers fought forest fires, cleared fire lanes, built hiking trails, planted trees on eroded hillsides, and otherwise improved tens of thousands of acres of wildlife habitat, from wetlands to mountain ridges. The program concluded with World War II, but while it prospered, the Civilian Conservation Corps employed more than 3 million men, revitalized overused landscape and certainly inspired the workers and others with a sense that human welfare and environmental health, which were inextricably linked. Although not considered the conservation visionary and crusader his cousin Theodore had been, Franklin Roosevelt clearly saw the imperative of sustaining the nation's renewable natural resources. "Conservation" said President Roosevelt shortly before his death, "is a basis for permanent peace" (Matthiessen 1959:219). *Photo courtesy of the U.S. Forest Service.*

wrote a series of articles between 1928 and 1931 that advocated formulation of an American game policy. These articles were expanded into the first textbook on wildlife management, published in 1933. Titled simply *Game Management,* Leopold's book proved a true classic, nearly as applicable today as it was 70 years ago. By codifying the underlying concepts fundamental to wildlife management, Leopold and others were able to influence legislation crucial to the funding of wildlife management, most notably, the Federal Aid in Wildlife Restoration Act (or Pittman-Robertson Act, named after its main sponsors, and often referred to as P-R Act).

The P-R program was based on an idea originated in 1925 to develop a feasible means of funding wildlife conservation (Williamson 1987). Approved by Congress in 1937, the law established an 11% manufacturer's excise tax on sporting rifles, shotguns and ammunition, and subsequently amended to include an 11% excise tax on archery equipment used in hunting and a 10% excise tax on handguns. The taxes were collected by the Treasury Department and transferred to the U.S. Fish and Wildlife Service. No more than 8% of funds collected could be used for administrative purposes. The remainder was to be returned to the states, using a formula based on state area and population.

States receiving P-R funds had to provide a match of 25% from state revenues, which the states derived (primarily) from the sale of hunting licenses and tags. This money would be used for either the purchase, development and management of land for wildlife restoration purposes, or for wildlife research directed to address problems affecting wildlife restoration. None could be used for wildlife law enforcement. The Act further coerced (some might say stimulated) the states by making any diversion of license and tag funding for any purpose other than wildlife management a reason for that state's wildlife agency to forfeit eligibility for P-R funding. This key provision helped ensure that all revenues derived from license and tag sales would be directed into wildlife management, rather than siphoned off for other, nonwildlife, purposes. The ploy worked across the board (Kallman et al. 1987).

With passage of the P-R Act, the burden of financial support for wildlife restoration was eased on state treasuries, as costs were shifted directly to persons who purchased sporting equipment as well as hunting licenses and tags. Elected state officials were relieved of the politically risky requirement to find funding sources within the general population to support state wildlife agencies. To a significant degree, this move depoliticized state wildlife agencies—but it also made state legislators less accountable to the public for their decisions affecting wildlife.

The new law, however, set up a dichotomy within agencies charged with both wildlife law enforcement and wildlife restoration. The law forced the agencies to divide license and tag income into two pools (one for law enforcement and another for the federal match). The effect on budgets was profound, and the results were nothing less than outstanding (Lyon and Thomas 1987). State wildlife management agencies were now able to translocate elk to many areas where herds had been extirpated (or nearly so), and to establish effective state law enforcement programs to enhance opportunities for newly established elk herds to expand and rebuild their numbers to levels that would support hunting.

However, there were unintended consequences. The newly established federal largess to state wildlife agencies sometimes resulted in the loss of all financial support from state general funds, as state legislators addressed more pressing concerns by "stealing from Peter to pay Paul." In addition, the provision in the P-R Act that protected hunting license and tag fees from diversion to other state purposes resulted in greater degrees of budgetary independence for state wildlife management agencies. This high degree of insulation from the state budgetary processes was furthered in some states by citizen initiatives designed to reduce the ability of state governors and legislatures to influence wildlife management decisions. Many state legislators and governors resented this loss of control, and that independence has been, in many states, gradually eroded over time.

Wildlife Management in the Mid-20th Century, 1940 to 1980

Conservation efforts were again put on the back burner in 1940, as the United States and Canada turned their attention to attaining victory in World War II. When the war ended in 1945, demand for hunting opportunities boomed. When servicemen returned to their homes, they bought licenses, tags and equipment, thereby swelling the coffers of state wildlife management agencies.

Several colleges and universities had developed training programs for wildlife professionals in the mid- to-late 1930s with the establishment of cooperative wildlife research units at select land-grant college campuses. Trained professionals, home from the wars, resumed their jobs in state and federal agencies. Their ranks were bolstered by veterans who entered college and university programs under the GI Bill, for professional training including wildlife management.

Progress in natural conservation efforts shifted from offense to defense during the presidency of Dwight Eisenhower (1952–1960) and his Secretary of Interior, Douglas McKay (Trefethen 1975). Budgets were tight, and Eisenhower focused most of his attention on domestic security. Conditions improved when McKay resigned in 1956, but subsequent battles over the use and development of public lands set the stage for massive changes in conservation policy (Trefethen 1975).

Those changes began following the election of John F. Kennedy in 1960. Kennedy (and subsequent presidents) ushered in programs focusing on domestic and environmental protection issues that complemented the maturing conservation movement.

The economic prosperity of the 1960s and 1970s and the

Funding provided by the Federal Aid in Wildlife Restoration (or Pittman-Robertson) Act of 1937 provided opportunities for state wildlife management agencies to conduct research and management studies essential to the restoration of elk and other wildlife. Such studies have used increasingly sophisticated equipment and analysis tools, net guns *(top)*, radio collars *(bottom left)* that allow biologists to track and locate animals, and immobilization drugs and delivery systems *(bottom right)* that enable efficient and safe handling of subject animals by experienced personnel. *Top photo by Milo Burcham. Bottom photos by Dale E. Toweill.*

increase in knowledge delivered by research scientists favored the rise of an environmental movement. It was based on public concerns about the concurrent loss of wild lands, renewable resources and the accelerating pace of technology (MacCleery and Le Master 1999). The growing public concerns translated into a flurry of legislation with emphasis on both conservation and preservation of remaining public resources. Many environmental laws were passed and signed into law during this period (1960–1980), and several deserve particular attention because of their ultimate influence on elk management.

Among these was the Multiple Use Sustained Yield (MUSY) Act of 1960. This Act, drafted and strongly supported by the Forest Service, was primarily an attempt to reaffirm conservation with a *multiple use mandate* that provided for management of natural resources on a sustainable basis. It also provided clear authority for the Forest Service to include fish and wildlife management and recreation, along with the already authorized management of timber, range and water, in forest management activities. One of the intents was to fend off continuing efforts to transfer Forest Service lands to the National Park Service. This ploy was largely successful and, by the 1990s, more recreational use, bolstered by hunting and fishing, occurred on national forests than on national parks.

In contrast to the Multiple Use Sustained Yield Act, which was a victory for conservationists, The Wilderness Act of 1964 was a clear victory for preservationists. It placed millions of acres of Forest Service land (much of it prime elk habitat) into permanent reserve status wherein road building and other human development was prohibited. However, in one sense, it preserved the status quo of human manipulations of elk habitat and back country hunting opportunities were concerned.

The National Environmental Policy Act (NEPA) that followed in 1969 was an effort to balance public lands decision making between the forces of protectionism and exploitation. This Act specifically directed federal agencies to use an interdisciplinary approach in decision making and to coordinate programs and plans regarding environmental protection. In addition, it directed federal agencies to consider explicitly impacts to amenity values as well as cost–benefit calculations in decisions. It also required that federal agencies develop and publish environmental impact statements related to the development and analysis of management alternatives for public review.

The impacts of National Environmental Policy Act were far-reaching. As a result, federal agencies greatly expanded their accountability for of environmental impacts, including those on wildlife and recreation opportunities associated with land management decisions. The disclosure of those impacts (and, in some cases, failure to disclose impacts that might have been anticipated) greatly increased public awareness and participation in management decision processes and prompted greater scrutiny of federal land management decisions. Increased federal litigation associated with noncompliance with the law became common.

However, no legislation contributed more directly to promote litigation over federal land management than did the Endangered Species Act (ESA) of 1973. This Act expanded and strengthened protection for endangered or threatened species as mandated by the Endangered Species Conservation Act of 1969. The Endangered Species Act directed federal agencies to protect and assist in the recovery of populations of rare species of animals and plants. The impacts of those requirements were to evolve disproportionately in their effect on the agencies' public land management capability.

The Endangered Species Act was a "trump act," because its requirements overrode other laws such as the Multiple Use Sustained Yield Act. Protection and recovery of animals and plants under the provision of the Endangered Species Act was mandated, resulting in actual and potential modification of all other uses of federal lands wherein such species occur. Failure to provide "adequate" protection from threatened and endangered species frequently resulted in appeals of land-use decisions and lawsuits precluding implementation of land management activities.

In addition, regulations issued pursuant to the National Forest Management Act of 1979 (NFMA) had the force of law and, in the case of national forests, were even more stringent than the requirements of the Endangered Species Act. The regulations (36 C.F.R. 219) stated that all native and desirable nonnative vertebrates were to be maintained in "viable numbers well-distributed in the planning area."

Federal agencies grappled with the consequences to traditional land management activities as they assessed environmental impacts of land management decisions required by National Environmental Policy Act, and to provide protection to threatened and endangered species as required by the Endangered Species Act. Managers struggled to organize the vast amount of information required to perform these assessments. This resulted in encyclopedic catalogs of wildlife species and habitats, as well as their interactions with a variety of management actions. The first of these, which appeared in 1979 (Thomas 1979b), specifically addressed elk management as a "featured species." The need to compile and present detailed information about abundant and widespread animals such as elk (as well as threatened and endangered species) was a major force that resulted in publication of *Elk of North America: Ecology and Management* (Thomas and Toweill 1982), which joined other volumes dealing with big game (Schmidt and Gilbert 1978), mule deer (Wallmo 1981), white-tailed deer (Halls 1984) and, some time later, moose (Franzmann and Schwartz 1997).

Actions Affecting Elk Management, 1980 to 2000

By 1980, the pendulum of conservation was clearly swinging back toward preservation, with the full impact of the myriad of poorly related case laws resulting from the environmental legislation of the 1960s and 1970s yet to come. The following discussions provide insights into a few of the major developments of the 1980s and 1990s. Although not exhaustive, they reflect land and wildlife management issues that have come to direct the future of elk management in North America. Those influences are expected to increase with time and be modified by political pressures and ever-evolving case law.

Timber Harvest on Public Lands

Ronald Reagan, elected as president of the United States 1980, attempted to reverse the pendulum swing of conservation by accelerating exploitation of public lands, including the national forests. When Reagan assumed office in 1981, he selected John Crowell as Undersecretary of Agriculture. Crowell (former chief counsel for Louisiana-Pacific Corporation, a wood products company) pushed the Forest Service hard to dramatically increase timber harvests using the plans being developed for each national forest as required by the National Forest Management Act. The Forest Service responded (albeit reluctantly), and by 1989 cutting of timber from the national forests had risen from less than 4 billion board feet per year to nearly 14 billion board feet per year—an increase of 350%.

However, this increase in annual timber cutting was not easily achieved—procedurally nor legally. National forest managers, required to comply with the legislation of the 1960s and 1970s, completed a stream of environmental analysis reports, land-use planning documents, and environmental impact statements in an attempt to simultaneously comply with the laws and meet the instructions from the Reagan Administration. These reports fueled a public increasingly dissatisfied with exploitation of natural resources—and provided the information necessary for judicial review of public policy.

The Clean Air Act of 1970 limited the use of fire as a management tool, further restricting management options. The Clean Water Act of 1972 required that buffers be provided along streams that might receive and transport sediment resulting from land management activities. Those requirements were reinforced with critical habitat restrictions if fish or other aquatic organisms deemed to be threatened or endangered were present either in or downstream from the site of any disturbance.

Faced with these and other restrictions on what had been routine management actions, forest managers found themselves increasingly unable to offer timber sales that did not conflict with legal mandates or face certain court challenges. Public land managers were increasingly caught in a vice between marching orders from the Administration they served (for increased timber harvests, liberalized grazing policies and enhanced mineral production) and environmental laws. There also was increasing pressure for employees deep in the agency's ranks to reconsider the capability of the forest to maintain these ordained timber harvest levels. Something had to give—and it did.

To compound the challenges faced by forest managers, public interest and participation in public land management expanded greatly over the period, fueled both by public support for environmental protection efforts (Dunlap and Mertig 1992, Cortner et al. 1999) and by President Reagan's directives to decentralize decision-making authority. Manager's discretion in decision making was replaced largely by requirements to withstand formal review of management decisions in courts of law. Administrative appeals and lawsuits proliferated (MacCleery and Le Master 1999) as parties favoring protection of resources and those favoring exploitation both appealed to the courts. The Forest Service was caught in the tightening vise.

One clear result of federal laws requiring public disclosure of more and more information was that, in the process, ever more issues were raised on which appellants could base administrative appeals and lawsuits. A new "conflict industry" of environmental analysts and writers emerged to face off with industry's spokespersons, lawyers and scientists. Public land management and regulatory agencies grappled with the information requirements of law and regulation in disputes about land management. More and more, such decisions were forcing land management agencies into federal court. What began as an effort by individual environmentalists engaged in pursuit of their interests through almost haphazard involvement with federal land management agencies soon coalesced into a more organized network of well-informed and like-minded activists.

"Amateur hour" on the part of both the agencies and the involved public came to an end as numerous individual groups and coalitions emerged and stepped up organizational efforts. Many of these groups began to receive financial backing from a widespread and diverse membership, which resulted in evolving organizations with paid leaders, executive officers, lawyers, fund-raisers, lobbyists, public relations specialists and the accouterments of large businesses. These groups learned to target land management agencies that failed to comply with the full range of environmental legislation passed in the 1960s and 1970s. Such organizations became increasingly effective in the pursuit of goals related to public lands management—reducing resource extraction and directing attention to long-ignored environmental problems. In doing so, they continued to build up memberships, resources and political power. Litigation was ever more effectively used as a means of ensuring that decisions complied with the letter of law. The outcome of many of the court decisions impressed land management agencies that the environmental legislation had teeth and meant just what it said (Parker 1995). Land managers began to spend more time with legal advisors to assure that the efforts of resource specialists would stand up to legal scrutiny.

This growth and development of environmental groups, and increasing effectiveness of those groups, galvanized those interested in resource extraction to improve coordination of their own efforts. These contingents, in contrast to environmental groups, had long been well organized, adequately funded by the extractive industries, well represented by corporate lawyers and often well-connected in state legislatures and Congress. The battle was for market share of extractable resources and the future of resource extraction. The struggle was waged in Congress, in land management agency directives, in public land planning policies, and—more and more—in the media, as opponents struggled to sway public opinion and support.

Although the two sides occasionally took aim at one another, they more commonly fought their battles through the surrogate action of attacking federal land management agencies—primarily the Forest Service. Such attacks were "safe" tactics to raise money and satisfy constituencies, because the agencies could not—or would not—counter effectively. Attacks on government agencies (and even on government employees in the performance of duties), no matter how outlandish, became a routine tactic in an increasingly discourteous political discourse. All too often, simplification of complex issues, demonization of the positions of opposing interests and personalities involved and selective ignorance of guiding laws and principles replaced informed debate.

Despite the legal wranglings, acceleration of timber harvest during the Reagan Administration proved beneficial to elk—at least for a time. Elk commonly flourish on the forage provided by clearcuts and openings in the forest canopy until the new forest closes the canopy. A continuous supply of forage resulted from new cutting units as older forage areas were diminished or lost due to developing tree stands. However, the reduction in cover related to timber cutting and the proliferation of roads associated with timber sales, sometimes at a density of 4 to 8 miles per square mile increased elk vulnerability to hunters (Heib 1976, Perry and Overly 1977, Lyon 1979a, Rost and Bailey 1979, Witmer and deCalesta 1985, Cole et al. 1997, Rowland et al. 2000, see also Chapters 13 and 18).

With William Clinton's defeat of George H. W. Bush in the presidential election of 1992, the pendulum began to swing back from emphasis on commercial aspects of public land management that had personified the Reagan Administration, and toward preservation and increased environmental concern. However, it should be recognized that this shift was due as much to forced compliance with environmental laws passed in the 1970s as to a shift in political philosophy. In fact, from its peak during the Reagan and Bush years, a large part of the timber harvest decline from national forests occurred *before* Clinton took office.

Despite the continuing shift in conservation focus—or perhaps because of it—the groups on both sides, the emerging conflict industry, continued to fight and even escalate the battle. The battle continued to center on federal land management agencies (Thomas 2000). But, to an increasing degree, the state wildlife management agencies became targets as well, as opponents began to home in on individual state legislative bodies and local economic issues. In an interesting twist, the State of Idaho sought to acquire some degree of management control (and any associated profits therefrom) over forest lands in Idaho in 1998 (Federal Lands Task Force 1998), just two years after the Idaho legislature passed H.B. 794 (1996, codified at *Idaho Code* Section 58-1201)—a bill wherein the state renounced its obligations as a trustee to protect the state's natural resources under the public trust doctrine. Although Blumm et al. (1997) and Horner (2000) argued that H.B. 794 violated the Idaho Constitution and various other statutes, promulgation of such an act, and the effort to gain profitability by assuming management of federal lands, reflected western discomfort with both federal land management policy and the state's responsibilities for protection of natural resources.

By the late 1990s, local people with interests in the conflict over management of public lands, both those favoring extraction and those favoring preservation, began to realize that continuous exacerbation of the decades-long struggle was playing havoc with the social fabric of resource-dependent communities. The toll on the agencies—particularly on those in field assignments—was obvious as well. More and more, veterans of the public land management "wars" realized the truth in the ancient adage from the Indian subcontinent that "When elephants fight, the grass suffers." Only the elephants—the groups vying for public support and political power that compose the conflict industry—benefitted from the struggle. At a national scale, the fallout from these ongoing struggles was small, but local people and the resources on which they were dependent suffered as active land management slowed. Timber sales in particular were dramatically reduced in number. Processes related to initiation of management actions were prolonged or postponed—sometimes for years. Associated costs skyrocketed—in terms of dollars and people power as well as in credibility and good will. Social capital was rapidly depleted (Knight and Landres 1998, Wondolleck and Yaffee 2000).

A number of efforts emerged across the West to push the conflict industry aside or at least into the background. Attempts were made to grasp more local control through various sorts of collaborative processes (Knight and Landres 1998, Cortner and Moote 1999). There was growing recognition that, in addition to the more traditional constructs of resource management agencies, natural resources must be managed as a social value (Kennedy and Thomas 1995).

Some collaborative efforts failed after promising starts, others succeeded to varying degree, and still others are still in the process. New efforts are on the horizon. Government land management agencies, knowing that they cannot hand off either authority or responsibility, are working with these groups to develop means and processes to marginalize the hard-core conflict industry. The means to achieve that end are the establishment and evolution of new processes incorporating collaborative planning and management and new expanded views of economics (Power 1995) that will fit under the umbrella of ecosystem management (Kessler and Salwasser 1995).

Public Land Grazing

Efforts to decentralize decision making during the Reagan Administration (1981–1989) were met with enthusiasm in the West. Logically, most enthusiastic were those with permits to graze livestock on public lands, typically under conditions prescribed by the Forest Service or Bureau of Land Management. These permits are considered a privilege by the federal government and the federal courts. Nevertheless, in the case of Forest Service, leases were passed from owner to owner of the "base property" to which the permit was assigned. For those with such permits, the federal grazing allotment formed an integral component of ranch operations. The Bureau of Land Management issues grazing permits on a 10-year basis (Cubbage et al. 1993).

Grazing fees imposed by the government are determined by a formula set by Congress. These fees, in recent years, have fluctuated from $1.20 to $1.50 per animal unit month. An animal unit month is equivalent to the amount of forage consumed by a cow/calf pair or one bull or seven sheep or one horse over a one-month period. While valid comparisons with fees paid for grazing on private lands are difficult, because of varying types of arrangements and circumstances, they are nearly always greater than the fees paid for public land grazing.

The differences between fees paid to graze on private land versus those paid for public land are often cited by opponents as evidence of a subsidy for permit holders. We believe that most opponents are more concerned about environmental effects of livestock grazing than about economic returns to the federal treasury. Bringing up subsidized grazing fees without full examination of the circumstances makes a good political play, ensuring an audience for discussion of public policy.

During the Reagan Administration, grazing permittees began to agitate not only for decentralization of decisions regarding public land use, but for privatization of grazing permits—in other words, the establishment of grazing on federal lands as a right rather than a privilege. In doing so, they cited both states' rights issues and the historic practice of treating the permits as property transferable with ranch base property. Some went so far as to demand that the federal government cede land ownership to the states or sell or deed that land to the private sector. This Sagebrush Rebellion privatization ploy was quelled by the courts, but it focused a great deal of attention on grazing policy and associated environmental impacts of public land grazing. These efforts produced a backlash from certain environmentalists, who then focused on the elimination of livestock use of federal lands (McDonnell and Bates 1993).

The proposal to eliminate livestock grazing from the federal lands was championed by many who sought restoration of "natural" conditions assumed to favor native wildlife (Ferguson and Ferguson 1983). Conversely, some opponents argued that elimination of federal land grazing would reduce elk and deer numbers, because livestock grazing on public lands occurred during the spring, summer and autumn on high elevation ranges of federal lands where forage was reasonably abundant. As accumulating snow made food on these ranges inaccessible, elk and mule deer moved to traditional, lower elevation winter ranges where snow depths were less and temperatures more moderate. Livestock were commonly moved to winter range a month or so earlier. Because most lower elevation winter ranges were in private ownership (often the base property tied to the federal land grazing permit), ranchers were obligated by circumstance to provide privately owned forage for elk and deer. This could be considered, to some degree, quid pro quo for the grazing of livestock on public lands at other times of the year.

In the booming economic times of the 1990s, this situation was quickly transformed into quite a different issue.

By the end of the 20th century, demand emerged for the elimination of all livestock grazing on public lands, proponents of which believed that this change would increase the amount of forage available for wildlife. On the contrary, such a move could have a variety of adverse impacts on wildlife. More intensive grazing by domestic livestock on low-elevation private lands would reduce the amount of forage available there during the winter. Faced with a reduction in the total amount of forage available for domestic livestock, ranchers might be less willing to allow elk to compete with their livestock for forage on winter ranges. Perhaps more important, ranchers might be forced to sell ranchland for commercial or housing developments, eliminating much of the critical low-elevation habitat necessary to support elk during winter. *Photo by A. Lorin Ward.*

This was a period during which western states experienced unprecedented population growth, as people left eastern and southern states for the climate, cleaner air, lower population densities and relatively relaxed lifestyles of the West. The population of many western states increased by 10% to 30% during this time (1980–2000). Three trends in the West became gradually apparent: (1) increased densities of people, (2) increased economic activities dependent on public lands access, and (3) significant changes in ecological conditions (Knight and Clark 1998). The changes in ecological conditions included changes in plant communities influenced by human activities and coincident invasions by non-native noxious species of plants, significant loss of low-elevation areas for winter big game animals due to development, and changes in the numbers and influence of predatory species.

The workings of Adam Smith's "invisible hand" of unfettered economics produced an economic godsend to many ranchers who were struggling to hold onto marginally profitable ranches. Increasing numbers of people, without the need for the land to produce income, purchased operational ranches for subdivision into ranchettes and retirement homes or for "hobby ranching" (Knight and Landres 1998).

Despite efforts by some states and counties to preserve open space by taxation of developers and institution of zoning management schemes to help maintain the economic and social viability of ranches, the press of newcomers on open spaces—particularly where those lands were adjacent to federal lands—was inexorable. Many counties had no open land protective measures in place. In keeping with the western code of "nobody tells me what I can or cannot do with my land," many counties still are devoid of zoning or planning.

Taxation, in many cases, became a primary culprit driving the conversion of open lands into development, as inheritance taxes ballooned when the values formerly attributed to marginal ranch operations were inflated by valuations based on potential for just such development. Sons and daughters—in many cases, literally the sons and daughters of the pioneers—often had no choice but to yield to the highest bidder. All too often the low elevation complement to the high elevation habitat was and is being lost to suburbs, golf courses, shopping malls, ranchettes and hobby ranches.

In the face of economic pressures, under which most people have opted for maximum economic return for their possessions and investments, others, in growing numbers, choose options that ensure the land they love remains undeveloped. The most common course of action in achieving that end is the implementation of a *conservation easement* as a means of simultaneously maintaining viable farms and open space. In such cases, some private or public entity purchases the development rights from the owner (or the owner might donate such rights to a recognized nonprofit entity), thereby ensuring that the property could never be developed. With development no longer an option, tax liability is reduced to correspond with designation as farmland or open land with no development potential. The returns from the sale of development rights can be used to finance continued operations. With a conservation easement in place, a landowner has the option of donating the easement to a land management agency or nonprofit conservation organization, thereby gaining a tax liability reduction equal to the difference between assessed value of the land before and after establishment of the easement.

Other mechanisms can assure (or at least enhance) the value of these private lands for wildlife and open space. These include state wildlife management agencies assuming fiscal responsibility for wildlife-associated damages, leasing of hunting rights, payments to landowners for allowing hunter access, and even providing landowners with tags for big game on their property that can be used for personal use or sold for profit. Although the programs differ from state to state, the rationale is constant: maintenance of open space for wildlife habitat and preservation of aesthetic values. And it provides for landowners to benefit emotionally and economically—a win–win–win scenario for wildlife, landowners and hunters. Even so, such proposals have set off a firestorm of controversy in some states. These controversies often take on overtones of class warfare, pitting wealthy landowners and wealthy hunters against antihunters and those who choose to believe that free hunting and access, even on the private land of others, is a birthright.

Access Management

The acceleration of timber harvest on national forests in the 1970s and 1980s was accompanied by rapid expansion of the system of roads needed to access timber for cutting and transport to mills. Elk managers had detected local declines in elk numbers that were attributed to a proliferation of roads and timber cuts during the period 1950 to 1980. This resulted in development of management guidelines for designing roads and timber sales. To maximize overall benefits from logging operations and minimize adverse impacts on elk herds and hunting experience, the guidelines determined timber cutting units through criteria for sizing, spacing and juxtapositions, along with some road closures (Thomas 1979, Thomas et al. 1988). Such approaches became widespread throughout public lands in the West outside of national parks.

By the end of the 1980s, the association between roads, timber harvests and local declines in elk numbers was obvious. The issue involved far more than the disturbances connected with timber harvest and the traffic on roads that elk now avoided. The environmental changes dramatically altered the vulnerability of elk to hunters during hunting seasons as well (see Chapters 13 and 18). Timber removal temporarily reduced the cover that once provided ability for elk to escape detection, and the vast network of roads associated with timber management allowed a greater number of hunters rapid access to places where elk could be intercepted. As vulnerability increased and hunter numbers were not reduced accordingly, mature bull elk were overharvested in many areas, resulting in reduced reproductive performance in some herds (Mitchell and Lincoln 1973, Hershey and Leege 1982, Freddy 1987a, Noyes et al. 1996). Circumstances surrounding hunting became less and less connected with concepts of fair chase as elk in some heavily cut-over regions almost literally had no place to hide from hunters during traditional elk hunting seasons.

Elk and hunter management is a prerogative of state wildlife management agencies, but habitat management (including road management) in the United States is the prerogative of the federal, state or private landowners. Some state agencies responded to the increasing vulnerability of elk and diminishing opportunity for fair chase hunting by shortening seasons and reducing hunter numbers. They appealed to forestland managers for assistance in reducing elk vulnerability by reducing the number of roads accessible to vehicular traffic.

The result was the development of access management programs, wherein state wildlife management agencies worked with federal land managers to select and close roads no longer needed for timber harvest or management either temporarily or long term. These road closures, whether during hunting season or year-round, reduced elk vulnerability to hunters as the animals could substitute terrain and distance for cover. Terrain, in the form of intervening ridges and hills, blocked elk from view from open roads, while walking distance from road closure barriers reduced the number and frequency of hunters and the speed with which they could venture into areas where roads were closed (Rowland et al. 2000).

Various road closure programs were deemed effective in reducing elk vulnerability to hunters, allowing state and federal agencies simultaneously and in collaboration to meet their jointly derived objectives for elk and timber management. Road closures also aided federal land management agencies to resolve other concerns emanating from the extensive road networks. In particular, closure of roads benefited federal agencies by simultaneously reducing sedimentation damage to rivers and streams resulting from vehicle travel on unprotected dirt and gravel roads (especially during the rain and snow events that often coincided with periods of high road use during fall hunting seasons) and reducing the annual costs of road maintenance.

The road system on national forests did, and do, have extensive maintenance backlogs. By the late 1980s, budget requests from federal land management agencies for road maintenance were routinely refused while new roads were routinely funded. Budget inadequacies translated directly into fewer people and resources available to maintain ever-increasing miles of roads—even while agencies were, at the same time, required by federal laws to reduce the impacts of a deteriorating road system. As a result, federal land management agencies, with no other choices available, became active partners in reducing the system of open roads. Unnecessary roads (evaluated in both short- and long-term bases) were closed and old road surfaces were revegetated. A serendipitous effect of these closures was further reduction of elk vulnerability to hunters, which made the habitat more effective for elk.

Closure of roads to vehicles on public lands were (and are) perceived by many citizens, particularly locals, as a federal "lock up" of public lands—a deliberate attempt to deny them access to lands that they, as citizens, own in part with all other citizens. Many had used the forest road system to reach favorite camping, hunting and fishing spots for years. A common message to forest managers across the West has been that federal land management agencies must ensure some level of access to public lands for the benefit of local communities and for recreation. This is a growing tension between the desire of some for totally unrestricted access and the need for a significant reduction in roads for environmental reasons, including enhancement of habitat effectiveness for such species as elk.

Since 1980, recreation on public lands has taken on an entirely new context with the development and popularity of efficient and reliable off-road vehicles (ORVs). These machines are immensely popular with recreationists (and are becoming more so) because of their ease of use, ability to navigate difficult terrain and affordability. Public lands, because of their expanse, availability and the tolerance of many public land managers, receive much of the impacts associated with the use of these vehicles. The impact of these vehicles can be far from benign. Off-road use by ORVs can destroy vegetation, cause development of ruts and soil erosion, and disturb wildlife and other recreational users. Damage from ORVs, similar to damage from unimproved roads, usually is greatest following rain and snow events typical of the autumn elk and deer hunting seasons.

ORVs have become a staple piece of hunting equipment for many hunters. ORVs allow hunters to transport their equipment far from standard roads, and to transport dead elk relatively easily from areas and distances that would and did present significant barriers to those hunting on foot. In short, these machines have increased elk vulnerability to hunters in much the same manner as the proliferation of roads did in the 1970s and 1980s.

However, damage to public lands associated with ORV use extends far beyond the impacts caused by hunters on foot or transported by horses confined to established trails. ORV users have proliferated tremendously as the population of Western states has increased—and those numbers continue to increase. ORV users are increasingly attracted to key parcels of public lands where access is readily available, concentrating both the use of ORVs and the potential damage associated with that use. Public land managers, faced with a fixed amount of land impacted by more people reflecting more diverse recreational interests, more use by (and damage associated with) ORV users, and reductions in budgets for rehabilitating landscapes, are scrambling to find a means of dealing with these issues. The ORV management problem is a classic vicious circle that will not go away. It will become more vicious over time for, in reality, it represents a clash of cultures.

The Office of Management and Budget and Congressional budget committees proved (until the mid-1990s) far

Off-road vehicles (ORVs) have become an increasingly important piece of equipment not only for hunters, but also for many other recreational users of public lands. These machines provide a valuable service to many people who would not otherwise have access to public lands. However, ORVs also provide headaches for land managers who must deal with damages that they cause to roads, trails and fragile landscapes and for wildlife management agencies concerned with increased in elk vulnerability as a result of more mobile hunters during elk hunting seasons. *Photo courtesy of the U.S. Bureau of Land Management.*

more willing to fund more roads to facilitate timber extraction than they were to fund road maintenance. Economists refer to these decisions not to face costs associated with an action as externalities—or costs not considered in the short term.

By the 1990s, these mounting externalities could no longer be ignored. The consequences of a road system that was not maintained were accumulating and becoming more and more obvious. Congress, in 1994, simply refused to continue to fund roads built to access timber that could not be brought to market at a profit for taxpayers. In the late 1990s, the Chief of the Forest Service, Michael Dombeck, ordered a review of roads on the National Forest System. Roads were to be inventoried and recommendations made for each road segment. Roads to be upgraded were to be identified, as were roads to be maintained and opened for use. Similarly, roads were to be identified for closure, abandonment with no maintenance and "putting to bed" (i.e., obliteration and revegetation).

Some ORV users have seen this effort, no matter how well founded from an environmental or wildlife management standpoint, as an attack on their recreational activities—and their "rights" to recreate on public land. Some have gone so far as to propose ulterior motives and sinister plots to lock up federal lands as the real motivation for these actions.

Unfortunately, in 2000, these fears were magnified by the simultaneous, although not directly related, instructions from President Clinton to the Forest Service to consider the status of all roadless areas of more than 5,000 acres and make recommendations as to their future status. The decision was made in late 2000 to maintain all such areas in roadless status. This was seen by some as complete verification of their worst suspicions. Shortly after his inauguration in 2001, President George W. Bush instructed that President Clinton's decision regarding roadless areas be held in abeyance pending review. And, lawsuits were filed in Idaho and Utah, maintaining that the process followed was in violation of the National Forest Management Act and the National Environmental Policy Act.

Conflicts over road management and protection of roadless areas will continue with significant importance to elk habitat effectiveness and elk vulnerability during hunting seasons. Our best advice is full participation of those interested in elk welfare and freedom to use ORVs in the next round of forest planning. The old adage of "Come, let us reason together" will produce better, more socially acceptable results than the political brouhaha that seems likely to erupt.

Unfortunately, relatively little progress has been made in regulating the use of these machines, particularly when they are used away from established roads. Management of the operators of these machines will require new collaborative approaches—perhaps including licensing the operators of these vehicles for off-road use.

Endangered Species

Attention to protection of threatened and endangered species was addressed in 1966 with the Endangered Species Preservation Act. Protection was expanded to include all native vertebrates, mollusks and crustaceans in 1969 with passage of the Endangered Species Conservation Act, and authority for the protection of threatened or endangered species was further enhanced in 1973 with passage of the Endangered Species Act (PL 93-205). The 1973 Act extended protection to subspecies and any "viable population segment thereof" (Czech and Krausman 2000).

The Endangered Species Act of 1973 greatly broadened the scope and authority of federal regulations for the protection of species listed as threatened and endangered. The Act was used extensively in the final two decades of the 20th century to push the conservation pendulum back toward preservation—and it was a push with considerable vigor (Czech and Krausman 2000).

In addition, the Forest Service promulgated regulations (which carry the force of law) under auspices of the National Forest Management Act of 1976, which calls for maintaining viable populations of all native and desirable nonnative species in a well-distributed fashion throughout planning areas. This requirement, related solely to National Forest System lands, is more stringent in terms of its requirements upon land managers than is the Endangered Species Act.

Proponents of preservation captured public sentiments that favored widespread restoration of native species that had fared poorly as a result of human activities. As a result, they promoted an agenda that featured protection for species that were never abundant, species that were adapted to particular rare or unusual habitat types or that occupied marginal habitats near the limits of their natural distribution. Protection for these species required protection or restoration of rare or declining types of habitat wherever found, and whether or not actually occupied by the species. The most celebrated instance was protection for the northern spotted owl, a reclusive bird associated with old-growth timber stands.

The northern spotted owl is an inhabitant primarily of forests west of the Cascades in Washington, Oregon, northern California and British Columbia. These forests are characterized by big, old trees—the very kind that are most profitable as timber. Such forests take at least a number of human generations to develop, and they then may persist for hundreds of years. Cutting of old growth has essentially amounted to "mining" this successional stage of the forest, because these trees were cut significantly faster than they could be replaced by new old-growth forests—even if that were planned. Although cutting of old-growth forests generated industry jobs and supported timber communities, the acreage of old growth was rapidly diminishing by 1980. This resulted in an outcry of concern and protest (Thomas et al. 1990).

Although the cut-over forests provided excellent foraging habitats for elk (at least until regenerating trees reached the pole/sapling stage, when shade reduced the production of grasses, forbs, and shrubs), species dependent on old growth (such as the spotted owl) were declining even faster that the old-growth timber was being cut. It was feared that spotted owls and other species associated with old-growth forests were unable to cross the ever-widening "seas" of young stands separating ever-smaller "islands" of old trees (Thomas et al. 1990).

The battle over the future of old-growth forest, particularly forests included in the timber base on National Forest System lands that were scheduled for harvest under operational forest plans, accelerated during the presidency of George H. W. Bush (1989–1993). The Directors of the U.S. Fish and Wildlife Service, Bureau of Land Management, National Park Service, and the Chief of the Forest Service were frustrated by the disconnect between the requirements of the Endangered Species Act and the Forest Service's regulations, and by the economic/social/political consequences of actions taken for complying with the law. The consequences of certain social and economic disruptions—of whatever magnitude—were simply too tough to face politically with the information at hand (Yaffee 1994).

The directors appointed a select team of scientists and biologists to develop an array of management alternatives, and to sort fact from rhetoric. This group, the Interagency Scientific Committee, proposed a strategy to assure continued viability of the northern spotted owl as mandated by the Endangered Species Act and the Forest Service's regulations (Thomas et al. 1990). The costs associated with this strategy, in terms of reduction in timber cut from the public lands, set off a political firestorm. Following initial acceptance of the strategy by all involved agency heads, the director of the Bureau of Land Management pulled out of the agreement and announced he had a better and less costly plan.

In the meantime, the House Agriculture Committee named a group of four scientists—pejoratively referred to by a timber industry spokesperson as the Gang of Four—to produce an array of alternatives for consideration by Congress. The alternatives, for the first time, considered the im-

pacts on threatened and endangered species of salmon, also due protection under provisions of the Endangered Species Act (Johnson et al. 1990). Looking at the report and judging the political climate, the House Agriculture Committee deferred addressing alternatives until after the presidential election of 1992.

Resolution of this issue became an issue of national attention during the presidential campaign of 1992, as candidates staked out differing positions. President George H. W. Bush, characterizing the issue as "owls versus jobs," supported the timber industry position. Independent candidate Ross Perot scathingly criticized all involved for their concerns about endangered species when humans would suffer significant consequences of management actions. William Clinton, the Democratic Party candidate, assumed a neutral stance, but promised, if elected, to resolve the issue within 6 months of assuming office.

Clinton was elected and, as promised, convened a regional "timber summit" to identify a conservation-based outcome. Following this summit, he appointed yet another team, the Forest Ecosystem Management Assessment Team and provided guidance for the delivery of an assessment of alternative management strategies for his consideration. When that report was delivered (Forest Ecosystem Management Assessment Team 1993), President Clinton selected an alternative promptly dubbed the President's Plan. That alternative reduced the amount of timber expected to be cut on federal lands in western Oregon and Washington from about 4 billion board feet per year to some 1 billion board feet per year. In reality, constraints added during subsequent processes of an environmental impact statement and a Record of Decision leading to final adoption of the plan reduced the actual amount of timber offered for sale to an average of about 250 million board feet per year from the plan's inception in 1993 through 2000.

Using this response to an "endangered species crisis" as an example, we ask: "How do such actions taken to protect various 'threatened' species affect elk?" Following timber harvest, each logged site is highly productive of forage for elk and deer for a relatively brief period. After 10 to 20 years, young growing trees will develop a forest canopy that will shade the ground, preventing vigorous growth of the grasses, forbs, and shrubs that flourished after the logging. This transitory stage, so valuable to elk for foraging areas, exists only for a relatively small portion of time between initial harvest and subsequent cutting in, say, 80 to 100 years. In a fully managed forest on an 80-year rotation cycle (the time between stand regeneration and final harvest of that stand), 12% to 25% of the area could be expected to produce a significant amount of forage for elk and deer each year.

However, the strategy selected to favor old-growth associated species and anadromous fish in the Pacific Northwest has set aside slightly more than 16 million acres (6.5 million ha) in reserves. These are areas where, to assure restoration of old forests, there will be *no* cutting of trees (beyond thinning to speed the development of large trees in stands less than 80 years old). Those acres make up some 67% of the federal land within the area considered—primarily federal lands west of the Cascades in Oregon, Washington, and northern California (Forest Ecosystem Management Assessment Team 1993). As a result, there will be much less area available to timber cutting and much less timber cut. This translates into diminishing areas of prime forage for elk and deer as time passes. Forage areas will be limited to natural openings created by natural processes such as wildfire, avalanche chutes, blowdown or trees killed by disease or pests—and these will be relatively rare compared with openings created by routine timber cutting. These sites are designated as high priority for protection from stand-replacing wildfire. Elk numbers in these areas are likely to decline as the forests become older and as forage production is diminished.

Overall, timber cutting on the national forests in this area has declined steadily since the late 1980s from over 4.5 billion board feet per year to approximately 250 million board feet per year in 2000. Assuming that the cutting rate of 1 million board feet per year (or likely less) is to become the norm, forested acres that can produce elk forage will dramatically decline in coming decades. Forage available and quality in forested areas can be expected to emerge rapidly as a significant limiting factor for elk and, in turn, elk hunting on national forests in those areas.

Timber cutting in mature and old-growth stands on adjacent private lands also may be effected by forced compliance with the recovery plans produced by the Fish and Wildlife Service, as directed by the Endangered Species Act. Where that occurs, there is a question of "takings" of private property by the government. These issues are still working their way through the federal court system (Meltz et al. 1999).

Other controversies of critical importance to elk management have arisen more recently relative to the Endangered Species Act. There are controversies that will continue to impact elk management well into the 21st century. Although wolves had dispersed from Canada into the northern Rocky Mountains for years, few if any found mates and formed packs in the United States. Following completion of the Northern Rocky Mountain Wolf Recovery Plan (U.S. Fish and Wildlife Service 1987) and completion of an Environmental Impact Statement (U.S. Fish and Wildlife Service 1994), wolves from Canada were introduced into Yellowstone National Park and central Idaho in 1995 and 1996.

Wolf reintroduction was highly controversial then, and remains so today. Introductions lacked support from nearby communities and faced active opposition from the livestock industry as well as from a significant number of hunters and political leaders. In Idaho, the legislature specifically banned the state wildlife management agency from any involvement in wolf reintroduction or management.

Some citizens expressed fear for the safety of their children as well as their livestock and pets. As federal land management and regulatory agencies took actions mandated by the Endangered Species Act to assure establishment of the species, significant numbers of Westerners came to see wolf introduction as a federal preservationist action imposed on an unwilling populace. State wildlife management agencies, dependent on income from sale of hunting licenses and tags, found their elk and deer resources beset to some unknown extent by a new population of predators.

Stable or declining agency budgets were increasingly devoted to burgeoning predator management demands. Widespread disgruntlement about wolf reintroduction persists in western states about the action itself and about the lack of adequate financial support to allow affected states to assume management of wolves without cutting funds from other, more traditional programs—"The feds take the action and the states have to deal with it."

Limited data have not demonstrated that wolves have significantly reduced elk numbers. Despite the facts that introduced wolves quickly established packs and wolf populations expanded so rapidly that the animals were proposed for delisting only 5 years after initial reintroduction, monitoring has yet to show a significant decline in either elk and deer populations or hunter harvests as a direct result. However, more important, wolf introduction has had significant impacts on elk management. State wildlife management agencies have been pushed by state legislators and the public to focus management attention on predators rather than on the underlying habitat issues that are much more important in determining elk population size and distribution.

Preservation of Federal Lands

As his second term ended in 2000, President Clinton moved to establish his conservation legacy as a preservationist. He used the Antiquities Act (originally passed in 1908 to provide authority for President Theodore Roosevelt and successors to set aside lands with a high priority for preservation) to protect key recreational lands as national monuments in states throughout the west—Arizona, California, Colorado, Montana, Oregon and Utah.

Also in 2000, the Forest Service moved to implement

President Clinton's policy of preserving all inventoried roadless areas greater than 5,000 acres (2,023 ha) within the national forests as permanently "roadless." Exact land uses in such areas were to be worked out on a forest-by-forest basis. Presently (2001), 54.3 million acres (22 million ha) of the 192-million-acre (77.7 million ha) National Forest System are to remain roadless under the planning authorities contained in the National Forest Management Act, but this proposal is still under legal review. Many of these roadless areas adjoin designated Wilderness Areas, and (if they remain roadless) will increase (and likely enhance) the value of the Wilderness System.

In one regard, the effect of this action will not change the status quo of these lands for elk. Designation of these lands as roadless does nothing to alter their present status as wildlife habitat. That they remain unroaded is simply a reflection of the fact that, in most instances, there is little or no convincing economic, ecological or political rationale for building roads into these areas.

State Wildlife Agency Management

State and provincial wildlife management agencies occur in a variety of forms, based on provisions of the individual state constitution and governmental organization. In a majority of Pacific and interior western states with large elk populations (Alaska, Arizona, Idaho, Montana, Oregon, Washington, Wyoming), wildlife management responsibilities are assigned to an independent state agency (Wildlife Management Institute 1997). However, wildlife management is a branch of a larger agency with wider responsibilities in California, Colorado, Nevada and Utah.

These varying organizational arrangements have implications for the management of elk. As discussed earlier, wildlife management at the beginning of the 20th century was largely dependent on revenues derived from the sale of licenses and tags, supplemented (after 1937) by federal excise taxes in the United States. In each of these states, license and tag fee changes must be approved by the state legislature. Four (Arizona, Colorado, Idaho and Wyoming) of the 11 states receive no supplemental income from their state's treasury, and at least two others (California, which receives less than 5% of its budget from the state treasury, and Montana, which receives state funds for management of parks only) receive only limited funding (Wildlife Management Institute 1997). Each of these states is, therefore, entirely dependent on license and tag fees to generate funds to support law enforcement related to wildlife and wildlife management. All lack the ability to regulate license fees, which is reserved to various legislatures that have trust responsibility to manage public resources, including wildlife.

This reliance on sportsman's dollars to fund elk management is a legacy of the 1930s, when there was less competition for wildlife resources, and hunters and anglers comprised a much larger portion of each state's (and the nation's) population. Passage of the Federal Aid in Wildlife Restoration Act in 1937 resulted in additional funding for wildlife restoration programs. Initially, this independence allowed state wildlife management agencies to focus, with a dampening of political interference, on wildlife restoration, because revenues derived from license sales and matching federal dollars could not be devoted to non-wildlife-related matters. However, this independence of state revenues set the stage for later burgeoning financial problems. Nearly all state wildlife management agencies would have to grapple almost continuously with budget concerns, when late in the 20th century, declines in hunting opportunities and access limited the growth of the hunting community and, therefore, license and tag sales, even as human populations burgeoned in urban communities in western states. In addition, wildlife management agencies faced increasing pressures to respond to urban sprawl and ranchette developments in formerly productive wildlife habitats.

Although the last two decades of the 20th century saw a decline in hunters and anglers as a percentage of the population, the number of big game hunters increased dramatically—from slightly more than 1.5 million in 1955 to over 11 million in 1996. In 1996, big game hunters spent more than 154 million recreation days afield, and in excess of $9.7 billion on big game hunting trips and associated expenditures (Kenyon and Duda 2000).

Despite the growth in numbers of big game hunters, many western state wildlife management agencies have seen the sales of hunting licenses and tags remain relatively stable, while increases in inflation have significantly outstripped real dollar increases in license and tag sale income. Faced with declining real income, many state wildlife management agencies in the West have been forced routinely to approach their state legislatures for increases in license and tag fees to make up the deficit. Most state legislators seem loath to raise fees for their constituents, and many seem to have developed an animosity to those state wildlife agencies that enjoy independence from legislative oversight. On the other hand, state legislators are quite willing to increase, routinely and significantly, the fees for nonresident hunters and anglers, who cannot vote for state legislators.

Legislators usually can gain political support by increasing fees for nonresidents. That support comes in part from resident hunters and anglers for helping the agency (and, perhaps more to the point, for not raising in-state fees). Additional support stems from resident hunters who do not want competition from nonresidents for hunting opportunities, and even from nonhunters who do not want nonresidents "congesting" the public lands. This view is myopic; out-of-state hunters are cash cows, milked at higher and higher rates but also discouraged from coming into the state. It would seem likely that such actions eventually will result in reduction of out-of-state hunters and the significant fees they pay at highly disproportiate rates compared with those in-state hunters, who they, in effect, subsidize.

Because the public lands are "owned" in part by all citizens of the United States (who share equally in the costs of managing these lands), there has been some opposition by nonresident hunters to pay increasingly and disproportionately higher fees. The U.S. Supreme Court has ruled that disproportionate charges for licenses and permits between residents and nonresidents are legal so long as the difference is rational (*Baldwin v. Montana Fish and Game Commission* 436 U.S. 371). The charges have steadily become more and more disproportionate since that ruling. But the specter of reopening the case has likely served as a damper on the rates of increase that might have occurred otherwise. At some point, we expect this matter to be revisited in the Courts.

Requests of state wildlife management agencies for resident license fee increases are routinely rejected, delayed or compromised. Some such increases have been held hostage to arrangements that provide increased gubernatorial or legislative oversight over programs and budgets of traditionally independent state wildlife commissions. Subsequent increases in fees often have been accompanied by a dictated program that is politically motivated, such as payment for wildlife damages to private lands from funds derived from hunting license sales—programs that have routinely siphoned off money intended to support wildlife restoration efforts. Such actions are used as clubs to punish state agencies for not satisfying wishes of legislators from rural areas who wield considerable power in relatively sparsely populated western states.

In western states, agricultural and timber constituencies retain power and political influence far in excess of their proportion to the population. Big game hunters while increasing in total numbers, are declining as a percentage of the population within these increasingly urbanized states. This does not invoke a bright vision of politicians remaining as closely attuned to the needs and desires of hunters in the future as they have in the past.

Because state wildlife management agencies must rely, whether heavily or solely, on revenues from sales of licenses and tags to support their activities, there is ever-present temptation to push the pendulum of management actions toward increased exploitation of such cash cows as elk

hunting where demand perennially exceeds supply. License and tag sales have been increased, in some cases, to near-tolerable or maximally tolerable limits to hunters. Consequently, the number of animals killed annually (particularly in the case of bull elk) have been excessive for optimal maintenance of herd productivity (Noyes et al. 1996). One way this has been done is by providing general hunts with minimal harvest restrictions (wherein anyone may buy a license and tag, and hunt where he or she pleases). The result is higher numbers of hunters pursuing the same or fewer number of elk, which produces lower hunter success rates, a higher number of animals killed relative to elk population size, and more unhappy hunters. If only antlered males are legal game, the average age of animals killed is inevitably and increasingly skewed toward younger elk.

Because most elk carry their first set of hardened antlers at 18 months of age (and, therefore, become legal game in many areas), in those elk herds subjected to a high annual rate of harvest, most bull elk are killed before they reach the age of 3 years. Few elk living on public lands commonly survive past the age of 3 to emerge from the raghorn stage with their first set of six-point antlers typical of bulls older than 4 years. Far fewer still will reach the ages of more than 5 years—the age at which a mature set of antlers typically develops.

Since 1980, irrefutable data began to emerge from research indicating that overharvest of young bull elk resulted in a very low ratio of bull elk—particularly mature bull elk—to cows in postseason. Such rates have been demonstrated to contribute to reduced calf crops and increased calf elk mortality (Guinness et al. 1978, Hines and Lemos 1979, Prothero et al. 1979, Hines et al. 1985, Squibb 1985, Ginsberg and Milner-Gulland 1994, Noyes et al. 1996). As a result, many state agencies have struggled to reduce the harvest of bulls—struggled, that is, to balance income from license sales and harvests, hunter demand and biological mandates to preserve enough older age bulls to ensure high herd productivity. However, reducing hunter numbers invariably leads to increased disgruntlement from many hunters consequently disallowed hunting opportunities.

One widespread management strategy, mentioned earlier in this and other chapters (see Chapters 13 and 18), has been an effort to reduce bull elk vulnerability to hunters by decreasing roads open to vehicular traffic. However, the ultimate possible solutions are inescapably bounded. Hunters must be increasingly handicapped by shorter seasons, limits on weapons or other measures such as restrictions on access.

Alternatively, the total number of hunters must be stabilized or reduced, despite adverse impacts on agency income and the creation of an increasingly disappointed constituency. To their credit, many state agencies have opted to

Most elk carry their first set of branched antlers at 2 or 3 years of age; their first set of six-point antlers at 4 years of age, and rarely produce the large antlers typical of a fully mature bull elk until age 8 years. Because most western states harvest bull elk heavily, relatively few bulls survive to produce the large antlers that most hunters desire. More important, few of these older bulls exist in most western elk herds, and an increasing body of evidence indicates that these prime animals are necessary for regulating the breeding season. *Photo by Leonard Lee Rue III.*

limit total numbers of elk hunters either by putting a cap on elk tag sales statewide or eliminating general hunting seasons for elk altogether in lieu of drawings for permits by designated area. Increasingly, general hunting seasons have been replaced by limiting hunters by management unit. Success in management of hunting often has come at the cost of a significant decline in revenue from license and tag sales. In turn, this has increased financial difficulties faced by most state wildlife management agencies that deal with elk management. It sets up a vicious circle, whereby required management actions to benefit elk and elk hunters produce a decline in revenue that results in decreased effectiveness of the agencies. As far as financial incentives are concerned, "right" decisions lead to reduced revenues and "wrong" decisions increase revenue.

The State Agency Decision-making Process

Obviously, any time an agency takes action to reduce supply (that is, the days of hunting permissible and the number of elk that can be killed by hunters each year) relative to hunter demand for elk hunting opportunity, that decision will create controversy and animosity toward the agency—and loss of revenue. Within agencies, the outcomes of such actions are that positions, equipment and even wildlife management programs are cut when agency budgets decrease due to lessening revenue and inexorable inflation. Externally, resulting controversies are a loss of agency support by hunters who feel that the agency has somehow let them down by reducing or restricting hunting opportunity.

Additional conflicts emerge when resident hunters find themselves competing not only with one another but also with nonresidents for a limited number of elk tags. Often, these controversies result in legislative reviews—and sometimes legislative actions—to modify or reverse decisions the agencies deemed necessary to achieve elk herd management objectives. As a result, agencies are sometimes forced back into the position of allowing high (and biologically inappropriate) elk harvests, and even having to defend decisions they recommended against.

To understand management of elk by state wildlife management agencies, it is essential to understand the decision-making process. The decision-making structure common to wildlife agencies in western states features an oversight board or commission comprised of five to nine members and an agency director. Members of the board are appointed by the governor of the state to staggered terms of 3 to 6 years (Wildlife Management Institute 1997). Requirements for appointment vary among states. In some states, appointees are selected to represent particular industry or interest groups. In other states, only an interest in wildlife management is required.

The board usually selects the agency director, although among major elk-producing states, governors appoint the directors in California, Colorado, Nevada and Utah (Wildlife Management Institute 1997). These appointments, as all political appointments, carry some measure of prestige. Such appointees often are particularly sensitive to the interests of the state's governor as well as the hunters and other wildlife interest groups they represent. The management agencies are responsible for the welfare of all wildlife species and are answerable to all the people. However, in reality, they focus the majority of their attention and resources on hunted species, the people who hunt them and the private landowners. Money is not everything—but it comes close.

Typically, the agency director, who is nominally responsible for agency operations and resources (staff and budget), is somewhat less sensitive to political pressures than is a board or commission. The board or commission is responsible for ensuring that the agency is responsive to citi-

(*Top left*) A royal (6 by 6 tines per antler) elk bull; (*bottom left*) an imperial (7 by 7) bull; and (*right*) a monarch (8 by 8). All are Rocky Mountain elk. *Photos by Leonard Lee Rue III.*

zen interests, on that basis, and establishes agency policy. The job of the director is to maintain a smoothly functioning organization that operates within policy guidelines and budget limits, and is able to identify and meet management challenges. However, there is a recent trend for governors and state legislatures to expand further their political control over decision making within state wildlife management agencies and, thereby, politicize agency decision making. In 1997, directors were selected by the governor in 16 of the 50 states (up from 11 of 50 in 1985). As one unidentified wag put it, "The Director is Captain of the ship, but he has no control of the weather."

State wildlife management agencies may be directed by the governor or state legislature to address and spend both time and money on politically popular programs, some of which are quite peripheral or even antithetical to wildlife welfare or to the benefit of hunters. To an increasing degree, such programs are accompanied by budget or program directives formulated on some political basis other than fulfilling the agency's trust responsibility as custodian of the state's wildlife resources.

In addition, the ability of state wildlife management agencies to manage wildlife may be directed by popular ballot, that is, based on the outcome of citizen ballot initiatives. Recent ballot initiatives have resulted in significant

Many state fish and wildlife management agencies are governed by a commission or board, whose members typically are businessmen selected to represent the public. Board members provide overall direction for the agency, and often are involved in establishing broad agency objectives and policies. *Photo courtesy of the Idaho Game and Fish Commission.*

limitations on hunting of mountain lions and black bears (both potential predators on elk) in California, Oregon and Washington. The precedent of setting regulations with initiative ballot is significant, because it has the effect of separating management decisions from scientific evidence. Voters are directed to choose an outcome often based on little more than emotional advertisements and philosophical positions.

Directors also have found that, to an ever-increasing degree, state wildlife management agency budget priorities ultimately are established outside of the agency. Agency budget priorities were established by the governor or cabinet in 27 of the 50 states in 1997 (up from 6 in 1985) and by legislative budget officers in 14 states (up from 1 in 1985) (Wildlife Management Institute 1997). In addition, much of state agency directors' decision-making authority over budgets and operations has been lost to oversight commissions.

Most western wildlife agencies faced dwindling budgets and reductions in staff during 1950 to 2000. At the same time, despite increases in big game hunters nationwide, the proportion of resident hunters in many western states have declined relative to total population (an effect of increasing populations and urbanization of western landscapes).

Agencies have coped with limitations on hunter numbers and in elk harvests—particularly of bulls—necessitated by management concerns. In turn, many have sought supplemental funding from state treasuries to pay for legislatively mandated activities assigned to them. Some of these activities have, by and large, only marginal associations with providing hunting and fishing opportunity (e.g., monitoring water quality, reviewing environmental documents, and attending to nongame and endangered species). Although some states have been successful in garnering additional resources to carry out these efforts, many have not.

Those that have been successful have often found that the additional funding and the new constituencies associated with such funds have limited interest in hunting, or even express opposition to hunting. As a result, there has been an erosion of decision-making authority related to management of hunting.

In the case of most state wildlife management agencies, recommendations for elk hunting seasons developed by staff commonly are presented to a board or commission for final approval. Whereas these recommendations usually are based on elk herd management data and concerns for hunters (numbers, distribution, harvest success, satisfaction, etc.), tempered by concerns for equitable and effective wildlife law enforcement, board decisions are influenced by such additional factors as public comments, agency budget considerations and political issues. Most public comments related to big game management, not surprisingly, come from hunters, outfitters and industries that are directly affected by agency decisions. Because the decision makers typically have been appointed and lack formal training in biological sciences, the social, economic and biological ramifications of their decisions loom large.

When it comes to setting elk hunting seasons and establishing management direction, hunters quite understandably consider themselves to be the primary constituents of the governing board and expect to exert a major influence within the realm of management options. These options are bounded on three sides by elk herd status, application of sound management practices related to biology, and social and political acceptability. Changes in management direction, whether or not they are supported by good technical information, can be extremely difficult to implement. This is particularly true if actions have the potential to adversely affect public land-based business interests (e.g., livestock grazing, timber harvest, outfitting), which can exert effective influence to maintain the status quo to provide greater stability in their planning for the future. Or, perhaps, "the devil you know is better than the devil you don't know." The net result is that new management direction is difficult to implement and, in the absence of needed adjustments made in a timely manner, hunter numbers and associated elk harvests often are expanded until the lowest common denominator (and highest harvest levels) are reached.

State Regulation of Elk Harvests

Most elk hunters want an opportunity to harvest a large, mature bull elk. Management biologists possess sufficient know-how to produce such animals, both in terms of habitat and herd management. However, to do so, information on the number and structure of elk populations and habitats is a necessary component of a manager's decision making. In some cases, habitats must be manipulated to provide the food, water and space to meet desired herd numbers with satisfactory recruitment rates of young animals into the herd. Those activities require funding and cooperation with landowners, whether federal, state, provincial or private. Obtaining the necessary information to meet acceptable statistical parameters, developing an approach to achieve management objectives and implementing actions necessary to achieve objectives all require time (at least several years, in the case of elk) and commitment of resources to retain adequately skilled and experienced personnel to do the work. To achieve such long-term objectives, agencies must have the ability to develop, conduct and monitor long-range planning.

Unfortunately, ill-advised political influence on wildlife management in several states since 1985 has significantly reduced the ability of those agencies to formulate and carry out long-range wildlife management plans in any consistent fashion. Since 1985, the number of states with comprehensive wildlife management plans declined from 43 to 29 and even fewer agencies have plans that are linked with agency budgets (Wildlife Management Institute 1997) and thus any significant probability that goals can be accomplished is unknown. The number of state wildlife agencies developing conservation plans declined from 34 to 16 between 1985 and 1997, and those with full-time planning staff declined from 25 to 16 (Wildlife Management Institute 1997).

Declines in long-range planning efforts reflect several factors, including increasing uncertainty about future budgets, loss of experienced personnel, and increasingly confused direction of agency actions dictated by people other than the agency director. Such situations change quickly and significantly as the players change. However, if agencies lack comprehensive plans or the ability to carry them out, agency personnel have difficulty formulating and communicating long-term management objectives and defending the courses of action necessary to achieve those objectives.

With regard to elk, herd management objectives that require short-term reductions or changes in hunt opportunity (and which may require years to accomplish) are difficult to justify to administrators, boards, and sportsmen and women unless objectives are well-defined in long-term

management plans. Without such long-range plans, management proposals are increasingly vulnerable to political intervention, and decisions often reflect short-term knee-jerk responses to changing facets of chronic problems. The ultimate effect is routine failure to achieve management objectives—and a growing distrust of agency professionals by the public and their elected representatives.

The Contribution of Elk Hunters and Private Landowners

Both federal and state agencies struggled to fulfill their responsibilities to management of wildlife resources in the last two decades of the 20th century. Hunters, once again at their position at the forefront of wildlife conservation efforts in North America, continue to carry nearly the entire financial burden of wildlife conservation—no matter what the species in question, whether hunted or not. As the 21st century begins, hunters, concerned about the future of big game and the hunting of same, have again banded together to address critical issues of elk management. As a result, the game of elk management is changing—and for the better.

As some traditional wildlife conservation groups broadened their focus and reduced their attention to hunting in favor of a more general environmental protection agenda, new organizations formed to fill the vacated niche. These organizations focused on the welfare of species that were hunted and the interests of those who did the hunting. Among these upstart organizations are Quail Unlimited, Ducks Unlimited, Pheasants Forever, the National Wild Turkey Federation and the Mule Deer Foundation. Most have patterned themselves after the highly successful model of Ducks Unlimited, Inc., founded in 1937.

Significant credit for the dramatic growth of elk herds throughout North America in the period 1985 to 2000 goes to the Rocky Mountain Elk Foundation, a nonprofit organization of persons interested in elk and elk hunting. Founded in 1984, the Rocky Mountain Elk Foundation is centered in Missoula, Montana, with a Canadian headquarters in Rocky Mountain House, Alberta. Begun as an organization of avid elk aficionados seeking ways to support elk management activities throughout North America, the Rocky Mountain Elk Foundation grew in 15 years to more than 115,000 members in the year 2000 (Rocky Mountain Elk Foundation 2000).

The Rocky Mountain Elk Foundation members and staff have focused their energies and dollars on preserving elk habitat and restoring elk populations. Through efforts of the Rocky Mountain Elk Foundation, more than 3 million acres (1.2 million ha) of wildlife habitat have been protected or enhanced since 1984. In addition, the organization has become a major supporter of agencies' wildlife management activities designed to benefit wild, free-ranging elk. It also has fostered cooperation and communication among federal, state, provincial agencies and private interests, and developed programs to educate its members and the general public about habitat conservation, elk management and hunting issues.

Much of the success of the Rocky Mountain Elk Foundation comes from its status as a private, nonprofit organization that can and does act quickly and decisively to seize opportunities to implement its goals and objectives. The organization's primary focus on wildlife habitat conservation has been a significant asset to elk management efforts. State, provincial, and federal wildlife and land management agencies often lack both immediate access to funds and the ability to act expeditiously to purchase critical lands and conservation easements that become available from willing sellers.

The Rocky Mountain Elk Foundation has not only helped identify such key habitats, but also has organized public support—political and monetary—for their protection. It then has provided critical funding (partial or total), evaluators, purchase negotiators and legal expertise to cinch the deals. In many cases, Rocky Mountain Elk Foundation held title to such lands (sometimes for several years) until it could be transferred to a federal land management agency, state wildlife management agency or private conservation-oriented organization. Title transfers can be slow processes, replete with myriad pitfalls. The Rocky Mountain Elk Foundation's ability to move quickly around and through red tape imposed on others can, has and does make a critical difference that separates success from failure.

The Rocky Mountain Elk Foundation has contributed to elk management in another and more subtle way. Many habitat management and elk translocation projects conducted by federal, state and provincial wildlife management agencies have been funded wholly or in part by the Rocky Mountain Elk Foundation. Often, these efforts have been bolstered by the direct assistance of volunteers from the organization's ranks. Without such funding and volunteer efforts, many of the projects would not have been possible.

This arrangement exemplifies the inverse of circumstance in European cultures from which the early settlers of North America came. Those pilgrims were so angered by their exclusion from the enjoyment of wildlife, hunting and otherwise, that they assured that wildlife in New World was owned by and managed for the people as a whole. This arrangement can be likened to a three-legged stool. One leg is the wildlife owned by the people. A second leg is the habitat owned by the landowner. The third leg is the landowner's prerogative to allow or not allow other people access to his land where the publicly owned wildlife may be found.

Ultimately, success for elk managers depends on maintaining the strength and balance of all three legs of the stool. They must be equally strong and of equal length, lest the stool wobble or collapse. Maintenance of the stool is the joint responsibility of landowners, management agencies and such conservation groups as Rocky Mountain Elk Foundation. Only they can effectively coordinate, regulate, collaborate, facilitate collaboration by others, provide information, and fund necessary general actions and activities. The future success of elk and elk management will increasingly rely on the sturdiness of that three-legged stool.

The abundance of public lands in the western states and provinces with most of the elk and elk habitat tends to overshadow the increasingly significant contributions that private landowners make toward elk conservation. Although citizens own the wildlife, landowners (federal or private) have nearly total responsibility for management of habitat. In addition, they have the right to limit access to their lands for whatever reason, including hunting. While this bipartite arrangement renders elk management by the state agencies more difficult, there is a flip side. In this era when elk refuges on public lands are rare, private lands owners often exercise a very stringent hunting management program or even exclude hunting altogether. Thus, these private lands often afford elk refuge from hunters not available elsewhere. These de facto or partial refuges on large private ownerships—where public access is limited and hunting, if allowed, is very conservative—are scattered widely across the landscape. Many private ranchlands afford refuge to bull elk and allow significant numbers of them to reach full maturity—a much less likely outcome for those that live entirely on more heavily hunted public lands.

Private lands often include the best and some of the most productive habitats at relatively low elevations—the very lands that elk need during periods of severe or prolonged winter weather. Elk facing winter's cold and deepening snows at higher elevations retire to these scattered parcels where temperatures are more moderate and snow depth is significantly less. There, they may be spared the experience of energy-draining harassment by winter recreationists. Many private landowners are zealously protective of wintering elk, despite the fact that elk may compete for forage with livestock and even consume supplemental feed provided for livestock.

Because private landowners exercise nearly complete control over the management of their lands, some state and provincial agencies have developed programs to reward landowners for harboring elk and for management practices that preserve or restore elk habitat. Incentives usually take the form of elk harvest permits valid for the lands at issue during the regular hunting season, cash incentives based on acreage occupied by elk or harvest by hunters selected by the state.

When elk damage private property, such as fences or emerging or stored crops, the state wildlife management agency usually is required to attempt alleviation of immediate damage and to lessen potential damages. In some states, the agencies must compensate the private landowner for damages incurred. Damage control often takes the form of physical barriers to protect stored crops (such as hay). The herd may be moved, either through hazing, trapping and translocating, or "shortstopping." Herds may be attracted with decoy crops planted and maintained by the responsible state or federal agency (as at the National Elk Refuge). Where these measures are ineffective, the only practical alternative may be to sacrifice or cull the offending animals—always a course of last resort, because it invariably brings significant public criticism. On rare occasions, the elk population occupying an extensive area of public land most of the year must be reduced significantly through hunter harvest, translocation or controlled shooting to address the concerns of a particular landowner who has suffered significant damages.

The Future of Elk and Elk Management

A New Policy and a New Paradigm for Federal Land Management

Historians may come to refer to the period of 1900 to 2000 as the century of conservation in North America. As westward expansion of Euro-Americans in the 19th century ended, thereby fulfilling the vision of "Manifest Destiny," the 20th century began in a time of extreme and damaging land use and wildlife exploitation. This led to formulation of a new land management policy—conservation. Neither unsustainable exploitation nor absolute preservation provided a means of protecting natural resources. As mentioned earlier, conservation (wise use) was coined and implemented with the Roosevelt Doctrine—a decision paradigm based on centralized decision making by experts using the best scientific information available (Leopold 1933).

Results that developed from the Progressive Era have been a source of continuing debate (Nelson 1999, Thomas and Burchfield 1999). At the least, so far as elk management is concerned, this paradigm paid remarkable dividends. But times are changing, and controversies over the management of public lands continue to abound and even seem to intensify. Many students of the subject suggest that a new era is dawning—one in which management will be deter-

mined at more local levels by coalitions of various interest groups with less authoritarian control by government experts (Wondolleck and Yaffee 2000).

The first years of the 21st century feature a new and still evolving land management paradigm—ecosystem management (Boyce and Haney 1997, Thomas 1997b). Ecosystem management as public policy germinated from federal government commitment to establish what were intended to be renewable forests in reserves (and later, national forests) under the leadership of Pinchot and Theodore Roosevelt. However, not much thought was given to the mechanisms of renewal and sustainability. Rather, most of the federal guidance for conservation was provided piecemeal, by laws designed to protect specific sites (e.g., forest reserves, national parks, wildlife refuges, wilderness areas, etc.), endangered species, clean water, and clean air (Keiter et al. 1999). Adoption of the National Environmental Policy Act of 1970 made federal land managers accountable for implementation of environmental legislation—and implementation of National Environmental Policy Act forced a realization that "everything is connected to everything else, and there is no such thing as a free lunch," as ecologist Paul Erlich once intoned. It soon was obvious that neither project nor jurisdictional boundaries were effective in assessing or containing project impacts on the environment.

During President Ronald Reagan's Administration, there were significant efforts to adjust to this new reality by decentralizing decision-making authority and promoting increased involvement in decision making by those outside of government. The policy was expanded by George H. W. Bush. Vocal members of the public demanded an enhanced role in the process and, despite past successes in restoration of natural resources, the public more and more frequently rejected "expert opinion" as the sole basis for decisions (Wondolleck and Yaffee 2000). Resource management agencies were increasingly forced out of the role of proposers of management alternatives, arbiters of public decisions or final authority and into a role of facilitator for collaborative decisions (Hummel and Freet 1999). With no designee as final authority, this modified niche has not shown dramatic success in either a technical or political sense. However, the current planning regulations for the National Forest System (made final in 2000) mandate collaboration, without being specific as to what such a process would entail. This nebulous requirement seems destined to attract legal actions from anyone not satisfied with the final result of a planning effort for a particular national forest.

In this new management paradigm, science is increasingly used to inform decision makers, and to identify and contrast potential outcomes within the constraints imposed by existing statute and evolving case law. Decisions about particular issues are considered adaptive, that is, decisions are routinely revisited and revamped as information accumulates about the results of management. Termed adaptive management, this supposedly new procedural construct for decision making requires gathering data about both the affected environment and about people's concerns and desires, and making "mid-course corrections" based on experience and new information (Bormann et al. 1999). Actually, adaptive management is ages old and could be more simply stated as "figure it out, do it, evaluate results, adjust the action, do it and so on and on." Practically, adaptive management often means that no decision can be thoroughly evaluated relative to its impacts over the long term.

In 1991, Forest Service Chief Dale Robertson announced that henceforth, the national forests would be managed under the concept of ecosystem management. Old ways of dealing with one project at a time, one national forest at a time, was producing a totally incomprehensible hodgepodge of overlapping plans that essentially boggled up all the decision space available to management. That concept was simply to recognize that management planning had to be expanded in terms of both time and space, that more variables (ecological, legal, social and economic) had to be considered and that people (their needs and desires) were part and parcel of ecosystem management. As might be expected, with such dramatic changes in management focus, there was pointed criticism. The most legitimate of these was the charge that ecosystem management is "fuzzy." That charge can be answered by recognizing that ecosystem management is a concept that must be placed in context of a single circumstance: the area to be considered is carefully defined and the definition explained; the operative time frames are delineated and justified; the variables and their interactions to be considered are listed and justified; the people and the requirements of law are defined in detail. Context definition erases fuzziness.

Cortner and Moote (1999) discussed ecosystem management as embracing four themes: (1) socially defined goals and objectives, (2) holistic, integrated science, (3) adaptable institutions, and (4) collaborative decision making. Cortner et al. (1999:5) suggested that the ultimate success of ecosystem management (as all other systems of natural resources management) will depend on, among other things, being simultaneously "politically and legally acceptable." Earlier, it was observed that paradoxes could be expected to be encountered frequently in instituting and carrying out ecosystem management (Cortner et al. 1999). Clearly, the requirement for public land management agencies to manage land (and wildlife) in a way that is simultaneously legal and politically acceptable is clearly a paradox in that both require-

ments are true and actions taken to comply with law as demanded by the courts are less and less politically acceptable.

The possibility of simultaneously accomplishing both objectives in public land management is inversely related to scale—both in the geographic sense and in terms of numbers of people involved. For example, management of public lands to provide increased protection of threatened species and increased protection of public lands through actions such as declaration of national monuments, are both legal and politically acceptable at the national level—but are often violently opposed at local or regional scales when individual and local economies are directly affected.

When the scale of consideration is narrowed down to the western states where the public lands are concentrated and where a minority of Americans live, the result is very different than when such actions are viewed in national perspective. Compliance with environmental laws has produced a situation in which elected officials in the western states object (some rather vehemently) to actions taken by land management and regulatory agencies to comply with law and court decisions. This leaves the management agencies in an awkward position of being criticized from both sides in the long-running debate between protection and exploitation. In many cases, due to confusion of inconsistent decisions or political direction from within the Administration above the agency level, desired management activities come to a halt as efforts are made to comply with the law. Then, in sheer frustration, budgets are threatened or actually reduced by western congressmen as punishment. Western members of Congress frequently make up the majority in and control of the key committees that deal with public land matters through membership on the committees or chairmanships, or both.

It seems likely that the described paradox will continue to influence adversely the capabilities of land management and regulatory agencies to move aggressively to bring management challenges into compliance with the law. Relief from the consequences of this paradox would seem to require a reconciliation of laws passed in the 1970s. Little or no consideration was then or has since been given to their interactions—particularly as interpretation by the courts and succeeding Administrations evolved. Nothing short of a dramatic effort to coordinate, streamline and set clear policy in a bipartisan manner seems apt to relieve the consequences of that ever-more apparent paradox as it progressively throttles active public land management. One scholar referred to the outdated laws, policies, and ideas that guide public land management today as the Lords of Yesterday (Wilkinson 1992). We most desperately need to develop the Lords of Today—and Tomorrow.

Despite certain reservations, we believe that the concept

of ecosystem management, by whatever name, will dominate land-use planning (particularly of public and associated lands) in the early decades of the 21st century (see Boyce and Haney 1997, Hunter 1999).

The Federal Lands and Elk in the 21st Century

Similar to the philosophy of conservation from which it evolved, ecosystem management is neither wholly preservationist nor exploitative. Instead, ecosystem management adds new dimensions to the old conservation paradigm that requires responsible decision makers to consider the impacts of their decisions on adjoining ownership. The long-term implications of land management decisions are assessed over longer time frames to ensure the viability of ecosystem processes and sustainability of renewable natural resources. Similar to conservation, ecosystem management is to be funded by its beneficiaries. And, unlike earlier views of conservation, the number of beneficiaries is expanded far beyond the immediate providers and users of extractable resources.

To begin an assessment of elk and elk management in the 21st century, we go back to where we started—and examination of the condition of the federal estate, which will continue to be the heart of elk country. Elk are a product of their environment. Their survival, like that of every other species, depends on the amount and arrangement of food, water, living space and, to some extent, shelter to escape predation—most specifically, the human predator.

Technological advances of the late 20th century have allowed compiling and obtaining information to guide land management information on a scale and in detail previously unimaginable. One of the largest efforts yet undertaken to compile and assess landscape-scale information on federal lands has been the Interior Columbia Basin Ecosystem Management Project. This project was an effort, chartered in 1994, to gather and present coordinated, scientifically sound, broad-scale, ecosystem-based land management data across the entire Columbia River Basin east of the summit of the Cascade Mountain Range (Interior Columbia Basin Ecosystem Management Project 1997, 2000). Although this area encompasses only a portion of the range occupied by elk in North America, that assessment revealed trends that are hugely informative about what has happened and is happening to elk habitat in the western United States.

The Interior Columbia Basin Ecosystem Management Project analysis area included approximately 72 million acres (29.1 million ha) of federal lands managed by the Forest Service and Bureau of Land Management, and associated private lands. Among the trends with direct implica-

tion to the future of elk is the significant—and ongoing—fragmentation of habitat caused by human action. This fragmentation is particularly evident in low elevation forests, shrub–steppe and riparian areas that are the very lands most critical to elk during periods of winter stress.

Remember, over much of the elk habitat in North America, elk are slowly starving on their winter ranges. Life for those animals on winter ranges is a race of time between death and spring greenup. That is, likely, as it has always been. Only 16% of the species' range demonstrated high ecological integrity—that is, low levels of human alteration of landscapes. Forested areas outside of designated wilderness areas were particularly affected (Quigley and Arbelbide 1997, Quigley and Bigler-Cole 1997). Only a part of the fragmentation was associated with timber harvests. Timber cuts can provide elk forage until closing tree canopies interfere significantly with light reaching the forest floor. Timber management activities on national forests in the area were reduced dramatically between 1985 and 2000. An increasing amount of the fragmentation has been associated with development of rural housing, roads and other activities and services that represent long-term diminution in habitat value or permanent loss of elk habitat.

Wildlife habitats were determined to be subject to increasing risk, with anticipated dramatic changes (Quigley and Arbelbide 1997). These changes include stand-replacing (lethal) wildfire, accelerated erosion associated with road construction and logging, and continued retrograde succession in plant communities (i.e., plant succession moving toward reduced site complexity and increased occurrence of "weed" species) related to continued heavy grazing by domestic livestock. Potential for stand-replacing wildfire was determined to be growing dramatically, integrity of native grasslands and shrublands was declining and invasions of non-native noxious weeds were expected to accelerate their spread. In addition, declines in a number of animal species (elk were not specifically assessed, although they surely would be affected negatively) were anticipated and associated with continuing conversion of pasture land to agriculture, and additive impacts of grazing by domestic livestock and wild ungulates. Nonsustainable timber cutting, introduction and rapid range expansion of exotic plant and animal species, increased recreational impacts, higher road densities, fire exclusion and mining were also identified (Quigley and Arbelbide 1997), and likely will have a long-term negative impact on elk populations. This effort is but one of a number of such efforts that were undertaken from 1990 to 2000 (Johnson et al. 1999).

The implications of these changes to the future of elk are individually negative and, both singly and collectively, could prove to be severe. Elk are large, mobile, highly

Wildfire is a natural event that can improve elk habitat by removing blocks of forest canopy and stimulating forage production. However, when fire frequency has been reduced by fire suppression efforts, allowing potential fuels to build up, wildfire can have devastating consequences. Hot wildfires can destroy massive amounts of timber, burn away groundcover plants and essential humus near the top of the soil profile (resulting in increased delivery of silt to clog rivers and streams), and expose large areas to invasion by noxious weeds. Although wildfires are generally considered dangerous, elk have been reported to be indifferent even to crown fires, and fire mortality of elk is rare. The large fires of 1988 in the greater Yellowstone area killed about 1% of the area's elk population (Singer and Schullery 1989). However, subsequent drought and fires produced a winter forage shortage, therefore overwinter elk mortality was high—as much as 40% at one location (Singer et al. 1989, Vales and Peek 1996). *Photo by John McColgan.*

adaptable animals, but they require relatively large areas of suitable habitat. When their habitat is fragmented by human activity, elk often attempt to adopt or at least adapt to human-altered habitats. As an example, elk are living or attempting to live amid rural subdivisions, feeding on agricultural crops, lawns and shrubs. Elk usually are short-lived in these situations because of human intolerance.

Elk populations can suffer when essential forage is nearly consumed by livestock and elk, opening the way for takeover of the site by invasive noxious weeds with low or no palliative or nutritive value. Foraging habitats—forest canopy openings caused by logging or fire—are increasingly eliminated by forest plant succession. As timber harvests continue to decline, such transitory range created by logging is becoming rarer on national forests. The future of active forest management on such lands is politically, economically and legally uncertain. Some habitats will be rendered less accessible to elk because of developing recreation, mining activities and road development.

Trends in vegetation at the landscape level showed an increasing proportion of mid-aged forests on both dry and moist sites—a reflection, in part, of dramatic declines in timber harvest from 1985 to 2000. The amount of potential fuel that will be burned in uncontrolled wildfires in many of these forests has increased beyond historic levels, largely due to very successful wildfire control efforts since 1940. The extant combination of high fuel loads and nearly continuous blocks of forest at mid and high elevations—where, in many cases, there are no roads—translates to a seriously elevating risk of extremely hot and damaging wildfire (Quigley and Arbelbide 1997). These trends carry the potential of a triple-whammy to elk welfare: (1) loss of forage areas as canopies close and timber harvest declines, (2) heightened risk of large-scale stand-replacing wildfire, and (3) seemingly inevitable proliferation of noxious weeds on public lands.

Although large-scale wildfire is a natural event that has altered forest vegetation on a broad scale historically, it is not necessarily desirable for elk. Despite the fact that large wildfires typically result in forest canopy removal and create abundant forage during the period of early succession, if closed canopy forests existed for a considerable period before the onset of fire, it is likely that area elk populations were depressed. Elk populations may require several generations of high productivity (10 years or more) to increase to the extent that they are in balance with available forage. Over that same period, regenerating forest may result in declines in forage productivity, leading to a cycle of boom or bust in elk numbers.

In contrast to such a scenario, forest managers have the capability to create forage areas of the desired size and distribution on a planned schedule, incorporating elk herd welfare considerations into a significant timber harvest program. The balance between habitat and elk numbers can then be, at least to some extent, regulated through controlled hunting. In other words, land and wildlife managers have some level of joint control of habitat, forest condition and elk numbers. When the creation of forage areas depends primarily or solely on wildlfire or other disturbance, such as blowdowns, the effect is considerably more random and much less subject to management control. Then, managers, essentially must replace a proactive management approach with a reactive approach.

The proliferation of noxious weeds is an even more difficult problem, both because weeds invade public lands by wind, water and transported by animals and people, and because there is an political impasse over appropriate control techniques. Noxious weeds can be controlled, in favorable circumstances, by herbicides or introduction of insects that feed on such vegetation. Mechanical control by hand pulling or grazing likely will not be sufficient. However, suitable control techniques (particularly herbicide application) on public lands have been and probably will continue to be controversial. As a result, large-scale stand-replacing wildfires may simplify instead of rejuvenate grassland/shrub communities, allowing unpalatable—perhaps even toxic—weeds to become permanent and, in some cases, dominant components of the vegetative community—a result that will directly reduce forage available during some or all seasons.

However, it is well to note the wildfire risks associated with forest canopy closure and fuel build-up can be offset, surprisingly, by judicious use of controlled burns to develop a "fire mosaic" of stands of differing ages. It is debatable as to how much controlled burning is acceptable over the long term, because of smoke, risks of uncontrolled wildlife, costs and risk factors from exotic weeds.

Developing an Action Plan for the Federal Lands

Acquiring and upgrading information on trends in federal land management actions that provide habitat for elk are only a prelude to ensuring the ability of federal lands to

Controlled burns have the potential to thin overcrowded stands of young trees, allowing older trees to grow more rapidly, while opening the canopy and promoting production of nutritious forage for elk. Characterized by many standing stems initially, such fires kill the smaller plants, and their ashes nourish the soil, providing access to nutrients eagerly sought by feeding elk and other animals. *Photo by Jim Zumbo.*

support future desired populations of elk and other wildlife. A review of the legal framework for implementation of ecosystem management on federal lands leads us to two conclusions.

First, provisions of the National Environmental Policy Act, the Endangered Species Act and regulations issued pursuant to the National Forest Management Act mandate that federal land managers implement ecosystem management, or something similar to meet simultaneous legal requirements in any fiscally reasonable fashion. Second, the interaction of a wide range of single purpose (and sometimes contradictory) laws, regulations developed pursuant to those laws by differing agencies, and a growing accumulation of poorly coordinated case law can make implementation of newly derived ecosystem management policies and processes—or any such land management policy—increasingly difficult and perhaps impossible (Keiter et al. 1999).

Although the legal basis and pragmatic requirement for

ecosystem management are in place, legal complexities and confounding agency actions are seemingly inevitable under existing legislation. These increasing legal and administrative complexities translate into significant delays and dramatically increased costs going from the initiation of a proposal for action to implementation.

One possible means of addressing the ever more complex issues of moving more efficiently and rapidly from proposals for land management actions to implementation is, obviously enough, reducing legal complexities. As legal maneuvering is especially commonplace in the United States, the following discussion is so directed. The president, in coordination with Congress, could implement a federal land law review. In this process, the entire body of law would be reviewed by a group of experts (*real* experts) who then would make recommendations to Congress in the form of draft legislation. Recommendations would address the intent of Congress in originally establishing the laws, identification of contradictions between original intent and status quo, and suggestions for alternative solutions. Pending action by Congress to amend or modify the existing body of law or the development and passage of new legislation (which is unlikely in the short term), all affected agencies should simultaneously promulgate—under guidance of a single "czar"—new regulations and policies consistent with legislation. The intent would be production of a body of regulations issued pursuant to extant enabling legislation and that encompasses the intent of the legislation but removes paradoxes and conflicts, streamlines processes and strives for compatibility between regulations (Thomas 2000). Regulations developed internally and in isolation by agencies with varying missions and that defend their turf and the independence of the individual agencies simply do not fit together in a coherent fashion. In the process suggested here, the regulation czar would mandated to overcome those tendencies.

Timber Harvest

During the final 20 years of the 20th century, timber cutting on federal lands became increasingly contentious. Alarmed about growing fragmentation of forests, the perceived ugliness of clearcuts and loss of particular forest components such as old-growth and associated plant and animal species, many people came to believe that only preservation (cessation of all extractive uses) of the nation's forested public lands could offer long-term protection. Simultaneously, congressional concerns over deficits resulted in reductions in budgets for land management agencies, while impacts of management actions and legally mandated additional tasks were increasing.

Clearly, the rising costs of environmental analysis and litigation were turning into an effective barrier to implementation of timber sales or other management actions (i.e., costs in personnel, time and money of making timber sales were increasing while timber yields were declining). Furthermore, below cost sales, made for whatever reason, were less and less acceptable to many in Congress and, one would assume, their constituents.

The most dramatic interactive effect of these laws and regulations was a drop of more than 90% of the amount of timber cut on federal lands in the Pacific Northwest west of the Cascades, where the highest site timberlands in the National Forest System were contained. This was related primarily to concerns with the status of such threatened species as the spotted owl, marbled murrelet and salmon. Similar drops in timber harvesting in the Intermountain West related to concerns with such threatened species as the bull trout, grizzly bear and lynx. Curtailment of timber cutting in the Southwest was related to concerns over goshawks, Mexican spotted owls and other species. Pending revisions in law and regulations, those curtailments are likely to become the order of the day.

Federal policy emerged during 1990 to 2000 that, when interpreted into action, placed on federal lands the brunt of complying with the Endangered Species Act to the extent possible (Johnson et al. 1990, Thomas et al. 1990, Forest Ecosystem Management Assessment Team 1993). Mandates to protect threatened and endangered species, unacceptable to private landowners, could be broadly applied to lands managed by federal agencies. This may have been inevitable for two reasons. The vast majority of the remnant lands not yet subjected to roading and timber extraction was in federal ownership (i.e., the best habitat for species associated with old forests was on federal lands). And except when it could not be avoided, nobody in power had the nerve to address restrictions on private land management.

Trends in Timber Harvest on Public Lands

Escalation in conflicts over actions of federal land management agencies, fueled by the conflict industry—hired hands that thrived on conflict from both extractive industries and environmental groups—that emerged full blown in the 1990s did little or nothing to aid in the resolution of the divisive issues explored. It has become more and more obvious with time that ever-exacerbating social/political conflict—no matter how well funded—cannot form the basis for long-term management with any real chance of reasonable stability or sustainability of land management action.

Clearly, the degree of economic, social and ecological stability that was believed possible, as a matter of faith, at mid-20th century has proven impossible to sustain over significant time periods (Thomas 1996). However, even while stability seems an impossible dream, it does seem worthwhile to reduce instability in the yield of forest products, goods and services to the extent practicable.

Therefore, it appears likely that there will be more attention to collaborative planning and management at local levels, with less power and less influence residing in the hands of the conflict industry except to define the boundaries of debate and decision space (Wondolleck and Jaffe 2000). Self-interest, limited resources and insatiable demands from a growing human population dictate that all interested or concerned parties must ultimately acknowledge the ancient wisdom and advice applied to debilitating conflict too long endured: "Come, let us reason together" (Thomas 2000b).

Although the concerns about forest fragmentation are both genuine and justified, the result of such dramatic reductions in timber harvest on public lands—particularly the national forests—do not bode well for elk that reside primarily in forested habitats on public lands. As discussed previously, closure of forest canopies results in loss of grasses, forbs and shrubs at ground level, and, therefore, loss of food for elk and other species dependent on early seral conditions. The concern is that the early seral stage of vegetation is very short lived (on the order of 10 to 20 years), compared with the time that trees can dominate sites (which can extend into hundreds of years for forests that are preserved and protected from fire). The period of optimum forage production is shorter still—5 to 10 years. If forest canopies are not opened routinely, providing for development of new forage growth, elk numbers likely will decline, and perhaps dramatically so. The potential for these early successional habitats to be dominated by invasive, noxious weeds of lesser palatability as forage for ungulates is not fully known, but it may well be of enormous significance. Also, domestic livestock that depends on transitory range will be a target for reduction in numbers and season of grazing. This will throw elk into competition, in terms of both available space and grazing.

In fact, widespread evidence of just such declines in elk numbers is emerging in widely scattered portions of the primary elk range in the western United States. For example, in Oregon, declining productivity of elk—both Rocky Mountain and Roosevelt subspecies—is reflected in long-term declines of calf/cow ratios in spring. Declines have been documented both in western Oregon's Roosevelt elk ranges where calf/cow ratios determined in the spring have declined by about 35% (to 31 to 40 calves per 100 cows) during the past 40 years, and in northeastern portions of the state where those have declined by half during the same period—from 50 to 55 calves per 100 cows in 1965 to 25 to 30 calves per 100 cows (Cook et al. 1999).

Declines in herd productivity have been most pronounced in the areas with the largest elk populations. Most elk herds in northeastern Oregon are well below management objectives (Carter 1992, Schommer 1991). Elk population declines in several Washington elk herds have been striking—elk numbers in the Olympic herd declined 40% since the early 1990s, and some herds in the North and South Rainier areas in Washington have declined 33% to 75% (Cook et al. 1999). Elk populations currently are 25% below management objectives in the Blue Mountains of southeastern Washington.

In Idaho, elk numbers in the Lolo Elk Zone (which includes the Clearwater elk herd, formerly one of the state's largest and most productive) have declined dramatically since 1996 (Compton 1999). In the Clearwater River drainage (Unit 10), elk herds have declined by 48%, and calf recruitment has declined from 30 to 40 calves per 100 cows before 1980 to consistently below 10 calves per 100 cows since that time (Compton 1999).

We believe that much of the documented increase in elk numbers during the period 1950 to 1990 was due to dramatically increased forage resulting from extensive timber harvest coordinated with elk habitat specifications. Significant declines of 75% and more in timber cut on public lands since the mid-1980s has led to declines in elk numbers because of forage reduction. Exotic weed problems will exacerbate the problem by further reducing forage availability.

President Clinton's decision to ensure the future roadless character of 54.3 million acres (22 million ha) of national forests can benefit or hurt elk populations, depending largely on actions taken to assure that a significant amount of disturbance (i.e., fire) will be allowed to occur on these lands. Fire management is a complicated business, as related to sizing, spacing and timing of controlled burns. Inevitably, some of the controlled burns will escape and become wildfires and, consequently, burn more ground than intended. An escaped controlled burn by the National Park Service in New Mexico (the Los Alamos fire) in 2000 destroyed hundreds of homes. Vast expanses of closed forest canopies (i.e., trees with canopies that touch those of their neighbors) interspersed with large fire-created openings of hundreds or even thousands of acres following wildfire probably will contribute much less to elk welfare than carefully spaced, sized and timed timber cuts (i.e., canopy removal).

In the case of roadless lands, habitat manipulations to benefit elk are and will be difficult and risky to achieve. Habitat manipulations largely confined to applications of controlled burns (including allowing wildfires to burn "under prescription") may be of limited usefulness in elk habitat management. These limitations are due to fire magnitude and intensity allowable in relation to control capability

Closed canopy forests fail to provide the amount and type of forage required to sustain elk. However, managed, uneven-aged timber stands can support healthy elk populations by providing essential foods and shelter. *Photo by Milo Burcham.*

(i.e., terrain in these areas is likely to be steep and varied). Accessibility (either for attack on the fire or rapid retreat for firefighters) is significantly limited by the absence of roads. As a result, fire, controlled or wild, will be allowed to have its way only when risks are judged to be very low. And low-risk fires rarely achieve a scale or intensity of treatment that is meaningful in terms of an entire elk population (Thomas 2000a).

The wildfire season of the summer of 2000, largely in Montana, clearly demonstrated that wildfire will likely be the wild card influencing the role of roadless areas in regard to elk habitat (Thomas 2000a). Oddly, the fire policy for these areas was not part of the debate over President Clinton's instructions to the Forest Service to implement roadless area designations. Perhaps an essential fire policy will evolve from forest-by-forest planning that the Forest Service will undertake from 2001 to 2010.

For the benefit of elk habitat on national forests and for the benefit of those forests overall, funds to address fire management must be adequate and assured on a continuing basis. A year after the fires of 2000, federal money is pouring into national forest coffers to address the described problems related to fire, both controlled and wild. But as time passes, if history provides any lessons, there will be a series of years when wildfires are minimal and years when they are significant. Political attention and interest are likely to wane in the quiet years and funds likely will be directed elsewhere.

In addition, public acceptance of continuous controlled burning and occasional escapes of controlled burns may well wane over time, particularly over a span of years when wildfire activity is low. Support for controlled burns, from both people and politicians, will likely lessen during such periods as other "emergencies" compete for attention—and funding.

Therefore, it is problematic whether political and public can be sustained for such a program of burning, decade after decade. Executing such programs successfully and on a sustainable basis will require increases in and retention of staff specifically trained to carry out the mission, including sustaining the necessary support or, at least, tolerance. The learning curves for new recruits and new fire bosses will be very steep, with lives and property on the line. Increased spending for adequate equipment (trucks, fire engines, helicopters, communications equipment and aircraft) will be required. Whether funding will keep pace with needs is uncertain.

Also, it is likely that the areas in the urban/wildland interface will receive most of the initial and continuing emphasis, and there certainly will be less attention to back country regions that provide most of the elk habitat for spring, summer and autumn. In addition, such manipulations of vegetation, in terms of effects on wildlife habitat, will not be benign. To the extent that attention will be primarily focused, at least initially, on relatively low elevation public land/urban interfaces, the most dramatic effects on wildlife habitat will occur there.

These manipulations of vegetation and the relative elevation at which they will take place have high potential of producing and maintaining high-quality winter range for elk and deer. In at least some cases, and inadvertently at this point, this will put the deer and elk habitat where the people are—for good or ill. Will concentrations of deer and elk in such areas be politically acceptable in light of inevitable damage to vegetation and fences, incompatibility with dogs and domestic livestock, automobile collisions, etc? And, in some cases, such predators as bears, cougars, wolves and coyotes can be expected to take advantage of winter concentrations of wild ungulates, with carcasses revealed each spring by melting snows. It is highly advisable to identify and deal with such management problems before they occur.

In the absence of fire (wild or controlled) on a massive basis, most roadless areas will become more and more vulnerable to wildfire over time, and less suited to plant species associated with early seral stages that produce forage for elk. Forest canopies will tend to close, preventing sunlight from reaching ground-level plants and shrubs, and dead limbs, dead trees and other biomass (living and dead) will accumulate. This accumulation is what fire ecologists and managers refer to as fuel, and it is measured by a fuel loading index.

When big fires occur—as they did in 2000 and inevitably will again when summer temperatures soar and fuel loading is high and moisture content low—the result will be burns hotter and perhaps much more extensive than have been experienced since 1910. The consequences may include soils temporarily rendered hydrophobic (water shedding), flooding due to quick run-off, erosion and delayed revegetation with extensive areas devoid of hiding cover for elk and deer for many years. The vulnerability of elk to hunters in those areas will increase significantly.

Managers will either accept what is to come or move ahead with actions to reduce the risk of stand-replacing fire by mechanical reduction of fuel and institution of controlled fire on a rotational basis. Therein lies huge opportunity for enhancement of elk forage and creation of habitat for wildlife species dependent on early seral vegetation. The fuel-control measures can be designed to achieve that goal through attention to location, sizing and spacing of treatments, and to reduce risk of broad and severe damage from *hot* stand-replacing fires that are otherwise inevitable. But such treatments will be very expensive and always risky in terms of unpredictable results and, possibly, explosion into fast-moving wildfire that burns what is not intended. Then, too, controlled burns must be repeated at regular intervals.

What about identified wilderness areas, where habitat manipulation is severely restricted or forbidden by law? Most wilderness areas are located at high elevation on lands of relatively low biomass. The combination of high elevation (with some areas above timberline), complex and rugged topography, shallow soils, deep snow accumulations, mechanical actions resulting from snowslides, relatively short growing seasons and extreme fluctuations in annual temperatures often results in a mosaic of vegetation that includes many natural openings. These produce the early seral vegetation favored by elk in late spring, summer and early autumn.

The contribution of wilderness or unroaded areas to elk habitat and, specifically, to quality elk hunting, is significant, but these lands do not provide sufficient forage for elk herds when viewed either year-round and over the long term. Snow accumulations force elk out of many high elevation areas during winter. Acreage of wilderness in the form of low elevation forests is limited. Wilderness lands are subject to naturally occurring wildfires that may be allowed to burn under prescription (i.e., if they burn within specified limits). These fires occur irregularly and may result in the aforementioned boom or bust cycles of elk forage availability. Extensive wildfires occur relatively rarely. But under certain circumstances, they may create, for a time, vast acreages conducive to forage production for elk. Without a doubt, wilderness and roadless areas produce unique hunting experiences much treasured by some hunters (including the authors). But these lands are limited in distribution and, therefore, in importance to elk populations (and most elk hunters) compared with forested lands that are at lower elevations and traditionally have been subject to roading and logging.

Grazing

Much like timber production, the grazing of domestic livestock (cattle, sheep, goats and horses) on public lands have become increasingly contentious during the closing decades of the 20th century. Opponents have argued—with increasing effect—for both significant reductions in allowable grazing of livestock and for higher grazing fees. The trend toward closing forest canopies will reduce forage for livestock as well as for elk, resulting in increased competition between elk and cattle on spring, summer and autumn ranges. Likely, this will result in reduced allocations for livestock use and, less likely, in reduced elk numbers.

Management decisions related to livestock grazing may well have a significant impact on elk numbers during the 21st century. Conventional wisdom equates reduction in livestock grazing to a lessening of potential competition with elk and, therefore, enhancement of elk welfare. When the situation is viewed at larger scale and with full consideration of relevant socioeconomic factors, there is no certainty that removal, in whole or in part, of livestock from federal lands will inevitability provide a benefit to elk over the long term.

Most permittees who graze livestock on federal lands cohabited by elk own properties whose boundaries are adjacent to national forests. These are the so-called base properties for allocation of grazing permits from the Forest Service. Most of these permittees are remarkably tolerant of wintering elk and mule deer on their private properties, despite the competition between the elk and their cattle for food (both natural and supplemental).

In many cases, deer and elk do not arrive in large numbers on winter ranges on private lands until after hunting

The immense network of roads constructed in elk habitat during the last few decades of the 20th century have posed thorny problems for managers of public lands. Some areas have been closed to motorized vehicles to provide security for elk during critical periods of the year for biological reasons, such as reducing the potential for disturbance during the winter, when food supplies are low or on critical portions of the calving area during calving season. Other closures have been implemented for social reasons, such as providing increased elk security during hunting seasons, or reducing the expense of annual upkeep and maintenance requirements. *Above photo by Milo Burcham. Right photo by J. Mark Higley.*

seasons are concluded. Accordingly, ranch owners have limited capability to control deer or elk through hunting, whether or not for a fee. Wintering elk and deer commonly damage fences and haystacks. If present on ranches during autumn hunting seasons, elk and deer can create an attractive nuisance, bringing hunters and, in some cases, disruption to normal ranch operations and economic loss if less-conscientious hunters leave livestock gates open. It may be that the tolerance of such landowners for elk and mule deer in large numbers on their lands in winter is a tacit and little recognized quid pro quo for the privilege of public land grazing at attractive prices.

Ranching under such conditions is commonly a marginal economic enterprise, wherein ranchers are "land rich but dollar poor." Economic failures seem more frequently to result in sale of the property for subdivision into ranchettes or hobby ranches for those with adequate means to ranch at the margin and absorb losses. We believe that the long-term viability of many ranches is significantly tied to continued availability of federal land grazing permits at relatively low costs (see also Knight and Landres 1998).

If grazing fees increase or livestock numbers decline significantly, as seems possible (if not likely), economic viability of many ranching operations will be adversely affected. That, in turn, would direct attention to efficiency,

competition and reduction of all unnecessary costs of the ranching business. Measures likely to occur include fences that exclude elk and mule deer, an increase in wildlife depredation complaints, demands for financial restitution from wildlife management agencies for damages incurred, commercialization of hunting opportunities where possible and exclusion of hunters and recreationists unless their activities can be made to pay. If these measures, in whatever combination, are not effective in making marginal ranching operations profitable, sale of ranches for ranchettes, subdivisions, second homes and hobby ranches seems almost inevitable. The resulting fragmentation of habitat cannot be considered good news for the well being and management of elk or mule deer over the long term.

Nevertheless, environmental activists have rolled up an impressive string of accomplishments since 1970. Among them have been drastic reductions of timber extraction and active management on federal lands. These victories have dramatically and steadily increased the costs of planning, assessments, protests and appeals of decisions, legal actions, land-use allocations, and political activities. The next area of contention surely will be livestock grazing on public lands. However, whether the future brings a moratorium against grazing on public lands or a workable solution to conflicting interests in these lands, the future of elk on these lands, where spring/summer/autumn range is in public ownership and winter range is in private ownership, will be a function of the continued availability of winter habitat for elk on private ranches and the ecological condition of these ranges.

The management issue of winter habitat for elk and deer must be addressed as part of the political issue of public land grazing. We believe that arrangements to ensure the future of adjoining open lands at low elevations as viable, operating ranches is a key to the future of elk in much of the West. That outcome is inescapably linked with the issue of economic viability of ranch operations, particularly in the face of increasing pressures for development of those lands. Increased fees for grazing or unnecessary constraints on livestock numbers that reduce the economic viability of ranch operations dependent on public land grazing seem likely to reduce the ability of elk to exist on high elevation public lands at levels approaching present numbers.

We believe the ultimate guiding principle for land managers in dealing with this dilemma is the larger issue of range condition. In the larger sense, it matters little whether grazing fees increase or decrease, as long as habitat conditions on public lands are satisfactory or at least improving. Even reduction of fees for grazing, if that results in improvement of range conditions, may yield significant improvement in the potential for elk to flourish where habitats are a mix of public and private lands.

Access Management

President Clinton's 2000 decision to maintain all unroaded areas on national forests of more than 5,000 acres (2,024 ha) in roadless status has triggered cries of indignation from the timber industry, ORV users and some political figures from affected areas, and the State of Idaho sued over the process used. Similar expressions of outrage have accompanied efforts to reduce road densities in roaded areas. These protests have taken up the war cry from the early 1900s that federal lands were being locked up (i.e., closed to access or use). So, roads and road management on public lands are contentious and significant land management issues. They are apt to become even more divisive in the future, as traditional means of back country access, hiking and packing with horses, mules, llamas and even dogs interact with ever-more sophisticated ORVs, such as four-wheel-drive trucks, trail machines, motorcycles, mountain bikes and snowmobiles.

Use of ORVs on roads closed to unrestricted motorized access will increase and cause problems on road systems that are rapidly deteriorating. Federal land management agencies are likely to look toward private organizations to assist in road and trail maintenance to accommodate ORV use. Nevertheless, the situation is likely to result in open an-

tagonism between different types of user groups (e.g., back country horsemen versus motorcyclists versus hikers, etc.).

Although competition and conflict over the management of road systems will continue to be controversial, ORV use of federally managed lands will prove even more resistant to regulation. The underlying issues are complex: increasing competition among various types of users for recreational opportunity; disturbance to wildlife; damage of trails; erosion; sedimentation of water courses; unsightliness; noise; costs associated with management and upkeep to roads and trails; rules enforcement; and other issues. ORVs facilitate and promote access to back country areas for some people who lack back country skills and appreciation of the impacts of their activities on the land. Motorized access to back country greatly changes the nature of the recreational experience. The main issue is not whether one form of recreation has higher moral or legal ground, but one of determining the point of jeopardy to public landscape and its natural features, including elk and other wildlife, to preclude or limit the public from pursuing certain forms of recreation that are lawful elsewhere.

The ORV use has significant potential to affect elk and elk management adversely. Access management was developed initially as a means of decreasing elk disturbance and harvest vulnerability with physical and visual barriers provided by terrain for forest cover. Off-road vehicle impacts on elk vulnerability are not yet definitive, but elk avoidance of roads open to motorized vehicles has been demonstrated repeatedly (Hieb 1976, Lyon 1979a, Rost and Bailey 1979, Witmer and deCalesta 1985, Cole et al. 1997, Johnson et al. 2000, Rowland et al. 2000).

Endangered Species

If past is prologue, responses to managing habitats for threatened or endangered species will fall disproportionately on federal lands (Thomas et al.1990, Forest Ecosystem Management Assessment Team 1993). For example, spotted owl recovery plans mandated under the Endangered Species Act have relied heavily on the establishment of reserves within which any manipulation of vegetation, particularly logging in any form, is controversial at best and may well be precluded. Considering all forested lands, examination of accumulating numbers of recovery plans for plants and animals is focused to the extent possible on the public lands. This growing patchwork of protected areas will have an increasingly dramatic, cumulative, negative influence on any active management of public lands. Ground disturbing activities, such as the manipulation of vegetation, road construction, logging, silviculture and controlled burning, will become more difficult or even impossible to execute over larger and larger areas.

The likely response to this complex management situation will be a forest-by-forest review of ecosystem protection obligations, resulting in a nested (i.e., zoned) ecosystem-based network of forest reserves. These reserves will be interspersed with areas established through forest planning or congressional action for emphasis on the efficient growing and extraction of forest products (such as timber) in a relatively predictable and sustainable fashion.

Although it is impossible to predict accurately the entire structure of such a management system, the system could be designed around a group of core, fully protected areas (e.g., rare habitats such as old-growth providing for the needs of rare species). These core areas could be surrounded and buffered by larger areas wherein complete protection is not required (i.e., stream protection zones) in which ground-disturbing activities must be minimized. Such a system would appear compatible with wilderness and roadless area management designations. However, there is no reason to expect that such arrangements would be optimal for production of elk.

In federal land management planning jargon, elk are referred to as featured species or even as management indicator species (see Chapter 11), categories that include any species that receives specific management attention. But required management attention to the needs of species declared to be threatened or endangered (as determined by the Fish and Wildlife Service or the National Marine Fisheries Service) trump any desire or demand to focus on production of featured species such as elk (Czech and Krausman 2001).

Experience with the management plans for maintenance or improvement of habitat for threatened or endangered species that rely on late successional forests (i.e., old growth) indicates that such a focus will seriously handicap land managers who wish to enhance habitat for elk through forest and associated road management. In such cases, most old growth and even relatively mature forests become off-limits to logging, as are those areas designated to mature into late successional forests over time. In effect, the average age, size and canopy closure of dominant trees in the forest tract in question will tend to increase, thereby reducing forage production.

As late as the 1960s, the dominant paradigm put forth by foresters, including those concerned with public lands, was the desirability of converting slow-growing or stagnant (older, mature) forest stands to younger, more vigorous stands that produced wood at an enhanced rate. To some degree, this paradigm has been replaced on public lands by an appreciation for the beauty and addition to the biodiversity of old-growth or mature forests. Given the high price of retention of old growth in terms of opportunity costs (i.e.,

the economic return that could have resulted from a particular action, say, the cutting of old growth or mature forest), such retention of older forests have been essentially relegated to public lands. This situation seems likely to continue as technology and economic factors make harvesting trees at younger ages and smaller sizes more feasible and economically attractive. Over time, this circumstance can be expected to result in declines in elk or elk use on public lands and an increase in elk use on private lands due to the latter's much greater admixture of cover and forage areas.

This shift in use patterns by elk can be anticipated and potential land management activities evaluated. One way to view the situation where economic return is of primary importance is to return harvested areas to tree cover of desired species with complete utilization of the growing space by trees. This will require immediate replanting and determined efforts (use of repellents, fencing or population control) to minimize damage by wild ungulates. Subsequent management (thinning, fertilization, insect and disease control) will be directed toward maximization of tree growth.

Under such intense management regimes, the presence of wild ungulates—elk or deer—in any significant numbers would be considered a negative influence. Such management regimes will likely be more feasible—economically and practically—on very high site timber lands, such as those west of the Cascade Mountains in northern California, Oregon, Washington and British Columbia, where moisture is abundant. This is, largely, the range of the Roosevelt elk subspecies.

However, on elk ranges east of the Cascades, which is primarily occupied by the Rocky Mountain elk subspecies, tree growing potential is significantly less due to site limitations, moisture conditions and terrain. Immediate reforestation and preclusion of ungulate damage to young trees will be much more expensive and less likely to be successful.

The outcome of such shifts could be profound in both impact on private land operations and opportunities for landowners, particularly large landowners such as corporate landholders. They may well capitalize on the situation by instituting commercial hunting operations to compensate for negative impacts of elk on intensive forest operations. After all, the corporate bottom line surely will focus on revenues in excess of costs—however that is accomplished.

Because dealing with elk and deer impacts on forestry operations will be expensive, continuous and problematical commercialization of hunting opportunities will become more attractive as elk and deer numbers decline on public lands and increase on private lands. Oddly, almost paradoxically, private lands have potential to become the multiple use lands that produce maximum revenue to stockholders as the public lands become more focused on single uses centered around focal species (especially threatened or endangered species).

Elk Management by the State Agencies

State agencies are likely to continue to have direct management responsibility for resident wildlife. But that is not a certainty. There will be continued efforts on the part of some—particularly animal rights, antihunting and antitrapping groups—for expansion of federal responsibility and control of wildlife on the public lands. Their moves will build on an expansion of the directed and focused management for the recovery of threatened or endangered species under provisions of Endangered Species Act. Supporters of increased federal control often believe (with good reason, we think) that federal control would afford them greater influence over wildlife management decisions on public lands than they currently enjoy. Although there appears little immediate likelihood that federal agencies will move into a position of preemption on issues of regulating hunting on public lands, the ability of state wildlife agencies to influence land management to benefit such game species as elk will likely be diminished in the 21st century as other powerful political forces become more involved in public land management.

This seems a likely outcome of many interacting factors, the most significant of which includes (1) an ever-expanding list of threatened and endangered species and the subsequent development of recovery plans for these species, (2) increases in demands for management and enhancement of the welfare of nongame and predatory wildlife, and (3) new sources of revenue to provide funding to both state and federal agencies for the management of wildlife species that are not hunted. The result is that hunting will be less and less the "bread and butter" of state wildlife agencies—and money does talk.

Some have argued that such expansions in the role and mission of state wildlife management agencies will diminish the responsiveness of agencies to hunters as their traditional constituency. This, we believe, is inevitable, as state wildlife management agencies are required to become more responsive to an ever-more diverse clientele. However, we do not believe that states will lose their traditional role as mangers of the wildlife resource or as providers of hunting opportunity. Although we address the future of hunting later in this chapter, it is well to note at this point that the number of hunters in America, particularly big game hunters, has grown in recent decades. That number likely will continue to grow for the first decade, at least, of the 21st century (Kenyon and Duda 2000). However, despite these gains in numbers, there is a decline in the percentage of the Americans who claim themselves to be hunters (i.e., the overall population is increasing even faster than the increase in hunter numbers). These trends—an ever-increasing demand for hunting opportunity and a declining voice of hunters as a percentage of the public—establish a tension that can tear traditional wildlife management agencies apart as new voices clamor for attention of decision makers. Hunting in the 21st century will become increasingly controversial as opponents challenge accepted practices and objectives. Wildlife managers must become more effective in identifying the biological basis for management of game species via hunting, as well as the use of hunting as a tool of wildlife management for the benefit and protection of private and public resources. The effectiveness of such evolving strategies will be determined largely by how astutely and effectively state fish and wildlife agencies react to the developing tensions described above.

State Agency Decision Making

State wildlife management agencies came into being largely as a result of the devastation of wildlife numbers and destruction of wildlife habitats during the 19th century. Wildlife, along with timber, grass, water and minerals, was viewed and treated then as commodities to be exploited within restriction. Wildlife restoration efforts initially focused on game species, and it was hunting license fees that funded (and, in most states, still fund) the vast majority of state wildlife agency operations. There was a heroic effort in the U.S. Congress in 2000 to enhance and broaden the base of funding for wildlife management issues in the new millennium. The mechanism was the Conservation and Reinvestment Act (CARA). Despite overwhelming bipartisan support from Congress and governors of the states, a few senators who held leadership positions on Budget Committees assured defeat of the effort. Their primary concern was with the appropriateness of guaranteed multiyear funding for any federal program. This defeat was a significant blow to increased and broadened activities for wildlife—particularly on the part of the states (Thomas 1999). This failure to match resources with the demands and expectations raised by the spate of environmental laws of the 1970s was a continuation of a long and sorry tradition.

The alternative action to Conservation and Reinvestment Act by the Clinton Administration was to fund the Land and Water Conservation Fund at its authorized level. Revenues from royalties to the federal government from off-shore oil and gas leases had long been authorized for conservation purposes. However, Congress routinely shifted those revenues to other uses. In his first budget speech to Congress in February 2001, President George W. Bush proposed that the royalties be allocated from the Land

and Water Conservation Fund to the extent authorized. Regardless of that outcome—and the conservation community is not holding its breath in great expectation—a great opportunity for wildlife and its management was foregone for inadequate reasons. And the tradition lives on.

Trends toward an expanded role of wildlife restoration efforts by the states to deal with *all* wildlife—as opposed to a continued near-total focus on game species—are wide and varied. In 1997, 47 state agencies reported having developed public areas for "watchable wildlife" (Wildlife Management Institute 1997). All (50) states reported trends away from traditional, concentrated monitoring of game animals and threatened and endangered species. Most (39) state agencies reported monitoring neotropical migratory birds. And nearly all (47) reported monitoring other nongame species. In contrast, there was a decline in the number of states (from 22 in 1985 to 12 in 1997) maintaining gamefarms (Wildlife Management Institute 1997)—an action, in our opinion, long overdue.

These changes coincided with expanded responsibilities of many state wildlife management agencies for more generalized environmental protection and enhancement. The shifts in focus produced an increased funding base, with at least a portion of the budget of some agencies being provided from general state revenues. Although this latter trend is less pronounced in the western elk-producing states, the move in this direction is inevitable, as sportsmen are increasingly unwilling or unable to carry the full burden for ecosystem protection and the broader spectrum of generalized wildlife management responsibilities. Furthermore, to expect hunters (and anglers) to carry that burden alone or mainly so seems patently unfair and increasingly politically unpalatable to citizen-hunters.

A revitalized Conservation and Reinvestment Act, or something akin to it, could provide much of the sustained financial assistance necessary to make the changes in the states' expanding conservation role related to all wildlife and associated recreation. Patterned after the Federal Aid in Wildlife Restoration Act, such a measure could provide a three to one match of federal to state funding to be directed toward restoration of those "species with the greatest conservation need."

The impacts of such new or enhanced sources of funding on elk management efforts by the states will remain unclear until wildlife conservation plans have been approved. The states will have to provide matching funds. Those state wildlife agencies that remain solely dependent on sales of hunting licenses and tags for support must develop new sources of funds to provide the match, or draw from funds already dedicated to wildlife law enforcement or existing wildlife management programs.

What will change, given such a boost in funding, is that state wildlife agencies are likely to increase dramatically in overall influence in the conservation arena as additional personnel, better suited to the new tasks, are hired. As they gain experience in implementation of new wildlife and associated recreation and education management programs, this will equate to broadened and intensified agency missions.

Concurrent with the passage of the necessary funding vehicle, demands will increase for western state wildlife management agencies to deal with the impacts of expanding (in both numbers and range) populations of predators, such as bears, wolves, coyotes and mountain lions, on both big game and livestock. While the primary "driver" for such programs results from successful introduction, establishment and range extension of wolves in many western elk ranges, the potential reintroduction of grizzly bears into northern Idaho and western Montana, and continuing expansion of mountain lion populations throughout western states, will also contribute to that demand. Many western states have been unable (because of provisions of the Endangered Species Act or statewide citizen initiatives) or unwilling (because of political sensitivity) to become heavily involved in management of predators. This reluctance—in many cases, an abdication of responsibility by the states—has left the field to federal agencies, such as the Wildlife Services program of the Animal and Plant Health Inspection Service, the Fish and Wildlife Service, and to nongovernmental entities and environmental activists.

However, the Fish and Wildlife Service's delisting of wolves (i.e., removal from the list of threatened or endangered species), and the demands of state legislatures for programs to address a perceived need to protect humans, their pets and wildlife from predators, makes future emphasis by state agencies on management of predators inevitable. This cup will not pass them by. Managers will be charged with assuring that populations of predators remain viable or those species will be relisted and responsibility for them will revert to the federal Fish and Wildlife Service. State wildlife management agencies face a "Hobson's choice." State agencies must either defer to federal control of predators (as pests or as threatened or endangered species), allow environmental activists to take control of predator management through initiative processes, or assume control (and responsibility) for those predators not protected by federal law. Some significant proaction by the states will be required. The credibility and effectiveness of state wildlife management agencies is rapidly dissipating as they delay taking decisive action to manage resident predators, with all of the attendant public concerns.

We believe that the net result of these diverse demands will be an evolving but fundamental change in the role of

Successful reintroduction of large predators onto public lands will require that state wildlife management agencies become increasingly involved with management of those species as they interact with the game animal populations that are the focus of most wildlife management agencies. Funding to offset the costs for these new management tasks, not only in manpower and equipment but also in the reduction (in some cases) of the number of game animals available for harvest by hunters, needs to be identified in federal land management and state wildlife management agency budgets. *Photo by Barbara Thomas.*

most state wildlife management agencies. Founded on the perception that wildlife resources are a commodity (game species) that should be maintained and rationed to customers (hunters), state wildlife management agencies now find their role in general wildlife management expanding—whether they like it or not—to include management of a wider range of species to meet a rapidly widening range of preservation, restoration and recreational demands. (This is akin to the experience of federal land management agencies that changed focus during 1985 to 2000, from an emphasis on commodity production to ecosystem management, wherein preservation of biodiversity and sustainability of ecosystem function processes are of overriding importance.) This expanded role of state agencies in the wildlife management arena, which seems inevitable, will require not only expanded sources of funding, but expansion of staff expertise beyond wildlife management, into the realm of human dimensions of such management decisions. Agencies will find themselves serving and answering to a new, larger, more diverse and more fickle clientele—one that will demand clear, biologically and socially accountable decisions.

These new demands will result in state wildlife agencies that are oriented (in addition to focus on game species and serving hunters) to a broader scope of wildlife species and management of a broader array of wildlife-associated recreation not related to hunting. These agencies will dis-

cover that their primary *product* (from the standpoint of revenue generation) is recreation, and that recreation can be packaged in many ways consistent with the state's trust responsibility for wildlife. Although recreation is "sellable," it will *not* allow the agencies to divorce themselves from either their trust responsibility for wildlife resources or from the demands of biologically intricate ecosystems. State agencies will always be required to manage wildlife, to ensure the viability of animal populations within some balance with available habitat and within guidelines to protect people and property. Hunting—removal of animals excess to population management guidelines, is likely to remain, as it is today, the best and most efficient and effective tool to manage populations of game animals—and as important, to create and maintain within the public a concern for and knowledge about wildlife management.

One result of an increasingly diverse constituency for wildlife management agencies, in the case of at least some western states, will be a merger of state wildlife management agencies with state land management agencies, state parks and recreation departments, or any combination. Mergers will create larger state departments of natural resources, already common in eastern and mid-western states and in some western states (Wildlife Management Institute 1997). It seems unlikely that many state wildlife agencies supported solely or primarily by traditional users (i.e., hunters) only (and federal matching funds derived from taxation on sporting firearms, ammunition, handguns and archery equipment) will continue to exist far into the 21st century.

State Agency Regulation of Elk Harvests

Whatever the future holds for the organization and mission of state fish and wildlife agencies, it seems clear that elk hunting, where it exists, will provide a major source of income for the wildlife management programs of state wildlife management agencies. Hunters have demonstrated their willingness and ability to fund wildlife management that includes opportunity to harvest wild animals within sound biological guidelines. Whatever new sources of funding may appear in the future, it is unlikely that they will replace hunter dollars as a key source of renewable income from a biologically renewable resource. Thus, elk management likely will remain central to wildlife management activities in these states.

State wildlife management agencies that are less dependent on hunting license and tag income are more able (and more likely) to provide a variety of wildlife-associated recreational experiences based on shifting public demand. In the case of elk hunting, such opportunities may range from signifying areas managed to produce a very low annual harvest, with significant chance to see or kill old-age bulls, or special opportunities to be in the field during the rut when elk are bugling. Opportunities to use hunters to control undesirable elk population expansion in numbers or range would be more feasible. Some significant areas may be set aside completely, whether primarily for elk or other species, where elk are habituated to the presence of humans and are readily and routinely seen by recreationists.

However, by and large, harvest of elk by hunters seems unlikely to change dramatically as a component of elk management programs during the next several decades. State agencies will continue to focus, as they have in past years, on many of the perennial management problems identified elsewhere in this book. When queried by Bunnell (1997), most wildlife management agencies of states with huntable elk populations identified elk habitat management as their primary concern and listed the following among current and anticipated elk management problems.

- Limitations to the public land habitat base (Alaska, Oklahoma, Pennsylvania, South Dakota, Texas).
- Urban sprawl and habitat conversion to human uses (California, Colorado, Minnesota, Nebraska, Oregon, Washington, Wyoming).
- Lack of openings in forest canopies (i.e., lack of early seral stages for forage production) in areas where forests have matured and timber harvests have declined

(Idaho, Michigan, Minnesota, Oklahoma, Oregon, Pennsylvania).
- Increased road densities or timber harvest practices (Alaska, California, Idaho, Kentucky, Oregon, South Dakota, Wyoming).
- Depredation or forage competition with domestic livestock (Arizona, Kansas, Nebraska, Nevada, New Mexico, North Dakota, South Dakota, Utah, Washington, Wyoming).
- Grazing impacts on riparian areas (Arizona).
- Land access for elk management (Colorado).
- Artificial feeding (Michigan).

Not surprisingly, in the wake of expansions in elk numbers and occupied range in the closing decades of the 20th century, four states identified efforts to decrease (Arizona, Montana, New Mexico, Oregon) or stabilize (Michigan, Minnesota, North Dakota, Washington) elk populations (Bunnell 1997). Arkansas, California, Nebraska, Nevada, Oregon, South Dakota and Utah identified areas for future expansion of elk herds. Increased hunter harvests were identified as desirable in California, Montana, New Mexico, South Dakota and Washington.

Another problem that will become more prevalent is the habituation (a behavioral response to an altered environment) of elk to living in proximity to humans (Thompson and Henderson 1998). Habituation occurs when animals alter their behavioral response to stimuli that provide neither positive nor negative reinforcement (Knight and Gutzwiller 1995). In the case of elk, habituation to humans usually takes the form of an animal (or group of animals) learning that human behavior is both predictable and nonthreatening. Such reactions facilitate coexistence with humans without elk demonstrating normal avoidance or stress responses to humans.

As pointed out by Thompson and Henderson (1998), habituation offers advantages to elk, especially on traditional winter habitats that have been fragmented by human development or activity, because it allows elk to share those habitats with humans. Habituated animals conserve energy by 'turning off' their normal tendencies to flee from humans and human activities.

By occupying private lands, parks, golf courses and even rural subdivisions during hunting seasons, some habituated elk learn to lessen or avoid risk of death or bodily injury and simultaneously maintain physical condition. Habituation allows elk to exploit otherwise inaccessible resources (including manicured lawns and shrubbery) when other food is unavailable or in short supply, and it may even allow individual elk a competitive survival advantage over non-habituated elk.

Although elk may benefit by habituating to human environments and activities, this adaptation presents a wide range of problems to federal, state and provincial wildlife management agencies and private landowners. Elk are large and inquisitive animals, whose very size can create problems as they wander through homeowners' yards or across rain-softened golf greens, leaving tracks that become muddy mini-craters. Foraging can destroy manicured yards and shrubbery as well as stored crops and foodstuffs such as hay. Elk crossing or along roads present a significant risk to drivers and themselves. And elk habituated to humans may injure people, pets and livestock or damage property if they feel threatened (Thompson and Henderson 1998).

It is because of such problems, and the fact that many state and provincial wildlife management agencies have an explicit mandate to resolve problems associated with human/wildlife interactions, that agencies often strive to reduce the potential for elk habituation. Such efforts often require reduction or elimination of elk in areas that would facilitate habituation. That typically means maximizing hunter numbers in rural areas near human occupation, especially those areas where traditional elk winter ranges have been encroached upon and fragmented by human development. Such reductions will continue to place the agencies in an awkward situation created by conflicting landowner desires and demands. Owners of residential lots or ranchettes of various sizes sometimes differ dramatically in their tolerance of habituated elk. Ultimately, most such situations require reducing elk herd numbers far below levels that might be supported during other seasons of the year to minimize risk to humans and property and to minimize agency investment in problem resolution. Alternatively, elk may be excluded from their former ranges by erection of fences. However, people who have hunted these areas or the associated spring/summer/autumn ranges may resent the resultant losses in hunting opportunities.

The Role of Sportsmen and Private Landowners

The role of nongovernmental organizations, such as the Rocky Mountain Elk Foundation, in elk management is likely to expand. The proliferation of game species oriented groups in the final decades of the 20th century (i.e., the Foundation for North American Wild Sheep, the Mule Deer Foundation, etc.) suggests to us that recreational hunters have become ever-more specialized or more focused on particular species. If investment of time and money by individuals is a reliable indicator of interest and commitment, the expansion of the Rocky Mountain Elk Foundation and other nongovernmental organizations bodes well for the future of elk management and hunting traditions.

As discussed earlier, relatively lower levels of timber cutting on public lands may cause elk to shift occupancy to habitats on private and corporate timber holdings where more active timber harvest programs and stand treatments such as thinning and harvesting on relatively short-term rotations provide a continuous supply of abundant forage. An increasing presence of large numbers of elk on private lands, with potential for damage to young trees, is likely to produce conflict. That conflict will require more attention to elk depredation or landowners will commercialize hunting opportunities to reduce losses and enhance their economic bottom line.

Habituation of elk to humans offers substantial advantages to elk, allowing elk to exploit the nutritious vegetation of lawns and shrubbery while enjoying relative security from natural predators and hunters. Such habituation also brings increased risk of elk-caused injury to humans and their pets, damages to private lands, and headaches for wildlife management agencies. *Photo by Kim Hart.*

Experience has shown that the only permanent or even semipermanent solutions to serious damage by wild ungulates to desired vegetation, whether crops, trees or ornamental shrubs or flowers, is the elimination of the damaging animals or excluding them. Both approaches are expensive, apt to be judged politically incorrect and attacked by significant numbers of people.

In the case of large forest tracts, taking the advantage of the situation through commercial hunting can provide an alternative source of income to offset losses and improving overall economic performance. Due to tradition and coupled with fear of political consequences, large forest landowners in the Northwest and Intermountain West have been slow to capitalize on this rapidly developing opportunity. Experiences elsewhere in the United States with deer, turkey, waterfowl and quail hunting have demonstrated the potential of leasing hunting opportunities to enhance financial returns.

Elk Farming

At the close of the 20th century, elk ranching was highly controversial. For some people, it was highly lucrative. Some scientists, notably Geist (1988, 1991b, 1993, 1995a), have argued eloquently and convincingly that elk ranching and other commercialization of wildlife erodes the very underlying foundation on which North American wildlife management was constructed (i.e., public ownership of wildlife). Other scientists have argued that involvement of private landowners in wildlife ranching can aid conservation efforts and promote wildlife habitat protection (Teer 1993).

We do not believe that the future of elk ranching is bright, based on many converging lines of evidence, management experience and current events.

The first and perhaps major issue involves the economic aspects of elk ranching. Although elk have been classified as livestock in many states, and provisions of legislation such as Alberta's 1984 Wildlife Act allow the government to sell elk into private ownership, the economics of buying and selling elk bear a disturbing resemblance to past markets in wildlife. History is replete with boom and bust accounts of farming foxes, mink, chinchillas, nutria, and ratite birds such as ostriches and emus. In nearly every instance, value of the animals soared to astronomic levels early in the boom phase, only to fall precipitously as stock became more commonly available and would-be entrepreneurs dealt with the difficulties of adequate containment, unusual feed requirements, veterinary care, and a host of disease problems. Costs associated with each of these issues (and more) undermined the profitability of most operations, because values of the products declined in response to easy

availability of competitive products and substitutes. In short, a saturated market eliminated the scarcity value of what had been a unique product.

The value of elk in an economic context is measured by the marketability of elk products. Although proponents identify markets for elk meat, that market, in reality, is a niche market currently buoyed by the uniqueness of the product. We can well attest that elk venison can be excellent, and most of it is untainted by agricultural chemicals and food additives, such as red dyes. Unfortunately, in a commercial marketplace those generalities do not apply— elk raised on commercial farms will be subjected to the entire range of chemicals, medicines and additives as are other commercial meats.

There has long been a flourishing market in elk antler products for traditional medicines of the Far East. A recent (2001) shopping trip into the Chinatown section of Washington, D.C., produced a wide range of elk antler products, including slices of velvet antler, pills, potions, elixers, and teas. Traditionally, such products have been identified as aids to male potency—a market that has been replaced to a substantial degree by prescribed chemical formulations such as Viagra. Also, the international trade in elk antler products was dealt a serious blow when, early in 2001, Korea banned the import of antlers and antler products, in an effort to reduce the risk of importation of foot and mouth disease and mad cow disease, following recent outbreaks in Europe.

In fact, the outbreak of mad cow disease, or bovine spongiform encephalopathy, in Europe likely sounded the death knell of gamefarming operations. Bovine spongiform encephalopathy is one of a host of diseases referred to as transmissible spongiform encephalopathies, including a human form (Creutzfelt-Jacob disease) whose impacts are similar to those of Alzheimer's disease, and a form that occurs in elk and mule deer (chronic wasting disease). All of these diseases can be fatal; 80 deaths in the United Kingdom during the first half of 2001 were attributed to mad cow disease. Transmission is believed to occur by body fluids, soils contaminated by fecal material and placental fluids, and by ingestion of bones (including antlers) of infected animals (see Chapter 6).

In Canada, chronic wasting disease was reported from gamefarm elk in Sasketchewan in 1996, and subsequent intensive monitoring revealed its presence on at least 19 gamefarms. More than 3,000 elk in Canada were destroyed in efforts to confine the disease. However, a case was reported in a free-ranging white-tailed deer in 2001. Chronic wasting disease also has been reported from wild ungulates in Colorado and Wyoming. Although it is not known whether chronic wasting disease, like mad cow disease, is

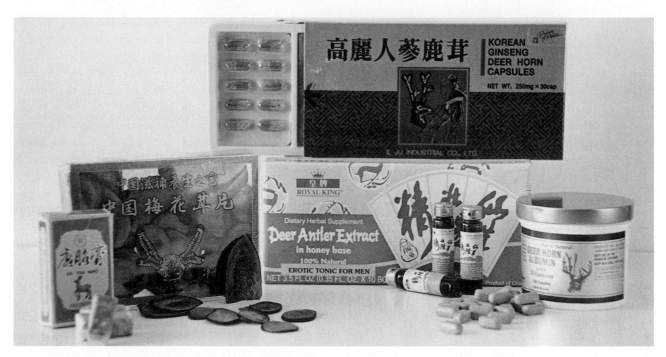

A wide variety of antler-based products derived from elk farming operations are readily available as traditional pharmaceutical aids in major cities around the world. This collection of velvet antler slices, elixirs, pills and potions was purchased in the Chinatown section of Washington, D.C., in February 2001. *Photo by Diane Ronayne.*

transferable to humans, the Colorado Division of Wildlife recommended that humans not eat elk venison suspected of being chronic wasting disease contaminated.

Unfortunately for gamefarm owners, there is no test for chronic wasting disease in living elk; confirmation of the disease is made by examination of the brain tissue of dead animals. The implications for game ranching are chilling— there is no way to ensure that interstate sale of living animals is not, in fact, spreading the disease nationally and internationally. Confirmed cases of chronic wasting disease provide case histories (trace-backs) of elk sold among game ranches in many states where the disease is not yet known to occur. Even if there was a means of nonlethal diagnosis, no treatment for chronic wasting disease exists beyond destruction and appropriate disposal of infected animals.

If transmissible spongiform encephalopathies sounded the death knell for game ranching, foot and mouth disease (FMD) provided the chorus. Foot and mouth disease is a highly contagious disease of livestock, but is not transmissible to humans. Still, there is a tremendous international effort currently underway to contain this disease and at tremendous cost to livestock owners and affected governments (i.e., taxpayers). Foot and mouth disease has occurred in the United States—Aldo Leopold (1933) identified Bureau of Animal Industry control of an outbreak among deer in California's Stanislaus National Forest in 1924 as the first effort at public arrest of a game disease epidemic in the

United States—but it is believed to have been eradicated. If foot and mouth disease should be found in the United States, wildlife management agencies will be involved in efforts to isolate any occurrences and prevent its spread by the same means as are used on agricultural practice— slaughter of exposed animals and incineration of carcasses. A memorandum on foot and mouth disease responsibility was circulated from the Southeastern Cooperative Wildlife Disease Study Group to state wildlife liaison officers in April 2001. It advised that, if foot and mouth disease was detected in the United States, the state wildlife liaison officer will be charged with conducting activities, including wildlife population reduction, that would result in surveillance and containment of the disease. This task was described as follows: "If wildlife is considered a risk factor for FMD [foot and mouth disease] persistence or dissemination, programs to reduce contact between infected livestock, wildlife, and uninfected domestic animals should begin as soon as possible. Containment of free-ranging wildlife to prevent the spread of disease is extremely difficult. It may be necessary to reduce local wildlife populations to a density at which FMD is unlikely. This requires immediate and aggressive actions that will have drastic effects on local wildlife. However, short-term and localized impact must be weighed against the long-term and widespread consequences of allowing FMD to persist in wildlife. Opposition to population reduction should be anticipated from interest groups as diverse as hunters and animal rights activists." Because of the ease by which foot and mouth disease may be spread, hunting seasons around the affected area will be closed.

The third member of this grisly disease trio is bovine tuberculosis, which *is* transmissible to humans and has been found in captive elk herds in North America.

Occurrences of these diseases in captive elk have already led to eradication of several entire herds of domestic elk and to quarantine of other elk farming operations that had received animals from the herds subsequently destroyed. Emergence of these diseases increases the potential for transmission between domestic and wild animals—and in some instances to humans.

Just as these diseases dramatically increase the risks of loss of capital investment in elk as livestock, those risks have resulted in the elimination of commercial markets for elk products. Disease risks also have increased the costs of maintaining elk, transferring them from owner to owner, and greatly increased the quality and cost of facilities necessary for elk production on private lands. Government regulatory agencies (livestock or wildlife agencies, depending on the state or province) will demand more and more assurance that *no* animals will escape the enclosures. There will also be increasing costs and red tape because of required testing of animals for disease. And almost certain to come is certification of the health of animals on a periodic basis, but because there currently is no test for chronic wasting disease, even a certification program may be inadequate.

Owners of elk farms are fighting back in the press and in the courts to protect their investments. The basis of such actions focus on the "takings" issue. Takings issue are matters wherein the government, in the name of the people, takes away a personal right or property without just and appropriate compensation. Whether or not that claim can be made to stand in the courts, it is difficult not to have some sympathy for people who pursued an alternative enterprise, with all its attendant risks.

We predict that, despite public aversion to takings, there will be increasing public animosity toward gamefarm operations. Passage in 2000 of a Montana citizens' initiative prohibited issuance of additional elk farming permits and denied the transmittal of existing permits to another person. Elk farm operators in Montana have sued to overturn the results of the initiative. No matter how the legal actions work out, there seems to be a tide of public opinion against elk farming. Supporting that tide is a century of game law founded on the belief that management of wildlife is a public trust responsibility of governments, and that markets in wildlife, wildlife products and parts are inimical to fulfill-

ment of that responsibility. Also, considerable case law clearly is against the kind of privatization of the resource that gamefarming represents. Initiatives and legal actions such as those in Montana are signals that the public envisions more risks associated with gamefarms than merely costs of their commercial operation.

Resolution of many of the issues relating to the operation of gamefarms will be in the courts. However, it is instructive to consider the position of the Rocky Mountain Elk Foundation on elk ranching. In its position, adopted in 1994, the Foundation discouraged elk ranching in states with free-ranging elk populations because of serious risks to the health and viability of those wild elk herds—risks associated with potential disease transmission and genetic pollution of native elk stocks (some captive "elk" have genes from red deer). The Rocky Mountain Elk Foundation statement supported additional research, regulation of gamefarm operations and involvement of state wildlife management agencies in regulation of the gamefarm industry. In addition, there was a statement of concern about the loss of habitat and migration corridors for native elk on public lands that might be associated with high fences surrounding private gamefarms.

Perhaps of most significance has been the transfer of regulatory authority over elk ranching from state wildlife agencies to state agencies dealing with livestock operations (i.e., agriculture, veterinary science). In such cases, there is great concern, however justified, that such agencies will favor elk ranches over the welfare and management of wild elk.

Elk Hunting

The future of big game hunting in the United States and Canada appears secure for the next quarter century. Although society has become increasingly urbanized since 1950, three of four citizens of the United States polled in a nationwide survey approved of legal hunting, and four of five believed that hunting should remain legal (Duda et al. 1995). However, support for legal hunting declines as the human population becomes increasingly urbanized. Although 83% of rural residents and 73% of residents of small cities or towns approved of hunting, fewer suburban residents (67%) and urban dwellers (65%) supported hunting (Duda et al. 1995). Approval of legal hunting was most highly correlated with associated variables such as white males living a rural lifestyle and familiar with hunting or hunters. Less support for hunting was attributed to those less able to participate in hunting because of lifestyle or surroundings. Among the latter were women, members of minority races, suburban and urban residents, single/divorced/widowed persons, disabled persons, those who have moved their residence over 100 miles within the previous year, persons with increasing levels of education beyond high school, and those with greater annual income. Even so, support for legal hunting among these groups ranged from 58% to 75% (Duda et al. 1998).

However, public attitudes toward hunting are far more complex than the mere support or lack thereof for legal hunting. Public opinion polls have shown that Americans care significantly about wildlife recreation and wildlife management. Whereas hunting for food is strongly supported, many Americans do not support hunting for trophies only, and nearly all strongly disapprove of illegal hunting (Duda et al. 1998).

It seems critical, therefore, that wildlife management programs in general, and elk management programs in particular, clearly identify the role of hunting in the broader scheme of wildlife and land management activities. Hunting programs should be designed to ensure that game animal populations are in numerical balance with their environment, harvest of animals by hunters is not detrimental to the long-term welfare of managed populations, harvest is as humane as possible, animals harvested are used as food, and hunters use safe and ethical practices.

However, as we have written elsewhere (Thomas and Toweill 1998), if the future of hunting is to be assured, hunters *absolutely must* be continuous and effective spokespersons for the conservation of all species and populations of wildlife—hunted and nonhunted. Hunters emerged as the prime movers for and supporters of wildlife restoration in the last decades of the 19th century and maintained those roles throughout the 20th century. Even today, as previously noted, hunters remain primarily responsible for underwriting the costs of all wildlife restoration and management efforts. They must retain their well-earned reputation as spokespersons for and champions of wildlife conservation. Nevertheless, the future of hunting lies in the hands of the majority—many of whom have never hunted and never will. Hunting will continue as an acceptable passion only as long as hunters are seen by the citizenry at large as true custodians and stewards of wildlife resources, and hunting is viewed as a legitimate, ethical and safe enterprise.

We believe that the 21st century will produce continued and accelerated attacks on hunting. The initial focus will be on hunting on public lands. This will occur through attempts at legislation at the national level and through the increasing use of ballot initiatives in those states where they are allowed. Almost inevitably, these attacks will be intertwined with the politically charged debates surrounding the private ownership and use of firearms.

Hunting on private lands will be put under the magnifying glass as well. On large tracts of private land where elk move freely among seasonal ranges, the owners who pro-vide adequate habitat for elk and limit harvest of elk within the framework of the state or provincial wildlife management agency likely will profit from public goodwill and from the opportunity for uncrowded hunting access. However, on some private lands and some elk farms, people are allowed to shoot bulls with trophy quality antlers for a significant fee. These so-called canned hunts are widely deplored as being devoid of any semblance of fair chase hunting under anything remotely resembling wild and free conditions (Norris et al. 2001). Such activities, in more extreme forms, cannot be considered hunting at all. As sensationally depicted on television, they tend to reflect poorly on all hunting and all hunters. Antihunting and antihunter groups will continue to exploit such images to discredit hunting in general. To be fair, such canned hunt operations are a predictable outgrowth of the privatization of wildlife and economic decisions. State wildlife agencies have no jurisdiction over such practices when the *hunted* animals, such as elk, are classified as agricultural stock and thus are removed from wildlife agency oversight. The distinction is certain to be lost—by default or design—by those opposed to hunting.

All of these debates will be intertwined with issues related to the holistic management of ecosystems. Opponents of hunting will characterize all hunting (not only elk hunting) simply as a form of natural resource exploitation that is unnecessary in ecosystems wherein predators such as coyotes, cougars, bobcats, lynx, wolves, and grizzly and black bears have been restored. This tactic is more likely to resonate with the portions of the public that have remained uninvolved to this point. Previous attempts to outlaw hunting were based more on ethical or puritanical grounds (although those arguments will no doubt be used again, whenever and wherever judged to be effective).

As the future of elk hunting is contemplated, it is well to remember that, in a democracy, decisions are made by the majority of the minority intensely concerned about a particular issue. The conflict between those who come down on the side of conservation versus those who espouse strict preservation will continue as it has since the days of Muir, Pinchot and Theodore Roosevelt about a century ago. A tilt toward preservation seems to be occurring as fewer and fewer North Americans spend time with anything but flooring and pavement beneath their feet. More and more, public connection with the things and places wild is through the printed page and images on television. For most non-hunters, hunting is a poor spectator sport.

It is in these interactions between the increasing unfamiliarity with the wild and the pure democratic process that the fears of John Hamilton, primary author of the Constitution of the United States could come true—the im-

In the future, hunting of elk and other game species likely will be viewed by the public with heightened apprehension and lessened tolerance. With greater urbanization and vocational specialization, perception of hunters as armed predators who find satisfaction in a recreation that has killing as its goal will gain in abstraction and perhaps in disfavor. For the sake of hunting, for the sake of science-based management of wildlife resources and for the sake of elk, hunters—unlike necessary respites in elk camp—cannot afford to relax their guard against antihunting/antimanagement campaigns of misinformation, political and bureaucratic maneuvers that threaten the amount and viability of wild lands, and behavior by other hunters and outdoor enthusiasts that damage wildlife resources or, in any other way, the hunting privilege. *Above left*, "taking five" on an elk hunt are book editors/compilers Dale Toweill (*on the left*) and Jack Ward Thomas. Few sounds so excite the hunter's notion of things and places wild as does the bugle of a bull elk (*right*). It is the sound of autumn where elk reside; it is a clarion call to elk hunters to embrace and ensure their sport and its traditions. *Left photo courtesy of Dale E. Toweill; right photo by Milo Burcham.*

position of the tyranny of the majority upon the minority. It was from that fear that the checks and balances of the Constitution arose, and the genius (or luck) of the founders became manifest. In time, many of the states made legal the process of making law through initiative petition. This phenomenon arose from a growing distrust of elected representatives—that is, republican government. Through initiative petition, the citizenry can make law directly through the ballot. The number required in the various states for

passage ranges from simple majority to some "super majority" of the vote.

It is in this process of making of law through initiative ballots that there may be much for hunters to fear. There will be more dueling over wildlife management issues through initiative ballots as time wears on. Regardless of the result, these repeated ballots will divert huge amounts of resources and energy that might be better used to benefit wildlife, including elk.

As North Americans become both more numerous and more bound to urban lifestyles, they will inevitably become less attuned to natural processes and rhythms, except from what is absorbed curiously or vicariously through media sources and other glass windows.

As a result, the evolutionary role of human as predator is destined to become more abstract. A critical task for hunters is to see that the role does not become too abstract. Hunters must demonstrate their commitment to wildlife conservation in general, sustainable natural resource management, ethical and humane behavior toward the wildlife they seek, and respect for other users of public lands and natural resources. To the extent that hunters do and live these things, the future of hunting will be secure.

We end this chapter as we began—with a return to the time when elk were teetering on the edge of extinction in North America. Then, almost miraculously, something truly remarkable happened. A very few dedicated people simply decided that the loss of this magnificent animal—the spirit of truly wild places in the West—was simply too much to be endured even in the name of progress. They rallied themselves, then they rallied others, mostly hunters, and began a long journey, now well over a century in progress. Today, the bugle of the elk bull is not a rarity in western landscapes. It is heard clearest by those who share a dedication to the animal and the conservation principles and practices that sustain it. Through the pages of this chapter and book, it has been our privilege to chronicle the journey to date. More so, it has been our privilege to be on that journey.

Some who peruse these pages will be daunted by the challenges that lie ahead, for those challenges are formidable. Other persons will see the challenges as opportunities to preserve and even expand our wildlife heritage. It is our fervent hope that the readers of this book will work to ensure the future of wildlands and free-ranging elk.

Common and Scientific Names of Plants Cited

Name format is genus (capitalized) and species if known. Many extinct species have no common name, and are identified in text by their scientific (generic) names. Those species do not appear in this listing.

Alder, American green   *Alnus crispa*
Alder, Sitka   *A. sinuata*
Alder, thinleaf   *A. tenuifolia*
Alder (red)   *A. rubra*
Alexanders, heart-leaved   *Zia aptera*
Alfalfa   *Medicago sativa*
Alkalimallow   *Sida hederacea*
Alumroot, smooth   *Heuchera glabella*
Apple, common   *Pyrus malus*
Arborvite, giant   *Thuja plicata*
Ash, American mountain   *Sorbus americana*
Ash, Greenes mountain   *S. scopulina*
Ash, western mountain   *S. occidentalis*
Aspen, quaking   *Populus tremuloides*
Avens, prariesmoke   *Geum triflorum*
Avens, Ross   *G. turbinatum*
Baccharis, kidneywhort   *Baccharis pilularis*
Bamboo   *Bambusa*
Barberry   *Berberis*
Barley, foxtail   *Hordeum jubatum*
Bassia, fivehook   *Bassia hyssopifolia*
Beadlily, queencup   *Clintonia uniflora*
Bearberry   *Arctostaphylos uva-ursi*
Beargrass, common   *Xerophyllum tenax*
Bedstraw, northern   *Galium boreale*
Bedstraw, rough   *G. asperrimum*
Bentgrass, Idaho   *Agrostis idahoensis*
Bentgrass, Oregon   *A. oregonensis*

Bentgrass, spike   *A. exarata*
Bergamot, wild   *Monarda fistulosa*
Betony, Mexican   *Stachys mexicana*
Birch, bog   *Betula glandulosa*
Birch, water   *B. fontinalis*
Bitterbrush, antelope   *Purshia tridentata*
Bittercherry   *Prunus emarginata*
Blackberry, cutleaf   *Rubus laciniatus*
Blackberry, Himalaya   *R. procerus*
Blazingstar   *Mentzelia*
Bleedingheart, Pacific   *Dicentra formosa*
Bluebells, mountain   *Mertensia cilata*
Blueberry, box   *Vaccinium ovatum*
Bluegrass, alpine   *Poa alpina*
Bluegrass, bulbous   *P. bulbosa*
Bluegrass, Canada   *P. compressa*
Bluegrass, Kentucky   *P. pratensis*
Bluegrass, pine   *P. scabrella*
Bluegrass, Sandberg   *P. secunda*
Bluegrass, skyline   *P. epilis*
Bluestem, big   *Andropogon gerardii*
Bluestem, little   *A. scoparius*
Bracken, western   *Pteridium aquilinum*
Brome, cheatgrass   *Bromus tectorum*
Brome, Columbia   *B. vulgaris*
Brome, mountain   *B. carinatus*
Brome, smooth   *B. inermis*
Buckthorn, cascara   *Rhamnus purshiana*

Buckwheat   *Fagopyrum*
Buffaloberry, russet   *Shepherdia canadensis*
Bunchberry   *Cornus canadensis*
Burnet, Sitka   *Sanguisorba sitchensis*
Bursage   *Franseria*
Buttercup, sagebrush   *Ranunculus glaberrimus*
Cabbage, skunk   *Lysichitum americanum*
Catsear, spotted   *Hypochoeris radicata*
Cattail   *Typha latifolia*
Ceanothus, jerseytea   *Ceanothus americanus*
Ceanothus, redstem   *C. sanguineus*
Ceanothus, snowbrush   *C. velutinus*
Cedar, western red   *Thuja plicata*
Cherry, pin   *Prunus pennsylvanica*
Chokecherry, common   *P. virginiana*
Cholla, pricklypear   *Opuntia phaeacantha*
Cinquefoil, bigflower   *Potentilla fissa*
Cinquefoil, bush   *P. fruticosa*
Cinquefoil, gland   *P. glandulosa*
Cinquefoil, northwest   *P. gracilis*
Cinquefoil, varileaf   *P. diversifolia*
Clover, Hayden   *Trifolium haydeni*
Clover, red   *T. pratense*
Clover, Rydberg   *T. rydergi*
Clover, whiproot   *T. dasyphyllum*
Clover, white   *T. repens*
Clubmoss, lesser   *Selaginella densa*
Cocklebur, common   *Xanthium strumarium*
Commandra, common   *Commandra umbellata*
Commandra, pale   *C. pallida*
Coralberry, Indiancurrant   *Symphoricarpos orbiculatus*
Corydalis, Scouler   *Corydalis scouleri*
Cowparsnip, common   *Heracleum lanatum*
Crabgrass, hairy   *Digitaria sanguinalis*
Crabgrass, smooth   *D. ischaemum*
Crazyweed, showy   *Oxytropis splendens*
Crazyweed, yellowhair   *O. viscidula*
Cryptantha   *Cryptantha*
Currant, gooseberry   *Ribes montigenum*
Currant, sticky   *R. viscosissimum*
Currant, wax   *R. cereum*
Currant, western black   *R. petiolare*
Dandelion, common   *Taraxacum officinale*
Danthonia, California   *Danthonia californica*
Danthonia, onespike   *D. unispicata*
Danthonia, Parry   *D. parryi*
Danthonia, timber   *D. intermedia*
Deathcamus, mountain   *Zigadenus elegans*
Deerfern   *Blechnum spicant*
Devilsclub, American   *Oplopanax horridus*
Dewberry, California   *Rubus ursinus*
Dewberry, grapeleaf California   *R. vitifolius*
Dogwood, bunchberry   *Cornus canadensis*
Dogwood, redosier   *C. stolonifera*
Douglas-fir   *Pseudotsuga menziesii*

Dropseed, pine   *Sporobolus oxytandrus*
Elaeagnus, silverberry   *Elaeagnus commutata*
Elder, blueberry   *Sambucus cerulea*
Elder, European red   *S. racemosa*
Elder, blackbead   *S. melanocarpa*
Eriogonum   *Eriogonum*
Eriogonum, rock   *E. fasciculifolium*
Eriogonum, sulfur   *E. umbellatum*
Eriogonum, Wyeth   *E. heracleoides*
Falsebugbane   *Trautvetteria carolinensis*
Falsehellebore, American   *Veratrum viride*
Falsehellebore, California   *V. californicum*
Falsehellebore, Eschscholtz   *V. eschscholtzii*
Fescue, Arizona   *Festuca arizonenica*
Fescue, Idaho   *F. idahoensis*
Fescue, meadow   *F. arundinaceae*
Fescue, Montana   *F. saximontana*
Fescue, red   *F. rubra*
Fescue, rough   *F. scabrella*
Fescue, sheep   *F. ovina*
Fescue, spike   *Hesperochloa kingii*
Fir, grand   *Abies grandis*
Fir, subalpine (alpine)   *A. lasiocarpa*
Fireweed   *Epilobium angustifolium*
Fleabane   *Erigeron*
Fleeceflower, pokeweed   *Polygonum phytolaccaefolium*
Foamflower, trefoil   *Tiarella trifoliata*
Forger-me-not, alpine   *Myosotis alpestris*
Foxglove   *Digitalis purpirea*
Gaillardia, common perennial   *Gaillardia aristata*
Galax   *Galax aphylla*
Galleta   *Hilaria jamesi*
Gayfeather, dotted   *Liatris punctata*
Geranium, Richardson   *Geranium richardsonii*
Geranium, sticky   *G. viscosissimum*
Gilia   *Gilia*
Globemallow, streambank   *Iliamna rivularis*
Goldaster, hairy   *Heterotheca villosa*
Goldenrod, creek   *Solidago elongata*
Goldthread, western   *Coptis occidentalis*
Gooseberry, Umatilla   *Ribes cognatum*
Grama, blue   *Bouteloua gracilis*
Greasewood, black   *Sarcobatus vermiculatus*
Gromwell, wayside   *Lithospermum ruderale*
Groundsel, arrowleaf   *Senecio triangularis*
Groundel, Columbian   *S. columbianus*
Hairgrass, mountain   *Deschampsia atropurpurea*
Hairgrass, slender   *D. elongata*
Hairgrass, tufted   *D. caespitosa*
Hawksbeard, low   *Crepis modocensus*
Hawkweed, houndstongue   *Hieracium cynoglossoides*
Hawkweed, western   *H. albertinum*
Hawkweed, white   *H. albiflorum*
Hemlock, eastern   *Tsuga canadensis*
Hemlock, Pacific (western)   *T. heterophylla*

Hemp   *Cannabis*
Hound's-tongue   *Cynoglossum officinale*
Honeysuckle, bearberry   *Lonicera involucrata*
Honeysuckle, Utah   *L. utahensis*
Horsetail   *Equisetum*
Horsemint   *Agastache*
Huckleberry, red   *Vaccinium parvifolium*
Indigo, false   *Amorpha canescens*
Ironwood   *Eusideroxylon*
Iris, Rocky Mountain   *Iris missouriensis*
Junegrass, prairie   *Koeleria cristata*
Juniper, common   *Juniperus communis*
Juniper, creeping   *J. horizonalis*
Juniper, Rocky Mountain   *J. scopulorum*
Juniper, Sierra   *J. occidentalis*
Knotgrass   *Paspalum distichum*
Ladder, Jacob's   *Polemonium delicatum*
Ladyfern   *Arthyrium cyclosorum*
Larkspur, little   *Delphinium bicolor*
Larkspur, Sierra   *D. scopulorum*
Larch, western   *Larix occidentalis*
Ledum, Labrodortea   *Ledum groenlandicum*
Lespedeza, Korean   *Lespedeza stipulacea*
Lettuce, chicory   *Lactuca pulchella*
Lettuce, Indian   *Montia*
Lettuce, prickly   *Lactuca serriola*
Licorice, American   *Gylcyrrhiza lepidota*
Licoriceroot, Canby's   *Ligusticum canbyi*
Licoriceroot, fernleaf   *L. tenufolium*
Licoriceroot, Grays   *L. grayi*
Locoweed   *Astragulus* or *Oxytropis*
Lomatium, biscuitroot   *Lomatium*
Lotus   *Lotus*
Lousewort, fernleaved   *Pedicularis cystopteridifolia*
Lovage, sea   *Ligusticum hultenii*
Loveroot, sharptooth   *Angelica carguta*
Lucerne   *Medicago*
Lupine, Nootka   *Lupinus nootkatensis*
Lupine, oread   *L. monticola*
Lupine, ornate   *L. ornatus*
Lupine, silky   *L. sericeus*
Lupine, velvet   *L. leucophyllus*
Mahonia, Cascades   *Berberis nervosa*
Mahonia, creeping   *B. repens*
Maize   *Zea mays*
Mannagrass, rattlesnake   *Poa canadensis* (= *Glyeria canadensis*)
Maple, bigleaf   *Acer macrophyllum*
Maple, mountain   *A. spicatum*
Maple, Rocky Mountain   *A. glabrum*
Maple, vine   *A. circinatum*
Mariposa, northwestern   *Calochortus elegans*
Menziesia, rusty   *Menziesia ferruginea*
Microseris   *Microseris*
Milkvetch   *Astragulus*
Miterwort   *Mitella stauropetala*

Mockorange, Lewis   *Philadelphus lewisii*
Montia, Siberian   *Montia sibirica*
Montia, cordleaved   *M. cordifolia*
Moss, Californian Spanish   *Ramalina reticulata*
Mountainmahogany, curleaf   *Cercocarpus ledifolius*
Mountainmahogany, true   *C. montanus*
Muhly, mountain   *Muhlenbergia montana*
Muhly, pullup   *M. filiformis*
Musineon, leafy   *Musineon divaricatum*
Mustard, tansy   *Descurainia pinnata*
Needle-and-thread   *Stipa comata*
Neddlegrass, desert   *S. speciosa*
Needlegrass, green   *S. viridula*
Needlegrass, subalpine   *S. columbiana*
Ninebark, mallow   *Physocarpus malvaceus*
Oak, cork   *Quercus suber*
Oak, Gambel   *Q. gambelii*
Oak, scarlet   *Q. coccinea*
Oak, northern red   *Q. rubra*
Onion   *Allium*
Oniongrass   *Melica bulbosa*
Oniongrass, Alaska   *M. subulata*
Oniongrass, showy   *M. spectabilia*
Orchardgrass   *Dactylis glomerata*
Oreoxis, alpine   *Oreoxis alpina*
Oxalis, Oregon   *Oxalis oregana*
Pahcistima   *Pachistima myrsinites*
Pearly-everlasting   *Anaphalis margaritaceae*
Peavine, aspen   *Lathyrus laetivirens*
Pedicularis, elephanthead   *Pedicularis groenlandica*
Pedicularis, sickletop   *P. racemosa*
Peppermint   *Mentha*
Penstemon, green   *Penstemon virens*
Penstemon, littleflower   *P. procerus*
Penstemon, sulfur   *P. attenuatus*
Penstemon, Wilcox   *P. pinetorum*
Penstemon, yellow   *P. confertus*
Phacelia, silverleaf   *Phacelia heterophylla, P. hastata*
Phlox, Hood's   *Phlox hoodii*
Pineapple weed   *Matricaria matricarioides*
Pinegrass   *Calamagrostis rubescens*
Pine, jack   *Pinus banksiana*
Pine, limber   *P. flexis*
Pine, lodgepole   *P. contorta*
Pine, pinyon   *P. edulis*
Pine, ponderosa   *P. ponderosa*
Pine, whitebark   *P. albicaulis*
Pipsissewa, common   *Chimaphila umbellata*
Plantain, buckthorn   *Plantago lanceolata*
Poison-hemlock   *Conium maculatum*
Poplar, California   *Populus trichocarpa*
Poplar, southern   *P. balsamifera*
Primrose, yellow-evening   *Oenothera flava*
Pussytoes, rose   *Antennaria microphylla*
Pyrola   *Pyrola*

Rabbitbrush, green   *Chrysothamnus viscidiflorus*
Rabbitbrush, rubber   *C. nauseosus*
Raspberry, red   *Rubus idaeus*
Raspberry, whitebark   *R. leucodermis*
Redtop   *Agrostis alba*
Reedgrass, bluejoint   *Calamagrostis hymenoides*
Ricegrass, Indian   *Oryzopsis hymenoides*
Rockspirea, creambrush   *Holodiscus discolor*
Rose, Arkansaas   *Rosa arkansana*
Rose, California   *R. californica*
Rose, Nootka   *R. nutkana*
Rose, prickly   *R. acicularis*
Rush, Baltic   *Juncus balticus*
Rush, Parry   *J. parryi*
Ryegrass, perennial   *Lolium perenne*
Sage, prairie   *Artemisia ludoviciana*
Sagebrush, big   *A. tridentata*
Sagebrush, silver   *A. cana*
Sagebrush, threetip   *A. tripartita*
Sagewort, fringed   *A. frigida*
Saintfoin   *Onobrychis viciaefolia*
Salal   *Gaultheria shallon*
Salmonberry   *Rubus spectabilis*
Salsify, yellow   *Tragopogon dubius*
Saltbush, big   *Atriplex lentiformis*
Saltgrass, inland   *Distichlis stricta*
Sandreed, prairie   *Calamovilfa longifolia*
Sandwort, bigleaf   *Arenaria macrophylla*
Saskatoonberry (Saskatoon serviceberry)   *Amalanchier alnifolia*
Sassafras, silky   *Sassafras varifolium*
Scalebud   *Anisocoma acaulis*
Seawatch   *Angelica lucida*
Sedge, cloud   *Carex nubicola*
Sedge, Dewey's   *C. leptopoda*
Sedge, elk   *C. geyeri*
Sedge, Raynolds   *C. raynoldsii*
Sedge, slough   *C. obnupta*
Sedge, threadleaf   *C. filifolia*
Sedge, windseed   *C. ablata*
Selfheal, common   *Prunella vulgaris*
Serviceberry, Saskatoon   *Amelanchier alnifolia*
Shootingstar, darkthroat   *Dodecatheon pauciflorum*
Shootingstar, slimpod   *D. conjugens*
Silktassel, Wrights   *Garrya wrighti*
Snowberry, common   *Symphoricarpos albus*
Snowberry, Utah   *S. utahensis*
Snowberry, western   *S. occidentalis*
Soapweed, small   *Yucca glauca*
Solomonplume, feather   *Smilacina racemosa*
Solomonplume, starry   *S. stellata*
Sorrel, mountain   *Rumex paucifolius*
Spirea, birchleaf   *Spiraea betulifolia*
Spirea, Menzies   *S. menziesii*
Spirea, shinyleaf   *S. lucida*
Spruce, Sitka   *Picea sitchensis*

Spruce, white   *P. glauca*
Squirreltail, bottlebrush   *Sitanion hystrix*
Starwort   *Stellaria*
Stonecrop   *Sedum spathulifolium*
Storks-bill   *Erodium*
Stonyhills   *Muhlenbergia cuspidata*
Strawberry, European   *Fragaria vesca*
Strawberry, Virginia   *F. virginiana*
Sumac, staghorn   *Rhus typhina*
Sunflower, common   *Helianthus annuus*
Sunflower, Maxmilian's   *H. maximilianii*
Sweetclover, white   *Meliotus albus*
Sweetclover, yellow   *M. officinalis*
Sweetvetch, sulfur   *Hedysarum sulphurescens*
Swordfern, western   *Polystichum munitum*
Thermopsis, mountain   *Thermopsis montana*
Thermopsis, pine   *T. pinetorum*
Thimbleberry, western   *Rubus parviflorus*
Thistle, Canada   *Cirsium canadensis*
Thistle, elk   *C. foliosum*
Threeawn, purple   *Aristida purpureae*
Tidytips   *Layia*
Timothy, alpine   *Phleum alpinum*
Tolmiea, Menzies   *Tolmiea menziesii*
Trisetum, spike   *Trisetum spicatum*
Trisetum, Wolf's   *T. wolfii*
Twinflower, American   *Linnaea borealis*
Usnea, bearded   *Usnea barbata*
Usnea, pleated   *U. plicata*
Valerian, Sitka   *Valeriana sitchensis*
Velvetgrass, common   *Holcus lanatus*
Vernalgrass   *Anthoxanthum odoratum*
Vetch, American   *Vicia americana*
Viburnum, moosewood   *Viburnum edule*
Violet, Nuttall   *Viola nuttallii*
Walnut   *Juglans*
Wapato   *Sagittaria*
Waterleaf, ballhead   *Hydrophyllum capitatum*
Wheatgrass, bearded   *Agropyron subsecundum*
Wheatgrass, bearded-bluebunch   *A. spicatum*
Wheatgrass, bluestem   *A. smithii*
Wheatgrass, crested   *A. cristatum*
Wheatgrass, Scribner   *A. scribneri*
Wheatgrass, thickspike   *A. trichophorum*
Wheatgrass, stiffhair   *A. dasystachyum*
Wheatgrass, slender   *A. caninum*
Whortleberry, big huckleberry   *Vaccinium membranaceum*
Whortleberry, grouse   *V. scoparium*
Whortleberry, ovalleaf   *V. ovalifolium*
Whortleberry, red   *V. parvifolium*
Wildrye, blue   *Elymus glaucus*
Wildrye, Canada   *E. canadensis*
Wildrye, fuzzyspike   *E. innovatus*
Wildrye, yellow   *E. flavescens*
Willow, Bebb   *Salix bebbiana*

Willow, blue   *S. subcoerulea*

Willow, coyote   *S. exigua*

Willow, dusky   *S. melanopsis*

Willow, Geyer   *S. geyeriana*

Willow, Scouler   *S. scouleriana*

Willow, Sitka   *S. sitchensis*

Willow, yellow   *S. lutea*

Willoweed, smooth   *Epilobium glaberrimum*

Willoweed, Watson   *E. watsonii*

Winterfat, common   *Eurotia lanata*

Wintergreen, checkerberry   *Gaultheria procumbens*

Woodrush, millet   *Luzula parviflora*

Woolyweed   *Hieracium chapacanum*

Wyethia   *Wyethia*

Yampa   *Perideridia gairdneri*

Yew, Pacific   *Taxus brevifolia*

Common and Scientific Names
of Animals Cited

Name format is genus (capitalized) and species if known. Many extinct species have no common name and are identified in text by their scientific (generic) names, but those species are not in this listing

Antelope, pronghorn (see Pronghorn)   *Antilocapra americana*

Antelope, sable   *Hippotragus niger*

Auk, great   *Pinguinus impennis*

Badger, European   *Meles meles*

Barasingha   *Rucervus duvauceli*

Bear, black   *Ursus americanus*

Bear, brown   *U. arctos*

Bear, grizzly   *U. arctos horribilis*

Bear, polar   *U. maritimus*

Beaver   *Castor canadensis*

Bison, American (plains, wood)   *Bison bison*

Bison, American long-horned   *B. latifrons*

Bison, Siberian long-horned   *B. priscus/occidentalis*

Bluebuck   *Boselaphus tragocamelus*

Boar, Russian wild   *Sus scrofa*

Bobcat   *Lynx rufus*

Bongo   *Boocercus eurycerus*

Buffalo   *Bubalus bubalis* (Old World); in North America, *Bison bison*

Camel   *Camelidae*

Caribou, barren ground   *Rangifer tarandus*

Caribou, woodland   *R. tarandus*

Cat, domestic   *Felis domestica*

Cat, saber-tooth   *Smilodon, Homotherium*

Cattle   *Bos taurus* and *B. indicus*

Chamois, alpine   *Rupicapra rupicapra*

Cheetah   *Acinonvx jubatus*

Chicken   *Gallus gallus*

Chinchilla   *Chinchilla*

Chital (see Deer, axis)   *Axis axis*

Cougar   *Felis concolor*

Coyote   *Canis latrans*

Deer, Andean   *Hippocamelus*

Deer, axis   *Axis axis*

Deer, black-tailed (see Deer, mule)   *Odocoileus hemionus*

Deer, brocket   *Mazama*

Deer, Columbian black-tailed   *Odocoileus hemionus*

Deer, Eld's   *Rucervus eldi*

Deer (red), Eurasian   *Cervus elaphus*

Deer (red), European   *C. elaphus*

Deer, fallow   *Dama dama*

Deer, hog   *Axis porcinus*

Deer, Key   *Odocoileus virginianus clavium*

Deer, mule   *O. hemionus*

Deer, musk   *Moschus moschiferus*

Deer, Père David's   *Elaphurus davidanus*

Deer (red), acoronate   *Cervus elaphus acoronatus*

Deer (red), Bactrian (Bukharen)   *C. e. bactrianus*

Deer (red), Barbary   *C. e. barbarus*

Deer (red), Caucasian   *C. e. maral*

Deer (red), Central European or Yugoslavian   *C. e. elaphus* (hippelaphus)

Deer (red), Corsican   *C. e. corsicanus*

Deer (red), Gansu   *C. e. kansuensis*

Deer (red), hangul (Kashmir)   *C. e. hanglu*

Deer (red), Norwegian   *C. e. atlanticus*

Deer (red), Scottish   *C. e. atlanticus (scoticus)*
Deer (red), shou (Wallichi's)   *C. e. wallichi (affinis)*
Deer (red), Spanish   *C. e. hispanicus*
Deer (red), Swedish   *C. e. (elaphus)*
Deer (red), Tarim (Yarkand)   *C. e. yarkandensis*
Deer (red), Tibetan   *C. e. kansuensis (macneilli)*
Deer, roe   *Capreolus capreolus*
Deer, rusa   *Cervus timorensis*
Deer, sambar   *C. unicolor*
Deer, sika   *C. nippon*
Deer, water   *Hydropotes inermis*
Deer, white-lipped   *Przewalskium albirostris*
Deer, white-tailed   *Odocoileus viginiananus*
Dhole or red dog   *Cuon alpinus*
Dingo   *Canis familiaris*
Dog, mastiff   *C. familiaris*
Duck, pintail   *Anas acuta*
Duck, shoveler   *A. clypeata*
Duck, black   *A. rubripes*
Duck, gadwall   *A. strepera*
Duck, green-winged teal   *A. carolinensis*
Duck, mallard   *A. platyrynchos*
Duck, wood   *Aix sponsa*
Duiker   *Cephalophus*
Eagle, wedgetailed   *Aquila audax*
Eel   Anguillidae
Eland   *Taurotragus oryx*
Elephant   Elephantidae
Elk, North American   *Cervus elaphus*
Elk, Alashan   *C. e. alashanicus*
Elk, Altai (maral)   *C. e. canadensis (sibiricus, asiaticus)*
Elk, eastern   *C. e. canadensis*
Elk, California (Tule)   *C. e. nannodes*
Elk, forest (Manchurian or Izubr)   *C. e. xanthopygus*
Elk, Gansu   *C. e. kansuensis*
Elk, Manchurian (isuber)   *C. e. xanthopylus*
Elk, Manitoban   *C. e. canadensis (manitobensis)*
Elk, Merriam's   *C. e. merriami*
Elk, M'Neill's   *C. e. kansuensis (macneilli)*
Elk, Rocky Mountian   *C. e. canadensis (nelsoni)*
Elk, Roosevelt (Olympic)   *C. e. canadensis (roosevelti)*
Elk, Tien Shan   *C. e. canadensis (songaricus)*
Elk, Tule   *C. e. nannodes*
Emu   *Promiceius novaehollandiae*
Ermine   *Mustela erminea*
Eucerathere   *Eucatherium*
Falcon   primarily *Falco*
Ferret   *Mustela putorius furo*
Fisher, Pacific   *Martes pennanti*
Flies, biting   primarily Tabanidae
Fluke, American (giant liver)   *Fascioloides magna*
Fox   *Vulpes* spp.
Gazelle, Thomson   *Gazella thomsonii*
Goat   *Capra hircus*
Goat, mountain   *Oreamnos americanus*

Goose, Canada   *Branta canadensis*
Goshawk   *Accipiter gentilis*
Greyhound   *Canis familiaris*
Grouse   Tetraonidae
Grouse, sage   *Centrocercus urophasianus*
Guanaco   *Lama guanicoe*
Hare   *Lepus* spp.
Horse   *Equus caballus*
Hound   *Canis familiaris*
Human   *Homo* spp.
Hydatid cyst   *Echinococcus granulosus*
Hyena, Pleistocene cave   *Crocuta spelaea*
Ibex   *Capra ibex*
Jackrabbit   *Lepus*
Jay, gray   *Perisoreus canadensis*
Kudu, greater   *Tragelaphus strepsiceros*
Kudu, lesser   *T. imberis*
Kulan   *Equus hemionus*
Leopard   *Panthera pardus*
Lion, African   *P. leo*
Lion, Pleistocene lions   *P. l. atrox (spelaea)*
Llama   *Lama glama*
Llama, big-headed   *Hemiauchenia macrocephala*
Lynx   *Felix lynx*
Mammoth   *Mammuthus* sp.
Mastodon   *Mammut* sp.
Maral   *Cervus elaphus canadensis (sibericus, asiaticus)*
Mazama   *Mazama*
Midges, no-see-ums   *Culicoides variipennis*
Mink   *Mustela vison*
Mites, psoroptic   *Psoroptes* sp.
Moose   *Alces alces*
Mouflon, European   *Ovis musimon*
Mountain lion (puma)   *Felis concolor*
Mule   *Equus caballus* H *E. asinus*
Muntjac, Chinese   *Muntjacus reevesi*
Muskox   *Ovibos moschatus*
Murrelet, marbled   *Brachyramphus marmoratus*
Muskrat   *Ondatra zibehicus*
Oryx, scimitar horned   *Oryx dammah*
Ostrich   *Struthio camelus*
Otter   *Lutra canadensis*
Owl, spotted   *Strix occidentalis*
Ox   *Bos taurus*
Oxen, American shrub   *Euceratherium collinum*
Oxen, forest musk   *Symbos cavifrons*
Peccary, collared   *Tayassu tajacu*
Pickerel   *Stizostedion vitreum*
Pig, domestic   *Sus scrofa*
Pigeon, passenger   *Ectopistes migratorius*
Pine marten   *Martes americana*
Porcupine   *Erethizon dorsaum*
Possum, brush-tailed   *Trichosurus vulpecula*
Prairie chicken   *Typanuchus cupido*
Pronghorn   *Antilocapra americana*

Pudu   *Pudu pudu*
Quail   Phasianidae
Rabbit   *Sylvilagus*
Raccoon   *Procyon lotor*
Rattlesnake   *Crotalus*
Rattlesnake, prairie   *C. viridis*
Reindeer   *Rangifer tarandus*
Rhinoceros   Rhinocerotidae
Salmon   Salmonidae
Serow   *Capricornis*
Sheep, blue   *Pseudois nayaur*
Sheep, domestic   *Ovis aries*
Sheep, bighorn   *O. canadensis*
Sheep, Marco Polo   *O. ammon poli*
Sheep, mountain   *O. canadensis*
Sheep, Stone's   *O. dalli stoni*
Sparrow   *Passer domesticus*
Squirrel, gray   *Sciurus carolinensis*
Squirrel, ground   Sciuridae
Stag, Buchara   *Cervus elaphus bactrianus*
Stag, English   *C. elaphus*
Stag, Izubr   *C. e.xanthopylus*

Stag, Kashmir   *C. e. hanglu*
Stag, Lop Nor   *C. e. yarkandensis*
Stag, Sikkim   *C. e. affinis*
Stag, Yarkand   *C. e. yarkandensis*
Stag-moose   *Cervalces scotti*
Swine   *Sus scrofa*
Tarpan   *Equus caballus*
Tick, winter   *Dermacentor albipictus*
Tick, scrub   *Ixodes holocyclus*
Tiger   *Panthera tieris*
Turkey   Meleagrididae
Whitefish   *Coregonus, Prosopium*
Wisent   *Bison bonasusWisentBison bonasus*
Wolf, gray   *Canis lupus*
Wolverine   *Gulo luscus*
Worm, arterial   *Elaeophora schneideri*
Worm, bladder   *Taenia* spp.
Worm, carotid artery   *Elaeophora schneideri*
Worm, lung   primarily *Dictyocaulus* spp.
Worm, meningeal   *Parelaphostrongylus tenuis*
Yak   *Bos grunniens*

References

Abbott, M. J., D. E. Ullrey, P. K. Ku, S. M. Schmitt, D. R. Romos and H. A. Tucker. 1984. Effect of photoperiod on growth and fat accretion in white-tailed doe fawns. J. Wildl. Manage. 48: 776–787.

Adam, C. L. and T. Atkinson. 1984. Effect of feeding melatonin to red deer (*Cervus elaphus*) on the onset of the breeding season. J. Reprod. Fert. 72: 463–466.

Adam, C. L. and C. E. Moir. 1985. Effect of winter nutrition of young farmed red deer on their subsequent growth on pasture. Anim. Prod. 40: 135–141.

Adam, C. L., C. E. Moir and T. Atkinson. 1985. Plasma concentrations of progesterone in female red deer (*Cervus elaphus*) during the breeding season, pregnancy and anoestrus. J. Reprod. Fert. 74: 631–636.

Adam, C. L., C. E. Moir and P. Shiach. 1989. Melatonin can induce year-round ovarian cyclicity in red deer (*Cervus elaphus*). J. Reprod. Fert. 87: 401–408.

Adam, C. L., I. MacDonald, C. E. Moir and K. Pennie. 1988a. Foetal development in red deer (*Cervus elaphus*). 1. Growth of the foetus and associated tissues. Anim. Prod. 46: 131–138.

Adam, C. L., I. MacDonald, C. E. Moir and R. I. Smart. 1988b. Foetal development in red deer (*Cervus elaphus*) . 2. Chemical composition of the foetus and associated tissues. Anim. Prod. 46: 139–146.

Adamczewski, J. Z., C. C. Gates and R. J. Hudson. 1987a. Fat distribution and indices of carcass composition in Coats Island caribou (*Rangifer tarandus groenlandicus*). Can. J. Zool. 65: 368–374.

Adamczewski, J. Z., C. C. Gates, R. J. Hudson and M. A. Price. 1987b. Seasonal changes in body composition of mature female caribou and calves (*Rangifer tarandus groenlandicus*) on an arctic island with limited winter resources. Can. J. Zool. 65: 1,149–1,157.

Adamczewski, J. Z., R. J. Hudson and C. C. Gates. 1993. Winter energy balance and activity of female caribou on Coats Island, Northwest Territories: The relative importance of foraging and body reserves. Can. J. Zool. 71: 1221–1229.

Adams, A. W. 1982. Migration. Pages 301–321 *in* J. W. Thomas and D. A. Toweill, eds. Elk of North America: Ecology and management. Stackpole Books, Harrisburg, Pennsylvania. 698 pp.

Adams, B. A. 1990. Prayers of smoke. Celestial Arts, Berkeley, California. 179 pp.

Adams, C. C. 1913. Guide to the study of animal ecology. Macmillan Co., New York. 183 pp.

Adams, J. L. 1979. Innervation and blood supply of the antler pedicle of red deer. New Zealand Vet. J. 27: 200–201.

Adcock, J. L. and R. E. Keiss. 1969. Locoism in elk, a disease resembling cerebral pseudolipidosis. Bull. Wildl. Dis. Assoc. 5: 121–124.

Adcock, J. L. and C. P. Hibler. 1969. Vascular and neuroophthalmic pathology of elaeophorosis in elk. Path. Vet. 6: 185–213.

Addison, E. M., J. Hoeve, D. G. Joachim and D. J. McLachlin. 1988. *Fascioloides magna* (Trematoda) and Taenia hydatigena (Cestoda) from white-tailed deer. Can. J. Zool. 66: 1359–1364.

Adrian, W. J. and R. E. Keiss. 1977. Survey of Colorado's wild ruminants for serologic titers to brucellosis and leptospirosis. J. Wildl. Dis. 13: 429–431.

Aflalo, F. G. 1904. The sportsman's book for India. Horace Marshall and Son, London, U.K. 567 pp.

———. 1910. Sport in Europe. E. P. Dutton and Co., New York. 483 pp.

Ager, A. and M. Hitchcock. 1992. Microcomputer software for calculating the western Oregon elk habitat effectiveness index. Gen. Tech. Rept. PNW-GTR–303. USDA For. Serv., Portland, Oregon. 12 pp.

———. 1994. HEICALC: Elk habitat-effectiveness index software. Wildl. Soc. Bull. 22: 126–128.

Ager, A. and R. McGaughey. 1997. UTOOLS: Microcomputer software for spatial analysis and landscape visualization. Gen. Tech. Rept. PNW-GTR–397. USDA For. Serv., Portland, Oregon. 15 pp.

Aguirre, A. A., D. E. Hansen, E. E. Starkey and R. G. McLean. 1995. Serologic survey of wild cervids for potential disease agents in selected national parks in the United States. Preventive Vet. Med. 21: 313–322.

Ahlen, I. 1965. Studies on the red deer, *Cervus elaphus* L., in Scandinavia. Viltrevy 3(2): 90–168.

Aho, R. W. and J. Hendrickson. 1989. Reproduction and mortality of moose translocated from Ontario to Michigan. Alces 25: 75–80.

Albers, P. and J. Kay. 1987. Sharing the land: A study in American Indian territoriality. Pages 47–91 *in* T. E. Ross and T. G. Moore, eds., A cultural geography of North American Indians. Westview Press, Boulder, Colorado. 331 pp.

Albon, T. F. and R. Langvatn. 1992. Plant phenology and the benefits of migration in a temperate ungulate. Oikos 65: 502–513.

Albon, S. D., T. H. Clutton-Brock and F. E. Guinness. 1983a. Influence of climatic variation on the birth weights of red deer. J. Zool. 200: 295–298.

Albon, S. D., B. Mitchell and B. W. Staines. 1983b. Fertility and body weight in female red deer: A density-dependent relationship. J. Anim. Ecol. 52: 969–980.

Albon, S. D., B. Mitchell, B. J. Huby and D. Brown. 1986. Fertility in female red deer (*Cervus elaphus*): The effects of body composition, age and reproductive status. J. Zool. (London) 209: 447–460.

Albon, S. D., T. H. Clutton-Brock and F. E. Guinness. 1987. Early development and population dynamics in red deer. II. Density-independent effects and cohort variation. J. Anim. Ecol. 56: 69–81.

Alderson, L. E. 1951. Internal parasites of the elk in Wyoming. Univ. Wyoming Publ. 16: 77–78.

Alexander, R. R. 1974. Silviculture of central and southern Rocky Mountain forests: A summary of the status of our knowledge by timber types. Res. Pap. RM–120. USDA For. Serv., Fort Collins, Colorado. 36 pp.

———. 1975. Partial cutting in old-growth lodgepole pine. Res. Pap. RM–136. USDA For. Serv., Fort Collins, Colorado. 17 pp.

Alexander, R. McN., A. S. Jayes and R. F. Ker. 1980. Estimates of energy cost for quadrupedal running gaits. J. Zool. London 190: 155–192.

Allard, M. W., M. M. Miyamoto, L. Jarecki, F. Kraus and M.R. Tennant. 1992. DNA systematics and evolution of the artiodactyl family Bovidae. Proc. Nat. Acad. Sci. 89: 3,972–3,976.

Allen, D. L. 1962. Our wildlife legacy. Funk and Wagnalls, New York. 422 pp.

———. 1967. The life of prairies and plains. Our Living World of Nature Series. McGraw-Hill Book Co., New York. 232 pp.

———. 1970. Historical perspective. Pages 1–28 *in* National Research Council, land use and wildlife resources. Nat. Acad. Sci., Washington, D.C. 262 pp.

Allen, E. O. 1968. Range use, foods, conditions, and productivity of white-tailed deer in Montana. J. Wildl. Manage. 32: 130–141.

———. 1971. Elk-logging relationships in the northern Rocky Mountains. The Wildl. Soc., Bozeman, Montana. 7 pp. Mimeo.

———. 1972. Elk and timber—A public land jigsaw. Montana Outdoors (Feb.): 38–40.

———. 1973. Calf: cow ratios—What do they really mean? Pages 80–89 *in* Proc. Biennial Conf. West. States Elk Workshop. Bozeman, Montana.

Allen, G. M. 1940. The mammals of China and Mongolia. Pages 621–1,350 *in* Natural history of central Asia. Amer. Mus. Natur. Hist., Vol. XI, Part 2.

———. 1942. Extinct and vanishing mammals of the Western Hemisphere. Spec. Publ. 11, Amer. Cmmtt. for Int. Wildl. Protection. The Intelligencer Print. Co., Lancaster, Pennsylvania. 620 pp.

Allen, J. A. 1871a. The fauna of the prairies. Amer. Naturalist 5: 47.

———. 1871b. Notes on the mammals of Iowa. Boston Soc. Natur. Hist. Proc. 13 (1869–1871): 178–194.

———. 1874. Notes on the mammals of portions of Kansas, Colorado, Wyoming, and Utah. Bull. Essex Inst. 6: 43–66.

———. 1876. Description of some remains of an extinct species of wolf and an extinct species of deer from the lead region of the Upper Mississippi. Amer. J. Sci. 3(11): 49.

———. 1877. History of the American bison, *Bison americanus*. Annu. Rept. U.S. Geol. Surv. 9:443–587.

———. 1893. List of mammals collected by Mr. Charles P. Rowley in the San Juan Region of Colorado, New Mexico and Utah, with descriptions of new species. Bull. Amer. Mus. Natur. Hist. 5(6): 69–84.

Allen, R. H. 1965. History and results of deer restocking in Alabama. Div. Game and Fish Bull. 6, Alabama Dept. Conserv., Montgomery. 50 pp.

Allen, R. W. 1973. The biology of *Thysanosoma actinioides* (Cestoda: Anoplocephalidae) a parasite of domestic and wild ruminants. Bull. 604. New Mexico Ag. Exp. Sta., Albuquerque. 68 pp.

Allred, W. J. 1950. Re-establishment of seasonal elk migration through transplanting. Trans. N. Amer. Wildl. Conf. 15: 597–611.

Allred, W. J., R. C. Brown and O. J. Murie 1944. Disease kills feedground elk. Wyoming Wildl. 9(2): 1–8, 27.

Alt, K. L., M. R. Frisina and F. J. King. 1992. Coordinated management of elk and cattle, a perspective. Wall Creek Wildlife Management Area. Rangelands 14(1): 12–15.

Altmann, M. 1952. Social behavior of elk, *Cervus canadensis nelsoni*, in the Jackson Hole area of Wyoming. Behavior 4(2): 116–143.

———. 1956a. Patterns of social behavior in big game. Trans. N. Amer. Wildl. Conf. 21: 538–545.

———. 1956b. Patterns of herd behavior in free-ranging elk of Wyoming, *Cervus canadensis nelsoni*. Zoologica 41(2): 65–71.

———. 1958. The flight distance in free-ranging big game. J. Wildl. Manage. 22(2) 207–209.

———. 1961. "Teenager" problems in the wilderness. Animal Kingdom 64(2): 41–44.

———. 1963a. Naturalistic studies of maternal care in moose and elk. Pages 233–253 *in* H. L. Rheingold, ed., Maternal behavior in mammals. J. Wiley and Sons, New York.

———. 1963b. Seniors of the wilderness. Animal Kingdom 66(12): 181–183.

Alvard, M. S. 1993. Testing the "Ecologically Noble Savage" hypothesis: Interspecific prey choice by piro hunters of Amazonian Peru. Human Ecol. 21: 355–387.

Anand, B. K. and J. F. Brobeck. 1951. Hypothalamic control of food intake. Yale J. Biol. Med. 24: 123–140.

Anderluh, G 1990 Jagdrechtliche aspekte von regionalplanungen. Pages 97–114 *in* H. Gossow, E. Donaubauer, F. Reimoser and J. Dieberger, eds., Tagungsbericht IURFO-Symposium regionalplanungskonzept, fur eine forstlich integrierte Schalenwildbewirtschaftung im Hoch- und Mittelgebirge. BOKU-reports on Wildlife Research and Game Management 1. Institut for Wildbiologie und Jagdwirtschaft, Universitat fur Bodenkultur, Wien.

Andersen, F. L., P. O. Wright and C. Mortensen. 1973. Prevalence of *Echinococcus granulosus* infections in dogs and sheep in central Utah. J. Amer. Vet. Med. Assoc. 163(10): 1,168–1,171.

Anderson, A. C. 1882. An appendix to British Columbia Directory 1882–1883. Climate and resources. R.T. Williams, Victoria, British Columbia. 26 pp.

Anderson, A. E. 1981. Morphological and physiological characteristics. Pages 27–97 *in* O. C. Wallmo, ed., Mule and black-tailed deer of North America. Univ. Nebraska Press, Lincoln. 605 pp.

Anderson, A. E., W. A. Snyder and G. W. Brown. 1965. Stomach content analyses related to condition of mule deer, Guadalupe Mountains, New Mexico. J. Wildl. Manage. 29: 352–366.

Anderson, A. E., D. E. Medin, and D. C. Bowden. 1972. Indices of carcass fat in a Colorado mule deer population. J. Wildl. Manage. 36: 579–594.

Anderson, A. E., D. E. Medin and D. C. Bowden. 1974. Growth and morphometry of the carcass, selected bones, organs and glands of mule deer. Wildl. Monogr. 39: 122.

Anderson, A. E., D. C. Bowden and D. E. Medin. 1990. Indexing the annual fat cycle in a mule deer population. J. Wildl. Manage. 54: 550–556.

Anderson, C. C. 1954. Migration studies of Jackson Hole's elk herd. Wyoming Wildl. 18(4): 26–34.

——. 1958. The elk of Jackson Hole: A review of Jackson elk studies. Bull. 10, Wyoming Game and Fish Commiss., Cheyenne. 184 pp.

Anderson, C. C., W. I. Crump and T. C. Baker. 1956. Food habits of antelope, elk, deer, and moose. Fed. Aid Compl. Rept. Proj. W–27-R–9, WP–1, J–1. Wyoming Game and Fish Commiss., Laramie.

Anderson, C. R., Jr., D. S. Moody, B. L. Smith, F. G. Lindzey and R. P. Lanka. 1998. Development and evaluation of sightability models for summer elk surveys. J. Wildl. Manage. 62: 1,055–1,066.

Anderson, D. R. 1993. Unpublished. Records on file, W. M. Samuel, Dept. Biol. Sci., Univ. Alberta, Edmonton.

Anderson, E. 1968. Fauna of the Little Box Elder Cave, Converse County, Wyoming. Pages 1–59 *in* The carnivore. Univ. Colorado Studies, Ser. Earth Sci., No. 6. Univ. Colorado, Boulder.

Anderson, E. W. and R.J. Scherzinger. 1975. Improving quality of winter forage for elk by cattle grazing. J. Range Manage. 28(2): 120–125.

Anderson, E. W., D. L. Franzen and J. E. Melland. 1990a. Prescribed grazing to benefit watershed–wildlife–livestock. Rangelands 12: 105–111.

Anderson, E. W., D. L. Franzen and J. E. Melland. 1990b. Forage quality as influenced by prescribed grazing. Pages 56–70 *in* K. E. Severson, ed., Can livestock be used as a tool to enhance wildlife habitat? Gen. Tech. Res. RM–194. USDA For. Serv., Washington, D.C.

Anderson, G. S. 1891. Report of the Superintendent of the Yellowstone National Park to the Secretary of the Interior. Govt. Print. Off., Washington, D.C. 21 pp.

——. 1892. Report of the Superintendent of the Yellowstone National Park to the Secretary of the Interior. Govt. Print. Off. Washington, D.C. 17 pp.

——. 1893. Report of the Superintendent of the Yellowstone National Park. Pages 613–630 *in* Report of the Secretary of the Interior. Govt. Print. Off., Washington, D.C. 773 pp.

——. 1894. Report of the Superintendent of the Yellowstone National Park. Park 651–672 *in* Report of the Secretary of the Interior, 1894, Vol. 3. Govt. Print. Off., Washington, D.C. 775 pp.

——. 1895. Report of the Acting Superintendent of the Yellowstone National Park to the Secretary of the Interior, 1895. Govt. Print. Off., Washington, D.C. 24 pp.

——. 1896. Report of the Acting Superintendent of the Yellowstone National Park to the Secretary of the Interior, 1896. Govt. Print. Off., Washington, D.C. 22 pp.

Anderson, R. C. 1964. Neurologic disease in moose infected experimentally with *Pneumostrongylus tenuis* from white-tailed deer. Pathol. Vet. 1: 89–322.

——. 1965a. The development of *Pneumostrongylus tenuis* in the central nervous system of white-tailed deer. Pathol. Vet. 2: 360–379.

——. 1965b. An examination of wild moose exhibiting neurologic signs in Ontario. Can. J. Zool. 43: 635–639.

——. 1970. Neurologic disease in reindeer (*Rangifer tarandus tarandus*) introduced into Ontario. Can. J. Zool. 49: 159–166.

——. 1971. Neurologic disease in reindeer (*Rangifer tarandus tarandus*) introduced into Ontario. Can. J. Zool. 49: 159–166.

——. 1972. The ecological relationships of meningeal worm and native cervids in North America. J. Wildl. Dis. 8: 304–309.

Anderson, R. C. and A. K. Prestwood. 1981. Lungworms. Pages 266–317 *in* W. R. Davidson, F. A. Hayes, V. F. Nettles and F. E. Kellogg, eds., Diseases and parasites of white-tailed deer. Misc. Publ. No. 7, Tall Timbers Res. Sta., Tallahassee, Florida. 458 pp.

Anderson, R. C. and U. R. Strelive. 1966. Experimental cerebrospinal nematodiasis (*Pneumostrongylus tenuis*) in sheep. Can. J. Zool. 44: 889–894.

Anderson, R. C. and U. R. Strelive. 1967. The penetration of *Pneumostrongylus tenuis* into the tissues of white-tailed deer. Can. J. Zool. 45: 285–289.

——. 1968. The experimental transmission of *Pneumostrongylus tenuis* to caribou Rangifer tarandus terraenovae. Can. J. Zool. 46: 503–510.

——. 1972. Experimental cerebrospinal nematodiasis in kids. J. Parasitol. 58: 816.

Anderson, R. C., M. W. Lankester and U. R. Strelive. 1966. Further experimental studies of *Pneumostrongylus tenuis* in cervids. Can. J. Zool. 44: 851–861.

Anderson, R. M. 1947. Catalogue of Canadian recent mammals. Bull. No. 102, Biol. Ser. No. 31. Ottawa, Ontario.

Anderson, S. 1972. Mammals of Chihuahua: Taxonomy and distribution. Bull. Amer. Mus. Natur. Hist., Vol. 148 (Article 2): 149–410.

Anderson, S. and R. Barlow. 1978. Taxonomic status of *Cervus elaphus merriami* (Cervidae). The Southwest. Naturalist 23(1): 63–70.

Anderson, S. and J. K. Jones, Jr., eds. 1967. Recent mammals of the world, a synopsis of families. Ronald Press Co., New York. 453 pp.

Andrews, C. L. 1969. Parasitism and other disease entities among selected populations of cottontail rabbits (*Sylvilagus floridanus*). Unpubl. Ph.D. Thesis, Univ. Georgia, Athens. 185 pp.

Aney, W. W. 1974. Estimating fish and wildlife harvest, a survey of methods used. Proc. West. Assoc. State Game and Fish Commiss. 54: 70–79.

Angstman, J. B. and J. E. Gaab. 1950. West Gallatin winter elk study, 1949–1950. Montana Fish and Game Commiss. Wildl. Restor. Div. Quart. Rept. 10: 33–34.

Angus, R. D. 1989. Preparation, dosage delivery, and stability of a *Brucella abortus* strain 19 vaccine ballistic implant. Proc. U.S. Anim. Health Assoc. 93: 656–666.

Anonymous. 1907. Renewal of the Fox war. Pages 86–91 *in* L. C. Draper, ed., Collections of the State Historical Society of Wisconsin. Vol. V. 432 pp. (Reprint of 1868 original issue.)

——. 1980. 110 years of fish and game history. Outdoor California July / August: 31–34.

——. 1982. Not extinct after all. Species Survival Commiss. Newsletter, New Series 1: 19.

——. 1993. Disadvantages of game farming; Position paper of the Alberta Chapter of The Wildlife Society. Pages 135–139 *in* J. B. Stelfox, Hoofed mammals of Alberta. Lone Pine Publ., Vancouver, British Columbia. 241 pp.

Anthony, H. E. 1957. The sportsman or the predator: Part II, But it's instinctive. Saturday Rev. Lit. (August 17.): 4, 9–10.

Apollonio, M., M. Festa-Bianchet and F. Mari. 1989. Correlates of copulation success in a fallow deer lek. Behav. Ecol. and Scoiobiol. 25: 89–97.

Archer (Stockwell, G. A.) 1877. Fauna of Michigan. Forest and Stream 8: 177, 192, 224, 241, 261, 281, 300, 361, 380; 9: 5.

Argo, C. M. and J. S. Smith. 1983. Relationships of energy requirements and seasonal cycles of food intake in Soay rams. J. Physiol. 343: 23–24.

Arizona Game and Fish Department. 1972. Arizona big game bulletin: Elk. Form 4038. Arizona Game and Fish Dept., Phoenix. 4 pp.

———. 1975. Comparative elk hunt data. Arizona Game and Fish Dept., Phoenix. 12 pp.

Arman, P. 1974. A note on parturition and maternal behavior in captive red deer (*Cervus elaphus* L.). J. Reprod. Fert. 37: 97–90.

Arman, P., R. N. B. Kay, E. D. Goodall and G. A. M. Sharman. 1974. The composition and yield of milk from captive red deer (*Cervus elaphus* L.) J. Reprod. Fert. 37: 67–84.

Arman, P., W. J. Hamilton and G. A. M. Sharman. 1978. Observations on the calving of free-ranging tame red deer (*Cervus elaphus* L.) J. Reprod. Fert. 54: 279–283.

Armstrong, D. M. 1972. Distribution of mammals in Colorado. Monogr. Mus. Natur. Hist. Univ. Kansas, Lawrence. 3: 415.

Arnett, E. B. 1990. Bighorn sheep habitat selection patterns and response to fire and timber harvest in southcentral Wyoming. M. S. Thesis, Univ. Wyoming, Laramie. 156 pp.

Arnold, J. E. 1950. Changes in ponderosa pine bunchgrass ranges in northern Oregon resulting from pine regeneration and grazing. J. Forestry 48: 118–126.

Arnon, N. S. and W. W. Hill. 1979. Santa Clara pueblo. Pages 296–307 *in* A. Ortiz, ed., Southwest. Handbook of North American Indians, Vol. 9. Smithsonian Instit., Washington, D.C. 701 pp.

Arsenault, A. A. 1998. Saskatchewan elk (*Cervus elaphus*) management strategy. Fish and Wildl. Tech. Rept. 97—Draft. Saskatchewan Environ. and Resour. Manage., Saskatoon. 91 pp.

Arthur, G. W. 1975. An introduction to the ecology of early communal bison hunting among the northern Plains Indians. Archaeol. Surv. Paper 37. 136 pp.

Arza, E., M. D. Salman and D. P. Warner. 1989. Summary of results of brucellosis testing following adult vaccination in Florida beef herds. Proc. U.S. Animal Health Assoc. 93: 153–156.

Aselson, R. and B. Moore. 1985. Dialogue with nature: Landscape and literature in nineteenth-century America. Corcoran Gall. of Art, Washington, D.C. 48 pp.

Ashbrook, F. G. and E. N. Sater. 1945. Cooking wild game. Orange Judd Publ. Co., Inc., New York. 358 pp.

Ashcroft, W.H. 1967. The socio-economics of recreational use of the Cache elk herd. M.S. Thesis. Utah State Univ., Logan. 77 pp.

Asher, G. W. 1990. Effect of subcutaneous melatonin implants on the seasonal attainment of puberty in female red deer (*Cervus elaphus*). Anim. Reprod. Sci. 22: 145–160.

Asher, G. W. and J. L. Adam. 1985. Reproduction of farmed red and fallow deer in northern New Zealand. Pages 217–224, *in* P. F. Fennessy and K. R. Drew, eds., Biology of Deer Production. The Royal Soc. of New Zealand, Wellington. 482 pp.

Asher, G. W., M. W. Fisher, P. F. Fennessy, C. G. Mackintosh, H. N. Jabbour and C. J. Morrow. 1993. Oestrus synchronization, semen collection and artificial insemination of farmed red deer (*Cervus elaphus*) and fallow deer (*Dama dama*). Anim. Reprod. Sci. 33: 241–265.

Asquith, T. N. and L. G. Butler. 1985. Use of a dye-labeled protein as a spectrophotometric assay for protein precipitants such as tannin. J. Chem. Ecol. 11: 1,535–1,544.

Audubon, J. J. and J. Bachman. 1851. The quadrupeds of North America. 3 vols. J. J. Audubon, New York.

Austin, C. R. 1975. Sperm fertility and persistence in the female tract. J. Reprod. Fert. Suppl. 22: 75–89.

Austin, D. D., R. A. Riggs, P. J. Urness, D. L. Turner and J. F. Kimball. 1989. Changes in mule deer size in Utah. Great Basin Naturalist 49: 31–35.

Austin, P. J., Suchar, C. T. Robbins and A. E. Hagerman. 1989. Tannin-binding proteins in saliva of deer and their absence in saliva of sheep and cattle. J. Chem. Ecol. 15: 1,335–1,348.

Autoine v. State of Washington, 420 U.S. 194 (1975).

Avise, J. C. 1989. A role for molecular genetics in the recognition and conservation of endangered species. Trends Ecol. Evol. 4: 279–281.

———. 1994. Molecular markers, natural history and evolution. Chapman and Hall, New York. 511 pp.

Axelrod, D. I. 1950. Evolution of desert vegetation in western North America. Pages 217–306 *in* Carnegie Inst. Publ. 590. Carnegie Inst., Washington, D.C.

Baas, J. M. 1988. Identifying some benefits of hunting: A study of young hunters in Oregon. Notes on People, Parks and Forests 1(3): 1–4.

Baccus, R., N. Ryman, M. H. Smith, C. Reuterwall and D. G. Cameron. 1983. Genetic variability and differentiation of large grazing mammals. J. Mammal. 64(1): 109–120.

Bachnová, L. and A. B. Bubenik. 1958. Pachove zlazy parohate zvere. Myslivost (Prague) November.

Badger, S. B. 1982. Infectious epiphysitis and valvular endocarditis in a red deer (*Cervus elaphus*). New Zealand Vet. J. 30: 17–18.

Bahnak, B. R., J. C. Holland, L. J. Verme and J. J. Ozoga. 1981. Seasonal and nutritional influences on growth hormone and thyroid activity in white-tailed deer. J. Wildl. Manage. 45: 140–147.

Baier, L.E. 1993. The Boone and Crockett Club: A 106-year retrospective. Pages 3–28 *in* J. Reneau and S. C. Reneau, eds., Records of North American big game 10th edition. Boone and Crockett Club, Missoula, Montana. 604 pp.

Bailey, C. B. and G. J. Mears. 1990. Birth weight in calves and its relation to growth rates from birth to weaning and weaning to slaughter. Can. J. Anim. Sci. 70: 167–173.

Bailey, J. A. 1980. Desert bighorn, forage competition, and zoogeography. Wildl. Soc. Bull. 8(3): 208–216.

Bailey, R. G. 1975. Ecological regionalization of the intermountain west. Presented at 75th Nat. Conv., Soc. Amer. For., Washington, D.C. [Abstract.]

Bailey, V. 1896. List of mammals of the District of Columbia. Biol. Soc. Washington, D.C. Proc. 10: 93–101.

———. 1905. Biological survey of Texas. North Amer. Fauna No. 25. USDA Bur. Biol. Surv., Washington, D.C. 222 pp.

———. 1926. A biological survey of North Dakota. I. Physiography and life zones. II. The mammals. North Amer. Fauna No. 49. USDA Bur. Biol. Surv., Washington, D.C. 226 pp.

———. 1931. Mammals of New Mexico. N. Amer. Fauna No. 53. USDA Bur. Biol. Surv., Washington, D.C. 412 pp.

———. 1935. A new name for the Rocky Mountain elk. Proc. Biol. Soc., Washington, D.C. 48: 187–189.

———. 1936. The mammals and life zones of Oregon. North Amer. Fauna No. 55. USDA Bur. Biol. Surv., Washington, D.C. 461 pp.

Baillie-Grohman, W.A. 1882. Camps in the Rockies. Gilbert and Rivington Ltd., London, U.K.. 438 pp.

———. 1896. Sport in the Alps. Charles Scribner's Sons, New York. 356 pp.

———. 1900. Fifteen years sport and life in the hunting grounds of western America and British Columbia. H. Cox, London, U.K. 403 pp.

———. 1910. Austria. Pages 19–43 *in* F. G. Aflalo, ed., Sport in Europe. E. P. Dutton and Co., New York. 483 pp.

Baillie-Grohman, W. A. and F. Baillie-Grohman, eds. 1909. The master of the game. Chatto and Windus, London, U.K. 438 pp.

Baird, D. 1975. Specialized hunting—specialized enforcement. Proc. West. Assoc. State Game and Fish Commiss. 55: 147–151.

Bakeless, J., compiler. 1964. The journals of Lewis and Clark. New Amer. Library, Inc., New York. 384 pp.

Baker, D. L. and D. R. Hansen. 1985. Comparative digestion of grass in mule deer and elk. J. Wildl. Manage. 49: 77–79.

Baker, D. L. and N. T. Hobbs. 1982. Composition and quality of elk summer diets in Colorado. J. Wildl. Manage. 46: 694–703.

Baker, D. L. and N. T. Hobbs. 1985. Emergency feeding of mule deer during winter: Tests of a supplemental ration. J. Wildl. Manage. 49: 934–942.

Baker, D. L. and N. T. Hobbs. 1987. Strategies of digestion: Digestive efficiency and retention time of forage diets in montane ungulates. Can. J. Zool. 65: 1,978–1,984.

Baker, D. L., D. E. Johnson, L. H. Carpenter, O. C. Wallmo and R. B. Gill. 1979. Energy requirements of mule deer fawns in winter. J. Wildl. Manage. 43: 162–169.

Baker, P. E. 1955. The forgotten Kutenai. Mountain States Press. Boise, Idaho. 64 pp.

Baker, R. 1978. Evolutionary ecology of animal migration. Holder and Stoughton, London, U.K. 1,098 pp.

Baker, R. H. 1956. Mammals of Coahuila, Mexico. Univ. Kansas Publ., Mus. Natur. Hist. 9(7): 125–335.

Baker, T. C., C. Anderson and W. I. Crump. 1953. Food habits study of game animals. Wyoming Wildl. 17(11): 24–31.

Baldwin, E. M. 1964. Geology of Oregon. 2nd ed. Univ. Oregon Coop. Bookstore, Eugene. 165 pp.

Baldwin, W. P. and C. P. Patton. 1938. A preliminary study of food habits of elk in Virginia. Trans. N. Amer. Wildl. Conf. 3: 747–755.

Bandy, P. J., Cowan, I. M. and Wood, A. J. 1970. Comparative growth in four races of black tailed deer. Part I. Growth in body weight. Can. J. Zool. 48: 1,401–1,410.

Banfield, A. W. F. 1949. An irruption of elk in Riding Mountain National Park, Manitoba. J. Wildl. Manage. 13: 127–134.

Banks, J. J., G. P. Epling, R. A. Kainer and R. W. Davis. 1968a. Antler growth and osteoporosis. I. Morphological and morphometric changes in the costal compacta during the antler growth cycle. Anat. Rec. 162(4): 387–397.

———. 1968b. II. Gravimetric and chemical changes in the costal compacta during the antler growth cycle. Anat. Rec. 162(4): 399–405.

Banks, W. J. and J. W. Newbrey. 1982. Light microscopic studies of the ossification process in developing antlers. Pages 231–260 in R. D. Brown, ed., Antler development in Cervidae. Caesar Kleberg Wildl. Res. Inst., Kingsville, Texas.

Bannikov, A. G. 1955. O biologicheskikh grupakh kopytnykh. Uchenye zapiski, 38(5): 13–22.

Banwell, D. B. 1991a. Wapitoid wrap up. The Deer Farmer. August 18–20.

———. 1991b. Wapiti viewing tour a success. The Deer Farmer. May 24–29.

———. 1993. Banwell on deer. Australian Deer 18(6): 17–21.

———. 2000. A suggested regrouping of the species *elaphus* of the genus *Cervus*, with a view to achieving acceptable standardization. Deer 11(6): 327–332.

Barber, T. L. and M. M. Jochim. 1975. Serotyping blue-tongue and epizootic hemorrhagic disease virus strains. Proc. Amer. Assoc. Vet. Lab. Diag. 18: 149–162.

Barclay, E. N. 1934. The red deer of the Caucasus. Proc. Zool. Soc. London, U.K. 789–798 pp.

Barnard, E. S., ed. 1977. Story of the great American West. The Reader's Digest Assoc., Inc., Pleasantville, New York. 384 pp.

Barnicoat, C. R., A. G. Logan and A. I. Grant. 1949. Milk-secretion studies with New Zealand Romney ewes. Parts I and II. J. Ag. Sci. 39: 44–55.

Baron, F. J., E. C. Nord, A. B. Evanko and W. J. Makel. 1966. Seeding conifers and buffer crops to reduce deer depredation. Res. Note PSW–100. USDA For. Serv., Berkeley, California. 8 pp.

Barr, R. 1997. Tally-no! Missoulian, Sunday, November 29. Page C1.

Barrell, G. K. and S. Bos. 1989. Changes in serum oestrone sulphate and progesterone levels of red deer hinds during pregnancy. New Zealand Vet. J. 37: 1–3.

Barrett, R. E. and D. E. Worley. 1966. The incidence of *Dictyocaulus* sp. in three populations of elk in south-central Montana. Bull. Wildl. Dis. Assoc. 2: 5–6.

Barrett, S. A. 1917. Pomo bear doctors. Univ. California Publ. in Amer. Archaeol. 12(11): 443–465.

Barrett, S. W. 1980. Indians and fire. Western Wildlands 6(3): 17–21.

Barrette, C. 1975. Social behavior of Muntjac. Ph.D. Thesis, Univ. Calgary, Canada. 234 pp.

———. 1977a. Some aspects of behavior of muntjacs in Wilpattu National Park. Mammalia 41: 1–34.

———. 1977b. The social behavior of captive muntjacs *Muntiacus reevesi* (Ogilby 1839). Zs. Tierpsychologie 43: 188–213.

———. 1977c. Fighting behavior of muntjac and the evolution of antlers. Evolution 31(1): 169–176.

Barrette, C. and D. Vandal. 1990a. Sparring, relative antler size, and assessment in male caribou. Behav. Ecol. Sociobiol. 26: 383–387.

Barrette, C. and D. Vandal. 1990b. Sparring and access to food in female caribou in winter. Animal Behavior 40: 1,183–1,185.

Barrow, A. S. (pseudonym Sabretache) 1948. Monarchy and the chase. Eyre and Spottiswoode, London, U.K. 185 pp.

Barry, T. N. and B. J. Blaney. 1987. Secondary compounds in plants. Pages 91–119 in J. B. Hacker and J. H. Ternouth, eds., The nutrition of herbivores. Academic Press, New York. 552 pp.

Barry, T. N. and P. R. Wilson. 1994. Venison production from farmed deer. J. Ag. Sci. 123: 159–165.

Barsness, L. 1985. Heads, hides and horns: The complete buffalo book. Texas Christian Univ. Press, Fort Worth. 233 pp.

Bartels, R. and R. Denney. 1969. Analysis of factors contributing toward declining elk populations in the Chesnimnus unit. Special Rept., Game Div., Wallowa District. Oregon State Game Commiss., Portland. 29 pp.

Bartholow, J. 1995. POP II system documentation. Fossil Creek Software, Fort Collins, Colorado. 48 pp.

Bartmann, R. M. 1983. Composition and quality of mule deer diets on pinyon–juniper winter range, Colorado. J. Wildl. Manage 36: 534–541.

Bartmann, R. M., G. C. White, L. H. Carpenter and R. A. Garrott. 1987. Aerial mark–recapture estimates of confined mule deer in pinyon–juniper woodland. Wildl. Soc. Bull. 14: 356–363.

Bartmann, R. M., G. C. White and L. H. Carpenter. 1992. Compensatory mortality in a Colorado mule deer population. Wildl. Monogr 121. 39 pp.

Barton, B. S. 1806. An account of the Cervus wapiti or southern elk of North America. Philadelphia Med. and Phys. J., March. Art. 7: 36–55.

Barton, K. and W. Fosburgh. 1986. The U.S. Forest Service. Pages 1–156 in Eno, Amos S., Roger L. DiSilvestro and William J. Chandler, compilers, Audubon Wildlife Report 1986. The National Audubon Soc., New York. 1,094 pp.

Bartoññ, L., V. Perner and B. Prochààzka. 1987. On relationship between social rank during the velvet period and antler growth parameters in a growing red deer stag. Acta Theriologica 33: 403–412.

Bartoññ, L. and S. Losos. 1997. Responses of antler growth to changing rank of fallow deer bucks during the velvet period. Can. J. Zool. 75: 1,934–1,939.

Bartos, L. 1980. The date of antler casting, age and social hierarchy relationships in the red deer stag. Behavioral Processes 5: 293–301.

———. 1985. Social activity and the antler cycle in red deer stags. Royal. Soc. New Zealand Bull. 22: 269–272.

Bartos, L. and Hyanek. 1982. Social position in the red deer stag. Pages

463–466 *in* R. D. Brown, ed., II. The relationship with developed antlers. Antler development in cervidae. Caesar Kleberg Wildlife Res. Inst., Texas A & M Univ., College Station.

Bartos, L. and V. Perner. 1991. Asynchronous antler casting in red deer. Pages 291–293 *in* B. Bobek, K. Perzanowski and W. L. Regelin, eds., Global trends in wildlife management. Congr. Int. Union Game Biol. 18: 291–293.

Bartos, L., D. Schams, U. Kierdorf, K. Fischer, G. A. Bubenik, J. Siler, S. Losos, M. Tomanek and J. Lastovkova. 2000. Cyproterone acetate reduced antler growth in surgically castrated fallow deer. J. Endocrinology 164: 87–95.

Bartram, W. 1928. The travels of William Bartram. Dover Publ., New York. 414 pp.

Bartsch, R. C., E. E. McConnell, G. D. Imes and J. M. Schmidt. 1977. A review of exertional rhabdomyolysis in wild and domestic animals and man. Vet. Pathol. 14: 314–324.

Basile, J. V. 1970. Fertilizing to improve elk winter range in Montana. Res. Note INT–113. USDA For. Serv., Ogden, Utah. 6 pp.

———. 1974. Judith road closure study. Pages 145–149 *in* Montana Coop. Elk/logging study, Prog. Rept. for the Period Jan. 1–Dec. 31, 1973, Montana Coop. Elk-Logging study., Bozeman, Montana. Mimeo.

Basile, J. V. and C. E. Jensen. 1971. Grazing potential on lodge-pole pine clearcuts in Montana. Res. Pap. INT–98. USDA For. Serv., Ogden, Utah. 11 pp.

Basile, J. V. and T. N. Lonner, 1979. Vehicle restrictions influence elk and hunter distribution in Montana. J. Forestry 77(3): 155–159.

Baskin, L. M. 1987. Behavior of moose in the USSR. Viltrevy Supplement 1(1): 377–387.

Bass, A. 1996. The Arapaho way. Clarkson N. Potter, Inc., New York. 80 pp.

Bassi, R. 1875. Jaundiced verminous cachexy or pus of the stag caused by *Distoma magnum*. Med. Vet. 4: 497–515. [Translated from Italian by G. Bonvini and published in the Southeastern Vet. 14: 103–112.].

———. 1893. *Distomum magnum* (Bassi) in Italia ed America. Mod. Zooiatro 4: 269–270.

Batcheler, C. L. 1968. Compensatory responses of artificially controlled mammal populations. Proc. New Zealand Ecol. Soc. 15: 25–30.

Batchelor, R. F. 1965. The Roosevelt elk in Alaska—Its ecology and management. Alaska Dept. Fish and Game, Juneau. 37 pp.

Bateman, J. A. 1971. Animal traps and trapping. Stackpole Books, Harrisburg, Pennsylvania. 286 pp.

Bateson, P. 1997. The behavioural and physiological effects of culling red deer. The National Trust., London, U.K.

Bateson, P. and E. L. Bradshaw. 1997. Physiological effects of hunting red deer (*Cervus elaphus*). Proceed.Royal Soc. London, U.K. (B)264: 1,707–1,714.

Bauer, E. A. 1974. Hunting with a camera, A world guide to wildlife photography. Winchester Press, New York. 322 pp.

Baumgartner, W., A. M. Zajac, B. L. Hull, F. Andrews and F. Garry. 1985. Parelaphostrongylosis in llamas. J. Amer. Vet. Med. Assoc. 187: 1,243–1,245.

Baumhoff, M.A. 1978. Environmental background. Pages 16–24 *in* R. F. Heizer, ed., California. Handbook of North American Indians, Vol. 8. Smithsonian Instit. Press, Washington, D.C. 800 pp.

Bayerische-Staatsforstverwaltung 1983 Verbesserung der nahrungsgrundlage des schalenwildes. Munchen. 30 pp.

Bayoumi, M. A. and A. D. Smith. 1976. Response of big game winter range vegetation to fertilization. J. Range Manage. 29(1): 44–48.

Beall, R. C. 1974. Winter habitat selection and use by a western Montana elk herd. Ph.D. Thesis, Univ. Montana, Missoula. 197 pp.

———. 1976. Elk habitat selection in relation to thermal radiation. Pages 97–100 *in* S. R. Hieb, ed., Proc. Elk-Logging-Roads Symp., Univ. Idaho, Moscow. 142 pp.

Bean, M. J. 1977a. The evolution of national wildlife law. U.S. Govt. Print. Off., Washington, D.C. 485 pp.

———. 1977b. The developing law of wildlife conservation on national forests and natural resource lands. J. Contemp. Law 4: 58–77.

———. 1978. Federal wildlife law. Pages 279–289 *in* H. P. Brokaw, ed., Wildlife and America: Contributions to understanding of American wildlife and its conservation. U.S. Govt. Print. Off., Washington, D.C. 532 pp.

———. 1983. The evolution of national wildlife law. Praeger, New York. 390 pp.

Bear, G. D., G. C. White, L. H. Carpenter, R. B. Gill and D. J. Essex. 1989. Evaluation of aerial mark-resighting estimates of elk populations. J. Wildl. Manage. 53: 908–915.

Beatson, N. S. 1985. Tuberculosis in red deer in New Zealand. Royal Soc. New Zealand Bull. 22: 147–150.

Beauchamp, W. M. 1902. Horn and bone implements of the New York Indians. New York State Mus. Bull. 50: 244–350.

Beaufort, The Duke of and M. Morris. 1885. Hunting. Longmans, Green and Co., London, U.K. 373 pp.

Becker, J. M., T. Q. and K. J. Raedeke. 1996. Seeding herbs to enhance cervid forage and reforestation in Pacific Northwest conifer forests: A review. J. Sustainable Forestry 3(2/3): 29–44.

Beck, T. 1996. A failure of the spirit. Pages 200–209 *in* D. Petersen, ed., A hunter's heart: Honest essays on blood sport. Henry Holt and Co., New York. 331 pp.

Bedell, D. M. and J. F. Miller. 1966. A report of the examination of 270 white-tailed deer, *Odocoileus virginianus,* from Anaplasmosis enzootic areas of southeastern United States for evidence of Anaplasmosis. Annu. Disease Rept., Univ. Georgia, Tifton. 8 pp.

Bedford, J. M. 1970. Sperm capacitation and fertilization in mammals. Biol. Reprod. Suppl. 2: 128.

———. 1974. Report of a workshop. Maturation of the fertilizing ability of mammalian spermatozoa in the male and female reproductive tract. Biol. Reprod. 11(3): 346–362.

———. 1976. Prospects of regulation of the post-testicular phase of sperm maturation. Pages 143–148 *in* C. H. Spillman et al., eds., Regulatory mechanisms of the male reproductive physiology. Excerpta Medical, Amsterdam.

Bedford, the Duke of and F. H. A. Marshall. 1942. On the incidence of the breeding season in mammals after transference to a new latitude. Proc. Royal Soc., London. B130: 396–399.

Beetle, A. A. 1962. Range survey in Teton County, Wyoming. III. Utilization and condition classes. Wyoming Ag. Bull. 400: 1–38.

———. 1979. Jackson Hole elk herd: A summary after 25 years of study. Pages 259–262 *in* M. S. Boyce and L. D. Hayden-Wing, eds., North American elk: Ecology, behavior and management. Univ. Wyoming, Laramie. 294 pp.

Behrensmeyer, A. K. and R.W. Hook. 1992. Paleoenvironmental contexts and taphonomic modes. Pages 15–136 *in* A. K. Behrensmeyer, J. D. Damuth, W. A. DiMichele, R. Potts, H-D. Sues and S. L. Wing, eds., Terrestrial ecosystems through time. Univ. Chicago Press, Chicago, Illinois. 568 pp.

Beier, P. 1987. Sex differences in quality of white-tailed deer diets. J. Mammal. 68: 323–329.

Bell, R. H. V. 1971. A grazing ecosystem in the Serengeti. Sci. Amer. 225(1): 86–93.

Bemmel, A. C. V. 1952. On the meaning of movable attachment of the incisiniform teeth in Ruminantia. Beaufortia (Amsterdam) 22: 1–3.

Bender, L. C. 1992. The Michigan elk herd: Ecology of a heavily exploited population. Ph.D. Diss., Michigan State Univ., East Lansing. 199 pp.

Bender, L. C. and R. D. Spencer. 1999. Estimating elk population size by reconstruction from harvest data and herd rations. Wildl. Soc. Bull. 27: 636–645.

Bender, L. C. and P. B. Hall. 1996. *Leptospira interrogans* exposure in free-ranging elk in Washington. J. Wildl. Dis. 32: 121–124.

Bender, L. G., G. J. Roloff and J. B. Haufler. 1994. Amer. Midland Naturalist 132(2): 401–404.

Benedict, R. F. 1923. The concept of the guardian spirit in North America. Mem. Amer. Anthropol. Assoc. 29: 5–85.

Benevolent and Protective Order of Elks. 1903. The protection of the elk. Proc. Grand Lodge of the Benevolent and Protective Order of Elks of the U.S.A. 39: 87–88.

———. 1904. Minutes of business meeting. Proc. Grand Lodge of the Benevolent and Protective Order of Elks of the U.S.A. 40: 268–269.

Beninde, J. 1937a. Zur Naturgeschichte des Rothirsches. Monographie der Wildsäugetiere. P. Schöps, Leipizg. 4: 223.

———. 1937b. Über die Edelhirschformen von Mosbach, Maur und Steinheim a.d. Murr. Paleontologische Zeitschrift, Berlin. 19: 79–116.

Benson, D. E. 1991. Commercialization of wildlife: a value-added incentive for conservation. Pages 539–553 in R. D. Brown, ed., The biology of deer. Springer-Verlag, New York.

Benson, H. C. 1910. Report of the Acting Superintendent of the Yellowstone National Park to the Secretary of the Interior, 1909. Govt. Print. Off, Washington, D.C. 18 pp.

———. 1911. Report of the Acting Superintendent of the Yellowstone National Park to the Secretary of the Interior, 1910. Govt. Print. Off., Washington, D.C. 18 pp.

Bentley, A. 1967. An introduction to deer of Australia. John Garner at the Hawthorn Press, Melbourne, Australia. 224 pp.

Bequaert, J. C. 1942. A monograph of the Melaphoginae, or ked-flies, of sheep, goats, deer, and antelopes. (Diptera: Hippoboscidea). Entomol. Amer. N. S. 22: 1–210.

Berg, A. B., 1970. Management of young growth Douglas-fir and western hemlock. Symp. Proc. Oregon State Univ, Corvallis. 145 pp.

Berg, R. T. and R. M. Butterfield. 1976. New concepts of cattle growth. Halstad Press, Wiley and Sons, New York. 240 pp.

Berg, W. E. 1975. Management implications of natural mortality of moose in northwestern Minnesota. Proc. N. Amer. Moose Conf. Workshop 11: 332–342.

Bergen, J. D. 1971. Vertical profiles of windspeed in a lodgepole pine stand. For. Sci. 17: 314–321.

———. 1974a. Variations of windspeed with canopy cover within a lodgepole pine stand. Res. Note RM–252. USDA For. Serv., Fort Collins, Colorado. 4 pp.

———. 1974b. Variations of air temperature and canopy closure in a lodgepole pine stand. Res. Note RM–253. USDA For. Serv., Fort Collins, Colorado. 3 pp.

Berger, M. E. 1974. Texas hunters: Characteristics, opinions, and facility preferences. Ph.D. Thesis, Texas A & M Univ., College Station. 131 pp.

Berger, J. and S. L. Cain. 1999. Reproductive synchrony in brucellosis-exposed bison in the southern greater Yellowstone ecosystem and in noninfected populations. Conserv. Biol. 12: 357–366.

Bergerud, A. 1974. Rutting behavior of Newfoundland caribou. Pages 395–435 in V. Geist and F. Walther, eds., The behavior of ungulates and its relation to management. Vol. 1, IUCN Publ. New Ser. 24, Morges, Switzerland.

Bergerud, A. T. 1985. Antipredator strategies of caribou: Dispersion along shore lines. Can. J. Zool. 63: 1,324–1,329.

Bergerud, A. T., H. E. Butler and D. R. Miller. 1984. Antipredator tactics of calving caribou: Dispersion in mountains. Can. J. Zool. 62: 1,566–1,575.

Bergerud, A. T. and W. B. Mercer. 1989. Caribou introductions in eastern North America. Wildl. Soc. Bull. 17: 111–120.

Bergerud, A. T. and L. Russell. 1964. Evaluation of rumen food analysis for Newfoundland caribou. J. Wildl. Manage. 28: 809–814.

Berglund, E. R. and R. J. Barney. 1977. Air temperature and wind profiles in an Alaskan lowland black spruce stand. Res. Note PNW–305. USDA For. Serv., Portland, Oregon. 12 pp.

Bergmann, F. 1976. Beitrage zur Kenntnis der Infrastrukturen beim Rotwild 2. Erste Versuche zur Klärung der genetischen Struktur von Rotwildpopulationen an Hand von Serumprotein-Polymorphismen. Z. Jagdwiss. 22(1): 28–35.

Bergstrom, R. C. 1968. Parasites of ungulates in the Jackson Hole area. In Annual report on the activities of the Jackson Hole Biological Research Station. Univ. Wyoming, Laramie. 4 pp.

———. 1975. Prevalence of Dictyocaulus viviparus infection in Rocky Mountain elk in Teton County, Wyoming. J. Wildl. Dis. 11: 40–44.

———. 1982. Lungworms of ruminants. Pages 206–213 in E. T. Thorne, N. Kingston, W. R. Jolley and R. C. Bergstrom, eds. Diseases of Wildlife in Wyoming, 2nd Edition. Wyoming Game and Fish Dept., Cheyenne. 353 pp.

Bergstrom, R. C. and R. Robbins. 1979. Lungworms, *Dictyocaulus viviparus* in various age classes of elk (*Cervus canadensis*) in the Tetons. Pages 221–223 in M. S. Boyce and L. D. Hayden-Wing, eds., North American elk: Ecology, behavior and management. Univ. Wyoming, Laramie. 294 pp.

Bergmann, V. F. 1976. Erste Versuche zur Klärung der genetichen Struktur von Rotwild populationen an Hand von Serumprotein-polymorphismen. Z. Jagdwiss. 22: 28–35.

Berkeley, G. C. G. F. 1861. The English sportsman in the western prairies. Hurst and Blackett, London. 431 pp.

Berlitz, L. 1973. Step-by-step brain tanning the Sioux way. Larry Berlitz, Hot Springs, South Dakota. 16 pp.

Bernard, R. 1963. Specific gravity, ash, calcium, and phosphorous content of antlers of Cervidae. Canadian Naturalist 90(12): 310–322.

Bernick, K. 1983. A site catchment analysis of the Little Qualicum River site, DiSc–1: A wet site on the east coast of Vancouver Island, B.C. Mercury 118, Ottawa. pp.

Berry, J. K. 1986. Learning computer-assisted map analysis. J. Forestry 84: 39–43.

Berry, K. H. 1986. Introduction: Development, testing, and application of wildlife-habitat models. Pages 3–5 in J. Verner, M. L. Morrison and C. J. Ralph, eds., Wildlife 2000 modeling habitat relationships of terrestrial vertebrates. Univ. Wisconsin Press, Madison.

Bettinger, R. L. and M. A. Baumhoff. 1982. The numeric spread: Great Basin cultures in competition. Amer. Antiquity 47: 485–503.

Bevins, M. I., R. S. Bond, T. J. Corcoran, K. D. McIntosh and R. J. McNeil. 1968. Characteristics of hunters and fishermen in six northeastern states. Ag. Exp. Sta. Bull. 656. Univ. Vermont, Burlington. 76 pp.

Beyer, D. E. and Haufler, J. B. 1994. Diurnal versus 24-hour sampling of habitat use. J. Wildl. Manage. 58(1): 178–180.

Bickler, M. 1995. Master hunter—the future of hunting? Pages 5–9 in Wildlife Forever. Proc., Fourth annual governor's symposium on North America's hunting heritage. Green Bay, Wisconsin. 215 pp.

Bider, J. R. and D. H. Pimlott. 1973. Access to hunting areas from major urban centres and big game kills in Quebec. North Amer. Moose Workshop and Conf. 9: 59–80.

Bidwell, J. 1937. A journey to California. J. H. Nash, San Francisco, California. 48 pp. (Reprinted from 1842 booklet in the Bancroft Library, Univ. California-Berkeley.)

Biggins, D. E. 1975. Seasonal habitat selection and movements of the Spotted Bear elk herd. M.S. Thesis. Univ. Montana, Missoula. 90 pp.

Bines, J. A. and S. V. Morant. 1983. The effect of body condition on metabolic changes associated with intake of food by the cow. British J. Nutr. 50: 81–89.

Binford, L. R. 1978. Nunamiut ethnoarchaeology. Academic Press, New York. 509 pp.

Birch, L. C. 1957. The meaning of competition. Amer. Nat. 91: 5–18.

Bird, R. D. 1933. A three-horned wapiti (*Cervus canadensis canadensis*). J. Mammal. 14(2): 164–166.

Bishop, C. A. 1970. The emergence of hunting territories among the Northern Ojibwa. Ethnol. 9: 1–15.

Bishopp, F. C. and H. L. Trembley. 1945. Distribution and hosts of certain North American ticks. J. Parasitol. 31: 1–54.

Bishopp, F. C. and H. P. Wood. 1913. The biology of some North American ticks of the genus *Dermacentor*. J. Parasitol. 6: 153–187.

Biswell, H. H. 1969. Prescribed burning for wildlife in California brushlands. Trans. N. Amer. Wildl. and Natur. Resour. Conf. 34: 438–446.

Bitterlich, W. 1961. Canopy density determination by the angle-count method. Holz-Kur. Wien. 16(35): 7–8.

Bjornn, T. C. and P. D. Dalke. 1975. A survey of behavior, preferences, and opinions of Idaho hunters. Boise: Idaho Dept. Fish and Game. 56 pp.

Bjugstad, A. J., H. S. Crawford and D. L. Neal. 1970. Determining forage consumption by direct observation of domestic grazing animals. Pages 101–104 *in* Range and wildlife habitat evaluation—a research symposium. Misc. Publ. 1147. USDA For. Serv., Washington, D.C.

Black, H. C., ed. 1969. Wildlife and reforestation in the Pacific Northwest. Symp. Proc. Oregon State Univ., Corvallis. 92 pp.

———, ed. 1974. Wildlife and forest management in the Pacific Northwest. Symp. Proc. Oregon State Univ., Corvallis. 236 pp.

Black, H. C., E. J. Dimock, II, W. E. Dodge and W. H. Lawrence. 1969. Survey of animal damage on forest plantations in Oregon and Washington. Trans. N. Amer. Wildl. and Natur. Resour. Conf. 34: 388–408.

Black, H. C., E. J. Dimock, II, J. Evans and J. A. Rochelle. 1979. Animal damage to coniferous plantations in Oregon and Washington-Part 1. A survey, 1963–1975. Res. Bull. 25. Oregon State Univ., Corvallis. 44 pp.

Black, H., Jr., R. J. Scherzinger and J. W. Thomas. 1976. Relationships of Rocky Mountain elk and Rocky Mountain mule deer habitat to timber management in the Blue Mountains of Oregon and Washington. Pages 11–31 *in* S. R. Heib, ed., Proc. Elk- Logging-Roads Symp., Univ. Idaho, Moscow. 142 pp.

Blackburn, T. C. and K. Anderson, eds. 1993. Before the wilderness: Environmental management by native Californians. Ballena Press, Menlo Park, California. 476 pp.

Blackshaw, A. W., D. Hamilton and P. F. Massey. 1973. Effect of scrotal heating on testicular enzymes and spermatogenesis in the rat. Austral. J. Biol. Sci. 26(6): 1935.

Blair, N. 1987. The history of wildlife management in Wyoming. Wyoming Game and Fish Dept., Cheyenne. 295 pp.

Blair, R. M. 1971. Forage production after hardwood control in a southern pine hardwood stand. For. Sci. 17(3): 279–284.

Blair, R. M., R. Alcaniz and A. Harrell. 1983. Shade intensity influences the nutrient quality and digestibility of southern deer browse leaves. J. Range Manage. 36: 257–264.

Blair, W. F. 1939. Faunal relationships and geographic distribution of mammals in Oklahoma. Amer. Midl. Natural. 22(1): 85–133.

Blaisdell, J. P. and J. F. Pechanec. 1949. Effects of herbage removal at various dates on vigor of bluebunch wheatgrass and arrowleaf balsamroot. Ecology 30: 298–305.

Blaser, R. E., R. C. Hames, Jr., H. T. Bryant, W. A. Hardison, J. P. Fontenot and R. W. Engel. 1960. The effect of selective grazing on animal output. Proc. Int. Grassland Congr. 8: 601–606.

Blaxter, K. L. 1961. Energy utilization in ruminants. Pages 183–197 *in* D. Lewis, ed., Digestive physiology and nutrition of the ruminant. Butterworth and Co., London, U.K.

———. 1967. Energy metabolism of ruminants. Hutchinson, London, U.K. 332 pp.

Blaxter, K. L. and W. J. Hamilton. 1980. Reproduction in farmed red deer. 2. Calf growth and mortality. J. Ag. Sci. (Cambridge) 95: 275–284.

Blaxter, K. L., R. N. B Kay,. G. A. M. Sharman, J. M. M. Cunningham and W. J. Hamilton. 1974. Growth and development. Pages 42–48 *in* Farming the red deer. Report of the Rowett Research Institute and Hill Farming Research Organisation. Dept. Agriculture and Fisheries, Scotland.

Blevins, W. 1993. Dictionary of the American West. Facts on File, New York. 400 pp.

Blish, H. H. 1967. A pictographic history of the Oglala Sioux. Univ. Nebraska Press, Lincoln. 530 pp.

Bliss, L. C. 1975. Tundra grasslands, herblands and shrublands and the role of herbivores. Geosci. and Man 10: 51–75.

Blood, D. A. 1966. Range relationships of elk and cattle in Riding Mountain National Park, Manitoba. Wildl. Manage. Bull. 1(19). Can. Wildl. Serv., Ottawa. 62 pp.

Blood, D. A. and A. L. Lovaas. 1966. Measurements and weight relationships in Manitoba elk. J. Wildl. Manage. 30(1): 135–140.

Blood, D. C. and O. M. Radostits. 1989. Veterinary medicine. Seventh ed. Baillière and Tindell, Philadelphia, Pennsylvania. 1,502 pp.

Blottner, S., O. Hingst and H. H. D. Meyer. 1995. Inverse relationship between testicular proliferation and poptosis in mammalian seasonal breeders. Theriogenology. 44: 321–328.

Blumm, M., H. Dunning and S. Reed. 1997. Renouncing the Public Trust Doctrine: An assessment of the validity of Idaho House Bill 794. Ecology Law Quart. 24: 461–504.

Blyth, C. B. 1995. Dynamics of ungulate populations in Elk Island National Park. M.S. Thesis, Dept. Ag., Food and Nutritional Sci., Univ. Alberta, Edmonton. 140 pp.

Bø, S. and O. Hjeljord. 1991. Do continental moose ranges improve during cloudy summers? Can. J. Zool. 69: 1,875–1,879.

Boas, R. 1906a. The tribes of the north Pacific coast. Pages 235–249 *in* Annu. Archaeol. Rept. 1905. Report of the Ontario Minister of Education. L. K. Cameron, Toronto. 249 pp.

———. 1906b. The Salish tribes of the interior of British Columbia. Pages 219–225 *in* Annu. Archaeol. Rept. 1905. Report of the Ontario Minister of Education. L. K. Cameron, Toronto. 249 pp.

Boddicker, M. L. and E. J. Hugghins. 1969. Helminths of big game animals in South Dakota. J. Parasitol. 55: 1,067–1,074.

Boer, A. E. 1997. Interspecific relationships. Pages 337–349 *in* A. E. Franzmann and C. E. Schwartz, eds., Ecology and management of the North American moose. Smithsonian Instit. Press, Washington, D.C. 733 pp.

Boertje, R. D. 1985. An energy model for adult female caribou of the Denali Herd, Alaska. J. Range Manage. 38: 468–473.

———. 1990. Diet quality and intake requirements of adult female caribou of the Denali herd, Alaska. J. Appl. Ecol. 27: 420–434.

Bohne, J. R. 1974. Food habits, seasonal distribution, and habitat utilization of elk in the South Fork of Fish Creek, Lolo National Forest, Montana. M.S. Thesis, Univ. Montana, Missoula. 197 pp.

Bolen, E. G. and W. L. Robinson. 1999. Wildlife ecology and management. Prentice Hall, Upper Saddle River, New Jersey. 605 pp.

Boll, L. A. 1958. Elk nutrition—the response of elk calves to various winter diets under controlled conditions. M.S. Thesis. Univ. Montana, Missoula. 99 pp.

Bolon, N. A. 1994. Estimates of the Values of Elk in the Blue Mountains of Oregon and Washington: Evidence from the Existing Literature. USDA For. Serv., Gen. Tech. Rept. PNW–316. Portland, Oregon. 38 pp.

Boltz, M. J. Unpublished. Impacts of prescribed burns and clearcuts upon summer elk food habits, diet quality, and distribution in Central Washington. 1979. M.S. Thesis, Washington State Univ., Pullman. 129 pp.

Bomar, L. K. 2000. Broad-scale patterns of elk recruitment in Idaho: Relationships with habitat quality and effect of data aggregation. M.S. Thesis, Univ. Idaho, Moscow.

Bond, G. C. and R. Lotti. 1995. Iceberg discharges into the North Atlantic on millennial time scales during the last glaciation. Science 267(5,200): 1,005–1,010.

Borland, H. 1975. The history of wildlife in America. Nat. Wildl. Fed., Washington, D.C. 208 pp.

Bormann, B. T., J. R. Martin, F. H. Wagner, G. T. Wood, J. Alegria, P. G. Cunningham, M. H. Brooks, P. Friesema, J. Berg and J. R. Henshaw. 1999. Adaptive management. Vol. 3. Pages 505–534 in R. C. Szaro, N. C. Johnson, W. T. Sexton and A. J. Malk, eds., Ecological stewardship: A common reference for ecosystem management. Elsevier Science Ltd., Kidlington, Oxford, U.K. 761 pp.

Bourke, J. 1891. On the border with Crook. Charles Scribner's Sons, New York. 491 pp.

Bourke, J. G. Unpublished. John Gregory Bourke diaries. Denver Public Library, 1480. Denver, Colorado. (Microfilm copies.)

Bourke, J. G. 1966. McKenzie's last fight with the Cheyennes: A winter campaign in Wyoming and Montana. Argonaut Press, New York. 56 pp.

Boutelle, F. A. 1890. Report of the Superintendent of the Yellowstone National Park to the Secretary of the Interior. Govt. Print. Off., Washington, D.C. 23 pp.

Bowyer, R. T. 1984. Sexual segregation in southern mule deer. Mammal. 65: 410–417.

Boyce, M. S. 1989. The Jackson elk herd: Intensive wildlife management in North America. Cambridge Univ. Press, New York. 306 pp.

———. 1991a. Migratory behavior and management of elk (*Cervus elaphus*). Appl. Animal Behavior Sci. 29: 1–4.

———. 1991b. Natural regulation or the control of nature? Pages 183–208 in R. B. Keiter and M. S. Boyce, eds., The Greater Yellowstone ecosystem: Redefining America's wilderness heritage. Yale Univ. Press, New Haven, Connecticut. 428 pp.

———. 1998. Ecological-process management and ungulates: Yellowstone's conservation paradigm. Wildl. Soc. Bull. 26: 391–398.

Boyce, M. S. and A. Haney. 1997. Ecosystem management: Applications for ecosystem management. Yale U. Press, New Haven, Connecticut. 361 pp.

Boyce, W. M. and R. N. Brown. 1991. Antigenic characterization of *Psoroptes* spp. (Acari: Psoroptidae) mites from different hosts. J. Parasitol. 77: 675–679.

Boyce, W., L. Elliott, R. Clark and D. Jessup. 1990. Morphometric analysis of *Psoroptes* spp. mites from bighorn sheep, mule deer, cattle, and rabbits. J. Parasitol. 76: 823–828.

Boyd, D. K., R. R. Ream, D. H. Pletscher and M. W. Fairchild. 1994. Prey taken by colonizing wolves and hunters in the Glacier National Park area. J. Wildl. Manage. 58: 289–295.

Boyd, R. J. 1968. Seasonal movements—Rio Grande elk herd. Pages 365–381 in Job. Prog. Repy. W–38-R–22, Colorado Div. Game, Fish and Parks, Denver.

———. 1970. Elk of the White River Plateau, Colorado. Colorado Div. Game, Fish and Parks. Denver. 126 pp.

———. 1972. Stomach contents data from the Rio Grande elk herd in southwestern Colorado. Unpublished on file. Coloorado Div. Game, Fish and Parks, Fort Collins.

———. 1978. American elk. Pages 11–29 in J. L. Schmidt and D. L. Gilbert, eds., Big game of North America: Ecology and management. Stackpole Books, Inc., Harrisburg, Pennsylvania. 512 pp.

Boyd, R. J. and J. F. Lipscomb. 1976. An evaluation of yearling bull elk hunting restrictions in Colorado. Wildl. Soc. Bull. 4(1): 3–10.

Boyle, S. H. and F. B. Samson. 1985. Effects of nonconsumptive recreation on wildlife: A review. Wildl. Soc. Bull. 13: 110–116.

Bracken, E. and J. Musser. 1993. Colockum elk study. Compl. Rept. Washington Dept. Wildlife, Olympia. 129 pp.

Bradley, J. H. 1966. Contributions to the Historical Society of Montana. J. S. Conner and Co., Inc., Boston, Massachusetts. IX: 349–350.

Bradshaw, H. and V. Bradshaw. 1959. Teach your son to hunt safely. Better Homes and Gardens 37(9): 32B, 34, 37.

Branch, E. D. 1962. The hunting of the buffalo. Univ. Nebraska Press, Lincoln. 240 pp.

Brander, M. 1971. Hunting and shooting. G. P. Putnam's Sons, New York. 255 pp.

Brands, H. W. 1997. TR: The last romantic. BasidBooks, New York, 897 pp.

Brazda, A. R. 1953. Elk migration patterns and some of the factors affecting movements in the Gallatin River Drainage, Montana. J. Wildl. Manage. 17(1): 9–23.

Breier, B. H., J. J. Bass, J. H. Butler and P. D. Gluckman. 1986. The somatotrophic axis in young steers: Influence of nutritional status on pulsatile release of growth hormone and circulating concentrates of insulin-like growth factor. J. Endocrinology 111: 209–215.

Brelurut, A., M. Theriez and G. Bechet. 1995. Effects of winter feeding level on the performance of red deer calves (*Cervus elaphus*). Anim. Sci. 60: 151–156.

Brett, L. M. 1912. Report of the Acting Superintendent of the Yellowstone National Park to the Secretary of the Interior, 1911. Govt. Print. Off., Washington, D.C. 20 pp.

———. 1913. Report of the Acting Superintendent of the Yellowstone National Park to the Secretary of the Interior, 1912. Govt. Print. Off., Washington, D.C. 22 pp.

———. 1914. Report of the Acting Superintendent of the Yellowstone National Park to the Secretary of the Interior, 1913. Govt. Print. Off., Washington, D.C. 21 pp.

———. 1915. Report of the Acting Superintendent of the Yellowstone National Park to the Secretary of the Interior, 1914. Govt. Print. Off., Washington, D.C. 29 pp.

———. 1916. Report of the Acting Superintendent of the Yellowstone National Park to the Secretary of the Interior, 1915. Govt. Print. Off., Washington, D.C. 39 pp.

Brewer, W. H. 1871. Animal life in the Rocky Mountains of Colorado. American Naturalist 5: 220–223.

Brickell, J. 1737. The natural history of North Carolina. James Carson, Dublin, Ireland. 417 pp.

Briedermann, L. 1986. Schwarzwild. Neumann-Neudamm. 539 pp.

Bright, W. 1978. Karok. Pages 180–189 in R. F. Heizer, ed., California. Handbook of North American Indians. Vol. 8. Smithsonian Instit. Press, Washington, D.C. 800 pp.

Brinklow, B. R. and A. S. I. Loudon. 1993. Gestation periods in the Pere

David's deer (*Elaphus davidianus*): Evidence for embryonic diapause or delayed development. Reprod. Fertil. Dev. 5: 567–575.

Brna, J. 1969. Fertility of hinds and postnatal mortality of young (*C. elaphus* L.) in Belje. Jelen (Beograd.) 1(8): 69–72.

Brockway, J. M. and G. M. O. Maloiy. 1967. Energy metabolism of the red deer. Proc. Physiol. Soc. 67: 22–24.

Brockway, J.M. and J.A. Gessaman. 1977. The energy cost of locomotion on the level and on gradients for the red deer (*Cervus elaphus*). Quart. J. Exp. Physiol. 62: 333–339.

Brody, S. 1945. Bioenergetics and growth. Reinhold Publishing Co., New York. 1,023 pp.

Bromley, P. T. 1976. Aspects of the behavioral ecology and sociobiology of the pronghorn (*Antilocapra americana*). Ph.D. Diss., Univ. Calgary, Alberta. 370 pp.

Brooks, F. E. 1911. The mammals of West Virginia: Notes on the distribution and habits of all our known native species. Pages 9–30 *in* West Virginia State Board Ag. Rept. for quarter ending December 30, 1910.

Brooks, H. V. and J. J. Cahill. 1985. The susceptibility of Canadian wapiti to ryegrass staggers. New Zealand Vet. J. 33: 126.

Brooks, R., C. S. Swanson and J. Duffield. 1991. Total economic value of elk in Montana: an emphasis on hunting values. Pages 186–195 *in* A. Christensen, J. Lyon and T. Lonner, eds., Proc., Elk Vulnerability Symp. Montana State Univ., Bozeman.

Brose, D. S. 1978. Late prehistory of the upper Great Lakes area. Pages 569–582 *in* B. G. Trigger, ed., Northeast. Handbook of North American Indians, Vol. 15. Smithsonian Instit. Press, Washington, D.C. 924 pp.

Brown, B. 1908. The Conard Fissure, a Pleistocene bone deposit in northern Arkansas: With descriptions of two new genera and twenty new species of mammals. Memoirs Amer. Mus. Natur. Hist. IX: 157–208.

Brown, C. 1985. The Sand Creek elk, northeastern Idaho—population status, movements, and distribution. Idaho Dept. Fish Game. Proj. No. W–160-R. 119 pp.

Brown, D. 1954. Methods of surveying and measuring vegetation. Commonwealth Bur. of Pastures and Field Crops Bull. 42. Commonwealth Agricultural Bureaux, Farnham Royal, U.K. 223 pp.

———. 1977. Hear that lonesome whistle blow. Holt, Rinehart and Winston, New York. 311 pp.

Brown, D. and A. Dimeo. 1976. Remote sensing for big game counts. USDA For. Serv., Missoula, Montana. 7 pp.

Brown, E. R. 1961. The black-tailed deer of western Washington. Biol. Bull. 13. Washington Game Dept., Olympia. 124 pp.

———. 1967. Preliminary elk management plan. Unpublished State of Washington big game management rept. on file at Washington Game Dept., Olympia. 4 pp.

Brown, E. R. and J. H. Mandery. 1962. Planting and fertilization as a possible means of controlling distribution of big game animals. J. Forestry 60(1): 33–35.

Brown, J. E. 1992. Animals of the soul. Element, Inc., Rockport, Massachusetts. 145 pp.

Brown, M. E. 1986. Reproductive disorders—female. Pages 112–113 *in* T. L. Alexander, ed., Management and disease of deer. Vet. Deer Soc., London, U.K.

Brown, O. J. 1899. Report of the Acting Superintendent of the Yellowstone National Park to the Secretary of the Interior, 1899. Govt. Print. Off., Washington, D.C. 18 pp.

Brown, P. T. 1988 Bragging bucks of Davis Island. Mississippi Game and Fish. Nov 1988: 28–29, 56–57.

Brown, R. D., ed. 1992. The biology of deer. Springer Verlag, New York. 596 pp.

Brown, R. D., C. C. Chao and L. W. Faulkner. 1983a. The endocrine con-

trol of the initiation and growth of antlers in white-tailed deer. Acta Endocrinol. 103: 138–144

Brown, R. D., C. C. Chao and L. W. Faulkner. 1983b. Hormone levels and antler development in white-tailed deer and sika fawns. Comp. Biochem. Physiol. 75A: 385–390.

Brown, R. E. 1990. Effects of a Savory grazing method on big game. Arizona Game and Fish Dept., Tech. Rept. 3: 33.

Brown, T. T., Jr., H. E. Jordan and C. N. Demorest. 1978. Cerebrospinal parelaphostrongylosis in llamas. J. Wildl. Dis. 14: 441–444.

Browning, M. 1859. Forty-four years of the life of a hunter. Winston Printing Co., Winston Salem, North Carolina. 400 pp.

Brüggemann, J. and H. Karg. 1967. Hormonal regulation of the rut in the male red-deer and roe-deer. Pages 73–79 *in* I. Isakovic, ed., Trans. 7th Congr. IUGB, Beograd-Ljubljana, September 1965. Beograd-Ljubljana. Union of Organizations of Game of Yugoslavia, Yugoslavia. 636 pp.

Brüggemann, J., U. Drescher-Kaden and K. Walser-Karst. 1973. Die Zusammensetzung der Rotwildmich 1. Mitt: Der Rohnahrstoffgehalt (Rohfett, Rohprotein, Lacotse and Rohasche). Z. Tierphsil., Tierernähr. and Futtermittelkunde 31(5): 227–238.

Brüggemann, J., D. Giesecke and K. Karst. 1965. Untersuchungen am Panseninhalt von Reh- und Rotwild. Pages 139–144 *in* Trans. 6th Congr. IUGB, Bournemouth England, 7–12 October 1965. Nature Conservancy, London. 394 pp.

Bruhin, H. 1953. Zur Biologie der Stirnaufsatze bei den Huftieren. Physiol. Comp. et Oecol. 3: 63–127.

Brunt, K. 1990. Application of a geographic information system (GIS) to test models of Vancouver Island Roosevelt Elk habitat suitability. Pages 1–7 *in* R. L. Callas, D. B. Koch and E. R. Loft, eds., Proc. Western States and Provinces Elk Workshop. California Dept. Fish and Game, Sacramento.

———. 1991. Testing models of the suitability of Roosevelt elk (*Cervus elaphus roosevelti*) seasonal ranges. M.S. Thesis, Univ. Victoria, British Columbia. 156 pp.

Brunt, K. and C. Ray. 1986. Seasonal range habitat suitability index models for Vancouver Island Roosevelt elk. Pages 117–144 *in* D. L. Eastman, ed., Proc. Western States and Provinces Elk Workshop. Oregon Dept. Fish and Wildlife, Portland.

Bryant, L. D. 1993. Quality of bluebunch wheatgrass (*Agropyron spicatum*) as a winter range forage for Rocky Mountain elk (*Cervus elaphus nelsoni*) in the Blue Mountains of Oregon. Ph.D. Thesis, Oregon State Univ., Corvallis. 147 pp.

Bryant, L. D. and C. Maser. 1982. Classification and distribution. Chapter 1. Pages 1–59 *in* J. W. Thomas and D. E. Toweill, eds., Elk of North America: Ecology and management. Stackpole Books, Harrisburg, Pennsylvania. 698 pp.

Bubenik, A. B. 1956. Prizpevek Kotazce vnitrodruhove rovnovahy jeleni zvere (Contribution to the intra specific balance in red deer). Lesnictvi, Prague. 29(1): 21–44.

———. 1959a. Rotwildgehe auf biologischer Grundlage. Z. f. Jagdwiss. 5(4): 121–132.

———. 1959b. Grundlagen der Wildernahrung. Berlin: Deutscher Bauernverlag. 300pp.

———. 1960a. Le rhythme nycthemeral et le regime journalier des ongules sauvages. Probleme theoretique. Rhythme d'activite du chevreuil. Mammalia 24(1): 1–59.

———. 1960b. Vom Betaubungsschlafdes Schalenwildes. Wild und Hund 63(3): 72.

———. 1962. Geweihmorphogenese im Lichte der neurohumoralen Forschung. Sympos. Theriologicum, CSAV, Brno. 1960: 59–66.

———. 1965. Beiträge zur Geburtskunde und zu den Mutter-Kind

Beziehungen des Reh (*Capreolus capreolus* L.) und Rotwildes (*Cervus elaphus* L.). Z. f. Saugetierkunde 30(2): 65–128.

————. 1966. Das Geweihe. P. Parey Verlag, Hamburg and Berlin. 214 pp.

————. 1971a. Geweihe und ihre biologische Funktion. Naturwiss. und Medizin (n + m) 8(36): 33–51.

————. 1971b. Social well-being as a special aspect of animal sociology. Presented at the 1st Int. Conf. on the behaviour of ungulates and its relation to management, Nov. 2–5, 1971, Univ. Calgary, Alberta, Canada. Mimeo.

————. 1971c. Rehwildhege und Rehwildbiologies. F. C. Mayer Verlag, München. 59 pp.

————. 1972. North American moose management in light of European experiences. Proc. N. Amer. Moose Conf. and Workshop 8: 276–295.

————. 1973. Antlers as a releaser and gestalt in the social life of animals. Abstract. 13th Int. Ecol. Conf., Washington, D.C.

————. 1974. Brennende Fragen der Schalenwildbewirtschaftung. BJV-Mitteilungen #6 (Müncher). 7 pp.

————. 1975. Significance of antlers in the social life of Barren Ground caribou. Pages 436–461 *in* 1st Int. Reindeer/Caribou Symp., College, Alaska August 9–11, 1972.

————. 1982. Physiology. Pages 125–179 *in* J. W. Thomas and D. E. Toweill, eds., Elk of North America: Ecology and management. Stackpole Books, Harrisburg, Pennsylvania. 698 pp.

————. 1983. The behavioral aspects of antlerogenesis. Pages 389–449 *in* Antler Development in Cervidae. Proc., First Int. Symp. Caesar Kleberg Wildl. Res. Inst., Texas A & M Univ., Kingsville, Texas. 480 pp.

————. 1984 Ernahrung, verhalten and umwelt des schalenwildes. BLV, Munchen, Wien, Zurich. 272 pp.

————. 1987. Behavior of moose (*Alces alces* spp) of North America. Viltrevy Supplement 1(1), 333–365.

————. In press. The behavioural physiology and nutrition of European large game, vol. 1. BLV Munich.

————. Unpublished. Data from FUST-Project Achental on sexual selection of red deer stags by hind under surplus of prime males. In author's file at Ontario Ministry of Natural Resources, Maple, Ontario.

————. Unpublished. Development and seasonal variation of organs in red deer (*Cervus elaphus*). In author's file at Ontario Ministry of Natural Resources, Maple, Ontario.

————. Unpublished. Morphophysiological responses in red deer (*Cervus elaphus*) to changes in population structure. In author's file at Ontario Ministry of Natural Resources, Maple, Ontario.

Bubenik, A. B. and T. J. Belihouse. In press. Brain volume of taiga moose (*Alces alces* sp.). N. Amer. Moose Conf. and Workshop 16.

Bubenik, A. B. and G. A. Bubenik. Unpublished. The dynamics of antler mineralization. In author's file at Ont. Min. of Natural Resources, Maple, Ontario.

Bubenik, A. B. and J. Bubenikova. 1966. 24-Std.-Periodik des Rotwildes (*Cervus elaphus* L.). Borlaufige Mitt. Annual Meeting of Conseil International de la Chasse, München.

Bubenik, A. B. and R. Pavlanský. 1965. Trophic responses to trauma in growing antlers. J. Exp. Zool. 159(3): 282–302.

Bubenik, A. B. and P. Schwab. 1974. Populationsstruktur des Gamswildes, ihre Simulierung und Bedeutung fur die Regulierung der Bestande. 1st Intern. Gamstreffen October 1974, Oberammergau. pp. 117–122.

Bubenik, A. B. and H. Wurtzinger. 1967. Beidseitiger erster Pramolar im Unterkiefer des Rehes, *Capreolus capreolus* Linne, 1758. Saugetierdkl. Mitt. 15(1): 35–39.

Bubenik, A. B., J. Bilek and K. Hynek. 1956. Permeability of the rumen wall of sheep for phosphate ions. Manuscript.

Bubenik, A. B., J. Lochman, I. Semizorova and Z. Fiser. 1957. Spasani

lesnich drevin parohatou zveri s hlediska jejich fysiologickych potreb. Lesnictvi, Czech Republic 3(4): 347–352.

Bubenik, A. B., M. Domalagian, J. W. Wheeler and O. Williams. 1979. The role of the tarsal glands in the olfactory communication of the Ontario moose—a preliminary report. Proc. N. Amer. Moose Conf. and Workshop (H. Cumming, ed.) 15: 119–147.

Bubenik, A. B., R. Tachezy and G. A. Bubenik. 1976. The role of the pituitary-adrenal-axis in the regulation of antler growth processes. Saugetierdkl. Mitt. 24(1): 1–5.

Bubenik, A. B., O. Williams and H. R. Timmermann. 1978. Significance of hooves in moose management—a preliminary report. Proc. N. Amer. Moose Conf. and Workshop (H. Cumming, ed.) 14: 209–226.

Bubenik, A. B., G. A. Bubenik and E. Bamberg. Unpublished. The development of hormonal secretion in red deer (*Cervus elaphus*) and chamois (*Rupicapra rupicapra*). Part II: Seasonal and sexual differences in sex hormone levels. In author's file at Ontario Ministry of Natural Resources, Maple, Ontario.

Bubenik, A. D. 1985. Reproductive strategies in cervids. Pages 367–373 *in* P. F. Fennessy and K. R. Drew, eds., Biology of deer production. The Royal Soc. of New Zealand, Wellington Bull. 22. 482 pp.

Bubenik, G. A. 1972. Seasonal variations of nuclear size of hypothalamic cells in the roe-buck. J. Anim. Sci. 35(5): 967–973.

————. 1982. The endocrine regulation of the antler cycle. Pages 73–107 *in* R. D. Brown, ed., Antler development in Cervidae. Caesar Kleberg Wildl. Res. Inst., Kingsville, Texas.

————. 1986. Regulation of seasonal endocrine rhythms in male boreal cervids. Pages 461–474 *in* I. Assenmacher and J. Boissin, eds., Endocrine regulations as adaptive mechanisms to the environment. Paris, France.

————. 1990a. Neuroendocrine regulation of the antler cycle. Pages 265–297 *in* G. A. Bubenik and A. B. Bubenik, eds., Horns, Pronghorns and Antlers. Springer-Verlag, New York. 562 pp.

————. 1990b. The role of the nervous system in the growth of antlers. Pages 339–358 *in* G. A. Bubenik and A. B. Bubenik, eds, Horns, Pronghorns and Antlers. Springer Verlag, New York. 562 pp.

————. 1992. Morphological differences in the antler velvet of cervidae. Pages 56–64 *in* N. Ohtaishi and H-I Sheng, eds., Deer of China: Biology and Management. Elsevier, Amsterdam.

————. Unpublished. The development of antlers in white-tailed doe (*Odocoileus virginianus*) by neurogenic stimulation of the pedicle. On file at Ontario Min. Nat. Res., Maple, Ontario.

Bubenik, G. A. and L. Bartos. 1993. Cortisol levels in red deer (*Cervus elaphus*) and fallow deer (*Dama dama*) after an acute ACTH administration. Can. J. Zool. 71: 2,258–2,261.

Bubenik, G. A. and A. B. Bubenik. 1967. Adrenal glands in roe deer (*Capreolus capreolus* L.). Pages 93–97 *in* I. Isakovic, ed., Trans. 7th Congr. IUGB, Beograd-Ljubljana, September 1965. Union of Organizations of Game of Yugoslavia, Beograd. 636 pp.

————. 1973. Effect of cyproterone acetate on the antler cycle. Amer. Zool. 13(4): 1,287. Abstr.

————. 1976. Effects of antiestrogens on the growth and mineralization of the antler bone. Proc. Can. Fed. Biol. Soc., pp. 50. Abstr.

————. 1978. Thyroxine levels in white-tailed deer (*Odocoileus virginianus*). Can. J. Physiol. Pharmacol. 56(6): 945–949.

————. 1990. Horns, pronghorns and antlers: Evolution, morphology, physiology, and social significance. Springer-Verlag, New York. 562 pp.

Bubenik, G. A., G. M. Brown, A. B. Bubenik and L. J. Grota. 1974. Immunohistological localization of testosterone in the growing antler of the white-tailed deer (*Odocoileus virginianus*). Calc. Tiss. Res. 14(2): 121–130.

Bubenik, G. A., G. M. Brown, A. Trenkle and D. A. Wilson. 1975a. Growth hormone and cortisol levels in the annual cycle of the white-tailed deer (*Odocoileus virginianus*). Can. J. Physiol. Pharmacol. 53: 787–792.

Bubenik, G. A., A. B. Bubenik, G. M. Brown and D. A. Wilson. 1975b. The role of sex hormones in the growth of antler bone tissue. I. Endocrine and metabolic effects of anti-androgen therapy. J. Exp. Zool. 194(2): 349–358.

Bubenik, G. A., G. M. Brown and L. J. Grota. 1976a. Differential localization of N-acetylated indole-alkylamines in CNS, and the Harderian gland using immunohistology. Brain Res. 118: 417–427.

Bubenik, G. A., A. B. Bubenik, A. Trenkle, D. A. Wilson and G. M. Brown. 1976b. Stress and short-term changes of cortisol, growth hormone, and insulin in plasma of white-tailed deer during the annual cycle. Prog. and Abstr., 58th Annu. Meet. Endocrin. Soc. 428: 271.

Bubenik, G. A., A. B. Bubenik, G. M. Brown and D. A. Wilson. 1977a. Sexual stimulation in normal, antiandrogen and antiestrogen treated white-tailed deer (*Odocoileus virginianus*) during annual cycle. Pages 377–386 *in* T. J. Peterle, ed., Trans. 13th Congr. IUGB, March 11–15, 1977, Atlanta, Georgia. The Wildl. Soc. and Wildl. Manage. Inst., Washington, D.C. 538 pp.

Bubenik, G. A., A. B. Bubenik, A. Trenkle, A. Sirek, D. A. Wilson and G. M. Brown. 1977b. Short-term changes in plasma concentration of cortisol, growth hormone, and insulin during the annual cycle of a male white-tailed deer (*Odocoileus virginianus*). Comp. Biochem. Physiol. 58A: 387–391.

Bubenik, G. A., A. B. Bubenik and J. Zamecnik. 1979. The development of circannual rhythm of estradiol in plasma of white-tailed deer (*Odocoileus virginianus*). Comp. Biochem. Physiol. 62A: 869–872.

Bubenik, G. A., J. M. Morris, D. Schams and A. Claus. 1982. Photoperiodicity and circannual levels of LH, FSH, and testosterone in normal and castrated male, white-tailed deer. Can. J. Physiol. and Pharmacol. 60: 788–793.

Bubenik, G. A., P. S. Smith and D. Schams. 1986. The effect of orally administered melatonin on the seasonality of deer pelage exchange, antler development, LH, FSH, prolactin, testosterone, T3, T4, cortisol and calkaline phosphatase. J. Pineal Res. 3: 331–349.

Bubenik, G. A., A. B. Bubenik and E. Bamberg. Unpublished. The development of hormonal secretion in red deer (*Cervus elaphus*) and chamois (*Rupicapra rupicapra*). Part I. Seasonal and sexual differences in cortisol levels. On file at Ontario Ministry of Natural Resources, Maple, Ontario.

Buechner, H. K. 1950. Life history, ecology, and range use of the pronghorn antelope in Trans-Pecos, Texas. Amer. Midl. Natur. 43(2): 257–354.

———. 1952. Winter-range utilization by elk and mule deer in southeastern Washington. J. Range Manage. 5(2): 76–80.

———. 1960. The bighorn sheep in the United States, its past, present, and future. Wildl. Monogr. No. 4. The Wildl. Soc., Washington, D.C. 174 pp.

Buechner, H. K. and C. V. Swanson. 1955. Increased natality resulting from lowered population density among elk in southeastern Washington. Trans. N. Amer. Wildl. Conf. 20: 560–567.

Buechner, H. K., Am. M. Harthoorn and J. A. Lock. 1960. Recent advances in field immobilization of large mammals with drugs. Trans. N. Amer. Wildl. Conf. 25: 415–422.

Bullock, K. D., J. K. Bertrand, L. L. Benyshek, S. E. Williams and D. G. Lust. 1991. Comparison of real-time ultrasound and other live measures to carcass measures as predictors of beef cow energy stores. J. Anim. Sci. 69: 3,908–3,916.

Bunch, T. D., R. W. Meadows, W. C. Foote, L. N. Egbert and J. J. Spillett.

1976. Identification of ungulate hemoglobins for law enforcement. J. Wildl. Manage. 40(3): 517–522.

Bunnage, R. J. and T. L. Church. 1991. Is game farming really all that bad? Can. Vet. J. 32: 70–72.

Bunnell, F. L. 1993. Advice, faith, and general relativity: Reaction to presentations on the commercialization of wildlife. Pages 103–116 *in* A. W. L. Hawley, ed., Commercialization and wildlife management: dancing with the devil. Kreiger Publ. Co., Malabar, Florida. 124 pp.

Bunnell, F. L., C. Galindo-Leal and A. Chan-McLeod. 1995. From wildlife management to conservation biology: A Canadian perspective. Pages 138–142 *in* J. A. Bissonette and P. R. Krausmann, eds., Integrating people and wildlife for a sustainable future. Proc. First International Wildlife Management Congress. The Wildl. Soc., Bethesda, Maryland. 697 pp.

Bunnell, S.D. 1997. Status of elk in North America: 1975–1995. Rocky Mountain Elk Found., Missoula, Montana. 27 pp.

Burbridge, W. R. and D. J. Neff. 1976. Conconino National Forest—Arizona Game and Fish Department Cooperative Roads—wildlife study. Pages 44–57 *in* S. R. Hieb, ed., Proc. Elk-Logging-Roads Symp., Univ. Idaho, Moscow. 142 pp.

Burch, J. B. and T. A. Pearce. 1990. Terrestrial gastropods. Page 201–309 *in* D. L. Dindal, ed., Soil biology guide. John Wiley and Sons, New York.

Burcham, M., W. D. Edge and C. L. Marcum. 1999. Elk use of private land refuges. Wildl. Soc. Bull. 27(3): 833–839

Burgoyne, G. E., Jr. 1981. Observations on a heavily exploited deer populations. Pages 403–413 *in* C. W. Fowler and T. D. Smith, eds., Dynamics of large mammal populations. John Wiley and Sons, New York. 477 pp.

Burnett, P. H. 1880. Recollections and opinions of an old pioneer. D. Appleton and Co., New York. 448 pp.

Burns, J. A. 1986. A 9,000-year-old wapiti (*Cervus elaphus*) skeleton from northern Alberta, and its implications for the early Holocene environment. Géographie Physique et Quaternaire 40: 105–108.

———. 1989. Fossil vertebrates from Rats Nest Cave, Alberta. Can. Caver, Spring 1989: 41–43.

Burris, O. E. and D. E. McKnight. 1973. Game transplants in Alaska. Wildl. Tech. Bull. 4. Alaska Dept. Fish and Game, Juneau. 58 pp.

Burroughs, R. D., ed., 1961. The natural history of the Lewis and Clark Expedition. Michigan State Univ. Press, East Lansing. 331 pp.

Burt, T., Jr. and G. H. Cates. 1959. Pecos elk reproductive and food habits studies. Fed. Aid Compl. Rept. Proj. W–93–R–1, WP–3, J–6. New Mexico Dept. Game and Fish, Albuquerque. 19 pp.

Burt, W. H. 1943. Territorial and home range concepts as applied to mammals. J. Mammal. 24(3): 346–352.

———. 1954. The subspecies category in mammals. Syst. Zool. 3(3): 99–104.

Burthey, F., A. Burthey, F. Sennaoui and N. Bensefia. 1992. The *Cervus elaphus barberus* (Gennett, 1833) in Algeria. Pages 271–276 *in* F. Spitz, G. Janeau, G. Gonzalez and S. Aulagner, eds., Ongulés/ungulates 91. Société Française pour L'Etude et la Protection des Mammifères, Paris. 661 pp.

Buss, M. E. 1967. Habitat utilization and early food habits of Michigan elk. M.S. Thesis. Univ. Michigan, Ann Arbor. 97 pp.

Buss, M. E. and J. D. Solf. 1959. Record of an antlered female elk. J. Mammal. 40(2): 252.

Butler, A. W. 1895. The mammals of Indiana. Proc. Indiana Acad. Sci., Indianapolis. 1894: 81–86.

Butler, W. J. 1938. Wild animal disease investigation. *In* Montana Livestock San. Board Rept., 1936–1938. Montana Livestock San. Board, Helena. 14 pp.

Bützler, W. 1972. Rotwild. Bayerischer Landwirtschafts Verlag, Munich. 165 pp.

———. 1974. Kampf- und Paarungsverhalten, Soziale Reihenordnung und Aktivitätsperiodik beim Rothirsch. Fortschritte der Verhaltensforschung Paul Pary Verlag, Berlin. 80 pp. (Supplement to the J. Compar. Ethol.).

———. 1986. Rotwild: Biologie, verhalten, umwelt, hege. BLV verlagsgesellschaft Munchen. 256 pp.

Byers, R. C., ed. 1998. 23rd big game awards. The Boone and Crockett Club, Missoula, Montana. 566 pp.

Caballero, y C. E. 1945. Morfologia posicion sistematica de Onchocerca cervipedis, Wehr & Dikmans, 1935. Rev. Brasil Biol. 5: 557–562.

Cahalane, V. H. 1939. Mammals of the Chiricahua Mountains, Cochise County, Arizona. J. Mammal. 20(4): 418–440.

———. 1947. Mammals of North America. The Macmillan Co., New York. 682 pp.

Cahn, A. R. 1937. The mammals of the Quetico Provincial Park of Ontario. J. Mammal. 18(1): 19–30.

Caillard, P. 1910. France. Pages 109–144 in F. G. Aflalo, ed., Sport in Europe. E. P. Dutton and Co., New York. 483 pp.

Calhoun, J. B. 1965. Ecological factors in the development of behavioral anomalies. Symp. Comp. Psycho-Pathol.—Anim. and Human. 65 pp. Mimeo.

Callaway, D., J. Janetski and O. C. Stewart. 1986. Ute. Pages 336–367 in W. L. D'Azevedo, ed., Great Basin. Vol. 11. Handbook of North American Indians. Smithsonian Instit. Press, Washington, D.C. 852 pp.

Cameron, A. E. 1923. Notes on buffalo: Anatomy, pathological conditions, and parasites. Vet. J. 79: 331–336.

Cameron, A. G. 1923. The wild red deer of Scotland. William Blackwood and Sons, Edinburgh and London, U.K. 248 pp.

Cameron, D. G. and E. R. Vyse. 1978. Heterozygosity in Yellowstone Park elk. Biochemical Genetics 16(7/8): 651–657.

Cameron, R. D. 1994. Reproductive pauses by female caribou. J. Mammalogy 75: 10–13.

Cameron, R. D., W. T. Smith, S. G. Fancy, G. L. Gerhart and R. G. White. 1993. Calving success of female caribou in relation to body weight. Can. J. Zool. 71: 480–486.

Cameron, T. W. M. 1935. Animal parasites and wildlife. Trans. Amer. Game Conf. 21: 412–417.

———. 1968. Northern sylvatic helminthiasis. Arch. Environ. Health. 17: 614–621.

Campbell, D. L. 1969. Plastic fabric to protect seedlings from animal damage. Pages 87–88 in H. C. Black, ed., Wildlife and reforestation in the Pacific Northwest. Symp. Proc. Oregon State Univ., Corvallis. 92 pp.

Campbell, D. L. and J. Evans. 1975. Improving wildlife habitat in young Douglas-fir plantations. Trans. N. Amer. Wildl. and Natur. Resour. Conf. 40: 202–208.

Canadian Wildlife Service. 1966. Parasites and diseases of Cervidae. Can. Wildl. Serv., Ottawa.

Canfield, J. E. 1988. Impact mitigation and monitoring of BPA 500 kV Garrison-Taft transmission line—effects on elk security and hunter opportunity. Final Report. Montana Dept. Fish, Wildl. and Parks, Missoula. 162 pp.

———. 1991. Applying radiotelemetry data to timber sale effects analysis in the Harvey-Eightmile drainages in west-central Montana. Pages 44–54 in A. G. Christensen, L. J. Lyon and T. N. Lonner, compilers, Proc. Elk Vulnerability Symp., Montana State Univ., Bozeman. 330 pp.

Cannon, K. P. 1992. A review of archeological and paleontological evidence for the prehistoric presence of wolf and related prey species in the northern and central Rockies physiographic province. Pages 177–265 in J. D. Varley and W. Brewster, eds., Wolves for Yellowstone? Vol. II. A report to U.S. Congress. Yellowstone Nat. Park, Wyoming.

Canon, S. K., P. J. Urness and N. V. DeByle. 1987. Habitat selection, foraging behavior, and dietary nutrition of elk in burned aspen forest. J. Range Manage. 40: 433–438.

Capp, J. 1967. Competition among bighorn sheep, elk and deer in Rocky Mountain National Park, Colorado. M.S. Thesis. Colorado State Univ., Fort Collins. 132 pp.

———. 1968. Bighorn sheep, elk, and mule deer range relationships. A review of literature. Fort Collins: Rocky Mountain Nature Assoc. and Dept. Fish and Wildl. Biol., Colorado State Univ. 75 pp.

Capps, B. 1973. The Indians. Time-LIFE Books, New York. 240 pp.

Caras, R.A. 1970. Death as a way of life. Little, Brown and Co., Boston, Massachusetts. 173 pp.

Carbyn, L. N. 1974. Wolf predation and behavioural interactions with elk and other ungulates in an area of high prey diversity. Ph.D. Thesis, Zoology. Univ. Alberta, Edmonton. 233 pp

———. 1975. Wolf predation and behavioral interactions with elk and other ungulates in an area of high prey diversity. Ph.D. Thesis, Univ. Alberta, Edmonton, Canada. 234 pp.

———. 1983. Wolf predation on elk in Riding Mountain National Park, Manitoba. J. Wildl. Manage. 47: 963–976.

Carlson, K. E. 1991. Elk tag/permit allocation as a revenue and management tool. Pages 182–185 in A. G. Christensen, L. J. Lyon, T. N. Lonner, compilers, Proc. Elk Vulnerability Symp., Montana State Univ., Bozeman. 330 pp.

Carlson, R. L. 1990. Cultural antecedents. Pages 60–69 in W. Suttles, ed., Northwest Coast. Handbook of North American Indians. Vol. 7. Smithsonian Instit. Press, Washington, D.C. 777 pp.

Carpenter, E. H., D. J. Witter, W. Shaw, L. Arthur and R. Gum. Unpublished. The aesthetic, existence, and consumptive value of wild animals: results of a national study. Written in 1977. On file at Dept. Ag. Econ., Univ. Arizona, Tucson. 11 pp. Mimeo.

Carpenter, J. W., H. E. Jordan and B. C. Ward. 1973. Neurologic disease in wapiti naturally infected with meningeal worms. J. Wildl. Dis. 9: 148–153.

Carpenter, L. H. 1991. Elk hunting regulations, the Colorado experience. Pages 16–22 in A. G. Christensen, L. J. Lyon and T. N. Lonner, eds., Elk Vulnerability Symp.. Montana State Univ., Bozeman, Montana. 330 pp.

Carpenter, L. H. and R. B. Gill. 1987. Antler point regulations: The good, the bad, and the ugly. Trans. West. Assoc. Game and Fish Commiss. 67: 94–107.

Carrasco, L., Y. Fierro, J. M. Sanchez-Castillejo, J. Hervas, J. Perez and J. C. Gomez-Villamandos. 1997. Abnormal antler growth associated with testicular hypogonadism in red deer. J. Wildl. Dis. 33: 670–672.

Carson, R. 1962. Silent spring. Houghton Mifflin and Riverside Press, Boston and Cambridge, Massachusetts. 368 pp.

Carter, B. 1992. Analysis of big game (elk) statistics 1965–1991: Umatilla, Malheur, Ochoco National Forests. USDA For. Serv., Umatilla Nat. For., Pendleton, Oregon.

Carter, G. R. and M. C. L. DeAlwis. 1989. Hemorrhagic septicemia. Pages 131–160 in C. Adlam and J. M. Rutter, eds., *Pasteurella* and pasteurellosis. Academic Press, New York. 341 pp.

Cartwright, M.E. 1995. Return of the elk. Arkansas Wildl. 26(4): 2–4.

Caruso, J. A. 1959. The Appalachian frontier; America's first surge westward. Bobbs-Merrill Co., New York. 408 pp.

Cary, M. 1911. A biological survey of Colorado. North Amer. Fauna 33. 256 pp.

———. 1917. Life zone investigations in Wyoming. North Amer. Fauna 42. 95 pp.

Case, G. W. 1938a. Influence of elk on deer populations. Proc. 1st and 2nd Idaho Game Manage. Conf. Univ. Idaho Bull. 33: 25–27.

———. 1938b. The use of salt in controlling the distribution of game. J. Wildl. Manage. 2: 79–81.

Case, R. L. 1994. Adaptations of northern ungulates to seasonal cycles in nitrogen intake. Ph.D. Thesis, Univ. Alberta, Edmonston. 128 pp.

Casebeer, R. L. 1961. Habitat of the Jackson Hole elk as a part of multiple resource planning, management and use. Trans. N. Amer. Wildl. and Natur. Resour. Conf. 26: 436–447.

Casgranda, L. and R. G. Janson. 1957. Wildlife investigations (Dist. 4): Big game surveys and investigations. Fed. Aid Compl. Rept. Proj. W–74–R–2, J-A1, pt. 3. Montana Dept. Fish and Game, Helena. 19 pp.

Cassirer, E. F., D. J. Freddy and E. D. Ables. 1992. Elk responses to disturbance by cross-country skiers in Yellowstone National Park. Wildl. Soc. Bull. 20: 375–381.

Catesby, M. 1754. The natural history of Carolina, Florida and the Bahama Islands . . . Vol. 2 London: Printed by author for C. Marsh.

Catlin, G. 1973. Letters and notes on the manners, customs, and conditions of the North American Indians. Vol. 2. Dover Publications, Inc., New York. 571 pp.

Caton, J. D. 1877. The antelope and deer and America. Forest and Stream Publ. Co., New York. 426 pp.

Catton, T. and L. Mighetto. 1998. The fish and wildlife job ob the national forests: A century of game and fish conservation, habitat protection, and ecosystem management. USDA For. Serv., Washington, D.C. 455 pp.

Caudill, S. J. 1976. Establishment of big game seasons in Colorado. Proc. West. Assoc. State Game and Fish Commiss. 56: 86–95.

Caughley, G. 1970. Eruption of ungulate populations, with emphasis on Himalayan thar in New Zealand. Ecology 51: 53–72.

———. 1971a. An investigation of hybridization between free-ranging wapiti and red deer in New Zealand. New Zealand J. Sci. 14(4): 993–1008.

———. 1971b. Demography, fat reserves, and body size of a population of red deer, *Cervus elaphus*, in New Zealand. Mammalia 35(3): 369–383.

———. 1974a. Reproduction of Shiras moose in Montana—productivity, offtake, and rate of increase. J. Wildl. Manage. 38(3): 566–567.

———. 1974b. Bias in aerial survey. J. Wildl. Manage. 38(4): 921–933.

———. 1976. Wildlife management and the dynamics of ungulate populations. Appl. Biol. 1: 183–246.

———. 1977. Analysis of vertebrate populations. John Wiley and Sons, New York. 234 pp.

———. 1980. What is this thing called carrying capacity? Pages 2–8 *in* M. S. Boyce and L. D. Hayden-Wing, eds., North American elk: ecology, behavior and management. Univ. Wyoming, Laramie. 294 pp.

———. 1983. The deer wars. Heinemann Publishers, Auckland, New Zealand. 187 pp.

Cause, M. L. 1995. A survey of economic values for recreational deer hunting in Australia. Pages 296–306 *in* G. Grigg, P. Hale and D. Lunnay, eds., Conservation through sustainable use of wildlife. Centre for Conserv. Biol., Univ. Queensland, Brisbane, Australia.

Causey, A. S. 1989. On the morality of hunting. Environ. Ethics 11(4): 327–343

Cayot, L. J., J. Prukop and D. R. Smith. 1979. Zootic climax vegetation and natural regulation of elk in Yellowstone National Park. Wildl. Soc. Bull. 7: 162–169.

Cederlund, G. and A. Nystrom. 1981. Seasonal differences between moose and roe deer in ability to digest browse. Holarctic Ecol. 4: 59–65.

Cederlund, G. N., R. J. Bergström and K. Danell. 1989. Seasonal variation in mandible marrow fat in moose. J. Wildl. Manage. 53: 587–592.

Cederlund, G. N., R. J. Berström, F. V. Stålfelt, K. Danell. 1986. Variability in mandible marrow fat in 3 moose populations in Sweden. J. Wildl. Manage. 50: 719–726.

Cederlund, G. N., H. K. G. Sand and A. Pehrson. 1991. Body mass dynamics of moose calves in relation to winter severity. J. Wildl. Manage. 55: 675–681.

Chabot, D. 1992. The relationship between heart rate and metabolic rate in wapiti (*Cervus elaphus canadensis*). Ph.D. Diss., Univ. of Calgary, Calgary, Alberta. 297 pp.

Chadwick, H. W. 1960. Plant succession and big game winter movements and feeding habits in a sand dune area in Fremont County, Idaho. Unpubl. M.S. Thesis, Univ. Idaho, Moscow. 121 pp.

Challies, C. N. 1985. Establishment, control, and commercial exploitation of wild deer in New Zealand. Pages 23–36 *in* P. F. Fennessy and K. R. Drew, eds., Biology of deer production. Royal Soc. New Zealand, Bull. 22, Wellington.

Chalmers, P. R. 1935. Deerstalking. Philip Allan, London, U.K. 253 pp.

Chamberlain, A. F. 1901. Signification of certain Algonkin animal names. Amer. Anthropologist. 3: 669–683.

———. 1906. The Kootenay Indians. Pages 178–187 *in* Annual Archaeological Report 1905. Report of the Ontario Minister of Education. L. K. Cameron, Toronto. 249 pp.

Chamrad, A. D. and T. W. Box. 1968. Food habits of white-tailed deer in south Texas. J. Range Manage. 21: 158–164.

Chapline, W. R. and M. W. Talbot. 1926. The use of salt in range management. USDA Circ. 379. U.S. Dept. Ag., Washington, D.C. 32 pp.

Chapman, A. B., L. E. Casida and A. Cote. 1938. Sex ratios of fetal calves. Proc. Amer. Soc. Anim. Prod. 1938: 303–304.

Chapman, D. G. 1951. Some properties of the hypergeometric distributions with applications to zoological censuses. Univ. Calif. Pub. Stat., 1: 131–180.

Chapman, D. I. 1975. Antlers—Bone of contention. Mammal Rev. 5(4): 121–172.

Charleston, W. A. G. 1980. Lungworm and lice of the red deer (*Cervus elaphus*) and the fallow deer (*Dama dama*)—a review. New Zealand Vet. J. 28: 150–152.

Chase, A. 1986. Playing God in Yellowstone. Atlantic Monthly Press, New York. 446 pp.

Chatham, R. 1976. Shooting elk in a barrel. Sports Illus. (Feb. 2): 62–63.

Cheatum, E. L. 1949. The use of corpora lutea for determining ovulation incidence in the fertility of the whitetailed deer. Cornell Vet. 39(3): 282–291.

———. 1952. Disease and parasite investigations. Final Rept., Fed. Aid in Wildl. Restor., Proj. 1-R, Suppl. E, Bur. Fish and Wildl. Invest., Div. Fish & Game. New York Conserv. Dept., Albany. 75 pp.

Cheatum, E. L. and J. E. Gaab. 1952. Productivity of north Yellowstone elk as indicated by ovary analysis. Proc. West. Assoc. State Game and Fish Commiss. 32: 174–177.

Chen, H., J. Ma, F. Li, Y. Wang, H. Wang and F. Li. 1993. Regional variation in winter diets of red deer in Heilongjiang, northeastern China. Pages 181–186 *in* N. Ohtaishi and H.-I. Sheng, eds., Deer of China. Elsevier, New York. 418 pp.

Cherokee Nation v. Georgia, 30 U.S. 1, 8 L. ed 25 (1831).

Child, B. 1990. Notes on the safari hunting industry. Pages 205–213 *in* A. Kiss, ed., Living with wildlife: Wildlife resource management with local participation in Africa. World Bank Tech. Paper 130, Africa Tech. Dept. Ser. The World Bank, Washington, D.C. 217 pp.

Chiodini, R. J., H. J. V. Kruiningen and R. Merkal. 1984. Ruminant paratuberculosis (Johne's disease): The current status and future prospects. Cornell Vet. 74: 218–262.

Chittenden, H. M. and A. T. Richardson, eds. 1969. Life, letters, and travels of Father Pierre-Jean De Smet, 1801–1873. Vol. 4. Arno Press, Inc., New York. 1,624 pp.

Chittenden H. R. 1935. The American fur trade of the far West. Vol. 2. Press of the Pioneers, Inc., New York. 1,014 pp.

Choquette, L. P. E. 1956. Significance of parasites in wildlife. Can. J. Comp. Med. 20: 418–426.

———. 1970. Anthrax. Pages 256–266 *in* J. Davis, L. Karstad and D. O. Trainer, eds., Infectious diseases of wild mammals. 1st edition. Iowa State Univ. Press, Ames. 421 pp.

Christensen, A.G., L. J. Lyon and T. N. Lonner, compilers. 1991. Proc. Elk Vulnerability Symp., Montana State Univ., Bozeman. 330 pp.

Christensen, A.G., L. J. Lyon and J. W. Unsworth. 1993. Elk management in the Northern Region: Considerations in forest plan updates or revisions. Gen. Tech. Rept. INT–303. USDA For. Serv., Ogden, Utah. 10 pp.

Christian, C. S. 1958. The concept of land units and land systems. *In* Proc. 9th pac. Sci. Congr., 1957. 20: 74–81.

Christian, C. S., G. A. Stewart and R. A. Perry. 1960. Land research in northern Australia. Austral. Geogr. 7: 217–231.

Christian, J. J. and S. A. Davis. 1971. Endocrines, behavior, and population. Pages 69–98 *in* I. A. McLaren, ed., Natural regulation of animal populations. Atherton Press, New York.

Christian, J. J., V. Flyger and D. E. Davis. 1960. Factors in the mass mortality of herd of Sika deer, *Cervus nippon*. Chesapeake Sci. 1(2): 79–95.

Christopherson, R. J. and B.A. Young. 1981. Heat flow between large terrestrial animals and the cold environment. Can. J. Chem. Engin. 59: 181–188.

Christopherson, R. J., R. J. Hudson and M. K. Christophersen. 1979. Seasonal energy expenditures and thermoregulatory responses of bison and cattle. Can. J. Anim. Sci. 59: 611–617.

Church, D. C. 1988. Salivary function and production. Pages 117–124 *in* D. C. Church, ed., The ruminant animal: digestive physiology and nutrition. Prentice-Hall, Englewood Cliffs, New Jersey. 564 pp.

Church, D. S. and W. H. Hines. 1978. Ruminoreticular characteristics of elk. J. Wildl. Manage. 42(3): 654–659.

Church, J. S. and R.J. Hudson. 1996. Calving behaviour of farmed wapiti (*Cervus elaphus*). Appl. Animal Behavior Sci. 46: 263–270.

Church, W. L. 1979. Private lands and public recreation. Nat. Assoc. of Conservation Districts, Washington, D.C. 33 pp.

Churcher, C. S. 1968. Pleistocene ungulates from the Bow River gravels at Cochrane, Alberta. Can. J. Earth Sci. 5(6): 1,467–1,488.

Cinq-mars, S. 1979. Bluefish Cave I: A late Pleistocene eastern Beringian cave deposit in the northern Yukon. Can. J. Archaeol. 3: 1–32.

Claar, J. J. 1973. Correlations of ungulate food habits and winter range conditions in the Idaho primitive area. J. M. S. Thesis, Univ. Idaho, Moscow. 96 pp.

Clark, F. G. 1961. A hemispherical forest photocanopy-meter. J. Forestry 59: 103–105.

Clark, J. G. D. 1952. Prehistoric Europe: The economic basis. Philosophical Library, New York. 349 pp.

Clark, P. E. 1996. Use of livestock to improve the quality of elk winter range forage in northeastern Oregon. Ph.D. Diss., Oregon State Univ., Corvallis. 179 pp.

Clarke, C. H. D. 1960. Moral and ethic aspects of hunting and angling for sport. Proc. World For. Cong. 5(3): 1,785–1,790.

Clarke, J. A., M. Edery, A. S. I. Loudon, V. A. Randall, M. C. Postel-Vinay, P. A. Kelly and H. N. Jabbour. 1995. Expression of the prolactin receptor gene during the breeding and non-breeding seasons in red deer (*Cervus elaphus*): Evidence for the expression of two forms in the testis. J. Endocrinology. 146: 313–321.

Clary, W. P. 1972. A treatment prescription for improving big game habi-

tat in ponderosa pine forests. Pages 25–28 *in* Proc. 16th Annu. Watershed Symp., Rept. No. 2. Arizona Water Commiss., Phoenix. 43 pp.

Clary, W. P. and P. F. Ffolliott. 1966. Differences in herbage–timber relationships between thinned and unthinned ponderosa pine stands. Note RM–74. USDA For. Serv., Fort Collins, Colorado. 4 pp.

Clary, W. P. and F. R. Larson. 1971. Elk and deer use are related to food sources in Arizona ponderosa pine. Res. Note RM–202. USDA For. Serv., Fort Collins, Colorado. 4 pp.

Clary, W. P., W. H. Kruse and F. R. Larson. 1975. Cattle grazing and wood production with different basal areas of ponderosa pine. J. Range Manage. 28(6): 434–437.

Claus, K. D. 1962. Survey of Clostridium hemolyticum in elk. Vet. Res. Lab., Montana State-Coll., Bozeman. 2 pp. (Unpubl. Lab notes)

Clawson, M. and J. Knetsch. 1966. Economics of Outdoor Recreation. Johns Hopkins Press, Baltimore, Maryland. 328 pp.

Cleland, C. E. 1966. The prehistoric animal ecology and ethnozoology of the upper Great Lakes region. Anthropol. Papers 29. Univ. Michigan, Mus. Anthrop., Ann Arbor. 294 pp.

Cliff, E. P. 1939. Relationship between elk and mule deer in the Blue Mountains of Oregon. Trans. N. Amer. Wildl. Conf. 4: 560–569.

Clifton, C. S. 1990. Elk where there used to be none: A quick history of Colorado elk. Bugle. Special edition, Colorado elk: 88–90.

Clifton, J. A. 1978. Potawatomi. Pages 725–742 *in* B. G. Trigger, ed., Northeast. Handbook of North American Indians, Vol. 15. Smithsonian Instit., Washington, D.C. 924 pp.

Clifton-Hadley, R. S. and J. W. Wilesmith. 1991. Tuberculosis in deer: A review. Vet. Rec. 129: 5–12.

Clifton-Hadley, R. S., J. W. Wilesmith and F. A. Stuart. 1993. *Mycobacterium bovis* in the European badger (*Meles meles*): Epidemiological findings in tuberculous badgers from naturally infected populations. Epidemiol. Infect. 111: 9–19.

Clouser, R. A. 1974. Man's intervention in the post-Wisconsin vegetational succession of the Great Plains. M. A. Thesis. Univ. Kansas, Lawrence.

Cluff, L. K., B. L. Welch, J. C. Pederson and J. D. Brotherson. 1982. Concentration of monoterpenoids in the rumen ingesta of wild mule deer. J. Range Manage. 35: 192–194.

Clutton-Brock, T. H. 1974. Why do animals live in groups. New Scientist 63(905): 72–74.

———. 1980. Antlers, body size and breeding group size in the Cervidae. Nature (London). 285: 565–567.

———. 1982. The functions of antlers. Behaviour 79: 108–125.

———. 1986. Red deer and man. Nat. Geogr. 170(4): 538–555.

Clutton-Brock, T. H. and S. D. Albon. 1979. The roaring of red deer and the evolution of honest advertisement. Behavior 69(3–4): 145–170.

Clutton-Brock, T. H. and S. D. Albon. 1989. Red deer in the highlands. BSP Professional Books, London, U.K. 260 pp.

Clutton-Brock, T. H. and F. E. Guinness. 1975. Behavior of red deer (*Cervus elaphus* L.) at calving time. Behavior 55: 287–300.

Clutton-Brock, T. H. and G. R. Iason. 1986. Sex ratio variation in mammals. Quart. Rev. Biol. 61: 339–374.

Clutton-Brock, T. H., S. D. Albon, R. M. Gibson and F. E. Guinness. 1979. The logical stag: Adaptive aspects of fighting in red deer (*Cervus elaphus* L.). Animal Behavior 27: 211–225.

Clutton-Brock, T. H., F. E. Guinness and S. D. Albon. 1982. Red deer: Behavior and ecology of two sexes. Univ. Chicago Press, Chicago, Illinois. 378 pp.

Clutton-Brock, T. H., G. R. Iason and F. E.Guiness. 1987a. Sexual segregation and density related changes in habitat use in male and female red deer (*Cervus elaphus*). J. Zool. 211: 275–289.

Clutton-Brock, T. H., M. Major, S. D. Albon and F. E. Guinness. 1987b.

Early development and population dynamics in red deer. I. Density-dependent effects on juvenile survival. J. Anim. Ecol. 56: 53–67.

Clutton-Brock, T. H., M. Hiraiwa-Hasegawa and A. Robertson. 1989. Mate choice on fallow deer leks. Nature 340: 463–465.

Cody, B. P. 1940. Pomo bear doctors. Masterkey 14(4): 132–137.

Coe, M. J., D. H. Cumming and J. Phillipson. 1976. Biomass and production of large African herbivores in relation to rainfall and primary production. Oecologia (Berlin) 22: 341–354.

Cogan, R. 1993. Elk population survey. Annu. Proj. Rept. Pennsylvania Game Commiss., Bur. Wildl. Manage., Res. Div., Harrisonburg, Pennsylvania. 12 pp.

Cogan, R. D. and D. R. Diefenbach. 1998. Effect of undercounting and model selection on a sightability-adjustment estimator for elk. J. Wildl. Manage. 62(1): 269–279.

Coggins, V. 1976. Controlled vehicle access during elk season in the Chesnimnus Area, Oregon. Pages 58–61 in S. R. Hieb, ed., Proc. Elk-Logging-Roads Symp., Univ. Idaho, Moscow. 142 pp.

Coggins, V. L. and G. G. Magera. 1973. Vehicle restrictions, elk harvest, and hunter behavior in the Chesnimnus Unit. Spec. Unpubl. Rept. Oregon Fish and Wildl. Dept., Salem. 25 pp.

Cohen, M. N. 1977. The food crisis in prehistory: Overpopulation and the origins of agricultural. Yale Univ. Press, New Haven. 341 pp.

Cohen, Y., C. T. Robbins and B. B. Davitt. 1978. Oxygen utlization by elk calves during horizontal and vertical locomotion compared to other species. Comp. Biochem. Physiol. 61A: 43–48.

Colbert, E.H. 1973. Wandering land and animals. E. P. Dutton and Co. Inc., New York. 323 pp.

Cole, E. K., M. D. Pope and R. G. Anthony. 1997. Effects of road management on movement and survival of Roosevelt elk. J. Wildl. Manage. 61: 1,115–1,126.

Cole, G. F. 1956. The pronghorn antelope—its range use and food habits in central Montana with special reference to alfalfa. Bull. 516. Montana Ag. Exp. Sta., Bozeman. 63 pp.

———. 1958. Big game–livestock competition on Montana's mountain rangelands. Montana Wildl. 1958: 24–30.

———. 1969. The elk of Grand Teton and Southern Yellowstone National parks. Res. Rept. GRTE-N–1. U.S. Nat. Park Serv., Washington, D.C. 192 pp.

———. 1971. An ecological rationale for the natural or artificial regulation of native ungulates in parks. Trans. N. Amer. Wildl. Conf. 36: 417–425.

———. 1972. Grizzly bear–elk relationships in Yellowstone National Park. J. Wildl. Manage. 36(2): 556–561.

———. 1983. A naturally regulated elk population. Pages 62–81 in F. L. Bunnell, D. S. Eastman and J. M. Peek, eds., Symposium on natural regulation of wildlife populations. Univ. Idaho, Moscow. 225 pp.

Cole, G. F. and I. J. Yorgason. 1964. Elk migration study. Jackson Hole elk herd. Nat. Park Serv., Moose, and Wyoming Game and Fish Commiss., Cheyenne. 18 pp.

Cole, R. S. 1974. Elk and bison management on the Oglala Sioux Game Range. J. Range Manage. 27(6): 484–485.

Colgrove, G. S., C. O. Thoen and B. O. Blackburn. 1989. Paratuberculosis in cattle: A comparison of three serologic tests with results of fecal culture. Vet. Microbiol. 19: 183–187.

Collins, H. F. and A. O. Fordyce, Jr. 1976. N X Bar hunting ranch, an ecological concept of range management. Rangeman's J. 3(3): 7274.

Collins, M. T., D. C. Sockett and S. Ridge. 1991. Evaluation of a commercial enzyme-linked immunosorbent assay for Johne's disease. J. Clin. Microbiol. 29: 272–276.

Collins, W. B. 1977. Diet composition and activities of elk on different habitat segments in the lodgepole pine type, Uinta Mountains, Utah. Pub. No. 77–18, Fed. Aid Proj. W–105-R–14. Utah Dept. of Natural Resources, Salt Lake City. 74 pp.

Collins, W. B. and P. J. Urness. 1979. Elk pellet group distributions and rates of deposition in aspen and lodgepole pine habitats. Pages 140–144 in M. S. Boyce and L. D. Hayden-Wing, eds., North American elk: Ecology, behavior, and management. Symposium Proc. Univ. Wyoming, Laramie. 294 pp.

Collins, W. B. and T. S. Smith. 1991. Effects of wind-hardened snow on foraging by reindeer (Rangifer tarandus). Arctic 44(3): 217–222.

Collins, W. B. and P. J. Urness. 1983. Feeding behavior and habitat selection of mule deer and elk on northern Utah summer ranges. J. Wildl. Manage. 47: 646–663.

Collins, W. B., P. J. Urness and D. D. Austin. 1978. Elk diets and activities on different lodge pole pine habitat segments. J. Wildl. Manage. 42(4): 799–810.

Colloredo-Mannsfeld, N. 1992 The deer–forest interaction and resulting conflicts and threats through human influences in the Austrian alpine region. BSc Thesis, Royal Agricultural College and Univ. Buckingham. 105 pp.

Colorado Department of Natural Resources. 1990. Elk harvest, number of license sales, and percent success, 1929–1989. Div.Wildl. Rept., Denver. 1 p.

Colorado Division of Wildlife. 1974. The strategy of today, for wildlife tomorrow—1975–1980. Vol. 1. Colorado Wildl. Comm, Denver. 103 pp.

Colorado Outdoors. 1991. Video: Colorado elk hunting. Colorado Division of Wildlife, Denver. 30 min.

Colwell, D. A. and J. S. Dunlap. 1975. Psoroptic mange in wapiti. J. Wildl. Dis. 11: 66–67.

Colwell, R. N. 1960. Manual of photographic interpretation. Amer. Soc. Photogram, Washington, D.C. 868 pp.

Comer, J. A., W. R. Davidson, A. K. Prestwood and V. F. Nettles. 1991. An update on the distribution of Parelaphostrongylus tenuis in the southeastern United States. J. Wildl. Dis. 27: 348–354.

Compton, B. B. 1999. White-tailed deer, mule deer and elk management plan. Idaho Dept. Fish and Game, Boise. 74 pp.

Compton, T. 1975. Mule deer–elk relationships in the western Sierra Madre area of southcentral Wyoming. Tech. Rept. No. 1. Wyoming Game and Fish Dept., Laramie. 125 pp.

Conaway, C. 1952. The age at sexual maturity in male elk (Cervus canadensis). J. Wildl. Manage. 16(3): 313–315.

Confederated Tribes of the Colville Indian Reservation v. State of Washington, No. C–75–146, Apr. 14, 1976.

Confederated Tribes of the Colville Indian Reservation v. State of Washington, No. 76–3286. U.S. Court of Appeals, Ninth Circuit. Feb. 16, 1979.

Conger, P. H. 1882. Report of the Superintendent of the Yellowstone National Park. Pages 995–1002 in Report of the Secretary of the Interior, Vol. 2. Govt. Print. Off., Washington, D.C. 1,076 pp.

———. 1883. Report of the Superintendent of the Yellowstone National Park. Pages 487–494 in Report of the Secretary of the Interior, vol. 2, Govt. Print. Off., Washington, D.C. 770 pp.

Conn, R. G. 1955. A classification of aboriginal North American clothing. M. S. Thesis. Univ. Washington, Seattle. 80 pp.

———. 1974. Robes of White Shell and Sunrise. Denver Art Mus., Denver, Colorado.

Conner, S. n.d. Elk antler piles made by Indians on the Northwestern Plains. Unpublished manuscript.

Connolly, G. E. 1981. Assessing populations. Pages 287–345 in O. C. Wallmo, ed., Mule and black-tailed deer of North America. Univ. Nebraska Press, Lincoln.

Conrad, G. S. 1980. The biostratigraphy and mammalian paleontology of the Glenns Ferry Formation from Hammet to Oreana, Idaho. Unpubl. Ph.D. Thesis, Idaho State Univ., Pocatello. pp.

Conrad, H. L. 1890. "Uncle Dick" Wootten. W. E. Dibble and Company, Chicago, Illinois. 472 pp.

Constan, K. J. 1972. Winter foods and range use of three species of ungulates. J. Wildl. Manage. 36(4): 1,068–1,076.

Converse, R. N. 1978. The Glacial Kame Indians. The Archaeol. Soc. of Ohio. 157 pp.

Cook, C. E., Jr. 1993. The historical biogeography and phylogeny of sika deer (Cervus nippon) in East Asia. Ph.D. Thesis, Univ. California, Berkeley. 141 pp.

Cook, C. W. 1959. The effect of site on the palatability and nutritive content of seeded wheatgrasses. J. Range Manage. 12: 289–292.

———. 1966. Factors affecting utilization of mountain slopes by cattle. J. Range Manage. 1(4): 200–211.

———. 1971. Comparative nutritive values of forbes, grasses and shrubs. Pages 303–310 in Wildland shrubs—their biology and utilization. Gen. Tech. Rept. INT–1, 1972. USDA For. Serv., Ogden, Utah.

Cook, J. G. 1990. Habitat, nutrition and population ecology of two transplanted bighorn sheep populations in southcentral Wyoming. Ph.D. Thesis, Univ. Wyoming, Laramie. 311 pp.

Cook, J. G., L. L. Irwin, L. D. Bryant and J. W. Thomas. 1994a. Fecal nitrogen and dietary quality relationships in juvenile elk. J. Wildl. Manage. 58: 46–53.

Cook, J. G., L. L. Irwin, L. D. Bryant, R. A. Riggs, D. A. Hengel and J. W. Thomas. 1994b. Studies of elk biology in northeast Oregon. 1993 Progress Rept. Nat. Counc. Pap. Indust. Air and Stream Improve., Corvallis, Oregon. 70 pp.

Cook, J. G., T. J. Hershey and L. L. Irwin. 1994c. Vegetative response to burning on Wyoming mountain-shrub big game ranges. J. Range Manage. 47: 296–302.

Cook, J. G., R. A. Riggs, A. R. Tiedemann, L. L. Irwin and L. D. Bryant. 1995. Large herbivore–vegetative feedback relations in the Blue Mountains Ecoregion. Pages 155–159 in W. D. Edge and S. L. Olson-Edge, eds., Proc. Symposium Sustaining Rangeland Ecosystems. SR953, Oregon State Univ., Corvallis. 213 pp.

Cook, J. G., L. J. Quinlan, L. L. Irwin, L. D. Bryant, R. A. Riggs and J. W. Thomas. 1996. Nutrition–growth relations of elk calves during late summer and fall. J. Wildl. Manage. 60: 528–541.

Cook, J. G., L. L. Irwin, L. D. Bryant, R. A. Riggs and J. W. Thomas. 1998. Relations of forest cover and condition of elk: A test of the thermal cover hypothesis in summer and winter. Wildl. Monogr. No. 141, The Wildl. Soc., Bethesda, Maryland. 61 pp.

Cook, J. G., L. Irwin, L. Bender, B. Johnson and D. Boyce, Jr. 1999. Assessing landscape-scale nutritional influences on elk herd productivity in the northwest. Unpubl. proposal for east and west-side studies.

Cook, J. R. 1907. The border and the buffalo. Crane and Co., Topeka, Kansas. 351 pp.

Cook, J. R. 1989. The border and the buffalo. State House Press, Austin, Texas. 362 pp.

Cook, R. C. 2000. Studies of body condition and reproductive physiology in Rocky Mountain elk. M.S. Thesis, Univ. Idaho, Moscow.

Cook, W., T. E. Cornish, S. Shideler, B. Lasley and M. T. Collins. 1997. Radiometric culture of Mycobacterium avium paratuberculosis from the feces of tule elk. J. Wildl. Dis. 33: 635–637.

Cool, N. and R. J. Hudson. 1996. Requirements for liveweight maintenance and gain of moose and wapiti calves during winter. Rangifer 16: 41–45.

Cool, N. L. 1992. Physiological indices of winter condition of wapiti and moose. M. S. Thesis, Univ. Alberta, Edmonton, Alberta. 58 pp.

Cooney, R. F. 1952. Elk problems in Montana. J. Range Manage. 5(1): 312.

Coop, K. J. 1971. Habitat use, distribution, movement and associated behavior of elk, Little Belt, Montana. Compl. Rept., Proj. No. W120-R–1 and 2. Montana Fish and Game Dept., Helena. 61 pp.

———. 1973. Habitat use and behavior of elk in relation to hunting. Pages 97–100 in West. States Elk Workshop Proc., Bozeman, Montana.

Cooper, A. B. 1994. Choosing a management option: The integration of economics and socio-political issues with elk ecology. Idaho Department of Fish and Game, Wildl. Bur., Boise. 23 pp.

———. 1995. Keeping people in mind while managing wildlife: integrating economics and socio-political issues with elk ecology. Idaho Wildlife, 15(6): 4–8.

———. 1996. Bridging the gap between humans and wildlife through management simulation models. Project W–160-R–23, Subproject No. 49. Idaho Dept. of Fish and Game. 33 pp.

Cooper, C. F. 1957. The variable plot methods for estimating shrub density. J. Range Manage. 10: 111–115.

———. 1961. The ecology of fire. Sci. Amer. 204(4): 150–160.

Cooper, J. G. 1860. [Reports of] exploration and surveys for a railroad route from the Mississippi River to the Pacific Ocean... Route near the 47th and 49th parallels, explored by I.I. Stevans. in1853–1855 12(II): 88.

Cooper, J. M. 1938. Snares, deadfalls and other traps of the northern Algonquians and northern Athapaskans. Anthropol. Ser. 5. Catholic Univ. America, Washington, D.C. 144 pp.

———. 1957. The Gros Ventres of Montana: Part II. Religion and ritual. R. Flannery, ed., Anthropol. Ser. 16. Catholic Univ. America, Washington, D.C. 423 pp.

Cooperrider, A. Y. 1982. Forage allocation for elk and cattle. Pages 142–149 in T. L. Britt and D. P. Theobald, eds., Proc. Western States Elk Workshop, Feb. 22–24, 1982. Flagstaff, Arizona.

Cooperrider, A.Y. and J. A. Bailey. 1984. A simulation approach to forage allocation. Pages 525–560 in Developing strategies for rangeland management. Westview Press, Boulder, Colorado.

Cope, E. D. 1870. Observations on the fauna of the Southern Alleghanies. American Naturalist 4(7): 392–402.

———. 1878. Descriptions of new vertebrata from the Upper Tertiary formations of the West. Proc. Amer. Philos. Soc. 17: 219–231.

———. 1889. The vertebrate fauna of the Equus beds. American Naturalist 23(266): 160–165.

Cordell, H. K., L. A. Hartmann, A. E. Watson, J. Fritschen, D. B. Propst and E. L. Siverts. 1987. The background and status of an interagency research effort: the Public Area Recreation Visitors Survey (PARVS). Pages 19–36 in Proc., Southeastern Recreation Res. Conf. Instit. of Community and Area Development, Univ. of Georgia, Athens.

Cordell, H. K., J. C. Bergstrom, L. A. Hartmann and D. B. K. English. 1990. An Analysis of the Outdoor Recreation and Wilderness Situation in the United States: 1989–2040. USDA For. Serv., Gen. Tech. Rept. RM–189. Fort Collins, Colorado. 112 pp.

Corner, A. H. and R. Connell. 1958. Brucellosis in bison, elk, and moose in Elk Island National Park, Alberta, Canada. Can. J. Comp. Med. 22: 9–21.

Corrigall, W. 1978. Naturally occurring leptospirosis (Leptospira ballum) in a red deer (Cervus elaphus). Vet. Rec. 103: 75–76.

Corrigall, W. and W. J. Hamilton. 1977. Reaction of red deer (Cervus elaphus L.) hinds to removal of their suckled calves for handrearing. Appl. Anim. Ecol. 3: 47–55.

Corrigall, W., R. R. Moody and J. C. Forbs. 1978. Foxglove (*Digitalis purpurea*) in farmed red deer (*Cervus elaphus*). Vet. Rec. 102: 119–122.

Corrin, K. C., C. E. Carter, R. C. Kissling and G. W. de Lisle. 1993. An evaluation of the comparative tuberculin skin test for detecting tuberculosis in farmed elk. New Zealand Vet. J. 41: 12–20.

Cortner, H. J. and M. A. Moote. 1999. The politics of ecosystem management. Island Press, Washington, D.C. and Covalo, California. 179 pp.

Cortner, H. J., J. C. Gordon, P. G. Risser, D. T. Teeguarden and J. W. Thomas. 1999. Ecosystem management: Evolving model for stewardship of the nation's natural resources. Vol. 2. Pages 3–19 in R. C. Szaro, N. C. Johnson, W. T. Sexton and A. J. Malk ed., Ecological stewardship: A common reference for ecosystem management. Elsevier Science Ltd., Kidlington, Oxford, UK. 741 pp.

Cottam, G. and J. T. Curtis. 1956. The use of distance measures in phytosociological sampling. Ecology 37(3): 451–460.

Coues, E., ed. 1893. History of the expedition under the command of Lewis and Clark . . . 1804-J–6. Vol 4. New York.

Coughenour, M. B. 1991. Biomass and nitrogen responses to grazing of upland steppe on Yellowstone's northern winter range. J. Applied Ecol. 28: 71–82.

Coughenour, M. B. and F. J. Singer. 1996. Elk population processes in Yellowstone National Park under the policy of natural regulation. Ecol. Appl. 6[2]: 573–593.

Courtright, A. M. 1959. Results of some detailed analyses of caribou rumen contents. Pages 28–35 in 10th Alaskan Science Conference Proc. Alaska Division, Amer. Assoc. for the Advancement of Science, Collge.

Coville, F. V., J. H. Hatton, F. H. Newell, G. Pinchot, A. F. Potter and W. A. Richards. 1905. Report of the Public Lands Commission with appendix. U.S. Senate. 58th Congress, 3rd Session Senate Doc. 189 (partial repts.: 58th Congress, 2nd Sess., Senate Doc. 188; 58th Congress, 3rd Sess. Senate Doc. 154).

Cowan, C. W. 1987. First farmers of the Ohio Valley: Fort Ancient societies, A.D. 1000–1670. Cincinnati Mus. Natur. Hist., Cincinnati, Ohio.

Cowan, I. McTaggart. 1936. Distribution and variation in deer (genus *Odocoileus*) of the Pacific Coast region of North America. Calif. Fish and Game. 22: 155–246.

———. 1947a. Range competition between mule deer, bighorn sheep and elk in Jasper Park, Alberta. Trans. N. Amer. Wildl. Conf. 12: 223–227.

———. 1947b. The timber wolf in the Rocky Mountain national parks of Canada. Can. J. Res. 25: 139–174.

———. 1948. The occurrence of the granular tapeworm (*Echinococcus granulosus*) in wild game in North America. J. Wildl. Manage. 12: 105–106.

———. 1950. Some vital statistics of big game on over-stocked mountain range. Trans. N. Amer. Wildl. Conf. 15: 581–588.

———. 1951. The disease and parasites of big game mammals of western Canada. Rept. Proc. Annu. Brit. Col. Game Conv. 5: 37–64.

———. 1995. Man wildlife and conservation in North America. Pages 277–308 in V. Geist and I. McTaggart-Cowan, eds., Wildlife Conservation Policies. Detselig, Calgary, Alberta.

Cowan, I. McTaggart and C. J. Guiguet. 1965. The mammals of British Columbia. 3rd ed. Dept. Recreation and Conserv. Handb. No. 11. British Columbia Prov. Mus., Victoria, British Columbia. 414 pp.

Cowan, I. McTaggart and C. W. Holloway. 1973. Threatened deer of the world: conservation status. Biol. Conserv. 5(4): 243–250.

Cowan, R. L., J. S. Jordan, J. L. Grimes and J. D. Gill. 1970. Comparative nutritive values of forage species. Pages 48–56 In Range and wildlife habitat evaluation—a research symposium. Misc. Publ. 1147. USDA For. Serv., Washington, D.C.

Cowie, G. M., Moore, G. H., Fisher, M. W. and M. J. Taylor. 1985. Calving behaviour of farmed red deer. Proc. of a Deer Course for Veterinarians 2: 143–154.

Craig, J. V. and R. A. Baruth. 1965. Inbreeding and social dominance ability of chickens. Animal Behavior 13: 109–113.

Craighead, F. C., J. J. Craighead, C. E. Cote and H. K. Buechner. 1972. Satellite and ground radiotracking of elk. Pages 99–111 in S. R. Galler, K. Schmidt-Koenig, C. J. Jacobs and R. E. Bellevelle, eds., Animal Orientation and Navigation. Scientific and Technical Information Office, National Aeronautics and Space Administration, Washington, D.C.

Craighead, J. J. 1952. A biological and economic appraisal of the Jackson Hole elk herd. New York Zool. Soc. and Conserv. Found., New York. 32 pp.

Craighead, J. J., G. Atwell and B. W. O'Gara. 1972. Elk migrations in and near Yellowstone National Park. Wildl. Monogr. No. 29. The Wildl. Soc., Washington, D.C. 48 pp.

Craighead, J. J., F. C. Craighead and R. L. Ruff and B. W. O'Gara. 1973. Home ranges and activity patterns of non-migratory elk of the Madison drainage herd as determined by biotelemetry. Wildl. Monogr. No. 33. The Wildl. Soc., Washington, D.C. 50 pp.

Crain, E. 1998. First southeast elk hunt. The Alaska Sportsman 64(2): 54.

Crampton, E. W. and L. E. Harris. 1969. Applied animal nutrition. 2nd ed. W. A. Freeman and Co., San Francisco. 753 pp.

Crampton, L. W. 1886. Hunting at army posts. Forest and Stream 26: 85.

Crawford, H. S. and J. B. Whelan. 1973. Estimating food intake by observing mastications by tractable deer. J. Range Manage. 26: 372–375.

Crawford, J. C. and D. C. Church. 1971. Response of black-tailed deer to various chemical taste stimuli. J. Wildl. Manage., 35: 210–215.

Crawford, L. F. 1926. Rekindling camp-fires. Capitol Book Co., Bismarck, North Dakota. 324 pp.

Crawford, R. P., J. D. Huber and B. S. Adams. 1990. Epidemiology and surveillance. Pages 131–151 in K. Nielsen and J. R. Duncan, eds., Animal brucellosis. CRC Press, Inc., Boca Raton, Florida. 453 pp.

Creech, G. T. 1930. *Brucella abortus* infection in a male bison. N. Amer. Vet. 11: 35–36.

Creed, W. A., F. Haberland, B. E. Kohn and K. R. McCaffery. 1984. Harvest management: The Wisconsin experience. Pages 243–260 in L. K. Halls, ed., White-tailed deer: Ecology and management. Stackpole Books, Harrisburg, Pennsylvania. 870 pp.

Crête, M. and J. Huot. 1993. Regulation of a large herd of migratory caribou: summer nutrition affects calf growth and body reserves of dams. Can. J. Zool. 71: 2,291–2,296.

Crissey, W. F. 1971. Some thoughts on wildlife research and management objectives. Wildl. Soc. News 134: 27–28.

Croft, A. R. and L. Ellison. 1960. Watershed and range conditions on Big Game Ridge and vicinity, Teton National Forest, Wyoming. USDA For. Serv., Ogden, Utah. 37 pp.

Croker, B. H. 1959. A method of estimating the botanical composition of the diet of sheep. New Zealand J. Ag. Res. 2: 72.

Cronin, M. A. 1991. Mitochondrial and nuclear genetic relationships of deer (*Odocoileus* spp.) in western North America. Can. J. Zool. 69: 1,270–1,279.

———. 1992a. Interspecific variation in mitochondrial DNA of North American cervids. J. Mammal. 73(1): 70–82.

———. 1992b. Mitochondrial-DNA phylogeny of deer (Cervidae). J. Mammal. 72(3): 553–566.

———. 1993. Mitochondrial DNA in wildlife taxonomy and conservation biology: Cautionary notes. Wildl. Soc. Bull. 21: 339–348.

Cronin, M. A.. L. Renecker, B. J. Pierson and J. C. Patton. 1995. Genetic variation in domestic reindeer and wild caribou in Alaska. Animal Genetics 26: 427–434.

Cronin, M. A., R. Stuart, B. J. Pierson and J. C. Patton. 1996. Kappa-casein gene phylogeny of higher ruminants (Pecora, Artiodactyla). Molecular Phylogenetics and Evolution 6(2): 295–311.

Cronon, W. 1983. Changes in the land. Hill and Wang, New York. 241 pp.

Crook, J. H., J. E. Ellis and J. D. Goss-Custard. 1976. Mammalian social systems: structure and function. Animal Behavior 24(2): 261–274.

Croon, G. W., D. R. McCullough, C. E. Olson, Jr. and L. M. Queal. 1968. Infrared scanning techniques for big game censusing. J. Wildl. Mange. 32: 751–759.

Cross, R. H., Jr. 1950. Virginia's elk herds. Virginia Wildl. 1(6): 10, 11, 22.

Crotty, M. J. 1975. Zoos and aquariums in the Americas. Amer. Assoc. Zool. Parks Aquariums, Wheeling, West Virginia. 222 pp.

Crouch, G. L. 1969. Animal damage to conifers on national forests in the Pacific Northwest region. Res. Pap. PNW–28. USDA For. Serv., Portland, Oregon. 13 pp.

Crouse, C. N. 1974. States' needs and responsibilities in non-game wildlife. Trans. N. Amer. Wildl. and Natur. Resour. Conf. 39: 77–80.

Cubbage, F. W., J. O'Laughlin, and Bullock. 1993. Forest resource policy. John Wiley and Sons, Inc., New York. 562 pp.

Culbreath, J. C. 1948. Colorado elk on increase Colorado Conserv. Comments 10: 7–8.

———. 1952. The role of public relations in wildlife management. Proc. West. Assoc. State Game and Fish Commiss. 32: 54–57.

Cumming, W. P., ed. 1958. The discoveries of John Lederer. Pp. 34–38. Univ. Virginia Press, Charlottesville.

Cummins, M. W. 1978. Tache-Yokuts. Pioneer Publ. Co., Fresno, California. 174 pp.

Cummins, R. A., R. N. Walsh, O. E. Budtz-Olson and T. Konstantionas. 1973. Environmentally-induced changes in the brain of elderly rats. Nature 243: 516–518.

Cunningham, E. B. 1971. A cougar kills an elk. Can. Field-Nat. 85(3): 253–254.

Cupal, J. J. 1974. A repeater type biotelemetry system for use on wild big game animals. Biomed. Sci. Instru. 10: 145–152.

Curlewis, J. D. 1992. Seasonal prolactin secretion and its role in seasonal reproduction: A review. Reprod. Fert. Dev. 4: 1–23.

Curlewis, J. D., A. S. Loudon, J.A. Milne and A. S. McNeilly. 1988. Effects of chronic long-acting bromocriptine treatment on liveweight, voluntary food intake, coat growth and breeding season in non-pregnant red deer hinds. J. Endocrin. 119: 413–420.

Curren, C. B. 1977. Prehistoric range extension of the elk: *Cervus canadensis*. Amer. Midl. Nat. 97(1): 230–232.

Curtis, E. S. 1970. The North American Indian: Being a series of volumes picturing and describing the Indians of the United States and Alaska. 20 vols. Johnson Reprint, New York.

Cuthbertson, T. A. 1851. Journal of an expedition to the mauvaises terres and the upper Missouri in 1850. Pages 84–145 *in* Smithsonian Institution. Fifth Annu. Rept., 1850. Smithsonian Instit., Washington, D.C.

Cutlip, S. M. and A. H. Center. 1964. Effective public relations. Prentice-Hall, Inc., Englewood Cliffs, New Jersey. 512 pp.

Czech, B. 1995. American Indians and wildlife conservation. Wildl Soc. Bull. 23(4): 568–573.

Czech, B. and P. R. Krausman. 2000. The Endangered Species Act: History, conservation biology, and public policy. John Hopkins U. Press. Baltimore, Maryland. 212 pp.

Dailey, T. V. and N. T. Hobbs 1989. Travel in alpine terrain: energy expenditures for locomotion by mountain goats and bighorn sheep. Can. J. Zool. 67: 2,368–2,375.

Dalke, P. D. 1937. The cover map in wildlife management. J. Wildl. Manage. 1: 100–106.

Dalke, P. D., R. D. Beeman, F. J. Kindel, R. J. Robel and T. R. Williams. 1965a. Use of salt by elk in Idaho. J. Wildl. Manage. 29: 319–332.

Dalke, P. D., R. D. Beeman, F. J. Kindel, R. J. Robel and T. R. Williams. 1965b. Seasonal movements of elk in the Selway River Drainage, Idaho. J. Wildl. Manage. 29: 333–338.

Dalquest, W. W. 1948. Mammals of Washington. Mus. Natur. Hist. 2. Univ. Kansas Publ., Lawrence. 444 pp.

Dalton, M. J. 1983. Outdoor recreation expenditures in Utah. Utah Tourism and Recreation Review 10(2): 1–4.

Daniel, M. J. 1963. Early fertility of red deer in New Zealand. Nature (London) 200(4,904): 380.

Daniels, S. E. and R. A. Riggs. 1988. Improving economic analysis of habitat management. Wildl. Soc. Bull. 16: 452–457.

Dansgaard, W., S. J. Johnsen, H. B. Clausen, D. Dahl-Jensen, N. S. Gunderstrup, C. U. Hammer, C. S. Hvidberg, J. P. Steffensen, A. E. Sveinbjornsdottir, J. Jouzel and G. Bond. 1993. Evidence for general instability of past climate from a 250-year ice-core record. Nature 364(6,249): 218–220.

Danvir, R. 1997. Personal communication. Member Utah Wildl. Board, Wildlife Program Manager, Deseret Land and Livestock, Woodruff, Utah 84086.

Darbyshire, J. H. and H. G. Pereira. 1964. An adenovirus precipitating antibody present in some sera of different animal species and its association with bovine respiratory disease. Nature 201: 895–897.

Darling, F. F. 1937. A herd of red deer. Oxford Univ. Press, London. 215 pp.

———. 1955. A herd of red deer: A study in animal behaviour. 2nd ed. Oxford Univ. Press, London. 215 pp.

Darwin, C. 1872. The expression of the emotions in man and animals. Univ. Chicago Press, Chicago, Illinois.

Dasmann, R. F. 1964. Wildlife biology. John Wiley and Sons, New York. 212 pp.

Dasmann, R. F. and R. D. Taber. 1956. Behavior of Columbian black-tailed deer with reference to population ecology. J. Mammal. 37: 143–164.

Dasmann, R. F., R. L. Hubbard, W. M. Longhurst, G. I. Ramstead, J. H. Harm and E. Calvert. 1967. Deer attractants: an approach to the deer damage problem. J. Forestry 65(8): 564–566.

Dasmann, W. P. 1971. If deer are to survive. Stackpole Books, Harrisburg, Pennsylvania. 128 pp.

———. 1975. Big game of California. California Dept. Fish and Game, Sacramento. 58 pp.

Dathe, H. 1966. Zum Mutter-Kind Verhalten bei Cerviden. Beiträge zur Jagd und Wildforschung 5: 83–93.

Daubenmire, R. 1959. A canopy-coverage method of vegetational analysis. Northwest Sci. 33: 43–64.

———. 1966. Vegetation: Identification of typal communities. Science 151(3708): 291–298.

Daubenmire, R. and J. B. Daubenmire. 1968. Forest vegetation in eastern Washington and northern Idaho. Tech. Bull. 60. Washington Ag. Exp. Sta., Pullman. 104 pp.

Dauphiné, T. C., Jr. 1975. Kidney weight fluctuations affecting the kidney fat index in caribou. J. Wildl. Manage. 39: 379–386.

Dauphine, T. C., Jr. and R. L. McClure. 1974. Synchronous mating in Canadian barren ground caribou. J. Wildl. Manage. 38(1): 54–66.

Davidson, R. W. and V. F. Nettles. 1992. Relocation of Wildlife: Identifying and evaluating disease risks. Trans. N. Amer. Wildl. and Natur. Resour. Conf. 57: 466–473.

Davies, R. B. and G. G. Clark. 1974. Trypanosomes from elk and horse flies in New Mexico. J. Wildl. Dis. 10: 63–65.

Davis, D. S. 1990. Brucellosis in wildlife. Pages 321–334 *in* K. Nielsen, J. R.

Nielsen and J. R. Duncan, eds., Animal brucellosis. CRC Press, Boca Raton, Florida. 453 pp.

Davis, D. S., W. J. Booer, J. P. Mims, F. C. Heck and L. G. Adams. 1979. *Brucella abortus* in coyotes. 1. A serologic and bacteriologic survey in eastern Texas. J. Wildl. Dis. 15(3): 367–372.

Davis, G. K. 1958. Metabolic function and practical use of cobalt in nutrition. Pages 193–211 *in* C. A. Lamb, O. G. Bentlby and J. M. Beattie, eds., Trace elements. Academic Press Inc., New York and London.

Davis, G. P., Jr. 1982. Man and wildlife in Arizona: The American exploration period. 1824–1865. Somers Graphics, Inc., Scottsdale, Arizona. 232 pp.

Davis, J. L. 1970. Elk use of spring and calving range during and after controlled logging. M.S. Thesis, Univ. Idaho, Moscow. 51 pp.

Davis, J. W. and K. G. Libke. 1971. Trematodes. Pages 235–257 *in*, J. W. Davis and R. C. Anderson, eds., Parasitic diseases of wild mammals. Iowa State Univ. Press., Ames. 364 pp.

Davis, L. B. 1973. Schmitt (24BW559): A middle period mine at the Missouri River headwaters, Montana. Paper presented at the Thirty-first Plains Conference, Columbia, Missouri.

Davis, R. B. 1952. The use of rumen contents data in a study of deer–cattle competition and "animal equivalence." Trans. N. Amer. Wildl. Conf. 17: 448–458.

Davis, R. C. ed. 1983a. Wildlife conservation. 1983. Pages 702–709 *in* Encyclopedia of Amercan forest and conservation history. Vol 2. Macmillan Publ. Co., New York. 871 pp.

———. 1983b. Yellowstone National Park. Pages 735–737 *in* Encyclopedia of American forest and conservation history. Vol 2. Macmillan Publ. Co., New York. 871 pp.

Davis, R. W., Y. Z. Abdelbaki and J. L. Adcock. 1966a. Investigations of diseases of elk. Job Compl. Rept., Fed. Aid in Wildl. Restor., Proj. W–78–R–9. Arizona Game and Fish Dept., Phoenix.

Davis, R. W., Y. Z. Abdelbaki, J. L. Adcock and C. P. Hibler. 1966b. Investigations of diseases of elk. Job Compl. Rept., Fed. Aid in Wildl. Restor., Proj. W–78–R–10. Arizona Game and Fish Dept., Phoenix.

Davis, T. A. 1962. Values of hunting and fishing in Arizona, 1960. Bur Bus. Publ, Res. Spec. Stud. No. 21. Univ. Arizona, Tucson. 61 pp.

———. 1967. Values of hunting and fishing in Arizona, 1965. Univ. Arizona, Coll. Bus. and Publ., Admin., Tucson. 91 pp.

———. 1987. Antler asymmetry caused by limb amputation and geophysical forces. Pages 223–229 *in* R. D. Brown, ed., Antler development in Cervidae. Caesar Kleberg Wildlife Research Institute, Texas A & M Univ., Kingsville, Texas.

Davitt, B. B. 1979. Elk summer diet composition and quality on the Colockum Multiple Use Research Unit, central Washington. Unpubl. M.S. Thesis, Washington State Univ., Pullman. 127 pp.

Dawson, M. R. 1967. Fossil history of the families of recent mammals. Pages 12–53 *in* S. Anderson and J. N. Jones, Jr., eds., Recent mammals of the world. Ronald Press Co., New York.

Dawson, M. R. and L. Krishtalka. 1984. Fossil history of the families of recent mammals. Pages 11–57 *in* S. Anderson and J. K. Jones, Jr., eds., Orders and families of recent mammals of the world. John Wiley and Sons, New York. 686 pp.

Day, G.M. 1953. The Indian as an ecological factor in the northeastern forest. Ecology 32: 329-346.

Day, T. A. 1973. Use of clearcuts by elk in the Little Belt Mountains, Montana. Final Rept., Proj. W–120–R–3 and 4, Job BG–3.oz(R). Montana Fish and Game Dept., Helena. 70 pp.

de Laguna, F. 1990. Tlingit. Pages 203–228 *in* Handbook of North American Indians, Vol. 7: Northwest coast. W. Suttles, ed. Smithsonian Instit. Press, Washington, D.C.

de Lisle, G. W. and D. M. Collins. 1995. Johne's disease in a red deer. Vet. Rec. 136: 336.

de Lisle, G. W., C. D. Anderson, A. L. R. Southern and A. J. Keay. 1988. Meningoencephalitis in farmed red deer (*Cervus elaphus*) caused by *Streptococcus zooepidemicus*. Vet. Rec. 122: 186–187.

de Smet, P. J. 1843. Letters and sketches. M. Fithian, Philadelphia, Pennsylvania. 244 pp.

de Vos, A. and H. S. Mosby. 1969. Habitat analysis and evaluation. Pages 135–172 *in* R. H. Giles, ed., Wildlife management techniques. The Wildl. Soc., Washington, D.C. 623 pp.

De Voto, B., ed. 1953. The journals of Lewis and Clark. Houghton, Mifflin and Co., Boston, Massachusetts. 504 pp.

Dealy, J. E. 1959. The influence of logging practices on Columbian blacktailed deer (*Odocoileus hemionus columbianus* Richardson) in the Blue River area of Oregon. M.S. Thesis, Oregon State Univ., Corvallis. 65 pp.

Dean, R. 1980. Some costs and benefits of elk in Wyoming. Pages 153–157 *in* K. Sumanik and W. Macgregor, eds., Proc. of the Western States Elk Workshop, 1980. Victoria, British Columbia. 174 pp.

Dean, R. E., E. T. Thorne and I. J. Yorgason. 1976. Weights of Rocky Mountain elk. J. Mammal. 57(1): 186–189.

deBuys, William. 1996. "GO Colorado" backs vision withe bold grants. Common Ground 7(5): 1,7.

DeCalesta, D. S., J. G. Nagy and J. A. Bailey. 1974. Some effects of starvation on mule deer rumen bacteria. J. Wildl. Manage. 38(4): 815–822.

Decker, D. and G. Goff, eds. 1986. Economic and Social Values of Wildlife. Westview Press, Boulder, Colorado. 424 pp.

Decker, D. J., J. W. Enck and T. L. Brown. 1993. The future of huntingCwill we pass on the heritage? Pages 22–46 *in* Proc., Second annual governor's symposium on North America's hunting heritage. Pierre, South Dakota. 199 pp.

Degen, A. A., M. Kam, R. W. Benjamin, R. König and K. Becker. 1990. Estimating body composition of lambs using bomb calorimetry. Can. J. Anim. Sci. 70: 1,127–1,129.

DeGraaf, R.M. and R.I. Miller. 1996. Importance of disturbance and land-use history in New England: Implication for forested landscapes and wildlife conservation. Pages 3-35 *in* R. M. DeGraaf and R. I. Miller, eds., Conservation of faunal diversity in forested landscapes. Chapman and Hall, New York. 633 pp.

Dehn, M. M. 1990. Vigilance for predators: detection and dilution effect. Behav. Ecol. and Sociobiol. 26: 337–342.

Deitscham, G. H. 1973. Mapping of habitat types throughout a national forest. Gen. Tech. Rept. INT–11. USDA For. Serv., Ogden, Utah. 15 pp.

DelGiudice, G. D. 1996. Assessing winter nutritional restriction of northern deer with urine in snow: Considerations, potential and limitations. Wildl. Soc. Bull. 23: 687–693.

DelGiudice, G. D. and J. E. Rodiek. 1984. Do elk need free water in Arizona? Wildl. Soc. 142–146.

DelGiudice, G. D. and U. S. Seal. 1988. Classifying winter undernutrition in deer via serum and urinary nitrogen. Wildl. Soc. Bull. 16: 27–32.

DelGiudice, G. D., L. D. Mech and U. S. Scal. 1989. Physiological assessment of deer populations by analysis of urine in snow. J. Wildl. Manage. 53: 284–291.

DelGiudice, G. D., L. D. Mech and U. S. Seal. 1990. Effects of winter undernutrition on body composition and physiological profiles of white-tailed deer. J. Wildl. Manage. 54: 539–550.

DelGiudice, G. D., U. S. Seal and L. D. Mech. 1991a. Indicators of severe undernutrition in urine of free-ranging elk during winter. Wildl. Soc. Bull. 19: 106–110.

DelGiudice, G. D., F. J. Singer and U. S. Seal. 1991b. Physiological assessment of winter nutritional deprivation of elk of Yellowstone National Park. J. Wildl. Manage. 55: 653–664.

Della-Bianca, L. and F. M. Johnson. 1965. Effect of an intensive cleaning on deer–browse production in the southern Appalachians. J. Wildl. Manage. 29(4): 729–733.

Deloria, E. C. 1932. Dakota text. Vol. 14. Public Amer. Ethnol. Soc. AMS Press, New York. 279 pp.

Deloria, E. C. and J. Brandon. 1961. The origin of the courting flute: A legend in the Santee dialect. Univ. South Dakota Mus. News 22(6): 1–7.

DeMalle, R. J., ed. 1984. The sixth grandfather: Black Elk's teachings given to John G. Niehardt. Univ. Nebraska Press, Lincoln. 452 pp.

Demidoff, Prince S.D. 1910. The Russian Empire. Pages 387–416 *in* F. G. Aflalo, ed., Sport in Europe. E.P. Dutton and Co., New York. 483 pp.

Denevan, W. M. 1992. The Native population of the Americas in 1492. 2nd ed. Univ. Wisconsin Press, Madison. 353 pp.

Dengler, H. 1923. American Indians. Albert and Chas. Boni, New York. 80 pp.

Denig, E. T. 1930. Indian tribes of the Upper Missouri. Pages 375–629 *in* J. N. B. Hewitt, ed., 46th Annual report of the Bureau of American Ethnology to the Secretary of the Interior, 1928–1929. Govt. Print. Off., Washington, D.C. 654 pp.

———. 1953. Of the Crow Nation. Anthropological Papers, No. 33, Bull. 151: 1–74. Bur. of Amer. Ethnol., Washington, D.C.

DeNio, R. M. 1938. Elk and deer foods and feeding habits. Trans. N. Amer. Wildl. Conf. 3: 421–427.

Denney, R. N. 1957. An indicated technique to determine the sex of dressed elk carcasses. Proc. West. Assoc. State Game and Fish. Commiss. 37: 211–217.

———. 1965a. Study of diseases and parasites (deer–elk). Job. Compl. Rept., Fed. Aid Pages 59–62 *in* Wildl. Restor., Proj. W–38–2–18. Colorado Dept. Game, Fish and Parks, Denver.

———. 1965b. A Colorado elk management plan, 1965–1975. Colorado Dept. Game, Fish and Parks, Fort Collins. 61 pp.

———. 1973. The hunter as seen by the nonhunter. Pages 20–22 *in* Proc. 4th Int. Big Game Hunter's and Fisherman's Conf. Game Conservation International, San Antonio, Texas.

Denney, R. N. and R. B. Gill. 1970. Annotated bibliography on mammal immobilization with drugs. Game Res. Sec., Spec. Rept. No. 15. Colorado Div. Game, Fish and Parks, Denver. 27 pp.

Denniston, R. H. 1956. Ecology, behavior and population dynamics of the Wyoming or Rocky Mountain moose, *Alces alces shirasi*. Zoologica 41: 105–118.

Denome, R. M. 1998. Genetic variation in North American populations of elk (*Cervus elaphus*). Wildl. Div. Rept. A–137A. North Dakota Game and Fish Dept., Bismarck. 19 pp.

Densmore, F. 1918. Teton Sioux music. Bur. of Amer. Ethnol., Bull. 61. Smithsonian Instit. Press, Washington, D.C. 561 pp.

Deschamps, A. M. 1989. Microbial degradation of tannins and related compounds. Pages 559–567 *in* N. G. Lewis and M. G. Paice, eds., Plant cell wall polymers. Amer. Chem. Soc., Washington, D.C.

DeSimone, R., J. Vore and T. Carlsen. 1993. Older bulls—who needs them? Pages 29–34 *in* J. D. Cada, J. G Petersen and T. N. Lonner, compilers, Proc. 1993 Western states and provinces elk workshop. Montana Dept. Fish, Wildl. and Parks, Helena. 72 pp.

Despain, D. D. Houston, M. Meagher and P. Schullerg. 1986. Wildlife in transition: Man and nature on Yellowstone's northern range. Roberts Rinehart, Boulder, Colorado. 142 pp.

Detling, L. E. 1968. Historical background of the flora of the Pacific Northwest. Mus. Natur. Hist., Bull. No. 13. Univ. Oregon, Eugene. 57 pp.

Devereux, S. 1976. Elk in British Columbia. British Columbia Fish and Wildl. Branch, Victoria. 4 pp.

Devlin, D. and W. Drake. 1989. Pennsylvania elk census –1989. Annu. Unpubl. Rept. Pennsylvania Game Commission, Harrisburg, Pennsylvania. 8 pp.

DeYoung, C. A. 1990 Inefficiency in trophy white-tailed deer harvest. Wildl. Soc. Bull 18: 7–12.

Di Stefano, G. and C. Petronio. 1992. Nuove osservazioni su *Cervus elaphus acoronatus* Beninde del Plsietocene Europeo. Bolletino della Societa Paleontologica Italiana 31: 295–315.

Dick, B. L. and P. J. Urness. 1991. Nutritional value of fresh Gambel oak browse for Spanish goats. J. Range Manage. 44: 361–364.

Dietrich, R. A., S. H. Amosson, R. P. Crawford and V. C. Beal. 1991. Relationship of strain 19 calfhood vaccination in beef herds and brucellosis reactor rates, duration of quarantine and number of tests. J. Am. Vet. Med. Assoc. 198: 78–80.

Dietz, D. R. 1970. Animal production and forage quality: definition and components of forage quality. Pages 1–9 *in* Range and wildlife habitat evaluation—a research symposium. Misc. Publ. 1147. USDA For. Serv., Washington, D.C.

Dikmans, G. 1939. Helminth parasites of North American semidomesticated and wild ruminants. Proc. Helminth Soc. Wash. 6(2): 97–101.

Dillon, L. S. 1956. Wisconsin climate and life zones in North America. Science 123(3188): 167–176.

Dimock, E. J. and H. C. Black. 1969. Scope and economic aspects of animal damage in Califomia, Oregon and Washington. Page 1,014 *in* H. C. Black, ed., Wildlife and reforestation in the Pacific Northwest. Symp. Proc. Oregon State Univ., Corvallis. 92 pp.

Dimock, E. J., II, R. R. Silen and V. E. Allen. 1976. Genetic resistance in Douglas-fir to damage by snowshoe hare and black-tailed deer. For. Sci. 22(2): 106–121.

Dinneford, B. 1995. Elk. Fed. Aid Wildl. Restor., Annu. Perform. Rept. Survey—Inventory Activities, 1 July 1994–30 June 1995. Grant W–24–3, Study 13.0, Proj. Title: Southeast Alaska elk management. Alaska Dept. Fish and Game, Div. Wildl. Manage., Juneau. 1 p.

Dix, R. L. 1961. An application of the point-centered quarter method to the sampling of grassland vegetation. J. Range Manage. 14: 63–69.

———. 1964. A history of biotic and climatic changes within the North American grassland. Pages 71–89 *in* D. J. Crisp, ed., Grazing in terrestrial and marine environments. Blackwells Sci. Publ., Dorking, U.K.

Dixon, R. B. 1905. The Northern Maidu. Bull. Amer. Mus. Natur. Hist. 17(3): 119–346.

Dixon, S. L. and R. L. Lyman. 1996. On the Holocene history of elk (*Cervus elaphus*) in eastern Washington. Northwest Sci. 70(3): 262–272.

Döbel, H. 1754. Neueröffnete Jager Practica. Oder der wohlgeübte und Erfahrene Jäger. Leipzig (2nd ed.)

Dobretzberger, F. 1980. Saison-und altersbedingte Veranderungen des Ovarium von *Cervus elaphus*-Untersuchungen zur Reproduktionsdynamik der Hirsch population einiger Reviere im Achental/Tirol. Ph.D. Thesis, Vet. Univ., Vienna. 58 pp.

Dobroruka, L.J. 1960. Der Karpatenhirsch, *Cervus elaphus montanus* Botezat 1903. Zoologisher Anzeiger 165: 481–483.

Dobyns, H. F. 1966. Estimating aboriginal American population. Current Anthropol. 7: 395–449.

———. 1983. Their numbers become thinned: Native American population dynamics in eastern North America. Univ. Tennessee Press, Knoxville. 378 pp.

———. 1988. Reassessing new world populations at the time of contact. Encuentro 4(4):8–9.

Dobzhansky, T. 1937. What is a species? Scientia 61(301–5): 280–286.

———. 1970. Genetics of the evolutionary process. Columbia Univ. Press, New York. 505 pp.

D'Occhio, M. J. and J. M. Suttie. 1992. The role of the pineal gland and melatonin in reproduction in male domestic ruminants. Anim. Reprod. Sci. 30: 135–155.

Dodge, O. 1898. Pioneer history of Coos and Curry Counties, Oregon. Capital Print. Co., Salem, Oregon. 103 pp.

Dodge, R. I. 1877. The plains of the great west and their inhabitants. G. P. Putnam Sons, New York. 448 pp.

———. 1882. Our wild Indians. A. D. Worthington, Hartford, Connecticut. 653 pp.

———. 1959. The plains of the great West. Archer House Inc., New York. 452 pp.

Dolan, J. M., Jr. 1988. A deer of many lands—A guide to the subspecies of the red deer *Cervus elaphus* L. Zoonooz 62(10): 4–34.

Dolan, J. M., Jr. and L. E. Killmar. 1988. The shou, *Cervus elaphus wallichi* Cuvier, 1825, a rare and little-known cervid, with remarks on three additional Asiatic elaphines. Zool. Garten 58(2,5): 84–96.

Doll, G. F. and C. Phillips. 1972. Wyoming's hunting and fishing resources, 1970. Div. Bus. Econ. Res., Univ. Wyoming, Laramie. 116 pp.

Dom, R. D. 1969. Relations of moose, cattle and willows in southwestern Montana. Unpubl. M.S. Thesis, Montana State Univ., Bozeman. 79 pp.

———. 1970. Moose and cattle food habits in southwestern Montana. J. Wildl. Manage. 34: 559–564.

Doman, E. R. and D. I. Rassmussen. 1944. Supplemental feeding of mule deer in northern Utah. J. Wildl. Manage. 317–338.

Domingue, B. M. F., D. W. Dellow, P. R. Wilson and T. N. Barry. 1991. Nitrogen metabolism, rumen fermentation and water absorptionin red deer, goats and sheep. New Zealand J. Ag. Res. 34: 391–400.

Domingue, B. M., P. R. Wilson, D. W. Dellow and T. N. Barry. 1992. Effects of subcutaneous melatonin implants during long daylength on voluntary feed intake, rumen capacity and heart rate of red deer (*Cervus elaphus*) fed on a forage diet. Brit. J. Nutr. 68: 77–88.

Donaubauer, E. 1990 Einflusse des wildes auf die waldvegetation- erhebungsmethode fur regionale beurteilungen: methoden und deren aussagekapazitat. Pages 260–171 *in* H. Gossow, E. Donaubauer, F. Reimoser and J. Dieberger, eds., Tagungsbericht IURFO-Symposium regionalplanungskonzept, fur eine forstlich integrierte Schalenwildbewirtschaftung im Hoch- und Mittelgebirge. BOKU-reports on Wildlife Research and Game Management 1. Institut for Wildbiologie und Jagdwirtschaft, Universitat fur Bodenkultur, Wien.

Donne, T. E. 1924. The game animals of New Zealand. John Murray, London, U.K. 322 pp.

Dorè, A. 1999. Canadian zoo sanitary situation in 1998. CAH Nef. Bull., 3rd ed. Canadian Food Inspect. Ag. (www.cahnet.org/cfa.htm).

Dorf, E. 1960. Climatic changes of the past and present. Amer. Sci. 48(3): 341–364.

Dorn, R. D. 1970. Moose and cattle food habits in southwestern Montana. J. Wildl. Manage. 34: 559–564.

Dorrance, M. J., P. J. Savage and D. E. Huff. 1975. Effects of snowmobiles on white-tailed deer. J. Wildl. Manage. 39: 563–569.

Dorsey, G. A. 1903. Indians of the Southwest. Atchison, Topeka, and Santa Fe Railway System, Topeka, Kansas. 223 pp.

———. 1904. Traditions of the Arikara. Publ. no. 7. Carnegi Inst. of Washington, Washington, D.C. 202 pp.

———. 1905. The Cheyenne: I. Ceremonial organization; II. The sun dance. Field Columbian Mus. Publ. 103. Anthro. Ser. 9 vols., no. 2. Chicago, Illinois.

Doster, G. L., ed. 1996. TB in Michigan whitetails. Southeastern Cooperative Wildlife Disease Study Briefs Athens, Georgia. 11(4): 1.

Doty, J. D. 1908. Northern Wisconsin in 1820. Pages 195–206 *in* L. C.

Draper, ed., Collections of the State Historical Society of Wisconsin. Vol 7. 492 pp. (Reprint of 1876 original issue.)

Douglas, M. J. W. 1971. Behavior responses of red deer and chamois to cessation of hunting. New Zealand J. Sci. 14: 507–518.

Dout, J. K. and J. C. Donaldson. 1959. An antlered doe with possible masculinizing tumor. J. Mammal. 40(2): 230–236.

Dowling, T. E., B. D. DeMarais, W. L. Minckley, M. E. Douglas and P. C. Marsh. 1992. Use of genetic characters in conservation biology. Conserv. Biol. 6(1): 7–8.

Drake, C. H. 1951. Mistaken diagnosis of actinomycosis for osteogenic sarcoma in an American elk (*Cervus canadensis*). J. Wildl. Manage. 15: 284–287.

Drake, F. 1653. Sir Francis Drake revived . . . being a summary and true relation of foure severall voyages made by the said Sir Francis Drake to the West-Indies . . . collected out of notes of the said Sir Francis Drake; Master Philip Nichols, Master Francis Fletcher, preacher; and the notes of divers other gentlemen, who went in the said voyages, carefully compared together. 3 parts. Nicholas Bourne, London.

Dratch, P. A. 1986. A marker for red deer–wapiti hybrids. Proc. New Zealand Soc. Animal Production 46: 179–182.

Dratch, P. A. and J. M. Pemberton. 1992. Application of biochemical genetics to deer management: What the gels tell. Pages 367–383 *in* R. D. Brown, ed., The biology of deer. Springer-Verlag, New York. 596 pp.

Dratch, P. A. and V. Gyllensten. 1985. Genetic differentiation of red deer and North American elk (wapiti). Pages 37–40 *in* P. F. Fennessy and K. R. Drew, eds., The biology of deer production. Royal Soc. of New Zealand, Wellington. Bull 22. 482 pp.

Dratch, P. A., M. Tate, G. J. Kraay and V. Gerwing. 1992. Plasma proteins differentiating European red deer and North American elk. Animal Genetics 23(suppl. 1): 32.

Drescher-Kaden, U. 1974. Vergleichend hamatologische Untersuchungen an wildlebenden Wiederkauern (Rotwild, Rehe, Gemsen, Rentiere). 3. Mitt. Z. f. Jagdwiss. 20(4): 192–201.

———. 1991. Ernahrungsphysiologie und futterungspraxis. Pages 68–102 *in* Bogner, H., ed., Damwild und rotwild in landwirtschaftlichen gehegen. Pary, Hamburg and Berlin.

Drescher-Kaden, U. and P. Hoppe. 1972. Vergleichend haematologische Untersuchungen an willebenden Wiederkauern (Rotwild, Rehe, Gemsen, Rentiere). 1. Mitt. Z. f. Jagdwiss. 18(3): 121–132.

Drescher-Kaden, U. and P. Hoppe. 1973. Vergleichend haematologische Untersuchungen an willebenden Wiederkauern (Rotwild, Rehe, Gemsen, Rentiere). 2. Mitt. Z. f. Jagdwiss. 19(2): 65–76.

Drew, K. R. 1985. Meat production from farmed deer. Pages 285–290 *in* P. F. Fennessy and K. R. Drew, eds., Biology of deer production. Royal Soc. of New Zealand, Wellington. 482 pp.

———. 1992. Venison and other deer products. Pages 225–232 *in* R. D. Brown, ed., The biology of deer. Springer Verlag, New York. 596 pp.

Drew, K. R. and D. L. Seman. 1987. The nutrient content of venison. Proc. Nutr. Soc. New Zealand 12: 49–55.

Drew, M. L., D. A. Jessup, A. A. Burr and C. E. Franti. 1992. Serologic survey for brucellosis in feral swine, wild ruminants and black bear of California, 1977–1988. J. Wildl. Dis. 28: 355–363.

Driscoll, R. S. 1963. Repellents reduce deer browsing on ponderosa pine seedlings. Res. Note PNW–5. USDA For. Serv., Portland, Oregon. 8 pp.

Driver, H. E. 1968. On the population nadir of Indians in the United States. Current Anthropol. 9: 330.

———. 1969. Indians of North America. Univ. Chicago Press, Chicago, Illinois. 632 pp.

Driver, H. E. and W. C. Massey. 1957. Comparative studies of North American Indians. Trans. Amer. Philos. Soc. 47: 165–456.

Driver, J. C. 1988. Late Pleistocene and Holocene vertebrates and paleo-environments from Charlie Lake Cave, northeast British Columbia. Can. J. Earth Sci. 25(10): 1,545–1,553.

Drucker, P. 1951. The Northern and Central Nootkan tribes. Bull. 144, Bur. Amer. Ethnol., Washington, D.C.

Du Creux, F. 1664. Historiac Canadensis sev. Novae-Franciae. Cramoisy, Paris, France. 830 pp.

DuBois, C. A. 1936. The wealth concept as an interrogative factor in the Tolowa-Tututni culture. Pages 46–65 in R. H. Lowie, ed., Essays in anthropology. Univ. California Press, Berkeley. 433 pp.

Duckworth, J. A. and G. K. Barrell. 1989. Effect of melatonin immunization on liveweight gain of red deer. Proc. NZ Soc. Anim. Prod. 49: 29–34.

Duda, M. D. and K. C. Young. 1994. Americans and Wildlife Diversity: Public Opinion, Attitudes, Interest and Participation in Wildlife Viewing and Wildlife Diversity Programs. Responsive Management. Harrisonburg, Viginia. 155 pp.

Duda, M. D., S. J. Bissell and K. C. Young. 1998. Wildlife and the American mind. Responsive Management, Harrisonburg, Virginia. 804 pp.

Dudley, W. H. 1886. The national park from the hurricane deck of a cayuse, or the Liederkranz expedition to geyserland. Frederick Loeber, Butte, Montana. 132 pp.

Duffield, J. W. 1992. Total valuation of wildlife and fishery resources: applications in the Northern Rockies. Pages 97–113 in C. Payne, J. M. Bowker and P. C. Reed, eds., The Economic Value of Wilderness: Proc. of the Conference; 1991 May 8–11; Jackson, Wyo. Gen. Tech. Rept. SE–78. USDA For. Serv., Asheville, North Carolina.

Duffus, D. A. and P. Dearden. 1990. Nonconsumptive wildlife-oriented recreation: A conceptual framework. Biol. Conserv. 53: 213–231.

Duffy, P. J. B. 1965. A forest land classification for the mixed wood section of Alberta. Dept. For. Publ. 1128. Queens Printer and Controller of Stationery, Ottawa, Canada.

Duke of Frias. 1910. Spain. Pages 307–331 in F. G. Aflalo, ed., Sport in Europe. E. P. Dutton and Co., New York. 483 pp.

Dulan Bureau of Agriculture and Animal Husbandry. 1987. A brief report and plan for Dulan International Hunting Reserve, Dulan. 9 pp. (In Chinese.)

Dunbar, C. O. 1949. Historical geology. John Wiley and Sons, Inc., New York. 567 pp.

Duncan, D. A. 1958. Weight methods for measuring herbage utilization. Pages 32–35 in Techniques and methods of measuring understory vegetation, Proc. Tifton Symp., Tifton, Georgia, Oct. 1958. USDA For. Serv., Washington, D.C.

Dunlap, R. and A. Mertig. 1992. American environmentalism: The U.S. environmental movement, 1970–1990. Taylor and Frances, Bristol, Pennsylvania.

Dunraven, Earl of. 1967. The great divide, travels in the Yellowstone in the summer of 1874. Univ. Nebraska Press, Lincoln. 377 pp.

Durrant, S. D. 1955. In defense of the subspecies. Syst. Zool. 4(4): 186–190.

Dusi, J. L. 1949. Methods for determination of food habits by plant microtechniques and histology and their applications to cottontail rabbits in Ohio. J. Wildl. Manage. 13(2): 289–295.

Dutson, V. J., J. N. Shaw and S. E. Knapp. 1967. Epizootiologic factors of Fascioloides magna (Trematoda) in Oregon and southern Washington. Amer. J. Vet. Res. 28: 853–860.

Duvall, D., D. Muller-Schwarze and R. M. Silverstein, eds. 1986. Chemical signals in vertebrates: 3. Ecology, evolution and comparative biology. Plenum Press. 742 pp.

Dyksterhuis, E. J. 1949. Condition and management of range based on quantitative ecology. J. Range Manage. 2: 104–115.

Dyrness, C. T. 1965. Soil surface condition following tractor and high-lead logging in the Oregon Cascades. J. Forestry 63(4): 273–275.

Dyson-Hudson, R. and E. A. Smith. 1978. Human territoriality: An ecological reassessment. Amer. Anthropol. 80: 21–41.

Dzieciolowski, R. 1967. Winter food of the red deer (Cervus elaphus L.) as determined by tracking techniques. Tom XV, Nr 11. Polish Acad. Sci., Warsaw, Poland. 21 pp.

———. 1969. The quantity, quality and seasonal variation of food resources available to red deer in various environmental conditions of forest management. Polish Acad. Sci., For. Res. Inst., Warsaw. 295 pp.

———. 1970. Relations between the age and size of red deer in Poland. Acta Theriologica 15(17): 253–268.

Eabry, S., ed. 1970. A glossary of deer terminology. Prepared by the terminology committee, northeastern deer study group. Wildlife Res. Lab., New York. 31 pp.

East African Agriculture and Forest Research Organization. 1969. Proc. of the workshop on the use of light aircraft in wildlife management in East Africa. Spec. Issue. East African Ag. and For. J. 111 pp.

East, B. 1937. Quarry of the camera. Animal Kingdom (N.Y. Zoological Soc.) 11(3): 89–96.

Easterbrook, D. J. and D. A. Rahm. 1970. Landforms of Washington. Union Print. Co., Bellingham, Washington. 156 pp.

Eastman, C. A. 1904. Red hunters and animal people. Harper and Brothers, New York. 248 pp.

Eastman, M. 1849. Dakotah; or life and legends of the Sioux around Fort Snelling. John Wiley, New York.

Eberhardt, L. E., L. L. Eberhardt, B. L. Tiller and L. L. Cadwell. 1996. Growth of an isolated elk population. J. Wildl. Manage. 60: 369–373.

Eberhardt, L. L. 1960. Estimation of vital characteristics of Michigan deer herds. Rept. 2282, Michigan Dept. Conserv., Game Div., East Lansing. 192 pp.

———. 1971. Population analysis. Pages 457–495 in R. H. Giles, ed., Wildlife management techniques. The Wildl. Soc., Washington D.C. 623 pp.

———. 1977. Optimal management policies for marine mammals. Wildl. Soc. Bull. 5: 162–169.

———. 1978. Appraising variability in population studies. J. Wildl. Manage. 42: 1–31.

———. 1985. Assessing the dynamics of wild populations. J. Wildl. Manage. 49: 997–1,012.

———. 1987. Population projections from simple models. J. Appl. Ecol. 24: 103–118.

Eberhardt, L. L., R. A. Garrott, P. J. White and P. J. Gogan. 1998. Alternative approaches to aerial censusing of elk. J. Wildl. Manage. 62: 1,046–1,055.

Ebling, F. J. P. and M.H. Hastings. 1992. The neural basis of seasonal reproduction. Annu. Zootech. 41: 239–246.

Eby, J. R. and L. R. Bright. 1986. A digital GIS based on LANDSAT and other data for elk habitat effectiveness analysis. Proc. 19th Int. Symp. on Remote Sensing of Environment, Ann Arbor, Michigan, Oct 21–25, 1985. Envir. Res. Inst. of Mich., Univ. Mich., Ann Arbor.

Eckroade, R. J., G. M. ZuRhein and W. Foreyt. 1970. Meningeal worm invasion of the brain of a naturally infected white-tailed deer. J. Wildl. Dis. 6: 430–436.

Eckstein, R. G., T. F. O'Brient, O. J. Rongstad and J. G. Bollinger. 1979. Snowmobile effects on movements of white-tailed deers: A case study. Environ. Cons. 6: 45–51.

Ecological Society of America. 1996. The report of the Ecological Society of America Committee on the Scientific Basis for Ecosystem Management. Ecological Applications 6(3): 665–691.

Edge, W. D. 1982. Distribution, habitat use and movements of elk in relation to roads and human disturbances in western Montana. M.S. Thesis, Univ. Montana, Missoula. 98 pp.

Edge, W. D. and C. L. Marcum. 1985a. Effects of logging activities on home range fidelity of elk. J. Wildl. Manage. 49: 741–744.

———. 1985b. Movements of elk in relation to logging disturbances. J.Wildl.Manage. 49: 926–930.

Edge, W. D. and C. L. Marcum. 1991. Topography ameliorates the effects of roads and human disturbance on elk. Pages 132–137 in A. G. Christiansen, L. J. Lyon and T. N. Loner, compilers, Proc. Elk Vulnerability Symp., Montana State Univ., Bozeman. 330 pp.

Edge, W. D., C. L. Marcum, S. L. Olson and J. F. Lehmkuhl. 1986. Nonmigratory cow elk herd ranges as management units. J. Wildl. Manage. 50: 660–663.

Edge, W. D., C. L. Marcum and S. L. Olson-Edge. 1988. Summer forage and feeding site selection by elk. J. Wildl. Manage. 52: 573–577.

Edge, W. D., S. L. Olson-Edge and L. L. Irwin. 1990. "In my opinion . . ." Planning for wildlife in national forests: elk and mule deer habitats as an example. Wildl. Soc. Bull. 18: 87–98.

Edgerton, P. J. 1972. Big game use and habitat changes in a recently logged mixed conifer forest in northeastern Oregon. Pages 239–246 in Western Proc. 52nd Annual Conference, Western Assoc. of State Game and Fish Commissioners, Portland, Oregon.

———. 1987. Influence of ungulates on the development of the shrub understory of an upper slope mixed conifer forest. Pages 162–167 in F. D. Provenza, J. T. Flinders and E. D. McArthur, compilers, Proc. symposium on plant–herbivore interactions. USDA For. Serv., Ogden, Utah.

Edgerton, P. J. and B. R. McConnell. 1976. Diurmal temperature regimes of logged and unlogged mixed conifer stands on elk summer range. Res. Note PNW–277. USDA For. Serv., Portland, Oregon. 6 pp.

Edgerton, P. J. and J. G. Smith. 1971. Seasonal forage use by deer and elk on the Starkey Experimental Forest and Range, Oregon. Res. Pap. PNW–122. USDA For. Serv., Portland, Oregon. 12 pp.

Edmonds, M. and E. E. Clark. 1989. Voices of the winds. Facts on File, Inc., New York. 368 pp.

Edson, M. A. 1954. Firearm safety through education. Idaho Wildl. Rev. 6(5): 6–8.

———. 1963. Idaho wildlife in the early days. Idaho Wildl. Rev. 16(1): 8–13.

Edwards, M. 1996. Searching for the Scythians. Nat. Geogr. 190(3): 54–79.

Edwards, R. Y. 1956. Snow depths and ungulate abundance in the mountains of western Canada. J. Wildl. Manage. 20(2): 159–168.

Efremov, J. A. 1940. Taphonomy: New branch of paleontology. Pan-Amer. Geol. 74: 81–93.

Egorov, O. V. 1965. Wild ungulates of Yakutia. (Translated from Russian.) Clearinghouse for Fed. Sci. and Tech. Info., U.S. Dept. Commerce, Springfield, Virginia. 204 pp.

Ehrenreich, J. H. and D. A. Murphy. 1962. A method of evaluating habitat for forest wildlife. Trans. N. Amer. Wildl. and Natur. Resour. Conf. 27: 376–383.

Ehrlich, P. R. and P. H. Raven. 1969. Differentiation of populations. Science 165(3899): 1,228–1,232.

Eibl-Eibesfeldt, I. 1970. Ethology, the biology of behavior. Holt, Rinehart and Winston, New York. 530 pp.

Eidmann, H. 1939. Untersuchungen am Gebiss des Rothirsches und anderen Cerviden. Verlag Schaper, Hannover.

Einarsen, A. S. 1946. Crude protein determination of deer food as an applied management technique. Trans. N. Amer. Wildl. Conf. 11: 309–312.

———. 1948. The pronghorn antelope and its management. The Stackpole Company, Harrisburg, Pennsylvania. 235 pp.

Eisenberg, J. F. 1987. The evolutionary history of the Cervidae with special reference to the South American radiation. Pages 60–64 in C. M. Wemmer, ed., Biology and management of the Cervidae. Smithsonian Instit. Press, Washington, D.C. 577 pp.

Eisfeld, D. 1990 Welchen sinn haben futterung und asungsverbesserung fur reh- und rotwild? Pages 16–20 in Wildforschungsstelle der landes Baden-Wurtemberg, ed., Futterung und asungsverbesserung fur reh- und rotwild. Schriftenreihe wildforschung in Baden-Wurttemberg 1. Aulendorf

Eldridge, B. F., C. H. Callisher, J. F. Fryer, L. Bright and D. J. Hobbs. 1987. Serological evidence of California serogroup virus activity in Oregon. J. Wildl. Dis. 23: 199–204.

Elk Status Report. 1996. Michigan Dept. Nat. Resour., Wildl. Div., Lansing. 8 pp. unpublished.

Elk Status Reports. 1995. Pages 71–92 in Idaho Dept. Fish and Game, Proc., Western States and Provinces 1995 joint deer and elk workshop. Boise, Idaho. 139 pp.

Ellerman, J. R. and T. C. S. Morrison-Scott. 1951. Checklist of Palaearctic and Indian mammals, 1758 to 1946. British Mus. Natur. Hist., London. 810 pp.

Ellig, L. 1975. Yellowstone elk: curse or blessing? Montana Outdoors 6(5): 26–30.

Elliott, J. L. 1994. Receptors for GH and IGFs in cartilage using antler as a model for bone growth. D. Phil Thesis, Univ. Waikato, Hamilton, New Zealand.

Elliott, J. L., J. M. Oldham, G. R. Ambler, J. J. Bass, G. S. G. Spencer, S. C. Hodgkinon, B. H. Breier, P. D. Gluckman and J. M. Suttie. 1992. Presence of insulin-like growth factor-I receptors and absence of growth hormone receptors in antler tip. Endocrinology 130: 2,513–2,520.

Elliott, J. L., J. M. Oldham, G. R. Ambler, P. C. Molan, G. S. G. Spencer, S. C. Hodgkinon, B. H. Breier, P. D. Gluckman, J. M. Suttie and J. J. Bass. 1993. Receptors for insulin-like growth factor-II in the growing tip of the deer antler. J. Endocrinology 138: 233–241.

Ellis, L. L., Jr. 1955. A survey of the ectoparasites of certain mammals in Oklahoma. Ecology 36(1): 12–18.

Ellison, R. 1974. Chamberlain Creek study.Pages 105–125 in Montana Coop. Elk-Logging study, Prog. Rept. for the period Jan. 1–Dec. 31, 1973. Mimeo. Montana Coop. Elk-Logging Study, Bozeman.

Elmendorf, W. M. 1960. The structure of Twana culture. Mono. Suppl. 2. Washington State Univ. Research Stud. 28(3).

Eloranta, E., J. Timisjarvi, M. Niemenen and O. Vakkuri. 1995. Seasonal onset and disappearance of diurnal rhythmicity in melatonin secretion in female reindeer. Amer. Zool. 35: 203–214.

Elsasser, B. A. 1978a. Wiyot. Pages 155–163 in R. F. Heizer, ed., California. Handbook of North American Indians. Vol. 8. Smithsonian Instit., Washington, D.C. 800 pp.

———. 1978b. Mattole, Nongatl, Sinkyone, Lassik and Wailaki. Pages 190–204 in R. F. Heizer, ed., California. Handbook of North American Indians, Vol. 8. Smithsonian Instit., Washington, D.C. 800 pp.

Elton, C. 1933. The ecology of animals. Methuen's Monographs on Biological Subjects. John Wiley and Sons, London, U.K.

———. 1947. Animal ecology. 3rd ed. MacMillan Co., New York. 209 pp.

Emerson, B. C. and M. L. Tate. 1993. Genetic analysis of evolutionary relationships among deer (subfamily Cervinae). J. Hered. 84(4): 266–273.

Emerson, K. 1988. Elkhorn Wildlife Area: Artificial feeding of elk. Pages 50–52 *in* M. Zahn, J. Pierce and R. Johnson, eds., Proc. Western States and Provinces Elk Workshop. Washington Dept. Wildl., Olympia. 249 pp.

Emerson, K. C. 1962. A tentative list of Mallophaga of North American mammals (north of Mexico). (Aug. 15). Dugway, Utah. 20 pp.

Engelmann, C. 1938. Üeber die Grossäuger Szetschwans, Sikongs und Osttibets. Zs. Säugetierkunde 13 (Sonderheft) 76 pp.

England, R. E. and A. de Vos. 1969. Influence of animals on pristine conditions on the Canadian grasslands. J. Range Manage. 22: 8,794.

Ennemoser, E. 1983. Unser rotwild. Schlusselverlag, Innsbruck. 160 pp.

Erepb, B. H. and H. G. Aeeb. 1994. Elk antler breeding. A manual for university students. Konoc, Moscow. 98 pp. (Partially translated from Russian by Alexander Borisov.)

Erhardova, B. 1961. *Fascioloides magna* in Europe. Helminthol. 3: 91–106.

Erhardova-Kotrla, B. 1971. The occurrence of *Fascioloides magna* (Bassi, 1875) in Czechoslovakia. Czech. Acad. Sci., Prague. 155 pp.

Erwin, J. B. 1898. Report of the Acting Superintendent of the Yellowstone National Park to the Secretary of the Interior, 1898. Govt. Print. Off., Washington, D.C. 59 pp.

Essey, M. A. 1992a. Bovine tuberculosis in captive Cervidae in the United States. Pages 1–5 *in* M. A. Essey, ed., Bovine tuberculosis in Cervidae: Proc. of a symposium. Misc. Publ. No. 1,506, USDA Animal and Plant Health Inspect. Serv., Denver, Colorado. 71 pp.

———, ed. 1992b. Bovine tuberculosis in Cervidae: Proceedings of a symposium. Misc. Publ. No. 1,506, USDA Animal and Plant Health Inspect. Serv., Denver, Colorado. 71 pp.

Estes, J.A. 1966. Predators and ecosystem management Wildl. Soc. Bull. 24: 390–396.

Estes, R. D. 1974. Social organization of the African Bovidae. Pages 166–205 *in* V. Geist and F. Walther, eds., The Behavior of ungulates in relation to management. IUCN Publ. NS 24. Morges. 940 pp.

Eustace, C. D. 1967. Food habits, range use and relationships between elk and livestock in the Gravelly Mountains, Montana. M.S. Thesis, Montana State Univ., Bozeman. 55 pp.

Evans, K. E., compiler. 1996. Sharing common ground on western rangelands: Proceeding of a livestock/big game symposium; 1996 February 26–28; Sparks, NV. Gen.Tech.Rept. INT-GTR–343. U.S. Dept. Ag., For. Serv., Ogden, Utah. 164 pp.

Eveland, J. F., J. L. George, N. V. Hunter, D. M. Forney and R. L. Harrison. 1979. A preliminary evaluation of the ecology of the elk in Pennsylvania. Pages 145–151 *in* M. S. Boyce and L. D. Hayden-Wing, eds., North American elk: Ecology, behavior and management. Univ. Wyoming, Laramie. 294 pp.

Eveleth, D. F. and F. M. Bolin. 1955. Parasitic gastritis of elk. J. Wildl. Manage. 19(1): 152.

Ewers, J. C. 1939. Plains Indian painting. Stanford Univ. Press, Stanford, California. 84 pp.

———. 1954. The Indian trade of the upper Missouri River before Lewis and Clark: An interpretation. Missouri Hist. Soc. Bull. 10: 429–446.

———. 1955. The horse in Blackfoot Indian culture. Bull. 159. Bur. Amer. Ethnol., Washington, D.C. 374 pp.

———. 1958. The Blackfeet: Raiders on the northwestern Plains. Univ. Oklahoma Press, Norman. 345 pp.

———. 1968. Indian life on the upper Missouri. Univ. Oklahoma Press, Norman. 222 pp.

———. 1974. Ethnological report on the Blackfeet and Gros Ventre tribes of Indians. Pages 26–206 *in* J. C. Ewers, ed., Blackfeet Indians. Garland Publ., Inc., New York. 312 pp.

Fagan, B. M. 1995. Ancient North America. Rev. ed. Thames and Hudson, Inc., New York. 528 pp.

Fahey, J. 1974. The Flathead Indians. Univ. Oklahoma Press, Norman. 366 pp.

Fahey, Jr., G. C. and L. L. Berger. 1988. Carbohydrate nutrition of ruminants. Pages 269–297 *in* D. C. Church, ed., The ruminant animal: Digestive physiology and nutrition. Prentice Hall, Englewood Cliffs, New Jersey. 564 pp.

Failing, O. 1951. Pigeon River elk. Michigan Conservation 20: 4–6, 23.

Fairbanks, W. S. 1993. Birthdate, birthweight and survival in pronghorn fawns. J. Mamm. 74: 129–135.

Fairley, R. A., D. R. Cooper, W. G. Guilford and L. M. Schollum. 1986. Haemolytic disease associated with *Leptospira interrogans* serovar *pomona* in red deer calves (*Cervus elaphus*). New Zealand Vet. J. 34: 116–117.

Fairley, R. A., L. M. Schollum and D. K. Blackmore. 1984. Leptospirosis associated with serovars *hardjo* and pomona in red deer calves (*Cervus elaphus*). New Zealand Vet. J. 32: 76–78.

Fancy, S. G. and R. G. White. 1985. Incremental cost of activity. Pages 143–160 *in* R. J. Hudson and R. G. White, eds., Bioenergetics of wild herbivores. CRC Press, Inc., Boca Raton, Florida. 314 pp.

Fancy, S. G. and R. G. White. 1987. Energy expenditures for locomotion by barren-ground caribou. Can. J. Zool. 65: 122–128.

Fancy, S. G., J. M. Blanchard, D. R. Holleman, K. J. Kokjer and R. G. White. 1986. Validation of doubly labeled water method using a ruminant. Am. J. Physiol. 251: R143–R149.

Fancy, S. G., L. F. Pank, K. R. Whitten and W. L. Regelin. 1989. Seasonal movements of caribou in Arctic Alaska as determined by satellite. Can. J. Zool. 67: 644–650.

Fane, D., I. Jacknis and C. M. Breen. 1991. Objects of myth and memory. Univ. Washington Press, Seattle. 320 pp.

Fanning, A. 1992. *Mycobacterium bovis* infection in humans exposed to tuberculous elk. Pages 21–25 *in* M. A. Essey, ed., Bovine tuberculosis in Cervidae: Proc. of symposium. Miscellaneous Publication No. 1506. U.S. Dept. Ag., Animal, Plant Health Inspection Service, Denver, Colorado. 71 pp.

Farragher, J. M. 1992. Daniel Boone: The life and legend of an American pioneer. Henry Holt and Co., New York. 429 pp.

Fashingbauer, B. A. 1965. The elk in Minnesota. Pages 99–132 *in* J. B. Moyle, ed., Big game in Minnesota. Tech. Bull. No. 9. Minnesota Dept. Conserv., St. Paul. 231 pp.

Faunmap Working Group. 1994. FAUNMAP—A database documenting late Quaternary distributions of mammal species in the United States. Illinois State Mus. Sci. Pap. 25 (Volumes 1 and 2).

———. 1996. Spatial response of mammals to late Quaternary environmental fluctuations. Science 272(5,268): 1,601–1,606.

Fay, L. D. 1970. Skin tumors of the Cervidae. Pages 385–392 *in* J. W. Davis, L. H. Karstad and D. O. Trainer, eds., Infectious diseases of wild mammals. Iowa State Univ. Press, Ames, Iowa. 446 pp.

Fay, L. D. and J. N. Stuht. 1973. Meningeal worms in association with neurologic disease in Michigan wapiti. Annu. Conf. Wildl. Dis. Assoc., Univ.Connecticut, Storrs. 32 pp.

Fayer, R. 1970. *Sarcocystis*: Development in cultured avian and mammalian cells. Science 168: 1,104–1,108.

———. 1972. Gametogony of *Sarcocystis* sp. in cell culture. Science 175: 65–67.

Featherstonhaugh, G. W. 1835. Geological report of an examination made in 1834, of the elevated country between the Missouri and Red rivers. Gales and Seaton, Washington, D.C. 96 pp.

Feder, N. 1958. Plains hair and roach ornaments. Amer. Indian Hobbyist 6(9 and 10): 83–88.

———. 1962. Bottom tab leggings. Amer. Indian Trad. 8(4): 148–159.

Feder, N. and M. G. Chandler. 1961. Grizzly claw necklaces. Amer. Indian Trad. 8(1): 7–16.

Federal Lands Task Force. 1998. New approaches for managing federally administered lands. A Report to the Idaho State Board of Land Commissioners. Boise, Idaho. 62 pp.

Feest, C. F. 1978. Virginia Algonquians. Pages 253–270 *in* B. G. Trigger, ed., Northeast. Handbook of North American Indians. Vol. 15. Smithsonian Instit., Washington, D.C. 924 pp.

Feest, J. E. and C. F. Feest. 1978. Ottawa. Pages 772–786 *in* B. G. Trigger, ed., Northeast. Handbook of North American Indians. Vol. 15. Smithsonian Instit., Washington, D.C. 924 pp.

Fehrenbach, T. R. 1967. Elkdom U.S.A. Benevolent and Protective Order of Elks of the U.S.A. Benevolent and Protective Order of Elks, Chicago. 93 pp.

Feit, H. A. 1987. North American native hunting and management of moose populations. Swedish Wildl. Res. (Suppl. 1): 25–42.

Feltskog, E. N., ed. 1969. Parkman—the Oregon Trail. Univ. Wisconsin Press, Madison. 758 pp.

Fenneman, N. M. 1931. Physiography of western United States. McGraw-Hill Book Co., New York and London. 534 pp.

Fennessy, P. F. 1991. Velvet antler: the product and pharmacology. Proc. Deer Course for Veterinarians, 8: 169–180.

Fennessy, P. F. and J. M. Suttie. 1985. Antler growth: nutritional and endocrine factors. Pages 239–250 *in* P. F. Fennessy and K. R. Drew, eds., Biology of Deer Production. Bulletin No. 22. The Royal Soc. New Zealand.

Fennessy, P. F., G. H. Moore and I. D. Corson. 1981. Energy requirements of red deer. Proc. New Zealand Soc. Anim. Prod. 41: 167–173.

Fennessy, P. F., J. M. Suttie and M. W. Fisher. 1985. Reproductive physiology of male red deer. Pages 101–106 *in* Proc. of a deer course for veterinarians. Vol. 2. Deer Branch of the New Zealand Vet. Assoc., Ashburton.

Fennessy, P. F., J. M. Suttie, S. F. Crosbie, I. D. Corson, H. J. Elgar and K. R. Lapwood. 1988. Plasma LH and testosterone responses to gonadotrophin-releasing hormone in adult red deer *(Cervus elaphus)* stags during the antler cycle. J. Endocr. 117: 35–41.

Fennessy, P. F., J. M. Thompson and J. M. Suttie. 1991. Season and growth strategy in red deer: evolutionary implications and nutritional management. Pages 495–502 *in* L. A. Renecker and R. J. Hudson, eds., Wildlife production: conservation and sustainable development. AFES Misc. Pub. 91–6. Univ. Alaska, Fairbanks. 601 pp.

Fenton, W. N. 1978. Northern Iroquoian culture patterns. Pages 296–321 *in* B. G. Trigger, ed., Northeast. Handbook of North American Indians. Vol. 15. Smithsonian Instit. Press, Washington, D.C. 924 pp.

Ferguson, D. and N. Ferguson. 1983. Sacred cows at the public trough. Maverick Publ., Bend, Oregon. 250 pp.

Ferguson, M. A. D. and L. B. Keith. 1982. Influence of Nordic skiing on distribution of moose and elk in Elk Island National Park, Alberta. Can. Field Nat. 96: 69–78.

Ferguson, R. B. 1972. Bitterbrush topping; shrub response and cost factors. Res. Pap. INT–125. USDA For. Serv., Ogden, Utah. 11 pp.

Ferrel, C. M. 1962. Miscellaneous food habit studies. Calif. Fed. Aid Proj. W–52-R–6, Job 4. California Dept. Fish and Game, Sacramento.

———. 1963. Miscellaneous food habit studies. Calif. Fed. Aid Proj. W52–7, Job 4. California Dept. Fish and Game, Sacramento.

Ferrel, C. M. and H. R. Leach. 1950. Food habits of a California deer herd. Calif. Fish and Game 36: 235–240.

Festa-Bianchet, M. 1988. Birthdate and survival in bighorn lambs *(Ovis canadensis)*. J. Zool., London 214: 653–661.

Festa-Bianchet, M., J. T. Jorgenson and D. Reale. 2000. Early development, adult mass, and reproductive success in bighorn sheep. Behavioral Ecology 11: 633-639.

Ffolliott, P. and W. Clary. 1972. A selected and annotated bibiography of understory–overstory vegetation relationships. Bull. 198. Ag. Exp. Sta.Tech., Univ. Arizona, Tucson. 33 pp.

Field, R. A., F. C. Smith and W. G. Hepworth. 1973a. The mule deer carcass. Bull. 489. Univ. Wyoming Ag. Exp. Sta., Laramie. 6 pp.

———. 1973b. The elk carcass. Bull. 594. Univ. Wyoming Ag. Exp. Sta., Lararamie. 8 pp.

Field, R. A., F. C. Smith and W. G. Hepworth. 1974. Quality and quantity of meat from elk carcasses in Wyoming. J. Wildl. Manage. 38(4): 947.

Finger, S. E., I. L. Brisbin, Jr., M. H. Smith and D. F. Urbston. 1981. Kidney fat as a predictor of body condition in white-tailed deer. J. Wildl. Manage. 45: 964–968.

Finlayson, W. D. 1977. The Saugeen Culture: A Middle Woodland Manifestation in southwestern Ontario. Mercury 61, Ottawa.

Fischer, A., and H. Gossow. 1987. Untersuchungen zur raum-zeit-nutzung des rotwildes angesichts menschlicher storeinflusse unter besonderer berucksichtigung der wintersituation: fallstudie St. Anton am Arlberg. Centralblatt fur das gesamte forstwesen 104/4: 191–218

Fishbein, S. L. 1989. Yellowstone country: The enduring wonder. Nat. Geogr. Soc., Washington, D.C. 198 pp.

Fisher, M. W. and P. F. Fennessy. 1985. Reproductive physiology of female red deer and elk. *In* Proc. of a deer course for veterinarians. Deer Branch of the New Zealand Vet. Assoc. 2: 88–100.

Fisher, M. W., P. F. Fennessy and J. D. Milne. 1988. Effects of melatonin on seasonal physiology of red deer. Proc. New Zealand Soc. Anim. Prod. 48: 113–116.

Fistiani, A. 1991. First record of a fossil *Cervus elaphus* L., 1758 from Albania. Z. Saugetierkunde 56(4): 248–251.

Fitch, C. P. 1934. Report on the committee on Bang's disease project. Proc. US Livest. Sanit. Assoc. 38: 311–317.

Fitzgerald, W.R. 1982. Lest the beaver run loose: the early 17th century Christianson site and trends in historic neutral archaeology. Mercury 111, Ottawa.

Flannery, R. 1953. The Gros Ventres of Montana: Part I, social life. Anthro. Ser. No. 15. Catholic Univ. Press, Washington, D.C. 217 pp.

———. 1975. The Gros Ventres of Montana: Part I. Social life. The Catholic Univ. Press, Washington, D.C. 221 pp.

Flather, C. H. and K. Cordell. 1995. Outdoor recreation: historical and anticipated trends. Pages 3–16 *in* R. L. Knight and K. J. Gutzwiller, eds., Wildlife and recreationists. Island Press, Washington, D.C. 373 pp.

Flerov, K. K. 1950. Morfologiya i ekologiya oleneobraznykh v processee ikh evolucii. *In* Materialy po chetvert. periodu SSSR. 2: 50–69. Moskva-Leningrad: AN SSSR.

———. 1952a. Musk deer and deer: Fauna of the USSR, Vol. 2. Mammals. Vol. 1, No. 2. Acad. Sci. USSR. (Translation, U.S. Dept. Commerce, Washington, D.C.). 257 pp.

———. 1952b. Kabargy i oleni. Fauna Sssr, Mlekopityushtchie I. Vol. 2. Nov. Ser. No. 55. Moskva-Leningrad: Zool. Inst. AN SSSR. 256 pp.

Fletcher, A. C. 1882. The elk mystery or festival: Ogallala Sioux. Peabody Mus. Rept. 3: 276–288.

Fletcher, A. C. and F. La Flesche. 1972. The Omaha Tribe. Vol 2. Univ. Nebraska Press, Lincoln. 660 pp.

Fletcher, T. J. 1974. The timing of reproduction in red deer J. Zool. (London) 172: 363–367.

———. 1978. The induction of male sexual behavior in red deer *(Cervus elaphus)* by the administration of testosterone of hinds and estradiol–17-B to stags. Hormones and Behav. 11(1): 74–88.

———. 1982. Management problems and disease in farmed deer. Vet. Rec. 111: 219–223.

Fletcher, T. J. and R. V. Short. 1974. Restoration of libido in castrated red deer stag (*Cervus elaphus*) with Oestradiol–17b. Nature 248: 616–618.

Flint, R. F. 1971. Glacial and Quaternary geology. John Wiley and Sons, Inc., New York. 892 pp.

Flook, D. R. 1962. Range relationships of some ungulates native to Banff and Jasper National Parks, Alberta. Pages 11–14 *in* Symposium on grazing. British Ecol. Soc., Bangor, North Wales.

———. 1964. Range relationships of some ungulates native to Banff and Jasper National Parks, Alberta. Pages 119–128 *in* D. J. Crisp, ed., Grazing in terrestrial and marine environments symposiumBritish Ecol. Soc. No. 4. Blackwell Sci. Publ., Oxford, U.K.

———. 1970a. A study of sex differential in the survival of wapiti. Can. Wildl. Serv. Rept., Ser. No. 11. Queens Printer, Ottawa, Ontario. 71 pp.

———. 1970b. Causes and implications of an observed sex differential in the survival of wapiti. Can. Wildl. Serv. Bull. Rept. Ser. 11. Can. Wildl. Serv., Ottawa. 71 pp.

Flook, D. R. and J. E. Stenton. 1969. Incidence and abundance of certain parasites in wapiti in the national parks of the Canadian Rockies. Can. J. Zool. 47: 795–803.

Flueck, von W. T. and J. M. Smith-Flueck. 1993. Über das in Argentinen angesiedelte Rotwild (*Cervus elaphus* L., 1758): Verbreitung und Tendenzen. Z. Jagdwiss. 9(3): 153–160.

Foldes, L. and H. Brull. 1972. Weidwerk der Gegenwart. Verlag Paul Parey, Hamburg and Berlin. 237 pp.

Folk, G. E., Jr. 1966. Introduction to environmental physiology. Lea and Febiger, Philadelphia, Pennsylvania. 308 pp.

Folkman, W. S. 1963. Levels and sources of forest fire prevention knowledge of California hunters. Res. Pap. PSW-II. USDA For. Serv., Berkeley, California. 22 pp.

Follis, T. B. 1972. Reproduction and hematology of the Cache Creek elk herd. Res. Publ. No. 72–8. Utah Div. Wildl. Resour., Salt Lake City. 147 pp.

Follis, T. B. and N. V. Hancock. 1975. Quadruplet embryos in an aged elk. J. Zoo An. Med. 6: 9–10.

Follis, T. B. and J. J. Spillett. 1974. Winter pregnancy rates and subsequent cow/calf ratios in elk. J. Wildl. Manage. 38(4): 789–791.

Fonda, J. H. 1907. Early Wisconsin. Pages 205–284 *in* L. C. Draper, ed., Collections of the State Historical Society of Wisconsin. Vol. 5. 432 pp. (Reprint of 1868 original issue.)

Fontana, F. and M. Rubini. 1990. Chromosomal evolution in Cervinae. Biosystems 24: 157–174.

Foos, K. M. 1989. Isolation of *Pilobolus* spp. from the northern elk herd in Yellowstone National Park. J. Wildl. Dis. 25: 302–304.

Ford, R. I. 1983. Inter-Indian exchange in the Southwest. Pages 711–722 *in* A. Ortiz, ed., Southwest. Vol. 10. Handbook of North American Indians. Smithsonian Instit. Press, Washington, D.C. 868 pp.

Ford-Robertson, F. C., ed. 1971. Terminology of forest science, technology practice and products. English language version. The Multilingual For. Terminol. Ser. No. 1. Soc. Amer. Foresters, Washington, D.C. 349 pp.

Forest and Stream. 1876. Large game in the territories. Forest and Stream 7(10): 152.

Forest Ecosystem Management Assessment Team. 1993. Forest ecosystem management: An ecological, economic and social assessment. USDA For. Serv., U.S. Dept. Commerce, National Oceanic and Atmospheric Administration, National Marine Fisheries Service, USDI Bureau of Land Managment, U.S. Fish and Wildlife Service, National Park Service and U.S. Environmental Portection Agency, Portland, Oregon.

Foreyt, W. J. 1981. Trematodes and cestodes. Pages 237–265 *in* W. R. Davidson, F. A. Hayes, V. F. Nettles and F. E. Kellogg, eds., Diseases and parasites of white-tailed deer. Misc. Publ. No. 7, Tall Timbers Res. Sta., Tallahassee, Florida.

———. 1993. Efficacy of in-feed formulation ivermectin against *Psoroptes* sp. in bighorn sheep. J. Wildl. Dis. 29: 85–89.

———. 1995. Experimental infections of *Sarcocystis* spp. in Rocky Mountain elk (*Cervus elaphus*) calves. J. Wildl. Dis. 31: 462–466.

———. 1996a. Susceptibility of bighorn sheep (*Ovis canadensis*) to experimentally-induced *Fascioloides magna* infections. J. Wildl. Dis. 32: 556–559.

———. 1996b. Mule deer (*Odocoileus hemionus*) and elk (*Cervus elaphus*) as experimental definitive hosts for *Fascioloides magna*. J. Wildl. Dis. 32: 603–606.

Foreyt, W. J. and J. E. Lagerquist. 1994. Experimental infections of *Eimeria wapiti* and *E. zuernii*-like oocysts in Rocky Mountain elk (*Cervus elaphus*) calves. J. Wildl. Dis. 30: 466–469.

Foreyt, W. J. and A. C. Todd. 1976. Development of the large American liver fluke, *Fascioloides magna*, in white-tailed deer, cattle and sheep. J. Parasitol. 62: 26–32.

Formozov, A. N. 1946. Snow cover as an integral factor of the environment and its importance in the ecology of mammals and birds. Fauna and flora of the USSR, New Series, Zoology, 5 (XX). Moscow Soc. Naturalists. Translated from Russian by W. Prychodko. Occas. Pap. 1. Boreal Inst., Univ. Alberta, Edmonton. 176 pp.

Foster, J. W. 1873. Prehistoric races of the United States of America. S. C. Griggs and Co., Chicago, Illinois. 415 pp.

Fowler, C. S. 1986. Subsistence. Pages 64–97 *in* W. L. D'Azevedo, ed., Great Basin. Vol. 11. Handbook of North American Indians. Smithsonian Instit. Press, Washington, D.C. 852 pp.

Fowler, C. W. 1981. Density dependence as related to life history strategy. Ecology 62: 602–610.

———. 1987. A review of density dependence in populations of large mammals. Pages 401–411 *in* H. H. Genoways, ed., Current Mammalogy. Vol. 1. Plenum, New York.

Fowler, G. H. 1894. Notes on some specimens of antlers of the fallow deer showing continuous variation and the effects of total or partial castration. Proc. Zool. Soc. London: 485–494.

Fox, H. 1928. Parasites. Rept. Lab. and Mus. Comp. Path. Zool. Soc., Philadelphia. Pages 31–33.

Frachtenberg, L. J. 1916. Quileute ethnology: Luipush, Washington. Field notebook no. 30 (W3a5) [Freeman no. 3,177]. Amer. Philos. Soc. Lib., Philadelphia, Pennsylvania.

Franchere, G. 1904. Narrative of a voyage to the northwest coast, 1811–1814. Pages 167–410 *in* R. G. Thwaites, ed., Early western travels, 1748–1846. Vol. 6. The A. H. Clark, Co., Cleveland, Ohio.

Frandson, R. D. and E. H. Whitten. 1981. Anatomy and physiology of farm animals. 3rd ed. Lea & Febiger, Philadelphia, Pennsylvania. 553 pp.

Frank, D. A. and S. J. McNaughton. 1992. The ecology of plants, large mammalian herbivores and drought in Yellowstone National Park. Ecology 73: 2,043–2,058.

Frank, J., T. Griffin, A. J. Thomson, J. P. Cross, G. S. Buchan and C. G. Mackintosh. 1991. The impact of domestication on red deer immunity and disease resistance. Pages 120–125 *in* R. D. Brown, ed., The biology of deer. Springer-Verlag, New York.

Frankenberger, Z. 1951. Prve zacatky vyvoje parohu u Cervidu. Biol. Listy, Suppl. 2: 127–147.

———. 1953. Studie o zubech cervidu, 2. Vyvoj mlecnych kelcu u jelena (*Cerrus elaphus* L.). Cs. Morfologie 1(2): 115–133.

———. 1954. Interstitialni bunky jelena (*Cervus elaphus* L.). Cs. Morfologie 2(1): 36–41.

———. 1957. Cirkumanalni a cirkumgenitalni zlazy nasich Cervidu. Cs. Morfologie 5(3): 255–265.

———. 1959. Une note sur le development des os metacarpiens chez les Cervidae. Cs. Morfologie 7(4): 363–374.

———. 1961. Some remarks on the mechanism of the shedding of the antlers in the deer. Cs. Morfologie 9(1): 41–45.

Franklin, W. L. and J. W. Lieb. 1979. The social organization of a sedentary population of North American elk: A model for understanding other populations. Pages 185–198 *in* M. S. Boyce and L. D. Hayden-Wing, eds., North American elk: Ecology, behavior and management. Univ. Wyoming, Laramie. 294 pp.

Franklin, W. L., A. S. Mossman and M. Dole. 1975. Social organization and home range of Roosevelt elk. J. Mammal. 56(1): 102–118.

Franson, J. C. and B. L. Smith. 1988. Septicemic pasteurellosis in elk (*Cervus elaphus*) on the United States National Elk Refuge, Wyoming. J. Wildl. Dis. 24: 715–717.

Franzmann, A. W. 1978. Moose. Pages 67–82 *in* J. L. Schmidt and D. L. Gilbert, eds., Big game of North America: Ecology and management. Stackpole Books, Harrisburg, Pennsylvania. 512 pp.

———. 1985. Assessment of nutritional status. Pages 239–260 *in* R. J. Hudson and R. G. White, eds., Bioenergetics of wild herbivores. CRC Press, Inc., Boca Raton, Florida. 314 pp.

Franzmann, A. W. and C. C. Schwartz. 1997. Ecology and management of the North American moose. Smithsonian Press, Washington, D.C. 733 pp.

Franzmann, A. W., A. Flynn and P. D. Arneson. 1975. Serum corticoid levels relative to handling stress in Alaskan moose. Can. J. Zool. 53(10): 1,424–1,426.

Fraser, H. M. and A. S. McNeilly. 1982. Effect of chronic immunoneutralization of thyrotropin-releasing hormone on the hypothalmic-pituitary-thyroid axis, prolactin and reproductive function in the ewe. Endocrinology 111: 1,964–1,973.

Freddy, D. J. 1977. Estimating survival rates of elk and developing techniques to estimate population size. Fed. Aid Wildl. Restor., Job Prog. Rept., Proj. W–153-R–10. Colorado Dept. Wildl., Denver. 25 pp.

———. 1985. Quantifying capacity of winter ranges to support deer—evaluation of thermal cover used by deer. Pages 13–36 *in* Colorado Div. Wildl., Wildl. Res. Rept., Denver, Co.

———. 1987a. Effect of elk harvest systems on elk breeding biology. Colorado Div. Wildl. Res. Rept. 01-03-047. Fort Collins, Colorado. 20 pp.

———. 1987b. The White River elk herd: a perspective, 1960–85. Colorado Div. Of Wildl. Tech. Pub. No. 37. Fort Collins. 64 pp.

French, C. E., L. C. McEwen, N. D. Magruder, R. H. Ingram and R. W. Swift. 1955. Nutritional requirements of white-tailed deer for growth and antler development. Bull. 600. Pennsylvania Ag. Exp. Sta., State College. 50 pp.

Freudenberger, D. O., C. J. Burns, K. Toyokawa and T. N. Barry. 1994a. Digestion and rumen metabolism of red clover and perennial rye grass/white clover forages by red deer. J. Ag. Sci. 122: 115–120.

Freudenberger, D. O., K. Toyakawa, T. N. Barry, A. J. Ball and J. M. Suttie. 1994b. Seasonality in digestion and rumen metabolism in red deer (*Cervus elaphus*) fed on a forage diet. Brit. J. Nutr. 71: 489–499.

Freundova, D. 1955. Stitna zlaza jelena (*Cervus elaphus* L.) a jeji souvislost s pohlavnim cyklem. Cs. Morfologie 3(3): 205–211.

Frevert, W. 1959. Rominten. Munich: Bayerischer Landwirtschufts Verlag. 227 pp.

———. 1977. Rominten. Bayerischer Landwirtschafts Verlag Munich. 225 pp.

Frick, C. 1937. Homed ruminants of North America. Amer. Mus. Natur. Hist. Bull. 69: 1–699.

Fried, B. M., R. M. Adams, R. P. Berrens and O. Bergland. 1995. Willingness to pay for a change in elk hunting quality. Wildl. Soc. Bull. 23: 680–686.

Friedel, B. A. and R. J. Hudson. 1993. Productive performance of farmed wapiti. North American Elk, Summer issue: 9–11.

Friedel, B. A. and R. J. Hudson. 1994. Productivity of farmed wapiti in Alberta (*Cervus elaphus canadensis*). Can. J. Anim. Sci. 74: 297–303.

Friederichs, K. 1943. Uber den Begriff "Umwelt" in der Biologie. Acta Biotheor. 7: 142–162.

———. 1950. Umwelt als Stufenbegriff und als Wirklichkeit. Stud. Gen. 3: 70–74.

———. 1957. Der Gegenstand der Okologie. Stud. Gen. 10: 112–124.

Frisina, M. R. 1986. Preliminary evaluation of elk habitat use within a three-pasture rest-rotation grazing system. Proc. Montana Acad. Sci. 46: 27–36.

———. 1992. Elk habitat use within a rest rotation grazing system. Rangelands. 14(2): 93–96.

Frisina, M. R. and J. M. Mariani. 1995. Wildlife and livestock as elements of grassland ecosystems. Rangelands 17: 23–25.

Frisina, M. R. and F. G. Morin. 1991. Grazing private and public land to improve the Fleecer Elk Winter Range. Rangelands. 13: 291–294.

Frison, G. C. 1967. The Piney Creek sites, Wyoming. Univ. Wyoming Publ. 33(1): 1–92.

———. 1971. Shoshonean antelope procurement in the Upper Green River Basin, Wyoming. Plains Anthro. 16: 258–284.

———. 1978. Prehistoric hunters of the high plains. Academic Press, New York. 457 pp.

Frison, G. C. and B. A. Bradley. 1981. Fluting of Folsom projectile points: Archeological evidence. Lithic Tech., vol. 1, no. 1. 12 pp.

Frison, G. C. and D. N. Walker, eds. 1984. The Dead Indian Creek site: An Archaic occupation in the Absoroka Mountains of northeastern Wyoming. Wyoming Archaeol. 27(1–2): 11–122.

Frodelius, R. B. 1973. Determination of anti-hunt organizations by content analysis of their literature. Ph.D. Thesis, New York State Univ., Syracuse. 259 pp.

Frölich, K. 1995. Bovine virus diarrhea and mucosal disease in free-ranging and captive deer (Cervidae) in Germany. J. Wildl. Dis. 31: 247–250.

Frost, L. A. 1964. The Custer album. Superior Publishing Co., Seattle. 192 pp.

Frye, G. H. and R. R. Hillman. 1997. National Cooperative Brucellosis Eradication Program. Pages 79–85 *in* E. T. Thorne, M. S. Boyce, P. Nicoletti and T. J. Kreeger, eds., Brucellosis, bison, elk and cattle in the Greater Yellowstone Area: defining the problem, exploring solutions. Wyoming Game and Fish Dept. and Greater Yellowstone Interagency Brucellosis Committee, Cheyenne. 219 pp.

Fryxell, J. M., J. Greever and A.R.E. Sinclair. 1988. Why are migrating ungulates so abundant? Amer. Nat. 131: 781–798.

Fundaburk, E. L. 1958. Southeastern Indians—Life portraits. Emma Lila Fundaburk, Publisher, Luverne, Alabama. 136 pp.

Furst, A. 1987. Die ernahrung des rotwildes im winter-winterfutterung. Anblick 9: 340–344.

———. 1990 Erfahrungen mit einem forstlich abgestimmten zonierungskonzept der rotwildbewirtschaftung in der Oststeiermark. Page 23–26 *in* H. Gossow, E. Donaubauer, F. Reimoser and J. Dieberger, eds., Tagungsbericht IURFO-Symposium regionalplanungskonzept, fur eine forstlich integrierte Schalenwildbewirtschaftung im Hoch- und Mittelgebirge. BOKU-reports on Wildlife Research and Game Management 1. Institut for Wildbiologie und Jagdwirtschaft, Universitat fur Bodenkultur, Wien.

Futuyama, D. J. 1979. Evolutionary biology. Sinaur Associates Inc., Sunderland, Massachusetts. 565 pp.

Fyffe, J. J. and M. J. Fyffe. 1995. Triplets in red deer (*Cervus elaphus*). Austr. Vet. J. 72: 469–470.

Fyvie, A. 1969. Manual of common parasites, diseases and anomalies of wildlife in Ontario. 2nd ed. Ontario Dept. Lands and For., Toronto. 102 pp.

Gabrielson, I. N. 1941. Wildlife conservation. MacMillan, New York. 250 pp.

Gaffney, W. S. 1941. The effects of winter elk browsing, south fork of the Flathead River, Montana. J. Wildl. Manage. 5(4): 427–453.

Gaillard, J. M., D. Delorme and J. M. Julien. 1993. Effects of cohort, sex and birth date on body development of roe deer (*Capreolus capreolus*) fawns. Oecologia 84: 57–61.

Gambaryan, P. P. 1974. How animals run. John Wiley and Sons, New York. 367 pp.

Gander, H. and P. Ingold. 1997. Reactions of male alpine chamois (*Rupicapra r. rupicapra*) to hikers, joggers and mountain bikers. Biol. Conserv. 79: 107–109

Gao, X. and D. Hu. 1993. Status of wild and farmed red deer in Xinjiang. Pages 159–164 *in* N. Ohtaishi and H.-I. Sheng, eds., Deer of China. Elsevier, New York. 418 pp.

Gard, W. 1959. The great buffalo hunt. Alfred A. Knopf, New York. 324 pp.

———. 1968. The great buffalo hunt. Univ. Nebraska Press, Lincoln. 336 pp.

Gardner, R. B. 1971. Forest road standards as related to economics and the environment. Res. Note INT–145. USDA For. Serv., Ogden, Utah. 4 pp.

Garner, D. L. and M. L. Wilton. 1993. The potential role of winter tick (*Dermacentor albipictus*) in the dynamics of a south central Ontario moose population. Alces 29: 169–173.

Garner, D. L., H. B. Underwood and W. F. Porter. 1995. The use of modern infrared thermography for wildlife population surveys. J. Environ. Manage. 19: 233–238.

Garrison, G. A. 1949. Uses and modifications of the "moosehorn" crown closure estimation. J. Forestry 47: 733–735.

Garrison, G. A. and J. G. Smith. 1974. Habitat of grazing animals. Pages Pl–P10 *In* O. P. Cramer, ed., Environmental effects of forest residues management in the Pacific Northwest. Gen. Tech. Rept. PNW–24. USDA For. Serv., Portland, Oregon.

Garrison, G. A., A. J. Bjugstad, D. A. Duncan, M. E. Lewis and D. R. Smith. 1977. Vegetation and environmental features of forest and range ecosystems. Ag. Handb. No. 475. USDA For. Serv., Washington, D.C. 68 pp.

Garrott, R. A., J. G. Cook, J. G. Berardinelli, P. J. White, S. Cherry and D. B. Vagnoni. 1997. Urinary allantoin: Creatinine ratios as a noninvasive dietary index for elk. Can. J. Zool. 75: 1,519–1,525.

Garrott, R. A., P. J. White, D. B. Vagnoni and D. M. Heisey. 1996. Purine derivatives in snow-urine as a dietary index for free-ranging elk. J. Wildl. Manage. 60: 735–743.

Garth, T. R. 1953. Atsugewi ethnography. Univ. of California Anthropol. Rec., Berkeley. 14(2): 129–212.

———. 1978. Atsugewi. Pages 236–248 *in* R. F. Heizer, ed., California. Handbook of North American Indians. Vol. 8. Smithsonian Instit., Washington, D.C. 800 pp.

Garton, G. A. and W. R. H. Duncan. 1971. Fatty acid composition and in-

tramolecular structure of triglycerides from adipose tissues of the red deer and the reindeer. J. Sci. Fd. Ag. 22: 29–33.

Garton, G. A., W. R. H., Duncan and E. H. McEwan. 1971. Composition of adipose tissue triglycerides of the elk (*Cervus canadensis*), caribou (*Rangifer tarandus groenlandicus*), moose (*Alces alces*) and white-tailed deer (*Odocoileus virginianus*). Can. J. Zool. 49: 1,159–1,162.

Gary, H. L. 1975. Watershed management problems and opportunities for the Colorado front range ponderosa pine zone: the status of our knowledge. Res. Pap. RM–139. USDA For. Serv., Fort Collins, Colorado. 32 pp.

Gasaway, W. A. and J. W. Coady. 1974. Review of energy requirements and rumen fermentation in moose and other ruminants. Naturaliste Canadien 101: 227–262.

Gasaway, W. C., R. D. Boertje, D. V. Grangaard, D. G. Kelleyhouse, R. O. Stephenson and D. G. Larsen. 1992. The role of predation in limiting moose at low densities in Alaska and Yukon and implications for conservation. Wildlife Monographs Number 120. 59 pp.

Gates, C. C. and R.J. Hudson. 1978. Energy costs of locomotion in wapiti. Acta Theriol. 23: 365–370.

———. 1979. Effects of posture and activity on metabolic responses of wapiti to cold. J. Wildl. Manage. 43(2): 564567.

———. 1981. Weight dynamics of wapiti in the boreal forest. Acta Theriol. 26: 407–418.

Gates, D. M. 1962. Energy exchange in the biosphere. Harper and Row, New York. 151 pp.

Gatesy, J., D. Yelon, R. DeSalle and E. S. Vrba. 1992. Phylogeny of the Bovidae (Artiodactyla, Mammalia), based on mitochondrial DNA sequences. Mol. Biol. Evol. 9(3): 433–446.

Gauch, H. G., Jr. 1973. The relationship between sample similarity and ecological distance. Ecology 54: 618–622.

Gause, G. F. 1934a. Experimental analysis of Vito Volterra's mathematical theory of the struggle for existence. Science 79: 1,617.

———. 1934b. The struggle for existence. Williams and Wilkins Publ. Co., Baltimore. 163 pp.

Gebhard, D. 1974. Indian art of the northern Plains. Standard Print. of Santa Barbara, Inc., Santa Barbara, California. 99 pp.

Gee, E.P. 1965. Report on the status of the Kashmir stag: October 1965. J. Bombay Natur. Hist. Soc. 62(3): 379–393.

Geiger, R. 1965. The climate near the ground. Harvard Univ. Press, Cambridge, Massachusetts. 611 pp.

Geis, A. F. 1954. The food requirements and relative digestibility of a variety of winter diets fed to elk (*Cervus canadensis nelsoni*) under controlled conditions. M. S. Thesis, Univ. Montana, Missoula. 68 pp.

Geist, V. 1963. On the behaviour of the North American moose *Alces alces andersoni*, Peterson 1950, in British Columbia. Behaviour 20: 377–416.

———. 1966a. Ethological observations on some North American cervids. Zoll. Beitrage (N.F.) 12: 219–250.

———. 1966b. The evolution of horn-like organs. Behavior 27: 175–214.

———. 1971a. On the relation of social evolution and dispersal in ungulates during the Pleistocene, with emphasis on the Old World deer and the genus Bison. Quat. Res. 1(3): 283–315.

———. 1971b. Is big game harassment harmful? Oil Week 14 (June): 12–13.

———. 1971c. Mountain sheep. A study in behavior and evolution. Univ. Chicago Press, Chicago, Illinois. 383 pp.

———. 1971d. A behavioural approach to the management of wild ungulates. Page 413–424 *in* E. Duffy and A. S. Watt, eds., The scientific management of animal and plant communities for conservation: 11th Symp. British Ecol. Soc., Blackwell Sci. Publ., Oxford, U.K.

———. 1971e. Bighorn sheep biology. Wildl. Soc. News 136: 61.

———. 1974a. On the relationship of social evolution and ecology in ungulates. Amer. Zool. 14: 205–220.

———. 1974b. On the relationship of ecology and behaviour in the evolution of ungulates: Theoretical considerations. Pages 235–246 *in* V. Geist and F. Walther, eds., The behaviour of ungulates and its relation to management. IUCN New Ser. Publ. No. 24, Vol. 1. IUCN, Morges, Switzerland. 511 pp.

———. 1974c. On the evolution of reproductive potential in moose. Canadian Naturalist 101: 527–537.

———. 1978a. Behavior. Pages 283–296 *in* J. L. Schmidt and D. L. Gilbert, eds., Big game of North America: Ecology and management. Stackpole Books, Inc., Harrisburg, Pennsylvania. 512 pp.

———. 1978b. Life strategies, human evolution, environmental design. Towards a biological theory of health. Springer-Verlag, New York. 495 pp.

———. 1978c. On weapons, combat and ecology. Pages 1–30 *in* L. Krames, ed., Advances in the study of communication and effect. Vol. 4. Plenum, New York.

———. 1981. Behavior: Adaptive strategies in mule deer. Pages 157–223 *in* O. C. Wallmo, ed., Mule and black-tailed deer of North America. Univ. Nebraska Press, Lincoln. 605 pp.

———. 1982. Adaptive behavioral strategies. Pages 219–277 *in* J. W. Thomas and D. E. Toweill, eds., Elk of North America: Ecology and management. Stackpole Books, Harrisburg, Pennsylvania. 698 pp.

———. 1985. Game ranching: Threat to wildlife conservation in North America. Wildl. Soc. Bull. 13(4): 594–598.

———. 1986a. New evidence of high frequency antler wounding in cervids. Can. J. Zool. 64: 380–384.

———. 1986b. The paradox of the great Irish stags. Natur. Hist. 95(3): 4–64.

———. 1986c. Super antlers and pre-world war II European research. Wildl. Soc. Bull. 14: 91–94 .

———. 1987a. On speciation in Ice Age mammals, with special reference to cervids and caprids. Can. J. Zool. 65(5): 1,067–1,084.

———. 1987b. Bergmann's rule is invalid. Can. J. Zool. 65: 1,035–1,038.

———. 1988. How markets in wildlife meat and parts, and the sale of hunting privileges, jeopardize wildlife conservation. Conserv. Biol. 2: 15–26.

———. 1989a. Legal trafficking and paid hunting threatens conservation. Trans. N. Amer. Wildl. and Natur. Resour. Conf. 54: 171–178.

———. 1989b. Environmentally guided phenotype plasticity in mammals and some of its consequences to theoretical and applied biology. Pages 153–176 *in* M. N. Burton, ed., Alternative life-history styles of animals. Kluwer Academic Publ., Dordrect, The Netherlands. 616 pp.

———. 1990a. Bergmann's rule is invalid: A reply to J. D. Paterson. Can. J. Zool. 68: 1,613–1,615.

———. 1990b. Elk speciation: Genetics or environment? Bugle Fall: 101–104, 106–108.

———. 1991a. Bones of contention revisited: Did antlers enlarge with sexual selection as a consequence of neonatal security strategies? Appl. Animal Behavior Sci. 29: 453–469.

———. 1991b. Deer ranching for products and paid hunting: Threat to conservation and biodiversity by luxury markets. Pages 554–561 *in* R. D. Brown, ed., The biology of deer. Springer-Verlag, New York.

———. 1991c. The big bull in the breeding biology of elk. Pages 6–9 *in* A. G. Christensen, L. J. Lyon and T. N. Lonner, eds., Elk vulnerability Symp. Montana State Univ., Bozeman. 330 pp.

———. 1991d. Phantom subspecies: The wood bison Bison bison "athabascae" Rhoads 1897 is not valid taxon, but an ecotype. Arctic 44(1): 283–300.

———. 1991e. Elk country. Northwood Press, Minocqua, Minnessota. 175 pp.

———. 1991f. On the taxonomy of the giant sheep (*Ovis ammon* Linnaeus, 1766). Can. J. Zool. 69(3): 706–723.

———. 1991g. Game-ranching: Menace to the survival of the North American elk. Pages 292–295 *in* A. G. Christensen, L. J. Lyon and T. N. Lonner, compilers, Proc Elk Vulnerability Symp., Montana State Univ., Bozeman.

———. 1991h. Spongiform encephalopathy (BSE) in elk from the western U.S.A. Unpubl ms. on file, Univ. Calgary, Alberta. 5 pp.

———. 1992. Endangered species and the law. Nature 357: 247–276.

———. 1993. Great achievements, great expectations: Successes of North American wildlife management. Pages 47–72 *in* A. W. L. Hawley, ed., Commercialization and wildlife management: Dancing with the devil. Krieger Publ. Co., Malabar, Florida. 124 pp.

———. 1994. Wildlife conservation as wealth. Nature 368(6,471): 491–492.

———. 1995a. North American policies of wildlife conservation. Pages 77–129 *in* V. Geist and I. McTaggart-Cowan, eds., Wildlife conservation policy. Detselig Enterprises, Ltd., Calgary, Alberta. 308 pp.

———. 1995b. Wildlife conservation American style creates biodiversity and wealth. Pages 279–282 *in* J. A. Bissonette and P. R. Krausman, eds., Integrating people and wildlife for a sustainable future. Proc. First International Wildlife Management Congress. The Wildl. Soc., Bethesda, Maryland. 715 pp.

———. 1996. Bison nation. Voyageur Press, Stillwater, Minnesota. 144 pp.

———. 1998. Deer of the world. Their evolution, behavior and ecology. Stackpole Books, Mechanicsburg, Pennsylvania. 448 pp.

———. In press. On the reproductive strategies in ungulates and some problems of adaptation. Proc. 2nd Int. Congress of Syst. and Evol. Biol.

Geist, V. and M. Bayer. 1988. Sexual dimorphism in the Cervidae and its relation to habitat. J. Zool. 214: 45–54.

Geist, V. and P. T. Bromley. 1978. Why deer shed antlers. Zs. Saugetierkunde 43: 223–232.

Geist, V. and M. H. Francis. 1991. Elk country. NorthWord Press, Inc., Minocqua, Wisconsin. 175 pp.

Geist, V. and R. Petocz. 1977. Bighorn sheep in winter: Do rams maximize reproductive fitness by spatial and habitat segregation from ewes? Can. J. Zool. 55(11): 1,802–1,810.

Gelbke, V. 1973. Materialuntersuchungen an Hirschgeweiben. Saugetierkdl. Mitt. 21(4): 348–359.

Gennadius, J. 1910. Greece. Pages 173–200 *in* F. G. Aflalo, ed., Sport in Europe. E. P. Dutton and Co., New York. 483 pp.

George, J. L. 1974. Pennsylvania elk. Pennsylvania For. Resour. No. 13. Coop. Ext. Serv., State College, Pennsylvania. 4 pp.

Georgiadis, N. 1985. Growth patterns, sexual dimorphism and reproduction in African ruminants. Afr. J. Ecol. 23: 75–87.

Geptner, V. G. and V. I. Tsalkin. 1947. Oleni SSSR. Izdat. Mogoobschchest. Prirody, Moskva. 176 pp.

Gerhardt, K. L., R. G. White, R. D. Cameron and D. E. Russell. 1996. Estimating fat content of caribou from body condition scores. J. Wildl. Manage. 60: 713–718.

Gerstell, R. 1936. The elk in Pennsylvania—its extermination and reintroduction. Pennsylvania Game News 7(7): 6–7, 26.

———. 1937. Winter deer losses. Pennsylvania Game News 8(7): 18–21.

Gese, E. M. and S. Grothe. 1995. Analysis of coyote predation on deer and elk during winter in Yellowstone National Park, Wyoming. Am. Midl. Nat. 133: 36–43.

Ghiselin, M. R. 1974. A radical solution to the species problem. Syst. Zool. 23(4): 536–544.

Giacometti, N. 1992. Nahrungsbedarf des hirschwildes im winter unter besonderer berucksichtigung der winterlichen asungsaufnahme im ratiken. Bundnerwald 3: 6–11.

Gibbs, E. P. J. and M. J. P. Lawman. 1977. Infection of British deer and farm animals with epizootic hemorrhagic disease of deer virus. J. Comp. Pathol. 87: 335–343.

Gibson, H. E. 1940. Animals in the writings of Shang. Pages 169–179 *in* A. deC. Sowerby, ed., Nature in Chinese art. The John Day Co., New York. 203 pp.

Gidley, J. W. and C. L. Gazin. 1938. The Pleistocene vertebrate fauna from Cumberland Cave, Maryland. Bull. U.S. Nat. Mus. 171 pp.

Gilbert, B. M. 1980. The Plains setting. Pages 8–16 *in* W. R. Wood and M. Liberty, eds., Anthropology on the Great Plains. Univ. Nebraska Press, Lincoln. 306 pp.

Gilbert, D. L. 1975. Natural resources and public relations. The Wildl. Soc., Washington, D.C. 320 pp.

———. 1978a. Evolution and taxonomy. Pages 1–9 *in* J. L. Schmidt and D. L. Gilbert, eds., Big game of North America: Ecology and management. Stackpole Books, Harrisburg, Pennsylvania. 494 pp.

———. 1978b. Sociological considerations in management. Pages 409–416 *in* J. L. Schmidt and D. L. Gilbert, eds., Big game of North America: Ecology and management. Stackpole Books, Inc., Harrisburg, Pennsylvania 512 pp.

Gilbert, F. F. 1993. The vision: Wildlife management in North America. Pages 23–33 *in* A. W. L. Hawley, ed., Commercialization and wildlife management. Krieger Publ. Co., Malabar, Florida. 124 pp.

Gilbert, F. F. and M. C. Bateman. 1983. Some effects of winter shelter conditions on white-tailed deer, *Odocoileus virginianus,* fawns. Canad. Field Natur. 97: 391–400.

Gilbert, P. F., O. C. Wallmo and R. B. Gill. 1970. Effect of snow depth on mule deer in Middle Park, Colorado. J. Wildl. Manage. 34: 15–23.

Giles, R.H., Jr. 1969. Population manipulation. Pages 521–526 *in* R.H. Giles, Jr., ed., Wildlife management techniques, 3rd ed. The Wildl. Soc., Washington, D.C. 623 pp.

Gill, J. D., J. W. Thomas, W. M. Healy, J. C. Pack and H. R. Sanderson. 1975. Comparison of seven forest types for game in West Virginia. J. Wildl. Manage. 39(4): 762–768.

Gill, M. 1991 Modelling nutrient supply and utilization by ruminants. Pages 225–236 *in* W. Haresign and D. J. A. Cole, eds., Recent advances in animal nutrition. Academic Press, New York.

Gill, R.B. and L.H. Carpenter. 1985. Winter feeding—a good idea? Proc. West. Assoc. Game and Fish Agen. 65: 57–66.

Gill, R. B., L. H. Carpenter, R. M. Bartmann, D. L. Baker and G. G. Schoonveld. 1983. Fecal analysis to estimate mule deer diets. J. Wildl. Manage. 47: 902–915.

Gill, R. M. A. 1986. Der gegenwartige stand und die bewirtschaftung des europaischen rotwildes. Pages 9–24 *in* S. Linn, ed., Rotwild-cerf rouge-red deer. Proc. CIC Symposium 1986 Munchen.

Gillespie, B. C. 1981. Major fauna in the traditional economy. Pages 15–18 *in* J. Helm, ed., Subarctic. Vol. 6. Handbook of North American Indians. Smithsonian Instit. Press, Washington, D.C. 837 pp.

Gillingham, M. P. and F. L. Bunnell. 1989. Effects of learning on food selection and searching behaviour of deer. Can. J. Zool. 67: 24–32.

Gilmer, D. S., S. E. Miller and L. M. Cowardin. 1973. Analysis of radiotracking data using digitized habitat maps. J. Wildl. Manage. 37(3): 404–409.

Gilmore, R. M. 1947. Report on a collection of mammal bones from archeologic cave-sites in Coahuila, Mexico. J. Mammal 28(2): 147–165.

Gilmour, N. J. L. 1984. Paratuberculosis. Pages 113–119 *in* H. W. Reid, ed., The management and health of farmed deer. Kluwer Academic Publications, Boston. 206 pp.

Gilpin, M. and F. J. Ayala. 1973. Global models of growth and competition. Proc. Nat. Acad. Sci. 70: 3,590–3,593.

Ginsert, J. R. and E. J. Milner-Gulland. 1994. Sex-based harvesting and population dynamics in ungulates: Implications for conservation and sustainable use. Conserv. Biol. 8:157–166.

Glaser, O. 1983. Wintergattermanagement. Fallstudien in obersteirischen rotwildgattern. unpubl. Diploma Thesis Univ. Agriculture, Vienna. 293 pp.

Gleason, H.A. 1922. The vegetational history of the Middle West. Annu. Assoc. Amer. Geograph. XII: 39–85.

Glenn, T. C. and D. R. Smith. 1993. Genetic variation and subspecific relationships of Michigan elk (*Cervus elaphus*). J. Mammal. 74(3): 782–792.

Glines, M. V. and W. M. Samuel. 1989. The effect of *Dermacentor albipictus* (Acarina: Ixodidae) on blood composition, weight gain and hair coat of the moose, *Alces alces*. Exp. Appl. Acarol. 6: 197–213.

Glover, G. J. 1985. Aspects of the reproductive physiology of female elk. MSc. Thesis, Univ. Saskatchewan. 159 pp.

Gluckman, P. D., B. H. Breier and S. R. Davis. 1987. Physiology of the somatotropic axis with particular reference to the ruminant. J. Dairy Sci. 70: 442–466.

Gochenour, W. S. 1924. Hemorrhagic septicemia studies. J. Am. Vet. Med. Assoc. 65: 433–441.

Goddard, P. E. 1924. Indians of the Northwest coast. Amer. Mus. Natur. Hist., New York. 177 pp.

———. 1975. Indians of the Southwest. Cooper Square Publ., Inc., New York. 205 pp.

Godman, J. D. 1828. Elk. Pages 294–305 *in* American natural history. Vol. 3. Key and Mielkie, Philadelphia. 957 pp.

Gogan, P. J. P. and R. H. Barrett. 1987. Comparative dynamics of introduced Tule elk populations. J. Wildl. Manage. 51: 20–27.

Gogan, P. J. P. and D. A. Jessup. 1985. Cleft palate in a tule elk calf. J. Wildl. Dis. 21: 463–466.

Gogan, P. J. P., D. A. Jessup and R. H. Barrett. 1988. Antler anomalies in tule elk. J. Wildl. Dis. 24: 656–662.

Gogan, P. J. P., D. A. Jessup and M. Akeson. 1989. Copper deficiency in tule elk at Point Reyes, California. J. Range Manage. 42: 233–238.

Gohre, K. and R. Lutzke. 1956. Der eingfluss von bestandesdichte und strucktur auf das kleinklima im Walde. Arch. fur Forstwes 5: 387–572.

Goldoni, D., M. Rubini and F. Fontana. 1984. Cytogenetic studies on *Cervus elaphus* L. Constitutive heterochromatin and nucleolus organizer regions. Caryologia 37(4): 439–443.

Goldschmidt, W. 1978. Nomlaki. Pages 341–349 *in* R. F. Heizer, ed., California. Handbook of North American Indians. Vol. 8. Smithsonian Instit. Press, Washington, D.C. 800 pp.

Gomes, W. R., W. R. Butler and A. D. Johnson. 1971. Effect of elevated ambient temperature and blood levels in vitro biosynthesis of testosterone in the ram. J. Anim. Sci. 33(4): 804–807.

Goodall, D. W. 1954. Vegetational classification and vegetational continua. Angew. PflSoziol. Aichinger Festschr. 1: 168–182.

Goode, G. W. 1900. Report of the Acting Superintendent of the Yellowstone National Park to the Secretary of the Interior, 1900. Govt. Print. Off., Washington, D.C. 20 pp.

Goodson, N. J., D. R. Stevens and J. A. Bailey. 1991a. Effects of snow on foraging ecology and nutrition of bighorn sheep. J. Wildl. Manage. 55: 214–222

Goodson, N. J., D. R. Stevens and J. A. Bailey. 1991b. Winter–spring foraging ecology and nutrition of bighorn sheep on montane ranges. J. Wildl. Manage. 55: 422–433.

Goodwin, G. G. 1935. The mammals of Connecticut. Bull 53. Connecticut Geol. and Natur. Hist. Surv., Hartford. 221 pp. + 33 plates.

Gordon, F. A. 1968a. Range relationships of elk and cattle on elk winter range, Crow Creek, Montana. M.S. Thesis, Montana State Univ., Bozeman. 52 pp.

————. 1968b. Range relationships of elk and cattle on elk winter range, Crow Creek, Montana. Job Compl. Rept., Proj. W–73-R–12, 13, 14 and W–98-R-R and 9. Montana Fish and Game Dept., Helena. 52 pp.

————. 1989. The interspecies allometry of reproduction: Do larger species invest relatively less in their offspring? Functional Ecology 3: 285–288.

Gordon, I. F. and A.W. Illius. 1988. Incisor arcade structure and diet selection in ruminants. Functional Ecology 2: 15–22.

Gordon, I. J. and A. W. Illius. 1994. The functional significance of the browser–grazer dichotomy in African ruminants. Oecologia 98(2): 167–175.

Gordon, Lord G. 1910. The British Isles. Pages 359–383 *in* F. G. Aflalo, ed., Sport in Europe. E. P. Dutton and Co., New York. 483 pp.

Gordon, M. S., ed. 1972. Animal physiology: Principles of adaptations. 2nd ed. MacMillan Publ. Corp., Inc., New York. 592 pp.

Gore, R. 1997. The first Europeans. Nat. Geogr. 192(1): 96–112.

Goslin, R. M. 1943. Animal remains. Ohio State Archaeol. and Hist. Quarter. 52(1): 45–51.

————. 1975. Food and the Edena people. Pages 45–46 *in* W. S. Webb and R. S. Baby, eds., The Edena people no. 2. The Ohio Hist. Soc., Columbus. 123 pp.

Goss, R. J. 1963. The deciduous nature of deer antlers. Pages 339–369 *in* Mechanisms of hard tissue destruction, Publ. No. 75. Amer. Assoc. Adv. Sci., Washington, D.C.

————. 1969a. Photoperiodic control of antler cycles in deer. I. Phase shift and frequency changes. J. Exp. Zool. 170(3): 311–324.

————. 1969b. Photoperiodic control of antler cycles in deer. II. Alterations in amplitude. J. Exp. Zool. 171(2): 233–234.

————. 1970. Problems of antlerogenesis. Clin. Orthop. No. 69: 277–238.

————. 1991. Induction of deer antlers by transplanted periosteum: III Orientation. J. Exp. Zool. 259: 246–251.

————. 1992. The mechanism of antler casting in the fallow deer. J. Exp. Zool. 264: 429–436.

Goss, R. J., C. E. Dinsmore, L. N. Grimes and J. Rosen. 1974. Expression and suppression of the circannual antler growth cycle in deer. Pages 393–421 *in* Circannual clocks: Annual biological rhythms. San Francisco.

Gossow, H. 1983. Zur geschichtlichen entwicklung der beziehungen zwischen jagd und waldwirtschaft. Centralblatt fur das gesamte forstwesen 100, 2–3: 191–207.

————. 1990. Futterungskonzept-Abschussplanung-waldpflege-bedarf. Pages 169–194 *in* H. Gossow, E. Donaubauer, F. Reimoser and J. Dieberger, eds., Tagungsbericht IURFO-Symposium regionalplanungskonzept, fur eine forstlich integrierte Schalenwildbewirtschaftung im Hoch- und Mittelgebirge. BOKU-reports on Wildlife Research and Game Management 1. Institut for Wildbiologie und Jagdwirtschaft, Universitat fur Bodenkultur, Wien.

Gossow, H. and J. Dieberger. 1989. Gutachten zur behandlung der wildtiere im bereich der sonderschutzgebiete des Nationalparks Hohe Tauern (Salzburger Teil). Typoscript Institute fur wildbiologie und jagdwirtschaft der universitat fur bodenkulture Wien. 356 pp.

Gottschlich, H. J. 1965. Biotop und wachsform—eine craniometrisch—allometrische studie und europaischen Populationen von *Cervus elaphus*. Pages 83–101 *in* Beitrage zur Jagd-und Wildforschung IV. Deutsche Akademie der Landwirtschafts wissen-schajten, Berlin.

Gove, N. E. 1997. Using age–harvest data to estimate demographic parameters for wildlife populations. M.S. Thesis, Univ. Washington, Seattle, Washington. 128 pp.

Gove, P. B., ed. 1969. Webster's Seventh New Collegiate Dictionary. G. and C. Merriam Co., Springfield, Massachusetts. 1,221 pp.

Grace, J. and N. Easterbee. 1979. The natural shelter for red deer (*Cervus elaphus*) in a Scottish glen. J. Applied Ecol. 16: 37–48.

Graf, W. 1943. Natural history of the Roosevelt elk. Ph.D.Thesis, Oregon State Univ., Corvallis. 222 pp.

————. 1955. The Roosevelt elk. *Port Angeles Evening News,* Port Angeles, Washington. 105 pp.

Graham, A. and C. Heimsch. 1960. Pollen studies of some Texas peat deposits. Ecology 41(4): 751–763.

Graham, E. A., R. Rainey, R. E. Kuhlman, E. H. Houghton and C. A. Moyer. 1962. Biochemical investigations of deer antler growth. Part I. Alterations of deer blood chemistry resulting from antlerogenesis. J. Bone and Joint Surg. 44-A(3): 482–488.

Graham, R. W. 1979. Paleoclimates and the late Pleistocene faunal provinces in North America. Pages 49–69 *in* Pre-Lllano cultures of the Americas: Paradoxes and possibilities. Anthropological Soc. of Washington, Washington, D.C. pp.

————. 1981. Preliminary report on the late Pleistocene vertebrates from the Selby and Dutton archeological/paleontological sites, Yuma County, Colorado. Contributions to Geol., Univ. Wyoming 20: 35–56.

————. 1987. Late Quaternary mammalian faunas and paleoenvironments of the southwestern plains of the United States. Pages 24–86 *in* R. W. Graham, H. A. Semken, Jr. and M. A.Graham, eds., Late Quaternary mammalian biogeography and environments of the Great Plains and Prairies. Illinois State Mus. Sci. Pap. 22 pp.

Graham, R. W. and J. I. Mead. 1987. Environmental fluctuations and evolution of mammalian faunas during the last deglaciation in North America. Pages 371–402 *in* W. F. Ruddiman and H. E. Wright, Jr., eds., North America and adjacent oceans during the last deglaciation, Geological Soc. of America, Boulder, Colorado. 501 pp.

Graham, S. A. 1945. Ecological classification of cover types. J. Wildl. Manage. 9(3): 182–190.

Grant, W. L., ed. 1907. Voyages of Samuel de Champlain, 1604–1618. Charles Scribner's Sons, New York. 374 pp.

Graphodatsky, A. S. and S. I. Radjabli. 1985. Chromosomes of three cervid species (mammalia). Zoologicleskii zhurnal 19: 1,275–1,279.

Gratson, M. W. and P. Zager. 1993. Lochsa elk ecology. Job progress report W–160-R–20. Idaho Dept. Fish and Game, Boise, Idaho. 24 pp.

Graves, H. S. and E. W. Nelson. 1919. A program for conserving the elk on national forests about the Yellowstone National Park. Dept. Circ. 51. U.S. Dept. Ag., Washington, D.C. 34 pp.

Gray, A. P. 1954. Mammalian hybrids. A checklist with bibliography. Tech. Commiss. No. 10 of the Commonwealth Bur. Anim. Breeding and Genetics, Edinburgh. Longbank Works. Robert Cunningham & Sons Ltd., Alva, Great Britain. 144 pp.

————. 1972. Mammalian hybrids. A checklist with bibliography. Tech. Commiss. 10 (Revised) Commonwealth Ag. Bur. R. Clark, Ltd., Edinburgh, Scotland. 262 pp.

Gray, P. B. and R. A. Servello. 1995. Energy intake relationships for white-tailed deer on winter browse diets. J. Wildl. Manage. 59: 147-152.

Green, H. U. 1933. The wapiti of the Riding Mountain, Manitoba. Can. Field-Nat. 47(6): 105–111.

————. 1946. The elk of Banff National Park. National Parks Branch, Ottawa. Mimeographed Report. Pages 795–803 *in* D. R. Flook and J. E. Stenton,ed., 1969. Incidence and abundance of certain parasites in wapiti in the national parks of the Canadian Rockies. Can. J. Zool. 47.

————. 1949a. Occurrence of *Echinococcus granulosus* in elk (*Cervus canadensis nelsoni*), Banff National Park. Can. Field-Nat. 63: 204–205.

————. 1949b. The bighorn sheep of Banff National Park. Nat. Park and

Hist. Sites Ser. Can. Dept. Res. and Devel., Ottawa, Ontario. 53 pp.

———. 1950. The productivity and sex survival of elk, Banff National Park, Alberta. Can. Field Natur. 64(1): 40–42.

Greenley, J. C. 1971. The effects of biopolitics on proper game management. Proc. West. Assoc. State Game and Fish Commiss. 51: 505–509.

Greenough, W. T. 1975. Experimental modifications of the developing brain. Amer. Sci. 63: 37–46.

Greer, K. R. 1959a. Analysis of 68 samples from the 1956 Gallatin Canyon elk "hunter kill." Pages 5–6 in Wildlife investigations—State: Wildlife Investigations Laboratory. Fed. Aid Compl. Rept. Proj. W83-R-2. All jobs. Montana Dept. Fish and Game, Helena.

———. 1959b. Analysis of 23 elk rumen samples collected during 1957 from the vicinity of Gardiner, Montana. Page 8 in Wildlife investigations—State: Wildlife Investigations Laboratory. Fed. Aid Compl. Rept. Proj. W–83-R–2. All jobs. Montana Dept. Fish and Game, Helena.

———. 1960a. Analysis of 21 elk rumens collected from the 1956 hunter-kill at Boyd Ranch, Missoula County. Page 14 in Wildlife investigations—State: Wildlife Investigations Laboratory. Fed. Aid Compl. Rept. Proj. W–83-R–3. All jobs. Montana Dept. Fish and Game, Helena.

———. 1960b. Analysis of 29 elk rumen samples collected during 1956–1957 from the Sun River Game Range, Lewis and Clark County, Montana. Pages 16–17 in Wildlife investigations—State: Wildlife Investigations Laboratory. Fed. Aid Compl. Rept. Proj. W–83-R–3. All jobs. Montana Dept. Fish and Game, Helena.

———. 1965. Collections from the Gallatin elk post season, 1964–1965. Job. Compl. Rept., Proj. No. W–83-R–8. Montana Dept. Fish and Game, Helena.

———. 1966. Fertility rates of the northern Yellowstone elk populations. Proc. West. Assoc. State Game and Fish Commiss. 46: 123–128.

———. 1967. Special collections—Yellowstone elk study, 1967–1968. Job. Compl. Rept., Proj. No. W–83-R–10. Montana Dept. Fish and Game, Helena.

———. 1968a. A compression method indicates fat content of elk (wapiti) femur marrows. J. Wildl. Manage. 32(4): 747–751.

——— R. 1968b. Yellowstone elk study, 1967–1968. Job. Compl. Rept., Fed. Aid in Wildl. Restor., Proj. W–83-R–11. Montana Dept. Fish and Game, Helena. 26 pp.

———. 1968c. Elk teeth as ornaments. Montana Wildl. (February): 14–17.

———. 1968d. Special collection—Yellowstone elk study, 1967–1968. Job. Compl. Rept., Proj. No. W–83-R–11. Montana Dept. Fish and Game, Helena. 26 pp.

Greer, K. R. and H. W. Hawkins. 1967. Determining pregnancy in elk by rectal palpation. J. Wildl. Manage. 31: 145–149.

Greer, K. R. and R. E. Howe. 1964. Winter weights of northern Yellowstone elk, 1961–1962. Trans. N. Amer. Wildl. Conf. 29: 237–248.

Greer, K. R. and H. W. Yeager. 1967. Sex and age indications from upper canine teeth of elk (wapiti). J. Wildl. Manage. 31(3): 408–417.

Greer, K. R., J. B. Kirsch and H. W. Yeagher. 1970. Seasonal food habits of the northern Yellowstone elk (wapiti) herds during 1957 and 1962–1967 as determined from 793 rumen samples. Fed. Aid Final Rept. Proj. W–83-R–12, J-B–1. Montana Dept. Fish and Game, Helena. 76 pp.

Greffenius, R. J. 1938. Results of the Copper Ridge Basin elk study. USDA For. Serv. Rocky Mountain Bull. 21: 14–15.

Greig-Smith, P. 1964. Quantitative plant ecology. 2nd ed. Butterworths, London. 256 pp.

Grelen, H. E., L. B. Whitaker and R. E. Lohrey. 1972. Herbage response to precommercial thinning in direct-seeded slash pine. J. Range Manage. 25(6): 435–437.

Greutter, E 1985 Einfluss der lage von rotwildfutterungen auf schalschaden. unpubl. Diploma Thesis, Univ. Agriculture, Vienna. 106 pp.

Grieb, J. R. and R. N. Denney. 1965. Game research in Colorado. White River Elk Study. Colorado Dept. Game, Fish and Parks, Denver. 35 pp.

Grier, B. 1995. Nebraska's elk: A plan for the future. Nebraskaland 73(7): 34–39.

Griffin, J. B. 1978. Late prehistory of the Ohio Valley. Pages 547–559 in B. G. Trigger, ed., Northeast. Handbook of North American Indians. Smithsonian Instit. Press, Washington, D.C. 924 pp.

Griffin, J. F. T. 1988. The aetiology of tuberculosis and mycobacterial diseases in farmed deer. Irish Vet. J. 42: 23–26.

Griffin, J. F. T. and J. P. Cross. 1989. Diagnosis of tuberculosis in New Zealand farmed deer: An evaluation of intradermal skin testing and laboratory techniques. Irish Vet. J. 42: 101–107.

Griffin, J. F. T. and A. J. Thomson. 1994. Immunological markers of stress and well-being in domestic animals. Proc. Deer Course for Veterinarians 11: 146–154.

Griffin, J. F. T., A. J. Thomson, J. P. Cross, G. S. Buchan and C. G. MacKintosh. 1992a. The impact of domestication on red reer immunity and disease resistance. Pages 120–125 in R. D. Brown, ed., The biology of deer. Springer-Verlag, New York.

Griffin, J. F. T., G. S. Buchan, J. P. Cross and C. R. Rogers. 1992b. New testing procedures for diagnosis of tuberculosis in Cervidae. Pages 15–20 in M. A. Essey, ed., Bovine tuberculosis in Cervidae: Proc. of a Symposium. Misc. Publ. No. 1,506. USDA Anim. and Plant Health Inspect. Serv., Denver, Colorado. 71 pp.

Griffin, J. F. T., L. Slobbe, J. Hesketh, Y-E Shi and G. Buchan 1992c. Techniques in molecular immunology for disease diagnosis in wildlife populations: A deer model. Pages 190–194 in W. van Hoven, H. Ebedes and A. Conroy, eds., Wildlife ranching: a celebration of diversity. Pretoria, South Africa. 400 pp.

Grimstad, P. R., S. M. Schmitt and D. G. Williams. 1986. Prevalence of neutralizing antibody to Jamestown Canyon virus (California group) in populations of elk and moose in northern Michigan and Ontario, Canada. J. Wildl. Dis. 22: 453–458.

Grinnell, G. B. 1961. Pawnee hero stories and folk tales. Univ. Nebraska Press, Lincoln. 417 pp.

———. 1962. Blackfoot lodge tales: The story of a prairie people. Univ. Nebraska Press, Lincoln. 310 pp.

———. 1972. The Cheyenne Indians: Their history and ways of life. 2 vols. Univ. Nebraska Press, Lincoln. 788 pp.

Grinnell, G.B. and T.R. Roosevelt, eds., 1897. Trail and camp-fire: The book of the Boone and Crockett Club. Harper and Brothers Publ., New York.

Grisez, T. J. 1960. Slash helps protect seedlings from deer browsing. J. Forestry 58(5): 385–387.

Grkovic, N. 1976. Montana–Idaho elk migration and key-use area study: Salmon, Beaverhead and Bitterroot national forests. M.S. Thesis, Univ. Montana, Missoula. 128 pp.

Grosenbaugh, L. R. 1952. Plotless timber estimates—new, fast, easy. J. Forestry 50: 32–37.

Gross, J. E. 1969. Optimum yield in deer and elk populations. Trans. N. Amer. Wildl. and Natur. Resour. Conf. 34: 372–387.

Gross, J. E., J. E. Roelle and G. L. Williams. 1972. Progress report—Program ONEPOP and information processor: A systems modeling and communications project. Colorado Coop. Wildl. Res. Unit., Fort Collins. 327 pp.

Gross, J. E., L. A. Shipley, N. T. Hobbs, D. E. Spalinger and B. A. Wunder. 1993. Functional response of herbivores in food-concentrated patches: tests of a mechanistic model. Ecology 74: 778–791.

Gross, W. M. and J. E. Hawkins. 1985. Radiometric selective inhibition tests for differentiation of *Mycobacterium tuberculosis, Mycobacterium bovis* and other mycobacteria. J. Clin. Microbiol. 21: 565–568.

Grover, K. E. and M. J. Thompson. 1986. Factors influencing spring feeding site selection by elk in the Elkhorn Mountains, Montana. J. Wildl. Manage. 50: 466–470.

Groves, C. P. and P. Grubb. 1987. Relationships of living deer. Pages 21–59 *in* C. M. Wemmer, ed., Biology and management of the Cervidae. Smithsonian Instit. Press, Washington, D.C. 577 pp.

Gruell, G. E. 1973. An ecological evaluation of Big Game Ridge. USDA For. Serv. Publ., Intermt. Reg., Teton Wilderness-Teton Nat. For. USDA For. Serv., Northwest, Wyoming. 62 pp.

———. 1980. Fire's influence on wildlife habitat on the Bridger-Teton National Forest, Wyoming. 2 vols. Res. Paper INT–252. USDA For. Serv., Ogden, Utah. 242 pp.

Gruell, G. E. and L. L. Loope. 1974. Relationships among aspen, fire and ungulate browsing in Jackson Hole, Wyoming. USDA For. Serv., Ogden, Utah. 33 pp.

Grumbine, R.E. 1994. What is ecosystem management? Conserv. Biol. 8: 27–38.

Guest, J. E. 1971. Carrying capacity of elk summer range. Ph.D.Thesis, Univ. Wyoming, Laramie. 131 pp.

Guggenberger, C. 1981. Raumlich-Zeitliche nutzung von wintergattern durch rotwild (*Cervus elaphus* L) im Nationalpark Bayrischer Wald. unpubl. Diploma Thesis, Univ. Agriculture, Vienna. 74 pp.

Guilday, J. E. 1971. Biological and archeological analysis of bones from a seventeenth century Indian village (43 Pu 31), Putnam County, West Virginia. Archeol. Invest. Rept. No. 4, West Virginia Geol. and Econ. Surv., Morgantown. 64 pp.

Guilday, J. E. and D. P. Tanner. 1965. Vertebrate remains from the Mount Corban Site (46 Fa 7), Fayette County, West Virginia. West Virginia Archeol. 18: 1–14.

Guilday, J. E., P. W. Parmalee and D. P. Tanner. 1962. Aboriginal butchering techniques at the Eschelman Site (36 La 12), Lancaster County, Pennsylvania. Pennsylvania Archaeol. 32(2): 59-83.

Guilday, J. E., P. W. Parmalee and H. W. Hamilton. 1977. The Clark's Cave bone deposit and the late Pleistocene palececology of the Central Appalachian Mountains of Virginia. Bull. No. 2. Carnegie Mus. Natur. Hist., Pittsburgh. 87 pp.

Guinness, F. E., S. D. Albon and T. H. Clutton-Brock. 1978a. Factors affecting reproduction in red deer (*Cervus elaphus*) hinds on Rhum. J. Reprod. Fert. 54: 325–334.

Guinness, F. E., R. M. Gibson and T. H. Clutton-Brock. 1978b. Calving times of red deer (*Cervus elaphus*) on Rhum. J. Zool., London 185: 105–114.

Guiness, F. E., T. H. Clutton-Brock and S. D. Albon. 1978c. Factors affecting calf mortality in red deer (*Cervus elaphus*). J. Anim. Ecol. 47: 817–832.

Guinness, F. E., G. A. Lincoln and R. V.Short. 1971. The reproductive cycle of the female red deer, *Cervus elaphus* L. J. Reprod. Fert. 27: 427–438.

Gunson, J. R. 1997. Draft management plan for elk in Alberta. Wildl. Manage. Planning Ser. 8. Alberta Envir. Protect., Natur. Resour. Serv., Wildl. Manage. Div., Edmonton. 184 pp.

Gunther, K. A. and R. A. Renkin. 1991. Grizzly bear predation on elk calves and other fauna of Yellowstone National Park. Int. Conf. Bear Res. and Manage. 8: 329–334.

Gupta, R. P. and H. C. Gibbs. 1971. Infectivity of *D. viviparus* (moose strain) to calves. Can. Vet. J. 56: 56.

Gustavsson, I. and C.O. Sundt. 1968. Karyotypes in five species of deer (*Alces alces* L., *Capreolus caprelous* L., *Cervus elaphus* L., *Cervus nippon nippon* Temm. and *Dama dama* L.). Hereditas 60(3): 233–248.

Guthrie, R. D. 1966. The extinct wapiti of Alaska and Yukon Territory. Can. J. Zool. 44(1): 47–57.

———. 1968a. Paleoecology of a late Pleistocene small mammal community from interior Alaska. Arctic 21(4): 223–244.

———. 1968b. Paleoecology of the large mammal community in interior Alaska during the late Pleistocene. Amer. Midl. Natur. 79(2): 346–363.

———. 1982. Mammals of the mammoth steppe as paleoenvironmental indicators. Pages 307–326 *in* D. M. Hopkins, J. M. Matthews, Jr., C. E. Schweger and S. B. Young, eds., Paleoecology of Beringia. Academic Press, New York.

Guthrie, R. D. and J. V. Matthews, Jr. 1971. The Cape Deceit fauna—early Pleistocene mammalian assemblage from the Alaskan arctic. Quaternary Res. 1(4): 474–510.

Gwynn, J. V. 1977. Elk stocking in Virginia. Unpubl. Rept., Virginia Dept. Game and Inland Fish., Richmond. 10 pp.

Gyllensten, V., N. Ryman, C. Reuterwall and P. Dratch. 1983. Genetic differentiation in four European subspecies of red deer (*Cervus elaphus* L.). Heredity 51(3): 561–580.

Habeck, J. R. 1961. The original vegetation of the mid-Willamette Valley, Oregon. Northwest Sci. 35: 65–77.

Habeck, J. R. and R. W. Mutch. 1973. Fire dependent forests in the northern Rocky Mountains. Quat. Res. 3: 408–424.

Haber, G. C. 1977. Socioecological dynamics of wolves and prey in a subarctic ecosystem. Ph.D. Diss., Univ. British Columbia, Vancouver. 786 pp.

Hadley, M. E. 1984. Endocrinology. Prentice-Hall, Inc., Englewood Cliffs, New Jersey. 547 pp.

Hadwen, S. 1932. "Notes." J. Parasitol. 19: 83.

———. 1942. Tuberculosis in the buffalo. J. Amer. Vet. Med. Assoc. 100: 19–22.

Haeberlin, H. K. and E. Gunther. 1930. The Indians of Puget Sound. Univ. Washington Publ. in Anthropol. 4(1): 1–83.

Hafsten, V. 1961. Pleistocene development of vegetation and climate in the Southern High Plains as evidenced by pollen analysis. Pages 59–91 *in* F. Wendorf, ed., Paleoecology of the Llano Estacado. Fort Burgwin Res. Cent. Publ. No. 1. Mus. of New Mexico Press, Santa Fe.

Hagerman, A. E. 1987. Radial diffusion method for extracting tannin in plant extracts. J. Chem. Ecol. 13: 437–449.

Hagerman, A. E., C. T. Robbins, Y. Weerasuriya, T. C. Wilson and C. McArthur. 1992. Tannin chemistry in relation to digestion. J. Range Manage. 45: 57–62.

Hagmeier, E. M. 1958. Inapplicability of the subspecies concept to North American marten. Syst. Zool. 7(1): 1–7.

Haigh, J. C. 1982. Reproductive seasonality of male wapiti. MSc.Thesis, Univ. Saskatchewan, Saskatoon. 131 pp.

———. 1987. Game farming practice; Notes for the game farming industry: Antlers. Univ. Saskatchewan, Saskatoon. 4 pp.

———. 1988. A preliminary examination of the gestation length of wapiti. 4th Int. Deer Biol. Congr., Kapsovar, Hungary. 49 pp.

———. 1991. Requirements for managing farmed deer. Pages 159–172 *in* R. D. Brown, ed., The biology of deer. Springer-Verlag, New York.

Haigh, J. C. and R. J. Hudson. 1993. Farming Wapiti and Red Deer. Mosby Year Book. St. Louis, Missouri. 369 pp.

Haigh, J. C., W. F. Cates, G. J. Glover and N. C. Rawlings. 1984. Relationships between seasonal changes in serum testosterone concentrations, scrotal circumference and sperm morphology of male elk (*Cervus elaphus*). J. Reprod. and Fert. 70: 413–418.

Hail, B. A. 1980. Hau, Kóla! The Plains Indian collection of the Haffenreffer. Mus. Anthropol., Brown Univ. Eastern Press, Inc., Bristol, Rhode Island. 256 pp.

Haines, F. 1938a. Where did the Plains Indians get their horse? Amer. Anthropologist 40: 112–117.

———. 1938b. The northward spread of horses among the Plains Indians. Amer. Anthropol. 40: 429–437.

———. 1955. Osborne Russell's journal of a trapper. Oregon Hist. Soc. and Champoeg Press, Portland, Oregon. 191pp.

———. 1970a. Indians of the Great Basin and Plateau. G. P. Putnam's Sons, New York. 224 pp.

———. 1970b. The buffalo. Thomas Y. Crowell Co., New York. 242 pp.

———. 1977. The Yellowstone story. Vol. 2. Yellowstone Library and Mus. Assoc., Yellowstone Nat. Park, Wyoming, in cooperation with Colorado Assoc. Univ. Press. 970 pp.

Halazon, G. C. and H. K. Buechner. 1956. Postconception ovulation in elk. Trans. N. Amer. Wildl. Conf. 21: 545–554.

Hale, J.P. 1886. Trans-Allegheny pioneers. The Graphic Press, Cincinnati, Ohio. 330 pp.

Haley, J. L. 1981. Apaches: A history and culture portrait. Doubleday and Co., New York. 453 pp.

Hall, E. R. and K. R. Kelson. 1959. The mammals of North America. Vol. 2. Ronald Press Co., New York. 531 pp.

Hall, F. C. 1973. Plant communities of the Blue Mountains in eastern Oregon and southeastern Washington. USDA For. Serv., Pac. Northwest Reg., R6 Area Guide 3–1. USDA For. Serv., Portland, Oregon. 62 pp.

Hall, J. M. 1952. Game–livestock relationship studies in Arizona. Arizona Game and Fish Comm, Phoenix. 5 pp.

———. 1955. Livestock and big game relationships. J. Range Manage. 8: 4–6.

Hall, M. C. 1930. Parasites of elk and other wild ruminants. J. Washington Acad. Sci. 20(5): 87–88.

Hall, M. U. 1926. A buffalo robe biography. Mus. J. XVII: 5–35, Univ. Pennsylvania, Philadelphia. 93 pp.

Halloran, A. F. 1963. History of the Wichita Mountains Wildlife Refuge elk herd. Okla. Acad. Sci. Proc. 43: 229–232.

Halloran, A. F. and B. P. Glass. 1959. The carnivores and ungulates of the Wichita Mountains Wildlife Refuge, Oklahoma. J. Mammal. 40(3): 360–370.

Halls, L. K. 1973. Managing deer habitat in loblolly–shortleaf pine forest. J. Forestry 71(12): 752–757.

———. 1978. White-tailed deer. Pages 43–66 in J. L. Schmidt and D. L. Gilbert, eds., Big game of North America: Ecology and management. Stackpole Books, Harrisburg, Pennsylvania. 512 pp.

———. ed. 1984. White-tailed deer: Ecology and management. Stackpole Books, Harrisburg, Pennsylvania. 870 pp.

Halls, L. K. and R. Alcaniz. 1971. Forage yields in an east Texas pine–hardwood forest. J. Forestry 69(1): 25–26.

Halls, L. K. and T. R. Dell. 1966. Trial of ranked-set sampling for forage yields. For. Sci. 12(1): 22–26.

Halls, L. K. and J. L. Schuster. 1965. Tree–herbage relations in pine–hardwood forest of Texas. J. Forestry 63(4): 282–283.

Haltenorth, T. 1963. Klassifikation der Saugetiere: Artiodactyla 1(18) Handb. d. Zoologie, ed. Helmcke, et al. Walter de Gruyter and Co., Berlin. 167 pp.

Hamalainen, P. 1983. Statistical testing of surface collected and excavated faunal samples from the Plater-Martin site. Ontario Archaeol. 39: 57–64.

Hamer, D. and S. Herrero. 1991. Elk, *Cervus elaphus*, calves as food for Grizzly bears, *Ursus arctos*, in Banff National Park, Alberta. Can. Field. Nat. 105: 101–103.

Hamerstrom, F. N. and L. F. Camburn. 1950. Weight relationship in the George Reserve deer herd. J. Mammal. 31(1): 5–17.

Hamerton, A. E. 1941. Report on the deaths occurring in the Society's gardens during 1939–1940. Proc. Zool. Soc. London 111: 150.

———. 1942. Report on the deaths occurring in the Society's gardens during 1941. Proc. Zool. Soc. London 112: 120.

Hamilton, W. J. 1947. Dressed weights of some game mammals. J. Wildl. Manage. 11(4): 349–350.

Hamilton, W. J. and K. L. Blaxter. 1980a. Reproduction in farmed red deer. 1. Hind and stag fertility. J. Ag. Sci., Cambridge 95: 261–273.

Hamilton, W. J. and K. L. Blaxter. 1980b. Reproduction in farmed red deer. 2. Calf growth and mortality. J. Ag. Sci., Cambridge. 95: 275–284.

Hamilton, W. J., III. 1973. Life's color code. McGraw- Hill, New York. 238 pp.

Hamilton, W. R. 1978. Fossil giraffes from the Miocene of Africa and a revision of the phylogeny of the Giraffoidea. Philos. Trans. Royal Soc., London (ser. B.) Biol. Sci. 282: 165–229.

Hamlin, K. 1990. Personal communication. Montana Dept. Fish, Wildl. and Parks, Bozeman.

Hamlin, K. L. and M. S. Ross. 1991. Varying definitions of the legal bull—the effects on hunters, hunting and elk populations. Pages 247–254 in A. G. Christensen, L. J. Lyon and T. N. Lonner, eds., Elk vulnerability Symp., Montana State Univ., Bozeman. 330 pp.

Hammitt, W.E. and D.N. Cole. 1987. Wildland recreation. John Wiley and Sons, New York. 341 pp.

Hampton, H.D. 1971. How the U.S. Cavalry saved our national parks. Indiana Univ. Press, Bloomington. 246 pp.

Hamr, J. and G. A. Bubenik. 1990. Seasonal thyroid hormone levels of free-ranging white-tailed deer (*Odocoileus virginianus*) in Ontario. Can. J. Zool. 68: 2,174–2,180.

Hancock, N. V. 1955. A management study of the Cache elk herd. Info. Bull. 22. Utah Dept. Fish and Game, Salt Lake City. 161 pp.

———. 1957. A preliminary report of elk reproduction in Utah with special reference to precociousness in yearling female. Proc. West. Assoc. State Game and Fish Commiss. 37: 195–197.

———. 1979. Summary of game and nongame wildlife damage questionnaire sent to all states in July, 1979. File Rept. Utah Div. Wildl. Resources, Salt Lake City. 6 pp.

Hancock, N. and S. D. Bunnell. 1985. Elk in Utah's past, present and future. *In* Western Elk Management: A Symposium. Utah State Univ., College of Natur. Resour., Logan. 213 pp.

Hancox, N. M. 1972. Biology of bone. Univ. Press, Cambridge. 199 pp.

Handley, C. O., Jr. and C. P. Patton. 1947. Wild mammals of Virginia. Virginia Commiss. Game and Inland Fish, Richmond. 220 pp.

Hanley, T. A. 1984. Habitat patches and their selection by wapiti and black-tailed deer in a coastal montane coniferous forest. J. Appl. Ecol. 21: 423–436.

———. 1997. A nutritional view of understanding and complexity in the problem of diet selection by deer (Cervidae). Oikos 9: 209-218.

Hanley, T. A. and J. D. McKendrick. 1983. Seasonal changes in chemical composition and nutritive value of native forages in a spruce–hemlock forest, southeastern Alaska. U.S. For. Serv., Res. Pap. PNW–312. 41 pp.

Hanley, T. A. and J. D. McKendrick. 1985. Potential nutritional limitations for black-tailed deer in a spruce–hemlock forest, southeastern Alaska. J. Wildl. Manage. 49: 103–114.

Hanley, T. A., R. G. Cates, B. Van Horne and J. D. McKendrick. 1987. Forest stand age-related differences in apparent nutritional quality of forage for deer in southeastern Alaska. Pages 9–17 in F. D. Provenza, J. T. Flinders and E. D. McArthur, compilers, Proc. Symp. on plant–herbivore interactions. U.S. For. Serv., Gen. Tech. Rept. INT–222. 179 pp.

Hanley, T. A., C. T. Robbins, A. E. Hagerman and C. McArthur. 1992.

Predicting digestible protein and digestible dry matter in tannin-containing forages consumed by ruminants. Ecology 73: 537–541.

Hanley, T. A., C. T. Robbins and D. E. Spalinger. 1989. Forest habitats and the nutritional ecology of Sitka black-tailed deer: A research synthesis with implications for forest management. U.S. For. Ser., Gen. Tech. Rept. PNW-GTR–230. 52 pp.

Hann, W. J., J. L. Jones, M. G. Karl, P. F. Hessburg, R. E. Kean, D. G. Long, J. P. Menakis, C. H. McNicoll, S. G. Leonard, R. A. Gravenmier and B. G. Smith. 1997. Landscape dynamics of the basin. *In* T. M. Quigley and S. J. Arebibide, Technical eds., An assessment of ecosystem components in the interior Columbia basin and portions of the Klamath and Great Basins: Vol. 2. Gen. Tech. Rept. PNW-GTR–405. USDA For. Serv., Portland, Oregon.

Hansen, L. E. 1969. Current research on leptospirosis. Pages 26–36 *in* Symposium on Leptospirosis. Oregon Vet. Med. Assoc., Salem.

Hansen, R. M. and L. D. Reid. 1975. Diet overlap of deer, elk and cattle in southern Colorado. J. Range Manage. 28(1): 43–47.

Hansen, R. M. and D. N. Ueckert. 1970. Dietary similarity of some primary consumers. Ecology 51: 640–648.

Hansen, R. M., D. G. Peden and R. W. Rice. 1973. Discerned fragments in feces indicates diet overlap. J. Range Manage. 26(2): 103–105.

Hanson, C. E., Jr. 1955. The Northwest gun. Publ. in Anthropol. No. 2. Nebraska State Hist. Soc., Lincoln. 85 pp.

———. 1960. The Plains rifle. Bramhall House, New York. 171 pp.

Hanson, W. R. 1952. Grazing use of forest lands. For. Chron. 28: 23–32.

———. 1963. Calculation of productivity, survival and abundance of selected vertebrates from sex and age ratios. Wildl. Monogr. No. 9. The Wildl. Soc., Washington, D.C. 60 pp.

Happe, P. J., K. J. Jenkins, E. E. Stankey and S. H. Sharrow. 1990. Nutritional quality and tannin astringency of browse in clearcuts and old-growth forests. J. Wildl. Manage. 54(4): 557–566.

Harder, J. D. and R. L. Kirkpatrick. 1994. Physiological methods in wildlife research. Pages 275–306 *in* T. A. Bookhout, ed., Research and management techniques for wildlife and habitats, fifth ed. The Wildl. Soc., Bethesda, Maryland. 740 pp.

Hardin, G. 1968. The tragedy of the commons. Science 162(3859): 1243–1248.

Harington, C. R. 1977. Pleistocene mammals of the Yukon Territory. Unpubl. Ph.D.Thesis, Univ. Alberta, Edmonton.

———. 1980. Pleistocene mammals from Lost Chicken Creek, Alaska. Can. J. Earth Sci. 17(2): 168–198.

———. 1988. Pleistocene vertebrate localities in the Yukon. Pages 93–98 *in* L. D. Carter, T. D. Hamilton and J. P. Galoway, eds., Late Cenozoic history of the interior basins of Alaska and the Yukon. U.S. Geol. Surv. Circ. 1026. 114 pp.

Haris, J. T. 1963. Population dynamics of the White River elk herd, Colorado. Ph.D.Thesis, Univ. Michigan, Ann Arbor. 200 pp.

Harland, W. R., R. A. Magonigle and H. W. Vaughn. 1979. Evaluation of the anaplasmosis rapid card agglutination test for detecting experimentally-infected elk. J. Wildl. Dis. 15: 379–386.

Harmel, D. 1983. The effects of genetics on antler quality in white-tailed deer (*Odocoileus virginianus*). *in* R. D. Brown, ed., Antler development in cervidae. Caeser Kleberg Wildl. Res. Inst., Kingsville, Texas. 480 pp.

Harper, J. A. 1962. Daytime feeding habits of Roosevelt elk on Boyes Prairies, California. J. Wildl. Manage. 26(1): 97–100.

———. 1964. Movement and associated behavior of Roosevelt elk in southwestern Oregon. proc. West. Assoc. State Game and Fish Commiss. 44: 139–141.

———. 1966. Ecological study of Roosevelt elk. Game Res. Rept. 1. Oregon Game Commiss., Portland. 29 pp.

———. 1971. Ecology of Roosevelt elk. PR W–59-R. Oregon State Game Commiss., Portland. 44 pp.

———. 1980. Wish you were here??? Oregon Wildlife 35(11): 3–5.

Harper, J. A., J. H. Ham, W. W. Bentley and C. F. Yocum. 1967. The status and ecology of the Roosevelt elk in California. Wildl. Monogr. No. 16. The Wildl. Soc., Bethesda, Maryland. 49 pp.

Harper, J. A. et al. 1985. Ecology and management of Roosevelt elk in Oregon, Revised edition. Oregon Dept. Fish and Wildlife, Portland. 70 pp.

Harper's Weekly. 1885. Evicted tenants. Harper's Weekly 29(1471): 136,139.

Harrington, R. 1973. Hybridization among deer and its implication for conservation. Irish Forester 30: 64–78.

———. 1985. Evolution and distribution of the Cervidae. Pages 3–11 *in* P. F. Fenessy and K. R. Drew, eds., The biology of deer production. Bull. 22. Royal Soc. New Zealand, Wellington. 482 pp.

Harris, J. T. 1958. Analysis of elk winter range, south fork of the White River, Colorado. M.S. Thesis, Colorado State Univ., Fort Collins. 136 pp.

———. 1963. Population dynamics of the White River elk herd, Colorado. Ph.D.Thesis, Univ. Michigan, Ann Arbor. 200 pp.

Harris, L. E., C. W. Cook and J. E. Butcher. 1959. Symposium of forage evaluation: V. Intake and digestibility techniques and supplemental feeding in range forage evaluation. Agron. J. 51: 226–234.

Harris, M. 1886. Report of the Superintendent of the Yellowstone National Park. Govt. Print. Off., Washington, D.C. 13 pp.

———. 1887. Report of the Superintendent of the Yellowstone National Park. Govt. Print. Off., Washington, D.C. 28 pp.

———. 1888. Report of the Superintendent of the Yellowstone National Park. Govt. Print. Off., Washington, D.C. 30 pp.

———. 1889. Report of the Superintendent of the Yellowstone National Park to the Secretary of the Interior. Govt. Print. Off., Washington, D.C. 35 pp.

Harris, R. B. 1995. Ecotourism versus trophy hunting; incentives toward conservation in Yeniugau, Tibetan Plateau, China. Pages 228–234 *in* J. A. Bissonette and P. R. Krausman, eds., Integrating people and wildlife for a sustainable future. Proc. First International Wildlife Management Congress, The Wildl. Soc., Bethesda, Maryland. 715 pp.

Harris, R. W. 1951. Use of aerial photographs and subsampling in range inventories. J. Range Manage. 4(4): 270–278.

Harrison, J. L. 1958. Range of movement of some Malagan rats. J. Mammal. 38: 190–206.

Harry, G. B. 1957. Winter food habits of moose in Jackson Hole, Wyoming. J. Wildl. Manage. 21: 53–57.

Harry, J., R. Gale and J. Hendee. 1969. Conservation: an upper middle class social movement. J. Leisure Res. 1(3): 246–254.

Hart, L. 1967. Strategy. Praeger, New York.

Hart, R. H., J. Bisso, M. J. Samuel and H. J. W. Waggoner, Jr. 1993. Grazing systems, pasture size and cattle grazing behavior, distribution and gains. J. Range Manage. 46: 81–87.

Hart, R. H., K. W. Hepworth, M. A. Smith and J. W. Waggoner, Jr. 1991. Cattle grazing behavior on a foothill elk winter range in southeastern Wyoming. J. Range Manage. 44: 262–266.

Hart-Davis, D. 1978. Monarch of the glen. J. Cape Ltd., London, U.K. 234 pp.

Harthoorn, A. M. 1965. Application of pharmacological and physiological principles in restraint of wild animals. Wildl. Monogr. No. 14. The Wildl. Soc., Washington, D.C. 78 pp.

Hartwig, H. 1968. Durch Periostverlagerung experimentellerzeugte, Heterotrope Stirnzapfenbildung beim Reh. Z. f. Saugetierkunde 33(4): 246–248.

Hartwig, H. and H. G. Hartwig. 1974. Uber die Milz der Gams. Erge-boisse quantitativ-morphologischer Untersuchungen. Tagungsberichte I. Internation. Gams-wildtreffen Oberammergau: 17–25.

Hartwig, H. and J. Schrudde. 1974. Experimentelle Untersuchungen zur Bildung der primaren Stirnauswuchse beim Reh (*Capreolus capreolus* L.). Z. f. Jagdwiss. 20(1): 1–13.

Hash, H. S. 1973. Movements and food habits of the Lochsa elk. M. S. Thesis, Univ. Idaho, Moscow. 85 pp.

Hasserick, R. B. 1964. The Sioux: Life and customs of a warrior society. Univ. Oklahoma Press, Norman. 374 pp.

Hastings, A. 1983. Age-dependent predation is not a simple process, I: Continuous time models. Theoret. Popul. Biol. 23: 347–362.

———. 1984. Age-dependent predation is not a simple process, II: Wolves, ungulates, and a discrete time model for predation on juveniles with a stabilizing tail. Theor. Popul. Biol. 26: 271–282.

Hatch, E. 1886. Hunting at army posts. Forest and Stream 26: 85.

Hatt, R.T. 1949. Wapiti in Delaware. J. Mammal. 30(2): 201.

Hatter, J. 1950. The moose of central British Columbia. Ph.D. Thesis, State College of Washington (Washington State Univ.), Pullman. 359 pp.

Haufler, J. B. and F. A. Servello. 1994. Technniques for wildlife nutritional analyses. Pages 307–323 *in* T. A. Bookout, ed., Research and management techniques for wildlife and habitats. Fifth ed. The Wildl. Soc., Bethesda, Md.

Haugen, A. O. 1966. Fetus resorption in elk. J. Mammal. 47(2): 332–334.

Hautaluoma, J. and P. J. Brown. 1978. Attributes of the deer hunting experience: a cluster–analytic study. Journal of Leisure Research. 10: 271–287.

Hawes, R. A. and R. J. Hudson. 1976. A method of regional landscape evaluation for wildlife. J. Soil and Water Conserv. (Sept.–Oct.): 209–211.

Hay, O. P. 1927. The Pleistocene of the western region of North America and its vertebrated animals. Carnegie Institute of Washington Publ. 322B. 346 pp.

Hayden, F. V. 1873. Sixth annual report of the United States Geological Survey of the Territories embracing portions of Montana, Idaho, Wyoming and Utah. Govt. Print. Off., Washington, D.C. 844 pp.

Hayden, S. S. 1942. The international protection of wild life. Columbia Univ., New York. 246 pp.

Hayden-Wing, L. D. 1979. Distribution of deer, elk and moose on a winter range in southeastern Idaho. Pages 122–131 *in* M. S. Boyce and L. D. Hayden-Wing, eds., North American elk: Ecology, behavior and management. Univ. Wyoming, Laramie. 294 pp.

Hayne, D. W. 1949. Calculation of size of home range. J. Mammal. 30: 1–18.

Hays, W. J. 1871. Notes on the range of some of the animals in America at the time of the arrival of the white men. American Naturalist 5(7): 387–392.

He, B. 1991. China on the edge. Translation by China Books and Periodicals, Inc., San Francisco, California. 208 pp.

Heady, H. F. 1975. Rangeland management. McGraw-Hill Book Co., New York. 460 pp.

Hearne, S. A. 1795. A joumey from Prince of Wales' Fort in Hudson's Bay to the Northern Ocean. A. Strahan and T. Cadell, London. 458 pp.

Heberlein, T. A. 1991. Changing attitudes and funding for wildlife—preserving the sport hunter. Wildl. Soc. Bull. 19(4): 528–534.

———. 1992. Reducing hunter perception of crowding through information. Wildl. Soc. Bull. 20: 372–374.

Heberlein, T. A. and E. Thomson. 1996. Changes in U.S. hunting participation, 1980–90. Human Dimensions of Wildlife 1(1): 85–86.

Hebert, D. M. 1973. Altitudinal migration as a factor in the nutrition of bighorn sheep. Ph.D. Diss., Univ. British Columbia, Vancouver. 356 pp.

Hebert, D., J. Hebert and M. Caskey. 1984. Fecal nitrogen as a determinant of animal condition in bighorn sheep. North. Wild Sheep and Goat Council 4: 317–340.

Heckewelder, J. 1796. Map and despription of northeasetern Ohio. [Reprinted from the Magazine of History 1984 — Western Reserve Hist. Soc., Cleveland.]

Hediger, H. 1934. Zur biologie und psychologie der flucht bei tieren. Biol. Zgl. 54: 1–2.

———. 1955. The psychology and behaviour of animals in zoos and circuses. Dover, New York.

———. 1969. Comparative observations on sleep. Proc. Royal Soc. Med. 62(2): 153–156.

Hedrick, P. W. and P. S. Miller. 1992. Conservation genetics: Techniques and fundamentals. Ecol. Appl. 2(1): 30–46.

Heffelfinger, J., J. R. Purdue and K.E. Nicholls. 1999. Detecting evidence of Merriam's elk in Arizona's extant elk herds through analysis of mtDNA. Fed. Aid. Rept. W–78–M–4–9. Arizona Game and Fish Dept., Phoenix. 3 pp.

Heidmann, L. J. 1963. Deer repellents are effective on ponderosa pine in the Southwest. J. Forestry 61(1): 53–54.

Hein, R. G., J. L. Musser and E. F. Bracken. 1991. Serologic, parasitic and pregnancy survey of the Colockum elk herd in Washington. Northwest Science 65: 217–222.

Heinselman, M. L. 1971. The natural role of fire in northern conifer forests. Pages 61–72 *in* C. W. Slaughter, R. J. Barney and G. M. Hansen, eds., Fire in the northern environment—a symposium. USDA For. Serv., Portland, Oregon.

Heintz, E. 1970. Les cervidés, villafranchiens de France et d'Espagne. Mémoires du Mus. National d'Histoire naturelle. Série C, 22: 1–303, + 40 plates.

Heizer, R. F. 1955. Primitive man as an ecological factor. Kroeber Anthropol. Soc. Paper 13: 1-31.

———, ed. 1978. California. Handbook of North American Indians, Vol. 8. Smithsonian Instit. Press, Washington, D.C. 800 pp.

Helm, J., ed. 1981. Subarctic. Vol. 6. Handbook of North American Indians. Smithsonian Instit. Press, Washington, D.C. 837 pp.

Helwig, L. L. 1957. The value of conifers as a winter feed for elk (*Cervus canadensis nelsoni*), determined under controlled conditions. M.S. Thesis, Univ. Montana, Missoula. 79 pp.

Hemming, J. E. 1971. The distribution and movement patterns of caribou in Alaska. Game Tech. Bull. No. 1. Alaska Dept. Fish Game, Juneau. 60 pp.

Hendee, J. C. 1974. A multiple-satisfactions approach to game management. Wildl. Soc. Bull. 2(3): 104–113.

Hendee, J. C. and D. R. Potter, 1971. Human behavior and wildlife management: Needed research. Trans. N. Amer. Wildl. and Natur. Resour. Conf. 36: 383–396.

Hendee, J. C. and D. R. Potter. 1976. Hunters and hunting: management implications of research. Pages 137–161 *in* Proc. Southern States Recreation Res., Applications Workshop, New Orleans, Louisana,. Gen. Tech. Rept. SE–9. USDA For. Serv., Asheville, North Carolina.

Henderson, A. B. 1872. The diaries kept by A. B. Henderson during his prospecting journeys in the Snake, Wind River and Yellowstone country during the years 1867–1872. West. Hist. Res. Cent., Univ. Wyoming, from original in Coe Collection, Yale Univ. Library, New Haven, Connecticut. 113 pp. Photocopy.

Henderson, R. E. and A. O'Herren. 1992. Winter ranges for elk and deer: Victims of uncontrolled subdivisions? Western Wildlands 18(1): 20–25.

Henderson, T. G. 1983. Yersiniosis in deer from the Otago-Southland region of New Zealand. New Zealand Vet. J. 31: 221–224.

Hendricks, J. H. 1968. Control burning for deer management in chaparral in California. Proc. Tall Timbers Fire Ecol. Conf. 8: 218–233.

Henry, A. and D. Thompson. 1897. New light on the early history of the greater Northwest. The manuscript journals of Alexander Henry and of David Thompson, 1799–1814. E. Coues, ed., Vol. 1. F. P. Harper, New York. 3 vols.

Henshaw, J. 1969. Antlers—Bones of contention. Nature 244: 1,036–1,037.

Heptner, V. G. and V. I. Tsalkin. 1947. Oleni SSSR (Deer of the USSR) mater. K Pozn. Fauni i flory SSSR, Mov. Ser., Otd. Zool. (New series, Zoological Division), 10. Moscow.

Heptner, V. G. and A. A. Nasimowitsch. 1967. Der Elch. Neue Brehm-Bucherei, Wittenberg. 231 pp.

Heptner, V. G., A. A. Nasimovisch and A. G. Bannikov. 1961a. Mammals of the Soviet Union. Vol.1, Artiodactyla and Perissodactyla. Vysshaya Shkola, Moscow. 1,147 pp. Translated and published for the Smithsonian Instit. libraries by Amerind Publ. Co. Pvt. Ltd., New Delhi, India.

Heptner, V. G., A. A. Nasimovitch and A. A. Bannikov. 1961b. Mammals of the Soviet Union. Gustav Fischer Verlag, Jena. 939 pp.

Hepworth, W. G. and G. M. Thomas. 1962. Attempts to transfer psoroptic mites from elk to cattle and sheep. J. Amer. Vet. Med. Assoc. 140: 689–690.

Herin, R. 1968a. Electrocardiographic data on Rocky Mountain elk. J. Mammal. 49: 790–791.

———. 1968b. Physiological studies in the Rocky Mountain elk. J. Mammal. 49: 762–764.

Herman, C. M. 1969. The impact of disease on wildlife populations. Bioscience 19: 321–325

Herman, D. J. Unpublished. A comparison of fecal analysis with forage utilization analysis in the determination of elk diets. 1978. M.S. Thesis, Washington State Univ., Pullman. 51 pp.

Hermann, R. K. and D. P. Cavender, eds. 1973. Even-aged management. Symp. Proc. Oregon State Univ., Corvallis. 250 pp.

Hernandez-Pacheco, F. 1919. Escena pictòriea con representacliònes de insectos de epocia Paleolitica. Pages 62-67 in Tome extraordinario del 50 aniversario de la Real Soc. esp de Hist. Natur., Madrid, Spain.

Hernbrode, R.D. 1984. Colorado's emergency winter feeding operation, 1983–84. Pages 67–74 in R. W. Nelson, ed., Proc. West. States and Provinces Elk Workshop. Alberta Fish and Wildlife Div., Edmonton. 218 pp.

Herriges, J. D., Jr. and E. S. Williams. 1986. Unpublished. Records on file Department of Vet. Sciences, Univ. Wyoming, Laramie.

Herriges, J. D., Jr., E. T. Thorne, S. L. Anderson and H. A. Dawson. 1989. Vaccination of elk in Wyoming with reduced dose strain 19 Brucella: Controlled studies and ballistic implant field trials. Proc. U.S. Animal Health Assoc. 93: 640–653.

Herriges, J. D., Jr., E. T. Thorne and S. L. Anderson. 1991. Brucellosis vaccination of free-ranging elk (Cervus elaphus) on western Wyoming feedgrounds. Pages 107–112 in R. D. Brown, ed., The biology of deer. Springer-Verlag, New York. 596 pp.

Hershey, T. J. and T. A. Leege. 1976. Influences of logging on elk on summer range in north-central Idaho. Pages 73–80 in S. R. Hieb, ed., Proc. Elk-Logging-Roads Symp., Idaho Univ., Moscow. 142 pp.

Hershey, T. J. and T. A. Leege. 1982. Elk movements and habitat use on a managed forest in north-central Idaho. Wildl. Bull. No. 10, Idaho Dept. of Fish and Game, Boise. 24 pp.

Herzog, S. 1987. The karyotype of the red deer (Cervus elaphus L.). Caryologia 40(4): 299–305.

———. 1988. Polymorphism and genetic control of erythrocyte 6-phosphogluconate dehydrogenase in the genus Cervus. Animal Genetics 19: 291–294.

———. 1991. Management implications of genetic differentiation in red deer (Cervus elaphus Linné) populations. Congress of the International Union of Game Biologists 20(2): 816–821.

Hess, D., ed. 1977. Today's strategy . . . tomorrow's wildlife. A comprehensive management plan for Colorado's wildlife. Colorado Div. Wildlife, Denver. 96 pp.

Hess, K., Jr. 1993. Rocky times in Rocky Mountain National Park: An unnatural history. Univ. Colorado Press, Niwot. 167 pp.

Hess, M. 1997. Rocky Mountain elk trapping, transplanting and monitoring. Job Performance Rept., Fed. Aid Wildl. Restor. Grant W–48–R–28, Subgrant III, Proj. 1; Job 1. Nevada Div. Wildl., Reno. 16 pp.

Hett, J., R. Taber, J. Long and J. Schoen. 1978. Forest management policies and elk summer carrying capacity in the Abies amabilis forest, western Washington. Environ. Manage. 2: 561–566.

Hewitt, C. G. 1921.The Conservation of the Wildlife of Canada. Charles Scribner's Sons, Toronto. 344 pp.

Hewitt, J. N. B., ed. 1970. Journal of Rudolph Frederich Kurz. Univ. Nebraska Press, Lincoln. 382 pp.

———. 1973. Eye-witnesses to wagon trains west. Charles Scribner's Sons, New York. 178 pp.

Heydon, M. J., J. A. Milne, B. R. Brinklow and A. S. I. Loudon. 1995. Manipulating melatonin in red deer (Cervus elaphus): Differences in the response to food restriction and lactation on the timing of the breeding season and prolactin-dependent pelage changes. J. Exp. Zool. 273(1): 12–20.

Hibbard, C. T. 1996. Devil's Kitchen management team: Real life and sharing common ground. Pages 136–138 in K. E. Evans, compiler, Sharing common ground on western rangelands: Proccedings of a livestock/big game symposium; February 1996. Gen. Tech. Rept. INT-GTR-343. USDA For. Serv., Intermountain Res. Sta., Ogden, Utah. 164 pp.

Hibbard, C. W. 1959. Late Cenozoic microtine rodents from Wyoming and Idaho. Papers of the Michigan Acad. Sci. 44: 3–40.

Hibbard, C. W., C. E. Ray, D. E. Savage, D. W. Taylor and J. E. Guilday. 1965. Quaternary mammals of North America. Pages 509–525 in H. E. Wright, Jr. and D. G. Frey, eds., The Quaternary of the United States. Princeton Univ. Press, Princeton, New Jersey. 922 pp.

Hibler, C. P. 1981. Diseases. Pages 129–155 in O. C. Wallmo, ed., Mule and black-tailed deer of North America. Univ. Nebraska Press, Lincoln. 605 pp.

Hibler, C. P. and J. L. Adcock. 1971. Elaeophorosis. Pages 263–278 in J. W. Davis and R. C. Anderson, eds., Parasitic diseases of wild mammals. Iowa State Univ. Press, Ames.

Hibler, C. P., J. L. Adcock, R. W. Davis and Y. Z. Abdelbaki. 1969. Elaeophorosis in deer and elk in the Gila National Forest, New Mexico. Bull. Wildl. Dis. Assoc. 5(1): 27–30.

Hicks, L., A. Warren and C. Hicks. 1996. Upper Muddy Creek coordinated research management. Pages 125–128 in K. E. Evans, compiler, Sharing common ground on western rangelands: Proccedings of a livestock/big game symposium; February 1996. Gen. Tech. Rept. INT-GTR-343. USDA For. Serv., Intermountain Res. Sta., Ogden, Utah. 164 pp.

Hieb, S. R., ed. 1976. Proceedings of the Elk-Logging-Roads Symp., Univ. Idaho, Moscow. 142 pp.

Higgins, K. F. 1986. Interpretation and compendium of historical fire accounts in the northern Great Plains. Resour. Publ. 161, U.S. Fish and Wildl. Serv., Washington, D.C. 39 pp.

Hildebrand, P. R. 1971. Biology of white-tailed deer on winter range in Swan Valley, Montana. Unpubl. M. S. Thesis. Univ. Montana, Missoula. 91 pp.

Hilderbrand, G. V., S. D. Farley and C. T. Robbins. 1998. Predicting body condition of bears via two field methods. J. Wildl. Manage. 62: 406–409.

Hilger, M. I. 1952. Arapaho child life and its cultural background. Bull. 148. Bur. of Amer. Ethnol. , Washington, D.C. 253 pp.

Hiller, H., H. Schildknecht, A. B. Bubenik and J. Hamer. In press. Mammalian pheromones and allomones in antorbital secretion in red deer (*Cervus elaphus hippelaphus*). Proc. 3rd Int. Conf. on Chem. Commiss.

Hillis, J. M., M. J. Thompson, J.E. Canfield, L. J. Lyon, C. L. Marcum, P. M. Dolan and D. W. McCleery. 1991. Defining elk security: the Hillis Paradigm. Pages 38–43 *in* A. G. Christensen, L. J. Lyon and T. N. Lonner, compilers, Proc. Elk Vulnerability Symp., Montana State Univ., Bozeman. 330 pp.

Hillman, B. R. and D. L. Thompson. 1994. Report of the committee on tuberculosis. Proc. U.S. Animal Health Assoc. 98: 556–560.

Hill-Tout, C. 1906. The Salish tribes of the coast and lower Fraser Delta. Pages 225–235 *in* Annual Archaeological Report. Report of the Ontario Minister of Education. L. K. Cameron, Toronto. 249 pp.

Hilmon, J. B. 1959. Determination of herbage weight by double sampling: weight estimate and actual weight. Pages 20–25 *in* Techniques and methods of measuring understory vegetation. Tifton Symp. Proc., Tifton, Georgia, Oct. 1958. USDA For. Serv., Atlanta, Georgia.

Hindar, K. 1996. Introductions at the level of genes and populations. Pages 81–85 *in* O. T. Sandlund, P. J. Schei and A. Viken, eds., Proc. Norway/UN Conf. on Alien Species. Trondheim, Norway. 233 pp.

Hines, W. W. 1970. Ecological study of Roosevelt elk. Prog. Rept. Fed. Aid Proj. W–59–R–7, Job 1. Oregon Game Commiss., Portland. 25 pp.

Hines, W. W. and J. C. Lemos. 1979. Reproductive performance by two age-classes of male Roosevelt elk in southwestern Oregon. Oregon Dept. Fish and Wildl. Res. Rept. No. 8. 54 pp.

Hines, W. W., J. C. Lemos and N. A. Hartman. 1985. Male breeding efficiency in Roosevelt elk of southwestern Oregon. Oregon. Dept. Fish and Wildl., Wildl. Res. Rept. No. 15. 25 pp.

Hitchcock, M. and A. Ager. 1992. Microcomputer software for calculating an elk habitat effectiveness index on Blue Mountain winter range. PNW-GTR–301. USDA For. Serv., Portland, Oregon. 13 pp.

Hoar, W. S. 1966. General and comparative physiology. Prentice-Hall Publ. Co., Englewood Cliffs, New Jersey. 815 pp.

Hobbs, N. T. 1987. Fecal indices to dietary quality: A critic. J. Wildl. Manage. 51: 317–320.

———. 1989. Linking energy balance to survival in mule deer: Development and test of a simulation model. Wildl. Monogr. 101. 39 pp.

———. 1996. Modification of ecosystems by ungulates. J. Wildl. Manage. 60: 695–715.

Hobbs, N. T. and T.A. Hanley. 1990. Habitat evaluation: do use/availability data reflect carrying capacity? J. Wildl. Manage. 54: 515–522.

Hobbs, N. T. and R. A. Spowart. 1984. Effects of prescribed fire on nutrition of mountain sheep and mule deer during winter and spring. J. Wildl. Manage. 48: 551–560.

Hobbs, N. T. and R. A. Swift. 1985. Estimates of habitat carrying capacity incorporating explicit nutritional constraints. J. Wildl. Manage. 49: 814–822.

Hobbs, N. T., D. L. Baker and R. B. Gill. 1983. Comparative nutritional ecology of montane ungulates during winter. J. Wildl Manage. 47: 1–15.

Hobbs, N. T., B. L. Welch and T. E. Remington. 1986. Effects of big sagebrush on *in vitro* digestion of grass cell wall. Pages 186–189 in E. D. McArthur and B. L. Welch, compilers, Proc. symp on the biology of *Artemisia* and *Chrysothamnus*. Gen. Tech. Rept. INT–200. U.S. For. Serv.

Hobbs, N. T., D. L. Baker, G. D. Bear and D. C. Bowden. 1996. Ungulate grazing in sagebrush grasslands—effects of resources competition on secondary production. Ecol. Appl. 6: 218–227.

Hobbs, N. T., D. L. Baker, J. E. Ellis and D. M. Swift. 1979. Composition and quality of elk diets during winter and summer: a preliminary analysis. Page 47–53 *in* M. S. Boyce and L. D. Hayden-Wing, eds., North American elk: ecology, behavior and management. Univ. Wyoming, Laramie. 294 pp.

Hobbs, N. T., D. L. Baker, J. E. Ellis and D. M. Swift. 1981. Composition and quality of elk winter diets in Colorado. J. Wildl. Manage. 45: 156–171.

Hobbs, N. T., D. L. Baker, J. E. Ellis, D. M. Swift and R. A. Green. 1982. Energy- and nitrogen-based estimates of elk winter-range carrying capacity. J. Wildl. Manage. 46: 12–21.

Hobson, N. P. N. 1974. Experimental studies of food intake and digestion. Pages 46–50 *in* M. M. Bannerman and K. L. Blaxter, eds., (b) Studies on the rumen metabolism and other features of red deer. Aberdeen Univ. Press, Scotland.

Hobson, N. P. N., S. O. Munn, R. Summers and B. W. Staines. 1975. Rumen function in red deer, hill sheep and reindeer in Scottish Highlands. Proc. R. Soc. Edinburgh (B.) 75: 181–198.

Hobusch, E. 1980. Fair game. Arco Publishing, Inc., New York. 280 pp.

Hochereau-de Reviers, M-T. and G.A. Lincoln. 1978. Seasonal variation in the histology of the testis of the red deer, *Cervus elaphus*. J. Reprod. Fert. 54: 209–213.

Hodge, F. W., ed. 1907. Handbook of North American Indians north of Mexico. Smithsonian Instit., Bur. of Amer. Ethnol., Bull. 30. Part 1. Govt. Print. Off., Washington, D.C. 972 pp.

———, ed. 1910. Handbook of North American Indians north of Mexico. Smithsonian Instit., Bur. of Amer. Ethnol., Bull. 30. Part 2. Govt. Print. Off., Washington, D.C. 1,221 pp.

Hodgeman, T. P. and T. P. Bowyer. 1986. Fecal crude protein relative to browsing intensity by white-tailed deer on wintering areas in Maine. Acta Theriol. 31: 347–353.

Hoebel, E.A. 1938. Bands and distribution of the eastern Shoshone. Amer. Anthropol. 40: 3.

———. 1962. The Cheyennes: Indians of the Great Plains. Holt, Rinehart and Winston, New York. 112 pp.

Hoefs, M. And U. Nowlan. 1994. Distorted sex ratios in young ungulates: the role of nutrition. J. Mamm. 75: 631–636.

Hofer, H. 1972. Prolegomena primatologiae. Pages 113–148 *in* H. Hofer and G. Altman, eds., Die Sonderstellung des Menschen. Fischer Verlag, Stuttgart.

Hoff, G. L. and D. O. Trainer. 1973. Experimental infection in North American elk with epizootic hemorrhagic disease virus. J. Wildl. Dis. 9: 129–132.

———. 1981. Hemorrhagic diseases of wild ruminants. Pages 45–53 *in* J. W. Davis, L. H. Karstad and D. O. Trainer, eds., Infectious diseases of wild mammals, 2nd Edition, Iowa State Univ. Press, Ames, Iowa. 446 pp.

Hoffecker, J. F., W. R. Powers and T. Goebel. 1993. The colonization of Beringia and the peopling of the New World. Science 259: 46–53.

Hoffman, W. J. 1896. The Menomini Indians. Annu. Rept. Bur. Amer. Ethnol. 14(1): 5–328.

Hoffmeister, D. F. 1989. Mammals of Illinois. Univ. Illinois Press, Urbana. 348 pp.

Hoffmeister, D. P. 1947. Early observations on the elk in Kansas. Trans. Kansas Acad. Sci. 50(1): 75–76.

Hoflinger, H. 1948. Das Ovar des Rindes in den verschiendenen Lebensperioden unter besonderer Berucksichtigung seiner funktionellen Feinstruktur. Acta Anatomica, Suppl. V. S. Karger, New York. 196 pp.

Hofmann, R. R. 1973. The ruminant stomach. East African Monogr. Biol. 2: 354. East African Lit. Bur., Nairobi, Kenya.

———. 1985. Digestive physiology of the deer—Their morphophysiological specialization and adaptation (Deer digestive system). Pages 393–408 *in* P. F. Fennessy and K. R. Drew, eds., Biology of deer production. Bull. 22. Royal Soc. New Zealand.

———. 1988. Anatomy of the gastro-intestinal tract. Pages 14–43 *in* D. C. Church, ed., The ruminant animal: digestive physiology and nutrition. Prentice Hall, Englewood Cliffs, New Jersey. 564 pp.

———. 1989. Evolutionary steps of ecophysiological adaptation and diversification of ruminants: A comparative view of their digestive system. Oecologia 78: 443–457.

Hofmann, R. R. and N. Kirsten 1982 Die herbstmastsimulation. Schriften des Arbeitskreises fur Wildbiologie und Jagdwissenshaft and der Justus-Liebig-Universitat Giessen, Heft 9. Enke, Stuttgart. 113 pp.

Hofmann, R. R. and D. R. Steward. 1972. Grazer or browser? A classification based on stomach structure and feeding habits of East African ruminants. Mammalia 36: 226–240.

Hofmann, R., G. Geiger and R. König. 1976. Vergleichend-anatomische Untersuchungen an der Vormagenschleimhaut von Rehwild und Rotwild. Z. f. Saugetierkunde. 41: 167–193.

Hoglmuller, P.M. 1983 Rotwild-wintergatter. Anblick 4: 131–136.

Holder, P. 1974. The hoe and the horse on the Plains. Univ. Nebraska Press, Lincoln. 176 pp.

Holechek. J. L., R. D. Pieper and C. H. Herbel. 1989. Range management principles and practices. Prentice Hall, Englewood cliffs, New Jersey. 501 pp.

Holechek, J. L., M. Vavra and J. Skovlin. 1981. Diet quality and performance of cattle on forest and grassland range. J. Anim. Sci. 53: 291–298.

Holechek, J. L., M. Vavra and R. D. Pieper. 1982. Methods for determining the nutritive quality of range ruminant diets: a review. J. Anim. Sci. 54: 363–375.

Holland, M. D. and K. G. Odde. 1992. Factors affecting calf birth weight: a review. Theriogenology 38: 769–798.

Hollister, N. 1912. Mammals of the Alpine Club Expedition to the Mount Robson region. Can. Alpine J., Spec. No. 76 pp.

Holmes, J. C. 1982 Impact of infectious disease agents on the population growth and geographical distribution of animals. Pages 37–51 *in* R. M. Anderson and R. M. May, eds., Population biology of infections diseases. Dahlem Konferienzen, Berlin. Springer-Verlag, Publ.

Holmes, W. H. 1906. Decorative art of the aborigines of North America. Pages 179–188 *in* Anthropological papers written in honor of Franz Boaz. New York.

Holter, J. G. and H. H. Hayes. 1977. Growth in white-tailed deer fawns fed varying energy and constant protein. J. Wildl. Manage. 41: 506–510.

Holter, J. B., W. E. Urban, Jr. and H. H. Hayes. 1977. Nutrition of northern white-tailed deer throughout the year. J. Anim. Sci. 45: 365–376.

Holter, J. B., H. H. Hayes and S. H. Smith. 1979a. Protein requirement of yearling white-tailed deer. J. Wildl. Manage. 43: 872–879.

Holter, J. B., W. E. Urban and H. H. Hayes. 1979b. Predicting energy and nitrogen retention in young white-tailed deer. J. Wildl. Manage. 43: 880–888.

Holthausen, R. S., M. J. Wisdom, J. Pierce, D. K. Edwards and M. M. Rowland. 1994. Using expert opinion to evaluate a habitat effectiveness model for elk in western Oregon and Washington. Res. Pap. PNW-RP–479. USDA For. Serv., Portland, Oregon. 16 pp.

Hones, W. 1906. Central Algonkin. Pages 136–146 *in* Annual Archaeological Report 1905. Report of the Ontario Minister of Education. L. K. Cameron, Toronto. 249 pp.

Honess, R. F. 1955. The *Eimeria* of elk, *Cervus canadensis nelsoni*, with a description of a new species. Wyoming Game and Fish Commiss. Bull. 8: 25–28.

Honess, R. F. and K. B. Winter. 1956. Diseases of wildlife in Wyoming. Bull. 9. Wyoming Game and Fish Commiss., Laramie. 279 pp.

Hood, B. R., M. C. Rognlie and S. E. Knapp. 1997. Fascioloidiasis in game-ranched elk from Montana. J. Wildl. Dis. 33: 882–885.

Hoon, H. H., T. Nakano, R. J. Hudson and J. S. Sim. 1995. Chemical composition of antlers from wapiti (*Cervus elaphus*). J. Ag. Food Chem. 43: 2,846–2,849.

Hooven, E. F. 1973. A wildlife brief for the clearcut logging of Douglas-fir. J. Forestry 71(4): 210–214.

Hoover, M. D. 1973. Watershed management in lodgepole pine ecosystems. Pages 569–580 *in* D. M. Baumgartner, ed., Management lodgepole pine ecosystem symposium proc.. Washington State Univ., Pullman.

Hopkins, D. M. 1959. Cenozoic history of the Bering Land Bridge. Science 129(3362): 1519–1528.

Hopkins, D. M. 1960. Some characteristics of the climate in forest and tundra regions in Alaska. Arctic 12(4): 215–220.

Horejsi, B. L. 1976. Suckling and feeding behaviour in relation to lamb survival in bighorn sheep. Ph.D.Thesis, Univ. Calgary. 265 pp.

Horn, W. P. 1992. Slings and arrows: Challenges to sport hunting and wildlife management. Pages 108–115 *in* Proc., Governor's Symposium on North America's Hunting Heritage. Montana State Univ., Bozeman. 232 pp.

Hornaday, W. T. 1913. Our vanishing wild life: Its extermination and preservation. C. Scribner's Sons, New York. 411 pp.

Horner, G. W., A. J. Robinson, R. Hunter, B. T. Cox and R. Smith. 1987. Parapoxvirus infections in New Zealand farmed red deer (*Cervus elaphus*). New Zealand Vet. J. 35: 41–45.

Horner, S. M. 2000. Embryo, not fossil: Breathing life into the public trust in wildlife. Land and Water Law Rev. 35: 23–75.

Hornocker, M. G. 1970. An analysis of mountain lion predation upon mule deer and elk in the Idaho Primitive Area. Wildl. Monog. No. 21, The Wildl. Soc., Bethesda, Maryland. 39 pp.

Horr, D. A., ed. 1974. Ute Indians I. Garland Publishing Inc., New York. 159 pp.

Horwitz, W. J., ed. 1965. Official methods of analysis. 10th ed. Assoc. Off. Ag. Chem., Washington, D.C. 975 pp.

Hoskins, L. W. 1952. Browse utilization studies on the Pocatello winter big game range. M.S. Thesis, Univ. Idaho, Moscow. 87 pp.

Hoskins, L. W. and P. D. Dalke. 1955. Winter browse on the Pocatello big game range in southwestern Idaho. J. Wildl. Manage. 19: 215–225.

Hoskinson, R. L. and J. R. Tester 1980 Migration behavior of pronghorn antelope in southeastern Idaho J. Wildl. Manage. 44: 132–144

Hosley, N. W. 1956. Management of white-tailed deer in its environment. Pages 187–259 *in* W. P. Taylor, ed., Deer of North America. Stackpole Books, Harrisburg, Pennsylvania. 668 pp.

Hourrigan, J. L. and A. L. Klingsporn. 1975. Epizootiology of bluetongue: the situation in the United States of America. Aust. Vet. J. 51: 203–208.

Houston, D. B. 1968. The Shiras moose in Jackson Hole. Grand Teton Nat. Hist. Assoc., Wyoming Tech. Bull. 1: 1–110.

———. 1971. Ecosystems of National Parks. Science 172: 648–651.

———. 1973. Wildfires in northern Yellowstone National Park. Ecology 54(5): 1,111–1,117.

———. 1974. The northern Yellowstone elk. Parts I and II. History and demography. Unpubl. file rept., Yellowstone Nat. Park. 185 pp. Mimeo.

———. 1975. A comment on the history of the northern Yellowstone elk. BioScience 25(9): 578–579.

———. 1979. The northern Yellowstone elk—winter distribution and management. Pages 263–272 *in* M. S. Boyce and L. D. Hayden-Wing, eds., North American elk: Ecology, behavior and management. Univ. Wyoming, Laramie. 294 pp.

———. 1982. The Northern Yellowstone elk: Ecology and management. Macmillan Publ. Co., Inc., New York. 474 pp.

Howard, J. H. 1960. The roach headdress. Amer. Indian Hobbyist. 6(7 and 8): 89–94.

———. 1995. The Ponca tribe. Univ. Nebraska Press, Lincoln. 191 pp.

Howe, D. L. 1964. Study of anaplasmosis in game animals. Job Compl. Rept., Fed. Aid in Wildl. Restor., Proj. FW–3-R–11. Wyoming Game and Fish Commiss., Laramie.

———. 1965a. Diagnosis of diseases in mammals and birds. Job Compl. Rept., Fed. Aid in Wildl. Restor., Proj. FW–3-R–12. Wyoming Game and Fish Commiss., Laramie.

———. 1965b. Study of scab mite in elk. Job Compl. Rept., Fed. Aid in Wildl. Restor., Proj. FW–3-R–12, Wyoming Game and Fish Commiss., Laramie.

———. 1981. Miscellaneous bacterial diseases. Pages 418–422 *in* J. W. Davis, L. H. and D. O. Trainer, eds., Infectious diseases of wild mammals, 2nd ed. Iowa State Univ. Press, Ames. 446 pp.

Howe, D. L. and W. G. Hepworth. 1965. Anaplasmosis in big game animals: Tests on wild populations in Wyoming. Am. J. Vet. Res. 26: 1,114–1,120.

Howe, D. L., W. G. Hepworth, F. M. Blunt and G. M. Thomas. 1964. Anaplasmosis in big game animals: Experimental infection and evaluation of serologic tests. Am. J. Vet. Res. 25: 1,271–1,275.

Howe, G. E. 1976. The evolutionary role of wildfire in the northern Rockies and implications for resource managers. Tall Timbers Fire Ecol. Conf. Proc. 14: 257–265.

Howe, O. 1953. An exhibition of original painting in tempura: A thesis. Unpubl. MFAThesis, Univ. Oklahoma, Norman. 111 pp.

Howell, A. B. 1921. The black bear as a destroyer of game. J. Mammal. 2: 36.

Howery, L. D. and J. A. Pfister. 1990. Dietary and fecal concentrations of nitrogen and phosphorus in penned white-tailed deer does. J. Wildl. Manage. 54: 383–389.

Howes, S. W. 1977. Evaluation of elk–cattle competition on Clockum Creek watershed, Washington. Unpublished M.S. Thesis. Washington State Univ., Pullman. 70 pp.

Hoxie, F. E., ed. 1996. Encyclopedia of North American Indians. Houghton Mifflin Co., Boston, Massachusetts. 756 pp.

Hsu, T. C. and K. Benirschke. 1967. An atlas of mammalian chromosomes. Vol. 1, Folios 42 and 43.

Hubbell, T. H. 1954. The naming of geographically variant populations. Syst. Zool. 3(3): 113–121.

Huber, F. 1938. Die Magenwurmseuche des Rehwildes. Beobachtungen und Untersuchungen über ihre Bekampfungsmoglichkeiten. P. Parey Verlag, Berlin. 22 pp.

Hucin, B. 1957. Histologische Veranderungen in Nebennierenrinde des Rothirsches. Cs. Morfologie, Prague. 5(4): 376–382.

Huck, R., A. Shand, P. J. Allsop and A. B. Patterson. 1961. Malignant catarrh of deer. Vet. Rec. 73: 457–465.

Hudkins, G. G. and T. P. Kistner. 1977. *Sarcocystis hemionilatrantis* (sp. n.): life cycle in mule deer and coyotes. J. Wildl. Dis. 13(1): 80–84.

Hudson, R. J. 1985. Body size, energetics and adaptive radiation. Pages 1–24 *in* R. J. Hudson and R. G. White, eds., Bioenergetics of wild herbivores. CRC Press, Inc., Boca Raton, Florida. 314 pp.

———. 1989. History and technology. Pages 11–27 *in* R. J. Hudson, K. R. Drew and L. M. Baskin, eds., Wildlife production systems: Economic utilization of wild ungulates. Cambridge Univ. Press, U.K. 469 pp.

———. 1993. Origins of wildlife management in the western world.

Pages 5–21 *in* A. W. L. Hawley, ed., Commercialization and wildlife management: Dancing with the devil. Krieger Publ. Co., Malabar, Florida. 124 pp.

Hudson, R. J. and J. Z. Adamczewski. 1990. Effect of supplementing summer ranges on lactation and growth of wapiti (*Cervus elaphus*). Can. J. Anim. Sci. 70: 551–560.

Hudson, R. J. and R. J. Christopherson. 1985. Maintenance metabolism. Pages 121–142 *in* R. J. Hudson and R. G. White, eds., Bioenergetics of wild herbivores. CRC Press, Inc., Boca Raton, Florida. 314 pp.

Hudson, R. J. and V. V. Dezhkin. 1989. Socioeconomic prospects and design constraints. Pages 424–445 *in* R. J. Hudson, K. R. Drew and L. M. Baskin, eds., Wildlife production systems. Cambridge Univ. Press, Cambridge, U.K.

Hudson, R. J. and M. T. Neitfeld. 1985. Effect of forage depletion on the feeding rate of wapiti. J. Range Manage. 38: 80–82.

Hudson, R. J. and W. G. Watkins. 1986. Foraging rates of wapiti on green and cured pastures. Can. J. Zool. 64: 1,705–1,708.

Hudson, R. J. and R. G. White, eds. 1985. Bioenergetics of wild herbivores. CRC Press, Inc., Boca Raton, Florida. 314 pp.

Hudson, R. J., D. M. Hebert and V. C. Brink. 1976. Occupational pattern of wildlife on a major east Kootenay winter–spring range. J. Range Manage. 29(1): 38–43.

Hudson, R. J., H. M. Kozak, J. Z. Adamczewski and C. D. Olsen. 1991. Reproductive performance of farmed wapiti (*Cervus elaphus nelsoni*). Small Ruminant Res. 4: 19–28.

Hudson, R. J., W. G. Watkins and R. W. Pauls. 1985. Seasonal bioenergetics of wapiti in western Canada. Pages 447–452 *in* P. F. Fennessy and K. R. Drew, eds., Biology of Deer Production. Bull. 22. Royal Soc. New Zealand, Wellington. 482 pp.

Huggard, D. J. 1993a. Prey selectivity of wolves in Banff National Park I. Prey species. Can J. Zool. 71: 130–139.

———. 1993b. Prey selectivity of wolves in Banff National Park II. Age, sex and condition of elk. Can. J. Zool. 71: 140–147.

Hughbanks, D. L. 1993. Evaluation of a spike only regulation in southeastern Idaho. M. S. Thesis, Montana State Univ., Bozeman. 85 pp.

Hughbanks, D. L. and L. R. Irby. 1993. Evaluation of a spike-only regulation in S.E. Idaho. Pages 45–49 *in* 1993 Western States and Provinces Elk Workshop.

Hughes, R. H. 1958. The weight-estimate method in herbage production determinations. Pages 17–19 *in* Techniques and methods of measuring understory vegetation. Tifton Symp. Proc. USDA For. Serv., Atlanta, Georgia.

Hultkrantz, A. 1974a. The Shoshones in the Rocky Mountain area. Pages 173–214 *in* D. A. Horr, ed., Shoshone Indians. Garland Publ. Inc., New York. 320 pp.

———. 1974b. The Indians in Yellowstone Park. Pages 215–256 *in* D. A. Horr, ed., Shoshone Indians. Garland Publishing Inc., New York. 320 pp.

Humane Society of the United States. 1981. Hunted wildlife: The war on wildlife. Washington D.C. 2 pp.

Humbird, J. 1975. Modern day elk more plentiful. Idaho Wildl. Rev. (Jan./Feb.): 16–17.

Humboldt, A. De. 1811. Essai politique sur le royaume de la nouvellespagne (Mexico). 5 vols. Paris.

Hummel, M and B. Freet. 1999. Collaborative processes for improving land stewardship and sustainability. Vol. 3. Pages 97–129 *in* R. C. Szaro, N. C. Johnson, W. T. Sexton and A. J. Malk, eds., Ecological stewardship: A common reference for ecosystem management. Elsevier Science Ltd., Kidlington, Oxford, UK. 761 pp.

Hungerford, C. R. 1952. The food consumption and weight response of elk (*Cervus canadensis nelsoni*) under winter conditions. M.S. Thesis, Univ. Montana, Missoula. 60 pp.

Hunt, D. C. 1982. Legacy of the West. Univ. Nebraska Press, Lincoln. 157 pp.

Hunt, H. M. 1979. Comparison of dry-weight methods for estimating elk femur marrow fat. J. Wildl. Manage. 43: 560–562.

Hunter, G. N. 1949. The utility of personal interviews in obtaining information on game and fish resources Trans. N. Amer. Wildl. Conf 14: 239–252.

———. 1957. The techniques used in Colorado to obtain hunter distribution. Trans. N. Amer. Wildl. Conf. 22: 584–593.

———. 1966. Colorado big game harvest, 1959 to 1965. Manage. Rept. No. 1. Colorado Game, Fish and Parks. Dept., Denver. 41 pp.

Hunter, M. L., Jr. 1996. Fundamentals of conservation biology. Blackwell Science, Cambridge, Massachusetts. 482 pp.

———. 1999. Maintaining biodiversity in forest ecosystems. Cambridge U. Press, Cambridge, Massachusetts, 698 pp.

Hurley, M. A. 1994. Summer–fall ecology of the Blackfoot-Clearwater elk herd of western Montana. M. S. Thesis, Univ. Montana, Missoula. 138 pp.

Hurley, M. A. and G. A. Sargeant. 1991. Effectings of hunting and land manageemnt on elk habitat use, movement patterns and mortality in western Montana. Pages 94–98, *in* A. G. Christensen, L. J. Lyon and T. L. Lonner, eds., Proc. Elk Vulnerability Symp., Montana State Univ., Bozeman, Montana. 330 pp.

Hurt, W. R. 1953. Report of the investigation of the Thomas Riggs Site, 39HU1, Hughes County. Archeol. Studies Circ. 5. South Dakota Archeol. Commiss., Pierre. 98 pp.

Huston, D. B. 1968. The Shiras moose in Jackson Hole. Grand Teton Nat. Hist.Assoc., Wyo. Tech Bull. 1: 1–10.

Huston, J. E., B. S. Rector, W. C. Ellis and M. L. Allen. 1986. Dynamics of digestion in cattle, sheep, goats and deer. J. Anim. Sci. 62: 208–215.

Hutchings, D. L. and S. H. Wilson. 1995. Evaluation of lymphocyte stimulation tests for diagnosis of bovine tuberculosis in elk (*Cervus elaphus*). Am. J. Vet. Res. 56: 27–33.

Hutchings, S. S. and J. E. Schmautz. 1969. A field test of the relative-weight-estimate method for detemmining herbage production. J. Range Manage. 22: 408–411.

Hutchins, M. 1983. The mother–offspring relationship in mountain goat (*Oreamnos americanus*). Ph.D. Thesis, Univ. Washington, Seattle.

Hutchinson, G. E. 1958. Concluding remarks. Symp. Quantitative Biol. 22: 415–427.

Hutto, R. L., S. Reel and P. B. Landres. 1987. A critical evaluation of the species approach to biological conservation. Endangered Species Update 4: 1–4.

Hutton, D. A. 1972. Variation in the skulls and antlers of wapiti (*Cervus elaphus nelsoni Bailey*). M.S. Thesis. Univ. Calgary, Alberta, Canada. 139 pp.

Hutton, J., H. Jenkins and S. Edwards. 1995. Conservation and development compromised by animal welfare. Pages 271–274 *in* J. A. Bissonette and P. R. Krausman, eds., Integrating people and wildlife for a sustainable future. Proc. First Int. Wildl. Manage. Congr. The Wildl. Soc., Bethesda, Maryland. 697 pp.

Huxley, J. S. 1931. The relative size of antlers in deer. Proc. Zool. Soc., London. 819–863.

Interior Columbia Basin Environmental Management Project (ICBEMP). 1997. Eastside and Upper Columbia River Basin Draft Environmental Impact Statement. UDSA For. Serv. and USDI Bur. of Land Manage., Washington, D.C. 3 vols. March 2000.

———. 2000. Interior Columbia Basin Supplemental Draft Environmental Impact Statement. UDSA For. Serv. and USDI Bur. of Land Manage., Washington, D.C. 3 vols. March 2000.

Idaho Department of Fish and Game. 1994. 1993–1994 annual harvest report. Job Prog. Rept. W–170-R–18. Boise, Idaho.

———. 1995. Special section: Issues in elk management. Idaho Wildlife, 15(6): 4–15.

Idaho Elk Management Team. 1997. A turning point for elk hunters and elk hunting. Idaho Wildlife, 17(1): 13–30.

Ingersoll, E. 1882. Knocking around the Rockies. Univ. Oklahoma Press, Norman. 220 pp.

Inglis, D. M., J. M. Bowie, M. J. Allen and P. F. Nettleton. 1983. Ocular disease in red deer calves associated with a herpesvirus infection. Vet. Rec. 113: 182.

Inman, H. 1897. The old Santa Fe trail. The Macmillan Co., New York. 493 pp.

Interagency Ecosystem Management Task Force. 1995. The ecosystem approach—healthy ecosystems and sustainable economies. Vol. I. Overview. National Technical Information Service, Springfield, Virginia. 55 pp.

Interagency Study Team. 1977a. Elk habitat / timber management relationships on eastside forests of the Northern Region, USFS. USDA For. Serv. and Montana Dept. Fish and Game, Helena. 43 pp.

———. 1977b. Elk habitat coordinating guidelines for northern Idaho. USDA For. Serv., Idaho Dept. Fish and Game, USDI Bur. of Land Manage. and Univ. Idaho. 73 pp. Mimeo.

———. 1978. Elk habitat / timber management relationships, Central Zone-Region One. Confederated Salish and Kootenai Tribe, Montana Detp. Fish and Game, USDA For. Serv. 20 pp. Mimeo.

International Hunter Education Association. 1995. Hunting accident report. Outdoor Empire Publishing, Inc., Seattle, Washington. 36 pp.

Irving, J. T. 1835. Indian sketches, taken during an expedition to the Pawnee Tribes, 1833. Vol. 2. Cary, Lea and Blanchard, Philadelphia.

Irving, W. 1843. Adventures of Captain Bonneville. The Knickerbocker Press, New York. 459 pp.

Irwin, D. M., T. D. Kocher and A. C. Wilson. 1991. Evolution of cytochrome b gene of mammals. J. Molecular Evol. 32(2): 128–144.

Irwin, L. L. 1976. Effects of intensive silviculture on big game forage sources in northern Idaho. Pages 135–142 *in* S. R. Hieb, ed., Proc. Elk-Logging-Roads Symp., Univ. Idaho, Moscow. 142 pp.

———. 1978. Relationships between intensive timber culture, big game habitats and elk habitat use patterns in Northern Idaho. Unpubl. Ph.D. Thesis, Univ. Idaho, Moscow. 282 pp.

Irwin, L. L. and J. M. Peek. 1979. Relationship between road closures and elk behavior in northern Idaho. Pages 199–204 *in* M. S. Boyce and L. D. Hayden-Wing, eds., North American elk: Ecology, behavior and management. Univ. Wyoming, Laramie. 294 pp.

Irwin, L. L. and J. M. Peek. 1983a. Elk, *Cervus elaphus,* foraging related to forest management and succession in Idaho. Can. Field-Nat. 97: 443–447.

Irwin, L. L. and J. M. Peek. 1983b. Elk habitat use relative to forest succession in Idaho. J. Wildl. Manage. 47: 664–672.

Irwin, L. L. and J. M. Peek. 1978. Food habits of elk related to succession in Northern Idaho. Pages 175–189 *in* L. L. Irwin ed., Relationships between intensive timber culture, big game habitats and elk habitat use patterns in Northern Idaho. Unpubl. Ph.D. Thesis, Univ. Idaho, Moscow. 282 pp.

Irwin, L. L., J. G. Cook, D. E. McWhirter, S. G. Smith and E. B. Arnett. 1993. Assessing winter dietary quality in bighorn sheep via fecal nitrogen. J. Wildl. Manage. 57: 413–421.

Irwin, L. L., J. G. Cook, R. A. Riggs and J. M. Skovlin. 1994. Effects of long-term grazing by big game and livestock in the Blue Mountains forest ecosystems. U.S. For. Serv., Gen. Tech. Rept. PNW-GTR–325. Portland, Oregon. 49 pp.

Isaac, L. A. 1963. Fire—a tool not a blanket rule in Douglas-fir ecology. Tall Timbers Fire Ecol. Conf. Proc. 2: 1–18.

Ise, J. 1961. Our national park policy—a critical history. Johns Hopkins Press, Baltimore, Maryland. 701 pp.

Ives, F. F. 1969. Special hunts to control deer and elk damage. Pages 91–92 *in* H. C. Black, ed., Wildlife and reforestation in the Pacific Northwest. Symp. Proc. Oregon State Univ., Corvallis. 92 pp.

Jablan-Pantic, O. and J. Brna. 1966. Vreme i radosled pojava osifikacionih centara u skeletu jelena. Jelen (Beograd) 1(4): 21–30.

Jackson Hole News. 1971. Teton Park becomes firing line. November 11, 1971. 2 pp.

Jackson, C. S. 1947. Picture maker of the Old West: William H. Jackson. Chas. Scribner's Sons, New York. 308 pp.

Jackson, H.T. 1961. Mammals of Wisconsin. Univ. Wisconsin Press, Madison. 504 pp.

Jackson, R., G. W. de Lisle and R. S. Morris. 1995. A study of the environmental survival of Mycobacterium bovis on a farm in New Zealand. New Zealand Vet. J. 43: 346–352.

Jackson, S.G. 1992. Relationships among birds, willows and native ungulates in and around northern Yellowstone National Park. M.S. Thesis, Utah State Univ., Logan. 74 pp.

Jacobs, G. H. 1993. The distribution and nature of colour vision among the mammals. Biol. Rev. 68: 413–471.

Jacobs, G. H., J. F. Deegan II, J. Neitz, B. P. Murphy, K. V. Miller and R. L. Marchinton. 1994. Electrophysiological measurements of spectral mechanisms in the retinas of two cervids: white-tailed deer (*Odocoileus virginianus*) and fallow deer (*Dama dama*). J. Comp. Physiol. A 174: 551–557.

Jaczewski, Z. 1954. The effect of changes in length of daylight on the growth of antlers in the deer (*Cervus elaphus* L.). Folia Biol. 2: 133–143.

———. 1976. The induction of antler growth in female red deer. Bull Polish Acad. Sci. C1. II. 24(1): 61–65.

———. 1979. Die Auswirkungen von progesteron auf den Geweihzyklus beim rotwild (*Cervus elaphus* L.). Sonderdruck aus Bd. H.3,S. 150–159

———. 1990. Experimental induction of antler growth. Pages 371–395 *in* G.A. Bubenik and A. B. Bubenik, eds., Horns, Pronghorns and Antlers. Springer Verlag, New York. 562 pp.

Jaczewski, Z. and T. Jasiorowski. 1974. Observations on electroejaculation in red deer. Acta Ther. 19(10): 151–157.

Jaczewski, Z. and K. Krzywinska. 1974. The induction of antler growth in a red deer male castrate before puberty by traumatization of pedicle. Bull. Polish Academy of Sci. Cl. V. 22(1): 67–72.

Jaczewski, Z. and J. Morstin. 1973. Collection of the semen of the red deer by electroejaculation. Pr. Mater. Zool. 3: 83–86.

Jagd und Fischereirecht *in* Steiermark 1986 ed. Amt der Steierm. Landesreg. Graz. 324 pp.

Jakimchuk, R. D., S. H. Ferguson and L. G. Sopuck. 1987. Differential habitat use and sexual segregation in Central Arctic caribou herd. Can. J. Zool. 65: 534–541.

Janis, C. M. and D. Ehrhardt. 1988. Correlation of relative muzzle width and relative incisor width with dietary preference in ungulates. Zool. J. Linn. Soc. 92: 267–284.

Janis, C. M. and M. Fortelius. 1988. On the means whereby mammals achieve increased functional durability of their dentitions, with special reference to limiting factors. Biol. Rev. 63: 197–230.

Janis, C. M. and K. M. Scott. 1987. The interrelationships of higher ruminant families with special emphasis on the members of the Cervoidea. Amer. Mus. Novitates 2,893: 1–85.

Janson, R. 1973. Montana's elk habitat—Administrative Region 2. Pages 35–37 *in* Proc. West. States Elk Workshop, Bozeman, Montana. (Mimeo.)

Jarman, P. 1983. Mating system and sexual dimorphism in large, terrestrial, mammalian herbivores. Biol. Rev. 58: 485–520.

Jeffrey, D. E. 1963. Factors influencing elk and cattle distribution on the Willow Creek summer range, Utah. M.S. Thesis, Utah State Univ., Logan. 46 pp.

Jenkins, K. J. and E. E. Starkey. 1991. Food habits of Roosevelt elk. Rangelands 13(6): 261–265.

Jenkins, K. J. and E. E. Starkey. 1993. Winter forages and diets of elk in old-growth and regenerating coniferous forest in western Washington. Am. Midl. Nat. 130: 299–313.

Jenkins, K. J. and R. G. Wright. 1988. Resource partitioning and competition among cervids in the northern Rocky Mountains. J. Appl. Ecol. 25: 11–24.

Jensen, H. E., J. B. Jorgensen and H. Schonheyder. 1989. Pulmonary mycosis in farmed deer: Allergic zygomycosis and invasive aspergillosis. J. Med. Vet. Mycol. 27: 329–334.

Jensen, R. and L. Seghetti. 1955. Elaeophorosis in sheep. J. Amer. Vet. Med. Assoc. 127: 499–505.

Jensen, R.E., R.E. Paul and J.E. Carter. 1991. Eyewitness at Wounded Knee. Univ. Nebraska Press, Lincoln. 210 pp.

Jerison, H. J. 1961. Quantitative analysis of evolution of the brain in mammals. Science 121: 1,012–1,014.

Jerrett, I. V., K. J. Slee and B. I. Robertson. 1990. Yersiniosis in farmed deer. Aust. Vet. J. 67: 212–214.

Jessup, D. A., B. Abbas, D. Behymer and P. Gogan. 1981. Paratuberculosis in Tule elk in California. J. Am. Vet. Med. Assoc. 179: 1,252–1,254.

Jessup, D. A., H. J. Boermans and N. D. Kock. 1986. Toxicosis in tule elk caused by ingestion of poison hemlock. J. Am. Vet. Med. Assoc. 189: 1,173–1,175.

Jewitt, J. R. 1815. A narrative of the adventures and sufferings of John R. Jewitt; Only survivor of the crew of the ship Boston, during a captivity of nearly three years among the savages of Nootka Sound. Seth Richards, Middletown, Connecticut. 203 pp.

Jiang, A. and R. J. Hudson. 1992. Estimating forage intake and energy requirements of free-ranging wapiti (*Cervus elaphus*). Can. J. Zool. 70: 675–679.

———. 1993. Optimal grazing of wapiti (*Cervus elaphus*) on grassland: Patch and feeding station departure rules. Evol. Ecology 7: 488–498.

Jiang, A. and R. J. Hudson. 1994. Seasonal energy requirements of wapiti (*Cervus elaphus*) for maintenance and growth. Can. J. Anim. Sci. 74: 97–102.

Jochle, W. 1975. Current research in coitus-induced ovulation: a review. J. Reprod. Fert. Suppl. 22: 165–207.

Johns, P. E., M. H. Smith and R. K. Chesser. 1984. Annual cycles of the kidney fat index in a southeastern white-tailed deer herd. J. Wildl. Manage. 48: 969–973.

Johnson, A. 1923. The elk and the tooth hunter. Amer. Wildl. 12(2): 3–4.

Johnson, A., L. M. Bezeau and S. Smoliaks. 1968. Chemical composition and in vitro digestibility of alpine tundra plants. J. Wildl. Manage. 32: 773–777.

Johnson, A. J., P. K. Hildebrandt and R. Fayer. 1975. Experimentally induced *Sarcocystis* infection in calves: Pathology. Amer. J. Vet. Res. 36: 995–999.

Johnson, B. K., A. Ager, S. A. Crim, M. J. Wisdom, S. L. Findholt and D. Sheehy. 1996. Allocating forage among wild and domestic ungulates—a new approach. Pages 166–169 *in* W. D. Edge and S. Olson-Edge, eds., Proc. Sustaining Rangeland Ecosystems Symposium, Blue Mountains Natural Resources Institute, La Grande, Oregon.

Johnson, B. K., J. H. Noyes, J. W. Thomas and L. D. Bryant. 1991. Overview of the Starkey Project: current measures of elk vulnerability. Pages 225–228 *in* A. G. Christensen, L. J. Lyon and T. N. Lonner, compilers, Proc. Elk Vulnerability Symp., Montana State Univ., Bozeman. 330 pp.

Johnson, B. K., J. W. Kern, M. J. Wisdon, S. L. Findholt, and J. G. Kie. 2000. Resources selection of mule deer and elk during spring. J. Wildl. Manage. 64:685–697.

Johnson, D. E. 1951. Biology of the elk calf, *Cervus canadensis nelsoni*. J. Wildl. Manage. 15(4): 396–410.

Johnson, D. H. 1980. The comparison of usage and availability measurements for evaluating resource preference. Ecol. 61: 65–71.

Johnson, E. 1972. Moulting cycles. Mammal Rev. 1(7/8): 198–208.

Johnson, F. 1951. Radiocarbon dating. Memoirs of the Soc. for Amer. Archaeology, No. 8. Soc. for Amer. Archaeol., Salt Lake City, Utah. 65 pp.

Johnson, F. W. and D. I. Rasmussen. 1946. Recreational considerations of western big game hunt management. J. Forestry 44(11): 902–906.

Johnson, K. N., F. Swanson, M. Herring, S. Greene. 1999. Bioregional assessments: Science at the crossroads of management and policy. Island Press, Washington, DC. 398 pp.

Johnson, M. L. 1968. Application of blood protein electrophoretic studies to problems in mammalian taxonomy. Syst. Zool. 17(1): 23–30.

Johnson, M. L. and M. J. Wicks. 1959. Serum protein electrophoresis in mammals—taxonomic implications. Syst. Zool. 8(2): 88–95.

Johnson, M. L., M. J. Wicks and J. Brenneman. 1958. Serum protein electrophoresis of some boreal mammals. Murrelet 39(3): 32–36.

Johnson, N. K., J. F. Franklin, J. W. Thomas, and J. Gordon. 1990. Alternatives for management of late-successional forests of the Pacific Northwest: A report to the Agriculture Committee and the Merchant Marine and Fisheries Committee of the U.S. House of Representatives. The Scientific Panel on Late Successional Forest Ecosystems. 59 pp.

Johnson, O. W. 1969. Flathead and Kootenay. The Arthur H. Clark Co., Glendale, California. 392 pp.

Johnson, P. J. 1978. Patwin. Pages 350–360 *in* R. F. Heizer, ed., Handbook of North American Indians, Vol. 8, California. Smithsonian Instit. Press, Washington, D.C. 800 pp.

Johnson, R. L. and G. V. Johnson, eds. 1990. Economic Valuation of Natural Resources. Westview Press, Boulder, Colorado. 220 pp.

Johnson, W. M. 1962. Vegetation of high-altitude ranges in Wyoming as related to use by game and domestic sheep. Univ. Wyo. Bull. 387. Univ. Wyoming Ag. Exp. Sta., Laramie.

Johnston, J. S. 1898. First exploration of Kentucky. John P. Morton and Co., Louisville, Kentucky. 222 pp.

Johnstone-Wallace, D. B. and K. Kennedy. 1944. Grazing management practices and their relationship to the behavior and grazing habits of cattle. J. Ag. Sci. 34(4): 191–197.

Jones, D. I. H. and A. D. Wilson. 1987. Nutritive quality of forage. Pages 65–89 *in* J. B. Hacker and J. H. Ternouth, eds., The nutrition of herbivores. Academic Press, New York.

Jones, E. 1989. The elk man: Myth, ritual and symbolism. Crosscurrents 3: 1–32.

Jones, J. K., Jr. 1964. Mammals of Nebraska. Univ. Kansas. Publ., Mus. Natur. Hist. 16(1): 308–311.

Jones, J. K., Jr., D. C. Carter and H. H. Genoways. 1973. Checklist of North American mammals north of Mexico. Texas Tech. Univ. Mus. Occ. Paper 12. 14 pp.

Jones, J. K., Jr., R. S. Hoffman, D. W. Rice, C. Jones, R. J. Baker and M. D. Engstrom. 1991. Revised checklist of North American mammals north of Mexico, 1991. Texas Tech. Univ. Mus. Occ. Paper 146: 1–23.

Jones, J. R. 1974. Silviculture of southwestern mixed conifers and aspen: The status of our knowledge. Res. Pap. RM–122. USDA For. Serv., Fort Collins, Colorado. 44 pp.

Jones, W. 1906. Central Algonkin. Pages 136–146 *in* Annual archaeological report 1905. Append. to Rept. of the Minister of Ed., Ontario. L. K. Cameron, Toronto, Ontario. 249 pp.

Jones, W. B. 1965. Response of major plant species to elk and cattle grazing in northwestern Wyoming. J. Range Manage. 18(4): 218–220.

Jonkel, C. 1963. Deer, elk and moose population trends, food habits and range relationships in northwestern Montana. Job Compl. Rept. W–98–R–3. Montana Fish and Game Dept., Helena. 8 pp.

Jopson, N. B., M. W. Fisher and J. M. Suttie. 1990. Plasma progesterone concentrations in cycling and in ovariectomised red deer hinds: the effect of progesterone supplementation and adrenal stimulation. Anim. Reprod. Sci. 23: 61–73.

Jordan, C. F. 1971. A world pattern in plant energetics. Amer. Scientist 59: 425–433.

Jordan, L. A. and J.P. Workman. 1990. Survey of fee hunting for deer and elk on private land in Utah. Utah State Univ. Cooperative Extension Service. EC439. 11 pp.

Jortner, B. S., H. F., Troutt, T. Collins and K. Scarratt. 1985. Lesions of spinal cord parelaphostrongylosis in sheep. Sequential changes following intramedullary larval migration. Vet. Pathol. 22: 137–140.

Jourdonnais, C. S. and D. J. Bedunah. 1988. Influence of prescribed fire and cattle grazing on an elk winter range in Montana. Northwest Sci. 62: 72 (abstract).

Jourdonnais, C. S. and D. J. Bedunah. 1990. Prescribed fire and cattle grazing on an elk winter rnage in Montana. Wildl. Soc. Bull. 18: 232–240.

Julander, O. 1955. Deer and cattle range relations in Utah. For. Sci. 1: 130–139.

———. 1958. Techniques in studying competition between big game and livestock. J. Range Manage. 11: 18–21.

Julander, O. and D. E. Jeffrey. 1964. Deer, elk and cattle range relations on summer range in Utah. Trans. N. Amer. Wildl. and Natur. Resour. Conf. 29: 404–413.

Julander, O., W. L. Robinette and D. A. Jones. 1961. Relation of summer range condition to mule deer herd productivity. J. Wildl. Manage. 25: 54–60.

Kahlke, H. D. 1956. Die Cervidenreste aus den Altpleistozänen Ilmkiesen von Süssenborn bei Weimar. Part 1. Akademie Verlag, Berlin, Germany. 62 pp.

———. 1959. Die Cervidenreste aus den Altpleistozänen Sanden von Mosbach (Biebrich-Weisbaden). Abhandlungen der Akademie der Wissenschaften zu Berlin, Klasse für Chemie, Geologie und Biologie 156(9): 1–51.

Kahls, J. and G Stadlmann. 1990. Auswirkungen der neuen jagd- und forstrechtlichen bestimmungen auf die rotwildbewirtschaftung in der Steiermark. Pages 115–128 *in* H. Gossow, E. Donaubauer, F. Reimoser and J. Dieberger, eds., Tagungsbericht IURFO-Symposium regionalplanungskonzept, fur eine forstlich integrierte Schalenwildbewirtschaftung im Hoch- und Mittelgebirge. BOKU-reports on Wildlife Research and Game Management 1. Institut for Wildbiologie und Jagdwirtschaft, Universitat fur Bodenkultur, Wien.

Kallman, H., C. P. Agee, W. R. Goforth and J. P. Linduska, eds. 1987. Restoring America's wildlife 1937–1987. USDI Fish and Wildl. Serv., Washington, D.C. 394 pp.

Kamps, G. F. 1969. White-tailed and mule deer relationships in the Snowy Mountains of central Montana. Unpubl. M.S. Thesis, Montana State Univ., Bozeman. 59 pp.

Kappas, A. and A. P. Alvares. 1975. How the liver metabolizes foreign substances. Sci. Amer. 232(6): 22–51.

Kappler, C. J. 1904. Indian affairs. Laws and treaties. vol. II. U.S. Govt. Print. Off., Washington, D.C. 1,099 pp.

Karns, P. D. 1966. *Pneumostrongylus tenuis* from elk (*Cervus canadensis*) in Minnesota. Bull. Wildl. Dis. Assoc. 2: 79–80.

———. 1967. *Pneumostrongylus tenuis* in deer in Minnesota and implications for moose. J. Wildl. Manage. 31: 299–303.

Karstad, L. 1964. Diseases of the cervidae: a partially annotated bibliography. Wildl. Dis. Microcard No. 43, 7 cards.

———. 1969. Diseases of the cervidae: bibliography supplement 1. Wildl. Dis. Microfiche No. 52, 2 cards.

Katz, E. 1957. The two-step flow of communication: an update report on an hypothesis. Public Opinion Quart. 21(1): 61–78.

Kay, C. E. 1985. Aspen reproduction in the Yellowstone Park-Jackson Hole area and its relationship to natural regulation of ungulates. Pages 131–160 *in* G. W. Workman, ed., Western elk management: A symposium. Utah State Univ., Logan.

———. 1990. Yellowstone's northern elk herd: A critical evaluation of the "natural regulation" paradigm. Ph.D. Diss., Utah State Univ., Logan, Utah. 423 pp.

———. 1994. Aboriginal overkill—the role of Native Americans in structuring western ecosystems. Human Nature 5: 359–398.

———. 1995a. Aboriginal overkill and native burning: Implications for modern ecosystem management. West. J. Appl. Forestry 10(4): 121–126.

———. 1995b. Browsing by native ungulates: Effects on shrub and seed production in the Greater Yellowstone Ecosystem. Page 310–320 *in* B. A. Roundy, E. D. McArthur, J. S. Haley and D. K. Mann, compilers, Proc. Wildland Shrub and Arid Land Restoration Symp. Gen. Tech. Rept. INT-GTR–315. USDA For. Serv., Washington, D.C. 384 pp.

———. 1995c. An alternative interpretation of the historical evidence relating to the abundance of wolves in the Yellowstone ecosystem. Pages 77–84 *in* L. D. Carbyn, S. H. Fritts and D. R. Seips, eds., Ecology and conservation of wolves in a changing world. Can. Circumpolar Inst., Edmonton, Alberta. 620 pp.

———. 1996. Ecosystems then and now: A historical–ecological approach to ecosystem management and ecological integrity. *In* W. D. Williams and J. F. Dormaar, eds., Proc. 4th Prairie Conservation and Endangered Species Workshop, Occasional Pap. 23. Prov. Mus. Alberta Nat. Hist., Edmonton.

———. 1998. Are ecosystems structured from the top-down or bottom-up: A new look at an old debate. Wildl. Soc. Bull. 26: 484–498.

Kay, C. E. and S. Chadde. 1992. Reduction of willow seed production by ungulate browsing in Yellowstone National Park. Pages 92–99 *in* W. P. Clary, E. D. McArthur, D. Bedunah and C. L. Wambolt, compilers, Proc. Symp. On ecology and management of riparian shrub communities. Gen. Tech. Rept. INT–289. USDA For. Serv., Washington, D.C.

Kay, C. E. and F. H. Wagner. 1994. Historical condition of woody vegetation on Yellowstone's northern range: A critical evaluation of the "natural regulation" paradigm. Pages 151–169 *in* D. G. DeSpain, ed., Plants and their environments: Proc. First Biennial Scientific Conference on the Greater Yellowstone Ecosystem. U.S. Nat. Park Serv., Washington, D.C. 347 pp.

Kay, C. E. and C. A. White. 1995. Long-term ecosystem states and processes in the central Canadian Rockies: A new perspective on ecological integrity and ecosystem management. Pages 119–133 *in* R. M. Linn, ed., Sustainable society and protected areas. The Geo. Wright Soc., Hancock, Michigan. 300 pp.

Kay, J. 1985a. Native Americans in the fur trade and wildlife depletion. Environ. Rev. 9: 118-130.

———. 1985b. Preconditions of natural resource conservation. Ag. Hist. 59: 124–135.

Kay, R. N. B. 1985. Body size, patterns of growth and efficiency of production in red deer. Bull. Royal Soc. New Zealand 22: 411–422.

———. 1987. Weights of salivary glands in some ruminant animals. J. Zool. 211: 431–436.

———. 1989. Adaptation of the ruminant digestive tract to diet. Pages 196–203 *in* E. Skadhauge and P. Norgaard, eds., Suppl. 86. Acta Vet. Scandinavia.

Kay, R. N. B. and E. D. Goodall. 1976. The intake, digestibility and retention time of roughage diets by red deer (*Cervus elaphus*) and sheep. Proc. Nutr. Soc. 35: 98A–99A.

Kay, R. N. B. and M. L. Ryder. 1978. Coat growth in red deer (*Cervus elaphus*) exposed to a day-length cycle of six months duration. J. Zool. (London) 185: 505–510.

Kay, R. N. B. and B. W. Staines. 1981. The nutrition of the red deer (*Cervus elaphus*). Nutr. Abstr. Rev., Series B, 51: 601–622.

Kay, R. N. B., G. A. M. Sharman, W. J. Hamilton, W. J. Goodall, E. D. Pennie and A. G. P. Coutts. 1981. Carcass characteristics of young red deer farmed on hill pasture. J. Ag. Sci. Cambridge 96: 79–87.

Kearl, S. 1997. Personal communication. Wildlife Biologist, Utah Div. Wildl. Resour., and member Board of Directors, Lost Creek Landowners Assoc., Echo, Summit Co., Utah.

Keay, J. A. 1977. Relationship of habitat use patterns and forage preferences of white-tailed and mule deer to post-fire vegetation, upper Selway River, Idaho. Unpubl. M.S. Thesis, Univ. Idaho, Moscow. 76 pp.

Keech, M. A., R. D. Boertje, R. T. Bowyer and B. W. Dale. 1999. Effects of birth weight on growth of young moose: Do low-weight neonates compensate? Alces 35: 51-57.

Keech, M. A., R. T. Bowyer, J. M. Ver Hoef, R. D. Boertje, B. W. Dale and T. R. Stephenson. 2000. Life-history consequences of maternal condition in Alaskan moose. J. Wildl. Manage. 64: 450-462.

Keem, M. D. 1974. Some aspects of sarcosporidiousis in Wyoming elk (*Cervus canadensis*). Unpubl. M.S. Thesis, Univ. Wyoming, Laramie.

Keim, De B.R. 1885. Sheridan's troopers on the borders. David McKay, Philadelphia, Pennsylvania. 308 pp.

Keiss, R. E. 1969. Comparison of eruption-wear patterns and cementum annuli as age criteria in elk. J. Wildl. Manage. 33(1): 175–180.

Keiter, R. B. 1997. Greater Yellowstone's bison: Unraveling of an early American wildlife conservation achievement. J. Wildl. Manage. 61: 1–11.

Keiter, R. B. and R. H. Froelicher. 1993. Bison, brucellosis and law in the Greater Yellowstone Ecosystem. Land and Water Law Review 28: 1–75.

Keiter, R. B., T. Boling and L. Milkman. 1999. Legal perspectives on ecosystem management: Legitimizing a new federal land management policy. Vol. 3. Pages 9–41 *in* R. C. Szaro, N. C. Johnson, W. T. Sexton and A. J. Malk, eds., Ecological stewardship: A common reference for ecosystem management. Elsevier Science Ltd., Kidlington, Oxford, UK. 761 pp.

Keith, G. 1890. Le bourgeois de la compagnie du Nord-Ouest: Récits de voyages, lettres et rapports inédits relatifs au Nord-ouest Canadien. L. R. Masson, ed. 2 vols. A. Coté, Quebec.

Keith, L. B. 1974. Some features of population dynamics in mammals. Pages 17–58 *in* I. Kjener and P. Bjurholm, eds., Trans. 11th Congr. IUGB. Stockholm, September, 1973. National Swedish Environment Protection Board, Stockholm. 631 pp.

Kelker, G. H. 1940. Estimating deer populations by a differential hunting loss in the sexes. Proc. Utah Acad. Sci., Arts and Letters 17: 65–69.

———. 1964. Appraisal of ideas advanced by Aldo Leopold thirty years ago. J. Wildl. Manage. 28(1): 180–185.

Kellert, S. 1980. Activities of the American public relating to animals. Govt. Print. Off., Washington, D.C.

———. 1985. Historical trends in perceptions and uses of animals in 20th century America. Environ. Rev. 9: 34–53.

———. 1996. The value of life. Island Press/Shearwater Books, Washington, D.C. 263 pp.

Kellogg, F. E., A. K. Prestwood and R. E. Noble. 1970. Anthrax epizootic in white-tailed deer. J. Wildl. Dis. 6(4): 226–228.

Kellogg, R. 1939. Annotated list of Tennessee mammals. U.S. National Mus. Proc. 86(3,051): 245–303.

———. 1956. What and where are the whitetails? Pages 31–35 in W. P. Taylor, ed., The deer of North America. Stackpole Co., Harrisburg, Pennsylania. 668 pp.

Kelly, F. 1993. My captivity among the Sioux Indians. Citadel Press, New York. 285 pp.

Kelly, R. W., K. P. McNatty, G. H. Moore, D. Ross and M. Gibb. 1982. Plasma concentrations of LH, prolactin, oestradiol and progesterone in female red deer (Cervus elaphus) during pregnancy. J. Reprod. Fert. 64: 475–783.

Kelsall, J. P. 1968. The migratory barren-ground caribou of Canada. Dept. Indian Affairs and Northern Development. Can. Wildl. Serv., Ottawa. 339 pp.

Kendeigh, S. C. 1961. Animal ecology. Prentice-Hall, Inc., Englewood Cliffs, New Jersey. 468 pp.

Kennedy, D. I. D. and R. T. Bouchard. 1990. Northern Coast Salish. Pages 441–452 in W. Suttles, ed., Northwest coast. Handbook of North American Indians. Vol. 7. Smithsonian Instit. Press, Washington, D.C. 777 pp.

Kennedy, J. J. 1973. Some effects of urbanization on big and small game management. Trans. N. Amer. Wildl. and Natur. Resour. Conf. 38: 248–255.

———. 1974. Attitudes and behavior of deer hunters in a Maryland Forest. J. Wildl. Manage. 38: 1–8.

Kennedy, J. J. and J. W. Thomas. 1995. Managing natural resources as a social value. Pages 311–322 in R. L. Knight and S. F. Bates, eds., A new century for natural resources management. Island Press, Washington, D.C.

Kenyon, S. and M. D. Duda. 2000. Big game hunting—The future of hunting in America. Dallas, Texas. 4 pp.

Kerasote, T. 1993. Bloodties: Nature, culture and the hunt. Random House, New York. 277 pp.

Kerr, D. E., B. Laarveld, M. I. Fehr and J. G. Manns. 1991. Profiles of serum IGF–1 concentrations in calves from birth to eighteen months of age and in cows throughout the lactation cycle. Can. J. Anim. Sci. 71: 695–705.

Kessler, W. B. and H. Salwasser. 1995. Natural resource agencies: Transforming from within. Pages 171–188 in R. L. Knight and S. F. Bates, eds., A new century for natural resources management. Island Press, Washington, D.C.

Keyser, J. D. 1987. A lexicon for historic Plains Indian rock art: Increasing interpretive analysis. Plains Anthropol. 32(115): 43–71.

———. 1992. Indian rock art of the Columbia Plateau. Univ. Washington Press, Seattle. 138 pp.

Kiddie, D. G. 1962. The Sika deer (Cervus nippon) in New Zealand. New Zealand For. Serv., Wellington. 35 pp.

Kie, J. G., M. White and D. L. Drawe. 1983. Condition parameters of white-tailed deer in Texas. J. Wildl. Manage. 47: 583–594.

Kiltie, R. A. 1988. Gestation as a constraint on the evolution of seasonal breeding in mammals. Pages 257–289 in M. S. Boyce, ed., Evolution of life histories in mammals. Yale Univ. Press, New Haven, Connecticut. 373 pp.

Kimball, D. and J. Kimball. 1969. The market hunter. Dillon Press, Minneapolis. 132 pp.

Kimball, J. F. and M. L. Wolfe. 1974. Population analysis of a northern Utah elk herd. J. Wildl. Manage. 38: 161–174.

———. 1979. Continuing studies of the demographics of a northern Utah elk population. Pages 20–28 in M. S. Boyce and L. D. Hayden-Wing, eds., North American elk: Ecology, behavior and management. Univ. Wyoming, Laramie. 294 pp.

Kimball, J. F. and M. L. Wolfe. 1985. Elk management opportunities in northern Utah: To feed or not to feed. Pages 191–197 in G. W. Workman, ed., Western elk management: A symposium. College of Natur. Res., Utah State Univ., Logan. 212 pp.

Kimball, T. L. 1955. The application of controlled hunting to the take of big game. Proc. Int. Assoc. Game, Fish and Conserv. Commiss. 45: 95–102.

———. 1957. Pros and cons of nonresident fees. Proc. Int. Assoc. Game, Fish and Conserv. Commiss. 47: 63–67.

Kinch, C. 1998. Nebraska's last elk. Nebraskaland 76(10): 4.

Kindel, F. J. 1958. Salt in the management of elk and other wildlife in the vicinity of Clearwater Ridge area of Idaho. Project Rept. W–85-R–8. Univ. Idaho, Moscow. 69 pp.

King, F. 1948. The management of man. Wis. Conserv. Bull. 13(9): 9–11.

King, T. S. 1962. A vacation among the Sierras: Yosemite in 1860. J. A. Hussey, ed. The Book Club of California, San Francisco. 78 pp.

Kingery, J. L., J. C. Mosley and K. C. Bordwell. 1996. Dietary overlap among cattle and cervids in northern Idaho forest. J. Range. Manage. 49: 8–15.

Kingscote, A. A. 1950. Liver rot (fasciolidiasis) in ruminants. Can. J. Comp. Med. 14: 203–208.

Kingscote, B. F., W. D. G. Yates and G. B. Tiffin. 1987. Diseases of wapiti utilizing cattle range in southwestern Alberta. J. Wildl. Dis. 23: 86–91.

Kingston, J. T. 1908. Early western days. Pages 297–341 in L. C. Draper, ed., Collections of the State Historical Society of Wisconsin. Vol. 7. 492 pp. (Reprint of 1876 original issue.)

Kingston, N. and J. K. Morton. 1975. Trypanosoma cervi sp. n. from elk (Cervus canadensis) in Wyoming. J. Parasitol. 61: 17–23.

Kinietz, V. 1940. Notes on the roached headdress of animal hair among the North American Indians. Pap. Michigan Acad. Sci., Arts and Letters XXVI: 463–467.

Kip, I.W. 1846. The early Jesuit missions in North America. Wiley and Putnam, New York. 321 pp.

Kirkpatrick, R. L., D. E. Buckland, W. A. Abler, P.F. Scanlon, J. B. Whelan and H. E. Burkhart. 1975. Energy and protein influences on blood urea nitrogen of white-tailed deer fawns. J. Wildl. Manage. 39: 692–698.

Kirkpatrick, T. O. 1965. The economic and social values of hunting and fishing in New Mexico. Albuquerque: Bur. Bus. Res., Univ. New Mexico. 94 pp.

Kirkwood, A. C. 1986. History, biology and control of sheep scab. Parasitol. Today 2: 302–307.

Kirsch, J. B. 1963. Range use, relationship to logging and food habits of the elk in the Little Belt Mountains, Montana. M.S. Thesis, Montana State Univ., Bozeman. 44 pp.

Kirsch, J. B. and K. R. Greer. 1968. Bibliography . . . Wapiti-American elk and European red deer. Fed. Aid in Wildl. Restor. W–83-R, Special Report No. 2. Montana Fish and Game Dept., Bozeman. 147 pp.

Kirtland, J. P. 1838. A catalogue of the Mammalia, birds, reptiles, fishes, Testacea and Crustacea in Ohio. Pages 157–200 in Second annual report of the Ohio Geological Survey. Samual Medary Print., Columbus, Ohio. 286 pp.

Kistner, T. P. 1982. Diseases and parasites. Pages 181–217 in J. W. Thomas and D. E. Toweill, eds. Elk of North America: Ecology and management. Stackpole Books, Harrisburg, Pennsylvania. 698 pp.

Kistner, T. P. and D. Wyse. 1975. Anthelmintic efficacy of injectible livamisole in sheep. Proc. Helm. Soc. Washington 42(2): 93–97.

Kistner, T. P., G. E. Reynolds, L. D. Koller, C. E. Trainer and D. L. Eastman. 1975. Clinical and serological findings on the distribution of bluetongue and epizootic hemorrhagic disease viruses in Oregon. Proc. Amer. Assoc. Vet. Lab. Diag. 18: 135–148.

Kistner, T. P., G. R. Johnson and G. A. Rilling. 1977. Naturally occurring neurologic disease in a fallow deer infected with meningeal worms. J. Wildl. Dis. 13: 55–58.

Kistner, T. P., C. E. Triner and N. A. Hartmann. 1980. A field technique for evaluating physical condition of deer. Wildl. Soc. Bull. 8: 11-17.

Kistner, T. P., K. R. Greer, D. E. Worley and O. A. Brunetti. 1982. Diseases and parasites. Pages 181–217 in J. W. Thomas and D. E. Toweill, eds., Elk of North America. Stackpole Books, Harrisburg, Pennsylvania. 698 pp.

Kitchen, D. and P. T. Bromley. 1974. Agonistic behaviour of territorial pronghorn bucks. Pages 365–381 in V. Geist and F. Walther, eds., The behaviour of ungulates and its relation to management. IUCN Publ., n. s. No. 24, Morges, Switzerland.

Kitchener, A. C. 1985. The effect of behaviour and body weight in the mechanical design of horns. J. Zool., London. 205: 191–203.

———. 1991. *The evolution and mechanical design of horns and antlers*. Biomechanics in Evolution. Cambridge Univ. Press, Cambridge.

Kittams, W. H. 1953. Reproduction of Yellowstone elk. J. Wildl. Manage. 17(2): 177–184.

———. 1959. Future of the Yellowstone wapiti. Naturalist 10(2): 30–39.

Klaphake, P. 1997. Trails to the future. Wapiti 12(3): A.

———, ed. 2000. WAPITI for volunteers. Rocky Mountain Elk Found., Missoula, Montana. 31 pp.

Kleiber, M. 1961. The fire of life—an introduction to animal energetics. J. Wiley and Sons, Inc., New York. 454 pp.

Klein, A. M. 1980. Plains economic analysis: the Marxist complement. Pages 129–140 in W. R. Wood and M. Liberty, eds., Anthropology on the Great Plains. Univ. Nebraska Press, Lincoln. 306 pp.

Klein, D. R. 1964. Range-related differences in growth of deer reflected in skeletal ratios. J. Mammal. 45(2): 226–235.

———. 1965a. Ecology of deer range in Alaska. Ecolog. Monogr. 35: 259–284.

———. 1965b. Postglacial distribution patterns of mammals in the southern coastal regions of Alaska. Arctic 18(1): 7–20.

———. 1970. Food selection by North American deer and their response to over-utilization of preferred plant species. Pages 25–44 in A. Watson, ed., Animal populations in relation to their food sources. Blackwell Scientific Publ., Oxford. 477 pp.

———. 1986. Latitudinal variation in foraging strategies. Pages 237–246 in O. Gudmundsson, ed., Grazing research at northern latitudes. Plenum, New York.

———. 1991. The status of deer in a changing world environment. Pages 3–12 in R. D. Brown, ed., The biology of deer. Springer-Verlag, New York.

Klein, D. R., M. Meldgaard and S. G. Fancy. 1987. Factors determining leg length in *Rangifer tarandus*. J. Mammal. 68(3): 642–655.

Klemmedson, J. O. 1967. Big-game winter range—a diminishing resource. Trans. N. Amer. Wildl. and Natur. Resour. Conf. 32: 259–269.

Kleppe v. State of New Mexico. 1976. CCH U.S. Supreme Court Bull. B–3328. Jan. 17.

Klessig, L. L. 1970. Hunting in Wisconsin: Initiation, desertion, activity patterns and attitudes as influenced by social class and residence. M.S. Thesis, Univ. Wisconsin, Madison. 152 pp.

Knaus, W. and W. Schroder. 1975. Das Gamswild. 2nd ed. Paul Parey, Berlin. 234 pp.

Kniffen, F. B. 1928. Achowmawi geography. Univ. of California (Berkeley) Publ. in Amer. Archaeol. and Ethnol. 23(5): 297–332.

Knight, R. L. and D. N. Cole. 1995. Wildlife responses to recreationists. Pages 51–69 in R. L. Knight and K. J. Gutzwiller, eds., Wildlife and recreationists. Island Press, Washington, D.C. 373 pp.

Knight, R. L. and K. J. Gutzwiller. 1995. Wildlife and recreationists: Coexistence through management and research. Island Press, Washington, D.C.

Knight, R. L. and P. B. Landres. 1998. Stewardship across boundaries. Island Press, Washington, D.C. 371 pp.

Knight, R. L. and T. W. Clark. 1998. Boundaries between public and private lands: Defining obstacles, finding solutions. Pates 1750191 in R. L. Knight and P. B. Landres, eds., Stewardship across boundaries, Island Press, Washington, DC.

Knight, R. R. 1966a. The effectiveness of neckbands for marking elk. J. Wildl. Manage. 30: 845–846.

———. 1966b. Bone characteristics associated with aging in elk. J. Wildl. Manage. 30: 369–374.

———. 1967. Elk population trends, food habits and range relationships in the Sun River area. Job Compl. Rept. Fed. Aid Proj. W–98–R–6 & 7, Job No. B–4. Montana Dept. Fish and Game, Helena. 237 pp.

———. 1970. The Sun River elk herd. Wildl. Monogr. No. 23. The Wildl. Soc., Washington, D.C. 66 pp.

———. 1972. The Lochsa elk herd. Idaho For. 23–25.

———. 1973. Calf:cow ratios in the Lochsa elk herd. Pages 90–91 in Proc. Biennial Conf. West. States Elk Workshop, Bozeman, Montana.

Knorre, E. P. 1974. Changes in the behavior of moose with age and during the process of domestication. Naturaliste Canadien 101: 371–377.

Knowles, C. J. 1975. Range relationships of mule deer, elk and cattle in a rest–rotation grazing system during summer and fall. Fed. Aid Proj. W–120-R, Job BG–10.01. Montana Dept. Fish and Game, Helena. 111 pp.

Knowles, C. J. and R. B. Campbell. 1987. Distribution of elk and cattle in a rest–rotation grazing system. Pages 46–60 in J. M. Peek and P. D. Dalke, eds., Wildlife–livestock Relationship Symposium: Proc. 10. Univ. Idaho, Wildl. and Range Exp. Sta., Moscow.

Knowlton, F. F. 1960. Food habits, movements and populations of moose in the Gravelly Mountains, Montana. J. Wildl. Manage. 24: 162–170.

Knox, M. V. B. 1875. Kansas mammalia. Trans. Kansas Acad. Sci. 4: 19–22.

Kocan, A. A. 1985. The use of ivermectin in the treatment and prevention of infection with *Parelaphostrongylus tenuis* (Dougherty) (Nematoda: Metastrongyloidea) in white-tailed dear (*Odocoileus virginianus* Zimmermann). J. Wildl. Dis. 21: 454–455.

Kocan, A. A., M. G. Shaw, K . A. Waldrup and G. J. Kubat. 1982. Distribution of *Parelaphostrongylus tenuis* (Nematoda: Metastrongyloidea) in white-tailed deer from Oklahoma. J. Wildl. Dis. 18: 457–460.

Koch, E. 1941. Big game in Montana from early historical records. J. Wildl. Manage. 5(4): 357–370.

Koch, R. P. 1977. Dress clothing of the Plains Indians. Univ. Oklahoma Press, Norman. 219 pp.

Kohl, J. G. 1860. Kitchi-Gami: Wanderings round Lake Superior. Translated by L. Wraxall. Chapman and Hall, London. 428 pp.

Kohlmann, S. G. 1999. Adaptive fetal sex allocation in elk: Evidence and implications. J. Wildl. Manage. 63: 1,109-1,117.

Komarek, E. V., Sr. 1976. Fire ecology review. Tall Timbers Fire Ecol. Conf. Proc. 14: 201–216.

Komarek, R. 1963. Fire and the changing wildlife habitat. Tall Timbers Fire Ecol. Conf. Proc. 2: 35–43.

Komberec, T. J. 1976a. Range relationships of mule deer, elk and cattle in a rest–rotation grazing system during winter and spring. Fed. Aid Proj. W–120-R, Job 2. Montana Dept. Fish and Game, Helena.

———. 1976b. Range relationships of mule deer, elk and cattle in the "breaks" habitat of eastern Montana. Job Compl. Rept., W–120-R–6–7. Montana Dept. Fish and Game, Helena. 79 pp.

Koong, L. J. C. L. Ferrell and J. A. Nienaber. 1985. Assessment of interrelationships among levels of intake and production, organ size and fasting heat production in growing animals. J. Nutr. 115: 1,383–1,390.

Kopcha, M., J. V. Marteniuk, R. Sills, B. Steficek and T. W. Schillhorn van Veen. 1989. Cerebrospinal nematodiasis in a goat herd. J. Am. Vet. Med. Assoc. 194: 1,439–1,442.

Korfhage, R. C. 1974. Summer food habits of elk in the Blue Mountains of northeastern Oregon based on fecal analysis. M.S. Thesis, Washington State Univ., Pullman. 117 pp.

Korfhage, R. C., J. R. Nelson and J. M. Skovlin. 1980. Summer diets of Rocky Mountain elk in northeastern Oregon. J. Wildl. Manage. 44(3): 746–750.

Kortright, F. H. 1962. The ducks, geese and swans of North America. Stackpole Books, Inc., Harrisburg, Pennsylvania. 476 pp.

Koulischer, L., J. Tiskens and J. Mortelmans. 1972. Mammalian cytogenetics VII. The chromosomes of *Cervis canadensis, Elaphurus davidianus, Cervus nippon nippon* (Temminck) and *Pudu pudu*. Acta. Zool. Pathol. Antverp 56: 25–30.

Kovalicky, T. and G. S. Blair. 1991. The role of the key land manager in influencing hunter opportunity. Pages 244–246 in A. G. Christensen, L. J. Lyon, T. N. Lonner, compilers, Proc. Elk Vulnerability Symp., Montana State Univ., Bozeman. 330 pp.

Kozak, H. M., R. J. Hudson and L. A. Renecker. 1994. Supplemental winter feeding. Rangelands 16: 153–156.

Kozak, H. M., R. J. Hudson, N. French and L. A. Renecker. 1995. Winter feeding, lactation and calf growth in farmed wapiti. Rangelands 17: 116–120.

Kozlowski, T. T. and C. E. Ahlgren, eds. 1974. Fire and ecosystems. Academic Press, New York. 542 pp.

Kraus, F. and M. M. Miyamoto. 1991. Rapid cladogenesis among the pecoran ruminants: Evidence from mitochondrial DNA sequences. Syst. Zool. 40(2): 117–130.

Krebs, C. J., M. S. Gains, B. L. Keller, J. H. Myres and R. H. Tamarin. 1973. Population cycles in small rodents. Science 179: 35–41.

Krech, D. M., M. R. Rosenzweig and E. L. Bennett. 1960. Effects of environmental complexity and training on brain chemistry. J. Comp. Physiol. Psychol. 53: 509–519.

Krech, S. III, ed. 1981. Indians, animals and the fur trade. Univ. Georgia Press, Athens. 207 pp.

Kristal, M. B. 1980. Placentophagia: A behavioural enigma. Neuroscience and Behavioural Reviews 4: 141–150.

Kroeber, A. L. 1902. The Arapaho. Amer. Mus. Natur. Hist. Bull. XVIII: 1–229. Part 1.

———. 1925. Handbook of the Indians of California. Bull. 78. Bur. Amer. Ethnol., Govt. Print. Off., Washington, D.C. 995 pp.

———. 1934. Native American population. Amer. Anthropol. 36: 1–25.

———. 1939. Cultural and natural areas of native North America. Univ. California Press, Berkeley. 242 pp.

Kröning, F. and F. Vorreyer. 1957. Untersuchungen uber Vermehrungsraten und Karpergewichte beim weiblichen Rotwild. Z. Jagdwiss. 3(4): 145–153.

Krueger, J. K. and D. J. Bedunah. 1988. Influence of forest site on total nonstructural carbohydrate reserves of pinegrass, elk sedge and snowberry. J. Range Manage. 41: 144–149.

Krueger, W. C. and A. H. Winward. 1974. Influence of cattle and big game grazing on understory structure of a Douglas-fir ponderosa pine-Kentucky bluegrass community. J. Range Manage. 27(6): 450–453.

Krumbiegel, J. 1954. Biologie der Saugetiere. Agis Verlag, Krefeld. 844 pp.

Kruska, D. 1970. Über die Evolution des Gehirns in der Ordnung Artiodactyla Owen 1848, ins besonder der Teilordnung Svina Gray 1868. Z. f. Saugetierkunde 35: 214–238.

Krzywinski, A. 1993. Hybridization of milu stags with red deer hinds using the imprinting phenomenon. Pages 242–246 in N. Ohtaishi and H.-I. Sheng, eds., Deer of China. Elsevier, New York. 418 pp.

Krzywinski, A. and Z. Jaczewski. 1978. Observations on the artificial breeding of red deer. Symp. Zool. Soc., London. 43: 271–287.

Kucera, T. E. 1991. Genetic variability in Tule elk. Calif. Fish and Game. 77(2): 70–78.

Küchler, A. W. 1964. Potential natural vegetation of the conterminous United States. Spec. Publ. No. 36. Amer. Geogr. Soc., Washington, D.C. 116 pp.

Kuck, L. 1993. Archery equipment restrictions in Idaho. Pages 79–81 in D. E. Guynn and D. E. Samuel, eds., Proc. Western Bowhunting Conference. Bozeman, Montana. 134 pp.

———. 1995. Elk surveys and inventories. Fed. Aid Wildl. Restor., Prog. Rept., Proj. W–160-R–19. Idaho Dept. Fish and Game, Boise. 13 pp.

Kuck, L., G. L. Hompland and E. H. Merrill. 1985. Elk calf response to simulated mine disturbance in southeast Idaho. J. Wildl. Manage. 49: 751–757.

Kuck, L., T. Hemker and G. L. Hompland. 1988. The effects of supplemental feeding on elk winter mortality patterns in southeast Idaho. Pages 42–49 in M. Zahn, J. Pierce and R. Johnson, eds., Proc. West. States and Provinces Elk Workshop. Washington Dept. Wildlife, Olympia. 249 pp.

Kuck, L., M. D. Scott and J. W. Unsworth. 1991. Accommodating hunter desires through hunting regulations in Idaho. Pages 30–37 in A. G. Christensen, L. J. Lyon and T. N. Lonner, compilers, Proc. Elk Vulnerability Symp., Montana State Univ., Bozeman. 330 pp.

Kufeld, R. C. 1973. Foods eaten by the Rocky Mountain elk. J. Range Manage. 26(2): 106–113.

Kulp, J. L. 1961. The geologic time scale. Science 133(3,459): 1,105–1,114.

Kunkel, K. E. 1997. Predation by wolves and other large carnivores in northwestern Montana and southeastern British Columbia. Ph.D. Diss., Univ. Montana, Missoula. 272 pp.

Kunkel, K. E. and D. H. Pletscher. 1999. Species-specific dynamics of cervids in a multipredator ecosystem. J. Wildl. Manage. 63: 1,082–1,093.

Kunkel, K. E., T. K. Ruth, D. H. Pletscher and M. G. Hornocker. 1999. Winter prey selection by wolves and cougars in and near Glacier National Park, Montana. J. Wildl. Manage. 63: 901–910.

Kurtén, B. 1968. Pleistocene mammals of Europe. Aldine Publ. Co., Chicago, Illinois. 317 pp.

Kurtén, B. and E. Anderson. 1980. Pleistocene mammals of North America. Columbia Univ. Press, New York. 442 pp.

Kuttler, K. L. 1984. Anaplasma infections in wild and domestic ruminants. J. Wildl. Dis. 20: 12–20.

La Farge, O. 1957. A pictorial history of the American Indian. Crown Publ., Inc., New York. 272 pp.

Lacate, D. S. 1966. Wildland inventory and mapping. For. Chron. 42: 184–194.

Laerm, J., E. J. Reitz and K. J. Roe. 1993. Records of the elk *Cervus elaphus*

Erxleben (Mammalia: Cervidae) in Georgia and adjacent regions of the Southeastern United States. Georgia J. Sci. 51(3): 141–149.

Laflamme, L. F. and M. L. Connor. 1992. Effect of postpartum nutrition and cow body condition at parturition on subsequent performance of beef cattle. Can. J. Anim. Sci. 72: 843–851.

LaFlesche, F. 1890. The Omaha buffalo medicine men. J. Amer. Folklore (3): 215–221.

Lahontan, Louis Armand de Lom d'Arce, baron de. 1703. New voyages to North-America. Printed for H. Bonwicke, T. Goodwin, M. Wotton, B. Tooke and S. Manship, London. 2 vol. in 1.

Lamprey, H. F. 1963. Ecological separation of the large mammal species in the Tarangire Game Reserve, Tanganyika. East African Wildl. J. 1: 63–92.

Lance, W. R., C. P. Hibler and J. DeMartini. 1983. Experimental contagious ecthyma in mule deer, white-tailed deer, pronghorn and wapiti. J. Wildl. Dis. 19: 165–169.

Lancia, R. A., J. D. Nichols and K. H. Pollock. 1994. Estimating the number of animals in wildlife populations. Pages 215–253 *in* T. A. Bookhout, ed., Research and management techniques for wildlife and habitats. The Wildl. Soc., Bethesda, Maryland. 740 pp.

Land, C. R. and D. James. 1989. Elk. Fed. Aid in Wildl. Restor. Annu. Rept. Survey—Inventory Activities. Vol. XIX, Part III, Proj. W–23–1, Study 13.0. Alaska Dept. Fish and Game, Div. Wildl. Conserv., Juneau. 7 pp.

Landon, M. 1931. Elk remains in Norfolk County. Can. Field Nat. 45(1): 40.

Landres, P. B., J. Verner and J. W. Thomas. 1988. Ecological uses of vertebrate indicator species: A critique. Conserv. Biol. 2(4): 316–328.

Lang, E. M. 1958. Elk of New Mexico. Bull. 8. New Mexico Dept. Fish and Game, Albuquerque. 33 pp.

Langbein, J. and S. J. Thirgood. 1989. Variation in mating systems of fallow deer (*Dama dama*) in relation to ecology. Ethol. 83: 195–214.

Lange, R. E. 1982. Psoroptic scabies. Pages 244–247 *in* E. T. Thorne, N. Kingston, W. R. Jolley and R. C. Bergstrom, eds., Diseases of wildlife in Wyoming, 2nd Edition, Wyoming Game and Fish Dept., Cheyenne. 353 pp.

Langvatn, R. 1992a. Seasonal and age-related changes in size of reproductive structures of red deer hinds (*Cervus elaphus* L.). Rangifer 12: 57–66.

———. 1992b. Analysis of ovaries in studies of reproduction in red deer (*Cervus elaphus* L.): Applications and limitations. Rangifer 12: 67–91.

Langvatn, R. and T. F. Albon. 1986. Geographic clines in body weight of Norwegian red deer: A novel explanation of Bergmann's rule? Holactic Ecology 9: 285–293.

Langvatn, R. and T. A. Hanley. 1993. Feeding patch choice by red deer in relation to foraging efficiency. Oecologia 95: 164–170.

Langvatn, R., O. Bakke and S. Engen. 1994. Retrospective studies of red deer reproduction using regressing luteal structures. J. Wildl. Manage. 58: 654–663.

Lankester, M. W. 1974. *Parelaphostrongylus tenuis* (Nematoda) and *Fascioloides magna* (Trematoda) in moose of southeastern Manitoba. Can. J. Zool. 52: 235–239.

Lankester, M. W. and R. C. Anderson. 1968. Gastropods as intermediate hosts of *Pneumostrongylus tenuis* Dougherty of white-tailed deer. Can. J. Zool. 46: 373–383.

Lankester, M. W. and D. Fong. 1989. Distribution of elaphostrongyline nematodes (Metastrongyloidea: Protostrongylidae) in Cervidae and possible effects of moving *Rangifer* spp. into and within North America. Alces 25: 133–145.

Lankester, M. W. and P. L. Hauta. 1989. *Parelaphostrongylus andersoni* (Nematoda: Elaphostrongylinae) in caribou (*Rangifer tarandus*) of northern and central Canada. Can. J. Zool. 67: 1,966–1,975.

Lankester, M. W. and S. Luttich. 1988. *Fascioloides magna* (Trematoda) in woodland caribou (*Rangifer tarandus caribou*) of the George River herd, Labrador. Can. J. Zool. 66: 475–479.

Lankester, M. W. and W. M. Samuel. 1997. Pests, parasites and diseases. *in* A. W. Franzmann and C. C. Schwartz, eds., Moose of North America: Ecology and management. Smithsonian Instit. Press, Washington, D.C. 733 pp.

Lansman, R. A., J. C. Avise, C. E. Aquadro, J. F. Shapira and S. W. Daniel. 1983. Extensive genetic variation in mitochondrial DNA's among geographic populations of the deer mouse, *Peromycus maniculatus*. Evolution 37(1): 1–16.

Lantz, D. E. 1910. Raising deer and other large game animals in the United States. Bull. No. 36. U.S. Bur. Biol. Surv., Washington, D.C.

Larocque, F. 1910. Journal of Larocque from the Assiniboine to the Yellowstone, 1805. Publ. No. 3. Canada Archives, Ottawa, Ontario. 82 pp.

Larsson, S. 1954. On the hypothalamic organization of the nervous mechanisms regulating food intake. Acta Physiol. Scandinav. 32. Suppl. 115: 1–63.

Lauber, R. and G. Lauber. 1977. Indian dances of North America. Norman: Univ. Oklahoma Press. 538 pp.

Lauckhart, J. B. 1954. Are we adequately harvesting our big game? Proc. West. Assoc. State Game and Fish Commiss. 34: 75–77.

Lawman, M. J. P., D. Evans, E. P. J. Gibbs and A. McDiarmid and L. Rowe. 1978. Br. Vet. J. 134: 85–91.

Laws, R. M. 1974. Behaviour, dynamics and management of elephant populations. Pages 513–529 *in* V. Geist and F. Walther, eds., The behaviour of ungulates and its relation to management. Vol. 2. IUCN Publ. New Ser. 24. IUCN, Morges, Switzerland. 941 pp.

Laycock, G. 1955. Teen-agers learn to hunt safely. Pop. Mech. 104(3): 126–130.

Laycock, W. A. and D. A. Price. 1970. Factors influencing forage quality: Environmental influences on nutritional value of forage plants. Pages 37–47 *in* Range and habitat evaluation—a research symposium. Publ. 1147. USDA For. Serv., Washington, D.C.

Laymon, S. A. and R. H. Barrett. 1986. Developing and testing habitat-capability models: Pitfalls and recommendations. Pages 87–91 *in* J. Verner, M. L. Morrison and C. J. Ralph, eds., Wildlife 2000 modeling habitat relationships of terrestrial vertebrates. Univ. Wisconsin Press, Madison.

Leaf, C. F. 1975. Watershed management in the central and southern Rocky Mountains; a summary of the status of our knowledge by vegetation types. Res. Pap. RM–142. USDA For. Serv., Fort Collins, Colorado. 28 pp.

Leaf, C. F. and R. R. Alexander. 1975. Simulating timber yields and hydrologic impacts resulting from timber harvest on subalpine watersheds. Res. Pap. RM–133. USDA For. Serv., Fort Collins, Colorado. 20 pp.

Lebedinsky, N. G. 1939. Beschleunigung der Geweihmetamorphose beim Reh (*Capreolus capreolus* L.) durch das Schilddrusenhormon. Acta Biol. Latvica IC: 125–134.

Leckenby, D. A. 1984. Elk use and availability of cover and forage habitat components in the Blue Mountains, northeast Oregon, 1976–82. Wild Res. Rept. No. 14, Ore. Dept. Fish and Wildl. 40 pp.

Leckenby, D. A., D. L. Isaccson and S. R. Thomas. 1985. Landsat application to elk habitat management in northeast Oregon. Wildl. Soc. Bull. 13: 130–134.

Leckenby, D. A., J. W. Thomas, M. G. Henjum and L. J. Erickson. 1986. An index to evaluate forage quantity and quality interactions: one of four variables proposed for modeling elk habitat effectiveness on winter ranges in the Blue Mountains of Oregon and Washington. Pages 195–212 *in* D. L. Eastman, ed., Proc. Western States and Provinces Elk Workshop. Oregon Dept. Fish and Wildl., Portland.

Leckenby, D. A., C. Wheaton and L. Bright. 1991. Elk vulnerability—the Oregon situation. Pages 89–93 *in* A. G. Christensen, L. J. Lyon and T. N. Lonner, eds., Proc. Elk Vulnerability Symp. Montana State Univ., Bozeman, Montana. 330 pp.

Ledger, H. P. and N. S. Smith. 1964. The carcass and body weight composition of the Uganda kob. J. Wildl. Manage. 28: 827–839.

Leege, T. A. 1968. Prescribed burning for elk in northern Idaho. Tall Timbers Fire Ecol. Conf. Proc. 8: 235–254.

———. 1969. Burning seral brush ranges for big game in northern Idaho. Trans. N. Amer. Wildl. and Natur. Resour. Conf. 34: 429–437.

———. 1975. Question: Timber or elk in northern Idaho. Idaho Wildl. Rev. 27(4): 3–17.

———. 1976. Relationship of logging to decline of Pete King elk herd. Pages 6–10 *in* S. R. Hieb, ed., Proc. Elk-Logging-Roads Symp., Univ. Idaho, Moscow. 142 pp.

———. 1984. Guidelines for evaluating and managing summer elk habitat in northern Idaho. Wildl. Bull. No. 11. Idaho Dept. Fish and Game, Boise. 38 pp.

Leege, T. A. and W. O. Hickey. 1971. Sprouting of northern Idaho shrubs after prescribed burning. J. Wildl. Manage. 35(3): 508–515.

Leege, T. A. and W. O. Hickey. 1977. Elk–snow–habitat relationships in the Pete King drainage, Idaho. Wildl. Bull. No. 6. Idaho Dept. Fish and Game, Boise. 23 pp.

Leege, T. A. and G. Godbolt. 1985. Herbaceous response following prescribed burning and seeding of elk range in Idaho. Northwest Science 59(2): 134–143.

Leege, T. A., J. R. Nelson and J. W. Thomas. 1977. Food habits and diet quality of North American elk. Pages 221–241 *in* M. Recheigl, Jr., ed., Diets, culture media and food supplements. Handbook Series in Nutrition and Food, Sect. G. CRC Press, Cleveland.

Leege, T. A., M. W. Schlegel and T. Hershey. 1975. Elk ecology. Proj. W–160–R–2, pp. 47–89. Idaho Dept. Fish and Game, Boise.

Leek, S. N. 1915. Elk tusk hunting. Outdoor Life 35: 149–151.

Lehmann, T. 1993. Ectoparasites: Direct impact on host fitness. Parasitol. Today 9: 8–13.

Leiby, P. D. and W. G. Dyer. 1971. Cyclophyllidean tapeworms of wild carnivora. Pages 174–234 *in* J. W. Davis and R. C. Anderson, eds., Parasitic diseases of wild mammals. Iowa State Univ. Press, Ames. 364 pp.

Leinders, J. J. M. and E. Heintz. 1980. The configuration of the lacrimal orifice in pecorans and tragulinds (Artiodactyla: Mammalia) and its significance for the distinction between Bovidae and Cervidae. Beaufortia 30(7): 155–160.

Lekagul, B. and J. A. McNeely. 1977. Mammals of Thailand. Kuruspha Ladproz Press, Bangkok, Thailand. 758 pp.

Lemke, T. 1989. Winterkill. Montana Outdoors. 20: 2–6.

———. 1994. Early winter 1993/94 Northern Yellowstone elk survey. Report, Jan.25, 1994 (files). Montana Dept. Fish, Wildl. and Parks, Bozeman 5 pp.

———. 1995. A Montana tradition. Montana Outdoors. 26: 2–9.

Lemke, T. O., J. A. Mack and D. B. Houston. 1998. Winter range expansion of the northern Yellowstone elk herd. Intermountain J. Sciences 4: 1–9.

Lemke, T. O., J. A. Mack and D. B. Houston. Submitted. The northern Yellowstone elk herd: Population counts, harvests and changes in winter distribution, 1975–1995. Submitted to Wildl. Soc. Bull.

Lemon, P. E. 1956. A spherical densiometer for estimating forest overstory density. For. Sci. 2: 314–320.

Lemos, J. C. and W. W. Hines. 1974. Ecological study of Roosevelt elk. Proj. No. W–70–R–4, Job Prog. Rept. Oregon Wildl. Commiss., Portland.

Lennox, P. A. 1981. The Hamilton site: a late historic neutral town. Mercury 103: 211–403.

———. 1984a. The Bogle I and Bogle II sites: Historical neutral hamlets of the northern tier. Mercury 121: 184–289.

———. 1984b. The Hood site: A historic neutral town of 1640 AD. Mercury 121: 1–183.

Lent, P. C. 1966. Calving and related social behaviour in the barren-ground caribou. Zs. Tierpsychologie 23: 701–756.

———. 1974. Mother–infant relationships in ungulates. Pages 14–55 *in* V. Geist and F. Walther, eds., The behaviour of ungulates and its relation to management. IUCN Publication 1973, No. 24, Vol. 1. IUCN, Morges, Switzerland. 511 pp.

Leonard, J. W. 1965. Moral, ethical. And fiscal aspects of wildlife management. Trans. N. Amer. Wildl. and Natur. Resour. Conf. 30: 422–425.

Leopold, A. 1933. Game management. Charles Scribner's Sons, New York. 481 pp.

———. 1936. Deer and Dauerwald in Gemmany. I. History. J. Forestry 34(4): 366–375.

———. 1947. Status of Mexican big-game herds. Trans. N. Amer. Wildl. Conf. 12: 436–448.

———. 1948. Why and how research? Trans. N. Amer. Wildl. Conf. 13: 44–48.

———. 1949. A sand county almanac and sketches here and there. Oxford Univ. Press, Oxford, New York. 228 pp.

———. 1959. Wildlife of Mexico. Univ. California Press, Berkeley. 581 pp.

Leopold, A., L. K. Sowls and D. L. Spencer. 1947. A survey of overpopulated deer ranges in the United States. J. Wildl. Manage. 11: 162–177.

Leopold, A. S. 1944. The nature of heritable wilderness in turkeys. Condor 46: 133–197.

———. 1947. Status of Mexican big-game herds. Trans. N. Amer. Wildl. Conf. 12: 436–448.

———. 1972. Wildlife of Mexico: The game birds and mammals. Univ. California Press, Berkeley. 568 pp.

Leopold, A. S., S. A. Cain, C. Cottam, I. N. Gabrielson and T. L. Kimball. 1963a. Study of wildlife problems in national parks. Trans. N. Amer. Wildl. and Natur. Resour. Conf. 28: 28–45.

Leopold, A. S., S. A. Cain, C. M. Cottam, I. N. Gabrielson and T. L. Kimball. 1963b. Wildlife management in the national parks. Trans. N. Amer. Wildl. and Natur. Resour. Conf. 28: 29–44.

Lepofsky, D., K. Kusmer, B. Hayden and K. P. Lertzman. 1996. Reconstructing prehistoric socioeconomies from paleoethnobotanical and zooarchaeological data: An example from the British Columbia Plateau. J. Ethnobiol. 16: 31–62.

Leptich, D. J. 1993. Idaho is elk country: A three-way partnership helps keep it that way. Idaho Wildlife, 13(6): 5–8.

Leptich, D. J. and P. Zager. 1991. Road access management effects on elk mortality and population dynamics. Pages 126–131 *in* A. G. Christensen, L. J. Lyon and T. N. Lonner, compilers, Proc. Elk Vulnerability Symp., Montana State Univ., Bozeman. 330 pp.

Leptich, D. J. and P. Zager. 1994. Coeur d'Alene elk ecology project. Study III: Elk habitat security characteristics and hunting season mortality rates. Fed. Aid Wildl. Restor., Job Prog. Rept., Proj. W–160–R–21. Idaho Dept. Fish and Game, Boise. 31 pp.

Leptich, D. J., S. G. Hayes and P. Zager. 1995. Coeur d'Alene elk ecology project. Study III: Elk habitat security characteristics and hunting season mortality rates. Fed. Aid Wildl. Restor., Job Prog. Rept., Proj. W–160–R–21. Idaho Dept. Fish and Game, Boise. 36 pp.

LeResche, R. E. 1974a. Social and ethical considerations in conservation. Idaho Wildl. Rev. 27(1): 7–9, 12–13.

———. 1974b. Hunters, anti-hunters and land managers: A time for unity. Alaska Dept. Fish and Game, Juneau. 8 pp.

LeResche, R. E. and R. A. Rausch. 1974. Accuracy and precision of aerial moose censusring. J. Wildl. Manage. 38: 175–182.

LeResche, R. E., U. S. Seal, P. D. Karns and A. W. Franzmann. 1974. A review of blood chemistry of moose and other Cervidae with emphasis on nutritional assessment. Canadian Naturalist 101: 263–290.

Leslie, Jr., D. M. and K. J. Jenkins. 1985. Rutting mortality among male Roosevelt elk. J. Mammal. 66: 163–164.

Leslie, Jr., D. M. and E. E. Starkey. 1985. Fecal indices of dietary quality of cervids in old-growth forests. J. Wildl. Manage. 49: 142–166.

Leslie, Jr., D. M., E. E. Starkey and B. G. Smith. 1987. Forage acquisition by sympatric cervids along an old-growth sere. J. Mammal. 68: 430–434.

Leslie, Jr., D. M., E. E. Starkey and M. Vavra. 1984. Elk and deer diets in old-growth forests in western Washington. J. Wildl. Manage. 48: 762–775.

Leslie, P. H. 1945. The use of matrices in certain population mathematics. Biometrika 33: 183–212.

———. 1948. Some further notes on the use of matrices in population mathematics. Biometrika 35: 213–245.

Levine, N. D. and V. Ivens. 1970. The coccidian parasites (Protozoa: Sporozoa) of ruminants. III. Biol. Monogr. 44. Univ. Illinois Press, Urbana. 278 pp.

Levy, R. 1978. Eastern Miwok. Pages 398–413 *in* R. F. Heizer, ed., California. Handbook of North American Indians, Vol. 8. Smithsonian Instit. Press, Washington, D.C. 800 pp.

Lewellyn, K. N. and E. A. Hoebel. 1941. The Cheyenne way: conflict and case law in primitive jurisprudence. Univ. Oklahoma Press, Norman. 360 pp.

Lewis, H. T. 1977. Makuta: The ecology of Indian fires in northern Alberta. West. Can. J. Anthropol. 7(15): 15–52.

Lewis, H. T. and T. A. Ferguson. 1988. Yards, corridors and mosaics: How to burn a boreal forest. Human Ecol. 16: 57–77.

Lewis, L. K. and G. K. Barrell. 1994. Regional distribution of estradiol receptors in growing antlers. Steroids 59: 490–492.

Lewis, R. J., G. A. Chalmers, M. W. Barrett and R. Bhatnagar. 1977. Capture myopathy in elk in Alberta, Canada: A report of three cases. J. Am. Vet. Med. Assoc. 171: 927–932.

Lexden. 1914. Across the continent in "the sixties." Forest and Stream 83: 333.

Li, C. 1987. Cytosol testosterone receptor in antler tissue of Sika deer: an assay based on isoelectric focusing in polyacrylamide gel. Chin. J. Zool. 22: 23–25.

Li, C. and J. M. Suttie. 1994. Light microscopic studies of pedicle and early first antler development in red deer (*Cervus elaphus*). Anatomical Record Anat. Rec. 239: 198–215.

———. 1996. Histological examination of antlerogenic region of red deer (*Cervus elaphus*) hummels. New Zealand Vet. J. 44: 126–130.

———. 2000. Histological studies of pedicle skin formation and its transformation to antler velvet in red deer (*Cervus elaphus*). The Anatomical Record 260: 62–71.

Li, C., P. W. Sheard, I. D. Corson and J. M. Suttie. 1993. Pedicle and antler development following sectioning of the sensory nerves to the anterogenic region of the red deer (*Cervus elaphus*). J. Exp. Zool. 267: 188–197.

Li, H., D. T. Shen, D. A. Jessup, D. P. Knowles, J. R. Gorham, T. Thorne, D. O'Toole and T. B. Crawford. 1996. Prevalence of antibody to malignant catarrhal fever virus in wild and domestic ruminants by competitive-inhibition ELISA. J. Wildl. Dis. 32: 437–443.

Li, C., J. M. Suttie and R. P. Littlejohn. 1994. The design and use of a device to detect deer pedicle growth. New Zealand Vet. J. 42: 9–15.

Li, M. 1996. Study of phylogeny among deer in China. Ph.D. Thesis, East China Normal Univ., Shanghai. English Abstract. 80 pp.

Li, W. and X. Zhao. 1989. China's nature reserves. Foreign Languages Press, Beijing, China. 191 pp.

Liddiker, W. Z. 1975. The role of dispersal in the demography of small mammals. Pages 103–134 *in* Small mammals: Their productivity and population dynamics. Int. Biol. Programme, Vol. 5.

Lieb, J. W. 1981. Activity, heart rate and associated energy expenditure of elk in western Montana. Ph.D. Thesis, Univ. Montana, Missoula. 200 pp.

Lieb, J. W. and C. L. Marcum. 1979. Biotelemetric monitoring of heart rate and activity in elk. Proc. Int. Conf. on Wildl. Biotelemetry 2: 21–32.

Lima-de-Faria, A., U. Arnason, B. Widegren, J. Essen-Möller, M. Isaksson, E. Olsson and H. Jaworska. 1984. Conservation of repetitive RNA sequences in deer species studied by southern blot transfer. J. Molecular Evol. 20: 17–24.

Lime, D. W. 1976. Wildlife is for nonhunters, too. J. Forestry 74(9): 600–604.

Lincoln, G. A. 1971a. The seasonal reproductive changes in the red deer stag (*Cervus elaphus*). J. Zool., London. 163: 105–123.

———. 1971b. Puberty in a seasonally breeding male, the red deer stag (*Cervus elaphus* L.). J. Reprod. Fert. 25(1): 41–54.

———. 1972a. Do red deer stags masturbate during the rut ? Deer. 2(9): 941–942.

———. 1972b. The role of antlers in the behaviour of red deer. J. Exp. Zool. 182: 233–250.

———. 1973. Appearance of antler pedicles in early foetal life in red deer. J. Embryol. and Exp. Morphol. 29(2): 431–437.

———. 1975. An effect of the epididymis on the growth of antlers of castrated red deer. J. Reprod. Fert. 42(1): 159–161.

———. 1985. Seasonal breeding in deer. Pages 165–180 *in* P. F. Fennessy. and K. R. Drew, eds., Biology of deer production. Bull. No. 22. Royal Soc. New Zealand, Wellington. 482 pp.

———. 1992. Biology of antlers. J. Zool. (London) 226: 517–528.

Lincoln, G. A. and F. E. Guinness. 1973. The sexual significance of the rut in red deer. J. Reprod. Fert. Suppl. 19: 475–489.

Lincoln, G. A. and T. J. Fletcher. 1976. Induction of antler growth in a congenitally polled Scottish red deer stag. J. Exp. Zool. 195(2): 247252.

Lincoln, G. A. and R. V. Short. 1969. History of a hummel. Deer 1(9): 372–373.

Lincoln, G. A., F. Guinnes and R. V. Short. 1971. The history of a hummel—Part 2. Deer 2(4): 630–631.

Lincoln, G. A., H. M. Fraser and T. J. Fletcher. 1984. Induction of early rutting in male red deer (*Cervus elaphus*) by melatonin and its dependence on LHRH. J. Reprod. Fert. 72: 339–343.

Lincoln, G. A., R. W. Youngson and R. V. Short. 1970. The social and sexual behaviour of the red deer stag. J. Reprod. Fert. Suppl. 11: 71–103.

Lindemann, W. 1956. Transplantation of game in Europe and Asia. J. Wildl. Manage. 20(1): 68–70.

Lindsley, C. A. 1917. Yellowstone National Park. Pages 774–789 *in* Reports of the Department of the Interior for the Fiscal Year ended June 30, 1916. Vol. 1. Govt. Print. Off., Washington, D.C. 837 pp.

———. 1918. Report of the Acting Superintendent of Yellowstone National Park. Pages 899–922 *in* Reports of the Department of the Interior for the Fiscal Year ended June 30, 1917. Vol. 1. Govt. Print. Off., Washington, D.C. 1,048 pp.

———. 1919. Yellowstone National Park. Pages 842–849 *in* Reports of the Dept. of the Interior for the Fiscal Year ended June 30, 1918. Vol. I. Govt. Print. Off., Washington, D.C. 1,085 pp.

Lindstedt, S. L. and M. S. Boyce. 1985. Seasonality, fasting endurance and body size in mammals. American Naturalist 125: 873–878.

Lindzey, J. S. 1967. Highlights of management. *in* O. H. Hewitt, ed., The wild turkey and its management, Valley Offset, Inc., Deposit, New York. 589 pp.

Linke, W. 1957. Der Rothirsch. Die Neue Brehm-Buderei No. 129. Wittenberg-Lutherstadt: A. ZiemsenVerlag. 128 pp.

Linn, S. 1987. Zum sozialen verhalten eines rotwildrudels (*Cervus elaphus*) am winter futterungsplatz unter besonderer berucksichtigung soziobiologischer hypothesen. Ph.D. Thesis, Univ. Geneve. 281 pp.

Linton, R. 1923. Purification of the sacred bundles, a ceremony of the Pawnee. Field Mus. Natur. Hist. Leaflet 7.

———. 1940. Acculturation in seven American Indian tribes. D. Appleton-Century, New York. 526 pp.

Lipp, W., G. Hager and A. B. Bubenik. 1977. Sexuale Reitung von Rothirsch im Lichte der Histologie der Qeschlechtsdrusen. 1977. Berichte von FUST-Bonn. In prept.

Lipscomb, J. F. 1973. Systems modeling big game populations. Pages 263–273 in Game research report, Part 3. Prog. Rept. P-R Proj. W–38-R–27, Work Plan 17, Job 1. Colorado Div. Wildl., Denver.

———. 1974. A modeling approach to harvest and trend data analysis. Proc. West. Assoc. State Game and Fish Commiss. 54: 5,661.

Lister, A. M. 1981. Evolutionary studies on Pleistocene deer. Ph.D. Thesis, Univ. Cambridge, U.K.

———. 1984. Evolutionary and ecological origins of British deer. The Royal Soc. of Edinburgh Proc. (B) 82(4): 205–229.

———. 1986. New results on deer from Swanscombe and the stratigraphical significance of deer in the Middle and Upper Pleistocene of Europe. J. Archaeol. Sci. 13: 319–338.

———. 1987. Diversity and evolution of antler form in Quaternary deer. Pages 81–98 in C. M. Wemmer, ed., Biology and management of the Cervidae. Smithsonian Instit. Press, Washington, D.C. 577 pp.

———. 1989. Rapid dwarfing of red deer on Jersey in the last interglacial. Nature 342(6,434): 539–542.

Little, E. L., Jr. 1971. Atlas of United States trees—Volume 1. Conifers and important hardwoods. Misc. Publ. No. 1146. USDA For. Serv., Washington, D.C. 9 pp.

Little, S. 1968. A Sioux woman's dentalium shell dress. Amer. Indian Crafts and Culture 2(10).

Liu, Y. 1993. International hunting and involvement of local people, Dulan, Qinghai, Peoples Republic of China. M.S. Thesis, Univ. Montana, Missoula. 72 pp.

———. 1995. International hunting and the involvement of local people, Dulan, Qinghai, Peoples Republic of China. Pages 63–67 in J. A. Bissonette and P. R. Krausman, eds., Integrating people and wildlife for a sustainable future. Proc. First International Wildlife Management Congress. The Wildl. Soc., Bethesda, Maryland. 697 pp.

Llewellyn, K. N. and A. E. Hoebel. 1941. The Cheyenne way: Conflict and case law in primitive jurisprudence. Univ. Oklahoma Press, Norman. 360 pp.

Lobley, G. E. 1992. Control of the metabolic fate of amino acids in ruminants: a review. J. Anim. Sci. 70: 3,264–3,275.

Lochman, J. 1965. Nektere vysledky pastevniho rezimu jeleni zvere a srnci zvere. Prace vyzk. ustavu lesn. 30: 103–140.

Lochman, J. and A. Barth. 1967. Influence de la structure des aliments sur la digestion des cervids. Pages 231–234 in Trans. 7th Congr. IUGB, ed. 1. Isakovic. Union of Organizations of Game of Yugoslavia, Beograd. 636 pp.

Lockwood, J. H. 1903. Early times and events in Wisconsin. Pages 98–196 in L. C. Draper., ed., Collections of the State Historical Society of Wisconsin. Vol. 2. 520 pp. (Reprint of 1856 original issue.)

Loftus, B. 1991. Bugling for bulls and the tragedy of the commons. Pages 272–274 in A. G. Christensen, L. J. Lyon, T. N. Lonner, compilers, Proc. Elk Vulnerability Symp., Montana State Univ., Bozeman. 330 pp.

Lohse, E. S. 1988. Trade goods. Pages 396–403 in W. E. Washburn, ed., History of Indian–White relations. Vol. 4. Handbook of North American Indians. Smithsonian Instit. Press, Washington, D.C. 838 pp.

Lojda, Z. 1956. Histogenesis of the antlers of our Cervidae and its histochemical picture. Cs. Morfologie, Prague. 4(1): 43–62.

Long, J. L. 1942. Land of Nakoda. Montana State Publ. Co., Helena. 186 pp.

Long, W. 1989. Habitat manipulations to prevent elk damage to private rangelands. Gen.Tech.Rept. RM–171. USDA For. Serv., Rocky Mtn. For. and Range Exp. Sta. 101–103, Ft. Collins, Colorado.

Longhurst, W. M. 1957. The effectiveness of hunting in controlling big-game populations in North America. Trans. N. Amer. Wildl. Conf. 22: 544–569.

Longhurst, W. M., A. S. Leopold and R. F. Dasmann. 1952. A survey of California deer herds: Their ranges and management problems. Game Bull. 6. California Dept. Natur. Resour., Div. Fish and Game, Sacramento. 136 pp.

Lonner, T. N. 1974. Ruby road closure study. Pages 127–143 in Montana Coop. Elk-Logging Study. Prog. Rept. for the period Jan. 1–Dec. 31, 1973. Montana Coop. Elk-Logging Study, Missoula. (mimeo).

———. 1975a. Elk and logging. Montana Outdoors 6(4): 38–42.

———. 1975b. Elk–cattle distribution and interspecific relationships. Long Tom Creek Study, Montana. Pages . 60–72 in Montana Coop. Elk-Logging Study Annu. Prog. Rept. Montana Coop. Elk-Logging Study, Bozeman.

———. 1976. Elk use–habitat type relationships on summer and fall range in Long Tom Creek, southwestern Montana. Pages 101–109 in S. R. Hieb, ed., Proc. Elk-Logging-Roads Symp., Univ. Idaho, Moscow. 142 pp.

———. 1977. Long Tom Creek Study. Pages 25–68 in Annu. Prog. Rept., Montana Coop. Elk-Logging Study. Montana Coop. Elk-Logging Study, Bozeman.

———. 1984. Modeling elk habitat use by probability. Page 117 in R. W. Nelson, ed., Proc. Western States and Provinces Elk Workshop. Alberta Fish and Wildlife Div., Alberta.

———. 1985. An elk–habitat use model based on probability. Page 117 in R. W. Nelson, ed., Proc. 1984 Western States Elk Workshop, Edmonton, Alberta, Can. (abstract).

———. 1991. Elk vulnerability and the biomodulator. Pages 2–5 in A. G. Christensen, L. J. Lyon and T. N. Lonner, compilers, Proc. Elk Vulnerability Symp., Montana State Univ., Bozeman. 330 p.

———. 1997. Elk vulnerability: What is it and how can it improve elk management? Bugle. 14 (2): 83–86.

Lonner, T. N. and J. D. Cada. 1982. Some effects of forest management on elk hunting opportunity. Pages 119–128 in T. L. Britt and D. P. Theobald, eds., Proc. Western States Elk Workshop. Arizona Fish and Game Dept., Phoenix.

Lonner, T. N. and R. J. Mackie. 1983. On the nature of competition between big game and livestock. Pages 53–58 in B. F. Roche, Jr. and D. M. Baumgarther, eds., Proc. Forestland Grazing Symp. Washington State Univ., Pullman.

Loomis, J. B. and R. G. Walsh. 1997. Recreation economic decisions. Venture Publ., State College, Pennsylvania. 438 pp.

Loomis, J. B., G. Peterson and C. Sorg. 1984. A field guide to wildlife economic analyses. Trans. N. Amer. Wildl. and Natur. Resour. Conf. 49: 315–324.

Loran, T., E. H. Kowal and A. A. Aarsenault. 1997. Status of the elk transplant program in Saskatchewan. Fish and Wildl. Tech. Rept. 97–2. Saskatchewan Environ. and Resour. Manage., Saskatoon. 17 pp.

Lord, J. K. 1866. The naturalist in Vancouver Island and British Columbia. Vol. 2. Richard Bentley, London, U.K. 375 pp.

Lorenz, K. 1966. On aggression. Harcourt, Brace & World, New York. 306 pp.

———. 1974. Analogy as a source of knowledge. Science 185: 229–234.

Loscheider, M. Unpublished. Indian fire practices of the northern Great

Plains and adjacent areas: An ethnohistorical account. 1975 paper, on file at Univ. Montana, Missoula.

Lostroh, A. J. 1976. Hormonal control of spermatogenesis. Pages 13–23 *in* C. H. Spilman et al., eds., Regulatory mechanisms of male reproductive physiology. Excerpta Medica, Amsterdam, Oxford. American Elsevier Publ. Co., New York.

Lothian, W. F. 1981. The history of Canada's National Parks, Vol. 4, Parks Canada Library. 155 pp.

Lotka, A. J. 1925. Elements of physical energy. Williams and Wilkins, Baltimore, Maryland. 460 pp.

Lott, D. F. 1979. Hair display loss in mature male American bison: a temperate zone adaptation. Zs. Tierpsychol. 49: 71–76.

Loudon, A. S. I. and B. R. Brinklow. 1992. Reproduction in deer: Adaptations for life in seasonal environments. Pages 261–278 *in* R. D. Brown, ed., The biology of deer. Springer-Verlag, New York. 596 pp.

Loudon, A. S. I. and J. D. Curlewis. 1988. Cycles of antler and testicular growth in an aseasonal tropical deer (*Axis axis*). J. Reprod. Fertil. 83: 729–738.

Loudon, A. S. I., A. D. Darroch and J. A. Milne. 1984. The lactation performance of red deer on hill and improved species pastures. J. Ag. Sci., Cambridge 102: 149–158.

Loudon, A. S. I., A. S. McNeilly and J. A. Milne. 1983. Nutrition and lactation control of fertility in red deer. Nature 302: 145–147.

Loudon, A. S. I., J. A. Milne, J. D. Curlewis and A. S. McNeilly. 1989. A comparison of the seasonal hormone changes and patterns of growth, voluntary food intake and reproduction in juvenile and adult red deer (*Cervus elaphus*) and Pere David's deer (*Elaphurus davidianus*) hinds. J. Endocrinol. 122: 733–746.

Lovaas, A. L. 1958. Mule deer food habits and range use, Little Belt Mountains, Montana. J. Wildl. Manage. 22: 275–283.

———. 1970. People and the Gallatin elk herd. Montana Fish and Game Dept., Helena. 44 pp.

———. 1973. A cooperative elk trapping program in Wind Cave National Park. Wildl. Soc. Bull. 1(2): 93–100.

———. 1976. Introduction of prescribed burning to Wind Cave National Park. Wildl. Soc. Bull. 4(2): 69–73.

Lovaas, A. L., J. L. Egan and R. R. Knight. 1966. Aerial counting of two Montana elk herds. J. Wildl. Manage. 30(2): 364–30.

Love, B. I. 1955. Personal observation in the care and management of an elk (wapiti) herd at Elk Island National Park, Alberta, Canada. Can. J. Comp. Med. 19: 184–192.

Loveless, C. M. 1964. Some relationships between wintering mule deer and the physical environment. Trans. N. Amer. Wildl. and Natur. Resour. Conf. 29: 415–431.

Low, J. B. 1951. The role of checking stations in student training and wildlife research. Proc. West. Assoc. State Game and Fish Commiss. 31: 142–144.

Lowe, V. P. W. 1966. Observations on the dispersal of red deer on Rhum. Pages 211–228 *in* P. A. Jewell and C. Loizos, eds., Play, exploration and territoriality in mammals. Zool. Soc. London. No. 18. London, Academic Press, London.

———. 1969. Population dynamics of the red deer (*Cervus elaphus* L.) on Rhum. J. Anim. Ecol. 38: 425–457.

Lowe, V. P. W. and A. S. Gardiner. 1974. A re-examination of the subspecies of red deer (*Cervus elaphus*) with particular reference to the stocks in Britain. J. Zool. London 174: 185–201.

Lowery, G. H., Jr. 1974. The mammals of Louisiana and its adjacent waters. Louisiana State Univ. Press, Baton Rouge. 565 pp.

Lowie, R. H. 1913. Societies of the Crow, Hidatsa and Mandan Indians. Amer. Mus. Natur. Hist. Anthropol. Pap. 6(3): 145–358.

———. 1920. The Tobacco Society of the Crow Indians. Amer. Mus. Natur. Hist. Anthropol. Pap. 21(2):100–201.

———. 1963. Indians of the Plains. Amer. Mus. Natur. Hist., The Natural History Press, Garden City, New York. 258 pp.

———. 1976. What about this anti-hunting thing? Conservationist (October): 2–4.

Lucas, C. 1969. Herd management suggestions on the basis of park Stock. Pages 32–38 *in* M. M. Bannerman and K. L. Blaxter, eds., The husbanding of red eer. Rowett Research Inst. Aberdeen, Scotland.

Ludlow, F. 1959. The shou or "Sikkim stag." J. Bombay Natur. Hist. Soc. 56(3): 626–627.

Ludlow, W. 1876. Report of a reconnaissance from Carroll, Montana Territory, on the upper Missouri, to the Yellowstone National Park and return, made in 1875. Govt. Print. Off., Washington, D.C. 155 pp.

Ludwig, J. 1975. Great Lakes Deer Group Meeting. Minist. Natur. Resour., Wildl. Serv., Maple, Ont. 14 pp. Mimeo.

Luman, D. and W. Neitro. 1980. Preservation of mature forest seral stages to provide wildlife habitat diversity. Trans. N. Amer. Wildl. and Natur. Resour. Conf. 45.

Lumsden, H. G. 1957. The problem of changing beliefs and attitudes. J. Wildl. Manage. 21(4): 463–65.

Lund, T. 1980. American wildlife law. Univ. California Press, Berkeley. 179 pp.

Lundbert, P. and R. T. Palo. 1993. Resource use, plant defenses and optimal digestion in ruminants. Oikos 68: 224–228.

Lundelius, E. L., Jr., R. W. Graham, E. Anderson, J. Guilday, J. A. Holman, D. W. Steadman and S. D. Webb. 1983. Terrestrial vertebrate faunas. Pages 311–353 *in* S. C. Porter, ed., Late Quaternary environments of the United States. Vol. 1, The Late Pleistocene. Univ. Minnesota Press, Minneapolis. 336 pp.

Lundelius, E. L., Jr., T. Downs, E. H. Lindsay, H. A. Semken, R. J. Zakrzewski, C. S. Churcher, C. R. Harington, G. E. Schultz and S. D. Webb. 1987. The North American Quaternary sequence. Pages 211–235 *in* M. O. Woodburne, ed., Cenozoic mammals of North America—Geochronology and biostratigraphy. Univ. California Press, Berkeley. 336 pp.

Lydekker, R. 1894. The royal natural history. Vol. 2. Frederick Warner and Co., London, U.K. 583 pp.

———. 1898. The deer of all lands. R. and R. Clark Ltd., Edinburgh, Scotland. 329 pp.

———. 1901. The great and small game of Europe, western and northern Asia and America; their distribution, habits and structure. R. Ward, Ltd., London. 445 pp.

———. 1915. Catalogue of the ungulate mammals in the British Museum (Natural History). Vol. 4, Artiodactyla. Reprinted 1966 by Johnson Reprint Corp., New York. 438 pp.

Lyford, Jr., S. J. 1988. Growth and development of the ruminant digestive system. Pages 44–63 *in* D. C. Church, ed., The ruminant animal: Digestive physiology and nutrition. Prentice Hall, Englewood Cliffs, New Jersey. 564 pp.

Lyford, Jr., S. J. and J. T. Huber. 1988. Digestion, metabolism and nutrient needs in preruminants. Pages 401–420 *in* D. C. Church, ed., The ruminant animal: digestive physiology and nutrition. Prentice-Hall, Englewood Cliffs, New Jersey. 564 pp.

Lyon, L. J. and P. F. Stickney. 1966. Two forest fires and some specific implications in big game habitat. Proc. West. Assoc. State Game and Fish Commiss. 46: 181–193. (Fig. 88)

Lyon, L. J. and M. G. Burcham. 1998. Tracking elk hunters with the global positioning system. U.S. Dept. Ag., For. Serv. Res. Pap. RMRS-RP–3, Rocky Mtn. Res. Sta., Fort Collins, Colorado. 6 pp.

Lyon, L. J. 1966. Problems of habitat management for deer and elk in the northern forests. Res. Pap. INT–24. USDA For. Serv., Ogden, Utah. 15 pp.

———. 1971a. Vegetal development following prescribed burning of Douglas-fir in south-central Idaho. Res. Pap. INT–105. USDA For. Serv., Ogden, Utah. 30 pp.

———. 1971b. A cooperative research program: Effects of logging on elk in Montana. Proc. West. Assoc. State Game and Fish Commiss. 51: 447–457.

———. 1973. Elk use of Burdette Creek. Pages 101–106 *in* West. States Elk Workshop Proc., Bozeman, Montana.

———. 1975. Coordinating forestry and elk management in Montana: Initial recommendations. Trans. N. Amer. Wildl. and Natur. Resour. Conf. 40: 193–201.

———. 1976. Elk use as related to characteristics of clearcuts in western Montana. Pages 69–72 *in* S. R. Hieb, ed., Proc. Elk-Logging-Roads Symp., Univ. Idaho, Moscow. 142 pp.

———. 1979a. Habitat effectiveness for elk as influenced by roads and cover. J. Forestry 77(10): 658–660.

———. 1979b. Influences of logging and weather on elk distribution in western Montana. Res. Pap. INT–236. USDA For. Serv., Ogden, Utah. 11 pp.

———. 1983. Road density models describing habitat effectiveness for elk. J. Forestry 81(9): 592–594, 613.

———. 1984. Field tests of elk/timber coordination guidelines. Res. Pap. INT–325. USDA For.Serv., Intermtn. Res. Sta. 10 pp.

———. 1986. Effects of thinning small-stem lodgepole pine stands on big game habitat. Pages 162–165 *in* R. L. Barger, compiler, Management of small-stem stands of lodgepole pine. Workshop Proc. Gen.Tech. Rept. INT–237. USDA For. Serv., Intermtn. Res. Sta. 172 pp.

Lyon, L. J. and M. G. Burcham. 1995. Tracking hunters with global positioning systems. Abstract *in* Proc. West. States and Prov. 1995 Joint Deer and Elk Workshop. (Avail. from Idaho Dept. Fish and Game, Boise.)

Lyon, L. J. and J. E. Canfield. 1991. Habitat selections by Rocky Mountain elk under hunting season stress. pp. 99–105 *in* A. G. Christensen, L. J. Lyon and T. N. Lonner, compilers, Proc. Elk Vulnerability Symp., Montana State Univ., Bozeman. 330 pp.

Lyon, L. J. and A. G. Christensen. 1990. Toward a workable glossary of elk management terms. West. States and Provinces Elk Workshop, Eureka, California.

Lyon, L. J. and A. G. Christensen. 1992. A partial glossary of elk management terms. Gen. Tech. Rept. INT–288. USDA For. Serv., Intermtn. Res. Sta. 6 pp.

Lyon, L. J. and C. E. Jensen. 1980. Management implications of elk and deer use of clearcuts in Montana. J. Wildl. Manage. 44(2): 352–362.

Lyon, L. J. and W. F. Mueggler. 1968. Herbicide treatment of north Idaho browse evaluated six years later. J. Wildl. Manage. 32(3): 538–541.

Lyon, L. J. and P. F. Stickney. 1966. Two forest fires and some specific implications in big game habitat management. Proc. West. Assoc. State Game and Fish Commiss. 46: 181–193.

Lyon, L. J. and P. F. Stickney. 1976. Early vegetal succession following large northern Rocky Mountain wildfires. Tall Timbers Fire Ecol. Conf. Proc. 14: 355–375.

Lyon, L. J. and J. W. Thomas. 1987. Elk: Rocky Mountain majesty. Pages 145–159 *in* H. Kallman, C. P. Agee, W. R. Goforth and J. P. Linduska, eds., Restoring America's Wildlife. USDI Fish and Wildl. Service, Washington, D.C. 394 pp.

Lyon, L. J. and A. L. Ward. 1982. Elk and land management. Pages 443–477 *in* J. W. Thomas and D. E. Toweill, eds., Elk of North America, ecology and management. Stackpole Books, Harrisburg, Pennsylvania. 698 pp.

Lyon, L. J., T. N. Lonner, J. P. Weigand, C. L. Marcum, W. D. Edge, J. D. Jones, D. R. McCleery and L. L. Hicks. 1985. Coordinating elk and timber management, Final report of the Montana Coop. Elk-Logging Study, 1970–1985. Montana Dept. Fish, Wildlife and Parks, Bozeman. 53 pp.

Lyon, M. W. Jr. 1936. Mammals of Indiana. Amer. Midland Naturalist 17(1): 1–384.

Lyon, R. B. 1969. Trouble on the winter range. Idaho Wildl. Rev. 21(4): 79.

Lyons, R. K. and J. W. Stuth. 1992. Fecal NIRS equations for predicting diet quality of free-ranging cattle. J. Range Manage. 45: 238–244.

MacArthur, R. A., V. Geist and R. H. Johnson. 1982. Physiological correlates of social behaviour in bighorn sheep: A field study using electrocardiogram telemetry. J. Zool. 196: 401–415.

MacCleery, D. W. and D. C. Le Master. 1999. The historical foundation and evolving context for natural resource management on federal lands. Vol. 2. Pages 517–556 *in* R. C. Szaro, N. C. Johnson, W. T. Sexton and A. J. Malk, eds., Ecological stewardship: A common reference for ecosystem management. Elsevier Science Ltd., Kidlington, Oxford, UK. 741 pp.

MacDougall, D. B., B. G. Shaw, G. F. Nute and D. N. Rhodes. 1979. Effect of pre-slaughter handling on the quality and microbiology of venison from farmed young red deer. J. Sci. Food Ag. 30: 1,160–1,167.

Mace, R. U. 1953. Big game harvest methods. Proc. West. Assoc. State Game and Fish Commiss. 33: 201–204.

———. 1956. Oregon's elk. Oregon State Game Commiss., Portland. 33 pp.

———. 1971. Oregon's elk. Wildl. Bull. No. 4. Oregon State Game Commiss., Portland. 29 pp.

Mace, R. U., R. Denny and R. Ingram. 1995. Big game history. Oregon Dept. Fish and Wildl., Portland. 40 pp.

MacGregor, G. 1946. Warriors without weapons. Univ. Chicago Press, Chicago, Illinois. 228 pp.

Mack, J. A. and F. J. Singer. 1993. Using POP-II models to predict effects of wolf predation and hunter harvests on elk, mule deer and moose on the Northern Range. Pages 49–74 *in* R. S. Cook, ed., Ecological issues on reintroducing wolves into Yellowstone National Park. U.S. Nat. Park Serv. Sci. Monogr. Ser. 93/22.

MacKay, K. 1998. Court ruling may spell doom for park wolves: Complex case threatens restored biodiversity in Yellowstone. Nat. Parks 72(3–4): 13

Mackie, R. J. 1970. Range ecology and relations of mule deer, elk and cattle in the Missouri River breaks. Montana Wildl. Monogr., The Wildl. Soc., Washington, D.C. 20: 1–79.

———. 1976. Interspecific competition between mule deer, other game animals and livestock. Pages 49–54 *in* J. B. Low, ed., Mule deer decline in the West: A symposium. Utah State Univ. Ag. Exp Sta., Logan. 125 pp.

———. 1978. Impacts of livestock grazing on wild ungulates. Trans. N. Amer. Wildl. and Natur. Resour. Conf. 43: 462–476.

———. 1991. Welcome and opening remarks. Page 1 *in* A. G. Christensen, L. J. Lyon, T. N. Lonner, compilers, Proc. Elk Vulnerability Symp., Montana State Univ., Bozeman. 330 pp.

Mackintosh, C. G., M. B. Orr, R. T. Gallagher and I. C. Harvey. 1982. Ryegrass staggers in Canadian wapiti deer. New Zealand Vet. J. 30: 106–107.

MacMillan, A. 1990. Conventional serologic tests. Pages 153–197 *in* K. Nielsen and J. R. Duncan, eds., Animal brucellosis. CRC Press, Inc., Boca Raton, Florida. 453 pp.

MacNally, L. 1970. Highland deer forest. J. M. Dent and Sons, Ltd., London, U.K. 107 pp.

MacNamara, M. and W. D. Eldridge. 1987. Behavior and reproduction in captive pudu (*Pudu pudu*) and red brocket (*Mazama americana*), descriptive and comparative analysis. Pages 371–387 *in* C. M. Wemmer, ed., Biology and management of the Cervidae. Smithsonian Instit. Press, Washington, D.C.

MacNeish, R. S. 1958. An introduction to the archaeology of southeast Manitoba. Bull. 157, Anthropol. Series 44. Nat. Mus. Canada, Ottawa, Ontario. 184 pp.

MacPherson, H. A. 1896. Red deer. Longmans, Green and Co., London, U.K. 281 pp.

Madsen, J. 1966. The elk. Conserv. Dept., Winchester-Western Div., Olin Corp., East Alton, Illinois. 125 pp.

———. 1976. What about this anti-hunting thing? Conservationist (October): 2–4.

———. 1992. Why men hunt. Pages 58–62 *in* The governor's symposium on North America's hunting heritage. Proc. Montana State Univ., Bozeman, Montana. 232 pp.

Madsen R.L. 1985. The history of supplemental feeding at the National Elk Refuge. Pages 45–49 *in* G. W. Workman, ed., Western elk management: A symposium. Utah State Univ., Logan.

Madson, C. 1993. State wildlife agencies and the future of hunting. Pages 64–71 *in* Proc., Second annual governor's symposium on North America's hunting heritage. Pierre, South Dakota. 199 pp.

Madson, J. and E. Kozicky. 1971. Game, gunners and biology, the scientific approach to wildlife management. Conserv. Dept., Winchester-Western Div., Olin Corp. Winchester Press, New York. 48 pp.

Magonigle, R. A. and W. P. Eckblad. 1979. Evaluation of the anaplasmosis rapid card test for detecting experimentally infected elk. Cornell Vet. pp. 402–410.

Magruder, N. D., C. E. French, L. C. McEwen and R. W. Swift. 1957. Nutritional requirements of white-tailed deer for growth and antler development. Ag. Exp. Sta. Bull. 628. Pennsylvania State Univ., University Park. 20 pp.

Mails, T. E. 1972. The mystic warriors of the plains. Doubleday and Co., Inc., Garden City, New York. 618 pp.

Majak, W. 1992. Metabolism and absorption of toxic glycosides by ruminants. J. Range Manage. 45: 67–71.

Makah Indian Tribes, et al. v. Schoettler, 192 F. 2d 224 (9th Circ., 1951).

Mallery, G. 1893. Picture-writing of the American Indians. Tenth annual report of the Bureau of Ethnology to the Secretary [J.W. Powell] of the Smithsonian Institution. U.S. Govt. Print. Off., Washington, D.C. 822 pp.

Maloney, A. B., ed. 1945. Fur brigade to Bonaventura: John Work's California Expedition, 1832–1833 for the Hudson's Bay Company. California Hist. Soc., San Francisco. 112 pp.

Malouf, C. I. 1966. Ethohistory in the Great Basin. Pages 1–38 *in* W. L. d'Azevedo, W. A. Davis, D. D. Fowler and W. Suttles, eds., The current status of anthropological research in the Great Basin: 1964. Tech. Rept. Series S-H. Desert Research Institute, Reno, Nevada. 379 pp.

———. 1974. The Gosiute Indians. Pages 25–172 *in* D. A. Horr, ed., Shoshone Indians. Garland Publ. Inc., New York. 320 pp.

Manners, G. D., J. A. Pfister, M. H. Ralphs, K. E. Panter and J. D. Olsen. 1992. Larkspur chemistry: Toxic alkaloids in tall larkspurs. J. Range Manage. 45: 63–67.

Manning, A. 1972. An introduction to animal behavior. 2nd ed. MacMillan of Canada, Toronto. 294 pp.

Manning, R. 1995. Grassland: the history, biology, politics and promise of the American prairie. Viking Penguin Books, New York. 306 pp.

Mansueti, R. 1950. Extinct and vanishing mammals of Maryland and District of Columbia. Maryland Natur. 20(1, 2): 1–48.

Marburger, R. G., R. M. Robinson, J. W. Thomas, M. J. Adregg and K. A. Clarke. 1972. Antler malformation produced by leg injury in white-tailed deer. J. Wildl. Dis. 8(4): 311–314.

Marcum, C. L. 1975. Summer–fall habitat selection and use by a western Montana elk herd. Ph.D. Thesis, Univ. Montana, Missoula. 188 pp.

———. 1976. Habitat selection and use during summer and fall months by a western Montana elk herd. Pages 91–96 *in* S. R. Hieb, ed., Proc. Elk-Logging-Roads Symp., Univ. Idaho, Moscow. 142 pp.

Marcum, C. L. 1979. Summer–fall food habits and forage preferences of a western Montana elk herd. Pages 54–62 *in* M. S. Boyce and L. D. Hayden-Wing, eds., North American elk: ecology, behavior and management. Univ. Wyoming, Laramie. 294 pp.

Marcum, C. L. and W. D. Edge. 1991. Sexual differences in distribution of elk relative to roads and logged areas in western Montana. Pages 142–148 *in* A. G. Christensen, L. J. Lyon and T. N. Lonner, compilers, Proc. Elk Vulnerability Symp., Montana State Univ., Bozeman. 330 pp.

Margalef, R. 1968. On certain unifying principles in ecology. Amer. Natur. 97: 357–374.

Margolin, J. H. and W. R. Jolley. 1979. Experimental infection of dogs with *Sarcosystis* from wapiti. J. Wildl. Dis. 15: 259–262.

Markgren, G. 1969. Reproduction of moose in Sweden. Viltrevy 6(3): 129–299.

Margry, P., ed. 1875–1886. Découvertes et établissements des francais dans l'ouest et dans le sud de l'Amérique septentrionale (1614–1754). Mémoires et documents originaux. 6 vols. D. Jouaust, Paris.

Marler, P. and W. J. Hamilton, III. 1966. Mechanisms of animal behavior. J. Wiley and Sons, New York. 771 pp.

Marquis, T. 1975. Custer, cavalry and Crows. The Old Army Press, Fort Collins, Colorado. 183 pp.

Marsh, J. 1840. Letter published 31 October 1840 in the *Daily Argus*, St. Louis, Missouri.

Marshall, A. G. 1977. Nez Perce social groups: An ecological perspective. Ph.D. Diss., Washington State Univ., Pullman.

Marshall, F. H. A. 1937. On the change over in the oestrus cycle in animals after transference across the equator, with further observations on the incidence of the breeding seasons and factors controlling sexual periodicity. Proc. Royal Soc. London. B122. 413–428.

Martin, C. 1978. Keepers of the game. Univ. California Press, Berkeley. 226 pp.

Martin, J. S. and M. M. Martin. 1982. Tannin assays in ecological studies. Lack of correlation between phenolics, proanthocyanidins and protein-precipitating constituents in mature foliage of six oak species. Oecologia 54: 205–211.

Martin, P. S. 1973. The discovery of America. Science 179: 646–974.

Martin, P. S. and R. G. Klein, Eds. 1984. Quaternary extinctions: A prehistoric revolution. The Univ. Arizona Press, Tucson.

Martin, P. S. and C. R. Szuter. 1999. War zone and game sinks in Lewis and Clark's West. Conserv. Biol. 13(1): 36–45.

Martin, P. S. and H. E. Wright, Jr., eds. 1967. Pleistocene extinctions. Yale Univ. Press, New Haven. 453 pp.

Martin, S. R. 1995. Preferences for Recreational Wildlife Viewing Experiences: A Survey of Nonresident Visitors to Montana. Research Rept. No. 38, Institute for Tourism and Recreation Research, Univ. Montana, Missoula.

Martinka, C. J. 1968. Habitat relationships of white-tailed and mule deer in northern Montana. J. Wildl. Manage. 32: 558–565.

———. 1969. Population ecology of summer resident elk in Jackson Hole, Wyoming. J. Wildl. Manage. 33(3): 465–481.

———. 1970. Winter food of white-tailed deer in Glacier National Park, Montana. Proc. West. Assoc. State Game and Fish Commiss. 6 pp.

———. 1976. Fire and elk in Glacier National Park. Proc. Tall Timbers Fire Ecol. Conf. 14: 377–389.

———. 1978. Ungulate populations in relation to wilderness in Glacier National Park, Montana. Trans. N. Amer. Wildl. and Natur. Resour. Conf. 43: 351–357.

Martyny, J. W. and R. G. Botzler. 1975. *Listeria monocytogenes* isolated from wapiti (*Cervus canadensis roosevelti*). J Wildl. Dis. 11: 330–334.

Martyny, J. W. and R. G. Botzler. 1976. Yersinae isolated from wapiti. J. Wildl. Dis. 12: 386–389.

Maser, C. 1990. On the "naturalness" of natural areas: A perspective for the future. Natural Areas Journal 10: 129–133.

Mason, O. P. 1889. The Ray collection from the Hupa Reservation. Pages 205–239 *in* Annual report of the Smithsonian Institution for 1886. Part 1. Smithsonian Instit., Washington, D.C. 878 pp.

Mason, P. 1994. Parasites of deer in New Zealand. New Zealand J. Zool. 21: 39–47.

Masson, L. 1889–90. Les bourgeois de la Compagnie du Nord-Ouest. Vol. 2. Impr. generale A. Còtè et cie, Quebec.

Matson, R. G. 1976. The Glenrose Cannery site. Mercury 52, Ottawa, Ontario. pp.

———. 1981. Prehistoric subsistence patterns in the Fraser Delta: The evidence from the Glenrose Cannery site. BC Studies 48(winter): 64–85.

Matthiessen, P. 1959. Wildlife in America. Viking Press, New York. 304 pp.

Mattson, D. J. 1997. Use of ungulates by Yellowstone grizzly bears (*Ursus arctos*). Biol. Cons. 81: 161–167.

Mauer, E. M. 1992. Visions of the people: A pictorial history of Plains Indian life. The Minneapolis Inst. of Arts, Minneapolis, Minnesota. 298 pp.

Mautz, W. W., U. S. Seal and C. B. Boardman. 1980. Blood serum analyses of chemically and physically restrained white-tailed deer. J. Wildl. Manage. 44: 343–351.

Mautz, W. W., J. Kanter and P. J. Pekins. 1992. Seasonal metabolic rhythms of captive female white-tailed deer: A re-examination. J. Wildl. Manage. 56: 656–661.

Maxwell, H. 1910. The use and abuse of forest by Virginia Indians. William and Mary Coll. Quart. Hist. Mag., Vol. 34. College of William and Mary, Williamsburg, Virginia. 296 pp.

Maxwell, J. A., ed. 1978. America's fascinating Indian heritage. The Reader's Digest Assoc., Inc., Pleasantville, New York. 416 pp.

Mayer, F. H. and C. B. Roth. 1958. The buffalo harvest. Sage Books, Denver, Colorado. 96 pp.

Mayer, H. 1977. Zur wiederherstellung eines okologischen gleichgewichtes zwischen wald und wild im Gebirge. Pages 77–84 *in* F. Wolkinger, ed., Natur und mensch im alpenraum. Ludwig Boltzmann-Institut f Umweltwissenschaften und Naturschutz Graz. Leykam AG Graz

Mayfield, T. J. 1929. San Joaquin primeval, Uncle Jeff story: A tale of a San Joaquin Valley pioneer and his life with the Yokuts Indians. Tulare Times Press, Tulare, California.

Maynard Smith, J. 1980. A new theory of sexual investment. Behav. Ecol. Sociobiol. 7: 247–51.

Maynard, J. and G. R. Price. 1973. The logic of animal conflict. Nature 246: 15–18.

Mayr, E. 1940. Speciation phenomena in birds. Amer. Natur. 74(752): 249–278.

———. 1949. The species concept: Semantics vs. semantics. Evolution 3(4): 371–372.

———. 1953. Concepts of classification and nomenclature in higher organisms and microorganisms. Ann. New York Acad. Sci. 56(3): 391–397.

———. 1954. Notes on nomenclature and classification. Syst. Zool. 3(2): 86–89.

———. 1963. Animal species and evolution. Belknap Press of Harvard Univ.Press, Cambridge, Massachusetts. 797 pp.

———. 1964. Systematics and the origin of species from the viewpoint of a zoologist. Dover Publ., New York. 334 pp.

———. 1970. Populations, species and evolution. The Belknap Press of Harvard Univ. Press, Cambridge, Massachusetts. 453 pp.

Mayr, E., E. G. Linsley and R. L. Usinger. 1953. Methods and principles of systematic zoology. McGraw-Hill Book Co., New York. 328 pp.

McAllum, H. J., A. S. Familton, R. A. Brown and P. Hemmingsen. 1978. Salmonellosis in red deer calves (*Cervus elaphus*). New Zealand Vet. J. 26: 130–131.

McArthur, C., C. T. Robbins, A. E. Hagerman and T. A. Hanley. 1993. Diet selection by a ruminant generalist browser in relation to plant chemistry. Can. J. Zool. 71: 2,236–2,243.

McArthur, M. B. 1977. Seasonal food habits and diet quality of the Colockum elk herd in central Washington. M.S. Thesis, Washington State Univ., Pullman. 88 pp.

McArthur, R. H. and R. H. Levins. 1967. The limiting similarity, convergence and divergence of coexisting species. Amer. Natur. 102: 377–385.

McAtee, W. L. 1918. A sketch of the natural history of the District of Columbia together with an indexed edition of the U.S. Geological Survey's 1917 map of Washington and vicinity. Press of H. L. and J. B. McQueen, Inc., Washington, D.C. 142 pp.

McBee, R. H., J. L. Johnson and M. P. Bryant. 1969. Ruminal microorganisms from elk. J. Wildl. Manage. 33: 181–186.

McBryde, G. L. 1995 Economics of supplemental feeding and food plots for white-tailed deer. Wildl. Soc. Bull. 23: 497–501

McCabe, R. E. 1982. Elk and Indians: Historical values and perspectives. Pages 61–123 *in* J. W. Thomas and D. E. Toweill, eds., Elk of North America: ecology and management. Stackpole Books, Inc., Harrisburg, Pennsylvania. 698 pp.

McCabe, R. E. and T. R. McCabe. 1984. Of slings and arrows: An historical retrospection. Pages 19–72 *in* L. K. Halls, ed., White-tailed deer: Ecology and management. Stackpole Books, Harrisburg, Pennsylvania. 870 pp.

McCall, T. 1996. Final environmental impact statement for the Washington State management plan for elk. Washington Dept. Fish and Wildl., Wildl. Manage. Program, Olympia. 217 pp.

McCann, L. J. 1956. Ecology of the mountain sheep. Amer. Midl. Natur. 56: 297–324.

McClintock, W. 1968. The old north trail, or life, legends and religion of the blackfeet Indians. Univ. Nebraska Press, Lincoln. 539 pp.

McClure, N. R. 1958. Grass seedlings on lodgepole pine burns in the Northwest. J. Range Manage. 11(4): 183–186.

McClymont, R. A. 1979. Skeletal muscle fatty acid composition of wild ungulates and forensic applications. MS. Thesis, Univ. Alberta, 168 pp.

McCollum, D. W., G. L. Peterson, J. R. Arnold, D. C. Markstrom and D. M. Hellerstein. 1990. The Net Economic Value of Recreation on the National Forests: Twelve Types of Primary Activity Trips Across Nine Forest Service Regions. Gen. Tech. Rept. RM–289. Rocky Mountain Forest and Range Experiment Station, Fort Collins, Colorado. 36 pp.

McComb, K. 1987. Roaring by red deer stags advances the date of oestrus in hinds. Nature, London. 330: 648–649.

———. 1991. Female choice for high roaring rates in red deer, *Cervus elaphus*. Animal Behaviour 41: 79–88.

McConnell, B. R. and J. G. Smith. 1965. Understory response three years after thinning pine. J. Range Manage. 18(3): 129–132.

McConnell, B. R. and J. G. Smith. 1970a. Frequency distributions of deer and elk pellet groups. J. Wildl. Manage. 34(1): 29–36.

McConnell, B. R. and J. G. Smith. 1970b. Response of understory vegetation to ponderosa pine thinning in eastern Washington. J. Range Manage. 23: 208–212.

McConnell, B. R. and J. G. Smith. 1971. Response of understory vegetation to ponderosa pine thinning in eastern Washington. J. Range Manage. 23(3): 203–212.

McConnell, J. 1993. Back in the U.S.A. Pembina Gorge. Bugle 10(4): 109–113.

McConnochie, A. I. 1923. The deer and deer forests of Scotland: Historical, descriptive, sporting. H. F. Witherby and G. Witherby, London, U.K. 336 pp.

McCool, S. F. 1996. Wildlife viewing, natural area protection and community sustainability and resiliency. Natural Areas Journal 16: 147–151.

McCorquodale, S. 1991a. Biased sex ratios and spike-only herds: Products of open bull hunting? Bugle. 8(1): 11–19.

———. 1991b. Energetic considerations and habitat quality for elk in arid grasslands and coniferous forests. J. Wildl. Manage. 55: 237–242.

———. 1993. Winter foraging behavior of elk in the shrub-steppe of Washington. J.Wildl.Manage. 57: 881–890.

McCorquodale, S. M. and R. F. DiGiacomo. 1985. The role of wild North American ungulates in the epidemiology of bovine brucellosis: A review. J. Wildl. Dis. 21: 351–357.

McCorquodale, S. M., K. J. Raedeke and R. D. Taber. 1986. Elk habitat use patterns in the shrub-steppe of Washington. J. Wildl. Manage. 50(4): 664–669.

McCorquodale, S. M., L. L. Eberhardt and L. E. Eberhardt. 1988. Dynamics of a colonizing elk population. J. Wildl. Manage. 52: 309–312.

McCorquodale, S. M., L. E. Eberhardt and G. A. Sargeant. 1989. Antler characteristics in a colonizing elk population. J. Wildl. Manage. 53(3): 618–621.

McCulloch, C. Y., Jr. 1955. Utilization of winter browse on wilderness big game range. J. Wildl. Manage. 19(2): 206–215.

McCullough, D. R. 1969. The Tule elk: Its history, behavior and ecology. Univ. California Publ. Zool. Vol 88. Univ. California Press, Berkeley. 209 pp.

———. 1971. The Tule elk: Its history, behavior, and ecology. Univ. California Publ. in Zoology 88. Univ. California Press, Berkeley. 209 pp.

———. 1979. The George Reserve deer herd: Population ecology of a K-selected species. Univ. Michigan Press, Ann Arbor. 271 pp.

———. 1984. Lessons from the George Reserve, Michigan. Pages 211–242 in L. K. Halls, White-tailed deer: Ecology and management. Stackpole Books, Inc., Harrisburg, Pennsylvania.

———. 1985. Long range movements of large terrestrial mammals. Pages 444–465 in M. A. Rankin, ed., Migration: Mechanisms and adaptive significance. Contrib. Mar. Sci. 27.

———. 1993. History and management of elk in North America. Pages 331–341 in N. Ohtaishi and H. -I. Sheng, eds., Deer of China. Elsevier Sci. Publ., New York. 418 pp.

———. 1994. What do herd composition counts tell us? Wildl. Soc. Bull. 22: 295–300.

McCullough, D. R. and D. E. Ullrey. 1983. Proximate mineral and gross energy composition of white-tailed deer. J. Wildl. Manage. 47: 30–441.

McCullough, D. R., J. K. Fisher and J. D. Ballou. 1996. From bottleneck to metapopulation: Recovery of the Tule elk in California. Pages 375–403 in D. R. McCullough, ed., Metapopulations and wildlife conservation. Island Press, Washington, D.C. 429 pp.

McDermott, J. F., ed. 1952. Journal of an expedition to the Mauvaises Terres and the Upper Missouri in 1850 by Thaddeus J. Cuthbertson.

Bur. of Amer. Ethnol., Bull. 147. Govt. Print. Off., Washington, D.C. 164 pp.

McDonald, A. 1917. A few items of the Old West. Washington Hist. Quart. (Tacoma) 8(3): 188–229.

McDonald, P., R. A. Edwards and J. F. D. Greenhalgh. 1973. Animal nutrition. 2nd ed. Hafner Publ. Co., New York. 479 pp.

McDonnell, L. G. and S. F. Bates. 1993. Natural resources policy and law: Trends and directions. Island Press, Washington, DC. 211 pp.

McDowell, R. D. and H. W. Pillsbury. 1959. Wildlife damage to crops in the United States. J. Wildl. Manage. 23(2): 240–241.

McElroy, C. J., ed., 1989. SCI Record Book of Trophy Animals. Ed. 6, Vol. 2. Walsworth Publ., Inc., Tucson, Arizona. 860 pp.

McEwan, E. H. and P. E. Whitehead. 1970. Seasonal changes in the energy and nitrogen intake in reindeer and caribou. Can. J. Zool. 48: 905–913.

McGarigal, K. and B.J. Marks. 1995. FRAGSTATS: Spatial pattern analysis program for quantifying landscape structure. Gen. Tech. Rept. PNW-GTR-351. USDA For. Serv., Pac. Northwest Sta., Portland, Oregon. 122 pp.

McGhie, C. J. and S. Watson. 1995. Queensland wild deer and their role in sustainable wildlife management. Pages 312–316 in G. Grigg, P. Hale and D. Lunney, eds., Conservation through sustainable use of wildlife. Centre for Conserv. Biol., Univ. Queensland, Brisbane, Auatralia. 362 pp.

McGinnis, B. S. 1966. cited in Anderson, R. C., M. W. Lankester and U. R. Strelive. 1966. Further experimental studies of *Pneumostrongylus tenuis* in cervids. Can. J. Zool. 44: 851–861.

McGuire, J. D. 1899. Pipes and smoking customs of the American aborigines, based on material in the U.S. National Museum. Pages 351–645 in Annual report of the board of regents of the Smithsonian Institution . . . for the year ending June 30, 1897. Part 1. Govt. Print. Off., Washington, D.C.

McGuire, M. A., J. C. Vicini, D. E. Bauman and J. J. Veenhuizen. 1992. Insulin-like growth factors and binding proteins in ruminants and their nutritional regulation. J. Anim. Sci. 70: 2901–2910.

McHugh, T. 1979. The time of the buffalo. Univ. Nebraska Press, Lincoln. 374 pp.

McIntyre, G. A. 1952. A method for unbiased selective sampling, using ranked sets. Aust. J. Ag. Res. 3(4): 385–390.

McKeel, R. 1988. Status of elk winter feeding. Pages 26–29 in M. Zahn, J. Pierce and R. Johnson, eds., Proc. of the 1988 West. States and Provinces Elk Workshop. Washington Dept. Wildl., Olympia. 249 pp.

McKenna, P. B., I. Mackenzie and D. D. Heath. 1980. Fatal hepatitis cysticercosis in a red deer fawn. New Zealand Vet. J. 28: 124.

McLaren, I. A., ed. 1971. Natural regulation of animal populations. Atherton, New York. 196 pp.

McLaughlin, R. F. and E. M. Addison. 1986. Tick (*Dermacentor albipictus*)-induced winter hair-loss in captive moose (*Alces alces*). J. Wildl. Dis. 22: 502–510.

McLaughlin, W. J., N. Sanyal, J. Tangen-Foster, J. F. Tynon, S. Allen and C. C. Harris. 1989. 1987–88 Idaho Rifle Elk Hunting Study. Volume 1: Results. Contribution No. 499, Idaho Forest, Wildlife and Range Exp. Sta., Moscow.

McLean, L. S. 1972. Movements and migrations of the Lochsa elk herd. M.S. Thesis, Univ. Idaho, Moscow. 63 pp.

McLellan, B. 1978. Relationships between elk, snow, habitat use and timber management in the White River drainage of southeastern British Columbia. File report. British Columbia Fish and Wildlife Branch, Victoria, British Columbia. 33 pp. Mimeo.

McLeod, W. C. 1936. Conservation among primitive peoples. Sci. Month. 43: 562–566.

McMahon, T. A. 1975. Allometry and biomechanics: Limb bones in adult ungulates. Amer. Natur. 109(969): 547–563.

McMichael, E. V. 1963. 1963 excavations at the Buffalo Site, 46 Pu 31. West Virginia Archeologist 16: 12–23.

McMillan, A.D. and D. E. St. Claire. 1982. Alberni prehistory: Archaeological and ethnographic investigations on western Vancouver Island. Alberni Valley Mus., Port Alberni, B.C., Canada. pp.

McMillan, J. F. 1953a. Measures of association between moose and elk on feeding grounds. J. Wildl. Manage. 17: 162–166.

———. 1953b. Some feeding habits of moose in Yellowstone National Park. Ecology 34: 102–110.

McNaughton, S. J. 1985. Ecology of a grazing system: the Serengeti. Ecol. Monogr. 55: 259–294.

McNaughton, S. J. 1991. Evolutionary ecology of large tropical herbivores. Pages 509–522 in P. W. Price, T. M. Lewinsohn, G. W. Fernandes and W. W. Bensen, eds., Plant–animal interactions: Evolutionary ecology in tropical and temperate regions. John Wiley and Sons, New York.

McNeel, W., Jr. and J. Kennedy. 1959. Prevention of browsing by deer in a pine plantation. J. Wildl. Manage. 23(4): 450–451.

McNeil, G. R. 1972. Elk management in the Clearwater Region. Idaho Wildl. Rev. 24(4): 3–6.

McNitt, F. 1962. The Indian traders. Univ. Okla. Press, Norman. 393 pp.

McReynolds, S. J. 1977. Seasonal elk food habits and diet quality in central Washington. M. S. Thesis. Washington State Univ., Pullman. 79 pp.

McReynolds, S. J. Unpublished. Seasonal elk food habits and diet quality in central Washington. 1977. M.S. Thesis. Washington State Univ., Pullman. 79 pp.

Mead, J. R. 1986. Hunting and trading on the Great Plains, 1859–1875. Univ. Oklahoma Press, Norman. 276 pp.

Meagher, M. M. 1978. Bison. Pages 123–134 in J. L. Schmidt and D. L. Gilbert, eds., Big game of North America: Ecology and management. Stackpole Books, Harrisburg, Pennsylvania. 512 pp.

Meagher, M. and M. E. Meyer. 1994. On the origin of brucellosis in bison of Yellowstone National Park: A review. Con. Biol. 8: 645–653.

Mealey, R. H. 1969. Nylon fencing to protect forest plantations from deer and elk. Pages 89–90 in H. C. Black, ed., Wildlife and reforestation in the Pacific Northwest, Symp. Proc. Oregon State Univ., Corvallis. 92 pp.

Mearns, E. A. 1907. Mammals of the Mexican boundary of the United States. Part 1. Families Didelphidae to Muridae. Bull. 56. U.S. Nat. Mus., Washington, D.C. 530 pp.

Mech, L. D. 1970. The wolf: the ecology and behavior of an endangered species. Natural History Press, New York. 384 pp.

———. 1975. A new profile for the wolf. Natur. Hist. 83(4): 26–31.

Mech, L. D. and G. D. DelGiudice. 1985. Limitations of the marrow–fat technique as an indicator of body condition. Wildl. Soc. Bull. 13: 204–206.

Mech, L. D., M. E. Nelson and R. E. McRoberts. 1991. Effects of maternal and grandmaternal nutrition on deer mass and vulnerability to wolf predation. J. Mammal. 72(1): 146–151.

Meddis, R. 1975. On the function of sheep. Animal Behavior 23(3): 676–691.

Medin, D. E. 1970. Stomach content analysis: collections from wild herbivores and birds. Pages 133–145 in Range and wildlife habitat evaluation—a research symposium. Misc. Publ. 1147. USDA For. Serv., Washington, D.C.

Meeker, L. L. 1901. Ogalala games. Bull. Free Mus. Science and Art 3.

Meffe, G. K. and C. R. Carroll. 1994. Principles of Conservation Biology. Sinauer Associates, Inc., Sunderland, Massachusetts. 600 pp.

Meier, A. H. 1977. Prolactin, the liporegulatory hormone. Adv. Exp. Med. Biol. 80: 153–171.

Meile, P. and A. B. Bubenik. 1979. Zur Bedeutung sozialer Ausloser fur das Sozialverhalten der Gemse, *Rupicapra rupicapra* (Linne, 1758). Mammal. Inform. Munich, 27 (Sonderheft Gemsen): 1–42.

Meister, W. 1956. Changes in histological structure of the long bones of white-tailed deer (*Odocoileus virginianus*) during the growth of the antlers. Anat. Rec. 116: 709–721.

Meleney, W. P. 1985. Mange mites and other parasitic mites. Pages 317–346. in S. M. Gaafar, W. E. Howard and R. E. Marsh, eds., Parasites, pests and predators. Elsevier Science Publ., B. V., Amsterdam. 575 pp.

Meltz, R., D. H., Merriam, and R. M. Frank. 1999. The takings issue: Constitutional limits on land use control and environmental regulations. Island Press, Washington, DC. 595 pp.

Menominee Tribe v. United States, 391 U.S. 404 (1968).

Merchen, N. R. 1988. Digestion, absorption and excretion in ruminants. Pages 172–201 in D. C. Church, ed., The ruminant animal: digestive physiology and nutrition. Prentice Hall, Englewood Cliffs, New Jersey. 564 pp.

Mereszczak, I. M., W. C. Krueger and M. Vavra. 1981. Effects of range improvement on Roosevelt elk winter nutrition. J. Range Manage. 34: 184–187.

Merriam, C. H. 1897. *Cervus roosevelti,* a new elk from the Olympics. Proc. Biol. Soc. Washington 11: 271–275.

———. 1905. A new elk from California, *Cervus nannodes.* Proc. Biol. Soc. Washington 18: 23–25.

Merrill, E. H. 1987. Population dynamics and habitat ecology of elk in the Mount St. Helens Blast Zone. Ph.D. Diss., Univ. Washington, Seattle. 246 pp.

———. 1991. Thermal constraints on use of cover types and activity time of elk. Applied Animal Behaviour Science 29: 251–267.

———. 1994. Summer foraging ecology of wapiti (*Cervus elaphus nelsoni*) in the Mount Saint Helens blast zone. Can. J. Zool. 72: 303–311.

Merrill, E. H. and M. S. Boyce. 1991. Summer range and elk population dynamics in Yellowstone National Park. Pages 263–274 in R. B. Keiter and M. S. Boyce, eds., The Greater Yellowstone ecosystem: redefining America's wilderness heritage. Yale Univ. Press, New Haven, Connecticut. 428 pp.

Merrill, E., K. J. Raedeke and R. D. Taber. 1987. The population dynamics and habitat ecology of elk in the Mount St. Helens blast zone. Wildl. Sci. Group, Coll. For. Resou., Univ. Washinton, Seatle. 186 pp.

Merrill, E. H., A. Callahan-Olson, K. J. Raedeke and R. D. Tabler. 1995. Elk (*Cervus elaphus roosevelti*) dietary composition and quality in the Mount St. Helens blast zone. Northw. Sci. 69: 9–18.

Merrill, S. 1916. The moose book. E. P. Dutton and Co., New York. 366 pp.

Merritt, A.S. 1988. Women's beaded robes: Artistic reflections of the Crow world. Pages 41–47 in Fr. P.J. Powell, To honor the Crow people. Found. for the Preserv. American Indian Art and Cult., Inc., Chicago, Illinois. 48 pp.

Merts, P. A. 1953. Rol zhaludei v kormovom balanse olenei voroniezhskogo sapovednika. Trudy Voron. Gosudarstv. Sapov. 4: 123–132.

Meslow, E. C. 1993. Failures in wildlife management: Opportunities for success. Pages 35–45 in A. W. L. Hawley, ed., Commercialization and wildlife management: Dancing with the devil. Krieger Publ. Co., Malabar, Florida. 124 pp.

Messier, F. 1994. Ungulate population models with predation: A case study with the North American Moose. Ecology 75: 478–488.

Messier, F., D. M. Desaulniers, A. K. Goff, R. Nault, R. Patenaude and M. Crete. 1990. Caribou pregnancy diagnosis from immunoreactive progestins and estrogens excreted in feces. J.Wildl.Manage. 54: 279–283.

Messier, F., M. E. Rau and M. A. McNeill. 1989. *Echinococcus granulosus* (Cestoda: Taeniidae) infections and moose–wolf population dynamics in southwestern Quebec. Can. J. Zool. 67: 216–219.

Meyer, R. W. 1977. The village Indians of the Upper Missouri. Univ. Nebraska Press, Lincoln. 354 pp.

Meyers, C. 1997. Elk on growth spurt at Arizona reservation. *The Denver Post.* 7 December 1997. Page 2C.

Michigan Department of Natural Resources. Unpublished. 1996 elk status report. Michigan Dept. Natur. Resour., Wildl. Div., Lansing. 8 pp.

Michod, R. E. 1979. Evolution of life histories in response to age-specific mortality factors. American Naturalist 113: 531–550.

Midwood, A. J., P. Haggarty, B. A. McGaw and J. J. Robinson. 1989. Methane production in ruminants: Its effect on the double-labelled water method. Am. J. Physiol. 26: R1488–R1495.

Milchunas, D. G., A. S. Varnamkhasti, W. K. Lauenroth and H. Goetz. 1995. Forage quality in relation to long-term grazing history, current-year defoliation and water resource. Oecologia 101: 366–374.

Milchunas, D. G., M. I. Dyer, O. C. Wallmo and D. E. Johnson. 1978. *In vivo/in vitro* relationships of Colorado mule deer forages. Colorado Div. of Wildlife, Spec. Rept. No. 43.

Miles, C. 1963. Indian and Eskimo artifacts of North America. Bonanza Books, New York. 244 pp.

Millais, J. G. 1915a. North America. Pages 234–403 *in* D. Caruthers, P. B. Van der Byl, R. L. Kennion, J. G. Millais, H. F. Wallace and F. G. Barclay, eds., The gun at home and abroad, big game of Asia and North America. The London and Counties Press Assoc., Ltd., London, U.K. 433 pp.

———. 1915b. Wapiti. Pages 281–300 *in* D. Caruthers et al., eds., The gun at home and abroad: The big game of Asia and North America. The London and Counties Press Assoc., Ltd., London, U.K. 433 pp.

Miller, D. H. 1985. Custer's fall. Univ. Nebraska Press, Lincoln. 271 pp.

Miller, G. S., Jr. and R. Kellogg. 1955. List of North American recent mammals. Bull. 205. U.S. Nat. Mus., Washington, D.C. 954 pp.

Miller, H. A. 1963. Use of fire in wildlife management. Proc. Tall Timbers Fire Ecol. Conf. 2: 18–30.

Miller, J. and W. R. Seaburg. 1990. Athapaskans of southwestern Oregon. Pages 580–588 *in* W. Suttles, ed., Northwest coast. Handbook of North American Indians. Vol. 7. Smithsonian Instit. Press, Washington, D.C. 777 pp.

Miller, K. V. and R. L. Marchinton, eds. 1995. Quality whitetails. Stackpole Books, Mechanicsburg, Pennsylvania. 322 pp.

Miller, M. W. and E. T. Thorne. 1993. Captive cervids as potential sources of disease for North America's wild cervid populations: Avenues, implications and preventive management. Trans. N. Amer. Wildl. and Natur. Resour. Conf. 58: 460–467.

Miller, M. W., M. A. Wild, B. J. Baker and A. T. Tu. 1989. Snakebite in captive Rocky Mountain elk (*Cervus elaphus nelsoni*). J. Wildl. Dis. 25: 392–396.

Miller, M. W., J. M. Williams, T. J. Schiefer and J. W. Seidel. 1991. Bovine tuberculosis in a captive elk herd in Colorado: Epizootiology, diagnosis and management. Proc. U.S. Animal Health Assoc. 95: 533–542.

Miller, M. W., E. S. Williams, C. W. McCarty, T. R. Spraker, T. J. Kreeger, C. T. Larsen and E. T. Thorne. 2000. Epidemiology of chronic wasting disease in free-ranging cervids. J. Wildl. Dis. 36: 676–690.

Miller, R. F. 1974. Spring, summer and fall use by cattle and big game on foothill rangelands. M.S. Thesis, Oregon State Univ., Corvallis. 126 pp.

Miller, R. S. 1967. Pattern and process in competition. Adv. Ecol. Res. 4: 1–74.

Miller, W. H., J. H. Brock and J. Horsly. 1995. Elk and cattle competition in central Arizona. Final Rept., Arizona Game and Fish Dept., Phoenix. 95 pp.

Mills, H. B. 1936. Observations on Yellowstone elk. J. Mammal. 17: 250–253.

Mills, L. S., M. E. Soule and D. F. Doak. 1993. The keystone species concept in ecology and conservation. BioScience 43: 219–224.

Mills, W. C. 1922. Exploration of the Mound City group. Ohio Archaeol. and Hist. Soc. Quarterly 31(4): 423–585.

Millspaugh, J. J. 1999. Behavioral and physiological responses of elk to human disturbances in the southern Black Hills, South Dakota. Ph.D. Diss., Univ. Washington, Seattle. 284 pp.

Millspaugh, J. J. and J. M. Marzluff, eds. 2001. Radio-tracking and animal populations. Academic Press, San Diego, California.

Milne, J. A., J. C. MacRae, A. M. Spence and S. Wilson. 1978. A comparison of the voluntary intake and digestion of a range of forages at different times of the year by the sheep and the red deer. Brit. J. Nutr. 40: 347–357.

Milne, J. A., A. M. Sibbald, H. A. McCormack and A. S. I. Loudon. 1987. The influences of nutrition and management on the growth of red deer calves from weaning to 16 months of age. Anim. Prod. 45: 511–522.

Milne, J. A., A. S. I. Loudon, A. M. Sibbald, J. D., Curlewis and A. S. McNeilly. 1990. Effects of melatonin and a dopamine agonist and antagonist on seasonal changes in voluntary intake, reproductive activity and plasma concentrations of prolactin and triiodothyronine in red deer hinds. J. Endocrin. 125: 241–250.

Milner, C. A., II. 1994. National initiatives. pages 155–193 *in* C. A. Milner, C. A. O'Connor and M. A. Sandweiss, eds., The Oxford history of the American West. Oxford Univ. Press, New York. 872 pp.

Minnesota long range management plan for elk. 1997 Draft. Minnesota Dept. Natur. Resour., Saint Paul. 9 pp.

Minson, D. J. 1990. Forage in ruminant nutrition. Academic Press, Inc., New York. 483 pp.

Minson, D. J. and J. R. Wilson. 1994. Prediction of intake as an element of forage quality. Pages 533–563 *in* G. C. Fahey, ed., Forage quality, evaluation and utilization. ASA, Madison, Wisconsin.

Miquelle, D. G. 1990. Why don't bull moose eat during the rut? Behav. Ecol. Sociobiol, 27: 145–151.

Mirarchi, R. E., B. E. Howland, R. L. Kirkpatrick and P. F. Scanlon. 1976. Seasonal changes in plasma LH and testosterone levels in captive and wild adult male white-tailed deer. Paper read at the 56th Annu. Meet. Amer. Soc. Mammal. Abstr. pp. 12–13.

Mishkin, B. 1940. Rank and warfare among the Plains Indians. J. J. Augustin, New York. 65 pp.

Mitchell, B. 1963. Determination of age in Scottish red deer from growth layers in dental cement. Nature. 198(4,578): 350–351.

———. 1973. The reproductive performance of wild Scottish red deer, *Cervus elaphus*. J. Reprod. Fert. 19: 271–285.

Mitchell, B. and D. Brown. 1974. The effects of age and body size on fertility in female red deer (*Cervus elaphus* L.). Pages 89–98 *in* I. Kjerner and P. Bjurholm, eds., Trans. 11th Congr. IUGB. Nat. Swedish Environ. Protect. Board, Stockholm. 631 pp.

Mitchell, B. and G. A. Lincoln. 1973. Conception dates in relation to age and condition in two populations of red deer in Scotland. J. Zool., London 171: 141–152.

Mitchell, B., B. W. Staines and D. Welch. 1977. Ecology of the red deer. Inst. Terrestrial Ecology, Cambridge, U.K. 74 pp.

Mitchell, B., B. W. Staines and D. Welch. 1977. Ecology of red deer: a research review relevant to their management in Scotland. Inst. Territorial Ecol., Banchory, Scotland. 74 pp.

Mitchell, B., D. McCowan and I. A. Nicholson. 1976. Annual cycles of body weight and condition in Scottish red deer. J. Zool. London 180: 107–27.

Mitchell, B., W. Grant and J. Cubby. 1981. Notes on the performance of red deer, *Cervus elaphus*, in woodland habitat. J. Zool., London. 194: 279–284.

Mitchell, G. E. and J. B. Lauckhart. 1948. Management of the Yakima Rocky Mountain elk herd. Trans. N. Amer. Wildl. Conf. 13: 401–409.

Mitchell, G. J. 1980. The pronghorn antelope in Alberta. Alberta Dept. Lands For., Fish and Wildl. Div. 165 pp.

Mitchell, J. G. 1979. The hunt. Alfred A. Knopf, New York. 243 pp.

———. 1992. Going after the hunt: An inventory and credo synopsis of the animal protection movement. Pages 100–107 *in* Montana State Univ., Proc., The governor's symposium on North America's hunting heritage. Bozeman, Montana. 232 pp.

Mitscherlich, E. and E. H. Marth. 1984. Microbial survival in the environment. Springer-Verlag, New York. 802 pp.

Miura, S. 1984 Social behavior and territoriality in male sika deer (*Cervus nippon* Temminck 1838). Z. Tierpsychol. 64: 33–73.

Moar, M. H. and W. F. Jarrett. 1985. A cutaneous fibropapilloma from a red deer (*Cervus elaphus*) associated with a papillomavirus. Intervirol. 24: 108–118.

Moen, A. N. 1968. Energy balance of white-tailed deer in the winter. Trans. N. Amer. Wildl. and Natur. Resour. Conf. 33: 224–236.

———. 1973. Wildlife ecology. W. H. Freeman and Co., San Francisco. 458 pp.

Moen, A. N. and F. L. Jacobsen. 1974. Changes in radiant temperature of animal surfaces with wind and radiation. J. Wildl. Manage. 38(2): 366–368.

Moffitt, J. 1934. History of the Yosemite elk herd. Calif. Fish and Game 20: 37–51.

Mohler, J. R. 1917. Annual report of the U.S. Bureau of Animal Industry. USDA, Washington, D.C. 106 pp.

Mohler, L. L. 1956. Idaho game management plans in relation to hunting pressure and hunter distribution. Proc. West. Assoc. State Game and Fish Commiss. 36: 132–137.

Mohler, L. L. 1959. How big game report cards contribute to better game management in Idaho. Proc. West. Assoc. State Game and Fish Commiss. 39: 219–221.

Mohler, L. L. 1962. Deer management units in Idaho. Proc. West. Assoc. State Game and Fish Commiss. 42: 67–68.

Mohler, L. L. and D. E. Toweill. 1982. Regulated elk populations and hunter harvests. Pages 561–597 *in* J. W. Thomas and D. E. Toweill, eds., Elk of North America: Ecology and management. Stackpole Books, Harrisburg, Pennsylvania. 698 pp.

Mohler, L. L., P. D. Dalke and W. M. Shaw. 1958. Elk and elk hunting in Idaho. Trans. N. Amer. Wildl. Conf. 23: 491–501.

Mohr, C. O. and W. A. Stumpf. 1966. Comparison of methods for calculating areas of animal activity. J. Wildl. Manage. 30(2): 293–303.

Moisey, N. and M. S. Yuan. 1990. Estimates of Economic Impact of Non-Resident Travelers to Montana. Research Report 11, Institute for Tourism and Recreation Research, Univ. Montana, Missoula.

Molyneux, R. J. and M. H. Ralphs. 1992. Plant toxins and palatability to herbivores. J. Range Manage. 45: 13–18.

Monks, G. G. 1977. An examination of relationships between artifact classes and food resource remains at Deep Bay, DiSe–7. Ph.D. Thesis, Dept. of Anthropology and Sociology, Univ. of British Columbia, Vancouver, Canada. pp.

Montana Department of Fish and Game. 1972. Montana Fish and Game Department environmental statement: Annual statewide harvest of big game animals. Game Div. Proj. No. FG–22. Montana Fish and Game Dept., Helena. 76 pp.

———. 1975. Can we afford natural regulation? Montana Outdoors 6(4): 36–37.

Montana Department of Fish, Wildlife and Parks. 1992. Montana Department of Fish, Wildlife and Parks environmental statement: annual statewide harvest of big game animals. Game Div. Proj. No. FG–22. Montana Dept. of Fish, Wildl. and Parks, Helena. 76 pp.

Montana Fish, Wildlife and Parks. 1997. Montana Big Game Hunting Regulations. Montana Dept. of Fish, Widl. and Parks, Helena. 70 pp.

Montana State University. 1975. Cooperative elk-logging study. Annu. Prog. Rept., Res. Committee. Montana State Univ., Bozeman. 146 pp.

Mooney, J. 1896. The Ghost Dance religion and Sioux outbreak of 1890. Pages 641–1,136 *in* Fourteenth Annual Report of the Bureau of Ethnology to the Secretary of the Smithsonian Institution, Part 2. Govt. Print. Off., Washington, D.C. 842 pp.

———. 1898. Calendar history of the Kiowa Indians. Annu. Rept. Bur. Amer. Ethnol. for Years 1895–1896. 17(1): 129–445.

———. 1928. The aboriginal populations of America north of Mexico. Smithsonian Instit. Misc. Coll. 80(7): 1–40.

Moore, C. T. 1972. Man and fire in central North American grassland, 1535–1890. Ph.D. Thesis, Univ. California, Los Angeles. 155 pp.

Moore, G. H. and G. M. Cowie. 1986. Advancement of breeding in non-lactating adult red deer hinds. Proc. NZ Soc. Anim. Prod. 46: 175–178.

Moore, K. L., ed. 1966. The sex chromatin. W. B. Saunders Co., Philadelphia. 474 pp.

Moorhead, W. K. 1899. Report of field work in various portions of Ohio. Ohio Archaeol. and Hist. Publ. 10: 471–472.

Moran, A. J. 1973. The Rocky Mountain elk in Michigan. Wildl. Div., Res. and Dev. Rept. 267. Dept. Natur. Resour., Lansing. 93 pp.

Moran, R. J. 1970. Precocious antler development and sexual maturity in a captive elk. J. Mammal. 51(4): 812–813.

———. 1973. The Rocky Mountain elk in Michigan. Wildl. Div. Res. and Dev. Rept. 267. Michigan Dept. Natur. Resour., Lansing. 93 pp.

Moran, R. J. and J. J. Ozoga. 1965. Elk calf pursued by coyotes in Michigan. J. Mammal. 46(3): 498.

More, T. A. 1970. Motivational attitudes of licensed Massachusetts hunters. M.S. Thesis, Univ. Massachusetts, Amherst. 50 pp.

———. 1973. Attitudes of Massachusetts hunters. Trans. N. Amer. Wildl. and Natur. Resour. Conf. 38: 230–234.

Morgan, D. L. and E. T. Harris, ed. 1967. The Rocky Mountain journals of William Marshall Anderson: The West in 1834. The Huntington Library, San Marino, California. 430 pp.

Morgantini, L. E. and R. J. Hudson. 1980. Human disturbance and habitat selection in elk. Pages 132–139 *in* M. S. Boyce and L. D. Hayden-Wing, eds., North American elk: Ecology, behavior and management. Second ed. Univ. Wyoming, Laramie. 294 pp.

———. 1988. Migratory patterns of the wapiti, *Cervus elaphus,* in Banff National Park, Alberta. Can. Field-Naturalist 102: 12–19.

Morgantini, L. E. and R. J. Hudson. 1989. Nutritional significance of wapiti (*Cervus elaphus*) migrations to alpine ranges in western Alberta, Canada. Arctic and Alpine Res. 21: 288–295.

Morlan, R. E., compiler. 1999. C14 database. Can. Archaeol. Assoc. and Can. Mus. Civilization. http://www.canadianarchaeology.com.

Morlan, R. E., R. McNeely and B. T. Schreiner. 1996. Saskatchewan radiocarbon dates and vertebrate faunas. Geol. Surv. of Canada Open File 3,366. pp.

Moroz, P. 1991. Managing access to affect elk vulnerability. Pages 138–141 *in* A. G. Christensen, L. J. Lyon, T. N. Lonner, compilers, Proc. Elk Vulnerability Symp., Montana State Univ., Bozeman. 330 pp.

Morrice, A. G. 1906. The Canadian Denes. Pages 187–218 *in* Annual Archeological Report 1905. Report of the Ontario Minister of Education. L. K. Cameron, Toronto, Ontario. 249 pp.

Morris, D. 1967. The naked ape. McGraw-Hill Book Co., New York. 252 pp.

Morris, J. M. 1980. Effects of androgens on antler development and blood biochemical profiles of male white-tailed deer (*Odocoileus virginianus*). M.S. Thesis, Univ. of Guelph, Guelph, Ontario. 70 pp.

Morris, M. S. 1956. Elk and livestock competition. J. Range Manage. 9(1): 11–14.

Morris, M. S. and J. E. Schwartz. 1957. Mule deer and elk food habits on the National Bison Range. J. Wildl. Manage. 21(2): 189–193.

Morris, R. S. and D. U. Pfeiffer. 1995. Directions and issues in bovine tuberculosis epidemiology and control in New Zealand. New Zealand Vet. J. 43: 256–265.

Morris, R. C. 1994. Radioecology and ecology publications of the Idaho National Engineering Laboratory: 1974–1994 Environmental Science and Research Foundation, Idaho Falls, Idaho. 35 pp.

Morrison, F. B. 1957. Feeds and feeding. 22nd ed. Morrison Publ. Co., Ithaca, New York. 1,165 pp.

Morrison, J. A. 1960a. Characteristics of estrus in captive elk. Behaviour 16(1–2): 84–92.

———. 1960b. Ovarian characteristics in elk of known breeding history. J. Wildl. Manage. 24(3): 297–307.

———. 1960c. Big game management problems in Idaho. Proc. West. Assoc. State Game and Fish Commiss. 40: 224–231.

Morrison, J. A., C. E. Trainer and P. L. Wright. 1959. Breeding season in elk as determined from known-age embryos. J. Wildl. Manage. 23(1): 27–34.

Morrison, J. R., W. J. de Vergie, A. W. Alldredge, A. E. Byrne and W. W. Andree. 1995. The effects of ski area expansion on elk. Wildl. Soc. Bull. 23(3): 481–489.

Morton, J. K. and E. T. Thorne. 1975. Long-term effects of brucellosis in elk and the role of venereal transmission. Wyo. Game and Fish Commiss. Job Compl. Rept., Fed. Aid in Wildl. Restor., Proj. FW–3-R21, pp. 17–21. Wyoming Game and Fish Commiss., Laramie.

Morton, J. K., E. T. Thorne and G. M. Thomas. 1981. Brucellosis in elk. III. Serologic evaluation. J. Wildl. Dis. 17: 23–31.

Morton, T. 1637. New English Canaan or New Canaan. J. F. Stam, Amsterdam. 188 pp.

———. 1883. New English Canaan, with introductory matter and notes by Charles Francis Adams, Jr. Vol. 14. The Prince Soc., Boston, Massachusetts. 381 pp.

Mott, T. D. 1960. Grazing pressure and measurement of pasture production. Proc. Int. Grassland Congr. 8: 606–611.

Mould, E. D. and C. T. Robbins. 1981. Nitrogen metabolism in elk. J. Wildl. Manage. 45: 323–334.

Mould, E. D. and C. T. Robbins. 1982. Digestive capabilities in elk compared to white-tailed deer. J. Wildl. Manage. 46: 22–29.

Moulton, G. E., ed. 1986–1999. The journals of the Lewis and Clark expedition. 12 vols. Univ. Nebraska Press, Lincoln.

Mower, K. J. and H. D. Smith. 1989. Diet similarity between elk and deer in Utah. Great Basin Naturalist 49: 552–555.

Mross, G. A. and R. F. Doolittle. 1967. Amino acid sequence studies on artiodactyl fibrinopeptides. II. Vicuna, elk, muntjak, pronghorn antelope and water buffalo. Archives of Biochem. and Biophysics 122(3): 674–684.

Mueggler, W. F. 1965. Cattle distribution on steep slopes. J. Range Manage. 18: 255–257.

———. 1966. Herbicide treatment of browse on a big-game winter range in northern Idaho. J. Wildl. Manage. 30(1): 141–151.

———. 1967a. Trees, shrubs and elk. Idaho Wildl. Rev. 19(4): 12–13.

———. 1967b. Response of mountain grassland vegetation to clipping in southwestern Montana. Ecology 48(6): 942–949.

———. 1971. Weather variations on a mountain grassland in southwestern Montana. Res. Pap. INT–99. USDA For. Serv., Ogden, Utah.

Mueller-Dombois, D. and H. Ellenberg. 1974. Aims and methods of vegetation ecology. John Wiley and Sons, Inc., New York. 547 pp.

Muir, P. D. and A. R. Sykes. 1988. Effect of winter nutrition on antler development in red deer (*Cervus elaphus*): A field study. New Zealand J. Ag. Res. 31: 145–150.

Muir, P. D., G. Semiadi, G. W. Asher, T. E. Broad, M. L. Tate and T. N. Barry. 1997. Interspecies hybridization of sambar deer (*Cervus unicolor*) and red deer (*Cervus elaphus*). J. Heredity 88(5): 366–372.

Mullan, J. 1861. Report on the construction of military road from Fort Benton to Fort Walla Walla. 36 Cong., 2ndSess., H.R. Exec. Doc. 44. Washington, D.C. 183 pp.

Mullarkey, B. 1996. Blue Mountains elk initiative: Management success through cooperation and cost saving. Pages 132–135 *in* K. E. Evans, compiler, Sharing common ground on western rangelands: Proceedings of a livestock/big game symposium; February 1996. Gen. Tech. Rept. INT-GTR–343. USDA For. Serv., Intermountain Res. Sta., Ogden, Utah. 164 pp.

Muller, R. A. 1971. Transmission components of solar radiation in pine stands in relation to climatic and stand variables. Res. Pap. PSW71. USDA For. Serv., Berkeley, California. 13 pp.

Muller-Schwarze, D. 1971. Pheromones in black-tailed deer (*Odocoileus hemionus columbianus*). Animal Behavior 19: 141142.

———. 1987. Evolution of cervid olfactory communication. Pages 223–234 *in* C.M. Wemmer, ed., Biology and Management of the Cervidae.

Muller-Schwarze, D., C. Muller-Schwarze, A. G. Singer and R. M. Silverstein. 1974. Mammalian pheromone: Identification of active component in the subauricular scent of the male pronghorn. Science 183(4127): 860–862.

Müller-Using, D., and R. Schloeth. 1967. Das Verhalten der Hirsche (*Cervidae*). Handbuch der Zoologie 8, 10(28): 1–60.

Mulloy, W. 1942. The Hagen site: A prehistoric village on the lower Yellowstone. Univ. Montana Publ. in Soc. Sci., No. 1. Univ. Montana, Missoula. 106 pp.

———. 1958. A preliminary historical outline for the Northwestern Plains. Univ. Wyoming Publications in Sciences. 22(1): 1–264.

Mumford, R. E. 1969. Distribution of the mammals of Indiana. Monogr. No. 1. Indiana Academy of Science, Indianapolis. 114 pp.

Mundy, K. R. D. and D. R. Flook. 1973. Background for managing grizzly bears in the national parks of Canada. Rept. Ser. 22. Can. Wildl. Serv., Ottawa. 35 pp.

Munro, J. A. 1947. Observations of birds and mammals in central British Columbia. Occas. Pap. British Columbia Prov. Mus. 6: 1–165.

Munro, R., A. R. Hunter, M. Bonniwell and W. Corrigall. 1985. Systemic mycosis in Scottish red deer (*Cervus elaphus*). J. Comp. Pathol. 95: 281–289.

Murata, H., H. Takahashi and H. Matsumoto. 1987. The effects of road transportation on peripheral blood lymphocyte sub populations, lymphocyte blastogenesis and neutrophil function in calves. Brit. Vet. J. 143: 166–174.

Murdock, G. P. and T. J. O'Leary. 1975. Ethnographic bibliography of North America. 5 vols. 4th ed. Human Relat. Area Files Press, New Haven, Connecticut.

Murie, A. 1940. Ecology of the coyote in the Yellowstone. Fauna of the Nat. Park of U.S. No. 4. U.S. Nat. Park Serv., Washington, D.C. 206 pp.

Murie, O. L. 1930. An epizootic disease of elk. J. Mammal. 11: 214–222

———. 1935. Food habits of the coyote in Jackson Hole, Wyoming. Circ. 362. USDA, Washington, D.C. 24 pp.

———. 1951. The elk of North America. Stackpole Co., Harrisburg, Pennsylvania. 376 pp.

———. 1954. A field guide to animal tracks. Houghton Mifflin Co., Boston, Massachusetts. 374 pp.

———. 1966. Appendix 3. Reproduction and hybridisation. Pages 151–154 *in* D. B. Banwell, ed., Wapiti in New Zealand, the story of the Fiordland Herd. A. H. & A. W. Reed, Wellington, New Zealand.

Murison, W. 1906. Notes on some specimens. Pages 10–35 *in* Annual Archaeological Report 1905. Report of the Ontario Minister of Education. L. K. Cameron, Toronto. 249 pp.

Murphy, D. A. 1963. A captive elk herd in Missouri. J. Wildl. Manage. 27(3): 411–414.

Murphy, D. A. and J. A. Coates. 1966. Effects of dietary protein on deer. Trans. N. Amer. Wildl. Conf. 31: 129–139.

Murphy, D. R. 1963. A captive elk herd in Missouri. J. Wildl. Manage. 27(3): 411–414.

Murphy, J. M. 1879. Sporting adventures in the far West. London: Samson Low, Marston, Searle and Rivington. 404 pp.

Murray, J. O. and D. O. Trainer. 1970. Bluetongue virus in North American elk. J. Wildl. Dis. 144–148.

Muschenheim, A. 1988. Ivermectin for the treatment of psoroptic scabies in elk (*Cervus elaphus nelsoni*) and Rocky Mountain bighorn sheep (*Ovis canadensis canadensis*). M. S. Thesis, Univ. Wyoming, Dept. of Zoology and Physiology, Laramie, Wyoming. 108 pp.

Musclow, R. W. 1984. Emergency big game feeding in Utah: past–present–future. Utah Dept. Natur. Resour., Salt Lake City. 69 pp.

Musgrave, R. S., J. A. Flynn-O'Brien, A. A. Smith and Y. D. Marinakis. 1998. Federal wildlife laws handbook with related laws. Govt. Inst., Rockville, Maryland. 679 pp.

Mutch, R. W. 1976. Fire management today: Tradition and change in the Forest Service. Proc. 1975 Nat. Comb. Soc. Amer. For. 189–202.

Muth, R. M. 1975. Applied research in the U.S. Forest Service: A program design for diffusion of innovation. Unpubl. M.S. Thesis, Univ. Washington, Seattle. 61 pp.

Myers, W. L., B. Lyndaker, P.E. Fowler and W. Moore. 1996. Investigations of calf elk mortalities in southeastern Washington: A progress report 1992–1996. Washington Dept. Fish and Wildl., Olympia, Washington. 14 pp.

Myers, W. L., Jr., R. D. Spencer, D. J. Pierce and P. E. Fowler. 1995. Aerial mark-resighting estimates of elk populations in southeast Washington using aerial paintball marking techniques. Progr. Rept., Washington Dept. Fish and Wildlife, Olympia. 10 pp.

Mykytowycz, R. and B. S. Goodrich. 1974. Skin glands as organs of communication in mammals. J. Invest. Derm. 62: 124–131.

Myrberget, S. 1991. Game management in Europe outside the Soviet Union. Pages 41–53 *in* B. Bobek, K. Perzanowski and W. L. Regelin, eds., Global trends in wildlife management. Eighteenth Int. Union of Game Biologists Congress, Kraków, Poland. 660 pp.

Mystkowska, E. T. 1966. Morphological variability of the skull and body weight of red deer. Acta Theriologica 31(5): 129–194.

Nagle, J. P. and G. A. Harris. 1966. Grazing compatibility of cattle and elk on mountain ranges. Proc. Int. Grassland Congr. (Helsinki, Finland) 10: 994–997.

Nagy, J. G. 1970. Biological relations of rumen flora and fauna. Pages 159–163 *in* Range and wildlife habitat evaluation—a research symposium. Misc. Publ. 1147. USDA For. Serv., Washington, D.C.

Nagy, J. G. and W. L. Regelin. 1975. Comparison of digestive organ size of three deer species. J. Wildl. Manage. 39: 621–624.

Nagy, K. A. 1983. The doubly labeled water (^{3}HH^{18}O) method: A guide to its use. UCLA Publ. 12–1417, Univ. California, Los Angeles. 45 pp.

Nagy, K. A. 1987. Field metabolic rate and food requirements scaling in mammals and birds. Ecol. Monogr. 57: 111–128.

Nandra, K. S., V. H. Oddy, J. F. Ayres, P. J. Nicholls, B. Langevad and W. Ly. 1995. The use of cell wall organic matter components and *in vitro* degradability characteristics to predict intake and digestibility of white clover for sheep. Aust. J. Ag. Res. 46: 1,111–1,120.

Nash, R., ed. 1968. The American environment: Readings in the history of conservation, second edition. Addison-Wesley Publ. Co., Reading, Massachusetts. 264 pp.

Nasimovich, A. A. 1955. The role of the regime of snow cover in the life of ungulates in the USSR. Moscow: Acad. Sci. USSR. (Translation by Can. Wildl. Serv., Ottawa). 290 pp.

National Academy of Sciences. 1962. Range research—basic problems and techniques. Natur. Resour. Counc., Publ. No. 890. Nat. Acad. Sci., Washington, D.C. 341 pp.

National Fish and Wildlife Foundation. 1994. USDA For. Serv., FY1995 Fisheries and wildlife assessment. Nat. Fish and Wildl. Found., Washington, D.C. 118 pp.

National Research Council. 1984. Nutrient requirements of cattle. Sixth ed. Nat. Acad. Press, Washington D.C. 90 pp.

———. 1985. Nutrient requirements of sheep. Sixth ed. Nat. Acad. Press, Washington, D.C. 99 pp.

National Rifle Association. 1972. Special annual big game survey. Pages 10–21 *in* National Rifle Association 1972 hunting annual. Nat. Rifle Assoc., Washington, D.C.

National Wildlife Refuge System Act. 1996. P.L. 89–669, 80 Stat. 926.

Naugle, D. E., J. A. Jenks and B. J. Kernohan. 1996. Use of thermal infrared sensing to estimate density of white-tailed deer. Wildl. Soc. Bull. 24: 37–43.

Neff, D. J. 1968. The pellet-group count technique for big game trend, census and distribution: A review. J. Wildl. Manage. 32(3): 597–614.

———. 1980. Effects of watershed treatments on deer and elk range use. Job Proj. Rept. W–78–R–4/5. Arizona Game and Fish Dept., Tucson. 28 pp.

Neff, D. J., O. C. Wallmo and D. C. Morrison. 1965. A determination of defecation rate for elk. J. Wildl. Manage. 29(2): 406–407.

Neihardt, J. G. 1959. Black Elk speaks: Being the life story of a holy man of the Oglala Sioux. Simon and Shuster, Inc., New York.

Neiland, K. A. 1970. Weight of dried marrow as indicator of fat in caribou femurs. J. Wildl. Manage. 34: 904–907.

Neiman, K. E. 1977. Relationship of canopy volume, biomass and utilization form class to annual production of *Amelanchier alnifolia*. M.S. Thesis, Washington State Univ., Pullman. 35 pp.

Neitzel, H. 1987. Chromosomal evolution of Cervidae. Pages 90–112 *in* G. Obe and A. Basler, eds., Cytogenetics. Springer Verlag, Berlin, Germany. 401 pp.

Nelson, E. W. 1902. A new species of elk from Arizona. Amer. Mus. Natur. Hist. Bull. 16(1): 1–12.

———. 1925. Status of the pronghorned antelope, 1922–1924. U.S. Dept. Ag. Bull. 1,346. 64 pp.

Nelson, J. R. 1976. Forest fire and big game in the Pacific Northwest. Proc. Tall Timbers Fire Ecology Conf. 15: 85–102.

———. 1977. Maximum stocking rates with common-use and proper-use grazing. Washington Ag. Res. Cen. Bull. 856: 1–6.

———. 1978. Maximizing mixed animal species stocking rates under proper-use management. J. Wildl. Manage. 42: 172–174.

———. 1982. Relationships of elk and other large herbivores. Pages 415–441 *in* J. W. Thomas and D. E. Toweill, eds., Elk of North America. Stackpole Books, Inc., Harrisburg, Pennsylvania.

———. 1984. A modeling approach to large herbivore competition. Pages 491–524 *in* Developing Strategies for Rangeland Management. Westview Press, Boulder, Colorado.

Nelson, J. R. and D. G. Burnell. 1975. Elk–cattle competition in central Washington *In* Range multiple use management. Univ. Idaho, Moscow. 172 pp.

Nelson, J. R. and D. G. Burnell. 1976. Elk–cattle competition in central Washington. Northwest Sect. Soc. Amer. For., Spokane. 8 pp.

Nelson, J. R. and T. A. Leege. 1982. Nutritional requirements and food habits. Pages 323–368 *in* J. W. Thomas and D. E. Toweill, eds., Elk of North America: Ecology and management. Stackpole Books, Inc., Harrisburg, Pennsylvania. 698 pp.

Nelson, J. R., A. N. Pell, P. Schofield and S. Zinder. 1995. Isolation and characterization of an anaerobic hydrolyzable tannin degrading bacterium. Appl. Environ. Microbiol. 61: 3,293–3,298.

Nelson, L. J. and J. M. Peek. 1982. Effect of survival and fecundity on rate of increase of elk. J. Wildl. Manage. 46: 535–540.

Nelson, N. C. 1942. Camping on ancient trails. Natur. Hist. 49: 262–267.

Nelson, R. H. 1999. The religion of forestry: Scientific management. J. For. 97(11):4–8.

Nelson, R. K. 1973. Hunters of the northern forest: Designs for survival among the Alaskan Kutchin. Univ. Chicago Press, Chicago, Illinois.

———. 1983. Make prayers to the raven. Univ. Chicago Press, Chicago, Illinois.

Nelson, T. 1991. License and Harvest Statistics. Pages 14.1–14.34 *in* R. Neslon and T. Powell, ed., A guide to elk hunting in Colorado, third edition. Elk Mountain Guide Books, Elk Rancho, Colorado.

Nerl, W. 1985. Der hirsch und sein review Ludwig verlag, Pfaffenhofen. 387 pp.

Netter, F. 1965. CIBA—collection of medical illustrations. Vol. 4. CIBA, New York. 287 pp.

Nettles, V. F. and D. E. Stallknecht. 1992. History and progress in the study of hemorrhagic disease of deer. Trans. N. Amer. Wildl. and Natur. Resour. Conf. 57: 499–516.

Nettles, V. F., A. K. Prestwood, R. G. Nichols and C. J. Whitehead. 1977a. Meningeal worm-induced neurologic disease in black-tailed deer. J. Wildl. Dis. 13: 137–143.

Nettles, V. F., A. K. Prestwood and R. D. Smith. 1977b. Cerebrospinal parelaphostrongylosis in fallow deer. J. Wildl. Dis. 13: 440–444.

Nettleton, P. F., J. A. Herring and W. Corrigall. 1980. Isolation of bovine virus diarrhoea virus from a Scottish red deer. Vet. Rec. 107: 425–426.

Nettleton, P. F., J. A. Sinclair, J. A. Herring, D. M. Inglis, T. J. Fletcher, H. M. Ross and M. A. Bonniwell. 1986. Prevalence of herpesvirus infection in British red deer and investigations of further disease outbreaks. Vet. Rec. 118: 267–270.

Neu, C. W., C. R. Byers and J. M. Peek. 1974. A technique for analysis of utilization-availability data. J. Wildl. Manage. 38(3): 541–545.

Neumann, A. 1968. Rotwild population Hohenbucko. Beiträge zur Jagd und Wildforschung VI, Deutsche Akademie der Landwirtschafts wisseuschajten, Berlin. pp. 93–101.

———. 1973. Alterserscheinungen beim Rotwild. Beitrage zur Jagd-und Wildforschung 8: 33–38.

Nevada Division of Wildlife. 1997. Nevada elk species management plan. Fed. Aid in Wildl. Restor. Grant W–48-R–28, Subgrant III, Planning Proj. 4: Job 1. Reno. 66 pp. + 17 pp. Appendices.

Nevada. 1991. Livestock/Big Game: Seeking common ground on Western rangelands. Nevada Cattlemen's Assoc., Elko (Abstracts).

Newby, F. E. 1975. Environmental impact statements on hunting seasons. Proc. West. Assoc. State Game and Fish Commiss. 55: 95–97.

Newcomb, W. W. 1955. A re-examination of the causes of Plains warfare. Amer. Anthropol. 52: 317–330.

Newcomb, W. W., Jr. 1961. The Indians of Texas. Univ. Texas Press, Austin. 404 pp.

Newman, C. C. 1958. Roosevelt elk of Olympic National Park. Nat. Park Serv., Olympic Natur. Hist. Assoc.

Newsholme, E. A. and A. R. Leech. 1983. Biochemistry for the medical sciences. John Wiley and Sons, New York. 952 pp.

New York ex rel Kennedy v. Backer, 89 Wash. 492, 154 P. 810, 155 P. 1041 (1916).

Ngugi, K. R., J. Powell, F. C. Hinds and R. A. Olson. 1992. Range animal diet composition in southcentral Wyoming. J. Range Manage. 45: 542–545.

New Zealand Department of Conservation. 1997. Issues and options for managing the impacts of deer on native forests and other ecosystems. Wright and Carmen, Ltd., Wellington, New Zealand. 55 pp.

Nichols, D. K., R. J. Montali, L. G. Phillips, T. P. Alvarado, M. Bush and L. Collins. 1986. *Parelaphostrongylus tenuis* in captive reindeer and sable antelope. J. Am. Vet. Med. Assoc. 188: 619–621.

Nichols, L., Jr. 1957a. Forage utilization by elk and domestic sheep in the White River National Forest. M.S. Thesis. Colorado State Univ., Fort Collins. 92 pp.

———. 1957b. Study of forage utilization by elk and domestic sheep on the South Fork of the White River. Compl. Rept., Proj. W–38-R–10. Colorado Fish and Game Dept., Denver. pp. 11–22.

Nicholson, J. R. and L. A. Donaldson. 1969. History of the Order of Elk, 1868–1967. Rev. edit. Nat. Memorial Publ. Commission of the Benevolent and Protective Order of Elks of the U.S.A., Chicago. 482 pp.

Nicoletti, P. 1990. Vaccination. Pages 283–299 *in* K. Nielson and J. R. Duncan, eds., Animal brucellosis. CRC Press, Boca Raton, Florida. 453 pp.

Nikolski, V. A. and D. Wallschlager. 1983. Intraspecific divergency of whistles of red deer (*Cervus elaphus*). Zool. Jahrbucher Physiol. 87: 353–357.

Nilssen, K. J., J. A. Sundsfjord and A. S. Blix. 1984. Regulation of metabolic rate in Svalbard and Norwegian reindeer. Am. J. Physiol. 247: R837–R841.

Nilsson, T. 1982. The Pleistocene. D. Reidel Publ. Co., Dordrect, Holland. 651 pp.

Nimmo, B. W. 1971. Population dynamics of a Wyoming pronghorn cohort from the Eden- Farson site, 48SW304. Plains Anthropol. 16: 285–288.

Noble, W. C. 1975. Van Beisen, a study in Glen Meyer development. Ontario Archaeol. 24: 3–95.

Norberg, E. R. and L. Trout. 1957. Clearwater game range study. Fed. Aid in Wildl. Restor. Final Rept., Proj. W–112-R. Idaho Fish and Game Dept., Boise. 171 pp.

Norris, D., N. Phelps and D. J. Schubert. 2001. Canned hunts: Unfair at any price. The Fund for Animals, New York. 64 pp.

Norris, J. J. 1943. Botanical analysis of stomach contents as a method of determining forage consumption of range sheep. Ecology 24: 244.

Norris, P. W. 1877. Report of the Superintendent of the Yellowstone National Park. Govt. Print. Off., Washington, D.C. 15 pp.

———. 1878. Report on the Yellowstone National Park. Pages 979–996 *in* Report of the Secretary of the Interior. Vol. 1. Govt. Print. Off., Washington, D.C. 1,283 pp.

———. 1880a. Report of the Superintendent of the Yellowstone National Park for the year 1879. Govt. Print. Off., Washington, D.C. 31 pp.

———. 1880b. Annual Report of the Superintendent of the Yellowstone National Park. Govt. Print. Off., Washington, D.C. 64 pp.

————. Unpublished. Meanderings of a mountaineer, or, the journals and musings (or storys) of a rambler over Prairie (or mountain) and Plain. Manuscript prepared from newspaper clippings (1870–1875) and annotated about 1885. On file in the P. W. Norris Collection (HM506), Henry E. Huntington Library, San Marino, California.

North Dakota Game and Fish Department. 1942. Elk to roam North Dakota Badlands. North Dakota Outdoors (March): 13–14.

Northrup, H. D. 1891. Indian horrors; or massacres by the red men. Nat. Publ. Co., Philadelphia, Pennsylvania.

Norton, T. E. 1974. The fur trade in colonial New York 1686–1776. Univ. Wisconsin Press, Madison. 243 pp.

Noss, R. F. and A. Y. Cooperrider. 1994. Saving nature's legacy—protecting and restoring biodiversity. Island Press, Covelo, Califonia. 416 pp.

Novellie, P. 1986. Relationships between rainfall, population density and the size of the bontebok lamb crop in the Bontebok National Park. S. Afr. J. Wildl. Resour. 16: 39–46.

Nowak, R. M. and J. L. Paradiso. 1983. Walker's mammals of the world, 4th edition, Vol. 2. The Johns Hopkins Univ. Press, Baltimore, Maryland. Pages 569–1,362.

Nowlin, R. A. 1974. Prescribed burning effects on in vitro digestibility of elk browse. M.S. Thesis, Univ. Idaho, Moscow. 27 pp.

Noyes, J. H., B. K. Johnson, L. D. Bryant, S. L. Findholt and J. W. Thomas. 1996. Effects of bull age on conception dates and pregnancy rates of cow elk. J. Wildl. Manage. 60(3): 508–517.

Nudds, T. D. 1977. Quantifying the vegetative structure of wildlife cover. Wildl. Soc. Bull. 5(3): 113–117.

Oberholser, H. C. 1905. The mammals and summer birds of western North Carolina. Biltmore For. School, Biltmore, North Carolina. 22 pp.

Obermaier, H. 1924. Fossil man in Spain. Yale Univ. Press, New Haven, Connecticut. 495 pp.

O'Brien, S. J. and E. Mayr. 1991. Bureaucratic mischief: Recognizing endangered species and subspecies. Science 251(4998): 1,187–1,188.

Odum, E. P. 1971. Fundamentals of ecology. 3rd ed. W. B. Saunders Co., Philadelphia. 574 pp.

Oertle, V. L. 1977. Elk hunting today—a comparison of 11 states. Outdoor Life 160(2): 85, 124–125.

Oftedal, O. 1985. Pregnancy and lactation. Pages 216–238 in Bioenergetics of Wild Herbivores. R. J. Hudson and R. G. White, eds., C.R.C. Press, Boca Raton, Florida. 314 pp.

O'Gara, B. W. 1988. Snow leopards and sport hunting in the Mongolian Peoples Republic. Int. Snow Leopard Symp. Proc. 5: 215–225.

O'Gara, B. W. and Z. Li. 1988. Overview of wildlife ranching in Asia. Int. Wildl. Ranching Symp. Proc. 1: 37–46.

O'Gara, B. W. and G. Matson. 1975. Growth and casting of horns by pronghorns and exfoliation of horns by bovids. J. Mammal. 56(4): 829–846.

Ogurlu, I. 1992. Wild ungulates in Turkey. Pages 575–577 in F. Spitz, G. Janeau, G. Gonzalez and S. Aulagner, eds., Ongulés/ungulates 91. Société Francaise pour L'Etude et la Protection des Mammifères, Paris. 661 pp.

Ohtaishi, N. and Y. Gao. 1990. A review of the distribution of all species of deer (Tragulidae, Moschinae and Cervidae) in China. Mammal Rev. 20(2/3): 125–144.

Okarma, H. 1984. The physical condition of red deer falling prey to the wolf and lynx and harvested in the Carpathian Mountains. ACTA Therlogica 29: 283–290.

Oldemeyer, J. L., R. L. Robbins and B. L. Smith. 1993. Effect of feeding level on elk weights and reproductive success at the National Elk Refuge. Pages 64–68 in 1990 Proc. West. States Prov. Elk Workshop. Calif. Fish and Game, Sacramento. 138 pp.

Oldemeyer, J. L., W. J. Barmore and D. L. Gilbert. 1971. Winter ecology of bighorn in Yellowstone National Park. J. Wildl. Manage. 35: 257–269.

Oldys, H. 1910. The game market to-day. Pages 243–254 in U.S. Department of Agriculture yearbook, 1910. U.S. Dept. Ag., Washington, D.C.

Olmsted, D. L. and O. C. Stewart. 1978. Achumawi. Pages 225–235 in R. F. Heizer, ed., California. Handbook of North American Indians. Vol. 8. Smithsonian Instit., Washington, D.C. 800 pp.

Oloff, H. B. 1951. Zur Biologie und Ökologie des Wildschweines. Verlag P. Schöps, Frankfurt/Main. 95 pp.

Olsen, A. 1989. The economic value of hunting and fishing in Montana. Transactions, North American Wildlife and Natural Resources Conference 54: 239–246.

Olsen, A. and A. Woolf. 1978. The development of clinical signs and the population significance of neurological disease in a captive wapiti herd. J. Wildl. Dis. 14: 263–268.

Olsen, F. W. and R. M. Hansen. 1977. Food relationships of wild free-roaming horses to livestock and big game, Red Desert, Wyoming. J. Range Manage. 30: 17–20.

Olsen, O. A. 1943. Big game in multiple land use in Utah. J. Forestry 41: 792–797.

Olson, G. 1991. Kansas City here I come! Pages 79–81 in A. G. Christensen, L. J. Lyon and T. N. Lonner, compilers, Proc. Elk Vulnerability Symp., Montana State Univ., Bozeman. 330 pp.

Olson, R. and A.M. Lewis. 1994. Winter big game feeding: an undesirable wildlife management practice. Bull B–1003, Univ. Wyoming Cooperative Extension Service, Laramie. 11 pp.

Onderscheka, K. 1986. Ist die futterung des rotwildes in der kulturlandschaft des alpinen Raumes eine biologische absurditat oder ein betrag zur erhaltung der funktion des okosystems? Pages 386–395 in S. Linn, ed., Rotwild-cerf rouge-red deer. Proc. CIC Sympos. 1986. Munchen.

Onderscheka, K. 1991. Wildtierernahrung-wildschaden. Oesterreichisches Weidwerk 6: 40–45, 7: 39–41

Onderscheka, K., F. Reimoser, F. Tataruch, T. Steineck, E. Klansek, F. Volk, R. Willing, and J. Zandl. 1989. Integrale schalenwildbewirtschaftung im Furstentum Liechtenstein unter besonderer berucksichtigung landschaftsokologischer zusammenhange Naturkundl. Forschung im Furstentum Liechtenstein 11, Vaduz. 265 pp.

Onderscheka, K., F. Reimoser, F. Volk, F. Tataruch, T. Steineck, E. Klansek, I. Vavra, R. Willing, and J. Zandl. 1990. Integrale schalenwildhege im ratikon (Herrschaft Prattigau/Graubunden) unter besonderer berucksichtigung der walderhaltung. Typoscript Institut fur Wildtierkunde, Veterinarmedizinische Universitat, Wien. 367 pp.

O'Neil, B. D. and H. J. Pharo. 1995. The control of bovine tuberculosis in New Zealand. New Zealand Vet. J. 43: 249–255.

Oosting. H. J. 1956. The study of plant communities. W. H. Freeman and Co., San Francisco, California. 440 pp.

Opler, M. E. 1941. An Apache life-way. Univ. Chicago Press, Chicago, Illinois. 500 pp.

Orchard, W. C. 1916. Technique of porcupine quill decoration among the North American Indians. Mus. of the Amer. Indian, Contributions IV(1). Amer. Mus. of Natur. Hist., New York. 53 pp.

Ordway, L. L. and P. R. Krausman. 1986. Habitat use by desert mule deer. J. Wildl. Manage. 50: 677–683.

Oregon Department of Fish and Wildlife. 1975. 1975 Annual Report. Oregon Dept. Fish and Wildl., Portland. 178 pp.

————. 1992. Responsible hunting: The Oregon hunter education manual, revised edition. Outdoor Empire Publishing, Inc., Seattle. 103 pp.

Ormiston, J. H. and J. R. Naumann. 1978. Guides for elk habitat objectives. Bitterroot Nat. For. USDA For. Serv., Hamilton, Montana. 40 pp. Mimeo.

Ortega y Gasset, J. 1972. Meditations on hunting. Charles Scribner's Sons, New York. 152 pp.

Ortiz, A., ed. 1979. Southwest. Handbook of North American Indians. Vol. 9. Smithsonian Instit., Washington, D.C. 701 pp.

———. 1983. Southwest. Handbook of North American Indians, Vol. 10.. Smithsonian Instit., Washington, D.C. 868 pp.

Oswalt, W. H. 1966. This land was theirs: A study of the North American Indian. John Wiley and Sons, Inc., New York. 560 pp.

Osuji, P. O. 1974. Physiology of eating and the energy expenditure of the ruminant at pasture. J. Range Manage. 27(6): 437–443.

Oswalt, W. H. 1966. This land was theirs: a study of the North American Indian. John Wiley and Sons, Inc., New York. 560 pp.

Otsyina, R., C. M. McKell and G. Van Epps. 1982. Use of range shrubs to meet nutrient requirements of sheep grazing on crested wheatgrass during fall and early winter. J. Range Manage. 35: 751–753.

Otten, M. R. M., J. B. Haufler, S. R. Winterstein and L. C. Bender. 1993. An aerial censusing procedure for elk in Michigan. Wildl. Soc. Bull. 21: 73–80.

Otway, W. 1985 Adaptation of red deer after transport from the United Kingdom to New Zealand. Pages 225–226 in P. F. Fennessy and K. R. Drew, eds., Biology of deer production. Bull. 22. The Royal Soc. of New Zealand. 482 pp.

Ovington, J. D. 1954. A comparison of rainfall in different woodlands. Forestry 27: 41–53.

Owens, F. N. and R. Zinn. 1988. Ruminal fermentation. Pages 227–249 in D. C. Church, ed., The ruminant animal: Digestive physiology and nutrition. Prentice Hall, Englewood Cliffs, New Jersey. 564 pp.

Owens, F. N., P. Dubeski and C. F. Hanson. 1993. Factors that alter the growth and development of ruminants. J. Anim. Sci. 71: 3,138–3,150.

Owen-Smith, R. N. 1988. Megaherbivores. Cambridge Univ. Press. 369 pp.

Ozoga, J. J. and L. W. Gysel. 1972. Response of white-tailed deer to winter weather. J. Wildl. Manage. 36(3): 892–896.

Ozoga, J. J. and L. J. Verme. 1982. Physical and reproductive characteristics of a supplementally fed white-tailed deer herd. J. Wildl. Manage. 46: 281–301.

Pace, C. P. 1958. Herbage production and composition under immature ponderosa pine stands in the Black Hills. J. Range Manage. 11(1): 238–243.

Pacher, A. 1987. Schaden mindern-wildgerecht futtern. Typoscript Raiffeisen verban Salzburg. 32 pp.

Packard, F. M. 1947. A study of the deer and elk herds of Rocky Mountain National Park, Colorado. J. Mammal. 28(1): 4–12.

Packer, P. E. 1963. Soil stability requirements for the Gallatin elk winter range. J. Wildl. Manage. 27(3): 401–410.

Paehlke, R. C. 1989. Environmentalism and the future of progressive politics. Yale Univ. Press, New Haven, Connecticut. 325 pp.

Paine, B. H. 1935. Pioneers, Indians and buffaloes. The Curtis Enterprise, Curtis, Nebraska. 192 pp.

Painter, G. G. 1980. Elk and cattle spatial interactions. Special M.S. Paper, Washington State Univ., Pullman. 93 pp.

Palmer, T. S. 1912. Chronology and index of the more important events in American game protection, 1776–1911. Bull. No. 41. USDA Bur. of Biol. Surv., Washington, D.C. 62 pp.

Pamilo, P. and M. Nei. 1988. Relationships between gene trees and species trees. Molecular Biol. Evol. 5(5): 568–583.

Panter, K. E., R. F. Keeler, L. F. James and T. D. Bunch. 1992. Impact of plant toxins on fetal and neonatal development: a review. J. Range Manage. 45: 52–57.

Papageorgiou, M., C. Neophytou, A. Spais and C. Vavalekas. 1981. Food preferences and protein and energy requirements for maintenance of roe deer. J. Wildl. Manage. 45: 728–732.

Paper, J. 1988. Offering smoke: The sacred pipe and Native American religion. Univ. Idaho Press, Moscow. 161 pp.

Paradiso, J. L. 1969. Mammals of Maryland. North Amer. Fauna No. 66. U.S. Bur. Sport Fisheries and Wildl., U.S. Govt. Print. Off., Washington, D.C. 193 pp.

Park, T.A., J. B. Loomis and M. Creel. 1991. Confidence intervals for evaluating benefits estimates from dichotomous choice contingent valuation studies. Land Economics 67: 64–73.

Parker, K. 1983. Ecological energetics of mule deer and elk: locomotion and thermoregulation. Ph.D. Diss., Dept. Zool. Wildl. Biol. Program. Washington State Univ., Pullman. 128 pp.

Parker, K. L. and C. T. Robbins. 1984. Thermoregulation in mule deer and elk. Can. J. Zool. 62: 1,409–1,422.

Parker, K. L. and M. P. Gillingham. 1990. Estimates of critical thermal environments for mule deer. J. Range Manage. 43: 73–81.

Parker, K. L., M. P. Gillingham and T. A. Hanley. 1993a. An accurate technique for estimating forage intake of tractable animals. Can. J. Zool. 71: 1462–1465.

Parker, K. L., M. P. Gillingham, T. A. Hanley and C. T. Robbins. 1993b. Seasonal patterns in body mass, body composition and water transfer rates of free-ranging and captive black-tailed deer (*Odocoileus hemionus sitkensis*) in Alaska. Can. J. Zool. 71: 1,397–1,404.

Parker, K. L., C. T. Robbins and T. A. Hanley. 1984. Energy expenditures for locomotion by mule deer and elk. J. Wildl. Manage. 48: 474–488.

Parker, K. L., M. P. Gillingham, T. A. Hanley and C. T. Robbins. 1999. Energy and protein balance of free-ranging black-tailed deer in a natural forest environment. Wildl. Mono. No. 143. 48 pp.

Parker, R. 1995. Open houses open doors of communication. Idaho Wildlife 15(6): 9.

Parker, V. 1995. Natural resources management by litigation. Pages 209–220 in R. L. Knight and S. F. Bates, eds., A new century for natural resources management. Island Press, Washington, D.C.

Parkes, K. C. 1955. Sympatry, allopatry and the subspecies in birds. Syst. Zool. 4(1): 35–40.

Parkhurst, J. A. 1997. A study of the feasibility of reintroducing elk (*Cervus elaphus*) to the Commonwealth of Virginia—a proposal for project funding (Draft). Dept. Fish and Wildl. Sci., Virginia Tech., Blacksburg. 7 pp.

Parkman, F. 1910. The Oregon Trail of Francis Parkman. Ginn and Co., Boston, Massachusetts. 433 pp.

Parks, D. R. 1996. Myth and traditions of Arikara Indians. Univ. Nebraska Press, Lincoln. 405 pp.

Parsons, L. D. 1975. The Monday elk opener. Rept. to Washington Game Commiss. Washington Dept. of Game, Olympia. 17 pp.

Parsons, S. D. and G. L. Hunter. 1967. Effect of the ram on duration of oestrus in the ewe. J. Reprod. Fert. 14: 61.

Pase, C. P. 1958. Herbage production and composition under an immature ponderosa pine stand in the Black Hills. J. Range Manage. 11: 238–243.

Paterrek, J. 1994. Encyclopedia of American Indian costume. W. W. Norton and Co., New York. 516 pp.

Patton, D. R. 1969. Deer and elk use of a ponderosa pine forest in Arizona before and after timber harvest. Res. Note RM–139. USDA For. Serv., Fort Collins, Colorado. 7 pp.

Patton, D. R. 1975. A diversity index for quantifying habitat "edge." Wildl. Soc. Bull. 3(4): 171–173.

Pauley, G. 1991. Sand Creek elk study. Idaho Dept . Fish Game, Boise. 86 pp.

Paulik, G. M. and D. S. Robson. 1969. Statistical calculations for change-in-ratio estimators of population parameters. J. Wildl. Manage. 33(1): 1–27.

Pauls, R. W., R. J. Hudson and S. Sylven. 1981 Energy expenditure of free-ranging wapiti. Feeders' Day Rept. 60: 87–91.

Paulsen, H. A., Jr. 1975. Range management in the central and southern Rocky Mountains: A summary of the status of our knowledge by range ecosystems. Res. Pap. RM–154. USDA For. Serv., Fort Collins, Colorado. 34 pp.

Payne, C., J. M. Bowker and P. C. Reed, eds. 1992. The Economic Value of Wilderness: Proc. of the Conference; 1991 May 8–11; Jackson, Wyoming. USDA For. Serv., Gen. Tech. Rept. SE–78. Southeastern Forest Exp. Sta., Asheville, North Carolina. 330 pp.

Pearse, A. J. 1992. Farming of wapiti and wapiti hybrids in New Zealand. Pages 73–79 *in* R. D. Brown, ed., The biology of deer. Springer-Verlag, New York. 596 pp.

Pearson, A. B. 1984. A possible cause for the "pink-eye-like" condition in red deer. New Zealand Vet. J. 32: 119.

Pearson, H. A. 1964. Studies of forage digestibility under ponderosa pine stands. Pages 71–73 *in* Proc. Soc. of American Foresters. Soc. Amer. Forest., Washington, D.C.

———. 1968. Thinning, clearcutting and reseeding affect deer and elk use of ponderosa pine forests in Arizona. Res. Note RM–119. USDA For. Serv., Fort Collins, Colorado. 4 pp.

Peart, J. N. 1968. Lactation studies with blackface ewes and their lambs. J. Ag. Sci., Cambridge 70: 87–94.

Pechanec, J. F. and G. D. Pickford. 1937a. A comparison of some methods used in determining percentage utilization of range grasses. J. Ag. Res. 54(10): 753–765.

Pechanec, J. F. and G. D. Pickford. 1937b. A weight estimate method for the determination of range or pasture production. J. Amer. Agron. 29: 894–904.

Pechanec, J. F. and G. Stewart. 1940. Sagebrush–grass range sampling studies: size and structure of sampling unit. J. Amer. Soc. Agron. 32(9): 669–682.

Peck, A. L. and E. S. Forster. 1961. Parts of animals. Loeb Classical Library 323. Harvard Univ. Press, Cambridge, Massachusetts. 555 pp.

Peck, V. R. and J. M. Peek. 1991. Elk, *Cervus elaphus*, habitat use related to prescribed fire, Tuchodi River, British Columbia. Can. Field-Natur. 105: 354–362.

Pedersen, R. J. 1979. Management and impacts of roads in relation to elk populations. Pages 169–173 *in* Recreational impact on wildlands. Conf. Proc. USDA For. Serv. and USDI Nat. Park Serv., Washington, D.C.

Pedersen, R. J. and A. W. Adams. 1974. Habitat use by elk. Prog. Rept., Proj. No. W–70-R–4. Oregon Dept. Fish and Wildl., Portland. 15 pp.

Pedersen, R. J. and A. W. Adams. 1976. Rocky Mountain elk research project progress report. Prog. Rept., Proj. No. W–70-R–6. Oregon Dept. Fish and Wildl., Portland. 19 pp.

Pedersen, R. J. and A. A. Pedersen. 1975. Blood chemistry and hematology of elk. J. Wildl. Manage. 39(3): 617–620.

Pedersen, R. J., A. W. Adams and W. Williams. 1974. Black bear predation on an elk calf. Murrelet 55(2): 28

Pedersen, R. J., A. W. Adams and J. Skovlin. 1979. Elk management in Blue Mountain habitats. Res. and Development Rept. W–70-R. Oregon Dept. Fish and Wildl., Portland. 27 pp.

Pedersen, R. J., A. W. Adams and J. M. Skovlin. 1980. Elk habitat use in an unlogged and logged forest environment. Res. Rept. No. 9. Oregon Dept. of Fish and Wildl., Portland. 121 pp.

Peek, J. M. 1963. Wildlife investigations (Dist. 3): Big game survey and investigation—summer of 1956–1960. Gravelly-Snowcrest rumen collections. Fed. Aid Compl. Rept. Proj. W–73-R–8, J-A–1. Montana Dept. Fish and Game, Helena. 11 pp.

———. 1974. A review of food habits of moose in North America. Can. Natur. 101: 195–215.

———. 1976. Proceedings of the Elk-Logging-Roads Symp., For., Wildl. and Range Exp. Sta., Univ. Idaho, Moscow. 142 pp.

———. 1985a. In defense of the old bull. Bugle 2(3): 36–39.

———. 1985b. On counting elk. Bugle 2: 46–47.

———. 1989. Another look at burning shrubs in northern Idaho. Pages 157–159 *in* D. M. Baumgartner, D. W. Breuer, B. A. Zamora, L. F. Neuenshwander and R. H. Wakimoto, eds., Proc. symposium on prescribed fire in the Intermountain Region, forest site preparation and range improvement. Washington State Univ., Pullman.

Peek, J. M. and A. L. Lovaas. 1968. Differential distribution of elk by sex and age on the Gallatin Winter Range, Montana. J. Wildl. Manage. 32(3): 553–557.

Peek, J. M. and E. O. Garton. 1987. Electronic harvest: the great computer hunt. Bugle 4: 82–89.

Peek, J. M., A. L. Lovaas and R. A. Rouse. 1967. Population changes within the Gallatin elk herd, 1932–1965. J. Wildl. Manage. 31: 304–315.

Peek, J. M., D. L. Urich and R. J. Mackie. 1976. Moose habitat selection and relationships to forest management in northeastern Minnesota. Wildl. Monogr. No. 48. The Wildl. Soc., Washington, D.C. 65 pp.

Peek, J. M., R. J. Pedersen and J. W. Thomas. 1982a. The future of elk and elk hunting. Pages 599–625 *in* J. W. Thomas and D. E. Toweill, eds., Elk of North America: Ecology and management. Stackpole Books, Harrisburg, Pennsylvania. 698 pp.

Peek, J. M., M. D. Scott, L. J. Nelson, D. J. Pierce and L. L. Irwin. 1982b. The role of cover in habitat management in Northwestern United States. Trans. N. Amer. Wildl. and Natur. Resour. Conf. 47: 363–373.

Peek, J. M., V. van Ballenberghe and D. G. Miquelle. 1986. Intensity of interactions between rutting bull moose in central Alaska. J. Mamm. 67, 423–426.

Peery, C. 1981. A taste for venison. Virginia Wildl. 42(1): 6.

Peet, R. L. and K. Hepworth. 1993. Enzootic ataxia in red deer, *Cervus elaphus*. Aust. Vet. J. 70: 395–396.

Peet, S. D. 1890. Emblematic mounds and animal effigies. Prehistoric America. Vol. 2. Amer. Antiquities Off., Chicago, Illinois. 351 pp.

Pekelharing, C. J. 1968. Molar duplication in red deer and wapiti. J. Mammal. 49(3): 524–526.

Pekins, P. J., W. M. Mautz and J. Kanter. 1992. Reevaluation of the basal metabolic cycle in white-tailed deer. Page 418–422 *in* R. D. Brown, ed., The biology of deer. Springer-Verlag, New York.

Pelabon, C. 1997. Is weight at birth a good predictor of weight in winter for fallow deer? J. Mammal. 78: 48-54.

Pengelly, W. L. 1961. Factors influencing production of white-tailed deer on the Coeur d'Alene National Forest, Idaho. USDA For. Serv., Missoula, Montana.

Pengelly, W. L. 1963a. Thunder on the Yellowstone. Naturalist (Natur. Hist. Soc., Minneapolis) 14(2): 18–25.

———. 1963b. Timberlands and deer in the Northern Rockies. J. Forestry 61(10): 734–740.

———. 1972. Clearcutting: Detrimental aspects for wildlife resources. J. Soil and Water Conserv. 27(6): 255–258.

Pennant, T. 1785. Arctic zoology. Vol. 1. H. Hugh, London. 185 pp.

Penney, D. W. 1992. Art of the American Indian frontier. Douglas and McIntyre, Vancouver, British Columbia. 368 pp.

Penrose, C. B. 1924. Removal of the testicle of a sika deer followed by deformity of antler on the opposite side. J. Mammal. 5: 116.

Pereladova, O. B. 1993. Bukchara deer in USSR. Pages 325–330 *in* N. Ohtaishi and H.-I. Sheng, eds., Deer of China. Elsevier, New York. 481 pp.

Perry, C. and R. Overly. 1976. Impact of roads on big game distribution in portions of the Blue Mountains of Washington. Pages 62–68 *in* S. R. Hieb, ed., Proc. Elk-Logging-Roads Symp., Univ. Idaho, Moscow. 142 pp.

Perry, C. and R. Overly. 1977. Impacts of roads on big game distribution in portions of the Blue Mountains of Washington, 1972–1973. Appl. Res. Sect. Bull. No. 11. Washington Game Dept., Olympia. 39 pp.

Perry, F. J. 1964. Progress report of the Vermont Fish and Game Department. Vermont Fish and Game Department, Montpelier. 75 pp.

Peterle, T. J. 1961. The hunter—who is he? Trans. N. Amer. Wildl. and Natur. Resour. Conf. 26: 254–266.

Peterle, T. J. 1967. Characteristics of some Ohio hunters. J. Wildl. Manage. 31(2): 375–389.

Peterle, T. J. 1977a. Changes in responses from identical Ohio hunters interviewed in 1960–61 and 1973–74. Trans. N. Amer. Wildl. and Natur. Resour. Conf. 42: 156–168.

Peterle, T. J. 1977b. Hunters, hunting, anti-hunting. Wildl. Soc. Bull. 5(4): 151–161.

Peters, J. A. 1954. Symposium: Subspecies and clines. Syst. Zool. 3(3): 97–125.

Petersen, D. 1989. Among the elk: Wilderness images. Singapore Nat. Printers, Singapore. 118 pp.

———. 1993. *Manitobans*: The forgotten elk of the north. Bugle 10(4): 100–108.

———. 1996. A hunter's heart: Honest essays on blood sport. Henry Holt and Company, New York. 331 pp.

Peterson, K. J. and T. P. Kistner. 1973. Epizootiologic studies of Anaplasmosis in Oregon mule deer. J. Wildl. Dis. 9: 314–319.

Peterson, R. A. and E. J. Woolfolk. 1955. Behavior of hereford cows and calves on short grass range. J. Range Manage. 8: 51–57.

Peterson, R. L. 1955. North American moose. Univ. Toronto Press, Toronto. 280 pp.

———. 1966. The mammals of eastern Canada. Oxford Univ. Press, Toronto. 465 pp.

Petrides, G. A. 1949. Sex and age determination in the oppossum. J. Mammal. 30(4): 364–378.

Petrides, G. A. 1954. Estimating the percentage kill in ringnecked pheasants and other game species. J. Wildl. Manage. 18(3): 294–297.

Péwé, T. 1975. Quaternary geology of Alaska. U.S. Geol. Surv. Prof. Pap. 835. pp.

Péwé, T. L. 1967. Permafrost and its effect on life in the North. Pages 27–65 *in* H. P. Hansen, ed., Arctic biology. Biol. Colloquium, Oreg. State Univ., Corvallis.

Péwé, T. L., D. M. Hopkins and J. L. Giddings. 1965. The Quaternary geology and archaeology of Alaska. Pages 355–374 *in* J. E. Wright, Jr. and D. G. Frey, eds., The Quaternary of the United States. Princeton Univ. Press, Princeton, New Jersey.

Pfandl, E. 1977. Ergebnisse aus den Achentaler Forschungsrevieren. Jagd in Tirol 29(1): 10–14.

Pfau, R.S. 1994. First record of a native American elk (*Cervus elaphus*) from Texas. Texas J. Sci. 46(2): 189–190.

Pfister, R. D., B. L. Kavalchik, S. F. Arno and R. C. Presby. 1974. Forest habitat types of Montana. USDA For. Serv., Ogden, Utah. 213 pp.

Phillippo, M., G. A. Lincoln and C. B. Lawrence. 1972. The relationship between thyroidal calcitonin and seasonal and reproductive change in stag (*Cervus elaphus*). J. Endocrin. 53: 48–49.

Phillips, B. 1992. Merriam's elk: Is the biggest American elk subspecies really extinct? Bugle 9(4): 38–39.

Phillips, C. and S. Ferguson. 1977. Hunting and fishing expenditure values and participation preferences in Wyoming, 1975. Univ. Wyoming, Water Resources Research Institute, Laramie. 184 pp.

Phillips, D. R., ed. 1974. The taming of the American West. Henry Regnery Co., Chicago, Illinois. 232 pp.

Phillips, E. A. 1959. Methods of vegetation study. Henry Holt and Co., Inc., New York. 107 pp.

Phillips, P. C., ed. 1940. W. A. Ferris: Life in the Rocky Mountains (diary of the wanderings of a trapper in the years 1831–1832). The Old West Publishing Co., Denver. 365 pp.

Phillips, P. C., and J. W. Smurr. 1961. The fur trade. Vol. 2. Univ. Oklahoma Press, Norman. 656 pp.

Phillips, T. A. 1966. Calf Drop Ridge elk calving ground survey. USDA For. Serv., Unpubl. Rept. on file at Salmon National Forest, Salmon, Idaho. 4 pp.

———. 1974. Characteristics of elk calving habitat on the Sawtooth N. F. Range Improvement Notes 19(1): 1–5.

Pickford, G. D. and E. H. Reid. 1943. Competition of elk and domestic livestock for summer range forage. J. Wildl. Manage. 7: 328–332.

Pickett, S. T. A. and R. S. Ostfeld. 1995. The shifting paradigm in ecology. Pages 261–268 *in* R. L. Knight and S. F. Bates, eds., A new century for natural resource management. Island Press, Washington, D.C. 398 pp.

Picton, H. D. 1960a. Migration patterns of the Sun River elk herd, Montana. J. Range Manage. 24(3): 279–290.

———. 1960b. A comparison of the results of feeding site examinations with teh vegetative composition of the sites in the Sun River Game Range. Page 9 *in* Wildlife inverstigations (Dist. 4): Big game surveys and investigations. Fed. Aid Compl. Rept., Proj. W–74–R–5, J-A–1. Montana Dept. Fish and Game, Helena.

———. 1961. Differential hunter harvest of elk in two Montana herds. J. Wildl. Manage. 25: 415–421.

———. 1974. The Gallatin wildlife community. Gallatin Canyon Res. Monogr. Montana State Univ., Bozeman. 9 pp.

———. 1984. Climate and the prediction of reproduction of three ungulate species. J. Appl. Ecol. 21: 869–879.

———. 1991. A brief history of elk: The hunt, research and management. Pages 10–15 *in* A. G. Christensen, L. J. Lyon and T. N. Lonner, compilers, Proc. Elk Vulnerability Symp., Montana State Univ., Bozeman. 330 pp.

Picton, H. D. and I. E. Picton. 1975. Saga of the sun—A history of the Sun River elk herd. Montana Dept. Fish and Game, Helena. 55 pp.

Pidgeon, W. 1853. Traditions of De-coo-dah. And antiquarian researches: Comprising extensive explorations, surveys and excavations of the wonderful and mysterious earthen remains of the mound builders in America. Thayer, Bridgman and Fanning, New York. 334 pp.

Pie, A. C., R. A. Garrott and J. J. Borkowski. 1999. Sampling and statistical analysis of snow-urine allantoin:creatinine ratios. J. Wildl. Manage 63: 1,118-1,132.

Pietrzak, J. 1991. Wildlife management in Poland. Int. Union of Game Biologists Congr. 18: 89–92.

Pinchot, G. 1947. Breaking new ground. Harcourt and Brace, New York. 522 pp.

Pinsker, W. 1978. Die Saisonveranderungen der Hoden und Nebenhoden von Hirschen verschiedener Altersstufen in der Vor-, Haupt- und Nachbrunft. Ph.D. Thesis. Vet. Univ., Vienna. 68 pp.

Pioneer Packing Co. v. Winslow, 159 Wash. 655, 294 P. 557 (1930).

Pitard, E. 1910. Switzerland, Pages 335–356 *in* F. G. Aflalo, ed., Sport in Europe. E. P. Dutton and Co., New York. 483 pp.

Pitcher, J. 1901. Report of the Acting Superintendent of the Yellowstone

National Park to the Secretary of the Interior, 1901. Govt. Print. Off., Washington, D.C. 21 pp.

———. 1902. Report of the Acting Superintendent of the Yellowstone National Park to the Secretary of the Interior, 1902. Govt. Print. Off., Washington, D.C. 22 pp.

———. 1903. Report of the Acting Superintendent of the Yellowstone National Park to the Secretary of the Interior, 1903. Govt. Print. Off., Washington, D.C. 19 pp.

———. 1904. Report of the Acting Superintendent of the Yellowstone National Park to the Secretary of the Interior, 1904. Govt. Print. Off., Washington, D.C. 25 pp.

———. 1905. Report of the Acting Superintendent of the Yellowstone National Park to the Secretary of the Interior, 1905. Govt. Print. Off., Washington, D.C. 27 pp.

———. 1906. Report of the Acting Superintendent of the Yellowstone National Park to the Secretary of the Interior, 1906. Govt. Print. Off., Washington, D.C. 22 pp.

Platt, R. M. and S. Soukup. 1977. Banding studies in four Artiodactyl and one primate species. Mammal. Chromos. Newslett. 18: 122–123.

Platt, S. 1993. Respectfully quoted: A dictionary of quotations. Barnes and Noble Books, New York, 520 pp.

Platt, T. R. and W. M. Samuel. 1978. *Parelaphostrongylus odocoilei*: Life cycle in experimentally infected cervids including the mule doer, *Odocoilei h. hemionus*. Exp. Parasitol. 46: 330–338.

Plog, F. 1979. Prehistory: Western Anasazi. Pages 108–130 *in* A. Ortiz, ed., Southwest. Handbook of American Indians. Vol. 9. Smithsonian Instit., Washington, D.C. 701 pp.

Plotka, E. D., U. S. Seal, L. J. Verme and J. J. Ozaga. 1980. Reproductive steroids in deer. III. Luteinizing hormone, estradiol and progesterone around estrus. Biol. Reprod. 22(3): 576–581.

Plummer, A. P., D. R. Christensen and S. B. Monsen. 1968. Restoring big-game range in Utah. Publ. No. 68–3. Utah Div. Fish and Game, Salt Lake City. 183 pp.

Plummer, J. J. 1844. Scraps in natural history (Quadrupeds). Amer. J. Sci. Arts 46(2): 236–249.

Pocock, R. I. 1912. On a rare stag (*Cervus wallichi*) from Nepal recently presented to the Zoological Soc. by His Majesty King George. Proc. Zool. Soc., London. 558–575.

Pocock, R.I. 1942. The larger deer of British India. J. of the Bombay Natural History Soc. 43(3): 298–317.

Poelker, R. J. 1972. The Shiras moose in Washington. Washington Game Dept., Olympia. 46 pp.

Pohrt, K. 1976. The boy. Northwest Rev. 15(2): 172–189.

Point, N. 1967. Wilderness kingdom—Indian life in the Rocky Mountains: 1840–1847. Translated and introduced by J. P. Donnelly. Holt, Rinehart and Winston, New York. 300 pp.

Pollard, J. C., R. P. Littlejohn and J. M. Suttie. 1992. Behaviour and weight change of red deer calves during different weaning procedures. Appl. Animal Behavior Sci. 35: 23–33.

Pollard, J. C., R. P. Littlejohn and J. R. Webster. 1994a. Quantification of temperament in weaned deer calves of two genotypes (*Cervus elaphus* and *Cervus elaphus x Elaphurus davidianus* hybrids). Appl. Animal Behavior Sci. 41: 229–241.

Pollard, J. C., R. P. Littlejohn, A. M. Cassidy and G.W. Asher. 1994b. Temperament assessment in red deer. Proc. Deer Course for Vet.. 11: 186–192.

Pollock, A. M. 1975. Seasonal changes in appetite and sexual condition in red deer stags maintained on a six-month photoperiod. J. Physiol. (London). 244: 95–96.

Pollock, K. H and W. L. Kendall. 1987. Visibility bias in aerial surveys: A review of estimation procedures. J. Wildl. Manage. 51: 502–510.

Polziehn, R. O. and C. Strobeck. 1998. Phylogeny of wapiti, red deer, sika deer, and other North American cervids as determined from mitochondrial DNA. Molecular Phylogenetics and Evolution 10(2): 249–258.

Polziehn, R. O., J. Hamr, F. F. Mallory and C. Strobeck. 1998. Phylogenetic status of North American wapiti (*Cervus elaphus*) subspecies. Can. J. Zool. 76(6): 998–1,010.

Poole, D. A. 1978. Foreword. Pages v–vii *in* J. L. Schmidt and D. L. Gilbert, eds., Big game of North America: Ecology and management. Stackpole Books, Harrisburg, Pennsylvania. 512 pp.

Poore, M. E. D. and V. C. Robertson. 1964. An approach to the rapid description and mapping of biological habitats. Int. Biol. Programme. 68 pp.

Pope, S. T. 1918. Yahi archery. Univ. of California (Berkeley) Publ. in Amer. Archaeol. and Ethnol. 13(3): 103–152.

Popov, B.H. and J.B. Low. 1950. Game, fur animal and fish introductions into Utah. Misc. Publ. 4. Utah Dept. Fish and Game, Salt Lake City. 85 pp.

Popovic, S. 1964. Mikrostruktura i fiziko-hemijska svojstva mesa jelena. Jelen (Beograd) 1(1): 93–101.

Posewitz, J. 1994. Beyond fair chase: The ethic and tradition of hunting. Falcon Press, Helena, Montana. 118 pp.

Post, G. and G. M. Thomas. 1961. A study of anaplasmosis in elk. J. Am. Vet. Med. Assoc. 139: 357–358.

Poston, J. P. 1993. Hunting ethics: original principles of the club. Pages 1–2 *in* J. Reneau and S. C. Reneau, eds., Records of North American big game 10th edition. Boone and Crockett Club, Missoula, Montana. 604 pp.

Potter, D. R. 1982. Recreational use of elk. Pages 509–559 *in* J. W. Thomas and D. E. Toweill, eds. Elk of North America: Ecology and management. Stackpole Books, Harrisburg, Pennsylvania. 698 pp.

Potter, D. R., J. C. Hendee and R. N. Clark. 1973. Hunting satisfaction: Game, guns, or nature? Trans. N. Amer. Wildl. and Natur. Resour. Conf. 38: 220–229.

Potter, M. A. 1968. Ohio's prehistoric peoples. The Ohio Historical Soc., Columbus. 76 pp.

Pottinger, Sir H. 1910. Scandinavia. Pages 279–304 *in* F. G. Aflalo, ed., Sport in Europe. E. P. Dutton and Co., New York. 483 pp.

Powell, P. J. 1992. Sacrifice transformed into victory: Standing Bear portrays Sitting Bull's sundance and the final summer of Lakota freedom. Pages 81–106 *in* E. Maurer, ed., Visions of the people: A pictorial history of Plains Indian Life. The Minneapolis Inst. of Arts, Minneapolis, Minnesota. 298 pp.

Power, S. B., J. Haagsma and D. P. Smyth. 1993. Paratuberculosis in red deer (*Cervus elaphus*) in Ireland. Vet. Rec. 132: 213–216.

Power, T. M. 1995. Thinking about natural resource-dependent economies: Moving beyond the folk economics of the rear-view mirror. Pages 235–253 *in* R. L. Knight and S. F. Bates, eds., A new century for natural resources management. Island Press, Washington, D.C.

Powers, W. K. 1978. The art of courtship among the Oglala. Amer. Indian Art Mag. 5(2): 40–47.

———. 1986. Sacred language: The nature of supernatural discourse in Lakota. Univ. Oklahoma Press, Norman. 247 pp.

———. 1988. Foolish words: Text and content in Lakota love songs. European Rev. Native Amer. Studies 2(2): 29–34.

Preble, E. A. 1908. A biological investigation of the Athabaska-Mackenzie region. North Amer. Fauna 27. U.S. Nat. Park Serv., Washington, D.C. 574 pp.

Preble, E. A. 1911. Report on condition of elk in Jackson Hole, Wyoming in 1911. Bull. 40. USDA Bur. Biol. Surv., Washington, D.C. 23 pp.

Presidente, P. J. A. and S. E. Knapp. 1973. Susceptibility of cattle to an isolate of *Dictyocaulus viviparus* from black-tailed deer. J. Wildl. Dis. 9: 41–43.

Presidente, P. J. A., D. E. Worley and J. E. Catlin. 1972. Cross-transmission experiments with *Dictyocaulus viviparus* isolates from Rocky Mountain elk and cattle. J. Wildl. Dis. 8: 57–62.

Presidente, P. J. A., S. E. Knapp and R. E. Dean. 1973. Treatment and control of *Dictyocaulus viviparus* in captive black-tailed deer. J. Wildl. Dis. 9: 34–40.

Presnall, C. C. 1938. Mammals of Zion-Bryce and Cedar Breaks. Zion-Bryce Mus., Bull. 2., National Park Service. 20 pp.

Prestwood, A. K. 1970. Neurologic disease in a white-tailed deer massively infected with meningeal worms. J. Wildl. Dis. 6: 84–86.

Prestwood, A. K. and T. R. Ridgeway. 1972. Elaeophorosis in whitetailed deer of the southeastern U.S.A.: case report and distribution. J. Wildl. Dis. 8: 233–236.

Price, J. S., B. O. Oyajobi, R. O. C. Oreffo and R. G. G. Russell. 1994. Cells cultured from the growing tip of red deer antler express alkaline-phosphatase and proliferate in response to insulin-like growth factor-I. J. Endocrinology. 143: R9–R16.

Price, M. A. and R. G. White. 1985. Growth and development. Pages 183–214 *in* R. J. Hudson and R. G. White, eds., Bioenergetics of wild herbivores. CRC Press, Inc., Boca Raton, Florida. 314 pp.

Primack, R. B. 1993. Essentials of Conservation Biology. Sinauer Associates, 564 pp.

Prins, H. H. T. 1989. Condition changes and choice of social environment in African buffalo bulls. Behaviour 108: 297–232.

Prins, R. A and M. J. H. Geelen. 1971. Rumen characteristics of red deer, fallow deer and roe deer. J. Wildl. Manage. 35(4): 673–680.

Prior, R. L. and D. B. Laster. 1979. Development of the bovine fetus. J. Anim. Sci. 48: 1,546–1,553.

Pritchard, J. A. 1999. Preserving Yellowstone's natural conditions. Univ. Nebraska Press, Lincoln. 370 pp.

Probasco, B. E. 1968. Diet preferences and utilization patterns of elk on the Bighorn Mountains, Wyoming. M.S. Thesis, Univ. Wyoming, Laramie. 294 pp.

Probst, G. F. 1737. Besonderes Gespräche von der Par-Force-Jagd. Leipzig (now Verlag P. Parey, Hamburg.) 40 pp.

Prothero, W. L. 1977. Rutting behavior in elk. M.S. Thesis. Utah State Univ., Logan. 48 pp.

Prothero, W. L., J. J. Spillett and D. F. Balph. 1979. Rutting behavior of yearling and mature bull elk: some implications for open bull hunting. Pages 160–165 *in* M. S. Boyce and L. D. Hayden-Wing, eds., North American elk: Ecology and management. Univ. Wyoming, Laramie. 294 pp.

Provenza, F. D. 1995. Postingestive feedback as an elementary determinant of food preference and intake in ruminants. J. Range Manage. 48: 2–17.

Provenza, F. D., J. A. Pfister and C. D. Cheney. 1992. Mechanisms of learning in diet selection with reference to phytotoxicosis in herbivores. J Range Manage. 45(1): 36–45.

Prufer, O. H. and D. H. McKenzie. 1967. Studies in Ohio archaeology. Press of West. Reserve Univ., Cleveland, Ohio. 368 pp.

Prusiner, S. B. 1991. Molecular biology of prion diseases. Science 252: 1,515–1,522.

Public Land Law Review Commission. 1970. One third of the nation's land. A report to the President and to the Congress by the Public Land Law Review Commission. U.S. Govt. Print. Off., Washington, D.C. 342 pp.

Pulliam, D. E., Jr. and J. R. Nelson. 1979. Determination of digestibility coefficients for quantification of fecal analysis with elk. Pages 240–246 *in* M. S. Boyce and L. D. Hayden-Wing, eds., North American elk: ecology, behavior and management. Univ. Wyoming, Laramie. 294 pp.

Purdue, J. R. and B. W. Styles. 1986. Dynamics of mammalian distribution in the Holocene of Illinois. Rept. of Investigations 41. Illinois State Mus. Soc., Springfield. 63 pp.

Pursglove, S. R., A. K. Prestwood, T. R. Ridgeway and F. A. Hayes. 1977. *Fascioloides magna* infection in white-tailed deer of southeastern United States. J. Am. Vet. Med. Assoc. 171: 936–938.

Putman, R. 1988. The natural history of deer. Comstock Publ. Assoc., Ithaca, New York. 191 pp.

Pybus, M. J. 1990a. Lungs and liver parasites of big game in Alberta, 1988. Wildlife Management Branch, Occasional Paper Series Number 6, Alberta Forestry, Lands and Wildlife, Edmonton. 21 pp.

———. 1990b. Survey of hepatic and pulmonary parasites of wild cervids in Alberta, Canada. J. Wildl. Dis. 26: 453–459.

———. 1997. Unpublished. Records on file, Natural Resources Services, Alberta Environmental Protection Branch, Edmonton, Alberta.

Pybus, M. J., D. K. Onderka and N. Cool. 1991. Efficacy of triclabendazole against natural infections of Fascioloides magna in wapiti. J. Wildl. Dis. 27: 599–605.

Pybus, M. J., W. M. Samuel and V. Crichton. 1989. Identification of dorsal spined larvae from free-ranging wapiti (*Cervus elaphus*) in southwestern Manitoba, Canada. J. Wildl. Dis. 25: 291–293.

Pybus, M. J., W. M. Samuel, D. A. Welch., J. Smits and J. C. Haigh. 1992. Mortality of fallow deer (*Dama dama*) experimentally-infected with meningeal worm, *Parelaphostrongylus tenuis*. J. Wildl. Dis. 28: 95–101.

Pybus, M. J., W. M. Samuel and S. Groom. 1996. Meningeal worm in experimentally-infected domestic and bighorn sheep. J. Wildl. Dis. 32: 614–618.

Pyne, S. J. 1982. Fire in America: A cultural history of wildlife and rural fire. Princeton Univ. Press, Princeton, New Jersey. 699 pp.

———. 1993. Keeper of the flame: A survey of anthropogenic fire. Pages 245–266 *in* P. J. Crutzen and J. G. Goldammer, eds., Fire in the environment: Its ecological, climatic, and atmosphere chemical importance. John Wiley and Sons, New York. 400 pp.

———. 1995. Vestal fires and virgin lands: A reburn. Pages 15–21 *in* J. K. Brown, R. W. Mutch, C. W. Spoon and R. H. Wakimoto, eds., Proc. Symp. on Fire in Wilderness and Park Manage. Gen. Tech. Rept. INT–320. USDA For. Serv., Ogden, Utah. 283 pp.

Quigley, T. M. and S. J. Arbelbide. 1997. An assessment of ecosystem components in the Interior Columbia Basin and portions of the Klamath and Great Basins. 4 vols.USDA For. Serv., Gen. Tech. Rept. PNW-GTR–405, Portland, Oregon. 2,066 pp.

Quigley, T. M. and H. Bigler Cole. 1997. Highlighted scientific findings of the Interior Columbia Basin Ecosystem Management Project. USDA For. Serv., Gen. Tech. Rept. PNW-GTR–404, Portland, Oregon. 34 pp.

Quigley, T. M., R. T. Graham and R. W. Haynes (tech. eds.) 1996. An integrated scientific assessment for ecosystem management in the interior Columbia Basin including portions of the Klamath and Great Basins. Gen. Tech. Rept., USDA For. Serv., Portland, Oregon.

Quimby, D. C. and J. E. Gaab. 1957. Mandibular dentition as an age indicator in Rocky Mountain elk. J. Wildl. Manage. 21(4): 435–451.

Quimby, D. C. and D. E. Johnson. 1951. Weights and measurements of Rocky Mountain elk. J. Wildl. Manage. 15(1): 57–62.

Quimby, G. I. 1952. The archaeology of the Great Lakes area. Pages 99–107 *in* J. B. Griffin, ed., Archaeology of eastern United States. Univ. Chicago Press, Chicago, Illinois. 392 pp.

Quinlan, J., J. H. R. Bishop and T. F. Adelaar. 1941. Bionomic studies on cattle in the semi-arid regions of the Union of South Africa: 4. The ovarian cycle of heifers during summer. Onderstepoort J. Vet. Sci. Anim. Ind. 16: 213.

Quinlan-Murphy, L. J. 1998. Influences of age, condition, nutrition and season on serum and urine chemistry of Rocky Mountain Elk. M.S. Thesis, Oregon State Univ., Corvallis. 165 pp.

Quirk, W. A. and D. J. Sykes. 1971. White spruce stringers in a fire-patterned landscape in interior Alaska. Pages 179–197 in C. W. Slaughter, R. J. Bamey and G. M. Hansen, eds., Fire in the northern environment—a symposium. USDA For. Serv., Pac. Northwest For. and Range Exp. Sta., Portland, Oregon.

Raedeke, J. K. and J. F. Lehmkuhl. 1986. A simulation procedure for modeling the relationships between wildlife and forest management. Pages 377–381 in J. Verner, M. L. Morrison and C. J. Ralph, eds., Wildlife 2000 modeling habitat relationships of terrestrial vertebrates. Univ. Wisconsin Press, Madison.

Raedeke, K. J. and R. D. Taber. 1985. Black-tailed deer population regulation through antlerless hunts in western Washington. Pages 139–147 in S. L. Beasom and S. F. Roberson, eds., Game harvest management. Caesar Kleberg Wildl. Resour. Inst., Kingsville, Texas.

Raedeke, K. J., J. J. Millspaugh, A. J. Renkert and N. K. Elston. 1998. Assessment of harvest strategies for Rocky Mountain elk. Rept. to the Ministry of the Environment, British Columbia, Canada. 54 pp.

Ralph, E. K. 1971. Carbon–14 dating. Pages 1–48 in H. N. Michael and E. K. Ralph, eds., Dating techniques for the archaeologist. Massachusetts Inst. Tech., Cambridge.

Ramsey, J. G. M. 1853. The annals of Tennessee to the end of the eighteenth century. Reprint edition 1971 by Arno Press, Inc., New York. 744 pp.

Ranching Systems Group. 1994. Grazing land applications information technology for improved resource management. Texas A and M Univ., College Station. 414 pp.

Randall, D. 1980. Wolves for Yellowstone: Experts say "yes," though cautiously, to reintroduction. Defenders 55: 188–190.

Ransom, A. B. 1965. Kidney and marrow fat as indicators of white-tailed deer condition. J. Wildl. Manage. 29: 397–398.

Ranta, B. 1998. The elk of Ontario. Bugle 15(6): 18–25.

Rapley, M. D. 1985. Behaviour of elk during the rut. Pages 357–362 in P. F. Fennessy and K.R. Drew, eds., Biology of deer production. Bull. 22. Roy. Soc. of New Zealand, Wellington. 482 pp.

Raskevitz, R. F., A. A. Kocan and J. H. Shaw. 1991. Gastropod availability and habitat utilization by wapiti and white-tailed deer sympatric on range enzootic for meningeal worm. J. Wildl. Dis. 27: 92–101.

Rasmussen, D. I. 1949. The American elk or wapiti—today. Trans. N. Amer. Wildl. Conf. 14: 513–526.

Rasmussen, D. I. and E. R. Doman. 1943. Census methods and their application in the management of mule deer. Trans. N. Amer. Wildl. Conf. 8: 369–379.

Rau, M. E. and F. R. Caron. 1979. Parasite-induced susceptibility of moose to hunting. Can. J. Zool. 57: 2,466–2,468.

Rausch, R. L. 1952. Hydatid disease in boreal regions. Arctic 5: 157.

Rausch, R. L. 1963. A review of the distribution of holarctic recent mammals. Pages 29–43 in J. L. Gressitt, ed., Pacific Basin biogeography. Bishop Mus. Press, Honolulu.

Rayner, V. and S. W. B. Ewen. 1981. Do the blood vessels of the antler velvet of red deer have an adrenergic innervation? Quart. J. Experim. Physiol. 66: 81–86.

Raynolds, F. W. 1868. Report on the exploration of the Yellowstone River in 1859–60. Senate Exec. Doc. 77, 40th Cong., 2nd Sess. Washington, D.C. 174 pp.

Reagan, A. B. 1922. Hunting and fishing of various tribes of Indians. Trans. Kansas Acad. Sci. 30: 443–448

Ream, C. H. 1979. Human–wildlife conflicts in back country: possible solutions. Pages 153–163 in R. Ittner, D. R. Potter and J. K. Agee, eds., Recreational impacts on wildlands. USDA For. Serv., Pacific Northwest Region, Seattle, Washington.

———. 1980. Impact of backcountry recreationists on wildlife. Gen. Tech. Rept. INT–84. USDA For. Serv., Ogden, Utah. 62 pp.

Redgate, R. M. 1978. Behavioural and ecological considerations in the management of elk in Camp 1, Athabasca Valley, Alberta. MEDS Thesis, Univ. Calgary, Alberta. 164 pp.

Reeves, H. M. and R. E. McCabe. 1997. Of moose and men. Pages 1–75 in C. E. Schwartz and A. W Franzmann, eds., Ecology and management of North American moose. Smithsonian Instit., Washington, D.C. 733 pp.

Regelin, W. L. 1991. Wildlife management in Canada and the United States. Pages 55–64 in B. Bobek, K. Perzanowski and W. L. Regelin, eds., Global trends in wildlife management. Eighteenth Int. Union of Game Biologists Congress, Kraków, Poland 660 pp.

Regelin, W. L. and O. C. Wallmo. 1978. Duration of deer forage benefits after clearcut logging of subalpine forest in Colorado. Res. Note RM–356. USDA For. Serv., Fort Collins, Colorado. 4 pp.

Regelin, W. L., O. C. Wallmo, J. Nagy and D. R. Dietz. 1974. Effect of logging on forage values for deer in Colorado. J.For. 72(5): 282–285.

Regelin, W. L., C. C. Schwartz and A.W. Franzmann. 1986. Energy cost of standing in adult moose. Alces 22: 83–90.

Reichelt, L. R. 1962. Effect of logging on understory vegetation and deer use in a ponderosa pine forest of Arizona. Res. Note RM–80. USDA For. Serv., Fort Collins, Colorado. 7 pp.

———. 1964a. Elk and deer habitat use of a pinyon–juniper woodland in southern New Mexico. Trans. N. Amer. Wildl. and Natur. Resour. Conf. 29: 438–444.

———. 1964b. Some livestock–wildlife habitat relations in Arizona and New Mexico. Amer. Soc. Range Manage., New Mexico Sec. 13 pp. Mimeo.

———. 1966a. Use of a ponderosa pine forest in Arizona by deer, elk and cattle. Res. Note RM–63. USDA For. Serv., Fort Collins, Colorado. 7 pp.

———. 1966b. Use of openings in spruce–fir forests of Arizona by elk, deer and cattle. Res. Note RM–66. USDA For. Serv., Fort Collins, Colorado. 4 pp.

———. 1966c. Slash cleanup in a ponderosa pine forest affects use by deer and cattle. Res. Note RM–64. USDA For. Serv., Fort Collins, Colorado. 3 pp.

———. 1969a. Aspen grove use by deer, elk and cattle in southwestern coniferous forests. Res. Note RM–138. USDA For. Serv., Fort Collins, Colorado. 4 pp.

———. 1969b. Improvement of deer habitat on southwestern forest lands. J. Forestry 67(11): 803–805.

———. 1973. Characteristics of elk calving sites along the West Fork of the Madison River, Montana. Job Final Rept., Prog. W–130-R–4. Montana Fish and Game Dept., Helena. 39 pp.

Reichert, D. W. 1972. Rearing and training deer for food habits studies. USDA For. Serv., Res. Note RM–208. Rocky Mt. For. and Range Exp. Sta., Fort Collins, Colorado. 7 pp.

Reid, D. K. 1987. Fire and habitat modification: An anthropological inquiry into the use of fire by indigenous people. M. A. Thesis, Univ. Alberta, Edmonton. 169 pp.

Reid, H. W., D. Buxton, W. Corrigall, A. R. Hunter, D. A. McMartin and R. Rushton. 1979. An outbreak of malignant catarrhal fever in red deer (Cervus elaphus). Vet. Rec. 104: 120–123.

Reid, H. W., R. M. Barlow and I. Pow. 1978. Isolation of louping-ill virus from red deer (Cervus elaphus). Vet. Rec. 102: 463–464.

Reid, T. C., H. J. F. McAllum and P. D. Johnstone. 1980. Liver copper concentrations in red deer (*Cervus elaphus*) and wapiti (*C. canadensis*) in New Zealand. Res. in Vet. Sci. 28: 261–262.

Reid, T. R. 1997. The world according to Rome. Nat. Geogr. 192(2): 55–83.

Reiger, J. F. 1975. American sportsmen and the origins of conservation. Univ. Oklahoma Press. 316 pp.

———. 1986. American sportsmen and the origins of conservation, revised edition. Univ. Oklahoma Press, Norman. 316 pp.

Reimers, E. 1983a. Reproduction in wild reindeer in Norway. Can. J. Zool. 61: 211–217.

———. 1983b. Growth rate and body size differences in *Rangifer*, a study of cause and effects. Rangifer 3: 3–15.

Reimoser, F. 1988a. Probleme der schalenwildbewirtschaftung in der alpenlandischen kulturlandschaft. Anblick 1988(8): 318–321, 1988(9): 376–380.

———. 1988b. Regionalplanungskonzept zur Schalenwildbewirtschaftung in Vorarlberg. Oesterr. Forstztg. 99: 58–61.

———. 1990. Grundsatzliche aspekte zue asungsverbesserung und futterung fur rot- und rehwild in der mittellandischen kulturlandschaft aus wildokologischer sicht. Futterung und asungsverbesserung fur reh- und rotwild. Schriftenreihe wildforschung in Baden-Wurttemberg 1: 26–36, 172–179.

———. 1996. Game-ecological area planning for ungulates in alpine regions. Proc. Biotopkartierung im Alpenraum 8: 207–220.

Reimoser, F. and H. Gossow. 1996. Impact of ungulates on forest vegetation and its dependence on the silvicultural system. For. Ecol. and Manage. 88: 107–119.

Reinders, E. 1960. Das Rotwild in Krongut Het Loo5. Int. Union of Game Biologists Congress, Arnhem/Oosterbeak 4: 216–218.

Reiter, R. J. 1991. Pineal melatonin: Cell biology of its synthesis and of its physiological interactions. Endocrine Rev. 12: 151–180.

Renaud, E. B. 1930. Prehistoric cultures of the Cimarron Valley, northeastern New Mexico and western Oklahoma. Proc. Colorado Sci. Soc. 12(5): 122–135.

Reneau, J. and S. C. Reneau, eds. 1993. Records of North American big game. 10th ed. Boone and Crockett Club, Missoula, Montana. 604 pp.

Reneau, J. and S. C. Reneau, eds. 1996. Records of North American elk and mule deer. 2nd ed. Boone and Crockett Club, Missoula, Montana. 339 pp.

Renecker, L. A. and R. J. Hudson. 1985. Estimation of dry matter intake of free-ranging moose. J. Wildl. Manage. 49: 785–792.

———. 1988. Seasonal quality of forages used by moose in the aspen-dominated boreal forest, central Alberta. Holarctic Ecology 11: 111–118.

———. 1990. Digestive kinetics of moose (*Alces alces*), wapiti (*Cervus elaphus*) and cattle. Anim. Prod. 50: 51–61.

———, eds. 1991. Wildlife production: Conservation and sustainable development. AFES Misc. Pub. 91–6. Univ. Alaska Fairbanks, Fairbanks. 601 pp.

———. 1993. Advantages of game farming. Pages 132–134 *in* J. B. Stelfox, ed., Hoofed mammals of Alberta. Lone Pine Publ. Vancouver, British Columbia.

Renecker, L. A. and W. M. Samuel. 1991. Growth and seasonal weight changes as they relate to spring and autumn set points in mule deer. Can. J. Zool. 69: 744–747.

Renecker, L. A. and R. Valdez. 1992. The wildlife ranching symposium: History, stucture, achievements, goals and implications for wildlife management. Pages 1–6 *in* W. van Hoven, H. Ebedes and A. Conroy, eds., Wildlife ranching: A celebration of diversity. Pretoria, South Africa.

Renecker, L. A., R. J. Hudson, M. K. Christophersen and C. Arelis. 1978. Effect of posture, feeding, low temperature and wind on energy ex-

penditures of moose calves. Pages 126–140 *in* North American Moose Conf. Workshop. Vol. 14.

Repenning, C. A. 1992. Allophaiomys and the age of the Olyor suite, Krestovka Sections, Yakutia. U.S. Geol. Surv. Bull. 2,037 pp.

Repenning, C. A. and F. Grady. 1988. The microtine rodents of the Cheetah Room fauna, Hamilton Cave, West Virginia and the spontaneous origin of Synaptomys. U.S. Geol. Surv. Bull. 1,853 pp.

Repenning, C. A., T. R. Weasma and G. R. Scott. 1995. The early Pleistocene (latest Blancan-Earliest Irvingtonian) Froman Ferry Fauna and history of the Glenns Ferry Formation, southwestern Idaho. U.S. Geol. Sur. Bull. 2,105 pp.

Rerabek, J. and A. B. Bubenik. 1963. U.S. Atomic Energy Commiss. Div. Tech. Inform. AEC-fr–5631. U.S. Atomic Energy Commiss., Washington, D.C. 51 pp.

Resler, R. A. 1972. Clearcutting: beneficial aspects for wildlife resources. J. Soil and Water Conserv. 27(6): 1,418–1,419.

Retfalvi, L. 1969. Sexual dimorphism in fetuses of wapiti, *Cervus canadensis*. Can. J. Zool. 47(6): 1,418–1,419.

Revol, B. and P. R. Wilson. 1991a. Foetal ageing in farmed red deer using real-time ultrasonography. Anim. Reprod. Sci. 25: 241–253.

Revol, B. and P. R. Wilson. 1991b. Ultrasonography of reproductive tract and early pregnancy in red deer. Vet. Rec. 229–233 pp.

Reyes, E., G. A. Bubenik, D. Schams, A. Lobos and R. Enriques. 1997. Seasonal changes of testicular parameters in southern pudu (*Pudu pudu*) in relationship to circannual variation in its reproductive hormones. Acta Theriol. 42: 25–35.

Reynolds, G. E. 1971. Clinical aspects of bluetongue in Oregon cattle. Proc. Annul Meet. U.S. Anim. Health Assoc. 75: 74–79.

Reynolds, H. G. 1962a. Use of natural openings in a ponderosa pine forest of Arizona by deer, elk and cattle. Res. Note RM–78. USDA For. Serv., Fort Collins, Colorado. 4 pp.

———. 1962b. Effect of logging on understory vegetation and deer use in a ponderosa pine forest of Arizona. Res. Note RM–80. USDA For.Serv., Fort Collins, Colorado. 7 pp.

———. 1964a. Elk and deer habitat use of a pinyon–juniper woodland in southern New Mexico. Trans. N. Amer. Wildl. and Natur. Resour. Conf. 29: 438–444.

———. 1964b. Some livestock–wildlife habitat relations in Arizona and New Mexico. Amer. Soc. Range Manage., New Mexico Section. 13 pp. (mimeo).

———. 1966a. Use of a ponderosa pine forest in Arizona by deer, elk and cattle. Res. Note RM–63. USDA For. Serv., Fort Collins, Colorado. 7 pp.

———. 1966b. Slash cleanup in a ponderosa pine forest affects use by deer and cattle. Res. Note RM–64. USDA For. Serv., Fort Collins, Colorado. 3 pp.

———. 1969. Aspen grove use by deer, elk and cattle in southwestern coniferous forests. Res. Note RM–138. USDA For. Serv., Fort Collins, Colorado. 4 pp.

Reynolds, R. D. Unpublished. Effect of natural fires and aboriginal burning upon the forests of central Sierra Nevada. 1959 M.A. Thesis, Univ. California, Berkeley.

Reynolds, T. D. 1984. Daily summer movements, activity patterns and home range of pronghorn. Northwest Science 58: 300–311

Rhoades, D. F. and R. G. Cates. 1976. Toward a general theory of plant antiherbivory chemistry. Recent Adv. Phytochem. 10: 168–213.

Rhoads, S. N. 1897. Contributions to the zoology of Tennessee. No. 3, Mammals. Acad. Natur. Sci. Phila. Proc. 1896: 175–205.

Rhode, W., T. Porstmann and G. Gorner. 1973. Migration of Y-bearing human spermatozoa in cervical mucus. J. Reprod. Fert. 33: 167.

Rhodes, B. D. and S. H. Sharrow. 1990. Effects of grazing by sheep on the quantity and quality of forage available to big game in Oregon's Coast Range. J. Range. Manage. 43: 235–237.

Rhyan, J. C. and D. A. Saari. 1995. A comparative study of the histopathologic features of bovine tuberculosis in cattle, fallow deer (*Dama dama*), sika deer (*Cervus nippon*) and red deer and elk (*Cervus elaphus*). Vet. Pathol. 32: 215–220.

Rhyan, J. C., D. A. Saari, E. S. Williams, M. W. Miller, A. J. Davis and A. J. Wilson. 1992. Gross and microscopic lesions of naturally occurring tuberculosis in a captive herd of wapiti (*Cervus elaphus nelsoni*) in Colorado. J. Vet. Diagn. Invest. 4: 428–433.

Rhyan, J. D., K. Aune, B. Hood, R. Clarke, J. Payeur, J. Jarnagin and L. Stackhouse. 1995. Bovine tuberculosis in a free-ranging mule deer (*Odocoileus hemionus*) from Montana. J. Wildl. Dis. 31: 432–435.

Rhyan, J. C., K. Aune, D. R. Ewalt, J. Marquardt, J. W. Mertins, J. B. Payeur, D. A. Saari, P. Schladweiler, E. J. Sheehan and D. Worley. 1997. Survey of free-ranging elk from Wyoming and Montana for selected pathogens. J. Wildl. Dis. 33: 290–298.

Rice, C. E. 1947. A survey of elk and buffallo herds for serologic activity and with two rickettsial antigens. Can. J. Comp. Med. 11: 299–301.

Rice, P. R. and D. C. Church. 1974. Taste responses of deer to browse extracts, organic acids and odors. J. Wildl. Manage. 38: 830–836.

Rice, R. W. 1970. Stomach content analyses: a comparison of the rumen vs. esophageal techniques. Pages 127–132 in Range and wildlife habitat evaluation—a research symposium. Misc. Publ. 1147. USDA For. Serv., Washington, D.C.

Rich, G. B. 1957. The ear tick, *Otobius megnini* (Duges) (Acarina: Argasidae) and its record in British Columbia. Can. J. Comp. Med. 21: 415–418.

Richards, M. R. 1975. Some experiences with comprehensive planning: Idaho's problems and progress. Trans. N. Amer. Wildl. and Natur. Resour. Conf. 40: 113–116.

Richardson, J. 1829. Fauna boreali—Americana, Part 1. Quadrupeds. J. Murray, London. 300 pp.

Richeson, A. R. 1977. Understory response to overstory thinning in stagnated mixed-conifer forests of central Washington. Unpubl. M.S. Thesis, Washington State Univ., Pullman. 42 pp.

Rickard, W. H., J. D. Hedlund and R. E. Fitzner. 1977. Elk in the shrub-steppe region of Washington: An authentic record. Science 196: 1,009–1,010.

Rickard, L. G., B. B. Smith, E. J. Gentz, A. A, Grank, E. G. Pearson, L. L. Walker and M. J. Pybus. 1994. Experimentally induced meningeal worm (*Parelaphostrongylus tenuis*) infection in the llama (*Lama glama*): Clinical evaluation and implications for parasite translocation. J. Zoo Wildl. Med. 25: 390–402.

Riddell, F. A. 1978. Maidu and Konkow. Pages 370–386 in R. F. Heizer, ed., California. Handbook of North American Indians, Vol. 8. Smithsonian Instit., Washington, D.C. 800 pp.

Riggs, R. A., J. G. Cook, L. A. Irwin and J. L. Spicer. 1993. Relating timber management to cover for big game on interior northwest winter range: Some thoughts on reducing conflict. Pages 18–36 in R. L. Callas, D. B. Koch and E. R. Loft, eds., Proc. Western States Provinces Elk Workshop. Calif. Dept. Fish and Game, Sacramento, California. 138 pp.

Riggs, R. A., P. J. Urness and K. A. Gonzalez. 1990. Effects of domestic goats on deer wintering in Utah oakbrush. J. Range Manage. 43: 229–234.

Riggs, R. A., S. C. Bunting and S. E. Daniels. 1996. Prescribed fire. Pages 295–320 in P. R. Krausman, ed., Rangeland Wildlife. The Soc. for Range Management, Denver, Co. 440 pp.

Riggs, R. A., J. G. Cook, L. L. Irwin and J. L. Spicer. 1993. Relating timber management to cover for big game on interior northwest winter range: Some thoughts on reducing conflict. Pages 18–36 in R. L. Callas, D. B. Koch and E. R. Loft, eds., Proc. of the Western States and Provinces Elk Workshop.

Riney, T. 1955. Evaluating condition of free-ranging red deer (*Cervus elaphus*), with special reference to New Zealand. Part I: Description of techniques for determination of condition of red deer. New Zealand J. Sci. and Tech., Sect. B. 36: 429–463.

Riney, T. 1964. The impact of introductions of large herbivores on the tropical environment. Pages 261–273 in The ecology of man in tropical environments. New Series Publ. No. 4. IUCN, Morges, Switzerland.

Ringberg, T. M., R. G. White, D. F. Holleman and J. R. Luick. 1981. Prediction of carcass composition in reindeer (*Rangifer tarandus tarandus* L.) by use of selected indicator bones and muscles. Can. J. Zool. 59: 583–588.

Riordan, L. E. 1948. The sexing of deer and elk by airplane in Colorado. Trans. N. Amer. Wildl. Conf. 13: 409–430.

Rippe, D. 1997. A question of values. Wyoming Wildl. 61(5): 6–9.

Ritchie, W. A. 1944. The pre-Iroquoian occupations of New York State. Memoir No. 1. Rochester Mus., Rochester, New York. 416 pp.

Roath, R. 1996. Ecosystem management: The Owl Mountain partnership. Pages 122–124 in K. E. Evans, compiler, Sharing common ground on western rangelands: Proccedings of a livestock/big game symposium; February 1996. Gen. Tech. Rept. INT-GTR–343. USDA For. Serv., Intermountain Res. Sta., Ogden, Utah. 164 pp.

Robbins, C. T. 1973. The biological basis for the determination of capacity. Ph.D. Thesis, Cornell Univ., Ithaca, New York.

———. 1983. Wildlife feeding and nutrition. Academic Press, Inc., Orlando, Florida. 343 pp.

Robbins, C. T. and B. L. Robbins. 1979. Fetal and neonatal growth patterns and maternal reproductive effort in ungulates and subungulates. Am. Natur. 114: 101–116.

Robbins, C. T., A. N. Moen and J. T. Reid. 1974. Body composition of white-tailed deer. J. Anim. Sci. 38: 871–876.

Robbins, C. T., Y. Cohen and B. B. Davitt. 1979. Energy expenditure by elk calves. J. Wildl. Manage. 43: 445–453.

Robbins, C. T., R. S. Podbielancik-Norman, D. L. Wilson and E. D. Mould. 1981. Growth and nutrient consumption of elk calves compared to other ungulate species. J. Wildl. Manage. 45: 172–186.

Robbins, C. T., A. E. Hagerman, P. J. Austin, C. McArthur and T. A. Hanley. 1991. Variation in mammalian physiological responses to a condensed tannin and its ecological implications. J. Mamm. 72: 480–486.

Robbins, C. T., T. A. Hanley, A. E. Hagerman, O. Hjeljord, D. L. Baker, C. C. Schwartz and W. W. Mautz. 1987a. Role of tannins in defending plants against ruminants: reduction in protein availability. Ecology 68: 98–107.

Robbins, C. T., S. Mole, A. E. Hagerman and T. A. Hanley. 1987b. Role of tannins in defending plants against ruminants: Reduction in dry matter digestion? Ecology 68: 1,606–1,615.

Robbins, C. T., D. E. Spalinger and W. van Hoven. 1995. Adaptation of ruminants to browse and grass diets: Are anatomical-based browser–grazer interpretations valid? Oecologia 103: 208–213.

Robbins, R. L. Unpublished. 1973 Prog. Rept. on Nat. Elk Refuge, Jackson, Wyoming. 91 pp.

Robbins, R.L. and J. Wilbrecht. 1979. Supplemental feeding of elk wintering on the National Elk Refuge. Pages 255–258 in M. S. Boyce and L. D. Hayden-Wing, eds., North American elk: Ecology, behavior and management. Univ. Wyoming, Laramie. 294 pp.

Robbins, R. L., D. E. Redfearn and C. P. Stone. 1982. Refuges and elk management. Pages 479–507 in J. W. Thomas and D. E. Toweill, eds.,

Elk of North America: Ecology and management. Stackpole Books, Harrisburg. Pennsylvania. 698 pp.

Robel, R. J. 1960a. Determining elk movements through periodic aerial counts. J. Wildl. Manage. 24(1): 103–104.

Robel, R. J. 1960b. Detection of elk migration through hunter interviews. J. Wildl. Manage. 24(3): 337–338.

Roberts, H. B. 1956. Food habits and reproductivity of white-tailed deer in the Hatter Creek enclosure. Unpubl. M.S. Thesis, Univ. Idaho, Moscow. 57 pp.

———. 1974. Effects of logging on elk calving habitat. Moyer Creek, Salmon National Forest, Idaho. 23 pp.

Robinette, W. L. 1958. Unusual dentition in mule deer. J. Mammal. 39(1): 156–157.

Robinette, W. L. and D. A. Jones. 1959. Antler anomalies of mule deer. J. Mammal. 49(1): 96–108.

Robinette, W. L., J. S. Gashwiler, D. A. Jones and H. S. Crane. 1955. Fertility of mule deer in Utah. J. Wildl. Manage. 19(1): 115–136.

Robinette, W. L., J. S. Gashwiler, J. B. Low and D. A. Jones. 1957. Differential mortality by sex and age among mule deer. J. Wildl. Manage. 21: 1–16.

Robinson, W. B. 1952. Some observations on coyote predation in Yellowstone National Park. J. Mammal. 33(4): 470–476.

Robinson, W. L. 1960. Test of shelter requirements of penned white-tailed deer. J. Wildl. Manage. 45: 293–313.

Rocky Mountain Elk Foundation. 1990. Marketing Survey. Canyon Consulting, Missoula, Montana. 40 pp.

———. 1997. Rocky Mountain Elk Foundation homepage. [http:www.elkfoundation.org], February 1997.

———. 2000. Tracking the Rocky Mountain Elk Foundation. Bugle: 17(2): 131–146.

Robbins, J. 1998. The elk of Yellowstone. Wildl. Conserv. 101(2): 36–45.

Roberts, L. 1989. Disease and death in the new world. Science 246: 1,245–1,247.

Roberts, R. K. 1932. Conservation as formerly practiced by the Klamatch River region. California Fish and Game 18: 283–290.

Roe, F. G. 1955. The Indian and the horse. Univ. Oklahoma Press, Norman. 434 pp.

Roedle, J. 1971. Wenn die Hirsche röhren. Franck'sche Verlagshandlung Stuttgart Kosmos, Stuttgart. 80 pp.

Roedel, P. M. 1975. Optimum sustainable yield as a concept in fisheries management. Amer. Fish. Soc. Spec. Publ. 9: 85.

Roelle, J. E. and J. M. Bartholow. 1977. User documentation—PROGRAM ONEPOP. Fort Collins, Colorado.

Rogers, E. M. 1962. Diffusion of innovations. The Free Press, New York. 476 pp.

Rogers, E. M. and F. F. Shoemaker. 1971. Communication of innovations, a cross cultural approach. The Free Press, New York. 367 pp.

Rogers, G., O. Julander and W. L. Robinette. 1958. Pellet-group counts for deer census and range-use index. J. Wildl. Manage. 22: 192–199.

Rogers, R. 1957. The St. Joe elk herd. Idaho Wildl. Rev. 10(1): 11–18.

Rognrud, M. and R. Janson. 1971. Elk. Pages 39–51 in T. W. Mussehl and F. W. Howell, eds., Game management in Montana. Montana Fish and Game Dept., Helena. 238 pp.

Rohonczy, E. B., A. V. Balachandran, T. W. Dukes, J. B. Payeur, J. C. Rhyan, D. A. Saari, T. L. Whiting, S. H. Wilson and J. L. Jarnagin. 1996. A comparison of gross pathology, histopathology and mycobacterial culture for the diagnosis of tuberculosis in elk (*Cervus elaphus*). Can. J. Vet. Res. 60: 108–114.

Rolf, H. J. and A. Enderle. 1999. Hard fallow deer antler: A living bone till antler casting? Anatomical Record 255: 69–77.

Rolf, H. J. and A. Enderle. 2000. Histomorphology and physiology of "living" hard antlers—evidence for substance transport into polished antlers via the vascular system. First Int. Symp. on Antler and Product Technology 2000: 18.

Roll, P., O. Schmut, M. E. Reich and H. Hofmann. 1979. Biochemical and electronmicroscopic investigations of the antler's collagen. Mikroskopie, Vienna. 35: 275–279.

Rollins, P. A. 1935. The discovery of the Oregon Trail. Charles Scribner's Sons, New York: 391 pp.

Romer, A. S. 1962. The vertebrate body. 2nd ed. W. B. Saunders Co., Philadelphia. 644 pp.

Romme, W. H., M. G. Turner, L. L. Wallace and J. S. Walker. 1995. Aspen, elk and fire in northern Yellowstone National Park. Ecology 76: 2,097–2,106.

Rommel, M., A. O. Heydorn and F. Gruber. 1972. Beitraze zum lebinszyklus der sarkosporidien. 1. Die Sporozysti von Sarcocystis tenella in den Fazes der Katze. Berl. Munch. Tierarztl. Wschr. 85: 101–105.

Ronayne, D. 1995. Idaho's boom and wildlife. Idaho Wildlife. 15(1): 4–5.

Rongstad, O. J. and R. A. McCabe, 1984. Capture techniques. Pages 655–676 in L. K. Hall, ed., White-tailed deer: Ecology and management. Stackpole Books, Harrisburg, Pennsylvania. 870 pp.

Roosevelt, T. R. 1893. The wilderness hunter: An account of the big game of the United States and its chase with horse, hound and rifle. G. P. Putnam's Sons, The Knickerbocker Press, New York and London. 279 pp.

———. 1896. Ranch life and the hunting-trail. The Century Co., New York. 186 pp.

———. 1900. Hunting trips on the prairie and in the mountains. G. P. Putnam's Sons, New York. 238 pp.

———. 1902. The wapiti, or round-horned elk. Pages 131–164 in T. Roosevelt, T. S. Van Dyke, D. G. Elliot and A. J. Stone, eds., The deer family. Macmillan, New York.

———. 1905. Outdoor pastimes of an American hunter. Charles Scribner's Sons, New York. 369 pp.

Roper, E. 1986. Steamboat elk–Carter leases mule deer–Subletle antelope project. Quart. Prog. Rept., November 1, 1985–February 15, 1986. Wyoming Game and Fish Dept., Green River.

Rorabacher, J. A. 1970. The American buffalo in transition. North Star Press, Saint Cloud, Minnesota. 146 pp.

Roseberry, J. L. and A. Woolf. 1991. A comparative evaluation of techniques for analyzing white-tailed deer harvest data. Wildlife Monograph 117. The Wildl. Soc., Bethesda, Maryland. 59 pp.

Rosen, M. N. 1981. Necrobacillosis foot root, hoof rot, *Fusobacterium necrophorum*. Pages 332–338 in Infectious diseases of wild mammals. 2nd ed.

Ross, C. 1975. Economic evaluation of resident big game hunting in Saskatchewan. Res. Rept. 1, Resour. Planning and Policy Branch. Saskatchewan Dept. Tourism and Renewable Resour, Regina. 90 pp.

Rossler, G. 1983. Theorie und wirklichkeit bei rotwildwintergattern. Fallstudie in Eisenerz. Unpubl. Diploma Thesis, Univ. Agriculture, Vienna. 69 pp.

Rost, G. R. and J. A. Bailey. 1974. Responses of deer and elk to roads on the Roosevelt National Forest. M.S. Thesis, Colorado State Univ., Fort Collins. 19 pp.

Rost, G. R. and J. A. Bailey. 1979. Distribution of mule deer and elk in relation to roads. J. Wildl. Manage. 43(3): 634–641.

Rounds, R. C. 1979. Height and species as factors determining browsing of shrubs by wapiti. J. Appl. Ecol. 16: 227–241.

Rouse, R. A. 1957. Elk food habits, range use and movements. Gravelly Mountains, Montana. M.S. Thesis, Montana State Univ., Bozeman. 29 pp.

Rouse, R. A. 1958. Wildlife investigations (Dist. 3): Elk investigations (elk–livestock relationships). Fed. Aid Compl. Rept. Proj. W–73-R–3, JA–2. Montana Dept. Fish and Game, Helena. 3 pp.

Rousseau, M. K. and T. Richards. 1988. The Oregon Jack Creek site (EdRi–6): A Lehman Phase site in the Thompson River Valley, British Columbia. Can. J. Archaeol. 12: 39–63.

Rowe, J. S. 1962. Soil, site and land classification. For. Chron. (Dec.): 420–432.

Rowland, M. M. 1981. Comparative winter nutrition of elk in the Jemez Mountains, New Mexico. M.S. Thesis, Colorado State Univ., Fort Collins. 83 pp.

Rowland, M. M., A. W. Alldredge, J. E. Ellis, B. J. Weber and G. C. White. 1983. Comparative winter diets of elk in New Mexico. J. Wildl. Manage. 47: 924–932.

Rowland, M. M., M. J. Wisdom, B. K. Johnson, and J. G. Kie. 2000. Elk distribution and modeling in relation to roads. J. Wildl Manage. 64:672–684.

Rowley, I. 1970. Lamb predation in Australia: Incidence, predisposing conditions and the identification of wounds. CSIRO Wildl. Resour. 15: 79–123.

Ruby, R. H. and J. A. Brown. 1972. The Cayuse Indians. Univ. Oklahoma Press, Norman. 345 pp.

Ruckebusch, Y. 1974. Motility of the ruminant stomach associated with states of sleep. Pages 77–90 in I. W. McDonald and A. C. I. Warner, eds., Proc., 4th Int. Symposium on Ruminant Physiology. Vol. 2,351. Univ. New England Pub. Unit, Annidale.

Ruckebusch, Y., R. W. Dougherty and H. M. Cook. 1974. Jaw movements and rumen motility as criteria for measurement of deep sleep in cattle. Amer. J. Vet. Res. 35(10): 1,309–1,312.

Rudd, W. J. 1982. Elk migrations and movements in relation to weather and hunting in the Absaroka Mountains, Wyoming. M.S. Thesis, Univ. Wyoming, Laramie. 238 pp.

Rudd, W. J., A. L. Ward and L. L. Irwin. 1983. Do split hunting seasons influence elk migrations from Yellowstone National Park? Wildl. Soc. Bull. 11: 328–331.

Ruddiman, W. F. and H. E. Wright, Jr. 1987. Introduction. Pages 1–12 in W. F. Ruddiman and H. E. Wright, Jr., eds., North America and adjacent oceans during the last deglaciation. Geological Soc. of America, Boulder, Colorado. 501 pp.

Ruediger, W. 1977. Guidelines for coordinating timber sales with big game winter range. USDA For. Serv. On file on Kootenai Nat. For., Libby, Montana 15 pp. Mimeo.

Rule, D. C., R. N. Arnold, E. J. Hentges and D. C. Beitz. 1986. Evaluation of urea dilution as a technique for estimating body composition of beef steers in vivo: Validation of published equations and comparison with chemical composition. J. Anim. Sci. 63: 1935–1948.

Rummell, R. S. 1951. Some effects of livestock grazing on ponderosa pine forest and range in central Washington. Ecology 32(4): 594–607.

Rush, W. M. 1932a. Northern Yellowstone elk study. Montana Fish and Game Commiss., Helena. 131 pp.

———. 1932b. Bang's disease in Yellowstone National Park buffalo and elk herds. J. Mammal. 13: 371–372.

Russell, M. S. 1981. Land of enchantment. Univ. New Mexico Press, Albuquerque. 163 pp.

Rust, H. J. 1946. Mammals of northern Idaho. J. Mammal. 27: 308–327.

Rutter, S. M., R. A. Champion and P. D. Penning. 1997. An automatic system to record foraging behaviour in free-ranging ruminants. Applied Animal Behaviour Science 54: 185-195.

Rybarczyk, W. B. and J. W. Unsworth. 1991. Elk sightability as a tool for implementing management change. Pages 119–122 in A. G. Christensen, L. J. Lyon and T. N. Lonner, compilers, Proc. Elk Vulnerability Symp., Montana State Univ., Bozeman. 330 pp.

Ryder, M. L. and R. N. B. Kay. 1973. Structure and seasonal change in the coat of red deer (*Cervus elaphus*). J. Zool. (London) 170: 69–77.

Ryder, O. A. 1986. Species conservation and systematics: The dilemma of subspecies. Trends in Ecol. and Evol. 1(1): 9–10.

Ryg, M. 1986. Physiological control of growth, reproduction and lactation in deer. Rangifer Spec. Issue 1: 261–266.

Ryg, M. and E. Jacobsen. 1982. Effect of thyroid hormone and prolactin on food intake and weight change in young male reindeer (*Rangifer tarandus tarandus*). Can. J. Zool. 60: 1,562–1,567.

Sackl, K. 1992. Erfahrungen mit der Kommissionierung von Rotwildfutterungen und rotwildwintergattern. umpubl. Diploma Thesis, Univ. Agriculture, Vienna. 834 pp.

Sadighi, M., S. R. Haines, A. Skottner, A. J. Harris and M. I. Suttie. 1994. Effects of insulin-like growth factor-1 (IGF-1) and IGF-11 on the growth of antlers in vivo. J. Endocrinol. 143: 461–469.

Sadlier, R. M. F. S. 1969. The ecology of reproduction in wild and domestic mammals. Methuen, London, U.K. 321 pp.

———. 1982. Energy consumption and subsequent partitioning in lactating black-tailed deer. Can. J. Zool. 60: 382–386.

———. 1987. Reproduction of female cervids. Pages 123–144 in C. M. Wemmer, ed., Biology and management of the Cervidae. Smithsonian Instit. Press, Washington, D.C. 577 pp.

Sæther, B. E. 1985. Annual variation in carcass weight of Norwegian moose in relation to climate along a latitudinal gradient. J. Wildl. Manage. 49: 977–983.

Sæther, B. E. and H. Haagenrud. 1983. Life history of moose (*Alces alces*): Fecundity rates in relation to age and carcass weight. J. Mammal. 64: 226–232.

Sæther, B. E. and M. Heim. 1993. Ecological correlates of individual variation in age at maturity in female moose (*Alces alces*): The effects of environmental variability. J. Anim. Ecol. 62: 482–489.

Saltz, D. and G. C. White. 1991. Urinary cortisol and urea nitrogen responses to winter stress in mule deer. J. Wildl. Manage. 55: 1–16.

Saltz, D., G. C. White and R. M. Bartmann. 1992. Urinary cortisol, urea nitrogen excretion and winter survival in mule deer fawns. J. Wildl. Manage. 56: 640–644.

Saltz, D., G. C. White and R. M. Bartmann. 1996. Assessing animal condition, nutrition and stress from urine in snow. Wildl. Soc. Bull. 23: 694–704.

Sams, M. G., R. L. Lochmiller, C. W. Qualls, Jr., D. M. Leslie, Jr. and M. E. Payton. 1996. Physiological correlates of neonatal mortality in an overpopulation herd of white- tailed deer. J. Mammal. 77: 179–190.

Samuel, M. D., E. O., Garton, M. W. Schlegel and R. G. Carson. 1987. Visibility bias during aerial surveys of elk in north central Idaho. J. Wildl. Manage. 51: 622–630.

Samuel, W. M. 1973, 1974, 1977, 1996. Unpublished. Records on file, Department of Biological Sciences, Univ. Alberta, Edmonton, Canada.

———. 1987. Moving the zoo or the potential introduction of a dangerous parasite into Alberta with its translocated host. Pages 85–92 in L. A. Renecker, ed., Focus on a new industry. Proc. Alberta Game Growers' Assoc. Conf. 110 pp.

———. 1994a. The parasites and diseases of whitetails. Pages 233–236 in D. Gerlach, S. Atwater and J. Schnell, eds., Deer. Stackpole Books, Mechanicsburg, Pennsylvania. 384 pp.

———. 1994b. The parasites and diseases of mule deer. Pages 334–336 in D. Gerlach, S. Atwater and J. Schnell, eds., Deer. Stackpole Books, Mechanicsburg, Pennsylvania. 384 pp.

Samuel, W. M. and M. J. Barker. 1979. The winter tick, *Dermacentor albipictus* (Packard, 1869) on moose, *Alces alces* (L.) of central Alberta. Proc. N. A. Moose Conf. Workshop. 15: 303–348.

Samuel, W. M. and S. Demarais. 1993. Conservation challenges concerning wildlife farming and ranching in North America. Trans. N. Amer. Wildl. and Natur. Resour. Conf. 58: 445–447.

Samuel, W. M. and J. B. Gray. 1988. Efficacy of ivermectin against *Parelaphostrongylus andersoni* (Nematoda: Metastrongyloidea) in white-tailed deer (*Odocoileus virginianus*). J. Wildl. Dis. 24: 491–495.

Samuel, W. M. and D. A. Welch. 1991. Winter ticks on moose and other ungulates: Factors influencing their population size. Alces 27: 169–182.

Samuel, W. M., M. W. Barrett and G. M. Lynch. 1976. Helminths in moose of Alberta. Can. J. Zool. 54: 307–312.

Samuel, W. M., D. A. Welch and B. L. Smith. 1991. Ectoparasites from elk (*Cervus elaphus nelsoni*) from Wyoming. J. Wildl. Dis. 27: 446–451.

Samuel, W. M., M. J. Pybus, D. A. Welch and C. J. Wilke. 1992. Elk as a potential host for meningeal worm: Implications for translocation. J. Wildl. Manage. 56: 629–639.

Sanchez-Hermosillo, M. and R. N. B. Kay. 1979. Retention time and digestibility of milled hay in sheep and red deer (*Cervus elaphus*). Proc. Nutr. Soc. 38: 123A.

Sandoz, M. 1978. The buffalo hunters. Univ. Nebraska Press, Lincoln. 372 pp.

Sandrey, R. A., S. T. Buccola and W. G. Brown. 1983. Pricing policies for antlerless elk hunting permits. Land Economics 59: 432–443.

Sanford, S. E. 1995. Outbreak of yersiniosis caused by *Yersinia pseudotuberculosis* in farmed cervids. J. Vet. Diagn. Invest. 7: 78–81.

Sanyal, N. and W. J. McLaughlin. 1993. The link between hunting goals and strategy and harvest outcome. Leisure Sciences 15: 189–204.

Sapir, E. 1916. Time perspective in aboriginal American culture, a study in method. Geological Survey of Canada, Mem. No. 90, Anthropol. Ser. No. 13. Govt. Print. Bur., Ottawa. 87 pp.

Sappington, R.L. 1994. The prehistory of the Clearwater River region, north central Idaho. Univ. Idaho Anthropol. Rept. 95. 422 pp.

Sappington, R.L. and C.D. Carley. 1989. Archeological investigations at the Beaver Flat and Pete King Creek sites, Lochsa River, north central Idaho. Univ. Idaho Anthropol. Rept. 89. 127 pp.

Sauer, C. O. 1975. Man's dominance by the use of fire. Geoscience and Man 10: 1–13.

Sauer, J. R. and M. S. Boyce. 1983. Density dependence and survival of elk in northwestern Wyoming. J. Wildl. Manage. 47: 31–37.

Sauer, R. H. and D. W. Uresk. 1976. Phenology of steppe plants in wet and dry years. Northwest Sci. 50: 133–139.

Sayama, K. 1952. *Sarcocystis* in deer and elk in California. Calif. Fish and Game 38: 99–104.

Schaafsma, P. 1994. The rock art of Utah. Univ. Utah Press, Salt Lake City. 170 pp.

Schafer, E. H. 1963. Hunting parks and animal enclosures in ancient China. J. Econ. and Social Hist. of the Orient 2: 318–343.

Schallenberger, A. 1965a. Big game forage competition in the Sun River Canyon, Montana. Fed. Aid Compl. Rept. Helena: Montana Fish and Game Dep. 44 pp.

———. 1965b. Big game forage competition in the Sun River Canyon. M.S. Thesis. Montana State Univ., Bozeman. 43 pp.

Schaller, G. B. 1967. The deer and the tiger. Univ. Chicago Press, Chicago, Illinois. 370 pp.

Schaller, G. B., W. Liu and X. Wang. 1996. Status of Tibet red deer. Oryx 30(4): 269–274.

Schally, A. V., A. Arimura and A. J. Kastin. 1973. Hypothalamic regulatory hormones. Science 179(4,071): 341–350.

Schectman, S.M. 1978. The "Bambi Syndrome": How NEPA's public participation in wildlife management is hurting the environment. Environ. Law 8: 611–643.

Scheffer, V. B. 1976. The future of wildlife management. Wildl. Soc. Bull. 4(2): 51–54.

Scheibler, Count. 1910. Italy. Pages 211–237 *in* F. G. Aflalo, ed., Sport in Europe. E. P. Dutton and Co., New York. 483 pp.

Scheunert, A. and A. Trautmann. 1976. Lehrbuch der Veterinar-Physiologie. 6. Aufl. Berlin and P. Parey Verlag, Hamburg. 988 pp.

Schingoethe, D. J. 1988. Nutrient needs during critical periods of the life cycle: effect of nutrition on fertility, reproduction and lactation. Pages 421–436 *in* D. C. Church, ed., The ruminant animal: Digestive physiology and nutrition. Prentice Hall, Englewood Cliffs, New Jersey. 564 pp.

Schladweiler, P. 1974. Ecology of Shiras moose in Montana. Big Game Res. Prog. W–98-R and W–120-R, Final Rept. Montana Dept. Fish and Game, Helena, Montana. 100 pp.

Schlegel, M. 1976. Factors affecting calf elk survival in north central Idaho. A Progress report. Proc. West. Assoc. State Game Fish Commiss. 56: 342–355.

Schlegel, M. W., T. A. Leege and R. F. Lapen. 1972. Injurious antler anomaly in a Rocky Mountain elk. J. Wildl. Dis. 8: 319.

Schloeth, R. 1961. Marierung und erstc Beobachtungen von Markenen Rotwild im Schweizerischen National Park und dessen Umgebung. Ereg. Wiss. Unters. Schweiz. Nat. Parks 7(N.F.): 197–227.

———. 1966. Verwandschaftliche Beziehungen und Rudelbildung beim Rothirsch (*Cervus elaphus* L.). Rev. Suisse. Zool. 73(24): 434–440.

Schmidt, J. L. 1974. Field care of big game. Colorado State Univ. Extension Serv., Service in Action Leafl. No. 6.503. Colorado State Univ., Extension Serv. n. p., Fort Collins.

———. 1978a. Care and use of the harvested animal. Pages 437–451 *in* J. L. Schmidt and D. L. Gilbert, eds., Big game of North America: Ecology and management. Stackpole Books, Harrisburg, Pennsylvania. 512 pp.

———. 1978b. Early management: Intentional and otherwise. Pages 257–270 *in* J. L. Schmidt and D. L. Gilbert, eds., Big game of North America: Ecology and management. Stackpole Books, Harrisburg, Pennsylvania. 512 pp.

Schmidt, J. L. and D. L. Gilbert., eds.1978. Big game of North America: Ecology and management. Stackpole Books, Harrisburg, Pennsylvania. 494 pp.

Schmidt, K. 1990. Zur winterokologie ostalpiner rotwildrudel. Ph.D. Thesis, Univ. Vienna. 93 pp.

———. 1992. Uber den einfluss von futterung und jagd auf das raum-zeit-verhalten von rotwild. Z Jagdwiss. 38: 88–100.

———. 1993. Winter ecology of non-migratory alpine red deer. Oecologia 95: 226–233.

Schmidt-Nielsen, L. 1975. Animal physiology: adaptation and environment. MacMillan of Canada, Toronto. 699 pp.

Schmitt, S. M., S. D. Fitzgerald, T. M. Cooley, C. S. Bruning-Fann, L. Sullivan, D. Berry, T. Carlson, R. B. Minnis, J. B. Payeur and J. Sikarskie. 1997. Bovine tuberculosis in free-ranging white-tailed deer from Michigan. J. Wildl. Dis. 33: 749–758.

Schoen, J. W. 1977. The ecological distribution and biology of wapiti, *Cervus elaphus nelsoni,* in the Cedar River watershed, Washington. Ph.D. Thesis, Univ. Washington, Seattle. 405 pp.

Schoenfeld, C. A. 1957. Public relations aspects of wildlife management. J. Wildl. Manage. 21(1): 70–74.

Schoening, H. W. 1956. Rabies. Pages 195–202 *in* Yearbook of Agriculture, Animal Diseases. USDA, Washington, D.C.

Schole, B. J. 1973. Hunter behavior, attitudes and philosophies. M.S. Thesis, Colorado State Univ., Fort Collins. 192 pp.

Schommer, T. 1991. Analysis of big game statistics 1965–1990: Walowa

National Forest. USDA For. Serv., Wallowa-Whitman Nat. For., Baker City, Oregon.

Schommer, T. J. 1978. Seasonal *in vitro* digestion coefficients for energy and protein of central Washington elk diets. M.S. Thesis, Washington State Univ., Pullman. 57 pp.

Schönberg, B. O. 1910. Germany. Pages 147–169 *in* F. G. Aflalo, ed., Sport in Europe. E. P. Dutton and Co., New York. 483 pp.

Schonewald, C. 1994. *Cervus canadensis* and *C. elaphus* subspecies and evaluation of clinal extremes. Acta Theriologica 39(4): 431–452.

Schonewald-Cox, C. M., J. W. Bayless and J. Schonewald. 1985. Cranial morphology of Pacific Coast elk. J. Mammal. 66(1): 63–74.

Schorger, A.W. 1954. The elk in early Wisconsin. Trans. Wisconsin Acad. Sci., Arts and Letters 43: 5–23.

Schramm, W. 1954. How communications works. Pages 3–26 *in* W. Schramm, ed., The process and effects of mass communications. Univ. Illinois Press, Urbana. 586 pp.

Schroder, W. 1985. Schalenwild futtern? Beilage zu wildtiere 4/1985. Infodienst wildbiologie und okologie, Zurich. 4 pp.

Schroer, G. L., K. J. Jenkins and B. B. Moorhead. 1993. Roosevelt elk selection of temperate rain forest seral stages in western Washington. Northwest Sci. 67(1): 23–29.

Schuerholz, G. 1974. Quantitative evaluation of edge from aerial photographs. J. Wildl. Manage. 38(4): 913–920.

Schuhmacher, V. M. 1939. Jagd und Biologie—Ein Grundriss der Wildkunde. J. Springer Verlag, Berlin. 136 pp.

Schuknecht, S. F. 2000. Wewukiyepuh (10-NO-336): Archaeolgical investigations of a Windust phase site on the Lower Snake River. M.A. Thesis, Univ. Idaho, Moscow. 155 pp.

Schullery, P., ed. 1996. The Yellowstone wolf: A guide and sourcebook. High Plains Publ. Co., Worland, Wyoming. 354 pp.

Schultz, A. M. 1956. The use of regression in range research. J. Range Manage. 9: 41–46.

Schultz, R. D. and J. A. Bailey. 1978. Responses of national park elk to human activity. J. Wildl. Manage. 42(1): 91–100.

Schultz, S. R. and M. K. Johnson. 1995. Effects of birth date and body mass at birth on adult body mass of male white-tailed deer. J. Mammal. 76(2): 575–579.

Schwab, P. 1975. Grundsatze wissenschaftlich funierter Regulierung der Schalenwildbestande. Allgem. ForstZtg 86(2): 58–60.

Schwartz, C. C. and N. T. Hobbs. 1985. Forage and range evaluation. Pages 25–52 *in* R. J. Hudson and R. G. White, eds., Bioenergetics of wild herbivores. CRC Press, Boca Raton, Florida. 314 pp.

Schwartz, C. C. and L. A. Renecker. 1997. Nutrition and energetics. Pages 441–478 *in* A. W. Franzmann and C. C. Schwartz, eds., Ecology and management of the North American moose. Smithsonian Instit. Press, Washington, D.C. 733 pp.

Schwartz, C. C., W. L. Regelin and A. W. Franzmann. 1987. Protein digestion in moose. J. Wildl. Manage. 51: 352–357.

Schwartz, C. C., M. E. Hubbert and A. W. Franzmann. 1988. Energy requirements of adult moose for winter maintenance. J. Wildl. Manage. 52: 26–33.

Schwartz, C. G., J. G. Nagy and S. M. Kerr. 1976. Rearing and training pronghorns for ecological studies. J. Wildl. Manage. 40: 464–468.

Schwartz, J. E. 1942. Range conditions and management of the Roosevelt elk on the Olympic Peninsula. USDA For. Serv., Washington, D.C. 65 pp.

Schwartz, J. E. and G. E. Mitchell. 1945. The Roosevelt elk on the Olympic Peninsula, Washington. J. Wildl. Manage. 9(4): 295–319.

Scott, J. M., B. Csuti, K. Smith, J. E. Estes and S. Caicco. 1988. Beyond endangered species: An integrated conservation strategy for the preservation of biological diversity. Endangered Species Update 5: 43–48.

Scott, M. D. 1981. Fluorescent orange discrimination by wapiti. Wildl. Soc. Bull. 9: 256–260.

Scotter, G. W. 1980. Management of wild ungulate habitat in the western United States and Canada: A review. J. Range. Manage. 33(1): 16–27.

Scottish Natural Heritage Policy Paper. 1994. Red deer and the Natural Heritage. Scottish Natural Heritage Publications and Graphics, Edinburgh, Scotland. 70 pp.

Seal, U. S. and R. L. Hoskinson. 1978. Metabolic indicators of habitat condition and capture stress in pronghorns. J. Wildl. Manage. 42: 755–763.

Seal, U. S., J. J. Ozoga, A. W. Erickson and L. J. Verme. 1972. Effects of immobilization on blood analyses of white-tailed deer. J. Wildl. Manage. 36(4): 1,034–1,040.

Seal, U. S., L. J. Verme, J. J., Ozoga and A. W. Erickson. 1972. Nutritional effects on thyroid activity and blood of white-tailed deer. J. Wildl. Manage. 36(4): 1,041–1,052.

Seal, U. S., L. J. Verme and J. J. Ozoga. 1978. Dietary protein and energy effects on deer fawn metabolic patterns. J. Wildl. Manage. 42: 776–790.

Seber, G. A. F. 1982. The estimation of animal abundance and relation parameters. Macmillan, New York. 654 pp.

Seefelt, S. and D. Helfer. 1980. Seminoma in an elk (*Cervus canadensis*). Vet. Pathol. 17: 248–249.

Seligmann, M. E. P. 1975. Helplessness: On depression, development and death. Freeman, San Francisco.

Sellars, R.W. 1997. Preserving nature in the National Parks. Yale Univ. Press, New Haven, Connecticut.

Selleck, D. M. and C. M. Hart. 1957. Calculating the percentage of kill from sex and age ratios. Calif. Fish and Game 43(4): 309–316.

Selye, H. 1973. The evolution of the stress concept. Am. Sci. 61: 692–699.

———. 1974. Stress without distress. J. B. Lippincot Co., New York. 171 pp.

Seman, D. L., K. R. Drew, P. A. Clarken and R. P. Littlejohn. 1988. Influence of packaging method and length of chilled storage on microflora, tenderness and color stability of venison loins. Meat Sci. 22: 267–282.

Sempere, A. J. and J. Boisson. 1982. Neuroendocrine and endocrine control of the antler cycle in roe deer. Pages 109–122 *in* R. D. Brown, ed., Antler Development in Cervidae. Caesar Kleberg Wildl. Res. Inst. Kingsville, Texas. 480 pp.

Seoane, J. R., C. Beaulieu, J. Florez and G. Dupuis. 1991. Evaluation of the nutritive value of grass hays for growing sheep. Can. J. Anim. Sci. 71: 1,135–1,147.

Seton, E. T. 1909. Life-histories of northern mammals. Vol. 1. Grasseaters. Charles Scribner's Sons, New York. 673 pp.

———. 1927. Lives of game animals. Vol. 3, part 1. Doubleday, Page and Co., Garden City, New York. 412 pp.

———. 1937. Lives of game animals. Vol. 3. Hoofed animals. Literary Guild of America, New York. 780 pp.

———. 1953. Lives of game animals. Vol. 3—Part 1, Hoofed animals. Charles T. Branford Co., Boston, Massachusetts. 412 pp.

Severinghaus, C. W. and R. W. Darrow. 1976. Failure of elk to survive in the Adirondacks. New York Fish and Game J. 23(1): 98–99.

Severson, K. E. 1981. Plains habitats. Pages 459–485 *in* O. C. Wallmo, ed., Mule and blacktailed deer of North America. Univ. Nebraska Press, Lincoln. 605 pp.

Shackleton, D. M. 1973. Population quality and bighorn sheep. Ph.D. Thesis, Univ. Calgary, Canada. 227 pp.

Shackleton, D. M. and L. V. Hills. 1977. Postglacial ungulates (*Cervus* and *Bison*) from Three Hills, Alberta. Can. J. Earth Sci. 14(5): 963–986.

Shae, J. G. 1908. Discovering the Mississippi. Pages 111–122 *in* L. C. Draper, ed., Collections of the State Historical Society of Wisconsin. Vol. 7. 492 pp. (Reprint of 1876 original issue.)

Shaffer, B. S. 1994. Appendix A: Analysis of the vertebrate remains. Pages 145–160 *in* R. C. Fields, E. F. Gadus, L. W. Klement and K. M. Gardner, eds., Excavations at the Spider Knoll site, Cooper Lake project, Delta County, Texas. Reports of Investigations, No. 96. Prewitt and Associates, Inc., Austin, Texas. 201 pp.

Shaffer, B. S., B. C. Yates and B. W. Baker. 1995. An additional record of the native American elk (*Cervus elaphus*) from North Texas. Texas J. Sci. 47: 159–160.

Shank, C. C. 1982. Age–sex differences in the diet of wintering Rocky Mountain bighorn sheep. Ecol. 63: 627–633.

Shaw, D. L. 1973. The hunting controversy: Attitudes and arguments. Ph.D. Thesis, Colorado State Univ., Fort Collins. 174 pp.

Shaw, W. W. 1977. A survey of hunting opponents. Wildl. Soc. Bull. 5(1): 19–24.

Sheehy, D. P. and M. Vavra. 1996. Ungulate foraging areas on seasonal rangeland in northeastern Oregon. J. Range Manage. 49: 16–23.

Shelby, B. and T. A. Heberlein. 1986. Carrying Capacity in Recreation Settings. Oregon State Univ. Press, Corvallis.

Shelford, V. E. 1963. The ecology of North America. Univ. Illinois Press, Urbana. 632 pp.

Shephard, P. 1973. The tender carnivore and the sacred game. New York: Charles Scribner's Sons. 302 pp.

Shephard, P., Jr. 1959. A theory on the value of hunting. Trans. N. Amer. Wildl. Conf. 24: 504–512.

Sher, A. 1984. The role of the Beringian Land in the development of Holarctic mammalian fauna in the Late Cenozoic. Pages 296–316 *in* V. L. Kontrimavichus, ed., Beringia in the Cenozoic Era. Amerind Publ. Co. Priv. Lmt., New Delhi. pp.

Sherratt, A., ed. 1980. Cambridge encyclopedia of archeology. Crown Publ. Inc., New York. 495 pp.

Shi, Z. D. and G. K. Barrell. 1992. Effects of thyroidectomy on seasonal patterns of liveweight, testicular function, antler development and molting in red deer. Pages 443–449 *in* R. D. Brown, ed., The biology of deer. Springer-Verlag, New York. 596 pp.

———. 1994. Thyroid hormones are required for the expression of seasonal changes in red deer (*Cervus elaphus*) stags. Reprod. Fert. and Dev. 6: 187–192.

Shields, G. F. and A. C. Wilson. 1987. Subspecies of the Canada goose have distinct mitochondrial DNAs. Evolution 41(3): 662–666.

Shields, G. O. 1888. Elk-hunting in the Rocky Mountains. Harper's Monthly Magazine 77: 856–863.

Shimwell, D. W. 1971. The description and classification of vegetation. Univ. Washington Press, Seattle. 322 pp.

Shiras, G., III. 1906. Photographing wild game with flashlight and camera. Nat. Geogr. 17(7): 366–423.

———. 1913. Wild animals that took their own pictures by day and by night. Nat. Geogr. 24(7): 762–834.

Shiverdecker, W., K. Rasmussen and L. Greenwood. 1996. Monroe Mountain livestock/big game demonstration project: "Seeking Common Ground." Pages 129–131 *in* K. E. Evans, compiler, Sharing common ground on western rangelands: Proccedings of a livestock/big game symposium; February 1996. Gen. Tech. Rept. INT-GTR-343. USDA For. Serv., Intermountain Res. Sta., Ogden, Utah. 164 pp.

Shoemaker, H. W. 1939. Vanished game. Pages 15–34 *in* A. Ely, H. E. Anthony and R. M. Carpenter, eds., North American big game. Charles Scribner's Sons, New York. 533 pp.

Shoesmith, M. W. 1978. Social organization of wapiti and woodland caribou. Ph.D. Thesis, Univ. Manitoba, Winnipeg. 155 pp.

Short, H. L. 1963. Rumen fermentations and energy relationships in white-tailed deer. J. Wildl. Manage. 27: 184–195.

———. 1981. Nutrition and metabolism. Pages 99–128 *in* O. C. Wallmo, ed., Mule and black-tailed deer of North America. Univ. Nebraska Press, Lincoln. 605 pp.

Short, H. L., D. E. Medin and A. E. Anderson. 1965. Ruminoreticular characteristics of mule deer. J. Mammal. 46(2): 196–199.

Short, H. L., E. E. Remmeng and C. E. Boyd. 1969. Variations in ruminoreticular contents of white-tailed deer. J. Wildl. Manage. 33(1): 189–191.

Short, H. L., W. Evans and E. L. Boeker. 1977. The use of natural and modified pinyon pine–juniper woodlands by deer and elk. J. Wildl. Manage. 41(3): 543–559.

Shostak, A. W. and W. M. Samuel. 1984. Moisture and temperature effects of survival and infectivity of first-stage larvae of *Parelaphostrongylus odocoilei* and *P. tenuis* (Nematoda: Metastrongylidea). J. Parasitol. 70: 261–269.

Shotwell, J. A. 1970. Pliocene mammals of southeast Oregon and adjacent Idaho. Bull. Mus. Natur. Hist. 17, Univ. Oregon, Eugene. pp.

Shriver, P.R. 1991. The elk and the Indian in the Ohio country. Ohio Archaeol. 41(1): 33–37

Shupe, J. L., A. E. Olson, H. B. Peterson and J. B. Low. 1984. Fluoride toxicosis in wild ungulates. J. Am. Vet. Med. Assoc. 185: 1,295–1,300.

Shure, D. J. and L. A. Wilson. 1993. Patch-size effects on plant phenolics in successional openings of the southern Appalachians. Ecology 74: 55–67.

Sibbald, A. M. and J. A. Milne. 1993. Physical characteristics of the alimentary tract in relation to seasonal changes in voluntary food intake by the red deer (*Cervus elaphus*). J. Ag. Sci. (Camb.). 120: 99–120.

Sibbald, A. M., P. D. Fenn, W. G. Kerr and A. S. I. Loudon. 1993. The influence of birth date on the development of seasonal cycles in red deer hinds (*Cervus elaphus*). J. Zool., London 230: 593–607.

Siegmund, O. H., ed. 1973. The Merck veterinary manual. Third edition. Merck and Co., Inc., Rahway, New Jersey. 1,686 pp.

Sikorski, J. 1991. Big game management in Poland—economical aspects and perspectives. Pages 93–96 *in* B. Bobek, K. Perzanowski and W. L. Regelin, eds., Global trends in wildlife management. Eighteenth Int. Union of Game Biologists Congress, Kraków, Poland. 660 pp.

Silver, H. 1957. Elk. Pages 215–221 *in* A history of New Hampshire game and furbearers. Surv. Rept. No. 6. New Hampshire Fish and Game Dept., Concord. 466 pp.

———. 1968. Deer nutrition studies. Pages 182–196 *in* H. R. Siegler, ed., The white-tailed deer of New Hampshire. Surv. Rept. No. 10. New Hampshire Fish and Game Dept., Concord.

Silver, S. 1978. Shastan peoples. Pages 211–224 *in* R. F. Heizer, ed., California. Handbook of North American Indians, Vol. 8. Smithsonian Instit., Washington, D.C. 800 pp.

Simkin, D. W. 1965. Reproduction and productivity of moose in northwestern Ontario. J. Wildl. Manage. 29(4): 740–750.

Simkiss, K. 1975. Bone and biomineralization. MacMillan of Canada, Toronto. 64 pp.

Simmons, C. A. 1974. Seasonal range use and migration patterns of elk using various portions of the lower South Fork, Flathead River, winter range. Montana Res. Proj. No. W–120-R–5 and 6. Montana Dept. Fish and Game, Helena. 99 pp.

Simms, S. R. 1984. Aboriginal Great Basin foraging strategies: An evolutionary analysis. Ph.D. Diss., Univ. Utah., Salt Lake City. 286 pp.

———. 1992. Wilderness as a human landscape. Pages 183–201 *in* S. I. Zeveloff, L. M. Vause and W. H. McVaugh, eds., Wilderness tapestry: An eclectic approach to preservation. Univ. Nevada Press, Reno. 306 pp.

Simpson, A. M., A. J. F. Webster, J. S. Smith and C. A. Simpson. 1978. The efficiency of utilization of dietary energy for growth in sheep (*Ovis aries*) and red deer (*Cervus elaphus*). Comp. Biochem. Physiol. 59A: 95–99.

Simpson, A. M., A. J. F. Webster, J. S. Smith and C. A. Simpson. 1978. Energy and nitrogen metabolism of red deer (*Cervus elaphus*) in cold environments: A comparison with cattle and sheep. Comp. Biochem Physiol. 60: 251–256.

Simpson, G. G. 1945. The principles of classification and a classification of mammals. Bull. Amer. Mus. Natur. Hist. 85: i-xvi and 1–350.

———. 1952. The species concept. Evolution 5(4): 285–298.

———. 1990. Principals of animal taxonomy. Columbia Univ. Press, New York. 247 pp.

Simpson, J. H. 1876. Report of explorations across the Great Basin of the Territory of Utah for a direct wagon-route from Camp Floyd to Genoa, in Carson Valley, 1859. Govt. Print. Off., Washington, D.C. 518 pp.

Sinclair, A. R. E. 1985. Does interspecific competition or predation shape the African ungulate community? J. Anim. Ecology 54: 899–918.

Singer, F. J. 1975. Wildfire and ungulates in the Glacier National Park area, northwestern Montana. M. S. Thesis, Univ. Idaho, Moscow. 64 pp.

Singer, F. J. and J. E. Norland. 1994. Niche relationships within a guild of ungulate species in Yellowstone National Park, Wyoming, following release from artificial controls. Can. J. Zool. 72: 1,383–1,394.

Singer, F. J. and E. O. Garton. 1994. Supercub, elk sightability model. Pages 47–49 *in* J. W. Unsworth, F. A. Leban, D. J. Leptich, E. O. Garton and P. Zager, eds., Aerial survey: User's manual. Idaho Fish and Game Dept., Boise. 84 pp.

Singer, F. J. and P. Schullery. 1989. Yellowstone wildlife: Populations in process. West. Wildlands 15(2):18–22.

Singer, F. J. and R. G. Cates. 1995. Response to comment: Ungulate herbivory on willows on Yellowstone's northern winter range. J. Range Manage. 48: 563–565.

Singer, F. J., L. Mack and R. G. Cates. 1994. Ungulate herbivory of willows on Yellowstone's northern winter range. J. Range Manage. 47: 435–443.

Singer, F. J., A. Harting, K. K. Symonds and M. B. Coughenour. 1997. Density dependence, compensation and enviornmental effects on elk calf mortality in Yellowstone National Park. J. Wildl. Manage. 61: 12–25.

Singer, F. J., W. Schreier, J. Oppenheim and E. O. Garton. 1989. Drought, fires and large mammals. BioScience 39: 716–722.

Singer, F. J., D. M. Swift, M. B. Coughenour, and J. D. Varley. 1998. Thunder on the Yellowstone revisited: An assessment of the management of native ungulates by natural regulation, 1968–1993. Wildl. Soc. Bull. 26: 375–390.

Sizer, B. 1974. Nonresident quotas and fees. Proc. West.

Skalski, J. R. and D. S. Robson. 1992. Techniques for wildlife investigations design and analysis of capture data. Academic Press, San Diego, California 237 pp.

Skinner, M. F. 1942. The fauna of Papago Springs Cave, Arizona, and a study of Stockocerus with three new Antiloceprines from Nebraska and Arizona. Bull. 80. American Mus. Natur. Hist., Washington, D.C. 60 pp.

Skinner, M. P. 1925. Migration routes in Yellowstone Park. J. Mammal. 6: 184–192.

———. 1928. The elk situation. J. Mammal. 9: 309–317.

———. 1936. Browsing of the Olympic Peninsula elk in early winter. J. Mammal. 17(3): 253–256.

Skogland, T. 1983. The effects of density-dependent resource limitation on size of wild reindeer. Oecologia 60: 156–168.

Skogland, T. 1989. Comparative social organization of wild reindeer in relation to food, mates and predator avoidance. Advances in Ethology No. 29. 74 pp.

Skovlin, J. and M. Vavra. 1979. Winter diets of elk and deer in the Blue Mountains, Oregon, Research Paper PNW–260. Pacific NW Forest and Range Exp. Sta., Portland, Oregon. 21 pp.

Skovlin, J. M. 1962. Cow and calf weight trends on mountain summer range. U.S. For. Serv., PNW RN–220. 7 pp.

Skovlin, J. M. 1967. Fluctuations in forage quality on summer range in the Blue Mountains. U.S. For. Serv., Res. Pap PNW–44. 20 pp.

Skovlin, J. M. 1982. Habitat requirements and evaluations. Pages 369–413 *in* J. W. Thomas and D. E. Toweill, eds., Elk of North America: Ecology and management. Stackpole Books, Inc., Harrisburg, Pennsylvania. 698 pp.

Skovlin, J. M. and R. W. Harris. 1970. Management of conifer woodland grazing resources for cattle, deer and elk. Proc. Int. Grassland Congr. 11: 75–78.

Skovlin, J. M., P. J. Edgerton and R. W. Harris. 1968. The influence of cattle management on deer and elk. Trans. N. Amer. Wildl. and Natur. Resour. Conf. 33: 169–181.

Skovlin, J. M., R. W. Harris, G. S. Strickler and G. A. Garrison. 1976. Effects of cattle grazing methods on ponderosa pine-bunchgrass range in the Pacific Northwest. Tech. Bull. 1531. USDA For. Serv., Washington, D.C. 40 pp.

Skovlin, J. M., P. J. Edgerton and B. R. McConnell. 1983. Elk use of winter range as affected by cattle grazing, fertilizing and burning in southeastern Washington. J. Range Manage. 36(2): 184–189.

Skovlin, J. M., L. D. Bryant and P. J. Edgerton. 1989. Timber harvest affects elk distribution in the Blue Mountains of Oregon. Res. Pap. PNW-RP–415, USDA For. Serv., Portland, Oregon. 10 pp.

Slabý, O. 1962. Morfogeneza autopodia nasich jelenovitych savcu. Cs. Morfologie 10(1): 94–106.

Slatkin, M. 1987. Gene flow and geographic structure of natural populations. Science 236(4,803): 787–792.

Smil, V. 1984. The bad earth: Environmental degradation in China. M. E. Sharp, Inc., Armonk, New York. 245 pp.

Smith, A. D. 1965. Determining common use grazing capacities by application of the key species concept. J. Range Manage. 18: 196–201.

———. 1974. Production and survival of pronghorn antelope on artificial diets with different protein levels. Pages 74–91 *in* Proc. 6th Antelope States Workshop. Salt Lake City, Utah.

Smith, A. M. C. 1974. Ethnography of the Northern Utes. Pap. in Anthropol. Mus. New Mexico, Santa Fe. 288 pp.

Smith, B. L. 1985. Scabies and elk mortalities on the National Elk Refuge, Wyoming. Pages 180–194 *in* Proc. 1984 West. States and Provinces Elk Workshop. Alberta Fish and Wildl. Div., Edmonton. 218 pp.

———. 1994a. Out-of-season births of elk calves in Wyoming. Prairie Natur. 26: 131–136.

———. 1994b. Population regulation of the Jackson elk herd. Ph.D. Diss., Univ. Wyoming, Laramie. 264 pp.

———. 1997. Antler size and winter mortality of elk: effects of environment, birth year and parasites. J. Mamm. 78: 26–39.

Smith, B. L. and R. L. Robbins. 1984. Pelleted alfalfa hay as supplemental winter feed for elk at the National Elk Refuge. U.S. Fish and Wildl. Serv., Nat. Elk Ref., Jackson, Wyoming. 73 pp.

Smith, B. L. and T. Roffe. 1994. Diseases among elk of the Yellowstone ecosystem. Pages 162–166 *in* W. Van-Hoven, H. Ebedes and A. Conroy, eds., Wildlife ranching: A celebration of diversity. Prod. 3rd Int. Wildl. Ranching Symp. Centre for Wildl. Manage., Univ. Pretoria, South Africa. 400 pp.

Smith, B. L. and R. L. Robbins. 1994. Migration and management of the Jackson elk herd. Res. Public. No. 199. U.S. Nat. Biol. Surv., Washington, D.C. 61 pp.

Smith, B. L. and S. H. Anderson. 1998. Juvenile survival and population regulation of the Jackson elk herd. J. Wildl. Manage. 62: 1,036–1,045.

Smith, B. L., R. L. Robbins and S. H. Anderson. 1996a. Patterns of neonatal mortality of elk in northwest Wyoming. Can. J. Zool. 74: 1,229–1,237.

Smith, B. L., R. L. Robbins and S. H. Anderson. 1996b. Adaptive sex ratios: Another example? J. Mamm. 77: 818–825.

Smith, B.L., R. L. Robbins and S. H. Anderson. 1997. Early development of supplementally fed, free-ranging elk. J. Wildl. Manage. 61: 27–39.

Smith, D. B. and M. S. Yuan. 1991. Modeling the effects of hunter caused elk mortality. Pages 204–208 in A. G. Christensen, L. J. Lyon and T. N. Lonner, eds., Montana State Univ., Elk Vulnerability Symp. Bozeman, Montana. 330 pp.

Smith, D. M. 1962. The practice of silviculture. 7th ed. John Wiley and Sons, Inc., New York. 578 pp.

Smith, D. R. 1961. Competition between cattle and game on elk winter range. Ag. Exp. Sta. Bull. 377. Univ. Wyoming, Laramie. pp. 1–15.

Smith, D. R. and R. L. Lang. 1962. Nitrogen fertilization of upland range in the Big Horn Mountains. Ag. Exp. Sta. Bull. 388. Univ. Wyoming, Laramie. 10 pp.

Smith, D. R., P. O. Currie, J. V. Basile and N. C. Frischknecht. 1962. Methods for measuring forage utilization and differentiating use by different classes of animals. Pages 93–102 in Range research methods. Misc. Publ. 940. USDA For. Serv., Washington, D.C.

Smith, E. H. 1798. Concerning the elk. Med. Repository 2(2): 168–173.

Smith, F. W. 1987. Elk hiding and thermal cover guidelines in the context of lodgeple pine stand density. Western Journal of Applied Forestry. 2(1): 6–10.

Smith, H. A., T. C. Jones and R. D. Hunt. 1972. Vet. pathology. 4th ed. Lea and Febiger, Philadelphia. 1,521 pp.

Smith, H. C. T. 1974. Biology and management of the wapiti (Cervus elaphus nelsoni) of Fjordland, New Zealand. New Zealand Deer Stalkers Assoc., Wellington. New Zealand. 253 pp.

Smith, J. G. 1952. Food habits of mule deer in Utah. J. Wildl. Manage. 16: 148–155.

Smith, J. G. and O. Julander. 1953. Deer and sheep competition in Utah. Journ. Wildl. Manage. 17: 101–112.

Smith, J. G. E. 1981. Western Woods Cree. Pages 256–270 in J. Helm, ed., Subarctic. Vol. 6. Handbook of North American Indians. Smithsonian Instit. Press, Washington, D.C. 837 pp.

Smith, J. L., 1980. Reproductive rates, age structure and management of Roosevelt elk in Washington's Olympic Mountains. Pages 67–111 in W. Macgregor, ed., Proc. of Western states elk workshop. B. C. Fish and Wildlife Branch, Cranbrook, British Columbia. 174 pp.

Smith, J. H. and G. A. Bubenik. 1990. Plasma concentration of glucocorticoids in white-tailed deer: The effect of acute ACTH and dexamethasone administration. Can. J. Zool. 68: 2,123–2,129.

Smith, K. and A. Peischel. 1991. Intensive wapiti production in the tropics: Hawaii. Pages 503–515 in L. A. Renecker and R. J. Hudson, eds., Wildlife production: Conservation and sustainable development. AFES Misc. Pub. 91–6. Univ. Alaska Fairbanks, Fairbanks. 601 pp.

Smith, L. H. 1901. The extinction of the elk in Ontario. Ottawa Natur. 15(5): 94–97.

Smith, M. C. T. 1974. Biology and management of the wapiti (Cervus elaphus nelsoni) of Fiordland, New Zealand. New Zealand Deerstalkers Assoc., Wellington, New Zealand. 253 pp.

Smith, N. S. 1962. The fall and winter ecology of the Shiras moose in Rock Creek drainage, Cranite County, Montana. Unpubl. M.S. Thesis, Univ. Montana, Missoula. 52 pp.

Smith, R. H. 1959. A hunter questionnaire for compiling hunt statistics. Proc. West. Assoc. State Game and Fish Commiss. 39: 213–218.

Smith, R. H., D. J. Neff and C. Y. McCulloch. 1969. A model for the installation and use of a deer pellet group survey. Spec. Rept. No. 1. Arizona Game and Fish Dept., Tucson. 30 pp.

Smith, S. G., S. Kilpatrick, A. D. Reese, B. L. Smith, T. Lemke and D. Hunter. 1997. Wildlife habitat, feedgrounds and brucellosis in the Greater Yellowstone Area. Pages 65–76 in E. T. Thorne, M. S. Boyce, P. Nicoletti and T. J. Kreeger, eds., Brucellosis, bison, elk and cattle in the Greater Yellowstone Area: defining the problem, exploring solutions. Wyoming Game and Fish Dept. and Greater Yellowstone Interagency Brucellosis Committee, Cheyenne. 219 pp.

Smith, S. H., J. B. Holter, H. H. Hayes and H. Silver. 1975. Protein requirement of white-tailed deer fawns. J. Wildl. Manage. 39: 582–589.

Smitman, G. E. Unpublished. An examination of laboratory techniques for quantification of elk fecal analysis. 1980 M.S. Thesis, Washington State Univ., Pullman. 58 pp.

Smits, J. E. G. 1991. A brief review of infectious and parasitic diseases of wapiti, with empasis on western Canada and the northwestern United States. Can. Vet. J. 32: 471–479.

Smits, J. E. G. 1992. Elk disease survey in western Canada and northwestern United States. Pages 101–106 in R. D. Brown, ed., The biology of deer. Springer-Verlag, New York, New York. 596 pp.

Snedecor, G. W. and W. G. Cochran. 1967. Statistical methods. 6th ed. Iowa State Univ. Press, Ames. 593 pp.

Snow, D. R. 1995. Microchronology and demographic evidence relating to the size of pre-Columbian North American Indian populations. Science 268: 1,601–1,604.

Snyder, R. 1969. Forage competition between cattle and elk in the Gird Creek drainage of western Montana. M.S. Thesis, Univ. Montana, Missoula. 86 pp.

Snyder, S. P., R. B. Davies and D. Stevens. 1981. Brain tumors in two free-ranging elk in Colorado. J. Wildl. Dis. 17: 101–104.

Snyder, S. P., R. B. Davies and R. E. Keiss. 1979a. Myxosarcoma in a wapiti. J. Wildl. Dis. 15: 307–308.

Snyder, S. P., R. B. Davies, T. R. Spraker and H. Browning. 1979b. Embryonal nephroma in a wapiti. J. Wildl. Dis. 15: 303–306.

Society of American Foresters. 1983. Terminology of forest science technology practice and products. F. C. Ford-Robertson and Robert K. Winters, eds., Second printing with addendum. Soc. of Amer. Foresters, Washington, D.C. 370 pp.

Sokal, R. R. 1973. The species problem reconsidered. Syst. Zool. 22(4): 360–374.

Sokolov, V. E. and L. M. Baskin. 1991. Game management in the USSR with special reference to the extent of landscape modification by man. Pages 81–88 in B. Bobek, K. Perzanowski and W. L. Regelin, eds., Global trends in wildlife management. Eighteenth Int. Union of Game Biologists Congress, Kraków, Poland 660 pp.

Solberg, E. J. and B. E. Sæther. 1994. Male traits as life-history variables: annual variation in body mass and antler size in moose (Alces alces). J. Mammal. 75: 1069–1079.

Soper, J. D. 1946. 1947. Observations on mammals and birds in the Rocky Mountains of Alberta. Can. Field Natur. 61(5): 143–173.

Soper, J. D. 1946. Mammals of the northern Great Plains along the international boundary in Canada. J. Mammal. 27(2): 127–153.

Sorg, C. F. and L. J. Nelson. 1986. Net economic value of elk hunting in Idaho. USDA For. Serv., Res. Bull RM–12. 21 pp.

Soulé, M.E. 1986. Conservation biology: The science of scarcity and diversity. Sinauer Associates, Sunderland, Massachusetts. 584 pp.

Sowell, B. F., J. D. Wallace, M. E. Branine, M. E. Hubbert, E. L. Fredrickson and J. G. P. Bowman. 1996. Effects of restricted suckling on forage intake of range calves. J. Range Manage. 49: 290–293.

Sowerby, A. de C. 1914. Fur and feather in north China. Tientsin Press Ltd., Tientsin, China. 190 pp.

———. 1917. A sportsman's miscellany. The Tientsin Press Ltd., Tientsin, China. 226 pp.

Sowerby, A. de C. 1922. The naturalist in Manchuria. Vol. I. Tientsin Press Ltd., Tientsin, China. 347 pp.

Spaeth, N. J. 1993. American Indian law deskbook. Univ. Press of Colorado, Niwot. 465 pp.

Spalding, D. J. 1992. The history of elk (*Cervus elaphus*) in British Columbia. Contrib. to Natur. Sci. No. 18. The Roy. British Columbia Mus., Victoria, Canada. 27 pp.

Spalinger, D. E. and C. T Robbins. 1992. The dynamics of particle flow in the rumen of mule deer (*Odocoileus hemionus hemionus*) and elk (*Cervus elaphus nelsoni*). Physiol. Zool. 65: 379–402.

Spalinger, D. E. and N. T. Hobbs. 1992. Mechanisms of foraging in mammalian herbivores: new models of functional response. Amer. Naturalist 140: 325–348.

Spalinger, D. E., C. T. Robbins and T. A. Hanley. 1986. The assessment of handling time in ruminants: The effect of plant chemical and physical structure on the rate of breakdown of plant particles in the rumen of mule deer and elk. Can. J. Zool. 64: 312–321.

Spalinger, D. E., C. T. Robbins and T. A. Hanley. 1993. Adaptive rumen function in elk (*Cervus elaphus nelsoni*) and mule deer (*Odocoileus hemionus hemionus*). Can. J. Zool. 71: 601–610.

Speck, F. G. 1913. The Indians and game preservation. Red Man 6: 21–25.

Spencer, R. D. 1997. GMU 485 Elk mark–recapture population estimate. Final Rept., Washington Dept. Fish and Wildlife, Olympia. 9 pp.

Spencer, R.F and J.D. Jennings. 1965. The Native Americans. Harper and Row Publ., New York. 539 pp.

Speth, J. D. 1987. Early hominid subsistence strategegies in seasonal habitats. J. Archaeol. Sci. 14: 13–29.

———. 1989. Early hominid hunting and scavenging: The role of meat as an energy source. J. Human Evol. 18: 329–343.

———. 1991. Protein selection and avoidance strategies of contemporary and ancestral foragers: Unresolved issues. Philosoph. Trans. Royal Soc. London (Series B) 334: 265–270.

Speth, J. D. and K. A. Spielmann. 1983. Energy source, protein metabolism, and hunter–gatherer subsistence strategies. J. Anthropol. Archaeol. 2: 1–31.

Spielmann, K. A. 1989. A review: Dietary restrictions on hunter–gatherer women and the implications for fertility and infant mortality. Human Ecol. 17: 321–345.

Spillett, J. J. 1969. Economics of wildlife conservation: Values of consumptive and non-consumptive uses of wildlife species. Pages 121–129 in IUCN New Series Publ. 17. IUCN, Morges, Switzerland.

Spinden, H. J. 1908. The Nez-Perce Indians. Mem. Amer. Anthropol. Assoc., Lancaster, Pennsylvania. 2(3): 165–274.

Spott, R. and A. L. Kroeber. 1942. Yurok narratives. Univ. California Publ. Amer. Archaeol. and Ethnol. 35(a): 143–256.

Spraker, T. R. 1993. Stress and capture myopathy in artiodactylids. Pages 481–488 in M. E. Fowler, ed., Zoo and wildlife medicine. W. B. Saunders, Philadelphia, Pennsylvania. 617 pp.

Spraker, T. R., M. W. Miller, E. S. Williams, D. M Getzy, W. J. Adrian, G. G. Schoonveld, R. A. Spowart, K. I. O'Rourke, J. M. Miller and P. A. Merz. 1997. Spongiform encephalopathy in free-ranging mule deer (*Odocoileus hemionus*), white-tailed deer (*Odocoileus virginianus*) and Rocky Mountain elk (*Cervus elaphus nelsoni*) in northcentral Colorado. J. Wildl. Dis. 33: 1–6.

Sproat, G. M. 1868. Scenes and studies of savage life. Smith, Elder, London.

Spurrell, J. A. 1917. An annotated list of the mammals of Sac County, Iowa. Iowa Acad. Sci. Proc. 24: 273–284.

Squibb, R. C., J. F. Kimball, Jr. and D. R. Anderson. 1986. Bimodal distribution of estimated conception dates in Rocky Mountain elk. J. Wildl. Manage. 50: 118–122.

Squibb, R. C., R. E. Danvir, J. F. Kimball, Jr., S. T. Davis and T. D. Bunch. 1991. Ecology of conception in a northern Utah elk herd. Pages 110–118 in A. G. Christensen, L. J. Lyon, T. N. Lonner, compilers, Proc. Elk Vulnerability Symp., Montana State Univ., Bozeman. 330 pp.

Stafford, K. J., C. S. W. Reid, T. N. Barry and J. M. Suttie. 1993. Ruminoreticular motility in red deer (*Cervus elaphus*) fed chaffed lucerne hay during winter and summer. New Zealand J. Ag. Res. 36: 465–473.

Stahl, D. 1979. Wild. lebendige umwelt. Orbis Academicus: problemgeschichte von naturschutz, landschaftspflege und humanokologie: Sonderbd 2,2. Alber Verlag Freiburg, Munchen. 349 pp.

Staines, B. W. 1978. The dynamics and performance of a declining population of red deer (*Cervus elaphus*). J. Zool. 184: 403–419.

Staines, B. W., J. M. Crisp and T. Parish. 1982. Differences in the quality of food eaten by red deer (*Cervus elaphus*) stags and hinds in winter. J. Appl. Ecol. 19: 65–77.

Stalling, D. 1989. The perils of elk farms. Bugle 15(4): 70–75.

———. 1994a. Making bulls less vulnerable: Road closed. Bugle 11(4): 107–115.

———. 1994b. Dark Canyon, then and now. Bugle 11(3): 21–28.

———. 1994c. Are they really extinct? Eastern elk. Bugle 11(2): 83–89.

———. 1995a. Regulating the hunt. Bugle 12(3): 97–104.

———. 1995b. Selling Big Bulls. Bugle 12(4): 115–125.

———. 1996a. Hunting the rut. Bugle 13(3): 109–116.

———. 1996b. Modeling the hunt. Bugle 13(2): 81–86.

———. 1996c. Space age technology, stone age pursuit. Pages 182–199 in D. Petersen, ed., A hunter's heart: Honest essays on blood sport. Henry Holt and Company, New York. 331 pp.

———. 1996d. Oregon's master hunters: a new breed of jagermeister. Bugle 13(4): 41–50.

———. 1996e. Bringing back the bulls. Bugle 14(1): 67–75.

———. 1996f. The variables of vulnerability. Bugle 13 (Spring): 82.

———. 1997. Bringing back the bulls. Bugle. 14 (1): 67–75.

———. 2000. Learning about wolves and elk. Bugle 17(5): 126–128.

Stands in Timber, J. and M. Liberty. 1967. Cheyenne memories. Yale Univ. Press, New Haven, Connecticut. 345 pp.

Stange, M. Z. 1997. Woman the hunter. Beacon Press, Boston, Massachusetts. 247 pp.

Stankey, G. H., R. C. Lucas and R. R. Ream. 1973. Relationships between hunting success and satisfaction. Transactions, N. Amer. Wildl. Natur. Resour. Conf. 38: 235–242.

Starfield, A. M. 1997. A pragmatic approach to modeling for wildlife management. J. Wildl. Manage. 61: 261–270.

Starfield, A. M. and A. L. Bleloch. 1991. Building models for conservation and wildlife management. Second ed. Burgess Int., Edina, Minnesota. 253 pp.

Starfield, A. M., K. A. Smith and A. L. Bleloch. 1994. How to model it: problem-solving for the computer age. Burgess Int., Edina, Minnesota. 206 pp.

Stark, R. H., Jr. 1973. Elk–cattle interrelations on the Colockum Creek watershed. M.S. Thesis. Washington State Univ., Pullman. 87 pp.

State of Washington v. Chambers. 1973. Wash., 506 P. 2d 311, No. 42450.

State of Washington v. Moses, Aukeen D. J. Ct. (1975).

State of Washington v. Starr et al., Pierce County Washington Cause No. 48753 (1976).

Stehn, T. V. 1973. Daily movements and activities of cow elk in the Sapphire Mountains of western Montana during summer and fall. Ph.D. Thesis, Univ. Montana, Missoula. 66 pp.

Stein, C. D. and G. B. Van Ness. 1956. Anthrax. *in* Animal diseases. Yearbook of Agriculture. USDA, Washington, D.C.

Stein, C. D. and M. G. Stoner. 1952. Anthrax in livestock during 1951 and comparative data on diseases from 1945 through 1951. Vet. Med. 49: 579–588.

Stein, M., R. C. Schiavi and M. Camerino. 1976. Influence of brain and behavior on the immune system. Science 191(4,226): 435–440.

Steinhoff, H. W., R. G. Walsh, T. J. Peterle and J. M. Petulla 1987 Evolution of the valuation of wildlife. Pages 34–49, *in* D. J. Decker and G. R. Goff, eds., Valuing wildlife, economic and social perspectives. Westview Press, Inc, Boulder, Colorado.

Steinmetz, P. B. 1984. The sacred pipe in American Indian religions. Amer. Indian Cult. And Research J. 8(3): 27–80.

Stelfox, J. G. 1962a. Effects on big game of harvesting coniferous forests in western Alberta. For. Chron. 38: 94–107.

Stelfox, J. G. 1962b. Liver, lungs and larvae parasites and diseases in moose, deer and elk in Alberta. Land-Forest-Wildl. 5(4): 5–12.

Stelfox, J. G. 1964. Elk in northwest Alberta. Land-Forest-Wildl. 6(5): 14–23.

Stemp, R. 1983. Heart rate responses of bighorn sheep to environmental factors and harassment. Masters Degree Project, Environmental Design, Univ. Calgary, Alberta. 314 pp +.

Stephens, H. B. 1890. Jacques Cartier and his four voyages to Canada. W. Drysdale and Co., Montreal. 163 pp.

Stephenson, T. R. 1995. Lipid reserves in female moose in relation to physiological and environmental variables. Ph.D. Thesis, Univ. of Idaho, Moscow.

Stephenson, T. R., K. J. Hundertmark, C. C. Schwartz and V. V. Ballenberghe. 1998. Predicting body fat and body mass in moose with ultrasonography. Can. J. Zool. 76: 717–722.

Stern, C. M., S. A. Miller and M. S. Schanfield. 1992. Differentiation of wapiti and Eurasian red deer by isoelectric focusing electrophoresis of GC on agrose gels. Animal Genetics 23(Suppl. 1): 32

Sternath, M. 1994. Rotwildfutterung- das angebot des marktes. Weidwerk 10/94: 18–19

Stevens, D. R. 1966. Range relationships of elk and livestock, Crow Creek Drainage, Montana. J. Wildl. Manage. 30: 349–363.

Stevens, D. R. 1967. Ecology of moose in southwestern Montana. Job. Compl. Rept. W–98–R–7. Montana Fish and Game Dept., Helena. 39 pp.

Stevens, D. R. 1970. Winter ecology of moose in the Gallatin Mountains, Montana. J. Wildl. Manage. 34: 37–46.

Stevens, D. R. 1974. Rocky Mountain elk–Shiras moose range relations. Can. Natur. 101: 505–516.

Stevenson, J. M., D. L. Seman and R. P. Littlejohn. 1992. Seasonal variation in venison quality of mature, farmed red deer stags in New Zealand. J. Anim. Sci. 70: 1,389–1,396.

Steward, J. H. 1941. Nevada Shoshoni. Culture element distribution XIII. Univ. California, Berkeley. 4(2): 209–259.

———. 1943. Culture element distribution: XXIII. Northern and Gosiute Shoshoni. Anthropol. Records , Univ. California, Berkeley. 8(3): 263–392.

Stewart, D. R. M. 1967. Analysis of plant epidermis in feces: A technique for studying the food preferences of grazing herbivores. J. Appl. Ecol. 4(1): 83–111.

Stewart, O. C. 1954. Forest fires with a purpose. Southwest. Lore 20(4): 59–64.

———. 1963. Barriers to understanding the influence of the use of fire by aborigines on vegetation. Proc. Tall Timbers Fire Ecol. Conf. 2: 117–126.

Stewart-Scott, I. A., P. D Pearce, G. H. Moore and P. F. Fennessy. 1990. Freemartinism in red deer (*Cervus elaphus* L.). Cytogenet. Cell Genet. 54: 58–59.

Stirton, R. A. 1944. Comments on the relationships of the Palaeomerycidae. Amer. J. Sci. 242: 633–655.

Stock, T. M. 1978. Gastro-intestinal helminths in white-tailed deer (*Odocoilei virginianus*) and mule deer (*Odocoilei hemionus*) of Alberta: A community approach. M. S. Thesis, Dept. of Zoology, Univ. Alberta, Edmonton, Alberta. 111 pp.

Stock, T. M. and M. W. Barrett. 1983. Helminth parasites of the gastrointestinal tracts and lungs of moose (*Alces alces*) and wapiti (*Cervus elaphus*) from Cypress Hills, Alberta, Canada. Proc. Helminthol. Soc. Wash. 50: 246–251.

Stockle, A. W., G. L. Doster and W. R. Davidson. 1978. Endogenous fat as indicator of physical condition of south-eastern white-tailed deer. Proc. Southeast. Assoc. Fish and Wildl. Agen. 32: 269–279.

Stockstad, D. S., M. S. Morris and E. C. Lory. 1953. Chemical characteristics of natural licks used by big game animals in western Montana. Trans. N. Amer. Wildl. Conf. 18: 247–258.

Stoddart, L. A. and A. D. Smith. 1955. Range management. McGraw-Hill Book Co., New York. 433 pp.

Stoddart, L. A., A. D. Smith and T. W. Box. 1975. Range management. McGraw-Hill Book Co., New York. 532 pp.

Stoenner, H. G. 1969. Epidemiological studies and evaluation of diagnostic tests. Pages 8–11 in Symposium on Leptospirosis. Oregon Vet. Med. Assoc., Salem.

Stone, J. L. 1971. Winter movements and distribution of moose in upper Rock Creek drainage, Granite County, Montana. Unpubl. M.S. Thesis, Univ. Montana, Missoula. 80 pp.

Stone, W. 1908. The mammals of New Jersey. New Jersey State Mus. Ann. Rept. 1907, Part 2: 33–110.

Stopp, M. P. 1985. An archaeological examination of the Baumann site: A 15th-century settlement in Simcoe County, Ontario. Ontario Archaeol. 43: 3–29.

Stothers, D. M. 1977. The Princess Point Complex. Mercury 58, Ottawa. pp.

Stoutenburgh, J. L. 1960. Dictionary of the American Indian. Philosophical Library, Inc., New York. 462 pp.

Straley, J. H. 1968. Population analysis of ear-tagged elk. Proc. W. Assoc. State Game and Fish Commiss. 48: 152–160.

Strandgaard, H. and V. Simonsen. 1993. Genetic differentiation in populations of red deer, *Cervus elaphus,* in Denmark. Hereditas 119(2): 171–177.

Striby, K. D., C. L. Wambolt, R. G. Kelsy and K. M. Havstad. 1987. Crude terpenoid influence on in vitro digestibility of sagebrush. J. Range Manage. 40: 244–248.

Strickland, M. D. and K. Diem. 1975. The impact of snow on mule deer. Pages *in* D. Knight, ed., Final report, Medicine Bow Ecology Project. Univ. Wyoming, Laramie. 380 pp.

Strickland, R. K., R. R. Gerrish, J. L. Hourrigan and G O. Schubert. 1976. Ticks of veterinary importance. APHIS, USDA. Ag. Handbook No. 485. USDA, Washington, D.C. 122 pp.

Strickler, G. S. 1959. Use of the densiometer to estimate density of forest canopy on permanent sample plots. Res. Note PNW–180. USDA For. Serv., Portland, Oregon. 5 pp.

Strohmeyer, D. C. and J. M. Peek. 1996. Wapiti home range and movement patterns in a sagebrush desert. Northwest Science 70(2): 79–87.

Stromberg, P. C. and W. F. Fisher. 1986. Dermatopathology and immunity in experimental *Psoroptes ovis* (Acari: Psoroptidae) infestation of native and previously exposed Hereford cattle. Am. J. Vet. Res. 47: 1,551–1,560.

Stromberg, P. C. and F. S. Guillot. 1989. Pathogenesis of psoroptic scabies in Hereford heifer calves. Am. J. Vet. Res. 50: 594–601.

Strong, P. T. 1979. Santa Ana Pueblo. Pages 398–406 *in* A. Ortiz, ed., Southwest. Handbook of North American Indians. Vol. 9. Smithsonian Instit., Washington, D.C. 701 pp.

Strong, W. D. 1933. The Plains cultural area in the light of archaeology. Amer. Archaeol. 35: 271–287.

Strong, W. E. 1876. A trip to the Yellowstone National Park in July, August and September 1875. Privately printed, Washington, D.C. 143 pp.

Struhsaker, H. T. 1967. Behavior of elk (*Cervus canadensis*) during the rut. Zeitschrift fur Tierpsycholigie. 24: 80–114.

Stuart, A. J. 1982. Pleistocene vertebrates in the British Isles. Longman, London, U.K.

Stubbe, C. 1972. Die Bedeutung von Bastgeweihen fuer die Jagdwirtschaft Sibiriens. Beitrage zur Jagd- und Wildforschung 8: 75–87.

Stubbe, C. and H. Passarge. 1979. Rehwild. Verlag Neumann-Neudamm, Berlin. 432 pp.

Stubblefield, S. S., R. J. Warren and B. R. Murphy. 1986. Hybridization of free-ranging white-tailed and mule deer in Texas. J. Wildl. Manage. 50(4): 688–690.

Stumpff, C. D. 1982. Epidemiologic study of an outbreak of bovine TB in confined elk herds. Proc. U.S. Animal Health Assoc. 86: 524–527.

Stumpff, C. D. 1992. Epidemiology of an outbreak of bovine tuberculosis in confined elk herds. Pages 31–32 *in* M. A. Essey, ed., Bovine tuberculosis in Cervidae: Proc. of a Symposium. Misc. Publ. No. 1,506. USDA Anim. and Plant Health Inspect. Serv., Denver, Colorado. 71 pp.

Stussy, R. J. 1993. The effects of forage improvement practices on Roosevelt elk in the Oregon Coast range. M.S. Thesis, Oregon State Univ., Corvallis 77 pp.

Stussy, R. J., W. D. Edge and T. A. O'Neil. 1994. Survival of resident and translocated female elk in the Cascade Mountains of Oregon. Wildl. Soc. Bull. 22: 242–247.

Stussy, R. J., S. L. Findholt, B. K. Johnson, J. H. Noyes and B. L. Dick. 2000. Selenium levels and productivity in three Oregon elk herds. Northwest Science 74: 97-101.

Sugden, L. G. 1961. The California bighorn in British Columbia, with particular reference to the Churn Creek herd. British Columbia Dept. Recreation and Conserv., Victoria. 58 pp.

Sukamar, R. and M. Gadgill. 1988. Male–female differences in foraging on crops by Asian elephants. Animal Behavior 36: 1,233–1,235.

Sundberg, J. P. and W. D. Lancaster. 1988. Deer papillomaviruses. Pages 279–291 *in* G. Darai, ed., Virus disease in laboratory and captive animals. Kluwer Academic Publishers, New York. 568 pp.

Sura, G. 1967. Desert elk. Wyoming Wildlife 31(4): 10–17.

Suttie, J. M. 1980. Influence of nutrition on growth and sexual maturation of captive red deer stags. Proc. Int. Reindeer/Caribou Symp. 2: 341–349.

———. 1990. Experimental manipulation of the neuronal control of antler growth. Pages 359–370 *in* G. A. Bubenik and A. B. Bubenik, eds., Horns, pronghorns and antlers. Springer Verlag, New York.

Suttie, J. M. and W. J. Hamilton. 1983. The effect of winter nutrition on growth of young Scottish red deer stags (*Cervus elaphus*). Brit. J. Nutr. 201: 153–159.

Suttie, J. M. and P. F. Fennessy. 1985. Regrowth of amputated velvet antlers with and without innervation. J. Exp. Zool. 234: 359–366.

———. 1992. Recent advances in the physiological control of velvet antler growth. Pages 471–486 *in* R. Brown, ed., The biology of deer. Springer Verlag Inc., New York. 596 pp.

Suttie, J. M. and J. R. Webster. 1995. Extreme seasonal growth in Arctic deer: Comparisons and control mechanisms. Amer. Zool. 35: 215–221.

Suttie, J. M., E. D. Goodall, K. Pennie and R. N. B. Kay. 1983. Winter food restriction and summer compensation in red deer stags (*Cervus elaphus*). Br. J. Nutr. 50: 737–747.

Suttie, J. M., G. A. Lincoln and R. N. B. Kay. 1984. Endocrine control of antler growth in red deer stags. J. Reprod. Fert. 71: 7–15.

Suttie, J. M., P. F. Fennessy, C. G. Mackintiosh, I. D. Corson, R. Christie and S. W. Heap. 1985. Sequential cranial angiography of young red deer stags. Pages 263–268 *in* P. F. Fennessy and K. R. Drew, eds., Biology of deer production. Bull. 22. Roy. Soc. of New Zealand, Wellington. 482 pp.

Suttie, J. M., P. F. Fennessy, B. A. VeenVliet, R. P. Littlejohn, M. W. Fisher, I. D. Corson and R. E. Labes. 1987. Energy nutrition of young red deer (*Cervus elaphus*) hinds and a comparison with young stags. Proc. NZ Soc. Anim. Prod. 47: 111–114.

Suttie, J. M., P. F. Fennessy, I. D. Corson, F. J. Laas, S. F. Crosbie, J. H. Butler and P. D. Gluckman. 1989. Pulsatile growth hormone, insulin-like growth factors and antler development in red deer (*Cervus elaphus scoticus*) stags. J. Endocrin. 121: 351–360.

Suttie, J. M., R. G. White, B. H. Breier and P. D. Gluckman. 1991a. Photoperiod-associated changes in insulin-like growth factor-1 in reindeer. Endocrinology 129: 679–682.

Suttie, J. M., P. F. Fennessy, S. F. Crosbie, I. D. Corson, F. J. Laas, H. J. Elgar and K. R. Lapwood. 1991b. Temporal changes in LH and testosterone and thier relationship with the first antler in red deer (*Cervus elaphus*) stags from 3 to 15 months of age. J. Endocrin. 131: 467–474.

Suttie, J. M., B. H. Breier, P. D. Gluckman, R. P. Littlejohn and J. R. Webster. 1992. Effects of mclatonin implants on insulin-like growth factor 1 in male red deer (*Cervus elaphus*). Gen. Comp. Endocrin. 111–119.

Suttie, J. M., C. Li, P. W. Sheard, I. D. Corson and K. A. Waldrup. 1995. Effects of unilateral cranial sympathectomy either alone or with sensory nerve sectioning on pedicle growth in red deer (*Cervus elaphus*). J. Exp. Zool. 271: 131–138.

Suttles, W., ed. 1990. Northwest coast. Vol. 7. Handbook of North American Indians. Smithsonian Instit. Press, Washington, D.C. 777 pp.

Swales, W. E. 1935. The life cycle of *Fascioloides magna* (Bass), 1875), the large liver fluke of ruminants, in Canada, with observations on the bionomics of the larval stages and the intermediate hosts, pathology of *Fasciolodiasis magna* and control measures. Can. J. Res. 12: 177–215.

Swales, W. E. 1936. Further studies on *Fascioloides magna* (Bassi, 1875) Ward, 1917, as a parasite of ruminants. Can. J. Res. 14 (D): 83–95.

Swank, W. G. 1962. Manipulation of hunting regulations as a management measure. J. Forestry 60(1): 30–32.

Swanson, D. O. 1970. Roosevelt elk–forest relationships in the Douglas-fir region of the southern Oregon coast range. Ph.D. Thesis, Univ. Michigan, Ann Arbor. 173 pp.

Swanson, E. B. Unpublished. The history of Minnesota game, 1850–1900. 1940 Ph.D. Thesis, Univ. Minnesota, St. Paul. 294 pp.

Swanson, G. A., J. T. Shields, W. H. Olson, E. Decker, R. B. Held, J. A. Strayer, R. Hill, G. Hunter and G. Perdue. 1969. Fish and wildlife resources on the public lands. Vol. 1. U.S. Dept. Commerce Clearinghouse for Fed. Sci. and Tech. Info., Springfield, Virginia. 213 pp.

Sweatman, G. K. 1958. On the life history and validity of the species in *Psoroptes*, a genus of mange mites. Can. J. Zool. 36: 905–929.

Sweatman, G. K. and T. C. Henshall. 1962. The comparative biology and morphology of *Taenia ovis* and *Taenia krabbei*, with observations on the development of *T. ovis* in domestic sheep. Can. J. Zool. 40: 1,287–1,311.

Sweatmen, G. K. 1958. On the life history and validity of the species in *Psoroptes*, a genus of mange mites. Can. J. Zool. 36: 905–929.

Sweeney, J. M. 1975. Elk movements and calving as related to snow cover. Ph.D. Thesis, Colorado State Univ., Fort Collins. 95 pp.

Sweeney, J. M. and H. W. Steinhoff. 1976. Elk movements and calving as related to snow cover. Pages 415–436 in H. W. Steinhoff and J. D. Ives, eds., Ecological impacts of snowpack augmentation in the San Juan Mountains, Colorado. Colorado State Univ., Fort Collins. 489 pp.

Sweeney, R. W., R. H. Whitlock and C. L. Buckley. 1995. Evaluation of a commercial enzyme-linked immunosorbent assay for the diagnosis of paratuberculosis in dairy cattle. J. Vet. Diagn. Invest. 7: 488–293.

Swenson, M. J., ed. 1977. Duke's physiology of domestic animals. 9th ed. Cornell Univ. Press, Ithaca, New York. 914 pp.

Swift, D. M., J. E. Ellis and N. T. Hobbs. 1980. Nitrogen and energy requirements of North American cervids in winter—a simulation study. Pages 244–251 in E. Reimers, E. Gaare and S. Skjenneberg, eds., Proc. 2nd Int. Reindeer/Carbou Symp. Ro/ros, Norway. Direktoratet for vilt og ferskvannsfisk, Trondheim.

Swift, L. W. 1945. A partial history of the elk herds of Colorado. J. Mammal. 26(2): 114–119.

Synder, R. 1969. Forage competition between cattle and elk in the Gird Creek drainage of western Montana. M.S. Thesis, Univ. Montana, Missoula. 86 pp.

Szaniawski, A. 1966. Osteologische Untersuchungen uber den Rothirsch in Polen. Acta Ther. 10(6): 195–267.

Széchényi, Count G. 1910. Hungary. Pages 47–74 in F. G. Aflalo, ed., Sport in Europe. E. P. Dutton and Co., New York. 483 pp.

Taber, R. D. 1976. Seasonal landscape use by elk in the managed forests of the Cedar River Drainage, western Washington. Final Rept. Washington Dept. Game Proj. FS-PNW-Grant #14, Olympia. 146 pp.

Taber, R. D. and K. J. Raedeke. 1987. The management of *Cervus* in North America. pp. 568–577 in C. M. Wemmer, ed., Biology and management of the Cervidae (conference at National Zool. Park, Front Royal, Virginia Aug. 1–5, 1982) Smithsonian Instit. Press, Washington, D.C. 577 pp.

Taber, R. D., K. J. Raedeke and D. A. McCaughran. 1982. Population characteristics. Pages 279–298 in J. W. Thomas and D. E. Toweill, eds., Elk of North America: Ecology and management. Stackpole Books, Inc., Harrisburg, Pennsylvania. 698 pp.

Tanner, D. 1965. The Big Wood River elk herd. Idaho Wildl. Rev. 18(3): 3–6.

Tate, M. L., H. C. Manly and K.M. McEwan. 1992. Genetic polymorphism of C3c in red deer and wapiti (*Cervus elaphus* subsp.). Animal Genetics 23(suppl. 1): 33

Tate, M.L., H.D. Mathias, P. F. Fennessy, K. G. Dodds, J. M. Penty and D. F. Hill. 1995. A new gene mapping resource: Interspecies hybrids between Père David's deer (*Elaphurus davidianus*) and red deer (*Cervus elaphus*). Genetics 139(3): 1,383–1,391.

Taverner, P.A. 1920. The test of subspecies. J. Mammal. 1(3): 124–127.

Taylor, C. 1957. The Plains Indian shirt. Amer. Indian Hobbyist 3(7&8): 61–65.

———. 1961. Plains Indians' leggings. English Westerner's Brand Book 3(2): 2–8.

———. 1975. The warriors of the Plains. The Hamlyn Publishing Group Ltd., New York. 144 pp.

Taylor, M. W. 1977. A comparison of three edge indexes. Wildl. Soc. Bull. 5: 192–193.

Taylor, W. P. and W. T. Shawl 1927. Mammals and birds of Mount Rainier National Park. U.S. Nat. Park Serv., Washington, D.C. 249 pp.

Taylor-Page, F. J. 1957. Field guide to British deer. Wyman and Sons Ltd, London. 80 pp.

Teer, J. G. 1993. Commercial utilization of wildlife: Has its time come? Pages 73–83 in A. W. L. Hawley, ed., Commercialization and wildlife management: Dancing with the devil. Krieger Publ. Co., Malabar, Florida. 124 pp.

Teit, J. H. 1928. The Middle Columbia Salish. Univ. Washington Publ. in Anthropol. 2: 83-128.

Telfer, E. S. and J. P. Kelsall. 1984. Adaptation of some large North American mammals for survival in snow. Ecology 65: 1,828–1,834.

Telfer, E. S. and A. Cairns. 1979. Bison–wapiti interrelationships in Elk Island National Park, Alberta. Pages 114–121 In M. S. Boyce and L. D. Hayden-Wing, eds., North American elk: ecology, behavior and management. Univ. Wyoming, Laramie. 294 pp.

Telfer, E. S. and G. W. Scotter. 1975. Potential for game ranching in boreal aspen forests of western Canada. J. Range Manage. 28(3): 172–180.

Telfer, E. S. and J. P. Kelsall. 1971. Morphological parameters for mammal locomotion in snow. Proc. 51st Annul Meet. Amer. Soc. Mammal., Univ. British Columbia, Vancouver. 12 pp.

———. 1979. Studies on morphological parameters affecting ungulate locomotion in snow. Can. J. Zool. 57: 2,153–2,159.

Temple, S. A. 1987. Do predators always capture substandard individuals disproportionately from pre populations? Ecol. 68: 669–674.

Tempelton, A. R. 1986. Coadaptation and outbreeding depression. Pages 105–121 in M. E. Soulé, ed., Conservation biology: The science of scarcity and diversity. Sinauer Associates, Inc., Sunderland, Massachusetts. 584 pp.

Tessaro, S. V. 1986. The existing and potential importance of brucellosis and tuberculosis in Canadian wildlife: A review. Can. Vet. J. 27: 119–124.

———. 1992. Bovine tuberculosis and brucellosis in animals, including man. Alberta 3: 207–224.

Tessaro, S. V., P. S. Carman and D. Deregt. 1999. Viremia and virus shedding in elk with type 1 and virulent type 2 bovine viral diarrhea virus. J. Wildl. Dis. 35: 671–677.

Testa,, J. W. and G. P. Adams. 1998. Body condition and adjustments to reproductive effort in female moose (Alces alces). J. Mammal. 79: 1,345-1,354.

Tester, J. R. and D. B. Siniff. 1965. Aspects of animal movements and home range data obtained by telemetry. Trans. N. Amer. Wildl. and Natur. Resour. Conf. 30: 379–392.

Texas Game, Fish and Oyster Commission. 1945. Principal game birds and mammals of Texas. Texas Game, Fish and Oyster Commiss., Austin. 149 pp.

Thelemann, W. and A. Hennig. 1973. Investigations with labeled urea on lactating ruminants. 3. Utilization of urea-nitrogen. Archiv. f. Thiernahrung 23(3): 175.

Thelen, T. H. 1991. Effects of harvest on antlers of simulated populations of elk. J. Wildl. Manage. 55: 243–249.

Thiessen, J. L. 1975. Big game aerial surveys. Idaho Dept. Fish and Game, Boise. 91 pp.

———. 1976. Some elk–logging relationships in southern Idaho. Proc. Elk-Logging-Roads Symp., Univ. Idaho, Moscow. 142 pp.

Thiry, E., M. Vercouter, J. Dubuisson, J. Barrat, C. Sepulchre, C. Gerardy, C. Meersschaert, B. Collin, J. Blancou and P. P. Pastoret. 1988. Serological survey of herpesvirus infections in wild ruminants of France and Belgium. J. Wildl. Dis. 24: 268–273.

Thoen, C. O. 1992. Pathogenesis of *Mycobacterium bovis* infection. Pages 7–10 in M. A. Essey, ed., Bovine tuberculosis in Cervidae: Proc. of a symposium. Miscellaneous Publication No. 1506. USDA, Animal and Plant Health Inspection Service, Denver, Colorado. 71 pp.

Thoen, C. O. and J. Haagsma. 1996. Molecular techniques in the diagnosis and control of paratuberculosis in cattle. J. Am. Vet. Med. Assoc. 209: 734–737.

Thoen, C. O. and E. M. Himes. 1986. Mycobacterium. Pages 26–37 in C. L. Gyles and C. O. Thoen, eds., Pathogenesis of bacterial infections in animals. Iowa State Univ. Press, Ames. 227 pp.

Thoen, C. O., W. J. Quinn, L. D. Miller, L. L. Stackhouse, B. F. Newcomb and J. M. Ferrell. 1992. Mycobacterium bovis infection in North American elk (Cervus elaphus). J. Vet. Diag. Investig. 4: 423–427.

Thomas, D. C. 1982. The relationship between fertility and fat reserves of Peary caribou. Can. J. Zool. 60: 597–602.

Thomas, D. and K. Ronnefeldt. 1976. People of the first man. E. P. Dutton & Co. Inc., New York. 256 pp.

Thomas, J. W. 1979. Preface. Page 6 in J. W. Thomas, ed., Wildlife habitats in managed forests: The Blue Mountains of Oregon and Washington. Ag. Handbook No. 553, USDA For. Serv., Portland, Oregon. 512 pp.

———. 1986. Elk management—new days and new ways. Pages 309–314 in D. L. Eastman, ed., Proc. 1986 West. States and Provinces Elk Workshop. Oregon Dept. Fish and Wildl., Portland. 315 pp.

———. 1991. Elk vulnerability—a conference perspective. Pages 318–319 in A. G. Christensen, L. J. Lyon and T. N. Lonner, compilers, Proc. Elk Vulnerability Symp., Montana State Univ., Bozeman. 330 pp.

———. 1996 Stability and predictability in federal forest management, some thoughts from the chief. Public Land and Res. Law Rev. 17:9–23.

———. 1997. On the yellow brick road to the 21st century. Bugle 14(2): 80–83.

———. 1999. From the center—the Boone and Crockett Club's role in conservation, then and now. Fair Chase 14(3):14–17.

———. 2000a. High stakes poker with the joker wild: Fire risks in roadless areas. Fair Chase 15(3):11–15.

———. 2000b. What now? From a former chief of the Forest Service. Pages 10–43 in R. A. Sedjo, ed., Forest Service: goals for the next century. Resour. for the Future, Washington, DC.

Thomas, J. W. and J. Burchfield. 1999. Comments on the "The Religion of Forestry: Scientific Forestry." J. Fore. 97(11):10–13.

Thomas, J. W. and R. M. DeGraaf. 1973. Non-game research in megalopolis: The Forest Service program. Gen. Tech. Rept. NE–4. USDA For. Serv., Upper Darby, Pennsylvania. 12 pp.

Thomas, J. W. and D. E. Toweill., eds. 1982. Elk of North America: Ecology and management. Stackpole Books, Inc., Harrisburg, Pennsylvania. 698 pp.

Thomas, J.W. and D.E. Toweill. 1998. The future of hunting. Pages 3–13 in C. R. Byers, ed., Boone and Crockett Club's 23rd Big Game Awards 1995–1997. 566 pp.

Thomas, J. W., J. C. Pack, W. M. Healy, J. D. Gill and H. R. Sanderson. 1973. Territoriality among hunters—the policy implications. Trans. N. Amer. Wildl. and Natur. Resour. Conf. 38: 274–280.

Thomas, J. W., R. J. Miller, H. Black, J. E. Rodiek and C. Maser. 1976. Guidelines for maintaining and enhancing wildlife habitat in forest management in the Blue Mountains of Oregon and Washington. Trans. N. Amer. Wildl. and Natur. Resour. Conf. 41: 452–476.

Thomas, J. W., C. Maser and J. E. Rodiek. 1979a. Edges. Pages 48–59 in J. W. Thomas, ed., Wildlife habitats in managed forests: The Blue Mountains of Oregon and Washington. Handbook No. 533, USDA, Portland, Oregon. 512 pp.

Thomas, J. W., H. Black, Jr., R. J. Scherzinger and R. J. Pederson. 1979b. Deer and elk. Pages 104–127 in J. W. Thomas, ed., Wildlife habitats in

managed forests: The Blue Mountains of Oregon and Washington. Handbook No. 533. USDA, Portland, Oregon. 512 pp.

Thomas, J. W., D. A. Leckenby, L. J. Erickson, S. R. Thomas, D. L. Isaacson and R. Murray. 1986. Wildlife habitat by design: national forests in the Blue mountains of Oregon and Washington. Trans. N. Amer. Wildl. and Natur. Resour. Conf. 51: 203–214.

Thomas, J. W., D. A. Leckenby, M. Henjum, R. J. Pedersen and L. D. Bryant. 1988a. Habitat-effectiveness index for elk on Blue Mountain winter ranges. U.S. For. Serv., Gen. Tech. Rept. PNW-GTR–218. 28 pp.

Thomas, J. W., D. A. Leckenby, L. J. Lyon, L. L. Hicks and C. L. Marcum. 1988b. Integrated management of timber–elk–cattle: interior forests of western North America. U.S. For. Serv., Gen. Tech. Rept. PNW-GTR–225. 12 pp.

Thomas, J. W., E. D. Forsman, J. D. Lint, E. C. Meslow, B. R. Noon and J. Verner. 1990. A conservation strategy for the Northern Spotted Owl. USDA For. Serv., USDI Bureau of Land Managment, USDI Fish and Wildlife Service and USDI National Park Service. Portland, Oregon. 427 pp.

Thomas, R. D. 1975. The status of Rocky Mountain elk in Kern County, 1974. Calif. Fish and Game 61(4): 239–241.

Thompkins, J. L., J. N. Stuht and J.E. Knight. 1977. Meningeal worm in deer and wapiti of Canada Creek Ranch. Wildl. Div. Rept. No. 2,775. Michigan Dept. Natur. Resour. 3 pp.

Thompson, D. 1916. David Thompson's narrative of his explorations in western America, 1784–1812. J. B. Tyrell, ed.. The Champlain Soc., Toronto, Ontario. 582 pp.

Thompson, D. A. (transl.) 1910. Aristotle (384–322 BC) The works of Aristotle. Volume IV. Historia Animalium. translated by D. A. Thompson, 1910. Oxford, at the Clarendon Press.

Thompson, D. L. and R. Willer. 1998. Report of the U.S. AHA Committee on tuberculosis. United States Animal Health Assoc. 102: 698–712.

Thompson, G. A. 1964. Fire in wilderness areas. Proc. Tall Timbers Fire Ecol. Conf. 3: 105–110.

Thompson, M. J. and R. E. Henderson. 1999. Elk habituation as a credibility challenge for wildlife professionals. Wildl. Soc. Bull. 26: 477–483.

Thompson, M. J., R. E. Henderson and R. Ortegon 1991. Do hunters support road closures to address elk security problems? Pages 275–279 in A. G. Christensen, L. J. Lyon, T. N. Lonner, compilers, Proc. Elk Vulnerability Symp., Montana State Univ., Bozeman. 330 pp.

Thompson, S. K. and G. F. Sever. 1996. Adaptive sampling. John Wiley and Sons, New York. 265 pp.

Thompson, W. K. 1951. The value of checking stations in wildlife research. Proc. West. Assoc. State Game and Fish Commiss. 31: 138–141.

Thompson, Z. 1853. Natural history of Vermont. Charles E. Tuttle Co., Rutland, Vermont. 286 pp.

Thorne, E. T. 1982a. Bluetongue. Pages 5–9 in E. T. Thorne, N. Kingston, W. R. Jolley and R. C. Bergstrom, eds., Diseases of wildlife in Wyoming, 2nd ed. Wyoming Game and Fish Dept., Cheyenne. 353 pp.

———. 1982b. Brucellosis. Pages 54–63 in E. T. Thorne, N. Kingston, W. R. Jolley and R. C. Bergstrom, eds., Diseases of wildlife in Wyoming, 2nd ed. Wyoming Game and Fish Dept., Cheyenne. 353 pp.

———. 1982c. Epizootic hemorrhagic disease. Pages 9–10 in E. T. Thorne, N. Kingston, W. R. Jolley and R. C. Bergstrom, eds., Diseases of wildlife in Wyoming, 2nd ed. Wyoming Game and Fish Dept., Cheyenne. 353 pp.

———. 1982d. Miscellaneous bacteria. Pages 29–45 in E. T. Thorne, N. Kingston, W. R. Jolley and R. C. Bergstrom, eds., Diseases of wildlife in Wyoming, 2nd ed. Wyoming Game and Fish Dept., Cheyenne. 353 pp.

———. 1982e. Pasteurellosis. Pages 72–77 in E. T. Thorne, N. Kingston,

W. R. Jolley and R. C. Bergstrom, eds., Diseases of wildlife in Wyoming, 2nd ed. Wyoming Game and Fish Dept., Cheyenne. 353 pp.

————. 1982f. Pseudotuberculosis (Yersiniosis). Pages 65–67 *in* E. T. Thorne, N. Kingston, W. R. Jolley and R. C. Bergstrom, eds., Diseases of wildlife in Wyoming, 2nd ed. Wyoming Game and Fish Dept., Cheyenne. 353 pp.

————. 1992. A plague on your elk. Wyoming Wildl. 55: 20–29.

Thorne, E. T. and G. Butler. 1976. Comparison of pelleted, cubed and baled alfalfa hay as winter feed for elk. Tech. Rept. 6. Wyoming Game and Fish Dept., Cheyenne. 38 pp.

Thorne, E. T. and J. D. Herriges, Jr. 1992. Brucellosis, wildlife and conflicts in the Greater Yellowstone Area. Trans. N. Amer. Wildl. and Natur. Resour. Conf. 57: 453–465.

Thorne, E. T. and J. K. Morton. 1975a. The incidence and importance of brucellosis in elk in northwestern Wyoming. Job Compl. Rept., Fed. Aid in Wildl. Restor., Proj. FW–3–R–21. Wyoming Game and Fish Commiss., Laramie.

————. 1975b. Brucellosis transmission between elk and domestic cattle. Job Compl. Rept., Fed Aid in Wildl. Restor., Proj. FW–3–R–21. Wyoming Game and Fish Commiss., Laramie.

Thorne, E. T., R. E. Dean and W. G. Hepworth. 1976. Nutrition during gestation in relation to successful reproduction in elk. J. Wildl. Manage. 40: 330–335.

Thorne, E. T., J. K. Morton and G. M. Thomas. 1978a. Brucellosis in elk. I. Serologic and bacteriologic survey in Wyoming. J. Wildl. Dis. 14: 74–81.

Thorne, E. T., J. K. Morton, F. M. Blunt and H. A. Dawson. 1978b. Brucellosis in elk. II. Clinical effects and means of transmission as determined through artificial infections. J. Wildl. Dis. 14: 280–291.

Thorne, E. T, J. K. Morton and W. C. Ray. 1979. Brucellosis, its effect and impact on elk in western Wyoming. Pages 212–220 *in* M. S. Boyce and L. D. Hayden-Wing, eds., North American elk: Ecology, behavior and management. Univ. Wyoming, Laramie. 294 pp.

Thorne, E. T., T. J. Walthall and H. A. Dawson. 1981. Vaccination of elk with strain 19 *Brucella abortus*. Proc. U.S. Anim. Health Assoc. 85: 359–374.

Thorne, E. T., J. D. Herriges and A. D. Reese. 1991a. Bovine brucellosis in elk: Conflicts in the Greater Yellowstone Area. Pages 296–303 *in* A. G. Christensen, L. J. Lyon and T. N. Lonner, compilers, Proc. Elk Vulnerability Symp., Montana State Univ., Bozeman. 330 pp.

Thorne, E. T., M. Meagher and R. Hillman. 1991b. Brucellosis in free-ranging bison: Three perspectives. Pages 275–287 *in* R. B. Keiter and M. S. Boyce, eds., The Greater Yellowstone ecosystem. Yale Univ. Press, New Haven, Connecticut. 428 pp.

Thorne, E. T., N. Kingston, W. R. Jolley and R. C. Bergstrom, eds. 1982. Diseases of wildlife in Wyoming. 2nd ed. Wyoming Game and Fish Dept., Cheyenne. 353 pp.

Thorne, E. T., E. S. Williams, T. R. Spraker, W. Helms and T. Segerstrom. 1988. Bluetongue in free-ranging pronghorn (*Antilocapra americana*) in Wyoming: 1976 and 1984. J. Wildl. Dis. 24: 113–119.

Thorne, E. T., M. W. Miller, D. L. Hunter and E. S. Williams. 1992. Wildlife management agency concerns about bovine tuberculosis in captive Cervidae. Pages 47–51 *in* M. A. Essey, ed., Bovine tuberculosis in Cervidae: Proc. of a symposium. Misc. Publ. No. 1,506. USDA Anim. Plant Health Inspect. Serv., Denver, Colorado. 71 pp.

Thorne, E. T, S. G. Smith, K. Aune, D. Hunter and T. J. Roffe. 1997. Brucellosis: The disease in elk. Pages 33–44 *in* E. T. Thorne, M. S. Boyce, P. Nicoletti and T. J. Kreeger, eds., Brucellosis, bison, elk and cattle in the Greater Yellowstone area: Defining the problem, exploring solutions. Wyoming Game and Fish Dept. and Greater Yellowstone Interagency Brucellosis Committee, Cheyenne. 219 pp.

Thorne, T. and G. Butler. 1976. Comparison of pelleted, cubed, and baled alfalfa hay as winter feed for elk. Wildl. Tech. Rept. No. 6. Wyoming Game and Fish Dept., Laramie. 38 pp.

Thornton, G. C., III. Unpublished. 1972 report on gun buying behavior and motivation research of Colorado big-game hunters. On file at Psychology Dept., Colorado State Univ., Fort Collins. 28 pp. Mimeo.

Thurston, H. and D. Attwater, eds. 1956. Butler's lives of the saints. Vol. IV. Christian Classics, Inc., Westminster, Maryland.

Thwaites, R. G., ed. 1966. Early western travels—1748–1846. Vol. 7. AMS Press, Inc., New York. 332 pp.

————, ed. 1969. Original journals of the Lewis and Clark expedition, 1804–1806. 8 vols. Arno Press, New York.

Tilden, F. 1964. Following the frontier with F. Jay Haynes. Alfred A. Knopf, New York. 414 pp.

Tileston, J. V. 1962. Big game research projects, 1937–1957, in Colorado. Colorado Game and Fish Dept., Denver, Tech. Bull. 9: 44–45.

Timoney, J. F., J. H. Gillespie, F. W. Scott and J. E. Barlough. 1988. Hagan and Bruner's Microbiology and Infectious Diseases of Domestic Animals. Comstock Publishing Associates, Ithaca, New York. 951 pp.

Todd, J. W. and R. M. Hansen. 1973. Plant fragments in the feces of bighorns as indicators of food habits. J. Wildl. Manage. 37(3): 363–366.

Toine, P. 1854. Pioneer Life; or thirty years a hunter. Aurand Press, Harrisburg, Pennsylvania. 173 pp.

Topinski, P. 1975. Abnormal antler cycle in deer as a result of stress-inducing factors. Acta Theriol. 20(15–23): 267–279.

Torbit, S. C., L. H. Carpenter, D.M. Swift and A. W. Alldredge. 1985a. Differential loss of fat and protein by mule deer during winter. J. Wildl. Manage. 49: 80–85.

Torbit, S. C., L. H. Carpenter, D. M. Swift and A. W. Alldredge. 1985b. Mule deer body composition—a comparison of methods. J. Wildl. Manage. 49: 86–91.

Torrence, G. 1994. The American Indian parfleche: A tradition of abstract painting. Univ. Washington Press, Seattle. 272 pp.

Torrey, B. 1906. Friends on the shelf. 2 vols. Houghton, Mifflin and Co., Boston, Massachusetts.

Toutain, P. L. and A. J. Webster. 1975. Equilibre energetique au cours du sommeil chez les ruminants. C. R. Acad. Sc. Paris 281: 1,605–1,608.

Toweill, D. E. 1999. Feeding wintering elk: A report to the Clearwater Elk Recovery Team (CERT). Idaho Dept. Fish and Game, Boise. 11 pp.

Toweill, D. E. and R. G. Anthony 1988. Coyote foods in a coniferous forest in Oregon. J. Wildl. Manage. 52: 507–512.

Toweill, D. E. and E. C. Meslow. 1977. Food habits of cougars in Oregon. J. Wildl. Manage. 41: 232–234.

Trainer, C. E. 1955. Progress reports on elk reproduction. Montana Coop. Wildl. Resour. Unit, Missoula. 15 pp.

————. 1969. Fertility study of Roosevelt elk. Job Compl. Rept., Fed. Aid in Wildl. Restor., Proj. W–59–R–6. Oregon Game Commiss., Portland. 25 pp.

————. 1971. The relationship of physical condition and fertility of female Roosevelt elk (*Cervus canadensis roosevelti*) in Oregon. M.S. Thesis, Oregon State Univ., Corvallis, Oregon. 93 pp.

Trainer, D. O. 1970. Bluetongue. Pages 55–59 *in* J. W. Davis, L. H. Karstad and D. O. Trainer, eds., Infectious diseases of wild mammals. Iowa State Univ. Press, Ames.

Trainer, D. O. and M. M. Jochim. 1969. Serologic evidence of bluetongue in wild ruminants of North America. Am. J. Vet. Res. 30: 2,007–2,011.

Trainer, D. O. and L. H. Karstad. 1970. Epizootic hemorrhagic disease. Pages 50–54 *in* J. W. Davis, L. H. Karstad and D. O. Trainer, eds., Infectious diseases of wild mammals. Iowa State Univ. Press, Ames. 421 pp.

Traylor, D. 1977. Bandelier: Excavation in the flood pool of Chochiti

Lake, New Mexico. Manuscript on file at the Southwest Cultural Resource Center, Santa Fe, New Mexico. 604 pp.

Trefethen, J. B. 1961. Crusade for wildlife: Highlights in conservation progress. Stackpole Co., Harrisburg, Pennsylvania. 377 pp.

———. 1975. An American crusade for wildlife. Winchester Press and the Boone and Crockett Club, New York. 409 pp.

Trense, W. 1989. The big game of the world. Verlag Paul Parey, Hamburg, Germany. 413 pp.

Trigger, B. G., ed. 1978. Northeast. Handbook of North American Indians. Vol. 15. Smithsonian Instit., Washington, D.C. 924 pp.

Trippensee, R. E. 1948. Wildlife management. Vol. 1. Upland game and general principles. McGraw-Hill Book Co., New York. 479 pp.

Trivers, R. L. and D. E. Willard. 1973. Natural selection of parental ability to vary the sex ratio of offspring. Science 179: 90–92.

Trout, L. C. and T. A. Leege. 1971. Are the northern Idaho elk herds doomed? Idaho Wildl. Rev. 24(3): 3–9.

Troyer, W. A. 1960. The Roosevelt elk on Afognak island, Alaska. J. Wildl. Manage. 24(1): 15–21.

Trudell, J. and R. G. White. 1981. The effect of forage structure and availability on food intake, biting rate, bite size and daily eating time of reindeer. J. Appl. Ecol. 18: 63–81.

True, W. F. 1883. A list of the vertebrate animals of South Carolina. South Carolina State Board Ag. Rept. 10: 209–216.

Tulee v. Washington, 315 U.S. 681, 62 S. Ct. 862, 86 L. Ed. 1115 (1942).

Tully, R. J. 1975. Costs and benefits of special seasons. Proc. West. Assoc. State Game and Fish Commiss. 55: 131–138.

Tully, R. J. 1976. Meeting future challenges in management of deer and elk hunting pressure. Proc. West. Assoc. State Game and Fish Commiss. 56: 328–341.

Tunnicliff, E. A. and H. Marsh. 1935. Bang's disease in bison and elk in the Yellowstone National Park and on the National Bison Range. J. Am. Vet. Med. Assoc. 86: 745–752.

Turbeville, G. 1576. The noble art of venerie or hunting. 1908 reprint. Clarendon Press. 250 pp.

Turner, M. G., Y. Wu, L. L. Wallace, W. H. Romme and A. Brenkert. 1994. Simulating winter interactions among ungulates, vegetation and fire in northern Yellowstone National Park. Ecol. Appl. 4: 472–496.

Turner, M. G., W. Yogang, W. H. Romme and L. L. Wallace. 1993. A landscape simulation model of winter foraging by large ungulates. Ecol. Model. 69: 163–184.

Turner, N. J. 1991. Burning mountain sides for better crops: Aboriginal landscape burning in British Columbia. Archaeol. in Montana. 32: 57–73.

Tyler, G. V., C. P. Hibler and A. K. Prestwood. 1980. Experimental infection of mule deer with *Parelaphostrongylus tenuis.* J. Wildl. Dis. 16: 533–540.

Tyrrell, J. B., ed. 1916. David Thompson's narrative of his explorations in western America, 1784–1812. Publ. No. 12. The Champlain Soc., Toronto, Ontario. 582 pp.

Ubelaker, D. H. 1988. North American Indian population size, A.D. 1500 to 1985. Amer. J. Phys. Anthropol. 77: 289–294.

Ueckermann, E. 1986. Die futterung des schalenwildes. Ernahrungsgrundlagen und anleitung fur die futterungstechnik in freier wildbahn und im gehege. Schriftenreihe der forschungsstelle fur jagdkunde und wildschadensverhutung des landes Nordrhein-Westfalen H.5. Parey, Hamburg, Berlin. 167 pp.

Ueckermann, E. 1987. Managing German red deer (*Cervus elaphus* L.) populations. Pages 505–516 in C. M. Wemmer, ed., Biology and management of the Cervidae. Smithsonian Instit. Press, Washington, D.C. 577 pp.

Ueckermann, E. 1990. Verlauf der winterfutterung des rotwildes in rheinland-pfalzischen forstamtern-Beziehung zu temperatur und schneetagen. Pages 26–36 und 172–179 in Wildforschungsstelle der landes Baden-Wurttemberg, ed., Futterung und asungsverbesserung fur reh- und rotwild. Schriftenreihe wildforschung in Baden-Wurttemberg. Vol. 1. Aulendorf.

Uexküll, J. V. 1921. Umwelt and Innenwelt der Tiere. 2. Aufl. Berlin 1937. Umweltforschung. Z. Tierpsychol. 1: 33–34.

Ullrey, D. E. 1983. Nutrition and antler development in white-tailed deer. Pages 49–59 in R. D. Brown, ed., Antler development in Cervidae. Caesar Kleberg Wildl. Res. Institute, Kingsville, Texas. 480 pp.

Ullrey, D. E., W. G. Youatt, H. E. Johnson, L. D. Fay and B. L. Bradley. 1967. Protein requirement of white-tailed deer fawns. J. Wildl. Manage. 31: 679–685.

Ullrey, D. E., W. G. Youatt, H. E. Johnson, L. D. Fay, B. L. Schoepke and W. T. Magee. 1970. Digestible and metabolizable energy requirements for winter maintenance of Michigan white-tailed does. J. Wildl. Manage. 34: 863–869

Ullrey, D. E., H. E. Johnson, W. G. Youatt, L. D. Fay, B. L. Schoepke and W. T. Magee. 1971. A basal diet for deer nutrition research. J. Wildl Manage 35: 57–62.

Underhill, R. 1944. Indians of the Pacific Northwest. Educational Div., U.S. Off. Indian Affairs, Washington, D.C. 232 pp.

U.S. Animal Health Association, Leptospirosis Committee. 1975. Annual report, Leptospirosis Committee. Proc. U.S. Anim. Health Assoc. 79: 126–145.

U.S. Army Corps of Engineers. 1956. Snow hydrology: Summary report of the snow investigation. North Pac. Div., U.S. Army Corps of Engineers, Portland, Oregon. 437 pp.

U.S. Bureau of Land Management. 1979. The Tule elk. Third Annu. Rept. to Congress. California State Dir., U.S. Bur. Land Manage., Sacramento. 32 pp.

———. 1980. The Tule elk in California. Fourth Annu. Rept. to Congress. U.S. Bur. Land Manage., Washington, D.C. 50 pp.

U.S. Department of Agriculture. 1958. Techniques and methods of measuring understory vegetation. Proc. Symp. at Tifton, Georgia, USDA For. Serv., Washington, D.C. 174 pp.

———. 1962. Range research methods. Misc. Publ. No. 940. USDA For. Serv., Washington, D.C. 172 pp.

———. 1967. National handbook for range and related grazing lands. USDA Soil Conserv. Serv., Washington, D.C. 54 pp.

———. 1970. Range and wildlife habitat evaluation: a research symposium. Misc. Publ. 1147. U.S. Forest Service, Washington, D.C. 220 pp.

———. 1976. Leptospirosis of domestic animals. Ag. Info. Bull. 394. USDA Ag. Resour. Serv., Washington, D.C. 9 pp.

———. 1994. Land areas of the National Forest System. FS–383. USDA For. Serv., Washington, D.C. 121 pp.

U.S. Animal and Plant Health Inspection Service, Veterinary Services. 1992. Brucellosis eradication uniform methods and rules. U.S. Animal and Plant Health Inspection Service, Vet. Serv., Washington, D.C. 100 pp.

U.S. Forest Service. 1972. Forest statistics for the United States, by state and region, 1970. U.S. Forest Service, Washington, D.C. 96 pp.

———. 1975a. RPA the nation's renewable resources—an assessment, 1975. U.S. Forest Service, Washington, D.C. 345 pp.

———. 1975b. Annual wildlife report. U.S. Forest Service, Washington, D.C. 22 pp.

———. 1990. The Forest Service Program for Forest and Rangeland Resources: A long-term strategic plan. Govt. Print. Off., Washington, D.C.

U.S. Department of Agriculture Office of Government and Public Affairs. 1982. Idaho diggings tell about an ancient way of life. News feature 494–82. U.S. DA News Center, Washington, D.C. 3 pp.

U.S. Department of the Interior. 1917. Proceedings of the National Parks Conference. Govt. Print Off., Washington, D.C. 364 pp.

———1976. Endangered and threatened wildlife and plants. Fed. Reg. 41(208): 47,179–47,198.

———. 1981. Standards for the development of suitability index models. Ecological Services Manual 103. USDI, Fish and Wildl. Serv., Div. Ecological Serv.. Govt. Print. Off., Washington, D.C. 68 pp., plus append.

U.S. Department of the Interior Fish and Wildlife Service. 1972. 1970 national survey of fishing and hunting. U.S. Department of the Interior Resour. Publ. 95. U.S. Fish and Wildl. Serv., Washington, D.C. 108 pp.

———. 1975. Federal aid in fish and wildlife restoration, 1974. Wildl. Manage. Inst. and Sport Fish. Inst. 138 pp.

———. 1977. 1975 national survey of hunting, fishing and wildlife-associated recreation. U.S. Fish and Wildl. Serv., Washington, D.C. 91 pp.

———. 1978. Operation of the federal aid in sport fishing and wildlife restoration program. U.S. Department of the Interior Environ. Impact State. U.S. Fish and Wildl. Serv., Washington, D.C. 425 pp.

———. 1993. 1991 national survey of fishing, hunting and wildlife-associated recreation. U.S. Govt. Print. Off., Washington, D.C. 124 pp.

———. 1994. An ecosystem approach to fish and wildlife conservation—an approach to more effectively conserve the nation's biodiversity. U.S. Fish and Wildl. Serv., Washington, D.C. 14 pp.

———. 1997. 1996 national survey of fishing, hunting and wildlife-associated recreation. National overview. U.S. Fish and Wildl. Serv., Washington, D.C. 176 pp.

U.S. Department of the Interior National Park Service. 1937. Yellowstone National Park–Wyoming. U.S. Govt. Print. Off., Washington, D.C. 32 pp.

———. 1994. Yellowstone's northern range: A critical evaluation of the "natural regulation" paradigm. Pages 151–169 *in* D. G. DeSpain, ed., Plants and their environments: Proc. First Biennial Scientific Conf. on Greater Yellowstone Ecosystem. Nat. Park Serv., Washington, D.C. 374 pp.

U.S. General Accounting Office. 1994. Ecosystem management—additional actions needed to adequately test a promising approach. Rept. GAO/RCED–94–11. U.S. Gen. Account. Off., Washington, D.C. 87 pp.

U.S. Government. 1872. Statutes at Large (Yellowstone Organic Act). Vol. 17, Chap. 24, Sec. 2: 32–33.

———. 1916. Statutes at Large (National Park Service Act). 16 U.S.C. 1 and 2–3 (1970).

U.S. Senate. 1976. Senate bill 3887. Congr. Rec. 94th Congr., 2nd sess. 122(151-part III): 3.

United States v. Winans, 198 U.S. 371, 26 S. Ct. 662, 49 L. Ed. 1089 (1905).

Unsworth, J. W., L. Kuck and E. O. Garton. 1990. Elk sightability model validation at National Bison Range, Montana. Wildl. Soc. Bull. 18: 113–115.

Unsworth J. W. and L. Kuck. 1991. Bull elk vulnerability in the clearwater drainage of north-central Idaho. Pages 85–88 *in* A. G. Christensen, L. J. Lyon, T. N. Lonner, compilers, Proc. Elk Vulnerability Symp., Montana State Univ., Bozeman. 330 pp.

Unsworth, J. W., L. Kuck, M. D. Scott and E. O. Garton. 1993. Elk mortality in the clearwater drainage of northcentral Idaho. J. Wildl. Manage. 57: 495–502.

Unsworth, J. W., L. Cuck, E. O. Garton and B. R. Butterfield. 1998. Elk habitat selection on the Clearwater National Forest, Idaho. Journal of Wildlife Management. 62:1255-1263.

Urness, P. J., D. D. Austin and L. C. Fierro. 1983. Nutritional value of crested wheatgrass for wintering mule deer. J. Range Manage. 36: 225–226.

Utah Division of Wildlife Resources. 1997. License sales report. 6 pp.

Utah Fish and Game Commission. 1920–1924. Biennial Report of the State Fish and Game Commission of the State of Utah. No. 14–16. Salt Lake City.

———. 1948. Biennial report of the State Fish and Game Commission of the State of Utah. 28:34.

———. 1954. Biennial report of the State Fish and Game Commission of the State of Utah. 31:34.

Utley, R.M. 1984. The Indian frontier of the American West, 1846–1890. Univ. New Mexico Press, Albuquerque. 325 pp.

———. 1993. The lance and the shield. Henry Holt and Co., New York. 413 pp.

Vacek, Z. 1955. Innervace lyci rostouciho parohu u Cervidu. Cs. Morfologie 3(3): 249–264.

Vacek, Z. 1966. Submikroskopicka struktura placenty savcu. Lynx (Prague) nova series 6: 173–178.

Vagnoni, D. B., R. A. Garrott, J. G. Cook, P. J. White and M. K. Clayton. 1996. Urinary allantoin: creatinine ratios as a dietary index for elk. J. Wildl. Manage. 60: 728–734.

Valdez, R. 1982. The wild sheep of the world. Wild Sheep and Goat Int.. Mesilla, New Mexico. 186 pp.

Valentincic, S. I. 1958. Beitrag zur Kenntnis der Reproduktion-serscheinungen beim Rotwild. Z. Jagdwiss. 4(4): 105–130.

Vales, D. J. 1996. User's manual for ELKVUN: an elk vulnerability, hunter and population projection program. Prog. Vers. 1, 14 Feb. 1996. Univ. of Idaho, Dept. of Fish and Wildl. Resour, Moscow. 25 pp.

Vales, D. J. and J. M. Peek. 1993. Estimating the relations between hunter harvest and gray wolf predation on the Gallatin, Montana and Sand Creek, Idaho, elk populations. Pages 118–172 *in* R. S. Cook, ed., Ecological issues on reintroducing wolves into Yellowstone National Park. U.S. Nat. Park Serv. Sci. Monogr. Ser. 93/22.

Vales, D. J. and J. M. Peek. 1996. Responses of elk to the 1988 Yellowstone fires and drought. Pages 159–167 *in* J. Greenlee, ed., Ecological implications of fire in Greater Yellowstone. Proc. 2nd Bienn. Sci. Conf. Greater Yellowstone Ecosystem. Int. Assoc. Wildland Fire, Fairfield, WA. 236 pp.

Vales, D. J., V. L. Coggins, P. Mathews,and R. A. Riggs. 1991. Analyzing options for improving bull: cow ratios of Rocky Mountain elk populations in northeast Oregon. Pages 174–181 *in* A. G. Christensen, L. J. Lyon, T. N. Lonner, compilers., Proc. Elk Vulnerability Symp., Montana State Univ., Bozeman. 330 pp.

Van Baran, D. C., E. P. Hoberg and R. G. Botzler. 1996. Abomasal parasites in Tule elk (*Cervus elaphus nannodes*) from Grizzly Island, California. J. Helminthol. Soc. Wash. 63: 222–225.

Van Campen, H. and E. S. Williams. 1996. Wildlife and bovine viral diarrhea virus. Pages 167–175 *in* E. J. Dubovi, ed., Proc. of the Int. Symposium, Bovine Viral Diarrhea Virus, a 50-year review. Cornell Univ., Ithaca, New York. 210 pp.

Van de Veen, H. 1979. Food selection and habitat use in the red deer (*Cervus elaphus L.*). Groningen, Netherlands, Riiksuniversitette Groningen, Proefochrift. 263 pp.

Van der Byl, P.B. 1915. The Indian Empire: The plains, hills and jungles. Pages 71–97 *in* D. Caruthers, P. B. Van der Byl, R. L. Kennion, J. G. Millais, H. F. Wallace and F. G. Barclay, eds., The gun at home and abroad: The big game of Asia and North America. The London and Counties Press Assoc. Ltd., London, U.K. 433 pp.

Van Dyke, F. G., W. C. Klein and S. T. Stewart. 1998. Long-term range fidelity in Rocky Mountain elk. J. Wildl. Manage. 62: 1,020–1,035.

Van Dyke, T. S. 1902. The elk of the pacific coast. Pages 167–257 *in* T. Roosevelt, T. S. Van Dyke, D. G. Elliot and A. J. Stone, eds., The deer family. Macmillan, New York.

Van Dyne, G. M., P. T. Kortopates and F. M. Smith, eds. 1984. Quantitative frameworks for forage allocation. Pages 289–416 *in* Developing strategies for rangeland management, National Research Council/National Academy of Sciences, Westview Press, Boulder, Colorado.

Van Horne, B., T. A. Hanley, R. G. Cates, J. D. McKendrick and J. D. Horner. 1988. Influence of seral stage and season on leaf chemistry of southeastern Alaska deer forage. Can. J. Forestry Res. 18: 90–99.

Van Soest, P. J. 1965. Symposium on factors influencing the voluntary intake of herbage ruminants: Voluntary intake in relation to chemical composition and digestibility. J. Anim. Sci. 23: 834–843.

———. 1982. Nutritional Ecology of the ruminant. O&B, Corvallis, Oregon. 374 pp.

———. 1994. Nutritional ecology of the ruminant. Second edition. Cornell Univ. Press, Ithaca, New York. 476 pp.

Van Soest, P. J., C. J. Sniffen and M. S. Allen. 1988. Rumen dynamics. Pages 21–42 in A. Dobson and M. J. Dobson, eds., Aspects of Digestive Physiology in Ruminants. M. J. Comstock Publishing Associates, Ithaca and London.

Van Valkenburgh, B. and F. Hertel. 1993. Tough times at La Brea: Tooth breakage in large carnivores of the late Pleistocene. Science 261: 456–459.

Van Wormer, J. 1969. The world of the American elk. J. B. Lippincott, New York. 154 pp.

Vandenbergh, J. 1976. Acceleration of sexual maturation in female rats by male stimulation. J. Reprod. Fert. 46(2): 451–453.

Vaske, J. J., M. P. Donnelly, T. A. Heberlein and B. Shelby. 1982. Differences in reported satisfaction ratings by consumptive and nonconsumptive recreationists. Journal of Leisure Research 14: 195–206.

Vaughn, H. W., R. R. Knight and F. W. Frank. 1973. A study of reproduction, disease and physiological blood and serum values in Idaho elk. J. Wildl. Dis. 9(4): 296–301.

Vaughn, H. W., H. W. Renshaw and F. W. Frank. 1976. Survey of anaplasmosis in elk in the Clearwater National Forest, Idaho. Am. J. Vet. Res. 37: 615–617.

Vavra, M. and R. L. Phillips. 1980. Drought effects on cattle performance, diet quality and intake. West. Section, Amer. Soc. of Anim. Sci. 31: 157–160.

Vavra, M., M. McInnis and D. Sheehy. 1989. Implications of dietary overlap to management of free-ranging large herbivores. Proc. Western Sec. Amer Soc. Anim. Sci. 40: 489–495.

Veblen, T.T. 1982. The effects of introduced wild animals on New Zealand Forests. Annu. Assoc. Amer. Geogr. 72:3 72–397.

Veblen, T.T., M. Mermoz, C. Martin and E. Ramilo. 1989. Effects of exotic deer on forest regeneration and composition in northern Patagonia. J. Appl. Ecol. 26: 711–724.

Veblen, T.T., M. Mermoz, C. Martin and T. Kitzberger. 1992. Ecological impact of introduced animals in Nahuel Huapi National Park, Argentina. Conserv. Biol. 6(1): 71–83.

Vereshchagin, N. K. 1967. The mammals of the Caucasus. Translated from Russian by the Israel Program for Scientific Translation. Jerusalem. 816 pp.

Verme, L. J. 1962. Mortality of white-tailed deer fawns in relation to nutrition. Deer Disease Symp. 1: 15–32.

———. 1963. Effect of nutrition on growth of white-tailed deer fawns. Trans. N. Amer. Wildl. and Natur. Resour. Conf. 28: 431–443.

———. 1965. Reproduction studies on penned white-tailed deer. J. Wildl. Manage. 29: 74–79.

———. 1969. Reproductive patterns of white-tailed deer related to nutritional plane. J. Wildl. Manage. 33: 881–887.

———. 1977. Assessment of natal mortality in upper Michigan deer. J. Wildl. Manage. 41: 700–708.

———. 1983. Sex ratio variation in Odocoileus: A critical review. J. Wildl. Manage. 47: 573–582.

———. 1988a. Niche selection by male white-tailed deer: An alternative hypotheses. Wildl. Soc. Bull. 16: 448–451.

———. 1988b. Lipogenesis in buck fawn white-tailed deer: Photoperiod effects. J. Mammal. 69: 67–70.

Verme, L. J. and J. C. Holland. 1973. Reagent-dry assay of marrow fat in white-tailed deer. J. Wildl. Manage. 37: 103–105.

Verme, L. J. and J. J. Ozoga. 1980a. Influence of protein-energy intake on deer fawns in autumn. J. Wildl. Manage. 44: 305–314.

Verme, L. J. and J. J. Ozoga. 1980b. Effects of diet on growth and lipogenesis in deer fawns. J. Wildl. Manage. 44: 315–324.

Verme, L. J. and D. E. Ullrey. 1984. Physiology and nutrition. Pages 91–108 in L. K. Halls, ed., White-tailed deer: Ecology and management. Stackpole Books, Inc., Harrisburg, Pennsylvania. 870 pp.

Verner, J., M. L. Morrison and C. J. Ralph, eds. 1986. Wildlife 2000: Modeling habitat relationships of terrestrial vertebrates. Univ. Wisconsin Press, Madison. 470 pp.

Vickers, C. 1945. Archeology in the Rock and Pelican Lake area of south-central Manitoba. Amer. Antiq. 11(2): 88–94.

Vikoren, T. and G. Stuve. 1996. Fluoride exposure in cervids inhabiting areas adjacent to aluminum smelters in Norway. II. Fluorosis. J. Wildl. Dis. 32: 181–189.

Vivian, R. G. and T. W. Mathews. 1964. Kin Kletso, a Pueblo III community in Chaco Canyon, New Mexico. Southwestern Monuments Assoc. Tech. Ser., Vol. 6, parts I and 2. Southwestern Monuments Assoc., Globe, Arizona. 214 pp.

Voegelin, C. F. 1938. Shawnee stems and the Jacob P. Dunn Miami dictionary. In Prehistory Research Series, vol. 1, No. 3, 5, 8. Indiana Hist. Soc., Indianapolis.

Voegelin, C. F. and F. M. Voegelin. 1966. Map of North American Indian languages. Publ. No. 20. Amer. Ethnological Soc. and Indiana Univ., Indianapolis.

Voegelin, E. 1942. Culture element distribution, XX: Northeast California. Univ. California, Berkeley. Anthropol. Rec. 2(1): 184.

Vogt, F. 1936. Neue Wege der Hege. Verlag Neumann-Neudamm, Berlin, Germany. 165 pp.

———. 1937. Neue wege der hege. Neumann-Neudamm, Wien. 165 pp.

———. 1947. Das Rotwild. Osterr. jagd- u. Fischerei-Verlag, Wein. 208 pp.

———. 1948. Das Rotwild. Osterreichischer Jagd und Fischerei Verlag, Vienna, Austria. 111 pp.

Volk, F. 1993. Uber die winterliche futter aufnahme des rotwildes als interpretationshilte fur botanische Panseninhaltsuntersuchungen. Anblick 11: 38–44.

Volterra, V. 1931. Lecons sur la theorie matematique de la lutte pour la vie. Gauthier- villars, Paris. 214 pp.

Von Raesfeld, F. 1920. Die hege in der freien wildbahn. Parey, Berlin 643 pp.

Von Raesfeld, F. and F. Vorreyer. 1957. Das Rotwild. 4. Aufl. P. Parey Verlag, Hamburg. 385 pp.

Von Raesfeld, F. and F. Vorreyer. 1964. Das Rotwild-Naturgeschichte, Hege und Jagd. (5th ed., revised by F. Vorreyer). P. Parey Verlag, Hamburg and Berlin. 386 pp.

Von Raesfeld, F. and G. V. Lettow-Vorbeck. 1965. Die hege in der freien wildbahn. Parey, Berlin. 309 pp.

Von Raesfeld, F. and F. Vorreyer 1978. Das Rotwild. Paul Parey Verlag, Berlin. 395 pp.

Von Raesfeld, F. and K. Reulecke. 1988. Das rotwild. Parey, Hamburg, Berlin. 416 pp.

Vore, J. 1990. Movements and distribution of some northern Yellowstone elk. M.S. Thesis, Montanan State Univ., Bozeman. 80 pp.

Vore J. and R. DeSimone. 1991. Effects of an innovative hunting regulation on elk populations and hunter attitudes. Pages 23–29 *in* A. G. Christensen, L. J. Lyon, T. N. Lonner, compilers, Proc. Elk Vulnerability Symp., Montana State Univ., Bozeman. 330 pp.

Wade, H. T. 1910. With boat and gun in the Yangtze Valley, second edition. Shanghai, China. 284 pp.

Wadsworth, W. A. 1902. The wapiti (*Cervus canadensis*). Annu. Rept. New York State For., Fish and Game Commiss. 7: 239–242.

Wagar, J. V. K. 1971. Quality in wildlife management. Pages 44–47 *in* R. D. Teague, ed., A manual of wildlife conservation. The Wildl. Soc., Washington, D.C. 206 pp.

Wagenknecht, E. 1980. Schalenwild. Landwirtschaftsverlag Berlin. 408 pp.

———. 1981. Das rotwild. Landwirtschaftsverlag Berlin. 484 pp.

———. 1992. Futterung im meinungsstreit. Unsere jagd 10/92: 10–20

Waggoner, G. A. 1904. Stories of old Oregon. Statesman Publ. Co., Salem, Oregon. 292 pp.

Wagner, F. H. 1978. Livestock grazing and the livestock industry. Pages 129–145 *in* H. Brokaw, ed., Wildlife in America. Council on Economic Quality, Washington, D.C.

———. 1994. Scientist says Yellowstone Park is being destroyed. High Country News 26(10): 14–15.

Wagner, F. H., R. B. Keigley and C. L. Wambolt. 1995. Comment: Ungulate herbivory of willows on Yellowstone's northern winter range: Response to Singer et al. (1994). J. Range Manage. 48: 475–477.

Wagner, F. W., R. Foresta, R. B. Gill, D. R. McCullough, M. R. Pelton, W. F. Porter and H. Salwasser. 1995. Wildlife policies in the U.S. national parks. Island Press, Washington. D.C. 242 pp.

Wairimu, S. and R. J. Hudson, 1993. Foraging dynamics of wapiti stags (*Cervus elaphus*) during compensatory growth. Appl. Animal Behavior Sci. 36: 65–79.

Wairimu, S., R. J. Hudson and M. A. Price. 1992. Catch-up growth of yearling wapiti stags (*Cervus elaphus*). Can. J. Anim. Sci. 72(3): 619–631.

Waldo, C. M., G. B. Wislocki and D. W. Fawcett. 1949. Observations on the blood supply of growing antlers. Amer. J. Anat. 84(1–3): 2751.

Waldrip, G. P. and J. H. Shaw. 1979. Movements and habitat use by cow and calf elk at the Wichita Mountains National Wildlife Refuge. Pages 177–184 *in* M. S. Boyce and L. D. Hayden-Wing, eds., North American elk: ecology, behavior and management. Univ. Wyoming, Laramie. 294 pp.

Walker, E. P., F. Warnick, S. E. Hamlet, K. I. Lange, M. A. Davis, H. E. Uible and P. F. Wright. 1975. Mammals of the world. Vol.2. 3 vols., 3rd ed. Johns Hopkins Univ. Press, Baltimore, Maryland. 1,500 pp.

Walker, J. R. 1905. Sioux games. J. Amer. Folklore 18: 277–290.

———. 1991. Lakota belief and ritual. R. J. DeMallie and E. A. Jahner, eds. Univ. Nebraska Press, Lincoln. 329 pp.

Walker, V. 1991. Photoperiod influences on the seasonal energy metabolism of ewes. Ph.D. Diss., Univ. Alberta. 188 pp.

Wall, G. and C. Wright. 1977. The environmental impact of outdoor recreation. Dept.Geogr. Publ. Ser. No. 11, Univ. Ontario, Waterloo. 69 pp.

Wallace, H. F. 1915a. The deer of Asia. Pages 192–207 *in* D. Caruthers, P. B. Van der Byl, R. L. Kennion, J. G. Millais, H. F. Wallace and F. G. Barclay, eds., The gun at home and abroad: The big game of Asia and North America. The London and Counties Press Assoc. Ltd., London, U.K. 433 pp.

———. 1915b. China. Pages 156–178 *in* D. Caruthers, P. B. Van der Byl, R. L. Kennion, J. G. Millais, H. F. Wallace and F. G. Barclay, eds., The gun at home and abroad: The big game of Asia and North America. The London and Counties Press Assoc. Ltd., London, U.K. 433 pp.

Wallace, L. R. 1948. The growth of lambs before and after birth in relation to level of nutrition, Part III. J. Ag. Sci. 38(4): 367–401.

Wallace, M. C. and P. R. Krausman. 1987. Elk, mule deer and cattle habitats in central Arizona. J. Range Manage. 40: 80–83.

Wallace, M. C. and P. R. Krausman. 1991. Neonatal elk habitat in Central Arizona. Pages 69–75 *in* R. D. Brown, ed., The biology of deer. Springer-Verlag, New York.

Wallace, M. C., J. Jojolla and P. R. Krausman. 1988. Unusual reproduction in an Arizona elk. Southwest Natur. 33: 249.

Wallace, R. S., M. Bush and R. J. Montali. 1987. Deaths from exertional myopathy at the National Zoological Park from 1975–1985. J. Wildl. Dis. 23: 454–462.

Wallace, V. and M. J. Birtles. 1985. The accessory sex glands of the red deer stag. Pages 193–196 *in* P. F. Fennessy and K. R. Drew, eds., The biology of deer production. Bull. 20. Royal Soc. of New Zealand, Wellington. 482 pp.

Wallace, W. J. 1978a. Hupa, Chilula and Whilkut. Pages 164–179 *in* R. F. Heinzer, ed., California. Handbook of North American Indians. Vol. 8. Smithsonian Instit., Washington, D.C. 800 pp.

———. 1978b. Southern Valley Yokuts. Pages 448–461 *in* R. F. Heizer, ed., California. Handbook of North American Indians. Vol. 8. Smithsonian Instit., Washington, D.C. 800 pp.

———. 1978c. Northern Valley Yokuts. Pages 362–470 *in* R. F. Heizer, ed., California. Handbook of North American Indians. Vol. 8. Smithsonian Instit., Washington, D.C. 800 pp.

Wallmo, O.C., ed. 1981. Mule and black-tailed deer of North America. Univ. Nebraska Press, Lincoln. 605 pp.

Wallmo, O. C. and D. J. Neff. 1970. Direct observations of tamed deer to measure their consumption of natural forage. Pages 105–110 *in* Range and wildlife habitat evaluation—a research symposium. Misc. Publ. 1147. USDA For. Serv., Washington, D.C.

Wallmo, O. C., L. H. Carpenter, W. L. Regelin, R. B. Gill and D. L. Baker. 1977. Evaluation of deer habitat on a nutritional basis. J. Range Manage. 30: 122–127.

Wallmo, O. C., R. B. Gill, L. H. Carpenter and D. W. Reichert. 1973. Accuracy of field estimates of deer food habits. J. Wildl. Manage. 37(4): 556–562.

Wallmo, O. C., W. L. Regelin and D. W. Reichert. 1972. Forage use by mule deer relative to logging in lodgepole pine–spruce–fir. J. Wildl. Manage. 36(4): 1,025–1,033.

Walsh, N. E., G. C. White and D. J. Freddy. 1991. Responses of bull elk to simulated elk vocalization during rut. J. Wildl. Manage. 55(3): 396–400.

Walsh, R. G., K. H. John, J. R. McKean and J. G. Hof. 1992. Effect of price on forecasts of participation in fish and wildlife recreation: An aggregate demand model. Journal of Leisure Research 24(2): 140–156.

Walters, C. 1986 Adaptive management of renewable resources. MacMillan Publ. Co., New York. 363 pp.

Walters, C. J. and P. J. Bandy. 1972. Periodic harvest as a method of increasing big game yields. J. Wildl. Manage. 36(1): 128–134.

Walters, C. J., M. Stocker and G. C. Haber. 1981. Simulation and optimization models for a wolf–ungulate system. Pages 317–337 *in* C. W. Fowler and T. D. Smith, eds., Dynamics of large mammal populations. John Wiley and Sons, New York. 477 pp.

Walther, F. 1968. Verhalten der Gazellen. Die Neue Brehm Bucherci No. 373. Wittenberg-Lutherstadt: A. Ziemsen Verlag. 144 pp.

———. 1977. Sex and activity dependency of distances between Thomson's gazelles (*Gazella thomsoni* Gunther 1884). Animal Behavior 25: 713–719.

———. 1984. Communication and expression in hoofed mammals. Indiana Univ. Press, Bloomington, Indiana. 423 pp.

Walther, F., E. C. Mungall and G. A. Grau. 1983. Gazelles and their relatives. A study in territorial behaviour. Noyes Publications, Park Ridge, New Jersey. 239 pp.

Wambolt, C. L. and A. F. McNeal. 1987. Selection of winter foraging sites by elk and mule deer. J. Envir. Manage. 25: 285–291.

Wang, X. and G. B. Schaller. 1996. Status of large mammals in western Inner Mongolia, China. J. East China Normal Univ. 12: 93–104.

Wang, Z. and R. Du. 1981. Polymorphism of karyotype of Bactrian wapiti in Beijing Zoo. Acta Genetica Sinica 8(4): 316–320.

Wang, Z., R. Du, J. Xu and Q. Che. 1982. Karyotypes of four species of deer. Acta Zool. Sin. 28(1): 35–40.

Ward v. Race Horse, 163 U.S. 504, 16 S. Ct. 1076.41 L. Ed. 244 (1896).

Ward, A. L. 1970. Stomach content and fecal analysis: Methods of forage identification. Pages 146–158 in Range and wildlife habitat evaluation—a research symposium, pp. Misc. Publ. No. 1147. USDA For. Serv., Washington, D.C.

———. 1971. In vitro digestibility of elk winter forage in southern Wyoming. J. Wildl. Manage. 35: 681–688.

———. 1973a. Elk behavior in relation to multiple uses on the Medicine Bow National Forest. Proc. West. Assoc. State Game and Fish Commiss. 53: 125–141.

———. 1973b. Sagebrush control with herbicide has little effect on elk calving behavior. Res. Note RM–240. USDA For. Serv., Fort Collins, Colorado. 4 pp.

———. 1976. Elk behavior in relation to timber harvest operations and traffic on the Medicine Bow range in south-central Wyoming. Pages 32–43 in S. R. Hieb, ed., Proc. Elk-Logging-Roads Symp., Univ. Idaho, Moscow. 142 pp.

Ward, A. L. and J. J. Cupal. 1979. Telemetered heart rate of three elk as affected by activity and human disturbance. Pages 47–56 in Dispersed recreation and natural resource management. Symp. Proc. Utah State Univ., Logan.

Ward, A. L., J. J. Cupal, A. L Lea, C. A. Walkey and R. W. Weeks. 1973. Elk behavior in relation to cattle grazing forest recreation and traffic. Trans. N. Amer. Wildl. and Natur. Resour. Conf. 38: 327–337.

Ward, A. L., K. Diem and R. W. Weeks. 1975. The impact of snow on elk. Pages 105–174 in D. Knight, ed., Final Rept. Medicine Bow Ecol. Proj. Univ. Wyoming, Laramie. 380 pp.

Ward, A. L., J. J. Cupal, G. A. Goodwin and H. D. Morris. 1976. Effects of highway construction and use on big game populations. Rept. No. FHWA-RD–76. Fed. Highway Admin., Washington, D.C. 92 pp.

Ward, A. L., N. E. Fornwalt, S. E. Henry and R. A. Hodorff. 1980. Effects of highway operation practices and facilities on elk, mule deer and pronghorn antelope. Rept. No. FHWA-RD–79–143. National Technical Information Service, Springfield, Virginia. 48 pp.

Warner, A. C. I. 1981. Rate of passage of digesta through the gut of mammals and birds. Nutr. Abstr. Rev. 55: 789–820.

Warner, J. A. 1975. The life and art of the North American Indians. Crescent Books, New York. 168 pp.

Wasel, S. M. 1995. Meningeal worm, Parelaphostrongylus tenuis (Nematoda), in Manitoba, Saskatchewan and North Dakota: Distribution and ecological correlates. Dept. of Zoology, Univ. Alberta, Edmonton, Alberta. 100 pp.

Washburn, W. E. 1973. The American Indian and the United States. A documentary history. Random House, Inc., New York. IV: 2,267 3,119.

———., ed. 1988. History of Indian–White relations. Vol. 4. Handbook of North American Indians. Smithsonian Instit. Press, Washington, D.C. 838 pp.

Washington Department of Game. 1979. Big game status report. Washington Game Dept., Olympia. 293 pp.

Water Resources Research Institute. 1975. Wyoming Game and Fish Department 1974 attitude survey—resident elk hunters. Univ. Wyoming, Water Resour. Res. Inst., Laramie. 52 pp. Mimeo.

Waterman, T. T. 1920. Yurok geography. Univ. California Publ. in Amer. Archaeol. and Ethnol. 8(6): 271–358.

Waters, J. H. and C. W. Mack. 1962. Note on former range of Cervus canadensis in New England. J. Mammal. 43(2): 266–267.

Wathen, G., L. Marcum, A. Peterson, D. Scott and B. Layton. 1997. Elk reintroduction in Tennessee: An evaluation of its potential. Tech. Rept. 97–7, Tennessee Wildl. Resour. Agen., Nashville. 13 pp. + 6 Appendices and 3 Attachments.

Watkins, B. E. 1980. Iodine status and thyroid activity of white-tailed deer. (Odocoileus virginianus borealis). Ph.D. Diss., Michigan State Univ., East Lansing.

Watkins, B. E., D. E. Ullrey, J. H. Witham and J. M. Jones. 1990. Field evaluation of deuterium oxide for estimating body composition of white-tailed deer (Odocoileus virginianus) fawns. J. Zoo Wildl. Medic. 21: 453–456

Watkins, B. E., J. H. Withan, D. E. Ullrey, D. J. Watkins and J. M. Jones. 1991. Body composition and condition evaluation of white-tailed deer fawns. J. Wildl. Manage. 55: 39–51.

Watkins, B. E., R. R. Nachreiner, S. M. Schmitt, T. M. Cooley and D. E. Ullrey. 1982. Thyroid function in fed and fasted white-tailed deer fawns. Can. J. Zool. 60: 1,331–1,338.

Watkins, W. G., R. J. Hudson and N. French. 1985. The composition and yield of wapiti milk in relation to winter feeding. Univ. Alberta Feeders Day Report 64: 73–75.

Watkins, W.G., R.J. Hudson and P. L. J. Fargey. 1991. Compensatory growth of wapiti (Cervus elaphus) on aspen parkland ranges. Can. J. Zool. 69(6): 1, 682–1,688.

Watson, A. and R. Moss. 1972. A current model of population dynamics in red grouse. Proc. Int. Ornithol. Congr. 15: 134–149. Brill, Leiden, Netherlands.

Watson, A. E. T., ed. 1896. Red deer. Longmans, Green and Co., London, U.K. 320 pp.

Watson, D. 1990. Red deer in Scotland—a resource out of control. Ecos 11(3): 22–24.

Wear, D. W. 1885. Report of the Superintendent of the Yellowstone National Park. Govt. Print. Off., Washington, D.C. 5 pp.

Weaver, H. 1974. Effects of fire on temperate forests: western United States. Pages 279–319 in T. T. Kozlowski and C. E. Ahlgren, eds., Fire and ecosystems. Academic Press, New York.

Webb, P. A., R. G. McLean, G. C. Smith, J. H. Ellenberger, D. B. Francy, T. E. Walton and T. P. Monath. 1987. Epizootic vesicular stomatitis in Colorado, 1982: Some observations on the possible role of wildlife populations in an enzootic maintenance cycle. J. Wildl. Dis. 23: 192–198.

Webb, W. S. 1950. The Carlson Annis Mound: Site 5, Butler County, Kentucky. Repts. in Anthropol. VII(4): 300–304.

Weber, B. J. and M. L. Wolfe. 1982. Use of serum progesterone levels to detect pregnancy in elk. J. Wildl. Manage. 46: 835–837.

Weber, B. U., M. L. Wolfe, G. C. White and M. M. Rowland. 1984. Physiologic response of elk to differences in winter range quality. J. Wildl. Manage. 48: 248–253.

Weber, H. 1942. Organismus und Umwelt. Biologe 77: 57–58.

———. 1949. Grundriss der Insektenkunde. 2. Aufl. Jena.

Weber, K. T. 1996. Identifying landscape elements in relation to elk kill sites in western Montana. M.S. Thesis, Univ. Montana, Missoula. 74 pp.

Weber, Y. B. 1973. Aspects of physiology and diseases of the North American elk. Unpubl. Ph.D. Thesis, Portland State Univ., Portland, Oregon. 166 pp.

Weber, Y. B. and L. Giacometti. 1972. Sickling phenomena in the erythrocytes of wapiti (*Cervus canadensis*). J. Mammal. 53(44): 917–919.

Weber, Y. B. and M. L. Bliss. 1972. Blood chemistry of Roosevelt elk (*Cervus canadensis* Roosevelti). Comp. Biochem. Physiol. 43A: 649–653.

Webster, A. J. F. 1971. Prediction of heat losses from cattle exposed to cold outdoor environments. J. Appl. Physiol. 30: 684–690.

Webster, G. S. 1983. Iroquoian hunting: An optimization approach. Ph.D. Diss., Pennsylvania State Univ., State College.

Webster, J. R. and G. K. Barrell. 1985. Advancement of reproductive activity, seasonal reduction in prolactin secretion and seasonal pelage changes in pubertal red deer hinds (*Cervus elaphus*) subjected to artificially shortened daily photoperiod or daily melatonin treatments. J. Reprod. Fert. 73: 255–260.

Weckerly, F. W. 1996. Roosevelt elk along the Prairie Creek drainage: An evaluation of estimating abundance and herd composition. California Fish and Game 82: 175–181.

Wedel, W. R. 1955. Archaeological materials from the vicinity of Mobridge, South Dakota. Anthropol. Papers. Bur. of Amer. Ethnol., Bull. 157. Smithsonian Instit., Washington, D.C. 45: 69–188.

———. 1961. Prehistoric man on the Great Plains. Univ. Oklahoma Press, Norman. 355 pp.

Wegge, P. 1974. Reproductive rates of red deer (*Cervus elaphus atlanticus* L.) in Norway. Pages 79–87 *in* I. Kjemer and P. Bjurholm, eds., Trans. 11th Congr. IUGB. Nat. Swedish Environ. Protect. Board, Stockholm. 631 pp.

Wegge, P. 1975. Reproduction and early calf mortality in Norwegian red deer. J. Wildl. Manage. 39: 92–100.

Wehausen, J. D. 1995. Fecal measures of diet quality in wild and domestic ruminants. J. Wildl. Manage. 59: 816–823.

Weigand, J. P. and R. J. Mackie. 1987. What's working and what's not: an overview to approaches to management for quality hunting. Trans. West. Assoc. Game and Fish Commiss. 67: 69–76.

Welch, A., M. J. Pybus, C. J. Wilke and W. M. Samuel. 1991a. Reliability of fecal examination for detecting infections of meningeal worm (*Parelaphostrongylus tenuis*) in elk. Wildl. Soc. Bull. 19: 26–331.

Welch, B. L. 1966. Projected assessment of new physiological indicators of population conditions in deer. Proc. Southeast. Assoc. Game and Fish Commiss. 19: 157–160.

Welch, D. A., W. M. Samuel and C. J. Wilke. 1991b. Suitability of moose, elk, mule deer and white-tailed deer as hosts for winter ticks (*Dermacentor albipictus*) Can. J. Zool. 69: 2,300–2,305.

Welch, J. 1994. Killing Custer. W. W. Norton & Co., New York. 320 pp.

Welch, J. G. and A. P. Hooper. 1988. Ingestion of feed and water. Pages 108–116 *in* D. C. Church, ed., The ruminant animal: digestive physiology and nutrition. Prentice Hall, Englewood Cliffs, New Jersey. 564 pp.

Wells, P. V. 1970. Postglacial vegetational history of the Great Plains. Science 167(3925): 1,574–1,582.

Weltfish, G. 1965. The lost universe. Univ. Nebraska Press, Lincoln. 506 pp.

Wesley, D. E., K. L. Knox and J. G. Nagy. 1973 Energy metabolism of pronghorn antelope. J. Wildl. Manage 37: 563–573

Wesson, J. A., P. F. Scanlon, R. L. Kirkpatrick and H. S. Mosby. 1979. Influence of chemical immobilization and physical restraint on packed cell volume, total protein, glucose and blood urea nitrogen in blood of white-tailed deer. Can. J. Zool. 57: 756–767.

West, N.E. 1993. Biodiversity of rangelands. J. Range Manage. 46: 2–13.

Westenskow-Wall, K. J., W. C. Krueger, L. D. Bryant and D. R. Thomas. 1994. Nutrient quality of bluebunch wheatgrass re-growth on elk winter range in relation to defoliation. J. Range Manage. 47: 240–244.

Weston, R. H. and D. P. Poppi. 1987. Comparitive aspects of food intake. Pages 133–161 *in* J. B. Hacker and J. H. Ternouth, eds., The nutrition of herbivores. Academic Press, New York.

Westra, R. 1977. Urea recycling in wapiti. Pages 42–53 *in* R. J. Hudson, co-ord., Wildlife productivity. Dept. of Anim. Sci., Univ. Alberta, Edmonton.

Westra, R. and R. J. Hudson. 1979. Urea recycling in wapiti. Pages 236–239, *in* M. S. Boyce and L. D. Hayden-Wing, eds. North American elk: ecology, behavior, and management. The Univ. Wyoming, Laramie. 294 pp.

Westra, R. and R. J. Hudson. 1981. Digestive function of wapiti calves. J. Wildl. Manage. 45: 148–155.

Wheat, J. B. 1972. The Olsen-Chubbuck site, a Paleo-Indian bison kill. Mem. of the Soc. for Amer. Archaeol. No. 26. Issued as Amer. Antiquity, Vol. 37, No. 1, Part 2. January 1972. 180 pp.

Wheaton, C., M. Pybus and K. Blakely. 1993. Agency perspectives on private ownership of wildlife in the United States and Canada. Trans. N. Amer. Wildl. and Natur. Resour. Conf. 58: 487–494.

Wheeler, K. 1976. The chroniclers. Time-LIFE Books, New York. 240 pp.

Whisker, J. B. 1981. The right to hunt. North River Press, Croton-on-Hudson, New York. 173 pp.

Whitacre D. and R. Whitacre. 1986. The Whitacre site (12D 246). Ohio Archaeol. 36(3): 27.

Whitaker, J. O., Jr. 1970. The biological subspecies: an adjunct of the biological species. Biologist 52(1): 12–15.

White, C. A., C. E. Olmsted, and C. E. Kay. 1998. Aspen, elk, and fire in the Rocky Mountain national parks of North America. Wildl. Soc. Bull. 26(3): 449–462.

White, G. C. 1985. Survival rates of wapiti (*Cervus elaphus nelsoni*) in the Jemez Mountains, New Mexico, U.S.A. Pages 51–54 *in* P. F. Fennesy and K. R. Drew, eds., Biology of Deer Production Bull. 22. The Roy. Soc. of New Zealand, Wellington. 482 pp.

White, K. L. 1958. Summer range ecology of Rattlesnake Creek mule deer in the spruce–fir zone. Unpubl. M.S. Thesis. Univ. Montana, Missoula. 95 pp.

White, L. M., D. A. Hosack, R. J. Warren and R. A. Fayrer-Hosken. 1995. Influence of mating on duration of estrus in captive white-tailed deer. J. Mammal. 76: 1,159–1,163.

White, P. J., R. A. Garrott, J. F. Kirkpatrick and E. V. Berkeley. 1995. Diagnosing pregnancy in free-ranging elk using fecal steroid metabolites. J. Wild. Dis. 31: 514–522.

White, P. J., R. A. Garrott, C. A. Vanderbilt White and G. A. Sargeant. 1996. Interpreting mean chemical ratios from simple random collections of snow-urine samples. Wildl. Soc. Bull. 23: 705–710.

White, R. 1975. Indian land use and environmental change. Island County, Washington—a case study. Arizona and the West. 17: 327–338.

White, R. G. 1983. Foraging patterns and their multiplier effects on productivity of northern ungulates. Oikos 40: 377–384.

———. 1992. Nutrition in relation to season, lactation and growth of North temperate deer. Pages 407–417 *in* R. D. Brown, ed., The biology of deer. Springer-Verlag, New York.

Whitehead, G. K. 1960. The deer stalking grounds of Great Britain and Ireland. Hollis and Carter, London, U.K. 556 pp.

———. 1964. The deer of Great Britain and Ireland. Routledge and Kegan Paul, London, U.K. 597 pp. + 95 plates.

———. 1972. The deer of the world. Constable, London. 194 pp.

———. 1980. Hunting and stalking deer in Britain through the ages. B. T. Batsford, London, U.K. 304 pp.

————. 1982. Hunting and stalking deer throughout the world. B.T. Batsford Ltd., London, U.K. 336 pp.

————. 1993. The Whitehead encyclopedia of deer. Susan Hill Press, Shrewsbury, U.K. 604 pp.

Whiting, T. L. and S. V. Tessaro. 1994. An abattoir study of tuberculosis in a herd of farmed elk. Can. Vet. J. 35: 497–501.

Whittaker, J. O., Jr. and W. J. Hamilton, Jr. 1998. Mammals of the eastern United States. Comstock Publ. Assoc., a division of Cornell Univ. Press, Ithaca, New York. 577 pp.

Whittaker, R. H. 1954. Plant populations and the basis of plant indication. Angew. Pflanzensoziol., Festschr. Aichinger 1: 183–206.

————. 1962. Classification of natural communities. Botan. Rev. 28: 1–239.

Whittaker, R. H., S. A. Levin and R. B. Root. 1973. Niche, habitat, ecotype. Amer. Natur. 107(955): 321–338.

Whittaker, R. H., S. A. Levin and R. B. Root. 1975. On the reasons for distinguishing "niche, habitat and ecotype." Amer. Natur. 109(968): 479–482.

Whitten, K. R., G. W. Garner, F. J. Mauer and R. B. Harris. 1992. Productivity and early calf survival in the Porcupine caribou herd. J. Wildl. Manage. 56: 201–212.

Whittleseg, L.H. 1998. Too many elk? Wildl. Conserv. 101(3): 66.

Wickler, W. 1965. Die Evolution von Mustern der Zeichnung und des Verhaltens. Naturwiss. 52: 335–341.

————. 1972. Verhalten und Umwelt. Hoffman und Campe Verlag, Hamburg. 193 pp.

Wicktrom, M. L., C. T. Robbins, T. A. Hanley, D. E. Spalinger and S. M. Parrish. 1984. Food intake and foraging energetics of elk and mule deer. J. Wildl. Manage. 48: 1,285–1,301.

Wied, Maximilian, Prince of. 1843. Travels in the interior of North America. Translated by H. Evans Lloyd. London: Ackemmann and Company. 520 pp.

————. 1906. Travels into the interior of North America, 1832–34. *in* R. G. Thwaites, ed., Early western travels, 1748–1846. Vol. 22. Burrows Bros., Cleveland, Ohio.

Wieselmann, H. 1994. Rotwildfutterung. Kernsatze, Details, Empfehlungen. ed. No Landesjagdverband. 28 pp.

Wight, H. M. 1938. Field and laboratory technique in wildlife management. Univ. Michigan Press., Ann Arbor. 105 pp.

Wilbert, D. E. 1963. Some effects of chemical sagebrush control on elk distribution. J. Range Manage. 16(2): 74–78.

Wilbrecht, J. and R. L. Robbins. 1979. History of the National Elk Refuge. Pages 248–258 *In* M. S. Boyce and L. D. Hayden-Wing, eds., North American elk: Ecology, behavior and management. Univ. Wyoming, Laramie. 294 pp.

Wilcove, D. S. 1987. From fragmentation to extinction. Natural Areas Journal 7: 23–29.

Wildforschung VII, ed. H. Stubbe, pp. 75–88. VEB Deutscher Landwirtschafts Verlag, Berlin.

Wildlife Management Institute. 1962. Clearwater elk study. Job Compl. Rept. W–85–R–13. Idaho Dept. Fish and Game, Boise. 49 pp.

————. 1971. Report to the Western Association of State Game and Fish Commissioners on nonresident hunting and angling. Wildl. Manage. Inst., Washington, D.C. 16 pp.

————. 1973a. National survey of state fish and wildlife funding. Wildl. Manage. Inst., Washington, D.C. 40 pp.

————. 1973b. Wildlife areas attract a million in California. Outdoor News Bull. 27(20): 4.

————. 1975. Current investments, projected needs and potential new sources of income for nongame fish and wildlife programs in the United States. Wildl. Manage. Inst., Washington, D.C. 116 pp.

————. 1976. Sportsmen's numbers and contributors increase. Outdoor News Bull. 30(13): 5.

————. 1997. Organization, authority, and programs of state fish and wildlife agencies. Wildlife Management Institute, Washington, DC. 164 pp.

Wildschut, W. 1975. Crow Indian medicine bundles. *In* J. C. Ewers, ed., Contributions from the Museum of the American Indian, Heye Foundation. Vol. 17, 2nd ed. Amer. Indian, Heye Foundation, New York. 55 pp.

Wildschut, W. and J.C. Ewers. 1959. Crow Indian beadwork: A descriptive and historical study. Contributions from the Museum of the American Indian. Vol. 16. Heye Foundation, New York.

Wilesmith, J. W., J. B. M. Ryan and M. J. Atkinson. 1991. Bovine spongiform encephalopathy: Epidemiological studies on the origin. Vet. Rec. 128: 199–203.

Will, R. G., J. W. Ironside, M. Zeidler, S. N. Cousens, K. Estibeiro, A. Alperovitch, S. Poser, M. Pocchiari, A. Hofman and P. G. Smith. 1996. A new variant of Creutzfeldt-Jakob disease in the U.K. The Lancet 347: 921–925.

Willard, S. T., R. G. Sasser, J. C. Gillespie, J. T. Jaques, T. H. Welsh and R. D. Dandle. 1994. Methods for pregnancy determination and the effects of body condition on pregnancy status in Rocky Mountain Elk *(Cervus elaphus nelsoni)*. Theriogenology 42: 1,095–1,102.

Williams, E. S. 1982. Neoplasia (tumors). Pages 261–274 *in* E. T. Thorne, N. Kingston, W. R. Jolley and R. C. Bergstrom, eds., Diseases of wildlife in Wyoming, 2nd Edition, Wyoming Game and Fish Dept., Cheyenne. 353 pp.

————. 1985. Unpublished. Records on file in author's file at Department of Vet.Sciences, Univ. Wyoming, Laramie.

————. 1993. Humane considerations in immobilization and study of free-ranging wildlife. Pages 64–67 *in* M. E. Fowler, ed., Zoo and wildlife medicine. W. B. Saunders, Philadelphia, Pennsylvania. 617 pp.

————. 1994. Unpublished. Records on file in author's file at Department of Vet.Sciences, Univ. Wyoming, Laramie.

Williams, E. S. and T. R. Spraker. 1979. Paratuberculosis in free-ranging bighorn sheep and a Rocky Mountain goat with a brief review of the disease in wild species. Pages 122–125 *in* Proceeding of the American Association of Zoo Veterinarians. Amer. Assoc. Zoo Veterinarians, Denver, Colorado. 132 pp.

Williams, E. S. and E. T. Thorne. 1996. Exertional myopathy (capture myopathy). Pages 181–193 *in* G. L. Hoff, A. Fairbrother and L. Locke, eds., Noninfectious diseases of wildlife. Iowa State Press, Ames. 219 pp.

Williams, E. S. and S. Young. 1980. Chronic wasting disease of captive mule deer: A spongiform encephalopathy. J. Wildl. Disease 16: 89–98.

Williams, E. S. and S. Young. 1982. Spongiform encephalopathy of Rocky Mountain elk. J. Wildl. Diseases 18: 465–471.

Williams, E. S. and S. Young. 1992. Spongiform encephalopathies in Cervidae. Revue Scientifique Technique Office International des Epizooties 11: 551–567.

Williams, E. S., S. P. Snyder and K. L. Martin. 1983a. Experimental infection of some North American wild ruminants and domestic sheep with *Mycobacterium paratuberculosis*: Clinical and bacteriological findings. J. Wildl. Dis. 19: 185–191.

Williams, E. S., S. P. Snyder and K. L. Martin. 1983b. Pathology of spontaneous and experimental infection of North American wild ruminants with *Mycobacterium paratuberculosis*. Vet. Path. 20: 274–291.

Williams, E. S., J. C. DeMartini and S. P. Snyder. 1985. Lymphocyte blastogenesis, complement fixation and fecal culture as diagnostic tests for paratuberculosis in North American wild ruminants and domestic sheep. Am. J. Vet. Res. 46: 2,317–2,321.

Williams, E. S., S. G. Smith, R. M. Meyer and E. T. Thorne. 1995. Three-year survey for bovine tuberculosis in hunter-killed free-ranging elk (*Cervus elaphus nelsoni*) in northwestern Wyoming. Proc. U.S. Anim. Health Assoc. 99: 631–637.

Williams, E. S., J. K. Kirkwood and M. W. Miller. In press. Transmissible spongiform encephalopathies. *in* E. S. Williams and I. K. Barker, eds., Infectious diseases of wild mammals. Iowa State Univ. Press, Ames.

Williams, G. L. 1981. An example of simulation models as decision tools in wildlife management. 9: 101–107.

Williams, J. D., W. F. Krueger and D. N. Harmel. 1994. Heritabilities for antler characteristics and body weight in yearling white-tailed deer. Heredity 73: 78–83.

Williams, T. R. 1960. The significance of salt and natural licks in elk management, Idaho County, Idaho. Proj. Compl. Rept. W–85-R-II. Univ. Idaho, Moscow. 9 pp.

———. 1962. Clearwater elk study. Job Compl. Rept. W–85-R–13. Idaho Dept. Fish and Game, Boise. 49 pp.

Williams, T. 1989. The elk–ranch boom. Bugle 15(4): 62–69.

Williamson, L. L. 1973. Decrease seen for wildlife habitat. Conserv. News: (Feb. 1): 3.

———. 1987. Evolution of landmark law. Pages 1–16 *in* H. Kallman, C. P. Agee, W. R. Goforth and J. P. Linduska, eds., Restoring America's wildlife. USDI Fish and Wildlife Service, Washington, D.C. 394 pp.

Williamson, P. 1974. The fine structure of ejaculated ram spermatozoa following scrotal heating. J. Reprod. Fert. 40(1): 191–195.

Wills, G. F. and H. J. Spinden. 1906. The Mandans: A study of their culture, archeology and language. Papers of the Peabody Mus. of Amer. Archeol. and Ethnol. 3(4): 81–219.

Wilm, H. G., D. F. Costello and G. E. Klipple. 1944. Estimating forage yield by the double-sampling method. J. Amer. Soc. Agron. 36: 194–203.

Wilman, E. A. 1984. Benefits to deer hunters from forest management practices. Transactions, North Amer. Wildlife and Natural Resources Conference 49: 334–344.

Wilmeth, R. 1978. Anahim Lake archaeology and the early historic Chilcotin Indians. Mercury 82, Ottawa. pp.

Wilmshurst, J. F. and J. M. Fryxell. 1995. Patch selection by red deer in relation to energy and protein intake: a re-evaluation of Langvatn and Hanley's (1993) results. Oecologia 104: 297–300.

Wilmshurst, J. F., J. M. Fryxell and R. J. Hudson. 1995. Forage quality and patch choice by wapiti (*Cervus elaphus*). Behav. Ecol. 6: 209–217.

Wilson, A. C., R. L. Cann, S. M. Carr, M. George, V. B. Gyllensten, K. M. Helm-Bychowski, R. G. Higuchi, S. R. Palumbi, E. M. Prager, R. D. Sage and M. Stoneking. 1985. Mitochondrial DNA and two prospectives on evolutionary genetics. Biol. J. Linnean Soc. 26: 375–400.

Wilson, D. E. 1971. Carrying capacity of the key browse species for moose on the north slopes of the Uinta Mountains, Utah. Utah State Div. Wildl. Resour. Publ. 71: 9. Utah Division of Wildl. Resour., Salt Lake City.

Wilson, D. E., S. M. Hirst and R. P. Ellis. 1977. Determination of feeding preferences in wild ruminants from trocar samples. J. Wildl. Manage. 41(1): 70–75.

Wilson, E. N. 1919. The White Indian Boy: The story of Uncle Nick among the Shoshones. Rev. and ed. by H. R. Driggs. World Book Co., Yonkers-on-Hudson, New York. 222 pp.

Wilson, E. N. 1971. Among the Shoshones. Repr. of 1910 edit. Pine Cone Publishers, Medford, Oregon. 222 pp.

Wilson, E. O. 1975. Sociobiology: The new synthesis. Belknap Press of Harvard Univ. Press, Cambridge, Massachusetts. 697 pp.

Wilson, E. O. and W. L. Brown, Jr. 1953. The subspecies concept and its taxonomic application. Syst. Zool. 2(3): 97–111.

Wilson, G. I. 1969. Some parasites of elk in New Mexico. Bull. Wildl. Dis. Assoc. 5: 23–24.

Wilson, G. L. 1924. The horse and dog in Hidatsa culture. Anthropol. Papers of the Amer. Mus. of Natur. Hist., New York. 15(2): 127–311.

Wilson, J. R. 1994. Cell wall characteristics in relation to forage digestion by ruminants. J. Ag. Sci., Cambridge 122: 173–182.

Wilson, M. A., R. M. Duncan, T. J. Roffe, G. E. Nordholm and B. M. Berlowski. Pasteurellosis in elk (*Cervus elaphus*): DNA fingerprinting of isolates. Vet. Rec. 137: 195–196.

Wilson, M. L. and A. H. Towne. 1978. Nisenan. Pages 387–397 *in* R. F. Heizer, ed., California. Handbook of North American Indians. Vol. 8. Smithsonian Instit., Washington, D.C. 800 pp.

Wilson, P. R., B. S. Cooper, S. B. Badger, A. J. Jopp and P. Abeynayake. 1981. Keratitis in red deer. New Zealand Vet. J. 29: 92–94.

Wilson, S. H. 1986. A naturalist in western China. Vols. I and II. Cadogan Books, London, U.K. 229 pp.

Winans, W. 1913. Deer breeding for fine heads. Rowland Ward, Ltd., London. 105 pp.

Winchell, N. H. 1884–1901. The geology of Minnesota. 6 vols. The Pioneer Press Co., St. Paul, Minnesota.

Wing, L. D. 1962. Big game and livestock browse utilization and feeding habits on a sandy range in southeastern Idaho. M.S. Thesis, Univ. Idaho, Moscow. 89 pp.

Winick, M. 1976. Malnutrition and brain development. Oxford Univ. Press, London. 169 pp.

Winn, D. S. 1976. Terrestrial vertebrate fauna and selected coniferous habitat types on the north slope of the Uinta Mountains. Wasatch Nat. For. Spec. Rept. USDA For. Serv., Salt Lake City. 145 pp.

Winner, C. 1996. The grandmother effect. Wyoming Wildl. 60(3): 10–15.

Wintemberg, W. J. 1906. Bone and horn harpoon heads of the Ontario Indians. Pages 33–56 *in* Annual Archaeological Report 1905. Report of the Ontario Minister of Education. L. K. Cameron, Toronto, Ontario. 249 pp.

———. 1926. Archaeological evidence of the presence of the wapiti in southwestern Ontario. Can. Field. Natur. 40(3): 58.

———. 1936. The Roebuck prehistoric village site, Grenville County, Ontario. Anthropol. Ser. 19, Bull. 83. Nat. Mus. of Canada, Ottawa, Ontario. 178 pp.

Wisdom, M. J. and J. W. Thomas. 1996. Elk. Pages 157–182 *in* P. R.Krausman, ed., Rangeland wildlife. Soc. for Range Manage., Denver, Colorado. 440 pp.

Wisdom, M. J. and J. G. Cook. 2000. North American elk. Pages 694–735 *in* S. Demarais and P. R. Krausman, eds., Ecology and management of large mammals in North America. Prentice Hall, Upper Saddle River, New Jersey. 778 pp.

Wisdom, M. J., L. R. Bright, C. G. Carey, W. W. Hines, R. J.Pederson, D. A. Smithey, J. W. Thomas and G. W. Witmer. 1986. A model to evaluate elk habitat in western Oregon. Publ. No. R6-F&WL–216–1986. USDA For. Serv., Portland, Oregon. 36 pp.

Wishart, W. D. 1981. January conception in an elk in Alberta. J. Wildl. Manage. 45: 544.

Wislizenus, F. A. 1912. A journey to the Rocky Mountains in the year 1839 by F. A. Wislizenus, M.D. Missouri Historical Soc., St. Louis. 162 pp.

Wislocki, G. B. 1942. Studies on the growth of deer antlers. I. Amer. J. Anat. 71(3): 371–415.

———. 1943. Studies on the growth of deer antlers. II. Pages 631–655 *in* Essays in Biology. Univ. Calif. Press, Berkeley.

———. 1954. Antlers in female deer, with a report of three cases in *Odocoileus*. J. Mammal. 35(4): 486–495.

Wislocki, G. B. and M. Singer. 1946. The occurrence and function of nerves in the growing antlers of deer. J. Comp. Neurol. 85: 1–19.

Wislocki, G. B., J. C. Aub and C. M. Waldo. 1947. The effects of gonadectomy and the administration of testosterone propionate on the growth of antlers in male and female deer. Endocrinol. 40: 202–224.

Wissler, C. 1902. Symbolism in the decorative art of the Sioux. Proc. Int. Congr. Americanists XIII.

———. 1905. The whirlwind and the elk of the mythology of the Dakota. J. Amer. Folklore 18: 256–268.

———. 1906. The Blackfoot Indians. Pages 162–178 in Annual Archaeological Report 1905. Report of the Ontario Minister of Education. L. K. Cameron, Toronto. 249 pp.

———. 1907. Some protective designs of the Dakota. Anthropol. Papers of the Amer. Mus. Natur. Hist. 1(2): 19–35.

———. 1910. Material culture of the Blackfoot Indians. Amer. Mus. of Natur. Hist. Anthropol. Papers. X(1): 3–99.

———. 1912a. Societies and ceremonial associations in the Oglala division of the Teton-Dakota. Amer. Mus. of Natur. Hist. Anthropol. Papers. XI(1): 3–99.

———. 1912b. Ceremonial bundles of the Blackfoot Indians. Anthropol. Papers of the Amer. Mus. Natur. Hist. 7(1): 65–298.

———. 1915. Costumes of the Plains Indians. Amer. Mus. of Natur. Hist. Anthropol. Papers, XVI(2): 39–91.

———. 1948. North American Indians of the Plains. 3rd ed. Handbook Ser. No. 1. Amer. Mus. of Natur. Hist., New York. 172 pp.

———. 1966. Indians of the United States. Doubleday and Co., Inc., Garden City, New York. 336 pp.

Wistar, I. J. 1914. Autobiography of Isaac Jones Wistar, 1827–1905. Wistar Inst. Anat. and Biol., Philadelphia, Pennsylvania. 2 vols.

Witmer, G. W. and D. S. deCalesta. 1983. Habitat use by female Roosevelt elk in the Oregon Coast range. J. Wildl. Manage. 47(4): 933–939.

Witmer, G. W. and D. S. deCalesta. 1985. Effect of forest roads on habitat use by Roosevelt elk. Northwest Sci. 59(2): 122–125.

Witmer, G. W., M. Wisdom, E. P. Harshman, R. J. Anderson, C. Carey, M. P. Kuttel, I. D. Luman, J. A. Rochelle, R. W. Scharpf and D. A. Smithey. 1985. E. R. Brown, ed., Deer and elk. Pages 231–258 in Management of wildlife and fish habitats in forests of western Oregon and Washington, part 1—chapter narratives. USDA For. Serv., Publ.No.R6-F&WL–192–1985. U.S. Govt. Print. Off., Washington, D.C. 332 pp.

Witter, J. F. and D. C. O'Meara. 1970. Brucellosis. Pages 249–255 in J. W. Davis, L. H., Karstad. and D. O. Trainer, eds., Infectious diseases of wild mammals. Iowa State Univ. Press., Ames. 421 pp.

Wobeser, G., A. A. Gajadhar and H. M. Hunt. 1985. Fascioloides magna: Occurrence in Saskatchewan and distribution in Canada. Can. Vet. J. 26: 241–244.

Wodzicki, K. A. 1950. Introduced mammals of New Zealand—An ecological and economic survey. Res. Bull. No. 98. New Zealand Dept. Sci. and Ind., Wellington. 255 pp.

Wofford, H., J. L. Holechek, M. L. Galyean, J. D. Wallace and M. Cardenas. 1985. Evaluation of fecal indices to predict cattle diet quality. J. Range Manage. 38: 450–454.

Wolfe, G. J. 1980. Elk management on a New Mexico ranch. Pages 26–32 in W. Macgregor, ed. Proc. West. States Elk Workshop. B. C. Fish and Wildl. Branch, Victoria. 174 pp.

———. 1983. The relationship between age and antler development in wapiti. Pages 29–36 in R. D. Brown, ed., Antler Development in Cervidae. Caesar Kleberg Wildlife Research Institute, Kingsville, Texas.

———. 1985. Population dynamics of the Vermejo Park elk herd, with special reference to trophy management. Ph.D. Thesis, Colorado State Univ., Fort Collins. 161 pp.

Wolfe, G. J. and W. R. Lance. 1984. Locoweed poisoning in a northern New Mexico elk herd. J. Range. Manag. 37: 59–63.

Wolfe, M. L. 1995. An overview of legal systems for managing wildlife. Pages 327–331 in J. A. Bissonette and P. R. Krausman, eds., Integrating people and wildlife for a sustainable future. Proc. First Int. Wildlife Management Congress. The Wildl. Soc., Bethesda, Maryland. 697 pp.

Wolfe, M. L. and F. C. Berg. 1988. Deer and forestry in Germany. J. Forestry 86: 25–31.

Wolfe, M. L., G. E. Simonds, R. Danvir and W. J. Hopkin. 1996. Integrating livestock production and wildlife in a sagebrush-grass ecosystem. Pages 73–77 in D. M. Finch, ed., Ecosystem disturbance and wildlife conservation in western grasslands—a symposium. Proc. Gen. Tech. Rept. RM-GTR–285. USDA For. Serv., Fort Collins, Colorado. 82 pp.

Wolfel, H. 1986. Erhalten statt masten. Anblick 5/1986: 202–204

Wolff, J. O. 1995. On the limitations of species–habitat association studies. Northw. Sci. 69: 72–76.

Wolfgang, R. W. and J. B. Poole. 1956. Distribution of Echinococcus disease in northwestern Canada. Amer. J. Trop. Med. Hyg. 5(5): 869–871.

Wolkers, J., T. Wensing and J. T. Schonewille. 1994. Effect of undernutrition on haematological and serum biochemical characteristics in red deer (Cervus elaphus). Can. J. Zool. 72: 1,291–1,296.

Wong-Quincey, J. 1939. Chinese hunter. The John Day Co., New York. 383 pp.

Wondolleck, J. M. and S. L. Yaffee. 2000. Making collaboration work: Lessons from innovation in natural resource management. Island Press, Washington, DC. 277 pp.

Wood, A. J., I. M. Cowan and H. C. Nordan. 1962. Periodicity of growth in ungulates as shown by deer of the genus Odocoileus. Can. J. Zool. 40: 593–603.

Wood, D. B. and J. J. Kennedy. 1973. Nonconsumptive uses of a Utah elk herd. Utah State Univ. Press, Logan. 22 pp.

Wood, R. K. 1943. The elk in Virginia. M.S. Thesis, Virginia Polytechnic Inst., Blacksburg. 272 pp.

Wood, W. 1957. Perforated elk teeth: A functional and historical analysis. Amer. Antiquity 22(4): 381–387.

Woodburne, M. O. 1987. Cenozoic mammals of North America. Univ. California Press, Berkeley and Los Angeles. 336 pp.

Woodbury, M. R. 1995. Antlers: Innervation studies and growth measurements. MS Thesis, Univ. Saskatchewan, Saskatoon. 89 pp.

Woodbury, M. R. and J. C. Haigh. 1996. Innervation and anaesthesia of the antler pedicle in wapiti and red deer. Can. Vet. J. 37: 486–489.

Woodbury, R. 1997. Arctic cats and buffalo. Time (March 17): 62–63. Wyoming Game and Fish Dept., Annual Report 1996.

Woodgerd, W. R. 1975. Comprehensive planning for improved management of wildlife and non-wildlife outdoor recreational resources in Montana: A director's viewpoint. Trans. N. Amer. Wildl. and Natur. Resour. Conf. 40: 103–108.

Woods, J. G. 1991. Ecology of a partially migratory elk population. Ph.D. Diss., Univ. British Columbia, Vancouver. 149 pp.

Woolf, A. 1974. The Yellowstone elk controversy. Pages 451–466 in J. A. Bailey, W. Elder and T. D. McKinney, eds., Readings in wildlife conservation. The Wildl. Soc., Washington, D.C. 722 pp.

Woolf, A. and J. D. Harder. 1979. Population dynamics of a captive white-tailed deer herd with emphasis on reproduction and mortality. Wildl. Monogr 67. 53 pp.

Woolf, A., C. A. Mason and D. Kradel. 1977. Prevalence and effects of Parelaphostrongylus tenuis in a captive wapiti population. J. Wildl. Dis. 13: 149–154.

Woolston, T. K. 1995. Isolation and characterization of anaerobic tannin-tolerant bacteria from elk rumen fluid. Senior Thesis, Cornell Univ., Ithaca, New York. 38 pp.

World Health Organization. 2000. WHO consultation on public health and animal transmissible spongiform encephalopathies: Epidemiology, risk and research requirements. (WHO/CDS/APH/2000.2) 52 pp.

Worley, D. E. 1975. Observations on epizootiology and distribution of *Elaeophora schneideri* in Montana ruminants. J. Wildl. Dis. 11: 486–488.

Worley, D. E. 1979. Parasites and parasitic diseases of elk in the northern Rocky Mountain region: A review. Pages 206–211 *in* M. S. Boyce and L. D. Hayden-Wing, eds., North American elk: Ecology, behavior and management. Univ. Wyoming, Laramie. 294 pp.

Worley, D. E. and K. R. Greer. 1976. Parasites and diseases of North American elk (*Cervus* spp.): An annotated bibliography. Joint Contribution of the Federal Aid Wildlife Restoration, Montana Project W–120-R(6083), Wildlife Laboratory and Vet.Research Laboratory, Agr. Exp. Sta., Montana State Univ., Bozeman. 48 pp.

Worley, D. E. and R. E. Barrett. 1964. Studies of the parasites of the northern Yellowstone elk herd. Pages 10–28 *in* R. H. McBee, ed., Rumen physiology and parasitology of the northern Yellowstone elk herd. Progress Report, National Park Service, Mammoth, Wyoming.

Worley, D. E., R. E. Barrett, P. J. A. Presidente and R. H. Jacobson. 1969. The Rocky Mountain elk as a reservoir host for parasites of domestic animals in western Montana. Bull. Wildl. Dis. Assoc. 5: 348–350.

Wormington, H. M. 1964. Prehistoric Indians of the Southwest. Popular Ser. No. 7. Denver Mus. Natur. Hist., Denver, Colorado. 191 pp.

Wotschikowsky, U. 1981 Wintergatter-ist das die losung? Jager 11: 42–47.

Wright, G. A. 1984. People of the high country: Jackson Hole before the settlers. Peter Lang, New York. 181 pp.

Wright, G. A. and S. J. Miller. 1976. Prehistoric hunting of New World wild sheep: Implications for the study of sheep domestication. Pages 293–312 *in* C. E. Cleland, ed., Cultural change and continuity: Essays in honor of James Bennett Griffin. Academic Press, New York. 378 pp.

Wright, H. E., Jr. and D. G. Frey, eds. 1965. The Quaternary of the United States. Princeton Univ. Press, Princeton, New Jersey. 922 pp.

Wright, J. F. 1958. Necrotic stomatitis in an American elk. Vet. Med. 53: 520–521.

Wright, J. V. and J. E. Anderson. 1963. The Donaldson site. Nat. Mus. Canada Bull. 184. 192 pp.

Wright, M. J. 1981. The Walker site. Mercury 103, Ottawa, Ontario.

Wright, R. G. 1998. A review of the relationship between visitors and ungulates in national parks. Wildl. Soc. Bull. 26(3): 471–476.

Wu, Y., M. G. Turner, L. L. Wallace and W. H. Romme. 1996. Elk survival following the 1988 Yellowstone Fires: A simulation experiment. Natural Areas J. 16: 198–207.

Wurster, D. H. and K. Benirschke. 1967. The chromosomes of twenty-three species of the Cervoidea and Bovoidea. Mammal. Chromos. Newslett. 8: 226–229.

Wydeven, A. P. and R. B. Dahlgren. 1983. Food habits of elk in the northern Great Plains. J. Wildl. Manage. 47: 916–923.

Wyman, J. 1868. An account of some Kjoekkenmoeddings, or shell heaps, in Maine and Massachusetts. Amer. Natur. 1: 561–584.

Wynne-Edwards, W. C. 1962. Animal dispersion in relation to social behaviour. Oliver and Boyd, Ltd., Edinburgh. 653 pp.

Wyoming Forest Study Team. 1971. Forest management in Wyoming: timber harvest and the environment on the Teton, Bridger, Shoshone and Bighorn National Forests. USDA For. Serv., Ogden, Utah and Denver, Colorado. 81 pp.

Wyoming Game and Fish Department. 1992. Unpublished. Reports on file Wyoming Game and Fish Dept., Vet. Section, Laramie, Wyoming.

Wyoming Game and Fish Department. 1996. Unpublished. Reports on file Wyoming Game and Fish Dept., Vet. Section, Laramie, Wyoming.

Wyoming State Legislature. 1907. Session laws of the state of Wyoming passed by the ninth state legislature. House Joint Memorial No. 1, pp. 196–197. State of Wyoming, Laramie.

Wyoming Territory. 1884. Laws pertaining to the Yellowstone National Park. The Leader Printing Co., Cheyenne, Wyoming.

Yaffee, S. L. 1982. Prohibitive policy: Implementing the Endangered Species Act. MIT Press, Cambridge, Massachusetts. 239 pp.

Yaffee, S. L. 1994. The wisdom of the spotted owl: Policy lessons for a new century. Island Press, May 7, 2001Washington, DC. 430 pp.

Yalow, R. S. and S. A. Berson. 1971. Fundamental principles of radioimmunoassay techniques in measurement of hormones. Pages 16–34 *in* Mattar et al., eds., Recent advances in endocrinology. Excerpta Medica, Amsterdam.

Yarmolloy, C., M. Bayer and V. Geist. 1988. Behavior response and reproduction of mule deer *Odocoileus hemionus,* does following experimental harassment with all-terrain vehicle. Can. Field Natur. 102(3): 425–429.

Yellon, S. M., D. L. Foster, L. D. Longo and J. M. Suttie. 1992. Ontogeny of the pineal melatonin rhythm and implications for reproductive development in domestic ruminants. Anim. Reprod. Sci. 30: 91–112.

Yeo, J. J., J. M. Peek, W. T. Wittinger and C. T. Kvale. 1993. Influence of rest–rotation cattle grazing on mule deer and elk habitat use in east-central Idaho. J.Range Manage. 46: 245–250.

Yerex, D. 1979. Deer farming in New Zealand. Deer Farm. Serv., Div. Ag., Wellington, New Zealand. 120 pp.

Yesner, D. R. 1996. Human adaptation at the Pleistocene–Holocene boundary (circa 13,000 to 8,000 BP) in eastern Beringia. Pages 255–276 *in* L. G. Strauss, B. V. Eriksen, J. M. Erlandson and D. R. Yesner, eds., Humans at the end of the Ice Age: The archeology of the Pleistocene–Holocene transition. Plenum Press, New York.

Yoakum, J. D. 1978. Pronghorn. Pages 103–122 *in* J. L. Schmidt and D. L. Gilbert, eds., Big game of North America: Ecology and management. Stackpole Books, Inc., Harrisburg, Pennsylvania. 512 pp.

Yorgason, I. J. and R. H. Bendt. 1960. Elk migration and distribution study, Jackson Hole elk herd. Nat. Park Serv., Moose, and Wyoming Game and Fish Commiss., Jackson. 8 pp.

Yorgason, I. J., G. E. Gruell, R. Johnson and C. Thompson. 1975. Gros Ventre cooperative elk study. Wyoming Game and Fish Dept. and Bridger-Teton Nat. For., Jackson. 28 pp.

Youmans, C. C. 1991. Analysis of long-term trends in elk vulnerability on the Bitterroot National Forest in relation to selected predictor variables. Pages 159–167 *in* A. G. Christensen, L. J. Lyon and T. N. Lonner, compilers, Proc. Elk Vulnerability Symp., Montana State Univ., Bozeman. 330 pp.

Youmans, H. B., compiler. 1992. Statewide elk management plan for Montana. Montana Dept. of Fish, Wildl. and Parks, Helena. 170 pp.

Young, C. C. 1932. On the Artiodactyla from the *Sinanthropus* site at Chouk'outien. Palaeontologia Sinica (c), 8(2): 1–158.

Young, S. B. M. 1897. Report of the Acting Superintendent of the Yellowstone National Park to the Secretary of the Interior, 1897. Govt. Print. Off., Washington, D.C. 34 pp.

Young, S. B. M. 1907. Annual Report of the Superintendent of the Yellowstone National Park to the Secretary of the Interior, 1907. Govt. Print. Off., Washington, D.C. 26 pp.

Young, S. B. M. 1908. Report of the Superintendent of the Yellowstone National Park to the Secretary of the Interior, 1908. Govt. Print. Off., Washington, D.C. 19 pp.

Young, S. P. 1956. The deer, the Indians and the American pioneers. Pages 1–27 *in* W. P. Taylor, ed., The deer of North America. Stackpole Books, Inc., Harrisburg, Pennsylvania. 668 pp.

Young, V. A. 1938. The carrying capacity of big game range. J. Wildl. Manage. 2: 131–134.

Young, V. A. and W. L. Robinette. 1939. Study of the range habits of elk on the Selway Game Preserve. Bull. 34. Univ. Idaho, Moscow. 47 pp.

Youngman, P. M. 1975. Mammals of the Yukon Territory. Nat. Mus. Can. Publ. in Zool. 10. 192 pp.

Youngson, R. W. 1970. Rearing red deer calves in captivity. J. Wildl. Manage. 34: 467–470.

Yount, H. 1881. Report of [Yellowstone National Park] gamekeeper. Pages 806–807 *in* Report of the Secretary of the Interior. Vol. 2. Govt. Print. Off., Washington, D.C. 1,132 pp.

Zager, P. and D. J. Leptich. 1991. Comparing two methods of calculating elk survival rates. Pages 106–109 *in* A. G. Christensen, L. J. Lyon, T. N. Lonner, compilers, Proc. Elk Vulnerability Symp., Montana State Univ., Bozeman. 330 pp.

Zahn, H. M. 1974. Seasonal movements of the Burdette Creek elk herd. Job Compl. Rept. W–120–R–4. Montana Fish and Game Dept., Helena. 70 pp.

Zar, J. H. 1984. Biostatistical analysis. Prentice-Hall, Inc., Englewood Cliffs, New Jersey. 718 pp.

Zaret, T. M. and A. S. Rand. 1971. Competition in tropical streams by fishes: Support for the competitive exclusion principle. Ecology 52: 336–342.

Zaugg, J. L. and K. L. Kuttler. 1985. *Anaplasma marginale* infections in American bison: Experimental infection and serologic study. Am. J. Vet. Res. 46: 438–441.

Zaugg, J. L., W. L. Goff, W. Foreyt and D. L. Hunter. 1996. Susceptibility of elk (*Cervus elaphus*) to experimental infection with *Anaplasma marginale* and *A. ovis*. J. Wildl. Dis. 32: 62–66.

Zebarth, G. 1995. Body condition scoring for elk cows. North Amer. Elk, Winter 1995: 54–56.

Zeiler, H. 1996. Jagd und Nachhaltigkkeit. Monographie 73, Umweltbundesamt/Federal Encivornent Agen., Wien.

Zeiler, H., and H. Gossow. 1990. Nationalpark Hohe Tauern (Salzburger Teil) und regionale schalenwild-planung Fuscher Tal. Pages 63–85 *in* H. Gossow, E. Donaubauer, F. Reimoser and J. Dieberger, eds., Tagungsbericht IURFO-Symposium regionalplanungskonzept, fur eine forstlich integrierte Schalenwildbewirtschaftung im Hoch- und Mittelgebirge. BOKU-reports on Wildlife Research and Game Management 1. Institut for Wildbiologie und Jagdwirtschaft, Universitat fur Bodenkultur, Wien.

Zeiler, H., M. Preleuthner, M. Grinner and H. Gossow. 1990. Zur bewirtschaftung und regulierung des schalenwildes im hegering fusch. Typoscript, Institut fur Wildbiologie und Jagdwirtschaft der Universitat fur Bodenkultur. Wien. 132 pp.

Zepelin, H. and A. Rechtsschaften. 1974. Mammalian sleep, longevity and energy metabolism. Brain, Behav. and Evol. 10(6): 425–470.

Zeuner, F. E. 1959. The Pleistocene Period. Hutchinson and Co., London, U.K.

Zhao, Q. C., H. Kiyohara, T. Nakai and H. Yamada. 1992. Structure of the complement-activating proteoglycan from the pilose antler from *Cervus nippon* Temminck. Carbohydrate Res. 230: 361–372.

Zhigunov, P. S., ed. 1961. Reindeer husbandry. 2nd ed. Translation from Russian. U.S. Dept. of Commerce, Springfield, Virginia. 348 pp.

Ziccardi, M. H., W. M. Boyce and I. A. Gardner. 1996. Seroprevalence of *Psoroptes* sp. mites in free-ranging elk (*Cervus elaphus*) as determined by kinetic elisa. J. Wildl. Dis. 32: 51–56.

Zimmerberg, B., S. D. Glick and T. Jerussi. 1974. Neurochemical correlate of spatial preference in rats. Science 185: 623–625.

Zipf, G. K. 1949. Human behaviour and the principle of least effort. Addison-Wesley, Cambridge, Massachusetts.

Contributors

Mark W. Brunson is an associate professor for the Forest Resources Department of Utah State University, Logan.

Anthony B. Bubenik, deceased, was a research scientist for the Wildlife Branch of the Ontario Department of Lands and Forests in Maple, Ontario.

S. Dwight Bunnell is a wildlife biologist for the Utah Division of Wildlife Resources, Salt Lake City.

Alan G. Christensen is group leader for watershed, fisheries and wildlife, USDA Forest Service, Portland, Oregon.

Patrick E. Clark is a range scientist for the USDA Agricultural Research Service, Boise, Idaho.

John G. Cook is a wildlife biologist for the National Council for Air and Stream Improvement, Inc., La Grande, Oregon.

Allen Y. Cooperrider, retired, served as a wildlife biologist for the U.S. Fish and Wildlife Service and currently resides in Ukiah, California.

Dan K. Crockett is the editor of the Rocky Mountain Elk Foundation's *Bugle* magazine, in Missoula, Montana.

Michael J. Dorrance is retired as head of the problem wildlife section, Alberta Agriculture Food and Rural Development, and currently is with Matheson Dorrance and Associates in Bridesville, British Columbia.

Robert G. Dundas is a lecturer in the Department of Earth and Environmental Sciences and the Department of Biology, California State University, Fresno.

Valerius Geist is professor emeritus, Faculty of the Environmental Design, University of Calgary, Alberta.

Jerry C. Haigh is a professor of veterinary medicine, specializing in wildlife and game ranching, at the Western College of Veterinary Medicine, University of Saskatchewan in Saskatoon.

Robert J. Hudson is a professor in the Department of Renewable Resources at the University of Alberta, Edmonton.

Larry L. Irwin is principal scientist with the National Council for Air and Stream Improvement, Inc., La Grande, Oregon, and he has adjunct faculty appointments at the University of Montana in Missoula and Oregon State University, Corvallis.

Bruce K. Johnson is a wildlife research biologist for the Oregon Department of Fish and Wildlife, La Grande.

John F. Kimball, Jr. is the director of the Utah Division of Wildlife Resources, Salt Lake City.

T. P. Kistner is a retired wildlife research veterinarian and professor of fisheries and wildlife at Oregon State University, Corvallis

L. Jack Lyon, retired, served as project leader and research scientist for wildlife habitat with the USDA Forest Service, Intermountain Research Station, Missoula, Montana.

Richard E. McCabe is vice-president of the Wildlife Management Institute, Washington, D.C.

William Miller works at the School of Agribusiness and Resource Management, Arizona State University, East Mesa.

Joshua J. Millspaugh is an assistant professor of wildlife conservation at the University of Missouri, Columbia.

Bart W. O'Gara, retired, served as leader of the Montana Cooperative Wildlife Research Unit at the University of Montana, Missoula, and he currently lives in Lolo, Montana.

James M. Peek is professor emeritus of wildlife resources, University of Idaho, Moscow.

Dale R. Potter, retired, worked for the USDA Forest Service, Seattle, Washington.

Kenneth J. Raedeke is a research associate professor of wildlife at the College of Forest Resources, University of Washington in Seattle, and president of Raedeke Associates, Inc., Seattle.

William M. Samuel is a professor in the Department of Biological Sciences and coordinator of the Challenge Grants in Biodiversity Program at the University of Alberta in Edmonton.

Gregory T. M. Schildwachter is a policy advisor for the Governor's Office of Species Conservation, Boise, Idaho.

Karoline T. Schmidt is a research scientist at the Research Institute of Wildlife Ecology, University of Veterinary Medicine, Vienna, Austria.

Jon M. Skovlin is wildlife and rangeland consultant, formerly research scientist Pacific Northwest Research Station, U.S. Department of Agriculture, Forest Service, La Grande, Oregon.

Bruce L. Smith is a wildlife biologist for the U.S. Fish and Wildlife Service on the National Elk Refuge, Jackson, Wyoming.

David H. Stalling is the conservation editor of the Rocky Mountain Elk Foundation's *Bugle* magazine, in Missoula, Montana.

Jack Ward Thomas is chief emeritus of the U.S. Forest Service and the Boone and Crockett Professor at the University of Montana, Missoula.

E. Tom Thorne is a wildlife veterinarian and chief of the Services Division, Wyoming Game and Fish Department, Cheyenne.

Dale E. Toweill is wildlife program coordinator for the Idaho Department of Fish and Game, Boise.

Elizabeth S. Williams is a wildlife veterinarian and veterinary pathologist with the Department of Veterinary Sciences, University of Wyoming, Laramie.

Gary J. Wolfe is president emeritus of the Rocky Mountain Elk Foundation in Missoula, Montana.

Michael L. Wolfe is a professor in the Department of Fisheries and Wildlife at Utah State University, Logan.

Peter Zager is a principal wildlife research biologist at Idaho Department of Fish and Game, Lewiston.

Index